HOLY
BIBLE
Uncovered

HOLY
BIBLE
Uncovered

NEW INTERNATIONAL VERSION

BIBLE SOCIETY

INTERNATIONAL BIBLE SOCIETY
PO BOX 62970, Colorado Springs, CO 80962-2970

Cased ISBN 0 564 09035 2
Hardback ISBN 0 564 09045 X

A catalogue record for this book is available from the British Library

This publication is not included under licences issued by the Copyright
Licensing Agency

Published by Bible Society, Stonehill Green, Westlea, Swindon SN5 7DG
Typeset by Autographics Inc., California, U.S.A.
Printed in Great Britain by Richard Clay Ltd, Bungay, Suffolk
Cover design by Creative Link, Edinburgh

CONTENTS

BOOKS OF THE OLD TESTAMENT

BOOKS OF THE NEW TESTAMENT

HOW BIG IS YOUR BIBLE?

Plato, Aristotle, and other Greek philosophers were some of the cleverest individuals this world has ever produced. They lived in the same century as one of the Bible's authors, Nehemiah. Nehemiah is not the Bible's most prominent character by a long, long way. But millions more people around the world have heard Nehemiah's words than Plato's. Why is there this power in the Bible? What is it?

"Well," people might say, "it's a book. God's book." Nearly right. It is actually God's library of books. It is two libraries; 39 books in the Old Testament and 27 in the New. Among some of its writers are a general, a shepherd, a king, a farmer, a fisherman, a doctor, and a taxman. The common bond that unites the books is that they all show how God interacts with his people, and how he constantly saves them. This culminates in his Son Jesus Christ. From beginning to end, four great themes thread their way through the 66 books. They are creation, the fall of the human race into sin, God's way of salvation, and the new heaven and new earth that Christ's return will bring in at the close of history.

If we can build a framework for our lives around God's revelation, we can establish our relationship to the universe, and as we read the Scriptures and prayerfully apply them to our lives, we shall come to know God in his Son Jesus Christ. We can expect to become more like him in character and outlook. In so doing, regardless of our achievements or failures in life, we shall be fulfilling the purpose for which we were born.

All that sounds like a lifetime of reading. Your Bible is, in reality, no bigger than your reading of it. Some people's Bibles consist of no more than a few psalms and a number of favourite stories and half-remembered texts from childhood days. It is better to be more purposeful than this. Where should you begin? Genesis? Perhaps not. Remember that you are dealing with two libraries; you are not obliged to work your way consecutively through its books. We are living on the AD side of history, so you can start with the life of Jesus. Beginning with Matthew? Not necessarily. You may wish to start with Luke, a book written by a Gentile (non-Jew) for Gentile readers. It is warm, human, and compassionate; a book that has helped millions fall in love with Jesus Christ.

At times Scripture is baffling, with thoughts and ideas that seem far-removed from our own times. Understanding will come with regular reading. Perhaps you could set a time — early in the morning, or in the evening, or both. You could plan an outline of reading for a month, or a year, with the help of the plans in this Bible, or various outlines and notes available from Bible bookshops. And all the time you will be growing in knowledge.

The Bible deals with everyday situations. It has examples, warnings, and promises, and it is important to turn those into prayer — for families, colleagues, friends, the world, and personal issues. With humility, we can come to the amazing realization that the Bible gives us something that the best of Plato or Aristotle cannot. It is the adventure of a lifetime.

The Revd Preb Richard Bewes
Rector, All Souls', Langham Place, London

HOW GREAT IS YOUR BIBLE?

Even when you are familiar with the Bible, it can be a daunting book. Its arrangement is complex, and it seems so long and difficult to understand. The early Christians did not have all that we have now, as the New Testament was only just in the process of being written. Yet they managed to be disciples of Jesus. So why should we bother with the Bible?

As disciples we have entered into a relationship with Jesus, not with a book. This relationship is brought alive by the Holy Spirit who, according to Jesus, was going to be the teacher who led his disciples to understand and obey the truth (John 16:12-15). So where does the Bible fit in, and why is it so important?

The answer is that the Bible is one of the tools the Holy Spirit uses to teach us what it is to be a disciple of Jesus. Some would want to say, as I myself would, that it is the primary tool. The Holy Spirit and the Bible are never in opposition but always in partnership (2 Timothy 1:13,14).

The Bible is a revealing book. As followers of Jesus, what can we know about him apart from what is in the Bible? It says so much about him. How would we know who he was, what he was like, what he taught, what he accomplished, and how he wanted his disciples to live, without it? Take it away and we are left with only guesswork.

The Bible is a living book. It should never be a dull book. It is our "growth hormone". We "have been born again. . . through the living and enduring word of God" (1 Peter 1:23). It is a word "planted in you" (James 1:21). It is "living and active" (Hebrews 4:12).

The Bible is an authoritative book. It is "useful for teaching, rebuking, correcting and training in righteousness" (2 Timothy 3:16). In other words it tells us what we should believe and what we should not believe. It tells us how we should behave and points out to us when we behave wrongly.

The Bible is an effective book. It is like a weapon we can use when faced with temptation, as Jesus did (Matthew 4:1-11). It is an instrument we can use in our witnessing to others. The book of Acts tells us repeatedly that the early Christians spread the word of the Lord — a shorthand expression for the message we now have written in the Bible.

The Bible is a sufficient book. In 2 Timothy 3:17 we read that this gift of God is given so that people "may be thoroughly equipped for every good work". Everything we need is found in it, and every aspect of our life is mirrored in it. It is able to help us become effective disciples.

Quite simply, the disciple of Jesus cannot do without the Bible. Growth will not take place, temptation will not be resisted, and witness will be ineffective. Read it, study it, learn it, live it, and let the spiritual "growth hormone" do its work.

The Revd Dr Derek Tidball
Secretary for Mission and Evangelism, Baptist Union

READING PLANS

Discovering the Bible for the first time can be a daunting business, especially when you are faced with a big collection of books which say different things and involve many different characters.

The purpose of these reading plans is to enable you to understand the content and message of the Bible over a period of time, and to discover how God's word in the Bible can speak to you today.

There are two kinds of reading plans in this Bible. The first group has sections to help you to discover different themes over a short period of time. Each section lasts not more than two weeks, so you can begin to build up a picture of the overall shape and content of the Bible by reading short passages. The second group helps you to understand the overall message of different books in the Bible, and it extends over a longer period of time, although, again, each section lasts no more than two weeks. You may well find yourself reading passages that you read in the first group, but don't worry! In this way you will be able to see where different themes and ideas about God fit into the overall shape and direction of the Bible.

Remember! If you come across any difficult words or ideas as you read the Bible, you will find help in the boxed section on that page. If you are still confused, don't be afraid to ask your minister or other members of your church — it's all part of the excitement of learning from the Bible.

Group 1

First Encounters with Jesus

Day 1	Luke 2:1–20
Day 2	Matthew 2:1–12
Day 3	Luke 2:21–35
Day 4	Mark 1:1–11
Day 5	Matthew 3:13–17
Day 6	John 1:19–34
Day 7	Mark 1:14–20

Recognizing and Responding

Day 1	Mark 3:7–19
Day 2	Matthew 4:18–25
Day 3	Luke 5:1–11
Day 4	John 1:35–51

Day 5	Acts 9:1–20
Day 6	Matthew 21:1–11
Day 7	Mark 1:21–24
Day 8	Ezekiel 2:1 — 3:4
Day 9	Jeremiah 1:4–10
Day 10	Isaiah 6:1–8
Day 11	1 Samuel 3:1–10
Day 12	Psalm 40:1–10
Day 13	Psalm 63:1–9
Day 14	Psalm 139:1–11

Finding Forgiveness

Day 1	Matthew 9:9–13
Day 2	Matthew 18:21–35
Day 3	Mark 2:13–17

Day 4	Luke 7:36–50
Day 5	Luke 15:11–32
Day 6	John 8:1–11
Day 7	Isaiah 58:1–8
Day 8	Joel 2:12–13
Day 9	Psalm 103:8–13
Day 10	Psalm 51
Day 11	Ezekiel 18:30–32
Day 12	Colossians 1:21–23
Day 13	Romans 8:1–6
Day 14	Revelation 1:12–18

The Way of Life

Day 1	Matthew 19:16–26
Day 2	Mark 12:28–34
Day 3	Luke 6:27, 28
Day 4	Exodus 20:1–17
Day 5	Deuteronomy 10:12–20
Day 6	Micah 6:8
Day 7	Psalm 119:1–16
Day 8	Psalm 119:17–32
Day 9	Psalm 119:33–56
Day 10	Psalm 119:105–112
Day 11	Ephesians 4:17–25, 32
Day 12	Ephesians 5:1–10
Day 13	Colossians 3:12–17
Day 14	Galatians 5:16–25

Sharing Good News

Day 1	Matthew 5:13–16
Day 2	Matthew 28:16–21
Day 3	Mark 6:7–13
Day 4	Luke 4:16–20
Day 5	John 3:16–20
Day 6	John 13:34, 35
Day 7	Acts 2:37–47
Day 8	Acts 4:8–12
Day 9	Acts 17:22–34

Day 10	2 Corinthians 4:1–10
Day 11	2 Corinthians 5:14–6:2
Day 12	Ephesians 2:13–22
Day 13	1 Thessalonians 2:3–8
Day 14	Psalm 113

Doubt and Uncertainty

Day 1	Isaiah 50:4–9a
Day 2	Jeremiah 20:7–11a
Day 3	Jonah 2:1–9
Day 4	Psalm 23
Day 5	Psalm 31:1–5
Day 6	Psalm 55:1–12, 18–20
Day 7	Psalm 121
Day 8	Matthew 7:7–12
Day 9	Mark 16:1–8
Day 10	John 20:19–26
Day 11	Romans 8:35–39
Day 12	1 Corinthians 15:51–58
Day 13	Philippians 4:4–7
Day 14	Revelation 21:1–4

Discovering God

Day 1	Genesis 32:22–32
Day 2	Exodus 3:1–14
Day 3	1 Samuel 3:1–21
Day 4	Psalm 46
Day 5	Isaiah 9:2–7
Day 6	Hosea 11:1–11
Day 7	Micah 6:6–8
Day 8	Matthew 16:13–28
Day 9	Mark 15:33–41
Day 10	Luke 4:14–21
Day 11	Luke 9:28–36
Day 12	John 19:16–37
Day 13	1 Corinthians 2:1–16
Day 14	Revelation 4:1–11

Group 2

The Gospel of Mark

Day 1	Mark 1
Day 2	Mark 2
Day 3	Mark 3
Day 4	Mark 4
Day 5	Mark 5
Day 6	Mark 6
Day 7	Mark 7

Day 8	Mark 8
Day 9	Mark 9
Day 10	Mark 10
Day 11	Mark 11, 12
Day 12	Mark 13
Day 13	Mark 14, 15
Day 14	Mark 16

The Gospels of Luke and Matthew

Day 1	Luke 1
Day 2	Luke 2
Day 3	Luke 4
Day 4	Luke 5:1–32
Day 5	Luke 10
Day 6	Luke 15
Day 7	Luke 16
Day 8	Matthew 5
Day 9	Matthew 12
Day 10	Matthew 13
Day 11	Matthew 18
Day 12	Matthew 26
Day 13	Matthew 27
Day 14	Matthew 28

The Gospel of John

Day 1	John 1
Day 2	John 2
Day 3	John 3
Day 4	John 6
Day 5	John 9
Day 6	John 10
Day 7	John 11
Day 8	John 12
Day 9	John 13
Day 10	John 14
Day 11	John 15
Day 12	John 16
Day 13	John 17
Day 14	John 20

The Acts of the Apostles

Day 1	Acts 1
Day 2	Acts 2
Day 3	Acts 4
Day 4	Acts 5
Day 5	Acts 6
Day 6	Acts 7
Day 7	Acts 9
Day 8	Acts 15
Day 9	Acts 16
Day 10	Acts 17
Day 11	Acts 21
Day 12	Acts 26
Day 13	Acts 27
Day 14	Acts 28

The Letters

Day 1	Romans 3
Day 2	Romans 7
Day 3	Romans 8
Day 4	Romans 9
Day 5	Romans 12
Day 6	1 Corinthians 1
Day 7	1 Corinthians 2
Day 8	1 Corinthians 12
Day 9	1 Corinthians 13
Day 10	1 Corinthians 14
Day 11	1 Corinthians 15
Day 12	2 Corinthians 4
Day 13	2 Corinthians 5
Day 14	2 Corinthians 12

The Letters

Day 1	Galatians 1
Day 2	Galatians 2
Day 3	Galatians 3
Day 4	Ephesians 2
Day 5	Ephesians 3
Day 6	Philippians 1
Day 7	Philippians 2
Day 8	Philippians 3
Day 9	Colossians 1
Day 10	1 Thessalonians 3
Day 11	1 Thessalonians 4
Day 12	2 Thessalonians 2
Day 13	1 Timothy 1
Day 14	1 Timothy 4

The Letters

Day 1	2 Timothy 1
Day 2	2 Timothy 2
Day 3	2 Timothy 4
Day 4	Titus 2
Day 5	Philemon
Day 6	Hebrews 1
Day 7	Hebrews 4:14—6:3
Day 8	Hebrews 10
Day 9	Hebrews 12
Day 10	James 1
Day 11	1 Peter 1
Day 12	1 John 1
Day 13	Jude
Day 14	Revelation 21

The Old Testament Story: The Beginning

Day 1	Genesis 1
Day 2	Genesis 3
Day 3	Genesis 22
Day 4	Genesis 37
Day 5	Exodus 3
Day 6	Exodus 10
Day 7	Exodus 11
Day 8	Exodus 14
Day 9	Exodus 15
Day 10	Exodus 19
Day 11	Exodus 20
Day 12	Exodus 24
Day 13	Exodus 32
Day 14	Exodus 40

The Old Testament Story: The Story Unfolds

Day 1	Numbers 1:1–19
Day 2	Numbers 11
Day 3	Numbers 14
Day 4	Deuteronomy 4
Day 5	Deuteronomy 8
Day 6	Deuteronomy 28
Day 7	Joshua 2
Day 8	Joshua 6
Day 9	Joshua 7
Day 10	Joshua 23, 24
Day 11	Judges 1
Day 12	Judges 6
Day 13	Judges 7
Day 14	Judges 16

The Old Testament Story: The Chronicles of History

Day 1	1 Samuel 3
Day 2	1 Samuel 16
Day 3	1 Samuel 17
Day 4	1 Samuel 20
Day 5	2 Samuel 6
Day 6	2 Samuel 11
Day 7	2 Samuel 12
Day 8	1 Kings 3
Day 9	1 Kings 8
Day 10	1 Kings 17
Day 11	1 Kings 18
Day 12	2 Kings 5
Day 13	2 Kings 17
Day 14	2 Kings 22

God's Word and the Prophets

Day 1	Isaiah 1
Day 2	Isaiah 6
Day 3	Isaiah 40
Day 4	Isaiah 52
Day 5	Isaiah 53
Day 6	Isaiah 61
Day 7	Jeremiah 2
Day 8	Jeremiah 11
Day 9	Jeremiah 15
Day 10	Jeremiah 31
Day 11	Jeremiah 33
Day 12	Jeremiah 38
Day 13	Jeremiah 39
Day 14	Lamentations 5

The Prophets

Day 1	Ezekiel 2, 3
Day 2	Ezekiel 37
Day 3	Daniel 1
Day 4	Daniel 6
Day 5	Hosea 2, 3
Day 6	Hosea 11
Day 7	Amos 4
Day 8	Obadiah
Day 9	Micah 6
Day 10	Nahum 1
Day 11	Habakkuk 1
Day 12	Zephaniah 3
Day 13	Zechariah 8
Day 14	Malachi 3

Memorable Poetry

Day 1	Psalm 1
Day 2	Psalm 23
Day 3	Psalm 51
Day 4	Psalm 67
Day 5	Psalm 84
Day 6	Psalm 101
Day 7	Psalm 145
Day 8	Proverbs 4
Day 9	Ecclesiastes 3
Day 10	Song of Songs 2
Day 11	Ecclesiastes 12
Day 12	Psalm 90
Day 13	Proverbs 2
Day 14	Psalm 119:1–6

PREFACE

to the New International Version

THE NEW INTERNATIONAL VERSION is a completely new translation of the Holy Bible made by over a hundred scholars working directly from the best available Hebrew, Aramaic and Greek texts. It had its beginning in 1965 when, after several years of exploratory study by committees from the Christian Reformed Church and the National Association of Evangelicals, a group of scholars met at Palos Heights, Illinois, and concurred in the need for a new translation of the Bible in contemporary English. This group, though not made up of official church representatives, was transdenominational. Its conclusion was endorsed by a large number of leaders from many denominations who met in Chicago in 1966.

Responsibility for the new version was delegated by the Palos Heights group to a self-governing body of fifteen, the Committee on Bible Translation, composed for the most part of biblical scholars from colleges, universities and seminaries. In 1967 the New York Bible Society (now the International Bible Society) generously undertook the financial sponsorship of the project — a sponsorship that made it possible to enlist the help of many distinguished scholars. The fact that participants from the United States, Great Britain, Canada, Australia and New Zealand worked together gave the project its international scope. That they were from many denominations — including Anglican, Assemblies of God, Baptist, Brethren, Christian Reformed, Church of Christ, Evangelical Free, Lutheran, Mennonite, Methodist, Nazarene, Presbyterian, Wesleyan and other churches — helped to safeguard the translation from sectarian bias.

How it was made helps to give the New International Version its distinctiveness. The translation of each book was assigned to a team of scholars. Next, one of the Intermediate Editorial Committees revised the initial translation, with constant reference to the Hebrew, Aramaic or Greek. Their work then went to one of the General Editorial Committees, which checked it in detail and made another thorough revision. This revision in turn was carefully reviewed by the Committee on Bible Translation, which made further changes and then released the final version for publication. In this way the entire Bible underwent three revisions, during each of which the translation was examined for its faithfulness to the original languages and for its English style.

All this involved many thousands of hours of research and discussion regarding the meaning of the texts and the precise way of putting them into

English. It may well be that no other translation has been made by a more thorough process of review and revision from committee to committee than this one.

From the beginning of the project, the Committee on Bible Translation held to certain goals for the New International Version: that it would be an accurate translation and one that would have clarity and literary quality and so prove suitable for public and private reading, teaching, preaching, memorising and liturgical use. The Committee also sought to preserve some measure of continuity with the long tradition of translating the Scriptures into English.

In working towards these goals, the translators were united in their commitment to the authority and infallibility of the Bible as God's Word in written form. They believe that it contains the divine answer to the deepest needs of humanity, that it sheds unique light on our path in a dark world, and that it sets forth the way to our eternal well-being.

The first concern of the translators has been the accuracy of the translation and its fidelity to the thought of the biblical writers. They have weighed the significance of the lexical and grammatical details of the Hebrew, Aramaic and Greek texts. At the same time, they have striven for more than a word-for-word translation. Because thought patterns and syntax differ from language to language, faithful communication of the meaning of the writers of the Bible demands frequent modifications in sentence structure and constant regard for the contextual meanings of words.

A sensitive feeling for style does not always accompany scholarship. Accordingly the Committee on Bible Translation submitted the developing version to a number of stylistic consultants. Two of them read every book of both Old and New Testaments twice — once before and once after the last major revision — and made invaluable suggestions. Samples of the translation were tested for clarity and ease of reading by various kinds of people — young and old, highly educated and less well educated, ministers and laymen.

Concern for clear and natural English — that the New International Version should be idiomatic but not idiosyncratic, contemporary but not dated — motivated the translators and consultants. At the same time, they tried to reflect the differing styles of the biblical writers. In view of the international use of English, the translators sought to avoid obvious Americanisms on the one hand and obvious Anglicisms on the other. A British edition reflects the comparatively few differences of significant idiom and of spelling.

As for the traditional pronouns "thou", "thee" and "thine" in reference to the Deity, the translators judged that to use these archaisms (along with old verb forms such as "doest", "wouldest" and "hadst") would violate accuracy in translation. Neither Hebrew, Aramaic nor Greek uses special pronouns for the persons of the Godhead. A present-day translation is not enhanced by forms that in the time of the King James Version were used in everyday speech, whether referring to God or man.

For the Old Testament the standard Hebrew text, the Masoretic Text as published in the latest editions of *Biblia Hebraica*, was used throughout. The Dead Sea Scrolls contain material bearing on an earlier stage of the Hebrew text. They were consulted, as were the Samaritan Pentateuch and the ancient scribal traditions relating to textual changes. Sometimes a variant Hebrew reading in the margin of the Masoretic Text was followed instead of the text itself. Such instances, being variants within the Masoretic tradition, are not specified by footnotes. In rare cases, words in the consonantal text were divided differently from the way they appear in the Masoretic Text. Footnotes indicate this. The translators also consulted the more important early versions — the Septuagint; Aquila, Symmachus and Theodotion; the Vulgate; the Syriac Peshitta; the Targums; and for the Psalms the *Juxta Hebraica* of Jerome. Readings from these versions were occasionally followed where the Masoretic Text seemed doubtful and where accepted principles of textual criticism showed that one or more of these textual witnesses appeared to provide the correct reading. Such instances are footnoted. Sometimes vowel letters and vowel signs did not, in the judgment of the translators, represent the correct vowels for the original consonantal text. Accordingly some words were read with a different set of vowels. These instances are usually not indicated by footnotes.

The Greek text used in translating the New Testament was an eclectic one. No other piece of ancient literature has such an abundance of manuscript witnesses as does the New Testament. Where existing manuscripts differ, the translators made their choice of readings according to accepted principles of New Testament textual criticism. Footnotes call attention to places where there was uncertainty about what the original text was. The best current printed texts of the Greek New Testament were used.

There is a sense in which the work of translation is never wholly finished. This applies to all great literature and uniquely so to the Bible. In 1973 the New Testament in the New International Version was published. Since then, suggestions for corrections and revisions have been received from various sources. The Committee on Bible Translation carefully considered the suggestions and adopted a number of them. These were incorporated in the first printing of the entire Bible in 1978. Additional revisions were made by the Committee on Bible Translation in 1983 and appear in printings after that date.

As in other ancient documents, the precise meaning of the biblical texts is sometimes uncertain. This is more often the case with the Hebrew and Aramaic texts than with the Greek text. Although archaeological and linguistic discoveries in this century aid in understanding difficult passages, some uncertainties remain. The more significant of these have been called to the reader's attention in the footnotes.

In regard to the divine name *YHWH*, commonly referred to as the *Tetragrammaton*, the translators adopted the device used in most English versions of rendering that name as "LORD" in capital letters to distinguish if from *Adonai*, another Hebrew word rendered "Lord", for which small letters are used. Wherever the two names stand together in the Old Testament as a compound name of God, they are rendered "Sovereign LORD".

Because for most readers today the phrases "the LORD of hosts" and "God of hosts" have little meaning, this version renders them "the LORD Almighty" and "God Almighty". These renderings convey the sense of the Hebrew, namely, "he who is sovereign over all the 'hosts' (powers) in heaven and on earth, especially over the 'hosts' (armies) of Israel." For readers unacquainted with Hebrew this does not make clear the distinction between *Sabaoth* ("hosts" or "Almighty") and *Shaddai* (which can also be translated "Almighty"), but the latter occurs infrequently and is always foot-noted. When *Adonai* and *YHWH Sabaoth* occur together, they are rendered "the Lord, the LORD Almighty".

As for other proper nouns, the familiar spellings of the Authorised Version are generally retained. Names traditionally spelled with "ch", except where it is final, are usually spelled in this translation with "k" or "c", since the biblical languages do not have the sound the "ch" frequently indicates in English — for example, in *chant.* For well-known names such as Zechariah, however, the traditional spelling has been retained. Variation in the spelling of names in the original languages has usually not been indicated. Where a person or place has two or more different names in the Hebrew, Aramaic or Greek texts, the more familiar one has generally been used, with footnotes where needed.

To achieve clarity the translators sometimes supplied words not in the original texts but required by the context. If there was uncertainty about such material, it is enclosed in brackets. Also for the sake of clarity or style, nouns, including some proper nouns, are sometimes substituted for pro-nouns, and vice versa. And though the Hebrew writers often shifted back and forth between first, second and third personal pronouns without change of antecedent, this translation often makes them uniform, in accordance with English style and without the use of footnotes.

Poetical passages are printed as poetry, that is, with indentation of lines and with separate stanzas. These are generally designed to reflect the struc-ture of Hebrew poetry. This poetry is normally characterised by parallelism in balanced lines. Most of the poetry in the Bible is in the Old Testament, and scholars differ regarding the scansion of Hebrew lines. The translators determined the stanza divisions for the most part by analysis of the subject matter. The stanzas therefore serve as poetic paragraphs.

As an aid to the reader, italicised sectional headings are inserted in most of the books. They are not to be regarded as part of the NIV text, are not for oral reading, and are not intended to dictate the interpretation of the sections they head.

The footnotes in this version are of several kinds, most of which need no explanation. Those giving alternative translations begin with "Or" and gen-erally introduce the alternative with the last word preceding it in the text, except when it is a single-word alternative; in poetry quoted in a footnote a slant mark indicates a line division. Footnotes introduced by "Or" do not have uniform significance. In some cases two possible translations were con-sidered to have about equal validity. In other cases, though the translators were convinced that the translation in the text was correct, they judged that another interpretation was possible and of sufficient importance to be rep-resented in a footnote.

In the New Testament, footnotes that refer to uncertainty regarding the original text are introduced by "Some manuscripts" or similar expressions. In the Old Testament, evidence for the reading chosen is given first and evidence for the alternative is added after a semicolon (for example: Sep-tuagint; Hebrew *father*). In such notes the term "Hebrew" refers to the Masoretic Text.

It should be noted that minerals, flora and fauna, architectural details, articles of clothing and jewellery, musical instruments and other articles cannot always be identified with precision. Also measures of capacity in the biblical period are particularly uncertain (see the table of weights and measures following the text).

Like all translations of the Bible, made as they are by imperfect man, this one undoubtedly falls short of its goals. Yet we are grateful to God for the extent to which he has enabled us to realise these goals and for the strength he has given us and our colleagues to complete our task. We offer this version of the Bible to him in whose name and for whose glory it has been made. We pray that it will lead many into a better understanding of the Holy Scriptures and a fuller knowledge of Jesus Christ the incarnate Word, of whom the Scriptures so faithfully testify.

The Committee on Bible Translation
June 1978
(Revised August 1983)
Names of the translators and editors may be secured
from the International Bible Society
PO Box 62970, Colorado Springs, CO 80962-2970, U.S.A.

CONTENTS AND DESCRIPTION OF BOOKS IN THE BIBLE

The Old Testament

Genesis How it all began. The creation of the world, the first man and woman, the faithfulness of the first people to respond to God's call.

Exodus The story of redemption. The leadership of Moses, an escape from slavery, the giving of the Law.

Leviticus Guidelines for life, prayer, and worship.

Numbers Rejection and rebellion. How God's chosen people rejected his laws, how they wandered as a homeless rabble in the wilderness, and how they finally entered a land that had been promised to them.

Deuteronomy Restating the Law. Looking back over the past, the good things and the bad things, and looking forward to the future.

Joshua Another great leader. The man who conquered the promised land after Moses' death.

Judges The trials and tribulations of a settled nation, and the calling of judges to maintain the Law.

Ruth Widowhood and rebirth. The woman who lost her husband and therefore her birthright in the dark and dismal days of war and agression.

1 Samuel Preparing for the king's arrival. Samuel acts as a "caretaker" leader of God's people before appointing Saul king. Political failure follows, and David appears to take the throne.

2 Samuel Great David. The ideal ruler, appointed by God, strengthens and brings unity to the nation. Political and moral scandal soon follow, and the future begins to look bleak.

1 Kings Solomon the Wise. David's son succeeds him as king in a reign that has its ups and downs. He is unable to maintain national unity, and those who succeed him are unable to maintain law and order.

2 Kings The saga continues. A divided kingdom, lacking in leadership, continues on the slippery slope towards defeat and disaster.

1 Chronicles Who's who? A comprehensive genealogy of people in the Bible so far, along with episodes from David's life from 2 Samuel.

2 Chronicles It wasn't all bad. The story of the good things achieved by the kings of Judah.

Ezra The priest taken hostage. Ezra leads the returning exiles home from Babylon to Jerusalem, where they rebuild the temple.

Nehemiah   The builder of the walls. Nehemiah returns from exile in Babylon to make Jerusalem secure, and calls the people to renew their faith.

Esther   A story of faith and hope amid persecution. Esther saves the exiled people of God from death and destruction.

Job   Why? A good man wrestles with the question of undeserved suffering.

Psalms   The hymn book of the Bible. A collection of hymns and poems which relate to every aspect of life.

Proverbs   Free advice. Memorable sayings which offer profound insights for all walks of life.

Ecclesiastes   Depressing or real? The Teacher considers the pleasures and relentless pressures of life and concludes that, without God, it is all a waste of time.

Song of Songs   A celebration of human life and the gift of human love.

Isaiah   Poetic eloquence. Isaiah combines straight-talking political comment with matchless prose, which looks forward to a future peace when God will come to redeem his waiting people.

Jeremiah   Keeping God's word alive in times of trouble. Jeremiah found that preaching the word of the Lord set him at odds with everyone around him, but he showed that his words were fulfilled as Jerusalem was invaded and ransacked by the Babylonians.

Lamentations   Raw grief. A collection of hymns and poems which express the sorrow of a nation at the the destruction of the temple and the holy city of Jerusalem.

Ezekiel   A voice from a far country. Ezekiel speaks to the exiled Jews in Babylon, often within the context of spectacular visions.

Daniel   High office in a foreign land. The exiled prophet combines practical issues with visions for the future of God's people.

Hosea   Parables and experience. As one who experienced for himself the pain of adultery, Hosea uses it as the basis for series of prophecies to describe Israel's unfaithfulness to God.

Joel   Sound the trumpet. Joel foretells the coming judgement upon the rebelliousness of Judah.

Amos   A judgement on materialism. Amos prophesies that Israel's prosperity will be the cause of its downfall.

Obadiah   A warning to big brother. Obadiah warns the neighbouring nation of Edom that their wickedness will bring disaster from God.

Jonah   Escaping from God. Jonah is reluctant to preach to an enemy nation, but God gets him there in the end.

Micah   Blowing their cover. Micah unearths the corruption and hypocrisy which eats away at the moral fabric of society, and promises that repentance will bring peace and forgiveness.

Nahum   Saying it again. Despite Jonah's earlier mission to the Assyrians, their aggression continues, and Nahum predicts their downfall.

Habakkuk   Why are things so unfair? Habakkuk wrestles with the questions of suffering and injustice.

Zephaniah   The Lord will come. The prophet tells of the way in which God will purify the people of Judah, and through them bless all the nations.

Haggai   The new temple. The returning exiles are encouraged to rebuild their city, starting first with the temple and placing God's dwelling place at the centre of all their activity.

Zechariah   A sign of God's presence. Zechariah, echoing much of Haggai, encourages the people to rebuild the temple as the place to which the Messiah will come.

Malachi   Waking the dead. Malachi faces the dispassionate response of a nation that has lost interest in God's promises of salvation.

The New Testament

Matthew   Writing for a mainly Jewish audience, Matthew seeks to show how Jesus was the fulfilment of all that was promised by Moses and the prophets.

Mark   A graphic and fast-moving account of the life of Jesus, aimed at a non-Jewish audience.

Luke   The story-teller's Gospel, including many events and parables of real human interest.

John   The "theological" Gospel, which seeks to reflect upon the significance of Jesus' words and actions.

Acts   The first steps of exploration by Jesus' followers after his death.

Romans   Paul writes about the nature of Christian belief, and covers fundamental issues like suffering and redemption, time and eternity, creation, grace, and forgiveness.

1 Corinthians   A plan of action for Christian living, addressed to a church beset with problems of morality and disunity.

2 Corinthians   A sequel to the first letter, in which Paul seeks to re-establish his integrity as an apostle in the face of false teaching from others.

Galatians   Covering some of the topics from Romans, Paul tells of the freedom that comes to us in Christ.

Ephesians   A joyful proclamation from prison, which tells how knowledge of Christ is able to transfigure our present sufferings.

Philippians   Continuing the theme of joy found in Ephesians, this letter helps us to discover the nature of Christ as the source of life.

Colossians   An antidote to those who impose beliefs from other sects and cults.

1 Thessalonians   An early letter from Paul, addressing specific issues with which the Thessalonian church was particularly concerned.

2 Thessalonians   A second letter which seeks to reinforce the points Paul raised in his first letter, and address the nature of Christ's second coming.

1 Timothy   A letter to plan for the future. Paul outlines the needs and priorities for the continuing pastoral work of the church.

2 Timothy   A personal message from Paul to Timothy, written before his death.

Titus   Practical advice for a young church, seeking to grow in difficult circumstances.

Philemon   A message to proclaim that all are equal in Christ, as Philemon is urged to forgive a runaway slave.

Hebrews   Probably written to a group of Jews (or those who had a good working knowledge of the Hebrew Scriptures), this letter seeks to encourage those who are being tempted to give up their new-found Christian faith.

James   James encourages his readers to match their faith with practical action.

1 Peter   Peter's letter faces the suffering and hardship that was a daily reality for many early Christians, and offers them encouragement and support.

2 Peter   This second letter moves away from problems coming from outside the church to address specific problems of belief within the church.

1 John   A letter explaining the basics of Christian belief, addressed to Christians who were probably from a non-Jewish background.

2 John   A shorter letter to re-emphasize the basics of faith and warn against those who are corrupting it by false teaching.

3 John   An even shorter letter, almost in the manner of a postscript, reminding the Christian community not to turn away those who have come bearing the good news about Christ.

Jude   A short but hard-hitting message, reminding the Christian community to maintain their faith and good lifestyle.

Revelation   A prophetic series of visions, which points to the future by showing how good will overcome evil. It brings the New Testament to an end by echoing the book of Genesis, describing the creation of a new heaven and a new earth.

THE
OLD TESTAMENT

Genesis

Chosen by God

The Jews as a nation have not been particularly significant in world history. They have been led by some dubious characters, and behaved in a fairly ungodly way, but they are convinced that God relies on them to show himself to the world. The Old Testament is the record of how God touched their lives. They found that nothing was outside his concern and that there was always something new to discover about him. So they used all sorts of ways to try to describe God: history, poetry, stories, proverbs and more, because there are never enough words.

Special

The people of Israel give a special place to the first five books of the Bible, which are often as a group called "The Pentateuch". The Jews call them "Torah", which literally means "law", but is perhaps better translated as "rule of life". In them they find everything they need for knowing and following God.

God Loves the World

The book of Genesis begins at the beginning by describing how the world was made and how the first human beings in it behaved. One of the main ideas in the minds of the people who wrote things that are in the Bible was that God loved his world, and wanted to be loved by the people he had put there. The only really important question for humans is, "How should we respond to God's love?" Stories like the one about how the world was made were not told for their own sake but as good ways of answering that great question.

Order—Not Chaos

A close look at the first two chapters of Genesis illustrates this. In chapter 1, God brought order out of watery chaos, called for the world to exist, and filled it with living things. He crowned his efforts by creating people who had a special job of keeping God's order in the world. In chapter 2 God started with desert land, watered and planted it, then put a man in it. Animals were made to keep man company, but he was only satisfied when he was given a female made out of his own flesh. The writer of Genesis chose to use both these two stories; not because he was trying to tell us what happened at the beginning of the world, but what God's original intentions for the world were. Each story has something to say about that and so they are both in Genesis. Chapter 1 tells how people are made in

God's image and are his representatives on earth. Chapter 2 concentrates on what the people's relationships were with each other and with God, and goes on to tell how those relationships developed.

A Promise to Care

The first eleven chapters of Genesis are stories about the early days of humankind. The writers often used popular stories from that part of the world (the Middle East) when they were helpful in telling great truths about God and his world. For example, the story of Noah tells us about God rescuing his spoilt world by choosing a special person to act for him. Then God made a solemn promise to care for Noah and his descendants for ever.

Abraham, Isaac, and Jacob

We begin to hear how God will carry out his promises when, in chapter twelve, we meet Abraham. The stage has narrowed, both in terms of people and places. From now on the action concerns only those people and nations who are involved with Abraham and his descendants.

A National Saga

The people of Israel knew who their ancestors were and where they had come from, but those who wrote down the national sagas made what can seem like surprising decisions when choosing what material to include. Why, for example, do we read so little about Isaac himself, when there are three stories about a wife being passed off as a sister? (12:10–20, 20:1–18, 26:6–11). Ancestor sagas from all countries are like this. When a nation speaks about its ancestors it is saying who it is and what hopes it has for the future. It thinks of the national character, looks at how it was in the past, and hopes that some of the characteristics will be passed on to future generations.

Faithfulness to God

The compilers of Genesis tried to show that the most important thing about Israel was the people's relationship with God. He had put them in the land of Canaan and promised always to care for them. So they should trust him, be faithful to him, and encourage other people to believe in him. All too often the Israelites failed; by worshipping other gods, putting their trust in foreign alliances, or being proud and nationalistic. So the stories had to concentrate on the people's faithfulness, and more importantly on how God fulfilled his promises even when things seemed hopeless. We see how Abraham left his homeland before he had a child. He and Isaac and Jacob did not own the land they lived in, yet they persisted in following God. And at the end of Genesis, the story of Joseph shows God's faithfulness in a situation which would have seemed impossible.

The Beginning

1 In the beginning God created the heavens and the earth. [2]Now the earth was[a] formless and empty, darkness was over the surface of the deep, and the Spirit of God was hovering over the waters.

[3]And God said, "Let there be light," and there was light. [4]God saw that the light was good, and he separated the light from the darkness. [5]God called the light "day", and the darkness he called "night". And there was evening, and there was morning—the first day.

[6]And God said, "Let there be an expanse between the waters to separate water from water." [7]So God made the expanse and separated the water under the expanse from the water above it. And it was so. [8]God called the expanse "sky". And there was evening, and there was morning—the second day.

[9]And God said, "Let the water under the sky be gathered to one place, and let dry ground appear." And it was so. [10]God called the dry ground "land", and the gathered waters he called "seas". And God saw that it was good.

[11]Then God said, "Let the land produce vegetation: seed-bearing plants and trees on the land that bear fruit with seed in it, according to their various kinds." And it was so. [12]The land produced vegetation: plants bearing seed according to their kinds and trees bearing fruit with seed in it according to their kinds. And God saw that it was good. [13]And there was evening, and there was morning—the third day.

[14]And God said, "Let there be lights in the expanse of the sky to separate the day from the night, and let them serve as signs to mark seasons and days and years, [15]and let them be lights in the expanse of the sky to give light on the earth." And it was so. [16]God made two great lights—the greater light to govern the day and the lesser light to govern the night. He also made the stars. [17]God set them in the expanse of the sky to give light on the earth, [18]to govern the day and the night, and to separate light from darkness. And God saw that it was good. [19]And there was evening, and there was morning—the fourth day.

[20]And God said, "Let the water teem with living creatures, and let birds fly above the earth across the expanse of the sky." [21]So God created the great creatures of the sea and every living and moving thing with which the water teems, according to their kinds, and every winged bird according to its kind. And God saw that it was good. [22]God blessed them and said, "Be fruitful and increase in number and fill the water in the seas, and let the birds increase on the earth." [23]And there was evening, and there was morning—the fifth day.

[24]And God said, "Let the land produce living creatures according to their kinds: livestock, creatures that move along the ground, and wild animals, each according to its kind." And it was so. [25]God made the wild animals according to their kinds, the livestock according to their kinds, and all the creatures that move along the ground according to their kinds. And God saw that it was good.

[26]Then God said, "Let us make man in our image, in our likeness, and let them rule over the fish of the sea and the birds of the air, over the livestock, over all the earth,[b] and over all the creatures that move along the ground."

[27]So God created man
in his own image,
in the image of God
he created him;
male and female
he created them.

[28]God blessed them and said to them, "Be fruitful and increase in number; fill the earth and subdue it. Rule over the fish of the sea and the birds of the air and over every living creature that moves on the ground."

[29]Then God said, "I give you every seed-bearing plant on the face of the whole earth and every tree that has fruit with seed in it. They will be yours for food. [30]And to all the beasts of the earth and all the birds of the air and all the creatures that move on the ground—everything that has the breath of life in it—I give every green plant for food." And it was so.

[31]God saw all that he had made, and it was very good. And there was evening, and there was morning—the sixth day.

2 Thus the heavens and the earth were completed in all their vast array.

[2]By the seventh day God had finished the work he had been doing; so on the seventh day he rested[a] from all his work. [3]And God blessed the seventh day and made it holy, because on it he rested from all the work of creating that he had done.

Adam and Eve

[4]This is the account of the heavens and the earth when they were created.

When the LORD God made the earth and the heavens—[5]and no shrub of the field had yet appeared on the earth[b] and no plant of the field had yet sprung up, for the LORD God had not sent rain on the earth[b] and there was no man to work the ground, [6]but streams[c] came up from the earth and watered the whole surface of the ground—[7]the LORD God formed the man[d] from the dust of the ground and breathed into his nostrils the breath of life, and the man became a living being.

[8]Now the LORD God had planted a garden in the east, in Eden; and there he put the man he had formed.

---

a2 Or possibly *became*   b26 Hebrew; Syriac *all the wild animals*   a2 Or *ceased*; also in verse 3
b5 Or *land*; also in verse 6   c6 Or *mist*
d7 The Hebrew for *man (adam)* sounds like and may be related to the Hebrew for *ground (adamah)*; it is also the name *Adam* (see Gen. 2:20).

⁹And the LORD God made all kinds of trees grow out of the ground — trees that were pleasing to the eye and good for food. In the middle of the garden were the tree of life and the tree of the knowledge of good and evil.

¹⁰A river watering the garden flowed from Eden; from there it was separated into four headwaters. ¹¹The name of the first is the Pishon; it winds through the entire land of Havilah, where there is gold. ¹²(The gold of that land is good; aromatic resin *e* and onyx are also there.) ¹³The name of the second river is the Gihon; it winds through the entire land of Cush. *f* ¹⁴The name of the third river is the Tigris; it runs along the east side of Asshur. And the fourth river is the Euphrates.

¹⁵The LORD God took the man and put him in the Garden of Eden to work it and take care of it. ¹⁶And the LORD God commanded the man, "You are free to eat from any tree in the garden; ¹⁷but you must not eat from the tree of the knowledge of good and evil, for when you eat of it you will surely die."

¹⁸The LORD God said, "It is not good for the man to be alone. I will make a helper suitable for him." ¹⁹Now the LORD God had formed out of the ground all the beasts of the field and all the birds of the air. He brought them to the man to see what he would name them; and whatever the man called each living creature, that was its name. ²⁰So the man gave names to all the livestock, the birds of the air and all the beasts of the field.

But for Adam *g* no suitable helper was found. ²¹So the LORD God caused the man to fall into a deep sleep; and while he was sleeping, he took one of the man's ribs *h* and closed up the place with flesh. ²²Then the LORD God made a woman from the rib *i* he had taken out of the man, and he brought her to the man.

²³The man said,

"This is now bone of my bones
    and flesh of my flesh;
she shall be called 'woman',*j*
    for she was taken out of man."

²⁴For this reason a man will leave his father and mother and be united to his wife, and they will become one flesh.

²⁵The man and his wife were both naked, and they felt no shame.

The Fall of Man

3 Now the serpent was more crafty than any of the wild animals the LORD God had made. He said to the woman, "Did God really say, 'You must not eat from any tree in the garden'?"

3:1   It was Adam and Eve's lack of trust in God which spoiled their relationship with him and with each other, with other creatures, and the earth itself (3:15–19).

---

²The woman said to the serpent, "We may eat fruit from the trees in the garden, ³but God did say, 'You must not eat fruit from the tree that is in the middle of the garden, and you must not touch it, or you will die.' "

⁴"You will not surely die," the serpent said to the woman. ⁵"For God knows that when you eat of it your eyes will be opened, and you will be like God, knowing good and evil."

⁶When the woman saw that the fruit of the tree was good for food and pleasing to the eye, and also desirable for gaining wisdom, she took some and ate it. She also gave some to her husband, who was with her, and he ate it. ⁷Then the eyes of both of them were opened, and they realised that they were naked; so they sewed fig leaves together and made coverings for themselves.

⁸Then the man and his wife heard the sound of the LORD God as he was walking in the garden in the cool of the day, and they hid from the LORD God among the trees of the garden. ⁹But the LORD God called to the man, "Where are you?"

¹⁰He answered, "I heard you in the garden, and I was afraid because I was naked; so I hid."

¹¹And he said, "Who told you that you were naked? Have you eaten from the tree from which I commanded you not to eat?"

¹²The man said, "The woman you put here with me — she gave me some fruit from the tree, and I ate it."

¹³Then the LORD God said to the woman, "What is this you have done?"

The woman said, "The serpent deceived me, and I ate."

¹⁴So the LORD God said to the serpent, "Because you have done this,

"Cursed are you above all the livestock
    and all the wild animals!
You will crawl on your belly
    and you will eat dust
    all the days of your life.
¹⁵And I will put enmity
    between you and the woman,
    and between your offspring *a* and hers;
he will crush *b* your head,
    and you will strike his heel."

¹⁶To the woman he said,

"I will greatly increase your pains in childbearing;
    with pain you will give birth to children.
Your desire will be for your husband,
    and he will rule over you."

¹⁷To Adam he said, "Because you listened to your wife and ate from the tree about which I commanded you, 'You must not eat of it,'

"Cursed is the ground because of you;
    through painful toil you will eat of it
    all the days of your life.
¹⁸It will produce thorns and thistles for you,
    and you will eat the plants of the field.
¹⁹By the sweat of your brow
    you will eat your food
until you return to the ground,
    since from it you were taken;

for dust you are
  and to dust you will return."

20Adam*c* named his wife Eve,*d* because she would become the mother of all the living.

21The LORD God made garments of skin for Adam and his wife and clothed them. 22And the LORD God said, "The man has now become like one of us, knowing good and evil. He must not be allowed to reach out his hand and take also from the tree of life and eat, and live for ever." 23So the LORD God banished him from the Garden of Eden to work the ground from which he had been taken. 24After he drove the man out, he placed on the east side*e* of the Garden of Eden cherubim and a flaming sword flashing back and forth to guard the way to the tree of life.

Cain and Abel

4 Adam*a* lay with his wife Eve, and she became pregnant and gave birth to Cain.*b* She said, "With the help of the LORD I have brought forth*c* a man." 2Later she gave birth to his brother Abel.

Now Abel kept flocks, and Cain worked the soil. 3In the course of time Cain brought some of the fruits of the soil as an offering to the LORD. 4But Abel brought fat portions from some of the firstborn of his flock. The LORD looked with favour on Abel and his offering, 5but on Cain and his offering he did not look with favour. So Cain was very angry, and his face was downcast.

4:5   Cain was upset that his offering was rejected. Even brothers can feel anger and jealousy towards one another, and in this case it led to violence. Jesus said that anger and lack of respect are very real sins because they are the motivation behind bad actions (Matthew 5:21–22).

6Then the LORD said to Cain, "Why are you angry? Why is your face downcast? 7If you do what is right, will you not be accepted? But if you do not do what is right, sin is crouching at your door; it desires to have you, but you must master it."

8Now Cain said to his brother Abel, "Let's go out to the field."*d* And while they were in the field, Cain attacked his brother Abel and killed him.

9Then the LORD said to Cain, "Where is your brother Abel?"

"I don't know," he replied. "Am I my brother's keeper?"

10The LORD said, "What have you done? Listen! Your brother's blood cries out to me from the ground. 11Now you are under a curse and driven from the ground, which opened its mouth to receive your brother's blood from your hand. 12When you work the ground, it will no longer yield its crops for you. You will be a restless wanderer on the earth."

13Cain said to the LORD, "My punishment is more than I can bear. 14Today you are driving me from the land, and I will be hidden from your presence; I will be a restless wanderer on the earth, and whoever finds me will kill me."

15But the LORD said to him, "Not so;*e* if anyone kills Cain, he will suffer vengeance seven times over." Then the LORD put a mark on Cain so that no-one who found him would kill him. 16So Cain went out from the LORD's presence and lived in the land of Nod,*f* east of Eden.

17Cain lay with his wife, and she became pregnant and gave birth to Enoch. Cain was then building a city, and he named it after his son Enoch. 18To Enoch was born Irad, and Irad was the father of Mehujael, and Mehujael was the father of Methushael, and Methushael was the father of Lamech.

19Lamech married two women, one named Adah and the other Zillah. 20Adah gave birth to Jabal; he was the father of those who live in tents and raise livestock. 21His brother's name was Jubal; he was the father of all who play the harp and flute. 22Zillah also had a son, Tubal-Cain, who forged all kinds of tools out of*g* bronze and iron. Tubal-Cain's sister was Naamah.

23Lamech said to his wives,

"Adah and Zillah, listen to me;
  wives of Lamech, hear my words.
I have killed*h* a man for wounding me,
  a young man for injuring me.
24If Cain is avenged seven times,
  then Lamech seventy-seven times."

25Adam lay with his wife again, and she gave birth to a son and named him Seth,*i* saying, "God has granted me another child in place of Abel, since Cain killed him." 26Seth also had a son, and he named him Enosh.

At that time men began to call on*j* the name of the LORD.

From Adam to Noah

5 This is the written account of Adam's line.

When God created man, he made him in the likeness of God. 2He created them male and female and blessed them. And when they were created, he called them "man".*a*

3When Adam had lived 130 years, he had a son in his own likeness, in his own image; and he named him Seth. 4After Seth was born, Adam lived 800 years and had other sons and daughters. 5Altogether, Adam lived 930 years, and then he died.

6When Seth had lived 105 years, he became the father*b* of Enosh. 7And after he became the father of Enosh, Seth lived 807 years and had other sons and daughters. 8Altogether, Seth lived 912 years, and then he died.

9When Enosh had lived 90 years, he became the

---

c20 Or *The man*   *d20 Eve* probably means *living.*   *e24* Or *placed in front*   *a1* Or *The man*
b1 Cain sounds like the Hebrew for *brought forth* or *acquired.*   *c1* Or *have acquired*
d8 Samaritan Pentateuch, Septuagint, Vulgate and Syriac; Masoretic Text does not have *"Let's go out to the field."*
e15 Septuagint, Vulgate and Syriac; Hebrew *Very well*   *f16 Nod* means *wandering* (see verses 12 and 14).
g22 Or *who instructed all who work in*   *h23* Or *I will kill*   *i25 Seth* probably means *granted.*
j26 Or *to proclaim*   *a2* Hebrew *adam*   *b6 Father* may mean *ancestor*; also in verses 7–26.

father of Kenan. ¹⁰And after he became the father of Kenan, Enosh lived 815 years and had other sons and daughters. ¹¹Altogether, Enosh lived 905 years, and then he died.

¹²When Kenan had lived 70 years, he became the father of Mahalalel. ¹³And after he became the father of Mahalalel, Kenan lived 840 years and had other sons and daughters. ¹⁴Altogether, Kenan lived 910 years, and then he died.

¹⁵When Mahalalel had lived 65 years, he became the father of Jared. ¹⁶And after he became the father of Jared, Mahalalel lived 830 years and had other sons and daughters. ¹⁷Altogether, Mahalalel lived 895 years, and then he died.

¹⁸When Jared had lived 162 years, he became the father of Enoch. ¹⁹And after he became the father of Enoch, Jared lived 800 years and had other sons and daughters. ²⁰Altogether, Jared lived 962 years, and then he died.

²¹When Enoch had lived 65 years, he became the father of Methuselah. ²²And after he became the father of Methuselah, Enoch walked with God 300 years and had other sons and daughters. ²³Altogether, Enoch lived 365 years. ²⁴Enoch walked with God; then he was no more, because God took him away.

²⁵When Methuselah had lived 187 years, he became the father of Lamech. ²⁶And after he became the father of Lamech, Methuselah lived 782 years and had other sons and daughters. ²⁷Altogether, Methuselah lived 969 years, and then he died.

²⁸When Lamech had lived 182 years, he had a son. ²⁹He named him Noah^c and said, "He will comfort us in the labour and painful toil of our hands caused by the ground the LORD has cursed." ³⁰After Noah was born, Lamech lived 595 years and had other sons and daughters. ³¹Altogether, Lamech lived 777 years, and then he died.

³²After Noah was 500 years old, he became the father of Shem, Ham and Japheth.

The Flood

6 When men began to increase in number on the earth and daughters were born to them, ²the sons of God saw that the daughters of men were beautiful, and they married any of them they chose. ³Then the LORD said, "My Spirit will not contend with^a man for ever, for he is mortal;^{b} his days will be a hundred and twenty years."

6:1–2   It is not clear whether these were angels or prehistoric men, but the point of this part of the story is clear. All the good instincts with which people were created, like the desire for faithful marriage (2:24), have been abused. There is nothing in the world which is not infected by sin.

---

⁴The Nephilim were on the earth in those days — and also afterwards — when the sons of God went to the daughters of men and had children by them. They were the heroes of old, men of renown.

⁵The LORD saw how great man's wickedness on the earth had become, and that every inclination of the thoughts of his heart was only evil all the time. ⁶The LORD was grieved that he had made man on the earth, and his heart was filled with pain. ⁷So the LORD said, "I will wipe mankind, whom I have created, from the face of the earth — men and animals, and creatures that move along the ground, and birds of the air — for I am grieved that I have made them." ⁸But Noah found favour in the eyes of the LORD.

⁹This is the account of Noah.

Noah was a righteous man, blameless among the people of his time, and he walked with God. ¹⁰Noah had three sons: Shem, Ham and Japheth.

¹¹Now the earth was corrupt in God's sight and was full of violence. ¹²God saw how corrupt the earth had become, for all the people on earth had corrupted their ways. ¹³So God said to Noah, "I am going to put an end to all people, for the earth is filled with violence because of them. I am surely going to destroy both them and the earth. ¹⁴So make yourself an ark of cypress^c wood; make rooms in it and coat it with pitch inside and out. ¹⁵This is how you are to build it: The ark is to be 450 feet long, 75 feet wide and 45 feet high.^{d} ¹⁶Make a roof for it and finish^e the ark to within 18 inches^f of the top. Put a door in the side of the ark and make lower, middle and upper decks. ¹⁷I am going to bring floodwaters on the earth to destroy all life under the heavens, every creature that has the breath of life in it. Everything on earth will perish. ¹⁸But I will establish my covenant with you, and you will enter the ark — you and your sons and your wife and your sons' wives with you. ¹⁹You are to bring into the ark two of all living creatures, male and female, to keep them alive with you. ²⁰Two of every kind of bird, of every kind of animal and of every kind of creature that moves along the ground will come to you to be kept alive. ²¹You are to take every kind of food that is to be eaten and store it away as food for you and for them."

²²Noah did everything just as God commanded him.

7 The LORD then said to Noah, "Go into the ark, you and your whole family, because I have found you righteous in this generation. ²Take with you seven^a of every kind of clean animal, a male and its mate, and two of every kind of unclean animal, a male and its mate, ³and also seven of every kind of bird, male and female, to keep their various kinds alive throughout the earth. ⁴Seven days from now I will send rain on the earth for forty days and forty nights, and I will wipe from the face of the earth every living creature I have made."

⁵And Noah did all that the LORD commanded him.

⁶Noah was six hundred years old when the floodwaters came on the earth. ⁷And Noah and his sons and

---

^{c}29 *Noah* sounds like the Hebrew for *comfort.*
^{c}14 The meaning of the Hebrew for this word is uncertain.
^{d}15 Hebrew *300 cubits long, 50 cubits wide and 30 cubits high* (about 140 metres long, 23 metres wide and 13.5 metres high)
^{e}16 Or *Make an opening for light by finishing* ^{f}16 Hebrew *a cubit* (about 0.5 metre)
^{a}3 Or *My spirit will not remain in* ^{b}3 Or *corrupt*
^{a}2 Or *seven pairs;* also in verse 3

his wife and his sons' wives entered the ark to escape the waters of the flood. [8]Pairs of clean and unclean animals, of birds and of all creatures that move along the ground, [9]male and female, came to Noah and entered the ark, as God had commanded Noah. [10]And after the seven days the floodwaters came on the earth.

[11]In the six hundredth year of Noah's life, on the seventeenth day of the second month—on that day all the springs of the great deep burst forth, and the floodgates of the heavens were opened. [12]And rain fell on the earth for forty days and forty nights.

[13]On that very day Noah and his sons, Shem, Ham and Japheth, together with his wife and the wives of his three sons, entered the ark. [14]They had with them every wild animal according to its kind, all livestock according to their kinds, every creature that moves along the ground according to its kind and every bird according to its kind, everything with wings. [15]Pairs of all creatures that have the breath of life in them came to Noah and entered the ark. [16]The animals going in were male and female of every living thing, as God had commanded Noah. Then the LORD shut him in.

[17]For forty days the flood kept coming on the earth, and as the waters increased they lifted the ark high above the earth. [18]The waters rose and increased greatly on the earth, and the ark floated on the surface of the water. [19]They rose greatly on the earth, and all the high mountains under the entire heavens were covered. [20]The waters rose and covered the mountains to a depth of more than twenty feet.[b,c] [21]Every living thing that moved on the earth perished—birds, livestock, wild animals, all the creatures that swarm over the earth, and all mankind. [22]Everything on dry land that had the breath of life in its nostrils died. [23]Every living thing on the face of the earth was wiped out; men and animals and the creatures that move along the ground and the birds of the air were wiped from the earth. Only Noah was left, and those with him in the ark.

7:18 There is an ancient Babylonian story of a flood, in which the waters are beyond the control of the gods. In this story, however, the continuation of night and day and the presence of the ark showed that God was in control. The chaos of water was only allowed to return because he allowed it to.

---

[24]The waters flooded the earth for a hundred and fifty days.

8 But God remembered Noah and all the wild animals and the livestock that were with him in the ark, and he sent a wind over the earth, and the waters receded. [2]Now the springs of the deep and the floodgates of the heavens had been closed, and the rain had stopped falling from the sky. [3]The water receded steadily from the earth. At the end of the hundred and fifty days the water had gone down, [4]and on the seventeenth day of the seventh month the ark came to rest on the mountains of Ararat. [5]The waters continued to recede until the tenth month, and on the first day of the tenth month the tops of the mountains became visible.

[6]After forty days Noah opened the window he had made in the ark [7]and sent out a raven, and it kept flying back and forth until the water had dried up from the earth. [8]Then he sent out a dove to see if the water had receded from the surface of the ground. [9]But the dove could find no place to set its feet because there was water over all the surface of the earth; so it returned to Noah in the ark. He reached out his hand and took the dove and brought it back to himself in the ark. [10]He waited seven more days and again sent out the dove from the ark. [11]When the dove returned to him in the evening, there in its beak was a freshly plucked olive leaf! Then Noah knew that the water had receded from the earth. [12]He waited seven more days and sent the dove out again, but this time it did not return to him.

[13]By the first day of the first month of Noah's six hundred and first year, the water had dried up from the earth. Noah then removed the covering from the ark and saw that the surface of the ground was dry. [14]By the twenty-seventh day of the second month the earth was completely dry.

[15]Then God said to Noah, [16]"Come out of the ark, you and your wife and your sons and their wives. [17]Bring out every kind of living creature that is with you—the birds, the animals, and all the creatures that move along the ground—so they can multiply on the earth and be fruitful and increase in number upon it."

[18]So Noah came out, together with his sons and his wife and his sons' wives. [19]All the animals and all the creatures that move along the ground and all the birds—everything that moves on the earth—came out of the ark, one kind after another.

[20]Then Noah built an altar to the LORD and, taking some of all the clean animals and clean birds, he sacrificed burnt offerings on it. [21]The LORD smelled the pleasing aroma and said in his heart: "Never again will I curse the ground because of man, even though[a] every inclination of his heart is evil from childhood. And never again will I destroy all living creatures, as I have done.

[22]"As long as the earth endures,
   seedtime and harvest,
   cold and heat,
   summer and winter,
   day and night
   will never cease."

God's Covenant With Noah

9 Then God blessed Noah and his sons, saying to them, "Be fruitful and increase in number and fill the earth. [2]The fear and dread of you will fall upon all the beasts of the earth and all the birds of the air, upon every creature that moves along the ground, and upon all the fish of the sea; they are given into your hands. [3]Everything that lives and moves will be food for you. Just as I gave you the green plants, I now give you everything.

---

b20 Hebrew *fifteen cubits* (about 6.9 metres)   c20 Or *rose more than twenty feet, and the mountains were covered*
a21 Or *man, for*

[4]"But you must not eat meat that has its lifeblood still in it. [5]And for your lifeblood I will surely demand an accounting. I will demand an accounting from every animal. And from each man, too, I will demand an accounting for the life of his fellow man.

[6]"Whoever sheds the blood of man,
   by man shall his blood be shed;
for in the image of God
   has God made man.

[7]As for you, be fruitful and increase in number; multiply on the earth and increase upon it."

[8]Then God said to Noah and to his sons with him: [9]"I now establish my covenant with you and with your descendants after you [10]and with every living creature that was with you—the birds, the livestock and all the wild animals, all those that came out of the ark with you—every living creature on earth. [11]I establish my covenant with you: Never again will all life be cut off by the waters of a flood; never again will there be a flood to destroy the earth."

[12]And God said, "This is the sign of the covenant I am making between me and you and every living creature with you, a covenant for all generations to come: [13]I have set my rainbow in the clouds, and it will be the sign of the covenant between me and the earth. [14]Whenever I bring clouds over the earth and the rainbow appears in the clouds, [15]I will remember my covenant between me and you and all living creatures of every kind. Never again will the waters become a flood to destroy all life. [16]Whenever the rainbow appears in the clouds, I will see it and remember the everlasting covenant between God and all living creatures of every kind on the earth."

9:15   A covenant is a binding agreement between two parties. It was a gracious act of God and a mark of his love to commit himself like this. Because he loves everything he has made, this first covenant was made between him and every living creature.

---

[17]So God said to Noah, "This is the sign of the covenant I have established between me and all life on the earth."

The Sons of Noah

[18]The sons of Noah who came out of the ark were Shem, Ham and Japheth. (Ham was the father of Canaan.) [19]These were the three sons of Noah, and from them came the people who were scattered over the earth.

[20]Noah, a man of the soil, proceeded[a] to plant a vineyard. [21]When he drank some of its wine, he became drunk and lay uncovered inside his tent. [22]Ham, the father of Canaan, saw his father's nakedness and told his two brothers outside. [23]But Shem and Japheth took a garment and laid it across their shoulders; then they walked in backwards and covered their father's nakedness. Their faces were turned the other way so that they would not see their father's nakedness.

[24]When Noah awoke from his wine and found out what his youngest son had done to him, [25]he said,

"Cursed be Canaan!
   The lowest of slaves
   will he be to his brothers."

[26]He also said,

"Blessed be the LORD, the God of Shem!
   May Canaan be the slave of Shem.[b]
[27]May God extend the territory of Japheth;[c]
   may Japheth live in the tents of Shem,
   and may Canaan be his[d] slave."

[28]After the flood Noah lived 350 years. [29]Altogether, Noah lived 950 years, and then he died.

The Table of Nations

10   This is the account of Shem, Ham and Japheth, Noah's sons, who themselves had sons after the flood.

The Japhethites

[2]The sons[a] of Japheth:
   Gomer, Magog, Madai, Javan, Tubal, Meshech and Tiras.
[3]The sons of Gomer:
   Ashkenaz, Riphath and Togarmah.
[4]The sons of Javan:
   Elishah, Tarshish, the Kittim and the Rodanim.[b] [5](From these the maritime peoples spread out into their territories by their clans within their nations, each with its own language.)

The Hamites

[6]The sons of Ham:
   Cush, Mizraim,[c] Put and Canaan.
[7]The sons of Cush:
   Seba, Havilah, Sabtah, Raamah and Sabteca.
The sons of Raamah:
   Sheba and Dedan.

[8]Cush was the father[d] of Nimrod, who grew to be a mighty warrior on the earth. [9]He was a mighty hunter before the LORD; that is why it is said, "Like Nimrod, a mighty hunter before the LORD." [10]The first centres of his kingdom were Babylon, Erech, Akkad and Calneh, in[e] Shinar.[f] [11]From that land he went to Assyria, where he built Nineveh, Rehoboth Ir,[g] Calah [12]and Resen, which is between Nineveh and Calah; that is the great city.

---

a 20 Or *soil, was the first*   *b 26* Or *be his slave*   *c 27 Japheth* sounds like the Hebrew for *extend.*
d 27 Or *their*   *a 2 Sons* may mean *descendants* or *successors* or *nations*; also in verses 3, 4, 6, 7, 20–23, 29 and 31.
b 4 Some manuscripts of the Masoretic Text and Samaritan Pentateuch (see also Septuagint and 1 Chron. 1:7); most manuscripts of the Masoretic Text *Dodanim*   *c 6* That is, Egypt; also in verse 13
d 8 Father may mean *ancestor* or *predecessor* or *founder*; also in verses 13, 15, 24 and 26.   *e 10* Or *Erech and Akkad—all of them in*
f 10 That is, Babylonia   *g 11* Or *Nineveh with its city squares*

[13]Mizraim was the father of
the Ludites, Anamites, Lehabites, Naphtuhites, [14]Pathrusites, Casluhites (from whom
the Philistines came) and Caphtorites.
[15]Canaan was the father of
Sidon his firstborn,[h] and of the Hittites,
[16]Jebusites, Amorites, Girgashites, [17]Hivites,
Arkites, Sinites, [18]Arvadites, Zemarites and
Hamathites.

Later the Canaanite clans scattered [19]and the borders of Canaan reached from Sidon towards Gerar as
far as Gaza, and then towards Sodom, Gomorrah,
Admah and Zeboiim, as far as Lasha.

[20]These are the sons of Ham by their clans and languages, in their territories and nations.

The Semites

[21]Sons were also born to Shem, whose older brother
was[i] Japheth; Shem was the ancestor of all the sons
of Eber.

[22]The sons of Shem:
Elam, Asshur, Arphaxad, Lud and Aram.
[23]The sons of Aram:
Uz, Hul, Gether and Meshech.[j]
[24]Arphaxad was the father of[k] Shelah,
and Shelah the father of Eber.
[25]Two sons were born to Eber:
One was named Peleg,[l] because in his time
the earth was divided; his brother was named
Joktan.
[26]Joktan was the father of
Almodad, Sheleph, Hazarmaveth, Jerah,
[27]Hadoram, Uzal, Diklah, [28]Obal, Abimael,
Sheba, [29]Ophir, Havilah and Jobab. All these
were sons of Joktan.

[30]The region where they lived stretched from Mesha
towards Sephar, in the eastern hill country.

[31]These are the sons of Shem by their clans and languages, in their territories and nations.

[32]These are the clans of Noah's sons, according to
their lines of descent, within their nations. From these
the nations spread out over the earth after the flood.

The Tower of Babel

11 Now the whole world had one language and
a common speech. [2]As men moved east-
ward,[a] they found a plain in Shinar[b] and settled
there.
[3]They said to each other, "Come, let's make bricks
and bake them thoroughly." They used brick instead of
stone, and bitumen for mortar. [4]Then they said,
"Come, let us build ourselves a city, with a tower that
reaches to the heavens, so that we may make a name

for ourselves and not be scattered over the face of the
whole earth."
[5]But the LORD came down to see the city and the
tower that the men were building. [6]The LORD said, "If
as one people speaking the same language they have
begun to do this, then nothing they plan to do will be
impossible for them. [7]Come, let us go down and confuse their language so they will not understand each
other."
[8]So the LORD scattered them from there over all the
earth, and they stopped building the city. [9]That is why
it was called Babel[c]—because there the LORD confused the language of the whole world. From there the
LORD scattered them over the face of the whole earth.

From Shem to Abram

[10]This is the account of Shem.

Two years after the flood, when Shem was 100 years
old, he became the father[d] of Arphaxad. [11]And after
he became the father of Arphaxad, Shem lived 500
years and had other sons and daughters.

11:10   Although the story of Babel shows
that people are ambitious and that they use
their resources to try to compete with God,
his intentions for the world are not frustrated. The family tree shows how the family
saved in the flood leads directly to Abraham.
Through him, all people will receive the
blessing that had been lost in the Garden of
Eden.

---

[12]When Arphaxad had lived 35 years, he became
the father of Shelah. [13]And after he became the father
of Shelah, Arphaxad lived 403 years and had other sons
and daughters.[e]
[14]When Shelah had lived 30 years, he became the
father of Eber. [15]And after he became the father of
Eber, Shelah lived 403 years and had other sons and
daughters.
[16]When Eber had lived 34 years, he became the
father of Peleg. [17]And after he became the father of
Peleg, Eber lived 430 years and had other sons and
daughters.
[18]When Peleg had lived 30 years, he became the
father of Reu. [19]And after he became the father of
Reu, Peleg lived 209 years and had other sons and
daughters.
[20]When Reu had lived 32 years, he became the
father of Serug. [21]And after he became the father of
Serug, Reu lived 207 years and had other sons and
daughters.
[22]When Serug had lived 30 years, he became the
father of Nahor. [23]And after he became the father of

h15 Or of the Sidonians, the foremost   i21 Or Shem, the older brother of
j23 See Septuagint and 1 Chron. 1:17; Hebrew Mash.   k24 Hebrew; Septuagint father of Cainan, and Cainan was the father of
l25 Peleg means division.   a2 Or from the east; or in the east   b2 That is, Babylonia
c9 That is, Babylon; Babel sounds like the Hebrew for confused.   d10 Father may mean ancestor; also in verses 11–25.
e12,13 Hebrew; Septuagint (see also Luke 3:35, 36 and note at Gen. 10:24) 35 years, he became the father of Cainan. 13And after he
became the father of Cainan, Arphaxad lived 430 years and had other sons and daughters, and then he died. When Cainan had lived 130
years, he became the father of Shelah. And after he became the father of Shelah, Cainan lived 330 years and had other sons and daughters

Nahor, Serug lived 200 years and had other sons and daughters.

²⁴When Nahor had lived 29 years, he became the father of Terah. ²⁵And after he became the father of Terah, Nahor lived 119 years and had other sons and daughters.

²⁶After Terah had lived 70 years, he became the father of Abram, Nahor and Haran.

²⁷This is the account of Terah.

Terah became the father of Abram, Nahor and Haran. And Haran became the father of Lot. ²⁸While his father Terah was still alive, Haran died in Ur of the Chaldeans, in the land of his birth. ²⁹Abram and Nahor both married. The name of Abram's wife was Sarai, and the name of Nahor's wife was Milcah; she was the daughter of Haran, the father of both Milcah and Iscah. ³⁰Now Sarai was barren; she had no children.

³¹Terah took his son Abram, his grandson Lot son of Haran, and his daughter-in-law Sarai, the wife of his son Abram, and together they set out from Ur of the Chaldeans to go to Canaan. But when they came to Haran, they settled there.

³²Terah lived 205 years, and he died in Haran.

The Call of Abram

12 The LORD had said to Abram, "Leave your country, your people and your father's household and go to the land I will show you.

²"I will make you into a great nation
   and I will bless you;
I will make your name great,
   and you will be a blessing.
³I will bless those who bless you,
   and whoever curses you I will curse;
and all peoples on earth
   will be blessed through you."

⁴So Abram left, as the LORD had told him; and Lot went with him. Abram was seventy-five years old when he set out from Haran. ⁵He took his wife Sarai, his nephew Lot, all the possessions they had accumulated and the people they had acquired in Haran, and they set out for the land of Canaan, and they arrived there.

⁶Abram travelled through the land as far as the site of the great tree of Moreh at Shechem. At that time the Canaanites were in the land. ⁷The LORD appeared to Abram and said, "To your offspringᵃ I will give this land." So he built an altar there to the LORD, who had appeared to him.

⁸From there he went on towards the hills east of Bethel and pitched his tent, with Bethel on the west and Ai on the east. There he built an altar to the LORD and called on the name of the LORD. ⁹Then Abram set out and continued towards the Negev.

Abram in Egypt

¹⁰Now there was a famine in the land, and Abram went down to Egypt to live there for a while because the famine was severe. ¹¹As he was about to enter Egypt, he said to his wife Sarai, "I know what a beautiful woman you are. ¹²When the Egyptians see you, they will say, 'This is his wife.' Then they will kill me but will let you live. ¹³Say you are my sister, so that I will be treated well for your sake and my life will be spared because of you."

12:8   Notice how often words are used which show that Abraham was on the move. Even when he had built an altar to worship God he left it. God can never be captured in one place or situation, and he is always calling people to discover him in new ways.

---

¹⁴When Abram came to Egypt, the Egyptians saw that she was a very beautiful woman. ¹⁵And when Pharaoh's officials saw her, they praised her to Pharaoh, and she was taken into his palace. ¹⁶He treated Abram well for her sake, and Abram acquired sheep and cattle, male and female donkeys, menservants and maidservants, and camels.

¹⁷But the LORD inflicted serious diseases on Pharaoh and his household because of Abram's wife Sarai. ¹⁸So Pharaoh summoned Abram. "What have you done to me?" he said. "Why didn't you tell me she was your wife? ¹⁹Why did you say, 'She is my sister,' so that I took her to be my wife? Now then, here is your wife. Take her and go!" ²⁰Then Pharaoh gave orders about Abram to his men, and they sent him on his way, with his wife and everything he had.

Abram and Lot Separate

13 So Abram went up from Egypt to the Negev, with his wife and everything he had, and Lot went with him. ²Abram had become very wealthy in livestock and in silver and gold.

³From the Negev he went from place to place until he came to Bethel, to the place between Bethel and Ai where his tent had been earlier ⁴and where he had first built an altar. There Abram called on the name of the LORD.

⁵Now Lot, who was moving about with Abram, also had flocks and herds and tents. ⁶But the land could not support them while they stayed together, for their possessions were so great that they were not able to stay together. ⁷And quarrelling arose between Abram's herdsmen and the herdsmen of Lot. The Canaanites and Perizzites were also living in the land at that time.

⁸So Abram said to Lot, "Let's not have any quarrelling between you and me, or between your herdsmen and mine, for we are brothers. ⁹Is not the whole land before you? Let's part company. If you go to the left, I'll go to the right; if you go to the right, I'll go to the left."

¹⁰Lot looked up and saw that the whole plain of the Jordan was well watered, like the garden of the LORD, like the land of Egypt, towards Zoar. (This was before the LORD destroyed Sodom and Gomorrah.) ¹¹So Lot chose for himself the whole plain of the Jordan and set out towards the east. The two men parted company:

ᵃ7 Or seed

¹²Abram lived in the land of Canaan, while Lot lived among the cities of the plain and pitched his tents near Sodom. ¹³Now the men of Sodom were wicked and were sinning greatly against the LORD.

¹⁴The LORD said to Abram after Lot had parted from him, "Lift up your eyes from where you are and look north and south, east and west. ¹⁵All the land that you see I will give to you and your offspring[a] for ever. ¹⁶I will make your offspring like the dust of the earth, so that if anyone could count the dust, then your off-spring could be counted. ¹⁷Go, walk through the length and breadth of the land, for I am giving it to you."

¹⁸So Abram moved his tents and went to live near the great trees of Mamre at Hebron, where he built an altar to the LORD.

Abram Rescues Lot

14 At this time Amraphel king of Shinar,[a] Arioch king of Ellasar, Kedorlaomer king of Elam and Tidal king of Goiim ²went to war against Bera king of Sodom, Birsha king of Gomorrah, Shinab king of Admah, Shemeber king of Zeboiim, and the king of Bela (that is, Zoar). ³All these latter kings joined forces in the Valley of Siddim (the Salt Sea[b]). ⁴For twelve years they had been subject to Kedorlaomer, but in the thirteenth year they rebelled.

⁵In the fourteenth year, Kedorlaomer and the kings allied with him went out and defeated the Rephaites in Ashteroth Karnaim, the Zuzites in Ham, the Emites in Shaveh Kiriathaim ⁶and the Horites in the hill country of Seir, as far as El Paran near the desert. ⁷Then they turned back and went to En Mishpat (that is, Kadesh), and they conquered the whole territory of the Amalekites, as well as the Amorites who were living in Hazezon Tamar.

⁸Then the king of Sodom, the king of Gomorrah, the king of Admah, the king of Zeboiim and the king of Bela (that is, Zoar) marched out and drew up their battle lines in the Valley of Siddim ⁹against Kedorlaomer king of Elam, Tidal king of Goiim, Amraphel king of Shinar and Arioch king of Ellasar — four kings against five. ¹⁰Now the Valley of Siddim was full of tar pits, and when the kings of Sodom and Gomorrah fled, some of the men fell into them and the rest fled to the hills. ¹¹The four kings seized all the goods of Sodom and Gomorrah and all their food; then they went away. ¹²They also carried off Abram's nephew Lot and his possessions, since he was living in Sodom.

¹³One who had escaped came and reported this to Abram the Hebrew. Now Abram was living near the great trees of Mamre the Amorite, a brother[c] of Eshcol and Aner, all of whom were allied with Abram. ¹⁴When Abram heard that his relative had been taken captive, he called out the 318 trained men born in his household and went in pursuit as far as Dan. ¹⁵During the night Abram divided his men to attack them and he routed them, pursuing them as far as Hobah, north of Damascus. ¹⁶He recovered all the goods and brought back his relative Lot and his possessions, together with the women and the other people.

¹⁷After Abram returned from defeating Kedorlaomer and the kings allied with him, the king of Sodom came out to meet him in the Valley of Shaveh (that is, the King's Valley).

¹⁸Then Melchizedek king of Salem[d] brought out bread and wine. He was priest of God Most High, ¹⁹and he blessed Abram, saying,

"Blessed be Abram by God Most High,
    Creator[e] of heaven and earth.

14:18   Salem (Jerusalem) stayed in the hands of the Canaanites until David captured it and made it his capital (probably around 960 BC). There is a tradition that the Jerusalem priests were related to Melchizedek.

---

²⁰And blessed be[f] God Most High,
    who delivered your enemies into your hand."

Then Abram gave him a tenth of everything.

²¹The king of Sodom said to Abram, "Give me the people and keep the goods for yourself."

²²But Abram said to the king of Sodom, "I have raised my hand to the LORD, God Most High, Creator of heaven and earth, and have taken an oath ²³that I will accept nothing belonging to you, not even a thread or the thong of a sandal, so that you will never be able to say, 'I made Abram rich.' ²⁴I will accept nothing but what my men have eaten and the share that belongs to the men who went with me — to Aner, Eshcol and Mamre. Let them have their share."

God's Covenant With Abram

15 After this, the word of the LORD came to Abram in a vision:

"Do not be afraid, Abram.
    I am your shield,[a]
    your very great reward."[b]

²But Abram said, "O Sovereign LORD, what can you give me since I remain childless and the one who will inherit[c] my estate is Eliezer of Damascus?" ³And Abram said, "You have given me no children; so a servant in my household will be my heir." ⁴Then the word of the LORD came to him: "This man will not be your heir, but a son coming from your own body will be your heir." ⁵He took him outside and said, "Look up at the heavens and count the stars — if indeed you can count them." Then he said to him, "So shall your offspring be."

⁶Abram believed the LORD, and he credited it to him as righteousness.

⁷He also said to him, "I am the LORD, who brought you out of Ur of the Chaldeans to give you this land to take possession of it."

⁸But Abram said, "O Sovereign LORD, how can I know that I shall gain possession of it?" ⁹So the LORD said to him, "Bring me a heifer, a goat

---

a 15 Or *seed*; also in verse 16   *a 1* That is, Babylonia; also in verse 9   *b 3* That is, the Dead Sea
c 13 Or *a relative*; or *an ally*   *d 18* That is, Jerusalem   *e 19* Or *Possessor*; also in verse 22   *f 20* Or *And praise be to*
a 1 Or *sovereign*   *b 1* Or *shield; / your reward will be very great*   *c 2* The meaning of the Hebrew for this phrase is uncertain.

and a ram, each three years old, along with a dove and a young pigeon."

15:6   Abraham had not earned credit with God. He put Sarah at risk in Egypt, and himself at risk in battle, but these things did not make him righteous. It was because he had faith in God that God accepted him. Three times in the New Testament this verse is quoted (Romans 4:3, Galatians 3:6, James 2:23). Salvation comes from faith, not from an ability to keep the Law perfectly. Coming as early as it does in the Old Testament is a reassurance to believers of how much God cares for them.

---

¹⁰Abram brought all these to him, cut them in two and arranged the halves opposite each other; the birds, however, he did not cut in half. ¹¹Then birds of prey came down on the carcasses, but Abram drove them away.

¹²As the sun was setting, Abram fell into a deep sleep, and a thick and dreadful darkness came over him. ¹³Then the LORD said to him, "Know for certain that your descendants will be strangers in a country not their own, and they will be enslaved and ill-treated four hundred years. ¹⁴But I will punish the nation they serve as slaves, and afterwards they will come out with great possessions. ¹⁵You, however, will go to your fathers in peace and be buried at a good old age. ¹⁶In the fourth generation your descendants will come back here, for the sin of the Amorites has not yet reached its full measure."

¹⁷When the sun had set and darkness had fallen, a smoking brazier with a blazing torch appeared and passed between the pieces. ¹⁸On that day the LORD made a covenant with Abram and said, "To your descendants I give this land, from the river*d* of Egypt to the great river, the Euphrates — ¹⁹the land of the Kenites, Kenizzites, Kadmonites, ²⁰Hittites, Perizzites, Rephaites, ²¹Amorites, Canaanites, Girgashites and Jebusites."

Hagar and Ishmael

16 Now Sarai, Abram's wife, had borne him no children. But she had an Egyptian maidservant named Hagar; ²so she said to Abram, "The LORD has kept me from having children. Go, sleep with my maidservant; perhaps I can build a family through her."

Abram agreed to what Sarai said. ³So after Abram had been living in Canaan ten years, Sarai his wife took her Egyptian maidservant Hagar and gave her to her husband to be his wife. ⁴He slept with Hagar, and she conceived.

When she knew she was pregnant, she began to despise her mistress. ⁵Then Sarai said to Abram, "You are responsible for the wrong I am suffering. I put my servant in your arms, and now that she knows she is

pregnant, she despises me. May the LORD judge between you and me."

⁶"Your servant is in your hands," Abram said. "Do with her whatever you think best." Then Sarai ill-treated Hagar; so she fled from her.

⁷The angel of the LORD found Hagar near a spring in the desert; it was the spring that is beside the road to Shur. ⁸And he said, "Hagar, servant of Sarai, where have you come from, and where are you going?"

"I'm running away from my mistress Sarai," she answered.

⁹Then the angel of the LORD told her, "Go back to your mistress and submit to her." ¹⁰The angel added, "I will so increase your descendants that they will be too numerous to count."

¹¹The angel of the LORD also said to her:

"You are now with child
    and you will have a son.
You shall name him Ishmael,*a*
    for the LORD has heard of your misery.
¹²He will be a wild donkey of a man;
    his hand will be against everyone
    and everyone's hand against him,
and he will live in hostility
    towards*b* all his brothers."

¹³She gave this name to the LORD who spoke to her: "You are the God who sees me," for she said, "I have now seen*c* the One who sees me." ¹⁴That is why the well was called Beer Lahai Roi;*d* it is still there, between Kadesh and Bered.

¹⁵So Hagar bore Abram a son, and Abram gave the name Ishmael to the son she had borne. ¹⁶Abram was eighty-six years old when Hagar bore him Ishmael.

The Covenant of Circumcision

17 When Abram was ninety-nine years old, the LORD appeared to him and said, "I am God Almighty;*a* walk before me and be blameless. ²I will confirm my covenant between me and you and will greatly increase your numbers."

³Abram fell face down, and God said to him, ⁴"As for me, this is my covenant with you: You will be the father of many nations. ⁵No longer will you be called Abram;*b* your name will be Abraham,*c* for I have made you a father of many nations. ⁶I will make you very fruitful; I will make nations of you, and kings will come from you. ⁷I will establish my covenant as an everlasting covenant between me and you and your descendants after you for the generations to come, to be your God and the God of your descendants after you. ⁸The whole land of Canaan, where you are now an alien, I will give as an everlasting possession to you and your descendants after you; and I will be their God."

⁹Then God said to Abraham, "As for you, you must keep my covenant, you and your descendants after you for the generations to come. ¹⁰This is my covenant with you and your descendants after you, the covenant you are to keep: Every male among you shall be circumcised. ¹¹You are to undergo circumcision, and it will be

---

*d*18 Or *Wadi*   *a*11 *Ishmael* means *God hears.*   *b*12 Or *live to the east / of*
*d*14 *Beer Lahai Roi* means *well of the Living One who sees me.*   *a*1 Hebrew *El-Shaddai*   *b*5 *Abram* means *exalted father.*
*c*5 *Abraham* means *father of many.*   *c*13 Or *seen the back of*

the sign of the covenant between me and you. [12]For the generations to come every male among you who is eight days old must be circumcised, including those born in your household or bought with money from a foreigner — those who are not your offspring. [13]Whether born in your household or bought with your money, they must be circumcised. My covenant in your flesh is to be an everlasting covenant. [14]Any uncircumcised male, who has not been circumcised in the flesh, will be cut off from his people; he has broken my covenant."

[15]God also said to Abraham, "As for Sarai your wife, you are no longer to call her Sarai; her name will be Sarah. [16]I will bless her and will surely give you a son by her. I will bless her so that she will be the mother of nations; kings of peoples will come from her."

[17]Abraham fell face down; he laughed and said to himself, "Will a son be born to a man a hundred years old? Will Sarah bear a child at the age of ninety?" [18]And Abraham said to God, "If only Ishmael might live under your blessing!"

17:17   Both Abraham and Sarah (18:12) laughed at God's ridiculous promise. When their son was born he was called Isaac, which comes from the Hebrew word for laughter. They were both far too old to have children, but despite this human weakness God made the child who was to restore his delight in creation.

---

[19]Then God said, "Yes, but your wife Sarah will bear you a son, and you will call him Isaac.[d] I will establish my covenant with him as an everlasting covenant for his descendants after him. [20]And as for Ishmael, I have heard you: I will surely bless him; I will make him fruitful and will greatly increase his numbers. He will be the father of twelve rulers, and I will make him into a great nation. [21]But my covenant I will establish with Isaac, whom Sarah will bear to you by this time next year." [22]When he had finished speaking with Abraham, God went up from him.

[23]On that very day Abraham took his son Ishmael and all those born in his household or bought with his money, every male in his household, and circumcised them, as God told him. [24]Abraham was ninety-nine years old when he was circumcised, [25]and his son Ishmael was thirteen; [26]Abraham and his son Ishmael were both circumcised on that same day. [27]And every male in Abraham's household, including those born in his household or bought from a foreigner, was circumcised with him.

The Three Visitors

18 The LORD appeared to Abraham near the great trees of Mamre while he was sitting at the entrance to his tent in the heat of the day. [2]Abraham looked up and saw three men standing nearby. When he saw them, he hurried from the entrance of his tent to meet them and bowed low to the ground.

[3]He said, "If I have found favour in your eyes, my lord,[a] do not pass your servant by. [4]Let a little water be brought, and then you may all wash your feet and rest under this tree. [5]Let me get you something to eat, so you can be refreshed and then go on your way — now that you have come to your servant."

"Very well," they answered, "do as you say."

[6]So Abraham hurried into the tent to Sarah. "Quick," he said, "get three seahs[b] of fine flour and knead it and bake some bread."

[7]Then he ran to the herd and selected a choice, tender calf and gave it to a servant, who hurried to prepare it. [8]He then brought some curds and milk and the calf that had been prepared, and set these before them. While they ate, he stood near them under a tree.

[9]"Where is your wife Sarah?" they asked him.

"There, in the tent," he said.

[10]Then the LORD[c] said, "I will surely return to you about this time next year, and Sarah your wife will have a son."

Now Sarah was listening at the entrance to the tent, which was behind him. [11]Abraham and Sarah were already old and well advanced in years, and Sarah was past the age of childbearing. [12]So Sarah laughed to herself as she thought, "After I am worn out and my master[d] is old, will I now have this pleasure?"

[13]Then the LORD said to Abraham, "Why did Sarah laugh and say, 'Will I really have a child, now that I am old?' [14]Is anything too hard for the LORD? I will return to you at the appointed time next year and Sarah will have a son."

[15]Sarah was afraid, so she lied and said, "I did not laugh."

But he said, "Yes, you did laugh."

Abraham Pleads for Sodom

[16]When the men got up to leave, they looked down towards Sodom, and Abraham walked along with them to see them on their way. [17]Then the LORD said, "Shall I hide from Abraham what I am about to do? [18]Abraham will surely become a great and powerful nation, and all nations on earth will be blessed through him. [19]For I have chosen him, so that he will direct his children and his household after him to keep the way of the LORD by doing what is right and just, so that the LORD will bring about for Abraham what he has promised him."

[20]Then the LORD said, "The outcry against Sodom and Gomorrah is so great and their sin so grievous [21]that I will go down and see if what they have done is as bad as the outcry that has reached me. If not, I will know."

[22]The men turned away and went towards Sodom, but Abraham remained standing before the LORD.[e] [23]Then Abraham approached him and said: "Will you sweep away the righteous with the wicked? [24]What if there are fifty righteous people in the city? Will you really sweep it away and not spare[f] the place for the

---

d 19 Isaac means he laughs.   *a 3 Or O Lord*   *b 6 That is, probably about 39 pints (about 22 litres)*
c 10 Hebrew Then he   *d 12 Or husband*
e 22 Masoretic Text; an ancient Hebrew scribal tradition but the LORD remained standing before Abraham
f 24 Or forgive; also in verse 26

sake of the fifty righteous people in it? ²⁵Far be it from you to do such a thing—to kill the righteous with the wicked, treating the righteous and the wicked alike. Far be it from you! Will not the Judge⁸ of all the earth do right?"

²⁶The LORD said, "If I find fifty righteous people in the city of Sodom, I will spare the whole place for their sake."

²⁷Then Abraham spoke up again: "Now that I have been so bold as to speak to the Lord, though I am nothing but dust and ashes, ²⁸what if the number of the righteous is five less than fifty? Will you destroy the whole city because of five people?"

"If I find forty-five there," he said, "I will not destroy it."

²⁹Once again he spoke to him, "What if only forty are found there?"

He said, "For the sake of forty, I will not do it."

³⁰Then he said, "May the Lord not be angry, but let me speak. What if only thirty can be found there?"

He answered, "I will not do it if I find thirty there."

³¹Abraham said, "Now that I have been so bold as to speak to the Lord, what if only twenty can be found there?"

He said, "For the sake of twenty, I will not destroy it."

³²Then he said, "May the Lord not be angry, but let me speak just once more. What if only ten can be found there?"

He answered, "For the sake of ten, I will not destroy it."

³³When the LORD had finished speaking with Abraham, he left, and Abraham returned home.

Sodom and Gomorrah Destroyed

19 The two angels arrived at Sodom in the evening, and Lot was sitting in the gateway of the city. When he saw them, he got up to meet them and bowed down with his face to the ground. ²"My lords," he said, "please turn aside to your servant's house. You can wash your feet and spend the night and then go on your way early in the morning."

"No," they answered, "we will spend the night in the square."

³But he insisted so strongly that they did go with him and entered his house. He prepared a meal for them, baking bread without yeast, and they ate. ⁴Before they had gone to bed, all the men from every part of the city of Sodom—both young and old—surrounded the house. ⁵They called to Lot, "Where are the men who came to you tonight? Bring them out to us so that we can have sex with them."

⁶Lot went outside to meet them and shut the door behind him ⁷and said, "No, my friends. Don't do this wicked thing. ⁸Look, I have two daughters who have never slept with a man. Let me bring them out to you, and you can do what you like with them. But don't do anything to these men, for they have come under the protection of my roof."

⁹"Get out of our way," they replied. And they said, "This fellow came here as an alien, and now he wants to play the judge! We'll treat you worse than them." They kept bringing pressure on Lot and moved forward to break down the door.

¹⁰But the men inside reached out and pulled Lot back into the house and shut the door. ¹¹Then they struck the men who were at the door of the house, young and old, with blindness so that they could not find the door.

¹²The two men said to Lot, "Do you have anyone else here—sons-in-law, sons or daughters, or anyone else in the city who belongs to you? Get them out of here, ¹³because we are going to destroy this place. The outcry to the LORD against its people is so great that he has sent us to destroy it."

¹⁴So Lot went out and spoke to his sons-in-law, who were pledged to marry⁴ his daughters. He said, "Hurry and get out of this place, because the LORD is about to destroy the city!" But his sons-in-law thought he was joking.

¹⁵With the coming of dawn, the angels urged Lot, saying, "Hurry! Take your wife and your two daughters who are here, or you will be swept away when the city is punished."

¹⁶When he hesitated, the men grasped his hand and the hands of his wife and of his two daughters and led them safely out of the city, for the LORD was merciful to them. ¹⁷As soon as they had brought them out, one of them said, "Flee for your lives! Don't look back, and don't stop anywhere in the plain! Flee to the mountains or you will be swept away!"

¹⁸But Lot said to them, "No, my lords,ᵇ please! ¹⁹Yourᶜ servant has found favour in yourᶜ eyes, and youᶜ have shown great kindness to me in sparing my life. But I can't flee to the mountains; this disaster will overtake me, and I'll die. ²⁰Look, here is a town near enough to run to, and it is small. Let me flee to it—it is very small, isn't it? Then my life will be spared."

²¹He said to him, "Very well, I will grant this request too; I will not overthrow the town you speak of. ²²But flee there quickly, because I cannot do anything until you reach it." (That is why the town was called Zoar.ᵈ)

²³By the time Lot reached Zoar, the sun had risen over the land. ²⁴Then the LORD rained down burning sulphur on Sodom and Gomorrah—from the LORD out of the heavens. ²⁵Thus he overthrew those cities and the entire plain, including all those living in the cities—and also the vegetation in the land. ²⁶But Lot's wife looked back, and she became a pillar of salt.

²⁷Early the next morning Abraham got up and returned to the place where he had stood before the LORD. ²⁸He looked down towards Sodom and Gomorrah, towards all the land of the plain, and he saw dense smoke rising from the land, like smoke from a furnace.

²⁹So when God destroyed the cities of the plain, he remembered Abraham, and he brought Lot out of the catastrophe that overthrew the cities where Lot had lived.

---

g 25 Or *Ruler*   *a 14* Or *were married to*   *b 18* Or *No, Lord*; or *No, my lord*   *c 19* The Hebrew is singular.
d 22 Zoar means *small.*

Lot and His Daughters

30Lot and his two daughters left Zoar and settled in the mountains, for he was afraid to stay in Zoar. He and his two daughters lived in a cave. 31One day the older daughter said to the younger, "Our father is old, and there is no man around here to lie with us, as is the custom all over the earth. 32Let's get our father to drink wine and then lie with him and preserve our family line through our father."

33That night they got their father to drink wine, and the older daughter went in and lay with him. He was not aware of it when she lay down or when she got up. 34The next day the older daughter said to the younger, "Last night I lay with my father. Let's get him to drink wine again tonight, and you go in and lie with him so we can preserve our family line through our father." 35So they got their father to drink wine that night also, and the younger daughter went and lay with him. Again he was not aware of it when she lay down or when she got up.

36So both of Lot's daughters became pregnant by their father. 37The older daughter had a son, and she named him Moab;e he is the father of the Moabites of today. 38The younger daughter also had a son, and she named him Ben-Ammi;f he is the father of the Ammonites of today.

19:36   When stories like this are featured, it shows that the Israelites recognized that they were of the same racial stock as many of the nations round about them. Despite this they were often at war.

Abraham and Abimelech

20 Now Abraham moved on from there into the region of the Negev and lived between Kadesh and Shur. For a while he stayed in Gerar, 2and there Abraham said of his wife Sarah, "She is my sister." Then Abimelech king of Gerar sent for Sarah and took her.

3But God came to Abimelech in a dream one night and said to him, "You are as good as dead because of the woman you have taken; she is a married woman."

4Now Abimelech had not gone near her, so he said, "Lord, will you destroy an innocent nation? 5Did he not say to me, 'She is my sister,' and didn't she also say, 'He is my brother'? I have done this with a clear conscience and clean hands."

6Then God said to him in the dream, "Yes, I know you did this with a clear conscience, and so I have kept you from sinning against me. That is why I did not let you touch her. 7Now return the man's wife, for he is a prophet, and he will pray for you and you will live. But if you do not return her, you may be sure that you and all yours will die."

8Early the next morning Abimelech summoned all his officials, and when he told them all that had happened, they were very much afraid. 9Then Abimelech

called Abraham in and said, "What have you done to us? How have I wronged you that you have brought such great guilt upon me and my kingdom? You have done things to me that should not be done." 10And Abimelech asked Abraham, "What was your reason for doing this?"

11Abraham replied, "I said to myself, 'There is surely no fear of God in this place, and they will kill me because of my wife.' 12Besides, she really is my sister, the daughter of my father though not of my mother; and she became my wife. 13And when God caused me to wander from my father's household, I said to her, 'This is how you can show your love to me: Everywhere we go, say of me, "He is my brother." ' "

14Then Abimelech brought sheep and cattle and male and female slaves and gave them to Abraham, and he returned Sarah his wife to him. 15And Abimelech said, "My land is before you; live wherever you like."

16To Sarah he said, "I am giving your brother a thousand shekelsa of silver. This is to cover the offence against you before all who are with you; you are completely vindicated."

17Then Abraham prayed to God, and God healed Abimelech, his wife and his slave girls so they could have children again, 18for the LORD had closed up every womb in Abimelech's household because of Abraham's wife Sarah.

The Birth of Isaac

21 Now the LORD was gracious to Sarah as he had said, and the LORD did for Sarah what he had promised. 2Sarah became pregnant and bore a son to Abraham in his old age, at the very time God had promised him. 3Abraham gave the name Isaaca to the son Sarah bore him. 4When his son Isaac was eight days old, Abraham circumcised him, as God commanded him. 5Abraham was a hundred years old when his son Isaac was born to him.

6Sarah said, "God has brought me laughter, and everyone who hears about this will laugh with me." 7And she added, "Who would have said to Abraham that Sarah would nurse children? Yet I have borne him a son in his old age."

Hagar and Ishmael Sent Away

8The child grew and was weaned, and on the day Isaac was weaned Abraham held a great feast. 9But Sarah saw that the son whom Hagar the Egyptian had borne to Abraham was mocking, 10and she said to Abraham, "Get rid of that slave woman and her son, for that slave woman's son will never share in the inheritance with my son Isaac."

11The matter distressed Abraham greatly because it concerned his son. 12But God said to him, "Do not be so distressed about the boy and your maidservant. Listen to whatever Sarah tells you, because it is through Isaac that your offspringb will be reckoned. 13I will make the son of the maidservant into a nation also, because he is your offspring."

14Early the next morning Abraham took some food

---

e37 Moab sounds like the Hebrew for from father.   f38 Ben-Ammi means son of my people.
a16 That is, about 25 pounds (about 11.5 kilograms)   a3 Isaac means he laughs.   b12 Or seed

and a skin of water and gave them to Hagar. He set them on her shoulders and then sent her off with the boy. She went on her way and wandered in the desert of Beersheba.

¹⁵When the water in the skin was gone, she put the boy under one of the bushes. ¹⁶Then she went off and sat down nearby, about a bow-shot away, for she thought, "I cannot watch the boy die." And as she sat there nearby, she c began to sob.

¹⁷God heard the boy crying, and the angel of God called to Hagar from heaven and said to her, "What is the matter, Hagar? Do not be afraid; God has heard the boy crying as he lies there. ¹⁸Lift the boy up and take him by the hand, for I will make him into a great nation."

¹⁹Then God opened her eyes and she saw a well of water. So she went and filled the skin with water and gave the boy a drink.

²⁰God was with the boy as he grew up. He lived in the desert and became an archer. ²¹While he was living in the Desert of Paran, his mother got a wife for him from Egypt.

The Treaty at Beersheba

²²At that time Abimelech and Phicol the commander of his forces said to Abraham, "God is with you in everything you do. ²³Now swear to me here before God that you will not deal falsely with me or my children or my descendants. Show to me and the country where you are living as an alien the same kindness I have shown to you."

²⁴Abraham said, "I swear it."

²⁵Then Abraham complained to Abimelech about a well of water that Abimelech's servants had seized. ²⁶But Abimelech said, "I don't know who has done this. You did not tell me, and I heard about it only today."

²⁷So Abraham brought sheep and cattle and gave them to Abimelech, and the two men made a treaty. ²⁸Abraham set apart seven ewe lambs from the flock, ²⁹and Abimelech asked Abraham, "What is the meaning of these seven ewe lambs you have set apart by themselves?"

³⁰He replied, "Accept these seven lambs from my hand as a witness that I dug this well."

³¹So that place was called Beersheba, d because the two men swore an oath there.

³²After the treaty had been made at Beersheba, Abimelech and Phicol the commander of his forces returned to the land of the Philistines. ³³Abraham planted a tamarisk tree in Beersheba, and there he called upon the name of the LORD, the Eternal God. ³⁴And Abraham stayed in the land of the Philistines for a long time.

Abraham Tested

22 Some time later God tested Abraham. He said to him, "Abraham!"
"Here I am," he replied.

²Then God said, "Take your son, your only son, Isaac, whom you love, and go to the region of Moriah. Sacrifice him there as a burnt offering on one of the mountains I will tell you about."

³Early the next morning Abraham got up and saddled his donkey. He took with him two of his servants and his son Isaac. When he had cut enough wood for the burnt offering, he set out for the place God had told him about. ⁴On the third day Abraham looked up and saw the place in the distance. ⁵He said to his servants, "Stay here with the donkey while I and the boy go over there. We will worship and then we will come back to you."

⁶Abraham took the wood for the burnt offering and placed it on his son Isaac, and he himself carried the fire and the knife. As the two of them went on together, ⁷Isaac spoke up and said to his father Abraham, "Father?"

"Yes, my son?" Abraham replied.

"The fire and wood are here," Isaac said, "but where is the lamb for the burnt offering?"

⁸Abraham answered, "God himself will provide the lamb for the burnt offering, my son." And the two of them went on together.

⁹When they reached the place God had told him about, Abraham built an altar there and arranged the wood on it. He bound his son Isaac and laid him on the altar, on top of the wood. ¹⁰Then he reached out his hand and took the knife to slay his son. ¹¹But the angel of the LORD called out to him from heaven, "Abraham! Abraham!"

"Here I am," he replied.

¹²"Do not lay a hand on the boy," he said. "Do not do anything to him. Now I know that you fear God, because you have not withheld from me your son, your only son."

¹³Abraham looked up and there in a thicket he saw a ram a caught by its horns. He went over and took the ram and sacrificed it as a burnt offering instead of his son. ¹⁴So Abraham called that place The LORD Will Provide. And to this day it is said, "On the mountain of the LORD it will be provided."

22:14   Isaac was a gift. His parents realized this before he was born. Now Abraham had to treat him as such, and this very difficult situation came about. Abraham was prepared to hand his only son over to God, so giving everything he had to him. God recognized Abraham's obedience, and in return made him a great promise. Abraham's name for the place, "The LORD will provide", is a fitting one.

---

¹⁵The angel of the LORD called to Abraham from heaven a second time ¹⁶and said, "I swear by myself, declares the LORD, that because you have done this and have not withheld your son, your only son, ¹⁷I will surely bless you and make your descendants as

---

c16 Hebrew; Septuagint *the child*   d31 *Beersheba* can mean *well of seven* or *well of the oath.*
a13 Many manuscripts of the Masoretic Text, Samaritan Pentateuch, Septuagint and Syriac; most manuscripts of the Masoretic Text *a ram behind ˌhim*

numerous as the stars in the sky and as the sand on the seashore. Your descendants will take possession of the cities of their enemies, [18]and through your offspring[b] all nations on earth will be blessed, because you have obeyed me."

[19]Then Abraham returned to his servants, and they set off together for Beersheba. And Abraham stayed in Beersheba.

Nahor's Sons

[20]Some time later Abraham was told, "Milcah is also a mother; she has borne sons to your brother Nahor: [21]Uz the firstborn, Buz his brother, Kemuel (the father of Aram), [22]Kesed, Hazo, Pildash, Jidlaph and Bethuel." [23]Bethuel became the father of Rebekah. Milcah bore these eight sons to Abraham's brother Nahor. [24]His concubine, whose name was Reumah, also had sons: Tebah, Gaham, Tahash and Maacah.

The Death of Sarah

23 Sarah lived to be a hundred and twenty-seven years old. [2]She died at Kiriath Arba (that is, Hebron) in the land of Canaan, and Abraham went to mourn for Sarah and to weep over her.

[3]Then Abraham rose from beside his dead wife and spoke to the Hittites.[a] He said, [4]"I am an alien and a stranger among you. Sell me some property for a burial site here so that I can bury my dead."

[5]The Hittites replied to Abraham, [6]"Sir, listen to us. You are a mighty prince among us. Bury your dead in the choicest of our tombs. None of us will refuse you his tomb for burying your dead."

[7]Then Abraham rose and bowed down before the people of the land, the Hittites. [8]He said to them, "If you are willing to let me bury my dead, then listen to me and intercede with Ephron son of Zohar on my behalf [9]so that he will sell me the cave of Machpelah, which belongs to him and is at the end of his field. Ask him to sell it to me for the full price as a burial site among you."

[10]Ephron the Hittite was sitting among his people and he replied to Abraham in the hearing of all the Hittites who had come to the gate of his city. [11]"No, my lord," he said. "Listen to me; I give[b] you the field, and I give[b] you the cave that is in it. I give[b] it to you in the presence of my people. Bury your dead."

[12]Again Abraham bowed down before the people of the land [13]and he said to Ephron in their hearing, "Listen to me, if you will. I will pay the price of the field. Accept it from me so that I can bury my dead there."

[14]Ephron answered Abraham, [15]"Listen to me, my lord; the land is worth four hundred shekels[c] of silver, but what is that between me and you? Bury your dead."

[16]Abraham agreed to Ephron's terms and weighed out for him the price he had named in the hearing of the Hittites: four hundred shekels of silver, according to the weight current among the merchants.

[17]So Ephron's field in Machpelah near Mamre — both the field and the cave in it, and all the trees within the borders of the field — was legally made over [18]to Abraham as his property in the presence of all the Hittites who had come to the gate of the city. [19]Afterwards Abraham buried his wife Sarah in the cave in the field of Machpelah near Mamre (which is at Hebron) in the land of Canaan. [20]So the field and the cave in it were legally made over to Abraham by the Hittites as a burial site.

23:15 In this typically Middle-Eastern piece of bartering, Abraham came off quite badly. We are reminded that he was all too human and that it was God who was in control. Ironically this was the first time Israel had possession in the promised land.

Isaac and Rebekah

24 Abraham was now old and well advanced in years, and the LORD had blessed him in every way. [2]He said to the chief[a] servant in his household, the one in charge of all that he had, "Put your hand under my thigh. [3]I want you to swear by the LORD, the God of heaven and the God of earth, that you will not get a wife for my son from the daughters of the Canaanites, among whom I am living, [4]but will go to my country and my own relatives and get a wife for my son Isaac."

[5]The servant asked him, "What if the woman is unwilling to come back with me to this land? Shall I then take your son back to the country you came from?"

[6]"Make sure that you do not take my son back there," Abraham said. [7]"The LORD, the God of heaven, who brought me out of my father's household and my native land and who spoke to me and promised me on oath, saying, 'To your offspring[b] I will give this land' — he will send his angel before you so that you can get a wife for my son from there. [8]If the woman is unwilling to come back with you, then you will be released from this oath of mine. Only do not take my son back there." [9]So the servant put his hand under the thigh of his master Abraham and swore an oath to him concerning this matter.

[10]Then the servant took ten of his master's camels and left, taking with him all kinds of good things from his master. He set out for Aram Naharaim[c] and made his way to the town of Nahor. [11]He made the camels kneel down near the well outside the town; it was towards evening, the time the women go out to draw water.

[12]Then he prayed, "O LORD, God of my master Abraham, give me success today, and show kindness to my master Abraham. [13]See, I am standing beside this spring, and the daughters of the townspeople are coming out to draw water. [14]May it be that when I say to a girl, 'Please let down your jar that I may have a drink,' and she says, 'Drink, and I'll water your camels too' — let her be the one you have chosen for your servant Isaac. By this I will know that you have shown kindness to my master."

---

[b]18 Or seed   [a]3 Or the sons of Heth; also in verses 5, 7, 10, 16, 18 and 20   [b]11 Or sell
[c]15 That is, about 10 pounds (about 4.5 kilograms)   [a]2 Or oldest   [b]7 Or seed   [c]10 That is, North-west Mesopotamia

[15]Before he had finished praying, Rebekah came out with her jar on her shoulder. She was the daughter of Bethuel son of Milcah, who was the wife of Abraham's brother Nahor. [16]The girl was very beautiful, a virgin; no man had ever lain with her. She went down to the spring, filled her jar and came up again.

[17]The servant hurried to meet her and said, "Please give me a little water from your jar."

[18]"Drink, my lord," she said, and quickly lowered the jar to her hands and gave him a drink.

[19]After she had given him a drink, she said, "I'll draw water for your camels too, until they have finished drinking." [20]So she quickly emptied her jar into the trough, ran back to the well to draw more water, and drew enough for all his camels. [21]Without saying a word, the man watched her closely to learn whether or not the LORD had made his journey successful.

[22]When the camels had finished drinking, the man took out a gold nose ring weighing a beka[d] and two gold bracelets weighing ten shekels.[e] [23]Then he asked, "Whose daughter are you? Please tell me, is there room in your father's house for us to spend the night?"

[24]She answered him, "I am the daughter of Bethuel, the son that Milcah bore to Nahor." [25]And she added, "We have plenty of straw and fodder, as well as room for you to spend the night."

[26]Then the man bowed down and worshipped the LORD, [27]saying, "Praise be to the LORD, the God of my master Abraham, who has not abandoned his kindness and faithfulness to my master. As for me, the LORD has led me on the journey to the house of my master's relatives."

[28]The girl ran and told her mother's household about these things. [29]Now Rebekah had a brother named Laban, and he hurried out to the man at the spring. [30]As soon as he had seen the nose ring, and the bracelets on his sister's arms, and had heard Rebekah tell what the man said to her, he went out to the man and found him standing by the camels near the spring. [31]"Come, you who are blessed by the LORD," he said. "Why are you standing out here? I have prepared the house and a place for the camels."

[32]So the man went to the house, and the camels were unloaded. Straw and fodder were brought for the camels, and water for him and his men to wash their feet. [33]Then food was set before him, but he said, "I will not eat until I have told you what I have to say."

"Then tell us," Laban said.

[34]So he said, "I am Abraham's servant. [35]The LORD has blessed my master abundantly, and he has become wealthy. He has given him sheep and cattle, silver and gold, menservants and maidservants, and camels and donkeys. [36]My master's wife Sarah has borne him a son in her[f] old age, and he has given him everything he owns. [37]And my master made me swear an oath, and said, 'You must not get a wife for my son from the daughters of the Canaanites, in whose land I live, [38]but go to my father's family and to my own clan, and get a wife for my son.'

[39]"Then I asked my master, 'What if the woman will not come back with me?'

[40]"He replied, 'The LORD, before whom I have walked, will send his angel with you and make your journey a success, so that you can get a wife for my son from my own clan and from my father's family. [41]Then, when you go to my clan, you will be released from my oath even if they refuse to give her to you—you will be released from my oath.'

24:38 The Israelites never forgot that their ancestors had come from Mesopotamia and had become nomads. When at last they were settled in Palestine and able to farm the land they recited at harvest thanksgiving "My father was a wandering Aramean. . ." (Deuteronomy 26:5) to remind themselves what God had done.

---

[42]"When I came to the spring today, I said, 'O LORD, God of my master Abraham, if you will, please grant success to the journey on which I have come. [43]See, I am standing beside this spring; if a maiden comes out to draw water and I say to her, "Please let me drink a little water from your jar," [44]and if she says to me, "Drink, and I'll draw water for your camels too," let her be the one the LORD has chosen for my master's son.'

[45]"Before I finished praying in my heart, Rebekah came out, with her jar on her shoulder. She went down to the spring and drew water, and I said to her, 'Please give me a drink.'

[46]"She quickly lowered her jar from her shoulder and said, 'Drink, and I'll water your camels too.' So I drank, and she watered the camels also.

[47]"I asked her, 'Whose daughter are you?'

"She said, 'The daughter of Bethuel son of Nahor, whom Milcah bore to him.'

"Then I put the ring in her nose and the bracelets on her arms, [48]and I bowed down and worshipped the LORD. I praised the LORD, the God of my master Abraham, who had led me on the right road to get the granddaughter of my master's brother for his son. [49]Now if you will show kindness and faithfulness to my master, tell me; and if not, tell me, so I may know which way to turn."

[50]Laban and Bethuel answered, "This is from the LORD; we can say nothing to you one way or the other. [51]Here is Rebekah; take her and go, and let her become the wife of your master's son, as the LORD has directed."

[52]When Abraham's servant heard what they said, he bowed down to the ground before the LORD. [53]Then the servant brought out gold and silver jewellery and articles of clothing and gave them to Rebekah; he also gave costly gifts to her brother and to her mother. [54]Then he and the men who were with him ate and drank and spent the night there.

When they got up the next morning, he said, "Send me on my way to my master."

[55]But her brother and her mother replied, "Let the

---

d22 That is, about ⅕ ounce (about 6 grams)   *e22* That is, about 4 ounces (about 115 grams)   *f36* Or *his* girl remain with us ten days or so; then you[g] may go."

⁵⁶But he said to them, "Do not detain me, now that the LORD has granted success to my journey. Send me on my way so I may go to my master."

⁵⁷Then they said, "Let's call the girl and ask her about it." ⁵⁸So they called Rebekah and asked her, "Will you go with this man?"

"I will go," she said.

⁵⁹So they sent their sister Rebekah on her way, along with her nurse and Abraham's servant and his men. ⁶⁰And they blessed Rebekah and said to her,

"Our sister, may you increase
    to thousands upon thousands;
may your offspring possess
    the gates of their enemies."

⁶¹Then Rebekah and her maids got ready and mounted their camels and went back with the man. So the servant took Rebekah and left.

⁶²Now Isaac had come from Beer Lahai Roi, for he was living in the Negev. ⁶³He went out to the field one evening to meditate,[h] and as he looked up, he saw camels approaching. ⁶⁴Rebekah also looked up and saw Isaac. She got down from her camel ⁶⁵and asked the servant, "Who is that man in the field coming to meet us?"

"He is my master," the servant answered. So she took her veil and covered herself.

⁶⁶Then the servant told Isaac all he had done. ⁶⁷Isaac brought her into the tent of his mother Sarah, and he married Rebekah. So she became his wife, and he loved her; and Isaac was comforted after his mother's death.

The Death of Abraham

25 Abraham took[a] another wife, whose name was Keturah. ²She bore him Zimran, Jokshan, Medan, Midian, Ishbak and Shuah. ³Jokshan was the father of Sheba and Dedan; the descendants of Dedan were the Asshurites, the Letushites and the Leummites. ⁴The sons of Midian were Ephah, Epher, Hanoch, Abida and Eldaah. All these were descendants of Keturah.

⁵Abraham left everything he owned to Isaac. ⁶But while he was still living, he gave gifts to the sons of his concubines and sent them away from his son Isaac to the land of the east.

⁷Altogether, Abraham lived a hundred and seventy-five years. ⁸Then Abraham breathed his last and died at a good old age, an old man and full of years; and he was gathered to his people. ⁹His sons Isaac and Ishmael buried him in the cave of Machpelah near Mamre, in the field of Ephron son of Zohar the Hittite, ¹⁰the field Abraham had bought from the Hittites.[b] There Abraham was buried with his wife Sarah. ¹¹After Abraham's death, God blessed his son Isaac, who then lived near Beer Lahai Roi.

Ishmael's Sons

¹²This is the account of Abraham's son Ishmael, whom Sarah's maidservant, Hagar the Egyptian, bore to Abraham.

¹³These are the names of the sons of Ishmael, listed in the order of their birth: Nebaioth the firstborn of Ishmael, Kedar, Adbeel, Mibsam, ¹⁴Mishma, Dumah, Massa, ¹⁵Hadad, Tema, Jetur, Naphish and Kedemah. ¹⁶These were the sons of Ishmael, and these are the names of the twelve tribal rulers according to their settlements and camps. ¹⁷Altogether, Ishmael lived a hundred and thirty-seven years. He breathed his last and died, and he was gathered to his people. ¹⁸His descendants settled in the area from Havilah to Shur, near the border of Egypt, as you go towards Asshur. And they lived in hostility towards[c] all their brothers.

Jacob and Esau

¹⁹This is the account of Abraham's son Isaac.

Abraham became the father of Isaac, ²⁰and Isaac was forty years old when he married Rebekah daughter of Bethuel the Aramean from Paddan Aram[d] and sister of Laban the Aramean.

²¹Isaac prayed to the LORD on behalf of his wife, because she was barren. The LORD answered his prayer, and his wife Rebekah became pregnant. ²²The babies jostled each other within her, and she said, "Why is this happening to me?" So she went to enquire of the LORD.

25:22 Before Jacob was even born we are given a hint of the life of struggle that he would lead. God is in control of events but he works through individuals and uses their personalities and talents for his purposes. By an accident of birth Esau had enormous advantages, namely the birthright. Jacob's progress depended on his wits, and the Bible is not afraid to paint him as a rogue and trickster.

---

²³The LORD said to her,

"Two nations are in your womb,
    and two peoples from within you will be
        separated;
one people will be stronger than the other,
    and the older will serve the younger."

²⁴When the time came for her to give birth, there were twin boys in her womb. ²⁵The first to come out was red, and his whole body was like a hairy garment; so they named him Esau.[e] ²⁶After this, his brother came out, with his hand grasping Esau's heel; so he was named Jacob.[f] Isaac was sixty years old when Rebekah gave birth to them.

²⁷The boys grew up, and Esau became a skilful

---

g 55 Or she   h 63 The meaning of the Hebrew for this word is uncertain.   a 1 Or had taken
b 10 Or the sons of Heth   c 18 Or lived to the east of   d 20 That is, North-west Mesopotamia
e 25 Esau may mean hairy; he was also called Edom, which means red.
f 26 Jacob means he grasps the heel (figuratively, he deceives).

hunter, a man of the open country, while Jacob was a quiet man, staying among the tents. [28]Isaac, who had a taste for wild game, loved Esau, but Rebekah loved Jacob.

[29]Once when Jacob was cooking some stew, Esau came in from the open country, famished. [30]He said to Jacob, "Quick, let me have some of that red stew! I'm famished!" (That is why he was also called Edom.[g])

[31]Jacob replied, "First sell me your birthright."

[32]"Look, I am about to die," Esau said. "What good is the birthright to me?"

[33]But Jacob said, "Swear to me first." So he swore an oath to him, selling his birthright to Jacob.

[34]Then Jacob gave Esau some bread and some lentil stew. He ate and drank, and then got up and left.

So Esau despised his birthright.

Isaac and Abimelech

26 Now there was a famine in the land—besides the earlier famine of Abraham's time—and Isaac went to Abimelech king of the Philistines in Gerar. [2]The LORD appeared to Isaac and said, "Do not go down to Egypt; live in the land where I tell you to live. [3]Stay in this land for a while, and I will be with you and will bless you. For to you and your descendants I will give all these lands and will confirm the oath I swore to your father Abraham. [4]I will make your descendants as numerous as the stars in the sky and will give them all these lands, and through your offspring[a] all nations on earth will be blessed, [5]because Abraham obeyed me and kept my requirements, my commands, my decrees and my laws." [6]So Isaac stayed in Gerar.

[7]When the men of that place asked him about his wife, he said, "She is my sister," because he was afraid to say, "She is my wife." He thought, "The men of this place might kill me on account of Rebekah, because she is beautiful."

[8]When Isaac had been there a long time, Abimelech king of the Philistines looked down from a window and saw Isaac caressing his wife Rebekah. [9]So Abimelech summoned Isaac and said, "She is really your wife! Why did you say, 'She is my sister'?"

Isaac answered him, "Because I thought I might lose my life on account of her."

[10]Then Abimelech said, "What is this you have done to us? One of the men might well have slept with your wife, and you would have brought guilt upon us."

[11]So Abimelech gave orders to all the people: "Anyone who molests this man or his wife shall surely be put to death."

[12]Isaac planted crops in that land and the same year reaped a hundredfold, because the LORD blessed him. [13]The man became rich, and his wealth continued to grow until he became very wealthy. [14]He had so many flocks and herds and servants that the Philistines envied him. [15]So all the wells that his father's servants had dug in the time of his father Abraham, the Philistines stopped up, filling them with earth.

[16]Then Abimelech said to Isaac, "Move away from us; you have become too powerful for us."

[17]So Isaac moved away from there and encamped in the Valley of Gerar and settled there. [18]Isaac reopened the wells that had been dug in the time of his father Abraham, which the Philistines had stopped up after Abraham died, and he gave them the same names his father had given them.

[19]Isaac's servants dug in the valley and discovered a well of fresh water there. [20]But the herdsmen of Gerar quarrelled with Isaac's herdsmen and said, "The water is ours!" So he named the well Esek,[b] because they disputed with him. [21]Then they dug another well, but they quarrelled over that one also; so he named it Sitnah.[c] [22]He moved on from there and dug another well, and no-one quarrelled over it. He named it Rehoboth,[d] saying, "Now the LORD has given us room and we will flourish in the land."

[23]From there he went up to Beersheba. [24]That night the LORD appeared to him and said, "I am the God of your father Abraham. Do not be afraid, for I am with you; I will bless you and will increase the number of your descendants for the sake of my servant Abraham."

[25]Isaac built an altar there and called on the name of the LORD. There he pitched his tent, and there his servants dug a well.

[26]Meanwhile, Abimelech had come to him from Gerar, with Ahuzzath his personal adviser and Phicol the commander of his forces. [27]Isaac asked them, "Why have you come to me, since you were hostile to me and sent me away?"

[28]They answered, "We saw clearly that the LORD was with you; so we said, 'There ought to be a sworn agreement between us'—between us and you. Let us make a treaty with you [29]that you will do us no harm, just as we did not molest you but always treated you well and sent you away in peace. And now you are blessed by the LORD."

[30]Isaac then made a feast for them, and they ate and drank. [31]Early the next morning the men swore an oath to each other. Then Isaac sent them on their way, and they left him in peace.

[32]That day Isaac's servants came and told him about the well they had dug. They said, "We've found water!" [33]He called it Shibah,[e] and to this day the name of the town has been Beersheba.[f]

[34]When Esau was forty years old, he married Judith daughter of Beeri the Hittite, and also Basemath daughter of Elon the Hittite. [35]They were a source of grief to Isaac and Rebekah.

Jacob Gets Isaac's Blessing

27 When Isaac was old and his eyes were so weak that he could no longer see, he called for Esau his older son and said to him, "My son."

"Here I am," he answered.

[2]Isaac said, "I am now an old man and don't know the day of my death. [3]Now then, get your weapons—your quiver and bow—and go out to the open country to hunt some wild game for me. [4]Prepare me the kind

---

[g]30 Edom means red.   [a]4 Or seed   [b]20 Esek means dispute.
[d]22 Rehoboth means room.   [e]33 Shibah can mean oath or seven.   [c]21 Sitnah means opposition.
[f]33 Beersheba can mean well of the oath or well of seven.

of tasty food I like and bring it to me to eat, so that I may give you my blessing before I die."

⁵Now Rebekah was listening as Isaac spoke to his son Esau. When Esau left for the open country to hunt game and bring it back, ⁶Rebekah said to her son Jacob, "Look, I overheard your father say to your brother Esau, ⁷'Bring me some game and prepare me some tasty food to eat, so that I may give you my blessing in the presence of the LORD before I die.' ⁸Now, my son, listen carefully and do what I tell you: ⁹Go out to the flock and bring me two choice young goats, so that I can prepare some tasty food for your father, just the way he likes it. ¹⁰Then take it to your father to eat, so that he may give you his blessing before he dies."

¹¹Jacob said to Rebekah his mother, "But my brother Esau is a hairy man, and I'm a man with smooth skin. ¹²What if my father touches me? I would appear to be tricking him and would bring down a curse on myself rather than a blessing."

¹³His mother said to him, "My son, let the curse fall on me. Just do what I say; go and get them for me." ¹⁴So he went and got them and brought them to his mother, and she prepared some tasty food, just the way his father liked it. ¹⁵Then Rebekah took the best clothes of Esau her older son, which she had in the house, and put them on her younger son Jacob. ¹⁶She also covered his hands and the smooth part of his neck with the goatskins. ¹⁷Then she handed to her son Jacob the tasty food and the bread she had made.

¹⁸He went to his father and said, "My father."

"Yes, my son," he answered. "Who is it?"

¹⁹Jacob said to his father, "I am Esau your firstborn. I have done as you told me. Please sit up and eat some of my game so that you may give me your blessing."

²⁰Isaac asked his son, "How did you find it so quickly, my son?"

"The LORD your God gave me success," he replied.

²¹Then Isaac said to Jacob, "Come near so I can touch you, my son, to know whether you really are my son Esau or not."

²²Jacob went close to his father Isaac, who touched him and said, "The voice is the voice of Jacob, but the hands are the hands of Esau." ²³He did not recognise him, for his hands were hairy like those of his brother Esau; so he blessed him. ²⁴"Are you really my son Esau?" he asked.

"I am," he replied.

²⁵Then he said, "My son, bring me some of your game to eat, so that I may give you my blessing."

Jacob brought it to him and he ate; and he brought some wine and he drank. ²⁶Then his father Isaac said to him, "Come here, my son, and kiss me."

²⁷So he went to him and kissed him. When Isaac caught the smell of his clothes, he blessed him and said,

"Ah, the smell of my son
    is like the smell of a field
    that the LORD has blessed.
²⁸May God give you of heaven's dew
    and of earth's richness—
    an abundance of grain and new wine.

²⁹May nations serve you
    and peoples bow down to you.
Be lord over your brothers,
    and may the sons of your mother bow down to
    you.
May those who curse you be cursed
    and those who bless you be blessed."

27:27   When making the world, God simply spoke and it was done. Even human speech in the Bible cannot be taken back, so by whatever means Isaac had been tricked his blessing could not now be removed from Jacob. A deathbed blessing had the force of a will, so now Jacob possessed legally what he had earlier got Esau to sell to him.

---

³⁰After Isaac finished blessing him and Jacob had scarcely left his father's presence, his brother Esau came in from hunting. ³¹He too prepared some tasty food and brought it to his father. Then he said to him, "My father, sit up and eat some of my game, so that you may give me your blessing."

³²His father Isaac asked him, "Who are you?"

"I am your son," he answered, "your firstborn, Esau."

³³Isaac trembled violently and said, "Who was it, then, that hunted game and brought it to me? I ate it just before you came and I blessed him—and indeed he will be blessed!"

³⁴When Esau heard his father's words, he burst out with a loud and bitter cry and said to his father, "Bless me—me too, my father!"

³⁵But he said, "Your brother came deceitfully and took your blessing."

³⁶Esau said, "Isn't he rightly named Jacob?ᵃ He has deceived me these two times: He took my birthright, and now he's taken my blessing!" Then he asked, "Haven't you reserved any blessing for me?"

³⁷Isaac answered Esau, "I have made him lord over you and have made all his relatives his servants, and I have sustained him with grain and new wine. So what can I possibly do for you, my son?"

³⁸Esau said to his father, "Do you have only one blessing, my father? Bless me too, my father!" Then Esau wept aloud.

³⁹His father Isaac answered him,

"Your dwelling will be
    away from the earth's richness,
    away from the dew of heaven above.
⁴⁰You will live by the sword
    and you will serve your brother.
But when you grow restless,
    you will throw his yoke
    from off your neck."

Jacob Flees to Laban

⁴¹Esau held a grudge against Jacob because of the blessing his father had given him. He said to himself,

---

ᵃ *36 Jacob* means *he grasps the heel* (figuratively, *he deceives*).

"The days of mourning for my father are near; then I will kill my brother Jacob."

42When Rebekah was told what her older son Esau had said, she sent for her younger son Jacob and said to him, "Your brother Esau is consoling himself with the thought of killing you. 43Now then, my son, do what I say: Flee at once to my brother Laban in Haran. 44Stay with him for a while until your brother's fury subsides. 45When your brother is no longer angry with you and forgets what you did to him, I'll send word for you to come back from there. Why should I lose both of you in one day?"

46Then Rebekah said to Isaac, "I'm disgusted with living because of these Hittite women. If Jacob takes a wife from among the women of this land, from Hittite women like these, my life will not be worth living."

28 So Isaac called for Jacob and blessed[a] him and commanded him: "Do not marry a Canaanite woman. 2Go at once to Paddan Aram,[b] to the house of your mother's father Bethuel. Take a wife for yourself there, from among the daughters of Laban, your mother's brother. 3May God Almighty[c] bless you and make you fruitful and increase your numbers until you become a community of peoples. 4May he give you and your descendants the blessing given to Abraham, so that you may take possession of the land where you now live as an alien, the land God gave to Abraham." 5Then Isaac sent Jacob on his way, and he went to Paddan Aram, to Laban son of Bethuel the Aramean, the brother of Rebekah, who was the mother of Jacob and Esau.

6Now Esau learned that Isaac had blessed Jacob and had sent him to Paddan Aram to take a wife from there, and that when he blessed him he commanded him, "Do not marry a Canaanite woman," 7and that Jacob had obeyed his father and mother and had gone to Paddan Aram. 8Esau then realised how displeasing the Canaanite women were to his father Isaac; 9so he went to Ishmael and married Mahalath, the sister of Nebaioth and daughter of Ishmael son of Abraham, in addition to the wives he already had.

Jacob's Dream at Bethel

10Jacob left Beersheba and set out for Haran. 11When he reached a certain place, he stopped for the night because the sun had set. Taking one of the stones there, he put it under his head and lay down to sleep. 12He had a dream in which he saw a stairway[d] resting on the earth, with its top reaching to heaven, and the angels of God were ascending and descending on it. 13There above it[e] stood the LORD, and he said: "I am the LORD, the God of your father Abraham and the God of Isaac. I will give you and your descendants the land on which you are lying. 14Your descendants will be like the dust of the earth, and you will spread out to the west and to the east, to the north and to the south. All peoples on earth will be blessed through you and your offspring. 15I am with you and will watch over you wherever you go, and I will bring you back to this land.

I will not leave you until I have done what I have promised you."

16When Jacob awoke from his sleep, he thought, "Surely the LORD is in this place, and I was not aware of it." 17He was afraid and said, "How awesome is this place! This is none other than the house of God; this is the gate of heaven."

28:16   God is not limited by our ideas of him. We often go to a holy place in order to meet God, but in fact he can meet us anywhere. God chose to go and meet Jacob and give him his blessing. Jacob was fleeing for his life away from the promised land, but he discovered that God had been with him all along.

18Early the next morning Jacob took the stone he had placed under his head and set it up as a pillar and poured oil on top of it. 19He called that place Bethel,[f] though the city used to be called Luz. 20Then Jacob made a vow, saying, "If God will be with me and will watch over me on this journey I am taking and will give me food to eat and clothes to wear 21so that I return safely to my father's house, then the LORD[g] will be my God 22and[h] this stone that I have set up as a pillar will be God's house, and of all that you give me I will give you a tenth."

Jacob Arrives in Paddan Aram

29 Then Jacob continued on his journey and came to the land of the eastern peoples. 2There he saw a well in the field, with three flocks of sheep lying near it because the flocks were watered from that well. The stone over the mouth of the well was large. 3When all the flocks were gathered there, the shepherds would roll the stone away from the well's mouth and water the sheep. Then they would return the stone to its place over the mouth of the well.

4Jacob asked the shepherds, "My brothers, where are you from?"

"We're from Haran," they replied.

5He said to them, "Do you know Laban, Nahor's grandson?"

"Yes, we know him," they answered.

6Then Jacob asked them, "Is he well?"

"Yes, he is," they said, "and here comes his daughter Rachel with the sheep."

7"Look," he said, "the sun is still high; it is not time for the flocks to be gathered. Water the sheep and take them back to pasture."

8"We can't," they replied, "until all the flocks are gathered and the stone has been rolled away from the mouth of the well. Then we will water the sheep."

9While he was still talking with them, Rachel came with her father's sheep, for she was a shepherdess. 10When Jacob saw Rachel daughter of Laban, his mother's brother, and Laban's sheep, he went over and

---

a 1 Or greeted   b 2 That is, North-west Mesopotamia; also in verses 5, 6 and 7   c 3 Hebrew El-Shaddai
d 12 Or ladder   e 13 Or There beside him   f 19 Bethel means house of God.
g 20,21 Or Since God ... father's house, the LORD   h 21,22 Or house, and the LORD will be my God, 22 then

rolled the stone away from the mouth of the well and watered his uncle's sheep. [11]Then Jacob kissed Rachel and began to weep aloud. [12]He had told Rachel that he was a relative of her father and a son of Rebekah. So she ran and told her father.

[13]As soon as Laban heard the news about Jacob, his sister's son, he hurried to meet him. He embraced him and kissed him and brought him to his home, and there Jacob told him all these things. [14]Then Laban said to him, "You are my own flesh and blood."

Jacob Marries Leah and Rachel

After Jacob had stayed with him for a whole month, [15]Laban said to him, "Just because you are a relative of mine, should you work for me for nothing? Tell me what your wages should be."

[16]Now Laban had two daughters; the name of the older was Leah, and the name of the younger was Rachel. [17]Leah had weak[a] eyes, but Rachel was lovely in form, and beautiful. [18]Jacob was in love with Rachel and said, "I'll work for you seven years in return for your younger daughter Rachel."

[19]Laban said, "It's better that I give her to you than to some other man. Stay here with me." [20]So Jacob served seven years to get Rachel, but they seemed like only a few days to him because of his love for her.

[21]Then Jacob said to Laban, "Give me my wife. My time is completed, and I want to lie with her."

[22]So Laban brought together all the people of the place and gave a feast. [23]But when evening came, he took his daughter Leah and gave her to Jacob, and Jacob lay with her. [24]And Laban gave his servant girl Zilpah to his daughter as her maidservant.

[25]When morning came, there was Leah! So Jacob said to Laban, "What is this you have done to me? I served you for Rachel, didn't I? Why have you deceived me?"

29:25 We are supposed to bring our sense of humour along with our piety when we read the Bible. The stories of Jacob meeting his match in his uncle Laban are told by a brilliant comic storyteller who, at the same time, manages effectively to sustain the theme of Jacob's struggle.

---

[26]Laban replied, "It is not our custom here to give the younger daughter in marriage before the older one. [27]Finish this daughter's bridal week; then we will give you the younger one also, in return for another seven years of work."

[28]And Jacob did so. He finished the week with Leah, and then Laban gave him his daughter Rachel to be his wife. [29]Laban gave his servant girl Bilhah to his daughter Rachel as her maidservant. [30]Jacob lay with Rachel also, and he loved Rachel more than Leah. And he worked for Laban another seven years.

Jacob's Children

[31]When the LORD saw that Leah was not loved, he opened her womb, but Rachel was barren. [32]Leah became pregnant and gave birth to a son. She named him Reuben,[b] for she said, "It is because the LORD has seen my misery. Surely my husband will love me now."

[33]She conceived again, and when she gave birth to a son she said, "Because the LORD heard that I am not loved, he gave me this one too." So she named him Simeon.[c]

[34]Again she conceived, and when she gave birth to a son she said, "Now at last my husband will become attached to me, because I have borne him three sons." So he was named Levi.[d]

[35]She conceived again, and when she gave birth to a son she said, "This time I will praise the LORD." So she named him Judah.[e] Then she stopped having children.

30 When Rachel saw that she was not bearing Jacob any children, she became jealous of her sister. So she said to Jacob, "Give me children, or I'll die!"

[2]Jacob became angry with her and said, "Am I in the place of God, who has kept you from having children?"

[3]Then she said, "Here is Bilhah, my maidservant. Sleep with her so that she can bear children for me and that through her I too can build a family."

[4]So she gave him her servant Bilhah as a wife. Jacob slept with her, [5]and she became pregnant and bore him a son. [6]Then Rachel said, "God has vindicated me; he has listened to my plea and given me a son." Because of this she named him Dan.[a]

[7]Rachel's servant Bilhah conceived again and bore Jacob a second son. [8]Then Rachel said, "I have had a great struggle with my sister, and I have won." So she named him Naphtali.[b]

[9]When Leah saw that she had stopped having children, she took her maidservant Zilpah and gave her to Jacob as a wife. [10]Leah's servant Zilpah bore Jacob a son. [11]Then Leah said, "What good fortune!"[c] So she named him Gad.[d]

[12]Leah's servant Zilpah bore Jacob a second son. [13]Then Leah said, "How happy I am! The women will call me happy." So she named him Asher.[e]

[14]During wheat harvest, Reuben went out into the fields and found some mandrake plants, which he brought to his mother Leah. Rachel said to Leah, "Please give me some of your son's mandrakes."

[15]But she said to her, "Wasn't it enough that you took away my husband? Will you take my son's mandrakes too?"

"Very well," Rachel said, "he can sleep with you tonight in return for your son's mandrakes."

[16]So when Jacob came in from the fields that evening, Leah went out to meet him. "You must sleep with me," she said. "I have hired you with my son's mandrakes." So he slept with her that night.

[17]God listened to Leah, and she became pregnant

---

a 17 Or *delicate*   *b* 32 *Reuben* sounds like the Hebrew for *he has seen my misery*; the name means *see, a son.*
c 33 *Simeon* probably means *one who hears.*   *d* 34 *Levi* sounds like and may be derived from the Hebrew for *attached.*
e 35 *Judah* sounds like and may be derived from the Hebrew for *praise.*   *a* 6 *Dan* here means *he has vindicated.*
b 8 *Naphtali* means *my struggle.*   *c* 11 Or *"A troop is coming!"*   *d* 11 *Gad* can mean *good fortune* or *a troop.*
e 13 *Asher* means *happy.*

and bore Jacob a fifth son. [18]Then Leah said, "God has rewarded me for giving my maidservant to my husband." So she named him Issachar.[f]

[19]Leah conceived again and bore Jacob a sixth son. [20]Then Leah said, "God has presented me with a precious gift. This time my husband will treat me with honour, because I have borne him six sons." So she named him Zebulun.[g]

[21]Some time later she gave birth to a daughter and named her Dinah.

[22]Then God remembered Rachel; he listened to her and opened her womb. [23]She became pregnant and gave birth to a son and said, "God has taken away my disgrace." [24]She named him Joseph,[h] and said, "May the LORD add to me another son."

Jacob's Flocks Increase

[25]After Rachel gave birth to Joseph, Jacob said to Laban, "Send me on my way so that I can go back to my own homeland. [26]Give me my wives and children, for whom I have served you, and I will be on my way. You know how much work I've done for you."

[27]But Laban said to him, "If I have found favour in your eyes, please stay. I have learned by divination that[i] the LORD has blessed me because of you." [28]He added, "Name your wages, and I will pay them."

[29]Jacob said to him, "You know how I have worked for you and how your livestock has fared under my care. [30]The little you had before I came has increased greatly, and the LORD has blessed you wherever I have been. But now, when may I do something for my own household?"

[31]"What shall I give you?" he asked.

"Don't give me anything," Jacob replied. "But if you will do this one thing for me, I will go on tending your flocks and watching over them: [32]Let me go through all your flocks today and remove from them every speckled or spotted sheep, every dark-coloured lamb and every spotted or speckled goat. They will be my wages. [33]And my honesty will testify for me in the future, whenever you check on the wages you have paid me. Any goat in my possession that is not speckled or spotted, or any lamb that is not dark-coloured, will be considered stolen."

[34]"Agreed," said Laban. "Let it be as you have said." [35]That same day he removed all the male goats that were streaked or spotted, and all the speckled or spotted female goats (all that had white on them) and all the dark-coloured lambs, and he placed them in the care of his sons. [36]Then he put a three-day journey between himself and Jacob, while Jacob continued to tend the rest of Laban's flocks.

[37]Jacob, however, took fresh-cut branches from poplar, almond and plane trees and made white stripes on them by peeling the bark and exposing the white inner wood of the branches. [38]Then he placed the peeled branches in all the watering troughs, so that they would be directly in front of the flocks when they came to drink. When the flocks were in heat and came to drink, [39]they mated in front of the branches. And they bore young that were streaked or speckled or spotted. [40]Jacob set apart the young of the flock by themselves, but made the rest face the streaked and dark-coloured animals that belonged to Laban. Thus he made separate flocks for himself and did not put them with Laban's animals. [41]Whenever the stronger females were in heat, Jacob would place the branches in the troughs in front of the animals so that they would mate near the branches, [42]but if the animals were weak, he would not place them there. So the weak animals went to Laban and the strong ones to Jacob. [43]In this way the man grew exceedingly prosperous and came to own large flocks, and maidservants and menservants, and camels and donkeys.

Jacob Flees From Laban

31 Jacob heard that Laban's sons were saying, "Jacob has taken everything our father owned and has gained all this wealth from what belonged to our father." [2]And Jacob noticed that Laban's attitude towards him was not what it had been.

[3]Then the LORD said to Jacob, "Go back to the land of your fathers and to your relatives, and I will be with you."

[4]So Jacob sent word to Rachel and Leah to come out to the fields where his flocks were. [5]He said to them, "I see that your father's attitude towards me is not what it was before, but the God of my father has been with me. [6]You know that I've worked for your father with all my strength, [7]yet your father has cheated me by changing my wages ten times. However, God has not allowed him to harm me. [8]If he said, 'The speckled ones will be your wages,' then all the flocks gave birth to speckled young; and if he said, 'The streaked ones will be your wages,' then all the flocks bore streaked young. [9]So God has taken away your father's livestock and has given them to me.

31:9 Jacob finally became wealthy despite Laban's wiles. The writer of this story will have believed that Jacob's system really did produce speckled sheep, but even he acknowledges that the real credit was God's. It was all within God's plan to re-set Jacob in the promised land (31:13).

---

[10]"In the breeding season I once had a dream in which I looked up and saw that the male goats mating with the flock were streaked, speckled or spotted. [11]The angel of God said to me in the dream, 'Jacob.' I answered, 'Here I am.' [12]And he said, 'Look up and see that all the male goats mating with the flock are streaked, speckled or spotted, for I have seen all that Laban has been doing to you. [13]I am the God of Bethel, where you anointed a pillar and where you made a vow to me. Now leave this land at once and go back to your native land.' "

[14]Then Rachel and Leah replied, "Do we still have any share in the inheritance of our father's estate?

---

f18 Issachar sounds like the Hebrew for *reward.*   *g20 Zebulun* probably means *honour.*   *h24 Joseph* means *may he add.*
i27 Or possibly *have become rich and*

[15] Does he not regard us as foreigners? Not only has he sold us, but he has used up what was paid for us. [16] Surely all the wealth that God took away from our father belongs to us and our children. So do whatever God has told you."

[17] Then Jacob put his children and his wives on camels, [18] and he drove all his livestock ahead of him, along with all the goods he had accumulated in Paddan Aram,[a] to go to his father Isaac in the land of Canaan. [19] When Laban had gone to shear his sheep, Rachel stole her father's household gods. [20] Moreover, Jacob deceived Laban the Aramean by not telling him he was running away. [21] So he fled with all he had, and crossing the River,[b] he headed for the hill country of Gilead.

Laban Pursues Jacob

[22] On the third day Laban was told that Jacob had fled. [23] Taking his relatives with him, he pursued Jacob for seven days and caught up with him in the hill country of Gilead. [24] Then God came to Laban the Aramean in a dream at night and said to him, "Be careful not to say anything to Jacob, either good or bad."

[25] Jacob had pitched his tent in the hill country of Gilead when Laban overtook him, and Laban and his relatives camped there too. [26] Then Laban said to Jacob, "What have you done? You've deceived me, and you've carried off my daughters like captives in war. [27] Why did you run off secretly and deceive me? Why didn't you tell me, so that I could send you away with joy and singing to the music of tambourines and harps? [28] You didn't even let me kiss my grandchildren and my daughters good-bye. You have done a foolish thing. [29] I have the power to harm you; but last night the God of your father said to me, 'Be careful not to say anything to Jacob, either good or bad.' [30] Now you have gone off because you longed to return to your father's house. But why did you steal my gods?"

[31] Jacob answered Laban, "I was afraid, because I thought you would take your daughters away from me by force. [32] But if you find anyone who has your gods, he shall not live. In the presence of our relatives, see for yourself whether there is anything of yours here with me; and if so, take it." Now Jacob did not know that Rachel had stolen the gods.

[33] So Laban went into Jacob's tent and into Leah's tent and into the tent of the two maidservants, but he found nothing. After he came out of Leah's tent, he entered Rachel's tent. [34] Now Rachel had taken the household gods and put them inside her camel's saddle and was sitting on them. Laban searched through everything in the tent but found nothing.

[35] Rachel said to her father, "Don't be angry, my lord, that I cannot stand up in your presence; I'm having my period." So he searched but could not find the household gods.

[36] Jacob was angry and took Laban to task. "What is my crime?" he asked Laban. "What sin have I committed that you hunt me down? [37] Now that you have searched through all my goods, what have you found that belongs to your household? Put it here in front of your relatives and mine, and let them judge between the two of us.

31:35 From contemporary documents we learn that these were some sort of small images. The person who possessed them had the right to inherit family property. Later, to own such things would be considered disloyalty to God, but in these early days it was thought that there were minor gods for small matters who were no threat to the great God.

---

[38] "I have been with you for twenty years now. Your sheep and goats have not miscarried, nor have I eaten rams from your flocks. [39] I did not bring you animals torn by wild beasts; I bore the loss myself. And you demanded payment from me for whatever was stolen by day or night. [40] This was my situation: The heat consumed me in the daytime and the cold at night, and sleep fled from my eyes. [41] It was like this for the twenty years I was in your household. I worked for you fourteen years for your two daughters and six years for your flocks, and you changed my wages ten times. [42] If the God of my father, the God of Abraham and the Fear of Isaac, had not been with me, you would surely have sent me away empty-handed. But God has seen my hardship and the toil of my hands, and last night he rebuked you."

[43] Laban answered Jacob, "The women are my daughters, the children are my children, and the flocks are my flocks. All you see is mine. Yet what can I do today about these daughters of mine, or about the children they have borne? [44] Come now, let's make a covenant, you and I, and let it serve as a witness between us."

[45] So Jacob took a stone and set it up as a pillar. [46] He said to his relatives, "Gather some stones." So they took stones and piled them in a heap, and they ate there by the heap. [47] Laban called it Jegar Sahadutha,[c] and Jacob called it Galeed.[d]

[48] Laban said, "This heap is a witness between you and me today." That is why it was called Galeed. [49] It was also called Mizpah,[e] because he said, "May the LORD keep watch between you and me when we are away from each other. [50] If you ill-treat my daughters or if you take any wives besides my daughters, even though no-one is with us, remember that God is a witness between you and me."

[51] Laban also said to Jacob, "Here is this heap, and here is this pillar I have set up between you and me. [52] This heap is a witness, and this pillar is a witness, that I will not go past this heap to your side to harm you and that you will not go past this heap and pillar to my side to harm me. [53] May the God of Abraham and the God of Nahor, the God of their father, judge between us."

So Jacob took an oath in the name of the Fear of his father Isaac. [54] He offered a sacrifice there in the hill country and invited his relatives to a meal. After they had eaten, they spent the night there.

---

a 18 That is, North-west Mesopotamia   *b 21* That is, the Euphrates   *c 47* The Aramaic *Jegar Sahadutha* means *witness heap.*
d 47 The Hebrew *Galeed* means *witness heap.*   *e 49* *Mizpah* means *watchtower.*

⁵⁵Early the next morning Laban kissed his grandchildren and his daughters and blessed them. Then he left and returned home.

Jacob Prepares to Meet Esau

32 Jacob also went on his way, and the angels of God met him. ²When Jacob saw them, he said, "This is the camp of God!" So he named that place Mahanaim.ᵃ

³Jacob sent messengers ahead of him to his brother Esau in the land of Seir, the country of Edom. ⁴He instructed them: "This is what you are to say to my master Esau: 'Your servant Jacob says, I have been staying with Laban and have remained there till now. ⁵I have cattle and donkeys, sheep and goats, menservants and maidservants. Now I am sending this message to my lord, that I may find favour in your eyes.' "

⁶When the messengers returned to Jacob, they said, "We went to your brother Esau, and now he is coming to meet you, and four hundred men are with him."

⁷In great fear and distress Jacob divided the people who were with him into two groups,ᵇ and the flocks and herds and camels as well. ⁸He thought, "If Esau comes and attacks one group,ᶜ the groupᶜ that is left may escape."

⁹Then Jacob prayed, "O God of my father Abraham, God of my father Isaac, O Lᴏʀᴅ, who said to me, 'Go back to your country and your relatives, and I will make you prosper,' ¹⁰I am unworthy of all the kindness and faithfulness you have shown your servant. I had only my staff when I crossed this Jordan, but now I have become two groups. ¹¹Save me, I pray, from the hand of my brother Esau, for I am afraid he will come and attack me, and also the mothers with their children. ¹²But you have said, 'I will surely make you prosper and will make your descendants like the sand of the sea, which cannot be counted.' "

¹³He spent the night there, and from what he had with him he selected a gift for his brother Esau: ¹⁴two hundred female goats and twenty male goats, two hundred ewes and twenty rams, ¹⁵thirty female camels with their young, forty cows and ten bulls, and twenty female donkeys and ten male donkeys. ¹⁶He put them in the care of his servants, each herd by itself, and said to his servants, "Go ahead of me, and keep some space between the herds."

¹⁷He instructed the one in the lead: "When my brother Esau meets you and asks, 'To whom do you belong, and where are you going, and who owns all these animals in front of you?' ¹⁸then you are to say, 'They belong to your servant Jacob. They are a gift sent to my lord Esau, and he is coming behind us.' "

¹⁹He also instructed the second, the third and all the others who followed the herds: "You are to say the same thing to Esau when you meet him. ²⁰And be sure to say, 'Your servant Jacob is coming behind us.' " For he thought, "I will pacify him with these gifts I am sending on ahead; later, when I see him, perhaps he will receive me." ²¹So Jacob's gifts went on ahead of him, but he himself spent the night in the camp.

Jacob Wrestles With God

²²That night Jacob got up and took his two wives, his two maidservants and his eleven sons and crossed the ford of the Jabbok. ²³After he had sent them across the stream, he sent over all his possessions. ²⁴So Jacob was left alone, and a man wrestled with him till daybreak. ²⁵When the man saw that he could not overpower him, he touched the socket of Jacob's hip so that his hip was wrenched as he wrestled with the man. ²⁶Then the man said, "Let me go, for it is daybreak."

But Jacob replied, "I will not let you go unless you bless me."

²⁷The man asked him, "What is your name?"

"Jacob," he answered.

²⁸Then the man said, "Your name will no longer be Jacob, but Israel,ᵈ because you have struggled with God and with men and have overcome."

²⁹Jacob said, "Please tell me your name."

But he replied, "Why do you ask my name?" Then he blessed him there.

³⁰So Jacob called the place Peniel,ᵉ saying, "It is because I saw God face to face, and yet my life was spared."

³¹The sun rose above him as he passed Peniel,ᶠ and he was limping because of his hip. ³²Therefore to this day the Israelites do not eat the tendon attached to the socket of the hip, because the socket of Jacob's hip was touched near the tendon.

Jacob Meets Esau

33 Jacob looked up and there was Esau, coming with his four hundred men; so he divided the children among Leah, Rachel and the two maidservants. ²He put the maidservants and their children in front, Leah and her children next, and Rachel and Joseph in the rear. ³He himself went on ahead and bowed down to the ground seven times as he approached his brother.

⁴But Esau ran to meet Jacob and embraced him; he threw his arms around his neck and kissed him. And they wept. ⁵Then Esau looked up and saw the women and children. "Who are these with you?" he asked.

Jacob answered, "They are the children God has graciously given your servant."

⁶Then the maidservants and their children approached and bowed down. ⁷Next, Leah and her children came and bowed down. Last of all came Joseph and Rachel, and they too bowed down.

⁸Esau asked, "What do you mean by all these droves I met?"

"To find favour in your eyes, my lord," he said.

⁹But Esau said, "I already have plenty, my brother. Keep what you have for yourself."

¹⁰"No, please!" said Jacob. "If I have found favour in your eyes, accept this gift from me. For to see your face is like seeing the face of God, now that you have received me favourably. ¹¹Please accept the present that was brought to you, for God has been gracious to

---

ᵃ2 *Mahanaim* means *two camps.*   ᵇ7 Or *camps*; also in verse 10   ᶜ8 Or *camp*
ᵈ28 *Israel* means *he struggles with God.*   ᵉ30 *Peniel* means *face of God.*   ᶠ31 Hebrew *Penuel*, a variant of *Peniel*

me and I have all I need." And because Jacob insisted, Esau accepted it.

¹²Then Esau said, "Let us be on our way; I'll accompany you."

¹³But Jacob said to him, "My lord knows that the children are tender and that I must care for the ewes and cows that are nursing their young. If they are driven hard just one day, all the animals will die. ¹⁴So let my lord go on ahead of his servant, while I move along slowly at the pace of the droves before me and that of the children, until I come to my lord in Seir."

¹⁵Esau said, "Then let me leave some of my men with you."

"But why do that?" Jacob asked. "Just let me find favour in the eyes of my lord."

¹⁶So that day Esau started on his way back to Seir. ¹⁷Jacob, however, went to Succoth, where he built a place for himself and made shelters for his livestock. That is why the place is called Succoth.ᵃ

¹⁸After Jacob came from Paddan Aram,ᵇ he arrived safely at theᶜ city of Shechem in Canaan and camped within sight of the city. ¹⁹For a hundred pieces of silver,ᵈ he bought from the sons of Hamor, the father of Shechem, the plot of ground where he pitched his tent. ²⁰There he set up an altar and called it El Elohe Israel.ᵉ

Dinah and the Shechemites

34 Now Dinah, the daughter Leah had borne to Jacob, went out to visit the women of the land. ²When Shechem son of Hamor the Hivite, the ruler of that area, saw her, he took her and raped her. ³His heart was drawn to Dinah daughter of Jacob, and he loved the girl and spoke tenderly to her. ⁴And Shechem said to his father Hamor, "Get me this girl as my wife."

⁵When Jacob heard that his daughter Dinah had been defiled, his sons were in the fields with his livestock; so he kept quiet about it until they came home.

⁶Then Shechem's father Hamor went out to talk with Jacob. ⁷Now Jacob's sons had come in from the fields as soon as they heard what had happened. They were filled with grief and fury, because Shechem had done a disgraceful thing inᵃ Israel by lying with Jacob's daughter—a thing that should not be done.

⁸But Hamor said to them, "My son Shechem has his heart set on your daughter. Please give her to him as his wife. ⁹Intermarry with us; give us your daughters and take our daughters for yourselves. ¹⁰You can settle among us; the land is open to you. Live in it, tradeᵇ in it, and acquire property in it."

¹¹Then Shechem said to Dinah's father and brothers, "Let me find favour in your eyes, and I will give you whatever you ask. ¹²Make the price for the bride and the gift I am to bring as great as you like, and I'll pay whatever you ask me. Only give me the girl as my wife."

¹³Because their sister Dinah had been defiled,

Jacob's sons replied deceitfully as they spoke to Shechem and his father Hamor. ¹⁴They said to them, "We can't do such a thing; we can't give our sister to a man who is not circumcised. That would be a disgrace to us. ¹⁵We will give you our consent to you on one condition only: that you become like us by circumcising all your males. ¹⁶Then we will give you our daughters and take your daughters for ourselves. We'll settle among you and become one people with you. ¹⁷But if you will not agree to be circumcised, we'll take our sisterᶜ and go."

¹⁸Their proposal seemed good to Hamor and his son Shechem. ¹⁹The young man, who was the most honoured of all his father's household, lost no time in doing what they said, because he was delighted with Jacob's daughter. ²⁰So Hamor and his son Shechem went to the gate of their city to speak to their fellow townsmen. ²¹"These men are friendly towards us," they said. "Let them live in our land and trade in it; the land has plenty of room for them. We can marry their daughters and they can marry ours. ²²But the men will consent to live with us as one people only on the condition that our males be circumcised, as they themselves are. ²³Won't their livestock, their property and all their other animals become ours? So let us give our consent to them, and they will settle among us."

²⁴All the men who went out of the city gate agreed with Hamor and his son Shechem, and every male in the city was circumcised.

²⁵Three days later, while all of them were still in pain, two of Jacob's sons, Simeon and Levi, Dinah's brothers, took their swords and attacked the unsuspecting city, killing every male. ²⁶They put Hamor and his son Shechem to the sword and took Dinah from Shechem's house and left. ²⁷The sons of Jacob came upon the dead bodies and looted the city whereᵈ their sister had been defiled. ²⁸They seized their flocks and herds and donkeys and everything else of theirs in the city and out in the fields. ²⁹They carried off all their wealth and all their women and children, taking as plunder everything in the houses.

34:25 By the time the Israelites were settled in Canaan, Simeon's clan had almost disappeared, and the Levites never possessed tribal territory. This story probably comes from a time when the two tribes were powerful, and is more a story about a tribal fight with Shechem than about the two brothers.

---

³⁰Then Jacob said to Simeon and Levi, "You have brought trouble on me by making me a stench to the Canaanites and Perizzites, the people living in this land. We are few in number, and if they join forces against me and attack me, I and my household will be destroyed."

³¹But they replied, "Should he have treated our sister like a prostitute?"

ᵃ17 *Succoth* means *shelters.*   ᵇ18 That is, North-west Mesopotamia   ᶜ18 Or *arrived at Shalem, a*
ᵈ19 Hebrew *hundred kesitahs*; a kesitah was a unit of money of unknown weight and value.
ᵉ20 *El Elohe Israel* can mean *God, the God of Israel* or *mighty is the God of Israel.*   ᵃ7 Or *against*
ᵇ10 Or *move about freely*; also in verse 21   ᶜ17 Hebrew *daughter*   ᵈ27 Or *because*

Jacob Returns to Bethel

35 Then God said to Jacob, "Go up to Bethel and settle there, and build an altar there to God, who appeared to you when you were fleeing from your brother Esau."

²So Jacob said to his household and to all who were with him, "Get rid of the foreign gods you have with you, and purify yourselves and change your clothes. ³Then come, let us go up to Bethel, where I will build an altar to God, who answered me in the day of my distress and who has been with me wherever I have gone." ⁴So they gave Jacob all the foreign gods they had and the rings in their ears, and Jacob buried them under the oak at Shechem. ⁵Then they set out, and the terror of God fell upon the towns all around them so that no-one pursued them.

⁶Jacob and all the people with him came to Luz (that is, Bethel) in the land of Canaan. ⁷There he built an altar, and he called the place El Bethel,ᵃ because it was there that God revealed himself to him when he was fleeing from his brother.

⁸Now Deborah, Rebekah's nurse, died and was buried under the oak below Bethel. So it was named Allon Bacuth.ᵇ

⁹After Jacob returned from Paddan Aram,ᶜ God appeared to him again and blessed him. ¹⁰God said to him, "Your name is Jacob,ᵈ but you will no longer be called Jacob; your name will be Israel."ᵉ So he named him Israel.

¹¹And God said to him, "I am God Almighty;ᶠ be fruitful and increase in number. A nation and a community of nations will come from you, and kings will come from your body. ¹²The land I gave to Abraham and Isaac I also give to you, and I will give this land to your descendants after you." ¹³Then God went up from him at the place where he had talked with him.

¹⁴Jacob set up a stone pillar at the place where God had talked with him, and he poured out a drink offering on it; he also poured oil on it. ¹⁵Jacob called the place where God had talked with him Bethel.ᵍ

The Deaths of Rachel and Isaac

¹⁶Then they moved on from Bethel. While they were still some distance from Ephrath, Rachel began to give birth and had great difficulty. ¹⁷And as she was having great difficulty in childbirth, the midwife said to her, "Don't be afraid, for you have another son." ¹⁸As she breathed her last—for she was dying—she named her son Ben-Oni.ʰ But his father named him Benjamin.ⁱ ¹⁹So Rachel died and was buried on the way to Ephrath (that is, Bethlehem). ²⁰Over her tomb Jacob set up a pillar, and to this day that pillar marks Rachel's tomb.

²¹Israel moved on again and pitched his tent beyond Migdal Eder. ²²While Israel was living in that region, Reuben went in and slept with his father's concubine Bilhah, and Israel heard of it.

Jacob had twelve sons:

²³The sons of Leah:
Reuben the firstborn of Jacob,
Simeon, Levi, Judah, Issachar and Zebulun.

²⁴The sons of Rachel:
Joseph and Benjamin.

²⁵The sons of Rachel's maidservant Bilhah:
Dan and Naphtali.

²⁶The sons of Leah's maidservant Zilpah:
Gad and Asher.

These were the sons of Jacob, who were born to him in Paddan Aram.

²⁷Jacob came home to his father Isaac in Mamre, near Kiriath Arba (that is, Hebron), where Abraham and Isaac had stayed. ²⁸Isaac lived a hundred and eighty years. ²⁹Then he breathed his last and died and was gathered to his people, old and full of years. And his sons Esau and Jacob buried him.

Esau's Descendants

36 This is the account of Esau (that is, Edom).

²Esau took his wives from the women of Canaan: Adah daughter of Elon the Hittite, and Oholibamah daughter of Anah and granddaughter of Zibeon the Hivite—³also Basemath daughter of Ishmael and sister of Nebaioth.

⁴Adah bore Eliphaz to Esau, Basemath bore Reuel, ⁵and Oholibamah bore Jeush, Jalam and Korah. These were the sons of Esau, who were born to him in Canaan.

⁶Esau took his wives and sons and daughters and all the members of his household, as well as his livestock and all his other animals and all the goods he had acquired in Canaan, and moved to a land some distance from his brother Jacob. ⁷Their possessions were too great for them to remain together; the land where they were staying could not support them both because of their livestock. ⁸So Esau (that is, Edom) settled in the hill country of Seir.

⁹This is the account of Esau the father of the Edomites in the hill country of Seir.

36:9 Edom is south of the Dead Sea. Its people are thought to be descended from Esau. For hundreds of years Israel and Edom were sworn enemies. David fought them, and when the Israelites were in exile Edom took over some of their territory (1 Kings 11). In New Testament times Edom was known as Idumea. King Herod was an Idumean.

ᵃ7 El Bethel means God of Bethel.   ᵇ8 Allon Bacuth means oak of weeping.
ᶜ9 That is, North-west Mesopotamia; also in verse 26   ᵈ10 Jacob means he grasps the heel (figuratively, he deceives).
ᵉ10 Israel means he struggles with God.   ᶠ11 Hebrew El-Shaddai   ᵍ15 Bethel means house of God.
ʰ18 Ben-Oni means son of my trouble.   ⁱ18 Benjamin means son of my right hand.

¹⁰These are the names of Esau's sons:
Eliphaz, the son of Esau's wife Adah, and Reuel, the son of Esau's wife Basemath.
¹¹The sons of Eliphaz:
Teman, Omar, Zepho, Gatam and Kenaz.
¹²Esau's son Eliphaz also had a concubine named Timna, who bore him Amalek. These were grandsons of Esau's wife Adah.
¹³The sons of Reuel:
Nahath, Zerah, Shammah and Mizzah. These were grandsons of Esau's wife Basemath.
¹⁴The sons of Esau's wife Oholibamah daughter of Anah and granddaughter of Zibeon, whom she bore to Esau:
Jeush, Jalam and Korah.

¹⁵These were the chiefs among Esau's descendants:
The sons of Eliphaz the firstborn of Esau:
Chiefs Teman, Omar, Zepho, Kenaz, ¹⁶Korah,ᵃ Gatam and Amalek. These were the chiefs descended from Eliphaz in Edom; they were grandsons of Adah.
¹⁷The sons of Esau's son Reuel:
Chiefs Nahath, Zerah, Shammah and Mizzah. These were the chiefs descended from Reuel in Edom; they were grandsons of Esau's wife Basemath.
¹⁸The sons of Esau's wife Oholibamah:
Chiefs Jeush, Jalam and Korah. These were the chiefs descended from Esau's wife Oholibamah daughter of Anah.
¹⁹These were the sons of Esau (that is, Edom), and these were their chiefs.

²⁰These were the sons of Seir the Horite, who were living in the region:
Lotan, Shobal, Zibeon, Anah, ²¹Dishon, Ezer and Dishan. These sons of Seir in Edom were Horite chiefs.
²²The sons of Lotan:
Hori and Homam.ᵇ Timna was Lotan's sister.
²³The sons of Shobal:
Alvan, Manahath, Ebal, Shepho and Onam.
²⁴The sons of Zibeon:
Aiah and Anah. This is the Anah who discovered the hot springsᶜ in the desert while he was grazing the donkeys of his father Zibeon.
²⁵The children of Anah:
Dishon and Oholibamah daughter of Anah.
²⁶The sons of Dishon:ᵈ
Hemdan, Eshban, Ithran and Keran.
²⁷The sons of Ezer:
Bilhan, Zaavan and Akan.
²⁸The sons of Dishan:
Uz and Aran.
²⁹These were the Horite chiefs:
Lotan, Shobal, Zibeon, Anah, ³⁰Dishon, Ezer and Dishan. These were the Horite chiefs, according to their divisions, in the land of Seir.

The Rulers of Edom

³¹These were the kings who reigned in Edom before any Israelite king reigned:ᵉ ³²Bela son of Beor became king of Edom. His city was named Dinhabah.
³³When Bela died, Jobab son of Zerah from Bozrah succeeded him as king.
³⁴When Jobab died, Husham from the land of the Temanites succeeded him as king.
³⁵When Husham died, Hadad son of Bedad, who defeated Midian in the country of Moab, succeeded him as king. His city was named Avith.
³⁶When Hadad died, Samlah from Masrekah succeeded him as king.
³⁷When Samlah died, Shaul from Rehoboth on the riverᶠ succeeded him as king.
³⁸When Shaul died, Baal-Hanan son of Acbor succeeded him as king.
³⁹When Baal-Hanan son of Acbor died, Hadadᵍ succeeded him as king. His city was named Pau, and his wife's name was Mehetabel daughter of Matred, the daughter of Me-Zahab.

⁴⁰These were the chiefs descended from Esau, by name, according to their clans and regions:
Timna, Alvah, Jetheth, ⁴¹Oholibamah, Elah, Pinon, ⁴²Kenaz, Teman, Mibzar, ⁴³Magdiel and Iram. These were the chiefs of Edom, according to their settlements in the land they occupied.

This was Esau the father of the Edomites.

Joseph's Dreams

37 Jacob lived in the land where his father had stayed, the land of Canaan.

²This is the account of Jacob.

Joseph, a young man of seventeen, was tending the flocks with his brothers, the sons of Bilhah and the sons of Zilpah, his father's wives, and he brought their father a bad report about them.

³Now Israel loved Joseph more than any of his other sons, because he had been born to him in his old age; and he made him a richly ornamentedᵃ robe for him. ⁴When his brothers saw that their father loved him more than any of them, they hated him and could not speak a kind word to him.

⁵Joseph had a dream, and when he told it to his brothers, they hated him all the more. ⁶He said to them, "Listen to this dream I had: ⁷We were binding sheaves of corn out in the field when suddenly my sheaf rose and stood upright, while your sheaves gathered round mine and bowed down to it."

⁸His brothers said to him, "Do you intend to reign over us? Will you actually rule us?" And they hated him all the more because of his dream and what he had said.

ᵃ16 Masoretic Text; Samaritan Pentateuch (see also Gen. 36:11 and 1 Chron. 1:36) does not have *Korah*.
ᵇ22 Hebrew *Hemam*, a variant of *Homam* (see 1 Chron. 1:39)
ᶜ24 Vulgate; Syriac *discovered water*; the meaning of the Hebrew for this word is uncertain.
ᵈ26 Hebrew *Dishan*, a variant of *Dishon*   ᵉ31 Or *before an Israelite king reigned over them*   ᶠ37 Possibly the Euphrates
ᵍ39 Many manuscripts of the Masoretic Text, Samaritan Pentateuch and Syriac (see also 1 Chron. 1:50); most manuscripts of the Masoretic Text *Hadar*   ᵃ3 The meaning of the Hebrew for *richly ornamented* is uncertain; also in verses 23 and 32.

[9]Then he had another dream, and he told it to his brothers. "Listen," he said, "I had another dream, and this time the sun and moon and eleven stars were bowing down to me."

37:3   Once again God's choice of leader is surprising. Joseph was one of the younger brothers, and the others hated him. The coat his father gave him was a sign that he was to be considered the heir of the family. Joseph could not be expected to spoil it by doing heavy work. This would have been the real reason for his brothers' jealousy.

---

[10]When he told his father as well as his brothers, his father rebuked him and said, "What is this dream you had? Will your mother and I and your brothers actually come and bow down to the ground before you?" [11]His brothers were jealous of him, but his father kept the matter in mind.

Joseph Sold by His Brothers

[12]Now his brothers had gone to graze their father's flocks near Shechem, [13]and Israel said to Joseph, "As you know, your brothers are grazing the flocks near Shechem. Come, I am going to send you to them."
"Very well," he replied.
[14]So he said to him, "Go and see if all is well with your brothers and with the flocks, and bring word back to me." Then he sent him off from the Valley of Hebron.
When Joseph arrived at Shechem, [15]a man found him wandering around in the fields and asked him, "What are you looking for?"
[16]He replied, "I'm looking for my brothers. Can you tell me where they are grazing their flocks?"
[17]"They have moved on from here," the man answered. "I heard them say, 'Let's go to Dothan.' "
So Joseph went after his brothers and found them near Dothan. [18]But they saw him in the distance, and before he reached them, they plotted to kill him.
[19]"Here comes that dreamer!" they said to each other. [20]"Come now, let's kill him and throw him into one of these cisterns and say that a ferocious animal devoured him. Then we'll see what comes of his dreams."
[21]When Reuben heard this, he tried to rescue him from their hands. "Let's not take his life," he said. [22]"Don't shed any blood. Throw him into this cistern here in the desert, but don't lay a hand on him." Reuben said this to rescue him from them and take him back to his father.
[23]So when Joseph came to his brothers, they stripped him of his robe — the richly ornamented robe he was wearing — [24]and they took him and threw him into the cistern. Now the cistern was empty; there was no water in it.
[25]As they sat down to eat their meal, they looked up and saw a caravan of Ishmaelites coming from Gilead.

Their camels were loaded with spices, balm and myrrh, and they were on their way to take them down to Egypt.
[26]Judah said to his brothers, "What will we gain if we kill our brother and cover up his blood? [27]Come, let's sell him to the Ishmaelites and not lay our hands on him; after all, he is our brother, our own flesh and blood." His brothers agreed.
[28]So when the Midianite merchants came by, his brothers pulled Joseph up out of the cistern and sold him for twenty shekels[b] of silver to the Ishmaelites, who took him to Egypt.
[29]When Reuben returned to the cistern and saw that Joseph was not there, he tore his clothes. [30]He went back to his brothers and said, "The boy isn't there! Where can I turn now?"
[31]Then they got Joseph's robe, slaughtered a goat and dipped the robe in the blood. [32]They took the ornamented robe back to their father and said, "We found this. Examine it to see whether it is your son's robe."
[33]He recognised it and said, "It is my son's robe! Some ferocious animal has devoured him. Joseph has surely been torn to pieces."
[34]Then Jacob tore his clothes, put on sackcloth and mourned for his son many days. [35]All his sons and daughters came to comfort him, but he refused to be comforted. "No," he said, "in mourning will I go down to the grave[c] to my son." So his father wept for him.
[36]Meanwhile, the Midianites[d] sold Joseph in Egypt to Potiphar, one of Pharaoh's officials, the captain of the guard.

Judah and Tamar

38   At that time, Judah left his brothers and went down to stay with a man of Adullam named Hirah. [2]There Judah met the daughter of a Canaanite man named Shua. He married her and lay with her; [3]she became pregnant and gave birth to a son, who was named Er. [4]She conceived again and gave birth to a son and named him Onan. [5]She gave birth to still another son and named him Shelah. It was at Kezib that she gave birth to him.
[6]Judah got a wife for Er, his firstborn, and her name was Tamar. [7]But Er, Judah's firstborn, was wicked in the LORD's sight; so the LORD put him to death.
[8]Then Judah said to Onan, "Lie with your brother's wife and fulfil your duty to her as a brother-in-law to produce offspring for your brother." [9]But Onan knew that the offspring would not be his; so whenever he lay with his brother's wife, he spilled his semen on the ground to keep from producing offspring for his brother. [10]What he did was wicked in the LORD's sight; so he put him to death also.
[11]Judah then said to his daughter-in-law Tamar, "Live as a widow in your father's house until my son Shelah grows up." For he thought, "He may die too, just like his brothers." So Tamar went to live in her father's house.
[12]After a long time Judah's wife, the daughter of Shua, died. When Judah had recovered from his grief,

---

[b]28 That is, about 8 ounces (about 0.2 kilogram)   [c]35 Hebrew *Sheol*
[d]36 Samaritan Pentateuch, Septuagint, Vulgate and Syriac (see also verse 28); Masoretic Text *Medanites*

he went up to Timnah, to the men who were shearing his sheep, and his friend Hirah the Adullamite went with him. ¹³When Tamar was told, "Your father-in-law is on his way to Timnah to shear his sheep," ¹⁴she took off her widow's clothes, covered herself with a veil to disguise herself, and then sat down at the entrance to Enaim, which is on the road to Timnah. For she saw that, though Shelah had now grown up, she had not been given to him as his wife.

¹⁵When Judah saw her, he thought she was a prostitute, for she had covered her face. ¹⁶Not realising that she was his daughter-in-law, he went over to her by the roadside and said, "Come now, let me sleep with you."

"And what will you give me to sleep with you?" she asked.

¹⁷"I'll send you a young goat from my flock," he said.

"Will you give me something as a pledge until you send it?" she asked.

¹⁸He said, "What pledge should I give you?"

"Your seal and its cord, and the staff in your hand," she answered. So he gave them to her and slept with her, and she became pregnant by him. ¹⁹After she left, she took off her veil and put on her widow's clothes again.

²⁰Meanwhile Judah sent the young goat by his friend the Adullamite in order to get his pledge back from the woman, but he did not find her. ²¹He asked the men who lived there, "Where is the shrine-prostitute who was beside the road at Enaim?"

"There hasn't been any shrine-prostitute here," they said.

²²So he went back to Judah and said, "I didn't find her. Besides, the men who lived there said, 'There hasn't been any shrine-prostitute here.' "

²³Then Judah said, "Let her keep what she has, or we will become a laughing-stock. After all, I did send her this young goat, but you didn't find her."

²⁴About three months later Judah was told, "Your daughter-in-law Tamar is guilty of prostitution, and as a result she is now pregnant."

Judah said, "Bring her out and have her burned to death!"

²⁵As she was being brought out, she sent a message to her father-in-law. "I am pregnant by the man who owns these," she said. And she added, "See if you recognise whose seal and cord and staff these are."

²⁶Judah recognised them and said, "She is more righteous than I, since I wouldn't give her to my son Shelah." And he did not sleep with her again.

²⁷When the time came for her to give birth, there were twin boys in her womb. ²⁸As she was giving birth, one of them put out his hand; so the midwife took a scarlet thread and tied it on his wrist and said, "This one came out first." ²⁹But when he drew back his hand, his brother came out, and she said, "So this is how you have broken out!" And he was named Perez.ᵃ ³⁰Then his brother, who had the scarlet thread on his wrist, came out and he was given the name Zerah.ᵇ

Joseph and Potiphar's Wife

39 Now Joseph had been taken down to Egypt. Potiphar, an Egyptian who was one of Pharaoh's officials, the captain of the guard, bought him from the Ishmaelites who had taken him there.

> **39:1** This verse, and 37:25,28,36, are confused about what happened to Joseph. Little muddles like this may well be a sign that the story was passed on by word of mouth for a long time before it was written down.

²The LORD was with Joseph and he prospered, and he lived in the house of his Egyptian master. ³When his master saw that the LORD was with him and that the LORD gave him success in everything he did, ⁴Joseph found favour in his eyes and became his attendant. Potiphar put him in charge of his household, and he entrusted to his care everything he owned. ⁵From the time he put him in charge of his household and of all that he owned, the LORD blessed the household of the Egyptian because of Joseph. The blessing of the LORD was on everything Potiphar had, both in the house and in the field. ⁶So he left in Joseph's care everything he had; with Joseph in charge, he did not concern himself with anything except the food he ate.

Now Joseph was well-built and handsome, ⁷and after a while his master's wife took notice of Joseph and said, "Come to bed with me!"

⁸But he refused. "With me in charge," he told her, "my master does not concern himself with anything in the house; everything he owns he has entrusted to my care. ⁹No-one is greater in this house than I am. My master has withheld nothing from me except you, because you are his wife. How then could I do such a wicked thing and sin against God?" ¹⁰And though she spoke to Joseph day after day, he refused to go to bed with her or even to be with her.

¹¹One day he went into the house to attend to his duties, and none of the household servants was inside. ¹²She caught him by his cloak and said, "Come to bed with me!" But he left his cloak in her hand and ran out of the house.

¹³When she saw that he had left his cloak in her hand and had run out of the house, ¹⁴she called her household servants. "Look," she said to them, "this Hebrew has been brought to us to make sport of us! He came in here to sleep with me, but I screamed. ¹⁵When he heard me scream for help, he left his cloak beside me and ran out of the house."

¹⁶She kept his cloak beside her until his master came home. ¹⁷Then she told him this story: "That Hebrew slave you brought us came to me to make sport of me. ¹⁸But as soon as I screamed for help, he left his cloak beside me and ran out of the house."

¹⁹When his master heard the story his wife told him, saying, "This is how your slave treated me," he burned with anger. ²⁰Joseph's master took him and put him

ᵃ29 Perez means breaking out. ᵇ30 Zerah can mean scarlet or brightness.

in prison, the place where the king's prisoners were confined.

But while Joseph was there in the prison, [21] the LORD was with him; he showed him kindness and granted him favour in the eyes of the prison warder. [22] So the warder put Joseph in charge of all those held in the prison, and he was made responsible for all that was done there. [23] The warder paid no attention to anything under Joseph's care, because the LORD was with Joseph and gave him success in whatever he did.

39:23   This verse underlines the point of the whole Joseph story. It was a necessary part of God's plan for humankind that his people should come to Egypt. The reader is told that God was with Joseph there, even though he did not know what was to become of him. People often find that when they look back on trying times they can see that some good has come out of the situation.

The Cupbearer and the Baker

40 Some time later, the cupbearer and the baker of the king of Egypt offended their master, the king of Egypt. [2] Pharaoh was angry with his two officials, the chief cupbearer and the chief baker, [3] and put them in custody in the house of the captain of the guard, in the same prison where Joseph was confined. [4] The captain of the guard assigned them to Joseph, and he attended them.

After they had been in custody for some time, [5] each of the two men — the cupbearer and the baker of the king of Egypt, who were being held in prison — had a dream the same night, and each dream had a meaning of its own.

[6] When Joseph came to them the next morning, he saw that they were dejected. [7] So he asked Pharaoh's officials who were in custody with him in his master's house, "Why are your faces so sad today?"

[8] "We both had dreams," they answered, "but there is no-one to interpret them."

Then Joseph said to them, "Do not interpretations belong to God? Tell me your dreams."

[9] So the chief cupbearer told Joseph his dream. He said to him, "In my dream I saw a vine in front of me, [10] and on the vine were three branches. As soon as it budded, it blossomed, and its clusters ripened into grapes. [11] Pharaoh's cup was in my hand, and I took the grapes, squeezed them into Pharaoh's cup and put the cup in his hand."

[12] "This is what it means," Joseph said to him. "The three branches are three days. [13] Within three days Pharaoh will lift up your head and restore you to your position, and you will put Pharaoh's cup in his hand, just as you used to do when you were his cupbearer. [14] But when all goes well with you, remember me and show me kindness; mention me to Pharaoh and get me out of this prison. [15] For I was forcibly carried off from the land of the Hebrews, and even here I have done nothing to deserve being put in a dungeon."

[16] When the chief baker saw that Joseph had given a favourable interpretation, he said to Joseph, "I too had a dream: On my head were three baskets of bread. [a] [17] In the top basket were all kinds of baked goods for Pharaoh, but the birds were eating them out of the basket on my head."

[18] "This is what it means," Joseph said. "The three baskets are three days. [19] Within three days Pharaoh will lift off your head and hang you on a tree. [b] And the birds will eat away your flesh."

[20] Now the third day was Pharaoh's birthday, and he gave a feast for all his officials. He lifted up the heads of the chief cupbearer and the chief baker in the presence of his officials: [21] He restored the chief cupbearer to his position, so that he once again put the cup into Pharaoh's hand, [22] but he hanged [c] the chief baker, just as Joseph had said to them in his interpretation.

[23] The chief cupbearer, however, did not remember Joseph; he forgot him.

Pharaoh's Dreams

41 When two full years had passed, Pharaoh had a dream: He was standing by the Nile, [2] when out of the river there came up seven cows, sleek and fat, and they grazed among the reeds. [3] After them, seven other cows, ugly and gaunt, came up out of the Nile and stood beside those on the riverbank. [4] And the cows that were ugly and gaunt ate up the seven sleek, fat cows. Then Pharaoh woke up.

[5] He fell asleep again and had a second dream: Seven ears of corn, healthy and good, were growing on a single stalk. [6] After them, seven other ears of corn sprouted — thin and scorched by the east wind. [7] The thin ears of corn swallowed up the seven healthy, full ears. Then Pharaoh woke up; it had been a dream.

[8] In the morning his mind was troubled, so he sent for all the magicians and wise men of Egypt. Pharaoh told them his dreams, but no-one could interpret them for him.

[9] Then the chief cupbearer said to Pharaoh, "Today I am reminded of my shortcomings. [10] Pharaoh was once angry with his servants, and he imprisoned me and the chief baker in the house of the captain of the guard. [11] Each of us had a dream the same night, and each dream had a meaning of its own. [12] Now a young Hebrew was there with us, a servant of the captain of the guard. We told him our dreams, and he interpreted them for us, giving each man the interpretation of his dream. [13] And things turned out exactly as he interpreted them to us: I was restored to my position, and the other man was hanged." [a]

[14] So Pharaoh sent for Joseph, and he was quickly brought from the dungeon. When he had shaved and changed his clothes, he came before Pharaoh.

[15] Pharaoh said to Joseph, "I had a dream, and no-one can interpret it. But I have heard it said of you that when you hear a dream you can interpret it."

[16] "I cannot do it," Joseph replied to Pharaoh, "but God will give Pharaoh the answer he desires."

---

a 16 Or *three wicker baskets*   *b* 19 Or *and impale you on a pole*   *c* 22 Or *impaled*   *a* 13 Or *impaled*

17Then Pharaoh said to Joseph, "In my dream I was standing on the bank of the Nile, 18when out of the river there came up seven cows, fat and sleek, and they grazed among the reeds. 19After them, seven other cows came up—scrawny and very ugly and lean. I had never seen such ugly cows in all the land of Egypt. 20The lean, ugly cows ate up the seven fat cows that came up first. 21But even after they ate them, no-one could tell that they had done so; they looked just as ugly as before. Then I woke up.

22"In my dreams I also saw seven ears of corn, full and good, growing on a single stalk. 23After them, seven other ears sprouted—withered and thin and scorched by the east wind. 24The thin ears of corn swallowed up the seven good ears. I told this to the magicians, but none could explain it to me."

25Then Joseph said to Pharaoh, "The dreams of Pharaoh are one and the same. God has revealed to Pharaoh what he is about to do. 26The seven good cows are seven years, and the seven good ears of corn are seven years; it is one and the same dream. 27The seven lean, ugly cows that came up afterwards are seven years, and so are the seven worthless ears of corn scorched by the east wind: They are seven years of famine.

28"It is just as I said to Pharaoh: God has shown Pharaoh what he is about to do. 29Seven years of great abundance are coming throughout the land of Egypt, 30but seven years of famine will follow them. Then all the abundance in Egypt will be forgotten, and the famine will ravage the land. 31The abundance in the land will not be remembered, because the famine that follows it will be so severe. 32The reason the dream was given to Pharaoh in two forms is that the matter has been firmly decided by God, and God will do it soon.

33"And now let Pharaoh look for a discerning and wise man and put him in charge of the land of Egypt. 34Let Pharaoh appoint commissioners over the land to take a fifth of the harvest of Egypt during the seven years of abundance. 35They should collect all the food of these good years that are coming and store up the grain under the authority of Pharaoh, to be kept in the cities for food. 36This food should be held in reserve for the country, to be used during the seven years of famine that will come upon Egypt, so that the country may not be ruined by the famine."

37The plan seemed good to Pharaoh and to all his officials. 38So Pharaoh asked them, "Can we find anyone like this man, one in whom is the spirit of God?"b

39Then Pharaoh said to Joseph, "Since God has made all this known to you, there is no-one so discerning and wise as you. 40You shall be in charge of my palace, and all my people are to submit to your orders. Only with respect to the throne will I be greater than you."

Joseph in Charge of Egypt

41So Pharaoh said to Joseph, "I hereby put you in charge of the whole land of Egypt." 42Then Pharaoh took his signet ring from his finger and put it on Joseph's finger. He dressed him in robes of fine linen and put a gold chain around his neck. 43He had him ride in a chariot as his second-in-command,c and men shouted before him, "Make way!"d Thus he put him in charge of the whole land of Egypt.

44Then Pharaoh said to Joseph, "I am Pharaoh, but without your word no-one will lift hand or foot in all Egypt." 45Pharaoh gave Joseph the name Zaphenath-Paneah and gave him Asenath daughter of Potiphera, priest of On,e to be his wife. And Joseph went throughout the land of Egypt.

41:45 It is not possible to say exactly when Joseph was in Egypt. If it was at the time when Semitic people ruled the country, they would have found it easier than native Egyptians to put Joseph into such a powerful position.

46Joseph was thirty years old when he entered the service of Pharaoh king of Egypt. And Joseph went out from Pharaoh's presence and travelled throughout Egypt. 47During the seven years of abundance the land produced plentifully. 48Joseph collected all the food produced in those seven years of abundance in Egypt and stored it in the cities. In each city he put the food grown in the fields surrounding it. 49Joseph stored up huge quantities of grain, like the sand of the sea; it was so much that he stopped keeping records because it was beyond measure.

50Before the years of famine came, two sons were born to Joseph by Asenath daughter of Potiphera, priest of On. 51Joseph named his firstborn Manassehf and said, "It is because God has made me forget all my trouble and all my father's household." 52The second son he named Ephraimg and said, "It is because God has made me fruitful in the land of my suffering."

53The seven years of abundance in Egypt came to an end, 54and the seven years of famine began, just as Joseph had said. There was famine in all the other lands, but in the whole land of Egypt there was food. 55When all Egypt began to feel the famine, the people cried to Pharaoh for food. Then Pharaoh told all the Egyptians, "Go to Joseph and do what he tells you." 56When the famine had spread over the whole country, Joseph opened the storehouses and sold grain to the Egyptians, for the famine was severe throughout Egypt. 57And all the countries came to Egypt to buy grain from Joseph, because the famine was severe in all the world.

Joseph's Brothers Go to Egypt

42 When Jacob learned that there was grain in Egypt, he said to his sons, "Why do you just keep looking at each other?" 2He continued, "I have heard that there is grain in Egypt. Go down there and buy some for us, so that we may live and not die."

3Then ten of Joseph's brothers went down to buy grain from Egypt. 4But Jacob did not send Benjamin, Joseph's brother, with the others, because he was afraid that harm might come to him. 5So Israel's sons

b38 Or of the gods   c43 Or in the chariot of his second-in-command; or in his second chariot   d43 Or Bow down
e45 That is, Heliopolis; also in verse 50   f51 Manasseh sounds like and may be derived from the Hebrew for forget.
g52 Ephraim sounds like the Hebrew for twice fruitful.

were among those who went to buy grain, for the famine was in the land of Canaan also.

[6]Now Joseph was the governor of the land, the one who sold grain to all its people. So when Joseph's brothers arrived, they bowed down to him with their faces to the ground. [7]As soon as Joseph saw his brothers, he recognised them, but he pretended to be a stranger and spoke harshly to them. "Where do you come from?" he asked.

"From the land of Canaan," they replied, "to buy food."

[8]Although Joseph recognised his brothers, they did not recognise him. [9]Then he remembered his dreams about them and said to them, "You are spies! You have come to see where our land is unprotected."

[10]"No, my lord," they answered. "Your servants have come to buy food. [11]We are all the sons of one man. Your servants are honest men, not spies."

[12]"No!" he said to them. "You have come to see where our land is unprotected."

[13]But they replied, "Your servants were twelve brothers, the sons of one man, who lives in the land of Canaan. The youngest is now with our father, and one is no more."

[14]Joseph said to them, "It is just as I told you: You are spies! [15]And this is how you will be tested: As surely as Pharaoh lives, you will not leave this place unless your youngest brother comes here. [16]Send one of your number to get your brother; the rest of you will be kept in prison, so that your words may be tested to see if you are telling the truth. If you are not, then as surely as Pharaoh lives, you are spies!" [17]And he put them all in custody for three days.

[18]On the third day, Joseph said to them, "Do this and you will live, for I fear God: [19]If you are honest men, let one of your brothers stay here in prison, while the rest of you go and take grain back for your starving households. [20]But you must bring your youngest brother to me, so that your words may be verified and that you may not die." This they proceeded to do.

[21]They said to one another, "Surely we are being punished because of our brother. We saw how distressed he was when he pleaded with us for his life, but we would not listen; that's why this distress has come upon us."

[22]Reuben replied, "Didn't I tell you not to sin against the boy? But you wouldn't listen! Now we must give an accounting for his blood." [23]They did not realise that Joseph could understand them, since he was using an interpreter.

[24]He turned away from them and began to weep, but then turned back and spoke to them again. He had Simeon taken from them and bound before their eyes.

[25]Joseph gave orders to fill their bags with grain, to put each man's silver back in his sack, and to give them provisions for their journey. After this was done for them, [26]they loaded their grain on their donkeys and left.

[27]At the place where they stopped for the night one of them opened his sack to get feed for his donkey, and he saw his silver in the mouth of his sack. [28]"My silver

has been returned," he said to his brothers. "Here it is in my sack."

Their hearts sank and they turned to each other trembling and said, "What is this that God has done to us?"

[29]When they came to their father Jacob in the land of Canaan, they told him all that had happened to them. They said, [30]"The man who is lord over the land spoke harshly to us and treated us as though we were spying on the land. [31]But we said to him, 'We are honest men; we are not spies. [32]We were twelve brothers, sons of one father. One is no more, and the youngest is now with our father in Canaan.'

[33]"Then the man who is lord over the land said to us, 'This is how I will know whether you are honest men: Leave one of your brothers here with me, and take food for your starving households and go. [34]But bring your youngest brother to me so I will know that you are not spies but honest men. Then I will give your brother back to you, and you can trade[a] in the land.' "

[35]As they were emptying their sacks, there in each man's sack was his pouch of silver! When they and their father saw the money pouches, they were frightened. [36]Their father Jacob said to them, "You have deprived me of my children. Joseph is no more and Simeon is no more, and now you want to take Benjamin. Everything is against me!"

[37]Then Reuben said to his father, "You may put both of my sons to death if I do not bring him back to you. Entrust him to my care, and I will bring him back."

42:37   The story of Joseph is so familiar it is easy to miss the drama of it. The storyteller's skill is marked here. Joseph thought that Reuben had allowed Jacob to suffer the loss of a son. Then he found himself risking the same grief for himself in order to save the whole family (43:8).

---

[38]But Jacob said, "My son will not go down there with you; his brother is dead and he is the only one left. If harm comes to him on the journey you are taking, you will bring my grey head down to the grave[b] in sorrow."

The Second Journey to Egypt

43 Now the famine was still severe in the land. [2]So when they had eaten all the grain they had brought from Egypt, their father said to them, "Go back and buy us a little more food."

[3]But Judah said to him, "The man warned us solemnly, 'You will not see my face again unless your brother is with you.' [4]If you will send our brother along with us, we will go down and buy food for you. [5]But if you will not send him, we will not go down, because the man said to us, 'You will not see my face again unless your brother is with you.' "

[6]Israel asked, "Why did you bring this trouble on me by telling the man you had another brother?"

[7]They replied, "The man questioned us closely

about ourselves and our family. 'Is your father still living?' he asked us. 'Do you have another brother?' We simply answered his questions. How were we to know he would say, 'Bring your brother down here'?"

[8]Then Judah said to Israel his father, "Send the boy along with me and we will go at once, so that we and you and our children may live and not die. [9]I myself will guarantee his safety; you can hold me personally responsible for him. If I do not bring him back to you and set him here before you, I will bear the blame before you all my life. [10]As it is, if we had not delayed, we could have gone and returned twice."

[11]Then their father Israel said to them, "If it must be, then do this: Put some of the best products of the land in your bags and take them down to the man as a gift — a little balm and a little honey, some spices and myrrh, some pistachio nuts and almonds. [12]Take double the amount of silver with you, for you must return the silver that was put back into the mouths of your sacks. Perhaps it was a mistake. [13]Take your brother also and go back to the man at once. [14]And may God Almighty[a] grant you mercy before the man so that he will let your other brother and Benjamin come back with you. As for me, if I am bereaved, I am bereaved."

[15]So the men took the gifts and double the amount of silver, and Benjamin also. They hurried down to Egypt and presented themselves to Joseph. [16]When Joseph saw Benjamin with them, he said to the steward of his house, "Take these men to my house, slaughter an animal and prepare dinner; they are to eat with me at noon."

[17]The man did as Joseph told him and took the men to Joseph's house. [18]Now the men were frightened when they were taken to his house. They thought, "We were brought here because of the silver that was put back into our sacks the first time. He wants to attack us and overpower us and seize us as slaves and take our donkeys."

[19]So they went up to Joseph's steward and spoke to him at the entrance to the house. [20]"Please, sir," they said, "we came down here the first time to buy food. [21]But at the place where we stopped for the night we opened our sacks and each of us found his silver — the exact weight — in the mouth of his sack. So we have brought it back with us. [22]We have also brought additional silver with us to buy food. We don't know who put our silver in our sacks."

[23]"It's all right," he said. "Don't be afraid. Your God, the God of your father, has given you treasure in your sacks; I received your silver." Then he brought Simeon out to them.

[24]The steward took the men into Joseph's house, gave them water to wash their feet and provided fodder for their donkeys. [25]They prepared their gifts for Joseph's arrival at noon, because they had heard that they were to eat there.

[26]When Joseph came home, they presented to him the gifts they had brought into the house, and they bowed down before him to the ground. [27]He asked them how they were, and then he said, "How is your aged father you told me about? Is he still living?"

[28]They replied, "Your servant our father is still alive

and well." And they bowed low to pay him honour.

[29]As he looked about and saw his brother Benjamin, his own mother's son, he asked, "Is this your youngest brother, the one you told me about?" And he said, "God be gracious to you, my son." [30]Deeply moved at the sight of his brother, Joseph hurried out and looked for a place to weep. He went into his private room and wept there.

[31]After he had washed his face, he came out and, controlling himself, said, "Serve the food."

[32]They served him by himself, the brothers by themselves, and the Egyptians who ate with him by themselves, because Egyptians could not eat with Hebrews, for that is detestable to Egyptians. [33]The men had been seated before him in the order of their ages, from the firstborn to the youngest; and they looked at each other in astonishment. [34]When portions were served to them from Joseph's table, Benjamin's portion was five times as much as anyone else's. So they feasted and drank freely with him.

43:32   The details of Egyptian life and customs throughout the story of Joseph are very accurate. This verse, which shows Egyptian prejudice over eating, seems to imply that the rulers of Egypt at this time were not Semitic people (see the note on 41:45). This shows how very difficult it is to discover when exactly Joseph lived.

A Silver Cup in a Sack

44   Now Joseph gave these instructions to the steward of his house: "Fill the men's sacks with as much food as they can carry, and put each man's silver in the mouth of his sack. [2]Then put my cup, the silver one, in the mouth of the youngest one's sack, along with the silver for his grain." And he did as Joseph said.

[3]As morning dawned, the men were sent on their way with their donkeys. [4]They had not gone far from the city when Joseph said to his steward, "Go after those men at once, and when you catch up with them, say to them, 'Why have you repaid good with evil? [5]Isn't this the cup my master drinks from and also uses for divination? This is a wicked thing you have done.' "

[6]When he caught up with them, he repeated these words to them. [7]But they said to him, "Why does my lord say such things? Far be it from your servants to do anything like that! [8]We even brought back to you from the land of Canaan the silver we found inside the mouths of our sacks. So why would we steal silver or gold from your master's house? [9]If any of your servants is found to have it, he will die; and the rest of us will become my lord's slaves."

[10]"Very well, then," he said, "let it be as you say. Whoever is found to have it will become my slave; the rest of you will be free from blame."

[11]Each of them quickly lowered his sack to the ground and opened it. [12]Then the steward proceeded

to search, beginning with the oldest and ending with the youngest. And the cup was found in Benjamin's sack. ¹³At this, they tore their clothes. Then they all loaded their donkeys and returned to the city.

¹⁴Joseph was still in the house when Judah and his brothers came in, and they threw themselves to the ground before him. ¹⁵Joseph said to them, "What is this you have done? Don't you know that a man like me can find things out by divination?"

¹⁶"What can we say to my lord?" Judah replied. "What can we say? How can we prove our innocence? God has uncovered your servants' guilt. We are now my lord's slaves — we ourselves and the one who was found to have the cup."

¹⁷But Joseph said, "Far be it from me to do such a thing! Only the man who was found to have the cup will become my slave. The rest of you, go back to your father in peace."

¹⁸Then Judah went up to him and said: "Please, my lord, let your servant speak a word to my lord. Do not be angry with your servant, though you are equal to Pharaoh himself. ¹⁹My lord asked his servants, 'Do you have a father or a brother?' ²⁰And we answered, 'We have an aged father, and there is a young son born to him in his old age. His brother is dead, and he is the only one of his mother's sons left, and his father loves him.'

²¹"Then you said to your servants, 'Bring him down to me so I can see him for myself.' ²²And we said to my lord, 'The boy cannot leave his father; if he leaves him, his father will die.' ²³But you told your servants, 'Unless your youngest brother comes down with you, you will not see my face again.' ²⁴When we went back to your servant my father, we told him what my lord had said.

²⁵"Then our father said, 'Go back and buy a little more food.' ²⁶But we said, 'We cannot go down. Only if our youngest brother is with us will we go. We cannot see the man's face unless our youngest brother is with us.'

²⁷"Your servant my father said to us, 'You know that my wife bore me two sons. ²⁸One of them went away from me, and I said, "He has surely been torn to pieces." And I have not seen him since. ²⁹If you take this one from me too and harm comes to him, you will bring my grey head down to the grave*a* in misery.'

³⁰"So now, if the boy is not with us when I go back to your servant my father and if my father, whose life is closely bound up with the boy's life, ³¹sees that the boy isn't there, he will die. Your servants will bring the grey head of our father down to the grave in sorrow. ³²Your servant guaranteed the boy's safety to my father. I said, 'If I do not bring him back to you, I will bear the blame before you, my father, all my life!'

³³"Now then, please let your servant remain here as my lord's slave in place of the boy, and let the boy return with his brothers. ³⁴How can I go back to my father if the boy is not with me? No! Do not let me see the misery that would come upon my father."

Joseph Makes Himself Known

45 Then Joseph could no longer control himself before all his attendants, and he cried out, "Make everyone leave my presence!" So there was no-one with Joseph when he made himself known to his brothers. ²And he wept so loudly that the Egyptians heard him, and Pharaoh's household heard about it.

³Joseph said to his brothers, "I am Joseph! Is my father still living?" But his brothers were not able to answer him, because they were terrified at his presence.

⁴Then Joseph said to his brothers, "Come close to me." When they had done so, he said, "I am your brother Joseph, the one you sold into Egypt! ⁵And now, do not be distressed and do not be angry with yourselves for selling me here, because it was to save lives that God sent me ahead of you. ⁶For two years now there has been famine in the land, and for the next five years there will not be ploughing and reaping. ⁷But God sent me ahead of you to preserve for you a remnant on earth and to save your lives by a great deliverance.*a*

⁸"So then, it was not you who sent me here, but God. He made me father to Pharaoh, lord of his entire household and ruler of all Egypt. ⁹Now hurry back to my father and say to him, 'This is what your son Joseph says: God has made me lord of all Egypt. Come down to me; don't delay. ¹⁰You shall live in the region of Goshen and be near me — you, your children and grandchildren, your flocks and herds, and all you have. ¹¹I will provide for you there, because five years of famine are still to come. Otherwise you and your household and all who belong to you will become destitute.'

¹²"You can see for yourselves, and so can my brother Benjamin, that it is really I who am speaking to you. ¹³Tell my father about all the honour accorded me in Egypt and about everything you have seen. And bring my father down here quickly."

¹⁴Then he threw his arms around his brother Benjamin and wept, and Benjamin embraced him, weeping. ¹⁵And he kissed all his brothers and wept over them. Afterwards his brothers talked with him.

¹⁶When the news reached Pharaoh's palace that Joseph's brothers had come, Pharaoh and all his officials were pleased. ¹⁷Pharaoh said to Joseph, "Tell your brothers, 'Do this: Load your animals and return to the land of Canaan, ¹⁸and bring your father and your families back to me. I will give you the best of the land of Egypt and you can enjoy the fat of the land.'

¹⁹"You are also directed to tell them, 'Do this: Take some carts from Egypt for your children and your wives, and get your father and come. ²⁰Never mind about your belongings, because the best of all Egypt will be yours.' "

²¹So the sons of Israel did this. Joseph gave them carts, as Pharaoh had commanded, and he also gave them provisions for their journey. ²²To each of them he gave new clothing, but to Benjamin he gave three hundred shekels*b* of silver and five sets of clothes. ²³And this is what he sent to his father: ten donkeys loaded

a29 Hebrew *Sheol*; also in verse 31   *a7* Or *save you as a great band of survivors*
b22 That is, about 7½ pounds (about 3.5 kilograms)

with the best things of Egypt, and ten female donkeys loaded with grain and bread and other provisions for his journey. ²⁴Then he sent his brothers away, and as they were leaving he said to them, "Don't quarrel on the way!"

²⁵So they went up out of Egypt and came to their father Jacob in the land of Canaan. ²⁶They told him, "Joseph is still alive! In fact, he is ruler of all Egypt." Jacob was stunned; he did not believe them. ²⁷But when they told him everything Joseph had said to them, and when he saw the carts Joseph had sent to carry him back, the spirit of their father Jacob revived. ²⁸And Israel said, "I'm convinced! My son Joseph is still alive. I will go and see him before I die."

Jacob Goes to Egypt

46 So Israel set out with all that was his, and when he reached Beersheba, he offered sacrifices to the God of his father Isaac.

²And God spoke to Israel in a vision at night and said, "Jacob! Jacob!"

"Here I am," he replied.

³"I am God, the God of your father," he said. "Do not be afraid to go down to Egypt, for I will make you into a great nation there. ⁴I will go down to Egypt with you, and I will surely bring you back again. And Joseph's own hand will close your eyes."

⁵Then Jacob left Beersheba, and Israel's sons took their father Jacob and their children and their wives in the carts that Pharaoh had sent to transport him. ⁶They also took with them their livestock and the possessions they had acquired in Canaan, and Jacob and all his offspring went to Egypt. ⁷He took with him to Egypt his sons and grandsons and his daughters and granddaughters—all his offspring.

⁸These are the names of the sons of Israel (Jacob and his descendants) who went to Egypt:

Reuben the firstborn of Jacob.
⁹The sons of Reuben:
Hanoch, Pallu, Hezron and Carmi.
¹⁰The sons of Simeon:
Jemuel, Jamin, Ohad, Jakin, Zohar and Shaul the son of a Canaanite woman.
¹¹The sons of Levi:
Gershon, Kohath and Merari.
¹²The sons of Judah:
Er, Onan, Shelah, Perez and Zerah (but Er and Onan had died in the land of Canaan).
The sons of Perez:
Hezron and Hamul.
¹³The sons of Issachar:
Tola, Puah,ª Jashubᵇ and Shimron.
¹⁴The sons of Zebulun:
Sered, Elon and Jahleel.
¹⁵These were the sons Leah bore to Jacob in Paddan Aram,ᶜ besides his daughter Dinah. These sons and daughters of his were thirty-three in all.

¹⁶The sons of Gad:
Zephon,ᵈ Haggi, Shuni, Ezbon, Eri, Arodi and Areli.
¹⁷The sons of Asher:
Imnah, Ishvah, Ishvi and Beriah.
Their sister was Serah.
The sons of Beriah:
Heber and Malkiel.
¹⁸These were the children born to Jacob by Zilpah, whom Laban had given to his daughter Leah—sixteen in all.

¹⁹The sons of Jacob's wife Rachel:
Joseph and Benjamin. ²⁰In Egypt, Manasseh and Ephraim were born to Joseph by Asenath daughter of Potiphera, priest of On.ᵉ
²¹The sons of Benjamin:
Bela, Beker, Ashbel, Gera, Naaman, Ehi, Rosh, Muppim, Huppim and Ard.
²²These were the sons of Rachel who were born to Jacob—fourteen in all.

²³The son of Dan:
Hushim.
²⁴The sons of Naphtali:
Jahziel, Guni, Jezer and Shillem.
²⁵These were the sons born to Jacob by Bilhah, whom Laban had given to his daughter Rachel—seven in all.

²⁶All those who went to Egypt with Jacob—those who were his direct descendants, not counting his sons' wives—numbered sixty-six persons. ²⁷With the two sonsᶠ who had been born to Joseph in Egypt, the members of Jacob's family, which went to Egypt, were seventyᵍ in all.

²⁸Now Jacob sent Judah ahead of him to Joseph to get directions to Goshen. When they arrived in the region of Goshen, ²⁹Joseph had his chariot made ready and went to Goshen to meet his father Israel. As soon as Joseph appeared before him, he threw his arms around his fatherʰ and wept for a long time.

³⁰Israel said to Joseph, "Now I am ready to die, since I have seen for myself that you are still alive."

³¹Then Joseph said to his brothers and to his father's household, "I will go up and speak to Pharaoh and will say to him, 'My brothers and my father's household, who were living in the land of Canaan, have come to me. ³²The men are shepherds; they tend livestock, and they have brought along their flocks and herds and everything they own.' ³³When Pharaoh calls you in and asks, 'What is your occupation?' ³⁴you should answer, 'Your servants have tended livestock from our boyhood on, just as our fathers did.' Then you will be allowed to settle in the region of Goshen, for all shepherds are detestable to the Egyptians."

47 Joseph went and told Pharaoh, "My father and brothers, with their flocks and herds and everything they own, have come from the land of

---

ª13 Samaritan Pentateuch and Syriac (see also 1 Chron. 7:1); Masoretic Text *Puvah*
ᵇ13 Samaritan Pentateuch and some Septuagint manuscripts (see also Num. 26:24 and 1 Chron. 7:1); Masoretic Text *Job*
ᶜ15 That is, North-west Mesopotamia   ᵈ16 Samaritan Pentateuch and Septuagint (see also Num. 26:15); Masoretic Text *Ziphion*
ᵉ20 That is, Heliopolis   ᶠ27 Hebrew; Septuagint *the nine children*
ᵍ27 Hebrew (see also Exodus 1:5 and footnote); Septuagint (see also Acts 7:14) *seventy-five*   ʰ29 Hebrew *around him*

Canaan and are now in Goshen." [2]He chose five of his brothers and presented them before Pharaoh.

[3]Pharaoh asked the brothers, "What is your occupation?"

"Your servants are shepherds," they replied to Pharaoh, "just as our fathers were." [4]They also said to him, "We have come to live here awhile, because the famine is severe in Canaan and your servants' flocks have no pasture. So now, please let your servants settle in Goshen."

[5]Pharaoh said to Joseph, "Your father and your brothers have come to you, [6]and the land of Egypt is before you; settle your father and your brothers in the best part of the land. Let them live in Goshen. And if you know of any among them with special ability, put them in charge of my own livestock."

[7]Then Joseph brought his father Jacob in and presented him before Pharaoh. After Jacob blessed[a] Pharaoh, [8]Pharaoh asked him, "How old are you?"

[9]And Jacob said to Pharaoh, "The years of my pilgrimage are a hundred and thirty. My years have been few and difficult, and they do not equal the years of the pilgrimage of my fathers." [10]Then Jacob blessed[b] Pharaoh and went out from his presence.

[11]So Joseph settled his father and his brothers in Egypt and gave them property in the best part of the land, the district of Rameses, as Pharaoh directed. [12]Joseph also provided his father and his brothers and all his father's household with food, according to the number of their children.

Joseph and the Famine

[13]There was no food, however, in the whole region because the famine was severe; both Egypt and Canaan wasted away because of the famine. [14]Joseph collected all the money that was to be found in Egypt and Canaan in payment for the grain they were buying, and he brought it to Pharaoh's palace. [15]When the money of the people of Egypt and Canaan was gone, all Egypt came to Joseph and said, "Give us food. Why should we die before your eyes? Our money is used up."

[16]"Then bring your livestock," said Joseph. "I will sell you food in exchange for your livestock, since your money is gone." [17]So they brought their livestock to Joseph, and he gave them food in exchange for their horses, their sheep and goats, their cattle and donkeys. And he brought them through that year with food in exchange for all their livestock.

[18]When that year was over, they came to him the following year and said, "We cannot hide from our lord the fact that since our money is gone and our livestock belongs to you, there is nothing left for our lord except our bodies and our land. [19]Why should we perish before your eyes—we and our land as well? Buy us and our land in exchange for food, and we with our land will be in bondage to Pharaoh. Give us seed so that we may live and not die, and that the land may not become desolate."

[20]So Joseph bought all the land in Egypt for Pharaoh. The Egyptians, one and all, sold their fields, because the famine was too severe for them. The land became Pharaoh's, [21]and Joseph reduced the people to servitude,[c] from one end of Egypt to the other. [22]However, he did not buy the land of the priests, because they received a regular allotment from Pharaoh and had food enough from the allotment Pharaoh gave them. That is why they did not sell their land.

[23]Joseph said to the people, "Now that I have bought you and your land today for Pharaoh, here is seed for you so you can plant the ground. [24]But when the crop comes in, give a fifth of it to Pharaoh. The other four-fifths you may keep as seed for the fields and as food for yourselves and your households and your children."

[25]"You have saved our lives," they said. "May we find favour in the eyes of our lord; we will be in bondage to Pharaoh."

[26]So Joseph established it as a law concerning land in Egypt—still in force today—that a fifth of the produce belongs to Pharaoh. It was only the land of the priests that did not become Pharaoh's.

[27]Now the Israelites settled in Egypt in the region of Goshen. They acquired property there and were fruitful and increased greatly in number.

[28]Jacob lived in Egypt seventeen years, and the years of his life were a hundred and forty-seven. [29]When the time drew near for Israel to die, he called for his son Joseph and said to him, "If I have found favour in your eyes, put your hand under my thigh and promise that you will show me kindness and faithfulness. Do not bury me in Egypt, [30]but when I rest with my fathers, carry me out of Egypt and bury me where they are buried."

"I will do as you say," he said.

[31]"Swear to me," he said. Then Joseph swore to him, and Israel worshipped as he leaned on the top of his staff.[d]

Manasseh and Ephraim

48 Some time later Joseph was told, "Your father is ill." So he took his two sons Manasseh and Ephraim along with him. [2]When Jacob was told, "Your son Joseph has come to you," Israel rallied his strength and sat up on the bed.

[3]Jacob said to Joseph, "God Almighty[a] appeared to me at Luz in the land of Canaan, and there he blessed me [4]and said to me, 'I am going to make you fruitful and will increase your numbers. I will make you a community of peoples, and I will give this land as an everlasting possession to your descendants after you.'

[5]"Now then, your two sons born to you in Egypt before I came to you here will be reckoned as mine; Ephraim and Manasseh will be mine, just as Reuben and Simeon are mine. [6]Any children born to you after them will be yours; in the territory they inherit they will be reckoned under the names of their brothers. [7]As I was returning from Paddan,[b] to my sorrow Rachel died in the land of Canaan while we were still on the way, a little distance from Ephrath. So I buried her there beside the road to Ephrath" (that is, Bethlehem).

---

[a]7 Or greeted   [b]10 Or said farewell to
[c]21 Samaritan Pentateuch and Septuagint (see also Vulgate); Masoretic Text and he moved the people into the cities
[d]31 Or Israel bowed down at the head of his bed   [a]3 Hebrew El-Shaddai   [b]7 That is, North-west Mesopotamia

[8]When Israel saw the sons of Joseph, he asked, "Who are these?"

[9]"They are the sons God has given me here," Joseph said to his father.

Then Israel said, "Bring them to me so that I may bless them."

[10]Now Israel's eyes were failing because of old age, and he could hardly see. So Joseph brought his sons close to him, and his father kissed them and embraced them.

[11]Israel said to Joseph, "I never expected to see your face again, and now God has allowed me to see your children too."

[12]Then Joseph removed them from Israel's knees and bowed down with his face to the ground. [13]And Joseph took both of them, Ephraim on his right towards Israel's left hand and Manasseh on his left towards Israel's right hand, and brought them close to him. [14]But Israel reached out his right hand and put it on Ephraim's head, though he was the younger, and crossing his arms, he put his left hand on Manasseh's head, even though Manasseh was the firstborn.

48:14   Isaac, Jacob, and Joseph were all younger brothers and yet received blessings which were normally restricted to the firstborn son. Now Ephraim, Joseph's younger son, too received the blessing. The writers could not emphasize strongly enough that God's blessing cannot be earned, nor is it a matter of position or privilege. It is a sheer and generous gift from God and as such is a mark of his very being. Above all God is a God of love and mercy.

---

[15]Then he blessed Joseph and said,

"May the God before whom my fathers
    Abraham and Isaac walked,
the God who has been my shepherd
    all my life to this day,
[16]the Angel who has delivered me from all harm
    —may he bless these boys.
May they be called by my name
    and the names of my fathers Abraham and
        Isaac,
and may they increase greatly
    upon the earth."

[17]When Joseph saw his father placing his right hand on Ephraim's head he was displeased; so he took hold of his father's hand to move it from Ephraim's head to Manasseh's head. [18]Joseph said to him, "No, my father, this one is the firstborn; put your right hand on his head."

[19]But his father refused and said, "I know, my son, I know. He too will become a people, and he too will become great. Nevertheless, his younger brother will be greater than he, and his descendants will become

a group of nations." [20]He blessed them that day and said,

"In your[c] name will Israel pronounce this
        blessing:
    'May God make you like Ephraim and
        Manasseh.' "

So he put Ephraim ahead of Manasseh.

[21]Then Israel said to Joseph, "I am about to die, but God will be with you[d] and take you[d] back to the land of your[d] fathers. [22]And to you, as one who is over your brothers, I give the ridge of land[e] I took from the Amorites with my sword and my bow."

Jacob Blesses His Sons

49 Then Jacob called for his sons and said: "Gather round so that I can tell you what will happen to you in days to come.

[2]"Assemble and listen, sons of Jacob;
    listen to your father Israel.

[3]"Reuben, you are my firstborn,
    my might, the first sign of my strength,
    excelling in honour, excelling in power.
[4]Turbulent as the waters, you will no longer excel,
    for you went up onto your father's bed,
    onto my couch and defiled it.

[5]"Simeon and Levi are brothers—
    their swords[a] are weapons of violence.
[6]Let me not enter their council,
    let me not join their assembly,
for they have killed men in their anger
    and hamstrung oxen as they pleased.
[7]Cursed be their anger, so fierce,
    and their fury, so cruel!
I will scatter them in Jacob
    and disperse them in Israel.

[8]"Judah,[b] your brothers will praise you;
    your hand will be on the neck of your enemies;
    your father's sons will bow down to you.
[9]You are a lion's cub, O Judah;
    you return from the prey, my son.
Like a lion he crouches and lies down,
    like a lioness—who dares to rouse him?
[10]The sceptre will not depart from Judah,
    nor the ruler's staff from between his feet,
until he comes to whom it belongs[c]
    and the obedience of the nations is his.
[11]He will tether his donkey to a vine,
    his colt to the choicest branch;
he will wash his garments in wine,
    his robes in the blood of grapes.
[12]His eyes will be darker than wine,
    his teeth whiter than milk.[d]

[13]"Zebulun will live by the seashore
    and become a haven for ships;
    his border will extend towards Sidon.

---

[c]20 The Hebrew is singular.   [d]21 The Hebrew is plural.
[e]22 Or *And to you I give one portion more than to your brothers—the portion*
[a]5 The meaning of the Hebrew for this word is uncertain.   [b]8 *Judah* sounds like and may be derived from the Hebrew for *praise*.
[c]10 Or *until Shiloh comes*; or *until he comes to whom tribute belongs*   [d]12 Or *will be dull from wine, / his teeth white from milk*

14"Issachar is a scrawny*e* donkey
   lying down between two saddlebags.*f*
15When he sees how good is his resting place
   and how pleasant is his land,
he will bend his shoulder to the burden
   and submit to forced labour.

16"Dan*g* will provide justice for his people
   as one of the tribes of Israel.
17Dan will be a serpent by the roadside,
   a viper along the path,
that bites the horse's heels
   so that its rider tumbles backwards.

18"I look for your deliverance, O LORD.

19"Gad*h* will be attacked by a band of raiders,
   but he will attack them at their heels.

20"Asher's food will be rich;
   he will provide delicacies fit for a king.

21"Naphtali is a doe set free
   that bears beautiful fawns.*i*

22"Joseph is a fruitful vine,
   a fruitful vine near a spring,
   whose branches climb over a wall.*j*
23With bitterness archers attacked him;
   they shot at him with hostility.
24But his bow remained steady,
   his strong arms stayed*k* supple,
because of the hand of the Mighty One of Jacob,
   because of the Shepherd, the Rock of Israel,
25because of your father's God, who helps you,
   because of the Almighty,*l* who blesses you
with blessings of the heavens above,
   blessings of the deep that lies below,
   blessings of the breast and womb.
26Your father's blessings are greater
   than the blessings of the ancient mountains,
   than*m* the bounty of the age-old hills.
Let all these rest on the head of Joseph,
   on the brow of the prince among*n* his
     brothers.

27"Benjamin is a ravenous wolf;
   in the morning he devours the prey,
   in the evening he divides the plunder."

28All these are the twelve tribes of Israel, and this is what their father said to them when he blessed them, giving each the blessing appropriate to him.

The Death of Jacob

29Then he gave them these instructions: "I am about to be gathered to my people. Bury me with my fathers in the cave in the field of Ephron the Hittite, 30the cave in the field of Machpelah, near Mamre in Canaan,

which Abraham bought as a burial place from Ephron the Hittite, along with the field. 31There Abraham and his wife Sarah were buried, there Isaac and his wife Rebekah were buried, and there I buried Leah. 32The field and the cave in it were bought from the Hittites."*o*

49:28   Jacob's blessings indicated what was to happen to his sons. Some of the blessings were rather obscure. We can understand a little more by reading the blessings of Moses (Deuteronomy 33) and the very ancient Song of Deborah (Judges 5).

33When Jacob had finished giving instructions to his sons, he drew his feet up into the bed, breathed his last and was gathered to his people.

50

Joseph threw himself upon his father and wept over him and kissed him. 2Then Joseph directed the physicians in his service to embalm his father Israel. So the physicians embalmed him, 3taking a full forty days, for that was the time required for embalming. And the Egyptians mourned for him seventy days.

4When the days of mourning had passed, Joseph said to Pharaoh's court, "If I have found favour in your eyes, speak to Pharaoh for me. Tell him, 5'My father made me swear an oath and said, "I am about to die; bury me in the tomb I dug for myself in the land of Canaan." Now let me go up and bury my father; then I will return.'"

6Pharaoh said, "Go up and bury your father, as he made you swear to do."

7So Joseph went up to bury his father. All Pharaoh's officials accompanied him—the dignitaries of his court and all the dignitaries of Egypt—8besides all the members of Joseph's household and his brothers and those belonging to his father's household. Only their children and their flocks and herds were left in Goshen. 9Chariots and horsemen*a* also went up with him. It was a very large company.

10When they reached the threshing-floor of Atad, near the Jordan, they lamented loudly and bitterly; and there Joseph observed a seven-day period of mourning for his father. 11When the Canaanites who lived there saw the mourning at the threshing-floor of Atad, they said, "The Egyptians are holding a solemn ceremony of mourning." That is why that place near the Jordan is called Abel Mizraim.*b*

12So Jacob's sons did as he had commanded them: 13They carried him to the land of Canaan and buried him in the cave in the field of Machpelah, near Mamre, which Abraham had bought as a burial place from Ephron the Hittite, along with the field. 14After burying his

---

*e*14 Or *strong*   *f*14 Or *campfires*   *g*16 *Dan* here means *he provides justice.*
*h*19 *Gad* can mean *attack* and *band of raiders.*   *i*21 Or *free;* / *he utters beautiful words*
*j*22 Or *Joseph is a wild colt, / a wild colt near a spring, / a wild donkey on a terraced hill*
*k*23,24 Or *archers will attack . . . will shoot . . . will remain . . . will stay*   *l*25 Hebrew *Shaddai*
*m*26 Or *of my progenitors, / as great as*   *n*26 Or *the one separated from*   *o*32 Or *the sons of Heth*
*a*9 Or *charioteers*   *b*11 *Abel Mizraim* means *mourning of the Egyptians.*

father, Joseph returned to Egypt, together with his brothers and all the others who had gone with him to bury his father.

Joseph Reassures His Brothers

[15]When Joseph's brothers saw that their father was dead, they said, "What if Joseph holds a grudge against us and pays us back for all the wrongs we did to him?" [16]So they sent word to Joseph, saying, "Your father left these instructions before he died: [17]'This is what you are to say to Joseph: I ask you to forgive your brothers the sins and the wrongs they committed in treating you so badly.' Now please forgive the sins of the servants of the God of your father." When their message came to him, Joseph wept.

[18]His brothers then came and threw themselves down before him. "We are your slaves," they said. [19]But Joseph said to them, "Don't be afraid. Am I in the place of God? [20]You intended to harm me, but God intended it for good to accomplish what is now being done, the saving of many lives. [21]So then, don't be afraid. I will provide for you and your children." And he reassured them and spoke kindly to them.

The Death of Joseph

[22]Joseph stayed in Egypt, along with all his father's family. He lived a hundred and ten years [23]and saw the third generation of Ephraim's children. Also the children of Makir son of Manasseh were placed at birth on Joseph's knees. [c]

[24]Then Joseph said to his brothers, "I am about to die. But God will surely come to your aid and take you up out of this land to the land he promised on oath to Abraham, Isaac and Jacob." [25]And Joseph made the sons of Israel swear an oath and said, "God will surely come to your aid, and then you must carry my bones up from this place."

[26]So Joseph died at the age of a hundred and ten. And after they embalmed him, he was placed in a coffin in Egypt.

[c]23 That is, were counted as his

Exodus

Freed by God

If there is a key to understanding the Old Testament it is to be found in Exodus 19. The people of Israel had been freed by God from years of slavery and came to Mount Sinai to meet him. There he revealed himself to them, in order that they should be able to choose whether or not to serve him.

God Is Known by His Love

God did not describe himself as God of the elements, or of war, or of fertility (although he had given plenty of evidence to the people and their ancestors of his power in those respects). He chose to describe himself as a God who, simply because he loved them, brought them out of Egypt. They must judge on this evidence that he is personally interested in them and is merciful to them. Faced with the forces and cycles of nature, or the horrors of war, people are all too often afraid, and resort to magic and superstition in an effort to please or control mysterious or hostile powers. But God does not want frightened slaves who are subject to what they think are his arbitrary whims. He wants people to be free to choose to love and serve him. God is clearly able to force himself on people, but instead he has chosen to free the slaves first and only then to offer himself to them.

A Love Story

The Old Testament is the story of this sort of relationship. It is a love story which started in Genesis when Adam and Eve, set free in a perfect world, a garden paradise, chose to betray the love of their maker and so sour all of creation. God's whole longing is to make everything he has made perfect once more, and here at Mount Sinai he offered Israel the chance of being the nation through whom he will set things right. Israel accepted the task.

The Covenant

The agreement between God and Israel was set in the form of a covenant. (Another word for this is testament, which is why we call the parts of the Bible Old and New Testament.) At the time the covenant was an accepted legal form, set in a religious ceremony during which an animal was sacrificed and its blood sprinkled on both parties involved in the agreement. The details of the covenant at Sinai are found in the Ten Commandments (chapter 20), but the more important basis of the covenant is in chapter 19. God declared, ". . . out of all nations you will be my treasured possession . . . you will be for me a kingdom of priests and a holy nation".

A Surprising Gift

God's gift of himself to Israel is breathtaking. Rather than one of the great nations of Mesopotamia and Egypt for example, he chose a stateless rabble of escaped slaves for his especial attention. But there are two sides to a covenant agreement, and in joining in this one the people of Israel took on a great task. They are to be a kingdom of priests and a holy nation. A priest stands between a person and God, representing each to the other. Every member of Israel must do this for the other people in the world, bringing them back to their creator, who wants to save them.

God's Holiness

Anything touched by God's holiness becomes itself pure and set apart and will infect with holiness everything that comes into contact with it. The Jews were chosen by God. They were to stand between God and his world, to be holy like him, and to help the world become as God intended it to be when he made it.

Moses Makes God Known

The rest of the Old Testament is the story of the covenant—of Israel's successes and failures and God's response. Some prophets spoke of Israel as God's bride, his city, his child, his vineyard. He is a God who cares passionately for his people. In chapter 3 Moses, who had been exiled from Egypt, was spending time alone looking after sheep in the Sinai wilderness. Here he encountered God in the form of a bush which was burning but not actually being destroyed. God gave him the task of freeing the Israelites from Egypt. Moses did not want to accept the task, and one of the things he wanted was to be told God's name. Even today we consider that to be able to call someone by their personal name means we are close to them. In the time of Moses, to know a name meant to understand a person's character, and so have power over them. So Moses was very bold to ask God's name, but God did answer him. He was told that this God was the same one who had led his ancestors. But no single word describes him, so his name is "I AM WHO I AM". The Hebrew word is "Yahweh", which is sometimes used in the Old Testament. An English version of it is "Jehovah".

Nothing Outside God's Control

It was to be many years before the Israelites realized that other gods actually did not exist. At this time they believed that others existed, but that they should only follow one. Moses led them in the name of God. Nothing they did or thought was outside God's control. What that meant in practice was something that took a long time to learn and could often only be understood through bitter experience. The Exodus stories of the escape from Egypt and the wanderings in the wilderness are the first chapters in the Bible's long account about the discovery of God.

The Israelites Oppressed

1 These are the names of the sons of Israel who went to Egypt with Jacob, each with his family: [2]Reuben, Simeon, Levi and Judah; [3]Issachar, Zebulun and Benjamin; [4]Dan and Naphtali; Gad and Asher. [5]The descendants of Jacob numbered seventy[a] in all; Joseph was already in Egypt.

[6]Now Joseph and all his brothers and all that generation died, [7]but the Israelites were fruitful and multiplied greatly and became exceedingly numerous, so that the land was filled with them.

[8]Then a new king, who did not know about Joseph, came to power in Egypt. [9]"Look," he said to his people, "the Israelites have become much too numerous for us. [10]Come, we must deal shrewdly with them or they will become even more numerous and, if war breaks out, will join our enemies, fight against us and leave the country."

[11]So they put slave masters over them to oppress them with forced labour, and they built Pithom and Rameses as store cities for Pharaoh. [12]But the more they were oppressed, the more they multiplied and spread; so the Egyptians came to dread the Israelites [13]and worked them ruthlessly. [14]They made their lives bitter with hard labour in brick and mortar and with all kinds of work in the fields; in all their hard labour the Egyptians used them ruthlessly.

[15]The king of Egypt said to the Hebrew midwives, whose names were Shiphrah and Puah, [16]"When you help the Hebrew women in childbirth and observe them on the delivery stool, if it is a boy, kill him; but if it is a girl, let her live." [17]The midwives, however, feared God and did not do what the king of Egypt had told them to do; they let the boys live. [18]Then the king of Egypt summoned the midwives and asked them, "Why have you done this? Why have you let the boys live?"

1:17 Because God had given freedom to his people, his plans depended on their faith in him and loyalty to him. Here the lives of Israelite boys, including Moses, depended on the godliness and bravery of two midwives. The storyteller underlines their importance by recording their names. He mixes drama with humour by relating their "economy with the truth" when they are summoned to Pharaoh to give an account of themselves.

---

[19]The midwives answered Pharaoh, "Hebrew women are not like Egyptian women; they are vigorous and give birth before the midwives arrive."

[20]So God was kind to the midwives and the people increased and became even more numerous. [21]And because the midwives feared God, he gave them families of their own.

[22]Then Pharaoh gave this order to all his people:

"Every boy that is born[b] you must throw into the Nile, but let every girl live."

The Birth of Moses

2 Now a man of the house of Levi married a Levite woman, [2]and she became pregnant and gave birth to a son. When she saw that he was a fine child, she hid him for three months. [3]But when she could hide him no longer, she got a papyrus basket for him and coated it with tar and pitch. Then she placed the child in it and put it among the reeds along the bank of the Nile. [4]His sister stood at a distance to see what would happen to him.

[5]Then Pharaoh's daughter went down to the Nile to bathe, and her attendants were walking along the river bank. She saw the basket among the reeds and sent her slave girl to get it. [6]She opened it and saw the baby. He was crying, and she felt sorry for him. "This is one of the Hebrew babies," she said.

[7]Then his sister asked Pharaoh's daughter, "Shall I go and get one of the Hebrew women to nurse the baby for you?"

[8]"Yes, go," she answered. And the girl went and got the baby's mother. [9]Pharaoh's daughter said to her, "Take this baby and nurse him for me, and I will pay you." So the woman took the baby and nursed him. [10]When the child grew older, she took him to Pharaoh's daughter and he became her son. She named him Moses,[a] saying, "I drew him out of the water."

Moses Flees to Midian

[11]One day, after Moses had grown up, he went out to where his own people were and watched them at their hard labour. He saw an Egyptian beating a Hebrew, one of his own people. [12]Glancing this way and that and seeing no-one, he killed the Egyptian and hid him in the sand. [13]The next day he went out and saw two Hebrews fighting. He asked the one in the wrong, "Why are you hitting your fellow Hebrew?"

[14]The man said, "Who made you ruler and judge over us? Are you thinking of killing me as you killed the Egyptian?" Then Moses was afraid and thought, "What I did must have become known."

[15]When Pharaoh heard of this, he tried to kill Moses, but Moses fled from Pharaoh and went to live in Midian, where he sat down by a well. [16]Now a priest of Midian had seven daughters, and they came to draw water and fill the troughs to water their father's flock. [17]Some shepherds came along and drove them away, but Moses got up and came to their rescue and watered their flock.

[18]When the girls returned to Reuel their father, he asked them, "Why have you returned so early today?"

[19]They answered, "An Egyptian rescued us from the shepherds. He even drew water for us and watered the flock."

[20]"And where is he?" he asked his daughters. "Why did you leave him? Invite him to have something to eat."

---

[a]5 Masoretic Text (see also Gen. 46:27); Dead Sea Scrolls and Septuagint (see also Acts 7:14 and note at Gen. 46:27) *seventy-five*
[b]22 Masoretic Text; Samaritan Pentateuch, Septuagint and Targums *born to the Hebrews*
[a]10 *Moses* sounds like the Hebrew for *draw out*.

²¹Moses agreed to stay with the man, who gave his daughter Zipporah to Moses in marriage. ²²Zipporah gave birth to a son, and Moses named him Gershom,ᵇ saying, "I have become an alien in a foreign land."

²³During that long period, the king of Egypt died. The Israelites groaned in their slavery and cried out, and their cry for help because of their slavery went up to God. ²⁴God heard their groaning and he remembered his covenant with Abraham, with Isaac and with Jacob. ²⁵So God looked on the Israelites and was concerned about them.

Moses and the Burning Bush

3 Now Moses was tending the flock of Jethro his father-in-law, the priest of Midian, and he led the flock to the far side of the desert and came to Horeb, the mountain of God. ²There the angel of the LORD appeared to him in flames of fire from within a bush. Moses saw that though the bush was on fire it did not burn up. ³So Moses thought, "I will go over and see this strange sight—why the bush does not burn up."

⁴When the LORD saw that he had gone over to look, God called to him from within the bush, "Moses! Moses!"

And Moses said, "Here I am."

⁵"Do not come any closer," God said. "Take off your sandals, for the place where you are standing is holy ground." ⁶Then he said, "I am the God of your father, the God of Abraham, the God of Isaac and the God of Jacob." At this, Moses hid his face, because he was afraid to look at God.

⁷The LORD said, "I have indeed seen the misery of my people in Egypt. I have heard them crying out because of their slave drivers, and I am concerned about their suffering. ⁸So I have come down to rescue them from the hand of the Egyptians and to bring them up out of that land into a good and spacious land, a land flowing with milk and honey—the home of the Canaanites, Hittites, Amorites, Perizzites, Hivites and Jebusites. ⁹And now the cry of the Israelites has reached me, and I have seen the way the Egyptians are oppressing them. ¹⁰So now, go. I am sending you to Pharaoh to bring my people the Israelites out of Egypt."

¹¹But Moses said to God, "Who am I, that I should go to Pharaoh and bring the Israelites out of Egypt?"

¹²And God said, "I will be with you. And this will be the sign to you that it is I who have sent you: When you have brought the people out of Egypt, youᵃ will worship God on this mountain."

¹³Moses said to God, "Suppose I go to the Israelites and say to them, 'The God of your fathers has sent me to you,' and they ask me, 'What is his name?' Then what shall I tell them?"

¹⁴God said to Moses, "I AM WHO I AM.ᵇ This is what you are to say to the Israelites: 'I AM has sent me to you.'"

¹⁵God also said to Moses, "Say to the Israelites, 'The LORD,ᶜ the God of your fathers—the God of Abraham, the God of Isaac and the God of Jacob—has sent me to you.' This is my name for ever, the name by which I

am to be remembered from generation to generation. ¹⁶"Go, assemble the elders of Israel and say to them, 'The LORD, the God of your fathers—the God of Abraham, Isaac and Jacob—appeared to me and said: I have watched over you and have seen what has been done to you in Egypt. ¹⁷And I have promised to bring you up out of your misery in Egypt into the land of the Canaanites, Hittites, Amorites, Perizzites, Hivites and Jebusites—a land flowing with milk and honey.'

3:11 Those who we know as the greatest leaders and prophets of Israel are the people who fought hardest against the call of God. Moses made five attempts to avoid becoming the liberator of his people (3:11,13; 4:1,10,13). He knew that he was incapable of such an enormous task. God knew it too. He showed at this point, and throughout Moses' life, that the power came from him. What God needed from Moses was the willingness to be used by him.

---

¹⁸"The elders of Israel will listen to you. Then you and the elders are to go to the king of Egypt and say to him, 'The LORD, the God of the Hebrews, has met with us. Let us take a three-day journey into the desert to offer sacrifices to the LORD our God.' ¹⁹But I know that the king of Egypt will not let you go unless a mighty hand compels him. ²⁰So I will stretch out my hand and strike the Egyptians with all the wonders that I will perform among them. After that, he will let you go. ²¹And I will make the Egyptians favourably disposed towards this people, so that when you leave you will not go empty-handed. ²²Every woman is to ask her neighbour and any woman living in her house for articles of silver and gold and for clothing, which you will put on your sons and daughters. And so you will plunder the Egyptians."

Signs for Moses

4 Moses answered, "What if they do not believe me or listen to me and say, 'The LORD did not appear to you'?"

²Then the LORD said to him, "What is that in your hand?"

"A staff," he replied.

³The LORD said, "Throw it on the ground."

Moses threw it on the ground and it became a snake, and he ran from it. ⁴Then the LORD said to him, "Reach out your hand and take it by the tail." So Moses reached out and took hold of the snake and it turned back into a staff in his hand. ⁵"This," said the LORD, "is so that they may believe that the LORD, the God of their fathers—the God of Abraham, the God of Isaac and the God of Jacob—has appeared to you."

⁶Then the LORD said, "Put your hand inside your cloak." So Moses put his hand into his cloak, and when he took it out, it was leprous,ᵃ like snow.

ᵇ22 Gershom sounds like the Hebrew for an alien there.   ᵃ12 The Hebrew is plural.   ᵇ14 Or I WILL BE WHAT I WILL BE
ᶜ15 The Hebrew for LORD sounds like and may be derived from the Hebrew for I AM in verse 14.
ᵃ6 The Hebrew word was used for various diseases affecting the skin—not necessarily leprosy.

7"Now put it back into your cloak," he said. So Moses put his hand back into his cloak, and when he took it out, it was restored, like the rest of his flesh.

8Then the LORD said, "If they do not believe you or pay attention to the first miraculous sign, they may believe the second. 9But if they do not believe these two signs or listen to you, take some water from the Nile and pour it on the dry ground. The water you take from the river will become blood on the ground."

10Moses said to the LORD, "O Lord, I have never been eloquent, neither in the past nor since you have spoken to your servant. I am slow of speech and tongue."

11The LORD said to him, "Who gave man his mouth? Who makes him deaf or mute? Who gives him sight or makes him blind? Is it not I, the LORD? 12Now go; I will help you speak and will teach you what to say."

13But Moses said, "O Lord, please send someone else to do it."

14Then the LORD's anger burned against Moses and he said, "What about your brother, Aaron the Levite? I know he can speak well. He is already on his way to meet you, and his heart will be glad when he sees you. 15You shall speak to him and put words in his mouth; I will help both of you speak and will teach you what to do. 16He will speak to the people for you, and it will be as if he were your mouth and as if you were God to him. 17But take this staff in your hand so that you can perform miraculous signs with it."

Moses Returns to Egypt

18Then Moses went back to Jethro his father-in-law and said to him, "Let me go back to my own people in Egypt to see if any of them are still alive."

Jethro said, "Go, and I wish you well."

19Now the LORD had said to Moses in Midian, "Go back to Egypt, for all the men who wanted to kill you are dead." 20So Moses took his wife and sons, put them on a donkey and started back to Egypt. And he took the staff of God in his hand.

21The LORD said to Moses, "When you return to Egypt, see that you perform before Pharaoh all the wonders I have given you the power to do. But I will harden his heart so that he will not let the people go. 22Then say to Pharaoh, 'This is what the LORD says: Israel is my firstborn son, 23and I told you, "Let my son go, so that he may worship me." But you refused to let him go; so I will kill your firstborn son.' "

24At a lodging place on the way, the LORD met Moses,b and was about to kill him. 25But Zipporah took a flint knife, cut off her son's foreskin and touched Moses', feet with it.c "Surely you are a bridegroom of blood to me," she said. 26So the LORD let him alone. (At that time she said "bridegroom of blood", referring to circumcision.)

27The LORD said to Aaron, "Go into the desert to meet Moses." So he met Moses at the mountain of God and kissed him. 28Then Moses told Aaron everything the LORD had sent him to say, and also about all the miraculous signs he had commanded him to perform.

29Moses and Aaron brought together all the elders of the Israelites, 30and Aaron told them everything the LORD had said to Moses. He also performed the signs before the people, 31and they believed. And when they heard that the LORD was concerned about them and had seen their misery, they bowed down and worshipped.

Bricks Without Straw

5 Afterwards Moses and Aaron went to Pharaoh and said, "This is what the LORD, the God of Israel, says: 'Let my people go, so that they may hold a festival to me in the desert.' "

2Pharaoh said, "Who is the LORD, that I should obey him and let Israel go? I do not know the LORD and I will not let Israel go."

3Then they said, "The God of the Hebrews has met with us. Now let us take a three-day journey into the desert to offer sacrifices to the LORD our God, or he may strike us with plagues or with the sword."

4But the king of Egypt said, "Moses and Aaron, why are you taking the people away from their labour? Get back to your work!" 5Then Pharaoh said, "Look, the people of the land are now numerous, and you are stopping them from working."

6That same day Pharaoh gave this order to the slave drivers and foremen in charge of the people: 7"You are no longer to supply the people with straw for making bricks; let them go and gather their own straw. 8But require them to make the same number of bricks as before; don't reduce the quota. They are lazy; that is why they are crying out, 'Let us go and sacrifice to our God.' 9Make the work harder for the men so that they keep working and pay no attention to lies."

10Then the slave drivers and the foremen went out and said to the people, "This is what Pharaoh says: 'I will not give you any more straw. 11Go and get your own straw wherever you can find it, but your work will not be reduced at all.' " 12So the people scattered all over Egypt to gather stubble to use for straw. 13The slave drivers kept pressing them, saying, "Complete the work required of you for each day, just as when you had straw." 14The Israelite foremen appointed by Pharaoh's slave drivers were beaten and were asked, "Why didn't you meet your quota of bricks yesterday or today, as before?"

15Then the Israelite foremen went and appealed to Pharaoh: "Why have you treated your servants this way? 16Your servants are given no straw, yet we are told, 'Make bricks!' Your servants are being beaten, but the fault is with your own people."

17Pharaoh said, "Lazy, that's what you are—lazy! That is why you keep saying, 'Let us go and sacrifice to the LORD.' 18Now get to work. You will not be given any straw, yet you must produce your full quota of bricks."

19The Israelite foremen realised they were in trouble when they were told, "You are not to reduce the number of bricks required of you for each day." 20When they left Pharaoh, they found Moses and Aaron waiting to meet them, 21and they said, "May the LORD

b24 Or ,Moses' son,; Hebrew him   c25 Or and drew near ,Moses', feet look upon you and judge you! You have made us a stench to Pharaoh and his officials and have put a sword in their hand to kill us."

5:21 It is known that Egypt used Semitic slaves for building projects in the Delta region where the Israelites lived. They were so oppressed that they lost the human spirit which longs for freedom, and the strength to fight for it. The height of their ambition was that their conditions should not get any worse.

God Promises Deliverance

22Moses returned to the LORD and said, "O Lord, why have you brought trouble upon this people? Is this why you sent me? 23Ever since I went to Pharaoh to speak in your name, he has brought trouble upon this people, and you have not rescued your people at all."

6 Then the LORD said to Moses, "Now you will see what I will do to Pharaoh: Because of my mighty hand he will let them go; because of my mighty hand he will drive them out of his country."

2God also said to Moses, "I am the LORD. 3I appeared to Abraham, to Isaac and to Jacob as God Almighty,*a* but by my name the LORD*b* I did not make myself known to them.*c* 4I also established my covenant with them to give them the land of Canaan, where they lived as aliens. 5Moreover, I have heard the groaning of the Israelites, whom the Egyptians are enslaving, and I have remembered my covenant.

6"Therefore, say to the Israelites: 'I am the LORD, and I will bring you out from under the yoke of the Egyptians. I will free you from being slaves to them, and I will redeem you with an outstretched arm and with mighty acts of judgment. 7I will take you as my own people, and I will be your God. Then you will know that I am the LORD your God, who brought you out from under the yoke of the Egyptians. 8And I will bring you to the land I swore with uplifted hand to give to Abraham, to Isaac and to Jacob. I will give it to you as a possession. I am the LORD.' "

9Moses reported this to the Israelites, but they did not listen to him because of their discouragement and cruel bondage.

10Then the LORD said to Moses, 11"Go, tell Pharaoh king of Egypt to let the Israelites go out of his country."

12But Moses said to the LORD, "If the Israelites will not listen to me, why would Pharaoh listen to me, since I speak with faltering lips?"*d*

Family Record of Moses and Aaron

13Now the LORD spoke to Moses and Aaron about the Israelites and Pharaoh king of Egypt, and he commanded them to bring the Israelites out of Egypt.

14These were the heads of their families:*e*

The sons of Reuben the firstborn son of Israel were Hanoch and Pallu, Hezron and Carmi. These were the clans of Reuben.

15The sons of Simeon were Jemuel, Jamin, Ohad, Jakin, Zohar and Shaul the son of a Canaanite woman. These were the clans of Simeon.

16These were the names of the sons of Levi according to their records: Gershon, Kohath and Merari. Levi lived 137 years.

17The sons of Gershon, by clans, were Libni and Shimei.

18The sons of Kohath were Amram, Izhar, Hebron and Uzziel. Kohath lived 133 years.

19The sons of Merari were Mahli and Mushi. These were the clans of Levi according to their records.

20Amram married his father's sister Jochebed, who bore him Aaron and Moses. Amram lived 137 years.

21The sons of Izhar were Korah, Nepheg and Zicri.

22The sons of Uzziel were Mishael, Elzaphan and Sithri.

23Aaron married Elisheba, daughter of Amminadab and sister of Nahshon, and she bore him Nadab and Abihu, Eleazar and Ithamar.

24The sons of Korah were Assir, Elkanah and Abiasaph. These were the Korahite clans.

25Eleazar son of Aaron married one of the daughters of Putiel, and she bore him Phinehas.

These were the heads of the Levite families, clan by clan.

26It was this same Aaron and Moses to whom the LORD said, "Bring the Israelites out of Egypt by their divisions." 27They were the ones who spoke to Pharaoh king of Egypt about bringing the Israelites out of Egypt. It was the same Moses and Aaron.

Aaron to Speak for Moses

28Now when the LORD spoke to Moses in Egypt, 29he said to him, "I am the LORD. Tell Pharaoh king of Egypt everything I tell you."

30But Moses said to the LORD, "Since I speak with faltering lips, why would Pharaoh listen to me?"

7 Then the LORD said to Moses, "See, I have made you like God to Pharaoh, and your brother Aaron will be your prophet. 2You are to say everything I command you, and your brother Aaron is to tell Pharaoh to let the Israelites go out of his country. 3But I will harden Pharaoh's heart, and though I multiply my miraculous signs and wonders in Egypt, 4he will not listen to you. Then I will lay my hand on Egypt and with mighty acts of judgment I will bring out my divisions, my people the Israelites. 5And the Egyptians will know that I am the LORD when I stretch out my hand against Egypt and bring the Israelites out of it."

---

a3 Hebrew *El-Shaddai*   *b3* See note at Exodus 3:15.
c3 Or *Almighty, and by my name the LORD did I not let myself be known to them?*
d12 Hebrew *I am uncircumcised of lips*; also in verse 30
e14 The Hebrew for *families* here and in verse 25 refers to units larger than clans.

6Moses and Aaron did just as the LORD commanded them. 7Moses was eighty years old and Aaron eighty-three when they spoke to Pharaoh.

Aaron's Staff Becomes a Snake

8The LORD said to Moses and Aaron, 9"When Pharaoh says to you, 'Perform a miracle,' then say to Aaron, 'Take your staff and throw it down before Pharaoh,' and it will become a snake."

10So Moses and Aaron went to Pharaoh and did just as the LORD commanded. Aaron threw his staff down in front of Pharaoh and his officials, and it became a snake. 11Pharaoh then summoned the wise men and sorcerers, and the Egyptian magicians also did the same things by their secret arts: 12Each one threw down his staff and it became a snake. But Aaron's staff swallowed up their staffs. 13Yet Pharaoh's heart became hard and he would not listen to them, just as the LORD had said.

The Plague of Blood

14Then the LORD said to Moses, "Pharaoh's heart is unyielding; he refuses to let the people go. 15Go to Pharaoh in the morning as he goes out to the water. Wait on the bank of the Nile to meet him, and take in your hand the staff that was changed into a snake. 16Then say to him, 'The LORD, the God of the Hebrews, has sent me to say to you: Let my people go, so that they may worship me in the desert. But until now you have not listened. 17This is what the LORD says: By this you will know that I am the LORD: With the staff that is in my hand I will strike the water of the Nile, and it will be changed into blood. 18The fish in the Nile will die, and the river will stink; the Egyptians will not be able to drink its water.' "

7:17   Many of the plagues can be explained as events which occur naturally in Egypt. When the Nile floods, its waters turn red because of the colour of silt brought down by the floods. The Bible does not distinguish between impossible miracles and natural events. It says that everything is controlled by God. What is important is that it is God's purpose for a thing to happen.

19The LORD said to Moses, "Tell Aaron, 'Take your staff and stretch out your hand over the waters of Egypt — over the streams and canals, over the ponds and all the reservoirs' — and they will turn to blood. Blood will be everywhere in Egypt, even in the wooden buckets and stone jars."

20Moses and Aaron did just as the LORD had commanded. He raised his staff in the presence of Pharaoh and his officials and struck the water of the Nile, and all the water was changed into blood. 21The fish in the Nile died, and the river smelled so bad that the Egyptians could not drink its water. Blood was everywhere in Egypt.

22But the Egyptian magicians did the same things by their secret arts, and Pharaoh's heart became hard; he would not listen to Moses and Aaron, just as the LORD had said. 23Instead, he turned and went into his palace, and did not take even this to heart. 24And all the Egyptians dug along the Nile to get drinking water, because they could not drink the water of the river.

The Plague of Frogs

25Seven days passed after the LORD struck the Nile.

8 1Then the LORD said to Moses, "Go to Pharaoh and say to him, 'This is what the LORD says: Let my people go, so that they may worship me. 2If you refuse to let them go, I will plague your whole country with frogs. 3The Nile will teem with frogs. They will come up into your palace and your bedroom and onto your bed, into the houses of your officials and on your people, and into your ovens and kneading troughs. 4The frogs will go up on you and your people and all your officials.' "

5Then the LORD said to Moses, "Tell Aaron, 'Stretch out your hand with your staff over the streams and canals and ponds, and make frogs come up on the land of Egypt.' "

6So Aaron stretched out his hand over the waters of Egypt, and the frogs came up and covered the land. 7But the magicians did the same things by their secret arts; they also made frogs come up on the land of Egypt.

8Pharaoh summoned Moses and Aaron and said, "Pray to the LORD to take the frogs away from me and my people, and I will let your people go to offer sacrifices to the LORD."

9Moses said to Pharaoh, "I leave to you the honour of setting the time for me to pray for you and your officials and your people that you and your houses may be rid of the frogs, except for those that remain in the Nile."

10"Tomorrow," Pharaoh said.

Moses replied, "It will be as you say, so that you may know there is no-one like the LORD our God. 11The frogs will leave you and your houses, your officials and your people; they will remain only in the Nile."

12After Moses and Aaron left Pharaoh, Moses cried out to the LORD about the frogs he had brought on Pharaoh. 13And the LORD did what Moses asked. The frogs died in the houses, in the courtyards and in the fields. 14They were piled into heaps, and the land reeked of them. 15But when Pharaoh saw that there was relief, he hardened his heart and would not listen to Moses and Aaron, just as the LORD had said.

The Plague of Gnats

16Then the LORD said to Moses, "Tell Aaron, 'Stretch out your staff and strike the dust of the ground,' and throughout the land of Egypt the dust will become gnats." 17They did this, and when Aaron stretched out his hand with the staff and struck the dust of the ground, gnats came upon men and animals. All the dust throughout the land of Egypt became gnats. 18But when the magicians tried to produce gnats by their secret arts, they could not. And the gnats were on men and animals.

19The magicians said to Pharaoh, "This is the finger of God." But Pharaoh's heart was hard and he would not listen, just as the LORD had said.

The Plague of Flies

[20]Then the LORD said to Moses, "Get up early in the morning and confront Pharaoh as he goes to the water and say to him, 'This is what the LORD says: Let my people go, so that they may worship me. [21]If you do not let my people go, I will send swarms of flies on you and your officials, on your people and into your houses. The houses of the Egyptians will be full of flies, and even the ground where they are.

[22]" 'But on that day I will deal differently with the land of Goshen, where my people live; no swarms of flies will be there, so that you will know that I, the LORD, am in this land. [23]I will make a distinction[a] between my people and your people. This miraculous sign will occur tomorrow.' "

[24]And the LORD did this. Dense swarms of flies poured into Pharaoh's palace and into the houses of his officials, and throughout Egypt the land was ruined by the flies.

[25]Then Pharaoh summoned Moses and Aaron and said, "Go, sacrifice to your God here in the land."

[26]But Moses said, "That would not be right. The sacrifices we offer the LORD our God would be detestable to the Egyptians. And if we offer sacrifices that are detestable in their eyes, will they not stone us? [27]We must take a three-day journey into the desert to offer sacrifices to the LORD our God, as he commands us."

[28]Pharaoh said, "I will let you go to offer sacrifices to the LORD your God in the desert, but you must not go very far. Now pray for me."

[29]Moses answered, "As soon as I leave you, I will pray to the LORD, and tomorrow the flies will leave Pharaoh and his officials and his people. Only be sure that Pharaoh does not act deceitfully again by not letting the people go to offer sacrifices to the LORD."

[30]Then Moses left Pharaoh and prayed to the LORD, [31]and the LORD did what Moses asked: The flies left Pharaoh and his officials and his people; not a fly remained. [32]But this time also Pharaoh hardened his heart and would not let the people go.

The Plague on Livestock

9 Then the LORD said to Moses, "Go to Pharaoh and say to him, 'This is what the LORD, the God of the Hebrews, says: Let my people go, so that they may worship me.' [2]If you refuse to let them go and continue to hold them back, [3]the hand of the LORD will bring a terrible plague on your livestock in the field—on your horses and donkeys and camels and on your cattle and sheep and goats. [4]But the LORD will make a distinction between the livestock of Israel and that of Egypt, so that no animal belonging to the Israelites will die.' "

[5]The LORD set a time and said, "Tomorrow the LORD will do this in the land." [6]And the next day the LORD did it: All the livestock of the Egyptians died, but not one animal belonging to the Israelites died. [7]Pharaoh sent men to investigate and found that not even one of the animals of the Israelites had died. Yet his heart was unyielding and he would not let the people go.

The Plague of Boils

[8]Then the LORD said to Moses and Aaron, "Take handfuls of soot from a furnace and have Moses toss it into the air in the presence of Pharaoh. [9]It will become fine dust over the whole land of Egypt, and festering boils will break out on men and animals throughout the land."

[10]So they took soot from a furnace and stood before Pharaoh. Moses tossed it into the air, and festering boils broke out on men and animals. [11]The magicians could not stand before Moses because of the boils that were on them and on all the Egyptians. [12]But the LORD hardened Pharaoh's heart and he would not listen to Moses and Aaron, just as the LORD had said to Moses.

The Plague of Hail

[13]Then the LORD said to Moses, "Get up early in the morning, confront Pharaoh and say to him, 'This is what the LORD, the God of the Hebrews, says: Let my people go, so that they may worship me, [14]or this time I will send the full force of my plagues against you and against your officials and your people, so you may know that there is no-one like me in all the earth. [15]For by now I could have stretched out my hand and struck you and your people with a plague that would have wiped you off the earth. [16]But I have raised you up[a] for this very purpose, that I might show you my power and that my name might be proclaimed in all the earth. [17]You still set yourself against my people and will not let them go. [18]Therefore, at this time tomorrow I will send the worst hailstorm that has ever fallen on Egypt, from the day it was founded till now. [19]Give an order now to bring your livestock and everything you have in the field to a place of shelter, because the hail will fall on every man and animal that has not been brought in and is still out in the field, and they will die.' "

[20]Those officials of Pharaoh who feared the word of the LORD hurried to bring their slaves and their livestock inside. [21]But those who ignored the word of the LORD left their slaves and livestock in the field.

[22]Then the LORD said to Moses, "Stretch out your hand towards the sky so that hail will fall all over Egypt—on men and animals and on everything growing in the fields of Egypt." [23]When Moses stretched out his staff towards the sky, the LORD sent thunder and hail, and lightning flashed down to the ground. So the LORD rained hail on the land of Egypt; [24]hail fell and lightning flashed back and forth. It was the worst storm in all the land of Egypt since it had become a nation. [25]Throughout Egypt hail struck everything in the fields—both men and animals; it beat down everything growing in the fields and stripped every tree. [26]The only place it did not hail was the land of Goshen, where the Israelites were.

[27]Then Pharaoh summoned Moses and Aaron. "This time I have sinned," he said to them. "The LORD is in the right, and I and my people are in the wrong. [28]Pray to the LORD, for we have had enough thunder and hail. I will let you go; you don't have to stay any longer."

[29]Moses replied, "When I have gone out of the city, I will spread out my hands in prayer to the LORD. The

---

[a]23 Septuagint and Vulgate; Hebrew will put a deliverance   [a]16 Or have spared you

thunder will stop and there will be no more hail, so you may know that the earth is the LORD's. ³⁰But I know that you and your officials still do not fear the LORD God."

³¹(The flax and barley were destroyed, since the barley was in the ear and the flax was in bloom. ³²The wheat and spelt, however, were not destroyed, because they ripen later.)

³³Then Moses left Pharaoh and went out of the city. He spread out his hands towards the LORD; the thunder and hail stopped, and the rain no longer poured down on the land. ³⁴When Pharaoh saw that the rain and hail and thunder had stopped, he sinned again: He and his officials hardened their hearts. ³⁵So Pharaoh's heart was hard and he would not let the Israelites go, just as the LORD had said through Moses.

The Plague of Locusts

10 Then the LORD said to Moses, "Go to Pharaoh, for I have hardened his heart and the hearts of his officials so that I may perform these miraculous signs of mine among them ²that you may tell your children and grandchildren how I dealt harshly with the Egyptians and how I performed my signs among them, and that you may know that I am the LORD."

10:1   People often say that God causes good things to happen, but not bad. The Old Testament does not say that. It says since there is no other power than God, everything must come from him. This makes suffering as difficult for the Israelites to understand as it is for us. The book of Job is a long meditation on the subject of "why?".

---

³So Moses and Aaron went to Pharaoh and said to him, "This is what the LORD, the God of the Hebrews, says: 'How long will you refuse to humble yourself before me? Let my people go, so that they may worship me. ⁴If you refuse to let them go, I will bring locusts into your country tomorrow. ⁵They will cover the face of the ground so that it cannot be seen. They will devour what little you have left after the hail, including every tree that is growing in your fields. ⁶They will fill your houses and those of all your officials and all the Egyptians — something neither your fathers nor your forefathers have ever seen from the day they settled in this land till now.'" Then Moses turned and left Pharaoh.

⁷Pharaoh's officials said to him, "How long will this man be a snare to us? Let the people go, so that they may worship the LORD their God. Do you not yet realise that Egypt is ruined?"

⁸Then Moses and Aaron were brought back to Pharaoh. "Go, worship the LORD your God," he said. "But just who will be going?"

⁹Moses answered, "We will go with our young and old, with our sons and daughters, and with our flocks and herds, because we are to celebrate a festival to the LORD."

¹⁰Pharaoh said, "The LORD be with you — if I let you go, along with your women and children! Clearly you are bent on evil.ᵃ ¹¹No! Let only the men go; and worship the LORD, since that's what you have been asking for." Then Moses and Aaron were driven out of Pharaoh's presence.

¹²And the LORD said to Moses, "Stretch out your hand over Egypt so that locusts will swarm over the land and devour everything growing in the fields, everything left by the hail."

¹³So Moses stretched out his staff over Egypt, and the LORD made an east wind blow across the land all that day and all that night. By morning the wind had brought the locusts; ¹⁴they invaded all Egypt and settled down in every area of the country in great numbers. Never before had there been such a plague of locusts, nor will there ever be again. ¹⁵They covered all the ground until it was black. They devoured all that was left after the hail — everything growing in the fields and the fruit on the trees. Nothing green remained on tree or plant in all the land of Egypt.

¹⁶Pharaoh quickly summoned Moses and Aaron and said, "I have sinned against the LORD your God and against you. ¹⁷Now forgive my sin once more and pray to the LORD your God to take this deadly plague away from me."

¹⁸Moses then left Pharaoh and prayed to the LORD. ¹⁹And the LORD changed the wind to a very strong west wind, which caught up the locusts and carried them into the Red Sea.ᵇ Not a locust was left anywhere in Egypt. ²⁰But the LORD hardened Pharaoh's heart, and he would not let the Israelites go.

The Plague of Darkness

²¹Then the LORD said to Moses, "Stretch out your hand towards the sky so that darkness will spread over Egypt — darkness that can be felt." ²²So Moses stretched out his hand towards the sky, and total darkness covered all Egypt for three days. ²³No-one could see anyone else or leave his place for three days. Yet all the Israelites had light in the places where they lived.

²⁴Then Pharaoh summoned Moses and said, "Go, worship the LORD. Even your women and children may go with you; only leave your flocks and herds behind."

²⁵But Moses said, "You must allow us to have sacrifices and burnt offerings to present to the LORD our God. ²⁶Our livestock too must go with us; not a hoof is to be left behind. We have to use some of them in worshipping the LORD our God, and until we get there we will not know what we are to use to worship the LORD."

²⁷But the LORD hardened Pharaoh's heart, and he was not willing to let them go. ²⁸Pharaoh said to Moses, "Get out of my sight! Make sure you do not appear before me again! The day you see my face you will die."

²⁹"Just as you say," Moses replied, "I will never appear before you again."

ᵃ 10 Or *Be careful, trouble is in store for you!*   ᵇ 19 Hebrew *Yam Suph*; that is, Sea of Reeds

The Plague on the Firstborn

11 Now the LORD said to Moses, "I will bring one more plague on Pharaoh and on Egypt. After that, he will let you go from here, and when he does, he will drive you out completely. [2]Tell the people that men and women alike are to ask their neighbours for articles of silver and gold." [3](The LORD made the Egyptians favourably disposed towards the people, and Moses himself was highly regarded in Egypt by Pharaoh's officials and by the people.)

[4]So Moses said, "This is what the LORD says: 'About midnight I will go throughout Egypt. [5]Every firstborn son in Egypt will die, from the firstborn son of Pharaoh, who sits on the throne, to the firstborn son of the slave girl, who is at her hand mill, and all the firstborn of the cattle as well. [6]There will be loud wailing throughout Egypt—worse than there has ever been or ever will be again. [7]But among the Israelites not a dog will bark at any man or animal.' Then you will know that the LORD makes a distinction between Egypt and Israel. [8]All these officials of yours will come to me, bowing down before me and saying, 'Go, you and all the people who follow you!' After that I will leave." Then Moses, hot with anger, left Pharaoh.

[9]The LORD had said to Moses, "Pharaoh will refuse to listen to you—so that my wonders may be multiplied in Egypt." [10]Moses and Aaron performed all these wonders before Pharaoh, but the LORD hardened Pharaoh's heart, and he would not let the Israelites go out of his country.

The Passover

12 The LORD said to Moses and Aaron in Egypt, [2]"This month is to be for you the first month, the first month of your year. [3]Tell the whole community of Israel that on the tenth day of this month each man is to take a lamb[a] for his family, one for each household. [4]If any household is too small for a whole lamb, they must share one with their nearest neighbour, having taken into account the number of people there are. You are to determine the amount of lamb needed in accordance with what each person will eat. [5]The animals you choose must be year-old males without defect, and you may take them from the sheep or the goats. [6]Take care of them until the fourteenth day of the month, when all the people of the community of Israel must slaughter them at twilight. [7]Then they are to take some of the blood and put it on the sides and tops of the door-frames of the houses where they eat the lambs. [8]That same night they are to eat the meat roasted over the fire, along with bitter herbs, and bread made without yeast. [9]Do not eat the meat raw or cooked in water, but roast it over the fire—head, legs and inner parts. [10]Do not leave any of it till morning; if some is left till morning, you must burn it. [11]This is how you are to eat it: with your cloak tucked into your belt, your sandals on your feet and your staff in your hand. Eat it in haste; it is the LORD's Passover.

[12]"On that same night I will pass through Egypt and strike down every firstborn—both men and animals—and I will bring judgment on all the gods of Egypt. I am

a 3 The Hebrew word can mean lamb *or* kid; *also in verse 4.*

the LORD. [13]The blood will be a sign for you on the houses where you are; and when I see the blood, I will pass over you. No destructive plague will touch you when I strike Egypt.

12:13 No nation invents stories about its own humiliation. It is certain that the Israelites were slaves in Egypt because they remember this event as they do no other. The way the account of the night is told here shows that the event was already celebrated each year. The total power of God is shown by his power over life and death, and the Israelites knew that being spared by him had far greater significance than just this one night. In the Garden of Eden humankind had lost the right to life with God, and here God presented the people with life. It is not their right, but it is a free and generous gift from him.

---

[14]"This is a day you are to commemorate; for the generations to come you shall celebrate it as a festival to the LORD—a lasting ordinance. [15]For seven days you are to eat bread made without yeast. On the first day remove the yeast from your houses, for whoever eats anything with yeast in it from the first day until the seventh must be cut off from Israel. [16]On the first day hold a sacred assembly, and another one on the seventh day. Do no work at all on these days, except to prepare food for everyone to eat—that is all you may do.

[17]"Celebrate the Feast of Unleavened Bread, because it was on this very day that I brought your divisions out of Egypt. Celebrate this day as a lasting ordinance for the generations to come. [18]In the first month you are to eat bread made without yeast, from the evening of the fourteenth day until the evening of the twenty-first day. [19]For seven days no yeast is to be found in your houses. And whoever eats anything with yeast in it must be cut off from the community of Israel, whether he is an alien or native-born. [20]Eat nothing made with yeast. Wherever you live, you must eat unleavened bread."

[21]Then Moses summoned all the elders of Israel and said to them, "Go at once and select the animals for your families and slaughter the Passover lamb. [22]Take a bunch of hyssop, dip it into the blood in the basin and put some of the blood on the top and on both sides of the door-frame. Not one of you shall go out of the door of his house until morning. [23]When the LORD goes through the land to strike down the Egyptians, he will see the blood on the top and sides of the door-frame and will pass over that doorway, and he will not permit the destroyer to enter your houses and strike you down.

[24]"Obey these instructions as a lasting ordinance for you and your descendants. [25]When you enter the land that the LORD will give you as he promised, observe this ceremony. [26]And when your children ask you, 'What

does this ceremony mean to you?' [27]then tell them, 'It is the Passover sacrifice to the LORD, who passed over the houses of the Israelites in Egypt and spared our homes when he struck down the Egyptians.' " Then the people bowed down and worshipped. [28]The Israelites did just what the LORD commanded Moses and Aaron.

[29]At midnight the LORD struck down all the firstborn in Egypt, from the firstborn of Pharaoh, who sat on the throne, to the firstborn of the prisoner, who was in the dungeon, and the firstborn of all the livestock as well. [30]Pharaoh and all his officials and all the Egyptians got up during the night, and there was loud wailing in Egypt, for there was not a house without someone dead.

The Exodus

[31]During the night Pharaoh summoned Moses and Aaron and said, "Up! Leave my people, you and the Israelites! Go, worship the LORD as you have requested. [32]Take your flocks and herds, as you have said, and go. And also bless me."

[33]The Egyptians urged the people to hurry and leave the country. "For otherwise," they said, "we will all die!" [34]So the people took their dough before the yeast was added, and carried it on their shoulders in kneading troughs wrapped in clothing. [35]The Israelites did as Moses instructed and asked the Egyptians for articles of silver and gold and for clothing. [36]The LORD had made the Egyptians favourably disposed towards the people, and they gave them what they asked for; so they plundered the Egyptians.

[37]The Israelites journeyed from Rameses to Succoth. There were about six hundred thousand men on foot, besides women and children. [38]Many other people went up with them, as well as large droves of livestock, both flocks and herds. [39]With the dough they had brought from Egypt, they baked cakes of unleavened bread. The dough was without yeast because they had been driven out of Egypt and did not have time to prepare food for themselves.

[40]Now the length of time the Israelite people lived in Egypt[b] was 430 years. [41]At the end of the 430 years, to the very day, all the LORD's divisions left Egypt. [42]Because the LORD kept vigil that night to bring them out of Egypt, on this night all the Israelites are to keep vigil to honour the LORD for the generations to come.

Passover Restrictions

[43]The LORD said to Moses and Aaron, "These are the regulations for the Passover:

"No foreigner is to eat of it. [44]Any slave you have bought may eat of it after you have circumcised him, [45]but a temporary resident and a hired worker may not eat of it.

[46]"It must be eaten inside one house; take none of the meat outside the house. Do not break any of the bones. [47]The whole community of Israel must celebrate it.

[48]"An alien living among you who wants to celebrate the LORD's Passover must have all the males in his household circumcised; then he may take part like one born in the land. No uncircumcised male may eat of it. [49]The same law applies to the native-born and to the alien living among you."

[50]All the Israelites did just what the LORD had commanded Moses and Aaron. [51]And on that very day the LORD brought the Israelites out of Egypt by their divisions.

Consecration of the Firstborn

13 The LORD said to Moses, [2]"Consecrate to me every firstborn male. The first offspring of every womb among the Israelites belongs to me, whether man or animal.

[3]Then Moses said to the people, "Commemorate this day, the day you came out of Egypt, out of the land of slavery, because the LORD brought you out of it with a mighty hand. Eat nothing containing yeast. [4]Today, in the month of Abib, you are leaving. [5]When the LORD brings you into the land of the Canaanites, Hittites, Amorites, Hivites and Jebusites—the land he swore to your forefathers to give you, a land flowing with milk and honey—you are to observe this ceremony in this month: [6]For seven days eat bread made without yeast and on the seventh day hold a festival to the LORD. [7]Eat unleavened bread during those seven days; nothing with yeast in it is to be seen among you, nor shall any yeast be seen anywhere within your borders. [8]On that day tell your son, 'I do this because of what the LORD did for me when I came out of Egypt.' [9]This observance will be for you like a sign on your hand and a reminder on your forehead that the law of the LORD is to be on your lips. For the LORD brought you out of Egypt with his mighty hand. [10]You must keep this ordinance at the appointed time year after year.

13:7 Many ceremonies in all religions are borrowed from ancient customs. When primitive people tried to understand God they often used very powerful symbols to express themselves and it was helpful to make use of those symbols. Yeast seemed to be able to make itself grow and live and so became a sign of life. To avoid using it was to recognize that life belongs to God.

---

[11]"After the LORD brings you into the land of the Canaanites and gives it to you, as he promised on oath to you and your forefathers, [12]you are to give over to the LORD the first offspring of every womb. All the first-born males of your livestock belong to the LORD. [13]Redeem with a lamb every firstborn donkey, but if you do not redeem it, break its neck. Redeem every firstborn among your sons.

[14]"In days to come when your son asks you, 'What does this mean?' say to him, 'With a mighty hand the LORD brought us out of Egypt, out of the land of slavery. [15]When Pharaoh stubbornly refused to let us go, the

LORD killed every firstborn in Egypt, both man and animal. This is why I sacrifice to the LORD the first male offspring of every womb and redeem each of my firstborn sons.' [16]And it will be like a sign on your hand and a symbol on your forehead that the LORD brought us out of Egypt with his mighty hand."

Crossing the Sea

[17]When Pharaoh let the people go, God did not lead them on the road through the Philistine country, though that was shorter. For God said, "If they face war, they might change their minds and return to Egypt." [18]So God led the people around by the desert road towards the Red Sea.[a] The Israelites went up out of Egypt armed for battle.

[19]Moses took the bones of Joseph with him because Joseph had made the sons of Israel swear an oath. He had said, "God will surely come to your aid, and then you must carry my bones up with you from this place."[b]

[20]After leaving Succoth they camped at Etham on the edge of the desert. [21]By day the LORD went ahead of them in a pillar of cloud to guide them on their way and by night in a pillar of fire to give them light, so that they could travel by day or night. [22]Neither the pillar of cloud by day nor the pillar of fire by night left its place in front of the people.

14 Then the LORD said to Moses, [2]"Tell the Israelites to turn back and camp near Pi Hahiroth, between Migdol and the sea. They are to camp by the sea, directly opposite Baal Zephon. [3]Pharaoh will think, 'The Israelites are wandering around the land in confusion, hemmed in by the desert.' [4]And I will harden Pharaoh's heart, and he will pursue them. But I will gain glory for myself through Pharaoh and all his army, and the Egyptians will know that I am the LORD." So the Israelites did this.

[5]When the king of Egypt was told that the people had fled, Pharaoh and his officials changed their minds about them and said, "What have we done? We have let the Israelites go and have lost their services!" [6]So he had his chariot made ready and took his army with him. [7]He took six hundred of the best chariots, along with all the other chariots of Egypt, with officers over all of them. [8]The LORD hardened the heart of Pharaoh king of Egypt, so that he pursued the Israelites, who were marching out boldly. [9]The Egyptians — all Pharaoh's horses and chariots, horsemen[a] and troops — pursued the Israelites and overtook them as they camped by the sea near Pi Hahiroth, opposite Baal Zephon.

[10]As Pharaoh approached, the Israelites looked up, and there were the Egyptians, marching after them. They were terrified and cried out to the LORD. [11]They said to Moses, "Was it because there were no graves in Egypt that you brought us to the desert to die? What have you done to us by bringing us out of Egypt? [12]Didn't we say to you in Egypt, 'Leave us alone; let us serve the Egyptians'? It would have been better for us to serve the Egyptians than to die in the desert!"

[13]Moses answered the people, "Do not be afraid. Stand firm and you will see the deliverance the LORD will bring you today. The Egyptians you see today you will never see again. [14]The LORD will fight for you; you need only to be still."

[15]Then the LORD said to Moses, "Why are you crying out to me? Tell the Israelites to move on. [16]Raise your staff and stretch out your hand over the sea to divide the water so that the Israelites can go through the sea on dry ground. [17]I will harden the hearts of the Egyptians so that they will go in after them. And I will gain glory through Pharaoh and all his army, through his chariots and his horsemen. [18]The Egyptians will know that I am the LORD when I gain glory through Pharaoh, his chariots and his horsemen."

[19]Then the angel of God, who had been travelling in front of Israel's army, withdrew and went behind them. The pillar of cloud also moved from in front and stood behind them, [20]coming between the armies of Egypt and Israel. Throughout the night the cloud brought darkness to the one side and light to the other; so neither went near the other all night long.

[21]Then Moses stretched out his hand over the sea, and all that night the LORD drove the sea back with a strong east wind and turned it into dry land. The waters were divided, [22]and the Israelites went through the sea on dry ground, with a wall of water on their right and on their left.

[23]The Egyptians pursued them, and all Pharaoh's horses and chariots and horsemen followed them into the sea. [24]During the last watch of the night the LORD looked down from the pillar of fire and cloud at the Egyptian army and threw it into confusion. [25]He made the wheels of their chariots come off[b] so that they had difficulty driving. And the Egyptians said, "Let's get away from the Israelites! The LORD is fighting for them against Egypt."

[26]Then the LORD said to Moses, "Stretch out your hand over the sea so that the waters may flow back over the Egyptians and their chariots and horsemen." [27]Moses stretched out his hand over the sea, and at daybreak the sea went back to its place. The Egyptians were fleeing towards[c] it, and the LORD swept them into the sea. [28]The water flowed back and covered the chariots and horsemen — the entire army of Pharaoh that had followed the Israelites into the sea. Not one of them survived.

[29]But the Israelites went through the sea on dry ground, with a wall of water on their right and on their left. [30]That day the LORD saved Israel from the hands of the Egyptians, and Israel saw the Egyptians lying dead on the shore. [31]And when the Israelites saw the great power the LORD displayed against the Egyptians, the people feared the LORD and put their trust in him and in Moses his servant.

The Song of Moses and Miriam

15 Then Moses and the Israelites sang this song to the LORD:

"I will sing to the LORD,
    for he is highly exalted.

---

[a]18 Hebrew *Yam Suph*; that is, Sea of Reeds   [b]19 See Gen. 50:25.   [a]9 Or *charioteers*; also in verses 17, 18, 23, 26 and 28
[b]25 Or *He jammed the wheels of their chariots* (see Samaritan Pentateuch, Septuagint and Syriac)   [c]27 Or *from*

The horse and its rider
    he has hurled into the sea.
[2]The LORD is my strength and my song;
    he has become my salvation.
He is my God, and I will praise him,
    my father's God, and I will exalt him.
[3]The LORD is a warrior;
    the LORD is his name.
[4]Pharaoh's chariots and his army
    he has hurled into the sea.
The best of Pharaoh's officers
    are drowned in the Red Sea.[a]
[5]The deep waters have covered them;
    they sank to the depths like a stone.

15:1   This exodus from Egypt has become a sign of hope to oppressed people ever since, who understand from it that God is on the side of the oppressed and that in the end they will be free. Later, Jews introduced a cautionary note. Realizing how easy it was for the oppressed to become oppressors, they tell how the angels joined in this freedom song and God silenced them, saying "How can you sing when my children are drowning?"

---

[6]"Your right hand, O LORD,
    was majestic in power.
Your right hand, O LORD,
    shattered the enemy.
[7]In the greatness of your majesty
    you threw down those who opposed you.
You unleashed your burning anger;
    it consumed them like stubble.
[8]By the blast of your nostrils
    the waters piled up.
The surging waters stood firm like a wall;
    the deep waters congealed in the heart of the
      sea.

[9]"The enemy boasted,
    'I will pursue, I will overtake them.
I will divide the spoils;
    I will gorge myself on them.
I will draw my sword
    and my hand will destroy them.'
[10]But you blew with your breath,
    and the sea covered them.
They sank like lead
    in the mighty waters.

[11]"Who among the gods is like you, O LORD?
    Who is like you—
      majestic in holiness,
      awesome in glory,
      working wonders?
[12]You stretched out your right hand
    and the earth swallowed them.

[13]"In your unfailing love you will lead
    the people you have redeemed.
In your strength you will guide them
    to your holy dwelling.
[14]The nations will hear and tremble;
    anguish will grip the people of Philistia.
[15]The chiefs of Edom will be terrified,
    the leaders of Moab will be seized with
      trembling,
the people[b] of Canaan will melt away;
[16] terror and dread will fall upon them.
By the power of your arm
    they will be as still as a stone—
until your people pass by, O LORD,
    until the people you bought[c] pass by.
[17]You will bring them in and plant them
    on the mountain of your inheritance—
the place, O LORD, you made for your dwelling,
    the sanctuary, O Lord, your hands established.
[18]The LORD will reign
    for ever and ever."

[19]When Pharaoh's horses, chariots and horsemen[d] went into the sea, the LORD brought the waters of the sea back over them, but the Israelites walked through the sea on dry ground. [20]Then Miriam the prophetess, Aaron's sister, took a tambourine in her hand, and all the women followed her, with tambourines and dancing. [21]Miriam sang to them:

"Sing to the LORD,
    for he is highly exalted.
The horse and its rider
    he has hurled into the sea."

The Waters of Marah and Elim

[22]Then Moses led Israel from the Red Sea and they went into the Desert of Shur. For three days they travelled in the desert without finding water. [23]When they came to Marah, they could not drink its water because it was bitter. (That is why the place is called Marah.[e]) [24]So the people grumbled against Moses, saying, "What are we to drink?"

[25]Then Moses cried out to the LORD, and the LORD showed him a piece of wood. He threw it into the water, and the water became sweet.

There the LORD made a decree and a law for them, and there he tested them. [26]He said, "If you listen carefully to the voice of the LORD your God and do what is right in his eyes, if you pay attention to his commands and keep all his decrees, I will not bring on you any of the diseases I brought on the Egyptians, for I am the LORD, who heals you."

[27]Then they came to Elim, where there were twelve springs and seventy palm trees, and they camped there near the water.

Manna and Quail

16 The whole Israelite community set out from Elim and came to the Desert of Sin, which is between Elim and Sinai, on the fifteenth day of the

---

[a]4 Hebrew *Yam Suph;* that is, Sea of Reeds; also in verse 22
[d]19 Or *charioteers*   [e]23 *Marah* means *bitter.*
[b]15 Or *rulers*   [c]16 Or *created*

second month after they had come out of Egypt. [2]In the desert the whole community grumbled against Moses and Aaron. [3]The Israelites said to them, "If only we had died by the LORD's hand in Egypt! There we sat round pots of meat and ate all the food we wanted, but you have brought us out into this desert to starve this entire assembly to death."

16:2 During their time in the wilderness the people grumbled many times. They soon forgot the times that God provided for them. The wilderness has now become a symbol for the times in life when God seems absent or unconcerned. Manna has become a symbol of the opposite. It is a sign that God is always there and cares about his people.

The miracle of quail, like many of the plagues in Egypt, may have a natural explanation. Quail migrate in huge numbers, are exhausted by their flight, and easily caught. God's provision is often through the natural world.

---

[4]Then the LORD said to Moses, "I will rain down bread from heaven for you. The people are to go out each day and gather enough for that day. In this way I will test them and see whether they will follow my instructions. [5]On the sixth day they are to prepare what they bring in, and that is to be twice as much as they gather on the other days."

[6]So Moses and Aaron said to all the Israelites, "In the evening you will know that it was the LORD who brought you out of Egypt, [7]and in the morning you will see the glory of the LORD, because he has heard your grumbling against him. Who are we, that you should grumble against us?" [8]Moses also said, "You will know that it was the LORD when he gives you meat to eat in the evening and all the bread you want in the morning, because he has heard your grumbling against him. Who are we? You are not grumbling against us, but against the LORD."

[9]Then Moses told Aaron, "Say to the entire Israelite community, 'Come before the LORD, for he has heard your grumbling.' "

[10]While Aaron was speaking to the whole Israelite community, they looked towards the desert, and there was the glory of the LORD appearing in the cloud.

[11]The LORD said to Moses, [12]"I have heard the grumbling of the Israelites. Tell them, 'At twilight you will eat meat, and in the morning you will be filled with bread. Then you will know that I am the LORD your God.' "

[13]That evening quail came and covered the camp, and in the morning there was a layer of dew around the camp. [14]When the dew was gone, thin flakes like frost on the ground appeared on the desert floor. [15]When the Israelites saw it, they said to each other, "What is it?" For they did not know what it was.

Moses said to them, "It is the bread the LORD has given you to eat. [16]This is what the LORD has commanded: 'Each one is to gather as much as he needs. Take an omer[a] for each person you have in your tent.' "

[17]The Israelites did as they were told; some gathered much, some little. [18]And when they measured it by the omer, he who gathered much did not have too much, and he who gathered little did not have too little. Each one gathered as much as he needed.

[19]Then Moses said to them, "No-one is to keep any of it until morning."

[20]However, some of them paid no attention to Moses; they kept part of it until morning, but it was full of maggots and began to smell. So Moses was angry with them.

[21]Each morning everyone gathered as much as he needed, and when the sun grew hot, it melted away. [22]On the sixth day, they gathered twice as much — two omers[b] for each person — and the leaders of the community came and reported this to Moses. [23]He said to them, "This is what the LORD commanded: 'Tomorrow is to be a day of rest, a holy Sabbath to the LORD. So bake what you want to bake and boil what you want to boil. Save whatever is left and keep it until morning.' "

[24]So they saved it until morning, as Moses commanded, and it did not stink or get maggots in it. [25]"Eat it today," Moses said, "because today is a Sabbath to the LORD. You will not find any of it on the ground today. [26]Six days you are to gather it, but on the seventh day, the Sabbath, there will not be any."

[27]Nevertheless, some of the people went out on the seventh day to gather it, but they found none. [28]Then the LORD said to Moses, "How long will you[c] refuse to keep my commands and my instructions? [29]Bear in mind that the LORD has given you the Sabbath; that is why on the sixth day he gives you bread for two days. Everyone is to stay where he is on the seventh day; no-one is to go out." [30]So the people rested on the seventh day.

[31]The people of Israel called the bread manna.[d] It was white like coriander seed and tasted like wafers made with honey. [32]Moses said, "This is what the LORD has commanded: 'Take an omer of manna and keep it for the generations to come, so they can see the bread I gave you to eat in the desert when I brought you out of Egypt.' "

[33]So Moses said to Aaron, "Take a jar and put an omer of manna in it. Then place it before the LORD to be kept for the generations to come."

[34]As the LORD commanded Moses, Aaron put the manna in front of the Testimony, that it might be kept. [35]The Israelites ate manna for forty years, until they came to a land that was settled; they ate manna until they reached the border of Canaan. [36](An omer is one tenth of an ephah.)

---

a16 That is, probably about 4 pints (about 2 litres); also in verses 18, 32, 33 and 36
b22 That is, probably about 7½ pints (about 4.5 litres)   c28 The Hebrew is plural.
d31 Manna means What is it? (see verse 15).

Water From the Rock

17 The whole Israelite community set out from the Desert of Sin, travelling from place to place as the LORD commanded. They camped at Rephidim, but there was no water for the people to drink. ²So they quarrelled with Moses and said, "Give us water to drink."

Moses replied, "Why do you quarrel with me? Why do you put the LORD to the test?"

³But the people were thirsty for water there, and they grumbled against Moses. They said, "Why did you bring us up out of Egypt to make us and our children and livestock die of thirst?"

⁴Then Moses cried out to the LORD, "What am I to do with these people? They are almost ready to stone me."

⁵The LORD answered Moses, "Walk on ahead of the people. Take with you some of the elders of Israel and take in your hand the staff with which you struck the Nile, and go. ⁶I will stand there before you by the rock at Horeb. Strike the rock, and water will come out of it for the people to drink." So Moses did this in the sight of the elders of Israel. ⁷And he called the place Massah*a* and Meribah*b* because the Israelites quarrelled and because they tested the LORD saying, "Is the LORD among us or not?"

The Amalekites Defeated

⁸The Amalekites came and attacked the Israelites at Rephidim. ⁹Moses said to Joshua, "Choose some of our men and go out to fight the Amalekites. Tomorrow I will stand on top of the hill with the staff of God in my hands."

¹⁰So Joshua fought the Amalekites as Moses had ordered, and Moses, Aaron and Hur went to the top of the hill. ¹¹As long as Moses held up his hands, the Israelites were winning, but whenever he lowered his hands, the Amalekites were winning. ¹²When Moses' hands grew tired, they took a stone and put it under him and he sat on it. Aaron and Hur held his hands up—one on one side, one on the other—so that his hands remained steady till sunset. ¹³So Joshua overcame the Amalekite army with the sword.

¹⁴Then the LORD said to Moses, "Write this on a scroll as something to be remembered and make sure that Joshua hears it, because I will completely blot out the memory of Amalek from under heaven."

¹⁵Moses built an altar and called it The LORD is my Banner. ¹⁶He said, "For hands were lifted up to the throne of the LORD. The*c* LORD will be at war against the Amalekites from generation to generation."

Jethro Visits Moses

18 Now Jethro, the priest of Midian and father-in-law of Moses, heard of everything God had done for Moses and for his people Israel, and how the LORD had brought Israel out of Egypt.

²After Moses had sent away his wife Zipporah, his father-in-law Jethro received her ³and her two sons.

One son was named Gershom,*a* for Moses said, "I have become an alien in a foreign land"; ⁴and the other was named Eliezer,*b* for he said, "My father's God was my helper; he saved me from the sword of Pharaoh."

⁵Jethro, Moses' father-in-law, together with Moses' sons and wife, came to him in the desert, where he was camped near the mountain of God. ⁶Jethro had sent word to him, "I, your father-in-law Jethro, am coming to you with your wife and her two sons."

⁷So Moses went out to meet his father-in-law and bowed down and kissed him. They greeted each other and then went into the tent. ⁸Moses told his father-in-law about everything the LORD had done to Pharaoh and the Egyptians for Israel's sake and about all the hardships they had met along the way and how the LORD had saved them.

⁹Jethro was delighted to hear about all the good things the LORD had done for Israel in rescuing them from the hand of the Egyptians. ¹⁰He said, "Praise be to the LORD, who rescued you from the hand of the Egyptians and of Pharaoh, and who rescued the people from the hand of the Egyptians. ¹¹Now I know that the LORD is greater than all other gods, for he did this to those who had treated Israel arrogantly." ¹²Then Jethro, Moses' father-in-law, brought a burnt offering and other sacrifices to God, and Aaron came with all the elders of Israel to eat bread with Moses' father-in-law in the presence of God.

18:12 Moses' father-in-law belonged to the Kenite tribe, who traced their ancestry back to Cain. It is clear here that Jethro worshipped the God of Israel. It may be that Moses learned much about God from Jethro, whose judgement he clearly respected (verses 17–24), and that it was a preparation for his vision of God at the burning bush (chapter 3).

---

¹³The next day Moses took his seat to serve as judge for the people, and they stood round him from morning till evening. ¹⁴When his father-in-law saw all that Moses was doing for the people, he said, "What is this you are doing for the people? Why do you alone sit as judge, while all these people stand round you from morning till evening?"

¹⁵Moses answered him, "Because the people come to me to seek God's will. ¹⁶Whenever they have a dispute, it is brought to me, and I decide between the parties and inform them of God's decrees and laws."

¹⁷Moses' father-in-law replied, "What you are doing is not good. ¹⁸You and these people who come to you will only wear yourselves out. The work is too heavy for you; you cannot handle it alone. ¹⁹Listen now to me and I will give you some advice, and may God be with you. You must be the people's representative before God and bring their disputes to him. ²⁰Teach them the decrees and laws, and show them the way to live and the duties they are to perform. ²¹But select capable men from all the people—men who fear God,

---

a 7 Massah means testing.　　　*b 7 Meribah means quarrelling.*　　　*c 16 Or "Because a hand was against the throne of the LORD, the*
a 3 Gershom sounds like the Hebrew for an alien there.　　　*b 4 Eliezer means my God is helper.*

trustworthy men who hate dishonest gain—and appoint them as officials over thousands, hundreds, fifties and tens. ²²Have them serve as judges for the people at all times, but have them bring every difficult case to you; the simple cases they can decide themselves. That will make your load lighter, because they will share it with you. ²³If you do this and God so commands, you will be able to stand the strain, and all these people will go home satisfied."

²⁴Moses listened to his father-in-law and did everything he said. ²⁵He chose capable men from all Israel and made them leaders of the people, officials over thousands, hundreds, fifties and tens. ²⁶They served as judges for the people at all times. The difficult cases they brought to Moses, but the simple ones they decided themselves.

²⁷Then Moses sent his father-in-law on his way, and Jethro returned to his own country.

At Mount Sinai

19 In the third month after the Israelites left Egypt—on the very day—they came to the Desert of Sinai. ²After they set out from Rephidim, they entered the Desert of Sinai, and Israel camped there in the desert in front of the mountain.

³Then Moses went up to God, and the LORD called to him from the mountain and said, "This is what you are to say to the house of Jacob and what you are to tell the people of Israel: ⁴'You yourselves have seen what I did to Egypt, and how I carried you on eagles' wings and brought you to myself. ⁵Now if you obey me fully and keep my covenant, then out of all nations you will be my treasured possession. Although the whole earth is mine, ⁶you^a will be for me a kingdom of priests and a holy nation.' These are the words you are to speak to the Israelites."

⁷So Moses went back and summoned the elders of the people and set before them all the words the LORD had commanded him to speak. ⁸The people all responded together, "We will do everything the LORD has said." So Moses brought their answer back to the LORD.

⁹The LORD said to Moses, "I am going to come to you in a dense cloud, so that the people will hear me speaking with you and will always put their trust in you." Then Moses told the LORD what the people had said.

¹⁰And the LORD said to Moses, "Go to the people and consecrate them today and tomorrow. Make them wash their clothes ¹¹and be ready by the third day, because on that day the LORD will come down on Mount Sinai in the sight of all the people. ¹²Put limits for the people around the mountain and tell them, 'Be careful that you do not go up the mountain or touch the foot of it. Whoever touches the mountain shall surely be put to death. ¹³He shall surely be stoned or shot with arrows; not a hand is to be laid on him. Whether man or animal, he shall not be permitted to live.' Only when the ram's horn sounds a long blast may they go up to the mountain."

¹⁴After Moses had gone down the mountain to the people, he consecrated them, and they washed their clothes. ¹⁵Then he said to the people, "Prepare yourselves for the third day. Abstain from sexual relations."

¹⁶On the morning of the third day there was thunder and lightning, with a thick cloud over the mountain, and a very loud trumpet blast. Everyone in the camp trembled. ¹⁷Then Moses led the people out of the camp to meet with God, and they stood at the foot of the mountain. ¹⁸Mount Sinai was covered with smoke, because the LORD descended on it in fire. The smoke billowed up from it like smoke from a furnace, the whole mountain^b trembled violently, ¹⁹and the sound of the trumpet grew louder and louder. Then Moses spoke and the voice of God answered him.^c

²⁰The LORD descended to the top of Mount Sinai and called Moses to the top of the mountain. So Moses went up ²¹and the LORD said to him, "Go down and warn the people so they do not force their way through to see the LORD and many of them perish. ²²Even the priests, who approach the LORD, must consecrate themselves, or the LORD will break out against them."

²³Moses said to the LORD, "The people cannot come up Mount Sinai, because you yourself warned us, 'Put limits around the mountain and set it apart as holy.' "

²⁴The LORD replied, "Go down and bring Aaron up with you. But the priests and the people must not force their way through to come up to the LORD, or he will break out against them."

²⁵So Moses went down to the people and told them.

The Ten Commandments

20 And God spoke all these words:

²"I am the LORD your God, who brought you out of Egypt, out of the land of slavery.

20:1 Having accepted God's offer of a covenant treaty with them, the people needed to learn how to live by it. These laws provided an outline of the spirit in which they must live. People of each generation and culture have to work out how to apply it to their own circumstances. More detailed rules are found in the other books of the Pentateuch and elsewhere in the Bible. One of the prophets' most frequent complaints was that people kept to the letter of the law, but broke the spirit of what it said.

---

³"You shall have no other gods before^a me.
⁴"You shall not make for yourself an idol in the form of anything in heaven above or on the earth beneath or in the waters below. ⁵You shall not bow down to them or worship them; for I, the LORD your God, am a jealous God, punishing the children for the sin of the fathers to the third and fourth generation of those who hate me,

⁶but showing love to a thousand ˻generations˼ of those who love me and keep my commandments.

⁷"You shall not misuse the name of the LORD your God, for the LORD will not hold anyone guiltless who misuses his name.

⁸"Remember the Sabbath day by keeping it holy. ⁹Six days you shall labour and do all your work, ¹⁰but the seventh day is a Sabbath to the LORD your God. On it you shall not do any work, neither you, nor your son or daughter, nor your manservant or maidservant, nor your animals, nor the alien within your gates. ¹¹For in six days the LORD made the heavens and the earth, the sea, and all that is in them, but he rested on the seventh day. Therefore the LORD blessed the Sabbath day and made it holy.

¹²"Honour your father and your mother, so that you may live long in the land the LORD your God is giving you.

¹³"You shall not murder.

¹⁴"You shall not commit adultery.

¹⁵"You shall not steal.

¹⁶"You shall not give false testimony against your neighbour.

¹⁷"You shall not covet your neighbour's house. You shall not covet your neighbour's wife, or his manservant or maidservant, his ox or donkey, or anything that belongs to your neighbour."

¹⁸When the people saw the thunder and lightning and heard the trumpet and saw the mountain in smoke, they trembled with fear. They stayed at a distance ¹⁹and said to Moses, "Speak to us yourself and we will listen. But do not have God speak to us or we will die."

²⁰Moses said to the people, "Do not be afraid. God has come to test you, so that the fear of God will be with you to keep you from sinning."

²¹The people remained at a distance, while Moses approached the thick darkness where God was.

Idols and Altars

²²Then the LORD said to Moses, "Tell the Israelites this: 'You have seen for yourselves that I have spoken to you from heaven: ²³Do not make any gods to be alongside me; do not make for yourselves gods of silver or gods of gold.

²⁴" 'Make an altar of earth for me and sacrifice on it your burnt offerings and fellowship offerings, ᵇ your sheep and goats and your cattle. Wherever I cause my name to be honoured, I will come to you and bless you. ²⁵If you make an altar of stones for me, do not build it with dressed stones, for you will defile it if you use a tool on it. ²⁶And do not go up to my altar on steps, lest your nakedness be exposed on it.'

21

"These are the laws you are to set before them:

Hebrew Servants

²"If you buy a Hebrew servant, he is to serve you for six years. But in the seventh year, he shall go free, without paying anything. ³If he comes alone, he is to go free alone; but if he has a wife when he comes, she is to go with him. ⁴If his master gives him a wife and she bears him sons or daughters, the woman and her children shall belong to her master, and only the man shall go free.

⁵"But if the servant declares, 'I love my master and my wife and children and do not want to go free,' ⁶then his master must take him before the judges. ᵃ He shall take him to the door or the door-post and pierce his ear with an awl. Then he will be his servant for life.

⁷"If a man sells his daughter as a servant, she is not to go free as menservants do. ⁸If she does not please the master who has selected her for himself, ᵇ he must let her be redeemed. He has no right to sell her to foreigners, because he has broken faith with her. ⁹If he selects her for his son, he must grant her the rights of a daughter. ¹⁰If he marries another woman, he must not deprive the first one of her food, clothing and marital rights. ¹¹If he does not provide her with these three things, she is to go free, without any payment of money.

Personal Injuries

¹²"Anyone who strikes a man and kills him shall surely be put to death. ¹³However, if he does not do it intentionally, but God lets it happen, he is to flee to a place I will designate. ¹⁴But if a man schemes and kills another man deliberately, take him away from my altar and put him to death.

¹⁵"Anyone who attacksᶜ his father or his mother must be put to death.

¹⁶"Anyone who kidnaps another and either sells him or still has him when he is caught must be put to death.

¹⁷"Anyone who curses his father or mother must be put to death.

¹⁸"If men quarrel and one hits the other with a stone or with his fistᵈ and he does not die but is confined to bed, ¹⁹the one who struck the blow will not be held responsible if the other gets up and walks around outside with his staff; however, he must pay the injured man for the loss of his time and see that he is completely healed.

²⁰"If a man beats his male or female slave with a rod and the slave dies as a direct result, he must be punished, ²¹but he is not to be punished if the slave gets up after a day or two, since the slave is his property.

²²"If men who are fighting hit a pregnant woman and she gives birth prematurelyᵉ but there is no serious injury, the offender must be fined whatever the woman's husband demands and the court allows. ²³But if there is serious injury, you are to take life for life, ²⁴eye for eye, tooth for tooth, hand for hand, foot for

---

ᵇ24 Traditionally peace offerings   ᵃ6 Or before God   ᵇ8 Or master so that he does not choose her
ᶜ15 Or kills   ᵈ18 Or with a tool   ᵉ22 Or she has a miscarriage

foot, [25]burn for burn, wound for wound, bruise for bruise.

21:21 This is a good example of an interpretation of the law which we would not follow today. At that time no one questioned the idea of slavery. Today we understand that God does not allow one person to own another, so we do not have a right to treat anyone in this way.

---

[26]"If a man hits a manservant or maidservant in the eye and destroys it, he must let the servant go free to compensate for the eye. [27]And if he knocks out the tooth of a manservant or maidservant, he must let the servant go free to compensate for the tooth.

[28]"If a bull gores a man or a woman to death, the bull must be stoned to death, and its meat must not be eaten. But the owner of the bull will not be held responsible. [29]If, however, the bull has had the habit of goring and the owner has been warned but has not kept it penned up and it kills a man or woman, the bull must be stoned and the owner also must be put to death. [30]However, if payment is demanded of him, he may redeem his life by paying whatever is demanded. [31]This law also applies if the bull gores a son or a daughter. [32]If the bull gores a male or female slave, the owner must pay thirty shekels[f] of silver to the master of the slave, and the bull must be stoned.

[33]"If a man uncovers a pit or digs one and fails to cover it and an ox or a donkey falls into it, [34]the owner of the pit must pay for the loss; he must pay its owner, and the dead animal will be his.

[35]"If a man's bull injures the bull of another and it dies, they are to sell the live one and divide both the money and the dead animal equally. [36]However, if it was known that the bull had the habit of goring, yet the owner did not keep it penned up, the owner must pay, animal for animal, and the dead animal will be his.

Protection of Property

22 "If a man steals an ox or a sheep and slaughters it or sells it, he must pay back five head of cattle for the ox and four sheep for the sheep.

[2]"If a thief is caught breaking in and is struck so that he dies, the defender is not guilty of bloodshed; [3]but if it happens[a] after sunrise, he is guilty of bloodshed.

"A thief must certainly make restitution, but if he has nothing, he must be sold to pay for his theft. [4]"If the stolen animal is found alive in his possession — whether ox or donkey or sheep — he must pay back double.

[5]"If a man grazes his livestock in a field or vineyard and lets them stray and they graze in another man's field, he must make restitution from the best of his own field or vineyard.

[6]"If a fire breaks out and spreads into thornbushes so that it burns shocks of grain or standing corn or the whole field, the one who started the fire must make restitution.

[7]"If a man gives his neighbour silver or goods for safekeeping and they are stolen from the neighbour's house, the thief, if he is caught, must pay back double. [8]But if the thief is not found, the owner of the house must appear before the judges[b] to determine whether he has laid his hands on the other man's property. [9]In all cases of illegal possession of an ox, a donkey, a sheep, a garment, or any other lost property about which somebody says, 'This is mine,' both parties are to bring their cases before the judges. The one whom the judges declare[c] guilty must pay back double to his neighbour.

[10]"If a man gives a donkey, an ox, a sheep or any other animal to his neighbour for safekeeping and it dies or is injured or is taken away while no-one is looking, [11]the issue between them will be settled by the taking of an oath before the Lord that the neighbour did not lay hands on the other person's property. The owner is to accept this, and no restitution is required. [12]But if the animal was stolen from the neighbour, he must make restitution to the owner. [13]If it was torn to pieces by a wild animal, he shall bring in the remains as evidence and he will not be required to pay for the torn animal.

[14]"If a man borrows an animal from his neighbour and it is injured or dies while the owner is not present, he must make restitution. [15]But if the owner is with the animal, the borrower will not have to pay. If the animal was hired, the money paid for the hire covers the loss.

Social Responsibility

[16]"If a man seduces a virgin who is not pledged to be married and sleeps with her, he must pay the bride-price, and she shall be his wife. [17]If her father absolutely refuses to give her to him, he must still pay the bride-price for virgins.

[18]"Do not allow a sorceress to live.

[19]"Anyone who has sexual relations with an animal must be put to death.

[20]"Whoever sacrifices to any god other than the Lord must be destroyed.[d]

[21]"Do not ill-treat an alien or oppress him, for you were aliens in Egypt.

[22]"Do not take advantage of a widow or an orphan. [23]If you do and they cry out to me, I will certainly hear their cry. [24]My anger will be aroused, and I will kill you with the sword; your wives will become widows and your children fatherless.

[25]"If you lend money to one of my people among you who is needy, do not be like a money-lender; charge him no interest.[e] [26]If you take your neighbour's cloak as a pledge, return it to him by sunset, [27]because his cloak is the only covering he has for his body. What else will he sleep in? When he cries out to me, I will hear, for I am compassionate.

[28]"Do not blaspheme God[f] or curse the ruler of your people.

---

[f]32 That is, about 12 ounces (about 0.3 kilogram)   [a]3 Or if he strikes him   [b]8 Or before God; also in verse 9
[c]9 Or whom God declares
[d]20 The Hebrew term refers to the irrevocable giving over of things or persons to the Lord, often by totally destroying them.
[e]25 Or excessive interest   [f]28 Or Do not revile the judges

29"Do not hold back offerings from your granaries or your vats.*g*

22:26   Many of the Israelites' laws are the same as are found in the law codes of other nations at the time. In some cases, however, Israelite law was more advanced, particularly when dealing with people. There is nothing to be lost or gained by observing this law, or caring for widows or orphans (22:22) or the poor (23:6). They are to do it because God is merciful and they are to be like him.

"You must give me the firstborn of your sons. 30Do the same with your cattle and your sheep. Let them stay with their mothers for seven days, but give them to me on the eighth day.

31"You are to be my holy people. So do not eat the meat of an animal torn by wild beasts; throw it to the dogs.

Laws of Justice and Mercy

23 "Do not spread false reports. Do not help a wicked man by being a malicious witness.

2"Do not follow the crowd in doing wrong. When you give testimony in a lawsuit, do not pervert justice by siding with the crowd, 3and do not show favouritism to a poor man in his lawsuit.

4"If you come across your enemy's ox or donkey wandering off, be sure to take it back to him. 5If you see the donkey of someone who hates you fallen down under its load, do not leave it there; be sure you help him with it.

6"Do not deny justice to your poor people in their lawsuits. 7Have nothing to do with a false charge and do not put an innocent or honest person to death, for I will not acquit the guilty.

8"Do not accept a bribe, for a bribe blinds those who see and twists the words of the righteous.

9"Do not oppress an alien; you yourselves know how it feels to be aliens, because you were aliens in Egypt.

Sabbath Laws

10"For six years you are to sow your fields and harvest the crops, 11but during the seventh year let the land lie unploughed and unused. Then the poor among your people may get food from it, and the wild animals may eat what they leave. Do the same with your vineyard and your olive grove.

12"Six days do your work, but on the seventh day do not work, so that your ox and your donkey may rest and the slave born in your household, and the alien as well, may be refreshed.

13"Be careful to do everything I have said to you. Do not invoke the names of other gods; do not let them be heard on your lips.

The Three Annual Festivals

14"Three times a year you are to celebrate a festival to me.

15"Celebrate the Feast of Unleavened Bread; for seven days eat bread made without yeast, as I commanded you. Do this at the appointed time in the month of Abib, for in that month you came out of Egypt.

"No-one is to appear before me empty-handed.

16"Celebrate the Feast of Harvest with the firstfruits of the crops you sow in your field.

"Celebrate the Feast of Ingathering at the end of the year, when you gather in your crops from the field.

17"Three times a year all the men are to appear before the Sovereign LORD.

18"Do not offer the blood of a sacrifice to me along with anything containing yeast.

"The fat of my festival offerings must not be kept until morning.

19"Bring the best of the firstfruits of your soil to the house of the LORD your God.

"Do not cook a young goat in its mother's milk.

God's Angel to Prepare the Way

20"See, I am sending an angel ahead of you to guard you along the way and to bring you to the place I have prepared. 21Pay attention to him and listen to what he says. Do not rebel against him; he will not forgive your rebellion, since my Name is in him. 22If you listen carefully to what he says and do all that I say, I will be an enemy to your enemies and will oppose those who oppose you. 23My angel will go ahead of you and bring you into the land of the Amorites, Hittites, Perizzites, Canaanites, Hivites and Jebusites, and I will wipe them out. 24Do not bow down before their gods or worship them or follow their practices. You must demolish them and break their sacred stones to pieces. 25Worship the LORD your God, and his blessing will be on your food and water. I will take away sickness from among you, 26and none will miscarry or be barren in your land. I will give you a full life span.

27"I will send my terror ahead of you and throw into confusion every nation you encounter. I will make all your enemies turn their backs and run. 28I will send the hornet ahead of you to drive the Hivites, Canaanites and Hittites out of your way. 29But I will not drive them out in a single year, because the land would become desolate and the wild animals too numerous for you. 30Little by little I will drive them out before you, until you have increased enough to take possession of the land.

31"I will establish your borders from the Red Sea*a* to the Sea of the Philistines,*b* and from the desert to the River.*c* I will hand over to you the people who live in the land and you will drive them out before you. 32Do not make a covenant with them or with their gods. 33Do not let them live in your land, or they will cause you to sin against me, because the worship of their gods will certainly be a snare to you."

---

g29 The meaning of the Hebrew for this phrase is uncertain.   *a31* Hebrew *Yam Suph;* that is, Sea of Reeds
b31 That is, the Mediterranean   *c31* That is, the Euphrates

The Covenant Confirmed

24 Then he said to Moses, "Come up to the LORD, you and Aaron, Nadab and Abihu, and seventy of the elders of Israel. You are to worship at a distance, ²but Moses alone is to approach the LORD; the others must not come near. And the people may not come up with him."

³When Moses went and told the people all the LORD's words and laws, they responded with one voice, "Everything the LORD has said we will do." ⁴Moses then wrote down everything the LORD had said.

He got up early the next morning and built an altar at the foot of the mountain and set up twelve stone pillars representing the twelve tribes of Israel. ⁵Then he sent young Israelite men, and they offered burnt offerings and sacrificed young bulls as fellowship offerings[a] to the LORD. ⁶Moses took half of the blood and put it in bowls, and the other half he sprinkled on the altar. ⁷Then he took the Book of the Covenant and read it to the people. They responded, "We will do everything the LORD has said; we will obey."

⁸Moses then took the blood, sprinkled it on the people and said, "This is the blood of the covenant that the LORD has made with you in accordance with all these words."

24:8 In this covenant a bull was killed and its blood sealed the agreement. This idea of sacrifice has become important in Christianity, because Jesus applied it to himself. He said that his life was sacrificed so that people's new relationship with God could be sealed. The wine at the Christian Eucharist (or Holy Communion) symbolizes his blood.

---

⁹Moses and Aaron, Nadab and Abihu, and the seventy elders of Israel went up ¹⁰and saw the God of Israel. Under his feet was something like a pavement made of sapphire,[b] clear as the sky itself. ¹¹But God did not raise his hand against these leaders of the Israelites; they saw God, and they ate and drank.

¹²The LORD said to Moses, "Come up to me on the mountain and stay here, and I will give you the tablets of stone, with the law and commands I have written for their instruction."

¹³Then Moses set out with Joshua his assistant, and Moses went up on the mountain of God. ¹⁴He said to the elders, "Wait here for us until we come back to you. Aaron and Hur are with you, and anyone involved in a dispute can go to them."

¹⁵When Moses went up on the mountain, the cloud covered it, ¹⁶and the glory of the LORD settled on Mount Sinai. For six days the cloud covered the mountain, and on the seventh day the LORD called to Moses from within the cloud. ¹⁷To the Israelites the glory of the LORD looked like a consuming fire on top of the mountain. ¹⁸Then Moses entered the cloud as he went on up the mountain. And he stayed on the mountain forty days and forty nights.

Offerings for the Tabernacle

25 The LORD said to Moses, ²"Tell the Israelites to bring me an offering. You are to receive the offering for me from each man whose heart prompts him to give. ³These are the offerings you are to receive from them: gold, silver and bronze; ⁴blue, purple and scarlet yarn and fine linen; goat hair; ⁵ram skins dyed red and hides of sea cows;[a] acacia wood; ⁶olive oil for the light; spices for the anointing oil and for the fragrant incense; ⁷and onyx stones and other gems to be mounted on the ephod and breastpiece.

⁸"Then have them make a sanctuary for me, and I will dwell among them. ⁹Make this tabernacle and all its furnishings exactly like the pattern I will show you.

The Ark

¹⁰"Have them make a chest of acacia wood—two and a half cubits long, a cubit and a half wide, and a cubit and a half high.[b] ¹¹Overlay it with pure gold, both inside and out, and make a gold moulding around it. ¹²Cast four gold rings for it and fasten them to its four feet, with two rings on one side and two rings on the other. ¹³Then make poles of acacia wood and overlay them with gold. ¹⁴Insert the poles into the rings on the sides of the chest to carry it. ¹⁵The poles are to remain in the rings of this ark; they are not to be removed. ¹⁶Then put in the ark the Testimony, which I will give you.

¹⁷"Make an atonement cover[c] of pure gold—two and a half cubits long and a cubit and a half wide.[d] ¹⁸And make two cherubim out of hammered gold at the ends of the cover. ¹⁹Make one cherub on one end and the second cherub on the other; make the cherubim of one piece with the cover, at the two ends. ²⁰The cherubim are to have their wings spread upwards, overshadowing the cover with them. The cherubim are to face each other, looking towards the cover. ²¹Place the cover on top of the ark and put in the ark the Testimony, which I will give you. ²²There, above the cover between the two cherubim that are over the ark of the Testimony, I will meet with you and give you all my commands for the Israelites.

The Table

²³"Make a table of acacia wood—two cubits long, a cubit wide and a cubit and a half high.[e] ²⁴Overlay it with pure gold and make a gold moulding around it. ²⁵Also make around it a rim a handbreadth[f] wide and put a gold moulding on the rim. ²⁶Make four gold rings for the table and fasten them to the four corners, where the four legs are. ²⁷The rings are to be close to the rim to hold the poles used in carrying the table. ²⁸Make the poles of acacia wood, overlay them with gold and carry

a5 Traditionally *peace offerings*   b10 Or *lapis lazuli*   a5 That is, large aquatic mammals
b10 That is, about 3¾ feet (about 1.1 metres) long and 2¼ feet (about 0.7 metre) wide and high   c17 Traditionally *a mercy seat*
d17 That is, about 3¾ feet (about 1.1 metres) long and 2¼ feet (about 0.7 metre) wide
e23 That is, about 3 feet (about 0.9 metre) long and 1½ feet (about 0.5 metre) wide and 2¼ feet (about 0.7 metre) high
f25 That is, about 3 inches (about 8 centimetres)

the table with them. ²⁹And make its plates and dishes of pure gold, as well as its pitchers and bowls for the pouring out of offerings. ³⁰Put the bread of the Presence on this table to be before me at all times.

The Lampstand

³¹"Make a lampstand of pure gold and hammer it out, base and shaft; its flowerlike cups, buds and blossoms shall be of one piece with it. ³²Six branches are to extend from the sides of the lampstand—three on one side and three on the other. ³³Three cups shaped like almond flowers with buds and blossoms are to be on one branch, three on the next branch, and the same for all six branches extending from the lampstand. ³⁴And on the lampstand there are to be four cups shaped like almond flowers with buds and blossoms. ³⁵One bud shall be under the first pair of branches extending from the lampstand, a second bud under the second pair, and a third bud under the third pair—six branches in all. ³⁶The buds and branches shall all be of one piece with the lampstand, hammered out of pure gold.

³⁷"Then make its seven lamps and set them up on it so that they light the space in front of it. ³⁸Its wick trimmers and trays are to be of pure gold. ³⁹A talent*g* of pure gold is to be used for the lampstand and all these accessories. ⁴⁰See that you make them according to the pattern shown you on the mountain.

The Tabernacle

26 "Make the tabernacle with ten curtains of finely twisted linen and blue, purple and scarlet yarn, with cherubim worked into them by a skilled craftsman. ²All the curtains are to be the same size— twenty-eight cubits long and four cubits wide.*a* ³Join five of the curtains together, and do the same with the other five. ⁴Make loops of blue material along the edge of the end curtain in one set, and do the same with the end curtain in the other set. ⁵Make fifty loops on one curtain and fifty loops on the end curtain of the other set, with the loops opposite each other. ⁶Then make fifty gold clasps and use them to fasten the curtains together so that the tabernacle is a unit.

⁷"Make curtains of goat hair for the tent over the tabernacle—eleven altogether. ⁸All eleven curtains are to be the same size—thirty cubits long and four cubits wide.*b* ⁹Join five of the curtains together into one set and the other six into another set. Fold the sixth curtain double at the front of the tent. ¹⁰Make fifty loops along the edge of the end curtain in one set and also along the edge of the end curtain in the other set. ¹¹Then make fifty bronze clasps and put them in the loops to fasten the tent together as a unit. ¹²As for the additional length of the tent curtains, the half curtain that is left over is to hang down at the rear of the tabernacle. ¹³The tent curtains will be a cubit*c* longer on both sides; what is left will hang over the sides of the tabernacle so as to cover it. ¹⁴Make for the tent a

covering of ram skins dyed red, and over that a covering of hides of sea cows.*d*

¹⁵"Make upright frames of acacia wood for the tabernacle. ¹⁶Each frame is to be ten cubits long and a cubit and a half wide,*e* ¹⁷with two projections set parallel to each other. Make all the frames of the tabernacle in this way. ¹⁸Make twenty frames for the south side of the tabernacle ¹⁹and make forty silver bases to go under them—two bases for each frame, one under each projection. ²⁰For the other side, the north side of the tabernacle, make twenty frames ²¹and forty silver bases—two under each frame. ²²Make six frames for the far end, that is, the west end of the tabernacle, ²³and make two frames for the corners at the far end. ²⁴At these two corners they must be double from the bottom all the way to the top, and fitted into a single ring; both shall be like that. ²⁵So there will be eight frames and sixteen silver bases—two under each frame.

²⁶"Also make crossbars of acacia wood: five for the frames on one side of the tabernacle, ²⁷five for those on the other side, and five for the frames on the west, at the far end of the tabernacle. ²⁸The centre crossbar is to extend from end to end at the middle of the frames. ²⁹Overlay the frames with gold and make gold rings to hold the crossbars. Also overlay the crossbars with gold.

³⁰"Set up the tabernacle according to the plan shown you on the mountain.

³¹"Make a curtain of blue, purple and scarlet yarn and finely twisted linen, with cherubim worked into it by a skilled craftsman. ³²Hang it with gold hooks on four posts of acacia wood overlaid with gold and standing on four silver bases. ³³Hang the curtain from the clasps and place the ark of the Testimony behind the curtain. The curtain will separate the Holy Place from the Most Holy Place. ³⁴Put the atonement cover on the ark of the Testimony in the Most Holy Place. ³⁵Place the table outside the curtain on the north side of the tabernacle and put the lampstand opposite it on the south side.

³⁶"For the entrance to the tent make a curtain of blue, purple and scarlet yarn and finely twisted linen— the work of an embroiderer. ³⁷Make gold hooks for this curtain and five posts of acacia wood overlaid with gold. And cast five bronze bases for them.

The Altar of Burnt Offering

27 "Build an altar of acacia wood, three cubits*a* high; it is to be square, five cubits long and five cubits wide.*b* ²Make a horn at each of the four corners, so that the horns and the altar are of one piece, and overlay the altar with bronze. ³Make all its utensils of bronze—its pots to remove the ashes, and its shovels, sprinkling bowls, meat forks and firepans. ⁴Make a grating for it, a bronze network, and make a bronze ring at each of the four corners of the network. ⁵Put it under the ledge of the altar so that it is halfway up the

---

g39 That is, about 75 pounds (about 34 kilograms)
a2 That is, about 42 feet (about 13 metres) long and 6 feet (about 1.8 metres) wide
b8 That is, about 45 feet (about 13.5 metres) long and 6 feet (about 1.8 metres) wide   *c13* That is, about 1½ feet (about 0.5 metre)
d14 That is, large aquatic mammals   *e16* That is, about 15 feet (about 4.5 metres) long and 2¼ feet (about 0.7 metre) wide
a1 That is, about 4½ feet (about 1.4 metres)   *b1* That is, about 7½ feet (about 2.3 metres) long and wide

altar. 6Make poles of acacia wood for the altar and overlay them with bronze. 7The poles are to be inserted into the rings so they will be on two sides of the altar when it is carried. 8Make the altar hollow, out of boards. It is to be made just as you were shown on the mountain.

The Courtyard

9"Make a courtyard for the tabernacle. The south side shall be a hundred cubits*c* long and is to have curtains of finely twisted linen, 10with twenty posts and twenty bronze bases and with silver hooks and bands on the posts. 11The north side shall also be a hundred cubits long and is to have curtains, with twenty posts and twenty bronze bases and with silver hooks and bands on the posts.

12"The west end of the courtyard shall be fifty cubits*d* wide and have curtains, with ten posts and ten bases. 13On the east end, towards the sunrise, the courtyard shall also be fifty cubits wide. 14Curtains fifteen cubits*e* long are to be on one side of the entrance, with three posts and three bases, 15and curtains fifteen cubits long are to be on the other side, with three posts and three bases.

16"For the entrance to the courtyard, provide a curtain twenty cubits*f* long, of blue, purple and scarlet yarn and finely twisted linen — the work of an embroiderer — with four posts and four bases. 17All the posts around the courtyard are to have silver bands and hooks, and bronze bases. 18The courtyard shall be a hundred cubits long and fifty cubits wide,*g* with curtains of finely twisted linen five cubits*h* high, and with bronze bases. 19All the other articles used in the service of the tabernacle, whatever their function, including all the tent pegs for it and those for the courtyard, are to be of bronze.

Oil for the Lampstand

20"Command the Israelites to bring you clear oil of pressed olives for the light so that the lamps may be kept burning. 21In the Tent of Meeting, outside the curtain that is in front of the Testimony, Aaron and his sons are to keep the lamps burning before the LORD from evening till morning. This is to be a lasting ordinance among the Israelites for the generations to come.

The Priestly Garments

28 "Have Aaron your brother brought to you from among the Israelites, with his sons Nadab and Abihu, Eleazar and Ithamar, so that they may serve me as priests. 2Make sacred garments for your brother Aaron, to give him dignity and honour. 3Tell all the skilled men to whom I have given wisdom in such matters that they are to make garments for Aaron, for his consecration, so that he may serve me as priest. 4These are the garments they are to make: a breastpiece, an ephod, a robe, a woven tunic, a turban and a sash. They

are to make these sacred garments for your brother Aaron and his sons, so that they may serve me as priests. 5Make them use gold, and blue, purple and scarlet yarn, and fine linen.

28:1   It is difficult to work out exactly how Aaron was dressed, but it is certain that whatever he wore was of the finest materials and most skilfully made. Verses 29 and 30 make it clear why. When Aaron entered the shrine he stood before the Lord representing all the people. Just as God's word has power, so does what he has in mind. If he "remembers" Israel, it means he will be working for them. They wanted Aaron to represent the best of themselves and to offer that to God.

The Ephod

6"Make the ephod of gold, and of blue, purple and scarlet yarn, and of finely twisted linen — the work of a skilled craftsman. 7It is to have two shoulder pieces attached to two of its corners, so that it can be fastened. 8Its skilfully woven waistband is to be like it — of one piece with the ephod and made with gold, and with blue, purple and scarlet yarn, and with finely twisted linen.

9"Take two onyx stones and engrave on them the names of the sons of Israel 10in the order of their birth — six names on one stone and the remaining six on the other. 11Engrave the names of the sons of Israel on the two stones the way a gem cutter engraves a seal. Then mount the stones in gold filigree settings 12and fasten them on the shoulder pieces of the ephod as memorial stones for the sons of Israel. Aaron is to bear the names on his shoulders as a memorial before the LORD. 13Make gold filigree settings 14and two braided chains of pure gold, like a rope, and attach the chains to the settings.

The Breastpiece

15"Fashion a breastpiece for making decisions — the work of a skilled craftsman. Make it like the ephod: of gold, and of blue, purple and scarlet yarn, and of finely twisted linen. 16It is to be square — a span*a* long and a span wide — and folded double. 17Then mount four rows of precious stones on it. In the first row there shall be a ruby, a topaz and a beryl; 18in the second row a turquoise, a sapphire*b* and an emerald; 19in the third row a jacinth, an agate and an amethyst; 20in the fourth row a chrysolite, an onyx and a jasper.*c* Mount them in gold filigree settings. 21There are to be twelve stones, one for each of the names of the sons of Israel, each engraved like a seal with the name of one of the twelve tribes.

c9 That is, about 150 feet (about 46 metres); also in verse 11
e14 That is, about 22½ feet (about 6.9 metres); also in verse 15
g18 That is, about 150 feet (about 46 metres) long and 75 feet (about 23 metres) wide
a16 That is, about 9 inches (about 23 centimetres)   b18 Or lapis lazuli
c20 The precise identification of some of these precious stones is uncertain.
d12 That is, about 75 feet (about 23 metres); also in verse 13
f16 That is, about 30 feet (about 9 metres)   h18 That is, about 7½ feet (about 2.3 metres)

22"For the breastpiece make braided chains of pure gold, like a rope. 23Make two gold rings for it and fasten them to two corners of the breastpiece. 24Fasten the two gold chains to the rings at the corners of the breastpiece, 25and the other ends of the chains to the two settings, attaching them to the shoulder pieces of the ephod at the front. 26Make two gold rings and attach them to the other two corners of the breastpiece on the inside edge next to the ephod. 27Make two more gold rings and attach them to the bottom of the shoulder pieces on the front of the ephod, close to the seam just above the waistband of the ephod. 28The rings of the breastpiece are to be tied to the rings of the ephod with blue cord, connecting it to the waistband, so that the breastpiece will not swing out from the ephod.

29"Whenever Aaron enters the Holy Place, he will bear the names of the sons of Israel over his heart on the breastpiece of decision as a continuing memorial before the LORD. 30Also put the Urim and the Thummim in the breastpiece, so they may be over Aaron's heart whenever he enters the presence of the LORD. Thus Aaron will always bear the means of making decisions for the Israelites over his heart before the LORD.

Other Priestly Garments

31"Make the robe of the ephod entirely of blue cloth, 32with an opening for the head in its centre. There shall be a woven edge like a collar*d* around this opening, so that it will not tear. 33Make pomegranates of blue, purple and scarlet yarn around the hem of the robe, with gold bells between them. 34The gold bells and the pomegranates are to alternate around the hem of the robe. 35Aaron must wear it when he ministers. The sound of the bells will be heard when he enters the Holy Place before the LORD and when he comes out, so that he will not die.

36"Make a plate of pure gold and engrave on it as on a seal: HOLY TO THE LORD. 37Fasten a blue cord to it to attach it to the turban; it is to be on the front of the turban. 38It will be on Aaron's forehead, and he will bear the guilt involved in the sacred gifts the Israelites consecrate, whatever their gifts may be. It will be on Aaron's forehead continually so that they will be acceptable to the LORD.

39"Weave the tunic of fine linen and make the turban of fine linen. The sash is to be the work of an embroiderer. 40Make tunics, sashes and headbands for Aaron's sons, to give them dignity and honour. 41After you put these clothes on your brother Aaron and his sons, anoint and ordain them. Consecrate them so they may serve me as priests.

42"Make linen undergarments as a covering for the body, reaching from the waist to the thigh. 43Aaron and his sons must wear them whenever they enter the Tent of Meeting or approach the altar to minister in the Holy Place, so that they will not incur guilt and die.

"This is to be a lasting ordinance for Aaron and his descendants.

Consecration of the Priests

29 "This is what you are to do to consecrate them, so that they may serve me as priests: Take a young bull and two rams without defect. 2And from fine wheat flour, without yeast, make bread, and cakes mixed with oil, and wafers spread with oil. 3Put them in a basket and present them in it—along with the bull and the two rams. 4Then bring Aaron and his sons to the entrance to the Tent of Meeting and wash them with water. 5Take the garments and dress Aaron with the tunic, the robe of the ephod, the ephod itself and the breastpiece. Fasten the ephod on him by its skilfully woven waistband. 6Put the turban on his head and attach the sacred diadem to the turban. 7Take the anointing oil and anoint him by pouring it on his head. 8Bring his sons and dress them in tunics 9and put headbands on them. Then tie sashes on Aaron and his sons.*a* The priesthood is theirs by a lasting ordinance. In this way you shall ordain Aaron and his sons.

10"Bring the bull to the front of the Tent of Meeting, and Aaron and his sons shall lay their hands on its head. 11Slaughter it in the LORD's presence at the entrance to the Tent of Meeting. 12Take some of the bull's blood and put it on the horns of the altar with your finger, and pour out the rest of it at the base of the altar. 13Then take all the fat around the inner parts, the covering of the liver, and both kidneys with the fat on them, and burn them on the altar. 14But burn the bull's flesh and its hide and its offal outside the camp. It is a sin offering.

15"Take one of the rams, and Aaron and his sons shall lay their hands on its head. 16Slaughter it and take the blood and sprinkle it against the altar on all sides. 17Cut the ram into pieces and wash the inner parts and the legs, putting them with the head and the other pieces. 18Then burn the entire ram on the altar. It is a burnt offering to the LORD, a pleasing aroma, an offering made to the LORD by fire.

19"Take the other ram, and Aaron and his sons shall lay their hands on its head. 20Slaughter it, take some of its blood and put it on the lobes of the right ears of Aaron and his sons, on the thumbs of their right hands, and on the big toes of their right feet. Then sprinkle blood against the altar on all sides. 21And take some of the blood on the altar and some of the anointing oil and sprinkle it on Aaron and his garments and on his sons and their garments. Then he and his sons and their garments will be consecrated.

29:20   Ritual worship was often elaborate, but was done with true religious feeling, and it symbolized something greater than just ritual. The priest's ears, hands, and feet were consecrated as a sign that he should constantly listen to God (ears), do his will (hands), and walk in his way (feet).

22"Take from this ram the fat, the fat tail, the fat around the inner parts, the covering of the liver, both kidneys with the fat on them, and the right thigh. (This

---

*d*32 The meaning of the Hebrew for this word is uncertain.   *a*9 Hebrew; Septuagint *on them* is the ram for the ordination.) 23From the basket of bread made without yeast, which is before the LORD, take a loaf, and a cake made with oil, and a wafer. 24Put all these in the hands of Aaron and his sons and wave them before the LORD as a wave offering. 25Then take them from their hands and burn them on the altar along with the burnt offering for a pleasing aroma to the LORD, an offering made to the LORD by fire. 26After you take the breast of the ram for Aaron's ordination, wave it before the LORD as a wave offering, and it will be your share.

27"Consecrate those parts of the ordination ram that belong to Aaron and his sons: the breast that was waved and the thigh that was presented. 28This is always to be the regular share from the Israelites for Aaron and his sons. It is the contribution the Israelites are to make to the LORD from their fellowship offerings.b

29"Aaron's sacred garments will belong to his descendants so that they can be anointed and ordained in them. 30The son who succeeds him as priest and comes to the Tent of Meeting to minister in the Holy Place is to wear them seven days.

31"Take the ram for the ordination and cook the meat in a sacred place. 32At the entrance to the Tent of Meeting, Aaron and his sons are to eat the meat of the ram and the bread that is in the basket. 33They are to eat these offerings by which atonement was made for their ordination and consecration. But no-one else may eat them, because they are sacred. 34And if any of the meat of the ordination ram or any bread is left over till morning, burn it up. It must not be eaten, because it is sacred.

35"Do for Aaron and his sons everything I have commanded you, taking seven days to ordain them. 36Sacrifice a bull each day as a sin offering to make atonement. Purify the altar by making atonement for it, and anoint it to consecrate it. 37For seven days make atonement for the altar and consecrate it. Then the altar will be most holy, and whatever touches it will be holy.

38"This is what you are to offer on the altar regularly each day: two lambs a year old. 39Offer one in the morning and the other at twilight. 40With the first lamb offer a tenth of an ephahc of fine flour mixed with a quarter of a hind of oil from pressed olives, and a quarter of a hin of wine as a drink offering. 41Sacrifice the other lamb at twilight with the same grain offering and its drink offering as in the morning—a pleasing aroma, an offering made to the LORD by fire.

42"For the generations to come this burnt offering is to be made regularly at the entrance to the Tent of Meeting before the LORD. There I will meet you and speak to you; 43there also I will meet with the Israelites, and the place will be consecrated by my glory.

44"So I will consecrate the Tent of Meeting and the altar and will consecrate Aaron and his sons to serve me as priests. 45Then I will dwell among the Israelites and be their God. 46They will know that I am the LORD

their God, who brought them out of Egypt so that I might dwell among them. I am the LORD their God.

The Altar of Incense

30 "Make an altar of acacia wood for burning incense. 2It is to be square, a cubit long and a cubit wide, and two cubits higha—its horns of one piece with it. 3Overlay the top and all the sides and the horns with pure gold, and make a gold moulding around it. 4Make two gold rings for the altar below the moulding—two on opposite sides—to hold the poles used to carry it. 5Make the poles of acacia wood and overlay them with gold. 6Put the altar in front of the curtain that is before the ark of the Testimony—before the atonement cover that is over the Testimony—where I will meet with you.

7"Aaron must burn fragrant incense on the altar every morning when he tends the lamps. 8He must burn incense again when he lights the lamps at twilight so that incense will burn regularly before the LORD for the generations to come. 9Do not offer on this altar any other incense or any burnt offering or grain offering, and do not pour a drink offering on it. 10Once a year Aaron shall make atonement on its horns. This annual atonement must be made with the blood of the atoning sin offering for the generations to come. It is most holy to the LORD."

Atonement Money

11Then the LORD said to Moses, 12"When you take a census of the Israelites to count them, each one must pay the LORD a ransom for his life at the time he is counted. Then no plague will come on them when you number them. 13Each one who crosses over to those already counted is to give a half shekel,b according to the sanctuary shekel, which weighs twenty gerahs. This half shekel is an offering to the LORD. 14All who cross over, those twenty years old or more, are to give an offering to the LORD. 15The rich are not to give more than a half shekel and the poor are not to give less when you make the offering to the LORD to atone for your lives. 16Receive the atonement money from the Israelites and use it for the service of the Tent of Meeting. It will be a memorial for the Israelites before the LORD, making atonement for your lives."

30:11 There was a persistent belief that to take a census was wrong. This relates partly to a primitive idea that if the gods knew how many people there were then they would have extra power over them. At the same time, the Israelites' experience told them that when a census had been taken it was often followed by increased taxation, conscription, or forced labour.

---

b28 Traditionally peace offerings   c40 That is, probably about 4 pints (about 2 litres)
d40 That is, probably about 1½ pints (about 1 litre)
a2 That is, about 1½ feet (about 0.5 metre) long and wide and about 3 feet (about 0.9 metre) high
b13 That is, about ⅕ ounce (about 6 grams); also in verse 15

Basin for Washing

17Then the LORD said to Moses, 18"Make a bronze basin, with its bronze stand, for washing. Place it between the Tent of Meeting and the altar, and put water in it. 19Aaron and his sons are to wash their hands and feet with water from it. 20Whenever they enter the Tent of Meeting, they shall wash with water so that they will not die. Also, when they approach the altar to minister by presenting an offering made to the LORD by fire, 21they shall wash their hands and feet so that they will not die. This is to be a lasting ordinance for Aaron and his descendants for the generations to come."

Anointing Oil

22Then the LORD said to Moses, 23"Take the following fine spices: 500 shekels*c* of liquid myrrh, half as much (that is, 250 shekels) of fragrant cinnamon, 250 shekels of fragrant cane, 24500 shekels of cassia—all according to the sanctuary shekel—and a hin*d* of olive oil. 25Make these into a sacred anointing oil, a fragrant blend, the work of a perfumer. It will be the sacred anointing oil. 26Then use it to anoint the Tent of Meeting, the ark of the Testimony, 27the table and all its articles, the lampstand and its accessories, the altar of incense, 28the altar of burnt offering and all its utensils, and the basin with its stand. 29You shall consecrate them so they will be most holy, and whatever touches them will be holy.

30"Anoint Aaron and his sons and consecrate them so they may serve me as priests. 31Say to the Israelites, 'This is to be my sacred anointing oil for the generations to come. 32Do not pour it on men's bodies and do not make any oil with the same formula. It is sacred, and you are to consider it sacred. 33Whoever makes perfume like it and whoever puts it on anyone other than a priest must be cut off from his people.' "

Incense

34Then the LORD said to Moses, "Take fragrant spices—gum resin, onycha and galbanum—and pure frankincense, all in equal amounts, 35and make a fragrant blend of incense, the work of a perfumer. It is to be salted and pure and sacred. 36Grind some of it to powder and place it in front of the Testimony in the Tent of Meeting, where I will meet with you. It shall be most holy to you. 37Do not make any incense with this formula for yourselves; consider it holy to the LORD. 38Whoever makes any like it to enjoy its fragrance must be cut off from his people."

Bezalel and Oholiab

31 Then the LORD said to Moses, 2"See I have chosen Bezalel son of Uri, the son of Hur, of the tribe of Judah, 3and I have filled him with the Spirit of God, with skill, ability and knowledge in all kinds of crafts—4to make artistic designs for work in gold, silver and bronze, 5to cut and set stones, to work in wood, and to engage in all kinds of craftsmanship. 6Moreover, I have appointed Oholiab son of Ahisamach, of the tribe of Dan, to help him. Also I have given skill to all the craftsmen to make everything I have commanded you: 7the Tent of Meeting, the ark of the Testimony with the atonement cover on it, and all the other furnishings of the tent—8the table and its articles, the pure gold lampstand and all its accessories, the altar of incense, 9the altar of burnt offering and all its utensils, the basin with its stand—10and also the woven garments, both the sacred garments for Aaron the priest and the garments for his sons when they serve as priests, 11and the anointing oil and fragrant incense for the Holy Place. They are to make them just as I commanded you."

The Sabbath

12Then the LORD said to Moses, 13"Say to the Israelites, 'You must observe my Sabbaths. This will be a sign between me and you for the generations to come, so that you may know that I am the LORD, who makes you holy.*a*

14" 'Observe the Sabbath, because it is holy to you. Anyone who desecrates it must be put to death; whoever does any work on that day must be cut off from his people. 15For six days, work is to be done, but the seventh day is a Sabbath of rest, holy to the LORD. Whoever does any work on the Sabbath day must be put to death. 16The Israelites are to observe the Sabbath, celebrating it for the generations to come as a lasting covenant. 17It will be a sign between me and the Israelites for ever, for in six days the LORD made the heavens and the earth, and on the seventh day he abstained from work and rested.' "

18When the LORD finished speaking to Moses on Mount Sinai, he gave him the two tablets of the Testimony, the tablets of stone inscribed by the finger of God.

The Golden Calf

32 When the people saw that Moses was so long in coming down from the mountain, they gathered round Aaron and said, "Come, make us gods*a* who will go before us. As for this fellow Moses who brought us up out of Egypt, we don't know what has happened to him."

2Aaron answered them, "Take off the gold ear-rings that your wives, your sons and your daughters are wearing, and bring them to me." 3So all the people took off their ear-rings and brought them to Aaron. 4He took what they handed him and made it into an idol cast in the shape of a calf, fashioning it with a tool. Then they said, "These are your gods,*b* O Israel, who brought you up out of Egypt."

5When Aaron saw this, he built an altar in front of the calf and announced, "Tomorrow there will be a festival to the LORD." 6So the next day the people rose early and sacrificed burnt offerings and presented

---

c23 That is, about 12½ pounds (about 6 kilograms)   *d24* That is, probably about 6½ pints (about 4 litres)
a13 Or *who sanctifies you*; or *who sets you apart as holy*   *a1* Or *a god*; also in verses 23 and 31
b4 Or *This is your god*; also in verse 8

fellowship offerings.*c* Afterwards they sat down to eat and drink and got up to indulge in revelry.

⁷Then the Lord said to Moses, "Go down, because your people, whom you brought up out of Egypt, have become corrupt. ⁸They have been quick to turn away from what I commanded them and have made themselves an idol cast in the shape of a calf. They have bowed down to it and sacrificed to it and have said, 'These are your gods, O Israel, who brought you up out of Egypt.'

⁹"I have seen these people," the Lord said to Moses, "and they are a stiff-necked people. ¹⁰Now leave me alone so that my anger may burn against them and that I may destroy them. Then I will make you into a great nation."

¹¹But Moses sought the favour of the Lord his God. "O Lord," he said, "why should your anger burn against your people, whom you brought out of Egypt with great power and a mighty hand? ¹²Why should the Egyptians say, 'It was with evil intent that he brought them out, to kill them in the mountains and to wipe them off the face of the earth'? Turn from your fierce anger; relent and do not bring disaster on your people. ¹³Remember your servants Abraham, Isaac and Israel, to whom you swore by your own self: 'I will make your descendants as numerous as the stars in the sky and I will give your descendants all this land I promised them, and it will be their inheritance for ever.'" ¹⁴Then the Lord relented and did not bring on his people the disaster he had threatened.

¹⁵Moses turned and went down the mountain with the two tablets of the Testimony in his hands. They were inscribed on both sides, front and back. ¹⁶The tablets were the work of God; the writing was the writing of God, engraved on the tablets.

¹⁷When Joshua heard the noise of the people shouting, he said to Moses, "There is the sound of war in the camp."

¹⁸Moses replied:

"It is not the sound of victory,
　it is not the sound of defeat;
　it is the sound of singing that I hear."

¹⁹When Moses approached the camp and saw the calf and the dancing, his anger burned and he threw the tablets out of his hands, breaking them to pieces at the foot of the mountain. ²⁰And he took the calf they had made and burned it in the fire; then he ground it to powder, scattered it on the water and made the Israelites drink it.

²¹He said to Aaron, "What did these people do to you, that you led them into such great sin?"

²²"Do not be angry, my lord," Aaron answered. "You know how prone these people are to evil. ²³They said to me, 'Make us gods who will go before us. As for this fellow Moses who brought us up out of Egypt, we don't know what has happened to him.' ²⁴So I told them, 'Whoever has any gold jewellery, take it off.' Then they gave me the gold, and I threw it into the fire, and out came this calf!"

²⁵Moses saw that the people were running wild and that Aaron had let them get out of control and so become a laughing-stock to their enemies. ²⁶So he stood at the entrance to the camp and said, "Whoever is for the Lord, come to me." And all the Levites rallied to him.

²⁷Then he said to them, "This is what the Lord, the God of Israel, says: 'Each man strap a sword to his side. Go back and forth through the camp from one end to the other, each killing his brother and friend and neighbour.'" ²⁸The Levites did as Moses commanded, and that day about three thousand of the people died. ²⁹Then Moses said, "You have been set apart to the Lord today, for you were against your own sons and brothers, and he has blessed you this day."

³⁰The next day Moses said to the people, "You have committed a great sin. But now I will go up to the Lord; perhaps I can make atonement for your sin."

³¹So Moses went back to the Lord and said, "Oh, what a great sin these people have committed! They have made themselves gods of gold. ³²But now, please forgive their sin—but if not, then blot me out of the book you have written."

32:32　　Three times in two chapters the greatness of Moses is demonstrated (32:11–14, 32:30–32, 33:12–18) as he pleaded for the people, and in this verse he identified with them so much that he did not want to live if they were going to be destroyed. When he pleaded he appealed to God's nature which he seemed to understand deeply; that God's leading characteristic is merciful love. It was to be many years before most Israelites understood this about God. In our own generation this part of God is all too often forgotten in favour of the idea of a stern God who practices uncompromising justice.

---

³³The Lord replied to Moses, "Whoever has sinned against me I will blot out of my book. ³⁴Now go, lead the people to the place I spoke of, and my angel will go before you. However, when the time comes for me to punish, I will punish them for their sin."

³⁵And the Lord struck the people with a plague because of what they did with the calf Aaron had made.

33 Then the Lord said to Moses, "Leave this place, you and the people you brought up out of Egypt, and go up to the land I promised on oath to Abraham, Isaac and Jacob, saying, 'I will give it to your descendants.' ²I will send an angel before you and drive out the Canaanites, Amorites, Hittites, Perizzites, Hivites and Jebusites. ³Go up to the land flowing with milk and honey. But I will not go with you, because you are a stiff-necked people and I might destroy you on the way."

⁴When the people heard these distressing words, they began to mourn and no-one put on any ornaments. ⁵For the Lord had said to Moses, "Tell the Israelites, 'You are a stiff-necked people. If I were to go with you even for a moment, I might destroy you. Now take off

c6 Traditionally peace offerings

your ornaments and I will decide what to do with you.' " 6So the Israelites stripped off their ornaments at Mount Horeb.

The Tent of Meeting

7Now Moses used to take a tent and pitch it outside the camp some distance away, calling it the "tent of meeting". Anyone enquiring of the LORD would go to the tent of meeting outside the camp. 8And whenever Moses went out to the tent, all the people rose and stood at the entrances to their tents, watching Moses until he entered the tent. 9As Moses went into the tent, the pillar of cloud would come down and stay at the entrance, while the LORD spoke with Moses. 10Whenever the people saw the pillar of cloud standing at the entrance to the tent, they all stood and worshipped, each at the entrance to his tent. 11The LORD would speak to Moses face to face, as a man speaks with his friend. Then Moses would return to the camp, but his young assistant Joshua son of Nun did not leave the tent.

Moses and the Glory of the LORD

12Moses said to the LORD, "You have been telling me, 'Lead these people,' but you have not let me know whom you will send with me. You have said, 'I know you by name and you have found favour with me.' 13If you are pleased with me, teach me your ways so I may know you and continue to find favour with you. Remember that this nation is your people."

14The LORD replied, "My Presence will go with you, and I will give you rest."

15Then Moses said to him, "If your Presence does not go with us, do not send us up from here. 16How will anyone know that you are pleased with me and with your people unless you go with us? What else will distinguish me and your people from all the other people on the face of the earth?"

17And the LORD said to Moses, "I will do the very thing you have asked, because I am pleased with you and I know you by name."

18Then Moses said, "Now show me your glory."

19And the LORD said, "I will cause all my goodness to pass in front of you, and I will proclaim my name, the LORD, in your presence. I will have mercy on whom I will have mercy, and I will have compassion on whom I will have compassion. 20But," he said, "you cannot see my face, for no-one may see me and live."

21Then the LORD said, "There is a place near me where you may stand on a rock. 22When my glory passes by, I will put you in a cleft in the rock and cover you with my hand until I have passed by. 23Then I will remove my hand and you will see my back; but my face must not be seen."

The New Stone Tablets

34 The LORD said to Moses, "Chisel out two stone tablets like the first ones, and I will write on them the words that were on the first tablets, which you broke. 2Be ready in the morning, and then come up on Mount Sinai. Present yourself to me there on top of the mountain. 3No-one is to come with you or be seen anywhere on the mountain; not even the flocks and herds may graze in front of the mountain."

4So Moses chiselled out two stone tablets like the first ones and went up Mount Sinai early in the morning, as the LORD had commanded him; and he carried the two stone tablets in his hands. 5Then the LORD came down in the cloud and stood there with him and proclaimed his name, the LORD. 6And he passed in front of Moses, proclaiming, "The LORD, the LORD, the compassionate and gracious God, slow to anger, abounding in love and faithfulness, 7maintaining love to thousands, and forgiving wickedness, rebellion and sin. Yet he does not leave the guilty unpunished; he punishes the children and their children for the sin of the fathers to the third and fourth generation."

8Moses bowed to the ground at once and worshipped. 9"O Lord, if I have found favour in your eyes," he said, "then let the Lord go with us. Although this is a stiff-necked people, forgive our wickedness and our sin, and take us as your inheritance."

10Then the LORD said: "I am making a covenant with you. Before all your people I will do wonders never before done in any nation in all the world. The people you live among will see how awesome is the work that I, the LORD, will do for you. 11Obey what I command you today. I will drive out before you the Amorites, Canaanites, Hittites, Perizzites, Hivites and Jebusites. 12Be careful not to make a treaty with those who live in the land where you are going, or they will be a snare among you. 13Break down their altars, smash their sacred stones and cut down their Asherah poles.*a* 14Do not worship any other god, for the LORD, whose name is Jealous, is a jealous God.

34:11   There are ten commandments here, but they are very different from those in chapter 20. These all concern ritual and religious matters. They remind the worshippers of God's greatness and distance, and the impossibility of making themselves holy enough for God. Only God can do that.

15"Be careful not to make a treaty with those who live in the land; for when they prostitute themselves to their gods and sacrifice to them, they will invite you and you will eat their sacrifices. 16And when you choose some of their daughters as wives for your sons and those daughters prostitute themselves to their gods, they will lead your sons to do the same.

17"Do not make cast idols.

18"Celebrate the Feast of Unleavened Bread. For seven days eat bread made without yeast, as I commanded you. Do this at the appointed time in the month of Abib, for in that month you came out of Egypt.

19"The first offspring of every womb belongs to me, including all the firstborn males of your livestock, whether from herd or flock. 20Redeem the firstborn

a 13 That is, symbols of the goddess Asherah

donkey with a lamb, but if you do not redeem it, break its neck. Redeem all your firstborn sons.

"No-one is to appear before me empty-handed.

21"Six days you shall labour, but on the seventh day you shall rest; even during the ploughing season and harvest you must rest.

22"Celebrate the Feast of Weeks with the firstfruits of the wheat harvest, and the Feast of Ingathering at the turn of the year.[b] 23Three times a year all your men are to appear before the Sovereign LORD, the God of Israel. 24I will drive out nations before you and enlarge your territory, and no-one will covet your land when you go up three times each year to appear before the LORD your God.

25"Do not offer the blood of a sacrifice to me along with anything containing yeast, and do not let any of the sacrifice from the Passover Feast remain until morning.

26"Bring the best of the firstfruits of your soil to the house of the LORD your God.

"Do not cook a young goat in its mother's milk."

27Then the LORD said to Moses, "Write down these words, for in accordance with these words I have made a covenant with you and with Israel." 28Moses was there with the LORD forty days and forty nights without eating bread or drinking water. And he wrote on the tablets the words of the covenant — the Ten Commandments.

The Radiant Face of Moses

29When Moses came down from Mount Sinai with the two tablets of the Testimony in his hands, he was not aware that his face was radiant because he had spoken with the LORD. 30When Aaron and all the Israelites saw Moses, his face was radiant, and they were afraid to come near him. 31But Moses called to them; so Aaron and all the leaders of the community came back to him, and he spoke to them. 32Afterwards all the Israelites came near him, and he gave them all the commands the LORD had given him on Mount Sinai.

33When Moses finished speaking to them, he put a veil over his face. 34But whenever he entered the LORD's presence to speak with him, he removed the veil until he came out. And when he came out and told the Israelites what he had been commanded, 35they saw that his face was radiant. Then Moses would put the veil back over his face until he went in to speak with the LORD.

Sabbath Regulations

35 Moses assembled the whole Israelite community and said to them, "These are the things the LORD has commanded you to do: 2For six days, work is to be done, but the seventh day shall be your holy day, a Sabbath of rest to the LORD. Whoever does any work on it must be put to death. 3Do not light a fire in any of your dwellings on the Sabbath day."

Materials for the Tabernacle

4Moses said to the whole Israelite community, "This is what the LORD has commanded: 5From what you have, take an offering for the LORD. Everyone who is willing is to bring to the LORD an offering of gold, silver and bronze; 6blue, purple and scarlet yarn and fine linen; goat hair; 7ram skins dyed red and hides of sea cows;[a] acacia wood; 8olive oil for the light; spices for the anointing oil and for the fragrant incense; 9and onyx stones and other gems to be mounted on the ephod and breastpiece.

10"All who are skilled among you are to come and make everything the LORD has commanded: 11the tabernacle with its tent and its covering, clasps, frames, crossbars, posts and bases; 12the ark with its poles and the atonement cover and the curtain that shields it; 13the table with its poles and all its articles and the bread of the Presence; 14the lampstand that is for light with its accessories, lamps and oil for the light; 15the altar of incense with its poles, the anointing oil and the fragrant incense; the curtain for the doorway at the entrance to the tabernacle; 16the altar of burnt offering with its bronze grating, its poles and all its utensils; the bronze basin with its stand; 17the curtains of the courtyard with its posts and bases, and the curtain for the entrance to the courtyard; 18the tent pegs for the tabernacle and for the courtyard, and their ropes; 19the woven garments worn for ministering in the sanctuary — both the sacred garments for Aaron the priest and the garments for his sons when they serve as priests."

35:21   God's work is not restricted to priests and theologians. Here in the building of the tabernacle, it was necessary for the whole community to dedicate itself to a task. The people then discovered the need for a wide variety of skills of a very practical nature. Priests are quite as dependent on the other workers as the community is on them.

20Then the whole Israelite community withdrew from Moses' presence, 21and everyone who was willing and whose heart moved him came and brought an offering to the LORD for the work on the Tent of Meeting, for all its service, and for the sacred garments. 22All who were willing, men and women alike, came and brought gold jewellery of all kinds: brooches, ear-rings, rings and ornaments. They all presented their gold as a wave offering to the LORD. 23Everyone who had blue, purple or scarlet yarn or fine linen, or goat hair, ram skins dyed red or hides of sea cows brought them. 24Those presenting an offering of silver or bronze brought it as an offering to the LORD, and everyone who had acacia wood for any part of the work brought it. 25Every skilled woman spun with her hands and brought what she had spun — blue, purple or scarlet yarn or fine linen. 26And all the women who were willing and had the skill spun the goat hair. 27The leaders brought onyx stones and other gems to be mounted on the ephod and breastpiece. 28They also brought spices

---

b22 That is, in the autumn   a7 That is, large aquatic mammals; also in verse 23 and olive oil for the light and for the anointing oil and for the fragrant incense. ²⁹All the Israelite men and women who were willing brought to the LORD freewill offerings for all the work the LORD through Moses had commanded them to do.

Bezalel and Oholiab

³⁰Then Moses said to the Israelites, "See, the LORD has chosen Bezalel son of Uri, the son of Hur, of the tribe of Judah, ³¹and he has filled him with the Spirit of God, with skill, ability and knowledge in all kinds of crafts—³²to make artistic designs for work in gold, silver and bronze, ³³to cut and set stones, to work in wood and to engage in all kinds of artistic craftsmanship. ³⁴And he has given both him and Oholiab son of Ahisamach, of the tribe of Dan, the ability to teach others. ³⁵He has filled them with skill to do all kinds of work as craftsmen, designers, embroiderers in blue, purple and scarlet yarn and fine linen, and weavers—

36 all of them master craftsmen and designers. ¹So Bezalel, Oholiab and every skilled person to whom the LORD has given skill and ability to know how to carry out all the work of constructing the sanctuary are to do the work just as the LORD has commanded."

²Then Moses summoned Bezalel and Oholiab and every skilled person to whom the LORD had given ability and who was willing to come and do the work. ³They received from Moses all the offerings the Israelites had brought to carry out the work of constructing the sanctuary. And the people continued to bring freewill offerings morning after morning. ⁴So all the skilled craftsmen who were doing all the work on the sanctuary left their work ⁵and said to Moses, "The people are bringing more than enough for doing the work the LORD commanded to be done."

⁶Then Moses gave an order and they sent this word throughout the camp: "No man or woman is to make anything else as an offering for the sanctuary." And so the people were restrained from bringing more, ⁷because what they already had was more than enough to do all the work.

The Tabernacle

⁸All the skilled men among the workmen made the tabernacle with ten curtains of finely twisted linen and blue, purple and scarlet yarn, with cherubim worked into them by a skilled craftsman. ⁹All the curtains were the same size—twenty-eight cubits long and four cubits wide.ᵃ ¹⁰They joined five of the curtains together and did the same with the other five. ¹¹Then they made loops of blue material along the edge of the end curtain in one set, and the same was done with the end curtain in the other set. ¹²They also made fifty loops on one curtain and fifty loops on the end curtain of the other set, with the loops opposite each other. ¹³Then they made fifty gold clasps and used them to fasten the two sets of curtains together so that the tabernacle was a unit.

¹⁴They made curtains of goat hair for the tent over the tabernacle—eleven altogether. ¹⁵All eleven curtains were the same size—thirty cubits long and four cubits wide.ᵇ ¹⁶They joined five of the curtains into one set and the other six into another set. ¹⁷Then they made fifty loops along the edge of the end curtain in one set and also along the edge of the end curtain in the other set. ¹⁸They made fifty bronze clasps to fasten the tent together as a unit. ¹⁹Then they made for the tent a covering of ram skins dyed red, and over that a covering of hides of sea cows.ᶜ

²⁰They made upright frames of acacia wood for the tabernacle. ²¹Each frame was ten cubits long and a cubit and a half wide,ᵈ ²²with two projections set parallel to each other. They made all the frames of the tabernacle in this way. ²³They made twenty frames for the south side of the tabernacle ²⁴and made forty silver bases to go under them—two bases for each frame, one under each projection. ²⁵For the other side, the north side of the tabernacle, they made twenty frames ²⁶and forty silver bases—two under each frame. ²⁷They made six frames for the far end, that is, the west end of the tabernacle, ²⁸and two frames were made for the corners of the tabernacle at the far end. ²⁹At these two corners the frames were double from the bottom all the way to the top and fitted into a single ring; both were made alike. ³⁰So there were eight frames and sixteen silver bases—two under each frame.

³¹They also made crossbars of acacia wood: five for the frames on one side of the tabernacle, ³²five for those on the other side, and five for the frames on the west, at the far end of the tabernacle. ³³They made the centre crossbar so that it extended from end to end at the middle of the frames. ³⁴They overlaid the frames with gold and made gold rings to hold the crossbars. They also overlaid the crossbars with gold.

³⁵They made the curtain of blue, purple and scarlet yarn and finely twisted linen, with cherubim worked into it by a skilled craftsman. ³⁶They made four posts of acacia wood for it and overlaid them with gold. They made gold hooks for them and cast their four silver bases. ³⁷For the entrance to the tent they made a curtain of blue, purple and scarlet yarn and finely twisted linen—the work of an embroiderer; ³⁸and they made five posts with hooks for them. They overlaid the tops of the posts and their bands with gold and made their five bases of bronze.

The Ark

37 Bezalel made the ark of acacia wood—two and a half cubits long, a cubit and a half wide, and a cubit and a half high.ᵃ ²He overlaid it with pure gold, both inside and out, and made a gold moulding around it. ³He cast four gold rings for it and fastened them to its four feet, with two rings on one side and two rings on the other. ⁴Then he made poles of acacia wood and overlaid them with gold. ⁵And he inserted the poles into the rings on the sides of the ark to carry it. ⁶He made the atonement cover of pure gold—two

---

ᵃ9 That is, about 42 feet (about 13 metres) long and 6 feet (about 1.8 metres) wide
ᵇ15 That is, about 45 feet (about 13.5 metres) long and 6 feet (about 1.8 metres) wide
ᵈ21 That is, about 15 feet (about 4.5 metres) long and 2¼ feet (about 0.7 metre) wide
ᵃ1 That is, about 3¾ feet (about 1.1 metres) long and 2¼ feet (about 0.7 metre) wide and high

ᶜ19 That is, large aquatic mammals

and a half cubits long and a cubit and a half wide.[b] [7]Then he made two cherubim out of hammered gold at the ends of the cover. [8]He made one cherub on one end and the second cherub on the other; at the two ends he made them of one piece with the cover. [9]The cherubim had their wings spread upwards, overshadowing the cover with them. The cherubim faced each other, looking towards the cover.

The Table

[10]They[c] made the table of acacia wood — two cubits long, a cubit wide, and a cubit and a half high.[d] [11]Then they overlaid it with pure gold and made a gold moulding around it. [12]They also made around it a rim a handbreadth[e] wide and put a gold moulding on the rim. [13]They cast four gold rings for the table and fastened them to the four corners, where the four legs were. [14]The rings were put close to the rim to hold the poles used in carrying the table. [15]The poles for carrying the table were made of acacia wood and were overlaid with gold. [16]And they made from pure gold the articles for the table — its plates and dishes and bowls and its pitchers for the pouring out of drink offerings.

The Lampstand

[17]They made the lampstand of pure gold and hammered it out, base and shaft; its flowerlike cups, buds and blossoms were of one piece with it. [18]Six branches extended from the sides of the lampstand — three on one side and three on the other. [19]Three cups shaped like almond flowers with buds and blossoms were on one branch, three on the next branch and the same for all six branches extending from the lampstand. [20]And on the lampstand were four cups shaped like almond flowers with buds and blossoms. [21]One bud was under the first pair of branches extending from the lampstand, a second bud under the second pair, and a third bud under the third pair — six branches in all. [22]The buds and the branches were all of one piece with the lampstand, hammered out of pure gold. [23]They made its seven lamps, as well as its wick trimmers and trays, of pure gold. [24]They made the lampstand and all its accessories from one talent[f] of pure gold.

The Altar of Incense

[25]They made the altar of incense out of acacia wood. It was square, a cubit long and a cubit wide, and two cubits high[g] — its horns of one piece with it. [26]They overlaid the top and all the sides and the horns with pure gold, and made a gold moulding around it. [27]They made two gold rings below the moulding — two on opposite sides — to hold the poles used to carry it. [28]They made the poles of acacia wood and overlaid them with gold.

[29]They also made the sacred anointing oil and the pure, fragrant incense — the work of a perfumer.

The Altar of Burnt Offering

38 They[a] built the altar of burnt offering of acacia wood, three cubits[b] high; it was square, five cubits long and five cubits wide.[c] [2]They made a horn at each of the four corners, so that the horns and the altar were of one piece, and they overlaid the altar with bronze. [3]They made all its utensils of bronze — its pots, shovels, sprinkling bowls, meat forks and firepans. [4]They made a grating for the altar, a bronze network, to be under its ledge, halfway up the altar. [5]They cast bronze rings to hold the poles for the four corners of the bronze grating. [6]They made the poles of acacia wood and overlaid them with bronze. [7]They inserted the poles into the rings so they would be on the sides of the altar for carrying it. They made it hollow, out of boards.

Basin for Washing

[8]They made the bronze basin and its bronze stand from the mirrors of the women who served at the entrance to the Tent of Meeting.

The Courtyard

[9]Next they made the courtyard. The south side was a hundred cubits[d] long and had curtains of finely twisted linen, [10]with twenty posts and twenty bronze bases, and with silver hooks and bands on the posts. [11]The north side was also a hundred cubits long and had twenty posts and twenty bronze bases, with silver hooks and bands on the posts. [12]The west end was fifty cubits[e] wide and had curtains, with ten posts and ten bases, with silver hooks and bands on the posts. [13]The east end, towards the sunrise, was also fifty cubits wide. [14]Curtains fifteen cubits[f] long were on one side of the entrance, with three posts and three bases, [15]and curtains fifteen cubits long were on the other side of the entrance to the courtyard, with three posts and three bases. [16]All the curtains around the courtyard were of finely twisted linen. [17]The bases for the posts were bronze. The hooks and bands on the posts were silver, and their tops were overlaid with silver; so all the posts of the courtyard had silver bands. [18]The curtain for the entrance to the courtyard was of blue, purple and scarlet yarn and finely twisted linen — the work of an embroiderer. It was twenty cubits[g] long and, like the curtains of the courtyard, five cubits[h] high, [19]with four posts and four bronze bases. Their hooks and bands were silver, and their tops were overlaid with silver. [20]All the tent pegs of the tabernacle and of the surrounding courtyard were bronze.

[b]6 That is, about 3¾ feet (about 1.1 metres) long and 2¼ feet (about 0.7 metre) wide   [c]10 Or *He*; also in verses 11–29
[d]10 That is, about 3 feet (about 0.9 metre) long, 1½ feet (about 0.5 metre) wide, and 2¼ feet (about 0.7 metre) high
[e]12 That is, about 3 inches (about 8 centimetres)   [f]24 That is, about 75 pounds (about 34 kilograms)
[g]25 That is, about 1½ feet (about 0.5 metre) long and wide, and about 3 feet (about 0.9 metre) high   [a]1 Or *He*; also in verses 2–9
[b]1 That is, about 4½ feet (about 1.4 metres)   [c]1 That is, about 7½ feet (about 2.3 metres) long and wide
[d]9 That is, about 150 feet (about 46 metres)   [e]12 That is, about 75 feet (about 23 metres)
[f]14 That is, about 22½ feet (about 6.9 metres)   [g]18 That is, about 30 feet (about 9 metres)
[h]18 That is, about 7½ feet (about 2.3 metres)

The Materials Used

21These are the amounts of the materials used for the tabernacle, the tabernacle of the Testimony, which were recorded at Moses' command by the Levites under the direction of Ithamar son of Aaron, the priest. 22(Bezalel son of Uri, the son of Hur, of the tribe of Judah, made everything the LORD commanded Moses; 23with him was Oholiab son of Ahisamach, of the tribe of Dan—a craftsman and designer, and an embroiderer in blue, purple and scarlet yarn and fine linen.) 24The total amount of the gold from the wave offering used for all the work on the sanctuary was 29 talents and 730 shekels,[i] according to the sanctuary shekel.

25The silver obtained from those of the community who were counted in the census was 100 talents and 1,775 shekels,[j] according to the sanctuary shekel— 26one beka per person, that is, half a shekel,[k] according to the sanctuary shekel, from everyone who had crossed over to those counted, twenty years old or more, a total of 603,550 men. 27The 100 talents[l] of silver were used to cast the bases for the sanctuary and for the curtain—100 bases from the 100 talents, one talent for each base. 28They used the 1,775 shekels[m] to make the hooks for the posts, to overlay the tops of the posts, and to make their bands.

29The bronze from the wave offering was 70 talents and 2,400 shekels.[n] 30They used it to make the bases for the entrance to the Tent of Meeting, the bronze altar with its bronze grating and all its utensils, 31the bases for the surrounding courtyard and those for its entrance and all the tent pegs for the tabernacle and those for the surrounding courtyard.

The Priestly Garments

39 From the blue, purple and scarlet yarn they made woven garments for ministering in the sanctuary. They also made sacred garments for Aaron, as the LORD commanded Moses.

The Ephod

2They[a] made the ephod of gold, and of blue, purple and scarlet yarn, and of finely twisted linen. 3They hammered out thin sheets of gold and cut strands to be worked into the blue, purple and scarlet yarn and fine linen—the work of a skilled craftsman. 4They made shoulder pieces for the ephod, which were attached to two of its corners, so that it could be fastened. 5Its skilfully woven waistband was like it—of one piece with the ephod and made with gold, and with blue, purple and scarlet yarn, and with finely twisted linen, as the LORD commanded Moses.

6They mounted the onyx stones in gold filigree settings and engraved them like a seal with the names of the sons of Israel. 7Then they fastened them on the shoulder pieces of the ephod as memorial stones for the sons of Israel, as the LORD commanded Moses.

The Breastpiece

8They fashioned the breastpiece—the work of a skilled craftsman. They made it like the ephod: of gold, and of blue, purple and scarlet yarn, and of finely twisted linen. 9It was square—a span[b] long and a span wide—and folded double. 10Then they mounted four rows of precious stones on it. In the first row there was a ruby, a topaz and a beryl; 11in the second row a turquoise, a sapphire[c] and an emerald; 12in the third row a jacinth, an agate and an amethyst; 13in the fourth row a chrysolite, an onyx and a jasper.[d] They were mounted in gold filigree settings. 14There were twelve stones, one for each of the names of the sons of Israel, each engraved like a seal with the name of one of the twelve tribes.

15For the breastpiece they made braided chains of pure gold, like a rope. 16They made two gold filigree settings and two gold rings, and fastened the rings to two of the corners of the breastpiece. 17They fastened the two gold chains to the rings at the corners of the breastpiece, 18and the other ends of the chains to the two settings, attaching them to the shoulder pieces of the ephod at the front. 19They made two gold rings and attached them to the other two corners of the breastpiece on the inside edge next to the ephod. 20Then they made two more gold rings and attached them to the bottom of the shoulder pieces on the front of the ephod, close to the seam just above the waistband of the ephod. 21They tied the rings of the breastpiece to the rings of the ephod with blue cord, connecting it to the waistband so that the breastpiece would not swing out from the ephod—as the LORD commanded Moses.

Other Priestly Garments

22They made the robe of the ephod entirely of blue cloth—the work of a weaver—23with an opening in the centre of the robe like the opening of a collar,[e] and a band around this opening, so that it would not tear. 24They made pomegranates of blue, purple and scarlet yarn and finely twisted linen around the hem of the robe. 25And they made bells of pure gold and attached them around the hem between the pomegranates. 26The bells and pomegranates alternated around the hem of the robe to be worn for ministering, as the LORD commanded Moses.

27For Aaron and his sons, they made tunics of fine linen—the work of a weaver—28and the turban of fine linen, the linen headbands and the undergarments of finely twisted linen. 29The sash was of finely twisted linen and blue, purple and scarlet yarn—the work of an embroiderer—as the LORD commanded Moses. 30They made the plate, the sacred diadem, out of pure gold and engraved on it, like an inscription on a seal: HOLY TO THE LORD. 31Then they fastened a blue cord to it to attach it to the turban, as the LORD commanded Moses.

---

i24 The weight of the gold was about one ton (about 1 metric ton).
j25 The weight of the silver was about 3⅓ tons (about 3.4 metric tons).
l27 That is, about 3⅓ tons (about 3.4 metric tons).   m28 That is, about 45 pounds (about 20 kilograms)
n29 The weight of the bronze was about 2⅓ tons (about 2.4 metric tons).
b9 That is, about 9 inches (about 23 centimetres)   c11 Or lapis lazuli
d13 The precise identification of some of these precious stones is uncertain.
e23 The meaning of the Hebrew for this word is uncertain.

k26 That is, about ⅕ ounce (about 6 grams)
a2 Or He; also in verses 7, 8 and 22

Moses Inspects the Tabernacle

32So all the work on the tabernacle, the Tent of Meeting, was completed. The Israelites did everything just as the LORD commanded Moses. 33Then they brought the tabernacle to Moses: the tent and all its furnishings, its clasps, frames, crossbars, posts and bases; 34the covering of ram skins dyed red, the covering of hides of sea cows*f* and the shielding curtain; 35the ark of the Testimony with its poles and the atonement cover; 36the table with all its articles and the bread of the Presence; 37the pure gold lampstand with its row of lamps and all its accessories, and the oil for the light; 38the gold altar, the anointing oil, the fragrant incense, and the curtain for the entrance to the tent; 39the bronze altar with its bronze grating, its poles and all its utensils; the basin with its stand; 40the curtains of the courtyard with its posts and bases, and the curtain for the entrance to the courtyard; the ropes and tent pegs for the courtyard; all the furnishings for the tabernacle, the Tent of Meeting; 41and the woven garments worn for ministering in the sanctuary, both the sacred garments for Aaron the priest and the garments for his sons when serving as priests.

39:32   A great deal of space is devoted to describing the making of the tent. It was of central importance because it symbolized the presence of God with his people wherever they were. This was an important idea. At the time, many other gods were considered to be restricted either to one place, or to one area of action like war or fertility. The tent was not replaced until Solomon built a temple. There tended to be an idea in Israel that it was a mistake to have a building, since God cannot be tied down.

42The Israelites had done all the work just as the LORD had commanded Moses. 43Moses inspected the work and saw that they had done it just as the LORD had commanded. So Moses blessed them.

Setting Up the Tabernacle

40 Then the LORD said to Moses: 2"Set up the tabernacle, the Tent of Meeting, on the first day of the first month. 3Place the ark of the Testimony in it and shield the ark with the curtain. 4Bring in the table and set out what belongs on it. Then bring in the lampstand and set up its lamps. 5Place the gold altar of incense in front of the ark of the Testimony and put the curtain at the entrance to the tabernacle.

6"Place the altar of burnt offering in front of the entrance to the tabernacle, the Tent of Meeting; 7place the basin between the Tent of Meeting and the altar and put water in it. 8Set up the courtyard around it and put the curtain at the entrance to the courtyard.

9"Take the anointing oil and anoint the tabernacle and everything in it; consecrate it and all its furnishings, and it will be holy. 10Then anoint the altar of burnt offering and all its utensils; consecrate the altar, and it will be most holy. 11Anoint the basin and its stand and consecrate them.

12"Bring Aaron and his sons to the entrance to the Tent of Meeting and wash them with water. 13Then dress Aaron in the sacred garments, anoint him and consecrate him so that he may serve me as priest. 14Bring his sons and dress them in tunics. 15Anoint them just as you anointed their father, so that they may serve me as priests. Their anointing will be to a priesthood that will continue for all generations to come." 16Moses did everything just as the LORD commanded him.

17So the tabernacle was set up on the first day of the first month in the second year. 18When Moses set up the tabernacle, he put the bases in place, erected the frames, inserted the crossbars and set up the posts. 19Then he spread the tent over the tabernacle and put the covering over the tent, as the LORD commanded him.

20He took the Testimony and placed it in the ark, attached the poles to the ark and put the atonement cover over it. 21Then he brought the ark into the tabernacle and hung the shielding curtain and shielded the ark of the Testimony, as the LORD commanded him.

22Moses placed the table in the Tent of Meeting on the north side of the tabernacle outside the curtain 23and set out the bread on it before the LORD, as the LORD commanded him.

24He placed the lampstand in the Tent of Meeting opposite the table on the south side of the tabernacle 25and set up the lamps before the LORD, as the LORD commanded him.

26Moses placed the gold altar in the Tent of Meeting in front of the curtain 27and burned fragrant incense on it, as the LORD commanded him. 28Then he put up the curtain at the entrance to the tabernacle.

29He set the altar of burnt offering near the entrance to the tabernacle, the Tent of Meeting, and offered on it burnt offerings and grain offerings, as the LORD commanded him.

30He placed the basin between the Tent of Meeting and the altar and put water in it for washing, 31and Moses and Aaron and his sons used it to wash their hands and feet. 32They washed whenever they entered the Tent of Meeting or approached the altar, as the LORD commanded Moses.

33Then Moses set up the courtyard around the tabernacle and altar and put up the curtain at the entrance to the courtyard. And so Moses finished the work.

The Glory of the LORD

34Then the cloud covered the Tent of Meeting, and the glory of the LORD filled the tabernacle. 35Moses

f34 That is, large aquatic mammals

could not enter the Tent of Meeting because the cloud had settled upon it, and the glory of the LORD filled the tabernacle.

[36]In all the travels of the Israelites, whenever the cloud lifted from above the tabernacle, they would set out; [37]but if the cloud did not lift, they did not set out — until the day it lifted. [38]So the cloud of the LORD was over the tabernacle by day, and fire was in the cloud by night, in the sight of all the house of Israel during all their travels.

Leviticus

A Different Book

Leviticus is different from the other four books of the Pentateuch. It is usually expected to be boring, or only to be interesting for the light it sheds on ancient customs. The fascinating tale of the people of Israel in Exodus and Numbers is interrupted by this collection of laws and regulations, mostly relating to priests and sacrifices and offerings. It is worth resisting the temptation to miss the book out. Originally, the books of the Pentateuch—Genesis, Exodus, Leviticus, Numbers, and Deuteronomy—were a single book. Those who produced them must have felt that Leviticus was a vital part of the whole work. Like all Old Testament writers, those who worked on the Pentateuch constantly "did theology", that is, they reflected all the time on their experiences to see where and how God was to be found in them. They became convinced that nothing could lie outside the interest of the God to whom the world belonged. He wanted a perfect world, so even small imperfections were to be avoided. The great majority of the rules and regulations in Leviticus concern a different way of life from ours and do not apply to us, but the principle on which they are based—that everything is important because it is of concern to God—is as relevant as ever.

The Worship of God

The contents of Leviticus are united by an interest in religious ritual and the conduct of worship. All worship begins when people recognize that God is holy and they are not. A feeling of awe in the presence of a greater power is common to all religions, and in order to show the difference between the things of God and the things of the world, the words "holy", and "common" or "profane" are used. People naturally feel that holy things (gods, spirits, or powers) are so totally separate from human beings that if they get too close they will be destroyed. One purpose of worship is to make it possible for common things to make contact with what is holy. People, places, and things can be set aside and consecrated to God—made holy. They in turn must then be treated with special reverence. Leviticus is concerned with worship which is right, because it is properly in awe of God. If God graciously allows himself to be approached it is only right to honour him by conscientious attention to the details of worship. There were prophets in Israel who condemned ritual which was done only for its own sake and ignored human suffering. They were right to say this, and to make the distinction between this and worship which is done with the right motivation.

A Reminder in Daily Life

The writers of Leviticus were concerned that, when worship was offered to God, it was worthy of him. They were also aware that God was not just present in holy places but in every part of life. They laid down rules for all sorts of situations so that the people were constantly reminded in their everyday lives that what they were doing was dedicated to God.

Israel's Canaanite neighbours thought that religious ritual had magic power. If performed correctly it automatically made the worshipper fit to be with God and ensured that God would answer the worshipper's prayer. The Israelites were often tempted to think the same, but they knew their God was not tied down by the cycles of nature. In historical acts like the exodus he had shown what he was like and that he was Lord of all things. He was loving and caring. If his people were to be fit for his presence they should be like him, so when he said "Be holy because I, the LORD your God, am holy" (Leviticus 19:2) he was telling them not just to be pure, but to be loving too. The consequences of this are drawn out in Leviticus 17—26. The section is called the Holiness Code because of its emphasis on holiness. It stresses that God is concerned with people's personal and social behaviour. If someone has hurt their neighbour, or been dishonest, they cannot truly worship God.

Every Moment Belongs to God

Leviticus is the book which shows us that every moment belongs to God. His power and majesty are honoured by his people worshipping him properly. His goodness and love are honoured by his people's care for all his creatures. Neither thing is sufficient on its own. It is only when we do both that we come close to God.

The Burnt Offering

1 The LORD called to Moses and spoke to him from the Tent of Meeting. He said, 2"Speak to the Israelites and say to them: 'When any of you brings an offering to the LORD, bring as your offering an animal from either the herd or the flock.

3" 'If the offering is a burnt offering from the herd, he is to offer a male without defect. He must present it at the entrance to the Tent of Meeting so that it*a* will be acceptable to the LORD. 4He is to lay his hand on the head of the burnt offering, and it will be accepted on his behalf to make atonement for him. 5He is to slaughter the young bull before the LORD, and then Aaron's sons the priests shall bring the blood and sprinkle it against the altar on all sides at the entrance to the Tent of Meeting. 6He is to skin the burnt offering and cut it into pieces. 7The sons of Aaron the priest are to put fire on the altar and arrange wood on the fire. 8Then Aaron's sons the priests shall arrange the pieces, including the head and the fat, on the burning wood that is on the altar. 9He is to wash the inner parts and the legs with water, and the priest is to burn all of it

on the altar. It is a burnt offering, an offering made by fire, an aroma pleasing to the LORD.

10" 'If the offering is a burnt offering from the flock, from either the sheep or the goats, he is to offer a male without defect. 11He is to slaughter it at the north side of the altar before the LORD, and Aaron's sons the priests shall sprinkle its blood against the altar on all sides. 12He is to cut it into pieces, and the priest shall arrange them, including the head and the fat, on the burning wood that is on the altar. 13He is to wash the inner parts and the legs with water, and the priest is to bring all of it and burn it on the altar. It is a burnt offering, an offering made by fire, an aroma pleasing to the LORD.

14" 'If the offering to the LORD is a burnt offering of birds, he is to offer a dove or a young pigeon. 15The priest shall bring it to the altar, wring off the head and burn it on the altar; its blood shall be drained out on the side of the altar. 16He is to remove the crop with its contents*b* and throw it to the east side of the altar, where the ashes are. 17He shall tear it open by the wings, not severing it completely, and then the priest shall burn it on the wood that is on the fire on the altar.

---

a3 Or *he* *b16* Or *crop and the feathers*; the meaning of the Hebrew for this word is uncertain.

It is a burnt offering, an offering made by fire, an aroma pleasing to the LORD.

The Grain Offering

2 " 'When someone brings a grain offering to the LORD, his offering is to be of fine flour. He is to pour oil on it, put incense on it ²and take it to Aaron's sons the priests. The priest shall take a handful of the fine flour and oil, together with all the incense, and burn this as a memorial portion on the altar, an offering made by fire, an aroma pleasing to the LORD. ³The rest of the grain offering belongs to Aaron and his sons; it is a most holy part of the offerings made to the LORD by fire.

2:1 Our offerings to God now are likely to be not of material objects, but of time, money, service, and skills. However, the principle established in Leviticus still holds good. Only the very best is good enough. Anything less indicates that we are not prepared to try to be as perfect as God, so the offering will not have the desired effect of bringing us closer to him.

---

⁴" 'If you bring a grain offering baked in an oven, it is to consist of fine flour: cakes made without yeast and mixed with oil, orᵃ wafers made without yeast and spread with oil. ⁵If your grain offering is prepared on a griddle, it is to be made of fine flour mixed with oil, and without yeast. ⁶Crumble it and pour oil on it; it is a grain offering. ⁷If your grain offering is cooked in a pan, it is to be made of fine flour and oil. ⁸Bring the grain offering made of these things to the LORD; present it to the priest, who shall take it to the altar. ⁹He shall take out the memorial portion from the grain offering and burn it on the altar as an offering made by fire, an aroma pleasing to the LORD. ¹⁰The rest of the grain offering belongs to Aaron and his sons; it is a most holy part of the offerings made to the LORD by fire.

¹¹" 'Every grain offering you bring to the LORD must be made without yeast, for you are not to burn any yeast or honey in an offering made to the LORD by fire. ¹²You may bring them to the LORD as an offering of the firstfruits, but they are not to be offered on the altar as a pleasing aroma. ¹³Season all your grain offerings with salt. Do not leave the salt of the covenant of your God out of your grain offerings; add salt to all your offerings.

¹⁴" 'If you bring a grain offering of firstfruits to the LORD, offer crushed heads of new grain roasted in the fire. ¹⁵Put oil and incense on it; it is a grain offering. ¹⁶The priest shall burn the memorial portion of the crushed grain and the oil, together with all the incense, as an offering made to the LORD by fire.

The Fellowship Offering

3 " 'If someone's offering is a fellowship offering,ᵃ and he offers an animal from the herd, whether male or female, he is to present before the LORD an animal without defect. ²He is to lay his hand on the head of his offering and slaughter it at the entrance to the Tent of Meeting. Then Aaron's sons the priests shall sprinkle the blood against the altar on all sides. ³From the fellowship offering he is to bring a sacrifice made to the LORD by fire: all the fat that covers the inner parts or is connected to them, ⁴both kidneys with the fat on them near the loins, and the covering of the liver, which he will remove with the kidneys. ⁵Then Aaron's sons are to burn it on the altar on top of the burnt offering that is on the burning wood, as an offering made by fire, an aroma pleasing to the LORD.

⁶" 'If he offers an animal from the flock as a fellowship offering to the LORD, he is to offer a male or female without defect. ⁷If he offers a lamb, he is to present it before the LORD. ⁸He is to lay his hand on the head of his offering and slaughter it in front of the Tent of Meeting. Then Aaron's sons shall sprinkle its blood against the altar on all sides. ⁹From the fellowship offering he is to bring a sacrifice made to the LORD by fire: its fat, the entire fat tail cut off close to the backbone, all the fat that covers the inner parts or is connected to them, ¹⁰both kidneys with the fat on them near the loins, and the covering of the liver, which he will remove with the kidneys. ¹¹The priest shall burn them on the altar as food, an offering made to the LORD by fire.

¹²" 'If his offering is a goat, he is to present it before the LORD. ¹³He is to lay his hand on its head and slaughter it in front of the Tent of Meeting. Then Aaron's sons shall sprinkle its blood against the altar on all sides. ¹⁴From what he offers he is to make this offering to the LORD by fire: all the fat that covers the inner parts or is connected to them, ¹⁵both kidneys with the fat on them near the loins, and the covering of the liver, which he will remove with the kidneys. ¹⁶The priest shall burn them on the altar as food, an offering made by fire, a pleasing aroma. All the fat is the LORD's.

¹⁷" 'This is a lasting ordinance for the generations to come, wherever you live: You must not eat any fat or any blood.' "

The Sin Offering

4 The LORD said to Moses, ²"Say to the Israelites: 'When anyone sins unintentionally and does what is forbidden in any of the LORD's commands—

³" 'If the anointed priest sins, bringing guilt on the people, he must bring to the LORD a young bull without defect as a sin offering for the sin he has committed. ⁴He is to present the bull at the entrance to the Tent of Meeting before the LORD. He is to lay his hand on its head and slaughter it before the LORD. ⁵Then the anointed priest shall take some of the bull's blood and carry it into the Tent of Meeting. ⁶He is to dip his finger into the blood and sprinkle some of it seven times before the LORD, in front of the curtain of the sanctuary. ⁷The priest shall then put some of the blood on the horns of the altar of fragrant incense that is before the LORD in the Tent of Meeting. The rest of the bull's blood he shall pour out at the base of the altar of burnt offering at the entrance to the Tent of Meeting. ⁸He shall remove all the fat from the bull of the sin

ᵃ4 Or and   ᵃ1 Traditionally *peace offering*; also in verses 3, 6 and 9 offering—the fat that covers the inner parts or is connected to them, ⁹both kidneys with the fat on them near the loins, and the covering of the liver, which he will remove with the kidneys—¹⁰just as the fat is removed from the ox*a* sacrificed as a fellowship offering.*b* Then the priest shall burn them on the altar of burnt offering. ¹¹But the hide of the bull and all its flesh, as well as the head and legs, the inner parts and offal—¹²that is, all the rest of the bull—he must take outside the camp to a place ceremonially clean, where the ashes are thrown, and burn it in a wood fire on the ash heap.

¹³" 'If the whole Israelite community sins unintentionally and does what is forbidden in any of the LORD's commands, even though the community is unaware of the matter, they are guilty. ¹⁴When they become aware of the sin they committed, the assembly must bring a young bull as a sin offering and present it before the Tent of Meeting. ¹⁵The elders of the community are to lay their hands on the bull's head before the LORD, and the bull shall be slaughtered before the LORD. ¹⁶Then the anointed priest is to take some of the bull's blood into the Tent of Meeting. ¹⁷He shall dip his finger into the blood and sprinkle it before the LORD seven times in front of the curtain. ¹⁸He is to put some of the blood on the horns of the altar that is before the LORD in the Tent of Meeting. The rest of the blood he shall pour out at the base of the altar of burnt offering at the entrance to the Tent of Meeting. ¹⁹He shall remove all the fat from it and burn it on the altar, ²⁰and do with this bull just as he did with the bull for the sin offering. In this way the priest will make atonement for them, and they will be forgiven. ²¹Then he shall take the bull outside the camp and burn it as he burned the first bull. This is the sin offering for the community.

4:13   It is a principle of the English legal system that ignorance of the law is no defence. Even if a person does not know something is against the law, wrongdoing usually causes harm to others, which can be foreseen. Dropping litter, for example, spoils the scenery, whether there is a law against it or not. Leviticus makes it clear that such sin should be acknowledged and an attempt made to make amends. For the Israelites this meant sacrificing an animal. Today, we would more probably try to right the wrong. In either case it is only when wrong is admitted that the offender's relationship with God can be set right.

---

²²" 'When a leader sins unintentionally and does what is forbidden in any of the commands of the LORD his God, he is guilty. ²³When he is made aware of the sin he committed, he must bring as his offering a male goat without defect. ²⁴He is to lay his hand on the goat's head and slaughter it at the place where the burnt offering is slaughtered before the LORD. It is a sin offering.

²⁵Then the priest shall take some of the blood of the sin offering with his finger and put it on the horns of the altar of burnt offering and pour out the rest of the blood at the base of the altar. ²⁶He shall burn all the fat on the altar as he burned the fat of the fellowship offering. In this way the priest will make atonement for the man's sin, and he will be forgiven.

²⁷" 'If a member of the community sins unintentionally and does what is forbidden in any of the LORD's commands, he is guilty. ²⁸When he is made aware of the sin he committed, he must bring as his offering for the sin he committed a female goat without defect. ²⁹He is to lay his hand on the head of the sin offering and slaughter it at the place of the burnt offering. ³⁰Then the priest is to take some of the blood with his finger and put it on the horns of the altar of burnt offering and pour out the rest of the blood at the base of the altar. ³¹He shall remove all the fat, just as the fat is removed from the fellowship offering, and the priest shall burn it on the altar as an aroma pleasing to the LORD. In this way the priest will make atonement for him, and he will be forgiven.

³²" 'If he brings a lamb as his sin offering, he is to bring a female without defect. ³³He is to lay his hand on its head and slaughter it for a sin offering at the place where the burnt offering is slaughtered. ³⁴Then the priest shall take some of the blood of the sin offering with his finger and put it on the horns of the altar of burnt offering and pour out the rest of the blood at the base of the altar. ³⁵He shall remove all the fat, just as the fat is removed from the lamb of the fellowship offering, and the priest shall burn it on the altar on top of the offerings made to the LORD by fire. In this way the priest will make atonement for him for the sin he has committed, and he will be forgiven.

5 " 'If a person sins because he does not speak up when he hears a public charge to testify regarding something he has seen or learned about, he will be held responsible.

²" 'Or if a person touches anything ceremonially unclean—whether the carcasses of unclean wild animals or of unclean livestock or of unclean creatures that move along the ground—even though he is unaware of it, he has become unclean and is guilty.

³" 'Or if he touches human uncleanness—anything that would make him unclean—even though he is unaware of it, when he learns of it he will be guilty.

⁴" 'Or if a person thoughtlessly takes an oath to do anything, whether good or evil—in any matter one might carelessly swear about—even though he is unaware of it, in any case when he learns of it he will be guilty.

⁵" 'When anyone is guilty in any of these ways, he must confess in what way he has sinned ⁶and, as a penalty for the sin he has committed, he must bring to the LORD a female lamb or goat from the flock as a sin offering; and the priest shall make atonement for him for his sin.

⁷" 'If he cannot afford a lamb, he is to bring two doves or two young pigeons to the LORD as a penalty for his sin—one for a sin offering and the other for a

---

a 10 The Hebrew word can include both male and female.   *b 10* Traditionally *peace offering*; also in verses 26, 31 and 35 burnt offering. ⁸He is to bring them to the priest, who shall first offer the one for the sin offering. He is to wring its head from its neck, not severing it completely, ⁹and is to sprinkle some of the blood of the sin offering against the side of the altar; the rest of the blood must be drained out at the base of the altar. It is a sin offering. ¹⁰The priest shall then offer the other as a burnt offering in the prescribed way and make atonement for him for the sin he has committed, and he will be forgiven.

¹¹" 'If, however, he cannot afford two doves or two young pigeons, he is to bring as an offering for his sin a tenth of an ephah*a* of fine flour for a sin offering. He must not put oil or incense on it, because it is a sin offering. ¹²He is to bring it to the priest, who shall take a handful of it as a memorial portion and burn it on the altar on top of the offerings made to the LORD by fire. It is a sin offering. ¹³In this way the priest will make atonement for him for any of these sins he has committed, and he will be forgiven. The rest of the offering will belong to the priest, as in the case of the grain offering.' "

The Guilt Offering

¹⁴The LORD said to Moses: ¹⁵"When a person commits a violation and sins unintentionally in regard to any of the LORD's holy things, he is to bring to the LORD as a penalty a ram from the flock, one without defect and of the proper value in silver, according to the sanctuary shekel.*b* It is a guilt offering. ¹⁶He must make restitution for what he has failed to do in regard to the holy things, add a fifth of the value to that and give it all to the priest, who will make atonement for him with the ram as a guilt offering, and he will be forgiven.

¹⁷"If a person sins and does what is forbidden in any of the LORD's commands, even though he does not know it, he is guilty and will be held responsible. ¹⁸He is to bring to the priest as a guilt offering a ram from the flock, one without defect and of the proper value. In this way the priest will make atonement for him for the wrong he has committed unintentionally, and he will be forgiven. ¹⁹It is a guilt offering; he has been guilty of*c* wrongdoing against the LORD."

6 The LORD said to Moses: ²"If anyone sins and is unfaithful to the LORD by deceiving his neighbour about something entrusted to him or left in his care or stolen, or if he cheats him, ³or if he finds lost property and lies about it, or if he swears falsely, or if he commits any such sin that people may do—⁴when he thus sins and becomes guilty, he must return what he has stolen or taken by extortion, or what was entrusted to him, or the lost property he found, ⁵or whatever it was he swore falsely about. He must make restitution in full, add a fifth of the value to it and give it all to the owner on the day he presents his guilt offering. ⁶And as a penalty he must bring to the priest, that is, to the LORD, his guilt offering, a ram from the flock, one without defect and of the proper value. ⁷In this way the priest will make atonement for him before the LORD, and he will be forgiven for any of these things he did that made him guilty."

6:2 Leviticus deals with the business of ritual and sacrifice. These practices may be unfamiliar to us, but we would recognize instantly the people that the book is talking to. Petty dishonesty and meanness were clearly the same then as now, and what we read in Leviticus shows that no amount of sacrifice can remove guilt for such sins unless the sacrifice is preceded by an attempt to right the wrong and to add damages as well.

The Burnt Offering

⁸The LORD said to Moses: ⁹"Give Aaron and his sons this command: 'These are the regulations for the burnt offering: The burnt offering is to remain on the altar hearth throughout the night, till morning, and the fire must be kept burning on the altar. ¹⁰The priest shall then put on his linen clothes, with linen undergarments next to his body, and shall remove the ashes of the burnt offering that the fire has consumed on the altar and place them beside the altar. ¹¹Then he is to take off these clothes and put on others, and carry the ashes outside the camp to a place that is ceremonially clean. ¹²The fire on the altar must be kept burning; it must not go out. Every morning the priest is to add firewood and arrange the burnt offering on the fire and burn the fat of the fellowship offerings*a* on it. ¹³The fire must be kept burning on the altar continuously; it must not go out.

The Grain Offering

¹⁴" 'These are the regulations for the grain offering: Aaron's sons are to bring it before the LORD, in front of the altar. ¹⁵The priest is to take a handful of fine flour and oil, together with all the incense on the grain offering, and burn the memorial portion on the altar as an aroma pleasing to the LORD. ¹⁶Aaron and his sons shall eat the rest of it, but it is to be eaten without yeast in a holy place; they are to eat it in the courtyard of the Tent of Meeting. ¹⁷It must not be baked with yeast; I have given it as their share of the offerings made to me by fire. Like the sin offering and the guilt offering, it is most holy. ¹⁸Any male descendant of Aaron may eat it. It is his regular share of the offerings made to the LORD by fire for the generations to come. Whatever touches it will become holy.' "*b*

¹⁹The LORD also said to Moses, ²⁰"This is the offering Aaron and his sons are to bring to the LORD on the day he*c* is anointed: a tenth of an ephah*d* of fine flour as a regular grain offering, half of it in the morning and half in the evening. ²¹Prepare it with oil on a griddle; bring it well-mixed and present the grain offering broken*e* in pieces as an aroma pleasing to the LORD. ²²The

---

a11 That is, probably about 4 pints (about 2 litres)   *b15* That is, about ⅔ ounce (about 11.5 grams)
c19 Or *has made full expiation for his*   *a12* Traditionally *peace offerings*
b18 Or *Whoever touches them must be holy*; similarly in verse 27   *c20* Or *each*   *d20* That is, probably about 4 pints
(about 2 litres)   *e21* The meaning of the Hebrew for this word is uncertain.

son who is to succeed him as anointed priest shall prepare it. It is the Lord's regular share and is to be burned completely. 23Every grain offering of a priest shall be burned completely; it must not be eaten."

The Sin Offering

24The Lord said to Moses, 25"Say to Aaron and his sons: 'These are the regulations for the sin offering: The sin offering is to be slaughtered before the Lord in the place where the burnt offering is slaughtered; it is most holy. 26The priest who offers it shall eat it; it is to be eaten in a holy place, in the courtyard of the Tent of Meeting. 27Whatever touches any of the flesh will become holy, and if any of the blood is spattered on a garment, you must wash it in a holy place. 28The clay pot that the meat is cooked in must be broken; but if it is cooked in a bronze pot, the pot is to be scoured and rinsed with water. 29Any male in a priest's family may eat it; it is most holy. 30But any sin offering whose blood is brought into the Tent of Meeting to make atonement in the Holy Place must not be eaten; it must be burned.

The Guilt Offering

7 " 'These are the regulations for the guilt offering, which is most holy: 2The guilt offering is to be slaughtered in the place where the burnt offering is slaughtered, and its blood is to be sprinkled against the altar on all sides. 3All its fat shall be offered: the fat tail and the fat that covers the inner parts, 4both kidneys with the fat on them near the loins, and the covering of the liver, which is to be removed with the kidneys. 5The priest shall burn them on the altar as an offering made to the Lord by fire. It is a guilt offering. 6Any male in a priest's family may eat it, but it must be eaten in a holy place; it is most holy.

7" 'The same law applies to both the sin offering and the guilt offering: They belong to the priest who makes atonement with them. 8The priest who offers a burnt offering for anyone may keep its hide for himself. 9Every grain offering baked in an oven or cooked in a pan or on a griddle belongs to the priest who offers it, 10and every grain offering, whether mixed with oil or dry, belongs equally to all the sons of Aaron.

The Fellowship Offering

11" 'These are the regulations for the fellowship offering*a* a person may present to the Lord:

12" 'If he offers it as an expression of thankfulness, then along with this thank-offering he is to offer cakes of bread made without yeast and mixed with oil, wafers made without yeast and spread with oil, and cakes of fine flour well-kneaded and mixed with oil. 13Along with his fellowship offering of thanksgiving he is to present an offering with cakes of bread made with yeast. 14He is to bring one of each kind as an offering, a contribution to the Lord; it belongs to the priest who sprinkles the blood of the fellowship offerings. 15The meat of his fellowship offering of thanksgiving must be

eaten on the day it is offered; he must leave none of it till morning.

16" 'If, however, his offering is the result of a vow or is a freewill offering, the sacrifice shall be eaten on the day he offers it, but anything left over may be eaten on the next day. 17Any meat of the sacrifice left over till the third day must be burned up. 18If any meat of the fellowship offering is eaten on the third day, it will not be accepted. It will not be credited to the one who offered it, for it is impure; the person who eats any of it will be held responsible.

19" 'Meat that touches anything ceremonially unclean must not be eaten; it must be burned up. As for other meat, anyone ceremonially clean may eat it. 20But if anyone who is unclean eats any meat of the fellowship offering belonging to the Lord, that person must be cut off from his people. 21If anyone touches something unclean—whether human uncleanness or an unclean animal or any unclean, detestable thing—and then eats any of the meat of the fellowship offering belonging to the Lord, that person must be cut off from his people.' "

Eating Fat and Blood Forbidden

22The Lord said to Moses, 23"Say to the Israelites: 'Do not eat any of the fat of cattle, sheep or goats. 24The fat of an animal found dead or torn by wild animals may be used for any other purpose, but you must not eat it. 25Anyone who eats the fat of an animal from which an offering by fire may be*b* made to the Lord must be cut off from his people. 26And wherever you live, you must not eat the blood of any bird or animal. 27If anyone eats blood, that person must be cut off from his people.' "

The Priests' Share

28The Lord said to Moses, 29"Say to the Israelites: 'Anyone who brings a fellowship offering to the Lord is to bring part of it as his sacrifice to the Lord. 30With his own hands he is to bring the offering made to the Lord by fire; he is to bring the fat, together with the breast, and wave the breast before the Lord as a wave offering. 31The priest shall burn the fat on the altar, but the breast belongs to Aaron and his sons. 32You are to give the right thigh of your fellowship offerings to the priest as a contribution. 33The son of Aaron who offers the blood and the fat of the fellowship offering shall have the right thigh as his share. 34From the fellowship offerings of the Israelites, I have taken the breast that is waved and the thigh that is presented and have given them to Aaron the priest and his sons as their regular share from the Israelites.' "

35This is the portion of the offerings made to the Lord by fire that were allotted to Aaron and his sons on the day they were presented to serve the Lord as priests. 36On the day they were anointed, the Lord commanded that the Israelites give this to them as their regular share for the generations to come.

37These, then, are the regulations for the burnt offering, the grain offering, the sin offering, the guilt offering, the ordination offering and the fellowship offering,

---

a 11 Traditionally *peace offering*; also in verses 13–37   *b 25* Or *fire is*

[38]which the LORD gave Moses on Mount Sinai on the day he commanded the Israelites to bring their offerings to the LORD, in the Desert of Sinai.

The Ordination of Aaron and His Sons

8 The LORD said to Moses, [2]"Bring Aaron and his sons, their garments, the anointing oil, the bull for the sin offering, the two rams and the basket containing bread made without yeast, [3]and gather the entire assembly at the entrance to the Tent of Meeting." [4]Moses did as the LORD commanded him, and the assembly gathered at the entrance to the Tent of Meeting.

[5]Moses said to the assembly, "This is what the LORD has commanded to be done." [6]Then Moses brought Aaron and his sons forward and washed them with water. [7]He put the tunic on Aaron, tied the sash around him, clothed him with the robe and put the ephod on him. He also tied the ephod to him by its skilfully woven waistband; so it was fastened on him. [8]He placed the breastpiece on him and put the Urim and Thummim in the breastpiece. [9]Then he placed the turban on Aaron's head and set the gold plate, the sacred diadem, on the front of it, as the LORD commanded Moses.

[10]Then Moses took the anointing oil and anointed the tabernacle and everything in it, and so consecrated them. [11]He sprinkled some of the oil on the altar seven times, anointing the altar and all its utensils and the basin with its stand, to consecrate them. [12]He poured some of the anointing oil on Aaron's head and anointed him to consecrate him. [13]Then he brought Aaron's sons forward, put tunics on them, tied sashes around them and put headbands on them, as the LORD commanded Moses.

[14]He then presented the bull for the sin offering, and Aaron and his sons laid their hands on its head. [15]Moses slaughtered the bull and took some of the blood, and with his finger he put it on all the horns of the altar to purify the altar. He poured out the rest of the blood at the base of the altar. So he consecrated it to make atonement for it. [16]Moses also took all the fat around the inner parts, the covering of the liver, and both kidneys and their fat, and burned it on the altar. [17]But the bull with its hide and its flesh and its offal he burned up outside the camp, as the LORD commanded Moses.

[18]He then presented the ram for the burnt offering, and Aaron and his sons laid their hands on its head. [19]Then Moses slaughtered the ram and sprinkled the blood against the altar on all sides. [20]He cut the ram into pieces and burned the head, the pieces and the fat. [21]He washed the inner parts and the legs with water and burned the whole ram on the altar as a burnt offering, a pleasing aroma, an offering made to the LORD by fire, as the LORD commanded Moses.

[22]He then presented the other ram, the ram for the ordination, and Aaron and his sons laid their hands on its head. [23]Moses slaughtered the ram and took some of its blood and put it on the lobe of Aaron's right ear, on the thumb of his right hand and on the big toe of his right foot. [24]Moses also brought Aaron's sons forward and put some of the blood on the lobes of their right ears, on the thumbs of their right hands and on the big toes of their right feet. Then he sprinkled blood against the altar on all sides. [25]He took the fat, the fat tail, all the fat around the inner parts, the covering of the liver, both kidneys and their fat and the right thigh. [26]Then from the basket of bread made without yeast, which was before the LORD, he took a cake of bread, and one made with oil, and a wafer; he put these on the fat portions and on the right thigh. [27]He put all these in the hands of Aaron and his sons and waved them before the LORD as a wave offering. [28]Then Moses took them from their hands and burned them on the altar on top of the burnt offering as an ordination offering, a pleasing aroma, an offering made to the LORD by fire. [29]He also took the breast—Moses' share of the ordination ram—and waved it before the LORD as a wave offering, as the LORD commanded Moses.

[30]Then Moses took some of the anointing oil and some of the blood from the altar and sprinkled them on Aaron and his garments and on his sons and their garments. So he consecrated Aaron and his garments and his sons and their garments.

[31]Moses then said to Aaron and his sons, "Cook the meat at the entrance to the Tent of Meeting and eat it there with the bread from the basket of ordination offerings, as I commanded, saying,[a] 'Aaron and his sons are to eat it.' [32]Then burn up the rest of the meat and the bread. [33]Do not leave the entrance to the Tent of Meeting for seven days, until the days of your ordination are completed, for your ordination will last seven days. [34]What has been done today was commanded by the LORD to make atonement for you. [35]You must stay at the entrance to the Tent of Meeting day and night for seven days and do what the LORD requires, so that you will not die; for that is what I have been commanded." [36]So Aaron and his sons did everything the LORD commanded through Moses.

The Priests Begin Their Ministry

9 On the eighth day Moses summoned Aaron and his sons and the elders of Israel. [2]He said to Aaron, "Take a bull calf for your sin offering and a ram for your burnt offering, both without defect, and present them before the LORD. [3]Then say to the Israelites: 'Take a male goat for a sin offering, a calf and a lamb—both a year old and without defect—for a burnt offering, [4]and an ox[a] and a ram for a fellowship offering[b] to sacrifice before the LORD, together with a grain offering mixed with oil. For today the LORD will appear to you.'"

[5]They took the things Moses commanded to the front of the Tent of Meeting, and the entire assembly came near and stood before the LORD. [6]Then Moses said, "This is what the LORD has commanded you to do, so that the glory of the LORD may appear to you."

---

[a]31 Or I was commanded: [a]4 The Hebrew word can include both male and female; also in verses 18 and 19.
[b]4 Traditionally peace offering; also in verses 18 and 22

7Moses said to Aaron, "Come to the altar and sacrifice your sin offering and your burnt offering and make atonement for yourself and the people; sacrifice the offering that is for the people and make atonement for them, as the LORD has commanded."

8So Aaron came to the altar and slaughtered the calf as a sin offering for himself. 9His sons brought the blood to him, and he dipped his finger into the blood and put it on the horns of the altar; the rest of the blood he poured out at the base of the altar. 10On the altar he burned the fat, the kidneys and the covering of the liver from the sin offering, as the LORD commanded Moses; 11the flesh and the hide he burned up outside the camp.

12Then he slaughtered the burnt offering. His sons handed him the blood, and he sprinkled it against the altar on all sides. 13They handed him the burnt offering piece by piece, including the head, and he burned them on the altar. 14He washed the inner parts and the legs and burned them on top of the burnt offering on the altar.

15Aaron then brought the offering that was for the people. He took the goat for the people's sin offering and slaughtered it and offered it for a sin offering as he did with the first one.

16He brought the burnt offering and offered it in the prescribed way. 17He also brought the grain offering, took a handful of it and burned it on the altar in addition to the morning's burnt offering.

18He slaughtered the ox and the ram as the fellowship offering for the people. His sons handed him the blood, and he sprinkled it against the altar on all sides. 19But the fat portions of the ox and the ram—the fat tail, the layer of fat, the kidneys and the covering of the liver—20these they laid on the breasts, and then Aaron burned the fat on the altar. 21Aaron waved the breasts and the right thigh before the LORD as a wave offering, as Moses commanded.

9:23 From the beginning of Genesis it has been clear that disregarding God's wishes brings increasing misery. Now the Israelites discovered that the opposite was also true. Once they were set right with God the people found that they could sense his presence and the result was not just natural awe, but also a profound joy.

22Then Aaron lifted his hands towards the people and blessed them. And having sacrificed the sin offering, the burnt offering and the fellowship offering, he stepped down.

23Moses and Aaron then went into the Tent of Meeting. When they came out, they blessed the people; and the glory of the LORD appeared to all the people. 24Fire came out from the presence of the LORD and consumed the burnt offering and the fat portions on the altar. And when all the people saw it, they shouted for joy and fell face down.

The Death of Nadab and Abihu

10 Aaron's sons Nadab and Abihu took their censers, put fire in them and added incense; and they offered unauthorised fire before the LORD, contrary to his command. 2So fire came out from the presence of the LORD and consumed them, and they died before the LORD. 3Moses then said to Aaron, "This is what the LORD spoke of when he said:

" 'Among those who approach me
I will show myself holy;
in the sight of all the people
I will be honoured.' "

Aaron remained silent.

4Moses summoned Mishael and Elzaphan, sons of Aaron's uncle Uzziel, and said to them, "Come here; carry your cousins outside the camp, away from the front of the sanctuary." 5So they came and carried them, still in their tunics, outside the camp, as Moses ordered.

6Then Moses said to Aaron and his sons Eleazar and Ithamar, "Do not let your hair become unkempt,a and do not tear your clothes, or you will die and the LORD will be angry with the whole community. But your relatives, all the house of Israel, may mourn for those the LORD has destroyed by fire. 7Do not leave the entrance to the Tent of Meeting or you will die, because the LORD's anointing oil is on you." So they did as Moses said.

8Then the LORD said to Aaron, 9"You and your sons are not to drink wine or other fermented drink whenever you go into the Tent of Meeting, or you will die. This is a lasting ordinance for the generations to come. 10You must distinguish between the holy and the common, between the unclean and the clean, 11and you must teach the Israelites all the decrees the LORD has given them through Moses."

12Moses said to Aaron and his remaining sons, Eleazar and Ithamar, "Take the grain offering left over from the offerings made to the LORD by fire and eat it prepared without yeast beside the altar, for it is most holy. 13Eat it in a holy place, because it is your share and your sons' share of the offerings made to the LORD by fire; for so I have been commanded. 14But you and your sons and your daughters may eat the breast that was waved and the thigh that was presented. Eat them in a ceremonially clean place; they have been given to you and your children as your share of the Israelites' fellowship offerings.b 15The thigh that was presented and the breast that was waved must be brought with the fat portions of the offerings made by fire, to be waved before the LORD as a wave offering. This will be the regular share for you and your children, as the LORD has commanded."

16When Moses enquired about the goat of the sin offering and found that it had been burned up, he was angry with Eleazar and Ithamar, Aaron's remaining sons, and asked, 17"Why didn't you eat the sin offering in the sanctuary area? It is most holy; it was given to you to take away the guilt of the community by making atonement for them before the LORD. 18Since its blood

---

a6 Or Do not uncover your heads   b14 Traditionally peace offerings was not taken into the Holy Place, you should have eaten the goat in the sanctuary area, as I commanded."

[19]Aaron replied to Moses, "Today they sacrificed their sin offering and their burnt offering before the LORD, but such things as this have happened to me. Would the LORD have been pleased if I had eaten the sin offering today?" [20]When Moses heard this, he was satisfied.

Clean and Unclean Food

11 The LORD said to Moses and Aaron, [2]"Say to the Israelites: 'Of all the animals that live on land, these are the ones you may eat: [3]You may eat any animal that has a split hoof completely divided and that chews the cud.

[4] 'There are some that only chew the cud or only have a split hoof, but you must not eat them. The camel, though it chews the cud, does not have a split hoof; it is ceremonially unclean for you. [5]The coney,[a] though it chews the cud, does not have a split hoof; it is unclean for you. [6]The rabbit, though it chews the cud, does not have a split hoof; it is unclean for you. [7]And the pig, though it has a split hoof completely divided, does not chew the cud; it is unclean for you. [8]You must not eat their meat or touch their carcasses; they are unclean for you.

[9] 'Of all the creatures living in the water of the seas and the streams, you may eat any that have fins and scales. [10]But all creatures in the seas or streams that do not have fins and scales—whether among all the swarming things or among all the other living creatures in the water—you are to detest. [11]And since you are to detest them, you must not eat their meat and you must detest their carcasses. [12]Anything living in the water that does not have fins and scales is to be detestable to you.

[13] 'These are the birds you are to detest and not eat because they are detestable: the eagle, the vulture, the black vulture, [14]the red kite, any kind of black kite, [15]any kind of raven, [16]the horned owl, the screech owl, the gull, any kind of hawk, [17]the little owl, the cormorant, the great owl, [18]the white owl, the desert owl, the osprey, [19]the stork, any kind of heron, the hoopoe and the bat.[b]

[20] 'All flying insects that walk on all fours are to be detestable to you. [21]There are, however, some winged creatures that walk on all fours that you may eat: those that have jointed legs for hopping on the ground. [22]Of these you may eat any kind of locust, katydid, cricket or grasshopper. [23]But all other winged creatures that have four legs you are to detest.

[24] 'You will make yourselves unclean by these; whoever touches their carcasses will be unclean till evening. [25]Whoever picks up one of their carcasses must wash his clothes, and he will be unclean till evening.

[26] 'Every animal that has a split hoof not completely divided or that does not chew the cud is unclean for you; whoever touches the carcass of any of them will be unclean. [27]Of all the animals that walk on all fours, those that walk on their paws are unclean for you; whoever touches their carcasses will be unclean till evening. [28]Anyone who picks up their carcasses must wash his clothes, and he will be unclean till evening. They are unclean for you.

[29] 'Of the animals that move about on the ground, these are unclean for you: the weasel, the rat, any kind of great lizard, [30]the gecko, the monitor lizard, the wall lizard, the skink and the chameleon. [31]Of all those that move along the ground, these are unclean for you. Whoever touches them when they are dead will be unclean till evening. [32]When one of them dies and falls on something, that article, whatever its use, will be unclean, whether it is made of wood, cloth, hide or sackcloth. Put it in water; it will be unclean till evening, and then it will be clean. [33]If one of them falls into a clay pot, everything in it will be unclean, and you must break the pot. [34]Any food that could be eaten but has water on it from such a pot is unclean, and any liquid that could be drunk from it is unclean. [35]Anything that one of their carcasses falls on becomes unclean; an oven or cooking pot must be broken up. They are unclean, and you are to regard them as unclean. [36]A spring, however, or a cistern for collecting water remains clean, but anyone who touches one of these carcasses is unclean. [37]If a carcass falls on any seeds that are to be planted, they remain clean. [38]But if water has been put on the seed and a carcass falls on it, it is unclean for you.

[39] 'If an animal that you are allowed to eat dies, anyone who touches the carcass will be unclean till evening. [40]Anyone who eats some of the carcass must wash his clothes, and he will be unclean till evening. Anyone who picks up the carcass must wash his clothes, and he will be unclean till evening.

[41] 'Every creature that moves about on the ground is detestable; it is not to be eaten. [42]You are not to eat any creature that moves about on the ground, whether it moves on its belly or walks on all fours or on many feet; it is detestable. [43]Do not defile yourselves by any of these creatures. Do not make yourselves unclean by means of them or be made unclean by them. [44]I am the LORD your God; consecrate yourselves and be holy, because I am holy. Do not make yourselves unclean by any creature that moves about on the ground. [45]I am the LORD who brought you up out of Egypt to be your God; therefore be holy, because I am holy.

[46] 'These are the regulations concerning animals, birds, every living thing that moves in the water and every creature that moves about on the ground. [47]You must distinguish between the unclean and the clean, between living creatures that may be eaten and those that may not be eaten.' "

Purification After Childbirth

12 The LORD said to Moses, [2]"Say to the Israelites: 'A woman who becomes pregnant and gives birth to a son will be ceremonially unclean for seven days, just as she is unclean during her monthly period. [3]On the eighth day the boy is to be circumcised.

---

[a]5 That is, the hyrax or rock badger

[b]19 The precise identification of some of the birds, insects and animals in this chapter is uncertain.

4Then the woman must wait thirty-three days to be purified from her bleeding. She must not touch anything sacred or go to the sanctuary until the days of her purification are over. 5If she gives birth to a daughter, for two weeks the woman will be unclean, as during her period. Then she must wait sixty-six days to be purified from her bleeding.

12:2   Blood was considered to carry the breath of life from God. Its mysterious loss was regarded with awe, and women losing blood were considered unclean. The principle behind this — of reverence for God's gift of life — was a sound one. We still have this reverence, but now that we understand the way the body works, we have no more reason to consider women as unclean than we do to sacrifice animals.

6" 'When the days of her purification for a son or daughter are over, she is to bring to the priest at the entrance to the Tent of Meeting a year-old lamb for a burnt offering and a young pigeon or a dove for a sin offering. 7He shall offer them before the LORD to make atonement for her, and then she will be ceremonially clean from her flow of blood.

" 'These are the regulations for the woman who gives birth to a boy or a girl. 8If she cannot afford a lamb, she is to bring two doves or two young pigeons, one for a burnt offering and the other for a sin offering. In this way the priest will make atonement for her, and she will be clean.' "

Regulations About Infectious Skin Diseases

13   The LORD said to Moses and Aaron, 2"When anyone has a swelling or a rash or a bright spot on his skin that may become an infectious skin disease,[a] he must be brought to Aaron the priest or to one of his sons[b] who is a priest. 3The priest is to examine the sore on his skin, and if the hair in the sore has turned white and the sore appears to be more than skin deep,[c] it is an infectious skin disease. When the priest examines him, he shall pronounce him ceremonially unclean. 4If the spot on his skin is white but does not appear to be more than skin deep and the hair in it has not turned white, the priest is to put the infected person in isolation for seven days. 5On the seventh day the priest is to examine him, and if he sees that the sore is unchanged and has not spread in the skin, he is to keep him in isolation another seven days. 6On the seventh day the priest is to examine him again, and if the sore has faded and has not spread in the skin, the priest shall pronounce him clean; it is only a rash. The man must wash his clothes, and he will be clean. 7But if the rash does spread in his skin after he has shown himself to the priest to be pronounced clean, he must appear before the priest again. 8The priest is to examine him, and if the rash has spread in the skin, he shall pronounce him unclean; it is an infectious disease.

9"When anyone has an infectious skin disease, he must be brought to the priest. 10The priest is to examine him, and if there is a white swelling in the skin that has turned the hair white and if there is raw flesh in the swelling, 11it is a chronic skin disease and the priest shall pronounce him unclean. He is not to put him in isolation, because he is already unclean.

12"If the disease breaks out all over his skin and, so far as the priest can see, it covers all the skin of the infected person from head to foot, 13the priest is to examine him, and if the disease has covered his whole body, he shall pronounce that person clean. Since it has all turned white, he is clean. 14But whenever raw flesh appears on him, he will be unclean. 15When the priest sees the raw flesh, he shall pronounce him unclean. The raw flesh is unclean; he has an infectious disease. 16Should the raw flesh change and turn white, he must go to the priest. 17The priest is to examine him, and if the sores have turned white, the priest shall pronounce the infected person clean; then he will be clean.

18"When someone has a boil on his skin and it heals, 19and in the place where the boil was, a white swelling or reddish-white spot appears, he must present himself to the priest. 20The priest is to examine it, and if it appears to be more than skin deep and the hair in it has turned white, the priest shall pronounce him unclean. It is an infectious skin disease that has broken out where the boil was. 21But if, when the priest examines it, there is no white hair in it and it is not more than skin deep and has faded, then the priest is to put him in isolation for seven days. 22If it is spreading in the skin, the priest shall pronounce him unclean; it is infectious. 23But if the spot is unchanged and has not spread, it is only a scar from the boil, and the priest shall pronounce him clean.

24"When someone has a burn on his skin and a reddish-white or white spot appears in the raw flesh of the burn, 25the priest is to examine the spot, and if the hair in it has turned white, and it appears to be more than skin deep, it is an infectious disease that has broken out in the burn. The priest shall pronounce him unclean; it is an infectious skin disease. 26But if the priest examines it and there is no white hair in the spot and if it is not more than skin deep and has faded, then the priest is to put him in isolation for seven days. 27On the seventh day the priest is to examine him, and if it is spreading in the skin, the priest shall pronounce him unclean; it is an infectious skin disease. 28If, however, the spot is unchanged and has not spread in the skin but has faded, it is a swelling from the burn, and the priest shall pronounce him clean; it is only a scar from the burn.

29"If a man or woman has a sore on the head or on the chin, 30the priest is to examine the sore, and if it appears to be more than skin deep and the hair in it is yellow and thin, the priest shall pronounce that person unclean; it is an itch, an infectious disease of the head or chin. 31But if, when the priest examines this kind of sore, it does not seem to be more than skin deep and there is no black hair in it, then the priest is to put the infected person in isolation for seven days. 32On

---

*a*2 Traditionally *leprosy*; the Hebrew word was used for various diseases affecting the skin — not necessarily leprosy; also elsewhere in this chapter.   *b*2 Or *descendants*   *c*3 Or *be lower than the rest of the skin*; also elsewhere in this chapter the seventh day the priest is to examine the sore, and if the itch has not spread and there is no yellow hair in it and it does not appear to be more than skin deep, 33he must be shaved except for the diseased area, and the priest is to keep him in isolation another seven days. 34On the seventh day the priest is to examine the itch, and if it has not spread in the skin and appears to be no more than skin deep, the priest shall pronounce him clean. He must wash his clothes, and he will be clean. 35But if the itch does spread in the skin after he is pronounced clean, 36the priest is to examine him, and if the itch has spread in the skin, the priest does not need to look for yellow hair; the person is unclean. 37If, however, in his judgment it is unchanged and black hair has grown in it, the itch is healed. He is clean, and the priest shall pronounce him clean.

38"When a man or woman has white spots on the skin, 39the priest is to examine them, and if the spots are dull white, it is a harmless rash that has broken out on the skin; that person is clean.

40"When a man has lost his hair and is bald, he is clean. 41If he has lost his hair from the front of his scalp and has a bald forehead, he is clean. 42But if he has a reddish-white sore on his bald head or forehead, it is an infectious disease breaking out on his head or forehead. 43The priest is to examine him, and if the swollen sore on his head or forehead is reddish-white like an infectious skin disease, 44the man is diseased and is unclean. The priest shall pronounce him unclean because of the sore on his head.

45"The person with such an infectious disease must wear torn clothes, let his hair be unkempt, d cover the lower part of his face and cry out, 'Unclean! Unclean!' 46As long as he has the infection he remains unclean. He must live alone; he must live outside the camp.

Regulations About Mildew

47"If any clothing is contaminated with mildew— any woollen or linen clothing, 48any woven or knitted material of linen or wool, any leather or anything made of leather — 49and if the contamination in the clothing, or leather, or woven or knitted material, or any leather article, is greenish or reddish, it is a spreading mildew and must be shown to the priest. 50The priest is to examine the mildew and isolate the affected article for seven days. 51On the seventh day he is to examine it, and if the mildew has spread in the clothing, or the woven or knitted material, or the leather, whatever its use, it is a destructive mildew; the article is unclean. 52He must burn up the clothing, or the woven or knitted material of wool or linen, or any leather article that has the contamination in it, because the mildew is destructive; the article must be burned up.

53"But if, when the priest examines it, the mildew has not spread in the clothing, or the woven or knitted material, or the leather article, 54he shall order that the contaminated article be washed. Then he is to isolate it for another seven days. 55After the affected article has been washed, the priest is to examine it, and if the mildew has not changed its appearance, even though

it has not spread, it is unclean. Burn it with fire, whether the mildew has affected one side or the other. 56If, when the priest examines it, the mildew has faded after the article has been washed, he is to tear the contaminated part out of the clothing, or the leather, or the woven or knitted material. 57But if it reappears in the clothing, or in the woven or knitted material, or in the leather article, it is spreading, and whatever has the mildew must be burned with fire. 58The clothing, or the woven or knitted material, or any leather article that has been washed and is rid of the mildew, must be washed again, and it will be clean."

13:52   Many of the regulations in Leviticus deal with practical matters and are the result of what happened in nature. This is true of the instructions for dealing with mildew. A number of Israel's food laws, such as pork being a forbidden food, came from seeing the harm that resulted from eating it in a hot climate, where it could easily go bad. Jewish people today keep such rules because the discipline is a constant reminder of God's presence in their lives.

59These are the regulations concerning contamination by mildew in woollen or linen clothing, woven or knitted material, or any leather article, for pronouncing them clean or unclean.

Cleansing From Infectious Skin Diseases

14 The LORD said to Moses, 2"These are the regulations for the diseased person at the time of his ceremonial cleansing, when he is brought to the priest: 3The priest is to go outside the camp and examine him. If the person has been healed of his infectious skin disease,a 4the priest shall order that two live clean birds and some cedar wood, scarlet yarn and hyssop be brought for the one to be cleansed. 5Then the priest shall order that one of the birds be killed over fresh water in a clay pot. 6He is then to take the live bird and dip it, together with the cedar wood, the scarlet yarn and the hyssop, into the blood of the bird that was killed over the fresh water. 7Seven times he shall sprinkle the one to be cleansed of the infectious disease and pronounce him clean. Then he is to release the live bird in the open fields.

8"The person to be cleansed must wash his clothes, shave off all his hair and bathe with water; then he will be ceremonially clean. After this he may come into the camp, but he must stay outside his tent for seven days. 9On the seventh day he must shave off all his hair; he must shave his head, his beard, his eyebrows and the rest of his hair. He must wash his clothes and bathe himself with water, and he will be clean.

10"On the eighth day he must bring two male lambs and one ewe lamb a year old, each without defect, along with three-tenths of an ephahb of fine flour

---

d45 Or clothes, uncover his head
a3 Traditionally leprosy; the Hebrew word was used for various diseases affecting the skin—not necessarily leprosy; also elsewhere in this chapter.   b10 That is, probably about 11½ pints (about 6.5 litres)

mixed with oil for a grain offering, and one log*c* of oil. [11] The priest who pronounces him clean shall present both the one to be cleansed and his offerings before the LORD at the entrance to the Tent of Meeting.

[12] "Then the priest is to take one of the male lambs and offer it as a guilt offering, along with the log of oil; he shall wave them before the LORD as a wave offering. [13] He is to slaughter the lamb in the holy place where the sin offering and the burnt offering are slaughtered. Like the sin offering, the guilt offering belongs to the priest; it is most holy. [14] The priest is to take some of the blood of the guilt offering and put it on the lobe of the right ear of the one to be cleansed, on the thumb of his right hand and on the big toe of his right foot. [15] The priest shall then take some of the log of oil, pour it in the palm of his own left hand, [16] dip his right forefinger into the oil in his palm, and with his finger sprinkle some of it before the LORD seven times. [17] The priest is to put some of the oil remaining in his palm on the lobe of the right ear of the one to be cleansed, on the thumb of his right hand and on the big toe of his right foot, on top of the blood of the guilt offering. [18] The rest of the oil in his palm the priest shall put on the head of the one to be cleansed and make atonement for him before the LORD.

[19] "Then the priest is to sacrifice the sin offering and make atonement for the one to be cleansed from his uncleanness. After that, the priest shall slaughter the burnt offering [20] and offer it on the altar, together with the grain offering, and make atonement for him, and he will be clean.

[21] "If, however, he is poor and cannot afford these, he must take one male lamb as a guilt offering to be waved to make atonement for him, together with a tenth of an ephah*d* of fine flour mixed with oil for a grain offering, a log of oil, [22] and two doves or two young pigeons, which he can afford, one for a sin offering and the other for a burnt offering.

[23] "On the eighth day he must bring them for his cleansing to the priest at the entrance to the Tent of Meeting, before the LORD. [24] The priest is to take the lamb for the guilt offering, together with the log of oil, and wave them before the LORD as a wave offering. [25] He shall slaughter the lamb for the guilt offering and take some of its blood and put it on the lobe of the right ear of the one to be cleansed, on the thumb of his right hand and on the big toe of his right foot. [26] The priest is to pour some of the oil into the palm of his own left hand, [27] and with his right forefinger sprinkle some of the oil from his palm seven times before the LORD. [28] Some of the oil in his palm he is to put on the same places he put the blood of the guilt offering—on the lobe of the right ear of the one to be cleansed, on the thumb of his right hand and on the big toe of his right foot. [29] The rest of the oil in his palm the priest shall put on the head of the one to be cleansed, to make atonement for him before the LORD. [30] Then he shall sacrifice the doves or the young pigeons, which the person can afford, [31] one*e* as a sin offering and the other as a burnt offering, together with the grain offering. In this way

the priest will make atonement before the LORD on behalf of the one to be cleansed."

[32] These are the regulations for anyone who has an infectious skin disease and who cannot afford the regular offerings for his cleansing.

Cleansing From Mildew

[33] The LORD said to Moses and Aaron, [34] "When you enter the land of Canaan, which I am giving you as your possession, and I put a spreading mildew in a house in that land, [35] the owner of the house must go and tell the priest, 'I have seen something that looks like mildew in my house.' [36] The priest is to order the house to be emptied before he goes in to examine the mildew, so that nothing in the house will be pronounced unclean. After this the priest is to go in and inspect the house. [37] He is to examine the mildew on the walls, and if it has greenish or reddish depressions that appear to be deeper than the surface of the wall, [38] the priest shall go out of the doorway of the house and close it up for seven days. [39] On the seventh day the priest shall return to inspect the house. If the mildew has spread on the walls, [40] he is to order that the contaminated stones be torn out and thrown into an unclean place outside the town. [41] He must have all the inside walls of the house scraped and the material that is scraped off dumped into an unclean place outside the town. [42] Then they are to take other stones to replace these and take new clay and plaster the house.

14:35 Israelite priests dealt with matters that we would send to a doctor or builder or other specialist. This shows that everything was a matter of God's concern and affected the whole community. There is a growing understanding today that we can only heal a sickness by treating the whole person. This can mean treating that person as part of society, not just as an individual.

[43] "If the mildew reappears in the house after the stones have been torn out and the house scraped and plastered, [44] the priest is to go and examine it and, if the mildew has spread in the house, it is a destructive mildew; the house is unclean. [45] It must be torn down—its stones, timbers and all the plaster—and taken out of the town to an unclean place.

[46] "Anyone who goes into the house while it is closed up will be unclean till evening. [47] Anyone who sleeps or eats in the house must wash his clothes.

[48] "But if the priest comes to examine it and the mildew has not spread after the house has been plastered, he shall pronounce the house clean, because the mildew is gone. [49] To purify the house he is to take two birds and some cedar wood, scarlet yarn and hyssop. [50] He shall kill one of the birds over fresh water in a clay pot. [51] Then he is to take the cedar wood, the hyssop, the scarlet yarn and the live bird, dip them into the blood of the dead bird and the fresh water, and sprinkle

---

c10 That is, probably about ½ pint (about 0.3 litre); also in verses 12, 15, 21 and 24
d21 That is, probably about 4 pints (about 2 litres)   *e31* Septuagint and Syriac; Hebrew *31 such as the person can afford, one*

the house seven times. [52]He shall purify the house with the bird's blood, the fresh water, the live bird, the cedar wood, the hyssop and the scarlet yarn. [53]Then he is to release the live bird in the open fields outside the town. In this way he will make atonement for the house, and it will be clean."

[54]These are the regulations for any infectious skin disease, for an itch, [55]for mildew in clothing or in a house, [56]and for a swelling, a rash or a bright spot, [57]to determine when something is clean or unclean.

These are the regulations for infectious skin diseases and mildew.

Discharges Causing Uncleanness

15 The LORD said to Moses and Aaron, [2]"Speak to the Israelites and say to them: 'When any man has a bodily discharge, the discharge is unclean. [3]Whether it continues flowing from his body or is blocked, it will make him unclean. This is how his discharge will bring about uncleanness:

[4]" 'Any bed the man with a discharge lies on will be unclean, and anything he sits on will be unclean. [5]Anyone who touches his bed must wash his clothes and bathe with water, and he will be unclean till evening. [6]Whoever sits on anything that the man with a discharge sat on must wash his clothes and bathe with water, and he will be unclean till evening.

[7]" 'Whoever touches the man who has a discharge must wash his clothes and bathe with water, and he will be unclean till evening.

[8]" 'If the man with the discharge spits on someone who is clean, that person must wash his clothes and bathe with water, and he will be unclean till evening.

[9]" 'Everything the man sits on when riding will be unclean, [10]and whoever touches any of the things that were under him will be unclean till evening; whoever picks up those things must wash his clothes and bathe with water, and he will be unclean till evening.

[11]" 'Anyone the man with a discharge touches without rinsing his hands with water must wash his clothes and bathe with water, and he will be unclean till evening.

[12]" 'A clay pot that the man touches must be broken, and any wooden article is to be rinsed with water.

[13]" 'When a man is cleansed from his discharge, he is to count off seven days for his ceremonial cleansing; he must wash his clothes and bathe himself with fresh water, and he will be clean. [14]On the eighth day he must take two doves or two young pigeons and come before the LORD to the entrance to the Tent of Meeting and give them to the priest. [15]The priest is to sacrifice them, the one for a sin offering and the other for a burnt offering. In this way he will make atonement before the LORD for the man because of his discharge.

[16]" 'When a man has an emission of semen, he must bathe his whole body with water, and he will be unclean till evening. [17]Any clothing or leather that has semen on it must be washed with water, and it will be unclean till evening. [18]When a man lies with a woman and there is an emission of semen, both must bathe with water, and they will be unclean till evening.

[19]" 'When a woman has her regular flow of blood, the impurity of her monthly period will last seven days, and anyone who touches her will be unclean till evening.

[20]" 'Anything she lies on during her period will be unclean, and anything she sits on will be unclean. [21]Whoever touches her bed must wash his clothes and bathe with water, and he will be unclean till evening. [22]Whoever touches anything she sits on must wash his clothes and bathe with water, and he will be unclean till evening. [23]Whether it is the bed or anything she was sitting on, when anyone touches it, he will be unclean till evening.

[24]" 'If a man lies with her and her monthly flow touches him, he will be unclean for seven days; any bed he lies on will be unclean.

[25]" 'When a woman has a discharge of blood for many days at a time other than her monthly period or has a discharge that continues beyond her period, she will be unclean as long as she has the discharge, just as in the days of her period. [26]Any bed she lies on while her discharge continues will be unclean, as is her bed during her monthly period, and anything she sits on will be unclean, as during her period. [27]Whoever touches them will be unclean; he must wash his clothes and bathe with water, and he will be unclean till evening.

[28]" 'When she is cleansed from her discharge, she must count off seven days, and after that she will be ceremonially clean. [29]On the eighth day she must take two doves or two young pigeons and bring them to the priest at the entrance to the Tent of Meeting. [30]The priest is to sacrifice one for a sin offering and the other for a burnt offering. In this way he will make atonement for her before the LORD for the uncleanness of her discharge.

[31]" 'You must keep the Israelites separate from things that make them unclean, so they will not die in their uncleanness for defiling my dwelling-place,[a] which is among them.' "

[32]These are the regulations for a man with a discharge, for anyone made unclean by an emission of semen, [33]for a woman in her monthly period, for a man or a woman with a discharge, and for a man who lies with a woman who is ceremonially unclean.

The Day of Atonement

16 The LORD spoke to Moses after the death of the two sons of Aaron who died when they approached the LORD. [2]The LORD said to Moses: "Tell your brother Aaron not to come whenever he chooses into the Most Holy Place behind the curtain in front of the atonement cover on the ark, or else he will die, because I appear in the cloud over the atonement cover.

[3]"This is how Aaron is to enter the sanctuary area: with a young bull for a sin offering and a ram for a burnt offering. [4]He is to put on the sacred linen tunic, with linen undergarments next to his body; he is to tie the linen sash around him and put on the linen turban. These are sacred garments; so he must bathe himself

[a]31 Or my tabernacle

with water before he puts them on. ⁵From the Israelite community he is to take two male goats for a sin offering and a ram for a burnt offering.

⁶"Aaron is to offer the bull for his own sin offering to make atonement for himself and his household. ⁷Then he is to take the two goats and present them before the LORD at the entrance to the Tent of Meeting. ⁸He is to cast lots for the two goats—one lot for the LORD and the other for the scapegoat.ᵃ ⁹Aaron shall bring the goat whose lot falls to the LORD and sacrifice it for a sin offering. ¹⁰But the goat chosen by lot as the scapegoat shall be presented alive before the LORD to be used for making atonement by sending it into the desert as a scapegoat.

¹¹"Aaron shall bring the bull for his own sin offering to make atonement for himself and his household, and he is to slaughter the bull for his own sin offering. ¹²He is to take a censer full of burning coals from the altar before the LORD and two handfuls of finely ground fragrant incense and take them behind the curtain. ¹³He is to put the incense on the fire before the LORD, and the smoke of the incense will conceal the atonement cover above the Testimony, so that he will not die. ¹⁴He is to take some of the bull's blood and with his finger sprinkle it on the front of the atonement cover; then he shall sprinkle some of it with his finger seven times before the atonement cover.

¹⁵"He shall then slaughter the goat for the sin offering for the people and take its blood behind the curtain and do with it as he did with the bull's blood: He shall sprinkle it on the atonement cover and in front of it. ¹⁶In this way he will make atonement for the Most Holy Place because of the uncleanness and rebellion of the Israelites, whatever their sins have been. He is to do the same for the Tent of Meeting, which is among them in the midst of their uncleanness. ¹⁷No-one is to be in the Tent of Meeting from the time Aaron goes in to make atonement in the Most Holy Place until he comes out, having made atonement for himself, his household and the whole community of Israel.

¹⁸"Then he shall come out to the altar that is before the LORD and make atonement for it. He shall take some of the bull's blood and some of the goat's blood and put it on all the horns of the altar. ¹⁹He shall sprinkle some of the blood on it with his finger seven times to cleanse it and consecrate it from the uncleanness of the Israelites.

²⁰"When Aaron has finished making atonement for the Most Holy Place, the Tent of Meeting and the altar, he shall bring forward the live goat. ²¹He is to lay both hands on the head of the live goat and confess over it all the wickedness and rebellion of the Israelites—all their sins—and put them on the goat's head. He shall send the goat away into the desert in the care of a man appointed for the task. ²²The goat will carry on itself all their sins to a solitary place; and the man shall release it in the desert.

²³"Then Aaron is to go into the Tent of Meeting and take off the linen garments he put on before he entered the Most Holy Place, and he is to leave them there. ²⁴He shall bathe himself with water in a holy place and put on his regular garments. Then he shall come out and sacrifice the burnt offering for himself and the burnt offering for the people, to make atonement for himself and for the people. ²⁵He shall also burn the fat of the sin offering on the altar.

16:21   The Day of Atonement (Yom Kippur) is still a very holy day of national repentance for the Jews. Christians use the idea of the scapegoat, which symbolically carried sins away into the desert, as a description of what Christ did in taking on himself the burden of human sin.

²⁶"The man who releases the goat as a scapegoat must wash his clothes and bathe himself with water; afterwards he may come into the camp. ²⁷The bull and the goat for the sin offerings, whose blood was brought into the Most Holy Place to make atonement, must be taken outside the camp; their hides, flesh and offal are to be burned up. ²⁸The man who burns them must wash his clothes and bathe himself with water; afterwards he may come into the camp.

²⁹"This is to be a lasting ordinance for you: On the tenth day of the seventh month you must deny yourselvesᵇ and not do any work—whether native-born or an alien living among you—³⁰because on this day atonement will be made for you, to cleanse you. Then, before the LORD, you will be clean from all your sins. ³¹It is a sabbath of rest, and you must deny yourselves; it is a lasting ordinance. ³²The priest who is anointed and ordained to succeed his father as high priest is to make atonement. He is to put on the sacred linen garments ³³and make atonement for the Most Holy Place, for the Tent of Meeting and the altar, and for the priests and all the people of the community.

³⁴"This is to be a lasting ordinance for you: Atonement is to be made once a year for all the sins of the Israelites."

And it was done, as the LORD commanded Moses.

Eating Blood Forbidden

17 The LORD said to Moses, ²"Speak to Aaron and his sons and to all the Israelites and say to them: 'This is what the LORD has commanded: ³Any Israelite who sacrifices an ox,ᵃ a lamb or a goat in the camp or outside of it ⁴instead of bringing it to the entrance to the Tent of Meeting to present it as an offering to the LORD in front of the tabernacle of the LORD—that man shall be considered guilty of bloodshed; he has shed blood and must be cut off from his people. ⁵This is so that the Israelites will bring to the LORD the sacrifices they are now making in the open fields. They must bring them to the priest, that is, to the LORD, at the entrance to the Tent of Meeting and sacrifice them as fellowship offerings.ᵇ ⁶The priest is to sprinkle the blood against the altar of the LORD at the entrance to the Tent of Meeting and burn the fat as an aroma pleasing to the LORD. ⁷They must no longer offer

---

ᵃ8 That is, the goat of removal; Hebrew *azazel*; also in verses 10 and 26
ᵃ3 The Hebrew word can include both male and female.

ᵇ29 Or *must fast*; also in verse 31
ᵇ5 Traditionally *peace offerings*

any of their sacrifices to the goat idols[c] to whom they prostitute themselves. This is to be a lasting ordinance for them and for the generations to come.'

[8]"Say to them: 'Any Israelite or any alien living among them who offers a burnt offering or sacrifice [9]and does not bring it to the entrance to the Tent of Meeting to sacrifice it to the LORD — that man must be cut off from his people.

[10]" 'Any Israelite or any alien living among them who eats any blood — I will set my face against that person who eats blood and will cut him off from his people. [11]For the life of a creature is in the blood, and I have given it to you to make atonement for yourselves on the altar; it is the blood that makes atonement for one's life. [12]Therefore I say to the Israelites, "None of you may eat blood, nor may an alien living among you eat blood."

[13]" 'Any Israelite or any alien living among you who hunts any animal or bird that may be eaten must drain out the blood and cover it with earth, [14]because the life of every creature is its blood. That is why I have said to the Israelites, "You must not eat the blood of any creature, because the life of every creature is its blood; anyone who eats it must be cut off."

[15]" 'Anyone, whether native-born or alien, who eats anything found dead or torn by wild animals must wash his clothes and bathe with water, and he will be ceremonially unclean till evening; then he will be clean. [16]But if he does not wash his clothes and bathe himself, he will be held responsible.' "

Unlawful Sexual Relations

18 The LORD said to Moses, [2]"Speak to the Israelites and say to them: 'I am the LORD your God. [3]You must not do as they do in Egypt, where you used to live, and you must not do as they do in the land of Canaan, where I am bringing you. Do not follow their practices. [4]You must obey my laws and be careful to follow my decrees. I am the LORD your God. [5]Keep my decrees and laws, for the man who obeys them will live by them. I am the LORD.

[6]" 'No-one is to approach any close relative to have sexual relations. I am the LORD.

18:6 Experience showed that sex with close relatives resulted in physical weakness in the children. It also demonstrated that open, happy family life is only possible when there is no question of sexual relations between any but the married couples in a household. When taboos against such relationships break down, enormous misery can result, as in cases of child abuse.

---

[7]" 'Do not dishonour your father by having sexual relations with your mother. She is your mother; do not have relations with her.

[8]" 'Do not have sexual relations with your father's wife; that would dishonour your father.

[9]" 'Do not have sexual relations with your sister, either your father's daughter or your mother's daughter, whether she was born in the same home or elsewhere.

[10]" 'Do not have sexual relations with your son's daughter or your daughter's daughter; that would dishonour you.

[11]" 'Do not have sexual relations with the daughter of your father's wife, born to your father; she is your sister.

[12]" 'Do not have sexual relations with your father's sister; she is your father's close relative.

[13]" 'Do not have sexual relations with your mother's sister, because she is your mother's close relative.

[14]" 'Do not dishonour your father's brother by approaching his wife to have sexual relations; she is your aunt.

[15]" 'Do not have sexual relations with your daughter-in-law. She is your son's wife; do not have relations with her.

[16]" 'Do not have sexual relations with your brother's wife; that would dishonour your brother.

[17]" 'Do not have sexual relations with both a woman and her daughter. Do not have sexual relations with either her son's daughter or her daughter's daughter; they are her close relatives. That is wickedness.

[18]" 'Do not take your wife's sister as a rival wife and have sexual relations with her while your wife is living.

[19]" 'Do not approach a woman to have sexual relations during the uncleanness of her monthly period.

[20]" 'Do not have sexual relations with your neighbour's wife and defile yourself with her.

[21]" 'Do not give any of your children to be sacrificed[a] to Molech, for you must not profane the name of your God. I am the LORD.

[22]" 'Do not lie with a man as one lies with a woman; that is detestable.

[23]" 'Do not have sexual relations with an animal and defile yourself with it. A woman must not present herself to an animal to have sexual relations with it; that is a perversion.

[24]" 'Do not defile yourselves in any of these ways, because this is how the nations that I am going to drive out before you became defiled. [25]Even the land was defiled; so I punished it for its sin, and the land vomited out its inhabitants. [26]But you must keep my decrees and my laws. The native-born and the aliens living among you must not do any of these detestable things, [27]for all these things were done by the people who lived in the land before you, and the land became defiled. [28]And if you defile the land, it will vomit you out as it vomited out the nations that were before you.

[29]" 'Everyone who does any of these detestable things — such persons must be cut off from their people. [30]Keep my requirements and do not follow any of the detestable customs that were practised before you came and do not defile yourselves with them. I am the LORD your God.' "

[c]7 Or *demons*   [a]21 Or *to be passed through the fire*

Various Laws

19 The LORD said to Moses, [2]"Speak to the entire assembly of Israel and say to them: 'Be holy because I, the LORD your God, am holy.

[3]" 'Each of you must respect his mother and father, and you must observe my Sabbaths. I am the LORD your God.

[4]" 'Do not turn to idols or make gods of cast metal for yourselves. I am the LORD your God.

[5]" 'When you sacrifice a fellowship offering[a] to the LORD, sacrifice it in such a way that it will be accepted on your behalf. [6]It shall be eaten on the day you sacrifice it or on the next day; anything left over until the third day must be burned up. [7]If any of it is eaten on the third day, it is impure and will not be accepted. [8]Whoever eats it will be held responsible because he has desecrated what is holy to the LORD; that person must be cut off from his people.

19:8   Obeying many of these laws does not have any obvious reward. They are for the protection of the poor and powerless. The command to love your neighbour as yourself shows what the point of the law often is. If there is common concern for the welfare of others, everybody can be happy. As always, Leviticus declares that it is because God cares in this way that he demands such behaviour from his people.

---

[9]" 'When you reap the harvest of your land, do not reap to the very edges of your field or gather the gleanings of your harvest. [10]Do not go over your vineyard a second time or pick up the grapes that have fallen. Leave them for the poor and the alien. I am the LORD your God.

[11]" 'Do not steal.

" 'Do not lie.

" 'Do not deceive one another.

[12]" 'Do not swear falsely by my name and so profane the name of your God. I am the LORD.

[13]" 'Do not defraud your neighbour or rob him.

" 'Do not hold back the wages of a hired man overnight.

[14]" 'Do not curse the deaf or put a stumbling-block in front of the blind, but fear your God. I am the LORD.

[15]" 'Do not pervert justice; do not show partiality to the poor or favouritism to the great, but judge your neighbour fairly.

[16]" 'Do not go about spreading slander among your people.

" 'Do not do anything that endangers your neighbour's life. I am the LORD.

[17]" 'Do not hate your brother in your heart. Rebuke your neighbour frankly so that you will not share in his guilt.

[18]" 'Do not seek revenge or bear a grudge against one of your people, but love your neighbour as yourself. I am the LORD.

[19]" 'Keep my decrees.

" 'Do not mate different kinds of animals.

" 'Do not plant your field with two kinds of seed.

" 'Do not wear clothing woven of two kinds of material.

[20]" 'If a man sleeps with a woman who is a slave girl promised to another man but who has not been ransomed or given her freedom, there must be due punishment. Yet they are not to be put to death, because she had not been freed. [21]The man, however, must bring a ram to the entrance to the Tent of Meeting for a guilt offering to the LORD. [22]With the ram of the guilt offering the priest is to make atonement for him before the LORD for the sin he has committed, and his sin will be forgiven.

[23]" 'When you enter the land and plant any kind of fruit tree, regard its fruit as forbidden.[b] For three years you are to consider it forbidden;[b] it must not be eaten. [24]In the fourth year all its fruit will be holy, an offering of praise to the LORD. [25]But in the fifth year you may eat its fruit. In this way your harvest will be increased. I am the LORD your God.

[26]" 'Do not eat any meat with the blood still in it.

" 'Do not practise divination or sorcery.

[27]" 'Do not cut the hair at the sides of your head or clip off the edges of your beard.

[28]" 'Do not cut your bodies for the dead or put tattoo marks on yourselves. I am the LORD.

[29]" 'Do not degrade your daughter by making her a prostitute, or the land will turn to prostitution and be filled with wickedness.

[30]" 'Observe my Sabbaths and have reverence for my sanctuary. I am the LORD.

[31]" 'Do not turn to mediums or seek out spiritists, for you will be defiled by them. I am the LORD your God.

[32]" 'Rise in the presence of the aged, show respect for the elderly and revere your God. I am the LORD.

[33]" 'When an alien lives with you in your land, do not ill-treat him. [34]The alien living with you must be treated as one of your native-born. Love him as yourself, for you were aliens in Egypt. I am the LORD your God.

[35]" 'Do not use dishonest standards when measuring length, weight or quantity. [36]Use honest scales and honest weights, an honest ephah[c] and an honest hin.[d] I am the LORD your God, who brought you out of Egypt.

[37]" 'Keep all my decrees and all my laws and follow them. I am the LORD.' "

Punishments for Sin

20 The LORD said to Moses, [2]"Say to the Israelites: 'Any Israelite or any alien living in Israel who gives[a] any of his children to Molech must be put to death. The people of the community are to stone him. [3]I will set my face against that man and I will cut him off from his people; for by giving his children to Molech, he has defiled my sanctuary and profaned my holy name. [4]If the people of the community close their

---

a5 Traditionally peace offering   *b23 Hebrew* uncircumcised   *c36 An ephah was a dry measure.*
d36 A hin was a liquid measure.   *a2 Or* sacrifices; *also in verses 3 and 4*

eyes when that man gives one of his children to Molech and they fail to put him to death, ⁵I will set my face against that man and his family and will cut off from their people both him and all who follow him in prostituting themselves to Molech.

⁶" 'I will set my face against the person who turns to mediums and spiritists to prostitute himself by following them, and I will cut him off from his people.

⁷" 'Consecrate yourselves and be holy, because I am the LORD your God. ⁸Keep my decrees and follow them. I am the LORD, who makes you holy.ᵇ

⁹" 'If anyone curses his father or mother, he must be put to death. He has cursed his father or his mother, and his blood will be on his own head.

¹⁰" 'If a man commits adultery with another man's wife—with the wife of his neighbour—both the adulterer and the adulteress must be put to death.

¹¹" 'If a man sleeps with his father's wife, he has dishonoured his father. Both the man and the woman must be put to death; their blood will be on their own heads.

¹²" 'If a man sleeps with his daughter-in-law, both of them must be put to death. What they have done is a perversion; their blood will be on their own heads.

¹³" 'If a man lies with a man as one lies with a woman, both of them have done what is detestable. They must be put to death; their blood will be on their own heads.

¹⁴" 'If a man marries both a woman and her mother, it is wicked. Both he and they must be burned in the fire, so that no wickedness will be among you.

¹⁵" 'If a man has sexual relations with an animal, he must be put to death, and you must kill the animal.

¹⁶" 'If a woman approaches an animal to have sexual relations with it, kill both the woman and the animal. They must be put to death; their blood will be on their own heads.

¹⁷" 'If a man marries his sister, the daughter of either his father or his mother, and they have sexual relations, it is a disgrace. They must be cut off before the eyes of their people. He has dishonoured his sister and will be held responsible.

¹⁸" 'If a man lies with a woman during her monthly period and has sexual relations with her, he has exposed the source of her flow, and she has also uncovered it. Both of them must be cut off from their people.

¹⁹" 'Do not have sexual relations with the sister of either your mother or your father, for that would dishonour a close relative; both of you would be held responsible.

²⁰" 'If a man sleeps with his aunt, he has dishonoured his uncle. They will be held responsible; they will die childless.

²¹" 'If a man marries his brother's wife, it is an act of impurity; he has dishonoured his brother. They will be childless.

²²" 'Keep all my decrees and laws and follow them, so that the land where I am bringing you to live may not vomit you out. ²³You must not live according to the customs of the nations I am going to drive out before

you. Because they did all these things, I abhorred them. ²⁴But I said to you, "You will possess their land; I will give it to you as an inheritance, a land flowing with milk and honey." I am the LORD your God, who has set you apart from the nations.

²⁵" 'You must therefore make a distinction between clean and unclean animals and between unclean and clean birds. Do not defile yourselves by any animal or bird or anything that moves along the ground—those which I have set apart as unclean for you. ²⁶You are to be holy to meᶜ because I, the LORD, am holy, and I have set you apart from the nations to be my own.

²⁷" 'A man or woman who is a medium or spiritist among you must be put to death. You are to stone them; their blood will be on their own heads.' "

20:27 These practices were common in Canaan, and never really died out. Saul got a witch to raise the spirit of the dead Samuel (1 Samuel 28:7–25). The fear and fatalism which go with such practices are destructive, whereas trust in God's care gives freedom and peace.

Rules for Priests

21 The LORD said to Moses, "Speak to the priests, the sons of Aaron, and say to them: 'A priest must not make himself ceremonially unclean for any of his people who die, ²except for a close relative, such as his mother or father, his son or daughter, his brother, ³or an unmarried sister who is dependent on him since she has no husband—for her he may make himself unclean. ⁴He must not make himself unclean for people related to him by marriage,ᵃ and so defile himself.

⁵" 'Priests must not shave their heads or shave off the edges of their beards or cut their bodies. ⁶They must be holy to their God and must not profane the name of their God. Because they present the offerings made to the LORD by fire, the food of their God, they are to be holy.

⁷" 'They must not marry women defiled by prostitution or divorced from their husbands, because priests are holy to their God. ⁸Regard them as holy, because they offer up the food of your God. Consider them holy, because I the LORD am holy—I who make you holy.ᵇ

⁹" 'If a priest's daughter defiles herself by becoming a prostitute, she disgraces her father; she must be burned in the fire.

¹⁰" 'The high priest, the one among his brothers who has had the anointing oil poured on his head and who has been ordained to wear the priestly garments, must not let his hair become unkemptᶜ or tear his clothes. ¹¹He must not enter a place where there is a dead body. He must not make himself unclean, even for his father or mother, ¹²nor leave the sanctuary of his God or desecrate it, because he has been dedicated by the anointing oil of his God. I am the LORD.

ᵇ8 Or who sanctifies you; or who sets you apart as holy　　ᶜ26 Or be my holy ones
ᵃ4 Or unclean as a leader among his people　　ᵇ8 Or who sanctify you; or who set you apart as holy
ᶜ10 Or not uncover his head

13" 'The woman he marries must be a virgin. 14He must not marry a widow, a divorced woman, or a woman defiled by prostitution, but only a virgin from his own people, 15so that he will not defile his offspring among his people. I am the LORD, who makes him holy.' " *d*

16The LORD said to Moses, 17"Say to Aaron: 'For the generations to come none of your descendants who has a defect may come near to offer the food of his God. 18No man who has any defect may come near: no man who is blind or lame, disfigured or deformed; 19no man with a crippled foot or hand, 20or who is hunchbacked or dwarfed, or who has any eye defect, or who has festering or running sores or damaged testicles. 21No descendant of Aaron the priest who has any defect is to come near to present the offerings made to the LORD by fire. He has a defect; he must not come near to offer the food of his God. 22He may eat the most holy food of his God, as well as the holy food; 23yet because of his defect, he must not go near the curtain or approach the altar, and so desecrate my sanctuary. I am the LORD, who makes them holy.' " *e*

24So Moses told this to Aaron and his sons and to all the Israelites.

22 The LORD said to Moses, 2"Tell Aaron and his sons to treat with respect the sacred offerings the Israelites consecrate to me, so that they will not profane my holy name. I am the LORD.

3"Say to them: 'For the generations to come, if any of your descendants is ceremonially unclean and yet comes near the sacred offerings that the Israelites consecrate to the LORD, that person must be cut off from my presence. I am the LORD.

4" 'If a descendant of Aaron has an infectious skin disease *a* or a bodily discharge, he may not eat the sacred offerings until he is cleansed. He will also be unclean if he touches something defiled by a corpse or by anyone who has an emission of semen, 5or if he touches any crawling thing that makes him unclean, or any person who makes him unclean, whatever the uncleanness may be. 6The one who touches any such thing will be unclean till evening. He must not eat any of the sacred offerings unless he has bathed himself with water. 7When the sun goes down, he will be clean, and after that he may eat the sacred offerings, for they are his food. 8He must not eat anything found dead or torn by wild animals, and so become unclean through it. I am the LORD.

9" 'The priests are to keep my requirements so that they do not become guilty and die for treating them with contempt. I am the LORD, who makes them holy. *b*

10" 'No-one outside a priest's family may eat the sacred offering, nor may the guest of a priest or his hired worker eat it. 11But if a priest buys a slave with money, or if a slave is born in his household, that slave may eat his food. 12If a priest's daughter marries anyone other than a priest, she may not eat any of the

sacred contributions. 13But if a priest's daughter becomes a widow or is divorced, yet has no children, and she returns to live in her father's house as in her youth, she may eat of her father's food. No unauthorised person, however, may eat any of it.

14" 'If anyone eats a sacred offering by mistake, he must make restitution to the priest for the offering and add a fifth of the value to it. 15The priests must not desecrate the sacred offerings the Israelites present to the LORD 16by allowing them to eat the sacred offerings and so bring upon them guilt requiring payment. I am the LORD, who makes them holy.' "

Unacceptable Sacrifices

17The LORD said to Moses, 18"Speak to Aaron and his sons and to all the Israelites and say to them: 'If any of you — either an Israelite or an alien living in Israel — presents a gift for a burnt offering to the LORD, either to fulfil a vow or as a freewill offering, 19you must present a male without defect from the cattle, sheep or goats in order that it may be accepted on your behalf. 20Do not bring anything with a defect, because it will not be accepted on your behalf. 21When anyone brings from the herd or flock a fellowship offering *c* to the LORD to fulfil a special vow or as a freewill offering, it must be without defect or blemish to be acceptable. 22Do not offer to the LORD the blind, the injured or the maimed, or anything with warts or festering or running sores. Do not place any of these on the altar as an offering made to the LORD by fire. 23You may, however, present as a freewill offering an ox *d* or a sheep that is deformed or stunted, but it will not be accepted in fulfilment of a vow. 24You must not offer to the LORD an animal whose testicles are bruised, crushed, torn or cut. You must not do this in your own land, 25and you must not accept such animals from the hand of a foreigner and offer them as the food of your God. They will not be accepted on your behalf, because they are deformed and have defects.' "

26The LORD said to Moses, 27"When a calf, a lamb or a goat is born, it is to remain with its mother for seven days. From the eighth day on, it will be acceptable as an offering made to the LORD by fire. 28Do not slaughter a cow or a sheep and its young on the same day.

29"When you sacrifice a thank-offering to the LORD, sacrifice it in such a way that it will be accepted on your behalf. 30It must be eaten that same day; leave none of it till morning. I am the LORD.

31"Keep my commands and follow them. I am the LORD. 32Do not profane my holy name. I must be acknowledged as holy by the Israelites. I am the LORD, who makes *e* you holy *f* 33and who brought you out of Egypt to be your God. I am the LORD."

23 The LORD said to Moses, 2"Speak to the Israelites and say to them: 'These are my appointed feasts, the appointed feasts of the LORD, which you are to proclaim as sacred assemblies.

---

d15 Or who sanctifies him; or who sets him apart as holy
a4 Traditionally leprosy; the Hebrew word was used for various diseases affecting the skin — not necessarily leprosy.
b9 Or who sanctifies them; or who sets them apart as holy; also in verse 16
d23 The Hebrew word can include both male and female.
f32 Or who sanctifies you; or who sets you apart as holy

e23 Or who sanctifies them; or who sets them apart as holy

c21 Traditionally peace offering
e32 Or made

The Sabbath

3" 'There are six days when you may work, but the seventh day is a Sabbath of rest, a day of sacred assembly. You are not to do any work; wherever you live, it is a Sabbath to the LORD.

The Passover and Unleavened Bread

4" 'These are the LORD's appointed feasts, the sacred assemblies you are to proclaim at their appointed times: 5The LORD's Passover begins at twilight on the fourteenth day of the first month. 6On the fifteenth day of that month the LORD's Feast of Unleavened Bread begins; for seven days you must eat bread made without yeast. 7On the first day hold a sacred assembly and do no regular work. 8For seven days present an offering made to the LORD by fire. And on the seventh day hold a sacred assembly and do no regular work.' "

Firstfruits

9The LORD said to Moses, 10"Speak to the Israelites and say to them: 'When you enter the land I am going to give you and you reap its harvest, bring to the priest a sheaf of the first grain you harvest. 11He is to wave the sheaf before the LORD so it will be accepted on your behalf; the priest is to wave it on the day after the Sabbath. 12On the day you wave the sheaf, you must sacrifice as a burnt offering to the LORD a lamb a year old without defect, 13together with its grain offering of two-tenths of an ephah*a* of fine flour mixed with oil — an offering made to the LORD by fire, a pleasing aroma — and its drink offering of a quarter of a hin*b* of wine. 14You must not eat any bread, or roasted or new grain, until the very day you bring this offering to your God. This is to be a lasting ordinance for the generations to come, wherever you live.

23:9 Every day belongs to God, but that is easier to remember if the year is punctuated with time specially set aside for him. Those days are a gift of the best of time just as a sacrifice was the gift of the best of the flock. During a festival the individual's faith is strengthened by being shared with others, there is time to enjoy worshipping God, and the community can review its commitment to following him.

Feast of Weeks

15" 'From the day after the Sabbath, the day you brought the sheaf of the wave offering, count off seven full weeks. 16Count off fifty days up to the day after the seventh Sabbath, and then present an offering of new grain to the LORD. 17From wherever you live, bring two loaves made of two-tenths of an ephah of fine flour, baked with yeast, as a wave offering of firstfruits to the LORD. 18Present with this bread seven male lambs, each a year old and without defect, one young bull and two rams. They will be a burnt offering to the LORD, together with their grain offerings and drink offerings — an offering made by fire, an aroma pleasing to the LORD. 19Then sacrifice one male goat for a sin offering and two lambs, each a year old, for a fellowship offering.*c* 20The priest is to wave the two lambs before the LORD as a wave offering, together with the bread of the firstfruits. They are a sacred offering to the LORD for the priest. 21On that same day you are to proclaim a sacred assembly and do no regular work. This is to be a lasting ordinance for the generations to come, wherever you live.

22" 'When you reap the harvest of your land, do not reap to the very edges of your field or gather the gleanings of your harvest. Leave them for the poor and the alien. I am the LORD your God.' "

Feast of Trumpets

23The LORD said to Moses, 24"Say to the Israelites: 'On the first day of the seventh month you are to have a day of rest, a sacred assembly commemorated with trumpet blasts. 25Do no regular work, but present an offering made to the LORD by fire.' "

Day of Atonement

26The LORD said to Moses, 27"The tenth day of this seventh month is the Day of Atonement. Hold a sacred assembly and deny yourselves,*d* and present an offering made to the LORD by fire. 28Do no work on that day, because it is the Day of Atonement, when atonement is made for you before the LORD your God. 29Anyone who does not deny himself on that day must be cut off from his people. 30I will destroy from among his people anyone who does any work on that day. 31You shall do no work at all. This is to be a lasting ordinance for the generations to come, wherever you live. 32It is a sabbath of rest for you, and you must deny yourselves. From the evening of the ninth day of the month until the following evening you are to observe your sabbath."

Feast of Tabernacles

33The LORD said to Moses, 34"Say to the Israelites: 'On the fifteenth day of the seventh month the LORD's Feast of Tabernacles begins, and it lasts for seven days. 35The first day is a sacred assembly; do no regular work. 36For seven days present offerings made to the LORD by fire, and on the eighth day hold a sacred assembly and present an offering made to the LORD by fire. It is the closing assembly; do no regular work.

37(" 'These are the LORD's appointed feasts, which you are to proclaim as sacred assemblies for bringing offerings made to the LORD by fire — the burnt offerings and grain offerings, sacrifices and drink offerings required for each day. 38These offerings are in addition to those for the LORD's Sabbaths and*e* in addition to your gifts and whatever you have vowed and all the freewill offerings you give to the LORD.)

---

a13 That is, probably about 7½ pints (about 4.5 litres); also in verse 17
c19 Traditionally *peace offering*   *d27* Or *and fast*; also in verses 29 and 32
e38 Or *These feasts are in addition to the LORD's Sabbaths, and these offerings are*

b13 That is, probably about 1½ pints (about 1 litre)

³⁹" 'So beginning with the fifteenth day of the seventh month, after you have gathered the crops of the land, celebrate the festival to the Lord for seven days; the first day is a day of rest, and the eighth day also is a day of rest. ⁴⁰On the first day you are to take choice fruit from the trees, and palm fronds, leafy branches and poplars, and rejoice before the Lord your God for seven days. ⁴¹Celebrate this as a festival to the Lord for seven days each year. This is to be a lasting ordinance for the generations to come; celebrate it in the seventh month. ⁴²Live in booths for seven days: All native-born Israelites are to live in booths ⁴³so that your descendants will know that I made the Israelites live in booths when I brought them out of Egypt. I am the Lord your God.' "

⁴⁴So Moses announced to the Israelites the appointed feasts of the Lord.

Oil and Bread Set Before the Lord

24 The Lord said to Moses, ²"Command the Israelites to bring you clear oil of pressed olives for the light so that the lamps may be kept burning continually. ³Outside the curtain of the Testimony in the Tent of Meeting, Aaron is to tend the lamps before the Lord from evening till morning, continually. This is to be a lasting ordinance for the generations to come. ⁴The lamps on the pure gold lampstand before the Lord must be tended continually.

⁵"Take fine flour and bake twelve loaves of bread, using two-tenths of an ephah*a* for each loaf. ⁶Set them in two rows, six in each row, on the table of pure gold before the Lord. ⁷Along each row put some pure incense as a memorial portion to represent the bread and to be an offering made to the Lord by fire. ⁸This bread is to be set out before the Lord regularly, Sabbath after Sabbath, on behalf of the Israelites, as a lasting covenant. ⁹It belongs to Aaron and his sons, who are to eat it in a holy place, because it is a most holy part of their regular share of the offerings made to the Lord by fire."

A Blasphemer Stoned

¹⁰Now the son of an Israelite mother and an Egyptian father went out among the Israelites, and a fight broke out in the camp between him and an Israelite. ¹¹The son of the Israelite woman blasphemed the Name with a curse; so they brought him to Moses. (His mother's name was Shelomith, the daughter of Dibri the Danite.) ¹²They put him in custody until the will of the Lord should be made clear to them.

¹³Then the Lord said to Moses: ¹⁴"Take the blasphemer outside the camp. All those who heard him are to lay their hands on his head, and the entire assembly is to stone him. ¹⁵Say to the Israelites: 'If anyone curses his God, he will be held responsible; ¹⁶anyone who blasphemes the name of the Lord must be put to death. The entire assembly must stone him. Whether an alien or native-born, when he blasphemes the Name, he must be put to death.

¹⁷" 'If anyone takes the life of a human being, he must be put to death. ¹⁸Anyone who takes the life of

someone's animal must make restitution—life for life. ¹⁹If anyone injures his neighbour, whatever he has done must be done to him: ²⁰fracture for fracture, eye for eye, tooth for tooth. As he has injured the other, so he is to be injured. ²¹Whoever kills an animal must make restitution, but whoever kills a man must be put to death. ²²You are to have the same law for the alien and the native-born. I am the Lord your God.' "

24:20   Vengeance for injuries could get out of hand. Longstanding blood feuds could cause terror over many years. This law was an advanced one for its time, limiting vengeance to an exact retaliation. Jesus took things much further, and made quite a startling claim. He said that far from taking revenge, we should show concern for our enemies just as we do for our friends.

---

²³Then Moses spoke to the Israelites, and they took the blasphemer outside the camp and stoned him. The Israelites did as the Lord commanded Moses.

The Sabbath Year

25 The Lord said to Moses on Mount Sinai, ²"Speak to the Israelites and say to them: 'When you enter the land I am going to give you, the land itself must observe a sabbath to the Lord. ³For six years sow your fields, and for six years prune your vineyards and gather their crops. ⁴But in the seventh year the land is to have a sabbath of rest, a sabbath to the Lord. Do not sow your fields or prune your vineyards. ⁵Do not reap what grows of itself or harvest the grapes of your untended vines. The land is to have a year of rest. ⁶Whatever the land yields during the sabbath year will be food for you—for yourself, your manservant and maidservant, and the hired worker and temporary resident who live among you, ⁷as well as for your livestock and the wild animals in your land. Whatever the land produces may be eaten.

The Year of Jubilee

⁸" 'Count off seven sabbaths of years—seven times seven years—so that the seven sabbaths of years amount to a period of forty-nine years. ⁹Then have the trumpet sounded everywhere on the tenth day of the seventh month; on the Day of Atonement sound the trumpet throughout your land. ¹⁰Consecrate the fiftieth year and proclaim liberty throughout the land to all its inhabitants. It shall be a jubilee for you; each one of you is to return to his family property and each to his own clan. ¹¹The fiftieth year shall be a jubilee for you; do not sow and do not reap what grows of itself or harvest the untended vines. ¹²For it is a jubilee and is to be holy for you; eat only what is taken directly from the fields.

¹³" 'In this Year of Jubilee everyone is to return to his own property.

¹⁴" 'If you sell land to one of your countrymen or buy

a5 That is, probably about 7½ pints (about 4.5 litres)

any from him, do not take advantage of each other. [15]You are to buy from your countryman on the basis of the number of years since the Jubilee. And he is to sell to you on the basis of the number of years left for harvesting crops. [16]When the years are many, you are to increase the price, and when the years are few, you are to decrease the price, because what he is really selling you is the number of crops. [17]Do not take advantage of each other, but fear your God. I am the LORD your God.

[18]" 'Follow my decrees and be careful to obey my laws, and you will live safely in the land. [19]Then the land will yield its fruit, and you will eat your fill and live there in safety. [20]You may ask, "What will we eat in the seventh year if we do not plant or harvest our crops?" [21]I will send you such a blessing in the sixth year that the land will yield enough for three years. [22]While you plant during the eighth year, you will eat from the old crop and will continue to eat from it until the harvest of the ninth year comes in.

[23]" 'The land must not be sold permanently, because the land is mine and you are but aliens and my tenants. [24]Throughout the country that you hold as a possession, you must provide for the redemption of the land.

[25]" 'If one of your countrymen becomes poor and sells some of his property, his nearest relative is to come and redeem what his countryman has sold. [26]If, however, a man has no-one to redeem it for him but he himself prospers and acquires sufficient means to redeem it, [27]he is to determine the value for the years since he sold it and refund the balance to the man to whom he sold it; he can then go back to his own property. [28]But if he does not acquire the means to repay him, what he sold will remain in the possession of the buyer until the Year of Jubilee. It will be returned in the Jubilee, and he can then go back to his property.

[29]" 'If a man sells a house in a walled city, he retains the right of redemption a full year after its sale. During that time he may redeem it. [30]If it is not redeemed before a full year has passed, the house in the walled city shall belong permanently to the buyer and his descendants. It is not to be returned in the Jubilee. [31]But houses in villages without walls round them are to be considered as open country. They can be redeemed, and they are to be returned in the Jubilee.

[32]" 'The Levites always have the right to redeem their houses in the Levitical towns, which they possess. [33]So the property of the Levites is redeemable — that is, a house sold in any town they hold — and is to be returned in the Jubilee, because the houses in the towns of the Levites are their property among the Israelites. [34]But the pasture-land belonging to their towns must not be sold; it is their permanent possession.

[35]" 'If one of your countrymen becomes poor and is unable to support himself among you, help him as you would an alien or a temporary resident, so that he can continue to live among you. [36]Do not take interest of any kind[a] from him, but fear your God, so that your countryman may continue to live among you. [37]You must not lend him money at interest or sell him food

at a profit. [38]I am the LORD your God, who brought you out of Egypt to give you the land of Canaan and to be your God.

[39]" 'If one of your countrymen becomes poor among you and sells himself to you, do not make him work as a slave. [40]He is to be treated as a hired worker or a temporary resident among you; he is to work for you until the Year of Jubilee. [41]Then he and his children are to be released, and he will go back to his own clan and to the property of his forefathers. [42]Because the Israelites are my servants, whom I brought out of Egypt, they must not be sold as slaves. [43]Do not rule over them ruthlessly, but fear your God.

[44]" 'Your male and female slaves are to come from the nations around you; from them you may buy slaves. [45]You may also buy some of the temporary residents living among you and members of their clans born in your country, and they will become your property. [46]You can will them to your children as inherited property and can make them slaves for life, but you must not rule over your fellow Israelites ruthlessly.

[47]" 'If an alien or a temporary resident among you becomes rich and one of your countrymen becomes poor and sells himself to the alien living among you or to a member of the alien's clan, [48]he retains the right of redemption after he has sold himself. One of his relatives may redeem him: [49]An uncle or a cousin or any blood-relative in his clan may redeem him. Or if he prospers, he may redeem himself. [50]He and his buyer are to count the time from the year he sold himself up to the Year of Jubilee. The price for his release is to be based on the rate paid to a hired man for that number of years. [51]If many years remain, he must pay for his redemption a larger share of the price paid for him. [52]If only a few years remain until the Year of Jubilee, he is to compute that and pay for his redemption accordingly. [53]He is to be treated as a man hired from year to year; you must see to it that his owner does not rule over him ruthlessly.

[54]" 'Even if he is not redeemed in any of these ways, he and his children are to be released in the Year of Jubilee, [55]for the Israelites belong to me as servants. They are my servants, whom I brought out of Egypt. I am the LORD your God.

Reward for Obedience

26 " 'Do not make idols or set up an image or a sacred stone for yourselves, and do not place a carved stone in your land to bow down before it. I am the LORD your God.

[2]" 'Observe my Sabbaths and have reverence for my sanctuary. I am the LORD.

[3]" 'If you follow my decrees and are careful to obey my commands, [4]I will send you rain in its season, and the ground will yield its crops and the trees of the field their fruit. [5]Your threshing will continue until grape harvest and the grape harvest will continue until planting, and you will eat all the food you want and live in safety in your land.

[a]36 Or take excessive interest; similarly in verse 37

⁶" 'I will grant peace in the land, and you will lie down and no-one will make you afraid. I will remove savage beasts from the land, and the sword will not pass through your country. ⁷You will pursue your enemies, and they will fall by the sword before you. ⁸Five of you will chase a hundred, and a hundred of you will chase ten thousand, and your enemies will fall by the sword before you.

⁹" 'I will look on you with favour and make you fruitful and increase your numbers, and I will keep my covenant with you. ¹⁰You will still be eating last year's harvest when you will have to move it out to make room for the new. ¹¹I will put my dwelling-placeᵃ among you, and I will not abhor you. ¹²I will walk among you and be your God, and you will be my people. ¹³I am the LORD your God, who brought you out of Egypt so that you would no longer be slaves to the Egyptians; I broke the bars of your yoke and enabled you to walk with heads held high.

Punishment for Disobedience

¹⁴" 'But if you will not listen to me and carry out all these commands, ¹⁵and if you reject my decrees and abhor my laws and fail to carry out all my commands and so violate my covenant, ¹⁶then I will do this to you: I will bring upon you sudden terror, wasting diseases and fever that will destroy your sight and drain away your life. You will plant seed in vain, because your enemies will eat it. ¹⁷I will set my face against you so that you will be defeated by your enemies; those who hate you will rule over you, and you will flee even when no-one is pursuing you.

¹⁸" 'If after all this you will not listen to me, I will punish you for your sins seven times over. ¹⁹I will break down your stubborn pride and make the sky above you like iron and the ground beneath you like bronze. ²⁰Your strength will be spent in vain, because your soil will not yield its crops, nor will the trees of the land yield their fruit.

²¹" 'If you remain hostile towards me and refuse to listen to me, I will multiply your afflictions seven times over, as your sins deserve. ²²I will send wild animals against you, and they will rob you of your children, destroy your cattle and make you so few in number that your roads will be deserted.

²³" 'If in spite of these things you do not accept my correction but continue to be hostile towards me, ²⁴I myself will be hostile towards you and will afflict you for your sins seven times over. ²⁵And I will bring the sword upon you to avenge the breaking of the covenant. When you withdraw into your cities, I will send a plague among you, and you will be given into enemy hands. ²⁶When I cut off your supply of bread, ten women will be able to bake your bread in one oven, and they will dole out the bread by weight. You will eat, but you will not be satisfied.

²⁷" 'If in spite of this you still do not listen to me but continue to be hostile towards me, ²⁸then in my anger I will be hostile towards you, and I myself will punish you for your sins seven times over. ²⁹You will eat the flesh of your sons and the flesh of your daughters. ³⁰I will destroy your high places, cut down your incense altars and pile your dead bodies on the lifeless forms of your idols, and I will abhor you. ³¹I will turn your cities into ruins and lay waste your sanctuaries, and I will take no delight in the pleasing aroma of your offerings. ³²I will lay waste the land, so that your enemies who live there will be appalled. ³³I will scatter you among the nations and will draw out my sword and pursue you. Your land will be laid waste, and your cities will lie in ruins. ³⁴Then the land will enjoy its sabbath years all the time that it lies desolate and you are in the country of your enemies; then the land will rest and enjoy its sabbaths. ³⁵All the time that it lies desolate, the land will have the rest it did not have during the sabbaths you lived in it.

³⁶" 'As for those of you who are left, I will make their hearts so fearful in the lands of their enemies that the sound of a wind-blown leaf will put them to flight. They will run as though fleeing from the sword, and they will fall, even though no-one is pursuing them. ³⁷They will stumble over one another as though fleeing from the sword, even though no-one is pursuing them. So you will not be able to stand before your enemies. ³⁸You will perish among the nations; the land of your enemies will devour you. ³⁹Those of you who are left will waste away in the lands of their enemies because of their sins; also because of their fathers' sins they will waste away.

⁴⁰" 'But if they will confess their sins and the sins of their fathers—their treachery against me and their hostility towards me, ⁴¹which made me hostile towards them so that I sent them into the land of their enemies—then when their uncircumcised hearts are humbled and they pay for their sin, ⁴²I will remember my covenant with Jacob and my covenant with Isaac and my covenant with Abraham, and I will remember the land. ⁴³For the land will be deserted by them and will enjoy its sabbaths while it lies desolate without them. They will pay for their sins because they rejected my laws and abhorred my decrees. ⁴⁴Yet in spite of this, when they are in the land of their enemies, I will not reject them or abhor them so as to destroy them completely, breaking my covenant with them. I am the LORD their God. ⁴⁵But for their sake I will remember the covenant with their ancestors whom I brought out of Egypt in the sight of the nations to be their God. I am the LORD.' "

26:45   When the Israelites were in exile from the promised land it would have been easy to despair. Leviticus constantly reminds its readers that God is perfect, not only in justice but also in mercy and faithfulness. He is his own guarantee that he will fulfil his promises.

---

⁴⁶These are the decrees, the laws and the regulations that the LORD established on Mount Sinai between himself and the Israelites through Moses.

ᵃ11 Or my tabernacle

Redeeming What Is the LORD's

27 The LORD said to Moses, [2]"Speak to the Israelites and say to them: 'If anyone makes a special vow to dedicate persons to the LORD by giving equivalent values, [3]set the value of a male between the ages of twenty and sixty at fifty shekels[a] of silver, according to the sanctuary shekel; [b] [4]and if it is a female, set her value at thirty shekels. [c] [5]If it is a person between the ages of five and twenty, set the value of a male at twenty shekels[d] and of a female at ten shekels. [e] [6]If it is a person between one month and five years, set the value of a male at five shekels[f] of silver and that of a female at three shekels[g] of silver. [7]If it is a person sixty years old or more, set the value of a male at fifteen shekels[h] and of a female at ten shekels. [8]If anyone making the vow is too poor to pay the specified amount, he is to present the person to the priest, who will set the value for him according to what the man making the vow can afford.

[9]"If what he vowed is an animal that is acceptable as an offering to the LORD, such an animal given to the LORD becomes holy. [10]He must not exchange it or substitute a good one for a bad one, or a bad one for a good one; if he should substitute one animal for another, both it and the substitute become holy. [11]If what he vowed is a ceremonially unclean animal—one that is not acceptable as an offering to the LORD—the animal must be presented to the priest, [12]who will judge its quality as good or bad. Whatever value the priest then sets, that is what it will be. [13]If the owner wishes to redeem the animal, he must add a fifth to its value.

[14]"If a man dedicates his house as something holy to the LORD, the priest will judge its quality as good or bad. Whatever value the priest then sets, so it will remain. [15]If the man who dedicates his house redeems it, he must add a fifth to its value, and the house will again become his.

[16]"If a man dedicates to the LORD part of his family land, its value is to be set according to the amount of seed required for it—fifty shekels of silver to a homer[i] of barley seed. [17]If he dedicates his field during the Year of Jubilee, the value that has been set remains. [18]But if he dedicates his field after the Jubilee, the priest will determine the value according to the number of years that remain until the next Year of Jubilee, and its set value will be reduced. [19]If the man who dedicates the field wishes to redeem it, he must add a fifth to its value, and the field will again become his. [20]If, however, he does not redeem the field, or if he has sold it to someone else, it can never be redeemed. [21]When the field is released in the Jubilee, it will become holy, like a field devoted to the LORD; it will become the property of the priests. [j]

[22]"If a man dedicates to the LORD a field he has bought, which is not part of his family land, [23]the priest will determine its value up to the Year of Jubilee, and the man must pay its value on that day as something holy to the LORD. [24]In the Year of Jubilee the field will revert to the person from whom he bought it, the one whose land it was. [25]Every value is to be set according to the sanctuary shekel, twenty gerahs to the shekel.

[26]"No-one, however, may dedicate the firstborn of an animal, since the firstborn already belongs to the LORD; whether an ox[k] or a sheep, it is the LORD's. [27]If it is one of the unclean animals, he may buy it back at its set value, adding a fifth of the value to it. If he does not redeem it, it is to be sold at its set value.

[28]"But nothing that a man owns and devotes[l] to the LORD—whether man or animal or family land—may be sold or redeemed; everything so devoted is most holy to the LORD.

[29]"No person devoted to destruction[m] may be ransomed; he must be put to death.

[30]"A tithe of everything from the land, whether grain from the soil or fruit from the trees, belongs to the LORD; it is holy to the LORD. [31]If a man redeems any of his tithe, he must add a fifth of the value to it. [32]The entire tithe of the herd and flock—every tenth animal that passes under the shepherd's rod—will be holy to the LORD. [33]He must not pick out the good from the bad or make any substitution. If he does make a substitution, both the animal and its substitute become holy and cannot be redeemed.' "

[34]These are the commands the LORD gave Moses on Mount Sinai for the Israelites.

---

a3 That is, about 1¼ pounds (about 0.6 kilogram); also in verse 16   *b3* That is, about ⅖ ounce (about 11.5 grams); also in verse 25
c4 That is, about 12 ounces (about 0.3 kilogram)   *d5* That is, about 8 ounces (about 0.2 kilogram)
e5 That is, about 4 ounces (about 115 grams); also in verse 7   *f6* That is, about 2 ounces (about 55 grams)
g6 That is, about 1¼ ounces (about 35 grams)   *h7* That is, about 6 ounces (about 170 grams)
i16 That is, probably about 6 bushels (about 220 litres)   *j21* Or *priest*
k26 The Hebrew word can include both male and female.
l28 The Hebrew term refers to the irrevocable giving over of things or persons to the LORD.
m29 The Hebrew term refers to the irrevocable giving over of things or persons to the LORD, often by totally destroying them.

Numbers

From a Rabble to a Great Nation

In Egypt there had been a group of slaves of Jewish descent who were dispirited and disaffected. They were held together only by their memories of a common ancestor, Joseph, who had a vision of a golden future in a promised land. In Palestine there was to be a nation possessing the land and united by their worship of God. The rabble had to become the nation. The book of Numbers records that transfiguration. It tells of the long time the process took — forty years (in other words, a generation) — and how it took place in the wilderness. The exodus was the greatest way God had shown himself in a historical act. In the wilderness he had shown himself just as clearly, but in the normal daily events of the group and in the lives of individuals. The exodus has become a symbol of God setting his people free so they can worship him fully. The wilderness is a picture of that life being lived out with all its successes and failures.

Beginning With a Census

At the beginning and end of the account the people are numbered for a census, hence the name of the book. The numbers given are absolutely huge. If it is an exaggeration, it expresses faith in the promises of God and a belief in his power to make those promises happen. In fact there was never a time when the twelve tribes united peacefully and sinlessly in worshipping God in Palestine. When, years later, the nation had been defeated, Jerusalem destroyed, and its people taken into exile, the people thought back to the wilderness period. They had lost the land that was promised. They needed to learn how to regain it, so they looked for inspiration to the time when their ancestors were trying to reach the land and they made the ancient struggles a pattern for their own.

Blunt Honesty

In all this period, Moses was at the centre of events. He was the channel through which God's words reached the people, so through him they learned what God is like. We are given a realistic picture of Moses, not an idealized one, so we are shown that his relationship with God was honest, and at times outspoken. None of the prophets tried to hide their feelings from God, perhaps because they were aware that he knows everything. In chapter 11 the people tired of the manna which they were once so grateful for. God was angry, and Moses responded irritably and with resentment to God. He wanted to throw the responsibility for the people back on God, and reckoned death would be preferable to dealing single-handedly with the troublesome Israelites. As is so often the case, he found that his problem didn't require a miracle to solve it, just simple management. He only needed to delegate responsibility and relieve the pressure on himself.

Close Encounters

Despite outbursts like this, Moses was very intimate with God. The Israelites were aware that their sinfulness put a great distance between them and the holiness of God. They recognized that sometimes special men and women bridged the divide, and that through such a person they felt closer to God and understood him better. In the case of Moses they described this by saying that when he had been in God's presence his face shone. On one occasion God makes Moses' privileged position clear himself.

"With him I speak face to face,
    clearly and not in riddles;
    he sees the form of the LORD."

(Numbers 12:8)

Something Important to Learn

Through Moses the Israelites learned something important about God. They knew that he was holy and that they must try to be like him. Because his holiness included goodness he required them to love their neighbours. Bitter experience had taught them that when they did wrong, their failures brought unhappiness to them and to others. They took this to be punishment from God. When (Numbers 13) the first spies went into Canaan, they told the people that its inhabitants were too strong to be conquered. The people lost all faith in God, and he was determined to destroy them. Moses found himself pleading for them and, as he realized that he cared for the people, he learned that God did too. God is not only good, but also loving, and that makes him merciful. Mercy is not weak. Only God himself can set aside his absolute laws of justice and choose to forgive people who are sorry. As Moses said, "Now may the Lord's strength be displayed, just as you have declared: 'The LORD is slow to anger, abounding in love . . .' In accordance with your great love, forgive the sin of these people." (Numbers 14:17–19)

The Census

1 The LORD spoke to Moses in the Tent of Meeting in the Desert of Sinai on the first day of the second month of the second year after the Israelites came out of Egypt. He said: ² "Take a census of the whole Israelite community by their clans and families, listing every man by name, one by one. ³You and Aaron are to number by their divisions all the men in Israel twenty years old or more who are able to serve in the army. ⁴One man from each tribe, each the head of his family, is to help you. ⁵These are the names of the men who are to assist you:

from Reuben, Elizur son of Shedeur;
⁶from Simeon, Shelumiel son of Zurishaddai;
⁷from Judah, Nahshon son of Amminadab;
⁸from Issachar, Nethanel son of Zuar;
⁹from Zebulun, Eliab son of Helon;
¹⁰from the sons of Joseph:
    from Ephraim, Elishama son of Ammihud;

from Manasseh, Gamaliel son of Pedahzur;
¹¹from Benjamin, Abidan son of Gideoni;
¹²from Dan, Ahiezer son of Ammishaddai;
¹³from Asher, Pagiel son of Ocran;
¹⁴from Gad, Eliasaph son of Deuel;
¹⁵from Naphtali, Ahira son of Enan."

¹⁶These were the men appointed from the community, the leaders of their ancestral tribes. They were the heads of the clans of Israel.

¹⁷Moses and Aaron took these men whose names had been given, ¹⁸and they called the whole community together on the first day of the second month. The people indicated their ancestry by their clans and families, and the men twenty years old or more were listed by name, one by one, ¹⁹as the LORD commanded Moses. And so he counted them in the Desert of Sinai:

²⁰From the descendants of Reuben the firstborn son of Israel:

All the men twenty years old or more who

were able to serve in the army were listed by name, one by one, according to the records of their clans and families. 21The number from the tribe of Reuben was 46,500.

22From the descendants of Simeon:

All the men twenty years old or more who were able to serve in the army were counted and listed by name, one by one, according to the records of their clans and families. 23The number from the tribe of Simeon was 59,300.

24From the descendants of Gad:

All the men twenty years old or more who were able to serve in the army were listed by name, according to the records of their clans and families. 25The number from the tribe of Gad was 45,650.

26From the descendants of Judah:

All the men twenty years old or more who were able to serve in the army were listed by name, according to the records of their clans and families. 27The number from the tribe of Judah was 74,600.

28From the descendants of Issachar:

All the men twenty years old or more who were able to serve in the army were listed by name, according to the records of their clans and families. 29The number from the tribe of Issachar was 54,400.

30From the descendants of Zebulun:

All the men twenty years old or more who were able to serve in the army were listed by name, according to the records of their clans and families. 31The number from the tribe of Zebulun was 57,400.

32From the sons of Joseph:

From the descendants of Ephraim:

All the men twenty years old or more who were able to serve in the army were listed by name, according to the records of their clans and families. 33The number from the tribe of Ephraim was 40,500.

34From the descendants of Manasseh:

All the men twenty years old or more who were able to serve in the army were listed by name, according to the records of their clans and families. 35The number from the tribe of Manasseh was 32,200.

36From the descendants of Benjamin:

All the men twenty years old or more who were able to serve in the army were listed by name, according to the records of their clans and families. 37The number from the tribe of Benjamin was 35,400.

38From the descendants of Dan:

All the men twenty years old or more who were able to serve in the army were listed by name, according to the records of their clans and families. 39The number from the tribe of Dan was 62,700.

40From the descendants of Asher:

All the men twenty years old or more who were able to serve in the army were listed by name, according to the records of their clans and families. 41The number from the tribe of Asher was 41,500.

42From the descendants of Naphtali:

All the men twenty years old or more who were able to serve in the army were listed by name, according to the records of their clans and families. 43The number from the tribe of Naphtali was 53,400.

44These were the men counted by Moses and Aaron and the twelve leaders of Israel, each one representing his family. 45All the Israelites twenty years old or more who were able to serve in Israel's army were counted according to their families. 46The total number was 603,550.

47The families of the tribe of Levi, however, were not counted along with the others. 48The LORD had said to Moses: 49"You must not count the tribe of Levi or include them in the census of the other Israelites. 50Instead, appoint the Levites to be in charge of the tabernacle of the Testimony—over all its furnishings and everything belonging to it. They are to carry the tabernacle and all its furnishings; they are to take care of it and encamp round it. 51Whenever the tabernacle is to move, the Levites are to take it down, and whenever the tabernacle is to be set up, the Levites shall do it. Anyone else who goes near it shall be put to death. 52The Israelites are to set up their tents by divisions, each man in his own camp under his own standard. 53The Levites, however, are to set up their tents round the tabernacle of the Testimony so that wrath will not fall on the Israelite community. The Levites are to be responsible for the care of the tabernacle of the Testimony."

54The Israelites did all this just as the LORD commanded Moses.

The Arrangement of the Tribal Camps

2 The LORD said to Moses and Aaron: 2"The Israelites are to camp round the Tent of Meeting some distance from it, each man under his standard with the banners of his family."

3On the east, towards the sunrise, the divisions of the camp of Judah are to encamp under their standard. The leader of the people of Judah is Nahshon son of Amminadab. 4His division numbers 74,600.

5The tribe of Issachar will camp next to them. The leader of the people of Issachar is Nethanel son of Zuar. 6His division numbers 54,400.

7The tribe of Zebulun will be next. The leader of the people of Zebulun is Eliab son of Helon. 8His division numbers 57,400.

9All the men assigned to the camp of Judah, according to their divisions, number 186,400. They will set out first.

10On the south will be the divisions of the camp of Reuben under their standard. The leader of the people of Reuben is Elizur son of Shedeur. ¹¹His division numbers 46,500.

¹²The tribe of Simeon will camp next to them. The leader of the people of Simeon is Shelumiel son of Zurishaddai. ¹³His division numbers 59,300.

¹⁴The tribe of Gad will be next. The leader of the people of Gad is Eliasaph son of Deuel.ᵃ ¹⁵His division numbers 45,650.

¹⁶All the men assigned to the camp of Reuben, according to their divisions, number 151,450. They will set out second.

¹⁷Then the Tent of Meeting and the camp of the Levites will set out in the middle of the camps. They will set out in the same order as they encamp, each in his own place under his standard.

¹⁸On the west will be the divisions of the camp of Ephraim under their standard. The leader of the people of Ephraim is Elishama son of Ammihud. ¹⁹His division numbers 40,500.

²⁰The tribe of Manasseh will be next to them. The leader of the people of Manasseh is Gamaliel son of Pedahzur. ²¹His division numbers 32,200.

²²The tribe of Benjamin will be next. The leader of the people of Benjamin is Abidan son of Gideoni. ²³His division numbers 35,400.

²⁴All the men assigned to the camp of Ephraim, according to their divisions, number 108,100. They will set out third.

²⁵On the north will be the divisions of the camp of Dan, under their standard. The leader of the people of Dan is Ahiezer son of Ammishaddai. ²⁶His division numbers 62,700.

²⁷The tribe of Asher will camp next to them. The leader of the people of Asher is Pagiel son of Ocran. ²⁸His division numbers 41,500.

²⁹The tribe of Naphtali will be next. The leader of the people of Naphtali is Ahira son of Enan. ³⁰His division numbers 53,400.

³¹All the men assigned to the camp of Dan number 157,600. They will set out last, under their standards.

2:32   If there were 603,550 fighting men in Israel, the whole body of people must have numbered about two million. Marching 50 abreast with a yard between each row, their column would have been 22 miles long. The numbers given represent an ideal. God had promised Abraham numerous descendants, and what God has said is so certain that it is in a sense already accomplished, even at the beginning of Israel's long history.

---

³²These are the Israelites, counted according to their families. All those in the camps, by their divisions, number 603,550. ³³The Levites, however, were not counted along with the other Israelites, as the LORD commanded Moses.

³⁴So the Israelites did everything the LORD commanded Moses; that is the way they encamped under their standards, and that is the way they set out, each with his clan and family.

The Levites

3 This is the account of the family of Aaron and Moses at the time the LORD talked with Moses on Mount Sinai.

²The names of the sons of Aaron were Nadab the firstborn and Abihu, Eleazar and Ithamar. ³Those were the names of Aaron's sons, the anointed priests, who were ordained to serve as priests. ⁴Nadab and Abihu, however, fell dead before the LORD when they made an offering with unauthorised fire before him in the Desert of Sinai. They had no sons; so only Eleazar and Ithamar served as priests during the lifetime of their father Aaron.

⁵The LORD said to Moses, ⁶"Bring the tribe of Levi and present them to Aaron the priest to assist him. ⁷They are to perform duties for him and for the whole community at the Tent of Meeting by doing the work of the tabernacle. ⁸They are to take care of all the furnishings of the Tent of Meeting, fulfilling the obligations of the Israelites by doing the work of the tabernacle. ⁹Give the Levites to Aaron and his sons; they are the Israelites who are to be given wholly to him.ᵃ ¹⁰Appoint Aaron and his sons to serve as priests; anyone else who approaches the sanctuary must be put to death."

¹¹The LORD also said to Moses, ¹²"I have taken the Levites from among the Israelites in place of the first male offspring of every Israelite woman. The Levites are mine, ¹³for all the firstborn are mine. When I struck down all the firstborn in Egypt, I set apart for myself every firstborn in Israel, whether man or animal. They are to be mine. I am the LORD."

¹⁴The LORD said to Moses in the Desert of Sinai, ¹⁵"Count the Levites by their families and clans. Count every male a month old or more." ¹⁶So Moses counted them, as he was commanded by the word of the LORD.

¹⁷These were the names of the sons of Levi:
Gershon, Kohath and Merari.
¹⁸These were the names of the Gershonite clans:
Libni and Shimei.
¹⁹The Kohathite clans:
Amram, Izhar, Hebron and Uzziel.
²⁰The Merarite clans:
Mahli and Mushi.
These were the Levite clans, according to their families.

²¹To Gershon belonged the clans of the Libnites and Shimeites; these were the Gershonite clans. ²²The number of all the males a month old or more who were

ᵃ14 Many manuscripts of the Masoretic Text, Samaritan Pentateuch and Vulgate (see also Num. 1:14); most manuscripts of the Masoretic Text *Reuel*   ᵃ9 Most manuscripts of the Masoretic Text; some manuscripts of the Masoretic Text, Samaritan Pentateuch and Septuagint (see also Num. 8:16) *to me* counted was 7,500. [23]The Gershonite clans were to camp on the west, behind the tabernacle. [24]The leader of the families of the Gershonites was Eliasaph son of Lael. [25]At the Tent of Meeting the Gershonites were responsible for the care of the tabernacle and tent, its coverings, the curtain at the entrance to the Tent of Meeting, [26]the curtains of the courtyard, the curtain at the entrance to the courtyard surrounding the tabernacle and altar, and the ropes — and everything related to their use.

[27]To Kohath belonged the clans of the Amramites, Izharites, Hebronites and Uzzielites; these were the Kohathite clans. [28]The number of all the males a month old or more was 8,600.[b] The Kohathites were responsible for the care of the sanctuary. [29]The Kohathite clans were to camp on the south side of the tabernacle. [30]The leader of the families of the Kohathite clans was Elizaphan son of Uzziel. [31]They were responsible for the care of the ark, the table, the lampstand, the altars, the articles of the sanctuary used in ministering, the curtain, and everything related to their use. [32]The chief leader of the Levites was Eleazar son of Aaron, the priest. He was appointed over those who were responsible for the care of the sanctuary.

[33]To Merari belonged the clans of the Mahlites and the Mushites; these were the Merarite clans. [34]The number of all the males a month old or more who were counted was 6,200. [35]The leader of the families of the Merarite clans was Zuriel son of Abihail; they were to camp on the north side of the tabernacle. [36]The Merarites were appointed to take care of the frames of the tabernacle, its crossbars, posts, bases, all its equipment, and everything related to their use, [37]as well as the posts of the surrounding courtyard with their bases, tent pegs and ropes.

[38]Moses and Aaron and his sons were to camp to the east of the tabernacle, towards the sunrise, in front of the Tent of Meeting. They were responsible for the care of the sanctuary on behalf of the Israelites. Anyone else who approached the sanctuary was to be put to death.

[39]The total number of Levites counted at the LORD's command by Moses and Aaron according to their clans, including every male a month old or more, was 22,000.

[40]The LORD said to Moses, "Count all the firstborn Israelite males who are a month old or more and make a list of their names. [41]Take the Levites for me in place of all the firstborn of the Israelites, and the livestock of the Levites in place of all the firstborn of the livestock of the Israelites. I am the LORD."

[42]So Moses counted all the firstborn of the Israelites, as the LORD commanded him. [43]The total number of firstborn males a month old or more, listed by name, was 22,273.

[44]The LORD also said to Moses, [45]"Take the Levites in place of all the firstborn of Israel, and the livestock of the Levites in place of their livestock. The Levites are to be mine. I am the LORD. [46]To redeem the 273 firstborn Israelites who exceed the number of the Levites, [47]collect five shekels[c] for each one, according to the sanctuary shekel, which weighs twenty gerahs. [48]Give the money for the redemption of the additional Israelites to Aaron and his sons."

3:44 The tribe of Levi never owned territory in the promised land. Its role was a priestly one. Priests represent the people they serve, and here that idea is enlarged. All things belong to God, and animal firstborn are sacrificed to him. The Levites are shown as giving up their ordinary place as a tribe, and taking the same role as firstborn Israelites.

---

[49]So Moses collected the redemption money from those who exceeded the number redeemed by the Levites. [50]From the firstborn of the Israelites he collected silver weighing 1,365 shekels,[d] according to the sanctuary shekel. [51]Moses gave the redemption money to Aaron and his sons, as he was commanded by the word of the LORD.

The Kohathites

4 The LORD said to Moses and Aaron: [2]"Take a census of the Kohathite branch of the Levites by their clans and families. [3]Count all the men from thirty to fifty years of age who come to serve in the work in the Tent of Meeting.

[4]"This is the work of the Kohathites in the Tent of Meeting: the care of the most holy things. [5]When the camp is to move, Aaron and his sons are to go in and take down the shielding curtain and cover the ark of the Testimony with it. [6]Then they are to cover this with hides of sea cows,[a] spread a cloth of solid blue over that and put the poles in place.

[7]"Over the table of the Presence they are to spread a blue cloth and put on it the plates, dishes and bowls, and the jars for drink offerings; the bread that is continually there is to remain on it. [8]Over these they are to spread a scarlet cloth, cover that with hides of sea cows and put its poles in place.

[9]"They are to take a blue cloth and cover the lampstand that is for light, together with its lamps, its wick trimmers and trays, and all its jars for the oil used to supply it. [10]Then they are to wrap it and all its accessories in a covering of hides of sea cows and put it on a carrying frame.

[11]"Over the gold altar they are to spread a blue cloth and cover that with hides of sea cows and put its poles in place.

[12]"They are to take all the articles used for ministering in the sanctuary, wrap them in a blue cloth, cover that with hides of sea cows and put them on a carrying frame.

---

[b]28 Hebrew; some Septuagint manuscripts 8,300   [c]47 That is, about 2 ounces (about 55 grams)
[d]50 That is, about 35 pounds (about 15.5 kilograms)   [a]6 That is, large aquatic mammals; also elsewhere in this chapter

¹³"They are to remove the ashes from the bronze altar and spread a purple cloth over it. ¹⁴Then they are to place on it all the utensils used for ministering at the altar, including the firepans, meat forks, shovels and sprinkling bowls. Over it they are to spread a covering of hides of sea cows and put its poles in place.

¹⁵"After Aaron and his sons have finished covering the holy furnishings and all the holy articles, and when the camp is ready to move, the Kohathites are to come to do the carrying. But they must not touch the holy things or they will die. The Kohathites are to carry those things that are in the Tent of Meeting.

¹⁶"Eleazar son of Aaron, the priest, is to have charge of the oil for the light, the fragrant incense, the regular grain offering and the anointing oil. He is to be in charge of the entire tabernacle and everything in it, including its holy furnishings and articles."

¹⁷The LORD said to Moses and Aaron, ¹⁸"See that the Kohathite tribal clans are not cut off from the Levites. ¹⁹So that they may live and not die when they come near the most holy things, do this for them: Aaron and his sons are to go into the sanctuary and assign to each man his work and what he is to carry. ²⁰But the Kohathites must not go in to look at the holy things, even for a moment, or they will die."

The Gershonites

²¹The LORD said to Moses, ²²"Take a census also of the Gershonites by their families and clans. ²³Count all the men from thirty to fifty years of age who come to serve in the work at the Tent of Meeting.

²⁴"This is the service of the Gershonite clans as they work and carry burdens: ²⁵They are to carry the curtains of the tabernacle, the Tent of Meeting, its covering and the outer covering of hides of sea cows, the curtains for the entrance to the Tent of Meeting, ²⁶the curtains of the courtyard surrounding the tabernacle and altar, the curtain for the entrance, the ropes and all the equipment used in its service. The Gershonites are to do all that needs to be done with these things. ²⁷All their service, whether carrying or doing other work, is to be done under the direction of Aaron and his sons. You shall assign to them as their responsibility all they are to carry. ²⁸This is the service of the Gershonite clans at the Tent of Meeting. Their duties are to be under the direction of Ithamar son of Aaron, the priest.

The Merarites

²⁹"Count the Merarites by their clans and families. ³⁰Count all the men from thirty to fifty years of age who come to serve in the work at the Tent of Meeting. ³¹This is their duty as they perform service at the Tent of Meeting: to carry the frames of the tabernacle, its crossbars, posts and bases, ³²as well as the posts of the surrounding courtyard with their bases, tent pegs, ropes, all their equipment and everything related to their use. Assign to each man the specific things he is to carry. ³³This is the service of the Merarite clans as

they work at the Tent of Meeting under the direction of Ithamar son of Aaron, the priest."

The Numbering of the Levite Clans

³⁴Moses, Aaron and the leaders of the community counted the Kohathites by their clans and families. ³⁵All the men from thirty to fifty years of age who came to serve in the work in the Tent of Meeting, ³⁶counted by clans, were 2,750. ³⁷This was the total of all those in the Kohathite clans who served in the Tent of Meeting. Moses and Aaron counted them according to the LORD's command through Moses.

³⁸The Gershonites were counted by their clans and families. ³⁹All the men from thirty to fifty years of age who came to serve in the work at the Tent of Meeting, ⁴⁰counted by their clans and families, were 2,630. ⁴¹This was the total of those in the Gershonite clans who served at the Tent of Meeting. Moses and Aaron counted them according to the LORD's command.

⁴²The Merarites were counted by their clans and families. ⁴³All the men from thirty to fifty years of age who came to serve in the work at the Tent of Meeting, ⁴⁴counted by their clans, were 3,200. ⁴⁵This was the total of those in the Merarite clans. Moses and Aaron counted them according to the LORD's command through Moses.

⁴⁶So Moses, Aaron and the leaders of Israel counted all the Levites by their clans and families. ⁴⁷All the men from thirty to fifty years of age who came to do the work of serving and carrying the Tent of Meeting ⁴⁸numbered 8,580. ⁴⁹At the LORD's command through Moses, each was assigned his work and told what to carry.

Thus they were counted, as the LORD commanded Moses.

The Purity of the Camp

5 The LORD said to Moses, ²"Command the Israelites to send away from the camp anyone who has an infectious skin disease*a* or a discharge of any kind, or who is ceremonially unclean because of a dead body. ³Send away male and female alike; send them outside the camp so that they will not defile their camp, where I dwell among them." ⁴The Israelites did this; they sent them outside the camp. They did just as the LORD had instructed Moses.

Restitution for Wrongs

⁵The LORD said to Moses, ⁶"Say to the Israelites: 'When a man or woman wrongs another in any way*b* and so is unfaithful to the LORD, that person is guilty ⁷and must confess the sin he has committed. He must make full restitution for his wrong, add one fifth to it and give it all to the person he has wronged. ⁸But if that person has no close relative to whom restitution can be made for the wrong, the restitution belongs to the LORD and must be given to the priest, along with the ram with which atonement is made for him. ⁹All the sacred contributions the Israelites bring to a priest will belong

a2 Traditionally *leprosy*; the Hebrew word was used for various diseases affecting the skin—not necessarily leprosy.
b6 Or *woman commits any wrong common to mankind*

to him. ¹⁰Each man's sacred gifts are his own, but what he gives to the priest will belong to the priest.' "

The Test for an Unfaithful Wife

¹¹Then the LORD said to Moses, ¹²"Speak to the Israelites and say to them: 'If a man's wife goes astray and is unfaithful to him ¹³by sleeping with another man, and this is hidden from her husband and her impurity is undetected (since there is no witness against her and she has not been caught in the act), ¹⁴and if feelings of jealousy come over her husband and he suspects his wife and she is impure—or if he is jealous and suspects her even though she is not impure— ¹⁵then he is to take his wife to the priest. He must also take an offering of a tenth of an ephah ᶜ of barley flour on her behalf. He must not pour oil on it or put incense on it, because it is a grain offering for jealousy, a reminder offering to draw attention to guilt.

¹⁶" 'The priest shall bring her and make her stand

5:14   The Hebrew word for the "feelings" of jealousy is the same as the word for God's spirit, and for wind—it indicates an emotion which is beyond human control. It may well be that some form of public trial was necessary to clear the name of a woman whose husband's feelings were so irrational. Trial by ordeal has been used in many cultures. In Israel it would have been thought that God could use it to reveal the truth.

---

before the LORD. ¹⁷Then he shall take some holy water in a clay jar and put some dust from the tabernacle floor into the water. ¹⁸After the priest has made the woman stand before the LORD, he shall loosen her hair and place in her hands the reminder offering, the grain offering for jealousy, while he himself holds the bitter water that brings a curse. ¹⁹Then the priest shall put the woman under oath and say to her, "If no other man has slept with you and you have not gone astray and become impure while married to your husband, may this bitter water that brings a curse not harm you. ²⁰But if you have gone astray while married to your husband and you have defiled yourself by sleeping with a man other than your husband"— ²¹here the priest is to put the woman under this curse of the oath—"may the LORD cause your people to curse and denounce you when he causes your thigh to waste away and your abdomen to swell.ᵈ ²²May this water that brings a curse enter your body so that your abdomen swells and your thigh wastes away."ᵉ

" 'Then the woman is to say, "Amen. So be it."

²³" 'The priest is to write these curses on a scroll and then wash them off into the bitter water. ²⁴He shall make the woman drink the bitter water that brings a curse, and this water will enter her and cause bitter suffering. ²⁵The priest is to take from her hands the grain offering for jealousy, wave it before the LORD and

bring it to the altar. ²⁶The priest is then to take a handful of the grain offering as a memorial offering and burn it on the altar; after that, he is to make the woman drink the water. ²⁷If she has defiled herself and been unfaithful to her husband, then when she is made to drink the water that brings a curse, it will go into her and cause bitter suffering; her abdomen will swell and her thigh waste away,ᶠ and she will become accursed among her people. ²⁸If, however, the woman has not defiled herself and is free from impurity, she will be cleared of guilt and will be able to have children.

²⁹" 'This, then, is the law of jealousy when a woman goes astray and defiles herself while married to her husband, ³⁰or when feelings of jealousy come over a man because he suspects his wife. The priest is to make her stand before the LORD and is to apply this entire law to her. ³¹The husband will be innocent of any wrongdoing, but the woman will bear the consequences of her sin.' "

The Nazirite

6 The LORD said to Moses, ²"Speak to the Israelites and say to them: 'If a man or woman wants to make a special vow, a vow of separation to the LORD as a Nazirite, ³he must abstain from wine and other fermented drink and must not drink vinegar made from wine or from other fermented drink. He must not drink grape juice or eat grapes or raisins. ⁴As long as he is a Nazirite, he must not eat anything that comes from the grapevine, not even the seeds or skins.

6:2   Samson and John the Baptist were both Nazirites. Paul took a Nazirite vow for a period (Acts 21). In almost all cultures the hair of holy people is sacred, perhaps because it grows and so it seems to contain the life-giving power of God.

---

⁵" 'During the entire period of his vow of separation no razor may be used on his head. He must be holy until the period of his separation to the LORD is over; he must let the hair of his head grow long. ⁶Throughout the period of his separation to the LORD he must not go near a dead body. ⁷Even if his own father or mother or brother or sister dies, he must not make himself ceremonially unclean on account of them, because the symbol of his separation to God is on his head. ⁸Throughout the period of his separation he is consecrated to the LORD.

⁹" 'If someone dies suddenly in his presence, thus defiling the hair he has dedicated, he must shave his head on the day of his cleansing—the seventh day. ¹⁰Then on the eighth day he must bring two doves or two young pigeons to the priest at the entrance to the Tent of Meeting. ¹¹The priest is to offer one as a sin offering and the other as a burnt offering to make atonement for him because he sinned by being in the presence of the dead body. That same day he is to consecrate his head. ¹²He must dedicate himself to the

---

c15 That is, probably about 4 pints (about 2 litres)   *d21 Or causes you to have a miscarrying womb and barrenness*
e22 Or body and cause you to be barren and have a miscarrying womb
f27 Or suffering; she will have barrenness and a miscarrying womb

LORD for the period of his separation and must bring a year-old male lamb as a guilt offering. The previous days do not count, because he became defiled during his separation.

13 " 'Now this is the law for the Nazirite when the period of his separation is over. He is to be brought to the entrance to the Tent of Meeting. 14There he is to present his offerings to the LORD: a year-old male lamb without defect for a burnt offering, a year-old ewe lamb without defect for a sin offering, a ram without defect for a fellowship offering,[a] 15together with their grain offerings and drink offerings, and a basket of bread made without yeast — cakes made of fine flour mixed with oil, and wafers spread with oil.

16 " 'The priest is to present them before the LORD and make the sin offering and the burnt offering. 17He is to present the basket of unleavened bread and is to sacrifice the ram as a fellowship offering to the LORD, together with its grain offering and drink offering.

18 " 'Then at the entrance to the Tent of Meeting, the Nazirite must shave off the hair that he dedicated. He is to take the hair and put it in the fire that is under the sacrifice of the fellowship offering.

19 " 'After the Nazirite has shaved off the hair of his dedication, the priest is to place in his hands a boiled shoulder of the ram, and a cake and a wafer from the basket, both made without yeast. 20The priest shall then wave them before the LORD as a wave offering; they are holy and belong to the priest, together with the breast that was waved and the thigh that was presented. After that, the Nazirite may drink wine.

21 " 'This is the law of the Nazirite who vows his offering to the LORD in accordance with his separation, in addition to whatever else he can afford. He must fulfil the vow he has made, according to the law of the Nazirite.' "

The Priestly Blessing

22The LORD said to Moses, 23 "Tell Aaron and his sons, 'This is how you are to bless the Israelites. Say to them:

6:23   This is an ancient blessing. Jewish tradition states that when it was pronounced in the temple each day, God's own name, Yahweh, was used. This would have greatly strengthened the sense that God himself was present. The "peace" he gives in Hebrew means much more than the absence of war. It means total well-being for individual people and for society.

---

24 " ' "The LORD bless you
    and keep you;
25the LORD make his face shine upon you
    and be gracious to you;
26the LORD turn his face towards you
    and give you peace." '

27 "So they will put my name on the Israelites, and I will bless them."

Offerings at the Dedication of the Tabernacle

7 When Moses finished setting up the tabernacle, he anointed it and consecrated it and all its furnishings. He also anointed and consecrated the altar and all its utensils. 2Then the leaders of Israel, the heads of families who were the tribal leaders in charge of those who were counted, made offerings. 3They brought as their gifts before the LORD six covered carts and twelve oxen — an ox from each leader and a cart from every two. These they presented before the tabernacle.

4The LORD said to Moses, 5 "Accept these from them, that they may be used in the work at the Tent of Meeting. Give them to the Levites as each man's work requires."

6So Moses took the carts and oxen and gave them to the Levites. 7He gave two carts and four oxen to the Gershonites, as their work required, 8and he gave four carts and eight oxen to the Merarites, as their work required. They were all under the direction of Ithamar son of Aaron, the priest. 9But Moses did not give any to the Kohathites, because they were to carry on their shoulders the holy things, for which they were responsible.

10When the altar was anointed, the leaders brought their offerings for its dedication and presented them before the altar. 11For the LORD had said to Moses, "Each day one leader is to bring his offering for the dedication of the altar."

12The one who brought his offering on the first day was Nahshon son of Amminadab of the tribe of Judah.

13His offering was one silver plate weighing a hundred and thirty shekels,[a] and one silver sprinkling bowl weighing seventy shekels,[b] both according to the sanctuary shekel, each filled with fine flour mixed with oil as a grain offering; 14one gold dish weighing ten shekels,[c] filled with incense; 15one young bull, one ram and one male lamb a year old, for a burnt offering; 16one male goat for a sin offering; 17and two oxen, five rams, five male goats and five male lambs a year old, to be sacrificed as a fellowship offering.[d] This was the offering of Nahshon son of Amminadab.

18On the second day Nethanel son of Zuar, the leader of Issachar, brought his offering.

19The offering he brought was one silver plate weighing a hundred and thirty shekels, and one silver sprinkling bowl weighing seventy shekels, both according to the sanctuary shekel, each filled with fine flour mixed with oil as a grain offering; 20one gold dish weighing ten shekels, filled with incense; 21one young bull, one ram and one male lamb a year old, for a burnt offering; 22one male goat for a sin offering; 23and two oxen, five rams,

---

a 14 Traditionally *peace offering*; also in verses 17 and 18
a 13 That is, about 3¼ pounds (about 1.5 kilograms); also elsewhere in this chapter
b 13 That is, about 1¾ pounds (about 0.8 kilogram); also elsewhere in this chapter
c 14 That is, about 4 ounces (about 115 grams); also elsewhere in this chapter
d 17 Traditionally *peace offering*; also elsewhere in this chapter

five male goats and five male lambs a year old, to be sacrificed as a fellowship offering. This was the offering of Nethanel son of Zuar.

24On the third day, Eliab son of Helon, the leader of the people of Zebulun, brought his offering. 25His offering was one silver plate weighing a hundred and thirty shekels, and one silver sprinkling bowl weighing seventy shekels, both according to the sanctuary shekel, each filled with fine flour mixed with oil as a grain offering; 26one gold dish weighing ten shekels, filled with incense; 27one young bull, one ram and one male lamb a year old, for a burnt offering; 28one male goat for a sin offering; 29and two oxen, five rams, five male goats and five male lambs a year old, to be sacrificed as a fellowship offering. This was the offering of Eliab son of Helon.

30On the fourth day Elizur son of Shedeur, the leader of the people of Reuben, brought his offering. 31His offering was one silver plate weighing a hundred and thirty shekels, and one silver sprinkling bowl weighing seventy shekels, both according to the sanctuary shekel, each filled with fine flour mixed with oil as a grain offering; 32one gold dish weighing ten shekels, filled with incense; 33one young bull, one ram and one male lamb a year old, for a burnt offering; 34one male goat for a sin offering; 35and two oxen, five rams, five male goats and five male lambs a year old, to be sacrificed as a fellowship offering. This was the offering of Elizur son of Shedeur.

36On the fifth day Shelumiel son of Zurishaddai, the leader of the people of Simeon, brought his offering. 37His offering was one silver plate weighing a hundred and thirty shekels, and one silver sprinkling bowl weighing seventy shekels, both according to the sanctuary shekel, each filled with fine flour mixed with oil as a grain offering; 38one gold dish weighing ten shekels, filled with incense; 39one young bull, one ram and one male lamb a year old, for a burnt offering; 40one male goat for a sin offering; 41and two oxen, five rams, five male goats and five male lambs a year old, to be sacrificed as a fellowship offering. This was the offering of Shelumiel son of Zurishaddai.

42On the sixth day Eliasaph son of Deuel, the leader of the people of Gad, brought his offering. 43His offering was one silver plate weighing a hundred and thirty shekels, and one silver sprinkling bowl weighing seventy shekels, both according to the sanctuary shekel, each filled with fine flour mixed with oil as a grain offering; 44one gold dish weighing ten shekels, filled with incense; 45one young bull, one ram and one male lamb a year old, for a burnt offering; 46one male goat for a sin offering; 47and two oxen, five rams, five male goats and five male lambs a year old, to be sacrificed as a fellowship offering. This was the offering of Eliasaph son of Deuel.

48On the seventh day Elishama son of Ammihud, the leader of the people of Ephraim, brought his offering.

49His offering was one silver plate weighing a hundred and thirty shekels, and one silver sprinkling bowl weighing seventy shekels, both according to the sanctuary shekel, each filled with fine flour mixed with oil as a grain offering; 50one gold dish weighing ten shekels, filled with incense; 51one young bull, one ram and one male lamb a year old, for a burnt offering; 52one male goat for a sin offering; 53and two oxen, five rams, five male goats and five male lambs a year old, to be sacrificed as a fellowship offering. This was the offering of Elishama son of Ammihud.

54On the eighth day Gamaliel son of Pedahzur, the leader of the people of Manasseh, brought his offering. 55His offering was one silver plate weighing a hundred and thirty shekels, and one silver sprinkling bowl weighing seventy shekels, both according to the sanctuary shekel, each filled with fine flour mixed with oil as a grain offering; 56one gold dish weighing ten shekels, filled with incense; 57one young bull, one ram and one male lamb a year old, for a burnt offering; 58one male goat for a sin offering; 59and two oxen, five rams, five male goats and five male lambs a year old, to be sacrificed as a fellowship offering. This was the offering of Gamaliel son of Pedahzur.

60On the ninth day Abidan son of Gideoni, the leader of the people of Benjamin, brought his offering. 61His offering was one silver plate weighing a hundred and thirty shekels, and one silver sprinkling bowl weighing seventy shekels, both according to the sanctuary shekel, each filled with fine flour mixed with oil as a grain offering; 62one gold dish weighing ten shekels, filled with incense; 63one young bull, one ram and one male lamb a year old, for a burnt offering; 64one male goat for a sin offering; 65and two oxen, five rams, five male goats and five male lambs a year old, to be sacrificed as a fellowship offering. This was the offering of Abidan son of Gideoni.

66On the tenth day Ahiezer son of Ammishaddai, the leader of the people of Dan, brought his offering. 67His offering was one silver plate weighing a hundred and thirty shekels, and one silver sprinkling bowl weighing seventy shekels, both according to the sanctuary shekel, each filled with fine flour mixed with oil as a grain offering; 68one gold dish weighing ten shekels, filled with incense; 69one young bull, one ram and one male lamb a year old, for a burnt offering; 70one male goat for a sin offering; 71and two oxen, five rams, five male goats and five male lambs a year old, to be sacrificed as a fellowship offering. This was the offering of Ahiezer son of Ammishaddai.

72On the eleventh day Pagiel son of Ocran, the leader of the people of Asher, brought his offering. 73His offering was one silver plate weighing a hundred and thirty shekels, and one silver sprinkling bowl weighing seventy shekels, both according to the sanctuary shekel, each filled with fine flour mixed with oil as a grain offering; 74one gold dish weighing ten shekels, filled with incense; 75one young bull, one ram and one male lamb a year old, for a burnt offering; 76one male goat for a sin offering; 77and two oxen, five rams, five male goats and five male lambs a year old, to be sacrificed as a fellowship offering. This was the offering of Pagiel son of Ocran.

78On the twelfth day Ahira son of Enan, the leader of the people of Naphtali, brought his offering.

79His offering was one silver plate weighing a hundred and thirty shekels, and one silver sprinkling bowl weighing seventy shekels, both according to the sanctuary shekel, each filled with fine flour mixed with oil as a grain offering; 80one gold dish weighing ten shekels, filled with incense; 81one young bull, one ram and one male lamb a year old, for a burnt offering; 82one male goat for a sin offering; 83and two oxen, five rams, five male goats and five male lambs a year old, to be sacrificed as a fellowship offering. This was the offering of Ahira son of Enan.

84These were the offerings of the Israelite leaders for the dedication of the altar when it was anointed: twelve silver plates, twelve silver sprinkling bowls and twelve gold dishes. 85Each silver plate weighed a hundred and thirty shekels, and each sprinkling bowl seventy shekels. Altogether, the silver dishes weighed two thousand four hundred shekels,*e* according to the sanctuary shekel. 86The twelve gold dishes filled with incense weighed ten shekels each, according to the sanctuary shekel. Altogether, the gold dishes weighed a hundred and twenty shekels.*f* 87The total number of animals for the burnt offering came to twelve young bulls, twelve rams and twelve male lambs a year old, together with their grain offering. Twelve male goats were used for the sin offering. 88The total number of animals for the sacrifice of the fellowship offering came to twenty-four oxen, sixty rams, sixty male goats and sixty male lambs a year old. These were the offerings for the dedication of the altar after it was anointed.

89When Moses entered the Tent of Meeting to speak with the LORD, he heard the voice speaking to him from between the two cherubim above the atonement cover on the ark of the Testimony. And he spoke with him.

Setting Up the Lamps

8 The LORD said to Moses, 2"Speak to Aaron and say to him, 'When you set up the seven lamps, they are to light the area in front of the lampstand.' "

3Aaron did so; he set up the lamps so that they faced forward on the lampstand, just as the LORD commanded Moses. 4This is how the lampstand was made: It was made of hammered gold—from its base to its blossoms. The lampstand was made exactly like the pattern the LORD had shown Moses.

The Setting Apart of the Levites

5The LORD said to Moses: 6"Take the Levites from among the other Israelites and make them

ceremonially clean. 7To purify them, do this: Sprinkle the water of cleansing on them; then make them shave their whole bodies and wash their clothes, and so purify themselves. 8Make them take a young bull with its grain offering of fine flour mixed with oil; then you are to take a second young bull for a sin offering. 9Bring the Levites to the front of the Tent of Meeting and assemble the whole Israelite community. 10You are to bring the Levites before the LORD, and the Israelites are to lay their hands on them. 11Aaron is to present the Levites before the LORD as a wave offering from the Israelites, so that they may be ready to do the work of the LORD.

12"After the Levites lay their hands on the heads of the bulls, use the one for a sin offering to the LORD and the other for a burnt offering, to make atonement for the Levites. 13Make the Levites stand in front of Aaron and his sons and then present them as a wave offering to the LORD. 14In this way you are to set the Levites apart from the other Israelites, and the Levites will be mine.

15"After you have purified the Levites and presented them as a wave offering, they are to come to do their work at the Tent of Meeting. 16They are the Israelites who are to be given wholly to me. I have taken them as my own in place of the firstborn, the first male offspring from every Israelite woman. 17Every firstborn male in Israel, whether man or animal, is mine. When I struck down all the firstborn in Egypt, I set them apart for myself. 18And I have taken the Levites in place of all the firstborn sons in Israel. 19Of all the Israelites, I have given the Levites as gifts to Aaron and his sons to do the work at the Tent of Meeting on behalf of the Israelites and to make atonement for them so that no plague will strike the Israelites when they go near the sanctuary."

20Moses, Aaron and the whole Israelite community did with the Levites just as the LORD commanded Moses. 21The Levites purified themselves and washed their clothes. Then Aaron presented them as a wave offering before the LORD and made atonement for them to purify them. 22After that, the Levites came to do their work at the Tent of Meeting under the supervision of Aaron and his sons. They did with the Levites just as the LORD commanded Moses.

23The LORD said to Moses, 24"This applies to the Levites: Men twenty-five years old or more shall come to take part in the work at the Tent of Meeting, 25but at the age of fifty, they must retire from their regular service and work no longer. 26They may assist their brothers in performing their duties at the Tent of Meeting, but they themselves must not do the work. This, then, is how you are to assign the responsibilities of the Levites."

The Passover

9 The LORD spoke to Moses in the Desert of Sinai in the first month of the second year after they came out of Egypt. He said, 2"Make the Israelites celebrate the Passover at the appointed time. 3Celebrate it at the appointed time, at twilight on the fourteenth

---

e 85 That is, about 61 pounds (about 28 kilograms)   *f 86* That is, about 3 pounds (about 1.4 kilograms) day of this month, in accordance with all its rules and regulations."

[4]So Moses told the Israelites to celebrate the Passover, [5]and they did so in the Desert of Sinai at twilight on the fourteenth day of the first month. The Israelites did everything just as the LORD commanded Moses.

[6]But some of them could not celebrate the Passover on that day because they were ceremonially unclean on account of a dead body. So they came to Moses and Aaron that same day [7]and said to Moses, "We have become unclean because of a dead body, but why should we be kept from presenting the LORD's offering with the other Israelites at the appointed time?"

[8]Moses answered them, "Wait until I find out what the LORD commands concerning you."

[9]Then the LORD said to Moses, [10]"Tell the Israelites: 'When any of you or your descendants are unclean because of a dead body or are away on a journey, they may still celebrate the LORD's Passover. [11]They are to celebrate it on the fourteenth day of the second month at twilight. They are to eat the lamb, together with unleavened bread and bitter herbs. [12]They must not leave any of it till morning or break any of its bones. When they celebrate the Passover, they must follow all the regulations. [13]But if a man who is ceremonially clean and not on a journey fails to celebrate the Passover, that person must be cut off from his people because he did not present the LORD's offering at the appointed time. That man will bear the consequences of his sin.

[14]" 'An alien living among you who wants to celebrate the LORD's Passover must do so in accordance with its rules and regulations. You must have the same regulations for the alien and the native-born.' "

The Cloud Above the Tabernacle

[15]On the day the tabernacle, the Tent of the Testimony, was set up, the cloud covered it. From evening till morning the cloud above the tabernacle looked like fire. [16]That is how it continued to be; the cloud covered it, and at night it looked like fire. [17]Whenever the cloud lifted from above the Tent, the Israelites set out; wherever the cloud settled, the Israelites encamped. [18]At the LORD's command the Israelites set out, and at his command they encamped. As long as the cloud stayed over the tabernacle, they remained in camp. [19]When the cloud remained over the tabernacle a long time, the Israelites obeyed the LORD's order and did not set out. [20]Sometimes the cloud was over the tabernacle only a few days; at the LORD's command they would encamp, and then at his command they would set out. [21]Sometimes the cloud stayed only from evening till morning, and when it lifted in the morning, they set out. Whether by day or by night, whenever the cloud lifted, they set out. [22]Whether the cloud stayed over the tabernacle for two days or a month or a year, the Israelites would remain in camp and not set out; but when it lifted, they would set out. [23]At the LORD's command they encamped, and at the LORD's command they set out. They obeyed the LORD's order, in accordance with his command through Moses.

The Silver Trumpets

10 The LORD said to Moses: [2]"Make two trumpets of hammered silver, and use them for calling the community together and for having the camps set out. [3]When both are sounded, the whole community is to assemble before you at the entrance to the Tent of Meeting. [4]If only one is sounded, the leaders—the heads of the clans of Israel—are to assemble before you. [5]When a trumpet blast is sounded, the tribes camping on the east are to set out. [6]At the sounding of a second blast, the camps on the south are to set out. The blast will be the signal for setting out. [7]To gather the assembly, blow the trumpets, but not with the same signal.

9:15　No matter how rebellious they were, the Israelites were constantly aware of the presence of God. This presence was symbolized by a cloud, which was also seen as a fire at night. Since the Israelites pictured heaven as a place above a flat earth, it made sense to picture that God was present in high clouds, like the ones which often cover the tops of mountains. The Bible contains many bold and vivid pictures of God, but never says that he is actually, for example, a cloud, or a rock.

---

[8]"The sons of Aaron, the priests, are to blow the trumpets. This is to be a lasting ordinance for you and the generations to come. [9]When you go into battle in your own land against an enemy who is oppressing you, sound a blast on the trumpets. Then you will be remembered by the LORD your God and rescued from your enemies. [10]Also at your times of rejoicing—your appointed feasts and New Moon festivals—you are to sound the trumpets over your burnt offerings and fellowship offerings,[a] and they will be a memorial for you before your God. I am the LORD your God."

The Israelites Leave Sinai

[11]On the twentieth day of the second month of the second year, the cloud lifted from above the tabernacle of the Testimony. [12]Then the Israelites set out from the Desert of Sinai and travelled from place to place until the cloud came to rest in the Desert of Paran. [13]They set out, this first time, at the LORD's command through Moses.

[14]The divisions of the camp of Judah went first, under their standard. Nahshon son of Amminadab was in command. [15]Nethanel son of Zuar was over the division of the tribe of Issachar, [16]and Eliab son of Helon was over the division of the tribe of Zebulun. [17]Then the tabernacle was taken down, and the Gershonites and Merarites, who carried it, set out.

[18]The divisions of the camp of Reuben went next, under their standard. Elizur son of Shedeur was in command. [19]Shelumiel son of Zurishaddai was over the division of the tribe of Simeon, [20]and Eliasaph son of Deuel

---

[a]10 Traditionally *peace offerings*

was over the division of the tribe of Gad. ²¹Then the Kohathites set out, carrying the holy things. The tabernacle was to be set up before they arrived.

²²The divisions of the camp of Ephraim went next, under their standard. Elishama son of Ammihud was in command. ²³Gamaliel son of Pedahzur was over the division of the tribe of Manasseh, ²⁴and Abidan son of Gideoni was over the division of the tribe of Benjamin.

²⁵Finally, as the rear guard for all the units, the divisions of the camp of Dan set out, under their standard. Ahiezer son of Ammishaddai was in command. ²⁶Pagiel son of Ocran was over the division of the tribe of Asher, ²⁷and Ahira son of Enan was over the division of the tribe of Naphtali. ²⁸This was the order of march for the Israelite divisions as they set out.

²⁹Now Moses said to Hobab son of Reuel the Midianite, Moses' father-in-law, "We are setting out for the place about which the LORD said, 'I will give it to you.' Come with us and we will treat you well, for the LORD has promised good things to Israel."

³⁰He answered, "No, I will not go; I am going back to my own land and my own people."

³¹But Moses said, "Please do not leave us. You know where we should camp in the desert, and you can be our eyes. ³²If you come with us, we will share with you whatever good things the LORD gives us."

³³So they set out from the mountain of the LORD and travelled for three days. The ark of the covenant of the LORD went before them during those three days to find them a place to rest. ³⁴The cloud of the LORD was over them by day when they set out from the camp.

³⁵Whenever the ark set out, Moses said,

"Rise up, O LORD!
May your enemies be scattered;
may your foes flee before you."

10:35   This prayer is still used in synagogue services when the scroll of the law is removed from its container. Like the priestly blessing (6:23), it uses God's own name, but the Jews never actually pronounce the name "Yahweh" as it is considered too holy. Instead, the title "LORD" is used.

---

³⁶Whenever it came to rest, he said,

"Return, O LORD,
to the countless thousands of Israel."

Fire From the LORD

11 Now the people complained about their hardships in the hearing of the LORD, and when he heard them his anger was aroused. Then fire from the LORD burned among them and consumed some of the outskirts of the camp. ²When the people cried out to Moses, he prayed to the LORD and the fire died down. ³So that place was called Taberah,^a because fire from the LORD had burned among them.

---

^a3 Taberah means burning.

Quail From the LORD

⁴The rabble with them began to crave other food, and again the Israelites started wailing and said, "If only we had meat to eat! ⁵We remember the fish we ate in Egypt at no cost—also the cucumbers, melons, leeks, onions and garlic. ⁶But now we have lost our appetite; we never see anything but this manna!"

⁷The manna was like coriander seed and looked like resin. ⁸The people went around gathering it, and then ground it in a hand mill or crushed it in a mortar. They cooked it in a pot or made it into cakes. And it tasted like something made with olive oil. ⁹When the dew settled on the camp at night, the manna also came down.

¹⁰Moses heard the people of every family wailing, each at the entrance to his tent. The LORD became exceedingly angry, and Moses was troubled. ¹¹He asked the LORD, "Why have you brought this trouble on your servant? What have I done to displease you that you put the burden of all these people on me? ¹²Did I conceive all these people? Did I give them birth? Why do you tell me to carry them in my arms, as a nurse carries an infant, to the land you promised on oath to their forefathers? ¹³Where can I get meat for all these people? They keep wailing to me, 'Give us meat to eat!' ¹⁴I cannot carry all these people by myself; the burden is too heavy for me. ¹⁵If this is how you are going to treat me, put me to death right now—if I have found favour in your eyes—and do not let me face my own ruin."

¹⁶The LORD said to Moses: "Bring me seventy of Israel's elders who are known to you as leaders and officials among the people. Make them come to the Tent of Meeting, that they may stand there with you. ¹⁷I will come down and speak with you there, and I will take of the Spirit that is on you and put the Spirit on them. They will help you carry the burden of the people so that you will not have to carry it alone.

11:16   In Exodus, it was Jethro's advice which led to Moses sharing the leadership which had become too much for him (Exodus 18:13ff). Here God's role in giving authority is emphasized. Moses' special gifts, his "Spirit", were put onto others too. Moses was aware of the great privilege and power which such a gift gave to a person. It was a mark of his great godliness that he was not jealous of others receiving his gifts. Rather, he wished they could be everyone's possession.

---

¹⁸"Tell the people: 'Consecrate yourselves in preparation for tomorrow, when you will eat meat. The LORD heard you when you wailed, "If only we had meat to eat! We were better off in Egypt!" Now the LORD will give you meat, and you will eat it. ¹⁹You will not eat it for just one day, or two days, or five, ten or twenty days, ²⁰but for a whole month—until it comes out of

your nostrils and you loathe it—because you have rejected the LORD, who is among you, and have wailed before him, saying, "Why did we ever leave Egypt?" ' "

²¹But Moses said, "Here I am among six hundred thousand men on foot, and you say, 'I will give them meat to eat for a whole month!' ²²Would they have enough if flocks and herds were slaughtered for them? Would they have enough if all the fish in the sea were caught for them?"

²³The LORD answered Moses, "Is the LORD's arm too short? You will now see whether or not what I say will come true for you."

²⁴So Moses went out and told the people what the LORD had said. He brought together seventy of their elders and made them stand round the Tent. ²⁵Then the LORD came down in the cloud and spoke with him, and he took of the Spirit that was on him and put the Spirit on the seventy elders. When the Spirit rested on them, they prophesied, but they did not do so again.^b

²⁶However, two men, whose names were Eldad and Medad, had remained in the camp. They were listed among the elders, but did not go out to the Tent. Yet the Spirit also rested on them, and they prophesied in the camp. ²⁷A young man ran and told Moses, "Eldad and Medad are prophesying in the camp."

²⁸Joshua son of Nun, who had been Moses' assistant since youth, spoke up and said, "Moses, my lord, stop them!"

²⁹But Moses replied, "Are you jealous for my sake? I wish that all the LORD's people were prophets and that the LORD would put his Spirit on them!" ³⁰Then Moses and the elders of Israel returned to the camp.

³¹Now a wind went out from the LORD and drove quail in from the sea. It brought them^c down all around the camp to about three feet^d above the ground, as far as a day's walk in any direction. ³²All that day and night and all the next day the people went out and gathered quail. No-one gathered less than ten homers.^e Then they spread them out all around the camp. ³³But while the meat was still between their teeth and before it could be consumed, the anger of the LORD burned against the people, and he struck them with a severe plague. ³⁴Therefore the place was named Kibroth Hattaavah,^f because there they buried the people who had craved other food.

³⁵From Kibroth Hattaavah the people travelled to Hazeroth and stayed there.

Miriam and Aaron Oppose Moses

12 Miriam and Aaron began to talk against Moses because of his Cushite wife, for he had married a Cushite. ²"Has the LORD spoken only through Moses?" they asked. "Hasn't he also spoken through us?" And the LORD heard this.

³(Now Moses was a very humble man, more humble than anyone else on the face of the earth.)

⁴At once the LORD said to Moses, Aaron and Miriam, "Come out to the Tent of Meeting, all three of you." So the three of them came out. ⁵Then the LORD came down in a pillar of cloud; he stood at the entrance to the Tent and summoned Aaron and Miriam. When both of them stepped forward, ⁶he said, "Listen to my words:

"When a prophet of the LORD is among you,
 I reveal myself to him in visions,
 I speak to him in dreams.
⁷But this is not true of my servant Moses;
 he is faithful in all my house.
⁸With him I speak face to face,
 clearly and not in riddles;
 he sees the form of the LORD.
Why then were you not afraid
 to speak against my servant Moses?"

⁹The anger of the LORD burned against them, and he left them.

¹⁰When the cloud lifted from above the Tent, there stood Miriam—leprous,^a like snow. Aaron turned towards her and saw that she had leprosy; ¹¹and he said to Moses, "Please, my lord, do not hold against us the sin we have so foolishly committed. ¹²Do not let her be like a stillborn infant coming from its mother's womb with its flesh half eaten away."

¹³So Moses cried out to the LORD, "O God, please heal her!"

¹⁴The LORD replied to Moses, "If her father had spat in her face, would she not have been in disgrace for seven days? Confine her outside the camp for seven days; after that she can be brought back." ¹⁵So Miriam was confined outside the camp for seven days, and the people did not move on till she was brought back. ¹⁶After that, the people left Hazeroth and encamped in the Desert of Paran.

Exploring Canaan

13 The LORD said to Moses, ²"Send some men to explore the land of Canaan, which I am giving to the Israelites. From each ancestral tribe send one of its leaders."

³So at the LORD's command Moses sent them out from the Desert of Paran. All of them were leaders of the Israelites. ⁴These are their names:

from the tribe of Reuben, Shammua son of Zaccur;
⁵from the tribe of Simeon, Shaphat son of Hori;
⁶from the tribe of Judah, Caleb son of Jephunneh;
⁷from the tribe of Issachar, Igal son of Joseph;
⁸from the tribe of Ephraim, Hoshea son of Nun;
⁹from the tribe of Benjamin, Palti son of Raphu;
¹⁰from the tribe of Zebulun, Gaddiel son of Sodi;
¹¹from the tribe of Manasseh (a tribe of Joseph), Gaddi son of Susi;
¹²from the tribe of Dan, Ammiel son of Gemalli;
¹³from the tribe of Asher, Sethur son of Michael;
¹⁴from the tribe of Naphtali, Nahbi son of Vophsi;
¹⁵from the tribe of Gad, Geuel son of Maki.

¹⁶These are the names of the men Moses sent to

---

^b25 Or prophesied and continued to do so   ^c31 Or They flew   ^d31 Hebrew two cubits (about 0.9 metre)
^e32 That is, probably about 60 bushels (about 2.2 kilolitres)   ^f34 Kibroth Hattaavah means graves of craving.
^a10 The Hebrew word was used for various diseases affecting the skin—not necessarily leprosy.

explore the land. (Moses gave Hoshea son of Nun the name Joshua.)

17When Moses sent them to explore Canaan, he said, "Go up through the Negev and on into the hill country. 18See what the land is like and whether the people who live there are strong or weak, few or many. 19What kind of land do they live in? Is it good or bad? What kind of towns do they live in? Are they unwalled or fortified? 20How is the soil? Is it fertile or poor? Are there trees on it or not? Do your best to bring back some of the fruit of the land." (It was the season for the first ripe grapes.)

21So they went up and explored the land from the Desert of Zin as far as Rehob, towards Lebo*a* Hamath. 22They went up through the Negev and came to Hebron, where Ahiman, Sheshai and Talmai, the descendants of Anak, lived. (Hebron had been built seven years before Zoan in Egypt.) 23When they reached the Valley of Eshcol,*b* they cut off a branch bearing a single cluster of grapes. Two of them carried it on a pole between them, along with some pomegranates and figs. 24That place was called the Valley of Eshcol because of the cluster of grapes the Israelites cut off there. 25At the end of forty days they returned from exploring the land.

Report on the Exploration

26They came back to Moses and Aaron and the whole Israelite community at Kadesh in the Desert of Paran. There they reported to them and to the whole assembly and showed them the fruit of the land. 27They gave Moses this account: "We went into the land to which you sent us, and it does flow with milk and honey! Here is its fruit. 28But the people who live there are powerful, and the cities are fortified and very large. We even saw descendants of Anak there. 29The Amalekites live in the Negev; the Hittites, Jebusites and Amorites live in the hill country; and the Canaanites live near the sea and along the Jordan."

30Then Caleb silenced the people before Moses and said, "We should go up and take possession of the land, for we can certainly do it."

31But the men who had gone up with him said, "We can't attack those people; they are stronger than we are." 32And they spread among the Israelites a bad report about the land they had explored. They said, "The land we explored devours those living in it. All the people we saw there are of great size. 33We saw the Nephilim there (the descendants of Anak come from the Nephilim). We seemed like grasshoppers in our own eyes, and we looked the same to them."

The People Rebel

14 That night all the people of the community raised their voices and wept aloud. 2All the Israelites grumbled against Moses and Aaron, and the whole assembly said to them, "If only we had died in Egypt! Or in this desert! 3Why is the LORD bringing us to this land only to let us fall by the sword? Our wives and children will be taken as plunder. Wouldn't it be better for us to go back to Egypt?" 4And they said to each other, "We should choose a leader and go back to Egypt."

5Then Moses and Aaron fell face down in front of the whole Israelite assembly gathered there. 6Joshua son of Nun and Caleb son of Jephunneh, who were among those who had explored the land, tore their clothes 7and said to the entire Israelite assembly, "The land we passed through and explored is exceedingly good. 8If the LORD is pleased with us, he will lead us into that land, a land flowing with milk and honey, and will give it to us. 9Only do not rebel against the LORD. And do not be afraid of the people of the land, because we will swallow them up. Their protection is gone, but the LORD is with us. Do not be afraid of them."

10But the whole assembly talked about stoning them. Then the glory of the LORD appeared at the Tent of Meeting to all the Israelites. 11The LORD said to Moses, "How long will these people treat me with contempt? How long will they refuse to believe in me, in spite of all the miraculous signs I have performed among them? 12I will strike them down with a plague and destroy them, but I will make you into a nation greater and stronger than they."

13Moses said to the LORD, "Then the Egyptians will hear about it! By your power you brought these people up from among them. 14And they will tell the inhabitants of this land about it. They have already heard that you, O LORD, are with these people and that you, O LORD, have been seen face to face, that your cloud stays over them, and that you go before them in a pillar of cloud by day and a pillar of fire by night. 15If you put these people to death all at one time, the nations who have heard this report about you will say, 16'The LORD was not able to bring these people into the land he promised them on oath; so he slaughtered them in the desert.'

17"Now may the Lord's strength be displayed, just as you have declared: 18'The LORD is slow to anger, abounding in love and forgiving sin and rebellion. Yet he does not leave the guilty unpunished; he punishes the children for the sin of the fathers to the third and fourth generation.' 19In accordance with your great love, forgive the sin of these people, just as you have pardoned them from the time they left Egypt until now."

20The LORD replied, "I have forgiven them, as you asked. 21Nevertheless, as surely as I live and as surely as the glory of the LORD fills the whole earth, 22not one of the men who saw my glory and the miraculous signs I performed in Egypt and in the desert but who disobeyed me and tested me ten times—23not one of them will ever see the land I promised on oath to their forefathers. No-one who has treated me with contempt will ever see it. 24But because my servant Caleb has a different spirit and follows me wholeheartedly, I will bring him into the land he went to, and his descendants will inherit it. 25Since the Amalekites and Canaanites are living in the valleys, turn back tomorrow and set out towards the desert along the route to the Red Sea."*a*

26The LORD said to Moses and Aaron: 27"How long will this wicked community grumble against me?

---

*a*21 Or *towards the entrance to*   *b*23 *Eshcol* means *cluster*; also in verse 24.   *a*25 Hebrew *Yam Suph*; that is, Sea of Reeds

I have heard the complaints of these grumbling Israelites. [28]So tell them, 'As surely as I live, declares the LORD, I will do to you the very things I heard you say: [29]In this desert your bodies will fall — every one of you twenty years old or more who was counted in the census and who has grumbled against me. [30]Not one of you will enter the land I swore with uplifted hand to make your home, except Caleb son of Jephunneh and Joshua son of Nun. [31]As for your children that you said would be taken as plunder, I will bring them in to enjoy the land you have rejected. [32]But you — your bodies will fall in this desert. [33]Your children will be shepherds here for forty years, suffering for your unfaithfulness, until the last of your bodies lies in the desert. [34]For forty years — one year for each of the forty days you explored the land — you will suffer for your sins and know what it is like to have me against you.' [35]I, the LORD, have spoken, and I will surely do these things to this whole wicked community, which has banded together against me. They will meet their end in this desert; here they will die."

14:23 God reveals himself in historical acts. These people had experienced his greatest power at the exodus, but at this point they did not trust him. As a result, God condemned them, but Moses appealed to him. So God decided that this generation would not die, but neither would it enter the promised land. The generation spent in the desert may have been necessary for the people's faith to develop so that when they were in Canaan they were not entirely seduced by its ways of life and worship.

---

[36]So the men Moses had sent to explore the land, who returned and made the whole community grumble against him by spreading a bad report about it — [37]these men responsible for spreading the bad report about the land were struck down and died of a plague before the LORD. [38]Of the men who went to explore the land, only Joshua son of Nun and Caleb son of Jephunneh survived.

[39]When Moses reported this to all the Israelites, they mourned bitterly. [40]Early the next morning they went up towards the high hill country. "We have sinned," they said. "We will go up to the place the LORD promised."

[41]But Moses said, "Why are you disobeying the LORD's command? This will not succeed! [42]Do not go up, because the LORD is not with you. You will be defeated by your enemies, [43]for the Amalekites and Canaanites will face you there. Because you have turned away from the LORD, he will not be with you and you will fall by the sword."

[44]Nevertheless, in their presumption they went up towards the high hill country, though neither Moses nor the ark of the LORD's covenant moved from the camp. [45]Then the Amalekites and Canaanites who lived in that hill country came down and attacked them and beat them down all the way to Hormah.

Supplementary Offerings

15 The LORD said to Moses, [2]"Speak to the Israelites and say to them: 'After you enter the land I am giving you as a home [3]and you present to the LORD offerings made by fire, from the herd or the flock, as an aroma pleasing to the LORD — whether burnt offerings or sacrifices, for special vows or freewill offerings or festival offerings — [4]then the one who brings his offering shall present to the LORD a grain offering of a tenth of an ephah[a] of fine flour mixed with a quarter of a hin[b] of oil. [5]With each lamb for the burnt offering or the sacrifice, prepare a quarter of a hin of wine as a drink offering.

[6]" 'With a ram prepare a grain offering of two-tenths of an ephah[c] of fine flour mixed with a third of a hin[d] of oil, [7]and a third of a hin of wine as a drink offering. Offer it as an aroma pleasing to the LORD.

[8]" 'When you prepare a young bull as a burnt offering or sacrifice, for a special vow or a fellowship offering[e] to the LORD, [9]bring with the bull a grain offering of three-tenths of an ephah[f] of fine flour mixed with half a hin[g] of oil. [10]Also bring half a hin of wine as a drink offering. It will be an offering made by fire, an aroma pleasing to the LORD. [11]Each bull or ram, each lamb or young goat, is to be prepared in this manner. [12]Do this for each one, for as many as you prepare.

[13]" 'Everyone who is native-born must do these things in this way when he brings an offering made by fire as an aroma pleasing to the LORD. [14]For the generations to come, whenever an alien or anyone else living among you presents an offering made by fire as an aroma pleasing to the LORD, he must do exactly as you do. [15]The community is to have the same rules for you and for the alien living among you; this is a lasting ordinance for the generations to come. You and the alien shall be the same before the LORD: [16]The same laws and regulations will apply both to you and to the alien living among you.' "

[17]The LORD said to Moses, [18]"Speak to the Israelites and say to them: 'When you enter the land to which I am taking you [19]and you eat the food of the land, present a portion as an offering to the LORD. [20]Present a cake from the first of your ground meal and present it as an offering from the threshing-floor. [21]Throughout the generations to come you are to give this offering to the LORD from the first of your ground meal.

Offerings for Unintentional Sins

[22]" 'Now if you unintentionally fail to keep any of these commands the LORD gave Moses — [23]any of the LORD's commands to you through him, from the day the LORD gave them and continuing through the generations to come — [24]and if this is done unintentionally without the community being aware of it, then the

---

[a]4 That is, probably about 4 pints (about 2 litres) [b]4 That is, probably about 1½ pints (about 1 litre); also in verse 5
[c]6 That is, probably about 7½ pints (about 4.5 litres) [d]6 That is, probably about 2¼ pints (about 1.2 litres); also in verse 7
[e]8 Traditionally *peace offering* [f]9 That is, probably about 11½ pints (about 6.5 litres)
[g]9 That is, probably about 3 pints (about 2 litres); also in verse 10

whole community is to offer a young bull for a burnt offering as an aroma pleasing to the LORD, along with its prescribed grain offering and drink offering, and a male goat for a sin offering. 25The priest is to make atonement for the whole Israelite community, and they will be forgiven, for it was not intentional and they have brought to the LORD for their wrong an offering made by fire and a sin offering. 26The whole Israelite community and the aliens living among them will be forgiven, because all the people were involved in the unintentional wrong.

27" 'But if just one person sins unintentionally, he must bring a year-old female goat for a sin offering. 28The priest is to make atonement before the LORD for the one who erred by sinning unintentionally, and when atonement has been made for him, he will be forgiven. 29One and the same law applies to everyone who sins unintentionally, whether he is a native-born Israelite or an alien.

30" 'But anyone who sins defiantly, whether native-born or alien, blasphemes the LORD, and that person must be cut off from his people. 31Because he has despised the LORD's word and broken his commands, that person must surely be cut off; his guilt remains on him.' "

The Sabbath-Breaker Put to Death

32While the Israelites were in the desert, a man was found gathering wood on the Sabbath day. 33Those who found him gathering wood brought him to Moses and Aaron and the whole assembly, 34and they kept him in custody, because it was not clear what should be done to him. 35Then the LORD said to Moses, "The man must die. The whole assembly must stone him outside the camp." 36So the assembly took him outside the camp and stoned him to death, as the LORD commanded Moses.

Tassels on Garments

37The LORD said to Moses, 38"Speak to the Israelites and say to them: 'Throughout the generations to come you are to make tassels on the corners of your garments, with a blue cord on each tassel. 39You will have these tassels to look at and so you will remember all the commands of the LORD, that you may obey them and not prostitute yourselves by going after the lusts of your own hearts and eyes. 40Then you will remember to obey all my commands and will be consecrated to your God. 41I am the LORD your God, who brought you out of Egypt to be your God. I am the LORD your God.' "

Korah, Dathan and Abiram

16 Korah son of Izhar, the son of Kohath, the son of Levi, and certain Reubenites—Dathan and Abiram, sons of Eliab, and On son of Peleth—became insolenta 2and rose up against Moses. With them were 250 Israelite men, well-known community leaders who had been appointed members of the council. 3They came as a group to oppose Moses and Aaron and said to them, "You have gone too far! The whole

community is holy, every one of them, and the LORD is with them. Why then do you set yourselves above the LORD's assembly?"

4When Moses heard this, he fell face down. 5Then he said to Korah and all his followers: "In the morning the LORD will show who belongs to him and who is holy, and he will make that person come near him. The man he chooses he will cause to come near him. 6You, Korah, and all your followers are to do this: Take censers 7and tomorrow put fire and incense in them before the LORD. The man the LORD chooses will be the one who is holy. You Levites have gone too far!"

8Moses also said to Korah, "Now listen, you Levites! 9Isn't it enough for you that the God of Israel has separated you from the rest of the Israelite community and brought you near himself to do the work at the LORD's tabernacle and to stand before the community and minister to them? 10He has brought you and all your fellow Levites near himself, but now you are trying to get the priesthood too. 11It is against the LORD that you and all your followers have banded together. Who is Aaron that you should grumble against him?"

12Then Moses summoned Dathan and Abiram, the sons of Eliab. But they said, "We will not come! 13Isn't it enough that you have brought us up out of a land flowing with milk and honey to kill us in the desert? And now you also want to lord it over us? 14Moreover, you haven't brought us into a land flowing with milk and honey or given us an inheritance of fields and vineyards. Will you gouge out the eyes ofb these men? No, we will not come!"

15Then Moses became very angry and said to the LORD, "Do not accept their offering. I have not taken so much as a donkey from them, nor have I wronged any of them."

16Moses said to Korah, "You and all your followers are to appear before the LORD tomorrow—you and they and Aaron. 17Each man is to take his censer and put incense in it—250 censers in all—and present it before the LORD. You and Aaron are to present your censers also." 18So each man took his censer, put fire and incense in it, and stood with Moses and Aaron at the entrance to the Tent of Meeting. 19When Korah had gathered all his followers in opposition to them at the entrance to the Tent of Meeting, the glory of the LORD appeared to the entire assembly. 20The LORD said to Moses and Aaron, 21"Separate yourselves from this assembly so that I can put an end to them at once."

22But Moses and Aaron fell face down and cried out, "O God, God of the spirits of all mankind, will you be angry with the entire assembly when only one man sins?"

23Then the LORD said to Moses, 24"Say to the assembly, 'Move away from the tents of Korah, Dathan and Abiram.' "

25Moses got up and went to Dathan and Abiram, and the elders of Israel followed him. 26He warned the assembly, "Move back from the tents of these wicked men! Do not touch anything belonging to them, or you will be swept away because of all their sins." 27So they moved away from the tents of Korah, Dathan and Abiram. Dathan and Abiram had come out and were

---

a 1 Or Peleth—took men   b 14 Or you make slaves of; or you deceive standing with their wives, children and little ones at the entrances to their tents.

16:22   The Israelites had a strong sense of communal responsibility. Often they were right to share the blame for an unjust or oppressive society. Nevertheless there are times when guilt (or innocence) belongs to a single person. Abraham believed that God would spare Sodom if there were a few good people there. So Moses and Aaron pleaded with God that only those who were guilty should suffer. It was to be many years before this idea was accepted as a general principle. Even here the families and households of the guilty men were destroyed.

---

²⁸Then Moses said, "This is how you will know that the LORD has sent me to do all these things and that it was not my idea: ²⁹If these men die a natural death and experience only what usually happens to men, then the LORD has not sent me. ³⁰But if the LORD brings about something totally new, and the earth opens its mouth and swallows them, with everything that belongs to them, and they go down alive into the grave,ᶜ then you will know that these men have treated the LORD with contempt."

³¹As soon as he finished saying all this, the ground under them split apart ³²and the earth opened its mouth and swallowed them, with their households and all Korah's men and all their possessions. ³³They went down alive into the grave, with everything they owned; the earth closed over them, and they perished and were gone from the community. ³⁴At their cries, all the Israelites around them fled, shouting, "The earth is going to swallow us too!"

³⁵And fire came out from the LORD and consumed the 250 men who were offering the incense.

³⁶The LORD said to Moses, ³⁷"Tell Eleazar son of Aaron, the priest, to take the censers out of the smouldering remains and scatter the coals some distance away, for the censers are holy—³⁸the censers of the men who sinned at the cost of their lives. Hammer the censers into sheets to overlay the altar, for they were presented before the LORD and have become holy. Let them be a sign to the Israelites."

³⁹So Eleazar the priest collected the bronze censers brought by those who had been burned up, and he had them hammered out to overlay the altar, ⁴⁰as the LORD directed him through Moses. This was to remind the Israelites that no-one except a descendant of Aaron should come to burn incense before the LORD, or he would become like Korah and his followers.

⁴¹The next day the whole Israelite community grumbled against Moses and Aaron. "You have killed the LORD's people," they said.

⁴²But when the assembly gathered in opposition to Moses and Aaron and turned towards the Tent of Meeting, suddenly the cloud covered it and the glory of the LORD appeared. ⁴³Then Moses and Aaron went to the front of the Tent of Meeting, ⁴⁴and the LORD said to Moses, ⁴⁵"Get away from this assembly so that I can put an end to them at once." And they fell face down.

⁴⁶Then Moses said to Aaron, "Take your censer and put incense in it, along with fire from the altar, and hurry to the assembly to make atonement for them. Wrath has come out from the LORD; the plague has started." ⁴⁷So Aaron did as Moses said, and ran into the midst of the assembly. The plague had already started among the people, but Aaron offered the incense and made atonement for them. ⁴⁸He stood between the living and the dead, and the plague stopped. ⁴⁹But 14,700 people died from the plague, in addition to those who had died because of Korah. ⁵⁰Then Aaron returned to Moses at the entrance to the Tent of Meeting, for the plague had stopped.

The Budding of Aaron's Staff

17 The LORD said to Moses, ²"Speak to the Israelites and get twelve staffs from them, one from the leader of each of their ancestral tribes. Write the name of each man on his staff. ³On the staff of Levi write Aaron's name, for there must be one staff for the head of each ancestral tribe. ⁴Place them in the Tent of Meeting in front of the Testimony, where I meet with you. ⁵The staff belonging to the man I choose will sprout, and I will rid myself of this constant grumbling against you by the Israelites."

⁶So Moses spoke to the Israelites, and their leaders gave him twelve staffs, one for the leader of each of their ancestral tribes, and Aaron's staff was among them. ⁷Moses placed the staffs before the LORD in the Tent of the Testimony.

⁸The next day Moses entered the Tent of the Testimony and saw that Aaron's staff, which represented the house of Levi, had not only sprouted but had budded, blossomed and produced almonds. ⁹Then Moses brought out all the staffs from the LORD's presence to all the Israelites. They looked at them, and each man took his own staff.

¹⁰The LORD said to Moses, "Put back Aaron's staff in front of the Testimony, to be kept as a sign to the rebellious. This will put an end to their grumbling against me, so that they will not die." ¹¹Moses did just as the LORD commanded him.

¹²The Israelites said to Moses, "We shall die! We are lost, we are all lost! ¹³Anyone who even comes near the tabernacle of the LORD will die. Are we all going to die?"

Duties of Priests and Levites

18 The LORD said to Aaron, "You, your sons and your father's family are to bear the responsibility for offences against the sanctuary, and you and your sons alone are to bear the responsibility for offences against the priesthood. ²Bring your fellow Levites from your ancestral tribe to join you and assist you when you and your sons minister before the Tent of the Testimony. ³They are to be responsible to you and are to perform all the duties of the Tent, but they must not go near the furnishings of the sanctuary or the altar, or

---

ᶜ30 Hebrew *Sheol*; also in verse 33

both they and you will die. [4]They are to join you and be responsible for the care of the Tent of Meeting—all the work at the Tent—and no-one else may come near where you are.

[5]"You are to be responsible for the care of the sanctuary and the altar, so that wrath will not fall on the Israelites again. [6]I myself have selected your fellow Levites from among the Israelites as a gift to you, dedicated to the LORD to do the work at the Tent of Meeting. [7]But only you and your sons may serve as priests in connection with everything at the altar and inside the curtain. I am giving you the service of the priesthood as a gift. Anyone else who comes near the sanctuary must be put to death."

Offerings for Priests and Levites

[8]Then the LORD said to Aaron, "I myself have put you in charge of the offerings presented to me; all the holy offerings the Israelites give me I give to you and your sons as your portion and regular share. [9]You are to have the part of the most holy offerings that is kept from the fire. From all the gifts they bring me as most holy offerings, whether grain or sin or guilt offerings, that part belongs to you and your sons. [10]Eat it as something most holy; every male shall eat it. You must regard it as holy.

[11]"This also is yours: whatever is set aside from the gifts of all the wave offerings of the Israelites. I give this to you and your sons and daughters as your regular share. Everyone in your household who is ceremonially clean may eat it.

[12]"I give you all the finest olive oil and all the finest new wine and grain they give to the LORD as the firstfruits of their harvest. [13]All the land's firstfruits that they bring to the LORD will be yours. Everyone in your household who is ceremonially clean may eat it.

[14]"Everything in Israel that is devoted[a] to the LORD is yours. [15]The first offspring of every womb, both man and animal, that is offered to the LORD is yours. But you must redeem every firstborn son and every firstborn male of unclean animals. [16]When they are a month old, you must redeem them at the redemption price set at five shekels[b] of silver, according to the sanctuary shekel, which weighs twenty gerahs.

[17]"But you must not redeem the firstborn of an ox, a sheep or a goat; they are holy. Sprinkle their blood on the altar and burn their fat as an offering made by fire, an aroma pleasing to the LORD. [18]Their meat is to be yours, just as the breast of the wave offering and the right thigh are yours. [19]Whatever is set aside from the holy offerings the Israelites present to the LORD I give to you and your sons and daughters as your regular share. It is an everlasting covenant of salt before the LORD for both you and your offspring."

[20]The LORD said to Aaron, "You will have no inheritance in their land, nor will you have any share among them; I am your share and your inheritance among the Israelites.

[21]"I give to the Levites all the tithes in Israel as their inheritance in return for the work they do while serving at the Tent of Meeting. [22]From now on the Israelites must not go near the Tent of Meeting, or they will bear the consequences of their sin and will die. [23]It is the Levites who are to do the work at the Tent of Meeting and bear the responsibility for offences against it. This is a lasting ordinance for the generations to come. They will receive no inheritance among the Israelites. [24]Instead, I give to the Levites as their inheritance the tithes that the Israelites present as an offering to the LORD. That is why I said concerning them: 'They will have no inheritance among the Israelites.' "

18:21   Since they weren't going to own any land, the Levites had to be supported by the people's offerings. If the worshippers didn't provide, then the ministers could suffer hardship. Equally, they could abuse their privileges and accumulate great wealth at the expense of the poor.

---

[25]The LORD said to Moses, [26]"Speak to the Levites and say to them: 'When you receive from the Israelites the tithe I give you as your inheritance, you must present a tenth of that tithe as the LORD's offering. [27]Your offering will be reckoned to you as grain from the threshing-floor or juice from the winepress. [28]In this way you also will present an offering to the LORD from all the tithes you receive from the Israelites. From these tithes you must give the LORD's portion to Aaron the priest. [29]You must present as the LORD's portion the best and holiest part of everything given to you.'

[30]"Say to the Levites: 'When you present the best part, it will be reckoned to you as the product of the threshing-floor or the winepress. [31]You and your households may eat the rest of it anywhere, for it is your wages for your work at the Tent of Meeting. [32]By presenting the best part of it you will not be guilty in this matter; then you will not defile the holy offerings of the Israelites, and you will not die.' "

The Water of Cleansing

19 The LORD said to Moses and Aaron: [2]"This is a requirement of the law that the LORD has commanded: Tell the Israelites to bring you a red heifer without defect or blemish and that has never been under a yoke. [3]Give it to Eleazar the priest; it is to be taken outside the camp and slaughtered in his presence. [4]Then Eleazar the priest is to take some of its blood on his finger and sprinkle it seven times towards the front of the Tent of Meeting. [5]While he watches, the heifer is to be burned—its hide, flesh, blood and offal. [6]The priest is to take some cedar wood, hyssop and scarlet wool and throw them onto the burning heifer. [7]After that, the priest must wash his clothes and bathe himself with water. He may then come into the camp, but he will be ceremonially unclean till evening. [8]The man who burns it must also wash his clothes and bathe with water, and he too will be unclean till evening.

---

[a] 14 The Hebrew term refers to the irrevocable giving over of things or persons to the LORD.
[b] 16 That is, about 2 ounces (about 55 grams)

⁹"A man who is clean shall gather up the ashes of the heifer and put them in a ceremonially clean place outside the camp. They shall be kept by the Israelite community for use in the water of cleansing; it is for purification from sin. ¹⁰The man who gathers up the ashes of the heifer must also wash his clothes, and he too will be unclean till evening. This will be a lasting ordinance both for the Israelites and for the aliens living among them.

¹¹"Whoever touches the dead body of anyone will be unclean for seven days. ¹²He must purify himself with the water on the third day and on the seventh day; then he will be clean. But if he does not purify himself on the third and seventh days, he will not be clean. ¹³Whoever touches the dead body of anyone and fails to purify himself defiles the LORD's tabernacle. That person must be cut off from Israel. Because the water of cleansing has not been sprinkled on him, he is unclean; his uncleanness remains on him.

¹⁴"This is the law that applies when a person dies in a tent: Anyone who enters the tent and anyone who is in it will be unclean for seven days, ¹⁵and every open container without a lid fastened on it will be unclean.

¹⁶"Anyone out in the open who touches someone who has been killed with a sword or someone who has died a natural death, or anyone who touches a human bone or a grave, will be unclean for seven days.

¹⁷"For the unclean person, put some ashes from the burned purification offering into a jar and pour fresh water over them. ¹⁸Then a man who is ceremonially clean is to take some hyssop, dip it in the water and sprinkle the tent and all the furnishings and the people who were there. He must also sprinkle anyone who has touched a human bone or a grave or someone who has been killed or someone who has died a natural death. ¹⁹The man who is clean is to sprinkle the unclean person on the third and seventh days, and on the seventh day he is to purify him. The person being cleansed must wash his clothes and bathe with water, and that evening he will be clean. ²⁰But if a person who is unclean does not purify himself, he must be cut off from the community, because he has defiled the sanctuary of the LORD. The water of cleansing has not been sprinkled on him, and he is unclean. ²¹This is a lasting ordinance for them.

"The man who sprinkles the water of cleansing must also wash his clothes, and anyone who touches the water of cleansing will be unclean till evening. ²²Anything that an unclean person touches becomes unclean, and anyone who touches it becomes unclean till evening."

Water From the Rock

20 In the first month the whole Israelite community arrived at the Desert of Zin, and they stayed at Kadesh. There Miriam died and was buried.

²Now there was no water for the community, and the people gathered in opposition to Moses and Aaron. ³They quarrelled with Moses and said, "If only we had died when our brothers fell dead before the LORD! ⁴Why did you bring the LORD's community into this desert, that we and our livestock should die here? ⁵Why did you bring us up out of Egypt to this terrible place? It has no grain or figs, grapevines or pomegranates. And there is no water to drink!"

⁶Moses and Aaron went from the assembly to the entrance to the Tent of Meeting and fell face down, and the glory of the LORD appeared to them. ⁷The LORD said to Moses, ⁸"Take the staff, and you and your brother Aaron gather the assembly together. Speak to that rock before their eyes and it will pour out its water. You will bring water out of the rock for the community so that they and their livestock can drink."

⁹So Moses took the staff from the LORD's presence, just as he commanded him. ¹⁰He and Aaron gathered the assembly together in front of the rock and Moses said to them, "Listen, you rebels, must we bring you water out of this rock?" ¹¹Then Moses raised his arm and struck the rock twice with his staff. Water gushed out, and the community and their livestock drank.

¹²But the LORD said to Moses and Aaron, "Because you did not trust in me enough to honour me as holy in the sight of the Israelites, you will not bring this community into the land I give them."

20:12   It is not clear what exactly was the fault which prevented Moses from entering Canaan. In practical terms it was probably better that he was not the leader of the entering tribes. A vigorous military campaign was necessary and it required a younger man with different skills.

---

¹³These were the waters of Meribah,ᵃ where the Israelites quarrelled with the LORD and where he showed himself holy among them.

Edom Denies Israel Passage

¹⁴Moses sent messengers from Kadesh to the king of Edom, saying:

"This is what your brother Israel says: You know about all the hardships that have come upon us. ¹⁵Our forefathers went down into Egypt, and we lived there many years. The Egyptians ill-treated us and our fathers, ¹⁶but when we cried out to the LORD, he heard our cry and sent an angel and brought us out of Egypt.

"Now we are here at Kadesh, a town on the edge of your territory. ¹⁷Please let us pass through your country. We will not go through any field or vineyard, or drink water from any well. We will travel along the king's highway and not turn to the right or to the left until we have passed through your territory."

¹⁸But Edom answered:

"You may not pass through here; if you try, we will march out and attack you with the sword."

¹⁹The Israelites replied:

"We will go along the main road, and if we or our livestock drink any of your water, we will pay

---

ᵃ13 *Meribah* means *quarrelling.*

for it. We only want to pass through on foot — nothing else."

²⁰Again they answered:

"You may not pass through."

Then Edom came out against them with a large and powerful army. ²¹Since Edom refused to let them go through their territory, Israel turned away from them.

The Death of Aaron

²²The whole Israelite community set out from Kadesh and came to Mount Hor. ²³At Mount Hor, near the border of Edom, the LORD said to Moses and Aaron, ²⁴"Aaron will be gathered to his people. He will not enter the land I give the Israelites, because both of you rebelled against my command at the waters of Meribah. ²⁵Call Aaron and his son Eleazar and take them up Mount Hor. ²⁶Remove Aaron's garments and put them on his son Eleazar, for Aaron will be gathered to his people; he will die there." ²⁷Moses did as the LORD commanded: They went up Mount Hor in the sight of the whole community. ²⁸Moses removed Aaron's garments and put them on his son Eleazar. And Aaron died there on top of the mountain. Then Moses and Eleazar came down from the mountain, ²⁹and when the whole community learned that Aaron had died, the entire house of Israel mourned for him thirty days.

Arad Destroyed

21 When the Canaanite king of Arad, who lived in the Negev, heard that Israel was coming along the road to Atharim, he attacked the Israelites and captured some of them. ²Then Israel made this vow to the LORD: "If you will deliver these people into our hands, we will totally destroy ᵃ their cities." ³The LORD listened to Israel's plea and gave the Canaanites over to them. They completely destroyed them and their towns; so the place was named Hormah. ᵇ

The Bronze Snake

⁴They travelled from Mount Hor along the route to the Red Sea, ᶜ to go round Edom. But the people grew impatient on the way; ⁵they spoke against God and against Moses, and said, "Why have you brought us up out of Egypt to die in the desert? There is no bread! There is no water! And we detest this miserable food!" ⁶Then the LORD sent venomous snakes among them; they bit the people and many Israelites died. ⁷The people came to Moses and said, "We sinned when we spoke against the LORD and against you. Pray that the LORD will take the snakes away from us." So Moses prayed for the people.

⁸The LORD said to Moses, "Make a snake and put it up on a pole; anyone who is bitten can look at it and live." ⁹So Moses made a bronze snake and put it up on a pole. Then when anyone was bitten by a snake and looked at the bronze snake, he lived.

The Journey to Moab

¹⁰The Israelites moved on and camped at Oboth. ¹¹Then they set out from Oboth and camped in Iye Abarim, in the desert that faces Moab towards the sunrise. ¹²From there they moved on and camped in the Zered Valley. ¹³They set out from there and camped alongside the Arnon, which is in the desert extending into Amorite territory. The Arnon is the border of Moab, between Moab and the Amorites. ¹⁴That is why the Book of the Wars of the LORD says:

> ". . . Waheb in Suphah ᵈ and the ravines,
>   the Arnon ¹⁵and ᵉ the slopes of the ravines
> that lead to the site of Ar
>   and lie along the border of Moab."

21:14 These songs are very ancient. It is a sign of the importance of the events in this chapter that the songs have been preserved. The defeat of Sihon and Og had double importance. Psychologically it gave a boost to the people's belief in their power to win battles. In tactical terms it gave them an important strategic base from which to cross the Jordan into Canaan.

---

¹⁶From there they continued on to Beer, the well where the LORD said to Moses, "Gather the people together and I will give them water."

¹⁷Then Israel sang this song:

> "Spring up, O well!
>   Sing about it,
> ¹⁸about the well that the princes dug,
>   that the nobles of the people sank—
>   the nobles with sceptres and staffs."

Then they went from the desert to Mattanah, ¹⁹from Mattanah to Nahaliel, from Nahaliel to Bamoth, ²⁰and from Bamoth to the valley in Moab where the top of Pisgah overlooks the wasteland.

Defeat of Sihon and Og

²¹Israel sent messengers to say to Sihon king of the Amorites:

²²"Let us pass through your country. We will not turn aside into any field or vineyard, or drink water from any well. We will travel along the king's highway until we have passed through your territory."

²³But Sihon would not let Israel pass through his territory. He mustered his entire army and marched out into the desert against Israel. When he reached Jahaz, he fought with Israel. ²⁴Israel, however, put him to the

---

ᵃ2 The Hebrew term refers to the irrevocable giving over of things or persons to the LORD, often by totally destroying them; also in verse 3.
ᵇ3 Hormah means destruction.   ᶜ4 Hebrew Yam Suph; that is, Sea of Reeds
ᵈ14 The meaning of the Hebrew for this phrase is uncertain.
ᵉ14,15 Or "I have been given from Suphah and the ravines / of the Arnon ¹⁵to

sword and took over his land from the Arnon to the Jabbok, but only as far as the Ammonites, because their border was fortified. [25]Israel captured all the cities of the Amorites and occupied them, including Heshbon and all its surrounding settlements. [26]Heshbon was the city of Sihon king of the Amorites, who had fought against the former king of Moab and had taken from him all his land as far as the Arnon.

[27]That is why the poets say:

"Come to Heshbon and let it be rebuilt;
let Sihon's city be restored.

[28]"Fire went out from Heshbon,
a blaze from the city of Sihon.
It consumed Ar of Moab,
the citizens of Arnon's heights.
[29]Woe to you, O Moab!
You are destroyed, O people of Chemosh!
He has given up his sons as fugitives
and his daughters as captives
to Sihon king of the Amorites.

[30]"But we have overthrown them;
Heshbon is destroyed all the way to Dibon.
We have demolished them as far as Nophah,
which extends to Medeba."

[31]So Israel settled in the land of the Amorites. [32]After Moses had sent spies to Jazer, the Israelites captured its surrounding settlements and drove out the Amorites who were there. [33]Then they turned and went up along the road towards Bashan, and Og king of Bashan and his whole army marched out to meet them in battle at Edrei.

[34]The LORD said to Moses, "Do not be afraid of him, for I have handed him over to you, with his whole army and his land. Do to him what you did to Sihon king of the Amorites, who reigned in Heshbon."

[35]So they struck him down, together with his sons and his whole army, leaving them no survivors. And they took possession of his land.

Balak Summons Balaam

22 Then the Israelites travelled to the plains of Moab and camped along the Jordan across from Jericho.[a]

[2]Now Balak son of Zippor saw all that Israel had done to the Amorites, [3]and Moab was terrified because there were so many people. Indeed, Moab was filled with dread because of the Israelites.

[4]The Moabites said to the elders of Midian, "This horde is going to lick up everything around us, as an ox licks up the grass of the field."

So Balak son of Zippor, who was king of Moab at that time, [5]sent messengers to summon Balaam son of Beor, who was at Pethor, near the River,[b] in his native land. Balak said:

"A people has come out of Egypt; they cover the face of the land and have settled next to me. [6]Now come and put a curse on these people, because they are too powerful for me. Perhaps then I will be able to defeat them and drive them

out of the country. For I know that those you bless are blessed, and those you curse are cursed."

[7]The elders of Moab and Midian left, taking with them the fee for divination. When they came to Balaam, they told him what Balak had said.

[8]"Spend the night here," Balaam said to them, "and I will bring you back the answer the LORD gives me." So the Moabite princes stayed with him.

[9]God came to Balaam and asked, "Who are these men with you?"

[10]Balaam said to God, "Balak son of Zippor, king of Moab, sent me this message: [11]'A people that has come out of Egypt covers the face of the land. Now come and put a curse on them for me. Perhaps then I will be able to fight them and drive them away.' "

[12]But God said to Balaam, "Do not go with them. You must not put a curse on those people, because they are blessed."

[13]The next morning Balaam got up and said to Balak's princes, "Go back to your own country, for the LORD has refused to let me go with you."

[14]So the Moabite princes returned to Balak and said, "Balaam refused to come with us."

[15]Then Balak sent other princes, more numerous and more distinguished than the first. [16]They came to Balaam and said:

"This is what Balak son of Zippor says: Do not let anything keep you from coming to me, [17]because I will reward you handsomely and do whatever you say. Come and put a curse on these people for me."

[18]But Balaam answered them, "Even if Balak gave me his palace filled with silver and gold, I could not do anything great or small to go beyond the command of the LORD my God. [19]Now stay here tonight as the others did, and I will find out what else the LORD will tell me."

[20]That night God came to Balaam and said, "Since these men have come to summon you, go with them, but do only what I tell you."

Balaam's Donkey

[21]Balaam got up in the morning, saddled his donkey and went with the princes of Moab. [22]But God was very angry when he went, and the angel of the LORD stood in the road to oppose him. Balaam was riding on his donkey, and his two servants were with him. [23]When the donkey saw the angel of the LORD standing in the road with a drawn sword in his hand, she turned off the road into a field. Balaam beat her to get her back on the road.

[24]Then the angel of the LORD stood in a narrow path between two vineyards, with walls on both sides. [25]When the donkey saw the angel of the LORD, she pressed close to the wall, crushing Balaam's foot against it. So he beat her again.

[26]Then the angel of the LORD moved on ahead and stood in a narrow place where there was no room to turn, either to the right or to the left. [27]When the donkey saw the angel of the LORD, she lay down under

---

[a]1 Hebrew *Jordan of Jericho;* possibly an ancient name for the Jordan River   [b]5 That is, the Euphrates

Balaam, and he was angry and beat her with his staff. [28]Then the LORD opened the donkey's mouth, and she said to Balaam, "What have I done to you to make you beat me these three times?"

[29]Balaam answered the donkey, "You have made a fool of me! If I had a sword in my hand, I would kill you right now."

[30]The donkey said to Balaam, "Am I not your own donkey, which you have always ridden, to this day? Have I been in the habit of doing this to you?"

"No," he said.

[31]Then the LORD opened Balaam's eyes, and he saw the angel of the LORD standing in the road with his sword drawn. So he bowed low and fell face down.

[32]The angel of the LORD asked him, "Why have you beaten your donkey these three times? I have come here to oppose you because your path is a reckless one before me.[c] [33]The donkey saw me and turned away from me these three times. If she had not turned away, I would certainly have killed you by now, but I would have spared her."

[34]Balaam said to the angel of the LORD, "I have sinned. I did not realise you were standing in the road to oppose me. Now if you are displeased, I will go back."

[35]The angel of the LORD said to Balaam, "Go with the men, but speak only what I tell you." So Balaam went with the princes of Balak.

[36]When Balak heard that Balaam was coming, he went out to meet him at the Moabite town on the Arnon border, at the edge of his territory. [37]Balak said to Balaam, "Did I not send you an urgent summons? Why didn't you come to me? Am I really not able to reward you?"

[38]"Well, I have come to you now," Balaam replied. "But can I say just anything? I must speak only what God puts in my mouth."

[39]Then Balaam went with Balak to Kiriath Huzoth. [40]Balak sacrificed cattle and sheep, and gave some to Balaam and the princes who were with him. [41]The next morning Balak took Balaam up to Bamoth Baal, and from there he saw part of the people.

Balaam's First Oracle

23 Balaam said, "Build me seven altars here, and prepare seven bulls and seven rams for me." [2]Balak did as Balaam said, and the two of them offered a bull and a ram on each altar.

[3]Then Balaam said to Balak, "Stay here beside your offering while I go aside. Perhaps the LORD will come to meet with me. Whatever he reveals to me I will tell you." Then he went off to a barren height.

[4]God met with him, and Balaam said, "I have prepared seven altars, and on each altar I have offered a bull and a ram."

[5]The LORD put a message in Balaam's mouth and said, "Go back to Balak and give him this message." [6]So he went back to him and found him standing beside his offering, with all the princes of Moab. [7]Then Balaam uttered his oracle:

"Balak brought me from Aram,
    the king of Moab from the eastern mountains.
'Come,' he said, 'curse Jacob for me;
    come, denounce Israel.'
[8]How can I curse
    those whom God has not cursed?
How can I denounce
    those whom the LORD has not denounced?

23:8   The story of Balak and Balaam is wittily told. Balaam is mentioned in seven books of the Bible. He was a professional pagan magician, and became a symbol for the way Israelite religion related to pagan cultures. Ironically he was used by God to deny the power of magic, and to bless those he had been paid to curse.

---

[9]From the rocky peaks I see them,
    from the heights I view them.
I see people who live apart
    and do not consider themselves one of the
        nations.
[10]Who can count the dust of Jacob
    or number the fourth part of Israel?
Let me die the death of the righteous,
    and may my end be like theirs!"

[11]Balak said to Balaam, "What have you done to me? I brought you to curse my enemies, but you have done nothing but bless them!"

[12]He answered, "Must I not speak what the LORD puts in my mouth?"

Balaam's Second Oracle

[13]Then Balak said to him, "Come with me to another place where you can see them; you will see only a part but not all of them. And from there, curse them for me." [14]So he took him to the field of Zophim on the top of Pisgah, and there he built seven altars and offered a bull and a ram on each altar.

[15]Balaam said to Balak, "Stay here beside your offering while I meet with him over there."

[16]The LORD met with Balaam and put a message in his mouth and said, "Go back to Balak and give him this message."

[17]So he went to him and found him standing beside his offering, with the princes of Moab. Balak asked him, "What did the LORD say?"

[18]Then he uttered his oracle:

"Arise, Balak, and listen;
    hear me, son of Zippor.
[19]God is not a man, that he should lie,
    nor a son of man, that he should change his
        mind.
Does he speak and then not act?
Does he promise and not fulfil?
[20]I have received a command to bless;
    he has blessed, and I cannot change it.

[c]32 The meaning of the Hebrew for this clause is uncertain.

²¹"No misfortune is seen in Jacob,
no misery observed in Israel.ᵃ
The Lᴏʀᴅ their God is with them;
the shout of the King is among them.
²²God brought them out of Egypt;
they have the strength of a wild ox.
²³There is no sorcery against Jacob,
no divination against Israel.
It will now be said of Jacob
and of Israel, 'See what God has done!'
²⁴The people rise like a lioness;
they rouse themselves like a lion
that does not rest till he devours his prey
and drinks the blood of his victims."

²⁵Then Balak said to Balaam, "Neither curse them at all nor bless them at all!"

²⁶Balaam answered, "Did I not tell you I must do whatever the Lᴏʀᴅ says?"

Balaam's Third Oracle

²⁷Then Balak said to Balaam, "Come, let me take you to another place. Perhaps it will please God to let you curse them for me from there." ²⁸And Balak took Balaam to the top of Peor, overlooking the wasteland. ²⁹Balaam said, "Build me seven altars here, and prepare seven bulls and seven rams for me." ³⁰Balak did as Balaam had said, and offered a bull and a ram on each altar.

24 Now when Balaam saw that it pleased the Lᴏʀᴅ to bless Israel, he did not resort to sorcery as at other times, but turned his face towards the desert. ²When Balaam looked out and saw Israel encamped tribe by tribe, the Spirit of God came upon him ³and he uttered his oracle:

"The oracle of Balaam son of Beor,
the oracle of one whose eye sees clearly,
⁴the oracle of one who hears the words of God,
who sees a vision from the Almighty,ᵃ
who falls prostrate, and whose eyes are opened:

⁵"How beautiful are your tents, O Jacob,
your dwelling-places, O Israel!

⁶"Like valleys they spread out,
like gardens beside a river,
like aloes planted by the Lᴏʀᴅ,
like cedars beside the waters.
⁷Water will flow from their buckets;
their seed will have abundant water.

"Their king will be greater than Agag;
their kingdom will be exalted.

⁸"God brought them out of Egypt;
they have the strength of a wild ox.
They devour hostile nations
and break their bones in pieces;
with their arrows they pierce them.
⁹Like a lion they crouch and lie down,
like a lioness—who dares to rouse them?

"May those who bless you be blessed
and those who curse you be cursed!"

¹⁰Then Balak's anger burned against Balaam. He struck his hands together and said to him, "I summoned you to curse my enemies, but you have blessed them these three times. ¹¹Now leave at once and go home! I said I would reward you handsomely, but the Lᴏʀᴅ has kept you from being rewarded."

¹²Balaam answered Balak, "Did I not tell the messengers you sent me, ¹³'Even if Balak gave me his palace filled with silver and gold, I could not do anything of my own accord, good or bad, to go beyond the command of the Lᴏʀᴅ—and I must say only what the Lᴏʀᴅ says'? ¹⁴Now I am going back to my people, but come, let me warn you of what this people will do to your people in days to come."

Balaam's Fourth Oracle

¹⁵Then he uttered his oracle:

"The oracle of Balaam son of Beor,
the oracle of one whose eye sees clearly,
¹⁶the oracle of one who hears the words of God,
who has knowledge from the Most High,
who sees a vision from the Almighty,
who falls prostrate, and whose eyes are opened:

¹⁷"I see him, but not now;
I behold him, but not near.
A star will come out of Jacob;
a sceptre will rise out of Israel.
He will crush the foreheads of Moab,
the skullsᵇ ofᶜ all the sons of Sheth.ᵈ

24:17   This prophecy of Balaam came true in David's reign when he defeated the nations of Moab and Edom. The star therefore became a symbol for David, a symbolism which continued after him for the second David, the Messiah, who would fulfil all of God's promises.

---

¹⁸Edom will be conquered;
Seir, his enemy, will be conquered,
but Israel will grow strong.
¹⁹A ruler will come out of Jacob
and destroy the survivors of the city."

Balaam's Final Oracles

²⁰Then Balaam saw Amalek and uttered his oracle:

"Amalek was first among the nations,
but he will come to ruin at last."

²¹Then he saw the Kenites and uttered his oracle:

"Your dwelling-place is secure,
your nest is set in a rock;
²²yet you Kenites will be destroyed
when Asshur takes you captive."

ᵃ21 Or He has not looked on Jacob's offences / or on the wrongs found in Israel.   ᵃ4 Hebrew Shaddai; also in verse 16
ᵇ17 Samaritan Pentateuch (see also Jer. 48:45); the meaning of the word in the Masoretic Text is uncertain.
ᶜ17 Or possibly Moab, / batter   ᵈ17 Or all the noisy boasters

23Then he uttered his oracle:

"Ah, who can live when God does this?*e*
24   Ships will come from the shores of Kittim;
   they will subdue Asshur and Eber,
      but they too will come to ruin."

25Then Balaam got up and returned home and Balak went his own way.

Moab Seduces Israel

25 While Israel was staying in Shittim, the men began to indulge in sexual immorality with Moabite women, 2who invited them to the sacrifices to their gods. The people ate and bowed down before these gods. 3So Israel joined in worshipping the Baal of Peor. And the LORD's anger burned against them.

4The LORD said to Moses, "Take all the leaders of these people, kill them and expose them in broad daylight before the LORD, so that the LORD's fierce anger may turn away from Israel."

5So Moses said to Israel's judges, "Each of you must put to death those of your men who have joined in worshipping the Baal of Peor."

6Then an Israelite man brought to his family a Midianite woman right before the eyes of Moses and the whole assembly of Israel while they were weeping at the entrance to the Tent of Meeting. 7When Phinehas son of Eleazar, the son of Aaron, the priest, saw this, he left the assembly, took a spear in his hand 8and followed the Israelite into the tent. He drove the spear through both of them—through the Israelite and into the woman's body. Then the plague against the Israelites was stopped; 9but those who died in the plague numbered 24,000.

10The LORD said to Moses, 11"Phinehas son of Eleazar, the son of Aaron, the priest, has turned my anger away from the Israelites; for he was as zealous as I am for my honour among them, so that in my zeal I did not put an end to them. 12Therefore tell him I am making my covenant of peace with him. 13He and his descendants will have a covenant of a lasting priesthood, because he was zealous for the honour of his God and made atonement for the Israelites."

14The name of the Israelite who was killed with the Midianite woman was Zimri son of Salu, the leader of a Simeonite family. 15And the name of the Midianite woman who was put to death was Cozbi daughter of Zur, a tribal chief of a Midianite family.

16The LORD said to Moses, 17"Treat the Midianites as enemies and kill them, 18because they treated you as enemies when they deceived you in the affair of Peor and their sister Cozbi, the daughter of a Midianite leader, the woman who was killed when the plague came as a result of Peor."

The Second Census

26 After the plague the LORD said to Moses and Eleazar son of Aaron, the priest, 2"Take a census of the whole Israelite community by families—all those twenty years old or more who are able to serve

in the army of Israel." 3So on the plains of Moab by the Jordan across from Jericho,*a* Moses and Eleazar the priest spoke with them and said, 4"Take a census of men twenty years old or more, as the LORD commanded Moses."

These were the Israelites who came out of Egypt:

5The descendants of Reuben, the firstborn son of Israel, were:
   through Hanoch, the Hanochite clan;
   through Pallu, the Palluite clan;
   6through Hezron, the Hezronite clan;
   through Carmi, the Carmite clan.
7These were the clans of Reuben; those numbered were 43,730.

8The son of Pallu was Eliab, 9and the sons of Eliab were Nemuel, Dathan and Abiram. The same Dathan and Abiram were the community officials who rebelled against Moses and Aaron and were among Korah's followers when they rebelled against the LORD. 10The earth opened its mouth and swallowed them along with Korah, whose followers died when the fire devoured the 250 men. And they served as a warning sign. 11The line of Korah, however, did not die out.

12The descendants of Simeon by their clans were:
   through Nemuel, the Nemuelite clan;
   through Jamin, the Jaminite clan;
   through Jakin, the Jakinite clan;
   13through Zerah, the Zerahite clan;
   through Shaul, the Shaulite clan.
14These were the clans of Simeon; there were 22,200 men.

15The descendants of Gad by their clans were:
   through Zephon, the Zephonite clan;
   through Haggi, the Haggite clan;
   through Shuni, the Shunite clan;
   16through Ozni, the Oznite clan;
   through Eri, the Erite clan;
   17through Arodi,*b* the Arodite clan;
   through Areli, the Arelite clan.
18These were the clans of Gad; those numbered were 40,500.

19Er and Onan were sons of Judah, but they died in Canaan. 20The descendants of Judah by their clans were:
   through Shelah, the Shelanite clan;
   through Perez, the Perezite clan;
   through Zerah, the Zerahite clan.
21The descendants of Perez were:
   through Hezron, the Hezronite clan;
   through Hamul, the Hamulite clan.
22These were the clans of Judah; those numbered were 76,500.

23The descendants of Issachar by their clans were:
   through Tola, the Tolaite clan;
   through Puah, the Puite*c* clan;
   24through Jashub, the Jashubite clan;

---

e23 Masoretic Text; with a different word division of the Hebrew A people will gather from the north.
a3 Hebrew Jordan of Jericho; possibly an ancient name for the Jordan River; also in verse 63
b17 Samaritan Pentateuch and Syriac (see also Gen. 46:16); Masoretic Text Arod
c23 Samaritan Pentateuch, Septuagint, Vulgate and Syriac (see also 1 Chron. 7:1); Masoretic Text through Puvah, the Punite

through Shimron, the Shimronite clan.
25These were the clans of Issachar; those numbered were 64,300.

26The descendants of Zebulun by their clans were:
through Sered, the Seredite clan;
through Elon, the Elonite clan;
through Jahleel, the Jahleelite clan.
27These were the clans of Zebulun; those numbered were 60,500.

28The descendants of Joseph by their clans through Manasseh and Ephraim were:

29The descendants of Manasseh:
through Makir, the Makirite clan (Makir was the father of Gilead);
through Gilead, the Gileadite clan.
30These were the descendants of Gilead:
through Iezer, the Iezerite clan;
through Helek, the Helekite clan;
31through Asriel, the Asrielite clan;
through Shechem, the Shechemite clan;
32through Shemida, the Shemidaite clan;
through Hepher, the Hepherite clan.
33(Zelophehad son of Hepher had no sons; he had only daughters, whose names were Mahlah, Noah, Hoglah, Milcah and Tirzah.)
34These were the clans of Manasseh; those numbered were 52,700.

35These were the descendants of Ephraim by their clans:
through Shuthelah, the Shuthelahite clan;
through Beker, the Bekerite clan;
through Tahan, the Tahanite clan.
36These were the descendants of Shuthelah:
through Eran, the Eranite clan.
37These were the clans of Ephraim; those numbered were 32,500.

These were the descendants of Joseph by their clans.

38The descendants of Benjamin by their clans were:
through Bela, the Belaite clan;
through Ashbel, the Ashbelite clan;
through Ahiram, the Ahiramite clan;
39through Shupham,d the Shuphamite clan;
through Hupham, the Huphamite clan.
40The descendants of Bela through Ard and Naaman were:
through Ard,e the Ardite clan;
through Naaman, the Naamite clan.
41These were the clans of Benjamin; those numbered were 45,600.

42These were the descendants of Dan by their clans:
through Shuham, the Shuhamite clan.
These were the clans of Dan: 43All of them were Shuhamite clans; and those numbered were 64,400.

44The descendants of Asher by their clans:
through Imnah, the Imnite clan;
through Ishvi, the Ishvite clan;
through Beriah, the Beriite clan;
45and through the descendants of Beriah:
through Heber, the Heberite clan;
through Malkiel, the Malkielite clan.
46(Asher had a daughter named Serah.)
47These were the clans of Asher; those numbered were 53,400.

48The descendants of Naphtali by their clans were:
through Jahzeel, the Jahzeelite clan;
through Guni, the Gunite clan;
49through Jezer, the Jezerite clan;
through Shillem, the Shillemite clan.
50These were the clans of Naphtali; those numbered were 45,400.

51The total number of the men of Israel was 601,730.

52The LORD said to Moses, 53"The land is to be allotted to them as an inheritance based on the number of names. 54To a larger group give a larger inheritance, and to a smaller group a smaller one; each is to receive its inheritance according to the number of those listed. 55Be sure that the land is distributed by lot. What each group inherits will be according to the names for its ancestral tribe. 56Each inheritance is to be distributed by lot among the larger and smaller groups."

57These were the Levites who were counted by their clans:
through Gershon, the Gershonite clan;
through Kohath, the Kohathite clan;
through Merari, the Merarite clan.
58These also were Levite clans:
the Libnite clan,
the Hebronite clan,
the Mahlite clan,
the Mushite clan,
the Korahite clan.
(Kohath was the forefather of Amram; 59the name of Amram's wife was Jochebed, a descendant of Levi, who was born to the Levitesf in Egypt. To Amram she bore Aaron, Moses and their sister Miriam. 60Aaron was the father of Nadab and Abihu, Eleazar and Ithamar. 61But Nadab and Abihu died when they made an offering before the LORD with unauthorised fire.)

62All the male Levites a month old or more numbered 23,000. They were not counted along with the other Israelites because they received no inheritance among them.

63These are the ones counted by Moses and Eleazar the priest when they counted the Israelites on the plains of Moab by the Jordan across from Jericho. 64Not one of them was among those counted by Moses and Aaron the priest when they counted the Israelites in the Desert of Sinai. 65For the LORD had told those Israelites they would surely die in the desert, and not one of them was left except Caleb son of Jephunneh and Joshua son of Nun.

---

d39 A few manuscripts of the Masoretic Text, Samaritan Pentateuch, Vulgate and Syriac (see also Septuagint); most manuscripts of the Masoretic Text Shephupham   e40 Samaritan Pentateuch and Vulgate (see also Septuagint); Masoretic Text does not have through Ard,
f59 Or Jochebed, a daughter of Levi, who was born to Levi

Zelophehad's Daughters

27 The daughters of Zelophehad son of Hepher, the son of Gilead, the son of Makir, the son of Manasseh, belonged to the clans of Manasseh son of Joseph. The names of the daughters were Mahlah, Noah, Hoglah, Milcah and Tirzah. They approached ²the entrance to the Tent of Meeting and stood before Moses, Eleazar the priest, the leaders and the whole assembly, and said, ³"Our father died in the desert. He was not among Korah's followers, who banded together against the LORD, but he died for his own sin and left no sons. ⁴Why should our father's name disappear from his clan because he had no son? Give us property among our father's relatives."

⁵So Moses brought their case before the LORD ⁶and the LORD said to him, ⁷"What Zelophehad's daughters are saying is right. You must certainly give them property as an inheritance among their father's relatives and give their father's inheritance over to them.

⁸"Say to the Israelites, 'If a man dies and leaves no son, give his inheritance over to his daughter. ⁹If he has no daughter, give his inheritance to his brothers. ¹⁰If he has no brothers, give his inheritance to his father's brothers. ¹¹If his father had no brothers, give his inheritance to the nearest relative in his clan, that he may possess it. This is to be a legal requirement for the Israelites, as the LORD commanded Moses.' "

Joshua to Succeed Moses

¹²Then the LORD said to Moses, "Go up this mountain in the Abarim Range and see the land I have given the Israelites. ¹³After you have seen it, you too will be gathered to your people, as your brother Aaron was, ¹⁴for when the community rebelled at the waters in the Desert of Zin, both of you disobeyed my command to honour me as holy before their eyes." (These were the waters of Meribah Kadesh, in the Desert of Zin.)

27:17   This is the first appearance of the person who was to become the most powerful symbol of Israel's leaders. We are given another insight into Moses' greatness as a leader. Even though he was being punished he cared so much about the people that he begged for a suitable successor for himself. Joshua had "spirit" — that more-than-human power which God bestows, but he was not a second Moses. He did not speak personally with God but through the priest who used the sacred oracle.

---

¹⁵Moses said to the LORD, ¹⁶"May the LORD, the God of the spirits of all mankind, appoint a man over this community ¹⁷to go out and come in before them, one who will lead them out and bring them in, so that the LORD's people will not be like sheep without a shepherd."

¹⁸So the LORD said to Moses, "Take Joshua son of Nun, a man in whom is the spirit,ᵃ and lay your hand on him. ¹⁹Make him stand before Eleazar the priest and the entire assembly and commission him in their presence. ²⁰Give him some of your authority so that the whole Israelite community will obey him. ²¹He is to stand before Eleazar the priest, who will obtain decisions for him by enquiring of the Urim before the LORD. At his command he and the entire community of the Israelites will go out, and at his command they will come in."

²²Moses did as the LORD commanded him. He took Joshua and made him stand before Eleazar the priest and the whole assembly. ²³Then he laid his hands on him and commissioned him, as the LORD instructed through Moses.

Daily Offerings

28 The LORD said to Moses, ²"Give this command to the Israelites and say to them: 'See that you present to me at the appointed time the food for my offerings made by fire, as an aroma pleasing to me.' ³Say to them: 'This is the offering made by fire that you are to present to the LORD: two lambs a year old without defect, as a regular burnt offering each day. ⁴Prepare one lamb in the morning and the other at twilight, ⁵together with a grain offering of a tenth of an ephahᵃ of fine flour mixed with a quarter of a hinᵇ of oil from pressed olives. ⁶This is the regular burnt offering instituted at Mount Sinai as a pleasing aroma, an offering made to the LORD by fire. ⁷The accompanying drink offering is to be a quarter of a hin of fermented drink with each lamb. Pour out the drink offering to the LORD at the sanctuary. ⁸Prepare the second lamb at twilight, along with the same kind of grain offering and drink offering that you prepare in the morning. This is an offering made by fire, an aroma pleasing to the LORD.

Sabbath Offerings

⁹" 'On the Sabbath day, make an offering of two lambs a year old without defect, together with its drink offering and a grain offering of two-tenths of an ephahᶜ of fine flour mixed with oil. ¹⁰This is the burnt offering for every Sabbath, in addition to the regular burnt offering and its drink offering.

Monthly Offerings

¹¹" 'On the first of every month, present to the LORD a burnt offering of two young bulls, one ram and seven male lambs a year old, all without defect. ¹²With each bull there is to be a grain offering of three-tenths of an ephahᵈ of fine flour mixed with oil; with the ram, a grain offering of two-tenths of an ephah of fine flour mixed with oil; ¹³and with each lamb, a grain offering of a tenth of an ephah of fine flour mixed with oil. This is for a burnt offering, a pleasing aroma, an offering made to the LORD by fire. ¹⁴With each bull there is to be a drink offering of half a hinᵉ of wine; with the

---

ᵃ18 Or *Spirit*   ᵃ5 That is, probably about 4 pints (about 2 litres); also in verses 13, 21 and 29
ᵇ5 That is, probably about 1½ pints (about 1 litre); also in verses 7 and 14
ᶜ9 That is, probably about 7½ pints (about 4.5 litres); also in verses 12, 20 and 28
ᵈ12 That is, probably about 11½ pints (about 6.5 litres); also in verses 20 and 28   ᵉ14 That is, probably about 3 pints (about 2 litres)

ram, a third of a hin;*f* and with each lamb, a quarter of a hin. This is the monthly burnt offering to be made at each new moon during the year. [15]Besides the regular burnt offering with its drink offering, one male goat is to be presented to the LORD as a sin offering.

The Passover

[16]" 'On the fourteenth day of the first month the LORD's Passover is to be held. [17]On the fifteenth day of this month there is to be a festival; for seven days eat bread made without yeast. [18]On the first day hold a sacred assembly and do no regular work. [19]Present to the LORD an offering made by fire, a burnt offering of two young bulls, one ram and seven male lambs a year old, all without defect. [20]With each bull prepare a grain offering of three-tenths of an ephah of fine flour mixed with oil; with the ram, two-tenths; [21]and with each of the seven lambs, one-tenth. [22]Include one male goat as a sin offering to make atonement for you. [23]Prepare these in addition to the regular morning burnt offering. [24]In this way prepare the food for the offering made by fire every day for seven days as an aroma pleasing to the LORD; it is to be prepared in addition to the regular burnt offering and its drink offering. [25]On the seventh day hold a sacred assembly and do no regular work.

Feast of Weeks

[26]" 'On the day of firstfruits, when you present to the LORD an offering of new grain during the Feast of Weeks, hold a sacred assembly and do no regular work. [27]Present a burnt offering of two young bulls, one ram and seven male lambs a year old as an aroma pleasing to the LORD. [28]With each bull there is to be a grain offering of three-tenths of an ephah of fine flour mixed with oil; with the ram, two-tenths; [29]and with each of the seven lambs, one-tenth. [30]Include one male goat to make atonement for you. [31]Prepare these together with their drink offerings, in addition to the regular burnt offering and its grain offering. Be sure the animals are without defect.

Feast of Trumpets

29 " 'On the first day of the seventh month hold a sacred assembly and do no regular work. It is a day for you to sound the trumpets. [2]As an aroma pleasing to the LORD, prepare a burnt offering of one young bull, one ram and seven male lambs a year old, all without defect. [3]With the bull prepare a grain offering of three-tenths of an ephah*a* of fine flour mixed with oil; with the ram, two-tenths;*b* [4]and with each of the seven lambs, one-tenth.*c* [5]Include one male goat as a sin offering to make atonement for you. [6]These are in addition to the monthly and daily burnt offerings with their grain offerings and drink offerings as specified. They are offerings made to the LORD by fire—a pleasing aroma.

Day of Atonement

[7]" 'On the tenth day of this seventh month hold a sacred assembly. You must deny yourselves*d* and do no work. [8]Present as an aroma pleasing to the LORD a burnt offering of one young bull, one ram and seven male lambs a year old, all without defect. [9]With the bull prepare a grain offering of three-tenths of an ephah of fine flour mixed with oil; with the ram, two-tenths; [10]and with each of the seven lambs, one-tenth. [11]Include one male goat as a sin offering, in addition to the sin offering for atonement and the regular burnt offering with its grain offering, and their drink offerings.

Feast of Tabernacles

[12]" 'On the fifteenth day of the seventh month, hold a sacred assembly and do no regular work. Celebrate a festival to the LORD for seven days. [13]Present an offering made by fire as an aroma pleasing to the LORD, a burnt offering of thirteen young bulls, two rams and fourteen male lambs a year old, all without defect. [14]With each of the thirteen bulls prepare a grain offering of three-tenths of an ephah of fine flour mixed with oil; with each of the two rams, two-tenths; [15]and with each of the fourteen lambs, one-tenth. [16]Include one male goat as a sin offering, in addition to the regular burnt offering with its grain offering and drink offering.

[17]" 'On the second day prepare twelve young bulls, two rams and fourteen male lambs a year old, all without defect. [18]With the bulls, rams and lambs, prepare their grain offerings and drink offerings according to the number specified. [19]Include one male goat as a sin offering, in addition to the regular burnt offering with its grain offering, and their drink offerings.

[20]" 'On the third day prepare eleven bulls, two rams and fourteen male lambs a year old, all without defect. [21]With the bulls, rams and lambs, prepare their grain offerings and drink offerings according to the number specified. [22]Include one male goat as a sin offering, in addition to the regular burnt offering with its grain offering and drink offering.

[23]" 'On the fourth day prepare ten bulls, two rams and fourteen male lambs a year old, all without defect. [24]With the bulls, rams and lambs, prepare their grain offerings and drink offerings according to the number specified. [25]Include one male goat as a sin offering, in addition to the regular burnt offering with its grain offering and drink offering.

[26]" 'On the fifth day prepare nine bulls, two rams and fourteen male lambs a year old, all without defect. [27]With the bulls, rams and lambs, prepare their grain offerings and drink offerings according to the number specified. [28]Include one male goat as a sin offering, in addition to the regular burnt offering with its grain offering and drink offering.

[29]" 'On the sixth day prepare eight bulls, two rams and fourteen male lambs a year old, all without defect. [30]With the bulls, rams and lambs, prepare their grain offerings and drink offerings according to the number

---

f14 That is, probably about 2¼ pints (about 1.2 litres)
b3 That is, probably about 7½ pints (about 4.5 litres); also in verses 9 and 14
c4 That is, probably about 4 pints (about 2 litres); also in verses 10 and 15
a3 That is, probably about 11½ pints (about 6.5 litres); also in verses 9 and 14
d7 Or must fast

specified. ³¹Include one male goat as a sin offering, in addition to the regular burnt offering with its grain offering and drink offering.

³²" 'On the seventh day prepare seven bulls, two rams and fourteen male lambs a year old, all without defect. ³³With the bulls, rams and lambs, prepare their grain offerings and drink offerings according to the number specified. ³⁴Include one male goat as a sin offering, in addition to the regular burnt offering with its grain offering and drink offering.

³⁵" 'On the eighth day hold an assembly and do no regular work. ³⁶Present an offering made by fire as an aroma pleasing to the LORD, a burnt offering of one bull, one ram and seven male lambs a year old, all without defect. ³⁷With the bull, the ram and the lambs, prepare their grain offerings and drink offerings according to the number specified. ³⁸Include one male goat as a sin offering, in addition to the regular burnt offering with its grain offering and drink offering.

³⁹" 'In addition to what you vow and your freewill offerings, prepare these for the LORD at your appointed feasts: your burnt offerings, grain offerings, drink offerings and fellowship offerings.' " *e*

⁴⁰Moses told the Israelites all that the LORD commanded him.

Vows

30 Moses said to the heads of the tribes of Israel: "This is what the LORD commands: ²When a man makes a vow to the LORD or takes an oath to bind himself by a pledge, he must not break his word but must do everything he said.

³"When a young woman still living in her father's house makes a vow to the LORD or binds herself by a pledge ⁴and her father hears about her vow or pledge but says nothing to her, then all her vows and every pledge by which she bound herself will stand. ⁵But if her father forbids her when he hears about it, none of her vows or the pledges by which she bound herself will stand; the LORD will release her because her father has forbidden her.

30:3 These regulations show that although a woman had some freedom to conduct her own affairs and take certain responsibilities on herself, she was ultimately under the control of the head of her household. Although the rules seem restrictive they were in fact more advanced than was current practice in the area. Most women of the time were treated in law as property with the same status as animals — except that in some cases they were actually considered less valuable!

---

⁶"If she marries after she makes a vow or after her lips utter a rash promise by which she binds herself ⁷and her husband hears about it but says nothing to her, then her vows or the pledges by which she bound

herself will stand. ⁸But if her husband forbids her when he hears about it, he nullifies the vow that binds her or the rash promise by which she binds herself, and the LORD will release her.

⁹"Any vow or obligation taken by a widow or divorced woman will be binding on her.

¹⁰"If a woman living with her husband makes a vow or binds herself by a pledge under oath ¹¹and her husband hears about it but says nothing to her and does not forbid her, then all her vows or the pledges by which she bound herself will stand. ¹²But if her husband nullifies them when he hears about them, then none of the vows or pledges that came from her lips will stand. Her husband has nullified them, and the LORD will release her. ¹³Her husband may confirm or nullify any vow she makes or any sworn pledge to deny herself. ¹⁴But if her husband says nothing to her about it from day to day, then he confirms all her vows or the pledges binding on her. He confirms them by saying nothing to her when he hears about them. ¹⁵If, however, he nullifies them some time after he hears about them, then he is responsible for her guilt."

¹⁶These are the regulations the LORD gave Moses concerning relationships between a man and his wife, and between a father and his young daughter still living in his house.

Vengeance on the Midianites

31 The LORD said to Moses, ²"Take vengeance on the Midianites for the Israelites. After that, you will be gathered to your people."

³So Moses said to the people, "Arm some of your men to go to war against the Midianites and to carry out the LORD's vengeance on them. ⁴Send into battle a thousand men from each of the tribes of Israel." ⁵So twelve thousand men armed for battle, a thousand from each tribe, were supplied from the clans of Israel. ⁶Moses sent them into battle, a thousand from each tribe, along with Phinehas son of Eleazar, the priest, who took with him articles from the sanctuary and the trumpets for signalling.

⁷They fought against Midian, as the LORD commanded Moses, and killed every man. ⁸Among their victims were Evi, Rekem, Zur, Hur and Reba — the five kings of Midian. They also killed Balaam son of Beor with the sword. ⁹The Israelites captured the Midianite women and children and took all the Midianite herds, flocks and goods as plunder. ¹⁰They burned all the towns where the Midianites had settled, as well as all their camps. ¹¹They took all the plunder and spoils, including the people and animals, ¹²and brought the captives, spoils and plunder to Moses and Eleazar the priest and the Israelite assembly at their camp on the plains of Moab, by the Jordan across from Jericho. *a*

¹³Moses, Eleazar the priest and all the leaders of the community went to meet them outside the camp. ¹⁴Moses was angry with the officers of the army — the commanders of thousands and commanders of hundreds — who returned from the battle. ¹⁵"Have you allowed all the women to live?" he asked them. ¹⁶"They were the ones who followed

---

e 39 Traditionally peace offerings   *a 12 Hebrew Jordan of Jericho; possibly an ancient name for the Jordan River*

Balaam's advice and were the means of turning the Israelites away from the LORD in what happened at Peor, so that a plague struck the LORD's people. [17]Now kill all the boys. And kill every woman who has slept with a man, [18]but save for yourselves every girl who has never slept with a man.

31:15 Like everything else, victory in war belonged to God, so all the spoils of war were his. When Israel fought a holy war everything belonging to the enemy was put under a ban. Living things had to be killed and property burned. It is possible to admire the Israelites' dedication to God and understanding of his holiness (it was a great sacrifice to give up all plunder), while recognizing that we have grown in our understanding of God. We do not think he demands death and destruction any more than we think we should offer him animal sacrifices. In the same way, there will no doubt be blindness in our understanding that will amaze our descendants.

---

[19]"All of you who have killed anyone or touched anyone who was killed must stay outside the camp seven days. On the third and seventh days you must purify yourselves and your captives. [20]Purify every garment as well as everything made of leather, goat hair or wood."

[21]Then Eleazar the priest said to the soldiers who had gone into battle, "This is the requirement of the law that the LORD gave Moses: [22]Gold, silver, bronze, iron, tin, lead [23]and anything else that can withstand fire must be put through the fire, and then it will be clean. But it must also be purified with the water of cleansing. And whatever cannot withstand fire must be put through that water. [24]On the seventh day wash your clothes and you will be clean. Then you may come into the camp."

Dividing the Spoils

[25]The LORD said to Moses, [26]"You and Eleazar the priest and the family heads of the community are to count all the people and animals that were captured. [27]Divide the spoils between the soldiers who took part in the battle and the rest of the community. [28]From the soldiers who fought in the battle, set apart as tribute for the LORD one out of every five hundred, whether persons, cattle, donkeys, sheep or goats. [29]Take this tribute from their half share and give it to Eleazar the priest as the LORD's part. [30]From the Israelites' half, select one out of every fifty, whether persons, cattle, donkeys, sheep, goats or other animals. Give them to the Levites, who are responsible for the care of the LORD's tabernacle." [31]So Moses and Eleazar the priest did as the LORD commanded Moses.

[32]The plunder remaining from the spoils that the soldiers took was 675,000 sheep, [33]72,000 cattle,

[34]61,000 donkeys [35]and 32,000 women who had never slept with a man.

[36]The half share of those who fought in the battle was:

337,500 sheep, [37]of which the tribute for the LORD was 675;

[38]36,000 cattle, of which the tribute for the LORD was 72;

[39]30,500 donkeys, of which the tribute for the LORD was 61;

[40]16,000 people, of which the tribute for the LORD was 32.

[41]Moses gave the tribute to Eleazar the priest as the LORD's part, as the LORD commanded Moses.

[42]The half belonging to the Israelites, which Moses set apart from that of the fighting men — [43]the community's half — was 337,500 sheep, [44]36,000 cattle, [45]30,500 donkeys [46]and 16,000 people. [47]From the Israelites' half, Moses selected one out of every fifty persons and animals, as the LORD commanded him, and gave them to the Levites, who were responsible for the care of the LORD's tabernacle.

[48]Then the officers who were over the units of the army — the commanders of thousands and commanders of hundreds — went to Moses [49]and said to him, "Your servants have counted the soldiers under our command, and not one is missing. [50]So we have brought as an offering to the LORD the gold articles each of us acquired — armlets, bracelets, signet rings, earrings and necklaces — to make atonement for ourselves before the LORD."

[51]Moses and Eleazar the priest accepted from them the gold — all the handcrafted articles. [52]All the gold from the commanders of thousands and commanders of hundreds that Moses and Eleazar presented as a gift to the LORD weighed 16,750 shekels. [b] [53]Each soldier had taken plunder for himself. [54]Moses and Eleazar the priest accepted the gold from the commanders of thousands and commanders of hundreds and brought it into the Tent of Meeting as a memorial for the Israelites before the LORD.

The Transjordan Tribes

32 The Reubenites and Gadites, who had very large herds and flocks, saw that the lands of Jazer and Gilead were suitable for livestock. [2]So they came to Moses and Eleazar the priest and to the leaders of the community, and said, [3]"Ataroth, Dibon, Jazer, Nimrah, Heshbon, Elealeh, Sebam, Nebo and Beon — [4]the land the LORD subdued before the people of Israel — are suitable for livestock, and your servants have livestock. [5]If we have found favour in your eyes," they said, "let this land be given to your servants as our possession. Do not make us cross the Jordan."

[6]Moses said to the Gadites and Reubenites, "Shall your countrymen go to war while you sit here? [7]Why do you discourage the Israelites from going over into the land the LORD has given them? [8]This is what your fathers did when I sent them from Kadesh Barnea to look over the land. [9]After they went up to the Valley

b52 That is, about 420 pounds (about 190 kilograms)

of Eshcol and viewed the land, they discouraged the Israelites from entering the land the LORD had given them. [10]The LORD's anger was aroused that day and he swore this oath: [11]'Because they have not followed me wholeheartedly, not one of the men twenty years old or more who came up out of Egypt will see the land I promised on oath to Abraham, Isaac and Jacob — [12]not one except Caleb son of Jephunneh the Kenizzite and Joshua son of Nun, for they followed the LORD wholeheartedly.' [13]The LORD's anger burned against Israel and he made them wander in the desert for forty years, until the whole generation of those who had done evil in his sight was gone.

32:5   The tribes of Reuben and Gad (and later half of Manasseh), who wanted to settle on the east bank of the Jordan, were choosing excellent cattle pasture. However, it was more difficult to defend than the other territory, because it did not have any natural borders. Most of the sites mentioned in verses 34–42 have been identified by archaeologists.

---

[14]"And here you are, a brood of sinners, standing in the place of your fathers and making the LORD even more angry with Israel. [15]If you turn away from following him, he will again leave all this people in the desert, and you will be the cause of their destruction."

[16]Then they came up to him and said, "We would like to build pens here for our livestock and cities for our women and children. [17]But we are ready to arm ourselves and go ahead of the Israelites until we have brought them to their place. Meanwhile our women and children will live in fortified cities, for protection from the inhabitants of the land. [18]We will not return to our homes until every Israelite has received his inheritance. [19]We will not receive any inheritance with them on the other side of the Jordan, because our inheritance has come to us on the east side of the Jordan."

[20]Then Moses said to them, "If you will do this — if you will arm yourselves before the LORD for battle, [21]and if all of you will go armed over the Jordan before the LORD until he has driven his enemies out before him — [22]then when the land is subdued before the LORD, you may return and be free from your obligation to the LORD and to Israel. And this land will be your possession before the LORD.

[23]"But if you fail to do this, you will be sinning against the LORD; and you may be sure that your sin will find you out. [24]Build cities for your women and children, and pens for your flocks, but do what you have promised."

[25]The Gadites and Reubenites said to Moses, "We your servants will do as our lord commands. [26]Our children and wives, our flocks and herds will remain here in the cities of Gilead. [27]But your servants, every man armed for battle, will cross over to fight before the LORD, just as our lord says."

[28]Then Moses gave orders about them to Eleazar the priest and Joshua son of Nun and to the family heads of the Israelite tribes. [29]He said to them, "If the Gadites and Reubenites, every man armed for battle, cross over the Jordan with you before the LORD, then when the land is subdued before you, give them the land of Gilead as their possession. [30]But if they do not cross over with you armed, they must accept their possession with you in Canaan."

[31]The Gadites and Reubenites answered, "Your servants will do what the LORD has said. [32]We will cross over before the LORD into Canaan armed, but the property we inherit will be on this side of the Jordan."

[33]Then Moses gave to the Gadites, the Reubenites and the half-tribe of Manasseh son of Joseph the kingdom of Sihon king of the Amorites and the kingdom of Og king of Bashan — the whole land with its cities and the territory around them.

[34]The Gadites built up Dibon, Ataroth, Aroer, [35]Atroth Shophan, Jazer, Jogbehah, [36]Beth Nimrah and Beth Haran as fortified cities, and built pens for their flocks. [37]And the Reubenites rebuilt Heshbon, Elealeh and Kiriathaim, [38]as well as Nebo and Baal Meon (these names were changed) and Sibmah. They gave names to the cities they rebuilt.

[39]The descendants of Makir son of Manasseh went to Gilead, captured it and drove out the Amorites who were there. [40]So Moses gave Gilead to the Makirites, the descendants of Manasseh, and they settled there. [41]Jair, a descendant of Manasseh, captured their settlements and called them Havvoth Jair.[a] [42]And Nobah captured Kenath and its surrounding settlements and called it Nobah after himself.

Stages in Israel's Journey

33 Here are the stages in the journey of the Israelites when they came out of Egypt by divisions under the leadership of Moses and Aaron. [2]At the LORD's command Moses recorded the stages in their journey. This is their journey by stages:

[3]The Israelites set out from Rameses on the fifteenth day of the first month, the day after the Passover. They marched out boldly in full view of all the Egyptians, [4]who were burying all their firstborn, whom the LORD had struck down among them; for the LORD had brought judgment on their gods.

[5]The Israelites left Rameses and camped at Succoth.

[6]They left Succoth and camped at Etham, on the edge of the desert.

[7]They left Etham, turned back to Pi Hahiroth, to the east of Baal Zephon, and camped near Migdol.

[8]They left Pi Hahiroth[a] and passed through the sea into the desert, and when they had

[a]41 Or *them the settlements of Jair*   [a]8 Many manuscripts of the Masoretic Text, Samaritan Pentateuch and Vulgate; most manuscripts of the Masoretic Text *left from before Hahiroth*

travelled for three days in the Desert of Etham, they camped at Marah.

9They left Marah and went to Elim, where there were twelve springs and seventy palm trees, and they camped there.

10They left Elim and camped by the Red Sea. *b*

11They left the Red Sea and camped in the Desert of Sin.

12They left the Desert of Sin and camped at Dophkah.

13They left Dophkah and camped at Alush.

14They left Alush and camped at Rephidim, where there was no water for the people to drink.

15They left Rephidim and camped in the Desert of Sinai.

16They left the Desert of Sinai and camped at Kibroth Hattaavah.

17They left Kibroth Hattaavah and camped at Hazeroth.

18They left Hazeroth and camped at Rithmah.

19They left Rithmah and camped at Rimmon Perez.

20They left Rimmon Perez and camped at Libnah.

21They left Libnah and camped at Rissah.

22They left Rissah and camped at Kehelathah.

23They left Kehelathah and camped at Mount Shepher.

24They left Mount Shepher and camped at Haradah.

25They left Haradah and camped at Makheloth.

26They left Makheloth and camped at Tahath.

27They left Tahath and camped at Terah.

28They left Terah and camped at Mithcah.

29They left Mithcah and camped at Hashmonah.

30They left Hashmonah and camped at Moseroth.

31They left Moseroth and camped at Bene Jaakan.

32They left Bene Jaakan and camped at Hor Haggidgad.

33They left Hor Haggidgad and camped at Jotbathah.

34They left Jotbathah and camped at Abronah.

35They left Abronah and camped at Ezion Geber.

36They left Ezion Geber and camped at Kadesh, in the Desert of Zin.

37They left Kadesh and camped at Mount Hor, on the border of Edom. 38At the LORD's command Aaron the priest went up Mount Hor, where he died on the first day of the fifth month of the fortieth year after the Israelites came out of Egypt. 39Aaron was a hundred and twenty-three years old when he died on Mount Hor.

40The Canaanite king of Arad, who lived in the Negev of Canaan, heard that the Israelites were coming.

41They left Mount Hor and camped at Zalmonah.

42They left Zalmonah and camped at Punon.

43They left Punon and camped at Oboth.

44They left Oboth and camped at Iye Abarim, on the border of Moab.

45They left Iyim *c* and camped at Dibon Gad.

46They left Dibon Gad and camped at Almon Diblathaim.

47They left Almon Diblathaim and camped in the mountains of Abarim, near Nebo.

48They left the mountains of Abarim and camped on the plains of Moab by the Jordan across from Jericho. *d* 49There on the plains of Moab they camped along the Jordan from Beth Jeshimoth to Abel Shittim.

50On the plains of Moab by the Jordan across from Jericho the LORD said to Moses, 51"Speak to the Israelites and say to them: 'When you cross the Jordan into Canaan, 52drive out all the inhabitants of the land before you. Destroy all their carved images and their cast idols, and demolish all their high places. 53Take possession of the land and settle in it, for I have given you the land to possess. 54Distribute the land by lot, according to your clans. To a larger group give a larger inheritance, and to a smaller group a smaller one. Whatever falls to them by lot will be theirs. Distribute it according to your ancestral tribes.

33:52   Throughout their history the Israelites were tempted into both the Canaanite ways of worship and their social practices. The prophets said that the two things were related. They could not worship God properly while being unjust to their fellow citizens. Equally, perverted ways of worship gave them a false picture of God and so they forgot their social obligations. Moses is therefore pictured advocating destruction of everything Canaanite, and a completely new start. This never happened. The Israelites lived alongside the Canaanites with all the difficulties that it caused.

55" 'But if you do not drive out the inhabitants of the land, those you allow to remain will become barbs in your eyes and thorns in your sides. They will give you trouble in the land where you will live. 56And then I will do to you what I plan to do to them.' "

Boundaries of Canaan

34 The LORD said to Moses, 2"Command the Israelites and say to them: 'When you enter Canaan, the land that will be allotted to you as an inheritance will have these boundaries:

3" 'Your southern side will include some of the Desert of Zin along the border of Edom. On the east, your southern boundary will start from the end of the

---

b10 Hebrew *Yam Suph*; that is, Sea of Reeds; also in verse 11   *c45* That is, Iye Abarim
d48 Hebrew *Jordan of Jericho*; possibly an ancient name for the Jordan River; also in verse 50

Salt Sea,[a] [4]cross south of Scorpion[b] Pass, continue on to Zin and go south of Kadesh Barnea. Then it will go to Hazar Addar and over to Azmon, [5]where it will turn, join the Wadi of Egypt and end at the Sea.[c]

[6]" 'Your western boundary will be the coast of the Great Sea. This will be your boundary on the west.

[7]" 'For your northern boundary, run a line from the Great Sea to Mount Hor [8]and from Mount Hor to Lebo[d] Hamath. Then the boundary will go to Zedad, [9]continue to Ziphron and end at Hazar Enan. This will be your boundary on the north.

[10]" 'For your eastern boundary, run a line from Hazar Enan to Shepham. [11]The boundary will go down from Shepham to Riblah on the east side of Ain and continue along the slopes east of the Sea of Kinnereth.[e] [12]Then the boundary will go down along the Jordan and end at the Salt Sea.

" 'This will be your land, with its boundaries on every side.' "

[13]Moses commanded the Israelites: "Assign this land by lot as an inheritance. The LORD has ordered that it be given to the nine and a half tribes, [14]because the families of the tribe of Reuben, the tribe of Gad and the half-tribe of Manasseh have received their inheritance. [15]These two and a half tribes have received their inheritance on the east side of the Jordan of Jericho,[f] towards the sunrise."

[16]The LORD said to Moses, [17]"These are the names of the men who are to assign the land for you as an inheritance: Eleazar the priest and Joshua son of Nun. [18]And appoint one leader from each tribe to help assign the land. [19]These are their names:

Caleb son of Jephunneh,
    from the tribe of Judah;
[20]Shemuel son of Ammihud,
    from the tribe of Simeon;
[21]Elidad son of Kislon,
    from the tribe of Benjamin;
[22]Bukki son of Jogli,
    the leader from the tribe of Dan;
[23]Hanniel son of Ephod,
    the leader from the tribe of Manasseh son of
    Joseph;
[24]Kemuel son of Shiphtan,
    the leader from the tribe of Ephraim son of
    Joseph;
[25]Elizaphan son of Parnach,
    the leader from the tribe of Zebulun;
[26]Paltiel son of Azzan,
    the leader from the tribe of Issachar;
[27]Ahihud son of Shelomi,
    the leader from the tribe of Asher;
[28]Pedahel son of Ammihud,
    the leader from the tribe of Naphtali."

[29]These are the men the LORD commanded to assign the inheritance to the Israelites in the land of Canaan.

Towns for the Levites

35 On the plains of Moab by the Jordan across from Jericho,[a] the LORD said to Moses, [2]"Command the Israelites to give the Levites towns to live in from the inheritance the Israelites will possess. And give them pasture-lands around the towns. [3]Then they will have towns to live in and pasture-lands for their cattle, flocks and all their other livestock.

[4]"The pasture-lands around the towns that you give the Levites will extend out fifteen hundred feet[b] from the town wall. [5]Outside the town, measure three thousand feet[c] on the east side, three thousand on the south side, three thousand on the west and three thousand on the north, with the town in the centre. They will have this area as pasture-land for the towns.

Cities of Refuge

[6]"Six of the towns you give the Levites will be cities of refuge, to which a person who has killed someone may flee. In addition, give them forty-two other towns. [7]In all you must give the Levites forty-eight towns, together with their pasture-lands. [8]The towns you give the Levites from the land the Israelites possess are to be given in proportion to the inheritance of each tribe: Take many towns from a tribe that has many, but few from one that has few."

35:6   Every general commandment requires interpretation. In this case, the law concerned murder, and distinguished between deliberate and accidental killing. Murder was a special case because a dead man's next-of-kin had a duty to avenge his death, so cities of refuge were established for the accused. If an alleged murderer could reach one he was assured of a safe trial.

---

[9]Then the LORD said to Moses: [10]"Speak to the Israelites and say to them: 'When you cross the Jordan into Canaan, [11]select some towns to be your cities of refuge, to which a person who has killed someone accidentally may flee. [12]They will be places of refuge from the avenger, so that a person accused of murder may not die before he stands trial before the assembly. [13]These six towns you give will be your cities of refuge. [14]Give three on this side of the Jordan and three in Canaan as cities of refuge. [15]These six towns will be a place of refuge for Israelites, aliens and any other people living among them, so that anyone who has killed another accidentally can flee there.

[16]" 'If a man strikes someone with an iron object so that he dies, he is a murderer; the murderer shall be put to death. [17]Or if anyone has a stone in his hand that could kill, and he strikes someone so that he dies, he is a murderer; the murderer shall be put to death. [18]Or if anyone has a wooden object in his hand that could kill, and he hits someone so that he dies, he is a

---

a3 That is, the Dead Sea; also in verse 12   *b4* Hebrew *Akrabbim*   *c5* That is, the Mediterranean; also in verses 6 and 7
d8 Or *to the entrance to*   *e11* That is, Galilee   *f15* *Jordan of Jericho* was possibly an ancient name for the Jordan River.
a1 Hebrew *Jordan of Jericho*; possibly an ancient name for the Jordan River   *b4* Hebrew *a thousand cubits* (about 450 metres)
c5 Hebrew *two thousand cubits* (about 900 metres)

murderer; the murderer shall be put to death. [19]The avenger of blood shall put the murderer to death; when he meets him, he shall put him to death. [20]If anyone with malice aforethought pushes another or throws something at him intentionally so that he dies [21]or if in hostility he hits him with his fist so that he dies, that person shall be put to death; he is a murderer. The avenger of blood shall put the murderer to death when he meets him.

[22]" 'But if without hostility someone suddenly pushes another or throws something at him unintentionally [23]or, without seeing him, drops a stone on him that could kill him, and he dies, then since he was not his enemy and he did not intend to harm him, [24]the assembly must judge between him and the avenger of blood according to these regulations. [25]The assembly must protect the one accused of murder from the avenger of blood and send him back to the city of refuge to which he fled. He must stay there until the death of the high priest, who was anointed with holy oil.

[26]" 'But if the accused ever goes outside the limits of the city of refuge to which he has fled [27]and the avenger of blood finds him outside the city, the avenger of blood may kill the accused without being guilty of murder. [28]The accused must stay in his city of refuge until the death of the high priest; only after the death of the high priest may he return to his own property.

[29]" 'These are to be legal requirements for you throughout the generations to come, wherever you live.

[30]" 'Anyone who kills a person is to be put to death as a murderer only on the testimony of witnesses. But no-one is to be put to death on the testimony of only one witness.

[31]" 'Do not accept a ransom for the life of a murderer, who deserves to die. He must surely be put to death.

[32]" 'Do not accept a ransom for anyone who has fled to a city of refuge and so allow him to go back and live on his own land before the death of the high priest.

[33]" 'Do not pollute the land where you are. Bloodshed pollutes the land, and atonement cannot be made for the land on which blood has been shed, except by the blood of the one who shed it. [34]Do not defile the land where you live and where I dwell, for I, the LORD, dwell among the Israelites.' "

Inheritance of Zelophehad's Daughters

36 The family heads of the clan of Gilead son of Makir, the son of Manasseh, who were from the clans of the descendants of Joseph, came and spoke before Moses and the leaders, the heads of the Israelite families. [2]They said, "When the LORD commanded my lord to give the land as an inheritance to the Israelites by lot, he ordered you to give the inheritance of our brother Zelophehad to his daughters. [3]Now suppose they marry men from other Israelite tribes; then their inheritance will be taken from our ancestral inheritance and added to that of the tribe they marry into. And so part of the inheritance allotted to us will be taken away. [4]When the Year of Jubilee for the Israelites comes, their inheritance will be added to that of the tribe into which they marry, and their property will be taken from the tribal inheritance of our forefathers."

[5]Then at the LORD's command Moses gave this order to the Israelites: "What the tribe of the descendants of Joseph is saying is right. [6]This is what the LORD commands for Zelophehad's daughters: They may marry anyone they please as long as they marry within the tribal clan of their father. [7]No inheritance in Israel is to pass from tribe to tribe, for every Israelite shall keep the tribal land inherited from his forefathers. [8]Every daughter who inherits land in any Israelite tribe must marry someone in her father's tribal clan, so that every Israelite will possess the inheritance of his fathers. [9]No inheritance may pass from tribe to tribe, for each Israelite tribe is to keep the land it inherits."

[10]So Zelophehad's daughters did as the LORD commanded Moses. [11]Zelophehad's daughters—Mahlah, Tirzah, Hoglah, Milcah and Noah—married their cousins on their father's side. [12]They married within the clans of the descendants of Manasseh son of Joseph, and their inheritance remained in their father's clan and tribe.

[13]These are the commands and regulations the LORD gave through Moses to the Israelites on the plains of Moab by the Jordan across from Jericho.[a]

---

[a]13 Hebrew *Jordan of Jericho*; possibly an ancient name for the Jordan River

Deuteronomy

Faith and Life's Demands

When simple faith meets complex living conditions there is little room for compromise. Faith finds that it must grow to allow for complications, otherwise it will die. God rules the world of science, technology, business, and the arts. The believer must find him in all these things, and discover how to worship him in all the confusion of good and bad. This is the situation which the book of Deuteronomy confronts. The people of Israel were on the point of entering Canaan. Canaan was prosperous; its people farmed successfully, traded abroad, and were more technically advanced than the Israelites. They had military expertise, and the freedom and wealth to practise the arts. They were also religious. Their prosperity depended on farming so they worshipped gods of nature. They believed that if they performed religious rituals correctly the gods would be compelled to keep nature in order and bless the harvest. The God of Israel had promised his people that their land would be rich. They were easily tempted to think that its wealth depended on living as the Canaanites did and worshipping in the Canaanite way. They would not abandon their God but would worship him alongside the gods of Canaan.

Going Along With the World?

The history of Israel is the story of the nation struggling to be successful as well as faithful. The questions they faced are common in human experience. If God promises prosperity, where is he in times of personal or national disaster? If riches and well-being are a sign of his blessing, then presumably people who are well-off are acting morally. The poor and sick must have themselves to blame. If God is powerful, how can his people be defeated in war? The Canaanite response (and a worldly response sometimes heard today), would be to say that we do live in a world of logical consequences. A person can succeed by understanding the ways of the world and the gods, and by their own efforts. Groups and nations who work together can reap benefits for the wider community. Why, then, did the people of Israel not simply accept this view? If they had, they would almost certainly have disappeared as a nation, along with the others of its day. The nation survives till today because there were always Israelites who demanded a different way of life. The writers of the book of Deuteronomy belong in this group.

God Offers a Choice

Israel's God did not reveal himself in recurring cycles of nature, but in historical events and in personal contact with individuals. He had shown himself to be holy and loving and merciful, and had asked the people of

Israel to show him to the world by living in his way. They had bound themselves to him by solemn covenant and their well-being as a nation and as individuals depended on them choosing to be obedient to this. Moses said "I am setting before you today a blessing and a curse" (11:26).

Life Lived in God's Way

The first choice to be made was to worship God alone. If anything else in life has rights over our time and property, it becomes an idol. It has power and influence over us. To worship the gods of Canaan was to believe that they had power in the world. By exclusively worshipping God, Israel could witness to others that he alone controls the world. From this, it makes sense that life must be lived in God's way. He demands that property is treated honestly and carefully and that all people are treated as God's people. God had cared for the Israelites when they were poor slaves, so they should look after the poor and powerless in their own society.

Community and international affairs should be conducted according to the same high standards. If the people relied on foreign alliances they would be failing to trust God. If there was a faulty system of justice in the land it could not administer God's standard of justice.

Keeping Loyal to God

The book of Deuteronomy is written as though spoken by Moses on the eve of the Israelites' entry to the promised land. It contains laws, but is in fact much more like a sermon. It says that the law is a way of life which can give life and blessing to the people. Much of what it contains may have come from Moses himself. As pious Israelites tried to live according to the law, they collected their reflections on it, and these too form part of the book. Deuteronomy was probably compiled by members of the priestly class, so it has a strong interest in temple worship. In all other respects it is very close to the great prophets of Israel and fights, like them, to keep the people loyal to their covenant with God.

Despite all that the best teachers could do, Israel eventually fell into defeat and exile. Deuteronomy reached its present form during the exile. It stands not only at the end of the biblical law books, but also as the beginning of a great history of Israel contained in the books of Joshua, Judges, Samuel, and Kings.

This history was composed by writers of the same mind as those of Deuteronomy. They reflected on the nation's history and the choices it made which had led to "death" in exile rather than "life" in the promised land. Because they still had faith in the love of God they offered Deuteronomy as a standard, a guide, and a commentary on their history, and as a rule which offered them a way out of exile—a new exodus to the promised land.

The Command to Leave Horeb

1 These are the words Moses spoke to all Israel in the desert east of the Jordan—that is, in the Arabah—opposite Suph, between Paran and Tophel, Laban, Hazeroth and Dizahab. ²(It takes eleven days to go from Horeb to Kadesh Barnea by the Mount Seir road.)

³In the fortieth year, on the first day of the eleventh month, Moses proclaimed to the Israelites all that the LORD had commanded him concerning them. ⁴This was after he had defeated Sihon king of the Amorites,

who reigned in Heshbon, and at Edrei had defeated Og king of Bashan, who reigned in Ashtaroth.

⁵East of the Jordan in the territory of Moab, Moses began to expound this law, saying:

1:5 These first three chapters of Deuteronomy are a good example of what Old Testament writers meant by "law". The chapters are a review of the history of Israel from the exodus to the borders of the promised land. They are law because they are evidence of how God wants his people to live. He had been revealing himself through the events.

---

⁶The LORD our God said to us at Horeb, "You have stayed long enough at this mountain. ⁷Break camp and advance into the hill country of the Amorites; go to all the neighbouring peoples in the Arabah, in the mountains, in the western foothills, in the Negev and along the coast, to the land of the Canaanites and to Lebanon, as far as the great river, the Euphrates. ⁸See, I have given you this land. Go in and take possession of the land that the LORD swore he would give to your fathers — to Abraham, Isaac and Jacob — and to their descendants after them."

The Appointment of Leaders

⁹At that time I said to you, "You are too heavy a burden for me to carry alone. ¹⁰The LORD your God has increased your numbers so that today you are as many as the stars in the sky. ¹¹May the LORD, the God of your fathers, increase you a thousand times and bless you as he has promised! ¹²But how can I bear your problems and your burdens and your disputes all by myself? ¹³Choose some wise, understanding and respected men from each of your tribes, and I will set them over you."

¹⁴You answered me, "What you propose to do is good."

¹⁵So I took the leading men of your tribes, wise and respected men, and appointed them to have authority over you — as commanders of thousands, of hundreds, of fifties and of tens and as tribal officials. ¹⁶And I charged your judges at that time: Hear the disputes between your brothers and judge fairly, whether the case is between brother Israelites or between one of them and an alien. ¹⁷Do not show partiality in judging; hear both small and great alike. Do not be afraid of any man, for judgment belongs to God. Bring me any case too hard for you, and I will hear it. ¹⁸And at that time I told you everything you were to do.

Spies Sent Out

¹⁹Then, as the LORD our God commanded us, we set out from Horeb and went towards the hill country of the Amorites through all that vast and dreadful desert that you have seen, and so we reached Kadesh Barnea. ²⁰Then I said to you, "You have reached the hill country of the Amorites, which the LORD our God is giving us. ²¹See, the LORD your God has given you the land. Go up and take possession of it as the LORD, the God of your fathers, told you. Do not be afraid; do not be discouraged."

²²Then all of you came to me and said, "Let us send men ahead to spy out the land for us and bring back a report about the route we are to take and the towns we will come to."

²³The idea seemed good to me; so I selected twelve of you, one man from each tribe. ²⁴They left and went up into the hill country, and came to the Valley of Eshcol and explored it. ²⁵Taking with them some of the fruit of the land, they brought it down to us and reported, "It is a good land that the LORD our God is giving us."

Rebellion Against the LORD

²⁶But you were unwilling to go up; you rebelled against the command of the LORD your God. ²⁷You grumbled in your tents and said, "The LORD hates us; so he brought us out of Egypt to deliver us into the hands of the Amorites to destroy us. ²⁸Where can we go? Our brothers have made us lose heart. They say, 'The people are stronger and taller than we are; the cities are large, with walls up to the sky. We even saw the Anakites there.'"

²⁹Then I said to you, "Do not be terrified; do not be afraid of them. ³⁰The LORD your God, who is going before you, will fight for you, as he did for you in Egypt, before your very eyes, ³¹and in the desert. There you saw how the LORD your God carried you, as a father carries his son, all the way you went until you reached this place."

³²In spite of this, you did not trust in the LORD your God, ³³who went ahead of you on your journey, in fire by night and in a cloud by day, to search out places for you to camp and to show you the way you should go.

³⁴When the LORD heard what you said, he was angry and solemnly swore: ³⁵"Not a man of this evil generation shall see the good land I swore to give your forefathers, ³⁶except Caleb son of Jephunneh. He will see it, and I will give him and his descendants the land he set his feet on, because he followed the LORD wholeheartedly."

³⁷Because of you the LORD became angry with me also and said, "You shall not enter it, either. ³⁸But your assistant, Joshua son of Nun, will enter it. Encourage him, because he will lead Israel to inherit it. ³⁹And the little ones that you said would be taken captive, your children who do not yet know good from bad — they will enter the land. I will give it to them and they will take possession of it. ⁴⁰But as for you, turn round and set out towards the desert along the route to the Red Sea."ᵃ

⁴¹Then you replied, "We have sinned against the LORD. We will go up and fight, as the LORD our God commanded us." So every one of you put on his

---

ᵃ 40 Hebrew *Yam Suph*; that is, Sea of Reeds

weapons, thinking it easy to go up into the hill country. [42]But the LORD said to me, "Tell them, 'Do not go up and fight, because I will not be with you. You will be defeated by your enemies.' "

[43]So I told you, but you would not listen. You rebelled against the LORD's command and in your arrogance you marched up into the hill country. [44]The Amorites who lived in those hills came out against you; they chased you like a swarm of bees and beat you down from Seir all the way to Hormah. [45]You came back and wept before the LORD, but he paid no attention to your weeping and turned a deaf ear to you. [46]And so you stayed in Kadesh many days — all the time you spent there.

Wanderings in the Desert

2 Then we turned back and set out towards the desert along the route to the Red Sea,[a] as the LORD had directed me. For a long time we made our way around the hill country of Seir.

[2]Then the LORD said to me, [3]"You have made your way around this hill country long enough; now turn north. [4]Give the people these orders: 'You are about to pass through the territory of your brothers the descendants of Esau, who live in Seir. They will be afraid of you, but be very careful. [5]Do not provoke them to war, for I will not give you any of their land, not even enough to put your foot on. I have given Esau the hill country of Seir as his own. [6]You are to pay them in silver for the food you eat and the water you drink.' "

[7]The LORD your God has blessed you in all the work of your hands. He has watched over your journey through this vast desert. These forty years the LORD your God has been with you, and you have not lacked anything.

[8]So we went on past our brothers the descendants of Esau, who live in Seir. We turned from the Arabah road, which comes up from Elath and Ezion Geber, and travelled along the desert road of Moab.

[9]Then the LORD said to me, "Do not harass the Moabites or provoke them to war, for I will not give you any part of their land. I have given Ar to the descendants of Lot as a possession."

[10](The Emites used to live there — a people strong and numerous, and as tall as the Anakites. [11]Like the Anakites, they too were considered Rephaites, but the Moabites called them Emites. [12]Horites used to live in Seir, but the descendants of Esau drove them out. They destroyed the Horites from before them and settled in their place, just as Israel did in the land the LORD gave them as their possession.)

[13]And the LORD said, "Now get up and cross the Zered Valley." So we crossed the valley.

[14]Thirty-eight years passed from the time we left Kadesh Barnea until we crossed the Zered Valley. By then, that entire generation of fighting men had perished from the camp, as the LORD had sworn to them. [15]The LORD's hand was against them until he had completely eliminated them from the camp.

[16]Now when the last of these fighting men among the people had died, [17]the LORD said to me, [18]"Today you are to pass by the region of Moab at Ar. [19]When you come to the Ammonites, do not harass them or provoke them to war, for I will not give you possession of any land belonging to the Ammonites. I have given it as a possession to the descendants of Lot."

[20](That too was considered a land of the Rephaites, who used to live there; but the Ammonites called them Zamzummites. [21]They were a people strong and numerous, and as tall as the Anakites. The LORD destroyed them from before the Ammonites, who drove them out and settled in their place. [22]The LORD had done the same for the descendants of Esau, who lived in Seir, when he destroyed the Horites from before them. They drove them out and have lived in their place to this day. [23]And as for the Avvites who lived in villages as far as Gaza, the Caphtorites coming out from Caphtor[b] destroyed them and settled in their place.)

Defeat of Sihon King of Heshbon

[24]"Set out now and cross the Arnon Gorge. See, I have given into your hand Sihon the Amorite, king of Heshbon, and his country. Begin to take possession of it and engage him in battle. [25]This very day I will begin to put the terror and fear of you on all the nations under heaven. They will hear reports of you and will tremble and be in anguish because of you."

[26]From the desert of Kedemoth I sent messengers to Sihon king of Heshbon offering peace and saying, [27]"Let us pass through your country. We will stay on the main road; we will not turn aside to the right or to the left. [28]Sell us food to eat and water to drink for their price in silver. Only let us pass through on foot — [29]as the descendants of Esau, who live in Seir, and the Moabites, who live in Ar, did for us — until we cross the Jordan into the land the LORD our God is giving us." [30]But Sihon king of Heshbon refused to let us pass through. For the LORD your God had made his spirit stubborn and his heart obstinate in order to give him into your hands, as he has now done.

[31]The LORD said to me, "See, I have begun to deliver Sihon and his country over to you. Now begin to conquer and possess his land."

[32]When Sihon and all his army came out to meet us in battle at Jahaz, [33]the LORD our God delivered him over to us and we struck him down, together with his sons and his whole army. [34]At that time we took all his towns and completely destroyed[c] them — men, women and children. We left no survivors. [35]But the livestock and the plunder from the towns we had captured we carried off for ourselves. [36]From Aroer on the rim of the Arnon Gorge, and from the town in the gorge, even as far as Gilead, not one town was too strong for us. The LORD our God gave us all of them. [37]But in accordance with the command of the LORD our God, you did not encroach on any of the land of the Ammonites, neither the land along the course of the Jabbok nor that around the towns in the hills.

[a]1 Hebrew Yam Suph; that is, Sea of Reeds   [b]23 That is, Crete
[c]34 The Hebrew term refers to the irrevocable giving over of things or persons to the LORD, often by totally destroying them.

Defeat of Og King of Bashan

3 Next we turned and went up along the road towards Bashan, and Og king of Bashan with his whole army marched out to meet us in battle at Edrei. [2]The LORD said to me, "Do not be afraid of him, for I have handed him over to you with his whole army and his land. Do to him what you did to Sihon king of the Amorites, who reigned in Heshbon."

[3]So the LORD our God also gave into our hands Og king of Bashan and all his army. We struck them down, leaving no survivors. [4]At that time we took all his cities. There was not one of the sixty cities that we did not take from them — the whole region of Argob, Og's kingdom in Bashan. [5]All these cities were fortified with high walls and with gates and bars, and there were also a great many unwalled villages. [6]We completely destroyed[a] them, as we had done with Sihon king of Heshbon, destroying[a] every city — men, women and children. [7]But all the livestock and the plunder from their cities we carried off for ourselves.

[8]So at that time we took from these two kings of the Amorites the territory east of the Jordan, from the Arnon Gorge as far as Mount Hermon. [9](Hermon is called Sirion by the Sidonians; the Amorites call it Senir.) [10]We took all the towns on the plateau, and all Gilead, and all Bashan as far as Salecah and Edrei, towns of Og's kingdom in Bashan. [11](Only Og king of Bashan was left of the remnant of the Rephaites. His bed[b] was made of iron and was more than thirteen feet long and six feet wide.[c] It is still in Rabbah of the Ammonites.)

Division of the Land

[12]Of the land that we took over at that time, I gave the Reubenites and the Gadites the territory north of Aroer by the Arnon Gorge, including half the hill country of Gilead, together with its towns. [13]The rest of Gilead and also all of Bashan, the kingdom of Og, I gave to the half-tribe of Manasseh. (The whole region of Argob in Bashan used to be known as a land of the Rephaites. [14]Jair, a descendant of Manasseh, took the whole region of Argob as far as the border of the Geshurites and the Maacathites; it was named after him, so that to this day Bashan is called Havvoth Jair.[d]) [15]And I gave Gilead to Makir. [16]But to the Reubenites and the Gadites I gave the territory extending from Gilead down to the Arnon Gorge (the middle of the gorge being the border) and out to the Jabbok River, which is the border of the Ammonites. [17]Its western border was the Jordan in the Arabah, from Kinnereth to the Sea of the Arabah (the Salt Sea[e]), below the slopes of Pisgah.

[18]I commanded you at that time: "The LORD your God has given you this land to take possession of it. But all your able-bodied men, armed for battle, must cross over ahead of your brother Israelites. [19]However, your wives, your children and your livestock (I know you have much livestock) may stay in the towns I have

given you, [20]until the LORD gives rest to your brothers as he has to you, and they too have taken over the land that the LORD your God is giving them, across the Jordan. After that, each of you may go back to the possession I have given you."

Moses Forbidden to Cross the Jordan

[21]At that time I commanded Joshua: "You have seen with your own eyes all that the LORD your God has done to these two kings. The LORD will do the same to all the kingdoms over there where you are going. [22]Do not be afraid of them; the LORD your God himself will fight for you."

[23]At that time I pleaded with the LORD: [24]"O Sovereign LORD, you have begun to show to your servant your greatness and your strong hand. For what god is there in heaven or on earth who can do the deeds and mighty works you do? [25]Let me go over and see the good land beyond the Jordan — that fine hill country and Lebanon."

[26]But because of you the LORD was angry with me and would not listen to me. "That is enough," the LORD said. "Do not speak to me any more about this matter. [27]Go up to the top of Pisgah and look west and north and south and east. Look at the land with your own eyes, since you are not going to cross this Jordan. [28]But commission Joshua, and encourage and strengthen him, for he will lead this people across and will cause them to inherit the land that you will see." [29]So we stayed in the valley near Beth Peor.

3:26 In Numbers it was unclear why God was angry with Moses. The same is true here, but earlier (1:37ff) Moses blamed the Israelites. It was because of their faithlessness that Moses had to suffer. Certainly he had identified himself with the people on a number of occasions. Once he said he wanted to die if God would not forgive the people (Exodus 32:32).

Obedience Commanded

4 Hear now, O Israel, the decrees and laws I am about to teach you. Follow them so that you may live and may go in and take possession of the land that the LORD, the God of your fathers, is giving you. [2]Do not add to what I command you and do not subtract from it, but keep the commands of the LORD your God that I give you.

[3]You saw with your own eyes what the LORD did at Baal Peor. The LORD your God destroyed from among you everyone who followed the Baal of Peor, [4]but all of you who held fast to the LORD your God are still alive today.

[5]See, I have taught you decrees and laws as the LORD my God commanded me, so that you may follow them

---

[a]6 The Hebrew term refers to the irrevocable giving over of things or persons to the LORD, often by totally destroying them.
[b]11 Or *sarcophagus*   [c]11 Hebrew *nine cubits long and four cubits wide* (about 4 metres long and 1.8 metres wide)
[d]14 Or *called the settlements of Jair*   [e]17 That is, the Dead Sea

in the land you are entering to take possession of it. ⁶Observe them carefully, for this will show your wisdom and understanding to the nations, who will hear about all these decrees and say, "Surely this great nation is a wise and understanding people." ⁷What other nation is so great as to have their gods near them the way the LORD our God is near us whenever we pray to him? ⁸And what other nation is so great as to have such righteous decrees and laws as this body of laws I am setting before you today?

4:7 Deuteronomy was given its final form when the nation was in exile. More than a century before that the northern tribes had been defeated and scattered. Israel did not have any claim to greatness by normal standards; Moses was using a very different yardstick. Israel is to be measured by the stature of its God. It is great because the greatest God allows the people close to him and because he gives them laws by which they can become like him. The central theme of Deuteronomy follows on from this: Israel's well-being depends on their obedience to the law.

---

⁹Only be careful, and watch yourselves closely so that you do not forget the things your eyes have seen or let them slip from your heart as long as you live. Teach them to your children and to their children after them. ¹⁰Remember the day you stood before the LORD your God at Horeb, when you said to me, "Assemble the people before me to hear my words so that they may learn to revere me as long as they live in the land and may teach them to their children." ¹¹You came near and stood at the foot of the mountain while it blazed with fire to the very heavens, with black clouds and deep darkness. ¹²Then the LORD spoke to you out of the fire. You heard the sound of words but saw no form; there was only a voice. ¹³He declared to you his covenant, the Ten Commandments, which he commanded you to follow and then wrote them on two stone tablets. ¹⁴And the LORD directed me at that time to teach you the decrees and laws you are to follow in the land that you are crossing the Jordan to possess.

Idolatry Forbidden

¹⁵You saw no form of any kind the day the LORD spoke to you at Horeb out of the fire. Therefore watch yourselves very carefully, ¹⁶so that you do not become corrupt and make for yourselves an idol, an image of any shape, whether formed like a man or a woman, ¹⁷or like any animal on earth or any bird that flies in the air, ¹⁸or like any creature that moves along the ground or any fish in the waters below. ¹⁹And when you look up to the sky and see the sun, the moon and the stars—all the heavenly array—do not be enticed into bowing down to them and worshiping things the LORD your God has apportioned to all the nations under heaven. ²⁰But as for you, the LORD took you and brought you out of the iron-smelting furnace, out of Egypt, to be the people of his inheritance, as you now are.

²¹The LORD was angry with me because of you, and he solemnly swore that I would not cross the Jordan and enter the good land the LORD your God is giving you as your inheritance. ²²I will die in this land; I will not cross the Jordan; but you are about to cross over and take possession of that good land. ²³Be careful not to forget the covenant of the LORD your God that he made with you; do not make for yourselves an idol in the form of anything the LORD your God has forbidden. ²⁴For the LORD your God is a consuming fire, a jealous God.

²⁵After you have had children and grandchildren and have lived in the land a long time—if you then become corrupt and make any kind of idol, doing evil in the eyes of the LORD your God and provoking him to anger, ²⁶I call heaven and earth as witnesses against you this day that you will quickly perish from the land that you are crossing the Jordan to possess. You will not live there long but will certainly be destroyed. ²⁷The LORD will scatter you among the peoples, and only a few of you will survive among the nations to which the LORD will drive you. ²⁸There you will worship manmade gods of wood and stone, which cannot see or hear or eat or smell. ²⁹But if from there you seek the LORD your God, you will find him if you look for him with all your heart and with all your soul. ³⁰When you are in distress and all these things have happened to you, then in later days you will return to the LORD your God and obey him. ³¹For the LORD your God is a merciful God; he will not abandon or destroy you or forget the covenant with your forefathers, which he confirmed to them by oath.

The LORD Is God

³²Ask now about the former days, long before your time, from the day God created man on the earth; ask from one end of the heavens to the other. Has anything so great as this ever happened, or has anything like it ever been heard of? ³³Has any other people heard the voice of God[a] speaking out of fire, as you have, and lived? ³⁴Has any god ever tried to take for himself one nation out of another nation, by testings, by miraculous signs and wonders, by war, by a mighty hand and an outstretched arm, or by great and awesome deeds, like all the things the LORD your God did for you in Egypt before your very eyes?

³⁵You were shown these things so that you might know that the LORD is God; besides him there is no other. ³⁶From heaven he made you hear his voice to discipline you. On earth he showed you his great fire, and you heard his words from out of the fire. ³⁷Because he loved your forefathers and chose their descendants after them, he brought you out of Egypt by his Presence and his great strength, ³⁸to drive out before you nations greater and stronger than you and to bring you into their land to give it to you for your inheritance, as it is today.

a33 Or of a god

[39]Acknowledge and take to heart this day that the LORD is God in heaven above and on the earth below. There is no other. [40]Keep his decrees and commands, which I am giving you today, so that it may go well with you and your children after you and that you may live long in the land the LORD your God gives you for all time.

Cities of Refuge

[41]Then Moses set aside three cities east of the Jordan, [42]to which anyone who had killed a person could flee if he had unintentionally killed his neighbour without malice aforethought. He could flee into one of these cities and save his life. [43]The cities were these: Bezer in the desert plateau, for the Reubenites; Ramoth in Gilead, for the Gadites; and Golan in Bashan, for the Manassites.

Introduction to the Law

[44]This is the law Moses set before the Israelites. [45]These are the stipulations, decrees and laws Moses gave them when they came out of Egypt [46]and were in the valley near Beth Peor east of the Jordan, in the land of Sihon king of the Amorites, who reigned in Heshbon and was defeated by Moses and the Israelites as they came out of Egypt. [47]They took possession of his land and the land of Og king of Bashan, the two Amorite kings east of the Jordan. [48]This land extended from Aroer on the rim of the Arnon Gorge to Mount Siyon[b] (that is, Hermon), [49]and included all the Arabah east of the Jordan, as far as the Sea of the Arabah,[c] below the slopes of Pisgah.

The Ten Commandments

5 Moses summoned all Israel and said:
Hear, O Israel, the decrees and the laws I declare in your hearing today. Learn them and be sure to follow them. [2]The LORD our God made a covenant with us at Horeb. [3]It was not with our fathers that the LORD made this covenant, but with us, with all of us who are alive here today. [4]The LORD spoke to you face to face out of the fire on the mountain. [5](At that time I stood between the LORD and you to declare to you the word of the LORD, because you were afraid of the fire and did not go up the mountain.) And he said:

[6]"I am the LORD your God, who brought you out of Egypt, out of the land of slavery.
[7]"You shall have no other gods before[a] me.
[8]"You shall not make for yourself an idol in the form of anything in heaven above or on the earth beneath or in the waters below. [9]You shall not bow down to them or worship them; for I, the LORD your God, am a jealous God, punishing the children for the sin of the fathers to the third and fourth generation of those who hate me, [10]but showing love to a thousand ⌞generations⌟ of those who love me and keep my commandments.

[11]"You shall not misuse the name of the LORD your God, for the LORD will not hold anyone guiltless who misuses his name.
[12]"Observe the Sabbath day by keeping it holy, as the LORD your God has commanded you. [13]Six days you shall labour and do all your work, [14]but the seventh day is a Sabbath to the LORD your God. On it you shall not do any work, neither you, nor your son or daughter, nor your manservant or maidservant, nor your ox, your donkey or any of your animals, nor the alien within your gates, so that your manservant and maidservant may rest, as you do. [15]Remember that you were slaves in Egypt and that the LORD your God brought you out of there with a mighty hand and an outstretched arm. Therefore the LORD your God has commanded you to observe the Sabbath day.
[16]"Honour your father and your mother, as the LORD your God has commanded you, so that you may live long and that it may go well with you in the land the LORD your God is giving you.
[17]"You shall not murder.
[18]"You shall not commit adultery.
[19]"You shall not steal.
[20]"You shall not give false testimony against your neighbour.
[21]"You shall not covet your neighbour's wife. You shall not set your desire on your neighbour's house or land, his manservant or maidservant, his ox or donkey, or anything that belongs to your neighbour."

5:8   The Hebrew word for jealous does not mean "envious". It is the same as the word for "zealous". It indicates God's claim to exclusive rights over all creation and people's worship. For a long time the Israelites had thought that other gods existed and they even worshipped them, but their greatest teachers and leaders were, to all intents and purposes, complete monotheists (that is, believing in one God).

---

[22]These are the commandments the LORD proclaimed in a loud voice to your whole assembly there on the mountain from out of the fire, the cloud and the deep darkness; and he added nothing more. Then he wrote them on two stone tablets and gave them to me.
[23]When you heard the voice out of the darkness, while the mountain was ablaze with fire, all the leading men of your tribes and your elders came to me. [24]And you said, "The LORD our God has shown us his glory and his majesty, and we have heard his voice from the fire. Today we have seen that a man can live even if God speaks with him. [25]But now, why should we die? This great fire will consume us, and we will die if we hear the voice of the LORD our God any longer. [26]For

---

[b]48 Hebrew; Syriac (see also Deut. 3:9) *Sirion*   [c]49 That is, the Dead Sea   [a]7 Or *besides*

what mortal man has ever heard the voice of the living God speaking out of fire, as we have, and survived? [27]Go near and listen to all that the LORD our God says. Then tell us whatever the LORD our God tells you. We will listen and obey."

[28]The LORD heard you when you spoke to me and the LORD said to me, "I have heard what this people said to you. Everything they said was good. [29]Oh, that their hearts would be inclined to fear me and keep all my commands always, so that it might go well with them and their children for ever!

[30]"Go, tell them to return to their tents. [31]But you stay here with me so that I may give you all the commands, decrees and laws that you are to teach them to follow in the land I am giving them to possess."

[32]So be careful to do what the LORD your God has commanded you; do not turn aside to the right or to the left. [33]Walk in all the way that the LORD your God has commanded you, so that you may live and prosper and prolong your days in the land that you will possess.

Love the LORD Your God

6 These are the commands, decrees and laws the LORD your God directed me to teach you to observe in the land that you are crossing the Jordan to possess, [2]so that you, your children and their children after them may fear the LORD your God as long as you live by keeping all his decrees and commands that I give you, and so that you may enjoy long life. [3]Hear, O Israel, and be careful to obey so that it may go well with you and that you may increase greatly in a land flowing with milk and honey, just as the LORD, the God of your fathers, promised you.

[4]Hear, O Israel: The LORD our God, the LORD is one.[a] [5]Love the LORD your God with all your heart and with all your soul and with all your strength. [6]These commandments that I give you today are to be upon your hearts. [7]Impress them on your children. Talk about them when you sit at home and when you walk along the road, when you lie down and when you get up. [8]Tie them as symbols on your hands and bind them on your foreheads. [9]Write them on the door-frames of your houses and on your gates.

6:4 Orthodox Jews still recite these verses (4–9) morning and evening and take literally the command to wear them and to have them written on the doorpost of their houses. They know that to love God totally would be a perfect way of life.

---

[10]When the LORD your God brings you into the land he swore to your fathers, to Abraham, Isaac and Jacob, to give you—a land with large, flourishing cities you did not build, [11]houses filled with all kinds of good things you did not provide, wells you did not dig, and vineyards and olive groves you did not plant—then when you eat and are satisfied, [12]be careful that you do not forget the LORD, who brought you out of Egypt, out of the land of slavery.

[13]Fear the LORD your God, serve him only and take your oaths in his name. [14]Do not follow other gods, the gods of the peoples around you; [15]for the LORD your God, who is among you, is a jealous God and his anger will burn against you, and he will destroy you from the face of the land. [16]Do not test the LORD your God as you did at Massah. [17]Be sure to keep the commands of the LORD your God and the stipulations and decrees he has given you. [18]Do what is right and good in the LORD's sight, so that it may go well with you and you may go in and take over the good land that the LORD promised on oath to your forefathers, [19]thrusting out all your enemies before you, as the LORD said.

[20]In the future, when your son asks you, "What is the meaning of the stipulations, decrees and laws the LORD our God has commanded you?" [21]tell him: "We were slaves of Pharaoh in Egypt, but the LORD brought us out of Egypt with a mighty hand. [22]Before our eyes the LORD sent miraculous signs and wonders—great and terrible—upon Egypt and Pharaoh and his whole household. [23]But he brought us out from there to bring us in and give us the land that he promised on oath to our forefathers. [24]The LORD commanded us to obey all these decrees and to fear the LORD our God, so that we might always prosper and be kept alive, as is the case today. [25]And if we are careful to obey all this law before the LORD our God, as he has commanded us, that will be our righteousness."

Driving Out the Nations

7 When the LORD your God brings you into the land you are entering to possess and drives out before you many nations—the Hittites, Girgashites, Amorites, Canaanites, Perizzites, Hivites and Jebusites, seven nations larger and stronger than you—[2]and when the LORD your God has delivered them over to you and you have defeated them, then you must destroy them totally.[a] Make no treaty with them, and show them no mercy. [3]Do not intermarry with them. Do not give your daughters to their sons or take their daughters for your sons, [4]for they will turn your sons away from following me to serve other gods, and the LORD's anger will burn against you and will quickly destroy you. [5]This is what you are to do to them: Break down their altars, smash their sacred stones, cut down their Asherah poles[b] and burn their idols in the fire. [6]For you are a people holy to the LORD your God. The LORD your God has chosen you out of all the peoples on the face of the earth to be his people, his treasured possession.

[7]The LORD did not set his affection on you and choose you because you were more numerous than other peoples, for you were the fewest of all peoples. [8]But it was because the LORD loved you and kept the oath he swore to your forefathers that he brought you out with a mighty hand and redeemed you from the land of slavery, from the power of Pharaoh king of Egypt. [9]Know therefore that the LORD your God is God;

---

[a]4 Or *The LORD our God is one LORD*; or *The LORD is our God, the LORD is one*; or *The LORD is our God, the LORD alone*
[a]2 The Hebrew term refers to the irrevocable giving over of things or persons to the LORD, often by totally destroying them; also in verse 26.
[b]5 That is, symbols of the goddess Asherah; here and elsewhere in Deuteronomy

he is the faithful God, keeping his covenant of love to a thousand generations of those who love him and keep his commands. [10]But

> those who hate him he will repay to their face by destruction;
> he will not be slow to repay to their face those who hate him.

7:10   Harsh passages like this make belief in the God of Israel difficult for many people. They sound even stronger next to passages which show God as deeply loving. Some later writers came to see that God's love extended to all people, but there is still a sense in which God's punishment is inevitable. If people use the freedom he has given them to separate themselves from him he will not force their obedience and they will find themselves suffering as a result.

---

[11]Therefore, take care to follow the commands, decrees and laws I give you today.

[12]If you pay attention to these laws and are careful to follow them, then the LORD your God will keep his covenant of love with you, as he swore to your forefathers. [13]He will love you and bless you and increase your numbers. He will bless the fruit of your womb, the crops of your land—your grain, new wine and oil—the calves of your herds and the lambs of your flocks in the land that he swore to your forefathers to give you. [14]You will be blessed more than any other people; none of your men or women will be childless, nor any of your livestock without young. [15]The LORD will keep you free from every disease. He will not inflict on you the horrible diseases you knew in Egypt, but he will inflict them on all who hate you. [16]You must destroy all the peoples the LORD your God gives over to you. Do not look on them with pity and do not serve their gods, for that will be a snare to you.

[17]You may say to yourselves, "These nations are stronger than we are. How can we drive them out?" [18]But do not be afraid of them; remember well what the LORD your God did to Pharaoh and to all Egypt. [19]You saw with your own eyes the great trials, the miraculous signs and wonders, the mighty hand and outstretched arm, with which the LORD your God brought you out. The LORD your God will do the same to all the peoples you now fear. [20]Moreover, the LORD your God will send the hornet among them until even the survivors who hide from you have perished. [21]Do not be terrified by them, for the LORD your God, who is among you, is a great and awesome God. [22]The LORD your God will drive out those nations before you, little by little. You will not be allowed to eliminate them all at once, or the wild animals will multiply around you. [23]But the LORD your God will deliver them over to you, throwing them into great confusion until they are destroyed. [24]He will give their kings into your hand, and you will wipe out their names from under heaven. No-one will be able to stand up against you; you will destroy them. [25]The images of their gods you are to burn in the fire.

Do not covet the silver and gold on them, and do not take it for yourselves, or you will be ensnared by it, for it is detestable to the LORD your God. [26]Do not bring a detestable thing into your house or you, like it, will be set apart for destruction. Utterly abhor and detest it, for it is set apart for destruction.

Do Not Forget the LORD

8 Be careful to follow every command I am giving you today, so that you may live and increase and may enter and possess the land that the LORD promised on oath to your forefathers. [2]Remember how the LORD your God led you all the way in the desert these forty years, to humble you and to test you in order to know what was in your heart, whether or not you would keep his commands. [3]He humbled you, causing you to hunger and then feeding you with manna, which neither you nor your fathers had known, to teach you that man does not live on bread alone but on every word that comes from the mouth of the LORD. [4]Your clothes did not wear out and your feet did not swell during these forty years. [5]Know then in your heart that as a man disciplines his son, so the LORD your God disciplines you.

[6]Observe the commands of the LORD your God, walking in his ways and revering him. [7]For the LORD your God is bringing you into a good land—a land with streams and pools of water, with springs flowing in the valleys and hills; [8]a land with wheat and barley, vines and fig-trees, pomegranates, olive oil and honey; [9]a land where bread will not be scarce and you will lack nothing; a land where the rocks are iron and you can dig copper out of the hills.

[10]When you have eaten and are satisfied, praise the LORD your God for the good land he has given you. [11]Be careful that you do not forget the LORD your God, failing to observe his commands, his laws and his decrees that I am giving you this day. [12]Otherwise, when you eat and are satisfied, when you build fine houses and settle down, [13]and when your herds and flocks grow large and your silver and gold increase and all you have is multiplied, [14]then your heart will become proud and you will forget the LORD your God, who brought you out of Egypt, out of the land of slavery. [15]He led you through the vast and dreadful desert, that thirsty and waterless land, with its venomous snakes and scorpions. He brought you water out of hard rock. [16]He gave you manna to eat in the desert, something your fathers had never known, to humble and to test you so that in the end it might go well with you. [17]You may say to yourself, "My power and the strength of my hands have produced this wealth for me." [18]But remember the LORD your God, for it is he who gives you the ability to produce wealth, and so confirms his covenant, which he swore to your forefathers, as it is today.

[19]If you ever forget the LORD your God and follow other gods and worship and bow down to them, I testify against you today that you will surely be destroyed. [20]Like the nations the LORD destroyed before you, so you will be destroyed for not obeying the LORD your God.

Not Because of Israel's Righteousness

9 Hear, O Israel. You are now about to cross the Jordan to go in and dispossess nations greater and stronger than you, with large cities that have walls up to the sky. ²The people are strong and tall—Anakites! You know about them and have heard it said: "Who can stand up against the Anakites?" ³But be assured today that the LORD your God is the one who goes across ahead of you like a devouring fire. He will destroy them; he will subdue them before you. And you will drive them out and annihilate them quickly, as the LORD has promised you.

8:17 However biblical writers view Israel's time in the wilderness, they always contrast it with the temptations the nation met in the promised land. Here the writer sees the desert time as a period of schooling, so that in Canaan the people would remember what God had done. It is easy to take the credit when things go well but then to criticize God when they do not. As always the writer said that God had shown himself to be active in the past in good and bad so the people should recognize him in the present.

---

⁴After the LORD your God has driven them out before you, do not say to yourself, "The LORD has brought me here to take possession of this land because of my righteousness." No, it is on account of the wickedness of these nations that the LORD is going to drive them out before you. ⁵It is not because of your righteousness or your integrity that you are going in to take possession of their land; but on account of the wickedness of these nations, the LORD your God will drive them out before you, to accomplish what he swore to your fathers, to Abraham, Isaac and Jacob. ⁶Understand, then, that it is not because of your righteousness that the LORD your God is giving you this good land to possess, for you are a stiff-necked people.

The Golden Calf

⁷Remember this and never forget how you provoked the LORD your God to anger in the desert. From the day you left Egypt until you arrived here, you have been rebellious against the LORD. ⁸At Horeb you aroused the LORD's wrath so that he was angry enough to destroy you. ⁹When I went up on the mountain to receive the tablets of stone, the tablets of the covenant that the LORD had made with you, I stayed on the mountain forty days and forty nights; I ate no bread and drank no water. ¹⁰The LORD gave me two stone tablets inscribed by the finger of God. On them were all the commandments the LORD proclaimed to you on the mountain out of the fire, on the day of the assembly.

¹¹At the end of the forty days and forty nights, the LORD gave me the two stone tablets, the tablets of the covenant. ¹²Then the LORD told me, "Go down from here at once, because your people whom you brought out of Egypt have become corrupt. They have turned away quickly from what I commanded them and have made a cast idol for themselves."

¹³And the LORD said to me, "I have seen this people, and they are a stiff-necked people indeed! ¹⁴Let me alone, so that I may destroy them and blot out their name from under heaven. And I will make you into a nation stronger and more numerous than they."

¹⁵So I turned and went down from the mountain while it was ablaze with fire. And the two tablets of the covenant were in my hands.ᵃ ¹⁶When I looked, I saw that you had sinned against the LORD your God; you had made for yourselves an idol cast in the shape of a calf. You had turned aside quickly from the way that the LORD had commanded you. ¹⁷So I took the two tablets and threw them out of my hands, breaking them to pieces before your eyes.

¹⁸Then once again I fell prostrate before the LORD for forty days and forty nights; I ate no bread and drank no water, because of all the sin you had committed, doing what was evil in the LORD's sight and so provoking him to anger. ¹⁹I feared the anger and wrath of the LORD, for he was angry enough with you to destroy you. But again the LORD listened to me. ²⁰And the LORD was angry enough with Aaron to destroy him, but at that time I prayed for Aaron too. ²¹Also I took that sinful thing of yours, the calf you had made, and burned it in the fire. Then I crushed it and ground it to powder as fine as dust and threw the dust into a stream that flowed down the mountain.

²²You also made the LORD angry at Taberah, at Massah and at Kibroth Hattaavah.

²³And when the LORD sent you out from Kadesh Barnea, he said, "Go up and take possession of the land I have given you." But you rebelled against the command of the LORD your God. You did not trust him or obey him. ²⁴You have been rebellious against the LORD ever since I have known you.

²⁵I lay prostrate before the LORD those forty days and forty nights because the LORD had said he would destroy you. ²⁶I prayed to the LORD and said, "O Sovereign LORD, do not destroy your people, your own inheritance that you redeemed by your great power and brought out of Egypt with a mighty hand. ²⁷Remember your servants Abraham, Isaac and Jacob. Overlook the stubbornness of this people, their wickedness and their sin. ²⁸Otherwise, the country from which you brought us will say, 'Because the LORD was not able to take them into the land he had promised them, and because he hated them, he brought them out to put them to death in the desert.' ²⁹But they are your people, your inheritance that you brought out by your great power and your outstretched arm."

Tablets Like the First Ones

10 At that time the LORD said to me, "Chisel out two stone tablets like the first ones and come up to me on the mountain. Also make a wooden chest.ᵃ ²I will write on the tablets the words that were on the first tablets, which you broke. Then you are to put them in the chest."

ᵃ15 Or And I had the two tablets of the covenant with me, one in each hand   ᵃ1 That is, an ark

³So I made the ark out of acacia wood and chiselled out two stone tablets like the first ones, and I went up on the mountain with the two tablets in my hands. ⁴The LORD wrote on these tablets what he had written before, the Ten Commandments he had proclaimed to you on the mountain, out of the fire, on the day of the assembly. And the LORD gave them to me. ⁵Then I came back down the mountain and put the tablets in the ark I had made, as the LORD commanded me, and they are there now.

⁶(The Israelites travelled from the wells of the Jaakanites to Moserah. There Aaron died and was buried, and Eleazar his son succeeded him as priest. ⁷From there they travelled to Gudgodah and on to Jotbathah, a land with streams of water. ⁸At that time the LORD set apart the tribe of Levi to carry the ark of the covenant of the LORD, to stand before the LORD to minister and to pronounce blessings in his name, as they still do today. ⁹That is why the Levites have no share or inheritance among their brothers; the LORD is their inheritance, as the LORD your God told them.)

¹⁰Now I had stayed on the mountain forty days and nights, as I did the first time, and the LORD listened to me at this time also. It was not his will to destroy you. ¹¹"Go," the LORD said to me, "and lead the people on their way, so that they may enter and possess the land that I swore to their fathers to give them."

10:16   All too often the Israelites abused the knowledge that God had chosen them. They claimed superiority over other nations and were complacent about God's care of them, ignoring all obligations on themselves. This notion is rejected here. Being a Jew and physically circumcised meant nothing. It is the inner attitude, here called circumcision of the heart, which dictates God's relationship with us.

Fear the LORD

¹²And now, O Israel, what does the LORD your God ask of you but to fear the LORD your God, to walk in all his ways, to love him, to serve the LORD your God with all your heart and with all your soul, ¹³and to observe the LORD's commands and decrees that I am giving you today for your own good?

¹⁴To the LORD your God belong the heavens, even the highest heavens, the earth and everything in it. ¹⁵Yet the LORD set his affection on your forefathers and loved them, and he chose you, their descendants, above all the nations, as it is today. ¹⁶Circumcise your hearts, therefore, and do not be stiff-necked any longer. ¹⁷For the LORD your God is God of gods and Lord of lords, the great God, mighty and awesome, who shows no partiality and accepts no bribes. ¹⁸He defends the cause of the fatherless and the widow, and loves the alien, giving him food and clothing. ¹⁹And you are to love those who are aliens, for you yourselves were aliens in Egypt. ²⁰Fear the LORD your God and serve

him. Hold fast to him and take your oaths in his name. ²¹He is your praise; he is your God, who performed for you those great and awesome wonders you saw with your own eyes. ²²Your forefathers who went down into Egypt were seventy in all, and now the LORD your God has made you as numerous as the stars in the sky.

Love and Obey the LORD

11 Love the LORD your God and keep his requirements, his decrees, his laws and his commands always. ²Remember today that your children were not the ones who saw and experienced the discipline of the LORD your God: his majesty, his mighty hand, his outstretched arm; ³the signs he performed and the things he did in the heart of Egypt, both to Pharaoh king of Egypt and to his whole country; ⁴what he did to the Egyptian army, to its horses and chariots, how he overwhelmed them with the waters of the Red Seaᵃ as they were pursuing you, and how the LORD brought lasting ruin on them. ⁵It was not your children who saw what he did for you in the desert until you arrived at this place, ⁶and what he did to Dathan and Abiram, sons of Eliab the Reubenite, when the earth opened its mouth right in the middle of all Israel and swallowed them up with their households, their tents and every living thing that belonged to them. ⁷But it was your own eyes that saw all these great things the LORD has done.

⁸Observe therefore all the commands I am giving you today, so that you may have the strength to go in and take over the land that you are crossing the Jordan to possess, ⁹and so that you may live long in the land that the LORD swore to your forefathers to give to them and their descendants, a land flowing with milk and honey. ¹⁰The land you are entering to take over is not like the land of Egypt, from which you have come, where you planted your seed and irrigated it by foot as in a vegetable garden. ¹¹But the land you are crossing the Jordan to take possession of is a land of mountains and valleys that drinks rain from heaven. ¹²It is a land the LORD your God cares for; the eyes of the LORD your God are continually on it from the beginning of the year to its end.

¹³So if you faithfully obey the commands I am giving you today — to love the LORD your God and to serve him with all your heart and with all your soul — ¹⁴then I will send rain on your land in its season, both autumn and spring rains, so that you may gather in your grain, new wine and oil. ¹⁵I will provide grass in the fields for your cattle, and you will eat and be satisfied.

¹⁶Be careful, or you will be enticed to turn away and worship other gods and bow down to them. ¹⁷Then the LORD's anger will burn against you, and he will shut the heavens so that it will not rain and the ground will yield no produce, and you will soon perish from the good land the LORD is giving you. ¹⁸Fix these words of mine in your hearts and minds; tie them as symbols on your hands and bind them on your foreheads. ¹⁹Teach them to your children, talking about them when you sit at home and when you walk along the road, when you lie

ᵃ4 Hebrew *Yam Suph*; that is, Sea of Reeds

down and when you get up. ²⁰Write them on the door-frames of your houses and on your gates, ²¹so that your days and the days of your children may be many in the land that the LORD swore to give your forefathers, as many as the days that the heavens are above the earth.

²²If you carefully observe all these commands I am giving you to follow — to love the LORD your God, to walk in all his ways and to hold fast to him — ²³then the LORD will drive out all these nations before you, and you will dispossess nations larger and stronger than you. ²⁴Every place where you set your foot will be yours: Your territory will extend from the desert to Lebanon, and from the Euphrates River to the western sea.ᵇ ²⁵No man will be able to stand against you. The LORD your God, as he promised you, will put the terror and fear of you on the whole land, wherever you go.

²⁶See, I am setting before you today a blessing and a curse — ²⁷the blessing if you obey the commands of the LORD your God that I am giving you today; ²⁸the curse if you disobey the commands of the LORD your God and turn from the way that I command you today by following other gods, which you have not known. ²⁹When the LORD your God has brought you into the land you are entering to possess, you are to proclaim on Mount Gerizim the blessings, and on Mount Ebal the curses. ³⁰As you know, these mountains are across the Jordan, west of the road,ᶜ towards the setting sun, near the great trees of Moreh, in the territory of those Canaanites living in the Arabah in the vicinity of Gilgal. ³¹You are about to cross the Jordan to enter and take possession of the land the LORD your God is giving you. When you have taken it over and are living there, ³²be sure that you obey all the decrees and laws I am setting before you today.

The One Place of Worship

12 These are the decrees and laws you must be careful to follow in the land that the LORD, the God of your fathers, has given you to possess — as long as you live in the land. ²Destroy completely all the places on the high mountains and on the hills and under every spreading tree where the nations you are dispossessing worship their gods. ³Break down their altars, smash their sacred stones and burn their Asherah poles in the fire; cut down the idols of their gods and wipe out their names from those places.

⁴You must not worship the LORD your God in their way. ⁵But you are to seek the place the LORD your God will choose from among all your tribes to put his Name there for his dwelling. To that place you must go; ⁶there bring your burnt offerings and sacrifices, your tithes and special gifts, what you have vowed to give and your freewill offerings, and the firstborn of your herds and flocks. ⁷There, in the presence of the LORD your God, you and your families shall eat and shall rejoice in everything you have put your hand to, because the LORD your God has blessed you.

⁸You are not to do as we do here today, everyone as he sees fit, ⁹since you have not yet reached the resting place and the inheritance the LORD your God is giving you. ¹⁰But you will cross the Jordan and settle in the

land the LORD your God is giving you as an inheritance, and he will give you rest from all your enemies around you so that you will live in safety. ¹¹Then to the place the LORD your God will choose as a dwelling for his Name — there you are to bring everything I command you: your burnt offerings and sacrifices, your tithes and special gifts, and all the choice possessions you have vowed to the LORD. ¹²And there rejoice before the LORD your God, you, your sons and daughters, your menservants and maidservants, and the Levites from your towns, who have no allotment or inheritance of their own. ¹³Be careful not to sacrifice your burnt offerings anywhere you please. ¹⁴Offer them only at the place the LORD will choose in one of your tribes, and there observe everything I command you.

12:5 Until the eighth century BC, worship was offered in many places. Gradually the idea grew that sacrifices could only be made in Jerusalem. This may be because many Israelite holy places were also significant for the Canaanite worshippers of Baal. In order to prevent people slipping into pagan ways of worship, Jerusalem was declared unique. This also put power into the hands of the priesthood in Jerusalem and the king who was closely associated with them.

¹⁵Nevertheless, you may slaughter your animals in any of your towns and eat as much of the meat as you want, as if it were gazelle or deer, according to the blessing the LORD your God gives you. Both the ceremonially unclean and the clean may eat it. ¹⁶But you must not eat the blood; pour it out on the ground like water. ¹⁷You must not eat in your own towns the tithe of your grain and new wine and oil, or the firstborn of your herds and flocks, or whatever you have vowed to give, or your freewill offerings or special gifts. ¹⁸Instead, you are to eat them in the presence of the LORD your God at the place the LORD your God will choose — you, your sons and daughters, your menservants and maidservants, and the Levites from your towns — and you are to rejoice before the LORD your God in everything you put your hand to. ¹⁹Be careful not to neglect the Levites as long as you live in your land.

²⁰When the LORD your God has enlarged your territory as he promised you, and you crave meat and say, "I would like some meat," then you may eat as much of it as you want. ²¹If the place where the LORD your God chooses to put his Name is too far away from you, you may slaughter animals from the herds and flocks the LORD has given you, as I have commanded you, and in your own towns you may eat as much of them as you want. ²²Eat them as you would gazelle or deer. Both the ceremonially unclean and the clean may eat. ²³But be sure you do not eat the blood, because the blood is the life, and you must not eat the life with the meat. ²⁴You must not eat the blood; pour it out on the ground like

ᵇ24 That is, the Mediterranean   ᶜ30 Or Jordan, westward water. 25Do not eat it, so that it may go well with you and your children after you, because you will be doing what is right in the eyes of the LORD.

26But take your consecrated things and whatever you have vowed to give, and go to the place the LORD will choose. 27Present your burnt offerings on the altar of the LORD your God, both the meat and the blood. The blood of your sacrifices must be poured beside the altar of the LORD your God, but you may eat the meat. 28Be careful to obey all these regulations I am giving you, so that it may always go well with you and your children after you, because you will be doing what is good and right in the eyes of the LORD your God.

29The LORD your God will cut off before you the nations you are about to invade and dispossess. But when you have driven them out and settled in their land, 30and after they have been destroyed before you, be careful not to be ensnared by enquiring about their gods, saying, "How do these nations serve their gods? We will do the same." 31You must not worship the LORD your God in their way, because in worshipping their gods, they do all kinds of detestable things the LORD hates. They even burn their sons and daughters in the fire as sacrifices to their gods.

32See that you do all I command you; do not add to it or take away from it.

13:2   Usually if a prediction came true the prophet was shown to be a true one, since only God could show him the future. But there was deeper truth, which the Israelites should have known in their hearts from experience—that there is only one God. A prophet who abused his powers to deny God was false and the writer says that God had only allowed him to prophesy as a test of the Israelites' faith.

Worshipping Other Gods

13 If a prophet, or one who foretells by dreams, appears among you and announces to you a miraculous sign or wonder, 2and if the sign or wonder of which he has spoken takes place, and he says, "Let us follow other gods" (gods you have not known) "and let us worship them," 3you must not listen to the words of that prophet or dreamer. The LORD your God is testing you to find out whether you love him with all your heart and with all your soul. 4It is the LORD your God you must follow, and him you must revere. Keep his commands and obey him; serve him and hold fast to him. 5That prophet or dreamer must be put to death, because he preached rebellion against the LORD your God, who brought you out of Egypt and redeemed you from the land of slavery; he has tried to turn you from the way the LORD your God commanded you to follow. You must purge the evil from among you.

6If your very own brother, or your son or daughter, or the wife you love, or your closest friend secretly

entices you, saying, "Let us go and worship other gods" (gods that neither you nor your fathers have known, 7gods of the peoples around you, whether near or far, from one end of the land to the other), 8do not yield to him or listen to him. Show him no pity. Do not spare him or shield him. 9You must certainly put him to death. Your hand must be the first in putting him to death, and then the hands of all the people. 10Stone him to death, because he tried to turn you away from the LORD your God, who brought you out of Egypt, out of the land of slavery. 11Then all Israel will hear and be afraid, and no-one among you will do such an evil thing again.

12If you hear it said about one of the towns the LORD your God is giving you to live in 13that wicked men have arisen among you and have led the people of their town astray, saying, "Let us go and worship other gods" (gods you have not known), 14then you must enquire, probe and investigate it thoroughly. And if it is true and it has been proved that this detestable thing has been done among you, 15you must certainly put to the sword all who live in that town. Destroy it completely, *a* both its people and its livestock. 16Gather all the plunder of the town into the middle of the public square and completely burn the town and all its plunder as a whole burnt offering to the LORD your God. It is to remain a ruin for ever, never to be rebuilt. 17None of those condemned things *a* shall be found in your hands, so that the LORD will turn from his fierce anger; he will show you mercy, have compassion on you, and increase your numbers, as he promised on oath to your forefathers, 18because you obey the LORD your God, keeping all his commands that I am giving you today and doing what is right in his eyes.

Clean and Unclean Food

14 You are the children of the LORD your God. Do not cut yourselves or shave the front of your heads for the dead, 2for you are a people holy to the LORD your God. Out of all the peoples on the face of the earth, the LORD has chosen you to be his treasured possession.

3Do not eat any detestable thing. 4These are the animals you may eat: the ox, the sheep, the goat, 5the deer, the gazelle, the roe deer, the wild goat, the ibex, the antelope and the mountain sheep. *a* 6You may eat any animal that has a split hoof divided in two and that chews the cud. 7However, of those that chew the cud or that have a split hoof completely divided you may not eat the camel, the rabbit or the coney. *b* Although they chew the cud, they do not have a split hoof; they are ceremonially unclean for you. 8The pig is also unclean; although it has a split hoof, it does not chew the cud. You are not to eat their meat or touch their carcasses.

9Of all the creatures living in the water, you may eat any that has fins and scales. 10But anything that does not have fins and scales you may not eat; for you it is unclean.

---

a 15,17 The Hebrew term refers to the irrevocable giving over of things or persons to the LORD, often by totally destroying them.
a 5 The precise identification of some of the birds and animals in this chapter is uncertain.   *b 7* That is, the hyrax or rock badger

[11]You may eat any clean bird. [12]But these you may not eat: the eagle, the vulture, the black vulture, [13]the red kite, the black kite, any kind of falcon, [14]any kind of raven, [15]the horned owl, the screech owl, the gull, any kind of hawk, [16]the little owl, the great owl, the white owl, [17]the desert owl, the osprey, the cormorant, [18]the stork, any kind of heron, the hoopoe and the bat.

[19]All flying insects that swarm are unclean to you; do not eat them. [20]But any winged creature that is clean you may eat.

[21]Do not eat anything you find already dead. You may give it to an alien living in any of your towns, and he may eat it, or you may sell it to a foreigner. But you are a people holy to the LORD your God.

Do not cook a young goat in its mother's milk.

Tithes

[22]Be sure to set aside a tenth of all that your fields produce each year. [23]Eat the tithe of your grain, new wine and oil, and the firstborn of your herds and flocks in the presence of the LORD your God at the place he will choose as a dwelling for his Name, so that you may learn to revere the LORD your God always. [24]But if that place is too distant and you have been blessed by the LORD your God and cannot carry your tithe (because the place where the LORD will choose to put his Name is so far away), [25]then exchange your tithe for silver, and take the silver with you and go to the place the LORD your God will choose. [26]Use the silver to buy whatever you like: cattle, sheep, wine or other fermented drink, or anything you wish. Then you and your household shall eat there in the presence of the LORD your God and rejoice. [27]And do not neglect the Levites living in your towns, for they have no allotment or inheritance of their own.

[28]At the end of every three years, bring all the tithes of that year's produce and store it in your towns, [29]so that the Levites (who have no allotment or inheritance of their own) and the aliens, the fatherless and the widows who live in your towns may come and eat and be satisfied, and so that the LORD your God may bless you in all the work of your hands.

The Year for Cancelling Debts

15 At the end of every seven years you must cancel debts. [2]This is how it is to be done: Every creditor shall cancel the loan he has made to his fellow Israelite. He shall not require payment from his fellow Israelite or brother, because the LORD's time for cancelling debts has been proclaimed. [3]You may require payment from a foreigner, but you must cancel any debt your brother owes you. [4]However, there should be no poor among you, for in the land the LORD your God is giving you to possess as your inheritance, he will richly bless you, [5]if only you fully obey the LORD your God and are careful to follow all these commands I am giving you today. [6]For the LORD your God will bless you as he has promised, and you will lend to many nations but will borrow from none. You will rule over many nations but none will rule over you.

[7]If there is a poor man among your brothers in any of the towns of the land that the LORD your God is giving you, do not be hard-hearted or tight-fisted towards your poor brother. [8]Rather be open-handed and freely lend him whatever he needs. [9]Be careful not to harbour this wicked thought: "The seventh year, the year for cancelling debts, is near," so that you do not show ill will towards your needy brother and give him nothing. He may then appeal to the LORD against you, and you will be found guilty of sin. [10]Give generously to him and do so without a grudging heart; then because of this the LORD your God will bless you in all your work and in everything you put your hand to. [11]There will always be poor people in the land. Therefore I command you to be open-handed towards your brothers and towards the poor and needy in your land.

15:4 The writer revealed the tension between the ideal state when there should not be any poor people if God's laws are obeyed, and the fact of experience; that there will always be poor (verse 11). Verse 9 goes a long way to explaining this. People find it very hard to be generous when they know they will suffer by that generosity. As always, the reason given for caring for the poor is because that is the godlike thing to do. It will bring the giver closer to God.

Freeing Servants

[12]If a fellow Hebrew, a man or woman, sells himself to you and serves you six years, in the seventh year you must let him go free. [13]And when you release him, do not send him away empty-handed. [14]Supply him liberally from your flock, your threshing-floor and your winepress. Give to him as the LORD your God has blessed you. [15]Remember that you were slaves in Egypt and the LORD your God redeemed you. That is why I give you this command today.

[16]But if your servant says to you, "I do not want to leave you," because he loves you and your family and is well off with you, [17]then take an awl and push it through his ear lobe into the door, and he will become your servant for life. Do the same for your maidservant.

[18]Do not consider it a hardship to set your servant free, because his service to you these six years has been worth twice as much as that of a hired hand. And the LORD your God will bless you in everything you do.

The Firstborn Animals

[19]Set apart for the LORD your God every firstborn male of your herds and flocks. Do not put the firstborn of your oxen to work, and do not shear the firstborn of your sheep. [20]Each year you and your family are to eat them in the presence of the LORD your God at the place he will choose. [21]If an animal has a defect, is lame or blind, or has any serious flaw, you must not sacrifice it to the LORD your God. [22]You are to eat it in your own towns. Both the ceremonially unclean and the clean may eat it, as if it were gazelle or deer. [23]But you must not eat the blood; pour it out on the ground like water.

Passover

16 Observe the month of Abib and celebrate the Passover of the LORD your God, because in the month of Abib he brought you out of Egypt by night. [2]Sacrifice as the Passover to the LORD your God an animal from your flock or herd at the place the LORD will choose as a dwelling for his Name. [3]Do not eat it with bread made with yeast, but for seven days eat unleavened bread, the bread of affliction, because you left Egypt in haste—so that all the days of your life you may remember the time of your departure from Egypt. [4]Let no yeast be found in your possession in all your land for seven days. Do not let any of the meat you sacrifice on the evening of the first day remain until morning.

16:1 Most of Israel's festivals originated as ancient agricultural feasts. The feast of Weeks, for example, celebrated the end of the cereal harvest, and Tabernacles the end of the gathering of all crops. Israel related each feast to an event in its history, so that at Weeks the giving of the law at Sinai was commemorated, and at Tabernacles the nomadic period in the desert.

---

[5]You must not sacrifice the Passover in any town the LORD your God gives you [6]except in the place he will choose as a dwelling for his Name. There you must sacrifice the Passover in the evening, when the sun goes down, on the anniversary[a] of your departure from Egypt. [7]Roast it and eat it at the place the LORD your God will choose. Then in the morning return to your tents. [8]For six days eat unleavened bread and on the seventh day hold an assembly to the LORD your God and do no work.

Feast of Weeks

[9]Count off seven weeks from the time you begin to put the sickle to the standing corn. [10]Then celebrate the Feast of Weeks to the LORD your God by giving a freewill offering in proportion to the blessings the LORD your God has given you. [11]And rejoice before the LORD your God at the place he will choose as a dwelling for his Name—you, your sons and daughters, your menservants and maidservants, the Levites in your towns, and the aliens, the fatherless and the widows living among you. [12]Remember that you were slaves in Egypt, and follow carefully these decrees.

Feast of Tabernacles

[13]Celebrate the Feast of Tabernacles for seven days after you have gathered the produce of your threshing-floor and your winepress. [14]Be joyful at your Feast—you, your sons and daughters, your menservants and maidservants, and the Levites, the aliens, the fatherless and the widows who live in your towns. [15]For seven days celebrate the Feast to the LORD your God at the place the LORD will choose. For the LORD your God will

bless you in all your harvest and in all the work of your hands, and your joy will be complete.

[16]Three times a year all your men must appear before the LORD your God at the place he will choose: at the Feast of Unleavened Bread, the Feast of Weeks and the Feast of Tabernacles. No man should appear before the LORD empty-handed: [17]Each of you must bring a gift in proportion to the way the LORD your God has blessed you.

Judges

[18]Appoint judges and officials for each of your tribes in every town the LORD your God is giving you, and they shall judge the people fairly. [19]Do not pervert justice or show partiality. Do not accept a bribe, for a bribe blinds the eyes of the wise and twists the words of the righteous. [20]Follow justice and justice alone, so that you may live and possess the land the LORD your God is giving you.

Worshipping Other Gods

[21]Do not set up any wooden Asherah pole[b] beside the altar you build to the LORD your God, [22]and do not erect a sacred stone, for these the LORD your God hates.

17 Do not sacrifice to the LORD your God an ox or a sheep that has any defect or flaw in it, for that would be detestable to him.

[2]If a man or woman living among you in one of the towns the LORD your God gives you is found doing evil in the eyes of the LORD your God in violation of his covenant, [3]and contrary to my command has worshipped other gods, bowing down to them or to the sun or the moon or the stars of the sky, [4]and this has been brought to your attention, then you must investigate it thoroughly. If it is true and it has been proved that this detestable thing has been done in Israel, [5]take the man or woman who has done this evil deed to your city gate and stone that person to death. [6]On the testimony of two or three witnesses a man shall be put to death, but no-one shall be put to death on the testimony of only one witness. [7]The hands of the witnesses must be the first in putting him to death, and then the hands of all the people. You must purge the evil from among you.

Law Courts

[8]If cases come before your courts that are too difficult for you to judge—whether bloodshed, lawsuits or assaults—take them to the place the LORD your God will choose. [9]Go to the priests, who are Levites, and to the judge who is in office at that time. Enquire of them and they will give you the verdict. [10]You must act according to the decisions they give you at the place the LORD will choose. Be careful to do everything they direct you to do. [11]Act according to the law they teach you and the decisions they give you. Do not turn aside from what they tell you, to the right or to the left. [12]The man who shows contempt for the judge or for the priest who stands ministering there to the LORD your God must be put to death. You must purge the evil from

---

[a]6 Or *down, at the time of day*   [b]21 Or *Do not plant any tree dedicated to Asherah*

Israel. [13]All the people will hear and be afraid, and will not be contemptuous again.

The King

[14]When you enter the land the LORD your God is giving you and have taken possession of it and settled in it, and you say, "Let us set a king over us like all the nations around us," [15]be sure to appoint over you the king the LORD your God chooses. He must be from among your own brothers. Do not place a foreigner over you, one who is not a brother Israelite. [16]The king, moreover, must not acquire great numbers of horses for himself or make the people return to Egypt to get more of them, for the LORD has told you, "You are not to go back that way again." [17]He must not take many wives, or his heart will be led astray. He must not accumulate large amounts of silver and gold.

17:14 Kings often assume absolute power, and rely on treaties with other states, so compromising their independence. The Bible is therefore ambivalent about whether Israel should have a king (See 1 Samuel 8:10–18). A good king could give a godlike example to his people. This possibility was reflected in the idea that one day God would send such a person, the Messiah, to lead Israel.

---

[18]When he takes the throne of his kingdom, he is to write for himself on a scroll a copy of this law, taken from that of the priests, who are Levites. [19]It is to be with him, and he is to read it all the days of his life so that he may learn to revere the LORD his God and follow carefully all the words of this law and these decrees [20]and not consider himself better than his brothers and turn from the law to the right or to the left. Then he and his descendants will reign a long time over his kingdom in Israel.

Offerings for Priests and Levites

18 The priests, who are Levites — indeed the whole tribe of Levi — are to have no allotment or inheritance with Israel. They shall live on the offerings made to the LORD by fire, for that is their inheritance. [2]They shall have no inheritance among their brothers; the LORD is their inheritance, as he promised them. [3]This is the share due to the priests from the people who sacrifice a bull or a sheep: the shoulder, the jowls and the inner parts. [4]You are to give them the firstfruits of your grain, new wine and oil, and the first wool from the shearing of your sheep, [5]for the LORD your God has chosen them and their descendants out of all your tribes to stand and minister in the LORD's name always. [6]If a Levite moves from one of your towns anywhere in Israel where he is living, and comes in all

earnestness to the place the LORD will choose, [7]he may minister in the name of the LORD his God like all his fellow Levites who serve there in the presence of the LORD. [8]He is to share equally in their benefits even though he has received money from the sale of family possessions.

Detestable Practices

[9]When you enter the land the LORD your God is giving you, do not learn to imitate the detestable ways of the nations there. [10]Let no-one be found among you who sacrifices his son or daughter in[a] the fire, who practises divination or sorcery, interprets omens, engages in witchcraft, [11]or casts spells, or who is a medium or spiritist or who consults the dead. [12]Anyone who does these things is detestable to the LORD, and because of these detestable practices the LORD your God will drive out those nations before you. [13]You must be blameless before the LORD your God.

The Prophet

[14]The nations you will dispossess listen to those who practise sorcery or divination. But as for you, the LORD your God has not permitted you to do so. [15]The LORD your God will raise up for you a prophet like me from among your own brothers. You must listen to him. [16]For this is what you asked of the LORD your God at Horeb on the day of the assembly when you said, "Let us not hear the voice of the LORD our God nor see this great fire any more, or we will die."

[17]The LORD said to me: "What they say is good. [18]I will raise up for them a prophet like you from among their brothers; I will put my words in his mouth, and he will tell them everything I command him. [19]If anyone does not listen to my words that the prophet speaks in my name, I myself will call him to account. [20]But a prophet who presumes to speak in my name anything I have not commanded him to say, or a prophet who speaks in the name of other gods, must be put to death."

18:18 The Hebrew language here makes it clear that there would be a succession of prophets sent by God whenever they were needed by the people. Later it was understood to mean that there would be one prophet, who would appear to prepare for the Messiah. The monks at Qu'mran, who lived at the time of Jesus, and who wrote the Dead Sea Scrolls, laid great emphasis on this idea.

---

[21]You may say to yourselves, "How can we know when a message has not been spoken by the LORD?" [22]If what a prophet proclaims in the name of the LORD does not take place or come true, that is a message the LORD has not spoken. That prophet has spoken presumptuously. Do not be afraid of him.

---

[a] 10 Or *who makes his son or daughter pass through*

Cities of Refuge

19 When the LORD your God has destroyed the nations whose land he is giving you, and when you have driven them out and settled in their towns and houses, [2]then set aside for yourselves three cities centrally located in the land the LORD your God is giving you to possess. [3]Build roads to them and divide into three parts the land the LORD your God is giving you as an inheritance, so that anyone who kills a man may flee there.

[4]This is the rule concerning the man who kills another and flees there to save his life — one who kills his neighbour unintentionally, without malice aforethought. [5]For instance, a man may go into the forest with his neighbour to cut wood, and as he swings his axe to fell a tree, the head may fly off and hit his neighbour and kill him. That man may flee to one of these cities and save his life. [6]Otherwise, the avenger of blood might pursue him in a rage, overtake him if the distance is too great, and kill him even though he is not deserving of death, since he did it to his neighbour without malice aforethought. [7]This is why I command you to set aside for yourselves three cities.

[8]If the LORD your God enlarges your territory, as he promised on oath to your forefathers, and gives you the whole land he promised them, [9]because you carefully follow all these laws I command you today — to love the LORD your God and to walk always in his ways — then you are to set aside three more cities. [10]Do this so that innocent blood will not be shed in your land, which the LORD your God is giving you as your inheritance, and so that you will not be guilty of bloodshed.

[11]But if a man hates his neighbour and lies in wait for him, assaults and kills him, and then flees to one of these cities, [12]the elders of his town shall send for him, bring him back from the city, and hand him over to the avenger of blood to die. [13]Show him no pity. You must purge from Israel the guilt of shedding innocent blood, so that it may go well with you.

[14]Do not move your neighbour's boundary stone set up by your predecessors in the inheritance you receive in the land the LORD your God is giving you to possess.

Witnesses

[15]One witness is not enough to convict a man accused of any crime or offence he may have committed. A matter must be established by the testimony of two or three witnesses.

[16]If a malicious witness takes the stand to accuse a man of a crime, [17]the two men involved in the dispute must stand in the presence of the LORD before the priests and the judges who are in office at the time. [18]The judges must make a thorough investigation, and if the witness proves to be a liar, giving false testimony against his brother, [19]then do to him as he intended to do to his brother. You must purge the evil from among you. [20]The rest of the people will hear of this and be afraid, and never again will such an evil thing be done among you. [21]Show no pity: life for life, eye for eye, tooth for tooth, hand for hand, foot for foot.

Going to War

20 When you go to war against your enemies and see horses and chariots and an army greater than yours, do not be afraid of them, because the LORD your God, who brought you up out of Egypt, will be with you. [2]When you are about to go into battle, the priest shall come forward and address the army. [3]He shall say: "Hear, O Israel, today you are going into battle against your enemies. Do not be faint-hearted or afraid; do not be terrified or give way to panic before them. [4]For the LORD your God is the one who goes with you to fight for you against your enemies to give you victory."

[5]The officers shall say to the army: "Has anyone built a new house and not dedicated it? Let him go home, or he may die in battle and someone else may dedicate it. [6]Has anyone planted a vineyard and not begun to enjoy it? Let him go home, or he may die in battle and someone else enjoy it. [7]Has anyone become pledged to a woman and not married her? Let him go home, or he may die in battle and someone else marry her." [8]Then the officers shall add, "Is any man afraid or faint-hearted? Let him go home so that his brothers will not become disheartened too." [9]When the officers have finished speaking to the army, they shall appoint commanders over it.

[10]When you march up to attack a city, make its people an offer of peace. [11]If they accept and open their gates, all the people in it shall be subject to forced labour and shall work for you. [12]If they refuse to make peace and they engage you in battle, lay siege to that city. [13]When the LORD your God delivers it into your hand, put to the sword all the men in it. [14]As for the women, the children, the livestock and everything else in the city, you may take these as plunder for yourselves. And you may use the plunder the LORD your God gives you from your enemies. [15]This is how you are to treat all the cities that are at a distance from you and do not belong to the nations nearby.

[16]However, in the cities of the nations the LORD your God is giving you as an inheritance, do not leave alive anything that breathes. [17]Completely destroy[a] them — the Hittites, Amorites, Canaanites, Perizzites, Hivites and Jebusites — as the LORD your God has commanded you. [18]Otherwise, they will teach you to follow all the detestable things they do in worshipping their gods, and you will sin against the LORD your God.

[19]When you lay siege to a city for a long time, fighting against it to capture it, do not destroy its trees by putting an axe to them, because you can eat their fruit. Do not cut them down. Are the trees of the field people, that you should besiege them?[b] [20]However, you may cut down trees that you know are not fruit trees and use them to build siege works until the city at war with you falls.

Atonement for an Unsolved Murder

21 If a man is found slain, lying in a field in the land the LORD your God is giving you to possess, and it is not known who killed him, [2]your elders

---

[a]17 The Hebrew term refers to the irrevocable giving over of things or persons to the LORD, often by totally destroying them.
[b]19 Or down to use in the siege, for the fruit trees are for the benefit of man.

and judges shall go out and measure the distance from the body to the neighbouring towns. [3]Then the elders of the town nearest the body shall take a heifer that has never been worked and has never worn a yoke [4]and lead her down to a valley that has not been ploughed or planted and where there is a flowing stream. There in the valley they are to break the heifer's neck. [5]The priests, the sons of Levi, shall step forward, for the LORD your God has chosen them to minister and to pronounce blessings in the name of the LORD and to decide all cases of dispute and assault. [6]Then all the elders of the town nearest the body shall wash their hands over the heifer whose neck was broken in the valley, [7]and they shall declare: "Our hands did not shed this blood, nor did our eyes see it done. [8]Accept this atonement for your people Israel, whom you have redeemed, O LORD, and do not hold your people guilty of the blood of an innocent man." And the bloodshed will be atoned for. [9]So you will purge from yourselves the guilt of shedding innocent blood, since you have done what is right in the eyes of the LORD.

Marrying a Captive Woman

[10]When you go to war against your enemies and the LORD your God delivers them into your hands and you take captives, [11]if you notice among the captives a beautiful woman and are attracted to her, you may take her as your wife. [12]Bring her into your home and make her shave her head, trim her nails [13]and put aside the clothes she was wearing when captured. After she has lived in your house and mourned her father and mother for a full month, then you may go to her and be her husband and she shall be your wife. [14]If you are not pleased with her, let her go wherever she wishes. You must not sell her or treat her as a slave, since you have dishonoured her.

21:14   This and the following chapter contain a series of laws about sexual and family matters, and relationships with neighbours. They demonstrate the people's sense of responsibility to each other, and of family survival. The second was important because the Israelites did not believe in life after death, so their future depended on heirs who could give honour to the family name.

The Right of the Firstborn

[15]If a man has two wives, and he loves one but not the other, and both bear him sons but the firstborn is the son of the wife he does not love, [16]when he wills his property to his sons, he must not give the rights of the firstborn to the son of the wife he loves in preference to his actual firstborn, the son of the wife he does not love. [17]He must acknowledge the son of his unloved wife as the firstborn by giving him a double share of all he has. That son is the first sign of his father's strength. The right of the firstborn belongs to him.

A Rebellious Son

[18]If a man has a stubborn and rebellious son who does not obey his father and mother and will not listen to them when they discipline him, [19]his father and mother shall take hold of him and bring him to the elders at the gate of his town. [20]They shall say to the elders, "This son of ours is stubborn and rebellious. He will not obey us. He is a profligate and a drunkard." [21]Then all the men of his town shall stone him to death. You must purge the evil from among you. All Israel will hear of it and be afraid.

Various Laws

[22]If a man guilty of a capital offence is put to death and his body is hung on a tree, [23]you must not leave his body on the tree overnight. Be sure to bury him that same day, because anyone who is hung on a tree is under God's curse. You must not desecrate the land the LORD your God is giving you as an inheritance.

22   If you see your brother's ox or sheep straying, do not ignore it but be sure to take it back to him. [2]If the brother does not live near you or if you do not know who he is, take it home with you and keep it until he comes looking for it. Then give it back to him. [3]Do the same if you find your brother's donkey or his cloak or anything he loses. Do not ignore it.

[4]If you see your brother's donkey or his ox fallen on the road, do not ignore it. Help him to get it to its feet.

[5]A woman must not wear men's clothing, nor a man wear women's clothing, for the LORD your God detests anyone who does this.

[6]If you come across a bird's nest beside the road, either in a tree or on the ground, and the mother is sitting on the young or on the eggs, do not take the mother with the young. [7]You may take the young, but be sure to let the mother go, so that it may go well with you and you may have a long life.

[8]When you build a new house, make a parapet around your roof so that you may not bring the guilt of bloodshed on your house if someone falls from the roof.

[9]Do not plant two kinds of seed in your vineyard; if you do, not only the crops you plant but also the fruit of the vineyard will be defiled.[a]

[10]Do not plough with an ox and a donkey yoked together.

[11]Do not wear clothes of wool and linen woven together.

[12]Make tassels on the four corners of the cloak you wear.

Marriage Violations

[13]If a man takes a wife and, after lying with her, dislikes her [14]and slanders her and gives her a bad name, saying, "I married this woman, but when I approached her, I did not find proof of her virginity," [15]then the girl's father and mother shall bring proof that she was a virgin to the town elders at the gate. [16]The girl's father will say to the elders, "I gave my daughter in marriage to this man, but he dislikes her. [17]Now he has slandered her and said, 'I did not find your daughter to

[a]9 Or be forfeited to the sanctuary

be a virgin.' But here is the proof of my daughter's virginity." Then her parents shall display the cloth before the elders of the town, [18]and the elders shall take the man and punish him. [19]They shall fine him a hundred shekels of silver[b] and give them to the girl's father, because this man has given an Israelite virgin a bad name. She shall continue to be his wife; he must not divorce her as long as he lives.

[20]If, however, the charge is true and no proof of the girl's virginity can be found, [21]she shall be brought to the door of her father's house and there the men of her town shall stone her to death. She has done a disgraceful thing in Israel by being promiscuous while still in her father's house. You must purge the evil from among you.

[22]If a man is found sleeping with another man's wife, both the man who slept with her and the woman must die. You must purge the evil from Israel.

[23]If a man happens to meet in a town a virgin pledged to be married and he sleeps with her, [24]you shall take both of them to the gate of that town and stone them to death—the girl because she was in a town and did not scream for help, and the man because he violated another man's wife. You must purge the evil from among you.

[25]But if out in the country a man happens to meet a girl pledged to be married and rapes her, only the man who has done this shall die. [26]Do nothing to the girl; she has committed no sin deserving death. This case is like that of someone who attacks and murders his neighbour, [27]for the man found the girl out in the country, and though the betrothed girl screamed, there was no-one to rescue her.

[28]If a man happens to meet a virgin who is not pledged to be married and rapes her and they are discovered, [29]he shall pay the girl's father fifty shekels of silver.[c] He must marry the girl, for he has violated her. He can never divorce her as long as he lives.

[30]A man is not to marry his father's wife; he must not dishonour his father's bed.

Exclusion From the Assembly

23 No-one who has been emasculated by crushing or cutting may enter the assembly of the LORD.

[2]No-one born of a forbidden marriage[a] nor any of his descendants may enter the assembly of the LORD, even down to the tenth generation.

[3]No Ammonite or Moabite or any of his descendants may enter the assembly of the LORD, even down to the tenth generation. [4]For they did not come to meet you with bread and water on your way when you came out of Egypt, and they hired Balaam son of Beor from Pethor in Aram Naharaim[b] to pronounce a curse on you. [5]However, the LORD your God would not listen to Balaam but turned the curse into a blessing for you, because the LORD your God loves you. [6]Do not seek a treaty of friendship with them as long as you live.

[7]Do not abhor an Edomite, for he is your brother. Do not abhor an Egyptian, because you lived as an alien in his country. [8]The third generation of children born to them may enter the assembly of the LORD.

Uncleanness in the Camp

[9]When you are encamped against your enemies, keep away from everything impure. [10]If one of your men is unclean because of a nocturnal emission, he is to go outside the camp and stay there. [11]But as evening approaches he is to wash himself, and at sunset he may return to the camp.

[12]Designate a place outside the camp where you can go to relieve yourself. [13]As part of your equipment have something to dig with, and when you relieve yourself, dig a hole and cover up your excrement. [14]For the LORD your God moves about in your camp to protect you and to deliver your enemies to you. Your camp must be holy, so that he will not see among you anything indecent and turn away from you.

Miscellaneous Laws

[15]If a slave has taken refuge with you, do not hand him over to his master. [16]Let him live among you wherever he likes and in whatever town he chooses. Do not oppress him.

[17]No Israelite man or woman is to become a shrine-prostitute. [18]You must not bring the earnings of a female prostitute or of a male prostitute[c] into the house of the LORD your God to pay any vow, because the LORD your God detests them both.

[19]Do not charge your brother interest, whether on money or food or anything else that may earn interest. [20]You may charge a foreigner interest, but not a brother Israelite, so that the LORD your God may bless you in everything you put your hand to in the land you are entering to possess.

[21]If you make a vow to the LORD your God, do not be slow to pay it, for the LORD your God will certainly demand it of you and you will be guilty of sin. [22]But if you refrain from making a vow, you will not be guilty. [23]Whatever your lips utter you must be sure to do, because you made your vow freely to the LORD your God with your own mouth.

[24]If you enter your neighbour's vineyard, you may eat all the grapes you want, but do not put any in your basket. [25]If you enter your neighbour's cornfield, you may pick the ears with your hands, but you must not put a sickle to his standing corn.

24 If a man marries a woman who becomes displeasing to him because he finds something indecent about her, and he writes her a certificate of divorce, gives it to her and sends her from his house, [2]and if after she leaves his house she becomes the wife of another man, [3]and her second husband dislikes her and writes her a certificate of divorce, gives it to her and sends her from his house, or if he dies, [4]then her first husband, who divorced her, is not allowed to marry her again after she has been defiled. That would be detestable in the eyes of the LORD. Do not bring sin upon the land the LORD your God is giving you as an inheritance.

---

[b]19 That is, about 2½ pounds (about 1 kilogram)   [c]29 That is, about 1¼ pounds (about 0.6 kilogram)
[a]2 Or one of illegitimate birth   [b]4 That is, North-west Mesopotamia   [c]18 Hebrew of a dog

[5]If a man has recently married, he must not be sent to war or have any other duty laid on him. For one year he is to be free to stay at home and bring happiness to the wife he has married.

[6]Do not take a pair of millstones—not even the upper one—as security for a debt, because that would be taking a man's livelihood as security.

24:6   Israelite law was very advanced in its treatment of people. God cares for all people, and requires them to care for each other. There is concern here not to destroy a man, even when he is in debt, by taking his means of livelihood (the millstone). Nor must his dignity be violated. The creditor has no rights to invade his privacy; his rights only involve repayment of the actual debt.

---

[7]If a man is caught kidnapping one of his brother Israelites and treats him as a slave or sells him, the kidnapper must die. You must purge the evil from among you.

[8]In cases of leprous[a] diseases be very careful to do exactly as the priests, who are Levites, instruct you. You must follow carefully what I have commanded them. [9]Remember what the LORD your God did to Miriam along the way after you came out of Egypt.

[10]When you make a loan of any kind to your neighbour, do not go into his house to get what he is offering as a pledge. [11]Stay outside and let the man to whom you are making the loan bring the pledge out to you. [12]If the man is poor, do not go to sleep with his pledge in your possession. [13]Return his cloak to him by sunset so that he may sleep in it. Then he will thank you, and it will be regarded as a righteous act in the sight of the LORD your God.

[14]Do not take advantage of a hired man who is poor and needy, whether he is a brother Israelite or an alien living in one of your towns. [15]Pay him his wages each day before sunset, because he is poor and is counting on it. Otherwise he may cry to the LORD against you, and you will be guilty of sin.

[16]Fathers shall not be put to death for their children, nor children put to death for their fathers; each is to die for his own sin.

[17]Do not deprive the alien or the fatherless of justice, or take the cloak of the widow as a pledge. [18]Remember that you were slaves in Egypt and the LORD your God redeemed you from there. That is why I command you to do this.

[19]When you are harvesting in your field and you overlook a sheaf, do not go back to get it. Leave it for the alien, the fatherless and the widow, so that the LORD your God may bless you in all the work of your hands. [20]When you beat the olives from your trees, do not go over the branches a second time. Leave what remains for the alien, the fatherless and the widow. [21]When you harvest the grapes in your vineyard, do not go over the vines again. Leave what remains for the alien, the fatherless and the widow. [22]Remember that

you were slaves in Egypt. That is why I command you to do this.

25 When men have a dispute, they are to take it to court and the judges will decide the case, acquitting the innocent and condemning the guilty. [2]If the guilty man deserves to be beaten, the judge shall make him lie down and have him flogged in his presence with the number of lashes his crime deserves, [3]but he must not give him more than forty lashes. If he is flogged more than that, your brother will be degraded in your eyes.

[4]Do not muzzle an ox while it is treading out the grain.

[5]If brothers are living together and one of them dies without a son, his widow must not marry outside the family. Her husband's brother shall take her and marry her and fulfil the duty of a brother-in-law to her. [6]The first son she bears shall carry on the name of the dead brother so that his name will not be blotted out from Israel.

[7]However, if a man does not want to marry his brother's wife, she shall go to the elders at the town gate and say, "My husband's brother refuses to carry on his brother's name in Israel. He will not fulfil the duty of a brother-in-law to me." [8]Then the elders of his town shall summon him and talk to him. If he persists in saying, "I do not want to marry her," [9]his brother's widow shall go up to him in the presence of the elders, take off one of his sandals, spit in his face and say, "This is what is done to the man who will not build up his brother's family line." [10]That man's line shall be known in Israel as The Family of the Unsandalled.

[11]If two men are fighting and the wife of one of them comes to rescue her husband from his assailant, and she reaches out and seizes him by his private parts, [12]you shall cut off her hand. Show her no pity.

[13]Do not have two differing weights in your bag—one heavy, one light. [14]Do not have two differing measures in your house—one large, one small. [15]You must have accurate and honest weights and measures, so that you may live long in the land the LORD your God is giving you. [16]For the LORD your God detests anyone who does these things, anyone who deals dishonestly.

[17]Remember what the Amalekites did to you along the way when you came out of Egypt. [18]When you were weary and worn out, they met you on your journey and cut off all who were lagging behind; they had no fear of God. [19]When the LORD your God gives you rest from all the enemies around you in the land he is giving you to possess as an inheritance, you shall blot out the memory of Amalek from under heaven. Do not forget!

Firstfruits and Tithes

26 When you have entered the land that the LORD your God is giving you as an inheritance and have taken possession of it and settled in it, [2]take some of the firstfruits of all that you produce from the soil of the land that the LORD your God is giving you and put them in a basket. Then go to the place that the LORD your God will choose as a dwelling for his Name [3]and say to the priest in office at the time, "I declare today

---

[a]8 The Hebrew word was used for various diseases affecting the skin—not necessarily leprosy.

to the Lᴏʀᴅ your God that I have come to the land that the Lᴏʀᴅ swore to our forefathers to give us." ⁴The priest shall take the basket from your hands and set it down in front of the altar of the Lᴏʀᴅ your God. ⁵Then you shall declare before the Lᴏʀᴅ your God: "My father was a wandering Aramean, and he went down into Egypt with a few people and lived there and became a great nation, powerful and numerous. ⁶But the Egyptians ill-treated us and made us suffer, putting us to hard labour. ⁷Then we cried out to the Lᴏʀᴅ, the God of our fathers, and the Lᴏʀᴅ heard our voice and saw our misery, toil and oppression. ⁸So the Lᴏʀᴅ brought us out of Egypt with a mighty hand and an outstretched arm, with great terror and with miraculous signs and wonders. ⁹He brought us to this place and gave us this land, a land flowing with milk and honey; ¹⁰and now I bring the firstfruits of the soil that you, O Lᴏʀᴅ, have given me." Place the basket before the Lᴏʀᴅ your God and bow down before him. ¹¹And you and the Levites and the aliens among you shall rejoice in all the good things the Lᴏʀᴅ your God has given to you and your household.

26:5   The declarations of belief in verses 5–10 and 13–15 are very ancient. They were probably part of a religious service, perhaps when Israel worshipped at the tabernacle before the temple was built. The statements summarize the contents of the Pentateuch, recalling God's work in history, and they sum up the laws' ritual and social obligations.

---

¹²When you have finished setting aside a tenth of all your produce in the third year, the year of the tithe, you shall give it to the Levite, the alien, the fatherless and the widow, so that they may eat in your towns and be satisfied. ¹³Then say to the Lᴏʀᴅ your God: "I have removed from my house the sacred portion and have given it to the Levite, the alien, the fatherless and the widow, according to all you commanded. I have not turned aside from your commands nor have I forgotten any of them. ¹⁴I have not eaten any of the sacred portion while I was in mourning, nor have I removed any of it while I was unclean, nor have I offered any of it to the dead. I have obeyed the Lᴏʀᴅ my God; I have done everything you commanded me. ¹⁵Look down from heaven, your holy dwelling-place, and bless your people Israel and the land you have given us as you promised on oath to our forefathers, a land flowing with milk and honey."

Follow the Lᴏʀᴅ's Commands

¹⁶The Lᴏʀᴅ your God commands you this day to follow these decrees and laws; carefully observe them with all your heart and with all your soul. ¹⁷You have declared this day that the Lᴏʀᴅ is your God and that you will walk in his ways, that you will keep his decrees, commands and laws, and that you will obey him. ¹⁸And the Lᴏʀᴅ has declared this day that you are

his people, his treasured possession as he promised, and that you are to keep all his commands. ¹⁹He has declared that he will set you in praise, fame and honour high above all the nations he has made and that you will be a people holy to the Lᴏʀᴅ your God, as he promised.

The Altar on Mount Ebal

27 Moses and the elders of Israel commanded the people: "Keep all these commands that I give you today. ²When you have crossed the Jordan into the land the Lᴏʀᴅ your God is giving you, set up some large stones and coat them with plaster. ³Write on them all the words of this law when you have crossed over to enter the land the Lᴏʀᴅ your God is giving you, a land flowing with milk and honey, just as the Lᴏʀᴅ, the God of your fathers, promised you. ⁴And when you have crossed the Jordan, set up these stones on Mount Ebal, as I command you today, and coat them with plaster. ⁵Build there an altar to the Lᴏʀᴅ your God, an altar of stones. Do not use any iron tool upon them. ⁶Build the altar of the Lᴏʀᴅ your God with stones from the field and offer burnt offerings on it to the Lᴏʀᴅ your God. ⁷Sacrifice fellowship offeringsᵃ there, eating them and rejoicing in the presence of the Lᴏʀᴅ your God. ⁸And you shall write very clearly all the words of this law on these stones you have set up."

Curses From Mount Ebal

⁹Then Moses and the priests, who are Levites, said to all Israel, "Be silent, O Israel, and listen! You have now become the people of the Lᴏʀᴅ your God. ¹⁰Obey the Lᴏʀᴅ your God and follow his commands and decrees that I give you today."

¹¹On the same day Moses commanded the people: ¹²When you have crossed the Jordan, these tribes shall stand on Mount Gerizim to bless the people: Simeon, Levi, Judah, Issachar, Joseph and Benjamin. ¹³And these tribes shall stand on Mount Ebal to pronounce curses: Reuben, Gad, Asher, Zebulun, Dan and Naphtali.

¹⁴The Levites shall recite to all the people of Israel in a loud voice:

27:14   Covenant treaties that were not religious had to contain some regulations for reward and punishment to enforce obedience. The curses here and blessings in chapter 28 were to be recited at a great covenant ceremony when the people entered the land. Most of the sins to be cursed are secret ones. Deuteronomy is showing that God knows how a person is living even if they hide their actions from others.

---

¹⁵"Cursed is the man who carves an image or casts an idol—a thing detestable to the Lᴏʀᴅ, the work of the craftsman's hands—and sets it up in secret."

Then all the people shall say,

"Amen!"

¹⁶"Cursed is the man who dishonours his father or his mother."

Then all the people shall say,

"Amen!"

¹⁷"Cursed is the man who moves his neighbour's boundary stone."

Then all the people shall say,

"Amen!"

¹⁸"Cursed is the man who leads the blind astray on the road."

Then all the people shall say,

"Amen!"

¹⁹"Cursed is the man who withholds justice from the alien, the fatherless or the widow."

Then all the people shall say,

"Amen!"

²⁰"Cursed is the man who sleeps with his father's wife, for he dishonours his father's bed."

Then all the people shall say,

"Amen!"

²¹"Cursed is the man who has sexual relations with any animal."

Then all the people shall say,

"Amen!"

²²"Cursed is the man who sleeps with his sister, the daughter of his father or the daughter of his mother."

Then all the people shall say,

"Amen!"

²³"Cursed is the man who sleeps with his mother-in-law."

Then all the people shall say,

"Amen!"

²⁴"Cursed is the man who kills his neighbour secretly."

Then all the people shall say,

"Amen!"

²⁵"Cursed is the man who accepts a bribe to kill an innocent person."

Then all the people shall say,

"Amen!"

²⁶"Cursed is the man who does not uphold the words of this law by carrying them out."

Then all the people shall say,

"Amen!"

Blessings for Obedience

28 If you fully obey the LORD your God and carefully follow all his commands that I give you today, the LORD your God will set you high above all the nations on earth. ²All these blessings will come upon you and accompany you if you obey the LORD your God:

³You will be blessed in the city and blessed in the country.

⁴The fruit of your womb will be blessed, and the crops of your land and the young of your livestock—the calves of your herds and the lambs of your flocks.

⁵Your basket and your kneading trough will be blessed.

⁶You will be blessed when you come in and blessed when you go out.

⁷The LORD will grant that the enemies who rise up against you will be defeated before you. They will come at you from one direction but flee from you in seven.

⁸The LORD will send a blessing on your barns and on everything you put your hand to. The LORD your God will bless you in the land he is giving you.

⁹The LORD will establish you as his holy people, as he promised you on oath, if you keep the commands of the LORD your God and walk in his ways. ¹⁰Then all the peoples on earth will see that you are called by the name of the LORD, and they will fear you. ¹¹The LORD will grant you abundant prosperity—in the fruit of your womb, the young of your livestock and the crops of your ground—in the land he swore to your forefathers to give you.

¹²The LORD will open the heavens, the storehouse of his bounty, to send rain on your land in season and to bless all the work of your hands. You will lend to many nations but will borrow from none. ¹³The LORD will make you the head, not the tail. If you pay attention to the commands of the LORD your God that I give you this day and carefully follow them, you will always be at the top, never at the bottom. ¹⁴Do not turn aside from any of the commands I give you today, to the right or to the left, following other gods and serving them.

Curses for Disobedience

¹⁵However, if you do not obey the LORD your God and do not carefully follow all his commands and decrees I am giving you today, all these curses will come upon you and overtake you:

¹⁶You will be cursed in the city and cursed in the country.

¹⁷Your basket and your kneading trough will be cursed.

¹⁸The fruit of your womb will be cursed, and the crops of your land, and the calves of your herds and the lambs of your flocks.

¹⁹You will be cursed when you come in and cursed when you go out.

²⁰The LORD will send on you curses, confusion and rebuke in everything you put your hand to, until you are destroyed and come to sudden ruin because of the evil you have done in forsaking him.ᵃ ²¹The LORD will plague you with diseases until he has destroyed you from the land you are entering to possess. ²²The LORD will strike you with wasting disease, with fever and inflammation, with scorching heat and drought, with blight and mildew, which will plague you until you perish. ²³The sky over your head will be bronze, the ground beneath you iron. ²⁴The LORD will turn the rain of your country into dust and powder; it will come down from the skies until you are destroyed.

ᵃ20 Hebrew me

25The LORD will cause you to be defeated before your enemies. You will come at them from one direction but flee from them in seven, and you will become a thing of horror to all the kingdoms on earth. 26Your carcasses will be food for all the birds of the air and the beasts of the earth, and there will be no-one to frighten them away. 27The LORD will afflict you with the boils of Egypt and with tumours, festering sores and the itch, from which you cannot be cured. 28The LORD will afflict you with madness, blindness and confusion of mind. 29At midday you will grope about like a blind man in the dark. You will be unsuccessful in everything you do; day after day you will be oppressed and robbed, with no-one to rescue you.

30You will be pledged to be married to a woman, but another will take her and ravish her. You will build a house, but you will not live in it. You will plant a vineyard, but you will not even begin to enjoy its fruit. 31Your ox will be slaughtered before your eyes, but you will eat none of it. Your donkey will be forcibly taken from you and will not be returned. Your sheep will be given to your enemies, and no-one will rescue them. 32Your sons and daughters will be given to another nation, and you will wear out your eyes watching for them day after day, powerless to lift a hand. 33A people that you do not know will eat what your land and labour produce, and you will have nothing but cruel oppression all your days. 34The sights you see will drive you mad. 35The LORD will afflict your knees and legs with painful boils that cannot be cured, spreading from the soles of your feet to the top of your head.

36The LORD will drive you and the king you set over you to a nation unknown to you or your fathers. There you will worship other gods, gods of wood and stone. 37You will become a thing of horror and an object of scorn and ridicule to all the nations where the LORD will drive you.

38You will sow much seed in the field but you will harvest little, because locusts will devour it. 39You will plant vineyards and cultivate them but you will not drink the wine or gather the grapes, because worms will eat them. 40You will have olive trees throughout your country but you will not use the oil, because the olives will drop off. 41You will have sons and daughters but you will not keep them, because they will go into captivity. 42Swarms of locusts will take over all your trees and the crops of your land.

43The alien who lives among you will rise above you higher and higher, but you will sink lower and lower. 44He will lend to you, but you will not lend to him. He will be the head, but you will be the tail.

45All these curses will come upon you. They will pursue you and overtake you until you are destroyed, because you did not obey the LORD your God and observe the commands and decrees he gave you. 46They will be a sign and a wonder to you and your descendants for ever. 47Because you did not serve the LORD your God joyfully and gladly in the time of prosperity, 48therefore in hunger and thirst, in nakedness and dire poverty, you will serve the enemies the LORD sends against you. He will put an iron yoke on your neck until he has destroyed you.

49The LORD will bring a nation against you from far away, from the ends of the earth, like an eagle swooping down, a nation whose language you will not understand, 50a fierce-looking nation without respect for the old or pity for the young. 51They will devour the young of your livestock and the crops of your land until you are destroyed. They will leave you no grain, new wine or oil, nor any calves of your herds or lambs of your flocks until you are ruined. 52They will lay siege to all the cities throughout your land until the high fortified walls in which you trust fall down. They will besiege all the cities throughout the land the LORD your God is giving you.

53Because of the suffering that your enemy will inflict on you during the siege, you will eat the fruit of the womb, the flesh of the sons and daughters the LORD your God has given you. 54Even the most gentle and sensitive man among you will have no compassion on his own brother or the wife he loves or his surviving children, 55and he will not give to one of them any of the flesh of his children that he is eating. It will be all he has left because of the suffering that your enemy will inflict on you during the siege of all your cities. 56The most gentle and sensitive woman among you — so sensitive and gentle that she would not venture to touch the ground with the sole of her foot — will begrudge the husband she loves and her own son or daughter 57the afterbirth from her womb and the children she bears. For she intends to eat them secretly during the siege and in the distress that your enemy will inflict on you in your cities.

58If you do not carefully follow all the words of this law, which are written in this book, and do not revere this glorious and awesome name — the LORD your God — 59the LORD will send fearful plagues on you and your descendants, harsh and prolonged disasters, and severe and lingering illnesses. 60He will bring upon you all the diseases of Egypt that you dreaded, and they will cling to you. 61The LORD will also bring on you every kind of sickness and disaster not recorded in this Book of the Law, until you are destroyed. 62You who were as numerous as the stars in the sky will be left but few in number, because you did not obey the LORD your God. 63Just as it pleased the LORD to make you prosper and increase in number, so it will please him to ruin and destroy you. You will be uprooted from the land you are entering to possess.

64Then the LORD will scatter you among all nations, from one end of the earth to the other. There you will worship other gods — gods of wood and stone, which neither you nor your fathers have known. 65Among those nations you will find no repose, no resting place for the sole of your foot. There the LORD will give you an anxious mind, eyes weary with longing, and a despairing heart. 66You will live in constant suspense, filled with dread both night and day, never sure of your life. 67In the morning you will say, "If only it were evening!" and in the evening, "If only it were morning!" — because of the terror that will fill your hearts and the sights that your eyes will see. 68The LORD will send you back in ships to Egypt on a journey I said you should never make again. There you will offer yourselves for sale to your enemies as male and female slaves, but no-one will buy you.

Renewal of the Covenant

29 These are the terms of the covenant the LORD commanded Moses to make with the Israelites in Moab, in addition to the covenant he had made with them at Horeb.

28:68 The theme of Deuteronomy is that obedience to the covenant brings life, and disobedience death. The terrible catalogue of disasters in this chapter culminates in the threat of returning to Egypt. If that were to happen God would have annulled the covenant and all possibility of future blessings would be gone.

---

²Moses summoned all the Israelites and said to them:

Your eyes have seen all that the LORD did in Egypt to Pharaoh, to all his officials and to all his land. ³With your own eyes you saw those great trials, those miraculous signs and great wonders. ⁴But to this day the LORD has not given you a mind that understands or eyes that see or ears that hear. ⁵During the forty years that I led you through the desert, your clothes did not wear out, nor did the sandals on your feet. ⁶You ate no bread and drank no wine or other fermented drink. I did this so that you might know that I am the LORD your God.

⁷When you reached this place, Sihon king of Heshbon and Og king of Bashan came out to fight against us, but we defeated them. ⁸We took their land and gave it as an inheritance to the Reubenites, the Gadites and the half-tribe of Manasseh.

⁹Carefully follow the terms of this covenant, so that you may prosper in everything you do. ¹⁰All of you are standing today in the presence of the LORD your God — your leaders and chief men, your elders and officials, and all the other men of Israel, ¹¹together with your children and your wives, and the aliens living in your camps who chop your wood and carry your water. ¹²You are standing here in order to enter into a covenant with the LORD your God, a covenant the LORD is making with you this day and sealing with an oath, ¹³to confirm you this day as his people, that he may be your God as he promised you and as he swore to your fathers, Abraham, Isaac and Jacob. ¹⁴I am making this covenant, with its oath, not only with you ¹⁵who are standing here with us today in the presence of the LORD our God but also with those who are not here today.

¹⁶You yourselves know how we lived in Egypt and how we passed through the countries on the way here. ¹⁷You saw among them their detestable images and idols of wood and stone, of silver and gold. ¹⁸Make sure there is no man or woman, clan or tribe among you today whose heart turns away from the LORD our God to go and worship the gods of those nations; make sure there is no root among you that produces such bitter poison.

¹⁹When such a person hears the words of this oath, he invokes a blessing on himself and therefore thinks,

"I will be safe, even though I persist in going my own way." This will bring disaster on the watered land as well as the dry.[a] ²⁰The LORD will never be willing to forgive him; his wrath and zeal will burn against that man. All the curses written in this book will fall upon him, and the LORD will blot out his name from under heaven. ²¹The LORD will single him out from all the tribes of Israel for disaster, according to all the curses of the covenant written in this Book of the Law.

²²Your children who follow you in later generations and foreigners who come from distant lands will see the calamities that have fallen on the land and the diseases with which the LORD has afflicted it. ²³The whole land will be a burning waste of salt and sulphur — nothing planted, nothing sprouting, no vegetation growing on it. It will be like the destruction of Sodom and Gomorrah, Admah and Zeboiim, which the LORD overthrew in fierce anger. ²⁴All the nations will ask: "Why has the LORD done this to this land? Why this fierce, burning anger?"

²⁵And the answer will be: "It is because this people abandoned the covenant of the LORD, the God of their fathers, the covenant he made with them when he brought them out of Egypt. ²⁶They went off and worshipped other gods and bowed down to them, gods they did not know, gods he had not given them. ²⁷Therefore the LORD's anger burned against this land, so that he brought on it all the curses written in this book. ²⁸In furious anger and in great wrath the LORD uprooted them from their land and thrust them into another land, as it is now."

²⁹The secret things belong to the LORD our God, but the things revealed belong to us and to our children for ever, that we may follow all the words of this law.

Prosperity After Turning to the LORD

30 When all these blessings and curses I have set before you come upon you and you take them to heart wherever the LORD your God disperses you among the nations, ²and when you and your children return to the LORD your God and obey him with all your heart and with all your soul according to everything I command you today, ³then the LORD your God will restore your fortunes[a] and have compassion on you and gather you again from all the nations where he scattered you. ⁴Even if you have been banished to the most distant land under the heavens, from there the LORD your God will gather you and bring you back. ⁵He will bring you to the land that belonged to your fathers, and you will take possession of it. He will make you more prosperous and numerous than your fathers. ⁶The LORD your God will circumcise your hearts and the hearts of your descendants, so that you may love him with all your heart and with all your soul, and live. ⁷The LORD your God will put all these curses on your enemies who hate and persecute you. ⁸You will again obey the LORD and follow all his commands I am giving you today. ⁹Then the LORD your God will make you most prosperous in all the work of your hands and in the fruit of your womb, the young of your livestock and the crops of your land. The LORD will again delight in

a19 Or way, in order to add drunkenness to thirst."   *a3 Or will bring you back from captivity* you and make you prosperous, just as he delighted in your fathers, [10]if you obey the Lord your God and keep his commands and decrees that are written in this Book of the Law and turn to the Lord your God with all your heart and with all your soul.

The Offer of Life or Death

[11]Now what I am commanding you today is not too difficult for you or beyond your reach. [12]It is not up in heaven, so that you have to ask, "Who will ascend into heaven to get it and proclaim it to us so that we may obey it?" [13]Nor is it beyond the sea, so that you have to ask, "Who will cross the sea to get it and proclaim it to us so that we may obey it?" [14]No, the word is very near you; it is in your mouth and in your heart so that you may obey it.

30:14   Often the Old Testament is thought to contain an impersonal and legalized religion. This verse is the exact opposite. Religious obligation does not come from anything external. It is known to each person in their own spirit. No one can claim to have a particularly special insight into the way to God. It is everyone's birthright, and carries with it duties which cannot be disclaimed.

---

[15]See, I set before you today life and prosperity, death and destruction. [16]For I command you today to love the Lord your God, to walk in his ways, and to keep his commands, decrees and laws; then you will live and increase, and the Lord your God will bless you in the land you are entering to possess.

[17]But if your heart turns away and you are not obedient, and if you are drawn away to bow down to other gods and worship them, [18]I declare to you this day that you will certainly be destroyed. You will not live long in the land you are crossing the Jordan to enter and possess.

[19]This day I call heaven and earth as witnesses against you that I have set before you life and death, blessings and curses. Now choose life, so that you and your children may live [20]and that you may love the Lord your God, listen to his voice, and hold fast to him. For the Lord is your life, and he will give you many years in the land he swore to give to your fathers, Abraham, Isaac and Jacob.

Joshua to Succeed Moses

31 Then Moses went out and spoke these words to all Israel: [2]"I am now a hundred and twenty years old and I am no longer able to lead you. The Lord has said to me, 'You shall not cross the Jordan.' [3]The Lord your God himself will cross over ahead of you. He will destroy these nations before you, and you will take possession of their land. Joshua also will cross over ahead of you, as the Lord said. [4]And the Lord will do to them what he did to Sihon and Og, the kings of the Amorites, whom he destroyed along with their land. [5]The Lord will deliver them to you, and you must do to them all that I have commanded you. [6]Be strong and courageous. Do not be afraid or terrified because of them, for the Lord your God goes with you; he will never leave you nor forsake you."

[7]Then Moses summoned Joshua and said to him in the presence of all Israel, "Be strong and courageous, for you must go with this people into the land that the Lord swore to their forefathers to give them, and you must divide it among them as their inheritance. [8]The Lord himself goes before you and will be with you; he will never leave you nor forsake you. Do not be afraid; do not be discouraged."

The Reading of the Law

[9]So Moses wrote down this law and gave it to the priests, the sons of Levi, who carried the ark of the covenant of the Lord, and to all the elders of Israel. [10]Then Moses commanded them: "At the end of every seven years, in the year for cancelling debts, during the Feast of Tabernacles, [11]when all Israel comes to appear before the Lord your God at the place he will choose, you shall read this law before them in their hearing. [12]Assemble the people—men, women and children, and the aliens living in your towns—so that they can listen and learn to fear the Lord your God and follow carefully all the words of this law. [13]Their children, who do not know this law, must hear it and learn to fear the Lord your God as long as you live in the land you are crossing the Jordan to possess."

Israel's Rebellion Predicted

[14]The Lord said to Moses, "Now the day of your death is near. Call Joshua and present yourselves at the Tent of Meeting, where I will commission him." So Moses and Joshua came and presented themselves at the Tent of Meeting.

[15]Then the Lord appeared at the Tent in a pillar of cloud, and the cloud stood over the entrance to the Tent. [16]And the Lord said to Moses: "You are going to rest with your fathers, and these people will soon prostitute themselves to the foreign gods of the land they are entering. They will forsake me and break the covenant I made with them. [17]On that day I will become angry with them and forsake them; I will hide my face from them, and they will be destroyed. Many disasters and difficulties will come upon them, and on that day they will ask, 'Have not these disasters come upon us because our God is not with us?' [18]And I will certainly hide my face on that day because of all their wickedness in turning to other gods.

[19]"Now write down for yourselves this song and teach it to the Israelites and make them sing it, so that it may be a witness for me against them. [20]When I have brought them into the land flowing with milk and honey, the land I promised on oath to their forefathers, and when they eat their fill and thrive, they will turn to other gods and worship them, rejecting me and breaking my covenant. [21]And when many disasters and difficulties come upon them, this song will testify against them, because it will not be forgotten by their descendants. I know what they are disposed to do, even before I bring them into the land I promised them on oath." [22]So Moses wrote down this song that day and taught it to the Israelites.

23The LORD gave this command to Joshua son of Nun: "Be strong and courageous, for you will bring the Israelites into the land I promised them on oath, and I myself will be with you."

24After Moses finished writing in a book the words of this law from beginning to end, 25he gave this command to the Levites who carried the ark of the covenant of the LORD: 26"Take this Book of the Law and place it beside the ark of the covenant of the LORD your God. There it will remain as a witness against you. 27For I know how rebellious and stiff-necked you are. If you have been rebellious against the LORD while I am still alive and with you, how much more will you rebel after I die! 28Assemble before me all the elders of your tribes and all your officials, so that I can speak these words in their hearing and call heaven and earth to testify against them. 29For I know that after my death you are sure to become utterly corrupt and to turn from the way I have commanded you. In days to come, disaster will fall upon you because you will do evil in the sight of the LORD and provoke him to anger by what your hands have made."

The Song of Moses

30And Moses recited the words of this song from beginning to end in the hearing of the whole assembly of Israel:

32 Listen, O heavens, and I will speak;
      hear, O earth, the words of my mouth.
2Let my teaching fall like rain
  and my words descend like dew,
like showers on new grass,
  like abundant rain on tender plants.

32:1 When covenant treaties were broken in the ancient world a lawsuit was brought against the offender. This song, which is thought to be an ancient one, is set out as God's lawsuit against Israel. Heaven and earth are called to hear the case and Israel is condemned and sentenced. The song differs from the normal pattern in that it offers grounds of hope for the future to the convicted party.

3I will proclaim the name of the LORD.
  Oh, praise the greatness of our God!
4He is the Rock, his works are perfect,
  and all his ways are just.
A faithful God who does no wrong,
  upright and just is he.

5They have acted corruptly towards him;
  to their shame they are no longer his children,
  but a warped and crooked generation.a
6Is this the way you repay the LORD,
  O foolish and unwise people?
Is he not your Father, your Creator,b
  who made you and formed you?

7Remember the days of old;
  consider the generations long past.
Ask your father and he will tell you,
  your elders, and they will explain to you.
8When the Most High gave the nations their inheritance,
  when he divided all mankind,
he set up boundaries for the peoples
  according to the number of the sons of Israel.c
9For the LORD's portion is his people,
  Jacob his allotted inheritance.

10In a desert land he found him,
  in a barren and howling waste.
He shielded him and cared for him;
  he guarded him as the apple of his eye,
11like an eagle that stirs up its nest
  and hovers over its young,
that spreads its wings to catch them
  and carries them on its pinions.
12The LORD alone led him;
  no foreign god was with him.

13He made him ride on the heights of the land
  and fed him with the fruit of the fields.
He nourished him with honey from the rock,
  and with oil from the flinty crag,
14with curds and milk from herd and flock
  and with fattened lambs and goats,
with choice rams of Bashan
  and the finest grains of wheat.
You drank the foaming blood of the grape.

15Jeshurund grew fat and kicked;
  filled with food, he became heavy and sleek.
He abandoned the God who made him
  and rejected the Rock his Saviour.
16They made him jealous with their foreign gods
  and angered him with their detestable idols.
17They sacrificed to demons, which are not God—
  gods they had not known,
  gods that recently appeared,
  gods your fathers did not fear.
18You deserted the Rock, who fathered you;
  you forgot the God who gave you birth.

19The LORD saw this and rejected them
  because he was angered by his sons and daughters.
20"I will hide my face from them," he said,
  "and see what their end will be;
for they are a perverse generation,
  children who are unfaithful.
21They made me jealous by what is no god
  and angered me with their worthless idols.
I will make them envious by those who are not a people;
  I will make them angry by a nation that has no understanding.
22For a fire has been kindled by my wrath,
  one that burns to the realm of deathe below.

---

a5 Or Corrupt are they and not his children, / a generation warped and twisted to their shame   b6 Or Father, who bought you
c8 Masoretic Text; Dead Sea Scrolls (see also Septuagint) sons of God   d15 Jeshurun means the upright one, that is, Israel.
e22 Hebrew to Sheol

It will devour the earth and its harvests
and set on fire the foundations of the
mountains.

23 "I will heap calamities upon them
and expend my arrows against them.
24 I will send wasting famine against them,
consuming pestilence and deadly plague;
I will send against them the fangs of wild beasts,
the venom of vipers that glide in the dust.
25 In the street the sword will make them childless;
in their homes terror will reign.
Young men and young women will perish,
infants and grey-haired men.
26 I said I would scatter them
and blot out their memory from mankind,
27 but I dreaded the taunt of the enemy,
lest the adversary misunderstand
and say, 'Our hand has triumphed;
the LORD has not done all this.' "

28 They are a nation without sense,
there is no discernment in them.
29 If only they were wise and would understand this
and discern what their end will be!
30 How could one man chase a thousand,
or two put ten thousand to flight,
unless their Rock had sold them,
unless the LORD had given them up?
31 For their rock is not like our Rock,
as even our enemies concede.
32 Their vine comes from the vine of Sodom
and from the fields of Gomorrah.
Their grapes are filled with poison,
and their clusters with bitterness.
33 Their wine is the venom of serpents,
the deadly poison of cobras.

34 "Have I not kept this in reserve
and sealed it in my vaults?
35 It is mine to avenge; I will repay.
In due time their foot will slip;
their day of disaster is near
and their doom rushes upon them."

36 The LORD will judge his people
and have compassion on his servants
when he sees their strength is gone
and no-one is left, slave or free.
37 He will say: "Now where are their gods,
the rock they took refuge in,
38 the gods who ate the fat of their sacrifices
and drank the wine of their drink offerings?
Let them rise up to help you!
Let them give you shelter!

39 "See now that I myself am He!
There is no god besides me.
I put to death and I bring to life,
I have wounded and I will heal,
and no-one can deliver out of my hand.
40 I lift my hand to heaven and declare:

As surely as I live for ever,
41 when I sharpen my flashing sword
and my hand grasps it in judgment,
I will take vengeance on my adversaries
and repay those who hate me.
42 I will make my arrows drunk with blood,
while my sword devours flesh:
the blood of the slain and the captives,
the heads of the enemy leaders."

43 Rejoice, O nations, with his people,^{f,g}
for he will avenge the blood of his servants;
he will take vengeance on his enemies
and make atonement for his land and people.

44 Moses came with Joshua^h son of Nun and spoke all the words of this song in the hearing of the people. 45 When Moses finished reciting all these words to all Israel, 46 he said to them, "Take to heart all the words I have solemnly declared to you this day, so that you may command your children to obey carefully all the words of this law. 47 They are not just idle words for you — they are your life. By them you will live long in the land you are crossing the Jordan to possess."

Moses to Die on Mount Nebo

48 On that same day the LORD told Moses, 49 "Go up into the Abarim Range to Mount Nebo in Moab, across from Jericho, and view Canaan, the land I am giving the Israelites as their own possession. 50 There on the mountain that you have climbed you will die and be gathered to your people, just as your brother Aaron died on Mount Hor and was gathered to his people. 51 This is because both of you broke faith with me in the presence of the Israelites at the waters of Meribah Kadesh in the Desert of Zin and because you did not uphold my holiness among the Israelites. 52 Therefore, you will see the land only from a distance; you will not enter the land I am giving to the people of Israel."

Moses Blesses the Tribes

33 This is the blessing that Moses the man of God pronounced on the Israelites before his death. 2 He said:

"The LORD came from Sinai
and dawned over them from Seir;
he shone forth from Mount Paran.
He came with^a myriads of holy ones
from the south, from his mountain slopes.^{b}
3 Surely it is you who love the people;
all the holy ones are in your hand.
At your feet they all bow down,
and from you receive instruction,
4 the law that Moses gave us,
the possession of the assembly of Jacob.
5 He was king over Jeshurun^c
when the leaders of the people assembled,
along with the tribes of Israel.

---

^{f}43 Or *Make his people rejoice, O nations*
^{g}43 Masoretic Text; Dead Sea Scrolls (see also Septuagint) *people, / and let all the angels worship him /*
^{h}44 Hebrew *Hoshea,* a variant of *Joshua* ^{a}2 Or *from* ^{b}2 The meaning of the Hebrew for this phrase is uncertain.
^{c}5 *Jeshurun* means *the upright one,* that is, Israel; also in verse 26.

⁶"Let Reuben live and not die,
    nor^d his men be few."

⁷And this he said about Judah:

"Hear, O LORD, the cry of Judah;
    bring him to his people.
With his own hands he defends his cause.
Oh, be his help against his foes!"

⁸About Levi he said:

"Your Thummim and Urim belong
    to the man you favoured.
You tested him at Massah;
    you contended with him at the waters of
        Meribah.
⁹He said of his father and mother,
    'I have no regard for them.'
He did not recognise his brothers
    or acknowledge his own children,
but he watched over your word
    and guarded your covenant.
¹⁰He teaches your precepts to Jacob
    and your law to Israel.
He offers incense before you
    and whole burnt offerings on your
        altar.
¹¹Bless all his skills, O LORD,
    and be pleased with the work of
        his hands.
Smite the loins of those who rise up
    against him;
strike his foes till they rise no
        more."

¹²About Benjamin he said:

"Let the beloved of the LORD rest secure
    in him,
for he shields him all day long,
    and the one the LORD loves rests between
        his shoulders."

¹³About Joseph he said:

"May the LORD bless his land
    with the precious dew from heaven above
    and with the deep waters that lie below;
¹⁴with the best the sun brings forth
    and the finest the moon can yield;
¹⁵with the choicest gifts of the ancient mountains
    and the fruitfulness of the everlasting hills;
¹⁶with the best gifts of the earth and its fulness
    and the favour of him who dwelt in the burning
        bush.
Let all these rest on the head of Joseph,
    on the brow of the prince among^e his
        brothers.
¹⁷In majesty he is like a firstborn bull;
    his horns are the horns of a wild ox.
With them he will gore the nations,
    even those at the ends of the earth.
Such are the ten thousands of Ephraim;
    such are the thousands of Manasseh."

¹⁸About Zebulun he said:

"Rejoice, Zebulun, in your going out,
    and you, Issachar, in your tents.
¹⁹They will summon peoples to the mountain
    and there offer sacrifices of righteousness;
they will feast on the abundance of the
        seas,
    on the treasures hidden in the sand."

²⁰About Gad he said:

"Blessed is he who enlarges Gad's
        domain!
Gad lives there like a lion,
    tearing at arm or head.
²¹He chose the best land for himself;
    the leader's portion was kept for him.
When the heads of the people assembled,
    he carried out the LORD's righteous will,
    and his judgments concerning Israel."

²²About Dan he said:

"Dan is a lion's cub,
    springing out of Bashan."

²³About Naphtali he said:

"Naphtali is abounding with the favour
        of the LORD
    and is full of his blessing;
he will inherit southward to the lake."

²⁴About Asher he said:

"Most blessed of sons is Asher;
    let him be favoured by his brothers,
    and let him bathe his feet in oil.
²⁵The bolts of your gates will be iron and
        bronze,
    and your strength will equal your
        days.

²⁶"There is no-one like the God of Jeshurun,
    who rides on the heavens to help you
    and on the clouds in his majesty.
²⁷The eternal God is your refuge,
    and underneath are the everlasting
        arms.
He will drive out your enemy before
        you,
    saying, 'Destroy him!'
²⁸So Israel will live in safety alone;
    Jacob's spring is secure
in a land of grain and new wine,
    where the heavens drop dew.
²⁹Blessed are you, O Israel!
    Who is like you,
    a people saved by the LORD?
He is your shield and helper
    and your glorious sword.
Your enemies will cower before you,
    and you will trample down their high
        places."^f

---

^d6 Or but let   ^e16 Or of the one separated from   ^f29 Or will tread upon their bodies

The Death of Moses

34 Then Moses climbed Mount Nebo from the plains of Moab to the top of Pisgah, across from Jericho. There the LORD showed him the whole land — from Gilead to Dan, ²all of Naphtali, the territory of Ephraim and Manasseh, all the land of Judah as far as the western sea,ª ³the Negev and the whole region from the Valley of Jericho, the City of Palms, as far as Zoar. ⁴Then the LORD said to him, "This is the land I promised on oath to Abraham, Isaac and Jacob when I said, 'I will give it to your descendants.' I have let you see it with your eyes, but you will not cross over into it."

⁵And Moses the servant of the LORD died there in Moab, as the LORD had said. ⁶He buried himᵇ in Moab, in the valley opposite Beth Peor, but to this day no-one knows where his grave is. ⁷Moses was a hundred and twenty years old when he died, yet his eyes were not weak nor his strength gone. ⁸The Israelites grieved for Moses in the plains of Moab thirty days, until the time of weeping and mourning was over.

⁹Now Joshua son of Nun was filled with the spiritᶜ of wisdom because Moses had laid his hands on him. So the Israelites listened to him and did what the LORD had commanded Moses.

34:7   The length of Moses' life — 120 years — is probably symbolic. It is three times forty years which is a way of saying three generations. The writer emphasized Moses' health and strength in order to show that he died neither of old age nor sickness, but when God willed it to happen. He died when his work was finished.

¹⁰Since then, no prophet has risen in Israel like Moses, whom the LORD knew face to face, ¹¹who did all those miraculous signs and wonders the LORD sent him to do in Egypt — to Pharaoh and to all his officials and to his whole land. ¹²For no-one has ever shown the mighty power or performed the awesome deeds that Moses did in the sight of all Israel.

ª2 That is, the Mediterranean   ᵇ6 Or *He was buried*   ᶜ9 Or *Spirit*

Joshua

Getting to Grips With History

The book of Joshua forms part of the second main section of the Old Testament (the first being the Pentateuch) which deals with a part of the history of Israel; from the time of the people's entry into the land of Canaan until the fall of Jerusalem to the Babylonians (see 2 Kings 25). Within this period, the book of Joshua focuses on Israel's attempt to settle in Canaan, the battles which occurred in the process, and the ultimate allocation of the land to the various tribal groups. It seems likely that the stories recorded in Joshua were written down in the early days of the monarchy, even before David had captured Jerusalem (which was around 960 BC). The main aim of the book is to highlight God's faithfulness in keeping his promises to his people.

What's in a Name?

In modern western culture people's names don't signify a great deal, they are just names—John, Julie, David—by which a person is called. But in Old Testament society, names were often very important. They conveyed information about a person (e.g. "Isaac": Genesis 21:3,6), or proclaimed some general truth. So it was with the name Joshua. The truth expressed in this Hebrew name is that "God (Yahweh) saves". So although the book is an account of the exploits of the military leader Joshua, it is also the story of God's saving acts on behalf of his people.

The Meaning of Salvation

Sometimes "salvation" is spoken of in only one aspect, that is God for-giving people's sins through the death of Jesus. This is true, of course, but the biblical view of salvation is actually much wider, and it includes God's active involvement in the lives of his people, here and now. And that is the lesson of Joshua for us today. God saves in the here and now, in a very practical and down-to-earth way, by getting involved in the lives of those people he has a personal relationship with.

There are three particular aspects of this salvation to look out for in the book of Joshua: God's promises, God's presence, and God's provision.

God's Promises

Genesis relates how God chose Abraham to be part of his saving purposes for the whole world. When God established a relationship with him, he gave him three promises (Genesis 12:2,3,7): that he would be the ancestor of a great nation, that through his line of descendants all the world would be blessed, and that the land of Canaan would be given to him and to his descendants. It is this last promise which is the focus of the book of Joshua.

No one is quite sure when exactly Abraham lived, or even exactly when the Israelites began to settle in the land of Canaan. Some suggest that the events recorded in Joshua occurred in the late fifteenth century BC, although a more popular view is that the main Israelite settlement took place in the mid to late thirteenth century BC. Whatever the precise date, we are told that the interval between the giving of the promise and its fulfilment was 400 years (Genesis 15:13). That is a long time by our reckoning, but it teaches us two things about God's way of working. Firstly, that his time scale is not the same as ours, and also that he always keeps his word no matter how long it takes.

God's Presence

Humanly speaking, Joshua faced a daunting task. It can't have been easy to take on the role of leader after someone as great as Moses, but Joshua was reassured by the promise of God's presence with his people (1:9). The symbol or visible sign of God's presence with his people was the ark of the covenant. The details of its construction are given in Exodus 25:10–21, but in appearance it was simply a box with a lid which could be carried on poles inserted through rings on its side. The ark may have been thought of as the invisible throne on which God sat. Certainly it was the place where God was considered to meet with his people (Exodus 25:22). Possessing the ark was a tangible reminder of God's presence with his people at all times (e.g. Joshua 3:3–17). However, the knowledge that God was present with them had important implications for Israel. Every personal relationship, whether it is between two people, or between God and humans, involves both privileges and responsibilities, rights and duties. God had chosen to enter into a covenant relationship with Israel and had made them his "people", a word which in Hebrew denotes a kinship relationship. It was as though God had made them his family, and in so doing had bound himself to protect and provide for them. They were to be loyal to him (like a wife to her husband), and obedient to him (as a son should be to his father). That was what being holy was all about—absolute loyalty and complete obedience. If Israel failed to be loyal and obedient, the people would have sinned, and God would discipline them. So God's presence with his people did not necessarily always mean success and victory. As they learned at Ai (Joshua 7:1–12), obedience to God's word was vital.

God's Provision

The account of Israel's victories in the book of Joshua is not the whole story. The whole land was not conquered in one fell swoop although various Canaanite settlements were taken and their rulers (called "kings" in the English translations) captured. In fact it was not until the time of David that all the land was included under Israelite rule. In the book of Joshua, attention is focused on three main areas of land: Jericho in the centre, Hazor in the north, and Beth-horon in the south, which guarded the approach to the central highlands from the coastal plain. Control of these areas meant that Israel gained a sure foothold in the hill-country, and some peace and stability was achieved.

The LORD Commands Joshua

1 After the death of Moses the servant of the LORD, the LORD said to Joshua son of Nun, Moses' assistant: [2]"Moses my servant is dead. Now then, you and all these people, get ready to cross the Jordan River into the land I am about to give to them—to the Israelites. [3]I will give you every place where you set your foot, as I promised Moses. [4]Your territory will extend from the desert to Lebanon, and from the great river, the Euphrates—all the Hittite country—to the Great Sea[a] on the west. [5]No-one will be able to stand up against you all the days of your life. As I was with Moses, so I will be with you; I will never leave you nor forsake you.

1:5 God never asks anyone to do anything for him without the promise that he will be there to strengthen and guide them.

---

[6]"Be strong and courageous, because you will lead these people to inherit the land I swore to their forefathers to give them. [7]Be strong and very courageous. Be careful to obey all the law my servant Moses gave you; do not turn from it to the right or to the left, that you may be successful wherever you go. [8]Do not let this Book of the Law depart from your mouth; meditate on it day and night, so that you may be careful to do everything written in it. Then you will be prosperous and successful. [9]Have I not commanded you? Be strong and courageous. Do not be terrified; do not be discouraged, for the LORD your God will be with you wherever you go."

[10]So Joshua ordered the officers of the people: [11]"Go through the camp and tell the people, 'Get your supplies ready. Three days from now you will cross the Jordan here to go in and take possession of the land the LORD your God is giving you for your own.'"

[12]But to the Reubenites, the Gadites and the half-tribe of Manasseh, Joshua said, [13]"Remember the command that Moses the servant of the LORD gave you: 'The LORD your God is giving you rest and has granted you this land.' [14]Your wives, your children and your livestock may stay in the land that Moses gave you east of the Jordan, but all your fighting men, fully armed, must cross over ahead of your brothers. You are to help your brothers [15]until the LORD gives them rest, as he has done for you, and until they too have taken possession of the land that the LORD your God is giving them. After that, you may go back and occupy your own land, which Moses the servant of the LORD gave you east of the Jordan towards the sunrise."

[16]Then they answered Joshua, "Whatever you have commanded us we will do, and wherever you send us we will go. [17]Just as we fully obeyed Moses, so we will obey you. Only may the LORD your God be with you as he was with Moses. [18]Whoever rebels against your word and does not obey your words, whatever you may command them, will be put to death. Only be strong and courageous!"

Rahab and the Spies

2 Then Joshua son of Nun secretly sent two spies from Shittim. "Go, look over the land," he said, "especially Jericho." So they went and entered the house of a prostitute[a] named Rahab and stayed there.

2:1 Rahab earned her living as a prostitute, and even in her own society she was almost certainly an outcast. She knew what God had done for his people, and she was prepared to act on this. Her faith was enough to bring salvation to her and her kin (Joshua 6:22–25; see also Hebrews 11:31; James 2:25). A faith which fails to lead to action is no real faith at all.

---

[2]The king of Jericho was told, "Look! Some of the Israelites have come here tonight to spy out the land." [3]So the king of Jericho sent this message to Rahab: "Bring out the men who came to you and entered your house, because they have come to spy out the whole land."

[4]But the woman had taken the two men and hidden them. She said, "Yes, the men came to me, but I did not know where they had come from. [5]At dusk, when it was time to close the city gate, the men left. I don't know which way they went. Go after them quickly. You may catch up with them." [6](But she had taken them up to the roof and hidden them under the stalks of flax she had laid out on the roof.) [7]So the men set out in pursuit of the spies on the road that leads to the fords of the Jordan, and as soon as the pursuers had gone out, the gate was shut.

[8]Before the spies lay down for the night, she went up on the roof [9]and said to them, "I know that the LORD has given this land to you and that a great fear of you has fallen on us, so that all who live in this country are melting in fear because of you. [10]We have heard how the LORD dried up the water of the Red Sea[b] for you when you came out of Egypt, and what you did to Sihon and Og, the two kings of the Amorites east of the Jordan, whom you completely destroyed.[c] [11]When we heard of it, our hearts sank[d] and everyone's courage failed because of you, for the LORD your God is God in heaven above and on the earth below. [12]Now then, please swear to me by the LORD that you will show kindness to my family, because I have shown kindness to you. Give me a sure sign [13]that you will spare the lives of my father and mother, my brothers and sisters, and all who belong to them, and that you will save us from death."

[14]"Our lives for your lives!" the men assured her. "If you don't tell what we are doing, we will treat you kindly and faithfully when the LORD gives us the land."

[15]So she let them down by a rope through the window, for the house she lived in was part of the city wall. [16]Now she had said to them, "Go to the hills so that the pursuers will not find you. Hide yourselves there

---

[a]4 That is, the Mediterranean   [a]1 Or possibly an innkeeper   [b]10 Hebrew Yam Suph; that is, Sea of Reeds
[c]10 The Hebrew term refers to the irrevocable giving over of things or persons to the LORD, often by totally destroying them.
[d]11 Hebrew melted

three days until they return, and then go on your way." ¹⁷The men said to her, "This oath you made us swear will not be binding on us ¹⁸unless, when we enter the land, you have tied this scarlet cord in the window through which you let us down, and unless you have brought your father and mother, your brothers and all your family into your house. ¹⁹If anyone goes outside your house into the street, his blood will be on his own head; we will not be responsible. As for anyone who is in the house with you, his blood will be on our head if a hand is laid on him. ²⁰But if you tell what we are doing, we will be released from the oath you made us swear."

²¹"Agreed," she replied. "Let it be as you say." So she sent them away and they departed. And she tied the scarlet cord in the window.

²²When they left, they went into the hills and stayed there three days, until the pursuers had searched all along the road and returned without finding them. ²³Then the two men started back. They went down out of the hills, forded the river and came to Joshua son of Nun and told him everything that had happened to them. ²⁴They said to Joshua, "The Lord has surely given the whole land into our hands; all the people are melting in fear because of us."

Crossing the Jordan

3 Early in the morning Joshua and all the Israelites set out from Shittim and went to the Jordan, where they camped before crossing over. ²After three days the officers went throughout the camp, ³giving orders to the people: "When you see the ark of the covenant of the Lord your God, and the priests, who are Levites, carrying it, you are to move out from your positions and follow it. ⁴Then you will know which way to go, since you have never been this way before. But keep a distance of about a thousand yards[a] between you and the ark; do not go near it."

3:3   The ark symbolized God's presence with his people. The Israelites were to follow it. That way, they would find a way through the difficulties they came up against.

---

⁵Joshua told the people, "Consecrate yourselves, for tomorrow the Lord will do amazing things among you."

⁶Joshua said to the priests, "Take up the ark of the covenant and pass on ahead of the people." So they took it up and went ahead of them.

⁷And the Lord said to Joshua, "Today I will begin to exalt you in the eyes of all Israel, so that they may know that I am with you as I was with Moses. ⁸Tell the priests who carry the ark of the covenant: 'When you reach the edge of the Jordan's waters, go and stand in the river.' "

⁹Joshua said to the Israelites, "Come here and listen to the words of the Lord your God. ¹⁰This is how you will know that the living God is among you and that he will certainly drive out before you the Canaanites,

Hittites, Hivites, Perizzites, Girgashites, Amorites and Jebusites. ¹¹See, the ark of the covenant of the Lord of all the earth will go into the Jordan ahead of you. ¹²Now then, choose twelve men from the tribes of Israel, one from each tribe. ¹³And as soon as the priests who carry the ark of the Lord—the Lord of all the earth—set foot in the Jordan, its waters flowing downstream will be cut off and stand up in a heap."

¹⁴So when the people broke camp to cross the Jordan, the priests carrying the ark of the covenant went ahead of them. ¹⁵Now the Jordan is in flood all during harvest. Yet as soon as the priests who carried the ark reached the Jordan and their feet touched the water's edge, ¹⁶the water from upstream stopped flowing. It piled up in a heap a great distance away, at a town called Adam in the vicinity of Zarethan, while the water flowing down to the Sea of the Arabah (the Salt Sea[b]) was completely cut off. So the people crossed over opposite Jericho. ¹⁷The priests who carried the ark of the covenant of the Lord stood firm on dry ground in the middle of the Jordan, while all Israel passed by until the whole nation had completed the crossing on dry ground.

3:16   One interpretation of this event is that a landslip occurred upriver which effectively dammed the river's flow for long enough to allow the Israelites to cross it. However it happened, the timing was perfect for Israel.

---

4 When the whole nation had finished crossing the Jordan, the Lord said to Joshua, ²"Choose twelve men from among the people, one from each tribe, ³and tell them to take up twelve stones from the middle of the Jordan from right where the priests stood and to carry them over with you and put them down at the place where you stay tonight."

⁴So Joshua called together the twelve men he had appointed from the Israelites, one from each tribe, ⁵and said to them, "Go over before the ark of the Lord your God into the middle of the Jordan. Each of you is to take up a stone on his shoulder, according to the number of the tribes of the Israelites, ⁶to serve as a sign among you. In the future, when your children ask you, 'What do these stones mean?' ⁷tell them that the flow of the Jordan was cut off before the ark of the covenant of the Lord. When it crossed the Jordan, the waters of the Jordan were cut off. These stones are to be a memorial to the people of Israel for ever."

⁸So the Israelites did as Joshua commanded them. They took twelve stones from the middle of the Jordan, according to the number of the tribes of the Israelites, as the Lord had told Joshua; and they carried them over with them to their camp, where they put them down. ⁹Joshua set up the twelve stones that had been[a] in the middle of the Jordan at the spot where the priests who carried the ark of the covenant had stood. And they are there to this day.

¹⁰Now the priests who carried the ark remained

---

a4 Hebrew *about two thousand cubits* (about 900 metres)   b16 That is, the Dead Sea
a9 Or *Joshua also set up twelve stones*

standing in the middle of the Jordan until everything the LORD had commanded Joshua was done by the people, just as Moses had directed Joshua. The people hurried over, [11]and as soon as all of them had crossed, the ark of the LORD and the priests came to the other side while the people watched. [12]The men of Reuben, Gad and the half-tribe of Manasseh crossed over, armed, in front of the Israelites, as Moses had directed them. [13]About forty thousand armed for battle crossed over before the LORD to the plains of Jericho for war.

[14]That day the LORD exalted Joshua in the sight of all Israel; and they revered him all the days of his life, just as they had revered Moses.

[15]Then the LORD said to Joshua, [16]"Command the priests carrying the ark of the Testimony to come up out of the Jordan."

[17]So Joshua commanded the priests, "Come up out of the Jordan."

[18]And the priests came up out of the river carrying the ark of the covenant of the LORD. No sooner had they set their feet on the dry ground than the waters of the Jordan returned to their place and ran in flood as before.

[19]On the tenth day of the first month the people went up from the Jordan and camped at Gilgal on the eastern border of Jericho. [20]And Joshua set up at Gilgal the twelve stones they had taken out of the Jordan. [21]He said to the Israelites, "In the future when your descendants ask their fathers, 'What do these stones mean?' [22]tell them, 'Israel crossed the Jordan on dry ground.' [23]For the LORD your God dried up the Jordan before you until you had crossed over. The LORD your God did to the Jordan just what he had done to the Red Sea[b] when he dried it up before us until we had crossed over. [24]He did this so that all the peoples of the earth might know that the hand of the LORD is powerful and so that you might always fear the LORD your God."

4:21 Those who follow God are called to live in the present, but (particularly if our present circumstances are difficult) it is also a good thing to remember God's faithfulness in the past and to tell other people about his power and love (e.g. 4:6,24).

Circumcision at Gilgal

5 Now when all the Amorite kings west of the Jordan and all the Canaanite kings along the coast heard how the LORD had dried up the Jordan before the Israelites until we had crossed over, their hearts sank[a] and they no longer had the courage to face the Israelites.

[2]At that time the LORD said to Joshua, "Make flint knives and circumcise the Israelites again." [3]So Joshua made flint knives and circumcised the Israelites at Gibeath Haaraloth.[b]

[4]Now this is why he did so: All those who came out of Egypt—all the men of military age—died in the desert on the way after leaving Egypt. [5]All the people that came out had been circumcised, but all the people born in the desert during the journey from Egypt had not. [6]The Israelites had moved about in the desert forty years until all the men who were of military age when they left Egypt had died, since they had not obeyed the LORD. For the LORD had sworn to them that they would not see the land that he had solemnly promised their fathers to give us, a land flowing with milk and honey. [7]So he raised up their sons in their place, and these were the ones Joshua circumcised. They were still uncircumcised because they had not been circumcised on the way. [8]And after the whole nation had been circumcised, they remained where they were in camp until they were healed.

5:2 When God established his covenant with Abraham, he instituted the rite of circumcision (Genesis 17:10,11), as a sign of the covenant relationship, and as a mark of membership of God's people. Here it is applied to the generation who had grown up in the interval between the exodus from Egypt and the entry into the land of Canaan. In the Old Testament, the covenant mark was external and only applied to men. In the New Testament God's mark on believers in Christ, both men and women, was the gift of his Holy Spirit in their lives (Ephesians 1:13).

---

[9]Then the LORD said to Joshua, "Today I have rolled away the reproach of Egypt from you." So the place has been called Gilgal[c] to this day.

[10]On the evening of the fourteenth day of the month, while camped at Gilgal on the plains of Jericho, the Israelites celebrated the Passover. [11]The day after the Passover, that very day, they ate some of the produce of the land: unleavened bread and roasted grain. [12]The manna stopped the day after[d] they ate this food from the land; there was no longer any manna for the Israelites, but that year they ate of the produce of Canaan.

5:10 Of all the Jewish festivals, the Passover is probably the one with the greatest historical significance. Although it may have already been a festival of some sort, from the time of the exodus it became inextricably linked with God's redemption of his people from slavery. It must have been strange to have had the land that God had promised to their ancestors, as they remembered all those in the previous generation who had failed to get to the promised land because of their lack of faith (Numbers 14:20–23).

---

b23 Hebrew *Yam Suph*; that is, Sea of Reeds
c9 *Gilgal* sounds like the Hebrew for *roll*.
a1 Hebrew *melted*
d12 Or *the day*
b3 *Gibeath Haaraloth* means *hill of foreskins*.

The Fall of Jericho

[13]Now when Joshua was near Jericho, he looked up and saw a man standing in front of him with a drawn sword in his hand. Joshua went up to him and asked, "Are you for us or for our enemies?"

[14]"Neither," he replied, "but as commander of the army of the LORD I have now come." Then Joshua fell face down to the ground in reverence, and asked him, "What message does my Lord[e] have for his servant?"

[15]The commander of the LORD's army replied, "Take off your sandals, for the place where you are standing is holy." And Joshua did so.

6 Now Jericho was tightly shut up because of the Israelites. No-one went out and no-one came in. [2]Then the LORD said to Joshua, "See, I have delivered Jericho into your hands, along with its king and its fighting men. [3]March around the city once with all the armed men. Do this for six days. [4]Make seven priests carry trumpets of rams' horns in front of the ark. On the seventh day, march around the city seven times, with the priests blowing the trumpets. [5]When you hear them sound a long blast on the trumpets, make all the people give a loud shout; then the wall of the city will collapse and the people will go up, every man straight in."

[6]So Joshua son of Nun called the priests and said to them, "Take up the ark of the covenant of the LORD and make seven priests carry trumpets in front of it." [7]And he ordered the people, "Advance! March around the city, with the armed guard going ahead of the ark of the LORD."

[8]When Joshua had spoken to the people, the seven priests carrying the seven trumpets before the LORD went forward, blowing their trumpets, and the ark of the LORD's covenant followed them. [9]The armed guard marched ahead of the priests who blew the trumpets, and the rear guard followed the ark. All this time the trumpets were sounding. [10]But Joshua had commanded the people, "Do not give a war cry, do not raise your voices, do not say a word until the day I tell you to shout. Then shout!" [11]So he had the ark of the LORD carried around the city, circling it once. Then the people returned to camp and spent the night there.

[12]Joshua got up early the next morning and the priests took up the ark of the LORD. [13]The seven priests carrying the seven trumpets went forward, marching before the ark of the LORD and blowing the trumpets. The armed men went ahead of them and the rear guard followed the ark of the LORD, while the trumpets kept sounding. [14]So on the second day they marched around the city once and returned to the camp. They did this for six days.

[15]On the seventh day, they got up at daybreak and marched around the city seven times in the same manner, except that on that day they circled the city seven times. [16]The seventh time around, when the priests sounded the trumpet blast, Joshua commanded the people, "Shout! For the LORD has given you the city! [17]The city and all that is in it are to be devoted[a] to the LORD. Only Rahab the prostitute[b] and all who are with

her in her house shall be spared, because she hid the spies we sent. [18]But keep away from the devoted things, so that you will not bring about your own destruction by taking any of them. Otherwise you will make the camp of Israel liable to destruction and bring trouble on it. [19]All the silver and gold and the articles of bronze and iron are sacred to the LORD and must go into his treasury."

6:17–19 The destruction of an entire settlement in order to "devote" everything to the Lord seems offensive. The thinking behind this idea appears to be the concept of Israel being involved in a "holy war", the purpose of which was not to spread their faith by force but rather to ensure their survival as God's people in the land promised to their ancestors. Because the Israelites' very existence was at stake, their enemies were thought of as God's enemies. On the other hand, the people believed that the wars they fought were God's war. He fought for Israel, and he himself would be present with them symbolically in the ark of the covenant.

---

[20]When the trumpets sounded, the people shouted, and at the sound of the trumpet, when the people gave a loud shout, the wall collapsed; so every man charged straight in, and they took the city. [21]They devoted the city to the LORD and destroyed with the sword every living thing in it—men and women, young and old, cattle, sheep and donkeys.

[22]Joshua said to the two men who had spied out the land, "Go into the prostitute's house and bring her out and all who belong to her, in accordance with your oath to her." [23]So the young men who had done the spying went in and brought out Rahab, her father and mother and brothers and all who belonged to her. They brought out her entire family and put them in a place outside the camp of Israel.

[24]Then they burned the whole city and everything in it, but they put the silver and gold and the articles of bronze and iron into the treasury of the LORD's house. [25]But Joshua spared Rahab the prostitute, with her family and all who belonged to her, because she hid the men Joshua had sent as spies to Jericho—and she lives among the Israelites to this day.

[26]At that time Joshua pronounced this solemn oath: "Cursed before the LORD is the man who undertakes to rebuild this city, Jericho:

"At the cost of his firstborn son
will he lay its foundations;
at the cost of his youngest
will he set up its gates."

[27]So the LORD was with Joshua, and his fame spread throughout the land.

---

[e]14 Or *lord*
[a]17 The Hebrew term refers to the irrevocable giving over of things or persons to the LORD, often by totally destroying them; also in verses 18 and 21.   [b]17 Or possibly *innkeeper*; also in verses 22 and 25

Achan's Sin

7 But the Israelites acted unfaithfully in regard to the devoted things;[a] Achan son of Carmi,[b] the son of Zimri,[b] the son of Zerah, of the tribe of Judah, took some of them. So the LORD's anger burned against Israel.

7:1 One man sinned and the whole people suffered defeat. Why? It seems that in its early stages Israelite society had a very real sense of corporate identity—of the whole group being one. This principle operated in different areas at different levels of social organization. In terms of their religion, the whole people were regarded as one "body" and therefore the behaviour of a single member was enough to affect everyone.

---

²Now Joshua sent men from Jericho to Ai, which is near Beth Aven to the east of Bethel, and told them, "Go up and spy out the region." So the men went up and spied out Ai.

³When they returned to Joshua, they said, "Not all the people will have to go up against Ai. Send two or three thousand men to take it and do not weary all the people, for only a few men are there." ⁴So about three thousand men went up; but they were routed by the men of Ai, ⁵who killed about thirty-six of them. They chased the Israelites from the city gate as far as the stone quarries[c] and struck them down on the slopes. At this the hearts of the people melted and became like water.

⁶Then Joshua tore his clothes and fell face down to the ground before the ark of the LORD, remaining there till evening. The elders of Israel did the same, and sprinkled dust on their heads. ⁷And Joshua said, "Ah, Sovereign LORD, why did you ever bring this people across the Jordan to deliver us into the hands of the Amorites to destroy us? If only we had been content to stay on the other side of the Jordan! ⁸O Lord, what can I say, now that Israel has been routed by its enemies? ⁹The Canaanites and the other people of the country will hear about this and they will surround us and wipe out our name from the earth. What then will you do for your own great name?"

¹⁰The LORD said to Joshua, "Stand up! What are you doing down on your face? ¹¹Israel has sinned; they have violated my covenant, which I commanded them to keep. They have taken some of the devoted things; they have stolen, they have lied, they have put them with their own possessions. ¹²That is why the Israelites cannot stand against their enemies; they turn their backs and run because they have been made liable to destruction. I will not be with you any more unless you destroy whatever among you is devoted to destruction. ¹³"Go, consecrate the people. Tell them, 'Consecrate yourselves in preparation for tomorrow; for this

is what the LORD, the God of Israel, says: That which is devoted is among you, O Israel. You cannot stand against your enemies until you remove it.

¹⁴" 'In the morning, present yourselves tribe by tribe. The tribe that the LORD takes shall come forward clan by clan; the clan that the LORD takes shall come forward family by family; and the family that the LORD takes shall come forward man by man. ¹⁵He who is caught with the devoted things shall be destroyed by fire, along with all that belongs to him. He has violated the covenant of the LORD and has done a disgraceful thing in Israel!' "

¹⁶Early the next morning Joshua had Israel come forward by tribes, and Judah was taken. ¹⁷The clans of Judah came forward, and he took the Zerahites. He had the clan of the Zerahites come forward by families, and Zimri was taken. ¹⁸Joshua had his family come forward man by man, and Achan son of Carmi, the son of Zimri, the son of Zerah, of the tribe of Judah, was taken.

7:16 Early Israelite society is often described as "tribal". The evidence suggests that membership of any group within Israel was based on direct descent from a particular ancestor. Genealogies were very important as they demonstrated a person's (male) right to belong to a particular group.

---

¹⁹Then Joshua said to Achan, "My son, give glory to the LORD,[d] the God of Israel, and give him the praise.[e] Tell me what you have done; do not hide it from me."

²⁰Achan replied, "It is true! I have sinned against the LORD, the God of Israel. This is what I have done: ²¹When I saw in the plunder a beautiful robe from Babylonia,[f] two hundred shekels[g] of silver and a wedge of gold weighing fifty shekels,[h] I coveted them and took them. They are hidden in the ground inside my tent, with the silver underneath."

²²So Joshua sent messengers, and they ran to the tent, and there it was, hidden in his tent, with the silver underneath. ²³They took the things from the tent, brought them to Joshua and all the Israelites and spread them out before the LORD.

²⁴Then Joshua, together with all Israel, took Achan son of Zerah, the silver, the robe, the gold wedge, his sons and daughters, his cattle, donkeys and sheep, his tent and all that he had, to the Valley of Achor. ²⁵Joshua said, "Why have you brought this trouble on us? The LORD will bring trouble on you today."

Then all Israel stoned him, and after they had stoned the rest, they burned them. ²⁶Over Achan they heaped up a large pile of rocks, which remains to this day. Then the LORD turned from his fierce anger. Therefore that place has been called the Valley of Achor[i] ever since.

---

a1 The Hebrew term refers to the irrevocable giving over of things or persons to the LORD, often by totally destroying them; also in verses 11, 12, 13 and 15.   b1 See Septuagint and 1 Chron. 2:6; Hebrew *Zabdi*; also in verses 17 and 18.   c5 Or *as far as Shebarim*
d19 A solemn charge to tell the truth   e19 Or *and confess to him*   f21 Hebrew *Shinar*
g21 That is, about 5 pounds (about 2.3 kilograms)   h21 That is, about 1¼ pounds (about 0.6 kilogram)
i26 *Achor* means *trouble*.

Ai Destroyed

8 Then the LORD said to Joshua, "Do not be afraid; do not be discouraged. Take the whole army with you, and go up and attack Ai. For I have delivered into your hands the king of Ai, his people, his city and his land. ²You shall do to Ai and its king as you did to Jericho and its king, except that you may carry off their plunder and livestock for yourselves. Set an ambush behind the city."

³So Joshua and the whole army moved out to attack Ai. He chose thirty thousand of his best fighting men and sent them out at night ⁴with these orders: "Listen carefully. You are to set an ambush behind the city. Don't go very far from it. All of you be on the alert. ⁵I and all those with me will advance on the city, and when the men come out against us, as they did before, we will flee from them. ⁶They will pursue us until we have lured them away from the city, for they will say, 'They are running away from us as they did before.' So when we flee from them, ⁷you are to rise up from ambush and take the city. The LORD your God will give it into your hand. ⁸When you have taken the city, set it on fire. Do what the LORD has commanded. See to it; you have my orders."

⁹Then Joshua sent them off, and they went to the place of ambush and lay in wait between Bethel and Ai, to the west of Ai — but Joshua spent that night with the people.

¹⁰Early the next morning Joshua mustered his men, and he and the leaders of Israel marched before them to Ai. ¹¹The entire force that was with him marched up and approached the city and arrived in front of it. They set up camp north of Ai, with the valley between them and the city. ¹²Joshua had taken about five thousand men and set them in ambush between Bethel and Ai, to the west of the city. ¹³They had the soldiers take up their positions — all those in the camp to the north of the city and the ambush to the west of it. That night Joshua went into the valley.

¹⁴When the king of Ai saw this, he and all the men of the city hurried out early in the morning to meet Israel in battle at a certain place overlooking the Arabah. But he did not know that an ambush had been set against him behind the city. ¹⁵Joshua and all Israel let themselves be driven back before them, and they fled towards the desert. ¹⁶All the men of Ai were called to pursue them, and they pursued Joshua and were lured away from the city. ¹⁷Not a man remained in Ai or Bethel who did not go after Israel. They left the city open and went in pursuit of Israel.

¹⁸Then the LORD said to Joshua, "Hold out towards Ai the javelin that is in your hand, for into your hand I will deliver the city." So Joshua held out his javelin towards Ai. ¹⁹As soon as he did this, the men in the ambush rose quickly from their position and rushed forward. They entered the city and captured it and quickly set it on fire.

²⁰The men of Ai looked back and saw the smoke of the city rising against the sky, but they had no chance to escape in any direction, for the Israelites who had been fleeing towards the desert had turned back against their pursuers. ²¹For when Joshua and all Israel saw that the ambush had taken the city and that smoke was going up from the city, they turned round and attacked the men of Ai. ²²The men of the ambush also came out of the city against them, so that they were caught in the middle, with Israelites on both sides. Israel cut them down, leaving them neither survivors nor fugitives. ²³But they took the king of Ai alive and brought him to Joshua.

²⁴When Israel had finished killing all the men of Ai in the fields and in the desert where they had chased them, and when every one of them had been put to the sword, all the Israelites returned to Ai and killed those who were in it. ²⁵Twelve thousand men and women fell that day — all the people of Ai. ²⁶For Joshua did not draw back the hand that held out his javelin until he had destroyed[a] all who lived in Ai. ²⁷But Israel did carry off for themselves the livestock and plunder of this city, as the LORD had instructed Joshua.

²⁸So Joshua burned Ai and made it a permanent heap of ruins, a desolate place to this day. ²⁹He hung the king of Ai on a tree and left him there until evening. At sunset, Joshua ordered them to take his body from the tree and throw it down at the entrance of the city gate. And they raised a large pile of rocks over it, which remains to this day.

The Covenant Renewed at Mount Ebal

³⁰Then Joshua built on Mount Ebal an altar to the LORD, the God of Israel, ³¹as Moses the servant of the LORD had commanded the Israelites. He built it according to what is written in the Book of the Law of Moses — an altar of uncut stones, on which no iron tool had been used. On it they offered to the LORD burnt offerings and sacrificed fellowship offerings.[b] ³²There, in the presence of the Israelites, Joshua copied on stones the law of Moses, which he had written. ³³All Israel, aliens and citizens alike, with their elders, officials and judges, were standing on both sides of the ark of the covenant of the LORD, facing those who carried it — the priests, who were Levites. Half of the people stood in front of Mount Gerizim and half of them in front of Mount Ebal, as Moses the servant of the LORD had formerly commanded when he gave instructions to bless the people of Israel.

³⁴Afterwards, Joshua read all the words of the law — the blessings and the curses — just as it is written in the Book of the Law. ³⁵There was not a word of all that Moses had commanded that Joshua did not read to the whole assembly of Israel, including the women and children, and the aliens who lived among them.

The Gibeonite Deception

9 Now when all the kings west of the Jordan heard about these things — those in the hill country, in the western foothills, and along the entire coast of the Great Sea[a] as far as Lebanon (the kings of the Hittites, Amorites, Canaanites, Perizzites, Hivites and

---

a 26 The Hebrew term refers to the irrevocable giving over of things or persons to the LORD, often by totally destroying them.
b 31 Traditionally *peace offerings*   *a 1* That is, the Mediterranean

Jebusites) — [2]they came together to make war against Joshua and Israel.

[3]However, when the people of Gibeon heard what Joshua had done to Jericho and Ai, [4]they resorted to a ruse: They went as a delegation whose donkeys were loaded[b] with worn-out sacks and old wineskins, cracked and mended. [5]The men put worn and patched sandals on their feet and wore old clothes. All the bread of their food supply was dry and mouldy. [6]Then they went to Joshua in the camp at Gilgal and said to him and the men of Israel, "We have come from a distant country; make a treaty with us."

9:3   Gibeon was an important city only about six miles north of Jerusalem — certainly not in "a very distant country" as the Gibeonites maintained (9:6,9). But even though Israel had been tricked into making a treaty of peace with them, the Israelites honoured their word (9:18). However, the Gibeonites were not granted full membership rights in the Israelite communities that they attached themselves to. They were only given access to water, the use of timber for construction purposes, and fuel. Because they had no right to a portion of agricultural land, the Gibeonites had to hire out their services to others (9:21).

---

[7]The men of Israel said to the Hivites, "But perhaps you live near us. How then can we make a treaty with you?"

[8]"We are your servants," they said to Joshua.

But Joshua asked, "Who are you and where do you come from?"

[9]They answered: "Your servants have come from a very distant country because of the fame of the Lord your God. For we have heard reports of him: all that he did in Egypt, [10]and all that he did to the two kings of the Amorites east of the Jordan — Sihon king of Heshbon, and Og king of Bashan, who reigned in Ashtaroth. [11]And our elders and all those living in our country said to us, 'Take provisions for your journey; go and meet them and say to them, "We are your servants; make a treaty with us." ' [12]This bread of ours was warm when we packed it at home on the day we left to come to you. But now see how dry and mouldy it is. [13]And these wineskins that we filled were new, but see how cracked they are. And our clothes and sandals are worn out by the very long journey."

[14]The men of Israel sampled their provisions but did not enquire of the Lord. [15]Then Joshua made a treaty of peace with them to let them live, and the leaders of the assembly ratified it by oath.

[16]Three days after they made the treaty with the Gibeonites, the Israelites heard that they were neighbours, living near them. [17]So the Israelites set out and on the third day came to their cities: Gibeon, Kephirah, Beeroth and Kiriath Jearim. [18]But the Israelites did not attack them, because the leaders of the assembly had sworn an oath to them by the Lord, the God of Israel.

The whole assembly grumbled against the leaders, [19]but all the leaders answered, "We have given them our oath by the Lord, the God of Israel, and we cannot touch them now. [20]This is what we will do to them: We will let them live, so that wrath will not fall on us for breaking the oath we swore to them." [21]They continued, "Let them live, but let them be woodcutters and water-carriers for the entire community." So the leaders' promise to them was kept.

[22]Then Joshua summoned the Gibeonites and said, "Why did you deceive us by saying, 'We live a long way from you,' while actually you live near us? [23]You are now under a curse: You will never cease to serve as woodcutters and water-carriers for the house of my God."

[24]They answered Joshua, "Your servants were clearly told how the Lord your God had commanded his servant Moses to give you the whole land and to wipe out all its inhabitants from before you. So we feared for our lives because of you, and that is why we did this. [25]We are now in your hands. Do to us whatever seems good and right to you."

[26]So Joshua saved them from the Israelites, and they did not kill them. [27]That day he made the Gibeonites woodcutters and water-carriers for the community and for the altar of the Lord at the place the Lord would choose. And that is what they are to this day.

The Sun Stands Still

10 Now Adoni-Zedek king of Jerusalem heard that Joshua had taken Ai and totally destroyed[a] it, doing to Ai and its king as he had done to Jericho and its king, and that the people of Gibeon had made a treaty of peace with Israel and were living near them. [2]He and his people were very much alarmed at this, because Gibeon was an important city, like one of the royal cities; it was larger than Ai, and all its men were good fighters. [3]So Adoni-Zedek king of Jerusalem appealed to Hoham king of Hebron, Piram king of Jarmuth, Japhia king of Lachish and Debir king of Eglon. [4]"Come up and help me attack Gibeon," he said, "because it has made peace with Joshua and the Israelites."

[5]Then the five kings of the Amorites — the kings of Jerusalem, Hebron, Jarmuth, Lachish and Eglon — joined forces. They moved up with all their troops and took up positions against Gibeon and attacked it.

[6]The Gibeonites then sent word to Joshua in the camp at Gilgal: "Do not abandon your servants. Come up to us quickly and save us! Help us, because all the Amorite kings from the hill country have joined forces against us."

[7]So Joshua marched up from Gilgal with his entire army, including all the best fighting men. [8]The Lord said to Joshua, "Do not be afraid of them; I have given

---

[b]4 Most Hebrew manuscripts; some Hebrew manuscripts, Vulgate and Syriac (see also Septuagint) *They prepared provisions and loaded their donkeys*   [a]1 The Hebrew term refers to the irrevocable giving over of things or persons to the Lord, often by totally destroying them; also in verses 28, 35, 37, 39 and 40.

them into your hand. Not one of them will be able to withstand you."

10:6   Because the Israelites had made a treaty with the people of Gibeon, they were duty-bound to go to their defence. The result of the battle against the five kings was that the whole of the south of the hill-country of Canaan lay open to the Israelites.

---

[9]After an all-night march from Gilgal, Joshua took them by surprise. [10]The LORD threw them into confusion before Israel, who defeated them in a great victory at Gibeon. Israel pursued them along the road going up to Beth Horon and cut them down all the way to Azekah and Makkedah. [11]As they fled before Israel on the road down from Beth Horon to Azekah, the LORD hurled large hailstones down on them from the sky, and more of them died from the hailstones than were killed by the swords of the Israelites.
[12]On the day the LORD gave the Amorites over to Israel, Joshua said to the LORD in the presence of Israel:

"O sun, stand still over Gibeon,
   O moon, over the Valley of Aijalon."
[13]So the sun stood still,
   and the moon stopped,
   till the nation avenged itself on[b] its enemies,

as it is written in the Book of Jashar.
The sun stopped in the middle of the sky and delayed going down about a full day. [14]There has never been a day like it before or since, a day when the LORD listened to a man. Surely the LORD was fighting for Israel!
[15]Then Joshua returned with all Israel to the camp at Gilgal.

10:13   This is sometimes described as the "longest day". The enemy would have seen that even the elements were on the Israelite's side, and so also the God who controlled the forces of nature. The underlying idea is that God can intervene in human affairs and can use even natural disasters to further his purposes.

Five Amorite Kings Killed

[16]Now the five kings had fled and hidden in the cave at Makkedah. [17]When Joshua was told that the five kings had been found hiding in the cave at Makkedah, [18]he said, "Roll large rocks up to the mouth of the cave, and post some men there to guard it. [19]But don't stop! Pursue your enemies, attack them from the rear and don't let them reach their cities, for the LORD your God has given them into your hand."
[20]So Joshua and the Israelites destroyed them completely — almost to a man — but the few who were left reached their fortified cities. [21]The whole army then returned safely to Joshua in the camp at Makkedah, and no-one uttered a word against the Israelites.
[22]Joshua said, "Open the mouth of the cave and bring those five kings out to me." [23]So they brought the five kings out of the cave — the kings of Jerusalem, Hebron, Jarmuth, Lachish and Eglon. [24]When they had brought these kings to Joshua, he summoned all the men of Israel and said to the army commanders who had come with him, "Come here and put your feet on the necks of these kings." So they came forward and placed their feet on their necks.
[25]Joshua said to them, "Do not be afraid; do not be discouraged. Be strong and courageous. This is what the LORD will do to all the enemies you are going to fight." [26]Then Joshua struck and killed the kings and hung them on five trees, and they were left hanging on the trees until evening.
[27]At sunset Joshua gave the order and they took them down from the trees and threw them into the cave where they had been hiding. At the mouth of the cave they placed large rocks, which are there to this day.
[28]That day Joshua took Makkedah. He put the city and its king to the sword and totally destroyed everyone in it. He left no survivors. And he did to the king of Makkedah as he had done to the king of Jericho.

Southern Cities Conquered

[29]Then Joshua and all Israel with him moved on from Makkedah to Libnah and attacked it. [30]The LORD also gave that city and its king into Israel's hand. The city and everyone in it Joshua put to the sword. He left no survivors there. And he did to its king as he had done to the king of Jericho.
[31]Then Joshua and all Israel with him moved on from Libnah to Lachish; he took up positions against it and attacked it. [32]The LORD handed Lachish over to Israel, and Joshua took it on the second day. The city and everyone in it he put to the sword, just as he had done to Libnah. [33]Meanwhile, Horam king of Gezer had come up to help Lachish, but Joshua defeated him and his army — until no survivors were left.
[34]Then Joshua and all Israel with him moved on from Lachish to Eglon; they took up positions against it and attacked it. [35]They captured it that same day and put it to the sword and totally destroyed everyone in it, just as they had done to Lachish.
[36]Then Joshua and all Israel with him went up from Eglon to Hebron and attacked it. [37]They took the city and put it to the sword, together with its king, its villages and everyone in it. They left no survivors. Just as at Eglon, they totally destroyed it and everyone in it.
[38]Then Joshua and all Israel with him turned round and attacked Debir. [39]They took the city, its king and its villages, and put them to the sword. Everyone in it they totally destroyed. They left no survivors. They did to Debir and its king as they had done to Libnah and its king and to Hebron.
[40]So Joshua subdued the whole region, including the hill country, the Negev, the western foothills and the mountain slopes, together with all their kings. He left

---

b13 Or nation triumphed over

no survivors. He totally destroyed all who breathed, just as the LORD, the God of Israel, had commanded. [41]Joshua subdued them from Kadesh Barnea to Gaza and from the whole region of Goshen to Gibeon. [42]All these kings and their lands Joshua conquered in one campaign, because the LORD, the God of Israel, fought for Israel.

[43]Then Joshua returned with all Israel to the camp at Gilgal.

Northern Kings Defeated

11 When Jabin king of Hazor heard of this, he sent word to Jobab king of Madon, to the kings of Shimron and Acshaph, [2]and to the northern kings who were in the mountains, in the Arabah south of Kinnereth, in the western foothills and in Naphoth Dor[a] on the west; [3]to the Canaanites in the east and west; to the Amorites, Hittites, Perizzites and Jebusites in the hill country; and to the Hivites below Hermon in the region of Mizpah. [4]They came out with all their troops and a large number of horses and chariots—a huge army, as numerous as the sand on the seashore. [5]All these kings joined forces and made camp together at the Waters of Merom, to fight against Israel.

11:1 Although the heyday of Hazor's glory lay in the past, it was still a formidable threat to Israelite settlement in the northern regions. Its destruction paved the way for Israel's eventual control of the entire area. This did not happen overnight. 11:16 is a summary of the general effect of Joshua's military campaigns, which happened over a long period (11:18). Pockets of resistance and unconquered territory still remained but Israel was established in the land, and God's promise to his people had been fulfilled.

---

[6]The LORD said to Joshua, "Do not be afraid of them, because by this time tomorrow I will hand all of them over to Israel, slain. You are to hamstring their horses and burn their chariots."

[7]So Joshua and his whole army came against them suddenly at the Waters of Merom and attacked them, [8]and the LORD gave them into the hand of Israel. They defeated them and pursued them all the way to Greater Sidon, to Misrephoth Maim, and to the Valley of Mizpah on the east, until no survivors were left. [9]Joshua did to them as the LORD had directed: He hamstrung their horses and burned their chariots.

[10]At that time Joshua turned back and captured Hazor and put its king to the sword. (Hazor had been the head of all these kingdoms.) [11]Everyone in it they put to the sword. They totally destroyed[b] them, not sparing anything that breathed, and he burned up Hazor itself.

[12]Joshua took all these royal cities and their kings and put them to the sword. He totally destroyed them,

as Moses the servant of the LORD had commanded. [13]Yet Israel did not burn any of the cities built on their mounds—except Hazor, which Joshua burned. [14]The Israelites carried off for themselves all the plunder and livestock of these cities, but all the people they put to the sword until they completely destroyed them, not sparing anyone that breathed. [15]As the LORD commanded his servant Moses, so Moses commanded Joshua, and Joshua did it; he left nothing undone of all that the LORD commanded Moses.

[16]So Joshua took this entire land: the hill country, all the Negev, the whole region of Goshen, the western foothills, the Arabah and the mountains of Israel with their foothills, [17]from Mount Halak, which rises towards Seir, to Baal Gad in the Valley of Lebanon below Mount Hermon. He captured all their kings and struck them down, putting them to death. [18]Joshua waged war against all these kings for a long time. [19]Except for the Hivites living in Gibeon, not one city made a treaty of peace with the Israelites, who took them all in battle. [20]For it was the LORD himself who hardened their hearts to wage war against Israel, so that he might destroy them totally, exterminating them without mercy, as the LORD had commanded Moses.

[21]At that time Joshua went and destroyed the Anakites from the hill country: from Hebron, Debir and Anab, from all the hill country of Judah, and from all the hill country of Israel. Joshua totally destroyed them and their towns. [22]No Anakites were left in Israelite territory; only in Gaza, Gath and Ashdod did any survive. [23]So Joshua took the entire land, just as the LORD had directed Moses, and he gave it as an inheritance to Israel according to their tribal divisions.

Then the land had rest from war.

List of Defeated Kings

12 These are the kings of the land whom the Israelites had defeated and whose territory they took over east of the Jordan, from the Arnon Gorge to Mount Hermon, including all the eastern side of the Arabah:

[2]Sihon king of the Amorites,
who reigned in Heshbon. He ruled from Aroer on the rim of the Arnon Gorge—from the middle of the gorge—to the Jabbok River, which is the border of the Ammonites. This included half of Gilead. [3]He also ruled over the eastern Arabah from the Sea of Kinnereth[a] to the Sea of the Arabah (the Salt Sea[b]), to Beth Jeshimoth, and then southward below the slopes of Pisgah.

[4]And the territory of Og king of Bashan,
one of the last of the Rephaites, who reigned in Ashtaroth and Edrei. [5]He ruled over Mount Hermon, Salecah, all of Bashan to the border of the people of Geshur and Maacah, and half of Gilead to the border of Sihon king of Heshbon.

[6]Moses, the servant of the LORD, and the Israelites conquered them. And Moses the servant of the LORD

---

[a]2 Or in the heights of Dor
[b]11 The Hebrew term refers to the irrevocable giving over of things or persons to the LORD, often by totally destroying them; also in verses 12, 20 and 21.   [a]3 That is, Galilee   [b]3 That is, the Dead Sea

gave their land to the Reubenites, the Gadites and the half-tribe of Manasseh to be their possession.

[7]These are the kings of the land that Joshua and the Israelites conquered on the west side of the Jordan, from Baal Gad in the Valley of Lebanon to Mount Halak, which rises towards Seir (their lands Joshua gave as an inheritance to the tribes of Israel according to their tribal divisions — [8]the hill country, the western foothills, the Arabah, the mountain slopes, the desert and the Negev — the lands of the Hittites, Amorites, Canaanites, Perizzites, Hivites and Jebusites):

[9]the king of Jericho	one
the king of Ai (near Bethel)	one
[10]the king of Jerusalem	one
the king of Hebron	one
[11]the king of Jarmuth	one
the king of Lachish	one
[12]the king of Eglon	one
the king of Gezer	one
[13]the king of Debir	one
the king of Geder	one
[14]the king of Hormah	one
the king of Arad	one
[15]the king of Libnah	one
the king of Adullam	one
[16]the king of Makkedah	one
the king of Bethel	one
[17]the king of Tappuah	one
the king of Hepher	one
[18]the king of Aphek	one
the king of Lasharon	one
[19]the king of Madon	one
the king of Hazor	one
[20]the king of Shimron Meron	one
the king of Acshaph	one
[21]the king of Taanach	one
the king of Megiddo	one
[22]the king of Kedesh	one
the king of Jokneam in Carmel	one
[23]the king of Dor (in Naphoth Dor[c])	one
the king of Goyim in Gilgal	one
[24]the king of Tirzah	one

thirty-one kings in all.

Land Still to Be Taken

13 When Joshua was old and well advanced in years, the LORD said to him, "You are very old, and there are still very large areas of land to be taken over.

[2]"This is the land that remains: all the regions of the Philistines and Geshurites: [3]from the Shihor River on the east of Egypt to the territory of Ekron on the north, all of it counted as Canaanite (the territory of the five Philistine rulers in Gaza, Ashdod, Ashkelon, Gath and Ekron — that of the Avvites); [4]from the south, all the land of the Canaanites, from Arah of the Sidonians as far as Aphek, the region of the Amorites, [5]the area of the Gebalites;[a] and all Lebanon to the east, from Baal Gad below Mount Hermon to Lebo[b] Hamath.

13:1 Within the territory controlled by each tribe the land was allotted to individual clans. Note the number of times the phrase "clan by clan" appears in this account. The allocation was by lot, a process which the people regarded as giving divine sanction to the whole nation. Each area was therefore regarded as God's gift to the local community. The important point in the allocation was that everyone was given access to a means of livelihood sufficient for their needs. The early Christians attempted to apply the same principle in their life together as the people of God (Acts 4:32–35) and various groups down through the years have attempted to operate in a similar way by sharing their resources.

---

[6]"As for all the inhabitants of the mountain regions from Lebanon to Misrephoth Maim, that is, all the Sidonians, I myself will drive them out before the Israelites. Be sure to allocate this land to Israel for an inheritance, as I have instructed you, [7]and divide it as an inheritance among the nine tribes and half of the tribe of Manasseh."

Division of the Land East of the Jordan

[8]The other half of Manasseh,[c] the Reubenites and the Gadites had received the inheritance that Moses had given them east of the Jordan, as he, the servant of the LORD, had assigned it to them.

[9]It extended from Aroer on the rim of the Arnon Gorge, and from the town in the middle of the gorge, and included the whole plateau of Medeba as far as Dibon, [10]and all the towns of Sihon king of the Amorites, who ruled in Heshbon, out to the border of the Ammonites. [11]It also included Gilead, the territory of the people of Geshur and Maacah, all of Mount Hermon and all Bashan as far as Salecah — [12]that is, the whole kingdom of Og in Bashan, who had reigned in Ashtaroth and Edrei and had survived as one of the last of the Rephaites. Moses had defeated them and taken over their land. [13]But the Israelites did not drive out the people of Geshur and Maacah, so they continue to live among the Israelites to this day.

[14]But to the tribe of Levi he gave no inheritance, since the offerings made by fire to the LORD, the God of Israel, are their inheritance, as he promised them.

[15]This is what Moses had given to the tribe of Reuben, clan by clan:

[16]The territory from Aroer on the rim of the Arnon Gorge, and from the town in the middle of the

---

gorge, and the whole plateau past Medeba [17]to Heshbon and all its towns on the plateau, including Dibon, Bamoth Baal, Beth Baal Meon, [18]Jahaz, Kedemoth, Mephaath, [19]Kiriathaim, Sibmah, Zereth Shahar on the hill in the valley, [20]Beth Peor, the slopes of Pisgah, and Beth Jeshimoth [21]—all the towns on the plateau and the entire realm of Sihon king of the Amorites, who ruled at Heshbon. Moses had defeated him and the Midianite chiefs, Evi, Rekem, Zur, Hur and Reba—princes allied with Sihon—who lived in that country. [22]In addition to those slain in battle, the Israelites had put to the sword Balaam son of Beor, who practised divination. [23]The boundary of the Reubenites was the bank of the Jordan. These towns and their villages were the inheritance of the Reubenites, clan by clan.

[24]This is what Moses had given to the tribe of Gad, clan by clan:

[25]The territory of Jazer, all the towns of Gilead and half the Ammonite country as far as Aroer, near Rabbah; [26]and from Heshbon to Ramath Mizpah and Betonim, and from Mahanaim to the territory of Debir; [27]and in the valley, Beth Haram, Beth Nimrah, Succoth and Zaphon with the rest of the realm of Sihon king of Heshbon (the east side of the Jordan, the territory up to the end of the Sea of Kinnereth [d]). [28]These towns and their villages were the inheritance of the Gadites, clan by clan.

[29]This is what Moses had given to the half-tribe of Manasseh, that is, to half the family of the descendants of Manasseh, clan by clan:

[30]The territory extending from Mahanaim and including all of Bashan, the entire realm of Og king of Bashan—all the settlements of Jair in Bashan, sixty towns, [31]half of Gilead, and Ashtaroth and Edrei (the royal cities of Og in Bashan). This was for the descendants of Makir son of Manasseh—for half of the sons of Makir, clan by clan.

[32]This is the inheritance Moses had given when he was in the plains of Moab across the Jordan east of Jericho. [33]But to the tribe of Levi, Moses had given no inheritance; the LORD, the God of Israel, is their inheritance, as he promised them.

Division of the Land West of the Jordan

14 Now these are the areas the Israelites received as an inheritance in the land of Canaan, which Eleazar the priest, Joshua son of Nun and the heads of the tribal clans of Israel allotted to them. [2]Their inheritances were assigned by lot to the nine-and-a-half tribes, as the LORD had commanded through Moses. [3]Moses had granted the two-and-a-half tribes their inheritance east of the Jordan but had not granted the Levites an inheritance among the rest, [4]for the sons of Joseph had become two tribes—Manasseh and Ephraim. The Levites received no share of the land but only towns

to live in, with pasture-lands for their flocks and herds. [5]So the Israelites divided the land, just as the LORD had commanded Moses.

Hebron Given to Caleb

[6]Now the men of Judah approached Joshua at Gilgal, and Caleb son of Jephunneh the Kenizzite said to him, "You know what the LORD said to Moses the man of God at Kadesh Barnea about you and me. [7]I was forty years old when Moses the servant of the LORD sent me from Kadesh Barnea to explore the land. And I brought him back a report according to my convictions, [8]but my brothers who went up with me made the hearts of the people sink.[a] I, however, followed the LORD my God wholeheartedly. [9]So on that day Moses swore to me, 'The land on which your feet have walked will be your inheritance and that of your children for ever, because you have followed the LORD my God wholeheartedly.'[b]

[10]"Now then, just as the LORD promised, he has kept me alive for forty-five years since the time he said this to Moses, while Israel moved about in the desert. So here I am today, eighty-five years old! [11]I am still as strong today as the day Moses sent me out; I'm just as vigorous to go out to battle now as I was then. [12]Now give me this hill country that the LORD promised me that day. You yourself heard then that the Anakites were there and their cities were large and fortified, but, the LORD helping me, I will drive them out just as he said."

[13]Then Joshua blessed Caleb son of Jephunneh and gave him Hebron as his inheritance. [14]So Hebron has belonged to Caleb son of Jephunneh the Kenizzite ever since, because he followed the LORD, the God of Israel, wholeheartedly. [15](Hebron used to be called Kiriath Arba after Arba, who was the greatest man among the Anakites.)

Then the land had rest from war.

Allotment for Judah

15 The allotment for the tribe of Judah, clan by clan, extended down to the territory of Edom, to the Desert of Zin in the extreme south.

[2]Their southern boundary started from the bay at the southern end of the Salt Sea,[a] [3]crossed south of Scorpion[b] Pass, continued on to Zin and went over to the south of Kadesh Barnea. Then it ran past Hezron up to Addar and curved around to Karka. [4]It then passed along to Azmon and joined the Wadi of Egypt, ending at the sea. This is their[c] southern boundary.

[5]The eastern boundary is the Salt Sea as far as the mouth of the Jordan.

The northern boundary started from the bay of the sea at the mouth of the Jordan, [6]went up to Beth Hoglah and continued north of Beth Arabah to the Stone of Bohan son of Reuben. [7]The boundary then went up to Debir from the Valley of Achor and turned north to Gilgal, which faces the Pass of Adummim south of the gorge. It continued

---

d27 That is, Galilee   *a8 Hebrew melt*   *b9 Deut. 1:36*   *a2 That is, the Dead Sea; also in verse 5*
b3 Hebrew Akrabbim   *c4 Hebrew your*

along to the waters of En Shemesh and came out at En Rogel. [8]Then it ran up the Valley of Ben Hinnom along the southern slope of the Jebusite city (that is, Jerusalem). From there it climbed to the top of the hill west of the Hinnom Valley at the northern end of the Valley of Rephaim. [9]From the hilltop the boundary headed towards the spring of the waters of Nephtoah, came out at the towns of Mount Ephron and went down towards Baalah (that is, Kiriath Jearim). [10]Then it curved westward from Baalah to Mount Seir, ran along the northern slope of Mount Jearim (that is, Kesalon), continued down to Beth Shemesh and crossed to Timnah. [11]It went to the northern slope of Ekron, turned towards Shikkeron, passed along to Mount Baalah and reached Jabneel. The boundary ended at the sea.

[12]The western boundary is the coastline of the Great Sea.[d]

These are the boundaries around the people of Judah by their clans.

[13]In accordance with the LORD's command to him, Joshua gave to Caleb son of Jephunneh a portion in Judah — Kiriath Arba, that is, Hebron. (Arba was the forefather of Anak.) [14]From Hebron Caleb drove out the three Anakites — Sheshai, Ahiman and Talmai — descendants of Anak. [15]From there he marched against the people living in Debir (formerly called Kiriath Sepher). [16]And Caleb said, "I will give my daughter Acsah in marriage to the man who attacks and captures Kiriath Sepher." [17]Othniel son of Kenaz, Caleb's brother, took it; so Caleb gave his daughter Acsah to him in marriage.

[18]One day when she came to Othniel, she urged him[e] to ask her father for a field. When she got off her donkey, Caleb asked her, "What can I do for you?"

[19]She replied, "Do me a special favour. Since you have given me land in the Negev, give me also springs of water." So Caleb gave her the upper and lower springs.

[20]This is the inheritance of the tribe of Judah, clan by clan:

[21]The southernmost towns of the tribe of Judah in the Negev towards the boundary of Edom were:

Kabzeel, Eder, Jagur, [22]Kinah, Dimonah, Adadah, [23]Kedesh, Hazor, Ithnan, [24]Ziph, Telem, Bealoth, [25]Hazor Hadattah, Kerioth Hezron (that is, Hazor), [26]Amam, Shema, Moladah, [27]Hazar Gaddah, Heshmon, Beth Pelet, [28]Hazar Shual, Beersheba, Biziothiah, [29]Baalah, Iim, Ezem, [30]Eltolad, Kesil, Hormah, [31]Ziklag, Madmannah, Sansannah, [32]Lebaoth, Shilhim, Ain and Rimmon — a total of twenty-nine towns and their villages.

[33]In the western foothills:

Eshtaol, Zorah, Ashnah, [34]Zanoah, En Gannim, Tappuah, Enam, [35]Jarmuth, Adullam, Socoh, Azekah, [36]Shaaraim, Adithaim and Gederah (or

Gederothaim)[f] — fourteen towns and their villages.

[37]Zenan, Hadashah, Migdal Gad, [38]Dilean, Mizpah, Joktheel, [39]Lachish, Bozkath, Eglon, [40]Cabbon, Lahmas, Kitlish, [41]Gederoth, Beth Dagon, Naamah and Makkedah — sixteen towns and their villages.

[42]Libnah, Ether, Ashan, [43]Iphtah, Ashnah, Nezib, [44]Keilah, Aczib and Mareshah — nine towns and their villages.

[45]Ekron, with its surrounding settlements and villages; [46]west of Ekron, all that were in the vicinity of Ashdod, together with their villages; [47]Ashdod, its surrounding settlements and villages; and Gaza, its settlements and villages, as far as the Wadi of Egypt and the coastline of the Great Sea.

[48]In the hill country:

Shamir, Jattir, Socoh, [49]Dannah, Kiriath Sannah (that is, Debir), [50]Anab, Eshtemoh, Anim, [51]Goshen, Holon and Giloh — eleven towns and their villages.

[52]Arab, Dumah, Eshan, [53]Janim, Beth Tappuah, Aphekah, [54]Humtah, Kiriath Arba (that is, Hebron) and Zior — nine towns and their villages.

[55]Maon, Carmel, Ziph, Juttah, [56]Jezreel, Jokdeam, Zanoah, [57]Kain, Gibeah and Timnah — ten towns and their villages.

[58]Halhul, Beth Zur, Gedor, [59]Maarath, Beth Anoth and Eltekon — six towns and their villages.

[60]Kiriath Baal (that is, Kiriath Jearim) and Rabbah — two towns and their villages.

[61]In the desert:

Beth Arabah, Middin, Secacah, [62]Nibshan, the City of Salt and En Gedi — six towns and their villages.

[63]Judah could not dislodge the Jebusites, who were living in Jerusalem; to this day the Jebusites live there with the people of Judah.

Allotment for Ephraim and Manasseh

16 The allotment for Joseph began at the Jordan of Jericho,[a] east of the waters of Jericho, and went up from there through the desert into the hill country of Bethel. [2]It went on from Bethel (that is, Luz),[b] crossed over to the territory of the Arkites in Ataroth, [3]descended westward to the territory of the Japhletites as far as the region of Lower Beth Horon and on to Gezer, ending at the sea.

[4]So Manasseh and Ephraim, the descendants of Joseph, received their inheritance.

[5]This was the territory of Ephraim, clan by clan:

The boundary of their inheritance went from Ataroth Addar in the east to Upper Beth Horon [6]and continued to the sea. From Micmethath on the north it curved eastward to Taanath Shiloh, passing by it to Janoah on the east. [7]Then it went

---

[d]12 That is, the Mediterranean; also in verse 47
[e]18 Hebrew and some Septuagint manuscripts; other Septuagint manuscripts (see also note at Judges 1:14) *Othniel, he urged her*
[f]36 Or *Gederah and Gederothaim*   [a]1 *Jordan of Jericho* was possibly an ancient name for the Jordan River.
[b]2 Septuagint; Hebrew *Bethel to Luz*

down from Janoah to Ataroth and Naarah, touched Jericho and came out at the Jordan. [8]From Tappuah the border went west to the Kanah Ravine and ended at the sea. This was the inheritance of the tribe of the Ephraimites, clan by clan. [9]It also included all the towns and their villages that were set aside for the Ephraimites within the inheritance of the Manassites.

[10]They did not dislodge the Canaanites living in Gezer; to this day the Canaanites live among the people of Ephraim but are required to do forced labour.

17 This was the allotment for the tribe of Manasseh as Joseph's firstborn, that is, for Makir, Manasseh's firstborn. Makir was the ancestor of the Gileadites, who had received Gilead and Bashan because the Makirites were great soldiers. [2]So this allotment was for the rest of the people of Manasseh — the clans of Abiezer, Helek, Asriel, Shechem, Hepher and Shemida. These are the other male descendants of Manasseh son of Joseph by their clans.

[3]Now Zelophehad son of Hepher, the son of Gilead, the son of Makir, the son of Manasseh, had no sons but only daughters, whose names were Mahlah, Noah, Hoglah, Milcah and Tirzah. [4]They went to Eleazar the priest, Joshua son of Nun, and the leaders and said, "The LORD commanded Moses to give us an inheritance among our brothers." So Joshua gave them an inheritance along with the brothers of their father, according to the LORD's command. [5]Manasseh's share consisted of ten tracts of land besides Gilead and Bashan east of the Jordan, [6]because the daughters of the tribe of Manasseh received an inheritance among the sons. The land of Gilead belonged to the rest of the descendants of Manasseh.

[7]The territory of Manasseh extended from Asher to Micmethath east of Shechem. The boundary ran southward from there to include the people living at En Tappuah. [8](Manasseh had the land of Tappuah, but Tappuah itself, on the boundary of Manasseh, belonged to the Ephraimites.) [9]Then the boundary continued south to the Kanah Ravine. There were towns belonging to Ephraim lying among the towns of Manasseh, but the boundary of Manasseh was the northern side of the ravine and ended at the sea. [10]On the south the land belonged to Ephraim, on the north to Manasseh. The territory of Manasseh reached the sea and bordered Asher on the north and Issachar on the east.

[11]Within Issachar and Asher, Manasseh also had Beth Shan, Ibleam and the people of Dor, Endor, Taanach and Megiddo, together with their surrounding settlements (the third in the list is Naphoth[a]).

[12]Yet the Manassites were not able to occupy these towns, for the Canaanites were determined to live in that region. [13]However, when the Israelites grew stronger, they subjected the Canaanites to forced labour but did not drive them out completely.

[14]The people of Joseph said to Joshua, "Why have you given us only one allotment and one portion for an inheritance? We are a numerous people and the LORD has blessed us abundantly."

[15]"If you are so numerous," Joshua answered, "and if the hill country of Ephraim is too small for you, go up into the forest and clear land for yourselves there in the land of the Perizzites and Rephaites."

[16]The people of Joseph replied, "The hill country is not enough for us, and all the Canaanites who live in the plain have iron chariots, both those in Beth Shan and its settlements and those in the Valley of Jezreel."

[17]But Joshua said to the house of Joseph — to Ephraim and Manasseh — "You are numerous and very powerful. You will have not only one allotment [18]but the forested hill country as well. Clear it, and its farthest limits will be yours; though the Canaanites have iron chariots and though they are strong, you can drive them out."

Division of the Rest of the Land

18 The whole assembly of the Israelites gathered at Shiloh and set up the Tent of Meeting there. The country was brought under their control, [2]but there were still seven Israelite tribes who had not yet received their inheritance.

[3]So Joshua said to the Israelites: "How long will you wait before you begin to take possession of the land that the LORD, the God of your fathers, has given you? [4]Appoint three men from each tribe. I will send them out to make a survey of the land and to write a description of it, according to the inheritance of each. Then they will return to me. [5]You are to divide the land into seven parts. Judah is to remain in its territory on the south and the house of Joseph in its territory on the north. [6]After you have written descriptions of the seven parts of the land, bring them here to me and I will cast lots for you in the presence of the LORD our God. [7]The Levites, however, do not get a portion among you, because the priestly service of the LORD is their inheritance. And Gad, Reuben and the half-tribe of Manasseh have already received their inheritance on the east side of the Jordan. Moses the servant of the LORD gave it to them."

[8]As the men started on their way to map out the land, Joshua instructed them, "Go and make a survey of the land and write a description of it. Then return to me, and I will cast lots for you here at Shiloh in the presence of the LORD." [9]So the men left and went through the land. They wrote its description on a scroll, town by town, in seven parts, and returned to Joshua in the camp at Shiloh. [10]Joshua then cast lots for them in Shiloh in the presence of the LORD, and there he distributed the land to the Israelites according to their tribal divisions.

Allotment for Benjamin

[11]The lot came up for the tribe of Benjamin, clan by clan. Their allotted territory lay between the tribes of Judah and Joseph:

[12]On the north side their boundary began at the Jordan, passed the northern slope of Jericho and headed west into the hill country, coming out at

---

_a11_ That is, Naphoth Dor

the desert of Beth Aven. [13]From there it crossed to the south slope of Luz (that is, Bethel) and went down to Ataroth Addar on the hill south of Lower Beth Horon.

[14]From the hill facing Beth Horon on the south the boundary turned south along the western side and came out at Kiriath Baal (that is, Kiriath Jearim), a town of the people of Judah. This was the western side.

[15]The southern side began at the outskirts of Kiriath Jearim on the west, and the boundary came out at the spring of the waters of Nephtoah. [16]The boundary went down to the foot of the hill facing the Valley of Ben Hinnom, north of the Valley of Rephaim. It continued down the Hinnom Valley along the southern slope of the Jebusite city and so to En Rogel. [17]It then curved north, went to En Shemesh, continued to Geliloth, which faces the Pass of Adummim, and ran down to the Stone of Bohan son of Reuben. [18]It continued to the northern slope of Beth Arabah[a] and on down into the Arabah. [19]It then went to the northern slope of Beth Hoglah and came out at the northern bay of the Salt Sea,[b] at the mouth of the Jordan in the south. This was the southern boundary.

[20]The Jordan formed the boundary on the eastern side.

These were the boundaries that marked out the inheritance of the clans of Benjamin on all sides.

[21]The tribe of Benjamin, clan by clan, had the following cities:

Jericho, Beth Hoglah, Emek Keziz, [22]Beth Arabah, Zemaraim, Bethel, [23]Avvim, Parah, Ophrah, [24]Kephar Ammoni, Ophni and Geba—twelve towns and their villages.

[25]Gibeon, Ramah, Beeroth, [26]Mizpah, Kephirah, Mozah, [27]Rekem, Irpeel, Taralah, [28]Zelah, Haeleph, the Jebusite city (that is, Jerusalem), Gibeah and Kiriath—fourteen towns and their villages.

This was the inheritance of Benjamin for its clans.

Allotment for Simeon

19 The second lot came out for the tribe of Simeon, clan by clan. Their inheritance lay within the territory of Judah. [2]It included:

Beersheba (or Sheba),[a] Moladah, [3]Hazar Shual, Balah, Ezem, [4]Eltolad, Bethul, Hormah, [5]Ziklag, Beth Marcaboth, Hazar Susah, [6]Beth Lebaoth and Sharuhen—thirteen towns and their villages;

[7]Ain, Rimmon, Ether and Ashan—four towns and their villages—[8]and all the villages around these towns as far as Baalath Beer (Ramah in the Negev).

This was the inheritance of the tribe of the Simeonites, clan by clan. [9]The inheritance of the Simeonites was taken from the share of Judah, because Judah's portion was more than they needed. So the Simeonites

received their inheritance within the territory of Judah.

Allotment for Zebulun

[10]The third lot came up for Zebulun, clan by clan:

The boundary of their inheritance went as far as Sarid. [11]Going west it ran to Maralah, touched Dabbesheth, and extended to the ravine near Jokneam. [12]It turned east from Sarid towards the sunrise to the territory of Kisloth Tabor and went on to Daberath and up to Japhia. [13]Then it continued eastward to Gath Hepher and Eth Kazin; it came out at Rimmon and turned towards Neah. [14]There the boundary went round on the north to Hannathon and ended at the Valley of Iphtah El. [15]Included were Kattath, Nahalal, Shimron, Idalah and Bethlehem. There were twelve towns and their villages.

[16]These towns and their villages were the inheritance of Zebulun, clan by clan.

Allotment for Issachar

[17]The fourth lot came out for Issachar, clan by clan. [18]Their territory included:

Jezreel, Kesulloth, Shunem, [19]Hapharaim, Shion, Anaharath, [20]Rabbith, Kishion, Ebez, [21]Remeth, En Gannim, En Haddah and Beth Pazzez. [22]The boundary touched Tabor, Shahazumah and Beth Shemesh, and ended at the Jordan. There were sixteen towns and their villages.

[23]These towns and their villages were the inheritance of the tribe of Issachar, clan by clan.

Allotment for Asher

[24]The fifth lot came out for the tribe of Asher, clan by clan. [25]Their territory included:

Helkath, Hali, Beten, Acshaph, [26]Allammelech, Amad and Mishal. On the west the boundary touched Carmel and Shihor Libnath. [27]It then turned east towards Beth Dagon, touched Zebulun and the Valley of Iphtah El, and went north to Beth Emek and Neiel, passing Cabul on the left. [28]It went to Abdon,[b] Rehob, Hammon and Kanah, as far as Greater Sidon. [29]The boundary then turned back towards Ramah and went to the fortified city of Tyre, turned towards Hosah and came out at the sea in the region of Aczib, [30]Ummah, Aphek and Rehob. There were twenty-two towns and their villages.

[31]These towns and their villages were the inheritance of the tribe of Asher, clan by clan.

Allotment for Naphtali

[32]The sixth lot came out for Naphtali, clan by clan: [33]Their boundary went from Heleph and the large tree in Zaanannim, passing Adami Nekeb and Jabneel to Lakkum and ending at the Jordan. [34]The boundary ran west through Aznoth Tabor

---

[a]18 Septuagint; Hebrew *slope facing the Arabah*   [b]19 That is, the Dead Sea
[a]2 Or *Beersheba, Sheba*; 1 Chron. 4:28 does not have *Sheba*.
[b]28 Some Hebrew manuscripts (see also Joshua 21:30); most Hebrew manuscripts *Ebron*

and came out at Hukkok. It touched Zebulun on the south, Asher on the west and the Jordan[c] on the east. [35]The fortified cities were Ziddim, Zer, Hammath, Rakkath, Kinnereth, [36]Adamah, Ramah, Hazor, [37]Kedesh, Edrei, En Hazor, [38]Iron, Migdal El, Horem, Beth Anath and Beth Shemesh. There were nineteen towns and their villages.

[39]These towns and their villages were the inheritance of the tribe of Naphtali, clan by clan.

Allotment for Dan

[40]The seventh lot came out for the tribe of Dan, clan by clan. [41]The territory of their inheritance included:
Zorah, Eshtaol, Ir Shemesh, [42]Shaalabbin, Aijalon, Ithlah, [43]Elon, Timnah, Ekron, [44]Eltekeh, Gibbethon, Baalath, [45]Jehud, Bene Berak, Gath Rimmon, [46]Me Jarkon and Rakkon, with the area facing Joppa.
[47](But the Danites had difficulty taking possession of their territory, so they went up and attacked Leshem, took it, put it to the sword and occupied it. They settled in Leshem and named it Dan after their forefather.) [48]These towns and their villages were the inheritance of the tribe of Dan, clan by clan.

Allotment for Joshua

[49]When they had finished dividing the land into its allotted portions, the Israelites gave Joshua son of Nun an inheritance among them, [50]as the LORD had commanded. They gave him the town he asked for—Timnath Serah[d] in the hill country of Ephraim. And he built up the town and settled there.

[51]These are the territories that Eleazar the priest, Joshua son of Nun and the heads of the tribal clans of Israel assigned by lot at Shiloh in the presence of the LORD at the entrance to the Tent of Meeting. And so they finished dividing the land.

Cities of Refuge

20 Then the LORD said to Joshua: [2]"Tell the Israelites to designate the cities of refuge, as I instructed you through Moses, [3]so that anyone who kills a person accidentally and unintentionally may flee there and find protection from the avenger of blood.

[4]"When he flees to one of these cities, he is to stand in the entrance of the city gate and state his case before the elders of that city. Then they are to admit him into their city and give him a place to live with them. [5]If the avenger of blood pursues him, they must not surrender the one accused, because he killed his neighbour unintentionally and without malice aforethought. [6]He is to stay in that city until he has stood trial before the assembly and until the death of the high priest who is serving at that time. Then he may go back to his own home in the town from which he fled."

[7]So they set apart Kedesh in Galilee in the hill country of Naphtali, Shechem in the hill country of Ephraim, and Kiriath Arba (that is, Hebron) in the hill country of Judah. [8]On the east side of the Jordan of Jericho[a] they designated Bezer in the desert on the plateau in the tribe of Reuben, Ramoth in Gilead in the tribe of Gad, and Golan in Bashan in the tribe of Manasseh. [9]Any of the Israelites or any alien living among them who killed someone accidentally could flee to these designated cities and not be killed by the avenger of blood prior to standing trial before the assembly.

20:2 The principle of corporate identity extended to the area of revenge for any wrong done to a group member. In the event of a group member's death, it was the responsibility of the victim's family to seek retribution on the murderer. But suppose the death was an accident—a case of manslaughter, not cold-blooded murder (see Deuteronomy 19:4–6). The cities of refuge which were dotted through the land were, as their name implies, a haven. They protected the person concerned within their limits and ensured there was a fair trial, rather than an automatic killing (see Numbers 35:9–28).

Towns for the Levites

21 Now the family heads of the Levites approached Eleazar the priest, Joshua son of Nun, and the heads of the other tribal families of Israel [2]at Shiloh in Canaan and said to them, "The LORD commanded through Moses that you give us towns to live in, with pasture-lands for our livestock." [3]So, as the LORD had commanded, the Israelites gave the Levites the following towns and pasture-lands out of their own inheritance:

[4]The first lot came out for the Kohathites, clan by clan. The Levites who were descendants of Aaron the priest were allotted thirteen towns from the tribes of Judah, Simeon and Benjamin. [5]The rest of Kohath's descendants were allotted ten towns from the clans of the tribes of Ephraim, Dan and half of Manasseh.

[6]The descendants of Gershon were allotted thirteen towns from the clans of the tribes of Issachar, Asher, Naphtali and the half-tribe of Manasseh in Bashan.

[7]The descendants of Merari, clan by clan, received twelve towns from the tribes of Reuben, Gad and Zebulun.

[8]So the Israelites allotted to the Levites these towns and their pasture-lands, as the LORD had commanded through Moses.

[9]From the tribes of Judah and Simeon they allotted the following towns by name [10](these towns were assigned to the descendants of Aaron who were from the Kohathite clans of the Levites, because the first lot fell to them):

[11]They gave them Kiriath Arba (that is, Hebron), with its surrounding pasture-land, in the hill country of Judah. (Arba was the forefather of Anak.) [12]But the fields and villages around the city

---

c34 Septuagint; Hebrew *west, and Judah, the Jordan,*   d50 Also known as *Timnath Heres* (see Judges 2:9)
a8 *Jordan of Jericho* was possibly an ancient name for the Jordan River.

they had given to Caleb son of Jephunneh as his possession.

21:8   The Levites weren't given anything in the initial allocation of agricultural land. Their livelihood was already provided for in the laws relating to sacrifices and tithes as certain portions were to be given to them. But now towns and pasture-lands were allocated to them so that they would have a place where they belonged and would be secure.

---

¹³So to the descendants of Aaron the priest they gave Hebron (a city of refuge for one accused of murder), Libnah, ¹⁴Jattir, Eshtemoa, ¹⁵Holon, Debir, ¹⁶Ain, Juttah and Beth Shemesh, together with their pasture-lands — nine towns from these two tribes.

¹⁷And from the tribe of Benjamin they gave them Gibeon, Geba, ¹⁸Anathoth and Almon, together with their pasture-lands — four towns.

¹⁹All the towns for the priests, the descendants of Aaron, were thirteen, together with their pasture-lands.

²⁰The rest of the Kohathite clans of the Levites were allotted towns from the tribe of Ephraim:

²¹In the hill country of Ephraim they were given Shechem (a city of refuge for one accused of murder) and Gezer, ²²Kibzaim and Beth Horon, together with their pasture-lands — four towns.

²³Also from the tribe of Dan they received Eltekeh, Gibbethon, ²⁴Aijalon and Gath Rimmon, together with their pasture-lands — four towns.

²⁵From half the tribe of Manasseh they received Taanach and Gath Rimmon, together with their pasture-lands — two towns.

²⁶All these ten towns and their pasture-lands were given to the rest of the Kohathite clans.

²⁷The Levite clans of the Gershonites were given:
from the half-tribe of Manasseh,
Golan in Bashan (a city of refuge for one accused of murder) and Be Eshtarah, together with their pasture-lands — two towns;
²⁸from the tribe of Issachar,
Kishion, Daberath, ²⁹Jarmuth and En Gannim, together with their pasture-lands — four towns;
³⁰from the tribe of Asher,
Mishal, Abdon, ³¹Helkath and Rehob, together with their pasture-lands — four towns;
³²from the tribe of Naphtali,
Kedesh in Galilee (a city of refuge for one accused of murder), Hammoth Dor and Kartan, together with their pasture-lands — three towns.

³³All the towns of the Gershonite clans were thirteen, together with their pasture-lands.

³⁴The Merarite clans (the rest of the Levites) were given:
from the tribe of Zebulun,
Jokneam, Kartah, ³⁵Dimnah and Nahalal, together with their pasture-lands — four towns;

³⁶from the tribe of Reuben,
Bezer, Jahaz, ³⁷Kedemoth and Mephaath, together with their pasture-lands — four towns;
³⁸from the tribe of Gad,
Ramoth in Gilead (a city of refuge for one accused of murder), Mahanaim, ³⁹Heshbon and Jazer, together with their pasture-lands — four towns in all.

⁴⁰All the towns allotted to the Merarite clans, who were the rest of the Levites, were twelve.

⁴¹The towns of the Levites in the territory held by the Israelites were forty-eight in all, together with their pasture-lands. ⁴²Each of these towns had pasture-lands surrounding it; this was true for all these towns.

⁴³So the LORD gave Israel all the land he had sworn to give their forefathers, and they took possession of it and settled there. ⁴⁴The LORD gave them rest on every side, just as he had sworn to their forefathers. Not one of their enemies withstood them; the LORD handed all their enemies over to them. ⁴⁵Not one of all the LORD's good promises to the house of Israel failed; every one was fulfilled.

Eastern Tribes Return Home

22 Then Joshua summoned the Reubenites, the Gadites and the half-tribe of Manasseh ²and said to them, "You have done all that Moses the servant of the LORD commanded, and you have obeyed me in everything I commanded. ³For a long time now — to this very day — you have not deserted your brothers but have carried out the mission the LORD your God gave you. ⁴Now that the LORD your God has given your brothers rest as he promised, return to your homes in the land that Moses the servant of the LORD gave you on the other side of the Jordan. ⁵But be very careful to keep the commandment and the law that Moses the servant of the LORD gave you: to love the LORD your God, to walk in all his ways, to obey his commands, to hold fast to him and to serve him with all your heart and all your soul."

22:4   The descendants of Reuben and Gad together with some of the descendants of Manasseh were mainly pastoral people and they had therefore asked for the rural land east of the Jordan (see Numbers 32:1–5). Their request had been granted on the condition that they joined forces with the rest of the Israelite tribes to help them in their battle with the inhabitants west of the Jordan. When the task had been accomplished, they were free of their obligation to their kin and to God (see Numbers 32:18–22) and were able to return home.

---

⁶Then Joshua blessed them and sent them away, and they went to their homes. ⁷(To the half-tribe of Manasseh Moses had given land in Bashan, and to the other half of the tribe Joshua gave land on the west side of the Jordan with their brothers.) When Joshua sent them home, he blessed them, ⁸saying, "Return to your

homes with your great wealth—with large herds of livestock, with silver, gold, bronze and iron, and a great quantity of clothing—and divide with your brothers the plunder from your enemies."

⁹So the Reubenites, the Gadites and the half-tribe of Manasseh left the Israelites at Shiloh in Canaan to return to Gilead, their own land, which they had acquired in accordance with the command of the LORD through Moses.

¹⁰When they came to Geliloth near the Jordan in the land of Canaan, the Reubenites, the Gadites and the half-tribe of Manasseh built an imposing altar there by the Jordan. ¹¹And when the Israelites heard that they had built the altar on the border of Canaan at Geliloth near the Jordan on the Israelite side, ¹²the whole assembly of Israel gathered at Shiloh to go to war against them.

¹³So the Israelites sent Phinehas son of Eleazar, the priest, to the land of Gilead—to Reuben, Gad and the half-tribe of Manasseh. ¹⁴With him they sent ten of the chief men, one for each of the tribes of Israel, each the head of a family division among the Israelite clans.

¹⁵When they went to Gilead—to Reuben, Gad and the half-tribe of Manasseh—they said to them: ¹⁶"The whole assembly of the LORD says: 'How could you break faith with the God of Israel like this? How could you turn away from the LORD and build yourselves an altar in rebellion against him now? ¹⁷Was not the sin of Peor enough for us? Up to this very day we have not cleansed ourselves from that sin, even though a plague fell on the community of the LORD! ¹⁸And are you now turning away from the LORD?

" 'If you rebel against the LORD today, tomorrow he will be angry with the whole community of Israel. ¹⁹If the land you possess is defiled, come over to the LORD's land, where the LORD's tabernacle stands, and share the land with us. But do not rebel against the LORD or against us by building an altar for yourselves, other than the altar of the LORD our God. ²⁰When Achan son of Zerah acted unfaithfully regarding the devoted things,ᵃ did not wrath come upon the whole community of Israel? He was not the only one who died for his sin.' "

²¹Then Reuben, Gad and the half-tribe of Manasseh replied to the heads of the clans of Israel: ²²"The Mighty One, God, the LORD! The Mighty One, God, the LORD! He knows! And let Israel know! If this has been in rebellion or disobedience to the LORD, do not spare us this day. ²³If we have built our own altar to turn away from the LORD and to offer burnt offerings and grain offerings, or to sacrifice fellowship offeringsᵇ on it, may the LORD himself call us to account.

²⁴"No! We did it for fear that some day your descendants might say to ours, 'What do you have to do with the LORD, the God of Israel? ²⁵The LORD has made the Jordan a boundary between us and you—you Reubenites and Gadites! You have no share in the LORD.' So your descendants might cause ours to stop fearing the LORD.

²⁶"That is why we said, 'Let us get ready and build an altar—but not for burnt offerings or sacrifices.' ²⁷On the contrary, it is to be a witness between us and you and the generations that follow, that we will worship the LORD at his sanctuary with our burnt offerings, sacrifices and fellowship offerings. Then in the future your descendants will not be able to say to ours, 'You have no share in the LORD.'

²⁸"And we said, 'If they ever say this to us, or to our descendants, we will answer: Look at the replica of the LORD's altar, which our fathers built, not for burnt offerings and sacrifices, but as a witness between us and you.'

²⁹"Far be it from us to rebel against the LORD and turn away from him today by building an altar for burnt offerings, grain offerings and sacrifices, other than the altar of the LORD our God that stands before his tabernacle."

³⁰When Phinehas the priest and the leaders of the community—the heads of the clans of the Israelites—heard what Reuben, Gad and Manasseh had to say, they were pleased. ³¹And Phinehas son of Eleazar, the priest, said to Reuben, Gad and Manasseh, "Today we know that the LORD is with us, because you have not acted unfaithfully towards the LORD in this matter. Now you have rescued the Israelites from the LORD's hand."

³²Then Phinehas son of Eleazar, the priest, and the leaders returned to Canaan from their meeting with the Reubenites and Gadites in Gilead and reported to the Israelites. ³³They were glad to hear the report and praised God. And they talked no more about going to war against them to devastate the country where the Reubenites and the Gadites lived.

³⁴And the Reubenites and the Gadites gave the altar this name: A Witness Between Us that the LORD is God.

Joshua's Farewell to the Leaders

23 After a long time had passed and the LORD had given Israel rest from all their enemies around them, Joshua, by then old and well advanced in years, ²summoned all Israel—their elders, leaders, judges and officials—and said to them: "I am old and well advanced in years. ³You yourselves have seen everything the LORD your God has done to all these nations for your sake; it was the LORD your God who fought for you. ⁴Remember how I have allotted as an inheritance for your tribes all the land of the nations that remain—the nations I conquered—between the Jordan and the Great Seaᵃ in the west. ⁵The LORD your God himself will drive them out of your way. He will push them out before you, and you will take possession of their land, as the LORD your God promised you.

⁶"Be very strong; be careful to obey all that is written in the Book of the Law of Moses, without turning aside to the right or to the left. ⁷Do not associate with these nations that remain among you; do not invoke the names of their gods or swear by them. You must not serve them or bow down to them. ⁸But you are to hold fast to the LORD your God, as you have until now.

⁹"The LORD has driven out before you great and powerful nations; to this day no-one has been able to

---

ᵃ20 The Hebrew term refers to the irrevocable giving over of things or persons to the LORD, often by totally destroying them.
ᵇ23 Traditionally peace offerings; also in verse 27   ᵃ4 That is, the Mediterranean

withstand you. ¹⁰One of you routs a thousand, because the LORD your God fights for you, just as he promised. ¹¹So be very careful to love the LORD your God.

23:3   The testimony of Joshua's lifetime was that God is faithful to his promises. Israel's response to such faithfulness ought to be to love God and to be loyal to him. Joshua warned the people to resist the temptation to form alliances with their pagan neighbours and adopt their ways, because such actions would only lead to spiritual disaster, moral ruin, and military defeat.

---

¹²"But if you turn away and ally yourselves with the survivors of these nations that remain among you and if you intermarry with them and associate with them, ¹³then you may be sure that the LORD your God will no longer drive out these nations before you. Instead, they will become snares and traps for you, whips on your backs and thorns in your eyes, until you perish from this good land, which the LORD your God has given you. ¹⁴"Now I am about to go the way of all the earth. You know with all your heart and soul that not one of all the good promises the LORD your God gave you has failed. Every promise has been fulfilled; not one has failed. ¹⁵But just as every good promise of the LORD your God has come true, so the LORD will bring on you all the evil he has threatened, until he has destroyed you from this good land he has given you. ¹⁶If you violate the covenant of the LORD your God, which he commanded you, and go and serve other gods and bow down to them, the LORD's anger will burn against you, and you will quickly perish from the good land he has given you."

The Covenant Renewed at Shechem

24 Then Joshua assembled all the tribes of Israel at Shechem. He summoned the elders, leaders, judges and officials of Israel, and they presented themselves before God.

²Joshua said to all the people, "This is what the LORD, the God of Israel, says: 'Long ago your forefathers, including Terah the father of Abraham and Nahor, lived beyond the River*a* and worshipped other gods. ³But I took your father Abraham from the land beyond the River and led him throughout Canaan and gave him many descendants. I gave him Isaac, ⁴and to Isaac I gave Jacob and Esau. I assigned the hill country of Seir to Esau, but Jacob and his sons went down to Egypt.

⁵" 'Then I sent Moses and Aaron, and I afflicted the Egyptians by what I did there, and I brought you out. ⁶When I brought your fathers out of Egypt, you came to the sea, and the Egyptians pursued them with chariots and horsemen*b* as far as the Red Sea.*c* ⁷But they cried to the LORD for help, and he put darkness between you and the Egyptians; he brought the sea over them and covered them. You saw with your own

eyes what I did to the Egyptians. Then you lived in the desert for a long time.

24:2   The theme of this chapter is God's faithfulness to his promises, and his saving activity for his people is the basis of his ongoing relationship with them. But every relationship has two sides and the Israelites had to choose whether they would remain faithful to God in terms of their loyalty and obedience. Failure to keep their promises would bring disaster; God was the perfect lover who wanted only the best for his people, and so he would use events in their lives to discipline them and bring them back to him. Absolute dependence on God was the only way they could really live their lives.

---

⁸" 'I brought you to the land of the Amorites who lived east of the Jordan. They fought against you, but I gave them into your hands. I destroyed them from before you, and you took possession of their land. ⁹When Balak son of Zippor, the king of Moab, prepared to fight against Israel, he sent for Balaam son of Beor to put a curse on you. ¹⁰But I would not listen to Balaam, so he blessed you again and again, and I delivered you out of his hand.

¹¹" 'Then you crossed the Jordan and came to Jericho. The citizens of Jericho fought against you, as did also the Amorites, Perizzites, Canaanites, Hittites, Girgashites, Hivites and Jebusites, but I gave them into your hands. ¹²I sent the hornet ahead of you, which drove them out before you—also the two Amorite kings. You did not do it with your own sword and bow. ¹³So I gave you a land on which you did not toil and cities you did not build; and you live in them and eat from vineyards and olive groves that you did not plant.'

¹⁴"Now fear the LORD and serve him with all faithfulness. Throw away the gods your forefathers worshipped beyond the River and in Egypt, and serve the LORD. ¹⁵But if serving the LORD seems undesirable to you, then choose for yourselves this day whom you will serve, whether the gods your forefathers served beyond the River, or the gods of the Amorites, in whose land you are living. But as for me and my household, we will serve the LORD."

¹⁶Then the people answered, "Far be it from us to forsake the LORD to serve other gods! ¹⁷It was the LORD our God himself who brought us and our fathers up out of Egypt, from that land of slavery, and performed those great signs before our eyes. He protected us on our entire journey and among all the nations through which we travelled. ¹⁸And the LORD drove out before us all the nations, including the Amorites, who lived in the land. We too will serve the LORD, because he is our God."

¹⁹Joshua said to the people, "You are not able to serve the LORD. He is a holy God; he is a jealous God. He will not forgive your rebellion and your sins. ²⁰If you forsake the LORD and serve foreign gods, he will turn

---

a2 That is, the Euphrates; also in verses 3, 14 and 15   *b6* Or *charioteers*   *c6* Hebrew *Yam Suph*; that is, Sea of Reeds and bring disaster on you and make an end of you, after he has been good to you."

²¹But the people said to Joshua, "No! We will serve the LORD."

²²Then Joshua said, "You are witnesses against yourselves that you have chosen to serve the LORD."

"Yes, we are witnesses," they replied.

²³"Now then," said Joshua, "throw away the foreign gods that are among you and yield your hearts to the LORD, the God of Israel."

²⁴And the people said to Joshua, "We will serve the LORD our God and obey him."

²⁵On that day Joshua made a covenant for the people, and there at Shechem he drew up for them decrees and laws. ²⁶And Joshua recorded these things in the Book of the Law of God. Then he took a large stone and set it up there under the oak near the holy place of the LORD.

²⁷"See!" he said to all the people. "This stone will be a witness against us. It has heard all the words the LORD has said to us. It will be a witness against you if you are untrue to your God."

d 30 Also known as *Timnath Heres* (see Judges 2:9)
e 32 Hebrew *hundred kesitahs*; a kesitah was a unit of money of unknown weight and value.

Buried in the Promised Land

²⁸Then Joshua sent the people away, each to his own inheritance.

²⁹After these things, Joshua son of Nun, the servant of the LORD, died at the age of a hundred and ten. ³⁰And they buried him in the land of his inheritance, at Timnath Serah *d* in the hill country of Ephraim, north of Mount Gaash.

³¹Israel served the LORD throughout the lifetime of Joshua and of the elders who outlived him and who had experienced everything the LORD had done for Israel.

³²And Joseph's bones, which the Israelites had brought up from Egypt, were buried at Shechem in the tract of land that Jacob bought for a hundred pieces of silver *e* from the sons of Hamor, the father of Shechem. This became the inheritance of Joseph's descendants.

³³And Eleazar son of Aaron died and was buried at Gibeah, which had been allotted to his son Phinehas in the hill country of Ephraim.

Judges

A Long Time Span

The book of Judges covers the period of some 200 years of Israelite history between Joshua's death and the rise of Samuel (roughly 1220–1050 BC). The book forms part of a much larger historical record which runs from the time of the arrival of the Israelites in Canaan under Joshua (after the death of Moses), right through to the fall of the kingdom of Judah to the Babylonians (see 2 Kings 25). When this larger historical record was put together, the writers used a number of different traditions and sources of information. The common aim of the account was to provide some grounds for why the exile had happened, so the history recorded is written from a particular point of view in which the disaster that had occurred is attributed ultimately to Israel's disobedience and rebellion against God. The incidents recorded are not the whole story but seem to have been selected to give a representative sample of conditions at different times and in different parts of the country.

The Lessons of History

Someone once said "History repeats itself: it has to because nobody listens." In the book of Judges it does seem as though Israel was deaf to the lessons of experience. A recurring cycle can be traced: disobedience leading to defeat and then divine discipline; repentance and dependence on God; and deliverance. Israel's disobedience was mainly the abandoning of the worship of God alone, and the adoption of pagan practices. God's discipline of them was both political and practical. It involved the people being oppressed by their neighbours. The turning point in the people's fortunes was always their repentance and return to God. They acknowledged their dependence on him, and appealed to his mercy. They relied on his faithfulness to his covenant promises. God's response to such an appeal was to appoint a deliverer, a charismatic figure inspired by him and (with the exception of Samson) capable of rallying the Israelite forces to deal with their opposition. After the deliverance, a period of peace usually followed, but the process of rebellion and turning away from God was repeated. This is the cycle to look out for as you read through the book, especially in the middle section between 1:1—2:5 and 17:1—21:25.

Three things stand out:

1. The natural sinfulness of human nature. Despite the privileges of their position as God's chosen people, time and again the Israelites ignored God's promises and tried to do things their own way.

2. God's faithfulness and constant love for his people. Despite Israel's sin and even though God knew they would fail him again (and again), he never refused to respond to their repentance and cry for help. That is what God's covenant love is all about—it keeps holding on no matter what.

3. The strangeness of God's choice of servants. The lives of some of the "judges" or "deliverers" left a lot to be desired. Ehud was an assassin; Samson for much of his life never got his act together and squandered his God-given ability, eventually leading to his own death; Jephthah made a rash vow which brought tragedy and a barbaric death to his only child, and so on. The Bible never attempts to whitewash its "heroes" and yet their lives were used by God. There is a mystery here but it is a mystery which offers hope to us all. If we were only of use to God when we were perfect then nothing could ever get done.

Israel Fights the Remaining Canaanites

1 After the death of Joshua, the Israelites asked the LORD, "Who will be the first to go up and fight for us against the Canaanites?"

²The LORD answered, "Judah is to go; I have given the land into their hands."

³Then the men of Judah said to the Simeonites their brothers, "Come up with us into the territory allotted to us, to fight against the Canaanites. We in turn will go with you into yours." So the Simeonites went with them.

⁴When Judah attacked, the LORD gave the Canaanites and Perizzites into their hands and they struck down ten thousand men at Bezek. ⁵It was there that they found Adoni-Bezek and fought against him, putting to rout the Canaanites and Perizzites. ⁶Adoni-Bezek fled, but they chased him and caught him, and cut off his thumbs and big toes.

⁷Then Adoni-Bezek said, "Seventy kings with their thumbs and big toes cut off have picked up scraps under my table. Now God has paid me back for what I did to them." They brought him to Jerusalem, and he died there.

⁸The men of Judah attacked Jerusalem also and took it. They put the city to the sword and set it on fire.

⁹After that, the men of Judah went down to fight against the Canaanites living in the hill country, the Negev and the western foothills. ¹⁰They advanced against the Canaanites living in Hebron (formerly called Kiriath Arba) and defeated Sheshai, Ahiman and Talmai.

¹¹From there they advanced against the people living in Debir (formerly called Kiriath Sepher). ¹²And Caleb said, "I will give my daughter Acsah in marriage to the man who attacks and captures Kiriath Sepher." ¹³Othniel son of Kenaz, Caleb's younger brother, took it; so Caleb gave his daughter Acsah to him in marriage.

¹⁴One day when she came to Othniel, she urged

him[a] to ask her father for a field. When she got off her donkey, Caleb asked her, "What can I do for you?"

[15]She replied, "Do me a special favour. Since you have given me land in the Negev, give me also springs of water." Then Caleb gave her the upper and lower springs.

[16]The descendants of Moses' father-in-law, the Kenite, went up from the City of Palms[b] with the men of Judah to live among the people of the Desert of Judah in the Negev near Arad.

[17]Then the men of Judah went with the Simeonites their brothers and attacked the Canaanites living in Zephath, and they totally destroyed[c] the city. Therefore it was called Hormah.[d] [18]The men of Judah also took[e] Gaza, Ashkelon and Ekron—each city with its territory.

[19]The LORD was with the men of Judah. They took possession of the hill country, but they were unable to drive the people from the plains, because they had iron chariots. [20]As Moses had promised, Hebron was given to Caleb, who drove from it the three sons of Anak. [21]The Benjamites, however, failed to dislodge the Jebusites, who were living in Jerusalem; to this day the Jebusites live there with the Benjamites.

[22]Now the house of Joseph attacked Bethel, and the LORD was with them. [23]When they sent men to spy out Bethel (formerly called Luz), [24]the spies saw a man coming out of the city and they said to him, "Show us how to get into the city and we will see that you are treated well." [25]So he showed them, and they put the city to the sword but spared the man and his whole family. [26]He then went to the land of the Hittites, where he built a city and called it Luz, which is its name to this day.

1:27   The Israelites kept failing to drive out the inhabitants of various localities in Canaan. This provides a balance to the picture given in Joshua, with its emphasis on the major victories which enabled Israel to gain an initial foothold in the land. The subjection of the whole area was only finally achieved under David (see 2 Samuel 5).

---

[27]But Manasseh did not drive out the people of Beth Shan or Taanach or Dor or Ibleam or Megiddo and their surrounding settlements, for the Canaanites were determined to live in that land. [28]When Israel became strong, they pressed the Canaanites into forced labour but never drove them out completely. [29]Nor did Ephraim drive out the Canaanites living in Gezer, but the Canaanites continued to live there among them. [30]Neither did Zebulun drive out the Canaanites living in Kitron or Nahalol, who remained among them; but they did subject them to forced labour. [31]Nor did Asher drive out those living in Acco or Sidon or Ahlab or Aczib or Helbah or Aphek or Rehob, [32]and because of this the people of Asher lived among the Canaanite inhabitants of the land. [33]Neither did Naphtali drive out those living in Beth Shemesh or Beth Anath; but

the Naphtalites too lived among the Canaanite inhabitants of the land, and those living in Beth Shemesh and Beth Anath became forced labourers for them. [34]The Amorites confined the Danites to the hill country, not allowing them to come down into the plain. [35]And the Amorites were determined also to hold out in Mount Heres, Aijalon and Shaalbim, but when the power of the house of Joseph increased, they too were pressed into forced labour. [36]The boundary of the Amorites was from Scorpion[f] Pass to Sela and beyond.

The Angel of the LORD at Bokim

2 The angel of the LORD went up from Gilgal to Bokim and said, "I brought you up out of Egypt and led you into the land that I swore to give to your forefathers. I said, 'I will never break my covenant with you, [2]and you shall not make a covenant with the people of this land, but you shall break down their altars.' Yet you have disobeyed me. Why have you done this? [3]Now therefore I tell you that I will not drive them out before you; they will be ‚thorns¡ in your sides and their gods will be a snare to you."

2:2   The call of God is always an uncompromising demand for total commitment. Israel's mistake was to imagine that it was possible to have the best of both worlds: a relationship with God at the same time as participating in the pagan life of their neighbours.

---

[4]When the angel of the LORD had spoken these things to all the Israelites, the people wept aloud, [5]and they called that place Bokim.[a] There they offered sacrifices to the LORD.

Disobedience and Defeat

[6]After Joshua had dismissed the Israelites, they went to take possession of the land, each to his own inheritance. [7]The people served the LORD throughout the lifetime of Joshua and of the elders who outlived him and who had seen all the great things the LORD had done for Israel.

[8]Joshua son of Nun, the servant of the LORD, died at the age of a hundred and ten. [9]And they buried him in the land of his inheritance, at Timnath Heres[b] in the hill country of Ephraim, north of Mount Gaash.

[10]After that whole generation had been gathered to their fathers, another generation grew up, who knew neither the LORD nor what he had done for Israel. [11]Then the Israelites did evil in the eyes of the LORD and served the Baals. [12]They forsook the LORD, the God of their fathers, who had brought them out of Egypt. They followed and worshipped various gods of the

---

a14 Hebrew; Septuagint and Vulgate *Othniel, he urged her*   b16 That is, Jericho
c17 The Hebrew term refers to the irrevocable giving over of things or persons to the LORD, often by totally destroying them.
d17 *Hormah* means *destruction*.   e18 Hebrew; Septuagint *Judah did not take*   f36 Hebrew *Akrabbim*
a5 *Bokim* means *weepers*.   b9 Also known as *Timnath Serah* (see Joshua 19:50 and 24:30)

peoples around them. They provoked the LORD to anger [13]because they forsook him and served Baal and the Ashtoreths. [14]In his anger against Israel the LORD handed them over to raiders who plundered them. He sold them to their enemies all around, whom they were no longer able to resist. [15]Whenever Israel went out to fight, the hand of the LORD was against them to defeat them, just as he had sworn to them. They were in great distress.

2:10   Every generation of God's people needs a personal experience of the reality of the power of God in their lives. Without such an experience they can easily drift into adopting the lifestyle and standards of those they live with.

---

[16]Then the LORD raised up judges,[c] who saved them out of the hands of these raiders. [17]Yet they would not listen to their judges but prostituted themselves to other gods and worshipped them. Unlike their fathers, they quickly turned from the way in which their fathers had walked, the way of obedience to the LORD's commands. [18]Whenever the LORD raised up a judge for them, he was with the judge and saved them out of the hands of their enemies as long as the judge lived; for the LORD had compassion on them as they groaned under those who oppressed and afflicted them. [19]But when the judge died, the people returned to ways even more corrupt than those of their fathers, following other gods and serving and worshipping them. They refused to give up their evil practices and stubborn ways.

2:16   The English word "judges" conjures up the picture of a person whose main job is to settle disputes. It is possible that some of the judges in Israel may have given advice in difficult cases (e.g. 4:5). However, the Hebrew concept of "justice" and "judgement" was much wider than the English. It included the idea of restoring a situation to the way it should be, and making sure that those who are oppressed are allowed their rights. So the role of the judges, whose stories form the central section of the book, was mainly to deliver the people from oppression. They were charismatic figures who successfully led Israel's forces against their enemies, and were usually considered to be blessed with God's own spirit of power and practical wisdom.

---

[20]Therefore the LORD was very angry with Israel and said, "Because this nation has violated the covenant that I laid down for their forefathers and has not listened to me, [21]I will no longer drive out before them

any of the nations Joshua left when he died. [22]I will use them to test Israel and see whether they will keep the way of the LORD and walk in it as their forefathers did." [23]The LORD had allowed those nations to remain; he did not drive them out at once by giving them into the hands of Joshua.

3 These are the nations the LORD left to test all those Israelites who had not experienced any of the wars in Canaan [2](he did this only to teach warfare to the descendants of the Israelites who had not had previous battle experience): [3]the five rulers of the Philistines, all the Canaanites, the Sidonians, and the Hivites living in the Lebanon mountains from Mount Baal Hermon to Lebo[a] Hamath. [4]They were left to test the Israelites to see whether they would obey the LORD's commands, which he had given their forefathers through Moses.

[5]The Israelites lived among the Canaanites, Hittites, Amorites, Perizzites, Hivites and Jebusites. [6]They took their daughters in marriage and gave their own daughters to their sons, and served their gods.

Othniel

[7]The Israelites did evil in the eyes of the LORD; they forgot the LORD their God and served the Baals and the Asherahs. [8]The anger of the LORD burned against Israel so that he sold them into the hands of Cushan-Rishathaim king of Aram Naharaim,[b] to whom the Israelites were subject for eight years. [9]But when they cried out to the LORD, he raised up for them a deliverer, Othniel son of Kenaz, Caleb's younger brother, who saved them. [10]The Spirit of the LORD came upon him, so that he became Israel's judge[c] and went to war. The LORD gave Cushan-Rishathaim king of Aram into the hands of Othniel, who overpowered him. [11]So the land had peace for forty years, until Othniel son of Kenaz died.

Ehud

[12]Once again the Israelites did evil in the eyes of the LORD, and because they did this evil the LORD gave Eglon king of Moab power over Israel. [13]Getting the Ammonites and Amalekites to join him, Eglon came and attacked Israel, and they took possession of the City of Palms.[d] [14]The Israelites were subject to Eglon king of Moab for eighteen years.

[15]Again the Israelites cried out to the LORD, and he gave them a deliverer—Ehud, a left-handed man, the son of Gera the Benjamite. The Israelites sent him with tribute to Eglon king of Moab. [16]Now Ehud had made a double-edged sword about a foot and a half[e] long, which he strapped to his right thigh under his clothing. [17]He presented the tribute to Eglon king of Moab, who was a very fat man. [18]After Ehud had presented the tribute, he sent on their way the men who had carried it. [19]At the idols[f] near Gilgal he himself turned back and said, "I have a secret message for you, O king."

The king said, "Quiet!" And all his attendants left him.

---

c16 Or leaders; similarly in verses 17–19   a3 Or to the entrance to   b8 That is, North-west Mesopotamia
c10 Or leader   d13 That is, Jericho   e16 Hebrew a cubit (about 0.5 metre)
f19 Or the stone quarries; also in verse 26

²⁰Ehud then approached him while he was sitting alone in the upper room of his summer palace*g* and said, "I have a message from God for you." As the king rose from his seat, ²¹Ehud reached with his left hand, drew the sword from his right thigh and plunged it into the king's belly. ²²Even the handle sank in after the blade, which came out of his back. Ehud did not pull the sword out, and the fat closed in over it. ²³Then Ehud went out to the porch; *h* he shut the doors of the upper room behind him and locked them.

²⁴After he had gone, the servants came and found the doors of the upper room locked. They said, "He must be relieving himself in the inner room of the house." ²⁵They waited to the point of embarrassment, but when he did not open the doors of the room, they took a key and unlocked them. There they saw their lord fallen to the floor, dead.

²⁶While they waited, Ehud got away. He passed by the idols and escaped to Seirah. ²⁷When he arrived there, he blew a trumpet in the hill country of Ephraim, and the Israelites went down with him from the hills, with him leading them.

²⁸"Follow me," he ordered, "for the LORD has given Moab, your enemy, into your hands." So they followed him down and, taking possession of the fords of the Jordan that led to Moab, they allowed no-one to cross over. ²⁹At that time they struck down about ten thousand Moabites, all vigorous and strong; not a man escaped. ³⁰That day Moab was made subject to Israel, and the land had peace for eighty years.

Shamgar

³¹After Ehud came Shamgar son of Anath, who struck down six hundred Philistines with an ox-goad. He too saved Israel.

Deborah

4 After Ehud died, the Israelites once again did evil in the eyes of the LORD. ²So the LORD sold them into the hands of Jabin, a king of Canaan, who reigned in Hazor. The commander of his army was Sisera, who lived in Harosheth Haggoyim. ³Because he had nine hundred iron chariots and had cruelly oppressed the Israelites for twenty years, they cried to the LORD for help.

4:2 The city of Hazor had been burned by Joshua's army almost a century before, but presumably was not actually occupied by the Israelites. After it was rebuilt by the Canaanites, its strategic position in the Esdraelon valley meant that it was a powerful enemy. The name Jabin, which is also mentioned in Joshua 11, may well be a hereditary title adopted by successive kings.

---

⁴Deborah, a prophetess, the wife of Lappidoth, was leading*a* Israel at that time. ⁵She held court under the Palm of Deborah between Ramah and Bethel in the hill country of Ephraim, and the Israelites came to her to have their disputes decided. ⁶She sent for Barak son of Abinoam from Kedesh in Naphtali and said to him, "The LORD, the God of Israel, commands you: 'Go, take with you ten thousand men of Naphtali and Zebulun and lead the way to Mount Tabor. ⁷I will lure Sisera, the commander of Jabin's army, with his chariots and his troops to the Kishon River and give him into your hands.' "

⁸Barak said to her, "If you go with me, I will go; but if you don't go with me, I won't go."

⁹"Very well," Deborah said, "I will go with you. But because of the way you are going about this,*b* the honour will not be yours, for the LORD will hand Sisera over to a woman." So Deborah went with Barak to Kedesh, ¹⁰where he summoned Zebulun and Naphtali. Ten thousand men followed him, and Deborah also went with him.

¹¹Now Heber the Kenite had left the other Kenites, the descendants of Hobab, Moses' brother-in-law,*c* and pitched his tent by the great tree in Zaanannim near Kedesh.

¹²When they told Sisera that Barak son of Abinoam had gone up to Mount Tabor, ¹³Sisera gathered together his nine hundred iron chariots and all the men with him, from Harosheth Haggoyim to the Kishon River.

¹⁴Then Deborah said to Barak, "Go! This is the day the LORD has given Sisera into your hands. Has not the LORD gone ahead of you?" So Barak went down Mount Tabor, followed by ten thousand men. ¹⁵At Barak's advance, the LORD routed Sisera and all his chariots and army by the sword, and Sisera abandoned his chariot and fled on foot. ¹⁶But Barak pursued the chariots and army as far as Harosheth Haggoyim. All the troops of Sisera fell by the sword; not a man was left.

¹⁷Sisera, however, fled on foot to the tent of Jael, the wife of Heber the Kenite, because there were friendly relations between Jabin king of Hazor and the clan of Heber the Kenite.

¹⁸Jael went out to meet Sisera and said to him, "Come, my lord, come right in. Don't be afraid." So he entered her tent, and she put a covering over him.

¹⁹"I'm thirsty," he said. "Please give me some water." She opened a skin of milk, gave him a drink, and covered him up.

²⁰"Stand in the doorway of the tent," he told her. "If someone comes by and asks you, 'Is anyone here?' say 'No.' "

²¹But Jael, Heber's wife, picked up a tent peg and a hammer and went quietly to him while he lay fast asleep, exhausted. She drove the peg through his temple into the ground, and he died.

²²Barak came by in pursuit of Sisera, and Jael went out to meet him. "Come," she said, "I will show you the man you're looking for." So he went in with her, and there lay Sisera with the tent peg through his temple—dead.

²³On that day God subdued Jabin, the Canaanite king, before the Israelites. ²⁴And the hand of the

---

g20 The meaning of the Hebrew for this phrase is uncertain.   *h23 The meaning of the Hebrew for this word is uncertain.*
a4 Traditionally judging   *b9 Or But on the expedition you are undertaking*   *c11 Or father-in-law*

Israelites grew stronger and stronger against Jabin, the Canaanite king, until they destroyed him.

The Song of Deborah

5 On that day Deborah and Barak son of Abinoam sang this song:

5:1 The Song of Deborah is one of the oldest poems in the Bible and tells us important things about the economic, social, political, and religious conditions of the period.

---

²"When the princes in Israel take the lead,
  when the people willingly offer themselves—
  praise the LORD!

³"Hear this, you kings! Listen, you rulers!
  I will sing to^a the LORD, I will sing;
  I will make music to^b the LORD, the God of
    Israel.

⁴"O LORD, when you went out from Seir,
  when you marched from the land of Edom,
the earth shook, the heavens poured,
  the clouds poured down water.
⁵The mountains quaked before the LORD, the One
    of Sinai,
  before the LORD, the God of Israel.

⁶"In the days of Shamgar son of Anath,
  in the days of Jael, the roads were abandoned;
  travellers took to winding paths.
⁷Village life^c in Israel ceased,
  ceased until I,^d Deborah, arose,
  arose a mother in Israel.
⁸When they chose new gods,
  war came to the city gates,
and not a shield or spear was seen
  among forty thousand in Israel.
⁹My heart is with Israel's princes,
  with the willing volunteers among the people.
  Praise the LORD!

¹⁰"You who ride on white donkeys,
  sitting on your saddle blankets,
  and you who walk along the road,
consider ¹¹the voice of the singers^e at the
    watering places.
  They recite the righteous acts of the LORD,
  the righteous acts of his warriors^f in Israel.

"Then the people of the LORD
  went down to the city gates.
¹²'Wake up, wake up, Deborah!
  Wake up, wake up, break out in song!
Arise, O Barak!
  Take captive your captives, O son of Abinoam.'

¹³"Then the men who were left
  came down to the nobles;
the people of the LORD
  came to me with the mighty.

¹⁴Some came from Ephraim, whose roots were in
    Amalek;
  Benjamin was with the people who followed
    you.
From Makir captains came down,
  from Zebulun those who bear a commander's
    staff.
¹⁵The princes of Issachar were with Deborah;
  yes, Issachar was with Barak,
  rushing after him into the valley.
In the districts of Reuben
  there was much searching of heart.
¹⁶Why did you stay among the campfires^g
  to hear the whistling for the flocks?
In the districts of Reuben
  there was much searching of heart.
¹⁷Gilead stayed beyond the Jordan.
  And Dan, why did he linger by the ships?
Asher remained on the coast
  and stayed in his coves.
¹⁸The people of Zebulun risked their very lives;
  so did Naphtali on the heights of the field.

¹⁹"Kings came, they fought;
  the kings of Canaan fought
at Taanach by the waters of Megiddo,
  but they carried off no silver, no plunder.
²⁰From the heavens the stars fought,
  from their courses they fought against Sisera.
²¹The river Kishon swept them away,
  the age-old river, the river Kishon.
  March on, my soul; be strong!
²²Then thundered the horses' hoofs—
  galloping, galloping go his mighty steeds.
²³'Curse Meroz,' said the angel of the LORD.
  'Curse its people bitterly,
because they did not come to help the LORD,
  to help the LORD against the mighty.'

²⁴"Most blessed of women be Jael,
  the wife of Heber the Kenite,
  most blessed of tent-dwelling women.
²⁵He asked for water, and she gave him milk;
  in a bowl fit for nobles she brought him curdled
    milk.
²⁶Her hand reached for the tent peg,
  her right hand for the workman's hammer.
She struck Sisera, she crushed his head,
  she shattered and pierced his temple.
²⁷At her feet he sank,
  he fell; there he lay.
At her feet he sank, he fell;
  where he sank, there he fell—dead.

²⁸"Through the window peered Sisera's mother;
  behind the lattice she cried out,
'Why is his chariot so long in coming?
  Why is the clatter of his chariots delayed?'
²⁹The wisest of her ladies answer her;
  indeed, she keeps saying to herself,

---

^a3 Or of   ^b3 Or / with song I will praise   ^c7 Or Warriors   ^d7 Or you
^e11 Or archers; the meaning of the Hebrew for this word is uncertain.   ^f11 Or villagers   ^g16 Or saddlebags

30'Are they not finding and dividing the spoils:
   a girl or two for each man,
   colourful garments as plunder for Sisera,
   colourful garments embroidered,
   highly embroidered garments for my neck—
all this as plunder?'

31"So may all your enemies perish, O LORD!
   But may they who love you be like the sun
   when it rises in its strength."

Then the land had peace for forty years.

Gideon

6 Again the Israelites did evil in the eyes of the LORD, and for seven years he gave them into the hands of the Midianites. 2Because the power of Midian was so oppressive, the Israelites prepared shelters for themselves in mountain clefts, caves and strongholds. 3Whenever the Israelites planted their crops, the Midianites, Amalekites and other eastern peoples invaded the country. 4They camped on the land and ruined the crops all the way to Gaza and did not spare a living thing for Israel, neither sheep nor cattle nor donkeys. 5They came up with their livestock and their tents like swarms of locusts. It was impossible to count the men and their camels; they invaded the land to ravage it. 6Midian so impoverished the Israelites that they cried out to the LORD for help.

6:3   The Midianites, Amalekites, and eastern peoples were semi-nomadic groups (groups which spent some time travelling) who conducted raids upon Israelite villages. They plundered both crops and livestock, and left the inhabitants facing starvation and death. This explains Gideon's unusual action of threshing wheat in a winepress instead of on the village threshing floor in the open. Such caution was typical of a man who required a lot of convincing that he was God's choice for the occasion (chapters 36—40).

7When the Israelites cried to the LORD because of Midian, 8he sent them a prophet, who said, "This is what the LORD, the God of Israel, says: I brought you up out of Egypt, out of the land of slavery. 9I snatched you from the power of Egypt and from the hand of all your oppressors. I drove them from before you and gave you their land. 10I said to you, 'I am the LORD your God; do not worship the gods of the Amorites, in whose land you live.' But you have not listened to me."

11The angel of the LORD came and sat down under the oak in Ophrah that belonged to Joash the Abiezrite, where his son Gideon was threshing wheat in a winepress to keep it from the Midianites. 12When the angel of the LORD appeared to Gideon, he said, "The LORD is with you, mighty warrior."

13"But sir," Gideon replied, "if the LORD is with us, why has all this happened to us? Where are all his wonders that our fathers told us about when they said, 'Did not the LORD bring us up out of Egypt?' But now the LORD has abandoned us and put us into the hand of Midian."

14The LORD turned to him and said, "Go in the strength you have and save Israel out of Midian's hand. Am I not sending you?"

15"But Lord,"a Gideon asked, "how can I save Israel? My clan is the weakest in Manasseh, and I am the least in my family."

16The LORD answered, "I will be with you, and you will strike down all the Midianites together."

17Gideon replied, "If now I have found favour in your eyes, give me a sign that it is really you talking to me. 18Please do not go away until I come back and bring my offering and set it before you."

And the LORD said, "I will wait until you return."

19Gideon went in, prepared a young goat, and from an ephahb of flour he made bread without yeast. Putting the meat in a basket and its broth in a pot, he brought them out and offered them to him under the oak.

20The angel of God said to him, "Take the meat and the unleavened bread, place them on this rock, and pour out the broth." And Gideon did so. 21With the tip of the staff that was in his hand, the angel of the LORD touched the meat and the unleavened bread. Fire flared from the rock, consuming the meat and the bread. And the angel of the LORD disappeared. 22When Gideon realised that it was the angel of the LORD, he exclaimed, "Ah, Sovereign LORD! I have seen the angel of the LORD face to face!"

23But the LORD said to him, "Peace! Do not be afraid. You are not going to die."

24So Gideon built an altar to the LORD there and called it The LORD is Peace. To this day it stands in Ophrah of the Abiezrites.

25That same night the LORD said to him, "Take the second bull from your father's herd, the one seven years old.c Tear down your father's altar to Baal and cut down the Asherah poled beside it. 26Then build a proper kind ofe altar to the LORD your God on the top of this height. Using the wood of the Asherah pole that you cut down, offer the secondf bull as a burnt offering."

27So Gideon took ten of his servants and did as the LORD told him. But because he was afraid of his family and the men of the town, he did it at night rather than in the daytime.

28In the morning when the men of the town got up, there was Baal's altar, demolished, with the Asherah pole beside it cut down and the second bull sacrificed on the newly-built altar!

29They asked each other, "Who did this?"

When they carefully investigated, they were told, "Gideon son of Joash did it."

30The men of the town demanded of Joash, "Bring out your son. He must die, because he has broken

---

a15 Or sir   b19 That is, probably about ⅗ bushel (about 22 litres)
c25 Or Take a full-grown, mature bull from your father's herd
d25 That is, a symbol of the goddess Asherah; here and elsewhere in Judges   e26 Or build with layers of stone an
f26 Or full-grown; also in verse 28

down Baal's altar and cut down the Asherah pole beside it."

³¹But Joash replied to the hostile crowd around him, "Are you going to plead Baal's cause? Are you trying to save him? Whoever fights for him shall be put to death by morning! If Baal really is a god, he can defend himself when someone breaks down his altar." ³²So that day they called Gideon "Jerub-Baal,*" saying, "Let Baal contend with him," because he broke down Baal's altar.

³³Now all the Midianites, Amalekites and other eastern peoples joined forces and crossed over the Jordan and camped in the Valley of Jezreel. ³⁴Then the Spirit of the LORD came upon Gideon, and he blew a trumpet, summoning the Abiezrites to follow him. ³⁵He sent messengers throughout Manasseh, calling them to arms, and also into Asher, Zebulun and Naphtali, so that they too went up to meet them.

6:34   The literal meaning of the Hebrew in this verse is that the Spirit of the Lord clothed himself with Gideon. So God revealed himself through Gideon.

---

³⁶Gideon said to God, "If you will save Israel by my hand as you have promised—³⁷look, I will place a wool fleece on the threshing-floor. If there is dew only on the fleece and all the ground is dry, then I will know that you will save Israel by my hand, as you said." ³⁸And that is what happened. Gideon rose early the next day; he squeezed the fleece and wrung out the dew—a bowlful of water.

³⁹Then Gideon said to God, "Do not be angry with me. Let me make just one more request. Allow me one more test with the fleece. This time make the fleece dry and the ground covered with dew." ⁴⁰That night God did so. Only the fleece was dry; all the ground was covered with dew.

Gideon Defeats the Midianites

7 Early in the morning, Jerub-Baal (that is, Gideon) and all his men camped at the spring of Harod. The camp of Midian was north of them in the valley near the hill of Moreh. ²The LORD said to Gideon, "You have too many men for me to deliver Midian into their hands. In order that Israel may not boast against me that her own strength has saved her, ³announce now to the people, 'Anyone who trembles with fear may turn back and leave Mount Gilead.'" So twenty-two thousand men left, while ten thousand remained.

⁴But the LORD said to Gideon, "There are still too many men. Take them down to the water, and I will sift them out for you there. If I say, 'This one shall go with you,' he shall go; but if I say, 'This one shall not go with you,' he shall not go."

⁵So Gideon took the men down to the water. There the LORD told him, "Separate those who lap the water with their tongues like a dog from those who kneel down to drink." ⁶Three hundred men lapped with their hands to their mouths. All the rest got down on their knees to drink.

⁷The LORD said to Gideon, "With the three hundred men that lapped I will save you and give the Midianites into your hands. Let all the other men go, each to his own place." ⁸So Gideon sent the rest of the Israelites to their tents but kept the three hundred, who took over the provisions and trumpets of the others.

Now the camp of Midian lay below him in the valley. ⁹During that night the LORD said to Gideon, "Get up, go down against the camp, because I am going to give it into your hands. ¹⁰If you are afraid to attack, go down to the camp with your servant Purah ¹¹and listen to what they are saying. Afterwards, you will be encouraged to attack the camp." So he and Purah his servant went down to the outposts of the camp. ¹²The Midianites, the Amalekites and all the other eastern peoples had settled in the valley, thick as locusts. Their camels could no more be counted than the sand on the seashore.

¹³Gideon arrived just as a man was telling a friend his dream. "I had a dream," he was saying. "A round loaf of barley bread came tumbling into the Midianite camp. It struck the tent with such force that the tent overturned and collapsed."

¹⁴His friend responded, "This can be nothing other than the sword of Gideon son of Joash, the Israelite. God has given the Midianites and the whole camp into his hands."

¹⁵When Gideon heard the dream and its interpretation, he worshipped God. He returned to the camp of Israel and called out, "Get up! The LORD has given the Midianite camp into your hands." ¹⁶Dividing the three hundred men into three companies, he placed trumpets and empty jars in the hands of all of them, with torches inside.

7:15   The Midianite soldier's dream and its interpretation was an unexpected source of encouragement for Gideon. He recognized that God was in charge of the events of his life, and he responded by worshipping God, and committing himself to what he had to do.

---

¹⁷"Watch me," he told them. "Follow my lead. When I get to the edge of the camp, do exactly as I do. ¹⁸When I and all who are with me blow our trumpets, then from all around the camp blow yours and shout, 'For the LORD and for Gideon.'"

¹⁹Gideon and the hundred men with him reached the edge of the camp at the beginning of the middle watch, just after they had changed the guard. They blew their trumpets and broke the jars that were in their hands. ²⁰The three companies blew the trumpets and smashed the jars. Grasping the torches in their left hands and holding in their right hands the trumpets they were to blow, they shouted, "A sword for the LORD and for Gideon!" ²¹While each man held his position around the camp, all the Midianites ran, crying out as they fled.

8 32 Jerub-Baal means *let Baal contend.*

22When the three hundred trumpets sounded, the LORD caused the men throughout the camp to turn on each other with their swords. The army fled to Beth Shittah towards Zererah as far as the border of Abel Meholah near Tabbath. 23Israelites from Naphtali, Asher and all Manasseh were called out, and they pursued the Midianites. 24Gideon sent messengers throughout the hill country of Ephraim, saying, "Come down against the Midianites and seize the waters of the Jordan ahead of them as far as Beth Barah."

So all the men of Ephraim were called out and they took the waters of the Jordan as far as Beth Barah. 25They also captured two of the Midianite leaders, Oreb and Zeeb. They killed Oreb at the rock of Oreb, and Zeeb at the winepress of Zeeb. They pursued the Midianites and brought the heads of Oreb and Zeeb to Gideon, who was by the Jordan.

Zebah and Zalmunna

8 Now the Ephraimites asked Gideon, "Why have you treated us like this? Why didn't you call us when you went to fight Midian?" And they criticised him sharply.

2But he answered them, "What have I accomplished compared to you? Aren't the gleanings of Ephraim's grapes better than the full grape harvest of Abiezer? 3God gave Oreb and Zeeb, the Midianite leaders, into your hands. What was I able to do compared to you?" At this, their resentment against him subsided.

4Gideon and his three hundred men, exhausted yet keeping up the pursuit, came to the Jordan and crossed it. 5He said to the men of Succoth, "Give my troops some bread; they are worn out, and I am still pursuing Zebah and Zalmunna, the kings of Midian."

6But the officials of Succoth said, "Do you already have the hands of Zebah and Zalmunna in your possession? Why should we give bread to your troops?"

7Then Gideon replied, "Just for that, when the LORD has given Zebah and Zalmunna into my hand, I will tear your flesh with desert thorns and briers."

8From there he went up to Peniel*a* and made the same request of them, but they answered as the men of Succoth had. 9So he said to the men of Peniel, "When I return in triumph, I will tear down this tower."

10Now Zebah and Zalmunna were in Karkor with a force of about fifteen thousand men, all that were left of the armies of the eastern peoples; a hundred and twenty thousand swordsmen had fallen. 11Gideon went up by the route of the nomads east of Nobah and Jogbehah and fell upon the unsuspecting army. 12Zebah and Zalmunna, the two kings of Midian, fled, but he pursued them and captured them, routing their entire army.

13Gideon son of Joash then returned from the battle by the Pass of Heres. 14He caught a young man of Succoth and questioned him, and the young man wrote down for him the names of the seventy-seven officials of Succoth, the elders of the town. 15Then Gideon came and said to the men of Succoth, "Here are Zebah and Zalmunna, about whom you taunted me by saying, 'Do you already have the hands of Zebah and Zalmunna in your possession? Why should we give bread to your exhausted men?'" 16He took the elders of the town and taught the men of Succoth a lesson by punishing them with desert thorns and briers. 17He also pulled down the tower of Peniel and killed the men of the town.

18Then he asked Zebah and Zalmunna, "What kind of men did you kill at Tabor?"

"Men like you," they answered, "each one with the bearing of a prince."

19Gideon replied, "Those were my brothers, the sons of my own mother. As surely as the LORD lives, if you had spared their lives, I would not kill you." 20Turning to Jether, his oldest son, he said, "Kill them!" But Jether did not draw his sword, because he was only a boy and was afraid.

21Zebah and Zalmunna said, "Come, do it yourself. 'As is the man, so is his strength.'" So Gideon stepped forward and killed them, and took the ornaments off their camels' necks.

Gideon's Ephod

22The Israelites said to Gideon, "Rule over us—you, your son and your grandson—because you have saved us out of the hand of Midian."

23But Gideon told them, "I will not rule over you, nor will my son rule over you. The LORD will rule over you." 24And he said, "I do have one request, that each of you give me an ear-ring from your share of the plunder." (It was the custom of the Ishmaelites to wear gold ear-rings.)

25They answered, "We'll be glad to give them." So they spread out a garment, and each man threw a ring from his plunder onto it. 26The weight of the gold rings he asked for came to seventeen hundred shekels,*b* not counting the ornaments, the pendants and the purple garments worn by the kings of Midian or the chains that were on their camels' necks. 27Gideon made the gold into an ephod, which he placed in Ophrah, his town. All Israel prostituted themselves by worshipping it there, and it became a snare to Gideon and his family.

Gideon's Death

28Thus Midian was subdued before the Israelites and did not raise its head again. During Gideon's lifetime, the land enjoyed peace for forty years.

8:28 The phrase "forty years" should probably be understood as a figure of speech denoting "a generation" or "a lifetime", since the average life span at this time was only about 40–45 years.

29Jerub-Baal son of Joash went back home to live. 30He had seventy sons of his own, for he had many wives. 31His concubine, who lived in Shechem, also bore him a son, whom he named Abimelech. 32Gideon son of Joash died at a good old age and was buried

---

*a*8 Hebrew *Penuel*, a variant of *Peniel*; also in verses 9 and 17   *b*26 That is, about 43 pounds (about 19.5 kilograms) in the tomb of his father Joash in Ophrah of the Abiezrites.

³³No sooner had Gideon died than the Israelites again prostituted themselves to the Baals. They set up Baal-Berith as their god and ³⁴did not remember the LORD their God, who had rescued them from the hands of all their enemies on every side. ³⁵They also failed to show kindness to the family of Jerub-Baal (that is, Gideon) for all the good things he had done for them.

Abimelech

9 Abimelech son of Jerub-Baal went to his mother's brothers in Shechem and said to them and to all his mother's clan, ²"Ask all the citizens of Shechem, 'Which is better for you: to have all seventy of Jerub-Baal's sons rule over you, or just one man?' Remember, I am your flesh and blood."

9:1 Kinship ties were very important in early Israel. Abimelech appealed to the clan in Shechem on the basis that his mother had originally belonged there.

---

³When the brothers repeated all this to the citizens of Shechem, they were inclined to follow Abimelech, for they said, "He is our brother." ⁴They gave him seventy shekels[a] of silver from the temple of Baal-Berith, and Abimelech used it to hire reckless adventurers, who became his followers. ⁵He went to his father's home in Ophrah and on one stone murdered his seventy brothers, the sons of Jerub-Baal. But Jotham, the youngest son of Jerub-Baal, escaped by hiding. ⁶Then all the citizens of Shechem and Beth Millo gathered beside the great tree at the pillar in Shechem to crown Abimelech king.

⁷When Jotham was told about this, he climbed up on the top of Mount Gerizim and shouted to them, "Listen to me, citizens of Shechem, so that God may listen to you. ⁸One day the trees went out to anoint a king for themselves. They said to the olive tree, 'Be our king.'

⁹"But the olive tree answered, 'Should I give up my oil, by which both gods and men are honoured, to hold sway over the trees?'

¹⁰"Next, the trees said to the fig-tree, 'Come and be our king.'

¹¹"But the fig-tree replied, 'Should I give up my fruit, so good and sweet, to hold sway over the trees?'

¹²"Then the trees said to the vine, 'Come and be our king.'

¹³"But the vine answered, 'Should I give up my wine, which cheers both gods and men, to hold sway over the trees?'

¹⁴"Finally all the trees said to the thornbush, 'Come and be our king.'

¹⁵"The thornbush said to the trees, 'If you really want to anoint me king over you, come and take refuge in my shade; but if not, then let fire come out of the thornbush and consume the cedars of Lebanon!'

¹⁶"Now if you have acted honourably and in good faith when you made Abimelech king, and if you have

been fair to Jerub-Baal and his family, and if you have treated him as he deserves — ¹⁷and to think that my father fought for you, risked his life to rescue you from the hand of Midian ¹⁸(but today you have revolted against my father's family, murdered his seventy sons on a single stone, and made Abimelech, the son of his slave girl, king over the citizens of Shechem because he is your brother) — ¹⁹if then you have acted honourably and in good faith towards Jerub-Baal and his family today, may Abimelech be your joy, and may you be his, too! ²⁰But if you have not, let fire come out from Abimelech and consume you, citizens of Shechem and Beth Millo, and let fire come out from you, citizens of Shechem and Beth Millo, and consume Abimelech!"

9:15 Jotham's parable is a warning of the likely consequences of appointing Abimelech as king. The Hebrew tree to which Jotham likens Abimelech was probably not a thornbush, because the branches grow so close to the ground that there would be no possibility of resting in its shade. It is more likely that it was a larger tree which had greater height and shade.

---

²¹Then Jotham fled, escaping to Beer, and he lived there because he was afraid of his brother Abimelech.

²²After Abimelech had governed Israel for three years, ²³God sent an evil spirit between Abimelech and the citizens of Shechem, who acted treacherously against Abimelech. ²⁴God did this in order that the crime against Jerub-Baal's seventy sons, the shedding of their blood, might be avenged on their brother Abimelech and on the citizens of Shechem, who had helped him murder his brothers. ²⁵In opposition to him these citizens of Shechem set men on the hilltops to ambush and rob everyone who passed by, and this was reported to Abimelech.

²⁶Now Gaal son of Ebed moved with his brothers into Shechem, and its citizens put their confidence in him. ²⁷After they had gone out into the fields and gathered the grapes and trodden them, they held a festival in the temple of their god. While they were eating and drinking, they cursed Abimelech. ²⁸Then Gaal son of Ebed said, "Who is Abimelech, and who is Shechem, that we should be subject to him? Isn't he Jerub-Baal's son, and isn't Zebul his deputy? Serve the men of Hamor, Shechem's father! Why should we serve Abimelech? ²⁹If only this people were under my command! Then I would get rid of him. I would say to Abimelech, 'Call out your whole army!' "[b]

³⁰When Zebul the governor of the city heard what Gaal son of Ebed said, he was very angry. ³¹Under cover he sent messengers to Abimelech, saying, "Gaal son of Ebed and his brothers have come to Shechem and are stirring up the city against you. ³²Now then, during the night you and your men should come and lie in wait in the fields. ³³In the morning at sunrise, advance against the city. When Gaal and his men come out against you, do whatever your hand finds to do."

---

a4 That is, about 1¾ pounds (about 0.8 kilogram)
b29 Septuagint; Hebrew him." Then he said to Abimelech, "Call out your whole army!"

³⁴So Abimelech and all his troops set out by night and took up concealed positions near Shechem in four companies. ³⁵Now Gaal son of Ebed had gone out and was standing at the entrance to the city gate just as Abimelech and his soldiers came out from their hiding-place.

³⁶When Gaal saw them, he said to Zebul, "Look, people are coming down from the tops of the mountains!"

Zebul replied, "You mistake the shadows of the mountains for men."

³⁷But Gaal spoke up again: "Look, people are coming down from the centre of the land, and a company is coming from the direction of the soothsayers' tree."

³⁸Then Zebul said to him, "Where is your big talk now, you who said, 'Who is Abimelech that we should be subject to him?' Aren't these the men you ridiculed? Go out and fight them!"

³⁹So Gaal led out*ᶜ* the citizens of Shechem and fought Abimelech. ⁴⁰Abimelech chased him, and many fell wounded in the flight — all the way to the entrance to the gate. ⁴¹Abimelech stayed in Arumah, and Zebul drove Gaal and his brothers out of Shechem.

⁴²The next day the people of Shechem went out to the fields, and this was reported to Abimelech. ⁴³So he took his men, divided them into three companies and set an ambush in the fields. When he saw the people coming out of the city, he rose to attack them. ⁴⁴Abimelech and the companies with him rushed forward to a position at the entrance to the city gate. Then two companies rushed upon those in the fields and struck them down. ⁴⁵All that day Abimelech pressed his attack against the city until he had captured it and killed its people. Then he destroyed the city and scattered salt over it.

⁴⁶On hearing this, the citizens in the tower of Shechem went into the stronghold of the temple of El-Berith. ⁴⁷When Abimelech heard that they had assembled there, ⁴⁸he and all his men went up Mount Zalmon. He took an axe and cut off some branches, which he lifted to his shoulders. He ordered the men with him, "Quick! Do what you have seen me do!" ⁴⁹So all the men cut branches and followed Abimelech. They piled them against the stronghold and set it on fire over the people inside. So all the people in the tower of Shechem, about a thousand men and women, also died.

⁵⁰Next Abimelech went to Thebez and besieged it and captured it. ⁵¹Inside the city, however, was a strong tower, to which all the men and women — all the people of the city — fled. They locked themselves in and climbed up on the tower roof. ⁵²Abimelech went to the tower and stormed it. But as he approached the entrance to the tower to set it on fire, ⁵³a woman dropped an upper millstone on his head and cracked his skull.

⁵⁴Hurriedly he called to his armour-bearer, "Draw your sword and kill me, so that they can't say, 'A woman killed him.' " So his servant ran him through, and he died. ⁵⁵When the Israelites saw that Abimelech was dead, they went home.

⁵⁶Thus God repaid the wickedness that Abimelech had done to his father by murdering his seventy brothers. ⁵⁷God also made the men of Shechem pay for all their wickedness. The curse of Jotham son of Jerub-Baal came on them.

9:53 Grain was ground between two heavy circular stone slabs which measured about eighteen inches across. The effect of even a slight blow can be imagined. In those days to meet death at a woman's hands was regarded as the ultimate humiliation.

Tola

10 After the time of Abimelech a man of Issachar, Tola son of Puah, the son of Dodo, rose to save Israel. He lived in Shamir, in the hill country of Ephraim. ²He led*ᵃ* Israel for twenty-three years; then he died, and was buried in Shamir.

Jair

³He was followed by Jair of Gilead, who led Israel for twenty-two years. ⁴He had thirty sons, who rode thirty donkeys. They controlled thirty towns in Gilead, which to this day are called Havvoth Jair.*ᵇ* ⁵When Jair died, he was buried in Kamon.

Jephthah

⁶Again the Israelites did evil in the eyes of the LORD. They served the Baals and the Ashtoreths, and the gods of Aram, the gods of Sidon, the gods of Moab, the gods of the Ammonites and the gods of the Philistines. And because the Israelites forsook the LORD and no longer served him, ⁷he became angry with them. He sold them into the hands of the Philistines and the Ammonites, ⁸who that year shattered and crushed them. For eighteen years they oppressed all the Israelites on the east side of the Jordan in Gilead, the land of the Amorites. ⁹The Ammonites also crossed the Jordan to fight against Judah, Benjamin and the house of Ephraim; and Israel was in great distress. ¹⁰Then the Israelites cried out to the LORD, "We have sinned against you, forsaking our God and serving the Baals."

¹¹The LORD replied, "When the Egyptians, the Amorites, the Ammonites, the Philistines, ¹²the Sidonians, the Amalekites and the Maonites*ᶜ* oppressed you and you cried to me for help, did I not save you from their hands? ¹³But you have forsaken me and served other gods, so I will no longer save you. ¹⁴Go and cry out to the gods you have chosen. Let them save you when you are in trouble!"

¹⁵But the Israelites said to the LORD, "We have sinned. Do with us whatever you think best, but please rescue us now." ¹⁶Then they got rid of the foreign gods among them and served the LORD. And he could bear Israel's misery no longer.

¹⁷When the Ammonites were called to arms and camped in Gilead, the Israelites assembled and camped

---

ᶜ*39* Or *Gaal went out in the sight of*   ᵃ*2* Traditionally *judged*; also in verse 3   ᵇ*4* Or *called the settlements of Jair*
ᶜ*12* Hebrew; some Septuagint manuscripts *Midianites*

at Mizpah. [18]The leaders of the people of Gilead said to each other, "Whoever will launch the attack against the Ammonites will be the head of all those living in Gilead."

11 Jephthah the Gileadite was a mighty warrior. His father was Gilead; his mother was a prostitute. [2]Gilead's wife also bore him sons, and when they were grown up, they drove Jephthah away. "You are not going to get any inheritance in our family," they said, "because you are the son of another woman." [3]So Jephthah fled from his brothers and settled in the land of Tob, where a group of adventurers gathered around him and followed him.

[4]Some time later, when the Ammonites made war on Israel, [5]the elders of Gilead went to get Jephthah from the land of Tob. [6]"Come," they said, "be our commander, so we can fight the Ammonites."

[7]Jephthah said to them, "Didn't you hate me and drive me from my father's house? Why do you come to me now, when you're in trouble?"

[8]The elders of Gilead said to him, "Nevertheless, we are turning to you now; come with us to fight the Ammonites, and you will be our head over all who live in Gilead."

[9]Jephthah answered, "Suppose you take me back to fight the Ammonites and the LORD gives them to me—will I really be your head?"

[10]The elders of Gilead replied, "The LORD is our witness; we will certainly do as you say." [11]So Jephthah went with the elders of Gilead, and the people made him head and commander over them. And he repeated all his words before the LORD in Mizpah.

[12]Then Jephthah sent messengers to the Ammonite king with the question: "What do you have against us that you have attacked our country?"

[13]The king of the Ammonites answered Jephthah's messengers, "When Israel came up out of Egypt, they took away my land from the Arnon to the Jabbok, all the way to the Jordan. Now give it back peaceably."

[14]Jephthah sent back messengers to the Ammonite king, [15]saying:

"This is what Jephthah says: Israel did not take the land of Moab or the land of the Ammonites. [16]But when they came up out of Egypt, Israel went through the desert to the Red Sea[a] and on to Kadesh. [17]Then Israel sent messengers to the king of Edom, saying, 'Give us permission to go through your country,' but the king of Edom would not listen. They sent also to the king of Moab, and he refused. So Israel stayed at Kadesh.

[18]"Next they travelled through the desert, skirted the lands of Edom and Moab, passed along the eastern side of the country of Moab, and camped on the other side of the Arnon. They did not enter the territory of Moab, for the Arnon was its border.

[19]"Then Israel sent messengers to Sihon king of the Amorites, who ruled in Heshbon, and said to him, 'Let us pass through your country to our own place.' [20]Sihon, however, did not trust Israel[b] to pass through his territory. He mustered all his men and encamped at Jahaz and fought with Israel.

[21]"Then the LORD, the God of Israel, gave Sihon and all his men into Israel's hands, and they defeated them. Israel took over all the land of the Amorites who lived in that country, [22]capturing all of it from the Arnon to the Jabbok and from the desert to the Jordan.

[23]"Now since the LORD, the God of Israel, has driven the Amorites out before his people Israel, what right have you to take it over? [24]Will you not take what your god Chemosh gives you? Likewise, whatever the LORD our God has given us, we will possess. [25]Are you better than Balak son of Zippor, king of Moab? Did he ever quarrel with Israel or fight with them? [26]For three hundred years Israel occupied Heshbon, Aroer, the surrounding settlements and all the towns along the Arnon. Why didn't you retake them during that time? [27]I have not wronged you, but you are doing me wrong by waging war against me. Let the LORD, the Judge,[c] decide the dispute this day between the Israelites and the Ammonites."

[28]The king of Ammon, however, paid no attention to the message Jephthah sent him.

[29]Then the Spirit of the LORD came upon Jephthah. He crossed Gilead and Manasseh, passed through Mizpah of Gilead, and from there he advanced against the Ammonites. [30]And Jephthah made a vow to the LORD: "If you give the Ammonites into my hands, [31]whatever comes out of the door of my house to meet me when I return in triumph from the Ammonites will be the LORD's, and I will sacrifice it as a burnt offering."

11:30 There were problems raised by Jephthah's vow. Vows are not unbiblical, although care should be taken to make sure that the person who makes the vow is capable of fulfilling it (e.g. Proverbs 20:25; Ecclesiastes 5:4–5), and does not go against the known will of God. That was the mistake that Jephthah made.

---

[32]Then Jephthah went over to fight the Ammonites, and the LORD gave them into his hands. [33]He devastated twenty towns from Aroer to the vicinity of Minnith, as far as Abel Keramim. Thus Israel subdued Ammon.

[34]When Jephthah returned to his home in Mizpah, who should come out to meet him but his daughter, dancing to the sound of tambourines! She was an only child. Except for her he had neither son nor daughter. [35]When he saw her, he tore his clothes and cried, "Oh! My daughter! You have made me miserable and wretched, because I have made a vow to the LORD that I cannot break."

[36]"My father," she replied, "you have given your word to the LORD. Do to me just as you promised, now

that the LORD has avenged you of your enemies, the Ammonites. [37]But grant me this one request," she said. "Give me two months to roam the hills and weep with my friends, because I will never marry."

[38]"You may go," he said. And he let her go for two months. She and the girls went into the hills and wept because she would never marry. [39]After the two months, she returned to her father and he did to her as he had vowed. And she was a virgin.

From this comes the Israelite custom [40]that each year the young women of Israel go out for four days to commemorate the daughter of Jephthah the Gileadite.

Jephthah and Ephraim

12 The men of Ephraim called out their forces, crossed over to Zaphon and said to Jephthah, "Why did you go to fight the Ammonites without calling us to go with you? We're going to burn down your house over your head."

[2]Jephthah answered, "I and my people were engaged in a great struggle with the Ammonites, and although I called, you didn't save me out of their hands. [3]When I saw that you wouldn't help, I took my life in my hands and crossed over to fight the Ammonites, and the LORD gave me the victory over them. Now why have you come up today to fight me?"

[4]Jephthah then called together the men of Gilead and fought against Ephraim. The Gileadites struck them down because the Ephraimites had said, "You Gileadites are renegades from Ephraim and Manasseh." [5]The Gileadites captured the fords of the Jordan leading to Ephraim, and whenever a survivor of Ephraim said, "Let me cross over," the men of Gilead asked him, "Are you an Ephraimite?" If he replied, "No," [6]they said, "All right, say 'Shibboleth'." If he said, "Sibboleth", because he could not pronounce the word correctly, they seized him and killed him at the fords of the Jordan. Forty-two thousand Ephraimites were killed at that time.

[7]Jephthah led[a] Israel for six years. Then Jephthah the Gileadite died, and was buried in a town in Gilead.

Ibzan, Elon and Abdon

[8]After him, Ibzan of Bethlehem led Israel. [9]He had thirty sons and thirty daughters. He gave his daughters away in marriage to those outside his clan, and for his sons he brought in thirty young women as wives from outside his clan. Ibzan led Israel for seven years. [10]Then Ibzan died, and was buried in Bethlehem.

[11]After him, Elon the Zebulunite led Israel for ten years. [12]Then Elon died, and was buried in Aijalon in the land of Zebulun.

[13]After him, Abdon son of Hillel, from Pirathon, led Israel. [14]He had forty sons and thirty grandsons, who rode on seventy donkeys. He led Israel for eight years. [15]Then Abdon son of Hillel died, and was buried at Pirathon in Ephraim, in the hill country of the Amalekites.

---

a 7 Traditionally judged; also in verses 8–14

The Birth of Samson

13 Again the Israelites did evil in the eyes of the LORD, so the LORD delivered them into the hands of the Philistines for forty years.

[2]A certain man of Zorah, named Manoah, from the clan of the Danites, had a wife who was sterile and remained childless. [3]The angel of the LORD appeared to her and said, "You are sterile and childless, but you are going to conceive and have a son. [4]Now see to it that you drink no wine or other fermented drink and that you do not eat anything unclean, [5]because you will conceive and give birth to a son. No razor may be used on his head, because the boy is to be a Nazirite, set apart to God from birth, and he will begin the deliverance of Israel from the hands of the Philistines."

13:2   In ancient Israel, the inability to have children was one of the greatest tragedies for a married couple. Children were not only an "insurance policy" for old age, but also the way that the family name was preserved. God sent the promise of his power into this situation. That way the despair was turned into hope.

---

[6]Then the woman went to her husband and told him, "A man of God came to me. He looked like an angel of God, very awesome. I didn't ask him where he came from, and he didn't tell me his name. [7]But he said to me, 'You will conceive and give birth to a son. Now then, drink no wine or other fermented drink and do not eat anything unclean, because the boy will be a Nazirite of God from birth until the day of his death.' "

[8]Then Manoah prayed to the LORD: "O Lord, I beg you, let the man of God you sent to us come again to teach us how to bring up the boy who is to be born."

[9]God heard Manoah, and the angel of God came again to the woman while she was out in the field; but her husband Manoah was not with her. [10]The woman hurried to tell her husband, "He's here! The man who appeared to me the other day!"

[11]Manoah got up and followed his wife. When he came to the man, he said, "Are you the one who talked to my wife?"

"I am," he said.

[12]So Manoah asked him, "When your words are fulfilled, what is to be the rule for the boy's life and work?"

[13]The angel of the LORD answered, "Your wife must do all that I have told her. [14]She must not eat anything that comes from the grapevine, nor drink any wine or other fermented drink nor eat anything unclean. She must do everything I have commanded her."

[15]Manoah said to the angel of the LORD, "We would like you to stay until we prepare a young goat for you."

[16]The angel of the LORD replied, "Even though you detain me, I will not eat any of your food. But if you prepare a burnt offering, offer it to the LORD." (Manoah did not realise that it was the angel of the LORD.)

[17]Then Manoah enquired of the angel of the LORD,

"What is your name, so that we may honour you when your word comes true?"

[18]He replied, "Why do you ask my name? It is beyond understanding."[a] [19]Then Manoah took a young goat, together with the grain offering, and sacrificed it on a rock to the LORD. And the LORD did an amazing thing while Manoah and his wife watched: [20]As the flame blazed up from the altar towards heaven, the angel of the LORD ascended in the flame. Seeing this, Manoah and his wife fell with their faces to the ground. [21]When the angel of the LORD did not show himself again to Manoah and his wife, Manoah realised that it was the angel of the LORD.

[22]"We are doomed to die!" he said to his wife. "We have seen God!"

[23]But his wife answered, "If the LORD had meant to kill us, he would not have accepted a burnt offering and grain offering from our hands, nor shown us all these things or now told us this."

[24]The woman gave birth to a boy and named him Samson. He grew and the LORD blessed him, [25]and the Spirit of the LORD began to stir him while he was in Mahaneh Dan, between Zorah and Eshtaol.

Samson's Marriage

14 Samson went down to Timnah and saw there a young Philistine woman. [2]When he returned, he said to his father and mother, "I have seen a Philistine woman in Timnah; now get her for me as my wife."

14:1 The stories about Samson have the early years of the Philistine oppression as their background. The Philistines had settled in large numbers on the coastal plain round about the same time as Israel had entered the land. They established themselves in five cities from which they could expand their control further inland. Unlike previous enemies, they posed a threat to the whole of Israel. The reaction of some of the men of Judah to Samson's exploits would suggest that the Israelites were not aware at first of how much danger there was so close. One of the more significant effects of Samson's "one-man campaign" against the Philistines was to bring the danger out into the open. This may be one reason why so many incidents in which he was involved are recorded.

---

[3]His father and mother replied, "Isn't there an acceptable woman among your relatives or among all our people? Must you go to the uncircumcised Philistines to get a wife?"

But Samson said to his father, "Get her for me. She's the right one for me." [4](His parents did not know that this was from the LORD, who was seeking an occasion to confront the Philistines; for at that time they were ruling over Israel.) [5]Samson went down to Timnah together with his father and mother. As they approached the vineyards of Timnah, suddenly a young lion came roaring towards him. [6]The Spirit of the LORD came upon him in power so that he tore the lion apart with his bare hands as he might have torn a young goat. But he told neither his father nor his mother what he had done. [7]Then he went down and talked with the woman, and he liked her.

[8]Some time later, when he went back to marry her, he turned aside to look at the lion's carcass. In it was a swarm of bees and some honey, [9]which he scooped out with his hands and ate as he went along. When he rejoined his parents, he gave them some, and they too ate it. But he did not tell them that he had taken the honey from the lion's carcass.

[10]Now his father went down to see the woman. And Samson made a feast there, as was customary for bridegrooms. [11]When he appeared, he was given thirty companions.

[12]"Let me tell you a riddle," Samson said to them. "If you can give me the answer within the seven days of the feast, I will give you thirty linen garments and thirty sets of clothes. [13]If you can't tell me the answer, you must give me thirty linen garments and thirty sets of clothes."

"Tell us your riddle," they said. "Let's hear it." [14]He replied,

"Out of the eater, something to eat;
    out of the strong, something sweet."

For three days they could not give the answer. [15]On the fourth[a] day, they said to Samson's wife, "Coax your husband into explaining the riddle for us, or we will burn you and your father's household to death. Did you invite us here to rob us?"

[16]Then Samson's wife threw herself on him, sobbing, "You hate me! You don't really love me. You've given my people a riddle, but you haven't told me the answer."

"I haven't even explained it to my father or mother," he replied, "so why should I explain it to you?" [17]She cried the whole seven days of the feast. So on the seventh day he finally told her, because she continued to press him. She in turn explained the riddle to her people.

[18]Before sunset on the seventh day the men of the town said to him,

"What is sweeter than honey?
    What is stronger than a lion?"

Samson said to them,

"If you had not ploughed with my heifer,
    you would not have solved my riddle."

[19]Then the Spirit of the LORD came upon him in power. He went down to Ashkelon, struck down thirty of their men, stripped them of their belongings and gave their clothes to those who had explained the riddle. Burning with anger, he went up to his father's house. [20]And Samson's wife was given to the friend who had attended him at his wedding.

---

[a] 18 Or is wonderful   [a] 15 Some Septuagint manuscripts and Syriac; Hebrew seventh

Samson's Vengeance on the Philistines

15 Later on, at the time of wheat harvest, Samson took a young goat and went to visit his wife. He said, "I'm going to my wife's room." But her father would not let him go in.

2"I was so sure you thoroughly hated her," he said, "that I gave her to your friend. Isn't her younger sister more attractive? Take her instead."

3Samson said to them, "This time I have a right to get even with the Philistines; I will really harm them." 4So he went out and caught three hundred foxes and tied them tail to tail in pairs. He then fastened a torch to every pair of tails, 5lit the torches and let the foxes loose in the standing corn of the Philistines. He burned up the shocks and standing corn, together with the vineyards and olive groves.

15:3 Samson's strength was God's gift. How he chose to use it was his responsibility. Many of his exploits read like the actions of a hooligan and his life as a whole is an example of the fact that a person with spiritual charisma still has to have self-control. Too often Samson seems to have used his strength at the expense of others for his own advantage and pleasure.

6When the Philistines asked, "Who did this?" they were told, "Samson, the Timnite's son-in-law, because his wife was given to his friend."

So the Philistines went up and burned her and her father to death. 7Samson said to them, "Since you've acted like this, I won't stop until I get my revenge on you." 8He attacked them viciously and slaughtered many of them. Then he went down and stayed in a cave in the rock of Etam.

9The Philistines went up and camped in Judah, spreading out near Lehi. 10The men of Judah asked, "Why have you come to fight us?"

"We have come to take Samson prisoner," they answered, "to do to him as he did to us."

11Then three thousand men from Judah went down to the cave in the rock of Etam and said to Samson, "Don't you realise that the Philistines are rulers over us? What have you done to us?"

He answered, "I merely did to them what they did to me."

12They said to him, "We've come to tie you up and hand you over to the Philistines."

Samson said, "Swear to me that you won't kill me yourselves."

13"Agreed," they answered. "We will only tie you up and hand you over to them. We will not kill you." So they bound him with two new ropes and led him up from the rock. 14As he approached Lehi, the Philistines came towards him shouting. The Spirit of the LORD came upon him in power. The ropes on his arms became like charred flax, and the bindings dropped

from his hands. 15Finding a fresh jaw-bone of a donkey, he grabbed it and struck down a thousand men.

16Then Samson said,

"With a donkey's jaw-bone
I have made donkeys of them.[a]
With a donkey's jaw-bone
I have killed a thousand men."

17When he finished speaking, he threw away the jaw-bone; and the place was called Ramath Lehi.[b] 18Because he was very thirsty, he cried out to the LORD, "You have given your servant this great victory. Must I now die of thirst and fall into the hands of the uncircumcised?" 19Then God opened up the hollow place in Lehi, and water came out of it. When Samson drank, his strength returned and he revived. So the spring was called En Hakkore,[c] and it is still there in Lehi.

20Samson led[d] Israel for twenty years in the days of the Philistines.

Samson and Delilah

16 One day Samson went to Gaza, where he saw a prostitute. He went in to spend the night with her. 2The people of Gaza were told, "Samson is here!" So they surrounded the place and lay in wait for him all night at the city gate. They made no move during the night, saying, "At dawn we'll kill him."

3But Samson lay there only until the middle of the night. Then he got up and took hold of the doors of the city gate, together with the two posts, and tore them loose, bar and all. He lifted them to his shoulders and carried them to the top of the hill that faces Hebron.

4Some time later, he fell in love with a woman in the Valley of Sorek whose name was Delilah. 5The rulers of the Philistines went to her and said, "See if you can lure him into showing you the secret of his great strength and how we can overpower him so that we may tie him up and subdue him. Each one of us will give you eleven hundred shekels[a] of silver."

6So Delilah said to Samson, "Tell me the secret of your great strength and how you can be tied up and subdued."

7Samson answered her, "If anyone ties me with seven fresh thongs[b] that have not been dried, I'll become as weak as any other man."

8Then the rulers of the Philistines brought her seven fresh thongs that had not been dried, and she tied him with them. 9With men hidden in the room, she called to him, "Samson, the Philistines are upon you!" But he snapped the thongs as easily as a piece of string snaps when it comes close to a flame. So the secret of his strength was not discovered.

10Then Delilah said to Samson, "You have made a fool of me; you lied to me. Come now, tell me how you can be tied."

11He said, "If anyone ties me securely with new ropes that have never been used, I'll become as weak as any other man."

12So Delilah took new ropes and tied him with them.

---

[a]16 Or made a heap or two; the Hebrew for donkey sounds like the Hebrew for heap.   [b]17 Ramath Lehi means jaw-bone hill.
[c]19 En Hakkore means caller's spring.   [d]20 Traditionally judged   [a]5 That is, about 28 pounds (about 13 kilograms)
[b]7 Or bow-strings; also in verses 8 and 9

Then, with men hidden in the room, she called to him, "Samson, the Philistines are upon you!" But he snapped the ropes off his arms as if they were threads.

[13]Delilah then said to Samson, "Until now, you have been making a fool of me and lying to me. Tell me how you can be tied."

He replied, "If you weave the seven braids of my head into the fabric ʟon the loomʟ and tighten it with the pin, I'll become as weak as any other man." So while he was sleeping, Delilah took the seven braids of his head, wove them into the fabric [14]and[c] tightened it with the pin.

Again she called to him, "Samson, the Philistines are upon you!" He awoke from his sleep and pulled up the pin and the loom, with the fabric.

[15]Then she said to him, "How can you say, 'I love you,' when you won't confide in me? This is the third time you have made a fool of me and haven't told me the secret of your great strength." [16]With such nagging she prodded him day after day until he was tired to death.

[17]So he told her everything. "No razor has ever been used on my head," he said, "because I have been a Nazirite set apart to God since birth. If my head were shaved, my strength would leave me, and I would become as weak as any other man."

[18]When Delilah saw that he had told her everything, she sent word to the rulers of the Philistines, "Come back once more; he has told me everything." So the rulers of the Philistines returned with the silver in their hands. [19]Having put him to sleep on her lap, she called a man to shave off the seven braids of his hair, and so began to subdue him.[d] And his strength left him.

[20]Then she called, "Samson, the Philistines are upon you!"

He awoke from his sleep and thought, "I'll go out as before and shake myself free." But he did not know that the Lord had left him.

[21]Then the Philistines seized him, gouged out his eyes and took him down to Gaza. Binding him with bronze shackles, they set him to grinding in the prison. [22]But the hair on his head began to grow again after it had been shaved.

The Death of Samson

[23]Now the rulers of the Philistines assembled to offer a great sacrifice to Dagon their god and to celebrate, saying, "Our god has delivered Samson, our enemy, into our hands."

[24]When the people saw him, they praised their god, saying,

"Our god has delivered our enemy
    into our hands,
the one who laid waste our land
    and multiplied our slain."

[25]While they were in high spirits, they shouted, "Bring out Samson to entertain us." So they called Samson out of the prison, and he performed for them.

When they stood him among the pillars, [26]Samson said to the servant who held his hand, "Put me where I can feel the pillars that support the temple, so that I may lean against them." [27]Now the temple was crowded with men and women; all the rulers of the Philistines were there, and on the roof were about three thousand men and women watching Samson perform. [28]Then Samson prayed to the Lord, "O Sovereign Lord, remember me. O God, please strengthen me just once more, and let me with one blow get revenge on the Philistines for my two eyes." [29]Then Samson reached towards the two central pillars on which the temple stood. Bracing himself against them, his right hand on the one and his left hand on the other, [30]Samson said, "Let me die with the Philistines!" Then he pushed with all his might, and down came the temple on the rulers and all the people in it. Thus he killed many more when he died than while he lived.

[31]Then his brothers and his father's whole family went down to get him. They brought him back and buried him between Zorah and Eshtaol in the tomb of Manoah his father. He had led[e] Israel for twenty years.

Micah's Idols

17 Now a man named Micah from the hill country of Ephraim [2]said to his mother, "The eleven hundred shekels[a] of silver that were taken from you and about which I heard you utter a curse—I have that silver with me; I took it."

Then his mother said, "The Lord bless you, my son!"

[3]When he returned the eleven hundred shekels of silver to his mother, she said, "I solemnly consecrate my silver to the Lord for my son to make a carved image and a cast idol. I will give it back to you."

[4]So he returned the silver to his mother, and she took two hundred shekels[b] of silver and gave them to a silversmith, who made them into the image and the idol. And they were put in Micah's house. [5]Now this man Micah had a shrine, and he made an ephod and some idols and installed one of his sons as his priest. [6]In those days Israel had no king; everyone did as he saw fit.

[7]A young Levite from Bethlehem in Judah, who had been living within the clan of Judah, [8]left that town in search of some other place to stay. On his way[c] he came to Micah's house in the hill country of Ephraim. [9]Micah asked him, "Where are you from?"

"I'm a Levite from Bethlehem in Judah," he said, "and I'm looking for a place to stay."

17:9   In the early days of the Israelite settlement the Levites may have had a travelling ministry offering their religious services as priests to local communities, or individual clans.

---

[c]13,14 Some Septuagint manuscripts; Hebrew *"I canʟ if you weave the seven braids of my head into the fabric ʟon the loom."* [14]*So she*
[d]19 Hebrew; some Septuagint manuscripts *and he began to weaken*   [e]31 Traditionally *judged*
[a]2 That is, about 28 pounds (about 13 kilograms)   [b]4 That is, about 5 pounds (about 2.3 kilograms)
[c]8 Or *To carry on his profession*

[10]Then Micah said to him, "Live with me and be my father and priest, and I'll give you ten shekels[d] of silver a year, your clothes and your food." [11]So the Levite agreed to live with him, and the young man was to him like one of his sons. [12]Then Micah installed the Levite, and the young man became his priest and lived in his house. [13]And Micah said, "Now I know that the LORD will be good to me, since this Levite has become my priest."

Danites Settle in Laish

18 In those days Israel had no king.

And in those days the tribe of the Danites was seeking a place of their own where they might settle, because they had not yet come into an inheritance among the tribes of Israel. [2]So the Danites sent five warriors from Zorah and Eshtaol to spy out the land and explore it. These men represented all their clans. They told them, "Go, explore the land."

18:1 At first the tribe of Dan had settled in the western foothills bordering the coastal plain. Pressure from other groups, particularly the Philistines, had made it impossible for them to establish themselves in that area. So they went to the far north of the country. The city named after their ancestor became an important religious centre in the northern kingdom of Israel (1 Kings 12:29,30).

The men entered the hill country of Ephraim and came to the house of Micah, where they spent the night. [3]When they were near Micah's house, they recognised the voice of the young Levite; so they turned in there and asked him, "Who brought you here? What are you doing in this place? Why are you here?"

[4]He told them what Micah had done for him, and said, "He has hired me and I am his priest."

[5]Then they said to him, "Please enquire of God to learn whether our journey will be successful."

[6]The priest answered them, "Go in peace. Your journey has the LORD's approval."

[7]So the five men left and came to Laish, where they saw that the people were living in safety, like the Sidonians, unsuspecting and secure. And since their land lacked nothing, they were prosperous.[a] Also, they lived a long way from the Sidonians and had no relationship with anyone else.[b]

[8]When they returned to Zorah and Eshtaol, their brothers asked them, "How did you find things?"

[9]They answered, "Come on, let's attack them! We have seen that the land is very good. Aren't you going to do something? Don't hesitate to go there and take it over. [10]When you get there, you will find an unsuspecting people and a spacious land that God has put into your hands, a land that lacks nothing whatever."

[11]Then six hundred men from the clan of the Danites, armed for battle, set out from Zorah and Eshtaol.

[12]On their way they set up camp near Kiriath Jearim in Judah. This is why the place west of Kiriath Jearim is called Mahaneh Dan[c] to this day. [13]From there they went on to the hill country of Ephraim and came to Micah's house.

[14]Then the five men who had spied out the land of Laish said to their brothers, "Do you know that one of these houses has an ephod, other household gods, a carved image and a cast idol? Now you know what to do." [15]So they turned in there and went to the house of the young Levite at Micah's place and greeted him. [16]The six hundred Danites, armed for battle, stood at the entrance to the gate. [17]The five men who had spied out the land went inside and took the carved image, the ephod, the other household gods and the cast idol while the priest and the six hundred armed men stood at the entrance to the gate.

[18]When these men went into Micah's house and took the carved image, the ephod, the other household gods and the cast idol, the priest said to them, "What are you doing?"

[19]They answered him, "Be quiet! Don't say a word. Come with us, and be our father and priest. Isn't it better that you serve a tribe and clan in Israel as priest rather than just one man's household?" [20]Then the priest was glad. He took the ephod, the other household gods and the carved image and went along with the people. [21]Putting their little children, their livestock and their possessions in front of them, they turned away and left.

[22]When they had gone some distance from Micah's house, the men who lived near Micah were called together and overtook the Danites. [23]As they shouted after them, the Danites turned and said to Micah, "What's the matter with you that you called out your men to fight?"

[24]He replied, "You took the gods I made, and my priest, and went away. What else do I have? How can you ask, 'What's the matter with you?' "

[25]The Danites answered, "Don't argue with us, or some hot-tempered men will attack you, and you and your family will lose your lives." [26]So the Danites went their way, and Micah, seeing that they were too strong for him, turned round and went back home.

[27]Then they took what Micah had made, and his priest, and went on to Laish, against a peaceful and unsuspecting people. They attacked them with the sword and burned down their city. [28]There was no-one to rescue them because they lived a long way from Sidon and had no relationship with anyone else. The city was in a valley near Beth Rehob.

The Danites rebuilt the city and settled there. [29]They named it Dan after their forefather Dan, who was born to Israel — though the city used to be called Laish. [30]There the Danites set up for themselves the idols, and Jonathan son of Gershom, the son of Moses,[d] and his sons were priests for the tribe of Dan until the time of the captivity of the land. [31]They continued to use the idols Micah had made, all the time the house of God was in Shiloh.

---

[d]10 That is, about 4 ounces (about 115 grams)   [a]7 The meaning of the Hebrew for this clause is uncertain.
[b]7 Hebrew; some Septuagint manuscripts *with the Arameans*   [c]12 *Mahaneh Dan* means *Dan's camp.*
[d]30 An ancient Hebrew scribal tradition, some Septuagint manuscripts and Vulgate; Masoretic Text *Manasseh*

A Levite and His Concubine

19 In those days Israel had no king.
Now a Levite who lived in a remote area in the hill country of Ephraim took a concubine from Bethlehem in Judah. [2]But she was unfaithful to him. She left him and went back to her father's house in Bethlehem, Judah. After she had been there for four months, [3]her husband went to her to persuade her to return. He had with him his servant and two donkeys. She took him into her father's house, and when her father saw him, he gladly welcomed him. [4]His father-in-law, the girl's father, prevailed upon him to stay; so he remained with him three days, eating and drinking, and sleeping there.

19:1 This incident shows how unsafe a person was when they were outside their own kinship area. Significantly, it was a man from the Levite's own home area (who was himself an outsider living in Gibeah) who took him in for the night. The harassment they experienced indicates the need there was for the special provision laid down in the law regarding the treatment of "aliens" (e.g. Exodus 23:9; Deuteronomy 24:14).

---

[5]On the fourth day they got up early and he prepared to leave, but the girl's father said to his son-in-law, "Refresh yourself with something to eat; then you can go." [6]So the two of them sat down to eat and drink together. Afterwards the girl's father said, "Please stay tonight and enjoy yourself." [7]And when the man got up to go, his father-in-law persuaded him, so he stayed there that night. [8]On the morning of the fifth day, when he rose to go, the girl's father said, "Refresh yourself. Wait till afternoon!" So the two of them ate together.
[9]Then when the man, with his concubine and his servant, got up to leave, his father-in-law, the girl's father, said, "Now look, it's almost evening. Spend the night here; the day is nearly over. Stay and enjoy yourself. Early tomorrow morning you can get up and be on your way home." [10]But, unwilling to stay another night, the man left and went towards Jebus (that is, Jerusalem), with his two saddled donkeys and his concubine.
[11]When they were near Jebus and the day was almost gone, the servant said to his master, "Come, let's stop at this city of the Jebusites and spend the night."
[12]His master replied, "No. We won't go into an alien city, whose people are not Israelites. We will go on to Gibeah." [13]He added, "Come, let's try to reach Gibeah or Ramah and spend the night in one of those places." [14]So they went on, and the sun set as they neared Gibeah in Benjamin. [15]There they stopped to spend the night. They went and sat in the city square, but no-one took them into his home for the night.

[16]That evening an old man from the hill country of Ephraim, who was living in Gibeah (the men of the place were Benjamites), came in from his work in the fields. [17]When he looked and saw the traveller in the city square, the old man asked, "Where are you going? Where did you come from?"
[18]He answered, "We are on our way from Bethlehem in Judah to a remote area in the hill country of Ephraim where I live. I have been to Bethlehem in Judah and now I am going to the house of the LORD. No-one has taken me into his house. [19]We have both straw and fodder for our donkeys and bread and wine for ourselves your servants—me, your maidservant, and the young man with us. We don't need anything."
[20]"You are welcome at my house," the old man said. "Let me supply whatever you need. Only don't spend the night in the square." [21]So he took him into his house and fed his donkeys. After they had washed their feet, they had something to eat and drink.
[22]While they were enjoying themselves, some of the wicked men of the city surrounded the house. Pounding on the door, they shouted to the old man who owned the house, "Bring out the man who came to your house so we can have sex with him."
[23]The owner of the house went outside and said to them, "No, my friends, don't be so vile. Since this man is my guest, don't do this disgraceful thing. [24]Look, here is my virgin daughter, and his concubine. I will bring them out to you now, and you can use them and do to them whatever you wish. But to this man, don't do such a disgraceful thing."
[25]But the men would not listen to him. So the man took his concubine and sent her outside to them, and they raped her and abused her throughout the night, and at dawn they let her go. [26]At daybreak the woman went back to the house where her master was staying, fell down at the door and lay there until daylight.
[27]When her master got up in the morning and opened the door of the house and stepped out to continue on his way, there lay his concubine, fallen in the doorway of the house, with her hands on the threshold. [28]He said to her, "Get up; let's go." But there was no answer. Then the man put her on his donkey and set out for home.
[29]When he reached home, he took a knife and cut up his concubine, limb by limb, into twelve parts and sent them into all the areas of Israel. [30]Everyone who saw it said, "Such a thing has never been seen or done, not since the day the Israelites came up out of Egypt. Think about it! Consider it! Tell us what to do!"

19:29 The Levite's response to the abuse of his concubine by the men of Gibeah seems horrific to us today, but it represents the only way in which he could be sure of getting justice for what had happened. It would have been no use appealing to the courts in Gibeah: the men who had committed the crime were the court, so he went above their heads to the higher authority of the tribes.

Israelites Fight the Benjamites

20 Then all the Israelites from Dan to Beersheba and from the land of Gilead came out as one man and assembled before the LORD in Mizpah. ²The leaders of all the people of the tribes of Israel took their places in the assembly of the people of God, four hundred thousand soldiers armed with swords. ³(The Benjamites heard that the Israelites had gone up to Mizpah.) Then the Israelites said, "Tell us how this awful thing happened."

⁴So the Levite, the husband of the murdered woman, said, "I and my concubine came to Gibeah in Benjamin to spend the night. ⁵During the night the men of Gibeah came after me and surrounded the house, intending to kill me. They raped my concubine, and she died. ⁶I took my concubine, cut her into pieces and sent one piece to each region of Israel's inheritance, because they committed this lewd and disgraceful act in Israel. ⁷Now, all you Israelites, speak up and give your verdict."

⁸All the people rose as one man, saying, "None of us will go home. No, not one of us will return to his house. ⁹But now this is what we'll do to Gibeah: We'll go up against it as the lot directs. ¹⁰We'll take ten men out of every hundred from all the tribes of Israel, and a hundred from a thousand, and a thousand from ten thousand, to get provisions for the army. Then, when the army arrives at Gibeah*a* in Benjamin, it can give them what they deserve for all this vileness done in Israel." ¹¹So all the men of Israel got together and united as one man against the city.

¹²The tribes of Israel sent men throughout the tribe of Benjamin, saying, "What about this awful crime that was committed among you? ¹³Now surrender those wicked men of Gibeah so that we may put them to death and purge the evil from Israel."

But the Benjamites would not listen to their fellow Israelites. ¹⁴From their towns they came together at Gibeah to fight against the Israelites. ¹⁵At once the Benjamites mobilised twenty-six thousand swordsmen from their towns, in addition to seven hundred chosen men from those living in Gibeah. ¹⁶Among all these soldiers there were seven hundred chosen men who were left-handed, each of whom could sling a stone at a hair and not miss.

20:14 The response of the Benjamites reflects the strength of kinship obligations in early Israel. Even though the men of Gibeah were in the wrong, their kinsmen were prepared to defend them to the death.

---

¹⁷Israel, apart from Benjamin, mustered four hundred thousand swordsmen, all of them fighting men.

¹⁸The Israelites went up to Bethel*b* and enquired of God. They said, "Who of us shall go first to fight against the Benjamites?"

The LORD replied, "Judah shall go first."

¹⁹The next morning the Israelites got up and pitched camp near Gibeah. ²⁰The men of Israel went out to fight the Benjamites and took up battle positions against them at Gibeah. ²¹The Benjamites came out of Gibeah and cut down twenty-two thousand Israelites on the battlefield that day. ²²But the men of Israel encouraged one another and again took up their positions where they had stationed themselves the first day. ²³The Israelites went up and wept before the LORD until evening, and they enquired of the LORD. They said, "Shall we go up again to battle against the Benjamites, our brothers?"

The LORD answered, "Go up against them."

²⁴Then the Israelites drew near to Benjamin the second day. ²⁵This time, when the Benjamites came out from Gibeah to oppose them, they cut down another eighteen thousand Israelites, all of them armed with swords.

²⁶Then the Israelites, all the people, went up to Bethel, and there they sat weeping before the LORD. They fasted that day until evening and presented burnt offerings and fellowship offerings*c* to the LORD. ²⁷And the Israelites enquired of the LORD. (In those days the ark of the covenant of God was there, ²⁸with Phinehas son of Eleazar, the son of Aaron, ministering before it.) They asked, "Shall we go up again to battle with Benjamin our brother, or not?"

The LORD responded, "Go, for tomorrow I will give them into your hands."

²⁹Then Israel set an ambush around Gibeah. ³⁰They went up against the Benjamites on the third day and took up positions against Gibeah as they had done before. ³¹The Benjamites came out to meet them and were drawn away from the city. They began to inflict casualties on the Israelites as before, so that about thirty men fell in the open field and on the roads — the one leading to Bethel and the other to Gibeah.

³²While the Benjamites were saying, "We are defeating them as before," the Israelites were saying, "Let's retreat and draw them away from the city to the roads."

³³All the men of Israel moved from their places and took up positions at Baal Tamar, and the Israelite ambush charged out of its place on the west*d* of Gibeah.*e* ³⁴Then ten thousand of Israel's finest men made a frontal attack on Gibeah. The fighting was so heavy that the Benjamites did not realise how near disaster was. ³⁵The LORD defeated Benjamin before Israel, and on that day the Israelites struck down 25,100 Benjamites, all armed with swords. ³⁶Then the Benjamites saw that they were beaten.

Now the men of Israel had given way before Benjamin, because they relied on the ambush they had set near Gibeah. ³⁷The men who had been in ambush made a sudden dash into Gibeah, spread out and put the whole city to the sword. ³⁸The men of Israel had arranged with the ambush that they should send up a great cloud of smoke from the city, ³⁹and then the men of Israel would turn in the battle.

The Benjamites had begun to inflict casualties on the

---

*a*10 One Hebrew manuscript; most Hebrew manuscripts *Geba*, a variant of *Gibeah*   *b*18 Or *to the house of God*; also in verse 26
*c*26 Traditionally *peace offerings*
*d*33 Some Septuagint manuscripts and Vulgate; the meaning of the Hebrew for this word is uncertain.
*e*33 Hebrew *Geba*, a variant of *Gibeah*

men of Israel (about thirty), and they said, "We are defeating them as in the first battle." [40]But when the column of smoke began to rise from the city, the Benjamites turned and saw the smoke of the whole city going up into the sky. [41]Then the men of Israel turned on them, and the men of Benjamin were terrified, because they realised that disaster had come upon them. [42]So they fled before the Israelites in the direction of the desert, but they could not escape the battle. And the men of Israel who came out of the towns cut them down there. [43]They surrounded the Benjamites, chased them and easily[f] overran them in the vicinity of Gibeah on the east. [44]Eighteen thousand Benjamites fell, all of them valiant fighters. [45]As they turned and fled towards the desert to the rock of Rimmon, the Israelites cut down five thousand men along the roads. They kept pressing after the Benjamites as far as Gidom and struck down two thousand more.

[46]On that day twenty-five thousand Benjamite swordsmen fell, all of them valiant fighters. [47]But six hundred men turned and fled into the desert to the rock of Rimmon, where they stayed for four months. [48]The men of Israel went back to Benjamin and put all the towns to the sword, including the animals and everything else they found. All the towns they came across they set on fire.

Wives for the Benjamites

21 The men of Israel had taken an oath at Mizpah: "Not one of us will give his daughter in marriage to a Benjamite."

[2]The people went to Bethel,[a] where they sat before God until evening, raising their voices and weeping bitterly. [3]"O LORD, the God of Israel," they cried, "why has this happened to Israel? Why should one tribe be missing from Israel today?"

[4]Early the next day the people built an altar and presented burnt offerings and fellowship offerings.[b]

[5]Then the Israelites asked, "Who from all the tribes of Israel has failed to assemble before the LORD?" For they had taken a solemn oath that anyone who failed to assemble before the LORD at Mizpah should certainly be put to death.

[6]Now the Israelites grieved for their brothers, the Benjamites. "Today one tribe is cut off from Israel," they said. [7]"How can we provide wives for those who are left, since we have taken an oath by the LORD not to give them any of our daughters in marriage?" [8]Then they asked, "Which one of the tribes of Israel failed to assemble before the LORD at Mizpah?" They discovered that no-one from Jabesh Gilead had come to the camp for the assembly. [9]For when they counted the people, they found that none of the people of Jabesh Gilead were there.

[10]So the assembly sent twelve thousand fighting men with instructions to go to Jabesh Gilead and put to the sword those living there, including the women

and children. [11]"This is what you are to do," they said. "Kill every male and every woman who is not a virgin." [12]They found among the people living in Jabesh Gilead four hundred young women who had never slept with a man, and they took them to the camp at Shiloh in Canaan.

21:6   The people of Israel had a problem. Justice demanded retribution against the tribe of Benjamin, but the obligations of kinship also meant making sure that the tribe did not altogether cease to exist. The way they ensured that the remaining Benjamites could have wives may seem questionable, but the principle of protecting the interests of those who, whatever they had done, were still "brothers", is still a good one.

---

[13]Then the whole assembly sent an offer of peace to the Benjamites at the rock of Rimmon. [14]So the Benjamites returned at that time and were given the women of Jabesh Gilead who had been spared. But there were not enough for all of them.

[15]The people grieved for Benjamin, because the LORD had made a gap in the tribes of Israel. [16]And the elders of the assembly said, "With the women of Benjamin destroyed, how shall we provide wives for the men who are left? [17]The Benjamin survivors must have heirs," they said, "so that a tribe of Israel will not be wiped out. [18]We can't give them our daughters as wives, since we Israelites have taken this oath: 'Cursed be anyone who gives a wife to a Benjamite.' [19]But look, there is the annual festival of the LORD in Shiloh, to the north of Bethel, and east of the road that goes from Bethel to Shechem, and to the south of Lebonah."

[20]So they instructed the Benjamites, saying, "Go and hide in the vineyards [21]and watch. When the girls of Shiloh come out to join in the dancing, then rush from the vineyards and each of you seize a wife from the girls of Shiloh and go to the land of Benjamin. [22]When their fathers or brothers complain to us, we will say to them, 'Do us a kindness by helping them, because we did not get wives for them during the war, and you are innocent, since you did not give your daughters to them.' "

[23]So that is what the Benjamites did. While the girls were dancing, each man caught one and carried her off to be his wife. Then they returned to their inheritance and rebuilt the towns and settled in them.

[24]At that time the Israelites left that place and went home to their tribes and clans, each to his own inheritance.

[25]In those days Israel had no king; everyone did as he saw fit.

[f]43 The meaning of the Hebrew for this word is uncertain.   [a]2 Or *to the house of God*   [b]4 Traditionally *peace offerings*

Ruth

The Bible's Best-Loved Mother-in-Law

The book of Ruth may at first seem an odd story. Set in the period following the judges, it focuses on the relationship between Ruth and her mother-in-law, Naomi. Yet this was no ordinary, clichéd caricature of the usual mother-in-law relationship; rather it demonstrates how faithfulness and love can flourish in human relationships, and the ways in which such a relationship can express faithfulness to the will of God.

Life Lived as It Should Be

The period following the judges was traumatic. The moral fabric of society was falling to pieces, idolatry was rife, and there was widespread rejection of God's laws. There was much internal political strife, and the threat of foreign invasion was hanging over the country. Against this depressing background, Ruth, Naomi, and Boaz (who Ruth eventually married), showed us how life could be lived under God, even when everything else around was falling to pieces, and the trends of the day made it easy to go along with the crowd.

God's Law and Daily Routine

Both Ruth and Naomi had been widowed and Ruth, rather than going her own way, decided to stay with Naomi and look after her. They journeyed from Moab to Bethlehem, where Boaz showed them his kindness. It is a moving picture of how God's laws, which may sound grand and lofty, can be worked out in life's daily routines. Respect for God becomes bound up with the way fellow human beings are respected and cared for.

Faithfulness and Love

But these expressions of kindness and love lead us on to a deeper level. When this book was written the Israelites understood themselves to be God's chosen people by virtue of their birth alone. But the book of Ruth challenges such a simplistic view of things. Ruth was born in neighbouring Moab (a long-standing enemy of Israel), yet she shows such steady faithfulness to God, and such selfless love towards her Jewish mother-in-law, that she showed what faithfulness to God was all about. The most important message of the book is this: salvation is not decided by being born at the right time and in the right place; it is freely given by God to people who want to do what is right, and to show their faithfulness to him in the way they live their lives and respect each other.

Naomi and Ruth

1 In the days when the judges ruled,[a] there was a famine in the land, and a man from Bethlehem in Judah, together with his wife and two sons, went to live for a while in the country of Moab. [2]The man's name was Elimelech, his wife's name Naomi, and the names of his two sons were Mahlon and Kilion. They were Ephrathites from Bethlehem, Judah. And they went to Moab and lived there.

[3]Now Elimelech, Naomi's husband, died, and she was left with her two sons. [4]They married Moabite women, one named Orpah and the other Ruth. After they had lived there about ten years, [5]both Mahlon and Kilion also died, and Naomi was left without her two sons and her husband.

[6]When she heard in Moab that the LORD had come to the aid of his people by providing food for them, Naomi and her daughters-in-law prepared to return home from there. [7]With her two daughters-in-law she left the place where she had been living and set out on the road that would take them back to the land of Judah.

[8]Then Naomi said to her two daughters-in-law, "Go back, each of you, to your mother's home. May the LORD show kindness to you, as you have shown to your dead and to me. [9]May the LORD grant that each of you will find rest in the home of another husband."

Then she kissed them and they wept aloud [10]and said to her, "We will go back with you to your people." [11]But Naomi said, "Return home, my daughters. Why would you come with me? Am I going to have any more sons, who could become your husbands? [12]Return home, my daughters; I am too old to have another husband. Even if I thought there was still hope for me — even if I had a husband tonight and then gave birth to sons — [13]would you wait until they grew up? Would you remain unmarried for them? No, my daughters. It is more bitter for me than for you, because the LORD's hand has gone out against me!"

[14]At this they wept again. Then Orpah kissed her mother-in-law good-bye, but Ruth clung to her.

[15]"Look," said Naomi, "your sister-in-law is going back to her people and her gods. Go back with her."

[16]But Ruth replied, "Don't urge me to leave you or to turn back from you. Where you go I will go, and where you stay I will stay. Your people will be my people and your God my God. [17]Where you die I will die, and there I will be buried. May the LORD deal with me, be it ever so severely, if anything but death separates you and me." [18]When Naomi realised that Ruth was determined to go with her, she stopped urging her.

[19]So the two women went on until they came to Bethlehem. When they arrived in Bethlehem, the whole town was stirred because of them, and the women exclaimed, "Can this be Naomi?"

[20]"Don't call me Naomi,"[b] she told them. "Call me Mara,[c] because the Almighty[d] has made my life very bitter. [21]I went away full, but the LORD has brought me back empty. Why call me Naomi? The LORD has

afflicted[e] me; the Almighty has brought misfortune upon me."

1:16 Ruth expressed her total devotion to Naomi. This went as far as pulling up her roots, leaving her own people, and discovering God in a strange land that was not her own. By such love and devotion to another human being, Ruth showed her love for God.

---

[22]So Naomi returned from Moab accompanied by Ruth the Moabitess, her daughter-in-law, arriving in Bethlehem as the barley harvest was beginning.

Ruth Meets Boaz

2 Now Naomi had a relative on her husband's side, from the clan of Elimelech, a man of standing, whose name was Boaz.

[2]And Ruth the Moabitess said to Naomi, "Let me go to the fields and pick up the leftover grain behind anyone in whose eyes I find favour."

Naomi said to her, "Go ahead, my daughter." [3]So she went out and began to glean in the fields behind the harvesters. As it turned out, she found herself working in a field belonging to Boaz, who was from the clan of Elimelech.

[4]Just then Boaz arrived from Bethlehem and greeted the harvesters, "The LORD be with you!"

"The LORD bless you!" they called back.

[5]Boaz asked the foreman of his harvesters, "Whose young woman is that?"

[6]The foreman replied, "She is the Moabitess who came back from Moab with Naomi. [7]She said, 'Please let me glean and gather among the sheaves behind the harvesters.' She went into the field and has worked steadily from morning till now, except for a short rest in the shelter."

[8]So Boaz said to Ruth, "My daughter, listen to me. Don't go and glean in another field and don't go away from here. Stay here with my servant girls. [9]Watch the field where the men are harvesting, and follow along after the girls. I have told the men not to touch you. And whenever you are thirsty, go and get a drink from the water jars the men have filled."

[10]At this, she bowed down with her face to the ground. She exclaimed, "Why have I found such favour in your eyes that you notice me — a foreigner?"

[11]Boaz replied, "I've been told all about what you have done for your mother-in-law since the death of your husband — how you left your father and mother and your homeland and came to live with a people you did not know before. [12]May the LORD repay you for what you have done. May you be richly rewarded by the LORD, the God of Israel, under whose wings you have come to take refuge."

[13]"May I continue to find favour in your eyes, my lord," she said. "You have given me comfort and have spoken kindly to your servant — though I do not have the standing of one of your servant girls."

---

[a]1 Traditionally judged   [b]20 Naomi means pleasant; also in verse 21.   [c]20 Mara means bitter.
[d]20 Hebrew Shaddai; also in verse 21   [e]21 Or has testified against

¹⁴At mealtime Boaz said to her, "Come over here. Have some bread and dip it in the wine vinegar."

When she sat down with the harvesters, he offered her some roasted grain. She ate all she wanted and had some left over. ¹⁵As she got up to glean, Boaz gave orders to his men, "Even if she gathers among the sheaves, don't embarrass her. ¹⁶Rather, pull out some stalks for her from the bundles and leave them for her to pick up, and don't rebuke her."

¹⁷So Ruth gleaned in the field until evening. Then she threshed the barley she had gathered, and it amounted to about an ephah.ᵃ ¹⁸She carried it back to town, and her mother-in-law saw how much she had gathered. Ruth also brought out and gave her what she had left over after she had eaten enough.

¹⁹Her mother-in-law asked her, "Where did you glean today? Where did you work? Blessed be the man who took notice of you!"

Then Ruth told her mother-in-law about the one at whose place she had been working. "The name of the man I worked with today is Boaz," she said.

²⁰"The LORD bless him!" Naomi said to her daughter-in-law. "He has not stopped showing his kindness to the living and the dead." She added, "That man is our close relative; he is one of our kinsman-redeemers."

²¹Then Ruth the Moabitess said, "He even said to me, 'Stay with my workers until they finish harvesting all my grain.' "

²²Naomi said to Ruth her daughter-in-law, "It will be good for you, my daughter, to go with his girls, because in someone else's field you might be harmed."

²³So Ruth stayed close to the servant girls of Boaz to glean until the barley and wheat harvests were finished. And she lived with her mother-in-law.

Ruth and Boaz at the Threshing-Floor

3 One day Naomi her mother-in-law said to her, "My daughter, should I not try to find a homeᵃ for you, where you will be well provided for? ²Is not Boaz, with whose servant girls you have been, a kinsman of ours? Tonight he will be winnowing barley on the threshing-floor. ³Wash and perfume yourself, and put on your best clothes. Then go down to the threshing-floor, but don't let him know you are there until he has finished eating and drinking. ⁴When he lies down, note the place where he is lying. Then go and uncover his feet and lie down. He will tell you what to do."

⁵"I will do whatever you say," Ruth answered. ⁶So she went down to the threshing-floor and did everything her mother-in-law told her to do.

⁷When Boaz had finished eating and drinking and was in good spirits, he went over to lie down at the far end of the grain pile. Ruth approached quietly, uncovered his feet and lay down. ⁸In the middle of the night something startled the man, and he turned and discovered a woman lying at his feet.

⁹"Who are you?" he asked.

"I am your servant Ruth," she said. "Spread the corner of your garment over me, since you are a kinsman-redeemer."

¹⁰"The LORD bless you, my daughter," he replied. "This kindness is greater than that which you showed earlier: You have not run after the younger men, whether rich or poor. ¹¹And now, my daughter, don't be afraid. I will do for you all you ask. All my fellow townsmen know that you are a woman of noble character. ¹²Although it is true that I am near of kin, there is a kinsman-redeemer nearer than I. ¹³Stay here for the night, and in the morning if he wants to redeem, good; let him redeem. But if he is not willing, as surely as the LORD lives I will do it. Lie here until morning."

¹⁴So she lay at his feet until morning, but got up before anyone could be recognised; and he said, "Don't let it be known that a woman came to the threshing-floor."

¹⁵He also said, "Bring me the shawl you are wearing and hold it out." When she did so, he poured into it six measures of barley and put it on her. Then heᵇ went back to town.

¹⁶When Ruth came to her mother-in-law, Naomi asked, "How did it go, my daughter?"

Then she told her everything Boaz had done for her ¹⁷and added, "He gave me these six measures of barley, saying, 'Don't go back to your mother-in-law empty-handed.' "

¹⁸Then Naomi said, "Wait, my daughter, until you find out what happens. For the man will not rest until the matter is settled today."

Boaz Marries Ruth

4 Meanwhile Boaz went up to the town gate and sat there. When the kinsman-redeemer he had mentioned came along, Boaz said, "Come over here, my friend, and sit down." So he went over and sat down. ²Boaz took ten of the elders of the town and said, "Sit here," and they did so. ³Then he said to the kinsman-redeemer, "Naomi, who has come back from Moab, is selling the piece of land that belonged to our brother Elimelech. ⁴I thought I should bring the matter to your attention and suggest that you buy it in the presence of these seated here and in the presence of the elders of my people. If you will redeem it, do so. But if youᵃ will not, tell me, so I will know. For no-one has the right to do it except you, and I am next in line."

"I will redeem it," he said.

⁵Then Boaz said, "On the day you buy the land from Naomi and from Ruth the Moabitess, you acquireᵇ the dead man's widow, in order to maintain the name of the dead with his property."

⁶At this, the kinsman-redeemer said, "Then I cannot redeem it because I might endanger my own estate. You redeem it yourself. I cannot do it."

⁷(Now in earlier times in Israel, for the redemption and transfer of property to become final, one party took off his sandal and gave it to the other. This was the method of legalising transactions in Israel.)

ᵃ17 That is, probably about ³⁄₅ bushel (about 22 litres)   ᵃ1 Hebrew find rest (see Ruth 1:9)
ᵇ15 Most Hebrew manuscripts; many Hebrew manuscripts, Vulgate and Syriac she
ᵃ4 Many Hebrew manuscripts, Septuagint, Vulgate and Syriac; most Hebrew manuscripts he
ᵇ5 Hebrew; Vulgate and Syriac Naomi, you acquire Ruth the Moabitess,

[8]So the kinsman-redeemer said to Boaz, "Buy it yourself." And he removed his sandal.

[9]Then Boaz announced to the elders and all the people, "Today you are witnesses that I have bought from Naomi all the property of Elimelech, Kilion and Mahlon. [10]I have also acquired Ruth the Moabitess, Mahlon's widow, as my wife, in order to maintain the name of the dead with his property, so that his name will not disappear from among his family or from the town records. Today you are witnesses!"

[11]Then the elders and all those at the gate said, "We are witnesses. May the Lord make the woman who is coming into your home like Rachel and Leah, who together built up the house of Israel. May you have standing in Ephrathah and be famous in Bethlehem. [12]Through the offspring the Lord gives you by this young woman, may your family be like that of Perez, whom Tamar bore to Judah."

The Genealogy of David

[13]So Boaz took Ruth and she became his wife. Then he went to her, and the Lord enabled her to conceive, and she gave birth to a son. [14]The women said to Naomi: "Praise be to the Lord, who this day has not left you without a kinsman-redeemer. May he become famous throughout Israel! [15]He will renew your life and sustain you in your old age. For your daughter-in-law, who loves you and who is better to you than seven sons, has given him birth."

[16]Then Naomi took the child, laid him in her lap and cared for him. [17]The women living there said, "Naomi has a son." And they named him Obed. He was the father of Jesse, the father of David.

4:18   Ruth was a foreigner from an enemy nation which threatened the people of God. Yet, by her love and kindness to others, she not only fulfilled all that God had commanded, but also became part of the royal line of David.

---

[18]This, then, is the family line of Perez:
Perez was the father of Hezron,

[19]Hezron the father of Ram,
Ram the father of Amminadab,

[20]Amminadab the father of Nahshon,
Nahshon the father of Salmon,[c]

[21]Salmon the father of Boaz,
Boaz the father of Obed,

[22]Obed the father of Jesse,
and Jesse the father of David.

---

[c]20 A few Hebrew manuscripts, some Septuagint manuscripts and Vulgate (see also verse 21 and Septuagint of 1 Chron. 2:11); most Hebrew manuscripts *Salma*

1 Samuel

Becoming a Nation

The book of 1 Samuel records an enormous change in the life of Israel, which occurred in the second half of the eleventh century BC, and which saw it move from the period of the judges (as described in the book of Judges) to the monarchy. During the period of the judges, Israel had existed as a loose alliance of twelve tribes, pledged to help each other in times of danger, and worshipping the same God. This book records how those tribes became joined as one nation under their king, and it is written around the experiences of three major characters: Samuel, Saul, and David.

God's Chosen Rulers

Samuel was portrayed as the last of the judges, and also described as both priest and prophet. He guided the nation through the time of great change and was responsible for anointing its first king, Saul. Samuel was a powerful character whose authority under God was never questioned. Under the leadership of its new king, Israel defeated the Philistines who had been threatening to overrun them. Saul's initial success did not last, however, and as he declined, David came to prominence as the man God had chosen to replace him. The book ends with the death of Saul, and with David poised to assume the throne.

The Importance of History

More important than the historical events recorded within the book is the activity of God that is behind them. The book sets out to interpret the events of history, and its purpose is to show how God is at work in the experiences of his people. This was achieved in a number of ways: prophets announced events in advance and God brought them to fulfilment; military success was ascribed directly to God, rather than to the military commander or king who led the campaign; the unusual circumstances of Samuel's birth and childhood underlined God's activity in raising and preparing him for his task; both David and Saul were presented as unlikely candidates for the monarchy, but were chosen in accordance with the will of the Lord; and the decline of Saul and rise of David came about because "the Lord was with David but had left Saul" (18:12). Saul's failure and David's success were both determined by their attitude towards God and had little to do with military competence or political wisdom.

The Ups and Downs of Being a King

The book shows mixed feelings about the institution of the monarchy. In the part which records the rise of the monarchy (chapters 7—12), both positive and negative aspects of having a king are recorded. The people's desire for a king is shown to have been sinful, but as a concession, God agreed to choose a king to rule over them (8:4–9). Ultimately, the people's desire for a king was sinful because the Lord is the true king of Israel. Once Saul had been anointed king, Samuel explained an important principle, one that underlies the book and which is essential for understanding the events that follow: both king and people must remain obedient to the Lord (12:14–15). It was not long before Saul was disobedient, and it is because of this that he was rejected as king by God. Once that rejection had been recorded, his decline began and David, chosen by God to replace him as king, came to prominence. Indeed, even though the latter half of the book is set during Saul's time as king, it reads more as an account of David's rise to power than an account of Saul's reign. The preference for David occurred despite the existence of Jonathan, Saul's natural heir and one well suited to the kingship. Jonathan became a close friend of David, who he recognized as God's chosen successor to his father, and protected him from Saul. Even though Saul attempted to kill David, he also knew that David would become king because he was the one the Lord had chosen.

Obedience

David remained obedient to the Lord throughout Saul's reign, refusing to take matters into his own hands even when he had the opportunity to kill Saul. This demonstrated the extent of David's trust in God, and confirmed him to be the one chosen by God to lead Israel. While reading the book, it is important to look for the way God is shown to be at work through earthly events. A key feature to notice in connection with this is the need for God's people to be obedient to the will of God as it has been made known to them.

The Birth of Samuel

1 There was a certain man from Ramathaim, a Zuphite[a] from the hill country of Ephraim, whose name was Elkanah son of Jeroham, the son of Elihu, the son of Tohu, the son of Zuph, an Ephraimite. [2]He had two wives; one was called Hannah and the other Peninnah. Peninnah had children, but Hannah had none.

[3]Year after year this man went up from his town to worship and sacrifice to the Lord Almighty at Shiloh, where Hophni and Phinehas, the two sons of Eli, were priests of the Lord. [4]Whenever the day came for Elkanah to sacrifice, he would give portions of the meat to his wife Peninnah and to all her sons and daughters. [5]But to Hannah he gave a double portion because he loved her, and the Lord had closed her womb. [6]And because the Lord had closed her womb, her rival kept provoking her in order to irritate her. [7]This went on year after year. Whenever Hannah went up to the house of the Lord, her rival provoked her till she wept and would not eat. [8]Elkanah her husband would say to her, "Hannah, why are you weeping? Why don't you eat? Why are you downhearted? Don't I mean more to you than ten sons?"

1:7   Childlessness was a disgrace for an eastern woman. This is made clear by Hannah's behaviour during the annual pilgrimage to Shiloh, an important holy place. Her promise that she would not cut her child's hair was a sign of total devotion to God and his service.

---

[9]Once when they had finished eating and drinking in Shiloh, Hannah stood up. Now Eli the priest was sitting on a chair by the doorpost of the Lord's temple.[b] [10]In bitterness of soul Hannah wept much and prayed to the Lord. [11]And she made a vow, saying, "O Lord Almighty, if you will only look upon your servant's misery and remember me, and not forget your servant but give her a son, then I will give him to the Lord for all the days of his life, and no razor will ever be used on his head."

[12]As she kept on praying to the Lord, Eli observed her mouth. [13]Hannah was praying in her heart, and her

---

a 1 Or from Ramathaim Zuphim   b 9 That is, tabernacle lips were moving but her voice was not heard. Eli thought she was drunk [14]and said to her, "How long will you keep on getting drunk? Get rid of your wine."

[15]"Not so, my lord," Hannah replied, "I am a woman who is deeply troubled. I have not been drinking wine or beer; I was pouring out my soul to the LORD. [16]Do not take your servant for a wicked woman; I have been praying here out of my great anguish and grief."

[17]Eli answered, "Go in peace, and may the God of Israel grant you what you have asked of him."

[18]She said, "May your servant find favour in your eyes." Then she went her way and ate something, and her face was no longer downcast.

[19]Early the next morning they arose and worshipped before the LORD and then went back to their home at Ramah. Elkanah lay with Hannah his wife, and the LORD remembered her. [20]So in the course of time Hannah conceived and gave birth to a son. She named him Samuel,[c] saying, "Because I asked the LORD for him."

1:20 The story of Samuel's birth is designed to show that God was at work in raising him up to direct this part of the history of his people.

Hannah Dedicates Samuel

[21]When the man Elkanah went up with all his family to offer the annual sacrifice to the LORD and to fulfil his vow, [22]Hannah did not go. She said to her husband, "After the boy is weaned, I will take him and present him before the LORD, and he will live there always."

[23]"Do what seems best to you," Elkanah her husband told her. "Stay here until you have weaned him; only may the LORD make good his[d] word." So the woman stayed at home and nursed her son until she had weaned him.

[24]After he was weaned, she took the boy with her, young as he was, along with a three-year-old bull,[e] an ephah[f] of flour and a skin of wine, and brought him to the house of the LORD at Shiloh. [25]When they had slaughtered the bull, they brought the boy to Eli, [26]and she said to him, "As surely as you live, my lord, I am the woman who stood here beside you praying to the LORD. [27]I prayed for this child, and the LORD has granted me what I asked of him. [28]So now I give him to the LORD. For his whole life he shall be given over to the LORD." And he worshipped the LORD there.

Hannah's Prayer

2 Then Hannah prayed and said:

"My heart rejoices in the LORD;
    in the LORD my horn[a] is lifted high.
My mouth boasts over my enemies,
    for I delight in your deliverance.

[2]"There is no-one holy[b] like the LORD;
    there is no-one besides you;
    there is no Rock like our God.

[3]"Do not keep talking so proudly
    or let your mouth speak such arrogance,
for the LORD is a God who knows,
    and by him deeds are weighed.

[4]"The bows of the warriors are broken,
    but those who stumbled are armed with
        strength.
[5]Those who were full hire themselves out for food,
    but those who were hungry hunger no more.
She who was barren has borne seven children,
    but she who has had many sons pines away.

[6]"The LORD brings death and makes alive;
    he brings down to the grave[c] and raises up.
[7]The LORD sends poverty and wealth;
    he humbles and he exalts.
[8]He raises the poor from the dust
    and lifts the needy from the ash heap;
he seats them with princes
    and has them inherit a throne of honour.

"For the foundations of the earth are the LORD's;
    upon them he has set the world.
[9]He will guard the feet of his saints,
    but the wicked will be silenced in darkness.

"It is not by strength that one prevails;
[10] those who oppose the LORD will be shattered.
He will thunder against them from heaven;
    the LORD will judge the ends of the earth.

"He will give strength to his king
    and exalt the horn of his anointed."

[11]Then Elkanah went home to Ramah, but the boy ministered before the LORD under Eli the priest.

Eli's Wicked Sons

[12]Eli's sons were wicked men; they had no regard for the LORD. [13]Now it was the practice of the priests with the people that whenever anyone offered a sacrifice and while the meat was being boiled, the servant of the priest would come with a three-pronged fork in his hand. [14]He would plunge it into the pan or kettle or cauldron or pot, and the priest would take for himself whatever the fork brought up. This is how they treated all the Israelites who came to Shiloh. [15]But even before the fat was burned, the servant of the priest would come and say to the man who was sacrificing, "Give the priest some meat to roast; he won't accept boiled meat from you, but only raw."

[16]If the man said to him, "Let the fat be burned up first, and then take whatever you want," the servant would then answer, "No, hand it over now; if you don't, I'll take it by force."

[17]This sin of the young men was very great in the LORD's sight, for they[d] were treating the LORD's offering with contempt.

---

c20 Samuel sounds like the Hebrew for heard of God.
e24 Dead Sea Scrolls, Septuagint and Syriac; Masoretic Text with three bulls
a1 Horn here symbolises strength; also in verse 10.
d17 Or men
d23 Masoretic Text; Dead Sea Scrolls, Septuagint and Syriac your
f24 That is, probably about ⅗ bushel (about 22 litres)
b2 Or no Holy One   c6 Hebrew Sheol

[18]But Samuel was ministering before the LORD—a boy wearing a linen ephod. [19]Each year his mother made him a little robe and took it to him when she went up with her husband to offer the annual sacrifice. [20]Eli would bless Elkanah and his wife, saying, "May the LORD give you children by this woman to take the place of the one she prayed for and gave to the LORD." Then they would go home. [21]And the LORD was gracious to Hannah; she conceived and gave birth to three sons and two daughters. Meanwhile, the boy Samuel grew up in the presence of the LORD.

[22]Now Eli, who was very old, heard about everything his sons were doing to all Israel and how they slept with the women who served at the entrance to the Tent of Meeting. [23]So he said to them, "Why do you do such things? I hear from all the people about these wicked deeds of yours. [24]No, my sons; it is not a good report that I hear spreading among the LORD's people. [25]If a man sins against another man, God[e] may mediate for him; but if a man sins against the LORD, who will intercede for him?" His sons, however, did not listen to their father's rebuke, for it was the LORD's will to put them to death.

2:25 The statement that Eli's sons disobeyed because "it was the LORD's will to put them to death" does not mean that God caused their disobedience. It is the writer's way of making clear that God was ultimately in control of the situation and that he was determined to judge their sin, which was very extensive (see 3:14). Eli's sons seemed to have reached a state of extreme sinfulness, and repentance had become a practical impossibility for them.

---

[26]And the boy Samuel continued to grow in stature and in favour with the LORD and with men.

Prophecy Against the House of Eli

[27]Now a man of God came to Eli and said to him, "This is what the LORD says: 'Did I not clearly reveal myself to your father's house when they were in Egypt under Pharaoh? [28]I chose your father out of all the tribes of Israel to be my priest, to go up to my altar, to burn incense, and to wear an ephod in my presence. I also gave your father's house all the offerings made with fire by the Israelites. [29]Why do you[f] scorn my sacrifice and offering that I prescribed for my dwelling? Why do you honour your sons more than me by fattening yourselves on the choice parts of every offering made by my people Israel?'

[30]"Therefore the LORD, the God of Israel, declares: 'I promised that your house and your father's house would minister before me for ever.' But now the LORD declares: 'Far be it from me! Those who honour me I will honour, but those who despise me will be disdained. [31]The time is coming when I will cut short your strength and the strength of your father's house, so that there will not be an old man in your family line [32]and you will see distress in my dwelling. Although good will be done to Israel, in your family line there will never be an old man. [33]Every one of you that I do not cut off from my altar will be spared only to blind your eyes with tears and to grieve your heart, and all your descendants will die in the prime of life.

[34]"'And what happens to your two sons, Hophni and Phinehas, will be a sign to you—they will both die on the same day. [35]I will raise up for myself a faithful priest, who will do according to what is in my heart and mind. I will firmly establish his house, and he will minister before my anointed one always. [36]Then everyone left in your family line will come and bow down before him for a piece of silver and a crust of bread and plead, "Appoint me to some priestly office so that I can have food to eat." '"

The LORD Calls Samuel

3 The boy Samuel ministered before the LORD under Eli. In those days the word of the LORD was rare; there were not many visions.

[2]One night Eli, whose eyes were becoming so weak that he could barely see, was lying down in his usual place. [3]The lamp of God had not yet gone out, and Samuel was lying down in the temple[a] of the LORD, where the ark of God was. [4]Then the LORD called Samuel.

Samuel answered, "Here I am." [5]And he ran to Eli and said, "Here I am; you called me."

But Eli said, "I did not call; go back and lie down." So he went and lay down.

[6]Again the LORD called, "Samuel!" And Samuel got up and went to Eli and said, "Here I am; you called me."

"My son," Eli said, "I did not call; go back and lie down."

[7]Now Samuel did not yet know the LORD: The word of the LORD had not yet been revealed to him.

[8]The LORD called Samuel a third time, and Samuel got up and went to Eli and said, "Here I am; you called me."

Then Eli realised that the LORD was calling the boy. [9]So Eli told Samuel, "Go and lie down, and if he calls you, say, 'Speak, LORD, for your servant is listening.' " So Samuel went and lay down in his place.

[10]The LORD came and stood there, calling as at the other times, "Samuel! Samuel!"

Then Samuel said, "Speak, for your servant is listening."

[11]And the LORD said to Samuel: "See, I am about to do something in Israel that will make the ears of everyone who hears of it tingle. [12]At that time I will carry out against Eli everything I spoke against his family—from beginning to end. [13]For I told him that I would judge his family for ever because of the sin he knew about; his sons made themselves contemptible,[b] and he failed to restrain them. [14]Therefore, I swore to the house of Eli, 'The guilt of Eli's house will never be atoned for by sacrifice or offering.' "

---

e25 Or *the judges*   *f29* The Hebrew is plural.   *a3* That is, tabernacle
b13 Masoretic Text; an ancient Hebrew scribal tradition and Septuagint *sons blasphemed God*

15Samuel lay down until morning and then opened the doors of the house of the LORD. He was afraid to tell Eli the vision, 16but Eli called him and said, "Samuel, my son."

3:14 Sacrifice and offering were the means of atonement (setting things right between God and people) in Old Testament times. However, deliberate sin against God could not be dealt with in this way (see Numbers 15:30).

Samuel answered, "Here I am."

17"What was it he said to you?" Eli asked. "Do not hide it from me. May God deal with you, be it ever so severely, if you hide from me anything he told you." 18So Samuel told him everything, hiding nothing from him. Then Eli said, "He is the LORD; let him do what is good in his eyes."

3:20 A prophet was called by God to speak his word to the people. This could be a dangerous and unpopular task, but Samuel had shown himself willing to declare whatever God told him (3:18).

19The LORD was with Samuel as he grew up, and he let none of his words fall to the ground. 20And all Israel from Dan to Beersheba recognised that Samuel was attested as a prophet of the LORD. 21The LORD continued to appear at Shiloh, and there he revealed himself to Samuel through his word.

4 And Samuel's word came to all Israel.

The Philistines Capture the Ark

Now the Israelites went out to fight against the Philistines. The Israelites camped at Ebenezer, and the Philistines at Aphek. 2The Philistines deployed their forces to meet Israel, and as the battle spread, Israel was defeated by the Philistines, who killed about four thousand of them on the battlefield. 3When the soldiers returned to camp, the elders of Israel asked, "Why did the LORD bring defeat upon us today before the Philistines? Let us bring the ark of the LORD's covenant from Shiloh, so that it*a* may go with us and save us from the hand of our enemies."

4:3 The ark of the Lord's covenant was primarily a chest containing the stone tablets on which the Ten Commandments were written. At the same time it served as a throne for the Lord, and represented his presence amongst his people.

4So the people sent men to Shiloh, and they brought back the ark of the covenant of the LORD Almighty, who is enthroned between the cherubim. And Eli's two sons, Hophni and Phinehas, were there with the ark of the covenant of God.

5When the ark of the LORD's covenant came into the camp, all Israel raised such a great shout that the ground shook. 6Hearing the uproar, the Philistines asked, "What's all this shouting in the Hebrew camp?"

When they learned that the ark of the LORD had come into the camp, 7the Philistines were afraid. "A god has come into the camp," they said. "We're in trouble! Nothing like this has happened before. 8Woe to us! Who will deliver us from the hand of these mighty gods? They are the gods who struck the Egyptians with all kinds of plagues in the desert. 9Be strong, Philistines! Be men, or you will be subject to the Hebrews, as they have been to you. Be men, and fight!"

10So the Philistines fought, and the Israelites were defeated and every man fled to his tent. The slaughter was very great; Israel lost thirty thousand foot soldiers. 11The ark of God was captured, and Eli's two sons, Hophni and Phinehas, died.

Death of Eli

12That same day a Benjamite ran from the battle line and went to Shiloh, his clothes torn and dust on his head. 13When he arrived, there was Eli sitting on his chair by the side of the road, watching, because his heart feared for the ark of God. When the man entered the town and told what had happened, the whole town sent up a cry.

14Eli heard the outcry and asked, "What is the meaning of this uproar?"

The man hurried over to Eli, 15who was ninety-eight years old and whose eyes were set so that he could not see. 16He told Eli, "I have just come from the battle line; I fled from it this very day."

Eli asked, "What happened, my son?"

17The man who brought the news replied, "Israel fled before the Philistines, and the army has suffered heavy losses. Also your two sons, Hophni and Phinehas, are dead, and the ark of God has been captured."

18When he mentioned the ark of God, Eli fell backwards off his chair by the side of the gate. His neck was broken and he died, for he was an old man and heavy. He had led*b* Israel for forty years.

19His daughter-in-law, the wife of Phinehas, was pregnant and near the time of delivery. When she heard the news that the ark of God had been captured and that her father-in-law and her husband were dead, she went into labour and gave birth, but was overcome by her labour pains. 20As she was dying, the women attending her said, "Don't despair; you have given birth to a son." But she did not respond or pay any attention.

21She named the boy Ichabod,*c* saying, "The glory has departed from Israel" — because of the capture of the ark of God and the deaths of her father-in-law and her husband. 22She said, "The glory has departed from Israel, for the ark of God has been captured."

---

a3 Or he   *b18* Traditionally *judged*   *c21* Ichabod means *no glory.*

The Ark in Ashdod and Ekron

5 After the Philistines had captured the ark of God, they took it from Ebenezer to Ashdod. [2]Then they carried the ark into Dagon's temple and set it beside Dagon. [3]When the people of Ashdod rose early the next day, there was Dagon, fallen on his face on the ground before the ark of the LORD! They took Dagon and put him back in his place. [4]But the following morning when they rose, there was Dagon, fallen on his face on the ground before the ark of the LORD! His head and hands had been broken off and were lying on the threshold; only his body remained. [5]That is why to this day neither the priests of Dagon nor any others who enter Dagon's temple at Ashdod step on the threshold.

[6]The LORD's hand was heavy upon the people of Ashdod and its vicinity; he brought devastation upon them and afflicted them with tumours.[a] [7]When the men of Ashdod saw what was happening, they said, "The ark of the god of Israel must not stay here with us, because his hand is heavy upon us and upon Dagon our god." [8]So they called together all the rulers of the Philistines and asked them, "What shall we do with the ark of the god of Israel?"

They answered, "Have the ark of the god of Israel moved to Gath." So they moved the ark of the God of Israel.

[9]But after they had moved it, the LORD's hand was against that city, throwing it into a great panic. He afflicted the people of the city, both young and old, with an outbreak of tumours.[b] [10]So they sent the ark of God to Ekron.

As the ark of God was entering Ekron, the people of Ekron cried out, "They have brought the ark of the god of Israel round to us to kill us and our people." [11]So they called together all the rulers of the Philistines and said, "Send the ark of the god of Israel away; let it go back to its own place, or it[c] will kill us and our people." For death had filled the city with panic; God's hand was very heavy upon it. [12]Those who did not die were afflicted with tumours, and the outcry of the city went up to heaven.

The Ark Returned to Israel

6 When the ark of the LORD had been in Philistine territory for seven months, [2]the Philistines called for the priests and the diviners and said, "What shall we do with the ark of the LORD? Tell us how we should send it back to its place."

[3]They answered, "If you return the ark of the god of Israel, do not send it away empty, but by all means send a guilt offering to him. Then you will be healed, and you will know why his hand has not been lifted from you."

[4]The Philistines asked, "What guilt offering should we send to him?"

They replied, "Five gold tumours and five gold rats, according to the number of the Philistine rulers, because the same plague has struck both you and your

rulers. [5]Make models of the tumours and of the rats that are destroying the country, and pay honour to Israel's god. Perhaps he will lift his hand from you and your gods and your land. [6]Why do you harden your hearts as the Egyptians and Pharaoh did? When he[a] treated them harshly, did they not send the Israelites out so that they could go on their way?

[7]"Now then, get a new cart ready, with two cows that have calved and have never been yoked. Hitch the cows to the cart, but take their calves away and pen them up. [8]Take the ark of the LORD and put it on the cart, and in a chest beside it put the gold objects you are sending back to him as a guilt offering. Send it on its way, [9]but keep watching it. If it goes up to its own territory, towards Beth Shemesh, then the LORD has brought this great disaster on us. But if it does not, then we shall know that it was not his hand that struck us and that it happened to us by chance."

6:7   This incident was a test designed so that the outcome would make clear whether God was at work in the situation.

---

[10]So they did this. They took two such cows and hitched them to the cart and penned up their calves. [11]They placed the ark of the LORD on the cart and along with it the chest containing the gold rats and the models of the tumours. [12]Then the cows went straight up towards Beth Shemesh, keeping on the road and lowing all the way; they did not turn to the right or to the left. The rulers of the Philistines followed them as far as the border of Beth Shemesh.

[13]Now the people of Beth Shemesh were harvesting their wheat in the valley, and when they looked up and saw the ark, they rejoiced at the sight. [14]The cart came to the field of Joshua of Beth Shemesh, and there it stopped beside a large rock. The people chopped up the wood of the cart and sacrificed the cows as a burnt offering to the LORD. [15]The Levites took down the ark of the LORD, together with the chest containing the gold objects, and placed them on the large rock. On that day the people of Beth Shemesh offered burnt offerings and made sacrifices to the LORD. [16]The five rulers of the Philistines saw all this and then returned that same day to Ekron.

[17]These are the gold tumours the Philistines sent as a guilt offering to the LORD — one each for Ashdod, Gaza, Ashkelon, Gath and Ekron. [18]And the number of the gold rats was according to the number of Philistine towns belonging to the five rulers — the fortified towns with their country villages. The large rock, on which[b] they set the ark of the LORD, is a witness to this day in the field of Joshua of Beth Shemesh.

[19]But God struck down some of the men of Beth Shemesh, putting seventy[c] of them to death because they had looked into the ark of the LORD. The people mourned because of the heavy blow the LORD had dealt them, [20]and the men of Beth Shemesh asked, "Who

---

[a]6 Hebrew; Septuagint and Vulgate *tumours. And rats appeared in their land, and death and destruction were throughout the city*
[b]9 Or *with tumours in the groin* (see Septuagint)   [c]11 Or *he*   [a]6 That is, God
[b]18 A few Hebrew manuscripts (see also Septuagint); most Hebrew manuscripts *villages as far as Greater Abel, where*
[c]19 A few Hebrew manuscripts; most Hebrew manuscripts and Septuagint *50,070*

can stand in the presence of the LORD, this holy God? To whom will the ark go up from here?"

6:19   Since the ark represented the presence of God, it was considered so holy that the people were forbidden either to touch it or even look at it. Frail humanity could not survive coming into direct contact with such a holy God.

21Then they sent messengers to the people of Kiriath Jearim, saying, "The Philistines have returned the ark of the LORD. Come down and take it up to your place."

7 1So the men of Kiriath Jearim came and took up the ark of the LORD. They took it to Abinadab's house on the hill and consecrated Eleazar his son to guard the ark of the LORD.

Samuel Subdues the Philistines at Mizpah

2It was a long time, twenty years in all, that the ark remained at Kiriath Jearim, and all the people of Israel mourned and sought after the LORD. 3And Samuel said to the whole house of Israel, "If you are returning to the LORD with all your hearts, then rid yourselves of the foreign gods and the Ashtoreths and commit yourselves to the LORD and serve him only, and he will deliver you out of the hand of the Philistines." 4So the Israelites put away their Baals and Ashtoreths, and served the LORD only.

7:4   The Baals and Ashtoreths were fertility gods and goddesses worshipped by the Canaanites, who had lived in the land prior to the Israelites. Some of the Israelites were tempted to worship them as well.

5Then Samuel said, "Assemble all Israel at Mizpah and I will intercede with the LORD for you." 6When they had assembled at Mizpah, they drew water and poured it out before the LORD. On that day they fasted and there they confessed, "We have sinned against the LORD." And Samuel was leader*a* of Israel at Mizpah. 7When the Philistines heard that Israel had assembled at Mizpah, the rulers of the Philistines came up to attack them. And when the Israelites heard of it, they were afraid because of the Philistines. 8They said to Samuel, "Do not stop crying out to the LORD our God for us, that he may rescue us from the hand of the Philistines." 9Then Samuel took a suckling lamb and offered it up as a whole burnt offering to the LORD. He cried out to the LORD on Israel's behalf, and the LORD answered him. 10While Samuel was sacrificing the burnt offering, the Philistines drew near to engage Israel in battle. But that day the LORD thundered with loud thunder against the Philistines and threw them into such a panic that they were routed before the Israelites. 11The men of Israel rushed out of Mizpah and pursued the Philistines, slaughtering them along the way to a point below Beth Car. 12Then Samuel took a stone and set it up between Mizpah and Shen. He named it Ebenezer,*b* saying, "Thus far has the LORD helped us." 13So the Philistines were subdued and did not invade Israelite territory again.

7:12   Ebenezer means "stone of help", and the comment "Thus far has the LORD helped us" sums up Israel's experience to this point in their history. It suggests that the request for a king came from their desire to be like the other nations and demonstrated a lack of faith in God who had led them without a king until now.

Throughout Samuel's lifetime, the hand of the LORD was against the Philistines. 14The towns from Ekron to Gath that the Philistines had captured from Israel were restored to her, and Israel delivered the neighbouring territory from the power of the Philistines. And there was peace between Israel and the Amorites. 15Samuel continued as judge over Israel all the days of his life. 16From year to year he went on a circuit from Bethel to Gilgal to Mizpah, judging Israel in all those places. 17But he always went back to Ramah, where his home was, and there he also judged Israel. And he built an altar there to the LORD.

Israel Asks for a King

8 When Samuel grew old, he appointed his sons as judges for Israel. 2The name of his firstborn was Joel and the name of his second was Abijah, and they served at Beersheba. 3But his sons did not walk in his ways. They turned aside after dishonest gain and accepted bribes and perverted justice.

4So all the elders of Israel gathered together and came to Samuel at Ramah. 5They said to him, "You are old, and your sons do not walk in your ways; now appoint a king to lead*a* us, such as all the other nations have."

6But when they said, "Give us a king to lead us," this displeased Samuel; so he prayed to the LORD. 7And the LORD told him: "Listen to all that the people are saying to you; it is not you they have rejected, but they have rejected me as their king. 8As they have done from the day I brought them up out of Egypt until this day, forsaking me and serving other gods, so they are doing to you. 9Now listen to them; but warn them solemnly and let them know what the king who will reign over them will do."

10Samuel told all the words of the LORD to the people who were asking him for a king. 11He said, "This is what the king who will reign over you will do: He will take your sons and make them serve with his chariots and horses, and they will run in front of his chariots. 12Some he will assign to be commanders of thousands and commanders of fifties, and others to plough his ground and reap his harvest, and still others to make

---

*a*6 Traditionally *judge*   *b*12 *Ebenezer* means *stone of help.*   *a*5 Traditionally *judge*; also in verses 6 and 20 weapons of war and equipment for his chariots. [13]He will take your daughters to be perfumers and cooks and bakers. [14]He will take the best of your fields and vineyards and olive groves and give them to his attendants. [15]He will take a tenth of your grain and of your vintage and give it to his officials and attendants. [16]Your menservants and maidservants and the best of your cattle[b] and donkeys he will take for his own use. [17]He will take a tenth of your flocks, and you yourselves will become his slaves. [18]When that day comes, you will cry out for relief from the king you have chosen, and the Lord will not answer you in that day."

[19]But the people refused to listen to Samuel. "No!" they said. "We want a king over us. [20]Then we shall be like all the other nations, with a king to lead us and to go out before us and fight our battles."

[21]When Samuel heard all that the people said, he repeated it before the Lord. [22]The Lord answered, "Listen to them and give them a king."

Then Samuel said to the men of Israel, "Everyone is to go back to his town."

Samuel Anoints Saul

9 There was a Benjamite, a man of standing, whose name was Kish son of Abiel, the son of Zeror, the son of Becorath, the son of Aphiah of Benjamin. [2]He had a son named Saul, an impressive young man without equal among the Israelites — a head taller than any of the others.

[3]Now the donkeys belonging to Saul's father Kish were lost, and Kish said to his son Saul, "Take one of the servants with you and go and look for the donkeys." [4]So he passed through the hill country of Ephraim and through the area around Shalisha, but they did not find them. They went on into the district of Shaalim, but the donkeys were not there. Then he passed through the territory of Benjamin, but they did not find them. [5]When they reached the district of Zuph, Saul said to the servant who was with him, "Come, let's go back, or my father will stop thinking about the donkeys and start worrying about us."

[6]But the servant replied, "Look, in this town there is a man of God; he is highly respected, and everything he says comes true. Let's go there now. Perhaps he will tell us what way to take."

[7]Saul said to his servant, "If we go, what can we give the man? The food in our sacks is gone. We have no gift to take to the man of God. What do we have?"

[8]The servant answered him again. "Look," he said, "I have a quarter of a shekel[a] of silver. I will give it to the man of God so that he will tell us what way to take." [9](Formerly in Israel, if a man went to enquire of God, he would say, "Come, let us go to the seer," because the prophet of today used to be called a seer.)

[10]"Good," Saul said to his servant. "Come, let's go." So they set out for the town where the man of God was.

[11]As they were going up the hill to the town, they met some girls coming out to draw water, and they asked them, "Is the seer here?"

[12]"He is," they answered. "He's ahead of you. Hurry now; he has just come to our town today, for the people

have a sacrifice at the high place. [13]As soon as you enter the town, you will find him before he goes up to the high place to eat. The people will not begin eating until he comes, because he must bless the sacrifice; afterwards, those who are invited will eat. Go up now; you should find him about this time."

[14]They went up to the town, and as they were entering it, there was Samuel, coming towards them on his way up to the high place.

[15]Now the day before Saul came, the Lord had revealed this to Samuel: [16]"About this time tomorrow I will send you a man from the land of Benjamin. Anoint him leader over my people Israel; he will deliver my people from the hand of the Philistines. I have looked upon my people, for their cry has reached me."

[17]When Samuel caught sight of Saul, the Lord said to him, "This is the man I spoke to you about; he will govern my people."

[18]Saul approached Samuel in the gateway and asked, "Would you please tell me where the seer's house is?"

[19]"I am the seer," Samuel replied. "Go up ahead of me to the high place, for today you are to eat with me, and in the morning I will let you go and will tell you all that is in your heart. [20]As for the donkeys you lost three days ago, do not worry about them; they have been found. And to whom is all the desire of Israel turned, if not to you and all your father's family?"

[21]Saul answered, "But am I not a Benjamite, from the smallest tribe of Israel, and is not my clan the least of all the clans of the tribe of Benjamin? Why do you say such a thing to me?"

9:21   Saul's question shows he considered himself to be an unlikely choice for king. This underlines the fact that he had been chosen for office by God, as was stated by Samuel in 10:24.

---

[22]Then Samuel brought Saul and his servant into the hall and seated them at the head of those who were invited — about thirty in number. [23]Samuel said to the cook, "Bring the piece of meat I gave you, the one I told you to lay aside."

[24]So the cook took up the leg with what was on it and set it in front of Saul. Samuel said, "Here is what has been kept for you. Eat, because it was set aside for you for this occasion, from the time I said, 'I have invited guests.' " And Saul dined with Samuel that day.

[25]After they came down from the high place to the town, Samuel talked with Saul on the roof of his house. [26]They rose about daybreak and Samuel called to Saul on the roof, "Get ready, and I will send you on your way." When Saul got ready, he and Samuel went outside together. [27]As they were going down to the edge of the town, Samuel said to Saul, "Tell the servant to go on ahead of us" — and the servant did so — "but you stay here awhile, so that I may give you a message from God."

---

b16 Septuagint; Hebrew *young men*   *a8* That is, about ¹⁄₁₀ ounce (about 3 grams)

10 Then Samuel took a flask of oil and poured it on Saul's head and kissed him, saying, "Has not the LORD anointed you leader over his inheritance?[a] ²When you leave me today, you will meet two men near Rachel's tomb, at Zelzah on the border of Benjamin. They will say to you, 'The donkeys you set out to look for have been found. And now your father has stopped thinking about them and is worried about you. He is asking, "What shall I do about my son?"'

³"Then you will go on from there until you reach the great tree of Tabor. Three men going up to God at Bethel will meet you there. One will be carrying three young goats, another three loaves of bread, and another a skin of wine. ⁴They will greet you and offer you two loaves of bread, which you will accept from them.

⁵"After that you will go to Gibeah of God, where there is a Philistine outpost. As you approach the town, you will meet a procession of prophets coming down from the high place with lyres, tambourines, flutes and harps being played before them, and they will be prophesying. ⁶The Spirit of the LORD will come upon you in power, and you will prophesy with them; and you will be changed into a different person. ⁷Once these signs are fulfilled, do whatever your hand finds to do, for God is with you.

⁸"Go down ahead of me to Gilgal. I will surely come down to you to sacrifice burnt offerings and fellowship offerings,[b] but you must wait seven days until I come to you and tell you what you are to do."

Saul Made King

⁹As Saul turned to leave Samuel, God changed Saul's heart, and all these signs were fulfilled that day. ¹⁰When they arrived at Gibeah, a procession of prophets met him; the Spirit of God came upon him in power, and he joined in their prophesying. ¹¹When all those who had formerly known him saw him prophesying with the prophets, they asked each other, "What is this that has happened to the son of Kish? Is Saul also among the prophets?"

¹²A man who lived there answered, "And who is their father?" So it became a saying: "Is Saul also among the prophets?" ¹³After Saul stopped prophesying, he went to the high place.

¹⁴Now Saul's uncle asked him and his servant, "Where have you been?"

"Looking for the donkeys," he said. "But when we saw they were not to be found, we went to Samuel."

¹⁵Saul's uncle said, "Tell me what Samuel said to you."

¹⁶Saul replied, "He assured us that the donkeys had been found." But he did not tell his uncle what Samuel had said about the kingship.

¹⁷Samuel summoned the people of Israel to the LORD at Mizpah ¹⁸and said to them, "This is what the LORD, the God of Israel, says: 'I brought Israel up out of Egypt, and I delivered you from the power of Egypt and all the kingdoms that oppressed you.' ¹⁹But you have now rejected your God, who saves you out of all your calamities and distresses. And you have said, 'No, set a king over us.' So now present yourselves before the LORD by your tribes and clans."

²⁰When Samuel brought all the tribes of Israel near, the tribe of Benjamin was chosen. ²¹Then he brought forward the tribe of Benjamin, clan by clan, and Matri's clan was chosen. Finally Saul son of Kish was chosen. But when they looked for him, he was not to be found. ²²So they enquired further of the LORD, "Has the man come here yet?"

And the LORD said, "Yes, he has hidden himself among the baggage."

²³They ran and brought him out, and as he stood among the people he was a head taller than any of the others. ²⁴Samuel said to all the people, "Do you see the man the LORD has chosen? There is no-one like him among all the people."

Then the people shouted, "Long live the king!"

²⁵Samuel explained to the people the regulations of the kingship. He wrote them down on a scroll and deposited it before the LORD. Then Samuel dismissed the people, each to his own home.

²⁶Saul also went to his home in Gibeah, accompanied by valiant men whose hearts God had touched. ²⁷But some troublemakers said, "How can this fellow save us?" They despised him and brought him no gifts. But Saul kept silent.

Saul Rescues the City of Jabesh

11 Nahash the Ammonite went up and besieged Jabesh Gilead. And all the men of Jabesh said to him, "Make a treaty with us, and we will be subject to you."

²But Nahash the Ammonite replied, "I will make a treaty with you only on the condition that I gouge out the right eye of every one of you and so bring disgrace on all Israel."

³The elders of Jabesh said to him, "Give us seven days so that we can send messengers throughout Israel; if no-one comes to rescue us, we will surrender to you."

⁴When the messengers came to Gibeah of Saul and reported these terms to the people, they all wept aloud. ⁵Just then Saul was returning from the fields, behind his oxen, and he asked, "What is wrong with the people? Why are they weeping?" Then they repeated to him what the men of Jabesh had said.

⁶When Saul heard their words, the Spirit of God came upon him in power, and he burned with anger. ⁷He took a pair of oxen, cut them into pieces, and sent the pieces by messengers throughout Israel, proclaiming, "This is what will be done to the oxen of anyone who does not follow Saul and Samuel." Then the terror of the LORD fell on the people, and they turned out as one man. ⁸When Saul mustered them at Bezek, the men of Israel numbered three hundred thousand and the men of Judah thirty thousand.

⁹They told the messengers who had come, "Say to the men of Jabesh Gilead, 'By the time the sun is hot tomorrow, you will be delivered.'" When the messengers went and reported this to the men of Jabesh, they

---

[a]1 Hebrew; Septuagint and Vulgate *over his people Israel? You will reign over the* LORD's *people and save them from the power of their enemies round about. And this will be a sign to you that the* LORD *has anointed you leader over his inheritance:*
[b]8 Traditionally *peace offerings*

were elated. [10]They said to the Ammonites, "Tomorrow we will surrender to you, and you can do to us whatever seems good to you."

[11]The next day Saul separated his men into three divisions; during the last watch of the night they broke into the camp of the Ammonites and slaughtered them until the heat of the day. Those who survived were scattered, so that no two of them were left together.

Saul Confirmed as King

[12]The people then said to Samuel, "Who was it that asked, 'Shall Saul reign over us?' Bring these men to us and we will put them to death."

[13]But Saul said, "No-one shall be put to death today, for this day the LORD has rescued Israel."

11:13 ". . . the LORD has rescued Israel." This statement makes clear one of the underlying concerns of the book: to show how God's saving activity is made known through the history of his people.

---

[14]Then Samuel said to the people, "Come, let us go to Gilgal and there reaffirm the kingship." [15]So all the people went to Gilgal and confirmed Saul as king in the presence of the LORD. There they sacrificed fellowship offerings[a] before the LORD, and Saul and all the Israelites held a great celebration.

Samuel's Farewell Speech

12 Samuel said to all Israel, "I have listened to everything you said to me and have set a king over you. [2]Now you have a king as your leader. As for me, I am old and grey, and my sons are here with you. I have been your leader from my youth until this day. [3]Here I stand. Testify against me in the presence of the LORD and his anointed. Whose ox have I taken? Whose donkey have I taken? Whom have I cheated? Whom have I oppressed? From whose hand have I accepted a bribe to make me shut my eyes? If I have done any of these, I will make it right."

[4]"You have not cheated or oppressed us," they replied. "You have not taken anything from anyone's hand."

[5]Samuel said to them, "The LORD is witness against you, and also his anointed is witness this day, that you have not found anything in my hand."

"He is witness," they said.

[6]Then Samuel said to the people, "It is the LORD who appointed Moses and Aaron and brought your forefathers up out of Egypt. [7]Now then, stand here, because I am going to confront you with evidence before the LORD as to all the righteous acts performed by the LORD for you and your fathers.

[8]"After Jacob entered Egypt, they cried to the LORD for help, and the LORD sent Moses and Aaron, who brought your forefathers out of Egypt and settled them in this place.

[9]"But they forgot the LORD their God; so he sold them into the hands of Sisera, the commander of the army of Hazor, and into the hands of the Philistines and the king of Moab, who fought against them. [10]They cried out to the LORD and said, 'We have sinned; we have forsaken the LORD and served the Baals and the Ashtoreths. But now deliver us from the hands of our enemies, and we will serve you.' [11]Then the LORD sent Jerub-Baal,[a] Barak,[b] Jephthah and Samuel,[c] and he delivered you from the hands of your enemies on every side, so that you lived securely.

[12]"But when you saw that Nahash king of the Ammonites was moving against you, you said to me, 'No, we want a king to rule over us' — even though the LORD your God was your king. [13]Now here is the king you have chosen, the one you asked for; see, the LORD has set a king over you. [14]If you fear the LORD and serve and obey him and do not rebel against his commands, and if both you and the king who reigns over you follow the LORD your God — good! [15]But if you do not obey the LORD, and if you rebel against his commands, his hand will be against you, as it was against your fathers.

[16]"Now then, stand still and see this great thing the LORD is about to do before your eyes! [17]Is it not wheat harvest now? I will call upon the LORD to send thunder and rain. And you will realise what an evil thing you did in the eyes of the LORD when you asked for a king."

[18]Then Samuel called upon the LORD, and that same day the LORD sent thunder and rain. So all the people stood in awe of the LORD and of Samuel.

[19]The people all said to Samuel, "Pray to the LORD your God for your servants so that we will not die, for we have added to all our other sins the evil of asking for a king."

[20]"Do not be afraid," Samuel replied. "You have done all this evil; yet do not turn away from the LORD, but serve the LORD with all your heart. [21]Do not turn away after useless idols. They can do you no good, nor can they rescue you, because they are useless. [22]For the sake of his great name the LORD will not reject his people, because the LORD was pleased to make you his own. [23]As for me, far be it from me that I should sin against the LORD by failing to pray for you. And I will teach you the way that is good and right. [24]But be sure to fear the LORD and serve him faithfully with all your heart; consider what great things he has done for you. [25]Yet if you persist in doing evil, both you and your king will be swept away."

Samuel Rebukes Saul

13 Saul was ⌜thirty⌟[a] years old when he became king, and he reigned over Israel for ⌜forty-⌟[b] two years.

[2]Saul[c] chose three thousand men from Israel; two thousand were with him at Michmash and in the hill country of Bethel, and a thousand were with Jonathan

---

a 15 Traditionally *peace offerings*   a 11 Also called *Gideon*
c 11 Hebrew; some Septuagint manuscripts and Syriac *Samson*
a 1 A few late manuscripts of the Septuagint; Hebrew does not have *thirty.*
b 1 See the round number in Acts 13:21; Hebrew does not have *forty-.*
c 1,2 Or *and when he had reigned over Israel for two years,* [2]*he*

b 11 Some Septuagint manuscripts and Syriac; Hebrew *Bedan*

at Gibeah in Benjamin. The rest of the men he sent back to their homes.

³Jonathan attacked the Philistine outpost at Geba, and the Philistines heard about it. Then Saul had the trumpet blown throughout the land and said, "Let the Hebrews hear!" ⁴So all Israel heard the news: "Saul has attacked the Philistine outpost, and now Israel has become an offence to the Philistines." And the people were summoned to join Saul at Gilgal.

⁵The Philistines assembled to fight Israel, with three thousand^d chariots, six thousand charioteers, and soldiers as numerous as the sand on the seashore. They went up and camped at Michmash, east of Beth Aven. ⁶When the men of Israel saw that their situation was critical and that their army was hard pressed, they hid in caves and thickets, among the rocks, and in pits and cisterns. ⁷Some Hebrews even crossed the Jordan to the land of Gad and Gilead.

Saul remained at Gilgal, and all the troops with him were quaking with fear. ⁸He waited for seven days, the time set by Samuel; but Samuel did not come to Gilgal, and Saul's men began to scatter. ⁹So he said, "Bring me the burnt offering and the fellowship offerings."^{e} And Saul offered up the burnt offering. ¹⁰Just as he finished making the offering, Samuel arrived, and Saul went out to greet him.

13:9   When Saul offered up the burnt offering he went against Samuel's instructions (10:8), and as a result he was told that the Lord would not establish his kingdom for ever, as had originally been promised (13:13–14). Here is a warning of the Lord's eventual rejection of Saul.

---

¹¹"What have you done?" asked Samuel.

Saul replied, "When I saw that the men were scattering, and that you did not come at the set time, and that the Philistines were assembling at Michmash, ¹²I thought, 'Now the Philistines will come down against me at Gilgal, and I have not sought the Lord's favour.' So I felt compelled to offer the burnt offering."

¹³"You acted foolishly," Samuel said. "You have not kept the command the Lord your God gave you; if you had, he would have established your kingdom over Israel for all time. ¹⁴But now your kingdom will not endure; the Lord has sought out a man after his own heart and appointed him leader of his people, because you have not kept the Lord's command."

¹⁵Then Samuel left Gilgal^f and went up to Gibeah in Benjamin, and Saul counted the men who were with him. They numbered about six hundred.

Israel Without Weapons

¹⁶Saul and his son Jonathan and the men with them were staying in Gibeah^g of Benjamin, while the Philistines camped at Michmash. ¹⁷Raiding parties went out from the Philistine camp in three detachments. One turned towards Ophrah in the vicinity of Shual, ¹⁸another towards Beth Horon, and the third towards the borderland overlooking the Valley of Zeboim facing the desert.

¹⁹Not a blacksmith could be found in the whole land of Israel, because the Philistines had said, "Otherwise the Hebrews will make swords or spears!" ²⁰So all Israel went down to the Philistines to have their ploughshares, mattocks, axes and sickles^h sharpened. ²¹The price was two thirds of a shekel^i for sharpening ploughshares and mattocks, and a third of a shekel^j for sharpening forks and axes and for repointing goads.

²²So on the day of the battle not a soldier with Saul and Jonathan had a sword or spear in his hand; only Saul and his son Jonathan had them.

Jonathan Attacks the Philistines

²³Now a detachment of Philistines had gone out to the pass at Michmash. **14** ¹One day Jonathan son of Saul said to the young man bearing his armour, "Come, let's go over to the Philistine outpost on the other side." But he did not tell his father.

²Saul was staying on the outskirts of Gibeah under a pomegranate tree in Migron. With him were about six hundred men, ³among whom was Ahijah, who was wearing an ephod. He was a son of Ichabod's brother Ahitub son of Phinehas, the son of Eli, the Lord's priest in Shiloh. No-one was aware that Jonathan had left.

⁴On each side of the pass that Jonathan intended to cross to reach the Philistine outpost was a cliff; one was called Bozez, and the other Seneh. ⁵One cliff stood to the north towards Michmash, the other to the south towards Geba.

⁶Jonathan said to his young armour-bearer, "Come, let's go over to the outpost of those uncircumcised fellows. Perhaps the Lord will act on our behalf. Nothing can hinder the Lord from saving, whether by many or by few."

⁷"Do all that you have in mind," his armour-bearer said. "Go ahead; I am with you heart and soul."

⁸Jonathan said, "Come, then; we will cross over towards the men and let them see us. ⁹If they say to us, 'Wait there until we come to you,' we will stay where we are and not go up to them. ¹⁰But if they say, 'Come up to us,' we will climb up, because that will be our sign that the Lord has given them into our hands."

¹¹So both of them showed themselves to the Philistine outpost. "Look!" said the Philistines. "The Hebrews are crawling out of the holes they were hiding in." ¹²The men of the outpost shouted to Jonathan and his armour-bearer, "Come up to us and we'll teach you a lesson."

So Jonathan said to his armour-bearer, "Climb up after me; the Lord has given them into the hand of Israel."

¹³Jonathan climbed up, using his hands and feet, with his armour-bearer right behind him. The Philistines fell before Jonathan, and his armour-bearer

---

^{d}5 Some Septuagint manuscripts and Syriac; Hebrew *thirty thousand*
^{f}15 Hebrew; Septuagint *Gilgal and went his way; the rest of the people went after Saul to meet the army, and they went out of Gilgal*
^{g}16 Two Hebrew manuscripts; most Hebrew manuscripts *Geba,* a variant of *Gibeah*
^{i}21 Hebrew *pim;* that is, about ¼ ounce (about 8 grams)
^{e}9 Traditionally *peace offerings*
^{h}20 Septuagint; Hebrew *ploughshares*
^{j}21 That is, about ⅛ ounce (about 4 grams)

followed and killed behind him. [14]In that first attack Jonathan and his armour-bearer killed some twenty men in an area of about half an acre.[a]

Israel Routs the Philistines

[15]Then panic struck the whole army—those in the camp and field, and those in the outposts and raiding parties—and the ground shook. It was a panic sent by God.[b]
[16]Saul's lookouts at Gibeah in Benjamin saw the army melting away in all directions. [17]Then Saul said to the men who were with him, "Muster the forces and see who has left us." When they did, it was Jonathan and his armour-bearer who were not there.
[18]Saul said to Ahijah, "Bring the ark of God." (At that time it was with the Israelites.)[c] [19]While Saul was talking to the priest, the tumult in the Philistine camp increased more and more. So Saul said to the priest, "Withdraw your hand."
[20]Then Saul and all his men assembled and went to the battle. They found the Philistines in total confusion, striking each other with their swords. [21]Those Hebrews who had previously been with the Philistines and had gone up with them to their camp went over to the Israelites who were with Saul and Jonathan. [22]When all the Israelites who had hidden in the hill country of Ephraim heard that the Philistines were on the run, they joined the battle in hot pursuit. [23]So the LORD rescued Israel that day, and the battle moved on beyond Beth Aven.

Jonathan Eats Honey

[24]Now the men of Israel were in distress that day, because Saul had bound the people under an oath, saying, "Cursed be any man who eats food before evening comes, before I have avenged myself on my enemies!" So none of the troops tasted food.
[25]The entire army[d] entered the woods, and there was honey on the ground. [26]When they went into the woods, they saw the honey oozing out, yet no-one put his hand to his mouth, because they feared the oath. [27]But Jonathan had not heard that his father had bound the people with the oath, so he reached out the end of the staff that was in his hand and dipped it into the honeycomb. He raised his hand to his mouth, and his eyes brightened.[e] [28]Then one of the soldiers told him, "Your father bound the army under a strict oath, saying, 'Cursed be any man who eats food today!' That is why the men are faint."
[29]Jonathan said, "My father has made trouble for the country. See how my eyes brightened[f] when I tasted a little of this honey. [30]How much better it would have been if the men had eaten today some of the plunder they took from their enemies. Would not the slaughter of the Philistines have been even greater?"
[31]That day, after the Israelites had struck down the Philistines from Michmash to Aijalon, they were exhausted. [32]They pounced on the plunder and, taking sheep, cattle and calves, they butchered them on the ground and ate them, together with the blood. [33]Then someone said to Saul, "Look, the men are sinning against the LORD by eating meat that has blood in it."

14:29 Jonathan was guilty of breaking the king's oath. However, his remark that his father has made trouble for the country indicates the real source of trouble for Israel.

"You have broken faith," he said. "Roll a large stone over here at once." [34]Then he said, "Go out among the men and tell them, 'Each of you bring me your cattle and sheep, and slaughter them here and eat them. Do not sin against the LORD by eating meat with blood still in it.' "
So everyone brought his ox that night and slaughtered it there. [35]Then Saul built an altar to the LORD; it was the first time he had done this.
[36]Saul said, "Let us go down after the Philistines by night and plunder them till dawn, and let us not leave one of them alive."
"Do whatever seems best to you," they replied.
But the priest said, "Let us enquire of God here."
[37]So Saul asked God, "Shall I go down after the Philistines? Will you give them into Israel's hand?" But God did not answer him that day.
[38]Saul therefore said, "Come here, all you who are leaders of the army, and let us find out what sin has been committed today. [39]As surely as the LORD who rescues Israel lives, even if it lies with my son Jonathan, he must die." But not one of the men said a word.
[40]Saul then said to all the Israelites, "You stand over there; I and Jonathan my son will stand over here."
"Do what seems best to you," the men replied.
[41]Then Saul prayed to the LORD, the God of Israel, "Give me the right answer."[g] And Jonathan and Saul were taken by lot, and the men were cleared. [42]Saul said, "Cast the lot between me and Jonathan my son." And Jonathan was taken.
[43]Then Saul said to Jonathan, "Tell me what you have done."
So Jonathan told him, "I merely tasted a little honey with the end of my staff. And now must I die?"
[44]Saul said, "May God deal with me, be it ever so severely, if you do not die, Jonathan."
[45]But the men said to Saul, "Should Jonathan die— he who has brought about this great deliverance in Israel? Never! As surely as the LORD lives, not a hair of his head shall fall to the ground, for he did this today with God's help." So the men rescued Jonathan, and he was not put to death.
[46]Then Saul stopped pursuing the Philistines, and they withdrew to their own land.
[47]After Saul had assumed rule over Israel, he fought against their enemies on every side: Moab, the Ammonites, Edom, the kings[h] of Zobah, and the Philistines. Wherever he turned, he inflicted punishment on

---

[a]14 Hebrew half a yoke; a "yoke" was the land ploughed by a yoke of oxen in one day.   [b]15 Or a terrible panic
[c]18 Hebrew; Septuagint "Bring the ephod." (At that time he wore the ephod before the Israelites.)
[d]25 Or Now all the people of the land   [e]27 Or his strength was renewed   [f]29 Or my strength was renewed
[g]41 Hebrew; Septuagint "Why have you not answered your servant today? If the fault is in me or my son Jonathan, respond with Urim, but if the men of Israel are at fault, respond with Thummim."   [h]47 Masoretic Text; Dead Sea Scrolls and Septuagint king

them.[i] [48]He fought valiantly and defeated the Amalekites, delivering Israel from the hands of those who had plundered them.

Saul's Family

[49]Saul's sons were Jonathan, Ishvi and Malki-Shua. The name of his older daughter was Merab, and that of the younger was Michal. [50]His wife's name was Ahinoam daughter of Ahimaaz. The name of the commander of Saul's army was Abner son of Ner, and Ner was Saul's uncle. [51]Saul's father Kish and Abner's father Ner were sons of Abiel.

[52]All the days of Saul there was bitter war with the Philistines, and whenever Saul saw a mighty or brave man, he took him into his service.

The LORD Rejects Saul as King

15 Samuel said to Saul, "I am the one the LORD sent to anoint you king over his people Israel; so listen now to the message from the LORD. [2]This is what the LORD Almighty says: 'I will punish the Amalekites for what they did to Israel when they waylaid them as they came up from Egypt. [3]Now go, attack the Amalekites and totally destroy[a] everything that belongs to them. Do not spare them; put to death men and women, children and infants, cattle and sheep, camels and donkeys.' "

15:3   The Amalekites had attacked Israel during the people's journey from Egypt to the land God had promised to give them. By doing so they became God's enemies and Moses declared that they would be wiped out (Exodus 17:8–16 Deuteronomy 25:17–19). This is why Saul was given the command to destroy the Amalekites. It was still a harsh command.

---

[4]So Saul summoned the men and mustered them at Telaim—two hundred thousand foot soldiers and ten thousand men from Judah. [5]Saul went to the city of Amalek and set an ambush in the ravine. [6]Then he said to the Kenites, "Go away, leave the Amalekites so that I do not destroy you along with them; for you showed kindness to all the Israelites when they came up out of Egypt." So the Kenites moved away from the Amalekites.

[7]Then Saul attacked the Amalekites all the way from Havilah to Shur, to the east of Egypt. [8]He took Agag king of the Amalekites alive, and all his people he totally destroyed with the sword. [9]But Saul and the army spared Agag and the best of the sheep and cattle, the fat calves[b] and lambs—everything that was good. These they were unwilling to destroy completely, but everything that was despised and weak they totally destroyed.

[10]Then the word of the LORD came to Samuel: [11]"I am grieved that I have made Saul king, because he has turned away from me and has not carried out my instructions." Samuel was troubled, and he cried out to the LORD all that night.

[12]Early in the morning Samuel got up and went to meet Saul, but he was told, "Saul has gone to Carmel. There he has set up a monument in his own honour and has turned and gone on down to Gilgal."

[13]When Samuel reached him, Saul said, "The LORD bless you! I have carried out the LORD's instructions."

[14]But Samuel said, "What then is this bleating of sheep in my ears? What is this lowing of cattle that I hear?"

[15]Saul answered, "The soldiers brought them from the Amalekites; they spared the best of the sheep and cattle to sacrifice to the LORD your God, but we totally destroyed the rest."

[16]"Stop!" Samuel said to Saul. "Let me tell you what the LORD said to me last night."

"Tell me," Saul replied.

[17]Samuel said, "Although you were once small in your own eyes, did you not become the head of the tribes of Israel? The LORD anointed you king over Israel. [18]And he sent you on a mission, saying, 'Go and completely destroy those wicked people, the Amalekites; make war on them until you have wiped them out.' [19]Why did you not obey the LORD? Why did you pounce on the plunder and do evil in the eyes of the LORD?"

[20]"But I did obey the LORD," Saul said. "I went on the mission the LORD assigned me. I completely destroyed the Amalekites and brought back Agag their king. [21]The soldiers took sheep and cattle from the plunder, the best of what was devoted to God, in order to sacrifice them to the LORD your God at Gilgal."

[22]But Samuel replied:

"Does the LORD delight in burnt offerings and
      sacrifices
   as much as in obeying the voice of the LORD?
To obey is better than sacrifice,
   and to heed is better than the fat of rams.
[23]For rebellion is like the sin of divination,
   and arrogance like the evil of idolatry.
Because you have rejected the word of the LORD,
   he has rejected you as king."

15:23   The reason why the Lord rejected Saul as king is given: he failed to obey completely the Lord's instructions. The remainder of the book, although describing the reign of Saul, reads more like an account of David's rise to power.

---

[24]Then Saul said to Samuel, "I have sinned. I violated the LORD's command and your instructions. I was afraid of the people and so I gave in to them. [25]Now I beg you, forgive my sin and come back with me, so that I may worship the LORD."

[26]But Samuel said to him, "I will not go back with

---

[i]47 Hebrew; Septuagint *he was victorious*
[a]3 The Hebrew term refers to the irrevocable giving of things or persons to the LORD, often by totally destroying them; also in verses 8, 9, 15, 18, 20 and 21.   [b]9 Or *the grown bulls*; the meaning of the Hebrew for this phrase is uncertain.

you. You have rejected the word of the LORD, and the LORD has rejected you as king over Israel!"

27As Samuel turned to leave, Saul caught hold of the hem of his robe, and it tore. 28Samuel said to him, "The LORD has torn the kingdom of Israel from you today and has given it to one of your neighbours — to one better than you. 29He who is the Glory of Israel does not lie or change his mind; for he is not a man, that he should change his mind."

30Saul replied, "I have sinned. But please honour me before the elders of my people and before Israel; come back with me, so that I may worship the LORD your God." 31So Samuel went back with Saul, and Saul worshipped the LORD.

32Then Samuel said, "Bring me Agag king of the Amalekites."

Agag came to him confidently,c thinking, "Surely the bitterness of death is past."

33But Samuel said,

"As your sword has made women childless,
    so will your mother be childless among
        women."

And Samuel put Agag to death before the LORD at Gilgal.

34Then Samuel left for Ramah, but Saul went up to his home in Gibeah of Saul. 35Until the day Samuel died, he did not go to see Saul again, though Samuel mourned for him. And the LORD was grieved that he had made Saul king over Israel.

Samuel Anoints David

16 The LORD said to Samuel, "How long will you mourn for Saul, since I have rejected him as king over Israel? Fill your horn with oil and be on your way; I am sending you to Jesse of Bethlehem. I have chosen one of his sons to be king."

2But Samuel said, "How can I go? Saul will hear about it and kill me."

The LORD said, "Take a heifer with you and say, 'I have come to sacrifice to the LORD.' 3Invite Jesse to the sacrifice, and I will show you what to do. You are to anoint for me the one I indicate."

4Samuel did what the LORD said. When he arrived at Bethlehem, the elders of the town trembled when they met him. They asked, "Do you come in peace?"

5Samuel replied, "Yes, in peace; I have come to sacrifice to the LORD. Consecrate yourselves and come to the sacrifice with me." Then he consecrated Jesse and his sons and invited them to the sacrifice.

6When they arrived, Samuel saw Eliab and thought, "Surely the LORD's anointed stands here before the LORD."

7But the LORD said to Samuel, "Do not consider his appearance or his height, for I have rejected him. The LORD does not look at the things man looks at. Man looks at the outward appearance, but the LORD looks at the heart."

8Then Jesse called Abinadab and made him pass in front of Samuel. But Samuel said, "The LORD has not

chosen this one either." 9Jesse then made Shammah pass by, but Samuel said, "Nor has the LORD chosen this one." 10Jesse made seven of his sons pass before Samuel, but Samuel said to him, "The LORD has not chosen these." 11So he asked Jesse, "Are these all the sons you have?"

"There is still the youngest," Jesse answered, "but he is tending the sheep."

Samuel said, "Send for him; we will not sit downa until he arrives."

12So he sent and had him brought in. He was ruddy, with a fine appearance and handsome features.

Then the LORD said, "Rise and anoint him; he is the one."

13So Samuel took the horn of oil and anointed him in the presence of his brothers, and from that day on the Spirit of the LORD came upon David in power. Samuel then went to Ramah.

David in Saul's Service

14Now the Spirit of the LORD had departed from Saul, and an evilb spirit from the LORD tormented him.

15Saul's attendants said to him, "See, an evil spirit from God is tormenting you. 16Let our lord command his servants here to search for someone who can play the harp. He will play when the evil spirit from God comes upon you, and you will feel better."

17So Saul said to his attendants, "Find someone who plays well and bring him to me."

18One of the servants answered, "I have seen a son of Jesse of Bethlehem who knows how to play the harp. He is a brave man and a warrior. He speaks well and is a fine-looking man. And the LORD is with him."

19Then Saul sent messengers to Jesse and said, "Send me your son David, who is with the sheep." 20So Jesse took a donkey loaded with bread, a skin of wine and a young goat and sent them with his son David to Saul.

21David came to Saul and entered his service. Saul liked him very much, and David became one of his armour-bearers. 22Then Saul sent word to Jesse, saying, "Allow David to remain in my service, for I am pleased with him."

23Whenever the spirit from God came upon Saul, David would take his harp and play. Then relief would come to Saul; he would feel better, and the evil spirit would leave him.

David and Goliath

17 Now the Philistines gathered their forces for war and assembled at Socoh in Judah. They pitched camp at Ephes Dammim, between Socoh and Azekah. 2Saul and the Israelites assembled and camped in the Valley of Elah and drew up their battle line to meet the Philistines. 3The Philistines occupied one hill and the Israelites another, with the valley between them.

4A champion named Goliath, who was from Gath, came out of the Philistine camp. He was over nine feeta tall. 5He had a bronze helmet on his head and

---

c32 Or him trembling, yet   a11 Some Septuagint manuscripts; Hebrew not gather round
b14 Or injurious; also in verses 15, 16 and 23   a4 Hebrew was six cubits and a span (about 3 metres)

wore a coat of scale armour of bronze weighing five thousand shekels;[b] [6]on his legs he wore bronze greaves, and a bronze javelin was slung on his back. [7]His spear shaft was like a weaver's rod, and its iron point weighed six hundred shekels.[c] His shield-bearer went ahead of him.

[8]Goliath stood and shouted to the ranks of Israel, "Why do you come out and line up for battle? Am I not a Philistine, and are you not the servants of Saul? Choose a man and have him come down to me. [9]If he is able to fight and kill me, we will become your subjects; but if I overcome him and kill him, you will become our subjects and serve us." [10]Then the Philistine said, "This day I defy the ranks of Israel! Give me a man and let us fight each other." [11]On hearing the Philistine's words, Saul and all the Israelites were dismayed and terrified.

[12]Now David was the son of an Ephrathite named Jesse, who was from Bethlehem in Judah. Jesse had eight sons, and in Saul's time he was old and well advanced in years. [13]Jesse's three oldest sons had followed Saul to the war: The firstborn was Eliab; the second, Abinadab; and the third, Shammah. [14]David was the youngest. The three oldest followed Saul, [15]but David went back and forth from Saul to tend his father's sheep at Bethlehem.

[16]For forty days the Philistine came forward every morning and evening and took his stand.

[17]Now Jesse said to his son David, "Take this ephah[d] of roasted grain and these ten loaves of bread for your brothers and hurry to their camp. [18]Take along these ten cheeses to the commander of their unit.[e] See how your brothers are and bring back some assurance[f] from them. [19]They are with Saul and all the men of Israel in the Valley of Elah, fighting against the Philistines."

[20]Early in the morning David left the flock with a shepherd, loaded up and set out, as Jesse had directed. He reached the camp as the army was going out to its battle positions, shouting the war cry. [21]Israel and the Philistines were drawing up their lines facing each other. [22]David left his things with the keeper of supplies, ran to the battle lines and greeted his brothers. [23]As he was talking with them, Goliath, the Philistine champion from Gath, stepped out from his lines and shouted his usual defiance, and David heard it. [24]When the Israelites saw the man, they all ran from him in great fear.

[25]Now the Israelites had been saying, "Do you see how this man keeps coming out? He comes out to defy Israel. The king will give great wealth to the man who kills him. He will also give him his daughter in marriage and will exempt his father's family from taxes in Israel."

[26]David asked the men standing near him, "What will be done for the man who kills this Philistine and removes this disgrace from Israel? Who is this uncircumcised Philistine that he should defy the armies of the living God?"

[27]They repeated to him what they had been saying and told him, "This is what will be done for the man who kills him."

[28]When Eliab, David's oldest brother, heard him speaking with the men, he burned with anger at him and asked, "Why have you come down here? And with whom did you leave those few sheep in the desert? I know how conceited you are and how wicked your heart is; you came down only to watch the battle."

[29]"Now what have I done?" said David. "Can't I even speak?" [30]He then turned away to someone else and brought up the same matter, and the men answered him as before. [31]What David said was overheard and reported to Saul, and Saul sent for him.

[32]David said to Saul, "Let no-one lose heart on account of this Philistine; your servant will go and fight him."

[33]Saul replied, "You are not able to go out against this Philistine and fight him; you are only a boy, and he has been a fighting man from his youth."

[34]But David said to Saul, "Your servant has been keeping his father's sheep. When a lion or a bear came and carried off a sheep from the flock, [35]I went after it, struck it and rescued the sheep from its mouth. When it turned on me, I seized it by its hair, struck it and killed it. [36]Your servant has killed both the lion and the bear; this uncircumcised Philistine will be like one of them, because he has defied the armies of the living God. [37]The LORD who delivered me from the paw of the lion and the paw of the bear will deliver me from the hand of this Philistine."

Saul said to David, "Go, and the LORD be with you."

[38]Then Saul dressed David in his own tunic. He put a coat of armour on him and a bronze helmet on his head. [39]David fastened on his sword over the tunic and tried walking around, because he was not used to them.

"I cannot go in these," he said to Saul, "because I am not used to them." So he took them off. [40]Then he took his staff in his hand, chose five smooth stones from the stream, put them in the pouch of his shepherd's bag and, with his sling in his hand, approached the Philistine.

[41]Meanwhile, the Philistine, with his shield-bearer in front of him, kept coming closer to David. [42]He looked David over and saw that he was only a boy, ruddy and handsome, and he despised him. [43]He said to David, "Am I a dog, that you come at me with sticks?" And the Philistine cursed David by his gods. [44]"Come here," he said, "and I'll give your flesh to the birds of the air and the beasts of the field!"

[45]David said to the Philistine, "You come against me with sword and spear and javelin, but I come against you in the name of the LORD Almighty, the God of the armies of Israel, whom you have defied. [46]This day the LORD will hand you over to me, and I'll strike you down and cut off your head. Today I will give the carcasses of the Philistine army to the birds of the air and the beasts of the earth, and the whole world will know that there is a God in Israel. [47]All those gathered here will know that it is not by sword or spear that the LORD

[b]5 That is, about 125 pounds (about 57 kilograms)
[c]7 That is, about 15 pounds (about 7 kilograms)
[d]17 That is, probably about ⅗ bushel (about 22 litres)
[e]18 Hebrew thousand
[f]18 Or some token; or some pledge of spoils

saves; for the battle is the Lord's, and he will give all of you into our hands."

⁴⁸As the Philistine moved closer to attack him, David ran quickly towards the battle line to meet him. ⁴⁹Reaching into his bag and taking out a stone, he slung it and struck the Philistine on the forehead. The stone sank into his forehead, and he fell face down on the ground.

⁵⁰So David triumphed over the Philistine with a sling and a stone; without a sword in his hand he struck down the Philistine and killed him.

⁵¹David ran and stood over him. He took hold of the Philistine's sword and drew it from the scabbard. After he killed him, he cut off his head with the sword.

When the Philistines saw that their hero was dead, they turned and ran. ⁵²Then the men of Israel and Judah surged forward with a shout and pursued the Philistines to the entrance of Gath*g* and to the gates of Ekron. Their dead were strewn along the Shaaraim road to Gath and Ekron. ⁵³When the Israelites returned from chasing the Philistines, they plundered their camp. ⁵⁴David took the Philistine's head and brought it to Jerusalem, and he put the Philistine's weapons in his own tent.

⁵⁵As Saul watched David going out to meet the Philistine, he said to Abner, commander of the army, "Abner, whose son is that young man?"

Abner replied, "As surely as you live, O king, I don't know."

⁵⁶The king said, "Find out whose son this young man is."

⁵⁷As soon as David returned from killing the Philistine, Abner took him and brought him before Saul, with David still holding the Philistine's head.

⁵⁸"Whose son are you, young man?" Saul asked him.

David said, "I am the son of your servant Jesse of Bethlehem."

Saul's Jealousy of David

18 After David had finished talking with Saul, Jonathan became one in spirit with David, and he loved him as himself. ²From that day Saul kept David with him and did not let him return to his father's house. ³And Jonathan made a covenant with David because he loved him as himself. ⁴Jonathan took off the robe he was wearing and gave it to David, along with his tunic, and even his sword, his bow and his belt.

⁵Whatever Saul sent him to do, David did it so successfully*a* that Saul gave him a high rank in the army. This pleased all the people, and Saul's officers as well.

⁶When the men were returning home after David had killed the Philistine, the women came out from all the towns of Israel to meet King Saul with singing and dancing, with joyful songs and with tambourines and lutes. ⁷As they danced, they sang:

"Saul has slain his thousands,
    and David his tens of thousands."

⁸Saul was very angry; this refrain galled him. "They

have credited David with tens of thousands," he thought, "but me with only thousands. What more can he get but the kingdom?" ⁹And from that time on Saul kept a jealous eye on David.

¹⁰The next day an evil*b* spirit from God came forcefully upon Saul. He was prophesying in his house, while David was playing the harp, as he usually did. Saul had a spear in his hand ¹¹and he hurled it, saying to himself, "I'll pin David to the wall." But David eluded him twice.

¹²Saul was afraid of David, because the Lord was with David but had left Saul. ¹³So he sent David away from him and gave him command over a thousand men, and David led the troops in their campaigns. ¹⁴In everything he did he had great success,*c* because the Lord was with him. ¹⁵When Saul saw how successful*d* he was, he was afraid of him. ¹⁶But all Israel and Judah loved David, because he led them in their campaigns.

18:12   An increasingly sharp contrast will be drawn between David and Saul in the following chapters, the reason for which is given here: the Lord was with David but had left Saul.

---

¹⁷Saul said to David, "Here is my older daughter Merab. I will give her to you in marriage; only serve me bravely and fight the battles of the Lord." For Saul said to himself, "I will not raise a hand against him. Let the Philistines do that!"

¹⁸But David said to Saul, "Who am I, and what is my family or my father's clan in Israel, that I should become the king's son-in-law?" ¹⁹So*e* when the time came for Merab, Saul's daughter, to be given to David, she was given in marriage to Adriel of Meholah.

²⁰Now Saul's daughter Michal was in love with David, and when they told Saul about it, he was pleased. ²¹"I will give her to him," he thought, "so that she may be a snare to him and so that the hand of the Philistines may be against him." So Saul said to David, "Now you have a second opportunity to become my son-in-law."

²²Then Saul ordered his attendants: "Speak to David privately and say, 'Look, the king is pleased with you, and his attendants all like you; now become his son-in-law.' "

²³They repeated these words to David. But David said, "Do you think it is a small matter to become the king's son-in-law? I'm only a poor man and little known."

²⁴When Saul's servants told him what David had said, ²⁵Saul replied, "Say to David, 'The king wants no other price for the bride than a hundred Philistine foreskins, to take revenge on his enemies.' " Saul's plan was to have David fall by the hands of the Philistines.

²⁶When the attendants told David these things, he was pleased to become the king's son-in-law. So before the allotted time elapsed, ²⁷David and his men went out and killed two hundred Philistines. He brought their foreskins and presented the full number to the

---

g 52 Some Septuagint manuscripts; Hebrew *a valley*   *a 5* Or *wisely*   *b 10* Or *injurious*   *c 14* Or *he was very wise*
d 15 Or *wise*   *e 19* Or *However,*

king so that he might become the king's son-in-law. Then Saul gave him his daughter Michal in marriage.

18:27   David's presentation of the fore-skins of his enemies to the king were proof that he had been in battle with, and killed, the numbers he claimed.

28When Saul realised that the LORD was with David and that his daughter Michal loved David, 29Saul became still more afraid of him, and he remained his enemy for the rest of his days.

30The Philistine commanders continued to go out to battle, and as often as they did, David met with more successf than the rest of Saul's officers, and his name became well known.

Saul Tries to Kill David

19 Saul told his son Jonathan and all the attend-ants to kill David. But Jonathan was very fond of David 2and warned him, "My father Saul is looking for a chance to kill you. Be on your guard tomorrow morning; go into hiding and stay there. 3I will go out and stand with my father in the field where you are. I'll speak to him about you and will tell you what I find out."

4Jonathan spoke well of David to Saul his father and said to him, "Let not the king do wrong to his servant David; he has not wronged you, and what he has done has benefited you greatly. 5He took his life in his hands when he killed the Philistine. The LORD won a great victory for all Israel, and you saw it and were glad. Why then would you do wrong to an innocent man like David by killing him for no reason?"

6Saul listened to Jonathan and took this oath: "As surely as the LORD lives, David will not be put to death."

7So Jonathan called David and told him the whole conversation. He brought him to Saul, and David was with Saul as before.

8Once more war broke out, and David went out and fought the Philistines. He struck them with such force that they fled before him.

9But an evila spirit from the LORD came upon Saul as he was sitting in his house with his spear in his hand. While David was playing the harp, 10Saul tried to pin him to the wall with his spear, but David eluded him as Saul drove the spear into the wall. That night David made good his escape.

11Saul sent men to David's house to watch it and to kill him in the morning. But Michal, David's wife, warned him, "If you don't run for your life tonight, tomorrow you'll be killed." 12So Michal let David down through a window, and he fled and escaped. 13Then Michal took an idolb and laid it on the bed, covering it with a garment and putting some goats' hair at the head.

14When Saul sent the men to capture David, Michal said, "He is ill."

15Then Saul sent the men back to see David and told them, "Bring him up to me in his bed so that I may kill him." 16But when the men entered, there was the idol in the bed, and at the head was some goats' hair.

17Saul said to Michal, "Why did you deceive me like this and send my enemy away so that he escaped?"

Michal told him, "He said to me, 'Let me get away. Why should I kill you?' "

18When David had fled and made his escape, he went to Samuel at Ramah and told him all that Saul had done to him. Then he and Samuel went to Naioth and stayed there. 19Word came to Saul: "David is in Naioth at Ramah"; 20so he sent men to capture him. But when they saw a group of prophets prophesying, with Samuel standing there as their leader, the Spirit of God came upon Saul's men and they also prophesied. 21Saul was told about it, and he sent more men, and they proph-esied too. Saul sent men a third time, and they also prophesied. 22Finally, he himself left for Ramah and went to the great cistern at Secu. And he asked, "Where are Samuel and David?"

"Over in Naioth at Ramah," they said.

23So Saul went to Naioth at Ramah. But the Spirit of God came even upon him, and he walked along proph-esying until he came to Naioth. 24He stripped off his robes and also prophesied in Samuel's presence. He lay that way all that day and night. This is why people say, "Is Saul also among the prophets?"

David and Jonathan

20 Then David fled from Naioth at Ramah and went to Jonathan and asked, "What have I done? What is my crime? How have I wronged your father, that he is trying to take my life?"

2"Never!" Jonathan replied. "You are not going to die! Look, my father doesn't do anything, great or small, without confiding in me. Why should he hide this from me? It's not so!"

3But David took an oath and said, "Your father knows very well that I have found favour in your eyes, and he has said to himself, 'Jonathan must not know this or he will be grieved.' Yet as surely as the LORD lives and as you live, there is only a step between me and death."

4Jonathan said to David, "Whatever you want me to do, I'll do for you."

5So David said, "Look, tomorrow is the New Moon festival, and I am supposed to dine with the king; but let me go and hide in the field until the evening of the day after tomorrow. 6If your father misses me at all, tell him, 'David earnestly asked my permission to hurry to Bethlehem, his home town, because an annual sacri-fice is being made there for his whole clan.' 7If he says, 'Very well,' then your servant is safe. But if he loses his temper, you can be sure that he is determined to harm me. 8As for you, show kindness to your servant, for you have brought him into a covenant with you before the LORD. If I am guilty, then kill me yourself! Why hand me over to your father?"

9"Never!" Jonathan said. "If I had the least inkling that my father was determined to harm you, wouldn't I tell you?"

---

f30 Or David acted more wisely   a9 Or injurious   b13 Hebrew teraphim; also in verse 16

¹⁰David asked, "Who will tell me if your father answers you harshly?"

¹¹"Come," Jonathan said, "let's go out into the field." So they went there together.

¹²Then Jonathan said to David: "By the LORD, the God of Israel, I will surely sound out my father by this time the day after tomorrow! If he is favourably disposed towards you, will I not send you word and let you know? ¹³But if my father is inclined to harm you, may the LORD deal with me, be it ever so severely, if I do not let you know and send you away safely. May the LORD be with you as he has been with my father. ¹⁴But show me unfailing kindness like that of the LORD as long as I live, so that I may not be killed, ¹⁵and do not ever cut off your kindness from my family — not even when the LORD has cut off every one of David's enemies from the face of the earth."

¹⁶So Jonathan made a covenant with the house of David, saying, "May the LORD call David's enemies to account." ¹⁷And Jonathan made David reaffirm his oath out of love for him, because he loved him as he loved himself.

¹⁸Then Jonathan said to David: "Tomorrow is the New Moon festival. You will be missed, because your seat will be empty. ¹⁹The day after tomorrow, towards evening, go to the place where you hid when this trouble began, and wait by the stone Ezel. ²⁰I will shoot three arrows to the side of it, as though I were shooting at a target. ²¹Then I will send a boy and say, 'Go, find the arrows.' If I say to him, 'Look, the arrows are on this side of you; bring them here,' then come, because, as surely as the LORD lives, you are safe; there is no danger. ²²But if I say to the boy, 'Look, the arrows are beyond you,' then you must go, because the LORD has sent you away. ²³And about the matter you and I discussed — remember, the LORD is witness between you and me for ever."

²⁴So David hid in the field, and when the New Moon festival came, the king sat down to eat. ²⁵He sat in his customary place by the wall, opposite Jonathan,ᵃ and Abner sat next to Saul, but David's place was empty. ²⁶Saul said nothing that day, for he thought, "Something must have happened to David to make him ceremonially unclean — surely he is unclean." ²⁷But the next day, the second day of the month, David's place was empty again. Then Saul said to his son Jonathan, "Why hasn't the son of Jesse come to the meal, either yesterday or today?"

²⁸Jonathan answered, "David earnestly asked me for permission to go to Bethlehem. ²⁹He said, 'Let me go, because our family is observing a sacrifice in the town and my brother has ordered me to be there. If I have found favour in your eyes, let me go to see my brothers.' That is why he has not come to the king's table."

³⁰Saul's anger flared up at Jonathan and he said to him, "You son of a perverse and rebellious woman! Don't I know that you have sided with the son of Jesse to your own shame and to the shame of the mother who bore you? ³¹As long as the son of Jesse lives on this earth, neither you nor your kingdom will be established. Now send and bring him to me, for he must die!"

³²"Why should he be put to death? What has he done?" Jonathan asked his father. ³³But Saul hurled his spear at him to kill him. Then Jonathan knew that his father intended to kill David.

³⁴Jonathan got up from the table in fierce anger; on that second day of the month he did not eat, because he was grieved at his father's shameful treatment of David.

³⁵In the morning Jonathan went out to the field for his meeting with David. He had a small boy with him, ³⁶and he said to the boy, "Run and find the arrows I shoot." As the boy ran, he shot an arrow beyond him. ³⁷When the boy came to the place where Jonathan's arrow had fallen, Jonathan called out after him, "Isn't the arrow beyond you?" ³⁸Then he shouted, "Hurry! Go quickly! Don't stop!" The boy picked up the arrow and returned to his master. ³⁹(The boy knew nothing of all this; only Jonathan and David knew.) ⁴⁰Then Jonathan gave his weapons to the boy and said, "Go, carry them back to town."

⁴¹After the boy had gone, David got up from the south side ˎof the stoneˎ and bowed down before Jonathan three times, with his face to the ground. Then they kissed each other and wept together — but David wept the most.

⁴²Jonathan said to David, "Go in peace, for we have sworn friendship with each other in the name of the LORD, saying, 'The LORD is witness between you and me, and between your descendants and my descendants for ever.'" Then David left, and Jonathan went back to the town.

David at Nob

21 David went to Nob, to Ahimelech the priest. Ahimelech trembled when he met him, and asked, "Why are you alone? Why is no-one with you?"

²David answered Ahimelech the priest, "The king charged me with a certain matter and said to me, 'No-one is to know anything about your mission and your instructions.' As for my men, I have told them to meet me at a certain place. ³Now then, what have you to hand? Give me five loaves of bread, or whatever you can find."

⁴But the priest answered David, "I don't have any ordinary bread to hand; however, there is some consecrated bread here — provided the men have kept themselves from women."

⁵David replied, "Indeed women have been kept from us, as usual wheneverᵃ I set out. The men's thingsᵇ are holy even on missions that are not holy. How much more so today!" ⁶So the priest gave him the consecrated bread, since there was no bread there except the bread of the Presence that had been removed from before the LORD and replaced by hot bread on the day it was taken away.

⁷Now one of Saul's servants was there that day, detained before the LORD; he was Doeg the Edomite, Saul's head shepherd.

⁸David asked Ahimelech, "Don't you have a spear or

ᵃ25 Septuagint; Hebrew *wall. Jonathan arose*   ᵃ5 Or *from us in the past few days since*   ᵇ5 Or *bodies* sword here? I haven't brought my sword or any other weapon, because the king's business was urgent."

⁹The priest replied, "The sword of Goliath the Philistine, whom you killed in the Valley of Elah, is here; it is wrapped in a cloth behind the ephod. If you want it, take it; there is no sword here but that one."

David said, "There is none like it; give it to me."

21:6 The bread of the Presence was holy, because it had been placed in the house of God as a cereal offering. Once it had been removed from the Lord's presence it was meant to be eaten only by the priests (Leviticus 24:9).

David at Gath

¹⁰That day David fled from Saul and went to Achish king of Gath. ¹¹But the servants of Achish said to him, "Isn't this David, the king of the land? Isn't he the one they sing about in their dances:

" 'Saul has slain his thousands,
    and David his tens of thousands'?"

¹²David took these words to heart and was very much afraid of Achish king of Gath. ¹³So he feigned insanity in their presence; and while he was in their hands he acted like a madman, making marks on the doors of the gate and letting saliva run down his beard.

¹⁴Achish said to his servants, "Look at the man! He is insane! Why bring him to me? ¹⁵Am I so short of madmen that you have to bring this fellow here to carry on like this in front of me? Must this man come into my house?"

David at Adullam and Mizpah

22 David left Gath and escaped to the cave of Adullam. When his brothers and his father's household heard about it, they went down to him there. ²All those who were in distress or in debt or discontented gathered round him, and he became their leader. About four hundred men were with him.

³From there David went to Mizpah in Moab and said to the king of Moab, "Would you let my father and mother come and stay with you until I learn what God will do for me?" ⁴So he left them with the king of Moab, and they stayed with him as long as David was in the stronghold.

⁵But the prophet Gad said to David, "Do not stay in the stronghold. Go into the land of Judah." So David left and went to the forest of Hereth.

Saul Kills the Priests of Nob

⁶Now Saul heard that David and his men had been discovered. And Saul, spear in hand, was seated under the tamarisk tree on the hill at Gibeah, with all his officials standing round him. ⁷Saul said to them, "Listen, men of Benjamin! Will the son of Jesse give all of you fields and vineyards? Will he make all of you commanders of thousands and commanders of hundreds?

⁸Is that why you have all conspired against me? No-one tells me when my son makes a covenant with the son of Jesse. None of you is concerned about me or tells me that my son has incited my servant to lie in wait for me, as he does today."

⁹But Doeg the Edomite, who was standing with Saul's officials, said, "I saw the son of Jesse come to Ahimelech son of Ahitub at Nob. ¹⁰Ahimelech enquired of the LORD for him; he also gave him provisions and the sword of Goliath the Philistine."

¹¹Then the king sent for the priest Ahimelech son of Ahitub and his father's whole family, who were the priests at Nob, and they all came to the king. ¹²Saul said, "Listen now, son of Ahitub."

"Yes, my lord," he answered.

¹³Saul said to him, "Why have you conspired against me, you and the son of Jesse, giving him bread and a sword and enquiring of God for him, so that he has rebelled against me and lies in wait for me, as he does today?"

¹⁴Ahimelech answered the king, "Who of all your servants is as loyal as David, the king's son-in-law, captain of your bodyguard and highly respected in your household? ¹⁵Was that day the first time I enquired of God for him? Of course not! Let not the king accuse your servant or any of his father's family, for your servant knows nothing at all about this whole affair."

¹⁶But the king said, "You shall surely die, Ahimelech, you and your father's whole family."

¹⁷Then the king ordered the guards at his side: "Turn and kill the priests of the LORD, because they too have sided with David. They knew he was fleeing, yet they did not tell me."

But the king's officials were not willing to raise a hand to strike the priests of the LORD.

¹⁸The king then ordered Doeg, "You turn and strike down the priests." So Doeg the Edomite turned and struck them down. That day he killed eighty-five men who wore the linen ephod. ¹⁹He also put to the sword Nob, the town of the priests, with its men and women, its children and infants, and its cattle, donkeys and sheep.

22:20 Abiathar was the sole survivor of Saul's slaughter of the priests at Nob. He went on to serve David throughout his reign. A descendant of Eli, he eventually fell from grace during the reign of Solomon, and so fulfilled the word of the Lord against the house of Eli (2:31–36; 1 Kings 2:26,27).

---

²⁰But Abiathar, son of Ahimelech son of Ahitub, escaped and fled to join David. ²¹He told David that Saul had killed the priests of the LORD. ²²Then David said to Abiathar: "That day, when Doeg the Edomite was there, I knew he would be sure to tell Saul. I am responsible for the death of your father's whole family. ²³Stay with me; don't be afraid; the man who is seeking your life is seeking mine also. You will be safe with me."

David Saves Keilah

23 When David was told, "Look, the Philistines are fighting against Keilah and are looting the threshing-floors," ²he enquired of the LORD, saying, "Shall I go and attack these Philistines?"

The LORD answered him, "Go, attack the Philistines and save Keilah."

³But David's men said to him, "Here in Judah we are afraid. How much more, then, if we go to Keilah against the Philistine forces!"

⁴Once again David enquired of the LORD, and the LORD answered him, "Go down to Keilah, for I am going to give the Philistines into your hand." ⁵So David and his men went to Keilah, fought the Philistines and carried off their livestock. He inflicted heavy losses on the Philistines and saved the people of Keilah. ⁶(Now Abiathar son of Ahimelech had brought the ephod down with him when he fled to David at Keilah.)

Saul Pursues David

⁷Saul was told that David had gone to Keilah, and he said, "God has handed him over to me, for David has imprisoned himself by entering a town with gates and bars." ⁸And Saul called up all his forces for battle, to go down to Keilah to besiege David and his men.

⁹When David learned that Saul was plotting against him, he said to Abiathar the priest, "Bring the ephod." ¹⁰David said, "O LORD, God of Israel, your servant has heard definitely that Saul plans to come to Keilah and destroy the town on account of me. ¹¹Will the citizens of Keilah surrender me to him? Will Saul come down, as your servant has heard? O LORD, God of Israel, tell your servant."

And the LORD said, "He will."

¹²Again David asked, "Will the citizens of Keilah surrender me and my men to Saul?"

And the LORD said, "They will."

¹³So David and his men, about six hundred in number, left Keilah and kept moving from place to place. When Saul was told that David had escaped from Keilah, he did not go there.

¹⁴David stayed in the desert strongholds and in the hills of the Desert of Ziph. Day after day Saul searched for him, but God did not give David into his hands.

¹⁵While David was at Horesh in the Desert of Ziph, he learned that Saul had come out to take his life. ¹⁶And Saul's son Jonathan went to David at Horesh and helped him to find strength in God. ¹⁷"Don't be afraid," he said. "My father Saul will not lay a hand on you. You shall be king over Israel, and I will be second to you. Even my father Saul knows this." ¹⁸The two of them made a covenant before the LORD. Then Jonathan went home, but David remained at Horesh.

¹⁹The Ziphites went up to Saul at Gibeah and said, "Is not David hiding among us in the strongholds at Horesh, on the hill of Hakilah, south of Jeshimon? ²⁰Now, O king, come down whenever it pleases you to do so, and we will be responsible for handing him over to the king."

²¹Saul replied, "The LORD bless you for your concern for me. ²²Go and make further preparation. Find out where David usually goes and who has seen him there. They tell me he is very crafty. ²³Find out about all the hiding-places he uses and come back to me with definite information.ᵃ Then I will go with you; if he is in the area, I will track him down among all the clans of Judah."

²⁴So they set out and went to Ziph ahead of Saul. Now David and his men were in the Desert of Maon, in the Arabah south of Jeshimon. ²⁵Saul and his men began the search, and when David was told about it, he went down to the rock and stayed in the Desert of Maon. When Saul heard this, he went into the Desert of Maon in pursuit of David.

²⁶Saul was going along one side of the mountain, and David and his men were on the other side, hurrying to get away from Saul. As Saul and his forces were closing in on David and his men to capture them, ²⁷a messenger came to Saul, saying, "Come quickly! The Philistines are raiding the land." ²⁸Then Saul broke off his pursuit of David and went to meet the Philistines. That is why they call this place Sela Hammahlekoth.ᵇ ²⁹And David went up from there and lived in the strongholds of En Gedi.

David Spares Saul's Life

24 After Saul returned from pursuing the Philistines, he was told, "David is in the Desert of En Gedi." ²So Saul took three thousand chosen men from all Israel and set out to look for David and his men near the Crags of the Wild Goats.

³He came to the sheep pens along the way; a cave was there, and Saul went in to relieve himself. David and his men were far back in the cave. ⁴The men said, "This is the day the LORD spoke of when he saidᵃ to you, 'I will give your enemy into your hands for you to deal with as you wish.'" Then David crept up unnoticed and cut off a corner of Saul's robe.

⁵Afterwards, David was conscience-stricken for having cut off a corner of his robe. ⁶He said to his men, "The LORD forbid that I should do such a thing to my master, the LORD's anointed, or lift my hand against him; for he is the anointed of the LORD." ⁷With these words David rebuked his men and did not allow them to attack Saul. And Saul left the cave and went his way.

24:5   To have harmed Saul would have laid David open to God's vengeance because Saul was the Lord's anointed. David recognized this and only cut Saul's robe. But such a humiliating action ought not to have been taken against the one chosen by God to be king. David realized this and was conscience-stricken as a result.

---

⁸Then David went out of the cave and called out to Saul, "My lord the king!" When Saul looked behind him, David bowed down and prostrated himself with his face to the ground. ⁹He said to Saul, "Why do you listen when men say, 'David is bent on harming you'? ¹⁰This day you have seen with your own eyes how the

ᵃ23 Or me at Nacon   ᵇ28 Sela Hammahlekoth means rock of parting.   ᵃ4 Or "Today the LORD is saying

LORD gave you into my hands in the cave. Some urged me to kill you, but I spared you; I said, 'I will not lift my hand against my master, because he is the LORD's anointed.' [11]See, my father, look at this piece of your robe in my hand! I cut off the corner of your robe but did not kill you. Now understand and recognise that I am not guilty of wrongdoing or rebellion. I have not wronged you, but you are hunting me down to take my life. [12]May the LORD judge between you and me. And may the LORD avenge the wrongs you have done to me, but my hand will not touch you. [13]As the old saying goes, 'From evildoers come evil deeds,' so my hand will not touch you.

[14]"Against whom has the king of Israel come out? Whom are you pursuing? A dead dog? A flea? [15]May the LORD be our judge and decide between us. May he consider my cause and uphold it; may he vindicate me by delivering me from your hand."

[16]When David finished saying this, Saul asked, "Is that your voice, David my son?" And he wept aloud. [17]"You are more righteous than I," he said. "You have treated me well, but I have treated you badly. [18]You have just now told me of the good you did to me; the LORD gave me into your hands, but you did not kill me. [19]When a man finds his enemy, does he let him get away unharmed? May the LORD reward you well for the way you treated me today. [20]I know that you will surely be king and that the kingdom of Israel will be established in your hands. [21]Now swear to me by the LORD that you will not cut off my descendants or wipe out my name from my father's family."

[22]So David gave his oath to Saul. Then Saul returned home, but David and his men went up to the stronghold.

David, Nabal and Abigail

25 Now Samuel died, and all Israel assembled and mourned for him; and they buried him at his home in Ramah.

Then David moved down into the Desert of Maon. [a] [2]A certain man in Maon, who had property there at Carmel, was very wealthy. He had a thousand goats and three thousand sheep, which he was shearing in Carmel. [3]His name was Nabal and his wife's name was Abigail. She was an intelligent and beautiful woman, but her husband, a Calebite, was surly and mean in his dealings.

[4]While David was in the desert, he heard that Nabal was shearing sheep. [5]So he sent ten young men and said to them, "Go up to Nabal at Carmel and greet him in my name. [6]Say to him: 'Long life to you! Good health to you and your household! And good health to all that is yours!

[7]" 'Now I hear that it is sheep-shearing time. When your shepherds were with us, we did not ill-treat them, and the whole time they were at Carmel nothing of theirs was missing. [8]Ask your own servants and they will tell you. Therefore be favourable towards my young men, since we come at a festive time. Please give

your servants and your son David whatever you can find for them.' "

[9]When David's men arrived, they gave Nabal this message in David's name. Then they waited.

[10]Nabal answered David's servants, "Who is this David? Who is this son of Jesse? Many servants are breaking away from their masters these days. [11]Why should I take my bread and water, and the meat I have slaughtered for my shearers, and give it to men coming from who knows where?"

[12]David's men turned round and went back. When they arrived, they reported every word. [13]David said to his men, "Put on your swords!" So they put on their swords, and David put on his. About four hundred men went up with David, while two hundred stayed with the supplies.

[14]One of the servants told Nabal's wife Abigail: "David sent messengers from the desert to give our master his greetings, but he hurled insults at them. [15]Yet these men were very good to us. They did not ill-treat us, and the whole time we were out in the fields near them nothing was missing. [16]Night and day they were a wall around us all the time we were herding our sheep near them. [17]Now think it over and see what you can do, because disaster is hanging over our master and his whole household. He is such a wicked man that no-one can talk to him."

[18]Abigail lost no time. She took two hundred loaves of bread, two skins of wine, five dressed sheep, five seahs[b] of roasted grain, a hundred cakes of raisins and two hundred cakes of pressed figs, and loaded them on donkeys. [19]Then she told her servants, "Go on ahead; I'll follow you." But she did not tell her husband Nabal.

[20]As she came riding her donkey into a mountain ravine, there were David and his men descending towards her, and she met them. [21]David had just said, "It's been useless—all my watching over this fellow's property in the desert so that nothing of his was missing. He has paid me back evil for good. [22]May God deal with David,[c] be it ever so severely, if by morning I leave alive one male of all who belong to him!"

[23]When Abigail saw David, she quickly got off her donkey and bowed down before David with her face to the ground. [24]She fell at his feet and said: "My lord, let the blame be on me alone. Please let your servant speak to you; hear what your servant has to say. [25]May my lord pay no attention to that wicked man Nabal. He is just like his name—his name is Fool, and folly goes with him. But as for me, your servant, I did not see the men my master sent.

[26]"Now since the LORD has kept you, my master, from bloodshed and from avenging yourself with your own hands, as surely as the LORD lives and as you live, may your enemies and all who intend to harm my master be like Nabal. [27]And let this gift, which your servant has brought to my master, be given to the men who follow you. [28]Please forgive your servant's offence, for the LORD will certainly make a lasting dynasty for my master, because he fights the LORD's battles. Let no wrongdoing be found in you as long as you live. [29]Even though someone is pursuing you to take your life, the

---

[a]1 Some Septuagint manuscripts; Hebrew *Paran*   [b]18 That is, probably about a bushel (about 37 litres)
[c]22 Some Septuagint manuscripts; Hebrew *with David's enemies*

life of my master will be bound securely in the bundle of the living by the LORD your God. But the lives of your enemies he will hurl away as from the pocket of a sling. 30When the LORD has done for my master every good thing he promised concerning him and has appointed him leader over Israel, 31my master will not have on his conscience the staggering burden of needless bloodshed or of having avenged himself. And when the LORD has brought my master success, remember your servant."

32David said to Abigail, "Praise be to the LORD, the God of Israel, who has sent you today to meet me. 33May you be blessed for your good judgment and for keeping me from bloodshed this day and from avenging myself with my own hands. 34Otherwise, as surely as the LORD, the God of Israel, lives, who has kept me from harming you, if you had not come quickly to meet me, not one male belonging to Nabal would have been left alive by daybreak."

35Then David accepted from her hand what she had brought to him and said, "Go home in peace. I have heard your words and granted your request."

36When Abigail went to Nabal, he was in the house holding a banquet like that of a king. He was in high spirits and very drunk. So she told him nothing until daybreak. 37Then in the morning, when Nabal was sober, his wife told him all these things, and his heart failed him and he became like a stone. 38About ten days later, the LORD struck Nabal and he died.

39When David heard that Nabal was dead, he said, "Praise be to the LORD, who has upheld my cause against Nabal for treating me with contempt. He has kept his servant from doing wrong and has brought Nabal's wrongdoing down on his own head."

Then David sent word to Abigail, asking her to become his wife. 40His servants went to Carmel and said to Abigail, "David has sent us to you to take you to become his wife."

41She bowed down with her face to the ground and said, "Here is your maidservant, ready to serve you and wash the feet of my master's servants." 42Abigail quickly got on a donkey and, attended by her five maids, went with David's messengers and became his wife. 43David had also married Ahinoam of Jezreel, and they both were his wives. 44But Saul had given his daughter Michal, David's wife, to Paltiel[d] son of Laish, who was from Gallim.

25:43 At this stage in Israel's history, the practice of a man having more than one wife at one time, seems to have been considered acceptable. It was used by kings to gain political and economic advantage, despite the warning against it in Deuteronomy 17:17.

David Again Spares Saul's Life

26 The Ziphites went to Saul at Gibeah and said, "Is not David hiding on the hill of Hakilah, which faces Jeshimon?"

2So Saul went down to the Desert of Ziph, with his three thousand chosen men of Israel, to search there for David. 3Saul made his camp beside the road on the hill of Hakilah facing Jeshimon, but David stayed in the desert. When he saw that Saul had followed him there, 4he sent out scouts and learned that Saul had definitely arrived.[a]

5Then David set out and went to the place where Saul had camped. He saw where Saul and Abner son of Ner, the commander of the army, had lain down. Saul was lying inside the camp, with the army encamped around him.

6David then asked Ahimelech the Hittite and Abishai son of Zeruiah, Joab's brother, "Who will go down into the camp with me to Saul?"

"I'll go with you," said Abishai.

7So David and Abishai went to the army by night, and there was Saul, lying asleep inside the camp with his spear stuck in the ground near his head. Abner and the soldiers were lying round him.

8Abishai said to David, "Today God has given your enemy into your hands. Now let me pin him to the ground with one thrust of my spear; I won't strike him twice."

9But David said to Abishai, "Don't destroy him! Who can lay a hand on the LORD's anointed and be guiltless? 10As surely as the LORD lives," he said, "the LORD himself will strike him; either his time will come and he will die, or he will go into battle and perish. 11But the LORD forbid that I should lay a hand on the LORD's anointed. Now get the spear and water jug that are near his head, and let's go."

12So David took the spear and water jug near Saul's head, and they left. No-one saw or knew about it, nor did anyone wake up. They were all sleeping, because the LORD had put them into a deep sleep.

13Then David crossed over to the other side and stood on top of the hill some distance away; there was a wide space between them. 14He called out to the army and to Abner son of Ner, "Aren't you going to answer me, Abner?"

Abner replied, "Who are you who calls to the king?"

15David said, "You're a man, aren't you? And who is like you in Israel? Why didn't you guard your lord the king? Someone came to destroy your lord the king. 16What you have done is not good. As surely as the LORD lives, you and your men deserve to die, because you did not guard your master, the LORD's anointed. Look around you. Where are the king's spear and water jug that were near his head?"

17Saul recognised David's voice and said, "Is that your voice, David my son?"

David replied, "Yes it is, my lord the king." 18And he added, "Why is my lord pursuing his servant? What have I done, and what wrong am I guilty of? 19Now let my lord the king listen to his servant's words. If the LORD has incited you against me, then may he accept an offering. If, however, men have done it, may they be cursed before the LORD! They have now driven me from my share in the LORD's inheritance and have said, 'Go, serve other gods.' 20Now do not let my blood fall to the ground far from the presence of the LORD. The

---

d44 Hebrew Palti, a variant of Paltiel   *a4 Or had come to Nacon* king of Israel has come out to look for a flea—as one hunts a partridge in the mountains."

21Then Saul said, "I have sinned. Come back, David my son. Because you considered my life precious today, I will not try to harm you again. Surely I have acted like a fool and have erred greatly."

22"Here is the king's spear," David answered. "Let one of your young men come over and get it. 23The LORD rewards every man for his righteousness and faithfulness. The LORD gave you into my hands today, but I would not lay a hand on the LORD's anointed. 24As surely as I valued your life today, so may the LORD value my life and deliver me from all trouble."

25Then Saul said to David, "May you be blessed, my son David; you will do great things and surely triumph."

So David went on his way, and Saul returned home.

David Among the Philistines

27 But David thought to himself, "One of these days I shall be destroyed by the hand of Saul. The best thing I can do is to escape to the land of the Philistines. Then Saul will give up searching for me anywhere in Israel, and I will slip out of his hand."

2So David and the six hundred men with him left and went over to Achish son of Maoch king of Gath. 3David and his men settled in Gath with Achish. Each man had his family with him, and David had his two wives: Ahinoam of Jezreel and Abigail of Carmel, the widow of Nabal. 4When Saul was told that David had fled to Gath, he no longer searched for him.

5Then David said to Achish, "If I have found favour in your eyes, let a place be assigned to me in one of the country towns, that I may live there. Why should your servant live in the royal city with you?"

6So on that day Achish gave him Ziklag, and it has belonged to the kings of Judah ever since. 7David lived in Philistine territory for a year and four months.

8Now David and his men went up and raided the Geshurites, the Girzites and the Amalekites. (From ancient times these peoples had lived in the land extending to Shur and Egypt.) 9Whenever David attacked an area, he did not leave a man or woman alive, but took sheep and cattle, donkeys and camels, and clothes. Then he returned to Achish.

27:8 The Philistines trusted that David was on their side to fight against his own people. In fact, he and his men raided various enemies of Israel but pretended that they were attacking their own people. In this way David kept in favour with the Philistines, and at the same time began the task of subduing Israel's neighbours, a job he would complete when he was king.

10When Achish asked, "Where did you go raiding today?" David would say, "Against the Negev of Judah" or "Against the Negev of Jerahmeel" or "Against the Negev of the Kenites." 11He did not leave a man or

woman alive to be brought to Gath, for he thought, "They might inform on us and say, 'This is what David did.' " And such was his practice as long as he lived in Philistine territory. 12Achish trusted David and said to himself, "He has become so odious to his people, the Israelites, that he will be my servant for ever."

Saul and the Witch of Endor

28 In those days the Philistines gathered their forces to fight against Israel. Achish said to David, "You must understand that you and your men will accompany me in the army."

2David said, "Then you will see for yourself what your servant can do."

Achish replied, "Very well, I will make you my body-guard for life."

3Now Samuel was dead, and all Israel had mourned for him and buried him in his own town of Ramah. Saul had expelled the mediums and spiritists from the land.

4The Philistines assembled and came and set up camp at Shunem, while Saul gathered all the Israelites and set up camp at Gilboa. 5When Saul saw the Philistine army, he was afraid; terror filled his heart. 6He enquired of the LORD, but the LORD did not answer him by dreams or Urim or prophets. 7Saul then said to his attendants, "Find me a woman who is a medium, so that I may go and enquire of her."

"There is one in Endor," they said.

28:4 Saul was terrified by the Philistine army, and wanted to seek God's guidance. The approved methods of discovering God's will: dreams, casting lots, and prophets, all provided no answer. So Saul turned to a medium, something which was forbidden by God, along with all occult practices (Deuteronomy 18:9–13).

8So Saul disguised himself, putting on other clothes, and at night he and two men went to the woman. "Consult a spirit for me," he said, "and bring up for me the one I name."

9But the woman said to him, "Surely you know what Saul has done. He has cut off the mediums and spiritists from the land. Why have you set a trap for my life to bring about my death?"

10Saul swore to her by the LORD, "As surely as the LORD lives, you will not be punished for this."

11Then the woman asked, "Whom shall I bring up for you?"

"Bring up Samuel," he said.

12When the woman saw Samuel, she cried out at the top of her voice and said to Saul, "Why have you deceived me? You are Saul!"

13The king said to her, "Don't be afraid. What do you see?"

The woman said, "I see a spirit a coming up out of the ground."

14"What does he look like?" he asked.

"An old man wearing a robe is coming up," she said.

a 13 Or see spirits; or see gods

Then Saul knew it was Samuel, and he bowed down and prostrated himself with his face to the ground. [15]Samuel said to Saul, "Why have you disturbed me by bringing me up?"

"I am in great distress," Saul said. "The Philistines are fighting against me, and God has turned away from me. He no longer answers me, either by prophets or by dreams. So I have called on you to tell me what to do."

[16]Samuel said, "Why do you consult me, now that the LORD has turned away from you and become your enemy? [17]The LORD has done what he predicted through me. The LORD has torn the kingdom out of your hands and given it to one of your neighbours — to David. [18]Because you did not obey the LORD or carry out his fierce wrath against the Amalekites, the LORD has done this to you today. [19]The LORD will hand over both Israel and you to the Philistines, and tomorrow you and your sons will be with me. The LORD will also hand over the army of Israel to the Philistines."

[20]Immediately Saul fell full length on the ground, filled with fear because of Samuel's words. His strength was gone, for he had eaten nothing all that day and night.

[21]When the woman came to Saul and saw that he was greatly shaken, she said, "Look, your maidservant has obeyed you. I took my life in my hands and did what you told me to do. [22]Now please listen to your servant and let me give you some food so that you may eat and have the strength to go on your way."

[23]He refused and said, "I will not eat."

But his men joined the woman in urging him, and he listened to them. He got up from the ground and sat on the couch.

[24]The woman had a fattened calf at the house, which she slaughtered at once. She took some flour, kneaded it and baked bread without yeast. [25]Then she set it before Saul and his men, and they ate. That same night they got up and left.

Achish Sends David Back to Ziklag

29 The Philistines gathered all their forces at Aphek, and Israel camped by the spring in Jezreel. [2]As the Philistine rulers marched with their units of hundreds and thousands, David and his men were marching at the rear with Achish. [3]The commanders of the Philistines asked, "What about these Hebrews?"

Achish replied, "Is this not David, who was an officer of Saul king of Israel? He has already been with me for over a year, and from the day he left Saul until now, I have found no fault in him."

[4]But the Philistine commanders were angry with him and said, "Send the man back, that he may return to the place you assigned him. He must not go with us into battle, or he will turn against us during the fighting. How better could he regain his master's favour than by taking the heads of our own men? [5]Isn't this the David they sang about in their dances:

" 'Saul has slain his thousands,
    and David his tens of thousands'?"

[6]So Achish called David and said to him, "As surely as the LORD lives, you have been reliable, and I would be pleased to have you serve with me in the army. From the day you came to me until now, I have found no fault in you, but the rulers don't approve of you. [7]Turn back and go in peace; do nothing to displease the Philistine rulers."

[8]"But what have I done?" asked David. "What have you found against your servant from the day I came to you until now? Why can't I go and fight against the enemies of my lord the king?"

[9]Achish answered, "I know that you have been as pleasing in my eyes as an angel of God; nevertheless, the Philistine commanders have said, 'He must not go up with us into battle.' [10]Now get up early, along with your master's servants who have come with you, and leave in the morning as soon as it is light."

[11]So David and his men got up early in the morning to go back to the land of the Philistines, and the Philistines went up to Jezreel.

David Destroys the Amalekites

30 David and his men reached Ziklag on the third day. Now the Amalekites had raided the Negev and Ziklag. They had attacked Ziklag and burned it, [2]and had taken captive the women and all who were in it, both young and old. They killed none of them, but carried them off as they went on their way.

[3]When David and his men came to Ziklag, they found it destroyed by fire and their wives and sons and daughters taken captive. [4]So David and his men wept aloud until they had no strength left to weep. [5]David's two wives had been captured — Ahinoam of Jezreel and Abigail, the widow of Nabal of Carmel. [6]David was greatly distressed because the men were talking of stoning him; each one was bitter in spirit because of his sons and daughters. But David found strength in the LORD his God.

[7]Then David said to Abiathar the priest, the son of Ahimelech, "Bring me the ephod." Abiathar brought it to him, [8]and David enquired of the LORD, "Shall I pursue this raiding party? Will I overtake them?"

"Pursue them," he answered. "You will certainly overtake them and succeed in the rescue."

[9]David and the six hundred men with him came to the Besor Ravine, where some stayed behind, [10]for two hundred men were too exhausted to cross the ravine. But David and four hundred men continued the pursuit.

[11]They found an Egyptian in a field and brought him to David. They gave him water to drink and food to eat — [12]part of a cake of pressed figs and two cakes of raisins. He ate and was revived, for he had not eaten any food or drunk any water for three days and three nights.

[13]David asked him, "To whom do you belong, and where do you come from?"

He said, "I am an Egyptian, the slave of an Amalekite. My master abandoned me when I became ill three days ago. [14]We raided the Negev of the Kerethites and the territory belonging to Judah and the Negev of Caleb. And we burned Ziklag."

[15]David asked him, "Can you lead me down to this raiding party?"

He answered, "Swear to me before God that you will not kill me or hand me over to my master, and I will take you down to them."

[16]He led David down, and there they were, scattered over the countryside, eating, drinking and revelling because of the great amount of plunder they had taken from the land of the Philistines and from Judah. [17]David fought them from dusk until the evening of the next day, and none of them got away, except four hundred young men who rode off on camels and fled. [18]David recovered everything the Amalekites had taken, including his two wives. [19]Nothing was missing: young or old, boy or girl, plunder or anything else they had taken. David brought everything back. [20]He took all the flocks and herds, and his men drove them ahead of the other livestock, saying, "This is David's plunder."

[21]Then David came to the two hundred men who had been too exhausted to follow him and who were left behind at the Besor Ravine. They came out to meet David and the people with him. As David and his men approached, he greeted them. [22]But all the evil men and troublemakers among David's followers said, "Because they did not go out with us, we will not share with them the plunder we recovered. However, each man may take his wife and children and go."

[23]David replied, "No, my brothers, you must not do that with what the LORD has given us. He has protected us and handed over to us the forces that came against us. [24]Who will listen to what you say? The share of the man who stayed with the supplies is to be the same as that of him who went down to the battle. All shall share alike." [25]David made this a statute and ordinance for Israel from that day to this.

[26]When David arrived in Ziklag, he sent some of the plunder to the elders of Judah, who were his friends, saying, "Here is a present for you from the plunder of the LORD's enemies."

[27]He sent it to those who were in Bethel, Ramoth Negev and Jattir; [28]to those in Aroer, Siphmoth, Eshtemoa [29]and Racal; to those in the towns of the Jerahmeelites and the Kenites; [30]to those in Hormah, Bor Ashan, Athach [31]and Hebron; and to those in all the other places where David and his men had roamed.

Saul Takes His Life

31 Now the Philistines fought against Israel; the Israelites fled before them, and many fell slain on Mount Gilboa. [2]The Philistines pressed hard after Saul and his sons, and they killed his sons Jonathan, Abinadab and Malki-Shua. [3]The fighting grew fierce around Saul, and when the archers overtook him, they wounded him critically.

[4]Saul said to his armour-bearer, "Draw your sword and run me through, or these uncircumcised fellows will come and run me through and abuse me."

But the armour-bearer was terrified and would not do it; so Saul took his own sword and fell on it. [5]When the armour-bearer saw that Saul was dead, he too fell on his sword and died with him. [6]So Saul and his three sons and his armour-bearer and all his men died together that same day.

[7]When the Israelites along the valley and those across the Jordan saw that the Israelite army had fled and that Saul and his sons had died, they abandoned their towns and fled. And the Philistines came and occupied them.

[8]The next day, when the Philistines came to strip the dead, they found Saul and his three sons fallen on Mount Gilboa. [9]They cut off his head and stripped off his armour, and they sent messengers throughout the land of the Philistines to proclaim the news in the temple of their idols and among their people. [10]They put his armour in the temple of the Ashtoreths and fastened his body to the wall of Beth Shan.

[11]When the people of Jabesh Gilead heard of what the Philistines had done to Saul, [12]all their valiant men journeyed through the night to Beth Shan. They took down the bodies of Saul and his sons from the wall of Beth Shan and went to Jabesh, where they burned them. [13]Then they took their bones and buried them under a tamarisk tree at Jabesh, and they fasted seven days.

31:11 Saul had saved Jabesh Gilead when he first became king (1 Samuel 11:1–11). It would have been a public disgrace for the bodies to have been left. So the people wanted to give Saul a decent burial.

---

2 Samuel

Continuing the Story

The book of 2 Samuel takes up the account of Israel's history from the point at which 1 Samuel left off, with David poised ready to assume the throne following the death of Saul. It is widely agreed that these two books were written originally as one work, bearing the name of Samuel, and were later divided. This accounts for the strange way in which 2 Samuel bears the name of a prophet who appears to have nothing to do with the book.

Major Events

The book is concerned with the events of David's reign from the time he heard of Saul's death until the time near the end of his life when he purchased the site for the Jerusalem temple, which his son Solomon was to build. A number of major events within the history of God's people occurred during the reign of David. Under his leadership the kingdoms of Israel and Judah were brought together to form one nation and Jerusalem, the city of David, became its capital. The ark of the covenant was brought to Jerusalem with great rejoicing. David's army defeated the Philistines, as well as subduing other troublesome neighbours. The resulting peace enabled the expansion of trade that produced Israel's golden age, which continued through the reign of Solomon, David's son and successor. All this reflected the blessing of God on David, his chosen king, who remained faithful to God throughout the years of his long reign.

Only Human

The book makes no attempt to hide the fact that Israel's ideal ruler was less than perfect. The account of David's adultery with Bathsheba, followed by the murder of her husband, Uriah, makes it very clear that David was as capable of sin as any other person. However, in response to the prophet Nathan's direct accusations, David confessed his sin and accepted the punishment sent by God. Such honesty before God indicates what a great man of faith David was, even when he had failed. David is also shown to be a clever military leader and shrewd politician who could be ruthless, but who could also show compassion when the situation needed it. The quality of the man portrayed in this book is such that later, when the Israelites were suffering times of national distress, they looked for a deliverer who would resemble this great man of God.

Always Faithful

The book also recounts the difficulties faced by David from within his own nation and family. The main one of these was the rebellion led by his own son, Absalom, which is recorded at some length. Through all the difficulties of his reign, however, David is shown to be faithful to God. Despite attempts to overthrow David, God continued to establish his reign.

The Promised Messiah

The most important passage of the book is contained within chapter seven, and it records God's great promise to David through the prophet Nathan. The promise to establish David's rule for ever would ultimately lead on to the Jewish hope of a Messiah who would come from the house of David. It is this hope which Christians understand to have been fulfilled in Jesus Christ.

God is in Control

As with 1 Samuel, it is important to notice God's activity, which underlines the events taking place in the history of his people. God is shown to be in ultimate control throughout the book, and we see him working out his purposes through a king who, despite his failures and the various difficulties he was faced with, remained faithful throughout the many years of his long reign over the people of God.

David Hears of Saul's Death

1 After the death of Saul, David returned from defeating the Amalekites and stayed in Ziklag two days. 2On the third day a man arrived from Saul's camp, with his clothes torn and with dust on his head. When he came to David, he fell to the ground to pay him honour.

3"Where have you come from?" David asked him.

He answered, "I have escaped from the Israelite camp."

4"What happened?" David asked. "Tell me."

He said, "The men fled from the battle. Many of them fell and died. And Saul and his son Jonathan are dead."

5Then David said to the young man who brought him the report, "How do you know that Saul and his son Jonathan are dead?"

6"I happened to be on Mount Gilboa," the young man said, "and there was Saul, leaning on his spear, with the chariots and riders almost upon him. 7When he turned round and saw me, he called out to me, and I said, 'What can I do?'

8"He asked me, 'Who are you?'

" 'An Amalekite,' I answered.

9"Then he said to me, 'Stand over me and kill me! I am in the throes of death, but I'm still alive.'

10"So I stood over him and killed him, because I knew that after he had fallen he could not survive. And I took the crown that was on his head and the band on his arm and have brought them here to my lord."

11Then David and all the men with him took hold of their clothes and tore them. 12They mourned and wept and fasted till evening for Saul and his son Jonathan, and for the army of the LORD and the house of Israel, because they had fallen by the sword.

13David said to the young man who brought him the report, "Where are you from?"

"I am the son of an alien, an Amalekite," he answered.

14David asked him, "Why were you not afraid to lift your hand to destroy the LORD's anointed?"

15Then David called one of his men and said, "Go, strike him down!" So he struck him down, and he died. 16For David had said to him, "Your blood be on your own head. Your own mouth testified against you when you said, 'I killed the LORD's anointed.' "

David's Lament for Saul and Jonathan

17David took up this lament concerning Saul and his son Jonathan, 18and ordered that the men of Judah be taught this lament of the bow (it is written in the Book of Jashar):

19"Your glory, O Israel, lies slain on your
        heights.
    How the mighty have fallen!

20"Tell it not in Gath,
        proclaim it not in the streets of Ashkelon,
    lest the daughters of the Philistines be glad,
    lest the daughters of the uncircumcised
        rejoice.

21"O mountains of Gilboa,
        may you have neither dew nor rain,
        nor fields that yield offerings ˌof grainˌ.
    For there the shield of the mighty was
        defiled,
        the shield of Saul—no longer rubbed with
        oil.

22From the blood of the slain,
        from the flesh of the mighty,

the bow of Jonathan did not turn back,
  the sword of Saul did not return
    unsatisfied.

²³"Saul and Jonathan—
    in life they were loved and gracious,
    and in death they were not parted.
  They were swifter than eagles,
    they were stronger than lions.

²⁴"O daughters of Israel,
    weep for Saul,
  who clothed you in scarlet and finery,
    who adorned your garments with
      ornaments of gold.

²⁵"How the mighty have fallen in battle!
    Jonathan lies slain on your heights.
²⁶I grieve for you, Jonathan my brother;
    you were very dear to me.
  Your love for me was wonderful,
    more wonderful than that of women.

²⁷"How the mighty have fallen!
    The weapons of war have perished!"

David Anointed King Over Judah

2 In the course of time, David enquired of the LORD. "Shall I go up to one of the towns of Judah?" he asked.

The LORD said, "Go up."

David asked, "Where shall I go?"

"To Hebron," the LORD answered.

²So David went up there with his two wives, Ahinoam of Jezreel and Abigail, the widow of Nabal of Carmel. ³David also took the men who were with him, each with his family, and they settled in Hebron and its towns. ⁴Then the men of Judah came to Hebron and there they anointed David king over the house of Judah.

When David was told that it was the men of Jabesh Gilead who had buried Saul, ⁵he sent messengers to the men of Jabesh Gilead to say to them, "The LORD bless you for showing this kindness to Saul your master by burying him. ⁶May the LORD now show you kindness and faithfulness, and I too will show you the same favour because you have done this. ⁷Now then, be strong and brave, for Saul your master is dead, and the house of Judah has anointed me king over them."

War Between the Houses of David and Saul

⁸Meanwhile, Abner son of Ner, the commander of Saul's army, had taken Ish-Bosheth son of Saul and brought him over to Mahanaim. ⁹He made him king over Gilead, Ashuri ᵃ and Jezreel, and also over Ephraim, Benjamin and all Israel.

¹⁰Ish-Bosheth son of Saul was forty years old when he became king over Israel, and he reigned two years. The house of Judah, however, followed David. ¹¹The length of time David was king in Hebron over the house of Judah was seven years and six months.

¹²Abner son of Ner, together with the men of Ish-Bosheth son of Saul, left Mahanaim and went to Gibeon. ¹³Joab son of Zeruiah and David's men went out and met them at the pool of Gibeon. One group sat down on one side of the pool and one group on the other side.

2:10 Following his death, Saul's kingdom was divided into two separate states for a time: Israel in the north, and Judah in the south. David would succeed in uniting them into one nation, over which both he and Solomon would rule. Following the death of Solomon, however, the kingdoms of Israel and Judah would separate once more.

---

¹⁴Then Abner said to Joab, "Let's have some of the young men get up and fight hand to hand in front of us."

"All right, let them do it," Joab said.

¹⁵So they stood up and were counted off—twelve men for Benjamin and Ish-Bosheth son of Saul, and twelve for David. ¹⁶Then each man grabbed his opponent by the head and thrust his dagger into his opponent's side, and they fell down together. So that place in Gibeon was called Helkath Hazzurim. ᵇ

¹⁷The battle that day was very fierce, and Abner and the men of Israel were defeated by David's men.

¹⁸The three sons of Zeruiah were there: Joab, Abishai and Asahel. Now Asahel was as fleet-footed as a wild gazelle. ¹⁹He chased Abner, turning neither to the right nor to the left as he pursued him. ²⁰Abner looked behind him and asked, "Is that you, Asahel?"

"It is," he answered.

²¹Then Abner said to him, "Turn aside to the right or to the left; take on one of the young men and strip him of his weapons." But Asahel would not stop chasing him.

²²Again Abner warned Asahel, "Stop chasing me! Why should I strike you down? How could I look your brother Joab in the face?"

²³But Asahel refused to give up the pursuit; so Abner thrust the butt of his spear into Asahel's stomach, and the spear came out through his back. He fell there and died on the spot. And every man stopped when he came to the place where Asahel had fallen and died.

²⁴But Joab and Abishai pursued Abner, and as the sun was setting, they came to the hill of Ammah, near Giah on the way to the wasteland of Gibeon. ²⁵Then the men of Benjamin rallied behind Abner. They formed themselves into a group and took their stand on top of a hill.

²⁶Abner called out to Joab, "Must the sword devour for ever? Don't you realise that this will end in bitterness? How long before you order your men to stop pursuing their brothers?"

²⁷Joab answered, "As surely as God lives, if you had not spoken, the men would have continued the pursuit of their brothers until morning." ᶜ

ᵃ9 Or Asher   ᵇ16 Helkath Hazzurim means field of daggers or field of hostilities.
ᶜ27 Or spoken this morning, the men would not have taken up the pursuit of their brothers; or spoken, the men would have given up the pursuit of their brothers by morning

²⁸So Joab blew the trumpet, and all the men came to a halt; they no longer pursued Israel, nor did they fight any more.

²⁹All that night Abner and his men marched through the Arabah. They crossed the Jordan, continued through the whole Bithron*d* and came to Mahanaim. ³⁰Then Joab returned from pursuing Abner and assembled all his men. Besides Asahel, nineteen of David's men were found missing. ³¹But David's men had killed 360 Benjamites who were with Abner. ³²They took Asahel and buried him in his father's tomb at Bethlehem. Then Joab and his men marched all night and arrived at Hebron by daybreak.

3 The war between the house of Saul and the house of David lasted a long time. David grew stronger and stronger, while the house of Saul grew weaker and weaker.

3:2   Sons were considered much more valuable than daughters, and the birth of so many sons to David at this time would have been considered a sign of God's blessing.

---

²Sons were born to David in Hebron:
His firstborn was Amnon the son of Ahinoam of Jezreel;
³his second, Kileab the son of Abigail the widow of Nabal of Carmel;
the third, Absalom the son of Maacah daughter of Talmai king of Geshur;
⁴the fourth, Adonijah the son of Haggith;
the fifth, Shephatiah the son of Abital;
⁵and the sixth, Ithream the son of David's wife Eglah.
These were born to David in Hebron.

Abner Goes Over to David

⁶During the war between the house of Saul and the house of David, Abner had been strengthening his own position in the house of Saul. ⁷Now Saul had had a concubine named Rizpah daughter of Aiah. And Ish-Bosheth said to Abner, "Why did you sleep with my father's concubine?"

3:7   Ish-Bosheth accused Abner of sleeping with Rizpah, Saul's concubine. This suggests that Abner had his eye on becoming Saul's replacement, that he wanted to become king.

---

⁸Abner was very angry because of what Ish-Bosheth said and he answered, "Am I a dog's head—on Judah's side? This very day I am loyal to the house of your father Saul and to his family and friends. I haven't handed you over to David. Yet now you accuse me of an offence involving this woman! ⁹May God deal with Abner, be it ever so severely, if I do not do for David what the LORD promised him on oath ¹⁰and transfer the kingdom from the house of Saul and establish David's

throne over Israel and Judah from Dan to Beersheba." ¹¹Ish-Bosheth did not dare to say another word to Abner, because he was afraid of him.

¹²Then Abner sent messengers on his behalf to say to David, "Whose land is it? Make an agreement with me, and I will help you bring all Israel over to you." ¹³"Good," said David. "I will make an agreement with you. But I demand one thing of you: Do not come into my presence unless you bring Michal daughter of Saul when you come to see me." ¹⁴Then David sent messengers to Ish-Bosheth son of Saul, demanding, "Give me my wife Michal, whom I betrothed to myself for the price of a hundred Philistine foreskins." ¹⁵So Ish-Bosheth gave orders and had her taken away from her husband Paltiel son of Laish. ¹⁶Her husband, however, went with her, weeping behind her all the way to Bahurim. Then Abner said to him, "Go back home!" So he went back.

¹⁷Abner conferred with the elders of Israel and said, "For some time you have wanted to make David your king. ¹⁸Now do it! For the LORD promised David, 'By my servant David I will rescue my people Israel from the hand of the Philistines and from the hand of all their enemies.' "

¹⁹Abner also spoke to the Benjamites in person. Then he went to Hebron to tell David everything that Israel and the whole house of Benjamin wanted to do. ²⁰When Abner, who had twenty men with him, came to David at Hebron, David prepared a feast for him and his men. ²¹Then Abner said to David, "Let me go at once and assemble all Israel for my lord the king, so that they may make a compact with you, and that you may rule over all that your heart desires." So David sent Abner away, and he went in peace.

Joab Murders Abner

²²Just then David's men and Joab returned from a raid and brought with them a great deal of plunder. But Abner was no longer with David in Hebron, because David had sent him away, and he had gone in peace. ²³When Joab and all the soldiers with him arrived, he was told that Abner son of Ner had come to the king and that the king had sent him away and that he had gone in peace.

²⁴So Joab went to the king and said, "What have you done? Look, Abner came to you. Why did you let him go? Now he is gone! ²⁵You know Abner son of Ner; he came to deceive you and observe your movements and find out everything you are doing."

²⁶Joab then left David and sent messengers after Abner, and they brought him back from the well of Sirah. But David did not know it. ²⁷Now when Abner returned to Hebron, Joab took him aside into the gateway, as though to speak with him privately. And there, to avenge the blood of his brother Asahel, Joab stabbed him in the stomach, and he died.

²⁸Later, when David heard about this, he said, "I and my kingdom are for ever innocent before the LORD concerning the blood of Abner son of Ner. ²⁹May his blood fall upon the head of Joab and upon all his father's house! May Joab's house never be without someone

---

d29 Or *morning*; or *ravine*; the meaning of the Hebrew for this word is uncertain.

who has a running sore or leprosy[a] or who leans on a crutch or who falls by the sword or who lacks food."

[30](Joab and his brother Abishai murdered Abner because he had killed their brother Asahel in the battle of Gibeon.)

[31]Then David said to Joab and all the people with him, "Tear your clothes and put on sackcloth and walk in mourning in front of Abner." King David himself walked behind the bier. [32]They buried Abner in Hebron, and the king wept aloud at Abner's tomb. All the people wept also.

[33]The king sang this lament for Abner:

"Should Abner have died as the lawless die?
[34]   Your hands were not bound,
        your feet were not fettered.
You fell as one falls before wicked men."

And all the people wept over him again.

[35]Then they all came and urged David to eat something while it was still day; but David took an oath, saying, "May God deal with me, be it ever so severely, if I taste bread or anything else before the sun sets!"

[36]All the people took note and were pleased; indeed, everything the king did pleased them. [37]So on that day all the people and all Israel knew that the king had no part in the murder of Abner son of Ner.

[38]Then the king said to his men, "Do you not realise that a prince and a great man has fallen in Israel this day? [39]And today, though I am the anointed king, I am weak, and these sons of Zeruiah are too strong for me. May the LORD repay the evildoer according to his evil deeds!"

Ish-Bosheth Murdered

4 When Ish-Bosheth son of Saul heard that Abner had died in Hebron, he lost courage, and all Israel became alarmed. [2]Now Saul's son had two men who were leaders of raiding bands. One was named Baanah and the other Recab; they were sons of Rimmon the Beerothite from the tribe of Benjamin — Beeroth is considered part of Benjamin, [3]because the people of Beeroth fled to Gittaim and have lived there as aliens to this day.

[4](Jonathan son of Saul had a son who was lame in both feet. He was five years old when the news about Saul and Jonathan came from Jezreel. His nurse picked him up and fled, but as she hurried to leave, he fell and became crippled. His name was Mephibosheth.)

[5]Now Recab and Baanah, the sons of Rimmon the Beerothite, set out for the house of Ish-Bosheth, and they arrived there in the heat of the day while he was taking his noonday rest. [6]They went into the inner part of the house as if to get some wheat, and they stabbed him in the stomach. Then Recab and his brother Baanah slipped away.

[7]They had gone into the house while he was lying on the bed in his bedroom. After they stabbed and killed him, they cut off his head. Taking it with them, they travelled all night by way of the Arabah. [8]They brought the head of Ish-Bosheth to David at Hebron

and said to the king, "Here is the head of Ish-Bosheth son of Saul, your enemy, who tried to take your life. This day the LORD has avenged my lord the king against Saul and his offspring."

[9]David answered Recab and his brother Baanah, the sons of Rimmon the Beerothite, "As surely as the LORD lives, who has delivered me out of all trouble, [10]when a man told me, 'Saul is dead,' and thought he was bringing good news, I seized him and put him to death in Ziklag. That was the reward I gave him for his news! [11]How much more — when wicked men have killed an innocent man in his own house and on his own bed — should I not now demand his blood from your hand and rid the earth of you!"

[12]So David gave an order to his men, and they killed them. They cut off their hands and feet and hung the bodies by the pool in Hebron. But they took the head of Ish-Bosheth and buried it in Abner's tomb at Hebron.

David Becomes King Over Israel

5 All the tribes of Israel came to David at Hebron and said, "We are your own flesh and blood. [2]In the past, while Saul was king over us, you were the one who led Israel on their military campaigns. And the LORD said to you, 'You shall shepherd my people Israel, and you shall become their ruler.' "

[3]When all the elders of Israel had come to King David at Hebron, the king made a compact with them at Hebron before the LORD, and they anointed David king over Israel.

[4]David was thirty years old when he became king, and he reigned for forty years. [5]In Hebron he reigned over Judah for seven years and six months, and in Jerusalem he reigned over all Israel and Judah for thirty-three years.

David Conquers Jerusalem

[6]The king and his men marched to Jerusalem to attack the Jebusites, who lived there. The Jebusites said to David, "You will not get in here; even the blind and the lame can ward you off." They thought, "David cannot get in here." [7]Nevertheless, David captured the fortress of Zion, the City of David.

5:6   Finding a capital city acceptable to both Israel and Judah was a major step towards uniting them into one nation. Jerusalem which was on the border between the two and belonged to neither, was the ideal place to become the City of David.

---

[8]On that day, David said, "Anyone who conquers the Jebusites will have to use the water shaft[a] to reach those 'lame and blind' who are David's enemies."[b] That is why they say, "The 'blind and lame' will not enter the palace."

[9]David then took up residence in the fortress and called it the City of David. He built up the area around

---

[a]29 The Hebrew word was used for various diseases affecting the skin—not necessarily leprosy.   [a]8 Or use scaling hooks
[b]8 Or are hated by David

it, from the supporting terraces[c] inward. 10And he became more and more powerful, because the LORD God Almighty was with him.

11Now Hiram king of Tyre sent messengers to David, along with cedar logs and carpenters and stonemasons, and they built a palace for David. 12And David knew that the LORD had established him as king over Israel and had exalted his kingdom for the sake of his people Israel.

13After he left Hebron, David took more concubines and wives in Jerusalem, and more sons and daughters were born to him. 14These are the names of the children born to him there: Shammua, Shobab, Nathan, Solomon, 15Ibhar, Elishua, Nepheg, Japhia, 16Elishama, Eliada and Eliphelet.

David Defeats the Philistines

17When the Philistines heard that David had been anointed king over Israel, they went up in full force to search for him, but David heard about it and went down to the stronghold. 18Now the Philistines had come and spread out in the Valley of Rephaim; 19so David enquired of the LORD, "Shall I go and attack the Philistines? Will you hand them over to me?"

The LORD answered him, "Go, for I will surely hand the Philistines over to you."

20So David went to Baal Perazim, and there he defeated them. He said, "As waters break out, the LORD has broken out against my enemies before me." So that place was called Baal Perazim.[d] 21The Philistines abandoned their idols there, and David and his men carried them off.

22Once more the Philistines came up and spread out in the Valley of Rephaim; 23so David enquired of the LORD, and he answered, "Do not go straight up, but circle round behind them and attack them in front of the balsam trees. 24As soon as you hear the sound of marching in the tops of the balsam trees, move quickly, because that will mean the LORD has gone out in front of you to strike the Philistine army." 25So David did as the LORD commanded him, and he struck down the Philistines all the way from Gibeon[e] to Gezer.

The Ark Brought to Jerusalem

6 David again brought together out of Israel chosen men, thirty thousand in all. 2He and all his men set out from Baalah of Judah[a] to bring up from there the ark of God, which is called by the Name,[b] the name of the LORD Almighty, who is enthroned between the cherubim that are on the ark. 3They set the ark of God on a new cart and brought it from the house of Abinadab, which was on the hill. Uzzah and Ahio, sons of Abinadab, were guiding the new cart 4with the ark of God on it,[c] and Ahio was walking in front of it. 5David and the whole house of Israel were celebrating with all their might before the LORD, with songs[d] and with harps, lyres, tambourines, sistrums and cymbals.

6:2 Since the ark represented the presence of God amongst his people, the bringing of the ark to Jerusalem, David's new capital city, was a sign that God had made David the true king over Israel.

6When they came to the threshing-floor of Nacon, Uzzah reached out and took hold of the ark of God, because the oxen stumbled. 7The LORD's anger burned against Uzzah because of his irreverent act; therefore God struck him down and he died there beside the ark of God.

6:6 By touching the ark Uzzah came into direct contact with God because the ark represented his presence. Uzzah may well have had the right intentions, but God's command not to touch the ark still stood. The inevitable consequence was death.

8Then David was angry because the LORD's wrath had broken out against Uzzah, and to this day that place is called Perez Uzzah.[e]

9David was afraid of the LORD that day and said, "How can the ark of the LORD ever come to me?" 10He was not willing to take the ark of the LORD to be with him in the City of David. Instead, he took it aside to the house of Obed-Edom the Gittite. 11The ark of the LORD remained in the house of Obed-Edom the Gittite for three months, and the LORD blessed him and his entire household.

12Now King David was told, "The LORD has blessed the household of Obed-Edom and everything he has, because of the ark of God." So David went down and brought up the ark of God from the house of Obed-Edom to the City of David with rejoicing. 13When those who were carrying the ark of the LORD had taken six steps, he sacrificed a bull and a fattened calf. 14David, wearing a linen ephod, danced before the LORD with all his might, 15while he and the entire house of Israel brought up the ark of the LORD with shouts and the sound of trumpets.

16As the ark of the LORD was entering the City of David, Michal daughter of Saul watched from a window. And when she saw King David leaping and dancing before the LORD, she despised him in her heart.

17They brought the ark of the LORD and set it in its place inside the tent that David had pitched for it, and David sacrificed burnt offerings and fellowship offerings[f] before the LORD. 18After he had finished sacrificing the burnt offerings and fellowship offerings, he blessed the people in the name of the LORD Almighty.

---

c9 Or the Millo   d20 Baal Perazim means the lord who breaks out.
a2 That is, Kiriath Jearim; Hebrew Baale Judah, a variant of Baalah of Judah
b2 Hebrew; Septuagint and Vulgate do not have the Name.
c3,4 Dead Sea Scrolls and some Septuagint manuscripts; Masoretic Text cart 4and they brought it with the ark of God from the house of Abinadab, which was on the hill
d5 See Dead Sea Scrolls, Septuagint and 1 Chron. 13:8; Masoretic Text celebrating before the LORD with all kinds of instruments made of pine.
e8 Perez Uzzah means the outbreak against Uzzah.   f17 Traditionally peace offerings; also in verse 18
e25 Septuagint (see also 1 Chron. 14:16); Hebrew Geba

[19]Then he gave a loaf of bread, a cake of dates and a cake of raisins to each person in the whole crowd of Israelites, both men and women. And all the people went to their homes.

[20]When David returned home to bless his household, Michal daughter of Saul came out to meet him and said, "How the king of Israel has distinguished himself today, disrobing in the sight of the slave girls of his servants as any vulgar fellow would."

[21]David said to Michal, "It was before the Lord, who chose me rather than your father or anyone from his house when he appointed me ruler over the Lord's people Israel — I will celebrate before the Lord. [22]I will become even more undignified than this, and I will be humiliated in my own eyes. But by these slave girls you spoke of, I will be held in honour."

[23]And Michal daughter of Saul had no children to the day of her death.

God's Promise to David

7 After the king was settled in his palace and the Lord had given him rest from all his enemies around him, [2]he said to Nathan the prophet, "Here I am, living in a palace of cedar, while the ark of God remains in a tent."

> **7:2**   As a prophet, Nathan was one of the most important counsellors in David's court. His speech in this chapter forms the most important passage in the whole of the two books of Samuel.

[3]Nathan replied to the king, "Whatever you have in mind, go ahead and do it, for the Lord is with you."

[4]That night the word of the Lord came to Nathan, saying:

[5]"Go and tell my servant David, 'This is what the Lord says: Are you the one to build me a house to dwell in? [6]I have not dwelt in a house from the day I brought the Israelites up out of Egypt to this day. I have been moving from place to place with a tent as my dwelling. [7]Wherever I have moved with all the Israelites, did I ever say to any of their rulers whom I commanded to shepherd my people Israel, "Why have you not built me a house of cedar?" '

[8]"Now then, tell my servant David, 'This is what the Lord Almighty says: I took you from the pasture and from following the flock to be ruler over my people Israel. [9]I have been with you wherever you have gone, and I have cut off all your enemies from before you. Now I will make your name great, like the names of the greatest men of the earth. [10]And I will provide a place for my people Israel and will plant them so that they can have a home of their own and no longer be disturbed. Wicked people shall not oppress them any more, as they did at the beginning [11]and have

done ever since the time I appointed leaders[a] over my people Israel. I will also give you rest from all your enemies.

> **7:11**   The Lord's promise to David that he would establish his throne for ever was of the utmost importance. The hope produced by this promise lived on in the people after Israel was conquered and they had been exiled. They had an expectation that God would send his Messiah from the house of David to deliver them from their enemies, and re-establish David's royal line.

" 'The Lord declares to you that the Lord himself will establish a house for you: [12]When your days are over and you rest with your fathers, I will raise up your offspring to succeed you, who will come from your own body, and I will establish his kingdom. [13]He is the one who will build a house for my Name, and I will establish the throne of his kingdom for ever. [14]I will be his father, and he shall be my son. When he does wrong, I will punish him with the rod of men, with floggings inflicted by men. [15]But my love will never be taken away from him, as I took it away from Saul, whom I removed from before you. [16]Your house and your kingdom shall endure for ever before me;[b] your throne shall be established for ever.' "

[17]Nathan reported to David all the words of this entire revelation.

David's Prayer

[18]Then King David went in and sat before the Lord, and he said:

"Who am I, O Sovereign Lord, and what is my family, that you have brought me this far? [19]And as if this were not enough in your sight, O Sovereign Lord, you have also spoken about the future of the house of your servant. Is this your usual way of dealing with man, O Sovereign Lord?

[20]"What more can David say to you? For you know your servant, O Sovereign Lord. [21]For the sake of your word and according to your will, you have done this great thing and made it known to your servant.

[22]"How great you are, O Sovereign Lord! There is no-one like you, and there is no God but you, as we have heard with our own ears. [23]And who is like your people Israel — the one nation on earth that God went out to redeem as a people for himself, and to make a name for himself, and to perform great and awesome wonders by driving out nations and their gods from before your people, whom you redeemed from Egypt?[c] [24]You have established your people Israel as your very own for ever, and you, O Lord, have become their God.

a11 Traditionally *judges*   *b16* Some Hebrew manuscripts and Septuagint; most Hebrew manuscripts *you*
c23 See Septuagint and 1 Chron. 17:21; Hebrew *wonders for your land and before your people, whom you redeemed from Egypt, from the nations and their gods.*

25"And now, LORD God, keep for ever the promise you have made concerning your servant and his house. Do as you promised, 26so that your name will be great for ever. Then men will say, 'The LORD Almighty is God over Israel!' And the house of your servant David will be established before you.

27"O LORD Almighty, God of Israel, you have revealed this to your servant, saying, 'I will build a house for you.' So your servant has found courage to offer you this prayer. 28O Sovereign LORD, you are God! Your words are trustworthy, and you have promised these good things to your servant. 29Now be pleased to bless the house of your servant, that it may continue for ever in your sight; for you, O Sovereign LORD, have spoken, and with your blessing the house of your servant will be blessed for ever."

David's Victories

8 In the course of time, David defeated the Philistines and subdued them, and he took Metheg Ammah from the control of the Philistines.

2David also defeated the Moabites. He made them lie down on the ground and measured them off with a length of cord. Every two lengths of them were put to death, and the third length was allowed to live. So the Moabites became subject to David and brought tribute.

3Moreover, David fought Hadadezer son of Rehob, king of Zobah, when he went to restore his control along the Euphrates River. 4David captured a thousand of his chariots, seven thousand charioteers*a* and twenty thousand foot soldiers. He hamstrung all but a hundred of the chariot horses.

5When the Arameans of Damascus came to help Hadadezer king of Zobah, David struck down twenty-two thousand of them. 6He put garrisons in the Aramean kingdom of Damascus, and the Arameans became subject to him and brought tribute. The LORD gave David victory wherever he went.

7David took the gold shields that belonged to the officers of Hadadezer and brought them to Jerusalem. 8From Tebah*b* and Berothai, towns that belonged to Hadadezer, King David took a great quantity of bronze.

9When Tou*c* king of Hamath heard that David had defeated the entire army of Hadadezer, 10he sent his son Joram*d* to King David to greet him and congratulate him on his victory in battle over Hadadezer, who had been at war with Tou. Joram brought with him articles of silver and gold and bronze.

11King David dedicated these articles to the LORD, as he had done with the silver and gold from all the nations he had subdued: 12Edom*e* and Moab, the Ammonites and the Philistines, and Amalek. He also dedicated the plunder taken from Hadadezer son of Rehob, king of Zobah.

13And David became famous after he returned from striking down eighteen thousand Edomites*f* in the Valley of Salt.

14He put garrisons throughout Edom, and all the Edomites became subject to David. The LORD gave David victory wherever he went.

David's Officials

15David reigned over all Israel, doing what was just and right for all his people. 16Joab son of Zeruiah was over the army; Jehoshaphat son of Ahilud was recorder; 17Zadok son of Ahitub and Ahimelech son of Abiathar were priests; Seraiah was secretary; 18Benaiah son of Jehoiada was over the Kerethites and Pelethites; and David's sons were royal advisers.*g*

David and Mephibosheth

9 David asked, "Is there anyone still left of the house of Saul to whom I can show kindness for Jonathan's sake?"

2Now there was a servant of Saul's household named Ziba. They called him to appear before David, and the king said to him, "Are you Ziba?"

"Your servant," he replied.

3The king asked, "Is there no-one still left of the house of Saul to whom I can show God's kindness?"

Ziba answered the king, "There is still a son of Jonathan; he is crippled in both feet."

4"Where is he?" the king asked.

Ziba answered, "He is at the house of Makir son of Ammiel in Lo Debar."

5So King David had him brought from Lo Debar, from the house of Makir son of Ammiel.

6When Mephibosheth son of Jonathan, the son of Saul, came to David, he bowed down to pay him honour.

David said, "Mephibosheth!"

"Your servant," he replied.

7"Don't be afraid," David said to him, "for I will surely show you kindness for the sake of your father Jonathan. I will restore to you all the land that belonged to your grandfather Saul, and you will always eat at my table."

8Mephibosheth bowed down and said, "What is your servant, that you should notice a dead dog like me?"

9Then the king summoned Ziba, Saul's servant, and said to him, "I have given your master's grandson everything that belonged to Saul and his family. 10You and your sons and your servants are to farm the land for him and bring in the crops, so that your master's grandson may be provided for. And Mephibosheth, grandson of your master, will always eat at my table." (Now Ziba had fifteen sons and twenty servants.)

11Then Ziba said to the king, "Your servant will do whatever my lord the king commands his servant to

---

a4 Septuagint (see also Dead Sea Scrolls and 1 Chron. 18:4); Masoretic Text *captured seventeen hundred of his charioteers*
b8 See some Septuagint manuscripts (see also 1 Chron. 18:8); Hebrew *Betah*.   *c9* Hebrew *Toi*, a variant of *Tou*; also in verse 10
d10 A variant of *Hadoram*
e12 Some Hebrew manuscripts, Septuagint and Syriac (see also 1 Chron. 18:11); most Hebrew manuscripts *Aram*
f13 A few Hebrew manuscripts, Septuagint and Syriac (see also 1 Chron. 18:12); most Hebrew manuscripts *Aram* (that is, Arameans)
g18 Or *were priests*

do." So Mephibosheth ate at David's[a] table like one of the king's sons.

[12]Mephibosheth had a young son named Mica, and all the members of Ziba's household were servants of Mephibosheth. [13]And Mephibosheth lived in Jerusalem, because he always ate at the king's table, and he was crippled in both feet.

David Defeats the Ammonites

10 In the course of time, the king of the Ammonites died, and his son Hanun succeeded him as king. [2]David thought, "I will show kindness to Hanun son of Nahash, just as his father showed kindness to me." So David sent a delegation to express his sympathy to Hanun concerning his father.

When David's men came to the land of the Ammonites, [3]the Ammonite nobles said to Hanun their lord, "Do you think David is honouring your father by sending men to you to express sympathy? Hasn't David sent them to you to explore the city and spy it out and overthrow it?" [4]So Hanun seized David's men, shaved off half of each man's beard, cut off their garments in the middle at the buttocks, and sent them away.

[5]When David was told about this, he sent messengers to meet the men, for they were greatly humiliated. The king said, "Stay at Jericho till your beards have grown, and then come back."

[6]When the Ammonites realised that they had become an offence to David's nostrils, they hired twenty thousand Aramean foot soldiers from Beth Rehob and Zobah, as well as the king of Maacah with a thousand men, and also twelve thousand men from Tob.

[7]On hearing this, David sent Joab out with the entire army of fighting men. [8]The Ammonites came out and drew up in battle formation at the entrance to their city gate, while the Arameans of Zobah and Rehob and the men of Tob and Maacah were by themselves in the open country.

[9]Joab saw that there were battle lines in front of him and behind him; so he selected some of the best troops in Israel and deployed them against the Arameans. [10]He put the rest of the men under the command of Abishai his brother and deployed them against the Ammonites. [11]Joab said, "If the Arameans are too strong for me, then you are to come to my rescue; but if the Ammonites are too strong for you, then I will come to rescue you. [12]Be strong and let us fight bravely for our people and the cities of our God. The LORD will do what is good in his sight."

[13]Then Joab and the troops with him advanced to fight the Arameans, and they fled before him. [14]When the Ammonites saw that the Arameans were fleeing, they fled before Abishai and went inside the city. So Joab returned from fighting the Ammonites and came to Jerusalem.

[15]After the Arameans saw that they had been routed by Israel, they regrouped. [16]Hadadezer had Arameans brought from beyond the River;[a] they went to Helam, with Shobach the commander of Hadadezer's army leading them.

[17]When David was told of this, he gathered all Israel, crossed the Jordan and went to Helam. The Arameans formed their battle lines to meet David and fought against him. [18]But they fled before Israel, and David killed seven hundred of their charioteers and forty thousand of their foot soldiers.[b] He also struck down Shobach the commander of their army, and he died there. [19]When all the kings who were vassals of Hadadezer saw that they had been defeated by Israel, they made peace with the Israelites and became subject to them.

So the Arameans were afraid to help the Ammonites any more.

David and Bathsheba

11 In the spring, at the time when kings go off to war, David sent Joab out with the king's men and the whole Israelite army. They destroyed the Ammonites and besieged Rabbah. But David remained in Jerusalem.

[2]One evening David got up from his bed and walked around on the roof of the palace. From the roof he saw a woman bathing. The woman was very beautiful, [3]and David sent someone to find out about her. The man said, "Isn't this Bathsheba, the daughter of Eliam and the wife of Uriah the Hittite?" [4]Then David sent messengers to get her. She came to him, and he slept with her. (She had purified herself from her uncleanness.) Then[a] she went back home. [5]The woman conceived and sent word to David, saying, "I am pregnant."

11:2   The story of David's adultery with Bathsheba, and his subsequent murder of Uriah, is remarkable for the way it demonstrates the openness of the Bible. Rather than pretending that God always works through blameless people, the writers show how God was able to carry out his will despite the sinfulness of the people that he works through.

---

[6]So David sent this word to Joab: "Send me Uriah the Hittite." And Joab sent him to David. [7]When Uriah came to him, David asked him how Joab was, how the soldiers were and how the war was going. [8]Then David said to Uriah, "Go down to your house and wash your feet." So Uriah left the palace, and a gift from the king was sent after him. [9]But Uriah slept at the entrance to the palace with all his master's servants and did not go down to his house.

[10]When David was told, "Uriah did not go home," he asked him, "Haven't you just come from a distance? Why didn't you go home?"

[11]Uriah said to David, "The ark and Israel and Judah are staying in tents, and my master Joab and my lord's men are camped in the open fields. How could I go to

---

a11 Septuagint; Hebrew *my*   *a16* That is, the Euphrates
b18 Some Septuagint manuscripts (see also 1 Chron. 19:18); Hebrew *horsemen*
a4 Or *with her. When she purified herself from her uncleanness,*

my house to eat and drink and lie with my wife? As surely as you live, I will not do such a thing!"

¹²Then David said to him, "Stay here one more day, and tomorrow I will send you back." So Uriah remained in Jerusalem that day and the next. ¹³At David's invitation, he ate and drank with him, and David made him drunk. But in the evening Uriah went out to sleep on his mat among his master's servants; he did not go home.

¹⁴In the morning David wrote a letter to Joab and sent it with Uriah. ¹⁵In it he wrote, "Put Uriah in the front line where the fighting is fiercest. Then withdraw from him so that he will be struck down and die."

¹⁶So while Joab had the city under siege, he put Uriah at a place where he knew the strongest defenders were. ¹⁷When the men of the city came out and fought against Joab, some of the men in David's army fell; moreover, Uriah the Hittite died.

¹⁸Joab sent David a full account of the battle. ¹⁹He instructed the messenger: "When you have finished giving the king this account of the battle, ²⁰the king's anger may flare up, and he may ask you, 'Why did you get so close to the city to fight? Didn't you know they would shoot arrows from the wall? ²¹Who killed Abimelech son of Jerub-Besheth?ᵇ Didn't a woman throw an upper millstone on him from the wall, so that he died in Thebez? Why did you get so close to the wall?' If he asks you this, then say to him, 'Also, your servant Uriah the Hittite is dead.' "

²²The messenger set out, and when he arrived he told David everything Joab had sent him to say. ²³The messenger said to David, "The men overpowered us and came out against us in the open, but we drove them back to the entrance to the city gate. ²⁴Then the archers shot arrows at your servants from the wall, and some of the king's men died. Moreover, your servant Uriah the Hittite is dead."

²⁵David told the messenger, "Say this to Joab: 'Don't let this upset you; the sword devours one as well as another. Press the attack against the city and destroy it.' Say this to encourage Joab."

²⁶When Uriah's wife heard that her husband was dead, she mourned for him. ²⁷After the time of mourning was over, David had her brought to his house, and she became his wife and bore him a son. But the thing David had done displeased the LORD.

Nathan Rebukes David

12 The LORD sent Nathan to David. When he came to him, he said, "There were two men in a certain town, one rich and the other poor. ²The rich man had a very large number of sheep and cattle, ³but the poor man had nothing except one little ewe lamb that he had bought. He raised it, and it grew up with him and his children. It shared his food, drank from his cup and even slept in his arms. It was like a daughter to him.

⁴"Now a traveller came to the rich man, but the rich man refrained from taking one of his own sheep or cattle to prepare a meal for the traveller who had come

to him. Instead, he took the ewe lamb that belonged to the poor man and prepared it for the one who had come to him."

⁵David burned with anger against the man and said to Nathan, "As surely as the LORD lives, the man who did this deserves to die! ⁶He must pay for that lamb four times over, because he did such a thing and had no pity."

⁷Then Nathan said to David, "You are the man! This is what the LORD, the God of Israel, says: 'I anointed you king over Israel, and I delivered you from the hand of Saul. ⁸I gave your master's house to you, and your master's wives into your arms. I gave you the house of Israel and Judah. And if all this had been too little, I would have given you even more. ⁹Why did you despise the word of the LORD by doing what is evil in his eyes? You struck down Uriah the Hittite with the sword and took his wife to be your own. You killed him with the sword of the Ammonites. ¹⁰Now, therefore, the sword shall never depart from your house, because you despised me and took the wife of Uriah the Hittite to be your own.'

12:7 Nathan's "You are the man!", demonstrates the authority that a prophet had, even over the king. David had already condemned himself by his own words (12:5), and Nathan confirmed this death sentence. It is only because of David's confession of guilt (12:13) that Nathan announced God's decision to spare David's life.

---

¹¹"This is what the LORD says: 'Out of your own household I am going to bring calamity upon you. Before your very eyes I will take your wives and give them to one who is close to you, and he will lie with your wives in broad daylight. ¹²You did it in secret, but I will do this thing in broad daylight before all Israel.' "

¹³Then David said to Nathan, "I have sinned against the LORD."

Nathan replied, "The LORD has taken away your sin. You are not going to die. ¹⁴But because by doing this you have made the enemies of the LORD show utter contempt,ᵃ the son born to you will die."

¹⁵After Nathan had gone home, the LORD struck the child that Uriah's wife had borne to David, and he became ill. ¹⁶David pleaded with God for the child. He fasted and went into his house and spent the nights lying on the ground. ¹⁷The elders of his household stood beside him to get him up from the ground, but he refused, and he would not eat any food with them.

¹⁸On the seventh day the child died. David's servants were afraid to tell him that the child was dead, for they thought, "While the child was still living, we spoke to David but he would not listen to us. How can we tell him the child is dead? He may do something desperate."

¹⁹David noticed that his servants were whispering among themselves and he realised that the child was dead. "Is the child dead?" he asked.

ᵇ21 Also known as Jerub-Baal (that is, Gideon)
ᵃ14 Masoretic Text; an ancient Hebrew scribal tradition *this you have shown utter contempt for the LORD*

"Yes," they replied, "he is dead."

²⁰Then David got up from the ground. After he had washed, put on lotions and changed his clothes, he went into the house of the LORD and worshipped. Then he went to his own house, and at his request they served him food, and he ate.

²¹His servants asked him, "Why are you acting in this way? While the child was alive, you fasted and wept, but now that the child is dead, you get up and eat!"

²²He answered, "While the child was still alive, I fasted and wept. I thought, 'Who knows? The LORD may be gracious to me and let the child live.' ²³But now that he is dead, why should I fast? Can I bring him back again? I will go to him, but he will not return to me."

²⁴Then David comforted his wife Bathsheba, and he went to her and lay with her. She gave birth to a son, and they named him Solomon. The LORD loved him; ²⁵and because the LORD loved him, he sent word through Nathan the prophet to name him Jedidiah. *b*

12:24   The name "Solomon" probably means "peaceful", and Jedidiah means "loved by the LORD". Both these things indicate that God's blessing had once again returned to David's house. It also showed the way God's blessing would be upon Israel during Solomon's reign (see 1 Kings).

---

²⁶Meanwhile Joab fought against Rabbah of the Ammonites and captured the royal citadel. ²⁷Joab then sent messengers to David, saying, "I have fought against Rabbah and taken its water supply. ²⁸Now muster the rest of the troops and besiege the city and capture it. Otherwise I shall take the city, and it will be named after me."

²⁹So David mustered the entire army and went to Rabbah, and attacked and captured it. ³⁰He took the crown from the head of their king*c*—its weight was a talent*d* of gold, and it was set with precious stones—and it was placed on David's head. He took a great quantity of plunder from the city ³¹and brought out the people who were there, consigning them to labour with saws and with iron picks and axes, and he made them work at brickmaking.*e* He did this to all the Ammonite towns. Then David and his entire army returned to Jerusalem.

Amnon and Tamar

13 In the course of time, Amnon son of David fell in love with Tamar, the beautiful sister of Absalom son of David.

²Amnon became frustrated to the point of illness on account of his sister Tamar, for she was a virgin, and it seemed impossible for him to do anything to her.

³Now Amnon had a friend named Jonadab son of Shimeah, David's brother. Jonadab was a very shrewd man. ⁴He asked Amnon, "Why do you, the king's son, look so haggard morning after morning? Won't you tell me?"

Amnon said to him, "I'm in love with Tamar, my brother Absalom's sister."

⁵"Go to bed and pretend to be ill," Jonadab said. "When your father comes to see you, say to him, 'I would like my sister Tamar to come and give me something to eat. Let her prepare the food in my sight so that I may watch her and then eat it from her hand.' "

⁶So Amnon lay down and pretended to be ill. When the king came to see him, Amnon said to him, "I would like my sister Tamar to come and make some special bread in my sight, so that I may eat from her hand."

⁷David sent word to Tamar at the palace: "Go to the house of your brother Amnon and prepare some food for him." ⁸So Tamar went to the house of her brother Amnon, who was lying down. She took some dough, kneaded it, made the bread in his sight and baked it. ⁹Then she took the pan and served him the bread, but he refused to eat.

"Send everyone out of here," Amnon said. So everyone left him. ¹⁰Then Amnon said to Tamar, "Bring the food here into my bedroom so that I may eat from your hand." And Tamar took the bread she had prepared and brought it to her brother Amnon in his bedroom. ¹¹But when she took it to him to eat, he grabbed her and said, "Come to bed with me, my sister."

¹²"Don't, my brother!" she said to him. "Don't force me. Such a thing should not be done in Israel! Don't do this wicked thing. ¹³What about me? Where could I get rid of my disgrace? And what about you? You would be like one of the wicked fools in Israel. Please speak to the king; he will not keep me from being married to you." ¹⁴But he refused to listen to her, and since he was stronger than she, he raped her.

¹⁵Then Amnon hated her with intense hatred. In fact, he hated her more than he had loved her. Amnon said to her, "Get up and get out!"

¹⁶"No!" she said to him. "Sending me away would be a greater wrong than what you have already done to me."

But he refused to listen to her. ¹⁷He called his personal servant and said, "Get this woman out of here and bolt the door after her." ¹⁸So his servant put her out and bolted the door after her. She was wearing a richly ornamented*a* robe, for this was the kind of garment the virgin daughters of the king wore. ¹⁹Tamar put ashes on her head and tore the ornamented robe she was wearing. She put her hand on her head and went away, weeping aloud as she went.

²⁰Her brother Absalom said to her, "Has that Amnon, your brother, been with you? Be quiet now, my sister; he is your brother. Don't take this thing to heart." And Tamar lived in her brother Absalom's house, a desolate woman.

²¹When King David heard all this, he was furious. ²²Absalom never said a word to Amnon, either good or bad; he hated Amnon because he had disgraced his sister Tamar.

---

b25 Jedidiah means *loved by the LORD.*   *c30* Or *of Milcom* (that is, Molech)
d30 That is, about 75 pounds (about 34 kilograms)   *e31* The meaning of the Hebrew for this clause is uncertain.
a18 The meaning of the Hebrew for this phrase is uncertain; also in verse 19.

Absalom Kills Amnon

23Two years later, when Absalom's sheep-shearers were at Baal Hazor near the border of Ephraim, he invited all the king's sons to come there. 24Absalom went to the king and said, "Your servant has had shearers come. Will the king and his officials please join me?"

25"No, my son," the king replied. "All of us should not go; we would only be a burden to you." Although Absalom urged him, he still refused to go, but gave him his blessing.

26Then Absalom said, "If not, please let my brother Amnon come with us."

The king asked him, "Why should he go with you?" 27But Absalom urged him, so he sent with him Amnon and the rest of the king's sons.

28Absalom ordered his men, "Listen! When Amnon is in high spirits from drinking wine and I say to you, 'Strike Amnon down,' then kill him. Don't be afraid. Have not I given you this order? Be strong and brave." 29So Absalom's men did to Amnon what Absalom had ordered. Then all the king's sons got up, mounted their mules and fled.

30While they were on their way, the report came to David: "Absalom has struck down all the king's sons; not one of them is left." 31The king stood up, tore his clothes and lay down on the ground; and all his servants stood by with their clothes torn.

32But Jonadab son of Shimeah, David's brother, said, "My lord should not think that they killed all the princes; only Amnon is dead. This has been Absalom's expressed intention ever since the day that Amnon raped his sister Tamar. 33My lord the king should not be concerned about the report that all the king's sons are dead. Only Amnon is dead."

34Meanwhile, Absalom had fled.

Now the man standing watch looked up and saw many people on the road west of him, coming down the side of the hill. The watchman went and told the king, "I see men in the direction of Horonaim, on the side of the hill."b

35Jonadab said to the king, "See, the king's sons are here; it has happened just as your servant said."

36As he finished speaking, the king's sons came in, wailing loudly. The king, too, and all his servants wept very bitterly.

37Absalom fled and went to Talmai son of Ammihud, the king of Geshur. But King David mourned for his son every day.

38After Absalom fled and went to Geshur, he stayed there for three years. 39And the spirit of the kingc longed to go to Absalom, for he was consoled concerning Amnon's death.

Absalom Returns to Jerusalem

14 Joab son of Zeruiah knew that the king's heart longed for Absalom. 2So Joab sent someone to Tekoa and had a wise woman brought from there. He said to her, "Pretend you are in mourning. Dress in mourning clothes, and don't use any cosmetic lotions. Act like a woman who has spent many days grieving for the dead. 3Then go to the king and speak these words to him." And Joab put the words in her mouth.

4When the woman from Tekoa wenta to the king, she fell with her face to the ground to pay him honour, and she said, "Help me, O king!"

5The king asked her, "What is troubling you?"

She said, "I am indeed a widow; my husband is dead. 6I your servant had two sons. They got into a fight with each other in the field, and no-one was there to separate them. One struck the other and killed him. 7Now the whole clan has risen up against your servant; they say, 'Hand over the one who struck his brother down, so that we may put him to death for the life of his brother whom he killed; then we will get rid of the heir as well.' They would put out the only burning coal I have left, leaving my husband neither name nor descendant on the face of the earth."

8The king said to the woman, "Go home, and I will issue an order on your behalf."

9But the woman from Tekoa said to him, "My lord the king, let the blame rest on me and on my father's family, and let the king and his throne be without guilt."

10The king replied, "If anyone says anything to you, bring him to me, and he will not bother you again."

11She said, "Then let the king invoke the LORD his God to prevent the avenger of blood from adding to the destruction, so that my son shall not be destroyed."

"As surely as the LORD lives," he said, "not one hair of your son's head will fall to the ground."

12Then the woman said, "Let your servant speak a word to my lord the king."

"Speak," he replied.

13The woman said, "Why then have you devised a thing like this against the people of God? When the king says this, does he not convict himself, for the king has not brought back his banished son? 14Like water spilled on the ground, which cannot be recovered, so we must die. But God does not take away life; instead, he devises ways so that a banished person may not remain estranged from him.

15"And now I have come to say this to my lord the king because the people have made me afraid. Your servant thought, 'I will speak to the king; perhaps he will do what his servant asks. 16Perhaps the king will agree to deliver his servant from the hand of the man who is trying to cut off both me and my son from the inheritance God gave us.'

17"And now your servant says, 'May the word of my lord the king bring me rest, for my lord the king is like an angel of God in discerning good and evil. May the LORD your God be with you.' "

18Then the king said to the woman, "Do not keep from me the answer to what I am going to ask you."

"Let my lord the king speak," the woman said.

19The king asked, "Isn't the hand of Joab with you in all this?"

The woman answered, "As surely as you live, my

---

b34 Septuagint; Hebrew does not have this sentence.
c39 Dead Sea Scrolls and some Septuagint manuscripts; Masoretic Text But ˌthe spirit of, David the king
a4 Many Hebrew manuscripts, Septuagint, Vulgate and Syriac; most Hebrew manuscripts spoke

lord the king, no-one can turn to the right or to the left from anything my lord the king says. Yes, it was your servant Joab who instructed me to do this and who put all these words into the mouth of your servant. 20Your servant Joab did this to change the present situation. My lord has wisdom like that of an angel of God — he knows everything that happens in the land."

21The king said to Joab, "Very well, I will do it. Go, bring back the young man Absalom."

22Joab fell with his face to the ground to pay him honour, and he blessed the king. Joab said, "Today your servant knows that he has found favour in your eyes, my lord the king, because the king has granted his servant's request."

23Then Joab went to Geshur and brought Absalom back to Jerusalem. 24But the king said, "He must go to his own house; he must not see my face." So Absalom went to his own house and did not see the face of the king.

25In all Israel there was not a man so highly praised for his handsome appearance as Absalom. From the top of his head to the sole of his foot there was no blemish in him. 26Whenever he cut the hair of his head — he used to cut his hair from time to time when it became too heavy for him — he would weigh it, and its weight was two hundred shekels[b] by the royal standard.

27Three sons and a daughter were born to Absalom. The daughter's name was Tamar, and she became a beautiful woman.

28Absalom lived for two years in Jerusalem without seeing the king's face. 29Then Absalom sent for Joab in order to send him to the king, but Joab refused to come to him. So he sent a second time, but he refused to come. 30Then he said to his servants, "Look, Joab's field is next to mine, and he has barley there. Go and set it on fire." So Absalom's servants set the field on fire.

31Then Joab did go to Absalom's house and he said to him, "Why have your servants set my field on fire?" 32Absalom said to Joab, "Look, I sent word to you and said, 'Come here so that I can send you to the king to ask, "Why have I come from Geshur? It would be better for me if I were still there!" ' Now then, I want to see the king's face, and if I am guilty of anything, let him put me to death."

33So Joab went to the king and told him this. Then the king summoned Absalom, and he came in and bowed down with his face to the ground before the king. And the king kissed Absalom.

Absalom's Conspiracy

15 In the course of time, Absalom provided himself with a chariot and horses and with fifty men to run ahead of him. 2He would get up early and stand by the side of the road leading to the city gate. Whenever anyone came with a complaint to be placed before the king for a decision, Absalom would call out to him, "What town are you from?" He would answer, "Your servant is from one of the tribes of Israel." 3Then Absalom would say to him, "Look, your claims are valid and proper, but there is no representative of the king

to hear you." 4And Absalom would add, "If only I were appointed judge in the land! Then everyone who has a complaint or case could come to me and I would see that he receives justice."

5Also, whenever anyone approached him to bow down before him, Absalom would reach out his hand, take hold of him and kiss him. 6Absalom behaved in this way towards all the Israelites who came to the king asking for justice, and so he stole the hearts of the men of Israel.

7At the end of four[a] years, Absalom said to the king, "Let me go to Hebron and fulfil a vow I made to the LORD. 8While your servant was living at Geshur in Aram, I made this vow: 'If the LORD takes me back to Jerusalem, I will worship the LORD in Hebron.' "[b]

9The king said to him, "Go in peace." So he went to Hebron.

10Then Absalom sent secret messengers throughout the tribes of Israel to say, "As soon as you hear the sound of the trumpets, then say, 'Absalom is king in Hebron.' " 11Two hundred men from Jerusalem had accompanied Absalom. They had been invited as guests and went quite innocently, knowing nothing about the matter. 12While Absalom was offering sacrifices, he also sent for Ahithophel the Gilonite, David's counsellor, to come from Giloh, his home town. And so the conspiracy gained strength, and Absalom's following kept on increasing.

David Flees

13A messenger came and told David, "The hearts of the men of Israel are with Absalom."

14Then David said to all his officials who were with him in Jerusalem, "Come! We must flee, or none of us will escape from Absalom. We must leave immediately, or he will move quickly to overtake us and bring ruin upon us and put the city to the sword."

15The king's officials answered him, "Your servants are ready to do whatever our lord the king chooses."

16The king set out, with his entire household following him; but he left ten concubines to take care of the palace. 17So the king set out, with all the people following him, and they halted at a place some distance away. 18All his men marched past him, along with all the Kerethites and Pelethites; and all the six hundred Gittites who had accompanied him from Gath marched before the king.

15:18   In addition to loyal Israelites, David's army contained a number of foreign mercenary (hired) soldiers drawn largely from nations David had conquered.

19The king said to Ittai the Gittite, "Why should you come along with us? Go back and stay with King Absalom. You are a foreigner, an exile from your homeland. 20You came only yesterday. And today shall I make you wander about with us, when I do not know where I am going? Go back, and take your countrymen. May kindness and faithfulness be with you."

---

[b]26 That is, about 5 pounds (about 2.3 kilograms)   [a]7 Some Septuagint manuscripts, Syriac and Josephus; Hebrew *forty*
[b]8 Some Septuagint manuscripts; Hebrew does not have *in Hebron.*

21But Ittai replied to the king, "As surely as the LORD lives, and as my lord the king lives, wherever my lord the king may be, whether it means life or death, there will your servant be."

22David said to Ittai, "Go ahead, march on." So Ittai the Gittite marched on with all his men and the families that were with him.

23The whole countryside wept aloud as all the people passed by. The king also crossed the Kidron Valley, and all the people moved on towards the desert.

24Zadok was there, too, and all the Levites who were with him were carrying the ark of the covenant of God. They set down the ark of God, and Abiathar offered sacrifices[c] until all the people had finished leaving the city.

15:24 Zadok is shown to have special responsibility for the ark, and Abiathar is David's court priest. When Solomon became King, Zadok replaced Abiathar, and his descendants became the most powerful priestly family in Jerusalem right down to the time of Jesus.

25Then the king said to Zadok, "Take the ark of God back into the city. If I find favour in the LORD's eyes, he will bring me back and let me see it and his dwelling-place again. 26But if he says, 'I am not pleased with you,' then I am ready; let him do to me whatever seems good to him."

27The king also said to Zadok the priest, "Aren't you a seer? Go back to the city in peace, with your son Ahimaaz and Jonathan son of Abiathar. You and Abiathar take your two sons with you. 28I will wait at the fords in the desert until word comes from you to inform me." 29So Zadok and Abiathar took the ark of God back to Jerusalem and stayed there.

30But David continued up the Mount of Olives, weeping as he went; his head was covered and he was barefoot. All the people with him covered their heads too and were weeping as they went up. 31Now David had been told, "Ahithophel is among the conspirators with Absalom." So David prayed, "O LORD, turn Ahithophel's counsel into foolishness."

15:30 David's head was covered and he was barefoot. Both these things were signs of mourning and humility before God, and they expressed his sorrow at the situation that had arisen and at his attitude before God. He hoped God would restore his rule over all Israel.

32When David arrived at the summit, where people used to worship God, Hushai the Arkite was there to meet him, his robe torn and dust on his head. 33David said to him, "If you go with me, you will be a burden to me. 34But if you return to the city and say to Absalom, 'I will be your servant, O king; I was your father's servant in the past, but now I will be your servant,' then you can help me by frustrating Ahithophel's advice. 35Won't the priests Zadok and Abiathar be there with you? Tell them anything you hear in the king's palace. 36Their two sons, Ahimaaz son of Zadok and Jonathan son of Abiathar, are there with them. Send them to me with anything you hear."

37So David's friend Hushai arrived at Jerusalem as Absalom was entering the city.

David and Ziba

16 When David had gone a short distance beyond the summit, there was Ziba, the steward of Mephibosheth, waiting to meet him. He had a string of donkeys saddled and loaded with two hundred loaves of bread, a hundred cakes of raisins, a hundred cakes of figs and a skin of wine.

2The king asked Ziba, "Why have you brought these?"

Ziba answered, "The donkeys are for the king's household to ride on, the bread and fruit are for the men to eat, and the wine is to refresh those who become exhausted in the desert."

3The king then asked, "Where is your master's grandson?"

Ziba said to him, "He is staying in Jerusalem, because he thinks, 'Today the house of Israel will give me back my grandfather's kingdom.'"

4Then the king said to Ziba, "All that belonged to Mephibosheth is now yours."

"I humbly bow," Ziba said. "May I find favour in your eyes, my lord the king."

Shimei Curses David

5As King David approached Bahurim, a man from the same clan as Saul's family came out from there. His name was Shimei son of Gera, and he cursed as he came out. 6He pelted David and all the king's officials with stones, though all the troops and the special guard were on David's right and left. 7As he cursed, Shimei said, "Get out, get out, you man of blood, you scoundrel! 8The LORD has repaid you for all the blood you shed in the household of Saul, in whose place you have reigned. The LORD has handed the kingdom over to your son Absalom. You have come to ruin because you are a man of blood!"

9Then Abishai son of Zeruiah said to the king, "Why should this dead dog curse my lord the king? Let me go over and cut off his head."

10But the king said, "What do you and I have in common, you sons of Zeruiah? If he is cursing because the LORD said to him, 'Curse David,' who can ask, 'Why do you do this?'"

11David then said to Abishai and all his officials, "My son, who is of my own flesh, is trying to take my life. How much more, then, this Benjamite! Leave him alone; let him curse, for the LORD has told him to. 12It may be that the LORD will see my distress and repay me with good for the cursing I am receiving today."

13So David and his men continued along the road while Shimei was going along the hillside opposite

*c*24 Or *Abiathar went up*

him, cursing as he went and throwing stones at him and showering him with dirt. [14]The king and all the people with him arrived at their destination exhausted. And there he refreshed himself.

The Advice of Hushai and Ahithophel

[15]Meanwhile, Absalom and all the men of Israel came to Jerusalem, and Ahithophel was with him. [16]Then Hushai the Arkite, David's friend, went to Absalom and said to him, "Long live the king! Long live the king!"

[17]Absalom asked Hushai, "Is this the love you show your friend? Why didn't you go with your friend?"

[18]Hushai said to Absalom, "No, the one chosen by the LORD, by these people and by all the men of Israel — his I will be, and I will remain with him. [19]Furthermore, whom should I serve? Should I not serve the son? Just as I served your father, so I will serve you."

[20]Absalom said to Ahithophel, "Give us your advice. What should we do?"

[21]Ahithophel answered, "Lie with your father's concubines whom he left to take care of the palace. Then all Israel will hear that you have made yourself an offence to your father's nostrils, and the hands of everyone with you will be strengthened." [22]So they pitched a tent for Absalom on the roof, and he lay with his father's concubines in the sight of all Israel.

16:22   The action of sleeping openly with David's concubines was deliberately calculated to be offensive to David (16:21) and indicated that the breach between the two men was final. David had behaved in a similar way when he replaced Saul (12:8). Such an act was equivalent to a declaration that the former king was dead and had been replaced.

---

[23]Now in those days the advice Ahithophel gave was like that of one who enquires of God. That was how both David and Absalom regarded all of Ahithophel's advice.

17 Ahithophel said to Absalom, "I would[a] choose twelve thousand men and set out tonight in pursuit of David. [2]I would[b] attack him while he is weary and weak. I would[b] strike him with terror, and then all the people with him will flee. I would[b] strike down only the king [3]and bring all the people back to you. The death of the man you seek will mean the return of all; all the people will be unharmed." [4]This plan seemed good to Absalom and to all the elders of Israel.

[5]But Absalom said, "Summon also Hushai the Arkite, so that we can hear what he has to say." [6]When Hushai came to him, Absalom said, "Ahithophel has given this advice. Should we do what he says? If not, give us your opinion."

[7]Hushai replied to Absalom, "The advice Ahithophel

has given is not good this time. [8]You know your father and his men; they are fighters, and as fierce as a wild bear robbed of her cubs. Besides, your father is an experienced fighter; he will not spend the night with the troops. [9]Even now, he is hidden in a cave or some other place. If he should attack your troops first,[c] whoever hears about it will say, 'There has been a slaughter among the troops who follow Absalom.' [10]Then even the bravest soldier, whose heart is like the heart of a lion, will melt with fear, for all Israel knows that your father is a fighter and that those with him are brave.

[11]"So I advise you: Let all Israel, from Dan to Beersheba — as numerous as the sand on the seashore — be gathered to you, with you yourself leading them into battle. [12]Then we will attack him wherever he may be found, and we will fall on him as dew settles on the ground. Neither he nor any of his men will be left alive. [13]If he withdraws into a city, then all Israel will bring ropes to that city, and we will drag it down to the valley until not even a piece of it can be found."

[14]Absalom and all the men of Israel said, "The advice of Hushai the Arkite is better than that of Ahithophel." For the LORD had determined to frustrate the good advice of Ahithophel in order to bring disaster on Absalom.

17:14   Behind the political plotting which is apparent in this chapter, here God is shown to be at work. Hushai, David's adviser, managed to flatter Absalom enough to trick him, and so David had enough time to gather support. So God brought about the circumstances that saw David restored as rightful king.

---

[15]Hushai told Zadok and Abiathar, the priests, "Ahithophel has advised Absalom and the elders of Israel to do such and such, but I have advised them to do so and so. [16]Now send a message immediately and tell David, 'Do not spend the night at the fords in the desert; cross over without fail, or the king and all the people with him will be swallowed up.' "

[17]Jonathan and Ahimaaz were staying at En Rogel. A servant girl was to go and inform them, and they were to go and tell King David, for they could not risk being seen entering the city. [18]But a young man saw them and told Absalom. So the two of them left quickly and went to the house of a man in Bahurim. He had a well in his courtyard, and they climbed down into it. [19]His wife took a covering and spread it out over the opening of the well and scattered grain over it. No-one knew anything about it.

[20]When Absalom's men came to the woman at the house, they asked, "Where are Ahimaaz and Jonathan?"

The woman answered them, "They crossed over the brook."[d] The men searched but found no-one, so they returned to Jerusalem.

[21]After the men had gone, the two climbed out of

---

the well and went to inform King David. They said to him, "Set out and cross the river at once; Ahithophel has advised such and such against you." 22So David and all the people with him set out and crossed the Jordan. By daybreak, no-one was left who had not crossed the Jordan.

23When Ahithophel saw that his advice had not been followed, he saddled his donkey and set out for his house in his home town. He put his house in order and then hanged himself. So he died and was buried in his father's tomb.

24David went to Mahanaim, and Absalom crossed the Jordan with all the men of Israel. 25Absalom had appointed Amasa over the army in place of Joab. Amasa was the son of a man named Jether,e an Israelitef who had married Abigail,g the daughter of Nahash and sister of Zeruiah the mother of Joab. 26The Israelites and Absalom camped in the land of Gilead.

27When David came to Mahanaim, Shobi son of Nahash from Rabbah of the Ammonites, and Makir son of Ammiel from Lo Debar, and Barzillai the Gileadite from Rogelim 28brought bedding and bowls and articles of pottery. They also brought wheat and barley, flour and roasted grain, beans and lentils,h 29honey and curds, sheep, and cheese from cows' milk for David and his people to eat. For they said, "The people have become hungry and tired and thirsty in the desert."

Absalom's Death

18 David mustered the men who were with him and appointed over them commanders of thousands and commanders of hundreds. 2David sent the troops out—a third under the command of Joab, a third under Joab's brother Abishai son of Zeruiah, and a third under Ittai the Gittite. The king told the troops, "I myself will surely march out with you."

3But the men said, "You must not go out; if we are forced to flee, they won't care about us. Even if half of us die, they won't care; but you are worth ten thousand of us.a It would be better now for you to give us support from the city."

4The king answered, "I will do whatever seems best to you."

So the king stood beside the gate while all the men marched out in units of hundreds and of thousands. 5The king commanded Joab, Abishai and Ittai, "Be gentle with the young man Absalom for my sake." And all the troops heard the king giving orders concerning Absalom to each of the commanders.

6The army marched into the field to fight Israel, and the battle took place in the forest of Ephraim. 7There the army of Israel was defeated by David's men, and the casualties that day were great—twenty thousand men. 8The battle spread out over the whole countryside, and the forest claimed more lives that day than the sword.

9Now Absalom happened to meet David's men. He was riding his mule, and as the mule went under the thick branches of a large oak, Absalom's head got caught in the tree. He was left hanging in mid-air, while the mule he was riding kept on going.

10When one of the men saw this, he told Joab, "I have just seen Absalom hanging in an oak tree."

11Joab said to the man who had told him this, "What! You saw him? Why didn't you strike him to the ground right there? Then I would have had to give you ten shekelsb of silver and a warrior's belt."

12But the man replied, "Even if a thousand shekelsc were weighed out into my hands, I would not lift my hand against the king's son. In our hearing the king commanded you and Abishai and Ittai, 'Protect the young man Absalom for my sake.'d 13And if I had put my life in jeopardye—and nothing is hidden from the king—you would have kept your distance from me."

14Joab said, "I am not going to wait like this for you." So he took three javelins in his hand and plunged them into Absalom's heart while Absalom was still alive in the oak tree. 15And ten of Joab's armour-bearers surrounded Absalom, struck him and killed him.

16Then Joab sounded the trumpet, and the troops stopped pursuing Israel, for Joab halted them. 17They took Absalom, threw him into a big pit in the forest and piled up a large heap of rocks over him. Meanwhile, all the Israelites fled to their homes.

18During his life-time Absalom had taken a pillar and erected it in the King's Valley as a monument to himself, for he thought, "I have no son to carry on the memory of my name." He named the pillar after himself, and it is called Absalom's Monument to this day.

David Mourns

19Now Ahimaaz son of Zadok said, "Let me run and take the news to the king that the LORD has delivered him from the hand of his enemies."

20"You are not the one to take the news today," Joab told him. "You may take the news another time, but you must not do so today, because the king's son is dead."

21Then Joab said to a Cushite, "Go, tell the king what you have seen." The Cushite bowed down before Joab and ran off.

22Ahimaaz son of Zadok again said to Joab, "Come what may, please let me run behind the Cushite."

But Joab replied, "My son, why do you want to go? You don't have any news that will bring you a reward."

23He said, "Come what may, I want to run."

So Joab said, "Run!" Then Ahimaaz ran by way of the plainf and outran the Cushite.

24While David was sitting between the inner and outer gates, the watchman went up to the roof of the gateway by the wall. As he looked out, he saw a man running alone. 25The watchman called out to the king and reported it.

e25 Hebrew Ithra, a variant of Jether
f25 Hebrew and some Septuagint manuscripts; other Septuagint manuscripts (see also 1 Chron. 2:17) Ishmaelite or Jezreelite
g25 Hebrew Abigal, a variant of Abigail   h28 Most Septuagint manuscripts and Syriac; Hebrew lentils, and roasted grain
a3 Two Hebrew manuscripts, some Septuagint manuscripts and Vulgate; most Hebrew manuscripts care; for now there are ten thousand
like us   b11 That is, about 4 ounces (about 115 grams)   c12 That is, about 25 pounds (about 11 kilograms)
d12 A few Hebrew manuscripts, Septuagint, Vulgate and Syriac; most Hebrew manuscripts may be translated Absalom, whoever you may be.
e13 Or Otherwise, if I had acted treacherously towards him   f23 That is, the plain of the Jordan

The king said, "If he is alone, he must have good news." And the man came closer and closer.

26Then the watchman saw another man running, and he called down to the gatekeeper, "Look, another man running alone!"

The king said, "He must be bringing good news, too."

27The watchman said, "It seems to me that the first one runs like Ahimaaz son of Zadok."

"He's a good man," the king said. "He comes with good news."

28Then Ahimaaz called out to the king, "All is well!" He bowed down before the king with his face to the ground and said, "Praise be to the LORD your God! He has delivered up the men who lifted their hands against my lord the king."

29The king asked, "Is the young man Absalom safe?"

Ahimaaz answered, "I saw great confusion just as Joab was about to send the king's servant and me, your servant, but I don't know what it was."

30The king said, "Stand aside and wait here." So he stepped aside and stood there.

31Then the Cushite arrived and said, "My lord the king, hear the good news! The LORD has delivered you today from all who rose up against you."

32The king asked the Cushite, "Is the young man Absalom safe?"

The Cushite replied, "May the enemies of my lord the king and all who rise up to harm you be like that young man."

33The king was shaken. He went up to the room over the gateway and wept. As he went, he said: "O my son Absalom! My son, my son Absalom! If only I had died instead of you—O Absalom, my son, my son!"

19 Joab was told, "The king is weeping and mourning for Absalom." 2And for the whole army the victory that day was turned into mourning, because on that day the troops heard it said, "The king is grieving for his son." 3The men stole into the city that day as men steal in who are ashamed when they flee from battle. 4The king covered his face and cried aloud, "O my son Absalom! O Absalom, my son, my son!"

5Then Joab went into the house to the king and said, "Today you have humiliated all your men, who have just saved your life and the lives of your sons and daughters and the lives of your wives and concubines. 6You love those who hate you and hate those who love you. You have made it clear today that the commanders and their men mean nothing to you. I see that you would be pleased if Absalom were alive today and all of us were dead. 7Now go out and encourage your men. I swear by the LORD that if you don't go out, not a man will be left with you by nightfall. This will be worse for you than all the calamities that have come upon you from your youth till now."

8So the king got up and took his seat in the gateway. When the men were told, "The king is sitting in the gateway," they all came before him.

David Returns to Jerusalem

Meanwhile, the Israelites had fled to their homes. 9Throughout the tribes of Israel, the people were all arguing with each other, saying, "The king delivered us from the hand of our enemies; he is the one who rescued us from the hand of the Philistines. But now he has fled the country because of Absalom; 10and Absalom, whom we anointed to rule over us, has died in battle. So why do you say nothing about bringing the king back?"

11King David sent this message to Zadok and Abiathar, the priests: "Ask the elders of Judah, 'Why should you be the last to bring the king back to his palace, since what is being said throughout Israel has reached the king at his quarters? 12You are my brothers, my own flesh and blood. So why should you be the last to bring back the king?' 13And say to Amasa, 'Are you not my own flesh and blood? May God deal with me, be it ever so severely, if from now on you are not the commander of my army in place of Joab.' "

14He won over the hearts of all the men of Judah as though they were one man. They sent word to the king, "Return, you and all your men." 15Then the king returned and went as far as the Jordan.

Now the men of Judah had come to Gilgal to go out and meet the king and bring him across the Jordan. 16Shimei son of Gera, the Benjamite from Bahurim, hurried down with the men of Judah to meet King David. 17With him were a thousand Benjamites, along with Ziba, the steward of Saul's household, and his fifteen sons and twenty servants. They rushed to the Jordan, where the king was. 18They crossed at the ford to take the king's household over and to do whatever he wished.

When Shimei son of Gera crossed the Jordan, he fell prostrate before the king 19and said to him, "May my lord not hold me guilty. Do not remember how your servant did wrong on the day my lord the king left Jerusalem. May the king put it out of his mind. 20For I your servant know that I have sinned, but today I have come here as the first of the whole house of Joseph to come down and meet my lord the king."

21Then Abishai son of Zeruiah said, "Shouldn't Shimei be put to death for this? He cursed the LORD's anointed."

22David replied, "What do you and I have in common, you sons of Zeruiah? This day you have become my adversaries! Should anyone be put to death in Israel today? Do I not know that today I am king over Israel?" 23So the king said to Shimei, "You shall not die." And the king promised him on oath.

24Mephibosheth, Saul's grandson, also went down to meet the king. He had not taken care of his feet or trimmed his moustache or washed his clothes from the day the king left until the day he returned safely. 25When he came from Jerusalem to meet the king, the king asked him, "Why didn't you go with me, Mephibosheth?"

26He said, "My lord the king, since I your servant am lame, I said, 'I will have my donkey saddled and will ride on it, so that I can go with the king.' But Ziba my servant betrayed me. 27And he has slandered your servant to my lord the king. My lord the king is like an angel of God; so do whatever pleases you. 28All my grandfather's descendants deserved nothing but death from my lord the king, but you gave your servant a place among those who eat at your table. So what right do I have to make any more appeals to the king?"

²⁹The king said to him, "Why say more? I order you and Ziba to divide the fields."

³⁰Mephibosheth said to the king, "Let him take everything, now that my lord the king has arrived home safely."

³¹Barzillai the Gileadite also came down from Rogelim to cross the Jordan with the king and to send him on his way from there. ³²Now Barzillai was a very old man, eighty years of age. He had provided for the king during his stay in Mahanaim, for he was a very wealthy man. ³³The king said to Barzillai, "Cross over with me and stay with me in Jerusalem, and I will provide for you."

³⁴But Barzillai answered the king, "How many more years shall I live, that I should go up to Jerusalem with the king? ³⁵I am now eighty years old. Can I tell the difference between what is good and what is not? Can your servant taste what he eats and drinks? Can I still hear the voices of men and women singers? Why should your servant be an added burden to my lord the king? ³⁶Your servant will cross over the Jordan with the king for a short distance, but why should the king reward me in this way? ³⁷Let your servant return, that I may die in my own town near the tomb of my father and mother. But here is your servant Kimham. Let him cross over with my lord the king. Do for him whatever pleases you."

³⁸The king said, "Kimham shall cross over with me, and I will do for him whatever pleases you. And anything you desire from me I will do for you."

³⁹So all the people crossed the Jordan, and then the king crossed over. The king kissed Barzillai and gave him his blessing, and Barzillai returned to his home.

⁴⁰When the king crossed over to Gilgal, Kimham crossed with him. All the troops of Judah and half the troops of Israel had taken the king over.

⁴¹Soon all the men of Israel were coming to the king and saying to him, "Why did our brothers, the men of Judah, steal the king away and bring him and his household across the Jordan, together with all his men?"

19:41   Even though David had united the kingdoms of Israel and Judah into one nation, division and suspicion still remained beneath the surface.

---

⁴²All the men of Judah answered the men of Israel, "We did this because the king is closely related to us. Why are you angry about it? Have we eaten any of the king's provisions? Have we taken anything for ourselves?"

⁴³Then the men of Israel answered the men of Judah, "We have ten shares in the king; and besides, we have a greater claim on David than you have. So why do you treat us with contempt? Were we not the first to speak of bringing back our king?"

But the men of Judah responded even more harshly than the men of Israel.

---

a 14 Or *Abel, even Beth Maacah*; also in verse 15

Sheba Rebels Against David

20 Now a troublemaker named Sheba son of Bicri, a Benjamite, happened to be there. He sounded the trumpet and shouted,

"We have no share in David,
    no part in Jesse's son!
Every man to his tent, O Israel!"

²So all the men of Israel deserted David to follow Sheba son of Bicri. But the men of Judah stayed by their king all the way from the Jordan to Jerusalem.

³When David returned to his palace in Jerusalem, he took the ten concubines he had left to take care of the palace and put them in a house under guard. He provided for them, but did not lie with them. They were kept in confinement till the day of their death, living as widows.

⁴Then the king said to Amasa, "Summon the men of Judah to come to me within three days, and be here yourself." ⁵But when Amasa went to summon Judah, he took longer than the time the king had set for him.

⁶David said to Abishai, "Now Sheba son of Bicri will do us more harm than Absalom did. Take your master's men and pursue him, or he will find fortified cities and escape from us." ⁷So Joab's men and the Kerethites and Pelethites and all the mighty warriors went out under the command of Abishai. They marched out from Jerusalem to pursue Sheba son of Bicri.

⁸While they were at the great rock in Gibeon, Amasa came to meet them. Joab was wearing his military tunic, and strapped over it at his waist was a belt with a dagger in its sheath. As he stepped forward, it dropped out of its sheath.

⁹Joab said to Amasa, "How are you, my brother?" Then Joab took Amasa by the beard with his right hand to kiss him. ¹⁰Amasa was not on his guard against the dagger in Joab's hand, and Joab plunged it into his belly, and his intestines spilled out on the ground. Without being stabbed again, Amasa died. Then Joab and his brother Abishai pursued Sheba son of Bicri.

¹¹One of Joab's men stood beside Amasa and said, "Whoever favours Joab, and whoever is for David, let him follow Joab!" ¹²Amasa lay wallowing in his blood in the middle of the road, and the man saw that all the troops came to a halt there. When he realised that everyone who came up to Amasa stopped, he dragged him from the road into a field and threw a garment over him. ¹³After Amasa had been removed from the road, all the men went on with Joab to pursue Sheba son of Bicri.

¹⁴Sheba passed through all the tribes of Israel to Abel Beth Maacahᵃ and through the entire region of the Berites, who gathered together and followed him. ¹⁵All the troops with Joab came and besieged Sheba in Abel Beth Maacah. They built a siege ramp up to the city, and it stood against the outer fortifications. While they were battering the wall to bring it down, ¹⁶a wise woman called from the city, "Listen! Listen! Tell Joab to come here so that I can speak to him." ¹⁷He went towards her, and she asked, "Are you Joab?"

"I am," he answered.

She said, "Listen to what your servant has to say."
"I'm listening," he said.

[18]She continued, "Long ago they used to say, 'Get your answer at Abel,' and that settled it. [19]We are the peaceful and faithful in Israel. You are trying to destroy a city that is a mother in Israel. Why do you want to swallow up the LORD's inheritance?"

[20]"Far be it from me!" Joab replied, "Far be it from me to swallow up or destroy! [21]That is not the case. A man named Sheba son of Bicri, from the hill country of Ephraim, has lifted up his hand against the king, against David. Hand over this one man, and I'll withdraw from the city."

The woman said to Joab, "His head will be thrown to you from the wall."

[22]Then the woman went to all the people with her wise advice, and they cut off the head of Sheba son of Bicri and threw it to Joab. So he sounded the trumpet, and his men dispersed from the city, each returning to his home. And Joab went back to the king in Jerusalem.

[23]Joab was over Israel's entire army; Benaiah son of Jehoiada was over the Kerethites and Pelethites; [24]Adoniram[b] was in charge of forced labour; Jehoshaphat son of Ahilud was recorder; [25]Sheva was secretary; Zadok and Abiathar were priests; [26]and Ira the Jairite was David's priest.

The Gibeonites Avenged

21 During the reign of David, there was a famine for three successive years; so David sought the face of the LORD. The LORD said, "It is on account of Saul and his blood-stained house; it is because he put the Gibeonites to death."

[2]The king summoned the Gibeonites and spoke to them. (Now the Gibeonites were not a part of Israel but were survivors of the Amorites; the Israelites had sworn to spare them, but Saul in his zeal for Israel and Judah had tried to annihilate them.) [3]David asked the Gibeonites, "What shall I do for you? How shall I make amends so that you will bless the LORD's inheritance?"

[4]The Gibeonites answered him, "We have no right to demand silver or gold from Saul or his family, nor do we have the right to put anyone in Israel to death."

"What do you want me to do for you?" David asked.

[5]They answered the king, "As for the man who destroyed us and plotted against us so that we have been decimated and have no place anywhere in Israel, [6]let seven of his male descendants be given to us to be killed and exposed before the LORD at Gibeah of Saul — the LORD's chosen one."

So the king said, "I will give them to you."

[7]The king spared Mephibosheth son of Jonathan, the son of Saul, because of the oath before the LORD between David and Jonathan son of Saul. [8]But the king took Armoni and Mephibosheth, the two sons of Aiah's daughter Rizpah, whom she had borne to Saul, together with the five sons of Saul's daughter Merab,[a] whom she had borne to Adriel son of Barzillai the Meholathite. [9]He handed them over to the Gibeonites,

who killed and exposed them on a hill before the LORD. All seven of them fell together; they were put to death during the first days of harvest, just as the barley harvest was beginning.

21:6   In ancient time, families shared responsibility for the crimes of one of their members. This helps explain how Saul's descendants could be punished for something he had done, even though they may not have shared personally in the crime.

---

[10]Rizpah daughter of Aiah took sackcloth and spread it out for herself on a rock. From the beginning of the harvest till the rain poured down from the heavens on the bodies, she did not let the birds of the air touch them by day or the wild animals by night. [11]When David was told what Aiah's daughter Rizpah, Saul's concubine, had done, [12]he went and took the bones of Saul and his son Jonathan from the citizens of Jabesh Gilead. (They had taken them secretly from the public square at Beth Shan, where the Philistines had hung them after they struck Saul down on Gilboa.) [13]David brought the bones of Saul and his son Jonathan from there, and the bones of those who had been killed and exposed were gathered up.

[14]They buried the bones of Saul and his son Jonathan in the tomb of Saul's father Kish, at Zela in Benjamin, and did everything the king commanded. After that, God answered prayer on behalf of the land.

21:14   The provision of a proper burial for Saul and his family reflected the respect that David showed for Saul throughout his life. He treated him as the one God originally chose to be king.

Wars Against the Philistines

[15]Once again there was a battle between the Philistines and Israel. David went down with his men to fight against the Philistines, and he became exhausted. [16]And Ishbi-Benob, one of the descendants of Rapha, whose bronze spearhead weighed three hundred shekels[b] and who was armed with a new sword, said he would kill David. [17]But Abishai son of Zeruiah came to David's rescue; he struck the Philistine down and killed him. Then David's men swore to him, saying, "Never again will you go out with us to battle, so that the lamp of Israel will not be extinguished."

[18]In the course of time, there was another battle with the Philistines, at Gob. At that time Sibbecai the Hushathite killed Saph, one of the descendants of Rapha.

[19]In another battle with the Philistines at Gob, Elhanan son of Jaare-Oregim[c] the Bethlehemite killed

---

b24 Some Septuagint manuscripts (see also 1 Kings 4:6 and 5:14); Hebrew Adoram   *a8 Two Hebrew manuscripts, some*
Septuagint manuscripts and Syriac (see also 1 Samuel 18:19); most Hebrew and Septuagint manuscripts *Michal*
b16 That is, about 7½ pounds (about 3.5 kilograms)   *c19 Or son of Jair the weaver*

Goliath *d* the Gittite, who had a spear with a shaft like a weaver's rod. ²⁰In still another battle, which took place at Gath, there was a huge man with six fingers on each hand and six toes on each foot—twenty-four in all. He also was descended from Rapha. ²¹When he taunted Israel, Jonathan son of Shimeah, David's brother, killed him. ²²These four were descendants of Rapha in Gath, and they fell at the hands of David and his men.

David's Song of Praise

22 David sang to the Lord the words of this song when the Lord delivered him from the hand of all his enemies and from the hand of Saul. ²He said:

22:1   The song of David recorded in this chapter appears also as Psalm 18. This is only one of a number of psalms associated with specific events in the life of David. The others are Psalms 3; 51; 52; 54; 56; 57; 59; 60; 63; 142. The introductory words to each of these psalms draw attention to the incident within David's life with which the psalm is associated.

"The Lord is my rock, my fortress and my
    deliverer;
³   my God is my rock, in whom I take refuge,
    my shield and the horn *a* of my salvation.
He is my stronghold, my refuge and my saviour—
    from violent men you save me.
⁴I call to the Lord, who is worthy of praise,
    and I am saved from my enemies.

⁵"The waves of death swirled about me;
    the torrents of destruction overwhelmed me.
⁶The cords of the grave *b* coiled around me;
    the snares of death confronted me.
⁷In my distress I called to the Lord;
    I called out to my God.
From his temple he heard my voice;
    my cry came to his ears.

⁸"The earth trembled and quaked,
    the foundations of the heavens *c* shook;
    they trembled because he was angry.
⁹Smoke rose from his nostrils;
    consuming fire came from his mouth,
    burning coals blazed out of it.
¹⁰He parted the heavens and came down;
    dark clouds were under his feet.
¹¹He mounted the cherubim and flew;
    he soared *d* on the wings of the wind.
¹²He made darkness his canopy around him—
    the dark *e* rain clouds of the sky.
¹³Out of the brightness of his presence
    bolts of lightning blazed forth.

¹⁴The Lord thundered from heaven;
    the voice of the Most High resounded.
¹⁵He shot arrows and scattered ,the enemies,,
    bolts of lightning and routed them.
¹⁶The valleys of the sea were exposed
    and the foundations of the earth laid bare
at the rebuke of the Lord,
    at the blast of breath from his nostrils.

¹⁷"He reached down from on high and took
        hold of me;
    he drew me out of deep waters.
¹⁸He rescued me from my powerful enemy,
    from my foes, who were too strong for me.
¹⁹They confronted me in the day of my disaster,
    but the Lord was my support.
²⁰He brought me out into a spacious place;
    he rescued me because he delighted in me.

²¹"The Lord has dealt with me according to my
        righteousness;
    according to the cleanness of my hands he has
        rewarded me.
²²For I have kept the ways of the Lord;
    I have not done evil by turning from my God.
²³All his laws are before me;
    I have not turned away from his decrees.
²⁴I have been blameless before him
    and have kept myself from sin.
²⁵The Lord has rewarded me according to my
        righteousness,
    according to my cleanness *f* in his sight.

²⁶"To the faithful you show yourself faithful,
    to the blameless you show yourself blameless,
²⁷to the pure you show yourself pure,
    but to the crooked you show yourself shrewd.
²⁸You save the humble,
    but your eyes are on the haughty to bring them
        low.
²⁹You are my lamp, O Lord;
    the Lord turns my darkness into light.
³⁰With your help I can advance against a troop; *g*
    with my God I can scale a wall.

³¹"As for God, his way is perfect;
    the word of the Lord is flawless.
He is a shield
    for all who take refuge in him.
³²For who is God besides the Lord?
    And who is the Rock except our God?
³³It is God who arms me with strength *h*
    and makes my way perfect.
³⁴He makes my feet like the feet of a deer;
    he enables me to stand on the heights.
³⁵He trains my hands for battle;
    my arms can bend a bow of bronze.
³⁶You give me your shield of victory;
    you stoop down to make me great.

---

d19 Hebrew and Septuagint; 1 Chron. 20:5 *son of Jair killed Lahmi the brother of Goliath*   *a3* *Horn* here symbolises strength.
b6 Hebrew *Sheol*   *c8* Hebrew; Vulgate and Syriac (see also Psalm 18:7) *mountains*
d11 Many Hebrew manuscripts (see also Psalm 18:10); most Hebrew manuscripts *appeared*
e12 Septuagint and Vulgate (see also Psalm 18:11); Hebrew *massed*
f25 Hebrew; Septuagint and Vulgate (see also Psalm 18:24) *to the cleanness of my hands*   *g30* Or *can run through a barricade*
h33 Dead Sea Scrolls, some Septuagint manuscripts, Vulgate and Syriac (see also Psalm 18:32); Masoretic Text *who is my strong refuge*

³⁷You broaden the path beneath me,
    so that my ankles do not turn over.

³⁸"I pursued my enemies and crushed them;
    I did not turn back till they were destroyed.
³⁹I crushed them completely, and they could not
    rise;
    they fell beneath my feet.
⁴⁰You armed me with strength for battle;
    you made my adversaries bow at my feet.
⁴¹You made my enemies turn their backs in flight,
    and I destroyed my foes.
⁴²They cried for help, but there was no-one to save
    them—
    to the LORD, but he did not answer.
⁴³I beat them as fine as the dust of the earth;
    I pounded and trampled them like mud in the
    streets.

⁴⁴"You have delivered me from the attacks of my
    people;
    you have preserved me as the head of nations.
People I did not know are subject to me,
⁴⁵ and foreigners come cringing to me;
    as soon as they hear me, they obey me.
⁴⁶They all lose heart;
    they come trembling[i] from their strongholds.

⁴⁷"The LORD lives! Praise be to my Rock!
    Exalted be God, the Rock, my Saviour!
⁴⁸He is the God who avenges me,
    who puts the nations under me,
⁴⁹ who sets me free from my enemies.
You exalted me above my foes;
    from violent men you rescued me.
⁵⁰Therefore I will praise you, O LORD, among the
    nations;
    I will sing praises to your name.
⁵¹He gives his king great victories;
    he shows unfailing kindness to his anointed,
    to David and his descendants for ever."

The Last Words of David

23 These are the last words of David:

"The oracle of David son of Jesse,
    the oracle of the man exalted by the Most High,
the man anointed by the God of Jacob,
    Israel's singer of songs:[a]

²"The Spirit of the LORD spoke through me;
    his word was on my tongue.
³The God of Israel spoke,
    the Rock of Israel said to me:
'When one rules over men in righteousness,
    when he rules in the fear of God,
⁴he is like the light of morning at sunrise
    on a cloudless morning,
like the brightness after rain
    that brings the grass from the earth.'

⁵"Is not my house right with God?
    Has he not made with me an everlasting
    covenant,
    arranged and secured in every part?
Will he not bring to fruition my salvation
    and grant me my every desire?
⁶But evil men are all to be cast aside like thorns,
    which are not gathered with the hand.
⁷Whoever touches thorns
    uses a tool of iron or the shaft of a spear;
    they are burned up where they lie."

David's Mighty Men

⁸These are the names of David's mighty men:

Josheb-Basshebeth,[b] a Tahkemonite,[c] was chief of the Three; he raised his spear against eight hundred men, whom he killed[d] in one encounter.

⁹Next to him was Eleazar son of Dodai the Ahohite. As one of the three mighty men, he was with David when they taunted the Philistines gathered at Pas Dammim,[e] for battle. Then the men of Israel retreated, ¹⁰but he stood his ground and struck down the Philistines till his hand grew tired and froze to the sword. The LORD brought about a great victory that day. The troops returned to Eleazar, but only to strip the dead.

¹¹Next to him was Shammah son of Agee the Hararite. When the Philistines banded together at a place where there was a field full of lentils, Israel's troops fled from them. ¹²But Shammah took his stand in the middle of the field. He defended it and struck the Philistines down, and the LORD brought about a great victory.

¹³During harvest time, three of the thirty chief men came down to David at the cave of Adullam, while a band of Philistines was encamped in the Valley of Rephaim. ¹⁴At that time David was in the stronghold, and the Philistine garrison was at Bethlehem. ¹⁵David longed for water and said, "Oh, that someone would get me a drink of water from the well near the gate of Bethlehem!" ¹⁶So the three mighty men broke through the Philistine lines, drew water from the well near the gate of Bethlehem and carried it back to David. But he refused to drink it; instead, he poured it out before the LORD. ¹⁷"Far be it from me, O LORD, to do this!" he said. "Is it not the blood of men who went at the risk of their lives?" And David would not drink it.

Such were the exploits of the three mighty men.

¹⁸Abishai the brother of Joab son of Zeruiah was chief of the Three.[f] He raised his spear against three hundred men, whom he killed, and so he became as famous as the Three. ¹⁹Was he not held in greater honour than the Three? He became their commander, even though he was not included among them.

²⁰Benaiah son of Jehoiada was a valiant fighter from

ⁱ46 Some Septuagint manuscripts and Vulgate (see also Psalm 18:45); Masoretic Text *they arm themselves.*
^a1 Or *Israel's beloved singer*
^b8 Hebrew; some Septuagint manuscripts suggest *Ish-Bosheth*, that is, *Esh-Baal* (see also 1 Chron. 11:11 *Jashobeam*).
^c8 Probably a variant of *Hacmonite* (see 1 Chron. 11:11)   ^d8 Some Septuagint manuscripts (see also 1 Chron. 11:11); Hebrew and other Septuagint manuscripts *Three; it was Adino the Eznite who killed eight hundred men*   ^e9 See 1 Chron. 11:13; Hebrew *gathered there.*   ^f18 Most Hebrew manuscripts (see also 1 Chron. 11:20); two Hebrew manuscripts and Syriac *Thirty*

Kabzeel, who performed great exploits. He struck down two of Moab's best men. He also went down into a pit on a snowy day and killed a lion. ²¹And he struck down a huge Egyptian. Although the Egyptian had a spear in his hand, Benaiah went against him with a club. He snatched the spear from the Egyptian's hand and killed him with his own spear. ²²Such were the exploits of Benaiah son of Jehoiada; he too was as famous as the three mighty men. ²³He was held in greater honour than any of the Thirty, but he was not included among the Three. And David put him in charge of his bodyguard.

²⁴Among the Thirty were:
    Asahel the brother of Joab,
    Elhanan son of Dodo from Bethlehem,
  ²⁵Shammah the Harodite,
    Elika the Harodite,
  ²⁶Helez the Paltite,
    Ira son of Ikkesh from Tekoa,
  ²⁷Abiezer from Anathoth,
    Mebunnaiᵍ the Hushathite,
  ²⁸Zalmon the Ahohite,
    Maharai the Netophathite,
  ²⁹Heledʰ son of Baanah the Netophathite,
    Ithai son of Ribai from Gibeah in Benjamin,
  ³⁰Benaiah the Pirathonite,
    Hiddaiⁱ from the ravines of Gaash,
  ³¹Abi-Albon the Arbathite,
    Azmaveth the Barhumite,
  ³²Eliahba the Shaalbonite,
    the sons of Jashen,
    Jonathan ³³son ofʲ Shammah the Hararite,
    Ahiam son of Shararᵏ the Hararite,
  ³⁴Eliphelet son of Ahasbai the Maacathite,
    Eliam son of Ahithophel the Gilonite,
  ³⁵Hezro the Carmelite,
    Paarai the Arbite,
  ³⁶Igal son of Nathan from Zobah,
    the son of Hagri,ˡ
  ³⁷Zelek the Ammonite,
    Naharai the Beerothite, the armour-bearer of
      Joab son of Zeruiah,
  ³⁸Ira the Ithrite,
    Gareb the Ithrite
  ³⁹and Uriah the Hittite.
  There were thirty-seven in all.

David Counts the Fighting Men

24 Again the anger of the LORD burned against Israel, and he incited David against them, saying, "Go and take a census of Israel and Judah."

²So the king said to Joab and the army commandersᵃ with him, "Go throughout the tribes of Israel from Dan to Beersheba and enrol the fighting men, so that I may know how many there are."

³But Joab replied to the king, "May the LORD your God multiply the troops a hundred times over, and may the eyes of my lord the king see it. But why does my lord the king want to do such a thing?"

24:1 The statement that the Lord incited David to take a census which he then confessed as a sin (24:10) is a strange situation. It reflects the belief that ultimately nothing happened unless God allowed it, and that God could work through evil to bring about good. He did here by using the incident to lead to the purchasing of the site for the Jerusalem temple. The writer of a parallel account suggested that Satan was responsible for inciting David (1 Chronicles 21:1). If this was the case, it does not take ultimate authority from God, since Satan could do only what God permitted him.

---

⁴The king's word, however, overruled Joab and the army commanders; so they left the presence of the king to enrol the fighting men of Israel.

⁵After crossing the Jordan, they camped near Aroer, south of the town in the gorge, and then went through Gad and on to Jazer. ⁶They went to Gilead and the region of Tahtim Hodshi, and on to Dan Jaan and around towards Sidon. ⁷Then they went towards the fortress of Tyre and all the towns of the Hivites and Canaanites. Finally, they went on to Beersheba in the Negev of Judah.

⁸After they had gone through the entire land, they came back to Jerusalem at the end of nine months and twenty days.

⁹Joab reported the number of the fighting men to the king: In Israel there were eight hundred thousand ablebodied men who could handle a sword, and in Judah five hundred thousand.

¹⁰David was conscience-stricken after he had counted the fighting men, and he said to the LORD, "I have sinned greatly in what I have done. Now, O LORD, I beg you, take away the guilt of your servant. I have done a very foolish thing."

¹¹Before David got up the next morning, the word of the LORD had come to Gad the prophet, David's seer: ¹²"Go and tell David, 'This is what the LORD says: I am giving you three options. Choose one of them for me to carry out against you.' "

¹³So Gad went to David and said to him, "Shall there come upon you threeᵇ years of famine in your land? Or three months of fleeing from your enemies while they pursue you? Or three days of plague in your land? Now then, think it over and decide how I should answer the one who sent me."

ᵍ27 Hebrew; some Septuagint manuscripts (see also 1 Chron. 11:29) *Sibbecai*
ʰ29 Some Hebrew manuscripts and Vulgate (see also 1 Chron. 11:30); most Hebrew manuscripts *Heleb*
ⁱ30 Hebrew; some Septuagint manuscripts (see also 1 Chron. 11:32) *Hurai*
ʲ33 Some Septuagint manuscripts (see also 1 Chron. 11:34); Hebrew does not have *son of*.
ᵏ33 Hebrew; some Septuagint manuscripts (see also 1 Chron. 11:35) *Sacar*
ˡ36 Some Septuagint manuscripts (see also 1 Chron. 11:38); Hebrew *Haggadi*
ᵃ2 Septuagint (see also verse 4 and 1 Chron. 21:2); Hebrew *Joab the army commander*
ᵇ13 Septuagint (see also 1 Chron. 21:12); Hebrew *seven*

[14]David said to Gad, "I am in deep distress. Let us fall into the hands of the LORD, for his mercy is great; but do not let me fall into the hands of men."

[15]So the LORD sent a plague on Israel from that morning until the end of the time designated, and seventy thousand of the people from Dan to Beersheba died. [16]When the angel stretched out his hand to destroy Jerusalem, the LORD was grieved because of the calamity and said to the angel who was afflicting the people, "Enough! Withdraw your hand." The angel of the LORD was then at the threshing-floor of Araunah the Jebusite.

[17]When David saw the angel who was striking down the people, he said to the LORD, "I am the one who has sinned and done wrong. These are but sheep. What have they done? Let your hand fall upon me and my family."

David Builds an Altar

[18]On that day Gad went to David and said to him, "Go up and build an altar to the LORD on the threshing-floor of Araunah the Jebusite." [19]So David went up, as the LORD had commanded through Gad. [20]When Araunah looked and saw the king and his men coming towards him, he went out and bowed down before the king with his face to the ground.

[21]Araunah said, "Why has my lord the king come to his servant?"

"To buy your threshing-floor," David answered, "so that I can build an altar to the LORD, that the plague on the people may be stopped."

[22]Araunah said to David, "Let my lord the king take whatever pleases him and offer it up. Here are oxen for the burnt offering, and here are threshing-sledges and ox yokes for the wood. [23]O king, Araunah gives all this to the king." Araunah also said to him, "May the LORD your God accept you."

[24]But the king replied to Araunah, "No, I insist on paying you for it. I will not sacrifice to the LORD my God burnt offerings that cost me nothing."

24:24 David would not offer something to God that had been gained cheaply. This is a good illustration that true worship can be very costly.

So David bought the threshing-floor and the oxen and paid fifty shekels[c] of silver for them. [25]David built an altar to the LORD there and sacrificed burnt offerings and fellowship offerings.[d] Then the LORD answered prayer on behalf of the land, and the plague on Israel was stopped.

1 Kings

Taking Up a Great Theme

The book of 1 Kings resumes the account of the history of God's people at the point at which 2 Samuel left off, with David about to be succeeded by Solomon. It gives an account of Solomon's reign before tracing the fortunes of the divided kingdoms of Israel and Judah down to the middle of the ninth century BC, at which point 2 Kings, which originally formed one work with this book, takes up the story.

The Reign of Solomon

The first half of the book focuses on the reign of Solomon, which continued the golden age brought in by the reign of David, his father. Once the early challenge of Adonijah, Solomon's elder brother, had been ended, Solomon's wise rule resulted in a time of unparalleled peace and prosperity for God's people. Chief among his achievements was the building of the Jerusalem temple on the site obtained by David. The dedication of the temple, with the ark of the covenant present there, marked the very height of Solomon's reign, since God could now be seen to dwell among his people.

National Division

Despite his legendary wisdom, Solomon's great liking of foreign women led to the worshipping of their gods. This resulted, following his death, in the division of the nation into two kingdoms (chapter 12); Israel in the north and Judah in the south. Rehoboam, Solomon's son, reigned over Judah from Jerusalem, but Jeroboam (one of David's sons) ruled over the Northern Kingdom.

Judging the Kings

The book traces the history of the two nations by giving a series of summaries of the reigns of each of their kings. The reign of each king is evaluated, not on the basis of his political achievements, but according to his religious stance. Jeroboam, who introduced alternative places of worship for the Northern Kingdom, was seen as the model of a wicked and rebellious king. David, whose royal house was linked with the Jerusalem temple, was the model of faithfulness and obedience to God. The kings of the north were all condemned, many being accused of "walking in the ways of Jeroboam" (e.g. 1 Kings 16:19); whereas there were a few kings of Judah who were judged to have ruled well on the basis of the religious reforms introduced during their reign.

Introducing Elijah

Chapters 17—19 introduce one of the great Old Testament prophets, Elijah. He is probably most famous for his contest with 450 prophets of Baal on Mount Carmel. He appeared in Israel during the reign of wicked King Ahab and his wife Jezebel. Whilst Elijah is portrayed as a great man of God, we are also shown the human side of the man in his great fear of Jezebel. This is a further reminder of the way God uses ordinary people to achieve great things.

The Importance of the Temple

The most important passages in the book are those which record Solomon's prayer at the dedication of the temple (8:22–61) and the Lord's response to it (9:1–9). The temple would be regarded by God's people as the place where God lived among them, but Solomon's prayer made it clear that God was too great to be contained in an earthly temple, however splendid it might be. In response, the Lord renewed the promise made to David (9:4,5), although he made it conditional on the behaviour of Solomon and his descendants. This condition is of especial importance for understanding the downward path of the two kingdoms in the second half of the book, and also throughout 2 Kings.

God's Presence in National Affairs

1 Kings does not set out to be a history book that simply records a series of events. Its purpose is to indicate that God was at work through all the changing circumstances within the life of his people. This is made especially clear by the many references to the way in which events fulfilled the word of the Lord that had been spoken by his prophets. It is also important to notice the strong link between the behaviour of the various kings and the fortunes of the nation. The king was understood to embody the life of the whole nation before God. Obedience to God and his laws on the part of the king would bring prosperity, but disobedience would bring disaster. This becomes very clear in the summaries of the reigns of many of the kings of both Israel and Judah. For later generations of God's people, this book would bring a reminder of the importance of obedience to God's laws, and of the harsh consequences of disobedience.

Adonijah Sets Himself Up as King

1 When King David was old and well advanced in years, he could not keep warm even when they put covers over him. [2]So his servants said to him, "Let us look for a young virgin to attend the king and take care of him. She can lie beside him so that our lord the king may keep warm."

[3]Then they searched throughout Israel for a beautiful girl and found Abishag, a Shunammite, and brought her to the king. [4]The girl was very beautiful; she took care of the king and waited on him, but the king had no intimate relations with her.

[5]Now Adonijah, whose mother was Haggith, put himself forward and said, "I will be king." So he got chariots and horses[a] ready, with fifty men to run ahead of him. [6](His father had never interfered with him by asking, "Why do you behave as you do?" He was also very handsome and was born next after Absalom.)

1:5   Adonijah was David's oldest surviving son and next in line to the throne. He appeared to be David's natural successor.

---

[7]Adonijah conferred with Joab son of Zeruiah and with Abiathar the priest, and they gave him their support. [8]But Zadok the priest, Benaiah son of Jehoiada,

[a]5 Or charioteers

Nathan the prophet, Shimei and Rei[b] and David's special guard did not join Adonijah.

9Adonijah then sacrificed sheep, cattle and fattened calves at the Stone of Zoheleth near En Rogel. He invited all his brothers, the king's sons, and all the men of Judah who were royal officials, 10but he did not invite Nathan the prophet or Benaiah or the special guard or his brother Solomon.

11Then Nathan asked Bathsheba, Solomon's mother, "Have you not heard that Adonijah, the son of Haggith, has become king without our lord David's knowing it? 12Now then, let me advise you how you can save your own life and the life of your son Solomon. 13Go in to King David and say to him, 'My lord the king, did you not swear to me your servant: "Surely Solomon your son shall be king after me, and he will sit on my throne"? Why then has Adonijah become king?' 14While you are still there talking to the king, I will come in and confirm what you have said."

15So Bathsheba went to see the aged king in his room, where Abishag the Shunammite was attending him. 16Bathsheba bowed low and knelt before the king.

"What is it you want?" the king asked.

17She said to him, "My lord, you yourself swore to me your servant by the LORD your God: 'Solomon your son shall become king after me, and he will sit on my throne.' 18But now Adonijah has become king, and you, my lord the king, do not know about it. 19He has sacrificed great numbers of cattle, fattened calves, and sheep, and has invited all the king's sons, Abiathar the priest and Joab the commander of the army, but he has not invited Solomon your servant. 20My lord the king, the eyes of all Israel are on you, to learn from you who will sit on the throne of my lord the king after him. 21Otherwise, as soon as my lord the king is laid to rest with his fathers, I and my son Solomon will be treated as criminals."

22While she was still speaking with the king, Nathan the prophet arrived. 23And they told the king, "Nathan the prophet is here." So he went before the king and bowed with his face to the ground.

24Nathan said, "Have you, my lord the king, declared that Adonijah shall be king after you, and that he will sit on your throne? 25Today he has gone down and sacrificed great numbers of cattle, fattened calves, and sheep. He has invited all the king's sons, the commanders of the army and Abiathar the priest. At this very moment they are eating and drinking with him and saying, 'Long live King Adonijah!' 26But me your servant, and Zadok the priest, and Benaiah son of Jehoiada, and your servant Solomon he did not invite. 27Is this something my lord the king has done without letting his servants know who should sit on the throne of my lord the king after him?"

David Makes Solomon King

28Then King David said, "Call in Bathsheba." So she came into the king's presence and stood before him. 29The king then took an oath: "As surely as the LORD lives, who has delivered me out of every trouble, 30I will surely carry out today what I swore to you by the LORD, the God of Israel: Solomon your son shall be king after me, and he will sit on my throne in my place."

31Then Bathsheba bowed low with her face to the ground and, kneeling before the king, said, "May my lord King David live for ever!"

32King David said, "Call in Zadok the priest, Nathan the prophet and Benaiah son of Jehoiada." When they came before the king, 33he said to them: "Take your lord's servants with you and set Solomon my son on my own mule and take him down to Gihon. 34There shall Zadok the priest and Nathan the prophet anoint him king over Israel. Blow the trumpet and shout, 'Long live King Solomon!' 35Then you are to go up with him, and he is to come and sit on my throne and reign in my place. I have appointed him ruler over Israel and Judah."

36Benaiah son of Jehoiada answered the king, "Amen! May the LORD, the God of my lord the king, so declare it. 37As the LORD was with my lord the king, so may he be with Solomon to make his throne even greater than the throne of my lord King David!"

38So Zadok the priest, Nathan the prophet, Benaiah son of Jehoiada, the Kerethites and the Pelethites went down and put Solomon on King David's mule and escorted him to Gihon. 39Zadok the priest took the horn of oil from the sacred tent and anointed Solomon. Then they sounded the trumpet and all the people shouted, "Long live King Solomon!" 40And all the people went up after him, playing flutes and rejoicing greatly, so that the ground shook with the sound.

41Adonijah and all the guests who were with him heard it as they were finishing their feast. On hearing the sound of the trumpet, Joab asked, "What's the meaning of all the noise in the city?"

42Even as he was speaking, Jonathan son of Abiathar the priest arrived. Adonijah said, "Come in. A worthy man like you must be bringing good news."

43"Not at all!" Jonathan answered. "Our lord King David has made Solomon king. 44The king has sent with him Zadok the priest, Nathan the prophet, Benaiah son of Jehoiada, the Kerethites and the Pelethites, and they have put him on the king's mule, 45and Zadok the priest and Nathan the prophet have anointed him king at Gihon. From there they have gone up cheering, and the city resounds with it. That's the noise you hear. 46Moreover, Solomon has taken his seat on the royal throne. 47Also, the royal officials have come to congratulate our lord King David, saying, 'May your God make Solomon's name more famous than yours and his throne greater than yours!' And the king bowed in worship on his bed 48and said, 'Praise be to the LORD, the God of Israel, who has allowed my eyes to see a successor on my throne today.' "

49At this, all Adonijah's guests rose in alarm and dispersed. 50But Adonijah, in fear of Solomon, went and took hold of the horns of the altar. 51Then Solomon was told, "Adonijah is afraid of King Solomon and is clinging to the horns of the altar. He says, 'Let King Solomon swear to me today that he will not put his servant to death with the sword.' "

52Solomon replied, "If he shows himself to be a

worthy man, not a hair of his head will fall to the ground; but if evil is found in him, he will die." ⁵³Then King Solomon sent men, and they brought him down from the altar. And Adonijah came and bowed down to King Solomon, and Solomon said, "Go to your home."

> **1:50**   Adonijah claimed sanctuary from the anger of Solomon by the action of taking hold of the horns of the altar.

David's Charge to Solomon

2 When the time drew near for David to die, he gave a charge to Solomon his son.

²"I am about to go the way of all the earth," he said. "So be strong, show yourself a man, ³and observe what the LORD your God requires: Walk in his ways, and keep his decrees and commands, his laws and requirements, as written in the Law of Moses, so that you may prosper in all you do and wherever you go, ⁴and that the LORD may keep his promise to me: 'If your descendants watch how they live, and if they walk faithfully before me with all their heart and soul, you will never fail to have a man on the throne of Israel.'

⁵"Now you yourself know what Joab son of Zeruiah did to me—what he did to the two commanders of Israel's armies, Abner son of Ner and Amasa son of Jether. He killed them, shedding their blood in peacetime as if in battle, and with that blood stained the belt round his waist and the sandals on his feet. ⁶Deal with him according to your wisdom, but do not let his grey head go down to the grave*ᵃ* in peace.

⁷"But show kindness to the sons of Barzillai of Gilead and let them be among those who eat at your table. They stood by me when I fled from your brother Absalom.

⁸"And remember, you have with you Shimei son of Gera, the Benjamite from Bahurim, who called down bitter curses on me the day I went to Mahanaim. When he came down to meet me at the Jordan, I swore to him by the LORD: 'I will not put you to death by the sword.' ⁹But now, do not consider him innocent. You are a man of wisdom; you will know what to do to him. Bring his grey head down to the grave in blood."

¹⁰Then David rested with his fathers and was buried in the City of David. ¹¹He had reigned for forty years over Israel—seven years in Hebron and thirty-three in Jerusalem. ¹²So Solomon sat on the throne of his father David, and his rule was firmly established.

Solomon's Throne Established

¹³Now Adonijah, the son of Haggith, went to Bathsheba, Solomon's mother. Bathsheba asked him, "Do you come peacefully?"

He answered, "Yes, peacefully." ¹⁴Then he added, "I have something to say to you."

"You may say it," she replied.

¹⁵"As you know," he said, "the kingdom was mine. All Israel looked to me as their king. But things changed, and the kingdom has gone to my brother; for

it has come to him from the LORD. ¹⁶Now I have one request to make of you. Do not refuse me."

"You may make it," she said.

¹⁷So he continued, "Please ask King Solomon—he will not refuse you—to give me Abishag the Shunammite as my wife."

¹⁸"Very well," Bathsheba replied, "I will speak to the king for you."

¹⁹When Bathsheba went to King Solomon to speak to him for Adonijah, the king stood up to meet her, bowed down to her and sat down on his throne. He had a throne brought for the king's mother, and she sat down at his right hand.

²⁰"I have one small request to make of you," she said. "Do not refuse me."

The king replied, "Make it, my mother; I will not refuse you."

²¹So she said, "Let Abishag the Shunammite be given in marriage to your brother Adonijah."

²²King Solomon answered his mother, "Why do you request Abishag the Shunammite for Adonijah? You might as well request the kingdom for him—after all, he is my older brother—yes, for him and for Abiathar the priest and Joab son of Zeruiah!"

²³Then King Solomon swore by the LORD: "May God deal with me, be it ever so severely, if Adonijah does not pay with his life for this request! ²⁴And now, as surely as the LORD lives—he who has established me securely on the throne of my father David and has founded a dynasty for me as he promised—Adonijah shall be put to death today!" ²⁵So King Solomon gave orders to Benaiah son of Jehoiada, and he struck down Adonijah and he died.

> **2:23**   Adonijah's request to be allowed to marry David's former companion was seen by Solomon as an indirect attempt to gain the throne. This explains his harsh response towards Adonijah. The episode also gave him the opportunity to remove Abiathar the priest from office in fulfilment of the prophecy recorded in 1 Samuel 2:27–36.

²⁶To Abiathar the priest the king said, "Go back to your fields in Anathoth. You deserve to die, but I will not put you to death now, because you carried the ark of the Sovereign LORD before my father David and shared all my father's hardships." ²⁷So Solomon removed Abiathar from the priesthood of the LORD, fulfilling the word the LORD had spoken at Shiloh about the house of Eli.

²⁸When the news reached Joab, who had conspired with Adonijah though not with Absalom, he fled to the tent of the LORD and took hold of the horns of the altar. ²⁹King Solomon was told that Joab had fled to the tent of the LORD and was beside the altar. Then Solomon ordered Benaiah son of Jehoiada, "Go, strike him down!"

³⁰So Benaiah entered the tent of the LORD and said to Joab, "The king says, 'Come out!' "

ᵃ6 Hebrew *Sheol*; also in verse 9

But he answered, "No, I will die here."

Benaiah reported to the king, "This is how Joab answered me."

³¹Then the king commanded Benaiah, "Do as he says. Strike him down and bury him, and so clear me and my father's house of the guilt of the innocent blood that Joab shed. ³²The LORD will repay him for the blood he shed, because without the knowledge of my father David he attacked two men and killed them with the sword. Both of them—Abner son of Ner, commander of Israel's army, and Amasa son of Jether, commander of Judah's army—were better men and more upright than he. ³³May the guilt of their blood rest on the head of Joab and his descendants for ever. But on David and his descendants, his house and his throne, may there be the LORD's peace for ever."

³⁴So Benaiah son of Jehoiada went up and struck down Joab and killed him, and he was buried on his own land ᵇ in the desert. ³⁵The king put Benaiah son of Jehoiada over the army in Joab's position and replaced Abiathar with Zadok the priest.

³⁶Then the king sent for Shimei and said to him, "Build yourself a house in Jerusalem and live there, but do not go anywhere else. ³⁷The day you leave and cross the Kidron Valley, you can be sure you will die; your blood will be on your own head."

³⁸Shimei answered the king, "What you say is good. Your servant will do as my lord the king has said." And Shimei stayed in Jerusalem for a long time.

³⁹But three years later, two of Shimei's slaves ran off to Achish son of Maacah, king of Gath, and Shimei was told, "Your slaves are in Gath." ⁴⁰At this, he saddled his donkey and went to Achish at Gath in search of his slaves. So Shimei went away and brought the slaves back from Gath.

⁴¹When Solomon was told that Shimei had gone from Jerusalem to Gath and had returned, ⁴²the king summoned Shimei and said to him, "Did I not make you swear by the LORD and warn you, 'On the day you leave to go anywhere else, you can be sure you will die'? At that time you said to me, 'What you say is good. I will obey.' ⁴³Why then did you not keep your oath to the LORD and obey the command I gave you?"

⁴⁴The king also said to Shimei, "You know in your heart all the wrong you did to my father David. Now the LORD will repay you for your wrongdoing. ⁴⁵But King Solomon will be blessed, and David's throne will remain secure before the LORD for ever."

⁴⁶Then the king gave the order to Benaiah son of Jehoiada, and he went out and struck Shimei down and killed him.

The kingdom was now firmly established in Solomon's hands.

Solomon Asks for Wisdom

3 Solomon made an alliance with Pharaoh king of Egypt and married his daughter. He brought her to the City of David until he finished building his palace and the temple of the LORD, and the wall around Jerusalem. ²The people, however, were still sacrificing at the high places, because a temple had not yet been built for the Name of the LORD. ³Solomon showed his love for the LORD by walking according to the statutes of his father David, except that he offered sacrifices and burned incense on the high places.

3:2 The high places were open-air places of worship, often associated with the fertility gods of the Canaanites who had lived in the land before the people of Israel.

---

⁴The king went to Gibeon to offer sacrifices, for that was the most important high place, and Solomon offered a thousand burnt offerings on that altar. ⁵At Gibeon the LORD appeared to Solomon during the night in a dream, and God said, "Ask for whatever you want me to give you."

⁶Solomon answered, "You have shown great kindness to your servant, my father David, because he was faithful to you and righteous and upright in heart. You have continued this great kindness to him and have given him a son to sit on his throne this very day.

⁷"Now, O LORD my God, you have made your servant king in place of my father David. But I am only a little child and do not know how to carry out my duties. ⁸Your servant is here among the people you have chosen, a great people, too numerous to count or number. ⁹So give your servant a discerning heart to govern your people and to distinguish between right and wrong. For who is able to govern this great people of yours?"

¹⁰The Lord was pleased that Solomon had asked for this. ¹¹So God said to him, "Since you have asked for this and not for long life or wealth for yourself, nor have asked for the death of your enemies but for discernment in administering justice, ¹²I will do what you have asked. I will give you a wise and discerning heart, so that there will never have been anyone like you, nor will there ever be. ¹³Moreover, I will give you what you have not asked for—both riches and honour—so that in your lifetime you will have no equal among kings. ¹⁴And if you walk in my ways and obey my statutes and commands as David your father did, I will give you a long life." ¹⁵Then Solomon awoke—and he realised it had been a dream.

He returned to Jerusalem, stood before the ark of the Lord's covenant and sacrificed burnt offerings and fellowship offerings.ᵃ Then he gave a feast for all his court.

A Wise Ruling

¹⁶Now two prostitutes came to the king and stood before him. ¹⁷One of them said, "My lord, this woman and I live in the same house. I had a baby while she was there with me. ¹⁸The third day after my child was born, this woman also had a baby. We were alone; there was no-one in the house but the two of us.

¹⁹"During the night this woman's son died because she lay on him. ²⁰So she got up in the middle of the night and took my son from my side while I your servant was asleep. She put him by her breast and put her dead son by my breast. ²¹The next morning, I got up

---

ᵇ 34 Or buried in his tomb   ᵃ 15 Traditionally peace offerings to nurse my son—and he was dead! But when I looked at him closely in the morning light, I saw that it wasn't the son I had borne."

²²The other woman said, "No! The living one is my son; the dead one is yours."

But the first one insisted, "No! The dead one is yours; the living one is mine." And so they argued before the king.

²³The king said, "This one says, 'My son is alive and your son is dead,' while that one says, 'No! Your son is dead and mine is alive.' "

²⁴Then the king said, "Bring me a sword." So they brought a sword for the king. ²⁵He then gave an order: "Cut the living child in two and give half to one and half to the other."

²⁶The woman whose son was alive was filled with compassion for her son and said to the king, "Please, my lord, give her the living baby! Don't kill him!"

But the other said, "Neither I nor you shall have him. Cut him in two!"

²⁷Then the king gave his ruling: "Give the living baby to the first woman. Do not kill him; she is his mother."

²⁸When all Israel heard the verdict the king had given, they held the king in awe, because they saw that he had wisdom from God to administer justice.

Solomon's Officials and Governors

4 So King Solomon ruled over all Israel. ²And these were his chief officials:

Azariah son of Zadok—the priest;
³Elihoreph and Ahijah, sons of Shisha—secretaries;
Jehoshaphat son of Ahilud—recorder;
⁴Benaiah son of Jehoiada—commander-in-chief;
Zadok and Abiathar—priests;
⁵Azariah son of Nathan—in charge of the district officers;
Zabud son of Nathan—a priest and personal adviser to the king;
⁶Ahishar—in charge of the palace;
Adoniram son of Abda—in charge of forced labour.

⁷Solomon also had twelve district governors over all Israel, who supplied provisions for the king and the royal household. Each one had to provide supplies for one month in the year. ⁸These are their names:

Ben-Hur—in the hill country of Ephraim;
⁹Ben-Deker—in Makaz, Shaalbim, Beth Shemesh and Elon Bethhanan;
¹⁰Ben-Hesed—in Arubboth (Socoh and all the land of Hepher were his);
¹¹Ben-Abinadab—in Naphoth Dor ᵃ (he was married to Taphath daughter of Solomon);
¹²Baana son of Ahilud—in Taanach and Megiddo, and in all of Beth Shan next to Zarethan below Jezreel, from Beth Shan to Abel Meholah across to Jokmeam;

¹³Ben-Geber—in Ramoth Gilead (the settlements of Jair son of Manasseh in Gilead were his, as well as the district of Argob in Bashan and its sixty large walled cities with bronze gate bars);
¹⁴Ahinadab son of Iddo—in Mahanaim;
¹⁵Ahimaaz—in Naphtali (he had married Basemath daughter of Solomon);
¹⁶Baana son of Hushai—in Asher and in Aloth;
¹⁷Jehoshaphat son of Paruah—in Issachar;
¹⁸Shimei son of Ela—in Benjamin;
¹⁹Geber son of Uri—in Gilead (the country of Sihon king of the Amorites and the country of Og king of Bashan). He was the only governor over the district.

Solomon's Daily Provisions

²⁰The people of Judah and Israel were as numerous as the sand on the seashore; they ate, they drank and they were happy. ²¹And Solomon ruled over all the kingdoms from the River ᵇ to the land of the Philistines, as far as the border of Egypt. These countries brought tribute and were Solomon's subjects all his life.

²²Solomon's daily provisions were thirty cors ᶜ of fine flour and sixty cors ᵈ of meal, ²³ten head of stall-fed cattle, twenty of pasture-fed cattle and a hundred sheep and goats, as well as deer, gazelles, roebucks and choice fowl. ²⁴For he ruled over all the kingdoms west of the River, from Tiphsah to Gaza, and had peace on all sides. ²⁵During Solomon's lifetime Judah and Israel, from Dan to Beersheba, lived in safety, each man under his own vine and fig-tree.

4:25 The picture of each man under his own vine and fig tree is a popular image for a time of peace.

---

²⁶Solomon had four ᵉ thousand stalls for chariot horses, and twelve thousand horses. ᶠ

²⁷The district officers, each in his month, supplied provisions for King Solomon and all who came to the king's table. They saw to it that nothing was lacking. ²⁸They also brought to the proper place their quotas of barley and straw for the chariot horses and the other horses.

Solomon's Wisdom

²⁹God gave Solomon wisdom and very great insight, and a breadth of understanding as measureless as the sand on the seashore. ³⁰Solomon's wisdom was greater than the wisdom of all the men of the East, and greater than all the wisdom of Egypt. ³¹He was wiser than any other man, including Ethan the Ezrahite—wiser than Heman, Calcol and Darda, the sons of Mahol. And his fame spread to all the surrounding nations. ³²He spoke three thousand proverbs and his songs numbered a thousand and five. ³³He described plant life, from the

---

ᵃ11 Or in the heights of Dor   ᵇ21 That is, the Euphrates; also in verse 24
ᶜ22 That is, probably about 180 bushels (about 6.6 kilolitres)   ᵈ22 That is, probably about 365 bushels (about 13.2 kilolitres)
ᵉ26 Some Septuagint manuscripts (see also 2 Chron. 9:25); Hebrew forty   ᶠ26 Or charioteers

cedar of Lebanon to the hyssop that grows out of walls. He also taught about animals and birds, reptiles and fish. [34]Men of all nations came to listen to Solomon's wisdom, sent by all the kings of the world, who had heard of his wisdom.

Preparations for Building the Temple

5 When Hiram king of Tyre heard that Solomon had been anointed king to succeed his father David, he sent his envoys to Solomon, because he had always been on friendly terms with David. [2]Solomon sent back this message to Hiram:

[3]"You know that because of the wars waged against my father David from all sides, he could not build a temple for the Name of the LORD his God until the LORD put his enemies under his feet. [4]But now the LORD my God has given me rest on every side, and there is no adversary or disaster. [5]I intend, therefore, to build a temple for the Name of the LORD my God, as the LORD told my father David, when he said, 'Your son whom I will put on the throne in your place will build the temple for my Name.'

[6]"So give orders that cedars of Lebanon be cut for me. My men will work with yours, and I will pay you for your men whatever wages you set. You know that we have no-one so skilled in felling timber as the Sidonians."

[7]When Hiram heard Solomon's message, he was greatly pleased and said, "Praise be to the LORD today, for he has given David a wise son to rule over this great nation."

[8]So Hiram sent word to Solomon:

"I have received the message you sent me and will do all you want in providing the cedar and pine logs. [9]My men will haul them down from Lebanon to the sea, and I will float them in rafts by sea to the place you specify. There I will separate them and you can take them away. And you are to grant my wish by providing food for my royal household."

[10]In this way Hiram kept Solomon supplied with all the cedar and pine logs he wanted, [11]and Solomon gave Hiram twenty thousand cors[a] of wheat as food for his household, in addition to twenty thousand baths[b,c] of pressed olive oil. Solomon continued to do this for Hiram year after year. [12]The LORD gave Solomon wisdom, just as he had promised him. There were peaceful relations between Hiram and Solomon, and the two of them made a treaty.

[13]King Solomon conscripted labourers from all Israel—thirty thousand men. [14]He sent them off to Lebanon in shifts of ten thousand a month, so that they spent one month in Lebanon and two months at home.

Adoniram was in charge of the forced labour. [15]Solomon had seventy thousand carriers and eighty thousand stonecutters in the hills, [16]as well as thirty-three hundred[d] foremen who supervised the project and directed the workmen. [17]At the king's command they removed from the quarry large blocks of quality stone to provide a foundation of dressed stone for the temple. [18]The craftsmen of Solomon and Hiram and the men of Gebal[e] cut and prepared the timber and stone for the building of the temple.

5:13   When the people had originally requested a king to rule over them (1 Samuel 8:11–18), the conscription of Israelites was one of the features of the monarchy Samuel had warned the people about.

Solomon Builds the Temple

6 In the four hundred and eightieth[a] year after the Israelites had come out of Egypt, in the fourth year of Solomon's reign over Israel, in the month of Ziv, the second month, he began to build the temple of the LORD.

[2]The temple that King Solomon built for the LORD was sixty cubits long, twenty wide and thirty high.[b] [3]The portico at the front of the main hall of the temple extended the width of the temple, that is twenty cubits,[c] and projected ten cubits[d] from the front of the temple. [4]He made narrow clerestory windows in the temple. [5]Against the walls of the main hall and inner sanctuary he built a structure around the building, in which there were side rooms. [6]The lowest floor was five cubits[e] wide, the middle floor six cubits[f] and the third floor seven.[g] He made offset ledges around the outside of the temple so that nothing would be inserted into the temple walls.

[7]In building the temple, only blocks dressed at the quarry were used, and no hammer, chisel or any other iron tool was heard at the temple site while it was being built.

[8]The entrance to the lowest[h] floor was on the south side of the temple; a stairway led up to the middle level and from there to the third. [9]So he built the temple and completed it, roofing it with beams and cedar planks. [10]And he built the side rooms all along the temple. The height of each was five cubits, and they were attached to the temple by beams of cedar.

[11]The word of the LORD came to Solomon: [12]"As for this temple you are building, if you follow my decrees, carry out my regulations and keep all my commands and obey them, I will fulfil through you the promise I gave to David your father. [13]And I will live among the Israelites and will not abandon my people Israel."

[14]So Solomon built the temple and completed it.

---

a11 That is, probably about 121,000 bushels (about 4,400 kilolitres)   *b11* Septuagint (see also 2 Chron. 2:10); Hebrew *twenty cors*
c11 That is, about 97,000 gallons (about 440 kilolitres)
d16 Hebrew; some Septuagint manuscripts (see also 2 Chron. 2:2, 18) *thirty-six hundred*   *e18* That is, Byblos
a1 Hebrew; Septuagint *four hundred and fortieth*
b2 That is, about 90 feet (about 27 metres) long and 30 feet (about 9 metres) wide and 45 feet (about 13.5 metres) high
c3 That is, about 30 feet (about 9 metres)   *d3* That is, about 15 feet (about 4.5 metres)
e6 That is, about 7½ feet (about 2.3 metres); also in verses 10 and 24   *f6* That is, about 9 feet (about 2.7 metres)
g6 That is, about 10½ feet (about 3.2 metres)   *h8* Septuagint; Hebrew *middle*

¹⁵He lined its interior walls with cedar boards, panelling them from the floor of the temple to the ceiling, and covered the floor of the temple with planks of pine. ¹⁶He partitioned off twenty cubits^i at the rear of the temple with cedar boards from floor to ceiling to form within the temple an inner sanctuary, the Most Holy Place. ¹⁷The main hall in front of this room was forty cubits^j long. ¹⁸The inside of the temple was cedar, carved with gourds and open flowers. Everything was cedar; no stone was to be seen.

6:12   God's promise to David (2 Samuel 7:12ff) was reaffirmed and made conditional on the continuing obedience of Solomon. The obedience of the king is an important feature in 1 and 2 Kings.

---

¹⁹He prepared the inner sanctuary within the temple to set the ark of the covenant of the LORD there. ²⁰The inner sanctuary was twenty cubits long, twenty wide and twenty high.^{k} He overlaid the inside with pure gold, and he also overlaid the altar of cedar. ²¹Solomon covered the inside of the temple with pure gold, and he extended gold chains across the front of the inner sanctuary, which was overlaid with gold. ²²So he overlaid the whole interior with gold. He also overlaid with gold the altar that belonged to the inner sanctuary.

²³In the inner sanctuary he made a pair of cherubim of olive wood, each ten cubits^l high. ²⁴One wing of the first cherub was five cubits long, and the other wing five cubits—ten cubits from wing tip to wing tip. ²⁵The second cherub also measured ten cubits, for the two cherubim were identical in size and shape. ²⁶The height of each cherub was ten cubits. ²⁷He placed the cherubim inside the innermost room of the temple, with their wings spread out. The wing of one cherub touched one wall, while the wing of the other touched the other wall, and their wings touched each other in the middle of the room. ²⁸He overlaid the cherubim with gold.

²⁹On the walls all round the temple, in both the inner and outer rooms, he carved cherubim, palm trees and open flowers. ³⁰He also covered the floors of both the inner and outer rooms of the temple with gold.

³¹For the entrance of the inner sanctuary he made doors of olive wood with five-sided jambs. ³²And on the two olive wood doors he carved cherubim, palm trees and open flowers, and overlaid the cherubim and palm trees with beaten gold. ³³In the same way he made four-sided jambs of olive wood for the entrance to the main hall. ³⁴He also made two pine doors, each having two leaves that turned in sockets. ³⁵He carved cherubim, palm trees and open flowers on them and overlaid them with gold hammered evenly over the carvings.

³⁶And he built the inner courtyard of three courses of dressed stone and one course of trimmed cedar beams.

³⁷The foundation of the temple of the LORD was laid in the fourth year, in the month of Ziv. ³⁸In the eleventh year in the month of Bul, the eighth month, the temple was finished in all its details according to its specifications. He had spent seven years building it.

Solomon Builds His Palace

7 It took Solomon thirteen years, however, to complete the construction of his palace. ²He built the Palace of the Forest of Lebanon a hundred cubits long, fifty wide and thirty high,^{a} with four rows of cedar columns supporting trimmed cedar beams. ³It was roofed with cedar above the beams that rested on the columns—forty-five beams, fifteen to a row. ⁴Its windows were placed high in sets of three, facing each other. ⁵All the doorways had rectangular frames; they were in the front part in sets of three, facing each other.^{b}

⁶He made a colonnade fifty cubits long and thirty wide.^{c} In front of it was a portico, and in front of that were pillars and an overhanging roof.

⁷He built the throne hall, the Hall of Justice, where he was to judge, and he covered it with cedar from floor to ceiling.^{d} ⁸And the palace in which he was to live, set farther back, was similar in design. Solomon also made a palace like this hall for Pharaoh's daughter, whom he had married.

⁹All these structures, from the outside to the great courtyard and from foundation to eaves, were made of blocks of high-grade stone cut to size and trimmed with a saw on their inner and outer faces. ¹⁰The foundations were laid with large stones of good quality, some measuring ten cubits^e and some eight.^{f} ¹¹Above were high-grade stones, cut to size, and cedar beams. ¹²The great courtyard was surrounded by a wall of three courses of dressed stone and one course of trimmed cedar beams, as was the inner courtyard of the temple of the LORD with its portico.

The Temple's Furnishings

¹³King Solomon sent to Tyre and brought Huram,^{g} ¹⁴whose mother was a widow from the tribe of Naphtali and whose father was a man of Tyre and a craftsman in bronze. Huram was highly skilled and experienced in all kinds of bronze work. He came to King Solomon and did all the work assigned to him.

¹⁵He cast two bronze pillars, each eighteen cubits high and twelve cubits round,^{h} by line. ¹⁶He also made two capitals of cast bronze to set on the tops of the pillars; each capital was five cubits^i high. ¹⁷A network of interwoven chains festooned the capitals on top of the pillars, seven for each capital. ¹⁸He made

---

^{i}16 That is, about 30 feet (about 9 metres) ^{j}17 That is, about 60 feet (about 18 metres)
^{k}20 That is, about 30 feet (about 9 metres) long, wide and high ^{l}23 That is, about 15 feet (about 4.5 metres)
^{a}2 That is, about 150 feet (about 46 metres) long, 75 feet (about 23 metres) wide and 45 feet (about 13.5 metres) high
^{b}5 The meaning of the Hebrew for this verse is uncertain.
^{c}6 That is, about 75 feet (about 23 metres) long and 45 feet (about 13.5 metres) wide ^{d}7 Vulgate and Syriac; Hebrew *floor*
^{e}10 That is, about 15 feet (about 4.5 metres) ^{f}10 That is, about 12 feet (about 3.7 metres)
^{g}13 Hebrew *Hiram*, a variant of *Huram*; also in verses 40 and 45
^{h}15 That is, about 27 feet (about 8.2 metres) high and 18 feet (about 5.5 metres) round
^{i}16 That is, about 7½ feet (about 2.3 metres); also in verse 23

pomegranates in two rows/ encircling each network to decorate the capitals on top of the pillars.* He did the same for each capital. ¹⁹The capitals on top of the pillars in the portico were in the shape of lilies, four cubits¹ high. ²⁰On the capitals of both pillars, above the bowl-shaped part next to the network, were the two hundred pomegranates in rows all around. ²¹He erected the pillars at the portico of the temple. The pillar to the south he named Jakin^m and the one to the north Boaz.^n ²²The capitals on top were in the shape of lilies. And so the work on the pillars was completed.

²³He made the Sea of cast metal, circular in shape, measuring ten cubits^o from rim to rim and five cubits high. It took a line of thirty cubits^p to measure round it. ²⁴Below the rim, gourds encircled it — ten to a cubit. The gourds were cast in two rows in one piece with the Sea.

²⁵The Sea stood on twelve bulls, three facing north, three facing west, three facing south and three facing east. The Sea rested on top of them, and their hindquarters were towards the centre. ²⁶It was a handbreadth^q in thickness, and its rim was like the rim of a cup, like a lily blossom. It held two thousand baths.^r

²⁷He also made ten movable stands of bronze; each was four cubits long, four wide and three high. ^s ²⁸This is how the stands were made: They had side panels attached to uprights. ²⁹On the panels between the uprights were lions, bulls and cherubim — and on the uprights as well. Above and below the lions and bulls were wreaths of hammered work. ³⁰Each stand had four bronze wheels with bronze axles, and each had a basin resting on four supports, cast with wreaths on each side. ³¹On the inside of the stand there was an opening that had a circular frame one cubit^t deep. This opening was round, and with its basework it measured a cubit and a half.^u Around its opening there was engraving. The panels of the stands were square, not round. ³²The four wheels were under the panels, and the axles of the wheels were attached to the stand. The diameter of each wheel was a cubit and a half. ³³The wheels were made like chariot wheels; the axles, rims, spokes and hubs were all of cast metal.

³⁴Each stand had four handles, one on each corner, projecting from the stand. ³⁵At the top of the stand there was a circular band half a cubit^v deep. The supports and panels were attached to the top of the stand. ³⁶He engraved cherubim, lions and palm trees on the surfaces of the supports and on the panels, in every available space, with wreaths all around. ³⁷This is the way he made the ten stands. They were all cast in the same moulds and were identical in size and shape.

³⁸He then made ten bronze basins, each holding forty baths^w and measuring four cubits across, one basin to go on each of the ten stands. ³⁹He placed five of the stands on the south side of the temple and five on the north. He placed the Sea on the south side, at the south-east corner of the temple. ⁴⁰He also made the basins and shovels and sprinkling bowls.

So Huram finished all the work he had undertaken for King Solomon in the temple of the Lord:

⁴¹the two pillars;
the two bowl-shaped capitals on top of the pillars;
the two sets of network decorating the two bowl-shaped capitals on top of the pillars;
⁴²the four hundred pomegranates for the two sets of network (two rows of pomegranates for each network, decorating the bowl-shaped capitals on top of the pillars);
⁴³the ten stands with their ten basins;
⁴⁴the Sea and the twelve bulls under it;
⁴⁵the pots, shovels and sprinkling bowls.

All these objects that Huram made for King Solomon for the temple of the Lord were of burnished bronze. ⁴⁶The king had them cast in clay moulds in the plain of the Jordan between Succoth and Zarethan. ⁴⁷Solomon left all these things unweighed, because there were so many; the weight of the bronze was not determined.

⁴⁸Solomon also made all the furnishings that were in the Lord's temple:

the golden altar;
the golden table on which was the bread of the Presence;
⁴⁹the lampstands of pure gold (five on the right and five on the left, in front of the inner sanctuary);
the gold floral work and lamps and tongs;
⁵⁰the pure gold dishes, wick trimmers, sprinkling bowls, dishes and censers;
and the gold sockets for the doors of the innermost room, the Most Holy Place, and also for the doors of the main hall of the temple.

⁵¹When all the work King Solomon had done for the temple of the Lord was finished, he brought in the things his father David had dedicated — the silver and gold and the furnishings — and he placed them in the treasuries of the Lord's temple.

The Ark Brought to the Temple

8 Then King Solomon summoned into his presence at Jerusalem the elders of Israel, all the heads of the tribes and the chiefs of the Israelite families, to bring up the ark of the Lord's covenant from Zion, the City of David. ²All the men of Israel came together to King Solomon at the time of the festival in the month of Ethanim, the seventh month.

³When all the elders of Israel had arrived, the priests took up the ark, ⁴and they brought up the ark of the Lord and the Tent of Meeting and all the sacred

---

/18 Two Hebrew manuscripts and Septuagint; most Hebrew manuscripts *made the pillars, and there were two rows*
k18 Many Hebrew manuscripts and Syriac; most Hebrew manuscripts *pomegranates*
l19 That is, about 6 feet (about 1.8 metres); also in verse 38   m21 *Jakin* probably means *he establishes.*
n21 *Boaz* probably means *in him is strength.*   o23 That is, about 15 feet (about 4.5 metres)
p23 That is, about 45 feet (about 13.7 metres)   q26 That is, about 3 inches (about 8 centimetres)
r26 That is, probably about 9,700 gallons (about 44 kilolitres); the Septuagint does not have this sentence.
s27 That is, about 6 feet (about 1.8 metres) long and wide and about 4½ feet (about 1.4 metres) high
t31 That is, about 1½ feet (about 0.5 metre)   u31 That is, about 2¼ feet (about 0.7 metre); also in verse 32
v35 That is, about ¾ foot (about 0.2 metre)   w38 That is, about 195 gallons (about 880 litres)

furnishings in it. The priests and Levites carried them up, ⁵and King Solomon and the entire assembly of Israel that had gathered about him were before the ark, sacrificing so many sheep and cattle that they could not be recorded or counted.

⁶The priests then brought the ark of the LORD's covenant to its place in the inner sanctuary of the temple, the Most Holy Place, and put it beneath the wings of the cherubim. ⁷The cherubim spread their wings over the place of the ark and overshadowed the ark and its carrying poles. ⁸These poles were so long that their ends could be seen from the Holy Place in front of the inner sanctuary, but not from outside the Holy Place; and they are still there today. ⁹There was nothing in the ark except the two stone tablets that Moses had placed in it at Horeb, where the LORD made a covenant with the Israelites after they came out of Egypt.

¹⁰When the priests withdrew from the Holy Place, the cloud filled the temple of the LORD. ¹¹And the priests could not perform their service because of the cloud, for the glory of the LORD filled his temple.

8:11   The cloud represented the presence of the Lord within the temple.

---

¹²Then Solomon said, "The LORD has said that he would dwell in a dark cloud; ¹³I have indeed built a magnificent temple for you, a place for you to dwell for ever."

¹⁴While the whole assembly of Israel was standing there, the king turned round and blessed them. ¹⁵Then he said:

"Praise be to the LORD, the God of Israel, who with his own hand has fulfilled what he promised with his own mouth to my father David. For he said, ¹⁶'Since the day I brought my people Israel out of Egypt, I have not chosen a city in any tribe of Israel to have a temple built for my Name to be there, but I have chosen David to rule my people Israel.'

¹⁷"My father David had it in his heart to build a temple for the Name of the LORD, the God of Israel. ¹⁸But the LORD said to my father David, 'Because it was in your heart to build a temple for my Name, you did well to have this in your heart. ¹⁹Nevertheless, you are not the one to build the temple, but your son, who is your own flesh and blood—he is the one who will build the temple for my Name.'

8:17   The reference to a temple for the Name of the Lord was a way of indicating that the Lord was present in the temple at the same time as being too great to be confined within an earthly place. This is emphasized in the words of Solomon's great prayer (8:27–30).

---

²⁰"The LORD has kept the promise he made: I have succeeded David my father and now I sit on the throne of Israel, just as the LORD promised,

and I have built the temple for the Name of the LORD, the God of Israel. ²¹I have provided a place there for the ark, in which is the covenant of the LORD that he made with our fathers when he brought them out of Egypt."

Solomon's Prayer of Dedication

²²Then Solomon stood before the altar of the LORD in front of the whole assembly of Israel, spread out his hands towards heaven ²³and said:

"O LORD, God of Israel, there is no God like you in heaven above or on earth below—you who keep your covenant of love with your servants who continue wholeheartedly in your way. ²⁴You have kept your promise to your servant David my father; with your mouth you have promised and with your hand you have fulfilled it—as it is today.

²⁵"Now LORD, God of Israel, keep for your servant David my father the promises you made to him when you said, 'You shall never fail to have a man to sit before me on the throne of Israel, if only your sons are careful in all they do to walk before me as you have done.' ²⁶And now, O God of Israel, let your word that you promised your servant David my father come true.

²⁷"But will God really dwell on earth? The heavens, even the highest heaven, cannot contain you. How much less this temple I have built! ²⁸Yet give attention to your servant's prayer and his plea for mercy, O LORD my God. Hear the cry and the prayer that your servant is praying in your presence this day. ²⁹May your eyes be open towards this temple night and day, this place of which you said, 'My Name shall be there,' so that you will hear the prayer your servant prays towards this place. ³⁰Hear the supplication of your servant and of your people Israel when they pray towards this place. Hear from heaven, your dwelling-place, and when you hear, forgive.

³¹"When a man wrongs his neighbour and is required to take an oath and he comes and swears the oath before your altar in this temple, ³²then hear from heaven and act. Judge between your servants, condemning the guilty and bringing down on his own head what he has done. Declare the innocent not guilty, and so establish his innocence.

³³"When your people Israel have been defeated by an enemy because they have sinned against you, and when they turn back to you and confess your name, praying and making supplication to you in this temple, ³⁴then hear from heaven and forgive the sin of your people Israel and bring them back to the land you gave to their fathers.

³⁵"When the heavens are shut up and there is no rain because your people have sinned against you, and when they pray towards this place and confess your name and turn from their sin because you have afflicted them, ³⁶then hear from heaven and forgive the sin of your servants, your people Israel. Teach them the right way to live, and send rain on the land you gave your people for an inheritance.

37"When famine or plague comes to the land, or blight or mildew, locusts or grasshoppers, or when an enemy besieges them in any of their cities, whatever disaster or disease may come, 38and when a prayer or plea is made by any of your people Israel—each one aware of the afflictions of his own heart, and spreading out his hands towards this temple—39then hear from heaven, your dwelling-place. Forgive and act; deal with each man according to all he does, since you know his heart (for you alone know the hearts of all men), 40so that they will fear you all the time they live in the land you gave our fathers.

41"As for the foreigner who does not belong to your people Israel but has come from a distant land because of your name—42for men will hear of your great name and your mighty hand and your outstretched arm—when he comes and prays towards this temple, 43then hear from heaven, your dwelling-place, and do whatever the foreigner asks of you, so that all the peoples of the earth may know your name and fear you, as do your own people Israel, and may know that this house I have built bears your Name.

44"When your people go to war against their enemies, wherever you send them, and when they pray to the Lord towards the city you have chosen and the temple I have built for your Name, 45then hear from heaven their prayer and their plea, and uphold their cause.

46"When they sin against you—for there is no-one who does not sin—and you become angry with them and give them over to the enemy, who takes them captive to his own land, far away or near; 47and if they have a change of heart in the land where they are held captive, and repent and plead with you in the land of their conquerors and say, 'We have sinned, we have done wrong, we have acted wickedly'; 48and if they turn back to you with all their heart and soul in the land of their enemies who took them captive, and pray to you towards the land you gave their fathers, towards the city you have chosen and the temple I have built for your Name; 49then from heaven, your dwelling-place, hear their prayer and their plea, and uphold their cause. 50And forgive your people, who have sinned against you; forgive all the offences they have committed against you, and cause their conquerors to show them mercy; 51for they are your people and your inheritance, whom you brought out of Egypt, out of that iron-smelting furnace.

52"May your eyes be open to your servant's plea and to the plea of your people Israel, and may you listen to them whenever they cry out to you. 53For you singled them out from all the nations of the world to be your own inheritance, just as you declared through your servant Moses when you, O Sovereign Lord, brought our fathers out of Egypt."

54When Solomon had finished all these prayers and supplications to the Lord, he rose from before the altar of the Lord, where he had been kneeling with his hands spread out towards heaven. 55He stood and blessed the whole assembly of Israel in a loud voice, saying:

56"Praise be to the Lord, who has given rest to his people Israel just as he promised. Not one word has failed of all the good promises he gave through his servant Moses. 57May the Lord our God be with us as he was with our fathers; may he never leave us nor forsake us. 58May he turn our hearts to him, to walk in all his ways and to keep the commands, decrees and regulations he gave our fathers. 59And may these words of mine, which I have prayed before the Lord, be near to the Lord our God day and night, that he may uphold the cause of his servant and the cause of his people Israel according to each day's need, 60so that all the peoples of the earth may know that the Lord is God and that there is no other. 61But your hearts must be fully committed to the Lord our God, to live by his decrees and obey his commands, as at this time."

The Dedication of the Temple

62Then the king and all Israel with him offered sacrifices before the Lord. 63Solomon offered a sacrifice of fellowship offerings*a* to the Lord: twenty-two thousand cattle and a hundred and twenty thousand sheep and goats. So the king and all the Israelites dedicated the temple of the Lord.

8:63   The huge numbers of animals sacrificed may well be exaggerated. This is not to say that the writer deliberately lied—it was a device to show how very important the occasion was.

64On that same day the king consecrated the middle part of the courtyard in front of the temple of the Lord, and there he offered burnt offerings, grain offerings and the fat of the fellowship offerings, because the bronze altar before the Lord was too small to hold the burnt offerings, the grain offerings and the fat of the fellowship offerings.

65So Solomon observed the festival at that time, and all Israel with him—a vast assembly, people from Lebo*b* Hamath to the Wadi of Egypt. They celebrated it before the Lord our God for seven days and seven days more, fourteen days in all. 66On the following day he sent the people away. They blessed the king and then went home, joyful and glad in heart for all the good things the Lord had done for his servant David and his people Israel.

The Lord Appears to Solomon

9 When Solomon had finished building the temple of the Lord and the royal palace, and had achieved all he had desired to do, 2the Lord appeared

---

a63 Traditionally peace offerings; also in verse 64   *b65 Or from the entrance to* to him a second time, as he had appeared to him at Gibeon. ³The Lord said to him:

"I have heard the prayer and plea you have made before me; I have consecrated this temple, which you have built, by putting my Name there for ever. My eyes and my heart will always be there.

9:3   The conditional promise of 6:11–13 was now extended to include Solomon's descendants. Here for the first time in this book we find a clear reference to the eventual exile of God's people.

---

⁴"As for you, if you walk before me in integrity of heart and uprightness, as David your father did, and do all I command and observe my decrees and laws, ⁵I will establish your royal throne over Israel for ever, as I promised David your father when I said, 'You shall never fail to have a man on the throne of Israel.'

⁶"But if you*ᵃ* or your sons turn away from me and do not observe the commands and decrees I have given you*ᵃ* and go off to serve other gods and worship them, ⁷then I will cut off Israel from the land I have given them and will reject this temple I have consecrated for my Name. Israel will then become a byword and an object of ridicule among all peoples. ⁸And though this temple is now imposing, all who pass by will be appalled and will scoff and say, 'Why has the Lord done such a thing to this land and to this temple?' ⁹People will answer, 'Because they have forsaken the Lord their God, who brought their fathers out of Egypt, and have embraced other gods, worshipping and serving them — that is why the Lord brought all this disaster on them.'"

Solomon's Other Activities

¹⁰At the end of twenty years, during which Solomon built these two buildings — the temple of the Lord and the royal palace — ¹¹King Solomon gave twenty towns in Galilee to Hiram king of Tyre, because Hiram had supplied him with all the cedar and pine and gold he wanted. ¹²But when Hiram went from Tyre to see the towns that Solomon had given him, he was not pleased with them. ¹³"What kind of towns are these you have given me, my brother?" he asked. And he called them the Land of Cabul,*ᵇ* a name they have to this day. ¹⁴Now Hiram had sent to the king 120 talents*ᶜ* of gold.

¹⁵Here is the account of the forced labour King Solomon conscripted to build the Lord's temple, his own palace, the supporting terraces,*ᵈ* the wall of Jerusalem, and Hazor, Megiddo and Gezer. ¹⁶(Pharaoh king of Egypt had attacked and captured Gezer. He had set

it on fire. He killed its Canaanite inhabitants and then gave it as a wedding gift to his daughter, Solomon's wife. ¹⁷And Solomon rebuilt Gezer.) He built up Lower Beth Horon, ¹⁸Baalath, and Tadmor*ᵉ* in the desert, within his land, ¹⁹as well as all his store cities and the towns for his chariots and for his horses*ᶠ*—whatever he desired to build in Jerusalem, in Lebanon and throughout all the territory he ruled.

²⁰All the people left from the Amorites, Hittites, Perizzites, Hivites and Jebusites (these peoples were not Israelites), ²¹that is, their descendants remaining in the land, whom the Israelites could not exterminate*ᵍ*—these Solomon conscripted for his slave labour force, as it is to this day. ²²But Solomon did not make slaves of any of the Israelites; they were his fighting men, his government officials, his officers, his captains, and the commanders of his chariots and charioteers. ²³They were also the chief officials in charge of Solomon's projects — 550 officials supervising the men who did the work.

²⁴After Pharaoh's daughter had come up from the City of David to the palace Solomon had built for her, he constructed the supporting terraces.

²⁵Three times a year Solomon sacrificed burnt offerings and fellowship offerings*ʰ* on the altar he had built for the Lord, burning incense before the Lord along with them, and so fulfilled the temple obligations.

²⁶King Solomon also built ships at Ezion Geber, which is near Elath in Edom, on the shore of the Red Sea.*ⁱ* ²⁷And Hiram sent his men — sailors who knew the sea — to serve in the fleet with Solomon's men. ²⁸They sailed to Ophir and brought back 420 talents*ʲ* of gold, which they delivered to King Solomon.

The Queen of Sheba Visits Solomon

10 When the queen of Sheba heard about the fame of Solomon and his relation to the name of the Lord, she came to test him with hard questions. ²Arriving at Jerusalem with a very great caravan — with camels carrying spices, large quantities of gold, and precious stones — she came to Solomon and talked with him about all that she had on her mind. ³Solomon answered all her questions; nothing was too hard for the king to explain to her. ⁴When the queen of Sheba saw all the wisdom of Solomon and the palace he had built, ⁵the food on his table, the seating of his officials, the attending servants in their robes, his cupbearers, and the burnt offerings he made at*ᵃ* the temple of the Lord, she was overwhelmed.

⁶She said to the king, "The report I heard in my own country about your achievements and your wisdom is true. ⁷But I did not believe these things until I came and saw with my own eyes. Indeed, not even half was told me; in wisdom and wealth you have far exceeded the report I heard. ⁸How happy your men must be! How happy your officials, who continually stand before you and hear your wisdom! ⁹Praise be to the Lord your

---

ᵃ6 The Hebrew is plural.   *ᵇ13 Cabul* sounds like the Hebrew for *good-for-nothing.*
ᶜ14 That is, about 4 tons (about 4 metric tons)   *ᵈ15* Or *the Millo;* also in verse 24
ᵉ18 The Hebrew may also be read *Tamar.*   *ᶠ19* Or *charioteers*
ᵍ21 The Hebrew term refers to the irrevocable giving over of things or persons to the Lord, often by totally destroying them.
ʰ25 Traditionally *peace offerings*   *ⁱ26* Hebrew *Yam Suph;* that is, Sea of Reeds
ʲ28 That is, about 14 tons (about 14.5 metric tons)   *ᵃ5* Or *the ascent by which he went up to*

God, who has delighted in you and placed you on the throne of Israel. Because of the LORD's eternal love for Israel, he has made you king, to maintain justice and righteousness."

10And she gave the king 120 talents[b] of gold, large quantities of spices, and precious stones. Never again were so many spices brought in as those the queen of Sheba gave to King Solomon.

11(Hiram's ships brought gold from Ophir; and from there they brought great cargoes of almug-wood[c] and precious stones. 12The king used the almug-wood to make supports for the temple of the LORD and for the royal palace, and to make harps and lyres for the musicians. So much almug-wood has never been imported or seen since that day.)

13King Solomon gave the queen of Sheba all she desired and asked for, besides what he had given her out of his royal bounty. Then she left and returned with her retinue to her own country.

Solomon's Splendour

14The weight of the gold that Solomon received yearly was 666 talents,[d] 15not including the revenues from merchants and traders and from all the Arabian kings and the governors of the land.

16King Solomon made two hundred large shields of hammered gold; six hundred bekas[e] of gold went into each shield. 17He also made three hundred small shields of hammered gold, with three minas[f] of gold in each shield. The king put them in the Palace of the Forest of Lebanon.

18Then the king made a great throne inlaid with ivory and overlaid with fine gold. 19The throne had six steps, and its back had a rounded top. On both sides of the seat were armrests, with a lion standing beside each of them. 20Twelve lions stood on the six steps, one at either end of each step. Nothing like it had ever been made for any other kingdom. 21All King Solomon's goblets were gold, and all the household articles in the Palace of the Forest of Lebanon were pure gold. Nothing was made of silver, because silver was considered of little value in Solomon's days. 22The king had a fleet of trading ships[g] at sea along with the ships of Hiram. Once every three years it returned carrying gold, silver and ivory, and apes and baboons.

23King Solomon was greater in riches and wisdom than all the other kings of the earth. 24The whole world sought audience with Solomon to hear the wisdom God had put in his heart. 25Year after year, everyone who came brought a gift—articles of silver and gold, robes, weapons and spices, and horses and mules.

26Solomon accumulated chariots and horses; he had fourteen hundred chariots and twelve thousand horses,[h] which he kept in the chariot cities and also with him in Jerusalem. 27The king made silver as common in Jerusalem as stones, and cedar as plentiful as sycamore-fig trees in the foothills. 28Solomon's horses were imported from Egypt[i] and from Kue[j]—the royal merchants purchased them from Kue.[j] 29They imported a chariot from Egypt for six hundred shekels[k] of silver, and a horse for a hundred and fifty.[l] They also exported them to all the kings of the Hittites and of the Arameans.

Solomon's Wives

11 King Solomon, however, loved many foreign women besides Pharaoh's daughter—Moabites, Ammonites, Edomites, Sidonians and Hittites. 2They were from nations about which the LORD had told the Israelites, "You must not intermarry with them, because they will surely turn your hearts after their gods." Nevertheless, Solomon held fast to them in love. 3He had seven hundred wives of royal birth and three hundred concubines, and his wives led him astray. 4As Solomon grew old, his wives turned his heart after other gods, and his heart was not fully devoted to the LORD his God, as the heart of David his father had been. 5He followed Ashtoreth the goddess of the Sidonians, and Molech[a] the detestable god of the Ammonites. 6So Solomon did evil in the eyes of the LORD; he did not follow the LORD completely, as David his father had done.

11:1 Solomon's disobedience in marrying foreign women and accepting their gods is described and condemned at the beginning of the chapter, which then describes the problems associated with his reign. In this way the writer makes it clear that the king's relationship with God affected the fortunes of the entire nation.

7On a hill east of Jerusalem, Solomon built a high place for Chemosh the detestable god of Moab, and for Molech the detestable god of the Ammonites. 8He did the same for all his foreign wives, who burned incense and offered sacrifices to their gods.

9The LORD became angry with Solomon because his heart had turned away from the LORD, the God of Israel, who had appeared to him twice. 10Although he had forbidden Solomon to follow other gods, Solomon did not keep the LORD's command. 11So the LORD said to Solomon, "Since this is your attitude and you have not kept my covenant and my decrees, which I commanded you, I will most certainly tear the kingdom away from you and give it to one of your subordinates. 12Nevertheless, for the sake of David your father, I will not do it during your lifetime. I will tear it out of the hand of your son. 13Yet I will not tear the whole kingdom from him, but will give him one tribe for the sake of David my servant and for the sake of Jerusalem, which I have chosen."

---

b 10 That is, about 4 tons (about 4 metric tons)
d 14 That is, about 22½ tons (about 23 metric tons)
f 17 That is, about 3¾ pounds (about 1.7 kilograms)
i 28 Or possibly Muzur, a region in Cilicia; also in verse 29
k 29 That is, about 15 pounds (about 7 kilograms)
a 5 Hebrew Milcom; also in verse 33

c 11 Probably a variant of algum-wood; also in verse 12
e 16 That is, about 7½ pounds (about 3.5 kilograms)
g 22 Hebrew of ships of Tarshish   h 26 Or charioteers
j 28 Probably Cilicia
l 29 That is, about 3¾ pounds (about 1.7 kilograms)

Solomon's Adversaries

[14]Then the LORD raised up against Solomon an adversary, Hadad the Edomite, from the royal line of Edom. [15]Earlier when David was fighting with Edom, Joab the commander of the army, who had gone up to bury the dead, had struck down all the men in Edom. [16]Joab and all the Israelites stayed there for six months, until they had destroyed all the men in Edom. [17]But Hadad, still only a boy, fled to Egypt with some Edomite officials who had served his father. [18]They set out from Midian and went to Paran. Then taking men from Paran with them, they went to Egypt, to Pharaoh king of Egypt, who gave Hadad a house and land and provided him with food.

[19]Pharaoh was so pleased with Hadad that he gave him a sister of his own wife, Queen Tahpenes, in marriage. [20]The sister of Tahpenes bore him a son named Genubath, whom Tahpenes brought up in the royal palace. There Genubath lived with Pharaoh's own children.

[21]While he was in Egypt, Hadad heard that David rested with his fathers and that Joab the commander of the army was also dead. Then Hadad said to Pharaoh, "Let me go, so that I may return to my own country."

[22]"What have you lacked here that you want to go back to your own country?" Pharaoh asked.

"Nothing," Hadad replied, "but do let me go!"

[23]And God raised up against Solomon another adversary, Rezon son of Eliada, who had fled from his master, Hadadezer king of Zobah. [24]He gathered men around him and became the leader of a band of rebels when David destroyed the forces[b] of Zobah; the rebels went to Damascus, where they settled and took control. [25]Rezon was Israel's adversary as long as Solomon lived, adding to the trouble caused by Hadad. So Rezon ruled in Aram and was hostile towards Israel.

Jeroboam Rebels Against Solomon

[26]Also, Jeroboam son of Nebat rebelled against the king. He was one of Solomon's officials, an Ephraimite from Zeredah, and his mother was a widow named Zeruah.

[27]Here is the account of how he rebelled against the king: Solomon had built the supporting terraces[c] and had filled in the gap in the wall of the city of David his father. [28]Now Jeroboam was a man of standing, and when Solomon saw how well the young man did his work, he put him in charge of the whole labour force of the house of Joseph.

[29]About that time Jeroboam was going out of Jerusalem, and Ahijah the prophet of Shiloh met him on the way, wearing a new cloak. The two of them were alone out in the country, [30]and Ahijah took hold of the new cloak he was wearing and tore it into twelve pieces. [31]Then he said to Jeroboam, "Take ten pieces for yourself, for this is what the LORD, the God of Israel, says: 'See, I am going to tear the kingdom out of Solomon's hand and give you ten tribes. [32]But for the sake of my servant David and the city of Jerusalem, which I have chosen out of all the tribes of Israel, he will have one

tribe. [33]I will do this because they have[d] forsaken me and worshipped Ashtoreth the goddess of the Sidonians, Chemosh the god of the Moabites, and Molech the god of the Ammonites, and have not walked in my ways, nor done what is right in my eyes, nor kept my statutes and laws as David, Solomon's father, did.

[34]" 'But I will not take the whole kingdom out of Solomon's hand; I have made him ruler all the days of his life for the sake of David my servant, whom I chose and who observed my commands and statutes. [35]I will take the kingdom from his son's hands and give you ten tribes. [36]I will give one tribe to his son so that David my servant may always have a lamp before me in Jerusalem, the city where I chose to put my Name. [37]However, as for you, I will take you, and you will rule over all that your heart desires; you will be king over Israel. [38]If you do whatever I command you and walk in my ways and do what is right in my eyes by keeping my statutes and commands, as David my servant did, I will be with you. I will build you a dynasty as enduring as the one I built for David and will give Israel to you. [39]I will humble David's descendants because of this, but not for ever.' "

[40]Solomon tried to kill Jeroboam, but Jeroboam fled to Egypt, to Shishak the king, and stayed there until Solomon's death.

Solomon's Death

[41]As for the other events of Solomon's reign—all he did and the wisdom he displayed—are they not written in the book of the annals of Solomon? [42]Solomon reigned in Jerusalem over all Israel for forty years. [43]Then he rested with his fathers and was buried in the city of David his father. And Rehoboam his son succeeded him as king.

11:41   The book of the annals of Solomon was used by the writer as a source of information. Also referred to in 1 Kings are the chronicles of the kings of Israel (15:31) and of Judah (22:45). Most of the other sources used in 1 and 2 Kings have not survived.

Israel Rebels Against Rehoboam

12 Rehoboam went to Shechem, for all the Israelites had gone there to make him king. [2]When Jeroboam son of Nebat heard this (he was still in Egypt, where he had fled from King Solomon), he returned from[a] Egypt. [3]So they sent for Jeroboam, and he and the whole assembly of Israel went to Rehoboam and said to him: [4]"Your father put a heavy yoke on us, but now lighten the harsh labour and the heavy yoke he put on us, and we will serve you."

[5]Rehoboam answered, "Go away for three days and then come back to me." So the people went away.

[6]Then King Rehoboam consulted the elders who had served his father Solomon during his lifetime. "How

---

b24 Hebrew *destroyed them*   c27 Or *the Millo*   d33 Hebrew; Septuagint, Vulgate and Syriac *because he has*
a2 Or *he remained in*

would you advise me to answer these people?" he asked.

⁷They replied, "If today you will be a servant to these people and serve them and give them a favourable answer, they will always be your servants."

⁸But Rehoboam rejected the advice the elders gave him and consulted the young men who had grown up with him and were serving him. ⁹He asked them, "What is your advice? How should we answer these people who say to me, 'Lighten the yoke your father put on us'?"

¹⁰The young men who had grown up with him replied, "Tell these people who have said to you, 'Your father put a heavy yoke on us, but make our yoke lighter'—tell them, 'My little finger is thicker than my father's waist. ¹¹My father laid on you a heavy yoke; I will make it even heavier. My father scourged you with whips; I will scourge you with scorpions.' "

¹²Three days later Jeroboam and all the people returned to Rehoboam, as the king had said, "Come back to me in three days." ¹³The king answered the people harshly. Rejecting the advice given him by the elders, ¹⁴he followed the advice of the young men and said, "My father made your yoke heavy; I will make it even heavier. My father scourged you with whips; I will scourge you with scorpions." ¹⁵So the king did not listen to the people, for this turn of events was from the LORD, to fulfil the word the LORD had spoken to Jeroboam son of Nebat through Ahijah the Shilonite.

12:15   This chapter marks a decisive turning point in the history of God's people as they divided into the two kingdoms of Israel and Judah. By describing the events as being from the Lord, the writer makes it clear that ultimately God was in control. The division occurred as a result of the people's disobedience, which was represented by the king's disobedience.

---

¹⁶When all Israel saw that the king refused to listen to them, they answered the king:

"What share do we have in David,
    what part in Jesse's son?
To your tents, O Israel!
Look after your own house, O David!"

So the Israelites went home. ¹⁷But as for the Israelites who were living in the towns of Judah, Rehoboam still ruled over them.

¹⁸King Rehoboam sent out Adoniram,ᵇ who was in charge of forced labour, but all Israel stoned him to death. King Rehoboam, however, managed to get into his chariot and escape to Jerusalem. ¹⁹So Israel has been in rebellion against the house of David to this day.

²⁰When all the Israelites heard that Jeroboam had returned, they sent and called him to the assembly and made him king over all Israel. Only the tribe of Judah remained loyal to the house of David.

²¹When Rehoboam arrived in Jerusalem, he mustered the whole house of Judah and the tribe of Benjamin—a hundred and eighty thousand fighting men—to make war against the house of Israel and to regain the kingdom for Rehoboam son of Solomon.

²²But this word of God came to Shemaiah the man of God: ²³"Say to Rehoboam son of Solomon king of Judah, to the whole house of Judah and Benjamin, and to the rest of the people, ²⁴'This is what the LORD says: Do not go up to fight against your brothers, the Israelites. Go home, every one of you, for this is my doing.' " So they obeyed the word of the LORD and went home again, as the LORD had ordered.

Golden Calves at Bethel and Dan

²⁵Then Jeroboam fortified Shechem in the hill country of Ephraim and lived there. From there he went out and built up Peniel.ᶜ

²⁶Jeroboam thought to himself, "The kingdom is now likely to revert to the house of David. ²⁷If these people go up to offer sacrifices at the temple of the LORD in Jerusalem, they will again give their allegiance to their lord, Rehoboam king of Judah. They will kill me and return to King Rehoboam."

²⁸After seeking advice, the king made two golden calves. He said to the people, "It is too much for you to go up to Jerusalem. Here are your gods, O Israel, who brought you up out of Egypt." ²⁹One he set up in Bethel, and the other in Dan. ³⁰And this thing became a sin; the people went even as far as Dan to worship the one there.

³¹Jeroboam built shrines on high places and appointed priests from all sorts of people, even though they were not Levites. ³²He instituted a festival on the fifteenth day of the eighth month, like the festival held in Judah, and offered sacrifices on the altar. This he did in Bethel, sacrificing to the calves he had made. And at Bethel he also installed priests at the high places he had made. ³³On the fifteenth day of the eighth month, a month of his own choosing, he offered sacrifices on the altar he had built at Bethel. So he instituted the festival for the Israelites and went up to the altar to make offerings.

The Man of God From Judah

13 By the word of the LORD a man of God came from Judah to Bethel, as Jeroboam was standing by the altar to make an offering. ²He cried out against the altar by the word of the LORD: "O altar, altar! This is what the LORD says: 'A son named Josiah will be born to the house of David. On you he will sacrifice the priests of the high places who now make offerings here, and human bones will be burned on you.' " ³That same day the man of God gave a sign: "This is the sign the LORD has declared: The altar will be split apart and the ashes on it will be poured out."

⁴When King Jeroboam heard what the man of God cried out against the altar at Bethel, he stretched out his hand from the altar and said, "Seize him!" But the hand he stretched out towards the man shrivelled up, so that he could not pull it back. ⁵Also, the altar was

ᵇ18 Some Septuagint manuscripts and Syriac (see also 1 Kings 4:6 and 5:14); Hebrew *Adoram*
ᶜ25 Hebrew *Penuel*, a variant of *Peniel*

split apart and its ashes poured out according to the sign given by the man of God by the word of the Lord.

6Then the king said to the man of God, "Intercede with the Lord your God and pray for me that my hand may be restored." So the man of God interceded with the Lord, and the king's hand was restored and became as it was before.

7The king said to the man of God, "Come home with me and have something to eat, and I will give you a gift."

8But the man of God answered the king, "Even if you were to give me half your possessions, I would not go with you, nor would I eat bread or drink water here. 9For I was commanded by the word of the Lord: 'You must not eat bread or drink water or return by the way you came.' " 10So he took another road and did not return by the way he had come to Bethel.

11Now there was a certain old prophet living in Bethel, whose sons came and told him all that the man of God had done there that day. They also told their father what he had said to the king. 12Their father asked them, "Which way did he go?" And his sons showed him which road the man of God from Judah had taken. 13So he said to his sons, "Saddle the donkey for me." And when they had saddled the donkey for him, he mounted it 14and rode after the man of God. He found him sitting under an oak tree and asked, "Are you the man of God who came from Judah?"

"I am," he replied.

15So the prophet said to him, "Come home with me and eat."

16The man of God said, "I cannot turn back and go with you, nor can I eat bread or drink water with you in this place. 17I have been told by the word of the Lord: 'You must not eat bread or drink water there or return by the way you came.' "

18The old prophet answered, "I too am a prophet, as you are. And an angel said to me by the word of the Lord: 'Bring him back with you to your house so that he may eat bread and drink water.' " (But he was lying to him.) 19So the man of God returned with him and ate and drank in his house.

20While they were sitting at the table, the word of the Lord came to the old prophet who had brought him back. 21He cried out to the man of God who had come from Judah, "This is what the Lord says: 'You have defied the word of the Lord and have not kept the command the Lord your God gave you. 22You came back and ate bread and drank water in the place where he told you not to eat or drink. Therefore your body will not be buried in the tomb of your fathers.' "

23When the man of God had finished eating and drinking, the prophet who had brought him back saddled his donkey for him. 24As he went on his way, a lion met him on the road and killed him, and his body was thrown down on the road, with both the donkey and the lion standing beside it. 25Some people who passed by saw the body thrown down there, with the lion standing beside the body, and they went and reported it in the city where the old prophet lived.

26When the prophet who had brought him back from his journey heard of it, he said, "It is the man of God who defied the word of the Lord. The Lord has given him over to the lion, which has mauled him and

killed him, as the word of the Lord had warned him."

27The prophet said to his sons, "Saddle the donkey for me," and they did so. 28Then he went out and found the body thrown down on the road, with the donkey and the lion standing beside it. The lion had neither eaten the body nor mauled the donkey. 29So the prophet picked up the body of the man of God, laid it on the donkey, and brought it back to his own city to mourn for him and bury him. 30Then he laid the body in his own tomb, and they mourned over him and said, "Oh, my brother!"

31After burying him, he said to his sons, "When I die, bury me in the grave where the man of God is buried; lay my bones beside his bones. 32For the message he declared by the word of the Lord against the altar in Bethel and against all the shrines on the high places in the towns of Samaria will certainly come true."

33Even after this, Jeroboam did not change his evil ways, but once more appointed priests for the high places from all sorts of people. Anyone who wanted to become a priest he consecrated for the high places. 34This was the sin of the house of Jeroboam that led to its downfall and to its destruction from the face of the earth.

Ahijah's Prophecy Against Jeroboam

14 At that time Abijah son of Jeroboam became ill, 2and Jeroboam said to his wife, "Go, disguise yourself, so that you won't be recognised as the wife of Jeroboam. Then go to Shiloh. Ahijah the prophet is there — the one who told me I would be king over this people. 3Take ten loaves of bread with you, some cakes and a jar of honey, and go to him. He will tell you what will happen to the boy." 4So Jeroboam's wife did what he said and went to Ahijah's house in Shiloh.

Now Ahijah could not see; his sight was gone because of his age. 5But the Lord had told Ahijah, "Jeroboam's wife is coming to ask you about her son, for he is ill, and you are to give her such and such an answer. When she arrives, she will pretend to be someone else."

6So when Ahijah heard the sound of her footsteps at the door, he said, "Come in, wife of Jeroboam. Why this pretence? I have been sent to you with bad news. 7Go, tell Jeroboam that this is what the Lord, the God of Israel, says: 'I raised you up from among the people and made you a leader over my people Israel. 8I tore the kingdom away from the house of David and gave it to you, but you have not been like my servant David, who kept my commands and followed me with all his heart, doing only what was right in my eyes. 9You have done more evil than all who lived before you. You have made for yourself other gods, idols made of metal; you have provoked me to anger and thrust me behind your back.

10" 'Because of this, I am going to bring disaster on the house of Jeroboam. I will cut off from Jeroboam every last male in Israel — slave or free. I will burn up the house of Jeroboam as one burns dung, until it is all gone. 11Dogs will eat those belonging to Jeroboam who die in the city, and the birds of the air will feed on those who die in the country. The LORD has spoken!'

¹²"As for you, go back home. When you set foot in your city, the boy will die. ¹³All Israel will mourn for him and bury him. He is the only one belonging to Jeroboam who will be buried, because he is the only one in the house of Jeroboam in whom the LORD, the God of Israel, has found anything good.

¹⁴"The LORD will raise up for himself a king over Israel who will cut off the family of Jeroboam. This is the day! What? Yes, even now.ᵃ ¹⁵And the LORD will strike Israel, so that it will be like a reed swaying in the water. He will uproot Israel from this good land that he gave to their forefathers and scatter them beyond the River,ᵇ because they provoked the LORD to anger by making Asherah poles.ᶜ ¹⁶And he will give Israel up because of the sins Jeroboam has committed and has caused Israel to commit."

¹⁷Then Jeroboam's wife got up and left and went to Tirzah. As soon as she stepped over the threshold of the house, the boy died. ¹⁸They buried him, and all Israel mourned for him, as the LORD had said through his servant the prophet Ahijah.

¹⁹The other events of Jeroboam's reign, his wars and how he ruled, are written in the book of the annals of the kings of Israel. ²⁰He reigned for twenty-two years and then rested with his fathers. And Nadab his son succeeded him as king.

Rehoboam King of Judah

²¹Rehoboam son of Solomon was king in Judah. He was forty-one years old when he became king, and he reigned for seventeen years in Jerusalem, the city LORD had chosen out of all the tribes of Israel in which to put his Name. His mother's name was Naamah; she was an Ammonite.

14:23 Asherah poles were used by the previous inhabitants of the land, the Canaanites, in their fertility-cult worship. Dedicated to the mother-goddess, their presence became symbolic of God's people becoming involved in idolatry. When the failures of various kings were summarized, they often included the observation that a king "did not remove the Asherah poles".

---

²²Judah did evil in the eyes of the LORD. By the sins they committed they stirred up his jealous anger more than their fathers had done. ²³They also set up for themselves high places, sacred stones and Asherah poles on every high hill and under every spreading tree. ²⁴There were even male shrine-prostitutes in the land; the people engaged in all the detestable practices of the nations the LORD had driven out before the Israelites.

²⁵In the fifth year of King Rehoboam, Shishak king of Egypt attacked Jerusalem. ²⁶He carried off the treasures of the temple of the LORD and the treasures of the royal palace. He took everything, including all the gold shields Solomon had made. ²⁷So King Rehoboam made bronze shields to replace them and assigned these to the commanders of the guard on duty at the entrance to the royal palace. ²⁸Whenever the king went to the LORD's temple, the guards bore the shields, and afterwards they returned them to the guardroom.

²⁹As for the other events of Rehoboam's reign, and all he did, are they not written in the book of the annals of the kings of Judah? ³⁰There was continual warfare between Rehoboam and Jeroboam. ³¹And Rehoboam rested with his fathers and was buried with them in the City of David. His mother's name was Naamah; she was an Ammonite. And Abijahᵈ his son succeeded him as king.

Abijah King of Judah

15 In the eighteenth year of the reign of Jeroboam son of Nebat, Abijahᵃ became king of Judah, ²and he reigned in Jerusalem for three years. His mother's name was Maacah daughter of Abishalom.ᵇ

³He committed all the sins his father had done before him; his heart was not fully devoted to the LORD his God, as the heart of David his forefather had been. ⁴Nevertheless, for David's sake the LORD his God gave him a lamp in Jerusalem by raising up a son to succeed him and by making Jerusalem strong. ⁵For David had done what was right in the eyes of the LORD and had not failed to keep any of the LORD's commands all the days of his life — except in the case of Uriah the Hittite.

15:4 The lamp symbolized the living representative of the house of David. This was a living reminder of God's faithfulness to his promise to David to establish his house (2 Samuel 7:11–16).

---

⁶There was war between Rehoboamᶜ and Jeroboam throughout ₗAbijah'sⅉ lifetime. ⁷As for the other events of Abijah's reign, and all he did, are they not written in the book of the annals of the kings of Judah? There was war between Abijah and Jeroboam. ⁸And Abijah rested with his fathers and was buried in the City of David. And Asa his son succeeded him as king.

Asa King of Judah

⁹In the twentieth year of Jeroboam king of Israel, Asa became king of Judah, ¹⁰and he reigned in Jerusalem for forty-one years. His grandmother's name was Maacah daughter of Abishalom.

¹¹Asa did what was right in the eyes of the LORD, as his father David had done. ¹²He expelled the male shrine-prostitutes from the land and got rid of all the

---

ᵃ14 The meaning of the Hebrew for this sentence is uncertain.　　ᵇ15 That is, the Euphrates
ᶜ15 That is, symbols of the goddess Asherah; here and elsewhere in 1 Kings
ᵈ31 Some Hebrew manuscripts and Septuagint (see also 2 Chron. 12:16); most Hebrew manuscripts Abijam
ᵃ1 Some Hebrew manuscripts and Septuagint (see also 2 Chron. 12:16); most Hebrew manuscripts Abijam; also in verses 7 and 8
ᵇ2 A variant of Absalom; also in verse 10
ᶜ6 Most Hebrew manuscripts; some Hebrew manuscripts and Syriac Abijam (that is, Abijah)

idols his fathers had made. [13]He even deposed his grandmother Maacah from her position as queen mother, because she had made a repulsive Asherah pole. Asa cut the pole down and burned it in the Kidron Valley. [14]Although he did not remove the high places, Asa's heart was fully committed to the LORD all his life. [15]He brought into the temple of the LORD the silver and gold and the articles that he and his father had dedicated.

[16]There was war between Asa and Baasha king of Israel throughout their reigns. [17]Baasha king of Israel went up against Judah and fortified Ramah to prevent anyone from leaving or entering the territory of Asa king of Judah.

[18]Asa then took all the silver and gold that was left in the treasuries of the LORD's temple and of his own palace. He entrusted it to his officials and sent them to Ben-Hadad son of Tabrimmon, the son of Hezion, the king of Aram, who was ruling in Damascus. [19]"Let there be a treaty between me and you," he said, "as there was between my father and your father. See, I am sending you a gift of silver and gold. Now break your treaty with Baasha king of Israel so that he will withdraw from me."

[20]Ben-Hadad agreed with King Asa and sent the commanders of his forces against the towns of Israel. He conquered Ijon, Dan, Abel Beth Maacah and all Kinnereth in addition to Naphtali. [21]When Baasha heard this, he stopped building Ramah and withdrew to Tirzah. [22]Then King Asa issued an order to all Judah — no one was exempt — and they carried away from Ramah the stones and timber Baasha had been using there. With them King Asa built up Geba in Benjamin, and also Mizpah.

[23]As for all the other events of Asa's reign, all his achievements, all he did and the cities he built, are they not written in the book of the annals of the kings of Judah? In his old age, however, his feet became diseased. [24]Then Asa rested with his fathers and was buried with them in the city of his father David. And Jehoshaphat his son succeeded him as king.

Nadab King of Israel

[25]Nadab son of Jeroboam became king of Israel in the second year of Asa king of Judah, and he reigned over Israel for two years. [26]He did evil in the eyes of the LORD, walking in the ways of his father and in his sin, which he had caused Israel to commit.

[27]Baasha son of Ahijah of the house of Issachar plotted against him, and he struck him down at Gibbethon, a Philistine town, while Nadab and all Israel were besieging it. [28]Baasha killed Nadab in the third year of Asa king of Judah and succeeded him as king.

[29]As soon as he began to reign, he killed Jeroboam's whole family. He did not leave Jeroboam anyone that breathed, but destroyed them all, according to the word of the LORD given through his servant Ahijah the Shilonite — [30]because of the sins Jeroboam had committed and had caused Israel to commit, and because he provoked the LORD, the God of Israel, to anger.

[31]As for the other events of Nadab's reign, and all he did, are they not written in the book of the annals of the kings of Israel? [32]There was war between Asa and Baasha king of Israel throughout their reigns.

Baasha King of Israel

[33]In the third year of Asa king of Judah, Baasha son of Ahijah became king of all Israel in Tirzah, and he reigned for twenty-four years. [34]He did evil in the eyes of the LORD, walking in the ways of Jeroboam and in his sin, which he had caused Israel to commit.

16 Then the word of the LORD came to Jehu son of Hanani against Baasha: [2]"I lifted you up from the dust and made you leader of my people Israel, but you walked in the ways of Jeroboam and caused my people Israel to sin and to provoke me to anger by their sins. [3]So I am about to consume Baasha and his house, and I will make your house like that of Jeroboam son of Nebat. [4]Dogs will eat those belonging to Baasha who die in the city, and the birds of the air will feed on those who die in the country."

[5]As for the other events of Baasha's reign, what he did and his achievements, are they not written in the book of the annals of the kings of Israel? [6]Baasha rested with his fathers and was buried in Tirzah. And Elah his son succeeded him as king.

[7]Moreover, the word of the LORD came through the prophet Jehu son of Hanani to Baasha and his house, because of all the evil he had done in the eyes of the LORD, provoking him to anger by the things he did, and becoming like the house of Jeroboam — and also because he destroyed it.

Elah King of Israel

[8]In the twenty-sixth year of Asa king of Judah, Elah son of Baasha became king of Israel, and he reigned in Tirzah for two years.

[9]Zimri, one of his officials, who had command of half his chariots, plotted against him. Elah was in Tirzah at the time, getting drunk in the home of Arza, the man in charge of the palace at Tirzah. [10]Zimri came in, struck him down and killed him in the twenty-seventh year of Asa king of Judah. Then he succeeded him as king.

[11]As soon as he began to reign and was seated on the throne, he killed off Baasha's whole family. He did not spare a single male, whether relative or friend. [12]So Zimri destroyed the whole family of Baasha, in accordance with the word of the LORD spoken against Baasha through the prophet Jehu — [13]because of all the sins Baasha and his son Elah had committed and had caused Israel to commit, so that they provoked the LORD, the God of Israel, to anger by their worthless idols.

[14]As for the other events of Elah's reign, and all he did, are they not written in the book of the annals of the kings of Israel?

Zimri King of Israel

[15]In the twenty-seventh year of Asa king of Judah, Zimri reigned in Tirzah for seven days. The army was encamped near Gibbethon, a Philistine town. [16]When the Israelites in the camp heard that Zimri had plotted against the king and murdered him, they proclaimed Omri, the commander of the army, king over Israel that

very day there in the camp. [17]Then Omri and all the Israelites with him withdrew from Gibbethon and laid siege to Tirzah. [18]When Zimri saw that the city was taken, he went into the citadel of the royal palace and set the palace on fire around him. So he died, [19]because of the sins he had committed, doing evil in the eyes of the LORD and walking in the ways of Jeroboam and in the sin he had committed and had caused Israel to commit.

[20]As for the other events of Zimri's reign, and the rebellion he carried out, are they not written in the book of the annals of the kings of Israel?

Omri King of Israel

[21]Then the people of Israel were split into two factions; half supported Tibni son of Ginath for king, and the other half supported Omri. [22]But Omri's followers proved stronger than those of Tibni son of Ginath. So Tibni died and Omri became king.

[23]In the thirty-first year of Asa king of Judah, Omri became king of Israel, and he reigned for twelve years, six of them in Tirzah. [24]He bought the hill of Samaria from Shemer for two talents[a] of silver and built a city on the hill, calling it Samaria, after Shemer, the name of the former owner of the hill.

[25]But Omri did evil in the eyes of the LORD and sinned more than all those before him. [26]He walked in all the ways of Jeroboam son of Nebat and in his sin, which he had caused Israel to commit, so that they provoked the LORD, the God of Israel, to anger by their worthless idols.

[27]As for the other events of Omri's reign, what he did and the things he achieved, are they not written in the book of the annals of the kings of Israel? [28]Omri rested with his fathers and was buried in Samaria. And Ahab his son succeeded him as king.

Ahab Becomes King of Israel

[29]In the thirty-eighth year of Asa king of Judah, Ahab son of Omri became king of Israel, and he reigned in Samaria over Israel for twenty-two years. [30]Ahab son of Omri did more evil in the eyes of the LORD than any of those before him. [31]He not only considered it trivial to commit the sins of Jeroboam son of Nebat, but he also married Jezebel daughter of Ethbaal king of the Sidonians, and began to serve Baal and worship him. [32]He set up an altar for Baal in the temple of Baal that he built in Samaria. [33]Ahab also made an Asherah pole and did more to provoke the LORD, the God of Israel, to anger than did all the kings of Israel before him.

16:31   The wickedness of Jezebel is legendary. Her name is still used today to describe a wicked woman. She promoted the worship of Baal with enthusiasm, and Ahab followed her lead.

---

[34]In Ahab's time, Hiel of Bethel rebuilt Jericho. He laid its foundations at the cost of his firstborn son Abiram, and he set up its gates at the cost of his youngest son Segub, in accordance with the word of the LORD spoken by Joshua son of Nun.

Elijah Fed by Ravens

17 Now Elijah the Tishbite, from Tishbe[a] in Gilead, said to Ahab, "As the LORD, the God of Israel, lives, whom I serve, there will be neither dew nor rain in the next few years except at my word."

17:1   Elijah, who appeared virtually without introduction, came to be seen as the ideal example of an Old Testament prophet. He also appeared with Jesus and Moses at the transfiguration as the representative of Old Testament prophecy (Matthew 17:3).

---

[2]Then the word of the LORD came to Elijah: [3]"Leave here, turn eastward and hide in the Kerith Ravine, east of the Jordan. [4]You will drink from the brook, and I have ordered the ravens to feed you there."

[5]So he did what the LORD had told him. He went to the Kerith Ravine, east of the Jordan, and stayed there. [6]The ravens brought him bread and meat in the morning and bread and meat in the evening, and he drank from the brook.

The Widow at Zarephath

[7]Some time later the brook dried up because there had been no rain in the land. [8]Then the word of the LORD came to him: [9]"Go at once to Zarephath of Sidon and stay there. I have commanded a widow in that place to supply you with food." [10]So he went to Zarephath. When he came to the town gate, a widow was there gathering sticks. He called to her and asked, "Would you bring me a little water in a jar so I may have a drink?" [11]As she was going to get it, he called, "And bring me, please, a piece of bread."

[12]"As surely as the LORD your God lives," she replied, "I don't have any bread—only a handful of flour in a jar and a little oil in a jug. I am gathering a few sticks to take home and make a meal for myself and my son, that we may eat it—and die."

[13]Elijah said to her, "Don't be afraid. Go home and do as you have said. But first make a small cake of bread for me from what you have and bring it to me, and then make something for yourself and your son. [14]For this is what the LORD, the God of Israel, says: 'The jar of flour will not be used up and the jug of oil will not run dry until the day the LORD gives rain on the land.' "

[15]She went away and did as Elijah had told her. So there was food every day for Elijah and for the woman and her family. [16]For the jar of flour was not used up and the jug of oil did not run dry, in keeping with the word of the LORD spoken by Elijah.

[17]Some time later the son of the woman who owned the house became ill. He grew worse and worse, and finally stopped breathing. [18]She said to Elijah, "What

---

[a]24 That is, about 150 pounds (about 70 kilograms)   [a]1 Or Tishbite, of the settlers

do you have against me, man of God? Did you come to remind me of my sin and kill my son?"

19"Give me your son," Elijah replied. He took him from her arms, carried him to the upper room where he was staying, and laid him on his bed. 20Then he cried out to the Lord, "O Lord my God, have you brought tragedy also upon this widow I am staying with, by causing her son to die?" 21Then he stretched himself out on the boy three times and cried to the Lord, "O Lord my God, let this boy's life return to him!"

22The Lord heard Elijah's cry, and the boy's life returned to him, and he lived. 23Elijah picked up the child and carried him down from the room into the house. He gave him to his mother and said, "Look, your son is alive!"

24Then the woman said to Elijah, "Now I know that you are a man of God and that the word of the Lord from your mouth is the truth."

Elijah and Obadiah

18 After a long time, in the third year, the word of the Lord came to Elijah: "Go and present yourself to Ahab, and I will send rain on the land." 2So Elijah went to present himself to Ahab.

Now the famine was severe in Samaria, 3and Ahab had summoned Obadiah, who was in charge of his palace. (Obadiah was a devout believer in the Lord. 4While Jezebel was killing off the Lord's prophets, Obadiah had taken a hundred prophets and hidden them in two caves, fifty in each, and had supplied them with food and water.) 5Ahab had said to Obadiah, "Go through the land to all the springs and valleys. Maybe we can find some grass to keep the horses and mules alive so we will not have to kill any of our animals." 6So they divided the land they were to cover, Ahab going in one direction and Obadiah in another.

7As Obadiah was walking along, Elijah met him. Obadiah recognised him, bowed down to the ground, and said, "Is it really you, my lord Elijah?"

8"Yes," he replied. "Go tell your master, 'Elijah is here.' "

9"What have I done wrong," asked Obadiah, "that you are handing your servant over to Ahab to be put to death? 10As surely as the Lord your God lives, there is not a nation or kingdom where my master has not sent someone to look for you. And whenever a nation or kingdom claimed you were not there, he made them swear they could not find you. 11But now you tell me to go to my master and say, 'Elijah is here.' 12I don't know where the Spirit of the Lord may carry you when I leave you. If I go and tell Ahab and he doesn't find you, he will kill me. Yet I your servant have worshipped the Lord since my youth. 13Haven't you heard, my lord, what I did while Jezebel was killing the prophets of the Lord? I hid a hundred of the Lord's prophets in two caves, fifty in each, and supplied them with food and water. 14And now you tell me to go to my master and say, 'Elijah is here.' He will kill me!"

15Elijah said, "As the Lord Almighty lives, whom I serve, I will surely present myself to Ahab today."

Elijah on Mount Carmel

16So Obadiah went to meet Ahab and told him, and Ahab went to meet Elijah. 17When he saw Elijah, he said to him, "Is that you, you troubler of Israel?"

18"I have not made trouble for Israel," Elijah replied. "But you and your father's family have. You have abandoned the Lord's commands and have followed the Baals. 19Now summon the people from all over Israel to meet me on Mount Carmel. And bring the four hundred and fifty prophets of Baal and the four hundred prophets of Asherah, who eat at Jezebel's table."

18:17 Ahab accused Elijah of being the troubler of Israel, since it was Elijah who had announced the drought over the land. As Elijah's response indicated, however, it was Ahab's rebellion against the Lord that made him the real cause of the trouble.

20So Ahab sent word throughout all Israel and assembled the prophets on Mount Carmel. 21Elijah went before the people and said, "How long will you waver between two opinions? If the Lord is God, follow him; but if Baal is God, follow him."

But the people said nothing.

22Then Elijah said to them, "I am the only one of the Lord's prophets left, but Baal has four hundred and fifty prophets. 23Get two bulls for us. Let them choose one for themselves, and let them cut it into pieces and put it on the wood but not set fire to it. I will prepare the other bull and put it on the wood but not set fire to it. 24Then you call on the name of your god, and I will call on the name of the Lord. The god who answers by fire — he is God."

Then all the people said, "What you say is good."

25Elijah said to the prophets of Baal, "Choose one of the bulls and prepare it first, since there are so many of you. Call on the name of your god, but do not light the fire." 26So they took the bull given them and prepared it.

Then they called on the name of Baal from morning till noon. "O Baal, answer us!" they shouted. But there was no response; no-one answered. And they danced around the altar they had made.

27At noon Elijah began to taunt them. "Shout louder!" he said. "Surely he is a god! Perhaps he is deep in thought, or busy, or travelling. Maybe he is sleeping and must be awakened." 28So they shouted louder and slashed themselves with swords and spears, as was their custom, until their blood flowed. 29Midday passed, and they continued their frantic prophesying until the time for the evening sacrifice. But there was no response, no-one answered, no-one paid attention.

30Then Elijah said to all the people, "Come here to me." They came to him, and he repaired the altar of the Lord, which was in ruins. 31Elijah took twelve stones, one for each of the tribes descended from Jacob, to whom the word of the Lord had come, saying, "Your name shall be Israel." 32With the stones he built an altar in the name of the Lord, and he dug a trench round it large enough to hold two seahs*a* of seed. ³³He arranged the wood, cut the bull into pieces and laid it on the wood. Then he said to them, "Fill four large jars with water and pour it on the offering and on the wood."

³⁴"Do it again," he said, and they did it again.

"Do it a third time," he ordered, and they did it the third time. ³⁵The water ran down around the altar and even filled the trench.

³⁶At the time of sacrifice, the prophet Elijah stepped forward and prayed: "O LORD, God of Abraham, Isaac and Israel, let it be known today that you are God in Israel and that I am your servant and have done all these things at your command. ³⁷Answer me, O LORD, answer me, so these people will know that you, O LORD, are God, and that you are turning their hearts back again."

³⁸Then the fire of the LORD fell and burned up the sacrifice, the wood, the stones and the soil, and also licked up the water in the trench.

³⁹When all the people saw this, they fell prostrate and cried, "The LORD—he is God! The LORD—he is God!"

⁴⁰Then Elijah commanded them, "Seize the prophets of Baal. Don't let anyone get away!" They seized them, and Elijah had them brought down to the Kishon Valley and slaughtered there.

⁴¹And Elijah said to Ahab, "Go, eat and drink, for there is the sound of a heavy rain." ⁴²So Ahab went off to eat and drink, but Elijah climbed to the top of Carmel, bent down to the ground and put his face between his knees.

⁴³"Go and look towards the sea," he told his servant. And he went up and looked.

"There is nothing there," he said.

Seven times Elijah said, "Go back."

⁴⁴The seventh time the servant reported, "A cloud as small as a man's hand is rising from the sea."

So Elijah said, "Go and tell Ahab, 'Hitch up your chariot and go down before the rain stops you.'"

⁴⁵Meanwhile, the sky grew black with clouds, the wind rose, a heavy rain came on and Ahab rode off to Jezreel. ⁴⁶The power of the LORD came upon Elijah and, tucking his cloak into his belt, he ran ahead of Ahab all the way to Jezreel.

Elijah Flees to Horeb

19 Now Ahab told Jezebel everything Elijah had done and how he had killed all the prophets with the sword. ²So Jezebel sent a messenger to Elijah to say, "May the gods deal with me, be it ever so severely, if by this time tomorrow I do not make your life like that of one of them."

³Elijah was afraid*a* and ran for his life. When he came to Beersheba in Judah, he left his servant there, ⁴while he himself went a day's journey into the desert. He came to a broom tree, sat down under it and prayed that he might die. "I have had enough, LORD," he said. "Take my life; I am no better than my ancestors." ⁵Then he lay down under the tree and fell asleep.

All at once an angel touched him and said, "Get up

and eat." ⁶He looked around, and there by his head was a cake of bread baked over hot coals, and a jar of water. He ate and drank and then lay down again.

⁷The angel of the LORD came back a second time and touched him and said, "Get up and eat, for the journey is too much for you." ⁸So he got up and ate and drank. Strengthened by that food, he travelled for forty days and forty nights until he reached Horeb, the mountain of God. ⁹There he went into a cave and spent the night.

The LORD Appears to Elijah

And the word of the LORD came to him: "What are you doing here, Elijah?"

¹⁰He replied, "I have been very zealous for the LORD God Almighty. The Israelites have rejected your covenant, broken down your altars, and put your prophets to death with the sword. I am the only one left, and now they are trying to kill me too."

¹¹The LORD said, "Go out and stand on the mountain in the presence of the LORD, for the LORD is about to pass by."

Then a great and powerful wind tore the mountains apart and shattered the rocks before the LORD, but the LORD was not in the wind. After the wind there was an earthquake, but the LORD was not in the earthquake. ¹²After the earthquake came a fire, but the LORD was not in the fire. And after the fire came a gentle whisper. ¹³When Elijah heard it, he pulled his cloak over his face and went out and stood at the mouth of the cave.

Then a voice said to him, "What are you doing here, Elijah?"

¹⁴He replied, "I have been very zealous for the LORD God Almighty. The Israelites have rejected your covenant, broken down your altars, and put your prophets to death with the sword. I am the only one left, and now they are trying to kill me too."

¹⁵The LORD said to him, "Go back the way you came, and go to the Desert of Damascus. When you get there, anoint Hazael king over Aram. ¹⁶Also, anoint Jehu son of Nimshi king over Israel, and anoint Elisha son of Shaphat from Abel Meholah to succeed you as prophet. ¹⁷Jehu will put to death any who escape the sword of Hazael, and Elisha will put to death any who escape the sword of Jehu. ¹⁸Yet I reserve seven thousand in Israel—all whose knees have not bowed down to Baal and all whose mouths have not kissed him."

The Call of Elisha

¹⁹So Elijah went from there and found Elisha son of Shaphat. He was ploughing with twelve yoke of oxen, and he himself was driving the twelfth pair. Elijah went up to him and threw his cloak around him. ²⁰Elisha then left his oxen and ran after Elijah. "Let me kiss my father and mother good-bye," he said, "and then I will come with you."

"Go back," Elijah replied. "What have I done to you?"

²¹So Elisha left him and went back. He took his yoke of oxen and slaughtered them. He burned the ploughing equipment to cook the meat and gave it to the

---

a32 That is, probably about 26 pints (about 15 litres)   *a3* Or *Elijah saw* people, and they ate. Then he set out to follow Elijah and became his attendant.

Ben-Hadad Attacks Samaria

20 Now Ben-Hadad king of Aram mustered his entire army. Accompanied by thirty-two kings with their horses and chariots, he went up and besieged Samaria and attacked it. ²He sent messengers into the city to Ahab king of Israel, saying, "This is what Ben-Hadad says: ³'Your silver and gold are mine, and the best of your wives and children are mine.' "

⁴The king of Israel answered, "Just as you say, my lord the king. I and all I have are yours."

⁵The messengers came again and said, "This is what Ben-Hadad says: 'I sent to demand your silver and gold, your wives and your children. ⁶But about this time tomorrow I am going to send my officials to search your palace and the houses of your officials. They will seize everything you value and carry it away.' "

⁷The king of Israel summoned all the elders of the land and said to them, "See how this man is looking for trouble! When he sent for my wives and my children, my silver and my gold, I did not refuse him."

⁸The elders and the people all answered, "Don't listen to him or agree to his demands."

⁹So he replied to Ben-Hadad's messengers, "Tell my lord the king, 'Your servant will do all you demanded the first time, but this demand I cannot meet.' " They left and took the answer back to Ben-Hadad.

¹⁰Then Ben-Hadad sent another message to Ahab: "May the gods deal with me, be it ever so severely, if enough dust remains in Samaria to give each of my men a handful."

¹¹The king of Israel answered, "Tell him: 'One who puts on his armour should not boast like one who takes it off.' "

¹²Ben-Hadad heard this message while he and the kings were drinking in their tents,ᵃ and he ordered his men: "Prepare to attack." So they prepared to attack the city.

Ahab Defeats Ben-Hadad

¹³Meanwhile a prophet came to Ahab king of Israel and announced, "This is what the LORD says: 'Do you see this vast army? I will give it into your hand today, and then you will know that I am the LORD.' "

¹⁴"But who will do this?" asked Ahab.

The prophet replied, "This is what the LORD says: 'The young officers of the provincial commanders will do it.' "

"And who will start the battle?" he asked.

The prophet answered, "You will."

¹⁵So Ahab summoned the young officers of the provincial commanders, 232 men. Then he assembled the rest of the Israelites, 7,000 in all. ¹⁶They set out at noon while Ben-Hadad and the 32 kings allied with him were in their tents getting drunk. ¹⁷The young officers of the provincial commanders went out first.

Now Ben-Hadad had dispatched scouts, who reported, "Men are advancing from Samaria."

¹⁸He said, "If they have come out for peace, take

them alive; if they have come out for war, take them alive."

¹⁹The young officers of the provincial commanders marched out of the city with the army behind them ²⁰and each one struck down his opponent. At that, the Arameans fled, with the Israelites in pursuit. But Ben-Hadad king of Aram escaped on horseback with some of his horsemen. ²¹The king of Israel advanced and overpowered the horses and chariots and inflicted heavy losses on the Arameans.

²²Afterwards, the prophet came to the king of Israel and said, "Strengthen your position and see what must be done, because next spring the king of Aram will attack you again."

²³Meanwhile, the officials of the king of Aram advised him, "Their gods are gods of the hills. That is why they were too strong for us. But if we fight them on the plains, surely we will be stronger than they. ²⁴Do this: Remove all the kings from their commands and replace them with other officers. ²⁵You must also raise an army like the one you lost — horse for horse and chariot for chariot — so we can fight Israel on the plains. Then surely we will be stronger than they." He agreed with them and acted accordingly.

²⁶The next spring Ben-Hadad mustered the Arameans and went up to Aphek to fight against Israel. ²⁷When the Israelites were also mustered and given provisions, they marched out to meet them. The Israelites camped opposite them like two small flocks of goats, while the Arameans covered the countryside.

²⁸The man of God came up and said to the king of Israel, "This is what the LORD says: 'Because the Arameans think the LORD is a god of the hills and not a god of the valleys, I will deliver this vast army into your hands, and you will know that I am the LORD.' "

²⁹For seven days they camped opposite each other, and on the seventh day the battle was joined. The Israelites inflicted a hundred thousand casualties on the Aramean foot soldiers in one day. ³⁰The rest of them escaped to the city of Aphek, where the wall collapsed on twenty-seven thousand of them. And Ben-Hadad fled to the city and hid in an inner room.

³¹His officials said to him, "Look, we have heard that the kings of the house of Israel are merciful. Let us go to the king of Israel with sackcloth round our waists and ropes round our heads. Perhaps he will spare your life."

20:32 The wearing of sackcloth around the waist was a sign of mourning or penitence, and the rope on the head a sign of a humble request for mercy.

---

³²Wearing sackcloth round their waists and ropes round their heads, they went to the king of Israel and said, "Your servant Ben-Hadad says: 'Please let me live.' "

The king answered, "Is he still alive? He is my brother."

ᵃ12 Or *in Succoth*; also in verse 16

33The men took this as a good sign and were quick to pick up his word. "Yes, your brother Ben-Hadad!" they said.

"Go and get him," the king said. When Ben-Hadad came out, Ahab had him come up into his chariot.

34"I will return the cities my father took from your father," Ben-Hadad offered. "You may set up your own market areas in Damascus, as my father did in Samaria."

¡Ahab said,¡¡ "On the basis of a treaty I will set you free." So he made a treaty with him, and let him go.

A Prophet Condemns Ahab

35By the word of the LORD one of the sons of the prophets said to his companion, "Strike me with your weapon," but the man refused.

36So the prophet said, "Because you have not obeyed the LORD, as soon as you leave me a lion will kill you." And after the man went away, a lion found him and killed him.

37The prophet found another man and said, "Strike me, please." So the man struck him and wounded him. 38Then the prophet went and stood by the road waiting for the king. He disguised himself with his headband down over his eyes. 39As the king passed by, the prophet called out to him, "Your servant went into the thick of the battle, and someone came to me with a captive and said, 'Guard this man. If he is missing, it will be your life for his life, or you must pay a talent[b] of silver.' 40While your servant was busy here and there, the man disappeared."

"That is your sentence," the king of Israel said. "You have pronounced it yourself."

41Then the prophet quickly removed the headband from his eyes, and the king of Israel recognised him as one of the prophets. 42He said to the king, "This is what the LORD says: 'You have set free a man I had determined should die.[c] Therefore it is your life for his life, your people for his people.' " 43Sullen and angry, the king of Israel went to his palace in Samaria.

Naboth's Vineyard

21 Some time later there was an incident involving a vineyard belonging to Naboth the Jezreelite. The vineyard was in Jezreel, close to the palace of Ahab king of Samaria. 2Ahab said to Naboth, "Let me have your vineyard to use for a vegetable garden, since it is close to my palace. In exchange I will give you a better vineyard or, if you prefer, I will pay you whatever it is worth."

3But Naboth replied, "The LORD forbid that I should give you the inheritance of my fathers."

4So Ahab went home, sullen and angry because Naboth the Jezreelite had said, "I will not give you the inheritance of my fathers." He lay on his bed sulking and refused to eat.

5His wife Jezebel came in and asked him, "Why are you so sullen? Why won't you eat?"

6He answered her, "Because I said to Naboth the Jezreelite, 'Sell me your vineyard; or if you prefer, I will

give you another vineyard in its place.' But he said, 'I will not give you my vineyard.' "

7Jezebel his wife said, "Is this how you act as king over Israel? Get up and eat! Cheer up. I'll get you the vineyard of Naboth the Jezreelite."

8So she wrote letters in Ahab's name, placed his seal on them, and sent them to the elders and nobles who lived in Naboth's city with him. 9In those letters she wrote:

"Proclaim a day of fasting and seat Naboth in a prominent place among the people. 10But seat two scoundrels opposite him and have them testify that he has cursed both God and the king. Then take him out and stone him to death."

11So the elders and nobles who lived in Naboth's city did as Jezebel directed in the letters she had written to them. 12They proclaimed a fast and seated Naboth in a prominent place among the people. 13Then two scoundrels came and sat opposite him and brought charges against Naboth before the people, saying, "Naboth has cursed both God and the king." So they took him outside the city and stoned him to death. 14Then they sent word to Jezebel: "Naboth has been stoned and is dead."

15As soon as Jezebel heard that Naboth had been stoned to death, she said to Ahab, "Get up and take possession of the vineyard of Naboth the Jezreelite that he refused to sell you. He is no longer alive, but dead." 16When Ahab heard that Naboth was dead, he got up and went down to take possession of Naboth's vineyard.

17Then the word of the LORD came to Elijah the Tishbite: 18"Go down to meet Ahab king of Israel, who rules in Samaria. He is now in Naboth's vineyard, where he has gone to take possession of it. 19Say to him, 'This is what the LORD says: Have you not murdered a man and seized his property?' Then say to him, 'This is what the LORD says: In the place where dogs licked up Naboth's blood, dogs will lick up your blood—yes, yours!' "

20Ahab said to Elijah, "So you have found me, my enemy!"

"I have found you," he answered, "because you have sold yourself to do evil in the eyes of the LORD. 21I am going to bring disaster on you. I will consume your descendants and cut off from Ahab every last male in Israel—slave or free. 22I will make your house like that of Jeroboam son of Nebat and that of Baasha son of Ahijah, because you have provoked me to anger and have caused Israel to sin.'

23"And also concerning Jezebel the LORD says: 'Dogs will devour Jezebel by the wall of[a] Jezreel.'

24"Dogs will eat those belonging to Ahab who die in the city, and the birds of the air will feed on those who die in the country."

25(There was never a man like Ahab, who sold himself to do evil in the eyes of the LORD, urged on by Jezebel his wife. 26He behaved in the vilest manner by

---

b39 That is, about 75 pounds (about 34 kilograms)
c42 The Hebrew term refers to the irrevocable giving over of things or persons to the LORD, often by totally destroying them.
a23 Most Hebrew manuscripts; a few Hebrew manuscripts, Vulgate and Syriac (see also 2 Kings 9:26) the plot of ground at

going after idols, like the Amorites the LORD drove out before Israel.)

27When Ahab heard these words, he tore his clothes, put on sackcloth and fasted. He lay in sackcloth and went around meekly.

28Then the word of the LORD came to Elijah the Tishbite: 29"Have you noticed how Ahab has humbled himself before me? Because he has humbled himself, I will not bring this disaster in his day, but I will bring it on his house in the days of his son."

Micaiah Prophesies Against Ahab

22 For three years there was no war between Aram and Israel. 2But in the third year Jehoshaphat king of Judah went down to see the king of Israel. 3The king of Israel had said to his officials, "Don't you know that Ramoth Gilead belongs to us and yet we are doing nothing to retake it from the king of Aram?"

4So he asked Jehoshaphat, "Will you go with me to fight against Ramoth Gilead?"

Jehoshaphat replied to the king of Israel, "I am as you are, my people as your people, my horses as your horses." 5But Jehoshaphat also said to the king of Israel, "First seek the counsel of the LORD."

6So the king of Israel brought together the prophets—about four hundred men—and asked them, "Shall I go to war against Ramoth Gilead, or shall I refrain?"

"Go," they answered, "for the Lord will give it into the king's hand."

7But Jehoshaphat asked, "Is there not a prophet of the LORD here whom we can enquire of?"

8The king of Israel answered Jehoshaphat, "There is still one man through whom we can enquire of the LORD, but I hate him because he never prophesies anything good about me, but always bad. He is Micaiah son of Imlah."

"The king should not say that," Jehoshaphat replied.

9So the king of Israel called one of his officials and said, "Bring Micaiah son of Imlah at once."

10Dressed in their royal robes, the king of Israel and Jehoshaphat king of Judah were sitting on their thrones at the threshing-floor by the entrance of the gate of Samaria, with all the prophets prophesying before them. 11Now Zedekiah son of Kenaanah had made iron horns and he declared, "This is what the LORD says: 'With these you will gore the Arameans until they are destroyed.'"

12All the other prophets were prophesying the same thing. "Attack Ramoth Gilead and be victorious," they said, "for the LORD will give it into the king's hand."

13The messenger who had gone to summon Micaiah said to him, "Look, as one man the other prophets are predicting success for the king. Let your word agree with theirs, and speak favourably."

14But Micaiah said, "As surely as the LORD lives, I can tell him only what the LORD tells me."

15When he arrived, the king asked him, "Micaiah, shall we go to war against Ramoth Gilead, or shall I refrain?"

"Attack and be victorious," he answered, "for the LORD will give it into the king's hand."

16The king said to him, "How many times must I make you swear to tell me nothing but the truth in the name of the LORD?"

17Then Micaiah answered, "I saw all Israel scattered on the hills like sheep without a shepherd, and the LORD said, 'These people have no master. Let each one go home in peace.'"

18The king of Israel said to Jehoshaphat, "Didn't I tell you that he never prophesies anything good about me, but only bad?"

19Micaiah continued, "Therefore hear the word of the LORD: I saw the LORD sitting on his throne with all the host of heaven standing round him on his right and on his left. 20And the LORD said, 'Who will entice Ahab into attacking Ramoth Gilead and going to his death there?'

"One suggested this, and another that. 21Finally, a spirit came forward, stood before the LORD and said, 'I will entice him.'

22"'By what means?' the LORD asked.

"'I will go out and be a lying spirit in the mouths of all his prophets,' he said.

"'You will succeed in enticing him,' said the LORD. 'Go and do it.'

23"So now the LORD has put a lying spirit in the mouths of all these prophets of yours. The LORD has decreed disaster for you."

24Then Zedekiah son of Kenaanah went up and slapped Micaiah in the face. "Which way did the spirit from[a] the LORD go when he went from me to speak to you?" he asked.

25Micaiah replied, "You will find out on the day you go to hide in an inner room."

26The king of Israel then ordered, "Take Micaiah and send him back to Amon the ruler of the city and to Joash the king's son 27and say, 'This is what the king says: Put this fellow in prison and give him nothing but bread and water until I return safely.'"

28Micaiah declared, "If you ever return safely, the LORD has not spoken through me." Then he added, "Mark my words, all you people!"

Ahab Killed at Ramoth Gilead

29So the king of Israel and Jehoshaphat king of Judah went up to Ramoth Gilead. 30The king of Israel said to Jehoshaphat, "I will enter the battle in disguise, but you wear your royal robes." So the king of Israel disguised himself and went into battle.

31Now the king of Aram had ordered his thirty-two chariot commanders, "Do not fight with anyone, small or great, except the king of Israel." 32When the chariot commanders saw Jehoshaphat, they thought, "Surely this is the king of Israel." So they turned to attack him, but when Jehoshaphat cried out, 33the chariot commanders saw that he was not the king of Israel and stopped pursuing him.

34But someone drew his bow at random and hit the king of Israel between the sections of his armour. The king told his chariot driver, "Wheel round and get me

a 24 Or Spirit of

out of the fighting. I've been wounded." [35]All day long the battle raged, and the king was propped up in his chariot facing the Arameans. The blood from his wound ran onto the floor of the chariot, and that evening he died. [36]As the sun was setting, a cry spread through the army: "Every man to his town; everyone to his land!"

[37]So the king died and was brought to Samaria, and they buried him there. [38]They washed the chariot at a pool in Samaria (where the prostitutes bathed),[b] and the dogs licked up his blood, as the word of the LORD had declared.

[39]As for the other events of Ahab's reign, including all he did, the palace he built and inlaid with ivory, and the cities he fortified, are they not written in the book of the annals of the kings of Israel? [40]Ahab rested with his fathers. And Ahaziah his son succeeded him as king.

Jehoshaphat King of Judah

[41]Jehoshaphat son of Asa became king of Judah in the fourth year of Ahab king of Israel. [42]Jehoshaphat was thirty-five years old when he became king, and he reigned in Jerusalem for twenty-five years. His mother's name was Azubah daughter of Shilhi. [43]In everything he walked in the ways of his father Asa and did not stray from them; he did what was right in the eyes of the LORD. The high places, however, were not removed, and the people continued to offer sacrifices and burn incense there. [44]Jehoshaphat was also at peace with the king of Israel.

[45]As for the other events of Jehoshaphat's reign, the things he achieved and his military exploits, are they not written in the book of the annals of the kings of Judah? [46]He rid the land of the rest of the male shrine-prostitutes who remained there even after the reign of his father Asa. [47]There was then no king in Edom; a deputy ruled.

[48]Now Jehoshaphat built a fleet of trading ships[c] to go to Ophir for gold, but they never set sail — they were wrecked at Ezion Geber. [49]At that time Ahaziah son of Ahab said to Jehoshaphat, "Let my men sail with your men," but Jehoshaphat refused.

[50]Then Jehoshaphat rested with his fathers and was buried with them in the city of David his father. And Jehoram his son succeeded him.

Ahaziah King of Israel

[51]Ahaziah son of Ahab became king of Israel in Samaria in the seventeenth year of Jehoshaphat king of Judah, and he reigned over Israel for two years. [52]He did evil in the eyes of the LORD, because he walked in the ways of his father and mother and in the ways of Jeroboam son of Nebat, who caused Israel to sin. [53]He served and worshipped Baal and provoked the LORD, the God of Israel, to anger, just as his father had done.

[b]38 Or Samaria and cleaned the weapons   [c]48 Hebrew of ships of Tarshish

2 Kings

Two Kingdoms

The book of 2 Kings takes up the story of the two kingdoms of Israel and Judah from the point at which 1 Kings left off. The book tells the sad story of the demise of both kingdoms. The Northern Kingdom of Israel fell to the Assyrians in 722 BC, and the Southern Kingdom of Judah fell to the Babylonians in 586 BC.

Elisha Tells of God's Power

In its early chapters the book concentrates on the activities of Elijah's successor, Elisha (chapters 1—8). The power of God was demonstrated through a number of dramatic miracles, at a time when the life of the people might otherwise have suggested that the Lord's power was lacking.

Apostasy and National Decline

There follows the account of the parallel histories of the two kingdoms of Israel and Judah from the middle of the ninth century BC to the fall of

Israel (chapters 8—17). The reign of each king was evaluated on the basis of his religious stance, and the Northern Kingdom was shown to be in steady and irreversible decline. The final result of the sin of the Northern Kingdom was their defeat by the Assyrians and their subsequent exile. This was followed by the resettling of the land, now called Samaria. The people mixed with foreign peoples who brought their own religious beliefs, and they became blended with certain aspects of Israelite belief. This mixture of beliefs gave rise to the deep mistrust and hatred between Jews and Samaritans (the name of some of the new residents of the north) that lasted through the New Testament period.

Disobedience and Defeat

The book continues with an account of the history of Judah until the time of its defeat and exile. Whereas there had been a steady decline of the Northern Kingdom on account of the consistently wicked behaviour of its kings, the decline of Judah was halted by the appearance of Hezekiah and Josiah. Both these men instituted religious reforms which had the effect of delaying God's judgement, although between them came Manasseh, the King of Judah whose ways were so wicked that the kingdom's eventual fall was ascribed directly to him. As had been the case with Israel, Judah's defeat and exile is shown to be due ultimately to disobedience to the law of God on the part of both king and people. The strong link between disobedience and judgement carried a strong message for the people of later generations about the necessity for obedience to the will of God which had been revealed to them.

Prophecy and Historic Fulfilment

It is important also to notice the strong link between the prophetic word of God and the events that are recorded as taking place in the history of his people. The defeat and exile of both kingdoms was announced in advance by the prophets, and their words were fulfilled in the course of time. This is not to suggest that the wicked kings or people never had the opportunity to repent. Rather, it indicates that God retained ultimate control, even when the fortunes of his people were in decline. Even in such disastrous circumstances as defeat and exile, God was at work, bringing his purposes to fulfilment.

Always Hope

The book ends with the people of God in exile, but there is still the possibility of hope. The closing verses refer to the release of Jehoiachin from prison in Babylon. Jehoiachin was of the house of David, the royal house established by God and through whom he had promised to bring his purposes to fulfilment. These closing verses of the book indicate that the royal line was still alive in exile, and the hopes of God's people lived on with it. Even in captivity within a strange land, God was at work.

The LORD's Judgment on Ahaziah

1 After Ahab's death, Moab rebelled against Israel. [2]Now Ahaziah had fallen through the lattice of his upper room in Samaria and injured himself. So he sent messengers, saying to them, "Go and consult Baal-Zebub, the god of Ekron, to see if I will recover from this injury."

[3]But the angel of the LORD said to Elijah the Tishbite, "Go up and meet the messengers of the king of Samaria and ask them, 'Is it because there is no God in Israel that you are going off to consult Baal-Zebub, the god of Ekron?' [4]Therefore this is what the LORD says: 'You will not leave the bed you are lying on. You will certainly die!' " So Elijah went.

[5]When the messengers returned to the king, he asked them, "Why have you come back?"

[6]"A man came to meet us," they replied. "And he said to us, 'Go back to the king who sent you and tell him, "This is what the LORD says: Is it because there is no God in Israel that you are sending men to consult Baal-Zebub, the god of Ekron? Therefore you will not leave the bed you are lying on. You will certainly die!" ' "

[7]The king asked them, "What kind of man was it who came to meet you and told you this?"

[8]They replied, "He was a man with a garment of hair and with a leather belt round his waist."

The king said, "That was Elijah the Tishbite."

[9]Then he sent to Elijah a captain with his company of fifty men. The captain went up to Elijah, who was sitting on the top of a hill, and said to him, "Man of God, the king says, 'Come down!' "

[10]Elijah answered the captain, "If I am a man of God, may fire come down from heaven and consume you and your fifty men!" Then the fire fell from heaven and consumed the captain and his men.

[11]At this the king sent to Elijah another captain with his fifty men. The captain said to him, "Man of God, this is what the king says, 'Come down at once!' "

[12]"If I am a man of God," Elijah replied, "may fire come down from heaven and consume you and your fifty men!" Then the fire of God fell from heaven and consumed him and his fifty men.

[13]So the king sent a third captain with his fifty men. This third captain went up and fell on his knees before Elijah. "Man of God," he begged, "please have respect for my life and the lives of these fifty men, your servants! [14]See, fire has fallen from heaven and consumed the first two captains and all their men. But now have respect for my life!"

[15]The angel of the LORD said to Elijah, "Go down with him; do not be afraid of him." So Elijah got up and went down with him to the king.

[16]He told the king, "This is what the LORD says: Is it because there is no God in Israel for you to consult that you have sent messengers to consult Baal-Zebub, the god of Ekron? Because you have done this, you will never leave the bed you are lying on. You will certainly die!" [17]So he died, according to the word of the LORD that Elijah had spoken.

Because Ahaziah had no son, Joram[a] succeeded

him as king in the second year of Jehoram son of Jehoshaphat king of Judah. [18]As for all the other events of Ahaziah's reign, and what he did, are they not written in the book of the annals of the kings of Israel?

Elijah Taken Up to Heaven

2 When the LORD was about to take Elijah up to heaven in a whirlwind, Elijah and Elisha were on their way from Gilgal. [2]Elijah said to Elisha, "Stay here; the LORD has sent me to Bethel."

But Elisha said, "As surely as the LORD lives and as you live, I will not leave you." So they went down to Bethel.

[3]The company of the prophets at Bethel came out to Elisha and asked, "Do you know that the LORD is going to take your master from you today?"

"Yes, I know," Elisha replied, "but do not speak of it."

[4]Then Elijah said to him, "Stay here, Elisha; the LORD has sent me to Jericho."

And he replied, "As surely as the LORD lives and as you live, I will not leave you." So they went to Jericho.

[5]The company of the prophets at Jericho went up to Elisha and asked him, "Do you know that the LORD is going to take your master from you today?"

"Yes, I know," he replied, "but do not speak of it."

[6]Then Elijah said to him, "Stay here; the LORD has sent me to the Jordan."

And he replied, "As surely as the LORD lives and as you live, I will not leave you." So the two of them walked on.

[7]Fifty men of the company of the prophets went and stood at a distance, facing the place where Elijah and Elisha had stopped at the Jordan. [8]Elijah took his cloak, rolled it up and struck the water with it. The water divided to the right and to the left, and the two of them crossed over on dry ground.

[9]When they had crossed, Elijah said to Elisha, "Tell me, what can I do for you before I am taken from you?"

"Let me inherit a double portion of your spirit," Elisha replied.

2:9 Elisha asked for a double portion of Elijah's spirit. By law a man's eldest son received a double portion of his father's estate. Elisha's request, therefore, is that he might become Elijah's true successor.

---

[10]"You have asked a difficult thing," Elijah said, "yet if you see me when I am taken from you, it will be yours—otherwise not."

[11]As they were walking along and talking together, suddenly a chariot of fire and horses of fire appeared and separated the two of them, and Elijah went up to heaven in a whirlwind. [12]Elisha saw this and cried out, "My father! My father! The chariots and horsemen of Israel!" And Elisha saw him no more. Then he took hold of his own clothes and tore them apart.

[13]He picked up the cloak that had fallen from Elijah and went back and stood on the bank of the Jordan.

---

a 17 Hebrew *Jehoram*, a variant of *Joram*

[14]Then he took the cloak that had fallen from him and struck the water with it. "Where now is the LORD, the God of Elijah?" he asked. When he struck the water, it divided to the right and to the left, and he crossed over.

2:12   "My father! My father! The chariots and horsemen of Israel!" The meaning of Elisha's last words to Elijah as he was taken up from him is obscure. They are perhaps a reference to the power of Elijah, something which the nation could not really afford to lose. Elisha expressed his own sense of loss by tearing off his clothes.

---

[15]The company of the prophets from Jericho, who were watching, said, "The spirit of Elijah is resting on Elisha." And they went to meet him and bowed to the ground before him. [16]"Look," they said, "we your servants have fifty able men. Let them go and look for your master. Perhaps the Spirit of the LORD has picked him up and set him down on some mountain or in some valley."

"No," Elisha replied, "do not send them."

[17]But they persisted until he was too ashamed to refuse. So he said, "Send them." And they sent fifty men, who searched for three days but did not find him. [18]When they returned to Elisha, who was staying in Jericho, he said to them, "Didn't I tell you not to go?"

Healing of the Water

[19]The men of the city said to Elisha, "Look, our lord, this town is well situated, as you can see, but the water is bad and the land is unproductive."

[20]"Bring me a new bowl," he said, "and put salt in it." So they brought it to him.

[21]Then he went out to the spring and threw the salt into it, saying, "This is what the LORD says: 'I have healed this water. Never again will it cause death or make the land unproductive.' " [22]And the water has remained wholesome to this day, according to the word Elisha had spoken.

Elisha Is Jeered

[23]From there Elisha went up to Bethel. As he was walking along the road, some youths came out of the town and jeered at him. "Go on up, you baldhead!" they said. "Go on up, you baldhead!" [24]He turned round, looked at them and called down a curse on them in the name of the LORD. Then two bears came out of the woods and mauled forty-two of the youths. [25]And he went on to Mount Carmel and from there returned to Samaria.

Moab Revolts

3 Joram[a] son of Ahab became king of Israel in Samaria in the eighteenth year of Jehoshaphat king of Judah, and he reigned for twelve years. [2]He did evil in the eyes of the LORD, but not as his father and mother had done. He got rid of the sacred stone of Baal that his father had made. [3]Nevertheless he clung to the sins of Jeroboam son of Nebat, which he had caused Israel to commit; he did not turn away from them.

2:23   The incident involving the bears causes the modern reader many difficulties, which are not easily solved. It is perhaps best to regard the incident as intended simply to underline the authority of the prophet, and although the bears killed the young people, there is no implication that Elisha's curse was related to this.

---

[4]Now Mesha king of Moab raised sheep, and he had to supply the king of Israel with a hundred thousand lambs and with the wool of a hundred thousand rams. [5]But after Ahab died, the king of Moab rebelled against the king of Israel. [6]So at that time King Joram set out from Samaria and mobilised all Israel. [7]He also sent this message to Jehoshaphat king of Judah: "The king of Moab has rebelled against me. Will you go with me to fight against Moab?"

"I will go with you," he replied. "I am as you are, my people as your people, my horses as your horses."

[8]"By what route shall we attack?" he asked.

"Through the Desert of Edom," he answered.

[9]So the king of Israel set out with the king of Judah and the king of Edom. After a roundabout march of seven days, the army had no more water for themselves or for the animals with them.

[10]"What!" exclaimed the king of Israel. "Has the LORD called us three kings together only to hand us over to Moab?"

[11]But Jehoshaphat asked, "Is there no prophet of the LORD here, that we may enquire of the LORD through him?"

An officer of the king of Israel answered, "Elisha son of Shaphat is here. He used to pour water on the hands of Elijah."[b]

[12]Jehoshaphat said, "The word of the LORD is with him." So the king of Israel and Jehoshaphat and the king of Edom went down to him.

[13]Elisha said to the king of Israel, "What do we have to do with each other? Go to the prophets of your father and the prophets of your mother."

"No," the king of Israel answered, "because it was the LORD who called us three kings together to hand us over to Moab."

[14]Elisha said, "As surely as the LORD Almighty lives, whom I serve, if I did not have respect for the presence of Jehoshaphat king of Judah, I would not look at you or even notice you. [15]But now bring me a harpist."

While the harpist was playing, the hand of the LORD came upon Elisha [16]and he said, "This is what the LORD says: Make this valley full of ditches. [17]For this is what the LORD says: You will see neither wind nor rain, yet this valley will be filled with water, and you, your cattle and your other animals will drink. [18]This is an easy thing in the eyes of the LORD; he will also hand Moab

---

[a]1 Hebrew *Jehoram*, a variant of *Joram*; also in verse 6   [b]11 That is, he was Elijah's personal servant.

over to you. 19You will overthrow every fortified city and every major town. You will cut down every good tree, stop up all the springs, and ruin every good field with stones."

20The next morning, about the time for offering the sacrifice, there it was—water flowing from the direction of Edom! And the land was filled with water.

21Now all the Moabites had heard that the kings had come to fight against them; so every man, young and old, who could bear arms was called up and stationed on the border. 22When they got up early in the morning, the sun was shining on the water. To the Moabites across the way, the water looked red—like blood. 23"That's blood!" they said. "Those kings must have fought and slaughtered each other. Now to the plunder, Moab!"

24But when the Moabites came to the camp of Israel, the Israelites rose up and fought them until they fled. And the Israelites invaded the land and slaughtered the Moabites. 25They destroyed the towns, and each man threw a stone on every good field until it was covered. They stopped up all the springs and cut down every good tree. Only Kir Hareseth was left with its stones in place, but men armed with slings surrounded it and attacked it as well.

26When the king of Moab saw that the battle had gone against him, he took with him seven hundred swordsmen to break through to the king of Edom, but they failed. 27Then he took his firstborn son, who was to succeed him as king, and offered him as a sacrifice on the city wall. The fury against Israel was great; they withdrew and returned to their own land.

The Widow's Oil

4 The wife of a man from the company of the prophets cried out to Elisha, "Your servant my husband is dead, and you know that he revered the LORD. But now his creditor is coming to take my two boys as his slaves."

2Elisha replied to her, "How can I help you? Tell me, what do you have in your house?"

"Your servant has nothing there at all," she said, "except a little oil."

3Elisha said, "Go round and ask all your neighbours for empty jars. Don't ask for just a few. 4Then go inside and shut the door behind you and your sons. Pour oil into all the jars, and as each is filled, put it to one side."

5She left him and afterwards shut the door behind her and her sons. They brought the jars to her and she kept pouring. 6When all the jars were full, she said to her son, "Bring me another one."

But he replied, "There is not a jar left." Then the oil stopped flowing.

7She went and told the man of God, and he said, "Go, sell the oil and pay your debts. You and your sons can live on what is left."

The Shunammite's Son Restored to Life

8One day Elisha went to Shunem. And a well-to-do woman was there, who urged him to stay for a meal. So whenever he came by, he stopped there to eat. 9She said to her husband, "I know that this man who often comes our way is a holy man of God. 10Let's make a

small room on the roof and put in it a bed and a table, a chair and a lamp for him. Then he can stay there whenever he comes to us."

11One day when Elisha came, he went up to his room and lay down there. 12He said to his servant Gehazi, "Call the Shunammite." So he called her, and she stood before him. 13Elisha said to him, "Tell her, 'You have gone to all this trouble for us. Now what can be done for you? Can we speak on your behalf to the king or the commander of the army?' "

She replied, "I have a home among my own people."

14"What can be done for her?" Elisha asked.

Gehazi said, "Well, she has no son and her husband is old."

15Then Elisha said, "Call her." So he called her, and she stood in the doorway. 16"About this time next year," Elisha said, "you will hold a son in your arms."

"No, my lord," she objected. "Don't mislead your servant, O man of God!"

17But the woman became pregnant, and the next year about that same time she gave birth to a son, just as Elisha had told her.

18The child grew, and one day he went out to his father, who was with the reapers. 19"My head! My head!" he said to his father.

His father told a servant, "Carry him to his mother." 20After the servant had lifted him up and carried him to his mother, the boy sat on her lap until noon, and then he died. 21She went up and laid him on the bed of the man of God, then shut the door and went out.

22She called her husband and said, "Please send me one of the servants and a donkey so I can go to the man of God quickly and return."

23"Why go to him today?" he asked. "It's not the New Moon or the Sabbath."

"It's all right," she said.

4:23   Both the New Moon and the Sabbath were occasions for the suspension of normal business (see Amos 8:5), and the Shunammite woman's journey to Elisha would normally have been reserved for such a day.

24She saddled the donkey and said to her servant, "Lead on; don't slow down for me unless I tell you." 25So she set out and came to the man of God at Mount Carmel.

When he saw her in the distance, the man of God said to his servant Gehazi, "Look! There's the Shunammite! 26Run to meet her and ask her, 'Are you all right? Is your husband all right? Is your child all right?' "

"Everything is all right," she said.

27When she reached the man of God at the mountain, she took hold of his feet. Gehazi came over to push her away, but the man of God said, "Leave her alone! She is in bitter distress, but the LORD has hidden it from me and has not told me why."

28"Did I ask you for a son, my lord?" she said. "Didn't I tell you, 'Don't raise my hopes'?"

29Elisha said to Gehazi, "Tuck your cloak into your belt, take my staff in your hand and run. If you meet anyone, do not greet him, and if anyone greets you, do not answer. Lay my staff on the boy's face."

[30]But the child's mother said, "As surely as the LORD lives and as you live, I will not leave you." So he got up and followed her.

[31]Gehazi went on ahead and laid the staff on the boy's face, but there was no sound or response. So Gehazi went back to meet Elisha and told him, "The boy has not awakened."

[32]When Elisha reached the house, there was the boy lying dead on his couch. [33]He went in, shut the door on the two of them and prayed to the LORD. [34]Then he got on the bed and lay upon the boy, mouth to mouth, eyes to eyes, hands to hands. As he stretched himself out upon him, the boy's body grew warm. [35]Elisha turned away and walked back and forth in the room and then got onto the bed and stretched out upon him once more. The boy sneezed seven times and opened his eyes.

[36]Elisha summoned Gehazi and said, "Call the Shunammite." And he did. When she came, he said, "Take your son." [37]She came in, fell at his feet and bowed to the ground. Then she took her son and went out.

Death in the Pot

[38]Elisha returned to Gilgal and there was a famine in that region. While the company of the prophets was meeting with him, he said to his servant, "Put on the large pot and cook some stew for these men."

[39]One of them went out into the fields to gather herbs and found a wild vine. He gathered some of its gourds and filled the fold of his cloak. When he returned, he cut them up into the pot of stew, though no-one knew what they were. [40]The stew was poured out for the men, but as they began to eat it, they cried out, "O man of God, there is death in the pot!" And they could not eat it.

[41]Elisha said, "Get some flour." He put it into the pot and said, "Serve it to the people to eat." And there was nothing harmful in the pot.

Feeding of a Hundred

[42]A man came from Baal Shalishah, bringing the man of God twenty loaves of barley bread baked from the first ripe corn, along with some ears of new corn. "Give it to the people to eat," Elisha said.

[43]"How can I set this before a hundred men?" his servant asked.

But Elisha answered, "Give it to the people to eat. For this is what the LORD says: 'They will eat and have some left over.' " [44]Then he set it before them, and they ate and had some left over, according to the word of the LORD.

Naaman Healed of Leprosy

5 Now Naaman was commander of the army of the king of Aram. He was a great man in the sight of his master and highly regarded, because through him the LORD had given victory to Aram. He was a valiant soldier, but he had leprosy. [a]

[2]Now bands from Aram had gone out and had taken captive a young girl from Israel, and she served Naaman's wife. [3]She said to her mistress, "If only my master would see the prophet who is in Samaria! He would cure him of his leprosy."

[4]Naaman went to his master and told him what the girl from Israel had said. [5]"By all means, go," the king of Aram replied. "I will send a letter to the king of Israel." So Naaman left, taking with him ten talents[b] of silver, six thousand shekels[c] of gold and ten sets of clothing. [6]The letter that he took to the king of Israel read: "With this letter I am sending my servant Naaman to you so that you may cure him of his leprosy."

[7]As soon as the king of Israel read the letter, he tore his robes and said, "Am I God? Can I kill and bring back to life? Why does this fellow send someone to me to be cured of his leprosy? See how he is trying to pick a quarrel with me!"

[8]When Elisha the man of God heard that the king of Israel had torn his robes, he sent him this message: "Why have you torn your robes? Make the man come to me and he will know that there is a prophet in Israel." [9]So Naaman went with his horses and chariots and stopped at the door of Elisha's house. [10]Elisha sent a messenger to say to him, "Go, wash yourself seven times in the Jordan, and your flesh will be restored and you will be cleansed."

[11]But Naaman went away angry and said, "I thought that he would surely come out to me and stand and call on the name of the LORD his God, wave his hand over the spot and cure me of my leprosy. [12]Are not Abana and Pharpar, the rivers of Damascus, better than any of the waters of Israel? Couldn't I wash in them and be cleansed?" So he turned and went off in a rage.

[13]Naaman's servants went to him and said, "My father, if the prophet had told you to do some great thing, would you not have done it? How much more, then, when he tells you, 'Wash and be cleansed'?" [14]So he went down and dipped himself in the Jordan seven times, as the man of God had told him, and his flesh was restored and became clean like that of a young boy.

[15]Then Naaman and all his attendants went back to the man of God. He stood before him and said, "Now I know that there is no God in all the world except in Israel. Please accept now a gift from your servant."

[16]The prophet answered, "As surely as the LORD lives, whom I serve, I will not accept a thing." And even though Naaman urged him, he refused.

[17]"If you will not," said Naaman, "please let me, your servant, be given as much earth as a pair of mules can carry, for your servant will never again make burnt offerings and sacrifices to any other god but the LORD. [18]But may the LORD forgive your servant for this one thing: When my master enters the temple of Rimmon to bow down and he is leaning on my arm and I bow there also—when I bow down in the temple of Rimmon, may the LORD forgive your servant for this."

[19]"Go in peace," Elisha said.

After Naaman had travelled some distance,

---

[a]*1* The Hebrew word was used for various diseases affecting the skin—not necessarily leprosy; also in verses 3, 6, 7, 11 and 27.
[b]*5* That is, about 750 pounds (about 340 kilograms)   [c]*5* That is, about 150 pounds (about 70 kilograms)

²⁰Gehazi, the servant of Elisha the man of God, said to himself, "My master was too easy on Naaman, this Aramean, by not accepting from him what he brought. As surely as the LORD lives, I will run after him and get something from him."

5:17   Naaman requested as much earth as a pair of mules could carry. This strange request reflects the belief that each god exercised power over its own territory and could only be worshipped on land which belonged to it. Naaman served Aram, Israel's enemy, and believed he needed Israelite soil if worship offered in Aram was to be acceptable to the God of Israel.

---

²¹So Gehazi hurried after Naaman. When Naaman saw him running towards him, he got down from the chariot to meet him. "Is everything all right?" he asked.

²²"Everything is all right," Gehazi answered. "My master sent me to say, 'Two young men from the company of the prophets have just come to me from the hill country of Ephraim. Please give them a talent^d of silver and two sets of clothing.' "

²³"By all means, take two talents," said Naaman. He urged Gehazi to accept them, and then tied up the two talents of silver in two bags, with two sets of clothing. He gave them to two of his servants, and they carried them ahead of Gehazi. ²⁴When Gehazi came to the hill, he took the things from the servants and put them away in the house. He sent the men away and they left. ²⁵Then he went in and stood before his master Elisha.

"Where have you been, Gehazi?" Elisha asked.

"Your servant didn't go anywhere," Gehazi answered.

²⁶But Elisha said to him, "Was not my spirit with you when the man got down from his chariot to meet you? Is this the time to take money, or to accept clothes, olive groves, vineyards, flocks, herds, or menservants and maidservants? ²⁷Naaman's leprosy will cling to you and to your descendants for ever." Then Gehazi went from Elisha's presence and he was leprous, as white as snow.

An Axe-Head Floats

6 The company of the prophets said to Elisha, "Look, the place where we meet with you is too small for us. ²Let us go to the Jordan, where each of us can get a pole; and let us build a place there for us to live."

And he said, "Go."

³Then one of them said, "Won't you please come with your servants?"

"I will," Elisha replied. ⁴And he went with them. They went to the Jordan and began to cut down trees. ⁵As one of them was cutting down a tree, the iron axe-head fell into the water. "Oh, my lord," he cried out, "it was borrowed!"

⁶The man of God asked, "Where did it fall?" When he showed him the place, Elisha cut a stick and threw it there, and made the iron float. ⁷"Lift it out," he said. Then the man reached out his hand and took it.

Elisha Traps Blinded Arameans

⁸Now the king of Aram was at war with Israel. After conferring with his officers, he said, "I will set up my camp in such and such a place."

⁹The man of God sent word to the king of Israel: "Beware of passing that place, because the Arameans are going down there." ¹⁰So the king of Israel checked on the place indicated by the man of God. Time and again Elisha warned the king, so that he was on his guard in such places.

¹¹This enraged the king of Aram. He summoned his officers and demanded of them, "Will you not tell me which of us is on the side of the king of Israel?"

¹²"None of us, my lord the king," said one of his officers, "but Elisha, the prophet who is in Israel, tells the king of Israel the very words you speak in your bedroom."

¹³"Go, find out where he is," the king ordered, "so that I can send men and capture him." The report came back: "He is in Dothan." ¹⁴Then he sent horses and chariots and a strong force there. They went by night and surrounded the city.

¹⁵When the servant of the man of God got up and went out early the next morning, an army with horses and chariots had surrounded the city. "Oh, my lord, what shall we do?" the servant asked.

¹⁶"Don't be afraid," the prophet answered. "Those who are with us are more than those who are with them."

¹⁷And Elisha prayed, "O LORD, open his eyes so that he may see." Then the LORD opened the servant's eyes, and he looked and saw the hills full of horses and chariots of fire all round Elisha.

¹⁸As the enemy came down towards him, Elisha prayed to the LORD, "Strike these people with blindness." So he struck them with blindness, as Elisha had asked.

¹⁹Elisha told them, "This is not the road and this is not the city. Follow me, and I will lead you to the man you are looking for." And he led them to Samaria.

²⁰After they entered the city, Elisha said, "LORD, open the eyes of these men so that they can see." Then the LORD opened their eyes and they looked, and there they were, inside Samaria.

²¹When the king of Israel saw them, he asked Elisha, "Shall I kill them, my father? Shall I kill them?"

²²"Do not kill them," he answered. "Would you kill men you have captured with your own sword or bow? Set food and water before them so that they may eat and drink and then go back to their master." ²³So he prepared a great feast for them, and after they had finished eating and drinking, he sent them away, and they returned to their master. So the bands from Aram stopped raiding Israel's territory.

^d22 That is, about 75 pounds (about 34 kilograms)

Famine in Besieged Samaria

24Some time later, Ben-Hadad king of Aram mobilised his entire army and marched up and laid siege to Samaria. 25There was a great famine in the city; the siege lasted so long that a donkey's head sold for eighty shekels*a* of silver, and a quarter of a cab*b* of seed pods*c* for five shekels.*d*

26As the king of Israel was passing by on the wall, a woman cried to him, "Help me, my lord the king!" 27The king replied, "If the LORD does not help you, where can I get help for you? From the threshing-floor? From the winepress?" 28Then he asked her, "What's the matter?"

She answered, "This woman said to me, 'Give up your son so that we may eat him today, and tomorrow we'll eat my son.' 29So we cooked my son and ate him. The next day I said to her, 'Give up your son so that we may eat him,' but she had hidden him."

30When the king heard the woman's words, he tore his robes. As he went along the wall, the people looked, and there, underneath, he had sackcloth on his body. 31He said, "May God deal with me, be it ever so severely, if the head of Elisha son of Shaphat remains on his shoulders today!"

32Now Elisha was sitting in his house, and the elders were sitting with him. The king sent a messenger ahead, but before he arrived, Elisha said to the elders, "Don't you see how this murderer is sending someone to cut off my head? Look, when the messenger comes, shut the door and hold it shut against him. Is not the sound of his master's footsteps behind him?" 33While he was still talking to them, the messenger came down to him. And the king, said, "This disaster is from the LORD. Why should I wait for the LORD any longer?"

7 Elisha said, "Hear the word of the LORD. This is what the LORD says: About this time tomorrow, a seah*a* of flour will sell for a shekel*b* and two seahs*c* of barley for a shekel at the gate of Samaria."

2The officer on whose arm the king was leaning said to the man of God, "Look, even if the LORD should open the floodgates of the heavens, could this happen?"

"You will see it with your own eyes," answered Elisha, "but you will not eat any of it!"

The Siege Lifted

3Now there were four men with leprosy*d* at the entrance of the city gate. They said to each other, "Why stay here until we die? 4If we say, 'We'll go into the city'—the famine is there, and we will die. And if we stay here, we will die. So let's go over to the camp of the Arameans and surrender. If they spare us, we live; if they kill us, then we die."

5At dusk they got up and went to the camp of the Arameans. When they reached the edge of the camp, not a man was there, 6for the Lord had caused the Arameans to hear the sound of chariots and horses and a great army, so that they said to one another, "Look, the king of Israel has hired the Hittite and Egyptian kings to attack us!" 7So they got up and fled in the dusk and abandoned their tents and their horses and donkeys. They left the camp as it was and ran for their lives.

8The men who had leprosy reached the edge of the camp and entered one of the tents. They ate and drank, and carried away silver, gold and clothes, and went off and hid them. They returned and entered another tent and took some things from it and hid them also.

9Then they said to each other, "We're not doing right. This is a day of good news and we are keeping it to ourselves. If we wait until daylight, punishment will overtake us. Let's go at once and report this to the royal palace."

10So they went and called out to the city gatekeepers and told them, "We went into the Aramean camp and not a man was there—not a sound of anyone—only tethered horses and donkeys, and the tents left just as they were." 11The gatekeepers shouted the news, and it was reported within the palace.

12The king got up in the night and said to his officers, "I will tell you what the Arameans have done to us. They know we are starving; so they have left the camp to hide in the countryside, thinking, 'They will surely come out, and then we will take them alive and get into the city.' "

13One of his officers answered, "Make some men take five of the horses that are left in the city. Their plight will be like that of all the Israelites left here—yes, they will only be like all these Israelites who are doomed. So let us send them to find out what happened."

14So they selected two chariots with their horses, and the king sent them after the Aramean army. He commanded the drivers, "Go and find out what has happened." 15They followed them as far as the Jordan, and they found the whole road strewn with the clothing and equipment the Arameans had thrown away in their headlong flight. So the messengers returned and reported to the king. 16Then the people went out and plundered the camp of the Arameans. So a seah of flour sold for a shekel, and two seahs of barley sold for a shekel, as the LORD had said.

17Now the king had put the officer on whose arm he leaned in charge of the gate, and the people trampled him in the gateway, and he died, just as the man of God had foretold when the king came down to his house. 18It happened as the man of God had said to the king: "About this time tomorrow, a seah of flour will sell for a shekel and two seahs of barley for a shekel at the gate of Samaria."

19The officer had said to the man of God, "Look, even if the LORD should open the floodgates of the heavens, could this happen?" The man of God had replied, "You will see it with your own eyes, but you

a25 That is, about 2 pounds (about 1 kilogram)   *b25* That is, probably about ½ pint (about 0.3 litre)
c25 Or *of dove's dung*   *d25* That is, about 2 ounces (about 55 grams)
a1 That is, probably about 13 pints (about 7.3 litres); also in verses 16 and 18
b1 That is, about ⅖ ounce (about 11 grams); also in verses 16 and 18
c1 That is, probably about 13 quarts (about 15 litres); also in verses 16 and 18
d3 The Hebrew word is used for various diseases affecting the skin—not necessarily leprosy; also in verse 8.

will not eat any of it!" ²⁰And that is exactly what happened to him, for the people trampled him in the gateway, and he died.

The Shunammite's Land Restored

8 Now Elisha had said to the woman whose son he had restored to life, "Go away with your family and stay for a while wherever you can, because the LORD has decreed a famine in the land that will last seven years." ²The woman proceeded to do as the man of God said. She and her family went away and stayed in the land of the Philistines for seven years.

³At the end of the seven years she came back from the land of the Philistines and went to the king to beg for her house and land. ⁴The king was talking to Gehazi, the servant of the man of God, and had said, "Tell me about all the great things Elisha has done." ⁵Just as Gehazi was telling the king how Elisha had restored the dead to life, the woman whose son Elisha had brought back to life came to beg the king for her house and land.

Gehazi said, "This is the woman, my lord the king, and this is her son whom Elisha restored to life." ⁶The king asked the woman about it, and she told him.

Then he assigned an official to her case and said to him, "Give back everything that belonged to her, including all the income from her land from the day she left the country until now."

Hazael Murders Ben-Hadad

⁷Elisha went to Damascus, and Ben-Hadad king of Aram was ill. When the king was told, "The man of God has come all the way up here," ⁸he said to Hazael, "Take a gift with you and go to meet the man of God. Consult the LORD through him; ask him, 'Will I recover from this illness?' "

⁹Hazael went to meet Elisha, taking with him as a gift forty camel-loads of all the finest wares of Damascus. He went in and stood before him, and said, "Your son Ben-Hadad king of Aram has sent me to ask, 'Will I recover from this illness?' "

¹⁰Elisha answered, "Go and say to him, 'You will certainly recover'; but^a the LORD has revealed to me that he will in fact die." ¹¹He stared at him with a fixed gaze until Hazael felt ashamed. Then the man of God began to weep.

¹²"Why is my lord weeping?" asked Hazael.

"Because I know the harm you will do to the Israelites," he answered. "You will set fire to their fortified places, kill their young men with the sword, dash their little children to the ground, and rip open their pregnant women."

¹³Hazael said, "How could your servant, a mere dog, accomplish such a feat?"

"The LORD has shown me that you will become king of Aram," answered Elisha.

¹⁴Then Hazael left Elisha and returned to his master. When Ben-Hadad asked, "What did Elisha say to you?" Hazael replied, "He told me that you would certainly recover." ¹⁵But the next day he took a thick cloth, soaked it in water and spread it over the king's face, so that he died. Then Hazael succeeded him as king.

Jehoram King of Judah

¹⁶In the fifth year of Joram son of Ahab king of Israel, when Jehoshaphat was king of Judah, Jehoram son of Jehoshaphat began his reign as king of Judah. ¹⁷He was thirty-two years old when he became king, and he reigned in Jerusalem for eight years. ¹⁸He walked in the ways of the kings of Israel, as the house of Ahab had done, for he married a daughter of Ahab. He did evil in the eyes of the LORD. ¹⁹Nevertheless, for the sake of his servant David, the LORD was not willing to destroy Judah. He had promised to maintain a lamp for David and his descendants for ever.

8:16 Joram ruled Israel and Jehoram (sometimes also written as Joram) ruled Judah at the same time. Another similar confusion can arise from the fact that both Judah and Israel had a king with the name Ahaziah, although it was at different times.

---

²⁰In the time of Jehoram, Edom rebelled against Judah and set up its own king. ²¹So Jehoram^b went to Zair with all his chariots. The Edomites surrounded him and his chariot commanders, but he rose up and broke through by night; his army, however, fled back home. ²²To this day Edom has been in rebellion against Judah. Libnah revolted at the same time.

²³As for the other events of Jehoram's reign, and all he did, are they not written in the book of the annals of the kings of Judah? ²⁴Jehoram rested with his fathers and was buried with them in the City of David. And Ahaziah his son succeeded him as king.

Ahaziah King of Judah

²⁵In the twelfth year of Joram son of Ahab king of Israel, Ahaziah son of Jehoram king of Judah began to reign. ²⁶Ahaziah was twenty-two years old when he became king, and he reigned in Jerusalem for one year. His mother's name was Athaliah, a granddaughter of Omri king of Israel. ²⁷He walked in the ways of the house of Ahab and did evil in the eyes of the LORD, as the house of Ahab had done, for he was related by marriage to Ahab's family.

²⁸Ahaziah went with Joram son of Ahab to war against Hazael king of Aram at Ramoth Gilead. The Arameans wounded Joram; ²⁹so King Joram returned to Jezreel to recover from the wounds the Arameans had inflicted on him at Ramoth^c in his battle with Hazael king of Aram.

Then Ahaziah son of Jehoram king of Judah went down to Jezreel to see Joram son of Ahab, because he had been wounded.

---

^a10 The Hebrew may also be read Go and say, 'You will certainly not recover,' for.
^b21 Hebrew Joram, a variant of Jehoram; also in verses 23 and 24
^c29 Hebrew Ramah, a variant of Ramoth

Jehu Anointed King of Israel

9 The prophet Elisha summoned a man from the company of the prophets and said to him, "Tuck your cloak into your belt, take this flask of oil with you and go to Ramoth Gilead. ²When you get there, look for Jehu son of Jehoshaphat, the son of Nimshi. Go to him, get him away from his companions and take him into an inner room. ³Then take the flask and pour the oil on his head and declare, 'This is what the LORD says: I anoint you king over Israel.' Then open the door and run; don't delay!"

⁴So the young man, the prophet, went to Ramoth Gilead. ⁵When he arrived, he found the army officers sitting together. "I have a message for you, commander," he said.

"For which of us?" asked Jehu.

"For you, commander," he replied.

⁶Jehu got up and went into the house. Then the prophet poured the oil on Jehu's head and declared, "This is what the LORD, the God of Israel, says: 'I anoint you king over the LORD's people Israel. ⁷You are to destroy the house of Ahab your master, and I will avenge the blood of my servants the prophets and the blood of all the LORD's servants shed by Jezebel. ⁸The whole house of Ahab will perish. I will cut off from Ahab every last male in Israel—slave or free. ⁹I will make the house of Ahab like the house of Jeroboam son of Nebat and like the house of Baasha son of Ahijah. ¹⁰As for Jezebel, dogs will devour her on the plot of ground at Jezreel, and no-one will bury her.' " Then he opened the door and ran.

¹¹When Jehu went out to his fellow officers, one of them asked him, "Is everything all right? Why did this madman come to you?"

"You know the man and the sort of things he says," Jehu replied.

¹²"That's not true!" they said. "Tell us."

Jehu said, "Here is what he told me: 'This is what the LORD says: I anoint you king over Israel.' "

¹³They hurried and took their cloaks and spread them under him on the bare steps. Then they blew the trumpet and shouted, "Jehu is king!"

Jehu Kills Joram and Ahaziah

¹⁴So Jehu son of Jehoshaphat, the son of Nimshi, conspired against Joram. (Now Joram and all Israel had been defending Ramoth Gilead against Hazael king of Aram, ¹⁵but King Joram[a] had returned to Jezreel to recover from the wounds the Arameans had inflicted on him in the battle with Hazael king of Aram.) Jehu said, "If this is the way you feel, don't let anyone slip out of the city to go and tell the news in Jezreel." ¹⁶Then he got into his chariot and rode to Jezreel, because Joram was resting there and Ahaziah king of Judah had gone down to see him.

¹⁷When the lookout standing on the tower in Jezreel saw Jehu's troops approaching, he called out, "I see some troops coming."

"Get a horseman," Joram ordered. "Send him to meet them and ask, 'Do you come in peace?' "

¹⁸The horseman rode off to meet Jehu and said, "This is what the king says: 'Do you come in peace?' "

"What do you have to do with peace?" Jehu replied. "Fall in behind me."

The lookout reported, "The messenger has reached them, but he isn't coming back."

¹⁹So the king sent out a second horseman. When he came to them he said, "This is what the king says: 'Do you come in peace?' "

Jehu replied, "What do you have to do with peace? Fall in behind me."

²⁰The lookout reported, "He has reached them, but he isn't coming back either. The driving is like that of Jehu son of Nimshi—he drives like a madman."

²¹"Hitch up my chariot," Joram ordered. And when it was hitched up, Joram king of Israel and Ahaziah king of Judah rode out, each in his own chariot, to meet Jehu. They met him at the plot of ground that had belonged to Naboth the Jezreelite. ²²When Joram saw Jehu he asked, "Have you come in peace, Jehu?"

"How can there be peace," Jehu replied, "as long as all the idolatry and witchcraft of your mother Jezebel abound?"

²³Joram turned about and fled, calling out to Ahaziah, "Treachery, Ahaziah!"

²⁴Then Jehu drew his bow and shot Joram between the shoulders. The arrow pierced his heart and he slumped down in his chariot. ²⁵Jehu said to Bidkar, his chariot officer, "Pick him up and throw him on the field that belonged to Naboth the Jezreelite. Remember how you and I were riding together in chariots behind Ahab his father when the LORD made this prophecy about him: ²⁶'Yesterday I saw the blood of Naboth and the blood of his sons, declares the LORD, and I will surely make you pay for it on this plot of ground, declares the LORD.'[b] Now then, pick him up and throw him on that plot, in accordance with the word of the LORD."

²⁷When Ahaziah king of Judah saw what had happened, he fled up the road to Beth Haggan.[c] Jehu chased him, shouting, "Kill him too!" They wounded him in his chariot on the way up to Gur near Ibleam, but he escaped to Megiddo and died there. ²⁸His servants took him by chariot to Jerusalem and buried him with his fathers in his tomb in the City of David. ²⁹(In the eleventh year of Joram son of Ahab, Ahaziah had become king of Judah.)

Jezebel Killed

³⁰Then Jehu went to Jezreel. When Jezebel heard about it, she painted her eyes, arranged her hair and looked out of a window. ³¹As Jehu entered the gate, she asked, "Have you come in peace, Zimri, you murderer of your master?"[d]

³²He looked up at the window and called out, "Who is on my side? Who?" Two or three eunuchs looked down at him. ³³"Throw her down!" Jehu said. So they threw her down, and some of her blood spattered the wall and the horses as they trampled her underfoot.

³⁴Jehu went in and ate and drank. "Take care of that cursed woman," he said, "and bury her, for she was a

---

a15 Hebrew *Jehoram*, a variant of *Joram*; also in verses 17 and 21–24   b26 See 1 Kings 21:19.
c27 Or *fled by way of the garden house*   d31 Or "Did Zimri have peace, who murdered his master?"

king's daughter." 35But when they went out to bury her, they found nothing except her skull, her feet and her hands. 36They went back and told Jehu, who said, "This is the word of the LORD that he spoke through his servant Elijah the Tishbite: On the plot of ground at Jezreel dogs will devour Jezebel's flesh.*e* 37Jezebel's body will be like refuse on the ground in the plot at Jezreel, so that no-one will be able to say, 'This is Jezebel.' "

Ahab's Family Killed

10 Now there were in Samaria seventy sons of the house of Ahab. So Jehu wrote letters and sent them to Samaria: to the officials of Jezreel,*a* to the elders and to the guardians of Ahab's children. He said, 2"As soon as this letter reaches you, since your master's sons are with you and you have chariots and horses, a fortified city and weapons, 3choose the best and most worthy of your master's sons and set him on his father's throne. Then fight for your master's house."

4But they were terrified and said, "If two kings could not resist him, how can we?"

5So the palace administrator, the city governor, the elders and the guardians sent this message to Jehu: "We are your servants and we will do anything you say. We will not appoint anyone as king; you do whatever you think best."

6Then Jehu wrote them a second letter, saying, "If you are on my side and will obey me, take the heads of your master's sons and come to me in Jezreel by this time tomorrow."

Now the royal princes, seventy of them, were with the leading men of the city, who were bringing them up. 7When the letter arrived, these men took the princes and slaughtered all seventy of them. They put their heads in baskets and sent them to Jehu in Jezreel. 8When the messenger arrived, he told Jehu, "They have brought the heads of the princes."

Then Jehu ordered, "Put them in two piles at the entrance of the city gate until morning."

9The next morning Jehu went out. He stood before all the people and said, "You are innocent. It was I who conspired against my master and killed him, but who killed all these? 10Know then, that not a word the LORD has spoken against the house of Ahab will fail. The LORD has done what he promised through his servant Elijah." 11So Jehu killed everyone in Jezreel who remained of the house of Ahab, as well as all his chief men, his close friends and his priests, leaving him no survivor.

12Jehu then set out and went towards Samaria. At Beth Eked of the Shepherds, 13he met some relatives of Ahaziah king of Judah and asked, "Who are you?"

They said, "We are relatives of Ahaziah, and we have come down to greet the families of the king and of the queen mother."

14"Take them alive!" he ordered. So they took them alive and slaughtered them by the well of Beth Eked — forty-two men. He left no survivor.

15After he left there, he came upon Jehonadab son of Recab, who was on his way to meet him. Jehu greeted him and said, "Are you in accord with me, as I am with you?"

"I am," Jehonadab answered.

"If so," said Jehu, "give me your hand." So he did, and Jehu helped him up into the chariot. 16Jehu said, "Come with me and see my zeal for the LORD." Then he made him ride in his chariot.

17When Jehu came to Samaria, he killed all who were left there of Ahab's family; he destroyed them, according to the word of the LORD spoken to Elijah.

Ministers of Baal Killed

18Then Jehu brought all the people together and said to them, "Ahab served Baal a little; Jehu will serve him much. 19Now summon all the prophets of Baal, all his ministers and all his priests. See that no-one is missing, because I am going to hold a great sacrifice for Baal. Anyone who fails to come will no longer live." But Jehu was acting deceptively in order to destroy the ministers of Baal.

20Jehu said, "Call an assembly in honour of Baal." So they proclaimed it. 21Then he sent word throughout Israel, and all the ministers of Baal came; not one stayed away. They crowded into the temple of Baal until it was full from one end to the other. 22And Jehu said to the keeper of the wardrobe, "Bring robes for all the ministers of Baal." So he brought out robes for them.

23Then Jehu and Jehonadab son of Recab went into the temple of Baal. Jehu said to the ministers of Baal, "Look around and see that no servants of the LORD are here with you — only ministers of Baal." 24So they went in to make sacrifices and burnt offerings. Now Jehu had posted eighty men outside with this warning: "If one of you lets any of the men I am placing in your hands escape, it will be your life for his life."

25As soon as Jehu had finished making the burnt offering, he ordered the guards and officers: "Go in and kill them; let no-one escape." So they cut them down with the sword. The guards and officers threw the bodies out and then entered the inner shrine of the temple of Baal. 26They brought the sacred stone out of the temple of Baal and burned it. 27They demolished the sacred stone of Baal and tore down the temple of Baal, and people have used it for a latrine to this day.

28So Jehu destroyed Baal worship in Israel. 29However, he did not turn away from the sins of Jeroboam son of Nebat, which he had caused Israel to commit — the worship of the golden calves at Bethel and Dan.

30The LORD said to Jehu, "Because you have done well in accomplishing what is right in my eyes and have done to the house of Ahab all I had in mind to do, your descendants will sit on the throne of Israel to the fourth generation." 31Yet Jehu was not careful to keep the law of the LORD, the God of Israel, with all his heart. He did not turn away from the sins of Jeroboam, which he had caused Israel to commit.

32In those days the LORD began to reduce the size of Israel. Hazael overpowered the Israelites throughout their territory 33east of the Jordan in all the land of

---

e 36 See 1 Kings 21:23.   *a 1* Hebrew; some Septuagint manuscripts and Vulgate *of the city*

Gilead (the region of Gad, Reuben and Manasseh), from Aroer by the Arnon Gorge through Gilead to Bashan.

10:32   The Lord began to reduce the size of Israel. The writers linked loss of territory in battle to God working out his purposes in response to the continued wickedness of Israel's kings.

---

[34]As for the other events of Jehu's reign, all he did, and all his achievements, are they not written in the book of the annals of the kings of Israel? [35]Jehu rested with his fathers and was buried in Samaria. And Jehoahaz his son succeeded him as king. [36]The time that Jehu reigned over Israel in Samaria was twenty-eight years.

Athaliah and Joash

11 When Athaliah the mother of Ahaziah saw that her son was dead, she proceeded to destroy the whole royal family. [2]But Jehosheba, the daughter of King Jehoram[a] and sister of Ahaziah, took Joash son of Ahaziah and stole him away from among the royal princes, who were about to be murdered. She put him and his nurse in a bedroom to hide him from Athaliah; so he was not killed. [3]He remained hidden with his nurse at the temple of the LORD for six years while Athaliah ruled the land.

11:2   The royal line of David, through which God had chosen to fulfil his purposes, was preserved by Joash being hidden from the murderous Queen Athaliah.

---

[4]In the seventh year Jehoiada sent for the commanders of units of a hundred, the Carites and the guards and had them brought to him at the temple of the LORD. He made a covenant with them and put them under oath at the temple of the LORD. Then he showed them the king's son. [5]He commanded them, saying, "This is what you are to do: You who are in the three companies that are going on duty on the Sabbath — a third of you guarding the royal palace, [6]a third at the Sur Gate, and a third at the gate behind the guard, who take turns guarding the temple — [7]and you who are in the other two companies that normally go off Sabbath duty are all to guard the temple for the king. [8]Station yourselves round the king, each man with his weapon in his hand. Anyone who approaches your ranks[b] must be put to death. Stay close to the king wherever he goes."

[9]The commanders of units of a hundred did just as Jehoiada the priest ordered. Each one took his men — those who were going on duty on the Sabbath and those who were going off duty — and came to Jehoiada the priest. [10]Then he gave the commanders the spears and shields that had belonged to King David and that were in the temple of the LORD. [11]The guards, each

with his weapon in his hand, stationed themselves round the king — near the altar and the temple, from the south side to the north side of the temple.

[12]Jehoiada brought out the king's son and put the crown on him; he presented him with a copy of the covenant and proclaimed him king. They anointed him, and the people clapped their hands and shouted, "Long live the king!"

[13]When Athaliah heard the noise made by the guards and the people, she went to the people at the temple of the LORD. [14]She looked and there was the king, standing by the pillar, as the custom was. The officers and the trumpeters were beside the king, and all the people of the land were rejoicing and blowing trumpets. Then Athaliah tore her robes and called out, "Treason! Treason!"

[15]Jehoiada the priest ordered the commanders of units of a hundred, who were in charge of the troops: "Bring her out between the ranks[c] and put to the sword anyone who follows her." For the priest had said, "She must not be put to death in the temple of the LORD." [16]So they seized her as she reached the place where the horses enter the palace grounds, and there she was put to death.

[17]Jehoiada then made a covenant between the LORD and the king and people that they would be the LORD's people. He also made a covenant between the king and the people. [18]All the people of the land went to the temple of Baal and tore it down. They smashed the altars and idols to pieces and killed Mattan the priest of Baal in front of the altars.

Then Jehoiada the priest posted guards at the temple of the LORD. [19]He took with him the commanders of hundreds, the Carites, the guards and all the people of the land, and together they brought the king down from the temple of the LORD and went into the palace, entering by way of the gate of the guards. The king then took his place on the royal throne, [20]and all the people of the land rejoiced. And the city was quiet, because Athaliah had been slain with the sword at the palace.

[21]Joash[d] was seven years old when he began his reign.

Joash Repairs the Temple

12 In the seventh year of Jehu, Joash[a] became king, and he reigned in Jerusalem for forty years. His mother's name was Zibiah; she was from Beersheba. [2]Joash did what was right in the eyes of the LORD all the years Jehoiada the priest instructed him. [3]The high places, however, were not removed; the people continued to offer sacrifices and burn incense there.

[4]Joash said to the priests, "Collect all the money that is brought as sacred offerings to the temple of the LORD — the money collected in the census, the money received from personal vows and the money brought voluntarily to the temple. [5]Let every priest receive the money from one of the treasurers, and let it be used to repair whatever damage is found in the temple." [6]But by the twenty-third year of King Joash the

---

a2 Hebrew Joram, a variant of Jehoram   *b8 Or approaches the precincts*   *c15 Or out from the precincts*
d21 Hebrew Jehoash, a variant of Joash   *a1 Hebrew Jehoash, a variant of Joash; also in verses 2, 4, 6, 7 and 18*

priests still had not repaired the temple. [7]Therefore King Joash summoned Jehoiada the priest and the other priests and asked them, "Why aren't you repairing the damage done to the temple? Take no more money from your treasurers, but hand it over for repairing the temple." [8]The priests agreed that they would not collect any more money from the people and that they would not repair the temple themselves.

[9]Jehoiada the priest took a chest and bored a hole in its lid. He placed it beside the altar, on the right side as one enters the temple of the LORD. The priests who guarded the entrance put into the chest all the money that was brought to the temple of the LORD. [10]Whenever they saw that there was a large amount of money in the chest, the royal secretary and the high priest came, counted the money that had been brought into the temple of the LORD and put it into bags. [11]When the amount had been determined, they gave the money to the men appointed to supervise the work on the temple. With it they paid those who worked on the temple of the LORD—the carpenters and builders, [12]the masons and stonecutters. They purchased timber and dressed stone for the repair of the temple of the LORD, and met all the other expenses of restoring the temple.

[13]The money brought into the temple was not spent for making silver basins, wick trimmers, sprinkling bowls, trumpets or any other articles of gold or silver for the temple of the LORD; [14]it was paid to the workmen, who used it to repair the temple. [15]They did not require an accounting from those to whom they gave the money to pay the workers, because they acted with complete honesty. [16]The money from the guilt offerings and sin offerings was not brought into the temple of the LORD; it belonged to the priests.

[17]About this time Hazael king of Aram went up and attacked Gath and captured it. Then he turned to attack Jerusalem. [18]But Joash king of Judah took all the sacred objects dedicated by his fathers—Jehoshaphat, Jehoram and Ahaziah, the kings of Judah—and the gifts he himself had dedicated and all the gold found in the treasuries of the temple of the LORD and of the royal palace, and he sent them to Hazael king of Aram, who then withdrew from Jerusalem.

[19]As for the other events of the reign of Joash, and all he did, are they not written in the book of the annals of the kings of Judah? [20]His officials conspired against him and assassinated him at Beth Millo, on the road down to Silla. [21]The officials who murdered him were Jozabad son of Shimeath and Jehozabad son of Shomer. He died and was buried with his fathers in the City of David. And Amaziah his son succeeded him as king.

Jehoahaz King of Israel

13 In the twenty-third year of Joash son of Ahaziah king of Judah, Jehoahaz son of Jehu became king of Israel in Samaria, and he reigned for seventeen years. [2]He did evil in the eyes of the LORD by following the sins of Jeroboam son of Nebat, which he had caused Israel to commit, and he did not turn away from them. [3]So the LORD's anger burned against Israel, and for a

long time he kept them under the power of Hazael king of Aram and Ben-Hadad his son.

[4]Then Jehoahaz sought the LORD's favour, and the LORD listened to him, for he saw how severely the king of Aram was oppressing Israel. [5]The LORD provided a deliverer for Israel, and they escaped from the power of Aram. So the Israelites lived in their own homes as they had before. [6]But they did not turn away from the sins of the house of Jeroboam, which he had caused Israel to commit; they continued in them. Also, the Asherah pole[a] remained standing in Samaria.

[7]Nothing had been left of the army of Jehoahaz except fifty horsemen, ten chariots and ten thousand foot soldiers, for the king of Aram had destroyed the rest and made them like the dust at threshing time.

[8]As for the other events of the reign of Jehoahaz, all he did and his achievements, are they not written in the book of the annals of the kings of Israel? [9]Jehoahaz rested with his fathers and was buried in Samaria. And Jehoash[b] his son succeeded him as king.

Jehoash King of Israel

[10]In the thirty-seventh year of Joash king of Judah, Jehoash son of Jehoahaz became king of Israel in Samaria, and he reigned for sixteen years. [11]He did evil in the eyes of the LORD and did not turn away from any of the sins of Jeroboam son of Nebat, which he had caused Israel to commit; he continued in them.

[12]As for the other events of the reign of Jehoash, all he did and his achievements, including his war against Amaziah king of Judah, are they not written in the book of the annals of the kings of Israel? [13]Jehoash rested with his fathers, and Jeroboam succeeded him on the throne. Jehoash was buried in Samaria with the kings of Israel.

[14]Now Elisha was suffering from the illness from which he died. Jehoash king of Israel went down to see him and wept over him. "My father! My father!" he cried. "The chariots and horsemen of Israel!"

[15]Elisha said, "Get a bow and some arrows," and he did so. [16]"Take the bow in your hands," he said to the king of Israel. When he had taken it, Elisha put his hands on the king's hands.

[17]"Open the east window," he said, and he opened it. "Shoot!" Elisha said, and he shot. "The LORD's arrow of victory, the arrow of victory over Aram!" Elisha declared. "You will completely destroy the Arameans at Aphek."

[18]Then he said, "Take the arrows," and the king took them. Elisha told him, "Strike the ground." He struck it three times and stopped. [19]The man of God was angry with him and said, "You should have struck the ground five or six times; then you would have defeated Aram and completely destroyed it. But now you will defeat it only three times."

[20]Elisha died and was buried.

Now Moabite raiders used to enter the country every spring. [21]Once while some Israelites were burying a man, suddenly they saw a band of raiders; so they threw the man's body into Elisha's tomb. When the

---

[a]6 That is, a symbol of the goddess Asherah; here and elsewhere in 2 Kings
[b]9 Hebrew Joash, a variant of Jehoash; also in verses 12–14 and 25

body touched Elisha's bones, the man came to life and stood up on his feet.

13:20 Like Aram, Moab was a small neighbouring kingdom that caused problems for both Israel and Judah from time to time. On other occasions these two small kingdoms formed an alliance in the face of threats from larger powers.

---

²²Hazael king of Aram oppressed Israel throughout the reign of Jehoahaz. ²³But the LORD was gracious to them and had compassion and showed concern for them because of his covenant with Abraham, Isaac and Jacob. To this day he has been unwilling to destroy them or banish them from his presence.

²⁴Hazael king of Aram died, and Ben-Hadad his son succeeded him as king. ²⁵Then Jehoash son of Jehoahaz recaptured from Ben-Hadad son of Hazael the towns he had taken in battle from his father Jehoahaz. Three times Jehoash defeated him, and so he recovered the Israelite towns.

Amaziah King of Judah

14 In the second year of Jehoash*ᵃ* son of Jehoahaz king of Israel, Amaziah son of Joash king of Judah began to reign. ²He was twenty-five years old when he became king, and he reigned in Jerusalem for twenty-nine years. His mother's name was Jehoaddin; she was from Jerusalem. ³He did what was right in the eyes of the LORD, but not as his father David had done. In everything he followed the example of his father Joash. ⁴The high places, however, were not removed; the people continued to offer sacrifices and burn incense there.

⁵After the kingdom was firmly in his grasp, he executed the officials who had murdered his father the king. ⁶Yet he did not put the sons of the assassins to death, in accordance with what is written in the Book of the Law of Moses where the LORD commanded: "Fathers shall not be put to death for their children, nor children put to death for their fathers; each is to die for his own sins."*ᵇ*

⁷He was the one who defeated ten thousand Edomites in the Valley of Salt and captured Sela in battle, calling it Joktheel, the name it has to this day.

⁸Then Amaziah sent messengers to Jehoash son of Jehoahaz, the son of Jehu, king of Israel, with the challenge: "Come, meet me face to face."

⁹But Jehoash king of Israel replied to Amaziah king of Judah: "A thistle in Lebanon sent a message to a cedar in Lebanon, 'Give your daughter to my son in marriage.' Then a wild beast in Lebanon came along and trampled the thistle underfoot. ¹⁰You have indeed defeated Edom and now you are arrogant. Glory in your victory, but stay at home! Why ask for trouble and cause your own downfall and that of Judah also?"

¹¹Amaziah, however, would not listen, so Jehoash

king of Israel attacked. He and Amaziah king of Judah faced each other at Beth Shemesh in Judah. ¹²Judah was routed by Israel, and every man fled to his home. ¹³Jehoash king of Israel captured Amaziah king of Judah, the son of Joash, the son of Ahaziah, at Beth Shemesh. Then Jehoash went to Jerusalem and broke down the wall of Jerusalem from the Ephraim Gate to the Corner Gate—a section about six hundred feet long.*ᶜ* ¹⁴He took all the gold and silver and all the articles found in the temple of the LORD and in the treasuries of the royal palace. He also took hostages and returned to Samaria.

¹⁵As for the other events of the reign of Jehoash, what he did and his achievements, including his war against Amaziah king of Judah, are they not written in the book of the annals of the kings of Israel? ¹⁶Jehoash rested with his fathers and was buried in Samaria with the kings of Israel. And Jeroboam his son succeeded him as king.

¹⁷Amaziah son of Joash king of Judah lived for fifteen years after the death of Jehoash son of Jehoahaz king of Israel. ¹⁸As for the other events of Amaziah's reign, are they not written in the book of the annals of the kings of Judah?

¹⁹They conspired against him in Jerusalem, and he fled to Lachish, but they sent men after him to Lachish and killed him there. ²⁰He was brought back by horse and was buried in Jerusalem with his fathers, in the City of David.

²¹Then all the people of Judah took Azariah,*ᵈ* who was sixteen years old, and made him king in place of his father Amaziah. ²²He was the one who rebuilt Elath and restored it to Judah after Amaziah rested with his fathers.

Jeroboam II King of Israel

²³In the fifteenth year of Amaziah son of Joash king of Judah, Jeroboam son of Jehoash king of Israel became king in Samaria, and he reigned for forty-one years. ²⁴He did evil in the eyes of the LORD and did not turn away from any of the sins of Jeroboam son of Nebat, which he had caused Israel to commit. ²⁵He was the one who restored the boundaries of Israel from Lebo*ᵉ* Hamath to the Sea of the Arabah,*ᶠ* in accordance with the word of the LORD, the God of Israel, spoken through his servant Jonah son of Amittai, the prophet from Gath Hepher.

²⁶The LORD had seen how bitterly everyone in Israel, whether slave or free, was suffering; there was no-one to help them. ²⁷And since the LORD had not said he would blot out the name of Israel from under heaven, he saved them by the hand of Jeroboam son of Jehoash.

²⁸As for the other events of Jeroboam's reign, all he did, and his military achievements, including how he recovered for Israel both Damascus and Hamath, which had belonged to Yaudi,*ᵍ* are they not written in the book of the annals of the kings of Israel? ²⁹Jeroboam rested with his fathers, the kings of Israel. And Zechariah his son succeeded him as king.

ᵃ 1 Hebrew *Joash*, a variant of *Jehoash*; also in verses 13, 23 and 27   *ᵇ 6* Deut. 24:16
ᶜ 13 Hebrew *four hundred cubits* (about 180 metres)   *ᵈ 21* Also called *Uzziah*   *ᵉ 25* Or *from the entrance to*
ᶠ 25 That is, the Dead Sea   *ᵍ 28* Or *Judah*

Azariah King of Judah

15 In the twenty-seventh year of Jeroboam king of Israel, Azariah son of Amaziah king of Judah began to reign. [2]He was sixteen years old when he became king, and he reigned in Jerusalem for fifty-two years. His mother's name was Jecoliah; she was from Jerusalem. [3]He did what was right in the eyes of the LORD, just as his father Amaziah had done. [4]The high places, however, were not removed; the people continued to offer sacrifices and burn incense there.

[5]The LORD afflicted the king with leprosy[a] until the day he died, and he lived in a separate house.[b] Jotham the king's son had charge of the palace and governed the people of the land.

[6]As for the other events of Azariah's reign, and all he did, are they not written in the book of the annals of the kings of Judah? [7]Azariah rested with his fathers and was buried near them in the City of David. And Jotham his son succeeded him as king.

Zechariah King of Israel

[8]In the thirty-eighth year of Azariah king of Judah, Zechariah son of Jeroboam became king of Israel in Samaria, and he reigned for six months. [9]He did evil in the eyes of the LORD, as his fathers had done. He did not turn away from the sins of Jeroboam son of Nebat, which he had caused Israel to commit.

[10]Shallum son of Jabesh conspired against Zechariah. He attacked him in front of the people,[c] assassinated him and succeeded him as king. [11]The other events of Zechariah's reign are written in the book of the annals of the kings of Israel. [12]So the word of the LORD spoken to Jehu was fulfilled: "Your descendants will sit on the throne of Israel to the fourth generation."[d]

Shallum King of Israel

[13]Shallum son of Jabesh became king in the thirty-ninth year of Uzziah king of Judah, and he reigned in Samaria for one month. [14]Then Menahem son of Gadi went from Tirzah up to Samaria. He attacked Shallum son of Jabesh in Samaria, assassinated him and succeeded him as king.

[15]The other events of Shallum's reign, and the conspiracy he led, are written in the book of the annals of the kings of Israel.

[16]At that time Menahem, starting out from Tirzah, attacked Tiphsah and everyone in the city and its vicinity, because they refused to open their gates. He sacked Tiphsah and ripped open all the pregnant women.

Menahem King of Israel

[17]In the thirty-ninth year of Azariah king of Judah, Menahem son of Gadi became king of Israel, and he reigned in Samaria for ten years. [18]He did evil in the eyes of the LORD. During his entire reign he did not turn away from the sins of Jeroboam son of Nebat, which he had caused Israel to commit.

[19]Then Pul[e] king of Assyria invaded the land, and Menahem gave him a thousand talents[f] of silver to gain his support and strengthen his own hold on the kingdom. [20]Menahem exacted this money from Israel. Every wealthy man had to contribute fifty shekels[g] of silver to be given to the king of Assyria. So the king of Assyria withdrew and stayed in the land no longer.

[21]As for the other events of Menahem's reign, and all he did, are they not written in the book of the annals of the kings of Israel? [22]Menahem rested with his fathers. And Pekahiah his son succeeded him as king.

Pekahiah King of Israel

[23]In the fiftieth year of Azariah king of Judah, Pekahiah son of Menahem became king of Israel in Samaria, and he reigned for two years. [24]Pekahiah did evil in the eyes of the LORD. He did not turn away from the sins of Jeroboam son of Nebat, which he had caused Israel to commit. [25]One of his chief officers, Pekah son of Remaliah, conspired against him. Taking fifty men of Gilead with him, he assassinated Pekahiah, along with Argob and Arieh, in the citadel of the royal palace at Samaria. So Pekah killed Pekahiah and succeeded him as king.

[26]The other events of Pekahiah's reign, and all he did, are written in the book of the annals of the kings of Israel.

Pekah King of Israel

[27]In the fifty-second year of Azariah king of Judah, Pekah son of Remaliah became king of Israel in Samaria, and he reigned for twenty years. [28]He did evil in the eyes of the LORD. He did not turn away from the sins of Jeroboam son of Nebat, which he had caused Israel to commit.

[29]In the time of Pekah king of Israel, Tiglath-Pileser king of Assyria came and took Ijon, Abel Beth Maacah, Janoah, Kedesh and Hazor. He took Gilead and Galilee, including all the land of Naphtali, and deported the people to Assyria. [30]Then Hoshea son of Elah conspired against Pekah son of Remaliah. He attacked and assassinated him, and then succeeded him as king in the twentieth year of Jotham son of Uzziah.

[31]As for the other events of Pekah's reign, and all he did, are they not written in the book of the annals of the kings of Israel?

Jotham King of Judah

[32]In the second year of Pekah son of Remaliah king of Israel, Jotham son of Uzziah king of Judah began to reign. [33]He was twenty-five years old when he became king, and he reigned in Jerusalem for sixteen years. His mother's name was Jerusha daughter of Zadok. [34]He did what was right in the eyes of the LORD, just as his father Uzziah had done. [35]The high places, however, were not removed; the people continued to offer

---

[a]5 The Hebrew word was used for various diseases affecting the skin—not necessarily leprosy.
[b]5 Or *in a house where he was relieved of responsibility*   [c]10 Hebrew; some Septuagint manuscripts *in Ibleam*
[d]12 2 Kings 10:30   [e]19 Also called *Tiglath-Pileser*   [f]19 That is, about 34 tons (about 34 metric tons)
[g]20 That is, about 1¼ pounds (about 0.6 kilogram)

sacrifices and burn incense there. Jotham rebuilt the Upper Gate of the temple of the LORD.

³⁶As for the other events of Jotham's reign, and what he did, are they not written in the book of the annals of the kings of Judah? ³⁷(In those days the LORD began to send Rezin king of Aram and Pekah son of Remaliah against Judah.) ³⁸Jotham rested with his fathers and was buried with them in the City of David, the city of his father. And Ahaz his son succeeded him as king.

Ahaz King of Judah

16 In the seventeenth year of Pekah son of Remaliah, Ahaz son of Jotham king of Judah began to reign. ²Ahaz was twenty years old when he became king, and he reigned in Jerusalem for sixteen years. Unlike David his father, he did not do what was right in the eyes of the LORD his God. ³He walked in the ways of the kings of Israel and even sacrificed his son in ᵃ the fire, following the detestable ways of the nations the LORD had driven out before the Israelites. ⁴He offered sacrifices and burned incense at the high places, on the hilltops and under every spreading tree.

⁵Then Rezin king of Aram and Pekah son of Remaliah king of Israel marched up to fight against Jerusalem and besieged Ahaz, but they could not overpower him. ⁶At that time, Rezin king of Aram recovered Elath for Aram by driving out the men of Judah. Edomites then moved into Elath and have lived there to this day.

⁷Ahaz sent messengers to say to Tiglath-Pileser king of Assyria, "I am your servant and vassal. Come up and save me out of the hand of the king of Aram and of the king of Israel who are attacking me." ⁸And Ahaz took the silver and gold found in the temple of the LORD and in the treasuries of the royal palace and sent it as a gift to the king of Assyria. ⁹The king of Assyria complied by attacking Damascus and capturing it. He deported its inhabitants to Kir and put Rezin to death.

16:7 The decision of Ahaz to appeal to Tiglath-Pileser, king of Assyria, for help had enormous consequences in the history of God's people. It paved the way for the defeat of Israel and the exile of its people. In addition to forming an alliance with Assyria against Israel, Ahaz also introduced pagan practices into Judah (16:3,4). His reign had disastrous consequences for both Israel and Judah.

---

¹⁰Then King Ahaz went to Damascus to meet Tiglath-Pileser king of Assyria. He saw an altar in Damascus and sent to Uriah the priest a sketch of the altar, with detailed plans for its construction. ¹¹So Uriah the priest built an altar in accordance with all the plans that King Ahaz had sent from Damascus and finished it before King Ahaz returned. ¹²When the king came back from Damascus and saw the altar, he approached it and presented offerings ᵇ on it. ¹³He offered up his burnt offering and grain offering, poured

out his drink offering, and sprinkled the blood of his fellowship offerings ᶜ on the altar. ¹⁴The bronze altar that stood before the LORD he brought from the front of the temple—from between the new altar and the temple of the LORD—and put it on the north side of the new altar.

¹⁵King Ahaz then gave these orders to Uriah the priest: "On the large new altar, offer the morning burnt offering and the evening grain offering, the king's burnt offering and his grain offering, and the burnt offering of all the people of the land, and their grain offering and their drink offering. Sprinkle on the altar all the blood of the burnt offerings and sacrifices. But I will use the bronze altar for seeking guidance." ¹⁶And Uriah the priest did just as King Ahaz had ordered.

¹⁷King Ahaz took away the side panels and removed the basins from the movable stands. He removed the Sea from the bronze bulls that supported it and set it on a stone base. ¹⁸He took away the Sabbath canopy ᵈ that had been built at the temple and removed the royal entrance outside the temple of the LORD, in deference to the king of Assyria.

¹⁹As for the other events of the reign of Ahaz, and what he did, are they not written in the book of the annals of the kings of Judah? ²⁰Ahaz rested with his fathers and was buried with them in the City of David. And Hezekiah his son succeeded him as king.

Hoshea Last King of Israel

17 In the twelfth year of Ahaz king of Judah, Hoshea son of Elah became king of Israel in Samaria, and he reigned for nine years. ²He did evil in the eyes of the LORD, but not like the kings of Israel who preceded him.

³Shalmaneser king of Assyria came up to attack Hoshea, who had been Shalmaneser's vassal and had paid him tribute. ⁴But the king of Assyria discovered that Hoshea was a traitor, for he had sent envoys to So ᵃ king of Egypt, and he no longer paid tribute to the king of Assyria, as he had done year by year. Therefore Shalmaneser seized him and put him in prison. ⁵The king of Assyria invaded the entire land, marched against Samaria and laid siege to it for three years. ⁶In the ninth year of Hoshea, the king of Assyria captured Samaria and deported the Israelites to Assyria. He settled them in Halah, in Gozan on the Habor River and in the towns of the Medes.

Israel Exiled Because of Sin

⁷All this took place because the Israelites had sinned against the LORD their God, who had brought them up out of Egypt from under the power of Pharaoh king of Egypt. They worshipped other gods ⁸and followed the practices of the nations the LORD had driven out before them, as well as the practices that the kings of Israel had introduced. ⁹The Israelites secretly did things against the LORD their God that were not right. From watchtower to fortified city they built themselves high places in all their towns. ¹⁰They set up sacred stones and Asherah poles on every high hill and under every

---

ᵃ3 Or even made his son pass through   ᵇ12 Or and went up   ᶜ13 Traditionally peace offerings
ᵈ18 Or the dais of his throne (see Septuagint)   ᵃ4 Or to Sais, to the; So is possibly an abbreviation for Osorkon.

spreading tree. [11]At every high place they burned incense, as the nations whom the LORD had driven out before them had done. They did wicked things that provoked the LORD to anger. [12]They worshipped idols, though the LORD had said, "You shall not do this."[b] [13]The LORD warned Israel and Judah through all his prophets and seers: "Turn from your evil ways. Observe my commands and decrees, in accordance with the entire Law that I commanded your fathers to obey and that I delivered to you through my servants the prophets."

[14]But they would not listen and were as stiff-necked as their fathers, who did not trust in the LORD their God. [15]They rejected his decrees and the covenant he had made with their fathers and the warnings he had given them. They followed worthless idols and themselves became worthless. They imitated the nations around them although the LORD had ordered them, "Do not do as they do," and they did the things the LORD had forbidden them to do.

[16]They forsook all the commands of the LORD their God and made for themselves two idols cast in the shape of calves, and an Asherah pole. They bowed down to all the starry hosts, and they worshipped Baal. [17]They sacrificed their sons and daughters in[c] the fire. They practised divination and sorcery and sold themselves to do evil in the eyes of the LORD, provoking him to anger.

[18]So the LORD was very angry with Israel and removed them from his presence. Only the tribe of Judah was left, [19]and even Judah did not keep the commands of the LORD their God. They followed the practices Israel had introduced. [20]Therefore the LORD rejected all the people of Israel; he afflicted them and gave them into the hands of plunderers, until he thrust them from his presence.

[21]When he tore Israel away from the house of David, they made Jeroboam son of Nebat their king. Jeroboam enticed Israel away from following the LORD and caused them to commit a great sin. [22]The Israelites persisted in all the sins of Jeroboam and did not turn away from them [23]until the LORD removed them from his presence, as he had warned through all his servants the prophets. So the people of Israel were taken from their homeland into exile in Assyria, and they are still there.

17:23 The exile of the people of Israel from their land by the Assyrians marked the end of the Northern Kingdom. The foreign people brought their own religious beliefs and practices, and also adopted parts of Israelite belief. This mixture gave rise to deep divisions between Jews and Samaritans that persisted into and beyond New Testament times.

Samaria Resettled

[24]The king of Assyria brought people from Babylon, Cuthah, Avva, Hamath and Sepharvaim and settled them in the towns of Samaria to replace the Israelites. They took over Samaria and lived in its towns. [25]When they first lived there, they did not worship the LORD; so he sent lions among them and they killed some of the people. [26]It was reported to the king of Assyria: "The people you deported and resettled in the towns of Samaria do not know what the god of that country requires. He has sent lions among them, which are killing them off, because the people do not know what he requires."

[27]Then the king of Assyria gave this order: "Make one of the priests you took captive from Samaria go back to live there and teach the people what the god of the land requires." [28]So one of the priests who had been exiled from Samaria came to live in Bethel and taught them how to worship the LORD.

[29]Nevertheless, each national group made its own gods in the several towns where they settled, and set them up in the shrines the people of Samaria had made at the high places. [30]The men from Babylon made Succoth Benoth, the men from Cuthah made Nergal, and the men from Hamath made Ashima; [31]the Avvites made Nibhaz and Tartak, and the Sepharvites burned their children in the fire as sacrifices to Adrammelech and Anammelech, the gods of Sepharvaim. [32]They worshipped the LORD, but they also appointed all sorts of their own people to officiate for them as priests in the shrines at the high places. [33]They worshipped the LORD, but they also served their own gods in accordance with the customs of the nations from which they had been brought.

[34]To this day they persist in their former practices. They neither worship the LORD nor adhere to the decrees and ordinances, the laws and commands that the LORD gave the descendants of Jacob, whom he named Israel. [35]When the LORD made a covenant with the Israelites, he commanded them: "Do not worship any other gods or bow down to them, serve them or sacrifice to them. [36]But the LORD, who brought you up out of Egypt with mighty power and outstretched arm, is the one you must worship. To him you shall bow down and to him offer sacrifices. [37]You must always be careful to keep the decrees and ordinances, the laws and commands he wrote for you. Do not worship other gods. [38]Do not forget the covenant I have made with you, and do not worship other gods. [39]Rather, worship the LORD your God; it is he who will deliver you from the hand of all your enemies."

[40]They would not listen, however, but persisted in their former practices. [41]Even while these people were worshipping the LORD, they were serving their idols. To this day their children and grandchildren continue to do as their fathers did.

Hezekiah King of Judah

18 In the third year of Hoshea son of Elah king of Israel, Hezekiah son of Ahaz king of Judah began to reign. [2]He was twenty-five years old when he became king, and he reigned in Jerusalem for twenty-nine years. His mother's name was Abijah[a] daughter of Zechariah. [3]He did what was right in the eyes of the

---

[b]12 Exodus 20:4, 5   [c]17 Or *They made their sons and daughters pass through*   [a]2 Hebrew *Abi*, a variant of *Abijah*

LORD, just as his father David had done. ⁴He removed the high places, smashed the sacred stones and cut down the Asherah poles. He broke into pieces the bronze snake Moses had made, for up to that time the Israelites had been burning incense to it. (It was called ᵇ Nehushtan. ᶜ)

⁵Hezekiah trusted in the LORD, the God of Israel. There was no-one like him among all the kings of Judah, either before him or after him. ⁶He held fast to the LORD and did not cease to follow him; he kept the commands the LORD had given Moses. ⁷And the LORD was with him; he was successful in whatever he undertook. He rebelled against the king of Assyria and did not serve him. ⁸From watchtower to fortified city, he defeated the Philistines, as far as Gaza and its territory.

⁹In King Hezekiah's fourth year, which was the seventh year of Hoshea son of Elah king of Israel, Shalmaneser king of Assyria marched against Samaria and laid siege to it. ¹⁰At the end of three years the Assyrians took it. So Samaria was captured in Hezekiah's sixth year, which was the ninth year of Hoshea king of Israel. ¹¹The king of Assyria deported Israel to Assyria and settled them in Halah, in Gozan on the Habor River, and in towns of the Medes. ¹²This happened because they had not obeyed the LORD their God, but had violated his covenant — all that Moses the servant of the LORD commanded. They neither listened to the commands nor carried them out.

¹³In the fourteenth year of King Hezekiah's reign, Sennacherib king of Assyria attacked all the fortified cities of Judah and captured them. ¹⁴So Hezekiah king of Judah sent this message to the king of Assyria at Lachish: "I have done wrong. Withdraw from me, and I will pay whatever you demand of me." The king of Assyria exacted from Hezekiah king of Judah three hundred talentsᵈ of silver and thirty talentsᵉ of gold. ¹⁵So Hezekiah gave him all the silver that was found in the temple of the LORD and in the treasuries of the royal palace.

¹⁶At this time Hezekiah king of Judah stripped off the gold with which he had covered the doors and doorposts of the temple of the LORD, and gave it to the king of Assyria.

Sennacherib Threatens Jerusalem

¹⁷The king of Assyria sent his supreme commander, his chief officer and his field commander with a large army, from Lachish to King Hezekiah at Jerusalem. They came up to Jerusalem and stopped at the aqueduct of the Upper Pool, on the road to the Washerman's Field. ¹⁸They called for the king; and Eliakim son of Hilkiah the palace administrator, Shebna the secretary, and Joah son of Asaph the recorder went out to them.

¹⁹The field commander said to them, "Tell Hezekiah:

" 'This is what the great king, the king of Assyria, says: On what are you basing this confidence of yours? ²⁰You say you have strategy and military strength — but you speak only empty words. On whom are you depending, that you rebel against me? ²¹Look now, you are depending on Egypt, that splintered reed of a staff, which pierces a man's hand and wounds him if he leans on it! Such is Pharaoh king of Egypt to all who depend on him. ²²And if you say to me, "We are depending on the LORD our God" — isn't he the one whose high places and altars Hezekiah removed, saying to Judah and Jerusalem, "You must worship before this altar in Jerusalem"?

²³" 'Come now, make a bargain with my master, the king of Assyria: I will give you two thousand horses — if you can put riders on them! ²⁴How can you repulse one officer of the least of my master's officials, even though you are depending on Egypt for chariots and horsemen?ᶠ ²⁵Furthermore, have I come to attack and destroy this place without word from the LORD? The LORD himself told me to march against this country and destroy it.' "

²⁶Then Eliakim son of Hilkiah, and Shebna and Joah said to the field commander, "Please speak to your servants in Aramaic, since we understand it. Don't speak to us in Hebrew in the hearing of the people on the wall."

²⁷But the commander replied, "Was it only to your master and you that my master sent me to say these things, and not to the men sitting on the wall — who, like you, will have to eat their own filth and drink their own urine?"

²⁸Then the commander stood and called out in Hebrew: "Hear the word of the great king, the king of Assyria! ²⁹This is what the king says: Do not let Hezekiah deceive you. He cannot deliver you from my hand. ³⁰Do not let Hezekiah persuade you to trust in the LORD when he says, 'The LORD will surely deliver us; this city will not be given into the hand of the king of Assyria.'

³¹"Do not listen to Hezekiah. This is what the king of Assyria says: Make peace with me and come out to me. Then every one of you will eat from his own vine and fig-tree and drink water from his own cistern, ³²until I come and take you to a land like your own, a land of grain and new wine, a land of bread and vineyards, a land of olive trees and honey. Choose life and not death!

"Do not listen to Hezekiah, for he is misleading you when he says, 'The LORD will deliver us.' ³³Has the god of any nation ever delivered his land from the hand of the king of Assyria? ³⁴Where are the gods of Hamath and Arpad? Where are the gods of Sepharvaim, Hena and Ivvah? Have they rescued Samaria from my hand? ³⁵Who of all the gods of these countries has been able to save his land from me? How then can the LORD deliver Jerusalem from my hand?"

³⁶But the people remained silent and said nothing in reply, because the king had commanded, "Do not answer him."

³⁷Then Eliakim son of Hilkiah the palace administrator, Shebna the secretary and Joah son of Asaph the recorder went to Hezekiah, with their clothes torn, and told him what the field commander had said.

ᵇ4 Or He called it   ᶜ4 Nehushtan sounds like the Hebrew for bronze and snake and unclean thing.
ᵈ14 That is, about 10 tons (about 10 metric tons)   ᵉ14 That is, about 1 ton (about 1 metric ton)   ᶠ24 Or charioteers

Jerusalem's Deliverance Foretold

19 When King Hezekiah heard this, he tore his clothes and put on sackcloth and went into the temple of the LORD. ²He sent Eliakim the palace administrator, Shebna the secretary and the leading priests, all wearing sackcloth, to the prophet Isaiah son of Amoz. ³They told him, "This is what Hezekiah says: This day is a day of distress and rebuke and disgrace, as when children come to the point of birth and there is no strength to deliver them. ⁴It may be that the LORD your God will hear all the words of the field commander, whom his master, the king of Assyria, has sent to ridicule the living God, and that he will rebuke him for the words the LORD your God has heard. Therefore pray for the remnant that still survives."

⁵When King Hezekiah's officials came to Isaiah, ⁶Isaiah said to them, "Tell your master, 'This is what the LORD says: Do not be afraid of what you have heard—those words with which the underlings of the king of Assyria have blasphemed me. ⁷Listen! I am going to put such a spirit in him that when he hears a certain report, he will return to his own country, and there I will have him cut down with the sword.' "

⁸When the field commander heard that the king of Assyria had left Lachish, he withdrew and found the king fighting against Libnah.

⁹Now Sennacherib received a report that Tirhakah, the Cushite[a] king of Egypt, was marching out to fight against him. So he again sent messengers to Hezekiah with this word: ¹⁰"Say to Hezekiah king of Judah: Do not let the god you depend on deceive you when he says, 'Jerusalem will not be handed over to the king of Assyria.' ¹¹Surely you have heard what the kings of Assyria have done to all the countries, destroying them completely. And will you be delivered? ¹²Did the gods of the nations that were destroyed by my forefathers deliver them: the gods of Gozan, Haran, Rezeph and the people of Eden who were in Tel Assar? ¹³Where is the king of Hamath, the king of Arpad, the king of the city of Sepharvaim, or of Hena or Ivvah?"

Hezekiah's Prayer

¹⁴Hezekiah received the letter from the messengers and read it. Then he went up to the temple of the LORD and spread it out before the LORD. ¹⁵And Hezekiah prayed to the LORD: "O LORD, God of Israel, enthroned between the cherubim, you alone are God over all the kingdoms of the earth. You have made heaven and earth. ¹⁶Give ear, O LORD, and hear; open your eyes, O LORD, and see; listen to the words Sennacherib has sent to insult the living God.

¹⁷"It is true, O LORD, that the Assyrian kings have laid waste these nations and their lands. ¹⁸They have thrown their gods into the fire and destroyed them, for they were not gods but only wood and stone, fashioned by men's hands. ¹⁹Now, O LORD our God, deliver us from his hand, so that all kingdoms on earth may know that you alone, O LORD, are God."

Isaiah Prophesies Sennacherib's Fall

²⁰Then Isaiah son of Amoz sent a message to Hezekiah: "This is what the LORD, the God of Israel, says: I have heard your prayer concerning Sennacherib king of Assyria. ²¹This is the word that the LORD has spoken against him:

" 'The Virgin Daughter of Zion
    despises you and mocks you.
The Daughter of Jerusalem
    tosses her head as you flee.
²²Who is it you have insulted and blasphemed?
    Against whom have you raised your voice
and lifted your eyes in pride?
    Against the Holy One of Israel!
²³By your messengers
    you have heaped insults on the Lord.
And you have said,
    "With my many chariots
I have ascended the heights of the mountains,
    the utmost heights of Lebanon.
I have cut down its tallest cedars,
    the choicest of its pines.
I have reached its remotest parts,
    the finest of its forests.
²⁴I have dug wells in foreign lands
    and drunk the water there.
With the soles of my feet
    I have dried up all the streams of Egypt."

²⁵" 'Have you not heard?
    Long ago I ordained it.
In days of old I planned it;
    now I have brought it to pass,
that you have turned fortified cities
    into piles of stone.
²⁶Their people, drained of power,
    are dismayed and put to shame.
They are like plants in the field,
    like tender green shoots,
like grass sprouting on the roof,
    scorched before it grows up.

²⁷" 'But I know where you stay
    and when you come and go
    and how you rage against me.
²⁸Because you rage against me
    and your insolence has reached my ears,
I will put my hook in your nose
    and my bit in your mouth,
and I will make you return
    by the way you came.'

²⁹"This will be the sign for you, O Hezekiah:

This year you will eat what grows by itself,
    and the second year what springs from that.
But in the third year sow and reap,
    plant vineyards and eat their fruit.
³⁰Once more a remnant of the house of Judah
    will take root below and bear fruit above.
³¹For out of Jerusalem will come a remnant,
    and out of Mount Zion a band of survivors.

---

a9 That is, from the upper Nile region

The zeal of the LORD Almighty will accomplish this.

³²"Therefore this is what the LORD says concerning the king of Assyria:

"He will not enter this city
or shoot an arrow here.
He will not come before it with shield
or build a siege ramp against it.
³³By the way that he came he will return;
he will not enter this city,
                                    declares the LORD.
³⁴I will defend this city and save it,
for my sake and for the sake of David my
    servant."

³⁵That night the angel of the LORD went out and put to death a hundred and eighty-five thousand men in the Assyrian camp. When the people got up the next morning—there were all the dead bodies! ³⁶So Sennacherib king of Assyria broke camp and withdrew. He returned to Nineveh and stayed there.

³⁷One day, while he was worshipping in the temple of his god Nisroch, his sons Adrammelech and Sharezer cut him down with the sword, and they escaped to the land of Ararat. And Esarhaddon his son succeeded him as king.

Hezekiah's Illness

20 In those days Hezekiah became ill and was at the point of death. The prophet Isaiah son of Amoz went to him and said, "This is what the LORD says: Put your house in order, because you are going to die; you will not recover."

²Hezekiah turned his face to the wall and prayed to the LORD, ³"Remember, O LORD, how I have walked before you faithfully and with wholehearted devotion and have done what is good in your eyes." And Hezekiah wept bitterly.

⁴Before Isaiah had left the middle court, the word of the LORD came to him: ⁵"Go back and tell Hezekiah, the leader of my people, 'This is what the LORD, the God of your father David, says: I have heard your prayer and seen your tears; I will heal you. On the third day from now you will go up to the temple of the LORD. ⁶I will add fifteen years to your life. And I will deliver you and this city from the hand of the king of Assyria. I will defend this city for my sake and for the sake of my servant David.' "

⁷Then Isaiah said, "Prepare a poultice of figs." They did so and applied it to the boil, and he recovered.

⁸Hezekiah had asked Isaiah, "What will be the sign that the LORD will heal me and that I will go up to the temple of the LORD on the third day from now?"

⁹Isaiah answered, "This is the LORD's sign to you that the LORD will do what he has promised: Shall the shadow go forward ten steps, or shall it go back ten steps?"

¹⁰"It is a simple matter for the shadow to go forward ten steps," said Hezekiah. "Rather, have it go back ten steps."

¹¹Then the prophet Isaiah called upon the LORD, and the LORD made the shadow go back the ten steps it had gone down on the stairway of Ahaz.

Envoys From Babylon

¹²At that time Merodach-Baladan son of Baladan king of Babylon sent Hezekiah letters and a gift, because he had heard of Hezekiah's illness. ¹³Hezekiah received the messengers and showed them all that was in his storehouses—the silver, the gold, the spices and the fine oil—his armoury and everything found among his treasures. There was nothing in his palace or in all his kingdom that Hezekiah did not show them.

¹⁴Then Isaiah the prophet went to King Hezekiah and asked, "What did those men say, and where did they come from?"

"From a distant land," Hezekiah replied. "They came from Babylon."

¹⁵The prophet asked, "What did they see in your palace?"

"They saw everything in my palace," Hezekiah said. "There is nothing among my treasures that I did not show them."

¹⁶Then Isaiah said to Hezekiah, "Hear the word of the LORD: ¹⁷The time will surely come when everything in your palace, and all that your fathers have stored up until this day, will be carried off to Babylon. Nothing will be left, says the LORD. ¹⁸And some of your descendants, your own flesh and blood, that will be born to you, will be taken away, and they will become eunuchs in the palace of the king of Babylon."

¹⁹"The word of the LORD you have spoken is good," Hezekiah replied. For he thought, "Will there not be peace and security in my lifetime?"

²⁰As for the other events of Hezekiah's reign, all his achievements and how he made the pool and the tunnel by which he brought water into the city, are they not written in the book of the annals of the kings of Judah? ²¹Hezekiah rested with his fathers. And Manasseh his son succeeded him as king.

20:20 Remains of the tunnel constructed by Hezekiah can be seen in Jerusalem to this day. This huge engineering operation made the city much less vulnerable to siege than before, when it had had no source of water within its walls. Hezekiah received a very favourable portrayal on account of the religious reforms he instituted.

Manasseh King of Judah

21 Manasseh was twelve years old when he became king, and he reigned in Jerusalem for fifty-five years. His mother's name was Hephzibah. ²He did evil in the eyes of the LORD, following the detestable practices of the nations the LORD had driven out before the Israelites. ³He rebuilt the high places his father Hezekiah had destroyed; he also erected altars to Baal and made an Asherah pole, as Ahab king of Israel had done. He bowed down to all the starry hosts and worshipped them. ⁴He built altars in the temple of the LORD, of which the LORD had said, "In Jerusalem I will put my Name." ⁵In both courts of the temple of the LORD, he built altars to all the starry hosts. ⁶He sacrificed his own son in ª the fire, practised sorcery and divination, and consulted mediums and spiritists. He did much evil in the eyes of the LORD, provoking him to anger.

⁷He took the carved Asherah pole he had made and put it in the temple, of which the LORD had said to David and to his son Solomon, "In this temple and in Jerusalem, which I have chosen out of all the tribes of Israel, I will put my Name for ever. ⁸I will not again make the feet of the Israelites wander from the land I gave their forefathers, if only they will be careful to do everything I commanded them and will keep the whole Law that my servant Moses gave them." ⁹But the people did not listen. Manasseh led them astray, so that they did more evil than the nations the LORD had destroyed before the Israelites.

¹⁰The LORD said through his servants the prophets: ¹¹"Manasseh king of Judah has committed these detestable sins. He has done more evil than the Amorites who preceded him and has led Judah into sin with his idols. ¹²Therefore this is what the LORD, the God of Israel, says: I am going to bring such disaster on Jerusalem and Judah that the ears of everyone who hears of it will tingle. ¹³I will stretch out over Jerusalem the measuring line used against Samaria and the plumbline used against the house of Ahab. I will wipe out Jerusalem as one wipes out a dish, wiping it and turning it upside-down. ¹⁴I will forsake the remnant of my inheritance and hand them over to their enemies. They will be looted and plundered by all their foes, ¹⁵because they have done evil in my eyes and have provoked me to anger from the day their forefathers came out of Egypt until this day."

21:10   In stark contrast to his father Hezekiah, Manasseh was a wicked king. As a result of the evil practices that went on in Judah during his reign, the prophets announced that Judah would be defeated and the people sent into exile.

---

¹⁶Moreover, Manasseh also shed so much innocent blood that he filled Jerusalem from end to end — besides the sin that he had caused Judah to commit, so that they did evil in the eyes of the LORD.

¹⁷As for the other events of Manasseh's reign, and all he did, including the sin he committed, are they not written in the book of the annals of the kings of Judah? ¹⁸Manasseh rested with his fathers and was buried in his palace garden, the garden of Uzza. And Amon his son succeeded him as king.

Amon King of Judah

¹⁹Amon was twenty-two years old when he became king, and he reigned in Jerusalem for two years. His mother's name was Meshullemeth daughter of Haruz; she was from Jotbah. ²⁰He did evil in the eyes of the LORD, as his father Manasseh had done. ²¹He walked in all the ways of his father; he worshipped the idols his father had worshipped, and bowed down to them.

ª6 Or *He made his own son pass through*

²²He forsook the LORD, the God of his fathers, and did not walk in the way of the LORD. ²³Amon's officials conspired against him and assassinated the king in his palace. ²⁴Then the people of the land killed all who had plotted against King Amon, and they made Josiah his son king in his place.

²⁵As for the other events of Amon's reign, and what he did, are they not written in the book of the annals of the kings of Judah? ²⁶He was buried in his grave in the garden of Uzza. And Josiah his son succeeded him as king.

The Book of the Law Found

22 Josiah was eight years old when he became king, and he reigned in Jerusalem for thirty-one years. His mother's name was Jedidah daughter of Adaiah; she was from Bozkath. ²He did what was right in the eyes of the LORD and walked in all the ways of his father David, not turning aside to the right or to the left.

³In the eighteenth year of his reign, King Josiah sent the secretary, Shaphan son of Azaliah, the son of Meshullam, to the temple of the LORD. He said: ⁴"Go up to Hilkiah the high priest and make him get ready the money that has been brought into the temple of the LORD, which the doorkeepers have collected from the people. ⁵Make them entrust it to the men appointed to supervise the work on the temple. And make these men pay the workers who repair the temple of the LORD — ⁶the carpenters, the builders and the masons. Also make them purchase timber and dressed stone to repair the temple. ⁷But they need not account for the money entrusted to them, because they are acting faithfully."

⁸Hilkiah the high priest said to Shaphan the secretary, "I have found the Book of the Law in the temple of the LORD." He gave it to Shaphan, who read it. ⁹Then Shaphan the secretary went to the king and reported to him: "Your officials have paid out the money that was in the temple of the LORD and have entrusted it to the workers and supervisors at the temple." ¹⁰Then Shaphan the secretary informed the king, "Hilkiah the priest has given me a book." And Shaphan read from it in the presence of the king.

22:11   Josiah instituted a reform based on the Book of the Law found in the temple, a book which many think may have been part of the book of Deuteronomy. As a result of his very thorough reforms, God's judgement on Judah was delayed until after Josiah's death (22:20).

---

¹¹When the king heard the words of the Book of the Law, he tore his robes. ¹²He gave these orders to Hilkiah the priest, Ahikam son of Shaphan, Acbor son of Micaiah, Shaphan the secretary and Asaiah the king's attendant: ¹³"Go and enquire of the LORD for me and for the people and for all Judah about what is written in this book that has been found. Great is

the LORD's anger that burns against us because our fathers have not obeyed the words of this book; they have not acted in accordance with all that is written there concerning us."

[14]Hilkiah the priest, Ahikam, Acbor, Shaphan and Asaiah went to speak to the prophetess Huldah, who was the wife of Shallum son of Tikvah, the son of Harhas, keeper of the wardrobe. She lived in Jerusalem, in the Second District.

[15]She said to them, "This is what the LORD, the God of Israel, says: Tell the man who sent you to me, [16]'This is what the LORD says: I am going to bring disaster on this place and its people, according to everything written in the book the king of Judah has read. [17]Because they have forsaken me and burned incense to other gods and provoked me to anger by all the idols their hands have made,[a] my anger will burn against this place and will not be quenched.' [18]Tell the king of Judah, who sent you to enquire of the LORD, 'This is what the LORD, the God of Israel, says concerning the words you heard: [19]Because your heart was responsive and you humbled yourself before the LORD when you heard what I have spoken against this place and its people, that they would become accursed and laid waste, and because you tore your robes and wept in my presence, I have heard you, declares the LORD. [20]Therefore I will gather you to your fathers, and you will be buried in peace. Your eyes will not see all the disaster I am going to bring on this place.' "

So they took her answer back to the king.

Josiah Renews the Covenant

23 Then the king called together all the elders of Judah and Jerusalem. [2]He went up to the temple of the LORD with the men of Judah, the people of Jerusalem, the priests and the prophets — all the people from the least to the greatest. He read in their hearing all the words of the Book of the Covenant, which had been found in the temple of the LORD. [3]The king stood by the pillar and renewed the covenant in the presence of the LORD — to follow the LORD and keep his commands, regulations and decrees with all his heart and all his soul, thus confirming the words of the covenant written in this book. Then all the people pledged themselves to the covenant.

[4]The king ordered Hilkiah the high priest, the priests next in rank and the doorkeepers to remove from the temple of the LORD all the articles made for Baal and Asherah and all the starry hosts. He burned them outside Jerusalem in the fields of the Kidron Valley and took the ashes to Bethel. [5]He did away with the pagan priests appointed by the kings of Judah to burn incense on the high places of the towns of Judah and on those around Jerusalem — those who burned incense to Baal, to the sun and moon, to the constellations and to all the starry hosts. [6]He took the Asherah pole from the temple of the LORD to the Kidron Valley outside Jerusalem and burned it there. He ground it to powder and scattered the dust over the graves of the common people. [7]He also tore down the quarters of the male shrine-prostitutes, which were in the temple of

the LORD and where women did weaving for Asherah.

[8]Josiah brought all the priests from the towns of Judah and desecrated the high places, from Geba to Beersheba, where the priests had burned incense. He broke down the shrines[a] at the gates — at the entrance to the Gate of Joshua, the city governor, which is on the left of the city gate. [9]Although the priests of the high places did not serve at the altar of the LORD in Jerusalem, they ate unleavened bread with their fellow priests.

[10]He desecrated Topheth, which was in the Valley of Ben Hinnom, so no-one could use it to sacrifice his son or daughter in[b] the fire to Molech. [11]He removed from the entrance to the temple of the LORD the horses that the kings of Judah had dedicated to the sun. They were in the court near the room of an official named Nathan-Melech. Josiah then burned the chariots dedicated to the sun.

23:10 The depth of wickedness in Judah against which Josiah contended is illustrated by the barbarous cult in which children were sacrificed to the god Molech.

---

[12]He pulled down the altars the kings of Judah had erected on the roof near the upper room of Ahaz, and the altars Manasseh had built in the two courts of the temple of the LORD. He removed them from there, smashed them to pieces and threw the rubble into the Kidron Valley. [13]The king also desecrated the high places that were east of Jerusalem on the south of the Hill of Corruption — the ones Solomon king of Israel had built for Ashtoreth the vile goddess of the Sidonians, for Chemosh the vile god of Moab, and for Molech[c] the detestable god of the people of Ammon. [14]Josiah smashed the sacred stones and cut down the Asherah poles and covered the sites with human bones.

[15]Even the altar at Bethel, the high place made by Jeroboam son of Nebat, who had caused Israel to sin — even that altar and high place he demolished. He burned the high place and ground it to powder, and burned the Asherah pole also. [16]Then Josiah looked around, and when he saw the tombs that were there on the hillside, he had the bones removed from them and burned on the altar to defile it, in accordance with the word of the LORD proclaimed by the man of God who foretold these things.

[17]The king asked, "What is that tombstone I see?"

The men of the city said, "It marks the tomb of the man of God who came from Judah and pronounced against the altar of Bethel the very things you have done to it."

[18]"Leave it alone," he said. "Don't let anyone disturb his bones." So they spared his bones and those of the prophet who had come from Samaria.

[19]Just as he had done at Bethel, Josiah removed and defiled all the shrines at the high places that the kings of Israel had built in the towns of Samaria that had provoked the LORD to anger. [20]Josiah slaughtered

---

[a]17 Or by everything they have done   [a]8 Or high places   [b]10 Or to make his son or daughter pass through
[c]13 Hebrew Milcom

all the priests of those high places on the altars and burned human bones on them. Then he went back to Jerusalem.

²¹The king gave this order to all the people: "Celebrate the Passover to the LORD your God, as it is written in this Book of the Covenant." ²²Not since the days of the judges who led Israel, nor throughout the days of the kings of Israel and the kings of Judah, had any such Passover been observed. ²³But in the eighteenth year of King Josiah, this Passover was celebrated to the LORD in Jerusalem.

²⁴Furthermore, Josiah got rid of the mediums and spiritists, the household gods, the idols and all the other detestable things seen in Judah and Jerusalem. This he did to fulfil the requirements of the law written in the book that Hilkiah the priest had discovered in the temple of the LORD. ²⁵Neither before nor after Josiah was there a king like him who turned to the LORD as he did—with all his heart and with all his soul and with all his strength, in accordance with all the Law of Moses.

²⁶Nevertheless, the LORD did not turn away from the heat of his fierce anger, which burned against Judah because of all that Manasseh had done to provoke him to anger. ²⁷So the LORD said, "I will remove Judah also from my presence as I removed Israel, and I will reject Jerusalem, the city I chose, and this temple, about which I said, 'There shall my Name be.'ᵈ"

²⁸As for the other events of Josiah's reign, and all he did, are they not written in the book of the annals of the kings of Judah?

²⁹While Josiah was king, Pharaoh Neco king of Egypt went up to the Euphrates River to help the king of Assyria. King Josiah marched out to meet him in battle, but Neco faced him and killed him at Megiddo. ³⁰Josiah's servants brought his body in a chariot from Megiddo to Jerusalem and buried him in his own tomb. And the people of the land took Jehoahaz son of Josiah and anointed him and made him king in place of his father.

Jehoahaz King of Judah

³¹Jehoahaz was twenty-three years old when he became king, and he reigned in Jerusalem for three months. His mother's name was Hamutal daughter of Jeremiah; she was from Libnah. ³²He did evil in the eyes of the LORD, just as his fathers had done. ³³Pharaoh Neco put him in chains at Riblah in the land of Hamathᵉ so that he might not reign in Jerusalem, and he imposed on Judah a levy of a hundred talentsᶠ of silver and a talentᵍ of gold. ³⁴Pharaoh Neco made Eliakim son of Josiah king in place of his father Josiah and changed Eliakim's name to Jehoiakim. But he took Jehoahaz and carried him off to Egypt, and there he died. ³⁵Jehoiakim paid Pharaoh Neco the silver and gold he demanded. In order to do so, he taxed the land and exacted the silver and gold from the people of the land according to their assessments.

Jehoiakim King of Judah

³⁶Jehoiakim was twenty-five years old when he became king, and he reigned in Jerusalem for eleven years. His mother's name was Zebidah daughter of Pedaiah; she was from Rumah. ³⁷And he did evil in the eyes of the LORD, just as his fathers had done.

24 During Jehoiakim's reign, Nebuchadnezzar king of Babylon invaded the land, and Jehoiakim became his vassal for three years. But then he changed his mind and rebelled against Nebuchadnezzar. ²The LORD sent Babylonian,ᵃ Aramean, Moabite and Ammonite raiders against him. He sent them to destroy Judah, in accordance with the word of the LORD proclaimed by his servants the prophets. ³Surely these things happened to Judah according to the LORD's command, in order to remove them from his presence because of the sins of Manasseh and all he had done, ⁴including the shedding of innocent blood. For he had filled Jerusalem with innocent blood, and the LORD was not willing to forgive.

24:2   The Lord's judgement on Judah as a result of the wickedness of the reign of Manasseh had been delayed. After Josiah's death, it began to take effect through the various foreign nations that attacked Judah.

---

⁵As for the other events of Jehoiakim's reign, and all he did, are they not written in the book of the annals of the kings of Judah? ⁶Jehoiakim rested with his fathers. And Jehoiachin his son succeeded him as king.

⁷The king of Egypt did not march out from his own country again, because the king of Babylon had taken all his territory, from the Wadi of Egypt to the Euphrates River.

Jehoiachin King of Judah

⁸Jehoiachin was eighteen years old when he became king, and he reigned in Jerusalem for three months. His mother's name was Nehushta daughter of Elnathan; she was from Jerusalem. ⁹He did evil in the eyes of the LORD, just as his father had done.

¹⁰At that time the officers of Nebuchadnezzar king of Babylon advanced on Jerusalem and laid siege to it, ¹¹and Nebuchadnezzar himself came up to the city while his officers were besieging it. ¹²Jehoiachin king of Judah, his mother, his attendants, his nobles and his officials all surrendered to him.

In the eighth year of the reign of the king of Babylon, he took Jehoiachin prisoner. ¹³As the LORD had declared, Nebuchadnezzar removed all the treasures from the temple of the LORD and from the royal palace, and took away all the gold articles that Solomon king of Israel had made for the temple of the LORD. ¹⁴He carried into exile all Jerusalem: all the officers and fighting men, and all the craftsmen and artisans—a total of ten thousand. Only the poorest people of the land were left.

ᵈ27 1 Kings 8:29   ᵉ33 Hebrew; Septuagint (see also 2 Chron. 36:3) *Neco at Riblah in Hamath removed him*
ᶠ33 That is, about 3½ tons (about 3.4 metric tons)   ᵍ33 That is, about 75 pounds (about 34 kilograms)
ᵃ2 Or *Chaldean*

15Nebuchadnezzar took Jehoiachin captive to Babylon. He also took from Jerusalem to Babylon the king's mother, his wives, his officials and the leading men of the land. 16The king of Babylon also deported to Babylon the entire force of seven thousand fighting men, strong and fit for war, and a thousand craftsmen and artisans. 17He made Mattaniah, Jehoiachin's uncle, king in his place and changed his name to Zedekiah.

Zedekiah King of Judah

18Zedekiah was twenty-one years old when he became king, and he reigned in Jerusalem for eleven years. His mother's name was Hamutal daughter of Jeremiah; she was from Libnah. 19He did evil in the eyes of the LORD, just as Jehoiakim had done. 20It was because of the LORD's anger that all this happened to Jerusalem and Judah, and in the end he thrust them from his presence.

The Fall of Jerusalem

25 Now Zedekiah rebelled against the king of Babylon. So in the ninth year of Zedekiah's reign, on the tenth day of the tenth month, Nebuchadnezzar king of Babylon marched against Jerusalem with his whole army. He encamped outside the city and built siege works all around it. 2The city was kept under siege until the eleventh year of King Zedekiah. 3By the ninth day of the ‚fourth‚a month the famine in the city had become so severe that there was no food for the people to eat. 4Then the city wall was broken through, and the whole army fled at night through the gate between the two walls near the king's garden, though the Babyloniansb were surrounding the city. They fled towards the Arabah,c 5but the Babyloniand army pursued the king and overtook him in the plains of Jericho. All his soldiers were separated from him and scattered, 6and he was captured. He was taken to the king of Babylon at Riblah, where sentence was pronounced on him. 7They killed the sons of Zedekiah before his eyes. Then they put out his eyes, bound him with bronze shackles and took him to Babylon.

8On the seventh day of the fifth month, in the nineteenth year of Nebuchadnezzar king of Babylon, Nebuzaradan commander of the imperial guard, an official of the king of Babylon, came to Jerusalem. 9He set fire to the temple of the LORD, the royal palace and all the houses of Jerusalem. Every important building he burned down. 10The whole Babylonian army, under the commander of the imperial guard, broke down the walls around Jerusalem. 11Nebuzaradan the commander of the guard carried into exile the people who remained in the city, along with the rest of the populace and those who had gone over to the king of Babylon. 12But the commander left behind some of the poorest people of the land to work the vineyards and fields.

13The Babylonians broke up the bronze pillars, the movable stands and the bronze Sea that were at the temple of the LORD and they carried the bronze to Babylon. 14They also took away the pots, shovels, wick trimmers, dishes and all the bronze articles used in the temple service. 15The commander of the imperial guard took away the censers and sprinkling bowls — all that were made of pure gold or silver.

16The bronze from the two pillars, the Sea and the movable stands, which Solomon had made for the temple of the LORD, was more than could be weighed. 17Each pillar was twenty-seven feete high. The bronze capital on top of one pillar was four and a half feetf high and was decorated with a network and pomegranates of bronze all around. The other pillar, with its network, was similar.

18The commander of the guard took as prisoners Seraiah the chief priest, Zephaniah the priest next in rank and the three doorkeepers. 19Of those still in the city, he took the officer in charge of the fighting men and five royal advisers. He also took the secretary who was chief officer in charge of conscripting the people of the land and sixty of his men who were found in the city. 20Nebuzaradan the commander took them all and brought them to the king of Babylon at Riblah. 21There at Riblah, in the land of Hamath, the king had them executed.

So Judah went into captivity, away from her land.

25:21   Judah went into exile as Israel had done before. The destruction of Jerusalem and its temple marked the lowest point in the history of God's people.

22Nebuchadnezzar king of Babylon appointed Gedaliah son of Ahikam, the son of Shaphan, to be over the people he had left behind in Judah. 23When all the army officers and their men heard that the king of Babylon had appointed Gedaliah as governor, they came to Gedaliah at Mizpah — Ishmael son of Nethaniah, Johanan son of Kareah, Seraiah son of Tanhumeth the Netophathite, Jaazaniah the son of the Maacathite, and their men. 24Gedaliah took an oath to reassure them and their men. "Do not be afraid of the Babylonian officials," he said. "Settle down in the land and serve the king of Babylon, and it will go well with you." 25In the seventh month, however, Ishmael son of Nethaniah, the son of Elishama, who was of royal blood, came with ten men and assassinated Gedaliah and also the men of Judah and the Babylonians who were with him at Mizpah. 26At this, all the people from the least to the greatest, together with the army officers, fled to Egypt for fear of the Babylonians.

Jehoiachin Released

27In the thirty-seventh year of the exile of Jehoiachin king of Judah, in the year Evil-Merodachg became

---

a3 See Jer. 52:6.   b4 Or Chaldeans; also in verses 13, 25 and 26   c4 Or the Jordan Valley
d5 Or Chaldean; also in verses 10 and 24   e17 Hebrew eighteen cubits (about 8.2 metres)
f17 Hebrew three cubits (about 1.4 metres)   g27 Also called Amel-Marduk

king of Babylon, he released Jehoiachin from prison on the twenty-seventh day of the twelfth month. ²⁸He spoke kindly to him and gave him a seat of honour higher than those of the other kings who were with him in Babylon. ²⁹So Jehoiachin put aside his prison clothes and for the rest of his life ate regularly at the king's table. ³⁰Day by day the king gave Jehoiachin a regular allowance as long as he lived.

25:27 The significance of the release of Jehoiachin is not clear, but it would seem to carry a seed of hope for the future. The royal house of David is shown still to be alive, and with it the hope of God's activity amongst his people, even in exile.

1 Chronicles

God's Chosen People

By our own standards of judgement the book of 1 Chronicles gets off to a very bad start. It presents us with nine chapters of family lists made up mostly of names which mean little to us. And yet if we are to understand the book we have to recognize the significance of these passages for the original readers. The opening sections of books are often the most revealing and the fact that 1 Chronicles begins in this way tells us that one of its major concerns is the establishment of Israel's identity as God's chosen people; this is what is achieved by tracing all the twelve tribes back to Abraham's family which God chose to bless and multiply. They are then traced back to Adam who was the first person God created. It is no surprise that the start of Genesis also relies heavily on genealogies; there the desire is to link Adam to Abraham, here it is to connect Adam first to David, the focus of the book, and then to those Israelites who had returned from exile. In an age before there was any accurate chronological dating system, the only way to grasp a sense of history and continuity from the past into the present was by mapping out the generations in this way.

A Sense of Belonging

We all need to be able to place ourselves in some context and to gain a sense of belonging to a community with a purpose in life, and this task was especially urgent for the Jews who had returned to a Jerusalem which was in ruins and a temple which had been destroyed. In a period of such great turmoil they needed to recapture their common heritage in a period of great turmoil and to renew their faith. By tracing the nation's common history the Chronicler began a process of reassurance, reminding the people of their great past which had been founded on the strong promises of God, and pointing them to a great future built on those same promises.

The House of David

Much of what we find in both 1 and 2 Chronicles is simply taken from the Old Testament's other great history books: 1 and 2 Samuel, and 1 and 2 Kings. But very often the Chronicler omitted certain passages or inserted fresh information to assist his own retelling of the national story. Certain themes were particularly important to him; most notably the house of David, the centrality of the temple, and the place for all Israel in God's plan.

National Pride

King David holds centre stage in 1 Chronicles. His line of descendants and the family tree of his own tribe, Judah, form one of the largest sections in the genealogical records. And from chapter 11 onwards we are concerned solely with David's reign, and particularly with his provisions for the ark and the temple. The Chronicler is careful to omit all the sins of David which we read about in Samuel; we hear nothing, for example, of his adultery with Bathsheba or of his murder of Uriah. The reason for this idealized picture of David is clear—his reign in about 1000 BC marked the high point in Israel's fortunes when national prestige was at its peak. Israelites of later centuries, after political independence had been lost, continually looked back to David for inspiration; he was a symbol to unite under and a powerful sign of God's blessing. Such high hopes in David were still present in the New Testament period when Jesus himself was hailed by some as the son of David and king of the Jews. For them, the hopes in David were finally fulfilled.

The Importance of the Temple

The role of the temple became a burning issue as soon as the Jews came back from Babylon, and the Chronicler belongs to the group which regarded the temple (here the second one, completed in 515 BC) as the only valid place in which to worship God. All that the writer said about the significance of the first temple planned by David and built by Solomon is applicable to the second temple. Once again the emphasis is on the people and their past.

National Unity

The Chronicler placed stress on "all Israel", as a response to the dilemma of the period after the exile. The Jewish nation was now scattered across many countries, and it had to decide who exactly made up the true people of God. Leaders such as Ezra and Nehemiah were concerned with the faithful people of Judah, but in 1 and 2 Chronicles the writer wanted to offer a place to even the rebellious tribes of the old Northern Kingdom. He persistently stressed the role of all twelve tribes in passages where his original sources do not; just as all the tribes were once united under David so there is the possibility that in the future all may again unite and enjoy God's blessings. (See 1 Chronicles 13 for a good example of this emphasis as compared to 2 Samuel 6).

An Optimistic Writer

We do not know the identity of the Chronicler. All we can safely say is that he lived in or near Jerusalem and had a close interest in the temple. He certainly shared a belief in the uniqueness of the temple and the sanctity of David's dynasty. Both these things were common themes in the Jerusalem of the fourth century BC, the most likely era in which the book was written. It is a tribute to the writer that he managed to produce a book which had such hope for the future in such dark times. There is a vision of unity for a divided nation which constantly celebrates God's firm promises to his children.

Historical Records From Adam to Abraham

To Noah's Sons

1 Adam, Seth, Enosh, [2]Kenan, Mahalalel, Jared, [3]Enoch, Methuselah, Lamech, Noah.

[4]The sons of Noah:[a]
Shem, Ham and Japheth.

The Japhethites

[5]The sons[b] of Japheth:
Gomer, Magog, Madai, Javan, Tubal, Meshech and Tiras.
[6]The sons of Gomer:
Ashkenaz, Riphath[c] and Togarmah.
[7]The sons of Javan:
Elishah, Tarshish, the Kittim and the Rodanim.

The Hamites

[8]The sons of Ham:
Cush, Mizraim,[d] Put and Canaan.
[9]The sons of Cush:
Seba, Havilah, Sabta, Raamah and Sabteca.
The sons of Raamah:
Sheba and Dedan.
[10]Cush was the father[e] of
Nimrod, who grew to be a mighty warrior on earth.
[11]Mizraim was the father of
the Ludites, Anamites, Lehabites, Naphtuhites, [12]Pathrusites, Casluhites (from whom the Philistines came) and Caphtorites.
[13]Canaan was the father of
Sidon his firstborn,[f] and of the Hittites, [14]Jebusites, Amorites, Girgashites, [15]Hivites, Arkites, Sinites, [16]Arvadites, Zemarites and Hamathites.

The Semites

[17]The sons of Shem:
Elam, Asshur, Arphaxad, Lud and Aram.
The sons of Aram:[g]
Uz, Hul, Gether and Meshech.
[18]Arphaxad was the father of Shelah, and Shelah the father of Eber.
[19]Two sons were born to Eber:
One was named Peleg,[h] because in his time the earth was divided; his brother was named Joktan.
[20]Joktan was the father of
Almodad, Sheleph, Hazarmaveth, Jerah, [21]Hadoram, Uzal, Diklah, [22]Obal,[i] Abimael,

Sheba, [23]Ophir, Havilah and Jobab. All these were sons of Joktan.

[24]Shem, Arphaxad,[j] Shelah,
[25]Eber, Peleg, Reu,
[26]Serug, Nahor, Terah
[27]and Abram (that is, Abraham).

The Family of Abraham

[28]The sons of Abraham:
Isaac and Ishmael.

Descendants of Hagar

[29]These were their descendants:
Nebaioth the firstborn of Ishmael, Kedar, Adbeel, Mibsam, [30]Mishma, Dumah, Massa, Hadad, Tema, [31]Jetur, Naphish and Kedemah. These were the sons of Ishmael.

Descendants of Keturah

[32]The sons born to Keturah, Abraham's concubine:
Zimran, Jokshan, Medan, Midian, Ishbak and Shuah.
The sons of Jokshan:
Sheba and Dedan.
[33]The sons of Midian:
Ephah, Epher, Hanoch, Abida and Eldaah.
All these were descendants of Keturah.

Descendants of Sarah

[34]Abraham was the father of Isaac.
The sons of Isaac:
Esau and Israel.

Esau's Sons

[35]The sons of Esau:
Eliphaz, Reuel, Jeush, Jalam and Korah.
[36]The sons of Eliphaz:
Teman, Omar, Zepho,[k] Gatam and Kenaz;
by Timna: Amalek.[l]
[37]The sons of Reuel:
Nahath, Zerah, Shammah and Mizzah.

The People of Seir in Edom

[38]The sons of Seir:
Lotan, Shobal, Zibeon, Anah, Dishon, Ezer and Dishan.
[39]The sons of Lotan:
Hori and Homam. Timna was Lotan's sister.
[40]The sons of Shobal:
Alvan,[m] Manahath, Ebal, Shepho and Onam.

---

[a]4 Septuagint; Hebrew does not have The sons of Noah:
[b]5 Sons may mean descendants or successors or nations; also in verses 6–10, 17 and 20.
[c]6 Many Hebrew manuscripts and Vulgate (see also Septuagint and Gen. 10:3); most Hebrew manuscripts Diphath
[d]8 That is, Egypt; also in verse 11   [e]10 Father may mean ancestor or predecessor or founder; also in verses 11, 13, 18 and 20.
[f]13 Or of the Sidonians, the foremost
[g]17 One Hebrew manuscript and some Septuagint manuscripts (see also Gen. 10:23); most Hebrew manuscripts do not have this line.
[h]19 Peleg means division.   [i]22 Some Hebrew manuscripts and Syriac (see also Gen. 10:28); most Hebrew manuscripts Ebal
[j]24 Hebrew; some Septuagint manuscripts Arphaxad, Cainan (see also note at Gen. 11:10)
[k]36 Many Hebrew manuscripts, some Septuagint manuscripts and Syriac (see also Gen. 36:11); most Hebrew manuscripts Zephi
[l]36 Some Septuagint manuscripts (see also Gen. 36:12); Hebrew Gatam, Kenaz, Timna and Amalek
[m]40 Many Hebrew manuscripts and some Septuagint manuscripts (see also Gen. 36:23); most Hebrew manuscripts Alian

The sons of Zibeon:
Aiah and Anah.
41The son of Anah:
Dishon.
The sons of Dishon:
Hemdan,[n] Eshban, Ithran and Keran.
42The sons of Ezer:
Bilhan, Zaavan and Akan.[o]
The sons of Dishan:[p]
Uz and Aran.

The Rulers of Edom

43These were the kings who reigned in Edom
before any Israelite king reigned:[q]
Bela son of Beor, whose city was named Dinhabah.
44When Bela died, Jobab son of Zerah from Bozrah
succeeded him as king.
45When Jobab died, Husham from the land of the
Temanites succeeded him as king.
46When Husham died, Hadad son of Bedad, who
defeated Midian in the country of Moab, succeeded him as king. His city was named Avith.
47When Hadad died, Samlah from Masrekah succeeded him as king.
48When Samlah died, Shaul from Rehoboth on the
river[r] succeeded him as king.
49When Shaul died, Baal-Hanan son of Acbor succeeded him as king.
50When Baal-Hanan died, Hadad succeeded him as
king. His city was named Pau,[s] and his wife's
name was Mehetabel daughter of Matred, the
daughter of Me-Zahab. 51Hadad also died.

The chiefs of Edom were:
Timna, Alvah, Jetheth, 52Oholibamah, Elah,
Pinon, 53Kenaz, Teman, Mibzar, 54Magdiel
and Iram. These were the chiefs of Edom.

Israel's Sons

2 These were the sons of Israel:
Reuben, Simeon, Levi, Judah, Issachar, Zebulun, 2Dan, Joseph, Benjamin, Naphtali, Gad
and Asher.

Judah

To Hezron's Sons

3The sons of Judah:
Er, Onan and Shelah. These three were born
to him by a Canaanite woman, the daughter of
Shua. Er, Judah's firstborn, was wicked in the
LORD's sight; so the LORD put him to death.
4Tamar, Judah's daughter-in-law, bore him
Perez and Zerah. Judah had five sons in all.

5The sons of Perez:
Hezron and Hamul.

2:1 The Chronicler nearly always called
Esau's brother Israel rather than Jacob,
because he wanted to stress the link with the
Israel of his own day. All the twelve tribes
which originated from the twelve sons of
Israel should take their place as God's chosen
people. Pride of place was still given to Judah
and Benjamin who became the loyal southern tribes, and to Levi who also supported
the Southern Kingdom.

6The sons of Zerah:
Zimri, Ethan, Heman, Calcol and Darda[a]—
five in all.
7The son of Carmi:
Achar,[b] who brought trouble on Israel by
violating the ban on taking devoted things.[c]
8The son of Ethan:
Azariah.
9The sons born to Hezron were:
Jerahmeel, Ram and Caleb.[d]

From Ram Son of Hezron

10Ram was the father of
Amminadab, and Amminadab the father of
Nahshon, the leader of the people of Judah.
11Nahshon was the father of Salmon,[e]
Salmon the father of Boaz, 12Boaz the father of
Obed and Obed the father of Jesse.
13Jesse was the father of
Eliab his firstborn; the second son was Abina-
dab, the third Shimea, 14the fourth Nethanel,
the fifth Raddai, 15the sixth Ozem and the sev-
enth David. 16Their sisters were Zeruiah and
Abigail. Zeruiah's three sons were Abishai,
Joab and Asahel. 17Abigail was the mother of
Amasa, whose father was Jether the Ishmaelite.

Caleb Son of Hezron

18Caleb son of Hezron had children by his wife
Azubah (and by Jerioth). These were her sons:
Jesher, Shobab and Ardon. 19When Azubah
died, Caleb married Ephrath, who bore him
Hur. 20Hur was the father of Uri, and Uri the
father of Bezalel.
21Later, Hezron lay with the daughter of Makir the
father of Gilead (he had married her when he

---

n41 Many Hebrew manuscripts and some Septuagint manuscripts (see also Gen. 36:26); most Hebrew manuscripts *Hamran*
o42 Many Hebrew and Septuagint manuscripts (see also Gen. 36:27); most Hebrew manuscripts *Zaavan, Jaakan*
p42 Hebrew *Dishon*, a variant of *Dishan*   q43 Or *before an Israelite king reigned over them*   r48 Possibly the Euphrates
s50 Many Hebrew manuscripts, some Septuagint manuscripts, Vulgate and Syriac (see also Gen. 36:39); most Hebrew manuscripts *Pai*
a6 Many Hebrew manuscripts, some Septuagint manuscripts and Syriac (see also 1 Kings 4:31); most Hebrew manuscripts *Dara*
b7 *Achar* means *trouble*; *Achar* is called *Achan* in Joshua.
c7 The Hebrew term refers to the irrevocable giving over of things or persons to the LORD, often by totally destroying them.
d9 Hebrew *Kelubai*, a variant of *Caleb*   e11 Septuagint (see also Ruth 4:21); Hebrew *Salma*

was sixty years old), and she bore him Segub. [22]Segub was the father of Jair, who controlled twenty-three towns in Gilead. [23](But Geshur and Aram captured Havvoth Jair,[f] as well as Kenath with its surrounding settlements— sixty towns.) All these were descendants of Makir the father of Gilead.

[24]After Hezron died in Caleb Ephrathah, Abijah the wife of Hezron bore him Ashhur the father[g] of Tekoa.

Jerahmeel Son of Hezron

[25]The sons of Jerahmeel the firstborn of Hezron:
Ram his firstborn, Bunah, Oren, Ozem and[h] Ahijah. [26]Jerahmeel had another wife, whose name was Atarah; she was the mother of Onam.
[27]The sons of Ram the firstborn of Jerahmeel:
Maaz, Jamin and Eker.
[28]The sons of Onam:
Shammai and Jada.
The sons of Shammai:
Nadab and Abishur.
[29]Abishur's wife was named Abihail, who bore him Ahban and Molid.
[30]The sons of Nadab:
Seled and Appaim. Seled died without children.
[31]The son of Appaim:
Ishi, who was the father of Sheshan.
Sheshan was the father of Ahlai.
[32]The sons of Jada, Shammai's brother:
Jether and Jonathan. Jether died without children.
[33]The sons of Jonathan:
Peleth and Zaza.
These were the descendants of Jerahmeel.
[34]Sheshan had no sons—only daughters.
He had an Egyptian servant named Jarha. [35]Sheshan gave his daughter in marriage to his servant Jarha, and she bore him Attai.
[36]Attai was the father of Nathan,
Nathan the father of Zabad,
[37]Zabad the father of Ephlal,
Ephlal the father of Obed,
[38]Obed the father of Jehu,
Jehu the father of Azariah,
[39]Azariah the father of Helez,
Helez the father of Eleasah,
[40]Eleasah the father of Sismai,
Sismai the father of Shallum,
[41]Shallum the father of Jekamiah, and Jekamiah the father of Elishama.

The Clans of Caleb

[42]The sons of Caleb the brother of Jerahmeel:
Mesha his firstborn, who was the father of

Ziph, and his son Mareshah,[i] who was the father of Hebron.
[43]The sons of Hebron:
Korah, Tappuah, Rekem and Shema. [44]Shema was the father of Raham, and Raham the father of Jorkeam. Rekem was the father of Shammai. [45]The son of Shammai was Maon, and Maon was the father of Beth Zur.
[46]Caleb's concubine Ephah was the mother of Haran, Moza and Gazez. Haran was the father of Gazez.
[47]The sons of Jahdai:
Regem, Jotham, Geshan, Pelet, Ephah and Shaaph.
[48]Caleb's concubine Maacah was the mother of Sheber and Tirhanah. [49]She also gave birth to Shaaph the father of Madmannah and to Sheva the father of Macbenah and Gibea. Caleb's daughter was Acsah. [50]These were the descendants of Caleb.

The sons of Hur the firstborn of Ephrathah:
Shobal the father of Kiriath Jearim, [51]Salma the father of Bethlehem, and Hareph the father of Beth Gader.
[52]The descendants of Shobal the father of Kiriath Jearim were:
Haroeh, half the Manahathites, [53]and the clans of Kiriath Jearim: the Ithrites, Puthites, Shumathites and Mishraites. From these descended the Zorathites and Eshtaolites.
[54]The descendants of Salma:
Bethlehem, the Netophathites, Atroth Beth Joab, half the Manahathites, the Zorites, [55]and the clans of scribes[j] who lived at Jabez: the Tirathites, Shimeathites and Sucathites. These are the Kenites who came from Hammath, the father of the house of Recab.[k]

The Sons of David

3 These were the sons of David born to him in Hebron:
The firstborn was Amnon the son of Ahinoam of Jezreel;
the second, Daniel the son of Abigail of Carmel;
[2]the third, Absalom the son of Maacah daughter of Talmai king of Geshur;
the fourth, Adonijah the son of Haggith;
[3]the fifth, Shephatiah the son of Abital;
and the sixth, Ithream, by his wife Eglah.
[4]These six were born to David in Hebron, where he reigned for seven years and six months.
David reigned in Jerusalem for thirty-three years, [5]and these were the children born to him there:
Shammua,[a] Shobab, Nathan and Solomon. These four were by Bathsheba[b] daughter of

---

[f]23 Or captured the settlements of Jair
[g]24 Father may mean civic leader or military leader; also in verses 42, 45, 49–52 and possibly elsewhere.
[h]25 Or Oren and Ozem, by   [i]42 The meaning of the Hebrew for this phrase is uncertain.   [j]55 Or of the Sopherites
[k]55 Or father of Beth Recab   [a]5 Hebrew Shimea, a variant of Shammua
[b]5 One Hebrew manuscript and Vulgate (see also Septuagint and 2 Sam. 11:3); most Hebrew manuscripts Bathshua

Ammiel. [6]There were also Ibhar, Elishua,[c] Eliphelet, [7]Nogah, Nepheg, Japhia, [8]Elishama, Eliada and Eliphelet—nine in all. [9]All these were the sons of David, besides his sons by his concubines. And Tamar was their sister.

The Kings of Judah

[10]Solomon's son was Rehoboam,
    Abijah his son,
    Asa his son,
    Jehoshaphat his son,

3:10   Chronicles was written to a people who no longer had a king, but it was still vital to recount the family tree of the Davidic line which ruled the Southern Kingdom of Judah after the nation split in two. The focus is on the continuity of the dynasty after the exile, showing that God's blessing towards David was still active. Zerubbabel (3:19) was a very important figure during the temple rebuilding (see Haggai).

---

[11]Jehoram[d] his son,
    Ahaziah his son,
    Joash his son,
[12]Amaziah his son,
    Azariah his son,
    Jotham his son,
[13]Ahaz his son,
    Hezekiah his son,
    Manasseh his son,
[14]Amon his son,
    Josiah his son.
[15]The sons of Josiah:
    Johanan the firstborn,
    Jehoiakim the second son,
    Zedekiah the third,
    Shallum the fourth.
[16]The successors of Jehoiakim:
    Jehoiachin[e] his son,
    and Zedekiah.

The Royal Line After the Exile

[17]The descendants of Jehoiachin the captive:
    Shealtiel his son, [18]Malkiram, Pedaiah, Shenazzar, Jekamiah, Hoshama and Nedabiah.
[19]The sons of Pedaiah:
    Zerubbabel and Shimei.
The sons of Zerubbabel:
    Meshullam and Hananiah.
Shelomith was their sister.
[20]There were also five others:
    Hashubah, Ohel, Berekiah, Hasadiah and Jushab-Hesed.

[21]The descendants of Hananiah:
    Pelatiah and Jeshaiah, and the sons of Rephaiah, of Arnan, of Obadiah and of Shecaniah.
[22]The descendants of Shecaniah:
    Shemaiah and his sons:
    Hattush, Igal, Bariah, Neariah and Shaphat—six in all.
[23]The sons of Neariah:
    Elioenai, Hizkiah and Azrikam—three in all.
[24]The sons of Elioenai:
    Hodaviah, Eliashib, Pelaiah, Akkub, Johanan, Delaiah and Anani—seven in all.

Other Clans of Judah

4   The descendants of Judah:
    Perez, Hezron, Carmi, Hur and Shobal.
[2]Reaiah son of Shobal was the father of Jahath, and Jahath the father of Ahumai and Lahad. These were the clans of the Zorathites.
[3]These were the sons[a] of Etam:
    Jezreel, Ishma and Idbash. Their sister was named Hazzelelponi. [4]Penuel was the father of Gedor, and Ezer the father of Hushah.
These were the descendants of Hur, the firstborn of Ephrathah and father[b] of Bethlehem.
[5]Ashhur the father of Tekoa had two wives, Helah and Naarah.
[6]Naarah bore him Ahuzzam, Hepher, Temeni and Haahashtari. These were the descendants of Naarah.
[7]The sons of Helah:
    Zereth, Zohar, Ethnan, [8]and Koz, who was the father of Anub and Hazzobebah and of the clans of Aharhel son of Harum.

[9]Jabez was more honourable than his brothers. His mother had named him Jabez,[c] saying, "I gave birth to him in pain." [10]Jabez cried out to the God of Israel, "Oh, that you would bless me and enlarge my territory! Let your hand be with me, and keep me from harm so that I will be free from pain." And God granted his request.

[11]Kelub, Shuhah's brother, was the father of Mehir, who was the father of Eshton. [12]Eshton was the father of Beth Rapha, Paseah and Tehinnah the father of Ir Nahash.[d] These were the men of Recah.

[13]The sons of Kenaz:
    Othniel and Seraiah.
The sons of Othniel:
    Hathath and Meonothai.[e] [14]Meonothai was the father of Ophrah.
Seraiah was the father of Joab,
    the father of Ge Harashim.[f] It was called this because its people were craftsmen.

---

[c]6 Two Hebrew manuscripts (see also 2 Sam. 5:15 and 1 Chron. 14:5); most Hebrew manuscripts *Elishama*
[d]11 Hebrew *Joram*, a variant of *Jehoram*   [e]16 Hebrew *Jeconiah*, a variant of *Jehoiachin*; also in verse 17
[a]3 Some Septuagint manuscripts (see also Vulgate); Hebrew *father*
[b]4 *Father* may mean *civic leader* or *military leader*; also in verses 12, 14, 17, 18 and possibly elsewhere.
[c]9 *Jabez* sounds like the Hebrew for *pain.*   [d]12 Or *of the city of Nahash*
[e]13 Some Septuagint manuscripts and Vulgate; Hebrew does not have *and Meonothai.*   [f]14 *Ge Harashim* means *valley of craftsmen.*

15The sons of Caleb son of Jephunneh:
   Iru, Elah and Naam.
The son of Elah:
   Kenaz.
16The sons of Jehallelel:
   Ziph, Ziphah, Tiria and Asarel.
17The sons of Ezrah:
   Jether, Mered, Epher and Jalon. One of
   Mered's wives gave birth to Miriam, Shammai
   and Ishbah the father of Eshtemoa. 18(His
   Judean wife gave birth to Jered the father of
   Gedor, Heber the father of Soco, and Jekuthiel
   the father of Zanoah.) These were the children
   of Pharaoh's daughter Bithiah, whom Mered
   had married.
19The sons of Hodiah's wife, the sister of Naham:
   the father of Keilah the Garmite, and Eshtemoa the Maacathite.
20The sons of Shimon:
   Amnon, Rinnah, Ben-Hanan and Tilon.
The descendants of Ishi:
   Zoheth and Ben-Zoheth.
21The sons of Shelah son of Judah:
   Er the father of Lecah, Laadah the father of
   Mareshah and the clans of the linen workers
   at Beth Ashbea, 22Jokim, the men of Cozeba,
   and Joash and Saraph, who ruled in Moab and
   Jashubi Lehem. (These records are from
   ancient times.) 23They were the potters who
   lived at Netaim and Gederah; they stayed
   there and worked for the king.

Simeon

24The descendants of Simeon:
   Nemuel, Jamin, Jarib, Zerah and Shaul;
   25Shallum was Shaul's son, Mibsam his son and
   Mishma his son.
26The descendants of Mishma:
   Hammuel his son, Zaccur his son and Shimei
   his son.
27Shimei had sixteen sons and six daughters, but his
brothers did not have many children; so their entire
clan did not become as numerous as the people of
Judah. 28They lived in Beersheba, Moladah, Hazar
Shual, 29Bilhah, Ezem, Tolad, 30Bethuel, Hormah, Ziklag, 31Beth Marcaboth, Hazar Susim, Beth Biri and
Shaaraim. These were their towns until the reign of
David. 32Their surrounding villages were Etam, Ain,
Rimmon, Token and Ashan — five towns — 33and all the
villages around these towns as far as Baalath.g These
were their settlements. And they kept a genealogical
record.

34Meshobab, Jamlech, Joshah son of Amaziah,
35Joel, Jehu son of Joshibiah, the son of Seraiah,
the son of Asiel, 36also Elioenai, Jaakobah, Jesho-
haiah, Asaiah, Adiel, Jesimiel, Benaiah, 37and Ziza
son of Shiphi, the son of Allon, the son of Jedaiah,
the son of Shimri, the son of Shemaiah.

38The men listed above by name were leaders of
their clans. Their families increased greatly, 39and they
went to the outskirts of Gedor to the east of the valley
in search of pasture for their flocks. 40They found rich,
good pasture, and the land was spacious, peaceful and
quiet. Some Hamites had lived there formerly.
41The men whose names were listed came in the
days of Hezekiah king of Judah. They attacked the Hamites in their dwellings and also the Meunites who were
there and completely destroyedh them, as is evident
to this day. Then they settled in their place, because
there was pasture for their flocks. 42And five hundred
of these Simeonites, led by Pelatiah, Neariah, Rephaiah
and Uzziel, the sons of Ishi, invaded the hill country of
Seir. 43They killed the remaining Amalekites who had
escaped, and they have lived there to this day.

Reuben

5 The sons of Reuben the firstborn of Israel (he was
   the firstborn, but when he defiled his father's
marriage bed, his rights as firstborn were given to the
sons of Joseph son of Israel; so he could not be listed
in the genealogical record in accordance with his birthright, 2and though Judah was the strongest of his
brothers and a ruler came from him, the rights of the
firstborn belonged to Joseph) — 3the sons of Reuben the
firstborn of Israel:
   Hanoch, Pallu, Hezron and Carmi.
4The descendants of Joel:
   Shemaiah his son, Gog his son,
   Shimei his son, 5Micah his son,
   Reaiah his son, Baal his son,
   6and Beerah his son, whom Tiglath-Pilesera
   king of Assyria took into exile. Beerah was a
   leader of the Reubenites.
7Their relatives by clans, listed according to their
   genealogical records:
   Jeiel the chief, Zechariah, 8and Bela son of
   Azaz, the son of Shema, the son of Joel. They
   settled in the area from Aroer to Nebo and Baal
   Meon. 9To the east they occupied the land up
   to the edge of the desert that extends to the
   Euphrates River, because their livestock had
   increased in Gilead.
   10During Saul's reign they waged war
   against the Hagrites, who were defeated at
   their hands; they occupied the dwellings of
   the Hagrites throughout the entire region east
   of Gilead.

Gad

11The Gadites lived next to them in Bashan, as far
   as Salecah:
   12Joel was the chief, Shapham the second, then
   Janai and Shaphat, in Bashan.
13Their relatives, by families, were:
   Michael, Meshullam, Sheba, Jorai, Jacan, Zia
   and Eber — seven in all.

g33 Some Septuagint manuscripts (see also Joshua 19:8); Hebrew Baal
h41 The Hebrew term refers to the irrevocable giving over of things or persons to the LORD, often by totally destroying them.
a6 Hebrew Tilgath-Pilneser, a variant of Tiglath-Pileser; also in verse 26

[14]These were the sons of Abihail son of Huri, the son of Jaroah, the son of Gilead, the son of Michael, the son of Jeshishai, the son of Jahdo, the son of Buz.

[15]Ahi son of Abdiel, the son of Guni, was head of their family.

[16]The Gadites lived in Gilead, in Bashan and its outlying villages, and on all the pasture-lands of Sharon as far as they extended.

[17]All these were entered in the genealogical records during the reigns of Jotham king of Judah and Jeroboam king of Israel.

[18]The Reubenites, the Gadites and the half-tribe of Manasseh had 44,760 men ready for military service — able-bodied men who could handle shield and sword, who could use a bow, and who were trained for battle. [19]They waged war against the Hagrites, Jetur, Naphish and Nodab. [20]They were helped in fighting them, and God handed the Hagrites and all their allies over to them, because they cried out to him during the battle. He answered their prayers, because they trusted in him. [21]They seized the livestock of the Hagrites — fifty thousand camels, two hundred and fifty thousand sheep and two thousand donkeys. They also took one hundred thousand people captive, [22]and many others fell slain, because the battle was God's. And they occupied the land until the exile.

The Half-Tribe of Manasseh

[23]The people of the half-tribe of Manasseh were numerous; they settled in the land from Bashan to Baal Hermon, that is, to Senir (Mount Hermon).

[24]These were the heads of their families: Epher, Ishi, Eliel, Azriel, Jeremiah, Hodaviah and Jahdiel. They were brave warriors, famous men, and heads of their families. [25]But they were unfaithful to the God of their fathers and prostituted themselves to the gods of the peoples of the land, whom God had destroyed before them. [26]So the God of Israel stirred up the spirit of Pul king of Assyria (that is, Tiglath-Pileser king of Assyria), who took the Reubenites, the Gadites and the half-tribe of Manasseh into exile. He took them to Halah, Habor, Hara and the river of Gozan, where they are to this day.

Levi

6 The sons of Levi:
Gershon, Kohath and Merari.

[2]The sons of Kohath:
Amram, Izhar, Hebron and Uzziel.

[3]The children of Amram:
Aaron, Moses and Miriam.
The sons of Aaron:
Nadab, Abihu, Eleazar and Ithamar.

[4]Eleazar was the father of Phinehas,
Phinehas the father of Abishua,

[5]Abishua the father of Bukki,
Bukki the father of Uzzi,

[6]Uzzi the father of Zerahiah,
Zerahiah the father of Meraioth,

[7]Meraioth the father of Amariah,
Amariah the father of Ahitub,

[8]Ahitub the father of Zadok,
Zadok the father of Ahimaaz,

[9]Ahimaaz the father of Azariah,
Azariah the father of Johanan,

[10]Johanan the father of Azariah (it was he who served as priest in the temple Solomon built in Jerusalem),

[11]Azariah the father of Amariah,
Amariah the father of Ahitub,

[12]Ahitub the father of Zadok,
Zadok the father of Shallum,

[13]Shallum the father of Hilkiah,
Hilkiah the father of Azariah,

[14]Azariah the father of Seraiah,
and Seraiah the father of Jehozadak.

[15]Jehozadak was deported when the LORD sent Judah and Jerusalem into exile by the hand of Nebuchadnezzar.

[16]The sons of Levi:
Gershon,[a] Kohath and Merari.

[17]These are the names of the sons of Gershon:
Libni and Shimei.

[18]The sons of Kohath:
Amram, Izhar, Hebron and Uzziel.

[19]The sons of Merari:
Mahli and Mushi.

These are the clans of the Levites listed according to their fathers:

[20]Of Gershon:
Libni his son, Jehath his son,
Zimmah his son, [21]Joah his son,
Iddo his son, Zerah his son
and Jeatherai his son.

[22]The descendants of Kohath:
Amminadab his son, Korah his son,
Assir his son, [23]Elkanah his son,
Ebiasaph his son, Assir his son,

[24]Tahath his son, Uriel his son,
Uzziah his son and Shaul his son.

[25]The descendants of Elkanah:
Amasai, Ahimoth,

[26]Elkanah his son,[b] Zophai his son,
Nahath his son, [27]Eliab his son,
Jeroham his son, Elkanah his son
and Samuel his son.[c]

[28]The sons of Samuel:
Joel[d] the firstborn
and Abijah the second son.

[29]The descendants of Merari:
Mahli, Libni his son,
Shimei his son, Uzzah his son,

[30]Shimea his son, Haggiah his son
and Asaiah his son.

---

[a]16 Hebrew *Gershom*, a variant of *Gershon*; also in verses 17, 20, 43, 62 and 71
[b]26 Some Hebrew manuscripts, Septuagint and Syriac; most Hebrew manuscripts *Ahimoth* [26]*and Elkanah. The sons of Elkanah:*
[c]27 Some Septuagint manuscripts (see also 1 Sam. 1:19, 20 and 1 Chron. 6:33, 34); Hebrew does not have *and Samuel his son.*
[d]28 Some Septuagint manuscripts and Syriac (see also 1 Sam. 8:2 and 1 Chron. 6:33); Hebrew does not have *Joel.*

The Temple Musicians

[31] These are the men David put in charge of the music in the house of the LORD after the ark came to rest there. [32] They ministered with music before the tabernacle, the Tent of Meeting, until Solomon built the temple of the LORD in Jerusalem. They performed their duties according to the regulations laid down for them.

[33] Here are the men who served, together with their sons:

From the Kohathites:

Heman, the musician,
the son of Joel, the son of Samuel,
[34] the son of Elkanah, the son of Jeroham,
the son of Eliel, the son of Toah,
[35] the son of Zuph, the son of Elkanah,
the son of Mahath, the son of Amasai,
[36] the son of Elkanah, the son of Joel,
the son of Azariah, the son of Zephaniah,
[37] the son of Tahath, the son of Assir,
the son of Ebiasaph, the son of Korah,
[38] the son of Izhar, the son of Kohath,
the son of Levi, the son of Israel;
[39] and Heman's associate Asaph, who served at his right hand:

Asaph son of Berekiah, the son of Shimea,
[40] the son of Michael, the son of Baaseiah, [e]
the son of Malkijah, [41] the son of Ethni,
the son of Zerah, the son of Adaiah,
[42] the son of Ethan, the son of Zimmah,
the son of Shimei, [43] the son of Jahath,
the son of Gershon, the son of Levi;

[44] and from their associates, the Merarites, at his left hand:

Ethan son of Kishi, the son of Abdi,
the son of Malluch, [45] the son of Hashabiah,
the son of Amaziah, the son of Hilkiah,
[46] the son of Amzi, the son of Bani,
the son of Shemer, [47] the son of Mahli,
the son of Mushi, the son of Merari,
the son of Levi.

[48] Their fellow Levites were assigned to all the other duties of the tabernacle, the house of God. [49] But Aaron and his descendants were the ones who presented offerings on the altar of burnt offering and on the altar of incense in connection with all that was done in the Most Holy Place, making atonement for Israel, in accordance with all that Moses the servant of God had commanded.

[50] These were the descendants of Aaron:

Eleazar his son, Phinehas his son,
Abishua his son, [51] Bukki his son,
Uzzi his son, Zerahiah his son,
[52] Meraioth his son, Amariah his son,
Ahitub his son, [53] Zadok his son
and Ahimaaz his son.

[54] These were the locations of their settlements allotted as their territory (they were assigned to the descendants of Aaron who were from the Kohathite clan, because the first lot was for them):

[55] They were given Hebron in Judah with its surrounding pasture-lands. [56] But the fields and villages around the city were given to Caleb son of Jephunneh.

[57] So the descendants of Aaron were given Hebron (a city of refuge), and Libnah, [f] Jattir, Eshtemoa, [58] Hilen, Debir, [59] Ashan, Juttah [g] and Beth Shemesh, together with their pasture-lands. [60] And from the tribe of Benjamin they were given Gibeon, [h] Geba, Alemeth and Anathoth, together with their pasture-lands.

These towns, which were distributed among the Kohathite clans, were thirteen in all.

[61] The rest of Kohath's descendants were allotted ten towns from the clans of half the tribe of Manasseh.

[62] The descendants of Gershon, clan by clan, were allotted thirteen towns from the tribes of Issachar, Asher and Naphtali, and from the part of the tribe of Manasseh that is in Bashan.

[63] The descendants of Merari, clan by clan, were allotted twelve towns from the tribes of Reuben, Gad and Zebulun.

[64] So the Israelites gave the Levites these towns and their pasture-lands. [65] From the tribes of Judah, Simeon and Benjamin they allotted the previously named towns.

[66] Some of the Kohathite clans were given as their territory towns from the tribe of Ephraim.

[67] In the hill country of Ephraim they were given Shechem (a city of refuge), and Gezer, [i] [68] Jokmeam, Beth Horon, [69] Aijalon and Gath Rimmon, together with their pasture-lands. [70] And from half the tribe of Manasseh the Israelites gave Aner and Bileam, together with their pasture-lands, to the rest of the Kohathite clans.

[71] The Gershonites received the following:

From the clan of the half-tribe of Manasseh
they received Golan in Bashan and also Ashtaroth, together with their pasture-lands;
[72] from the tribe of Issachar
they received Kedesh, Daberath, [73] Ramoth and Anem, together with their pasture-lands;
[74] from the tribe of Asher
they received Mashal, Abdon, [75] Hukok and Rehob, together with their pasture-lands;
[76] and from the tribe of Naphtali
they received Kedesh in Galilee, Hammon and Kiriathaim, together with their pasture-lands.

[77] The Merarites (the rest of the Levites) received the following:

From the tribe of Zebulun
they received Jokneam, Kartah, [j] Rimmono and Tabor, together with their pasture-lands;

---

[e] 40 Most Hebrew manuscripts; some Hebrew manuscripts, one Septuagint manuscript and Syriac *Maaseiah*
[f] 57 See Joshua 21:13; Hebrew *given the cities of refuge: Hebron, Libnah.*
[g] 59 Syriac (see also Septuagint and Joshua 21:16); Hebrew does not have *Juttah.*
[h] 60 See Joshua 21:17; Hebrew does not have *Gibeon.*   [i] 67 See Joshua 21:21; Hebrew *given the cities of refuge: Shechem, Gezer.*
[j] 77 See Septuagint and Joshua 21:34; Hebrew does not have *Jokneam, Kartah.*

78from the tribe of Reuben across the Jordan east
of Jericho
they received Bezer in the desert, Jahzah,
79Kedemoth and Mephaath, together with
their pasture-lands;
80and from the tribe of Gad
they received Ramoth in Gilead, Mahanaim,
81Heshbon and Jazer, together with their
pasture-lands.

Issachar

7 The sons of Issachar:
Tola, Puah, Jashub and Shimron—four in all.
2The sons of Tola:
Uzzi, Rephaiah, Jeriel, Jahmai, Ibsam and
Samuel—heads of their families. During the
reign of David, the descendants of Tola listed
as fighting men in their genealogy numbered
22,600.
3The son of Uzzi:
Izrahiah.
The sons of Izrahiah:
Michael, Obadiah, Joel and Isshiah. All five of
them were chiefs. 4According to their family
genealogy, they had 36,000 men ready for
battle, for they had many wives and children.
5The relatives who were fighting men belonging
to all the clans of Issachar, as listed in their
genealogy, were 87,000 in all.

Benjamin

6Three sons of Benjamin:
Bela, Beker and Jediael.
7The sons of Bela:
Ezbon, Uzzi, Uzziel, Jerimoth and Iri, heads of
families—five in all. Their genealogical record
listed 22,034 fighting men.
8The sons of Beker:
Zemirah, Joash, Eliezer, Elioenai, Omri, Jeremoth, Abijah, Anathoth and Alemeth. All
these were the sons of Beker. 9Their genealogical record listed the heads of families and
20,200 fighting men.
10The son of Jediael:
Bilhan.
The sons of Bilhan:
Jeush, Benjamin, Ehud, Kenaanah, Zethan,
Tarshish and Ahishahar. 11All these sons of
Jediael were heads of families. There were
17,200 fighting men ready to go out to war.
12The Shuppites and Huppites were the descendants of Ir, and the Hushites the descendants of
Aher.

Naphtali

13The sons of Naphtali:
Jahziel, Guni, Jezer and Shillem a—the
descendants of Bilhah.

Manasseh

14The descendants of Manasseh:
Asriel was his descendant through his Aramean concubine. She gave birth to Makir the
father of Gilead. 15Makir took a wife from among
the Huppites and Shuppites. His sister's name
was Maacah.
Another descendant was named Zelophehad,
who had only daughters.
16Makir's wife Maacah gave birth to a son
and named him Peresh. His brother was
named Sheresh, and his sons were Ulam and
Rakem.
17The son of Ulam:
Bedan.
These were the sons of Gilead son of Makir, the
son of Manasseh. 18His sister Hammoleketh
gave birth to Ishhod, Abiezer and Mahlah.
19The sons of Shemida were:
Ahian, Shechem, Likhi and Aniam.

Ephraim

20The descendants of Ephraim:
Shuthelah, Bered his son,
Tahath his son, Eleadah his son,
Tahath his son, 21Zabad his son
and Shuthelah his son.
Ezer and Elead were killed by the native-born
men of Gath, when they went down to seize
their livestock. 22Their father Ephraim mourned
for them many days, and his relatives came to
comfort him. 23Then he lay with his wife again,
and she became pregnant and gave birth to a son.
He named him Beriah, b because there had been
misfortune in his family. 24His daughter was
Sheerah, who built Lower and Upper Beth Horon
as well as Uzzen Sheerah.
25Rephah was his son, Resheph his son, c
Telah his son, Tahan his son,
26Ladan his son, Ammihud his son,
Elishama his son, 27Nun his son
and Joshua his son.
28Their lands and settlements included Bethel and
its surrounding villages, Naaran to the east, Gezer and
its villages to the west, and Shechem and its villages all
the way to Ayyah and its villages. 29Along the borders
of Manasseh were Beth Shan, Taanach, Megiddo and
Dor, together with their villages. The descendants of
Joseph son of Israel lived in these towns.

Asher

30The sons of Asher:
Imnah, Ishvah, Ishvi and Beriah. Their sister
was Serah.
31The sons of Beriah:
Heber and Malkiel, who was the father of
Birzaith.
32Heber was the father of Japhlet, Shomer and
Hotham and of their sister Shua.

a13 Some Hebrew and Septuagint manuscripts (see also Gen. 46:24 and Num. 26:49); most Hebrew manuscripts *Shallum*
b23 *Beriah* sounds like the Hebrew for *misfortune.*   c25 Some Septuagint manuscripts; Hebrew does not have *his son.*

33The sons of Japhlet:
Pasach, Bimhal and Ashvath.
These were Japhlet's sons.
34The sons of Shomer:
Ahi, Rohgah,*d* Hubbah and Aram.
35The sons of his brother Helem:
Zophah, Imna, Shelesh and Amal.
36The sons of Zophah:
Suah, Harnepher, Shual, Beri, Imrah, 37Bezer,
Hod, Shamma, Shilshah, Ithran*e* and Beera.
38The sons of Jether:
Jephunneh, Pispah and Ara.
39The sons of Ulla:
Arah, Hanniel and Rizia.
40All these were descendants of Asher—heads of families, choice men, brave warriors and outstanding leaders. The number of men ready for battle, as listed in their genealogy, was 26,000.

The Genealogy of Saul the Benjamite

8 Benjamin was the father of Bela his firstborn, Ashbel the second son, Aharah the third, 2Nohah the fourth and Rapha the fifth.
3The sons of Bela were:
Addar, Gera, Abihud,*a* 4Abishua, Naaman, Ahoah, 5Gera, Shephuphan and Huram.
6These were the descendants of Ehud, who were heads of families of those living in Geba and were deported to Manahath:
7Naaman, Ahijah and Gera, who deported them and who was the father of Uzza and Ahihud.
8Sons were born to Shaharaim in Moab after he had divorced his wives Hushim and Baara. 9By his wife Hodesh he had Jobab, Zibia, Mesha, Malcam, 10Jeuz, Sakia and Mirmah. These were his sons, heads of families. 11By Hushim he had Abitub and Elpaal.
12The sons of Elpaal:
Eber, Misham, Shemed (who built Ono and Lod with its surrounding villages), 13and Beriah and Shema, who were heads of families of those living in Aijalon and who drove out the inhabitants of Gath.
14Ahio, Shashak, Jeremoth, 15Zebadiah, Arad, Eder, 16Michael, Ishpah and Joha were the sons of Beriah.
17Zebadiah, Meshullam, Hizki, Heber, 18Ishmerai, Izliah and Jobab were the sons of Elpaal.
19Jakim, Zicri, Zabdi, 20Elienai, Zillethai, Eliel, 21Adaiah, Beraiah and Shimrath were the sons of Shimei.
22Ishpan, Eber, Eliel, 23Abdon, Zicri, Hanan, 24Hananiah, Elam, Anthothijah, 25Iphdeiah and Penuel were the sons of Shashak.
26Shamsherai, Shehariah, Athaliah, 27Jaareshiah, Elijah and Zicri were the sons of Jeroham.

28All these were heads of families, chiefs as listed in their genealogy, and they lived in Jerusalem.
29Jeiel*b* the father*c* of Gibeon lived in Gibeon. His wife's name was Maacah, 30and his firstborn son was Abdon, followed by Zur, Kish, Baal, Ner,*d* Nadab, 31Gedor, Ahio, Zeker 32and Mikloth, who was the father of Shimeah. They too lived near their relatives in Jerusalem.
33Ner was the father of Kish, Kish the father of Saul, and Saul the father of Jonathan, Malki-Shua, Abinadab and Esh-Baal.*e*
34The son of Jonathan:
Merib-Baal,*f* who was the father of Micah.
35The sons of Micah:
Pithon, Melech, Tarea and Ahaz.
36Ahaz was the father of Jehoaddah, Jehoaddah was the father of Alemeth, Azmaveth and Zimri, and Zimri was the father of Moza. 37Moza was the father of Binea; Raphah was his son, Eleasah his son and Azel his son.
38Azel had six sons, and these were their names: Azrikam, Bokeru, Ishmael, Sheariah, Obadiah and Hanan. All these were the sons of Azel.
39The sons of his brother Eshek:
Ulam his firstborn, Jeush the second son and Eliphelet the third. 40The sons of Ulam were brave warriors who could handle the bow. They had many sons and grandsons—150 in all.
All these were the descendants of Benjamin.

9 All Israel was listed in the genealogies in the book of the kings of Israel.

9:1 In 1 and 2 Chronicles, which started life as one book, about 14 different sources are mentioned from which the author gathered together his information. We hear about community genealogies, the records of various prophets, royal archives and so on. Many documents were probably lost during the fall of Jerusalem and those that did survive became vital in determining national identity.

The People in Jerusalem

The people of Judah were taken captive to Babylon because of their unfaithfulness. 2Now the first to resettle on their own property in their own towns were some Israelites, priests, Levites and temple servants.
3Those from Judah, from Benjamin, and from Ephraim and Manasseh who lived in Jerusalem were:
4Uthai son of Ammihud, the son of Omri, the son of Imri, the son of Bani, a descendant of Perez son of Judah.

d34 Or *of his brother Shomer: Rohgah*   *e37* Possibly a variant of *Jether*   *a3* Or *Gera the father of Ehud*
b29 Some Septuagint manuscripts (see also 1 Chron. 9:35); Hebrew does not have *Jeiel.*
c29 *Father* may mean *civic leader* or *military leader.*
d30 Some Septuagint manuscripts (see also 1 Chron. 9:36); Hebrew does not have *Ner.*   *e33* Also known as *Ish-Bosheth*
f34 Also known as *Mephibosheth*

⁵Of the Shilonites:

Asaiah the firstborn and his sons.

⁶Of the Zerahites:

Jeuel.

The people from Judah numbered 690.

⁷Of the Benjamites:

Sallu son of Meshullam, the son of Hodaviah, the son of Hassenuah;

⁸Ibneiah son of Jeroham; Elah son of Uzzi, the son of Micri; and Meshullam son of Shephatiah, the son of Reuel, the son of Ibnijah.

⁹The people from Benjamin, as listed in their genealogy, numbered 956. All these men were heads of their families.

¹⁰Of the priests:

Jedaiah; Jehoiarib; Jakin;

¹¹Azariah son of Hilkiah, the son of Meshullam, the son of Zadok, the son of Meraioth, the son of Ahitub, the official in charge of the house of God;

¹²Adaiah son of Jeroham, the son of Pashhur, the son of Malkijah; and Maasai son of Adiel, the son of Jahzerah, the son of Meshullam, the son of Meshillemith, the son of Immer.

¹³The priests, who were heads of families, numbered 1,760. They were able men, responsible for ministering in the house of God.

¹⁴Of the Levites:

Shemaiah son of Hasshub, the son of Azrikam, the son of Hashabiah, a Merarite; ¹⁵Bakbakkar, Heresh, Galal and Mattaniah son of Mica, the son of Zicri, the son of Asaph; ¹⁶Obadiah son of Shemaiah, the son of Galal, the son of Jeduthun; and Berekiah son of Asa, the son of Elkanah, who lived in the villages of the Netophathites.

¹⁷The gatekeepers:

Shallum, Akkub, Talmon, Ahiman and their brothers, Shallum their chief ¹⁸being stationed at the King's Gate on the east, up to the present time. These were the gatekeepers belonging to the camp of the Levites. ¹⁹Shallum son of Kore, the son of Ebiasaph, the son of Korah, and his fellow gatekeepers from his family (the Korahites) were responsible for guarding the thresholds of the Tent*a* just as their fathers had been responsible for guarding the entrance to the dwelling of the LORD. ²⁰In earlier times Phinehas son of Eleazar was in charge of the gatekeepers, and the LORD was with him. ²¹Zechariah son of Meshelemiah was the gatekeeper at the entrance to the Tent of Meeting.

²²Altogether, those chosen to be gatekeepers at the thresholds numbered 212. They were registered by genealogy in their villages. The gatekeepers had been assigned to their positions of trust by David and Samuel the seer. ²³They and their descendants were in charge of guarding the gates of the house of the LORD—the

house called the Tent. ²⁴The gatekeepers were on the four sides: east, west, north and south. ²⁵Their brothers in their villages had to come from time to time and share their duties for seven-day periods. ²⁶But the four principal gatekeepers, who were Levites, were entrusted with the responsibility for the rooms and treasuries in the house of God. ²⁷They would spend the night stationed round the house of God, because they had to guard it; and they had charge of the key for opening it each morning.

²⁸Some of them were in charge of the articles used in the temple service; they counted them when they were brought in and when they were taken out. ²⁹Others were assigned to take care of the furnishings and all the other articles of the sanctuary, as well as the flour and wine, and the oil, incense and spices. ³⁰But some of the priests took care of mixing the spices. ³¹A Levite named Mattithiah, the firstborn son of Shallum the Korahite, was entrusted with the responsibility for baking the offering bread. ³²Some of their Kohathite brothers were in charge of preparing for every Sabbath the bread set out on the table.

³³Those who were musicians, heads of Levite families, stayed in the rooms of the temple and were exempt from other duties because they were responsible for the work day and night.

³⁴All these were heads of Levite families, chiefs as listed in their genealogy, and they lived in Jerusalem.

The Genealogy of Saul

³⁵Jeiel the father*b* of Gibeon lived in Gibeon.

His wife's name was Maacah, ³⁶and his firstborn son was Abdon, followed by Zur, Kish, Baal, Ner, Nadab, ³⁷Gedor, Ahio, Zechariah and Mikloth. ³⁸Mikloth was the father of Shimeam. They too lived near their relatives in Jerusalem.

³⁹Ner was the father of Kish, Kish the father of Saul, and Saul the father of Jonathan, Malki-Shua, Abinadab and Esh-Baal.*c*

⁴⁰The son of Jonathan:

Merib-Baal,*d* who was the father of Micah.

⁴¹The sons of Micah:

Pithon, Melech, Tahrea and Ahaz.*e*

⁴²Ahaz was the father of Jadah, Jadah*f* was the father of Alemeth, Azmaveth and Zimri, and Zimri was the father of Moza. ⁴³Moza was the father of Binea; Rephaiah was his son, Eleasah his son and Azel his son.

⁴⁴Azel had six sons, and these were their names:

Azrikam, Bokeru, Ishmael, Sheariah, Obadiah and Hanan. These were the sons of Azel.

Saul Takes His Life

10 Now the Philistines fought against Israel; the Israelites fled before them, and many fell slain on Mount Gilboa. ²The Philistines pressed hard after Saul and his sons, and they killed his sons Jonathan,

---

a19 That is, the temple; also in verses 21 and 23   *b35 Father* may mean *civic leader* or *military leader.*
c39 Also known as *Ish-Bosheth*   *d40* Also known as *Mephibosheth*
e41 Vulgate and Syriac (see also Septuagint and 1 Chron. 8:35); Hebrew does not have *and Ahaz.*
f42 Some Hebrew manuscripts and Septuagint (see also 1 Chron. 8:36); most Hebrew manuscripts *Jarah, Jarah*

Abinadab and Malki-Shua. [3]The fighting grew fierce around Saul, and when the archers overtook him, they wounded him.

10:1 The Chronicler could not avoid mentioning Israel's first king, but only speaks of his failure in contrast to David's success (compare the full treatment Saul gets in 1 Samuel 9—31). The writer wanted us to see the despair at the end of Saul's rule, and the hope heralded by David, as a parallel to the gloom of exile and the joy of the return to Israel. God was seen at work in both instances, punishing unfaithfulness and then graciously restoring the country's fortunes.

---

[4]Saul said to his armour-bearer, "Draw your sword and run me through, or these uncircumcised fellows will come and abuse me."

But his armour-bearer was terrified and would not do it; so Saul took his own sword and fell on it. [5]When the armour-bearer saw that Saul was dead, he too fell on his sword and died. [6]So Saul and his three sons died, and all his house died together.

[7]When all the Israelites in the valley saw that the army had fled and that Saul and his sons had died, they abandoned their towns and fled. And the Philistines came and occupied them.

[8]The next day, when the Philistines came to strip the dead, they found Saul and his sons fallen on Mount Gilboa. [9]They stripped him and took his head and his armour, and sent messengers throughout the land of the Philistines to proclaim the news among their idols and their people. [10]They put his armour in the temple of their gods and hung up his head in the temple of Dagon.

[11]When all the inhabitants of Jabesh Gilead heard of everything the Philistines had done to Saul, [12]all their valiant men went and took the bodies of Saul and his sons and brought them to Jabesh. Then they buried their bones under the great tree in Jabesh, and they fasted seven days.

[13]Saul died because he was unfaithful to the LORD; he did not keep the word of the LORD, and even consulted a medium for guidance, [14]and did not enquire of the LORD. So the LORD put him to death and turned the kingdom over to David son of Jesse.

David Becomes King Over Israel

11 All Israel came together to David at Hebron and said, "We are your own flesh and blood. [2]In the past, even while Saul was king, you were the one who led Israel on their military campaigns. And the LORD your God said to you, 'You will shepherd my people Israel, and you will become their ruler.' "

[3]When all the elders of Israel had come to King David at Hebron, he made a compact with them at Hebron before the LORD, and they anointed David king over Israel, as the LORD had promised through Samuel.

David Conquers Jerusalem

[4]David and all the Israelites marched to Jerusalem (that is, Jebus). The Jebusites who lived there [5]said to David, "You will not get in here." Nevertheless, David captured the fortress of Zion, the City of David.

[6]David had said, "Whoever leads the attack on the Jebusites will become commander-in-chief." Joab son of Zeruiah went up first, and so he received the command.

[7]David then took up residence in the fortress, and so it was called the City of David. [8]He built up the city around it, from the supporting terraces[a] to the surrounding wall, while Joab restored the rest of the city. [9]And David became more and more powerful, because the LORD Almighty was with him.

David's Mighty Men

[10]These were the chiefs of David's mighty men—they, together with all Israel, gave his kingship strong support to extend it over the whole land, as the LORD had promised— [11]this is the list of David's mighty men:

Jashobeam,[b] a Hacmonite, was chief of the officers;[c] he raised his spear against three hundred men, whom he killed in one encounter.

[12]Next to him was Eleazar son of Dodai the Ahohite, one of the three mighty men. [13]He was with David at Pas Dammim when the Philistines gathered there for battle. At a place where there was a field full of barley, the troops fled from the Philistines. [14]But they took their stand in the middle of the field. They defended it and struck the Philistines down, and the LORD brought about a great victory.

[15]Three of the thirty chiefs came down to David to the rock at the cave of Adullam, while a band of Philistines was encamped in the Valley of Rephaim. [16]At that time David was in the stronghold, and the Philistine garrison was at Bethlehem. [17]David longed for water and said, "Oh, that someone would get me a drink of water from the well near the gate of Bethlehem!" [18]So the Three broke through the Philistine lines, drew water from the well near the gate of Bethlehem and carried it back to David. But he refused to drink it; instead, he poured it out before the LORD. [19]"God forbid that I should do this!" he said. "Should I drink the blood of these men who went at the risk of their lives?" Because they risked their lives to bring it back, David would not drink it.

Such were the exploits of the three mighty men.

[20]Abishai the brother of Joab was chief of the Three. He raised his spear against three hundred men, whom he killed, and so he became as famous as the Three. [21]He was doubly honoured above the Three and became their commander, even though he was not included among them.

[22]Benaiah son of Jehoiada was a valiant fighter from Kabzeel, who performed great exploits. He struck down two of Moab's best men. He also went down into a pit on a snowy day and killed a lion. [23]And he struck down an Egyptian who was seven and a half feet[d] tall. Although the Egyptian had a spear like a weaver's rod

---

[a]8 Or the Millo   [b]11 Possibly a variant of Jashob-Baal
[c]11 Or Thirty; some Septuagint manuscripts Three (see also 2 Sam. 23:8)   [d]23 Hebrew five cubits (about 2.3 metres)

in his hand, Benaiah went against him with a club. He snatched the spear from the Egyptian's hand and killed him with his own spear. 24Such were the exploits of Benaiah son of Jehoiada; he too was as famous as the three mighty men. 25He was held in greater honour than any of the Thirty, but he was not included among the Three. And David put him in charge of his bodyguard.

26The mighty men were:

Asahel the brother of Joab,
Elhanan son of Dodo from Bethlehem,
27Shammoth the Harorite,
Helez the Pelonite,
28Ira son of Ikkesh from Tekoa,
Abiezer from Anathoth,
29Sibbecai the Hushathite,
Ilai the Ahohite,
30Maharai the Netophathite,
Heled son of Baanah the Netophathite,
31Ithai son of Ribai from Gibeah in Benjamin,
Benaiah the Pirathonite,
32Hurai from the ravines of Gaash,
Abiel the Arbathite,
33Azmaveth the Baharumite,
Eliahba the Shaalbonite,
34the sons of Hashem the Gizonite,
Jonathan son of Shagee the Hararite,
35Ahiam son of Sacar the Hararite,
Eliphal son of Ur,
36Hepher the Mekerathite,
Ahijah the Pelonite,
37Hezro the Carmelite,
Naarai son of Ezbai,
38Joel the brother of Nathan,
Mibhar son of Hagri,
39Zelek the Ammonite,
Naharai the Berothite, the armour-bearer of Joab son of Zeruiah,
40Ira the Ithrite,
Gareb the Ithrite,
41Uriah the Hittite,
Zabad son of Ahlai,
42Adina son of Shiza the Reubenite, who was chief of the Reubenites, and the thirty with him,
43Hanan son of Maacah,
Joshaphat the Mithnite,
44Uzzia the Ashterathite,
Shama and Jeiel the sons of Hotham the Aroerite,
45Jediael son of Shimri,
his brother Joha the Tizite,
46Eliel the Mahavite,
Jeribai and Joshaviah the sons of Elnaam,
Ithmah the Moabite,
47Eliel, Obed and Jaasiel the Mezobaite.

Warriors Join David

12 These were the men who came to David at Ziklag, while he was banished from the presence of Saul son of Kish (they were among the warriors who helped him in battle; 2they were armed with bows and were able to shoot arrows or to sling stones right-handed or left-handed; they were kinsmen of Saul from the tribe of Benjamin):

3Ahiezer their chief and Joash the sons of Shemaah the Gibeathite; Jeziel and Pelet the sons of Azmaveth; Beracah, Jehu the Anathothite, 4and Ishmaiah the Gibeonite, a mighty man among the Thirty, who was a leader of the Thirty; Jeremiah, Jahaziel, Johanan, Jozabad the Gederathite, 5Eluzai, Jerimoth, Bealiah, Shemariah and Shephatiah the Haruphite; 6Elkanah, Isshiah, Azarel, Joezer and Jashobeam the Korahites; 7and Joelah and Zebadiah the sons of Jeroham from Gedor.

8Some Gadites defected to David at his stronghold in the desert. They were brave warriors, ready for battle and able to handle the shield and spear. Their faces were the faces of lions, and they were as swift as gazelles in the mountains.

9Ezer was the chief,
Obadiah the second in command, Eliab the third,
10Mishmannah the fourth, Jeremiah the fifth,
11Attai the sixth, Eliel the seventh,
12Johanan the eighth, Elzabad the ninth,
13Jeremiah the tenth and Macbannai the eleventh.

14These Gadites were army commanders; the least was a match for a hundred, and the greatest for a thousand. 15It was they who crossed the Jordan in the first month when it was overflowing all its banks, and they put to flight everyone living in the valleys, to the east and to the west.

16Other Benjamites and some men from Judah also came to David in his stronghold. 17David went out to meet them and said to them, "If you have come to me in peace, to help me, I am ready to have you unite with me. But if you have come to betray me to my enemies when my hands are free from violence, may the God of our fathers see it and judge you."

18Then the Spirit came upon Amasai, chief of the Thirty, and he said:

"We are yours, O David!
We are with you, O son of Jesse!
Success, success to you,
and success to those who help you,
for your God will help you."

So David received them and made them leaders of his raiding bands.

19Some of the men of Manasseh defected to David when he went with the Philistines to fight against Saul. (He and his men did not help the Philistines because, after consultation, their rulers sent him away. They said, "It will cost us our heads if he deserts to his master Saul.") 20When David went to Ziklag, these were the men of Manasseh who defected to him: Adnah, Jozabad, Jediael, Michael, Jozabad, Elihu and Zillethai, leaders of units of a thousand in Manasseh. 21They helped David against raiding bands, for all of them were brave warriors, and they were commanders in his army. 22Day after day men came to help David, until he had a great army, like the army of God.a

---

a22 Or *a great and mighty army*

Others Join David at Hebron

²³These are the numbers of the men armed for battle who came to David at Hebron to turn Saul's kingdom over to him, as the LORD had said:

²⁴men of Judah, carrying shield and spear — 6,800 armed for battle;

²⁵men of Simeon, warriors ready for battle — 7,100;

²⁶men of Levi — 4,600, ²⁷including Jehoiada, leader of the family of Aaron with 3,700 men, ²⁸and Zadok, a brave young warrior, with 22 officers from his family;

²⁹men of Benjamin, Saul's kinsmen — 3,000, most of whom had remained loyal to Saul's house until then;

³⁰men of Ephraim, brave warriors, famous in their own clans — 20,800;

³¹men of half the tribe of Manasseh, designated by name to come and make David king — 18,000;

³²men of Issachar, who understood the times and knew what Israel should do — 200 chiefs, with all their relatives under their command;

³³men of Zebulun, experienced soldiers prepared for battle with every type of weapon, to help David with undivided loyalty — 50,000;

³⁴men of Naphtali — 1,000 officers, together with 37,000 men carrying shields and spears;

³⁵men of Dan, ready for battle — 28,600;

³⁶men of Asher, experienced soldiers prepared for battle — 40,000;

³⁷and from east of the Jordan, men of Reuben, Gad, and the half-tribe of Manasseh, armed with every type of weapon — 120,000.

³⁸All these were fighting men who volunteered to serve in the ranks. They came to Hebron fully determined to make David king over all Israel. All the rest of the Israelites were also of one mind to make David king. ³⁹The men spent three days there with David, eating and drinking, for their families had supplied provisions for them. ⁴⁰Also, their neighbours from as far away as Issachar, Zebulun and Naphtali came bringing food on donkeys, camels, mules and oxen. There were plentiful supplies of flour, fig cakes, raisin cakes, wine, oil, cattle and sheep, for there was joy in Israel.

Bringing Back the Ark

13 David conferred with each of his officers, the commanders of thousands and commanders of hundreds. ²He then said to the whole assembly of Israel, "If it seems good to you and if it is the will of the LORD our God, let us send word far and wide to the rest of our brothers throughout the territories of Israel, and also to the priests and Levites who are with them in their towns and pasture-lands, to come and join us. ³Let us bring the ark of our God back to us, for we did not enquire of ª itᵇ during the reign of Saul." ⁴The whole assembly agreed to do this, because it seemed right to all the people.

⁵So David assembled all the Israelites, from the Shihor River in Egypt to Lebo ᶜ Hamath, to bring the ark of God from Kiriath Jearim. ⁶David and all the Israelites with him went to Baalah of Judah (Kiriath Jearim) to bring up from there the ark of God the LORD, who is enthroned between the cherubim — the ark that is called by the Name.

13:3 The ark was the most important sacred object of the Israelites and contained the tablets of stone bearing the Ten Commandments, which were the basis of God's covenant with his people in the wilderness. By bringing the ark into his new capital city, David ensured that Jerusalem became the focus for Israel's faith. The death of Uzzah in verse 9 is blamed on the irregular manner in which the ark was moved (15:13). It reminds us that God's holiness, as it was seen in the Old Testament, was a dangerous thing (compare Exodus 19:20ff).

---

⁷They moved the ark of God from Abinadab's house on a new cart, with Uzzah and Ahio guiding it. ⁸David and all the Israelites were celebrating with all their might before God, with songs and with harps, lyres, tambourines, cymbals and trumpets.

⁹When they came to the threshing-floor of Kidon, Uzzah reached out his hand to steady the ark, because the oxen stumbled. ¹⁰The LORD's anger burned against Uzzah, and he struck him down because he had put his hand on the ark. So he died there before God.

¹¹Then David was angry because the LORD's wrath had broken out against Uzzah, and to this day that place is called Perez Uzzah. ᵈ

¹²David was afraid of God that day and asked, "How can I ever bring the ark of God to me?" ¹³He did not take the ark to be with him in the City of David. Instead, he took it aside to the house of Obed-Edom the Gittite. ¹⁴The ark of God remained with the family of Obed-Edom in his house for three months, and the LORD blessed his household and everything he had.

David's House and Family

14 Now Hiram king of Tyre sent messengers to David, along with cedar logs, stonemasons and carpenters to build a palace for him. ²And David knew that the LORD had established him as king over Israel and that his kingdom had been highly exalted for the sake of his people Israel.

³In Jerusalem David took more wives and became the father of more sons and daughters. ⁴These are the names of the children born to him there: Shammua, Shobab, Nathan, Solomon, ⁵Ibhar, Elishua, Elpelet, ⁶Nogah, Nepheg, Japhia, ⁷Elishama, Beeliadaª and Eliphelet.

David Defeats the Philistines

⁸When the Philistines heard that David had been anointed king over all Israel, they went up in full force

---

ª3 Or we neglected   ᵇ3 Or him   ᶜ5 Or to the entrance to   ᵈ11 Perez Uzzah means outbreak against Uzzah.
ª7 A variant of Eliada

to search for him, but David heard about it and went out to meet them. ⁹Now the Philistines had come and raided the Valley of Rephaim; ¹⁰so David enquired of God: "Shall I go and attack the Philistines? Will you hand them over to me?"

The LORD answered him, "Go, I will hand them over to you."

¹¹So David and his men went up to Baal Perazim, and there he defeated them. He said, "As waters break out, God has broken out against my enemies by my hand." So that place was called Baal Perazim.ᵇ ¹²The Philistines had abandoned their gods there, and David gave orders to burn them in the fire.

¹³Once more the Philistines raided the valley; ¹⁴so David enquired of God again, and God answered him, "Do not go straight up, but circle round them and attack them in front of the balsam trees. ¹⁵As soon as you hear the sound of marching in the tops of the balsam trees, move out to battle, because that will mean God has gone out in front of you to strike the Philistine army." ¹⁶So David did as God commanded him, and they struck down the Philistine army, all the way from Gibeon to Gezer.

¹⁷So David's fame spread throughout every land, and the LORD made all the nations fear him.

The Ark Brought to Jerusalem

15 After David had constructed buildings for himself in the City of David, he prepared a place for the ark of God and pitched a tent for it. ²Then David said, "No-one but the Levites may carry the ark of God, because the LORD chose them to carry the ark of the LORD and to minister before him for ever."

³David assembled all Israel in Jerusalem to bring up the ark of the LORD to the place he had prepared for it. ⁴He called together the descendants of Aaron and the Levites:

⁵From the descendants of Kohath,
  Uriel the leader and 120 relatives;
⁶from the descendants of Merari,
  Asaiah the leader and 220 relatives;
⁷from the descendants of Gershon,ᵃ
  Joel the leader and 130 relatives;
⁸from the descendants of Elizaphan,
  Shemaiah the leader and 200 relatives;
⁹from the descendants of Hebron,
  Eliel the leader and 80 relatives;
¹⁰from the descendants of Uzziel,
  Amminadab the leader and 112 relatives.

¹¹Then David summoned Zadok and Abiathar the priests, and Uriel, Asaiah, Joel, Shemaiah, Eliel and Amminadab the Levites. ¹²He said to them, "You are the heads of the Levitical families; you and your fellow Levites are to consecrate yourselves and bring up the ark of the LORD, the God of Israel, to the place I have prepared for it. ¹³It was because you, the Levites, did not bring it up the first time that the LORD our God broke out in anger against us. We did not enquire of him about how to do it in the prescribed way." ¹⁴So the

priests and Levites consecrated themselves in order to bring up the ark of the LORD, the God of Israel. ¹⁵And the Levites carried the ark of God with the poles on their shoulders, as Moses had commanded in accordance with the word of the LORD.

¹⁶David told the leaders of the Levites to appoint their brothers as singers to sing joyful songs, accompanied by musical instruments: lyres, harps and cymbals.

¹⁷So the Levites appointed Heman son of Joel; from his brothers, Asaph son of Berekiah; and from their brothers the Merarites, Ethan son of Kushaiah; ¹⁸and with them their brothers next in rank: Zechariah,ᵇ Jaaziel, Shemiramoth, Jehiel, Unni, Eliab, Benaiah, Maaseiah, Mattithiah, Eliphelehu, Mikneiah, Obed-Edom and Jeiel,ᶜ the gatekeepers.

¹⁹The musicians Heman, Asaph and Ethan were to sound the bronze cymbals; ²⁰Zechariah, Aziel, Shemiramoth, Jehiel, Unni, Eliab, Maaseiah and Benaiah were to play the lyres according to alamoth,ᵈ ²¹and Mattithiah, Eliphelehu, Mikneiah, Obed-Edom, Jeiel and Azaziah were to play the harps, directing according to sheminith.ᵉ ²²Kenaniah the head Levite was in charge of the singing; that was his responsibility because he was skilful at it.

²³Berekiah and Elkanah were to be doorkeepers for the ark. ²⁴Shebaniah, Joshaphat, Nethanel, Amasai, Zechariah, Benaiah and Eliezer the priests were to blow trumpets before the ark of God. Obed-Edom and Jehiah were also to be doorkeepers for the ark.

²⁵So David and the elders of Israel and the commanders of units of a thousand went to bring up the ark of the covenant of the LORD from the house of Obed-Edom, with rejoicing. ²⁶Because God had helped the Levites who were carrying the ark of the covenant of the LORD, seven bulls and seven rams were sacrificed. ²⁷Now David was clothed in a robe of fine linen, as were all the Levites who were carrying the ark, and as were the singers, and Kenaniah, who was in charge of the singing of the choirs. David also wore a linen ephod. ²⁸So all Israel brought up the ark of the covenant of the LORD with shouts, with the sounding of rams' horns and trumpets, and of cymbals, and the playing of lyres and harps.

²⁹As the ark of the covenant of the LORD was entering the City of David, Michal daughter of Saul watched from a window. And when she saw King David dancing and celebrating, she despised him in her heart.

16 They brought the ark of God and set it inside the tent that David had pitched for it, and they presented burnt offerings and fellowship offeringsᵃ before God. ²After David had finished sacrificing the burnt offerings and fellowship offerings, he blessed the people in the name of the LORD. ³Then he gave a loaf of bread, a cake of dates and a cake of raisins to each Israelite man and woman.

⁴He appointed some of the Levites to minister before the ark of the LORD, to make petition, to give thanks, and to praise the LORD, the God of Israel: ⁵Asaph was the chief, Zechariah second, then Jeiel, Shemiramoth,

---

ᵇ11 Baal Perazim means the lord who breaks out.   ᵃ7 Hebrew Gershom, a variant of Gershon
ᵇ18 Three Hebrew manuscripts and most Septuagint manuscripts (see also verse 20 and 1 Chron. 16:5); most Hebrew manuscripts Zechariah
son and or Zechariah, Ben and   ᶜ18 Hebrew; Septuagint (see also verse 21) Jeiel and Azaziah   ᵈ20 Probably a musical term
ᵉ21 Probably a musical term   ᵃ1 Traditionally peace offerings; also in verse 2

Jehiel, Mattithiah, Eliab, Benaiah, Obed-Edom and Jeiel. They were to play the lyres and harps, Asaph was to sound the cymbals, [6]and Benaiah and Jahaziel the priests were to blow the trumpets regularly before the ark of the covenant of God.

David's Psalm of Thanks

[7]That day David first committed to Asaph and his associates this psalm of thanks to the LORD:

[8]Give thanks to the LORD, call on his name;
  make known among the nations what he has
    done.
[9]Sing to him, sing praise to him;
  tell of all his wonderful acts.
[10]Glory in his holy name;
  let the hearts of those who seek the LORD
    rejoice.
[11]Look to the LORD and his strength;
  seek his face always.
[12]Remember the wonders he has done,
  his miracles, and the judgments he pronounced,
[13]O descendants of Israel his servant,
  O sons of Jacob, his chosen ones.

[14]He is the LORD our God;
  his judgments are in all the earth.
[15]He remembers[b] his covenant for ever,
  the word he commanded, for a thousand
    generations,
[16]the covenant he made with Abraham,
  the oath he swore to Isaac.
[17]He confirmed it to Jacob as a decree,
  to Israel as an everlasting covenant:
[18]"To you I will give the land of Canaan
  as the portion you will inherit."

16:19   God did not choose Israel to be his people because they were a great and right-eous nation. At regular intervals in their his-tory they had to be reminded that it was God's grace alone, and not their own virtue, that caused their election (see Deuteronomy 7:7).

---

[19]When they were but few in number,
  few indeed, and strangers in it,
[20]they[c] wandered from nation to nation,
  from one kingdom to another.
[21]He allowed no man to oppress them;
  for their sake he rebuked kings:
[22]"Do not touch my anointed ones;
  do my prophets no harm."

[23]Sing to the LORD, all the earth;
  proclaim his salvation day after day.

[24]Declare his glory among the nations,
  his marvellous deeds among all peoples.
[25]For great is the LORD and most worthy of praise;
  he is to be feared above all gods.
[26]For all the gods of the nations are idols,
  but the LORD made the heavens.
[27]Splendour and majesty are before him;
  strength and joy in his dwelling-place.
[28]Ascribe to the LORD, O families of nations,
  ascribe to the LORD glory and strength,
[29] ascribe to the LORD the glory due to his name.
  Bring an offering and come before him;
  worship the LORD in the splendour of his[d]
    holiness.
[30]Tremble before him, all the earth!
  The world is firmly established; it cannot be
    moved.
[31]Let the heavens rejoice, let the earth be glad;
  let them say among the nations, "The LORD
    reigns!"
[32]Let the sea resound, and all that is in it;
  let the fields be jubilant, and everything in
    them!
[33]Then the trees of the forest will sing,
  they will sing for joy before the LORD,
  for he comes to judge the earth.

[34]Give thanks to the LORD, for he is good;
  his love endures for ever.
[35]Cry out, "Save us, O God our Saviour;
  gather us and deliver us from the nations,
  that we may give thanks to your holy name,
  that we may glory in your praise."
[36]Praise be to the LORD, the God of Israel,
  from everlasting to everlasting.

Then all the people said "Amen" and "Praise the LORD."

16:39   It was not until Solomon's time that worship was centralized in the temple of Jerusalem. Before his day two tabernacles were the focus for sacrifices. The new taber-nacle built by David housed the ark of the covenant in Jerusalem, but the old taberna-cle still stood at Gibeon, five miles away, and it is to this that the passage refers.

---

[37]David left Asaph and his associates before the ark of the covenant of the LORD to minister there regularly, according to each day's requirements. [38]He also left Obed-Edom and his sixty-eight associates to minister with them. Obed-Edom son of Jeduthun, and also Hosah, were gatekeepers.

[39]David left Zadok the priest and his fellow priests before the tabernacle of the LORD at the high place in Gibeon [40]to present burnt offerings to the LORD on the altar of burnt offering regularly, morning and evening,

---

[b]15 Some Septuagint manuscripts (see also Psalm 105:8); Hebrew *Remember*
[c]18–20 One Hebrew manuscript, Septuagint and Vulgate (see also Psalm 105:12); most Hebrew manuscripts *inherit,* / [19]*though you are but few in number,* / *few indeed, and strangers in it."* / [20]*They*   [d]29 Or LORD *with the splendour of*

in accordance with everything written in the Law of the LORD, which he had given Israel. ⁴¹With them were Heman and Jeduthun and the rest of those chosen and designated by name to give thanks to the LORD, "for his love endures for ever." ⁴²Heman and Jeduthun were responsible for the sounding of the trumpets and cymbals and for the playing of the other instruments for sacred song. The sons of Jeduthun were stationed at the gate.

⁴³Then all the people left, each for his own home, and David returned home to bless his family.

God's Promise to David

17 After David was settled in his palace, he said to Nathan the prophet, "Here I am, living in a palace of cedar, while the ark of the covenant of the LORD is under a tent."

²Nathan replied to David, "Whatever you have in mind, do it, for God is with you."

³That night the word of God came to Nathan, saying:

17:3 This is the Chronicler's version of the great covenant that God made with David to establish his throne forever. The original account can be found in 2 Samuel 7, and the same theme forms the basis for Psalm 89, where it is said that God will bless David's line regardless of the wicked behaviour of its kings! 1 Chronicles 28:9 makes it clear, however, that Solomon must seek God with devotion to enjoy this blessing.

---

⁴"Go and tell my servant David, 'This is what the LORD says: You are not the one to build me a house to dwell in. ⁵I have not dwelt in a house from the day I brought Israel up out of Egypt to this day. I have moved from one tent site to another, from one dwelling-place to another. ⁶Wherever I have moved with all the Israelites, did I ever say to any of their leadersᵃ whom I commanded to shepherd my people, "Why have you not built me a house of cedar?" '

⁷"Now then, tell my servant David, 'This is what the LORD Almighty says: I took you from the pasture and from following the flock, to be ruler over my people Israel. ⁸I have been with you wherever you have gone, and I have cut off all your enemies from before you. Now I will make your name like the names of the greatest men of the earth. ⁹And I will provide a place for my people Israel and will plant them so that they can have a home of their own and no longer be disturbed. Wicked people will not oppress them any more, as they did at the beginning ¹⁰and have done ever since the time I appointed leaders over my people Israel. I will also subdue all your enemies.

" 'I declare to you that the LORD will build a house for you: ¹¹When your days are over and you go to be with your fathers, I will raise up your offspring to succeed you, one of your own sons,

and I will establish his kingdom. ¹²He is the one who will build a house for me, and I will establish his throne for ever. ¹³I will be his father, and he will be my son. I will never take my love away from him, as I took it away from your predecessor. ¹⁴I will set him over my house and my kingdom for ever; his throne will be established for ever.' "

¹⁵Nathan reported to David all the words of this entire revelation.

David's Prayer

¹⁶Then King David went in and sat before the LORD, and he said:

"Who am I, O LORD God, and what is my family, that you have brought me this far? ¹⁷And as if this were not enough in your sight, O God, you have spoken about the future of the house of your servant. You have looked on me as though I were the most exalted of men, O LORD God.

¹⁸"What more can David say to you for honouring your servant? For you know your servant, ¹⁹O LORD. For the sake of your servant and according to your will, you have done this great thing and made known all these great promises.

²⁰"There is no-one like you, O LORD, and there is no God but you, as we have heard with our own ears. ²¹And who is like your people Israel—the one nation on earth whose God went out to redeem a people for himself, and to make a name for yourself, and to perform great and awesome wonders by driving out nations from before your people, whom you redeemed from Egypt? ²²You made your people Israel your very own for ever, and you, O LORD, have become their God.

²³"And now, LORD, let the promise you have made concerning your servant and his house be established for ever. Do as you promised, ²⁴so that it will be established and that your name will be great for ever. Then men will say, 'The LORD Almighty, the God over Israel, is Israel's God!' And the house of your servant David will be established before you.

²⁵"You, my God, have revealed to your servant that you will build a house for him. So your servant has found courage to pray to you. ²⁶O LORD, you are God! You have promised these good things to your servant. ²⁷Now you have been pleased to bless the house of your servant, that it may continue for ever in your sight; for you, O LORD, have blessed it, and it will be blessed for ever."

David's Victories

18 In the course of time, David defeated the Philistines and subdued them, and he took Gath and its surrounding villages from the control of the Philistines.

²David also defeated the Moabites, and they became subject to him and brought tribute.

³Moreover, David fought Hadadezer king of Zobah, as far as Hamath, when he went to establish his control

---

ᵃ 6 Traditionally *judges*; also in verse 10

along the Euphrates River. ⁴David captured a thousand of his chariots, seven thousand charioteers and twenty thousand foot soldiers. He hamstrung all but a hundred of the chariot horses.

⁵When the Arameans of Damascus came to help Hadadezer king of Zobah, David struck down twenty-two thousand of them. ⁶He put garrisons in the Aramean kingdom of Damascus, and the Arameans became subject to him and brought tribute. The LORD gave David victory everywhere he went.

⁷David took the gold shields carried by the officers of Hadadezer and brought them to Jerusalem. ⁸From Tebah[a] and Cun, towns that belonged to Hadadezer, David took a great quantity of bronze, which Solomon used to make the bronze Sea, the pillars and various bronze articles.

⁹When Tou king of Hamath heard that David had defeated the entire army of Hadadezer king of Zobah, ¹⁰he sent his son Hadoram to King David to greet him and congratulate him on his victory in battle over Hadadezer, who had been at war with Tou. Hadoram brought all kinds of articles of gold and silver and bronze.

¹¹King David dedicated these articles to the LORD, as he had done with the silver and gold he had taken from all these nations: Edom and Moab, the Ammonites and the Philistines, and Amalek.

¹²Abishai son of Zeruiah struck down eighteen thousand Edomites in the Valley of Salt. ¹³He put garrisons in Edom, and all the Edomites became subject to David. The LORD gave David victory everywhere he went.

David's Officials

¹⁴David reigned over all Israel, doing what was just and right for all his people. ¹⁵Joab son of Zeruiah was over the army; Jehoshaphat son of Ahilud was recorder; ¹⁶Zadok son of Ahitub and Ahimelech[b] son of Abiathar were priests; Shavsha was secretary; ¹⁷Benaiah son of Jehoiada was over the Kerethites and Pelethites; and David's sons were chief officials at the king's side.

The Battle Against the Ammonites

19 In the course of time, Nahash king of the Ammonites died, and his son succeeded him as king. ²David thought, "I will show kindness to Hanun son of Nahash, because his father showed kindness to me." So David sent a delegation to express his sympathy to Hanun concerning his father.

When David's men came to Hanun in the land of the Ammonites to express sympathy to him, ³the Ammonite nobles said to Hanun, "Do you think David is honouring your father by sending men to you to express sympathy? Haven't his men come to you to explore and spy out the country and overthrow it?" ⁴So Hanun seized David's men, shaved them, cut off their garments in the middle at the buttocks, and sent them away.

⁵When someone came and told David about the men, he sent messengers to meet them, for they were greatly humiliated. The king said, "Stay at Jericho till your beards have grown, and then come back."

⁶When the Ammonites realised that they had become an offence to David's nostrils, Hanun and the Ammonites sent a thousand talents[a] of silver to hire chariots and charioteers from Aram Naharaim,[b] Aram Maacah and Zobah. ⁷They hired thirty-two thousand chariots and charioteers, as well as the king of Maacah with his troops, who came and camped near Medeba, while the Ammonites were mustered from their towns and moved out for battle.

⁸On hearing this, David sent Joab out with the entire army of fighting men. ⁹The Ammonites came out and drew up in battle formation at the entrance to their city, while the kings who had come were by themselves in the open country.

¹⁰Joab saw that there were battle lines in front of him and behind him; so he selected some of the best troops in Israel and deployed them against the Arameans. ¹¹He put the rest of the men under the command of Abishai his brother, and they were deployed against the Ammonites. ¹²Joab said, "If the Arameans are too strong for me, then you are to rescue me; but if the Ammonites are too strong for you, then I will rescue you. ¹³Be strong and let us fight bravely for our people and the cities of our God. The LORD will do what is good in his sight."

¹⁴Then Joab and the troops with him advanced to fight the Arameans, and they fled before him. ¹⁵When the Ammonites saw that the Arameans were fleeing, they too fled before his brother Abishai and went inside the city. So Joab went back to Jerusalem.

¹⁶After the Arameans saw that they had been routed by Israel, they sent messengers and had Arameans brought from beyond the River,[c] with Shophach the commander of Hadadezer's army leading them.

¹⁷When David was told of this, he gathered all Israel and crossed the Jordan; he advanced against them and formed his battle lines opposite them. David formed his lines to meet the Arameans in battle, and they fought against him. ¹⁸But they fled before Israel, and David killed seven thousand of their charioteers and forty thousand of their foot soldiers. He also killed Shophach the commander of their army.

¹⁹When the vassals of Hadadezer saw that they had been defeated by Israel, they made peace with David and became subject to him.

So the Arameans were not willing to help the Ammonites any more.

The Capture of Rabbah

20 In the spring, at the time when kings go off to war, Joab led out the armed forces. He laid waste the land of the Ammonites and went to Rabbah and besieged it, but David remained in Jerusalem. Joab attacked Rabbah and left it in ruins. ²David took the crown from the head of their king[a]—its weight was

a 8 Hebrew *Tibhath*, a variant of *Tebah*
b 16 Some Hebrew manuscripts, Vulgate and Syriac (see also 2 Sam. 8:17); most Hebrew manuscripts *Abimelech*
a 6 That is, about 34 tons (about 34 metric tons)   *b* 6 That is, North-west Mesopotamia   *c* 16 That is, the Euphrates
a 2 Or *of Milcom*, that is, Molech

found to be a talent^b of gold, and it was set with precious stones—and it was placed on David's head. He took a great quantity of plunder from the city ³and brought out the people who were there, consigning them to labour with saws and with iron picks and axes. David did this to all the Ammonite towns. Then David and his entire army returned to Jerusalem.

War With the Philistines

⁴In the course of time, war broke out with the Philistines, at Gezer. At that time Sibbecai the Hushathite killed Sippai, one of the descendants of the Rephaites, and the Philistines were subjugated.

⁵In another battle with the Philistines, Elhanan son of Jair killed Lahmi the brother of Goliath the Gittite, who had a spear with a shaft like a weaver's rod.

⁶In still another battle, which took place at Gath, there was a huge man with six fingers on each hand and six toes on each foot—twenty-four in all. He also was descended from Rapha. ⁷When he taunted Israel, Jonathan son of Shimea, David's brother, killed him.

⁸These were descendants of Rapha in Gath, and they fell at the hands of David and his men.

David Numbers the Fighting Men

21 Satan rose up against Israel and incited David to take a census of Israel. ²So David said to Joab and the commanders of the troops, "Go and count the Israelites from Beersheba to Dan. Then report back to me so that I may know how many there are."

21:1 Satan is only mentioned three times in the Old Testament. The name means "the one who accuses". He played this very role against Joshua the high priest (Zechariah 3), and in Job 1,2 he is among the angels accusing Job before God. In 2 Samuel 24, which was the source for the passage here, it was the anger of the Lord that incited David to take a census. Here the Chronicler chose to replace this idea with that of Satan, and we can begin to see the development of Satan into the more familiar character of the New Testament.

---

³But Joab replied, "May the LORD multiply his troops a hundred times over. My lord the king, are they not all my lord's subjects? Why does my lord want to do this? Why should he bring guilt on Israel?"

⁴The king's word, however, overruled Joab; so Joab left and went throughout Israel and then came back to Jerusalem. ⁵Joab reported the number of the fighting men to David: In all Israel there were one million one hundred thousand men who could handle a sword, including four hundred and seventy thousand in Judah.

⁶But Joab did not include Levi and Benjamin in the numbering, because the king's command was

repulsive to him. ⁷This command was also evil in the sight of God; so he punished Israel.

⁸Then David said to God, "I have sinned greatly by doing this. Now, I beg you, take away the guilt of your servant. I have done a very foolish thing."

⁹The LORD said to Gad, David's seer, ¹⁰"Go and tell David, 'This is what the LORD says: I am giving you three options. Choose one of them for me to carry out against you.' "

¹¹So Gad went to David and said to him, "This is what the LORD says: 'Take your choice: ¹²three years of famine, three months of being swept away^a before your enemies, with their swords overtaking you, or three days of the sword of the LORD—days of plague in the land, with the angel of the LORD ravaging every part of Israel.' Now then, decide how I should answer the one who sent me."

¹³David said to Gad, "I am in deep distress. Let me fall into the hands of the LORD, for his mercy is very great; but do not let me fall into the hands of men."

¹⁴So the LORD sent a plague on Israel, and seventy thousand men of Israel fell dead. ¹⁵And God sent an angel to destroy Jerusalem. But as the angel was doing so, the LORD saw it and was grieved because of the calamity and said to the angel who was destroying the people, "Enough! Withdraw your hand." The angel of the LORD was then standing at the threshing-floor of Araunah^b the Jebusite.

¹⁶David looked up and saw the angel of the LORD standing between heaven and earth, with a drawn sword in his hand extended over Jerusalem. Then David and the elders, clothed in sackcloth, fell face down.

¹⁷David said to God, "Was it not I who ordered the fighting men to be counted? I am the one who has sinned and done wrong. These are but sheep. What have they done? O LORD my God, let your hand fall upon me and my family, but do not let this plague remain on your people."

¹⁸Then the angel of the LORD ordered Gad to tell David to go up and build an altar to the LORD on the threshing-floor of Araunah the Jebusite. ¹⁹So David went up in obedience to the word that Gad had spoken in the name of the LORD.

²⁰While Araunah was threshing wheat, he turned and saw the angel; his four sons who were with him hid themselves. ²¹Then David approached, and when Araunah looked and saw him, he left the threshing-floor and bowed down before David with his face to the ground.

²²David said to him, "Let me have the site of your threshing-floor so that I can build an altar to the LORD, that the plague on the people may be stopped. Sell it to me at the full price."

²³Araunah said to David, "Take it! Let my lord the king do whatever pleases him. Look, I will give the oxen for the burnt offerings, the threshing-sledges for the wood, and the wheat for the grain offering. I will give all this."

²⁴But King David replied to Araunah, "No, I insist on paying the full price. I will not take for the LORD

---

^{b}2 That is, about 75 pounds (about 34 kilograms) ^{a}12 Hebrew; Septuagint and Vulgate (see also 2 Sam. 24:13) of fleeing
^{b}15 Hebrew Ornan, a variant of Araunah; also in verses 18–28

what is yours, or sacrifice a burnt offering that costs me nothing."

²⁵So David paid Araunah six hundred shekels[c] of gold for the site. ²⁶David built an altar to the LORD there and sacrificed burnt offerings and fellowship offerings.[d] He called on the LORD, and the LORD answered him with fire from heaven on the altar of burnt offering.

²⁷Then the LORD spoke to the angel, and he put his sword back into its sheath. ²⁸At that time, when David saw that the LORD had answered him on the threshing-floor of Araunah the Jebusite, he offered sacrifices there. ²⁹The tabernacle of the LORD, which Moses had made in the desert, and the altar of burnt offering were at that time on the high place at Gibeon. ³⁰But David could not go before it to enquire of God, because he was afraid of the sword of the angel of the LORD.

22 Then David said, "The house of the LORD God is to be here, and also the altar of burnt offering for Israel."

Preparations for the Temple

²So David gave orders to assemble the aliens living in Israel, and from among them he appointed stone-cutters to prepare dressed stone for building the house of God. ³He provided a large amount of iron to make nails for the doors of the gateways and for the fittings, and more bronze than could be weighed. ⁴He also provided more cedar logs than could be counted, for the Sidonians and Tyrians had brought large numbers of them to David.

⁵David said, "My son Solomon is young and inexperienced, and the house to be built for the LORD should be of great magnificence and fame and splendour in the sight of all the nations. Therefore I will make preparations for it." So David made extensive preparations before his death.

⁶Then he called for his son Solomon and charged him to build a house for the LORD, the God of Israel. ⁷David said to Solomon: "My son, I had it in my heart to build a house for the Name of the LORD my God. ⁸But this word of the LORD came to me: 'You have shed much blood and have fought many wars. You are not to build a house for my Name, because you have shed much blood on the earth in my sight. ⁹But you will have a son who will be a man of peace and rest, and I will give him rest from all his enemies on every side. His name will be Solomon,[a] and I will grant Israel peace and quiet during his reign. ¹⁰He is the one who will build a house for my Name. He will be my son, and I will be his father. And I will establish the throne of his kingdom over Israel for ever.'

¹¹"Now, my son, the LORD be with you, and may you have success and build the house of the LORD your God, as he said you would. ¹²May the LORD give you discretion and understanding when he puts you in command over Israel, so that you may keep the law of the LORD your God. ¹³Then you will have success if you are careful to observe the decrees and laws that the LORD gave

to Moses for Israel. Be strong and courageous. Do not be afraid or discouraged.

¹⁴"I have taken great pains to provide for the temple of the LORD a hundred thousand talents[b] of gold, a million talents[c] of silver, quantities of bronze and iron too great to be weighed, and wood and stone. And you may add to them. ¹⁵You have many workmen: stone-cutters, masons and carpenters, as well as men skilled in every kind of work ¹⁶in gold and silver, bronze and iron—craftsmen beyond number. Now begin the work, and the LORD be with you."

¹⁷Then David ordered all the leaders of Israel to help his son Solomon. ¹⁸He said to them, "Is not the LORD your God with you? And has he not granted you rest on every side? For he has handed the inhabitants of the land over to me, and the land is subject to the LORD and to his people. ¹⁹Now devote your heart and soul to seeking the LORD your God. Begin to build the sanctuary of the LORD God, so that you may bring the ark of the covenant of the LORD and the sacred articles belonging to God into the temple that will be built for the Name of the LORD."

23:1 In accordance with the Chronicler's desire to present David and Solomon's reigns as a smooth unit, he did not mention here the many dynastic battles that marred the later years of David's rule and the early years of Solomon's. (See, for example, the rebellions of Absalom in 2 Samuel 13 and of Adonijah in 1 Kings 1.) At a time when peace and unity needed to be preached, the writer realized that some affairs of the past were best forgotten.

The Levites

23 When David was old and full of years, he made his son Solomon king over Israel.

²He also gathered together all the leaders of Israel, as well as the priests and Levites. ³The Levites thirty years old or more were counted, and the total number of men was thirty-eight thousand. ⁴David said, "Of these, twenty-four thousand are to supervise the work of the temple of the LORD and six thousand are to be officials and judges. ⁵Four thousand are to be gatekeepers and four thousand are to praise the LORD with the musical instruments I have provided for that purpose."

⁶David divided the Levites into groups corresponding to the sons of Levi: Gershon, Kohath and Merari.

Gershonites

⁷Belonging to the Gershonites:
    Ladan and Shimei.
⁸The sons of Ladan:
    Jehiel the first, Zetham and Joel—three in all.
⁹The sons of Shimei:
    Shelomoth, Haziel and Haran—three in all.

---

c25 That is, about 15 pounds (about 7 kilograms)   d26 Traditionally peace offerings
a9 Solomon sounds like and may be derived from the Hebrew for peace.   b14 That is, about 3,395 tons (about 3,450 metric tons)
c14 That is, about 33,950 tons (about 34,500 metric tons)

23:6 Once the temple had been completed and the ark permanently laid to rest in its holiest place there was need for a reorganization of the religious duties of the Levites. Since Moses' day they had been responsible for looking after the tabernacle, but now this portable tent had been replaced by a fixed building the Levites had to adapt to meet the fresh demands of the new situation. Chapters 23 — 26 describe the new jobs they undertook.

These were the heads of the families of Ladan.
[10]And the sons of Shimei:
Jahath, Ziza,[a] Jeush and Beriah.
These were the sons of Shimei—four in all.
[11]Jahath was the first and Ziza the second, but Jeush and Beriah did not have many sons; so they were counted as one family with one assignment.

Kohathites

[12]The sons of Kohath:
Amram, Izhar, Hebron and Uzziel—four in all.
[13]The sons of Amram:
Aaron and Moses.
Aaron was set apart, he and his descendants for ever, to consecrate the most holy things, to offer sacrifices before the LORD, to minister before him and to pronounce blessings in his name for ever. [14]The sons of Moses the man of God were counted as part of the tribe of Levi.
[15]The sons of Moses:
Gershom and Eliezer.
[16]The descendants of Gershom:
Shubael was the first.
[17]The descendants of Eliezer:
Rehabiah was the first.
Eliezer had no other sons, but the sons of Rehabiah were very numerous.
[18]The sons of Izhar:
Shelomith was the first.
[19]The sons of Hebron:
Jeriah the first, Amariah the second, Jahaziel the third and Jekameam the fourth.
[20]The sons of Uzziel:
Micah the first and Isshiah the second.

Merarites

[21]The sons of Merari:
Mahli and Mushi.
The sons of Mahli:
Eleazar and Kish.
[22]Eleazar died without having sons: he had only daughters. Their cousins, the sons of Kish, married them.

[23]The sons of Mushi:
Mahli, Eder and Jerimoth—three in all.

[24]These were the descendants of Levi by their families—the heads of families as they were registered under their names and counted individually, that is, the workers twenty years old or more who served in the temple of the LORD. [25]For David had said, "Since the LORD, the God of Israel, has granted rest to his people and has come to dwell in Jerusalem for ever, [26]the Levites no longer need to carry the tabernacle or any of the articles used in its service." [27]According to the last instructions of David, the Levites were counted from those twenty years old or more.

[28]The duty of the Levites was to help Aaron's descendants in the service of the temple of the LORD: to be in charge of the courtyards, the side rooms, the purification of all sacred things and the performance of other duties at the house of God. [29]They were in charge of the bread set out on the table, the flour for the grain offerings, the unleavened wafers, the baking and the mixing, and all measurements of quantity and size. [30]They were also to stand every morning to thank and praise the LORD. They were to do the same in the evening [31]and whenever burnt offerings were presented to the LORD on Sabbaths at New Moon festivals and at appointed feasts. They were to serve before the LORD regularly in the proper number and in the way prescribed for them.

[32]And so the Levites carried out their responsibilities for the Tent of Meeting, for the Holy Place and, under their brothers the descendants of Aaron, for the service of the temple of the LORD.

The Divisions of Priests

24 These were the divisions of the sons of Aaron:
The sons of Aaron were Nadab, Abihu, Eleazar and Ithamar. [2]But Nadab and Abihu died before their father did, and they had no sons; so Eleazar and Ithamar served as the priests. [3]With the help of Zadok a descendant of Eleazar and Ahimelech a descendant of Ithamar, David separated them into divisions for their appointed order of ministering. [4]A larger number of leaders were found among Eleazar's descendants than among Ithamar's, and they were divided accordingly: sixteen heads of families from Eleazar's descendants and eight heads of families from Ithamar's descendants. [5]They divided them impartially by drawing lots, for there were officials of the sanctuary and officials of God among the descendants of both Eleazar and Ithamar.

[6]The scribe Shemaiah son of Nethanel, a Levite, recorded their names in the presence of the king and of the officials: Zadok the priest, Ahimelech son of Abiathar and the heads of families of the priests and of the Levites—one family being taken from Eleazar and then one from Ithamar.

[7]The first lot fell to Jehoiarib,
the second to Jedaiah,
[8]the third to Harim,
the fourth to Seorim,

[a] 10 One Hebrew manuscript, Septuagint and Vulgate (see also verse 11); most Hebrew manuscripts Zina

⁹the fifth to Malkijah,
  the sixth to Mijamin,
¹⁰the seventh to Hakkoz,
  the eighth to Abijah,
¹¹the ninth to Jeshua,
  the tenth to Shecaniah,
¹²the eleventh to Eliashib,
  the twelfth to Jakim,
¹³the thirteenth to Huppah,
  the fourteenth to Jeshebeab,
¹⁴the fifteenth to Bilgah,
  the sixteenth to Immer,
¹⁵the seventeenth to Hezir,
  the eighteenth to Happizzez,
¹⁶the nineteenth to Pethahiah,
  the twentieth to Jehezkel,
¹⁷the twenty-first to Jakin,
  the twenty-second to Gamul,
¹⁸the twenty-third to Delaiah
  and the twenty-fourth to Maaziah.

¹⁹This was their appointed order of ministering when they entered the temple of the LORD, according to the regulations prescribed for them by their forefather Aaron, as the LORD, the God of Israel, had commanded him.

The Rest of the Levites

²⁰As for the rest of the descendants of Levi:
  from the sons of Amram: Shubael;
  from the sons of Shubael: Jehdeiah.
  ²¹As for Rehabiah, from his sons:
  Isshiah was the first.
²²From the Izharites: Shelomoth;
  from the sons of Shelomoth: Jahath.
²³The sons of Hebron: Jeriah the first,ᵃ Amariah the second, Jahaziel the third and Jekameam the fourth.
²⁴The son of Uzziel: Micah;
  from the sons of Micah: Shamir.
  ²⁵The brother of Micah: Isshiah;
  from the sons of Isshiah: Zechariah.
²⁶The sons of Merari: Mahli and Mushi.
  The son of Jaaziah: Beno.
²⁷The sons of Merari:
  from Jaaziah: Beno, Shoham, Zaccur and Ibri.
²⁸From Mahli: Eleazar, who had no sons.
²⁹From Kish: the son of Kish:
  Jerahmeel.
³⁰And the sons of Mushi: Mahli, Eder and Jerimoth.

These were the Levites, according to their families. ³¹They also cast lots, just as their brothers the descendants of Aaron did, in the presence of King David and of Zadok, Ahimelech, and the heads of families of the priests and of the Levites. The families of the oldest brother were treated the same as those of the youngest.

The Singers

25 David, together with the commanders of the army, set apart some of the sons of Asaph, Heman and Jeduthun for the ministry of prophesying, accompanied by harps, lyres and cymbals. Here is the list of the men who performed this service:

²From the sons of Asaph:
  Zaccur, Joseph, Nethaniah and Asarelah. The sons of Asaph were under the supervision of Asaph, who prophesied under the king's supervision.
³As for Jeduthun, from his sons:
  Gedaliah, Zeri, Jeshaiah, Shimei,ᵃ Hashabiah and Mattithiah, six in all, under the supervision of their father Jeduthun, who prophesied, using the harp in thanking and praising the LORD.
⁴As for Heman, from his sons:
  Bukkiah, Mattaniah, Uzziel, Shubael and Jerimoth; Hananiah, Hanani, Eliathah, Giddalti and Romamti-Ezer; Joshbekashah, Mallothi, Hothir and Mahazioth. ⁵All these were sons of Heman the king's seer. They were given to him through the promises of God to exalt him.ᵇ God gave Heman fourteen sons and three daughters.

⁶All these men were under the supervision of their fathers for the music of the temple of the LORD, with cymbals, lyres and harps, for the ministry at the house of God. Asaph, Jeduthun and Heman were under the supervision of the king. ⁷Along with their relatives — all of them trained and skilled in music for the LORD — they numbered 288. ⁸Young and old alike, teacher as well as student, cast lots for their duties.

⁹The first lot, which was for Asaph, fell to
  Joseph,
    his sons and relatives,ᶜ   12ᵈ
  the second to Gedaliah,
    he and his relatives and sons,   12
¹⁰the third to Zaccur,
    his sons and relatives,   12
¹¹the fourth to Izri,ᵉ
    his sons and relatives,   12
¹²the fifth to Nethaniah,
    his sons and relatives,   12
¹³the sixth to Bukkiah,
    his sons and relatives,   12
¹⁴the seventh to Jesarelah,ᶠ
    his sons and relatives,   12
¹⁵the eighth to Jeshaiah,
    his sons and relatives,   12
¹⁶the ninth to Mattaniah,
    his sons and relatives,   12
¹⁷the tenth to Shimei,
    his sons and relatives,   12
¹⁸the eleventh to Azarel,ᵍ
    his sons and relatives,   12

ᵃ23 Two Hebrew manuscripts and some Septuagint manuscripts (see also 1 Chron. 23:19); most Hebrew manuscripts *The sons of Jeriah:*
ᵃ3 One Hebrew manuscript and some Septuagint manuscripts (see also verse 17); most Hebrew manuscripts do not have *Shimei.*
ᵇ5 Hebrew *exalt the horn*   ᶜ9 See Septuagint; Hebrew does not have *his sons and relatives.*
ᵈ9 See the total in verse 7; Hebrew does not have *twelve.*   ᵉ11 A variant of *Zeri*   ᶠ14 A variant of *Asarelah*
ᵍ18 A variant of *Uzziel*

¹⁹the twelfth to Hashabiah,
 his sons and relatives,   12
²⁰the thirteenth to Shubael,
 his sons and relatives,   12
²¹the fourteenth to Mattithiah,
 his sons and relatives,   12
²²the fifteenth to Jerimoth,
 his sons and relatives,   12
²³the sixteenth to Hananiah,
 his sons and relatives,   12
²⁴the seventeenth to Joshbekashah,
 his sons and relatives,   12
²⁵the eighteenth to Hanani,
 his sons and relatives,   12
²⁶the nineteenth to Mallothi,
 his sons and relatives,   12
²⁷the twentieth to Eliathah,
 his sons and relatives,   12
²⁸the twenty-first to Hothir,
 his sons and relatives,   12
²⁹the twenty-second to Giddalti,
 his sons and relatives,   12
³⁰the twenty-third to Mahazioth,
 his sons and relatives,   12
³¹the twenty-fourth to Romamti-Ezer,
 his sons and relatives.   12

The Gatekeepers

26 The divisions of the gatekeepers:

From the Korahites: Meshelemiah son of Kore, one of the sons of Asaph.

²Meshelemiah had sons:
 Zechariah the firstborn,
 Jediael the second,
 Zebadiah the third,
 Jathniel the fourth,
 ³Elam the fifth,
 Jehohanan the sixth
 and Eliehoenai the seventh.
⁴Obed-Edom also had sons:
 Shemaiah the firstborn,
 Jehozabad the second,
 Joah the third,
 Sacar the fourth,
 Nethanel the fifth,
 ⁵Ammiel the sixth,
 Issachar the seventh
 and Peullethai the eighth.
 (For God had blessed Obed-Edom.)

⁶His son Shemaiah also had sons, who were leaders in their father's family because they were very capable men. ⁷The sons of Shemaiah: Othni, Rephael, Obed and Elzabad; his relatives Elihu and Semakiah were also able men. ⁸All these were descendants of Obed-Edom; they and their sons and their relatives were capable men with the strength to do the work — descendants of Obed-Edom, 62 in all.
⁹Meshelemiah had sons and relatives, who were able men — 18 in all.

¹⁰Hosah the Merarite had sons: Shimri the first (although he was not the firstborn, his father had appointed him the first), ¹¹Hilkiah the second, Tabaliah the third and Zechariah the fourth. The sons and relatives of Hosah were 13 in all.

¹²These divisions of the gatekeepers, through their chief men, had duties for ministering in the temple of the Lᴏʀᴅ, just as their relatives had. ¹³Lots were cast for each gate, according to their families, young and old alike.

¹⁴The lot for the East Gate fell to Shelemiah.ᵃ Then lots were cast for his son Zechariah, a wise counsellor, and the lot for the North Gate fell to him. ¹⁵The lot for the South Gate fell to Obed-Edom, and the lot for the storehouse fell to his sons. ¹⁶The lots for the West Gate and the Shalleketh Gate on the upper road fell to Shuppim and Hosah.

Guard was alongside guard: ¹⁷There were six Levites a day on the east, four a day on the north, four a day on the south and two at a time at the storehouse. ¹⁸As for the court to the west, there were four at the road and two at the court itself.

¹⁹These were the divisions of the gatekeepers who were descendants of Korah and Merari.

The Treasurers and Other Officials

²⁰Their fellow Levites wereᵇ in charge of the treasuries of the house of God and the treasuries for the dedicated things.

²¹The descendants of Ladan, who were Gershonites through Ladan and who were heads of families belonging to Ladan the Gershonite, were Jehieli, ²²the sons of Jehieli, Zetham and his brother Joel. They were in charge of the treasuries of the temple of the Lᴏʀᴅ.

²³From the Amramites, the Izharites, the Hebronites and the Uzzielites:

²⁴Shubael, a descendant of Gershom son of Moses, was the officer in charge of the treasuries. ²⁵His relatives through Eliezer: Rehabiah his son, Jeshaiah his son, Joram his son, Zicri his son and Shelomith his son. ²⁶Shelomith and his relatives were in charge of all the treasuries for the things dedicated by King David, by the heads of families who were the commanders of thousands and commanders of hundreds, and by the other army commanders. ²⁷Some of the plunder taken in battle they dedicated for the repair of the temple of the Lᴏʀᴅ. ²⁸And everything dedicated by Samuel the seer and by Saul son of Kish, Abner son of Ner and Joab son of Zeruiah, and all the other dedicated things were in the care of Shelomith and his relatives.

²⁹From the Izharites: Kenaniah and his sons were assigned duties away from the temple, as officials and judges over Israel.

³⁰From the Hebronites: Hashabiah and his relatives — seventeen hundred able men — were responsible in Israel west of the Jordan for all the work of the Lᴏʀᴅ and for the king's service. ³¹As for the Hebronites, Jeriah was their

---

ᵃ 14 A variant of *Meshelemiah*   ᵇ 20 Septuagint; Hebrew *As for the Levites, Ahijah was* chief according to the genealogical records of their families. In the fortieth year of David's reign a search was made in the records, and capable men among the Hebronites were found at Jazer in Gilead. [32]Jeriah had two thousand seven hundred relatives, who were able men and heads of families, and King David put them in charge of the Reubenites, the Gadites and the half-tribe of Manasseh for every matter pertaining to God and for the affairs of the king.

Army Divisions

27 This is the list of the Israelites — heads of families, commanders of thousands and commanders of hundreds, and their officers, who served the king in all that concerned the army divisions that were on duty month by month throughout the year. Each division consisted of 24,000 men.

[2]In charge of the first division, for the first month, was Jashobeam son of Zabdiel. There were 24,000 men in his division. [3]He was a descendant of Perez and chief of all the army officers for the first month.

[4]In charge of the division for the second month was Dodai the Ahohite; Mikloth was the leader of his division. There were 24,000 men in his division. [5]The third army commander, for the third month, was Benaiah son of Jehoiada the priest. He was chief and there were 24,000 men in his division. [6]This was the Benaiah who was a mighty man among the Thirty and was over the Thirty. His son Ammizabad was in charge of his division. [7]The fourth, for the fourth month, was Asahel the brother of Joab; his son Zebadiah was his successor. There were 24,000 men in his division.

[8]The fifth, for the fifth month, was the commander Shamhuth the Izrahite. There were 24,000 men in his division. [9]The sixth, for the sixth month, was Ira the son of Ikkesh the Tekoite. There were 24,000 men in his division. [10]The seventh, for the seventh month, was Helez the Pelonite, an Ephraimite. There were 24,000 men in his division. [11]The eighth, for the eighth month, was Sibbecai the Hushathite, a Zerahite. There were 24,000 men in his division. [12]The ninth, for the ninth month, was Abiezer the Anathothite, a Benjamite. There were 24,000 men in his division. [13]The tenth, for the tenth month, was Maharai the Netophathite, a Zerahite. There were 24,000 men in his division. [14]The eleventh, for the eleventh month, was Benaiah the Pirathonite, an Ephraimite. There were 24,000 men in his division. [15]The twelfth, for the twelfth month, was Heldai the Netophathite, from the family of Othniel. There were 24,000 men in his division.

Officers of the Tribes

[16]The officers over the tribes of Israel:

over the Reubenites: Eliezer son of Zicri;
over the Simeonites: Shephatiah son of Maacah;
[17]over Levi: Hashabiah son of Kemuel;
over Aaron: Zadok;
[18]over Judah: Elihu, a brother of David;
over Issachar: Omri son of Michael;
[19]over Zebulun: Ishmaiah son of Obadiah;
over Naphtali: Jerimoth son of Azriel;
[20]over the Ephraimites: Hoshea son of Azaziah;
over half the tribe of Manasseh: Joel son of Pedaiah;
[21]over the half-tribe of Manasseh in Gilead: Iddo son of Zechariah;
over Benjamin: Jaasiel son of Abner;
[22]over Dan: Azarel son of Jeroham.
These were the officers over the tribes of Israel.

[23]David did not take the number of the men twenty years old or less, because the LORD had promised to make Israel as numerous as the stars in the sky. [24]Joab son of Zeruiah began to count the men but did not finish. Wrath came on Israel on account of this numbering, and the number was not entered in the book[a] of the annals of King David.

The King's Overseers

[25]Azmaveth son of Adiel was in charge of the royal storehouses.

Jonathan son of Uzziah was in charge of the storehouses in the outlying districts, in the towns, the villages and the watchtowers.

[26]Ezri son of Kelub was in charge of the field workers who farmed the land.

[27]Shimei the Ramathite was in charge of the vineyards.

Zabdi the Shiphmite was in charge of the produce of the vineyards for the wine vats.

[28]Baal-Hanan the Gederite was in charge of the olive and sycamore-fig trees in the western foothills.

Joash was in charge of the supplies of olive oil.

[29]Shitrai the Sharonite was in charge of the herds grazing in Sharon.

Shaphat son of Adlai was in charge of the herds in the valleys.

[30]Obil the Ishmaelite was in charge of the camels.

Jehdeiah the Meronothite was in charge of the donkeys.

[31]Jaziz the Hagrite was in charge of the flocks.

All these were the officials in charge of King David's property.

[32]Jonathan, David's uncle, was a counsellor, a man of insight and a scribe. Jehiel son of Hacmoni took care of the king's sons.

[33]Ahithophel was the king's counsellor.

Hushai the Arkite was the king's friend. [34]Ahithophel was succeeded by Jehoiada son of Benaiah and by Abiathar.

Joab was the commander of the royal army.

[a] 24 Septuagint; Hebrew *number*

David's Plans for the Temple

28 David summoned all the officials of Israel to assemble at Jerusalem: the officers over the tribes, the commanders of the divisions in the service of the king, the commanders of thousands and commanders of hundreds, and the officials in charge of all the property and livestock belonging to the king and his sons, together with the palace officials, the mighty men and all the brave warriors.

28:1 The Chronicler made a great deal of the fact that David had made every possible provision for the temple's construction and had simply left Solomon to carry out his plans. This is how the author stressed the close link between David and the temple. In actual fact, as 2 Samuel shows, David's hopes to build a temple were quickly suppressed and we are never led to believe that he made any detailed provisions such as we find here in 1 Chronicles 22,28 and 29. In 1 Kings 5ff we are led to believe that it is Solomon alone who controlled the design and execution of the temple project.

---

²King David rose to his feet and said: "Listen to me, my brothers and my people. I had it in my heart to build a house as a place of rest for the ark of the covenant of the LORD, for the footstool of our God, and I made plans to build it. ³But God said to me, 'You are not to build a house for my Name, because you are a warrior and have shed blood.'

⁴"Yet the LORD, the God of Israel, chose me from my whole family to be king over Israel for ever. He chose Judah as leader, and from the house of Judah he chose my family, and from my father's sons he was pleased to make me king over all Israel. ⁵Of all my sons — and the LORD has given me many — he has chosen my son Solomon to sit on the throne of the kingdom of the LORD over Israel. ⁶He said to me, 'Solomon your son is the one who will build my house and my courts, for I have chosen him to be my son, and I will be his father. ⁷I will establish his kingdom for ever if he is unswerving in carrying out my commands and laws, as is being done at this time.'

⁸"So now I charge you in the sight of all Israel and of the assembly of the LORD, and in the hearing of our God: Be careful to follow all the commands of the LORD your God, that you may possess this good land and pass it on as an inheritance to your descendants for ever. ⁹"And you, my son Solomon, acknowledge the God of your father, and serve him with wholehearted devotion and with a willing mind, for the LORD searches every heart and understands every motive behind the thoughts. If you seek him, he will be found by you; but if you forsake him, he will reject you for ever. ¹⁰Consider now, for the LORD has chosen you to build a temple as a sanctuary. Be strong and do the work."

¹¹Then David gave his son Solomon the plans for the portico of the temple, its buildings, its storerooms, its upper parts, its inner rooms and the place of atonement. ¹²He gave him the plans of all that the Spirit had put in his mind for the courts of the temple of the LORD and all the surrounding rooms, for the treasuries of the temple of God and for the treasuries for the dedicated things. ¹³He gave him instructions for the divisions of the priests and Levites, and for all the work of serving in the temple of the LORD, as well as for all the articles to be used in its service. ¹⁴He designated the weight of gold for all the gold articles to be used in various kinds of service, and the weight of silver for all the silver articles to be used in various kinds of service: ¹⁵the weight of gold for the gold lampstands and their lamps, with the weight for each lampstand and its lamps; and the weight of silver for each silver lampstand and its lamps, according to the use of each lampstand; ¹⁶the weight of gold for each table for consecrated bread; the weight of silver for the silver tables; ¹⁷the weight of pure gold for the forks, sprinkling bowls and pitchers; the weight of gold for each gold dish; the weight of silver for each silver dish; ¹⁸and the weight of the refined gold for the altar of incense. He also gave him the plan for the chariot, that is, the cherubim of gold that spread their wings and shelter the ark of the covenant of the LORD.

¹⁹"All this," David said, "I have in writing from the hand of the LORD upon me, and he gave me understanding in all the details of the plan."

²⁰David also said to Solomon his son, "Be strong and courageous, and do the work. Do not be afraid or discouraged, for the LORD God, my God, is with you. He will not fail you or forsake you until all the work for the service of the temple of the LORD is finished. ²¹The divisions of the priests and Levites are ready for all the work on the temple of God, and every willing man skilled in any craft will help you in all the work. The officials and all the people will obey your every command."

Gifts for Building the Temple

29 Then King David said to the whole assembly: "My son Solomon, the one whom God has chosen, is young and inexperienced. The task is great, because this palatial structure is not for man but for the LORD God. ²With all my resources I have provided for the temple of my God — gold for the gold work, silver for the silver, bronze for the bronze, iron for the iron and wood for the wood, as well as onyx for the settings, turquoise,ᵃ stones of various colours, and all kinds of fine stone and marble — all of these in large quantities. ³Besides, in my devotion to the temple of my God I now give my personal treasures of gold and silver for the temple of my God, over and above everything I have provided for this holy temple: ⁴three thousand talentsᵇ of gold (gold of Ophir) and seven thousand talentsᶜ of refined silver, for the overlaying of the walls of the buildings, ⁵for the gold work and the silver work, and for all the work to be done by the craftsmen. Now,

---

ᵃ2 The meaning of the Hebrew for this word is uncertain.   ᵇ4 That is, about 100 tons (about 100 metric tons)
ᶜ4 That is, about 240 tons (about 240 metric tons)

who is willing to consecrate himself today to the LORD?"

⁶Then the leaders of families, the officers of the tribes of Israel, the commanders of thousands and commanders of hundreds, and the officials in charge of the king's work gave willingly. ⁷They gave towards the work on the temple of God five thousand talents *d* and ten thousand darics *e* of gold, ten thousand talents *f* of silver, eighteen thousand talents *g* of bronze and a hundred thousand talents *h* of iron. ⁸Any who had precious stones gave them to the treasury of the temple of the LORD in the custody of Jehiel the Gershonite. ⁹The people rejoiced at the willing response of their leaders, for they had given freely and wholeheartedly to the LORD. David the king also rejoiced greatly.

David's Prayer

¹⁰David praised the LORD in the presence of the whole assembly, saying,

"Praise be to you, O LORD,
    God of our father Israel,
    from everlasting to everlasting.
¹¹Yours, O LORD, is the greatness and the power
    and the glory and the majesty and the
        splendour,
    for everything in heaven and earth is yours.
Yours, O LORD, is the kingdom;
    you are exalted as head over all.
¹²Wealth and honour come from you;
    you are the ruler of all things.
In your hands are strength and power
    to exalt and give strength to all.
¹³Now, our God, we give you thanks,
    and praise your glorious name.

¹⁴"But who am I, and who are my people, that we should be able to give as generously as this? Everything comes from you, and we have given you only what comes from your hand. ¹⁵We are aliens and strangers in your sight, as were all our forefathers. Our days on earth are like a shadow, without hope. ¹⁶O LORD our God, as for all this abundance that we have provided for building you a temple for your Holy Name, it comes from your hand, and all of it belongs to you. ¹⁷I know, my God, that you test the heart and are pleased with integrity. All these things have I given willingly and with honest intent. And now I have seen with joy how willingly your people who are here have given to you. ¹⁸O LORD, God of our fathers Abraham, Isaac and Israel, keep this desire in the hearts of your people for ever, and keep their hearts loyal to you. ¹⁹And give my son Solomon the wholehearted devotion to keep your commands, requirements and decrees and to do everything to build the palatial structure for which I have provided."

²⁰Then David said to the whole assembly, "Praise the LORD your God." So they all praised the LORD, the God of their fathers; they bowed low and fell prostrate before the LORD and the king.

Solomon Acknowledged as King

²¹The next day they made sacrifices to the LORD and presented burnt offerings to him: a thousand bulls, a thousand rams and a thousand male lambs, together with their drink offerings, and other sacrifices in abundance for all Israel. ²²They ate and drank with great joy in the presence of the LORD that day.

Then they acknowledged Solomon son of David as king a second time, anointing him before the LORD to be ruler and Zadok to be priest. ²³So Solomon sat on the throne of the LORD as king in place of his father David. He prospered and all Israel obeyed him. ²⁴All the officers and mighty men, as well as all of King David's sons, pledged their submission to King Solomon.

²⁵The LORD highly exalted Solomon in the sight of all Israel and bestowed on him royal splendour such as no king over Israel ever had before.

The Death of David

²⁶David son of Jesse was king over all Israel. ²⁷He ruled over Israel for forty years — seven in Hebron and thirty-three in Jerusalem. ²⁸He died at a good old age, having enjoyed long life, wealth and honour. His son Solomon succeeded him as king.

²⁹As for the events of King David's reign, from beginning to end, they are written in the records of Samuel the seer, the records of Nathan the prophet and the records of Gad the seer, ³⁰together with the details of his reign and power, and the circumstances that surrounded him and Israel and the kingdoms of all the other lands.

---

d7 That is, about 170 tons (about 170 metric tons)
f7 That is, about 340 tons (about 345 metric tons)
h7 That is, about 3,400 tons (about 3,450 metric tons)

e7 That is, about 185 pounds (about 84 kilograms)
g7 That is, about 610 tons (about 620 metric tons)

2 Chronicles

A Message of Hope and Prosperity

The book of 2 Chronicles continues to preach the message of hope begun by the first (this is not surprising since they originally formed a single book). It starts with nine chapters about Solomon's reign which are quite selective. His harsh rule is mentioned only briefly, and the fact that the rebellion of the northern tribes was planned whilst Solomon was still king is played down. Just as 1 Chronicles passed over the sins of David, so 2 Chronicles omits critical details about Solomon. Instead the focus is on the building and dedication of the temple. The son is seen to finish the work which was begun by the father, and in doing so he cemented the covenant between God and David's house. The temple appears regularly throughout the book, often acting as a kind of judge of the religious commitment of the monarch: Uzziah defied its sanctity and was struck with leprosy, and Josiah repaired its walls after previous neglect, and brought in an age of prosperity. The book ends as it began; with the temple. The first temple had been built and now it was being destroyed, but the writer leaves us with the promise of a new temple.

A Royal Portrait Gallery

2 Chronicles offers a sweeping review of all Judah's kings from Solomon to the exile. We are presented with a clear-cut method of judging and categorizing them. The two categories of good and bad never mixed; rulers were either entirely good, like Josiah, or entirely bad, like Ahaz, or otherwise they started good and turned bad, like Asa, or started bad and turned good, like Manasseh. No king is ever portrayed as a realistic blend of good and bad at the same time, sometimes doing the right thing and sometimes the wrong. We should be careful, therefore, before turning the Chronicler's system into a general rule which states that anyone who prospers is enjoying God's blessing and anyone who suffers is being punished by God. This would be to misunderstand the author's aim and to ignore the many other different voices that the Bible offers on this problem (see, for example, the book of Job, the complaints in parts of Jeremiah and some psalms, and the words of Jesus in Luke 13). The Chronicler's main purpose was not to give a comprehensive explanation of personal suffering and prosperity, but to direct the nation to God by promoting his worship in the temple. The writer was also talking about kings and not ordinary people; the king was God's representative on earth, he was a son of God (Psalm 2), and his actions directly affected the fortunes of the whole nation. This is why the writer felt that the complicated course of history could be assessed by a very simple analysis of the behaviour of the kings. And finally, the Chronicler was writing in Judah about Judah for Judah; he was not interested in the

history of the rebellious Northern Kingdom which was destroyed in the eighth century; he omitted, for example, the career of Elisha and gave Elijah only the briefest mention. His attitude is summed up at 10:19: "So Israel has been in rebellion against the house of David to this day." In 2 Chronicles the rulers of the Northern Kingdom are simply foreign leaders used by God to punish Judah in the same way as any pagan king (e.g. 28:5ff).

An Offer of Repentance

Despite this distortion of history there is no doubt that the Chronicler's work provided a big boost for the people who had returned to Jerusalem; they needed a sense of God's calling and a focus for their faith, and the Chronicler offered them both. Furthermore, in contrast to his harsh treatment of the northern tribes, he constantly held out the hope of reconciliation; his account of Hezekiah's Passover celebrations makes it clear that there was still a welcome in Judah for the old tribes if they repented. This offer was refused by many of the people in Samaria, which explains the existence even to this day of a large number of Samaritans who still regard themselves as the true Jews.

The Chronicler, however, remained firm in the belief that God would be merciful and forgive all those who repented. Nowhere is this more powerfully shown than in his account of Manasseh. This monarch had the worst reputation of all Judah's kings; Jeremiah once placed all the blame for the fall of Jerusalem on his shoulders alone (Jeremiah 15:1–4). And yet the Chronicler reported that after Manasseh's humiliating capture by Assyria he repented of his evil ways, realizing at last that the Lord was God, and on his return to the throne he lived a devout and peaceful life. Such forgiveness and mercy is surely one of the Chronicler's most wonderful and enduring messages for us today.

Solomon Asks for Wisdom

1 Solomon son of David established himself firmly over his kingdom, for the LORD his God was with him and made him exceedingly great.

²Then Solomon spoke to all Israel — to the commanders of thousands and commanders of hundreds, to the judges and to all the leaders in Israel, the heads of families — ³and Solomon and the whole assembly went to the high place at Gibeon, for God's Tent of Meeting was there, which Moses the LORD's servant had made in the desert. ⁴Now David had brought up the ark of God from Kiriath Jearim to the place he had prepared for it, because he had pitched a tent for it in Jerusalem. ⁵But the bronze altar that Bezalel son of Uri, the son of Hur, had made was in Gibeon in front of the tabernacle of the LORD; so Solomon and the assembly enquired of him there. ⁶Solomon went up to the bronze altar before the LORD in the Tent of Meeting and offered a thousand burnt offerings on it.

⁷That night God appeared to Solomon and said to him, "Ask for whatever you want me to give you."

⁸Solomon answered God, "You have shown great kindness to David my father and have made me king in his place. ⁹Now, LORD God, let your promise to my father David be confirmed, for you have made me king over a people who are as numerous as the dust of the earth. ¹⁰Give me wisdom and knowledge, that I may lead this people, for who is able to govern this great people of yours?"

¹¹God said to Solomon, "Since this is your heart's desire and you have not asked for wealth, riches or honour, nor for the death of your enemies, and since you have not asked for a long life but for wisdom and knowledge to govern my people over whom I have made you king, ¹²therefore wisdom and knowledge will be given you. And I will also give you wealth, riches and honour, such as no king who was before you ever had and none after you will have."

¹³Then Solomon went to Jerusalem from the high place at Gibeon, from before the Tent of Meeting. And he reigned over Israel.

¹⁴Solomon accumulated chariots and horses; he had fourteen hundred chariots and twelve thousand horses,ᵃ which he kept in the chariot cities and also with him in Jerusalem. ¹⁵The king made silver and gold as common in Jerusalem as stones, and cedar as plentiful as sycamore-fig trees in the foothills. ¹⁶Solomon's

---

ᵃ14 Or charioteers

horses were imported from Egypt[b] and from Kue[c]— the royal merchants purchased them from Kue. [17]They imported a chariot from Egypt for six hundred shekels[d] of silver, and a horse for a hundred and fifty.[e] They also exported them to all the kings of the Hittites and of the Arameans.

1:14 When the Israelites first asked for a king, the prophet Samuel warned them that a king would accumulate wealth and abuse his power (1 Samuel 8:10–17). Samuel's words can be seen as a comment upon the later experience of the nation under Solomon. Solomon's use of forced labour was the heavy yoke which caused the rebellion of the northern tribes (see 2 Chronicles 10). The Chronicler failed to point out that Solomon's palace was more costly than the temple.

Preparations for Building the Temple

2 Solomon gave orders to build a temple for the Name of the LORD and a royal palace for himself. [2]He conscripted seventy thousand men as carriers and eighty thousand as stonecutters in the hills and thirty-six hundred as foremen over them. [3]Solomon sent this message to Hiram[a] king of Tyre:

"Send me cedar logs as you did for my father David when you sent him cedar to build a palace to live in. [4]Now I am about to build a temple for the Name of the LORD my God and to dedicate it to him for burning fragrant incense before him, for setting out the consecrated bread regularly, and for making burnt offerings every morning and evening and on Sabbaths and New Moons and at the appointed feasts of the LORD our God. This is a lasting ordinance for Israel.

[5]"The temple I am going to build will be great, because our God is greater than all other gods. [6]But who is able to build a temple for him, since the heavens, even the highest heavens, cannot contain him? Who then am I to build a temple for him, except as a place to burn sacrifices before him?

[7]"Send me, therefore, a man skilled to work in gold and silver, bronze and iron, and in purple, crimson and blue yarn, and experienced in the art of engraving, to work in Judah and Jerusalem with my skilled craftsmen, whom my father David provided.

[8]"Send me also cedar, pine and algum[b] logs from Lebanon, for I know that your men are skilled in cutting timber there. My men shall work with yours [9]to provide me with plenty of timber, because the temple I build must be large and

magnificent. [10]I will give your servants, the woodsmen who cut the timber, twenty thousand cors[c] of ground wheat, twenty thousand cors of barley, twenty thousand baths[d] of wine and twenty thousand baths of olive oil."

[11]Hiram king of Tyre replied by letter to Solomon:

"Because the LORD loves his people, he has made you their king."

[12]And Hiram added:

"Praise be to the LORD, the God of Israel, who made heaven and earth! He has given King David a wise son, endowed with intelligence and discernment, who will build a temple for the LORD and a palace for himself.

[13]"I am sending you Huram-Abi, a man of great skill, [14]whose mother was from Dan and whose father was from Tyre. He is trained to work in gold and silver, bronze and iron, stone and wood, and with purple and blue and crimson yarn and fine linen. He is experienced in all kinds of engraving and can execute any design given to him. He will work with your craftsmen and with those of my lord, David your father.

[15]"Now let my lord send his servants the wheat and barley and the olive oil and wine he promised, [16]and we will cut all the logs from Lebanon that you need and will float them in rafts by sea down to Joppa. You can then take them up to Jerusalem."

[17]Solomon took a census of all the aliens who were in Israel, after the census his father David had taken; and they were found to be 153,600. [18]He assigned 70,000 of them to be carriers and 80,000 to be stonecutters in the hills, with 3,600 foremen over them to keep the people working.

Solomon Builds the Temple

3 Then Solomon began to build the temple of the LORD in Jerusalem on Mount Moriah, where the LORD had appeared to his father David. It was on the threshing-floor of Araunah[a] the Jebusite, the place provided by David. [2]He began building on the second day of the second month in the fourth year of his reign.

[3]The foundation Solomon laid for building the temple of God was sixty cubits long and twenty cubits wide[b] (using the cubit of the old standard). [4]The portico at the front of the temple was twenty cubits[c] long across the width of the building and twenty cubits[d] high.

He overlaid the inside with pure gold. [5]He panelled the main hall with pine and covered it with fine gold and decorated it with palm tree and chain designs. [6]He adorned the temple with precious stones. And the gold he used was gold of Parvaim. [7]He overlaid the ceiling

---

b16 Or possibly *Muzur*, a region in Cilicia; also in verse 17   *c16* Probably Cilicia
d17 That is, about 15 pounds (about 7 kilograms)   *e17* That is, about 3¾ pounds (about 1.7 kilograms)
a3 Hebrew *Huram*, a variant of *Hiram*; also in verses 11 and 12   *b8* Probably a variant of *almug*; possibly juniper
c10 That is, probably about 120,000 bushels (about 4,400 kilolitres)   *d10* That is, probably about 95,000 gallons (about 440 kilolitres)
a1 Hebrew *Ornan*, a variant of *Araunah*   *b3* That is, about 90 feet (about 27 metres) long and 30 feet (about 9 metres) wide
c4 That is, about 30 feet (about 9 metres); also in verses 8, 11 and 13
d4 Some Septuagint and Syriac manuscripts; Hebrew *and a hundred and twenty*

beams, door-frames, walls and doors of the temple with gold, and he carved cherubim on the walls.

⁸He built the Most Holy Place, its length corresponding to the width of the temple — twenty cubits long and twenty cubits wide. He overlaid the inside with six hundred talents*e* of fine gold. ⁹The gold nails weighed fifty shekels.*f* He also overlaid the upper parts with gold.

¹⁰In the Most Holy Place he made a pair of sculptured cherubim and overlaid them with gold. ¹¹The total wing-span of the cherubim was twenty cubits. One wing of the first cherub was five cubits*g* long and touched the temple wall, while its other wing, also five cubits long, touched the wing of the other cherub. ¹²Similarly one wing of the second cherub was five cubits long and touched the other temple wall, and its other wing, also five cubits long, touched the wing of the first cherub. ¹³The wings of these cherubim extended twenty cubits. They stood on their feet, facing the main hall.*h*

¹⁴He made the curtain of blue, purple and crimson yarn and fine linen, with cherubim worked into it.

3:14   The curtain in the temple separated the Holy Place from the Most Holy Place where the ark was kept. Only the high priest could go behind this curtain, and then only once a year on the great Day of Atonement. In the desert the ark had been placed behind a curtain in the tabernacle (Exodus 26:31–33). The curtain, therefore, symbolized the distance between the holy God and his people. The miraculous tearing of the curtain in two at the moment when Jesus died on the cross signified that this gap had been bridged (Hebrews 9).

¹⁵In the front of the temple he made two pillars, which together, were thirty-five cubits*i* long, each with a capital on top measuring five cubits. ¹⁶He made interwoven chains*j* and put them on top of the pillars. He also made a hundred pomegranates and attached them to the chains. ¹⁷He erected the pillars in the front of the temple, one to the south and one to the north. The one to the south he named Jakin*k* and the one to the north Boaz.*l*

The Temple's Furnishings

4 He made a bronze altar twenty cubits long, twenty cubits wide and ten cubits high.*a* ²He made the Sea of cast metal, circular in shape, measuring ten cubits from rim to rim and five cubits*b* high. It took a line of thirty cubits*c* to measure round it.

³Below the rim, figures of bulls encircled it — ten to a cubit.*d* The bulls were cast in two rows in one piece with the Sea.

4:2   It is generally agreed that this piece of metalwork represented the cosmic Sea, "the deep", which, according to Jewish thought, God had conquered before creating the world (Genesis 1:2). The control of God over the sea was often cited as an example of his almighty power (e.g. Psalm 89:9), and the water contained within the Sea in the temple was a reminder of the God who shut up the sea within his chosen limits so the world could come into being (Job 38:8). Like most of the temple's treasures, the Sea was carried off by the Babylonians (2 Kings 25:13).

⁴The Sea stood on twelve bulls, three facing north, three facing west, three facing south and three facing east. The Sea rested on top of them, and their hindquarters were towards the centre. ⁵It was a handbreadth*e* in thickness, and its rim was like the rim of a cup, like a lily blossom. It held three thousand baths.*f*

⁶He then made ten basins for washing and placed five on the south side and five on the north. In them the things to be used for the burnt offerings were rinsed, but the Sea was to be used by the priests for washing.

⁷He made ten gold lampstands according to the specifications for them and placed them in the temple, five on the south side and five on the north. ⁸He made ten tables and placed them in the temple, five on the south side and five on the north. He also made a hundred gold sprinkling bowls.

⁹He made the courtyard of the priests, and the large court and the doors for the court, and overlaid the doors with bronze. ¹⁰He placed the Sea on the south side, at the south-east corner.

¹¹He also made the pots and shovels and sprinkling bowls.

So Huram finished the work he had undertaken for King Solomon in the temple of God:

¹²the two pillars;
the two bowl-shaped capitals on top of the pillars;
the two sets of network decorating the two bowl-shaped capitals on top of the pillars;
¹³the four hundred pomegranates for the two sets of network (two rows of pomegranates for each network, decorating the bowl-shaped capitals on top of the pillars);

e8 That is, about 20 tons (about 21 metric tons) 	*f9 That is, about 1¼ pounds (about 0.6 kilogram)*
g11 That is, about 7½ feet (about 2.3 metres); also in verse 15 	*h13 Or facing inward*
i15 That is, about 52 feet (about 16 metres)
j16 Or possibly made chains in the inner sanctuary; the meaning of the Hebrew for this phrase is uncertain.
k17 Jakin probably means he establishes. 	*l17 Boaz probably means in him is strength.*
a1 That is, about 30 feet (about 9 metres) long and wide, and about 15 feet (about 4.5 metres) high
b2 That is, about 7½ feet (about 2.3 metres) 	*c2 That is, about 45 feet (about 13.5 metres)*
d3 That is, about 1½ feet (about 0.5 metre) 	*e5 That is, about 3 inches (about 8 centimetres)*
f5 That is, about 14,500 gallons (about 66 kilolitres)

¹⁴the stands with their basins;
¹⁵the Sea and the twelve bulls under it;
¹⁶the pots, shovels, meat forks and all related articles.

All the objects that Huram-Abi made for King Solomon for the temple of the LORD were of polished bronze. ¹⁷The king had them cast in clay moulds in the plain of the Jordan between Succoth and Zarethan.ᵍ ¹⁸All these things that Solomon made amounted to so much that the weight of the bronze was not determined.

¹⁹Solomon also made all the furnishings that were in God's temple:

the golden altar;
the tables on which was the bread of the Presence;
²⁰the lampstands of pure gold with their lamps, to burn in front of the inner sanctuary as prescribed;
²¹the gold floral work and lamps and tongs (they were solid gold);
²²the pure gold wick trimmers, sprinkling bowls, dishes and censers; and the gold doors of the temple: the inner doors to the Most Holy Place and the doors of the main hall.

5 When all the work Solomon had done for the temple of the LORD was finished, he brought in the things his father David had dedicated — the silver and gold and all the furnishings — and he placed them in the treasuries of God's temple.

The Ark Brought to the Temple

²Then Solomon summoned to Jerusalem the elders of Israel, all the heads of the tribes and the chiefs of the Israelite families, to bring up the ark of the LORD's covenant from Zion, the City of David. ³And all the men of Israel came together to the king at the time of the festival in the seventh month.

⁴When all the elders of Israel had arrived, the Levites took up the ark, ⁵and they brought up the ark and the Tent of Meeting and all the sacred furnishings in it. The priests, who were Levites, carried them up; ⁶and King Solomon and the entire assembly of Israel that had gathered about him were before the ark, sacrificing so many sheep and cattle that they could not be recorded or counted.

⁷The priests then brought the ark of the LORD's covenant to its place in the inner sanctuary of the temple, the Most Holy Place, and put it beneath the wings of the cherubim. ⁸The cherubim spread their wings over the place of the ark and covered the ark and its carrying poles. ⁹These poles were so long that their ends, extending from the ark, could be seen from in front of the inner sanctuary, but not from outside the Holy Place; and they are still there today. ¹⁰There was nothing in the ark except the two tablets that Moses had placed in it at Horeb, where the LORD made a covenant with the Israelites after they came out of Egypt.

¹¹The priests then withdrew from the Holy Place. All the priests who were there had consecrated themselves, regardless of their divisions. ¹²All the Levites who were musicians — Asaph, Heman, Jeduthun and their sons and relatives — stood on the east side of the altar, dressed in fine linen and playing cymbals, harps and lyres. They were accompanied by 120 priests sounding trumpets. ¹³The trumpeters and singers joined in unison, as with one voice, to give praise and thanks to the LORD. Accompanied by trumpets, cymbals and other instruments, they raised their voices in praise to the LORD and sang:

5:9 The confident assertion that the ark poles were still in existence serves only to underline the tragic loss of the ark itself. We are never told exactly what happened to this most sacred box, which contained the Ten Commandments, but we have to assume it was lost during the fall of Jerusalem to the Babylonians in 568 BC.

"He is good;
his love endures for ever."

Then the temple of the LORD was filled with a cloud, ¹⁴and the priests could not perform their service because of the cloud, for the glory of the LORD filled the temple of God.

5:13 Throughout the Bible the cloud is one of the two most powerful symbols of God's presence; the other is the fire (see chapter 7). In the wilderness God guided the Israelites on their way by a pillar of cloud by day, and a pillar of fire by night (Exodus 13:21). The cloud is mentioned at the transfiguration and the ascension of Jesus, and the fire at Pentecost. All these occurrences were a witness to God's presence.

6 Then Solomon said, "The LORD has said that he would dwell in a dark cloud; ²I have built a magnificent temple for you, a place for you to dwell for ever."

³While the whole assembly of Israel was standing there, the king turned round and blessed them. ⁴Then he said:

"Praise be to the LORD, the God of Israel, who with his hands has fulfilled what he promised with his mouth to my father David. For he said, ⁵'Since the day I brought my people out of Egypt, I have not chosen a city in any tribe of Israel to have a temple built for my Name to be there, nor have I chosen anyone to be the leader over my people Israel. ⁶But now I have chosen Jerusalem for my Name to be there, and I have chosen David to rule my people Israel.'

⁷"My father David had it in his heart to build a temple for the Name of the LORD, the God of Israel. ⁸But the LORD said to my father David,

---

ᵍ17 Hebrew Zeredatha, a variant of Zarethan

'Because it was in your heart to build a temple for my Name, you did well to have this in your heart. ⁹Nevertheless, you are not the one to build the temple, but your son, who is your own flesh and blood — he is the one who will build the temple for my Name.'

¹⁰"The LORD has kept the promise he made. I have succeeded David my father and now I sit on the throne of Israel, just as the LORD promised, and I have built the temple for the Name of the LORD, the God of Israel. ¹¹There I have placed the ark, in which is the covenant of the LORD that he made with the people of Israel."

Solomon's Prayer of Dedication

¹²Then Solomon stood before the altar of the LORD in front of the whole assembly of Israel and spread out his hands. ¹³Now he had made a bronze platform, five cubits*a* long, five cubits wide and three cubits*b* high, and had placed it in the centre of the outer court. He stood on the platform and then knelt down before the whole assembly of Israel and spread out his hands towards heaven. ¹⁴He said:

"O LORD, God of Israel, there is no God like you in heaven or on earth — you who keep your covenant of love with your servants who continue wholeheartedly in your way. ¹⁵You have kept your promise to your servant David my father; with your mouth you have promised and with your hand you have fulfilled it — as it is today.

¹⁶"Now LORD, God of Israel, keep for your servant David my father the promises you made to him when you said, 'You shall never fail to have a man to sit before me on the throne of Israel, if only your sons are careful in all they do to walk before me according to my law, as you have done.' ¹⁷And now, O LORD, God of Israel, let your word that you promised your servant David come true.

¹⁸"But will God really dwell on earth with men? The heavens, even the highest heavens, cannot contain you. How much less this temple that I have built! ¹⁹Yet give attention to your servant's prayer and his plea for mercy, O LORD my God. Hear the cry and the prayer that your servant is praying in your presence. ²⁰May your eyes be open towards this temple day and night, this place of which you said you would put your Name there. May you hear the prayer your servant prays towards this place. ²¹Hear the supplications of your servant and of your people Israel when they pray towards this place. Hear from heaven, your dwelling-place; and when you hear, forgive.

²²"When a man wrongs his neighbour and is required to take an oath and he comes and swears the oath before your altar in this temple, ²³then hear from heaven and act. Judge between your servants, repaying the guilty by bringing down on his own head what he has done. Declare the innocent not guilty and so establish his innocence.

²⁴"When your people Israel have been defeated by an enemy because they have sinned against you and when they turn back and confess your name, praying and making supplication before you in this temple, ²⁵then hear from heaven and forgive the sin of your people Israel and bring them back to the land you gave to them and their fathers.

²⁶"When the heavens are shut up and there is no rain because your people have sinned against you, and when they pray towards this place and confess your name and turn from their sin because you have afflicted them, ²⁷then hear from heaven and forgive the sin of your servants, your people Israel. Teach them the right way to live, and send rain on the land that you gave your people for an inheritance.

²⁸"When famine or plague comes to the land, or blight or mildew, locusts or grasshoppers, or when enemies besiege them in any of their cities, whatever disaster or disease may come, ²⁹and when a prayer or plea is made by any of your people Israel — each one aware of his afflictions and pains, and spreading out his hands towards this temple — ³⁰then hear from heaven, your dwelling-place. Forgive, and deal with each man according to all he does, since you know his heart (for you alone know the hearts of men), ³¹so that they will fear you and walk in your ways all the time they live in the land that you gave our fathers.

³²"As for the foreigner who does not belong to your people Israel but has come from a distant land because of your great name and your mighty hand and your outstretched arm — when he comes and prays towards this temple, ³³then hear from heaven, your dwelling-place, and do whatever the foreigner asks of you, so that all the peoples of the earth may know your name and fear you, as do your own people Israel, and may know that this house that I have built bears your Name.

³⁴"When your people go to war against their enemies, wherever you send them, and when they pray to you towards this city you have chosen and the temple I have built for your Name, ³⁵then hear from heaven their prayer and their plea, and uphold their cause.

³⁶"When they sin against you — for there is no-one who does not sin — and you become angry with them and give them over to the enemy, who takes them captive to a land far away or near; ³⁷and if they have a change of heart in the land where they are held captive, and repent and plead with you in the land of their captivity and say, 'We have sinned, we have done wrong and acted wickedly'; ³⁸and if they turn back to you with all their heart and soul in the land of their captivity where they were taken, and pray towards the land that you gave their fathers, towards the city you have chosen and towards the temple that I have built for your Name; ³⁹then from heaven, your dwelling-place, hear their prayer and their pleas, and uphold their cause. And forgive your people, who have sinned against you.

⁴⁰"Now, my God, may your eyes be open and

---

a 13 That is, about 7½ feet (about 2.3 metres)　　　*b 13* That is, about 4½ feet (about 1.4 metres) your ears attentive to the prayers offered in this place.

⁴¹"Now arise, O Lᴏʀᴅ God, and come to your
  resting place,
  you and the ark of your might.
May your priests, O Lᴏʀᴅ God, be clothed
  with salvation,
  may your saints rejoice in your goodness.
⁴²O Lᴏʀᴅ God, do not reject your anointed
  one.
Remember the great love promised to
  David your servant."

The Dedication of the Temple

7 When Solomon finished praying, fire came down from heaven and consumed the burnt offering and the sacrifices, and the glory of the Lᴏʀᴅ filled the temple. ²The priests could not enter the temple of the Lᴏʀᴅ because the glory of the Lᴏʀᴅ filled it. ³When all the Israelites saw the fire coming down and the glory of the Lᴏʀᴅ above the temple, they knelt on the pavement with their faces to the ground, and they worshipped and gave thanks to the Lᴏʀᴅ, saying,

"He is good;
  his love endures for ever."

⁴Then the king and all the people offered sacrifices before the Lᴏʀᴅ. ⁵And King Solomon offered a sacrifice of twenty-two thousand head of cattle and a hundred and twenty thousand sheep and goats. So the king and all the people dedicated the temple of God. ⁶The priests took their positions, as did the Levites with the Lᴏʀᴅ's musical instruments, which King David had made for praising the Lᴏʀᴅ and which were used when he gave thanks, saying, "His love endures for ever." Opposite the Levites, the priests blew their trumpets, and all the Israelites were standing.

⁷Solomon consecrated the middle part of the courtyard in front of the temple of the Lᴏʀᴅ, and there he offered burnt offerings and the fat of the fellowship offerings,ᵃ because the bronze altar he had made could not hold the burnt offerings, the grain offerings and the fat portions.

⁸So Solomon observed the festival at that time for seven days, and all Israel with him—a vast assembly, people from Leboᵇ Hamath to the Wadi of Egypt. ⁹On the eighth day they held an assembly, for they had celebrated the dedication of the altar for seven days and the festival for seven days more. ¹⁰On the twenty-third day of the seventh month he sent the people to their homes, joyful and glad in heart for the good things the Lᴏʀᴅ had done for David and Solomon and for his people Israel.

The Lᴏʀᴅ Appears to Solomon

¹¹When Solomon had finished the temple of the Lᴏʀᴅ and the royal palace, and had succeeded in carrying out all he had in mind to do in the temple of the Lᴏʀᴅ and in his own palace, ¹²the Lᴏʀᴅ appeared to him at night and said:

"I have heard your prayer and have chosen this place for myself as a temple for sacrifices.

¹³"When I shut up the heavens so that there is no rain, or command locusts to devour the land or send a plague among my people, ¹⁴if my people, who are called by my name, will humble themselves and pray and seek my face and turn from their wicked ways, then will I hear from heaven and will forgive their sin and will heal their land. ¹⁵Now my eyes will be open and my ears attentive to the prayers offered in this place. ¹⁶I have chosen and consecrated this temple so that my Name may be there for ever. My eyes and my heart will always be there.

¹⁷"As for you, if you walk before me as David your father did, and do all I command, and observe my decrees and laws, ¹⁸I will establish your royal throne, as I covenanted with David your father when I said, 'You shall never fail to have a man to rule over Israel.'

¹⁹"But if youᶜ turn away and forsake the decrees and commands I have given youᶜ and go off to serve other gods and worship them, ²⁰then I will uproot Israel from my land, which I have given them, and will reject this temple which I have consecrated for my Name. I will make it a byword and an object of ridicule among all peoples. ²¹And though this temple is now so imposing, all who pass by will be appalled and say, 'Why has the Lᴏʀᴅ done such a thing to this land and to this temple?' ²²People will answer, 'Because they have forsaken the Lᴏʀᴅ, the God of their fathers, who brought them out of Egypt, and have embraced other gods, worshipping and serving them—that is why he brought all this disaster on them.'"

Solomon's Other Activities

8 At the end of twenty years, during which Solomon built the temple of the Lᴏʀᴅ and his own palace, ²Solomon rebuilt the villages that Hiramᵃ had given him, and settled Israelites in them. ³Solomon then went to Hamath Zobah and captured it. ⁴He also built up Tadmor in the desert and all the store cities he had built in Hamath. ⁵He rebuilt Upper Beth Horon and Lower Beth Horon as fortified cities, with walls and with gates and bars, ⁶as well as Baalath and all his store cities, and all the cities for his chariots and for his horsesᵇ—whatever he desired to build in Jerusalem, in Lebanon and throughout all the territory that he ruled.

⁷All the people left from the Hittites, Amorites, Perizzites, Hivites and Jebusites (these peoples were not Israelites), ⁸that is, their descendants remaining in the land, whom the Israelites had not destroyed—these Solomon conscripted for his slave labour force, as it is to this day. ⁹But Solomon did not make slaves of the Israelites for his work; they were his fighting men, commanders of his captains, and commanders of his chariots and charioteers. ¹⁰They were also King

---

ᵃ7 Traditionally *peace offerings*   ᵇ8 Or *from the entrance to*   ᶜ19 The Hebrew is plural.
ᵃ2 Hebrew *Huram*, a variant of *Hiram*; also in verse 18   ᵇ6 Or *charioteers*

Solomon's chief officials—two hundred and fifty officials supervising the men.

[11]Solomon brought Pharaoh's daughter up from the City of David to the palace he had built for her, for he said, "My wife must not live in the palace of David king of Israel, because the places the ark of the LORD has entered are holy."

8:11 Solomon married many foreign wives to help him secure the alliances of neighbouring states. Although this made sense politically, it opened him up to influences which he was unable to control. Just as the Chronicler introduced a pious explanation for Solomon's action, so he omitted any reference to the manner in which Solomon's wives led him away from God in later life (1 Kings 11).

---

[12]On the altar of the LORD that he had built in front of the portico, Solomon sacrificed burnt offerings to the LORD, [13]according to the daily requirement for offerings commanded by Moses for Sabbaths, New Moons and the three annual feasts—the Feast of Unleavened Bread, the Feast of Weeks and the Feast of Tabernacles. [14]In keeping with the ordinance of his father David, he appointed the divisions of the priests for their duties and the Levites to lead the praise and to assist the priests according to each day's requirement. He also appointed the gatekeepers by divisions for the various gates, because this was what David the man of God had ordered. [15]They did not deviate from the king's commands to the priests or to the Levites in any matter, including that of the treasuries.

[16]All Solomon's work was carried out, from the day the foundation of the temple of the LORD was laid until its completion. So the temple of the LORD was finished.

[17]Then Solomon went to Ezion Geber and Elath on the coast of Edom. [18]And Hiram sent him ships commanded by his own officers, men who knew the sea. These, with Solomon's men, sailed to Ophir and brought back four hundred and fifty talents[c] of gold, which they delivered to King Solomon.

The Queen of Sheba Visits Solomon

9 When the queen of Sheba heard of Solomon's fame, she came to Jerusalem to test him with hard questions. Arriving with a very great caravan—with camels carrying spices, large quantities of gold, and precious stones—she came to Solomon and talked with him about all she had on her mind. [2]Solomon answered all her questions; nothing was too hard for him to explain to her. [3]When the queen of Sheba saw the wisdom of Solomon, as well as the palace he had built, [4]the food on his table, the seating of his officials, the attending servants in their robes, the cupbearers in

their robes and the burnt offerings he made at[a] the temple of the LORD, she was overwhelmed.

[5]She said to the king, "The report I heard in my own country about your achievements and your wisdom is true. [6]But I did not believe what they said until I came and saw with my own eyes. Indeed, not even half the greatness of your wisdom was told me; you have far exceeded the report I heard. [7]How happy your men must be! How happy your officials, who continually stand before you and hear your wisdom! [8]Praise be to the LORD your God, who has delighted in you and placed you on his throne as king to rule for the LORD your God. Because of the love of your God for Israel and his desire to uphold them for ever, he has made you king over them, to maintain justice and righteousness."

[9]Then she gave the king 120 talents[b] of gold, large quantities of spices, and precious stones. There had never been such spices as those the queen of Sheba gave to King Solomon.

[10](The men of Hiram and the men of Solomon brought gold from Ophir; they also brought algum-wood[c] and precious stones. [11]The king used the algum-wood to make steps for the temple of the LORD and for the royal palace, and to make harps and lyres for the musicians. Nothing like them had ever been seen in Judah.)

[12]King Solomon gave the queen of Sheba all she desired and asked for; he gave her more than she had brought to him. Then she left and returned with her retinue to her own country.

Solomon's Splendour

[13]The weight of the gold that Solomon received yearly was 666 talents,[d] [14]not including the revenues brought in by merchants and traders. Also all the kings of Arabia and the governors of the land brought gold and silver to Solomon.

[15]King Solomon made two hundred large shields of hammered gold; six hundred bekas[e] of hammered gold went into each shield. [16]He also made three hundred small shields of hammered gold, with three hundred bekas[f] of gold in each shield. The king put them in the Palace of the Forest of Lebanon.

[17]Then the king made a great throne inlaid with ivory and overlaid with pure gold. [18]The throne had six steps, and a footstool of gold was attached to it. On both sides of the seat were armrests, with a lion standing beside each of them. [19]Twelve lions stood on the six steps, one at either end of each step. Nothing like it had ever been made for any other kingdom. [20]All King Solomon's goblets were gold, and all the household articles in the Palace of the Forest of Lebanon were pure gold. Nothing was made of silver, because silver was considered of little value in Solomon's day. [21]The king had a fleet of trading ships[g] manned by Hiram's[h] men. Once every three years it returned, carrying gold, silver and ivory, and apes and baboons.

---

c18 That is, about 17 tons (about 16 metric tons)
b9 That is, about 4 tons (about 4 metric tons)
d13 That is, about 23 tons (about 23 metric tons)
f16 That is, about 3¾ pounds (about 1.7 kilograms)
h21 Hebrew Huram, a variant of Hiram

a4 Or the ascent by which he went up to
c10 Probably a variant of almug-wood
e15 That is, about 7½ pounds (about 3.5 kilograms)
g21 Hebrew of ships that could go to Tarshish

22King Solomon was greater in riches and wisdom than all the other kings of the earth. 23All the kings of the earth sought audience with Solomon to hear the wisdom God had put in his heart. 24Year after year, everyone who came brought a gift—articles of silver and gold, and robes, weapons and spices, and horses and mules.

25Solomon had four thousand stalls for horses and chariots, and twelve thousand horses,*i* which he kept in the chariot cities and also with him in Jerusalem. 26He ruled over all the kings from the River*j* to the land of the Philistines, as far as the border of Egypt. 27The king made silver as common in Jerusalem as stones, and cedar as plentiful as sycamore-fig trees in the foothills. 28Solomon's horses were imported from Egypt*k* and from all other countries.

Solomon's Death

29As for the other events of Solomon's reign, from beginning to end, are they not written in the records of Nathan the prophet, in the prophecy of Ahijah the Shilonite and in the visions of Iddo the seer concerning Jeroboam son of Nebat? 30Solomon reigned in Jerusalem over all Israel for forty years. 31Then he rested with his fathers and was buried in the city of David his father. And Rehoboam his son succeeded him as king.

Israel Rebels Against Rehoboam

10 Rehoboam went to Shechem, for all the Israelites had gone there to make him king. 2When Jeroboam son of Nebat heard this (he was in Egypt, where he had fled from King Solomon), he returned from Egypt. 3So they sent for Jeroboam, and he and all Israel went to Rehoboam and said to him: 4"Your father put a heavy yoke on us, but now lighten the harsh labour and the heavy yoke he put on us, and we will serve you."

5Rehoboam answered, "Come back to me in three days." So the people went away.

6Then King Rehoboam consulted the elders who had served his father Solomon during his lifetime. "How would you advise me to answer these people?" he asked.

7They replied, "If you will be kind to these people and please them and give them a favourable answer, they will always be your servants."

8But Rehoboam rejected the advice the elders gave him and consulted the young men who had grown up with him and were serving him. 9He asked them, "What is your advice? How should we answer these people who say to me, 'Lighten the yoke your father put on us'?"

10The young men who had grown up with him replied, "Tell the people who have said to you, 'Your father put a heavy yoke on us, but make our yoke lighter'—tell them, 'My little finger is thicker than my father's waist. 11My father laid on you a heavy yoke; I will make it even heavier. My father scourged you with whips; I will scourge you with scorpions.'"

12Three days later Jeroboam and all the people returned to Rehoboam, as the king had said, "Come back to me in three days." 13The king answered them harshly. Rejecting the advice of the elders, 14he followed the advice of the young men and said, "My father made your yoke heavy; I will make it even heavier. My father scourged you with whips; I will scourge you with scorpions." 15So the king did not listen to the people, for this turn of events was from God, to fulfil the word that the LORD had spoken to Jeroboam son of Nebat through Ahijah the Shilonite.

16When all Israel saw that the king refused to listen to them, they answered the king:

"What share do we have in David,
    what part in Jesse's son?
To your tents, O Israel!
    Look after your own house, O David!"

So all the Israelites went home. 17But as for the Israelites who were living in the towns of Judah, Rehoboam still ruled over them.

18King Rehoboam sent out Adoniram,*a* who was in charge of forced labour, but the Israelites stoned him to death. King Rehoboam, however, managed to get into his chariot and escape to Jerusalem. 19So Israel has been in rebellion against the house of David to this day.

10:19 Although the writer of Kings shared this negative view (see 2 Kings 17:34), he nevertheless included Ahijah's powerful prophecy to show clearly that the revolt against Solomon and his son was ordained by God (1 Kings 11:27ff). The Chronicler, however, passed over this episode as quickly as possible in accordance with his dislike of the northern tribes who had broken up the glorious united kingdom of David.

---

11 When Rehoboam arrived in Jerusalem, he mustered the house of Judah and Benjamin—a hundred and eighty thousand fighting men—to make war against Israel and to regain the kingdom for Rehoboam.

2But this word of the LORD came to Shemaiah the man of God: 3"Say to Rehoboam son of Solomon king of Judah and to all the Israelites in Judah and Benjamin, 4'This is what the LORD says: Do not go up to fight against your brothers. Go home, every one of you, for this is my doing.'" So they obeyed the words of the LORD and turned back from marching against Jeroboam.

Rehoboam Fortifies Judah

5Rehoboam lived in Jerusalem and built up towns for defence in Judah: 6Bethlehem, Etam, Tekoa, 7Beth Zur, Soco, Adullam, 8Gath, Mareshah, Ziph, 9Adoraim, Lachish, Azekah, 10Zorah, Aijalon and Hebron. These were fortified cities in Judah and Benjamin. 11He strengthened their defences and put commanders in

i25 Or *charioteers*   *j26* That is, the Euphrates   *k28* Or possibly *Muzur*, a region in Cilicia
a18 Hebrew *Hadoram*, a variant of *Adoniram*

them, with supplies of food, olive oil and wine. [12]He put shields and spears in all the cities, and made them very strong. So Judah and Benjamin were his.

[13]The priests and Levites from all their districts throughout Israel sided with him. [14]The Levites even abandoned their pasture-lands and property, and came to Judah and Jerusalem because Jeroboam and his sons had rejected them as priests of the LORD. [15]And he appointed his own priests for the high places and for the goat and calf idols he had made. [16]Those from every tribe of Israel who set their hearts on seeking the LORD, the God of Israel, followed the Levites to Jerusalem to offer sacrifices to the LORD, the God of their fathers. [17]They strengthened the kingdom of Judah and supported Rehoboam son of Solomon for three years, walking in the ways of David and Solomon during this time.

Rehoboam's Family

[18]Rehoboam married Mahalath, who was the daughter of David's son Jerimoth and of Abihail, the daughter of Jesse's son Eliab. [19]She bore him sons: Jeush, Shemariah and Zaham. [20]Then he married Maacah daughter of Absalom, who bore him Abijah, Attai, Ziza and Shelomith. [21]Rehoboam loved Maacah daughter of Absalom more than any of his other wives and concubines. In all he had eighteen wives and sixty concubines, twenty-eight sons and sixty daughters.

[22]Rehoboam appointed Abijah son of Maacah to be the chief prince among his brothers, in order to make him king. [23]He acted wisely, dispersing some of his sons throughout the districts of Judah and Benjamin, and to all the fortified cities. He gave them abundant provisions and took many wives for them.

Shishak Attacks Jerusalem

12 After Rehoboam's position as king was established and he had become strong, he and all Israel[a] with him abandoned the law of the LORD. [2]Because they had been unfaithful to the LORD, Shishak king of Egypt attacked Jerusalem in the fifth year of King Rehoboam. [3]With twelve hundred chariots and sixty thousand horsemen and the innumerable troops of Libyans, Sukkites and Cushites[b] that came with him from Egypt, [4]he captured the fortified cities of Judah and came as far as Jerusalem.

[5]Then the prophet Shemaiah came to Rehoboam and to the leaders of Judah who had assembled in Jerusalem for fear of Shishak, and he said to them, "This is what the LORD says: 'You have abandoned me; therefore I now abandon you to Shishak.' "

[6]The leaders of Israel and the king humbled themselves and said, "The LORD is just."

[7]When the LORD saw that they humbled themselves, this word of the LORD came to Shemaiah: "Since they have humbled themselves, I will not destroy them but will soon give them deliverance. My wrath will not be poured out on Jerusalem through Shishak. [8]They will, however, become subject to him, so that they may learn the difference between serving me and serving the kings of other lands."

[9]When Shishak king of Egypt attacked Jerusalem, he carried off the treasures of the temple of the LORD and the treasures of the royal palace. He took everything, including the gold shields that Solomon had made. [10]So King Rehoboam made bronze shields to replace them and assigned these to the commanders of the guard on duty at the entrance to the royal palace. [11]Whenever the king went to the LORD's temple, the guards went with him, bearing the shields, and afterwards they returned them to the guardroom.

[12]Because Rehoboam humbled himself, the LORD's anger turned from him, and he was not totally destroyed. Indeed, there was some good in Judah.

[13]King Rehoboam established himself firmly in Jerusalem and continued as king. He was forty-one years old when he became king, and he reigned for seventeen years in Jerusalem, the city the LORD had chosen out of all the tribes of Israel in which to put his Name. His mother's name was Naamah; she was an Ammonite. [14]He did evil because he had not set his heart on seeking the LORD.

[15]As for the events of Rehoboam's reign, from beginning to end, are they not written in the records of Shemaiah the prophet and of Iddo the seer that deal with genealogies? There was continual warfare between Rehoboam and Jeroboam. [16]Rehoboam rested with his fathers and was buried in the City of David. And Abijah his son succeeded him as king.

Abijah King of Judah

13 In the eighteenth year of the reign of Jeroboam, Abijah became king of Judah, [2]and he reigned in Jerusalem for three years. His mother's name was Maacah,[a] a daughter[b] of Uriel of Gibeah.

There was war between Abijah and Jeroboam. [3]Abijah went into battle with a force of four hundred thousand able fighting men, and Jeroboam drew up a battle line against him with eight hundred thousand able troops.

13:4 There continues to be a favourable portrayal of the southern rulers even when the parallel history in Kings is less than glowing. This long and stirring speech is missing from 1 Kings 15, where Abijah's short rule is written off as wicked.

---

[4]Abijah stood on Mount Zemaraim, in the hill country of Ephraim, and said, "Jeroboam and all Israel, listen to me! [5]Don't you know that the LORD, the God of Israel, has given the kingship of Israel to David and his descendants for ever by a covenant of salt? [6]Yet Jeroboam son of Nebat, an official of Solomon son of David, rebelled against his master. [7]Some worthless scoundrels gathered around him and opposed Rehoboam son of Solomon when he was young and indecisive and not strong enough to resist them.

[8]"And now you plan to resist the kingdom of the LORD, which is in the hands of David's descendants.

---

[a]1 That is, Judah, as frequently in 2 Chronicles   [b]3 That is, people from the upper Nile region
[a]2 Most Septuagint manuscripts and Syriac (see also 2 Chron. 11:20 and 1 Kings 15:2); Hebrew *Micaiah*   [b]2 Or *granddaughter*

You are indeed a vast army and have with you the golden calves that Jeroboam made to be your gods. ⁹But didn't you drive out the priests of the LORD, the sons of Aaron, and the Levites, and make priests of your own as the peoples of other lands do? Whoever comes to consecrate himself with a young bull and seven rams may become a priest of what are not gods.

¹⁰"As for us, the LORD is our God, and we have not forsaken him. The priests who serve the LORD are sons of Aaron, and the Levites assist them. ¹¹Every morning and evening they present burnt offerings and fragrant incense to the LORD. They set out the bread on the ceremonially clean table and light the lamps on the gold lampstand every evening. We are observing the requirements of the LORD our God. But you have forsaken him. ¹²God is with us; he is our leader. His priests with their trumpets will sound the battle cry against you. Men of Israel, do not fight against the LORD, the God of your fathers, for you will not succeed."

¹³Now Jeroboam had sent troops round to the rear, so that while he was in front of Judah the ambush was behind them. ¹⁴Judah turned and saw that they were being attacked at both front and rear. Then they cried out to the LORD. The priests blew their trumpets ¹⁵and the men of Judah raised the battle cry. At the sound of their battle cry, God routed Jeroboam and all Israel before Abijah and Judah. ¹⁶The Israelites fled before Judah, and God delivered them into their hands. ¹⁷Abijah and his men inflicted heavy losses on them, so that there were five hundred thousand casualties among Israel's able men. ¹⁸The men of Israel were subdued on that occasion, and the men of Judah were victorious because they relied on the LORD, the God of their fathers.

¹⁹Abijah pursued Jeroboam and took from him the towns of Bethel, Jeshanah and Ephron, with their surrounding villages. ²⁰Jeroboam did not regain power during the time of Abijah. And the LORD struck him down and he died.

²¹But Abijah grew in strength. He married fourteen wives and had twenty-two sons and sixteen daughters. ²²The other events of Abijah's reign, what he did and what he said, are written in the annotations of the prophet Iddo.

14 And Abijah rested with his fathers and was buried in the City of David. Asa his son succeeded him as king, and in his days the country was at peace for ten years.

Asa King of Judah

²Asa did what was good and right in the eyes of the LORD his God. ³He removed the foreign altars and the high places, smashed the sacred stones and cut down the Asherah poles.ᵃ ⁴He commanded Judah to seek the LORD, the God of their fathers, and to obey his laws and commands. ⁵He removed the high places and incense altars in every town in Judah, and the kingdom was at peace under him. ⁶He built up the fortified cities of Judah, since the land was at peace. No-one was at war with him during those years, for the LORD gave him rest.

⁷"Let us build up these towns," he said to Judah, "and put walls round them, with towers, gates and bars. The land is still ours, because we have sought the LORD our God; we sought him and he has given us rest on every side." So they built and prospered.

⁸Asa had an army of three hundred thousand men from Judah, equipped with large shields and with spears, and two hundred and eighty thousand from Benjamin, armed with small shields and with bows. All these were brave fighting men.

⁹Zerah the Cushite marched out against them with a vast armyᵇ and three hundred chariots, and came as far as Mareshah. ¹⁰Asa went out to meet him, and they took up battle positions in the Valley of Zephathah near Mareshah.

¹¹Then Asa called to the LORD his God and said, "LORD, there is no-one like you to help the powerless against the mighty. Help us, O LORD our God, for we rely on you, and in your name we have come against this vast army. O LORD, you are our God; do not let man prevail against you."

¹²The LORD struck down the Cushites before Asa and Judah. The Cushites fled, ¹³and Asa and his army pursued them as far as Gerar. Such a great number of Cushites fell that they could not recover; they were crushed before the LORD and his forces. The men of Judah carried off a large amount of plunder. ¹⁴They destroyed all the villages around Gerar, for the terror of the LORD had fallen upon them. They plundered all these villages, since there was much booty there. ¹⁵They also attacked the camps of the herdsmen and carried off droves of sheep and goats and camels. Then they returned to Jerusalem.

Asa's Reform

15 The Spirit of God came upon Azariah son of Oded. ²He went out to meet Asa and said to him, "Listen to me, Asa and all Judah and Benjamin. The LORD is with you when you are with him. If you seek him, he will be found by you, but if you forsake him, he will forsake you. ³For a long time Israel was without the true God, without a priest to teach and without the law. ⁴But in their distress they turned to the LORD, the God of Israel, and sought him, and he was found by them. ⁵In those days it was not safe to travel about, for all the inhabitants of the lands were in great turmoil. ⁶One nation was being crushed by another and one city by another, because God was troubling them with every kind of distress. ⁷But as for you, be strong and do not give up, for your work will be rewarded."

⁸When Asa heard these words and the prophecy of Azariah son ofᵃ Oded the prophet, he took courage. He removed the detestable idols from the whole land of Judah and Benjamin and from the towns he had captured in the hills of Ephraim. He repaired the altar of the LORD that was in front of the portico of the LORD's temple.

ᵃ3 That is, symbols of the goddess Asherah; here and elsewhere in 2 Chronicles
ᵇ9 Hebrew *with an army of a thousand thousands* or *with an army of thousands upon thousands*
ᵃ8 Vulgate and Syriac (see also Septuagint and verse 1); Hebrew does not have *Azariah son of.*

⁹Then he assembled all Judah and Benjamin and the people from Ephraim, Manasseh and Simeon who had settled among them, for large numbers had come over to him from Israel when they saw that the LORD his God was with him.

15:9 For fifty years after Jeroboam's revolt, Israel and Judah fought a civil war. The two southern tribes were outnumbered but had a strong rallying point in the temple. Many of the northern kings built alternative sanctuaries on the "high places" to dissuade their people from going to Jerusalem to the temple. These sites were often called idolatrous, although this may be the slander of southern writers. However, when Asa launched a religious revival in the south some of the northern tribes did come over to Jerusalem.

---

¹⁰They assembled at Jerusalem in the third month of the fifteenth year of Asa's reign. ¹¹At that time they sacrificed to the LORD seven hundred head of cattle and seven thousand sheep and goats from the plunder they had brought back. ¹²They entered into a covenant to seek the LORD, the God of their fathers, with all their heart and soul. ¹³All who would not seek the LORD, the God of Israel, were to be put to death, whether small or great, man or woman. ¹⁴They took an oath to the LORD with loud acclamation, with shouting and with trumpets and horns. ¹⁵All Judah rejoiced about the oath because they had sworn it wholeheartedly. They sought God eagerly, and he was found by them. So the LORD gave them rest on every side.

¹⁶King Asa also deposed his grandmother Maacah from her position as queen mother, because she had made a repulsive Asherah pole. Asa cut the pole down, broke it up and burned it in the Kidron Valley. ¹⁷Although he did not remove the high places from Israel, Asa's heart was fully committed to the LORD all his life. ¹⁸He brought into the temple of God the silver and gold and the articles that he and his father had dedicated.

¹⁹There was no more war until the thirty-fifth year of Asa's reign.

Asa's Last Years

16 In the thirty-sixth year of Asa's reign Baasha king of Israel went up against Judah and fortified Ramah to prevent anyone from leaving or entering the territory of Asa king of Judah.

²Asa then took the silver and gold out of the treasuries of the LORD's temple and of his own palace and sent it to Ben-Hadad king of Aram, who was ruling in Damascus. ³"Let there be a treaty between me and you," he said, "as there was between my father and your father. See, I am sending you silver and gold. Now break your treaty with Baasha king of Israel so that he will withdraw from me."

⁴Ben-Hadad agreed with King Asa and sent the commanders of his forces against the towns of Israel. They conquered Ijon, Dan, Abel Maim*ᵃ* and all the store cities of Naphtali. ⁵When Baasha heard this, he stopped building Ramah and abandoned his work. ⁶Then King Asa brought all the men of Judah, and they carried away from Ramah the stones and timber Baasha had been using. With them he built up Geba and Mizpah.

⁷At that time Hanani the seer came to Asa king of Judah and said to him: "Because you relied on the king of Aram and not on the LORD your God, the army of the king of Aram has escaped from your hand. ⁸Were not the Cushites*ᵇ* and Libyans a mighty army with great numbers of chariots and horsemen*ᶜ*? Yet when you relied on the LORD, he delivered them into your hand. ⁹For the eyes of the LORD range throughout the earth to strengthen those whose hearts are fully committed to him. You have done a foolish thing, and from now on you will be at war."

¹⁰Asa was angry with the seer because of this; he was so enraged that he put him in prison. At the same time Asa brutally oppressed some of the people. ¹¹The events of Asa's reign, from beginning to end, are written in the book of the kings of Judah and Israel. ¹²In the thirty-ninth year of his reign Asa was afflicted with a disease in his feet. Though his disease was severe, even in his illness he did not seek help from the LORD, but only from the physicians. ¹³Then in the forty-first year of his reign Asa died and rested with his fathers. ¹⁴They buried him in the tomb that he had cut out for himself in the City of David. They laid him on a bier covered with spices and various blended perfumes, and they made a huge fire in his honour.

Jehoshaphat King of Judah

17 Jehoshaphat his son succeeded him as king and strengthened himself against Israel. ²He stationed troops in all the fortified cities of Judah and put garrisons in Judah and in the towns of Ephraim that his father Asa had captured.

³The LORD was with Jehoshaphat because in his early years he walked in the ways that his father David had followed. He did not consult the Baals ⁴but sought the God of his father and followed his commands rather than the practices of Israel. ⁵The LORD established the kingdom under his control; and all Judah brought gifts to Jehoshaphat, so that he had great wealth and honour. ⁶His heart was devoted to the ways of the LORD; furthermore, he removed the high places and the Asherah poles from Judah.

⁷In the third year of his reign he sent his officials Ben-Hail, Obadiah, Zechariah, Nethanel and Micaiah to teach in the towns of Judah. ⁸With them were certain Levites—Shemaiah, Nethaniah, Zebadiah, Asahel, Shemiramoth, Jehonathan, Adonijah, Tobijah and Tob-Adonijah—and the priests Elishama and Jehoram. ⁹They taught throughout Judah, taking with them the Book of the Law of the LORD; they went round to all the towns of Judah and taught the people.

¹⁰The fear of the LORD fell on all the kingdoms of the lands surrounding Judah, so that they did not make war

---

ᵃ4 Also known as *Abel Beth Maacah*   *ᵇ8* That is, people from the upper Nile region   *ᶜ8* Or *charioteers* with Jehoshaphat. [11]Some Philistines brought Jehoshaphat gifts and silver as tribute, and the Arabs brought him flocks: seven thousand seven hundred rams and seven thousand seven hundred goats.

[12]Jehoshaphat became more and more powerful; he built forts and store cities in Judah [13]and had large supplies in the towns of Judah. He also kept experienced fighting men in Jerusalem. [14]Their enrolment by families was as follows:

From Judah, commanders of units of 1,000:
Adnah the commander, with 300,000 fighting men;
[15]next, Jehohanan the commander, with 280,000;
[16]next, Amasiah son of Zicri, who volunteered himself for the service of the LORD, with 200,000;
[17]From Benjamin:
Eliada, a valiant soldier, with 200,000 men armed with bows and shields;
[18]next, Jehozabad, with 180,000 men armed for battle.

[19]These were the men who served the king, besides those he stationed in the fortified cities throughout Judah.

Micaiah Prophesies Against Ahab

18 Now Jehoshaphat had great wealth and honour, and he allied himself with Ahab by marriage. [2]Some years later he went down to visit Ahab in Samaria. Ahab slaughtered many sheep and cattle for him and the people with him and urged him to attack Ramoth Gilead. [3]Ahab king of Israel asked Jehoshaphat king of Judah, "Will you go with me against Ramoth Gilead?"

Jehoshaphat replied, "I am as you are, and my people as your people; we will join you in the war." [4]But Jehoshaphat also said to the king of Israel, "First seek the counsel of the LORD."

[5]So the king of Israel brought together the prophets — four hundred men — and asked them, "Shall we go to war against Ramoth Gilead, or shall I refrain?"

"Go," they answered, "for God will give it into the king's hand."

[6]But Jehoshaphat asked, "Is there not a prophet of the LORD here whom we can enquire of?"

[7]The king of Israel answered Jehoshaphat, "There is still one man through whom we can enquire of the LORD, but I hate him because he never prophesies anything good about me, but always bad. He is Micaiah son of Imlah."

"The king should not say that," Jehoshaphat replied.

[8]So the king of Israel called one of his officials and said, "Bring Micaiah son of Imlah at once."

[9]Dressed in their royal robes, the king of Israel and Jehoshaphat king of Judah were sitting on their thrones at the threshing-floor by the entrance to the gate of Samaria, with all the prophets prophesying before them. [10]Now Zedekiah son of Kenaanah had made iron horns, and he declared, "This is what the LORD says: 'With these you will gore the Arameans until they are destroyed.' "

[11]All the other prophets were prophesying the same thing. "Attack Ramoth Gilead and be victorious," they said, "for the LORD will give it into the king's hand."

18:6 The problem of distinguishing between a true and a false prophet was encountered time and time again in the Old Testament. Deuteronomy gives advice on how to tell the difference (Deuteronomy 18:22), and the clash between Jeremiah and Hananiah is also a useful guide (Jeremiah 28). But the essential problem was never solved satisfactorily. Micaiah claimed authority because he had seen into the heavenly council chamber. However, the idea of God sending a lying spirit to make the prophets speak falsely is an altogether confusing and unhelpful one.

---

[12]The messenger who had gone to summon Micaiah said to him, "Look, as one man the other prophets are predicting success for the king. Let your word agree with theirs, and speak favourably."

[13]But Micaiah said, "As surely as the LORD lives, I can tell him only what my God says."

[14]When he arrived, the king asked him, "Micaiah, shall we go to war against Ramoth Gilead, or shall I refrain?"

"Attack and be victorious," he answered, "for they will be given into your hand."

[15]The king said to him, "How many times must I make you swear to tell me nothing but the truth in the name of the LORD?"

[16]Then Micaiah answered, "I saw all Israel scattered on the hills like sheep without a shepherd, and the LORD said, 'These people have no master. Let each one go home in peace.' "

[17]The king of Israel said to Jehoshaphat, "Didn't I tell you that he never prophesies anything good about me, but only bad?"

[18]Micaiah continued, "Therefore hear the word of the LORD: I saw the LORD sitting on his throne with all the host of heaven standing on his right and on his left. [19]And the LORD said, 'Who will entice Ahab king of Israel into attacking Ramoth Gilead and going to his death there?'

"One suggested this, and another that. [20]Finally, a spirit came forward, stood before the LORD and said, 'I will entice him.'

" 'By what means?' the LORD asked.

[21]" 'I will go and be a lying spirit in the mouths of all his prophets,' he said.

" 'You will succeed in enticing him,' said the LORD. 'Go and do it.'

[22]"So now the LORD has put a lying spirit in the mouths of these prophets of yours. The LORD has decreed disaster for you."

[23]Then Zedekiah son of Kenaanah went up and slapped Micaiah in the face. "Which way did the spirit

from[a] the LORD go when he went from me to speak to you?" he asked.

24Micaiah replied, "You will find out on the day you go to hide in an inner room."

25The king of Israel then ordered, "Take Micaiah and send him back to Amon the ruler of the city and to Joash the king's son, 26and say, 'This is what the king says: Put this fellow in prison and give him nothing but bread and water until I return safely.' "

27Micaiah declared, "If you ever return safely, the LORD has not spoken through me." Then he added, "Mark my words, all you people!"

Ahab Killed at Ramoth Gilead

28So the king of Israel and Jehoshaphat king of Judah went up to Ramoth Gilead. 29The king of Israel said to Jehoshaphat, "I will enter the battle in disguise, but you wear your royal robes." So the king of Israel disguised himself and went into battle.

30Now the king of Aram had ordered his chariot commanders, "Do not fight with anyone, small or great, except the king of Israel." 31When the chariot commanders saw Jehoshaphat, they thought, "This is the king of Israel." So they turned to attack him, but Jehoshaphat cried out, and the LORD helped him. God drew them away from him, 32for when the chariot commanders saw that he was not the king of Israel, they stopped pursuing him.

33But someone drew his bow at random and hit the king of Israel between the sections of his armour. The king told the chariot driver, "Wheel around and get me out of the fighting. I've been wounded." 34All day long the battle raged, and the king of Israel propped himself up in his chariot facing the Arameans until evening. Then at sunset he died.

19 When Jehoshaphat king of Judah returned safely to his palace in Jerusalem, 2Jehu the seer, the son of Hanani, went out to meet him and said to the king, "Should you help the wicked and love[a] those who hate the LORD? Because of this, the wrath of the LORD is upon you. 3There is, however, some good in you, for you have rid the land of the Asherah poles and have set your heart on seeking God."

Jehoshaphat Appoints Judges

4Jehoshaphat lived in Jerusalem, and he went out again among the people from Beersheba to the hill country of Ephraim and turned them back to the LORD, the God of their fathers. 5He appointed judges in the land, in each of the fortified cities of Judah. 6He told them, "Consider carefully what you do, because you are not judging for man but for the LORD, who is with you whenever you give a verdict. 7Now let the fear of the LORD be upon you. Judge carefully, for with the LORD our God there is no injustice or partiality or bribery."

8In Jerusalem also, Jehoshaphat appointed some of the Levites, priests and heads of Israelite families to administer the law of the LORD and to settle disputes. And they lived in Jerusalem. 9He gave them these

orders: "You must serve faithfully and wholeheartedly in the fear of the LORD. 10In every case that comes before you from your fellow countrymen who live in the cities — whether bloodshed or other concerns of the law, commands, decrees or ordinances — you are to warn them not to sin against the LORD; otherwise his wrath will come on you and your brothers. Do this, and you will not sin.

11"Amariah the chief priest will be over you in any matter concerning the LORD, and Zebadiah son of Ishmael, the leader of the tribe of Judah, will be over you in any matter concerning the king, and the Levites will serve as officials before you. Act with courage, and may the LORD be with those who do well."

Jehoshaphat Defeats Moab and Ammon

20 After this, the Moabites and Ammonites with some of the Meunites[a] came to make war on Jehoshaphat.

2Some men came and told Jehoshaphat, "A vast army is coming against you from Edom,[b] from the other side of the Sea.[c] It is already in Hazezon Tamar" (that is, En Gedi). 3Alarmed, Jehoshaphat resolved to enquire of the LORD, and he proclaimed a fast for all Judah. 4The people of Judah came together to seek help from the LORD; indeed, they came from every town in Judah to seek him.

5Then Jehoshaphat stood up in the assembly of Judah and Jerusalem at the temple of the LORD in the front of the new courtyard 6and said:

20:6 There are two prayers in 2 Chronicles. The first is that of Solomon on the occasion of the dedication of the temple (6:14ff), and the second is this one of Jehoshaphat. Both were offered up in public worship in the temple, and reflected the important religious role of the king. They relied heavily on the people's loyalty to the temple as a guarantee that God would answer their prayer. This obviously had a contemporary message for the writer's own audience who based their faith on the second temple.

"O LORD, God of our fathers, are you not the God who is in heaven? You rule over all the kingdoms of the nations. Power and might are in your hand, and no-one can withstand you. 7O our God, did you not drive out the inhabitants of this land before your people Israel and give it for ever to the descendants of Abraham your friend? 8They have lived in it and have built in it a sanctuary for your Name, saying, 9'If calamity comes upon us, whether the sword of judgment, or plague or famine, we will stand in your presence before this temple that bears your Name and will cry out to you in our distress, and you will hear us and save us.'

---

a23 Or Spirit of　　　a2 Or and make alliances with　　　a1 Some Septuagint manuscripts; Hebrew Ammonites
b2 One Hebrew manuscript; most Hebrew manuscripts, Septuagint and Vulgate Aram　　　c2 That is, the Dead Sea

¹⁰"But now here are men from Ammon, Moab and Mount Seir, whose territory you would not allow Israel to invade when they came from Egypt; so they turned away from them and did not destroy them. ¹¹See how they are repaying us by coming to drive us out of the possession you gave us as an inheritance. ¹²O our God, will you not judge them? For we have no power to face this vast army that is attacking us. We do not know what to do, but our eyes are upon you."

¹³All the men of Judah, with their wives and children and little ones, stood there before the LORD.

¹⁴Then the Spirit of the LORD came upon Jahaziel son of Zechariah, the son of Benaiah, the son of Jeiel, the son of Mattaniah, a Levite and descendant of Asaph, as he stood in the assembly. ¹⁵He said: "Listen, King Jehoshaphat and all who live in Judah and Jerusalem! This is what the LORD says to you: 'Do not be afraid or discouraged because of this vast army. For the battle is not yours, but God's. ¹⁶Tomorrow march down against them. They will be climbing up by the Pass of Ziz, and you will find them at the end of the gorge in the Desert of Jeruel. ¹⁷You will not have to fight this battle. Take up your positions; stand firm and see the deliverance the LORD will give you, O Judah and Jerusalem. Do not be afraid; do not be discouraged. Go out to face them tomorrow, and the LORD will be with you.' "

¹⁸Jehoshaphat bowed with his face to the ground, and all the people of Judah and Jerusalem fell down in worship before the LORD. ¹⁹Then some Levites from the Kohathites and Korahites stood up and praised the LORD, the God of Israel, with a very loud voice.

²⁰Early in the morning they left for the Desert of Tekoa. As they set out, Jehoshaphat stood and said, "Listen to me, Judah and people of Jerusalem! Have faith in the LORD your God and you will be upheld; have faith in his prophets and you will be successful." ²¹After consulting the people, Jehoshaphat appointed men to sing to the LORD and to praise him for the splendour of his ^{d} holiness as they went out at the head of the army, saying:

"Give thanks to the LORD,
  for his love endures for ever."

²²As they began to sing and praise, the LORD set ambushes against the men of Ammon and Moab and Mount Seir who were invading Judah, and they were defeated. ²³The men of Ammon and Moab rose up against the men from Mount Seir to destroy and annihilate them. After they finished slaughtering the men from Seir, they helped to destroy one another. ²⁴When the men of Judah came to the place that overlooks the desert and looked towards the vast army, they saw only dead bodies lying on the ground; no-one had escaped. ²⁵So Jehoshaphat and his men went to carry off their plunder, and they found among them a great amount of equipment and clothing ^{e} and also articles of value—more than they could take away. There was so much plunder that it took three days to collect it. ²⁶On the fourth day they assembled in the Valley of Beracah, where they praised the LORD. This is why it is called the Valley of Beracah ^{f} to this day.

²⁷Then, led by Jehoshaphat, all the men of Judah and Jerusalem returned joyfully to Jerusalem, for the LORD had given them cause to rejoice over their enemies. ²⁸They entered Jerusalem and went to the temple of the LORD with harps and lutes and trumpets. ²⁹The fear of God came upon all the kingdoms of the countries when they heard how the LORD had fought against the enemies of Israel. ³⁰And the kingdom of Jehoshaphat was at peace, for his God had given him rest on every side.

The End of Jehoshaphat's Reign

³¹So Jehoshaphat reigned over Judah. He was thirty-five years old when he became king of Judah, and he reigned in Jerusalem for twenty-five years. His mother's name was Azubah daughter of Shilhi. ³²He walked in the ways of his father Asa and did not stray from them; he did what was right in the eyes of the LORD. ³³The high places, however, were not removed, and the people still had not set their hearts on the God of their fathers.

³⁴The other events of Jehoshaphat's reign, from beginning to end, are written in the annals of Jehu son of Hanani, which are recorded in the book of the kings of Israel.

³⁵Later, Jehoshaphat king of Judah made an alliance with Ahaziah king of Israel, who was guilty of wickedness. ³⁶He agreed with him to construct a fleet of trading ships. ^{g} After these were built at Ezion Geber, ³⁷Eliezer son of Dodavahu of Mareshah prophesied against Jehoshaphat, saying, "Because you have made an alliance with Ahaziah, the LORD will destroy what you have made." The ships were wrecked and were not able to set sail to trade. ^{h}

21 Then Jehoshaphat rested with his fathers and was buried with them in the City of David. And Jehoram his son succeeded him as king. ²Jehoram's brothers, the sons of Jehoshaphat, were Azariah, Jehiel, Zechariah, Azariahu, Michael and Shephatiah. All these were sons of Jehoshaphat king of Israel. ^{a} ³Their father had given them many gifts of silver and gold and articles of value, as well as fortified cities in Judah, but he had given the kingdom to Jehoram because he was his firstborn son.

Jehoram King of Judah

⁴When Jehoram established himself firmly over his father's kingdom, he put all his brothers to the sword along with some of the princes of Israel. ⁵Jehoram was thirty-two years old when he became king, and he reigned in Jerusalem for eight years. ⁶He walked in the ways of the kings of Israel, as the house of Ahab had done, for he married a daughter of Ahab. He did evil in the eyes of the LORD. ⁷Nevertheless, because of the covenant the LORD had made with David, the LORD was not willing to destroy the house of David. He had

---

^{d}21 Or him with the splendour of ^{e}25 Some Hebrew manuscripts and Vulgate; most Hebrew manuscripts corpses
^{f}26 Beracah means praise. ^{g}36 Hebrew of ships that could go to Tarshish ^{h}37 Hebrew sail for Tarshish
^{a}2 That is, Judah, as frequently in 2 Chronicles

promised to maintain a lamp for him and his descendants forever.

[8]In the time of Jehoram, Edom rebelled against Judah and set up its own king. [9]So Jehoram went there with his officers and all his chariots. The Edomites surrounded him and his chariot commanders, but he rose up and broke through by night. [10]To this day Edom has been in rebellion against Judah.

Libnah revolted at the same time, because Jehoram had forsaken the LORD, the God of his fathers. [11]He had also built high places on the hills of Judah and had caused the people of Jerusalem to prostitute themselves and had led Judah astray.

[12]Jehoram received a letter from Elijah the prophet, which said:

"This is what the LORD, the God of your father David, says: 'You have not walked in the ways of your father Jehoshaphat or of Asa king of Judah. [13]But you have walked in the ways of the kings of Israel, and you have led Judah and the people of Jerusalem to prostitute themselves, just as the house of Ahab did. You have also murdered your own brothers, members of your father's house, men who were better than you. [14]So now the LORD is about to strike your people, your sons, your wives and everything that is yours, with a heavy blow. [15]You yourself will be very ill with a lingering disease of the bowels, until the disease causes your bowels to come out.' "

[16]The LORD aroused against Jehoram the hostility of the Philistines and of the Arabs who lived near the Cushites. [17]They attacked Judah, invaded it and carried off all the goods found in the king's palace, together with his sons and wives. Not a son was left to him except Ahaziah,[b] the youngest.

[18]After all this, the LORD afflicted Jehoram with an incurable disease of the bowels. [19]In the course of time, at the end of the second year, his bowels came out because of the disease, and he died in great pain. His people made no fire in his honour, as they had for his fathers.

[20]Jehoram was thirty-two years old when he became king, and he reigned in Jerusalem for eight years. He passed away, to no-one's regret, and was buried in the City of David, but not in the tombs of the kings.

Ahaziah King of Judah

22 The people of Jerusalem made Ahaziah, Jehoram's youngest son, king in his place, since the raiders, who came with the Arabs into the camp, had killed all the older sons. So Ahaziah son of Jehoram king of Judah began to reign.

[2]Ahaziah was twenty-two[a] years old when he became king, and he reigned in Jerusalem for one year. His mother's name was Athaliah, a granddaughter of Omri.

[3]He too walked in the ways of the house of Ahab, for his mother encouraged him in doing wrong. [4]He did evil in the eyes of the LORD, as the house of Ahab had done, for after his father's death they became his advisers, to his undoing. [5]He also followed their counsel when he went with Joram[b] son of Ahab king of Israel to war against Hazael king of Aram at Ramoth Gilead. The Arameans wounded Joram; [6]so he returned to Jezreel to recover from the wounds they had inflicted on him at Ramoth[c] in his battle with Hazael king of Aram.

Then Ahaziah[d] son of Jehoram king of Judah went down to Jezreel to see Joram son of Ahab because he had been wounded.

[7]Through Ahaziah's visit to Joram, God brought about Ahaziah's downfall. When Ahaziah arrived, he went out with Joram to meet Jehu son of Nimshi, whom the LORD had anointed to destroy the house of Ahab. [8]While Jehu was executing judgment on the house of Ahab, he found the princes of Judah and the sons of Ahaziah's relatives, who had been attending Ahaziah, and he killed them. [9]He then went in search of Ahaziah, and his men captured him while he was hiding in Samaria. He was brought to Jehu and put to death. They buried him, for they said, "He was a son of Jehoshaphat, who sought the LORD with all his heart." So there was no-one in the house of Ahaziah powerful enough to retain the kingdom.

Athaliah and Joash

[10]When Athaliah the mother of Ahaziah saw that her son was dead, she proceeded to destroy the whole royal family of the house of Judah. [11]But Jehosheba,[e] the daughter of King Jehoram, took Joash son of Ahaziah and stole him away from among the royal princes who were about to be murdered and put him and his nurse in a bedroom. Because Jehosheba,[e] the daughter of King Jehoram and wife of the priest Jehoiada, was Ahaziah's sister, she hid the child from Athaliah so that she could not kill him. [12]He remained hidden with them at the temple of God for six years while Athaliah ruled the land.

23 In the seventh year Jehoiada showed his strength. He made a covenant with the commanders of units of a hundred: Azariah son of Jeroham, Ishmael son of Jehohanan, Azariah son of Obed, Maaseiah son of Adaiah, and Elishaphat son of Zicri. [2]They went throughout Judah and gathered the Levites and the heads of Israelite families from all the towns. When they came to Jerusalem, [3]the whole assembly made a covenant with the king at the temple of God.

Jehoiada said to them, "The king's son shall reign, as the LORD promised concerning the descendants of David. [4]Now this is what you are to do: A third of you priests and Levites who are going on duty on the Sabbath are to keep watch at the doors, [5]a third of you at the royal palace and a third at the Foundation Gate, and all the other men are to be in the courtyards of the temple of the LORD. [6]No-one is to enter the temple of the LORD except the priests and Levites on duty; they may enter because they are consecrated, but all the

---

[b]17 Hebrew *Jehoahaz*, a variant of *Ahaziah*   [a]2 Some Septuagint manuscripts and Syriac (see also 2 Kings 8:26); Hebrew *forty-two*
[b]5 Hebrew *Jehoram*, a variant of *Joram*; also in verses 6 and 7   [c]6 Hebrew *Ramah*, a variant of *Ramoth*
[d]6 Some Hebrew manuscripts, Septuagint, Vulgate and Syriac (see also 2 Kings 8:29); most Hebrew manuscripts *Azariah*
[e]11 Hebrew *Jehoshabeath*, a variant of *Jehosheba*

other men are to guard what the LORD has assigned to them.[a] [7]The Levites are to station themselves round the king, each man with his weapons in his hand. Anyone who enters the temple must be put to death. Stay close to the king wherever he goes."

[8]The Levites and all the men of Judah did just as Jehoiada the priest ordered. Each one took his men — those who were going on duty on the Sabbath and those who were going off duty — for Jehoiada the priest had not released any of the divisions. [9]Then he gave the commanders of units of a hundred the spears and the large and small shields that had belonged to King David and that were in the temple of God. [10]He stationed all the men, each with his weapon in his hand, round the king — near the altar and the temple, from the south side to the north side of the temple.

[11]Jehoiada and his sons brought out the king's son and put the crown on him; they presented him with a copy of the covenant and proclaimed him king. They anointed him and shouted, "Long live the king!"

23:11 The coronation of Joash includes two important elements: the presentation of a copy of the covenant to him, and his anointing. These two acts underlined the role of the monarch as God's agent on earth. The copy of the covenant either refers to God's covenant with David's house, or to the Law of Moses (see Deuteronomy 17:18). The anointing with oil marked Joash as chosen by God for special service; only priests, prophets, and kings were anointed in this way. Jesus the Messiah (Messiah means "the anointed one") fulfilled each of these three roles.

---

[12]When Athaliah heard the noise of the people running and cheering the king, she went to them at the temple of the LORD. [13]She looked, and there was the king, standing by his pillar at the entrance. The officers and the trumpeters were beside the king, and all the people of the land were rejoicing and blowing trumpets, and singers with musical instruments were leading the praises. Then Athaliah tore her robes and shouted, "Treason! Treason!"

[14]Jehoiada the priest sent out the commanders of units of a hundred, who were in charge of the troops, and said to them: "Bring her out between the ranks[b] and put to the sword anyone who follows her." For the priest had said, "Do not put her to death at the temple of the LORD." [15]So they seized her as she reached the entrance of the Horse Gate on the palace grounds, and there they put her to death.

[16]Jehoiada then made a covenant that he and the people and the king[c] would be the LORD's people. [17]All the people went to the temple of Baal and tore it down. They smashed the altars and idols and killed Mattan the priest of Baal in front of the altars. [18]Then Jehoiada placed the oversight of the temple

of the LORD in the hands of the priests, who were Levites, to whom David had made assignments in the temple, to present the burnt offerings of the LORD as written in the Law of Moses, with rejoicing and singing, as David had ordered. [19]He also stationed doorkeepers at the gates of the LORD's temple so that no-one who was in any way unclean might enter.

[20]He took with him the commanders of hundreds, the nobles, the rulers of the people and all the people of the land and brought the king down from the temple of the LORD. They went into the palace through the Upper Gate and seated the king on the royal throne, [21]and all the people of the land rejoiced. And the city was quiet, because Athaliah had been slain with the sword.

Joash Repairs the Temple

24 Joash was seven years old when he became king, and he reigned in Jerusalem for forty years. His mother's name was Zibiah; she was from Beersheba. [2]Joash did what was right in the eyes of the LORD all the years of Jehoiada the priest. [3]Jehoiada chose two wives for him, and he had sons and daughters.

[4]Some time later Joash decided to restore the temple of the LORD. [5]He called together the priests and Levites and said to them, "Go to the towns of Judah and collect the money due annually from all Israel, to repair the temple of your God. Do it now." But the Levites did not act at once.

[6]Therefore the king summoned Jehoiada the chief priest and said to him, "Why haven't you required the Levites to bring in from Judah and Jerusalem the tax imposed by Moses the servant of the LORD and by the assembly of Israel for the Tent of the Testimony?"

[7]Now the sons of that wicked woman Athaliah had broken into the temple of God and had used even its sacred objects for the Baals.

[8]At the king's command, a chest was made and placed outside, at the gate of the temple of the LORD. [9]A proclamation was then issued in Judah and Jerusalem that they should bring to the LORD the tax that Moses the servant of God had required of Israel in the desert. [10]All the officials and all the people brought their contributions gladly, dropping them into the chest until it was full. [11]Whenever the chest was brought in by the Levites to the king's officials and they saw that there was a large amount of money, the royal secretary and the officer of the chief priest would come and empty the chest and carry it back to its place. They did this regularly and collected a great amount of money. [12]The king and Jehoiada gave it to the men who carried out the work required for the temple of the LORD. They hired masons and carpenters to restore the LORD's temple, and also workers in iron and bronze to repair the temple.

[13]The men in charge of the work were diligent, and the repairs progressed under them. They rebuilt the temple of God according to its original design and reinforced it. [14]When they had finished, they brought

---

[a] 6 Or to observe the LORD's command not to enter;   [b] 14 Or out from the precincts
[c] 16 Or covenant between the LORD, and the people and the king that they (see 2 Kings 11:17)

the rest of the money to the king and Jehoiada, and with it were made articles for the LORD's temple: articles for the service and for the burnt offerings, and also dishes and other objects of gold and silver. As long as Jehoiada lived, burnt offerings were presented continually in the temple of the LORD.

¹⁵Now Jehoiada was old and full of years, and he died at the age of a hundred and thirty. ¹⁶He was buried with the kings in the City of David, because of the good he had done in Israel for God and his temple.

The Wickedness of Joash

¹⁷After the death of Jehoiada, the officials of Judah came and paid homage to the king, and he listened to them. ¹⁸They abandoned the temple of the LORD, the God of their fathers, and worshipped Asherah poles and idols. Because of their guilt, God's anger came upon Judah and Jerusalem. ¹⁹Although the LORD sent prophets to the people to bring them back to him, and though they testified against them, they would not listen.

²⁰Then the Spirit of God came upon Zechariah son of Jehoiada the priest. He stood before the people and said, "This is what God says: 'Why do you disobey the LORD's commands? You will not prosper. Because you have forsaken the LORD, he has forsaken you.'"

²¹But they plotted against him, and by order of the king they stoned him to death in the courtyard of the LORD's temple. ²²King Joash did not remember the kindness Zechariah's father Jehoiada had shown him but killed his son, who said as he lay dying, "May the LORD see this and call you to account."

24:21   It may well have been the death of Zechariah which Jesus referred to in Luke 11:51 and Matthew 23:25. He summed up the long and sad history of bloodshed against God's messengers by citing Abel (in Genesis) and Zechariah. This may indicate that 2 Chronicles had taken its place as the last book in the Hebrew Bible, where it remains today. A constant theme in the Old and New Testaments is that God's prophets were ignored and often killed. Luke showed that this was a strong idea that shaped Jesus' ministry (Luke 13:33).

---

²³At the turn of the year,ᵃ the army of Aram marched against Joash; it invaded Judah and Jerusalem and killed all the leaders of the people. They sent all the plunder to their king in Damascus. ²⁴Although the Aramean army had come with only a few men, the LORD delivered into their hands a much larger army. Because Judah had forsaken the LORD, the God of their fathers, judgment was executed on Joash. ²⁵When the Arameans withdrew, they left Joash severely wounded. His officials conspired against him for murdering the son of Jehoiada the priest, and they killed him in his

bed. So he died and was buried in the City of David, but not in the tombs of the kings.

²⁶Those who conspired against him were Zabad,ᵇ son of Shimeath an Ammonite woman, and Jehozabad, son of Shimrithᶜ a Moabite woman. ²⁷The account of his sons, the many prophecies about him, and the record of the restoration of the temple of God are written in the annotations on the book of the kings. And Amaziah his son succeeded him as king.

Amaziah King of Judah

25 Amaziah was twenty-five years old when he became king, and he reigned in Jerusalem for twenty-nine years. His mother's name was Jehoaddin;ᵃ she was from Jerusalem. ²He did what was right in the eyes of the LORD, but not wholeheartedly. ³After the kingdom was firmly in his control, he executed the officials who had murdered his father the king. ⁴Yet he did not put their sons to death, but acted in accordance with what is written in the Law, in the Book of Moses, where the LORD commanded: "Fathers shall not be put to death for their children, nor children put to death for their fathers; each is to die for his own sins."ᵇ

⁵Amaziah called the people of Judah together and assigned them according to their families to commanders of thousands and commanders of hundreds for all Judah and Benjamin. He then mustered those twenty years old or more and found that there were three hundred thousand men ready for military service, able to handle the spear and shield. ⁶He also hired a hundred thousand fighting men from Israel for a hundred talentsᶜ of silver.

⁷But a man of God came to him and said, "O king, these troops from Israel must not march with you, for the LORD is not with Israel—not with any of the people of Ephraim. ⁸Even if you go and fight courageously in battle, God will overthrow you before the enemy, for God has the power to help or to overthrow."

⁹Amaziah asked the man of God, "But what about the hundred talents I paid for these Israelite troops?"

The man of God replied, "The LORD can give you much more than that."

¹⁰So Amaziah dismissed the troops who had come to him from Ephraim and sent them home. They were furious with Judah and left for home in a great rage.

¹¹Amaziah then marshalled his strength and led his army to the Valley of Salt, where he killed ten thousand men of Seir. ¹²The army of Judah also captured ten thousand men alive, took them to the top of a cliff and threw them down so that all were dashed to pieces.

¹³Meanwhile the troops that Amaziah had sent back and had not allowed to take part in the war raided Judean towns from Samaria to Beth Horon. They killed three thousand people and carried off great quantities of plunder.

¹⁴When Amaziah returned from slaughtering the Edomites, he brought back the gods of the people of Seir. He set them up as his own gods, bowed down to them and burned sacrifices to them. ¹⁵The anger of the LORD burned against Amaziah, and he sent a prophet

---

ᵃ23 Probably in the spring   ᵇ26 A variant of Jozabad   ᶜ26 A variant of Shomer
ᵃ1 Hebrew Jehoaddan, a variant of Jehoaddin   ᵇ4 Deut. 24:16
ᶜ6 That is, about 3½ tons (about 3.4 metric tons); also in verse 9

to him, who said, "Why do you consult this people's gods, which could not save their own people from your hand?"

[16]While he was still speaking, the king said to him, "Have we appointed you an adviser to the king? Stop! Why be struck down?"

So the prophet stopped but said, "I know that God has determined to destroy you, because you have done this and have not listened to my counsel."

[17]After Amaziah king of Judah consulted his advisers, he sent this challenge to Jehoash[d] son of Jehoahaz, the son of Jehu, king of Israel: "Come, meet me face to face."

[18]But Jehoash king of Israel replied to Amaziah king of Judah, "A thistle in Lebanon sent a message to a cedar in Lebanon, 'Give your daughter to my son in marriage.' Then a wild beast in Lebanon came along and trampled the thistle underfoot. [19]You say to yourself that you have defeated Edom, and now you are arrogant and proud. But stay at home! Why ask for trouble and cause your own downfall and that of Judah also?"

[20]Amaziah, however, would not listen, for God so worked that he might hand them over to ⌊Jehoash⌋, because they sought the gods of Edom. [21]So Jehoash king of Israel attacked. He and Amaziah king of Judah faced each other at Beth Shemesh in Judah. [22]Judah was routed by Israel, and every man fled to his home. [23]Jehoash king of Israel captured Amaziah king of Judah, the son of Joash, the son of Ahaziah,[e] at Beth Shemesh. Then Jehoash brought him to Jerusalem and broke down the wall of Jerusalem from the Ephraim Gate to the Corner Gate — a section about six hundred feet[f] long. [24]He took all the gold and silver and all the articles found in the temple of God that had been in the care of Obed-Edom, together with the palace treasures and the hostages, and returned to Samaria.

[25]Amaziah son of Joash king of Judah lived for fifteen years after the death of Jehoash son of Jehoahaz king of Israel. [26]As for the other events of Amaziah's reign, from beginning to end, are they not written in the book of the kings of Judah and Israel? [27]From the time that Amaziah turned away from following the LORD, they conspired against him in Jerusalem and he fled to Lachish, but they sent men after him to Lachish and killed him there. [28]He was brought back by horse and was buried with his fathers in the City of Judah.

Uzziah King of Judah

26 Then all the people of Judah took Uzziah,[a] who was sixteen years old, and made him king in place of his father Amaziah. [2]He was the one who rebuilt Elath and restored it to Judah after Amaziah rested with his fathers.

[3]Uzziah was sixteen years old when he became king, and he reigned in Jerusalem for fifty-two years. His mother's name was Jecoliah; she was from Jerusalem. [4]He did what was right in the eyes of the LORD,

just as his father Amaziah had done. [5]He sought God during the days of Zechariah, who instructed him in the fear[b] of God. As long as he sought the LORD, God gave him success.

[6]He went to war against the Philistines and broke down the walls of Gath, Jabneh and Ashdod. He then rebuilt towns near Ashdod and elsewhere among the Philistines. [7]God helped him against the Philistines and against the Arabs who lived in Gur Baal and against the Meunites. [8]The Ammonites brought tribute to Uzziah, and his fame spread as far as the border of Egypt, because he had become very powerful.

[9]Uzziah built towers in Jerusalem at the Corner Gate, at the Valley Gate and at the angle of the wall, and he fortified them. [10]He also built towers in the desert and dug many cisterns, because he had much livestock in the foothills and in the plain. He had people working his fields and vineyards in the hills and in the fertile lands, for he loved the soil.

[11]Uzziah had a well-trained army, ready to go out by divisions according to their numbers as mustered by Jeiel the secretary and Maaseiah the officer under the direction of Hananiah, one of the royal officials. [12]The total number of family leaders over the fighting men was 2,600. [13]Under their command was an army of 307,500 men trained for war, a powerful force to support the king against his enemies. [14]Uzziah provided shields, spears, helmets, coats of armour, bows and slingstones for the entire army. [15]In Jerusalem he made machines designed by skilful men for use on the towers and on the corner defences to shoot arrows and hurl large stones. His fame spread far and wide, for he was greatly helped until he became powerful.

[16]But after Uzziah became powerful, his pride led to his downfall. He was unfaithful to the LORD his God, and entered the temple of the LORD to burn incense on the altar of incense. [17]Azariah the priest with eighty other courageous priests of the LORD followed him in. [18]They confronted him and said, "It is not right for you, Uzziah, to burn incense to the LORD. That is for the priests, the descendants of Aaron, who have been consecrated to burn incense. Leave the sanctuary, for you have been unfaithful; and you will not be honoured by the LORD God."

[19]Uzziah, who had a censer in his hand ready to burn incense, became angry. While he was raging at the priests in their presence before the incense altar in the LORD's temple, leprosy[c] broke out on his forehead. [20]When Azariah the chief priest and all the other priests looked at him, they saw that he had leprosy on his forehead, so they hurried him out. Indeed, he himself was eager to leave, because the LORD had afflicted him.

[21]King Uzziah had leprosy until the day he died. He lived in a separate house[d] — leprous, and excluded from the temple of the LORD. Jotham his son had charge of the palace and governed the people of the land.

[22]The other events of Uzziah's reign, from beginning to end, are recorded by the prophet Isaiah son of

---

[d]17 Hebrew *Joash*, a variant of *Jehoash*; also in verses 18, 21, 23 and 25   [e]23 Hebrew *Jehoahaz*, a variant of *Ahaziah*
[f]23 Hebrew *four hundred cubits* (about 180 metres)   [a]1 Also called *Azariah*
[b]5 Many Hebrew manuscripts, Septuagint and Syriac; other Hebrew manuscripts *vision*
[c]19 The Hebrew word was used for various diseases affecting the skin — not necessarily leprosy; also in verses 20, 21 and 23.
[d]21 Or *in a house where he was relieved of responsibilities*

Amoz. [23]Uzziah rested with his fathers and was buried near them in a field for burial that belonged to the kings, for people said, "He had leprosy." And Jotham his son succeeded him as king.

26:22 This is the prophet whose name stands at the head of the book Isaiah — a book that the Chronicler clearly had access to in some form. Isaiah prophesied during the reigns of Uzziah, Jotham, and Hezekiah, and his famous vision of God enthroned in glory in the temple is dated to the year when Uzziah died (Isaiah 6). Most scholars agree that it is only the first thirty-nine chapters of the book of Isaiah that belong to this man; the rest consists of later prophecies.

Jotham King of Judah

27 Jotham was twenty-five years old when he became king, and he reigned in Jerusalem for sixteen years. His mother's name was Jerusha daughter of Zadok. [2]He did what was right in the eyes of the LORD, just as his father Uzziah had done, but unlike him he did not enter the temple of the LORD. The people, however, continued their corrupt practices. [3]Jotham rebuilt the Upper Gate of the temple of the LORD and did extensive work on the wall at the hill of Ophel. [4]He built towns in the Judean hills and forts and towers in the wooded areas.

[5]Jotham made war on the king of the Ammonites and conquered them. That year the Ammonites paid him a hundred talents[a] of silver, ten thousand cors[b] of wheat and ten thousand cors of barley. The Ammonites brought him the same amount also in the second and third years.

[6]Jotham grew powerful because he walked steadfastly before the LORD his God.

[7]The other events in Jotham's reign, including all his wars and the other things he did, are written in the book of the kings of Israel and Judah. [8]He was twenty-five years old when he became king, and he reigned in Jerusalem for sixteen years. [9]Jotham rested with his fathers and was buried in the City of David. And Ahaz his son succeeded him as king.

Ahaz King of Judah

28 Ahaz was twenty years old when he became king, and he reigned in Jerusalem for sixteen years. Unlike David his father, he did not do what was right in the eyes of the LORD. [2]He walked in the ways of the kings of Israel and also made cast idols for worshipping the Baals. [3]He burned sacrifices in the Valley of Ben Hinnom and sacrificed his sons in the fire, following the detestable ways of the nations that the LORD had driven out before the Israelites. [4]He offered sacrifices and burned incense at the high places, on the hilltops and under every spreading tree.

[5]Therefore the LORD his God handed him over to the king of Aram. The Arameans defeated him and took many of his people as prisoners and brought them to Damascus.

He was also given into the hands of the king of Israel, who inflicted heavy casualties on him. [6]In one day Pekah son of Remaliah killed a hundred and twenty thousand soldiers in Judah — because Judah had forsaken the LORD, the God of their fathers. [7]Zicri, an Ephraimite warrior, killed Maaseiah the king's son, Azrikam the officer in charge of the palace, and Elkanah, second to the king. [8]The Israelites took captive from their kinsmen two hundred thousand wives, sons and daughters. They also took a great deal of plunder, which they carried back to Samaria.

[9]But a prophet of the LORD named Oded was there, and he went out to meet the army when it returned to Samaria. He said to them, "Because the LORD, the God of your fathers, was angry with Judah, he gave them into your hand. But you have slaughtered them in a rage that reaches to heaven. [10]And now you intend to make the men and women of Judah and Jerusalem your slaves. But aren't you also guilty of sins against the LORD your God? [11]Now listen to me! Send back your fellow countrymen that you have taken as prisoners, for the LORD's fierce anger rests on you."

28:9 Israel's army went too far in its prosecution of this "just" war, and the people were rebuked for the cruel way they punished the southern tribes. In a similar fashion, the people of Babylon did God's will when they seized Jerusalem, but their arrogance grew too great (Isaiah 47), and their fate was sealed. In this passage from 2 Chronicles we have one of the few positive comments about the Northern Kingdom; they gave up their plunder and prisoners, and made reparations for what they had done.

---

[12]Then some of the leaders in Ephraim — Azariah son of Jehohanan, Berekiah son of Meshillemoth, Jehizkiah son of Shallum, and Amasa son of Hadlai — confronted those who were arriving from the war. [13]"You must not bring those prisoners here," they said, "or we will be guilty before the LORD. Do you intend to add to our sin and guilt? For our guilt is already great, and his fierce anger rests on Israel."

[14]So the soldiers gave up the prisoners and plunder in the presence of the officials and all the assembly. [15]The men designated by name took the prisoners, and from the plunder they clothed all who were naked. They provided them with clothes and sandals, food and drink, and healing balm. All those who were weak they put on donkeys. So they took them back to their fellow countrymen at Jericho, the City of Palms, and returned to Samaria.

[16]At that time King Ahaz sent to the king[a] of Assyria for help. [17]The Edomites had again come and attacked Judah and carried away prisoners, [18]while the

---

a5 That is, about 3½ tons (about 3.4 metric tons)   *b5* That is, probably about 60,500 bushels (about 2,200 kilolitres)
a16 One Hebrew manuscript, Septuagint and Vulgate (see also 2 Kings 16:7); most Hebrew manuscripts *kings*

Philistines had raided towns in the foothills and in the Negev of Judah. They captured and occupied Beth Shemesh, Aijalon and Gederoth, as well as Soco, Timnah and Gimzo, with their surrounding villages. ¹⁹The LORD had humbled Judah because of Ahaz king of Israel,ᵇ for he had promoted wickedness in Judah and had been most unfaithful to the LORD. ²⁰Tiglath-Pileserᶜ king of Assyria came to him, but gave him trouble instead of help. ²¹Ahaz took some of the things from the temple of the LORD and from the royal palace and from the princes and presented them to the king of Assyria, but that did not help him.

²²In his time of trouble King Ahaz became even more unfaithful to the LORD. ²³He offered sacrifices to the gods of Damascus, who had defeated him; for he thought, "Since the gods of the kings of Aram have helped them, I will sacrifice to them so that they will help me." But they were his downfall and the downfall of all Israel.

²⁴Ahaz gathered together the furnishings from the temple of God and took them away.ᵈ He shut the doors of the LORD's temple and set up altars at every street corner in Jerusalem. ²⁵In every town in Judah he built high places to burn sacrifices to other gods and provoked the LORD, the God of his fathers, to anger.

²⁶The other events of his reign and all his ways, from beginning to end, are written in the book of the kings of Judah and Israel. ²⁷Ahaz rested with his fathers and was buried in the city of Jerusalem, but he was not placed in the tombs of the kings of Israel. And Hezekiah his son succeeded him as king.

Hezekiah Purifies the Temple

29 Hezekiah was twenty-five years old when he became king, and he reigned in Jerusalem for twenty-nine years. His mother's name was Abijah daughter of Zechariah. ²He did what was right in the eyes of the LORD, just as his father David had done.

³In the first month of the first year of his reign, he opened the doors of the temple of the LORD and repaired them. ⁴He brought in the priests and the Levites, assembled them in the square on the east side ⁵and said, "Listen to me, Levites! Consecrate yourselves now and consecrate the temple of the LORD, the God of your fathers. Remove all defilement from the sanctuary. ⁶Our fathers were unfaithful; they did evil in the eyes of the LORD our God and forsook him. They turned their faces away from the LORD's dwelling-place and turned their backs on him. ⁷They also shut the doors of the portico and put out the lamps. They did not burn incense or present any burnt offerings at the sanctuary to the God of Israel. ⁸Therefore, the anger of the LORD has fallen on Judah and Jerusalem; he has made them an object of dread and horror and scorn, as you can see with your own eyes. ⁹This is why our fathers have fallen by the sword and why our sons and daughters and our wives are in captivity. ¹⁰Now I intend to make a covenant with the LORD, the God of Israel, so that his fierce anger will turn away from us.

¹¹My sons, do not be negligent now, for the LORD has chosen you to stand before him and serve him, to minister before him and to burn incense."

¹²Then these Levites set to work:

from the Kohathites,
    Mahath son of Amasai and Joel son of Azariah;
from the Merarites,
    Kish son of Abdi and Azariah son of Jehallelel;
from the Gershonites,
    Joah son of Zimmah and Eden son of Joah;
¹³from the descendants of Elizaphan,
    Shimri and Jeiel;
from the descendants of Asaph,
    Zechariah and Mattaniah;
¹⁴from the descendants of Heman,
    Jehiel and Shimei;
from the descendants of Jeduthun,
    Shemaiah and Uzziel.

¹⁵When they had assembled their brothers and consecrated themselves, they went in to purify the temple of the LORD, as the king had ordered, following the word of the LORD. ¹⁶The priests went into the sanctuary of the LORD to purify it. They brought out to the courtyard of the LORD's temple everything unclean that they found in the temple of the LORD. The Levites took it and carried it out to the Kidron Valley. ¹⁷They began the consecration on the first day of the first month, and by the eighth day of the month they reached the portico of the LORD. For eight more days they consecrated the temple of the LORD itself, finishing in the sixteenth day of the first month.

¹⁸Then they went in to King Hezekiah and reported: "We have purified the entire temple of the LORD, the altar of burnt offering with all its utensils, and the table for setting out the consecrated bread, with all its articles. ¹⁹We have prepared and consecrated all the articles that King Ahaz removed in his unfaithfulness while he was king. They are now in front of the LORD's altar."

²⁰Early the next morning King Hezekiah gathered the city officials together and went up to the temple of the LORD. ²¹They brought seven bulls, seven rams, seven male lambs and seven male goats as a sin offering for the kingdom, for the sanctuary and for Judah. The king commanded the priests, the descendants of Aaron, to offer these on the altar of the LORD. ²²So they slaughtered the bulls, and the priests took the blood and sprinkled it on the altar; next they slaughtered the rams and sprinkled their blood on the altar; then they slaughtered the lambs and sprinkled their blood on the altar. ²³The goats for the sin offering were brought before the king and the assembly, and they laid their hands on them. ²⁴The priests then slaughtered the goats and presented their blood on the altar for a sin offering to atone for all Israel, because the king had ordered the burnt offering and the sin offering for all Israel.

²⁵He stationed the Levites in the temple of the LORD with cymbals, harps and lyres in the way prescribed by David and Gad the king's seer and Nathan the prophet; this was commanded by the LORD through his

ᵇ19 That is, Judah, as frequently in 2 Chronicles   ᶜ20 Hebrew Tilgath-Pilneser, a variant of Tiglath-Pileser
ᵈ24 Or and cut them up

prophets. [26]So the Levites stood ready with David's instruments, and the priests with their trumpets. [27]Hezekiah gave the order to sacrifice the burnt offering on the altar. As the offering began, singing to the LORD began also, accompanied by trumpets and the instruments of David king of Israel. [28]The whole assembly bowed in worship, while the singers sang and the trumpeters played. All this continued until the sacrifice of the burnt offering was completed.

[29]When the offerings were finished, the king and everyone present with him knelt down and worshipped. [30]King Hezekiah and his officials ordered the Levites to praise the LORD with the words of David and of Asaph the seer. So they sang praises with gladness and bowed their heads and worshipped.

[31]Then Hezekiah said, "You have now dedicated yourselves to the LORD. Come and bring sacrifices and thank-offerings to the temple of the LORD." So the assembly brought sacrifices and thank-offerings, and all whose hearts were willing brought burnt offerings.

[32]The number of burnt offerings the assembly brought was seventy bulls, a hundred rams and two hundred male lambs — all of them for burnt offerings to the LORD. [33]The animals consecrated as sacrifices amounted to six hundred bulls and three thousand sheep and goats. [34]The priests, however, were too few to skin all the burnt offerings; so their kinsmen the Levites helped them until the task was finished and until other priests had been consecrated, for the Levites had been more conscientious in consecrating themselves than the priests had been. [35]There were burnt offerings in abundance, together with the fat of the fellowship offerings[a] and the drink offerings that accompanied the burnt offerings.

So the service of the temple of the LORD was reestablished. [36]Hezekiah and all the people rejoiced at what God had brought about for his people, because it was done so quickly.

Hezekiah Celebrates the Passover

30 Hezekiah sent word to all Israel and Judah and also wrote letters to Ephraim and Manasseh, inviting them to come to the temple of the LORD in Jerusalem and celebrate the Passover to the LORD, the God of Israel. [2]The king and his officials and the whole assembly in Jerusalem decided to celebrate the Passover in the second month. [3]They had not been able to celebrate it at the regular time because not enough priests had consecrated themselves and the people had not assembled in Jerusalem. [4]The plan seemed right both to the king and to the whole assembly. [5]They decided to send a proclamation throughout Israel, from Beersheba to Dan, calling the people to come to Jerusalem and celebrate the Passover to the LORD, the God of Israel. It had not been celebrated in large numbers according to what was written.

[6]At the king's command, couriers went throughout Israel and Judah with letters from the king and from his officials, which read:

"People of Israel, return to the LORD, the God of Abraham, Isaac and Israel, that he may return to you who are left, who have escaped from the hand of the kings of Assyria. [7]Do not be like your fathers and brothers, who were unfaithful to the LORD, the God of their fathers, so that he made them an object of horror, as you see. [8]Do not be stiff-necked, as your fathers were; submit to the LORD. Come to the sanctuary, which he has consecrated for ever. Serve the LORD your God, so that his fierce anger will turn away from you. [9]If you return to the LORD, then your brothers and your children will be shown compassion by their captors and will come back to this land, for the LORD your God is gracious and compassionate. He will not turn his face from you if you return to him."

[10]The couriers went from town to town in Ephraim and Manasseh, as far as Zebulun, but the people scorned and ridiculed them. [11]Nevertheless, some men of Asher, Manasseh and Zebulun humbled themselves and went to Jerusalem. [12]Also in Judah the hand of God was on the people to give them unity of mind to carry out what the king and his officials had ordered, following the word of the LORD.

[13]A very large crowd of people assembled in Jerusalem to celebrate the Feast of Unleavened Bread in the second month. [14]They removed the altars in Jerusalem and cleared away the incense altars and threw them into the Kidron Valley.

[15]They slaughtered the Passover lamb on the fourteenth day of the second month. The priests and the Levites were ashamed and consecrated themselves and brought burnt offerings to the temple of the LORD. [16]Then they took up their regular positions as prescribed in the Law of Moses the man of God. The priests sprinkled the blood handed to them by the Levites. [17]Since many in the crowd had not consecrated themselves, the Levites had to kill the Passover lambs for all those who were not ceremonially clean and could not consecrate their lambs to the LORD. [18]Although most of the many people who came from Ephraim, Manasseh, Issachar and Zebulun had not purified themselves, yet they ate the Passover, contrary to what was written. But Hezekiah prayed for them, saying, "May the LORD, who is good, pardon everyone [19]who sets his heart on seeking God — the LORD, the God of his fathers — even if he is not clean according to the rules of the sanctuary." [20]And the LORD heard Hezekiah and healed the people.

[21]The Israelites who were present in Jerusalem celebrated the Feast of Unleavened Bread for seven days with great rejoicing, while the Levites and priests sang to the LORD every day, accompanied by the LORD's instruments of praise.[a]

[22]Hezekiah spoke encouragingly to all the Levites, who showed good understanding of the service of the LORD. For the seven days they ate their assigned portion and offered fellowship offerings[b] and praised the LORD, the God of their fathers.

[23]The whole assembly then agreed to celebrate the festival seven more days; so for another seven days they celebrated joyfully. [24]Hezekiah king of Judah provided a thousand bulls and seven thousand sheep and

goats for the assembly, and the officials provided them with a thousand bulls and ten thousand sheep and goats. A great number of priests consecrated themselves. ²⁵The entire assembly of Judah rejoiced, along with the priests and Levites and all who had assembled from Israel, including the aliens who had come from Israel and those who lived in Judah. ²⁶There was great joy in Jerusalem, for since the days of Solomon son of David king of Israel there had been nothing like this in Jerusalem. ²⁷The priests and the Levites stood to bless the people, and God heard them, for their prayer reached heaven, his holy dwelling-place.

31 When all this had ended, the Israelites who were there went out to the towns of Judah, smashed the sacred stones and cut down the Asherah poles. They destroyed the high places and the altars throughout Judah and Benjamin and in Ephraim and Manasseh. After they had destroyed all of them, the Israelites returned to their own towns and to their own property.

Contributions for Worship

²Hezekiah assigned the priests and Levites to divisions — each of them according to their duties as priests or Levites — to offer burnt offerings and fellowship offerings,ª to minister, to give thanks and to sing praises at the gates of the LORD's dwelling. ³The king contributed from his own possessions for the morning and evening burnt offerings and for the burnt offerings on the Sabbaths, New Moons and appointed feasts as written in the Law of the LORD. ⁴He ordered the people living in Jerusalem to give the portion due to the priests and Levites so that they could devote themselves to the Law of the LORD. ⁵As soon as the order went out, the Israelites generously gave the firstfruits of their grain, new wine, oil and honey and all that the fields produced. They brought a great amount, a tithe of everything. ⁶The men of Israel and Judah who lived in the towns of Judah also brought a tithe of their herds and flocks and a tithe of the holy things dedicated to the LORD their God, and they piled them in heaps. ⁷They began doing this in the third month and finished in the seventh month. ⁸When Hezekiah and his officials came and saw the heaps, they praised the LORD and blessed his people Israel.

⁹Hezekiah asked the priests and Levites about the heaps; ¹⁰and Azariah the chief priest, from the family of Zadok, answered, "Since the people began to bring their contributions to the temple of the LORD, we have had enough to eat and plenty to spare, because the LORD has blessed his people, and this great amount is left over."

¹¹Hezekiah gave orders to prepare storerooms in the temple of the LORD, and this was done. ¹²Then they faithfully brought in the contributions, tithes and dedicated gifts. Conaniah, a Levite, was in charge of these things, and his brother Shimei was next in rank. ¹³Jehiel, Azaziah, Nahath, Asahel, Jerimoth, Jozabad, Eliel, Ismakiah, Mahath and Benaiah were supervisors under Conaniah and Shimei his brother, by

appointment of King Hezekiah and Azariah the official in charge of the temple of God.

¹⁴Kore son of Imnah the Levite, keeper of the East Gate, was in charge of the freewill offerings given to God, distributing the contributions made to the LORD and also the consecrated gifts. ¹⁵Eden, Miniamin, Jeshua, Shemaiah, Amariah and Shecaniah assisted him faithfully in the towns of the priests, distributing to their fellow priests according to their divisions, old and young alike.

¹⁶In addition, they distributed to the males three years old or more whose names were in the genealogical records — all who would enter the temple of the LORD to perform the daily duties of their various tasks, according to their responsibilities and their divisions. ¹⁷And they distributed to the priests enrolled by their families in the genealogical records and likewise to the Levites twenty years old or more, according to their responsibilities and their divisions. ¹⁸They included all the little ones, the wives, and the sons and daughters of the whole community listed in these genealogical records. For they were faithful in consecrating themselves.

¹⁹As for the priests, the descendants of Aaron, who lived on the farm lands around their towns or in any other towns, men were designated by name to distribute portions to every male among them and to all who were recorded in the genealogies of the Levites.

²⁰This is what Hezekiah did throughout Judah, doing what was good and right and faithful before the LORD his God. ²¹In everything that he undertook in the service of God's temple and in obedience to the law and the commands, he sought his God and worked wholeheartedly. And so he prospered.

Sennacherib Threatens Jerusalem

32 After all that Hezekiah had so faithfully done, Sennacherib king of Assyria came and invaded Judah. He laid siege to the fortified cities, thinking to conquer them for himself. ²When Hezekiah saw that Sennacherib had come and that he intended to make war on Jerusalem, ³he consulted with his officials and military staff about blocking off the water from the springs outside the city, and they helped him. ⁴A large force of men assembled, and they blocked all the springs and the stream that flowed through the land. "Why should the kingsª of Assyria come and find plenty of water?" they said. ⁵Then he worked hard repairing all the broken sections of the wall and building towers on it. He built another wall outside that one and reinforced the supporting terracesᵇ of the City of David. He also made large numbers of weapons and shields.

⁶He appointed military officers over the people and assembled them before him in the square at the city gate and encouraged them with these words: ⁷"Be strong and courageous. Do not be afraid or discouraged because of the king of Assyria and the vast army with him, for there is a greater power with us than with him. ⁸With him is only the arm of flesh, but with us is the LORD our God to help us and to fight our battles."

ª2 Traditionally *peace offerings*   ª4 Hebrew; Septuagint and Syriac *king*   ᵇ5 Or *the Millo*

And the people gained confidence from what Hezekiah the king of Judah said.

⁹Later, when Sennacherib king of Assyria and all his forces were laying siege to Lachish, he sent his officers to Jerusalem with this message for Hezekiah king of Judah and for all the people of Judah who were there:

¹⁰"This is what Sennacherib king of Assyria says: On what are you basing your confidence, that you remain in Jerusalem under siege? ¹¹When Hezekiah says, 'The LORD our God will save us from the hand of the king of Assyria,' he is misleading you, to let you die of hunger and thirst. ¹²Did not Hezekiah himself remove this god's high places and altars, saying to Judah and Jerusalem, 'You must worship before one altar and burn sacrifices on it'?

¹³"Do you not know what I and my fathers have done to all the peoples of the other lands? Were the gods of those nations ever able to deliver their land from my hand? ¹⁴Who of all the gods of these nations that my fathers destroyed has been able to save his people from me? How then can your god deliver you from my hand? ¹⁵Now do not let Hezekiah deceive you and mislead you like this. Do not believe him, for no god of any nation or kingdom has been able to deliver his people from my hand or the hand of my fathers. How much less will your god deliver you from my hand!"

¹⁶Sennacherib's officers spoke further against the LORD God and against his servant Hezekiah. ¹⁷The king also wrote letters insulting the LORD, the God of Israel, and saying this against him: "Just as the gods of the peoples of the other lands did not rescue their people from my hand, so the god of Hezekiah will not rescue his people from my hand." ¹⁸Then they called out in Hebrew to the people of Jerusalem who were on the wall, to terrify them and make them afraid in order to capture the city. ¹⁹They spoke about the God of Jerusalem as they did about the gods of the other peoples of the world—the work of men's hands.

²⁰King Hezekiah and the prophet Isaiah son of Amoz cried out in prayer to heaven about this. ²¹And the LORD sent an angel, who annihilated all the fighting men and the leaders and officers in the camp of the Assyrian king. So he withdrew to his own land in disgrace. And when he went into the temple of his god, some of his sons cut him down with the sword.

²²So the LORD saved Hezekiah and the people of Jerusalem from the hand of Sennacherib king of Assyria and from the hand of all others. He took care of themᶜ on every side. ²³Many brought offerings to Jerusalem for the LORD and valuable gifts for Hezekiah king of Judah. From then on he was highly regarded by all the nations.

Hezekiah's Pride, Success and Death

²⁴In those days Hezekiah became ill and was at the point of death. He prayed to the LORD, who answered him and gave him a miraculous sign. ²⁵But Hezekiah's heart was proud and he did not respond to the kindness shown him; therefore the LORD's wrath was on him and on Judah and Jerusalem. ²⁶Then Hezekiah repented of the pride of his heart, as did the people of Jerusalem; therefore the LORD's wrath did not come upon them during the days of Hezekiah.

²⁷Hezekiah had very great riches and honour, and he made treasuries for his silver and gold and for his precious stones, spices, shields and all kinds of valuables. ²⁸He also made buildings to store the harvest of grain, new wine and oil; and he made stalls for various kinds of cattle, and pens for the flocks. ²⁹He built villages and acquired great numbers of flocks and herds, for God had given him very great riches.

³⁰It was Hezekiah who blocked the upper outlet of the Gihon spring and channelled the water down to the west side of the City of David. He succeeded in everything he undertook. ³¹But when envoys were sent by the rulers of Babylon to ask him about the miraculous sign that had occurred in the land, God left him to test him and to know everything that was in his heart.

32:30   The building projects of Hezekiah mentioned here (and also in 2 Kings 20:20,21) have been proved by archaeology to be authentic. The tunnel which brought the water of Gihon into the pool of Siloam within the city walls has been beautifully preserved in all its 1,749-foot length. It still performs its original function. An inscription discovered in 1880 cut into the tunnel wall tells of the exciting moment when the diggers, coming from opposite ends, finally met up.

---

³²The other events of Hezekiah's reign and his acts of devotion are written in the vision of the prophet Isaiah son of Amoz in the book of the kings of Judah and Israel. ³³Hezekiah rested with his fathers and was buried on the hill where the tombs of David's descendants are. All Judah and the people of Jerusalem honoured him when he died. And Manasseh his son succeeded him as king.

Manasseh King of Judah

33 Manasseh was twelve years old when he became king, and he reigned in Jerusalem for fifty-five years. ²He did evil in the eyes of the LORD, following the detestable practices of the nations the LORD had driven out before the Israelites. ³He rebuilt the high places his father Hezekiah had demolished; he also erected altars to the Baals and made Asherah poles. He bowed down to all the starry hosts and worshipped them. ⁴He built altars in the temple of the LORD, of which the LORD had said, "My Name will remain in Jerusalem for ever." ⁵In both courts of the temple of the LORD, he built altars to all the starry hosts. ⁶He sacrificed his sons inᵃ the fire in the Valley of Ben Hinnom, practised sorcery, divination and witchcraft, and

---

ᶜ22 Hebrew; Septuagint and Vulgate *He gave them rest*   ᵃ6 Or *He made his sons pass through* consulted mediums and spiritists. He did much evil in the eyes of the LORD, provoking him to anger.

[7]He took the carved image he had made and put it in God's temple, of which God had said to David and to his son Solomon, "In this temple and in Jerusalem, which I have chosen out of all the tribes of Israel, I will put my Name for ever. [8]I will not again make the feet of the Israelites leave the land I assigned to your forefathers, if only they will be careful to do everything that I commanded them concerning all the laws, decrees and ordinances given through Moses." [9]But Manasseh led Judah and the people of Jerusalem astray, so that they did more evil than the nations the LORD had destroyed before the Israelites.

[10]The LORD spoke to Manasseh and his people, but they paid no attention. [11]So the LORD brought against them the army commanders of the king of Assyria, who took Manasseh prisoner, put a hook in his nose, bound him with bronze shackles and took him to Babylon. [12]In his distress he sought the favour of the LORD his God and humbled himself greatly before the God of his fathers. [13]And when he prayed to him, the LORD was moved by his entreaty and listened to his plea; so he brought him back to Jerusalem and to his kingdom. Then Manasseh knew that the LORD is God.

[14]Afterwards he rebuilt the outer wall of the City of David, west of the Gihon spring in the valley, as far as the entrance of the Fish Gate and encircling the hill of Ophel; he also made it much higher. He stationed military commanders in all the fortified cities in Judah.

[15]He got rid of the foreign gods and removed the image from the temple of the LORD, as well as all the altars he had built on the temple hill and in Jerusalem; and he threw them out of the city. [16]Then he restored the altar of the LORD and sacrificed fellowship offerings[b] and thank-offerings on it, and told Judah to serve the LORD, the God of Israel. [17]The people, however, continued to sacrifice at the high places, but only to the LORD their God.

[18]The other events of Manasseh's reign, including his prayer to his God and the words the seers spoke to him in the name of the LORD, the God of Israel, are written in the annals of the kings of Israel.[c] [19]His prayer and how God was moved by his entreaty, as well as all his sins and unfaithfulness, and the sites where he built high places and set up Asherah poles and idols before he humbled himself—all are written in the records of the seers.[d] [20]Manasseh rested with his fathers and was buried in his palace. And Amon his son succeeded him as king.

Amon King of Judah

[21]Amon was twenty-two years old when he became king, and he reigned in Jerusalem for two years. [22]He did evil in the eyes of the LORD, as his father Manasseh had done. Amon worshipped and offered sacrifices to all the idols Manasseh had made. [23]But unlike his father Manasseh, he did not humble himself before the LORD; Amon increased his guilt.

[24]Amon's officials conspired against him and assassinated him in his palace. [25]Then the people of the land killed all who had plotted against King Amon, and they made Josiah his son king in his place.

Josiah's Reforms

34 Josiah was eight years old when he became king, and he reigned in Jerusalem for thirty-one years. [2]He did what was right in the eyes of the LORD and walked in the ways of his father David, not turning aside to the right or to the left.

[3]In the eighth year of his reign, while he was still young, he began to seek the God of his father David. In his twelfth year he began to purge Judah and Jerusalem of high places, Asherah poles, carved idols and cast images. [4]Under his direction the altars of the Baals were torn down; he cut to pieces the incense altars that were above them, and smashed the Asherah poles, the idols and the images. These he broke to pieces and scattered over the graves of those who had sacrificed to them. [5]He burned the bones of the priests on their altars, and so he purged Judah and Jerusalem. [6]In the towns of Manasseh, Ephraim and Simeon, as far as Naphtali, and in the ruins around them, [7]he tore down the altars and the Asherah poles and crushed the idols to powder and cut to pieces all the incense altars throughout Israel. Then he went back to Jerusalem.

[8]In the eighteenth year of Josiah's reign, to purify the land and the temple, he sent Shaphan son of Azaliah and Maaseiah the ruler of the city, with Joah son of Joahaz, the recorder, to repair the temple of the LORD his God.

34:9   After the fall of Samaria to the Assyrians in 722 BC and the collapse of the Northern Kingdom, many Jews were deported to the east (27,290 according to the Assyrian records). However, many remained and some moved south into Judah when the Assyrians resettled Israel with foreigners (2 Kings 17); these are the remnant of Israel mentioned here. The Chronicler has tried to show as large a section of the Jewish nation as possible serving the temple's needs.

---

[9]They went to Hilkiah the high priest and gave him the money that had been brought into the temple of God, which the Levites who were the doorkeepers had collected from the people of Manasseh, Ephraim and the entire remnant of Israel and from all the people of Judah and Benjamin and the inhabitants of Jerusalem. [10]Then they entrusted it to the men appointed to supervise the work on the LORD's temple. These men paid the workers who repaired and restored the temple. [11]They also gave money to the carpenters and builders to purchase dressed stone, and timber for joists and beams for the buildings that the kings of Judah had allowed to fall into ruin. [12]The men did the work faithfully. Over them to direct them were Jahath and Obadiah, Levites

---

b16 Traditionally *peace offerings*   c18 That is, Judah, as frequently in 2 Chronicles
d19 One Hebrew manuscript and Septuagint; most Hebrew manuscripts *of Hozai*

descended from Merari, and Zechariah and Meshullam, descended from Kohath. The Levites — all who were skilled in playing musical instruments — [13]had charge of the labourers and supervised all the workers from job to job. Some of the Levites were secretaries, scribes and doorkeepers.

The Book of the Law Found

[14]While they were bringing out the money that had been taken into the temple of the Lord, Hilkiah the priest found the Book of the Law of the Lord that had been given through Moses. [15]Hilkiah said to Shaphan the secretary, "I have found the Book of the Law in the temple of the Lord." He gave it to Shaphan.

[16]Then Shaphan took the book to the king and reported to him: "Your officials are doing everything that has been committed to them. [17]They have paid out the money that was in the temple of the Lord and have entrusted it to the supervisors and workers." [18]Then Shaphan the secretary informed the king, "Hilkiah the priest has given me a book." And Shaphan read from it in the presence of the king.

[19]When the king heard the words of the Law, he tore his robes. [20]He gave these orders to Hilkiah, Ahikam son of Shaphan, Abdon son of Micah,[a] Shaphan the secretary and Asaiah the king's attendant: [21]"Go and enquire of the Lord for me and for the remnant in Israel and Judah about what is written in this book that has been found. Great is the Lord's anger that is poured out on us because our fathers have not kept the word of the Lord; they have not acted in accordance with all that is written in this book."

[22]Hilkiah and those the king had sent with him[b] went to speak to the prophetess Huldah, who was the wife of Shallum son of Tokhath,[c] the son of Hasrah,[d] keeper of the wardrobe. She lived in Jerusalem, in the Second District.

[23]She said to them, "This is what the Lord, the God of Israel, says: Tell the man who sent you to me, [24]'This is what the Lord says: I am going to bring disaster on this place and its people — all the curses written in the book that has been read in the presence of the king of Judah. [25]Because they have forsaken me and burned incense to other gods and provoked me to anger by all that their hands have made,[e] my anger will be poured out on this place and will not be quenched.' [26]Tell the king of Judah, who sent you to enquire of the Lord, 'This is what the Lord, the God of Israel, says concerning the words you heard: [27]Because your heart was responsive and you humbled yourself before God when you heard what he spoke against this place and its people, and because you humbled yourself before me and tore your robes and wept in my presence, I have heard you, declares the Lord. [28]Now I will gather you to your fathers, and you will be buried in peace. Your eyes will not see all the disaster I am going to bring on this place and on those who live here.' "

So they took her answer back to the king.

[29]Then the king called together all the elders of Judah and Jerusalem. [30]He went up to the temple of the Lord with the men of Judah, the people of Jerusalem, the priests and the Levites — all the people from the least to the greatest. He read in their hearing all the words of the Book of the Covenant, which had been found in the temple of the Lord. [31]The king stood by his pillar and renewed the covenant in the presence of the Lord — to follow the Lord and keep his commands, regulations and decrees with all his heart and all his soul, and to obey the words of the covenant written in this book.

[32]Then he made everyone in Jerusalem and Benjamin pledge themselves to it; the people of Jerusalem did this in accordance with the covenant of God, the God of their fathers.

[33]Josiah removed all the detestable idols from all the territory belonging to the Israelites, and he made all who were present in Israel serve the Lord their God. As long as he lived, they did not fail to follow the Lord, the God of their fathers.

Josiah Celebrates the Passover

35 Josiah celebrated the Passover to the Lord in Jerusalem, and the Passover lamb was slaughtered on the fourteenth day of the first month. [2]He appointed the priests to their duties and encouraged them in the service of the Lord's temple. [3]He said to the Levites, who instructed all Israel and who had been consecrated to the Lord: "Put the sacred ark in the temple that Solomon son of David king of Israel built. It is not to be carried about on your shoulders. Now serve the Lord your God and his people Israel. [4]Prepare yourselves by families in your divisions, according to the directions written by David king of Israel and by his son Solomon.

[5]"Stand in the holy place with a group of Levites for each sub-division of the families of your fellow countrymen, the lay people. [6]Slaughter the Passover lambs, consecrate yourselves and prepare the lambs for your fellow countrymen, doing what the Lord commanded through Moses."

[7]Josiah provided for all the lay people who were there a total of thirty thousand sheep and goats for the Passover offerings, and also three thousand cattle — all from the king's own possessions.

[8]His officials also contributed voluntarily to the people and the priests and Levites. Hilkiah, Zechariah and Jehiel, the administrators of God's temple, gave the priests two thousand six hundred Passover offerings and three hundred cattle. [9]Also Conaniah along with Shemaiah and Nethanel, his brothers, and Hashabiah, Jeiel and Jozabad, the leaders of the Levites, provided five thousand Passover offerings and five hundred head of cattle for the Levites.

[10]The service was arranged and the priests stood in their places with the Levites in their divisions as the king had ordered. [11]The Passover lambs were slaughtered, and the priests sprinkled the blood handed to them, while the Levites skinned the animals. [12]They set aside the burnt offerings to give them to the

[a]20 Also called Acbor son of Micaiah
[b]22 One Hebrew manuscript, Vulgate and Syriac; most Hebrew manuscripts do not have had sent with him.
[c]22 Also called Tikvah   [d]22 Also called Harhas   [e]25 Or by everything they have done

subdivisions of the families of the people to offer to the LORD, as is written in the Book of Moses. They did the same with the cattle. ¹³They roasted the Passover animals over the fire as prescribed, and boiled the holy offerings in pots, cauldrons and pans and served them quickly to all the people. ¹⁴After this, they made preparations for themselves and for the priests, because the priests, the descendants of Aaron, were sacrificing the burnt offerings and the fat portions until nightfall. So the Levites made preparations for themselves and for the Aaronic priests.

¹⁵The musicians, the descendants of Asaph, were in the places prescribed by David, Asaph, Heman and Jeduthun the king's seer. The gatekeepers at each gate did not need to leave their posts, because their fellow Levites made the preparations for them.

¹⁶So at that time the entire service of the LORD was carried out for the celebration of the Passover and the offering of burnt offerings on the altar of the LORD, as King Josiah had ordered. ¹⁷The Israelites who were present celebrated the Passover at that time and observed the Feast of Unleavened Bread for seven days. ¹⁸The Passover had not been observed like this in Israel since the days of the prophet Samuel; and none of the kings of Israel had ever celebrated such a Passover as did Josiah, with the priests, the Levites and all Judah and Israel who were there with the people of Jerusalem. ¹⁹This Passover was celebrated in the eighteenth year of Josiah's reign.

The Death of Josiah

²⁰After all this, when Josiah had set the temple in order, Neco king of Egypt went up to fight at Carchemish on the Euphrates, and Josiah marched out to meet him in battle. ²¹But Neco sent messengers to him saying, "What quarrel is there between you and me, O king of Judah? It is not you I am attacking at this time, but the house with which I am at war. God has told me to hurry; so stop opposing God, who is with me, or he will destroy you."

²²Josiah, however, would not turn away from him, but disguised himself to engage him in battle. He would not listen to what Neco had said at God's command but went to fight him on the plain of Megiddo.

²³Archers shot King Josiah, and he told his officers, "Take me away; I am badly wounded." ²⁴So they took him out of his chariot, put him in the other chariot he had and brought him to Jerusalem, where he died. He was buried in the tombs of his fathers, and all Judah and Jerusalem mourned for him.

²⁵Jeremiah composed laments for Josiah, and to this day all the men and women singers commemorate Josiah in the laments. These became a tradition in Israel and are written in the Laments.

²⁶The other events of Josiah's reign and his acts of devotion, according to what is written in the Law of the LORD—²⁷all the events, from beginning to end, are written in the book of the kings of Israel and Judah.

36 ¹And the people of the land took Jehoahaz son of Josiah and made him king in Jerusalem in place of his father.

Jehoahaz King of Judah

²Jehoahaz[a] was twenty-three years old when he became king, and he reigned in Jerusalem for three months. ³The king of Egypt dethroned him in Jerusalem and imposed on Judah a levy of a hundred talents[b] of silver and a talent[c] of gold. ⁴The king of Egypt made Eliakim, a brother of Jehoahaz, king over Judah and Jerusalem and changed Eliakim's name to Jehoiakim. But Neco took Eliakim's brother Jehoahaz and carried him off to Egypt.

35:24 The Chronicler's simple system of judging good and bad kings never has its weaknesses more clearly exposed than in the account of Josiah's death. Both 2 Chronicles and 2 Kings make it clear that there was never such an upright king as Josiah. Why then did he die so young at the height of his power? 2 Kings cannot provide an explanation and 2 Chronicles produces the incident with Neco, which is a poor attempt at accounting for the sudden end of Judah's noblest monarch.

Jehoiakim King of Judah

⁵Jehoiakim was twenty-five years old when he became king, and he reigned in Jerusalem for eleven years. He did evil in the eyes of the LORD his God. ⁶Nebuchadnezzar king of Babylon attacked him and bound him with bronze shackles to take him to Babylon. ⁷Nebuchadnezzar also took to Babylon articles from the temple of the LORD and put them in his temple[d] there.

⁸The other events of Jehoiakim's reign, the detestable things he did and all that was found against him, are written in the book of the kings of Israel and Judah. And Jehoiachin his son succeeded him as king.

Jehoiachin King of Judah

⁹Jehoiachin was eighteen[e] years old when he became king, and he reigned in Jerusalem for three months and ten days. He did evil in the eyes of the LORD. ¹⁰In the spring, King Nebuchadnezzar sent for him and brought him to Babylon, together with articles of value from the temple of the LORD, and he made Jehoiachin's uncle,[f] Zedekiah, king over Judah and Jerusalem.

---

a2 Hebrew *Joahaz*, a variant of *Jehoahaz*; also in verse 4   b3 That is, about 3⅓ tons (about 3.4 metric tons)
c3 That is, about 75 pounds (about 34 kilograms)   d7 Or *palace*
e9 One Hebrew manuscript, some Septuagint manuscripts and Syriac (see also 2 Kings 24:8); most Hebrew manuscripts *eight*
f10 Hebrew *brother*, that is, relative (see 2 Kings 24:17)

Zedekiah King of Judah

[11]Zedekiah was twenty-one years old when he became king, and he reigned in Jerusalem for eleven years. [12]He did evil in the eyes of the LORD his God and did not humble himself before Jeremiah the prophet, who spoke the word of the LORD. [13]He also rebelled against King Nebuchadnezzar, who had made him take an oath in God's name. He became stiff-necked and hardened his heart and would not turn to the LORD, the God of Israel. [14]Furthermore, all the leaders of the priests and the people became more and more unfaithful, following all the detestable practices of the nations and defiling the temple of the LORD, which he had consecrated in Jerusalem.

The Fall of Jerusalem

[15]The LORD, the God of their fathers, sent word to them through his messengers again and again, because he had pity on his people and on his dwelling-place. [16]But they mocked God's messengers, despised his words and scoffed at his prophets until the wrath of the LORD was aroused against his people and there was no remedy. [17]He brought up against them the king of the Babylonians,[g] who killed their young men with the sword in the sanctuary, and spared neither young man nor young woman, old man or aged. God handed all of them over to Nebuchadnezzar. [18]He carried to Babylon all the articles from the temple of God, both large and small, and the treasures of the LORD's temple and the treasures of the king and his officials. [19]They set fire to God's temple and broke down the wall of Jerusalem; they burned all the palaces and destroyed everything of value there.

36:19   When the temple in Jerusalem was burned down by the Babylonians there was no replacement put up for about 70 years. During this time it is likely that synagogues developed to provide people with a place in which to pray and study their scriptures. The final verse of 2 Chronicles points forward to a time when the temple would once again stand tall and so the book closes on a hopeful note. The fact that the book of Ezra begins by repeating these verses gives weight to the argument that Chronicles and Ezra and Nehemiah were originally joined together.

[20]He carried into exile to Babylon the remnant who escaped from the sword, and they became servants to him and his sons until the kingdom of Persia came to power. [21]The land enjoyed its sabbath rests; all the time of its desolation it rested, until the seventy years were completed in fulfilment of the word of the LORD spoken by Jeremiah.

[22]In the first year of Cyrus king of Persia, in order to fulfil the word of the LORD spoken by Jeremiah, the LORD moved the heart of Cyrus king of Persia to make a proclamation throughout his realm and to put it in writing:

[23]"This is what Cyrus king of Persia says:

" 'The LORD, the God of heaven, has given me all the kingdoms of the earth and he has appointed me to build a temple for him at Jerusalem in Judah. Anyone of his people among you—may the LORD his God be with him, and let him go up.' "

Ezra

The Story Continues

The book of Ezra picks up exactly where 2 Chronicles left off. There is a repetition of the words of Cyrus the Persian king, already quoted in 2 Chronicles 36. The simplest and best conclusion to draw is that Ezra was probably written by the Chronicler as a continuation of his history of the people of Israel. The beginning of half a century of exile in Babylon is recorded at the close of 2 Chronicles, but is not dwelt upon here; instead Ezra begins by moving briskly on to the glorious new opportunities for God's people that were made available by the arrival of the conquering Cyrus in 539 BC. Cyrus' capture of Babylon and his release of the exiles is seen as the direct intervention of God, and the fulfilment of the prophecy recounted in Jeremiah 25:11. The opening six chapters of Ezra focus on the temple: first an altar was set up and proper sacrifices restored, then the foundations themselves were laid amid great thanksgiving for God's enduring love towards Israel. Finally, despite persistent opposition during which work was halted for almost twenty years, the people won their right to complete the temple and replaced the treasures stolen by the Babylonians. The first half of Ezra closes with two jubilant scenes: the dedication of the new temple and the first celebration of the Passover back on home soil; the year is 515 BC.

God's Ambassador

It is only in chapter 7 that Ezra himself appears. He was sent by the Persian king Artaxerxes to lead another party of Jews home, to take more treasure for the temple, and to promote the Jewish law. Unfortunately we do not know exactly which king is referred to here and so the date of Ezra's journey could be either 458 or 398 BC—either way it is certainly a long time after the events of chapters 1—6 and shows how many problems still needed to be solved in Jerusalem. The momentous occasion of Ezra's reading of the law is found in the book of Nehemiah, and the final chapters of Ezra deal with the correction of the widespread practice of Jews intermarrying with non-Jews. Ezra called upon the men of God to separate themselves from their foreign wives in obedience to a similar command given by Moses to the tribes of Israel before they entered the promised land (Deuteronomy 7:3). This call must be seen in the light of the long influence of foreign idol-worship in Israel which had so often perverted the people's faith; in exile there must have been a great temptation to embrace Babylon's gods (see Isaiah 46). The book ends with the successful suppression of intermarriage.

Faithfulness to the Law

Unlike 1 and 2 Chronicles, Ezra and Nehemiah make no reference to other biblical books or known historical texts and this means they are our sole witnesses to this era. They do both use a rich variety of other sources: personal memoirs, imperial edicts, family lists, temple inventories, and so on. However, the dates given in Ezra and Nehemiah do not always agree. Despite such problems, Ezra is clearly the figure who is presented as the one who rescued the Jewish law from being lost forever, and it is for this that he is still revered by modern Jews.

Maintaining Identity

Ezra is, therefore, a book about change and continuity. But this is not for everyone; the lists in chapters 2 and 8 are a reminder that at such moments there was a pressing need to re-establish who was the true Israel, and so who could share in the benefits of this new age. The book was written for the Jews who returned from exile and centred their lives on the temple at Jerusalem. The Jews who stayed in Babylon were not considered to be part of God's plan (although those who came home with Ezra at least eighty years after the first group were clearly welcomed), nor were the non-Jews who worshipped the Jewish God; they formed the group that came into sharp conflict with the exiles in chapter 4. It is only the exiles who went back to Jerusalem who shared in God's plan—it is they who fulfilled Jeremiah's prophecy, they who rebuilt the temple and so inherited the promises of David, they who had to remain pure from their neighbours, and they who had behind them the authority of the Persian king. Here there is a lesson that goes beyond some of the narrow opinions of the book of Ezra. The firm belief of the writer that God is ruler of all peoples is demonstrated in the way the Persian kings, who followed a different religion, respected and acknowledged God's power. God's transforming action in the world can be found, therefore, not just among his own people. Nor is God at work simply in the area of individual human relationships, such as husbands and wives, but also in the grand sweep of world affairs. Ezra reminds us how surprising God can be.

Cyrus Helps the Exiles to Return

1 In the first year of Cyrus king of Persia, in order to fulfil the word of the LORD spoken by Jeremiah, the LORD moved the heart of Cyrus king of Persia to make a proclamation throughout his realm and to put it in writing:

1:1 Unlike the Babylonians, the Persians had a policy of religious tolerance. Cyrus was the greatest of the Persian kings; he was regarded by Isaiah as God's chosen instrument for the salvation of the Jews in exile (Isaiah 45).

---

[2]"This is what Cyrus king of Persia says:
"'The LORD, the God of heaven, has given me all the kingdoms of the earth and he has appointed me to build a temple for him at Jerusalem in Judah. [3]Anyone of his people among you—may his God be with him, and let him go up to Jerusalem in Judah and build the temple of the LORD, the God of Israel, the God who is in Jerusalem. [4]And the people of any place where survivors may now be living are to provide him with silver and gold, with goods and livestock, and with freewill offerings for the temple of God in Jerusalem.'"

[5]Then the family heads of Judah and Benjamin, and the priests and Levites—everyone whose heart God had moved—prepared to go up and build the house of the LORD in Jerusalem. [6]All their neighbours assisted them with articles of silver and gold, with goods and livestock, and with valuable gifts, in addition to all the freewill offerings. [7]Moreover, King Cyrus brought out the articles belonging to the temple of the LORD, which Nebuchadnezzar had carried away from Jerusalem and

had placed in the temple of his god. *ᵃ* ⁸Cyrus king of Persia had them brought by Mithredath the treasurer, who counted them out to Sheshbazzar the prince of Judah.

⁹This was the inventory:

gold dishes	30
silver dishes	1,000
silver pansᵇ	29
¹⁰gold bowls	30
matching silver bowls	410
other articles	1,000

¹¹In all, there were 5,400 articles of gold and of silver. Sheshbazzar brought all these along when the exiles came up from Babylon to Jerusalem.

The List of the Exiles Who Returned

2 Now these are the people of the province who came up from the captivity of the exiles, whom Nebuchadnezzar king of Babylon had taken captive to Babylon (they returned to Jerusalem and Judah, each to his own town, ²in company with Zerubbabel, Jeshua, Nehemiah, Seraiah, Reelaiah, Mordecai, Bilshan, Mispar, Bigvai, Rehum and Baanah):

2:1 These lists show that most Jews preserved their family records and their places of origin back home while they were in exile. Those that failed to produce these records could not prove their heritage, and were in danger of losing their place in the returning community. The priests in verse 61 had to wait for a special ceremony using the mysterious Urim and Thummim (probably some sort of sacred dice) to see if their claims to the priesthood could be validated.

The list of the men of the people of Israel:

³the descendants of Parosh	2,172
⁴of Shephatiah	372
⁵of Arah	775
⁶of Pahath-Moab (through the line of Jeshua and Joab)	2,812
⁷of Elam	1,254
⁸of Zattu	945
⁹of Zaccai	760
¹⁰of Bani	642
¹¹of Bebai	623
¹²of Azgad	1,222
¹³of Adonikam	666
¹⁴of Bigvai	2,056
¹⁵of Adin	454
¹⁶of Ater (through Hezekiah)	98
¹⁷of Bezai	323
¹⁸of Jorah	112
¹⁹of Hashum	223
²⁰of Gibbar	95

²¹the men of Bethlehem	123
²²of Netophah	56
²³of Anathoth	128
²⁴of Azmaveth	42
²⁵of Kiriath Jearim,ᵃ Kephirah and Beeroth	743
²⁶of Ramah and Geba	621
²⁷of Michmash	122
²⁸of Bethel and Ai	223
²⁹of Nebo	52
³⁰of Magbish	156
³¹of the other Elam	1,254
³²of Harim	320
³³of Lod, Hadid and Ono	725
³⁴of Jericho	345
³⁵of Senaah	3,630

³⁶The priests:

the descendants of Jedaiah (through the family of Jeshua)	973
³⁷of Immer	1,052
³⁸of Pashhur	1,247
³⁹of Harim	1,017

⁴⁰The Levites:

the descendants of Jeshua and Kadmiel (through the line of Hodaviah)	74

⁴¹The singers:

the descendants of Asaph	128

⁴²The gatekeepers of the temple:

the descendants of Shallum, Ater, Talmon, Akkub, Hatita and Shobai	139

⁴³The temple servants:

the descendants of Ziha, Hasupha, Tabbaoth, ⁴⁴Keros, Siaha, Padon, ⁴⁵Lebanah, Hagabah, Akkub, ⁴⁶Hagab, Shalmai, Hanan, ⁴⁷Giddel, Gahar, Reaiah, ⁴⁸Rezin, Nekoda, Gazzam, ⁴⁹Uzza, Paseah, Besai, ⁵⁰Asnah, Meunim, Nephussim, ⁵¹Bakbuk, Hakupha, Harhur, ⁵²Bazluth, Mehida, Harsha, ⁵³Barkos, Sisera, Temah, ⁵⁴Neziah and Hatipha

⁵⁵The descendants of the servants of Solomon:

the descendants of Sotai, Hassophereth, Peruda, ⁵⁶Jaala, Darkon, Giddel, ⁵⁷Shephatiah, Hattil, Pokereth-Hazzebaim and Ami

⁵⁸The temple servants and the descendants of the servants of Solomon	392

⁵⁹The following came up from the towns of Tel Melah, Tel Harsha, Kerub, Addon and Immer, but

---

ᵃ7 Or gods   ᵇ9 The meaning of the Hebrew for this word is uncertain.
ᵃ25 See Septuagint (see also Neh. 7:29); Hebrew Kiriath Arim.

they could not show that their families were descended from Israel:

60The descendants of
Delaiah, Tobiah and Nekoda   652

61And from among the priests:

The descendants of
Hobaiah, Hakkoz and Barzillai (a man who had married a daughter of Barzillai the Gileadite and was called by that name). 62These searched for their family records, but they could not find them and so were excluded from the priesthood as unclean. 63The governor ordered them not to eat any of the most sacred food until there was a priest ministering with the Urim and Thummim.

64The whole company numbered 42,360, 65besides their 7,337 menservants and maidservants; and they also had 200 men and women singers. 66They had 736 horses, 245 mules, 67435 camels and 6,720 donkeys.

68When they arrived at the house of the LORD in Jerusalem, some of the heads of the families gave freewill offerings towards the rebuilding of the house of God on its site. 69According to their ability they gave to the treasury for this work 61,000 drachmas[b] of gold, 5,000 minas[c] of silver and 100 priestly garments.

2:68 It was very important that the second temple was built on the original site of the first temple; in this way after the exile the Jews would inherit all the blessings that God had promised to David and Solomon (recorded in 1 and 2 Chronicles). Ezra 3 continues to emphasize that everything was done in accordance with Scripture, and that the worship followed the pattern prescribed by David himself. Continuity of tradition was vital for the new community.

70The priests, the Levites, the singers, the gatekeepers and the temple servants settled in their own towns, along with some of the other people, and the rest of the Israelites settled in their towns.

Rebuilding the Altar

3 When the seventh month came and the Israelites had settled in their towns, the people assembled as one man in Jerusalem. 2Then Jeshua son of Jozadak and his fellow priests and Zerubbabel son of Shealtiel and his associates began to build the altar of the God of Israel to sacrifice burnt offerings on it, in accordance with what is written in the Law of Moses the man of God. 3Despite their fear of the peoples around them, they built the altar on its foundation and sacrificed burnt offerings on it to the LORD, both the morning and evening sacrifices. 4Then in accordance with what is written, they celebrated the Feast of Tabernacles with the required number of burnt offerings prescribed for each day. 5After that, they presented the regular burnt offerings, the New Moon sacrifices and the sacrifices for all the appointed sacred feasts of the LORD, as well as those brought as freewill offerings to the LORD. 6On the first day of the seventh month they began to offer burnt offerings to the LORD, though the foundation of the LORD's temple had not yet been laid.

3:2 It is odd that the author who takes such a great interest in the house of David made no special mention of who Zerubbabel was; he was the sole remaining representative of the Davidic dynasty, as he was the grandson of Jehoiachin, the exiled king. There is in Ezra the beginning of a movement away from the hopes that had been placed in the kingly figure towards a community ideal focused on the new temple.

Rebuilding the Temple

7Then they gave money to the masons and carpenters, and gave food and drink and oil to the people of Sidon and Tyre, so that they would bring cedar logs by sea from Lebanon to Joppa, as authorised by Cyrus king of Persia.

8In the second month of the second year after their arrival at the house of God in Jerusalem, Zerubbabel son of Shealtiel, Jeshua son of Jozadak and the rest of their brothers (the priests and the Levites and all who had returned from the captivity to Jerusalem) began the work, appointing Levites twenty years of age and older to supervise the building of the house of the LORD. 9Jeshua and his sons and brothers and Kadmiel and his sons (descendants of Hodaviah[a]) and the sons of Henadad and their sons and brothers — all Levites — joined together in supervising those working on the house of God.

10When the builders laid the foundation of the temple of the LORD, the priests in their vestments and with trumpets, and the Levites (the sons of Asaph) with cymbals, took their places to praise the LORD, as prescribed by David king of Israel. 11With praise and thanksgiving they sang to the LORD:

"He is good;
his love to Israel endures for ever."

And all the people gave a great shout of praise to the LORD, because the foundation of the house of the LORD was laid. 12But many of the older priests and Levites and family heads, who had seen the former temple, wept aloud when they saw the foundation of this temple being laid, while many others shouted for joy. 13No-one could distinguish the sound of the shouts of joy from the sound of weeping, because the people made so much noise. And the sound was heard far away.

---

b69 That is, about 1,100 pounds (about 500 kilograms)   c69 That is, about 2⅘ tons (about 2.9 metric tons)
a9 Hebrew Yehudah, probably a variant of Hodaviah

Opposition to the Rebuilding

4 When the enemies of Judah and Benjamin heard that the exiles were building a temple for the LORD, the God of Israel, [2]they came to Zerubbabel and to the heads of the families and said, "Let us help you build because, like you, we seek your God and have been sacrificing to him since the time of Esarhaddon king of Assyria, who brought us here."

[3]But Zerubbabel, Jeshua and the rest of the heads of the families of Israel answered, "You have no part with us in building a temple to our God. We alone will build it for the LORD, the God of Israel, as King Cyrus, the king of Persia, commanded us."

[4]Then the peoples around them set out to discourage the people of Judah and make them afraid to go on building.[a] [5]They hired counsellors to work against them and frustrate their plans during the entire reign of Cyrus king of Persia and down to the reign of Darius king of Persia.

Later Opposition Under Xerxes and Artaxerxes

[6]At the beginning of the reign of Xerxes,[b] they lodged an accusation against the people of Judah and Jerusalem.

[7]And in the days of Artaxerxes king of Persia, Bishlam, Mithredath, Tabeel and the rest of his associates wrote a letter to Artaxerxes. The letter was written in Aramaic script and in the Aramaic language.[c,d]

4:7 The reference to Aramaic shows that here the writer was using a new source. Since Aramaic was the official diplomatic language of the Persian empire it is not surprising to find that these documents were not translated into Hebrew, which was the common tongue of the Jewish nation. Aramaic became more and more widespread and by the time of Jesus it was the everyday language for many Jews.

---

[8]Rehum the commanding officer and Shimshai the secretary wrote a letter against Jerusalem to Artaxerxes the king as follows:

[9]Rehum the commanding officer and Shimshai the secretary, together with the rest of their associates — the judges and officials over the men from Tripolis, Persia,[e] Erech and Babylon, the Elamites of Susa, [10]and the other people whom the great and honourable Ashurbanipal[f] deported and settled in the city of Samaria and elsewhere in Trans-Euphrates.

[11](This is a copy of the letter they sent him.)

To King Artaxerxes,

From your servants, the men of Trans-Euphrates:

[12]The king should know that the Jews who came up to us from you have gone to Jerusalem and are rebuilding that rebellious and wicked city. They are restoring the walls and repairing the foundations.

[13]Furthermore, the king should know that if this city is built and its walls are restored, no more taxes, tribute or duty will be paid, and the royal revenues will suffer. [14]Now since we are under obligation to the palace and it is not proper for us to see the king dishonoured, we are sending this message to inform the king, [15]so that a search may be made in the archives of your predecessors. In these records you will find that this city is a rebellious city, troublesome to kings and provinces, a place of rebellion from ancient times. That is why this city was destroyed. [16]We inform the king that if this city is built and its walls are restored, you will be left with nothing in Trans-Euphrates.

[17]The king sent this reply:

To Rehum the commanding officer, Shimshai the secretary and the rest of their associates living in Samaria and elsewhere in Trans-Euphrates:

Greetings.

[18]The letter you sent us has been read and translated in my presence. [19]I issued an order and a search was made, and it was found that this city has a long history of revolt against kings and has been a place of rebellion and sedition. [20]Jerusalem has had powerful kings ruling over the whole of Trans-Euphrates, and taxes, tribute and duty were paid to them. [21]Now issue an order to these men to stop work, so that this city will not be rebuilt until I so order. [22]Be careful not to neglect this matter. Why let this threat grow, to the detriment of the royal interests?

[23]As soon as the copy of the letter of King Artaxerxes was read to Rehum and Shimshai the secretary and their associates, they went immediately to the Jews in Jerusalem and compelled them by force to stop.

[24]Thus the work on the house of God in Jerusalem came to a standstill until the second year of the reign of Darius king of Persia.

Tattenai's Letter to Darius

5 Now Haggai the prophet and Zechariah the prophet, a descendant of Iddo, prophesied to the Jews in Judah and Jerusalem in the name of the God of Israel, who was over them. [2]Then Zerubbabel son of Shealtiel and Jeshua son of Jozadak set to work to rebuild the house of God in Jerusalem. And the prophets of God were with them, helping them.

[3]At that time Tattenai, governor of Trans-Euphrates, and Shethar-Bozenai and their associates went to them and asked, "Who authorised you to rebuild this temple and restore this structure?" [4]They also asked, "What

---

a4 Or *and troubled them as they built*   *b6* Hebrew *Ahasuerus,* a variant of Xerxes' Persian name
c7 Or *written in Aramaic and translated*   *d7* The text of Ezra 4:8–6:18 is in Aramaic.
e9 Or *officials, magistrates and governors over the men from*   *f10* Aramaic *Osnappar,* a variant of *Ashurbanipal*

are the names of the men constructing this building?"[a] [5]But the eye of their God was watching over the elders of the Jews, and they were not stopped until a report could go to Darius and his written reply be received.

[6]This is a copy of the letter that Tattenai, governor of Trans-Euphrates, and Shethar-Bozenai and their associates, the officials of Trans-Euphrates, sent to King Darius. [7]The report they sent him read as follows:

To King Darius:

Cordial greetings.

[8]The king should know that we went to the district of Judah, to the temple of the great God. The people are building it with large stones and placing the timbers in the walls. The work is being carried on with diligence and is making rapid progress under their direction.

[9]We questioned the elders and asked them, "Who authorised you to rebuild this temple and restore this structure?" [10]We also asked them their names, so that we could write down the names of their leaders for your information.

[11]This is the answer they gave us:

"We are the servants of the God of heaven and earth, and we are rebuilding the temple that was built many years ago, one that a great king of Israel built and finished. [12]But because our fathers angered the God of heaven, he handed them over to Nebuchadnezzar the Chaldean, king of Babylon, who destroyed this temple and deported the people to Babylon.

[13]"However, in the first year of Cyrus king of Babylon, King Cyrus issued a decree to rebuild this house of God. [14]He even removed from the temple[b] of Babylon the gold and silver articles of the house of God, which Nebuchadnezzar had taken from the temple in Jerusalem and brought to the temple[b] in Babylon.

"Then King Cyrus gave them to a man named Sheshbazzar, whom he had appointed governor, [15]and he told him, 'Take these articles and go and deposit them in the temple in Jerusalem. And rebuild the house of God on its site.' [16]So this Sheshbazzar came and laid the foundations of the house of God in Jerusalem. From that day to the present it has been under construction but is not yet finished."

[17]Now if it pleases the king, let a search be made in the royal archives of Babylon to see if King Cyrus did in fact issue a decree to rebuild this house of God in Jerusalem. Then let the king send us his decision in this matter.

The Decree of Darius

6 King Darius then issued an order, and they searched in the archives stored in the treasury at Babylon. [2]A scroll was found in the citadel of Ecbatana in the province of Media, and this was written on it:

Memorandum:

[3]In the first year of King Cyrus, the king issued a decree concerning the temple of God in Jerusalem:

Let the temple be rebuilt as a place to present sacrifices, and let its foundations be laid. It is to be ninety feet[a] high and ninety feet wide, [4]with three courses of large stones and one of timbers. The costs are to be paid by the royal treasury. [5]Also, the gold and silver articles of the house of God, which Nebuchadnezzar took from the temple in Jerusalem and brought to Babylon, are to be returned to their places in the temple in Jerusalem; they are to be deposited in the house of God.

[6]Now then, Tattenai, governor of Trans-Euphrates, and Shethar-Bozenai and you, their fellow officials of that province, stay away from there. [7]Do not interfere with the work on this temple of God. Let the governor of the Jews and the Jewish elders rebuild this house of God on its site.

[8]Moreover, I hereby decree what you are to do for these elders of the Jews in the construction of this house of God:
The expenses of these men are to be fully paid out of the royal treasury, from the revenues of Trans-Euphrates, so that the work will not stop. [9]Whatever is needed—young bulls, rams, male lambs for burnt offerings to the God of heaven, and wheat, salt, wine and oil, as requested by the priests in Jerusalem—must be given them daily without fail, [10]so that they may offer sacrifices pleasing to the God of heaven and pray for the well-being of the king and his sons.

6:10 A ruler like the Persian king was not unaware of the benefits of getting his subjects to pray for him—at the least it was a mark of respect and goodwill. This practice continued into the Roman period and the Emperor allowed the Jews to continue their temple worship as long as they prayed for the health of the empire and its leaders. According to the Jewish historian Josephus, it was the refusal to offer this sacrifice that made war with Rome inevitable in 66 AD.

---

[11]Furthermore, I decree that if anyone changes this edict, a beam is to be pulled from his house and he is to be lifted up and impaled on it. And for this crime his house is to be made a pile of rubble. [12]May God, who has caused his Name to dwell there, overthrow any king or people who lifts a hand to change this decree or to destroy this temple in Jerusalem.

I Darius have decreed it. Let it be carried out with diligence.

---

[a]4 See Septuagint; Aramaic [4]We told them the names of the men constructing this building.   [b]14 Or palace
[a]3 Aramaic sixty cubits (about 27 metres)

Completion and Dedication of the Temple

13Then, because of the decree King Darius had sent, Tattenai, governor of Trans-Euphrates, and Shethar-Bozenai and their associates carried it out with diligence. 14So the elders of the Jews continued to build and prosper under the preaching of Haggai the prophet and Zechariah, a descendant of Iddo. They finished building the temple according to the command of the God of Israel and the decrees of Cyrus, Darius and Artaxerxes, kings of Persia. 15The temple was completed on the third day of the month Adar, in the sixth year of the reign of King Darius.

16Then the people of Israel—the priests, the Levites and the rest of the exiles—celebrated the dedication of the house of God with joy. 17For the dedication of this house of God they offered a hundred bulls, two hundred rams, four hundred male lambs and, as a sin offering for all Israel, twelve male goats, one for each of the tribes of Israel. 18And they installed the priests in their divisions and the Levites in their groups for the service of God at Jerusalem, according to what is written in the Book of Moses.

The Passover

19On the fourteenth day of the first month, the exiles celebrated the Passover. 20The priests and Levites had purified themselves and were all ceremonially clean. The Levites slaughtered the Passover lamb for all the exiles, for their brothers the priests and for themselves. 21So the Israelites who had returned from the exile ate it, together with all who had separated themselves from the unclean practices of their Gentile neighbours in order to seek the LORD, the God of Israel. 22For seven days they celebrated with joy the Feast of Unleavened Bread, because the LORD had filled them with joy by changing the attitude of the king of Assyria, so that he assisted them in the work on the house of God, the God of Israel.

Ezra Comes to Jerusalem

7 After these things, during the reign of Artaxerxes king of Persia, Ezra son of Seraiah, the son of Azariah, the son of Hilkiah, 2the son of Shallum, the son of Zadok, the son of Ahitub, 3the son of Amariah, the son of Azariah, the son of Meraioth, 4the son of Zerahiah, the son of Uzzi, the son of Bukki, 5the son of Abishua, the son of Phinehas, the son of Eleazar, the son of Aaron the chief priest—6this Ezra came up from Babylon. He was a teacher well versed in the Law of Moses, which the LORD, the God of Israel, had given. The king had granted him everything he asked, for the hand of the LORD his God was on him. 7Some of the Israelites, including priests, Levites, singers, gatekeepers and temple servants, also came up to Jerusalem in the seventh year of King Artaxerxes.

8Ezra arrived in Jerusalem in the fifth month of the seventh year of the king. 9He had begun his journey from Babylon on the first day of the first month, and he arrived in Jerusalem on the first day of the fifth month, for the gracious hand of his God was on him. 10For Ezra had devoted himself to the study and observance of the Law of the LORD, and to teaching its decrees and laws in Israel.

7:1   Ezra's status and rank are established by a genealogy listing sixteen names, going back as far as Moses' brother Aaron, the first of the Jewish nation. Ezra was a priest and his major role was that of a teacher. Elsewhere he is referred to as a scribe, which was a high office of court rather than a simple pen-pushing job (a secretary of state rather than a secretary). It was these special talents that made him best suited to teach the law to the Jews.

King Artaxerxes' Letter to Ezra

11This is a copy of the letter King Artaxerxes had given to Ezra the priest and teacher, a man learned in matters concerning the commands and decrees of the LORD for Israel:

12aArtaxerxes, king of kings,

To Ezra the priest, a teacher of the Law of the God of heaven:

Greetings.

13Now I decree that any of the Israelites in my kingdom, including priests and Levites, who wish to go to Jerusalem with you, may go. 14You are sent by the king and his seven advisers to enquire about Judah and Jerusalem with regard to the Law of your God, which is in your hand. 15Moreover, you are to take with you the silver and gold that the king and his advisers have freely given to the God of Israel, whose dwelling is in Jerusalem, 16together with all the silver and gold you may obtain from the province of Babylon, as well as the freewill offerings of the people and priests for the temple of their God in Jerusalem. 17With this money be sure to buy bulls, rams and male lambs, together with their grain offerings and drink offerings, and sacrifice them on the altar of the temple of your God in Jerusalem.

18You and your brother Jews may then do whatever seems best with the rest of the silver and gold, in accordance with the will of your God. 19Deliver to the God of Jerusalem all the articles entrusted to you for worship in the temple of your God. 20And anything else needed for the temple of your God that you may have occasion to supply, you may provide from the royal treasury.

21Now I, King Artaxerxes, order all the treasurers of Trans-Euphrates to provide with diligence whatever Ezra the priest, a teacher of the Law of the God of heaven, may ask of you—22up to a hundred talentsb of silver, a hundred corsc of

---

a12 The text of Ezra 7:12–26 is in Aramaic.   b22 That is, about 3⅓ tons (about 3.4 metric tons)
c22 That is, probably about 600 bushels (about 22 kilolitres)

wheat, a hundred baths^d of wine, a hundred baths^d of olive oil, and salt without limit. ^{23}Whatever the God of heaven has prescribed, let it be done with diligence for the temple of the God of heaven. Why should there be wrath against the realm of the king and of his sons? ^{24}You are also to know that you have no authority to impose taxes, tribute or duty on any of the priests, Levites, singers, gatekeepers, temple servants or other workers at this house of God.

^{25}And you, Ezra, in accordance with the wisdom of your God, which you possess, appoint magistrates and judges to administer justice to all the people of Trans-Euphrates — all who know the laws of your God. And you are to teach any who do not know them. ^{26}Whoever does not obey the law of your God and the law of the king must surely be punished by death, banishment, confiscation of property, or imprisonment.

^{27}Praise be to the LORD, the God of our fathers, who has put it into the king's heart to bring honour to the house of the LORD in Jerusalem in this way ^{28}and who has extended his good favour to me before the king and his advisers and all the king's powerful officials. Because the hand of the LORD my God was on me, I took courage and gathered leading men from Israel to go up with me.

List of the Family Heads Returning With Ezra

8 These are the family heads and those registered with them who came up with me from Babylon during the reign of King Artaxerxes:

^{2}of the descendants of Phinehas, Gershom;
of the descendants of Ithamar, Daniel;
of the descendants of David, Hattush ^{3}of the descendants of Shecaniah;

of the descendants of Parosh, Zechariah, and with him were registered 150 men;
^{4}of the descendants of Pahath-Moab, Eliehoenai son of Zerahiah, and with him 200 men;
^{5}of the descendants of Zattu,^{a} Shecaniah son of Jahaziel, and with him 300 men;
^{6}of the descendants of Adin, Ebed son of Jonathan, and with him 50 men;
^{7}of the descendants of Elam, Jeshaiah son of Athaliah, and with him 70 men;
^{8}of the descendants of Shephatiah, Zebadiah son of Michael, and with him 80 men;
^{9}of the descendants of Joab, Obadiah son of Jehiel, and with him 218 men;
^{10}of the descendants of Bani,^{b} Shelomith son of Josiphiah, and with him 160 men;
^{11}of the descendants of Bebai, Zechariah son of Bebai, and with him 28 men;
^{12}of the descendants of Azgad, Johanan son of Hakkatan, and with him 110 men;
^{13}of the descendants of Adonikam, the last ones, whose names were Eliphelet, Jeuel and Shemaiah, and with them 60 men;
^{14}of the descendants of Bigvai, Uthai and Zaccur, and with them 70 men.

The Return to Jerusalem

^{15}I assembled them at the canal that flows towards Ahava, and we camped there three days. When I checked among the people and the priests, I found no Levites there. ^{16}So I summoned Eliezer, Ariel, Shemaiah, Elnathan, Jarib, Elnathan, Nathan, Zechariah and Meshullam, who were leaders, and Joiarib and Elnathan, who were men of learning, ^{17}and I sent them to Iddo, the leader in Casiphia. I told them what to say to Iddo and his kinsmen, the temple servants in Casiphia, so that they might bring attendants to us for the house of our God. ^{18}Because the gracious hand of our God was on us, they brought us Sherebiah, a capable man, from the descendants of Mahli son of Levi, the son of Israel, and Sherebiah's sons and brothers, 18 men; ^{19}and Hashabiah, together with Jeshaiah from the descendants of Merari, and his brothers and nephews, 20 men. ^{20}They also brought 220 of the temple servants — a body that David and the officials had established to assist the Levites. All were registered by name.

^{21}There, by the Ahava Canal, I proclaimed a fast, so that we might humble ourselves before our God and ask him for a safe journey for us and our children, with all our possessions. ^{22}I was ashamed to ask the king for soldiers and horsemen to protect us from enemies on the road, because we had told the king, "The gracious hand of our God is on everyone who looks to him, but his great anger is against all who forsake him." ^{23}So we fasted and petitioned our God about this, and he answered our prayer.

^{24}Then I set apart twelve of the leading priests, together with Sherebiah, Hashabiah and ten of their brothers, ^{25}and I weighed out to them the offering of silver and gold and the articles that the king, his advisers, his officials and all Israel present there had donated for the house of our God. ^{26}I weighed out to them 650 talents^c of silver, silver articles weighing 100 talents,^{d} 100 talents^d of gold, ^{27}20 bowls of gold valued at 1,000 darics,^{e} and two fine articles of polished bronze, as precious as gold.

^{28}I said to them, "You as well as these articles are consecrated to the LORD. The silver and gold are a freewill offering to the LORD, the God of your fathers. ^{29}Guard them carefully until you weigh them out in the chambers of the house of the LORD in Jerusalem before the leading priests and the Levites and the family heads of Israel." ^{30}Then the priests and Levites received the silver and gold and sacred articles that had been weighed out to be taken to the house of our God in Jerusalem.

^{31}On the twelfth day of the first month we set out from the Ahava Canal to go to Jerusalem. The hand of

---

^{d}22 That is, probably about 500 gallons (about 2.2 kilolitres)
^{a}5 Some Septuagint manuscripts (also 1 Esdras 8:32); Hebrew does not have Zattu.
^{b}10 Some Septuagint manuscripts (also 1 Esdras 8:36); Hebrew does not have Bani.
^{c}26 That is, about 22 tons (about 22 metric tons) ^{d}26 That is, about 3⅓ tons (about 3.4 metric tons)
^{e}27 That is, about 19 pounds (about 8.5 kilograms)

our God was on us, and he protected us from enemies and bandits along the way. ³²So we arrived in Jerusalem, where we rested three days.

³³On the fourth day, in the house of our God, we weighed out the silver and gold and the sacred articles into the hands of Meremoth son of Uriah, the priest. Eleazar son of Phinehas was with him, and so were the Levites Jozabad son of Jeshua and Noadiah son of Binnui. ³⁴Everything was accounted for by number and weight, and the entire weight was recorded at that time.

³⁵Then the exiles who had returned from captivity sacrificed burnt offerings to the God of Israel: twelve bulls for all Israel, ninety-six rams, seventy-seven male lambs and, as a sin offering, twelve male goats. All this was a burnt offering to the LORD. ³⁶They also delivered the king's orders to the royal satraps and to the governors of Trans-Euphrates who then gave assistance to the people and to the house of God.

Ezra's Prayer About Intermarriage

9 After these things had been done, the leaders came to me and said, "The people of Israel, including the priests and the Levites, have not kept themselves separate from the neighbouring peoples with their detestable practices, like those of the Canaanites, Hittites, Perizzites, Jebusites, Ammonites, Moabites, Egyptians and Amorites. ²They have taken some of their daughters as wives for themselves and their sons, and have mingled the holy race with the peoples around them. And the leaders and officials have led the way in this unfaithfulness."

³When I heard this, I tore my tunic and cloak, pulled hair from my head and beard and sat down appalled. ⁴Then everyone who trembled at the words of the God of Israel gathered round me because of this unfaithfulness of the exiles. And I sat there appalled until the evening sacrifice.

⁵Then, at the evening sacrifice, I rose from my self-abasement, with my tunic and cloak torn, and fell on my knees with my hands spread out to the LORD my God ⁶and prayed:

"O my God, I am too ashamed and disgraced to lift up my face to you, my God, because our sins are higher than our heads and our guilt has reached to the heavens. ⁷From the days of our forefathers until now, our guilt has been great. Because of our sins, we and our kings and our priests have been subjected to the sword and captivity, to pillage and humiliation at the hand of foreign kings, as it is today.

⁸"But now, for a brief moment, the LORD our God has been gracious in leaving us a remnant and giving us a firm place in his sanctuary, and so our God gives light to our eyes and a little relief in our bondage. ⁹Though we are slaves, our God has not deserted us in our bondage. He has shown us kindness in the sight of the kings of Persia: He has granted us new life to rebuild the house of our God and repair its ruins, and he has given us a wall of protection in Judah and Jerusalem.

¹⁰"But now, O our God, what can we say after this? For we have disregarded the commands

¹¹you gave through your servants the prophets when you said: 'The land you are entering to possess is a land polluted by the corruption of its peoples. By their detestable practices they have filled it with their impurity from one end to the other. ¹²Therefore, do not give your daughters in marriage to their sons or take their daughters for your sons. Do not seek a treaty of friendship with them at any time, that you may be strong and eat the good things of the land and leave it to your children as an everlasting inheritance.'

9:12   We cannot help but notice that the advice Ezra gives here is completely opposite to that given to those going into exile in Babylon in Jeremiah 29. Jeremiah told the exiles to intermarry and have children, and to seek the prosperity of the Babylonian people. Now, in changed circumstances, Ezra called on the Jews who had come back from Babylon to separate themselves off completely from their neighbours.

---

¹³"What has happened to us is a result of our evil deeds and our great guilt, and yet, our God, you have punished us less than our sins have deserved and have given us a remnant like this. ¹⁴Shall we again break your commands and intermarry with the peoples who commit such detestable practices? Would you not be angry enough with us to destroy us, leaving us no remnant or survivor? ¹⁵O LORD, God of Israel, you are righteous! We are left this day as a remnant. Here we are before you in our guilt, though because of it not one of us can stand in your presence."

The People's Confession of Sin

10 While Ezra was praying and confessing, weeping and throwing himself down before the house of God, a large crowd of Israelites — men, women and children — gathered round him. They too wept bitterly. ²Then Shecaniah son of Jehiel, one of the descendants of Elam, said to Ezra, "We have been unfaithful to our God by marrying foreign women from the peoples around us. But in spite of this, there is still hope for Israel. ³Now let us make a covenant before our God to send away all these women and their children, in accordance with the counsel of my lord and of those who fear the commands of our God. Let it be done according to the Law. ⁴Rise up; this matter is in your hands. We will support you, so take courage and do it."

⁵So Ezra rose up and put the leading priests and Levites and all Israel under oath to do what had been suggested. And they took the oath. ⁶Then Ezra withdrew from before the house of God and went to the room of Jehohanan son of Eliashib. While he was there, he ate no food and drank no water, because he continued to mourn over the unfaithfulness of the exiles. ⁷A proclamation was then issued throughout Judah and Jerusalem for all the exiles to assemble in Jerusalem. ⁸Anyone who failed to appear within three days

would forfeit all his property, in accordance with the decision of the officials and elders, and would himself be expelled from the assembly of the exiles.

⁹Within the three days, all the men of Judah and Benjamin had gathered in Jerusalem. And on the twentieth day of the ninth month, all the people were sitting in the square before the house of God, greatly distressed by the occasion and because of the rain. ¹⁰Then Ezra the priest stood up and said to them, "You have been unfaithful; you have married foreign women, adding to Israel's guilt. ¹¹Now make confession to the Lord, the God of your fathers, and do his will. Separate yourselves from the peoples around you and from your foreign wives."

¹²The whole assembly responded with a loud voice: "You are right! We must do as you say. ¹³But there are many people here and it is the rainy season; so we cannot stand outside. Besides, this matter cannot be taken care of in a day or two, because we have sinned greatly in this thing. ¹⁴Let our officials act for the whole assembly. Then let everyone in our towns who has married a foreign woman come at a set time, along with the elders and judges of each town, until the fierce anger of our God in this matter is turned away from us." ¹⁵Only Jonathan son of Asahel and Jahzeiah son of Tikvah, supported by Meshullam and Shabbethai the Levite, opposed this.

¹⁶So the exiles did as was proposed. Ezra the priest selected men who were family heads, one from each family division, and all of them designated by name. On the first day of the tenth month they sat down to investigate the cases, ¹⁷and by the first day of the first month they finished dealing with all the men who had married foreign women.

10:17   The list of those Jews who had intermarried shows that the problem affected all levels of society, even the priests and the Levites who were expected to set an example as the religious leaders of the day. The first time the harm caused by intermarriage is mentioned it is in relation to the kings of Israel, Solomon being the worst culprit (see 1 Kings 11 and Nehemiah 13).

Those Guilty of Intermarriage

¹⁸Among the descendants of the priests, the following had married foreign women:

From the descendants of Jeshua son of Jozadak, and his brothers:
Maaseiah, Eliezer, Jarib and Gedaliah. ¹⁹(They all gave their hands in pledge to put away their wives, and for their guilt they each presented a ram from the flock as a guilt offering.)
²⁰From the descendants of Immer:
Hanani and Zebadiah.
²¹From the descendants of Harim:
Maaseiah, Elijah, Shemaiah, Jehiel and Uzziah.
²²From the descendants of Pashhur:
Elioenai, Maaseiah, Ishmael, Nethanel, Jozabad and Elasah.

²³Among the Levites:

Jozabad, Shimei, Kelaiah (that is Kelita), Pethahiah, Judah and Eliezer.
²⁴From the singers:
Eliashib.
From the gatekeepers:
Shallum, Telem and Uri.

²⁵And among the other Israelites:

From the descendants of Parosh:
Ramiah, Izziah, Malkijah, Mijamin, Eleazar, Malkijah and Benaiah.
²⁶From the descendants of Elam:
Mattaniah, Zechariah, Jehiel, Abdi, Jeremoth and Elijah.
²⁷From the descendants of Zattu:
Elioenai, Eliashib, Mattaniah, Jeremoth, Zabad and Aziza.
²⁸From the descendants of Bebai:
Jehohanan, Hananiah, Zabbai and Athlai.
²⁹From the descendants of Bani:
Meshullam, Malluch, Adaiah, Jashub, Sheal and Jeremoth.
³⁰From the descendants of Pahath-Moab:
Adna, Kelal, Benaiah, Maaseiah, Mattaniah, Bezalel, Binnui and Manasseh.
³¹From the descendants of Harim:
Eliezer, Ishijah, Malkijah, Shemaiah, Shimeon, ³²Benjamin, Malluch and Shemariah.
³³From the descendants of Hashum:
Mattenai, Mattattah, Zabad, Eliphelet, Jeremai, Manasseh and Shimei.
³⁴From the descendants of Bani:
Maadai, Amram, Uel, ³⁵Benaiah, Bedeiah, Keluhi, ³⁶Vaniah, Meremoth, Eliashib, ³⁷Mattaniah, Mattenai and Jaasu.
³⁸From the descendants of Binnui:ᵃ
Shimei, ³⁹Shelemiah, Nathan, Adaiah, ⁴⁰Macnadebai, Shashai, Sharai, ⁴¹Azarel, Shelemiah, Shemariah, ⁴²Shallum, Amariah and Joseph.
⁴³From the descendants of Nebo:
Jeiel, Mattithiah, Zabad, Zebina, Jaddai, Joel and Benaiah.

⁴⁴All these had married foreign women, and some of them had children by these wives.ᵇ

ᵃ37,38 See Septuagint (also 1 Esdras 9:34); Hebrew *Jaasu* 38*and Bani and Binnui,*
ᵇ44 Or *and they sent them away with their children*

Nehemiah

Jerusalem: City Centre

Nehemiah is the final book written by the Chronicler, and like 1 and 2 Chronicles and Ezra his interests remained much the same: the centre of activity is still Jerusalem, the holy city, and he was only concerned with the fortunes of the exiles who returned home. Nehemiah's lament on hearing about the state of the walls of Jerusalem is a dramatic opening to the book. He responded by interceding for the people with a prayer of confession which regretted their lack of faith and asked for mercy, as Ezra did when he heard about the crisis which had been caused by intermarriage.

Nehemiah to the Rescue

Ezra and Nehemiah were similar characters; both gave up their good jobs in the Persian court to return home and to press through measures to aid the suffering Jewish remnant there. Nehemiah struggled to rebuild the city walls in the face of opposition far fiercer than was ever raised against the rebuilding of the temple 70 years before. Building the walls up could easily have been seen as an act of rebellion, and opponents of the project often raised this objection (e.g. Ezra 4:12). Yet Nehemiah accomplished his task in just 52 days (although excavations suggest he only actually enclosed a small part of the city around the temple area) and also put an end to the oppressive debts and taxes by which the rich were crushing the poor. Like Ezra, his reforms were quickly accepted and his gentle rule for 12 years between 445 and 433 BC explains his popularity.

Two Great Men

Ezra himself took centre stage when he presented the Law of Moses to the assembly (chapter 8). This passage, it seems, originally belonged to the book of Ezra and the mention of Nehemiah in verse 9 may be the Chronicler's attempt to link the careers of these two great men; in truth we cannot be certain that they were active in Jerusalem at the same time. Following the reading of the law there was a great public confession which traces Israel's behaviour from the earliest times down to the exile. It is a powerful demonstration of how Israel made sense of God's action towards his people; the prayer recalls how God continually forgave them and refused to desert them despite their rebellion against him. God's generous love in the past, therefore, gave them strong hope in their present troubles and they pledged to change their ways.

A Song of Rejoicing

The closing chapters of Nehemiah recall both the settling of Jerusalem and the dedication of the new walls, when the sound of rejoicing could be heard far and wide. At the end a second governorship of Nehemiah is mentioned when he put an end to several abuses including cultic malpractice, infringements of sabbath laws, and intermarriage. At this point, with a typical request for God to remember him with favour, the book stops.

An Important Message

Nehemiah is important because, like Ezra, it shows how long it took to rebuild the nation; it was not simply a case of re-erecting the temple. The optimism of people like the prophet Zechariah, who wrote when the temple was being put up, seems to have been misplaced. Within a couple of generations Nehemiah heard of a land that was in great trouble and disgrace — walls needed to be constructed, people rehoused, a community put back together ready to face the world. Notice the strength of Nehemiah's comment in chapter 6: he refused to seek refuge in the temple as if it were some magic lifesaver. To find this sentiment in a book written by the Chronicler who had set such store by the temple is a sober reminder of two things: firstly that God is not confined to any building made by human hands (in Nehemiah God was worshipped in the city squares, on its walls, at its gates, and even far away in the Persian capital); secondly that God calls upon us all to work in partnership with him; for example, in chapter 4 when the work on the wall was under severe threat from its enemies Nehemiah did not just pray and he did not just post guards. He did both.

Working Together

The book also reminds us of the need for the physical to go hand in hand with the spiritual. Alongside the spiritual renewal which came from Ezra's reading of the law went the concrete improvements in social conditions; the wall offered peace and security to the inhabitants, the poor were delivered from their harsh and unjust burdens, and those in a position to exploit their power refrained from doing so. The result was a community which learned to pull together towards a common goal. It was led by a person of vision and courage, and inspired by a firm belief that what they were doing was divinely willed. It was only this powerful combination that enabled the Jews to overcome all the obstacles in their way and to fulfil the purposes of God.

Nehemiah's Prayer

1 The words of Nehemiah son of Hacaliah:

In the month of Kislev in the twentieth year, while I was in the citadel of Susa, ²Hanani, one of my brothers, came from Judah with some other men, and I questioned them about the Jewish remnant that survived the exile, and also about Jerusalem.

³They said to me, "Those who survived the exile and are back in the province are in great trouble and disgrace. The wall of Jerusalem is broken down, and its gates have been burned with fire."

⁴When I heard these things, I sat down and wept. For some days I mourned and fasted and prayed before the God of heaven. ⁵Then I said:

"O Lord, God of heaven, the great and awesome God, who keeps his covenant of love with those who love him and obey his commands, ⁶let your ear be attentive and your eyes open to hear the prayer your servant is praying before you day and night for your servants, the people of Israel. I confess the sins we Israelites, including myself and my father's house, have committed against you. ⁷We have acted very wickedly towards you.

We have not obeyed the commands, decrees and laws you gave your servant Moses.

[8]"Remember the instruction you gave your servant Moses, saying, 'If you are unfaithful, I will scatter you among the nations, [9]but if you return to me and obey my commands, then even if your exiled people are at the farthest horizon, I will gather them from there and bring them to the place I have chosen as a dwelling for my Name.'

[10]"They are your servants and your people, whom you redeemed by your great strength and your mighty hand. [11]O Lord, let your ear be attentive to the prayer of this your servant and to the prayer of your servants who delight in revering your name. Give your servant success today by granting him favour in the presence of this man."

I was cupbearer to the king.

Artaxerxes Sends Nehemiah to Jerusalem

2 In the month of Nisan in the twentieth year of King Artaxerxes, when wine was brought for him, I took the wine and gave it to the king. I had not been sad in his presence before; [2]so the king asked me, "Why does your face look so sad when you are not ill? This can be nothing but sadness of heart."

I was very much afraid, [3]but I said to the king, "May the king live for ever! Why should my face not look sad when the city where my fathers are buried lies in ruins, and its gates have been destroyed by fire?"

[4]The king said to me, "What is it you want?"

Then I prayed to the God of heaven, [5]and I answered the king, "If it pleases the king and if your servant has found favour in his sight, let him send me to the city in Judah where my fathers are buried so that I can rebuild it."

[6]Then the king, with the queen sitting beside him, asked me, "How long will your journey take, and when will you get back?" It pleased the king to send me; so I set a time.

[7]I also said to him, "If it pleases the king, may I have letters to the governors of Trans-Euphrates, so that they will provide me safe-conduct until I arrive in Judah? [8]And may I have a letter to Asaph, keeper of the king's forest, so he will give me timber to make beams for the gates of the citadel by the temple and for the city wall and for the residence I will occupy?" And because the gracious hand of my God was upon me, the king granted my requests. [9]So I went to the governors of Trans-Euphrates and gave them the king's letters. The king had also sent army officers and cavalry with me.

[10]When Sanballat the Horonite and Tobiah the Ammonite official heard about this, they were very much disturbed that someone had come to promote the welfare of the Israelites.

Nehemiah Inspects Jerusalem's Walls

[11]I went to Jerusalem, and after staying there three days [12]I set out during the night with a few men. I had not told anyone what my God had put in my heart to do for Jerusalem. There were no mounts with me except the one I was riding on.

[13]By night I went out through the Valley Gate towards the Jackal[a] Well and the Dung Gate, examining the walls of Jerusalem, which had been broken down, and its gates, which had been destroyed by fire. [14]Then I moved on towards the Fountain Gate and the King's Pool, but there was not enough room for my mount to get through; [15]so I went up the valley by night, examining the wall. Finally, I turned back and re-entered through the Valley Gate. [16]The officials did not know where I had gone or what I was doing, because as yet I had said nothing to the Jews or the priests or nobles or officials or any others who would be doing the work.

2:13 Some have suggested that Jerusalem suffered a disaster in the first half of the fifth century BC which left the city in this ruined state after the original exiles had repaired its damage. Since there is so little information about this era we can never be certain, but some think that the Edomites attacked the city, and that the curse against them in Psalm 137 refers to this event and not to the great fall of Jerusalem.

---

[17]Then I said to them, "You see the trouble we are in: Jerusalem lies in ruins, and its gates have been burned with fire. Come, let us rebuild the wall of Jerusalem, and we will no longer be in disgrace." [18]I also told them about the gracious hand of my God upon me and what the king had said to me.

They replied, "Let us start rebuilding." So they began this good work.

[19]But when Sanballat the Horonite, Tobiah the Ammonite official and Geshem the Arab heard about it, they mocked and ridiculed us. "What is this you are doing?" they asked. "Are you rebelling against the king?"

[20]I answered them by saying, "The God of heaven will give us success. We his servants will start rebuilding, but as for you, you have no share in Jerusalem or any claim or historic right to it."

Builders of the Wall

3 Eliashib the high priest and his fellow priests went to work and rebuilt the Sheep Gate. They dedicated it and set its doors in place, building as far as the Tower of the Hundred, which they dedicated, and as far as the Tower of Hananel. [2]The men of Jericho built the adjoining section, and Zaccur son of Imri built next to them.

[3]The Fish Gate was rebuilt by the sons of Hassenaah. They laid its beams and put its doors and bolts and bars in place. [4]Meremoth son of Uriah, the son of Hakkoz, repaired the next section. Next to him Meshullam son of Berekiah, the son of Meshezabel, made repairs, and next to him Zadok son of Baana also made repairs. [5]The

---

[a] 13 Or Serpent or Fig

next section was repaired by the men of Tekoa, but their nobles would not put their shoulders to the work under their supervisors.[a]

6The Jeshanah[b] Gate was repaired by Joiada son of Paseah and Meshullam son of Besodeiah. They laid its beams and put its doors and bolts and bars in place. 7Next to him, repairs were made by men from Gibeon and Mizpah—Melatiah of Gibeon and Jadon of Meronoth—places under the authority of the governor of Trans-Euphrates. 8Uzziel son of Harhaiah, one of the goldsmiths, repaired the next section; and Hananiah, one of the perfume-makers, made repairs next to that. They restored[c] Jerusalem as far as the Broad Wall. 9Rephaiah son of Hur, ruler of a half-district of Jerusalem, repaired the next section. 10Adjoining this, Jedaiah son of Harumaph made repairs opposite his house, and Hattush son of Hashabneiah made repairs next to him. 11Malkijah son of Harim and Hasshub son of Pahath-Moab repaired another section and the Tower of the Ovens. 12Shallum son of Hallohesh, ruler of a half-district of Jerusalem, repaired the next section with the help of his daughters.

13The Valley Gate was repaired by Hanun and the residents of Zanoah. They rebuilt it and put its doors and bolts and bars in place. They also repaired five hundred yards[d] of the wall as far as the Dung Gate.

14The Dung Gate was repaired by Malkijah son of Recab, ruler of the district of Beth Hakkerem. He rebuilt it and put its doors and bolts and bars in place.

15The Fountain Gate was repaired by Shallun son of Col-Hozeh, ruler of the district of Mizpah. He rebuilt it, roofing it over and putting its doors and bolts and bars in place. He also repaired the wall of the Pool of Siloam,[e] by the King's Garden, as far as the steps going down from the City of David. 16Beyond him, Nehemiah son of Azbuk, ruler of a half-district of Beth Zur, made repairs up to a point opposite the tombs[f] of David, as far as the artificial pool and the House of the Heroes.

17Next to him, the repairs were made by the Levites under Rehum son of Bani. Beside him, Hashabiah, ruler of half the district of Keilah, carried out repairs for his district. 18Next to him, the repairs were made by their countrymen under Binnui[g] son of Henadad, ruler of the other half-district of Keilah. 19Next to him, Ezer son of Jeshua, ruler of Mizpah, repaired another section, from a point facing the ascent to the armoury as far as the angle. 20Next to him, Baruch son of Zabbai zealously repaired another section, from the angle to the entrance of the house of Eliashib the high priest. 21Next to him, Meremoth son of Uriah, the son of Hakkoz, repaired another section, from the entrance of Eliashib's house to the end of it.

22The repairs next to him were made by the priests from the surrounding region. 23Beyond them, Benjamin and Hasshub made repairs in front of their house; and next to them, Azariah son of Maaseiah, the son of

Ananiah, made repairs beside his house. 24Next to him, Binnui son of Henadad repaired another section, from Azariah's house to the angle and the corner, 25and Palal son of Uzai worked opposite the angle and the tower projecting from the upper palace near the court of the guard. Next to him, Pedaiah son of Parosh 26and the temple servants living on the hill of Ophel made repairs up to a point opposite the Water Gate towards the east and the projecting tower. 27Next to them, the men of Tekoa repaired another section, from the great projecting tower to the wall of Ophel.

28Above the Horse Gate, the priests made repairs, each in front of his own house. 29Next to them, Zadok son of Immer made repairs opposite his house. Next to him, Shemaiah son of Shecaniah, the guard at the East Gate, made repairs. 30Next to him, Hananiah son of Shelemiah, and Hanun, the sixth son of Zalaph, repaired another section. Next to them, Meshullam son of Berekiah made repairs opposite his living quarters. 31Next to him, Malkijah, one of the goldsmiths, made repairs as far as the house of the temple servants and the merchants, opposite the Inspection Gate, and as far as the room above the corner; 32and between the room above the corner and the Sheep Gate the goldsmiths and merchants made repairs.

Opposition to the Rebuilding

4 When Sanballat heard that we were rebuilding the wall, he became angry and was greatly incensed. He ridiculed the Jews, 2and in the presence of his associates and the army of Samaria, he said, "What are those feeble Jews doing? Will they restore their wall? Will they offer sacrifices? Will they finish in a day? Can they bring the stones back to life from those heaps of rubble—burned as they are?"

3Tobiah the Ammonite, who was at his side, said, "What they are building—if even a fox climbed up on it, he would break down their wall of stones!"

4Hear us, O our God, for we are despised. Turn their insults back on their own heads. Give them over as plunder in a land of captivity. 5Do not cover up their guilt or blot out their sins from your sight, for they have thrown insults in the face of[a] the builders.

6So we rebuilt the wall till all of it reached half its height, for the people worked with all their heart.

7But when Sanballat, Tobiah, the Arabs, the Ammonites and the men of Ashdod heard that the repairs to Jerusalem's walls had gone ahead and that the gaps were being closed, they were very angry. 8They all plotted together to come and fight against Jerusalem and stir up trouble against it. 9But we prayed to our God and posted a guard day and night to meet this threat.

10Meanwhile, the people in Judah said, "The strength of the labourers is giving out, and there is so much rubble that we cannot rebuild the wall."

11Also our enemies said, "Before they know it or see

---

a5 Or their Lord or the governor   b6 Or Old   c8 Or They left out part of
d13 Hebrew a thousand cubits (about 450 metres)   e15 Hebrew Shelah, a variant of Shiloah, that is, Siloam
f16 Hebrew; Septuagint, some Vulgate manuscripts and Syriac tomb
g18 Two Hebrew manuscripts and Syriac (see also Septuagint and verse 24); most Hebrew manuscripts Bavvai
a5 Or have provoked you to anger before

us, we will be right there among them and will kill them and put an end to the work."

¹²Then the Jews who lived near them came and told us ten times over, "Wherever you turn, they will attack us."

¹³Therefore I stationed some of the people behind the lowest points of the wall at the exposed places, posting them by families, with their swords, spears and bows. ¹⁴After I looked things over, I stood up and said to the nobles, the officials and the rest of the people, "Don't be afraid of them. Remember the Lord, who is great and awesome, and fight for your brothers, your sons and your daughters, your wives and your homes."

¹⁵When our enemies heard that we were aware of their plot and that God had frustrated it, we all returned to the wall, each to his own work.

¹⁶From that day on, half of my men did the work, while the other half were equipped with spears, shields, bows and armour. The officers posted themselves behind all the people of Judah ¹⁷who were building the wall. Those who carried materials did their work with one hand and held a weapon in the other, ¹⁸and each of the builders wore his sword at his side as he worked. But the man who sounded the trumpet stayed with me.

¹⁹Then I said to the nobles, the officials and the rest of the people, "The work is extensive and spread out, and we are widely separated from each other along the wall. ²⁰Wherever you hear the sound of the trumpet, join us there. Our God will fight for us!"

²¹So we continued the work with half the men holding spears, from the first light of dawn till the stars came out. ²²At that time I also said to the people, "Have every man and his helper stay inside Jerusalem at night, so that they can serve us as guards by night and workmen by day." ²³Neither I nor my brothers nor my men nor the guards with me took off our clothes; each had his weapon, even when he went for water.[b]

Nehemiah Helps the Poor

5 Now the men and their wives raised a great outcry against their Jewish brothers. ²Some were saying, "We and our sons and daughters are numerous; in order for us to eat and stay alive, we must get grain."

³Others were saying, "We are mortgaging our fields, our vineyards and our homes to get grain during the famine."

⁴Still others were saying, "We have had to borrow money to pay the king's tax on our fields and vineyards. ⁵Although we are of the same flesh and blood as our countrymen and though our sons are as good as theirs, yet we have to subject our sons and daughters to slavery. Some of our daughters have already been enslaved, but we are powerless, because our fields and our vineyards belong to others."

⁶When I heard their outcry and these charges, I was very angry. ⁷I pondered them in my mind and then accused the nobles and officials. I told them, "You are exacting usury from your own countrymen!" So I called together a large meeting to deal with them ⁸and said:

"As far as possible, we have bought back our Jewish brothers who were sold to the Gentiles. Now you are selling your brothers, only for them to be sold back to us!" They kept quiet, because they could find nothing to say.

⁹So I continued, "What you are doing is not right. Shouldn't you walk in the fear of our God to avoid the reproach of our Gentile enemies? ¹⁰I and my brothers and my men are also lending the people money and grain. But let the exacting of usury stop! ¹¹Give back to them immediately their fields, vineyards, olive groves and houses, and also the usury you are charging them — the hundredth part of the money, grain, new wine and oil."

¹²"We will give it back," they said. "And we will not demand anything more from them. We will do as you say."

Then I summoned the priests and made the nobles and officials take an oath to do what they had promised. ¹³I also shook out the folds of my robe and said, "In this way may God shake out of his house and possessions every man who does not keep this promise. So may such a man be shaken out and emptied!"

At this the whole assembly said, "Amen," and praised the Lord. And the people did as they had promised.

¹⁴Moreover, from the twentieth year of King Artaxerxes, when I was appointed to be their governor in the land of Judah, until his thirty-second year — twelve years — neither I nor my brothers ate the food allotted to the governor. ¹⁵But the earlier governors — those preceding me — placed a heavy burden on the people and took forty shekels[a] of silver from them in addition to food and wine. Their assistants also lorded it over the people. But out of reverence for God I did not act like that. ¹⁶Instead, I devoted myself to the work on this wall. All my men were assembled there for the work; we[b] did not acquire any land.

5:14 It is typical of Nehemiah that he did not exploit his position as governor to make personal gains in land or money. The allowance for a governor was a very large amount and on top of other taxes could easily overburden the common people. It was Nehemiah's sense of true religion that prevented him abusing his authority, since he realized that he owed his position to God and not to his own righteousness.

---

¹⁷Furthermore, a hundred and fifty Jews and officials ate at my table, as well as those who came to us from the surrounding nations. ¹⁸Each day one ox, six choice sheep and some poultry were prepared for me, and every ten days an abundant supply of wine of all kinds. In spite of all this, I never demanded the food allotted to the governor, because the demands were heavy on these people.

---

b23 The meaning of the Hebrew for this clause is uncertain.
b16 Most Hebrew manuscripts; some Hebrew manuscripts, Septuagint, Vulgate and Syriac *I*

a15 That is, about 1 pound (about 0.5 kilogram)

[19]Remember me with favour, O my God, for all I have done for these people.

Further Opposition to the Rebuilding

6 When word came to Sanballat, Tobiah, Geshem the Arab and the rest of our enemies that I had rebuilt the wall and not a gap was left in it — though up to that time I had not set the doors in the gates — [2]Sanballat and Geshem sent me this message: "Come, let us meet together in one of the villages[a] on the plain of Ono."

But they were scheming to harm me; [3]so I sent messengers to them with this reply: "I am carrying on a great project and cannot go down. Why should the work stop while I leave it and go down to you?" [4]Four times they sent me the same message, and each time I gave them the same answer.

[5]Then, the fifth time, Sanballat sent his assistant to me with the same message, and in his hand was an unsealed letter [6]in which was written:

"It is reported among the nations — and Geshem[b] says it is true — that you and the Jews are plotting to revolt, and therefore you are building the wall. Moreover, according to these reports you are about to become their king [7]and have even appointed prophets to make this proclamation about you in Jerusalem: 'There is a king in Judah!' Now this report will get back to the king; so come, let us confer together."

[8]I sent him this reply: "Nothing like what you are saying is happening; you are just making it up out of your head."

[9]They were all trying to frighten us, thinking, "Their hands will get too weak for the work, and it will not be completed."

But I prayed, "Now strengthen my hands."

[10]One day I went to the house of Shemaiah son of Delaiah, the son of Mehetabel, who was shut in at his home. He said, "Let us meet in the house of God, inside the temple, and let us close the temple doors, because men are coming to kill you — by night they are coming to kill you."

[11]But I said, "Should a man like me run away? Or should one like me go into the temple to save his life? I will not go!" [12]I realised that God had not sent him, but that he had prophesied against me because Tobiah and Sanballat had hired him. [13]He had been hired to intimidate me so that I would commit a sin by doing this, and then they would give me a bad name to discredit me.

[14]Remember Tobiah and Sanballat, O my God, because of what they have done; remember also the prophetess Noadiah and the rest of the prophets who have been trying to intimidate me.

The Completion of the Wall

[15]So the wall was completed on the twenty-fifth of Elul, in fifty-two days. [16]When all our enemies heard about this, all the surrounding nations were afraid and lost their self-confidence, because they realised that this work had been done with the help of our God.

6:14 There were always dishonest prophets who would support the establishment and oppose any movement that might lead to a change in the normal way of life. Jeremiah fought a constant battle against such "yes" people (e.g. Jeremiah 14:13ff), who did not speak God's word but who were able to sway the crowds. It was often said that God's true prophets had been rejected and ignored throughout history (9:26) and this was seen as a mark of Israel's rebellious behaviour.

---

[17]Also, in those days the nobles of Judah were sending many letters to Tobiah, and replies from Tobiah kept coming to them. [18]For many in Judah were under oath to him, since he was son-in-law to Shecaniah son of Arah, and his son Jehohanan had married the daughter of Meshullam son of Berekiah. [19]Moreover, they kept reporting to me his good deeds and then telling him what I said. And Tobiah sent letters to intimidate me.

7 After the wall had been rebuilt and I had set the doors in place, the gatekeepers and the singers and the Levites were appointed. [2]I put in charge of Jerusalem my brother Hanani, along with[a] Hananiah the commander of the citadel, because he was a man of integrity and feared God more than most men do. [3]I said to them, "The gates of Jerusalem are not to be opened until the sun is hot. While the gatekeepers are still on duty, make them shut the doors and bar them. Also appoint residents of Jerusalem as guards, some at their posts and some near their own houses."

The List of the Exiles Who Returned

[4]Now the city was large and spacious, but there were few people in it, and the houses had not yet been rebuilt. [5]So my God put it into my heart to assemble the nobles, the officials and the common people for registration by families. I found the genealogical record of those who had been the first to return. This is what I found written there:

[6]These are the people of the province who came up from the captivity of the exiles whom Nebuchadnezzar king of Babylon had taken captive (they returned to Jerusalem and Judah, each

---

7:6 Because it was vital to establish the identity of the true Israel, the Jews who returned from exile kept careful track of their roots. The list in Nehemiah is almost exactly the same as the one in Ezra 2, reflecting the overlapping sources of the two books.

---

[a]2 Or in Kephirim   [b]6 Hebrew Gashmu, a variant of Geshem   [a]2 Or Hanani, that is,

to his own town, [7]in company with Zerubbabel, Jeshua, Nehemiah, Azariah, Raamiah, Nahamani, Mordecai, Bilshan, Mispereth, Bigvai, Nehum and Baanah):

The list of the men of Israel:

[8]the descendants of Parosh	2,172
[9]of Shephatiah	372
[10]of Arah	652
[11]of Pahath-Moab (through the line of Jeshua and Joab)	2,818
[12]of Elam	1,254
[13]of Zattu	845
[14]of Zaccai	760
[15]of Binnui	648
[16]of Bebai	628
[17]of Azgad	2,322
[18]of Adonikam	667
[19]of Bigvai	2,067
[20]of Adin	655
[21]of Ater (through Hezekiah)	98
[22]of Hashum	328
[23]of Bezai	324
[24]of Hariph	112
[25]of Gibeon	95
[26]the men of Bethlehem and Netophah	188
[27]of Anathoth	128
[28]of Beth Azmaveth	42
[29]of Kiriath Jearim, Kephirah and Beeroth	743
[30]of Ramah and Geba	621
[31]of Michmash	122
[32]of Bethel and Ai	123
[33]of the other Nebo	52
[34]of the other Elam	1,254
[35]of Harim	320
[36]of Jericho	345
[37]of Lod, Hadid and Ono	721
[38]of Senaah	3,930

[39]The priests:

the descendants of Jedaiah (through the family of Jeshua)	973
[40]of Immer	1,052
[41]of Pashhur	1,247
[42]of Harim	1,017

[43]The Levites:

the descendants of Jeshua (through Kadmiel through the line of Hodaviah)	74

[44]The singers:

the descendants of Asaph	148

[45]The gatekeepers:

the descendants of Shallum, Ater, Talmon, Akkub, Hatita and Shobai	138

[46]The temple servants:

the descendants of Ziha, Hasupha, Tabbaoth, [47]Keros, Sia, Padon, [48]Lebana, Hagaba, Shalmai, [49]Hanan, Giddel, Gahar, [50]Reaiah, Rezin, Nekoda, [51]Gazzam, Uzza, Paseah, [52]Besai, Meunim, Nephussim, [53]Bakbuk, Hakupha, Harhur, [54]Bazluth, Mehida, Harsha, [55]Barkos, Sisera, Temah, [56]Neziah and Hatipha

[57]The descendants of the servants of Solomon:

the descendants of Sotai, Sophereth, Perida, [58]Jaala, Darkon, Giddel, [59]Shephatiah, Hattil, Pokereth-Hazzebaim and Amon

[60]The temple servants and the descendants of the servants of Solomon	392

[61]The following came up from the towns of Tel Melah, Tel Harsha, Kerub, Addon and Immer, but they could not show that their families were descended from Israel:

[62]the descendants of Delaiah, Tobiah and Nekoda	642

[63]And from among the priests:

the descendants of Hobaiah, Hakkoz and Barzillai (a man who had married a daughter of Barzillai the Gileadite and was called by that name).

[64]These searched for their family records, but they could not find them and so were excluded from the priesthood as unclean. [65]The governor, therefore, ordered them not to eat any of the most sacred food until there should be a priest ministering with the Urim and Thummim.

[66]The whole company numbered 42,360, [67]besides their 7,337 menservants and maidservants; and they also had 245 men and women singers. [68]There were 736 horses, 245 mules,[b] [69]435 camels and 6,720 donkeys.

[70]Some of the heads of the families contributed to the work. The governor gave to the treasury 1,000 drachmas[c] of gold, 50 bowls and 530 garments for priests. [71]Some of the heads of the families gave to the treasury for the work 20,000 drachmas[d] of gold and 2,200 minas[e] of silver. [72]The total given by the rest of the people was 20,000 drachmas of gold, 2,000 minas[f] of silver and 67 garments for priests.

[73]The priests, the Levites, the gatekeepers, the singers and the temple servants, along with certain of the people and the rest of the Israelites, settled in their own towns.

[b]68 Some Hebrew manuscripts (see also Ezra 2:66); most Hebrew manuscripts do not have this verse.
[c]70 That is, about 19 pounds (about 8.5 kilograms)
[d]71 That is, about 375 pounds (about 170 kilograms); also in verse 72
[e]71 That is, about 1¼ tons (about 1.3 metric tons)
[f]72 That is, about 1 ton (about 1.1 metric tons)

Ezra Reads the Law

8 When the seventh month came and the Israelites had settled in their towns, [1]all the people assembled as one man in the square before the Water Gate. They told Ezra the scribe to bring out the Book of the Law of Moses, which the LORD had commanded for Israel.

[2]So on the first day of the seventh month, Ezra the priest brought the Law before the assembly, which was made up of men and women and all who were able to understand. [3]He read it aloud from daybreak till noon as he faced the square before the Water Gate in the presence of the men, women and others who could understand. And all the people listened attentively to the Book of the Law.

8:2   The "first day of the seventh month" was the holy day at the start of the month which contained the most important Jewish festival, and the book that Ezra read was probably similar to what is called the Pentateuch; the first five books of the Old Testament. It is important to note that all the community was there—women as well as men. The procedure that followed may reflect early synagogue practice which had begun to develop in exile when the people had to make do without the temple. A holy day was a holiday and the people were told not to weep but to rejoice.

---

[4]Ezra the scribe stood on a high wooden platform built for the occasion. Beside him on his right stood Mattithiah, Shema, Anaiah, Uriah, Hilkiah and Maaseiah; and on his left were Pedaiah, Mishael, Malkijah, Hashum, Hashbaddanah, Zechariah and Meshullam.

[5]Ezra opened the book. All the people could see him because he was standing above them; and as he opened it, the people all stood up. [6]Ezra praised the LORD, the great God; and all the people lifted their hands and responded, "Amen! Amen!" Then they bowed down and worshipped the LORD with their faces to the ground.

[7]The Levites—Jeshua, Bani, Sherebiah, Jamin, Akkub, Shabbethai, Hodiah, Maaseiah, Kelita, Azariah, Jozabad, Hanan and Pelaiah—instructed the people in the Law while the people were standing there. [8]They read from the Book of the Law of God, making it clear[a] and giving the meaning so that the people could understand what was being read.

[9]Then Nehemiah the governor, Ezra the priest and scribe, and the Levites who were instructing the people said to them all, "This day is sacred to the LORD your God. Do not mourn or weep." For all the people had been weeping as they listened to the words of the Law.

[10]Nehemiah said, "Go and enjoy choice food and sweet drinks, and send some to those who have nothing prepared. This day is sacred to our Lord. Do not grieve, for the joy of the LORD is your strength."

[11]The Levites calmed all the people, saying, "Be still, for this is a sacred day. Do not grieve."

[12]Then all the people went away to eat and drink, to send portions of food and to celebrate with great joy, because they now understood the words that had been made known to them.

[13]On the second day of the month, the heads of all the families, along with the priests and the Levites, gathered round Ezra the scribe to give attention to the words of the Law. [14]They found written in the Law, which the LORD had commanded through Moses, that the Israelites were to live in booths during the feast of the seventh month [15]and that they should proclaim this word and spread it throughout their towns and in Jerusalem: "Go out into the hill country and bring back branches from olive and wild olive trees, and from myrtles, palms and shade trees, to make booths"—as it is written.[b]

[16]So the people went out and brought back branches and built themselves booths on their own roofs, in their courtyards, in the courts of the house of God and in the square by the Water Gate and the one by the Gate of Ephraim. [17]The whole company that had returned from exile built booths and lived in them. From the days of Joshua son of Nun until that day, the Israelites had not celebrated it like this. And their joy was very great.

[18]Day after day, from the first day to the last, Ezra read from the Book of the Law of God. They celebrated the feast for seven days, and on the eighth day, in accordance with the regulation, there was an assembly.

The Israelites Confess Their Sins

9 On the twenty-fourth day of the same month, the Israelites gathered together, fasting and wearing sackcloth and having dust on their heads. [2]Those of Israelite descent had separated themselves from all foreigners. They stood in their places and confessed their sins and the wickedness of their fathers. [3]They stood where they were and read from the Book of the Law of the LORD their God for a quarter of the day, and spent another quarter in confession and in worshipping the LORD their God. [4]Standing on the stairs were the Levites—Jeshua, Bani, Kadmiel, Shebaniah, Bunni, Sherebiah, Bani and Kenani—who called with loud voices to the LORD their God. [5]And the Levites—Jeshua, Kadmiel, Bani, Hashabneiah, Sherebiah, Hodiah, Shebaniah and Pethahiah—said: "Stand up and praise the LORD your God, who is from everlasting to everlasting."[a]

"Blessed be your glorious name, and may it be exalted above all blessing and praise. [6]You alone are the LORD. You made the heavens, even the highest heavens, and all their starry host, the earth and all that is on it, the seas and all that is in them. You give life to everything, and the multitudes of heaven worship you.

[7]"You are the LORD God, who chose Abram and

---

a8 Or *God, translating it*   *b15* See Lev. 23:37–40.   *a5* Or *God for ever and ever* brought him out of Ur of the Chaldeans and named him Abraham. [8]You found his heart faithful to you, and you made a covenant with him to give to his descendants the land of the Canaanites, Hittites, Amorites, Perizzites, Jebusites and Girgashites. You have kept your promise because you are righteous.

[9]"You saw the suffering of our forefathers in Egypt; you heard their cry at the Red Sea.[b] [10]You sent miraculous signs and wonders against Pharaoh, against all his officials and all the people of his land, for you knew how arrogantly the Egyptians treated them. You made a name for yourself, which remains to this day. [11]You divided the sea before them, so that they passed through it on dry ground, but you hurled their pursuers into the depths, like a stone into mighty waters. [12]By day you led them with a pillar of cloud, and by night with a pillar of fire to give them light on the way they were to take.

[13]"You came down on Mount Sinai; you spoke to them from heaven. You gave them regulations and laws that are just and right, and decrees and commands that are good. [14]You made known to them your holy Sabbath and gave them commands, decrees and laws through your servant Moses. [15]In their hunger you gave them bread from heaven and in their thirst you brought them water from the rock; you told them to go in and take possession of the land you had sworn with uplifted hand to give them.

[16]"But they, our forefathers, became arrogant and stiff-necked, and did not obey your commands. [17]They refused to listen and failed to remember the miracles you performed among them. They became stiff-necked and in their rebellion appointed a leader in order to return to their slavery. But you are a forgiving God, gracious and compassionate, slow to anger and abounding in love. Therefore you did not desert them, [18]even when they cast for themselves an image of a calf and said, 'This is your god, who brought you up out of Egypt,' or when they committed awful blasphemies.

[19]"Because of your great compassion you did not abandon them in the desert. By day the pillar of cloud did not cease to guide them on their path, nor the pillar of fire by night to shine on the way they were to take. [20]You gave your good Spirit to instruct them. You did not withhold your manna from their mouths, and you gave them water for their thirst. [21]For forty years you sustained them in the desert; they lacked nothing, their clothes did not wear out nor did their feet become swollen.

[22]"You gave them kingdoms and nations, allotting to them even the remotest frontiers. They took over the country of Sihon[c] king of Heshbon and the country of Og king of Bashan. [23]You made their sons as numerous as the stars in the sky, and you brought them into the land that you told their fathers to enter and possess. [24]Their sons went in and took possession of the land. You subdued before them the Canaanites, who lived in the land; you handed the Canaanites over to them, along with their kings and the peoples of the land, to deal with them as they pleased. [25]They captured fortified cities and fertile land; they took possession of houses filled with all kinds of good things, wells already dug, vineyards, olive groves and fruit trees in abundance. They ate to the full and were well-nourished; they revelled in your great goodness.

[26]"But they were disobedient and rebelled against you; they put your law behind their backs. They killed your prophets, who had admonished them in order to turn them back to you; they committed awful blasphemies. [27]So you handed them over to their enemies, who oppressed them. But when they were oppressed they cried out to you. From heaven you heard them, and in your great compassion you gave them deliverers, who rescued them from the hand of their enemies.

[28]"But as soon as they were at rest, they again did what was evil in your sight. Then you abandoned them to the hand of their enemies so that they ruled over them. And when they cried out to you again, you heard from heaven, and in your compassion you delivered them time after time.

[29]"You warned them to return to your law, but they became arrogant and disobeyed your commands. They sinned against your ordinances, by which a man will live if he obeys them. Stubbornly they turned their backs on you, became stiff-necked and refused to listen. [30]For many years you were patient with them. By your Spirit you admonished them through your prophets. Yet they paid no attention, so you handed them over to the neighbouring peoples. [31]But in your great mercy you did not put an end to them or abandon them, for you are a gracious and merciful God.

[32]"Now therefore, O our God, the great, mighty and awesome God, who keeps his covenant of love, do not let all this hardship seem trifling in your eyes—the hardship that has come upon us, upon our kings and leaders, upon our priests and prophets, upon our fathers and all your people, from the days of the kings of Assyria until today. [33]In all that has happened to us, you have been just; you have acted faithfully, while we did wrong. [34]Our kings, our leaders, our priests and our fathers did not follow your law; they did not pay attention to your commands or the warnings you gave them. [35]Even while they were in their kingdom, enjoying your great goodness to them in the spacious and fertile land you gave them, they did not serve you or turn from their evil ways.

[36]"But see, we are slaves today, slaves in the land you gave our forefathers so that they could eat its fruit and the other good things it produces. [37]Because of our sins, its abundant harvest goes to the kings you have placed over us. They rule over

---

[b]9 Hebrew *Yam Suph*; that is, Sea of Reeds
[c]22 One Hebrew manuscript and Septuagint; most Hebrew manuscripts *Sihon, that is, the country of the*

our bodies and our cattle as they please. We are in great distress.

The Agreement of the People

38 "In view of all this, we are making a binding agreement, putting it in writing, and our leaders, our Levites and our priests are affixing their seals to it."

10

Those who sealed it were:

Nehemiah the governor, the son of Hacaliah.

Zedekiah, 2Seraiah, Azariah, Jeremiah, 3Pashhur, Amariah, Malkijah, 4Hattush, Shebaniah, Malluch, 5Harim, Meremoth, Obadiah, 6Daniel, Ginnethon, Baruch, 7Meshullam, Abijah, Mijamin, 8Maaziah, Bilgai and Shemaiah. These were the priests.

9The Levites:

Jeshua son of Azaniah,
    Binnui of the sons of Henadad, Kadmiel, 10and their associates:
Shebaniah, Hodiah, Kelita, Pelaiah, Hanan, 11Mica, Rehob, Hashabiah, 12Zaccur, Sherebiah, Shebaniah, 13Hodiah, Bani and Beninu.

14The leaders of the people:

Parosh, Pahath-Moab, Elam, Zattu, Bani, 15Bunni, Azgad, Bebai, 16Adonijah, Bigvai, Adin, 17Ater, Hezekiah, Azzur, 18Hodiah, Hashum, Bezai, 19Hariph, Anathoth, Nebai, 20Magpiash, Meshullam, Hezir, 21Meshezabel, Zadok, Jaddua, 22Pelatiah, Hanan, Anaiah, 23Hoshea, Hananiah, Hasshub, 24Hallohesh, Pilha, Shobek, 25Rehum, Hashabnah, Maaseiah, 26Ahiah, Hanan, Anan, 27Malluch, Harim and Baanah.

28 "The rest of the people—priests, Levites, gatekeepers, singers, temple servants and all who separated themselves from the neighbouring peoples for the sake of the Law of God, together with their wives and all their sons and daughters who are able to understand—29all these now join their brothers the nobles, and bind themselves with a curse and an oath to follow the Law of God given through Moses the servant of God and to obey carefully all the commands, regulations and decrees of the Lord our Lord.

30 "We promise not to give our daughters in marriage to the peoples around us or take their daughters for our sons.

31 "When the neighbouring peoples bring merchandise or grain to sell on the Sabbath, we will not buy from them on the Sabbath or on any holy day. Every seventh year we will forgo working the land and will cancel all debts.

32 "We assume the responsibility for carrying out the commands to give a third of a shekel[a] each year for the service of the house of our God: 33for the bread set out on the table; for the regular grain offerings and burnt offerings; for the offerings on the Sabbaths, New Moon festivals and appointed feasts; for the holy offerings; for sin offerings to make atonement for Israel; and for all the duties of the house of our God.

10:31 According to the law, Jews were not meant to do any work on the seventh day—the sabbath. Also, every seventh year was a sabbath year when the farmers were supposed to let the land rest and everyone was to cancel all the debts owed them. These rules were to help bring together national identity and community spirit, and had their origins traced to the creation of the world (Genesis 2:2). Unfortunately, the laws were not always obeyed in practice.

---

34 "We—the priests, the Levites and the people—have cast lots to determine when each of our families is to bring to the house of our God at set times each year a contribution of wood to burn on the altar of the Lord our God, as it is written in the Law.

35 "We also assume responsibility for bringing to the house of the Lord each year the firstfruits of our crops and of every fruit tree.

36 "As it is also written in the Law, we will bring the firstborn of our sons and of our cattle, of our herds and of our flocks to the house of our God, to the priests ministering there.

37 "Moreover, we will bring to the storerooms of the house of our God, to the priests, the first of our ground meal, of our grain offerings, of the fruit of all our trees and of our new wine and oil. And we will bring a tithe of our crops to the Levites, for it is the Levites who collect the tithes in all the towns where we work. 38A priest descended from Aaron is to accompany the Levites when they receive the tithes, and the Levites are to bring a tenth of the tithes up to the house of our God, to the storerooms of the treasury. 39The people of Israel, including the Levites, are to bring their contributions of grain, new wine and oil to the storerooms where the articles for the sanctuary are kept and where the ministering priests, the gatekeepers and the singers stay.

"We will not neglect the house of our God."

The New Residents of Jerusalem

11

Now the leaders of the people settled in Jerusalem, and the rest of the people cast lots to bring one out of every ten to live in Jerusalem, the holy

---

a32 That is, about 1/8 ounce (about 4 grams)

city, while the remaining nine were to stay in their own towns. [2]The people commended all the men who volunteered to live in Jerusalem.

[3]These are the provincial leaders who settled in Jerusalem (now some Israelites, priests, Levites, temple servants and descendants of Solomon's servants lived in the towns of Judah, each on his own property in the various towns, [4]while other people from both Judah and Benjamin lived in Jerusalem):

From the descendants of Judah:

Athaiah son of Uzziah, the son of Zechariah, the son of Amariah, the son of Shephatiah, the son of Mahalalel, a descendant of Perez; [5]and Maaseiah son of Baruch, the son of Col-Hozeh, the son of Hazaiah, the son of Adaiah, the son of Joiarib, the son of Zechariah, a descendant of Shelah. [6]The descendants of Perez who lived in Jerusalem totalled 468 able men.

[7]From the descendants of Benjamin:

Sallu son of Meshullam, the son of Joed, the son of Pedaiah, the son of Kolaiah, the son of Maaseiah, the son of Ithiel, the son of Jeshaiah, [8]and his followers, Gabbai and Sallai — 928 men. [9]Joel son of Zicri was their chief officer, and Judah son of Hassenuah was over the Second District of the city.

[10]From the priests:

Jedaiah; the son of Joiarib; Jakin; [11]Seraiah son of Hilkiah, the son of Meshullam, the son of Zadok, the son of Meraioth, the son of Ahitub, supervisor in the house of God, [12]and their associates, who carried on work for the temple — 822 men; Adaiah son of Jeroham, the son of Pelaliah, the son of Amzi, the son of Zechariah, the son of Pashhur, the son of Malkijah, [13]and his associates, who were heads of families — 242 men; Amashsai son of Azarel, the son of Ahzai, the son of Meshillemoth, the son of Immer, [14]and his[a] associates, who were able men — 128 men. Their chief officer was Zabdiel son of Haggedolim.

[15]From the Levites:

Shemaiah son of Hasshub, the son of Azrikam, the son of Hashabiah, the son of Bunni; [16]Shabbethai and Jozabad, two of the heads of the Levites, who had charge of the outside work of the house of God; [17]Mattaniah son of Mica, the son of Zabdi, the son of Asaph, the director who led in thanksgiving and prayer; Bakbukiah, second among his associates; and Abda son of Shammua, the son of Galal, the son of Jeduthun. [18]The Levites in the holy city totalled 284.

[19]The gatekeepers:

Akkub, Talmon and their associates, who kept watch at the gates — 172 men.

[20]The rest of the Israelites, with the priests and Levites, were in all the towns of Judah, each on his ancestral property.

[21]The temple servants lived on the hill of Ophel, and Ziha and Gishpa were in charge of them.

[22]The chief officer of the Levites in Jerusalem was Uzzi son of Bani, the son of Hashabiah, the son of Mattaniah, the son of Mica. Uzzi was one of Asaph's descendants, who were the singers responsible for the service of the house of God. [23]The singers were under the king's orders, which regulated their daily activity.

[24]Pethahiah son of Meshezabel, one of the descendants of Zerah son of Judah, was the king's agent in all affairs relating to the people.

[25]As for the villages with their fields, some of the people of Judah lived in Kiriath Arba and its surrounding settlements, in Dibon and its settlements, in Jekabzeel and its villages, [26]in Jeshua, in Moladah, in Beth Pelet, [27]in Hazar Shual, in Beersheba and its settlements, [28]in Ziklag, in Meconah and its settlements, [29]in En Rimmon, in Zorah, in Jarmuth, [30]Zanoah, Adullam and their villages, in Lachish and its fields, and in Azekah and its settlements. So they were living all the way from Beersheba to the Valley of Hinnom.

[31]The descendants of the Benjamites from Geba lived in Michmash, Aija, Bethel and its settlements, [32]in Anathoth, Nob and Ananiah, [33]in Hazor, Ramah and Gittaim, [34]in Hadid, Zeboim and Neballat, [35]in Lod and Ono, and in the Valley of the Craftsmen.

[36]Some of the divisions of the Levites of Judah settled in Benjamin.

Priests and Levites

12 These were the priests and Levites who returned with Zerubbabel son of Shealtiel and with Jeshua:

Seraiah, Jeremiah, Ezra,
[2]Amariah, Malluch, Hattush,
[3]Shecaniah, Rehum, Meremoth,
[4]Iddo, Ginnethon,[a] Abijah,
[5]Mijamin,[b] Moadiah, Bilgah,
[6]Shemaiah, Joiarib, Jedaiah,
[7]Sallu, Amok, Hilkiah and Jedaiah.

These were the leaders of the priests and their associates in the days of Jeshua.

[8]The Levites were Jeshua, Binnui, Kadmiel, Sherebiah, Judah, and also Mattaniah, who, together with his associates, was in charge of the songs of thanksgiving. [9]Bakbukiah and Unni, their associates, stood opposite them in the services.

[10]Jeshua was the father of Joiakim, Joiakim the father of Eliashib, Eliashib the father of Joiada, [11]Joiada the father of Jonathan, and Jonathan the father of Jaddua.

[12]In the days of Joiakim, these were the heads of the priestly families:

of Seraiah's family, Meraiah;
of Jeremiah's, Hananiah;
[13]of Ezra's, Meshullam;
of Amariah's, Jehohanan;

---

a14 Most Septuagint manuscripts; Hebrew *their*
a4 Many Hebrew manuscripts and Vulgate (see also Neh. 12:16); most Hebrew manuscripts *Ginnethoi*   b5 A variant of *Miniamin*

[14]of Malluch's, Jonathan;
  of Shecaniah's,[c] Joseph;
[15]of Harim's, Adna;
  of Meremoth's,[d] Helkai;
[16]of Iddo's, Zechariah;
  of Ginnethon's, Meshullam;
[17]of Abijah's, Zicri;
  of Miniamin's and of Moadiah's, Piltai;
[18]of Bilgah's, Shammua;
  of Shemaiah's, Jehonathan;
[19]of Joiarib's, Mattenai;
  of Jedaiah's, Uzzi;
[20]of Sallu's, Kallai;
  of Amok's, Eber;
[21]of Hilkiah's, Hashabiah;
  of Jedaiah's, Nethanel.

[22]The family heads of the Levites in the days of Eliashib, Joiada, Johanan and Jaddua, as well as those of the priests, were recorded in the reign of Darius the Persian. [23]The family heads among the descendants of Levi up to the time of Johanan son of Eliashib were recorded in the book of the annals. [24]And the leaders of the Levites were Hashabiah, Sherebiah, Jeshua son of Kadmiel, and their associates, who stood opposite them to give praise and thanksgiving, one section responding to the other, as prescribed by David the man of God.

[25]Mattaniah, Bakbukiah, Obadiah, Meshullam, Talmon and Akkub were gatekeepers who guarded the storerooms at the gates. [26]They served in the days of Joiakim son of Jeshua, the son of Jozadak, and in the days of Nehemiah the governor and of Ezra the priest and scribe.

Dedication of the Wall of Jerusalem

[27]At the dedication of the wall of Jerusalem, the Levites were sought out from where they lived and were brought to Jerusalem to celebrate joyfully the dedication with songs of thanksgiving and with the music of cymbals, harps and lyres. [28]The singers also were brought together from the region around Jerusalem — from the villages of the Netophathites, [29]from Beth Gilgal, and from the area of Geba and Azmaveth, for the singers had built villages for themselves around Jerusalem. [30]When the priests and Levites had purified themselves ceremonially, they purified the people, the gates and the wall.

[31]I had the leaders of Judah go up on top[e] of the wall. I also assigned two large choirs to give thanks. One was to proceed on top[f] of the wall to the right, towards the Dung Gate. [32]Hoshaiah and half the leaders of Judah followed them, [33]along with Azariah, Ezra, Meshullam, [34]Judah, Benjamin, Shemaiah, Jeremiah, [35]as well as some priests with trumpets, and also Zechariah son of Jonathan, the son of Shemaiah, the son of Mattaniah, the son of Micaiah, the son of Zaccur, the son of Asaph, [36]and his associates — Shemaiah, Azarel, Milalai, Gilalai, Maai, Nethanel, Judah and Hanani — with musical instruments ⌊prescribed by⌋ David the man of God. Ezra the scribe led the procession. [37]At the Fountain Gate they continued directly up the steps of the City of David on the ascent to the wall and passed above the house of David to the Water Gate on the east.

[38]The second choir proceeded in the opposite direction. I followed them on top[g] of the wall, together with half the people — past the Tower of the Ovens to the Broad Wall, [39]over the Gate of Ephraim, the Jeshanah[h] Gate, the Fish Gate, the Tower of Hananel and the Tower of the Hundred, as far as the Sheep Gate. At the Gate of the Guard they stopped.

[40]The two choirs that gave thanks then took their places in the house of God; so did I, together with half the officials, [41]as well as the priests — Eliakim, Maaseiah, Miniamin, Micaiah, Elioenai, Zechariah and Hananiah with their trumpets — [42]and also Maaseiah, Shemaiah, Eleazar, Uzzi, Jehohanan, Malkijah, Elam and Ezer. The choirs sang under the direction of Jezrahiah. [43]And on that day they offered great sacrifices, rejoicing because God had given them great joy. The women and children also rejoiced. The sound of rejoicing in Jerusalem could be heard far away.

[44]At that time men were appointed to be in charge of the storerooms for the contributions, firstfruits and tithes. From the fields around the towns they were to bring into the storerooms the portions required by the Law for the priests and the Levites, for Judah was pleased with the ministering priests and Levites. [45]They performed the service of their God and the service of purification, as did also the singers and gatekeepers, according to the commands of David and his son Solomon. [46]For long ago, in the days of David and Asaph, there had been directors for the singers and for the songs of praise and thanksgiving to God. [47]So in the days of Zerubbabel and of Nehemiah, all Israel contributed the daily portions for the singers and gatekeepers. They also set aside the portion for the other Levites, and the Levites set aside the portion for the descendants of Aaron.

13:2 The reference here is to incidents which are related in Numbers 21ff, including the famous story of the speaking donkey. Balaam was famed for his curses but could only speak what God put in his mouth, and ended up blessing the Jews instead of cursing them. His fourth oracle included one of the most important biblical prophecies about a Jewish messiah (Numbers 24:17).

Nehemiah's Final Reforms

13 On that day the Book of Moses was read aloud in the hearing of the people and there it was found written that no Ammonite or Moabite should ever be admitted into the assembly of God, [2]because they had not met the Israelites with food and water but had hired Balaam to call a curse down on them. (Our God, however, turned the curse into a blessing.) [3]When the people heard this law, they excluded from Israel all who were of foreign descent.

---

[c]14 Very many Hebrew manuscripts, some Septuagint manuscripts and Syriac (see also Neh. 12:3); most Hebrew manuscripts *Shebaniah's*
[d]15 Some Septuagint manuscripts (see also Neh. 12:3); Hebrew *Meraioth's*   [e]31 Or *go alongside*   [f]31 Or *proceed alongside*
[g]38 Or *them alongside*   [h]39 Or *Old*

4Before this, Eliashib the priest had been put in charge of the storerooms of the house of our God. He was closely associated with Tobiah, 5and he had provided him with a large room formerly used to store the grain offerings and incense and temple articles, and also the tithes of grain, new wine and oil prescribed for the Levites, singers and gatekeepers, as well as the contributions for the priests.

6But while all this was going on, I was not in Jerusalem, for in the thirty-second year of Artaxerxes king of Babylon I had returned to the king. Some time later I asked his permission 7and came back to Jerusalem. Here I learned about the evil thing Eliashib had done in providing Tobiah a room in the courts of the house of God. 8I was greatly displeased and threw all Tobiah's household goods out of the room. 9I gave orders to purify the rooms, and then I put back into them the equipment of the house of God, with the grain offerings and the incense.

10I also learned that the portions assigned to the Levites had not been given to them, and that all the Levites and singers responsible for the service had gone back to their own fields. 11So I rebuked the officials and asked them, "Why is the house of God neglected?" Then I called them together and stationed them at their posts.

12All Judah brought the tithes of grain, new wine and oil into the storerooms. 13I put Shelemiah the priest, Zadok the scribe, and a Levite named Pedaiah in charge of the storerooms and made Hanan son of Zaccur, the son of Mattaniah, their assistant, because these men were considered trustworthy. They were made responsible for distributing the supplies to their brothers.

14Remember me for this, O my God, and do not blot out what I have so faithfully done for the house of my God and its services.

15In those days I saw men in Judah treading winepresses on the Sabbath and bringing in grain and loading it on donkeys, together with wine, grapes, figs and all other kinds of loads. And they were bringing all this into Jerusalem on the Sabbath. Therefore I warned them against selling food on that day. 16Men from Tyre who lived in Jerusalem were bringing in fish and all kinds of merchandise and selling them in Jerusalem on the Sabbath to the people of Judah. 17I rebuked the nobles of Judah and said to them, "What is this wicked thing you are doing—desecrating the Sabbath day?

18Didn't your forefathers do the same things, so that our God brought all this calamity upon us and upon this city? Now you are stirring up more wrath against Israel by desecrating the Sabbath."

19When evening shadows fell on the gates of Jerusalem before the Sabbath, I ordered the doors to be shut and not opened until the Sabbath was over. I stationed some of my own men at the gates so that no load could be brought in on the Sabbath day. 20Once or twice the merchants and sellers of all kinds of goods spent the night outside Jerusalem. 21But I warned them and said, "Why do you spend the night by the wall? If you do this again, I will lay hands on you." From that time on they no longer came on the Sabbath. 22Then I commanded the Levites to purify themselves and go and guard the gates in order to keep the Sabbath day holy.

Remember me for this also, O my God, and show mercy to me according to your great love.

23Moreover, in those days I saw men of Judah who had married women from Ashdod, Ammon and Moab. 24Half of their children spoke the language of Ashdod or the language of one of the other peoples, and did not know how to speak the language of Judah. 25I rebuked them and called curses down on them. I beat some of the men and pulled out their hair. I made them take an oath in God's name and said: "You are not to give your daughters in marriage to their sons, nor are you to take their daughters in marriage for your sons or for yourselves. 26Was it not because of marriages like these that Solomon king of Israel sinned? Among the many nations there was no king like him. He was loved by his God, and God made him king over all Israel, but even he was led into sin by foreign women. 27Must we hear now that you too are doing all this terrible wickedness and are being unfaithful to our God by marrying foreign women?"

28One of the sons of Joiada son of Eliashib the high priest was son-in-law to Sanballat the Horonite. And I drove him away from me.

29Remember them, O my God, because they defiled the priestly office and the covenant of the priesthood and of the Levites.

30So I purified the priests and the Levites of everything foreign, and assigned them duties, each to his own task. 31I also made provision for contributions of wood at designated times, and for the firstfruits.

Remember me with favour, O my God.

Esther

A Strange Saga

Martin Luther, one of the most famous Protestant reformers, once said of the book of Esther, "I am so hostile to it that I wish it did not exist." Many others have reacted in a similar way to a story that at times looks more like something out of the tales of the Arabian nights than a book of the Bible. It contains, for a start, all the necessary characters for a good pantomime: the utterly wicked Haman, the persistently heroic Mordecai, the foolishly weak Xerxes, and the beautifully resourceful Esther. Together these people react and inter-react to provide us with an entertaining tale full of drama and suspense which tells of the Jews in the Persian empire escaping, in the nick of time, an attempted programme of annihilation. This is all good stuff, but should it be in the Bible? On top of this we have to cope with the book's failure to mention God even once; this is unique to the Bible and explains why some early Jews and Christians wanted the book left out. Such embarrassment is shown by the fact that in later Greek versions of Esther long prayers to God were inserted to help raise the religious tone.

Salvation for God's People

But in spite of these objections it would be very wrong to dismiss Esther as simply a piece of romantic fiction that has no deeper message. The story celebrates one of the Old Testament's most enduring and uplifting themes — the salvation of God's people from imminent destruction (think for example of Jerusalem's rescue from the army of Assyria in Isaiah 36—37 or, more famously, the exodus from Egypt across the Red Sea). Nor is it ever doubted that behind the bravery and ingenuity of Mordecai and his cousin Esther, and the apparently unlikely coincidences of the book, lies the hidden yet watchful love of God for his people. To believers all deliverance from danger is the deliverance of God, and chance events can always take on far deeper meanings. This is surely how we are meant to read Esther, ever aware that the book is offered as an explanation of the origins of one of the Jews' great annual festivals, Purim. This carnival-like festival is still observed today with all the enthusiasm expected of a celebration of God's saving power.

A Different Expression of Faith

It is right, therefore, that Esther has its place in the Bible for it not only adds to the rich variety of literature there, but also offers us a different expression of faith. It is one that does not need to mention God in order to demonstrate his love for his people; taking God for granted in this way is not to ignore him but rather faithfully to acknowledge his gracious action in the world. This kind of "implicit" faith which underlies Esther was one foundation on which the Jews could build their new lives in the east under first Babylonian and then Persian rule. And one of the major issues of the book concerns this very problem: how should the Jews relate to their foreign masters, who on the one hand offered security and protection but on the other threatened them with persecution and destruction? This dilemma faces many people of faith today who are fighting to keep hold of their identity in a secular age that fails to understand them. There is no simple answer to the problem. The solution that the anonymous author of Esther provides differs greatly from that offered by the writer of Ezra and Nehemiah. This is a powerful reminder that Esther, written sometime during or after the middle of the fifth century BC, originates from the Jewish community that did not go back to their homeland but stayed on in Babylon. For them there was no return from exile, and since they decided to stay abroad they tried to establish a more positive relationship with their host countries. They took the advice of Jeremiah 29 and integrated with their non-Jewish neighbours, whereas those who returned to Jerusalem found the need to separate themselves from those who were not of their own faith (see Ezra 9 and Nehemiah 13). The message of Esther, therefore, is that it is indeed possible to be a faithful Jew in a foreign land without the temple, and still rest assured in God's deliverance from persecution. It is no surprise in this kind of atmosphere that we come across a Jewish queen of Persia, and watch the Jew Mordecai, like Joseph in Egypt before him, reach a position second only to the king.

God's Scattered People

It is easy when reading the Bible to forget the importance of the Diaspora Jews—those Jews who were scattered throughout the Middle Eastern lands—because the focus is so often on Jerusalem, and so many of the Old Testament books were written in Jerusalem by people who regarded themselves as the only true Jews. Esther displays the influence of those other Jewish communities, for it is from the Persian Jews that the command goes out for all Jews everywhere to observe Purim, an order which was obeyed, as the survival of the festival proves.

God at Work in His World

The book of Esther then is an example to us of the continual Jewish struggle for existence and identity. And in this battle, as the success of Esther and Mordecai shows, God is on the side of the weak and oppressed. To modern Jews the book records the beginning of organized anti-Semitism (Gentile hatred for the Jews), the sad history of which has followed us down to the present day. It is in the light of such unjust persecution, aimed at a small group of strangers living in a foreign land, that we have to read the book of Esther and understand its very basic yet powerful message. God is indeed at work in the world saving his people.

Queen Vashti Deposed

1 This is what happened during the time of Xerxes,[a] the Xerxes who ruled over 127 provinces stretching from India to Cush:[b] [2]At that time King Xerxes reigned from his royal throne in the citadel of Susa, [3]and in the third year of his reign he gave a banquet for all his nobles and officials. The military leaders of Persia and Media, the princes, and the nobles of the provinces were present.

1:1 Xerxes ruled the Persian empire from 485–465 BC and is renowned for his unsuccessful attempt to conquer Greece. The dates in Esther fit well with what we know of Xerxes' reign from other sources — the banquet in the third year would fall into the period before Xerxes left for Greece, and the four years mentioned in 2:1 coincided with his absence on that campaign. Esther captures well the legendary wealth and extravagance of the Persian court and the king's great love of drinking.

---

[4]For a full 180 days he displayed the vast wealth of his kingdom and the splendour and glory of his majesty. [5]When these days were over, the king gave a banquet, lasting seven days, in the enclosed garden of the king's palace, for all the people from the least to the greatest, who were in the citadel of Susa. [6]The garden had hangings of white and blue linen, fastened with cords of white linen and purple material to silver rings on marble pillars. There were couches of gold and silver on a mosaic pavement of porphyry, marble, mother-of-pearl and other costly stones. [7]Wine was served in goblets of gold, each one different from the other, and the royal wine was abundant, in keeping with the king's liberality. [8]By the king's command each guest was allowed to drink in his own way, for the king instructed all the wine stewards to serve each man what he wished.

1:7 Jehoiachin had been king for only three months in 597 BC when the Babylonians captured Jerusalem and sacked the temple. He was taken off into exile along with the leading citizens and never returned (2 Kings 24:8–17).

---

[9]Queen Vashti also gave a banquet for the women in the royal palace of King Xerxes.

[10]On the seventh day, when King Xerxes was in high spirits from wine, he commanded the seven eunuchs who served him — Mehuman, Biztha, Harbona, Bigtha, Abagtha, Zethar and Carcas — [11]to bring before him Queen Vashti, wearing her royal crown, in order to display her beauty to the people and nobles, for she was lovely to look at. [12]But when the attendants delivered the king's command, Queen Vashti refused to come. Then the king became furious and burned with anger.

[13]Since it was customary for the king to consult experts in matters of law and justice, he spoke with the wise men who understood the times [14]and were closest to the king — Carshena, Shethar, Admatha, Tarshish, Meres, Marsena and Memucan, the seven nobles of Persia and Media who had special access to the king and were highest in the kingdom.

[15]"According to law, what must be done to Queen Vashti?" he asked. "She has not obeyed the command of King Xerxes that the eunuchs have taken to her."

[16]Then Memucan replied in the presence of the king and the nobles, "Queen Vashti has done wrong, not only against the king but also against all the nobles and the peoples of all the provinces of King Xerxes. [17]For the queen's conduct will become known to all the women, and so they will despise their husbands and say, 'King Xerxes commanded Queen Vashti to be brought before him, but she would not come.' [18]This very day the Persian and Median women of the nobility who have heard about the queen's conduct will respond to all the king's nobles in the same way. There will be no end of disrespect and discord.

[19]"Therefore, if it pleases the king, let him issue a royal decree and let it be written in the laws of Persia and Media, which cannot be repealed, that Vashti is never again to enter the presence of King Xerxes. Also let the king give her royal position to someone else who is better than she. [20]Then when the king's edict is proclaimed throughout all his vast realm, all the women will respect their husbands, from the least to the greatest."

[21]The king and his nobles were pleased with this advice, so the king did as Memucan proposed. [22]He sent dispatches to all parts of the kingdom, to each province in its own script and to each people in its own language, proclaiming in each people's tongue that every man should be ruler over his own household.

Esther Made Queen

2 Later when the anger of King Xerxes had subsided, he remembered Vashti and what she had done and what he had decreed about her. [2]Then the king's personal attendants proposed, "Let a search be made for beautiful young virgins for the king. [3]Let the king appoint commissioners in every province of his realm to bring all these beautiful girls into the harem at the citadel of Susa. Let them be placed under the care of Hegai, the king's eunuch, who is in charge of the women; and let beauty treatments be given to them. [4]Then let the girl who pleases the king be queen instead of Vashti." This advice appealed to the king, and he followed it.

[5]Now there was in the citadel of Susa a Jew of the tribe of Benjamin, named Mordecai son of Jair, the son of Shimei, the son of Kish, [6]who had been carried into exile from Jerusalem by Nebuchadnezzar king of Babylon, among those taken captive with Jehoiachin[a] king of Judah. [7]Mordecai had a cousin named

---

[a]1 Hebrew *Ahasuerus*, a variant of Xerxes' Persian name; here and throughout Esther
[a]6 Hebrew *Jeconiah*, a variant of *Jehoiachin*

[b]1 That is, the upper Nile region

Hadassah, whom he had brought up because she had neither father nor mother. This girl, who was also known as Esther, was lovely in form and features, and Mordecai had taken her as his own daughter when her father and mother died.

8When the king's order and edict had been proclaimed, many girls were brought to the citadel of Susa and put under the care of Hegai. Esther also was taken to the king's palace and entrusted to Hegai, who had charge of the harem. 9The girl pleased him and won his favour. Immediately he provided her with her beauty treatments and special food. He assigned to her seven maids selected from the king's palace and moved her and her maids into the best place in the harem.

10Esther had not revealed her nationality and family background, because Mordecai had forbidden her to do so. 11Every day he walked to and fro near the courtyard of the harem to find out how Esther was and what was happening to her.

12Before a girl's turn came to go in to King Xerxes, she had to complete twelve months of beauty treatments prescribed for the women, six months with oil of myrrh and six with perfumes and cosmetics. 13And this is how she would go to the king: Anything she wanted was given to her to take with her from the harem to the king's palace. 14In the evening she would go there and in the morning return to another part of the harem to the care of Shaashgaz, the king's eunuch who was in charge of the concubines. She would not return to the king unless he was pleased with her and summoned her by name.

15When the turn came for Esther (the girl Mordecai had adopted, the daughter of his uncle Abihail) to go to the king, she asked for nothing other than what Hegai, the king's eunuch who was in charge of the harem, suggested. And Esther won the favour of everyone who saw her. 16She was taken to King Xerxes in the royal residence in the tenth month, the month of Tebeth, in the seventh year of his reign.

17Now the king was attracted to Esther more than to any of the other women, and she won his favour and approval more than any of the other virgins. So he set a royal crown on her head and made her queen instead of Vashti. 18And the king gave a great banquet, Esther's banquet, for all his nobles and officials. He proclaimed a holiday throughout the provinces and distributed gifts with royal liberality.

Mordecai Uncovers a Conspiracy

19When the virgins were assembled a second time, Mordecai was sitting at the king's gate. 20But Esther had kept secret her family background and nationality just as Mordecai had told her to do, for she continued to follow Mordecai's instructions as she had done when he was bringing her up.

21During the time Mordecai was sitting at the king's gate, Bigthanab and Teresh, two of the king's officers who guarded the doorway, became angry and conspired to assassinate King Xerxes. 22But Mordecai found out about the plot and told Queen Esther, who in turn reported it to the king, giving credit to Mordecai. 23And when the report was investigated and found to be true, the two officials were hanged on a gallows.c All this was recorded in the book of the annals in the presence of the king.

Haman's Plot to Destroy the Jews

3 After these events, King Xerxes honoured Haman son of Hammedatha, the Agagite, elevating him and giving him a seat of honour higher than that of all the other nobles. 2All the royal officials at the king's gate knelt down and paid honour to Haman, for the king had commanded this concerning him. But Mordecai would not kneel down or pay him honour.

3:2 The Greek historian, Herodotus, talked about the custom where people were expected to prostrate themselves in front of their superiors. This practice offended those who regarded prostration as a reverential act only to be performed before God, and this explains Mordecai's refusal. Herodotus relates the story about a Greek man who avoided compromising his principles by dropping his ring in front of the king and picking it up, thus satisfying both himself and the monarch.

3Then the royal officials at the king's gate asked Mordecai, "Why do you disobey the king's command?" 4Day after day they spoke to him but he refused to comply. Therefore they told Haman about it to see whether Mordecai's behaviour would be tolerated, for he had told them he was a Jew.

5When Haman saw that Mordecai would not kneel down or pay him honour, he was enraged. 6Yet having learned who Mordecai's people were, he scorned the idea of killing only Mordecai. Instead Haman looked for a way to destroy all Mordecai's people, the Jews, throughout the whole kingdom of Xerxes.

7In the twelfth year of King Xerxes, in the first month, the month of Nisan, they cast the pur (that is, the lot) in the presence of Haman to select a day and month. And the lot fell ona the twelfth month, the month of Adar.

8Then Haman said to King Xerxes, "There is a certain people dispersed and scattered among the peoples in all the provinces of your kingdom whose customs are different from those of all other people and who do not obey the king's laws; it is not in the king's best interest to tolerate them. 9If it pleases the king, let a decree be issued to destroy them, and I will put ten thousand talentsb of silver into the royal treasury for the men who carry out this business."

10So the king took his signet ring from his finger and gave it to Haman son of Hammedatha, the Agagite, the enemy of the Jews. 11"Keep the money," the king said to Haman, "and do with the people as you please." 12Then on the thirteenth day of the first month the

b21 Hebrew Bigthan, a variant of Bigthana   c23 Or were hung (or impaled) on poles; similarly elsewhere in Esther
a7 Septuagint; Hebrew does not have And the lot fell on.   b9 That is, about 340 tons (about 345 metric tons)

royal secretaries were summoned. They wrote out in the script of each province and in the language of each people all Haman's orders to the king's satraps, the governors of the various provinces and the nobles of the various peoples. These were written in the name of King Xerxes himself and sealed with his own ring. [13]Dispatches were sent by couriers to all the king's provinces with the order to destroy, kill and annihilate all the Jews — young and old, women and little children — on a single day, the thirteenth day of the twelfth month, the month of Adar, and to plunder their goods. [14]A copy of the text of the edict was to be issued as law in every province and made known to the people of every nationality so that they would be ready for that day.

3:8   The Jewish way of life with its concern for ritual purity, special foods, sabbath observations and so on, meant that the people often marked themselves off from the society in which they lived. On many occasions in their history this was interpreted, by those who did not know better, as an arrogant refusal to integrate, and it led to their slander and persecution.

---

[15]Spurred on by the king's command, the couriers went out, and the edict was issued in the citadel of Susa. The king and Haman sat down to drink, but the city of Susa was bewildered.

Mordecai Persuades Esther to Help

4 When Mordecai learned of all that had been done, he tore his clothes, put on sackcloth and ashes, and went out into the city, wailing loudly and bitterly. [2]But he went only as far as the king's gate, because no-one clothed in sackcloth was allowed to enter it. [3]In every province to which the edict and order of the king came, there was great mourning among the Jews, with fasting, weeping and wailing. Many lay in sackcloth and ashes.

[4]When Esther's maids and eunuchs came and told her about Mordecai, she was in great distress. She sent clothes for him to put on instead of his sackcloth, but he would not accept them. [5]Then Esther summoned Hathach, one of the king's eunuchs assigned to attend her, and ordered him to find out what was troubling Mordecai and why. [6]So Hathach went out to Mordecai in the open square of the city in front of the king's gate. [7]Mordecai told him everything that had happened to him, including the exact amount of money Haman had promised to pay into the royal treasury for the destruction of the Jews. [8]He also gave him a copy of the text of the edict for their annihilation, which had been published in Susa, to show to Esther and explain it to her, and he told him to urge her to go into the king's presence to beg for mercy and plead with him for her people. [9]Hathach went back and reported to Esther what Mordecai had said. [10]Then she instructed him to say to Mordecai, [11]"All the king's officials and the people of the royal provinces know that for any man or woman

who approaches the king in the inner court without being summoned the king has but one law: that he be put to death. The only exception to this is for the king to extend the gold sceptre to him and spare his life. But thirty days have passed since I was called to go to the king."

[12]When Esther's words were reported to Mordecai, [13]he sent back this answer: "Do not think that because you are in the king's house you alone of all the Jews will escape. [14]For if you remain silent at this time, relief and deliverance for the Jews will arise from another place, but you and your father's family will perish. And who knows but that you have come to royal position for such a time as this?"

4:16   Fasting is often found as an accompaniment to prayer in the Bible: in Ezra a fast was ordered to ask God for a safe journey (Ezra 8:21), and the people of Nineveh fasted in the hope that God would not destroy their city (Jonah 3:6–10). The three-day fasts usually lasted only from morning to night, and reflected the acuteness of the danger facing the Jews in Susa.

---

[15]Then Esther sent this reply to Mordecai: [16]"Go, gather together all the Jews who are in Susa, and fast for me. Do not eat or drink for three days, night or day. I and my maids will fast as you do. When this is done, I will go to the king, even though it is against the law. And if I perish, I perish." [17]So Mordecai went away and carried out all of Esther's instructions.

Esther's Request to the King

5 On the third day Esther put on her royal robes and stood in the inner court of the palace, in front of the king's hall. The king was sitting on his royal throne in the hall, facing the entrance. [2]When he saw Queen Esther standing in the court, he was pleased with her and held out to her the gold sceptre that was in his hand. So Esther approached and touched the tip of the sceptre.

[3]Then the king asked, "What is it, Queen Esther? What is your request? Even up to half the kingdom, it will be given you."

[4]"If it pleases the king," replied Esther, "let the king, together with Haman, come today to a banquet I have prepared for him."

[5]"Bring Haman at once," the king said, "so that we may do what Esther asks."

So the king and Haman went to the banquet Esther had prepared. [6]As they were drinking wine, the king again asked Esther, "Now what is your petition? It will be given you. And what is your request? Even up to half the kingdom, it will be granted."

[7]Esther replied, "My petition and my request is this: [8]If the king regards me with favour and if it pleases the king to grant my petition and fulfil my request, let the king and Haman come tomorrow to the banquet I will prepare for them. Then I will answer the king's question."

Haman's Rage Against Mordecai

⁹Haman went out that day happy and in high spirits. But when he saw Mordecai at the king's gate and observed that he neither rose nor showed fear in his presence, he was filled with rage against Mordecai. ¹⁰Nevertheless, Haman restrained himself and went home.

Calling together his friends and Zeresh, his wife, ¹¹Haman boasted to them about his vast wealth, his many sons, and all the ways the king had honoured him and how he had elevated him above the other nobles and officials. ¹²"And that's not all," Haman added. "I'm the only person Queen Esther invited to accompany the king to the banquet she gave. And she has invited me along with the king tomorrow. ¹³But all this gives me no satisfaction as long as I see that Jew Mordecai sitting at the king's gate."

¹⁴His wife Zeresh and all his friends said to him, "Have a gallows built, seventy-five feet[a] high, and ask the king in the morning to have Mordecai hanged on it. Then go with the king to the dinner and be happy." This suggestion delighted Haman, and he had the gallows built.

Mordecai Honoured

6 That night the king could not sleep; so he ordered the book of the chronicles, the record of his reign, to be brought in and read to him. ²It was found recorded there that Mordecai had exposed Bigthana and Teresh, two of the king's officers who guarded the doorway, who had conspired to assassinate King Xerxes.

6:1 The progression of events relied totally upon coincidence: the king could not sleep; he happened to open the official records at the page about Mordecai; it happened that Mordecai had not yet been rewarded; Haman happened to appear on the scene just when the king needed some advice. All of these important events occurred by pure chance, but in the context of the book we are left in no doubt that this is divine providence at work in the Jews' favour.

---

³"What honour and recognition has Mordecai received for this?" the king asked.

"Nothing has been done for him," his attendants answered.

⁴The king said, "Who is in the court?" Now Haman had just entered the outer court of the palace to speak to the king about hanging Mordecai on the gallows he had erected for him.

⁵His attendants answered, "Haman is standing in the court."

"Bring him in," the king ordered.

⁶When Haman entered, the king asked him, "What should be done for the man the king delights to honour?"

Now Haman thought to himself, "Who is there that the king would rather honour than me?" ⁷So he answered the king, "For the man the king delights to honour, ⁸have them bring a royal robe the king has worn and a horse the king has ridden, one with a royal crest placed on its head. ⁹Then let the robe and horse be entrusted to one of the king's most noble princes. Let them robe the man the king delights to honour, and lead him on the horse through the city streets, proclaiming before him, 'This is what is done for the man the king delights to honour!' "

¹⁰"Go at once," the king commanded Haman. "Get the robe and the horse and do just as you have suggested for Mordecai the Jew, who sits at the king's gate. Do not neglect anything you have recommended."

¹¹So Haman got the robe and the horse. He robed Mordecai, and led him on horseback through the city streets, proclaiming before him, "This is what is done for the man the king delights to honour!"

¹²Afterwards Mordecai returned to the king's gate. But Haman rushed home, with his head covered, in grief, ¹³and told Zeresh his wife and all his friends everything that had happened to him.

His advisers and his wife Zeresh said to him, "Since Mordecai, before whom your downfall has started, is of Jewish origin, you cannot stand against him — you will surely come to ruin!" ¹⁴While they were still talking with him, the king's eunuchs arrived and hurried Haman away to the banquet Esther had prepared.

Haman Hanged

7 So the king and Haman went to dine with Queen Esther, ²and as they were drinking wine on that second day, the king again asked, "Queen Esther, what is your petition? It will be given you. What is your request? Even up to half the kingdom, it will be granted."

³Then Queen Esther answered, "If I have found favour with you, O king, and if it pleases your majesty, grant me my life — this is my petition. And spare my people — this is my request. ⁴For I and my people have been sold for destruction and slaughter and annihilation. If we had merely been sold as male and female slaves, I would have kept quiet, because no such distress would justify disturbing the king."[a]

⁵King Xerxes asked Queen Esther, "Who is he? Where is the man who has dared to do such a thing?"

⁶Esther said, "The adversary and enemy is this vile Haman."

Then Haman was terrified before the king and queen. ⁷The king got up in a rage, left his wine and went out into the palace garden. But Haman, realising that the king had already decided his fate, stayed behind to beg Queen Esther for his life.

⁸Just as the king returned from the palace garden to the banquet hall, Haman was falling on the couch where Esther was reclining.

---

a 14 Hebrew *fifty cubits* (about 23 metres)
a 4 Or *quiet, but the compensation our adversary offers cannot be compared with the loss the king would suffer*

The king exclaimed, "Will he even molest the queen while she is with me in the house?"

As soon as the word left the king's mouth, they covered Haman's face. [9]Then Harbona, one of the eunuchs attending the king, said, "A gallows seventy-five feet[b] high stands by Haman's house. He had it made for Mordecai, who spoke up to help the king."

The king said, "Hang him on it!" [10]So they hanged Haman on the gallows he had prepared for Mordecai. Then the king's fury subsided.

The King's Edict on Behalf of the Jews

8 That same day King Xerxes gave Queen Esther the estate of Haman, the enemy of the Jews. And Mordecai came into the presence of the king, for Esther had told how he was related to her. [2]The king took off his signet ring, which he had reclaimed from Haman, and presented it to Mordecai. And Esther appointed him over Haman's estate.

[3]Esther again pleaded with the king, falling at his feet and weeping. She begged him to put an end to the evil plan of Haman the Agagite, which he had devised against the Jews. [4]Then the king extended the gold sceptre to Esther and she arose and stood before him.

[5]"If it pleases the king," she said, "and if he regards me with favour and thinks it the right thing to do, and if he is pleased with me, let an order be written overruling the dispatches that Haman son of Hammedatha, the Agagite, devised and wrote to destroy the Jews in all the king's provinces. [6]For how can I bear to see disaster fall on my people? How can I bear to see the destruction of my family?"

[7]King Xerxes replied to Queen Esther and to Mordecai the Jew, "Because Haman attacked the Jews, I have given his estate to Esther, and they have hanged him on the gallows. [8]Now write another decree in the king's name on behalf of the Jews as seems best to you, and seal it with the king's signet ring—for no document written in the king's name and sealed with his ring can be revoked."

[9]At once the royal secretaries were summoned—on the twenty-third day of the third month, the month of Sivan. They wrote out all Mordecai's orders to the Jews, and to the satraps, governors and nobles of the 127 provinces stretching from India to Cush.[a] These orders were written in the script of each province and the language of each people and also to the Jews in their own script and language. [10]Mordecai wrote in the name of King Xerxes, sealed the dispatches with the king's signet ring, and sent them by mounted couriers, who rode fast horses especially bred for the king.

[11]The king's edict granted the Jews in every city the right to assemble and protect themselves; to destroy, kill and annihilate any armed force of any nationality or province that might attack them and their women and children; and to plunder the property of their enemies. [12]The day appointed for the Jews to do this in all the provinces of King Xerxes was the thirteenth day of the twelfth month, the month of Adar. [13]A copy of the text of the edict was to be issued as law in every province and made known to the people of every nationality so that the Jews would be ready on that day to avenge themselves on their enemies.

[14]The couriers, riding the royal horses, raced out, spurred on by the king's command. And the edict was also issued in the citadel of Susa.

[15]Mordecai left the king's presence wearing royal garments of blue and white, a large crown of gold and a purple robe of fine linen. And the city of Susa held a joyous celebration. [16]For the Jews it was a time of happiness and joy, gladness and honour. [17]In every province and in every city, wherever the edict of the king went, there was joy and gladness among the Jews, with feasting and celebrating. And many people of other nationalities became Jews because fear of the Jews had seized them.

8:17   It is possible that this is the original end to the story of Esther before a later editor added the passages about Purim. Indeed, to have many people converting to the Jewish faith would be a satisfying conclusion to Haman's downfall. The fear that seized the people should not be regarded as fear of persecution at the hands of the Jews but rather as a religious sense of awe, similar to what is found, for example, in Joshua.

Triumph of the Jews

9 On the thirteenth day of the twelfth month, the month of Adar, the edict commanded by the king was to be carried out. On this day the enemies of the Jews had hoped to overpower them, but now the tables were turned and the Jews got the upper hand over those who hated them. [2]The Jews assembled in their cities in all the provinces of King Xerxes to attack those seeking their destruction. No-one could stand against them, because the people of all the other nationalities were afraid of them. [3]And all the nobles of the provinces, the satraps, the governors and the king's administrators helped the Jews, because fear of Mordecai had seized them. [4]Mordecai was prominent in the palace; his reputation spread throughout the provinces, and he became more and more powerful.

[5]The Jews struck down all their enemies with the sword, killing and destroying them, and they did what they pleased to those who hated them. [6]In the citadel of Susa, the Jews killed and destroyed five hundred men. [7]They also killed Parshandatha, Dalphon, Aspatha, [8]Poratha, Adalia, Aridatha, [9]Parmashta, Arisai, Aridai and Vaizatha, [10]the ten sons of Haman son of Hammedatha, the enemy of the Jews. But they did not lay their hands on the plunder.

[11]The number of those slain in the citadel of Susa was reported to the king that same day. [12]The king said to Queen Esther, "The Jews have killed and destroyed five hundred men and the ten sons of Haman in the citadel of Susa. What have they done in the rest of the king's provinces? Now what is your petition? It will be

---

b9 Hebrew *fifty cubits* (about 23 metres)   a9 That is, the upper Nile region given you. What is your request? It will also be granted."

[13]"If it pleases the king," Esther answered, "give the Jews in Susa permission to carry out this day's edict tomorrow also, and let Haman's ten sons be hanged on gallows."

[14]So the king commanded that this be done. An edict was issued in Susa, and they hanged the ten sons of Haman. [15]The Jews in Susa came together on the fourteenth day of the month of Adar, and they put to death in Susa three hundred men, but they did not lay their hands on the plunder.

[16]Meanwhile, the remainder of the Jews who were in the king's provinces also assembled to protect themselves and get relief from their enemies. They killed seventy-five thousand of them but did not lay their hands on the plunder. [17]This happened on the thirteenth day of the month of Adar, and on the fourteenth they rested and made it a day of feasting and joy.

Purim Celebrated

[18]The Jews in Susa, however, had assembled on the thirteenth and fourteenth, and then on the fifteenth they rested and made it a day of feasting and joy.

[19]That is why rural Jews — those living in villages — observe the fourteenth of the month of Adar as a day of joy and feasting, a day for giving presents to each other.

[20]Mordecai recorded these events, and he sent letters to all the Jews throughout the provinces of King Xerxes, near and far, [21]to have them celebrate annually the fourteenth and fifteenth days of the month of Adar [22]as the time when the Jews got relief from their enemies, and as the month when their sorrow was turned into joy and their mourning into a day of celebration. He wrote to them to observe the days as days of feasting and joy and giving presents of food to one another and gifts to the poor.

[23]So the Jews agreed to continue the celebration they had begun, doing what Mordecai had written to them. [24]For Haman son of Hammedatha, the Agagite, the enemy of all the Jews, had plotted against the Jews to destroy them and had cast the *pur* (that is, the lot) for their ruin and destruction. [25]But when the plot came to the king's attention,[a] he issued written orders that the evil scheme Haman had devised against the Jews should come back on to his own head, and that he and his sons should be hanged on the gallows. [26](Therefore these days were called Purim, from the word *pur*.) Because of everything written in this letter and because of what they had seen and what had happened to them, [27]the Jews took it upon themselves to establish the custom that they and their descendants and all who join them should without fail observe these two days every year, in the way prescribed and at the time appointed. [28]These days should be remembered and observed in every generation by every family, and in every province and in every city. And these days of Purim should never cease to be celebrated by the Jews, nor should the memory of them die out among their descendants.

[29]So Queen Esther, daughter of Abihail, along with Mordecai the Jew, wrote with full authority to confirm this second letter concerning Purim. [30]And Mordecai sent letters to all the Jews in the 127 provinces of the kingdom of Xerxes — words of goodwill and assurance — [31]to establish these days of Purim at their designated times, as Mordecai the Jew and Queen Esther had decreed for them, and as they had established for themselves and their descendants in regard to their times of fasting and lamentation. [32]Esther's decree confirmed these regulations about Purim, and it was written down in the records.

The Greatness of Mordecai

10 King Xerxes imposed tribute throughout the empire, to its distant shores. [2]And all his acts of power and might, together with a full account of the greatness of Mordecai to which the king had raised him, are they not written in the book of the annals of the kings of Media and Persia? [3]Mordecai the Jew was second in rank to King Xerxes, pre-eminent among the Jews, and held in high esteem by his many fellow Jews, because he worked for the good of his people and spoke up for the welfare of all the Jews.

10:3   Mordecai and Esther reached high status in a foreign country; they were like Joseph in Egypt (Genesis 41) or Daniel at the court of Belshazzar (Daniel 6:28). On each occasion that the Old Testament records such successful careers it makes it clear that this was God's doing and that the high rank brought with it the challenge of great responsibility. Joseph told his brothers as much in Genesis 45:7, and Mordecai reminded Esther of the same (4:14). As Jesus said, "From everyone who has been given much, much will be demanded" (Luke 12:48).

Job

A Great Theme

One of the great themes in the Old Testament is the issue of undeserved suffering. Good people who follow God's laws seem to bear the brunt of all that life can possibly throw at them. One disaster follows another, and these faithful people cry out with their prayers of protest, but God is silent and there is no comfort to be found in their dilemmas.

Bad Things Happening to Good People

The book of Job is the story of a man who had all the good things of life. He was one of life's successful people who had consistently demonstrated his faithfulness towards God, but suddenly experienced his whole life crashing down around him. His belongings were stolen and his servants killed; his sheep were burned by fire; his house was blown away in a hurricane with his sons and daughters still inside; and finally, Job was afflicted by disease.

The Accuser

The plot is intriguing, and begins in heaven with Satan throwing down the gauntlet and challenging God to a theological battle of wits. At this particular time in the history of God's people, Satan was understood as the cynical one who skulked around the place criticizing and accusing others. He saw Job, his wealth, and his faithfulness to God, and accused him of being faithful to God only for the good things he would get in return. It was almost like saying that it's good to be religious because things will work out for you. Satan was calling God's integrity into question.

God's response was to set out to show Satan that Job's faithfulness was total, and he went to extraordinary lengths to prove it. The only way of testing Job's true motives was to take away all those good things which Satan was so sure were the real motives for his love for God.

Struggling With the Truth

As each disaster struck, three of Job's friends ("comforters") appeared: Eliphaz, Bildad, and Zophar. At first they sympathized with him, but then they began to accuse him. They suggested that he must have done something to deserve what was happening. They challenged him to confess his sins, but Job knew he was innocent, and refused. At the same time he still showed unswerving faithfulness to God. Job's three friends, unable to get him to confess any sins, gave up in the end, and a fourth friend, Elihu, tried to persuade Job to confess. But he got no answer.

Why?

Throughout the book, Job's mood and position were changing: sometimes he was confident in his innocence, at other times he cried out in protest; sometimes he burst out in anger; at other times he was depressed by self-pity. Behind all his shifts and changes of mood, there was one burning question: Why? He had done nothing to deserve all this suffering, he even remained faithful to God, yet the suffering grew and grew. Why?

The only one who could answer him was God, who appeared at the end in a mighty whirlwind to vindicate Job and restore him to wealth and happiness.

Job's Story Today

To the present-day reader, the book of Job can look hard-going. The plot unfolds by means of a series of long speeches, and reads more like Prime Minister's Question Time than an intriguing thriller. Of course, it is recognized as a great literary masterpiece, combining moving poetry with a slick-moving narrative. The essence of the story is summarized in chapters 1, 2, and 42, while the rest of the book is taken up with speeches. Yet if read in small sections, the real, heartbreaking reality of Job's predicament is brought home, and the discovery of God's goodness and Job's unfailing trust at the end is all the more telling.

Faithfulness and Trust

By being familiar with all the details of Job's story, we can begin to follow his example of faithfulness and trust, whatever life throws at us. We will ask questions, we will protest, we will probably not understand why things are as they are. But God, who knows us so much better than we do ourselves, will bring us through the pain and uncertainty, and show that he is truly the God of love.

Prologue

1 In the land of Uz there lived a man whose name was Job. This man was blameless and upright; he feared God and shunned evil. [2]He had seven sons and three daughters, [3]and he owned seven thousand sheep, three thousand camels, five hundred yoke of oxen and five hundred donkeys, and had a large number of servants. He was the greatest man among all the people of the East.

[4]His sons used to take turns holding feasts in their homes, and they would invite their three sisters to eat and drink with them. [5]When a period of feasting had run its course, Job would send and have them purified. Early in the morning he would sacrifice a burnt offering for each of them, thinking, "Perhaps my children have sinned and cursed God in their hearts." This was Job's regular custom.

Job's First Test

[6]One day the angels[a] came to present themselves before the Lord, and Satan[b] also came with them. [7]The Lord said to Satan, "Where have you come from?"

Satan answered the Lord, "From roaming through the earth and going to and fro in it."

[8]Then the Lord said to Satan, "Have you considered my servant Job? There is no-one on earth like him; he is blameless and upright, a man who fears God and shuns evil."

[9]"Does Job fear God for nothing?" Satan replied. [10]"Have you not put a hedge around him and his household and everything he has? You have blessed the work of his hands, so that his flocks and herds are spread throughout the land. [11]But stretch out your hand and strike everything he has, and he will surely curse you to your face."

¹²The LORD said to Satan, "Very well, then, everything he has is in your hands; but on the man himself do not lay a finger."

Then Satan went out from the presence of the LORD.

¹³One day when Job's sons and daughters were feasting and drinking wine at the oldest brother's house, ¹⁴a messenger came to Job and said, "The oxen were ploughing and the donkeys were grazing nearby, ¹⁵and the Sabeans attacked and carried them off. They put the servants to the sword, and I am the only one who has escaped to tell you!"

¹⁶While he was still speaking, another messenger came and said, "The fire of God fell from the sky and burned up the sheep and the servants, and I am the only one who has escaped to tell you!"

¹⁷While he was still speaking, another messenger came and said, "The Chaldeans formed three raiding parties and swept down on your camels and carried them off. They put the servants to the sword, and I am the only one who has escaped to tell you!"

¹⁸While he was still speaking, yet another messenger came and said, "Your sons and daughters were feasting and drinking wine at the oldest brother's house, ¹⁹when suddenly a mighty wind swept in from the desert and struck the four corners of the house. It collapsed on them and they are dead, and I am the only one who has escaped to tell you!"

²⁰At this, Job got up and tore his robe and shaved his head. Then he fell to the ground in worship ²¹and said:

"Naked I came from my mother's womb,
    and naked I shall depart.ᶜ
The LORD gave and the LORD has taken away;
    may the name of the LORD be praised."

1:21   How do you protest against injustice? Job's answer was to praise God. Throughout history, in many tragic situations, the Jews have praised God. To praise God in such dire circumstances is to say "I refuse to believe that God is not good." Praise became Job's protest against evil.

---

²²In all this, Job did not sin by charging God with wrongdoing.

Job's Second Test

2 On another day the angelsᵃ came to present themselves before the LORD, and Satan also came with them to present himself before him. ²And the LORD said to Satan, "Where have you come from?"

Satan answered the LORD, "From roaming through the earth and going to and fro in it."

³Then the LORD said to Satan, "Have you considered my servant Job? There is no-one on earth like him; he is blameless and upright, a man who fears God and shuns evil. And he still maintains his integrity, though you incited me against him to ruin him without any reason."

⁴"Skin for skin!" Satan replied. "A man will give all he has for his own life. ⁵But stretch out your hand and strike his flesh and bones, and he will surely curse you to your face."

⁶The LORD said to Satan, "Very well, then, he is in your hands; but you must spare his life."

⁷So Satan went out from the presence of the LORD and afflicted Job with painful sores from the soles of his feet to the top of his head. ⁸Then Job took a piece of broken pottery and scraped himself with it as he sat among the ashes.

⁹His wife said to him, "Are you still holding on to your integrity? Curse God and die!"

¹⁰He replied, "You are talking like a foolishᵇ woman. Shall we accept good from God, and not trouble?"

In all this, Job did not sin in what he said.

Job's Three Friends

¹¹When Job's three friends, Eliphaz the Temanite, Bildad the Shuhite and Zophar the Naamathite, heard about all the troubles that had come upon him, they set out from their homes and met together by agreement to go and sympathise with him and comfort him. ¹²When they saw him from a distance, they could hardly recognise him; they began to weep aloud, and they tore their robes and sprinkled dust on their heads. ¹³Then they sat on the ground with him for seven days and seven nights. No-one said a word to him, because they saw how great his suffering was.

Job Speaks

3 After this, Job opened his mouth and cursed the day of his birth. ²He said:

3:3   Job's praise turned to a desperate wish that he had never been born, as he touched upon one of the most profound human questions: "Why is life so unfair?"

---

³"May the day of my birth perish,
    and the night it was said, 'A boy is born!'
⁴That day—may it turn to darkness;
    may God above not care about it;
    may no light shine upon it.
⁵May darkness and deep shadowᵃ claim it once
        more;
    may a cloud settle over it;
    may blackness overwhelm its light.
⁶That night—may thick darkness seize it;
    may it not be included among the days of the
        year
    nor be entered in any of the months.
⁷May that night be barren;
    may no shout of joy be heard in it.
⁸May those who curse daysᵇ curse that day,
    those who are ready to rouse Leviathan.
⁹May its morning stars become dark;
    may it wait for daylight in vain
    and not see the first rays of dawn,

ᶜ21 Or shall return there   ᵃ1 Hebrew the sons of God
ᵃ5 Or and the shadow of death   ᵇ9 Or the sea   ᵇ10 The Hebrew word rendered foolish denotes moral deficiency.

¹⁰for it did not shut the doors of the womb on me
  to hide trouble from my eyes.

¹¹"Why did I not perish at birth,
  and die as I came from the womb?
¹²Why were there knees to receive me
  and breasts that I might be nursed?
¹³For now I would be lying down in peace;
  I would be asleep and at rest
¹⁴with kings and counsellors of the earth,
  who built for themselves places now lying in
    ruins,
¹⁵with rulers who had gold,
  who filled their houses with silver.
¹⁶Or why was I not hidden in the ground like a
    stillborn child,
  like an infant who never saw the light of
    day?
¹⁷There the wicked cease from turmoil,
  and there the weary are at rest.
¹⁸Captives also enjoy their ease;
  they no longer hear the slave driver's shout.
¹⁹The small and the great are there,
  and the slave is freed from his master.

²⁰"Why is light given to those in misery,
  and life to the bitter of soul,
²¹to those who long for death that does not come,
  who search for it more than for hidden
    treasure,
²²who are filled with gladness
  and rejoice when they reach the grave?
²³Why is life given to a man
  whose way is hidden,
  whom God has hedged in?
²⁴For sighing comes to me instead of food;
  my groans pour out like water.
²⁵What I feared has come upon me;
  what I dreaded has happened to me.
²⁶I have no peace, no quietness;
  I have no rest, but only turmoil."

Eliphaz

4 Then Eliphaz the Temanite replied:

²"If someone ventures a word with you, will you
  be impatient?
  But who can keep from speaking?
³Think how you have instructed many,
  how you have strengthened feeble hands.
⁴Your words have supported those who stumbled;
  you have strengthened faltering knees.
⁵But now trouble comes to you, and you are
    discouraged;
  it strikes you, and you are dismayed.
⁶Should not your piety be your confidence
  and your blameless ways your hope?

⁷"Consider now: Who, being innocent, has ever
    perished?
  Where were the upright ever destroyed?
⁸As I have observed, those who plough evil
  and those who sow trouble reap it.

⁹At the breath of God they are destroyed;
  at the blast of his anger they perish.
¹⁰The lions may roar and growl,
  yet the teeth of the great lions are broken.
¹¹The lion perishes for lack of prey,
  and the cubs of the lioness are scattered.

4:7   Eliphaz began by reassuring Job, but became much more cynical. If Job were a good man, he argued, no trouble would have come upon him. But he had begun to wonder whether Job had sinned, and was simply getting all that he deserved.

---

¹²"A word was secretly brought to me,
  my ears caught a whisper of it.
¹³Amid disquieting dreams in the night,
  when deep sleep falls on men,
¹⁴fear and trembling seized me
  and made all my bones shake.
¹⁵A spirit glided past my face,
  and the hair on my body stood on end.
¹⁶It stopped,
  but I could not tell what it was.
  A form stood before my eyes,
  and I heard a hushed voice:
¹⁷'Can a mortal be more righteous than God?
  Can a man be more pure than his Maker?
¹⁸If God places no trust in his servants,
  if he charges his angels with error,
¹⁹how much more those who live in houses of clay,
  whose foundations are in the dust,
  who are crushed more readily than a moth!
²⁰Between dawn and dusk they are broken to
    pieces;
  unnoticed, they perish for ever.
²¹Are not the cords of their tent pulled up,
  so that they die without wisdom?'ᵃ

5 "Call if you will, but who will answer you?
  To which of the holy ones will you turn?
²Resentment kills a fool,
  and envy slays the simple.
³I myself have seen a fool taking root,
  but suddenly his house was cursed.
⁴His children are far from safety,
  crushed in court without a defender.
⁵The hungry consume his harvest,
  taking it even from among thorns,
  and the thirsty pant after his wealth.
⁶For hardship does not spring from the soil,
  nor does trouble sprout from the ground.
⁷Yet man is born to trouble
  as surely as sparks fly upward.

⁸"But if it were I, I would appeal to God;
  I would lay my cause before him.
⁹He performs wonders that cannot be fathomed,
  miracles that cannot be counted.
¹⁰He bestows rain on the earth;
  he sends water upon the countryside.

ᵃ21 Some interpreters end the quotation after verse 17.

[11]The lowly he sets on high,
and those who mourn are lifted to safety.
[12]He thwarts the plans of the crafty,
so that their hands achieve no success.
[13]He catches the wise in their craftiness,
and the schemes of the wily are swept away.
[14]Darkness comes upon them in the daytime;
at noon they grope as in the night.
[15]He saves the needy from the sword in their
mouth;
he saves them from the clutches of the
powerful.
[16]So the poor have hope,
and injustice shuts its mouth.

5:8   A good piece of advice! If Job had
sinned, as Eliphaz believed he had, he should
turn to God and repent his sins. Eliphaz
reinforced this point by going on to list God's
attributes of wisdom and might.

---

[17]"Blessed is the man whom God corrects;
so do not despise the discipline of the
Almighty.[a]
[18]For he wounds, but he also binds up;
he injures, but his hands also heal.
[19]From six calamities he will rescue you;
in seven no harm will befall you.
[20]In famine he will ransom you from death,
and in battle from the stroke of the sword.
[21]You will be protected from the lash of the tongue,
and need not fear when destruction comes.
[22]You will laugh at destruction and famine,
and need not fear the beasts of the earth.
[23]For you will have a covenant with the stones of
the field,
and the wild animals will be at peace with you.
[24]You will know that your tent is secure;
you will take stock of your property and find
nothing missing.
[25]You will know that your children will be many,
and your descendants like the grass of the
earth.
[26]You will come to the grave in full vigour,
like sheaves gathered in season.

[27]"We have examined this, and it is true.
So hear it and apply it to yourself."

Job

6   Then Job replied:

[2]"If only my anguish could be weighed
and all my misery be placed on the scales!
[3]It would surely outweigh the sand of the seas—
no wonder my words have been impetuous.
[4]The arrows of the Almighty are in me,
my spirit drinks in their poison;
God's terrors are marshalled against me.

[5]Does a wild donkey bray when it has grass,
or an ox bellow when it has fodder?
[6]Is tasteless food eaten without salt,
or is there flavour in the white of an egg?[a]
[7]I refuse to touch it;
such food makes me ill.

[8]"Oh, that I might have my request,
that God would grant what I hope for,
[9]that God would be willing to crush me,
to let loose his hand and cut me off!
[10]Then I would still have this consolation—
my joy in unrelenting pain—
that I had not denied the words of the Holy One.

[11]"What strength do I have, that I should still hope?
What prospects, that I should be patient?
[12]Do I have the strength of stone?
Is my flesh bronze?
[13]Do I have any power to help myself,
now that success has been driven from me?

6:14   Job's protest was not just confined
to God. He felt vexed by his friends, too. Like
a stream in the desert which flows irregularly
and is dry when most needed, all they
offered Job in his misery was disappointment
rather than comfort.

---

[14]"A despairing man should have the devotion of
his friends,
even though he forsakes the fear of the
Almighty.
[15]But my brothers are as undependable as
intermittent streams,
as the streams that overflow
[16]when darkened by thawing ice
and swollen with melting snow,
[17]but that cease to flow in the dry season,
and in the heat vanish from their channels.
[18]Caravans turn aside from their routes;
they go up into the wasteland and perish.
[19]The caravans of Tema look for water,
the travelling merchants of Sheba look in hope.
[20]They are distressed, because they had been
confident;
they arrive there, only to be disappointed.
[21]Now you too have proved to be of no help;
you see something dreadful and are afraid.
[22]Have I ever said, 'Give something on my behalf,
pay a ransom for me from your wealth,
[23]deliver me from the hand of the enemy,
ransom me from the clutches of the ruthless'?

[24]"Teach me, and I will be quiet;
show me where I have been wrong.
[25]How painful are honest words!
But what do your arguments prove?
[26]Do you mean to correct what I say,
and treat the words of a despairing man as
wind?

---

[a]17 Hebrew *Shaddai*; here and throughout Job   [a]6 The meaning of the Hebrew for this phrase is uncertain.

²⁷You would even cast lots for the fatherless
 and barter away your friend.

²⁸"But now be so kind as to look at me.
 Would I lie to your face?
²⁹Relent, do not be unjust;
 reconsider, for my integrity is at stake.ᵇ
³⁰Is there any wickedness on my lips?
 Can my mouth not discern malice?

7 "Does not man have hard service on earth?
 Are not his days like those of a hired man?
²Like a slave longing for the evening shadows,
 or a hired man waiting eagerly for his wages,
³so I have been allotted months of futility,
 and nights of misery have been assigned to me.
⁴When I lie down I think, 'How long before I get
 up?'
 The night drags on, and I toss till dawn.
⁵My body is clothed with worms and scabs,
 my skin is broken and festering.

⁶"My days are swifter than a weaver's shuttle,
 and they come to an end without hope.
⁷Remember, O God, that my life is but a breath;
 my eyes will never see happiness again.
⁸The eye that now sees me will see me no longer;
 you will look for me, but I will be no more.
⁹As a cloud vanishes and is gone,
 so he who goes down to the graveᵃ does not
 return.
¹⁰He will never come to his house again;
 his place will know him no more.

7:20   Job's cries of protest took another
twist as he threw down the gauntlet to God.
If God was so wise and all-knowing, how
was it that the sin of which Job was accused
could not be identified? If God was so good
and loving and just, why should a good person have to live in such misery?

---

¹¹"Therefore I will not keep silent;
 I will speak out in the anguish of my spirit,
 I will complain in the bitterness of my soul.
¹²Am I the sea, or the monster of the deep,
 that you put me under guard?
¹³When I think my bed will comfort me
 and my couch will ease my complaint,
¹⁴even then you frighten me with dreams
 and terrify me with visions,
¹⁵so that I prefer strangling and death,
 rather than this body of mine.
¹⁶I despise my life; I would not live for ever.
 Let me alone; my days have no meaning.

¹⁷"What is man that you make so much of him,
 that you give him so much attention,
¹⁸that you examine him every morning
 and test him every moment?

¹⁹Will you never look away from me,
 or let me alone even for an instant?
²⁰If I have sinned, what have I done to you,
 O watcher of men?
 Why have you made me your target?
 Have I become a burden to you?ᵇ
²¹Why do you not pardon my offences
 and forgive my sins?
 For I shall soon lie down in the dust;
 you will search for me, but I shall be no more."

Bildad

8 Then Bildad the Shuhite replied:

²"How long will you say such things?
 Your words are a blustering wind.
³Does God pervert justice?
 Does the Almighty pervert what is right?
⁴When your children sinned against him,
 he gave them over to the penalty of their sin.
⁵But if you will look to God
 and plead with the Almighty,
⁶if you are pure and upright,
 even now he will rouse himself on your behalf
 and restore you to your rightful place.
⁷Your beginnings will seem humble,
 so prosperous will your future be.

⁸"Ask the former generations
 and find out what their fathers learned,
⁹for we were born only yesterday and know
 nothing,
 and our days on earth are but a shadow.
¹⁰Will they not instruct you and tell you?
 Will they not bring forth words from their
 understanding?
¹¹Can papyrus grow tall where there is no marsh?
 Can reeds thrive without water?
¹²While still growing and uncut,
 they wither more quickly than grass.
¹³Such is the destiny of all who forget God;
 so perishes the hope of the godless.
¹⁴What he trusts in is fragile;ᵃ
 what he relies on is a spider's web.
¹⁵He leans on his web, but it gives way;
 he clings to it, but it does not hold.
¹⁶He is like a well-watered plant in the sunshine,
 spreading its shoots over the garden;
¹⁷it entwines its roots around a pile of rocks
 and looks for a place among the stones.
¹⁸But when it is torn from its spot,
 that place disowns it and says, 'I never saw
 you.'
¹⁹Surely its life withers away,
 andᵇ from the soil other plants grow.

²⁰"Surely God does not reject a blameless man
 or strengthen the hands of evildoers.
²¹He will yet fill your mouth with laughter
 and your lips with shouts of joy.

ᵇ29 Or *my righteousness still stands*   ᵃ9 Hebrew *Sheol*
ᵇ20 A few manuscripts of the Masoretic Text, an ancient Hebrew scribal tradition and Septuagint; most manuscripts of the Masoretic Text *I
have become a burden to myself.*   ᵃ14 The meaning of the Hebrew for this word is uncertain.
ᵇ19 Or *Surely all the joy it has / is that*

²²Your enemies will be clothed in shame,
and the tents of the wicked will be no more."

Job

9 Then Job replied:

²"Indeed, I know that this is true.
But how can a mortal be righteous before God?
³Though one wished to dispute with him,
he could not answer him one time out of a
thousand.
⁴His wisdom is profound, his power is vast.
Who has resisted him and come out unscathed?
⁵He moves mountains without their knowing it
and overturns them in his anger.
⁶He shakes the earth from its place
and makes its pillars tremble.
⁷He speaks to the sun and it does not shine;
he seals off the light of the stars.
⁸He alone stretches out the heavens
and treads on the waves of the sea.
⁹He is the Maker of the Bear and Orion,
the Pleiades and the constellations of the south.
¹⁰He performs wonders that cannot be fathomed,
miracles that cannot be counted.
¹¹When he passes me, I cannot see him;
when he goes by, I cannot perceive him.
¹²If he snatches away, who can stop him?
Who can say to him, 'What are you doing?'
¹³God does not restrain his anger;
even the cohorts of Rahab cowered at his feet.

¹⁴"How then can I dispute with him?
How can I find words to argue with him?
¹⁵Though I were innocent, I could not answer him;
I could only plead with my Judge for mercy.
¹⁶Even if I summoned him and he responded,
I do not believe he would give me a hearing.
¹⁷He would crush me with a storm
and multiply my wounds for no reason.
¹⁸He would not let me regain my breath
but would overwhelm me with misery.
¹⁹If it is a matter of strength, he is mighty!
And if it is a matter of justice, who will
summon him?ᵃ
²⁰Even if I were innocent, my mouth would
condemn me;
if I were blameless, it would pronounce me
guilty.

²¹"Although I am blameless,
I have no concern for myself;
I despise my own life.
²²It is all the same; that is why I say,
'He destroys both the blameless and the
wicked.'
²³When a scourge brings sudden death,
he mocks the despair of the innocent.
²⁴When a land falls into the hands of the wicked,
he blindfolds its judges.
If it is not he, then who is it?

²⁵"My days are swifter than a runner;
they fly away without a glimpse of joy.
²⁶They skim past like boats of papyrus,
like eagles swooping down on their prey.
²⁷If I say, 'I will forget my complaint,
I will change my expression, and smile,'
²⁸I still dread all my sufferings,
for I know you will not hold me innocent.
²⁹Since I am already found guilty,
why should I struggle in vain?
³⁰Even if I washed myself with soapᵇ
and my hands with washing soda,
³¹you would plunge me into a slime pit
so that even my clothes would detest me.

³²"He is not a man like me that I might answer
him,
that we might confront each other in court.
³³If only there were someone to arbitrate between
us,
to lay his hand upon us both,
³⁴someone to remove God's rod from me,
so that his terror would frighten me no more.
³⁵Then I would speak up without fear of him,
but as it now stands with me, I cannot.

9:33   Here we reach an important point
in the book with the introduction of a mysterious figure to act as an umpire. Much of
the developing arguments and counter-
arguments will depend on him.

---

10   "I loathe my very life;
therefore I will give free rein to my
complaint
and speak out in the bitterness of my soul.
²I will say to God: Do not condemn me,
but tell me what charges you have against me.
³Does it please you to oppress me,
to spurn the work of your hands,
while you smile on the schemes of the wicked?
⁴Do you have eyes of flesh?
Do you see as a mortal sees?
⁵Are your days like those of a mortal
or your years like those of a man,
⁶that you must search out my faults
and probe after my sin—
⁷though you know that I am not guilty
and that no-one can rescue me from your hand?

⁸"Your hands shaped me and made me.
Will you now turn and destroy me?
⁹Remember that you moulded me like clay.
Will you now turn me to dust again?
¹⁰Did you not pour me out like milk
and curdle me like cheese,
¹¹clothe me with skin and flesh
and knit me together with bones and sinews?
¹²You gave me life and showed me kindness,
and in your providence watched over my spirit.

¹³"But this is what you concealed in your heart,
and I know that this was in your mind:

ᵃ 19 See Septuagint; Hebrew *me*.   ᵇ 30 Or *snow*

14If I sinned, you would be watching me
    and would not let my offence go unpunished.
15If I am guilty—woe to me!
    Even if I am innocent, I cannot lift my head,
  for I am full of shame
    and drowned in a my affliction.
16If I hold my head high, you stalk me like a lion
    and again display your awesome power against
      me.
17You bring new witnesses against me
    and increase your anger towards me;
    your forces come against me wave upon wave.

18"Why then did you bring me out of the womb?
    I wish I had died before any eye saw me.
19If only I had never come into being,
    or had been carried straight from the womb to
      the grave!
20Are not my few days almost over?
    Turn away from me so that I can have a
      moment's joy
21before I go to the place of no return,
    to the land of gloom and deep shadow, b
22to the land of deepest night,
    of deep shadow and disorder,
    where even the light is like darkness."

Zophar

11
Then Zophar the Naamathite replied:

2"Are all these words to go unanswered?
    Is this talker to be vindicated?
3Will your idle talk reduce men to silence?
    Will no-one rebuke you when you mock?
4You say to God, 'My beliefs are flawless
    and I am pure in your sight.'
5Oh, how I wish that God would speak,
    that he would open his lips against you
6and disclose to you the secrets of wisdom,
    for true wisdom has two sides.
  Know this: God has even forgotten some of
    your sin.

7"Can you fathom the mysteries of God?
    Can you probe the limits of the Almighty?
8They are higher than the heavens—what can you
      do?
  They are deeper than the depths of the
    grave a—what can you know?
9Their measure is longer than the earth
    and wider than the sea.

10"If he comes along and confines you in prison
    and convenes a court, who can oppose him?
11Surely he recognises deceitful men;
    and when he sees evil, does he not take note?
12But a witless man can no more become wise
    than a wild donkey's colt can be born a man. b

13"Yet if you devote your heart to him
    and stretch out your hands to him,
14if you put away the sin that is in your hand
    and allow no evil to dwell in your tent,

15then you will lift up your face without shame;
    you will stand firm and without fear.
16You will surely forget your trouble,
    recalling it only as waters gone by.
17Life will be brighter than noonday,
    and darkness will become like morning.
18You will be secure, because there is hope;
    you will look about you and take your rest in
      safety.
19You will lie down, with no-one to make you
      afraid,
    and many will court your favour.
20But the eyes of the wicked will fail,
    and escape will elude them;
    their hope will become a dying gasp."

11:12   Zophar, like his two friends, continued to accuse Job of having sinned. Throughout the Hebrew Scriptures, there is a strong belief that wisdom is equated with righteousness, and that foolishness is equated with moral deficiency and lack of belief (see Psalm 14:1).

Job

12
Then Job replied:

2"Doubtless you are the people,
    and wisdom will die with you!
3But I have a mind as well as you;
    I am not inferior to you.
  Who does not know all these things?

4"I have become a laughing-stock to my friends,
    though I called upon God and he answered—
  a mere laughing-stock, though righteous and
    blameless!
5Men at ease have contempt for misfortune
    as the fate of those whose feet are slipping.
6The tents of marauders are undisturbed,
    and those who provoke God are secure—
    those who carry their god in their hands. a

7"But ask the animals, and they will teach you,
    or the birds of the air, and they will tell you;
8or speak to the earth, and it will teach you,
    or let the fish of the sea inform you.
9Which of all these does not know
    that the hand of the LORD has done this?
10In his hand is the life of every creature
    and the breath of all mankind.
11Does not the ear test words
    as the tongue tastes food?
12Is not wisdom found among the aged?
    Does not long life bring understanding?

13"To God belong wisdom and power;
    counsel and understanding are his.
14What he tears down cannot be rebuilt;
    the man he imprisons cannot be released.

---

a 15 Or and aware of   b 21 Or and the shadow of death; also in verse 22   a 8 Hebrew than Sheol
b 12 Or wild donkey can be born tame   a 6 Or secure / in what God's hand brings them

¹⁵If he holds back the waters, there is drought;
  if he lets them loose, they devastate the land.
¹⁶To him belong strength and victory;
  both deceived and deceiver are his.
¹⁷He leads counsellors away stripped
  and makes fools of judges.
¹⁸He takes off the shackles put on by kings
  and ties a loincloth^b round their waist.
¹⁹He leads priests away stripped
  and overthrows men long established.
²⁰He silences the lips of trusted advisers
  and takes away the discernment of elders.
²¹He pours contempt on nobles
  and disarms the mighty.
²²He reveals the deep things of darkness
  and brings deep shadows into the light.
²³He makes nations great, and destroys them;
  he enlarges nations, and disperses them.
²⁴He deprives the leaders of the earth of their
    reason;
  he sends them wandering through a trackless
    waste.
²⁵They grope in darkness with no light;
  he makes them stagger like drunkards.

13 "My eyes have seen all this,
  my ears have heard and understood it.
²What you know, I also know;
  I am not inferior to you.
³But I desire to speak to the Almighty
  and to argue my case with God.
⁴You, however, smear me with lies;
  you are worthless physicians, all of you!
⁵If only you would be altogether silent!
  For you, that would be wisdom.
⁶Hear now my argument;
  listen to the plea of my lips.
⁷Will you speak wickedly on God's behalf?
  Will you speak deceitfully for him?
⁸Will you show him partiality?
  Will you argue the case for God?
⁹Would it turn out well if he examined you?
  Could you deceive him as you might deceive
    men?
¹⁰He would surely rebuke you
  if you secretly showed partiality.
¹¹Would not his splendour terrify you?
  Would not the dread of him fall on you?
¹²Your maxims are proverbs of ashes;
  your defences are defences of clay.

¹³"Keep silent and let me speak;
  then let come to me what may.
¹⁴Why do I put myself in jeopardy
  and take my life in my hands?
¹⁵Though he slay me, yet will I hope in him;
  I will surely^a defend my ways to his face.
¹⁶Indeed, this will turn out for my deliverance,
  for no godless man would dare come before
    him!
¹⁷Listen carefully to my words;
  let your ears take in what I say.

¹⁸Now that I have prepared my case,
  I know I will be vindicated.
¹⁹Can anyone bring charges against me?
  If so, I will be silent and die.
²⁰"Only grant me these two things, O God,
  and then I will not hide from you:
²¹Withdraw your hand far from me,
  and stop frightening me with your terrors.
²²Then summon me and I will answer,
  or let me speak, and you reply.
²³How many wrongs and sins have I committed?
  Show me my offence and my sin.
²⁴Why do you hide your face
  and consider me your enemy?
²⁵Will you torment a wind-blown leaf?
  Will you chase after dry chaff?
²⁶For you write down bitter things against me
  and make me inherit the sins of my youth.
²⁷You fasten my feet in shackles;
  you keep close watch on all my paths
  by putting marks on the soles of my feet.

²⁸"So man wastes away like something rotten,
  like a garment eaten by moths.

14:2 Job's misery brought him face to face with his own vulnerability to death, and he asked whether God would show any regard for him. There are many other passages in the Old Testament which express this sense of human mortality (see Psalm 103:15–17).

---

14 "Man born of woman
  is of few days and full of trouble.
²He springs up like a flower and withers away;
  like a fleeting shadow, he does not endure.
³Do you fix your eye on such a one?
  Will you bring him^a before you for judgment?
⁴Who can bring what is pure from the impure?
  No-one!
⁵Man's days are determined;
  you have decreed the number of his months
  and have set limits he cannot exceed.
⁶So look away from him and let him alone,
  till he has put in his time like a hired man.

⁷"At least there is hope for a tree:
  If it is cut down, it will sprout again,
  and its new shoots will not fail.
⁸Its roots may grow old in the ground
  and its stump die in the soil,
⁹yet at the scent of water it will bud
  and put forth shoots like a plant.
¹⁰But man dies and is laid low;
  he breathes his last and is no more.
¹¹As water disappears from the sea
  or a river bed becomes parched and dry,

^b18 Or *shackles of kings / and ties a belt*
^a3 Septuagint, Vulgate and Syriac; Hebrew *me*

^a15 Or *He will surely slay me; I have no hope — / yet I will*

12so man lies down and does not rise;
  till the heavens are no more, men will not
    awake
  or be roused from their sleep.
13"If only you would hide me in the grave[b]
  and conceal me till your anger has passed!
  If only you would set me a time
  and then remember me!
14If a man dies, will he live again?
  All the days of my hard service
  I will wait for my renewal[c] to come.
15You will call and I will answer you;
  you will long for the creature your hands have
    made.
16Surely then you will count my steps
  but not keep track of my sin.
17My offences will be sealed up in a bag;
  you will cover over my sin.
18"But as a mountain erodes and crumbles
  and as a rock is moved from its place,
19as water wears away stones
  and torrents wash away the soil,
  so you destroy man's hope.
20You overpower him once for all, and he is gone;
  you change his countenance and send him
    away.
21If his sons are honoured, he does not know it;
  if they are brought low, he does not see it.
22He feels but the pain of his own body
  and mourns only for himself."

Eliphaz

15 Then Eliphaz the Temanite replied:

2"Would a wise man answer with empty notions
  or fill his belly with the hot east wind?
3Would he argue with useless words,
  with speeches that have no value?
4But you even undermine piety
  and hinder devotion to God.
5Your sin prompts your mouth;
  you adopt the tongue of the crafty.
6Your own mouth condemns you, not mine;
  your own lips testify against you.

15:4 Eliphaz intensified his argument against Job, this time pointing out his lack of piety and devotion to God. His foolishness was there for everyone to see because of the way in which he appeared to think for himself. Surely God's wisdom was beyond dispute.

7"Are you the first man ever born?
  Were you brought forth before the hills?
8Do you listen in on God's council?
  Do you limit wisdom to yourself?
9What do you know that we do not know?
  What insights do you have that we do not have?
10The grey-haired and the aged are on our side,
  men even older than your father.

11Are God's consolations not enough for you,
  words spoken gently to you?
12Why has your heart carried you away,
  and why do your eyes flash,
13so that you vent your rage against God
  and pour out such words from your mouth?
14"What is man, that he could be pure,
  or one born of woman, that he could be
    righteous?
15If God places no trust in his holy ones,
  if even the heavens are not pure in his eyes,
16how much less man, who is vile and corrupt,
  who drinks up evil like water!

17"Listen to me and I will explain to you;
  let me tell you what I have seen,
18what wise men have declared,
  hiding nothing received from their fathers
19(to whom alone the land was given
  when no alien passed among them):
20All his days the wicked man suffers torment,
  the ruthless through all the years stored up for
    him.
21Terrifying sounds fill his ears;
  when all seems well, marauders attack him.
22He despairs of escaping the darkness;
  he is marked for the sword.
23He wanders about—food for vultures;[a]
  he knows the day of darkness is at hand.
24Distress and anguish fill him with terror;
  they overwhelm him, like a king poised to
    attack,
25because he shakes his fist at God
  and vaunts himself against the Almighty,
26defiantly charging against him
  with a thick, strong shield.

27"Though his face is covered with fat
  and his waist bulges with flesh,
28he will inhabit ruined towns
  and houses where no-one lives,
  houses crumbling to rubble.
29He will no longer be rich and his wealth will not
    endure,
  nor will his possessions spread over the land.
30He will not escape the darkness;
  a flame will wither his shoots,
  and the breath of God's mouth will carry him
    away.
31Let him not deceive himself by trusting what is
    worthless,
  for he will get nothing in return.
32Before his time he will be paid in full,
  and his branches will not flourish.
33He will be like a vine stripped of its unripe
    grapes,
  like an olive tree shedding its blossoms.
34For the company of the godless will be barren,
  and fire will consume the tents of those who
    love bribes.

---

b13 Hebrew *Sheol*   c14 Or *release*   a23 Or *about, looking for food*

35They conceive trouble and give birth to evil;
  their womb fashions deceit."

Job

16 Then Job replied:

2"I have heard many things like these;
  miserable comforters are you all!
3Will your long-winded speeches never end?
  What ails you that you keep on arguing?
4I also could speak like you,
  if you were in my place;
  I could make fine speeches against you
  and shake my head at you.
5But my mouth would encourage you;
  comfort from my lips would bring you relief.

6"Yet if I speak, my pain is not relieved;
  and if I refrain, it does not go away.
7Surely, O God, you have worn me out;
  you have devastated my entire household.
8You have bound me—and it has become a
    witness;
  my gauntness rises up and testifies against me.
9God assails me and tears me in his anger
  and gnashes his teeth at me;
  my opponent fastens on me his piercing eyes.
10Men open their mouths to jeer at me;
  they strike my cheek in scorn
  and unite together against me.
11God has turned me over to evil men
  and thrown me into the clutches of the wicked.
12All was well with me, but he shattered me;
  he seized me by the neck and crushed me.
  He has made me his target;
13 his archers surround me.
  Without pity, he pierces my kidneys
  and spills my gall on the ground.
14Again and again he bursts upon me;
  he rushes at me like a warrior.

15"I have sewed sackcloth over my skin
  and buried my brow in the dust.
16My face is red with weeping,
  deep shadows ring my eyes;
17yet my hands have been free of violence
  and my prayer is pure.

18"O earth, do not cover my blood;
  may my cry never be laid to rest!
19Even now my witness is in heaven;
  my advocate is on high.
20My intercessor is my friend[a]
  as my eyes pour out tears to God;
21on behalf of a man he pleads with God
  as a man pleads for his friend.

22"Only a few years will pass
  before I go on the journey of no return.

17 1My spirit is broken,
    my days are cut short,
  the grave awaits me.

2Surely mockers surround me;
  my eyes must dwell on their hostility.

3"Give me, O God, the pledge you demand.
  Who else will put up security for me?
4You have closed their minds to understanding;
  therefore you will not let them triumph.
5If a man denounces his friends for reward,
  the eyes of his children will fail.

6"God has made me a byword to everyone,
  a man in whose face people spit.
7My eyes have grown dim with grief;
  my whole frame is but a shadow.
8Upright men are appalled at this;
  the innocent are aroused against the ungodly.
9Nevertheless, the righteous will hold to their
    ways,
  and those with clean hands will grow stronger.

17:10 Job protested that his friends would never know the truth of his faithfulness to God. They were as mortal as he was, and he knew that there was hope even beyond the darkness of death.

10"But come on, all of you, try again!
  I will not find a wise man among you.
11My days have passed, my plans are shattered,
  and so are the desires of my heart.
12These men turn night into day;
  in the face of darkness they say, 'Light is near.'
13If the only home I hope for is the grave,[a]
  if I spread out my bed in darkness,
14if I say to corruption, 'You are my father,'
  and to the worm, 'My mother' or 'My sister',
15where then is my hope?
  Who can see any hope for me?
16Will it go down to the gates of death?[b]
  Will we descend together into the dust?"

Bildad

18 Then Bildad the Shuhite replied:

2"When will you end these speeches?
  Be sensible, and then we can talk.
3Why are we regarded as cattle
  and considered stupid in your sight?
4You who tear yourself to pieces in your anger,
  is the earth to be abandoned for your sake?
  Or must the rocks be moved from their place?

5"The lamp of the wicked is snuffed out;
  the flame of his fire stops burning.
6The light in his tent becomes dark;
  the lamp beside him goes out.
7The vigour of his step is weakened;
  his own schemes throw him down.
8His feet thrust him into a net
  and he wanders into its mesh.

---

a20 Or *My friends treat me with scorn*   a13 Hebrew *Sheol*   b16 Hebrew *to Sheol*

⁹A trap seizes him by the heel;
    a snare holds him fast.
¹⁰A noose is hidden for him on the ground;
    a trap lies in his path.
¹¹Terrors startle him on every side
    and dog his every step.
¹²Calamity is hungry for him;
    disaster is ready for him when he falls.
¹³It eats away parts of his skin;
    death's firstborn devours his limbs.
¹⁴He is torn from the security of his tent
    and marched off to the king of terrors.
¹⁵Fire resides*a* in his tent;
    burning sulphur is scattered over his dwelling.
¹⁶His roots dry up below
    and his branches wither above.
¹⁷The memory of him perishes from the earth;
    he has no name in the land.
¹⁸He is driven from light into darkness
    and is banished from the world.
¹⁹He has no offspring or descendants among his
    people,
    no survivor where once he lived.
²⁰Men of the west are appalled at his fate;
    men of the east are seized with horror.
²¹Surely such is the dwelling of an evil man;
    such is the place of one who knows not God."

Job

19

Then Job replied:

²"How long will you torment me
    and crush me with words?
³Ten times now you have reproached me;
    shamelessly you attack me.
⁴If it is true that I have gone astray,
    my error remains my concern alone.
⁵If indeed you would exalt yourselves above me
    and use my humiliation against me,
⁶then know that God has wronged me
    and drawn his net around me.

⁷"Though I cry, 'I've been wronged!' I get no
    response;
    though I call for help, there is no justice.
⁸He has blocked my way so that I cannot pass;
    he has shrouded my paths in darkness.
⁹He has stripped me of my honour
    and removed the crown from my head.
¹⁰He tears me down on every side till I am gone;
    he uproots my hope like a tree.
¹¹His anger burns against me;
    he counts me among his enemies.
¹²His troops advance in force;
    they build a siege ramp against me
    and encamp around my tent.

¹³"He has alienated my brothers from me;
    my acquaintances are completely estranged
    from me.

¹⁴My kinsmen have gone away;
    my friends have forgotten me.
¹⁵My guests and my maidservants count me a
    stranger;
    they look upon me as an alien.
¹⁶I summon my servant, but he does not answer,
    though I beg him with my own mouth.
¹⁷My breath is offensive to my wife;
    I am loathsome to my own brothers.
¹⁸Even the little boys scorn me;
    when I appear, they ridicule me.
¹⁹All my intimate friends detest me;
    those I love have turned against me.
²⁰I am nothing but skin and bones;
    I have escaped by only the skin of my teeth.*a*

²¹"Have pity on me, my friends, have pity,
    for the hand of God has struck me.
²²Why do you pursue me as God does?
    Will you never get enough of my flesh?

²³"Oh, that my words were recorded,
    that they were written on a scroll,
²⁴that they were inscribed with an iron tool on*b*
    lead,
    or engraved in rock for ever!
²⁵I know that my Redeemer*c* lives,
    and that in the end he will stand upon the
    earth.*d*
²⁶And after my skin has been destroyed,
    yet*e* in*f* my flesh I will see God;
²⁷I myself will see him
    with my own eyes—I, and not another.
    How my heart yearns within me!

19:25   Job's belief that there was hope beyond the grave is powerfully expressed in these famous words. Previously Job had asked, many times, that he should die to be relieved from his suffering. Now, returning to a note of praise, he longed to see God who would vindicate him.

---

²⁸"If you say, 'How we will hound him,
    since the root of the trouble lies in him,'*g*
²⁹you should fear the sword yourselves;
    for wrath will bring punishment by the sword,
    and then you will know that there is
    judgment."*h*

Zophar

20

Then Zophar the Naamathite replied:

²"My troubled thoughts prompt me to answer
    because I am greatly disturbed.
³I hear a rebuke that dishonours me,
    and my understanding inspires me to reply.

---

a 15 Or *Nothing he had remains*   *a 20* Or *only my gums*   *b 24* Or *and*   *c 25* Or *defender*
d 25 Or *upon my grave*   *e 26* Or *And after I awake, / though this body has been destroyed, / then*   *f 26* Or / *apart from*
g 28 Many Hebrew manuscripts, Septuagint and Vulgate; most Hebrew manuscripts *me*
h 29 Or / *that you may come to know the Almighty*

4"Surely you know how it has been from of old,
  ever since man[a] was placed on the earth,
5that the mirth of the wicked is brief,
  the joy of the godless lasts but a moment.
6Though his pride reaches to the heavens
  and his head touches the clouds,
7he will perish for ever, like his own dung;
  those who have seen him will say, 'Where is
  he?'
8Like a dream he flies away, no more to be found,
  banished like a vision of the night.
9The eye that saw him will not see him again;
  his place will look on him no more.
10His children must make amends to the poor;
  his own hands must give back his wealth.
11The youthful vigour that fills his bones
  will lie with him in the dust.

12"Though evil is sweet in his mouth
  and he hides it under his tongue,
13though he cannot bear to let it go
  and keeps it in his mouth,
14yet his food will turn sour in his stomach;
  it will become the venom of serpents within
  him.
15He will spit out the riches he swallowed;
  God will make his stomach vomit them up.
16He will suck the poison of serpents;
  the fangs of an adder will kill him.
17He will not enjoy the streams,
  the rivers flowing with honey and cream.
18What he toiled for he must give back uneaten;
  he will not enjoy the profit from his trading.
19For he has oppressed the poor and left them
  destitute;
  he has seized houses he did not build.

20"Surely he will have no respite from his craving;
  he cannot save himself by his treasure.
21Nothing is left for him to devour;
  his prosperity will not endure.
22In the midst of his plenty, distress will overtake
  him;
  the full force of misery will come upon him.
23When he has filled his belly,
  God will vent his burning anger against him
  and rain down his blows upon him.
24Though he flees from an iron weapon,
  a bronze-tipped arrow pierces him.
25He pulls it out of his back,
  the gleaming point out of his liver.
  Terrors will come over him;
26 total darkness lies in wait for his treasures.
  A fire unfanned will consume him
  and devour what is left in his tent.
27The heavens will expose his guilt;
  the earth will rise up against him.
28A flood will carry off his house,
  rushing waters[b] on the day of God's wrath.
29Such is the fate God allots the wicked,
  the heritage appointed for them by God."

Job

21
Then Job replied:

2"Listen carefully to my words;
  let this be the consolation you give me.
3Bear with me while I speak,
  and after I have spoken, mock on.

4"Is my complaint directed to man?
  Why should I not be impatient?
5Look at me and be astonished;
  clap your hand over your mouth.
6When I think about this, I am terrified;
  trembling seizes my body.
7Why do the wicked live on,
  growing old and increasing in power?
8They see their children established around them,
  their offspring before their eyes.
9Their homes are safe and free from fear;
  the rod of God is not upon them.
10Their bulls never fail to breed;
  their cows calve and do not miscarry.
11They send forth their children as a flock;
  their little ones dance about.
12They sing to the music of tambourine and harp;
  they make merry to the sound of the flute.
13They spend their years in prosperity
  and go down to the grave[a] in peace.[b]
14Yet they say to God, 'Leave us alone!
  We have no desire to know your ways.
15Who is the Almighty, that we should serve him?
  What would we gain by praying to him?'
16But their prosperity is not in their own hands,
  so I stand aloof from the counsel of the wicked.

21:7 Job began to question the very basis of his friends' arguments. If they were so sure that the wicked are punished in this world, how is it that in fact they still lived and gathered riches, enjoyed secure homes, and sang and danced as they enjoyed their prosperity?

17"Yet how often is the lamp of the wicked snuffed
  out?
  How often does calamity come upon them,
  the fate God allots in his anger?
18How often are they like straw before the wind,
  like chaff swept away by a gale?
19It is said,┐ 'God stores up a man's punishment for
  his sons.'
  Let him repay the man himself, so that he will
  know it!
20Let his own eyes see his destruction;
  let him drink of the wrath of the Almighty.[c]
21For what does he care about the family he leaves
  behind
  when his allotted months come to an end?

22"Can anyone teach knowledge to God,
  since he judges even the highest?

---

[a]4 Or Adam [b]28 Or The possessions in his house will be carried off, / washed away [a]13 Hebrew Sheol
[b]13 Or in an instant [c]17–20 Verses 17 and 18 may be taken as exclamations and 19 and 20 as declarations.

²³One man dies in full vigour,
  completely secure and at ease,
²⁴his body*d* well nourished,
  his bones rich with marrow.
²⁵Another man dies in bitterness of soul,
  never having enjoyed anything good.
²⁶Side by side they lie in the dust,
  and worms cover them both.

²⁷"I know full well what you are thinking,
  the schemes by which you would wrong me.
²⁸You say, 'Where now is the great man's house,
  the tents where wicked men lived?'
²⁹Have you never questioned those who travel?
  Have you paid no regard to their accounts—
³⁰that the evil man is spared from the day of
    calamity,
  that he is delivered from*e* the day of wrath?
³¹Who denounces his conduct to his face?
  Who repays him for what he has done?
³²He is carried to the grave,
  and watch is kept over his tomb.
³³The soil in the valley is sweet to him;
  all men follow after him,
  and a countless throng goes*f* before him.

³⁴"So how can you console me with your nonsense?
  Nothing is left of your answers but falsehood!"

Eliphaz

22

Then Eliphaz the Temanite replied:

²"Can a man be of benefit to God?
  Can even a wise man benefit him?
³What pleasure would it give the Almighty if you
    were righteous?
  What would he gain if your ways were
    blameless?

22:4   Eliphaz started to be more personal
in his charges against Job, and reached the
point of repeating the accusation that Satan
had made against Job in chapter 1.

---

⁴"Is it for your piety that he rebukes you
  and brings charges against you?
⁵Is not your wickedness great?
  Are not your sins endless?
⁶You demanded security from your brothers for no
    reason;
  you stripped men of their clothing, leaving them
    naked.
⁷You gave no water to the weary
  and you withheld food from the hungry,
⁸though you were a powerful man, owning land—
  an honoured man, living on it.
⁹And you sent widows away empty-handed
  and broke the strength of the fatherless.
¹⁰That is why snares are all around you,
  why sudden peril terrifies you,

¹¹why it is so dark that you cannot see,
  and why a flood of water covers you.
¹²"Is not God in the heights of heaven?
  And see how lofty are the highest stars!
¹³Yet you say, 'What does God know?
  Does he judge through such darkness?
¹⁴Thick clouds veil him, so he does not see us
  as he goes about in the vaulted heavens.'
¹⁵Will you keep to the old path
  that evil men have trod?
¹⁶They were carried off before their time,
  their foundations washed away by a flood.
¹⁷They said to God, 'Leave us alone!
  What can the Almighty do to us?'
¹⁸Yet it was he who filled their houses with good
    things,
  so I stand aloof from the counsel of the wicked.

¹⁹"The righteous see their ruin and rejoice;
  the innocent mock them, saying,
²⁰'Surely our foes are destroyed,
  and fire devours their wealth.'

²¹"Submit to God and be at peace with him;
  in this way prosperity will come to you.
²²Accept instruction from his mouth
  and lay up his words in your heart.
²³If you return to the Almighty, you will be
    restored:
  If you remove wickedness far from your tent
²⁴and assign your nuggets to the dust,
  your gold of Ophir to the rocks in the ravines,
²⁵then the Almighty will be your gold,
  the choicest silver for you.
²⁶Surely then you will find delight in the Almighty
  and will lift up your face to God.
²⁷You will pray to him, and he will hear you,
  and you will fulfil your vows.
²⁸What you decide on will be done,
  and light will shine on your ways.
²⁹When men are brought low and you say, 'Lift
    them up!'
  then he will save the downcast.
³⁰He will deliver even one who is not innocent,
  who will be delivered through the cleanness of
    your hands."

Job

23

Then Job replied:

²"Even today my complaint is bitter;
  his hand*a* is heavy in spite of*b* my groaning.
³If only I knew where to find him;
  if only I could go to his dwelling!
⁴I would state my case before him
  and fill my mouth with arguments.
⁵I would find out what he would answer me,
  and consider what he would say.
⁶Would he oppose me with great power?
  No, he would not press charges against me.

---

d24 The meaning of the Hebrew for this word is uncertain.
e30 Or *man is reserved for the day of calamity, / that he is brought forth to*
a2 Septuagint and Syriac; Hebrew / *the hand on me*   *b2* Or *heavy on me in*
f33 Or / *as a countless throng went*

7There an upright man could present his case
    before him,
  and I would be delivered for ever from my
    judge.

8"But if I go to the east, he is not there;
  if I go to the west, I do not find him.
9When he is at work in the north, I do not see
    him;
  when he turns to the south, I catch no glimpse
    of him.
10But he knows the way that I take;
  when he has tested me, I shall come forth as
    gold.
11My feet have closely followed his steps;
  I have kept to his way without turning aside.
12I have not departed from the commands of his
    lips;
  I have treasured the words of his mouth more
    than my daily bread.

13"But he stands alone, and who can oppose him?
  He does whatever he pleases.
14He carries out his decree against me,
  and many such plans he still has in store.
15That is why I am terrified before him;
  when I think of all this, I fear him.
16God has made my heart faint;
  the Almighty has terrified me.
17Yet I am not silenced by the darkness,
  by the thick darkness that covers my face.

24 "Why does the Almighty not set times for
    judgment?
  Why must those who know him look in vain for
    such days?
2Men move boundary stones;
  they pasture flocks they have stolen.
3They drive away the orphan's donkey
  and take the widow's ox in pledge.
4They thrust the needy from the path
  and force all the poor of the land into hiding.
5Like wild donkeys in the desert,
  the poor go about their labour of foraging food;
  the wasteland provides food for their children.
6They gather fodder in the fields
  and glean in the vineyards of the wicked.
7Lacking clothes, they spend the night naked;
  they have nothing to cover themselves in the
    cold.
8They are drenched by mountain rains
  and hug the rocks for lack of shelter.
9The fatherless child is snatched from the breast;
  the infant of the poor is seized for a debt.
10Lacking clothes, they go about naked;
  they carry the sheaves, but still go hungry.
11They crush olives among the terraces;a
  they tread the winepresses, yet suffer thirst.
12The groans of the dying rise from the city,
  and the souls of the wounded cry out for help.
  But God charges no-one with wrongdoing.

13"There are those who rebel against the light,
  who do not know its ways
  or stay in its paths.
14When daylight is gone, the murderer rises up
  and kills the poor and needy;
  in the night he steals forth like a thief.
15The eye of the adulterer watches for dusk;
  he thinks, 'No eye will see me,'
  and he keeps his face concealed.
16In the dark, men break into houses,
  but by day they shut themselves in;
  they want nothing to do with the light.
17For all of them, deep darkness is their morning;b
  they make friends with the terrors of
    darkness.c

18"Yet they are foam on the surface of the water;
  their portion of the land is cursed,
  so that no-one goes to the vineyards.
19As heat and drought snatch away the melted
    snow,
  so the graved snatches away those who have
    sinned.
20The womb forgets them,
  the worm feasts on them;
  evil men are no longer remembered
  but are broken like a tree.
21They prey on the barren and childless woman,
  and to the widow show no kindness.
22But God drags away the mighty by his power;
  though they become established, they have no
    assurance of life.
23He may let them rest in a feeling of security,
  but his eyes are on their ways.
24For a little while they are exalted, and then they
    are gone;
  they are brought low and gathered up like all
    others;
  they are cut off like ears of corn.

25"If this is not so, who can prove me false
  and reduce my words to nothing?"

25:2   Bildad reminded Job that he was no
match for God, who is the creator of all. It
was another plea for Job to give up, and has
a similar theme to Ecclesiastes 12.

Bildad

25 Then Bildad the Shuhite replied:

2"Dominion and awe belong to God;
  he establishes order in the heights of heaven.
3Can his forces be numbered?
  Upon whom does his light not rise?
4How then can a man be righteous before God?
  How can one born of woman be pure?
5If even the moon is not bright
  and the stars are not pure in his eyes,
6how much less man, who is but a maggot—
  a son of man, who is only a worm!"

---

a11 Or olives between the millstones; the meaning of the Hebrew for this word is uncertain.
b17 Or them, their morning is like the shadow of death　　　c17 Or of the shadow of death　　　d19 Hebrew Sheol

Job

26

Then Job replied:

2"How you have helped the powerless!
How you have saved the arm that is feeble!
3What advice you have offered to one without
wisdom!
And what great insight you have displayed!
4Who has helped you utter these words?
And whose spirit spoke from your mouth?

26:2   Job replied on a hopeful note. Job
was aware that God's justice and power was
so great that he could not fail to show justice
towards the righteous. If he didn't, then how
could he be God?

5"The dead are in deep anguish,
those beneath the waters and all that live in
them.
6Death[a] is naked before God;
Destruction[b] lies uncovered.
7He spreads out the northern skies over empty
space;
he suspends the earth over nothing.
8He wraps up the waters in his clouds,
yet the clouds do not burst under their weight.
9He covers the face of the full moon,
spreading his clouds over it.
10He marks out the horizon on the face of the
waters
for a boundary between light and darkness.
11The pillars of the heavens quake,
aghast at his rebuke.
12By his power he churned up the sea;
by his wisdom he cut Rahab to pieces.
13By his breath the skies became fair;
his hand pierced the gliding serpent.
14And these are but the outer fringe of his works;
how faint the whisper we hear of him!
Who then can understand the thunder of his
power?"

27

And Job continued his discourse:

2"As surely as God lives, who has denied me
justice,
the Almighty, who has made me taste bitterness
of soul,
3as long as I have life within me,
the breath of God in my nostrils,
4my lips will not speak wickedness,
and my tongue will utter no deceit.
5I will never admit you are in the right;
till I die, I will not deny my integrity.
6I will maintain my righteousness and never let go
of it;
my conscience will not reproach me as long as I
live.

7"May my enemies be like the wicked,
my adversaries like the unjust!
8For what hope has the godless when he is cut off,
when God takes away his life?
9Does God listen to his cry
when distress comes upon him?
10Will he find delight in the Almighty?
Will he call upon God at all times?

11"I will teach you about the power of God;
the ways of the Almighty I will not conceal.
12You have all seen this yourselves.
Why then this meaningless talk?

13"Here is the fate God allots to the wicked,
the heritage a ruthless man receives from the
Almighty:
14However many his children, their fate is the
sword;
his offspring will never have enough to eat.
15The plague will bury those who survive him,
and their widows will not weep for them.
16Though he heaps up silver like dust
and clothes like piles of clay,
17what he lays up the righteous will wear,
and the innocent will divide his silver.
18The house he builds is like a moth's cocoon,
like a hut made by a watchman.
19He lies down wealthy, but will do so no more;
when he opens his eyes, all is gone.
20Terrors overtake him like a flood;
a tempest snatches him away in the night.
21The east wind carries him off, and he is gone;
it sweeps him out of his place.
22It hurls itself against him without mercy
as he flees headlong from its power.
23It claps its hands in derision
and hisses him out of his place.

28

"There is a mine for silver
and a place where gold is refined.
2Iron is taken from the earth,
and copper is smelted from ore.
3Man puts an end to the darkness;
he searches the farthest recesses
for ore in the blackest darkness.
4Far from where people dwell he cuts a shaft,
in places forgotten by the foot of man;
far from men he dangles and sways.
5The earth, from which food comes,
is transformed below as by fire;
6sapphires[a] come from its rocks,
and its dust contains nuggets of gold.
7No bird of prey knows that hidden path,
no falcon's eye has seen it.
8Proud beasts do not set foot on it,
and no lion prowls there.
9Man's hand assaults the flinty rock
and lays bare the roots of the mountains.
10He tunnels through the rock;
his eyes see all its treasures.
11He searches[b] the sources of the rivers
and brings hidden things to light.

---

a6 Hebrew *Sheol*   *b6* Hebrew *Abaddon*   *a6* Or *lapis lazuli*; also in verse 16
b11 Septuagint, Aquila and Vulgate; Hebrew *He dams up*

¹²"But where can wisdom be found?
  Where does understanding dwell?
¹³Man does not comprehend its worth;
  it cannot be found in the land of the living.
¹⁴The deep says, 'It is not in me';
  the sea says, 'It is not with me.'
¹⁵It cannot be bought with the finest gold,
  nor can its price be weighed in silver.
¹⁶It cannot be bought with the gold of Ophir,
  with precious onyx or sapphires.
¹⁷Neither gold nor crystal can compare with it,
  nor can it be had for jewels of gold.
¹⁸Coral and jasper are not worthy of mention;
  the price of wisdom is beyond rubies.
¹⁹The topaz of Cush cannot compare with it;
  it cannot be bought with pure gold.

²⁰"Where then does wisdom come from?
  Where does understanding dwell?
²¹It is hidden from the eyes of every living thing,
  concealed even from the birds of the air.
²²Destruction^c and Death say,
  'Only a rumour of it has reached our ears.'
²³God understands the way to it
  and he alone knows where it dwells,
²⁴for he views the ends of the earth
  and sees everything under the heavens.
²⁵When he established the force of the wind
  and measured out the waters,
²⁶when he made a decree for the rain
  and a path for the thunderstorm,
²⁷then he looked at wisdom and appraised it;
  he confirmed it and tested it.
²⁸And he said to man,
  'The fear of the Lord—that is wisdom,
  and to shun evil is understanding.' "

29 Job continued his discourse:

²"How I long for the months gone by,
  for the days when God watched over me,
³when his lamp shone upon my head
  and by his light I walked through darkness!
⁴Oh, for the days when I was in my prime,
  when God's intimate friendship blessed my
    house,
⁵when the Almighty was still with me
  and my children were around me,
⁶when my path was drenched with cream
  and the rock poured out for me streams of olive
    oil.

⁷"When I went to the gate of the city
  and took my seat in the public square,
⁸the young men saw me and stepped aside
  and the old men rose to their feet;
⁹the chief men refrained from speaking
  and covered their mouths with their hands;
¹⁰the voices of the nobles were hushed,
  and their tongues stuck to the roof of their
    mouths.

¹¹Whoever heard me spoke well of me,
  and those who saw me commended me,
¹²because I rescued the poor who cried for help,
  and the fatherless who had none to assist him.
¹³The man who was dying blessed me;
  I made the widow's heart sing.
¹⁴I put on righteousness as my clothing;
  justice was my robe and my turban.
¹⁵I was eyes to the blind
  and feet to the lame.
¹⁶I was a father to the needy;
  I took up the case of the stranger.
¹⁷I broke the fangs of the wicked
  and snatched the victims from their teeth.

29:12 Job continued to protest his innocence, and reminded his friends of his righteous acts in the past.

¹⁸"I thought, 'I shall die in my own house,
  my days as numerous as the grains of sand.
¹⁹My roots will reach to the water,
  and the dew will lie all night on my branches.
²⁰My glory will remain fresh in me,
  the bow ever new in my hand.'

²¹"Men listened to me expectantly,
  waiting in silence for my counsel.
²²After I had spoken, they spoke no more;
  my words fell gently on their ears.
²³They waited for me as for showers
  and drank in my words as the spring rain.
²⁴When I smiled at them, they scarcely believed it;
  the light of my face was precious to them.^{a}
²⁵I chose the way for them and sat as their chief;
  I dwelt as a king among his troops;
  I was like one who comforts mourners.

30:1 Despite his past righteousness, Job
believed that those he had helped were turning against him for no reason. We are left
with no answers, only a hope that the tension may be resolved by God.

30 "But now they mock me,
  men younger than I,
  whose fathers I would have disdained
    to put with my sheep dogs.
²Of what use was the strength of their hands to
    me,
  since their vigour had gone from them?
³Haggard from want and hunger,
  they roamed^a the parched land
  in desolate wastelands at night.
⁴In the brush they gathered salt herbs,
  and their food^b was the root of the broom
    tree.
⁵They were banished from their fellow-men,
  shouted at as if they were thieves.

---

^{c}22 Hebrew *Abaddon* ^{a}24 The meaning of the Hebrew for this clause is uncertain. ^{a}3 Or *gnawed* ^{b}4 Or *fuel*

6They were forced to live in the dry stream beds,
  among the rocks and in holes in the ground.
7They brayed among the bushes
  and huddled in the undergrowth.
8A base and nameless brood,
  they were driven out of the land.

9"And now their sons mock me in song;
  I have become a byword among them.
10They detest me and keep their distance;
  they do not hesitate to spit in my face.
11Now that God has unstrung my bow and afflicted
  me,
  they throw off restraint in my presence.
12On my right the tribe*c* attacks;
  they lay snares for my feet,
  they build their siege ramps against me.
13They break up my road;
  they succeed in destroying me —
  without anyone's helping them.*d*
14They advance as through a gaping breach;
  amid the ruins they come rolling in.
15Terrors overwhelm me;
  my dignity is driven away as by the wind,
  my safety vanishes like a cloud.

16"And now my life ebbs away;
  days of suffering grip me.
17Night pierces my bones;
  my gnawing pains never rest.
18In his great power ⸢God⸣ becomes like clothing to
  me;*e*
  he binds me like the neck of my garment.
19He throws me into the mud,
  and I am reduced to dust and ashes.

20"I cry out to you, O God, but you do not answer;
  I stand up, but you merely look at me.
21You turn on me ruthlessly;
  with the might of your hand you attack me.
22You snatch me up and drive me before the wind;
  you toss me about in the storm.
23I know you will bring me down to death,
  to the place appointed for all the living.

24"Surely no-one lays a hand on a broken man
  when he cries for help in his distress.
25Have I not wept for those in trouble?
  Has not my soul grieved for the poor?
26Yet when I hoped for good, evil came;
  when I looked for light, then came darkness.
27The churning inside me never stops;
  days of suffering confront me.
28I go about blackened, but not by the sun;
  I stand up in the assembly and cry for help.
29I have become a brother of jackals,
  a companion of owls.
30My skin grows black and peels;
  my body burns with fever.
31My harp is tuned to mourning,
  and my flute to the sound of wailing.

31 "I made a covenant with my eyes
       not to look lustfully at a girl.
2For what is man's lot from God above,
  his heritage from the Almighty on high?
3Is it not ruin for the wicked,
  disaster for those who do wrong?
4Does he not see my ways
  and count my every step?

5"If I have walked in falsehood
  or my foot has hurried after deceit —
6let God weigh me in honest scales
  and he will know that I am blameless —
7if my steps have turned from the path,
  if my heart has been led by my eyes,
  or if my hands have been defiled,
8then may others eat what I have sown,
  and may my crops be uprooted.

9"If my heart has been enticed by a woman,
  or if I have lurked at my neighbour's door,
10then may my wife grind another man's grain,
  and may other men sleep with her.
11For that would have been shameful,
  a sin to be judged.
12It is a fire that burns to Destruction;*a*
  it would have uprooted my harvest.

13"If I have denied justice to my menservants and
      maidservants
  when they had a grievance against me,
14what will I do when God confronts me?
  What will I answer when called to account?
15Did not he who made me in the womb make
      them?
  Did not the same one form us both within our
      mothers?

16"If I have denied the desires of the poor
  or let the eyes of the widow grow weary,
17if I have kept my bread to myself,
  not sharing it with the fatherless —
18but from my youth I reared him as would a
      father,
  and from my birth I guided the widow —
19if I have seen anyone perishing for lack of
      clothing,
  or a needy man without a garment,
20and his heart did not bless me
  for warming him with the fleece from my
      sheep,
21if I have raised my hand against the fatherless,
  knowing that I had influence in court,
22then let my arm fall from the shoulder,
  let it be broken off at the joint.
23For I dreaded destruction from God,
  and for fear of his splendour I could not do such
      things.

24"If I have put my trust in gold
  or said to pure gold, 'You are my security,'
25if I have rejoiced over my great wealth,
  the fortune my hands had gained,

---

c12 The meaning of the Hebrew for this word is uncertain.   *d13* Or me. / 'No-one can help him,' they say,
e18 Hebrew; Septuagint ⸢God⸣ grasps my clothing   *a12* Hebrew Abaddon

²⁶if I have regarded the sun in its radiance
  or the moon moving in splendour,
²⁷so that my heart was secretly enticed
  and my hand offered them a kiss of homage,
²⁸then these also would be sins to be judged,
  for I would have been unfaithful to God on
    high.

²⁹"If I have rejoiced at my enemy's misfortune
  or gloated over the trouble that came to him—
³⁰I have not allowed my mouth to sin
  by invoking a curse against his life—
³¹if the men of my household have never said,
  'Who has not had his fill of Job's meat?'—
³²but no stranger had to spend the night in the
    street,
  for my door was always open to the traveller—
³³if I have concealed my sin as men do,ᵇ
  by hiding my guilt in my heart
³⁴because I so feared the crowd
  and so dreaded the contempt of the clans
  that I kept silent and would not go outside—

³⁵("Oh, that I had someone to hear me!
  I sign now my defence—let the Almighty
    answer me;
  let my accuser put his indictment in writing.
³⁶Surely I would wear it on my shoulder,
  I would put it on like a crown.
³⁷I would give him an account of my every step;
  like a prince I would approach him.)—

³⁸"if my land cries out against me
  and all its furrows are wet with tears,
³⁹if I have devoured its yield without payment
  or broken the spirit of its tenants,
⁴⁰then let briers come up instead of wheat
  and weeds instead of barley."

The words of Job are ended.

Elihu

32 So these three men stopped answering Job,
      because he was righteous in his own eyes.
²But Elihu son of Barakel the Buzite, of the family of
Ram, became very angry with Job for justifying himself
rather than God. ³He was also angry with the three
friends, because they had found no way to refute Job,
and yet had condemned him.ᵃ ⁴Now Elihu had waited
before speaking to Job because they were older than
he. ⁵But when he saw that the three men had nothing
more to say, his anger was aroused.

⁶So Elihu son of Barakel the Buzite said:

"I am young in years,
  and you are old;
that is why I was fearful,
  not daring to tell you what I know.
⁷I thought, 'Age should speak;
  advanced years should teach wisdom.'
⁸But it is the spiritᵇ in a man,
  the breath of the Almighty, that gives him
    understanding.

⁹It is not only the oldᶜ who are wise,
  not only the aged who understand what is right.

¹⁰"Therefore I say: Listen to me;
  I too will tell you what I know.
¹¹I waited while you spoke,
  I listened to your reasoning;
while you were searching for words,
¹² I gave you my full attention.
But not one of you has proved Job wrong;
  none of you has answered his arguments.
¹³Do not say, 'We have found wisdom;
  let God refute him, not man.'
¹⁴But Job has not marshalled his words against me,
  and I will not answer him with your arguments.

¹⁵"They are dismayed and have no more to say;
  words have failed them.
¹⁶Must I wait, now that they are silent,
  now that they stand there with no reply?
¹⁷I too will have my say;
  I too will tell what I know.
¹⁸For I am full of words,
  and the spirit within me compels me;
¹⁹inside I am like bottled-up wine,
  like new wineskins ready to burst.
²⁰I must speak and find relief;
  I must open my lips and reply.
²¹I will show partiality to no-one,
  nor will I flatter any man;
²²for if I were skilled in flattery,
  my Maker would soon take me away.

32:19   Elihu expressed his impatience
with Job's other three friends. He could contain himself no longer, and spoke with integrity and impartiality. He spoke of God's
justice (chapters 33—37), until God finally
revealed himself (chapter 38).

---

33 "But now, Job, listen to my words;
      pay attention to everything I say.
²I am about to open my mouth;
  my words are on the tip of my tongue.
³My words come from an upright heart;
  my lips sincerely speak what I know.
⁴The Spirit of God has made me;
  the breath of the Almighty gives me life.
⁵Answer me then, if you can;
  prepare yourself and confront me.
⁶I am just like you before God;
  I too have been taken from clay.
⁷No fear of me should alarm you,
  nor should my hand be heavy upon you.

⁸"But you have said in my hearing—
  I heard the very words—
⁹'I am pure and without sin;
  I am clean and free from guilt.
¹⁰Yet God has found fault with me;
  he considers me his enemy.

ᵇ33 Or as Adam did   ᵃ3 Masoretic Text; an ancient Hebrew scribal tradition *Job, and so had condemned God*
ᵇ8 Or *Spirit*; also in verse 18   ᶜ9 Or *many*; or *great*

11He fastens my feet in shackles;
   he keeps close watch on all my paths.'

12"But I tell you, in this you are not right,
   for God is greater than man.
13Why do you complain to him
   that he answers none of man's words?a
14For God does speak—now one way, now
      another—
   though man may not perceive it.
15In a dream, in a vision of the night,
   when deep sleep falls on men
   as they slumber in their beds,
16he may speak in their ears
   and terrify them with warnings,
17to turn man from wrongdoing
   and keep him from pride,
18to preserve his soul from the pit,b
   his life from perishing by the sword.c
19Or a man may be chastened on a bed of pain
   with constant distress in his bones,
20so that his very being finds food repulsive
   and his soul loathes the choicest meal.
21His flesh wastes away to nothing,
   and his bones, once hidden, now stick out.
22His soul draws near to the pit,d
   and his life to the messengers of death.e

23"Yet if there is an angel on his side
   as a mediator, one out of a thousand,
   to tell a man what is right for him,
24to be gracious to him and say,
   'Spare him from going down to the pit;f
   I have found a ransom for him'—
25then his flesh is renewed like a child's;
   it is restored as in the days of his youth.
26He prays to God and finds favour with him,
   he sees God's face and shouts for joy;
   he is restored by God to his righteous state.
27Then he comes to men and says,
   'I have sinned, and perverted what was right,
   but I did not get what I deserved.
28He redeemed my soul from going down to the
      pit,g
   and I shall live to enjoy the light.'

29"God does all these things to a man—
   twice, even three times—
30to turn back his soul from the pit,h
   that the light of life may shine on him.

31"Pay attention, Job, and listen to me;
   be silent, and I will speak.
32If you have anything to say, answer me;
   speak up, for I want you to be cleared.
33But if not, then listen to me;
   be silent, and I will teach you wisdom."

34 Then Elihu said:

2"Hear my words, you wise men;
   listen to me, you men of learning.

3For the ear tests words
   as the tongue tastes food.
4Let us discern for ourselves what is right;
   let us learn together what is good.

5"Job says, 'I am innocent,
   but God denies me justice.
6Although I am right,
   I am considered a liar;
   although I am guiltless,
   his arrow inflicts an incurable wound.'
7What man is like Job,
   who drinks scorn like water?
8He keeps company with evildoers;
   he associates with wicked men.
9For he says, 'It profits a man nothing
   when he tries to please God.'

10"So listen to me, you men of understanding.
   Far be it from God to do evil,
   from the Almighty to do wrong.
11He repays a man for what he has done;
   he brings upon him what his conduct deserves.
12It is unthinkable that God would do wrong,
   that the Almighty would pervert justice.
13Who appointed him over the earth?
   Who put him in charge of the whole world?
14If it were his intention
   and he withdrew his spirita and breath,
15all mankind would perish together
   and man would return to the dust.

16"If you have understanding, hear this;
   listen to what I say.
17Can he who hates justice govern?
   Will you condemn the just and mighty One?
18Is he not the One who says to kings, 'You are
      worthless,'
   and to nobles, 'You are wicked,'
19who shows no partiality to princes
   and does not favour the rich over the poor,
   for they are all the work of his hands?
20They die in an instant, in the middle of the night;
   the people are shaken and they pass away;
   the mighty are removed without human hand.

21"His eyes are on the ways of men;
   he sees their every step.
22There is no dark place, no deep shadow,
   where evildoers can hide.
23God has no need to examine men further,
   that they should come before him for judgment.
24Without enquiry he shatters the mighty
   and sets up others in their place.
25Because he takes note of their deeds,
   he overthrows them in the night and they are
      crushed.
26He punishes them for their wickedness
   where everyone can see them,
27because they turned from following him
   and had no regard for any of his ways.

---

a13 Or that he does not answer for any of his actions   b18 Or preserve him from the grave   c18 Or from crossing the River
d22 Or He draws near to the grave   e22 Or to the dead   f24 Or grave
g28 Or redeemed me from going down to the grave   h30 Or turn him back from the grave   a14 Or Spirit

28They caused the cry of the poor to come before him,
  so that he heard the cry of the needy.
29But if he remains silent, who can condemn him?
  If he hides his face, who can see him?
  Yet he is over man and nation alike,
30 to keep a godless man from ruling,
  from laying snares for the people.

31"Suppose a man says to God,
  'I am guilty but will offend no more.
32Teach me what I cannot see;
  if I have done wrong, I will not do so again.'
33Should God then reward you on your terms,
  when you refuse to repent?
  You must decide, not I;
  so tell me what you know.

34"Men of understanding declare,
  wise men who hear me say to me,
35'Job speaks without knowledge;
  his words lack insight.'
36Oh, that Job might be tested to the utmost
  for answering like a wicked man!
37To his sin he adds rebellion;
  scornfully he claps his hands among us
  and multiplies his words against God."

35 Then Elihu said:

2"Do you think this is just?
  You say, 'I shall be cleared by God.'a
3Yet you ask him, 'What profit is it to me,b
  and what do I gain by not sinning?'

4"I would like to reply to you
  and to your friends with you.
5Look up at the heavens and see;
  gaze at the clouds so high above you.
6If you sin, how does that affect him?
  If your sins are many, what does that do to him?
7If you are righteous, what do you give to him,
  or what does he receive from your hand?
8Your wickedness affects only a man like yourself,
  and your righteousness only the sons of men.

9"Men cry out under a load of oppression;
  they plead for relief from the arm of the powerful.
10But no-one says, 'Where is God my Maker,
  who gives songs in the night,
11who teaches more to us than toc the beasts of the earth
  and makes us wiser thand the birds of the air?'
12He does not answer when men cry out
  because of the arrogance of the wicked.
13Indeed, God does not listen to their empty plea;
  the Almighty pays no attention to it.
14How much less, then, will he listen
  when you say that you do not see him,
  that your case is before him
  and you must wait for him,

15and further, that his anger never punishes
  and he does not take the least notice of wickedness.e
16So Job opens his mouth with empty talk;
  without knowledge he multiplies words."

36 Elihu continued:

2"Bear with me a little longer and I will show you
  that there is more to be said on God's behalf.
3I get my knowledge from afar;
  I will ascribe justice to my Maker.
4Be assured that my words are not false;
  one perfect in knowledge is with you.

5"God is mighty, but does not despise men;
  he is mighty, and firm in his purpose.
6He does not keep the wicked alive
  but gives the afflicted their rights.
7He does not take his eyes off the righteous;
  he enthrones them with kings
  and exalts them for ever.
8But if men are bound in chains,
  held fast by cords of affliction,
9he tells them what they have done—
  that they have sinned arrogantly.
10He makes them listen to correction
  and commands them to repent of their evil.
11If they obey and serve him,
  they will spend the rest of their days in prosperity
  and their years in contentment.
12But if they do not listen,
  they will perish by the sworda
  and die without knowledge.

13"The godless in heart harbour resentment;
  even when he fetters them, they do not cry for help.
14They die in their youth,
  among male prostitutes of the shrines.
15But those who suffer he delivers in their suffering;
  he speaks to them in their affliction.

16"He is wooing you from the jaws of distress
  to a spacious place free from restriction,
  to the comfort of your table laden with choice food.
17But now you are laden with the judgment due to the wicked;
  judgment and justice have taken hold of you.
18Be careful that no-one entices you by riches;
  do not let a large bribe turn you aside.
19Would your wealth
  or even all your mighty efforts
  sustain you so you would not be in distress?
20Do not long for the night,
  to drag people away from their homes.b
21Beware of turning to evil,
  which you seem to prefer to affliction.

a2 Or My righteousness is more than God's   b3 Or you   c11 Or teaches us by   d11 Or us wise by
e15 Symmachus, Theodotion and Vulgate; the meaning of the Hebrew for this word is uncertain.   a12 Or will cross the River
b20 The meaning of the Hebrew for verses 18–20 is uncertain.

22"God is exalted in his power.
Who is a teacher like him?
23Who has prescribed his ways for him,
or said to him, 'You have done wrong'?
24Remember to extol his work,
which men have praised in song.
25All mankind has seen it;
men gaze on it from afar.
26How great is God—beyond our understanding!
The number of his years is past finding out.

27"He draws up the drops of water,
which distil as rain to the streams; c
28the clouds pour down their moisture
and abundant showers fall on mankind.
29Who can understand how he spreads out the
clouds,
how he thunders from his pavilion?
30See how he scatters his lightning about him,
bathing the depths of the sea.
31This is the way he governs d the nations
and provides food in abundance.
32He fills his hands with lightning
and commands it to strike its mark.
33His thunder announces the coming storm;
even the cattle make known its approach. e

37

"At this my heart pounds
and leaps from its place.
2Listen! Listen to the roar of his voice,
to the rumbling that comes from his mouth.
3He unleashes his lightning beneath the whole
heaven
and sends it to the ends of the earth.
4After that comes the sound of his roar;
he thunders with his majestic voice.
When his voice resounds,
he holds nothing back.
5God's voice thunders in marvellous ways;
he does great things beyond our understanding.
6He says to the snow, 'Fall on the earth,'
and to the rain shower, 'Be a mighty
downpour.'
7So that all men he has made may know his work,
he stops every man from his labour. a
8The animals take cover;
they remain in their dens.
9The tempest comes out from its chamber,
the cold from the driving winds.
10The breath of God produces ice,
and the broad waters become frozen.
11He loads the clouds with moisture;
he scatters his lightning through them.
12At his direction they swirl around
over the face of the whole earth
to do whatever he commands them.
13He brings the clouds to punish men,
or to water his earth b and show his love.

14"Listen to this, Job;
stop and consider God's wonders.

15Do you know how God controls the clouds
and makes his lightning flash?
16Do you know how the clouds hang poised,
those wonders of him who is perfect in
knowledge?
17You who swelter in your clothes
when the land lies hushed under the south
wind,
18can you join him in spreading out the skies,
hard as a mirror of cast bronze?

19"Tell us what we should say to him;
we cannot draw up our case because of our
darkness.
20Should he be told that I want to speak?
Would any man ask to be swallowed up?
21Now no-one can look at the sun,
bright as it is in the skies
after the wind has swept them clean.
22Out of the north he comes in golden splendour;
God comes in awesome majesty.
23The Almighty is beyond our reach and exalted in
power;
in his justice and great righteousness, he does
not oppress.
24Therefore, men revere him,
for does he not have regard for all the wise in
heart?" c

The LORD Speaks

38

Then the LORD answered Job out of the storm.
He said:

2"Who is this that darkens my counsel
with words without knowledge?
3Brace yourself like a man;
I will question you,
and you shall answer me.

38:5 God declared himself, finally, to
Job. He reminded Job that he is not like
humans. He is more powerful, more wise,
and his creation is a witness to this. In other
words, God is in charge, and he knows what
he is doing.

4"Where were you when I laid the earth's
foundation?
Tell me, if you understand.
5Who marked off its dimensions? Surely you know!
Who stretched a measuring line across it?
6On what were its footings set,
or who laid its cornerstone—
7while the morning stars sang together
and all the angels a shouted for joy?

8"Who shut up the sea behind doors
when it burst forth from the womb,
9when I made the clouds its garment
and wrapped it in thick darkness,

---

c27 Or distil from the mist as rain   d31 Or nourishes   e33 Or announces his coming— / the One zealous against evil
a7 Or / he fills all men with fear by his power   b13 Or to favour them
c24 Or for he does not have regard for any who think they are wise.   a7 Hebrew the sons of God

¹⁰when I fixed limits for it
  and set its doors and bars in place,
¹¹when I said, 'This far you may come and no
      farther;
  here is where your proud waves halt'?

¹²"Have you ever given orders to the morning,
  or shown the dawn its place,
¹³that it might take the earth by the edges
  and shake the wicked out of it?
¹⁴The earth takes shape like clay under a seal;
  its features stand out like those of a garment.
¹⁵The wicked are denied their light,
  and their upraised arm is broken.

¹⁶"Have you journeyed to the springs of the sea
  or walked in the recesses of the deep?
¹⁷Have the gates of death been shown to you?
  Have you seen the gates of the shadow of
      death?ᵇ
¹⁸Have you comprehended the vast expanses of the
      earth?
  Tell me, if you know all this.

¹⁹"What is the way to the abode of light?
  And where does darkness reside?
²⁰Can you take them to their places?
  Do you know the paths to their dwellings?
²¹Surely you know, for you were already born!
  You have lived so many years!

²²"Have you entered the storehouses of the snow
  or seen the storehouses of the hail,
²³which I reserve for times of trouble,
  for days of war and battle?
²⁴What is the way to the place where the lightning
      is dispersed,
  or the place where the east winds are scattered
      over the earth?
²⁵Who cuts a channel for the torrents of rain,
  and a path for the thunderstorm,
²⁶to water a land where no man lives,
  a desert with no-one in it,
²⁷to satisfy a desolate wasteland
  and make it sprout with grass?
²⁸Does the rain have a father?
  Who fathers the drops of dew?
²⁹From whose womb comes the ice?
  Who gives birth to the frost from the heavens
³⁰when the waters become hard as stone,
  when the surface of the deep is frozen?

³¹"Can you bind the beautifulᶜ Pleiades?
  Can you loose the cords of Orion?
³²Can you bring forth the constellations in their
      seasonsᵈ
  or lead out the Bearᵉ with its cubs?
³³Do you know the laws of the heavens?
  Can you set up ⌊God's⌋ dominion over the
      earth?

³⁴"Can you raise your voice to the clouds
  and cover yourself with a flood of water?

³⁵Do you send the lightning bolts on their way?
  Do they report to you, 'Here we are'?
³⁶Who endowed the heartᵍ with wisdom
  or gave understanding to the mind?ʰ
³⁷Who has the wisdom to count the clouds?
  Who can tip over the water jars of the heavens
³⁸when the dust becomes hard
  and the clods of earth stick together?

³⁹"Do you hunt the prey for the lioness
  and satisfy the hunger of the lions
⁴⁰when they crouch in their dens
  or lie in wait in a thicket?
⁴¹Who provides food for the raven
  when its young cry out to God
  and wander about for lack of food?

39 "Do you know when the mountain goats
      give birth?
  Do you watch when the doe bears her fawn?
²Do you count the months till they bear?
  Do you know the time they give birth?
³They crouch down and bring forth their young;
  their labour pains are ended.
⁴Their young thrive and grow strong in the wilds;
  they leave and do not return.

⁵"Who let the wild donkey go free?
  Who untied his ropes?
⁶I gave him the wasteland as his home,
  the salt flats as his habitat.
⁷He laughs at the commotion in the town;
  he does not hear a driver's shout.
⁸He ranges the hills for his pasture
  and searches for any green thing.

⁹"Will the wild ox consent to serve you?
  Will he stay by your manger at night?
¹⁰Can you hold him to the furrow with a harness?
  Will he till the valleys behind you?
¹¹Will you rely on him for his great strength?
  Will you leave your heavy work to him?
¹²Can you trust him to bring in your grain
  and gather it to your threshing-floor?

¹³"The wings of the ostrich flap joyfully,
  but they cannot compare with the pinions and
      feathers of the stork.
¹⁴She lays her eggs on the ground
  and lets them warm in the sand,
¹⁵unmindful that a foot may crush them,
  that some wild animal may trample them.
¹⁶She treats her young harshly, as if they were not
      hers;
  she cares not that her labour was in vain,
¹⁷for God did not endow her with wisdom
  or give her a share of good sense.
¹⁸Yet when she spreads her feathers to run,
  she laughs at horse and rider.

¹⁹"Do you give the horse his strength
  or clothe his neck with a flowing mane?
²⁰Do you make him leap like a locust,
  striking terror with his proud snorting?

ᵇ17 Or gates of deep shadows   ᶜ31 Or the twinkling; or the chains of the   ᵈ32 Or the morning star in its season
ᵉ32 Or out Leo   ᶠ33 Or his; or their   ᵍ36 The meaning of the Hebrew for this word is uncertain.
ʰ36 The meaning of the Hebrew for this word is uncertain.

21He paws fiercely, rejoicing in his strength,
  and charges into the fray.
22He laughs at fear, afraid of nothing;
  he does not shy away from the sword.
23The quiver rattles against his side,
  along with the flashing spear and lance.
24In frenzied excitement he eats up the ground;
  he cannot stand still when the trumpet sounds.
25At the blast of the trumpet he snorts, 'Aha!'
  He catches the scent of battle from afar,
  the shout of commanders and the battle cry.

26"Does the hawk take flight by your wisdom
  and spread his wings towards the south?
27Does the eagle soar at your command
  and build his nest on high?
28He dwells on a cliff and stays there at night;
  a rocky crag is his stronghold.
29From there he seeks out his food;
  his eyes detect it from afar.
30His young ones feast on blood,
  and where the slain are, there is he."

40 The LORD said to Job:

2"Will the one who contends with the Almighty
    correct him?
  Let him who accuses God answer him!"

3Then Job answered the LORD:

4"I am unworthy—how can I reply to you?
  I put my hand over my mouth.
5I spoke once, but I have no answer—
  twice, but I will say no more."

6Then the LORD spoke to Job out of the storm:

7"Brace yourself like a man;
  I will question you,
  and you shall answer me.

8"Would you discredit my justice?
  Would you condemn me to justify yourself?
9Do you have an arm like God's,
  and can your voice thunder like his?
10Then adorn yourself with glory and splendour,
  and clothe yourself in honour and majesty.
11Unleash the fury of your wrath,
  look at every proud man and bring him low,
12look at every proud man and humble him,
  crush the wicked where they stand.
13Bury them all in the dust together;
  shroud their faces in the grave.
14Then I myself will admit to you
  that your own right hand can save you.

15"Look at the behemoth,a
  which I made along with you
  and which feeds on grass like an ox.
16What strength he has in his loins,
  what power in the muscles of his belly!
17His tailb sways like a cedar;
  the sinews of his thighs are close-knit.

18His bones are tubes of bronze,
  his limbs like rods of iron.
19He ranks first among the works of God,
  yet his Maker can approach him with his
    sword.
20The hills bring him their produce,
  and all the wild animals play nearby.
21Under the lotus plant he lies,
  hidden among the reeds in the marsh.
22The lotuses conceal him in their shadow;
  the poplars by the stream surround him.
23When the river rages, he is not alarmed;
  he is secure, though the Jordan should surge
    against his mouth.
24Can anyone capture him by the eyes,c
  or trap him and pierce his nose?

41 "Can you pull in the leviathana with a
    fishhook
  or tie down his tongue with a rope?
2Can you put a cord through his nose
  or pierce his jaw with a hook?
3Will he keep begging you for mercy?
  Will he speak to you with gentle words?
4Will he make an agreement with you
  for you to take him as your slave for life?
5Can you make a pet of him like a bird
  or put him on a leash for your girls?
6Will traders barter for him?
  Will they divide him up among the merchants?
7Can you fill his hide with harpoons
  or his head with fishing spears?
8If you lay a hand on him,
  you will remember the struggle and never do it
    again!
9Any hope of subduing him is false;
  the mere sight of him is overpowering.
10No-one is fierce enough to rouse him.
  Who then is able to stand against me?
11Who has a claim against me that I must pay?
  Everything under heaven belongs to me.

12"I will not fail to speak of his limbs,
  his strength and his graceful form.
13Who can strip off his outer coat?
  Who would approach him with a bridle?
14Who dares open the doors of his mouth,
  ringed about with his fearsome teeth?
15His back hasb rows of shields
  tightly sealed together;
16each is so close to the next
  that no air can pass between.
17They are joined fast to one another;
  they cling together and cannot be parted.
18His snorting throws out flashes of light;
  his eyes are like the rays of dawn.
19Firebrands stream from his mouth;
  sparks of fire shoot out.
20Smoke pours from his nostrils
  as from a boiling pot over a fire of reeds.
21His breath sets coals ablaze,
  and flames dart from his mouth.

a15 Possibly the hippopotamus or the elephant   b17 Possibly trunk   c24 Or by a water hole
a1 Possibly the crocodile   b15 Or His pride is his

²²Strength resides in his neck;
   dismay goes before him.
²³The folds of his flesh are tightly joined;
   they are firm and immovable.
²⁴His chest is hard as rock,
   hard as a lower millstone.
²⁵When he rises up, the mighty are terrified;
   they retreat before his thrashing.
²⁶The sword that reaches him has no effect,
   nor does the spear or the dart or the javelin.
²⁷Iron he treats like straw
   and bronze like rotten wood.
²⁸Arrows do not make him flee;
   slingstones are like chaff to him.
²⁹A club seems to him but a piece of straw;
   he laughs at the rattling of the lance.
³⁰His undersides are jagged potsherds,
   leaving a trail in the mud like a
      threshing-sledge.
³¹He makes the depths churn like a boiling
      cauldron
   and stirs up the sea like a pot of ointment.
³²Behind him he leaves a glistening wake;
   one would think the deep had white hair.
³³Nothing on earth is his equal—
   a creature without fear.
³⁴He looks down on all that are haughty;
   he is king over all that are proud."

42:2   Job declared his faithfulness to God,
and acknowledged his justice and sovereignty. He soon discovered that God is faithful, too, and rewards those who love him.

Job

42

Then Job replied to the Lᴏʀᴅ:

²"I know that you can do all things;
   no plan of yours can be thwarted.

³You asked,ᴸ 'Who is this that obscures my counsel
   without knowledge?'

Surely I spoke of things I did not understand,
   things too wonderful for me to know.

⁴ᴸ"You said,ᴸ 'Listen now, and I will speak;
   I will question you,
   and you shall answer me.'
⁵My ears had heard of you
   but now my eyes have seen you.
⁶Therefore I despise myself
   and repent in dust and ashes."

Epilogue

⁷After the Lᴏʀᴅ had said these things to Job, he said
to Eliphaz the Temanite, "I am angry with you and your
two friends, because you have not spoken of me what
is right, as my servant Job has. ⁸So now take seven bulls
and seven rams and go to my servant Job and sacrifice
a burnt offering for yourselves. My servant Job will pray
for you, and I will accept his prayer and not deal with
you according to your folly. You have not spoken of me
what is right, as my servant Job has." ⁹So Eliphaz the
Temanite, Bildad the Shuhite and Zophar the Naamathite did what the Lᴏʀᴅ told them; and the Lᴏʀᴅ
accepted Job's prayer.

¹⁰After Job had prayed for his friends, the Lᴏʀᴅ made
him prosperous again and gave him twice as much as
he had before. ¹¹All his brothers and sisters and everyone who had known him before came and ate with him
in his house. They comforted and consoled him over
all the trouble the Lᴏʀᴅ had brought upon him, and
each one gave him a piece of silverᵃ and a gold ring.
¹²The Lᴏʀᴅ blessed the latter part of Job's life more
than the first. He had fourteen thousand sheep, six
thousand camels, a thousand yoke of oxen and a thousand donkeys. ¹³And he also had seven sons and three
daughters. ¹⁴The first daughter he named Jemimah,
the second Keziah and the third Keren-Happuch.
¹⁵Nowhere in all the land were there found women as
beautiful as Job's daughters, and their father granted
them an inheritance along with their brothers.

¹⁶After this, Job lived a hundred and forty years; he
saw his children and their children to the fourth generation. ¹⁷And so he died, old and full of years.

ᵃ 11 Hebrew *him a kesitah*; a kesitah was a unit of money of unknown weight and value.

Psalms

Poems Without Rhythm

At the heart of the Old Testament is a collection of writings that are a bit like poems and a bit like hymns. The book of Psalms contains a huge variety of material, expresses a wide range of emotions, and springs from many different situations in Israel's history.

The Psalms are basically poems although they are written in a style that would not easily be recognized as "poetry", as the original Hebrew of the psalms does not use any rhyme or strict rhythm. Rather, a short statement is made and then the idea is expanded. Sometimes in the second line the original idea is extended, or an opposite thought is made, and sometimes three lines are used. This kind of structure is easy to capture in translation so that the flavour of the original Hebrew poetry can be maintained.

Pictures From Everyday Life

One striking feature of the poetry is the use of imagery. The psalmists used very vivid concrete images to say what they meant about God. One of the gifts of the psalmist was the ability to take pictures from everyday life and say something profoundly spiritual with them. Warfare provided many images, as being at war was such a common experience for the people. God was likened to a shield, a rock, a strong fortress, a military leader, and a trainer of soldiers. The natural world and agriculture, family life and domestic matters also provided a rich ground for the psalmists' word plays. As well as being beautiful imagery these pictures give an insight into what ordinary life was like in ancient Israel. One of the secrets of reading and meditating on the psalms is to let these powerful images unfold.

On a deeper level, the psalms express and wrestle with a whole range of human emotion: great joy, deep bitterness, anger, despair, and grief. Many times the psalmists captured their happiness in joyful words of praise. At other times all is dark, God is silent, and the words are despairing. The writers had a real ability to be honest in expressing their feelings. Life was not all easy, God was not always evidently present, yet the writers managed to maintain their faith in God at the same time as expressing how difficult everything was.

Songs for Worship

With such a variety of emotion it is possible to find a suitable psalm for every kind of situation; the psalms have enriched Jewish and Christian worship down the centuries. In fact the collection has been called "the hymn book of the second temple". This was the period after the exile when the survivors returned from Babylon and rebuilt the ruined city of Jerusalem and the temple on Mount Zion. Scholars have tried to categorize the psalms according to their use in the worship of the temple. They are seen as hymns of praise, hymns of thanksgiving, national laments for use in time of national disaster, and individual laments for times of personal crisis. It is not always easy to locate a particular situation for each psalm in this way. Often there are not many clues. The headings that go with the psalms are not a lot of help as the terms are either imprecise or not well understood, particularly in the case of the musical directions.

Real Human Experience

Nevertheless, like hymns of today the psalms were first written by individuals out of their own experience and understanding, or through their observation of what was happening in the nation. The ones that were used in worship, either personal or communal, survived. The headings show that various smaller collections were made first, for example the psalms ascribed to David, or to the sons of Korah, or the songs of ascents. Eventually these were organized into the present five books with the David collection first.

Psalms of David?

Exactly how many psalms go back to David himself is open to question. It is thought that the headings which attempt to locate particular psalms in David's story were added much later on. However, David was renowned as a singer of songs and some psalms are reminiscent of incidents in his life. His story is found in 1 Samuel 16—31, 2 Samuel and 1 Kings 1, 2. Whether linked to David or not, the psalms make many connections with the rest of the Old Testament. All other kinds of writings are reflected in various psalms including those to do with history, the writings with priestly concerns, the ideas of Deuteronomy, the prophets, and the Wisdom Literature like Job and Proverbs. The psalms are a good place to start reading the Old Testament.

God Is King

Several major ideas run through almost all the psalms. The first is that the God of Israel is Lord both of creation and of the affairs of human beings (especially those of Israel). Alongside this conviction is the sense that the temple on Mount Zion in Jerusalem was the dwelling place of God on earth. As long as it stood all would be well and the Israelites would be blessed because God was with them. The psalmists suffered great anguish when the temple was destroyed. It took the experience of the exile for the people to come to a deeper understanding of how God was present in the world.

Human Sin Brings Destruction

A third conviction in most of the psalms is that disaster and calamity resulted from wrongdoing. If people were experiencing difficulties then they had done something wrong and they were being punished for their sins. Because of the strong sense of God's kingship over everything it was difficult to accept that things simply just went wrong for no human reason. However, some psalms do acknowledge that people could suffer unjustly and undeservedly.

Prayers We Can Make Our Own

The psalms therefore have a major place among the books of the Old Testament. But to read them straight through is a daunting task—there are so many and some seem very repetitive while others have depressing ideas. However, the best way to read these ancient prayers is to make them your own and speak them directly to God. So many of them catch deep human feelings that it is impossible to avoid being moved by them. The richest lessons that come from the psalms may be in the particularly difficult ones that you have to read again and again until you begin to see what the author had in mind.

BOOK I
Psalms 1–41

Psalm 1

[1]Blessed is the man
  who does not walk in the counsel of the wicked
  or stand in the way of sinners
  or sit in the seat of mockers.
[2]But his delight is in the law of the LORD,
  and on his law he meditates day and night.
[3]He is like a tree planted by streams of water,
  which yields its fruit in season
and whose leaf does not wither.
  Whatever he does prospers.

1:4 The psalmist believed that there were two kinds of people: those who were righteous and those who were wicked. The righteous ones followed the law of the Lord, the wicked rejected it. The first way led to success, the second to destruction. The pictures of a fruitful well-watered tree and worthless winnowed chaff express this contrast well.

[4]Not so the wicked!
  They are like chaff
  that the wind blows away.
[5]Therefore the wicked will not stand in the judgment,
  nor sinners in the assembly of the righteous.

[6]For the LORD watches over the way of the righteous,
  but the way of the wicked will perish.

Psalm 2

[1]Why do the nations conspire[a]
  and the peoples plot in vain?
[2]The kings of the earth take their stand
  and the rulers gather together against the LORD
  and against his Anointed One.[b]

[3]"Let us break their chains," they say,
  "and throw off their fetters."

[4]The One enthroned in heaven laughs;
  the Lord scoffs at them.
[5]Then he rebukes them in his anger
  and terrifies them in his wrath, saying,
[6]"I have installed my King[c]
  on Zion, my holy hill."

2:6 This psalm was probably used when kings were enthroned in Jerusalem. It has the extravagant language which was appropriate at such ceremonies. Becoming king was seen as being adopted as a son of God. A sign of this special relationship was for the king to be anointed with oil (see 1 Kings 1:34–35). The Hebrew word for "anoint" gives us the word "Messiah". In the New Testament this psalm is believed to refer to Jesus. He fulfilled the role of God's anointed Son in a way that Israelite kings never did. See Mark 1:10–11; John 1:34; Acts 4:25–26; 13:33; Hebrews 1:5; 5:5; Revelation 2:27.

[7]I will proclaim the decree of the LORD:

He said to me, "You are my Son;[d]
  today I have become your Father.[e]
[8]Ask of me,
  and I will make the nations your inheritance,
  the ends of the earth your possession.
[9]You will rule them with an iron sceptre;[f]
  you will dash them to pieces like pottery."

[10]Therefore, you kings, be wise;
  be warned, you rulers of the earth.
[11]Serve the LORD with fear
  and rejoice with trembling.
[12]Kiss the Son, lest he be angry
  and you be destroyed in your way,
  for his wrath can flare up in a moment.
  Blessed are all who take refuge in him.

---

a1 Hebrew; Septuagint *rage*   b2 Or *anointed one*   c6 Or *king*   d7 Or *son*; also in verse 12
e7 Or *have begotten you*   f9 Or *will break them with a rod of iron*

Psalm 3

A psalm of David. When he fled from his son Absalom.

[1]O LORD, how many are my foes!
How many rise up against me!
[2]Many are saying of me,
"God will not deliver him."   Selah[a]

[3]But you are a shield around me, O LORD;
you bestow glory on me and lift[b] up
my head.
[4]To the LORD I cry aloud,
and he answers me from his holy hill.   Selah

[5]I lie down and sleep;
I wake again, because the LORD sustains me.
[6]I will not fear the tens of thousands
drawn up against me on every side.

[7]Arise, O LORD!
Deliver me, O my God!
Strike all my enemies on the jaw;
break the teeth of the wicked.

[8]From the LORD comes deliverance.
May your blessing be on your people.   Selah

Psalm 4

For the director of music. With stringed instruments. A psalm
of David.

[1]Answer me when I call to you,
O my righteous God.
Give me relief from my distress;
be merciful to me and hear my prayer.

[2]How long, O men, will you turn my glory into
shame?[a]
How long will you love delusions and seek false
gods?[b]   Selah
[3]Know that the LORD has set apart the godly for
himself;
the LORD will hear when I call to him.

[4]In your anger do not sin;
when you are on your beds,
search your hearts and be silent.   Selah
[5]Offer right sacrifices
and trust in the LORD.

[6]Many are asking, "Who can show us any good?"
Let the light of your face shine upon us,
O LORD.
[7]You have filled my heart with greater joy
than when their grain and new wine abound.
[8]I will lie down and sleep in peace,
for you alone, O LORD,
make me dwell in safety.

Psalm 5

For the director of music. For flutes. A psalm of David.

[1]Give ear to my words, O LORD,
consider my sighing.
[2]Listen to my cry for help,
my King and my God,
for to you I pray.
[3]In the morning, O LORD, you hear my voice;
in the morning I lay my requests before you
and wait in expectation.

[4]You are not a God who takes pleasure in evil;
with you the wicked cannot dwell.
[5]The arrogant cannot stand in your presence;
you hate all who do wrong.
[6]You destroy those who tell lies;
bloodthirsty and deceitful men
the LORD abhors.

[7]But I, by your great mercy,
will come into your house;
in reverence will I bow down
towards your holy temple.
[8]Lead me, O LORD, in your righteousness
because of my enemies—
make straight your way before me.

[9]Not a word from their mouth can be trusted;
their heart is filled with destruction.
Their throat is an open grave;
with their tongue they speak deceit.
[10]Declare them guilty, O God!
Let their intrigues be their downfall.
Banish them for their many sins,
for they have rebelled against you.

[11]But let all who take refuge in you be glad;
let them ever sing for joy.
Spread your protection over them,
that those who love your name may rejoice in
you.
[12]For surely, O LORD, you bless the righteous;
you surround them with your favour as with a
shield.

Psalm 6

For the director of music. With stringed instruments. According
to sheminith.[a] A psalm of David.

[1]O LORD, do not rebuke me in your anger
or discipline me in your wrath.
[2]Be merciful to me, LORD, for I am faint;
O LORD, heal me, for my bones are in agony.
[3]My soul is in anguish.
How long, O LORD, how long?

[4]Turn, O LORD, and deliver me;
save me because of your unfailing love.
[5]No-one remembers you when he is dead.
Who praises you from his grave?[b]

---

[a]2 A word of uncertain meaning, occurring frequently in the Psalms; possibly a musical term
[b]3 Or LORD, / my Glorious One, who lifts   [a]2 Or you dishonour my Glorious One   [b]2 Or seek lies
[a]Title: Probably a musical term   [b]5 Hebrew Sheol

⁶I am worn out from groaning;
  all night long I flood my bed with weeping
  and drench my couch with tears.
⁷My eyes grow weak with sorrow;
  they fail because of all my foes.

⁸Away from me, all you who do evil,
  for the LORD has heard my weeping.
⁹The LORD has heard my cry for mercy;
  the LORD accepts my prayer.
¹⁰All my enemies will be ashamed and dismayed;
  they will turn back in sudden disgrace.

Psalm 7

A *shiggaion*^a of David, which he sang to the LORD concerning
Cush, a Benjamite.

¹O LORD my God, I take refuge in you;
  save and deliver me from all who pursue me,
²or they will tear me like a lion
  and rip me to pieces with no-one to rescue me.

³O LORD my God, if I have done this
  and there is guilt on my hands—
⁴if I have done evil to him who is at peace
    with me
  or without cause have robbed my foe—
⁵then let my enemy pursue and overtake me;
  let him trample my life to the ground
  and make me sleep in the dust. *Selah*

⁶Arise, O LORD, in your anger;
  rise up against the rage of my enemies.
  Awake, my God; decree justice.
⁷Let the assembled peoples gather round you.
  Rule over them from on high;
⁸ let the LORD judge the peoples.
Judge me, O LORD, according to my righteousness,
  according to my integrity, O Most High.
⁹O righteous God,
  who searches minds and hearts,
bring to an end the violence of the wicked
  and make the righteous secure.

7:10 Military life was a familiar experience, and the psalmist used many pictures drawn from it to talk about God. The war shield was a large all-encompassing protective screen. God protected those who put their trust in him. "Rock", "refuge", "fortress", and "stronghold" are all similar terms from warfare used to describe God's protection of his people.

---

¹⁰My shield^b is God Most High,
  who saves the upright in heart.
¹¹God is a righteous judge,
  a God who expresses his wrath every day.

¹²If he does not relent,
  he^c will sharpen his sword;
  he will bend and string his bow.
¹³He has prepared his deadly weapons;
  he makes ready his flaming arrows.

¹⁴He who is pregnant with evil
  and conceives trouble gives birth to
    disillusionment.
¹⁵He who digs a hole and scoops it out
  falls into the pit he has made.
¹⁶The trouble he causes recoils on himself;
  his violence comes down on his own
    head.

¹⁷I will give thanks to the LORD because of his
    righteousness
  and will sing praise to the name of the LORD
    Most High.

Psalm 8

For the director of music. According to *gittith*.^a A psalm
of David.

¹O LORD, our Lord,
  how majestic is your name in all the earth!

You have set your glory
  above the heavens.
²From the lips of children and infants
  you have ordained praise^b
because of your enemies,
  to silence the foe and the avenger.

³When I consider your heavens,
  the work of your fingers,
the moon and the stars,
  which you have set in place,
⁴what is man that you are mindful of him,
  the son of man that you care for him?
⁵You made him a little lower than the heavenly
    beings^c
  and crowned him with glory and honour.

⁶You made him ruler over the works of your
    hands;
  you put everything under his feet:
⁷all flocks and herds,
  and the beasts of the field,
⁸the birds of the air,
  and the fish of the sea,
  all that swim the paths of the seas.

⁹O LORD, our Lord,
  how majestic is your name in all the earth!

Psalm 9^a

For the director of music. To ˌthe tune of˴ "The Death of the
Son". A psalm of David.

¹I will praise you, O LORD, with all my heart;
  I will tell of all your wonders.

---

^aTitle: Probably a literary or musical term   ^b10 Or *sovereign*   ^c12 Or *If a man does not repent, / God*
^aTitle: Probably a musical term   ^b2 Or *strength*   ^c5 Or *than God*
^aPsalms 9 and 10 may have been originally a single acrostic poem, the stanzas of which begin with the successive letters of the Hebrew alphabet. In the Septuagint they constitute one psalm.

²I will be glad and rejoice in you;
  I will sing praise to your name, O Most High.

³My enemies turn back;
  they stumble and perish before you.
⁴For you have upheld my right and my cause;
  you have sat on your throne, judging
    righteously.
⁵You have rebuked the nations and destroyed the
    wicked;
  you have blotted out their name for ever and
    ever.
⁶Endless ruin has overtaken the enemy,
  you have uprooted their cities;
  even the memory of them has perished.

⁷The LORD reigns for ever;
  he has established his throne for judgment.
⁸He will judge the world in righteousness;
  he will govern the peoples with justice.
⁹The LORD is a refuge for the oppressed,
  a stronghold in times of trouble.
¹⁰Those who know your name will trust in you,
  for you, LORD, have never forsaken those who
    seek you.

¹¹Sing praises to the LORD, enthroned in Zion;
  proclaim among the nations what he has done.
¹²For he who avenges blood remembers;
  he does not ignore the cry of the afflicted.

¹³O LORD, see how my enemies persecute me!
  Have mercy and lift me up from the gates of
    death,
¹⁴that I may declare your praises
  in the gates of the Daughter of Zion
  and there rejoice in your salvation.
¹⁵The nations have fallen into the pit they have
    dug;
  their feet are caught in the net they have
    hidden.
¹⁶The LORD is known by his justice;
  the wicked are ensnared by the work of their
    hands.   *Higgaion.*ᵇ *Selah*

¹⁷The wicked return to the grave,ᶜ
  all the nations that forget God.
¹⁸But the needy will not always be forgotten,
  nor the hope of the afflicted ever perish.

¹⁹Arise, O LORD, let not man triumph;
  let the nations be judged in your presence.
²⁰Strike them with terror, O LORD;
  let the nations know they are but men.   *Selah*

Psalm 10ᵃ

¹Why, O LORD, do you stand far off?
  Why do you hide yourself in times of trouble?

²In his arrogance the wicked man hunts down the
    weak,
  who are caught in the schemes he devises.

³He boasts of the cravings of his heart;
  he blesses the greedy and reviles the LORD.
⁴In his pride the wicked does not seek him;
  in all his thoughts there is no room for God.
⁵His ways are always prosperous;
  he is haughty and your laws are far from him;
  he sneers at all his enemies.
⁶He says to himself, "Nothing will shake me;
  I'll always be happy and never have trouble."
⁷His mouth is full of curses and lies and threats;
  trouble and evil are under his tongue.
⁸He lies in wait near the villages;
  from ambush he murders the innocent,
  watching in secret for his victims.
⁹He lies in wait like a lion in cover;
  he lies in wait to catch the helpless;
  he catches the helpless and drags them off in
    his net.
¹⁰His victims are crushed, they collapse;
  they fall under his strength.
¹¹He says to himself, "God has forgotten;
  he covers his face and never sees."

10:1 Sometimes it looks as if God has not seen people's predicaments. The idea of the wicked prospering is very difficult to understand. The psalmist expressed his frustration, but his faith that God would act is not shaken.

¹²Arise, LORD! Lift up your hand, O God.
  Do not forget the helpless.
¹³Why does the wicked man revile God?
  Why does he say to himself,
  "He won't call me to account"?
¹⁴But you, O God, do see trouble and grief;
  you consider it to take it in hand.
  The victim commits himself to you;
  you are the helper of the fatherless.
¹⁵Break the arm of the wicked and evil man;
  call him to account for his wickedness
  that would not be found out.

¹⁶The LORD is King for ever and ever;
  the nations will perish from his land.
¹⁷You hear, O LORD, the desire of the afflicted;
  you encourage them, and you listen to their cry,
¹⁸defending the fatherless and the oppressed,
  in order that man, who is of the earth, may
    terrify no more.

Psalm 11

For the director of music. Of David.

¹In the LORD I take refuge.
  How then can you say to me:
  "Flee like a bird to your mountain.
²For look, the wicked bend their bows;
  they set their arrows against the strings

ᵇ16 Or *Meditation*; possibly a musical notation   ᶜ17 Hebrew *Sheol*
ᵃPsalms 9 and 10 may have been originally a single acrostic poem, the stanzas of which begin with the successive letters of the Hebrew alphabet. In the Septuagint they constitute one psalm.

to shoot from the shadows
    at the upright in heart.
3When the foundations are being destroyed,
    what can the righteous do?"ᵃ

4The LORD is in his holy temple;
    the LORD is on his heavenly throne.
He observes the sons of men;
    his eyes examine them.
5The LORD examines the righteous,
    but the wickedᵇ and those who love violence
    his soul hates.
6On the wicked he will rain
    fiery coals and burning sulphur;
    a scorching wind will be their lot.

7For the LORD is righteous,
    he loves justice;
    upright men will see his face.

Psalm 12

For the director of music. According to *sheminith*.ᵃ A psalm
of David.

1Help, LORD, for the godly are no more;
    the faithful have vanished from among men.
2Everyone lies to his neighbour;
    their flattering lips speak with deception.

3May the LORD cut off all flattering lips
    and every boastful tongue
4that says, "We will triumph with our tongues;
    we own our lipsᵇ—who is our master?"

5"Because of the oppression of the weak
    and the groaning of the needy,
I will now arise," says the LORD.
    "I will protect them from those who malign
    them."
6And the words of the LORD are flawless,
    like silver refined in a furnace of clay,
    purified seven times.

12:6   In contrast with human speech
God's words are pure, like silver which has
been completely refined. Human words can
be the cause of much suffering, but God's
words protect and support. Those who follow him should speak in the same way.

7O LORD, you will keep us safe
    and protect us from such people for ever.
8The wicked freely strut about
    when what is vile is honoured among men.

Psalm 13

For the director of music. A psalm of David.

1How long, O LORD? Will you forget me for ever?
    How long will you hide your face from me?

2How long must I wrestle with my thoughts
    and every day have sorrow in my heart?
    How long will my enemy triumph over me?

3Look on me and answer, O LORD my God.
    Give light to my eyes, or I will sleep in
    death;
4my enemy will say, "I have overcome him,"
    and my foes will rejoice when I fall.

5But I trust in your unfailing love;
    my heart rejoices in your salvation.
6I will sing to the LORD,
    for he has been good to me.

Psalm 14

For the director of music. Of David.

1The foolᵃ says in his heart,
    "There is no God."
They are corrupt, their deeds are vile;
    there is no-one who does good.

2The LORD looks down from heaven
    on the sons of men
to see if there are any who understand,
    any who seek God.
3All have turned aside,
    they have together become corrupt;
there is no-one who does good,
    not even one.

14:3   The psalmist's view of human life
was entirely negative. No one did good and
everyone had rejected God, even his own
people. Paul used this verse (in Romans
3:10–12) to show that no one could make
themselves righteous by their own actions.

4Will evildoers never learn—
    those who devour my people as men eat bread
    and who do not call on the LORD?
5There they are, overwhelmed with dread,
    for God is present in the company of the
    righteous.
6You evildoers frustrate the plans of the poor,
    but the LORD is their refuge.

7Oh, that salvation for Israel would come out of
    Zion!
    When the LORD restores the fortunes of his
    people,
    let Jacob rejoice and Israel be glad!

Psalm 15

A psalm of David.

1LORD, who may dwell in your sanctuary?
    Who may live on your holy hill?

ᵃ3 Or *what is the Righteous One doing*   ᵇ5 Or *The LORD, the Righteous One, examines the wicked, /*
ᵃTitle: Probably a musical term   ᵇ4 Or */ our lips are our ploughshares*
ᵃ1 The Hebrew words rendered *fool* in Psalms denote one who is morally deficient.

²He whose walk is blameless
and who does what is righteous,
who speaks the truth from his heart
³ and has no slander on his tongue,
who does his neighbour no wrong
and casts no slur on his fellow-man,
⁴who despises a vile man
but honours those who fear the LORD,
who keeps his oath
even when it hurts,
⁵who lends his money without usury
and does not accept a bribe against the
innocent.

15:1   Originally this was an exchange
between would-be worshippers and priests
about what qualifications were needed to
enter the temple. Only the person who is
obedient to the moral law is fit to spend time
in God's presence. Contrary to popular
belief, truly religious people are more concerned about the way they treat their neighbours than the "correctness" of worship.

He who does these things
will never be shaken.

Psalm 16

A miktamᵃ of David.

¹Keep me safe, O God,
for in you I take refuge.

²I said to the LORD, "You are my Lord;
apart from you I have no good thing."
³As for the saints who are in the land,
they are the glorious ones in whom is all my
delight.ᵇ
⁴The sorrows of those will increase
who run after other gods.
I will not pour out their libations of blood
or take up their names on my lips.

⁵LORD, you have assigned me my portion and my
cup;
you have made my lot secure.
⁶The boundary lines have fallen for me in pleasant
places;
surely I have a delightful inheritance.

⁷I will praise the LORD, who counsels me;
even at night my heart instructs me.
⁸I have set the LORD always before me.
Because he is at my right hand,
I shall not be shaken.

⁹Therefore my heart is glad and my tongue
rejoices;
my body also will rest secure,

¹⁰because you will not abandon me to the grave,ᶜ
nor will you let your Holy Oneᵈ see decay.
¹¹You have made knownᵉ to me the path of life;
you will fill me with joy in your presence,
with eternal pleasures at your right hand.

Psalm 17

A prayer of David.

¹Hear, O LORD, my righteous plea;
listen to my cry.
Give ear to my prayer—
it does not rise from deceitful lips.
²May my vindication come from you;
may your eyes see what is right.

³Though you probe my heart and examine me
at night,
though you test me, you will find
nothing;
I have resolved that my mouth will
not sin.
⁴As for the deeds of men—
by the word of your lips
I have kept myself
from the ways of the violent.
⁵My steps have held to your paths;
my feet have not slipped.

⁶I call on you, O God, for you will answer me;
give ear to me and hear my prayer.
⁷Show the wonder of your great love,
you who save by your right hand
those who take refuge in you from their
foes.

⁸Keep me as the apple of your eye;
hide me in the shadow of your wings
⁹from the wicked who assail me,
from my mortal enemies who surround
me.

¹⁰They close up their callous hearts,
and their mouths speak with arrogance.
¹¹They have tracked me down, they now
surround me,
with eyes alert, to throw me to the ground.
¹²They are like a lion hungry for prey,
like a great lion crouching in cover.
¹³Rise up, O LORD, confront them, bring them
down;
rescue me from the wicked by your sword.
¹⁴O LORD, by your hand save me from such men,
from men of this world whose reward is in this
life.

You still the hunger of those you cherish;
their sons have plenty,
and they store up wealth for their children.
¹⁵And I—in righteousness I shall see your face;
when I awake, I shall be satisfied with seeing
your likeness.

ᵃTitle: Probably a literary or musical term
ᵇ3 Or *As for the pagan priests who are in the land / and the nobles in whom all delight, I said:*   ᶜ10 Hebrew *Sheol*
ᵈ10 Or *your faithful one*   ᵉ11 Or *You will make known*

Psalm 18

For the director of music. Of David the servant of the LORD. He sang to the LORD the words of this song when the LORD delivered him from the hand of all his enemies and from the hand of Saul. He said:

[1] I love you, O LORD, my strength.

[2] The LORD is my rock, my fortress and my
      deliverer;
    my God is my rock, in whom I take refuge.
    He is my shield and the horn[a] of my salvation,
      my stronghold.
[3] I call to the LORD, who is worthy of praise,
    and I am saved from my enemies.

[4] The cords of death entangled me;
    the torrents of destruction overwhelmed me.
[5] The cords of the grave[b] coiled around me;
    the snares of death confronted me.
[6] In my distress I called to the LORD;
    I cried to my God for help.
    From his temple he heard my voice;
    my cry came before him, into his ears.

18:7   The tremendous power of God is beyond logical comprehension. Using images from violent natural events such as earthquakes, volcanoes, storms, thunder and lightning, all help towards understanding it. Although this power has great force, God still comes to the rescue of individuals who are in trouble.

---

[7] The earth trembled and quaked,
    and the foundations of the mountains shook;
    they trembled because he was angry.
[8] Smoke rose from his nostrils;
    consuming fire came from his mouth,
    burning coals blazed out of it.
[9] He parted the heavens and came down;
    dark clouds were under his feet.
[10] He mounted the cherubim and flew;
    he soared on the wings of the wind.
[11] He made darkness his covering, his canopy
      around him—
    the dark rain clouds of the sky.
[12] Out of the brightness of his presence clouds
      advanced,
    with hailstones and bolts of lightning.
[13] The LORD thundered from heaven;
    the voice of the Most High resounded.[c]
[14] He shot his arrows and scattered the enemies,
    great bolts of lightning and routed them.
[15] The valleys of the sea were exposed
    and the foundations of the earth laid bare
    at your rebuke, O LORD,
    at the blast of breath from your nostrils.

[16] He reached down from on high and took hold of
      me;
    he drew me out of deep waters.
[17] He rescued me from my powerful enemy,
    from my foes, who were too strong for me.
[18] They confronted me in the day of my disaster,
    but the LORD was my support.
[19] He brought me out into a spacious place;
    he rescued me because he delighted in me.

[20] The LORD has dealt with me according to my
      righteousness;
    according to the cleanness of my hands he has
      rewarded me.
[21] For I have kept the ways of the LORD;
    I have not done evil by turning from my God.
[22] All his laws are before me;
    I have not turned away from his decrees.
[23] I have been blameless before him
    and have kept myself from sin.
[24] The LORD has rewarded me according to my
      righteousness,
    according to the cleanness of my hands in his
      sight.

[25] To the faithful you show yourself faithful,
    to the blameless you show yourself blameless,
[26] to the pure you show yourself pure,
    but to the crooked you show yourself shrewd.
[27] You save the humble
    but bring low those whose eyes are haughty.
[28] You, O LORD, keep my lamp burning;
    my God turns my darkness into light.
[29] With your help I can advance against a troop;[d]
    with my God I can scale a wall.

[30] As for God, his way is perfect;
    the word of the LORD is flawless.
    He is a shield
    for all who take refuge in him.
[31] For who is God besides the LORD?
    And who is the Rock except our God?
[32] It is God who arms me with strength
    and makes my way perfect.
[33] He makes my feet like the feet of a deer;
    he enables me to stand on the heights.
[34] He trains my hands for battle;
    my arms can bend a bow of bronze.
[35] You give me your shield of victory,
    and your right hand sustains me;
    you stoop down to make me great.
[36] You broaden the path beneath me,
    so that my ankles do not turn over.

[37] I pursued my enemies and overtook them;
    I did not turn back till they were destroyed.
[38] I crushed them so that they could not rise;
    they fell beneath my feet.
[39] You armed me with strength for battle;
    you made my adversaries bow at my feet.
[40] You made my enemies turn their backs in flight,
    and I destroyed my foes.

---

a2 Horn here symbolises strength.   *b5* Hebrew *Sheol*
c13 Some Hebrew manuscripts and Septuagint (see also 2 Samuel 22:14); most Hebrew manuscripts *resounded, / amid hailstones and bolts of lightning*   *d29* Or *can run through a barricade*

⁴¹They cried for help, but there was no-one to save them —
  to the LORD, but he did not answer.
⁴²I beat them as fine as dust borne on the wind;
  I poured them out like mud in the streets.

⁴³You have delivered me from the attacks of the people;
  you have made me the head of nations;
  people I did not know are subject to me.
⁴⁴As soon as they hear me, they obey me;
  foreigners cringe before me.
⁴⁵They all lose heart;
  they come trembling from their strongholds.

⁴⁶The LORD lives! Praise be to my Rock!
  Exalted be God my Saviour!
⁴⁷He is the God who avenges me,
  who subdues nations under me,
⁴⁸ who saves me from my enemies.
  You exalted me above my foes;
  from violent men you rescued me.
⁴⁹Therefore I will praise you among the nations,
    O LORD;
  I will sing praises to your name.
⁵⁰He gives his king great victories;
  he shows unfailing kindness to his anointed,
  to David and his descendants for ever.

Psalm 19

For the director of music. A psalm of David.

¹The heavens declare the glory of God;
  the skies proclaim the work of his hands.
²Day after day they pour forth speech;
  night after night they display knowledge.
³There is no speech or language
  where their voice is not heard.ᵃ
⁴Their voiceᵇ goes out into all the earth,
  their words to the ends of the world.

19:1 God can be recognized in two ways. The natural universe reflects his glory as its creator, and the law given to his people shows his moral nature. Obedience to the law of the Lord leads to a personal knowledge of God. When the psalmist referred to God in this personal way, he used the name "Yahweh", translated "the LORD" (see Moses' encounter with God in Exodus 3:15).

In the heavens he has pitched a tent for the sun,
⁵ which is like a bridegroom coming forth from his pavilion,
  like a champion rejoicing to run his course.
⁶It rises at one end of the heavens
  and makes its circuit to the other;
  nothing is hidden from its heat.

⁷The law of the LORD is perfect,
  reviving the soul.
The statutes of the LORD are trustworthy,
  making wise the simple.
⁸The precepts of the LORD are right,
  giving joy to the heart.
The commands of the LORD are radiant,
  giving light to the eyes.
⁹The fear of the LORD is pure,
  enduring for ever.
The ordinances of the LORD are sure
  and altogether righteous.
¹⁰They are more precious than gold,
  than much pure gold;
they are sweeter than honey,
  than honey from the comb.
¹¹By them is your servant warned;
  in keeping them there is great reward.

¹²Who can discern his errors?
  Forgive my hidden faults.
¹³Keep your servant also from wilful sins;
  may they not rule over me.
Then will I be blameless,
  innocent of great transgression.

¹⁴May the words of my mouth and the meditation of my heart
  be pleasing in your sight,
  O LORD, my Rock and my Redeemer.

Psalm 20

For the director of music. A psalm of David.

¹May the LORD answer you when you are in distress;
  may the name of the God of Jacob protect you.
²May he send you help from the sanctuary
  and grant you support from Zion.
³May he remember all your sacrifices
  and accept your burnt offerings.   *Selah*
⁴May he give you the desire of your heart
  and make all your plans succeed.
⁵We will shout for joy when you are victorious
  and will lift up our banners in the name of our God.
May the LORD grant all your requests.

20:7 True security lay in the God who the Israelites knew was on their side. Chariots and horses were known to fail in the heat of battle but God could be relied upon to help his people. God's protection is worth more than anything that human beings can provide for their own security.

---

⁶Now I know that the LORD saves his anointed;
  he answers him from his holy heaven
  with the saving power of his right hand.
⁷Some trust in chariots and some in horses,
  but we trust in the name of the LORD our God.

ᵃ3 Or *They have no speech, there are no words; / no sound is heard from them*   ᵇ4 Septuagint, Jerome and Syriac; Hebrew *line*

⁸They are brought to their knees and fall,
but we rise up and stand firm.

⁹O LORD, save the king!
Answerᵃ us when we call!

Psalm 21

For the director of music. A psalm of David.

¹O LORD, the king rejoices in your strength.
How great is his joy in the victories you give!
²You have granted him the desire of his heart
and have not withheld the request of his lips.
Selah

³You welcomed him with rich blessings
and placed a crown of pure gold on his head.
⁴He asked you for life, and you gave it to him—
length of days, for ever and ever.
⁵Through the victories you gave, his glory is great;
you have bestowed on him splendour and
majesty.
⁶Surely you have granted him eternal blessings
and made him glad with the joy of your
presence.
⁷For the king trusts in the LORD;
through the unfailing love of the Most High
he will not be shaken.

⁸Your hand will lay hold on all your enemies;
your right hand will seize your foes.
⁹At the time of your appearing
you will make them like a fiery furnace.
In his wrath the LORD will swallow them up,
and his fire will consume them.
¹⁰You will destroy their descendants from the earth,
their posterity from mankind.
¹¹Though they plot evil against you
and devise wicked schemes, they cannot
succeed;
¹²for you will make them turn their backs
when you aim at them with drawn bow.

¹³Be exalted, O LORD, in your strength;
we will sing and praise your might.

Psalm 22

*For the director of music. To the tune of, "The Doe of the
Morning". A psalm of David.*

¹My God, my God, why have you forsaken me?
Why are you so far from saving me,
so far from the words of my groaning?
²O my God, I cry out by day, but you do not
answer,
by night, and am not silent.

³Yet you are enthroned as the Holy One;
you are the praise of Israel.ᵃ
⁴In you our fathers put their trust;
they trusted and you delivered them.
⁵They cried to you and were saved;
in you they trusted and were not disappointed.

⁶But I am a worm and not a man,
scorned by men and despised by the people.
⁷All who see me mock me;
they hurl insults, shaking their heads:
⁸"He trusts in the LORD;
let the LORD rescue him.
Let him deliver him,
since he delights in him."

22:1 Sometimes being one of God's faithful servants is not a pleasant experience. Many people are ready to mock and persecute those who have faith in God. Isaiah wrote more fully about the servant of God who suffers in his "Servant Songs" (see Isaiah 42:1–4; 49:1–6; 50:4–9; 52:13–53:12). Jesus used these words from Psalm 22 when he was dying on the cross (see Matthew 27:46). They expressed how he felt cut off from God at that particular moment. The New Testament writers saw Jesus as the innocent suffering servant who, through his suffering, brought eternal salvation to humanity.

⁹Yet you brought me out of the womb;
you made me trust in you
even at my mother's breast.
¹⁰From birth I was cast upon you;
from my mother's womb you have been my
God.
¹¹Do not be far from me,
for trouble is near
and there is no-one to help.

¹²Many bulls surround me;
strong bulls of Bashan encircle me.
¹³Roaring lions tearing their prey
open their mouths wide against me.
¹⁴I am poured out like water,
and all my bones are out of joint.
My heart has turned to wax;
it has melted away within me.
¹⁵My strength is dried up like a potsherd,
and my tongue sticks to the roof of my mouth;
you lay meᵇ in the dust of death.
¹⁶Dogs have surrounded me;
a band of evil men has encircled me,
they have piercedᶜ my hands and my feet.
¹⁷I can count all my bones;
people stare and gloat over me.
¹⁸They divide my garments among them
and cast lots for my clothing.

¹⁹But you, O LORD, be not far off;
O my Strength, come quickly to help me.
²⁰Deliver my life from the sword,
my precious life from the power of the dogs.
²¹Rescue me from the mouth of the lions;
saveᵈ me from the horns of the wild oxen.

ᵃ9 Or save! / O King, answer   ᵃ3 Or Yet you are holy, / enthroned on the praises of Israel   ᵇ15 Or / I am laid
ᶜ16 Some Hebrew manuscripts, Septuagint and Syriac; most Hebrew manuscripts / like the lion,   ᵈ21 Or / you have heard

[22] I will declare your name to my brothers;
  in the congregation I will praise you.
[23] You who fear the LORD, praise him!
  All you descendants of Jacob, honour him!
  Revere him, all you descendants of Israel!
[24] For he has not despised or disdained
  the suffering of the afflicted one;
  he has not hidden his face from him
  but has listened to his cry for help.

[25] From you comes the theme of my praise in the
    great assembly;
  before those who fear you[e] will I fulfil my
    vows.
[26] The poor will eat and be satisfied;
  they who seek the LORD will praise him—
  may your hearts live for ever!
[27] All the ends of the earth
  will remember and turn to the LORD,
  and all the families of the nations
  will bow down before him,
[28] for dominion belongs to the LORD
  and he rules over the nations.
[29] All the rich of the earth will feast and worship;
  all who go down to the dust will kneel before
    him—
  those who cannot keep themselves alive.
[30] Posterity will serve him;
  future generations will be told about the Lord.
[31] They will proclaim his righteousness
  to a people yet unborn—
  for he has done it.

23:1   The writer of this famous psalm likened himself to a sheep which enjoyed the caring protection of its shepherd. Whatever situation it got into the shepherd was on hand to rescue it. Life will certainly have its moments of pain and grief but there is always the opportunity to rely on God.

Psalm 23

A psalm of David.

[1] The LORD is my shepherd, I shall not be in want.
[2]   He makes me lie down in green pastures,
  he leads me beside quiet waters,
[3]   he restores my soul.
  He guides me in paths of righteousness
  for his name's sake.
[4] Even though I walk
  through the valley of the shadow of death,[a]
  I will fear no evil,
  for you are with me;
  your rod and your staff,
  they comfort me.

[5] You prepare a table before me
  in the presence of my enemies.
  You anoint my head with oil;
  my cup overflows.
[6] Surely goodness and love will follow me
  all the days of my life,
  and I will dwell in the house of the LORD
  for ever.

Psalm 24

Of David. A psalm.

[1] The earth is the LORD's, and everything in it,
  the world, and all who live in it;
[2] for he founded it upon the seas
  and established it upon the waters.

[3] Who may ascend the hill of the LORD?
  Who may stand in his holy place?
[4] He who has clean hands and a pure heart,
  who does not lift up his soul to an idol
  or swear by what is false.[a]
[5] He will receive blessing from the LORD
  and vindication from God his Saviour.
[6] Such is the generation of those who seek him,
  who seek your face, O God of Jacob.[b]   Selah

24:7   The image of God here is of a mighty king who is coming to his palace having been a hero in battle. The psalmist could draw on the pharaohs of Egypt and the kings of Assyria for examples of such figures. The Israelite worshippers may well have acted out the divine victory parade, led by priests and the ark of the covenant, in a procession around the city and into the temple (see Psalm 47:5 and 68:24–27).

---

[7] Lift up your heads, O you gates;
  be lifted up, you ancient doors,
  that the King of glory may come in.
[8] Who is this King of glory?
  The LORD strong and mighty,
  the LORD mighty in battle.
[9] Lift up your heads, O you gates;
  lift them up, you ancient doors,
  that the King of glory may come in.
[10] Who is he, this King of glory?
  The LORD Almighty—
  he is the King of glory.   Selah

Psalm 25[a]

Of David.

[1] To you, O LORD, I lift up my soul;
[2]   in you I trust, O my God.
  Do not let me be put to shame,
  nor let my enemies triumph over me.

---

[e]25 Hebrew him   [a]4 Or through the darkest valley   [a]4 Or swear falsely
[b]6 Two Hebrew manuscripts and Syriac (see also Septuagint); most Hebrew manuscripts face, Jacob
[a]This psalm is an acrostic poem, the verses of which begin with the successive letters of the Hebrew alphabet.

³No-one whose hope is in you
  will ever be put to shame,
but they will be put to shame
  who are treacherous without excuse.

25:4 The image of walking along the right path is used throughout the psalms as a metaphor for living a life which is pleasing to God. Going the right way means hearing and doing the words of God. This very often involved caring for others, and particularly looking after those in difficulties, such as the poor (see Leviticus 19:9–19).

---

⁴Show me your ways, O Lord,
  teach me your paths;
⁵guide me in your truth and teach me,
  for you are God my Saviour,
  and my hope is in you all day long.
⁶Remember, O Lord, your great mercy and love,
  for they are from of old.
⁷Remember not the sins of my youth
  and my rebellious ways;
according to your love remember me,
  for you are good, O Lord.

⁸Good and upright is the Lord;
  therefore he instructs sinners in his ways.
⁹He guides the humble in what is right
  and teaches them his way.
¹⁰All the ways of the Lord are loving and faithful
  for those who keep the demands of his
    covenant.
¹¹For the sake of your name, O Lord,
  forgive my iniquity, though it is great.
¹²Who, then, is the man that fears the Lord?
  He will instruct him in the way chosen for him.
¹³He will spend his days in prosperity,
  and his descendants will inherit the land.
¹⁴The Lord confides in those who fear him;
  he makes his covenant known to them.
¹⁵My eyes are ever on the Lord,
  for only he will release my feet from the snare.

¹⁶Turn to me and be gracious to me,
  for I am lonely and afflicted.
¹⁷The troubles of my heart have multiplied;
  free me from my anguish.
¹⁸Look upon my affliction and my distress
  and take away all my sins.
¹⁹See how my enemies have increased
  and how fiercely they hate me!
²⁰Guard my life and rescue me;
  let me not be put to shame,
  for I take refuge in you.
²¹May integrity and uprightness protect me,
  because my hope is in you.

²²Redeem Israel, O God,
  from all their troubles!

---

a 2 Or to slander me

Psalm 26

Of David.

¹Vindicate me, O Lord,
  for I have led a blameless life;
I have trusted in the Lord
  without wavering.
²Test me, O Lord, and try me,
  examine my heart and my mind;
³for your love is ever before me,
  and I walk continually in your truth.
⁴I do not sit with deceitful men,
  nor do I consort with hypocrites;
⁵I abhor the assembly of evildoers
  and refuse to sit with the wicked.
⁶I wash my hands in innocence,
  and go about your altar, O Lord,
⁷proclaiming aloud your praise
  and telling of all your wonderful deeds.
⁸I love the house where you live, O Lord,
  the place where your glory dwells.

⁹Do not take away my soul along with sinners,
  my life with bloodthirsty men,
¹⁰in whose hands are wicked schemes,
  whose right hands are full of bribes.
¹¹But I lead a blameless life;
  redeem me and be merciful to me.
¹²My feet stand on level ground;
  in the great assembly I will praise the Lord.

27:1 People who put their trust in God have absolutely nothing to fear. Even when circumstances are really hard, it is important to remember God's strength. It takes great faith to live out this ideal, and the writer of this psalm knew that he must spend plenty of time in God's presence to keep that faith going.

Psalm 27

Of David.

¹The Lord is my light and my salvation —
  whom shall I fear?
The Lord is the stronghold of my life —
  of whom shall I be afraid?
²When evil men advance against me
  to devour my flesh,ᵃ
when my enemies and my foes attack me,
  they will stumble and fall.
³Though an army besiege me,
  my heart will not fear;
though war break out against me,
  even then will I be confident.

⁴One thing I ask of the Lord,
  this is what I seek:

that I may dwell in the house of the LORD
  all the days of my life,
to gaze upon the beauty of the LORD
  and to seek him in his temple.
⁵For in the day of trouble
  he will keep me safe in his dwelling;
he will hide me in the shelter of his
    tabernacle
  and set me high upon a rock.
⁶Then my head will be exalted
  above the enemies who surround me;
at his tabernacle will I sacrifice with shouts of
    joy;
  I will sing and make music to the LORD.

⁷Hear my voice when I call, O LORD;
  be merciful to me and answer me.
⁸My heart says of you, "Seek his ᵇ face!"
  Your face, LORD, I will seek.
⁹Do not hide your face from me,
  do not turn your servant away in anger;
  you have been my helper.
Do not reject me or forsake me,
  O God my Saviour.
¹⁰Though my father and mother forsake me,
  the LORD will receive me.
¹¹Teach me your way, O LORD;
  lead me in a straight path
  because of my oppressors.
¹²Do not hand me over to the desire of my
    foes,
  for false witnesses rise up against me,
  breathing out violence.

¹³I am still confident of this:
  I will see the goodness of the LORD
  in the land of the living.
¹⁴Wait for the LORD;
  be strong and take heart
  and wait for the LORD.

Psalm 28

Of David.

¹To you I call, O LORD my Rock;
  do not turn a deaf ear to me.
For if you remain silent,
  I shall be like those who have gone down
    to the pit.
²Hear my cry for mercy
  as I call to you for help,
as I lift up my hands
  towards your Most Holy Place.

³Do not drag me away with the wicked,
  with those who do evil,
who speak cordially with their neighbours
  but harbour malice in their hearts.
⁴Repay them for their deeds
  and for their evil work;
repay them for what their hands have done
  and bring back upon them what they deserve.

⁵Since they show no regard for the works of the
    LORD
  and what his hands have done,
he will tear them down
  and never build them up again.

⁶Praise be to the LORD,
  for he has heard my cry for mercy.
⁷The LORD is my strength and my shield;
  my heart trusts in him, and I am helped.
My heart leaps for joy
  and I will give thanks to him in song.

⁸The LORD is the strength of his people,
  a fortress of salvation for his anointed
    one.
⁹Save your people and bless your inheritance;
  be their shepherd and carry them for ever.

Psalm 29

A psalm of David.

¹Ascribe to the LORD, O mighty ones,
  ascribe to the LORD glory and strength.
²Ascribe to the LORD the glory due to his name;
  worship the LORD in the splendour of his ᵃ
    holiness.

29:3   People of the ancient world looked
for divine explanations of natural events.
They thought that it was the gods who controlled storms, winds, sun, fertility and so on.
The Israelite psalmist believed that his God
was behind all these things, and took great
encouragement from this.

---

³The voice of the LORD is over the waters;
  the God of glory thunders,
  the LORD thunders over the mighty waters.
⁴The voice of the LORD is powerful;
  the voice of the LORD is majestic.
⁵The voice of the LORD breaks the cedars;
  the LORD breaks in pieces the cedars of
    Lebanon.
⁶He makes Lebanon skip like a calf,
  Sirion ᵇ like a young wild ox.
⁷The voice of the LORD strikes
  with flashes of lightning.
⁸The voice of the LORD shakes the desert;
  the LORD shakes the Desert of Kadesh.
⁹The voice of the LORD twists the oaks ᶜ
  and strips the forests bare.
And in his temple all cry, "Glory!"

¹⁰The LORD sits ᵈ enthroned over the flood;
  the LORD is enthroned as King for ever.
¹¹The LORD gives strength to his people;
  the LORD blesses his people with peace.

ᵇ8 Or *To you, O my heart, he has said, "Seek my*   ᵃ2 Or *LORD with the splendour of*   ᵇ6 That is, Mount Hermon
ᶜ9 Or *LORD makes the deer give birth*   ᵈ10 Or *sat*

Psalm 30

A psalm. A song. For the dedication of the temple.[a] Of David.

[1]I will exalt you, O LORD,
   for you lifted me out of the depths
   and did not let my enemies gloat over me.
[2]O LORD my God, I called to you for help
   and you healed me.
[3]O LORD, you brought me up from the grave;[b]
   you spared me from going down into the pit.

[4]Sing to the LORD, you saints of his;
   praise his holy name.
[5]For his anger lasts only a moment,
   but his favour lasts a lifetime;
weeping may remain for a night,
   but rejoicing comes in the morning.

[6]When I felt secure, I said,
   "I shall never be shaken."
[7]O LORD, when you favoured me,
   you made my mountain[c] stand firm;
but when you hid your face,
   I was dismayed.

[8]To you, O LORD, I called;
   to the Lord I cried for mercy:
[9]"What gain is there in my destruction,[d]
   in my going down into the pit?
Will the dust praise you?
   Will it proclaim your faithfulness?
[10]Hear, O LORD, and be merciful to me;
   O LORD, be my help."

[11]You turned my wailing into dancing;
   you removed my sackcloth and clothed me
      with joy,
[12]that my heart may sing to you and not be silent.
   O LORD my God, I will give you thanks for
      ever.

Psalm 31

For the director of music. A psalm of David.

[1]In you, O LORD, I have taken refuge;
   let me never be put to shame;
   deliver me in your righteousness.
[2]Turn your ear to me,
   come quickly to my rescue;
be my rock of refuge,
   a strong fortress to save me.
[3]Since you are my rock and my fortress,
   for the sake of your name lead and guide me.
[4]Free me from the trap that is set for me,
   for you are my refuge.
[5]Into your hands I commit my spirit;
   redeem me, O LORD, the God of truth.

[6]I hate those who cling to worthless idols;
   I trust in the LORD.
[7]I will be glad and rejoice in your love,
   for you saw my affliction
   and knew the anguish of my soul.

[8]You have not handed me over to the enemy
   but have set my feet in a spacious place.

[9]Be merciful to me, O LORD, for I am in
      distress;
   my eyes grow weak with sorrow,
   my soul and my body with grief.
[10]My life is consumed by anguish
   and my years by groaning;
my strength fails because of my affliction,[a]
   and my bones grow weak.
[11]Because of all my enemies,
   I am the utter contempt of my neighbours;
I am a dread to my friends—
   those who see me on the street flee from
      me.
[12]I am forgotten by them as though I were
      dead;
   I have become like broken pottery.
[13]For I hear the slander of many;
   there is terror on every side;
they conspire against me
   and plot to take my life.

[14]But I trust in you, O LORD;
   I say, "You are my God."
[15]My times are in your hands;
   deliver me from my enemies
   and from those who pursue me.
[16]Let your face shine on your servant;
   save me in your unfailing love.
[17]Let me not be put to shame, O LORD,
   for I have cried out to you;
but let the wicked be put to shame
   and lie silent in the grave.[b]
[18]Let their lying lips be silenced,
   for with pride and contempt
   they speak arrogantly against the
      righteous.

[19]How great is your goodness,
   which you have stored up for those who
      fear you,
which you bestow in the sight of men
   on those who take refuge in you.
[20]In the shelter of your presence you hide
      them
   from the intrigues of men;
in your dwelling you keep them safe
   from accusing tongues.

[21]Praise be to the LORD,
   for he showed his wonderful love to me
   when I was in a besieged city.
[22]In my alarm I said,
   "I am cut off from your sight!"
Yet you heard my cry for mercy
   when I called to you for help.

[23]Love the LORD, all his saints!
   The LORD preserves the faithful,
   but the proud he pays back in full.
[24]Be strong and take heart,
   all you who hope in the LORD.

[a]Title: Or palace   [b]3 Hebrew Sheol   [c]7 Or hill country   [d]9 Or there if I am silenced
[a]10 Or guilt   [b]17 Hebrew Sheol

Psalm 32

Of David. A *maskil.* [a]

[1] Blessed is he
   whose transgressions are forgiven,
   whose sins are covered.
[2] Blessed is the man
   whose sin the LORD does not count against him
   and in whose spirit is no deceit.

[3] When I kept silent,
   my bones wasted away
   through my groaning all day long.
[4] For day and night
   your hand was heavy upon me;
   my strength was sapped
   as in the heat of summer.   *Selah*
[5] Then I acknowledged my sin to you
   and did not cover up my iniquity.
   I said, "I will confess
   my transgressions to the LORD" —
   and you forgave
   the guilt of my sin.   *Selah*

[6] Therefore let everyone who is godly pray to you
   while you may be found;
   surely when the mighty waters rise,
   they will not reach him.
[7] You are my hiding-place;
   you will protect me from trouble
   and surround me with songs of deliverance.   *Selah*

[8] I will instruct you and teach you in the way you
      should go;
   I will counsel you and watch over you.
[9] Do not be like the horse or the mule,
   which have no understanding
   but must be controlled by bit and bridle
   or they will not come to you.
[10] Many are the woes of the wicked,
   but the LORD's unfailing love
   surrounds the man who trusts in him.

[11] Rejoice in the LORD and be glad, you righteous;
   sing, all you who are upright in heart!

Psalm 33

[1] Sing joyfully to the LORD, you righteous;
   it is fitting for the upright to praise him.
[2] Praise the LORD with the harp;
   make music to him on the ten-stringed lyre.
[3] Sing to him a new song;
   play skilfully, and shout for joy.

[4] For the word of the LORD is right and true;
   he is faithful in all he does.
[5] The LORD loves righteousness and justice;
   the earth is full of his unfailing love.

[6] By the word of the LORD were the heavens made,
   their starry host by the breath of his mouth.

[7] He gathers the waters of the sea into jars; [a]
   he puts the deep into storehouses.
[8] Let all the earth fear the LORD;
   let all the people of the world revere him.
[9] For he spoke, and it came to be;
   he commanded, and it stood firm.
[10] The LORD foils the plans of the nations;
   he thwarts the purposes of the peoples.
[11] But the plans of the LORD stand firm for ever,
   the purposes of his heart through all
      generations.

[12] Blessed is the nation whose God is the LORD,
   the people he chose for his inheritance.
[13] From heaven the LORD looks down
   and sees all mankind;
[14] from his dwelling-place he watches
   all who live on earth —
[15] he who forms the hearts of all,
   who considers everything they do.

[16] No king is saved by the size of his army;
   no warrior escapes by his great strength.
[17] A horse is a vain hope for deliverance;
   despite all its great strength it cannot save.
[18] But the eyes of the LORD are on those who fear
      him,
   on those whose hope is in his unfailing love,
[19] to deliver them from death
   and keep them alive in famine.

[20] We wait in hope for the LORD;
   he is our help and our shield.
[21] In him our hearts rejoice,
   for we trust in his holy name.
[22] May your unfailing love rest upon us, O LORD,
   even as we put our hope in you.

Psalm 34 [a]

Of David. When he pretended to be insane before Abimelech,
who drove him away, and he left.

[1] I will extol the LORD at all times;
   his praise will always be on my lips.
[2] My soul will boast in the LORD;
   let the afflicted hear and rejoice.
[3] Glorify the LORD with me:
   let us exalt his name together.

[4] I sought the LORD, and he answered me;
   he delivered me from all my fears.
[5] Those who look to him are radiant;
   their faces are never covered with shame.
[6] This poor man called, and the LORD heard him;
   he saved him out of all his troubles.
[7] The angel of the LORD encamps around those who
      fear him,
   and he delivers them.

[8] Taste and see that the LORD is good;
   blessed is the man who takes refuge in him.
[9] Fear the LORD, you his saints,
   for those who fear him lack nothing.

---

[a] Title: Probably a literary or musical term   [a] 7 Or *sea as into a heap*
[a] This psalm is an acrostic poem, the verses of which begin with the successive letters of the Hebrew alphabet.

¹⁰The lions may grow weak and hungry,
  but those who seek the LORD lack no good
  thing.

34:9   Fear is usually connected with being afraid of an actual thing; a person, place, situation and so on. However, in the Bible it means having a proper attitude towards God; treating him with appropriate reverence. He may seem frighteningly powerful, but in fact he reaches out to those who seek him, and is a safe haven for those who praise him.

---

¹¹Come, my children, listen to me;
  I will teach you the fear of the LORD.
¹²Whoever of you loves life
  and desires to see many good days,
¹³keep your tongue from evil
  and your lips from speaking lies.
¹⁴Turn from evil and do good;
  seek peace and pursue it.

¹⁵The eyes of the LORD are on the righteous
  and his ears are attentive to their cry;
¹⁶the face of the LORD is against those who do evil,
  to cut off the memory of them from the earth.

¹⁷The righteous cry out, and the LORD hears them;
  he delivers them from all their troubles.
¹⁸The LORD is close to the broken-hearted
  and saves those who are crushed in spirit.

¹⁹A righteous man may have many troubles,
  but the LORD delivers him from them all;
²⁰he protects all his bones,
  not one of them will be broken.

²¹Evil will slay the wicked;
  the foes of the righteous will be condemned.
²²The LORD redeems his servants;
  no-one will be condemned who takes refuge in
  him.

Psalm 35

Of David.

¹Contend, O LORD, with those who contend with
  me;
  fight against those who fight against me.
²Take up shield and buckler;
  arise and come to my aid.
³Brandish spear and javelin[a]
  against those who pursue me.
  Say to my soul,
  "I am your salvation."

⁴May those who seek my life
  be disgraced and put to shame;
  may those who plot my ruin
  be turned back in dismay.
⁵May they be like chaff before the wind,
  with the angel of the LORD driving them away;

⁶may their path be dark and slippery,
  with the angel of the LORD pursuing them.
⁷Since they hid their net for me without cause
  and without cause dug a pit for me,
⁸may ruin overtake them by surprise —
  may the net they hid entangle them,
  may they fall into the pit, to their ruin.
⁹Then my soul will rejoice in the LORD
  and delight in his salvation.
¹⁰My whole being will exclaim,
  "Who is like you, O LORD?
  You rescue the poor from those too strong for
  them,
  the poor and needy from those who rob them."

35:4   The writer was so upset by the attitude of those he had previously helped (verses 12–14) that he poured out his frustration and anger before God, and begged him to exact revenge against them. In the Old Testament there was a need for immediate justice to be done, and so anger and bitterness were openly expressed before God.

---

¹¹Ruthless witnesses come forward;
  they question me on things I know nothing
  about.
¹²They repay me evil for good
  and leave my soul forlorn.
¹³Yet when they were ill, I put on sackcloth
  and humbled myself with fasting.
  When my prayers returned to me unanswered,
¹⁴ I went about mourning
  as though for my friend or brother.
  I bowed my head in grief
  as though weeping for my mother.
¹⁵But when I stumbled, they gathered in glee;
  attackers gathered against me when I was
  unaware.
  They slandered me without ceasing.
¹⁶Like the ungodly they maliciously mocked;[b]
  they gnashed their teeth at me.
¹⁷O Lord, how long will you look on?
  Rescue my life from their ravages,
  my precious life from these lions.
¹⁸I will give you thanks in the great assembly;
  among throngs of people I will praise you.

¹⁹Let not those gloat over me
  who are my enemies without cause;
  let not those who hate me without reason
  maliciously wink the eye.
²⁰They do not speak peaceably,
  but devise false accusations
  against those who live quietly in the land.
²¹They gape at me and say, "Aha! Aha!
  With our own eyes we have seen it."

²²O LORD, you have seen this; be not silent.
  Do not be far from me, O Lord.

---

a 3 Or and block the way   b 16 Septuagint; Hebrew may mean *ungodly circle of mockers.*

²³Awake, and rise to my defence!
  Contend for me, my God and Lord.
²⁴Vindicate me in your righteousness, O LORD my
    God;
  do not let them gloat over me.
²⁵Do not let them think, "Aha, just what we
    wanted!"
  or say, "We have swallowed him up."

²⁶May all who gloat over my distress
  be put to shame and confusion;
  may all who exalt themselves over me
  be clothed with shame and disgrace.
²⁷May those who delight in my vindication
  shout for joy and gladness;
  may they always say, "The LORD be exalted,
  who delights in the well-being of his servant."
²⁸My tongue will speak of your righteousness
  and of your praises all day long.

Psalm 36

For the director of music. Of David the servant of the LORD.

¹An oracle is within my heart
  concerning the sinfulness of the wicked:ᵃ
There is no fear of God
  before his eyes.
²For in his own eyes he flatters himself
  too much to detect or hate his sin.
³The words of his mouth are wicked and deceitful;
  he has ceased to be wise and to do good.
⁴Even on his bed he plots evil;
  he commits himself to a sinful course
  and does not reject what is wrong.

⁵Your love, O LORD, reaches to the heavens,
  your faithfulness to the skies.
⁶Your righteousness is like the mighty mountains,
  your justice like the great deep.
O LORD, you preserve both man and beast.
⁷ How priceless is your unfailing love!
Both high and low among men
  findᵇ refuge in the shadow of your wings.
⁸They feast in the abundance of your house;
  you give them drink from your river of delights.
⁹For with you is the fountain of life;
  in your light we see light.

¹⁰Continue your love to those who know you,
  your righteousness to the upright in heart.
¹¹May the foot of the proud not come against me,
  nor the hand of the wicked drive me away.
¹²See how the evildoers lie fallen—
  thrown down, not able to rise!

Psalm 37ᵃ

Of David.

¹Do not fret because of evil men
  or be envious of those who do wrong;
²for like the grass they will soon wither,
  like green plants they will soon die away.

³Trust in the LORD and do good;
  dwell in the land and enjoy safe pasture.
⁴Delight yourself in the LORD
  and he will give you the desires of your heart.

⁵Commit your way to the LORD;
  trust in him and he will do this:
⁶He will make your righteousness shine like the
    dawn,
  the justice of your cause like the noonday sun.

⁷Be still before the LORD and wait patiently for
    him;
  do not fret when men succeed in their ways,
  when they carry out their wicked schemes.

⁸Refrain from anger and turn from wrath;
  do not fret—it leads only to evil.
⁹For evil men will be cut off,
  but those who hope in the LORD will inherit the
    land.

¹⁰A little while, and the wicked will be no more;
  though you look for them, they will not be
    found.
¹¹But the meek will inherit the land
  and enjoy great peace.

¹²The wicked plot against the righteous
  and gnash their teeth at them;
¹³but the Lord laughs at the wicked,
  for he knows their day is coming.

¹⁴The wicked draw the sword
  and bend the bow
to bring down the poor and needy,
  to slay those whose ways are upright.
¹⁵But their swords will pierce their own hearts,
  and their bows will be broken.

¹⁶Better the little that the righteous have
  than the wealth of many wicked;
¹⁷for the power of the wicked will be broken,
  but the LORD upholds the righteous.

¹⁸The days of the blameless are known to the LORD,
  and their inheritance will endure for ever.
¹⁹In times of disaster they will not wither;
  in days of famine they will enjoy plenty.

²⁰But the wicked will perish:
  The LORD's enemies will be like the beauty of
    the fields,
  they will vanish—vanish like smoke.

²¹The wicked borrow and do not repay,
  but the righteous give generously;
²²those the LORD blesses will inherit the land,
  but those he curses will be cut off.

²³If the LORD delights in a man's way,
  he makes his steps firm;
²⁴though he stumble, he will not fall,
  for the LORD upholds him with his hand.

ᵃ1 Or heart: / Sin proceeds from the wicked.   ᵇ7 Or love, O God! / Men find; or love! / Both heavenly beings and men / find
ᵃThis psalm is an acrostic poem, the stanzas of which begin with the successive letters of the Hebrew alphabet.

25I was young and now I am old,
  yet I have never seen the righteous forsaken
  or their children begging bread.
26They are always generous and lend freely;
  their children will be blessed.
27Turn from evil and do good;
  then you will dwell in the land for ever.
28For the LORD loves the just
  and will not forsake his faithful ones.

  They will be protected for ever,
  but the offspring of the wicked will be cut off;
29the righteous will inherit the land
  and dwell in it for ever.

30The mouth of the righteous man utters wisdom,
  and his tongue speaks what is just.
31The law of his God is in his heart;
  his feet do not slip.
32The wicked lie in wait for the righteous,
  seeking their very lives;
33but the LORD will not leave them in their power
  or let them be condemned when brought to
  trial.

34Wait for the LORD
  and keep his way.
  He will exalt you to inherit the land;
  when the wicked are cut off, you will see it.

35I have seen a wicked and ruthless man
  flourishing like a green tree in its native soil,
36but he soon passed away and was no more;
  though I looked for him, he could not be found.

37Consider the blameless, observe the upright;
  there is a future[b] for the man of peace.
38But all sinners will be destroyed;
  the future[c] of the wicked will be cut off.

39The salvation of the righteous comes from the
  LORD;
  he is their stronghold in time of trouble.
40The LORD helps them and delivers them;
  he delivers them from the wicked and saves
  them,
  because they take refuge in him.

Psalm 38

A psalm of David. A petition.

1O LORD, do not rebuke me in your anger
  or discipline me in your wrath.
2For your arrows have pierced me,
  and your hand has come down upon me.
3Because of your wrath there is no health in my
  body;
  my bones have no soundness because of my sin.
4My guilt has overwhelmed me
  like a burden too heavy to bear.
5My wounds fester and are loathsome
  because of my sinful folly.
6I am bowed down and brought very low;
  all day long I go about mourning.

7My back is filled with searing pain;
  there is no health in my body.
8I am feeble and utterly crushed;
  I groan in anguish of heart.

38:2 The writer used an image of being struck by God with arrows. It is possible to experience life, in which things often do go wrong, in a way which makes it seem as if God is against us. The writer had obviously suffered a great deal.

9All my longings lie open before you, O Lord:
  my sighing is not hidden from you.
10My heart pounds, my strength fails me;
  even the light has gone from my eyes.
11My friends and companions avoid me because of
  my wounds;
  my neighbours stay far away.
12Those who seek my life set their traps,
  those who would harm me talk of my ruin;
  all day long they plot deception.

13I am like a deaf man, who cannot hear,
  like a mute, who cannot open his mouth;
14I have become like a man who does not hear,
  whose mouth can offer no reply.
15I wait for you, O LORD;
  you will answer, O Lord my God.
16For I said, "Do not let them gloat
  or exalt themselves over me when my foot
  slips."

17For I am about to fall,
  and my pain is ever with me.
18I confess my iniquity;
  I am troubled by my sin.
19Many are those who are my vigorous enemies;
  those who hate me without reason are
  numerous.
20Those who repay my good with evil
  slander me when I pursue what is good.

21O LORD, do not forsake me;
  be not far from me, O my God.
22Come quickly to help me,
  O Lord my Saviour.

Psalm 39

For the director of music. For Jeduthun. A psalm of David.

1I said, "I will watch my ways
  and keep my tongue from sin;
  I will put a muzzle on my mouth
  as long as the wicked are in my presence."
2But when I was silent and still,
  not even saying anything good,
  my anguish increased.
3My heart grew hot within me,
  and as I meditated, the fire burned;
  then I spoke with my tongue:

b37 Or there will be posterity   c38 Or posterity

⁴"Show me, O Lᴏʀᴅ, my life's end
and the number of my days;
let me know how fleeting is my life.
⁵You have made my days a mere handbreadth;
the span of my years is as nothing before you.
Each man's life is but a breath.   *Selah*
⁶Man is a mere phantom as he goes to and fro:
He bustles about, but only in vain;
he heaps up wealth, not knowing who will get
it.
⁷"But now, Lord, what do I look for?
My hope is in you.
⁸Save me from all my transgressions;
do not make me the scorn of fools.
⁹I was silent; I would not open my mouth,
for you are the one who has done this.
¹⁰Remove your scourge from me;
I am overcome by the blow of your hand.
¹¹You rebuke and discipline men for their sin;
you consume their wealth like a moth—
each man is but a breath.   *Selah*

39:10   Sometimes life for the writer was
just too much. It seemed hardly worth living,
and would be better if it were soon over. The
psalms have no easy answers. All that can be
done at such times is to turn imploringly to
God in prayer.

¹²"Hear my prayer, O Lᴏʀᴅ,
listen to my cry for help;
be not deaf to my weeping.
For I dwell with you as an alien,
a stranger, as all my fathers were.
¹³Look away from me, that I may rejoice again
before I depart and am no more."

Psalm 40

For the director of music. Of David. A psalm.

¹I waited patiently for the Lᴏʀᴅ;
he turned to me and heard my cry.
²He lifted me out of the slimy pit,
out of the mud and mire;
he set my feet on a rock
and gave me a firm place to stand.
³He put a new song in my mouth,
a hymn of praise to our God.
Many will see and fear
and put their trust in the Lᴏʀᴅ.

⁴Blessed is the man
who makes the Lᴏʀᴅ his trust,
who does not look to the proud,
to those who turn aside to false gods.ᵃ
⁵Many, O Lᴏʀᴅ my God,
are the wonders you have done.
The things you planned for us
no-one can recount to you;

were I to speak and tell of them,
they would be too many to declare.
⁶Sacrifice and offering you did not desire,
but my ears you have pierced;ᵇ,ᶜ
burnt offerings and sin offerings
you did not require.
⁷Then I said, "Here I am, I have come—
it is written about me in the scroll.ᵈ
⁸I desire to do your will, O my God;
your law is within my heart."
⁹I proclaim righteousness in the great assembly;
I do not seal my lips,
as you know, O Lᴏʀᴅ.
¹⁰I do not hide your righteousness in my heart;
I speak of your faithfulness and salvation.
I do not conceal your love and your truth
from the great assembly.

¹¹Do not withhold your mercy from me, O Lᴏʀᴅ;
may your love and your truth always protect
me.
¹²For troubles without number surround me;
my sins have overtaken me, and I cannot see.
They are more than the hairs of my head,
and my heart fails within me.

¹³Be pleased, O Lᴏʀᴅ, to save me;
O Lᴏʀᴅ, come quickly to help me.
¹⁴May all who seek to take my life
be put to shame and confusion;
may all who desire my ruin
be turned back in disgrace.
¹⁵May those who say to me, "Aha! Aha!"
be appalled at their own shame.
¹⁶But may all who seek you
rejoice and be glad in you;
may those who love your salvation always say,
"The Lᴏʀᴅ be exalted!"

¹⁷Yet I am poor and needy;
may the Lord think of me.
You are my help and my deliverer;
O my God, do not delay.

Psalm 41

For the director of music. A psalm of David.

¹Blessed is he who has regard for the weak;
the Lᴏʀᴅ delivers him in times of trouble.
²The Lᴏʀᴅ will protect him and preserve his life;
he will bless him in the land
and not surrender him to the desire of his foes.
³The Lᴏʀᴅ will sustain him on his sick-bed
and restore him from his bed of illness.
⁴I said, "O Lᴏʀᴅ, have mercy on me;
heal me, for I have sinned against you."
⁵My enemies say in malice,
"When will he die and his name perish?"

ᵃ4 Or *to falsehood*   ᵇ6 Hebrew; Septuagint *but a body you have prepared for me* (see also Symmachus and Theodotion)
ᶜ6 Or *opened*   ᵈ7 Or *come / with the scroll written for me*

⁶Whenever one comes to see me,
  he speaks falsely, while his heart gathers
    slander;
  then he goes out and spreads it abroad.

⁷All my enemies whisper together against me;
  they imagine the worst for me, saying,
⁸"A vile disease has beset him;
  he will never get up from the place where he
    lies."
⁹Even my close friend, whom I trusted,
  he who shared my bread,
  has lifted up his heel against me.

¹⁰But you, O LORD, have mercy on me;
  raise me up, that I may repay them.
¹¹I know that you are pleased with me,
  for my enemy does not triumph over me.
¹²In my integrity you uphold me
  and set me in your presence for ever.

¹³Praise be to the LORD, the God of Israel,
  from everlasting to everlasting.
        Amen and Amen.

42:1   The second book of psalms starts
with an evocative image of the human need
to experience God. After a good start the
experience of God had faded. The writer's
initial enthusiasm for worship had withered
as a deep longing for the presence of God had
gone unrequited.

BOOK II

Psalms 42–72

Psalm 42ᵃ

For the director of music. A *maskil*ᵇ of the Sons of Korah.

¹As the deer pants for streams of water,
  so my soul pants for you, O God.
²My soul thirsts for God, for the living God.
  When can I go and meet with God?
³My tears have been my food
    day and night,
  while men say to me all day long,
    "Where is your God?"
⁴These things I remember
    as I pour out my soul:
  how I used to go with the multitude,
  leading the procession to the house of God,
  with shouts of joy and thanksgiving
    among the festive throng.

⁵Why are you downcast, O my soul?
  Why so disturbed within me?
  Put your hope in God,
    for I will yet praise him,
    my Saviour and ⁶my God.

Myᶜ soul is downcast within me;
  therefore I will remember you
from the land of the Jordan,
  the heights of Hermon—from Mount Mizar.
⁷Deep calls to deep
  in the roar of your waterfalls;
all your waves and breakers
  have swept over me.

⁸By day the LORD directs his love,
  at night his song is with me—
  a prayer to the God of my life.

⁹I say to God my Rock,
  "Why have you forgotten me?
Why must I go about mourning,
  oppressed by the enemy?"
¹⁰My bones suffer mortal agony
  as my foes taunt me,
saying to me all day long,
  "Where is your God?"

¹¹Why are you downcast, O my soul?
  Why so disturbed within me?
  Put your hope in God,
    for I will yet praise him,
    my Saviour and my God.

Psalm 43ᵃ

¹Vindicate me, O God,
  and plead my cause against an ungodly nation;
  rescue me from deceitful and wicked men.
²You are God my stronghold.
  Why have you rejected me?
Why must I go about mourning,
  oppressed by the enemy?
³Send forth your light and your truth,
  let them guide me;
let them bring me to your holy mountain,
  to the place where you dwell.
⁴Then will I go to the altar of God,
  to God, my joy and my delight.
I will praise you with the harp,
  O God, my God.

⁵Why are you downcast, O my soul?
  Why so disturbed within me?
  Put your hope in God,
    for I will yet praise him,
    my Saviour and my God.

Psalm 44

For the director of music. Of the Sons of Korah. A *maskil*.ᵃ

¹We have heard with our ears, O God;
  our fathers have told us
what you did in their days,
  in days long ago.
²With your hand you drove out the nations
  and planted our fathers;

ᵃIn many Hebrew manuscripts Psalms 42 and 43 constitute one psalm.
ᶜ5,6 A few Hebrew manuscripts, Septuagint and Syriac; most Hebrew manuscripts *praise him for his saving help.* / ⁶O my God, my
ᵃIn many Hebrew manuscripts Psalms 42 and 43 constitute one psalm.

ᵇTitle: Probably a literary or musical term
ᵃTitle: Probably a literary or musical term

you crushed the peoples
and made our fathers flourish.
[3]It was not by their sword that they won the land,
nor did their arm bring them victory;
it was your right hand, your arm,
and the light of your face, for you loved them.

[4]You are my King and my God,
who decrees[b] victories for Jacob.
[5]Through you we push back our enemies;
through your name we trample our foes.
[6]I do not trust in my bow,
my sword does not bring me victory;
[7]but you give us victory over our enemies,
you put our adversaries to shame.
[8]In God we make our boast all day long,
and we will praise your name for ever.   *Selah*

[9]But now you have rejected and humbled us;
you no longer go out with our armies.
[10]You made us retreat before the enemy,
and our adversaries have plundered us.
[11]You gave us up to be devoured like sheep
and have scattered us among the nations.
[12]You sold your people for a pittance,
gaining nothing from their sale.

[13]You have made us a reproach to our neighbours,
the scorn and derision of those around us.
[14]You have made us a byword among the nations;
the peoples shake their heads at us.
[15]My disgrace is before me all day long,
and my face is covered with shame
[16]at the taunts of those who reproach and revile
me,
because of the enemy, who is bent on revenge.

44:23   Once more God was silent in the
face of difficulties for the people. Why did he
let such things happen to his chosen people?
Defeat in war was a common experience,
but unfortunately defeat for the army was
often seen as defeat for the gods of the nation
as well. The psalmist was afraid that the
same thing had happened to his God too.

---

[17]All this happened to us,
though we had not forgotten you
or been false to your covenant.
[18]Our hearts had not turned back;
our feet had not strayed from your path.
[19]But you crushed us and made us a haunt for
jackals
and covered us over with deep darkness.

[20]If we had forgotten the name of our God
or spread out our hands to a foreign god,
[21]would not God have discovered it,
since he knows the secrets of the heart?

[b]4 Septuagint, Aquila and Syriac; Hebrew *King, O God;* / *command*
[b]12 Or *A Tyrian robe is among the gifts*

[22]Yet for your sake we face death all day long;
we are considered as sheep to be slaughtered.

[23]Awake, O Lord! Why do you sleep?
Rouse yourself! Do not reject us for ever.
[24]Why do you hide your face
and forget our misery and oppression?

[25]We are brought down to the dust;
our bodies cling to the ground.
[26]Rise up and help us;
redeem us because of your unfailing love.

Psalm 45

For the director of music. To ˌthe tune ofˌ "Lilies". Of the Sons of
Korah. A *maskil*.[a] A wedding song.

[1]My heart is stirred by a noble theme
as I recite my verses for the king;
my tongue is the pen of a skilful writer.

[2]You are the most excellent of men
and your lips have been anointed with grace,
since God has blessed you for ever.
[3]Gird your sword upon your side, O mighty one;
clothe yourself with splendour and majesty.
[4]In your majesty ride forth victoriously
on behalf of truth, humility and righteousness;
let your right hand display awesome deeds.
[5]Let your sharp arrows pierce the hearts of the
king's enemies;
let the nations fall beneath your feet.
[6]Your throne, O God, will last for ever and ever;
a sceptre of justice will be the sceptre of your
kingdom.
[7]You love righteousness and hate wickedness;
therefore God, your God, has set you above
your companions
by anointing you with the oil of joy.
[8]All your robes are fragrant with myrrh and aloes
and cassia;
from palaces adorned with ivory
the music of the strings makes you glad.
[9]Daughters of kings are among your honoured
women;
at your right hand is the royal bride in gold of
Ophir.

[10]Listen, O daughter, consider and give ear:
Forget your people and your father's house.
[11]The king is enthralled by your beauty;
honour him, for he is your lord.
[12]The Daughter of Tyre will come with a gift,[b]
men of wealth will seek your favour.

[13]All glorious is the princess within ˌher chamberˌ;
her gown is interwoven with gold.
[14]In embroidered garments she is led to the king;
her virgin companions follow her
and are brought to you.
[15]They are led in with joy and gladness;
they enter the palace of the king.

[a]Title: Probably a literary or musical term

16Your sons will take the place of your fathers;
  you will make them princes throughout the
  land.
17I will perpetuate your memory through all
  generations;
  therefore the nations will praise you for ever
  and ever.

Psalm 46

For the director of music. Of the Sons of Korah. According to
alamoth.^a A song.

1God is our refuge and strength,
  an ever-present help in trouble.
2Therefore we will not fear, though the earth give
  way
  and the mountains fall into the heart of the sea,
3though its waters roar and foam
  and the mountains quake with their surging.
                                        Selah

4There is a river whose streams make glad the city
  of God,
  the holy place where the Most High dwells.
5God is within her, she will not fall;
  God will help her at break of day.
6Nations are in uproar, kingdoms fall;
  he lifts his voice, the earth melts.

46:5 The temple and its surroundings
were thought to be the special dwelling place
of God. The people believed that as long as
the temple stood the city which contained it
would stand too, protected by God. In fact
this only worked as long as the people of God
reflected the holiness of God in their lives
(see Jeremiah 7:3–11).

7The LORD Almighty is with us;
  the God of Jacob is our fortress.   *Selah*

8Come and see the works of the LORD,
  the desolations he has brought on the earth.
9He makes wars cease to the ends of the earth;
  he breaks the bow and shatters the spear,
  he burns the shields^b with fire.
10"Be still, and know that I am God;
  I will be exalted among the nations,
  I will be exalted in the earth."

11The LORD Almighty is with us;
  the God of Jacob is our fortress.   *Selah*

Psalm 47

For the director of music. Of the Sons of Korah. A psalm.

1Clap your hands, all you nations;
  shout to God with cries of joy.

2How awesome is the LORD Most High,
  the great King over all the earth!
3He subdued nations under us,
  peoples under our feet.
4He chose our inheritance for us,
  the pride of Jacob, whom he loved.   *Selah*

5God has ascended amid shouts of joy,
  the LORD amid the sounding of trumpets.
6Sing praises to God, sing praises;
  sing praises to our King, sing praises.

7For God is the King of all the earth;
  sing to him a psalm^a of praise.
8God reigns over the nations;
  God is seated on his holy throne.
9The nobles of the nations assemble
  as the people of the God of Abraham,
  for the kings^b of the earth belong to God;
  he is greatly exalted.

Psalm 48

A song. A psalm of the Sons of Korah.

1Great is the LORD, and most worthy of praise,
  in the city of our God, his holy mountain.
2It is beautiful in its loftiness,
  the joy of the whole earth.
  Like the utmost heights of Zaphon^a is Mount
    Zion,
  the^b city of the Great King.
3God is in her citadels;
  he has shown himself to be her fortress.

48:2 "The Great King" was a title used
of the Assyrian kings. The psalmist used this
phrase to talk about God as it was the most
powerful image he knew to suggest what
God was like. As the Great Kings had their
palaces so did the God of Israel. His was on
Mount Zion, the temple mountain in Jerusalem.

4When the kings joined forces,
  when they advanced together,
5they saw ʟher⌋ and were astounded;
  they fled in terror.
6Trembling seized them there,
  pain like that of a woman in labour.
7You destroyed them like ships of Tarshish
  shattered by an east wind.

8As we have heard,
  so have we seen
in the city of the LORD Almighty,
  in the city of our God:
  God makes her secure for ever.   *Selah*

9Within your temple, O God,
  we meditate on your unfailing love.

---

^aTitle: Probably a musical term   ^b9 Or *chariots*   ^a7 Or a *maskil* (probably a literary or musical term)
^b9 Or *shields*   ^a2 Zaphon can refer to a sacred mountain or the direction north.
^b2 Or *earth, / Mount Zion, on the northern side / of the*

[10]Like your name, O God,
  your praise reaches to the ends of the earth;
  your right hand is filled with righteousness.
[11]Mount Zion rejoices,
  the villages of Judah are glad
  because of your judgments.

[12]Walk about Zion, go round her,
  count her towers,
[13]consider well her ramparts,
  view her citadels,
  that you may tell of them to the next
    generation.
[14]For this God is our God for ever and ever;
  he will be our guide even to the end.

Psalm 49

For the director of music. Of the Sons of Korah. A psalm.

[1]Hear this, all you peoples;
  listen, all who live in this world,
[2]both low and high,
  rich and poor alike:
[3]My mouth will speak words of wisdom;
  the utterance from my heart will give
    understanding.
[4]I will turn my ear to a proverb;
  with the harp I will expound my riddle:

[5]Why should I fear when evil days come,
  when wicked deceivers surround me—
[6]those who trust in their wealth
  and boast of their great riches?
[7]No man can redeem the life of another
  or give to God a ransom for him—
[8]the ransom for a life is costly,
  no payment is ever enough—
[9]that he should live on for ever
  and not see decay.

[10]For all can see that wise men die;
  the foolish and the senseless alike perish
  and leave their wealth to others.
[11]Their tombs will remain their houses[a] for ever,
  their dwellings for endless generations,
  though they had[b] named lands after
    themselves.

[12]But man, despite his riches, does not endure;
  he is[c] like the beasts that perish.

[13]This is the fate of those who trust in themselves,
  and of their followers, who approve their
    sayings.   *Selah*
[14]Like sheep they are destined for the grave,[d]
  and death will feed on them.
  The upright will rule over them in the morning;
  their forms will decay in the grave,[d]
  far from their princely mansions.
[15]But God will redeem my life[e] from the grave;
  he will surely take me to himself.   *Selah*

[16]Do not be overawed when a man grows rich,
  when the splendour of his house increases;
[17]for he will take nothing with him when he dies,
  his splendour will not descend with him.
[18]Though while he lived he counted himself
    blessed—
  and men praise you when you prosper—
[19]he will join the generation of his fathers,
  who will never see the light ¡of life¿.

[20]A man who has riches without understanding
  is like the beasts that perish.

Psalm 50

A psalm of Asaph.

[1]The Mighty One, God, the LORD,
  speaks and summons the earth
  from the rising of the sun to the place where it
    sets.
[2]From Zion, perfect in beauty,
  God shines forth.
[3]Our God comes and will not be silent;
  a fire devours before him,
  and around him a tempest rages.
[4]He summons the heavens above,
  and the earth, that he may judge his people:
[5]"Gather to me my consecrated ones,
  who made a covenant with me by sacrifice."
[6]And the heavens proclaim his righteousness,
  for God himself is judge.   *Selah*

50:4 God summoned the heavenly law court to try the case of Israel. God was prosecutor, chief witness, and judge in this court. The people of Israel were accused of hypocrisy for reciting God's words but failing to act on them. God suspended punishment to see if they would mend their ways. Action, not words, is God's first requirement from his people.

---

[7]"Hear, O my people, and I will speak,
  O Israel, and I will testify against you:
  I am God, your God.
[8]I do not rebuke you for your sacrifices
  or your burnt offerings, which are ever before
    me.
[9]I have no need of a bull from your stall
  or of goats from your pens,
[10]for every animal of the forest is mine,
  and the cattle on a thousand hills.
[11]I know every bird in the mountains,
  and the creatures of the field are mine.
[12]If I were hungry I would not tell you,
  for the world is mine, and all that is in it.
[13]Do I eat the flesh of bulls
  or drink the blood of goats?

---

a 11 Septuagint and Syriac; Hebrew *In their thoughts their houses will remain*
c 12 Hebrew; Septuagint and Syriac read verse 12 the same as verse 20.
e 15 Or *soul*

b 11 Or / *for they have*
d 14 Hebrew *Sheol*; also in verse 15

¹⁴Sacrifice thank-offerings to God,
  fulfil your vows to the Most High,
¹⁵and call upon me in the day of trouble;
  I will deliver you, and you will honour me."

¹⁶But to the wicked, God says:

"What right have you to recite my laws
  or take my covenant on your lips?
¹⁷You hate my instruction
  and cast my words behind you.
¹⁸When you see a thief, you join with him;
  you throw in your lot with adulterers.
¹⁹You use your mouth for evil
  and harness your tongue to deceit.
²⁰You speak continually against your brother
  and slander your own mother's son.
²¹These things you have done and I kept silent;
  you thought I was altogether* like you.
  But I will rebuke you
  and accuse you to your face.

²²"Consider this, you who forget God,
  or I will tear you to pieces, with none to
  rescue:
²³He who sacrifices thank-offerings honours me,
  and he prepares the way
  so that I may show him*b* the salvation of God."

Psalm 51

For the director of music. A psalm of David. When the prophet
Nathan came to him after David had committed adultery with
Bathsheba.

¹Have mercy on me, O God,
  according to your unfailing love;
according to your great compassion
  blot out my transgressions.
²Wash away all my iniquity
  and cleanse me from my sin.

³For I know my transgressions,
  and my sin is always before me.
⁴Against you, you only, have I sinned
  and done what is evil in your sight,
so that you are proved right when you speak
  and justified when you judge.
⁵Surely I was sinful at birth,
  sinful from the time my mother conceived me.
⁶Surely you desire truth in the inner parts;*a*
  you teach*b* me wisdom in the inmost place.

⁷Cleanse me with hyssop, and I shall be clean;
  wash me, and I shall be whiter than snow.
⁸Let me hear joy and gladness;
  let the bones you have crushed rejoice.
⁹Hide your face from my sins
  and blot out all my iniquity.

¹⁰Create in me a pure heart, O God,
  and renew a steadfast spirit within me.
¹¹Do not cast me from your presence
  or take your Holy Spirit from me.

¹²Restore to me the joy of your salvation
  and grant me a willing spirit, to sustain me.

51:10   This psalm is linked to one of the
worst incidents in David's chequered career.
After his adultery with Bathsheba he was
rebuked by the prophet Nathan (see
2 Samuel 11 and 12). He learned the hard
way that God is concerned with what is
going on inside a person's heart and not in
an outward show of religion.

¹³Then I will teach transgressors your ways,
  and sinners will turn back to you.
¹⁴Save me from bloodguilt, O God,
  the God who saves me,
  and my tongue will sing of your righteousness.
¹⁵O Lord, open my lips,
  and my mouth will declare your praise.
¹⁶You do not delight in sacrifice, or I would bring it;
  you do not take pleasure in burnt offerings.
¹⁷The sacrifices of God are*c* a broken spirit;
  a broken and contrite heart,
  O God, you will not despise.

¹⁸In your good pleasure make Zion prosper;
  build up the walls of Jerusalem.
¹⁹Then there will be righteous sacrifices,
  whole burnt offerings to delight you;
  then bulls will be offered on your altar.

Psalm 52

For the director of music. A *maskil*ᵃ of David. When Doeg the
Edomite had gone to Saul and told him: "David has gone to the
house of Ahimelech."

¹Why do you boast of evil, you mighty man?
  Why do you boast all day long,
  you who are a disgrace in the eyes of God?
²Your tongue plots destruction;
  it is like a sharpened razor,
  you who practise deceit.
³You love evil rather than good,
  falsehood rather than speaking the truth.   *Selah*
⁴You love every harmful word,
  O you deceitful tongue!

⁵Surely God will bring you down to everlasting
  ruin:
  He will snatch you up and tear you from your
  tent;
  he will uproot you from the land of the living.
                                            Selah
⁶The righteous will see and fear;
  they will laugh at him, saying,
⁷"Here now is the man
  who did not make God his stronghold
but trusted in his great wealth
  and grew strong by destroying others!"

---

*a*21 Or thought the 'I AM' was   *b*23 Or and to him who considers his way / I will show
*a*6 The meaning of the Hebrew for this phrase is uncertain.   *b*6 Or you desired . . . ; / you taught
*c*17 Or My sacrifice, O God, is   *a*Title: Probably a literary or musical term

8But I am like an olive tree
  flourishing in the house of God;
I trust in God's unfailing love
  for ever and ever.
9I will praise you for ever for what you have done;
  in your name I will hope, for your name is
    good.
I will praise you in the presence of your saints.

52:5 The Israelites had a strong sense of
natural justice. If someone had done something wrong they would surely suffer the
consequences. Even if evil people seemed to
be benefiting from their actions they would
eventually be brought to nothing. The person
who spends time in God's presence instead
of exploiting the poor will eventually prosper.

Psalm 53

For the director of music. According to *mahalath.*[a] A *maskil*[b]
of David.

1The fool says in his heart,
  "There is no God."
They are corrupt, and their ways are vile;
  there is no-one who does good.

2God looks down from heaven
  on the sons of men
to see if there are any who understand,
  any who seek God.
3Everyone has turned away,
  they have together become corrupt;
there is no-one who does good,
  not even one.

4Will the evildoers never learn—
  those who devour my people as men eat bread
  and who do not call on God?
5There they were, overwhelmed with dread,
  where there was nothing to dread.
God scattered the bones of those who attacked
    you;
  you put them to shame, for God despised them.

6Oh, that salvation for Israel would come out of
    Zion!
  When God restores the fortunes of his people,
  let Jacob rejoice and Israel be glad!

Psalm 54

For the director of music. With stringed instruments. A *maskil*[a]
of David. When the Ziphites had gone to Saul and said, "Is not
David hiding among us?"

1Save me, O God, by your name;
  vindicate me by your might.

2Hear my prayer, O God;
  listen to the words of my mouth.

3Strangers are attacking me;
  ruthless men seek my life—
  men without regard for God.   *Selah*

4Surely God is my help;
  the Lord is the one who sustains me.

5Let evil recoil on those who slander me;
  in your faithfulness destroy them.

6I will sacrifice a freewill offering to you;
  I will praise your name, O LORD,
  for it is good.
7For he has delivered me from all my troubles,
  and my eyes have looked in triumph on my foes.

Psalm 55

For the director of music. With stringed instruments. A *maskil*[a]
of David.

1Listen to my prayer, O God,
  do not ignore my plea;
2 hear me and answer me.
My thoughts trouble me and I am distraught
3 at the voice of the enemy,
  at the stares of the wicked;
for they bring down suffering upon me
  and revile me in their anger.

4My heart is in anguish within me;
  the terrors of death assail me.
5Fear and trembling have beset me;
  horror has overwhelmed me.
6I said, "Oh, that I had the wings of a dove!
  I would fly away and be at rest—
7I would flee far away
  and stay in the desert;   *Selah*
8I would hurry to my place of shelter,
  far from the tempest and storm."

9Confuse the wicked, O Lord, confound their
    speech,
  for I see violence and strife in the city.
10Day and night they prowl about on its walls;
  malice and abuse are within it.
11Destructive forces are at work in the city;
  threats and lies never leave its streets.

12If an enemy were insulting me,
  I could endure it;
if a foe were raising himself against me,
  I could hide from him.
13But it is you, a man like myself,
  my companion, my close friend,
14with whom I once enjoyed sweet fellowship
  as we walked with the throng at the house of
    God.

15Let death take my enemies by surprise;
  let them go down alive to the grave,[b]
  for evil finds lodging among them.

---

[a]Title: Probably a musical term   [b]Title: Probably a literary or musical term   [a]Title: Probably a literary or musical term
[a]Title: Probably a literary or musical term   [b]15 Hebrew *Sheol*

16But I call to God,
and the LORD saves me.
17Evening, morning and noon
I cry out in distress,
and he hears my voice.
18He ransoms me unharmed
from the battle waged against me,
even though many oppose me.
19God, who is enthroned for ever,
will hear them and afflict them—   *Selah*
men who never change their ways
and have no fear of God.

20My companion attacks his friends;
he violates his covenant.
21His speech is smooth as butter,
yet war is in his heart;
his words are more soothing than oil,
yet they are drawn swords.

22Cast your cares on the LORD
and he will sustain you;
he will never let the righteous fall.
23But you, O God, will bring down the wicked
into the pit of corruption;
bloodthirsty and deceitful men
will not live out half their days.

But as for me, I trust in you.

Psalm 56

For the director of music. To the tune of, "A Dove on Distant
Oaks". Of David. A *miktam.* ª When the Philistines had seized
him in Gath.

1Be merciful to me, O God, for men hotly pursue
me;
all day long they press their attack.
2My slanderers pursue me all day long;
many are attacking me in their pride.

3When I am afraid,
I will trust in you.
4In God, whose word I praise,
in God I trust; I will not be afraid.
What can mortal man do to me?

5All day long they twist my words;
they are always plotting to harm me.
6They conspire, they lurk,
they watch my steps,
eager to take my life.

7On no account let them escape;
in your anger, O God, bring down the nations.
8Record my lament;
list my tears on your scrollᵇ—
are they not in your record?

9Then my enemies will turn back
when I call for help.
By this I will know that God is for me.
10In God, whose word I praise,
in the LORD, whose word I praise—

11in God I trust; I will not be afraid.
What can man do to me?

12I am under vows to you, O God;
I will present my thank-offerings to you.
13For you have delivered meᶜ from death
and my feet from stumbling,
that I may walk before God
in the light of life. ᵈ

Psalm 57

For the director of music. To the tune of, "Do Not Destroy". Of
David. A *miktam.* ª When he had fled from Saul into the cave.

1Have mercy on me, O God, have mercy on me,
for in you my soul takes refuge.
I will take refuge in the shadow of your wings
until the disaster has passed.

2I cry out to God Most High,
to God, who fulfils his purpose for me.
3He sends from heaven and saves me,
rebuking those who hotly pursue me;   *Selah*
God sends his love and his faithfulness.

4I am in the midst of lions;
I lie among ravenous beasts—
men whose teeth are spears and arrows,
whose tongues are sharp swords.

5Be exalted, O God, above the heavens;
let your glory be over all the earth.

6They spread a net for my feet—
I was bowed down in distress.
They dug a pit in my path—
but they have fallen into it themselves.   *Selah*

7My heart is steadfast, O God,
my heart is steadfast;
I will sing and make music.
8Awake, my soul!
Awake, harp and lyre!
I will awaken the dawn.

9I will praise you, O Lord, among the nations;
I will sing of you among the peoples.
10For great is your love, reaching to the heavens;
your faithfulness reaches to the skies.

11Be exalted, O God, above the heavens;
let your glory be over all the earth.

Psalm 58

For the director of music. To the tune of, "Do Not Destroy".
Of David. A *miktam.* ª

1Do you rulers indeed speak justly?
Do you judge uprightly among men?
2No, in your heart you devise injustice,
and your hands mete out violence on the earth.
3Even from birth the wicked go astray;
from the womb they are wayward and speak
lies.

ªTitle: Probably a literary or musical term   ᵇ8 Or / put my tears in your wineskin   ᶜ13 Or my soul
ᵈ13 Or the land of the living   ªTitle: Probably a literary or musical term   ªTitle: Probably a literary or musical term

⁴Their venom is like the venom of a snake,
  like that of a cobra that has stopped its ears,
⁵that will not heed the tune of the charmer,
  however skilful the enchanter may be.

⁶Break the teeth in their mouths, O God;
  tear out, O LORD, the fangs of the lions!
⁷Let them vanish like water that flows away;
  when they draw the bow, let their arrows be
    blunted.
⁸Like a slug melting away as it moves along,
  like a stillborn child, may they not see the sun.

58:8 Here, another graphic description captures the sense of outrage felt by the writer as he experienced the injustice of Israel's rulers. This outrage led to violent language at the end of the psalm when the writer used the image of the righteous bathing their feet in the blood of the wicked. Canaanite poets described their goddess of love and war doing the same thing in the blood of her enemies.

---

⁹Before your pots can feel ₍the heat of₎ the
    thorns —
  whether they be green or dry — the wicked will
    be swept away.ᵇ
¹⁰The righteous will be glad when they are
    avenged,
  when they bathe their feet in the blood of the
    wicked.
¹¹Then men will say,
  "Surely the righteous still are rewarded;
  surely there is a God who judges the earth."

Psalm 59

For the director of music. ₍To the tune of₎ "Do Not Destroy". Of David. A *miktam.*ᵃ When Saul had sent men to watch David's house in order to kill him.

¹Deliver me from my enemies, O God;
  protect me from those who rise up against me.
²Deliver me from evildoers
  and save me from bloodthirsty men.

³See how they lie in wait for me!
  Fierce men conspire against me
  for no offence or sin of mine, O LORD.
⁴I have done no wrong, yet they are ready to
    attack me.
  Arise to help me; look on my plight!
⁵O LORD God Almighty, the God of Israel,
  rouse yourself to punish all the nations;
  show no mercy to wicked traitors.   *Selah*

⁶They return at evening,
  snarling like dogs,
  and prowl about the city.

⁷See what they spew from their mouths —
  they spew out swords from their lips,
  and they say, "Who can hear us?"
⁸But you, O LORD, laugh at them;
  you scoff at all those nations.

⁹O my Strength, I watch for you;
  you, O God, are my fortress, ¹⁰my loving God.

God will go before me
  and will let me gloat over those who slander
    me.
¹¹But do not kill them, O Lord our shield,ᵇ
  or my people will forget.
In your might make them wander about,
  and bring them down.
¹²For the sins of their mouths,
  for the words of their lips,
  let them be caught in their pride.
For the curses and lies they utter,
¹³ consume them in wrath,
  consume them till they are no more.
Then it will be known to the ends of the earth
  that God rules over Jacob.   *Selah*

59:14 Here, vivid descriptions are used again. Hungry snarling dogs provided a suitably vicious image for the writer to describe his enemies. He was not afraid to call on God to deal with those who opposed him, and he did not have any concept of love for his enemies. But his troubles did lead him to praise God for his protection.

---

¹⁴They return at evening,
  snarling like dogs,
  and prowl about the city.
¹⁵They wander about for food
  and howl if not satisfied.
¹⁶But I will sing of your strength,
  in the morning I will sing of your love;
for you are my fortress,
  my refuge in times of trouble.

¹⁷O my Strength, I sing praise to you;
  you, O God, are my fortress, my loving God.

Psalm 60

For the director of music. To ₍the tune of₎ "The Lily of the Covenant". A *miktam*ᵃ of David. For teaching. When he fought Aram Naharaimᵇ and Aram Zobah,ᶜ and when Joab returned and struck down twelve thousand Edomites in the Valley of Salt.

¹You have rejected us, O God, and burst forth
    upon us;
  you have been angry — now restore us!
²You have shaken the land and torn it open;
  mend its fractures, for it is quaking.
³You have shown your people desperate times;
  you have given us wine that makes us stagger.

ᵇ9 The meaning of the Hebrew for this verse is uncertain.
ᵇ11 Or *sovereign*   ᵃTitle: Probably a literary or musical term
ᶜTitle: That is, Arameans of central Syria

ᵃTitle: Probably a literary or musical term
ᵇTitle: That is, Arameans of North-west Mesopotamia

4But for those who fear you, you have raised a
banner
  to be unfurled against the bow.   *Selah*

5Save us and help us with your right hand,
  that those you love may be delivered.
6God has spoken from his sanctuary:
  "In triumph I will parcel out Shechem
  and measure off the Valley of Succoth.
7Gilead is mine, and Manasseh is mine;
  Ephraim is my helmet,
  Judah my sceptre.
8Moab is my washbasin,
  upon Edom I toss my sandal;
  over Philistia I shout in triumph."

9Who will bring me to the fortified city?
  Who will lead me to Edom?
10Is it not you, O God, you who have rejected us
  and no longer go out with our armies?
11Give us aid against the enemy,
  for the help of man is worthless.
12With God we shall gain the victory,
  and he will trample down our enemies.

Psalm 61

For the director of music. With stringed instruments. Of David.

1Hear my cry, O God;
  listen to my prayer.

2From the ends of the earth I call to you,
  I call as my heart grows faint;
  lead me to the rock that is higher than I.
3For you have been my refuge,
  a strong tower against the foe.

4I long to dwell in your tent for ever
  and take refuge in the shelter of your wings.
                                               Selah

5For you have heard my vows, O God;
  you have given me the heritage of those who
  fear your name.

6Increase the days of the king's life,
  his years for many generations.
7May he be enthroned in God's presence for ever;
  appoint your love and faithfulness to protect
  him.

8Then will I ever sing praise to your name
  and fulfil my vows day after day.

Psalm 62

For the director of music. For Jeduthun. A psalm of David.

1My soul finds rest in God alone;
  my salvation comes from him.
2He alone is my rock and my salvation;
  he is my fortress, I shall never be shaken.

3How long will you assault a man?
  Would all of you throw him down—
  this leaning wall, this tottering fence?

4They fully intend to topple him
  from his lofty place;
  they take delight in lies.
With their mouths they bless,
  but in their hearts they curse.   *Selah*

5Find rest, O my soul, in God alone;
  my hope comes from him.
6He alone is my rock and my salvation;
  he is my fortress, I shall not be shaken.
7My salvation and my honour depend on God;[a]
  he is my mighty rock, my refuge.
8Trust in him at all times, O people;
  pour out your hearts to him,
  for God is our refuge.   *Selah*

9Lowborn men are but a breath,
  the highborn are but a lie;
  if weighed on a balance, they are nothing;
  together they are only a breath.
10Do not trust in extortion
  or take pride in stolen goods;
  though your riches increase,
  do not set your heart on them.

11One thing God has spoken,
  two things have I heard:
  that you, O God, are strong,
12 and that you, O Lord, are loving.
Surely you will reward each person
  according to what he has done.

Psalm 63

A psalm of David. When he was in the Desert of Judah.

1O God, you are my God,
  earnestly I seek you;
  my soul thirsts for you,
  my body longs for you,
  in a dry and weary land
  where there is no water.

63:1   Anyone who has spent time in the
desert will know it is wonderful to have
water. The psalmist expressed his longing for
God in the image of someone desperate for
a sip of water.

2I have seen you in the sanctuary
  and beheld your power and your glory.
3Because your love is better than life,
  my lips will glorify you.
4I will praise you as long as I live,
  and in your name I will lift up my hands.
5My soul will be satisfied as with the richest of
  foods;
  with singing lips my mouth will praise you.

6On my bed I remember you;
  I think of you through the watches of the night.
7Because you are my help,
  I sing in the shadow of your wings.

---

a 7 Or / God Most High is my salvation and my honour

[8]My soul clings to you;
  your right hand upholds me.

[9]They who seek my life will be destroyed;
  they will go down to the depths of the earth.
[10]They will be given over to the sword
  and become food for jackals.

[11]But the king will rejoice in God;
  all who swear by God's name will praise him,
  while the mouths of liars will be silenced.

Psalm 64

For the director of music. A psalm of David.

[1]Hear me, O God, as I voice my complaint;
  protect my life from the threat of the enemy.
[2]Hide me from the conspiracy of the wicked,
  from that noisy crowd of evildoers.

[3]They sharpen their tongues like swords
  and aim their words like deadly arrows.
[4]They shoot from ambush at the innocent man;
  they shoot at him suddenly, without fear.

[5]They encourage each other in evil plans,
  they talk about hiding their snares;
  they say, "Who will see them?"[a]
[6]They plot injustice and say,
  "We have devised a perfect plan!"
  Surely the mind and heart of man are cunning.

[7]But God will shoot them with arrows;
  suddenly they will be struck down.
[8]He will turn their own tongues against them
  and bring them to ruin;
  all who see them will shake their heads in
    scorn.

[9]All mankind will fear;
  they will proclaim the works of God
  and ponder what he has done.
[10]Let the righteous rejoice in the LORD
  and take refuge in him;
  let all the upright in heart praise him!

Psalm 65

For the director of music. A psalm of David. A song.

[1]Praise awaits[a] you, O God, in Zion;
  to you our vows will be fulfilled.
[2]O you who hear prayer,
  to you all men will come.
[3]When we were overwhelmed by sins,
  you forgave[b] our transgressions.
[4]Blessed are those you choose
  and bring near to live in your courts!
  We are filled with the good things of your house,
  of your holy temple.

[5]You answer us with awesome deeds of
    righteousness,
  O God our Saviour,

the hope of all the ends of the earth
  and of the farthest seas,
[6]who formed the mountains by your power,
  having armed yourself with strength,
[7]who stilled the roaring of the seas,
  the roaring of their waves,
  and the turmoil of the nations.
[8]Those living far away fear your wonders;
  where morning dawns and evening fades
  you call forth songs of joy.

65:9 A plentiful harvest was a sign of God's blessing. In a time without mechanical or chemical aids farmers were very much at the mercy of natural forces. In fact it was not nature but God who was seen to be directly responsible for the productivity of the land.

---

[9]You care for the land and water it;
  you enrich it abundantly.
  The streams of God are filled with water
  to provide the people with corn,
  for so you have ordained it.[c]
[10]You drench its furrows
  and level its ridges;
  you soften it with showers
  and bless its crops.
[11]You crown the year with your bounty,
  and your carts overflow with abundance.
[12]The grasslands of the desert overflow;
  the hills are clothed with gladness.
[13]The meadows are covered with flocks
  and the valleys are mantled with corn;
  they shout for joy and sing.

Psalm 66

For the director of music. A song. A psalm.

[1]Shout with joy to God, all the earth!
[2] Sing the glory of his name;
  make his praise glorious!
[3]Say to God, "How awesome are your deeds!
  So great is your power
  that your enemies cringe before you.
[4]All the earth bows down to you;
  they sing praise to you,
  they sing praise to your name."   *Selah*

[5]Come and see what God has done,
  how awesome his works on man's behalf!
[6]He turned the sea into dry land,
  they passed through the waters on foot—
  come, let us rejoice in him.
[7]He rules for ever by his power,
  his eyes watch the nations—
  let not the rebellious rise up against him. *Selah*

[8]Praise our God, O peoples,
  let the sound of his praise be heard;
[9]he has preserved our lives
  and kept our feet from slipping.

---

a5 Or *us*   *a1* Or *befits*; the meaning of the Hebrew for this word is uncertain.   *b3* Or *made atonement for*
c9 Or *for that is how you prepare the land*

¹⁰For you, O God, tested us;
　　you refined us like silver.
¹¹You brought us into prison
　　and laid burdens on our backs.
¹²You let men ride over our heads;
　　we went through fire and water,
　　but you brought us to a place of abundance.

¹³I will come to your temple with burnt offerings
　　and fulfil my vows to you—
¹⁴vows my lips promised and my mouth spoke
　　when I was in trouble.
¹⁵I will sacrifice fat animals to you
　　and an offering of rams;
　　I will offer bulls and goats.   Selah

66:16   The people of Israel experienced
at least as much trouble as any other small
nation in those times. But the psalmist was
able to look back to the exodus and his own
experience to see that God had been with
the people all the time. The difficulties they
experienced were a test of faith in their Lord.

---

¹⁶Come and listen, all you who fear God;
　　let me tell you what he has done for me.
¹⁷I cried out to him with my mouth;
　　his praise was on my tongue.
¹⁸If I had cherished sin in my heart,
　　the Lord would not have listened;
¹⁹but God has surely listened
　　and heard my voice in prayer.
²⁰Praise be to God,
　　who has not rejected my prayer
　　or withheld his love from me!

Psalm 67

For the director of music. With stringed instruments. A psalm.
A song.

¹May God be gracious to us and bless us
　　and make his face shine upon us,   Selah
²that your ways may be known on earth,
　　your salvation among all nations.

³May the peoples praise you, O God;
　　may all the peoples praise you.
⁴May the nations be glad and sing for joy,
　　for you rule the peoples justly
　　and guide the nations of the earth.   Selah
⁵May the peoples praise you, O God;
　　may all the peoples praise you.

⁶Then the land will yield its harvest,
　　and God, our God, will bless us.
⁷God will bless us,
　　and all the ends of the earth will fear him.

Psalm 68

For the director of music. Of David. A psalm. A song.

¹May God arise, may his enemies be scattered;
　　may his foes flee before him.
²As smoke is blown away by the wind,
　　may you blow them away;
as wax melts before the fire,
　　may the wicked perish before God.
³But may the righteous be glad
　　and rejoice before God;
　　may they be happy and joyful.

⁴Sing to God, sing praise to his name,
　　extol him who rides on the clouds[a]—
his name is the Lord—
　　and rejoice before him.
⁵A father to the fatherless, a defender of widows,
　　is God in his holy dwelling.
⁶God sets the lonely in families,[b]
　　he leads forth the prisoners with singing;
　　but the rebellious live in a sun-scorched land.

⁷When you went out before your people, O God,
　　when you marched through the wasteland,
　　　　　　　　　　　　　　　　　　　Selah
⁸the earth shook,
　　the heavens poured down rain,
before God, the One of Sinai,
　　before God, the God of Israel.
⁹You gave abundant showers, O God;
　　you refreshed your weary inheritance.
¹⁰Your people settled in it,
　　and from your bounty, O God, you provided for
　　the poor.

¹¹The Lord announced the word,
　　and great was the company of those who
　　proclaimed it:
¹²"Kings and armies flee in haste;
　　in the camps men divide the plunder.
¹³Even while you sleep among the campfires,[c]
　　the wings of ⌐my⌐ dove are sheathed with silver,
　　its feathers with shining gold."
¹⁴When the Almighty[d] scattered the kings in the
　　land,
　　it was like snow fallen on Zalmon.

¹⁵The mountains of Bashan are majestic mountains;
　　rugged are the mountains of Bashan.
¹⁶Why gaze in envy, O rugged mountains,
　　at the mountain where God chooses to reign,
　　where the Lord himself will dwell for ever?
¹⁷The chariots of God are tens of thousands
　　and thousands of thousands;
　　the Lord ⌐has come⌐ from Sinai into his
　　sanctuary.
¹⁸When you ascended on high,
　　you led captives in your train;
　　you received gifts from men,
even from[e] the rebellious—
　　that you,[f] O Lord God, might dwell there.

ᵃ4 Or / prepare the way for him who rides through the deserts   ᵇ6 Or the desolate in a homeland   ᶜ13 Or saddlebags
ᵈ14 Hebrew Shaddai   ᵉ18 Or gifts for men, / even   ᶠ18 Or they

¹⁹Praise be to the Lord, to God our Saviour,
    who daily bears our burdens.   *Selah*
²⁰Our God is a God who saves;
    from the Sovereign LORD comes escape from
    death.

²¹Surely God will crush the heads of his enemies,
    the hairy crowns of those who go on in their
    sins.
²²The Lord says, "I will bring them from Bashan;
    I will bring them from the depths of the sea,
²³that you may plunge your feet in the blood of
    your foes,
    while the tongues of your dogs have their
    share."

68:24   It is very probable that many of
the psalms were sung in worship in the temple. Quite how they were used is difficult to
determine. Their construction allows some
to be sung in two parts, half a verse at a time.
Others have a chorus (e.g. Psalm 136) or a
repeated verse. There were other major festival occasions involving processions of singers
and musicians. Such processions were led by
a symbol of the presence of the Lord, probably the ark of the covenant from the innermost part of the temple (see 2 Samuel
6:3–5).

---

²⁴Your procession has come into view, O God,
    the procession of my God and King into the
    sanctuary.
²⁵In front are the singers, after them the musicians;
    with them are the maidens playing tambourines.
²⁶Praise God in the great congregation;
    praise the LORD in the assembly of Israel.
²⁷There is the little tribe of Benjamin, leading
    them,
    there the great throng of Judah's princes,
    and there the princes of Zebulun and of
    Naphtali.

²⁸Summon your power, O God;^g
    show us your strength, O God, as you have
    done before.
²⁹Because of your temple at Jerusalem
    kings will bring you gifts.
³⁰Rebuke the beast among the reeds,
    the herd of bulls among the calves of the
    nations.
Humbled, may it bring bars of silver.
Scatter the nations who delight in war.
³¹Envoys will come from Egypt;
    Cush^h will submit herself to God.

³²Sing to God, O kingdoms of the earth,
    sing praise to the Lord,   *Selah*
³³to him who rides the ancient skies above,
    who thunders with mighty voice.

³⁴Proclaim the power of God,
    whose majesty is over Israel,
    whose power is in the skies.
³⁵You are awesome, O God, in your sanctuary;
    the God of Israel gives power and strength to
    his people.

Praise be to God!

Psalm 69

For the director of music. To ˏthe tune of̡ "Lilies". Of David.

¹Save me, O God,
    for the waters have come up to my neck.
²I sink in the miry depths,
    where there is no foothold.
I have come into the deep waters;
    the floods engulf me.
³I am worn out calling for help;
    my throat is parched.
My eyes fail,
    looking for my God.
⁴Those who hate me without reason
    outnumber the hairs of my head;
many are my enemies without cause,
    those who seek to destroy me.
I am forced to restore
    what I did not steal.

⁵You know my folly, O God;
    my guilt is not hidden from you.

69:9   This psalm records the desolate cry
of a righteous person who was suffering
because of his devotion to God and his temple. Even his family had rejected him. Like
many other psalms it is attributed to David,
one of the heroes of Israel. None of David's
glorious deeds are mentioned here. Rather,
he is portrayed as a helpless victim because
of his faith. This psalm was seized on by New
Testament writers to give meaning to Jesus'
suffering and rejection (see John 2:17 and
Romans 15:3). However, Jesus asked for forgiveness for his enemies rather than heaping
curses on them as this psalmist does.

---

⁶May those who hope in you
    not be disgraced because of me,
    O Lord, the LORD Almighty;
may those who seek you
    not be put to shame because of me,
    O God of Israel.
⁷For I endure scorn for your sake,
    and shame covers my face.
⁸I am a stranger to my brothers,
    an alien to my own mother's sons;
⁹for zeal for your house consumes me,
    and the insults of those who insult you fall on
    me.

---

g28 Many Hebrew manuscripts, Septuagint and Syriac; most Hebrew manuscripts *Your God has summoned power for you*
h31 That is, the upper Nile region

¹⁰When I weep and fast,
　　I must endure scorn;
¹¹when I put on sackcloth,
　　people make sport of me.
¹²Those who sit at the gate mock me,
　　and I am the song of the drunkards.

¹³But I pray to you, O Lᴏʀᴅ,
　　in the time of your favour;
　in your great love, O God,
　　answer me with your sure salvation.
¹⁴Rescue me from the mire,
　　do not let me sink;
　deliver me from those who hate me,
　　from the deep waters.
¹⁵Do not let the floodwaters engulf me
　　or the depths swallow me up
　　or the pit close its mouth over me.
¹⁶Answer me, O Lᴏʀᴅ, out of the goodness of your
　　love;
　in your great mercy turn to me.
¹⁷Do not hide your face from your servant;
　　answer me quickly, for I am in trouble.
¹⁸Come near and rescue me;
　　redeem me because of my foes.

¹⁹You know how I am scorned, disgraced and
　　shamed;
　all my enemies are before you.
²⁰Scorn has broken my heart
　　and has left me helpless;
　I looked for sympathy, but there was none,
　　for comforters, but I found none.
²¹They put gall in my food
　　and gave me vinegar for my thirst.

²²May the table set before them become a snare;
　　may it become retribution andᵃ a trap.
²³May their eyes be darkened so that they cannot
　　see,
　and their backs be bent for ever.
²⁴Pour out your wrath on them;
　　let your fierce anger overtake them.
²⁵May their place be deserted;
　　let there be no-one to dwell in their tents.
²⁶For they persecute those you wound
　　and talk about the pain of those you hurt.
²⁷Charge them with crime upon crime;
　　do not let them share in your salvation.
²⁸May they be blotted out of the book of life
　　and not be listed with the righteous.

²⁹I am in pain and distress;
　　may your salvation, O God, protect me.

³⁰I will praise God's name in song
　　and glorify him with thanksgiving.
³¹This will please the Lᴏʀᴅ more than an ox,
　　more than a bull with its horns and hoofs.
³²The poor will see and be glad—
　　you who seek God, may your hearts live!
³³The Lᴏʀᴅ hears the needy
　　and does not despise his captive people.

³⁴Let heaven and earth praise him,
　　the seas and all that move in them,
³⁵for God will save Zion
　　and rebuild the cities of Judah.
Then people will settle there and possess it;
³⁶　the children of his servants will inherit it,
　　and those who love his name will dwell there.

Psalm 70

For the director of music. Of David. A petition.

¹Hasten, O God, to save me;
　O Lᴏʀᴅ, come quickly to help me.
²May those who seek my life
　　be put to shame and confusion;
　may all who desire my ruin
　　be turned back in disgrace.
³May those who say to me, "Aha! Aha!"
　　turn back because of their shame.
⁴But may all who seek you
　　rejoice and be glad in you;
　may those who love your salvation always say,
　　"Let God be exalted!"

⁵Yet I am poor and needy;
　　come quickly to me, O God.
You are my help and my deliverer;
　O Lᴏʀᴅ, do not delay.

Psalm 71

¹In you, O Lᴏʀᴅ, I have taken refuge;
　　let me never be put to shame.
²Rescue me and deliver me in your righteousness;
　　turn your ear to me and save me.
³Be my rock of refuge,
　　to which I can always go;
　give the command to save me,
　　for you are my rock and my fortress.
⁴Deliver me, O my God, from the hand of the
　　wicked,
　　from the grasp of evil and cruel men.

71:2　　On a memorial stone which was
found in an ancient Egyptian temple the local
god is represented as a pair of ears. Beneath
the ears is the name of the dead person who
had been heard and was thankful. Other
stones like this were intended to encourage
prayers. The writer's long years of experience confirmed that the God of Israel heard
and answered prayers.

---

⁵For you have been my hope, O Sovereign Lᴏʀᴅ,
　　my confidence since my youth.
⁶From my birth I have relied on you;
　　you brought me forth from my mother's womb.
　I will ever praise you.
⁷I have become like a portent to many,
　　but you are my strong refuge.

ᵃ22 Or snare / and their fellowship become

⁸My mouth is filled with your praise,
  declaring your splendour all day long.

⁹Do not cast me away when I am old;
  do not forsake me when my strength is gone.
¹⁰For my enemies speak against me;
  those who wait to kill me conspire together.
¹¹They say, "God has forsaken him;
  pursue him and seize him,
  for no-one will rescue him."
¹²Be not far from me, O God;
  come quickly, O my God, to help me.
¹³May my accusers perish in shame;
  may those who want to harm me
  be covered with scorn and disgrace.

¹⁴But as for me, I shall always have hope;
  I will praise you more and more.
¹⁵My mouth will tell of your righteousness,
  of your salvation all day long,
  though I know not its measure.
¹⁶I will come and proclaim your mighty acts,
  O Sovereign LORD;
  I will proclaim your righteousness, yours alone.
¹⁷Since my youth, O God, you have taught me,
  and to this day I declare your marvellous deeds.
¹⁸Even when I am old and grey,
  do not forsake me, O God,
  till I declare your power to the next generation,
  your might to all who are to come.

¹⁹Your righteousness reaches to the skies, O God,
  you who have done great things.
  Who, O God, is like you?
²⁰Though you have made me see troubles, many
      and bitter,
  you will restore my life again;
  from the depths of the earth
  you will again bring me up.
²¹You will increase my honour
  and comfort me once again.

²²I will praise you with the harp
  for your faithfulness, O my God;
  I will sing praise to you with the lyre,
  O Holy One of Israel.
²³My lips will shout for joy
  when I sing praise to you—
  I, whom you have redeemed.
²⁴My tongue will tell of your righteous acts
  all day long,
  for those who wanted to harm me
  have been put to shame and confusion.

Psalm 72

Of Solomon.

¹Endow the king with your justice, O God,
  the royal son with your righteousness.
²He willᵃ judge your people in righteousness,
  your afflicted ones with justice.

³The mountains will bring prosperity to the
      people,
  the hills the fruit of righteousness.
⁴He will defend the afflicted among the people
  and save the children of the needy;
  he will crush the oppressor.

72:1   This psalm is attributed to Solomon. It certainly reflects some of the aspects of the story of Solomon in 1 Kings. However, it could easily be applied to any of the kings of Israel on the day of coronation when such hopes and aspirations for a powerful and successful reign could be voiced.

---

⁵He will endureᵇ as long as the sun,
  as long as the moon, through all generations.
⁶He will be like rain falling on a mown field,
  like showers watering the earth.
⁷In his days the righteous will flourish;
  prosperity will abound till the moon is no more.

⁸He will rule from sea to sea
  and from the Riverᶜ to the ends of the earth.ᵈ
⁹The desert tribes will bow before him
  and his enemies will lick the dust.
¹⁰The kings of Tarshish and of distant shores
  will bring tribute to him;
  the kings of Sheba and Seba
  will present him gifts.
¹¹All kings will bow down to him
  and all nations will serve him.

¹²For he will deliver the needy who cry out,
  the afflicted who have no-one to help.
¹³He will take pity on the weak and the needy
  and save the needy from death.
¹⁴He will rescue them from oppression and
      violence,
  for precious is their blood in his sight.

¹⁵Long may he live!
  May gold from Sheba be given to him.
  May people ever pray for him
  and bless him all day long.
¹⁶Let corn abound throughout the land;
  on the tops of the hills may it sway.
  Let its fruit flourish like Lebanon;
  let it thrive like the grass of the field.
¹⁷May his name endure for ever;
  may it continue as long as the sun.

  All nations will be blessed through him,
  and they will call him blessed.

¹⁸Praise be to the LORD God, the God of Israel,
  who alone does marvellous deeds.
¹⁹Praise be to his glorious name for ever;
  may the whole earth be filled with his glory.
          Amen and Amen.

ᵃ2 Or *May he*; similarly in verses 3–11 and 17   ᵇ5 Septuagint; Hebrew *You will be feared*   ᶜ8 That is, the Euphrates
ᵈ8 Or *the end of the land*

20This concludes the prayers of David son of Jesse.

BOOK III

Psalms 73–89

Psalm 73

A psalm of Asaph.

1Surely God is good to Israel,
to those who are pure in heart.

2But as for me, my feet had almost slipped;
I had nearly lost my foothold.

3For I envied the arrogant
when I saw the prosperity of the wicked.

73:2   It is difficult to avoid envying the material prosperity of others who are better off. It is even harder to cope with when they obviously don't care about God. Wickedness does pay—or does it? Material wealth and possessions can be destroyed as quickly as they are acquired. Real prosperity is to be found only in the presence of God.

4They have no struggles;
their bodies are healthy and strong.ᵃ

5They are free from the burdens common to man;
they are not plagued by human ills.

6Therefore pride is their necklace;
they clothe themselves with violence.

7From their callous hearts comes iniquity;ᵇ
the evil conceits of their minds know no limits.

8They scoff, and speak with malice;
in their arrogance they threaten oppression.

9Their mouths lay claim to heaven,
and their tongues take possession of the earth.

10Therefore their people turn to them
and drink up waters in abundance.ᶜ

11They say, "How can God know?
Does the Most High have knowledge?"

12This is what the wicked are like—
always carefree, they increase in wealth.

13Surely in vain have I kept my heart pure;
in vain have I washed my hands in innocence.

14All day long I have been plagued;
I have been punished every morning.

15If I had said, "I will speak thus,"
I would have betrayed your children.

16When I tried to understand all this,
it was oppressive to me

17till I entered the sanctuary of God;
then I understood their final destiny.

18Surely you place them on slippery ground;
you cast them down to ruin.

19How suddenly are they destroyed,
completely swept away by terrors!

20As a dream when one awakes,
so when you arise, O Lord,
you will despise them as fantasies.

21When my heart was grieved
and my spirit embittered,

22I was senseless and ignorant;
I was a brute beast before you.

23Yet I am always with you;
you hold me by my right hand.

24You guide me with your counsel,
and afterwards you will take me into glory.

25Whom have I in heaven but you?
And earth has nothing I desire besides you.

26My flesh and my heart may fail,
but God is the strength of my heart
and my portion for ever.

27Those who are far from you will perish;
you destroy all who are unfaithful to you.

28But as for me, it is good to be near God.
I have made the Sovereign LORD my refuge;
I will tell of all your deeds.

Psalm 74

A maskilᵃ of Asaph.

1Why have you rejected us for ever, O God?
Why does your anger smoulder against the
sheep of your pasture?

2Remember the people you purchased of old,
the tribe of your inheritance, whom you
redeemed—
Mount Zion, where you dwelt.

3Turn your steps towards these everlasting ruins,
all this destruction the enemy has brought on
the sanctuary.

74:3   The idea that God would always protect his people because his Name dwelt in the temple on Mount Zion (1 Kings 8:17) was severely shaken when it was destroyed by enemy soldiers. The psalmist, like the prophet Isaiah, realized that God was not limited to one particular spot by a building. His authority was over the whole world and he could defeat any enemy if he wanted to (see Isaiah chapters 45 and 46).

4Your foes roared in the place where you met with
us;
they set up their standards as signs.

5They behaved like men wielding axes
to cut through a thicket of trees.

6They smashed all the carved panelling
with their axes and hatchets.

ᵃ4 With a different word division of the Hebrew; Masoretic Text *struggles at their death; / their bodies are healthy*
ᵇ7 Syriac (see also Septuagint); Hebrew *Their eyes bulge with fat*   ᶜ10 The meaning of the Hebrew for this verse is uncertain.
ᵃTitle: Probably a literary or musical term

[7]They burned your sanctuary to the ground;
  they defiled the dwelling-place of your Name.
[8]They said in their hearts, "We will crush them
    completely!"
  They burned every place where God was
    worshipped in the land.
[9]We are given no miraculous signs;
  no prophets are left,
  and none of us knows how long this will be.

[10]How long will the enemy mock you, O God?
  Will the foe revile your name for ever?
[11]Why do you hold back your hand, your right
    hand?
  Take it from the folds of your garment and
    destroy them!

[12]But you, O God, are my king from of old;
  you bring salvation upon the earth.
[13]It was you who split open the sea by your power;
  you broke the heads of the monster in the
    waters.
[14]It was you who crushed the heads of Leviathan
  and gave him as food to the creatures of the
    desert.
[15]It was you who opened up springs and streams;
  you dried up the ever-flowing rivers.
[16]The day is yours, and yours also the night;
  you established the sun and moon.
[17]It was you who set all the boundaries of the
    earth;
  you made both summer and winter.

[18]Remember how the enemy has mocked you,
    O LORD,
  how foolish people have reviled your name.
[19]Do not hand over the life of your dove to wild
    beasts;
  do not forget the lives of your afflicted people
    for ever.
[20]Have regard for your covenant,
  because haunts of violence fill the dark places of
    the land.
[21]Do not let the oppressed retreat in disgrace;
  may the poor and needy praise your name.

[22]Rise up, O God, and defend your cause;
  remember how fools mock you all day long.
[23]Do not ignore the clamour of your adversaries,
  the uproar of your enemies, which rises
    continually.

Psalm 75

For the director of music. To the tune of, "Do Not Destroy". A
psalm of Asaph. A song.

[1]We give thanks to you, O God,
  we give thanks, for your Name is near;
  men tell of your wonderful deeds.

[2]You say, "I choose the appointed time;
  it is I who judge uprightly.
[3]When the earth and all its people quake,
  it is I who hold its pillars firm.   *Selah*

[4]To the arrogant I say, 'Boast no more,'
  and to the wicked, 'Do not lift up your horns.
[5]Do not lift your horns against heaven;
  do not speak with outstretched neck.' "
[6]No-one from the east or the west
  or from the desert can exalt a man.
[7]But it is God who judges:
  He brings one down, he exalts another.
[8]In the hand of the LORD is a cup
  full of foaming wine mixed with spices;
  he pours it out, and all the wicked of the earth
  drink it down to its very dregs.
[9]As for me, I will declare this for ever;
  I will sing praise to the God of Jacob.
[10]I will cut off the horns of all the wicked,
  but the horns of the righteous shall be lifted
    up.

Psalm 76

For the director of music. With stringed instruments. A psalm of
Asaph. A song.

[1]In Judah God is known;
  his name is great in Israel.
[2]His tent is in Salem,
  his dwelling-place in Zion.
[3]There he broke the flashing arrows,
  the shields and the swords, the weapons of war.
                                                    Selah

[4]You are resplendent with light,
  more majestic than mountains rich with game.
[5]Valiant men lie plundered,
  they sleep their last sleep;
  not one of the warriors
  can lift his hands.
[6]At your rebuke, O God of Jacob,
  both horse and chariot lie still.
[7]You alone are to be feared.
  Who can stand before you when you are angry?
[8]From heaven you pronounced judgment,
  and the land feared and was quiet—
[9]when you, O God, rose up to judge,
  to save all the afflicted of the land.   *Selah*
[10]Surely your wrath against men brings you praise,
  and the survivors of your wrath are
    restrained. [a]
[11]Make vows to the LORD your God and fulfil them;
  let all the neighbouring lands
  bring gifts to the One to be feared.
[12]He breaks the spirit of rulers;
  he is feared by the kings of the earth.

Psalm 77

For the director of music. For Jeduthun. Of Asaph. A psalm.

[1]I cried out to God for help;
  I cried out to God to hear me.
[2]When I was in distress, I sought the Lord;
  at night I stretched out untiring hands
  and my soul refused to be comforted.

---

[a] 10 Or *Surely the wrath of men brings you praise, / and with the remainder of wrath you arm yourself*

³I remembered you, O God, and I groaned;
  I mused, and my spirit grew faint.   *Selah*
⁴You kept my eyes from closing;
  I was too troubled to speak.
⁵I thought about the former days,
  the years of long ago;
⁶I remembered my songs in the night.
  My heart mused and my spirit enquired:

77:2 Like millions of people, this psalmist could not sleep. There were things on his mind and God seemed to have forgotten him in his troubles. In despair he started to think about what God had done in the past. As he remembered great events in Israel's history and God's involvement in them, he was caught up in the power of God and was able to forget his anxiety.

---

⁷"Will the Lord reject for ever?
  Will he never show his favour again?
⁸Has his unfailing love vanished for ever?
  Has his promise failed for all time?
⁹Has God forgotten to be merciful?
  Has he in anger withheld his
    compassion?"   *Selah*
¹⁰Then I thought, "To this I will appeal:
  the years of the right hand of the Most
    High."
¹¹I will remember the deeds of the LORD;
  yes, I will remember your miracles of long
    ago.
¹²I will meditate on all your works
  and consider all your mighty deeds.

¹³Your ways, O God, are holy.
  What god is so great as our God?
¹⁴You are the God who performs miracles;
  you display your power among the peoples.
¹⁵With your mighty arm you redeemed your
    people,
  the descendants of Jacob and Joseph.   *Selah*

¹⁶The waters saw you, O God,
  the waters saw you and writhed;
  the very depths were convulsed.
¹⁷The clouds poured down water,
  the skies resounded with thunder;
  your arrows flashed back and forth.
¹⁸Your thunder was heard in the whirlwind,
  your lightning lit up the world;
  the earth trembled and quaked.
¹⁹Your path led through the sea,
  your way through the mighty waters,
  though your footprints were not seen.

²⁰You led your people like a flock
  by the hand of Moses and Aaron.

Psalm 78

A *maskil*[a] of Asaph.

¹O my people, hear my teaching;
  listen to the words of my mouth.
²I will open my mouth in parables,
  I will utter hidden things, things from of old—
³what we have heard and known,
  what our fathers have told us.
⁴We will not hide them from their children;
  we will tell the next generation
  the praiseworthy deeds of the LORD,
  his power, and the wonders he has done.
⁵He decreed statutes for Jacob
  and established the law in Israel,
  which he commanded our forefathers
  to teach their children,
⁶so that the next generation would know them,
  even the children yet to be born,
  and they in turn would tell their children.
⁷Then they would put their trust in God
  and would not forget his deeds
  but would keep his commands.
⁸They would not be like their forefathers—
  a stubborn and rebellious generation,
  whose hearts were not loyal to God,
  whose spirits were not faithful to him.

⁹The men of Ephraim, though armed with bows,
  turned back on the day of battle;
¹⁰they did not keep God's covenant
  and refused to live by his law.
¹¹They forgot what he had done,
  the wonders he had shown them.
¹²He did miracles in the sight of their fathers
  in the land of Egypt, in the region of Zoan.
¹³He divided the sea and led them through;
  he made the water stand firm like a wall.
¹⁴He guided them with the cloud by day
  and with light from the fire all night.
¹⁵He split the rocks in the desert
  and gave them water as abundant as the seas;
¹⁶he brought streams out of a rocky crag
  and made water flow down like rivers.

¹⁷But they continued to sin against him,
  rebelling in the desert against the Most High.
¹⁸They wilfully put God to the test
  by demanding the food they craved.
¹⁹They spoke against God, saying,
  "Can God spread a table in the desert?
²⁰When he struck the rock, water gushed out,
  and streams flowed abundantly.
  But can he also give us food?
  Can he supply meat for his people?"
²¹When the LORD heard them, he was very angry;
  his fire broke out against Jacob,
  and his wrath rose against Israel,
²²for they did not believe in God
  or trust in his deliverance.
²³Yet he gave a command to the skies above
  and opened the doors of the heavens;

ᵃTitle: Probably a literary or musical term

²⁴he rained down manna for the people to eat,
  he gave them the grain of heaven.
²⁵Men ate the bread of angels;
  he sent them all the food they could eat.
²⁶He let loose the east wind from the heavens
  and led forth the south wind by his power.
²⁷He rained meat down on them like dust,
  flying birds like sand on the seashore.
²⁸He made them come down inside their camp,
  all around their tents.
²⁹They ate till they had more than enough,
  for he had given them what they craved.
³⁰But before they turned from the food they craved,
  even while it was still in their mouths,
³¹God's anger rose against them;
  he put to death the sturdiest among them,
  cutting down the young men of Israel.

³²In spite of all this, they kept on sinning;
  in spite of his wonders, they did not believe.
³³So he ended their days in futility
  and their years in terror.
³⁴Whenever God slew them, they would seek him;
  they eagerly turned to him again.
³⁵They remembered that God was their Rock,
  that God Most High was their Redeemer.
³⁶But then they would flatter him with their
    mouths,
  lying to him with their tongues;
³⁷their hearts were not loyal to him,
  they were not faithful to his covenant.
³⁸Yet he was merciful;
  he forgave their iniquities
  and did not destroy them.
Time after time he restrained his anger
  and did not stir up his full wrath.
³⁹He remembered that they were but flesh,
  a passing breeze that does not return.

78:41 The people of the northern tribes of Israel rejected God time and time again, despite many acts on their behalf. In exasperation God turned away from them and his favour fell on Judah, Jerusalem, and David. This psalm sounds rather one-sided. There is another similar explanation in 2 Kings 17:7–23.

⁴⁰How often they rebelled against him in the desert
  and grieved him in the wasteland!
⁴¹Again and again they put God to the test;
  they vexed the Holy One of Israel.
⁴²They did not remember his power—
  the day he redeemed them from the oppressor,
⁴³the day he displayed his miraculous signs in
    Egypt,
  his wonders in the region of Zoan.
⁴⁴He turned their rivers to blood;
  they could not drink from their streams.
⁴⁵He sent swarms of flies that devoured them,
  and frogs that devastated them.
⁴⁶He gave their crops to the grasshopper,
  their produce to the locust.

⁴⁷He destroyed their vines with hail
  and their sycamore-figs with sleet.
⁴⁸He gave over their cattle to the hail,
  their livestock to bolts of lightning.
⁴⁹He unleashed against them his hot anger,
  his wrath, indignation and hostility—
  a band of destroying angels.
⁵⁰He prepared a path for his anger;
  he did not spare them from death
  but gave them over to the plague.
⁵¹He struck down all the firstborn of Egypt,
  the firstfruits of manhood in the tents of
    Ham.
⁵²But he brought his people out like a flock;
  he led them like sheep through the desert.
⁵³He guided them safely, so they were unafraid;
  but the sea engulfed their enemies.
⁵⁴Thus he brought them to the border of his holy
    land,
  to the hill country his right hand had taken.
⁵⁵He drove out nations before them
  and allotted their lands to them as an
    inheritance;
  he settled the tribes of Israel in their
    homes.

⁵⁶But they put God to the test
  and rebelled against the Most High;
  they did not keep his statutes.
⁵⁷Like their fathers they were disloyal and
    faithless,
  as unreliable as a faulty bow.
⁵⁸They angered him with their high places;
  they aroused his jealousy with their idols.
⁵⁹When God heard them, he was very angry;
  he rejected Israel completely.
⁶⁰He abandoned the tabernacle of Shiloh,
  the tent he had set up among men.
⁶¹He sent the ark of his might into captivity,
  his splendour into the hands of the enemy.
⁶²He gave his people over to the sword;
  he was very angry with his inheritance.
⁶³Fire consumed their young men,
  and their maidens had no wedding songs;
⁶⁴their priests were put to the sword,
  and their widows could not weep.

⁶⁵Then the Lord awoke as from sleep,
  as a man wakes from the stupor of wine.
⁶⁶He beat back his enemies;
  he put them to everlasting shame.
⁶⁷Then he rejected the tents of Joseph,
  he did not choose the tribe of Ephraim;
⁶⁸but he chose the tribe of Judah,
  Mount Zion, which he loved.
⁶⁹He built his sanctuary like the heights,
  like the earth that he established for ever.
⁷⁰He chose David his servant
  and took him from the sheep pens;
⁷¹from tending the sheep he brought him
  to be the shepherd of his people Jacob,
  of Israel his inheritance.
⁷²And David shepherded them with integrity of
    heart;
  with skilful hands he led them.

Psalm 79

A psalm of Asaph.

¹O God, the nations have invaded your
     inheritance;
  they have defiled your holy temple,
  they have reduced Jerusalem to rubble.
²They have given the dead bodies of your servants
     as food to the birds of the air,
  the flesh of your saints to the beasts of the
     earth.
³They have poured out blood like water
     all around Jerusalem,
  and there is no-one to bury the dead.
⁴We are objects of reproach to our neighbours,
  of scorn and derision to those around us.

79:5   Ancient people often linked the
destruction of their temples with weakness
of their god. The psalmist, however, saw it
as a sign of God's displeasure with his people.
The Israelites believed that disasters were a
sign of God's judgement for wrongdoing.
Many people still link personal misfortunes
with God's displeasure, but often things go
wrong for no reason. How we overcome
them is more important than linking them
with sin and punishment.

---

⁵How long, O Lord? Will you be angry for ever?
  How long will your jealousy burn like fire?
⁶Pour out your wrath on the nations
     that do not acknowledge you,
  on the kingdoms
     that do not call on your name;
⁷for they have devoured Jacob
  and destroyed his homeland.
⁸Do not hold against us the sins of the fathers;
  may your mercy come quickly to meet us,
  for we are in desperate need.

⁹Help us, O God our Saviour,
  for the glory of your name;
  deliver us and forgive our sins
  for your name's sake.
¹⁰Why should the nations say,
     "Where is their God?"
  Before our eyes, make known among the nations
  that you avenge the outpoured blood of your
     servants.
¹¹May the groans of the prisoners come before you;
  by the strength of your arm
  preserve those condemned to die.

¹²Pay back into the laps of our neighbours seven
     times
  the reproach they have hurled at you, O Lord.
¹³Then we your people, the sheep of your pasture,
  will praise you for ever;
  from generation to generation
  we will recount your praise.

Psalm 80

*For the director of music. To the tune of, "The Lilies of the
Covenant". Of Asaph. A psalm.*

¹Hear us, O Shepherd of Israel,
  you who lead Joseph like a flock;
  you who sit enthroned between the cherubim,
     shine forth
² before Ephraim, Benjamin and Manasseh.
  Awaken your might;
  come and save us.

80:1   The shepherd was an ancient symbol of kingship. A good king was like a shepherd who looked after his flock. God is
pictured as a king more than anything else.
Kings have thrones, and the Lord God of
Israel is no exception. His throne is the ark
of the covenant, with cherubim on both sides
like the mythical animals which sat on the
arms of the Assyrian king's throne (see
Exodus 37:7–9).

---

³Restore us, O God;
  make your face shine upon us,
  that we may be saved.

⁴O Lord God Almighty,
  how long will your anger smoulder
  against the prayers of your people?
⁵You have fed them with the bread of tears;
  you have made them drink tears by the bowlful.
⁶You have made us a source of contention to our
     neighbours,
  and our enemies mock us.

⁷Restore us, O God Almighty;
  make your face shine upon us,
  that we may be saved.

⁸You brought a vine out of Egypt;
  you drove out the nations and planted it.
⁹You cleared the ground for it,
  and it took root and filled the land.
¹⁰The mountains were covered with its shade,
  the mighty cedars with its branches.
¹¹It sent out its boughs to the Sea,ᵃ
  its shoots as far as the River.ᵇ

¹²Why have you broken down its walls
  so that all who pass by pick its grapes?
¹³Boars from the forest ravage it
  and the creatures of the field feed on it.
¹⁴Return to us, O God Almighty!
  Look down from heaven and see!
  Watch over this vine,
¹⁵ the root your right hand has planted,
  the sonᶜ you have raised up for yourself.

¹⁶Your vine is cut down, it is burned with fire;
  at your rebuke your people perish.
¹⁷Let your hand rest on the man at your right hand,
  the son of man you have raised up for yourself.

ᵃ11 Probably the Mediterranean   *ᵇ11 That is, the Euphrates*   *ᶜ15 Or branch*

¹⁸Then we will not turn away from you;
  revive us, and we will call on your name.

¹⁹Restore us, O Lord God Almighty;
  make your face shine upon us,
  that we may be saved.

Psalm 81

For the director of music. According to *gittith.*[a] Of Asaph.

¹Sing for joy to God our strength;
  shout aloud to the God of Jacob!
²Begin the music, strike the tambourine,
  play the melodious harp and lyre.

³Sound the ram's horn at the New Moon,
  and when the moon is full, on the day of our
    Feast;
⁴this is a decree for Israel,
  an ordinance of the God of Jacob.
⁵He established it as a statute for Joseph
  when he went out against Egypt,
  where we heard a language we did not
    understand.[b]

⁶He says, "I removed the burden from their
    shoulders;
  their hands were set free from the basket.
⁷In your distress you called and I rescued you,
  I answered you out of a thundercloud;
  I tested you at the waters of Meribah.   *Selah*

⁸"Hear, O my people, and I will warn you—
  if you would but listen to me, O Israel!
⁹You shall have no foreign god among you;
  you shall not bow down to an alien god.
¹⁰I am the Lord your God,
  who brought you up out of Egypt.
  Open wide your mouth and I will fill it.

81:9   The Israelite prophets continually
warned against the temptation to worship
the gods of the surrounding nations, particularly those of the Canaanites like Baal. Forbidding the acceptance and worship of other
gods ties in with the first of the Ten Commandments (Exodus 20:3).

---

¹¹"But my people would not listen to me;
  Israel would not submit to me.
¹²So I gave them over to their stubborn hearts
  to follow their own devices.

¹³"If my people would but listen to me,
  if Israel would follow my ways,
¹⁴how quickly would I subdue their enemies
  and turn my hand against their foes!
¹⁵Those who hate the Lord would cringe before
    him,
  and their punishment would last for ever.
¹⁶But you would be fed with the finest of wheat;
  with honey from the rock I would satisfy you."

Psalm 82

A psalm of Asaph.

¹God presides in the great assembly;
  he gives judgment among the "gods":

82:1   This psalm is concerned with
another of the functions of kingship; the
exercise of justice. Those God had given the
authority to judge on his behalf and misused
their power were called to account for what
they had done. Israel often had a strong sense
when the rights of the disadvantaged were
being neglected. Such failures could be an
indication of the king's spiritual weakness.
Whether the "gods" in this psalm were
human judges who had risen above their
position or divine beings which god had
demoted is not clear.

---

²"How long will you[a] defend the unjust
  and show partiality to the wicked?   *Selah*
³Defend the cause of the weak and fatherless;
  maintain the rights of the poor and
    oppressed.
⁴Rescue the weak and needy;
  deliver them from the hand of the wicked.

⁵"They know nothing, they understand
    nothing.
  They walk about in darkness;
  all the foundations of the earth are
    shaken.

⁶"I said, 'You are "gods";
  you are all sons of the Most High.'
⁷But you will die like mere men;
  you will fall like every other ruler."

⁸Rise up, O God, judge the earth,
  for all the nations are your inheritance.

Psalm 83

A song. A psalm of Asaph.

¹O God, do not keep silent;
  be not quiet, O God, be not still.
²See how your enemies are astir,
  how your foes rear their heads.
³With cunning they conspire against your people;
  they plot against those you cherish.
⁴"Come," they say, "let us destroy them as a
    nation,
  that the name of Israel be remembered no
    more."

⁵With one mind they plot together;
  they form an alliance against you—
⁶the tents of Edom and the Ishmaelites,
  of Moab and the Hagrites,

---

aTitle: Probably a musical term   b5 Or / and we heard a voice we had not known   a2 The Hebrew is plural.

⁷Gebal,ᵃ Ammon and Amalek,
  Philistia, with the people of Tyre.
⁸Even Assyria has joined them
  to lend strength to the descendants of Lot. *Selah*

⁹Do to them as you did to Midian,
  as you did to Sisera and Jabin at the river
    Kishon,
¹⁰who perished at Endor
  and became like refuse on the ground.
¹¹Make their nobles like Oreb and Zeeb,
  all their princes like Zebah and Zalmunna,
¹²who said, "Let us take possession
  of the pasture-lands of God."

¹³Make them like tumble-weed, O my God,
  like chaff before the wind.
¹⁴As fire consumes the forest
  or a flame sets the mountains ablaze,
¹⁵so pursue them with your tempest
  and terrify them with your storm.
¹⁶Cover their faces with shame
  so that men will seek your name, O LORD.

¹⁷May they ever be ashamed and dismayed;
  may they perish in disgrace.
¹⁸Let them know that you, whose name is the
    LORD—
  that you alone are the Most High over all the
    earth.

Psalm 84

For the director of music. According to *gittith.*ᵃ Of the Sons of
Korah. A psalm.

¹How lovely is your dwelling-place,
  O LORD Almighty!
²My soul yearns, even faints,
  for the courts of the LORD;
my heart and my flesh cry out
  for the living God.

³Even the sparrow has found a home,
  and the swallow a nest for herself,
  where she may have her young—
a place near your altar,
  O LORD Almighty, my King and my God.
⁴Blessed are those who dwell in your house;
  they are ever praising you.   *Selah*

⁵Blessed are those whose strength is in you,
  who have set their hearts on pilgrimage.
⁶As they pass through the Valley of Baca,
  they make it a place of springs;
  the autumn rains also cover it with pools.ᵇ
⁷They go from strength to strength,
  till each appears before God in Zion.

⁸Hear my prayer, O LORD God Almighty;
  listen to me, O God of Jacob.   *Selah*
⁹Look upon our shield,ᶜ O God;
  look with favour on your anointed one.

¹⁰Better is one day in your courts
  than a thousand elsewhere;

I would rather be a doorkeeper in the house of
    my God
  than dwell in the tents of the wicked.

84:10 The temple in Israel was thought
to be the especially holy place where the
Glory of the Lord resided (see Isaiah 6:1 for
an account of a vision of God which happened in the temple). Pilgrimage brought the
worshipper into the presence of God. Everyone needs a special place to go to where they
can find God. It does not have to be a religious building, but often these are filled with
a sense of the holy through many years of
devoted worship.

¹¹For the LORD God is a sun and shield;
  the LORD bestows favour and honour;
no good thing does he withhold
  from those whose walk is blameless.

¹²O LORD Almighty,
  blessed is the man who trusts in you.

Psalm 85

For the director of music. Of the Sons of Korah. A psalm.

¹You showed favour to your land, O LORD;
  you restored the fortunes of Jacob.
²You forgave the iniquity of your people
  and covered all their sins.   *Selah*
³You set aside all your wrath
  and turned from your fierce anger.

⁴Restore us again, O God our Saviour,
  and put away your displeasure towards us.
⁵Will you be angry with us for ever?
  Will you prolong your anger through all
    generations?
⁶Will you not revive us again,
  that your people may rejoice in you?
⁷Show us your unfailing love, O LORD,
  and grant us your salvation.

⁸I will listen to what God the LORD will say;
  he promises peace to his people, his saints—
  but let them not return to folly.
⁹Surely his salvation is near those who fear him,
  that his glory may dwell in our land.

¹⁰Love and faithfulness meet together;
  righteousness and peace kiss each other.
¹¹Faithfulness springs forth from the earth,
  and righteousness looks down from heaven.
¹²The LORD will indeed give what is good,
  and our land will yield its harvest.
¹³Righteousness goes before him
  and prepares the way for his steps.

ᵃ7 That is, Byblos   ᵃTitle: Probably a musical term   ᵇ6 Or *blessings*   ᶜ9 Or *sovereign*

Psalm 86

A prayer of David.

[1]Hear, O LORD, and answer me,
  for I am poor and needy.
[2]Guard my life, for I am devoted to you.
  You are my God; save your servant
  who trusts in you.
[3]Have mercy on me, O Lord,
  for I call to you all day long.
[4]Bring joy to your servant,
  for to you, O Lord,
  I lift up my soul.

86:5   This psalm is pervaded by a faithful
trust in God. The writer has a deep knowledge of the God who is compassionate, gracious, slow to anger, and abounding in love
and faithfulness. A lifetime spent in God's
presence through both good and bad experiences has brought him to this point. It takes
time to get to know God in this way, and
many never achieve it. It takes great humility
to make this much progress.

[5]You are forgiving and good, O Lord,
  abounding in love to all who call to you.
[6]Hear my prayer, O LORD;
  listen to my cry for mercy.
[7]In the day of my trouble I will call to you,
  for you will answer me.

[8]Among the gods there is none like you, O Lord;
  no deeds can compare with yours.
[9]All the nations you have made
  will come and worship before you, O Lord;
  they will bring glory to your name.
[10]For you are great and do marvellous deeds;
  you alone are God.

[11]Teach me your way, O LORD,
  and I will walk in your truth;
give me an undivided heart,
  that I may fear your name.
[12]I will praise you, O Lord my God, with all my
  heart;
  I will glorify your name for ever.
[13]For great is your love towards me;
  you have delivered me from the depths of the
  grave.[a]

[14]The arrogant are attacking me, O God;
  a band of ruthless men seeks my life —
  men without regard for you.
[15]But you, O Lord, are a compassionate and
  gracious God,
  slow to anger, abounding in love and
  faithfulness.

[16]Turn to me and have mercy on me;
  grant your strength to your servant
  and save the son of your maidservant.[b]
[17]Give me a sign of your goodness,
  that my enemies may see it and be put to
  shame,
  for you, O LORD, have helped me and comforted
  me.

Psalm 87

Of the Sons of Korah. A psalm. A song.

[1]He has set his foundation on the holy mountain;
[2] the LORD loves the gates of Zion
  more than all the dwellings of Jacob.
[3]Glorious things are said of you,
  O city of God: *Selah*
[4]"I will record Rahab[a] and Babylon
  among those who acknowledge me —
Philistia too, and Tyre, along with Cush[b] —
  and will say, 'This[c] one was born in Zion.' "

[5]Indeed, of Zion it will be said,
  "This one and that one were born in her,
  and the Most High himself will establish her."
[6]The LORD will write in the register of the
  peoples:
  "This one was born in Zion."   *Selah*
[7]As they make music they will sing,
  "All my fountains are in you."

Psalm 88

A song. A psalm of the Sons of Korah. For the director of music.
According to mahalath leannoth.[a] *A* maskil[b] *of Heman the*
Ezrahite.

[1]O LORD, the God who saves me,
  day and night I cry out before you.
[2]May my prayer come before you;
  turn your ear to my cry.

[3]For my soul is full of trouble
  and my life draws near the grave.[c]
[4]I am counted among those who go down to the
  pit;
  I am like a man without strength.
[5]I am set apart with the dead,
  like the slain who lie in the grave,
whom you remember no more,
  who are cut off from your care.

[6]You have put me in the lowest pit,
  in the darkest depths.
[7]Your wrath lies heavily upon me;
  you have overwhelmed me with all your waves.
                                             Selah
[8]You have taken from me my closest friends
  and have made me repulsive to them.
  I am confined and cannot escape;
[9] my eyes are dim with grief.

---

[a]13 Hebrew *Sheol*   [b]16 Or *save your faithful son*   [a]4 A poetic name for Egypt   [b]4 That is, the upper Nile region
[c]4 Or "*O Rahab and Babylon, / Philistia, Tyre and Cush, / I will record concerning those who acknowledge me: / 'This*
[a]Title: Possibly a tune, "The Suffering of Affliction"   [b]Title: Probably a literary or musical term   [c]3 Hebrew *Sheol*

I call to you, O Lord, every day;
   I spread out my hands to you.
¹⁰Do you show your wonders to the dead?
   Do those who are dead rise up and praise you?
                                                    Selah

88:6   This psalm is full of unrelieved gloom. The source of the trouble may have been a chronic illness that had lasted a number of years (verse 15). Whatever the cause, the psalmist had really been dragged down. This is not a very positive psalm but it illustrates very well how to be honest in a relationship with God.

---

¹¹Is your love declared in the grave,
   your faithfulness in Destruction?ᵈ
¹²Are your wonders known in the place of darkness,
   or your righteous deeds in the land of oblivion?
¹³But I cry to you for help, O Lord;
   in the morning my prayer comes before you.
¹⁴Why, O Lord, do you reject me
   and hide your face from me?
¹⁵From my youth I have been afflicted and close to death;
   I have suffered your terrors and am in despair.
¹⁶Your wrath has swept over me;
   your terrors have destroyed me.
¹⁷All day long they surround me like a flood;
   they have completely engulfed me.
¹⁸You have taken my companions and loved ones from me;
   the darkness is my closest friend.

Psalm 89

A *maskil*ᵃ of Ethan the Ezrahite.

¹I will sing of the Lord's great love for ever;
   with my mouth I will make your faithfulness known through all generations.
²I will declare that your love stands firm for ever,
   that you established your faithfulness in heaven itself.
³You said, "I have made a covenant with my chosen one,
   I have sworn to David my servant,
⁴'I will establish your line for ever
   and make your throne firm through all generations.'"
                                                    Selah
⁵The heavens praise your wonders, O Lord,
   your faithfulness too, in the assembly of the holy ones.
⁶For who in the skies above can compare with the Lord?
   Who is like the Lord among the heavenly beings?

⁷In the council of the holy ones God is greatly feared;
   he is more awesome than all who surround him.
⁸O Lord God Almighty, who is like you?
   You are mighty, O Lord, and your faithfulness surrounds you.
⁹You rule over the surging sea;
   when its waves mount up, you still them.
¹⁰You crushed Rahab like one of the slain;
   with your strong arm you scattered your enemies.
¹¹The heavens are yours, and yours also the earth;
   you founded the world and all that is in it.
¹²You created the north and the south;
   Tabor and Hermon sing for joy at your name.
¹³Your arm is endued with power;
   your hand is strong, your right hand exalted.
¹⁴Righteousness and justice are the foundation of your throne;
   love and faithfulness go before you.
¹⁵Blessed are those who have learned to acclaim you,
   who walk in the light of your presence, O Lord.
¹⁶They rejoice in your name all day long;
   they exult in your righteousness.
¹⁷For you are their glory and strength,
   and by your favour you exalt our horn.ᵇ
¹⁸Indeed, our shieldᶜ belongs to the Lord,
   our king to the Holy One of Israel.
¹⁹Once you spoke in a vision,
   to your faithful people you said:
   "I have bestowed strength on a warrior;
   I have exalted a young man from among the people.
²⁰I have found David my servant;
   with my sacred oil I have anointed him.
²¹My hand will sustain him;
   surely my arm will strengthen him.
²²No enemy will subject him to tribute;
   no wicked man will oppress him.
²³I will crush his foes before him
   and strike down his adversaries.
²⁴My faithful love will be with him,
   and through my name his hornᵈ will be exalted.
²⁵I will set his hand over the sea,
   his right hand over the rivers.
²⁶He will call out to me, 'You are my Father,
   my God, the Rock my Saviour.'
²⁷I will also appoint him my firstborn,
   the most exalted of the kings of the earth.
²⁸I will maintain my love to him for ever,
   and my covenant with him will never fail.
²⁹I will establish his line for ever,
   his throne as long as the heavens endure.
³⁰"If his sons forsake my law
   and do not follow my statutes,

ᵈ11 Hebrew *Abaddon*   ᵃTitle: Probably a literary or musical term   ᵇ17 *Horn* here symbolises strong one.
ᶜ18 Or *sovereign*   ᵈ24 *Horn* here symbolises strength.

³¹if they violate my decrees
  and fail to keep my commands,
³²I will punish their sin with the rod,
  their iniquity with flogging;
³³but I will not take my love from him,
  nor will I ever betray my faithfulness.
³⁴I will not violate my covenant
  or alter what my lips have uttered.
³⁵Once for all, I have sworn by my holiness—
  and I will not lie to David—
³⁶that his line will continue for ever
  and his throne endure before me like the sun;
³⁷it will be established for ever like the moon,
  the faithful witness in the sky."   *Selah*

89:39 When the king Jehoiachin and the
people of Judah were deported to Babylon,
all God's promises seem to have been worthless. God had failed to fulfil his promise
(verses 27, 28, 33–37) to keep a king of
David's line on the throne for ever. In his
complaint about the experience of downfall
and destruction in Jerusalem the psalmist
appealed to God's supreme power as creator
and to his promises to David. At least he was
honest in expressing his disgust with what
God had done and his lack of understanding.
During the exile Israelite thinkers tried to
work out what it meant to be God's people
and still trust in him despite disaster.

---

³⁸But you have rejected, you have spurned,
  you have been very angry with your anointed
    one.
³⁹You have renounced the covenant with your
    servant
  and have defiled his crown in the dust.
⁴⁰You have broken through all his walls
  and reduced his strongholds to ruins.
⁴¹All who pass by have plundered him;
  he has become the scorn of his neighbours.
⁴²You have exalted the right hand of his foes;
  you have made all his enemies rejoice.
⁴³You have turned back the edge of his sword
  and have not supported him in battle.
⁴⁴You have put an end to his splendour
  and cast his throne to the ground.
⁴⁵You have cut short the days of his youth;
  you have covered him with a mantle of shame.
                                            Selah

⁴⁶How long, O LORD? Will you hide yourself for
    ever?
  How long will your wrath burn like fire?
⁴⁷Remember how fleeting is my life.
  For what futility you have created all men!
⁴⁸What man can live and not see death,
  or save himself from the power of the grave?ᵉ
                                            Selah

⁴⁹O Lord, where is your former great love,
  which in your faithfulness you swore to David?
⁵⁰Remember, Lord, how your servant hasᶠ been
    mocked,
  how I bear in my heart the taunts of all the
    nations,
⁵¹the taunts with which your enemies have
    mocked, O LORD,
  with which they have mocked every step of
    your anointed one.

⁵²Praise be to the LORD for ever!
  Amen and Amen.

BOOK IV

Psalms 90–106

Psalm 90

A prayer of Moses the man of God.

¹Lord, you have been our dwelling-place
  throughout all generations.
²Before the mountains were born
  or you brought forth the earth and the world,
  from everlasting to everlasting you are God.

³You turn men back to dust,
  saying, "Return to dust, O sons of men."
⁴For a thousand years in your sight
  are like a day that has just gone by,
  or like a watch in the night.
⁵You sweep men away in the sleep of death;
  they are like the new grass of the morning—
⁶though in the morning it springs up new,
  by evening it is dry and withered.

90:7 The psalmist was never able to
reject God. He was firmly convinced of
God's power as creator and his relationship
with Israel. Yet he did not always appreciate
how that relationship worked out. It is only
possible to speculate why the psalmist understood that God was so angry with the people.
Anger, wrath, and indignation are not emotions that we readily attribute to God but it
helps to be aware of God's reactions to people's sin.

---

⁷We are consumed by your anger
  and terrified by your indignation.
⁸You have set our iniquities before you,
  our secret sins in the light of your presence.
⁹All our days pass away under your wrath;
  we finish our years with a moan.
¹⁰The length of our days is seventy years—
  or eighty, if we have the strength;
  yet their spanᵃ is but trouble and sorrow,
  for they quickly pass, and we fly away.

ᵉ 48 Hebrew *Sheol*   ᶠ 50 Or *your servants have*   ᵃ 10 Or *yet the best of them*

11Who knows the power of your anger?
  For your wrath is as great as the fear that is due
    to you.
12Teach us to number our days aright,
  that we may gain a heart of wisdom.

13Relent, O LORD! How long will it be?
  Have compassion on your servants.
14Satisfy us in the morning with your unfailing love,
  that we may sing for joy and be glad all our
    days.
15Make us glad for as many days as you have
    afflicted us,
  for as many years as we have seen trouble.
16May your deeds be shown to your servants,
  your splendour to their children.

17May the favour*b* of the Lord our God rest upon
    us;
  establish the work of our hands for us—
  yes, establish the work of our hands.

Psalm 91

1He who dwells in the shelter of the Most High
  will rest in the shadow of the Almighty.*a*
2I will say*b* of the LORD, "He is my refuge and my
    fortress,
  my God, in whom I trust."

3Surely he will save you from the fowler's snare
  and from the deadly pestilence.
4He will cover you with his feathers,
  and under his wings you will find refuge;
  his faithfulness will be your shield and rampart.
5You will not fear the terror of night,
  nor the arrow that flies by day,
6nor the pestilence that stalks in the darkness,
  nor the plague that destroys at midday.
7A thousand may fall at your side,
  ten thousand at your right hand,
  but it will not come near you.
8You will only observe with your eyes
  and see the punishment of the wicked.

9If you make the Most High your dwelling—
  even the LORD, who is my refuge—
10then no harm will befall you,
  no disaster will come near your tent.
11For he will command his angels concerning you
  to guard you in all your ways;
12they will lift you up in their hands,
  so that you will not strike your foot against a
    stone.
13You will tread upon the lion and the cobra;
  you will trample the great lion and the serpent.

14"Because he loves me," says the LORD, "I will
    rescue him;
  I will protect him, for he acknowledges my
    name.
15He will call upon me, and I will answer him;
  I will be with him in trouble,
  I will deliver him and honour him.

16With long life will I satisfy him
  and show him my salvation."

Psalm 92

A psalm. A song. For the Sabbath day.

1It is good to praise the LORD
  and make music to your name, O Most High,
2to proclaim your love in the morning
  and your faithfulness at night,
3to the music of the ten-stringed lyre
  and the melody of the harp.

4For you make me glad by your deeds, O LORD;
  I sing for joy at the work of your hands.
5How great are your works, O LORD,
  how profound your thoughts!
6The senseless man does not know,
  fools do not understand,
7that though the wicked spring up like grass
  and all evildoers flourish,
  they will be for ever destroyed.

8But you, O LORD, are exalted for ever.

9For surely your enemies, O LORD,
  surely your enemies will perish;
  all evildoers will be scattered.
10You have exalted my horn*a* like that of a wild
    ox;
  fine oils have been poured upon me.
11My eyes have seen the defeat of my adversaries;
  my ears have heard the rout of my wicked foes.

12The righteous will flourish like a palm tree,
  they will grow like a cedar of Lebanon;
13planted in the house of the LORD,
  they will flourish in the courts of our God.
14They will still bear fruit in old age,
  they will stay fresh and green,
15proclaiming, "The LORD is upright;
  he is my Rock, and there is no wickedness in
    him."

Psalm 93

1The LORD reigns, he is robed in majesty;
  the LORD is robed in majesty
  and is armed with strength.
  The world is firmly established;
  it cannot be moved.
2Your throne was established long ago;
  you are from all eternity.

3The seas have lifted up, O LORD,
  the seas have lifted up their voice;
  the seas have lifted up their pounding waves.
4Mightier than the thunder of the great waters,
  mightier than the breakers of the sea—
  the LORD on high is mighty.

5Your statutes stand firm;
  holiness adorns your house
  for endless days, O LORD.

b 17 Or beauty   *a 1 Hebrew Shaddai*   *b 2 Or He says*   *a 10 Horn here symbolises strength.*

Psalm 94

[1]O LORD, the God who avenges,
  O God who avenges, shine forth.
[2]Rise up, O Judge of the earth;
  pay back to the proud what they deserve.
[3]How long will the wicked, O LORD,
  how long will the wicked be jubilant?

[4]They pour out arrogant words;
  all the evildoers are full of boasting.
[5]They crush your people, O LORD;
  they oppress your inheritance.
[6]They slay the widow and the alien;
  they murder the fatherless.
[7]They say, "The LORD does not see;
  the God of Jacob pays no heed."

[8]Take heed, you senseless ones among the people;
  you fools, when will you become wise?
[9]Does he who implanted the ear not hear?
  Does he who formed the eye not see?
[10]Does he who disciplines nations not punish?
  Does he who teaches man lack knowledge?
[11]The LORD knows the thoughts of man;
  he knows that they are futile.

[12]Blessed is the man you discipline, O LORD,
  the man you teach from your law;
[13]you grant him relief from days of trouble,
  till a pit is dug for the wicked.
[14]For the LORD will not reject his people;
  he will never forsake his inheritance.
[15]Judgment will again be founded on righteousness,
  and all the upright in heart will follow it.

[16]Who will rise up for me against the wicked?
  Who will take a stand for me against evildoers?
[17]Unless the LORD had given me help,
  I would soon have dwelt in the silence of death.
[18]When I said, "My foot is slipping,"
  your love, O LORD, supported me.
[19]When anxiety was great within me,
  your consolation brought joy to my soul.

[20]Can a corrupt throne be allied with you—
  one that brings on misery by its decrees?
[21]They band together against the righteous
  and condemn the innocent to death.
[22]But the LORD has become my fortress,
  and my God the rock in whom I take refuge.
[23]He will repay them for their sins
  and destroy them for their wickedness;
  the LORD our God will destroy them.

Psalm 95

[1]Come, let us sing for joy to the LORD;
  let us shout aloud to the Rock of our salvation.
[2]Let us come before him with thanksgiving
  and extol him with music and song.

[3]For the LORD is the great God,
  the great King above all gods.

[4]In his hand are the depths of the earth,
  and the mountain peaks belong to him.
[5]The sea is his, for he made it,
  and his hands formed the dry land.

[6]Come, let us bow down in worship,
  let us kneel before the LORD our Maker;
[7]for he is our God
  and we are the people of his pasture,
  the flock under his care.

95:8 The rebellion of the children of Israel against Moses and God in the desert at Meribah and Massah was burned into the memory of the nation (see also Psalm 106:32–33). After a difficult journey the Israelites ran out of water and were very angry and frustrated. They were condemned to forty years wandering in the wilderness for their lack of faith (see Exodus 17:1–7). This wilderness experience was used to warn succeeding generations of Israelites not to make the same mistake.

Today, if you hear his voice,
[8] do not harden your hearts as you did at
      Meribah,[a]
  as you did that day at Massah[b] in the desert,
[9]where your fathers tested and tried me,
  though they had seen what I did.
[10]For forty years I was angry with that generation;
  I said, "They are a people whose hearts go
      astray,
  and they have not known my ways."
[11]So I declared on oath in my anger,
  "They shall never enter my rest."

Psalm 96

[1]Sing to the LORD a new song;
  sing to the LORD, all the earth.
[2]Sing to the LORD, praise his name;
  proclaim his salvation day after day.
[3]Declare his glory among the nations,
  his marvellous deeds among all peoples.

[4]For great is the LORD and most worthy of praise;
  he is to be feared above all gods.
[5]For all the gods of the nations are idols,
  but the LORD made the heavens.
[6]Splendour and majesty are before him;
  strength and glory are in his sanctuary.

[7]Ascribe to the LORD, O families of nations,
  ascribe to the LORD glory and strength.
[8]Ascribe to the LORD the glory due to his name;
  bring an offering and come into his courts.
[9]Worship the LORD in the splendour of his[a]
      holiness;
  tremble before him, all the earth.

---

[a]8 Meribah means quarrelling.   [b]8 Massah means testing.   [a]9 Or LORD with the splendour of

¹⁰Say among the nations, "The LORD reigns."
  The world is firmly established, it cannot be
    moved;
  he will judge the peoples with equity.

96:9 Holiness is the essence of the character of God. It is associated with words like glory, beauty, majesty, power, and might. God's holiness was certainly very powerful in its effects; see for example what happened to Uzzah when he touched the ark of God (2 Samuel 6:6–7). Priests underwent special rituals to be protected from the power of God's holiness. Needless to say it was also important for Israel, as God's holy people, to live lives that reflected God's holiness.

---

¹¹Let the heavens rejoice, let the earth be glad;
  let the sea resound, and all that is in it;
¹² let the fields be jubilant, and everything in
    them.
  Then all the trees of the forest will sing for joy;
¹³ they will sing before the LORD, for he comes,
  he comes to judge the earth.
  He will judge the world in righteousness
  and the peoples in his truth.

Psalm 97

¹The LORD reigns, let the earth be glad;
  let the distant shores rejoice.

²Clouds and thick darkness surround him;
  righteousness and justice are the foundation of
    his throne.
³Fire goes before him
  and consumes his foes on every side.
⁴His lightning lights up the world;
  the earth sees and trembles.
⁵The mountains melt like wax before the LORD,
  before the Lord of all the earth.
⁶The heavens proclaim his righteousness,
  and all the peoples see his glory.

⁷All who worship images are put to shame,
  those who boast in idols—
  worship him, all you gods!

⁸Zion hears and rejoices
  and the villages of Judah are glad
  because of your judgments, O LORD.
⁹For you, O LORD, are the Most High over all the
    earth;
  you are exalted far above all gods.

¹⁰Let those who love the LORD hate evil,
  for he guards the lives of his faithful ones
  and delivers them from the hand of the wicked.
¹¹Light is shed upon the righteous
  and joy on the upright in heart.
¹²Rejoice in the LORD, you who are righteous,
  and praise his holy name.

Psalm 98

A psalm.

¹Sing to the LORD a new song,
  for he has done marvellous things;
  his right hand and his holy arm
  have worked salvation for him.
²The LORD has made his salvation known
  and revealed his righteousness to the
    nations.
³He has remembered his love
  and his faithfulness to the house of Israel;
  all the ends of the earth have seen
  the salvation of our God.

⁴Shout for joy to the LORD, all the earth,
  burst into jubilant song with music;
⁵make music to the LORD with the harp,
  with the harp and the sound of singing,
⁶with trumpets and the blast of the ram's horn—
  shout for joy before the LORD, the King.

⁷Let the sea resound, and everything in it,
  the world, and all who live in it.
⁸Let the rivers clap their hands,
  let the mountains sing together for joy;
⁹let them sing before the LORD,
  for he comes to judge the earth.
  He will judge the world in righteousness
  and the peoples with equity.

Psalm 99

¹The LORD reigns,
  let the nations tremble;
  he sits enthroned between the cherubim,
  let the earth shake.
²Great is the LORD in Zion;
  he is exalted over all the nations.
³Let them praise your great and awesome name—
  he is holy.

⁴The King is mighty, he loves justice—
  you have established equity;
  in Jacob you have done
  what is just and right.
⁵Exalt the LORD our God
  and worship at his footstool;
  he is holy.

⁶Moses and Aaron were among his priests,
  Samuel was among those who called on his
    name;
  they called on the LORD
  and he answered them.
⁷He spoke to them from the pillar of cloud;
  they kept his statutes and the decrees he gave
    them.

⁸O LORD our God,
  you answered them;
  you were to Israel ᵃ a forgiving God,
  though you punished their misdeeds. ᵇ

ᵃ8 Hebrew *them*   ᵇ8 Or / *an avenger of the wrongs done to them*

[9]Exalt the LORD our God
and worship at his holy mountain,
for the LORD our God is holy.

Psalm 100

A psalm. For giving thanks.

[1]Shout for joy to the LORD, all the earth.
[2] Worship the LORD with gladness;
come before him with joyful songs.
[3]Know that the LORD is God.
It is he who made us, and we are his;[a]
we are his people, the sheep of his
pasture.

[4]Enter his gates with thanksgiving
and his courts with praise;
give thanks to him and praise his name.
[5]For the LORD is good and his love endures for
ever;
his faithfulness continues through all
generations.

Psalm 101

Of David. A psalm.

[1]I will sing of your love and justice;
to you, O LORD, I will sing praise.
[2]I will be careful to lead a blameless life —
when will you come to me?

I will walk in my house
with blameless heart.
[3]I will set before my eyes
no vile thing.

The deeds of faithless men I hate;
they shall not cling to me.
[4]Men of perverse heart shall be far from
me;
I will have nothing to do with evil.

101:7 The king promised to rule with
integrity and to surround himself with truthful and honest advisers. Politics, though,
often involves compromise and dealings with
people whose standards and values are different. It is difficult to maintain high standards
of integrity and honesty. The Israelite king
derived his strength from his worship of God.
When this relationship failed so too did the
nation.

---

[5]Whoever slanders his neighbour in
secret,
him will I put to silence;
whoever has haughty eyes and a proud
heart,
him will I not endure.

[6]My eyes will be on the faithful in the
land,

that they may dwell with me;
he whose walk is blameless
will minister to me.
[7]No-one who practises deceit
will dwell in my house;
no-one who speaks falsely
will stand in my presence.

[8]Every morning I will put to silence
all the wicked in the land;
I will cut off every evildoer
from the city of the LORD.

Psalm 102

A prayer of an afflicted man. When he is faint and pours out his
lament before the LORD.

[1]Hear my prayer, O LORD;
let my cry for help come to you.
[2]Do not hide your face from me
when I am in distress.
Turn your ear to me;
when I call, answer me quickly.

[3]For my days vanish like smoke;
my bones burn like glowing embers.
[4]My heart is blighted and withered like grass;
I forget to eat my food.
[5]Because of my loud groaning
I am reduced to skin and bones.
[6]I am like a desert owl,
like an owl among the ruins.
[7]I lie awake; I have become
like a bird alone on a roof.
[8]All day long my enemies taunt me;
those who rail against me use my name as a
curse.
[9]For I eat ashes as my food
and mingle my drink with tears
[10]because of your great wrath,
for you have taken me up and thrown me aside.
[11]My days are like the evening shadow;
I wither away like grass.

[12]But you, O LORD, sit enthroned for ever;
your renown endures through all generations.
[13]You will arise and have compassion on Zion,
for it is time to show favour to her;
the appointed time has come.
[14]For her stones are dear to your servants;
her very dust moves them to pity.
[15]The nations will fear the name of the LORD,
all the kings of the earth will revere your glory.
[16]For the LORD will rebuild Zion
and appear in his glory.
[17]He will respond to the prayer of the destitute;
he will not despise their plea.

[18]Let this be written for a future generation,
that a people not yet created may praise the
LORD:

---

[a]3 Or *and not we ourselves*

19"The LORD looked down from his sanctuary on high,
  from heaven he viewed the earth,
20to hear the groans of the prisoners
  and release those condemned to death."
21So the name of the LORD will be declared in Zion
  and his praise in Jerusalem
22when the peoples and the kingdoms
  assemble to worship the LORD.

102:26 The psalmist compared the permanence of God with the temporary nature of everything else in the world. Even the universe itself, which God has made, will eventually pass away and be discarded like worn-out clothes. The writer's own life is particularly short, like grass which is quickly dried up in the hot sun. Yet God's commitment to his people will never change.

23In the course of my life^a he broke my strength;
  he cut short my days.
24So I said:
  "Do not take me away, O my God, in the midst of my days;
  your years go on through all generations.
25In the beginning you laid the foundations of the earth,
  and the heavens are the work of your hands.
26They will perish, but you remain;
  they will all wear out like a garment.
  Like clothing you will change them
  and they will be discarded.
27But you remain the same,
  and your years will never end.
28The children of your servants will live in your presence;
  their descendants will be established before you."

Psalm 103

Of David.

1Praise the LORD, O my soul;
  all my inmost being, praise his holy name.
2Praise the LORD, O my soul,
  and forget not all his benefits —
3who forgives all your sins
  and heals all your diseases,
4who redeems your life from the pit
  and crowns you with love and compassion,
5who satisfies your desires with good things
  so that your youth is renewed like the eagle's.

6The LORD works righteousness
  and justice for all the oppressed.

7He made known his ways to Moses,
  his deeds to the people of Israel:
8The LORD is compassionate and gracious,
  slow to anger, abounding in love.

9He will not always accuse,
  nor will he harbour his anger for ever;
10he does not treat us as our sins deserve
  or repay us according to our iniquities.
11For as high as the heavens are above the earth,
  so great is his love for those who fear him;
12as far as the east is from the west,
  so far has he removed our transgressions from us.
13As a father has compassion on his children,
  so the LORD has compassion on those who fear him;
14for he knows how we are formed,
  he remembers that we are dust.
15As for man, his days are like grass,
  he flourishes like a flower of the field;
16the wind blows over it and it is gone,
  and its place remembers it no more.
17But from everlasting to everlasting
  the LORD's love is with those who fear him,
  and his righteousness with their children's children —
18with those who keep his covenant
  and remember to obey his precepts.

19The LORD has established his throne in heaven,
  and his kingdom rules over all.

20Praise the LORD, you his angels,
  you mighty ones who do his bidding,
  who obey his word.
21Praise the LORD, all his heavenly hosts,
  you his servants who do his will.
22Praise the LORD, all his works
  everywhere in his dominion.

Praise the LORD, O my soul.

Psalm 104

1Praise the LORD, O my soul.

O LORD my God, you are very great;
  you are clothed with splendour and majesty.
2He wraps himself in light as with a garment;
  he stretches out the heavens like a tent
3 and lays the beams of his upper chambers on their waters.
  He makes the clouds his chariot
  and rides on the wings of the wind.
4He makes winds his messengers,^a
  flames of fire his servants.
5He set the earth on its foundations;
  it can never be moved.
6You covered it with the deep as with a garment;
  the waters stood above the mountains.
7But at your rebuke the waters fled,
  at the sound of your thunder they took to flight;
8they flowed over the mountains,
  they went down into the valleys,
  to the place you assigned for them.
9You set a boundary they cannot cross;
  never again will they cover the earth.

---

^a23 Or By his power   ^a4 Or angels

[10]He makes springs pour water into the ravines;
   it flows between the mountains.
[11]They give water to all the beasts of the field;
   the wild donkeys quench their thirst.
[12]The birds of the air nest by the waters;
   they sing among the branches.
[13]He waters the mountains from his upper
      chambers;
   the earth is satisfied by the fruit of his work.
[14]He makes grass grow for the cattle,
   and plants for man to cultivate—
   bringing forth food from the earth:
[15]wine that gladdens the heart of man,
   oil to make his face shine,
   and bread that sustains his heart.
[16]The trees of the LORD are well watered,
   the cedars of Lebanon that he planted.
[17]There the birds make their nests;
   the stork has its home in the pine trees.
[18]The high mountains belong to the wild goats;
   the crags are a refuge for the conies.[b]

[19]The moon marks off the seasons,
   and the sun knows when to go down.
[20]You bring darkness, it becomes night,
   and all the beasts of the forest prowl.
[21]The lions roar for their prey
   and seek their food from God.
[22]The sun rises, and they steal away;
   they return and lie down in their dens.
[23]Then man goes out to his work,
   to his labour until evening.

104:22   This hymn of praise to God who
has made the universe is a comprehensive
description of the ancient Israelites' natural
world. They would not have understood
nature to be a power separate from God, but
rather that it was controlled by God. In this
psalm God is seen as the divine master architect, builder, and craftsman who has made
everything. Human beings should respond
with praise and with care for the world.

[24]How many are your works, O LORD!
   In wisdom you made them all;
   the earth is full of your creatures.
[25]There is the sea, vast and spacious,
   teeming with creatures beyond number—
   living things both large and small.
[26]There the ships go to and fro,
   and the leviathan, which you formed to frolic
      there.
[27]These all look to you
   to give them their food at the proper time.
[28]When you give it to them,
   they gather it up;
   when you open your hand,
   they are satisfied with good things.

[29]When you hide your face,
   they are terrified;
   when you take away their breath,
   they die and return to the dust.
[30]When you send your Spirit,
   they are created,
   and you renew the face of the earth.

[31]May the glory of the LORD endure for ever;
   may the LORD rejoice in his works—
[32]he who looks at the earth, and it trembles,
   who touches the mountains, and they smoke.

[33]I will sing to the LORD all my life;
   I will sing praise to my God as long as I live.
[34]May my meditation be pleasing to him,
   as I rejoice in the LORD.
[35]But may sinners vanish from the earth
   and the wicked be no more.

Praise the LORD, O my soul.

Praise the LORD.[c]

Psalm 105

[1]Give thanks to the LORD, call on his name;
   make known among the nations what he has
      done.
[2]Sing to him, sing praise to him;
   tell of all his wonderful acts.
[3]Glory in his holy name;
   let the hearts of those who seek the LORD
      rejoice.
[4]Look to the LORD and his strength;
   seek his face always.

105:5   When situations were difficult the
Israelite psalmist looked back to the things
that God had done in the past. In particular
the stories about Abraham, Isaac, Joseph,
Jacob, and Moses and the exodus encouraged him to go on trusting God in the
present. Christians too can look back at what
God has done in the past, especially through
Jesus, and feel motivated to go on.

[5]Remember the wonders he has done,
   his miracles, and the judgments he pronounced,
[6]O descendants of Abraham his servant,
   O sons of Jacob, his chosen ones.
[7]He is the LORD our God;
   his judgments are in all the earth.

[8]He remembers his covenant for ever,
   the word he commanded, for a thousand
      generations,
[9]the covenant he made with Abraham,
   the oath he swore to Isaac.
[10]He confirmed it to Jacob as a decree,
   to Israel as an everlasting covenant:
[11]"To you I will give the land of Canaan
   as the portion you will inherit."

[b]18 That is, the hyrax or rock badger   [c]35 Hebrew *Hallelu Yah*; in the Septuagint this line stands at the beginning of Psalm 105.

¹²When they were but few in number,
  few indeed, and strangers in it,
¹³they wandered from nation to nation,
  from one kingdom to another.
¹⁴He allowed no-one to oppress them;
  for their sake he rebuked kings:
¹⁵"Do not touch my anointed ones;
  do my prophets no harm."

¹⁶He called down famine on the land
  and destroyed all their supplies of food;
¹⁷and he sent a man before them—
  Joseph, sold as a slave.
¹⁸They bruised his feet with shackles,
  his neck was put in irons,
¹⁹till what he foretold came to pass,
  till the word of the LORD proved him true.
²⁰The king sent and released him,
  the ruler of peoples set him free.
²¹He made him master of his household,
  ruler over all he possessed,
²²to instruct his princes as he pleased
  and teach his elders wisdom.

²³Then Israel entered Egypt;
  Jacob lived as an alien in the land of Ham.
²⁴The LORD made his people very fruitful;
  he made them too numerous for their foes,
²⁵whose hearts he turned to hate his people,
  to conspire against his servants.
²⁶He sent Moses his servant,
  and Aaron, whom he had chosen.
²⁷They performed his miraculous signs among
    them,
  his wonders in the land of Ham.
²⁸He sent darkness and made the land dark—
  for had they not rebelled against his words?
²⁹He turned their waters into blood,
  causing their fish to die.
³⁰Their land teemed with frogs,
  which went up into the bedrooms of their
    rulers.
³¹He spoke, and there came swarms of flies,
  and gnats throughout their country.
³²He turned their rain into hail,
  with lightning throughout their land;
³³he struck down their vines and fig-trees
  and shattered the trees of their country.
³⁴He spoke, and the locusts came,
  grasshoppers without number;
³⁵they ate up every green thing in their land,
  ate up the produce of their soil.
³⁶Then he struck down all the firstborn in their
    land,
  the firstfruits of all their manhood.

³⁷He brought out Israel, laden with silver and gold,
  and from among their tribes no-one faltered.
³⁸Egypt was glad when they left,
  because dread of Israel had fallen on them.
³⁹He spread out a cloud as a covering,
  and a fire to give light at night.

⁴⁰They asked, and he brought them quail
  and satisfied them with the bread of heaven.
⁴¹He opened the rock, and water gushed out;
  like a river it flowed in the desert.

⁴²For he remembered his holy promise
  given to his servant Abraham.
⁴³He brought out his people with rejoicing,
  his chosen ones with shouts of joy;
⁴⁴he gave them the lands of the nations,
  and they fell heir to what others had toiled
    for—
⁴⁵that they might keep his precepts
  and observe his laws.

Praise the LORD.ᵃ

Psalm 106

¹Praise the LORD.ᵃ

Give thanks to the LORD, for he is good;
  his love endures for ever.
²Who can proclaim the mighty acts of the LORD
  or fully declare his praise?
³Blessed are they who maintain justice,
  who constantly do what is right.
⁴Remember me, O LORD, when you show favour to
    your people,
  come to my aid when you save them,
⁵that I may enjoy the prosperity of your chosen
    ones,
  that I may share in the joy of your nation
  and join your inheritance in giving praise.

106:6   The writer did not trace the history of the people for historical interest but to help his audience understand their present plight in exile. Many times the people had spurned the things that God had done for them. It was not surprising that his patience had run out and they found themselves being subject to other nations. However, God had been long-suffering, merciful, and forgiving rather than concerned with punishing and judging the people. Maybe he would relent again. Such loving characteristics should also be found in the people of God.

---

⁶We have sinned, even as our fathers did;
  we have done wrong and acted wickedly.
⁷When our fathers were in Egypt,
  they gave no thought to your miracles;
  they did not remember your many kindnesses,
  and they rebelled by the sea, the Red Sea.ᵇ
⁸Yet he saved them for his name's sake,
  to make his mighty power known.
⁹He rebuked the Red Sea, and it dried up;
  he led them through the depths as through a
    desert.

ᵃ45 Hebrew *Hallelu Yah*   ᵃ1 Hebrew *Hallelu Yah*; also in verse 48
ᵇ7 Hebrew *Yam Suph*; that is, Sea of Reeds; also in verses 9 and 22

¹⁰He saved them from the hand of the foe;
　from the hand of the enemy he redeemed them.
¹¹The waters covered their adversaries;
　not one of them survived.
¹²Then they believed his promises
　and sang his praise.

¹³But they soon forgot what he had done
　and did not wait for his counsel.
¹⁴In the desert they gave in to their craving;
　in the wasteland they put God to the test.
¹⁵So he gave them what they asked for,
　but sent a wasting disease upon them.

¹⁶In the camp they grew envious of Moses
　and of Aaron, who was consecrated to the
　　LORD.
¹⁷The earth opened up and swallowed Dathan;
　it buried the company of Abiram.
¹⁸Fire blazed among their followers;
　a flame consumed the wicked.

¹⁹At Horeb they made a calf
　and worshipped an idol cast from metal.
²⁰They exchanged their Glory
　for an image of a bull, which eats grass.
²¹They forgot the God who saved them,
　who had done great things in Egypt,
²²miracles in the land of Ham
　and awesome deeds by the Red Sea.
²³So he said he would destroy them—
　had not Moses, his chosen one,
　stood in the breach before him
　to keep his wrath from destroying them.

²⁴Then they despised the pleasant land;
　they did not believe his promise.
²⁵They grumbled in their tents
　and did not obey the LORD.
²⁶So he swore to them with uplifted hand
　that he would make them fall in the desert,
²⁷make their descendants fall among the nations
　and scatter them throughout the lands.

²⁸They yoked themselves to the Baal of Peor
　and ate sacrifices offered to lifeless gods;
²⁹they provoked the LORD to anger by their wicked
　　deeds,
　and a plague broke out among them.
³⁰But Phinehas stood up and intervened,
　and the plague was checked.
³¹This was credited to him as righteousness
　for endless generations to come.

³²By the waters of Meribah they angered the LORD,
　and trouble came to Moses because of them;
³³for they rebelled against the Spirit of God,
　and rash words came from Moses' lips.ᶜ

³⁴They did not destroy the peoples
　as the LORD had commanded them,
³⁵but they mingled with the nations
　and adopted their customs.
³⁶They worshipped their idols,
　which became a snare to them.

³⁷They sacrificed their sons
　and their daughters to demons.
³⁸They shed innocent blood,
　the blood of their sons and daughters,
　whom they sacrificed to the idols of Canaan,
　and the land was desecrated by their blood.
³⁹They defiled themselves by what they did;
　by their deeds they prostituted themselves.

⁴⁰Therefore the LORD was angry with his people
　and abhorred his inheritance.
⁴¹He handed them over to the nations,
　and their foes ruled over them.
⁴²Their enemies oppressed them
　and subjected them to their power.
⁴³Many times he delivered them,
　but they were bent on rebellion
　and they wasted away in their sin.

⁴⁴But he took note of their distress
　when he heard their cry;
⁴⁵for their sake he remembered his covenant
　and out of his great love he relented.
⁴⁶He caused them to be pitied
　by all who held them captive.

⁴⁷Save us, O LORD our God,
　and gather us from the nations,
　that we may give thanks to your holy name
　and glory in your praise.

⁴⁸Praise be to the LORD, the God of Israel,
　from everlasting to everlasting.
　Let all the people say, "Amen!"

Praise the LORD.

BOOK V

Psalms 107–150

Psalm 107

¹Give thanks to the LORD, for he is good;
　his love endures for ever.
²Let the redeemed of the LORD say this—
　those he redeemed from the hand of the foe,
³those he gathered from the lands,
　from east and west, from north and south.ᵃ

⁴Some wandered in desert wastelands,
　finding no way to a city where they could
　　settle.
⁵They were hungry and thirsty,
　and their lives ebbed away.
⁶Then they cried out to the LORD in their trouble,
　and he delivered them from their distress.
⁷He led them by a straight way
　to a city where they could settle.
⁸Let them give thanks to the LORD for his unfailing
　　love
　and his wonderful deeds for men,
⁹for he satisfies the thirsty
　and fills the hungry with good things.

ᶜ33 Or against his spirit, / and rash words came from his lips   ᵃ3 Hebrew north and the sea

¹⁰Some sat in darkness and the deepest gloom,
  prisoners suffering in iron chains,
¹¹for they had rebelled against the words of God
  and despised the counsel of the Most High.
¹²So he subjected them to bitter labour;
  they stumbled, and there was no-one to help.
¹³Then they cried to the LORD in their trouble,
  and he saved them from their distress.
¹⁴He brought them out of darkness and the deepest
  gloom
  and broke away their chains.
¹⁵Let them give thanks to the LORD for his unfailing
  love
  and his wonderful deeds for men,
¹⁶for he breaks down gates of bronze
  and cuts through bars of iron.

107:8   The psalmist thought about things
that went on in the world, especially in the
life of Israel. He concluded that God was con-
tinuously at work watching out for those in
trouble, rescuing them from disasters, and
teaching them to learn from their mistakes.
God works continually in the lives of human
beings, and believing that this is so can make
us more aware of his activity.

---

¹⁷Some became fools through their rebellious ways
  and suffered affliction because of their
    iniquities.
¹⁸They loathed all food
  and drew near the gates of death.
¹⁹Then they cried to the LORD in their trouble,
  and he saved them from their distress.
²⁰He sent forth his word and healed them;
  he rescued them from the grave.
²¹Let them give thanks to the LORD for his unfailing
  love
  and his wonderful deeds for men.
²²Let them sacrifice thank-offerings
  and tell of his works with songs of joy.

²³Others went out on the sea in ships;
  they were merchants on the mighty waters.
²⁴They saw the works of the LORD,
  his wonderful deeds in the deep.
²⁵For he spoke and stirred up a tempest
  that lifted high the waves.
²⁶They mounted up to the heavens and went down
    to the depths;
  in their peril their courage melted away.
²⁷They reeled and staggered like drunken men;
  they were at their wits' end.
²⁸Then they cried out to the LORD in their trouble,
  and he brought them out of their distress.
²⁹He stilled the storm to a whisper;
  the waves of the sea were hushed.
³⁰They were glad when it grew calm,
  and he guided them to their desired haven.
³¹Let them give thanks to the LORD for his unfailing
  love
  and his wonderful deeds for men.

³²Let them exalt him in the assembly of the people
  and praise him in the council of the elders.

³³He turned rivers into a desert,
  flowing springs into thirsty ground,
³⁴and fruitful land into a salt waste,
  because of the wickedness of those who lived
    there.
³⁵He turned the desert into pools of water
  and the parched ground into flowing springs;
³⁶there he brought the hungry to live,
  and they founded a city where they could settle.
³⁷They sowed fields and planted vineyards
  that yielded a fruitful harvest;
³⁸he blessed them, and their numbers greatly
    increased,
  and he did not let their herds diminish.

³⁹Then their numbers decreased, and they were
    humbled
  by oppression, calamity and sorrow;
⁴⁰he who pours contempt on nobles
  made them wander in a trackless waste.
⁴¹But he lifted the needy out of their affliction
  and increased their families like flocks.
⁴²The upright see and rejoice,
  but all the wicked shut their mouths.

⁴³Whoever is wise, let him heed these things
  and consider the great love of the LORD.

Psalm 108

A song. A psalm of David.

¹My heart is steadfast, O God;
  I will sing and make music with all my soul.
²Awake, harp and lyre!
  I will awaken the dawn.
³I will praise you, O LORD, among the nations;
  I will sing of you among the peoples.
⁴For great is your love, higher than the heavens;
  your faithfulness reaches to the skies.
⁵Be exalted, O God, above the heavens,
  and let your glory be over all the earth.

⁶Save us and help us with your right hand,
  that those you love may be delivered.
⁷God has spoken from his sanctuary:
  "In triumph I will parcel out Shechem
  and measure off the Valley of Succoth.
⁸Gilead is mine, Manasseh is mine;
  Ephraim is my helmet,
  Judah my sceptre.
⁹Moab is my washbasin,
  upon Edom I toss my sandal;
  over Philistia I shout in triumph."

¹⁰Who will bring me to the fortified city?
  Who will lead me to Edom?
¹¹Is it not you, O God, you who have rejected us
  and no longer go out with our armies?
¹²Give us aid against the enemy,
  for the help of man is worthless.
¹³With God we shall gain the victory,
  and he will trample down our enemies.

Psalm 109

For the director of music. Of David. A psalm.

[1]O God, whom I praise,
    do not remain silent,
[2]for wicked and deceitful men
    have opened their mouths against me;
    they have spoken against me with lying
        tongues.
[3]With words of hatred they surround me;
    they attack me without cause.
[4]In return for my friendship they accuse me,
    but I am a man of prayer.
[5]They repay me evil for good,
    and hatred for my friendship.

109:8 The psalmist had very bitter feelings about being betrayed by his friends; one of the worst experiences possible. The New Testament applies this verse to Judas' betrayal of Jesus (see Acts 1:20), and that was foreshadowed by David's similar plight. Unwarranted and unexplained suffering comes often to God's most faithful servants but it is harder to bear when caused by those thought to be friends.

---

[6]Appoint[a] an evil man[b] to oppose him;
    let an accuser[c] stand at his right hand.
[7]When he is tried, let him be found guilty,
    and may his prayers condemn him.
[8]May his days be few;
    may another take his place of leadership.
[9]May his children be fatherless
    and his wife a widow.
[10]May his children be wandering beggars;
    may they be driven[d] from their ruined homes.
[11]May a creditor seize all he has;
    may strangers plunder the fruits of his labour.
[12]May no-one extend kindness to him
    or take pity on his fatherless children.
[13]May his descendants be cut off,
    their names blotted out from the next
        generation.
[14]May the iniquity of his fathers be remembered
        before the LORD;
    may the sin of his mother never be blotted out.
[15]May their sins always remain before the LORD,
    that he may cut off the memory of them from
        the earth.

[16]For he never thought of doing a kindness,
    but hounded to death the poor
    and the needy and the broken-hearted.
[17]He loved to pronounce a curse—
    may it[e] come on him;
    he found no pleasure in blessing—
    may it be[f] far from him.

[18]He wore cursing as his garment;
    it entered into his body like water,
    into his bones like oil.
[19]May it be like a cloak wrapped about him,
    like a belt tied for ever round him.
[20]May this be the LORD's payment to my accusers,
    to those who speak evil of me.

[21]But you, O Sovereign LORD,
    deal well with me for your name's sake;
    out of the goodness of your love, deliver me.
[22]For I am poor and needy,
    and my heart is wounded within me.
[23]I fade away like an evening shadow;
    I am shaken off like a locust.
[24]My knees give way from fasting;
    my body is thin and gaunt.
[25]I am an object of scorn to my accusers;
    when they see me, they shake their heads.

[26]Help me, O LORD my God;
    save me in accordance with your love.
[27]Let them know that it is your hand,
    that you, O LORD, have done it.
[28]They may curse, but you will bless;
    when they attack they will be put to shame,
    but your servant will rejoice.
[29]My accusers will be clothed with disgrace
    and wrapped in shame as in a cloak.

[30]With my mouth I will greatly extol the LORD;
    in the great throng I will praise him.
[31]For he stands at the right hand of the needy one,
    to save his life from those who condemn him.

Psalm 110

Of David. A psalm.

[1]The LORD says to my Lord:
    "Sit at my right hand
until I make your enemies
    a footstool for your feet."

[2]The LORD will extend your mighty sceptre from
        Zion;
    you will rule in the midst of your enemies.
[3]Your troops will be willing
    on your day of battle.
Arrayed in holy majesty,
    from the womb of the dawn
    you will receive the dew of your youth.[a]

[4]The LORD has sworn
    and will not change his mind:
"You are a priest for ever,
    in the order of Melchizedek."

[5]The Lord is at your right hand;
    he will crush kings on the day of his wrath.
[6]He will judge nations, heaping up the dead
    and crushing the rulers of the whole earth.
[7]He will drink from a brook beside the way;[b]
    therefore he will lift up his head.

---

*a*6 Or *They say:*, *"Appoint* (with quotation marks at the end of verse 19)   *b*6 Or *the Evil One*   *c*6 Or *let Satan*
*d*10 Septuagint; Hebrew *sought*   *e*17 Or *curse, / and it has*   *f*17 Or *blessing, / and it is*
*a*3 Or / *your young men will come to you like the dew*   *b*7 Or / *The One who grants succession will set him in authority*

110:4   Melchizedek was the King of Salem (i.e. Jerusalem), and was also designated as "priest of God Most High", and Abraham acknowledged his authority (see Genesis 14). Here David, or the Davidic king, as king in Jerusalem was seen to be Melchizedek's successor as a priest as well. Kings in Jerusalem did play a role in the worship of the temple (see 2 Samuel 6:14–18) but probably not on a regular basis. The writer of the letter to the Hebrews used Melchizedek as a model to establish Jesus' own priesthood (see Hebrews 5:6; 7:17). Other New Testament writers believed that David, rather than an anonymous psalmist, was the speaker of the words of verse 1 of this psalm. They found a hint there that David was looking towards a future Messiah.

Psalm 111 [a]

[1] Praise the LORD. [b]

I will extol the LORD with all my heart
   in the council of the upright and in the assembly.

[2] Great are the works of the LORD;
   they are pondered by all who delight in them.
[3] Glorious and majestic are his deeds,
   and his righteousness endures for ever.
[4] He has caused his wonders to be remembered;
   the LORD is gracious and compassionate.
[5] He provides food for those who fear him;
   he remembers his covenant for ever.
[6] He has shown his people the power of his works,
   giving them the lands of other nations.
[7] The works of his hands are faithful and just;
   all his precepts are trustworthy.
[8] They are steadfast for ever and ever,
   done in faithfulness and uprightness.
[9] He provided redemption for his people;
   he ordained his covenant for ever —
   holy and awesome is his name.

[10] The fear of the LORD is the beginning of wisdom;
   all who follow his precepts have good understanding.
   To him belongs eternal praise.

Psalm 112 [a]

[1] Praise the LORD. [b]

Blessed is the man who fears the LORD,
   who finds great delight in his commands.

[2] His children will be mighty in the land;
   the generation of the upright will be blessed.

[3] Wealth and riches are in his house,
   and his righteousness endures for ever.
[4] Even in darkness light dawns for the upright,
   for the gracious and compassionate and righteous man. [c]
[5] Good will come to him who is generous and lends freely,
   who conducts his affairs with justice.
[6] Surely he will never be shaken;
   a righteous man will be remembered for ever.
[7] He will have no fear of bad news;
   his heart is steadfast, trusting in the LORD.
[8] His heart is secure, he will have no fear;
   in the end he will look in triumph on his foes.
[9] He has scattered abroad his gifts to the poor,
   his righteousness endures for ever;
   his horn [d] will be lifted high in honour.

[10] The wicked man will see and be vexed,
   he will gnash his teeth and waste away;
   the longings of the wicked will come to nothing.

Psalm 113

[1] Praise the LORD. [a]

Praise, O servants of the LORD,
   praise the name of the LORD.
[2] Let the name of the LORD be praised,
   both now and for evermore.
[3] From the rising of the sun to the place where it sets,
   the name of the LORD is to be praised.

113:1   Psalms 113–118 are known as the "Hallel" psalms, a name which comes from the Hebrew word meaning "praise" ("Hallelujah" means "Praise the Lord"). These psalms were traditionally sung at the Passover meal; the first two before the meal and the last four after it. Jesus and his disciples may well have sung them at the Last Supper (see Matthew 26:30).

[4] The LORD is exalted over all the nations,
   his glory above the heavens.
[5] Who is like the LORD our God,
   the One who sits enthroned on high,
[6] who stoops down to look
   on the heavens and the earth?

[7] He raises the poor from the dust
   and lifts the needy from the ash heap;
[8] he seats them with princes,
   with the princes of their people.

---

[a] This psalm is an acrostic poem, the lines of which begin with the successive letters of the Hebrew alphabet.
[b] 1 Hebrew *Hallelu Yah*
[b] 1 Hebrew *Hallelu Yah*
[d] 9 *Horn* here symbolises dignity.
[a] This psalm is an acrostic poem, the lines of which begin with the successive letters of the Hebrew alphabet.
[c] 4 Or / *for the* LORD *is gracious and compassionate and righteous*
[a] 1 Hebrew *Hallelu Yah*; also in verse 9

⁹He settles the barren woman in her home
  as a happy mother of children.

Praise the LORD.

Psalm 114

¹When Israel came out of Egypt,
  the house of Jacob from a people of foreign
    tongue,
²Judah became God's sanctuary,
  Israel his dominion.

³The sea looked and fled,
  the Jordan turned back;
⁴the mountains skipped like rams,
  the hills like lambs.

⁵Why was it, O sea, that you fled,
  O Jordan, that you turned back,
⁶you mountains, that you skipped like rams,
  you hills, like lambs?

⁷Tremble, O earth, at the presence of the Lord,
  at the presence of the God of Jacob,
⁸who turned the rock into a pool,
  the hard rock into springs of water.

Psalm 115

¹Not to us, O LORD, not to us
  but to your name be the glory,
  because of your love and faithfulness.

²Why do the nations say,
  "Where is their God?"
³Our God is in heaven;
  he does whatever pleases him.
⁴But their idols are silver and gold,
  made by the hands of men.
⁵They have mouths, but cannot speak,
  eyes, but they cannot see;
⁶they have ears, but cannot hear,
  noses, but they cannot smell;
⁷they have hands, but cannot feel,
  feet, but they cannot walk;
  nor can they utter a sound with their throats.
⁸Those who make them will be like them,
  and so will all who trust in them.

115:8   In the midst of trouble, when the
people were probably being oppressed by foreign nations, the psalmist encouraged them
with a call to trust in the God of heaven. The
other nations may have mocked the Israelites
for not having an image of God in the temple,
but idols are only powerless figures made by
humans. It is folly to trust in such things. God
is the creator who has complete power over
all things.

---

⁹O house of Israel, trust in the LORD —
  he is their help and shield.

¹⁰O house of Aaron, trust in the LORD —
  he is their help and shield.
¹¹You who fear him, trust in the LORD —
  he is their help and shield.

¹²The LORD remembers us and will bless us:
  He will bless the house of Israel,
  he will bless the house of Aaron,
¹³he will bless those who fear the LORD —
  small and great alike.

¹⁴May the LORD make you increase,
  both you and your children.
¹⁵May you be blessed by the LORD,
  the Maker of heaven and earth.

¹⁶The highest heavens belong to the LORD,
  but the earth he has given to man.
¹⁷It is not the dead who praise the LORD,
  those who go down to silence;
¹⁸it is we who extol the LORD,
  both now and for evermore.

Praise the LORD. ᵃ

Psalm 116

¹I love the LORD, for he heard my voice;
  he heard my cry for mercy.
²Because he turned his ear to me,
  I will call on him as long as I live.

³The cords of death entangled me,
  the anguish of the grave ᵃ came upon me;
  I was overcome by trouble and sorrow.
⁴Then I called on the name of the LORD:
  "O LORD, save me!"

⁵The LORD is gracious and righteous;
  our God is full of compassion.
⁶The LORD protects the simple-hearted;
  when I was in great need, he saved me.

⁷Be at rest once more, O my soul,
  for the LORD has been good to you.

⁸For you, O LORD, have delivered my soul from
    death,
  my eyes from tears,
  my feet from stumbling,
⁹that I may walk before the LORD
  in the land of the living.
¹⁰I believed; therefore ᵇ I said,
  "I am greatly afflicted."
¹¹And in my dismay I said,
  "All men are liars."

¹²How can I repay the LORD
  for all his goodness to me?
¹³I will lift up the cup of salvation
  and call on the name of the LORD.
¹⁴I will fulfil my vows to the LORD
  in the presence of all his people.

¹⁵Precious in the sight of the LORD
  is the death of his saints.

ᵃ18 Hebrew Hallelu Yah   ᵃ3 Hebrew Sheol   ᵇ10 Or believed even when

16O LORD, truly I am your servant;
    I am your servant, the son of your
        maidservant; c
    you have freed me from my chains.

17I will sacrifice a thank-offering to you
    and call on the name of the LORD.
18I will fulfil my vows to the LORD
    in the presence of all his people,
19in the courts of the house of the LORD—
    in your midst, O Jerusalem.

Praise the LORD. d

Psalm 117

1Praise the LORD, all you nations;
    extol him, all you peoples.
2For great is his love towards us,
    and the faithfulness of the LORD endures for
        ever.

Praise the LORD. d

Psalm 118

1Give thanks to the LORD, for he is good;
    his love endures for ever.

2Let Israel say:
    "His love endures for ever."
3Let the house of Aaron say:
    "His love endures for ever."
4Let those who fear the LORD say:
    "His love endures for ever."

5In my anguish I cried to the LORD,
    and he answered by setting me free.
6The LORD is with me; I will not be afraid.
    What can man do to me?
7The LORD is with me; he is my helper.
    I will look in triumph on my enemies.

8It is better to take refuge in the LORD
    than to trust in man.
9It is better to take refuge in the LORD
    than to trust in princes.

10All the nations surrounded me,
    but in the name of the LORD I cut them off.
11They surrounded me on every side,
    but in the name of the LORD I cut them off.
12They swarmed around me like bees,
    but they died out as quickly as burning thorns;
    in the name of the LORD I cut them off.

13I was pushed back and about to fall,
    but the LORD helped me.
14The LORD is my strength and my song;
    he has become my salvation.

15Shouts of joy and victory
    resound in the tents of the righteous:

"The LORD's right hand has done mighty things!
16 The LORD's right hand is lifted high;
    the LORD's right hand has done mighty things!"

118:15   Representations of ancient kings
from Egypt, Assyria, Babylon, and elsewhere
regularly show the kings with an outstretched right hand clasping a sword or a
club, about to kill an enemy. The right hand
was a sign of kingly authority and power. As
elsewhere in the Old Testament, God here is
thought of like the mighty kings of the day.
The psalmist had gone from hard circumstances to victory. He wanted to recognize
God's major part in all this by going to the
temple to give thanks.

17I will not die but live,
    and will proclaim what the LORD has done.
18The LORD has chastened me severely,
    but he has not given me over to death.

19Open for me the gates of righteousness;
    I will enter and give thanks to the LORD.
20This is the gate of the LORD
    through which the righteous may enter.
21I will give you thanks, for you answered me;
    you have become my salvation.

22The stone the builders rejected
    has become the capstone;
23the LORD has done this,
    and it is marvellous in our eyes.
24This is the day the LORD has made;
    let us rejoice and be glad in it.

25O LORD, save us;
    O LORD, grant us success.
26Blessed is he who comes in the name of the
        LORD.
    From the house of the LORD we bless you. a
27The LORD is God,
    and he has made his light shine upon us.
    With boughs in hand, join in the festal procession
    up b to the horns of the altar.

28You are my God, and I will give thanks;
    you are my God, and I will exalt you.

29Give thanks to the LORD, for he is good;
    his love endures for ever.

Psalm 119 a

א Aleph

1Blessed are they whose ways are blameless,
    who walk according to the law of the LORD.
2Blessed are they who keep his statutes
    and seek him with all their heart.
3They do nothing wrong;
    they walk in his ways.

---

c16 Or servant, your faithful son   d19, 2 Hebrew Hallelu Yah
b27 Or Bind the festal sacrifice with ropes / and take it
aThis psalm is an acrostic poem; the verses of each stanza begin with the same letter of the Hebrew alphabet.

a26 The Hebrew is plural.

⁴You have laid down precepts
    that are to be fully obeyed.
⁵Oh, that my ways were steadfast
    in obeying your decrees!
⁶Then I would not be put to shame
    when I consider all your commands.
⁷I will praise you with an upright heart
    as I learn your righteous laws.
⁸I will obey your decrees;
    do not utterly forsake me.

119:1   The person who is favoured by God is the one who meditates on the law of God day and night. Psalm 119 is an extended meditation on the theme of the goodness of this law. It is cleverly constructed. There are twenty-two sections (the number of Hebrew letters), and every line of a section begins with the same letter as the others in that particular section.

ב   Beth

⁹How can a young man keep his way pure?
    By living according to your word.
¹⁰I seek you with all my heart;
    do not let me stray from your commands.
¹¹I have hidden your word in my heart
    that I might not sin against you.
¹²Praise be to you, O Lᴏʀᴅ;
    teach me your decrees.
¹³With my lips I recount
    all the laws that come from your mouth.
¹⁴I rejoice in following your statutes
    as one rejoices in great riches.
¹⁵I meditate on your precepts
    and consider your ways.
¹⁶I delight in your decrees;
    I will not neglect your word.

ג   Gimel

¹⁷Do good to your servant, and I will live;
    I will obey your word.
¹⁸Open my eyes that I may see
    wonderful things in your law.
¹⁹I am a stranger on earth;
    do not hide your commands from me.
²⁰My soul is consumed with longing
    for your laws at all times.
²¹You rebuke the arrogant, who are cursed
    and who stray from your commands.
²²Remove from me scorn and contempt,
    for I keep your statutes.
²³Though rulers sit together and slander me,
    your servant will meditate on your decrees.
²⁴Your statutes are my delight;
    they are my counsellors.

ד   Daleth

²⁵I am laid low in the dust;
    preserve my life according to your word.
²⁶I recounted my ways and you answered me;
    teach me your decrees.
²⁷Let me understand the teaching of your precepts;
    then I will meditate on your wonders.
²⁸My soul is weary with sorrow;
    strengthen me according to your word.
²⁹Keep me from deceitful ways;
    be gracious to me through your law.
³⁰I have chosen the way of truth;
    I have set my heart on your laws.
³¹I hold fast to your statutes, O Lᴏʀᴅ;
    do not let me be put to shame.
³²I run in the path of your commands,
    for you have set my heart free.

ה   He

³³Teach me, O Lᴏʀᴅ, to follow your decrees;
    then I will keep them to the end.
³⁴Give me understanding, and I will keep your law
    and obey it with all my heart.
³⁵Direct me in the path of your commands,
    for there I find delight.
³⁶Turn my heart towards your statutes
    and not towards selfish gain.
³⁷Turn my eyes away from worthless things;
    preserve my life according to your word.ᵇ
³⁸Fulfil your promise to your servant,
    so that you may be feared.
³⁹Take away the disgrace I dread,
    for your laws are good.
⁴⁰How I long for your precepts!
    Preserve my life in your righteousness.

119:34   For the Israelites the law was not something negative. It did involve rules, obedience, punishment, and penalties but it was much more than that. "Torah" is the Hebrew word for law and it means something like "instruction". A favourite image used to describe the law was a pathway along which one should walk through life. The psalmist used the same eight synonyms for law in each section, here translated as decrees, law, commands, statutes, word, promise, laws (a different word), and precepts.

ו   Waw

⁴¹May your unfailing love come to me, O Lᴏʀᴅ,
    your salvation according to your promise;
⁴²then I will answer the one who taunts me,
    for I trust in your word.
⁴³Do not snatch the word of truth from my mouth,
    for I have put my hope in your laws.

ᵇ37 Two manuscripts of the Masoretic Text and Dead Sea Scrolls; most manuscripts of the Masoretic Text *life in your way*

⁴⁴I will always obey your law,
  for ever and ever.
⁴⁵I will walk about in freedom,
  for I have sought out your precepts.
⁴⁶I will speak of your statutes before kings
  and will not be put to shame,
⁴⁷for I delight in your commands
  because I love them.
⁴⁸I lift up my hands toᶜ your commands, which I
  love,
  and I meditate on your decrees.

ז   Zayin

⁴⁹Remember your word to your servant,
  for you have given me hope.
⁵⁰My comfort in my suffering is this:
  Your promise preserves my life.
⁵¹The arrogant mock me without restraint,
  but I do not turn from your law.
⁵²I remember your ancient laws, O LORD,
  and I find comfort in them.
⁵³Indignation grips me because of the wicked,
  who have forsaken your law.
⁵⁴Your decrees are the theme of my song
  wherever I lodge.
⁵⁵In the night I remember your name, O LORD,
  and I will keep your law.
⁵⁶This has been my practice:
  I obey your precepts.

ח   Heth

⁵⁷You are my portion, O LORD;
  I have promised to obey your words.
⁵⁸I have sought your face with all my heart;
  be gracious to me according to your promise.
⁵⁹I have considered my ways
  and have turned my steps to your statutes.
⁶⁰I will hasten and not delay
  to obey your commands.
⁶¹Though the wicked bind me with ropes,
  I will not forget your law.
⁶²At midnight I rise to give you thanks
  for your righteous laws.
⁶³I am a friend to all who fear you,
  to all who follow your precepts.
⁶⁴The earth is filled with your love, O LORD;
  teach me your decrees.

ט   Teth

⁶⁵Do good to your servant
  according to your word, O LORD.
⁶⁶Teach me knowledge and good judgment,
  for I believe in your commands.
⁶⁷Before I was afflicted I went astray,
  but now I obey your word.
⁶⁸You are good, and what you do is good;
  teach me your decrees.
⁶⁹Though the arrogant have smeared me with
  lies,
  I keep your precepts with all my heart.

⁷⁰Their hearts are callous and unfeeling,
  but I delight in your law.
⁷¹It was good for me to be afflicted
  so that I might learn your decrees.
⁷²The law from your mouth is more precious
    to me
  than thousands of pieces of silver and gold.

י   Yodh

⁷³Your hands made me and formed me;
  give me understanding to learn your commands.
⁷⁴May those who fear you rejoice when they see
    me,
  for I have put my hope in your word.
⁷⁵I know, O LORD, that your laws are righteous,
  and in faithfulness you have afflicted me.
⁷⁶May your unfailing love be my comfort,
  according to your promise to your servant.
⁷⁷Let your compassion come to me that I may
    live,
  for your law is my delight.
⁷⁸May the arrogant be put to shame for wronging
    me without cause;
  but I will meditate on your precepts.
⁷⁹May those who fear you turn to me,
  those who understand your statutes.
⁸⁰May my heart be blameless towards your decrees,
  that I may not be put to shame.

כ   Kaph

⁸¹My soul faints with longing for your salvation,
  but I have put my hope in your word.
⁸²My eyes fail, looking for your promise;
  I say, "When will you comfort me?"
⁸³Though I am like a wineskin in the smoke,
  I do not forget your decrees.
⁸⁴How long must your servant wait?
  When will you punish my persecutors?
⁸⁵The arrogant dig pitfalls for me,
  contrary to your law.
⁸⁶All your commands are trustworthy;
  help me, for men persecute me without cause.
⁸⁷They almost wiped me from the earth,
  but I have not forsaken your precepts.
⁸⁸Preserve my life according to your love,
  and I will obey the statutes of your mouth.

119:83   The psalms give clues to the life
and times of the ancient Israelites. The writers usually took their images from everyday
life. Here the writer used the image of wine,
which was stored in leather skins and hung
from a roof, to talk about his life. The smoke
from the open cooking fire would turn the
skins black, shrivelled, and unsightly over a
period of time. It is a picture of discomfort,
but despite the writer's unpleasant experience, he continued to trust God's law.

ᶜ48 Or for

ל Lamedh

89Your word, O Lord, is eternal;
   it stands firm in the heavens.
90Your faithfulness continues through all
      generations;
   you established the earth, and it endures.
91Your laws endure to this day,
   for all things serve you.
92If your law had not been my delight,
   I would have perished in my affliction.
93I will never forget your precepts,
   for by them you have preserved my life.
94Save me, for I am yours;
   I have sought out your precepts.
95The wicked are waiting to destroy me,
   but I will ponder your statutes.
96To all perfection I see a limit;
   but your commands are boundless.

מ Mem

97Oh, how I love your law!
   I meditate on it all day long.
98Your commands make me wiser than my
      enemies,
   for they are ever with me.
99I have more insight than all my teachers,
   for I meditate on your statutes.
100I have more understanding than the elders,
   for I obey your precepts.
101I have kept my feet from every evil path
   so that I might obey your word.
102I have not departed from your laws,
   for you yourself have taught me.
103How sweet are your words to my taste,
   sweeter than honey to my mouth!
104I gain understanding from your precepts;
   therefore I hate every wrong path.

נ Nun

105Your word is a lamp to my feet
   and a light for my path.
106I have taken an oath and confirmed it,
   that I will follow your righteous laws.
107I have suffered much;
   preserve my life, O Lord, according to your
      word.
108Accept, O Lord, the willing praise of my mouth,
   and teach me your laws.
109Though I constantly take my life in my hands,
   I will not forget your law.
110The wicked have set a snare for me,
   but I have not strayed from your precepts.
111Your statutes are my heritage for ever;
   they are the joy of my heart.
112My heart is set on keeping your decrees
   to the very end.

ס Samekh

113I hate double-minded men,
   but I love your law.
114You are my refuge and my shield;
   I have put my hope in your word.

115Away from me, you evildoers,
   that I may keep the commands of my God!
116Sustain me according to your promise, and I shall
      live;
   do not let my hopes be dashed.
117Uphold me, and I shall be delivered;
   I shall always have regard for your decrees.
118You reject all who stray from your decrees,
   for their deceitfulness is in vain.
119All the wicked of the earth you discard like
      dross;
   therefore I love your statutes.
120My flesh trembles in fear of you;
   I stand in awe of your laws.

ע Ayin

121I have done what is righteous and just;
   do not leave me to my oppressors.
122Ensure your servant's well-being;
   let not the arrogant oppress me.
123My eyes fail, looking for your salvation,
   looking for your righteous promise.
124Deal with your servant according to your love
   and teach me your decrees.
125I am your servant; give me discernment
   that I may understand your statutes.
126It is time for you to act, O Lord;
   your law is being broken.
127Because I love your commands
   more than gold, more than pure gold,
128and because I consider all your precepts right,
   I hate every wrong path.

פ Pe

129Your statutes are wonderful;
   therefore I obey them.
130The unfolding of your words gives light;
   it gives understanding to the simple.
131I open my mouth and pant,
   longing for your commands.
132Turn to me and have mercy on me,
   as you always do to those who love your name.
133Direct my footsteps according to your word;
   let no sin rule over me.
134Redeem me from the oppression of men,
   that I may obey your precepts.
135Make your face shine upon your servant
   and teach me your decrees.
136Streams of tears flow from my eyes,
   for your law is not obeyed.

צ Tsadhe

137Righteous are you, O Lord,
   and your laws are right.
138The statutes you have laid down are righteous;
   they are fully trustworthy.
139My zeal wears me out,
   for my enemies ignore your words.
140Your promises have been thoroughly tested,
   and your servant loves them.
141Though I am lowly and despised,
   I do not forget your precepts.

¹⁴²Your righteousness is everlasting
  and your law is true.
¹⁴³Trouble and distress have come upon me,
  but your commands are my delight.
¹⁴⁴Your statutes are for ever right;
  give me understanding that I may live.

ק Qoph

¹⁴⁵I call with all my heart; answer me, O LORD,
  and I will obey your decrees.
¹⁴⁶I call out to you; save me
  and I will keep your statutes.
¹⁴⁷I rise before dawn and cry for help;
  I have put my hope in your word.
¹⁴⁸My eyes stay open through the watches of the
    night,
  that I may meditate on your promises.
¹⁴⁹Hear my voice in accordance with your love;
  preserve my life, O LORD, according to your
    laws.
¹⁵⁰Those who devise wicked schemes are near,
  but they are far from your law.
¹⁵¹Yet you are near, O LORD,
  and all your commands are true.
¹⁵²Long ago I learned from your statutes
  that you established them to last for ever.

ר Resh

¹⁵³Look upon my suffering and deliver me,
  for I have not forgotten your law.
¹⁵⁴Defend my cause and redeem me;
  preserve my life according to your promise.
¹⁵⁵Salvation is far from the wicked,
  for they do not seek out your decrees.
¹⁵⁶Your compassion is great, O LORD;
  preserve my life according to your laws.
¹⁵⁷Many are the foes who persecute me,
  but I have not turned from your statutes.
¹⁵⁸I look on the faithless with loathing,
  for they do not obey your word.
¹⁵⁹See how I love your precepts;
  preserve my life, O LORD, according to your
    love.
¹⁶⁰All your words are true;
  all your righteous laws are eternal.

ש Sin and Shin

¹⁶¹Rulers persecute me without cause,
  but my heart trembles at your word.
¹⁶²I rejoice in your promise
  like one who finds great spoil.
¹⁶³I hate and abhor falsehood
  but I love your law.
¹⁶⁴Seven times a day I praise you
  for your righteous laws.
¹⁶⁵Great peace have they who love your law,
  and nothing can make them stumble.
¹⁶⁶I wait for your salvation, O LORD,
  and I follow your commands.
¹⁶⁷I obey your statutes,
  for I love them greatly.

¹⁶⁸I obey your precepts and your statutes,
  for all my ways are known to you.

ת Taw

¹⁶⁹May my cry come before you, O LORD;
  give me understanding according to your word.
¹⁷⁰May my supplication come before you;
  deliver me according to your promise.
¹⁷¹May my lips overflow with praise,
  for you teach me your decrees.
¹⁷²May my tongue sing of your word,
  for all your commands are righteous.
¹⁷³May your hand be ready to help me,
  for I have chosen your precepts.
¹⁷⁴I long for your salvation, O LORD,
  and your law is my delight.
¹⁷⁵Let me live that I may praise you,
  and may your laws sustain me.
¹⁷⁶I have strayed like a lost sheep.
  Seek your servant,
  for I have not forgotten your commands.

Psalm 120

A song of ascents.

¹I call on the LORD in my distress,
  and he answers me.
²Save me, O LORD, from lying lips
  and from deceitful tongues.

120:1 Psalm 120 is the first of the group of psalms (120—134) which all have the title "A song of ascents". It is most likely that "ascents" referred to the use of these psalms by pilgrims on their way to the Jerusalem temple. The word translated "ascents" was often used about going on a pilgrimage or for the processional ascent to the temple.

---

³What will he do to you,
  and what more besides, O deceitful tongue?
⁴He will punish you with a warrior's sharp arrows,
  with burning coals of the broom tree.

⁵Woe to me that I dwell in Meshech,
  that I live among the tents of Kedar!
⁶Too long have I lived
  among those who hate peace.
⁷I am a man of peace;
  but when I speak, they are for war.

Psalm 121

A song of ascents.

¹I lift up my eyes to the hills—
  where does my help come from?
²My help comes from the LORD,
  the Maker of heaven and earth.

³He will not let your foot slip—
  he who watches over you will not slumber;

[4]indeed, he who watches over Israel
  will neither slumber nor sleep.

[5]The LORD watches over you—
  the LORD is your shade at your right hand;
[6]the sun will not harm you by day,
  nor the moon by night.

121:7 This psalm is one of the most popular of this group of pilgrim songs. It records the words of a pilgrim just setting out on a journey. He was contemplating the difficult route through the mountains and was sent on his way with these words of blessing. He was quite possibly actually on his way home with these words from the priest to encourage him on his journey. Life itself can be seen as a pilgrimage and this psalm gives encouragement for those on the spiritual journey towards the city of God (see Hebrews 11:10).

---

[7]The LORD will keep you from all harm—
  he will watch over your life;
[8]the LORD will watch over your coming and going
  both now and for evermore.

Psalm 122

A song of ascents. Of David.

[1]I rejoiced with those who said to me,
  "Let us go to the house of the LORD."
[2]Our feet are standing
  in your gates, O Jerusalem.

[3]Jerusalem is built like a city
  that is closely compacted together.
[4]That is where the tribes go up,
  the tribes of the LORD,
to praise the name of the LORD
  according to the statute given to Israel.
[5]There the thrones for judgment stand,
  the thrones of the house of David.

[6]Pray for the peace of Jerusalem:
  "May those who love you be secure.
[7]May there be peace within your walls
  and security within your citadels."
[8]For the sake of my brothers and friends,
  I will say, "Peace be within you."
[9]For the sake of the house of the LORD our God,
  I will seek your prosperity.

Psalm 123

A song of ascents.

[1]I lift up my eyes to you,
  to you whose throne is in heaven.
[2]As the eyes of slaves look to the hand of their
    master,
  as the eyes of a maid look to the hand of her
    mistress,

so our eyes look to the LORD our God,
  till he shows us his mercy.

[3]Have mercy on us, O LORD, have mercy on us,
  for we have endured much contempt.
[4]We have endured much ridicule from the proud,
  much contempt from the arrogant.

Psalm 124

A song of ascents. Of David.

[1]If the LORD had not been on our side—
  let Israel say—
[2]if the LORD had not been on our side
  when men attacked us,
[3]when their anger flared against us,
  they would have swallowed us alive;
[4]the flood would have engulfed us,
  the torrent would have swept over us,
[5]the raging waters
  would have swept us away.

[6]Praise be to the LORD,
  who has not let us be torn by their teeth.
[7]We have escaped like a bird
  out of the fowler's snare;
the snare has been broken,
  and we have escaped.
[8]Our help is in the name of the LORD,
  the Maker of heaven and earth.

Psalm 125

A song of ascents.

[1]Those who trust in the LORD are like Mount Zion,
  which cannot be shaken but endures for ever.
[2]As the mountains surround Jerusalem,
  so the LORD surrounds his people
  both now and for evermore.

[3]The sceptre of the wicked will not remain
  over the land allotted to the righteous,
for then the righteous might use
  their hands to do evil.

125:3 The sceptre, like the mace carried by mayors, was a symbol of office indicating the power of the king. Here the "sceptre of the wicked" refers to the jurisdiction of a foreign people, like the Assyrians, over Israel. The psalmist was looking forward to the overthrow of these people before they had a bad effect on the people of God.

---

[4]Do good, O LORD, to those who are good,
  to those who are upright in heart.
[5]But those who turn to crooked ways
  the LORD will banish with the evildoers.

Peace be upon Israel.

Psalm 126

A song of ascents.

¹When the LORD brought back the captives to ᵃ
Zion,
  we were like men who dreamed. ᵇ
²Our mouths were filled with laughter,
  our tongues with songs of joy.
Then it was said among the nations,
  "The LORD has done great things for them."
³The LORD has done great things for us,
  and we are filled with joy.

⁴Restore our fortunes, ᶜ O LORD,
  like streams in the Negev.
⁵Those who sow in tears
  will reap with songs of joy.
⁶He who goes out weeping,
  carrying seed to sow,
will return with songs of joy,
  carrying sheaves with him.

Psalm 127

A song of ascents. Of Solomon.

¹Unless the LORD builds the house,
  its builders labour in vain.
Unless the LORD watches over the city,
  the watchmen stand guard in vain.
²In vain you rise early
  and stay up late,
toiling for food to eat —
  for he grants sleep to ᵈ those he loves.

³Sons are a heritage from the LORD,
  children a reward from him.
⁴Like arrows in the hands of a warrior
  are sons born in one's youth.
⁵Blessed is the man
  whose quiver is full of them.
They will not be put to shame
  when they contend with their enemies in the
    gate.

Psalm 128

A song of ascents.

¹Blessed are all who fear the LORD,
  who walk in his ways.
²You will eat the fruit of your labour;
  blessings and prosperity will be yours.
³Your wife will be like a fruitful vine
  within your house;
your sons will be like olive shoots
  round your table.
⁴Thus is the man blessed
  who fears the LORD.

⁵May the LORD bless you from Zion
  all the days of your life;

may you see the prosperity of Jerusalem,
⁶ and may you live to see your children's
  children.

Peace be upon Israel.

Psalm 129

A song of ascents.

¹They have greatly oppressed me from my youth —
  let Israel say —
²they have greatly oppressed me from my youth,
  but they have not gained the victory over me.
³Ploughmen have ploughed my back
  and made their furrows long.
⁴But the LORD is righteous;
  he has cut me free from the cords of the
    wicked.

⁵May all who hate Zion
  be turned back in shame.
⁶May they be like grass on the roof,
  which withers before it can grow;
⁷with it the reaper cannot fill his hands,
  nor the one who gathers fill his arms.
⁸May those who pass by not say,
  "The blessing of the LORD be upon you;
  we bless you in the name of the LORD."

Psalm 130

A song of ascents.

¹Out of the depths I cry to you, O LORD;
² O Lord, hear my voice.
Let your ears be attentive
  to my cry for mercy.

³If you, O LORD, kept a record of sins,
  O Lord, who could stand?
⁴But with you there is forgiveness;
  therefore you are feared.

⁵I wait for the LORD, my soul waits,
  and in his word I put my hope.
⁶My soul waits for the Lord
  more than watchmen wait for the morning,
  more than watchmen wait for the morning.

⁷O Israel, put your hope in the LORD,
  for with the LORD is unfailing love
  and with him is full redemption.
⁸He himself will redeem Israel
  from all their sins.

Psalm 131

A song of ascents. Of David.

¹My heart is not proud, O LORD,
  my eyes are not haughty;
I do not concern myself with great matters
  or things too wonderful for me.

ᵃ1 Or LORD restored the fortunes of   ᵇ1 Or men restored to health
ᵃ2 Or eat— / for while they sleep he provides for   ᶜ4 Or Bring back our captives

[2]But I have stilled and quietened my soul;
  like a weaned child with its mother,
  like a weaned child is my soul within me.

131:2   Here, two stages in the growth of a child are compared. A newborn child does not know how to be patient. It cries whenever it feels the need for something. An older child has established a deeper trust and learned to be more patient when its mother does not immediately respond. As Paul said in Philippians 4:12 "I have learned the secret of being content in any and every situation". This quality of life was of greater value to the psalmist than being involved in affairs of state.

---

[3]O Israel, put your hope in the Lord
  both now and for evermore.

Psalm 132

A song of ascents.

[1]O Lord, remember David
  and all the hardships he endured.

[2]He swore an oath to the Lord
  and made a vow to the Mighty One of Jacob:
[3]"I will not enter my house
  or go to my bed—
[4]I will allow no sleep to my eyes,
  no slumber to my eyelids,
[5]till I find a place for the Lord,
  a dwelling for the Mighty One of Jacob."

[6]We heard it in Ephrathah,
  we came upon it in the fields of Jaar:[a,b]
[7]"Let us go to his dwelling-place;
  let us worship at his footstool—
[8]arise, O Lord, and come to your resting place,
  you and the ark of your might.
[9]May your priests be clothed with righteousness;
  may your saints sing for joy."

[10]For the sake of David your servant,
  do not reject your anointed one.

[11]The Lord swore an oath to David,
  a sure oath that he will not revoke:
"One of your own descendants
  I will place on your throne—
[12]if your sons keep my covenant
  and the statutes I teach them,
then their sons shall sit
  on your throne for ever and ever."

[13]For the Lord has chosen Zion,
  he has desired it for his dwelling:
[14]"This is my resting place for ever and ever;
  here I will sit enthroned, for I have desired it—

[15]I will bless her with abundant provisions;
  her poor will I satisfy with food.
[16]I will clothe her priests with salvation,
  and her saints shall ever sing for joy.

132:13   Drawing on the traditions of the ark of the covenant in 1 Samuel, this psalm underlines what the people in Jerusalem thought about their security with God during the period of the kings who followed David. The temple would always be a guarantee of blessing because God dwelled in it. When the temple was destroyed and the people exiled they found it difficult to understand how God had deserted them. They forgot that the guarantee contained a conditional promise: "if your sons keep my covenant and the statutes I teach them. . .".

---

[17]"Here I will make a horn[c] grow for David
  and set up a lamp for my anointed one.
[18]I will clothe his enemies with shame,
  but the crown on his head shall be
  resplendent."

Psalm 133

A song of ascents. Of David.

[1]How good and pleasant it is
  when brothers live together in unity!
[2]It is like precious oil poured on the head,
  running down on the beard,
running down on Aaron's beard,
  down upon the collar of his robes.
[3]It is as if the dew of Hermon
  were falling on Mount Zion.
For there the Lord bestows his blessing,
  even life for evermore.

Psalm 134

A song of ascents.

[1]Praise the Lord, all you servants of the Lord
  who minister by night in the house of the
  Lord.
[2]Lift up your hands in the sanctuary
  and praise the Lord.

[3]May the Lord, the Maker of heaven and earth,
  bless you from Zion.

Psalm 135

[1]Praise the Lord.[a]

Praise the name of the Lord;
  praise him, you servants of the Lord,
[2]you who minister in the house of the Lord,
  in the courts of the house of our God.

---

[a]6 That is, Kiriath Jearim
[b]6 Or *heard of it in Ephrathah, / we found it in the fields of Jaar.* (and no quotation marks around verses 7–9)
[c]17 *Horn* here symbolises strong one, that is, king.   [a]1 Hebrew *Hallelu Yah*; also in verses 3 and 21

³Praise the LORD, for the LORD is good;
  sing praise to his name, for that is pleasant.
⁴For the LORD has chosen Jacob to be his own,
  Israel to be his treasured possession.

⁵I know that the LORD is great,
  that our Lord is greater than all gods.
⁶The LORD does whatever pleases him,
  in the heavens and on the earth,
  in the seas and all their depths.
⁷He makes clouds rise from the ends of the earth;
  he sends lightning with the rain
  and brings out the wind from his storehouses.

⁸He struck down the firstborn of Egypt,
  the firstborn of men and animals.
⁹He sent his signs and wonders into your midst, O
  Egypt,
  against Pharaoh and all his servants.
¹⁰He struck down many nations
  and killed mighty kings—
¹¹Sihon king of the Amorites,
  Og king of Bashan
  and all the kings of Canaan—
¹²and he gave their land as an inheritance,
  an inheritance to his people Israel.

¹³Your name, O LORD, endures for ever,
  your renown, O LORD, through all generations.
¹⁴For the LORD will vindicate his people
  and have compassion on his servants.

¹⁵The idols of the nations are silver and gold,
  made by the hands of men.
¹⁶They have mouths, but cannot speak,
  eyes, but they cannot see;
¹⁷they have ears, but cannot hear,
  nor is there breath in their mouths.
¹⁸Those who make them will be like them,
  and so will all who trust in them.

¹⁹O house of Israel, praise the LORD;
  O house of Aaron, praise the LORD;
²⁰O house of Levi, praise the LORD;
  you who fear him, praise the LORD.
²¹Praise be to the LORD from Zion,
  to him who dwells in Jerusalem.

  Praise the LORD.

Psalm 136

¹Give thanks to the LORD, for he is good.
        His love endures for ever.
²Give thanks to the God of gods.
        His love endures for ever.
³Give thanks to the Lord of lords:
        His love endures for ever.

⁴to him who alone does great wonders,
        His love endures for ever.
⁵who by his understanding made the heavens,
        His love endures for ever.

⁶who spread out the earth upon the waters,
        His love endures for ever.
⁷who made the great lights—
        His love endures for ever.
⁸the sun to govern the day,
        His love endures for ever.
⁹the moon and stars to govern the night;
        His love endures for ever.

136:1   Occasionally it is possible to see
how a psalm was used in the worship of the
temple. Clearly the refrain running through
this psalm was intended to be sung by a choir
in response to a single priest, or by the congregation in response to a choir. The history
of God's dealings with his people has been
turned into an opportunity for worship.

---

¹⁰to him who struck down the firstborn of Egypt
        His love endures for ever.
¹¹and brought Israel out from among them
        His love endures for ever.
¹²with a mighty hand and outstretched arm;
        His love endures for ever.
¹³to him who divided the Red Sea ͣ asunder
        His love endures for ever.
¹⁴and brought Israel through the midst of it,
        His love endures for ever.
¹⁵but swept Pharaoh and his army into the Red Sea;
        His love endures for ever.
¹⁶to him who led his people through the desert,
        His love endures for ever.
¹⁷who struck down great kings,
        His love endures for ever.
¹⁸and killed mighty kings—
        His love endures for ever.
¹⁹Sihon king of the Amorites
        His love endures for ever.
²⁰and Og king of Bashan—
        His love endures for ever.
²¹and gave their land as an inheritance,
        His love endures for ever.
²²an inheritance to his servant Israel;
        His love endures for ever.
²³to the One who remembered us in our low estate
        His love endures for ever.
²⁴and freed us from our enemies,
        His love endures for ever.
²⁵and who gives food to every creature.
        His love endures for ever.

²⁶Give thanks to the God of heaven.
        His love endures for ever.

Psalm 137

¹By the rivers of Babylon we sat and wept
  when we remembered Zion.
²There on the poplars
  we hung our harps,

ͣ 13 Hebrew *Yam Suph*; that is, Sea of Reeds; also in verse 15

³for there our captors asked us for songs,
  our tormentors demanded songs of joy;
  they said, "Sing us one of the songs of Zion!"

137:4   Music was a way for the people to express their joy in the Lord. Now there was no reason whatsoever to be happy, and in the depths of despair the psalmist expressed his grief at the loss of homeland. The exiles' bitter feelings spilled over into intense hatred of their captors. Warfare was always brutal, and the killing of babies was an accepted, although shocking, part of the fate of defeated peoples. The ideal of loving one's enemies is difficult to sustain in such extreme circumstances. Jesus' "Father forgive them. . ." from the cross (see Luke 23:34) is something that goes against the impulse of normal human nature.

---

⁴How can we sing the songs of the LORD
  while in a foreign land?
⁵If I forget you, O Jerusalem,
  may my right hand forget its skill.
⁶May my tongue cling to the roof of my mouth
  if I do not remember you,
  if I do not consider Jerusalem
  my highest joy.

⁷Remember, O LORD, what the Edomites did
  on the day Jerusalem fell.
"Tear it down," they cried,
  "tear it down to its foundations!"

⁸O Daughter of Babylon, doomed to destruction,
  happy is he who repays you
  for what you have done to us—
⁹he who seizes your infants
  and dashes them against the rocks.

Psalm 138

Of David.

¹I will praise you, O LORD, with all my heart;
  before the "gods" I will sing your praise.
²I will bow down towards your holy temple
  and will praise your name
  for your love and your faithfulness,
for you have exalted above all things
  your name and your word.
³When I called, you answered me;
  you made me bold and stout-hearted.

⁴May all the kings of the earth praise you, O LORD,
  when they hear the words of your mouth.
⁵May they sing of the ways of the LORD,
  for the glory of the LORD is great.

⁶Though the LORD is on high, he looks upon the
  lowly,
  but the proud he knows from afar.
⁷Though I walk in the midst of trouble,
  you preserve my life;
you stretch out your hand against the anger of my
  foes,
  with your right hand you save me.
⁸The LORD will fulfil his purpose for me;
  your love, O LORD, endures for ever—
  do not abandon the works of your hands.

Psalm 139

For the director of music. Of David. A psalm.

¹O LORD, you have searched me
  and you know me.
²You know when I sit and when I rise;
  you perceive my thoughts from afar.
³You discern my going out and my lying down;
  you are familiar with all my ways.
⁴Before a word is on my tongue
  you know it completely, O LORD.

⁵You hem me in—behind and before;
  you have laid your hand upon me.
⁶Such knowledge is too wonderful for me,
  too lofty for me to attain.

⁷Where can I go from your Spirit?
  Where can I flee from your presence?
⁸If I go up to the heavens, you are there;
  if I make my bed in the depths,ᵃ you are
  there.
⁹If I rise on the wings of the dawn,
  if I settle on the far side of the sea,
¹⁰even there your hand will guide me,
  your right hand will hold me fast.

¹¹If I say, "Surely the darkness will hide me
  and the light become night around me,"
¹²even the darkness will not be dark to you;
  the night will shine like the day,
  for darkness is as light to you.

¹³For you created my inmost being;
  you knit me together in my mother's womb.
¹⁴I praise you because I am fearfully and
    wonderfully made;
  your works are wonderful,
  I know that full well.
¹⁵My frame was not hidden from you
  when I was made in the secret place.
When I was woven together in the depths of the
  earth,
¹⁶ your eyes saw my unformed body.
  All the days ordained for me
  were written in your book
  before one of them came to be.

¹⁷How precious toᵇ me are your thoughts, O God!
  How vast is the sum of them!

ᵃ8 Hebrew *Sheol*   ᵇ17 Or *concerning*

18Were I to count them,
  they would outnumber the grains of sand.
When I awake,
  I am still with you.

19If only you would slay the wicked, O God!
  Away from me, you bloodthirsty men!
20They speak of you with evil intent;
  your adversaries misuse your name.
21Do I not hate those who hate you, O Lord,
  and abhor those who rise up against you?
22I have nothing but hatred for them;
  I count them my enemies.

23Search me, O God, and know my heart;
  test me and know my anxious thoughts.
24See if there is any offensive way in me,
  and lead me in the way everlasting.

Psalm 140

For the director of music. A psalm of David.

1Rescue me, O Lord, from evil men;
  protect me from men of violence,
2who devise evil plans in their hearts
  and stir up war every day.
3They make their tongues as sharp as a serpent's;
  the poison of vipers is on their lips.   Selah

4Keep me, O Lord, from the hands of the wicked;
  protect me from men of violence
  who plan to trip my feet.
5Proud men have hidden a snare for me;
  they have spread out the cords of their net
  and have set traps for me along my path.   Selah

6O Lord, I say to you, "You are my God."
  Hear, O Lord, my cry for mercy.
7O Sovereign Lord, my strong deliverer,
  who shields my head in the day of battle—
8do not grant the wicked their desires, O Lord;
  do not let their plans succeed,
  or they will become proud.   Selah

9Let the heads of those who surround me
  be covered with the trouble their lips have
     caused.
10Let burning coals fall upon them;
  may they be thrown into the fire,
  into miry pits, never to rise.
11Let slanderers not be established in the land;
  may disaster hunt down men of violence.

12I know that the Lord secures justice for the poor
  and upholds the cause of the needy.
13Surely the righteous will praise your name
  and the upright will live before you.

Psalm 141

A psalm of David.

1O Lord, I call to you; come quickly to me.
  Hear my voice when I call to you.

2May my prayer be set before you like incense;
  may the lifting up of my hands be like the
     evening sacrifice.

3Set a guard over my mouth, O Lord;
  keep watch over the door of my lips.
4Let not my heart be drawn to what is evil,
  to take part in wicked deeds
with men who are evildoers;
  let me not eat of their delicacies.

141:3   So much trouble can be caused by
the wrong word at the wrong time. The
psalmist asked God to help guard his speech.
There are repeated images about "guarding"
in Hebrew scripture, for example God is
referred to as a watchman and a shepherd.
These images were also applied to speech;
taking care over what you said was considered to be a blessing and a virtue.

5Let a righteous man*a* strike me—it is a
     kindness;
  let him rebuke me—it is oil on my head.
  My head will not refuse it.

Yet my prayer is ever against the deeds of
     evildoers;
6 their rulers will be thrown down from the cliffs,
  and the wicked will learn that my words were
     well spoken.
7They will say, "As one ploughs and breaks up the
     earth,
  so our bones have been scattered at the mouth
     of the grave."*b*

8But my eyes are fixed on you, O Sovereign Lord;
  in you I take refuge—do not give me over to
     death.
9Keep me from the snares they have laid for me,
  from the traps set by evildoers.
10Let the wicked fall into their own nets,
  while I pass by in safety.

Psalm 142

A *maskil*a of David. When he was in the cave. A prayer.

1I cry aloud to the Lord;
  I lift up my voice to the Lord for mercy.
2I pour out my complaint before him;
  before him I tell my trouble.

3When my spirit grows faint within me,
  it is you who know my way.
In the path where I walk
  men have hidden a snare for me.
4Look to my right and see;
  no-one is concerned for me.
I have no refuge;
  no-one cares for my life.

5I cry to you, O Lord;
  I say, "You are my refuge,
  my portion in the land of the living."

---

a5 Or *Let the Righteous One*   b7 Hebrew *Sheol*   aTitle: Probably a literary or musical term

⁶Listen to my cry,
for I am in desperate need;
rescue me from those who pursue me,
for they are too strong for me.
⁷Set me free from my prison,
that I may praise your name.

Then the righteous will gather about me
because of your goodness to me.

Psalm 143

A psalm of David.

¹O LORD, hear my prayer,
listen to my cry for mercy;
in your faithfulness and righteousness
come to my relief.
²Do not bring your servant into judgment,
for no-one living is righteous before you.

³The enemy pursues me,
he crushes me to the ground;
he makes me dwell in darkness
like those long dead.
⁴So my spirit grows faint within me;
my heart within me is dismayed.
⁵I remember the days of long ago;
I meditate on all your works
and consider what your hands have done.
⁶I spread out my hands to you;
my soul thirsts for you like a parched land. *Selah*

⁷Answer me quickly, O LORD;
my spirit fails.
Do not hide your face from me
or I will be like those who go down to the pit.
⁸Let the morning bring me word of your unfailing
love,
for I have put my trust in you.
Show me the way I should go,
for to you I lift up my soul.
⁹Rescue me from my enemies, O LORD,
for I hide myself in you.
¹⁰Teach me to do your will,
for you are my God;
may your good Spirit
lead me on level ground.

¹¹For your name's sake, O LORD, preserve my life;
in your righteousness, bring me out of trouble.
¹²In your unfailing love, silence my enemies;
destroy all my foes,
for I am your servant.

Psalm 144

Of David.

¹Praise be to the LORD my Rock,
who trains my hands for war,
my fingers for battle.

²He is my loving God and my fortress,
my stronghold and my deliverer,
my shield, in whom I take refuge,
who subdues peoples[a] under me.

³O LORD, what is man that you care for him,
the son of man that you think of him?
⁴Man is like a breath;
his days are like a fleeting shadow.

144:4 Whatever human beings think about their own value, the truth is that each person is only a temporary being when compared to the enormity of time and space. Yet this did not stop the psalm writer considering himself as an individual worthy of being loved, protected, and rescued by God. The amazing thing is that each human being can have an individual relationship with God the creator.

---

⁵Part your heavens, O LORD, and come down;
touch the mountains, so that they smoke.
⁶Send forth lightning and scatter ‚the enemies‚;
shoot your arrows and rout them.
⁷Reach down your hand from on high;
deliver me and rescue me
from the mighty waters,
from the hands of foreigners
⁸whose mouths are full of lies,
whose right hands are deceitful.

⁹I will sing a new song to you, O God;
on the ten-stringed lyre I will make music to
you,
¹⁰to the One who gives victory to kings,
who delivers his servant David from the deadly
sword.

¹¹Deliver me and rescue me
from the hands of foreigners
whose mouths are full of lies,
whose right hands are deceitful.

¹²Then our sons in their youth
will be like well-nurtured plants,
and our daughters will be like pillars
carved to adorn a palace.
¹³Our barns will be filled
with every kind of provision.
Our sheep will increase by thousands,
by tens of thousands in our fields;
¹⁴ our oxen will draw heavy loads.[b]
There will be no breaching of walls,
no going into captivity,
no cry of distress in our streets.

¹⁵Blessed are the people of whom this is true;
blessed are the people whose God is the LORD.

---

a2 Many manuscripts of the Masoretic Text, Dead Sea Scrolls, Aquila, Jerome and Syriac; most manuscripts of the Masoretic Text subdues my people   b14 Or our chieftains will be firmly established

Psalm 145[a]

A psalm of praise. Of David.

[1]I will exalt you, my God the King;
  I will praise your name for ever and ever.
[2]Every day I will praise you
  and extol your name for ever and ever.

[3]Great is the LORD and most worthy of praise;
  his greatness no-one can fathom.
[4]One generation will commend your works to
    another;
  they will tell of your mighty acts.
[5]They will speak of the glorious splendour of your
    majesty,
  and I will meditate on your wonderful works.[b]
[6]They will tell of the power of your awesome
    works,
  and I will proclaim your great deeds.
[7]They will celebrate your abundant goodness
  and joyfully sing of your righteousness.

[8]The LORD is gracious and compassionate,
  slow to anger and rich in love.
[9]The LORD is good to all;
  he has compassion on all he has made.
[10]All you have made will praise you, O LORD;
  your saints will extol you.
[11]They will tell of the glory of your kingdom
  and speak of your might,
[12]so that all men may know of your mighty acts
  and the glorious splendour of your kingdom.
[13]Your kingdom is an everlasting kingdom,
  and your dominion endures through all
    generations.

145:14 One of the major themes of the Old Testament is care for the weak, the disadvantaged, and the oppressed. This verse shows that that concern comes from God himself. God is especially interested in those who are finding things difficult. He is always ready to listen to those who, recognizing their need, call upon him.

The LORD is faithful to all his promises
  and loving towards all he has made.[c]
[14]The LORD upholds all those who fall
  and lifts up all who are bowed down.
[15]The eyes of all look to you,
  and you give them their food at the proper
    time.
[16]You open your hand
  and satisfy the desires of every living thing.

[17]The LORD is righteous in all his ways
  and loving towards all he has made.
[18]The LORD is near to all who call on him,
  to all who call on him in truth.

[19]He fulfils the desires of those who fear him;
  he hears their cry and saves them.
[20]The LORD watches over all who love him,
  but all the wicked he will destroy.

[21]My mouth will speak in praise of the LORD.
  Let every creature praise his holy name
  for ever and ever.

Psalm 146

[1]Praise the LORD.[a]

Praise the LORD, O my soul.
[2] I will praise the LORD all my life;
  I will sing praise to my God as long as I live.

[3]Do not put your trust in princes,
  in mortal men, who cannot save.
[4]When their spirit departs, they return to the
    ground;
  on that very day their plans come to nothing.

[5]Blessed is he whose help is the God of Jacob,
  whose hope is in the LORD his God,
[6]the Maker of heaven and earth,
  the sea, and everything in them —
  the LORD, who remains faithful for ever.
[7]He upholds the cause of the oppressed
  and gives food to the hungry.
The LORD sets prisoners free,
[8] the LORD gives sight to the blind,
the LORD lifts up those who are bowed down,
  the LORD loves the righteous.
[9]The LORD watches over the alien
  and sustains the fatherless and the widow,
  but he frustrates the ways of the wicked.

[10]The LORD reigns for ever,
  your God, O Zion, for all generations.

Praise the LORD.

147:2 This psalm captures the mood of a people who have been restored to their beloved Jerusalem. This has not happened because of human power or wisdom, but through God's protection and guidance. Here, the people's grateful response is expressed in a song of praise.

Psalm 147

[1]Praise the LORD.[a]

How good it is to sing praises to our God,
  how pleasant and fitting to praise him!

[2]The LORD builds up Jerusalem;
  he gathers the exiles of Israel.

---

[a]This psalm is an acrostic poem, the verses of which (including verse 13b) begin with the successive letters of the Hebrew alphabet.
[b]5 Dead Sea Scrolls and Syriac (see also Septuagint); Masoretic Text *On the glorious splendour of your majesty / and on your wonderful works I will meditate*
[c]13 One manuscript of the Masoretic Text, Dead Sea Scrolls and Syriac (see also Septuagint); most manuscripts of the Masoretic Text do not have the last two lines of verse 13.   [a]1 Hebrew *Hallelu Yah*; also in verse 10   [a]1 Hebrew *Hallelu Yah*; also in verse 20

3He heals the broken-hearted
and binds up their wounds.
4He determines the number of the stars
and calls them each by name.
5Great is our Lord and mighty in power;
his understanding has no limit.
6The Lord sustains the humble
but casts the wicked to the ground.

7Sing to the Lord with thanksgiving;
make music to our God on the harp.
8He covers the sky with clouds;
he supplies the earth with rain
and makes grass grow on the hills.
9He provides food for the cattle
and for the young ravens when they call.

10His pleasure is not in the strength of the
horse,
nor his delight in the legs of a man;
11the Lord delights in those who fear him,
who put their hope in his unfailing love.

12Extol the Lord, O Jerusalem;
praise your God, O Zion,
13for he strengthens the bars of your gates
and blesses your people within you.
14He grants peace to your borders
and satisfies you with the finest of wheat.

15He sends his command to the earth;
his word runs swiftly.
16He spreads the snow like wool
and scatters the frost like ashes.
17He hurls down hail like pebbles.
Who can withstand his icy blast?
18He sends his word and melts them;
he stirs up his breezes, and the waters
flow.

19He has revealed his word to Jacob,
his laws and decrees to Israel.
20He has done this for no other nation;
they do not know his laws.

Praise the Lord.

Psalm 148

1Praise the Lord.ᵃ

Praise the Lord from the heavens,
praise him in the heights above.
2Praise him, all his angels,
praise him, all his heavenly hosts.
3Praise him, sun and moon,
praise him, all you shining stars.
4Praise him, you highest heavens
and you waters above the skies.
5Let them praise the name of the Lord,
for he commanded and they were created.
6He set them in place for ever and ever;
he gave a decree that will never pass away.

7Praise the Lord from the earth,
you great sea creatures and all ocean depths,
8lightning and hail, snow and clouds,
stormy winds that do his bidding,
9you mountains and all hills,
fruit trees and all cedars,
10wild animals and all cattle,
small creatures and flying birds,
11kings of the earth and all nations,
you princes and all rulers on earth,
12young men and maidens,
old men and children.

13Let them praise the name of the Lord,
for his name alone is exalted;
his splendour is above the earth and the
heavens.
14He has raised up for his people a horn,ᵇ
the praise of all his saints,
of Israel, the people close to his heart.

Praise the Lord.

Psalm 149

1Praise the Lord.ᵃ

Sing to the Lord a new song,
his praise in the assembly of the saints.

2Let Israel rejoice in their Maker;
let the people of Zion be glad in their
King.
3Let them praise his name with dancing
and make music to him with tambourine
and harp.
4For the Lord takes delight in his people;
he crowns the humble with salvation.
5Let the saints rejoice in this honour
and sing for joy on their beds.

6May the praise of God be in their
mouths
and a double-edged sword in their
hands,
7to inflict vengeance on the nations
and punishment on the peoples,
8to bind their kings with fetters,
their nobles with shackles of iron,
9to carry out the sentence written against
them.
This is the glory of all his saints.

Praise the Lord.

Psalm 150

1Praise the Lord.ᵃ

Praise God in his sanctuary;
praise him in his mighty heavens.
2Praise him for his acts of power;
praise him for his surpassing greatness.

ᵃ1 Hebrew *Hallelu Yah*; also in verse 14
ᵃ1 Hebrew *Hallelu Yah*; also in verse 9
ᵇ14 *Horn* here symbolises strong one, that is, king.
ᵃ1 Hebrew *Hallelu Yah*; also in verse 6

³Praise him with the sounding of the trumpet,
  praise him with the harp and lyre,
⁴praise him with the tambourine and dancing,
  praise him with the strings and flute,
⁵praise him with the clash of cymbals,
  praise him with resounding cymbals.

⁶Let everything that has breath praise
  the LORD.

Praise the LORD.

150:6 This psalm is a suitably exuberant, noisy psalm to finish the collection. All the music makers of the temple are called on to take part in glorifying God. Everyone else can join in too; not just the "professionals". Anyone who has breath, which is the gift of being alive and comes from God himself, is invited to take part.

Proverbs

Understanding God

A growing relationship with God involves prayer, obedience, discipline, and knowledge. Knowledge enables us to come closer to God, to understand his ways, his nature, and the way he speaks to us through the Bible. It helps us to recognize God's activity in every aspect of life and to keep things in perspective. Knowledge also equips us to learn more about life, our relationships with others, and the plans we have for the future.

Practical and Down to Earth

The book of Proverbs is a collection of short, pithy sayings, full of practical advice for those who want to increase their knowledge of God, and to put into practice what he teaches. It is made clear throughout the book that knowledge must be worked out in the real world, because it is only in this way that it can become wisdom. The range of subjects covered in Proverbs is very wide indeed. Some things are big issues such as marriage and business decisions, others are the sort of things that form part of daily routines, for example talking to people and visiting the neighbours. There is no aspect of life which is beyond God's concern, and Proverbs deals with many.

Three Categories

The book of Proverbs falls into three broad sections, addressing different groups of people. The first section (chapters 1—9) is in the form of a father giving advice to his son. However it should not be interpreted so narrowly today. Think of it as advice for all young people, offered by someone who has been through life and has experienced many things and seen God at work in many situations.

The second section (Proverbs 10—24) was aimed at a more general audience. The short proverbs in this section encouraged the people to make connections between what they knew about God and the demands of daily life. The third section (Proverbs 25—31) was aimed at the king, and offered wisdom to all who held positions of authority, as well as those who wanted to be leaders in community and national life.

At first sight, Proverbs may look like one of the easiest books in the Bible, containing short, straightforward statements. It might be tempting to say "I've heard it all before," but this misses the whole point of the proverbs. It is the easiest thing in the world to read something and agree with it. It is more costly to actually do what it says, to turn our practical routine upside down and respond to God's call. Yet this is what Proverbs is all about.

Prologue: Purpose and Theme

1 The proverbs of Solomon son of David, king of Israel:

[2] for attaining wisdom and discipline;
   for understanding words of insight;
[3] for acquiring a disciplined and prudent life,
   doing what is right and just and fair;
[4] for giving prudence to the simple,
   knowledge and discretion to the young—
[5] let the wise listen and add to their learning,
   and let the discerning get guidance—
[6] for understanding proverbs and parables,
   the sayings and riddles of the wise.

[7] The fear of the LORD is the beginning of knowledge,
   but fools[a] despise wisdom and discipline.

1:7 The fear of the Lord is a phrase that comes up frequently. It should not be an unpleasant, scary emotion. It is a sense of reverence and respect for God.

Exhortations to Embrace Wisdom

Warning Against Enticement

[8] Listen, my son, to your father's instruction
   and do not forsake your mother's teaching.
[9] They will be a garland to grace your head
   and a chain to adorn your neck.

[10] My son, if sinners entice you,
   do not give in to them.
[11] If they say, "Come along with us;
   let's lie in wait for someone's blood,
   let's waylay some harmless soul;
[12] let's swallow them alive, like the grave,[b]
   and whole, like those who go down to the pit;
[13] we will get all sorts of valuable things
   and fill our houses with plunder;
[14] throw in your lot with us,
   and we will share a common purse"—
[15] my son, do not go along with them,
   do not set foot on their paths;
[16] for their feet rush into sin,
   they are swift to shed blood.
[17] How useless to spread a net
   in full view of all the birds!
[18] These men lie in wait for their own blood;
   they waylay only themselves!
[19] Such is the end of all who go after ill-gotten gain;
   it takes away the lives of those who get it.

Warning Against Rejecting Wisdom

[20] Wisdom calls aloud in the street,
   she raises her voice in the public squares;
[21] at the head of the noisy streets[c] she cries out,
   in the gateways of the city she makes her speech:

[22] "How long will you simple ones[d] love your simple ways?
   How long will mockers delight in mockery
   and fools hate knowledge?
[23] If you had responded to my rebuke,
   I would have poured out my heart to you
   and made my thoughts known to you.
[24] But since you rejected me when I called
   and no-one gave heed when I stretched out my hand,
[25] since you ignored all my advice
   and would not accept my rebuke,
[26] I in turn will laugh at your disaster;
   I will mock when calamity overtakes you—
[27] when calamity overtakes you like a storm,
   when disaster sweeps over you like a whirlwind,
   when distress and trouble overwhelm you.

[28] "Then they will call to me but I will not answer;
   they will look for me but will not find me.
[29] Since they hated knowledge
   and did not choose to fear the LORD,
[30] since they would not accept my advice
   and spurned my rebuke,
[31] they will eat the fruit of their ways
   and be filled with the fruit of their schemes.
[32] For the waywardness of the simple will kill them,
   and the complacency of fools will destroy them;
[33] but whoever listens to me will live in safety
   and be at ease, without fear of harm."

Moral Benefits of Wisdom

2 My son, if you accept my words
   and store up my commands within you,
[2] turning your ear to wisdom
   and applying your heart to understanding,
[3] and if you call out for insight
   and cry aloud for understanding,
[4] and if you look for it as for silver
   and search for it as for hidden treasure,
[5] then you will understand the fear of the LORD
   and find the knowledge of God.
[6] For the LORD gives wisdom,
   and from his mouth come knowledge and understanding.
[7] He holds victory in store for the upright,
   he is a shield to those whose walk is blameless,
[8] for he guards the course of the just
   and protects the way of his faithful ones.

[9] Then you will understand what is right and just and fair—every good path.
[10] For wisdom will enter your heart,
   and knowledge will be pleasant to your soul.
[11] Discretion will protect you,
   and understanding will guard you.

---

[a]7 The Hebrew words rendered *fool* in Proverbs, and often elsewhere in the Old Testament, denote one who is morally deficient.
[b]12 Hebrew *Sheol*   [c]21 Hebrew; Septuagint */ on the tops of the walls*
[d]22 The Hebrew word rendered *simple* in Proverbs generally denotes one without moral direction and inclined to evil.

¹²Wisdom will save you from the ways of wicked
    men,
    from men whose words are perverse,
¹³who leave the straight paths
    to walk in dark ways,
¹⁴who delight in doing wrong
    and rejoice in the perverseness of evil,
¹⁵whose paths are crooked
    and who are devious in their ways.

¹⁶It will save you also from the adulteress,
    from the wayward wife with her seductive
        words,
¹⁷who has left the partner of her youth
    and ignored the covenant she made before God. ᵃ
¹⁸For her house leads down to death
    and her paths to the spirits of the dead.
¹⁹None who go to her return
    or attain the paths of life.

²⁰Thus you will walk in the ways of good men
    and keep to the paths of the righteous.
²¹For the upright will live in the land,
    and the blameless will remain in it;
²²but the wicked will be cut off from the land,
    and the unfaithful will be torn from it.

Further Benefits of Wisdom

3 My son, do not forget my teaching,
    but keep my commands in your heart,
²for they will prolong your life many years
    and bring you prosperity.

³Let love and faithfulness never leave you;
    bind them around your neck,
    write them on the tablet of your heart.
⁴Then you will win favour and a good name
    in the sight of God and man.

⁵Trust in the LORD with all your heart
    and lean not on your own understanding;
⁶in all your ways acknowledge him,
    and he will make your paths straight. ᵃ

⁷Do not be wise in your own eyes;
    fear the LORD and shun evil.
⁸This will bring health to your body
    and nourishment to your bones.

⁹Honour the LORD with your wealth,
    with the firstfruits of all your crops;
¹⁰then your barns will be filled to overflowing,
    and your vats will brim over with new wine.

¹¹My son, do not despise the LORD's discipline
    and do not resent his rebuke,
¹²because the LORD disciplines those he loves,
    as a father ᵇ the son he delights in.

¹³Blessed is the man who finds wisdom,
    the man who gains understanding,
¹⁴for she is more profitable than silver
    and yields better returns than gold.
¹⁵She is more precious than rubies;
    nothing you desire can compare with her.

¹⁶Long life is in her right hand;
    in her left hand are riches and honour.
¹⁷Her ways are pleasant ways,
    and all her paths are peace.
¹⁸She is a tree of life to those who embrace her;
    those who lay hold of her will be blessed.

3:14   Wisdom is very costly, and to look
for and find it is a great discovery. Its benefits far outweigh anything that is purely
material.

---

¹⁹By wisdom the LORD laid the earth's foundations,
    by understanding he set the heavens in place;
²⁰by his knowledge the deeps were divided,
    and the clouds let drop the dew.

²¹My son, preserve sound judgment and
        discernment,
    do not let them out of your sight;
²²they will be life for you,
    an ornament to grace your neck.
²³Then you will go on your way in safety,
    and your foot will not stumble;
²⁴when you lie down, you will not be afraid;
    when you lie down, your sleep will be sweet.
²⁵Have no fear of sudden disaster
    or of the ruin that overtakes the wicked,
²⁶for the LORD will be your confidence
    and will keep your foot from being snared.

²⁷Do not withhold good from those who deserve it,
    when it is in your power to act.
²⁸Do not say to your neighbour,
    "Come back later; I'll give it tomorrow"—
    when you now have it with you.

²⁹Do not plot harm against your neighbour,
    who lives trustfully near you.
³⁰Do not accuse a man for no reason—
    when he has done you no harm.

³¹Do not envy a violent man
    or choose any of his ways,
³²for the LORD detests a perverse man
    but takes the upright into his confidence.

³³The LORD's curse is on the house of the wicked,
    but he blesses the home of the righteous.
³⁴He mocks proud mockers
    but gives grace to the humble.
³⁵The wise inherit honour,
    but fools he holds up to shame.

Wisdom Is Supreme

4 Listen, my sons, to a father's instruction;
    pay attention and gain understanding.
²I give you sound learning,
    so do not forsake my teaching.
³When I was a boy in my father's house,
    still tender, and an only child of my mother,

ᵃ17 Or *covenant of her God*   ᵃ6 Or *will direct your paths.*   ᵇ12 Hebrew; Septuagint / *and he punishes*

4he taught me and said,
"Lay hold of my words with all your heart;
keep my commands and you will live.
5Get wisdom, get understanding;
do not forget my words or swerve from them.
6Do not forsake wisdom, and she will protect you;
love her, and she will watch over you.
7Wisdom is supreme; therefore get wisdom.
Though it cost all you have,[a] get
understanding.
8Esteem her, and she will exalt you;
embrace her, and she will honour you.
9She will set a garland of grace on your head
and present you with a crown of splendour."

10Listen, my son, accept what I say,
and the years of your life will be many.
11I guide you in the way of wisdom
and lead you along straight paths.
12When you walk, your steps will not be hampered;
when you run, you will not stumble.
13Hold on to instruction, do not let it go;
guard it well, for it is your life.
14Do not set foot on the path of the wicked
or walk in the way of evil men.
15Avoid it, do not travel on it;
turn from it and go on your way.
16For they cannot sleep till they do evil;
they are robbed of slumber till they make
someone fall.
17They eat the bread of wickedness
and drink the wine of violence.

18The path of the righteous is like the first gleam of
dawn,
shining ever brighter till the full light of day.
19But the way of the wicked is like deep darkness;
they do not know what makes them stumble.

20My son, pay attention to what I say;
listen closely to my words.
21Do not let them out of your sight,
keep them within your heart;
22for they are life to those who find them
and health to a man's whole body.
23Above all else, guard your heart,
for it is the wellspring of life.
24Put away perversity from your mouth;
keep corrupt talk far from your lips.
25Let your eyes look straight ahead,
fix your gaze directly before you.
26Make level[b] paths for your feet
and take only ways that are firm.
27Do not swerve to the right or the left;
keep your foot from evil.

Warning Against Adultery

5 My son, pay attention to my wisdom,
listen well to my words of insight,
2that you may maintain discretion
and your lips may preserve knowledge.
3For the lips of an adulteress drip honey,
and her speech is smoother than oil;

4but in the end she is bitter as gall,
sharp as a double-edged sword.
5Her feet go down to death;
her steps lead straight to the grave.[a]
6She gives no thought to the way of life;
her paths are crooked, but she knows it not.

5:3 To turn away from wisdom is like
committing adultery. We reject and break
the vows between ourselves and God, and go
off after things that do not last. Some prophets compare the sinful actions of those who
reject God and worship idols with those of
people who commit adultery.

7Now then, my sons, listen to me;
do not turn aside from what I say.
8Keep to a path far from her,
do not go near the door of her house,
9lest you give your best strength to others
and your years to one who is cruel,
10lest strangers feast on your wealth
and your toil enrich another man's house.
11At the end of your life you will groan,
when your flesh and body are spent.
12You will say, "How I hated discipline!
How my heart spurned correction!
13I would not obey my teachers
or listen to my instructors.
14I have come to the brink of utter ruin
in the midst of the whole assembly."

15Drink water from your own cistern,
running water from your own well.
16Should your springs overflow in the streets,
your streams of water in the public squares?
17Let them be yours alone,
never to be shared with strangers.
18May your fountain be blessed,
and may you rejoice in the wife of your youth.
19A loving doe, a graceful deer—
may her breasts satisfy you always,
may you ever be captivated by her love.
20Why be captivated, my son, by an adulteress?
Why embrace the bosom of another man's wife?

21For a man's ways are in full view of the Lord,
and he examines all his paths.
22The evil deeds of a wicked man ensnare him;
the cords of his sin hold him fast.
23He will die for lack of discipline,
led astray by his own great folly.

Warnings Against Folly

6 My son, if you have put up security for your
neighbour,
if you have struck hands in pledge for another,
2if you have been trapped by what you said,
ensnared by the words of your mouth,

---

a7 Or Whatever else you get   b26 Or Consider the   a5 Hebrew Sheol

3then do this, my son, to free yourself,
  since you have fallen into your neighbour's
    hands:
 Go and humble yourself;
  press your plea with your neighbour!
4Allow no sleep to your eyes,
  no slumber to your eyelids.
5Free yourself, like a gazelle from the hand of the
    hunter,
  like a bird from the snare of the fowler.

6Go to the ant, you sluggard;
  consider its ways and be wise!
7It has no commander,
  no overseer or ruler,
8yet it stores its provisions in summer
  and gathers its food at harvest.

9How long will you lie there, you sluggard?
  When will you get up from your sleep?
10A little sleep, a little slumber,
  a little folding of the hands to rest—
11and poverty will come on you like a bandit
  and scarcity like an armed man.ᵃ

12A scoundrel and villain,
  who goes about with a corrupt mouth,
13 who winks with his eye,
    signals with his feet
    and motions with his fingers,
14 who plots evil with deceit in his heart—
  he always stirs up dissension.
15Therefore disaster will overtake him in an instant;
  he will suddenly be destroyed—without
    remedy.

16There are six things the LORD hates,
  seven that are detestable to him:
17 haughty eyes,
    a lying tongue,
    hands that shed innocent blood,
18 a heart that devises wicked schemes,
    feet that are quick to rush into evil,
19 a false witness who pours out lies
    and a man who stirs up dissension among
      brothers.

Warning Against Adultery

20My son, keep your father's commands
  and do not forsake your mother's teaching.
21Bind them upon your heart for ever;
  fasten them around your neck.
22When you walk, they will guide you;
  when you sleep, they will watch over you;
  when you awake, they will speak to you.
23For these commands are a lamp,
  this teaching is a light,
 and the corrections of discipline
  are the way to life,
24keeping you from the immoral woman,
  from the smooth tongue of the wayward wife.
25Do not lust in your heart after her beauty
  or let her captivate you with her eyes,

ᵃ11 Or like a vagrant / and scarcity like a beggar

26for the prostitute reduces you to a loaf of bread,
  and the adulteress preys upon your very life.
27Can a man scoop fire into his lap
  without his clothes being burned?
28Can a man walk on hot coals
  without his feet being scorched?
29So is he who sleeps with another man's wife;
  no-one who touches her will go unpunished.

30Men do not despise a thief if he steals
  to satisfy his hunger when he is starving.
31Yet if he is caught, he must pay sevenfold,
  though it costs him all the wealth of his house.
32But a man who commits adultery lacks judgment;
  whoever does so destroys himself.
33Blows and disgrace are his lot,
  and his shame will never be wiped away;
34for jealousy arouses a husband's fury,
  and he will show no mercy when he takes
    revenge.
35He will not accept any compensation;
  he will refuse the bribe, however great it is.

Warning Against the Adulteress

7 My son, keep my words
  and store up my commands within you.
2Keep my commands and you will live;
  guard my teachings as the apple of your eye.
3Bind them on your fingers;
  write them on the tablet of your heart.
4Say to wisdom, "You are my sister,"
  and call understanding your kinsman;
5they will keep you from the adulteress,
  from the wayward wife with her seductive
    words.

6At the window of my house
  I looked out through the lattice.
7I saw among the simple,
  I noticed among the young men,
  a youth who lacked judgment.
8He was going down the street near her corner,
  walking along in the direction of her house
9at twilight, as the day was fading,
  as the dark of night set in.

7:10 Many distractions exist to tempt us away from growing in knowledge and fear of the Lord. Those who turn away from wisdom are foolish, like a young man who thinks he can find love and fulfilment in a one-night stand with a prostitute.

10Then out came a woman to meet him,
  dressed like a prostitute and with crafty intent.
11(She is loud and defiant,
  her feet never stay at home;
12now in the street, now in the squares,
  at every corner she lurks.)
13She took hold of him and kissed him
  and with a brazen face she said:

¹⁴"I have fellowship offerings^a at home;
  today I fulfilled my vows.
¹⁵So I came out to meet you;
  I looked for you and have found you!
¹⁶I have covered my bed
  with coloured linens from Egypt.
¹⁷I have perfumed my bed
  with myrrh, aloes and cinnamon.
¹⁸Come, let's drink deep of love till morning;
  let's enjoy ourselves with love!
¹⁹My husband is not at home;
  he has gone on a long journey.
²⁰He took his purse filled with money
  and will not be home till full moon."

²¹With persuasive words she led him astray;
  she seduced him with her smooth talk.
²²All at once he followed her
  like an ox going to the slaughter,
  like a deer^b stepping into a noose^c
²³ till an arrow pierces his liver,
  like a bird darting into a snare,
  little knowing it will cost him his life.

²⁴Now then, my sons, listen to me;
  pay attention to what I say.
²⁵Do not let your heart turn to her ways
  or stray into her paths.
²⁶Many are the victims she has brought down;
  her slain are a mighty throng.
²⁷Her house is a highway to the grave,^d
  leading down to the chambers of death.

Wisdom's Call

8 Does not wisdom call out?
  Does not understanding raise her voice?
²On the heights along the way,
  where the paths meet, she takes her stand;
³beside the gates leading into the city,
  at the entrances, she cries aloud:
⁴"To you, O men, I call out;
  I raise my voice to all mankind.
⁵You who are simple, gain prudence;
  you who are foolish, gain understanding.
⁶Listen, for I have worthy things to say;
  I open my lips to speak what is right.
⁷My mouth speaks what is true,
  for my lips detest wickedness.
⁸All the words of my mouth are just;
  none of them is crooked or perverse.
⁹To the discerning all of them are right;
  they are faultless to those who have knowledge.
¹⁰Choose my instruction instead of silver,
  knowledge rather than choice gold,
¹¹for wisdom is more precious than rubies,
  and nothing you desire can compare with
  her.

¹²"I, wisdom, dwell together with prudence;
  I possess knowledge and discretion.

¹³To fear the LORD is to hate evil;
  I hate pride and arrogance,
  evil behaviour and perverse speech.
¹⁴Counsel and sound judgment are mine;
  I have understanding and power.
¹⁵By me kings reign
  and rulers make laws that are just;
¹⁶by me princes govern,
  and all nobles who rule on earth.^a
¹⁷I love those who love me,
  and those who seek me find me.
¹⁸With me are riches and honour,
  enduring wealth and prosperity.
¹⁹My fruit is better than fine gold;
  what I yield surpasses choice silver.
²⁰I walk in the way of righteousness,
  along the paths of justice,
²¹bestowing wealth on those who love me
  and making their treasuries full.

²²"The LORD brought me forth as the first of his
  works,^{b,c}
  before his deeds of old;
²³I was appointed^d from eternity,
  from the beginning, before the world began.
²⁴When there were no oceans, I was given
  birth,
  when there were no springs abounding with
  water;
²⁵before the mountains were settled in place,
  before the hills, I was given birth,
²⁶before he made the earth or its fields
  or any of the dust of the world.
²⁷I was there when he set the heavens in place,
  when he marked out the horizon on the face of
  the deep,
²⁸when he established the clouds above
  and fixed securely the fountains of the deep,
²⁹when he gave the sea its boundary
  so that the waters would not overstep his
  command,
  and when he marked out the foundations of the
  earth.
³⁰ Then I was the craftsman at his side.
  I was filled with delight day after day,
  rejoicing always in his presence,
³¹rejoicing in his whole world
  and delighting in mankind.

³²"Now then, my sons, listen to me;
  blessed are those who keep my ways.
³³Listen to my instruction and be wise;
  do not ignore it.
³⁴Blessed is the man who listens to me,
  watching daily at my doors,
  waiting at my doorway.
³⁵For whoever finds me finds life
  and receives favour from the LORD.
³⁶But whoever fails to find me harms himself;
  all who hate me love death."

---

^a14 Traditionally *peace offerings*   ^b22 Syriac (see also Septuagint); Hebrew *fool*
^c22 The meaning of the Hebrew for this line is uncertain.   ^d27 Hebrew *Sheol*
^a16 Many Hebrew manuscripts and Septuagint; most Hebrew manuscripts *and nobles—all righteous rulers*   ^b22 Or *way*; or *dominion*
^c22 Or *The LORD possessed me at the beginning of his work*; or *The LORD brought me forth at the beginning of his work*
^d23 Or *fashioned*

Invitations of Wisdom and of Folly

9 Wisdom has built her house;
she has hewn out its seven pillars.
[2] She has prepared her meat and mixed her wine;
she has also set her table.
[3] She has sent out her maids, and she calls
from the highest point of the city.
[4] "Let all who are simple come in here!"
she says to those who lack judgment.
[5] "Come, eat my food
and drink the wine I have mixed.
[6] Leave your simple ways and you will live;
walk in the way of understanding.

8:35 To choose wisdom is to choose life,
and those who follow God wrestle with that
choice everyday. A right relationship with
God — the "fear of the Lord" — demands
conviction and dedication in all choices and
decisions.

[7] "Whoever corrects a mocker invites insult;
whoever rebukes a wicked man incurs abuse.
[8] Do not rebuke a mocker or he will hate you;
rebuke a wise man and he will love you.
[9] Instruct a wise man and he will be wiser still;
teach a righteous man and he will add to his
learning.
[10] "The fear of the Lord is the beginning of wisdom,
and knowledge of the Holy One is
understanding.
[11] For through me your days will be many,
and years will be added to your life.
[12] If you are wise, your wisdom will reward you;
if you are a mocker, you alone will suffer."

[13] The woman Folly is loud;
she is undisciplined and without knowledge.
[14] She sits at the door of her house,
on a seat at the highest point of the city,
[15] calling out to those who pass by,
who go straight on their way.
[16] "Let all who are simple come in here!"
she says to those who lack judgment.
[17] "Stolen water is sweet;
food eaten in secret is delicious!"
[18] But little do they know that the dead are there,
that her guests are in the depths of the grave. [a]

Proverbs of Solomon

10 The proverbs of Solomon:

A wise son brings joy to his father,
but a foolish son grief to his mother.

[2] Ill-gotten treasures are of no value,
but righteousness delivers from death.

[3] The Lord does not let the righteous go hungry
but he thwarts the craving of the wicked.

[4] Lazy hands make a man poor,
but diligent hands bring wealth.

[5] He who gathers crops in summer is a wise son,
but he who sleeps during harvest is a
disgraceful son.

[6] Blessings crown the head of the righteous,
but violence overwhelms the mouth of the
wicked. [a]

[7] The memory of the righteous will be a blessing,
but the name of the wicked will rot.

[8] The wise in heart accept commands,
but a chattering fool comes to ruin.

[9] The man of integrity walks securely,
but he who takes crooked paths will be found
out.

[10] He who winks maliciously causes grief,
and a chattering fool comes to ruin.

[11] The mouth of the righteous is a fountain of life,
but violence overwhelms the mouth of the
wicked.

[12] Hatred stirs up dissension,
but love covers over all wrongs.

[13] Wisdom is found on the lips of the discerning,
but a rod is for the back of him who lacks
judgment.

[14] Wise men store up knowledge,
but the mouth of a fool invites ruin.

[15] The wealth of the rich is their fortified city,
but poverty is the ruin of the poor.

[16] The wages of the righteous bring them life,
but the income of the wicked brings them
punishment.

[17] He who heeds discipline shows the way to life,
but whoever ignores correction leads others
astray.

[18] He who conceals his hatred has lying lips,
and whoever spreads slander is a fool.

[19] When words are many, sin is not absent,
but he who holds his tongue is wise.

[20] The tongue of the righteous is choice silver,
but the heart of the wicked is of little value.

[21] The lips of the righteous nourish many,
but fools die for lack of judgment.

[22] The blessing of the Lord brings wealth,
and he adds no trouble to it.

[23] A fool finds pleasure in evil conduct,
but a man of understanding delights in wisdom.

[24] What the wicked dreads will overtake him;
what the righteous desire will be granted.

[25] When the storm has swept by, the wicked are
gone,
but the righteous stand firm for ever.

[a] 18 Hebrew *Sheol*   [a] 6 Or *but the mouth of the wicked conceals violence*; also in verse 11

²⁶As vinegar to the teeth and smoke to the eyes,
   so is a sluggard to those who send him.

²⁷The fear of the LORD adds length to life,
   but the years of the wicked are cut short.

²⁸The prospect of the righteous is joy,
   but the hopes of the wicked come to nothing.

²⁹The way of the LORD is a refuge for the righteous,
   but it is the ruin of those who do evil.

³⁰The righteous will never be uprooted,
   but the wicked will not remain in the land.

³¹The mouth of the righteous brings forth wisdom,
   but a perverse tongue will be cut out.

³²The lips of the righteous know what is fitting,
   but the mouth of the wicked only what is
   perverse.

11 The LORD abhors dishonest scales,
   but accurate weights are his delight.

²When pride comes, then comes disgrace,
   but with humility comes wisdom.

³The integrity of the upright guides them,
   but the unfaithful are destroyed by their
   duplicity.

⁴Wealth is worthless in the day of wrath,
   but righteousness delivers from death.

⁵The righteousness of the blameless makes a
   straight way for them,
   but the wicked are brought down by their own
   wickedness.

⁶The righteousness of the upright delivers them,
   but the unfaithful are trapped by evil desires.

⁷When a wicked man dies, his hope perishes;
   all he expected from his power comes to
   nothing.

⁸The righteous man is rescued from trouble,
   and it comes on the wicked instead.

⁹With his mouth the godless destroys his
   neighbour,
   but through knowledge the righteous escape.

¹⁰When the righteous prosper, the city rejoices;
   when the wicked perish, there are shouts of
   joy.

¹¹Through the blessing of the upright a city is
   exalted,
   but by the mouth of the wicked it is destroyed.

¹²A man who lacks judgment derides his neighbour,
   but a man of understanding holds his tongue.

¹³A gossip betrays a confidence,
   but a trustworthy man keeps a secret.

¹⁴For lack of guidance a nation falls,
   but many advisers make victory sure.

¹⁵He who puts up security for another will surely
   suffer,
   but whoever refuses to strike hands in pledge is
   safe.

¹⁶A kind-hearted woman gains respect,
   but ruthless men gain only wealth.

¹⁷A kind man benefits himself,
   but a cruel man brings trouble on himself.

¹⁸The wicked man earns deceptive wages,
   but he who sows righteousness reaps a sure
   reward.

¹⁹The truly righteous man attains life,
   but he who pursues evil goes to his death.

²⁰The LORD detests men of perverse heart
   but he delights in those whose ways are
   blameless.

²¹Be sure of this: The wicked will not go
   unpunished,
   but those who are righteous will go free.

²²Like a gold ring in a pig's snout
   is a beautiful woman who shows no discretion.

²³The desire of the righteous ends only in good,
   but the hope of the wicked only in wrath.

²⁴One man gives freely, yet gains even more;
   another withholds unduly, but comes to
   poverty.

²⁵A generous man will prosper;
   he who refreshes others will himself be
   refreshed.

²⁶People curse the man who hoards grain,
   but blessing crowns him who is willing to sell.

²⁷He who seeks good finds goodwill,
   but evil comes to him who searches for it.

²⁸Whoever trusts in his riches will fall,
   but the righteous will thrive like a green leaf.

²⁹He who brings trouble on his family will inherit
   only wind,
   and the fool will be servant to the wise.

³⁰The fruit of the righteous is a tree of life,
   and he who wins souls is wise.

³¹If the righteous receive their due on earth,
   how much more the ungodly and the sinner!

12 Whoever loves discipline loves knowledge,
   but he who hates correction is stupid.

²A good man obtains favour from the LORD,
   but the LORD condemns a crafty man.

³A man cannot be established through wickedness,
   but the righteous cannot be uprooted.

⁴A wife of noble character is her husband's crown,
   but a disgraceful wife is like decay in his bones.

⁵The plans of the righteous are just,
   but the advice of the wicked is deceitful.

⁶The words of the wicked lie in wait for blood,
   but the speech of the upright rescues them.

⁷Wicked men are overthrown and are no more,
  but the house of the righteous stands firm.

⁸A man is praised according to his wisdom,
  but men with warped minds are despised.

⁹Better to be a nobody and yet have a servant
  than pretend to be somebody and have no food.

12:9   In Proverbs, if a person was hungry
or poor, or was disreputable, then they were
regarded as lazy. But if they worked hard
then they would discover the riches of life.
The search for wisdom demands hard work
from all of us.

---

¹⁰A righteous man cares for the needs of his
    animal,
  but the kindest acts of the wicked are cruel.

¹¹He who works his land will have abundant food,
  but he who chases fantasies lacks judgment.

¹²The wicked desire the plunder of evil men,
  but the root of the righteous flourishes.

¹³An evil man is trapped by his sinful talk,
  but a righteous man escapes trouble.

¹⁴From the fruit of his lips a man is filled with good
    things
  as surely as the work of his hands rewards him.

¹⁵The way of a fool seems right to him,
  but a wise man listens to advice.

¹⁶A fool shows his annoyance at once,
  but a prudent man overlooks an insult.

¹⁷A truthful witness gives honest testimony,
  but a false witness tells lies.

¹⁸Reckless words pierce like a sword,
  but the tongue of the wise brings healing.

¹⁹Truthful lips endure for ever,
  but a lying tongue lasts only a moment.

²⁰There is deceit in the hearts of those who plot
    evil,
  but joy for those who promote peace.

²¹No harm befalls the righteous,
  but the wicked have their fill of trouble.

²²The LORD detests lying lips,
  but he delights in men who are truthful.

²³A prudent man keeps his knowledge to himself,
  but the heart of fools blurts out folly.

²⁴Diligent hands will rule,
  but laziness ends in slave labour.

²⁵An anxious heart weighs a man down,
  but a kind word cheers him up.

²⁶A righteous man is cautious in friendship,ᵃ
  but the way of the wicked leads them astray.

²⁷The lazy man does not roastᵇ his game,
  but the diligent man prizes his possessions.

²⁸In the way of righteousness there is life;
  along that path is immortality.

13   A wise son heeds his father's instruction,
      but a mocker does not listen to rebuke.

²From the fruit of his lips a man enjoys good
    things,
  but the unfaithful have a craving for violence.

³He who guards his lips guards his life,
  but he who speaks rashly will come to ruin.

⁴The sluggard craves and gets nothing,
  but the desires of the diligent are fully satisfied.

⁵The righteous hate what is false,
  but the wicked bring shame and disgrace.

⁶Righteousness guards the man of integrity,
  but wickedness overthrows the sinner.

⁷One man pretends to be rich, yet has nothing;
  another pretends to be poor, yet has great
    wealth.

⁸A man's riches may ransom his life,
  but a poor man hears no threat.

⁹The light of the righteous shines brightly,
  but the lamp of the wicked is snuffed out.

¹⁰Pride only breeds quarrels,
  but wisdom is found in those who take advice.

¹¹Dishonest money dwindles away,
  but he who gathers money little by little makes
    it grow.

¹²Hope deferred makes the heart sick,
  but a longing fulfilled is a tree of life.

¹³He who scorns instruction will pay for it,
  but he who respects a command is rewarded.

¹⁴The teaching of the wise is a fountain of life,
  turning a man from the snares of death.

¹⁵Good understanding wins favour,
  but the way of the unfaithful is hard.ᵃ

¹⁶Every prudent man acts out of knowledge,
  but a fool exposes his folly.

¹⁷A wicked messenger falls into trouble,
  but a trustworthy envoy brings healing.

¹⁸He who ignores discipline comes to poverty and
    shame,
  but whoever heeds correction is honoured.

¹⁹A longing fulfilled is sweet to the soul,
  but fools detest turning from evil.

²⁰He who walks with the wise grows wise,
  but a companion of fools suffers harm.

²¹Misfortune pursues the sinner,
  but prosperity is the reward of the righteous.

ᵃ26 Or *man is a guide to his neighbour*   ᵇ27 The meaning of the Hebrew for this word is uncertain.
ᵃ15 Or *unfaithful does not endure*

²²A good man leaves an inheritance for his
  children's children,
  but a sinner's wealth is stored up for the
    righteous.

²³A poor man's field may produce abundant food,
  but injustice sweeps it away.

²⁴He who spares the rod hates his son,
  but he who loves him is careful to discipline
    him.

²⁵The righteous eat to their hearts' content,
  but the stomach of the wicked goes hungry.

14 The wise woman builds her house,
  but with her own hands the foolish one
    tears hers down.

²He whose walk is upright fears the LORD,
  but he whose ways are devious despises him.

³A fool's talk brings a rod to his back,
  but the lips of the wise protect them.

⁴Where there are no oxen, the manger is empty,
  but from the strength of an ox comes an
    abundant harvest.

⁵A truthful witness does not deceive,
  but a false witness pours out lies.

⁶The mocker seeks wisdom and finds none,
  but knowledge comes easily to the discerning.

⁷Stay away from a foolish man,
  for you will not find knowledge on his lips.

⁸The wisdom of the prudent is to give thought to
    their ways,
  but the folly of fools is deception.

⁹Fools mock at making amends for sin,
  but goodwill is found among the upright.

¹⁰Each heart knows its own bitterness,
  and no-one else can share its joy.

¹¹The house of the wicked will be destroyed,
  but the tent of the upright will flourish.

¹²There is a way that seems right to a man,
  but in the end it leads to death.

¹³Even in laughter the heart may ache,
  and joy may end in grief.

¹⁴The faithless will be fully repaid for their ways,
  and the good man rewarded for his.

¹⁵A simple man believes anything,
  but a prudent man gives thought to his steps.

¹⁶A wise man fears the LORD and shuns evil,
  but a fool is hotheaded and reckless.

¹⁷A quick-tempered man does foolish things,
  and a crafty man is hated.

¹⁸The simple inherit folly,
  but the prudent are crowned with knowledge.

¹⁹Evil men will bow down in the presence of the
    good,
  and the wicked at the gates of the righteous.

²⁰The poor are shunned even by their neighbours,
  but the rich have many friends.

²¹He who despises his neighbour sins,
  but blessed is he who is kind to the needy.

²²Do not those who plot evil go astray?
  But those who plan what is good find*ᵃ* love
    and faithfulness.

²³All hard work brings a profit,
  but mere talk leads only to poverty.

²⁴The wealth of the wise is their crown,
  but the folly of fools yields folly.

²⁵A truthful witness saves lives,
  but a false witness is deceitful.

²⁶He who fears the LORD has a secure fortress,
  and for his children it will be a refuge.

²⁷The fear of the LORD is a fountain of life,
  turning a man from the snares of death.

²⁸A large population is a king's glory,
  but without subjects a prince is ruined.

²⁹A patient man has great understanding,
  but a quick-tempered man displays folly.

³⁰A heart at peace gives life to the body,
  but envy rots the bones.

³¹He who oppresses the poor shows contempt for
    their Maker,
  but whoever is kind to the needy honours God.

³²When calamity comes, the wicked are brought
    down,
  but even in death the righteous have a refuge.

³³Wisdom reposes in the heart of the discerning
  and even among fools she lets herself be
    known.*ᵇ*

³⁴Righteousness exalts a nation,
  but sin is a disgrace to any people.

³⁵A king delights in a wise servant,
  but a shameful servant incurs his wrath.

15 A gentle answer turns away wrath,
  but a harsh word stirs up anger.

²The tongue of the wise commends knowledge,
  but the mouth of the fool gushes folly.

15:1   Wise people do not lose their temper and behave irrationally, but act with discernment. Wisdom is not just knowledge, it
is self control.

---

³The eyes of the LORD are everywhere,
  keeping watch on the wicked and the good.

ᵃ22 Or show   ᵇ33 Hebrew; Septuagint and Syriac / but in the heart of fools she is not known

4The tongue that brings healing is a tree of life,
  but a deceitful tongue crushes the spirit.

5A fool spurns his father's discipline,
  but whoever heeds correction shows prudence.

6The house of the righteous contains great
    treasure,
  but the income of the wicked brings them
    trouble.

7The lips of the wise spread knowledge;
  not so the hearts of fools.

8The LORD detests the sacrifice of the wicked,
  but the prayer of the upright pleases him.

9The LORD detests the way of the wicked
  but he loves those who pursue righteousness.

10Stern discipline awaits him who leaves the path;
  he who hates correction will die.

11Death and Destruction[a] lie open before the
    LORD—
  how much more the hearts of men!

12A mocker resents correction;
  he will not consult the wise.

13A happy heart makes the face cheerful,
  but heartache crushes the spirit.

14The discerning heart seeks knowledge,
  but the mouth of a fool feeds on folly.

15All the days of the oppressed are wretched,
  but the cheerful heart has a continual feast.

16Better a little with the fear of the LORD
  than great wealth with turmoil.

17Better a meal of vegetables where there is love
  than a fattened calf with hatred.

18A hot-tempered man stirs up dissension,
  but a patient man calms a quarrel.

19The way of the sluggard is blocked with thorns,
  but the path of the upright is a highway.

20A wise son brings joy to his father,
  but a foolish man despises his mother.

21Folly delights a man who lacks judgment,
  but a man of understanding keeps a straight
    course.

22Plans fail for lack of counsel,
  but with many advisers they succeed.

23A man finds joy in giving an apt reply—
  and how good is a timely word!

24The path of life leads upward for the wise
  to keep him from going down to the grave.[b]

25The LORD tears down the proud man's house
  but he keeps the widow's boundaries intact.

26The LORD detests the thoughts of the wicked,
  but those of the pure are pleasing to him.

27A greedy man brings trouble to his family,
  but he who hates bribes will live.

28The heart of the righteous weighs its answers,
  but the mouth of the wicked gushes evil.

29The LORD is far from the wicked
  but he hears the prayer of the righteous.

30A cheerful look brings joy to the heart,
  and good news gives health to the bones.

31He who listens to a life-giving rebuke
  will be at home among the wise.

32He who ignores discipline despises himself,
  but whoever heeds correction gains
    understanding.

33The fear of the LORD teaches a man wisdom,[c]
  and humility comes before honour.

16 To man belong the plans of the heart,
  but from the LORD comes the reply of the
    tongue.

2All a man's ways seem innocent to him,
  but motives are weighed by the LORD.

3Commit to the LORD whatever you do,
  and your plans will succeed.

4The LORD works out everything for his own
    ends—
  even the wicked for a day of disaster.

5The LORD detests all the proud of heart.
  Be sure of this: They will not go unpunished.

6Through love and faithfulness sin is atoned for;
  through the fear of the LORD a man avoids evil.

7When a man's ways are pleasing to the LORD,
  he makes even his enemies live at peace with
    him.

8Better a little with righteousness
  than much gain with injustice.

9In his heart a man plans his course,
  but the LORD determines his steps.

10The lips of a king speak as an oracle,
  and his mouth should not betray justice.

11Honest scales and balances are from the LORD;
  all the weights in the bag are of his making.

12Kings detest wrongdoing,
  for a throne is established through
    righteousness.

13Kings take pleasure in honest lips;
  they value a man who speaks the truth.

14A king's wrath is a messenger of death,
  but a wise man will appease it.

15When a king's face brightens, it means life;
  his favour is like a rain cloud in spring.

16How much better to get wisdom than gold,
  to choose understanding rather than silver!

a 11 Hebrew *Sheol and Abaddon*   b 24 Hebrew *Sheol*   c 33 Or *Wisdom teaches the fear of the* LORD

17The highway of the upright avoids evil;
   he who guards his way guards his life.

18Pride goes before destruction,
   a haughty spirit before a fall.

19Better to be lowly in spirit and among the
      oppressed
   than to share plunder with the proud.

20Whoever gives heed to instruction prospers,
   and blessed is he who trusts in the LORD.

21The wise in heart are called discerning,
   and pleasant words promote instruction.*a*

22Understanding is a fountain of life to those who
      have it,
   but folly brings punishment to fools.

23A wise man's heart guides his mouth,
   and his lips promote instruction.*b*

24Pleasant words are a honeycomb,
   sweet to the soul and healing to the bones.

25There is a way that seems right to a man,
   but in the end it leads to death.

26The labourer's appetite works for him;
   his hunger drives him on.

27A scoundrel plots evil,
   and his speech is like a scorching fire.

28A perverse man stirs up dissension,
   and a gossip separates close friends.

29A violent man entices his neighbour
   and leads him down a path that is not good.

30He who winks with his eye is plotting perversity;
   he who purses his lips is bent on evil.

31Grey hair is a crown of splendour;
   it is attained by a righteous life.

32Better a patient man than a warrior,
   a man who controls his temper than one who
      takes a city.

33The lot is cast into the lap,
   but its every decision is from the LORD.

17 Better a dry crust with peace and quiet
      than a house full of feasting,*a* with strife.

2A wise servant will rule over a disgraceful son,
   and will share the inheritance as one of the
      brothers.

3The crucible for silver and the furnace for gold,
   but the LORD tests the heart.

4A wicked man listens to evil lips;
   a liar pays attention to a malicious tongue.

5He who mocks the poor shows contempt for their
      Maker;
   whoever gloats over disaster will not go
      unpunished.

6Children's children are a crown to the aged,
   and parents are the pride of their children.

7Arrogant*b* lips are unsuited to a fool—
   how much worse lying lips to a ruler!

8A bribe is a charm to the one who gives it;
   wherever he turns, he succeeds.

9He who covers over an offence promotes love,
   but whoever repeats the matter separates close
      friends.

10A rebuke impresses a man of discernment
   more than a hundred lashes a fool.

11An evil man is bent only on rebellion;
   a merciless official will be sent against him.

12Better to meet a bear robbed of her cubs
   than a fool in his folly.

13If a man pays back evil for good,
   evil will never leave his house.

14Starting a quarrel is like breaching a dam;
   so drop the matter before a dispute breaks out.

15Acquitting the guilty and condemning the
      innocent—
   the LORD detests them both.

16Of what use is money in the hand of a fool,
   since he has no desire to get wisdom?

17A friend loves at all times,
   and a brother is born for adversity.

18A man lacking in judgment strikes hands in
      pledge
   and puts up security for his neighbour.

19He who loves a quarrel loves sin;
   he who builds a high gate invites destruction.

20A man of perverse heart does not prosper;
   he whose tongue is deceitful falls into trouble.

21To have a fool for a son brings grief;
   there is no joy for the father of a fool.

22A cheerful heart is good medicine,
   but a crushed spirit dries up the bones.

23A wicked man accepts a bribe in secret
   to pervert the course of justice.

24A discerning man keeps wisdom in view,
   but a fool's eyes wander to the ends of the
      earth.

25A foolish son brings grief to his father
   and bitterness to the one who bore him.

26It is not good to punish an innocent man,
   or to flog officials for their integrity.

27A man of knowledge uses words with restraint,
   and a man of understanding is even-tempered.

28Even a fool is thought wise if he keeps silent,
   and discerning if he holds his tongue.

---

a21 Or words make a man persuasive   *b23 Or mouth / and makes his lips persuasive*   *a1 Hebrew sacrifices*
b7 Or Eloquent

18 An unfriendly man pursues selfish ends;
he defies all sound judgment.

2A fool finds no pleasure in understanding
but delights in airing his own opinions.

3When wickedness comes, so does contempt,
and with shame comes disgrace.

4The words of a man's mouth are deep waters,
but the fountain of wisdom is a bubbling brook.

5It is not good to be partial to the wicked
or to deprive the innocent of justice.

6A fool's lips bring him strife,
and his mouth invites a beating.

7A fool's mouth is his undoing,
and his lips are a snare to his soul.

8The words of a gossip are like choice morsels;
they go down to a man's inmost parts.

9One who is slack in his work
is brother to one who destroys.

10The name of the LORD is a strong tower;
the righteous run to it and are safe.

11The wealth of the rich is their fortified city;
they imagine it an unscalable wall.

12Before his downfall a man's heart is proud,
but humility comes before honour.

13He who answers before listening—
that is his folly and his shame.

14A man's spirit sustains him in sickness,
but a crushed spirit who can bear?

15The heart of the discerning acquires knowledge;
the ears of the wise seek it out.

16A gift opens the way for the giver
and ushers him into the presence of the great.

17The first to present his case seems right,
till another comes forward and questions him.

18Casting the lot settles disputes
and keeps strong opponents apart.

19An offended brother is more unyielding than a
fortified city,
and disputes are like the barred gates of a
citadel.

20From the fruit of his mouth a man's stomach is
filled;
with the harvest from his lips he is satisfied.

21The tongue has the power of life and death,
and those who love it will eat its fruit.

22He who finds a wife finds what is good
and receives favour from the LORD.

23A poor man pleads for mercy,
but a rich man answers harshly.

24A man of many companions may come to ruin,
but there is a friend who sticks closer than a
brother.

18:22   If a man finds a good wife, then
he is wise and discerning. A good wife is honoured for the good she brings to her husband
and her family, and demonstrates her love by
diligence and devotion to her work.

---

19 Better a poor man whose walk is
blameless
than a fool whose lips are perverse.
2It is not good to have zeal without knowledge,
nor to be hasty and miss the way.

3A man's own folly ruins his life,
yet his heart rages against the LORD.

4Wealth brings many friends,
but a poor man's friend deserts him.

5A false witness will not go unpunished,
and he who pours out lies will not go free.

6Many curry favour with a ruler,
and everyone is the friend of a man who gives
gifts.

7A poor man is shunned by all his relatives—
how much more do his friends avoid him!
Though he pursues them with pleading,
they are nowhere to be found. [a]

8He who gets wisdom loves his own soul;
he who cherishes understanding prospers.

9A false witness will not go unpunished,
and he who pours out lies will perish.

10It is not fitting for a fool to live in luxury—
how much worse for a slave to rule over
princes!

11A man's wisdom gives him patience;
it is to his glory to overlook an offence.

12A king's rage is like the roar of a lion,
but his favour is like dew on the grass.

13A foolish son is his father's ruin,
and a quarrelsome wife is like a constant
dripping.

14Houses and wealth are inherited from parents,
but a prudent wife is from the LORD.

15Laziness brings on deep sleep,
and the shiftless man goes hungry.

16He who obeys instructions guards his life,
but he who is contemptuous of his ways will
die.

17He who is kind to the poor lends to the LORD,
and he will reward him for what he has done.

18Discipline your son, for in that there is hope;
do not be a willing party to his death.

a7 The meaning of the Hebrew for this sentence is uncertain.

¹⁹A hot-tempered man must pay the penalty;
  if you rescue him, you will have to do it again.

²⁰Listen to advice and accept instruction,
  and in the end you will be wise.

²¹Many are the plans in a man's heart,
  but it is the LORD's purpose that prevails.

²²What a man desires is unfailing love;ᵇ
  better to be poor than a liar.

²³The fear of the LORD leads to life:
  Then one rests content, untouched by trouble.

²⁴The sluggard buries his hand in the dish;
  he will not even bring it back to his mouth!

²⁵Flog a mocker, and the simple will learn
    prudence;
  rebuke a discerning man, and he will gain
    knowledge.

²⁶He who robs his father and drives out his mother
  is a son who brings shame and disgrace.

²⁷Stop listening to instruction, my son,
  and you will stray from the words of
    knowledge.

²⁸A corrupt witness mocks at justice,
  and the mouth of the wicked gulps down evil.

²⁹Penalties are prepared for mockers,
  and beatings for the backs of fools.

20 Wine is a mocker and beer a brawler;
       whoever is led astray by them is not wise.

²A king's wrath is like the roar of a lion;
  he who angers him forfeits his life.

³It is to a man's honour to avoid strife,
  but every fool is quick to quarrel.

⁴A sluggard does not plough in season;
  so at harvest time he looks but finds nothing.

⁵The purposes of a man's heart are deep waters,
  but a man of understanding draws them out.

⁶Many a man claims to have unfailing love,
  but a faithful man who can find?

⁷The righteous man leads a blameless life;
  blessed are his children after him.

⁸When a king sits on his throne to judge,
  he winnows out all evil with his eyes.

⁹Who can say, "I have kept my heart pure;
  I am clean and without sin"?

¹⁰Differing weights and differing measures—
  the LORD detests them both.

¹¹Even a child is known by his actions,
  by whether his conduct is pure and right.

¹²Ears that hear and eyes that see—
  the LORD has made them both.

¹³Do not love sleep or you will grow poor;
  stay awake and you will have food to spare.

¹⁴"It's no good, it's no good!" says the buyer;
  then off he goes and boasts about his purchase.

¹⁵Gold there is, and rubies in abundance,
  but lips that speak knowledge are a rare jewel.

¹⁶Take the garment of one who puts up security for
    a stranger;
  hold it in pledge if he does it for a wayward
    woman.

¹⁷Food gained by fraud tastes sweet to a man,
  but he ends up with a mouth full of gravel.

¹⁸Make plans by seeking advice;
  if you wage war, obtain guidance.

¹⁹A gossip betrays a confidence;
  so avoid a man who talks too much.

²⁰If a man curses his father or mother,
  his lamp will be snuffed out in pitch darkness.

²¹An inheritance quickly gained at the beginning
  will not be blessed at the end.

²²Do not say, "I'll pay you back for this wrong!"
  Wait for the LORD, and he will deliver you.

²³The LORD detests differing weights,
  and dishonest scales do not please him.

²⁴A man's steps are directed by the LORD.
  How then can anyone understand his own way?

²⁵It is a trap for a man to dedicate something rashly
  and only later to consider his vows.

²⁶A wise king winnows out the wicked;
  he drives the threshing wheel over them.

²⁷The lamp of the LORD searches the spirit of a
    man;ᵃ
  it searches out his inmost being.

²⁸Love and faithfulness keep a king safe;
  through love his throne is made secure.

²⁹The glory of young men is their strength,
  grey hair the splendour of the old.

³⁰Blows and wounds cleanse away evil,
  and beatings purge the inmost being.

21 The king's heart is in the hand of the
       LORD;
     he directs it like a watercourse wherever he
       pleases.

21:1 The king was God's chosen servant,
and deserved respect. He judged in the name
of God, and made God's will known to the
people.

---

²All a man's ways seem right to him,
  but the LORD weighs the heart.

³To do what is right and just
  is more acceptable to the LORD than sacrifice.

ᵇ22 Or *A man's greed is his shame*   ᵃ27 Or *The spirit of man is the LORD's lamp*

⁴Haughty eyes and a proud heart,
   the lamp of the wicked, are sin!

⁵The plans of the diligent lead to profit
   as surely as haste leads to poverty.

⁶A fortune made by a lying tongue
   is a fleeting vapour and a deadly snare.ᵃ

⁷The violence of the wicked will drag them away,
   for they refuse to do what is right.

⁸The way of the guilty is devious,
   but the conduct of the innocent is upright.

⁹Better to live on a corner of the roof
   than share a house with a quarrelsome wife.

¹⁰The wicked man craves evil;
   his neighbour gets no mercy from him.

¹¹When a mocker is punished, the simple gain
      wisdom;
   when a wise man is instructed, he gets
      knowledge.

¹²The Righteous Oneᵇ takes note of the house of
      the wicked
   and brings the wicked to ruin.

¹³If a man shuts his ears to the cry of the poor,
   he too will cry out and not be answered.

¹⁴A gift given in secret soothes anger,
   and a bribe concealed in the cloak pacifies great
      wrath.

¹⁵When justice is done, it brings joy to the
      righteous
   but terror to evildoers.

¹⁶A man who strays from the path of understanding
   comes to rest in the company of the dead.

¹⁷He who loves pleasure will become poor;
   whoever loves wine and oil will never be rich.

¹⁸The wicked become a ransom for the righteous,
   and the unfaithful for the upright.

¹⁹Better to live in a desert
   than with a quarrelsome and ill-tempered wife.

²⁰In the house of the wise are stores of choice food
      and oil,
   but a foolish man devours all he has.

²¹He who pursues righteousness and love
   finds life, prosperityᶜ and honour.

²²A wise man attacks the city of the mighty
   and pulls down the stronghold in which they
      trust.

²³He who guards his mouth and his tongue
   keeps himself from calamity.

²⁴The proud and arrogant man—"Mocker" is his
      name;
   he behaves with overweening pride.

²⁵The sluggard's craving will be the death of him,
   because his hands refuse to work.

²⁶All day long he craves for more,
   but the righteous give without sparing.

²⁷The sacrifice of the wicked is detestable—
   how much more so when brought with evil
      intent!

²⁸A false witness will perish,
   and whoever listens to him will be destroyed
      for ever.ᵈ

²⁹A wicked man puts up a bold front,
   but an upright man gives thought to his ways.

³⁰There is no wisdom, no insight, no plan
   that can succeed against the LORD.

³¹The horse is made ready for the day of battle,
   but victory rests with the LORD.

22 A good name is more desirable than great
      riches;
   to be esteemed is better than silver or gold.

²Rich and poor have this in common:
   The LORD is the Maker of them all.

³A prudent man sees danger and takes refuge,
   but the simple keep going and suffer for it.

⁴Humility and the fear of the LORD
   bring wealth and honour and life.

⁵In the paths of the wicked lie thorns and snares,
   but he who guards his soul stays far from them.

⁶Trainᵃ a child in the way he should go,
   and when he is old he will not turn from it.

⁷The rich rule over the poor,
   and the borrower is servant to the lender.

⁸He who sows wickedness reaps trouble,
   and the rod of his fury will be destroyed.

⁹A generous man will himself be blessed,
   for he shares his food with the poor.

¹⁰Drive out the mocker, and out goes strife;
   quarrels and insults are ended.

¹¹He who loves a pure heart and whose speech is
      gracious
   will have the king for his friend.

¹²The eyes of the LORD keep watch over
      knowledge,
   but he frustrates the words of the unfaithful.

¹³The sluggard says, "There is a lion outside!"
   or, "I will be murdered in the streets!"

¹⁴The mouth of an adulteress is a deep pit;
   he who is under the LORD's wrath will fall into
      it.

¹⁵Folly is bound up in the heart of a child,
   but the rod of discipline will drive it far from
      him.

ᵃ6 Some Hebrew manuscripts, Septuagint and Vulgate; most Hebrew manuscripts *vapour for those who seek death*
ᵇ12 Or *The righteous man*   ᶜ21 Or *righteousness*   ᵈ28 Or / *but the words of an obedient man will live on*
ᵃ6 Or *Start*

¹⁶He who oppresses the poor to increase his wealth
and he who gives gifts to the rich—both come
to poverty.

Sayings of the Wise

¹⁷Pay attention and listen to the sayings of the
wise;
apply your heart to what I teach,
¹⁸for it is pleasing when you keep them in your
heart
and have all of them ready on your lips.
¹⁹So that your trust may be in the LORD,
I teach you today, even you.
²⁰Have I not written thirty ᵇ sayings for you,
sayings of counsel and knowledge,
²¹teaching you true and reliable words,
so that you can give sound answers
to him who sent you?

²²Do not exploit the poor because they are poor
and do not crush the needy in court,
²³for the LORD will take up their case
and will plunder those who plunder them.

22:22   Concern for the poor and practical
action to relieve suffering are at the heart of
true faith in God throughout Hebrew Scripture. A person cannot worship God and at
the same time despise men and women who
are made in his image.

---

²⁴Do not make friends with a hot-tempered man,
do not associate with one easily angered,
²⁵or you may learn his ways
and get yourself ensnared.

²⁶Do not be a man who strikes hands in pledge
or puts up security for debts;
²⁷if you lack the means to pay,
your very bed will be snatched from under you.

²⁸Do not move an ancient boundary stone
set up by your forefathers.

²⁹Do you see a man skilled in his work?
He will serve before kings;
he will not serve before obscure men.

23 When you sit to dine with a ruler,
note well what ᵃ is before you,
²and put a knife to your throat
if you are given to gluttony.
³Do not crave his delicacies,
for that food is deceptive.

⁴Do not wear yourself out to get rich;
have the wisdom to show restraint.
⁵Cast but a glance at riches, and they are gone,
for they will surely sprout wings
and fly off to the sky like an eagle.

⁶Do not eat the food of a stingy man,
do not crave his delicacies;
⁷for he is the kind of man
who is always thinking about the cost. ᵇ
"Eat and drink," he says to you,
but his heart is not with you.
⁸You will vomit up the little you have eaten
and will have wasted your compliments.

⁹Do not speak to a fool,
for he will scorn the wisdom of your words.

¹⁰Do not move an ancient boundary stone
or encroach on the fields of the fatherless,
¹¹for their Defender is strong;
he will take up their case against you.

¹²Apply your heart to instruction
and your ears to words of knowledge.

¹³Do not withhold discipline from a child;
if you punish him with the rod, he will not die.
¹⁴Punish him with the rod
and save his soul from death. ᶜ

¹⁵My son, if your heart is wise,
then my heart will be glad;
¹⁶my inmost being will rejoice
when your lips speak what is right.

¹⁷Do not let your heart envy sinners,
but always be zealous for the fear of the LORD.
¹⁸There is surely a future hope for you,
and your hope will not be cut off.

¹⁹Listen, my son, and be wise,
and keep your heart on the right path.
²⁰Do not join those who drink too much wine
or gorge themselves on meat,
²¹for drunkards and gluttons become poor,
and drowsiness clothes them in rags.

²²Listen to your father, who gave you life,
and do not despise your mother when she is
old.
²³Buy the truth and do not sell it;
get wisdom, discipline and understanding.
²⁴The father of a righteous man has great joy;
he who has a wise son delights in him.
²⁵May your father and mother be glad;
may she who gave you birth rejoice!

²⁶My son, give me your heart
and let your eyes keep to my ways,
²⁷for a prostitute is a deep pit
and a wayward wife is a narrow well.
²⁸Like a bandit she lies in wait,
and multiplies the unfaithful among men.

²⁹Who has woe? Who has sorrow?
Who has strife? Who has complaints?
Who has needless bruises? Who has bloodshot
eyes?
³⁰Those who linger over wine,
who go to sample bowls of mixed wine.

ᵇ20 Or *not formerly written*; or *not written excellent*   ᵃ1 Or *who*
ᵇ7 Or *for as he thinks within himself, / so he is*; or *for as he puts on a feast, / so he is*   ᶜ14 Hebrew *Sheol*

³¹Do not gaze at wine when it is red,
  when it sparkles in the cup,
  when it goes down smoothly!
³²In the end it bites like a snake
  and poisons like a viper.
³³Your eyes will see strange sights
  and your mind imagine confusing things.
³⁴You will be like one sleeping on the high seas,
  lying on top of the rigging.
³⁵"They hit me," you will say, "but I'm not hurt!
  They beat me, but I don't feel it!
  When will I wake up
  so I can find another drink?"

24 Do not envy wicked men,
  do not desire their company;
²for their hearts plot violence,
  and their lips talk about making trouble.

³By wisdom a house is built,
  and through understanding it is established;
⁴through knowledge its rooms are filled
  with rare and beautiful treasures.

⁵A wise man has great power,
  and a man of knowledge increases strength;
⁶for waging war you need guidance,
  and for victory many advisers.

⁷Wisdom is too high for a fool;
  in the assembly at the gate he has nothing to
  say.

⁸He who plots evil
  will be known as a schemer.
⁹The schemes of folly are sin,
  and men detest a mocker.

¹⁰If you falter in times of trouble,
  how small is your strength!

¹¹Rescue those being led away to death;
  hold back those staggering towards slaughter.
¹²If you say, "But we knew nothing about this,"
  does not he who weighs the heart perceive it?
  Does not he who guards your life know it?
  Will he not repay each person according to
  what he has done?

24:13 Those who search for wisdom
must not only act and think in the right way,
they must also eat things that will help them
to grow. Honey was traditionally regarded as
symbolic of wisdom.

---

¹³Eat honey, my son, for it is good;
  honey from the comb is sweet to your taste.
¹⁴Know also that wisdom is sweet to your soul;
  if you find it, there is a future hope for you,
  and your hope will not be cut off.

¹⁵Do not lie in wait like an outlaw against a
  righteous man's house,
  do not raid his dwelling-place;

¹⁶for though a righteous man falls seven times, he
  rises again,
  but the wicked are brought down by calamity.

¹⁷Do not gloat when your enemy falls;
  when he stumbles, do not let your heart rejoice,
¹⁸or the LORD will see and disapprove
  and turn his wrath away from him.

¹⁹Do not fret because of evil men
  or be envious of the wicked,
²⁰for the evil man has no future hope,
  and the lamp of the wicked will be snuffed out.

²¹Fear the LORD and the king, my son,
  and do not join with the rebellious,
²²for those two will send sudden destruction upon
  them,
  and who knows what calamities they can bring?

Further Sayings of the Wise

²³These also are sayings of the wise:

To show partiality in judging is not good:
²⁴Whoever says to the guilty, "You are innocent" —
  peoples will curse him and nations denounce
  him.
²⁵But it will go well with those who convict the
  guilty,
  and rich blessing will come upon them.

²⁶An honest answer
  is like a kiss on the lips.

²⁷Finish your outdoor work
  and get your fields ready;
  after that, build your house.

²⁸Do not testify against your neighbour without
  cause,
  or use your lips to deceive.
²⁹Do not say, "I'll do to him as he has done to me;
  I'll pay that man back for what he did."

³⁰I went past the field of the sluggard,
  past the vineyard of the man who lacks
  judgment;
³¹thorns had come up everywhere,
  the ground was covered with weeds,
  and the stone wall was in ruins.
³²I applied my heart to what I observed
  and learned a lesson from what I saw:
³³A little sleep, a little slumber,
  a little folding of the hands to rest —
³⁴and poverty will come on you like a bandit
  and scarcity like an armed man. ᵃ

More Proverbs of Solomon

25 These are more proverbs of Solomon, copied
  by the men of Hezekiah king of Judah:

²It is the glory of God to conceal a matter;
  to search out a matter is the glory of kings.

ᵃ34 Or *like a vagrant / and scarcity like a beggar*

³As the heavens are high and the earth is deep,
  so the hearts of kings are unsearchable.

⁴Remove the dross from the silver,
  and out comes material for^a the silversmith;
⁵remove the wicked from the king's presence,
  and his throne will be established through
  righteousness.

⁶Do not exalt yourself in the king's presence,
  and do not claim a place among great men;
⁷it is better for him to say to you, "Come up
  here,"
  than for him to humiliate you before a
  nobleman.

What you have seen with your eyes
⁸ do not bring^b hastily to court,
for what will you do in the end
  if your neighbour puts you to shame?

⁹If you argue your case with a neighbour,
  do not betray another man's confidence,
¹⁰or he who hears it may shame you
  and you will never lose your bad reputation.

¹¹A word aptly spoken
  is like apples of gold in settings of silver.

¹²Like an ear-ring of gold or an ornament of fine
  gold
  is a wise man's rebuke to a listening ear.

¹³Like the coolness of snow at harvest time
  is a trustworthy messenger to those who send
  him;
  he refreshes the spirit of his masters.

¹⁴Like clouds and wind without rain
  is a man who boasts of gifts he does not give.

¹⁵Through patience a ruler can be persuaded,
  and a gentle tongue can break a bone.

¹⁶If you find honey, eat just enough —
  too much of it, and you will vomit.
¹⁷Seldom set foot in your neighbour's house —
  too much of you, and he will hate you.

¹⁸Like a club or a sword or a sharp arrow
  is the man who gives false testimony against his
  neighbour.

¹⁹Like a bad tooth or a lame foot
  is reliance on the unfaithful in times of trouble.

²⁰Like one who takes away a garment on a cold
  day,
  or like vinegar poured on soda,
  is one who sings songs to a heavy heart.

²¹If your enemy is hungry, give him food to eat;
  if he is thirsty, give him water to drink.
²²In doing this, you will heap burning coals on his
  head,
  and the LORD will reward you.

²³As a north wind brings rain,
  so a sly tongue brings angry looks.

²⁴Better to live on a corner of the roof
  than share a house with a quarrelsome wife.

²⁵Like cold water to a weary soul
  is good news from a distant land.

²⁶Like a muddied spring or a polluted well
  is a righteous man who gives way to the
  wicked.

²⁷It is not good to eat too much honey,
  nor is it honourable to seek one's own honour.

²⁸Like a city whose walls are broken down
  is a man who lacks self-control.

26 Like snow in summer or rain in harvest,
  honour is not fitting for a fool.

²Like a fluttering sparrow or a darting swallow,
  an undeserved curse does not come to rest.

³A whip for the horse, a halter for the donkey,
  and a rod for the backs of fools!

⁴Do not answer a fool according to his folly,
  or you will be like him yourself.

⁵Answer a fool according to his folly,
  or he will be wise in his own eyes.

⁶Like cutting off one's feet or drinking violence
  is the sending of a message by the hand of a
  fool.

⁷Like a lame man's legs that hang limp
  is a proverb in the mouth of a fool.

26:7   If you say something, you must
believe it from the heart. What use is a proverb if you proclaim it, but don't live by it?

---

⁸Like tying a stone in a sling
  is the giving of honour to a fool.

⁹Like a thornbush in a drunkard's hand
  is a proverb in the mouth of a fool.

¹⁰Like an archer who wounds at random
  is he who hires a fool or any passer-by.

¹¹As a dog returns to its vomit,
  so a fool repeats his folly.

¹²Do you see a man wise in his own eyes?
  There is more hope for a fool than for him.

¹³The sluggard says, "There is a lion in the road,
  a fierce lion roaming the streets!"

¹⁴As a door turns on its hinges,
  so a sluggard turns on his bed.

¹⁵The sluggard buries his hand in the dish;
  he is too lazy to bring it back to his mouth.

¹⁶The sluggard is wiser in his own eyes
  than seven men who answer discreetly.

¹⁷Like one who seizes a dog by the ears
  is a passer-by who meddles in a quarrel not his
  own.

_a4 Or comes a vessel from   ^b7, 8 Or nobleman / on whom you had set your eyes. / ⁸Do not go

¹⁸Like a madman shooting
firebrands or deadly arrows
¹⁹is a man who deceives his neighbour
and says, "I was only joking!"

²⁰Without wood a fire goes out;
without gossip a quarrel dies down.

²¹As charcoal to embers and as wood to fire,
so is a quarrelsome man for kindling strife.

²²The words of a gossip are like choice morsels;
they go down to a man's inmost parts.

²³Like a coating of glaze[a] over earthenware
are fervent lips with an evil heart.

²⁴A malicious man disguises himself with his lips,
but in his heart he harbours deceit.
²⁵Though his speech is charming, do not believe
him,
for seven abominations fill his heart.
²⁶His malice may be concealed by deception,
but his wickedness will be exposed in the
assembly.

²⁷If a man digs a pit, he will fall into it;
if a man rolls a stone, it will roll back on him.

²⁸A lying tongue hates those it hurts,
and a flattering mouth works ruin.

27 Do not boast about tomorrow,
for you do not know what a day may
bring forth.

²Let another praise you, and not your own mouth;
someone else, and not your own lips.

³Stone is heavy and sand a burden,
but provocation by a fool is heavier than both.

⁴Anger is cruel and fury overwhelming,
but who can stand before jealousy?

⁵Better is open rebuke
than hidden love.

⁶Wounds from a friend can be trusted,
but an enemy multiplies kisses.

⁷He who is full loathes honey,
but to the hungry even what is bitter tastes
sweet.

⁸Like a bird that strays from its nest
is a man who strays from his home.

⁹Perfume and incense bring joy to the heart,
and the pleasantness of one's friend springs
from his earnest counsel.

¹⁰Do not forsake your friend and the friend of your
father,
and do not go to your brother's house when
disaster strikes you—
better a neighbour nearby than a brother far
away.

¹¹Be wise, my son, and bring joy to my heart;
then I can answer anyone who treats me with
contempt.

¹²The prudent see danger and take refuge,
but the simple keep going and suffer for it.

¹³Take the garment of one who puts up security for
a stranger;
hold it in pledge if he does it for a wayward
woman.

¹⁴If a man loudly blesses his neighbour early in the
morning,
it will be taken as a curse.

¹⁵A quarrelsome wife is like
a constant dripping on a rainy day;
¹⁶restraining her is like restraining the wind
or grasping oil with the hand.

¹⁷As iron sharpens iron,
so one man sharpens another.

¹⁸He who tends a fig-tree will eat its fruit,
and he who looks after his master will be
honoured.

¹⁹As water reflects a face,
so a man's heart reflects the man.

²⁰Death and Destruction[a] are never satisfied,
and neither are the eyes of man.

²¹The crucible for silver and the furnace for gold,
but man is tested by the praise he receives.

²²Though you grind a fool in a mortar,
grinding him like grain with a pestle,
you will not remove his folly from him.

²³Be sure you know the condition of your flocks,
give careful attention to your herds;
²⁴for riches do not endure for ever,
and a crown is not secure for all generations.
²⁵When the hay is removed and new growth
appears
and the grass from the hills is gathered in,
²⁶the lambs will provide you with clothing,
and the goats with the price of a field.
²⁷You will have plenty of goats' milk
to feed you and your family
and to nourish your servant girls.

28 The wicked man flees though no-one
pursues,
but the righteous are as bold as a lion.

²When a country is rebellious, it has many rulers,
but a man of understanding and knowledge
maintains order.

³A ruler[a] who oppresses the poor
is like a driving rain that leaves no crops.

⁴Those who forsake the law praise the wicked,
but those who keep the law resist them.

---

a 23 With a different word division of the Hebrew; Masoretic Text *of silver dross*   *a 20* Hebrew *Sheol and Abaddon*
a 3 Or *A poor man*

5Evil men do not understand justice,
  but those who seek the LORD understand it
    fully.

6Better a poor man whose walk is blameless
  than a rich man whose ways are perverse.

7He who keeps the law is a discerning son,
  but a companion of gluttons disgraces his father.

8He who increases his wealth by exorbitant
    interest
  amasses it for another, who will be kind to the
    poor.

9If anyone turns a deaf ear to the law,
  even his prayers are detestable.

10He who leads the upright along an evil path
  will fall into his own trap,
  but the blameless will receive a good
    inheritance.

11A rich man may be wise in his own eyes,
  but a poor man who has discernment sees
    through him.

12When the righteous triumph, there is great
    elation;
  but when the wicked rise to power, men go
    into hiding.

13He who conceals his sins does not prosper,
  but whoever confesses and renounces them
    finds mercy.

14Blessed is the man who always fears the LORD,
  but he who hardens his heart falls into trouble.

15Like a roaring lion or a charging bear
  is a wicked man ruling over a helpless people.

16A tyrannical ruler lacks judgment,
  but he who hates ill-gotten gain will enjoy a
    long life.

17A man tormented by the guilt of murder
  will be a fugitive till death;
  let no-one support him.

18He whose walk is blameless is kept safe,
  but he whose ways are perverse will suddenly
    fall.

19He who works his land will have abundant food,
  but the one who chases fantasies will have his
    fill of poverty.

20A faithful man will be richly blessed,
  but one eager to get rich will not go
    unpunished.

21To show partiality is not good —
  yet a man will do wrong for a piece of bread.

22A stingy man is eager to get rich
  and is unaware that poverty awaits him.

23He who rebukes a man will in the end gain more
    favour
  than he who has a flattering tongue.

24He who robs his father or mother
  and says, "It's not wrong" —
  he is partner to him who destroys.

25A greedy man stirs up dissension,
  but he who trusts in the LORD will prosper.

26He who trusts in himself is a fool,
  but he who walks in wisdom is kept safe.

27He who gives to the poor will lack nothing,
  but he who closes his eyes to them receives
    many curses.

28When the wicked rise to power, people go into
    hiding;
  but when the wicked perish, the righteous
    thrive.

29 A man who remains stiff-necked after
    many rebukes
  will suddenly be destroyed — without remedy.

2When the righteous thrive, the people rejoice;
  when the wicked rule, the people groan.

3A man who loves wisdom brings joy to his father,
  but a companion of prostitutes squanders his
    wealth.

4By justice a king gives a country stability,
  but one who is greedy for bribes tears it down.

5Whoever flatters his neighbour
  is spreading a net for his feet.

6An evil man is snared by his own sin,
  but a righteous one can sing and be glad.

7The righteous care about justice for the poor,
  but the wicked have no such concern.

8Mockers stir up a city,
  but wise men turn away anger.

9If a wise man goes to court with a fool,
  the fool rages and scoffs, and there is no peace.

29:9 Reasoning with fools is a waste of time. They do not fear God, and cannot share any worthwhile knowledge. If you spend time with a fool, you become like one, and this leads to disaster and death.

10Bloodthirsty men hate a man of integrity
  and seek to kill the upright.

11A fool gives full vent to his anger,
  but a wise man keeps himself under control.

12If a ruler listens to lies,
  all his officials become wicked.

13The poor man and the oppressor have this in
    common:
  The LORD gives sight to the eyes of both.

14If a king judges the poor with fairness,
  his throne will always be secure.

15The rod of correction imparts wisdom,
  but a child left to himself disgraces his mother.

16When the wicked thrive, so does sin,
   but the righteous will see their downfall.

17Discipline your son, and he will give you peace;
   he will bring delight to your soul.

18Where there is no revelation, the people cast off
      restraint;
   but blessed is he who keeps the law.

19A servant cannot be corrected by mere words;
   though he understands, he will not respond.

20Do you see a man who speaks in haste?
   There is more hope for a fool than for him.

21If a man pampers his servant from youth,
   he will bring grief a in the end.

22An angry man stirs up dissension,
   and a hot-tempered one commits many sins.

23A man's pride brings him low,
   but a man of lowly spirit gains honour.

24The accomplice of a thief is his own enemy;
   he is put under oath and dare not testify.

25Fear of man will prove to be a snare,
   but whoever trusts in the LORD is kept safe.

26Many seek an audience with a ruler,
   but it is from the LORD that man gets justice.

27The righteous detest the dishonest;
   the wicked detest the upright.

Sayings of Agur

30 The sayings of Agur son of Jakeh—an oracle: a

This man declared to Ithiel,
   to Ithiel and to Ucal: b

2"I am the most ignorant of men;
   I do not have a man's understanding.
3I have not learned wisdom,
   nor have I knowledge of the Holy One.
4Who has gone up to heaven and come down?
   Who has gathered up the wind in the hollow of
      his hands?
Who has wrapped up the waters in his cloak?
Who has established all the ends of the earth?
What is his name, and the name of his son?
   Tell me if you know!

5"Every word of God is flawless;
   he is a shield to those who take refuge in him.
6Do not add to his words,
   or he will rebuke you and prove you a liar.

7"Two things I ask of you, O LORD;
   do not refuse me before I die:
8Keep falsehood and lies far from me;
   give me neither poverty nor riches,
   but give me only my daily bread.

9Otherwise, I may have too much and disown you
   and say, 'Who is the LORD?'
Or I may become poor and steal,
   and so dishonour the name of my God.

10"Do not slander a servant to his master,
   or he will curse you, and you will pay for it.

11"There are those who curse their fathers
   and do not bless their mothers;
12those who are pure in their own eyes
   and yet are not cleansed of their filth;
13those whose eyes are ever so haughty,
   whose glances are so disdainful;
14those whose teeth are swords
   and whose jaws are set with knives
to devour the poor from the earth,
   the needy from among mankind.

15"The leech has two daughters.
   'Give! Give!' they cry.

"There are three things that are never satisfied,
   four that never say, 'Enough!':
16the grave, c the barren womb,
   land, which is never satisfied with water,
   and fire, which never says, 'Enough!'

17"The eye that mocks a father,
   that scorns obedience to a mother,
will be pecked out by the ravens of the valley,
   will be eaten by the vultures.

18"There are three things that are too amazing for
      me,
   four that I do not understand:
19the way of an eagle in the sky,
   the way of a snake on a rock,
the way of a ship on the high seas,
   and the way of a man with a maiden.

20"This is the way of an adulteress:
   She eats and wipes her mouth
   and says, 'I've done nothing wrong.'

21"Under three things the earth trembles,
   under four it cannot bear up:
22a servant who becomes king,
   a fool who is full of food,
23an unloved woman who is married,
   and a maidservant who displaces her mistress.

24"Four things on earth are small,
   yet they are extremely wise:
25Ants are creatures of little strength,
   yet they store up their food in the summer;
26conies d are creatures of little power,
   yet they make their home in the crags;
27locusts have no king,
   yet they advance together in ranks;
28a lizard can be caught with the hand,
   yet it is found in kings' palaces.

29"There are three things that are stately in their
      stride,
   four that move with stately bearing:

---

a21 The meaning of the Hebrew for this word is uncertain.   a1 Or Jakeh of Massa
b1 Masoretic Text; with a different word division of the Hebrew declared, "I am weary, O God; / I am weary, O God, and faint.
c16 Hebrew Sheol   d26 That is, the hyrax or rock badger

³⁰a lion, mighty among beasts,
who retreats before nothing;
³¹a strutting cock, a he-goat,
and a king with his army around him.^e

³²"If you have played the fool and exalted
yourself,
or if you have planned evil,
clap your hand over your mouth!
³³For as churning the milk produces butter,
and as twisting the nose produces blood,
so stirring up anger produces strife."

Sayings of King Lemuel

31 The sayings of King Lemuel—an oracle^a his
mother taught him:

²"O my son, O son of my womb,
O son of my vows,^b
³do not spend your strength on women,
your vigour on those who ruin kings.

⁴"It is not for kings, O Lemuel—
not for kings to drink wine,
not for rulers to crave beer,
⁵lest they drink and forget what the law
decrees,
and deprive all the oppressed of their rights.
⁶Give beer to those who are perishing,
wine to those who are in anguish;
⁷let them drink and forget their poverty
and remember their misery no more.

⁸"Speak up for those who cannot speak for
themselves,
for the rights of all who are destitute.
⁹Speak up and judge fairly;
defend the rights of the poor and needy."

Epilogue: The Wife of Noble Character

¹⁰^cA wife of noble character who can find?
She is worth far more than rubies.
¹¹Her husband has full confidence in her
and lacks nothing of value.

¹²She brings him good, not harm,
all the days of her life.
¹³She selects wool and flax
and works with eager hands.
¹⁴She is like the merchant ships,
bringing her food from afar.
¹⁵She gets up while it is still dark;
she provides food for her family
and portions for her servant girls.
¹⁶She considers a field and buys it;
out of her earnings she plants a vineyard.
¹⁷She sets about her work vigorously;
her arms are strong for her tasks.
¹⁸She sees that her trading is profitable,
and her lamp does not go out at night.
¹⁹In her hand she holds the distaff
and grasps the spindle with her fingers.
²⁰She opens her arms to the poor
and extends her hands to the needy.
²¹When it snows, she has no fear for her
household;
for all of them are clothed in scarlet.
²²She makes coverings for her bed;
she is clothed in fine linen and purple.
²³Her husband is respected at the city gate,
where he takes his seat among the elders of the
land.
²⁴She makes linen garments and sells them,
and supplies the merchants with sashes.
²⁵She is clothed with strength and dignity;
she can laugh at the days to come.
²⁶She speaks with wisdom,
and faithful instruction is on her tongue.
²⁷She watches over the affairs of her household
and does not eat the bread of idleness.
²⁸Her children arise and call her blessed;
her husband also, and he praises her:
²⁹"Many women do noble things,
but you surpass them all."
³⁰Charm is deceptive, and beauty is fleeting;
but a woman who fears the LORD is to be
praised.
³¹Give her the reward she has earned,
and let her works bring her praise at the city
gate.

---

e31 Or king secure against revolt.   *a1 Or of Lemuel king of Massa, which*   *b2 Or / the answer to my prayers*
c10 Verses 10–31 are an acrostic, each verse beginning with a successive letter of the Hebrew alphabet.

Ecclesiastes

A Paradox

"Paradox" is one of those great religious words that everyone loves to use. But what does it mean to you and me? We probably come across paradoxes all the time, only we give them different names like "contradictions". Like everyday life, faith is full of contradictions, and the book of Ecclesiastes is a profound and moving consideration of the "opposites" that are part and parcel of faith in God.

Advice From One Who Knows About Life

The author of this book, called the Teacher, was a rich, wise, and famous man. He shared his raw experience of life with the reader, and concluded that despite all the good things he had, life was utterly meaningless. He had discovered the real paradox of life: he had everything, yet he had nothing. He had been through life, seen everything there was to see, and yet was left with nothing.

It is easy to conclude that Ecclesiastes is just a series of depressing oracles from a man who no longer had faith in God or life; some may even want to ask what it is doing in the Bible at all. Yet a little probing will show that Ecclesiastes is much more than that.

A Sense of Priorities

First of all, it is a warning to us to get our priorities right. Most of us spend our time chasing after wealth and success, often working ourselves into the ground to get more and more and more, and for what? Material things just perish and money loses its value. If we think we can find fulfilment in wealth and power, we had better think again.

You Can't Take it With You

Secondly, it is a reminder to us to remember our own mortality. One day we will die, we don't know when, and we will be brought to utter nothingness. We can't take our earthly riches with us, and our frantic search for pleasure in wealth will have been futile.

Sharing Experience

Thirdly, it allows us to share the experience of another human being who has been through it all himself, and offers us the benefit of his wisdom and all he learned from hard experience. He spared no punches; he knew how superficial the glitter and glamour of life could be. Ecclesiastes constantly confronts us with that haunting paradox: you may have everything, but really you've got nothing.

The True Source of Happiness

Most importantly, of course, the Teacher in Ecclesiastes points us to the true source of happiness in life. Without God there is no ultimate meaning to life. Our pursuit of wealth and material pleasure is just another way of running away from God, of avoiding a living relationship with our creator. We are reminded about how life should be lived, and that all we enjoy here on earth will one day come to an end. God's laws and God's plans are eternal, and we can become part of them if only we recognize their true worth in our lives today.

Everything Is Meaningless

1 The words of the Teacher,ᵃ son of David, king of Jerusalem:

²"Meaningless! Meaningless!"
  says the Teacher.
"Utterly meaningless!
  Everything is meaningless."

1:2 The Teacher believed that almost everything in life was "meaningless". The Hebrew root of the word could be translated today as "hot air", and suggests that all our strivings are a worthless waste of time.

---

³What does man gain from all his labour
  at which he toils under the sun?
⁴Generations come and generations go,
  but the earth remains for ever.
⁵The sun rises and the sun sets,
  and hurries back to where it rises.
⁶The wind blows to the south
  and turns to the north;
round and round it goes,
  ever returning on its course.
⁷All streams flow into the sea,
  yet the sea is never full.
To the place the streams come from,
  there they return again.
⁸All things are wearisome,
  more than one can say.
The eye never has enough of seeing,
  nor the ear its fill of hearing.
⁹What has been will be again,
  what has been done will be done again;
there is nothing new under the sun.
¹⁰Is there anything of which one can say,
  "Look! This is something new"?
It was here already, long ago;
  it was here before our time.
¹¹There is no remembrance of men of old,
  and even those who are yet to
      come
will not be remembered
  by those who follow.

Wisdom Is Meaningless

¹²I, the Teacher, was king over Israel in Jerusalem. ¹³I devoted myself to study and to explore by wisdom all that is done under heaven. What a heavy burden God has laid on men! ¹⁴I have seen all the things that are done under the sun; all of them are meaningless, a chasing after the wind.

¹⁵What is twisted cannot be straightened;
  what is lacking cannot be counted.

¹⁶I thought to myself, "Look, I have grown and increased in wisdom more than anyone who has ruled over Jerusalem before me; I have experienced much of wisdom and knowledge." ¹⁷Then I applied myself to the understanding of wisdom, and also of madness and folly, but I learned that this, too, is a chasing after the wind.

¹⁸For with much wisdom comes much sorrow;
  the more knowledge, the more grief.

Pleasures Are Meaningless

2 I thought in my heart, "Come now, I will test you with pleasure to find out what is good." But that also proved to be meaningless. ²"Laughter," I said, "is foolish. And what does pleasure accomplish?" ³I tried cheering myself with wine, and embracing folly — my mind still guiding me with wisdom. I wanted to see what was worth while for men to do under heaven during the few days of their lives.

⁴I undertook great projects: I built houses for myself and planted vineyards. ⁵I made gardens and parks and planted all kinds of fruit trees in them. ⁶I made reservoirs to water groves of flourishing trees. ⁷I bought male and female slaves and had other slaves who were born in my house. I also owned more herds and flocks than anyone in Jerusalem before me. ⁸I amassed silver and gold for myself, and the treasure of kings and provinces. I acquired men and women singers, and a haremᵃ as well — the delights of the heart of man. ⁹I became greater by far than anyone in Jerusalem before me. In all this my wisdom stayed with me.

¹⁰I denied myself nothing my eyes desired;
  I refused my heart no pleasure.
My heart took delight in all my work,
  and this was the reward for all my labour.

ᵃ1 Or *leader of the assembly*; also in verses 2 and 12   ᵃ8 The meaning of the Hebrew for this phrase is uncertain.

[11]Yet when I surveyed all that my hands had done
  and what I had toiled to achieve,
everything was meaningless, a chasing after the
  wind;
  nothing was gained under the sun.

Wisdom and Folly Are Meaningless

[12]Then I turned my thoughts to consider wisdom,
  and also madness and folly.
What more can the king's successor do
  than what has already been done?
[13]I saw that wisdom is better than folly,
  just as light is better than darkness.
[14]The wise man has eyes in his head,
  while the fool walks in the darkness;
but I came to realise
  that the same fate overtakes them both.

[15]Then I thought in my heart,

"The fate of the fool will overtake me also.
  What then do I gain by being wise?"
I said in my heart,
  "This too is meaningless."
[16]For the wise man, like the fool, will not be long
  remembered;
  in days to come both will be forgotten.
Like the fool, the wise man too must die!

Toil Is Meaningless

[17]So I hated life, because the work that is done under
the sun was grievous to me. All of it is meaningless, a
chasing after the wind. [18]I hated all the things I had
toiled for under the sun, because I must leave them to
the one who comes after me. [19]And who knows
whether he will be a wise man or a fool? Yet he will
have control over all the work into which I have poured
my effort and skill under the sun. This too is meaningless. [20]So my heart began to despair over all my toilsome labour under the sun. [21]For a man may do his
work with wisdom, knowledge and skill, and then he
must leave all he owns to someone who has not worked
for it. This too is meaningless and a great misfortune.
[22]What does a man get for all the toil and anxious striving with which he labours under the sun? [23]All his days
his work is pain and grief; even at night his mind does
not rest. This too is meaningless.

[24]A man can do nothing better than to eat and drink
and find satisfaction in his work. This too, I see, is from
the hand of God, [25]for without him, who can eat or find
enjoyment? [26]To the man who pleases him, God gives
wisdom, knowledge and happiness, but to the sinner
he gives the task of gathering and storing up wealth to
hand it over to the one who pleases God. This too is
meaningless, a chasing after the wind.

A Time for Everything

3 There is a time for everything,
  and a season for every activity under heaven:

[2] a time to be born and a time to die,
     a time to plant and a time to uproot,
[3] a time to kill and a time to heal,
     a time to tear down and a time to build,
[4] a time to weep and a time to laugh,
     a time to mourn and a time to dance,
[5] a time to scatter stones and a time to gather
     them,
     a time to embrace and a time to refrain,
[6] a time to search and a time to give up,
     a time to keep and a time to throw away,
[7] a time to tear and a time to mend,
     a time to be silent and a time to speak,
[8] a time to love and a time to hate,
     a time for war and a time for peace.

3:1   The turning of the seasons describes
the worthlessness of human effort. Try as we
might, we cannot alter the rhythm of life:
even the cycles of time are already set.

---

[9]What does the worker gain from his toil? [10]I have
seen the burden God has laid on men. [11]He has made
everything beautiful in its time. He has also set eternity
in the hearts of men; yet they cannot fathom what God
has done from beginning to end. [12]I know that there
is nothing better for men than to be happy and do good
while they live. [13]That everyone may eat and drink,
and find satisfaction in all his toil—this is the gift of
God. [14]I know that everything God does will endure
for ever; nothing can be added to it and nothing taken
from it. God does it so that men will revere him.

[15]Whatever is has already been,
  and what will be has been before;
  and God will call the past to account.[a]

[16]And I saw something else under the sun:

In the place of judgment—wickedness was there,
  in the place of justice—wickedness was there.

[17]I thought in my heart,

"God will bring to judgment
  both the righteous and the wicked,
for there will be a time for every activity,
  a time for every deed."

[18]I also thought, "As for men, God tests them so that
they may see that they are like the animals. [19]Man's
fate is like that of the animals; the same fate awaits
them both: As one dies, so dies the other. All have the
same breath;[b] man has no advantage over the animal.
Everything is meaningless. [20]All go to the same place;
all come from dust, and to dust all return. [21]Who knows
if the spirit of man rises upward and if the spirit of the
animal[c] goes down into the earth?"
[22]So I saw that there is nothing better for a man than
to enjoy his work, because that is his lot. For who can
bring him to see what will happen after him?

---

[a]15 Or *God calls back the past*   [b]19 Or *spirit*
[c]21 Or *Who knows the spirit of man, which rises upward, or the spirit of the animal, which*

Oppression, Toil, Friendlessness

4 Again I looked and saw all the oppression that was
taking place under the sun:

I saw the tears of the oppressed—
  and they have no comforter;
power was on the side of their oppressors—
  and they have no comforter.
2And I declared that the dead,
  who had already died,
are happier than the living,
  who are still alive.
3But better than both
  is he who has not yet been,
who has not seen the evil
  that is done under the sun.

4And I saw that all labour and all achievement spring
from man's envy of his neighbour. This too is meaningless, a chasing after the wind.

5The fool folds his hands
  and ruins himself.
6Better one handful with tranquillity
  than two handfuls with toil
  and chasing after the wind.

7Again I saw something meaningless under the sun:

8There was a man all alone;
  he had neither son nor brother.
There was no end to his toil,
  yet his eyes were not content with his
    wealth.
"For whom am I toiling," he asked,
  "and why am I depriving myself of
    enjoyment?"
This too is meaningless—
  a miserable business!

9Two are better than one,
  because they have a good return for their
    work:
10If one falls down,
  his friend can help him up.
But pity the man who falls
  and has no-one to help him up!
11Also, if two lie down together, they will keep
    warm.
  But how can one keep warm alone?
12Though one may be overpowered,
  two can defend themselves.
A cord of three strands is not quickly broken.

Advancement Is Meaningless

13Better a poor but wise youth than an old but foolish
king who no longer knows how to take warning. 14The
youth may have come from prison to the kingship, or
he may have been born in poverty within his kingdom.
15I saw that all who lived and walked under the sun
followed the youth, the king's successor. 16There was
no end to all the people who were before them. But
those who came later were not pleased with the successor. This too is meaningless, a chasing after the
wind.

Stand in Awe of God

5 Guard your steps when you go to the house of
God. Go near to listen rather than to offer the sacrifice of fools, who do not know that they do wrong.

2Do not be quick with your mouth,
  do not be hasty in your heart
  to utter anything before God.
God is in heaven
  and you are on earth,
  so let your words be few.
3As a dream comes when there are many cares,
  so the speech of a fool when there are many
    words.

4When you make a vow to God, do not delay in fulfilling it. He has no pleasure in fools; fulfil your vow.
5It is better not to vow than to make a vow and not fulfil
it. 6Do not let your mouth lead you into sin. And do not
protest to the ,temple, messenger, "My vow was a mistake." Why should God be angry at what you say and
destroy the work of your hands? 7Much dreaming and
many words are meaningless. Therefore stand in awe
of God.

Riches Are Meaningless

8If you see the poor oppressed in a district, and justice and rights denied, do not be surprised at such
things; for one official is eyed by a higher one, and over
them both are others higher still. 9The increase from
the land is taken by all; the king himself profits from
the fields.

10Whoever loves money never has money enough;
  whoever loves wealth is never satisfied with his
    income.
  This too is meaningless.

5:10 All human striving is meaningless,
even the accumulation of wealth. Riches are
gifts bestowed by God, and not gained by
our own effort. Those who store up riches
are like officials who are corrupt and exploit
the poor.

11As goods increase,
  so do those who consume them.
And what benefit are they to the owner
  except to feast his eyes on them?

12The sleep of a labourer is sweet,
  whether he eats little or much,
but the abundance of a rich man
  permits him no sleep.

13I have seen a grievous evil under the sun:

wealth hoarded to the harm of its owner,
14 or wealth lost through some misfortune,
so that when he has a son
  there is nothing left for him.
15Naked a man comes from his mother's womb,
  and as he comes, so he departs.
He takes nothing from his labour
  that he can carry in his hand.

¹⁶This too is a grievous evil:

As a man comes, so he departs,
and what does he gain,
since he toils for the wind?
¹⁷All his days he eats in darkness,
with great frustration, affliction and anger.

¹⁸Then I realised that it is good and proper for a man to eat and drink, and to find satisfaction in his toilsome labour under the sun during the few days of life God has given him—for this is his lot. ¹⁹Moreover, when God gives any man wealth and possessions, and enables him to enjoy them, to accept his lot and be happy in his work—this is a gift of God. ²⁰He seldom reflects on the days of his life, because God keeps him occupied with gladness of heart.

6 I have seen another evil under the sun, and it weighs heavily on men: ²God gives a man wealth, possessions and honour, so that he lacks nothing his heart desires, but God does not enable him to enjoy them, and a stranger enjoys them instead. This is meaningless, a grievous evil.

³A man may have a hundred children and live many years; yet no matter how long he lives, if he cannot enjoy his prosperity and does not receive proper burial, I say that a stillborn child is better off than he. ⁴It comes without meaning, it departs in darkness, and in darkness its name is shrouded. ⁵Though it never saw the sun or knew anything, it has more rest than does that man—⁶even if he lives a thousand years twice over but fails to enjoy his prosperity. Do not all go to the same place?

6:3 To die without proper ritual ceremonial and burial was abhorrent to Jewish law and custom. Even long life, therefore, did not mean that a person was guaranteed honour.

---

⁷All man's efforts are for his mouth,
yet his appetite is never satisfied.
⁸What advantage has a wise man
over a fool?
What does a poor man gain
by knowing how to conduct himself before
others?
⁹Better what the eye sees
than the roving of the appetite.
This too is meaningless,
a chasing after the wind.

¹⁰Whatever exists has already been named,
and what man is has been known;
no man can contend
with one who is stronger than he.
¹¹The more the words,
the less the meaning,
and how does that profit anyone?

¹²For who knows what is good for a man in life, during the few and meaningless days he passes through like a shadow? Who can tell him what will happen under the sun after he is gone?

Wisdom

7 A good name is better than fine perfume,
and the day of death better than the day of
birth.
²It is better to go to a house of mourning
than to go to a house of feasting,
for death is the destiny of every man;
the living should take this to heart.
³Sorrow is better than laughter,
because a sad face is good for the heart.
⁴The heart of the wise is in the house of
mourning,
but the heart of fools is in the house of
pleasure.
⁵It is better to heed a wise man's rebuke
than to listen to the song of fools.
⁶Like the crackling of thorns under the pot,
so is the laughter of fools.
This too is meaningless.

⁷Extortion turns a wise man into a fool,
and a bribe corrupts the heart.

⁸The end of a matter is better than its beginning,
and patience is better than pride.
⁹Do not be quickly provoked in your spirit,
for anger resides in the lap of fools.

¹⁰Do not say, "Why were the old days better than
these?"
For it is not wise to ask such questions.

¹¹Wisdom, like an inheritance, is a good thing
and benefits those who see the sun.
¹²Wisdom is a shelter
as money is a shelter,
but the advantage of knowledge is this:
that wisdom preserves the life of its possessor.

¹³Consider what God has done:

Who can straighten
what he has made crooked?
¹⁴When times are good, be happy;
but when times are bad, consider:
God has made the one
as well as the other.
Therefore, a man cannot discover
anything about his future.

¹⁵In this meaningless life of mine I have seen both of these:

a righteous man perishing in his righteousness,
and a wicked man living long in his
wickedness.
¹⁶Do not be over-righteous,
neither be overwise—
why destroy yourself?
¹⁷Do not be overwicked,
and do not be a fool—
why die before your time?
¹⁸It is good to grasp the one
and not let go of the other.

The man who fears God will avoid all
extremes. [a]

[19] Wisdom makes one wise man more powerful
than ten rulers in a city.

[20] There is not a righteous man on earth
who does what is right and never sins.

[21] Do not pay attention to every word people say,
or you may hear your servant cursing you —
[22] for you know in your heart
that many times you yourself have cursed
others.

[23] All this I tested by wisdom and I said,

"I am determined to be wise" —
but this was beyond me.
[24] Whatever wisdom may be,
it is far off and most profound —
who can discover it?
[25] So I turned my mind to understand,
to investigate and to search out wisdom and the
scheme of things
and to understand the stupidity of wickedness
and the madness of folly.

[26] I find more bitter than death
the woman who is a snare,
whose heart is a trap
and whose hands are chains.
The man who pleases God will escape her,
but the sinner she will ensnare.

[27] "Look," says the Teacher,[b] "this is what I have
discovered:

"Adding one thing to another to discover the
scheme of things —
[28]   while I was still searching
but not finding —
I found one upright man among a thousand,
but not one upright woman among them all.
[29] This only have I found:
God made mankind upright,
but men have gone in search of many
schemes."

8 Who is like the wise man?
Who knows the explanation of things?
Wisdom brightens a man's face
and changes its hard appearance.

Obey the King

[2] Obey the king's command, I say, because you took
an oath before God. [3] Do not be in a hurry to leave the
king's presence. Do not stand up for a bad cause, for
he will do whatever he pleases. [4] Since a king's word
is supreme, who can say to him, "What are you doing?"

[5] Whoever obeys his command will come to no
harm,
and the wise heart will know the proper time
and procedure.

[6] For there is a proper time and procedure for
every matter,
though a man's misery weighs heavily upon
him.

[7] Since no man knows the future,
who can tell him what is to come?
[8] No man has power over the wind to contain it;[a]
so no-one has power over the day of his death.
As no-one is discharged in time of war,
so wickedness will not release those who
practise it.

[9] All this I saw, as I applied my mind to everything
done under the sun. There is a time when a man lords
it over others to his own[b] hurt. [10] Then too, I saw the
wicked buried — those who used to come and go from
the holy place and receive praise[c] in the city where
they did this. This too is meaningless.
[11] When the sentence for a crime is not quickly carried out, the hearts of the people are filled with
schemes to do wrong. [12] Although a wicked man commits a hundred crimes and still lives a long time, I
know that it will go better with God-fearing men, who
are reverent before God. [13] Yet because the wicked do
not fear God, it will not go well with them, and their
days will not lengthen like a shadow.
[14] There is something else meaningless that occurs
on earth: righteous men who get what the wicked
deserve, and wicked men who get what the righteous
deserve. This too, I say, is meaningless. [15] So I commend the enjoyment of life, because nothing is better
for a man under the sun than to eat and drink and be
glad. Then joy will accompany him in his work all the
days of the life God has given him under the sun.
[16] When I applied my mind to know wisdom and to
observe man's labour on earth — his eyes not seeing
sleep day or night — [17] then I saw all that God has done.
No-one can comprehend what goes on under the sun.
Despite all his efforts to search it out, man cannot discover its meaning. Even if a wise man claims he knows,
he cannot really comprehend it.

A Common Destiny for All

9 So I reflected on all this and concluded that the
righteous and the wise and what they do are in
God's hands, but no man knows whether love or hate
awaits him. [2] All share a common destiny — the righteous and the wicked, the good and the bad,[a] the clean
and the unclean, those who offer sacrifices and those
who do not.

As it is with the good man,
so with the sinner;
as it is with those who take oaths,
so with those who are afraid to take them.

[3] This is the evil in everything that happens under
the sun: The same destiny overtakes all. The hearts of
men, moreover, are full of evil and there is madness in
their hearts while they live, and afterwards they join
the dead. [4] Anyone who is among the living has

---

[a] 18 Or will follow them both   [b] 27 Or leader of the assembly   [a] 8 Or over his spirit to retain it
[b] 9 Or to their   [c] 10 Some Hebrew manuscripts and Septuagint (Aquila); most Hebrew manuscripts and are forgotten
[a] 2 Septuagint (Aquila), Vulgate and Syriac; Hebrew does not have and the bad

hope[b]—even a live dog is better off than a dead lion!

9:2 Everyone shares a common destiny whether people are good or bad. We can do nothing for ourselves, except rely on the mercy of God. It is better to enjoy life to the full, for we do not know when death will come.

---

[5]For the living know that they will die,
   but the dead know nothing;
they have no further reward,
   and even the memory of them is forgotten.
[6]Their love, their hate
   and their jealousy have long since vanished;
never again will they have a part
   in anything that happens under the sun.

[7]Go, eat your food with gladness, and drink your wine with a joyful heart, for it is now that God favours what you do. [8]Always be clothed in white, and always anoint your head with oil. [9]Enjoy life with your wife, whom you love, all the days of this meaningless life that God has given you under the sun—all your meaningless days. For this is your lot in life and in your toilsome labour under the sun. [10]Whatever your hand finds to do, do it with all your might, for in the grave,[c] where you are going, there is neither working nor planning nor knowledge nor wisdom.

[11]I have seen something else under the sun:

The race is not to the swift
   or the battle to the strong,
nor does food come to the wise
   or wealth to the brilliant
   or favour to the learned;
but time and chance happen to them all.

[12]Moreover, no man knows when his hour will come:

As fish are caught in a cruel net,
   or birds are taken in a snare,
so men are trapped by evil times
   that fall unexpectedly upon them.

Wisdom Better Than Folly

[13]I also saw under the sun this example of wisdom that greatly impressed me: [14]There was once a small city with only a few people in it. And a powerful king came against it, surrounded it and built huge siege-works against it. [15]Now there lived in that city a man poor but wise, and he saved the city by his wisdom. But nobody remembered that poor man. [16]So I said, "Wisdom is better than strength." But the poor man's wisdom is despised, and his words are no longer heeded.

[17]The quiet words of the wise are more to be heeded
   than the shouts of a ruler of fools.
[18]Wisdom is better than weapons of war,
   but one sinner destroys much good.

10 As dead flies give perfume a bad smell,
   so a little folly outweighs wisdom and honour.
[2]The heart of the wise inclines to the right,
   but the heart of the fool to the left.
[3]Even as he walks along the road,
   the fool lacks sense
   and shows everyone how stupid he is.
[4]If a ruler's anger rises against you,
   do not leave your post;
   calmness can lay great errors to rest.

[5]There is an evil I have seen under the sun,
   the sort of error that arises from a ruler:
[6]Fools are put in many high positions,
   while the rich occupy the low ones.
[7]I have seen slaves on horseback,
   while princes go on foot like slaves.

[8]Whoever digs a pit may fall into it;
   whoever breaks through a wall may be bitten by a snake.
[9]Whoever quarries stones may be injured by them;
   whoever splits logs may be endangered by them.

[10]If the axe is dull
   and its edge unsharpened,
more strength is needed
   but skill will bring success.

[11]If a snake bites before it is charmed,
   there is no profit for the charmer.

[12]Words from a wise man's mouth are gracious,
   but a fool is consumed by his own lips.
[13]At the beginning his words are folly;
   at the end they are wicked madness—
[14]   and the fool multiplies words.

No-one knows what is coming—
   who can tell him what will happen after him?

[15]A fool's work wearies him;
   he does not know the way to town.

[16]Woe to you, O land whose king was a servant[a]
   and whose princes feast in the morning.
[17]Blessed are you, O land whose king is of noble birth
   and whose princes eat at a proper time—
   for strength and not for drunkenness.

[18]If a man is lazy, the rafters sag;
   if his hands are idle, the house leaks.

[19]A feast is made for laughter,
   and wine makes life merry,
   but money is the answer for everything.

[20]Do not revile the king even in your thoughts,
   or curse the rich in your bedroom,
because a bird of the air may carry your words,
   and a bird on the wing may report what you say.

---

[b]4 Or *What then is to be chosen? With all who live, there is hope*   [c]10 Hebrew *Sheol*   [a]16 Or *king is a child*

Bread Upon the Waters

11 Cast your bread upon the waters,
for after many days you will find it again.
²Give portions to seven, yes to eight,
for you do not know what disaster may come
upon the land.

³If clouds are full of water,
they pour rain upon the earth.
Whether a tree falls to the south or to the north,
in the place where it falls, there will it lie.
⁴Whoever watches the wind will not plant;
whoever looks at the clouds will not reap.

⁵As you do not know the path of the wind,
or how the body is formed ᵃ in a mother's
womb,
so you cannot understand the work of God,
the Maker of all things.

⁶Sow your seed in the morning,
and at evening let not your hands be idle,
for you do not know which will succeed,
whether this or that,
or whether both will do equally well.

Remember Your Creator While Young

⁷Light is sweet,
and it pleases the eyes to see the sun.
⁸However many years a man may live,
let him enjoy them all.
But let him remember the days of darkness,
for they will be many.
Everything to come is meaningless.

⁹Be happy, young man, while you are young,
and let your heart give you joy in the days of
your youth.
Follow the ways of your heart
and whatever your eyes see,
but know that for all these things
God will bring you to judgment.
¹⁰So then, banish anxiety from your heart
and cast off the troubles of your body,
for youth and vigour are meaningless.

12 Remember your Creator
in the days of your youth,
before the days of trouble come
and the years approach when you will say,
"I find no pleasure in them" —
²before the sun and the light
and the moon and the stars grow dark,
and the clouds return after the rain;
³when the keepers of the house tremble,
and the strong men stoop,
when the grinders cease because they are few,

and those looking through the windows grow
dim;
⁴when the doors to the street are closed
and the sound of grinding fades;
when men rise up at the sound of birds,
but all their songs grow faint;
⁵when men are afraid of heights
and of dangers in the streets;
when the almond tree blossoms
and the grasshopper drags himself along
and desire no longer is stirred.
Then man goes to his eternal home
and mourners go about the streets.

12:5 The Teacher used metaphors of old age — failing eyesight, weak limbs, loss of teeth, and increasing deafness — to describe the progress of human life toward death. It is essential to remember the commandments of God and keep them while you are young, rather than reach old age and have great regrets.

---

⁶Remember him — before the silver cord is severed,
or the golden bowl is broken;
before the pitcher is shattered at the spring,
or the wheel broken at the well,
⁷and the dust returns to the ground it came from,
and the spirit returns to God who gave it.

⁸"Meaningless! Meaningless!" says the Teacher. ᵃ
"Everything is meaningless!"

The Conclusion of the Matter

⁹Not only was the Teacher wise, but also he imparted knowledge to the people. He pondered and searched out and set in order many proverbs. ¹⁰The Teacher searched to find just the right words, and what he wrote was upright and true.

¹¹The words of the wise are like goads, their collected sayings like firmly embedded nails — given by one Shepherd. ¹²Be warned, my son, of anything in addition to them.

Of making many books there is no end, and much study wearies the body.

¹³Now all has been heard;
here is the conclusion of the matter:
Fear God and keep his commandments,
for this is the whole ˌduty, of man.
¹⁴For God will bring every deed into judgment,
including every hidden thing,
whether it is good or evil.

ᵃ5 Or know how life (or the spirit) / enters the body being formed   ᵃ8 Or the leader of the assembly; also in verses 9 and 10

Song of Songs

Eroticism or Allegory?

The Song of Songs is the one book of the Bible that can be relied upon to provoke strong feelings. Many people are perplexed by the fact that a succession of highly erotic love poems, which may seem more appropriate in an "18" film, are included in the Bible.

In the past some commentators have tried to treat this book in an allegorical way. That means that they have tried to explain the language and imagery as representative of something; and some have said that it represents the sort of love between God and his people, or in Christian terms, between Christ and the Church. But where else in the Bible does God relate to his people in such an explicitly sexual way? If this view is right, and most scholars now dispute it, it does seem out of character with the way God reveals himself throughout the rest of the Bible. Whatever your view, the question still remains: why include such graphic love songs in the Bible?

God-Given Gift

Firstly, love and sexual expression between two people are recognized as being God-given gifts. They are not taboo subjects, but beautiful and worth celebrating. Within a relationship, two people can begin to explore every part of each other, and that includes their bodies.

Secondly, it demonstrates equality between men and women. As you read the Song of Songs, you soon realize that there are none of the stereotyped images of male dominance and female passiveness that have become such a strong part of all our thinking about human relationships. Instead, we are given an insight into a level of mutual respect that affirms the God-given nature of human relationships.

As Strong as Death

Thirdly, it challenges us to treat human love with the greatest respect. To fall in love with someone is to enjoy a gift from God. It is a risky undertaking and it makes great demands and sacrifices. In its own words, "love is as strong as death," (8:6). In other words, you have got to be ready for love, both physically and emotionally. It is not a game to be played by those who are too selfish or too frightened to be committed to it.

In translation, the Song of Songs retains all the original metaphors and images from the original Hebrew, which may be difficult to understand at first. The metaphors would have been well-known, colloquial (informal) phrases to the original readers. To have used modern colloquialisms in translation might have made it sound flippant and superficial. So how can we understand what they mean? The descriptions in the Song of Songs are not meant to be pictures so much as emotions. Don't think about what a fountain, for example, looks like, but what it makes you feel. The Hebrew metaphors help the modern reader to understand how the Lover and the Beloved felt as they shared the love which God has so freely given to all of us.

1

Solomon's Song of Songs.

Beloved[a]

[2]Let him kiss me with the kisses of his mouth —
  for your love is more delightful than wine.
[3]Pleasing is the fragrance of your perfumes;
  your name is like perfume poured out.
  No wonder the maidens love you!
[4]Take me away with you — let us hurry!
  Let the king bring me into his chambers.

Friends

We rejoice and delight in you;[b]
  we will praise your love more than wine.

Beloved

How right they are to adore you!

[5]Dark am I, yet lovely,
  O daughters of Jerusalem,
  dark like the tents of Kedar,
  like the tent curtains of Solomon.[c]
[6]Do not stare at me because I am dark,
  because I am darkened by the sun.
My mother's sons were angry with me
  and made me take care of the vineyards;
  my own vineyard I have neglected.
[7]Tell me, you whom I love, where you graze your
    flock
  and where you rest your sheep at midday.
Why should I be like a veiled woman
  beside the flocks of your friends?

Friends

[8]If you do not know, most beautiful of women,
  follow the tracks of the sheep
and graze your young goats
  by the tents of the shepherds.

Lover

[9]I liken you, my darling, to a mare
  harnessed to one of the chariots of Pharaoh.
[10]Your cheeks are beautiful with ear-rings,
  your neck with strings of jewels.
[11]We will make you ear-rings of gold,
  studded with silver.

Beloved

[12]While the king was at his table,
  my perfume spread its fragrance.
[13]My lover is to me a sachet of myrrh
  resting between my breasts.
[14]My lover is to me a cluster of henna blossoms
  from the vineyards of En Gedi.

Lover

[15]How beautiful you are, my darling!
  Oh, how beautiful!
  Your eyes are doves.

Beloved

[16]How handsome you are, my lover!
  Oh, how charming!
  And our bed is verdant.

Lover

[17]The beams of our house are cedars;
  our rafters are firs.

Beloved[a]

2

I am a rose[b] of Sharon,
  a lily of the valleys.

Lover

[2]Like a lily among thorns
  is my darling among the maidens.

Beloved

[3]Like an apple tree among the trees of the forest
  is my lover among the young men.
I delight to sit in his shade,
  and his fruit is sweet to my taste.
[4]He has taken me to the banquet hall,
  and his banner over me is love.
[5]Strengthen me with raisins,
  refresh me with apples,
  for I am faint with love.
[6]His left arm is under my head,
  and his right arm embraces me.
[7]Daughters of Jerusalem, I charge you
  by the gazelles and by the does of the field:
Do not arouse or awaken love
  until it so desires.

[8]Listen! My lover!
  Look! Here he comes,

---

a2 Primarily on the basis of the gender of the Hebrew pronouns used, male and female speakers are indicated in the margins by the captions Lover and Beloved respectively. The words of others are marked Friends. In some instances the divisions and their captions are debatable.
b4 The Hebrew is masculine singular.   c5 Or Salma   a1 Or Lover   b1 Possibly a member of the crocus family

leaping across the mountains,
  bounding over the hills.
⁹My lover is like a gazelle or a young stag.
  Look! There he stands behind our wall,
gazing through the windows,
  peering through the lattice.
¹⁰My lover spoke and said to me,
  "Arise, my darling,
  my beautiful one, and come with me.
¹¹See! The winter is past;
  the rains are over and gone.
¹²Flowers appear on the earth;
  the season of singing has come,
the cooing of doves
  is heard in our land.
¹³The fig-tree forms its early fruit;
  the blossoming vines spread their fragrance.
Arise, come, my darling;
  my beautiful one, come with me."

2:13   All the signs of new life and a new
beginning come with love, like spring coming after winter. Christians have often used
the images in this passage to describe the
new life that comes with Christ's resurrection at Easter.

Lover

¹⁴My dove in the clefts of the rock,
  in the hiding-places on the mountainside,
show me your face,
  let me hear your voice;
for your voice is sweet,
  and your face is lovely.
¹⁵Catch us the foxes,
  the little foxes
that ruin the vineyards,
  our vineyards that are in bloom.

Beloved

¹⁶My lover is mine and I am his;
  he browses among the lilies.
¹⁷Until the day breaks
  and the shadows flee,
turn, my lover,
  and be like a gazelle
or like a young stag
  on the rugged hills. ᶜ

3 All night long on my bed
  I looked for the one my heart loves;
  I looked for him but did not find him.
²I will get up now and go about the city,
  through its streets and squares;
I will search for the one my heart loves.
  So I looked for him but did not find him.
³The watchmen found me
  as they made their rounds in the city.
  "Have you seen the one my heart loves?"

⁴Scarcely had I passed them
  when I found the one my heart loves.
I held him and would not let him go
  till I had brought him to my mother's house,
  to the room of the one who conceived me.
⁵Daughters of Jerusalem, I charge you
  by the gazelles and by the does of the field:
Do not arouse or awaken love
  until it so desires.

⁶Who is this coming up from the desert
  like a column of smoke,
perfumed with myrrh and incense
  made from all the spices of the merchant?
⁷Look! It is Solomon's carriage,
  escorted by sixty warriors,
  the noblest of Israel,
⁸all of them wearing the sword,
  all experienced in battle,
each with his sword at his side,
  prepared for the terrors of the night.
⁹King Solomon made for himself the carriage;
  he made it of wood from Lebanon.
¹⁰Its posts he made of silver,
  its base of gold.
Its seat was upholstered with purple,
  its interior lovingly inlaid
  byᵃ the daughters of Jerusalem.
¹¹Come out, you daughters of Zion,
  and look at King Solomon wearing the crown,
  the crown with which his mother crowned him
on the day of his wedding,
  the day his heart rejoiced.

Lover

4 How beautiful you are, my darling!
  Oh, how beautiful!
  Your eyes behind your veil are doves.
Your hair is like a flock of goats
  descending from Mount Gilead.
²Your teeth are like a flock of sheep just shorn,
  coming up from the washing.
Each has its twin;
  not one of them is alone.
³Your lips are like a scarlet ribbon;
  your mouth is lovely.
Your temples behind your veil
  are like the halves of a pomegranate.
⁴Your neck is like the tower of David,
  built with elegance; ᵃ
on it hang a thousand shields,
  all of them shields of warriors.
⁵Your two breasts are like two fawns,
  like twin fawns of a gazelle
  that browse among the lilies.
⁶Until the day breaks
  and the shadows flee,
I will go to the mountain of myrrh
  and to the hill of incense.
⁷All beautiful you are, my darling;
  there is no flaw in you.

ᶜ17 Or *the hills of Bether*   ᵃ10 Or *its inlaid interior a gift of love / from*
ᵃ4 The meaning of the Hebrew for this word is uncertain.

4:8   The Lover became anxious at the absence of his Beloved in far away places, and called her to return to him. While she was away, he imagined that she might be in danger from wild animals. Like all human lovers, he found it difficult not to worry about the absence of his partner.

---

[8]Come with me from Lebanon, my bride,
    come with me from Lebanon.
Descend from the crest of Amana,
    from the top of Senir, the summit of Hermon,
from the lions' dens
    and the mountain haunts of the leopards.
[9]You have stolen my heart, my sister, my bride;
    you have stolen my heart
with one glance of your eyes,
    with one jewel of your necklace.
[10]How delightful is your love, my sister, my bride!
    How much more pleasing is your love than wine,
    and the fragrance of your perfume than any spice!
[11]Your lips drop sweetness as the honeycomb, my bride;
    milk and honey are under your tongue.
The fragrance of your garments is like that of Lebanon.
[12]You are a garden locked up, my sister, my bride;
    you are a spring enclosed, a sealed fountain.
[13]Your plants are an orchard of pomegranates
    with choice fruits,
    with henna and nard,
[14]   nard and saffron,
    calamus and cinnamon,
    with every kind of incense tree,
    with myrrh and aloes
    and all the finest spices.
[15]You are[b] a garden fountain,
    a well of flowing water
    streaming down from Lebanon.

Beloved

[16]Awake, north wind,
    and come, south wind!
Blow on my garden,
    that its fragrance may spread abroad.
Let my lover come into his garden
    and taste its choice fruits.

Lover

5 I have come into my garden, my sister, my bride;
    I have gathered my myrrh with my spice.
I have eaten my honeycomb and my honey;
    I have drunk my wine and my milk.

Friends

Eat, O friends, and drink;
    drink your fill, O lovers.

Beloved

[2]I slept but my heart was awake.
    Listen! My lover is knocking:
"Open to me, my sister, my darling,
    my dove, my flawless one.
My head is drenched with dew,
    my hair with the dampness of the night."
[3]I have taken off my robe—
    must I put it on again?
I have washed my feet—
    must I soil them again?
[4]My lover thrust his hand through the latch-opening;
    my heart began to pound for him.
[5]I arose to open for my lover,
    and my hands dripped with myrrh,
my fingers with flowing myrrh,
    on the handles of the lock.
[6]I opened for my lover,
    but my lover had left; he was gone.
    My heart sank at his departure.[a]
I looked for him but did not find him.
    I called him but he did not answer.
[7]The watchmen found me
    as they made their rounds in the city.
They beat me, they bruised me;
    they took away my cloak,
    those watchmen of the walls!
[8]O daughters of Jerusalem, I charge you—
    if you find my lover,
    what will you tell him?
    Tell him I am faint with love.

Friends

[9]How is your beloved better than others,
    most beautiful of women?
How is your beloved better than others,
    that you charge us so?

Beloved

[10]My lover is radiant and ruddy,
    outstanding among ten thousand.
[11]His head is purest gold;
    his hair is wavy
    and black as a raven.
[12]His eyes are like doves
    by the water streams,
washed in milk,
    mounted like jewels.
[13]His cheeks are like beds of spice
    yielding perfume.
His lips are like lilies
    dripping with myrrh.
[14]His arms are rods of gold
    set with chrysolite.

---

[b]15 Or *I am* (spoken by the *Beloved*)   [a]6 Or *heart had gone out to him when he spoke*

His body is like polished ivory
   decorated with sapphires.[b]
15His legs are pillars of marble
   set on bases of pure gold.
His appearance is like Lebanon,
   choice as its cedars.
16His mouth is sweetness itself;
   he is altogether lovely.
This is my lover, this my friend,
   O daughters of Jerusalem.

Friends

6 Where has your lover gone,
   most beautiful of women?
Which way did your lover turn,
   that we may look for him with you?

Beloved

2My lover has gone down to his garden,
   to the beds of spices,
to browse in the gardens
   and to gather lilies.
3I am my lover's and my lover is mine;
   he browses among the lilies.

6:4   The Lover likened his Beloved to the
cities of Tirzah (the old capital of Israel) and
Jerusalem. Cities often have romantic
associations, like Paris in spring and Venice
in summer.

Lover

4You are beautiful, my darling, as Tirzah,
   lovely as Jerusalem,
   majestic as troops with banners.
5Turn your eyes from me;
   they overwhelm me.
Your hair is like a flock of goats
   descending from Gilead.
6Your teeth are like a flock of sheep
   coming up from the washing.
Each has its twin,
   not one of them is alone.
7Your temples behind your veil
   are like the halves of a pomegranate.
8Sixty queens there may be,
   and eighty concubines,
   and virgins beyond number;
9but my dove, my perfect one, is unique,
   the only daughter of her mother,
   the favourite of the one who bore her.
The maidens saw her and called her
   blessed;
   the queens and concubines praised her.

Friends

10Who is this that appears like the dawn,
   fair as the moon, bright as the sun,
   majestic as the stars in procession?

Lover

11I went down to the grove of nut trees
   to look at the new growth in the valley,
to see if the vines had budded
   or the pomegranates were in bloom.
12Before I realised it,
   my desire set me among the royal chariots of
      my people.[a]

Friends

13Come back, come back, O Shulammite;
   come back, come back, that we may gaze on
      you!

Lover

Why would you gaze on the Shulammite
   as on the dance of Mahanaim?

7 How beautiful your sandalled feet,
   O prince's daughter!
Your graceful legs are like jewels,
   the work of a craftsman's hands.
2Your navel is a rounded goblet
   that never lacks blended wine.
Your waist is a mound of wheat
   encircled by lilies.
3Your breasts are like two fawns,
   twins of a gazelle.
4Your neck is like an ivory tower.
Your eyes are the pools of Heshbon
   by the gate of Bath Rabbim.
Your nose is like the tower of Lebanon
   looking towards Damascus.
5Your head crowns you like Mount Carmel.
   Your hair is like royal tapestry;
   the king is held captive by its tresses.
6How beautiful you are and how pleasing,
   O love, with your delights!
7Your stature is like that of the palm,
   and your breasts like clusters of fruit.
8I said, "I will climb the palm tree;
   I will take hold of its fruit."
May your breasts be like the clusters of the vine,
   the fragrance of your breath like apples,
9   and your mouth like the best wine.

Beloved

May the wine go straight to my lover,
   flowing gently over lips and teeth.[a]
10I belong to my lover,
   and his desire is for me.
11Come, my lover, let us go to the countryside,
   let us spend the night in the villages.[b]
12Let us go early to the vineyards
   to see if the vines have budded,
if their blossoms have opened,
   and if the pomegranates are in bloom—
      there I will give you my love.

---

b14 Or lapis lazuli   a12 Or among the chariots of Amminadab; or among the chariots of the people of the prince
a9 Septuagint, Aquila, Vulgate and Syriac; Hebrew lips of sleepers   b11 Or henna bushes

¹³The mandrakes send out their fragrance,
　and at our door is every delicacy,
both new and old,
　that I have stored up for you, my lover.

8 If only you were to me like a brother,
　who was nursed at my mother's breasts!
Then, if I found you outside,
　I would kiss you,
　and no-one would despise me.
²I would lead you
　and bring you to my mother's house—
　she who has taught me.
I would give you spiced wine to drink,
　the nectar of my pomegranates.
³His left arm is under my head
　and his right arm embraces me.
⁴Daughters of Jerusalem, I charge you:
　Do not arouse or awaken love
　until it so desires.

Friends

⁵Who is this coming up from the desert
　leaning on her lover?

Beloved

Under the apple tree I roused you;
　there your mother conceived you,
　there she who was in labour gave you birth.
⁶Place me like a seal over your heart,
　like a seal on your arm;
for love is as strong as death,
　its jealousy[a] unyielding as the grave.[b]
It burns like blazing fire,
　like a mighty flame.[c]
⁷Many waters cannot quench love;
　rivers cannot wash it away.
If one were to give
　all the wealth of his house for love,
　it[d] would be utterly scorned.

Friends

⁸We have a young sister,
　and her breasts are not yet grown.

8:6　　The Beloved brings us right to the heart of the matter. Love is a costly business, and those who embark upon it must know what they are doing, for it is as strong as death and as dangerous as a fire that cannot be put out.

What shall we do for our sister
　for the day she is spoken for?
⁹If she is a wall,
　we will build towers of silver on her.
If she is a door,
　we will enclose her with panels of cedar.

Beloved

¹⁰I am a wall,
　and my breasts are like towers.
Thus I have become in his eyes
　like one bringing contentment.
¹¹Solomon had a vineyard in Baal Hamon;
　he let out his vineyard to tenants.
Each was to bring for its fruit
　a thousand shekels[e] of silver.
¹²But my own vineyard is mine to give;
　the thousand shekels are for you, O Solomon,
　and two hundred[f] are for those who tend its
　　fruit.

Lover

¹³You who dwell in the gardens
　with friends in attendance,
　let me hear your voice!

Beloved

¹⁴Come away, my lover,
　and be like a gazelle
or like a young stag
　on the spice-laden mountains.

---

[a]6 Or ardour　　[b]6 Hebrew Sheol　　[c]6 Or / like the very flame of the LORD　　[d]7 Or he
[e]11 That is, about 25 pounds (about 11.5 kilograms); also in verse 12　　[f]12 That is, about 5 pounds (about 2.3 kilograms)

Isaiah

What Is a Prophet?

We tend to think of prophecy as being about the future. But the Old Testament prophets didn't look at spiritual crystal balls. They were "forth-tellers" rather than "fore-tellers"; speaking God's word to their own generation. Prophets were a well-known phenomenon in many ancient Near-Eastern religions, but unlike them most of the Old Testament prophets were not "professionals". Some of them seemed at first glance rather unsuited to their task; Jeremiah had enormous self-doubt, and Amos and Micah were both very ordinary people. We know little or nothing about most of the others because their whole lives were dedicated to bringing God's message to the people and drawing their attention to him, rather than talking about themselves.

An Immediate Message

The books from Isaiah onwards in the Old Testament are generally known as the Prophets. They contain the words of some of the most important prophets in the history of the Israelite people. Their messages from God weren't written down at first, but as the political and social situation got worse the importance of what they said was recognized and written down for a wider audience to hear. The first of these books (though not the first to be written) is Isaiah. It is also the largest and most complex. The Jewish Scriptures regard the historical books (Joshua, Judges, 1 and 2 Samuel, 1 and 2 Kings) as part of the Prophets. Their words certainly had implications for the future of Israel. However, they had an immediate meaning too because they looked at the current social and political situation in the light of what God had revealed to the people. Part of the prophets' task was to help the Israelites apply God's laws to their own circumstances. The first of the prophets to have his message written down was Amos (around 750 BC) and the last was probably Malachi (around 450 BC). The messages in Isaiah cover much of that turbulent period including wars, invasions, sieges, the exile, and finally the return from Babylon. As a result it is probably the most complex of the prophetic books.

A Privileged Prophet

The book has two distinct parts. The first 39 chapters are quite different in tone and content to chapters 40—66. Most scholars now agree that the first part was written by the prophet Isaiah in early Jerusalem, mostly during the reign of King Hezekiah (715–687 BC). He is usually known as Isaiah of Jerusalem, and from his writing we know he was a city dweller. He probably moved in privileged circles, and had access to the royal court and government. Because of these connections he was keen to emphasize the importance of David as God's chosen ruler over his people. More than the other prophets he spoke about a future king, descended from David's line, who would bring God's salvation to Israel. This idea was picked up by the writers of the New Testament who frequently used the Old Testament, and Isaiah in particular, to show how Jesus, a descendant of David, was God's chosen Messiah ("Anointed One").

Not Afraid to Speak Out

For all his royal contacts, Isaiah recognized that only God was Israel's true king. He emphasized Israel's rebelliousness, wrong worship, self indulgence and political incompetence. Despite being involved with the top people, Isaiah was never afraid to denounce the evil and hypocrisy he saw around him. One of the most famous passages of condemnation is the vineyard oracle in chapter five, an image used by Jesus in his parables.

Comfort and Hope

In complete contrast, chapter 40 starts with the theme of comfort. Chapters 40—56 are full of hope and reassurance to a people in despair. Most scholars now agree that chapters 40—66 date from a period about 150 years after the prophetic ministry of Isaiah of Jerusalem. There is no mention of Isaiah after chapter 39, and more importantly the historical background of these chapters indicates that the exile prophesied earlier in the book had now come about. These chapters are thought to be written by an author who is referred to as Second Isaiah. We have no idea who he actually was, but his messages may have been added to those of Isaiah of Jerusalem because he was part of a school of prophets who followed him (see 8:16).

Isaiah of Jerusalem had been speaking against the backdrop of the mighty Assyrian empire which was threatening Judah's northern borders — the Northern Kingdom had already been taken over in 721 BC. But even the Assyrian empire disintegrated over a relatively short period as the Babylonian empire grew in power. Under Nebuchadnezzar, in 587 BC, it took the people of Israel into exile leaving the promised land deserted and devastated. The historical details of these events can be found towards the end of 2 Kings. Until the exile, God's people didn't believe that he would allow such a thing to happen. After that they were in despair about their future. Then a message of hope was spoken to the exiles not long before their return to the promised land. Cyrus king of Persia was mentioned (45:1); he had jurisdiction over Jerusalem and he authorized the rebuilding of the temple when the Jews were returned to Jerusalem. The Babylonian empire was itself tottering by the time Second Isaiah's prophecies were written down.

A Message Full of Relevance for Today

Isaiah is not an easy book to come to terms with. The whole book has raised lots of questions for scholars, and many are unanswerable. But for all its complexities, the message of this book is unmistakable. It gives us many insights into God's will and ways, and his relationship with his people. Our own world is as complex and alarming as that of ancient Israel, but God's message is just as relevant to us as it was then. We have to take the consequences of our disobedience, but even in the darkest times there is hope if we return to God.

1

The vision concerning Judah and Jerusalem that Isaiah son of Amoz saw during the reigns of Uzziah, Jotham, Ahaz and Hezekiah, kings of Judah.

A Rebellious Nation

[2]Hear, O heavens! Listen, O earth!
   For the LORD has spoken:
"I reared children and brought them up,
   but they have rebelled against me.
[3]The ox knows his master,
   the donkey his owner's manger,
but Israel does not know,
   my people do not understand."

[4]Ah, sinful nation,
   a people loaded with guilt,
a brood of evildoers,
   children given to corruption!
They have forsaken the LORD;
   they have spurned the Holy One of Israel
   and turned their backs on him.

[5]Why should you be beaten any more?
   Why do you persist in rebellion?
Your whole head is injured,
   your whole heart afflicted.
[6]From the sole of your foot to the top of your head
   there is no soundness—
only wounds and bruises
   and open sores,
not cleansed or bandaged
   or soothed with oil.

[7]Your country is desolate,
   your cities burned with fire;
your fields are being stripped by foreigners
   right before you,
   laid waste as when overthrown by strangers.
[8]The Daughter of Zion is left
   like a shelter in a vineyard,
like a hut in a field of melons,
   like a city under siege.
[9]Unless the LORD Almighty
   had left us some survivors,
we would have become like Sodom,
   we would have been like Gomorrah.

[10]Hear the word of the LORD,
   you rulers of Sodom;
listen to the law of our God,
   you people of Gomorrah!
[11]"The multitude of your sacrifices—
   what are they to me?" says the LORD.

"I have more than enough of burnt offerings,
   of rams and the fat of fattened animals;
I have no pleasure
   in the blood of bulls and lambs and goats.
[12]When you come to appear before me,
   who has asked this of you,
   this trampling of my courts?
[13]Stop bringing meaningless offerings!
   Your incense is detestable to me.
New Moons, Sabbaths and convocations—
   I cannot bear your evil assemblies.
[14]Your New Moon festivals and your appointed feasts
   my soul hates.
They have become a burden to me;
   I am weary of bearing them.
[15]When you spread out your hands in prayer,
   I will hide my eyes from you;
even if you offer many prayers,
   I will not listen.
Your hands are full of blood;
[16] wash and make yourselves clean.
Take your evil deeds
   out of my sight!
Stop doing wrong,
[17] learn to do right!
Seek justice,
   encourage the oppressed.[a]
Defend the cause of the fatherless,
   plead the case of the widow.

1:18   Scarlet and crimson are both fast colours—they are very difficult to wash out. Only God can deal with Israel's sinfulness. There is a strong sense in this chapter of God's people breaking their covenant with God.

---

[18]"Come now, let us reason together,"
   says the LORD.
"Though your sins are like scarlet,
   they shall be as white as snow;
though they are red as crimson,
   they shall be like wool.
[19]If you are willing and obedient,
   you will eat the best from the land;
[20]but if you resist and rebel,
   you will be devoured by the sword."
       For the mouth of the LORD has spoken.

[21]See how the faithful city
   has become a harlot!

---

a 17 Or / rebuke the oppressor

She once was full of justice;
righteousness used to dwell in her—
but now murderers!
22Your silver has become dross,
your choice wine is diluted with water.
23Your rulers are rebels,
companions of thieves;
they all love bribes
and chase after gifts.
They do not defend the cause of the fatherless;
the widow's case does not come before them.
24Therefore the Lord, the LORD Almighty,
the Mighty One of Israel, declares:
"Ah, I will get relief from my foes
and avenge myself on my enemies.
25I will turn my hand against you;
I will thoroughly purge away your dross
and remove all your impurities.
26I will restore your judges as in days of old,
your counsellors as at the beginning.
Afterwards you will be called
the City of Righteousness,
the Faithful City."

27Zion will be redeemed with justice,
her penitent ones with righteousness.
28But rebels and sinners will both be broken,
and those who forsake the LORD will perish.

1:29   The "sacred oaks" were the cultivated areas where Canaanite rites took place.
The Israelites' basic problem was not that
they had abandoned worshipping God, but
that they had incorporated many other local
religious practices into it, most of which had
been forbidden by God (child sacrifice, for
example). This mixing of practices had also
happened through political alliances.

29"You will be ashamed because of the sacred oaks
in which you have delighted;
you will be disgraced because of the gardens
that you have chosen.
30You will be like an oak with fading leaves,
like a garden without water.
31The mighty man will become tinder
and his work a spark;
both will burn together,
with no-one to quench the fire."

The Mountain of the LORD

2 This is what Isaiah son of Amoz saw concerning
Judah and Jerusalem:

2In the last days

the mountain of the LORD's temple will be
established
as chief among the mountains;
it will be raised above the hills,
and all nations will stream to it.

3Many peoples will come and say,

"Come, let us go up to the mountain of the LORD,
to the house of the God of Jacob.
He will teach us his ways,
so that we may walk in his paths."
The law will go out from Zion,
the word of the LORD from Jerusalem.
4He will judge between the nations
and will settle disputes for many peoples.
They will beat their swords into ploughshares
and their spears into pruning hooks.
Nation will not take up sword against nation,
nor will they train for war any more.

5Come, O house of Jacob,
let us walk in the light of the LORD.

The Day of the LORD

6You have abandoned your people,
the house of Jacob.
They are full of superstitions from the East;
they practise divination like the Philistines
and clasp hands with pagans.
7Their land is full of silver and gold;
there is no end to their treasures.
Their land is full of horses;
there is no end to the chariots.
8Their land is full of idols;
they bow down to the work of their hands,
to what their fingers have made.
9So man will be brought low
and mankind humbled—
do not forgive them.a

10Go into the rocks,
hide in the ground
from dread of the LORD
and the splendour of his majesty!
11The eyes of the arrogant man will be humbled
and the pride of men brought low;
the LORD alone will be exalted in that day.

2:13   These trees, and the other things in
this passage, were symbols of the nation's
economic prosperity and pride. The trading
ships are "ships of Tarshish" in the Hebrew,
which means "refinery". Their trade contributed greatly to Judah's wealth.

12The LORD Almighty has a day in store
for all the proud and lofty,
for all that is exalted
(and they will be humbled),
13for all the cedars of Lebanon, tall and lofty,
and all the oaks of Bashan,
14for all the towering mountains
and all the high hills,
15for every lofty tower
and every fortified wall,
16for every trading shipb
and every stately vessel.

---

a9 Or not raise them up   b16 Hebrew every ship of Tarshish

¹⁷The arrogance of man will be brought low
   and the pride of men humbled;
the L<small>ORD</small> alone will be exalted in that day,
¹⁸ and the idols will totally disappear.

¹⁹Men will flee to caves in the rocks
   and to holes in the ground
from the dread of the L<small>ORD</small>
   and the splendour of his majesty,
   when he rises to shake the earth.
²⁰In that day men will throw away
   to the rodents and bats
their idols of silver and idols of gold,
   which they made to worship.
²¹They will flee to caverns in the rocks
   and to the overhanging crags
from dread of the L<small>ORD</small>
   and the splendour of his majesty,
   when he rises to shake the earth.

²²Stop trusting in man,
   who has but a breath in his nostrils.
Of what account is he?

Judgment on Jerusalem and Judah

3 See now, the Lord,
   the L<small>ORD</small> Almighty,
is about to take from Jerusalem and Judah
   both supply and support:
all supplies of food and all supplies of water,
² the hero and warrior,
   the judge and prophet,
   the soothsayer and elder,
³the captain of fifty and man of rank,
   the counsellor, skilled craftsman and clever
      enchanter.

⁴I will make boys their officials;
   mere children will govern them.
⁵People will oppress each other—
   man against man, neighbour against neighbour.
The young will rise up against the old,
   the base against the honourable.

3:5   As a result of the nation's rebellion
and disobedience there would be complete
social chaos. Leaders would be chosen in
desperation and economic decline would
lead to political instability.

---

⁶A man will seize one of his brothers
   at his father's home, and say,
"You have a cloak, you be our leader;
   take charge of this heap of ruins!"
⁷But in that day he will cry out,
   "I have no remedy.
I have no food or clothing in my house;
   do not make me the leader of the people."

⁸Jerusalem staggers,
   Judah is falling;
their words and deeds are against the L<small>ORD</small>,
   defying his glorious presence.

⁹The look on their faces testifies against them;
   they parade their sin like Sodom;
   they do not hide it.
Woe to them!
   They have brought disaster upon themselves.

¹⁰Tell the righteous it will be well with them,
   for they will enjoy the fruit of their deeds.
¹¹Woe to the wicked! Disaster is upon them!
   They will be paid back for what their hands
      have done.

¹²Youths oppress my people,
   women rule over them.
O my people, your guides lead you astray;
   they turn you from the path.

¹³The L<small>ORD</small> takes his place in court;
   he rises to judge the people.
¹⁴The L<small>ORD</small> enters into judgment
   against the elders and leaders of his people:
"It is you who have ruined my vineyard;
   the plunder from the poor is in your houses.
¹⁵What do you mean by crushing my people
   and grinding the faces of the poor?"
                  declares the Lord, the L<small>ORD</small> Almighty.

¹⁶The L<small>ORD</small> says,
   "The women of Zion are haughty,
walking along with outstretched necks,
   flirting with their eyes,
tripping along with mincing steps,
   with ornaments jingling on their ankles.
¹⁷Therefore the Lord will bring sores on the heads
   of the women of Zion;
   the L<small>ORD</small> will make their scalps bald."

¹⁸In that day the Lord will snatch away their finery:
the bangles and headbands and crescent necklaces,
¹⁹the ear-rings and bracelets and veils, ²⁰the head-
dresses and ankle chains and sashes, the perfume
bottles and charms, ²¹the signet rings and nose rings,
²²the fine robes and the capes and cloaks, the purses
²³and mirrors, and the linen garments and tiaras and
shawls.

²⁴Instead of fragrance there will be a stench;
   instead of a sash, a rope;
instead of well-dressed hair, baldness;
   instead of fine clothing, sackcloth;
   instead of beauty, branding.
²⁵Your men will fall by the sword,
   your warriors in battle.
²⁶The gates of Zion will lament and mourn;
   destitute, she will sit on the ground.

4 In that day seven women
   will take hold of one man
and say, "We will eat our own food
   and provide our own clothes;
only let us be called by your name.
   Take away our disgrace!"

The Branch of the L<small>ORD</small>

²In that day the Branch of the L<small>ORD</small> will be beautiful
and glorious, and the fruit of the land will be the pride

and glory of the survivors in Israel. ³Those who are left in Zion, who remain in Jerusalem, will be called holy, all who are recorded among the living in Jerusalem. ⁴The Lord will wash away the filth of the women of Zion; he will cleanse the bloodstains from Jerusalem by a spirit*a* of judgment and a spirit*a* of fire. ⁵Then the LORD will create over all of Mount Zion and over those who assemble there a cloud of smoke by day and a glow of flaming fire by night; over all the glory will be a canopy. ⁶It will be a shelter and shade from the heat of the day, and a refuge and hiding-place from the storm and rain.

The Song of the Vineyard

5 I will sing for the one I love
  a song about his vineyard:
My loved one had a vineyard
  on a fertile hillside.
²He dug it up and cleared it of stones
  and planted it with the choicest vines.
He built a watchtower in it
  and cut out a winepress as well.
Then he looked for a crop of good grapes,
  but it yielded only bad fruit.

5:1 Several times Judah is called "God's vineyard". In this famous oracle it is very unproductive. God had done all he could for his people, but the fruit they were bearing was not worthy of him. Jesus used a similar image (e.g. Matthew 21:33–46; John 15:1–17) to talk about God's relationship with humankind.

---

³"Now you dwellers in Jerusalem and men of Judah,
  judge between me and my vineyard.
⁴What more could have been done for my vineyard
  than I have done for it?
When I looked for good grapes,
  why did it yield only bad?
⁵Now I will tell you
  what I am going to do to my vineyard:
I will take away its hedge,
  and it will be destroyed;
I will break down its wall,
  and it will be trampled.
⁶I will make it a wasteland,
  neither pruned nor cultivated,
  and briers and thorns will grow there.
I will command the clouds
  not to rain on it."

⁷The vineyard of the LORD Almighty
  is the house of Israel,
and the men of Judah
  are the garden of his delight.

And he looked for justice, but saw bloodshed;
  for righteousness, but heard cries of distress.

Woes and Judgments

⁸Woe to you who add house to house
  and join field to field
till no space is left
  and you live alone in the land.

⁹The LORD Almighty has declared in my hearing:

"Surely the great houses will become desolate,
  the fine mansions left without occupants.
¹⁰A ten-acre*a* vineyard will produce only a bath*b*
    of wine,
  a homer*c* of seed only an ephah*d* of grain."

¹¹Woe to those who rise early in the morning
  to run after their drinks,
who stay up late at night
  till they are inflamed with wine.
¹²They have harps and lyres at their banquets,
  tambourines and flutes and wine,
but they have no regard for the deeds of the
    LORD,
  no respect for the work of his hands.
¹³Therefore my people will go into exile
  for lack of understanding;
their men of rank will die of hunger
  and their masses will be parched with thirst.
¹⁴Therefore the grave*e* enlarges its appetite
  and opens its mouth without limit;
into it will descend their nobles and masses
  with all their brawlers and revellers.
¹⁵So man will be brought low
  and mankind humbled,
  the eyes of the arrogant humbled.
¹⁶But the LORD Almighty will be exalted by his
    justice,
  and the holy God will show himself holy by his
    righteousness.
¹⁷Then sheep will graze as in their own pasture;
  lambs will feed*f* among the ruins of the rich.

¹⁸Woe to those who draw sin along with cords of
    deceit,
  and wickedness as with cart ropes,
¹⁹to those who say, "Let God hurry,
  let him hasten his work
  so that we may see it.
Let it approach,
  let the plan of the Holy One of Israel come,
  so that we may know it."

²⁰Woe to those who call evil good
  and good evil,
who put darkness for light
  and light for darkness,
who put bitter for sweet
  and sweet for bitter.
²¹Woe to those who are wise in their own eyes
  and clever in their own sight.

---

a4 Or *the Spirit*   *a10* Hebrew *ten-yoke,* that is, the land ploughed by 10 yoke of oxen in one day
b10 That is, probably about 5 gallons (about 22 litres)   *c10* That is, probably about 6 bushels (about 220 litres)
d10 That is, probably about ⅗ bushel (about 22 litres)   *e14* Hebrew *Sheol*   *f17* Septuagint; Hebrew */ strangers will eat*

²²Woe to those who are heroes at drinking wine
 and champions at mixing drinks,
²³who acquit the guilty for a bribe,
 but deny justice to the innocent.
²⁴Therefore, as tongues of fire lick up straw
 and as dry grass sinks down in the flames,
so their roots will decay
 and their flowers blow away like dust;
for they have rejected the law of the LORD
 Almighty
 and spurned the word of the Holy One of Israel.
²⁵Therefore the LORD's anger burns against his
 people;
 his hand is raised and he strikes them down.
The mountains shake,
 and the dead bodies are like refuse in the
 streets.

Yet for all this, his anger is not turned away,
 his hand is still upraised.

²⁶He lifts up a banner for the distant nations,
 he whistles for those at the ends of the earth.
Here they come,
 swiftly and speedily!
²⁷Not one of them grows tired or stumbles,
 not one slumbers or sleeps;
not a belt is loosened at the waist,
 not a sandal thong is broken.
²⁸Their arrows are sharp,
 all their bows are strung;
their horses' hoofs seem like flint,
 their chariot wheels like a whirlwind.
²⁹Their roar is like that of the lion,
 they roar like young lions;
they growl as they seize their prey
 and carry it off with no-one to rescue.
³⁰In that day they will roar over it
 like the roaring of the sea.
And if one looks at the land,
 he will see darkness and distress;
 even the light will be darkened by the clouds.

Isaiah's Commission

6 In the year that King Uzziah died, I saw the Lord
seated on a throne, high and exalted, and the train
of his robe filled the temple. ²Above him were seraphs,
each with six wings: With two wings they covered
their faces, with two they covered their feet, and with
two they were flying. ³And they were calling to one
another:

"Holy, holy, holy is the LORD Almighty;
 the whole earth is full of his glory."

⁴At the sound of their voices the doorposts and thresholds shook and the temple was filled with smoke.

⁵"Woe to me!" I cried. "I am ruined! For I am a man
of unclean lips, and I live among a people of unclean
lips, and my eyes have seen the King, the LORD
Almighty."

⁶Then one of the seraphs flew to me with a live coal

in his hand, which he had taken with tongs from the
altar. ⁷With it he touched my mouth and said, "See,
this has touched your lips; your guilt is taken away and
your sin atoned for."

6:1 This is perhaps the best known passage in the Bible describing a call from God.
Isaiah's greatest vision of God was the one
which motivated his whole ministry. It was
this experience of God's greatness, and his
own unworthiness in comparison, that sustained Isaiah throughout the many years of
his prophetic task.

---

⁸Then I heard the voice of the Lord saying, "Whom
shall I send? And who will go for us?"
 And I said, "Here am I. Send me!"
 ⁹He said, "Go and tell this people:

" 'Be ever hearing, but never understanding;
 be ever seeing, but never perceiving.'
¹⁰Make the heart of this people calloused;
 make their ears dull
 and close their eyes.ᵃ
Otherwise they might see with their eyes,
 hear with their ears,
 understand with their hearts,
and turn and be healed."

¹¹Then I said, "For how long, O Lord?"
 And he answered:

"Until the cities lie ruined
 and without inhabitant,
until the houses are left deserted
 and the fields ruined and ravaged,
¹²until the LORD has sent everyone far away
 and the land is utterly forsaken.
¹³And though a tenth remains in the land,
 it will again be laid waste.
But as the terebinth and oak
 leave stumps when they are cut down,
 so the holy seed will be the stump in the land."

The Sign of Immanuel

7 When Ahaz son of Jotham, the son of Uzziah, was
king of Judah, King Rezin of Aram and Pekah son
of Remaliah king of Israel marched up to fight against
Jerusalem, but they could not overpower it.

²Now the house of David was told, "Aram has allied
itself withᵃ Ephraim"; so the hearts of Ahaz and his
people were shaken, as the trees of the forest are
shaken by the wind.

³Then the LORD said to Isaiah, "Go out, you and your
son Shear-Jashub,ᵇ to meet Ahaz at the end of the
aqueduct of the Upper Pool, on the road to the Washerman's Field. ⁴Say to him, 'Be careful, keep calm and
don't be afraid. Do not lose heart because of these two
smouldering stubs of firewood—because of the fierce
anger of Rezin and Aram and of the son of Remaliah.

ᵃ9, 10 Hebrew; Septuagint 'You will be ever hearing, but never understanding; / you will be ever seeing, but never perceiving.' / ¹⁰This
people's heart has become calloused; / they hardly hear with their ears, / and they have closed their eyes   ᵃ2 Or has set up camp in
ᵇ3 Shear-Jashub means a remnant will return.

[5]Aram, Ephraim and Remaliah's son have plotted your ruin, saying, [6]"Let us invade Judah; let us tear it apart and divide it among ourselves, and make the son of Tabeel king over it." [7]Yet this is what the Sovereign Lord says:

" 'It will not take place,
  it will not happen,
[8]for the head of Aram is Damascus,
  and the head of Damascus is only Rezin.
Within sixty-five years
  Ephraim will be too shattered to be a people.
[9]The head of Ephraim is Samaria,
  and the head of Samaria is only Remaliah's son.
If you do not stand firm in your faith,
  you will not stand at all.' "

[10]Again the Lord spoke to Ahaz, [11]"Ask the Lord your God for a sign, whether in the deepest depths or in the highest heights."

[12]But Ahaz said, "I will not ask; I will not put the Lord to the test."

[13]Then Isaiah said, "Hear now, you house of David! Is it not enough to try the patience of men? Will you try the patience of my God also? [14]Therefore the Lord himself will give you[c] a sign: The virgin will be with child and will give birth to a son, and[d] will call him Immanuel.[e] [15]He will eat curds and honey when he knows enough to reject the wrong and choose the right. [16]But before the boy knows enough to reject the wrong and choose the right, the land of the two kings you dread will be laid waste. [17]The Lord will bring on you and on your people and on the house of your father a time unlike any since Ephraim broke away from Judah—he will bring the king of Assyria."

7:14 King Ahaz, like the rest of Judah, was anxious about the political situation, but he refused to ask God for a sign that the nation would be secure. He was a weak man, and decided that it was better to have an alliance with Assyria than to be overrun, but he was turned into a puppet ruler and had to adopt Assyria's religious practices. The sign Isaiah gave him indicated that before the child grew up Judah's enemies would cease to be a threat. The New Testament writers saw the ultimate fulfilment of this prophecy in the birth of Jesus.

---

[18]In that day the Lord will whistle for flies from the distant streams of Egypt and for bees from the land of Assyria. [19]They will all come and settle in the steep ravines and in the crevices in the rocks, on all the thornbushes and at all the water holes. [20]In that day the Lord will use a razor hired from beyond the River[f]—the king of Assyria—to shave your head and the hair of your legs, and to take off your beards also. [21]In that day, a man will keep alive a young cow and two goats. [22]And because of the abundance of the milk they give, he will have curds to eat. All who remain in the land will eat curds and honey. [23]In that day, in every place where there were a thousand vines worth a thousand silver shekels,[g] there will be only briers and thorns. [24]Men will go there with bow and arrow, for the land will be covered with briers and thorns. [25]As for all the hills once cultivated by the hoe, you will no longer go there for fear of the briers and thorns; they will become places where cattle are turned loose and where sheep run.

Assyria, the Lord's Instrument

8 The Lord said to me, "Take a large scroll and write on it with an ordinary pen: Maher-Shalal-Hash-Baz.[a] [2]And I will call in Uriah the priest and Zechariah son of Jeberekiah as reliable witnesses for me."

[3]Then I went to the prophetess, and she conceived and gave birth to a son. And the Lord said to me, "Name him Maher-Shalal-Hash-Baz. [4]Before the boy knows how to say 'My father' or 'My mother', the wealth of Damascus and the plunder of Samaria will be carried off by the king of Assyria."

[5]The Lord spoke to me again:

[6]"Because this people has rejected
  the gently flowing waters of Shiloah
and rejoices over Rezin
  and the son of Remaliah,
[7]therefore the Lord is about to bring against them
  the mighty floodwaters of the River[b]—
  the king of Assyria with all his pomp.
It will overflow all its channels,
  run over all its banks
[8]and sweep on into Judah, swirling over it,
  passing through it and reaching up to the neck.
Its outspread wings will cover the breadth of your
    land,
  O Immanuel!"[c]

[9]Raise the war cry,[d] you nations, and be
    shattered!
Listen, all you distant lands.
Prepare for battle, and be shattered!
Prepare for battle, and be shattered!
[10]Devise your strategy, but it will be thwarted;
  propose your plan, but it will not stand,
for God is with us.[e]

Fear God

[11]The Lord spoke to me with his strong hand upon me, warning me not to follow the way of this people. He said:

[12]"Do not call conspiracy
  everything that these people call conspiracy;[f]
do not fear what they fear,
  and do not dread it.

---

[c]14 The Hebrew is plural.   [d]14 Masoretic Text; Dead Sea Scrolls *and he* or *and they*   [e]14 *Immanuel* means *God with us.*
[f]20 That is, the Euphrates   [g]23 That is, about 25 pounds (about 11.5 kilograms)
[a]1 *Maher-Shalal-Hash-Baz* means *quick to the plunder, swift to the spoil*; also in verse 3.   [b]7 That is, the Euphrates
[c]8 *Immanuel* means *God with us.*   [d]9 Or *Do your worst*   [e]10 Hebrew *Immanuel*
[f]12 Or *Do not call for a treaty / every time these people call for a treaty*

¹³The LORD Almighty is the one you are to regard
    as holy,
he is the one you are to fear,
he is the one you are to dread,
¹⁴and he will be a sanctuary;
but for both houses of Israel he will be
a stone that causes men to stumble
and a rock that makes them fall.
And for the people of Jerusalem he will be
a trap and a snare.
¹⁵Many of them will stumble;
they will fall and be broken,
they will be snared and captured."

¹⁶Bind up the testimony
and seal up the law among my disciples.
¹⁷I will wait for the LORD,
who is hiding his face from the house of Jacob.
I will put my trust in him.

¹⁸Here am I, and the children the LORD has given me. We are signs and symbols in Israel from the LORD Almighty, who dwells on Mount Zion. ¹⁹When men tell you to consult mediums and spiritists, who whisper and mutter, should not a people enquire of their God? Why consult the dead on behalf of the living? ²⁰To the law and to the testimony! If they do not speak according to this word, they have no light of dawn. ²¹Distressed and hungry, they will roam through the land; when they are famished, they will become enraged and, looking upward, will curse their king and their God. ²²Then they will look towards the earth and see only distress and darkness and fearful gloom, and they will be thrust into utter darkness.

To Us a Child Is Born

9 Nevertheless, there will be no more gloom for those who were in distress. In the past he humbled the land of Zebulun and the land of Naphtali, but in the future he will honour Galilee of the Gentiles, by the way of the sea, along the Jordan—

²The people walking in darkness
have seen a great light;
on those living in the land of the shadow of
    death ᵃ
a light has dawned.
³You have enlarged the nation
and increased their joy;
they rejoice before you
as people rejoice at the harvest,
as men rejoice
when dividing the plunder.
⁴For as in the day of Midian's defeat,
you have shattered
the yoke that burdens them,
the bar across their shoulders,
the rod of their oppressor.
⁵Every warrior's boot used in battle
and every garment rolled in blood
will be destined for burning,
will be fuel for the fire.

⁶For to us a child is born,
to us a son is given,
and the government will be on his shoulders.
And he will be called
Wonderful Counsellor,ᵇ Mighty God,
Everlasting Father, Prince of Peace.
⁷Of the increase of his government and peace
there will be no end.
He will reign on David's throne
and over his kingdom,
establishing and upholding it
with justice and righteousness
from that time on and for ever.
The zeal of the LORD Almighty
will accomplish this.

9:6   Isaiah was the prophet who most looked forward to the coming Messiah. Isaiah may have written this as an oracle for the accession of Hezekiah, one of Judah's greatest monarchs. But this prophecy wasn't completely fulfilled in his reign, and its application to the birth of Jesus is clear. Like many Old Testament prophecies, it has both present and future significance.

The LORD's Anger Against Israel

⁸The Lord has sent a message against Jacob;
it will fall on Israel.
⁹All the people will know it—
Ephraim and the inhabitants of Samaria—
who say with pride
and arrogance of heart,
¹⁰"The bricks have fallen down,
but we will rebuild with dressed stone;
the fig-trees have been felled,
but we will replace them with cedars."
¹¹But the LORD has strengthened Rezin's foes
against them
and has spurred their enemies on.
¹²Arameans from the east and Philistines from the
    west
have devoured Israel with open mouth.

Yet for all this, his anger is not turned away,
his hand is still upraised.

¹³But the people have not returned to him who
struck them,
nor have they sought the LORD Almighty.
¹⁴So the LORD will cut off from Israel both head and
tail,
both palm branch and reed in a single day;
¹⁵the elders and prominent men are the head,
the prophets who teach lies are the tail.
¹⁶Those who guide this people mislead them,
and those who are guided are led astray.
¹⁷Therefore the Lord will take no pleasure in the
young men,
nor will he pity the fatherless and widows,

ᵃ2 Or land of darkness   ᵇ6 Or Wonderful, Counsellor

for everyone is ungodly and wicked,
   every mouth speaks vileness.

Yet for all this, his anger is not turned away,
   his hand is still upraised.

[18] Surely wickedness burns like a fire;
   it consumes briers and thorns,
it sets the forest thickets ablaze,
   so that it rolls upward in a column of smoke.
[19] By the wrath of the LORD Almighty
   the land will be scorched
and the people will be fuel for the fire;
   no-one will spare his brother.
[20] On the right they will devour,
   but still be hungry;
on the left they will eat,
   but not be satisfied.
Each will feed on the flesh of his own offspring: [c]
[21]   Manasseh will feed on Ephraim, and Ephraim
      on Manasseh;
   together they will turn against Judah.

Yet for all this, his anger is not turned away,
   his hand is still upraised.

10   Woe to those who make unjust laws,
      to those who issue oppressive decrees,
[2] to deprive the poor of their rights
   and withhold justice from the oppressed of my
      people,
making widows their prey
   and robbing the fatherless.
[3] What will you do on the day of reckoning,
   when disaster comes from afar?
To whom will you run for help?
   Where will you leave your riches?
[4] Nothing will remain but to cringe among the
      captives
   or fall among the slain.

Yet for all this, his anger is not turned away,
   his hand is still upraised.

God's Judgment on Assyria

[5] "Woe to the Assyrian, the rod of my anger,
   in whose hand is the club of my wrath!
[6] I send him against a godless nation,
   I dispatch him against a people who anger me,
to seize loot and snatch plunder,
   and to trample them down like mud in the
      streets.
[7] But this is not what he intends,
   this is not what he has in mind;
his purpose is to destroy,
   to put an end to many nations.
[8] 'Are not my commanders all kings?' he says.
[9]   'Has not Calno fared like Carchemish?
Is not Hamath like Arpad,
   and Samaria like Damascus?
[10] As my hand seized the kingdoms of the idols,
   kingdoms whose images excelled those of
      Jerusalem and Samaria—

[11] shall I not deal with Jerusalem and her images
   as I dealt with Samaria and her idols?' "

10:9   All these cities had been devastated, but the Lord would finally deal with
the wickedness of the Assyrians. They
had not reckoned with the power of the
living God, and would be punished for their
atrocities.

---

[12] When the Lord has finished all his work against
Mount Zion and Jerusalem, he will say, "I will punish
the king of Assyria for the wilful pride of his heart and
the haughty look in his eyes. [13] For he says:

" 'By the strength of my hand I have done this,
   and by my wisdom, because I have
      understanding.
I removed the boundaries of nations,
   I plundered their treasures;
like a mighty one I subdued [a] their kings.
[14] As one reaches into a nest,
   so my hand reached for the wealth of the
      nations;
as men gather abandoned eggs,
   so I gathered all the countries;
not one flapped a wing,
   or opened its mouth to chirp.' "

[15] Does the axe raise itself above him who swings it,
   or the saw boast against him who uses it?
As if a rod were to wield him who lifts it up,
   or a club brandish him who is not wood!
[16] Therefore, the Lord, the LORD Almighty,
   will send a wasting disease upon his sturdy
      warriors;
under his pomp a fire will be kindled
   like a blazing flame.
[17] The Light of Israel will become a fire,
   their Holy One a flame;
in a single day it will burn and consume
   his thorns and his briers.
[18] The splendour of his forests and fertile fields
   it will completely destroy,
   as when a sick man wastes away.
[19] And the remaining trees of his forests will be so
      few
   that a child could write them down.

The Remnant of Israel

[20] In that day the remnant of Israel,
   the survivors of the house of Jacob,
will no longer rely on him
   who struck them down
but will truly rely on the LORD,
   the Holy One of Israel.
[21] A remnant will return, [b] a remnant of Jacob
   will return to the Mighty God.
[22] Though your people, O Israel, be like the sand by
      the sea,
   only a remnant will return.

---

[c] 20 Or arm   [a] 13 Or / I subdued the mighty,   [b] 21 Hebrew shear-jashub; also in verse 22

Destruction has been decreed,
    overwhelming and righteous.
[23]The Lord, the LORD Almighty, will carry out
    the destruction decreed upon the whole land.

[24]Therefore, this is what the Lord, the LORD
Almighty, says:

"O my people who live in Zion,
    do not be afraid of the Assyrians,
who beat you with a rod
    and lift up a club against you, as Egypt did.
[25]Very soon my anger against you will end
    and my wrath will be directed to their
        destruction."

[26]The LORD Almighty will lash them with a whip,
    as when he struck down Midian at the rock of
        Oreb;
and he will raise his staff over the waters,
    as he did in Egypt.
[27]In that day their burden will be lifted from your
        shoulders,
    their yoke from your neck;
the yoke will be broken
    because you have grown so fat.[c]

[28]They enter Aiath;
    they pass through Migron;
    they store supplies at Michmash.
[29]They go over the pass, and say,
    "We will camp overnight at Geba."
Ramah trembles;
    Gibeah of Saul flees.
[30]Cry out, O Daughter of Gallim!
    Listen, O Laishah!
    Poor Anathoth!
[31]Madmenah is in flight;
    the people of Gebim take cover.
[32]This day they will halt at Nob;
    they will shake their fist
at the mount of the Daughter of Zion,
    at the hill of Jerusalem.

[33]See, the Lord, the LORD Almighty,
    will lop off the boughs with great power.
The lofty trees will be felled,
    the tall ones will be brought low.
[34]He will cut down the forest thickets with an axe;
    Lebanon will fall before the Mighty One.

The Branch From Jesse

11

[1]A shoot will come up from the stump of
Jesse;
    from his roots a Branch will bear fruit.
[2]The Spirit of the LORD will rest on him—
    the Spirit of wisdom and of understanding,
    the Spirit of counsel and of power,
    the Spirit of knowledge and of the fear of the
        LORD—
[3]and he will delight in the fear of the LORD.

He will not judge by what he sees with his eyes,
    or decide by what he hears with his ears;
[4]but with righteousness he will judge the needy,
    with justice he will give decisions for the poor
        of the earth.
He will strike the earth with the rod of his
        mouth;
    with the breath of his lips he will slay the
        wicked.
[5]Righteousness will be his belt
    and faithfulness the sash round his waist.

11:1   Jesse, David's father, is here
depicted as the stump of a tree—the Davidic
monarchy had hit hard times. But from that
stump a totally new branch will emerge—a
king endowed with God's Holy Spirit and the
gifts he needs to lead the nation in the ways
of God. This is yet another prophecy which
the New Testament writers saw as being fulfilled in Jesus.

[6]The wolf will live with the lamb,
    the leopard will lie down with the goat,
the calf and the lion and the yearling[a] together;
    and a little child will lead them.
[7]The cow will feed with the bear,
    their young will lie down together,
    and the lion will eat straw like the ox.
[8]The infant will play near the hole of the cobra,
    and the young child put his hand into the
        viper's nest.
[9]They will neither harm nor destroy
    on all my holy mountain,
for the earth will be full of the knowledge of the
        LORD
    as the waters cover the sea.

[10]In that day the Root of Jesse will stand as a banner
for the peoples; the nations will rally to him, and his
place of rest will be glorious. [11]In that day the Lord will
reach out his hand a second time to reclaim the remnant that is left of his people from Assyria, from Lower
Egypt, from Upper Egypt,[b] from Cush,[c] from Elam,
from Babylonia,[d] from Hamath and from the islands
of the sea.

[12]He will raise a banner for the nations
    and gather the exiles of Israel;
he will assemble the scattered people of Judah
    from the four quarters of the earth.
[13]Ephraim's jealousy will vanish,
    and Judah's enemies[e] will be cut off;
Ephraim will not be jealous of Judah,
    nor Judah hostile towards Ephraim.
[14]They will swoop down on the slopes of Philistia
    to the west;
together they will plunder the people to the
        east.
They will lay hands on Edom and Moab,
    and the Ammonites will be subject to them.

¹⁵The LORD will dry up
  the gulf of the Egyptian sea;
with a scorching wind he will sweep his hand
  over the Euphrates River.ᶠ
He will break it up into seven streams
  so that men can cross over in sandals.
¹⁶There will be a highway for the remnant of his
    people
  that is left from Assyria,
as there was for Israel
  when they came up from Egypt.

Songs of Praise

12 In that day you will say:

"I will praise you, O LORD.
  Although you were angry with me,
your anger has turned away
  and you have comforted me.
²Surely God is my salvation;
  I will trust and not be afraid.
The LORD, the LORD, is my strength and my song;
  he has become my salvation."
³With joy you will draw water
  from the wells of salvation.

⁴In that day you will say:

"Give thanks to the LORD, call on his name;
  make known among the nations what he has
    done,
  and proclaim that his name is exalted.
⁵Sing to the LORD, for he has done glorious things;
  let this be known to all the world.
⁶Shout aloud and sing for joy, people of Zion,
  for great is the Holy One of Israel among you."

12:6   The messages of hope already contained within Isaiah's oracles are here summed up in a hymn of praise, which concludes the first section of the book. In this radical new kingdom there will be no more evil or hatred, and God's people will be gathered together to worship him. The phrase "Holy One of Israel" is used rarely in the rest of the Old Testament, but many times in Isaiah. It points to the covenant relationship between God and his people.

A Prophecy Against Babylon

13 An oracle concerning Babylon that Isaiah son of Amoz saw:

²Raise a banner on a bare hilltop,
  shout to them;
beckon to them
  to enter the gates of the nobles.
³I have commanded my holy ones;
  I have summoned my warriors to carry out my
    wrath—
  those who rejoice in my triumph.

⁴Listen, a noise on the mountains,
  like that of a great multitude!
Listen, an uproar among the kingdoms,
  like nations massing together!
The LORD Almighty is mustering
  an army for war.
⁵They come from faraway lands,
  from the ends of the heavens—
the LORD and the weapons of his wrath—
  to destroy the whole country.

⁶Wail, for the day of the LORD is near;
  it will come like destruction from the
    Almighty.ᵃ
⁷Because of this, all hands will go limp,
  every man's heart will melt.
⁸Terror will seize them,
  pain and anguish will grip them;
  they will writhe like a woman in labour.
They will look aghast at each other,
  their faces aflame.

⁹See, the day of the LORD is coming—
  a cruel day, with wrath and fierce anger—
to make the land desolate
  and destroy the sinners within it.
¹⁰The stars of heaven and their constellations
  will not show their light.
The rising sun will be darkened
  and the moon will not give its light.
¹¹I will punish the world for its evil,
  the wicked for their sins.
I will put an end to the arrogance of the haughty
  and will humble the pride of the ruthless.
¹²I will make man scarcer than pure gold,
  more rare than the gold of Ophir.
¹³Therefore I will make the heavens tremble;
  and the earth will shake from its place
at the wrath of the LORD Almighty,
  in the day of his burning anger.

¹⁴Like a hunted gazelle,
  like sheep without a shepherd,
each will return to his own people,
  each will flee to his native land.
¹⁵Whoever is captured will be thrust through;
  all who are caught will fall by the sword.
¹⁶Their infants will be dashed to pieces before their
    eyes;
  their houses will be looted and their wives
    ravished.

¹⁷See, I will stir up against them the Medes,
  who do not care for silver
  and have no delight in gold.
¹⁸Their bows will strike down the young men;
  they will have no mercy on infants
  nor will they look with compassion on children.
¹⁹Babylon, the jewel of kingdoms,
  the glory of the Babylonians'ᵇ pride,
will be overthrown by God
  like Sodom and Gomorrah.

ᶠ15 Hebrew *the River*   ᵃ6 Hebrew *Shaddai*   ᵇ19 Or *Chaldeans'*

²⁰She will never be inhabited
  or lived in through all generations;
no Arab will pitch his tent there,
  no shepherd will rest his flocks there.
²¹But desert creatures will lie there,
  jackals will fill her houses;
there the owls will dwell,
  and there the wild goats will leap about.
²²Hyenas will howl in her strongholds,
  jackals in her luxurious palaces.
Her time is at hand,
  and her days will not be prolonged.

13:19   Babylon was a small but growing
force at the height of the Assyrian empire's
power. The New Testament writers made
Babylon the representative of all that was evil
and in rebellion against God.

---

14 The LORD will have compassion on Jacob;
  once again he will choose Israel
and will settle them in their own land.
Aliens will join them
  and unite with the house of Jacob.
²Nations will take them
  and bring them to their own place.
And the house of Israel will possess the nations
  as menservants and maidservants in the LORD's
  land.
They will make captives of their captors
  and rule over their oppressors.

³On the day the LORD gives you relief from suffering
and turmoil and cruel bondage, ⁴you will take up this
taunt against the king of Babylon:

How the oppressor has come to an end!
  How his fury^a has ended!
⁵The LORD has broken the rod of the wicked,
  the sceptre of the rulers,
⁶which in anger struck down peoples
  with unceasing blows,
and in fury subdued nations
  with relentless aggression.
⁷All the lands are at rest and at peace;
  they break into singing.
⁸Even the pine trees and the cedars of Lebanon
  exult over you and say,
"Now that you have been laid low,
  no woodsman comes to cut us down."

⁹The grave^b below is all astir
  to meet you at your coming;
it rouses the spirits of the departed to greet you—
  all those who were leaders in the world;
it makes them rise from their thrones—
  all those who were kings over the nations.
¹⁰They will all respond,
  they will say to you,

"You also have become weak, as we are;
  you have become like us."
¹¹All your pomp has been brought down to the
  grave,
  along with the noise of your harps;
maggots are spread out beneath you
  and worms cover you.

¹²How you have fallen from heaven,
  O morning star, son of the dawn!
You have been cast down to the earth,
  you who once laid low the nations!
¹³You said in your heart,
  "I will ascend to heaven;
I will raise my throne
  above the stars of God;
I will sit enthroned on the mount of
  assembly,
  on the utmost heights of the sacred
  mountain.^c
¹⁴I will ascend above the tops of the clouds;
  I will make myself like the Most High."
¹⁵But you are brought down to the grave,
  to the depths of the pit.

¹⁶Those who see you stare at you,
  they ponder your fate:
"Is this the man who shook the earth
  and made kingdoms tremble,
¹⁷the man who made the world a desert,
  who overthrew its cities
  and would not let his captives go home?"

¹⁸All the kings of the nations lie in state,
  each in his own tomb.
¹⁹But you are cast out of your tomb
  like a rejected branch;
you are covered with the slain,
  with those pierced by the sword,
  those who descend to the stones of the
  pit.
Like a corpse trampled underfoot,
²⁰ you will not join them in burial,
for you have destroyed your land
  and killed your people.

The offspring of the wicked
  will never be mentioned again.
²¹Prepare a place to slaughter his sons
  for the sins of their forefathers;
they are not to rise to inherit the land
  and cover the earth with their cities.

²²"I will rise up against them,"
  declares the LORD Almighty.
"I will cut off from Babylon her name and
  survivors,
  her offspring and descendants,"
                              declares the LORD.
²³"I will turn her into a place for owls
  and into swampland;
I will sweep her with the broom of destruction,"
  declares the LORD Almighty.

---

^a4 Dead Sea Scrolls, Septuagint and Syriac; the meaning of the word in the Masoretic Text is uncertain.
^b9 Hebrew Sheol; also in verses 11 and 15   ^c13 Or the north; Hebrew Zaphon

A Prophecy Against Assyria

24The LORD Almighty has sworn,

"Surely, as I have planned, so it will be,
   and as I have purposed, so it will stand.
25I will crush the Assyrian in my land;
   on my mountains I will trample him down.
His yoke will be taken from my people,
   and his burden removed from their shoulders."

26This is the plan determined for the whole world;
   this is the hand stretched out over all nations.
27For the LORD Almighty has purposed, and who
   can thwart him?
His hand is stretched out, and who can turn it
   back?

14:27   Chapters 13—23 show that God's purposes and sovereignty extend over all people and nations. Yet however great these empires may have been, however terrifying their ability in war, they could never block what God intended to accomplish. The prophecy against Philistia (the coastal region of Palestine) dates from around 716 BC, when it tried to bring Judah into an alliance against the Assyrians who were then weak. But they too would suffer the consequences of their wickedness—God's people must trust in him alone.

A Prophecy Against the Philistines

28This oracle came in the year King Ahaz died:

29Do not rejoice, all you Philistines,
   that the rod that struck you is broken;
from the root of that snake will spring up a viper,
   its fruit will be a darting, venomous serpent.
30The poorest of the poor will find pasture,
   and the needy will lie down in safety.
But your root I will destroy by famine;
   it will slay your survivors.
31Wail, O gate! Howl, O city!
   Melt away, all you Philistines!
A cloud of smoke comes from the north,
   and there is not a straggler in its ranks.
32What answer shall be given
   to the envoys of that nation?
"The LORD has established Zion,
   and in her his afflicted people will find refuge."

A Prophecy Against Moab

15 An oracle concerning Moab:

Ar in Moab is ruined,
   destroyed in a night!
Kir in Moab is ruined,
   destroyed in a night!

2Dibon goes up to its temple,
   to its high places to weep;
Moab wails over Nebo and Medeba.
Every head is shaved
   and every beard cut off.
3In the streets they wear sackcloth;
   on the roofs and in the public squares
they all wail,
   prostrate with weeping.
4Heshbon and Elealeh cry out,
   their voices are heard all the way to Jahaz.
Therefore the armed men of Moab cry out,
   and their hearts are faint.

5My heart cries out over Moab;
   her fugitives flee as far as Zoar,
   as far as Eglath Shelishiyah.
They go up the way to Luhith,
   weeping as they go;
on the road to Horonaim
   they lament their destruction.
6The waters of Nimrim are dried up
   and the grass is withered;
the vegetation is gone
   and nothing green is left.
7So the wealth they have acquired and stored up
   they carry away over the Ravine of the Poplars.
8Their outcry echoes along the border of Moab;
   their wailing reaches as far as Eglaim,
   their lamentation as far as Beer Elim.
9Dimon's[a] waters are full of blood,
   but I will bring still more upon Dimon[a]—
a lion upon the fugitives of Moab
   and upon those who remain in the land.

16 Send lambs as tribute
   to the ruler of the land,
from Sela, across the desert,
   to the mount of the Daughter of Zion.
2Like fluttering birds
   pushed from the nest,
so are the women of Moab
   at the fords of the Arnon.

3"Give us counsel,
   render a decision.
Make your shadow like night—
   at high noon.
Hide the fugitives,
   do not betray the refugees.
4Let the Moabite fugitives stay with you;
   be their shelter from the destroyer."

The oppressor will come to an end,
   and destruction will cease;
   the aggressor will vanish from the land.
5In love a throne will be established;
   in faithfulness a man will sit on it—
   one from the house[a] of David—
one who in judging seeks justice
   and speeds the cause of righteousness.

6We have heard of Moab's pride—
   her overweening pride and conceit,

---

a9 Masoretic Text; Dead Sea Scrolls, some Septuagint manuscripts and Vulgate *Dibon*   a5 Hebrew *tent*

her pride and her insolence—
but her boasts are empty.
[7]Therefore the Moabites wail,
they wail together for Moab.
Lament and grieve
for the men[b] of Kir Hareseth.
[8]The fields of Heshbon wither,
the vines of Sibmah also.
The rulers of the nations
have trampled down the choicest vines,
which once reached Jazer
and spread towards the desert.
Their shoots spread out
and went as far as the sea.
[9]So I weep, as Jazer weeps,
for the vines of Sibmah.
O Heshbon, O Elealeh,
I drench you with tears!
The shouts of joy over your ripened fruit
and over your harvests have been stilled.
[10]Joy and gladness are taken away from the
orchards;
no-one sings or shouts in the vineyards;
no-one treads out wine at the presses,
for I have put an end to the shouting.
[11]My heart laments for Moab like a harp,
my inmost being for Kir Hareseth.
[12]When Moab appears at her high place,
she only wears herself out;
when she goes to her shrine to pray,
it is to no avail.

[13]This is the word the LORD has already spoken concerning Moab. [14]But now the LORD says: "Within three years, as a servant bound by contract would count them, Moab's splendour and all her many people will be despised, and her survivors will be very few and feeble."

An Oracle Against Damascus

17 An oracle concerning Damascus:

"See, Damascus will no longer be a city
but will become a heap of ruins.
[2]The cities of Aroer will be deserted
and left to flocks, which will lie down,
with no-one to make them afraid.
[3]The fortified city will disappear from Ephraim,
and royal power from Damascus;
the remnant of Aram will be
like the glory of the Israelites,"
declares the LORD Almighty.

[4]"In that day the glory of Jacob will fade;
the fat of his body will waste away.
[5]It will be as when a reaper gathers the standing
corn
and harvests the corn with his arm—
as when a man gleans ears of corn
in the Valley of Rephaim.
[6]Yet some gleanings will remain,
as when an olive tree is beaten,

leaving two or three olives on the topmost
branches,
four or five on the fruitful boughs,"
declares the LORD, the God of Israel.

[7]In that day men will look to their Maker
and turn their eyes to the Holy One of Israel.
[8]They will not look to the altars,
the work of their hands,
and they will have no regard for the Asherah
poles[a]
and the incense altars their fingers have made.

[9]In that day their strong cities, which they left because of the Israelites, will be like places abandoned to thickets and undergrowth. And all will be desolation.

[10]You have forgotten God your Saviour;
you have not remembered the Rock, your
fortress.
Therefore, though you set out the finest plants
and plant imported vines,
[11]though on the day you set them out, you make
them grow,
and on the morning when you plant them, you
bring them to bud,
yet the harvest will be as nothing
in the day of disease and incurable pain.

[12]Oh, the raging of many nations—
they rage like the raging sea!
Oh, the uproar of the peoples—
they roar like the roaring of great waters!
[13]Although the peoples roar like the roar of surging
waters,
when he rebukes them they flee far away,
driven before the wind like chaff on the hills,
like tumble-weed before a gale.
[14]In the evening, sudden terror!
Before the morning, they are gone!
This is the portion of those who loot us,
the lot of those who plunder us.

A Prophecy Against Cush

18 Woe to the land of whirring wings[a]
along the rivers of Cush,[b]
[2]which sends envoys by sea
in papyrus boats over the water.

18:1   Cush is the area which is near Sudan or Ethiopia. Ahaz was often tempted to make alliances in this direction too, but Isaiah said that both nations would meet disaster.

Go, swift messengers,
to a people tall and smooth-skinned,
to a people feared far and wide,
an aggressive nation of strange speech,
whose land is divided by rivers.

b7 Or "raisin cakes," a word play   a8 That is, symbols of the goddess Asherah   a1 Or of locusts
b1 That is, the upper Nile region

3All you people of the world,
    you who live on the earth,
when a banner is raised on the mountains,
    you will see it,
and when a trumpet sounds,
    you will hear it.
4This is what the LORD says to me:
"I will remain quiet and will look on from my
    dwelling-place,
like shimmering heat in the sunshine,
like a cloud of dew in the heat of harvest."
5For, before the harvest, when the blossom is gone
    and the flower becomes a ripening grape,
he will cut off the shoots with pruning knives,
    and cut down and take away the spreading
    branches.
6They will all be left to the mountain birds of prey
    and to the wild animals;
the birds will feed on them all summer,
    the wild animals all winter.

7At that time gifts will be brought to the LORD
Almighty

from a people tall and smooth-skinned,
    from a people feared far and wide,
an aggressive nation of strange speech,
    whose land is divided by rivers—

the gifts will be brought to Mount Zion, the place of the
Name of the LORD Almighty.

A Prophecy About Egypt

19
An oracle concerning Egypt:

See, the LORD rides on a swift cloud
    and is coming to Egypt.
The idols of Egypt tremble before him,
    and the hearts of the Egyptians melt within
    them.

19:1   Isaiah announced the virtual disin-
tegration of the Egyptian empire, which
would be brought on by internal fighting. In
663 BC the Assyrians overthrew Thebes, the
capital of Egypt.

2"I will stir up Egyptian against Egyptian—
    brother will fight against brother,
    neighbour against neighbour,
    city against city,
    kingdom against kingdom.
3The Egyptians will lose heart,
    and I will bring their plans to nothing;
they will consult the idols and the spirits of the
    dead,
    the mediums and the spiritists.
4I will hand the Egyptians over
    to the power of a cruel master,
and a fierce king will rule over them,"
    declares the Lord, the LORD Almighty.

5The waters of the river will dry up,
    and the river bed will be parched and dry.
6The canals will stink;
    the streams of Egypt will dwindle and dry up.
The reeds and rushes will wither,
7   also the plants along the Nile,
    at the mouth of the river.
Every sown field along the Nile
    will become parched, will blow away and be no
    more.
8The fishermen will groan and lament,
    all who cast hooks into the Nile;
those who throw nets on the water
    will pine away.
9Those who work with combed flax will despair,
    the weavers of fine linen will lose hope.
10The workers in cloth will be dejected,
    and all the wage earners will be sick at heart.

11The officials of Zoan are nothing but fools;
    the wise counsellors of Pharaoh give senseless
    advice.
How can you say to Pharaoh,
    "I am one of the wise men,
    a disciple of the ancient kings"?

12Where are your wise men now?
    Let them show you and make known
what the LORD Almighty
    has planned against Egypt.
13The officials of Zoan have become fools,
    the leaders of Memphisa are deceived;
the cornerstones of her peoples
    have led Egypt astray.
14The LORD has poured into them
    a spirit of dizziness;
they make Egypt stagger in all that she does,
    as a drunkard staggers around in his vomit.
15There is nothing Egypt can do—
    head or tail, palm branch or reed.

16In that day the Egyptians will be like women. They
will shudder with fear at the uplifted hand that the
LORD Almighty raises against them. 17And the land of
Judah will bring terror to the Egyptians; everyone to
whom Judah is mentioned will be terrified, because of
what the LORD Almighty is planning against them.

18In that day five cities in Egypt will speak the lan-
guage of Canaan and swear allegiance to the LORD
Almighty. One of them will be called the City of
Destruction.b

19In that day there will be an altar to the LORD in the
heart of Egypt, and a monument to the LORD at its border. 20It will be a sign and witness to the LORD Almighty
in the land of Egypt. When they cry out to the LORD
because of their oppressors, he will send them a
saviour and defender, and he will rescue them. 21So the
LORD will make himself known to the Egyptians, and
in that day they will acknowledge the LORD. They will
worship with sacrifices and grain offerings; they will

---

a13 Hebrew Noph   b18 Most manuscripts of the Masoretic Text; some manuscripts of the Masoretic Text, Dead Sea Scrolls and
Vulgate City of the Sun (that is, Heliopolis)

make vows to the LORD and keep them. ²²The LORD will strike Egypt with a plague; he will strike them and heal them. They will turn to the LORD, and he will respond to their pleas and heal them.

²³In that day there will be a highway from Egypt to Assyria. The Assyrians will go to Egypt and the Egyptians to Assyria. The Egyptians and Assyrians will worship together. ²⁴In that day Israel will be the third, along with Egypt and Assyria, a blessing on the earth. ²⁵The LORD Almighty will bless them, saying, "Blessed be Egypt my people, Assyria my handiwork, and Israel my inheritance."

A Prophecy Against Egypt and Cush

20 In the year that the supreme commander, sent by Sargon king of Assyria, came to Ashdod and attacked and captured it — ²at that time the LORD spoke through Isaiah son of Amoz. He said to him, "Take off the sackcloth from your body and the sandals from your feet." And he did so, going around stripped and barefoot.

20:2   The year in question was 711 BC when the Assyrians defeated Philistia at Ashdod. Isaiah was instructed to act the part of a slave to illustrate Egypt's coming captivity. The prophets were often asked by God to dramatize his message in a visual way. It must have been very shocking for the people to see Isaiah in this state for three years.

---

³Then the LORD said, "Just as my servant Isaiah has gone stripped and barefoot for three years, as a sign and portent against Egypt and Cush,[a] ⁴so the king of Assyria will lead away stripped and barefoot the Egyptian captives and Cushite exiles, young and old, with buttocks bared — to Egypt's shame. ⁵Those who trusted in Cush and boasted in Egypt will be afraid and put to shame. ⁶In that day the people who live on this coast will say, 'See what has happened to those we relied on, those we fled to for help and deliverance from the king of Assyria! How then can we escape?' "

A Prophecy Against Babylon

21 An oracle concerning the Desert by the Sea:

Like whirlwinds sweeping through the
    southland,
an invader comes from the desert,
    from a land of terror.

²A dire vision has been shown to me:
    The traitor betrays, the looter takes loot.
Elam, attack! Media, lay siege!
    I will bring to an end all the groaning she
      caused.

³At this my body is racked with pain,
    pangs seize me, like those of a woman in
      labour;

I am staggered by what I hear,
    I am bewildered by what I see.
⁴My heart falters,
    fear makes me tremble;
the twilight I longed for
    has become a horror to me.

⁵They set the tables,
    they spread the rugs,
    they eat, they drink!
Get up, you officers,
    oil the shields!

⁶This is what the Lord says to me:

"Go, post a lookout
    and have him report what he sees.
⁷When he sees chariots
    with teams of horses,
riders on donkeys
    or riders on camels,
let him be alert,
    fully alert."

⁸And the lookout[a] shouted,

"Day after day, my lord, I stand on the
    watchtower;
every night I stay at my post.
⁹Look, here comes a man in a chariot
    with a team of horses.
And he gives back the answer:
    'Babylon has fallen, has fallen!
All the images of its gods
    lie shattered on the ground!' "

¹⁰O my people, crushed on the threshing-floor,
    I tell you what I have heard
from the LORD Almighty,
    from the God of Israel.

A Prophecy Against Edom

¹¹An oracle concerning Dumah:[b]

Someone calls to me from Seir,
    "Watchman, what is left of the night?
Watchman, what is left of the night?"
¹²The watchman replies,
    "Morning is coming, but also the night.
If you would ask, then ask;
    and come back yet again."

A Prophecy Against Arabia

¹³An oracle concerning Arabia:

You caravans of Dedanites,
    who camp in the thickets of Arabia,
¹⁴ bring water for the thirsty;
you who live in Tema,
    bring food for the fugitives.
¹⁵They flee from the sword,
    from the drawn sword,
from the bent bow
    and from the heat of battle.

---

a3 That is, the upper Nile region; also in verse 5   a8 Dead Sea Scrolls and Syriac; Masoretic Text *A lion*
b11 *Dumah* means *silence* or *stillness*, a word play on *Edom*.

[16]This is what the Lord says to me: "Within one year, as a servant bound by contract would count it, all the pomp of Kedar will come to an end. [17]The survivors of the bowmen, the warriors of Kedar, will be few." The LORD, the God of Israel, has spoken.

22:1   The Valley of Vision is Jerusalem, possibly a particular place used by Isaiah to listen to God's message. The inhabitants, thinking that they would not be beaten, had built water reservoirs and strengthened a few defences in case of war, but had not come to God for help (see 2 Chronicles 32).

A Prophecy About Jerusalem

22 An oracle concerning the Valley of Vision:

What troubles you now,
    that you have all gone up on the roofs,
[2]O town full of commotion,
    O city of tumult and revelry?
Your slain were not killed by the sword,
    nor did they die in battle.
[3]All your leaders have fled together;
    they have been captured without using the
        bow.
All you who were caught were taken prisoner
    together,
    having fled while the enemy was still far away.
[4]Therefore I said, "Turn away from me;
    let me weep bitterly.
Do not try to console me
    over the destruction of my people."

[5]The Lord, the LORD Almighty, has a day
    of tumult and trampling and terror
    in the Valley of Vision,
a day of battering down walls
    and of crying out to the mountains.
[6]Elam takes up the quiver,
    with her charioteers and horses;
    Kir uncovers the shield.
[7]Your choicest valleys are full of chariots,
    and horsemen are posted at the city gates;
[8] the defences of Judah are stripped away.

And you looked in that day
    to the weapons in the Palace of the Forest;
[9]you saw that the City of David
    had many breaches in its defences;
you stored up water
    in the Lower Pool.
[10]You counted the buildings in Jerusalem
    and tore down houses to strengthen the wall.
[11]You built a reservoir between the two walls
    for the water of the Old Pool,
but you did not look to the One who made it,
    or have regard for the One who planned it long
        ago.

[12]The Lord, the LORD Almighty,
    called you on that day
to weep and to wail,
    to tear out your hair and put on sackcloth.
[13]But see, there is joy and revelry,
    slaughtering of cattle and killing of sheep,
    eating of meat and drinking of wine!
"Let us eat and drink," you say,
    "for tomorrow we die!"

[14]The LORD Almighty has revealed this in my hearing: "Till your dying day this sin will not be atoned for," says the Lord, the LORD Almighty.

[15]This is what the Lord, the LORD Almighty, says:

"Go, say to this steward,
    to Shebna, who is in charge of the palace:
[16]What are you doing here and who gave you
        permission
    to cut out a grave for yourself here,
hewing your grave on the height
    and chiselling your resting place in the rock?

[17]"Beware, the LORD is about to take firm hold of
        you
    and hurl you away, O you mighty man.
[18]He will roll you up tightly like a ball
    and throw you into a large country.
There you will die
    and there your splendid chariots will remain—
    you disgrace to your master's house!
[19]I will depose you from your office,
    and you will be ousted from your position.

[20]"In that day I will summon my servant, Eliakim son of Hilkiah. [21]I will clothe him with your robe and fasten your sash around him and hand your authority over to him. He will be a father to those who live in Jerusalem and to the house of Judah. [22]I will place on his shoulder the key to the house of David; what he opens no-one can shut, and what he shuts no-one can open. [23]I will drive him like a peg into a firm place; he will be a seat[a] of honour for the house of his father. [24]All the glory of his family will hang on him: its offspring and offshoots—all its lesser vessels, from the bowls to all the jars.

[25]"In that day," declares the LORD Almighty, "the peg driven into the firm place will give way; it will be sheared off and will fall, and the load hanging on it will be cut down." The LORD has spoken.

A Prophecy About Tyre

23 An oracle concerning Tyre:

Wail, O ships of Tarshish!
    For Tyre is destroyed
    and left without house or harbour.
From the land of Cyprus[a]
    word has come to them.

[2]Be silent, you people of the island
    and you merchants of Sidon,
    whom the seafarers have enriched.

---

[a]23 Or throne   [a]1 Hebrew Kittim

³On the great waters
  came the grain of the Shihor;
the harvest of the Nile*ᵇ* was the revenue of
    Tyre,
and she became the market-place of the nations.

⁴Be ashamed, O Sidon, and you, O fortress of the
    sea,
  for the sea has spoken:
"I have neither been in labour nor given birth;
  I have neither reared sons nor brought up
    daughters."
⁵When word comes to Egypt,
  they will be in anguish at the report from Tyre.

⁶Cross over to Tarshish;
  wail, you people of the island.
⁷Is this your city of revelry,
  the old, old city,
  whose feet have taken her
  to settle in far-off lands?
⁸Who planned this against Tyre,
  the bestower of crowns,
  whose merchants are princes,
  whose traders are renowned in the earth?
⁹The LORD Almighty planned it,
  to bring low the pride of all glory
  and to humble all who are renowned on the
    earth.

23:8   In Isaiah's time Tyre was a great
trading city in Lebanon with many colonies,
including Cyprus. Merchants from Tyre
sailed as far as the English Channel, and even
to the Indian Ocean. The city was corrupted
by wealth and success, and overrun by
Assyria in 701 BC.

---

¹⁰Till*ᶜ* your land as along the Nile,
  O Daughter of Tarshish,
  for you no longer have a harbour.
¹¹The LORD has stretched out his hand over the sea
  and made its kingdoms tremble.
He has given an order concerning Phoenicia*ᵈ*
  that her fortresses be destroyed.
¹²He said, "No more of your revelling,
  O Virgin Daughter of Sidon, now crushed!

"Up, cross over to Cyprus;*ᵉ*
  even there you will find no rest."
¹³Look at the land of the Babylonians,*ᶠ*
  this people that is now of no account!
The Assyrians have made it
  a place for desert creatures;
they raised up their siege towers,
  they stripped its fortresses bare
  and turned it into a ruin.

¹⁴Wail, you ships of Tarshish;
  your fortress is destroyed!

¹⁵At that time Tyre will be forgotten for seventy
years, the span of a king's life. But at the end of these
seventy years, it will happen to Tyre as in the song of
the prostitute:

¹⁶"Take up a harp, walk through the city,
  O prostitute forgotten;
play the harp well, sing many a song,
  so that you will be remembered."

¹⁷At the end of seventy years, the LORD will deal
with Tyre. She will return to her hire as a prostitute
and will ply her trade with all the kingdoms on the face
of the earth. ¹⁸Yet her profit and her earnings will be
set apart for the LORD; they will not be stored up or
hoarded. Her profits will go to those who live before
the LORD, for abundant food and fine clothes.

The LORD's Devastation of the Earth

24 See, the LORD is going to lay waste the
earth
  and devastate it;
he will ruin its face
  and scatter its inhabitants—
²it will be the same
  for priest as for people,
  for master as for servant,
  for mistress as for maid,
  for seller as for buyer,
  for borrower as for lender,
  for debtor as for creditor.
³The earth will be completely laid waste
  and totally plundered.
            The LORD has spoken this word.

⁴The earth dries up and withers,
  the world languishes and withers,
  the exalted of the earth languish.
⁵The earth is defiled by its people;
  they have disobeyed the laws,
violated the statutes
  and broken the everlasting covenant.
⁶Therefore a curse consumes the earth;
  its people must bear their guilt.
Therefore earth's inhabitants are burned up,
  and very few are left.
⁷The new wine dries up and the vine withers;
  all the merrymakers groan.
⁸The gaiety of the tambourines is stilled,
  the noise of the revellers has stopped,
  the joyful harp is silent.
⁹No longer do they drink wine with a song;
  the beer is bitter to its drinkers.
¹⁰The ruined city lies desolate;
  the entrance to every house is barred.
¹¹In the streets they cry out for wine;
  all joy turns to gloom,
  all gaiety is banished from the earth.
¹²The city is left in ruins,
  its gate is battered to pieces.
¹³So will it be on the earth
  and among the nations,

ᵇ2, 3 Masoretic Text; one Dead Sea Scroll *Sidon, / who cross over the sea; / your envoys ³are on the great waters. / The grain of the Shihor,*
/ the harvest of the Nile,   *ᶜ10* Dead Sea Scrolls and some Septuagint manuscripts; Masoretic Text *Go through*
ᵈ11 Hebrew *Canaan*   *ᵉ12* Hebrew *Kittim*   *ᶠ13* Or *Chaldeans*

as when an olive tree is beaten,
  or as when gleanings are left after the grape
    harvest.

[14]They raise their voices, they shout for joy;
  from the west they acclaim the LORD's majesty.
[15]Therefore in the east give glory to the LORD;
  exalt the name of the LORD, the God of Israel,
  in the islands of the sea.
[16]From the ends of the earth we hear singing:
  "Glory to the Righteous One."

But I said, "I waste away, I waste away!
  Woe to me!
The treacherous betray!
  With treachery the treacherous betray!"
[17]Terror and pit and snare await you,
  O people of the earth.
[18]Whoever flees at the sound of terror
  will fall into a pit;
whoever climbs out of the pit
  will be caught in a snare.

The floodgates of the heavens are opened,
  the foundations of the earth shake.
[19]The earth is broken up,
  the earth is split asunder,
  the earth is thoroughly shaken.
[20]The earth reels like a drunkard,
  it sways like a hut in the wind;
so heavy upon it is the guilt of its rebellion
  that it falls—never to rise again.

24:21   After a long section of prophecies against specific nations, this is a universal oracle. It talks of God's judgement on the whole earth. The event described will be a violent upheaval and indicates a final showdown with the forces of evil.

---

[21]In that day the LORD will punish
  the powers in the heavens above
  and the kings on the earth below.
[22]They will be herded together
  like prisoners bound in a dungeon;
they will be shut up in prison
  and be punished[a] after many days.
[23]The moon will be abashed, the sun ashamed;
  for the LORD Almighty will reign
on Mount Zion and in Jerusalem,
  and before its elders, gloriously.

Praise to the LORD

25 O LORD, you are my God;
  I will exalt you and praise your name,
for in perfect faithfulness
  you have done marvellous things,
  things planned long ago.
[2]You have made the city a heap of rubble,
  the fortified town a ruin,
the foreigners' stronghold a city no more;
  it will never be rebuilt.

[3]Therefore strong peoples will honour you;
  cities of ruthless nations will revere you.
[4]You have been a refuge for the poor,
  a refuge for the needy in his distress,
a shelter from the storm
  and a shade from the heat.
For the breath of the ruthless
  is like a storm driving against a wall
[5] and like the heat of the desert.
You silence the uproar of foreigners;
  as heat is reduced by the shadow of a cloud,
so the song of the ruthless is stilled.

25:6   This famous prophecy depicts a glorious future. The idea of a resurrection from death appeared very late in Old Testament times, so it can be argued that the first phrase of verse 8 might have been added by a later editor. There are many biblical images of banquets to describe life in God's kingdom (e.g. Luke 14:15–24). This one could be a picture of celebrations following the restoration of Jerusalem, but it also implies the covenant relationship with God based on Mount Sinai (Exodus 24:9–11).

---

[6]On this mountain the LORD Almighty will prepare
  a feast of rich food for all peoples,
a banquet of aged wine—
  the best of meats and the finest of wines.
[7]On this mountain he will destroy
  the shroud that enfolds all peoples,
the sheet that covers all nations;
[8] he will swallow up death for ever.
The Sovereign LORD will wipe away the tears
  from all faces;
he will remove the disgrace of his people
  from all the earth.
                  The LORD has spoken.

[9]In that day they will say,

"Surely this is our God;
  we trusted in him, and he saved us.
This is the LORD, we trusted in him;
  let us rejoice and be glad in his salvation."

[10]The hand of the LORD will rest on this mountain;
  but Moab will be trampled under him
  as straw is trampled down in the manure.
[11]They will spread out their hands in it,
  as a swimmer spreads out his hands to swim.
God will bring down their pride
  despite the cleverness[a] of their hands.
[12]He will bring down your high fortified walls
  and lay them low;
he will bring them down to the ground,
  to the very dust.

---

a 22 Or *released*   a 11 The meaning of the Hebrew for this word is uncertain.

A Song of Praise

26 In that day this song will be sung in the land of Judah:

We have a strong city;
  God makes salvation
  its walls and ramparts.
²Open the gates
  that the righteous nation may enter,
  the nation that keeps faith.
³You will keep in perfect peace
  him whose mind is steadfast,
  because he trusts in you.
⁴Trust in the LORD for ever,
  for the LORD, the LORD, is the Rock eternal.
⁵He humbles those who dwell on high,
  he lays the lofty city low;
he levels it to the ground
  and casts it down to the dust.
⁶Feet trample it down—
  the feet of the oppressed,
  the footsteps of the poor.

⁷The path of the righteous is level;
  O upright One, you make the way of the
    righteous smooth.
⁸Yes, LORD, walking in the way of your laws,ᵃ
  we wait for you;
your name and renown
  are the desire of our hearts.
⁹My soul yearns for you in the night;
  in the morning my spirit longs for you.
When your judgments come upon the earth,
  the people of the world learn righteousness.
¹⁰Though grace is shown to the wicked,
  they do not learn righteousness;
even in a land of uprightness they go on doing
    evil
  and regard not the majesty of the LORD.
¹¹O LORD, your hand is lifted high,
  but they do not see it.
Let them see your zeal for your people and be put
    to shame;
  let the fire reserved for your enemies consume
    them.

¹²LORD, you establish peace for us;
  all that we have accomplished you have done
    for us.
¹³O LORD, our God, other lords besides you have
    ruled over us,
  but your name alone do we honour.
¹⁴They are now dead, they live no more;
  those departed spirits do not rise.
You punished them and brought them to ruin;
  you wiped out all memory of them.
¹⁵You have enlarged the nation, O LORD;
  you have enlarged the nation.
You have gained glory for yourself;
  you have extended all the borders of the land.

¹⁶LORD, they came to you in their distress;
  when you disciplined them,
  they could barely whisper a prayer.ᵇ

¹⁷As a woman with child and about to give birth
  writhes and cries out in her pain,
  so were we in your presence, O LORD.
¹⁸We were with child, we writhed in pain,
  but we gave birth to wind.
We have not brought salvation to the earth;
  we have not given birth to people of the world.

¹⁹But your dead will live;
  their bodies will rise.
You who dwell in the dust,
  wake up and shout for joy.
Your dew is like the dew of the morning;
  the earth will give birth to her dead.

²⁰Go, my people, enter your rooms
  and shut the doors behind you;
hide yourselves for a little while
  until his wrath has passed by.
²¹See, the LORD is coming out of his dwelling
  to punish the people of the earth for their sins.
The earth will disclose the blood shed upon her;
  she will conceal her slain no longer.

Deliverance of Israel

27 In that day,

the LORD will punish with his sword,
  his fierce, great and powerful sword,
Leviathan the gliding serpent,
  Leviathan the coiling serpent;
he will slay the monster of the sea.

27:1 Leviathan, the sea-monster of pagan mythology, represented the spiritual realm of evil, which would be as thoroughly brought down as the empires around Judah. Notice that God's people will now be a "fruitful vineyard".

---

²In that day—
"Sing about a fruitful vineyard:
³ I, the LORD, watch over it;
  I water it continually.
I guard it day and night
  so that no-one may harm it.
⁴ I am not angry.
If only there were briers and thorns confronting
    me!
  I would march against them in battle;
  I would set them all on fire.
⁵Or else let them come to me for refuge;
  let them make peace with me,
  yes, let them make peace with me."

⁶In days to come Jacob will take root,
  Israel will bud and blossom
  and fill all the world with fruit.

⁷Has ‚the LORD‚ struck her
  as he struck down those who struck her?

ᵃ8 Or judgments   ᵇ16 The meaning of the Hebrew for this clause is uncertain.

Has she been killed
as those were killed who killed her?
[8]By warfare[a] and exile you contend with her—
with his fierce blast he drives her out,
as on a day the east wind blows.
[9]By this, then, will Jacob's guilt be atoned for,
and this will be the full fruitage of the removal
of his sin:
When he makes all the altar stones
to be like chalk stones crushed to pieces,
no Asherah poles[b] or incense altars
will be left standing.
[10]The fortified city stands desolate,
an abandoned settlement, forsaken like the
desert;
there the calves graze,
there they lie down;
they strip its branches bare.
[11]When its twigs are dry, they are broken off
and women come and make fires with them.
For this is a people without understanding;
so their Maker has no compassion on them,
and their Creator shows them no favour.

[12]In that day the LORD will thresh from the flowing
Euphrates[c] to the Wadi of Egypt, and you, O Israelites,
will be gathered up one by one. [13]And in that day a
great trumpet will sound. Those who were perishing
in Assyria and those who were exiled in Egypt will
come and worship the LORD on the holy mountain in
Jerusalem.

Woe to Ephraim

28 Woe to that wreath, the pride of
Ephraim's drunkards,
to the fading flower, his glorious beauty,
set on the head of a fertile valley—
to that city, the pride of those laid low by wine!
[2]See, the Lord has one who is powerful and
strong.
Like a hailstorm and a destructive wind,
like a driving rain and a flooding downpour,
he will throw it forcefully to the ground.
[3]That wreath, the pride of Ephraim's drunkards,
will be trampled underfoot.
[4]That fading flower, his glorious beauty,
set on the head of a fertile valley,
will be like a fig ripe before harvest—
as soon as someone sees it and takes it in his
hand,
he swallows it.

[5]In that day the LORD Almighty
will be a glorious crown,
a beautiful wreath
for the remnant of his people.
[6]He will be a spirit of justice
to him who sits in judgment,
a source of strength
to those who turn back the battle at the gate.

[7]And these also stagger from wine
and reel from beer:
Priests and prophets stagger from beer
and are befuddled with wine;
they reel from beer,
they stagger when seeing visions,
they stumble when rendering decisions.
[8]All the tables are covered with vomit
and there is not a spot without filth.

[9]"Who is it he is trying to teach?
To whom is he explaining his message?
To children weaned from their milk,
to those just taken from the breast?
[10]For it is:
Do and do, do and do,
rule on rule, rule on rule;[a]
a little here, a little there."

28:10 Ephraim (verse 3) represents
Israel. This passage shows the way Isaiah's
hearers sneered at God's message. Next
time, said the prophet with irony, the message will come in a foreign language that
sounds like gibberish!

---

[11]Very well then, with foreign lips and strange
tongues
God will speak to this people,
[12]to whom he said,
"This is the resting-place, let the weary rest";
and, "This is the place of repose"—
but they would not listen.
[13]So then, the word of the LORD to them will
become:
Do and do, do and do,
rule on rule, rule on rule;
a little here, a little there—
so that they will go and fall backwards,
be injured and snared and captured.

[14]Therefore hear the word of the LORD, you scoffers
who rule this people in Jerusalem.
[15]You boast, "We have entered into a covenant
with death,
with the grave[b] we have made an agreement.
When an overwhelming scourge sweeps by,
it cannot touch us,
for we have made a lie our refuge
and falsehood[c] our hiding-place."

[16]So this is what the Sovereign LORD says:

"See, I lay a stone in Zion,
a tested stone,
a precious cornerstone for a sure foundation;
the one who trusts will never be dismayed.
[17]I will make justice the measuring line
and righteousness the plumb-line;
hail will sweep away your refuge, the lie,
and water will overflow your hiding-place.

---

[a]8 See Septuagint; the meaning of the Hebrew for this word is uncertain. [b]9 That is, symbols of the goddess Asherah
[c]12 Hebrew River
[a]10 Hebrew / sav lasav sav lasav / kav lakav kav lakav (possibly meaningless sounds; perhaps a mimicking of the prophet's words); also in
verse 13 [b]15 Hebrew Sheol; also in verse 18 [c]15 Or false gods

18Your covenant with death will be annulled;
your agreement with the grave will not stand.
When the overwhelming scourge sweeps by,
you will be beaten down by it.
19As often as it comes it will carry you away;
morning after morning, by day and by night,
it will sweep through."

The understanding of this message
will bring sheer terror.
20The bed is too short to stretch out on,
the blanket too narrow to wrap around you.
21The LORD will rise up as he did at Mount
Perazim,
he will rouse himself as in the Valley of
Gibeon—
to do his work, his strange work,
and perform his task, his alien task.
22Now stop your mocking,
or your chains will become heavier;
the Lord, the LORD Almighty, has told me
of the destruction decreed against the whole
land.

23Listen and hear my voice;
pay attention and hear what I say.
24When a farmer ploughs for planting, does he
plough continually?
Does he keep on breaking up and harrowing
the soil?
25When he has levelled the surface,
does he not sow caraway and scatter cummin?
Does he not plant wheat in its place,*d*
barley in its plot,*d*
and spelt in its field?
26His God instructs him
and teaches him the right way.

27Caraway is not threshed with a sledge,
nor is a cartwheel rolled over cummin;
caraway is beaten out with a rod,
and cummin with a stick.
28Grain must be ground to make bread;
so one does not go on threshing it for ever.
Though he drives the wheels of his threshing-cart
over it,
his horses do not grind it.
29All this also comes from the LORD Almighty,
wonderful in counsel and magnificent in
wisdom.

Woe to David's City

29 Woe to you, Ariel, Ariel,
the city where David settled!
Add year to year
and let your cycle of festivals go on.
2Yet I will besiege Ariel;
she will mourn and lament,
she will be to me like an altar hearth.*a*
3I will encamp against you all around;
I will encircle you with towers
and set up my siege works against you.

4Brought low, you will speak from the ground;
your speech will mumble out of the dust.
Your voice will come ghostlike from the earth;
out of the dust your speech will whisper.

5But your many enemies will become like fine
dust,
the ruthless hordes like blown chaff.
Suddenly, in an instant,
6 the LORD Almighty will come
with thunder and earthquake and great noise,
with windstorm and tempest and flames of a
devouring fire.
7Then the hordes of all the nations that fight
against Ariel,
that attack her and her fortress and besiege her,
will be as it is with a dream,
with a vision in the night—
8as when a hungry man dreams that he is eating,
but he awakens, and his hunger remains;
as when a thirsty man dreams that he is drinking,
but he awakens faint, with his thirst
unquenched.
So will it be with the hordes of all the nations
that fight against Mount Zion.

9Be stunned and amazed,
blind yourselves and be sightless;
be drunk, but not from wine,
stagger, but not from beer.
10The LORD has brought over you a deep sleep:
He has sealed your eyes (the prophets);
he has covered your heads (the seers).

11For you this whole vision is nothing but words
sealed in a scroll. And if you give the scroll to someone
who can read, and say to him, "Read this, please," he
will answer, "I can't; it is sealed." 12Or if you give the
scroll to someone who cannot read, and say, "Read
this, please," he will answer, "I don't know how to
read."

13The Lord says:

"These people come near to me with their mouth
and honour me with their lips,
but their hearts are far from me.
Their worship of me
is made up only of rules taught by men.*b*
14Therefore once more I will astound these people
with wonder upon wonder;
the wisdom of the wise will perish,
the intelligence of the intelligent will vanish."
15Woe to those who go to great depths
to hide their plans from the LORD,
who do their work in darkness and think,
"Who sees us? Who will know?"
16You turn things upside down,
as if the potter were thought to be like the clay!
Shall what is formed say to him who formed it,
"He did not make me"?
Can the pot say of the potter,
"He knows nothing"?

d25 The meaning of the Hebrew for this word is uncertain.
b13 Hebrew; Septuagint *They worship me in vain; / their teachings are but rules taught by men*
a2 The Hebrew for *altar hearth* sounds like the Hebrew for *Ariel.*

17In a very short time, will not Lebanon be turned
    into a fertile field
    and the fertile field seem like a forest?
18In that day the deaf will hear the words of the
    scroll,
    and out of gloom and darkness
    the eyes of the blind will see.
19Once more the humble will rejoice in the LORD;
    the needy will rejoice in the Holy One of Israel.
20The ruthless will vanish,
    the mockers will disappear,
    and all who have an eye for evil will be cut
    down—
21those who with a word make a man out to be
    guilty,
    who ensnare the defender in court
    and with false testimony deprive the innocent
    of justice.

22Therefore this is what the LORD, who redeemed
Abraham, says to the house of Jacob:

"No longer will Jacob be ashamed;
    no longer will their faces grow pale.
23When they see among them their children,
    the work of my hands,
they will keep my name holy;
    they will acknowledge the holiness of the Holy
    One of Jacob,
    and will stand in awe of the God of Israel.
24Those who are wayward in spirit will gain
    understanding;
    those who complain will accept instruction."

Woe to the Obstinate Nation

30 "Woe to the obstinate children,"
    declares the LORD,
    "to those who carry out plans that are not mine,
    forming an alliance, but not by my Spirit,
    heaping sin upon sin;
2who go down to Egypt
    without consulting me;
who look for help to Pharaoh's protection,
    to Egypt's shade for refuge.
3But Pharaoh's protection will be to your shame,
    Egypt's shade will bring you disgrace.
4Though they have officials in Zoan
    and their envoys have arrived in Hanes,
5everyone will be put to shame
    because of a people useless to them,
who bring neither help nor advantage,
    but only shame and disgrace."

6An oracle concerning the animals of the Negev:

Through a land of hardship and distress,
    of lions and lionesses,
    of adders and darting snakes,
the envoys carry their riches on donkeys' backs,
    their treasures on the humps of camels,
to that unprofitable nation,
7   to Egypt, whose help is utterly useless.
Therefore I call her
    Rahab the Do-Nothing.

8Go now, write it on a tablet for them,
    inscribe it on a scroll,
that for the days to come
    it may be an everlasting witness.
9These are rebellious people, deceitful children,
    children unwilling to listen to the LORD's
    instruction.
10They say to the seers,
    "See no more visions!"
and to the prophets,
    "Give us no more visions of what is right!
Tell us pleasant things,
    prophesy illusions.
11Leave this way,
    get off this path,
and stop confronting us
    with the Holy One of Israel!"

30:7 Hezekiah failed to listen to Isaiah,
and thought that an alliance with Egypt
would see off the Assyrians. In fact Egypt was
a useless ally, and Sennacherib the Assyrian
king sent his armies to destroy all Judah's fortified cities, demanding vast sums of money
from Hezekiah (see chapters 36 and 37).
There is no point trusting in military might
rather than the Lord, the Holy One of Israel.
Despite the rebellion, God longed to show
mercy to his people (verse 18).

12Therefore, this is what the Holy One of Israel says:

"Because you have rejected this message,
    relied on oppression
    and depended on deceit,
13this sin will become for you
    like a high wall, cracked and bulging,
    that collapses suddenly, in an instant.
14It will break in pieces like pottery,
    shattered so mercilessly
that among its pieces not a fragment will be
    found
    for taking coals from a hearth
    or scooping water out of a cistern."

15This is what the Sovereign LORD, the Holy One of
Israel, says:

"In repentance and rest is your salvation,
    in quietness and trust is your strength,
    but you would have none of it.
16You said, 'No, we will flee on horses.'
    Therefore you will flee!
You said, 'We will ride off on swift horses.'
    Therefore your pursuers will be swift!
17A thousand will flee
    at the threat of one;
at the threat of five
    you will all flee away,
till you are left
    like a flagstaff on a mountaintop,
    like a banner on a hill."

[18]Yet the LORD longs to be gracious to you;
he rises to show you compassion.
For the LORD is a God of justice.
Blessed are all who wait for him!

[19]O people of Zion, who live in Jerusalem, you will weep no more. How gracious he will be when you cry for help! As soon as he hears, he will answer you. [20]Although the Lord gives you the bread of adversity and the water of affliction, your teachers will be hidden no more; with your own eyes you will see them. [21]Whether you turn to the right or to the left, your ears will hear a voice behind you, saying, "This is the way; walk in it." [22]Then you will defile your idols overlaid with silver and your images covered with gold; you will throw them away like a menstrual cloth and say to them, "Away with you!"

[23]He will also send you rain for the seed you sow in the ground, and the food that comes from the land will be rich and plentiful. In that day your cattle will graze in broad meadows. [24]The oxen and donkeys that work the soil will eat fodder and mash, spread out with fork and shovel. [25]In the day of great slaughter, when the towers fall, streams of water will flow on every high mountain and every lofty hill. [26]The moon will shine like the sun, and the sunlight will be seven times brighter, like the light of seven full days, when the LORD binds up the bruises of his people and heals the wounds he inflicted.

[27]See, the Name of the LORD comes from afar,
with burning anger and dense clouds of smoke;
his lips are full of wrath,
and his tongue is a consuming fire.
[28]His breath is like a rushing torrent,
rising up to the neck.
He shakes the nations in the sieve of destruction;
he places in the jaws of the peoples
a bit that leads them astray.
[29]And you will sing
as on the night you celebrate a holy festival;
your hearts will rejoice
as when people go up with flutes
to the mountain of the LORD,
to the Rock of Israel.
[30]The LORD will cause men to hear his majestic voice
and will make them see his arm coming down
with raging anger and consuming fire,
with cloudburst, thunderstorm and hail.
[31]The voice of the LORD will shatter Assyria;
with his sceptre he will strike them down.
[32]Every stroke the LORD lays on them
with his punishing rod
will be to the music of tambourines and harps,
as he fights them in battle with the blows of his arm.
[33]Topheth has long been prepared;
it has been made ready for the king.
Its fire pit has been made deep and wide,
with an abundance of fire and wood;
the breath of the LORD,
like a stream of burning sulphur,
sets it ablaze.

Woe to Those Who Rely on Egypt

31 Woe to those who go down to Egypt for help,
who rely on horses,
who trust in the multitude of their chariots
and in the great strength of their horsemen,
but do not look to the Holy One of Israel,
or seek help from the LORD.
[2]Yet he too is wise and can bring disaster;
he does not take back his words.
He will rise up against the house of the wicked,
against those who help evildoers.
[3]But the Egyptians are men and not God;
their horses are flesh and not spirit.
When the LORD stretches out his hand,
he who helps will stumble,
he who is helped will fall;
both will perish together.

[4]This is what the LORD says to me:

"As a lion growls,
a great lion over his prey—
and though a whole band of shepherds
is called together against him,
he is not frightened by their shouts
or disturbed by their clamour—
so the LORD Almighty will come down
to do battle on Mount Zion and on its heights.
[5]Like birds hovering overhead,
the LORD Almighty will shield Jerusalem;
he will shield it and deliver it,
he will 'pass over' it and will rescue it."

[6]Return to him you have so greatly revolted against, O Israelites. [7]For in that day every one of you will reject the idols of silver and gold your sinful hands have made.

[8]"Assyria will fall by a sword that is not of man;
a sword, not of mortals, will devour them.
They will flee before the sword
and their young men will be put to forced labour.
[9]Their stronghold will fall because of terror;
at sight of the battle standard their commanders will panic,"
declares the LORD,
whose fire is in Zion,
whose furnace is in Jerusalem.

The Kingdom of Righteousness

32 See, a king will reign in righteousness
and rulers will rule with justice.
[2]Each man will be like a shelter from the wind
and a refuge from the storm,
like streams of water in the desert
and the shadow of a great rock in a thirsty land.

[3]Then the eyes of those who see will no longer be closed,
and the ears of those who hear will listen.
[4]The mind of the rash will know and understand,
and the stammering tongue will be fluent and clear.

⁵No longer will the fool be called noble
    nor the scoundrel be highly respected.
⁶For the fool speaks folly,
    his mind is busy with evil:
He practises ungodliness
    and spreads error concerning the LORD;
the hungry he leaves empty
    and from the thirsty he withholds water.
⁷The scoundrel's methods are wicked,
    he makes up evil schemes
to destroy the poor with lies,
    even when the plea of the needy is just.
⁸But the noble man makes noble plans,
    and by noble deeds he stands.

The Women of Jerusalem

⁹You women who are so complacent,
    rise up and listen to me;
you daughters who feel secure,
    hear what I have to say!
¹⁰In little more than a year
    you who feel secure will tremble;
the grape harvest will fail,
    and the harvest of fruit will not come.
¹¹Tremble, you complacent women;
    shudder, you daughters who feel secure!
Strip off your clothes,
    put sackcloth round your waists.
¹²Beat your breasts for the pleasant fields,
    for the fruitful vines
¹³and for the land of my people,
    a land overgrown with thorns and briers—
yes, mourn for all houses of merriment
    and for this city of revelry.
¹⁴The fortress will be abandoned,
    the noisy city deserted;
citadel and watchtower will become a wasteland
    for ever,
    the delight of donkeys, a pasture for flocks,
¹⁵till the Spirit is poured upon us from on high,
    and the desert becomes a fertile field,
    and the fertile field seems like a forest.
¹⁶Justice will dwell in the desert
    and righteousness live in the fertile field.
¹⁷The fruit of righteousness will be peace;
    the effect of righteousness will be quietness and
        confidence for ever.
¹⁸My people will live in peaceful dwelling-places,
    in secure homes,
    in undisturbed places of rest.
¹⁹Though hail flattens the forest
    and the city is levelled completely,
²⁰how blessed you will be,
    sowing your seed by every stream,
    and letting your cattle and donkeys range free.

Distress and Help

33
Woe to you, O destroyer,
    you who have not been destroyed!
Woe to you, O traitor,
    you who have not been betrayed!

When you stop destroying,
    you will be destroyed;
when you stop betraying,
    you will be betrayed.

²O LORD, be gracious to us;
    we long for you.
Be our strength every morning,
    our salvation in time of distress.
³At the thunder of your voice, the peoples flee;
    when you rise up, the nations scatter.
⁴Your plunder, O nations, is harvested as by young
        locusts;
    like a swarm of locusts men pounce on it.

33:5 This chapter contains a number of
oracles, some of which may have been used
in temple worship as liturgies. The message
is clear—God never deserts those who walk
in his ways and his defence is far greater than
any humanly-made fortification.

---

⁵The LORD is exalted, for he dwells on high;
    he will fill Zion with justice and righteousness.
⁶He will be the sure foundation for your times,
    a rich store of salvation and wisdom and
        knowledge;
    the fear of the LORD is the key to this
        treasure.ᵃ

⁷Look, their brave men cry aloud in the streets;
    the envoys of peace weep bitterly.
⁸The highways are deserted,
    no travellers are on the roads.
The treaty is broken,
    its witnessesᵇ are despised,
    no-one is respected.
⁹The land mournsᶜ and wastes away,
    Lebanon is ashamed and withers;
    Sharon is like the Arabah,
    and Bashan and Carmel drop their leaves.

¹⁰"Now will I arise," says the LORD.
    "Now will I be exalted;
    now will I be lifted up.
¹¹You conceive chaff,
    you give birth to straw;
    your breath is a fire that consumes you.
¹²The peoples will be burned as if to lime;
    like cut thornbushes they will be set ablaze."

¹³You who are far away, hear what I have done;
    you who are near, acknowledge my power!
¹⁴The sinners in Zion are terrified;
    trembling grips the godless:
"Who of us can dwell with the consuming fire?
    Who of us can dwell with everlasting burning?"
¹⁵He who walks righteously
    and speaks what is right,
who rejects gain from extortion
    and keeps his hand from accepting bribes,
who stops his ears against plots of murder
    and shuts his eyes against contemplating evil—

ᵃ6 Or is a treasure from him   ᵇ8 Dead Sea Scrolls; Masoretic Text / the cities   ᶜ9 Or dries up

¹⁶this is the man who will dwell on the heights,
  whose refuge will be the mountain fortress.
His bread will be supplied,
  and water will not fail him.

¹⁷Your eyes will see the king in his beauty
  and view a land that stretches afar.
¹⁸In your thoughts you will ponder the former
      terror:
  "Where is that chief officer?
  Where is the one who took the revenue?
  Where is the officer in charge of the towers?"
¹⁹You will see those arrogant people no more,
  those people of an obscure speech,
  with their strange, incomprehensible tongue.

²⁰Look upon Zion, the city of our festivals;
  your eyes will see Jerusalem,
  a peaceful abode, a tent that will not be moved;
  its stakes will never be pulled up,
  nor any of its ropes broken.
²¹There the LORD will be our Mighty One.
  It will be like a place of broad rivers and
      streams.
No galley with oars will ride them,
  no mighty ship will sail them.
²²For the LORD is our judge,
  the LORD is our lawgiver,
  the LORD is our king;
  it is he who will save us.

²³Your rigging hangs loose:
  The mast is not held secure,
  the sail is not spread.
Then an abundance of spoils will be divided
  and even the lame will carry off plunder.
²⁴No-one living in Zion will say, "I am ill";
  and the sins of those who dwell there will be
      forgiven.

34:1   Those who ill-treat God's people
will suffer for their wicked behaviour.
Isaiah's vision of the nations was very broad.
He seems to have the surest grasp of history
and politics of all the prophets.

Judgment Against the Nations

34 Come near, you nations, and listen;
      pay attention, you peoples!
Let the earth hear, and all that is in it,
  the world, and all that comes out of it!
²The LORD is angry with all nations;
  his wrath is upon all their armies.
He will totally destroy*a* them,
  he will give them over to slaughter.
³Their slain will be thrown out,
  their dead bodies will send up a stench;
  the mountains will be soaked with their blood.
⁴All the stars of the heavens will be dissolved
  and the sky rolled up like a scroll;

all the starry host will fall
  like withered leaves from the vine,
  like shrivelled figs from the fig-tree.

⁵My sword has drunk its fill in the heavens;
  see, it descends in judgment on Edom,
  the people I have totally destroyed.
⁶The sword of the LORD is bathed in blood,
  it is covered with fat—
  the blood of lambs and goats,
  fat from the kidneys of rams.
For the LORD has a sacrifice in Bozrah
  and a great slaughter in Edom.
⁷And the wild oxen will fall with them,
  the bull calves and the great bulls.
Their land will be drenched with blood,
  and the dust will be soaked with fat.

⁸For the LORD has a day of vengeance,
  a year of retribution, to uphold Zion's cause.
⁹Edom's streams will be turned into pitch,
  her dust into burning sulphur;
  her land will become blazing pitch!
¹⁰It will not be quenched night and day;
  its smoke will rise for ever.
From generation to generation it will lie desolate;
  no-one will ever pass through it again.
¹¹The desert owl*b* and screech owl*b* will possess
      it;
  the great owl*b* and the raven will nest there.
God will stretch out over Edom
  the measuring line of chaos
  and the plumb-line of desolation.
¹²Her nobles will have nothing there to be called a
      kingdom,
  all her princes will vanish away.
¹³Thorns will overrun her citadels,
  nettles and brambles her strongholds.
She will become a haunt for jackals,
  a home for owls.
¹⁴Desert creatures will meet with hyenas,
  and wild goats will bleat to each other;
  there the night creatures will also repose
  and find for themselves places of rest.
¹⁵The owl will nest there and lay eggs,
  she will hatch them, and care for her young
      under the shadow of her wings;
  there also the falcons will gather,
  each with its mate.

¹⁶Look in the scroll of the LORD and read:

None of these will be missing,
  not one will lack her mate.
For it is his mouth that has given the order,
  and his Spirit will gather them together.
¹⁷He allots their portions;
  his hand distributes them by measure.
They will possess it for ever
  and dwell there from generation to generation.

---

a2 The Hebrew term refers to the irrevocable giving over of things or persons to the LORD, often by totally destroying them; also in verse 5.
b11 The precise identification of these birds is uncertain.

Joy of the Redeemed

35 The desert and the parched land will be
glad;
    the wilderness will rejoice and blossom.
Like the crocus, ²it will burst into bloom;
    it will rejoice greatly and shout for joy.
The glory of Lebanon will be given to it,
    the splendour of Carmel and Sharon;
they will see the glory of the LORD,
    the splendour of our God.

³Strengthen the feeble hands,
    steady the knees that give way;
⁴say to those with fearful hearts,
    "Be strong, do not fear;
your God will come,
    he will come with vengeance;
with divine retribution
    he will come to save you."

⁵Then will the eyes of the blind be opened
    and the ears of the deaf unstopped.
⁶Then will the lame leap like a deer,
    and the mute tongue shout for joy.
Water will gush forth in the wilderness
    and streams in the desert.
⁷The burning sand will become a pool,
    the thirsty ground bubbling springs.
In the haunts where jackals once lay,
    grass and reeds and papyrus will grow.

⁸And a highway will be there;
    it will be called the Way of Holiness.
The unclean will not journey on it;
    it will be for those who walk in that Way;
    wicked fools will not go about on it.ᵃ
⁹No lion will be there,
    nor will any ferocious beast get up on it;
    they will not be found there.
But only the redeemed will walk there,
¹⁰ and the ransomed of the LORD will return.
They will enter Zion with singing;
    everlasting joy will crown their heads.
Gladness and joy will overtake them,
    and sorrow and sighing will flee away.

35:10   This is a clear picture of God
bringing his people safely home after the
destruction and doom. This chapter, full of
joy, hope, and new life, concludes the prophetic section of Isaiah of Jerusalem. Chapters 36—39 are largely historical narrative.

Sennacherib Threatens Jerusalem

36 In the fourteenth year of King Hezekiah's
reign, Sennacherib king of Assyria attacked all
the fortified cities of Judah and captured them. ²Then
the king of Assyria sent his field commander with a
large army from Lachish to King Hezekiah at Jerusalem.
When the commander stopped at the aqueduct of the
Upper Pool, on the road to the Washerman's Field, ³Eli-
akim son of Hilkiah the palace administrator, Shebna
the secretary, and Joah son of Asaph the recorder went
out to him.

⁴The field commander said to them, "Tell Hezekiah,

" 'This is what the great king, the king of
Assyria, says: On what are you basing this confidence of yours? ⁵You say you have strategy and
military strength—but you speak only empty
words. On whom are you depending, that you
rebel against me? ⁶Look now, you are depending
on Egypt, that splintered reed of a staff, which
pierces a man's hand and wounds him if he leans
on it! Such is Pharaoh king of Egypt to all who
depend on him. ⁷And if you say to me, "We are
depending on the LORD our God"—isn't he the
one whose high places and altars Hezekiah
removed, saying to Judah and Jerusalem, "You
must worship before this altar"?

⁸" 'Come now, make a bargain with my master,
the king of Assyria: I will give you two thousand
horses—if you can put riders on them! ⁹How then
can you repulse one officer of the least of my master's officials, even though you are depending on
Egypt for chariots and horsemen? ¹⁰Furthermore,
have I come to attack and destroy this land without the LORD? The LORD himself told me to march
against this country and destroy it.' "

¹¹Then Eliakim, Shebna and Joah said to the field
commander, "Please speak to your servants in Aramaic, since we understand it. Don't speak to us in
Hebrew in the hearing of the people on the wall."

¹²But the commander replied, "Was it only to your
master and you that my master sent me to say these
things, and not to the men sitting on the wall—who,
like you, will have to eat their own filth and drink their
own urine?"

¹³Then the commander stood and called out in
Hebrew, "Hear the words of the great king, the king
of Assyria! ¹⁴This is what the king says: Do not let Hezekiah deceive you. He cannot deliver you! ¹⁵Do not let
Hezekiah persuade you to trust in the LORD when he
says, 'The LORD will surely deliver us; this city will not
be given into the hand of the king of Assyria.'

¹⁶"Do not listen to Hezekiah. This is what the king
of Assyria says: Make peace with me and come out to
me. Then every one of you will eat from his own vine
and fig-tree and drink water from his own cistern,
¹⁷until I come and take you to a land like your own—a
land of corn and new wine, a land of bread and vineyards.

¹⁸"Do not let Hezekiah mislead you when he says,
'The LORD will deliver us.' Has the god of any nation
ever delivered his land from the hand of the king of
Assyria? ¹⁹Where are the gods of Hamath and Arpad?
Where are the gods of Sepharvaim? Have they rescued
Samaria from my hand? ²⁰Who of all the gods of these
countries has been able to save his land from me? How
then can the LORD deliver Jerusalem from my hand?"

²¹But the people remained silent and said nothing in

ᵃ8 Or / the simple will not stray from it

reply, because the king had commanded, "Do not answer him."

²²Then Eliakim son of Hilkiah the palace administrator, Shebna the secretary, and Joah son of Asaph the recorder went to Hezekiah, with their clothes torn, and told him what the field commander had said.

Jerusalem's Deliverance Foretold

37 When King Hezekiah heard this, he tore his clothes and put on sackcloth and went into the temple of the LORD. ²He sent Eliakim the palace administrator, Shebna the secretary, and the leading priests, all wearing sackcloth, to the prophet Isaiah son of Amoz. ³They told him, "This is what Hezekiah says: This day is a day of distress and rebuke and disgrace, as when children come to the point of birth and there is no strength to deliver them. ⁴It may be that the LORD your God will hear the words of the field commander, whom his master, the king of Assyria, has sent to ridicule the living God, and that he will rebuke him for the words the LORD your God has heard. Therefore pray for the remnant that still survives."

⁵When King Hezekiah's officials came to Isaiah, ⁶Isaiah said to them, "Tell your master, 'This is what the LORD says: Do not be afraid of what you have heard—those words with which the underlings of the king of Assyria have blasphemed me. ⁷Listen! I am going to put a spirit in him so that when he hears a certain report, he will return to his own country, and there I will have him cut down with the sword.' "

⁸When the field commander heard that the king of Assyria had left Lachish, he withdrew and found the king fighting against Libnah.

⁹Now Sennacherib received a report that Tirhakah, the Cushite[a] king ₍of Egypt₎, was marching out to fight against him. When he heard it, he sent messengers to Hezekiah with this word: ¹⁰"Say to Hezekiah king of Judah: Do not let the god you depend on deceive you when he says, 'Jerusalem will not be handed over to the king of Assyria.' ¹¹Surely you have heard what the kings of Assyria have done to all the countries, destroying them completely. And will you be delivered? ¹²Did the gods of the nations that were destroyed by my forefathers deliver them—the gods of Gozan, Haran, Rezeph and the people of Eden who were in Tel Assar? ¹³Where is the king of Hamath, the king of Arpad, the king of the city of Sepharvaim, or of Hena or Ivvah?"

Hezekiah's Prayer

¹⁴Hezekiah received the letter from the messengers and read it. Then he went up to the temple of the LORD and spread it out before the LORD. ¹⁵And Hezekiah prayed to the LORD: ¹⁶"O LORD Almighty, God of Israel, enthroned between the cherubim, you alone are God over all the kingdoms of the earth. You have made heaven and earth. ¹⁷Give ear, O LORD, and hear; open your eyes, O LORD, and see; listen to all the words Sennacherib has sent to insult the living God.

¹⁸"It is true, O LORD, that the Assyrian kings have laid waste all these peoples and their lands. ¹⁹They have thrown their gods into the fire and destroyed them, for they were not gods but only wood and stone, fashioned by human hands. ²⁰Now, O LORD our God, deliver us from his hand, so that all kingdoms on earth may know that you alone, O LORD, are God."[b]

Sennacherib's Fall

²¹Then Isaiah son of Amoz sent a message to Hezekiah: "This is what the LORD, the God of Israel, says: Because you have prayed to me concerning Sennacherib king of Assyria, ²²this is the word the LORD has spoken against him:

37:21 Isaiah could see that although the Assyrian threat seemed massive, it would die away. Instead a Babylonian threat started to emerge (chapter 39) which was to lead to the exile in 587 BC, and the prophecies towards the end of that time which are contained in chapters 40—66. This section of narrative largely parallels 2 Kings 18:19—20:19, and it may well have been inserted into the prophetic sections by a later editor to explain the historical background.

"The Virgin Daughter of Zion
  despises and mocks you.
The Daughter of Jerusalem
  tosses her head as you flee.
²³Who is it you have insulted and blasphemed?
  Against whom have you raised your voice
and lifted your eyes in pride?
  Against the Holy One of Israel!
²⁴By your messengers
  you have heaped insults on the Lord.
And you have said,
  'With my many chariots
I have ascended the heights of the mountains,
  the utmost heights of Lebanon.
I have cut down its tallest cedars,
  the choicest of its pines.
I have reached its remotest heights,
  the finest of its forests.
²⁵I have dug wells in foreign lands[c]
  and drunk the water there.
With the soles of my feet
  I have dried up all the streams of Egypt.'
²⁶"Have you not heard?
  Long ago I ordained it.
In days of old I planned it;
  now I have brought it to pass,
that you have turned fortified cities
  into piles of stone.
²⁷Their people, drained of power,
  are dismayed and put to shame.
They are like plants in the field,
  like tender green shoots,
like grass sprouting on the roof,
  scorched[d] before it grows up.

---

[a]9 That is, from the upper Nile region   [b]20 Dead Sea Scrolls (see also 2 Kings 19:19); Masoretic Text *alone are the LORD*
[c]25 Dead Sea Scrolls (see also 2 Kings 19:24); Masoretic Text does not have *in foreign lands.*
[d]27 Some manuscripts of the Masoretic Text, Dead Sea Scrolls and some Septuagint manuscripts (see also 2 Kings 19:26); most manuscripts of the Masoretic Text *roof / and terraced fields*

28"But I know where you stay
and when you come and go
and how you rage against me.
29Because you rage against me
and because your insolence has reached my
ears,
I will put my hook in your nose
and my bit in your mouth,
and I will make you return
by the way you came.

30"This will be the sign for you, O Hezekiah:

"This year you will eat what grows by itself,
and the second year what springs from that.
But in the third year sow and reap,
plant vineyards and eat their fruit.
31Once more a remnant of the house of Judah
will take root below and bear fruit above.
32For out of Jerusalem will come a remnant,
and out of Mount Zion a band of survivors.
The zeal of the LORD Almighty
will accomplish this.

33"Therefore this is what the LORD says concerning
the king of Assyria:

"He will not enter this city
or shoot an arrow here.
He will not come before it with shield
or build a siege ramp against it.
34By the way that he came he will return;
he will not enter this city,"
declares the LORD.
35"I will defend this city and save it,
for my sake and for the sake of David my
servant!"

36Then the angel of the LORD went out and put to
death a hundred and eighty-five thousand men in the
Assyrian camp. When the people got up the next morning—there were all the dead bodies! 37So Sennacherib
king of Assyria broke camp and withdrew. He returned
to Nineveh and stayed there.

38One day, while he was worshipping in the temple
of his god Nisroch, his sons Adrammelech and Sharezer cut him down with the sword, and they escaped
to the land of Ararat. And Esarhaddon his son succeeded him as king.

Hezekiah's Illness

38 In those days Hezekiah became ill and was at
the point of death. The prophet Isaiah son of
Amoz went to him and said, "This is what the LORD
says: Put your house in order, because you are going
to die; you will not recover."

2Hezekiah turned his face to the wall and prayed to
the LORD, 3"Remember, O LORD, how I have walked
before you faithfully and with wholehearted devotion
and have done what is good in your eyes." And Hezekiah wept bitterly.

4Then the word of the LORD came to Isaiah: 5"Go
and tell Hezekiah, 'This is what the LORD, the God of
your father David, says: I have heard your prayer and
seen your tears; I will add fifteen years to your life.
6And I will deliver you and this city from the hand of
the king of Assyria. I will defend this city.

7" 'This is the LORD's sign to you that the LORD will
do what he has promised: 8I will make the shadow cast
by the sun go back the ten steps it has gone down on
the stairway of Ahaz.' " So the sunlight went back the
ten steps it had gone down.

9A writing of Hezekiah king of Judah after his illness
and recovery:

10I said, "In the prime of my life
must I go through the gates of death ª
and be robbed of the rest of my years?"
11I said, "I will not again see the LORD,
the LORD, in the land of the living;
no longer will I look on mankind,
or be with those who now dwell in this
world. ᵇ
12Like a shepherd's tent my house
has been pulled down and taken from me.
Like a weaver I have rolled up my life,
and he has cut me off from the loom;
day and night you made an end of me.
13I waited patiently till dawn,
but like a lion he broke all my bones;
day and night you made an end of me.
14I cried like a swift or thrush,
I moaned like a mourning dove.
My eyes grew weak as I looked to the heavens.
I am troubled; O Lord, come to my aid!"

15But what can I say?
He has spoken to me, and he himself has done
this.
I will walk humbly all my years
because of this anguish of my soul.
16Lord, by such things men live;
and my spirit finds life in them too.
You restored me to health
and let me live.
17Surely it was for my benefit
that I suffered such anguish.
In your love you kept me
from the pit of destruction;
you have put all my sins
behind your back.
18For the grave ᶜ cannot praise you,
death cannot sing your praise;
those who go down to the pit
cannot hope for your faithfulness.
19The living, the living—they praise you,
as I am doing today;
fathers tell their children
about your faithfulness.

20The LORD will save me,
and we will sing with stringed instruments

ª 10 Hebrew *Sheol*   ᵇ 11 A few Hebrew manuscripts; most Hebrew manuscripts *in the place of cessation*
ᶜ 18 Hebrew *Sheol*

all the days of our lives
  in the temple of the Lord.

²¹Isaiah had said, "Prepare a poultice of figs and apply it to the boil, and he will recover."

²²Hezekiah had asked, "What will be the sign that I will go up to the temple of the Lord?"

Envoys From Babylon

39 At that time Merodach-Baladan son of Baladan king of Babylon sent Hezekiah letters and a gift, because he had heard of his illness and recovery. ²Hezekiah received the envoys gladly and showed them what was in his storehouses—the silver, the gold, the spices, the fine oil, his entire armoury and everything found among his treasures. There was nothing in his palace or in all his kingdom that Hezekiah did not show them.

³Then Isaiah the prophet went to King Hezekiah and asked, "What did those men say, and where did they come from?"

"From a distant land," Hezekiah replied. "They came to me from Babylon."

⁴The prophet asked, "What did they see in your palace?"

"They saw everything in my palace," Hezekiah said. "There is nothing among my treasures that I did not show them."

⁵Then Isaiah said to Hezekiah, "Hear the word of the Lord Almighty: ⁶The time will surely come when everything in your palace, and all that your fathers have stored up until this day, will be carried off to Babylon. Nothing will be left, says the Lord. ⁷And some of your descendants, your own flesh and blood who will be born to you, will be taken away, and they will become eunuchs in the palace of the king of Babylon."

⁸"The word of the Lord you have spoken is good," Hezekiah replied. For he thought, "There will be peace and security in my lifetime."

40:1 The change in theme is sudden and dramatic. Comfort and hope, rather than judgement and doom, are now the focus. The Assyrian threat had vanished, and Judah was in ruins, laid waste by Babylon. The Jews were no longer confident, but frightened and in despair. Had God really broken his eternal covenant? Was his promise to David's throne abandoned? Why had he allowed this to happen? These questions are about to be dealt with.

Comfort for God's People

40 Comfort, comfort my people,
  says your God.
²Speak tenderly to Jerusalem,
  and proclaim to her

that her hard service has been completed,
  that her sin has been paid for,
that she has received from the Lord's hand
  double for all her sins.

³A voice of one calling:
"In the desert prepare
  the way for the Lord;ᵃ
make straight in the wilderness
  a highway for our God.ᵇ
⁴Every valley shall be raised up,
  every mountain and hill made low;
the rough ground shall become level,
  the rugged places a plain.
⁵And the glory of the Lord will be revealed,
  and all mankind together will see it.
    For the mouth of the Lord has spoken."

⁶A voice says, "Cry out."
  And I said, "What shall I cry?"

"All men are like grass,
  and all their glory is like the flowers of the field.
⁷The grass withers and the flowers fall,
  because the breath of the Lord blows on them.
  Surely the people are grass.
⁸The grass withers and the flowers fall,
  but the word of our God stands for ever."

⁹You who bring good tidings to Zion,
  go up on a high mountain.
You who bring good tidings to Jerusalem,ᶜ
  lift up your voice with a shout,
lift it up, do not be afraid;
  say to the towns of Judah,
  "Here is your God!"
¹⁰See, the Sovereign Lord comes with power,
  and his arm rules for him.
See, his reward is with him,
  and his recompense accompanies him.
¹¹He tends his flock like a shepherd:
  He gathers the lambs in his arms
and carries them close to his heart;
  he gently leads those that have young.

¹²Who has measured the waters in the hollow of his hand,
  or with the breadth of his hand marked off the heavens?
Who has held the dust of the earth in a basket,
  or weighed the mountains on the scales
  and the hills in a balance?
¹³Who has understood the mindᵈ of the Lord,
  or instructed him as his counsellor?
¹⁴Whom did the Lord consult to enlighten him,
  and who taught him the right way?
Who was it that taught him knowledge
  or showed him the path of understanding?

¹⁵Surely the nations are like a drop in a bucket;
  they are regarded as dust on the scales;

ᵃ3 Or A voice of one calling in the desert: / "Prepare the way for the Lord
ᵇ3 Hebrew; Septuagint make straight the paths of our God
ᶜ9 Or O Zion, bringer of good tidings, / go up on a high mountain. / O Jerusalem, bringer of good tidings
ᵈ13 Or Spirit; or spirit

he weighs the islands as though they were fine
dust.
16Lebanon is not sufficient for altar fires,
nor its animals enough for burnt offerings.
17Before him all the nations are as nothing;
they are regarded by him as worthless
and less than nothing.

18To whom, then, will you compare God?
What image will you compare him to?
19As for an idol, a craftsman casts it,
and a goldsmith overlays it with gold
and fashions silver chains for it.
20A man too poor to present such an offering
selects wood that will not rot.
He looks for a skilled craftsman
to set up an idol that will not topple.

21Do you not know?
Have you not heard?
Has it not been told you from the beginning?
Have you not understood since the earth was
founded?
22He sits enthroned above the circle of the earth,
and its people are like grasshoppers.
He stretches out the heavens like a canopy,
and spreads them out like a tent to live in.
23He brings princes to naught
and reduces the rulers of this world to nothing.
24No sooner are they planted,
no sooner are they sown,
no sooner do they take root in the ground,
than he blows on them and they wither,
and a whirlwind sweeps them away like chaff.

25"To whom will you compare me?
Or who is my equal?" says the Holy One.
26Lift your eyes and look to the heavens:
Who created all these?
He who brings out the starry host one by one,
and calls them each by name.
Because of his great power and mighty strength,
not one of them is missing.

27Why do you say, O Jacob,
and complain, O Israel,
"My way is hidden from the LORD;
my cause is disregarded by my God"?
28Do you not know?
Have you not heard?
The LORD is the everlasting God,
the Creator of the ends of the earth.
He will not grow tired or weary,
and his understanding no-one can fathom.
29He gives strength to the weary
and increases the power of the weak.
30Even youths grow tired and weary,
and young men stumble and fall;
31but those who hope in the LORD
will renew their strength.
They will soar on wings like eagles;
they will run and not grow weary,
they will walk and not be faint.

a2 Or / whom victory meets at every step

The Helper of Israel

41 "Be silent before me, you islands!
Let the nations renew their strength!
Let them come forward and speak;
let us meet together at the place of judgment.

2"Who has stirred up one from the east,
calling him in righteousness to his service?a
He hands nations over to him
and subdues kings before him.
He turns them to dust with his sword,
to wind-blown chaff with his bow.
3He pursues them and moves on unscathed,
by a path his feet have not travelled before.
4Who has done this and carried it through,
calling forth the generations from the
beginning?
I, the LORD—with the first of them
and with the last—I am he."

41:2 "One from the east" is probably
Cyrus of Persia (he is mentioned by name in
44:28). "One from the north" (verse 25) is
also Cyrus. He would have taken a northerly
route before turning east.

5The islands have seen it and fear;
the ends of the earth tremble.
They approach and come forward;
6 each helps the other
and says to his brother, "Be strong!"
7The craftsman encourages the goldsmith,
and he who smooths with the hammer
spurs on him who strikes the anvil.
He says of the welding, "It is good."
He nails down the idol so that it will not topple.

8"But you, O Israel, my servant,
Jacob, whom I have chosen,
you descendants of Abraham my friend,
9I took you from the ends of the earth,
from its farthest corners I called you.
I said, 'You are my servant';
I have chosen you and have not rejected you.
10So do not fear, for I am with you;
do not be dismayed, for I am your God.
I will strengthen you and help you;
I will uphold you with my righteous right hand.

11"All who rage against you
will surely be ashamed and disgraced;
those who oppose you
will be as nothing and perish.
12Though you search for your enemies,
you will not find them.
Those who wage war against you
will be as nothing at all.
13For I am the LORD, your God,
who takes hold of your right hand
and says to you, Do not fear;
I will help you.

¹⁴Do not be afraid, O worm Jacob,
  O little Israel,
for I myself will help you," declares the LORD,
  your Redeemer, the Holy One of Israel.
¹⁵"See, I will make you into a threshing-sledge,
  new and sharp, with many teeth.
You will thresh the mountains and crush them,
  and reduce the hills to chaff.
¹⁶You will winnow them, the wind will pick them
  up,
  and a gale will blow them away.
But you will rejoice in the LORD
  and glory in the Holy One of Israel.

¹⁷"The poor and needy search for water,
  but there is none;
  their tongues are parched with thirst.
But I the LORD will answer them;
  I, the God of Israel, will not forsake them.
¹⁸I will make rivers flow on barren heights,
  and springs within the valleys.
I will turn the desert into pools of water,
  and the parched ground into springs.
¹⁹I will put in the desert
  the cedar and the acacia, the myrtle and the
  olive.
I will set pines in the wasteland,
  the fir and the cypress together,
²⁰so that people may see and know,
  may consider and understand,
that the hand of the LORD has done this,
  that the Holy One of Israel has created it.

41:21   The prophet wanted to focus the
people's eyes on the living God, Yahweh. He
alone could deliver them from exile. He is set
in contrast to the humanly-made gods of the
surrounding nations, which are unable to do
anything.

---

²¹"Present your case," says the LORD.
  "Set forth your arguments," says Jacob's King.
²²"Bring in ˻your idols˼ to tell us
  what is going to happen.
Tell us what the former things were,
  so that we may consider them
  and know their final outcome.
Or declare to us the things to come,
²³ tell us what the future holds,
  so that we may know you are gods.
Do something, whether good or bad,
  so that we will be dismayed and filled with fear.
²⁴But you are less than nothing
  and your works are utterly worthless;
  he who chooses you is detestable.

²⁵"I have stirred up one from the north, and he
  comes—
  one from the rising sun who calls on my name.
He treads on rulers as if they were mortar,
  as if he were a potter treading the clay.
²⁶Who told of this from the beginning, so that we
  could know,

or beforehand, so that we could say, 'He was
  right'?
No-one told of this,
  no-one foretold it,
  no-one heard any words from you.
²⁷I was the first to tell Zion, 'Look, here they are!'
  I gave to Jerusalem a messenger of good tidings.
²⁸I look but there is no-one—
  no-one among them to give counsel,
  no-one to give answer when I ask them.
²⁹See, they are all false!
  Their deeds amount to nothing;
  their images are but wind and confusion.

The Servant of the LORD

42 "Here is my servant, whom I uphold,
  my chosen one in whom I delight;
I will put my Spirit on him
  and he will bring justice to the nations.
²He will not shout or cry out,
  or raise his voice in the streets.
³A bruised reed he will not break,
  and a smouldering wick he will not snuff out.
In faithfulness he will bring forth justice;
⁴ he will not falter or be discouraged
  till he establishes justice on earth.
  In his law the islands will put their hope."

42:1   This is the first of the four "Servant
Songs". Originally it probably referred to
God's confidence in a messenger at the time.
However, the coming kingdom of justice
which is foreseen puts the prophecy into a
wider context. Israel as God's servant had
failed in all these areas. The New Testament
writers believed that these words found their
ultimate fulfilment in Jesus Christ.

---

⁵This is what God the LORD says—
he who created the heavens and stretched them
  out,
  who spread out the earth and all that comes out
  of it,
who gives breath to its people,
  and life to those who walk on it:
⁶"I, the LORD, have called you in righteousness;
  I will take hold of your hand.
I will keep you and will make you
  to be a covenant for the people
  and a light for the Gentiles,
⁷to open eyes that are blind,
  to free captives from prison
  and to release from the dungeon those who sit
  in darkness.

⁸"I am the LORD; that is my name!
  I will not give my glory to another
  or my praise to idols.
⁹See, the former things have taken place,
  and new things I declare;
before they spring into being
  I announce them to you."

Song of Praise to the LORD

¹⁰Sing to the LORD a new song,
  his praise from the ends of the earth,
you who go down to the sea, and all that is in it,
  you islands, and all who live in them.
¹¹Let the desert and its towns raise their voices;
  let the settlements where Kedar lives rejoice.
Let the people of Sela sing for joy;
  let them shout from the mountaintops.
¹²Let them give glory to the LORD
  and proclaim his praise in the islands.
¹³The LORD will march out like a mighty man,
  like a warrior he will stir up his zeal;
with a shout he will raise the battle cry
  and will triumph over his enemies.

¹⁴"For a long time I have kept silent,
  I have been quiet and held myself back.
But now, like a woman in childbirth,
  I cry out, I gasp and pant.
¹⁵I will lay waste the mountains and hills
  and dry up all their vegetation;
I will turn rivers into islands
  and dry up the pools.
¹⁶I will lead the blind by ways they have not
    known,
  along unfamiliar paths I will guide them;
I will turn the darkness into light before them
  and make the rough places smooth.
These are the things I will do;
  I will not forsake them.
¹⁷But those who trust in idols,
  who say to images, 'You are our gods,'
  will be turned back in utter shame.

Israel Blind and Deaf

¹⁸"Hear, you deaf;
  look, you blind, and see!
¹⁹Who is blind but my servant,
  and deaf like the messenger I send?
Who is blind like the one committed to me,
  blind like the servant of the LORD?
²⁰You have seen many things, but have paid no
    attention;
  your ears are open, but you hear nothing."
²¹It pleased the LORD
  for the sake of his righteousness
  to make his law great and glorious.
²²But this is a people plundered and looted,
  all of them trapped in pits
  or hidden away in prisons.
They have become plunder,
  with no-one to rescue them;
they have been made loot,
  with no-one to say, "Send them back."

²³Which of you will listen to this
  or pay close attention in time to come?
²⁴Who handed Jacob over to become loot,
  and Israel to the plunderers?
Was it not the LORD,
  against whom we have sinned?

For they would not follow his ways;
  they did not obey his law.
²⁵So he poured out on them his burning anger,
  the violence of war.
It enveloped them in flames, yet they did not
    understand;
  it consumed them, but they did not take it to
    heart.

Israel's Only Saviour

43 But now, this is what the LORD says—
  he who created you, O Jacob,
  he who formed you, O Israel:
"Fear not, for I have redeemed you;
  I have summoned you by name; you are mine.
²When you pass through the waters,
  I will be with you;
and when you pass through the rivers,
  they will not sweep over you.
When you walk through the fire,
  you will not be burned;
  the flames will not set you ablaze.
³For I am the LORD, your God,
  the Holy One of Israel, your Saviour;
I give Egypt for your ransom,
  Cush ᵃ and Seba in your stead.
⁴Since you are precious and honoured in my sight,
  and because I love you,
I will give men in exchange for you,
  and people in exchange for your life.
⁵Do not be afraid, for I am with you;
  I will bring your children from the east
  and gather you from the west.
⁶I will say to the north, 'Give them up!'
  and to the south, 'Do not hold them back.'
Bring my sons from afar
  and my daughters from the ends of the earth—
⁷everyone who is called by my name,
  whom I created for my glory,
  whom I formed and made."

⁸Lead out those who have eyes but are blind,
  who have ears but are deaf.
⁹All the nations gather together
  and the peoples assemble.
Which of them foretold this
  and proclaimed to us the former things?
Let them bring in their witnesses to prove they
    were right,
  so that others may hear and say, "It is true."
¹⁰"You are my witnesses," declares the LORD,
  "and my servant whom I have chosen,
so that you may know and believe me
  and understand that I am he.
Before me no god was formed,
  nor will there be one after me.
¹¹I, even I, am the LORD,
  and apart from me there is no saviour.
¹²I have revealed and saved and proclaimed—
  I, and not some foreign god among you.
You are my witnesses," declares the LORD, "that I
  am God.

ᵃ3 That is, the upper Nile region

¹³ Yes, and from ancient days I am he.
No-one can deliver out of my hand.
When I act, who can reverse it?"

43:9   The prophets sometimes used the language of a legal trial to highlight God's message. Here, Israel is called to account as a witness to testify to Yahweh. There is a summons to the hearing (verse 8, 9), a confirmation of the witnesses (verse 10), and Yahweh's speech in his defence (verses 10–13). The absence of any counter argument suggests that there was no convincing answer (see 44:8) against God.

God's Mercy and Israel's Unfaithfulness

¹⁴This is what the LORD says—
your Redeemer, the Holy One of Israel:
"For your sake I will send to Babylon
and bring down as fugitives all the
Babylonians,ᵇ
in the ships in which they took pride.
¹⁵I am the LORD, your Holy One,
Israel's Creator, your King."

¹⁶This is what the LORD says—
he who made a way through the sea,
a path through the mighty waters,
¹⁷who drew out the chariots and horses,
the army and reinforcements together,
and they lay there, never to rise again,
extinguished, snuffed out like a wick:
¹⁸"Forget the former things;
do not dwell on the past.
¹⁹See, I am doing a new thing!
Now it springs up; do you not perceive it?
I am making a way in the desert
and streams in the wasteland.
²⁰The wild animals honour me,
the jackals and the owls,
because I provide water in the desert
and streams in the wasteland,
to give drink to my people, my chosen,
²¹ the people I formed for myself
that they may proclaim my praise.

²²"Yet you have not called upon me, O Jacob,
you have not wearied yourselves for me,
O Israel.
²³You have not brought me sheep for burnt
offerings,
nor honoured me with your sacrifices.
I have not burdened you with grain offerings
nor wearied you with demands for incense.
²⁴You have not bought any fragrant calamus for me,
or lavished on me the fat of your sacrifices.
But you have burdened me with your sins
and wearied me with your offences.

²⁵"I, even I, am he who blots out
your transgressions, for my own sake,
and remembers your sins no more.
²⁶Review the past for me,
let us argue the matter together;
state the case for your innocence.
²⁷Your first father sinned;
your spokesmen rebelled against me.
²⁸So I will disgrace the dignitaries of your temple,
and I will consign Jacob to destructionᶜ
and Israel to scorn.

Israel the Chosen

44 "But now listen, O Jacob, my servant,
Israel, whom I have chosen.
²This is what the LORD says—
he who made you, who formed you in the
womb,
and who will help you:
Do not be afraid, O Jacob, my servant,
Jeshurun, whom I have chosen.
³For I will pour water on the thirsty land,
and streams on the dry ground;
I will pour out my Spirit on your offspring,
and my blessing on your descendants.
⁴They will spring up like grass in a meadow,
like poplar trees by flowing streams.
⁵One will say, 'I belong to the LORD';
another will call himself by the name of Jacob;
still another will write on his hand, 'The LORD's',
and will take the name Israel.

The LORD, Not Idols

⁶"This is what the LORD says—
Israel's King and Redeemer, the LORD Almighty:
I am the first and I am the last;
apart from me there is no God.
⁷Who then is like me? Let him proclaim it.
Let him declare and lay out before me
what has happened since I established my ancient
people,
and what is yet to come—
yes, let him foretell what will come.
⁸Do not tremble, do not be afraid.
Did I not proclaim this and foretell it long ago?
You are my witnesses. Is there any God besides
me?
No, there is no other Rock; I know not one."

44:8   God is often pictured as a rock or a fortress, most notably in the Psalms. It emphasizes his strength and invincibility, and also his protection (as here).

---

⁹All who make idols are nothing,
and the things they treasure are worthless.
Those who would speak up for them are blind;
they are ignorant, to their own shame.
¹⁰Who shapes a god and casts an idol,
which can profit him nothing?

ᵇ14 Or Chaldeans
ᶜ28 The Hebrew term refers to the irrevocable giving over of things or persons to the LORD, often by totally destroying them.

11He and his kind will be put to shame;
craftsmen are nothing but men.
Let them all come together and take their stand;
they will be brought down to terror and infamy.

12The blacksmith takes a tool
and works with it in the coals;
he shapes an idol with hammers,
he forges it with the might of his arm.
He gets hungry and loses his strength;
he drinks no water and grows faint.
13The carpenter measures with a line
and makes an outline with a marker;
he roughs it out with chisels
and marks it with compasses.
He shapes it in the form of man,
of man in all his glory,
that it may dwell in a shrine.
14He cut down cedars,
or perhaps took a cypress or oak.
He let it grow among the trees of the forest,
or planted a pine, and the rain made it grow.
15It is man's fuel for burning;
some of it he takes and warms himself,
he kindles a fire and bakes bread.
But he also fashions a god and worships it;
he makes an idol and bows down to it.
16Half of the wood he burns in the fire;
over it he prepares his meal,
he roasts his meat and eats his fill.
He also warms himself and says,
"Ah! I am warm; I see the fire."
17From the rest he makes a god, his idol;
he bows down to it and worships.
He prays to it and says,
"Save me; you are my god."
18They know nothing, they understand nothing;
their eyes are plastered over so that they cannot
see,
and their minds closed so that they cannot
understand.
19No-one stops to think,
no-one has the knowledge or understanding to
say,
"Half of it I used for fuel;
I even baked bread over its coals,
I roasted meat and I ate.
Shall I make a detestable thing from what is left?
Shall I bow down to a block of wood?"
20He feeds on ashes, a deluded heart misleads him;
he cannot save himself, or say,
"Is not this thing in my right hand a lie?"

21"Remember these things, O Jacob,
for you are my servant, O Israel.
I have made you, you are my servant;
O Israel, I will not forget you.
22I have swept away your offences like a cloud,
your sins like the morning mist.
Return to me,
for I have redeemed you."

23Sing for joy, O heavens, for the LORD has done
this;
shout aloud, O earth beneath.
Burst into song, you mountains,
you forests and all your trees,
for the LORD has redeemed Jacob,
he displays his glory in Israel.

Jerusalem to Be Inhabited

24"This is what the LORD says—
your Redeemer, who formed you in the womb:

I am the LORD,
who has made all things,
who alone stretched out the heavens,
who spread out the earth by myself,

25who foils the signs of false prophets
and makes fools of diviners,
who overthrows the learning of the wise
and turns it into nonsense,
26who carries out the words of his servants
and fulfils the predictions of his messengers,

who says of Jerusalem, 'It shall be inhabited,'
of the towns of Judah, 'They shall be built,'
and of their ruins, 'I will restore them,'
27who says to the watery deep, 'Be dry,
and I will dry up your streams,'
28who says of Cyrus, 'He is my shepherd
and will accomplish all that I please;
he will say of Jerusalem, "Let it be rebuilt,"
and of the temple, "Let its foundations be
laid." '

45 "This is what the LORD says to his
anointed,
to Cyrus, whose right hand I take hold of
to subdue nations before him
and to strip kings of their armour,
to open doors before him
so that gates will not be shut:
2I will go before you
and will level the mountains;a
I will break down gates of bronze
and cut through bars of iron.
3I will give you the treasures of darkness,
riches stored in secret places,
so that you may know that I am the LORD,
the God of Israel, who summons you by name.
4For the sake of Jacob my servant,
of Israel my chosen,
I summon you by name
and bestow on you a title of honour,
though you do not acknowledge me.
5I am the LORD, and there is no other;
apart from me there is no God.
I will strengthen you,
though you have not acknowledged me,
6so that from the rising of the sun
to the place of its setting
men may know there is none besides me.
I am the LORD, and there is no other.

a2 Dead Sea Scrolls and Septuagint; the meaning of the word in the Masoretic Text is uncertain.

⁷I form the light and create darkness,
  I bring prosperity and create disaster;
  I, the LORD, do all these things.

⁸"You heavens above, rain down righteousness;
  let the clouds shower it down.
Let the earth open wide,
  let salvation spring up,
let righteousness grow with it;
  I, the LORD, have created it.

⁹"Woe to him who quarrels with his Maker,
  to him who is but a potsherd among the
    potsherds on the ground.
Does the clay say to the potter,
  'What are you making?'
Does your work say,
  'He has no hands'?
¹⁰Woe to him who says to his father,
  'What have you begotten?'
or to his mother,
  'What have you brought to birth?'

¹¹"This is what the LORD says—
  the Holy One of Israel, and its Maker:
Concerning things to come,
  do you question me about my children,
  or give me orders about the work of my hands?
¹²It is I who made the earth
  and created mankind upon it.
My own hands stretched out the heavens;
  I marshalled their starry hosts.
¹³I will raise up Cyrus^b in my righteousness:
  I will make all his ways straight.
He will rebuild my city
  and set my exiles free,
but not for a price or reward,
  says the LORD Almighty."

¹⁴This is what the LORD says:

"The products of Egypt and the merchandise of
    Cush,^c
  and those tall Sabeans—
they will come over to you
  and will be yours;
they will trudge behind you,
  coming over to you in chains.
They will bow down before you
  and plead with you, saying,
'Surely God is with you, and there is no other;
  there is no other god.' "

¹⁵Truly you are a God who hides himself,
  O God and Saviour of Israel.
¹⁶All the makers of idols will be put to shame and
    disgraced;
  they will go off into disgrace together.
¹⁷But Israel will be saved by the LORD
  with an everlasting salvation;
you will never be put to shame or disgraced,
  to ages everlasting.
¹⁸For this is what the LORD says—
  he who created the heavens,

he is God;
he who fashioned and made the earth,
  he founded it;
he did not create it to be empty,
  but formed it to be inhabited—
he says:
"I am the LORD,
  and there is no other.
¹⁹I have not spoken in secret,
  from somewhere in a land of darkness;
I have not said to Jacob's descendants,
  'Seek me in vain.'
I, the LORD, speak the truth;
  I declare what is right.

²⁰"Gather together and come;
  assemble, you fugitives from the nations.
Ignorant are those who carry about idols of wood,
  who pray to gods that cannot save.
²¹Declare what is to be, present it—
  let them take counsel together.
Who foretold this long ago,
  who declared it from the distant past?
Was it not I, the LORD?
  And there is no God apart from me,
a righteous God and a Saviour;
  there is none but me.

²²"Turn to me and be saved,
  all you ends of the earth;
for I am God, and there is no other.
²³By myself I have sworn,
  my mouth has uttered in all integrity
  a word that will not be revoked:
Before me every knee will bow;
  by me every tongue will swear.
²⁴They will say of me, 'In the LORD alone
  are righteousness and strength.' "
All who have raged against him
  will come to him and be put to shame.
²⁵But in the LORD all the descendants of Israel
  will be found righteous and will exult.

Gods of Babylon

46 Bel bows down, Nebo stoops low;
      their idols are borne by beasts of
      burden.^a
The images that are carried about are
    burdensome,
  a burden for the weary.
²They stoop and bow down together;
  unable to rescue the burden,
  they themselves go off into captivity.

³"Listen to me, O house of Jacob,
  all you who remain of the house of Israel,
you whom I have upheld since you were
    conceived,
  and have carried since your birth.
⁴Even to your old age and grey hairs
  I am he, I am he who will sustain you.
I have made you and I will carry you;
  I will sustain you and I will rescue you.

^b13 Hebrew *him*   ^c14 That is, the upper Nile region   ^a1 Or *are but beasts and cattle*

5"To whom will you compare me or count me
    equal?
To whom will you liken me that we may be
    compared?
6Some pour out gold from their bags
    and weigh out silver on the scales;
they hire a goldsmith to make it into a god,
    and they bow down and worship it.
7They lift it to their shoulders and carry it;
    they set it up in its place, and there it stands.
From that spot it cannot move.
Though one cries out to it, it does not answer;
    it cannot save him from his troubles.

8"Remember this, fix it in mind,
    take it to heart, you rebels.
9Remember the former things, those of long ago;
    I am God, and there is no other;
    I am God, and there is none like me.
10I make known the end from the beginning,
    from ancient times, what is still to come.
I say: My purpose will stand,
    and I will do all that I please.
11From the east I summon a bird of prey;
    from a far-off land, a man to fulfil my purpose.
What I have said, that will I bring about;
    what I have planned, that will I do.
12Listen to me, you stubborn-hearted,
    you who are far from righteousness.
13I am bringing my righteousness near,
    it is not far away;
    and my salvation will not be delayed.
I will grant salvation to Zion,
    my splendour to Israel.

47:1   To the Israelites, the Babylonians
were evil personified. At the top of their list
of crimes was the desecration and destruction of the temple. The "Virgin Daughter"
represents the city of Babylon itself. Bel and
Nebo (46:1) were its gods.

The Fall of Babylon

47 "Go down, sit in the dust,
    Virgin Daughter of Babylon;
sit on the ground without a throne,
    Daughter of the Babylonians.ᵃ
No more will you be called
    tender or delicate.
2Take millstones and grind flour;
    take off your veil.
Lift up your skirts, bare your legs,
    and wade through the streams.
3Your nakedness will be exposed
    and your shame uncovered.
I will take vengeance;
    I will spare no-one."

4Our Redeemer—the LORD Almighty is his name—
    is the Holy One of Israel.

5"Sit in silence, go into darkness,
    Daughter of the Babylonians;
no more will you be called
    queen of kingdoms.
6I was angry with my people
    and desecrated my inheritance;
I gave them into your hand,
    and you showed them no mercy.
Even on the aged
    you laid a very heavy yoke.
7You said, 'I will continue for ever—
    the eternal queen!'
But you did not consider these things
    or reflect on what might happen.

8"Now then, listen, you wanton creature,
    lounging in your security
and saying to yourself,
    'I am, and there is none besides me.
I will never be a widow
    or suffer the loss of children.'
9Both of these will overtake you
    in a moment, on a single day:
    loss of children and widowhood.
They will come upon you in full measure,
    in spite of your many sorceries
    and all your potent spells.
10You have trusted in your wickedness
    and have said, 'No-one sees me.'
Your wisdom and knowledge mislead you
    when you say to yourself,
    'I am, and there is none besides me.'
11Disaster will come upon you,
    and you will not know how to conjure it away.
A calamity will fall upon you
    that you cannot ward off with a ransom;
a catastrophe you cannot foresee
    will suddenly come upon you.

47:12   This passage (verses 12–15) combines elements of a mocking song and a
funeral song. The Babylonians were great
astrologers, but it would do them no good
when disaster struck.

12"Keep on, then, with your magic spells
    and with your many sorceries,
    which you have laboured at since childhood.
Perhaps you will succeed,
    perhaps you will cause terror.
13All the counsel you have received has only worn
        you out!
Let your astrologers come forward,
    those stargazers who make predictions month by
        month,
    let them save you from what is coming upon
        you.
14Surely they are like stubble;
    the fire will burn them up.
They cannot even save themselves
    from the power of the flame.

ᵃ1 Or *Chaldeans*; also in verse 5

Here are no coals to warm anyone;
here is no fire to sit by.
[15]That is all they can do for you—
these you have laboured with
and trafficked with since childhood.
Each of them goes on in his error;
there is not one that can save you.

Stubborn Israel

48 "Listen to this, O house of Jacob,
you who are called by the name of Israel
and come from the line of Judah,
you who take oaths in the name of the LORD
and invoke the God of Israel—
but not in truth or righteousness—
[2]you who call yourselves citizens of the holy city
and rely on the God of Israel—
the LORD Almighty is his name:
[3]I foretold the former things long ago,
my mouth announced them and I made them
known;
then suddenly I acted, and they came to pass.
[4]For I knew how stubborn you were;
the sinews of your neck were iron,
your forehead was bronze.
[5]Therefore I told you these things long ago;
before they happened I announced them to you
so that you could not say,
'My idols did them;
my wooden image and metal god ordained
them.'
[6]You have heard these things; look at them all.
Will you not admit them?

"From now on I will tell you of new things,
of hidden things unknown to you.
[7]They are created now, and not long ago;
you have not heard of them before today.
So you cannot say,
'Yes, I knew of them.'
[8]You have neither heard nor understood;
from of old your ear has not been open.
Well do I know how treacherous you are;
you were called a rebel from birth.
[9]For my own name's sake I delay my wrath;
for the sake of my praise I hold it back from
you,
so as not to cut you off.
[10]See, I have refined you, though not as silver;
I have tested you in the furnace of affliction.
[11]For my own sake, for my own sake, I do this.
How can I let myself be defamed?
I will not yield my glory to another.

Israel Freed

[12]"Listen to me, O Jacob,
Israel, whom I have called:
I am he;
I am the first and I am the last.
[13]My own hand laid the foundations of the earth,
and my right hand spread out the heavens;

when I summon them,
they all stand up together.

[14]"Come together, all of you, and listen:
Which of the idols has foretold these things?
The LORD's chosen ally
will carry out his purpose against Babylon;
his arm will be against the Babylonians.[a]
[15]I, even I, have spoken;
yes, I have called him.
I will bring him,
and he will succeed in his mission.

[16]"Come near me and listen to this:

"From the first announcement I have not spoken
in secret;
at the time it happens, I am there."

And now the Sovereign LORD has sent me,
with his Spirit.

[17]This is what the LORD says—
your Redeemer, the Holy One of Israel:
"I am the LORD your God,
who teaches you what is best for you,
who directs you in the way you should go.
[18]If only you had paid attention to my commands,
your peace would have been like a river,
your righteousness like the waves of the sea.
[19]Your descendants would have been like the sand,
your children like its numberless grains;
their name would never be cut off
nor destroyed from before me."

48:20 "Leave Babylon" is a military command. The prophet was projecting his hearers into the future to experience what God has promised to do. There is a comparison with the exodus, when God delivered his people from slavery in Egypt. What God has achieved once he can do again.

---

[20]Leave Babylon,
flee from the Babylonians!
Announce this with shouts of joy
and proclaim it.
Send it out to the ends of the earth;
say, "The LORD has redeemed his servant
Jacob."
[21]They did not thirst when he led them through
the deserts;
he made water flow for them from the rock;
he split the rock
and water gushed out.
[22]"There is no peace," says the LORD, "for the
wicked."

The Servant of the LORD

49 Listen to me, you islands;
hear this, you distant nations:
Before I was born the LORD called me;

[a]14 Or Chaldeans; also in verse 20

from my birth he has made mention of my
　　name.
[2]He made my mouth like a sharpened sword,
　　in the shadow of his hand he hid me;
he made me into a polished arrow
　　and concealed me in his quiver.
[3]He said to me, "You are my servant,
　　Israel, in whom I will display my splendour."
[4]But I said, "I have laboured to no purpose;
　　I have spent my strength in vain and for
　　　nothing.
Yet what is due to me is in the LORD's hand,
　　and my reward is with my God."

[5]And now the LORD says—
　　he who formed me in the womb to be his
　　　servant
to bring Jacob back to him
　　and gather Israel to himself,
for I am honoured in the eyes of the LORD
　　and my God has been my strength—
[6]he says:
"It is too small a thing for you to be my servant
　　to restore the tribes of Jacob
　　and bring back those of Israel I have kept.
I will also make you a light for the Gentiles,
　　that you may bring my salvation to the ends of
　　　the earth."

49:6　　The figure in this second Servant
Song (verses 1–6) may refer both to a
prophet and to the "idealized Israel". God's
Servant here is given a mission to bring salvation to all peoples, so that they will recognize
God's sovereignty over the earth. The words
are strikingly reminiscent of the Nunc Dimit-
tis—the words that Simeon used when Jesus
was dedicated at the temple (Luke
2:29–32).

---

[7]This is what the LORD says—
　　the Redeemer and Holy One of Israel—
to him who was despised and abhorred by the
　　nation,
　　to the servant of rulers:
"Kings will see you and rise up,
　　princes will see and bow down,
because of the LORD, who is faithful,
　　the Holy One of Israel, who has chosen you."

Restoration of Israel

[8]This is what the LORD says:

"In the time of my favour I will answer you,
　　and in the day of salvation I will help you;
I will keep you and will make you
　　to be a covenant for the people,
to restore the land
　　and to reassign its desolate inheritances,
[9]to say to the captives, 'Come out,'
　　and to those in darkness, 'Be free!'

"They will feed beside the roads
　　and find pasture on every barren hill.
[10]They will neither hunger nor thirst,
　　nor will the desert heat or the sun beat upon
　　　them.
He who has compassion on them will guide them
　　and lead them beside springs of water.
[11]I will turn all my mountains into roads,
　　and my highways will be raised up.
[12]See, they will come from afar—
　　some from the north, some from the west,
　　some from the region of Aswan."[a]

[13]Shout for joy, O heavens;
　　rejoice, O earth;
　　burst into song, O mountains!
For the LORD comforts his people
　　and will have compassion on his afflicted ones.

[14]But Zion said, "The LORD has forsaken me,
　　the Lord has forgotten me."

[15]"Can a mother forget the baby at her breast
　　and have no compassion on the child she has
　　　borne?
Though she may forget,
　　I will not forget you!
[16]See, I have engraved you on the palms of my
　　　hands;
　　your walls are ever before me.
[17]Your sons hasten back,
　　and those who laid you waste depart from you.
[18]Lift up your eyes and look around;
　　all your sons gather and come to you.
As surely as I live," declares the LORD,
　　"you will wear them all as ornaments;
　　you will put them on, like a bride.

[19]"Though you were ruined and made desolate
　　and your land laid waste,
now you will be too small for your people,
　　and those who devoured you will be far away.
[20]The children born during your bereavement
　　will yet say in your hearing,
'This place is too small for us;
　　give us more space to live in.'
[21]Then you will say in your heart,
　　'Who bore me these?
I was bereaved and barren;
　　I was exiled and rejected.
Who brought these up?
I was left all alone,
　　but these—where have they come from?' "

[22]This is what the Sovereign LORD says:

"See, I will beckon to the Gentiles,
　　I will lift up my banner to the peoples;
they will bring your sons in their arms
　　and carry your daughters on their shoulders.
[23]Kings will be your foster fathers,
　　and their queens your nursing mothers.

---

[a]12 Dead Sea Scrolls; Masoretic Text *Sinim*

They will bow down before you with their faces
    to the ground;
  they will lick the dust at your feet.
Then you will know that I am the LORD;
  those who hope in me will not be
    disappointed."

24Can plunder be taken from warriors,
  or captives rescued from the fierce?*b*

25But this is what the LORD says:

"Yes, captives will be taken from warriors,
  and plunder retrieved from the fierce;
I will contend with those who contend with you,
  and your children I will save.
26I will make your oppressors eat their own flesh;
  they will be drunk on their own blood, as with
    wine.
Then all mankind will know
  that I, the LORD, am your Saviour,
  your Redeemer, the Mighty One of Jacob."

Israel's Sin and the Servant's Obedience

50 This is what the LORD says:

"Where is your mother's certificate of
    divorce
  with which I sent her away?
Or to which of my creditors
  did I sell you?
Because of your sins you were sold;
  because of your transgressions your mother was
    sent away.
2When I came, why was there no-one?
  When I called, why was there no-one to
    answer?
Was my arm too short to ransom you?
  Do I lack the strength to rescue you?
By a mere rebuke I dry up the sea,
  I turn rivers into a desert;
their fish rot for lack of water
  and die of thirst.
3I clothe the sky with darkness
  and make sackcloth its covering."

4The Sovereign LORD has given me an instructed
    tongue,
  to know the word that sustains the weary.
He wakens me morning by morning,
  wakens my ear to listen like one being taught.
5The Sovereign LORD has opened my ears,
  and I have not been rebellious;
  I have not drawn back.
6I offered my back to those who beat me,
  my cheeks to those who pulled out my beard;
I did not hide my face
  from mocking and spitting.
7Because the Sovereign LORD helps me,
  I will not be disgraced.
Therefore have I set my face like flint,
  and I know I will not be put to shame.
8He who vindicates me is near.
  Who then will bring charges against me?
  Let us face each other!

Who is my accuser?
  Let him confront me!
9It is the Sovereign LORD who helps me.
  Who is he who will condemn me?
They will all wear out like a garment;
  the moths will eat them up.

50:6   The third Servant Song could also
be seen as referring to the prophet. It is likely
that he, like Jeremiah and many others, was
ill-treated and made a laughing stock for
faithfully proclaiming God's message. There
are some parallels here with Jesus' trial (see
Matthew 26:67).

10Who among you fears the LORD
  and obeys the word of his servant?
Let him who walks in the dark,
  who has no light,
trust in the name of the LORD
  and rely on his God.
11But now, all you who light fires
  and provide yourselves with flaming torches,
go, walk in the light of your fires
  and of the torches you have set ablaze.
This is what you shall receive from my hand:
  You will lie down in torment.

Everlasting Salvation for Zion

51   "Listen to me, you who pursue
        righteousness
  and who seek the LORD:
Look to the rock from which you were cut
  and to the quarry from which you were hewn;
2look to Abraham, your father,
  and to Sarah, who gave you birth.
When I called him he was but one,
  and I blessed him and made him many.
3The LORD will surely comfort Zion
  and will look with compassion on all her ruins;
he will make her deserts like Eden,
  her wastelands like the garden of the LORD.
Joy and gladness will be found in her,
  thanksgiving and the sound of singing.

4"Listen to me, my people;
  hear me, my nation:
The law will go out from me;
  my justice will become a light to the nations.
5My righteousness draws near speedily,
  my salvation is on the way,
  and my arm will bring justice to the nations.
The islands will look to me
  and wait in hope for my arm.
6Lift up your eyes to the heavens,
  look at the earth beneath;
the heavens will vanish like smoke,
  the earth will wear out like a garment
  and its inhabitants die like flies.
But my salvation will last for ever,
  my righteousness will never fail.

---

*b*24 Dead Sea Scrolls, Vulgate and Syriac (see also Septuagint and verse 25); Masoretic Text *righteous*

7"Hear me, you who know what is right,
  you people who have my law in your hearts:
Do not fear the reproach of men
  or be terrified by their insults.
8For the moth will eat them up like a garment;
  the worm will devour them like wool.
But my righteousness will last for ever,
  my salvation through all generations."

51:9   This Rahab is not the woman who saved Joshua's spies (Joshua 2). Rahab was a mythological sea monster which lived around the area of the Nile river, so the name refers to Egypt.

9Awake, awake! Clothe yourself with strength,
  O arm of the LORD;
awake, as in days gone by,
  as in generations of old.
Was it not you who cut Rahab to pieces,
  who pierced that monster through?
10Was it not you who dried up the sea,
  the waters of the great deep,
who made a road in the depths of the sea
  so that the redeemed might cross over?
11The ransomed of the LORD will return.
  They will enter Zion with singing;
  everlasting joy will crown their heads.
Gladness and joy will overtake them,
  and sorrow and sighing will flee away.

12"I, even I, am he who comforts you.
  Who are you that you fear mortal men,
  the sons of men, who are but grass,
13that you forget the LORD your Maker,
  who stretched out the heavens
  and laid the foundations of the earth,
that you live in constant terror every day
  because of the wrath of the oppressor,
  who is bent on destruction?
For where is the wrath of the oppressor?
14   The cowering prisoners will soon be set free;
  they will not die in their dungeon,
  nor will they lack bread.
15For I am the LORD your God,
  who churns up the sea so that its waves roar—
  the LORD Almighty is his name.
16I have put my words in your mouth
  and covered you with the shadow of my hand—
I who set the heavens in place,
  who laid the foundations of the earth,
  and who say to Zion, 'You are my people.' "

The Cup of the LORD's Wrath

17Awake, awake!
  Rise up, O Jerusalem,
you who have drunk from the hand of the LORD
  the cup of his wrath,
you who have drained to its dregs
  the goblet that makes men stagger.

18Of all the sons she bore
  there was none to guide her;
of all the sons she brought up
  there was none to take her by the hand.
19These double calamities have come upon you—
  who can comfort you?—
ruin and destruction, famine and sword—
  who can*a* console you?
20Your sons have fainted;
  they lie at the head of every street,
  like antelope caught in a net.
They are filled with the wrath of the LORD
  and the rebuke of your God.

51:17   The image of God's anger as a cup of wine which "makes men stagger" was a common one in prophecy of this period (Jeremiah 25:15 and Ezekiel 23:32 are good examples). Here, Judah had already drunk its fill from this cup, and its enemies would drink from it instead.

21Therefore hear this, you afflicted one,
  made drunk, but not with wine.
22This is what your Sovereign LORD says,
  your God, who defends his people:
"See, I have taken out of your hand
  the cup that made you stagger;
from that cup, the goblet of my wrath,
  you will never drink again.
23I will put it into the hands of your tormentors,
  who said to you,
  'Fall prostrate that we may walk over you.'
And you made your back like the ground,
  like a street to be walked over."

52   Awake, awake, O Zion,
  clothe yourself with strength.
Put on your garments of splendour,
  O Jerusalem, the holy city.
The uncircumcised and defiled
  will not enter you again.
2Shake off your dust;
  rise up, sit enthroned, O Jerusalem.
Free yourself from the chains on your neck,
  O captive Daughter of Zion.

3For this is what the LORD says:

"You were sold for nothing,
  and without money you will be redeemed."

4For this is what the Sovereign LORD says:

"At first my people went down to Egypt to live;
  lately, Assyria has oppressed them.

5"And now what do I have here?" declares the LORD.

"For my people have been taken away for
  nothing,

---

a 19 Dead Sea Scrolls, Septuagint, Vulgate and Syriac; Masoretic Text / *how can I*

and those who rule them mock,"[a]
                              declares the LORD.
"And all day long
    my name is constantly blasphemed.
[6]Therefore my people will know my name;
    therefore in that day they will know
that it is I who foretold it.
    Yes, it is I."

[7]How beautiful on the mountains
    are the feet of those who bring good news,
who proclaim peace,
    who bring good tidings,
    who proclaim salvation,
who say to Zion,
    "Your God reigns!"
[8]Listen! Your watchmen lift up their voices;
    together they shout for joy.
When the LORD returns to Zion,
    they will see it with their own eyes.
[9]Burst into songs of joy together,
    you ruins of Jerusalem,
for the LORD has comforted his people,
    he has redeemed Jerusalem.
[10]The LORD will lay bare his holy arm
    in the sight of all the nations,
and all the ends of the earth will see
    the salvation of our God.

[11]Depart, depart, go out from there!
    Touch no unclean thing!
Come out from it and be pure,
    you who carry the vessels of the LORD.
[12]But you will not leave in haste
    or go in flight;
for the LORD will go before you,
    the God of Israel will be your rear guard.

52:13   This is the start of the fourth and
greatest Servant Song (52:13 — 53:12). After
the people's joyful return home (51 and
52:1–12) the cost of making the homecoming possible is explained. The lonely figure
of the one who pays the price is here portrayed
as being rejected, scorned, abused, and
killed. Astonishingly he is restored to life
and finally exalted. Among the many New
Testament passages which allude to this
prophecy in relation to Jesus are Matthew
27, Romans 5:6–9, Philippians 2:5–11, and
1 Peter 2:21–24.

The Suffering and Glory of the Servant

[13]See, my servant will act wisely;[b]
    he will be raised and lifted up and highly
        exalted.

[14]Just as there were many who were appalled at
        him[c]—
    his appearance was so disfigured beyond that of
        any man
    and his form marred beyond human likeness—
[15]so will he sprinkle many nations,[d]
    and kings will shut their mouths because of
        him.
For what they were not told, they will see,
    and what they have not heard, they will
        understand.

53 Who has believed our message
        and to whom has the arm of the LORD
        been revealed?
[2]He grew up before him like a tender shoot,
    and like a root out of dry ground.
He had no beauty or majesty to attract us to him,
    nothing in his appearance that we should desire
        him.
[3]He was despised and rejected by men,
    a man of sorrows, and familiar with suffering.
Like one from whom men hide their faces
    he was despised, and we esteemed him not.

[4]Surely he took up our infirmities
    and carried our sorrows,
yet we considered him stricken by God,
    smitten by him, and afflicted.
[5]But he was pierced for our transgressions,
    he was crushed for our iniquities;
the punishment that brought us peace was upon
        him,
    and by his wounds we are healed.
[6]We all, like sheep, have gone astray,
    each of us has turned to his own way;
and the LORD has laid on him
    the iniquity of us all.

[7]He was oppressed and afflicted,
    yet he did not open his mouth;
he was led like a lamb to the slaughter,
    and as a sheep before her shearers is silent,
    so he did not open his mouth.
[8]By oppression[a] and judgment he was taken
        away.
    And who can speak of his descendants?
For he was cut off from the land of the living;
    for the transgression of my people he was
        stricken.[b]
[9]He was assigned a grave with the wicked,
    and with the rich in his death,
though he had done no violence,
    nor was any deceit in his mouth.

[10]Yet it was the LORD's will to crush him and cause
        him to suffer,
    and though the LORD makes[c] his life a guilt
        offering,

---

[a]5 Dead Sea Scrolls and Vulgate; Masoretic Text *wail*   [b]13 Or *will prosper*   [c]14 Hebrew *you*
[d]15 Hebrew; Septuagint *so will many nations marvel at him*   [a]8 Or *From arrest*
[b]8 Or *away. / Yet who of his generation considered / that he was cut off from the land of the living / for the transgression of my people,
/to whom the blow was due?*   [c]10 Hebrew *though you make*

he will see his offspring and prolong his days,
    and the will of the LORD will prosper in his
    hand.
[11]After the suffering of his soul,
    he will see the light ,of life,[d] and be satisfied;[e]
by his knowledge[f] my righteous servant will
    justify many,
    and he will bear their iniquities.
[12]Therefore I will give him a portion among the
    great,[g]
    and he will divide the spoils with the strong,[h]
because he poured out his life unto death,
    and was numbered with the transgressors.
For he bore the sin of many,
    and made intercession for the transgressors.

The Future Glory of Zion

54 "Sing, O barren woman,
    you who never bore a child;
burst into song, shout for joy,
    you who were never in labour;
because more are the children of the desolate
    woman
    than of her who has a husband,"
                          says the LORD.
[2]"Enlarge the place of your tent,
    stretch your tent curtains wide,
    do not hold back;
lengthen your cords,
    strengthen your stakes.
[3]For you will spread out to the right and to the
    left;
    your descendants will dispossess nations
    and settle in their desolate cities.

[4]"Do not be afraid; you will not suffer shame.
    Do not fear disgrace; you will not be
    humiliated.
You will forget the shame of your youth
    and remember no more the reproach of your
    widowhood.
[5]For your Maker is your husband—
    the LORD Almighty is his name—
the Holy One of Israel is your Redeemer;
    he is called the God of all the earth.
[6]The LORD will call you back
    as if you were a wife deserted and distressed in
    spirit—
a wife who married young,
    only to be rejected," says your God.
[7]"For a brief moment I abandoned you,
    but with deep compassion I will bring you back.
[8]In a surge of anger
    I hid my face from you for a moment,
but with everlasting kindness
    I will have compassion on you,"
    says the LORD your Redeemer.

[9]"To me this is like the days of Noah,
    when I swore that the waters of Noah would
    never again cover the earth.

So now I have sworn not to be angry with you,
    never to rebuke you again.
[10]Though the mountains be shaken
    and the hills be removed,
yet my unfailing love for you will not be shaken
    nor my covenant of peace be removed,"
    says the LORD, who has compassion on you.

54:11   This description of the newly rebuilt Jerusalem may well have inspired the writer of Revelation (see 21:15–21). It is picture language, but seems to refer to something beyond the actual place the exiles would return to. This ideal city will be characterized by justice and righteousness.

---

[11]"O afflicted city, lashed by storms and not
    comforted,
    I will build you with stones of turquoise,[a]
    your foundations with sapphires.[b]
[12]I will make your battlements of rubies,
    your gates of sparkling jewels,
    and all your walls of precious stones.
[13]All your sons will be taught by the LORD,
    and great will be your children's peace.
[14]In righteousness you will be established:
Tyranny will be far from you;
    you will have nothing to fear.
Terror will be far removed;
    it will not come near you.
[15]If anyone does attack you, it will not be my
    doing;
    whoever attacks you will surrender to you.

[16]"See, it is I who created the blacksmith
    who fans the coals into flame
    and forges a weapon fit for its work.
And it is I who have created the destroyer to
    work havoc;
[17] no weapon forged against you will prevail,
    and you will refute every tongue that accuses
    you.
This is the heritage of the servants of the LORD,
    and this is their vindication from me,"
                        declares the LORD.

Invitation to the Thirsty

55 "Come, all you who are thirsty,
    come to the waters;
and you who have no money,
    come, buy and eat!
Come, buy wine and milk
    without money and without cost.
[2]Why spend money on what is not bread,
    and your labour on what does not satisfy?
Listen, listen to me, and eat what is good,
    and your soul will delight in the richest of fare.
[3]Give ear and come to me;
    hear me, that your soul may live.

---

[d]11 Dead Sea Scrolls (see also Septuagint); Masoretic Text does not have the light ,of life,.
[e]11 Or (with Masoretic Text) [11]He will see the result of the suffering of his soul / and be satisfied   [f]11 Or by knowledge of him
[g]12 Or many   [h]12 Or numerous   [a]11 The meaning of the Hebrew for this word is uncertain.
[b]11 Or lapis lazuli

I will make an everlasting covenant with you,
my faithful love promised to David.
4See, I have made him a witness to the peoples,
a leader and commander of the peoples.
5Surely you will summon nations you know not,
and nations that do not know you will hasten to you,
because of the LORD your God,
the Holy One of Israel,
for he has endowed you with splendour."

6Seek the LORD while he may be found;
call on him while he is near.
7Let the wicked forsake his way
and the evil man his thoughts.
Let him turn to the LORD, and he will have mercy on him,
and to our God, for he will freely pardon.

55:6 The prophet has summarized chapters 40—55, and called the exiles to attention by telling them to enter into God's promises while there was the opportunity. If they repented and turned back to God and his ways they would be ready to return to the promised land.

8"For my thoughts are not your thoughts,
neither are your ways my ways,"
declares the LORD.
9"As the heavens are higher than the earth,
so are my ways higher than your ways
and my thoughts than your thoughts.
10As the rain and the snow
come down from heaven,
and do not return to it
without watering the earth
and making it bud and flourish,
so that it yields seed for the sower and bread for the eater,
11so is my word that goes out from my mouth:
It will not return to me empty,
but will accomplish what I desire
and achieve the purpose for which I sent it.
12You will go out in joy
and be led forth in peace;
the mountains and hills
will burst into song before you,
and all the trees of the field
will clap their hands.
13Instead of the thornbush will grow the pine tree,
and instead of briers the myrtle will grow.
This will be for the LORD's renown,
for an everlasting sign,
which will not be destroyed."

Salvation for Others

56 This is what the LORD says:

"Maintain justice
and do what is right,
for my salvation is close at hand
and my righteousness will soon be revealed.
2Blessed is the man who does this,
the man who holds it fast,
who keeps the Sabbath without desecrating it,
and keeps his hand from doing any evil."

3Let no foreigner who has bound himself to the LORD say,
"The LORD will surely exclude me from his people."
And let not any eunuch complain,
"I am only a dry tree."

4For this is what the LORD says:

"To the eunuchs who keep my Sabbaths,
who choose what pleases me
and hold fast to my covenant—
5to them I will give within my temple and its walls
a memorial and a name
better than sons and daughters;
I will give them an everlasting name
that will not be cut off.
6And foreigners who bind themselves to the LORD
to serve him,
to love the name of the LORD,
and to worship him,
all who keep the Sabbath without desecrating it
and who hold fast to my covenant—
7these I will bring to my holy mountain
and give them joy in my house of prayer.
Their burnt offerings and sacrifices
will be accepted on my altar;
for my house will be called
a house of prayer for all nations."
8The Sovereign LORD declares—
he who gathers the exiles of Israel:
"I will gather still others to them
besides those already gathered."

56:10 Judah's spiritual leadership had been one of the root causes of all its problems and suffering. The priests had been corrupt, selfish, and materialistic, and had failed completely to fulfil what God had required of them. Instead of speaking the truth they had uttered empty promises.

God's Accusation Against the Wicked

9Come, all you beasts of the field,
come and devour, all you beasts of the forest!
10Israel's watchmen are blind,
they all lack knowledge;
they are all mute dogs,
they cannot bark;
they lie around and dream,
they love to sleep.
11They are dogs with mighty appetites;
they never have enough.
They are shepherds who lack understanding;
they all turn to their own way,
each seeks his own gain.

12"Come," each one cries, "let me get wine!
  Let us drink our fill of beer!
And tomorrow will be like today,
  or even far better."

57 The righteous perish,
       and no-one ponders it in his heart;
  devout men are taken away,
    and no-one understands
  that the righteous are taken away
    to be spared from evil.
2Those who walk uprightly
    enter into peace;
  they find rest as they lie in death.

3"But you—come here, you sons of a sorceress,
    you offspring of adulterers and prostitutes!
4Whom are you mocking?
  At whom do you sneer
    and stick out your tongue?
  Are you not a brood of rebels,
    the offspring of liars?
5You burn with lust among the oaks
    and under every spreading tree;
  you sacrifice your children in the ravines
    and under the overhanging crags.
6The idols among the smooth stones of the
        ravines are your portion;
  they, they are your lot.
  Yes, to them you have poured out drink offerings
    and offered grain offerings.
  In the light of these things, should I relent?
7You have made your bed on a high and lofty hill;
    there you went up to offer your sacrifices.
8Behind your doors and your doorposts
    you have put your pagan symbols.
  Forsaking me, you uncovered your bed,
    you climbed into it and opened it wide;
  you made a pact with those whose beds you love,
    and you looked on their nakedness.
9You went to Molech[a] with olive oil
    and increased your perfumes.
  You sent your ambassadors[b] far away;
    you descended to the grave[c] itself!
10You were wearied by all your ways,
    but you would not say, 'It is hopeless.'
  You found renewal of your strength,
    and so you did not faint.

11"Whom have you so dreaded and feared
    that you have been false to me,
  and have neither remembered me
    nor pondered this in your hearts?
  Is it not because I have long been silent
    that you do not fear me?
12I will expose your righteousness and your works,
    and they will not benefit you.
13When you cry out for help,
    let your collection of idols save you!
  The wind will carry all of them off,
    a mere breath will blow them away.

But the man who makes me his refuge
  will inherit the land
  and possess my holy mountain."

Comfort for the Contrite

14And it will be said:

"Build up, build up, prepare the road!
  Remove the obstacles out of the way of my
      people."
15For this is what the high and lofty One says—
  he who lives for ever, whose name is holy:
"I live in a high and holy place,
  but also with him who is contrite and lowly in
      spirit,
to revive the spirit of the lowly
  and to revive the heart of the contrite.
16I will not accuse for ever,
  nor will I always be angry,
for then the spirit of man would grow faint before
      me—
  the breath of man that I have created.
17I was enraged by his sinful greed;
  I punished him, and hid my face in anger,
  yet he kept on in his wilful ways.
18I have seen his ways, but I will heal him;
  I will guide him and restore comfort to him,
19 creating praise on the lips of the mourners in
      Israel.
Peace, peace, to those far and near,"
  says the LORD. "And I will heal them."
20But the wicked are like the tossing sea,
  which cannot rest,
  whose waves cast up mire and mud.
21"There is no peace," says my God, "for the
      wicked."

True Fasting

58 "Shout it aloud, do not hold back.
       Raise your voice like a trumpet.
  Declare to my people their rebellion
    and to the house of Jacob their sins.
2For day after day they seek me out;
    they seem eager to know my ways,
  as if they were a nation that does what is right
    and has not forsaken the commands of its God.
  They ask me for just decisions
    and seem eager for God to come near them.
3'Why have we fasted,' they say,
    'and you have not seen it?
  Why have we humbled ourselves,
    and you have not noticed?'

"Yet on the day of your fasting, you do as you
      please
  and exploit all your workers.
4Your fasting ends in quarrelling and strife,
    and in striking each other with wicked fists.
  You cannot fast as you do today
    and expect your voice to be heard on high.
5Is this the kind of fast I have chosen,
    only a day for a man to humble himself?

a9 Or to the king   b9 Or idols   c9 Hebrew Sheol

Is it only for bowing one's head like a reed
    and for lying on sackcloth and ashes?
Is that what you call a fast,
    a day acceptable to the LORD?

[6]"Is not this the kind of fasting I have chosen:
    to loose the chains of injustice
    and untie the cords of the yoke,
to set the oppressed free
    and break every yoke?
[7]Is it not to share your food with the hungry
    and to provide the poor wanderer with
        shelter—
when you see the naked, to clothe him,
    and not to turn away from your own flesh and
        blood?
[8]Then your light will break forth like the dawn,
    and your healing will quickly appear;
then your righteousness[a] will go before you,
    and the glory of the LORD will be your rear
        guard.
[9]Then you will call, and the LORD will answer;
    you will cry for help, and he will say: Here am I.

"If you do away with the yoke of oppression,
    with the pointing finger and malicious talk,
[10]and if you spend yourselves on behalf of the
        hungry
    and satisfy the needs of the oppressed,
then your light will rise in the darkness,
    and your night will become like the noonday.
[11]The LORD will guide you always;
    he will satisfy your needs in a sun-scorched land
    and will strengthen your frame.
You will be like a well-watered garden,
    like a spring whose waters never fail.
[12]Your people will rebuild the ancient ruins
    and will raise up the age-old foundations;
you will be called Repairer of Broken Walls,
    Restorer of Streets with Dwellings.

58:12   The exiles were to return home
and start to make the land and city inhabita-
ble. But they needed to do more than rebuild
walls. According to God's laws the whole of
society must be rebuilt, and previous evil
practices must be renounced and put aside.

---

[13]"If you keep your feet from breaking the Sabbath
    and from doing as you please on my holy day,
if you call the Sabbath a delight
    and the LORD's holy day honourable,
and if you honour it by not going your own way
    and not doing as you please or speaking idle
        words,
[14]then you will find your joy in the LORD,
    and I will cause you to ride on the heights of
        the land
    and to feast on the inheritance of your father
        Jacob."
        The mouth of the LORD has spoken.

[a] 8 Or *your righteous One*

Sin, Confession and Redemption

59 Surely the arm of the LORD is not too
    short to save,
    nor his ear too dull to hear.
[2]But your iniquities have separated
    you from your God;
your sins have hidden his face from you,
    so that he will not hear.
[3]For your hands are stained with blood,
    your fingers with guilt.
Your lips have spoken lies,
    and your tongue mutters wicked things.
[4]No-one calls for justice;
    no-one pleads his case with integrity.
They rely on empty arguments and speak lies;
    they conceive trouble and give birth to evil.
[5]They hatch the eggs of vipers
    and spin a spider's web.
Whoever eats their eggs will die,
    and when one is broken, an adder is hatched.
[6]Their cobwebs are useless for clothing;
    they cannot cover themselves with what they
        make.
Their deeds are evil deeds,
    and acts of violence are in their hands.
[7]Their feet rush into sin;
    they are swift to shed innocent blood.
Their thoughts are evil thoughts;
    ruin and destruction mark their ways.
[8]The way of peace they do not know;
    there is no justice in their paths.
They have turned them into crooked roads;
    no-one who walks in them will know
        peace.

[9]So justice is far from us,
    and righteousness does not reach us.
We look for light, but all is darkness;
    for brightness, but we walk in deep shadows.
[10]Like the blind we grope along the wall,
    feeling our way like men without eyes.
At midday we stumble as if it were twilight;
    among the strong, we are like the dead.
[11]We all growl like bears;
    we moan mournfully like doves.
We look for justice, but find none;
    for deliverance, but it is far away.

[12]For our offences are many in your sight,
    and our sins testify against us.
Our offences are ever with us,
    and we acknowledge our iniquities:
[13]rebellion and treachery against the LORD,
    turning our backs on our God,
fomenting oppression and revolt,
    uttering lies our hearts have conceived.
[14]So justice is driven back,
    and righteousness stands at a distance;
truth has stumbled in the streets,
    honesty cannot enter.
[15]Truth is nowhere to be found,
    and whoever shuns evil becomes a prey.

The LORD looked and was displeased
that there was no justice.

59:14   The law courts were in the public
squares. However, their prominence had not
prevented justice from falling apart. So God
dealt with the situation on his own initiative.
The images in verse 17 may have moved
Paul to write his famous passage about the
"full armour of God" (Ephesians 6:10–20).

16He saw that there was no-one,
he was appalled that there was no-one to
intervene;
so his own arm worked salvation for him,
and his own righteousness sustained him.
17He put on righteousness as his breastplate,
and the helmet of salvation on his head;
he put on the garments of vengeance
and wrapped himself in zeal as in a cloak.
18According to what they have done,
so will he repay
wrath to his enemies
and retribution to his foes;
he will repay the islands their due.
19From the west, men will fear the name of the LORD,
and from the rising of the sun, they will revere
his glory.
For he will come like a pent-up flood
that the breath of the LORD drives along.a

20"The Redeemer will come to Zion,
to those in Jacob who repent of their sins,"
declares the LORD.

21"As for me, this is my covenant with them," says
the LORD. "My Spirit, who is on you, and my words that
I have put in your mouth will not depart from your
mouth, or from the mouths of your children, or from
the mouths of their descendants from this time on and
for ever," says the LORD.

The Glory of Zion

60   "Arise, shine, for your light has come,
and the glory of the LORD rises upon you.
2See, darkness covers the earth
and thick darkness is over the peoples,
but the LORD rises upon you
and his glory appears over you.
3Nations will come to your light,
and kings to the brightness of your dawn.

4"Lift up your eyes and look about you:
All assemble and come to you;
your sons come from afar,
and your daughters are carried on the arm.
5Then you will look and be radiant,
your heart will throb and swell with joy;
the wealth on the seas will be brought to you,
to you the riches of the nations will come.
6Herds of camels will cover your land,
young camels of Midian and Ephah.

And all from Sheba will come,
bearing gold and incense
and proclaiming the praise of the LORD.
7All Kedar's flocks will be gathered to you,
the rams of Nebaioth will serve you;
they will be accepted as offerings on my altar,
and I will adorn my glorious temple.

8"Who are these that fly along like clouds,
like doves to their nests?
9Surely the islands look to me;
in the lead are the ships of Tarshish,a
bringing your sons from afar,
with their silver and gold,
to the honour of the LORD your God,
the Holy One of Israel,
for he has endowed you with splendour.

10"Foreigners will rebuild your walls,
and their kings will serve you.
Though in anger I struck you,
in favour I will show you compassion.
11Your gates will always stand open,
they will never be shut, day or night,
so that men may bring you the wealth of the
nations—
their kings led in triumphal procession.
12For the nation or kingdom that will not serve you
will perish;
it will be utterly ruined.

13"The glory of Lebanon will come to you,
the pine, the fir and the cypress together,
to adorn the place of my sanctuary;
and I will glorify the place of my feet.
14The sons of your oppressors will come bowing
before you;
all who despise you will bow down at your feet
and will call you the City of the LORD,
Zion of the Holy One of Israel.

15"Although you have been forsaken and hated,
with no-one travelling through,
I will make you the everlasting pride
and the joy of all generations.
16You will drink the milk of nations
and be nursed at royal breasts.
Then you will know that I, the LORD, am your
Saviour,
your Redeemer, the Mighty One of Jacob.
17Instead of bronze I will bring you gold,
and silver in place of iron.
Instead of wood I will bring you bronze,
and iron in place of stones.
I will make peace your governor
and righteousness your ruler.
18No longer will violence be heard in your land,
nor ruin or destruction within your borders,
but you will call your walls Salvation
and your gates Praise.
19The sun will no more be your light by day,
nor will the brightness of the moon shine on
you,

---

a19 Or When the enemy comes in like a flood, / the Spirit of the LORD will put him to flight   a9 Or the trading ships

for the LORD will be your everlasting light,
    and your God will be your glory.
²⁰Your sun will never set again,
    and your moon will wane no more;
the LORD will be your everlasting light,
    and your days of sorrow will end.
²¹Then will all your people be righteous
    and they will possess the land for ever.
They are the shoot I have planted,
    the work of my hands,
    for the display of my splendour.
²²The least of you will become a thousand,
    the smallest a mighty nation.
I am the LORD;
    in its time I will do this swiftly."

The Year of the LORD's Favour

61 The Spirit of the Sovereign LORD is on
me,
    because the LORD has anointed me
    to preach good news to the poor.
He has sent me to bind up the broken-hearted,
    to proclaim freedom for the captives
    and release from darkness for the prisoners,ᵃ
²to proclaim the year of the LORD's favour
    and the day of vengeance of our God,
to comfort all who mourn,
³ and provide for those who grieve in Zion—
to bestow on them a crown of beauty
    instead of ashes,
the oil of gladness
    instead of mourning,
and a garment of praise
    instead of a spirit of despair.
They will be called oaks of righteousness,
    a planting of the LORD
    for the display of his splendour.

61:1 This is not a Servant Song, but could be called a Servant Oracle. The "Spirit of the Lord" appears many times in these latter chapters of Isaiah. The mark of a prophet was that he was anointed for his ministry and recognized to have the Spirit of God on him. Jesus quoted these words in the synagogue at the outset of his ministry (Luke 4:18,19). He omitted "the day of vengeance of our God," (verse 2), because his mission was to bring peace and reconciliation.

---

⁴They will rebuild the ancient ruins
    and restore the places long devastated;
they will renew the ruined cities
    that have been devastated for generations.
⁵Aliens will shepherd your flocks;
    foreigners will work your fields and vineyards.
⁶And you will be called priests of the LORD,
    you will be named ministers of our God.

You will feed on the wealth of nations,
    and in their riches you will boast.
⁷Instead of their shame
    my people will receive a double portion,
and instead of disgrace
    they will rejoice in their inheritance;
and so they will inherit a double portion in their
        land,
    and everlasting joy will be theirs.

⁸"For I, the LORD, love justice;
    I hate robbery and iniquity.
In my faithfulness I will reward them
    and make an everlasting covenant with them.
⁹Their descendants will be known among the
        nations
    and their offspring among the peoples.
All who see them will acknowledge
    that they are a people the LORD has blessed."

¹⁰I delight greatly in the LORD;
    my soul rejoices in my God.
For he has clothed me with garments of salvation
    and arrayed me in a robe of righteousness,
as a bridegroom adorns his head like a priest,
    and as a bride adorns herself with her jewels.
¹¹For as the soil makes the young plant come up
    and a garden causes seeds to grow,
so the Sovereign LORD will make righteousness
        and praise
    spring up before all nations.

Zion's New Name

62 For Zion's sake I will not keep silent,
    for Jerusalem's sake I will not remain
        quiet,
till her righteousness shines out like the dawn,
    her salvation like a blazing torch.
²The nations will see your righteousness,
    and all kings your glory;
you will be called by a new name
    that the mouth of the LORD will bestow.
³You will be a crown of splendour in the LORD's
        hand,
    a royal diadem in the hand of your God.
⁴No longer will they call you Deserted,
    or name your land Desolate.
But you will be called Hephzibah,ᵃ
    and your land Beulah;ᵇ
for the LORD will take delight in you,
    and your land will be married.
⁵As a young man marries a maiden,
    so will your sonsᶜ marry you;
as a bridegroom rejoices over his bride,
    so will your God rejoice over you.

⁶I have posted watchmen on your walls,
    O Jerusalem;
they will never be silent day or night.
You who call on the LORD,
    give yourselves no rest,

ᵃ1 Hebrew; Septuagint *the blind*   ᵃ4 Hephzibah means *my delight is in her.*   ᵇ4 Beulah means *married.*
ᶜ5 Or *Builder*

7and give him no rest till he establishes Jerusalem
  and makes her the praise of the earth.

8The LORD has sworn by his right hand
  and by his mighty arm:
"Never again will I give your grain
  as food for your enemies,
and never again will foreigners drink the new
  wine
for which you have toiled;
9but those who harvest it will eat it
  and praise the LORD,
and those who gather the grapes will drink it
  in the courts of my sanctuary."

10Pass through, pass through the gates!
  Prepare the way for the people.
Build up, build up the highway!
  Remove the stones.
Raise a banner for the nations.

11The LORD has made proclamation
  to the ends of the earth:
"Say to the Daughter of Zion,
  'See, your Saviour comes!
See, his reward is with him,
  and his recompense accompanies him.' "
12They will be called the Holy People,
  the Redeemed of the LORD;
and you will be called Sought After,
  the City No Longer Deserted.

God's Day of Vengeance and Redemption

63 Who is this coming from Edom,
  from Bozrah, with his garments stained
  crimson?
Who is this, robed in splendour,
  striding forward in the greatness of his
  strength?

"It is I, speaking in righteousness,
  mighty to save."

2Why are your garments red,
  like those of one treading the winepress?

3"I have trodden the winepress alone;
  from the nations no-one was with me.
I trampled them in my anger
  and trod them down in my wrath;
their blood spattered my garments,
  and I stained all my clothing.
4For the day of vengeance was in my heart,
  and the year of my redemption has come.
5I looked, but there was no-one to help,
  I was appalled that no-one gave support;
so my own arm worked salvation for me,
  and my own wrath sustained me.
6I trampled the nations in my anger;
  in my wrath I made them drunk
and poured their blood on the ground."

Praise and Prayer

7I will tell of the kindnesses of the LORD,
  the deeds for which he is to be praised,
  according to all the LORD has done for us—
yes, the many good things he has done
  for the house of Israel,
  according to his compassion and many
  kindnesses.
8He said, "Surely they are my people,
  sons who will not be false to me";
  and so he became their Saviour.
9In all their distress he too was distressed,
  and the angel of his presence saved them.
In his love and mercy he redeemed them;
  he lifted them up and carried them
  all the days of old.
10Yet they rebelled
  and grieved his Holy Spirit.
So he turned and became their enemy
  and he himself fought against them.

63:7 The prophet recounted all God's mighty acts of the past. The Jews could hardly be blamed for wondering if God had forgotten them. Could he still be trusted? Was the covenant still worth anything? Had he totally abandoned them? This oracle set the record straight. God had never yet broken his promises, and would not do so now.

11Then his people recalled[a] the days of old,
  the days of Moses and his people—
where is he who brought them through the sea,
  with the shepherd of his flock?
Where is he who set
  his Holy Spirit among them,
12who sent his glorious arm of power
  to be at Moses' right hand,
who divided the waters before them,
  to gain for himself everlasting renown,
13who led them through the depths?
Like a horse in open country,
  they did not stumble;
14like cattle that go down to the plain,
  they were given rest by the Spirit of the LORD.
This is how you guided your people
  to make for yourself a glorious name.

15Look down from heaven and see
  from your lofty throne, holy and glorious.
Where are your zeal and your might?
  Your tenderness and compassion are withheld
  from us.
16But you are our Father,
  though Abraham does not know us
  or Israel acknowledge us;
you, O LORD, are our Father,
  our Redeemer from of old is your name.
17Why, O LORD, do you make us wander from your
  ways
  and harden our hearts so we do not revere you?

a 11 Or But may he recall

Return for the sake of your servants,
  the tribes that are your inheritance.
¹⁸For a little while your people possessed your holy
    place,
  but now our enemies have trampled down your
    sanctuary.
¹⁹We are yours from of old;
  but you have not ruled over them,
  they have not been called by your name.ᵇ

64 Oh, that you would rend the heavens and
    come down,
  that the mountains would tremble before you!
²As when fire sets twigs ablaze
  and causes water to boil,
  come down to make your name known to your
    enemies
  and cause the nations to quake before you!
³For when you did awesome things that we did
    not expect,
  you came down, and the mountains trembled
    before you.
⁴Since ancient times no-one has heard,
  no ear has perceived,
  no eye has seen any God besides you,
  who acts on behalf of those who wait for
    him.
⁵You come to the help of those who gladly do
    right,
  who remember your ways.
  But when we continued to sin against them,
  you were angry.
  How then can we be saved?
⁶All of us have become like one who is unclean,
  and all our righteous acts are like filthy
    rags;
  we all shrivel up like a leaf,
  and like the wind our sins sweep us away.
⁷No-one calls on your name
  or strives to lay hold of you;
  for you have hidden your face from us
  and made us waste away because of our
    sins.

⁸Yet, O LORD, you are our Father.
  We are the clay, you are the potter;
  we are all the work of your hand.
⁹Do not be angry beyond measure, O LORD;
  do not remember our sins for ever.
  Oh, look upon us we pray,
  for we are all your people.
¹⁰Your sacred cities have become a desert;
  even Zion is a desert, Jerusalem a desolation.
¹¹Our holy and glorious temple, where our fathers
    praised you,
  has been burned with fire,
  and all that we treasured lies in ruins.
¹²After all this, O LORD, will you hold yourself
    back?
  Will you keep silent and punish us beyond
    measure?

Judgment and Salvation

65 "I revealed myself to those who did not
    ask for me;
  I was found by those who did not seek me.
  To a nation that did not call on my name,
  I said, 'Here am I, here am I.'
²All day long I have held out my hands
  to an obstinate people,
  who walk in ways not good,
  pursuing their own imaginations—
³a people who continually provoke me
  to my very face,
  offering sacrifices in gardens
  and burning incense on altars of brick;
⁴who sit among the graves
  and spend their nights keeping secret vigil;
  who eat the flesh of pigs,
  and whose pots hold broth of unclean meat;
⁵who say, 'Keep away; don't come near me,
  for I am too sacred for you!'
  Such people are smoke in my nostrils,
  a fire that keeps burning all day.

⁶"See, it stands written before me;
  I will not keep silent but will pay back in full;
  I will pay it back into their laps—
⁷both your sins and the sins of your fathers,"
    says the LORD.
  "Because they burned sacrifices on the mountains
  and defied me on the hills,
  I will measure into their laps
  the full payment for their former deeds."

⁸This is what the LORD says:

"As when juice is still found in a cluster of grapes
  and men say, 'Don't destroy it,
  there is yet some good in it,'
  so will I do on behalf of my servants;
  I will not destroy them all.
⁹I will bring forth descendants from Jacob,
  and from Judah those who will possess my
    mountains;
  my chosen people will inherit them,
  and there will my servants live.
¹⁰Sharon will become a pasture for flocks,
  and the Valley of Achor a resting place for
    herds,
  for my people who seek me.

¹¹"But as for you who forsake the LORD
  and forget my holy mountain,
  who spread a table for Fortune
  and fill bowls of mixed wine for Destiny,
¹²I will destine you for the sword,
  and you will all bend down for the slaughter;
  for I called but you did not answer,
  I spoke but you did not listen.
  You did evil in my sight
  and chose what displeases me."

¹³Therefore this is what the Sovereign LORD says:

"My servants will eat,
  but you will go hungry;

ᵇ19 Or *We are like those you have never ruled, / like those never called by your name*

my servants will drink,
  but you will go thirsty;
my servants will rejoice,
  but you will be put to shame.
¹⁴My servants will sing
  out of the joy of their hearts,
but you will cry out
  from anguish of heart
  and wail in brokenness of spirit.
¹⁵You will leave your name
  to my chosen ones as a curse;
the Sovereign LORD will put you to death,
  but to his servants he will give another name.
¹⁶Whoever invokes a blessing in the land
  will do so by the God of truth;
he who takes an oath in the land
  will swear by the God of truth.
For the past troubles will be forgotten
  and hidden from my eyes.

New Heavens and a New Earth

¹⁷"Behold, I will create
  new heavens and a new earth.
The former things will not be remembered,
  nor will they come to mind.
¹⁸But be glad and rejoice for ever
  in what I will create,
for I will create Jerusalem to be a delight
  and its people a joy.
¹⁹I will rejoice over Jerusalem
  and take delight in my people;
the sound of weeping and of crying
  will be heard in it no more.

65:18 The new Jerusalem will be more than just a city. It represents a whole new order, and is a vision of what God will ultimately bring about. Long life was a special sign of God's favour to the Jews, and it will be perfectly normal, as will be the prosperity of the land. Even absolute enemies will be at peace (verse 25).

---

²⁰"Never again will there be in it
  an infant who lives but a few days,
  or an old man who does not live out his years;
he who dies at a hundred
  will be thought a mere youth;
he who fails to reach ᵃ a hundred
  will be considered accursed.
²¹They will build houses and dwell in them;
  they will plant vineyards and eat their fruit.
²²No longer will they build houses and others live
      in them,
  or plant and others eat.
For as the days of a tree,
  so will be the days of my people;
my chosen ones will long enjoy
  the works of their hands.

ᵃ20 Or / the sinner who reaches

²³They will not toil in vain
  or bear children doomed to misfortune;
for they will be a people blessed by the LORD,
  they and their descendants with them.
²⁴Before they call I will answer;
  while they are still speaking I will hear.
²⁵The wolf and the lamb will feed together,
  and the lion will eat straw like the ox,
  but dust will be the serpent's food.
They will neither harm nor destroy
  on all my holy mountain,"
                              says the LORD.

Judgment and Hope

66 This is what the LORD says:

"Heaven is my throne,
  and the earth is my footstool.
Where is the house you will build for me?
  Where will my resting place be?
²Has not my hand made all these things,
  and so they came into being?"
                              declares the LORD.

"This is the one I esteem:
  he who is humble and contrite in spirit,
  and trembles at my word.
³But whoever sacrifices a bull
  is like one who kills a man,
and whoever offers a lamb,
  like one who breaks a dog's neck;
whoever makes a grain offering
  is like one who presents pig's blood,
and whoever burns memorial incense,
  like one who worships an idol.
They have chosen their own ways,
  and their souls delight in their abominations;
⁴so I also will choose harsh treatment for them
  and will bring upon them what they dread.
For when I called, no-one answered,
  when I spoke, no-one listened.
They did evil in my sight
  and chose what displeases me."

⁵Hear the word of the LORD,
  you who tremble at his word;
"Your brothers who hate you,
  and exclude you because of my name, have
      said,
'Let the LORD be glorified,
  that we may see your joy!'
Yet they will be put to shame.
⁶Hear that uproar from the city,
  hear that noise from the temple!
It is the sound of the LORD
  repaying his enemies all they deserve.

⁷"Before she goes into labour,
  she gives birth;
before the pains come upon her,
  she delivers a son.
⁸Who has ever heard of such a thing?
  Who has ever seen such things?

Can a country be born in a day
or a nation be brought forth in a moment?
Yet no sooner is Zion in labour
than she gives birth to her children.
⁹Do I bring to the moment of birth
and not give delivery?" says the Lord.
"Do I close up the womb
when I bring to delivery?" says your God.
¹⁰"Rejoice with Jerusalem and be glad for her,
all you who love her;
rejoice greatly with her,
all you who mourn over her.
¹¹For you will nurse and be satisfied
at her comforting breasts;
you will drink deeply
and delight in her overflowing abundance."

¹²For this is what the Lord says:

"I will extend peace to her like a river,
and the wealth of nations like a flooding stream;
you will nurse and be carried on her arm
and dandled on her knees.
¹³As a mother comforts her child,
so will I comfort you;
and you will be comforted over Jerusalem."

¹⁴When you see this, your heart will rejoice
and you will flourish like grass;
the hand of the Lord will be made known to his
servants,
but his fury will be shown to his foes.
¹⁵See, the Lord is coming with fire,
and his chariots are like a whirlwind;
he will bring down his anger with fury,
and his rebuke with flames of fire.

¹⁶For with fire and with his sword
the Lord will execute judgment upon all men,
and many will be those slain by the Lord.

¹⁷"Those who consecrate and purify themselves to go into the gardens, following the one in the midst of[a] those who eat the flesh of pigs and rats and other abominable things—they will meet their end together," declares the Lord.

¹⁸"And I, because of their actions and their imaginations, am about to come[b] and gather all nations and tongues, and they will come and see my glory.

¹⁹"I will set a sign among them, and I will send some of those who survive to the nations—to Tarshish, to the Libyans[c] and Lydians (famous as archers), to Tubal and Greece, and to the distant islands that have not heard of my fame or seen my glory. They will proclaim my glory among the nations. ²⁰And they will bring all your brothers, from all the nations, to my holy mountain in Jerusalem as an offering to the Lord—on horses, in chariots and wagons, and on mules and camels," says the Lord. "They will bring them, as the Israelites bring their grain offerings, to the temple of the Lord in ceremonially clean vessels. ²¹And I will select some of them also to be priests and Levites," says the Lord.

²²"As the new heavens and the new earth that I make will endure before me," declares the Lord, "so will your name and descendants endure. ²³From one New Moon to another and from one Sabbath to another, all mankind will come and bow down before me," says the Lord. ²⁴"And they will go out and look upon the dead bodies of those who rebelled against me; their worm will not die, nor will their fire be quenched, and they will be loathsome to all mankind."

a17 Or gardens behind one of your temples, and   b18 The meaning of the Hebrew for this clause is uncertain.
c19 Some Septuagint manuscripts Put (Libyans); Hebrew Pul

Jeremiah

A Fascinating Character

Jeremiah is probably one of the most fascinating of all the Hebrew prophets. He was active during a particularly eventful period in the history of God's people: his ministry spanned the reign of no fewer than five different kings; it included the time when Daniel and Ezekiel were taken captive; and ended with the fall of Jerusalem to the Babylonians in 586 BC. 2 Kings 23—25 and 2 Chronicles 34—36 provide the historical background to Jeremiah's ministry, and help put many of his prophecies into some sort of context.

Calling the Reluctant

Like the other prophets, Jeremiah's ministry began with a call from God. Like Isaiah, he expressed his reluctance to be a prophet and his unworthiness for the task. This initial expression of doubt is important, because throughout his ministry, Jeremiah showed many signs of insecurity, of being ignored and misunderstood. In fact, by today's standards of job efficiency, Jeremiah was a complete failure.

Words Which Fell on Deaf Ears

He spoke perceptively about the events of his day, but no one listened. He predicted catastrophic events for Judah and Jerusalem, but he was ridiculed and isolated. He spoke out against the nation's rulers who had rejected God's laws, and they imprisoned him and burned his writings. The reader can gain a marvellous insight into Jeremiah's feelings as he protested against God and was offered no respite, just a simple promise that God would stand by him.

Destruction of Our Own Making

Jeremiah offers us a superb example of what it means to keep going against all the odds, to believe that what you are doing and what you are saying—despite the unpopularity of it all—is God's will for you and his people. Jeremiah was quite clear that the sins of individuals and communities were at the heart of Judah's downfall, and he made no bones about the sort of punishment that would befall those who had rejected God's law. In a long series of oracles, which dated from different periods of his ministry, he proclaimed God's sovereignty over the world, and called the people to renew their faithfulness to God; if they did not, then they should expect the worst to happen.

Prophecies Fulfilled

Jeremiah began his ministry during the reign of King Josiah (about 627 BC). The king had tried to introduce reform of Judah's political and religious life, but it failed because the people rejected God. Jeremiah's ministry ended with a graphic fulfilment of all the destruction and disaster that he had prophesied would take place if the people continued to reject God. It may sound very harsh, but the lesson is quite simple: if we continue to ignore what is in front of our own eyes, if we refuse to face up to our responsibilities, the problem gets bigger. Recognizing our need of God and our responsibility to his commands is the starting point to renewing our lives, our homes, and our communities.

---

1 The words of Jeremiah son of Hilkiah, one of the priests at Anathoth in the territory of Benjamin. ²The word of the Lᴏʀᴅ came to him in the thirteenth year of the reign of Josiah son of Amon king of Judah, ³and through the reign of Jehoiakim son of Josiah king of Judah, down to the fifth month of the eleventh year of Zedekiah son of Josiah king of Judah, when the people of Jerusalem went into exile.

The Call of Jeremiah

⁴The word of the Lᴏʀᴅ came to me, saying,

1:4 Like Amos, Hosea, Ezekiel, and Isaiah, Jeremiah began his ministry with a call from God. Despite his own feelings of unworthiness, Jeremiah could not turn away from the task that God was calling him to. Human weakness is the starting place that God chooses again and again.

---

⁵"Before I formed you in the womb I knew*ᵃ* you,
    before you were born I set you apart;
    I appointed you as a prophet to the nations."

⁶"Ah, Sovereign Lᴏʀᴅ," I said, "I do not know how to speak; I am only a child." ⁷But the Lᴏʀᴅ said to me, "Do not say, 'I am only a child.' You must go to everyone I send you to and say whatever I command you. ⁸Do not be afraid of them, for I am with you and will rescue you," declares the Lᴏʀᴅ.

⁹Then the Lᴏʀᴅ reached out his hand and touched my mouth and said to me, "Now, I have put my words in your mouth. ¹⁰See, today I appoint you over nations and kingdoms to uproot and tear down, to destroy and overthrow, to build and to plant."

¹¹The word of the Lᴏʀᴅ came to me: "What do you see, Jeremiah?"

"I see the branch of an almond tree," I replied.

¹²The Lᴏʀᴅ said to me, "You have seen correctly, for I am watching*ᵇ* to see that my word is fulfilled."

¹³The word of the Lᴏʀᴅ came to me again: "What do you see?"

"I see a boiling pot, tilting away from the north," I answered.

¹⁴The Lᴏʀᴅ said to me, "From the north disaster will be poured out on all who live in the land. ¹⁵I am about to summon all the peoples of the northern kingdoms," declares the Lᴏʀᴅ.

"Their kings will come and set up their thrones
    in the entrance of the gates of Jerusalem;
they will come against all her surrounding walls
    and against all the towns of Judah.
¹⁶I will pronounce my judgments on my people
    because of their wickedness in forsaking me,
in burning incense to other gods
    and in worshipping what their hands have
        made.

¹⁷"Get yourself ready! Stand up and say to them whatever I command you. Do not be terrified by them, or I will terrify you before them. ¹⁸Today I have made you a fortified city, an iron pillar and a bronze wall to stand against the whole land—against the kings of Judah, its officials, its priests and the people of the land. ¹⁹They will fight against you but will not overcome you, for I am with you and will rescue you," declares the Lᴏʀᴅ.

Israel Forsakes God

2 The word of the Lᴏʀᴅ came to me: ²"Go and proclaim in the hearing of Jerusalem:

" 'I remember the devotion of your youth,
    how as a bride you loved me
and followed me through the desert,
    through a land not sown.
³Israel was holy to the Lᴏʀᴅ,
    the firstfruits of his harvest;
all who devoured her were held guilty,
    and disaster overtook them,' "
                                    declares the Lᴏʀᴅ.

⁴Hear the word of the Lᴏʀᴅ, O house of Jacob,
    all you clans of the house of Israel.

⁵This is what the Lᴏʀᴅ says:

"What fault did your fathers find in me,
    that they strayed so far from me?
They followed worthless idols
    and became worthless themselves.
⁶They did not ask, 'Where is the Lᴏʀᴅ,
    who brought us up out of Egypt
and led us through the barren wilderness,
    through a land of deserts and rifts,

ᵃ5 Or *chose*   *ᵇ12* The Hebrew for *watching* sounds like the Hebrew for *almond tree.*

a land of drought and darkness,[a]
a land where no-one travels and no-one lives?'
[7]I brought you into a fertile land
to eat its fruit and rich produce.
But you came and defiled my land
and made my inheritance detestable.
[8]The priests did not ask,
'Where is the LORD?'
Those who deal with the law did not know me;
the leaders rebelled against me.
The prophets prophesied by Baal,
following worthless idols.

[9]"Therefore I bring charges against you again,"
declares the LORD.
"And I will bring charges against your children's
children.
[10]Cross over to the coasts of Kittim[b] and look,
send to Kedar[c] and observe closely;
see if there has ever been anything like this:
[11]Has a nation ever changed its gods?
(Yet they are not gods at all.)
But my people have exchanged their[d] Glory
for worthless idols.
[12]Be appalled at this, O heavens,
and shudder with great horror,"
declares the LORD.
[13]"My people have committed two sins:
They have forsaken me,
the spring of living water,
and have dug their own cisterns,
broken cisterns that cannot hold water.
[14]Is Israel a servant, a slave by birth?
Why then has he become plunder?
[15]Lions have roared;
they have growled at him.
They have laid waste his land;
his towns are burned and deserted.
[16]Also, the men of Memphis[e] and Tahpanhes
have shaved the crown of your head.[f]
[17]Have you not brought this on yourselves
by forsaking the LORD your God
when he led you in the way?
[18]Now why go to Egypt
to drink water from the Shihor?[g]
And why go to Assyria
to drink water from the River?[h]
[19]Your wickedness will punish you;
your backsliding will rebuke you.
Consider then and realise
how evil and bitter it is for you
when you forsake the LORD your God
and have no awe of me,"
declares the Lord, the LORD Almighty.

[20]"Long ago you broke off your yoke
and tore off your bonds;
you said, 'I will not serve you!'
Indeed, on every high hill
and under every spreading tree
you lay down as a prostitute.

[21]I had planted you like a choice vine
of sound and reliable stock.
How then did you turn against me
into a corrupt, wild vine?
[22]Although you wash yourself with soda
and use an abundance of soap,
the stain of your guilt is still before me,"
declares the Sovereign LORD.
[23]"How can you say, 'I am not defiled;
I have not run after the Baals'?
See how you behaved in the valley;
consider what you have done.
You are a swift she-camel
running here and there,
[24]a wild donkey accustomed to the desert,
sniffing the wind in her craving—
in her heat who can restrain her?
Any males that pursue her need not tire
themselves;
at mating time they will find her.
[25]Do not run until your feet are bare
and your throat is dry.
But you said, 'It's no use!
I love foreign gods,
and I must go after them.'

[26]"As a thief is disgraced when he is caught,
so the house of Israel is disgraced—
they, their kings and their officials,
their priests and their prophets.
[27]They say to wood, 'You are my father,'
and to stone, 'You gave me birth.'
They have turned their backs to me
and not their faces;
yet when they are in trouble, they say,
'Come and save us!'
[28]Where then are the gods you made for
yourselves?
Let them come if they can save you
when you are in trouble!
For you have as many gods
as you have towns, O Judah.

[29]"Why do you bring charges against me?
You have all rebelled against me,"
declares the LORD.
[30]"In vain I punished your people;
they did not respond to correction.
Your sword has devoured your prophets
like a ravening lion.

[31]"You of this generation, consider the word of the
LORD:

"Have I been a desert to Israel
or a land of great darkness?
Why do my people say, 'We are free to roam;
we will come to you no more'?
[32]Does a maiden forget her jewellery,
a bride her wedding ornaments?
Yet my people have forgotten me,
days without number.

---

[a]6 Or and the shadow of death   [b]10 That is, Cyprus and western coastlands
[c]10 The home of Bedouin tribes in the Syro-Arabian desert   [d]11 Masoretic Text; an ancient Hebrew scribal tradition my
[e]16 Hebrew Noph   [f]16 Or have cracked your skull   [g]18 That is, a branch of the Nile   [h]18 That is, the Euphrates

33How skilled you are at pursuing love!
  Even the worst of women can learn from your
    ways.
34On your clothes men find
  the lifeblood of the innocent poor,
  though you did not catch them breaking in.
  Yet in spite of all this
35 you say, 'I am innocent;
    he is not angry with me.'
  But I will pass judgment on you
    because you say, 'I have not sinned.'
36Why do you go about so much,
    changing your ways?
  You will be disappointed by Egypt
    as you were by Assyria.
37You will also leave that place
    with your hands on your head,
  for the LORD has rejected those you trust;
    you will not be helped by them.

2:32   Israel had forgotten the Lord, and
he was no longer central to the nation's way
of life. Like a bride and groom making vows,
God made a covenant with his people,
but they had forsaken him and the close
bond that existed between them had
disintegrated.

---

3   "If a man divorces his wife
      and she leaves him and marries another man,
  should he return to her again?
  Would not the land be completely defiled?
  But you have lived as a prostitute with many
    lovers—
  would you now return to me?"

                              declares the LORD.
2"Look up to the barren heights and see.
  Is there any place where you have not been
    ravished?
  By the roadside you sat waiting for lovers,
    sat like a nomad*a* in the desert.
  You have defiled the land
    with your prostitution and wickedness.
3Therefore the showers have been withheld,
    and no spring rains have fallen.
  Yet you have the brazen look of a prostitute;
    you refuse to blush with shame.
4Have you not just called to me:
  'My Father, my friend from my youth,
5will you always be angry?
  Will your wrath continue for ever?'
  This is how you talk,
    but you do all the evil you can."

Unfaithful Israel

6During the reign of King Josiah, the LORD said to
me, "Have you seen what faithless Israel has done? She
has gone up on every high hill and under every spreading tree and has committed adultery there. 7I thought
that after she had done all this she would return to me

but she did not, and her unfaithful sister Judah saw it.
8I gave faithless Israel her certificate of divorce and
sent her away because of all her adulteries. Yet I saw
that her unfaithful sister Judah had no fear; she also
went out and committed adultery. 9Because Israel's
immorality mattered so little to her, she defiled the
land and committed adultery with stone and wood. 10In
spite of all this, her unfaithful sister Judah did not
return to me with all her heart, but only in pretence,"
declares the LORD.

11The LORD said to me, "Faithless Israel is more
righteous than unfaithful Judah. 12Go, proclaim this
message towards the north:

  " 'Return, faithless Israel,' declares the LORD,
    'I will frown on you no longer,
  for I am merciful,' declares the LORD,
    'I will not be angry for ever.
13Only acknowledge your guilt—
    you have rebelled against the LORD your God,
  you have scattered your favours to foreign gods
    under every spreading tree,
    and have not obeyed me,' "

                              declares the LORD.

14"Return, faithless people," declares the LORD, "for
I am your husband. I will choose you—one from a town
and two from a clan—and bring you to Zion. 15Then I
will give you shepherds after my own heart, who will
lead you with knowledge and understanding. 16In
those days, when your numbers have increased greatly
in the land," declares the LORD, "men will no longer
say, 'The ark of the covenant of the LORD.' It will never
enter their minds or be remembered; it will not be
missed, nor will another one be made. 17At that time
they will call Jerusalem The Throne of the LORD, and
all nations will gather in Jerusalem to honour the name
of the LORD. No longer will they follow the stubbornness of their evil hearts. 18In those days the house of
Judah will join the house of Israel, and together they
will come from a northern land to the land I gave your
forefathers as an inheritance.

19"I myself said,

  " 'How gladly would I treat you like sons
    and give you a desirable land,
    the most beautiful inheritance of any nation.'
  I thought you would call me 'Father'
    and not turn away from following me.
20But like a woman unfaithful to her husband,
    so you have been unfaithful to me, O house of
      Israel,"

                              declares the LORD.

21A cry is heard on the barren heights,
  the weeping and pleading of the people of
    Israel,
because they have perverted their ways
  and have forgotten the LORD their God.

22"Return, faithless people;
  I will cure you of backsliding."

  "Yes, we will come to you,
    for you are the LORD our God.

---

a 2 Or an Arab

23Surely the ,idolatrous, commotion on the hills
    and mountains is a deception;
surely in the LORD our God
    is the salvation of Israel.
24From our youth shameful gods have consumed
    the fruits of our fathers' labour—
their flocks and herds,
    their sons and daughters.
25Let us lie down in our shame,
    and let our disgrace cover us.
We have sinned against the LORD our God,
    both we and our fathers;
from our youth till this day
    we have not obeyed the LORD our God."

4 "If you will return, O Israel,
    return to me,"
                              declares the LORD.
"If you put your detestable idols out of my sight
    and no longer go astray,
2and if in a truthful, just and righteous way
    you swear, 'As surely as the LORD lives,'
then the nations will be blessed by him
    and in him they will glory."

4:1   God's compassion never fails. He
was already offering his sinful people the
chance to turn back from their wickedness.
God was prepared to renew his covenant
with his people if they truly repented. Such
repentance should not just be an outward
show, but a renewal of inward spirit.

3This is what the LORD says to the men of Judah and
to Jerusalem:

"Break up your unploughed ground
    and do not sow among thorns.
4Circumcise yourselves to the LORD,
    circumcise your hearts,
you men of Judah and people of Jerusalem,
or my wrath will break out and burn like fire
    because of the evil you have done—
    burn with no-one to quench it.

Disaster From the North

5"Announce in Judah and proclaim in Jerusalem
    and say:
'Sound the trumpet throughout the land!'
Cry aloud and say:
'Gather together!
    Let us flee to the fortified cities!'
6Raise the signal to go to Zion!
    Flee for safety without delay!
For I am bringing disaster from the north,
    even terrible destruction."

7A lion has come out of his lair;
    a destroyer of nations has set out.
He has left his place
    to lay waste your land.

Your towns will lie in ruins
    without inhabitant.
8So put on sackcloth,
    lament and wail,
for the fierce anger of the LORD
    has not turned away from us.

9"In that day," declares the LORD,
    "the king and the officials will lose heart,
the priests will be horrified,
    and the prophets will be appalled."

10Then I said, "Ah, Sovereign LORD, how completely
you have deceived this people and Jerusalem by saying,
'You will have peace,' when the sword is at our
throats."

11At that time this people and Jerusalem will be told,
"A scorching wind from the barren heights in the
desert blows towards my people, but not to winnow or
cleanse; 12a wind too strong for that comes from me.ᵃ
Now I pronounce my judgments against them."

13Look! He advances like the clouds,
    his chariots come like a whirlwind,
his horses are swifter than eagles.
    Woe to us! We are ruined!
14O Jerusalem, wash the evil from your heart and
    be saved.
How long will you harbour wicked thoughts?
15A voice is announcing from Dan,
    proclaiming disaster from the hills of Ephraim.
16"Tell this to the nations,
    proclaim it to Jerusalem:
'A besieging army is coming from a distant land,
    raising a war cry against the cities of Judah.
17They surround her like men guarding a field,
    because she has rebelled against me,' "
                              declares the LORD.
18"Your own conduct and actions
    have brought this upon you.
This is your punishment.
    How bitter it is!
    How it pierces to the heart!"

4:16   The prophet warned his hearers
that the enemy troops surrounding Judah
would invade and destroy them. The cause
of this action lay on their own doorsteps:
their sinfulness and lack of regard for the law
of God always resulted in tragedy.

19Oh, my anguish, my anguish!
    I writhe in pain.
Oh, the agony of my heart!
    My heart pounds within me,
    I cannot keep silent.
For I have heard the sound of the trumpet;
    I have heard the battle cry.
20Disaster follows disaster;
    the whole land lies in ruins.
In an instant my tents are destroyed,
    my shelter in a moment.

ᵃ12 Or *comes at my command*

²¹How long must I see the battle standard
   and hear the sound of the trumpet?

²²"My people are fools;
   they do not know me.
They are senseless children;
   they have no understanding.
They are skilled in doing evil;
   they know not how to do good."

²³I looked at the earth,
   and it was formless and empty;
and at the heavens,
   and their light was gone.
²⁴I looked at the mountains,
   and they were quaking;
all the hills were swaying.
²⁵I looked, and there were no people;
   every bird in the sky had flown away.
²⁶I looked, and the fruitful land was a desert;
   all its towns lay in ruins
before the LORD, before his fierce anger.

²⁷This is what the LORD says:

"The whole land will be ruined,
   though I will not destroy it completely.
²⁸Therefore the earth will mourn
   and the heavens above grow dark,
because I have spoken and will not relent,
   I have decided and will not turn back."

²⁹At the sound of horsemen and archers
   every town takes to flight.
Some go into the thickets;
   some climb up among the rocks.
All the towns are deserted;
   no-one lives in them.

³⁰What are you doing, O devastated one?
   Why dress yourself in scarlet
   and put on jewels of gold?
Why shade your eyes with paint?
   You adorn yourself in vain.
Your lovers despise you;
   they seek your life.

³¹I hear a cry as of a woman in labour,
   a groan as of one bearing her first child —
the cry of the Daughter of Zion gasping for
      breath,
   stretching out her hands and saying,
"Alas! I am fainting;
   my life is given over to murderers."

Not One Is Upright

5 "Go up and down the streets of Jerusalem,
   look around and consider,
search through her squares.
If you can find but one person
   who deals honestly and seeks the truth,
   I will forgive this city.
²Although they say, 'As surely as the LORD lives,'
   still they are swearing falsely."

³O LORD, do not your eyes look for truth?
   You struck them, but they felt no pain;
   you crushed them but they refused correction.

They made their faces harder than stone
   and refused to repent.
⁴I thought, "These are only the poor;
   they are foolish,
for they do not know the way of the LORD,
   the requirements of their God.
⁵So I will go to the leaders
   and speak to them;
surely they know the way of the LORD,
   the requirements of their God."
But with one accord they too had broken off the
      yoke
   and torn off the bonds.
⁶Therefore a lion from the forest will attack them,
   a wolf from the desert will ravage them,
a leopard will lie in wait near their towns
   to tear to pieces any who venture out,
for their rebellion is great
   and their backslidings many.

⁷"Why should I forgive you?
   Your children have forsaken me
   and sworn by gods that are not gods.
I supplied all their needs,
   yet they committed adultery
   and thronged to the houses of prostitutes.
⁸They are well-fed, lusty stallions,
   each neighing for another man's wife.
⁹Should I not punish them for this?"
   declares the LORD.
"Should I not avenge myself
   on such a nation as this?

5:8   Jeremiah went into the city and
despaired at what he saw. He warned the
people that such widespread rejection
of God's laws could only result in kindling
his anger. Soon the people would know
for themselves the power of God's wrath
(verse 10).

---

¹⁰"Go through her vineyards and ravage them,
   but do not destroy them completely.
Strip off her branches,
   for these people do not belong to the LORD.
¹¹The house of Israel and the house of Judah
   have been utterly unfaithful to me,"
                           declares the LORD.

¹²They have lied about the LORD;
   they said, "He will do nothing!
No harm will come to us;
   we will never see sword or famine.
¹³The prophets are but wind
   and the word is not in them;
   so let what they say be done to them."

¹⁴Therefore this is what the LORD God Almighty
says:

"Because the people have spoken these words,
   I will make my words in your mouth a fire
   and these people the wood it consumes.

15O house of Israel," declares the LORD,
"I am bringing a distant nation against you—
an ancient and enduring nation,
a people whose language you do not know,
whose speech you do not understand.
16Their quivers are like an open grave;
all of them are mighty warriors.
17They will devour your harvests and food,
devour your sons and daughters;
they will devour your flocks and herds,
devour your vines and fig-trees.
With the sword they will destroy
the fortified cities in which you trust.

18"Yet even in those days," declares the LORD, "I will
not destroy you completely. 19And when the people
ask, 'Why has the LORD our God done all this to us?'
you will tell them, 'As you have forsaken me and served
foreign gods in your own land, so now you will serve
foreigners in a land not your own.'

20"Announce this to the house of Jacob
and proclaim it in Judah:
21Hear this, you foolish and senseless people,
who have eyes but do not see,
who have ears but do not hear:
22Should you not fear me?" declares the LORD.
"Should you not tremble in my presence?
I made the sand a boundary for the sea,
an everlasting barrier it cannot cross.
The waves may roll, but they cannot prevail;
they may roar, but they cannot cross it.
23But these people have stubborn and rebellious
hearts;
they have turned aside and gone away.
24They do not say to themselves,
'Let us fear the LORD our God,
who gives autumn and spring rains in season,
who assures us of the regular weeks of harvest.'
25Your wrongdoings have kept these away;
your sins have deprived you of good.

26"Among my people are wicked men
who lie in wait like men who snare birds
and like those who set traps to catch men.
27Like cages full of birds,
their houses are full of deceit;
they have become rich and powerful
28   and have grown fat and sleek.
Their evil deeds have no limit;
they do not plead the case of the fatherless to
win it,
they do not defend the rights of the poor.
29Should I not punish them for this?"
declares the LORD.
"Should I not avenge myself
on such a nation as this?

30"A horrible and shocking thing
has happened in the land:
31The prophets prophesy lies,
the priests rule by their own authority,
and my people love it this way.
But what will you do in the end?

a 10 Hebrew uncircumcised

Jerusalem Under Siege

6 "Flee for safety, people of Benjamin!
Flee from Jerusalem!
Sound the trumpet in Tekoa!
Raise the signal over Beth Hakkerem!
For disaster looms out of the north,
even terrible destruction.
2I will destroy the Daughter of Zion,
so beautiful and delicate.
3Shepherds with their flocks will come against her;
they will pitch their tents round her,
each tending his own portion."

4"Prepare for battle against her!
Arise, let us attack at noon!
But, alas, the daylight is fading,
and the shadows of evening grow long.
5So arise, let us attack at night
and destroy her fortresses!"

6This is what the LORD Almighty says:

"Cut down the trees
and build siege ramps against Jerusalem.
This city must be punished;
it is filled with oppression.
7As a well pours out its water,
so she pours out her wickedness.
Violence and destruction resound in her;
her sickness and wounds are ever before me.
8Take warning, O Jerusalem,
or I will turn away from you
and make your land desolate
so that no-one can live in it."

9This is what the LORD Almighty says:

"Let them glean the remnant of Israel
as thoroughly as a vine;
pass your hand over the branches again,
like one gathering grapes."

10To whom can I speak and give warning?
Who will listen to me?
Their ears are closed a
so that they cannot hear.
The word of the LORD is offensive to them;
they find no pleasure in it.
11But I am full of the wrath of the LORD,
and I cannot hold it in.

"Pour it out on the children in the street
and on the young men gathered together;
both husband and wife will be caught in it,
and the old, those weighed down with years.
12Their houses will be turned over to others,
together with their fields and their wives,
when I stretch out my hand
against those who live in the land,"
declares the LORD.
13"From the least to the greatest,
all are greedy for gain;
prophets and priests alike,
all practise deceit.

14They dress the wound of my people
  as though it were not serious.
'Peace, peace,' they say,
  when there is no peace.
15Are they ashamed of their loathsome conduct?
  No, they have no shame at all;
  they do not even know how to blush.
So they will fall among the fallen;
  they will be brought down when I punish
    them,"
                                    says the LORD.

16This is what the LORD says:

"Stand at the crossroads and look;
  ask for the ancient paths,
ask where the good way is, and walk in it,
  and you will find rest for your souls.
But you said, 'We will not walk in it.'
17I appointed watchmen over you and said,
  'Listen to the sound of the trumpet!'
But you said, 'We will not listen.'
18Therefore hear, O nations;
  observe, O witnesses,
  what will happen to them.
19Hear, O earth:
  I am bringing disaster on this people,
  the fruit of their schemes,
because they have not listened to my words
  and have rejected my law.
20What do I care about incense from Sheba
  or sweet calamus from a distant land?
Your burnt offerings are not acceptable;
  your sacrifices do not please me."

21Therefore this is what the LORD says:

"I will put obstacles before this people.
Fathers and sons alike will stumble over them;
neighbours and friends will perish."

22This is what the LORD says:

"Look, an army is coming
  from the land of the north;
a great nation is being stirred up
  from the ends of the earth.
23They are armed with bow and spear;
  they are cruel and show no mercy.
They sound like the roaring sea
  as they ride on their horses;
they come like men in battle formation
  to attack you, O Daughter of Zion."

24We have heard reports about them,
  and our hands hang limp.
Anguish has gripped us,
  pain like that of a woman in labour.
25Do not go out to the fields
  or walk on the roads,
for the enemy has a sword,
  and there is terror on every side.
26O my people, put on sackcloth
  and roll in ashes;
mourn with bitter wailing
  as for an only son,

for suddenly the destroyer
  will come upon us.

27"I have made you a tester of metals
  and my people the ore,
that you may observe
  and test their ways.
28They are all hardened rebels,
  going about to slander.
They are bronze and iron;
  they all act corruptly.
29The bellows blow fiercely
  to burn away the lead with fire,
but the refining goes on in vain;
  the wicked are not purged out.
30They are called rejected silver,
  because the LORD has rejected them."

False Religion Worthless

7 This is the word that came to Jeremiah from the
  LORD: 2"Stand at the gate of the LORD's house and
there proclaim this message:

" 'Hear the word of the LORD, all you people of Judah
who come through these gates to worship the LORD.
3This is what the LORD Almighty, the God of Israel,
says: Reform your ways and your actions, and I will let
you live in this place. 4Do not trust in deceptive words
and say, "This is the temple of the LORD, the temple
of the LORD, the temple of the LORD!" 5If you really
change your ways and your actions and deal with each
other justly, 6if you do not oppress the alien, the fatherless or the widow and do not shed innocent blood in
this place, and if you do not follow other gods to your
own harm, 7then I will let you live in this place, in the
land I gave to your forefathers for ever and ever. 8But
look, you are trusting in deceptive words that are
worthless.

9" 'Will you steal and murder, commit adultery and
perjury,a burn incense to Baal and follow other gods
you have not known, 10and then come and stand before
me in this house, which bears my Name, and say, "We
are safe" — safe to do all these detestable things? 11Has
this house, which bears my Name, become a den of
robbers to you? But I have been watching! declares the
LORD.

12" 'Go now to the place in Shiloh where I first made
a dwelling for my Name, and see what I did to it
because of the wickedness of my people Israel. 13While
you were doing all these things, declares the LORD, I
spoke to you again and again, but you did not listen;
I called you, but you did not answer. 14Therefore, what
I did to Shiloh I will now do to the house that bears my
Name, the temple you trust in, the place I gave to you
and your fathers. 15I will thrust you from my presence,
just as I did all your brothers, the people of Ephraim.'

16"So do not pray for this people nor offer any plea
or petition for them; do not plead with me, for I will
not listen to you. 17Do you not see what they are doing
in the towns of Judah and in the streets of Jerusalem?
18The children gather wood, the fathers light the fire,
and the women knead the dough and make cakes of
bread for the Queen of Heaven. They pour out drink

a 9 Or and swear by false gods

offerings to other gods to provoke me to anger. ¹⁹But am I the one they are provoking? declares the LORD. Are they not rather harming themselves, to their own shame?

7:19 The rejection of God by his people happened in many ways, not least through their adoption of heathen worship to the Queen of Heaven, Ishthar. Their action brought God's wrath to boiling point: they were so keen to worship a false goddess and bring offerings to her that they forgot that God, who redeemed them and made a covenant with them, was jealous. No amount of prayer and entreaty could save them now.

---

²⁰" 'Therefore this is what the Sovereign LORD says: My anger and my wrath will be poured out on this place, on man and beast, on the trees of the field and on the fruit of the ground, and it will burn and not be quenched.
²¹" 'This is what the LORD Almighty, the God of Israel, says: Go ahead, add your burnt offerings to your other sacrifices and eat the meat yourselves! ²²For when I brought your forefathers out of Egypt and spoke to them, I did not just give them commands about burnt offerings and sacrifices, ²³but I gave them this command: Obey me, and I will be your God and you will be my people. Walk in all the ways I command you, that it may go well with you. ²⁴But they did not listen or pay attention; instead, they followed the stubborn inclinations of their evil hearts. They went backward and not forward. ²⁵From the time your forefathers left Egypt until now, day after day, again and again I sent you my servants the prophets. ²⁶But they did not listen to me or pay attention. They were stiff-necked and did more evil than their forefathers.'
²⁷"When you tell them all this, they will not listen to you; when you call to them, they will not answer. ²⁸Therefore say to them, 'This is the nation that has not obeyed the LORD its God or responded to correction. Truth has perished; it has vanished from their lips. ²⁹Cut off your hair and throw it away; take up a lament on the barren heights, for the LORD has rejected and abandoned this generation that is under his wrath.

The Valley of Slaughter

³⁰" 'The people of Judah have done evil in my eyes, declares the LORD. They have set up their detestable idols in the house that bears my Name and have defiled it. ³¹They have built the high places of Topheth in the Valley of Ben Hinnom to burn their sons and daughters in the fire—something I did not command, nor did it enter my mind. ³²So beware, the days are coming, declares the LORD, when people will no longer call it Topheth or the Valley of Ben Hinnom, but the Valley of Slaughter, for they will bury the dead in Topheth until there is no more room. ³³Then the carcasses of this people will become food for the birds of the air and the beasts of the earth, and there will be no-one to frighten them away. ³⁴I will bring an end to the sounds of joy and gladness and to the voices of bride and bridegroom in the towns of Judah and the streets of Jerusalem, for the land will become desolate.

8 " 'At that time, declares the LORD, the bones of the kings and officials of Judah, the bones of the priests and prophets, and the bones of the people of Jerusalem will be removed from their graves. ²They will be exposed to the sun and the moon and all the stars of the heavens, which they have loved and served and which they have followed and consulted and worshipped. They will not be gathered up or buried, but will be like refuse lying on the ground. ³Wherever I banish them, all the survivors of this evil nation will prefer death to life, declares the LORD Almighty.'

Sin and Punishment

⁴"Say to them, 'This is what the LORD says:

" 'When men fall down, do they not get up?
When a man turns away, does he not return?
⁵Why then have these people turned away?
Why does Jerusalem always turn away?
They cling to deceit;
they refuse to return.
⁶I have listened attentively,
but they do not say what is right.
No-one repents of his wickedness,
saying, "What have I done?"
Each pursues his own course
like a horse charging into battle.
⁷Even the stork in the sky
knows her appointed seasons,
and the dove, the swift and the thrush
observe the time of their migration.
But my people do not know
the requirements of the LORD.

⁸" 'How can you say, "We are wise,
for we have the law of the LORD,"
when actually the lying pen of the scribes
has handled it falsely?
⁹The wise will be put to shame;
they will be dismayed and trapped.
Since they have rejected the word of the LORD,
what kind of wisdom do they have?
¹⁰Therefore I will give their wives to other men
and their fields to new owners.
From the least to the greatest,
all are greedy for gain;
prophets and priests alike,
all practise deceit.
¹¹They dress the wound of my people
as though it were not serious.
"Peace, peace," they say,
when there is no peace.
¹²Are they ashamed of their loathsome conduct?
No, they have no shame at all;
they do not even know how to blush.
So they will fall among the fallen;
they will be brought down when they are
    punished,
                              says the LORD.

¹³" 'I will take away their harvest,
                              declares the LORD.
There will be no grapes on the vine.

There will be no figs on the tree,
  and their leaves will wither.
What I have given them
  will be taken from them.' " ᵃ

14"Why are we sitting here?
  Gather together!
Let us flee to the fortified cities
  and perish there!
For the LORD our God has doomed us to perish
  and given us poisoned water to drink,
  because we have sinned against him.
15We hoped for peace
  but no good has come,
for a time of healing
  but there was only terror.
16The snorting of the enemy's horses
  is heard from Dan;
at the neighing of their stallions
  the whole land trembles.
They have come to devour
  the land and everything in it,
  the city and all who live there."

17"See, I will send venomous snakes among you,
  vipers that cannot be charmed,
  and they will bite you,"
                    declares the LORD.

18O my Comforterᵇ in sorrow,
  my heart is faint within me.
19Listen to the cry of my people
  from a land far away:
"Is the LORD not in Zion?
  Is her King no longer there?"

"Why have they provoked me to anger with their
    images,
  with their worthless foreign idols?"

20"The harvest is past,
  the summer has ended,
  and we are not saved."

8:20   There were two harvests in the agricultural life of near-Eastern communities. The grain harvest was gathered during the late spring and early summer, and if that failed, there was also the summer harvest— the fruit harvest—to fall back on. If they both failed, then economic and political disaster struck.

21Since my people are crushed, I am crushed;
  I mourn, and horror grips me.
22Is there no balm in Gilead?
  Is there no physician there?
Why then is there no healing
  for the wound of my people?

9   ¹Oh, that my head were a spring of water
      and my eyes a fountain of tears!
I would weep day and night
  for the slain of my people.
²Oh, that I had in the desert
  a lodging place for travellers,
so that I might leave my people
  and go away from them;
for they are all adulterers,
  a crowd of unfaithful people.

³"They make ready their tongue
  like a bow, to shoot lies;
it is not by truth
  that they triumphᵃ in the land.
They go from one sin to another;
  they do not acknowledge me,"
                    declares the LORD.
⁴"Beware of your friends;
  do not trust your brothers.
For every brother is a deceiver,ᵇ
  and every friend a slanderer.
⁵Friend deceives friend,
  and no-one speaks the truth.
They have taught their tongues to lie;
  they weary themselves with sinning.
⁶Youᶜ live in the midst of deception;
  in their deceit they refuse to acknowledge me,"
                    declares the LORD.

⁷Therefore this is what the LORD Almighty says:

"See, I will refine and test them,
  for what else can I do
because of the sin of my people?
⁸Their tongue is a deadly arrow;
  it speaks with deceit.
With his mouth each speaks cordially to his
    neighbour,
but in his heart he sets a trap for him.
⁹Should I not punish them for this?"
  declares the LORD.
"Should I not avenge myself
  on such a nation as this?"

10I will weep and wail for the mountains
  and take up a lament concerning the desert
    pastures.
They are desolate and untravelled,
  and the lowing of cattle is not heard.
The birds of the air have fled
  and the animals are gone.

11"I will make Jerusalem a heap of ruins,
  a haunt of jackals;
and I will lay waste the towns of Judah
  so that no-one can live there."

12What man is wise enough to understand this? Who has been instructed by the LORD and can explain it? Why has the land been ruined and laid waste like a desert that no-one can cross?
13The LORD said, "It is because they have forsaken my law, which I set before them; they have not obeyed

---

ᵃ13 The meaning of the Hebrew for this sentence is uncertain.
ᵃ3 Or lies; / they are not valiant for truth   ᵇ4 Or a deceiving Jacob

ᵇ18 The meaning of the Hebrew for this word is uncertain.
ᶜ6 That is, Jeremiah (the Hebrew is singular)

me or followed my law. [14]Instead, they have followed the stubbornness of their hearts; they have followed the Baals, as their fathers taught them." [15]Therefore, this is what the LORD Almighty, the God of Israel, says: "See, I will make this people eat bitter food and drink poisoned water. [16]I will scatter them among nations that neither they nor their fathers have known, and I will pursue them with the sword until I have destroyed them."

[17]This is what the LORD Almighty says:

"Consider now! Call for the wailing women to
    come;
  send for the most skilful of them.
[18]Let them come quickly
    and wail over us
  till our eyes overflow with tears
    and water streams from our eyelids.
[19]The sound of wailing is heard from Zion:
  'How ruined we are!
  How great is our shame!
  We must leave our land
    because our houses are in ruins.' "

[20]Now, O women, hear the word of the LORD;
  open your ears to the words of his mouth.
Teach your daughters how to wail;
  teach one another a lament.
[21]Death has climbed in through our windows
    and has entered our fortresses;
  it has cut off the children from the streets
    and the young men from the public squares.

[22]Say, "This is what the LORD declares:

" 'The dead bodies of men will lie
  like refuse on the open field,
  like cut corn behind the reaper,
    with no-one to gather them.' "

[23]This is what the LORD says:

"Let not the wise man boast of his wisdom
  or the strong man boast of his strength
  or the rich man boast of his riches,
[24]but let him who boasts boast about this:
  that he understands and knows me,
  that I am the LORD, who exercises kindness,
  justice and righteousness on earth,
    for in these I delight,"
                                        declares the LORD.

[25]"The days are coming," declares the LORD, "when I will punish all who are circumcised only in the flesh — [26]Egypt, Judah, Edom, Ammon, Moab and all who live in the desert in distant places. [d] For all these nations are really uncircumcised, and even the whole house of Israel is uncircumcised in heart."

God and Idols

10 Hear what the LORD says to you, O house of Israel. [2]This is what the LORD says:

"Do not learn the ways of the nations
  or be terrified by signs in the sky,
  though the nations are terrified by them.
[3]For the customs of the peoples are worthless;
  they cut a tree out of the forest,
  and a craftsman shapes it with his
    chisel.
[4]They adorn it with silver and gold;
  they fasten it with hammer and nails
  so that it will not totter.
[5]Like a scarecrow in a melon patch,
  their idols cannot speak;
they must be carried
  because they cannot walk.
Do not fear them;
  they can do no harm
  nor can they do any good."

[6]No-one is like you, O LORD;
  you are great,
  and your name is mighty in power.
[7]Who should not revere you,
  O King of the nations?
  This is your due.
Among all the wise men of the nations
  and in all their kingdoms,
  there is no-one like you.
[8]They are all senseless and foolish;
  they are taught by worthless wooden
    idols.
[9]Hammered silver is brought from Tarshish
  and gold from Uphaz.
What the craftsman and goldsmith have made
  is then dressed in blue and purple —
  all made by skilled workers.
[10]But the LORD is the true God;
  he is the living God, the eternal King.
When he is angry, the earth trembles;
  the nations cannot endure his wrath.

[11]"Tell them this: 'These gods, who did not make the heavens and the earth, will perish from the earth and from under the heavens.' " [a]

[12]But God made the earth by his power;
  he founded the world by his wisdom
  and stretched out the heavens by his
    understanding.
[13]When he thunders, the waters in the heavens
    roar;
  he makes clouds rise from the ends of the
    earth.
He sends lightning with the rain
  and brings out the wind from his storehouses.

[14]Everyone is senseless and without knowledge;
  every goldsmith is shamed by his idols.
His images are a fraud;
  they have no breath in them.
[15]They are worthless, the objects of mockery;
  when their judgment comes, they will
    perish.
[16]He who is the Portion of Jacob is not like these,
  for he is the Maker of all things,
  including Israel, the tribe of his inheritance —
    the LORD Almighty is his name.

d 26 Or desert and who clip the hair by their foreheads   _a 11 The text of this verse is in Aramaic._

Coming Destruction

17Gather up your belongings to leave the land,
   you who live under siege.
18For this is what the LORD says:
   "At this time I will hurl out
   those who live in this land;
I will bring distress on them
   so that they may be captured."

19Woe to me because of my injury!
   My wound is incurable!
Yet I said to myself,
   "This is my sickness, and I must endure it."
20My tent is destroyed;
   all its ropes are snapped.
My sons are gone from me and are no more;
   no-one is left now to pitch my tent
   or to set up my shelter.
21The shepherds are senseless
   and do not enquire of the LORD;
so they do not prosper
   and all their flock is scattered.
22Listen! The report is coming —
   a great commotion from the land of the north!
It will make the towns of Judah desolate,
   a haunt of jackals.

Jeremiah's Prayer

23I know, O LORD, that a man's life is not his own;
   it is not for man to direct his steps.
24Correct me, LORD, but only with justice —
   not in your anger,
   lest you reduce me to nothing.
25Pour out your wrath on the nations
   that do not acknowledge you,
   on the peoples who do not call on your name.
For they have devoured Jacob;
   they have devoured him completely
   and destroyed his homeland.

10:23   Jeremiah began his prayer by acknowledging the inadequacy of men and women to achieve anything by themselves. To abandon God and go it alone brings moral and spiritual misdirection.

The Covenant Is Broken

11 This is the word that came to Jeremiah from the LORD: 2"Listen to the terms of this covenant and tell them to the people of Judah and to those who live in Jerusalem. 3Tell them that this is what the LORD, the God of Israel, says: 'Cursed is the man who does not obey the terms of this covenant — 4the terms I commanded your forefathers when I brought them out of Egypt, out of the iron-smelting furnace.' I said, 'Obey me and do everything I command you, and you will be my people, and I will be your God. 5Then I will fulfil the oath I swore to your forefathers, to give them

a land flowing with milk and honey' — the land you possess today."
   I answered, "Amen, LORD."
6The LORD said to me, "Proclaim all these words in the towns of Judah and in the streets of Jerusalem: 'Listen to the terms of this covenant and follow them. 7From the time I brought your forefathers up from Egypt until today, I warned them again and again, saying, "Obey me." 8But they did not listen or pay attention; instead, they followed the stubbornness of their evil hearts. So I brought on them all the curses of the covenant I had commanded them to follow but that they did not keep.' "
   9Then the LORD said to me, "There is a conspiracy among the people of Judah and those who live in Jerusalem. 10They have returned to the sins of their forefathers, who refused to listen to my words. They have followed other gods to serve them. Both the house of Israel and the house of Judah have broken the covenant I made with their forefathers. 11Therefore this is what the LORD says: 'I will bring on them a disaster they cannot escape. Although they cry out to me, I will not listen to them. 12The towns of Judah and the people of Jerusalem will go and cry out to the gods to whom they burn incense, but they will not help them at all when disaster strikes. 13You have as many gods as you have towns, O Judah; and the altars you have set up to burn incense to that shameful god Baal are as many as the streets of Jerusalem.'
   14"Do not pray for this people nor offer any plea or petition for them, because I will not listen when they call to me in the time of their distress.

15"What is my beloved doing in my temple
   as she works out her evil schemes with many?
Can consecrated meat avert ⌊your punishment⌋?
When you engage in your wickedness,
   then you rejoice." a

16The LORD called you a thriving olive tree
   with fruit beautiful in form.
But with the roar of a mighty storm
   he will set it on fire,
   and its branches will be broken.

17The LORD Almighty, who planted you, has decreed disaster for you, because the house of Israel and the house of Judah have done evil and provoked me to anger by burning incense to Baal.

Plot Against Jeremiah

18Because the LORD revealed their plot to me, I knew it, for at that time he showed me what they were doing. 19I had been like a gentle lamb led to the slaughter; I did not realise that they had plotted against me, saying,

"Let us destroy the tree and its fruit;
   let us cut him off from the land of the living,
   that his name be remembered no more."
20But, O LORD Almighty, you who judge righteously
   and test the heart and mind,
let me see your vengeance upon them,
   for to you I have committed my cause.

---

a 15 Or Could consecrated meat avert your punishment? / Then you would rejoice

21"Therefore this is what the LORD says about the men of Anathoth who are seeking your life and saying, 'Do not prophesy in the name of the LORD or you will die by our hands' —22therefore this is what the LORD Almighty says: 'I will punish them. Their young men will die by the sword, their sons and daughters by famine. 23Not even a remnant will be left to them, because I will bring disaster on the men of Anathoth in the year of their punishment.' "

Jeremiah's Complaint

12 You are always righteous, O LORD,
   when I bring a case before you.
Yet I would speak with you about your justice:
   Why does the way of the wicked prosper?
   Why do all the faithless live at ease?
2You have planted them, and they have taken root;
   they grow and bear fruit.
You are always on their lips
   but far from their hearts.
3Yet you know me, O LORD;
   you see me and test my thoughts about you.
Drag them off like sheep to be butchered!
   Set them apart for the day of slaughter!
4How long will the land lie parched[a]
   and the grass in every field be withered?
Because those who live in it are wicked,
   the animals and birds have perished.
Moreover, the people are saying,
   "He will not see what happens to us."

God's Answer

5"If you have raced with men on foot
   and they have worn you out,
   how can you compete with horses?
If you stumble in safe country,[b]
   how will you manage in the thickets by[c] the
      Jordan?
6Your brothers, your own family —
   even they have betrayed you;
   they have raised a loud cry against you.
Do not trust them,
   though they speak well of you.

12:5 Jeremiah learned the hard truth about his ministry, as Jesus would much later, that a prophet is without honour among his own people. If he came unstuck in his own land, how would he cope among the wild animals — a reference to neighbouring hostile powers — in the jungle alongside the Jordan?

7"I will forsake my house,
   abandon my inheritance;
I will give the one I love
   into the hands of her enemies.
8My inheritance has become to me
   like a lion in the forest.

She roars at me;
   therefore I hate her.
9Has not my inheritance become to me
   like a speckled bird of prey
   that other birds of prey surround and attack?
Go and gather all the wild beasts;
   bring them to devour.
10Many shepherds will ruin my vineyard
   and trample down my field;
they will turn my pleasant field
   into a desolate wasteland.
11It will be made a wasteland,
   parched and desolate before me;
the whole land will be laid waste
   because there is no-one who cares.
12Over all the barren heights in the desert
   destroyers will swarm,
for the sword of the LORD will devour
   from one end of the land to the other;
   no-one will be safe.
13They will sow wheat but reap thorns;
   they will wear themselves out but gain nothing.
So bear the shame of your harvest
   because of the LORD's fierce anger."

14This is what the LORD says: "As for all my wicked neighbours who seize the inheritance I gave to my people Israel, I will uproot them from their lands and I will uproot the house of Judah from among them. 15But after I uproot them, I will again have compassion and will bring each of them back to his own inheritance and his own country. 16And if they learn well the ways of my people and swear by my name, saying, 'As surely as the LORD lives' — even as they once taught my people to swear by Baal — then they will be established among my people. 17But if any nation does not listen, I will completely uproot and destroy it," declares the LORD.

A Linen Belt

13 This is what the LORD said to me: "Go and buy a linen belt and put it round your waist, but do not let it touch water." 2So I bought a belt, as the LORD directed, and put it round my waist.

3Then the word of the LORD came to me a second time: 4"Take the belt you bought and are wearing round your waist, and go now to Perath[a] and hide it there in a crevice in the rocks." 5So I went and hid it at Perath, as the LORD told me.

6Many days later the LORD said to me, "Go now to Perath and get the belt I told you to hide there." 7So I went to Perath and dug up the belt and took it from the place where I had hidden it, but now it was ruined and completely useless.

8Then the word of the LORD came to me: 9"This is what the LORD says: 'In the same way I will ruin the pride of Judah and the great pride of Jerusalem. 10These wicked people, who refuse to listen to my words, who follow the stubbornness of their hearts and go after other gods to serve and worship them, will be like this

---

a4 Or land mourn   b5 Or If you put your trust in a land of safety   c5 Or the flooding of
a4 Or possibly the Euphrates; also in verses 5–7

belt—completely useless! [11]For as a belt is bound round a man's waist, so I bound the whole house of Israel and the whole house of Judah to me,' declares the LORD, 'to be my people for my renown and praise and honour. But they have not listened.'

Wineskins

[12]"Say to them: 'This is what the LORD, the God of Israel, says: Every wineskin should be filled with wine.' And if they say to you, 'Don't we know that every wineskin should be filled with wine?' [13]then tell them, 'This is what the LORD says: I am going to fill with drunkenness all who live in this land, including the kings who sit on David's throne, the priests, the prophets and all those living in Jerusalem. [14]I will smash them one against the other, fathers and sons alike, declares the LORD. I will allow no pity or mercy or compassion to keep me from destroying them.' "

13:12   By making reference to wineskins and drunkenness, Jeremiah turned a well-known colloquial saying to his own advantage, and declared that, as they drank, the people would be filled with the anger of God, who would not allow such a dangerous cocktail to be mixed with any mercy.

Threat of Captivity

[15]Hear and pay attention,
    do not be arrogant,
    for the LORD has spoken.
[16]Give glory to the LORD your God
    before he brings the darkness,
before your feet stumble
    on the darkening hills.
You hope for light,
    but he will turn it to thick darkness
    and change it to deep gloom.
[17]But if you do not listen,
    I will weep in secret
    because of your pride;
my eyes will weep bitterly,
    overflowing with tears,
    because the LORD's flock will be taken captive.

[18]Say to the king and to the queen mother,
    "Come down from your thrones,
    for your glorious crowns
    will fall from your heads."
[19]The cities in the Negev will be shut up,
    and there will be no-one to open them.
All Judah will be carried into exile,
    carried completely away.

[20]Lift up your eyes and see
    those who are coming from the north.
Where is the flock that was entrusted to you,
    the sheep of which you boasted?
[21]What will you say when the LORD sets over you
    those you cultivated as your special allies?

Will not pain grip you
    like that of a woman in labour?
[22]And if you ask yourself,
    "Why has this happened to me?" —
it is because of your many sins
    that your skirts have been torn off
    and your body ill-treated.
[23]Can the Ethiopian[b] change his skin
    or the leopard its spots?
Neither can you do good
    who are accustomed to doing evil.

[24]"I will scatter you like chaff
    driven by the desert wind.
[25]This is your lot,
    the portion I have decreed for you,"
                        declares the LORD,
    "because you have forgotten me
    and trusted in false gods.
[26]I will pull up your skirts over your face
    that your shame may be seen—
[27]your adulteries and lustful neighings,
    your shameless prostitution!
I have seen your detestable acts
    on the hills and in the fields.
Woe to you, O Jerusalem!
    How long will you be unclean?"

Drought, Famine, Sword

14 This is the word of the LORD to Jeremiah concerning the drought:

[2]"Judah mourns,
    her cities languish;
they wail for the land,
    and a cry goes up from Jerusalem.
[3]The nobles send their servants for water;
    they go to the cisterns
    but find no water.
They return with their jars unfilled;
    dismayed and despairing,
    they cover their heads.
[4]The ground is cracked
    because there is no rain in the land;
the farmers are dismayed
    and cover their heads.
[5]Even the doe in the field
    deserts her newborn fawn
    because there is no grass.
[6]Wild donkeys stand on the barren heights
    and pant like jackals;
their eyesight fails
    for lack of pasture."

[7]Although our sins testify against us,
    O LORD, do something for the sake of your
    name.
For our backsliding is great;
    we have sinned against you.
[8]O Hope of Israel,
    its Saviour in times of distress,
why are you like a stranger in the land,
    like a traveller who stays only a night?

---

[b]23 Hebrew *Cushite* (probably a person from the upper Nile region)

⁹Why are you like a man taken by surprise,
    like a warrior powerless to save?
You are among us, O Lord,
    and we bear your name;
    do not forsake us!

¹⁰This is what the Lord says about this people:

"They greatly love to wander;
    they do not restrain their feet.
So the Lord does not accept them;
    he will now remember their wickedness
    and punish them for their sins."

¹¹Then the Lord said to me, "Do not pray for the well-being of this people. ¹²Although they fast, I will not listen to their cry; though they offer burnt offerings and grain offerings, I will not accept them. Instead, I will destroy them with the sword, famine and plague."

¹³But I said, "Ah, Sovereign Lord, the prophets keep telling them, 'You will not see the sword or suffer famine. Indeed, I will give you lasting peace in this place.' "

¹⁴Then the Lord said to me, "The prophets are prophesying lies in my name. I have not sent them or appointed them or spoken to them. They are prophesying to you false visions, divinations, idolatriesᵃ and the delusions of their own minds. ¹⁵Therefore, this is what the Lord says about the prophets who are prophesying in my name: I did not send them, yet they are saying, 'No sword or famine will touch this land.' Those same prophets will perish by sword and famine. ¹⁶And the people they are prophesying to will be thrown out into the streets of Jerusalem because of the famine and sword. There will be no-one to bury them or their wives, their sons or their daughters. I will pour out on them the calamity they deserve.

¹⁷"Speak this word to them:

" 'Let my eyes overflow with tears
    night and day without ceasing;
for my virgin daughter—my people—
    has suffered a grievous wound,
    a crushing blow.
¹⁸If I go into the country,
    I see those slain by the sword;
if I go into the city,
    I see the ravages of famine.
Both prophet and priest
    have gone to a land they know not.' "

¹⁹Have you rejected Judah completely?
    Do you despise Zion?
Why have you afflicted us
    so that we cannot be healed?
We hoped for peace
    but no good has come,
for a time of healing
    but there is only terror.
²⁰O Lord, we acknowledge our wickedness
    and the guilt of our fathers;
    we have indeed sinned against you.
²¹For the sake of your name do not despise us;
    do not dishonour your glorious throne.

Remember your covenant with us
    and do not break it.
²²Do any of the worthless idols of the nations bring
        rain?
    Do the skies themselves send down showers?
No, it is you, O Lord our God.
    Therefore our hope is in you,
    for you are the one who does all this.

15 Then the Lord said to me: "Even if Moses and Samuel were to stand before me, my heart would not go out to this people. Send them away from my presence! Let them go! ²And if they ask you, 'Where shall we go?' tell them, 'This is what the Lord says:

" 'Those destined for death, to death;
    those for the sword, to the sword;
    those for starvation, to starvation;
    those for captivity, to captivity.'

³"I will send four kinds of destroyers against them," declares the Lord, "the sword to kill and the dogs to drag away and the birds of the air and the beasts of the earth to devour and destroy. ⁴I will make them abhorrent to all the kingdoms of the earth because of what Manasseh son of Hezekiah king of Judah did in Jerusalem.

⁵"Who will have pity on you, O Jerusalem?
    Who will mourn for you?
    Who will stop to ask how you are?
⁶You have rejected me," declares the Lord.
    "You keep on backsliding.
So I will lay hands on you and destroy you;
    I can no longer show compassion.

15:6   "Backsliding" is used here not as a metaphor for laziness, but as a way of saying that the people were forever going back on their promises, returning to their old ways, and worshipping idols.

---

⁷I will winnow them with a winnowing fork
    at the city gates of the land.
I will bring bereavement and destruction on my
        people,
    for they have not changed their ways.
⁸I will make their widows more numerous
    than the sand of the sea.
At midday I will bring a destroyer
    against the mothers of their young men;
suddenly I will bring down on them
    anguish and terror.
⁹The mother of seven will grow faint
    and breathe her last.
Her sun will set while it is still day;
    she will be disgraced and humiliated.
I will put the survivors to the sword
    before their enemies,"
                                    declares the Lord.

ᵃ14 Or visions, worthless divinations

[10]Alas, my mother, that you gave me birth,
    a man with whom the whole land strives and
        contends!
I have neither lent nor borrowed,
    yet everyone curses me.

[11]The LORD said,

"Surely I will deliver you for a good purpose;
    surely I will make your enemies plead with you
    in times of disaster and times of distress.

[12]"Can a man break iron —
    iron from the north — or bronze?
[13]Your wealth and your treasures
    I will give as plunder, without charge,
because of all your sins
    throughout your country.
[14]I will enslave you to your enemies
    in[a] a land you do not know,
for my anger will kindle a fire
    that will burn against you."

[15]You understand, O LORD;
    remember me and care for me.
Avenge me on my persecutors.
You are long-suffering — do not take me away;
    think of how I suffer reproach for your sake.
[16]When your words came, I ate them;
    they were my joy and my heart's delight,
for I bear your name,
    O LORD God Almighty.
[17]I never sat in the company of revellers,
    never made merry with them;
I sat alone because your hand was on me
    and you had filled me with indignation.
[18]Why is my pain unending
    and my wound grievous and incurable?
Will you be to me like a deceptive brook,
    like a spring that fails?

[19]Therefore this is what the LORD says:

"If you repent, I will restore you
    that you may serve me;
if you utter worthy, not worthless, words,
    you will be my spokesman.
Let this people turn to you,
    but you must not turn to them.
[20]I will make you a wall to this people,
    a fortified wall of bronze;
they will fight against you
    but will not overcome you,
for I am with you
    to rescue and save you,"
                        declares the LORD.
[21]"I will save you from the hands of the wicked
    and redeem you from the grasp of the cruel."

Day of Disaster

16

Then the word of the LORD came to me: [2]"You must not marry and have sons or daughters in this place." [3]For this is what the LORD says about the sons and daughters born in this land and about the women who are their mothers and the men who are their fathers: [4]"They will die of deadly diseases. They will not be mourned or buried but will be like refuse lying on the ground. They will perish by sword and famine, and their dead bodies will become food for the birds of the air and the beasts of the earth."

[5]For this is what the LORD says: "Do not enter a house where there is a funeral meal; do not go to mourn or show sympathy, because I have withdrawn my blessing, my love and my pity from this people," declares the LORD. [6]"Both high and low will die in this land. They will not be buried or mourned, and no-one will cut himself or shave his head for them. [7]No-one will offer food to comfort those who mourn for the dead — not even for a father or a mother — nor will anyone give them a drink to console them.

[8]"And do not enter a house where there is feasting and sit down to eat and drink. [9]For this is what the LORD Almighty, the God of Israel, says: Before your eyes and in your days I will bring an end to the sounds of joy and gladness and to the voices of bride and bridegroom in this place.

[10]"When you tell these people all this and they ask you, 'Why has the LORD decreed such a great disaster against us? What wrong have we done? What sin have we committed against the LORD our God?' [11]then say to them, 'It is because your fathers forsook me,' declares the LORD, 'and followed other gods and served and worshipped them. They forsook me and did not keep my law. [12]But you have behaved more wickedly than your fathers. See how each of you is following the stubbornness of his evil heart instead of obeying me. [13]So I will throw you out of this land into a land neither you nor your fathers have known, and there you will serve other gods day and night, for I will show you no favour.'

[14]"However, the days are coming," declares the LORD, "when men will no longer say, 'As surely as the LORD lives, who brought the Israelites up out of Egypt,' [15]but they will say, 'As surely as the LORD lives, who brought the Israelites up out of the land of the north and out of all the countries where he had banished them.' For I will restore them to the land I gave to their forefathers.

[16]"But now I will send for many fishermen," declares the LORD, "and they will catch them. After that I will send for many hunters, and they will hunt them down on every mountain and hill and from the crevices of the rocks. [17]My eyes are on all their ways; they are not hidden from me, nor is their sin concealed from my eyes. [18]I will repay them double for their wickedness and their sin, because they have defiled my land with the lifeless forms of their vile images and have filled my inheritance with their detestable idols."

[19]O LORD, my strength and my fortress,
    my refuge in time of distress,
to you the nations will come
    from the ends of the earth and say,
"Our fathers possessed nothing but false gods,
    worthless idols that did them no good.

---

[a]14 Some Hebrew manuscripts, Septuagint and Syriac (see also Jer. 17:4); most Hebrew manuscripts *I will cause your enemies to bring you / into*

²⁰Do men make their own gods?
　　Yes, but they are not gods!"

²¹"Therefore I will teach them—
　　this time I will teach them
　　my power and might.
　Then they will know
　　that my name is the LORD.

17 "Judah's sin is engraved with an iron tool,
　　inscribed with a flint point,
on the tablets of their hearts
　and on the horns of their altars.
²Even their children remember
　　their altars and Asherah poles*ᵃ*
beside the spreading trees
　and on the high hills.
³My mountain in the land
　and your*ᵇ* wealth and all your treasures
I will give away as plunder,
　together with your high places,
　because of sin throughout your country.
⁴Through your own fault you will lose
　　the inheritance I gave you.
I will enslave you to your enemies
　in a land you do not know,
for you have kindled my anger,
　and it will burn for ever."

⁵This is what the LORD says:

"Cursed is the one who trusts in man,
　who depends on flesh for his strength
　and whose heart turns away from the LORD.
⁶He will be like a bush in the wastelands;
　he will not see prosperity when it comes.
He will dwell in the parched places of the desert,
　in a salt land where no-one lives.

⁷"But blessed is the man who trusts in the LORD,
　whose confidence is in him.
⁸He will be like a tree planted by the water
　that sends out its roots by the stream.
It does not fear when heat comes;
　its leaves are always green.
It has no worries in a year of drought
　and never fails to bear fruit."

⁹The heart is deceitful above all things
　and beyond cure.
　Who can understand it?

¹⁰"I the LORD search the heart
　and examine the mind,
to reward a man according to his conduct,
　according to what his deeds deserve."

¹¹Like a partridge that hatches eggs it did not lay
　is the man who gains riches by unjust means.
When his life is half gone, they will desert him,
　and in the end he will prove to be a fool.

¹²A glorious throne, exalted from the beginning,
　is the place of our sanctuary.
¹³O LORD, the hope of Israel,
　all who forsake you will be put to shame.

Those who turn away from you will be written in
　the dust
because they have forsaken the LORD,
　the spring of living water.

17:13 Dust is a potent symbol of human sinfulness and mortality (see Genesis 3:19), and those who turn away from God will return to dust. Those who remain faithful to him will have their names written not in dust, but in the book of life.

---

¹⁴Heal me, O LORD, and I shall be healed;
　save me and I shall be saved,
　for you are the one I praise.
¹⁵They keep saying to me,
　"Where is the word of the LORD?
　Let it now be fulfilled!"
¹⁶I have not run away from being your shepherd;
　you know I have not desired the day of despair.
　What passes my lips is open before you.
¹⁷Do not be a terror to me;
　you are my refuge in the day of disaster.
¹⁸Let my persecutors be put to shame,
　but keep me from shame;
let them be terrified,
　but keep me from terror.
Bring on them the day of disaster;
　destroy them with double destruction.

Keeping the Sabbath Holy

¹⁹This is what the LORD said to me: "Go and stand at the gate of the people, through which the kings of Judah go in and out; stand also at all the other gates of Jerusalem. ²⁰Say to them, 'Hear the word of the LORD, O kings of Judah and all people of Judah and everyone living in Jerusalem who come through these gates. ²¹This is what the LORD says: Be careful not to carry a load on the Sabbath day or bring it through the gates of Jerusalem. ²²Do not bring a load out of your houses or do any work on the Sabbath, but keep the Sabbath day holy, as I commanded your forefathers. ²³Yet they did not listen or pay attention; they were stiff-necked and would not listen or respond to discipline. ²⁴But if you are careful to obey me, declares the LORD, and bring no load through the gates of this city on the Sabbath, but keep the Sabbath day holy by not doing any work on it, ²⁵then kings who sit on David's throne will come through the gates of this city with their officials. They and their officials will come riding in chariots and on horses, accompanied by the men of Judah and those living in Jerusalem, and this city will be inhabited for ever. ²⁶People will come from the towns of Judah and the villages around Jerusalem, from the territory of Benjamin and the western foothills, from the hill country and the Negev, bringing burnt offerings and sacrifices, grain offerings, incense and thank-offerings to the house of the LORD. ²⁷But if you do not obey me to keep the Sabbath day holy by not carrying any load as

---

ᵃ2 That is, symbols of the goddess Asherah　　*ᵇ2, 3 Or hills / ³and the mountains of the land. / Your* you come through the gates of Jerusalem on the Sabbath day, then I will kindle an unquenchable fire in the gates of Jerusalem that will consume her fortresses.' "

At the Potter's House

18 This is the word that came to Jeremiah from the LORD: 2"Go down to the potter's house, and there I will give you my message." 3So I went down to the potter's house, and I saw him working at the wheel. 4But the pot he was shaping from the clay was marred in his hands; so the potter formed it into another pot, shaping it as it seemed best to him.

5Then the word of the LORD came to me: 6"O house of Israel, can I not do with you as this potter does?" declares the LORD. "Like clay in the hand of the potter, so are you in my hand, O house of Israel. 7If at any time I announce that a nation or kingdom is to be uprooted, torn down and destroyed, 8and if that nation I warned repents of its evil, then I will relent and not inflict on it the disaster I had planned. 9And if at another time I announce that a nation or kingdom is to be built up and planted, 10and if it does evil in my sight and does not obey me, then I will reconsider the good I had intended to do for it.

11"Now therefore say to the people of Judah and those living in Jerusalem, 'This is what the LORD says: Look! I am preparing a disaster for you and devising a plan against you. So turn from your evil ways, each one of you, and reform your ways and your actions.' 12But they will reply, 'It's no use. We will continue with our own plans; each of us will follow the stubbornness of his evil heart.' "

13Therefore this is what the LORD says:

"Enquire among the nations:
  Who has ever heard anything like this?
A most horrible thing has been done
  by Virgin Israel.
14Does the snow of Lebanon
  ever vanish from its rocky slopes?
Do its cool waters from distant sources
  ever cease to flow?*a*
15Yet my people have forgotten me;
  they burn incense to worthless idols,
which made them stumble in their ways
  and in the ancient paths.
They made them walk in bypaths
  and on roads not built up.
16Their land will be laid waste,
  an object of lasting scorn;
all who pass by will be appalled
  and will shake their heads.
17Like a wind from the east,
  I will scatter them before their enemies;
I will show them my back and not my face
  in the day of their disaster."

18They said, "Come, let's make plans against Jeremiah; for the teaching of the law by the priest will not be lost, nor will counsel from the wise, nor the word

from the prophets. So come, let's attack him with our tongues and pay no attention to anything he says."

19Listen to me, O LORD;
  hear what my accusers are saying!
20Should good be repaid with evil?
  Yet they have dug a pit for me.
Remember that I stood before you
  and spoke on their behalf
  to turn your wrath away from them.
21So give their children over to famine;
  hand them over to the power of the sword.
Let their wives be made childless and widows;
  let their men be put to death,
  their young men slain by the sword in battle.
22Let a cry be heard from their houses
  when you suddenly bring invaders against them,
for they have dug a pit to capture me
  and have hidden snares for my feet.
23But you know, O LORD,
  all their plots to kill me.
Do not forgive their crimes
  or blot out their sins from your sight.
Let them be overthrown before you;
  deal with them in the time of your anger.

19 This is what the LORD says: "Go and buy a clay jar from a potter. Take along some of the elders of the people and of the priests 2and go out to the Valley of Ben Hinnom, near the entrance of the Potsherd Gate. There proclaim the words I tell you, 3and say, 'Hear the word of the LORD, O kings of Judah and people of Jerusalem. This is what the LORD Almighty, the God of Israel, says: Listen! I am going to bring a disaster on this place that will make the ears of everyone who hears of it tingle. 4For they have forsaken me and made this a place of foreign gods; they have burned sacrifices in it to gods that neither they nor their fathers nor the kings of Judah ever knew, and they have filled this place with the blood of the innocent. 5They have built the high places of Baal to burn their sons in the fire as offerings to Baal—something I did not command or mention, nor did it enter my mind. 6So beware, the days are coming, declares the LORD, when people will no longer call this place Topheth or the Valley of Ben Hinnom, but the Valley of Slaughter.

7" 'In this place I will ruin*a* the plans of Judah and Jerusalem. I will make them fall by the sword before their enemies, at the hands of those who seek their lives, and I will give their carcasses as food to the birds of the air and the beasts of the earth. 8I will devastate this city and make it an object of scorn; all who pass by will be appalled and will scoff because of all its wounds. 9I will make them eat the flesh of their sons and daughters, and they will eat one another's flesh during the stress of the siege imposed on them by the enemies who seek their lives.'

10"Then break the jar while those who go with you are watching, 11and say to them, 'This is what the LORD Almighty says: I will smash this nation and this city just as this potter's jar is smashed and cannot be repaired.

---

a 14 The meaning of the Hebrew for this sentence is uncertain.
a 7 The Hebrew for *ruin* sounds like the Hebrew for *jar* (see verses 1 and 10).

They will bury the dead in Topheth until there is no more room. 12This is what I will do to this place and to those who live here, declares the LORD. I will make this city like Topheth. 13The houses in Jerusalem and those of the kings of Judah will be defiled like this place, Topheth—all the houses where they burned incense on the roofs to all the starry hosts and poured out drink offerings to other gods.' "

14Jeremiah then returned from Topheth, where the LORD had sent him to prophesy, and stood in the court of the LORD's temple and said to all the people, 15"This is what the LORD Almighty, the God of Israel, says: 'Listen! I am going to bring on this city and the villages around it every disaster I pronounced against them, because they were stiff-necked and would not listen to my words.' "

Jeremiah and Pashhur

20 When the priest Pashhur son of Immer, the chief officer in the temple of the LORD, heard Jeremiah prophesying these things, 2he had Jeremiah the prophet beaten and put in the stocks at the Upper Gate of Benjamin at the LORD's temple. 3The next day, when Pashhur released him from the stocks, Jeremiah said to him, "The LORD's name for you is not Pashhur, but Magor-Missabib.ᵃ 4For this is what the LORD says: 'I will make you a terror to yourself and to all your friends; with your own eyes you will see them fall by the sword of their enemies. I will hand all Judah over to the king of Babylon, who will carry them away to Babylon or put them to the sword. 5I will hand over to their enemies all the wealth of this city—all its products, all its valuables and all the treasures of the kings of Judah. They will take it away as plunder and carry it off to Babylon. 6And you, Pashhur, and all who live in your house will go into exile to Babylon. There you will die and be buried, you and all your friends to whom you have prophesied lies.' "

20:7   Jeremiah was brought to the point of desperation. His lack of confidence is quite clear. He had done all that God commanded him to do (chapter 19) and all he got in return was public condemnation.

Jeremiah's Complaint

7O LORD, you deceivedᵇ me, and I was
     deceived;ᵇ
  you overpowered me and prevailed.
  I am ridiculed all day long;
     everyone mocks me.
8Whenever I speak, I cry out
  proclaiming violence and destruction.
  So the word of the LORD has brought me
     insult and reproach all day long.
9But if I say, "I will not mention him
  or speak any more in his name,"

his word is in my heart like a fire,
  a fire shut up in my bones.
I am weary of holding it in;
  indeed, I cannot.
10I hear many whispering,
  "Terror on every side!
  Report him! Let's report him!"
All my friends
  are waiting for me to slip, saying,
"Perhaps he will be deceived;
  then we will prevail over him
  and take our revenge on him."

11But the LORD is with me like a mighty warrior;
  so my persecutors will stumble and not prevail.
They will fail and be thoroughly disgraced;
  their dishonour will never be forgotten.
12O LORD Almighty, you who examine the righteous
  and probe the heart and mind,
let me see your vengeance upon them,
  for to you I have committed my cause.

13Sing to the LORD!
  Give praise to the LORD!
He rescues the life of the needy
  from the hands of the wicked.

14Cursed be the day I was born!
  May the day my mother bore me not be blessed!
15Cursed be the man who brought my father the
     news,
  who made him very glad, saying,
  "A child is born to you—a son!"
16May that man be like the towns
  the LORD overthrew without pity.
May he hear wailing in the morning,
  a battle cry at noon.
17For he did not kill me in the womb,
  with my mother as my grave,
  her womb enlarged for ever.
18Why did I ever come out of the womb
  to see trouble and sorrow
  and to end my days in shame?

God Rejects Zedekiah's Request

21 The word came to Jeremiah from the LORD when King Zedekiah sent to him Pashhur son of Malkijah and the priest Zephaniah son of Maaseiah. They said: 2"Enquire now of the LORD for us because Nebuchadnezzarᵃ king of Babylon is attacking us. Perhaps the LORD will perform wonders for us as in times past so that he will withdraw from us."

3But Jeremiah answered them, "Tell Zedekiah, 4'This is what the LORD, the God of Israel, says: I am about to turn against you the weapons of war that are in your hands, which you are using to fight the king of Babylon and the Babyloniansᵇ who are outside the wall besieging you. And I will gather them inside this city. 5I myself will fight against you with an outstretched hand and a mighty arm in anger and fury and great wrath. 6I will strike down those who live in this

---

ᵃ3 *Magor-Missabib* means *terror on every side.*   ᵇ7 Or *persuaded*
ᵃ2 Hebrew *Nebuchadrezzar,* of which *Nebuchadnezzar* is a variant; here and often in Jeremiah and Ezekiel
ᵇ4 Or *Chaldeans;* also in verse 9

city—both men and animals—and they will die of a terrible plague. [7]After that, declares the LORD, I will hand over Zedekiah king of Judah, his officials and the people in this city who survive the plague, sword and famine, to Nebuchadnezzar king of Babylon and to their enemies who seek their lives. He will put them to the sword; he will show them no mercy or pity or compassion.'

[8]"Furthermore, tell the people, 'This is what the LORD says: See, I am setting before you the way of life and the way of death. [9]Whoever stays in this city will die by the sword, famine or plague. But whoever goes out and surrenders to the Babylonians who are besieging you will live; he will escape with his life. [10]I have determined to do this city harm and not good, declares the LORD. It will be given into the hands of the king of Babylon, and he will destroy it with fire.'

[11]"Moreover, say to the royal house of Judah, 'Hear the word of the LORD; [12]O house of David, this is what the LORD says:

" 'Administer justice every morning;
    rescue from the hand of his oppressor
    the one who has been robbed,
or my wrath will break out and burn like fire
    because of the evil you have done—
    burn with no-one to quench it.
[13]I am against you, ₍Jerusalem,₎
    you who live above this valley
    on the rocky plateau,
                          declares the LORD—
you who say, "Who can come against us?
    Who can enter our refuge?"
[14]I will punish you as your deeds deserve,
                          declares the LORD.
I will kindle a fire in your forests
    that will consume everything around you.' "

Judgment Against Evil Kings

22 This is what the LORD says: "Go down to the palace of the king of Judah and proclaim this message there: [2]'Hear the word of the LORD, O king of Judah, you who sit on David's throne—you, your officials and your people who come through these gates. [3]This is what the LORD says: Do what is just and right. Rescue from the hand of his oppressor the one who has been robbed. Do no wrong or violence to the alien, the fatherless or the widow, and do not shed innocent blood in this place. [4]For if you are careful to carry out these commands, then kings who sit on David's throne will come through the gates of this palace, riding in chariots and on horses, accompanied by their officials and their people. [5]But if you do not obey these commands, declares the LORD, I swear by myself that this palace will become a ruin.' "

[6]For this is what the LORD says about the palace of the king of Judah:

"Though you are like Gilead to me,
    like the summit of Lebanon,
I will surely make you like a desert,
    like towns not inhabited.

[7]I will send destroyers against you,
    each man with his weapons,
and they will cut up your fine cedar beams
    and throw them into the fire.

[8]"People from many nations will pass by this city and will ask one another, 'Why has the LORD done such a thing to this great city?' [9]And the answer will be: 'Because they have forsaken the covenant of the LORD their God and have worshipped and served other gods.' "

[10]Do not weep for the dead ₍king₎ or mourn his loss;
    rather, weep bitterly for him who is exiled,
because he will never return
    nor see his native land again.

[11]For this is what the LORD says about Shallum[a] son of Josiah, who succeeded his father as king of Judah but has gone from this place: "He will never return. [12]He will die in the place where they have led him captive; he will not see this land again."

[13]"Woe to him who builds his palace by
        unrighteousness,
    his upper rooms by injustice,
making his countrymen work for nothing,
    not paying them for their labour.
[14]He says, 'I will build myself a great palace
    with spacious upper rooms.'
So he makes large windows in it,
    panels it with cedar
    and decorates it in red.

22:16 Jeremiah boldly spoke out against Shallum (or Jehoahaz), the ungodly son of the godly reformer, Josiah. He built fine buildings and styled himself as a great emperor, but ignored the plight of the poor. Jeremiah, along with all the prophets, stressed again and again that true worship of God goes hand in hand with a concern for the poor.

---

[15]"Does it make you a king
    to have more and more cedar?
Did not your father have food and drink?
    He did what was right and just,
    so all went well with him.
[16]He defended the cause of the poor and needy,
    and so all went well.
Is that not what it means to know me?"
    declares the LORD.
[17]"But your eyes and your heart
    are set only on dishonest gain,
on shedding innocent blood
    and on oppression and extortion."

[18]Therefore this is what the LORD says about Jehoiakim son of Josiah king of Judah:

"They will not mourn for him:
    'Alas, my brother! Alas, my sister!'

---

[a] 11 Also called Jehoahaz

They will not mourn for him:
'Alas, my master! Alas, his splendour!'
19He will have the burial of a donkey—
dragged away and thrown
outside the gates of Jerusalem."

20"Go up to Lebanon and cry out,
let your voice be heard in Bashan,
cry out from Abarim,
for all your allies are crushed.
21I warned you when you felt secure,
but you said, 'I will not listen!'
This has been your way from your youth;
you have not obeyed me.
22The wind will drive all your shepherds away,
and your allies will go into exile.
Then you will be ashamed and disgraced
because of all your wickedness.
23You who live in 'Lebanon',b
who are nestled in cedar buildings,
how you will groan when pangs come upon you,
pain like that of a woman in labour!

24"As surely as I live," declares the LORD, "even if you, Jehoiachinc son of Jehoiakim king of Judah, were a signet ring on my right hand, I would still pull you off. 25I will hand you over to those who seek your life, those you fear—to Nebuchadnezzar king of Babylon and to the Babylonians.d 26I will hurl you and the mother who gave you birth into another country, where neither of you was born, and there you both will die. 27You will never come back to the land you long to return to."

28Is this man Jehoiachin a despised, broken pot,
an object no-one wants?
Why will he and his children be hurled out,
cast into a land they do not know?
29O land, land, land,
hear the word of the LORD!
30This is what the LORD says:
"Record this man as if childless,
a man who will not prosper in his lifetime,
for none of his offspring will prosper,
none will sit on the throne of David
or rule any more in Judah."

The Righteous Branch

23 "Woe to the shepherds who are destroying and scattering the sheep of my pasture!" declares the LORD. 2Therefore this is what the LORD, the God of Israel, says to the shepherds who tend my people: "Because you have scattered my flock and driven them away and have not bestowed care on them, I will bestow punishment on you for the evil you have done," declares the LORD. 3"I myself will gather the remnant of my flock out of all the countries where I have driven them and will bring them back to their pasture, where they will be fruitful and increase in number. 4I will place shepherds over them who will tend them, and they will no longer be afraid or terrified, nor will any be missing," declares the LORD.

5"The days are coming," declares the LORD,
"when I will raise up to Davida a righteous
Branch,
a King who will reign wisely
and do what is just and right in the land.
6In his days Judah will be saved
and Israel will live in safety.
This is the name by which he will be called:
The LORD Our Righteousness.

7"So then, the days are coming," declares the LORD, "when people will no longer say, 'As surely as the LORD lives, who brought the Israelites up out of Egypt,' 8but they will say, 'As surely as the LORD lives, who brought the descendants of Israel up out of the land of the north and out of all the countries where he had banished them.' Then they will live in their own land."

Lying Prophets

9Concerning the prophets:

My heart is broken within me;
all my bones tremble.
I am like a drunken man,
like a man overcome by wine,
because of the LORD
and his holy words.
10The land is full of adulterers;
because of the curseb the land lies parchedc
and the pastures in the desert are withered.
The ⌊prophets⌋ follow an evil course
and use their power unjustly.

11"Both prophet and priest are godless;
even in my temple I find their wickedness,"
declares the LORD.
12"Therefore their path will become slippery;
they will be banished to darkness
and there they will fall.
I will bring disaster on them
in the year they are punished,"
declares the LORD.

13"Among the prophets of Samaria
I saw this repulsive thing:
They prophesied by Baal
and led my people Israel astray.
14And among the prophets of Jerusalem
I have seen something horrible:
They commit adultery and live a lie.
They strengthen the hands of evildoers,
so that no-one turns from his wickedness.
They are all like Sodom to me;
the people of Jerusalem are like Gomorrah."

15Therefore, this is what the LORD Almighty says concerning the prophets:

"I will make them eat bitter food
and drink poisoned water,
because from the prophets of Jerusalem
ungodliness has spread throughout the land."

---

b23 That is, the palace in Jerusalem (see 1 Kings 7:2)
d25 Or Chaldeans   a5 Or up from David's line
c24 Hebrew Coniah, a variant of Jehoiachin; also in verse 28
b10 Or because of these things   c10 Or land mourns

¹⁶This is what the LORD Almighty says:

"Do not listen to what the prophets are
    prophesying to you;
  they fill you with false hopes.
They speak visions from their own minds,
  not from the mouth of the LORD.
¹⁷They keep saying to those who despise me,
    'The LORD says: You will have peace.'
And to all who follow the stubbornness of their
    hearts
  they say, 'No harm will come to you.'
¹⁸But which of them has stood in the council of the
    LORD
  to see or to hear his word?
Who has listened and heard his word?
¹⁹See, the storm of the LORD
  will burst out in wrath,
a whirlwind swirling down
  on the heads of the wicked.
²⁰The anger of the LORD will not turn back
  until he fully accomplishes
  the purposes of his heart.
In days to come
  you will understand it clearly.
²¹I did not send these prophets,
  yet they have run with their message;
I did not speak to them,
  yet they have prophesied.
²²But if they had stood in my council,
  they would have proclaimed my words to my
    people
and would have turned them from their evil ways
  and from their evil deeds.

²³"Am I only a God nearby,"
                                    declares the LORD,
  "and not a God far away?
²⁴Can anyone hide in secret places
  so that I cannot see him?"
                                    declares the LORD.
"Do not I fill heaven and earth?"
                                    declares the LORD.

²⁵"I have heard what the prophets say who prophesy lies in my name. They say, 'I had a dream! I had a dream!' ²⁶How long will this continue in the hearts of these lying prophets, who prophesy the delusions of their own minds? ²⁷They think the dreams they tell one another will make my people forget my name, just as their fathers forgot my name through Baal worship. ²⁸Let the prophet who has a dream tell his dream, but let the one who has my word speak it faithfully. For what has straw to do with grain?" declares the LORD. ²⁹"Is not my word like fire," declares the LORD, "and like a hammer that breaks a rock in pieces?

³⁰"Therefore," declares the LORD, "I am against the prophets who steal from one another words supposedly from me. ³¹Yes," declares the LORD, "I am against the prophets who wag their own tongues and yet declare, 'The LORD declares.' ³²Indeed, I am against those who

prophesy false dreams," declares the LORD. "They tell them and lead my people astray with their reckless lies, yet I did not send or appoint them. They do not benefit these people in the least," declares the LORD.

False Oracles and False Prophets

³³"When these people, or a prophet or a priest, ask you, 'What is the oracle^d of the LORD?' say to them, 'What oracle?^e I will forsake you, declares the LORD.' ³⁴If a prophet or a priest or anyone else claims, 'This is the oracle of the LORD,' I will punish that man and his household. ³⁵This is what each of you keeps on saying to his friend or relative: 'What is the LORD's answer?' or 'What has the LORD spoken?' ³⁶But you must not mention 'the oracle of the LORD' again, because every man's own word becomes his oracle and so you distort the words of the living God, the LORD Almighty, our God. ³⁷This is what you keep saying to a prophet: 'What is the LORD's answer to you?' or 'What has the LORD spoken?' ³⁸Although you claim, 'This is the oracle of the LORD,' this is what the LORD says: You used the words, 'This is the oracle of the LORD,' even though I told you that you must not claim, 'This is the oracle of the LORD.' ³⁹Therefore, I will surely forget you and cast you out of my presence along with the city I gave to you and your fathers. ⁴⁰I will bring upon you everlasting disgrace—everlasting shame that will not be forgotten."

Two Baskets of Figs

24 After Jehoiachin^a son of Jehoiakim king of Judah and the officials, the craftsmen and the artisans of Judah were carried into exile from Jerusalem to Babylon by Nebuchadnezzar king of Babylon, the LORD showed me two baskets of figs placed in front of the temple of the LORD. ²One basket had very good figs, like those that ripen early; the other basket had very poor figs, so bad that they could not be eaten.

24:1   Disaster finally struck, and those who would have provided leadership and national cohesion—the political and religious leaders, and the captains of industry—were taken away, leaving a disaffected group of uncoordinated people.

---

³Then the LORD asked me, "What do you see, Jeremiah?"

"Figs," I answered. "The good ones are very good, but the poor ones are so bad that they cannot be eaten."

⁴Then the word of the LORD came to me: ⁵"This is what the LORD, the God of Israel, says: 'Like these good figs, I regard as good the exiles from Judah, whom I sent away from this place to the land of the Babylonians.^b ⁶My eyes will watch over them for their good, and I will bring them back to this land. I will build them up and not tear them down; I will plant them and not

---

^d33 Or burden (see Septuagint and Vulgate)
^e33 Hebrew; Septuagint and Vulgate 'You are the burden; the Hebrew for oracle and burden is the same.
^a1 Hebrew Jeconiah, a variant of Jehoiachin   ^b5 Or Chaldeans

uproot them. ⁷I will give them a heart to know me, that I am the LORD. They will be my people, and I will be their God, for they will return to me with all their heart.

⁸" 'But like the poor figs, which are so bad that they cannot be eaten,' says the LORD, 'so will I deal with Zedekiah king of Judah, his officials and the survivors from Jerusalem, whether they remain in this land or live in Egypt. ⁹I will make them abhorrent and an offence to all the kingdoms of the earth, a reproach and a byword, an object of ridicule and cursing, wherever I banish them. ¹⁰I will send the sword, famine and plague against them until they are destroyed from the land I gave to them and their fathers.' "

24:10   God poured cold water on the self-righteous complacency of those who were left in Jerusalem. They thought that they must be the favoured ones because they had been left in the holy city, and that those who were exiled were reaping the harvest of their sins. The parable of the baskets of figs tells a different story (verse 8).

Seventy Years of Captivity

25 The word came to Jeremiah concerning all the people of Judah in the fourth year of Jehoiakim son of Josiah king of Judah, which was the first year of Nebuchadnezzar king of Babylon. ²So Jeremiah the prophet said to all the people of Judah and to all those living in Jerusalem: ³For twenty-three years — from the thirteenth year of Josiah son of Amon king of Judah until this very day — the word of the LORD has come to me and I have spoken to you again and again, but you have not listened.

⁴And though the LORD has sent all his servants the prophets to you again and again, you have not listened or paid any attention. ⁵They said, "Turn now, each of you, from your evil ways and your evil practices, and you can stay in the land the LORD gave to you and your fathers for ever and ever. ⁶Do not follow other gods to serve and worship them; do not provoke me to anger with what your hands have made. Then I will not harm you."

⁷"But you did not listen to me," declares the LORD, "and you have provoked me with what your hands have made, and you have brought harm to yourselves."

⁸Therefore the LORD Almighty says this: "Because you have not listened to my words, ⁹I will summon all the peoples of the north and my servant Nebuchadnezzar king of Babylon," declares the LORD, "and I will bring them against this land and its inhabitants and against all the surrounding nations. I will completely destroy[a] them and make them an object of horror and scorn, and an everlasting ruin. ¹⁰I will banish from them the sounds of joy and gladness, the voices of bride and bridegroom, the sound of millstones and the light of the lamp. ¹¹This whole country will become a desolate wasteland, and these nations will serve the king of Babylon for seventy years.

¹²"But when the seventy years are fulfilled, I will punish the king of Babylon and his nation, the land of the Babylonians,[b] for their guilt," declares the LORD, "and will make it desolate for ever. ¹³I will bring upon that land all the things I have spoken against it, all that are written in this book and prophesied by Jeremiah against all the nations. ¹⁴They themselves will be enslaved by many nations and great kings; I will repay them according to their deeds and the work of their hands."

The Cup of God's Wrath

¹⁵This is what the LORD, the God of Israel, said to me: "Take from my hand this cup filled with the wine of my wrath and make all the nations to whom I send you drink it. ¹⁶When they drink it, they will stagger and go mad because of the sword I will send among them."

¹⁷So I took the cup from the LORD's hand and made all the nations to whom he sent me drink it: ¹⁸Jerusalem and the towns of Judah, its kings and officials, to make them a ruin and an object of horror and scorn and cursing, as they are today; ¹⁹Pharaoh king of Egypt, his attendants, his officials and all his people, ²⁰and all the foreign people there; all the kings of Uz; all the kings of the Philistines (those of Ashkelon, Gaza, Ekron, and the people left at Ashdod); ²¹Edom, Moab and Ammon; ²²all the kings of Tyre and Sidon; the kings of the coastlands across the sea; ²³Dedan, Tema, Buz and all who are in distant places;[c] ²⁴all the kings of Arabia and all the kings of the foreign people who live in the desert; ²⁵all the kings of Zimri, Elam and Media; ²⁶and all the kings of the north, near and far, one after the other — all the kingdoms on the face of the earth. And after all of them, the king of Sheshach[d] will drink it too.

²⁷"Then tell them, 'This is what the LORD Almighty, the God of Israel, says: Drink, get drunk and vomit, and fall to rise no more because of the sword I will send among you.' ²⁸But if they refuse to take the cup from your hand and drink, tell them, 'This is what the LORD Almighty says: You must drink it! ²⁹See, I am beginning to bring disaster on the city that bears my Name, and will you indeed go unpunished? You will not go unpunished, for I am calling down a sword upon all who live on the earth, declares the LORD Almighty.'

³⁰"Now prophesy all these words against them and say to them:

" 'The LORD will roar from on high;
  he will thunder from his holy dwelling
  and roar mightily against his land.
He will shout like those who tread the grapes,
  shout against all who live on the earth.
³¹The tumult will resound to the ends of the earth,
  for the LORD will bring charges against the
    nations;
he will bring judgment on all mankind
  and put the wicked to the sword,' "
                              declares the LORD.

---

a9 The Hebrew term refers to the irrevocable giving over of things or persons to the LORD, often by totally destroying them.
b12 Or Chaldeans   c23 Or who clip the hair by their foreheads   d26 Sheshach is a cryptogram for Babylon.

32This is what the Lord Almighty says:

"Look! Disaster is spreading
    from nation to nation;
a mighty storm is rising
    from the ends of the earth."

33At that time those slain by the Lord will be every-where—from one end of the earth to the other. They will not be mourned or gathered up or buried, but will be like refuse lying on the ground.

34Weep and wail, you shepherds;
    roll in the dust, you leaders of the flock.
For your time to be slaughtered has come;
    you will fall and be shattered like fine pottery.
35The shepherds will have nowhere to flee,
    the leaders of the flock no place to escape.
36Hear the cry of the shepherds,
    the wailing of the leaders of the flock,
    for the Lord is destroying their pasture.
37The peaceful meadows will be laid waste
    because of the fierce anger of the Lord.
38Like a lion he will leave his lair,
    and their land will become desolate
because of the sword*e* of the oppressor
    and because of the Lord's fierce anger.

Jeremiah Threatened With Death

26 Early in the reign of Jehoiakim son of Josiah king of Judah, this word came from the Lord: 2"This is what the Lord says: Stand in the courtyard of the Lord's house and speak to all the people of the towns of Judah who come to worship in the house of the Lord. Tell them everything I command you; do not omit a word. 3Perhaps they will listen and each will turn from his evil way. Then I will relent and not bring on them the disaster I was planning because of the evil they have done. 4Say to them, 'This is what the Lord says: If you do not listen to me and follow my law, which I have set before you, 5and if you do not listen to the words of my servants the prophets, whom I have sent to you again and again (though you have not listened), 6then I will make this house like Shiloh and this city an object of cursing among all the nations of the earth.' "

7The priests, the prophets and all the people heard Jeremiah speak these words in the house of the Lord. 8But as soon as Jeremiah finished telling all the people everything the Lord had commanded him to say, the priests, the prophets and all the people seized him and said, "You must die! 9Why do you prophesy in the Lord's name that this house will be like Shiloh and this city will be desolate and deserted?" And all the people crowded around Jeremiah in the house of the Lord.

10When the officials of Judah heard about these things, they went up from the royal palace to the house of the Lord and took their places at the entrance of the New Gate of the Lord's house. 11Then the priests and the prophets said to the officials and all the people, "This man should be sentenced to death because he

has prophesied against this city. You have heard it with your own ears!"

12Then Jeremiah said to all the officials and all the people: "The Lord sent me to prophesy against this house and this city all the things you have heard. 13Now reform your ways and your actions and obey the Lord your God. Then the Lord will relent and not bring the disaster he has pronounced against you. 14As for me, I am in your hands; do with me whatever you think is good and right. 15Be assured, however, that if you put me to death, you will bring the guilt of innocent blood on yourselves and on this city and on those who live in it, for in truth the Lord has sent me to you to speak all these words in your hearing."

26:15 Jeremiah called the people to repentance. He decided to hit at a very sensitive nerve—"this city" meant the temple. Jewish zeal for the dwelling place of God was so strong that by speaking against it, Jeremiah risked being charged for blasphemy, an offence punishable by death.

16Then the officials and all the people said to the priests and the prophets, "This man should not be sentenced to death! He has spoken to us in the name of the Lord our God."

17Some of the elders of the land stepped forward and said to the entire assembly of people, 18"Micah of Moresheth prophesied in the days of Hezekiah king of Judah. He told all the people of Judah, 'This is what the Lord Almighty says:

" 'Zion will be ploughed like a field,
    Jerusalem will become a heap of rubble,
    the temple hill a mound overgrown with
        thickets.'*a*

19"Did Hezekiah king of Judah or anyone else in Judah put him to death? Did not Hezekiah fear the Lord and seek his favour? And did not the Lord relent, so that he did not bring the disaster he pronounced against them? We are about to bring a terrible disaster on ourselves!"

20(Now Uriah son of Shemaiah from Kiriath Jearim was another man who prophesied in the name of the Lord; he prophesied the same things against this city and this land as Jeremiah did. 21When King Jehoiakim and all his officers and officials heard his words, the king sought to put him to death. But Uriah heard of it and fled in fear to Egypt. 22King Jehoiakim, however, sent Elnathan son of Acbor to Egypt, along with some other men. 23They brought Uriah out of Egypt and took him to King Jehoiakim, who had him struck down with a sword and his body thrown into the burial place of the common people.)

24Furthermore, Ahikam son of Shaphan supported Jeremiah, and so he was not handed over to the people to be put to death.

---

e 38 Some Hebrew manuscripts and Septuagint (see also Jer. 46:16 and 50:16); most Hebrew manuscripts *anger*
a 18 Micah 3:12

Judah to Serve Nebuchadnezzar

27 Early in the reign of Zedekiah[a] son of Josiah king of Judah, this word came to Jeremiah from the LORD: ²This is what the LORD said to me: "Make a yoke out of straps and crossbars and put it on your neck. ³Then send word to the kings of Edom, Moab, Ammon, Tyre and Sidon through the envoys who have come to Jerusalem to Zedekiah king of Judah. ⁴Give them a message for their masters and say, 'This is what the LORD Almighty, the God of Israel, says: "Tell this to your masters: ⁵With my great power and outstretched arm I made the earth and its people and the animals that are on it, and I give it to anyone I please. ⁶Now I will hand all your countries over to my servant Nebuchadnezzar king of Babylon; I will make even the wild animals subject to him. ⁷All nations will serve him and his son and his grandson until the time for his land comes; then many nations and great kings will subjugate him.

⁸" ' "If, however, any nation or kingdom will not serve Nebuchadnezzar king of Babylon or bow its neck under his yoke, I will punish that nation with the sword, famine and plague, declares the LORD, until I destroy it by his hand. ⁹So do not listen to your prophets, your diviners, your interpreters of dreams, your mediums or your sorcerers who tell you, 'You will not serve the king of Babylon.' ¹⁰They prophesy lies to you that will only serve to remove you far from your lands; I will banish you and you will perish. ¹¹But if any nation will bow its neck under the yoke of the king of Babylon and serve him, I will let that nation remain in its own land to till it and to live there, declares the LORD." ' "

¹²I gave the same message to Zedekiah king of Judah. I said, "Bow your neck under the yoke of the king of Babylon; serve him and his people, and you will live. ¹³Why will you and your people die by the sword, famine and plague with which the LORD has threatened any nation that will not serve the king of Babylon? ¹⁴Do not listen to the words of the prophets who say to you, 'You will not serve the king of Babylon,' for they are prophesying lies to you. ¹⁵'I have not sent them,' declares the LORD. 'They are prophesying lies in my name. Therefore, I will banish you and you will perish, both you and the prophets who prophesy to you.' "

¹⁶Then I said to the priests and all these people, "This is what the LORD says: Do not listen to the prophets who say, 'Very soon now the articles from the LORD's house will be brought back from Babylon.' They are prophesying lies to you. ¹⁷Do not listen to them. Serve the king of Babylon, and you will live. Why should this city become a ruin? ¹⁸If they are prophets and have the word of the LORD, let them plead with the LORD Almighty that the furnishings remaining in the house of the LORD and in the palace of the king of Judah and in Jerusalem not be taken to Babylon. ¹⁹For this is what the LORD Almighty says about the pillars, the Sea, the movable stands and the other furnishings that are left in this city, ²⁰which Nebuchadnezzar king of Babylon did not take away when he carried Jehoiachin[b]

son of Jehoiakim king of Judah into exile from Jerusalem to Babylon, along with all the nobles of Judah and Jerusalem — ²¹yes, this is what the LORD Almighty, the God of Israel, says about the things that are left in the house of the LORD and in the palace of the king of Judah and in Jerusalem: ²²'They will be taken to Babylon and there they will remain until the day I come for them,' declares the LORD. 'Then I will bring them back and restore them to this place.' "

The False Prophet Hananiah

28 In the fifth month of that same year, the fourth year, early in the reign of Zedekiah king of Judah, the prophet Hananiah son of Azzur, who was from Gibeon, said to me in the house of the LORD in the presence of the priests and all the people: ²"This is what the LORD Almighty, the God of Israel, says: 'I will break the yoke of the king of Babylon. ³Within two years I will bring back to this place all the articles of the LORD's house that Nebuchadnezzar king of Babylon removed from here and took to Babylon. ⁴I will also bring back to this place Jehoiachin son of Jehoiakim king of Judah and all the other exiles from Judah who went to Babylon,' declares the LORD, 'for I will break the yoke of the king of Babylon.' "

⁵Then the prophet Jeremiah replied to the prophet Hananiah before the priests and all the people who were standing in the house of the LORD. ⁶He said, "Amen! May the LORD do so! May the LORD fulfil the words you have prophesied by bringing the articles of the LORD's house and all the exiles back to this place from Babylon. ⁷Nevertheless, listen to what I have to say in your hearing and in the hearing of all the people: ⁸From early times the prophets who preceded you and me have prophesied war, disaster and plague against many countries and great kingdoms. ⁹But the prophet who prophesies peace will be recognised as one truly sent by the LORD only if his prediction comes true."

¹⁰Then the prophet Hananiah took the yoke off the neck of the prophet Jeremiah and broke it, ¹¹and he said before all the people, "This is what the LORD says: 'In the same way will I break the yoke of Nebuchadnezzar king of Babylon off the neck of all the nations within two years.' " At this, the prophet Jeremiah went on his way.

¹²Shortly after the prophet Hananiah had broken the yoke off the neck of the prophet Jeremiah, the word of the LORD came to Jeremiah: ¹³"Go and tell Hananiah, 'This is what the LORD says: You have broken a wooden yoke, but in its place you will get a yoke of iron. ¹⁴This is what the LORD Almighty, the God of Israel, says: I will put an iron yoke on the necks of all these nations to make them serve Nebuchadnezzar king of Babylon, and they will serve him. I will even give him control over the wild animals.' "

¹⁵Then the prophet Jeremiah said to Hananiah the prophet, "Listen, Hananiah! The LORD has not sent you, yet you have persuaded this nation to trust in lies. ¹⁶Therefore, this is what the LORD says: 'I am about to remove you from the face of the earth. This very year

---

[a] *1* A few Hebrew manuscripts and Syriac (see also Jer. 27:3, 12 and 28:1); most Hebrew manuscripts *Jehoiakim* (most Septuagint manuscripts do not have this verse.)   [b] *20* Hebrew *Jeconiah*, a variant of *Jehoiachin*; also in 28:4 and 29:2

you are going to die, because you have preached rebellion against the LORD.' "

[17]In the seventh month of that same year, Hananiah the prophet died.

A Letter to the Exiles

29 This is the text of the letter that the prophet Jeremiah sent from Jerusalem to the surviving elders among the exiles and to the priests, the prophets and all the other people Nebuchadnezzar had carried into exile from Jerusalem to Babylon. [2](This was after King Jehoiachin and the queen mother, the court officials and the leaders of Judah and Jerusalem, the craftsmen and the artisans had gone into exile from Jerusalem.) [3]He entrusted the letter to Elasah son of Shaphan and to Gemariah son of Hilkiah, whom Zedekiah king of Judah sent to King Nebuchadnezzar in Babylon. It said:

[4]This is what the LORD Almighty, the God of Israel, says to all those I carried into exile from Jerusalem to Babylon: [5]"Build houses and settle down; plant gardens and eat what they produce. [6]Marry and have sons and daughters; find wives for your sons and give your daughters in marriage, so that they too may have sons and daughters. Increase in number there; do not decrease. [7]Also, seek the peace and prosperity of the city to which I have carried you into exile. Pray to the LORD for it, because if it prospers, you too will prosper." [8]Yes, this is what the LORD Almighty, the God of Israel, says: "Do not let the prophets and diviners among you deceive you. Do not listen to the dreams you encourage them to have. [9]They are prophesying lies to you in my name. I have not sent them," declares the LORD.

[10]This is what the LORD says: "When seventy years are completed for Babylon, I will come to you and fulfil my gracious promise to bring you back to this place. [11]For I know the plans I have for you," declares the LORD, "plans to prosper you and not to harm you, plans to give you hope and a future. [12]Then you will call upon me and come and pray to me, and I will listen to you. [13]You will seek me and find me when you seek me with all your heart. [14]I will be found by you," declares the LORD, "and will bring you back from captivity.[a] I will gather you from all the nations and places where I have banished you," declares the LORD, "and will bring you back to the place from which I carried you into exile."

[15]You may say, "The LORD has raised up prophets for us in Babylon," [16]but this is what the LORD says about the king who sits on David's throne and all the people who remain in this city, your countrymen who did not go with you into exile — [17]yes, this is what the LORD Almighty says: "I will send the sword, famine and plague against them and I will make them like poor figs that are so bad they cannot be eaten. [18]I will pursue them with the sword, famine and plague and will make them abhorrent to all the kingdoms of the earth and an

object of cursing and horror, of scorn and reproach, among all the nations where I drive them. [19]For they have not listened to my words," declares the LORD, "words that I sent to them again and again by my servants the prophets. And you exiles have not listened either," declares the LORD.

29:11   Jeremiah assured the people that God knew what he was doing, and that they should trust him. The Jews were desperate to return to Jerusalem, for they knew that, having the temple, it was the only place where God could be worshipped. Such desperation had led to great unrest and the death of other prophets. Jeremiah reminded the exiles that the whole world is God's and that he can be found amid the life of his people beyond Jerusalem — even in Babylon.

---

[20]Therefore, hear the word of the LORD, all you exiles whom I have sent away from Jerusalem to Babylon. [21]This is what the LORD Almighty, the God of Israel, says about Ahab son of Kolaiah and Zedekiah son of Maaseiah, who are prophesying lies to you in my name: "I will hand them over to Nebuchadnezzar king of Babylon, and he will put them to death before your very eyes. [22]Because of them, all the exiles from Judah who are in Babylon will use this curse: 'The LORD treat you like Zedekiah and Ahab, whom the king of Babylon burned in the fire.' [23]For they have done outrageous things in Israel; they have committed adultery with their neighbours' wives and in my name have spoken lies, which I did not tell them to do. I know it and am a witness to it," declares the LORD.

Message to Shemaiah

[24]Tell Shemaiah the Nehelamite, [25]"This is what the LORD Almighty, the God of Israel, says: You sent letters in your own name to all the people in Jerusalem, to Zephaniah son of Maaseiah the priest, and to all the other priests. You said to Zephaniah, [26]'The LORD has appointed you priest in place of Jehoiada to be in charge of the house of the LORD; you should put any madman who acts like a prophet into the stocks and neck-irons. [27]So why have you not reprimanded Jeremiah from Anathoth, who poses as a prophet among you? [28]He has sent this message to us in Babylon: It will be a long time. Therefore build houses and settle down; plant gardens and eat what they produce.' "

[29]Zephaniah the priest, however, read the letter to Jeremiah the prophet. [30]Then the word of the LORD came to Jeremiah: [31]"Send this message to all the exiles: 'This is what the LORD says about Shemaiah the Nehelamite: Because Shemaiah has prophesied to you, even though I did not send him, and has led you to believe a lie, [32]this is what the LORD says: I will surely punish Shemaiah the Nehelamite and his descendants.

[a]14 Or will restore your fortunes

He will have no-one left among this people, nor will he see the good things I will do for my people, declares the LORD, because he has preached rebellion against me.' "

Restoration of Israel

30 This is the word that came to Jeremiah from the LORD: ²"This is what the LORD, the God of Israel, says: 'Write in a book all the words I have spoken to you. ³The days are coming,' declares the LORD, 'when I will bring my people Israel and Judah back from captivity*ᵃ* and restore them to the land I gave to their forefathers to possess,' says the LORD."

⁴These are the words the LORD spoke concerning Israel and Judah: ⁵"This is what the LORD says:

" 'Cries of fear are heard—
    terror, not peace.
⁶Ask and see:
    Can a man bear children?
Then why do I see every strong man
    with his hands on his stomach like a woman in
        labour,
    every face turned deathly pale?
⁷How awful that day will be!
    None will be like it.
It will be a time of trouble for Jacob,
    but he will be saved out of it.

⁸" 'In that day,' declares the LORD Almighty,
    'I will break the yoke off their necks
and will tear off their bonds;
    no longer will foreigners enslave them.
⁹Instead, they will serve the LORD their God
    and David their king,
    whom I will raise up for them.

¹⁰" 'So do not fear, O Jacob my servant;
    do not be dismayed, O Israel,'
                            declares the LORD.
'I will surely save you out of a distant place,
    your descendants from the land of their exile.
Jacob will again have peace and security,
    and no-one will make him afraid.
¹¹I am with you and will save you,'
                            declares the LORD.
'Though I completely destroy all the nations
    among which I scatter you,
    I will not completely destroy you.
I will discipline you but only with justice;
    I will not let you go entirely unpunished.'

¹²"This is what the LORD says:

" 'Your wound is incurable,
    your injury beyond healing.
¹³There is no-one to plead your cause,
    no remedy for your sore,
    no healing for you.
¹⁴All your allies have forgotten you;
    they care nothing for you.
I have struck you as an enemy would
    and punished you as would the cruel,
because your guilt is so great
    and your sins so many.

¹⁵Why do you cry out over your wound,
    your pain that has no cure?
Because of your great guilt and many sins
    I have done these things to you.

¹⁶" 'But all who devour you will be devoured;
    all your enemies will go into exile.
Those who plunder you will be plundered;
    all who make spoil of you I will despoil.
¹⁷But I will restore you to health
    and heal your wounds,'
                            declares the LORD,
'because you are called an outcast,
    Zion for whom no-one cares.'

¹⁸"This is what the LORD says:

" 'I will restore the fortunes of Jacob's tents
    and have compassion on his dwellings;
the city will be rebuilt on her ruins,
    and the palace will stand in its proper place.
¹⁹From them will come songs of thanksgiving
    and the sound of rejoicing.
I will add to their numbers,
    and they will not be decreased;
I will bring them honour,
    and they will not be disdained.
²⁰Their children will be as in days of old,
    and their community will be established before
        me;
    I will punish all who oppress them.
²¹Their leader will be one of their own;
    their ruler will arise from among them.
I will bring him near and he will come close to
        me,
    for who is he who will devote himself
    to be close to me?'
                            declares the LORD.
²²" 'So you will be my people,
    and I will be your God.' "

²³See, the storm of the LORD
    will burst out in wrath,
a driving wind swirling down
    on the heads of the wicked.
²⁴The fierce anger of the LORD will not turn back
    until he fully accomplishes
    the purposes of his heart.
In days to come
    you will understand this.

31 "At that time," declares the LORD, "I will be the God of all the clans of Israel, and they will be my people."

²This is what the LORD says:

"The people who survive the sword
    will find favour in the desert;
    I will come to give rest to Israel."

³The LORD appeared to us in the past,*ᵃ* saying:

"I have loved you with an everlasting love;
    I have drawn you with loving-kindness.
⁴I will build you up again
    and you will be rebuilt, O Virgin Israel.

---

*ᵃ*3 Or *will restore the fortunes of my people Israel and Judah*   *ᵃ*3 Or *LORD has appeared to us from afar*

Again you will take up your tambourines
   and go out to dance with the joyful.
⁵Again you will plant vineyards
   on the hills of Samaria;
the farmers will plant them
   and enjoy their fruit.
⁶There will be a day when watchmen cry out
   on the hills of Ephraim,
'Come, let us go up to Zion,
   to the LORD our God.' "

⁷This is what the LORD says:

"Sing with joy for Jacob;
   shout for the foremost of the nations.
Make your praises heard, and say,
   'O LORD, save your people,
   the remnant of Israel.'
⁸See, I will bring them from the land of the north
   and gather them from the ends of the earth.
Among them will be the blind and the lame,
   expectant mothers and women in labour;
   a great throng will return.
⁹They will come with weeping;
   they will pray as I bring them back.
I will lead them beside streams of water
   on a level path where they will not stumble,
because I am Israel's father,
   and Ephraim is my firstborn son.

31:9 Jeremiah declared God's readiness
to restore his exiled people. In one of the
most graphic passages in the book, the
prophet portrayed the homecoming as a
great party in which the whole world is
invited to share.

---

¹⁰"Hear the word of the LORD, O nations;
   proclaim it in distant coastlands:
'He who scattered Israel will gather them
   and will watch over his flock like a shepherd.'
¹¹For the LORD will ransom Jacob
   and redeem them from the hand of those
      stronger than they.
¹²They will come and shout for joy on the heights
      of Zion;
   they will rejoice in the bounty of the LORD—
the grain, the new wine and the oil,
   the young of the flocks and herds.
They will be like a well-watered garden,
   and they will sorrow no more.
¹³Then maidens will dance and be glad,
   young men and old as well.
I will turn their mourning into gladness;
   I will give them comfort and joy instead of
      sorrow.
¹⁴I will satisfy the priests with abundance,
   and my people will be filled with my bounty,"
                                 declares the LORD.

¹⁵This is what the LORD says:

"A voice is heard in Ramah,
   mourning and great weeping,
Rachel weeping for her children
   and refusing to be comforted,
   because her children are no more."

¹⁶This is what the LORD says:

"Restrain your voice from weeping
   and your eyes from tears,
for your work will be rewarded,"
                                 declares the LORD.
   "They will return from the land of the enemy.
¹⁷So there is hope for your future,"
                                 declares the LORD.
   "Your children will return to their own land.

¹⁸"I have surely heard Ephraim's moaning:
   'You disciplined me like an unruly calf,
   and I have been disciplined.
Restore me, and I will return,
   because you are the LORD my God.
¹⁹After I strayed,
   I repented;
after I came to understand,
   I beat my breast.
I was ashamed and humiliated
   because I bore the disgrace of my youth.'
²⁰Is not Ephraim my dear son,
   the child in whom I delight?
Though I often speak against him,
   I still remember him.
Therefore my heart yearns for him;
   I have great compassion for him,"
                                 declares the LORD.

²¹"Set up road signs;
   put up guideposts.
Take note of the highway,
   the road that you take.
Return, O Virgin Israel,
   return to your towns.
²²How long will you wander,
   O unfaithful daughter?
The LORD will create a new thing on earth—
   a woman will surround^b a man."

²³This is what the LORD Almighty, the God of Israel,
says: "When I bring them back from captivity,^c the
people in the land of Judah and in its towns will once
again use these words: 'The LORD bless you, O righteous dwelling, O sacred mountain.' ²⁴People will live
together in Judah and all its towns—farmers and those
who move about with their flocks. ²⁵I will refresh the
weary and satisfy the faint."
   ²⁶At this I awoke and looked around. My sleep had
been pleasant to me.
   ²⁷"The days are coming," declares the LORD, "when
I will plant the house of Israel and the house of Judah
with the offspring of men and of animals. ²⁸Just as I
watched over them to uproot and tear down, and to
overthrow, destroy and bring disaster, so I will watch
over them to build and to plant," declares the LORD.
²⁹"In those days people will no longer say,

ᵇ22 Or *will go about ⸜seeking⸝*; or *will protect*   ᶜ23 Or *I restore their fortunes*

'The fathers have eaten sour grapes,
and the children's teeth are set on edge.'

30Instead, everyone will die for his own sin; whoever eats sour grapes—his own teeth will be set on edge.

31"The time is coming," declares the LORD,
"when I will make a new covenant
with the house of Israel
and with the house of Judah.
32It will not be like the covenant
I made with their forefathers
when I took them by the hand
to lead them out of Egypt,
because they broke my covenant,
though I was a husband to*d* them,"*e*
                              declares the LORD.
33"This is the covenant that I will make with the
house of Israel
after that time," declares the LORD.
"I will put my law in their minds
and write it on their hearts.
I will be their God,
and they will be my people.
34No longer will a man teach his neighbour,
or a man his brother, saying, 'Know the LORD,'
because they will all know me,
from the least of them to the greatest,"
                              declares the LORD.
"For I will forgive their wickedness
and will remember their sins no more."

35This is what the LORD says,

he who appoints the sun
to shine by day,
who decrees the moon and stars
to shine by night,
who stirs up the sea
so that its waves roar—
the LORD Almighty is his name:
36"Only if these decrees vanish from my sight,"
declares the LORD,
"will the descendants of Israel ever cease
to be a nation before me."

37This is what the LORD says:

"Only if the heavens above can be measured
and the foundations of the earth below be
searched out
will I reject all the descendants of Israel
because of all they have done,"
                              declares the LORD.

38"The days are coming," declares the LORD, "when this city will be rebuilt for me from the Tower of Hananel to the Corner Gate. 39The measuring line will stretch from there straight to the hill of Gareb and then turn to Goah. 40The whole valley where dead bodies and ashes are thrown, and all the terraces out to the Kidron Valley on the east as far as the corner of the Horse Gate, will be holy to the LORD. The city will never again be uprooted or demolished."

Jeremiah Buys a Field

32 This is the word that came to Jeremiah from the LORD in the tenth year of Zedekiah king of Judah, which was the eighteenth year of Nebuchadnezzar. 2The army of the king of Babylon was then besieging Jerusalem, and Jeremiah the prophet was confined in the courtyard of the guard in the royal palace of Judah.

3Now Zedekiah king of Judah had imprisoned him there, saying, "Why do you prophesy as you do? You say, 'This is what the LORD says: I am about to hand this city over to the king of Babylon, and he will capture it. 4Zedekiah king of Judah will not escape out of the hands of the Babylonians*a* but will certainly be handed over to the king of Babylon, and will speak with him face to face and see him with his own eyes. 5He will take Zedekiah to Babylon, where he will remain until I deal with him, declares the LORD. If you fight against the Babylonians, you will not succeed.'"

6Jeremiah said, "The word of the LORD came to me: 7Hanamel son of Shallum your uncle is going to come to you and say, 'Buy my field at Anathoth, because as nearest relative it is your right and duty to buy it.'

8"Then, just as the LORD had said, my cousin Hanamel came to me in the courtyard of the guard and said, 'Buy my field at Anathoth in the territory of Benjamin. Since it is your right to redeem it and possess it, buy it for yourself.'

"I knew that this was the word of the LORD; 9so I bought the field at Anathoth from my cousin Hanamel and weighed out for him seventeen shekels*b* of silver. 10I signed and sealed the deed, had it witnessed, and weighed out the silver on the scales. 11I took the deed of purchase—the sealed copy containing the terms and conditions, as well as the unsealed copy—12and I gave this deed to Baruch son of Neriah, the son of Mahseiah, in the presence of my cousin Hanamel and of the witnesses who had signed the deed and of all the Jews sitting in the courtyard of the guard.

13"In their presence I gave Baruch these instructions: 14'This is what the LORD Almighty, the God of Israel, says: Take these documents, both the sealed and unsealed copies of the deed of purchase, and put them in a clay jar so that they will last a long time. 15For this is what the LORD Almighty, the God of Israel, says: Houses, fields and vineyards will again be bought in this land.'

16"After I had given the deed of purchase to Baruch son of Neriah, I prayed to the LORD:

17"Ah, Sovereign LORD, you have made the heavens and the earth by your great power and outstretched arm. Nothing is too hard for you. 18You show love to thousands but bring the punishment for the fathers' sins into the laps of their children after them. O great and powerful God, whose name is the LORD Almighty, 19great are your purposes and mighty are your deeds. Your eyes are open to all the ways of men; you reward everyone according to his conduct and as his deeds deserve. 20You performed miraculous signs and wonders in

---

*d*32 Hebrew; Septuagint and Syriac *covenant, / and I turned away from*   *e*32 Or *was their master*
*a*4 Or *Chaldeans*; also in verses 5, 24, 25, 28, 29 and 43   *b*9 That is, about 7 ounces (about 200 grams)

Egypt and have continued them to this day, both in Israel and among all mankind, and have gained the renown that is still yours. [21]You brought your people Israel out of Egypt with signs and wonders, by a mighty hand and an outstretched arm and with great terror. [22]You gave them this land you had sworn to give to their forefathers, a land flowing with milk and honey. [23]They came in and took possession of it, but they did not obey you or follow your law; they did not do what you commanded them to do. So you brought all this disaster upon them.

[24]"See how the siege ramps are built up to take the city. Because of the sword, famine and plague, the city will be handed over to the Babylonians who are attacking it. What you said has happened, as you now see. [25]And though the city will be handed over to the Babylonians, you, O Sovereign LORD, say to me, 'Buy the field with silver and have the transaction witnessed.' "

[26]Then the word of the LORD came to Jeremiah: [27]"I am the LORD, the God of all mankind. Is anything too hard for me? [28]Therefore, this is what the LORD says: I am about to hand this city over to the Babylonians and to Nebuchadnezzar king of Babylon, who will capture it. [29]The Babylonians who are attacking this city will come in and set it on fire; they will burn it down, along with the houses where the people provoked me to anger by burning incense on the roofs to Baal and by pouring out drink offerings to other gods.

[30]"The people of Israel and Judah have done nothing but evil in my sight from their youth; indeed, the people of Israel have done nothing but provoke me with what their hands have made, declares the LORD. [31]From the day it was built until now, this city has so aroused my anger and wrath that I must remove it from my sight. [32]The people of Israel and Judah have provoked me by all the evil they have done—they, their kings and officials, their priests and prophets, the men of Judah and the people of Jerusalem. [33]They turned their backs to me and not their faces; though I taught them again and again, they would not listen or respond to discipline. [34]They set up their abominable idols in the house that bears my Name and defiled it. [35]They built high places for Baal in the Valley of Ben Hinnom to sacrifice their sons and daughters[c] to Molech, though I never commanded, nor did it enter my mind, that they should do such a detestable thing and so make Judah sin.

[36]"You are saying about this city, 'By the sword, famine and plague it will be handed over to the king of Babylon'; but this is what the LORD, the God of Israel, says: [37]I will surely gather them from all the lands where I banish them in my furious anger and great wrath; I will bring them back to this place and let them live in safety. [38]They will be my people, and I will be their God. [39]I will give them singleness of heart and action, so that they will always fear me for their own good and the good of their children after them. [40]I will make an everlasting covenant with them: I will never

stop doing good to them, and I will inspire them to fear me, so that they will never turn away from me. [41]I will rejoice in doing them good and will assuredly plant them in this land with all my heart and soul.

[42]"This is what the LORD says: As I have brought all this great calamity on this people, so I will give them all the prosperity I have promised them. [43]Once more fields will be bought in this land of which you say, 'It is a desolate waste, without men or animals, for it has been handed over to the Babylonians.' [44]Fields will be bought for silver, and deeds will be signed, sealed and witnessed in the territory of Benjamin, in the villages around Jerusalem, in the towns of Judah and in the towns of the hill country, of the western foothills and of the Negev, because I will restore their fortunes,[d] declares the LORD."

32:44   As surely as God can bring calamity, so he can bring prosperity, and, in the form of a new covenant, he offered the hand of partnership and friendship to his people. Jeremiah was keen to stress the down-to-earth nature of this covenant, by reference to immediate political concerns.

Promise of Restoration

33 While Jeremiah was still confined in the courtyard of the guard, the word of the LORD came to him a second time: [2]"This is what the LORD says, he who made the earth, the LORD who formed it and established it—the LORD is his name: [3]'Call to me and I will answer you and tell you great and unsearchable things you do not know.' [4]For this is what the LORD, the God of Israel, says about the houses in this city and the royal palaces of Judah that have been torn down to be used against the siege ramps and the sword [5]in the fight with the Babylonians:[a] 'They will be filled with the dead bodies of the men I will slay in my anger and wrath. I will hide my face from this city because of all its wickedness.

[6]" 'Nevertheless, I will bring health and healing to it; I will heal my people and will let them enjoy abundant peace and security. [7]I will bring Judah and Israel back from captivity[b] and will rebuild them as they were before. [8]I will cleanse them from all the sin they have committed against me and will forgive all their sins of rebellion against me. [9]Then this city will bring me renown, joy, praise and honour before all nations on earth that hear of all the good things I do for it; and they will be in awe and will tremble at the abundant prosperity and peace I provide for it.'

[10]"This is what the LORD says: 'You say about this place, "It is a desolate waste, without men or animals." Yet in the towns of Judah and the streets of Jerusalem that are deserted, inhabited by neither men nor animals, there will be heard once more [11]the sounds of joy and gladness, the voices of bride and bridegroom, and

---

c35 Or to make their sons and daughters pass through ⎣the fire⎦   d44 Or will bring them back from captivity
a5 Or Chaldeans   b7 Or will restore the fortunes of Judah and Israel

the voices of those who bring thank-offerings to the house of the LORD, saying,

"Give thanks to the LORD Almighty,
for the LORD is good;
his love endures for ever."

For I will restore the fortunes of the land as they were before,' says the LORD.

12"This is what the LORD Almighty says: 'In this place, desolate and without men or animals—in all its towns there will again be pastures for shepherds to rest their flocks. 13In the towns of the hill country, of the western foothills and of the Negev, in the territory of Benjamin, in the villages around Jerusalem and in the towns of Judah, flocks will again pass under the hand of the one who counts them,' says the LORD.

14" 'The days are coming,' declares the LORD, 'when I will fulfil the gracious promise I made to the house of Israel and to the house of Judah.

15" 'In those days and at that time
I will make a righteous Branch sprout from
David's line;
he will do what is just and right in the land.
16In those days Judah will be saved
and Jerusalem will live in safety.
This is the name by which it c will be called:
The LORD Our Righteousness.'

17For this is what the LORD says: 'David will never fail to have a man to sit on the throne of the house of Israel, 18nor will the priests, who are Levites, ever fail to have a man to stand before me continually to offer burnt offerings, to burn grain offerings and to present sacrifices.' "

19The word of the LORD came to Jeremiah: 20"This is what the LORD says: 'If you can break my covenant with the day and my covenant with the night, so that day and night no longer come at their appointed time, 21then my covenant with David my servant—and my covenant with the Levites who are priests ministering before me—can be broken and David will no longer have a descendant to reign on his throne. 22I will make the descendants of David my servant and the Levites who minister before me as countless as the stars of the sky and as measureless as the sand on the seashore.' "

23The word of the LORD came to Jeremiah: 24"Have you not noticed that these people are saying, 'The LORD has rejected the two kingdomsd he chose'? So they despise my people and no longer regard them as a nation. 25This is what the LORD says: 'If I have not established my covenant with day and night and the fixed laws of heaven and earth, 26then I will reject the descendants of Jacob and David my servant and will not choose one of his sons to rule over the descendants of Abraham, Isaac and Jacob. For I will restore their fortunese and have compassion on them.' "

Warning to Zedekiah

34 While Nebuchadnezzar king of Babylon and all his army and all the kingdoms and peoples in the empire he ruled were fighting against Jerusalem and all its surrounding towns, this word came to Jeremiah from the LORD: 2"This is what the LORD, the God of Israel, says: Go to Zedekiah king of Judah and tell him, 'This is what the LORD says: I am about to hand this city over to the king of Babylon, and he will burn it down. 3You will not escape from his grasp but will surely be captured and handed over to him. You will see the king of Babylon with your own eyes, and he will speak with you face to face. And you will go to Babylon.

4" 'Yet hear the promise of the LORD, O Zedekiah king of Judah. This is what the LORD says concerning you: You will not die by the sword; 5you will die peacefully. As people made a funeral fire in honour of your fathers, the former kings who preceded you, so they will make a fire in your honour and lament, "Alas, O master!" I myself make this promise, declares the LORD.' "

6Then Jeremiah the prophet told all this to Zedekiah king of Judah, in Jerusalem, 7while the army of the king of Babylon was fighting against Jerusalem and the other cities of Judah that were still holding out—Lachish and Azekah. These were the only fortified cities left in Judah.

Freedom for Slaves

8The word came to Jeremiah from the LORD after King Zedekiah had made a covenant with all the people in Jerusalem to proclaim freedom for the slaves. 9Everyone was to free his Hebrew slaves, both male and female; no-one was to hold a fellow Jew in bondage. 10So all the officials and people who entered into this covenant agreed that they would free their male and female slaves and no longer hold them in bondage. They agreed, and set them free. 11But afterwards they changed their minds and took back the slaves they had freed and enslaved them again.

12Then the word of the LORD came to Jeremiah: 13"This is what the LORD, the God of Israel, says: I made a covenant with your forefathers when I brought them out of Egypt, out of the land of slavery. I said, 14'Every seventh year each of you must free any fellow Hebrew who has sold himself to you. After he has served you for six years, you must let him go free.' a Your fathers, however, did not listen to me or pay attention to me. 15Recently you repented and did what is right in my sight: Each of you proclaimed freedom to his countrymen. You even made a covenant before me in the house that bears my Name. 16But now you have turned round and profaned my name; each of you has taken back the male and female slaves you had set free to go where they wished. You have forced them to become your slaves again.

17"Therefore, this is what the LORD says: You have not obeyed me; you have not proclaimed freedom for your fellow countrymen. So I now proclaim 'freedom' for you, declares the LORD—'freedom' to fall by the sword, plague and famine. I will make you abhorrent to all the kingdoms of the earth. 18The men who have violated my covenant and have not fulfilled the terms of the covenant they made before me, I will treat like

c16 Or he   d24 Or families   e26 Or will bring them back from captivity   a14 Deut. 15:12

the calf they cut in two and then walked between its pieces. [19]The leaders of Judah and Jerusalem, the court officials, the priests and all the people of the land who walked between the pieces of the calf, [20]I will hand over to their enemies who seek their lives. Their dead bodies will become food for the birds of the air and the beasts of the earth.

[21]"I will hand Zedekiah king of Judah and his officials over to their enemies who seek their lives, to the army of the king of Babylon, which has withdrawn from you. [22]I am going to give the order, declares the LORD, and I will bring them back to this city. They will fight against it, take it and burn it down. And I will lay waste the towns of Judah so that no-one can live there."

The Recabites

35 This is the word that came to Jeremiah from the LORD during the reign of Jehoiakim son of Josiah king of Judah: [2]"Go to the Recabite family and invite them to come to one of the side rooms of the house of the LORD and give them wine to drink."

[3]So I went to get Jaazaniah son of Jeremiah, the son of Habazziniah, and his brothers and all his sons—the whole family of the Recabites. [4]I brought them into the house of the LORD, into the room of the sons of Hanan son of Igdaliah the man of God. It was next to the room of the officials, which was over that of Maaseiah son of Shallum the door-keeper. [5]Then I set bowls full of wine and some cups before the men of the Recabite family and said to them, "Drink some wine."

[6]But they replied, "We do not drink wine, because our forefather Jonadab son of Recab gave us this command: 'Neither you nor your descendants must ever drink wine. [7]Also you must never build houses, sow seed or plant vineyards; you must never have any of these things, but must always live in tents. Then you will live a long time in the land where you are nomads.' [8]We have obeyed everything our forefather Jonadab son of Recab commanded us. Neither we nor our wives nor our sons and daughters have ever drunk wine [9]or built houses to live in or had vineyards, fields or crops. [10]We have lived in tents and have fully obeyed everything our forefather Jonadab commanded us. [11]But when Nebuchadnezzar king of Babylon invaded this land, we said, 'Come, we must go to Jerusalem to escape the Babylonian[a] and Aramean armies.' So we have remained in Jerusalem."

[12]Then the word of the LORD came to Jeremiah, saying: [13]"This is what the LORD Almighty, the God of Israel, says: Go and tell the men of Judah and the people of Jerusalem, 'Will you not learn a lesson and obey my words?' declares the LORD. [14]'Jonadab son of Recab ordered his sons not to drink wine and this command has been kept. To this day they do not drink wine, because they obey their forefather's command. But I have spoken to you again and again, yet you have not obeyed me. [15]Again and again I sent all my servants the prophets to you. They said, "Each of you must turn from your wicked ways and reform your actions; do not follow other gods to serve them. Then you shall live in the land I have given to you and your fathers." But you have not paid attention or listened to me. [16]The descendants of Jonadab son of Recab have carried out the command their forefather gave them, but these people have not obeyed me.'

[17]"Therefore, this is what the LORD God Almighty, the God of Israel, says: 'Listen! I am going to bring on Judah and on everyone living in Jerusalem every disaster I pronounced against them. I spoke to them, but they did not listen; I called to them, but they did not answer.' "

[18]Then Jeremiah said to the family of the Recabites, "This is what the LORD Almighty, the God of Israel, says: 'You have obeyed the command of your forefather Jonadab and have followed all his instructions and have done everything he ordered.' [19]Therefore, this is what the LORD Almighty, the God of Israel, says: 'Jonadab son of Recab shall never fail to have a man to serve me.' "

Jehoiakim Burns Jeremiah's Scroll

36 In the fourth year of Jehoiakim son of Josiah king of Judah, this word came to Jeremiah from the LORD: [2]"Take a scroll and write on it all the words I have spoken to you concerning Israel, Judah and all the other nations from the time I began speaking to you in the reign of Josiah till now. [3]Perhaps when the people of Judah hear about every disaster I plan to inflict on them, each of them will turn from his wicked way; then I will forgive their wickedness and their sin."

[4]So Jeremiah called Baruch son of Neriah, and while Jeremiah dictated all the words the LORD had spoken to him, Baruch wrote them on the scroll. [5]Then Jeremiah told Baruch, "I am restricted; I cannot go to the LORD's temple. [6]So you go to the house of the LORD on a day of fasting and read to the people from the scroll the words of the LORD that you wrote as I dictated. Read them to all the people of Judah who come in from their towns. [7]Perhaps they will bring their petition before the LORD, and each will turn from his wicked ways, for the anger and wrath pronounced against this people by the LORD are great."

[8]Baruch son of Neriah did everything Jeremiah the prophet told him to do; at the LORD's temple he read the words of the LORD from the scroll. [9]In the ninth month of the fifth year of Jehoiakim son of Josiah king of Judah, a time of fasting before the LORD was proclaimed for all the people in Jerusalem and those who had come from the towns of Judah. [10]From the room of Gemariah son of Shaphan the secretary, which was in the upper courtyard at the entrance of the New Gate of the temple, Baruch read to all the people at the LORD's temple the words of Jeremiah from the scroll.

[11]When Micaiah son of Gemariah, the son of Shaphan, heard all the words of the LORD from the scroll, [12]he went down to the secretary's room in the royal palace, where all the officials were sitting: Elishama the secretary, Delaiah son of Shemaiah, Elnathan son of Acbor, Gemariah son of Shaphan, Zedekiah son of

Hananiah, and all the other officials. ¹³After Micaiah told them everything he had heard Baruch read to the people from the scroll, ¹⁴all the officials sent Jehudi son of Nethaniah, the son of Shelemiah, the son of Cushi, to say to Baruch, "Bring the scroll from which you have read to the people and come." So Baruch son of Neriah went to them with the scroll in his hand. ¹⁵They said to him, "Sit down, please, and read it to us."

So Baruch read it to them. ¹⁶When they heard all these words, they looked at each other in fear and said to Baruch, "We must report all these words to the king." ¹⁷Then they asked Baruch, "Tell us, how did you come to write all this? Did Jeremiah dictate it?"

¹⁸"Yes," Baruch replied, "he dictated all these words to me, and I wrote them in ink on the scroll."

¹⁹Then the officials said to Baruch, "You and Jeremiah, go and hide. Don't let anyone know where you are."

²⁰After they put the scroll in the room of Elishama the secretary, they went to the king in the courtyard and reported everything to him. ²¹The king sent Jehudi to get the scroll, and Jehudi brought it from the room of Elishama the secretary and read it to the king and all the officials standing beside him. ²²It was the ninth month and the king was sitting in the winter apartment, with a fire burning in the brazier in front of him. ²³Whenever Jehudi had read three or four columns of the scroll, the king cut them off with a scribe's knife and threw them into the brazier, until the entire scroll was burned in the fire. ²⁴The king and all his attendants who heard all these words showed no fear, nor did they tear their clothes. ²⁵Even though Elnathan, Delaiah and Gemariah urged the king not to burn the scroll, he would not listen to them. ²⁶Instead, the king commanded Jerahmeel, a son of the king, Seraiah son of Azriel and Shelemiah son of Abdeel to arrest Baruch the scribe and Jeremiah the prophet. But the LORD had hidden them.

²⁷After the king burned the scroll containing the words that Baruch had written at Jeremiah's dictation, the word of the LORD came to Jeremiah: ²⁸"Take another scroll and write on it all the words that were on the first scroll, which Jehoiakim king of Judah burned up. ²⁹Also tell Jehoiakim king of Judah, 'This is what the LORD says: You burned that scroll and said, "Why did you write on it that the king of Babylon would certainly come and destroy this land and cut off both men and animals from it?" ³⁰Therefore, this is what the LORD says about Jehoiakim king of Judah: He will have no-one to sit on the throne of David; his body will be thrown out and exposed to the heat by day and the frost by night. ³¹I will punish him and his children and his attendants for their wickedness; I will bring on them and those living in Jerusalem and the people of Judah every disaster I pronounced against them, because they have not listened.' "

³²So Jeremiah took another scroll and gave it to the scribe Baruch son of Neriah, and as Jeremiah dictated, Baruch wrote on it all the words of the scroll that Jehoiakim king of Judah had burned in the fire. And many similar words were added to them.

Jeremiah in Prison

37 Zedekiah son of Josiah was made king of Judah by Nebuchadnezzar king of Babylon; he reigned in place of Jehoiachin[a] son of Jehoiakim. ²Neither he nor his attendants nor the people of the land paid any attention to the words the LORD had spoken through Jeremiah the prophet.

³King Zedekiah, however, sent Jehucal son of Shelemiah with the priest Zephaniah son of Maaseiah to Jeremiah the prophet with this message: "Please pray to the LORD our God for us."

⁴Now Jeremiah was free to come and go among the people, for he had not yet been put in prison. ⁵Pharaoh's army had marched out of Egypt, and when the Babylonians[b] who were besieging Jerusalem heard the report about them, they withdrew from Jerusalem.

⁶Then the word of the LORD came to Jeremiah the prophet: ⁷"This is what the LORD, the God of Israel, says: Tell the king of Judah, who sent you to enquire of me, 'Pharaoh's army, which has marched out to support you, will go back to its own land, to Egypt. ⁸Then the Babylonians will return and attack this city; they will capture it and burn it down.'

⁹"This is what the LORD says: Do not deceive yourselves, thinking, 'The Babylonians will surely leave us.' They will not! ¹⁰Even if you were to defeat the entire Babylonian[c] army that is attacking you and only wounded men were left in their tents, they would come out and burn this city down."

¹¹After the Babylonian army had withdrawn from Jerusalem because of Pharaoh's army, ¹²Jeremiah started to leave the city to go to the territory of Benjamin to get his share of the property among the people there. ¹³But when he reached the Benjamin Gate, the captain of the guard, whose name was Irijah son of Shelemiah, the son of Hananiah, arrested him and said, "You are deserting to the Babylonians!"

¹⁴"That's not true!" Jeremiah said. "I am not deserting to the Babylonians." But Irijah would not listen to him; instead, he arrested Jeremiah and brought him to the officials. ¹⁵They were angry with Jeremiah and had him beaten and imprisoned in the house of Jonathan the secretary, which they had made into a prison.

¹⁶Jeremiah was put into a vaulted cell in a dungeon, where he remained a long time. ¹⁷Then King Zedekiah sent for him and had him brought to the palace, where he asked him privately, "Is there any word from the LORD?"

"Yes," Jeremiah replied, "you will be handed over to the king of Babylon."

¹⁸Then Jeremiah said to King Zedekiah, "What crime have I committed against you or your officials or this people, that you have put me in prison? ¹⁹Where are your prophets who prophesied to you, 'The king of Babylon will not attack you or this land'? ²⁰But now, my lord the king, please listen. Let me bring my petition before you: Do not send me back to the house of Jonathan the secretary, or I shall die there."

²¹King Zedekiah then gave orders for Jeremiah to be placed in the courtyard of the guard and given bread

a 1 Hebrew Coniah, a variant of Jehoiachin   b 5 Or Chaldeans; also in verses 8, 9, 13 and 14
c 10 Or Chaldean; also in verse 11

from the street of the bakers each day until all the bread in the city was gone. So Jeremiah remained in the courtyard of the guard.

Jeremiah Thrown Into a Cistern

38 Shephatiah son of Mattan, Gedaliah son of Pashhur, Jehucal[a] son of Shelemiah, and Pashhur son of Malkijah heard what Jeremiah was telling all the people when he said, ²"This is what the LORD says: 'Whoever stays in this city will die by the sword, famine or plague, but whoever goes over to the Babylonians[b] will live. He will escape with his life; he will live.' ³And this is what the LORD says: 'This city will certainly be handed over to the army of the king of Babylon, who will capture it.' "

⁴Then the officials said to the king, "This man should be put to death. He is discouraging the soldiers who are left in this city, as well as all the people, by the things he is saying to them. This man is not seeking the good of these people but their ruin."

⁵"He is in your hands," King Zedekiah answered. "The king can do nothing to oppose you."

⁶So they took Jeremiah and put him into the cistern of Malkijah, the king's son, which was in the courtyard of the guard. They lowered Jeremiah by ropes into the cistern; it had no water in it, only mud, and Jeremiah sank down into the mud.

⁷But Ebed-Melech, a Cushite,[c] an official[d] in the royal palace, heard that they had put Jeremiah into the cistern. While the king was sitting in the Benjamin Gate, ⁸Ebed-Melech went out of the palace and said to him, ⁹"My lord the king, these men have acted wickedly in all they have done to Jeremiah the prophet. They have thrown him into a cistern, where he will starve to death when there is no longer any bread in the city."

¹⁰Then the king commanded Ebed-Melech the Cushite, "Take thirty men from here with you and lift Jeremiah the prophet out of the cistern before he dies."

¹¹So Ebed-Melech took the men with him and went to a room under the treasury in the palace. He took some old rags and worn-out clothes from there and let them down with ropes to Jeremiah in the cistern. ¹²Ebed-Melech the Cushite said to Jeremiah, "Put these old rags and worn-out clothes under your arms to pad the ropes." Jeremiah did so, ¹³and they pulled him up with the ropes and lifted him out of the cistern. And Jeremiah remained in the courtyard of the guard.

Zedekiah Questions Jeremiah Again

¹⁴Then King Zedekiah sent for Jeremiah the prophet and had him brought to the third entrance to the temple of the LORD. "I am going to ask you something," the king said to Jeremiah. "Do not hide anything from me."

¹⁵Jeremiah said to Zedekiah, "If I give you an answer, will you not kill me? Even if I did give you counsel, you would not listen to me."

¹⁶But King Zedekiah swore this oath secretly to Jeremiah: "As surely as the LORD lives, who has given us

breath, I will neither kill you nor hand you over to those who are seeking your life."

¹⁷Then Jeremiah said to Zedekiah, "This is what the LORD God Almighty, the God of Israel, says: 'If you surrender to the officers of the king of Babylon, your life will be spared and this city will not be burned down; you and your family will live. ¹⁸But if you will not surrender to the officers of the king of Babylon, this city will be handed over to the Babylonians and they will burn it down; you yourself will not escape from their hands.' "

¹⁹King Zedekiah said to Jeremiah, "I am afraid of the Jews who have gone over to the Babylonians, for the Babylonians may hand me over to them and they will ill-treat me."

²⁰"They will not hand you over," Jeremiah replied. "Obey the LORD by doing what I tell you. Then it will go well with you, and your life will be spared. ²¹But if you refuse to surrender, this is what the LORD has revealed to me: ²²All the women left in the palace of the king of Judah will be brought out to the officials of the king of Babylon. Those women will say to you:

" 'They misled you and overcame you —
　　those trusted friends of yours.
Your feet are sunk in the mud;
　　your friends have deserted you.'

38:22　　King Zedekiah was in a mess, and sought a meeting with Jeremiah to try and get some assurance that no harm would befall him. Jeremiah had no false comfort to offer him, just the plain truth!

---

²³"All your wives and children will be brought out to the Babylonians. You yourself will not escape from their hands but will be captured by the king of Babylon; and this city will[e] be burned down."

²⁴Then Zedekiah said to Jeremiah, "Do not let anyone know about this conversation, or you may die. ²⁵If the officials hear that I talked with you, and they come to you and say, 'Tell us what you said to the king and what the king said to you; do not hide it from us or we will kill you,' ²⁶then tell them, 'I was pleading with the king not to send me back to Jonathan's house to die there.' "

²⁷All the officials did come to Jeremiah and question him, and he told them everything the king had ordered him to say. So they said no more to him, for no-one had heard his conversation with the king.

²⁸And Jeremiah remained in the courtyard of the guard until the day Jerusalem was captured.

The Fall of Jerusalem

39 This is how Jerusalem was taken: ¹In the ninth year of Zedekiah king of Judah, in the tenth month, Nebuchadnezzar king of Babylon marched against Jerusalem with his whole army and laid siege to it. ²And on the ninth day of the fourth month of Zedekiah's eleventh year, the city wall was broken

---

a 1 Hebrew *Jucal*, a variant of *Jehucal*　　b 2 Or *Chaldeans*; also in verses 18, 19 and 23
c 7 Probably from the upper Nile region　　d 7 Or *a eunuch*　　e 23 Or *and you will cause this city to*

through. [3]Then all the officials of the king of Babylon came and took seats in the Middle Gate: Nergal-Sharezer of Samgar, Nebo-Sarsekim[a] a chief officer, Nergal-Sharezer a high official and all the other officials of the king of Babylon. [4]When Zedekiah king of Judah and all the soldiers saw them, they fled; they left the city at night by way of the king's garden, through the gate between the two walls, and headed towards the Arabah.[b]

[5]But the Babylonian[c] army pursued them and overtook Zedekiah in the plains of Jericho. They captured him and took him to Nebuchadnezzar king of Babylon at Riblah in the land of Hamath, where he pronounced sentence on him. [6]There at Riblah the king of Babylon slaughtered the sons of Zedekiah before his eyes and also killed all the nobles of Judah. [7]Then he put out Zedekiah's eyes and bound him with bronze shackles to take him to Babylon.

[8]The Babylonians[d] set fire to the royal palace and the houses of the people and broke down the walls of Jerusalem. [9]Nebuzaradan commander of the imperial guard carried into exile to Babylon the people who remained in the city, along with those who had gone over to him, and the rest of the people. [10]But Nebuzaradan the commander of the guard left behind in the land of Judah some of the poor people, who owned nothing; and at that time he gave them vineyards and fields.

[11]Now Nebuchadnezzar king of Babylon had given these orders about Jeremiah through Nebuzaradan commander of the imperial guard: [12]"Take him and look after him; don't harm him but do for him whatever he asks." [13]So Nebuzaradan the commander of the guard, Nebushazban a chief officer, Nergal-Sharezer a high official and all the other officers of the king of Babylon [14]sent and had Jeremiah taken out of the courtyard of the guard. They handed him over to Gedaliah son of Ahikam, the son of Shaphan, to take him back to his home. So he remained among his own people.

[15]While Jeremiah had been confined in the courtyard of the guard, the word of the LORD came to him: [16]"Go and tell Ebed-Melech the Cushite, 'This is what the LORD Almighty, the God of Israel, says: I am about to fulfil my words against this city through disaster, not prosperity. At that time they will be fulfilled before your eyes. [17]But I will rescue you on that day, declares the LORD; you will not be handed over to those you fear. [18]I will save you; you will not fall by the sword but will escape with your life, because you trust in me, declares the LORD.'"

Jeremiah Freed

40 The word came to Jeremiah from the LORD after Nebuzaradan commander of the imperial guard had released him at Ramah. He had found Jeremiah bound in chains among all the captives from Jerusalem and Judah who were being carried into exile to Babylon. [2]When the commander of the guard found Jeremiah, he said to him, "The LORD your God decreed this disaster for this place. [3]And now the LORD has

brought it about; he has done just as he said he would. All this happened because you people sinned against the LORD and did not obey him. [4]But today I am freeing you from the chains on your wrists. Come with me to Babylon, if you like, and I will look after you; but if you do not want to, then don't come. Look, the whole country lies before you; go wherever you please." [5]However, before Jeremiah turned to go,[a] Nebuzaradan added, "Go back to Gedaliah son of Ahikam, the son of Shaphan, whom the king of Babylon has appointed over the towns of Judah, and live with him among the people, or go anywhere else you please."

Then the commander gave him provisions and a present and let him go. [6]So Jeremiah went to Gedaliah son of Ahikam at Mizpah and stayed with him among the people who were left behind in the land.

Gedaliah Assassinated

[7]When all the army officers and their men who were still in the open country heard that the king of Babylon had appointed Gedaliah son of Ahikam as governor over the land and had put him in charge of the men, women and children who were the poorest in the land and who had not been carried into exile to Babylon, [8]they came to Gedaliah at Mizpah—Ishmael son of Nethaniah, Johanan and Jonathan the sons of Kareah, Seraiah son of Tanhumeth, the sons of Ephai the Netophathite, and Jaazaniah[b] the son of the Maacathite, and their men. [9]Gedaliah son of Ahikam, the son of Shaphan, took an oath to reassure them and their men. "Do not be afraid to serve the Babylonians,"[c] he said. "Settle down in the land and serve the king of Babylon, and it will go well with you. [10]I myself will stay in Mizpah to represent you before the Babylonians who come to us, but you are to harvest the wine, summer fruit and oil, and put them in your storage jars, and live in the towns you have taken over."

[11]When all the Jews in Moab, Ammon, Edom and all the other countries heard that the king of Babylon had left a remnant in Judah and had appointed Gedaliah son of Ahikam, the son of Shaphan, as governor over them, [12]they all came back to the land of Judah, to Gedaliah at Mizpah, from all the countries where they had been scattered. And they harvested an abundance of wine and summer fruit.

[13]Johanan son of Kareah and all the army officers still in the open country came to Gedaliah at Mizpah [14]and said to him, "Don't you know that Baalis king of the Ammonites has sent Ishmael son of Nethaniah to take your life?" But Gedaliah son of Ahikam did not believe them.

[15]Then Johanan son of Kareah said privately to Gedaliah in Mizpah, "Let me go and kill Ishmael son of Nethaniah, and no-one will know it. Why should he take your life and cause all the Jews who are gathered around you to be scattered and the remnant of Judah to perish?"

[16]But Gedaliah son of Ahikam said to Johanan son of Kareah, "Don't do such a thing! What you are saying about Ishmael is not true."

---

a3 Or Nergal-Sharezer, Samgar-Nebo, Sarsekim   b4 Or the Jordan Valley   c5 Or Chaldean   d8 Or Chaldeans
a5 Or Jeremiah answered   b8 Hebrew Jezaniah, a variant of Jaazaniah   c9 Or Chaldeans; also in verse 10

41 In the seventh month Ishmael son of Nethaniah, the son of Elishama, who was of royal blood and had been one of the king's officers, came with ten men to Gedaliah son of Ahikam at Mizpah. While they were eating together there, ²Ishmael son of Nethaniah and the ten men who were with him got up and struck down Gedaliah son of Ahikam, the son of Shaphan, with the sword, killing the one whom the king of Babylon had appointed as governor over the land. ³Ishmael also killed all the Jews who were with Gedaliah at Mizpah, as well as the Babylonian^a soldiers who were there.

⁴The day after Gedaliah's assassination, before anyone knew about it, ⁵eighty men who had shaved off their beards, torn their clothes and cut themselves came from Shechem, Shiloh and Samaria, bringing grain offerings and incense with them to the house of the LORD. ⁶Ishmael son of Nethaniah went out from Mizpah to meet them, weeping as he went. When he met them, he said, "Come to Gedaliah son of Ahikam." ⁷When they went into the city, Ishmael son of Nethaniah and the men who were with him slaughtered them and threw them into a cistern. ⁸But ten of them said to Ishmael, "Don't kill us! We have wheat and barley, oil and honey, hidden in a field." So he let them alone and did not kill them with the others. ⁹Now the cistern where he threw all the bodies of the men he had killed along with Gedaliah was the one King Asa had made as part of his defence against Baasha king of Israel. Ishmael son of Nethaniah filled it with the dead.

¹⁰Ishmael made captives of all the rest of the people who were in Mizpah — the king's daughters along with all the others who were left there, over whom Nebuzaradan commander of the imperial guard had appointed Gedaliah son of Ahikam. Ishmael son of Nethaniah took them captive and set out to cross over to the Ammonites.

¹¹When Johanan son of Kareah and all the army officers who were with him heard about all the crimes Ishmael son of Nethaniah had committed, ¹²they took all their men and went to fight Ishmael son of Nethaniah. They caught up with him near the great pool in Gibeon. ¹³When all the people Ishmael had with him saw Johanan son of Kareah and the army officers who were with him, they were glad. ¹⁴All the people Ishmael had taken captive at Mizpah turned and went over to Johanan son of Kareah. ¹⁵But Ishmael son of Nethaniah and eight of his men escaped from Johanan and fled to the Ammonites.

Flight to Egypt

¹⁶Then Johanan son of Kareah and all the army officers who were with him led away all the survivors from Mizpah whom he had recovered from Ishmael son of Nethaniah after he had assassinated Gedaliah son of Ahikam: the soldiers, women, children and court officials he had brought from Gibeon. ¹⁷And they went on, stopping at Geruth Kimham near Bethlehem on their way to Egypt ¹⁸to escape the Babylonians.^b They were afraid of them because Ishmael son of Nethaniah had

killed Gedaliah son of Ahikam, whom the king of Babylon had appointed as governor over the land.

42 Then all the army officers, including Johanan son of Kareah and Jezaniah^a son of Hoshaiah, and all the people from the least to the greatest approached ²Jeremiah the prophet and said to him, "Please hear our petition and pray to the LORD your God for this entire remnant. For as you now see, though we were once many, now only a few are left. ³Pray that the LORD your God will tell us where we should go and what we should do."

⁴"I have heard you," replied Jeremiah the prophet. "I will certainly pray to the LORD your God as you have requested; I will tell you everything the LORD says and will keep nothing back from you."

42:4 Jeremiah, once despised by the officials and rulers of Judah, was now seen as their major asset in such different circumstances.

---

⁵Then they said to Jeremiah, "May the LORD be a true and faithful witness against us if we do not act in accordance with everything the LORD your God sends you to tell us. ⁶Whether it is favourable or unfavourable, we will obey the LORD our God, to whom we are sending you, so that it will go well with us, for we will obey the LORD our God."

⁷Ten days later the word of the LORD came to Jeremiah. ⁸So he called together Johanan son of Kareah and all the army officers who were with him and all the people from the least to the greatest. ⁹He said to them, "This is what the LORD, the God of Israel, to whom you sent me to present your petition, says: ¹⁰'If you stay in this land, I will build you up and not tear you down; I will plant you and not uproot you, for I am grieved over the disaster I have inflicted on you. ¹¹Do not be afraid of the king of Babylon, whom you now fear. Do not be afraid of him, declares the LORD, for I am with you and will save you and deliver you from his hands. ¹²I will show you compassion so that he will have compassion on you and restore you to your land.'

¹³"However, if you say, 'We will not stay in this land,' and so disobey the LORD your God, ¹⁴and if you say, 'No, we will go and live in Egypt, where we will not see war or hear the trumpet or be hungry for bread,' ¹⁵then hear the word of the LORD, O remnant of Judah. This is what the LORD Almighty, the God of Israel, says: 'If you are determined to go to Egypt and you do go to settle there, ¹⁶then the sword you fear will overtake you there, and the famine you dread will follow you into Egypt, and there you will die. ¹⁷Indeed, all who are determined to go to Egypt to settle there will die by the sword, famine and plague; not one of them will survive or escape the disaster I will bring on them.' ¹⁸This is what the LORD Almighty, the God of Israel, says: 'As my anger and wrath have been poured out on those who lived in Jerusalem, so will my wrath be poured out on you when you go to Egypt. You will be an object of cursing and horror, of condemnation and reproach; you will never see this place again.'

---

^a3 Or *Chaldean*   ^b18 Or *Chaldeans*   ^a1 Hebrew; Septuagint (see also 43:2) *Azariah*

¹⁹"O remnant of Judah, the LORD has told you, 'Do not go to Egypt.' Be sure of this: I warn you today ²⁰that you made a fatal mistake*b* when you sent me to the LORD your God and said, 'Pray to the LORD our God for us; tell us everything he says and we will do it.' ²¹I have told you today, but you still have not obeyed the LORD your God in all he sent me to tell you. ²²So now, be sure of this: You will die by the sword, famine and plague in the place where you want to go to settle."

43

When Jeremiah finished telling the people all the words of the LORD their God—everything the LORD had sent him to tell them—²Azariah son of Hoshaiah and Johanan son of Kareah and all the arrogant men said to Jeremiah, "You are lying! The LORD our God has not sent you to say, 'You must not go to Egypt to settle there.' ³But Baruch son of Neriah is inciting you against us to hand us over to the Babylonians,*a* so that they may kill us or carry us into exile to Babylon."

⁴So Johanan son of Kareah and all the army officers and all the people disobeyed the LORD's command to stay in the land of Judah. ⁵Instead, Johanan son of Kareah and all the army officers led away all the remnant of Judah who had come back to live in the land of Judah from all the nations where they had been scattered. ⁶They also led away all the men, women and children and the king's daughters whom Nebuzaradan commander of the imperial guard had left with Gedaliah son of Ahikam, the son of Shaphan, and Jeremiah the prophet and Baruch son of Neriah. ⁷So they entered Egypt in disobedience to the LORD and went as far as Tahpanhes.

⁸In Tahpanhes the word of the LORD came to Jeremiah: ⁹"While the Jews are watching, take some large stones with you and bury them in clay in the brick pavement at the entrance to Pharaoh's palace in Tahpanhes. ¹⁰Then say to them, 'This is what the LORD Almighty, the God of Israel, says: I will send for my servant Nebuchadnezzar king of Babylon, and I will set his throne over these stones I have buried here; he will spread his royal canopy above them. ¹¹He will come and attack Egypt, bringing death to those destined for death, captivity to those destined for captivity, and the sword to those destined for the sword. ¹²He*b* will set fire to the temples of the gods of Egypt; he will burn their temples and take their gods captive. As a shepherd wraps his garment round him, so will he wrap Egypt round himself and depart from there unscathed. ¹³There in the temple of the sun*c* in Egypt he will demolish the sacred pillars and will burn down the temples of the gods of Egypt.' "

Disaster Because of Idolatry

44

This word came to Jeremiah concerning all the Jews living in Lower Egypt—in Migdol, Tahpanhes and Memphis*a*—and in Upper Egypt:*b* ²"This is what the LORD Almighty, the God of Israel, says: You saw the great disaster I brought on Jerusalem and on all the towns of Judah. Today they lie deserted and in ruins ³because of the evil they have done. They provoked me to anger by burning incense to and by worshipping other gods that neither they nor you nor your fathers ever knew. ⁴Again and again I sent my servants the prophets, who said, 'Do not do this detestable thing that I hate!' ⁵But they did not listen or pay attention; they did not turn from their wickedness or stop burning incense to other gods. ⁶Therefore, my fierce anger was poured out; it raged against the towns of Judah and the streets of Jerusalem and made them the desolate ruins they are today.

⁷"Now this is what the LORD God Almighty, the God of Israel, says: Why bring such great disaster on yourselves by cutting off from Judah the men and women, the children and infants, and so leave yourselves without a remnant? ⁸Why provoke me to anger with what your hands have made, burning incense to other gods in Egypt, where you have come to live? You will destroy yourselves and make yourselves an object of cursing and reproach among all the nations on earth. ⁹Have you forgotten the wickedness committed by your fathers and by the kings and queens of Judah and the wickedness committed by you and your wives in the land of Judah and the streets of Jerusalem? ¹⁰To this day they have not humbled themselves or shown reverence, nor have they followed my law and the decrees I set before you and your fathers.

¹¹"Therefore, this is what the LORD Almighty, the God of Israel, says: I am determined to bring disaster on you and to destroy all Judah. ¹²I will take away the remnant of Judah who were determined to go to Egypt to settle there. They will all perish in Egypt; they will fall by the sword or die from famine. From the least to the greatest, they will die by sword or famine. They will become an object of cursing and horror, of condemnation and reproach. ¹³I will punish those who live in Egypt with the sword, famine and plague, as I punished Jerusalem. ¹⁴None of the remnant of Judah who have gone to live in Egypt will escape or survive to return to the land of Judah, to which they long to return and live; none will return except a few fugitives."

¹⁵Then all the men who knew that their wives were burning incense to other gods, along with all the women who were present—a large assembly—and all the people living in Lower and Upper Egypt,*c* said to Jeremiah, ¹⁶"We will not listen to the message you have spoken to us in the name of the LORD! ¹⁷We will certainly do everything we said we would: We will burn incense to the Queen of Heaven and will pour out drink offerings to her just as we and our fathers, our kings and our officials did in the towns of Judah and in the streets of Jerusalem. At that time we had plenty of food and were well off and suffered no harm. ¹⁸But ever since we stopped burning incense to the Queen of Heaven and pouring out drink offerings to her, we have had nothing and have been perishing by sword and famine."

¹⁹The women added, "When we burned incense to the Queen of Heaven and poured out drink offerings to her, did not our husbands know that we were making

---

*b*20 Or *you erred in your hearts*   *a*3 Or *Chaldeans*   *b*12 Or *I*   *c*13 Or *in Heliopolis*
*a*1 Hebrew *Noph*   *b*1 Hebrew *in Pathros*   *c*15 Hebrew *in Egypt and Pathros*

cakes like her image and pouring out drink offerings to her?"

44:18　Again, the people believed that their fortunes would be revived by worshipping Ishthar, the Queen of Heaven. They reflected upon the fact that a series of major disasters had befallen them. Instead of realizing that this was because they had forsaken the law of God, they concluded that their misfortune came because they stopped making sacrifices to the goddess and no longer burned incense to her honour.

[20]Then Jeremiah said to all the people, both men and women, who were answering him, [21]"Did not the LORD remember and think about the incense burned in the towns of Judah and the streets of Jerusalem by you and your fathers, your kings and your officials and the people of the land? [22]When the LORD could no longer endure your wicked actions and the detestable things you did, your land became an object of cursing and a desolate waste without inhabitants, as it is today. [23]Because you have burned incense and have sinned against the LORD and have not obeyed him or followed his law or his decrees or his stipulations, this disaster has come upon you, as you now see."

[24]Then Jeremiah said to all the people, including the women, "Hear the word of the LORD, all you people of Judah in Egypt. [25]This is what the LORD Almighty, the God of Israel, says: You and your wives have shown by your actions what you promised when you said, 'We will certainly carry out the vows we made to burn incense and pour out drink offerings to the Queen of Heaven.'

"Go ahead then, do what you promised! Keep your vows! [26]But hear the word of the LORD, all Jews living in Egypt: 'I swear by my great name,' says the LORD, 'that no-one from Judah living anywhere in Egypt shall ever again invoke my name or swear, "As surely as the Sovereign LORD lives." [27]For I am watching over them for harm, not for good; the Jews in Egypt will perish by sword and famine until they are all destroyed. [28]Those who escape the sword and return to the land of Judah from Egypt will be very few. Then the whole remnant of Judah who came to live in Egypt will know whose word will stand — mine or theirs.

[29]" 'This will be the sign to you that I will punish you in this place,' declares the LORD, 'so that you will know that my threats of harm against you will surely stand.' [30]This is what the LORD says: 'I am going to hand Pharaoh Hophra king of Egypt over to his enemies who seek his life, just as I handed Zedekiah king of Judah over to Nebuchadnezzar king of Babylon, the enemy who was seeking his life.' "

A Message to Baruch

45　This is what Jeremiah the prophet told Baruch son of Neriah in the fourth year of Jehoiakim son of Josiah king of Judah, after Baruch had written on a scroll the words Jeremiah was then dictating: [2]"This

is what the LORD, the God of Israel, says to you, Baruch: [3]You said, 'Woe to me! The LORD has added sorrow to my pain; I am worn out with groaning and find no rest.' "

[4]The LORD said, "Say this to him: 'This is what the LORD says: I will overthrow what I have built and uproot what I have planted, throughout the land. [5]Should you then seek great things for yourself? Seek them not. For I will bring disaster on all people, declares the LORD, but wherever you go I will let you escape with your life.' "

A Message About Egypt

46　This is the word of the LORD that came to Jeremiah the prophet concerning the nations:

[2]Concerning Egypt:

This is the message against the army of Pharaoh Neco king of Egypt, which was defeated at Carchemish on the Euphrates River by Nebuchadnezzar king of Babylon in the fourth year of Jehoiakim son of Josiah king of Judah:

46:2　True to the tradition of the Prophets, Jeremiah related God's word to the events of the world around him. In this first oracle about the nations, he described how Egypt was defeated at the Battle of Carcamesh in 605 BC by the Babylonians. This event was pivotal in shaping the politics and national boundaries of the ancient world at the time, and Jeremiah showed how the Lord was active in bringing the proud and ruthless Egyptian Pharaoh, Neco, to a sticky end.

[3]"Prepare your shields, both large and small,
　and march out for battle!
[4]Harness the horses,
　mount the steeds!
Take your positions
　with helmets on!
Polish your spears,
　put on your armour!
[5]What do I see?
　They are terrified,
they are retreating,
　their warriors are defeated.
They flee in haste
　without looking back,
　and there is terror on every side,"
　　　　　　　　　　　declares the LORD.
[6]"The swift cannot flee
　nor the strong escape.
In the north by the River Euphrates
　they stumble and fall.

[7]"Who is this that rises like the Nile,
　like rivers of surging waters?
[8]Egypt rises like the Nile,
　like rivers of surging waters.

She says, 'I will rise and cover the earth;
  I will destroy cities and their people.'
⁹Charge, O horses!
  Drive furiously, O charioteers!
March on, O warriors—
  men of Cush ᵃ and Put who carry shields,
  men of Lydia who draw the bow.
¹⁰But that day belongs to the Lord, the LORD
      Almighty—
  a day of vengeance, for vengeance on his foes.
The sword will devour till it is satisfied,
  till it has quenched its thirst with blood.
For the Lord, the LORD Almighty, will offer
      sacrifice
  in the land of the north by the River Euphrates.

¹¹"Go up to Gilead and get balm,
  O Virgin Daughter of Egypt.
But you multiply remedies in vain;
  there is no healing for you.
¹²The nations will hear of your shame;
  your cries will fill the earth.
One warrior will stumble over another;
  both will fall down together."

¹³This is the message the LORD spoke to Jeremiah
the prophet about the coming of Nebuchadnezzar king
of Babylon to attack Egypt:

¹⁴"Announce this in Egypt, and proclaim it in
      Migdol;
  proclaim it also in Memphis ᵇ and Tahpanhes:
'Take your positions and get ready,
  for the sword devours those around you.'
¹⁵Why will your warriors be laid low?
  They cannot stand, for the LORD will push them
      down.
¹⁶They will stumble repeatedly;
  they will fall over each other.
They will say, 'Get up, let us go back
  to our own people and our native lands,
  away from the sword of the oppressor.'
¹⁷There they will exclaim,
'Pharaoh king of Egypt is only a loud noise;
  he has missed his opportunity.'

¹⁸"As surely as I live," declares the King,
  whose name is the LORD Almighty,
"one will come who is like Tabor among the
      mountains,
  like Carmel by the sea.
¹⁹Pack your belongings for exile,
  you who live in Egypt,
for Memphis will be laid waste
  and lie in ruins without inhabitant.

²⁰"Egypt is a beautiful heifer,
  but a gadfly is coming
  against her from the north.
²¹The mercenaries in her ranks
  are like fattened calves.
They too will turn and flee together,
  they will not stand their ground,

for the day of disaster is coming upon them,
  the time for them to be punished.
²²Egypt will hiss like a fleeing serpent
  as the enemy advances in force;
they will come against her with axes,
  like men who cut down trees.
²³They will chop down her forest,"
                          declares the LORD,
"dense though it be.
They are more numerous than locusts,
  they cannot be counted.
²⁴The Daughter of Egypt will be put to shame,
  handed over to the people of the north."

²⁵The LORD Almighty, the God of Israel, says: "I am
about to bring punishment on Amon god of Thebes, ᶜ
on Pharaoh, on Egypt and her gods and her kings, and
on those who rely on Pharaoh. ²⁶I will hand them over
to those who seek their lives, to Nebuchadnezzar king
of Babylon and his officers. Later, however, Egypt will
be inhabited as in times past," declares the LORD.

²⁷"Do not fear, O Jacob my servant;
  do not be dismayed, O Israel.
I will surely save you out of a distant place,
  and your descendants from the land of their
      exile.
Jacob will again have peace and security,
  and no-one will make him afraid.
²⁸Do not fear, O Jacob my servant,
  for I am with you," declares the LORD.
"Though I completely destroy all the nations
  among which I scatter you,
I will not completely destroy you.
I will discipline you but only with justice;
  I will not let you go entirely unpunished."

A Message About the Philistines

47 This is the word of the LORD that came to Jeremiah the prophet concerning the Philistines
before Pharaoh attacked Gaza:

47:1   In his oracle about the Philistines,
Jeremiah kept up his contemporary feel by
describing the downfall of the Philistines by
Pharaoh Neco as he retreated from the Battle
of Carcamesh. Again, Jeremiah showed how
God's hand was active in bringing Israel's
enemies to ultimate defeat.

---

²This is what the LORD says:

"See how the waters are rising in the north;
  they will become an overflowing torrent.
They will overflow the land and everything in it,
  the towns and those who live in them.
The people will cry out;
  all who dwell in the land will wail
³at the sound of the hoofs of galloping steeds,
  at the noise of enemy chariots
  and the rumble of their wheels.
Fathers will not turn to help their children;
  their hands will hang limp.

ᵃ9 That is, the upper Nile region   ᵇ14 Hebrew Noph; also in verse 19   ᶜ25 Hebrew No

⁴For the day has come
  to destroy all the Philistines
and to cut off all survivors
  who could help Tyre and Sidon.
The LORD is about to destroy the Philistines,
  the remnant from the coasts of Caphtor.ᵃ
⁵Gaza will shave her head in mourning;
  Ashkelon will be silenced.
O remnant on the plain,
  how long will you cut yourselves?

⁶" 'Ah, sword of the LORD,' ˌyou cry,ˌ
  'how long till you rest?
Return to your scabbard;
  cease and be still.'
⁷But how can it rest
  when the LORD has commanded it,
when he has ordered it
  to attack Ashkelon and the coast?"

A Message About Moab

48 Concerning Moab:

This is what the LORD Almighty, the God of Israel,
says:

"Woe to Nebo, for it will be ruined.
  Kiriathaim will be disgraced and captured;
  the strongholdᵃ will be disgraced and
    shattered.
²Moab will be praised no more;
  in Heshbonᵇ men will plot her downfall:
  'Come, let us put an end to that nation.'
You too, O Madmen,ᶜ will be silenced;
  the sword will pursue you.
³Listen to the cries from Horonaim,
  cries of great havoc and destruction.
⁴Moab will be broken;
  her little ones will cry out.ᵈ
⁵They go up the way to Luhith,
  weeping bitterly as they go;
on the road down to Horonaim
  anguished cries over the destruction are heard.
⁶Flee! Run for your lives;
  become like a bushᵉ in the desert.
⁷Since you trust in your deeds and riches,
  you too will be taken captive,
and Chemosh will go into exile,
  together with his priests and officials.
⁸The destroyer will come against every town,
  and not a town will escape.
The valley will be ruined
  and the plateau destroyed,
because the LORD has spoken.
⁹Put salt on Moab,
  for she will be laid waste;ᶠ
her towns will become desolate,
  with no-one to live in them.

¹⁰"A curse on him who is lax in doing the LORD's
  work!
A curse on him who keeps his sword from
  bloodshed!

¹¹"Moab has been at rest from youth,
  like wine left on its dregs,
not poured from one jar to another—
  she has not gone into exile.
So she tastes as she did,
  and her aroma is unchanged.
¹²But days are coming,"
  declares the LORD,
"when I will send men who pour from jars,
  and they will pour her out;
they will empty her jars
  and smash her jugs.
¹³Then Moab will be ashamed of Chemosh,
  as the house of Israel was ashamed
when they trusted in Bethel.

¹⁴"How can you say, 'We are warriors,
  men valiant in battle'?
¹⁵Moab will be destroyed and her towns invaded;
  her finest young men will go down in the
    slaughter,"
  declares the King, whose name is the LORD
    Almighty.
¹⁶"The fall of Moab is at hand;
  her calamity will come quickly.
¹⁷Mourn for her, all who live around her,
  all who know her fame;
say, 'How broken is the mighty sceptre,
  how broken the glorious staff!'

¹⁸"Come down from your glory
  and sit on the parched ground,
O inhabitants of the Daughter of Dibon,
for he who destroys Moab
  will come up against you
  and ruin your fortified cities.
¹⁹Stand by the road and watch,
  you who live in Aroer.
Ask the man fleeing and the woman escaping,
  ask them, 'What has happened?'
²⁰Moab is disgraced, for she is shattered.
  Wail and cry out!
Announce by the Arnon
  that Moab is destroyed.
²¹Judgment has come to the plateau—
  to Holon, Jahzah and Mephaath,
²² to Dibon, Nebo and Beth Diblathaim,
²³ to Kiriathaim, Beth Gamul and Beth Meon,
²⁴ to Kerioth and Bozrah—
  to all the towns of Moab, far and near.
²⁵Moab's hornᵍ is cut off;
  her arm is broken,"
                                        declares the LORD.

²⁶"Make her drunk,
  for she has defied the LORD.
Let Moab wallow in her vomit;
  let her be an object of ridicule.

ᵃ4 That is, Crete   ᵃ1 Or / Misgab   ᵇ2 The Hebrew for Heshbon sounds like the Hebrew for plot.
ᶜ2 The name of the Moabite town Madmen sounds like the Hebrew for be silenced.   ᵈ4 Hebrew; Septuagint / proclaim it to Zoar
ᵉ6 Or like Aroer   ᶠ9 Or Give wings to Moab, / for she will fly away   ᵍ25 Horn here symbolises strength.

27Was not Israel the object of your ridicule?
    Was she caught among thieves,
  that you shake your head in scorn
    whenever you speak of her?
28Abandon your towns and dwell among the rocks,
    you who live in Moab.
  Be like a dove that makes its nest
    at the mouth of a cave.

29"We have heard of Moab's pride—
    her overweening pride and conceit,
  her pride and arrogance
    and the haughtiness of her heart.
30I know her insolence but it is futile,"
                    declares the LORD,
  "and her boasts accomplish nothing.
31Therefore I wail over Moab,
    for all Moab I cry out,
  I moan for the men of Kir Hareseth.
32I weep for you, as Jazer weeps,
    O vines of Sibmah.
  Your branches spread as far as the sea;
    they reached as far as the sea of Jazer.
  The destroyer has fallen
    on your ripened fruit and grapes.
33Joy and gladness are gone
    from the orchards and fields of Moab.
  I have stopped the flow of wine from the presses;
    no-one treads them with shouts of joy.
  Although there are shouts,
    they are not shouts of joy.

34"The sound of their cry rises
    from Heshbon to Elealeh and Jahaz,
  from Zoar as far as Horonaim and Eglath
    Shelishiyah,
  for even the waters of Nimrim are dried up.
35In Moab I will put an end
    to those who make offerings on the high places
    and burn incense to their gods,"
                    declares the LORD.
36"So my heart laments for Moab like a flute;
    it laments like a flute for the men of Kir
      Hareseth.
  The wealth they acquired is gone.
37Every head is shaved
    and every beard cut off;
  every hand is slashed
    and every waist is covered with sackcloth.
38On all the roofs in Moab
    and in the public squares
  there is nothing but mourning,
  for I have broken Moab
    like a jar that no-one wants,"
                    declares the LORD.
39"How shattered she is! How they wail!
  How Moab turns her back in shame!
  Moab has become an object of ridicule,
    an object of horror to all those around her."

40This is what the LORD says:

  "Look! An eagle is swooping down,
    spreading its wings over Moab.

41Kerioth[h] will be captured
    and the strongholds taken.
  In that day the hearts of Moab's warriors
    will be like the heart of a woman in labour.
42Moab will be destroyed as a nation
    because she defied the LORD.
43Terror and pit and snare await you,
    O people of Moab,"
                    declares the LORD.
44"Whoever flees from the terror
    will fall into a pit,
  whoever climbs out of the pit
    will be caught in a snare;
  for I will bring upon Moab
    the year of her punishment,"
                    declares the LORD.

45"In the shadow of Heshbon
    the fugitives stand helpless,
  for a fire has gone out from Heshbon,
    a blaze from the midst of Sihon;
  it burns the foreheads of Moab,
    the skulls of the noisy boasters.
46Woe to you, O Moab!
  The people of Chemosh are destroyed;
  your sons are taken into exile
    and your daughters into captivity.

47"Yet I will restore the fortunes of Moab
    in days to come,"
                    declares the LORD.

Here ends the judgment on Moab.

A Message About Ammon

49 Concerning the Ammonites:

This is what the LORD says:

  "Has Israel no sons?
    Has she no heirs?
  Why then has Molech[a] taken possession of Gad?
    Why do his people live in its towns?
2But the days are coming,"
    declares the LORD,
  "when I will sound the battle cry
    against Rabbah of the Ammonites;
  it will become a mound of ruins,
    and its surrounding villages will be set on fire.
  Then Israel will drive out
    those who drove her out,"
                    says the LORD.
3"Wail, O Heshbon, for Ai is destroyed!
    Cry out, O inhabitants of Rabbah!
  Put on sackcloth and mourn;
    rush here and there inside the walls,
  for Molech will go into exile,
    together with his priests and officials.
4Why do you boast of your valleys,
    boast of your valleys so fruitful?
  O unfaithful daughter,
    you trust in your riches and say,
    'Who will attack me?'

---

h41 Or The cities   a1 Or their king; Hebrew malcam; also in verse 3

⁵I will bring terror on you
    from all those around you,"
                                           declares the Lord,
                                            the LORD Almighty.
"Every one of you will be driven away,
    and no-one will gather the fugitives.

⁶"Yet afterwards, I will restore the fortunes of the
    Ammonites,"
                                           declares the LORD.

A Message About Edom

⁷Concerning Edom:

This is what the LORD Almighty says:

"Is there no longer wisdom in Teman?
    Has counsel perished from the prudent?
    Has their wisdom decayed?
⁸Turn and flee, hide in deep caves,
    you who live in Dedan,
for I will bring disaster on Esau
    at the time I punish him.
⁹If grape-pickers came to you,
    would they not leave a few grapes?
If thieves came during the night,
    would they not steal only as much as they
        wanted?
¹⁰But I will strip Esau bare;
    I will uncover his hiding-places,
    so that he cannot conceal himself.
His children, relatives and neighbours will perish,
    and he will be no more.
¹¹Leave your orphans; I will protect their lives.
    Your widows too can trust in me."

¹²This is what the LORD says: "If those who do not
deserve to drink the cup must drink it, why should you
go unpunished? You will not go unpunished, but must
drink it. ¹³I swear by myself," declares the LORD, "that
Bozrah will become a ruin and an object of horror, of
reproach and of cursing; and all its towns will be in
ruins for ever."

¹⁴I have heard a message from the LORD:
    An envoy was sent to the nations to say,
"Assemble yourselves to attack it!
    Rise up for battle!"

¹⁵"Now I will make you small among the nations,
    despised among men.
¹⁶The terror you inspire
    and the pride of your heart have deceived you,
you who live in the clefts of the rocks,
    who occupy the heights of the hill.
Though you build your nest as high as the eagle's,
    from there I will bring you down,"
                                           declares the LORD.
¹⁷"Edom will become an object of horror;
    all who pass by will be appalled and will scoff
    because of all its wounds.
¹⁸As Sodom and Gomorrah were overthrown,
    along with their neighbouring towns,"
                                           says the LORD,

"so no-one will live there;
    no man will dwell in it.

¹⁹"Like a lion coming up from Jordan's thickets
    to a rich pasture-land,
I will chase Edom from its land in an instant.
    Who is the chosen one I will appoint for this?
Who is like me and who can challenge me?
    And what shepherd can stand against me?"
²⁰Therefore, hear what the LORD has planned
        against Edom,
    what he has purposed against those who live in
        Teman:
The young of the flock will be dragged away;
    he will completely destroy their pasture because
        of them.
²¹At the sound of their fall the earth will tremble;
    their cry will resound to the Red Sea.ᵇ
²²Look! An eagle will soar and swoop down,
    spreading its wings over Bozrah.
In that day the hearts of Edom's warriors
    will be like the heart of a woman in labour.

A Message About Damascus

²³Concerning Damascus:

"Hamath and Arpad are dismayed,
    for they have heard bad news.
They are disheartened,
    troubled likeᶜ the restless sea.
²⁴Damascus has become feeble,
    she has turned to flee
    and panic has gripped her;
anguish and pain have seized her,
    pain like that of a woman in labour.
²⁵Why has the city of renown not been abandoned,
    the town in which I delight?
²⁶Surely, her young men will fall in the streets;
    all her soldiers will be silenced in that day,"
                                           declares the LORD Almighty.
²⁷"I will set fire to the walls of Damascus;
    it will consume the fortresses of Ben-Hadad."

A Message About Kedar and Hazor

²⁸Concerning Kedar and the kingdoms of Hazor,
which Nebuchadnezzar king of Babylon attacked:

This is what the LORD says:

"Arise, and attack Kedar
    and destroy the people of the East.
²⁹Their tents and their flocks will be taken;
    their shelters will be carried off
    with all their goods and camels.
Men will shout to them,
    'Terror on every side!'

³⁰"Flee quickly away!
    Stay in deep caves, you who live in Hazor,"
                                           declares the LORD.
"Nebuchadnezzar king of Babylon has plotted
        against you;
    he has devised a plan against you.

ᵇ21 Hebrew *Yam Suph*; that is, Sea of Reeds   ᶜ23 Hebrew *on* or *by*

31"Arise and attack a nation at ease,
    which lives in confidence,"
                    declares the LORD,
"a nation that has neither gates nor bars;
    its people live alone.
32Their camels will become plunder,
    and their large herds will be booty.
I will scatter to the winds those who are in
        distant places[d]
    and will bring disaster on them from every
        side,"
                    declares the LORD.
33"Hazor will become a haunt of jackals,
    a desolate place for ever.
No-one will live there;
    no man will dwell in it."

A Message About Elam

34This is the word of the LORD that came to Jeremiah
the prophet concerning Elam, early in the reign of Zedekiah king of Judah:

35This is what the LORD Almighty says:

"See, I will break the bow of Elam,
    the mainstay of their might.
36I will bring against Elam the four winds
    from the four quarters of the heavens;
I will scatter them to the four winds,
    and there will not be a nation
    where Elam's exiles do not go.
37I will shatter Elam before their foes,
    before those who seek their lives;
I will bring disaster upon them,
    even my fierce anger,"
                    declares the LORD.
"I will pursue them with the sword
    until I have made an end of them.
38I will set my throne in Elam
    and destroy her king and officials,"
                    declares the LORD.

39"Yet I will restore the fortunes of Elam
    in days to come,"
                    declares the LORD.

A Message About Babylon

50 This is the word the LORD spoke through Jeremiah the prophet concerning Babylon and the
land of the Babylonians:[a]

50:1 Jeremiah reserved his greatest
judgement for Babylon for this final oracle,
which runs to two chapters in length! The
repetitive style emphasizes Jeremiah's anger
and Israel's utter contempt for the nation
that destroyed Jerusalem and God's dwelling
place in the temple.

2"Announce and proclaim among the nations,
    lift up a banner and proclaim it;
    keep nothing back, but say,

'Babylon will be captured;
    Bel will be put to shame,
    Marduk filled with terror.
Her images will be put to shame
    and her idols filled with terror.'
3A nation from the north will attack her
    and lay waste her land.
No-one will live in it;
    both men and animals will flee away.

4"In those days, at that time,"
    declares the LORD,
"the people of Israel and the people of Judah
        together
    will go in tears to seek the LORD their God.
5They will ask the way to Zion
    and turn their faces towards it.
They will come and bind themselves to the LORD
    in an everlasting covenant
    that will not be forgotten.

6"My people have been lost sheep;
    their shepherds have led them astray
    and caused them to roam on the mountains.
They wandered over mountain and hill
    and forgot their own resting place.
7Whoever found them devoured them;
    their enemies said, 'We are not guilty,
for they sinned against the LORD, their true
        pasture,
    the LORD, the hope of their fathers.'

8"Flee out of Babylon;
    leave the land of the Babylonians,
    and be like the goats that lead the flock.
9For I will stir up and bring against Babylon
    an alliance of great nations from the land of the
        north.
They will take up their positions against her,
    and from the north she will be captured.
Their arrows will be like skilled warriors
    who do not return empty-handed.
10So Babylonia[b] will be plundered;
    all who plunder her will have their fill,"
                    declares the LORD.

11"Because you rejoice and are glad,
    you who pillage my inheritance,
because you frolic like a heifer threshing corn
    and neigh like stallions,
12your mother will be greatly ashamed;
    she who gave you birth will be disgraced.
She will be the least of the nations—
    a wilderness, a dry land, a desert.
13Because of the LORD's anger she will not be
        inhabited
    but will be completely desolate.
All who pass Babylon will be horrified and scoff
    because of all her wounds.

14"Take up your positions round Babylon,
    all you who draw the bow.
Shoot at her! Spare no arrows,
    for she has sinned against the LORD.

---

[d]32 Or who clip the hair by their foreheads   [a]1 Or Chaldeans; also in verses 8, 25, 35 and 45   [b]10 Or Chaldea

¹⁵Shout against her on every side!
    She surrenders, her towers fall,
    her walls are torn down.
Since this is the vengeance of the LORD,
    take vengeance on her;
    do to her as she has done to others.
¹⁶Cut off from Babylon the sower,
    and the reaper with his sickle at harvest.
Because of the sword of the oppressor
    let everyone return to his own people,
    let everyone flee to his own land.

¹⁷"Israel is a scattered flock
    that lions have chased away.
The first to devour him
    was the king of Assyria;
the last to crush his bones
    was Nebuchadnezzar king of Babylon."

¹⁸Therefore this is what the LORD Almighty, the God
of Israel, says:

"I will punish the king of Babylon and his land
    as I punished the king of Assyria.
¹⁹But I will bring Israel back to his own pasture
    and he will graze on Carmel and Bashan;
his appetite will be satisfied
    on the hills of Ephraim and Gilead.
²⁰In those days, at that time,"
    declares the LORD,
"search will be made for Israel's guilt,
    but there will be none,
and for the sins of Judah,
    but none will be found,
    for I will forgive the remnant I spare.

²¹"Attack the land of Merathaim
    and those who live in Pekod.
Pursue, kill and completely destroy[c] them,"
                            declares the LORD.
    "Do everything I have commanded you.
²²The noise of battle is in the land,
    the noise of great destruction!
²³How broken and shattered
    is the hammer of the whole earth!
How desolate is Babylon
    among the nations!
²⁴I set a trap for you, O Babylon,
    and you were caught before you knew it;
you were found and captured
    because you opposed the LORD.
²⁵The LORD has opened his arsenal
    and brought out the weapons of his wrath,
for the Sovereign LORD Almighty has work to do
    in the land of the Babylonians.
²⁶Come against her from afar.
    Break open her granaries;
    pile her up like heaps of grain.
Completely destroy her
    and leave her no remnant.
²⁷Kill all her young bulls;
    let them go down to the slaughter!

Woe to them! For their day has come,
    the time for them to be punished.
²⁸Listen to the fugitives and refugees from Babylon
    declaring in Zion
how the LORD our God has taken vengeance,
    vengeance for his temple.

²⁹"Summon archers against Babylon,
    all those who draw the bow.
Encamp all round her;
    let no-one escape.
Repay her for her deeds;
    do to her as she has done.
For she defied the LORD,
    the Holy One of Israel.
³⁰Therefore, her young men will fall in the streets;
    all her soldiers will be silenced in that day,"
                            declares the LORD.
³¹"See, I am against you, O arrogant one,"
    declares the Lord, the LORD Almighty,
"for your day has come,
    the time for you to be punished.
³²The arrogant one will stumble and fall
    and no-one will help her up;
I will kindle a fire in her towns
    that will consume all who are around her."

³³This is what the LORD Almighty says:

"The people of Israel are oppressed,
    and the people of Judah as well.
All their captors hold them fast,
    refusing to let them go.
³⁴Yet their Redeemer is strong;
    the LORD Almighty is his name.
He will vigorously defend their cause
    so that he may bring rest to their land,
    but unrest to those who live in Babylon.

³⁵"A sword against the Babylonians!"
    declares the LORD —
"against those who live in Babylon
    and against her officials and wise men!
³⁶A sword against her false prophets!
    They will become fools.
A sword against her warriors!
    They will be filled with terror.
³⁷A sword against her horses and chariots
    and all the foreigners in her ranks!
    They will become women.
A sword against her treasures!
    They will be plundered.
³⁸A drought on[d] her waters!
    They will dry up.
For it is a land of idols,
    idols that will go mad with terror.

³⁹"So desert creatures and hyenas will live there,
    and there the owl will dwell.
It will never again be inhabited
    or lived in from generation to generation.
⁴⁰As God overthrew Sodom and Gomorrah
    along with their neighbouring towns,"
                            declares the LORD,

---

c21 The Hebrew term refers to the irrevocable giving over of things or persons to the LORD, often by totally destroying them; also in verse 26.
d38 Or *A sword against*

"so no-one will live there;
no man will dwell in it.

41"Look! An army is coming from the north;
a great nation and many kings
are being stirred up from the ends of the earth.
42They are armed with bows and spears;
they are cruel and without mercy.
They sound like the roaring sea
as they ride on their horses;
they come like men in battle formation
to attack you, O Daughter of Babylon.
43The king of Babylon has heard reports about
them,
and his hands hang limp.
Anguish has gripped him,
pain like that of a woman in labour.
44Like a lion coming up from Jordan's thickets
to a rich pasture-land,
I will chase Babylon from its land in an instant.
Who is the chosen one I will appoint for this?
Who is like me and who can challenge me?
And what shepherd can stand against me?"
45Therefore, hear what the LORD has planned
against Babylon,
what he has purposed against the land of the
Babylonians:
The young of the flock will be dragged away;
he will completely destroy their pasture because
of them.
46At the sound of Babylon's capture the earth will
tremble;
its cry will resound among the nations.

51

This is what the LORD says:

"See, I will stir up the spirit of a destroyer
against Babylon and the people of Leb Kamai.[a]
2I will send foreigners to Babylon
to winnow her and to devastate her land;
they will oppose her on every side
in the day of her disaster.
3Let not the archer string his bow,
nor let him put on his armour.
Do not spare her young men;
completely destroy[b] her army.
4They will fall down slain in Babylon,[c]
fatally wounded in her streets.
5For Israel and Judah have not been forsaken
by their God, the LORD Almighty,
though their land[d] is full of guilt
before the Holy One of Israel.

6"Flee from Babylon!
Run for your lives!
Do not be destroyed because of her sins.
It is time for the LORD's vengeance;
he will pay her what she deserves.
7Babylon was a gold cup in the LORD's hand;
she made the whole earth drunk.
The nations drank her wine;
therefore they have now gone mad.

8Babylon will suddenly fall and be broken.
Wail over her!
Get balm for her pain;
perhaps she can be healed.
9" 'We would have healed Babylon,
but she cannot be healed;
let us leave her and each go to his own land,
for her judgment reaches to the skies,
it rises as high as the clouds.'
10" 'The LORD has vindicated us;
come, let us tell in Zion
what the LORD our God has done.'
11"Sharpen the arrows,
take up the shields!
The LORD has stirred up the kings of the Medes,
because his purpose is to destroy Babylon.
The LORD will take vengeance,
vengeance for his temple.
12Lift up a banner against the walls of Babylon!
Reinforce the guard,
station the watchmen,
prepare an ambush!
The LORD will carry out his purpose,
his decree against the people of Babylon.
13You who live by many waters
and are rich in treasures,
your end has come,
the time for you to be cut off.
14The LORD Almighty has sworn by himself:
I will surely fill you with men, as with a swarm
of locusts,
and they will shout in triumph over you.

15"He made the earth by his power;
he founded the world by his wisdom
and stretched out the heavens by his
understanding.
16When he thunders, the waters in the heavens
roar;
he makes clouds rise from the ends of the
earth.
He sends lightning with the rain
and brings out the wind from his storehouses.
17"Every man is senseless and without knowledge;
every goldsmith is shamed by his idols.
His images are a fraud;
they have no breath in them.
18They are worthless, the objects of mockery;
when their judgment comes, they will perish.
19He who is the Portion of Jacob is not like these,
for he is the Maker of all things,
including the tribe of his inheritance—
the LORD Almighty is his name.
20"You are my war club,
my weapon for battle—
with you I shatter nations,
with you I destroy kingdoms,

---

a1 Leb Kamai is a cryptogram for Chaldea, that is, Babylonia.
b3 The Hebrew term refers to the irrevocable giving over of things or persons to the LORD, often by totally destroying them.
c4 Or Chaldea   d5 Or / and the land of the Babylonians,

21with you I shatter horse and rider,
  with you I shatter chariot and driver,
22with you I shatter man and woman,
  with you I shatter old man and youth,
  with you I shatter young man and maiden,
23with you I shatter shepherd and flock,
  with you I shatter farmer and oxen,
  with you I shatter governors and officials.

24"Before your eyes I will repay Babylon and all who live in Babylonia^e for all the wrong they have done in Zion," declares the LORD.

25"I am against you, O destroying mountain,
  you who destroy the whole earth,"
                                                    declares the LORD.
  "I will stretch out my hand against you,
  roll you off the cliffs,
  and make you a burnt-out mountain.
26No rock will be taken from you for a cornerstone,
  nor any stone for a foundation,
  for you will be desolate for ever,"
                                                    declares the LORD.

27"Lift up a banner in the land!
  Blow the trumpet among the nations!
Prepare the nations for battle against her;
  summon against her these kingdoms:
  Ararat, Minni and Ashkenaz.
Appoint a commander against her;
  send up horses like a swarm of locusts.
28Prepare the nations for battle against her—
  the kings of the Medes,
  their governors and all their officials,
  and all the countries they rule.
29The land trembles and writhes,
  for the LORD's purposes against Babylon stand—
to lay waste the land of Babylon
  so that no-one will live there.
30Babylon's warriors have stopped fighting;
  they remain in their strongholds.
  Their strength is exhausted;
  they have become like women.
  Her dwellings are set on fire;
  the bars of her gates are broken.
31One courier follows another
  and messenger follows messenger
to announce to the king of Babylon
  that his entire city is captured,
32the river crossings seized,
  the marshes set on fire,
  and the soldiers terrified."

33This is what the LORD Almighty, the God of Israel, says:

"The Daughter of Babylon is like a threshing-floor
  at the time it is trampled;
  the time to harvest her will soon come."

34"Nebuchadnezzar king of Babylon has devoured us,
  he has thrown us into confusion,
  he has made us an empty jar.

Like a serpent he has swallowed us
  and filled his stomach with our delicacies,
  and then has spewed us out.
35May the violence done to our flesh^f be upon Babylon,"
  say the inhabitants of Zion.
"May our blood be on those who live in Babylonia,"
  says Jerusalem.

36Therefore, this is what the LORD says:

"See, I will defend your cause
  and avenge you;
I will dry up her sea
  and make her springs dry.
37Babylon will be a heap of ruins,
  a haunt of jackals,
  an object of horror and scorn,
  a place where no-one lives.
38Her people all roar like young lions,
  they growl like lion cubs.
39But while they are aroused,
  I will set out a feast for them
  and make them drunk,
so that they shout with laughter—
  then sleep for ever and not awake,"
                                                    declares the LORD.
40"I will bring them down
  like lambs to the slaughter,
  like rams and goats.

41"How Sheshach^g will be captured,
  the boast of the whole earth seized!
What a horror Babylon will be
  among the nations!
42The sea will rise over Babylon;
  its roaring waves will cover her.
43Her towns will be desolate,
  a dry and desert land,
a land where no-one lives,
  through which no man travels.
44I will punish Bel in Babylon
  and make him spew out what he has swallowed.
The nations will no longer stream to him.
  And the wall of Babylon will fall.

45"Come out of her, my people!
  Run for your lives!
  Run from the fierce anger of the LORD.
46Do not lose heart or be afraid
  when rumours are heard in the land;
one rumour comes this year, another the next,
  rumours of violence in the land
  and of ruler against ruler.
47For the time will surely come
  when I will punish the idols of Babylon;
her whole land will be disgraced
  and her slain will all lie fallen within her.
48Then heaven and earth and all that is in them
  will shout for joy over Babylon,
for out of the north
  destroyers will attack her,"
                                                    declares the LORD.

---

^e24 Or *Chaldea*; also in verse 35   ^f35 Or *done to us and to our children*   ^g41 *Sheshach* is a cryptogram for Babylon.

49"Babylon must fall because of Israel's slain,
    just as the slain in all the earth
    have fallen because of Babylon.
50You who have escaped the sword,
    leave and do not linger!
Remember the LORD in a distant land,
    and think on Jerusalem."

51"We are disgraced,
    for we have been insulted
    and shame covers our faces,
because foreigners have entered
    the holy places of the LORD's house."

52"But days are coming," declares the LORD,
    "when I will punish her idols,
and throughout her land
    the wounded will groan.
53Even if Babylon reaches the sky
    and fortifies her lofty stronghold,
    I will send destroyers against her,"
                        declares the LORD.

54"The sound of a cry comes from Babylon,
    the sound of great destruction
    from the land of the Babylonians.ʰ
55The LORD will destroy Babylon;
    he will silence her noisy din.
Waves ₍of enemies₎ will rage like great waters;
    the roar of their voices will resound.
56A destroyer will come against Babylon;
    her warriors will be captured,
    and their bows will be broken.
For the LORD is a God of retribution;
    he will repay in full.
57I will make her officials and wise men drunk,
    her governors, officers and warriors as well;
they will sleep for ever and not awake,"
    declares the King, whose name is the LORD
        Almighty.

58This is what the LORD Almighty says:

"Babylon's thick wall will be levelled
    and her high gates set on fire;
the peoples exhaust themselves for nothing,
    the nations' labour is only fuel for the flames."

59This is the message Jeremiah gave to the staff officer Seraiah son of Neriah, the son of Mahseiah, when he went to Babylon with Zedekiah king of Judah in the fourth year of his reign. 60Jeremiah had written on a scroll about all the disasters that would come upon Babylon—all that had been recorded concerning Babylon. 61He said to Seraiah, "When you get to Babylon, see that you read all these words aloud. 62Then say, 'O LORD, you have said you will destroy this place, so that neither man nor animal will live in it; it will be desolate for ever.' 63When you finish reading this scroll, tie a stone to it and throw it into the Euphrates. 64Then say, 'So will Babylon sink to rise no more because of the disaster I will bring upon her. And her people will fall.' "

The words of Jeremiah end here.

The Fall of Jerusalem

52 Zedekiah was twenty-one years old when he became king, and he reigned in Jerusalem for eleven years. His mother's name was Hamutal daughter of Jeremiah; she was from Libnah. 2He did evil in the eyes of the LORD, just as Jehoiakim had done. 3It was because of the LORD's anger that all this happened to Jerusalem and Judah, and in the end he thrust them from his presence.

Now Zedekiah rebelled against the king of Babylon.

4So in the ninth year of Zedekiah's reign, on the tenth day of the tenth month, Nebuchadnezzar king of Babylon marched against Jerusalem with his whole army. They camped outside the city and built siege works all around it. 5The city was kept under siege until the eleventh year of King Zedekiah.

52:4 Here, and in similar passages up to the end of the book, there is a body of material which is closely echoed in 2 Kings 24 and 25. With this historical dimension to the end of the book, the words of Jeremiah are rooted in the history of God's people.

6By the ninth day of the fourth month the famine in the city had become so severe that there was no food for the people to eat. 7Then the city wall was broken through, and the whole army fled. They left the city at night through the gate between the two walls near the king's garden, though the Babyloniansᵃ were surrounding the city. They fled towards the Arabah,ᵇ 8but the Babylonianᶜ army pursued King Zedekiah and overtook him in the plains of Jericho. All his soldiers were separated from him and scattered, 9and he was captured.

He was taken to the king of Babylon at Riblah in the land of Hamath, where he pronounced sentence on him. 10There at Riblah the king of Babylon slaughtered the sons of Zedekiah before his eyes; he also killed all the officials of Judah. 11Then he put out Zedekiah's eyes, bound him with bronze shackles and took him to Babylon, where he put him in prison till the day of his death.

12On the tenth day of the fifth month, in the nineteenth year of Nebuchadnezzar king of Babylon, Nebuzaradan commander of the imperial guard, who served the king of Babylon, came to Jerusalem. 13He set fire to the temple of the LORD, the royal palace and all the houses of Jerusalem. Every important building he burned down. 14The whole Babylonian army under the commander of the imperial guard broke down all the walls around Jerusalem. 15Nebuzaradan the commander of the guard carried into exile some of the poorest people and those who remained in the city, along with the rest of the craftsmenᵈ and those who had gone over to the king of Babylon. 16But Nebuzaradan left behind the rest of the poorest people of the land to work the vineyards and fields.

17The Babylonians broke up the bronze pillars, the

ʰ54 Or Chaldeans   ᵃ7 Or Chaldeans; also in verse 17   ᵇ7 Or the Jordan Valley   ᶜ8 Or Chaldean; also in verse 14
ᵈ15 Or populace

movable stands and the bronze Sea that were at the temple of the LORD and they carried all the bronze to Babylon. ¹⁸They also took away the pots, shovels, wick trimmers, sprinkling bowls, dishes and all the bronze articles used in the temple service. ¹⁹The commander of the imperial guard took away the basins, censers, sprinkling bowls, pots, lampstands, dishes and bowls used for drink offerings—all that were made of pure gold or silver.

²⁰The bronze from the two pillars, the Sea and the twelve bronze bulls under it, and the movable stands, which King Solomon had made for the temple of the LORD, was more than could be weighed. ²¹Each of the pillars was eighteen cubits high and twelve cubits in circumference;ᵉ each was four fingers thick, and hollow. ²²The bronze capital on the top of the one pillar was five cubitsᶠ high and was decorated with a network and pomegranates of bronze all around. The other pillar, with its pomegranates, was similar. ²³There were ninety-six pomegranates on the sides; the total number of pomegranates above the surrounding network was a hundred.

²⁴The commander of the guard took as prisoners Seraiah the chief priest, Zephaniah the priest next in rank and the three doorkeepers. ²⁵Of those still in the city, he took the officer in charge of the fighting men, and seven royal advisers. He also took the secretary who was chief officer in charge of conscripting the people of the land and sixty of his men who were found in the city. ²⁶Nebuzaradan the commander took them all and brought them to the king of Babylon at Riblah. ²⁷There at Riblah, in the land of Hamath, the king had them executed.

So Judah went into captivity, away from her land. ²⁸This is the number of the people Nebuchadnezzar carried into exile:

in the seventh year, 3,023 Jews;
²⁹in Nebuchadnezzar's eighteenth year,
    832 people from Jerusalem;
³⁰in his twenty-third year,
    745 Jews taken into exile by Nebuzaradan the
    commander of the imperial guard.
There were 4,600 people in all.

Jehoiachin Released

³¹In the thirty-seventh year of the exile of Jehoiachin king of Judah, in the year Evil-Merodachᵍ became king of Babylon, he released Jehoiachin king of Judah and freed him from prison on the twenty-fifth day of the twelfth month. ³²He spoke kindly to him and gave him a seat of honour higher than those of the other kings who were with him in Babylon. ³³So Jehoiachin put aside his prison clothes and for the rest of his life ate regularly at the king's table. ³⁴Day by day the king of Babylon gave Jehoiachin a regular allowance as long as he lived, till the day of his death.

ᵉ21 That is, about 27 feet (about 8.1 metres) high and 18 feet (about 5.5 metres) in circumference
ᶠ22 That is, about 7 ½ feet (about 2.3 metres)   ᵍ31 Also called Amel-Marduk

Lamentations

A Terrible Situation

Throughout the Old Testament there are calamities, and situations of total loss and defeat. The usual response to such events is to protest and ask "Why?" There are, however, situations so overwhelming, so terrible, that even protests will not do, and all that is left is a desire for some space in which to grieve and cry. Lamentations is such a book. It was probably written around the period 586—540 BC, and movingly expresses the grief of God's people as they witnessed and came to terms with one of the most devastating events in their history: the ransacking of Jerusalem by the Babylonians in 586 BC (see 2 Kings 25 for the historical background).

The Tradition of Jeremiah

Tradition links the book's authorship with Jeremiah. He was active during the reign of King Josiah, who had been responsible for reforming the life and faith of Israel. This included placing Jerusalem at the centre of the nation's political and religious life, with the temple as its focus. The original Hebrew, however, makes no suggestion that Jeremiah is the author, and it is probably more likely that these poetic laments were composed by prophets (and possibly priests) who followed the teachings and traditions of Jeremiah.

A Massive Invasion

When the Babylonian armies came crashing into Jerusalem in 586 BC, they destroyed the temple along with all the other principal buildings in the city. The cost in terms of human life was huge, and most of those that survived the brutal killings became part of a mass deportation into Babylon, where they became slaves. With the temple in ruins, and no political leadership, those who remained in Jerusalem felt that they had been forsaken by God. Indeed, they believed, all these terrible things came about by the will of God who was angry at his people for turning away from his laws. This theme is powerfully expressed at the beginning of the book (1:5):

"Her foes have become her masters;
 her enemies are at ease.
The Lord has brought her grief
 because of her many sins.
Her children have gone into exile,
 captive before the foe."

Sorrow and Hope

Without God or king or national identity, all the people could do was grieve and express the way they had been forsaken as they considered the traumatic events. As they became absorbed into the devotional life of Judaism, the Lamentations were given a place in Jewish liturgy, and were read at the site of the temple on the east to commemorate its destruction. For many centuries, Christians used these poems during the week from Palm Sunday to Easter Day, to express great sorrow at the suffering and death of Christ.

Was there hope, then, which could come out of great calamity? In Hebrew thought, God was king over all the earth, no matter how tragic life seemed. He was judge, too, and called his people to face up to their misdoings and repent. This called for a renewal of life, both personal and national, to provide a stable basis for society. The final chapter of the book eloquently expresses such sentiments, as acknowledgement of past sin gives way to a recognition of God's sovereignty and a prayer of renewal (5:21):

"Restore us to yourself, O Lord, that we may return;
 renew our days as of old".

1[a] How deserted lies the city,
  once so full of people!
How like a widow is she,
  who once was great among the nations!
She who was queen among the provinces
  has now become a slave.

2Bitterly she weeps at night,
  tears are upon her cheeks.
Among all her lovers
  there is none to comfort her.
All her friends have betrayed her;
  they have become her enemies.

[a]This chapter is an acrostic poem, the verses of which begin with the successive letters of the Hebrew alphabet.

3After affliction and harsh labour,
    Judah has gone into exile.
She dwells among the nations;
    she finds no resting place.
All who pursue her have overtaken her
    in the midst of her distress.

4The roads to Zion mourn,
    for no-one comes to her appointed feasts.
All her gateways are desolate,
    her priests groan,
her maidens grieve,
    and she is in bitter anguish.

5Her foes have become her masters;
    her enemies are at ease.
The LORD has brought her grief
    because of her many sins.
Her children have gone into exile,
    captive before the foe.

6All the splendour has departed
    from the Daughter of Zion.
Her princes are like deer
    that find no pasture;
in weakness they have fled
    before the pursuer.

7In the days of her affliction and wandering
    Jerusalem remembers all the treasures
    that were hers in days of old.
When her people fell into enemy hands,
    there was no-one to help her.
Her enemies looked at her
    and laughed at her destruction.

8Jerusalem has sinned greatly
    and so has become unclean.
All who honoured her despise her,
    for they have seen her nakedness;
she herself groans
    and turns away.

9Her filthiness clung to her skirts;
    she did not consider her future.
Her fall was astounding;
    there was none to comfort her.
"Look, O LORD, on my affliction,
    for the enemy has triumphed."

10The enemy laid hands
    on all her treasures;
she saw pagan nations
    enter her sanctuary—
those you had forbidden
    to enter your assembly.

11All her people groan
    as they search for bread;
they barter their treasures for food
    to keep themselves alive.
"Look, O LORD, and consider,
    for I am despised."

12"Is it nothing to you, all you who pass by?
    Look around and see.

Is any suffering like my suffering
    that was inflicted on me,
that the LORD brought on me
    in the day of his fierce anger?

13"From on high he sent fire,
    sent it down into my bones.
He spread a net for my feet
    and turned me back.
He made me desolate,
    faint all the day long.

14"My sins have been bound into a yoke; b
    by his hands they were woven together.
They have come upon my neck
    and the Lord has sapped my strength.
He has handed me over
    to those I cannot withstand.

15"The Lord has rejected
    all the warriors in my midst;
he has summoned an army against me
    to c crush my young men.
In his winepress the Lord has trampled
    the Virgin Daughter of Judah.

16"This is why I weep
    and my eyes overflow with tears.
No-one is near to comfort me,
    no-one to restore my spirit.
My children are destitute
    because the enemy has prevailed."

17Zion stretches out her hands,
    but there is no-one to comfort her.
The LORD has decreed for Jacob
    that his neighbours become his foes;
Jerusalem has become
    an unclean thing among them.

18"The LORD is righteous,
    yet I rebelled against his command.
Listen, all you peoples;
    look upon my suffering.
My young men and maidens
    have gone into exile.

19"I called to my allies
    but they betrayed me.
My priests and my elders
    perished in the city
while they searched for food
    to keep themselves alive.

20"See, O LORD, how distressed I am!
    I am in torment within,
and in my heart I am disturbed,
    for I have been most rebellious.
Outside, the sword bereaves;
    inside, there is only death.

21"People have heard my groaning,
    but there is no-one to comfort me.
All my enemies have heard of my distress;
    they rejoice at what you have done.
May you bring the day you have announced
    so that they may become like me.

b14 Most Hebrew manuscripts; Septuagint He kept watch over my sins   c15 Or has set a time for me / when he will

²²"Let all their wickedness come before you;
    deal with them
as you have dealt with me
    because of all my sins.
My groans are many
    and my heart is faint."

2 ᵃ How the Lord has covered the Daughter of
        Zion
    with the cloud of his anger!ᵇ
He has hurled down the splendour of Israel
    from heaven to earth;
he has not remembered his footstool
    in the day of his anger.

²Without pity the Lord has swallowed up
    all the dwellings of Jacob;
in his wrath he has torn down
    the strongholds of the Daughter of Judah.
He has brought her kingdom and its princes
    down to the ground in dishonour.

³In fierce anger he has cut off
    every hornᶜ of Israel.
He has withdrawn his right hand
    at the approach of the enemy.
He has burned in Jacob like a flaming fire
    that consumes everything around it.

⁴Like an enemy he has strung his bow;
    his right hand is ready.
Like a foe he has slain
    all who were pleasing to the eye;
he has poured out his wrath like fire
    on the tent of the Daughter of Zion.

⁵The Lord is like an enemy;
    he has swallowed up Israel.
He has swallowed up all her palaces
    and destroyed her strongholds.
He has multiplied mourning and lamentation
    for the Daughter of Judah.

⁶He has laid waste his dwelling like a garden;
    he has destroyed his place of meeting.
The Lord has made Zion forget
    her appointed feasts and her Sabbaths;
in his fierce anger he has spurned
    both king and priest.

⁷The Lord has rejected his altar
    and abandoned his sanctuary.
He has handed over to the enemy
    the walls of her palaces;
they have raised a shout in the house of the Lord
    as on the day of an appointed feast.

⁸The Lord determined to tear down
    the wall around the Daughter of Zion.
He stretched out a measuring line
    and did not withhold his hand from destroying.
He made ramparts and walls lament;
    together they wasted away.

⁹Her gates have sunk into the ground;
    their bars he has broken and destroyed.
Her king and her princes are exiled among the
        nations,
    the law is no more,
and her prophets no longer find
    visions from the Lord.

¹⁰The elders of the Daughter of Zion
    sit on the ground in silence;
they have sprinkled dust on their heads
    and put on sackcloth.
The young women of Jerusalem
    have bowed their heads to the ground.

¹¹My eyes fail from weeping,
    I am in torment within,
my heart is poured out on the ground
    because my people are destroyed,
because children and infants faint
    in the streets of the city.

¹²They say to their mothers,
    "Where is bread and wine?"
as they faint like wounded men
    in the streets of the city,
as their lives ebb away
    in their mothers' arms.

¹³What can I say for you?
    With what can I compare you,
    O Daughter of Jerusalem?
To what can I liken you,
    that I may comfort you,
    O Virgin Daughter of Zion?
Your wound is as deep as the sea.
    Who can heal you?

¹⁴The visions of your prophets
    were false and worthless;
they did not expose your sin
    to ward off your captivity.
The oracles they gave you
    were false and misleading.

¹⁵All who pass your way
    clap their hands at you;
they scoff and shake their heads
    at the Daughter of Jerusalem:
"Is this the city that was called
    the perfection of beauty,
    the joy of the whole earth?"

¹⁶All your enemies open their mouths
    wide against you;
they scoff and gnash their teeth
    and say, "We have swallowed her up.
This is the day we have waited for;
    we have lived to see it."

¹⁷The Lord has done what he planned;
    he has fulfilled his word,
    which he decreed long ago.

ᵃThis chapter is an acrostic poem, the verses of which begin with the successive letters of the Hebrew alphabet.
ᵇ1 Or How the Lord in his anger / has treated the Daughter of Zion with contempt!
ᶜ3 Or / all the strength; or every king; horn here symbolises strength.

He has overthrown you without pity,
he has let the enemy gloat over you,
he has exalted the horn[d] of your foes.

18The hearts of the people
cry out to the Lord.
O wall of the Daughter of Zion,
let your tears flow like a river
day and night;
give yourself no relief,
your eyes no rest.

19Arise, cry out in the night,
as the watches of the night begin;
pour out your heart like water
in the presence of the Lord.
Lift up your hands to him
for the lives of your children,
who faint from hunger
at the head of every street.

20"Look, O LORD, and consider:
Whom have you ever treated like this?
Should women eat their offspring,
the children they have cared for?
Should priest and prophet be killed
in the sanctuary of the Lord?

21"Young and old lie together
in the dust of the streets;
my young men and maidens
have fallen by the sword.
You have slain them in the day of your anger;
you have slaughtered them without pity.

22"As you summon to a feast day,
so you summoned against me terrors on every
side.
In the day of the LORD's anger
no-one escaped or survived;
those I cared for and reared,
my enemy has destroyed."

3 ^a I am the man who has seen affliction
by the rod of his wrath.
2He has driven me away and made me walk
in darkness rather than light;
3indeed, he has turned his hand against me
again and again, all day long.

4He has made my skin and my flesh grow old
and has broken my bones.
5He has besieged me and surrounded me
with bitterness and hardship.
6He has made me dwell in darkness
like those long dead.

7He has walled me in so that I cannot escape;
he has weighed me down with chains.
8Even when I call out or cry for help,
he shuts out my prayer.
9He has barred my way with blocks of stone;
he has made my paths crooked.

10Like a bear lying in wait,
like a lion in hiding,
11he dragged me from the path and mangled me
and left me without help.
12He drew his bow
and made me the target for his arrows.
13He pierced my heart
with arrows from his quiver.
14I became the laughing-stock of all my people;
they mock me in song all day long.
15He has filled me with bitter herbs
and sated me with gall.

16He has broken my teeth with gravel;
he has trampled me in the dust.
17I have been deprived of peace;
I have forgotten what prosperity is.
18So I say, "My splendour is gone
and all that I had hoped from the LORD."

19I remember my affliction and my wandering,
the bitterness and the gall.
20I well remember them,
and my soul is downcast within me.
21Yet this I call to mind
and therefore I have hope:

22Because of the LORD's great love we are not
consumed,
for his compassions never fail.
23They are new every morning;
great is your faithfulness.
24I say to myself, "The LORD is my portion;
therefore I will wait for him."

25The LORD is good to those whose hope is in him,
to the one who seeks him;
26it is good to wait quietly
for the salvation of the LORD.
27It is good for a man to bear the yoke
while he is young.

28Let him sit alone in silence,
for the LORD has laid it on him.
29Let him bury his face in the dust—
there may yet be hope.
30Let him offer his cheek to one who would strike
him,
and let him be filled with disgrace.

31For men are not cast off
by the Lord for ever.
32Though he brings grief, he will show compassion,
so great is his unfailing love.
33For he does not willingly bring affliction
or grief to the children of men.

34To crush underfoot
all prisoners in the land,
35to deny a man his rights
before the Most High,
36to deprive a man of justice—
would not the Lord see such things?

d17 Horn here symbolises strength.
aThis chapter is an acrostic poem; the verses of each stanza begin with the successive letters of the Hebrew alphabet, and the verses within each stanza begin with the same letter.

³⁷Who can speak and have it happen
    if the Lord has not decreed it?
³⁸Is it not from the mouth of the Most High
    that both calamities and good things come?
³⁹Why should any living man complain
    when punished for his sins?

⁴⁰Let us examine our ways and test them,
    and let us return to the LORD.
⁴¹Let us lift up our hearts and our hands
    to God in heaven, and say:
⁴²"We have sinned and rebelled
    and you have not forgiven.

⁴³"You have covered yourself with anger and
        pursued us;
    you have slain without pity.
⁴⁴You have covered yourself with a cloud
    so that no prayer can get through.
⁴⁵You have made us scum and refuse
    among the nations.

⁴⁶"All our enemies have opened their mouths
    wide against us.
⁴⁷We have suffered terror and pitfalls,
    ruin and destruction."
⁴⁸Streams of tears flow from my eyes
    because my people are destroyed.

⁴⁹My eyes will flow unceasingly,
    without relief,
⁵⁰until the LORD looks down
    from heaven and sees.
⁵¹What I see brings grief to my soul
    because of all the women of my city.

⁵²Those who were my enemies without cause
    hunted me like a bird.
⁵³They tried to end my life in a pit
    and threw stones at me;
⁵⁴the waters closed over my head,
    and I thought I was about to be cut off.

⁵⁵I called on your name, O LORD,
    from the depths of the pit.
⁵⁶You heard my plea: "Do not close your ears
    to my cry for relief."
⁵⁷You came near when I called you,
    and you said, "Do not fear."

⁵⁸O Lord, you took up my case;
    you redeemed my life.
⁵⁹You have seen, O LORD, the wrong done to me.
    Uphold my cause!
⁶⁰You have seen the depth of their vengeance,
    all their plots against me.

⁶¹O LORD, you have heard their insults,
    all their plots against me—
⁶²what my enemies whisper and mutter
    against me all day long.
⁶³Look at them! Sitting or standing,
    they mock me in their songs.

⁶⁴Pay them back what they deserve, O LORD,
    for what their hands have done.
⁶⁵Put a veil over their hearts,
    and may your curse be on them!
⁶⁶Pursue them in anger and destroy them
    from under the heavens of the LORD.

4^a How the gold has lost its lustre,
    the fine gold become dull!
The sacred gems are scattered
    at the head of every street.

²How the precious sons of Zion,
    once worth their weight in gold,
are now considered as pots of clay,
    the work of a potter's hands!

³Even jackals offer their breasts
    to nurse their young,
but my people have become heartless
    like ostriches in the desert.

⁴Because of thirst the infant's tongue
    sticks to the roof of its mouth;
the children beg for bread,
    but no-one gives it to them.

⁵Those who once ate delicacies
    are destitute in the streets.
Those nurtured in purple
    now lie on ash heaps.

⁶The punishment of my people
    is greater than that of Sodom,
which was overthrown in a moment
    without a hand turned to help her.

⁷Their princes were brighter than snow
    and whiter than milk,
their bodies more ruddy than rubies,
    their appearance like sapphires.^b

⁸But now they are blacker than soot;
    they are not recognised in the streets.
Their skin has shrivelled on their bones;
    it has become as dry as a stick.

⁹Those killed by the sword are better off
    than those who die of famine;
racked with hunger, they waste away
    for lack of food from the field.

¹⁰With their own hands compassionate women
    have cooked their own children,
who became their food
    when my people were destroyed.

¹¹The LORD has given full vent to his wrath;
    he has poured out his fierce anger.
He kindled a fire in Zion
    that consumed her foundations.

¹²The kings of the earth did not believe,
    nor did any of the world's people,
that enemies and foes could enter
    the gates of Jerusalem.

---

^aThis chapter is an acrostic poem, the verses of which begin with the successive letters of the Hebrew alphabet.
^b7 Or *lapis lazuli*

¹³But it happened because of the sins of her
  prophets
  and the iniquities of her priests,
who shed within her
  the blood of the righteous.

¹⁴Now they grope through the streets
  like men who are blind.
They are so defiled with blood
  that no-one dares to touch their garments.

¹⁵"Go away! You are unclean!" men cry to them.
  "Away! Away! Don't touch us!"
When they flee and wander about,
  people among the nations say,
  "They can stay here no longer."

¹⁶The LORD himself has scattered them;
  he no longer watches over them.
The priests are shown no honour,
  the elders no favour.

¹⁷Moreover, our eyes failed,
  looking in vain for help;
from our towers we watched
  for a nation that could not save us.

¹⁸Men stalked us at every step,
  so we could not walk in our streets.
Our end was near, our days were numbered,
  for our end had come.

¹⁹Our pursuers were swifter
  than eagles in the sky;
they chased us over the mountains
  and lay in wait for us in the desert.

²⁰The LORD's anointed, our very life breath,
  was caught in their traps.
We thought that under his shadow
  we would live among the nations.

²¹Rejoice and be glad, O Daughter of Edom,
  you who live in the land of Uz.
But to you also the cup will be passed;
  you will be drunk and stripped naked.

²²O Daughter of Zion, your punishment will end;
  he will not prolong your exile.
But, O Daughter of Edom, he will punish your sin
  and expose your wickedness.

5 Remember, O LORD, what has happened to us;
  look, and see our disgrace.
²Our inheritance has been turned over to aliens,
  our homes to foreigners.
³We have become orphans and fatherless,
  our mothers like widows.
⁴We must buy the water we drink;
  our wood can be had only at a price.
⁵Those who pursue us are at our heels;
  we are weary and find no rest.
⁶We submitted to Egypt and Assyria
  to get enough bread.
⁷Our fathers sinned and are no more,
  and we bear their punishment.
⁸Slaves rule over us,
  and there is none to free us from their hands.
⁹We get our bread at the risk of our lives
  because of the sword in the desert.
¹⁰Our skin is hot as an oven,
  feverish from hunger.
¹¹Women have been ravished in Zion,
  and virgins in the towns of Judah.
¹²Princes have been hung up by their hands;
  elders are shown no respect.
¹³Young men toil at the millstones;
  boys stagger under loads of wood.
¹⁴The elders are gone from the city gate;
  the young men have stopped their music.
¹⁵Joy is gone from our hearts;
  our dancing has turned to mourning.
¹⁶The crown has fallen from our head.
  Woe to us, for we have sinned!
¹⁷Because of this our hearts are faint;
  because of these things our eyes grow dim
¹⁸for Mount Zion, which lies desolate,
  with jackals prowling over it.
¹⁹You, O LORD, reign for ever;
  your throne endures from generation to
  generation.
²⁰Why do you always forget us?
  Why do you forsake us so long?
²¹Restore us to yourself, O LORD, that we may
  return;
  renew our days as of old
²²unless you have utterly rejected us
  and are angry with us beyond measure.

Ezekiel

Ordinary Person or out of this World?

If you look at the lives of the prophets it is clear that on the whole they were very down—to—earth people, experiencing everything that other humans experience, and that most of them had an overbearing sense of their own inadequacy to do the job of a prophet. Ezekiel, however, was different. He was one of those people who is "larger than life". His vision of God's glory and his message to God's people often seemed "out of this world" by comparison with other prophets.

Working with the Deported

His ministry began around 586 BC when Jerusalem was invaded by the Babylonians, and large numbers of Jews, including Ezekiel, were deported as slaves to Babylon. He was active at the same time as Jeremiah—indeed the two prophets could be said to have been working in tandem with one another: Ezekiel with the exiles and Jeremiah with the remnant in Jerusalem.

A Sense of God's Holiness

From the outset, however, it is clear that Ezekiel was completely different to Jeremiah. He had a different personality, an extra dimension to his words and thoughts. He had a strong sense of God's holiness and described his visions in very graphic language. Coupled with this sense of God's holiness was an underlying firmness and awareness of the demands of God's law. He was quite uncompromising in his belief that God is active in the suffering of his people, and is calling them to repent and return to him.

A Priestly Prophet

The belief that Ezekiel was a priest (see 1:3) gives us a clue to what lay behind a lot of his words and thoughts. A priest ministered in the temple, and only priests were permitted to enter that part of the temple called the Holy of Holies—the place where God dwelt. They would be thoroughly versed in the Holiness Code (Leviticus 17—27) and the Priestly Code (Exodus 25—40; Leviticus 1—16), and fulfilled the function of acting as a bridge between God, who was absolutely holy, and his people, who were sinful and not permitted to look upon God. Ezekiel was following this priestly tradition with its strong emphasis upon God's holiness. In the later part of the book, when he looked forward to a restored and renewed Jerusalem, his hopes focused on the temple, and his working knowledge of the temple is very much at the forefront.

Radical

Ezekiel's priestly roots must not, however, allow us to be side-tracked from how radical he was. He was not just simply speaking and acting from the confines of a tradition. At times he turned the theology of his day on its head. Traditionally, it was believed that God's dwelling place was the temple, and that Jerusalem was the place where true worship of God took place. As a priest, Ezekiel would have upheld that tradition. But now he was not in Jerusalem, and neither were the majority of the Jews. Their holy city had been destroyed and the temple with it. Had God abandoned his people? Could God be worshipped somewhere other than the temple?

Changing Belief

Ezekiel answered such questions with great firmness, and showed that religious belief is not something that remains static but is always moving on and responding to new circumstances. Ezekiel argued that God had not abandoned his people. He was holy, and he was sovereign, too. It was his world, and there was nowhere that he could not be found. Even in Babylon, a nation of paganism, God could be known and worshipped. Throughout the book you will find that his oracles contain the punchline "They will know that I am the LORD." It was this awareness of God's holiness and his availability which inspired Ezekiel's ministry.

The Living Creatures and the Glory of the LORD

1 In the[a] thirtieth year, in the fourth month on the fifth day, while I was among the exiles by the Kebar River, the heavens were opened and I saw visions of God.

²On the fifth of the month—it was the fifth year of the exile of King Jehoiachin—³the word of the LORD came to Ezekiel the priest, the son of Buzi,[b] by the Kebar River in the land of the Babylonians.[c] There the hand of the LORD was upon him.

⁴I looked, and I saw a windstorm coming out of the north—an immense cloud with flashing lightning and surrounded by brilliant light. The centre of the fire looked like glowing metal, ⁵and in the fire was what looked like four living creatures. In appearance their form was that of a man, ⁶but each of them had four faces and four wings. ⁷Their legs were straight; their feet were like those of a calf and gleamed like burnished bronze. ⁸Under their wings on their four sides they had the hands of a man. All four of them had faces and wings, ⁹and their wings touched one another. Each one went straight ahead; they did not turn as they moved.

¹⁰Their faces looked like this: Each of the four had the face of a man, and on the right side each had the face of a lion, and on the left the face of an ox; each also had the face of an eagle. ¹¹Such were their faces. Their wings were spread out upwards; each had two

wings, one touching the wing of another creature on either side, and two wings covering its body. ¹²Each one went straight ahead. Wherever the spirit would go, they would go, without turning as they went. ¹³The appearance of the living creatures was like burning coals of fire or like torches. Fire moved back and forth among the creatures; it was bright, and lightning flashed out of it. ¹⁴The creatures sped back and forth like flashes of lightning.

¹⁵As I looked at the living creatures, I saw a wheel on the ground beside each creature with its four faces. ¹⁶This was the appearance and structure of the wheels: They sparkled like chrysolite, and all four looked alike. Each appeared to be made like a wheel intersecting a wheel. ¹⁷As they moved, they would go in any one of the four directions the creatures faced; the wheels did not turn about[d] as the creatures went. ¹⁸Their rims were high and awesome, and all four rims were full of eyes all around.

1:18 Compare Ezekiel's vision of God's glory with that of Isaiah (6:1–8). Ezekiel was much more graphic, and used language which is uncommon in the prophets. In this "out of this world" vision, Ezekiel did not attempt to describe God—for no one has ever seen him—but compared him with mighty things.

---

a1 Or *my*,   b3 Or *Ezekiel son of Buzi the priest*   c3 Or *Chaldeans*   d17 Or *aside*

¹⁹When the living creatures moved, the wheels beside them moved; and when the living creatures rose from the ground, the wheels also rose. ²⁰Wherever the spirit would go, they would go, and the wheels would rise along with them, because the spirit of the living creatures was in the wheels. ²¹When the creatures moved, they also moved; when the creatures stood still, they also stood still; and when the creatures rose from the ground, the wheels rose along with them, because the spirit of the living creatures was in the wheels.

²²Spread out above the heads of the living creatures was what looked like an expanse, sparkling like ice, and awesome. ²³Under the expanse their wings were stretched out one towards the other, and each had two wings covering its body. ²⁴When the creatures moved, I heard the sound of their wings, like the roar of rushing waters, like the voice of the Almighty,ᵉ like the tumult of an army. When they stood still, they lowered their wings.

²⁵Then there came a voice from above the expanse over their heads as they stood with lowered wings. ²⁶Above the expanse over their heads was what looked like a throne of sapphire,ᶠ and high above on the throne was a figure like that of a man. ²⁷I saw that from what appeared to be his waist up he looked like glowing metal, as if full of fire, and that from there down he looked like fire; and brilliant light surrounded him. ²⁸Like the appearance of a rainbow in the clouds on a rainy day, so was the radiance around him.

This was the appearance of the likeness of the glory of the Lᴏʀᴅ. When I saw it, I fell face down, and I heard the voice of one speaking.

Ezekiel's Call

2 He said to me, "Son of man, stand up on your feet and I will speak to you." ²As he spoke, the Spirit came into me and raised me to my feet, and I heard him speaking to me.

³He said: "Son of man, I am sending you to the Israelites, to a rebellious nation that has rebelled against me; they and their fathers have been in revolt against me to this very day. ⁴The people to whom I am sending you are obstinate and stubborn. Say to them, 'This is what the Sovereign Lᴏʀᴅ says.' ⁵And whether they listen or fail to listen—for they are a rebellious house—they will know that a prophet has been among them. ⁶And you, son of man, do not be afraid of them or their words. Do not be afraid, though briers and thorns are all around you and you live among scorpions. Do not be afraid of what they say or terrified by them, though they are a rebellious house. ⁷You must speak my words to them, whether they listen or fail to listen, for they are rebellious. ⁸But you, son of man, listen to what I say to you. Do not rebel like that rebellious house; open your mouth and eat what I give you."

⁹Then I looked, and I saw a hand stretched out to me. In it was a scroll, ¹⁰which he unrolled before me. On both sides of it were written words of lament and mourning and woe.

3 And he said to me, "Son of man, eat what is before you, eat this scroll; then go and speak to the house of Israel." ²So I opened my mouth, and he gave me the scroll to eat.

³Then he said to me, "Son of man, eat this scroll I am giving you and fill your stomach with it." So I ate it, and it tasted as sweet as honey in my mouth.

⁴He then said to me: "Son of man, go now to the house of Israel and speak my words to them. ⁵You are not being sent to a people of obscure speech and difficult language, but to the house of Israel—⁶not to many peoples of obscure speech and difficult language, whose words you cannot understand. Surely if I had sent you to them, they would have listened to you. ⁷But the house of Israel is not willing to listen to you because they are not willing to listen to me, for the whole house of Israel is hardened and obstinate. ⁸But I will make you as unyielding and hardened as they are. ⁹I will make your forehead like the hardest stone, harder than flint. Do not be afraid of them or terrified by them, though they are a rebellious house."

¹⁰And he said to me, "Son of man, listen carefully and take to heart all the words I speak to you. ¹¹Go now to your countrymen in exile and speak to them. Say to them, 'This is what the Sovereign Lᴏʀᴅ says,' whether they listen or fail to listen."

¹²Then the Spirit lifted me up, and I heard behind me a loud rumbling sound—May the glory of the Lᴏʀᴅ be praised in his dwelling-place!—¹³the sound of the wings of the living creatures brushing against each other and the sound of the wheels beside them, a loud rumbling sound. ¹⁴The Spirit then lifted me up and took me away, and I went in bitterness and in the anger of my spirit, with the strong hand of the Lᴏʀᴅ upon me. ¹⁵I came to the exiles who lived at Tel Abib near the Kebar River. And there, where they were living, I sat among them for seven days—overwhelmed.

3:15   After such a momentous vision, and such a great commission and call from God Ezekiel was, to all intents and purposes, flabbergasted! He did not rush out to get on with the Lord's work — rather he needed to sit down and take in all that had happened.

Warning to Israel

¹⁶At the end of seven days the word of the Lᴏʀᴅ came to me: ¹⁷"Son of man, I have made you a watchman for the house of Israel; so hear the word I speak and give them warning from me. ¹⁸When I say to a wicked man, 'You will surely die,' and you do not warn him or speak out to dissuade him from his evil ways in order to save his life, that wicked man will die forᵃ his sin, and I will hold you accountable for his blood. ¹⁹But if you do warn the wicked man and he does not turn from his wickedness or from his evil ways, he will die for his sin; but you will have saved yourself. ²⁰"Again, when a righteous man turns from his righteousness and does evil, and I put a stumbling-

---

ᵉ24 Hebrew *Shaddai*   ᶠ26 Or *lapis lazuli*   ᵃ18 Or *in*; also in verses 19 and 20 block before him, he will die. Since you did not warn him, he will die for his sin. The righteous things he did will not be remembered, and I will hold you accountable for his blood. 21But if you do warn the righteous man not to sin and he does not sin, he will surely live because he took warning, and you will have saved yourself."

22The hand of the LORD was upon me there, and he said to me, "Get up and go out to the plain, and there I will speak to you." 23So I got up and went out to the plain. And the glory of the LORD was standing there, like the glory I had seen by the Kebar River, and I fell face down.

24Then the Spirit came into me and raised me to my feet. He spoke to me and said: "Go, shut yourself inside your house. 25And you, son of man, they will tie with ropes; you will be bound so that you cannot go out among the people. 26I will make your tongue stick to the roof of your mouth so that you will be silent and unable to rebuke them, though they are a rebellious house. 27But when I speak to you, I will open your mouth and you shall say to them, 'This is what the Sovereign LORD says.' Whoever will listen let him listen, and whoever will refuse let him refuse; for they are a rebellious house.

Siege of Jerusalem Symbolised

4 "Now, son of man, take a clay tablet, put it in front of you and draw the city of Jerusalem on it. 2Then lay siege to it: Erect siege works against it, build a ramp up to it, set up camps against it and put battering-rams around it. 3Then take an iron pan, place it as an iron wall between you and the city and turn your face towards it. It will be under siege, and you shall besiege it. This will be a sign to the house of Israel.

4"Then lie on your left side and put the sin of the house of Israel upon yourself.ᵃ You are to bear their sin for the number of days you lie on your side. 5I have assigned you the same number of days as the years of their sin. So for 390 days you will bear the sin of the house of Israel.

6"After you have finished this, lie down again, this time on your right side, and bear the sin of the house of Judah. I have assigned you 40 days, a day for each year. 7Turn your face towards the siege of Jerusalem and with bared arm prophesy against her. 8I will tie you up with ropes so that you cannot turn from one side to the other until you have finished the days of your siege.

9"Take wheat and barley, beans and lentils, millet and spelt; put them in a storage jar and use them to make bread for yourself. You are to eat it during the 390 days you lie on your side. 10Weigh out twenty shekelsᵇ of food to eat each day and eat it at set times. 11Also measure out a sixth of a hinᶜ of water and drink it at set times. 12Eat the food as you would a barley cake; bake it in the sight of the people, using human excrement for fuel." 13The LORD said, "In this way the people of Israel will eat defiled food among the nations where I will drive them."

14Then I said, "Not so, Sovereign LORD! I have never defiled myself. From my youth until now I have never eaten anything found dead or torn by wild animals. No unclean meat has ever entered my mouth."

15"Very well," he said, "I will let you bake your bread over cow manure instead of human excrement."

16He then said to me: "Son of man, I will cut off the supply of food in Jerusalem. The people will eat rationed food in anxiety and drink rationed water in despair, 17for food and water will be scarce. They will be appalled at the sight of each other and will waste away because ofᵈ their sin.

5 "Now, son of man, take a sharp sword and use it as a barber's razor to shave your head and your beard. Then take a set of scales and divide up the hair. 2When the days of your siege come to an end, burn a third of the hair with fire inside the city. Take a third and strike it with the sword all around the city. And scatter a third to the wind. For I will pursue them with drawn sword. 3But take a few strands of hair and tuck them away in the folds of your garment. 4Again, take a few of these and throw them into the fire and burn them up. A fire will spread from there to the whole house of Israel.

5"This is what the Sovereign LORD says: This is Jerusalem, which I have set in the centre of the nations, with countries all around her. 6Yet in her wickedness she has rebelled against my laws and decrees more than the nations and countries around her. She has rejected my laws and has not followed my decrees.

7"Therefore this is what the Sovereign LORD says: You have been more unruly than the nations around you and have not followed my decrees or kept my laws. You have not evenᵃ conformed to the standards of the nations around you.

5:7   Not only had God's people sinned and rejected the Law, but their behaviour had been so bad that they had sinned worse than the surrounding heathen nations, who had no knowledge of God's laws. In the remaining verses of this chapter, God's punishment for such sinfulness is spelt out in detail.

8"Therefore this is what the Sovereign LORD says: I myself am against you, Jerusalem, and I will inflict punishment on you in the sight of the nations. 9Because of all your detestable idols, I will do to you what I have never done before and will never do again. 10Therefore in your midst fathers will eat their children, and children will eat their fathers. I will inflict punishment on you and will scatter all your survivors to the winds. 11Therefore as surely as I live, declares the Sovereign LORD, because you have defiled my sanctuary with all your vile images and detestable practices, I myself will withdraw my favour; I will not look on you with pity or spare you. 12A third of your people will die of the plague or perish by famine inside you; a third will fall

---

ᵃ4 Or your side   ᵇ10 That is, about 8 ounces (about 0.2 kilogram)   ᶜ11 That is, about 1 pint (about 0.6 litre)
ᵈ17 Or away in   ᵃ7 Most Hebrew manuscripts; some Hebrew manuscripts and Syriac You have

by the sword outside your walls; and a third I will scatter to the winds and pursue with drawn sword.

13 "Then my anger will cease and my wrath against them will subside, and I will be avenged. And when I have spent my wrath upon them, they will know that I the LORD have spoken in my zeal.

14 "I will make you a ruin and a reproach among the nations around you, in the sight of all who pass by. 15 You will be a reproach and a taunt, a warning and an object of horror to the nations around you when I inflict punishment on you in anger and in wrath and with stinging rebuke. I the LORD have spoken. 16 When I shoot at you with my deadly and destructive arrows of famine, I will shoot to destroy you. I will bring more and more famine upon you and cut off your supply of food. 17 I will send famine and wild beasts against you, and they will leave you childless. Plague and bloodshed will sweep through you, and I will bring the sword against you. I the LORD have spoken."

A Prophecy Against the Mountains of Israel

6 The word of the LORD came to me: 2 "Son of man, set your face against the mountains of Israel; prophesy against them 3 and say: 'O mountains of Israel, hear the word of the Sovereign LORD. This is what the Sovereign LORD says to the mountains and hills, to the ravines and valleys: I am about to bring a sword against you, and I will destroy your high places. 4 Your altars will be demolished and your incense altars will be smashed; and I will slay your people in front of your idols. 5 I will lay the dead bodies of the Israelites in front of their idols, and I will scatter your bones around your altars. 6 Wherever you live, the towns will be laid waste and the high places demolished, so that your altars will be laid waste and devastated, your idols smashed and ruined, your incense altars broken down, and what you have made wiped out. 7 Your people will fall slain among you, and you will know that I am the LORD.

8 " 'But I will spare some, for some of you will escape the sword when you are scattered among the lands and nations. 9 Then in the nations where they have been carried captive, those who escape will remember me — how I have been grieved by their adulterous hearts, which have turned away from me, and by their eyes, which have lusted after their idols. They will loathe themselves for the evil they have done and for all their detestable practices. 10 And they will know that I am the LORD; I did not threaten in vain to bring this calamity on them.

11 " 'This is what the Sovereign LORD says: Strike your hands together and stamp your feet and cry out "Alas!" because of all the wicked and detestable practices of the house of Israel, for they will fall by the sword, famine and plague. 12 He that is far away will die of the plague, and he that is near will fall by the sword, and he that survives and is spared will die of famine. So will I spend my wrath upon them. 13 And they will know that I am the LORD, when their people lie slain among their idols around their altars, on every high hill

and on all the mountaintops, under every spreading tree and every leafy oak — places where they offered fragrant incense to all their idols. 14 And I will stretch out my hand against them and make the land a desolate waste from the desert to Diblah[a] — wherever they live. Then they will know that I am the LORD.' "

The End Has Come

7 The word of the LORD came to me: 2 "Son of man, this is what the Sovereign LORD says to the land of Israel: The end! The end has come upon the four corners of the land. 3 The end is now upon you and I will unleash my anger against you. I will judge you according to your conduct and repay you for all your detestable practices. 4 I will not look on you with pity or spare you; I will surely repay you for your conduct and the detestable practices among you. Then you will know that I am the LORD.

5 "This is what the Sovereign LORD says: Disaster! An unheard-of[a] disaster is coming. 6 The end has come! The end has come! It has roused itself against you. It has come! 7 Doom has come upon you — you who dwell in the land. The time has come, the day is near; there is panic, not joy, upon the mountains. 8 I am about to pour out my wrath on you and spend my anger against you; I will judge you according to your conduct and repay you for all your detestable practices. 9 I will not look on you with pity or spare you; I will repay you in accordance with your conduct and the detestable practices among you. Then you will know that it is I the LORD who strikes the blow.

10 "The day is here! It has come! Doom has burst forth, the rod has budded, arrogance has blossomed! 11 Violence has grown into[b] a rod to punish wickedness; none of the people will be left, none of that crowd — no wealth, nothing of value. 12 The time has come, the day has arrived. Let not the buyer rejoice nor the seller grieve, for wrath is upon the whole crowd. 13 The seller will not recover the land he has sold as long as both of them live, for the vision concerning the whole crowd will not be reversed. Because of their sins, not one of them will preserve his life. 14 Though they blow the trumpet and get everything ready, no-one will go into battle, for my wrath is upon the whole crowd.

15 "Outside is the sword, inside are plague and famine; those in the country will die by the sword, and those in the city will be devoured by famine and plague. 16 All who survive and escape will be in the mountains, moaning like doves of the valleys, each because of his sins. 17 Every hand will go limp, and every knee will become as weak as water. 18 They will put on sackcloth and be clothed with terror. Their faces will be covered with shame and their heads will be shaved. 19 They will throw their silver into the streets, and their gold will be an unclean thing. Their silver and gold will not be able to save them in the day of the LORD's wrath. They will not satisfy their hunger or fill their stomachs with it, for it has made them stumble into sin. 20 They were proud of their beautiful jewellery

---

a 14 Most Hebrew manuscripts; a few Hebrew manuscripts *Riblah*
a 5 Most Hebrew manuscripts; some Hebrew manuscripts and Syriac *Disaster after*　　　　b 11 Or *The violent one has become*

and used it to make their detestable idols and vile images. Therefore I will turn these into an unclean thing for them. ²¹I will hand it all over as plunder to foreigners and as loot to the wicked of the earth, and they will defile it. ²²I will turn my face away from them, and they will desecrate my treasured place; robbers will enter it and desecrate it.

²³"Prepare chains, because the land is full of bloodshed and the city is full of violence. ²⁴I will bring the most wicked of the nations to take possession of their houses; I will put an end to the pride of the mighty, and their sanctuaries will be desecrated. ²⁵When terror comes, they will seek peace, but there will be none. ²⁶Calamity upon calamity will come, and rumour upon rumour. They will try to get a vision from the prophet; the teaching of the law by the priest will be lost, as will the counsel of the elders. ²⁷The king will mourn, the prince will be clothed with despair, and the hands of the people of the land will tremble. I will deal with them according to their conduct, and by their own standards I will judge them. Then they will know that I am the LORD."

Idolatry in the Temple

8 In the sixth year, in the sixth month on the fifth day, while I was sitting in my house and the elders of Judah were sitting before me, the hand of the Sovereign LORD came upon me there. ²I looked, and I saw a figure like that of a man.ᵃ From what appeared to be his waist down he was like fire, and from there up his appearance was as bright as glowing metal. ³He stretched out what looked like a hand and took me by the hair of my head. The Spirit lifted me up between earth and heaven and in visions of God he took me to Jerusalem, to the entrance to the north gate of the inner court, where the idol that provokes to jealousy stood. ⁴And there before me was the glory of the God of Israel, as in the vision I had seen in the plain.

⁵Then he said to me, "Son of man, look towards the north." So I looked, and in the entrance north of the gate of the altar I saw this idol of jealousy.

⁶And he said to me, "Son of man, do you see what they are doing—the utterly detestable things the house of Israel is doing here, things that will drive me far from my sanctuary? But you will see things that are even more detestable."

8:6 Ezekiel had another vision. This time, however, he looked not upon God's holiness, but upon idols which had replaced God in the temple. God's holiness had been profaned, and he was jealous with rage. Chapter 9 talks about the consequences of provoking God to anger.

---

⁷Then he brought me to the entrance to the court. I looked, and I saw a hole in the wall. ⁸He said to me, "Son of man, now dig into the wall." So I dug into the wall and saw a doorway there.

⁹And he said to me, "Go in and see the wicked and detestable things they are doing here." ¹⁰So I went in and looked, and I saw portrayed all over the walls all kinds of crawling things and detestable animals and all the idols of the house of Israel. ¹¹In front of them stood seventy elders of the house of Israel, and Jaazaniah son of Shaphan was standing among them. Each had a censer in his hand, and a fragrant cloud of incense was rising.

¹²He said to me, "Son of man, have you seen what the elders of the house of Israel are doing in the darkness, each at the shrine of his own idol? They say, 'The LORD does not see us; the LORD has forsaken the land.' " ¹³Again, he said, "You will see them doing things that are even more detestable."

¹⁴Then he brought me to the entrance to the north gate of the house of the LORD, and I saw women sitting there, mourning for Tammuz. ¹⁵He said to me, "Do you see this, son of man? You will see things that are even more detestable than this."

¹⁶He then brought me into the inner court of the house of the LORD, and there at the entrance to the temple, between the portico and the altar, were about twenty-five men. With their backs towards the temple of the LORD and their faces towards the east, they were bowing down to the sun in the east.

¹⁷He said to me, "Have you seen this, son of man? Is it a trivial matter for the house of Judah to do the detestable things they are doing here? Must they also fill the land with violence and continually provoke me to anger? Look at them putting the branch to their nose! ¹⁸Therefore I will deal with them in anger; I will not look on them with pity or spare them. Although they shout in my ears, I will not listen to them."

Idolaters Killed

9 Then I heard him call out in a loud voice, "Bring the guards of the city here, each with a weapon in his hand." ²And I saw six men coming from the direction of the upper gate, which faces north, each with a deadly weapon in his hand. With them was a man clothed in linen who had a writing kit at his side. They came in and stood beside the bronze altar.

³Now the glory of the God of Israel went up from above the cherubim, where it had been, and moved to the threshold of the temple. Then the LORD called to the man clothed in linen who had the writing kit at his side ⁴and said to him, "Go throughout the city of Jerusalem and put a mark on the foreheads of those who grieve and lament over all the detestable things that are done in it."

⁵As I listened, he said to the others, "Follow him through the city and kill, without showing pity or compassion. ⁶Slaughter old men, young men and maidens, women and children, but do not touch anyone who has the mark. Begin at my sanctuary." So they began with the elders who were in front of the temple.

⁷Then he said to them, "Defile the temple and fill the courts with the slain. Go!" So they went out and began killing throughout the city. ⁸While they were killing and I was left alone, I fell face down, crying out,

---

ᵃ2 Or *saw a fiery figure*

"Ah, Sovereign LORD! Are you going to destroy the entire remnant of Israel in this outpouring of your wrath on Jerusalem?"

⁹He answered me, "The sin of the house of Israel and Judah is exceedingly great; the land is full of bloodshed and the city is full of injustice. They say, 'The LORD has forsaken the land; the LORD does not see.' ¹⁰So I will not look on them with pity or spare them, but I will bring down on their own heads what they have done."

¹¹Then the man in linen with the writing kit at his side brought back word, saying, "I have done as you commanded."

The Glory Departs From the Temple

10 I looked, and I saw the likeness of a throne of sapphire[a] above the expanse that was over the heads of the cherubim. ²The LORD said to the man clothed in linen, "Go in among the wheels beneath the cherubim. Fill your hands with burning coals from among the cherubim and scatter them over the city." And as I watched, he went in.

³Now the cherubim were standing on the south side of the temple when the man went in, and a cloud filled the inner court. ⁴Then the glory of the LORD rose from above the cherubim and moved to the threshold of the temple. The cloud filled the temple, and the court was full of the radiance of the glory of the LORD. ⁵The sound of the wings of the cherubim could be heard as far away as the outer court, like the voice of God Almighty[b] when he speaks.

⁶When the LORD commanded the man in linen, "Take fire from among the wheels, from among the cherubim," the man went in and stood beside a wheel. ⁷Then one of the cherubim reached out his hand to the fire that was among them. He took up some of it and put it into the hands of the man in linen, who took it and went out. ⁸(Under the wings of the cherubim could be seen what looked like the hands of a man.)

⁹I looked, and I saw beside the cherubim four wheels, one beside each of the cherubim; the wheels sparkled like chrysolite. ¹⁰As for their appearance, the four of them looked alike; each was like a wheel intersecting a wheel. ¹¹As they moved, they would go in any one of the four directions the cherubim faced; the wheels did not turn about[c] as the cherubim went. The cherubim went in whatever direction the head faced, without turning as they went. ¹²Their entire bodies, including their backs, their hands and their wings, were completely full of eyes, as were their four wheels. ¹³I heard the wheels being called "the whirling wheels". ¹⁴Each of the cherubim had four faces: One face was that of a cherub, the second the face of a man, the third the face of a lion, and the fourth the face of an eagle.

¹⁵Then the cherubim rose upwards. These were the living creatures I had seen by the Kebar River. ¹⁶When the cherubim moved, the wheels beside them moved; and when the cherubim spread their wings to rise from the ground, the wheels did not leave their side. ¹⁷When the cherubim stood still, they also stood still; and when the cherubim rose, they rose with them, because the spirit of the living creatures was in them.

¹⁸Then the glory of the LORD departed from over the threshold of the temple and stopped above the cherubim. ¹⁹While I watched, the cherubim spread their wings and rose from the ground, and as they went, the wheels went with them. They stopped at the entrance to the east gate of the LORD's house, and the glory of the God of Israel was above them.

²⁰These were the living creatures I had seen beneath the God of Israel by the Kebar River, and I realised that they were cherubim. ²¹Each had four faces and four wings, and under their wings was what looked like the hands of a man. ²²Their faces had the same appearance as those I had seen by the Kebar River. Each one went straight ahead.

Judgment on Israel's Leaders

11 Then the Spirit lifted me up and brought me to the gate of the house of the LORD that faces east. There at the entrance to the gate were twenty-five men, and I saw among them Jaazaniah son of Azzur and Pelatiah son of Benaiah, leaders of the people. ²The LORD said to me, "Son of man, these are the men who are plotting evil and giving wicked advice in this city. ³They say, 'Will it not soon be time to build houses?[a] This city is a cooking pot, and we are the meat.' ⁴Therefore prophesy against them; prophesy, son of man."

⁵Then the Spirit of the LORD came upon me, and he told me to say: "This is what the LORD says: That is what you are saying, O house of Israel, but I know what is going through your mind. ⁶You have killed many people in this city and filled its streets with the dead.

⁷"Therefore this is what the Sovereign LORD says: The bodies you have thrown there are the meat and this city is the pot, but I will drive you out of it. ⁸You fear the sword, and the sword is what I will bring against you, declares the Sovereign LORD. ⁹I will drive you out of the city and hand you over to foreigners and inflict punishment on you. ¹⁰You will fall by the sword, and I will execute judgment on you at the borders of Israel. Then you will know that I am the LORD. ¹¹This city will not be a pot for you, nor will you be the meat in it; I will execute judgment on you at the borders of Israel. ¹²And you will know that I am the LORD, for you have not followed my decrees or kept my laws but have conformed to the standards of the nations around you."

¹³Now as I was prophesying, Pelatiah son of Benaiah died. Then I fell face down and cried out in a loud voice, "Ah, Sovereign LORD! Will you completely destroy the remnant of Israel?"

¹⁴The word of the LORD came to me: ¹⁵"Son of man, your brothers—your brothers who are your blood-relatives[b] and the whole house of Israel—are those of whom the people of Jerusalem have said, 'They are[c] far away from the LORD; this land was given to us as our possession.'

---

a1 Or *lapis lazuli*   *b5* Hebrew *El-Shaddai*   *c11* Or *aside*   *a3* Or *This is not the time to build houses.*
b15 Or *are in exile with you* (see Septuagint and Syriac)   *c15* Or *those to whom the people of Jerusalem have said, 'Stay*

Promised Return of Israel

16"Therefore say: 'This is what the Sovereign LORD says: Although I sent them far away among the nations and scattered them among the countries, yet for a little while I have been a sanctuary for them in the countries where they have gone.'

17"Therefore say: 'This is what the Sovereign LORD says: I will gather you from the nations and bring you back from the countries where you have been scattered, and I will give you back the land of Israel again.'

11:17   Despite being scattered from the city where God had been worshipped, and even though they had been unable to observe the rites of their religion, the Jews found God amid the traumas of exile. But God would restore them to Jerusalem (verse 18) so they should renew their hearts and motives to follow and obey God as they removed the idols from the temple and renewed their worship.

18"They will return to it and remove all its vile images and detestable idols. 19I will give them an undivided heart and put a new spirit in them; I will remove from them their heart of stone and give them a heart of flesh. 20Then they will follow my decrees and be careful to keep my laws. They will be my people, and I will be their God. 21But as for those whose hearts are devoted to their vile images and detestable idols, I will bring down on their own heads what they have done, declares the Sovereign LORD."

22Then the cherubim, with the wheels beside them, spread their wings, and the glory of the God of Israel was above them. 23The glory of the LORD went up from within the city and stopped above the mountain east of it. 24The Spirit lifted me up and brought me to the exiles in Babylonia*d* in the vision given by the Spirit of God.

Then the vision I had seen went up from me, 25and I told the exiles everything the LORD had shown me.

The Exile Symbolised

12 The word of the LORD came to me: 2"Son of man, you are living among a rebellious people. They have eyes to see but do not see and ears to hear but do not hear, for they are a rebellious people.

3"Therefore, son of man, pack your belongings for exile and in the daytime, as they watch, set out and go from where you are to another place. Perhaps they will understand, though they are a rebellious house. 4During the daytime, while they watch, bring out your belongings packed for exile. Then in the evening, while they are watching, go out like those who go into exile. 5While they watch, dig through the wall and take your belongings out through it. 6Put them on your shoulder as they are watching and carry them out at dusk. Cover your face so that you cannot see the land, for I have made you a sign to the house of Israel."

7So I did as I was commanded. During the day I brought out my things packed for exile. Then in the evening I dug through the wall with my hands. I took my belongings out at dusk, carrying them on my shoulders while they watched.

8In the morning the word of the LORD came to me: 9"Son of man, did not that rebellious house of Israel ask you, 'What are you doing?'

10"Say to them, 'This is what the Sovereign LORD says: This oracle concerns the prince in Jerusalem and the whole house of Israel who are there.' 11Say to them, 'I am a sign to you.'

"As I have done, so it will be done to them. They will go into exile as captives.

12"The prince among them will put his things on his shoulder at dusk and leave, and a hole will be dug in the wall for him to go through. He will cover his face so that he cannot see the land. 13I will spread my net for him, and he will be caught in my snare; I will bring him to Babylonia, the land of the Chaldeans, but he will not see it, and there he will die. 14I will scatter to the winds all those around him—his staff and all his troops—and I will pursue them with drawn sword.

15"They will know that I am the LORD, when I disperse them among the nations and scatter them through the countries. 16But I will spare a few of them from the sword, famine and plague, so that in the nations where they go they may acknowledge all their detestable practices. Then they will know that I am the LORD."

17The word of the LORD came to me: 18"Son of man, tremble as you eat your food, and shudder in fear as you drink your water. 19Say to the people of the land: 'This is what the Sovereign LORD says about those living in Jerusalem and in the land of Israel: They will eat their food in anxiety and drink their water in despair, for their land will be stripped of everything in it because of the violence of all who live there. 20The inhabited towns will be laid waste and the land will be desolate. Then you will know that I am the LORD.' "

21The word of the LORD came to me: 22"Son of man, what is this proverb you have in the land of Israel: 'The days go by and every vision comes to nothing'? 23Say to them, 'This is what the Sovereign LORD says: I am going to put an end to this proverb, and they will no longer quote it in Israel.' Say to them, 'The days are near when every vision will be fulfilled. 24For there will be no more false visions or flattering divinations among the people of Israel. 25But I the LORD will speak what I will, and it shall be fulfilled without delay. For in your days, you rebellious house, I will fulfil whatever I say, declares the Sovereign LORD.' "

26The word of the LORD came to me: 27"Son of man, the house of Israel is saying, 'The vision he sees is for many years from now, and he prophesies about the distant future.'

28"Therefore say to them, 'This is what the Sovereign LORD says: None of my words will be delayed any longer; whatever I say will be fulfilled, declares the Sovereign LORD.' "

d24 Or *Chaldea*

False Prophets Condemned

13 The word of the LORD came to me: 2"Son of man, prophesy against the prophets of Israel who are now prophesying. Say to those who prophesy out of their own imagination: 'Hear the word of the LORD! 3This is what the Sovereign LORD says: Woe to the foolish[a] prophets who follow their own spirit and have seen nothing! 4Your prophets, O Israel, are like jackals among ruins. 5You have not gone up to the breaks in the wall to repair it for the house of Israel so that it will stand firm in the battle on the day of the LORD. 6Their visions are false and their divinations a lie. They say, "The LORD declares", when the LORD has not sent them; yet they expect their words to be fulfilled. 7Have you not seen false visions and uttered lying divinations when you say, "The LORD declares", though I have not spoken?

8" 'Therefore this is what the Sovereign LORD says: Because of your false words and lying visions, I am against you, declares the Sovereign LORD. 9My hand will be against the prophets who see false visions and utter lying divinations. They will not belong to the council of my people or be listed in the records of the house of Israel, nor will they enter the land of Israel. Then you will know that I am the Sovereign LORD.

10" 'Because they lead my people astray, saying, "Peace", when there is no peace, and because, when a flimsy wall is built, they cover it with whitewash, 11therefore tell those who cover it with whitewash that it is going to fall. Rain will come in torrents, and I will send hailstones hurtling down, and violent winds will burst forth. 12When the wall collapses, will people not ask you, "Where is the whitewash you covered it with?"

13" 'Therefore this is what the Sovereign LORD says: In my wrath I will unleash a violent wind, and in my anger hailstones and torrents of rain will fall with destructive fury. 14I will tear down the wall you have covered with whitewash and will level it to the ground so that its foundation will be laid bare. When it[b] falls, you will be destroyed in it; and you will know that I am the LORD. 15So I will spend my wrath against the wall and against those who covered it with whitewash. I will say to you, "The wall is gone and so are those who whitewashed it, 16those prophets of Israel who prophesied to Jerusalem and saw visions of peace for her when there was no peace, declares the Sovereign LORD." '

13:16 Like the other prophets, Ezekiel spoke out against false prophets. We know that they were false prophets because their words did not measure up to the word of the LORD. A true prophet of God speaks not from personal opinions, but from the word addressed to them by God.

17"Now, son of man, set your face against the daughters of your people who prophesy out of their own imagination. Prophesy against them 18and say, 'This is what the Sovereign LORD says: Woe to the women who sew magic charms on all their wrists and make veils of various lengths for their heads in order to ensnare people. Will you ensnare the lives of my people but preserve your own? 19You have profaned me among my people for a few handfuls of barley and scraps of bread. By lying to my people, who listen to lies, you have killed those who should not have died and have spared those who should not live.

20" 'Therefore this is what the Sovereign LORD says: I am against your magic charms with which you ensnare people like birds and I will tear them from your arms; I will set free the people that you ensnare like birds. 21I will tear off your veils and save my people from your hands, and they will no longer fall prey to your power. Then you will know that I am the LORD. 22Because you disheartened the righteous with your lies, when I had brought them no grief, and because you encouraged the wicked not to turn from their evil ways and so save their lives, 23therefore you will no longer see false visions or practise divination. I will save my people from your hands. And then you will know that I am the LORD.' "

Idolaters Condemned

14 Some of the elders of Israel came to me and sat down in front of me. 2Then the word of the LORD came to me: 3"Son of man, these men have set up idols in their hearts and put wicked stumbling-blocks before their faces. Should I let them enquire of me at all? 4Therefore speak to them and tell them, 'This is what the Sovereign LORD says: When any Israelite sets up idols in his heart and puts a wicked stumbling-block before his face and then goes to a prophet, I the LORD will answer him myself in keeping with his great idolatry. 5I will do this to recapture the hearts of the people of Israel, who have all deserted me for their idols.'

6"Therefore say to the house of Israel, 'This is what the Sovereign LORD says: Repent! Turn from your idols and renounce all your detestable practices!

7" 'When any Israelite or any alien living in Israel separates himself from me and sets up idols in his heart and puts a wicked stumbling-block before his face and then goes to a prophet to enquire of me, I the LORD will answer him myself. 8I will set my face against that man and make him an example and a byword. I will cut him off from my people. Then you will know that I am the LORD.

9" 'And if the prophet is enticed to utter a prophecy, I the LORD have enticed that prophet, and I will stretch out my hand against him and destroy him from among my people Israel. 10They will bear their guilt—the prophet will be as guilty as the one who consults him. 11Then the people of Israel will no longer stray from me, nor will they defile themselves any more with all their sins. They will be my people, and I will be their God, declares the Sovereign LORD.' "

---

a3 Or wicked   b14 Or the city

Judgment Inescapable

[12]The word of the LORD came to me: [13]"Son of man, if a country sins against me by being unfaithful and I stretch out my hand against it to cut off its food supply and send famine upon it and kill its men and their animals, [14]even if these three men—Noah, Daniel[a] and Job—were in it, they could save only themselves by their righteousness, declares the Sovereign LORD.

[15]"Or if I send wild beasts through that country and they leave it childless and it becomes desolate so that no-one can pass through it because of the beasts, [16]as surely as I live, declares the Sovereign LORD, even if these three men were in it, they could not save their own sons or daughters. They alone would be saved, but the land would be desolate.

[17]"Or if I bring a sword against that country and say, 'Let the sword pass throughout the land,' and I kill its men and their animals, [18]as surely as I live, declares the Sovereign LORD, even if these three men were in it, they could not save their own sons or daughters. They alone would be saved.

[19]"Or if I send a plague into that land and pour out my wrath upon it through bloodshed, killing its men and their animals, [20]as surely as I live, declares the Sovereign LORD, even if Noah, Daniel and Job were in it, they could save neither son nor daughter. They would save only themselves by their righteousness.

[21]"For this is what the Sovereign LORD says: How much worse will it be when I send against Jerusalem my four dreadful judgments—sword and famine and wild beasts and plague—to kill its men and their animals! [22]Yet there will be some survivors—sons and daughters who will be brought out of it. They will come to you, and when you see their conduct and their actions, you will be consoled regarding the disaster I have brought upon Jerusalem—every disaster I have brought upon it. [23]You will be consoled when you see their conduct and their actions, for you will know that I have done nothing in it without cause, declares the Sovereign LORD."

Jerusalem, a Useless Vine

15 The word of the LORD came to me: [2]"Son of man, how is the wood of a vine better than that of a branch on any of the trees in the forest? [3]Is wood ever taken from it to make anything useful? Do they make pegs from it to hang things on? [4]And after it is thrown on the fire as fuel and the fire burns both ends and chars the middle, is it then useful for anything? [5]If it was not useful for anything when it was whole, how much less can it be made into something useful when the fire has burned it and it is charred?

[6]"Therefore this is what the Sovereign LORD says: As I have given the wood of the vine among the trees of the forest as fuel for the fire, so will I treat the people living in Jerusalem. [7]I will set my face against them. Although they have come out of the fire, the fire will yet consume them. And when I set my face against

them, you will know that I am the LORD. [8]I will make the land desolate because they have been unfaithful, declares the Sovereign LORD."

15:6   A vine is tame, cultivated with care to produce fruit and wood for making things. But the wood of the forest is wild and no good for anything except burning. Israel is like the wood of the forest and will be burned, and all that will be left is a desolate land.

An Allegory of Unfaithful Jerusalem

16 The word of the LORD came to me: [2]"Son of man, confront Jerusalem with her detestable practices [3]and say, 'This is what the Sovereign LORD says to Jerusalem: Your ancestry and birth were in the land of the Canaanites; your father was an Amorite and your mother a Hittite. [4]On the day you were born your cord was not cut, nor were you washed with water to make you clean, nor were you rubbed with salt or wrapped in cloths. [5]No-one looked on you with pity or had compassion enough to do any of these things for you. Rather, you were thrown out into the open field, for on the day you were born you were despised.

[6]" 'Then I passed by and saw you kicking about in your blood, and as you lay there in your blood I said to you, "Live!"[a] [7]I made you grow like a plant of the field. You grew up and developed and became the most beautiful of jewels.[b] Your breasts were formed and your hair grew, you who were naked and bare.

[8]" 'Later I passed by, and when I looked at you and saw that you were old enough for love, I spread the corner of my garment over you and covered your nakedness. I gave you my solemn oath and entered into a covenant with you, declares the Sovereign LORD, and you became mine.

[9]" 'I bathed[c] you with water and washed the blood from you and put ointments on you. [10]I clothed you with an embroidered dress and put leather sandals on you. I dressed you in fine linen and covered you with costly garments. [11]I adorned you with jewellery: I put bracelets on your arms and a necklace around your neck, [12]and I put a ring on your nose, ear-rings on your ears and a beautiful crown on your head. [13]So you were adorned with gold and silver; your clothes were of fine linen and costly fabric and embroidered cloth. Your food was fine flour, honey and olive oil. You became very beautiful and rose to be a queen. [14]And your fame spread among the nations on account of your beauty, because the splendour I had given you made your beauty perfect, declares the Sovereign LORD.

[15]" 'But you trusted in your beauty and used your fame to become a prostitute. You lavished your favours on anyone who passed by and your beauty became his.[d] [16]You took some of your garments to make gaudy high places, where you carried on your prostitution.

---

a[14] Or *Danel*; the Hebrew spelling may suggest a person other than the prophet Daniel; also in verse 20.
a[6] A few Hebrew manuscripts, Septuagint and Syriac; most Hebrew manuscripts *"Live!" And as you lay there in your blood I said to you,* "Live!"   b[7] Or *became mature*   c[9] Or *I had bathed*
d[15] Most Hebrew manuscripts; one Hebrew manuscript (see some Septuagint manuscripts) *by. Such a thing should not happen*

Such things should not happen, nor should they ever occur. [17]You also took the fine jewellery I gave you, the jewellery made of my gold and silver, and you made for yourself male idols and engaged in prostitution with them. [18]And you took your embroidered clothes to put on them, and you offered my oil and incense before them. [19]Also the food I provided for you — the fine flour, olive oil and honey I gave you to eat — you offered as fragrant incense before them. That is what happened, declares the Sovereign LORD.

[20] 'And you took your sons and daughters whom you bore to me and sacrificed them as food to the idols. Was your prostitution not enough? [21]You slaughtered my children and sacrificed them[e] to the idols. [22]In all your detestable practices and your prostitution you did not remember the days of your youth, when you were naked and bare, kicking about in your blood.

[23] 'Woe! Woe to you, declares the Sovereign LORD. In addition to all your other wickedness, [24]you built a mound for yourself and made a lofty shrine in every public square. [25]At the head of every street you built your lofty shrines and degraded your beauty, offering your body with increasing promiscuity to anyone who passed by. [26]You engaged in prostitution with the Egyptians, your lustful neighbours, and provoked me to anger with your increasing promiscuity. [27]So I stretched out my hand against you and reduced your territory; I gave you over to the greed of your enemies, the daughters of the Philistines, who were shocked by your lewd conduct. [28]You engaged in prostitution with the Assyrians too, because you were insatiable; and even after that, you still were not satisfied. [29]Then you increased your promiscuity to include Babylonia,[f] a land of merchants, but even with this you were not satisfied.

[30] 'How weak-willed you are, declares the Sovereign LORD, when you do all these things, acting like a brazen prostitute! [31]When you built your mounds at the head of every street and made your lofty shrines in every public square, you were unlike a prostitute, because you scorned payment.

[32] 'You adulterous wife! You prefer strangers to your own husband! [33]Every prostitute receives a fee, but you give gifts to all your lovers, bribing them to come to you from everywhere for your illicit favours. [34]So in your prostitution you are the opposite of others; no-one runs after you for your favours. You are the very opposite, for you give payment and none is given to you.

[35] 'Therefore, you prostitute, hear the word of the LORD! [36]This is what the Sovereign LORD says: Because you poured out your wealth[g] and exposed your nakedness in your promiscuity with your lovers, and because of all your detestable idols, and because you gave them your children's blood, [37]therefore I am going to gather all your lovers, with whom you found pleasure, those you loved as well as those you hated. I will gather them against you from all around and will strip you in front of them, and they will see all your nakedness. [38]I will sentence you to the punishment of women who commit adultery and who shed blood; I will bring upon you the blood vengeance of my wrath and jealous anger. [39]Then I will hand you over to your lovers, and they will tear down your mounds and destroy your lofty shrines. They will strip you of your clothes and take your fine jewellery and leave you naked and bare. [40]They will bring a mob against you, who will stone you and hack you to pieces with their swords. [41]They will burn down your houses and inflict punishment on you in the sight of many women. I will put a stop to your prostitution, and you will no longer pay your lovers. [42]Then my wrath against you will subside and my jealous anger will turn away from you; I will be calm and no longer angry.

[43] 'Because you did not remember the days of your youth but enraged me with all these things, I will surely bring down on your head what you have done, declares the Sovereign LORD. Did you not add lewdness to all your other detestable practices?

[44] 'Everyone who quotes proverbs will quote this proverb about you: "Like mother, like daughter." [45]You are a true daughter of your mother, who despised her husband and her children; and you are a true sister of your sisters, who despised their husbands and their children. Your mother was a Hittite and your father an Amorite. [46]Your older sister was Samaria, who lived to the north of you with her daughters; and your younger sister, who lived to the south of you with her daughters, was Sodom. [47]You not only walked in their ways and copied their detestable practices, but in all your ways you soon became more depraved than they. [48]As surely as I live, declares the Sovereign LORD, your sister Sodom and her daughters never did what you and your daughters have done.

[49] 'Now this was the sin of your sister Sodom: She and her daughters were arrogant, overfed and unconcerned; they did not help the poor and needy. [50]They were haughty and did detestable things before me. Therefore I did away with them as you have seen. [51]Samaria did not commit half the sins you did. You have done more detestable things than they, and have made your sisters seem righteous by all these things you have done. [52]Bear your disgrace, for you have furnished some justification for your sisters. Because your sins were more vile than theirs, they appear more righteous than you. So then, be ashamed and bear your disgrace, for you have made your sisters appear righteous.

[53] 'However, I will restore the fortunes of Sodom and her daughters and of Samaria and her daughters, and your fortunes along with them, [54]so that you may bear your disgrace and be ashamed of all you have done in giving them comfort. [55]And your sisters, Sodom with her daughters and Samaria with her daughters, will return to what they were before; and you and your daughters will return to what you were before. [56]You would not even mention your sister Sodom in the day of your pride, [57]before your wickedness was uncovered. Even so, you are now scorned by the daughters of Edom[h] and all her neighbours and the daughters of the Philistines — all those around you who despise you.

---

e21 Or *and made them pass through the fire*   *f29* Or *Chaldea*   *g36* Or *lust*
h57 Many Hebrew manuscripts and Syriac; most Hebrew manuscripts, Septuagint and Vulgate *Aram*

[58]You will bear the consequences of your lewdness and your detestable practices, declares the LORD.

[59]" 'This is what the Sovereign LORD says: I will deal with you as you deserve, because you have despised my oath by breaking the covenant. [60]Yet I will remember the covenant I made with you in the days of your youth, and I will establish an everlasting covenant with you. [61]Then you will remember your ways and be ashamed when you receive your sisters, both those who are older than you and those who are younger. I will give them to you as daughters, but not on the basis of my covenant with you. [62]So I will establish my covenant with you, and you will know that I am the LORD. [63]Then, when I make atonement for you for all you have done, you will remember and be ashamed and never again open your mouth because of your humiliation, declares the Sovereign LORD.' "

Two Eagles and a Vine

17 The word of the LORD came to me: [2]"Son of man, set forth an allegory and tell the house of Israel a parable. [3]Say to them, 'This is what the Sovereign LORD says: A great eagle with powerful wings, long feathers and full plumage of varied colours came to Lebanon. Taking hold of the top of a cedar, [4]he broke off its topmost shoot and carried it away to a land of merchants, where he planted it in a city of traders.

[5]" 'He took some of the seed of your land and put it in fertile soil. He planted it like a willow by abundant water, [6]and it sprouted and became a low, spreading vine. Its branches turned towards him, but its roots remained under it. So it became a vine and produced branches and put out leafy boughs.

[7]" 'But there was another great eagle with powerful wings and full plumage. The vine now sent out its roots towards him from the plot where it was planted and stretched out its branches to him for water. [8]It had been planted in good soil by abundant water so that it would produce branches, bear fruit and become a splendid vine.'

[9]"Say to them, 'This is what the Sovereign LORD says: Will it thrive? Will it not be uprooted and stripped of its fruit so that it withers? All its new growth will wither. It will not take a strong arm or many people to pull it up by the roots. [10]Even if it is transplanted, will it thrive? Will it not wither completely when the east wind strikes it—wither away in the plot where it grew?' "

[11]Then the word of the LORD came to me: [12]"Say to this rebellious house, 'Do you not know what these things mean?' Say to them: 'The king of Babylon went to Jerusalem and carried off her king and her nobles, bringing them back with him to Babylon. [13]Then he took a member of the royal family and made a treaty with him, putting him under oath. He also carried away the leading men of the land, [14]so that the kingdom would be brought low, unable to rise again, surviving only by keeping his treaty. [15]But the king rebelled against him by sending his envoys to Egypt to get horses and a large army. Will he succeed? Will he who does such things escape? Will he break the treaty and yet escape?

[16]" 'As surely as I live, declares the Sovereign LORD,

he shall die in Babylon, in the land of the king who put him on the throne, whose oath he despised and whose treaty he broke. [17]Pharaoh with his mighty army and great horde will be of no help to him in war, when ramps are built and siege works erected to destroy many lives. [18]He despised the oath by breaking the covenant. Because he had given his hand in pledge and yet did all these things, he shall not escape.

[19]" 'Therefore this is what the Sovereign LORD says: As surely as I live, I will bring down on his head my oath that he despised and my covenant that he broke. [20]I will spread my net for him, and he will be caught in my snare. I will bring him to Babylon and execute judgment upon him there because he was unfaithful to me. [21]All his fleeing troops will fall by the sword, and the survivors will be scattered to the winds. Then you will know that I the LORD have spoken.

[22]" 'This is what the Sovereign LORD says: I myself will take a shoot from the very top of a cedar and plant it; I will break off a tender sprig from its topmost shoots and plant it on a high and lofty mountain. [23]On the mountain heights of Israel I will plant it; it will produce branches and bear fruit and become a splendid cedar. Birds of every kind will nest in it; they will find shelter in the shade of its branches. [24]All the trees of the field will know that I the LORD bring down the tall tree and make the low tree grow tall. I dry up the green tree and make the dry tree flourish.

" 'I the LORD have spoken, and I will do it.' "

17:22   The cedar tree is a symbol of the family tree of David, and the mountain on which the sprig will be planted is Mount Zion. In language which resembles Isaiah 11:1, the prophet announced that God would bring great glory to the vulnerable nation of Israel (the low tree), and restore his people to Jerusalem, and thwart Babylon (the tall tree).

The Soul Who Sins Will Die

18 The word of the LORD came to me: [2]"What do you people mean by quoting this proverb about the land of Israel:

" 'The fathers eat sour grapes,
    and the children's teeth are set on edge'?

[3]"As surely as I live, declares the Sovereign LORD, you will no longer quote this proverb in Israel. [4]For every living soul belongs to me, the father as well as the son—both alike belong to me. The soul who sins is the one who will die.

[5]"Suppose there is a righteous man
    who does what is just and right.
[6]He does not eat at the mountain shrines
    or look to the idols of the house of Israel.
He does not defile his neighbour's wife
    or lie with a woman during her period.
[7]He does not oppress anyone,
    but returns what he took in pledge for a loan.

He does not commit robbery,
  but gives his food to the hungry
  and provides clothing for the naked.
[8]He does not lend at usury
  or take excessive interest.[a]
He withholds his hand from doing wrong
  and judges fairly between man and man.
[9]He follows my decrees
  and faithfully keeps my laws.
That man is righteous;
  he will surely live,
                    declares the Sovereign LORD.

[10]"Suppose he has a violent son, who sheds blood or
does any of these other things[b] [11](though the father
has done none of them):

"He eats at the mountain shrines.
He defiles his neighbour's wife.
[12]He oppresses the poor and needy.
He commits robbery.
He does not return what he took in pledge.
He looks to the idols.
He does detestable things.
[13]He lends at usury and takes excessive interest.

Will such a man live? He will not! Because he has done
all these detestable things, he will surely be put to
death and his blood will be on his own head.

[14]"But suppose this son has a son who sees all the
sins his father commits, and though he sees them, he
does not do such things:

[15]"He does not eat at the mountain shrines
  or look to the idols of the house of Israel.
He does not defile his neighbour's wife.
[16]He does not oppress anyone
  or require a pledge for a loan.
He does not commit robbery,
  but gives his food to the hungry
  and provides clothing for the naked.
[17]He withholds his hand from sin[c]
  and takes no usury or excessive interest.
He keeps my laws and follows my decrees.

He will not die for his father's sin; he will surely live.
[18]But his father will die for his own sin, because he
practised extortion, robbed his brother and did what
was wrong among his people.

[19]"Yet you ask, 'Why does the son not share the guilt
of his father?' Since the son has done what is just and
right and has been careful to keep all my decrees, he
will surely live. [20]The soul who sins is the one who will
die. The son will not share the guilt of the father, nor
will the father share the guilt of the son. The righteousness of the righteous man will be credited to him, and
the wickedness of the wicked will be charged against
him.

[21]"But if a wicked man turns away from all the sins
he has committed and keeps all my decrees and does
what is just and right, he will surely live; he will not
die. [22]None of the offences he has committed will
be remembered against him. Because of the righteous things he has done, he will live. [23]Do I take any

pleasure in the death of the wicked? declares the Sovereign LORD. Rather, am I not pleased when they
turn from their ways and live?

[24]"But if a righteous man turns from his righteousness and commits sin and does the same detestable
things the wicked man does, will he live? None of the
righteous things he has done will be remembered.
Because of the unfaithfulness he is guilty of and
because of the sins he has committed, he will die.
[25]"Yet you say, 'The way of the Lord is not just.'
Hear, O house of Israel: Is my way unjust? Is it not your
ways that are unjust? [26]If a righteous man turns from
his righteousness and commits sin, he will die for it;
because of the sin he has committed he will die. [27]But
if a wicked man turns away from the wickedness he has
committed and does what is just and right, he will save
his life. [28]Because he considers all the offences he has
committed and turns away from them, he will surely
live; he will not die. [29]Yet the house of Israel says, 'The
way of the Lord is not just.' Are my ways unjust, O
house of Israel? Is it not your ways that are unjust?
[30]"Therefore, O house of Israel, I will judge you,
each one according to his ways, declares the Sovereign
LORD. Repent! Turn away from all your offences; then
sin will not be your downfall. [31]Rid yourselves of all the
offences you have committed, and get a new heart and
a new spirit. Why will you die, O house of Israel? [32]For
I take no pleasure in the death of anyone, declares the
Sovereign LORD. Repent and live!

A Lament for Israel's Princes

19 "Take up a lament concerning the princes of
Israel [2]and say:

" 'What a lioness was your mother
  among the lions!
She lay down among the young lions
  and reared her cubs.
[3]She brought up one of her cubs,
  and he became a strong lion.
He learned to tear the prey
  and he devoured men.
[4]The nations heard about him,
  and he was trapped in their pit.
They led him with hooks
  to the land of Egypt.

[5]" 'When she saw her hope unfulfilled,
  her expectation gone,
she took another of her cubs
  and made him a strong lion.
[6]He prowled among the lions,
  for he was now a strong lion.
He learned to tear the prey
  and he devoured men.
[7]He broke down[a] their strongholds
  and devastated their towns.
The land and all who were in it
  were terrified by his roaring.
[8]Then the nations came against him,
  those from regions round about.

---

[a]8 Or *take interest*; similarly in verses 13 and 17   [b]10 Or *things to a brother*
[c]17 Septuagint (see also verse 8); Hebrew *from the poor*   [a]7 Targum (see Septuagint); Hebrew *He knew*

They spread their net for him,
and he was trapped in their pit.
⁹With hooks they pulled him into a cage
and brought him to the king of Babylon.
They put him in prison,
so his roar was heard no longer
on the mountains of Israel.

¹⁰" 'Your mother was like a vine in your vineyard ᵇ
planted by the water;
it was fruitful and full of branches
because of abundant water.
¹¹Its branches were strong,
fit for a ruler's sceptre.
It towered high
above the thick foliage,
conspicuous for its height
and for its many branches.
¹²But it was uprooted in fury
and thrown to the ground.
The east wind made it shrivel,
it was stripped of its fruit;
its strong branches withered
and fire consumed them.
¹³Now it is planted in the desert,
in a dry and thirsty land.
¹⁴Fire spread from one of its main ᶜ branches
and consumed its fruit.
No strong branch is left on it
fit for a ruler's sceptre.'

This is a lament and is to be used as a lament."

Rebellious Israel

20 In the seventh year, in the fifth month on the
tenth day, some of the elders of Israel came to
enquire of the LORD, and they sat down in front of me.
²Then the word of the LORD came to me: ³"Son of
man, speak to the elders of Israel and say to them, 'This
is what the Sovereign LORD says: Have you come to
enquire of me? As surely as I live, I will not let you
enquire of me, declares the Sovereign LORD.'

⁴"Will you judge them? Will you judge them, son of
man? Then confront them with the detestable practices of their fathers ⁵and say to them: 'This is what the
Sovereign LORD says: On the day I chose Israel, I swore
with uplifted hand to the descendants of the house of
Jacob and revealed myself to them in Egypt. With
uplifted hand I said to them, "I am the LORD your God."
⁶On that day I swore to them that I would bring them
out of Egypt into a land I had searched out for them,
a land flowing with milk and honey, the most beautiful
of all lands. ⁷And I said to them, 'Each of you, get rid
of the vile images you have set your eyes on, and do
not defile yourselves with the idols of Egypt. I am the
LORD your God."

⁸" 'But they rebelled against me and would not listen to me; they did not get rid of the vile images they
had set their eyes on, nor did they forsake the idols of
Egypt. So I said I would pour out my wrath on them and
spend my anger against them in Egypt. ⁹But for the
sake of my name I did what would keep it from being

profaned in the eyes of the nations they lived among
and in whose sight I had revealed myself to the Israelites by bringing them out of Egypt. ¹⁰Therefore I led
them out of Egypt and brought them into the desert.
¹¹I gave them my decrees and made known to them my
laws, for the man who obeys them will live by them.
¹²Also I gave them my Sabbaths as a sign between us,
so they would know that I the LORD made them holy.

20:12 Ezekiel's concern with the Law,
particularly as it was likely to affect the temple or the observance of worship, is reflected
in his concern with the Sabbath. At the time
of Ezekiel, the Sabbath was not surrounded
by much of the stringent legalism of the later,
New Testament period (see Matthew
12:1–14). Instead, it was seen as a gift from
God to his people, and by keeping the Sabbath Israel was able to show that it was God's
holy people, called and chosen by him.

---

¹³" 'Yet the people of Israel rebelled against me in
the desert. They did not follow my decrees but rejected
my laws—although the man who obeys them will live
by them—and they utterly desecrated my Sabbaths. So
I said I would pour out my wrath on them and destroy
them in the desert. ¹⁴But for the sake of my name I did
what would keep it from being profaned in the eyes of
the nations in whose sight I had brought them out.
¹⁵Also with uplifted hand I swore to them in the desert
that I would not bring them into the land I had given
them—a land flowing with milk and honey, most
beautiful of all lands—¹⁶because they rejected my laws
and did not follow my decrees and desecrated my Sabbaths. For their hearts were devoted to their idols.
¹⁷Yet I looked on them with pity and did not destroy
them or put an end to them in the desert. ¹⁸I said to
their children in the desert, "Do not follow the statutes
of your fathers or keep their laws or defile yourselves
with their idols. ¹⁹I am the LORD your God; follow my
decrees and be careful to keep my laws. ²⁰Keep my Sabbaths holy, that they may be a sign between us. Then
you will know that I am the LORD your God."

²¹" 'But the children rebelled against me: They did
not follow my decrees, they were not careful to keep
my laws—although the man who obeys them will live
by them—and they desecrated my Sabbaths. So I said
I would pour out my wrath on them and spend my
anger against them in the desert. ²²But I withheld my
hand, and for the sake of my name I did what would
keep it from being profaned in the eyes of the nations
in whose sight I had brought them out. ²³Also with
uplifted hand I swore to them in the desert that I would
disperse them among the nations and scatter them
through the countries, ²⁴because they had not obeyed
my laws but had rejected my decrees and desecrated
my Sabbaths, and their eyes lusted after their fathers'
idols. ²⁵I also gave them over to statutes that were not
good and laws they could not live by; ²⁶I let them
become defiled through their gifts—the sacrifice of

ᵇ10 Two Hebrew manuscripts; most Hebrew manuscripts *your blood*   ᶜ14 Or *from under its* every firstborn*—that I might fill them with horror so that they would know that I am the LORD.'

27"Therefore, son of man, speak to the people of Israel and say to them, 'This is what the Sovereign LORD says: In this also your fathers blasphemed me by forsaking me: 28When I brought them into the land I had sworn to give them and they saw any high hill or any leafy tree, there they offered their sacrifices, made offerings that provoked me to anger, presented their fragrant incense and poured out their drink offerings. 29Then I said to them: What is this high place you go to?' " (It is called Bamah*b* to this day.)

Judgment and Restoration

30"Therefore say to the house of Israel: 'This is what the Sovereign LORD says: Will you defile yourselves the way your fathers did and lust after their vile images? 31When you offer your gifts—the sacrifice of your sons in*c* the fire—you continue to defile yourselves with all your idols to this day. Am I to let you enquire of me, O house of Israel? As surely as I live, declares the Sovereign LORD, I will not let you enquire of me.

32" 'You say, "We want to be like the nations, like the peoples of the world, who serve wood and stone." But what you have in mind will never happen. 33As surely as I live, declares the Sovereign LORD, I will rule over you with a mighty hand and an outstretched arm and with outpoured wrath. 34I will bring you from the nations and gather you from the countries where you have been scattered—with a mighty hand and an outstretched arm and with outpoured wrath. 35I will bring you into the desert of the nations and there, face to face, I will execute judgment upon you. 36As I judged your fathers in the desert of the land of Egypt, so I will judge you, declares the Sovereign LORD. 37I will take note of you as you pass under my rod, and I will bring you into the bond of the covenant. 38I will purge you of those who revolt and rebel against me. Although I will bring them out of the land where they are living, yet they will not enter the land of Israel. Then you will know that I am the LORD.

39" 'As for you, O house of Israel, this is what the Sovereign LORD says: Go and serve your idols, every one of you! But afterwards you will surely listen to me and no longer profane my holy name with your gifts and idols. 40For on my holy mountain, the high mountain of Israel, declares the Sovereign LORD, there in the land the entire house of Israel will serve me, and there I will accept them. There I will require your offerings and your choice gifts,*d* along with all your holy sacrifices. 41I will accept you as fragrant incense when I bring you out from the nations and gather you from the countries where you have been scattered, and I will show myself holy among you in the sight of the nations. 42Then you will know that I am the LORD, when I bring you into the land of Israel, the land I had sworn with uplifted hand to give to your fathers. 43There you will remember your conduct and all the actions by which you have defiled yourselves, and you will loathe yourselves for all the evil you have done. 44You will know

that I am the LORD, when I deal with you for my name's sake and not according to your evil ways and your corrupt practices, O house of Israel, declares the Sovereign LORD.' "

Prophecy Against the South

45The word of the LORD came to me: 46"Son of man, set your face towards the south; preach against the south and prophesy against the forest of the southland. 47Say to the southern forest: 'Hear the word of the LORD. This is what the Sovereign LORD says: I am about to set fire to you, and it will consume all your trees, both green and dry. The blazing flame will not be quenched, and every face from south to north will be scorched by it. 48Everyone will see that I the LORD have kindled it; it will not be quenched.' "

49Then I said, "Ah, Sovereign LORD! They are saying of me, 'Isn't he just telling parables?' "

Babylon, God's Sword of Judgment

21 The word of the LORD came to me: 2"Son of man, set your face against Jerusalem and preach against the sanctuary. Prophesy against the land of Israel 3and say to her: 'This is what the LORD says: I am against you. I will draw my sword from its scabbard and cut off from you both the righteous and the wicked. 4Because I am going to cut off the righteous and the wicked, my sword will be unsheathed against everyone from south to north. 5Then all people will know that I the LORD have drawn my sword from its scabbard; it will not return again.'

6"Therefore groan, son of man! Groan before them with broken heart and bitter grief. 7And when they ask you, 'Why are you groaning?' you shall say, 'Because of the news that is coming. Every heart will melt and every hand go limp; every spirit will become faint and every knee become as weak as water.' It is coming! It will surely take place, declares the Sovereign LORD."

8The word of the LORD came to me: 9"Son of man, prophesy and say, 'This is what the Lord says:

" 'A sword, a sword,
    sharpened and polished—
10sharpened for the slaughter,
    polished to flash like lightning!

" 'Shall we rejoice in the sceptre of my son ⌊Judah⌋?
The sword despises every such stick.

11" 'The sword is appointed to be polished,
    to be grasped with the hand;
it is sharpened and polished,
    made ready for the hand of the slayer.
12Cry out and wail, son of man,
    for it is against my people;
    it is against all the princes of Israel.
They are thrown to the sword
    along with my people.
Therefore beat your breast.

---

a 26 Or—making every firstborn pass through ⌊the fire⌋   *b 29 Bamah means high place.*
c 31 Or—making your sons pass through   *d 40 Or and the gifts of your firstfruits*

13 " 'Testing will surely come. And what if the sceptre ˌof Judah,, which the sword despises, does not continue? declares the Sovereign LORD.'

14 "So then, son of man, prophesy
and strike your hands together.
Let the sword strike twice,
even three times.
It is a sword for slaughter—
a sword for great slaughter,
closing in on them from every side.
15 So that hearts may melt
and the fallen be many,
I have stationed the sword for slaughter[a]
at all their gates.
Oh! It is made to flash like lightning,
it is grasped for slaughter.
16 O sword, slash to the right,
then to the left,
wherever your blade is turned.
17 I too will strike my hands together,
and my wrath will subside.
I the LORD have spoken."

18 The word of the LORD came to me: 19 "Son of man, mark out two roads for the sword of the king of Babylon to take, both starting from the same country. Make a signpost where the road branches off to the city. 20 Mark out one road for the sword to come against Rabbah of the Ammonites and another against Judah and fortified Jerusalem. 21 For the king of Babylon will stop at the fork in the road, at the junction of the two roads, to seek an omen: He will cast lots with arrows, he will consult his idols, he will examine the liver. 22 Into his right hand will come the lot for Jerusalem, where he is to set up battering-rams, to give the command to slaughter, to sound the battle cry, to set battering-rams against the gates, to build a ramp and to erect siege works. 23 It will seem like a false omen to those who have sworn allegiance to him, but he will remind them of their guilt and take them captive.

24 "Therefore this is what the Sovereign LORD says: 'Because you people have brought to mind your guilt by your open rebellion, revealing your sins in all that you do—because you have done this, you will be taken captive.

25 " 'O profane and wicked prince of Israel, whose day has come, whose time of punishment has reached its climax, 26 this is what the Sovereign LORD says: Take off the turban, remove the crown. It will not be as it was: The lowly will be exalted and the exalted will be brought low. 27 A ruin! A ruin! I will make it a ruin! It will not be restored until he comes to whom it rightfully belongs; to him I will give it.'

28 "And you, son of man, prophesy and say, 'This is what the Sovereign LORD says about the Ammonites and their insults:

" 'A sword, a sword,
drawn for the slaughter,
polished to consume
and to flash like lightning!
29 Despite false visions concerning you
and lying divinations about you,

it will be laid on the necks
of the wicked who are to be slain,
whose day has come,
whose time of punishment has reached its
climax.
30 Return the sword to its scabbard.
In the place where you were created,
in the land of your ancestry,
I will judge you.
31 I will pour out my wrath upon you
and breathe out my fiery anger against you;
I will hand you over to brutal men,
men skilled in destruction.
32 You will be fuel for the fire,
your blood will be shed in your land,
you will be remembered no more;
for I the LORD have spoken.' "

Jerusalem's Sins

22 The word of the LORD came to me: 2 "Son of man, will you judge her? Will you judge this city of bloodshed? Then confront her with all her detestable practices 3 and say: 'This is what the Sovereign LORD says: O city that brings on herself doom by shedding blood in her midst and defiles herself by making idols, 4 you have become guilty because of the blood you have shed and have become defiled by the idols you have made. You have brought your days to a close, and the end of your years has come. Therefore I will make you an object of scorn to the nations and a laughing-stock to all the countries. 5 Those who are near and those who are far away will mock you, O infamous city, full of turmoil.

6 " 'See how each of the princes of Israel who are in you uses his power to shed blood. 7 In you they have treated father and mother with contempt; in you they have oppressed the alien and ill-treated the fatherless and the widow. 8 You have despised my holy things and desecrated my Sabbaths. 9 In you are slanderous men bent on shedding blood; in you are those who eat at the mountain shrines and commit lewd acts. 10 In you are those who dishonour their fathers' bed; in you are those who violate women during their period, when they are ceremonially unclean. 11 In you one man commits a detestable offence with his neighbour's wife, another shamefully defiles his daughter-in-law, and another violates his sister, his own father's daughter. 12 In you men accept bribes to shed blood; you take usury and excessive interest[a] and make unjust gain from your neighbours by extortion. And you have forgotten me, declares the Sovereign LORD.

13 " 'I will surely strike my hands together at the unjust gain you have made and at the blood you have shed in your midst. 14 Will your courage endure or your hands be strong in the day I deal with you? I the LORD have spoken, and I will do it. 15 I will disperse you among the nations and scatter you through the countries; and I will put an end to your uncleanness. 16 When you have been defiled[b] in the eyes of the nations, you will know that I am the LORD.' "

---

[a] 15 Septuagint; the meaning of the Hebrew for this word is uncertain.
[b] 16 Or When I have allotted you your inheritance

[a] 12 Or usury and interest

[17]Then the word of the LORD came to me: [18]"Son of man, the house of Israel has become dross to me; all of them are the copper, tin, iron and lead left inside a furnace. They are but the dross of silver. [19]Therefore this is what the Sovereign LORD says: 'Because you have all become dross, I will gather you into Jerusalem. [20]As men gather silver, copper, iron, lead and tin into a furnace to melt it with a fiery blast, so will I gather you in my anger and my wrath and put you inside the city and melt you. [21]I will gather you and I will blow on you with my fiery wrath, and you will be melted inside her. [22]As silver is melted in a furnace, so you will be melted inside her, and you will know that I the LORD have poured out my wrath upon you.' "

[23]Again the word of the LORD came to me: [24]"Son of man, say to the land, 'You are a land that has had no rain or showers[c] in the day of wrath.' [25]There is a conspiracy of her princes[d] within her like a roaring lion tearing its prey; they devour people, take treasures and precious things and make many widows within her. [26]Her priests do violence to my law and profane my holy things; they do not distinguish between the holy and the common; they teach that there is no difference between the unclean and the clean; and they shut their eyes to the keeping of my Sabbaths, so that I am profaned among them. [27]Her officials within her are like wolves tearing their prey; they shed blood and kill people to make unjust gain. [28]Her prophets whitewash these deeds for them by false visions and lying divinations. They say, 'This is what the Sovereign LORD says'—when the LORD has not spoken. [29]The people of the land practise extortion and commit robbery; they oppress the poor and needy and ill-treat the alien, denying them justice.

[30]"I looked for a man among them who would build up the wall and stand before me in the gap on behalf of the land so that I would not have to destroy it, but I found none. [31]So I will pour out my wrath on them and consume them with my fiery anger, bringing down on their own heads all they have done, declares the Sovereign LORD."

Two Adulterous Sisters

23 The word of the LORD came to me: [2]"Son of man, there were two women, daughters of the same mother. [3]They became prostitutes in Egypt, engaging in prostitution from their youth. In that land their breasts were fondled and their virgin bosoms caressed. [4]The older was named Oholah, and her sister was Oholibah. They were mine and gave birth to sons and daughters. Oholah is Samaria, and Oholibah is Jerusalem.

[5]"Oholah engaged in prostitution while she was still mine; and she lusted after her lovers, the Assyrians— [6]warriors clothed in blue, governors and commanders, all of them handsome young men, and mounted horsemen. [7]She gave herself as a prostitute to all the elite of the Assyrians and defiled herself with all the idols of everyone she lusted after. [8]She did not give up the prostitution she began in Egypt, when during her youth

men slept with her, caressed her virgin bosom and poured out their lust upon her.

[9]"Therefore I handed her over to her lovers, the Assyrians, for whom she lusted. [10]They stripped her naked, took away her sons and daughters and killed her with the sword. She became a byword among women, and punishment was inflicted on her.

[11]"Her sister Oholibah saw this, yet in her lust and prostitution she was more depraved than her sister. [12]She too lusted after the Assyrians—governors and commanders, warriors in full dress, mounted horsemen, all handsome young men. [13]I saw that she too defiled herself; both of them went the same way.

[14]"But she carried her prostitution still further. She saw men portrayed on a wall, figures of Chaldeans[a] portrayed in red, [15]with belts round their waists and flowing turbans on their heads; all of them looked like Babylonian chariot officers, natives of Chaldea.[b] [16]As soon as she saw them, she lusted after them and sent messengers to them in Chaldea. [17]Then the Babylonians came to her, to the bed of love, and in their lust they defiled her. After she had been defiled by them, she turned away from them in disgust. [18]When she carried on her prostitution openly and exposed her nakedness, I turned away from her in disgust, just as I had turned away from her sister. [19]Yet she became more and more promiscuous as she recalled the days of her youth, when she was a prostitute in Egypt. [20]There she lusted after her lovers, whose genitals were like those of donkeys and whose emission was like that of horses. [21]So you longed for the lewdness of your youth, when in Egypt your bosom was caressed and your young breasts fondled.[c]

[22]"Therefore, Oholibah, this is what the Sovereign LORD says: I will stir up your lovers against you, those you turned away from in disgust, and I will bring them against you from every side—[23]the Babylonians and all the Chaldeans, the men of Pekod and Shoa and Koa, and all the Assyrians with them, handsome young men, all of them governors and commanders, chariot officers and men of high rank, all mounted on horses. [24]They will come against you with weapons,[d] chariots and wagons and with a throng of people; they will take up positions against you on every side with large and small shields and with helmets. I will turn you over to them for punishment, and they will punish you according to their standards. [25]I will direct my jealous anger against you, and they will deal with you in fury. They will cut off your noses and your ears, and those of you who are left will fall by the sword. They will take away your sons and daughters, and those of you who are left will be consumed by fire. [26]They will also strip you of your clothes and take away your fine jewellery. [27]So I will put a stop to the lewdness and prostitution you began in Egypt. You will not look on these things with longing or remember Egypt any more.

[28]"For this is what the Sovereign LORD says: I am about to hand you over to those you hate, to those you turned away from in disgust. [29]They will deal with you in hatred and take away everything you have worked

---

c24 Septuagint; Hebrew *has not been cleansed or rained on*   d25 Septuagint; Hebrew *prophets*   a14 Or *Babylonians*
b15 Or *Babylonia*; also in verse 16   c21 Syriac (see also verse 3); Hebrew *caressed because of your young breasts*
d24 The meaning of the Hebrew for this word is uncertain.

for. They will leave you naked and bare, and the shame of your prostitution will be exposed. Your lewdness and promiscuity [30]have brought this upon you, because you lusted after the nations and defiled yourself with their idols. [31]You have gone the way of your sister; so I will put her cup into your hand.

[32]"This is what the Sovereign LORD says:

"You will drink your sister's cup,
    a cup large and deep;
it will bring scorn and derision,
    for it holds so much.
[33]You will be filled with drunkenness and sorrow,
    the cup of ruin and desolation,
    the cup of your sister Samaria.
[34]You will drink it and drain it dry;
    you will dash it to pieces
    and tear your breasts.

I have spoken, declares the Sovereign LORD.

[35]"Therefore this is what the Sovereign LORD says: Since you have forgotten me and thrust me behind your back, you must bear the consequences of your lewdness and prostitution."

[36]The LORD said to me: "Son of man, will you judge Oholah and Oholibah? Then confront them with their detestable practices, [37]for they have committed adultery and blood is on their hands. They committed adultery with their idols; they even sacrificed their children, whom they bore to me,[e] as food for them. [38]They have also done this to me: At that same time they defiled my sanctuary and desecrated my Sabbaths. [39]On the very day they sacrificed their children to their idols, they entered my sanctuary and desecrated it. That is what they did in my house.

[40]"They even sent messengers for men who came from far away, and when they arrived you bathed yourself for them, painted your eyes and put on your jewellery. [41]You sat on an elegant couch, with a table spread before it on which you had placed the incense and oil that belonged to me.

[42]"The noise of a carefree crowd was around her; Sabeans[f] were brought from the desert along with men from the rabble, and they put bracelets on the arms of the woman and her sister and beautiful crowns on their heads. [43]Then I said about the one worn out by adultery, 'Now let them use her as a prostitute, for that is all she is.' [44]And they slept with her. As men sleep with a prostitute, so they slept with those lewd women, Oholah and Oholibah. [45]But righteous men will sentence them to the punishment of women who commit adultery and shed blood, because they are adulterous and blood is on their hands.

[46]"This is what the Sovereign LORD says: Bring a mob against them and give them over to terror and plunder. [47]The mob will stone them and cut them down with their swords; they will kill their sons and daughters and burn down their houses.

[48]"So I will put an end to lewdness in the land, that all women may take warning and not imitate you. [49]You will suffer the penalty for your lewdness and bear the consequences of your sins of idolatry. Then you will know that I am the Sovereign LORD."

The Cooking Pot

24 In the ninth year, in the tenth month on the tenth day, the word of the LORD came to me: [2]"Son of man, record this date, this very date, because the king of Babylon has laid siege to Jerusalem this very day. [3]Tell this rebellious house a parable and say to them: 'This is what the Sovereign LORD says:

" 'Put on the cooking pot; put it on
    and pour water into it.
[4]Put into it the pieces of meat,
    all the choice pieces—the leg and the shoulder.
Fill it with the best of these bones;
[5] take the pick of the flock.
Pile wood beneath it for the bones;
    bring it to the boil
    and cook the bones in it.

[6]" 'For this is what the Sovereign LORD says:

" 'Woe to the city of bloodshed,
    to the pot now encrusted,
    whose deposit will not go away!
Empty it piece by piece
    without casting lots for them.

[7]" 'For the blood she shed is in her midst:
    She poured it on the bare rock;
she did not pour it on the ground,
    where the dust would cover it.
[8]To stir up wrath and take revenge
    I put her blood on the bare rock,
    so that it would not be covered.

[9]" 'Therefore this is what the Sovereign LORD says:

" 'Woe to the city of bloodshed!
    I, too, will pile the wood high.
[10]So heap on the wood
    and kindle the fire.
Cook the meat well,
    mixing in the spices;
    and let the bones be charred.
[11]Then set the empty pot on the coals
    till it becomes hot and its copper glows
so its impurities may be melted
    and its deposit burned away.
[12]It has frustrated all efforts;
    its heavy deposit has not been removed,
    not even by fire.

24:12   By using a cooking pot as a symbol of Jerusalem, God reminded his people of the significance of the fall of the city. Its contents are the people of Jerusalem who will be taken out of it. The encrusted pot (verse 6) symbolized the guilt of the people. The meat and the bones (the people) will be burned and the pot itself finally consumed by fire.

---

e 37 Or even made the children they bore to me pass through ˌthe fireˌ   f 42 Or drunkards

[13] " 'Now your impurity is lewdness. Because I tried to cleanse you but you would not be cleansed from your impurity, you will not be clean again until my wrath against you has subsided.

[14] " 'I the LORD have spoken. The time has come for me to act. I will not hold back; I will not have pity, nor will I relent. You will be judged according to your conduct and your actions, declares the Sovereign LORD.' "

Ezekiel's Wife Dies

[15] The word of the LORD came to me: [16] "Son of man, with one blow I am about to take away from you the delight of your eyes. Yet do not lament or weep or shed any tears. [17] Groan quietly; do not mourn for the dead. Keep your turban fastened and your sandals on your feet; do not cover the lower part of your face or eat the customary food ‚of mourners‚."

[18] So I spoke to the people in the morning, and in the evening my wife died. The next morning I did as I had been commanded.

[19] Then the people asked me, "Won't you tell us what these things have to do with us?"

[20] So I said to them, "The word of the LORD came to me: [21] Say to the house of Israel, 'This is what the Sovereign LORD says: I am about to desecrate my sanctuary—the stronghold in which you take pride, the delight of your eyes, the object of your affection. The sons and daughters you left behind will fall by the sword. [22] And you will do as I have done. You will not cover the lower part of your face or eat the customary food ‚of mourners‚. [23] You will keep your turbans on your heads and your sandals on your feet. You will not mourn or weep but will waste away because of[a] your sins and groan among yourselves. [24] Ezekiel will be a sign to you; you will do just as he has done. When this happens, you will know that I am the Sovereign LORD.'

[25] "And you, son of man, on the day I take away their stronghold, their joy and glory, the delight of their eyes, their heart's desire, and their sons and daughters as well—[26] on that day a fugitive will come to tell you the news. [27] At that time your mouth will be opened; you will speak with him and will no longer be silent. So you will be a sign to them, and they will know that I am the LORD."

A Prophecy Against Ammon

25 The word of the LORD came to me: [2] "Son of man, set your face against the Ammonites and prophesy against them. [3] Say to them, 'Hear the word of the Sovereign LORD. This is what the Sovereign LORD says: Because you said "Aha!" over my sanctuary when it was desecrated and over the land of Israel when it was laid waste and over the people of Judah when they went into exile, [4] therefore I am going to give you to the people of the East as a possession. They will set up their camps and pitch their tents among you; they will eat your fruit and drink your milk. [5] I will turn Rabbah into a pasture for camels and Ammon into a resting place for sheep. Then you will know that I am the LORD. [6] For

this is what the Sovereign LORD says: Because you have clapped your hands and stamped your feet, rejoicing with all the malice of your heart against the land of Israel, [7] therefore I will stretch out my hand against you and give you as plunder to the nations. I will cut you off from the nations and exterminate you from the countries. I will destroy you, and you will know that I am the LORD.' "

A Prophecy Against Moab

[8] "This is what the Sovereign LORD says: 'Because Moab and Seir said, "Look, the house of Judah has become like all the other nations," [9] therefore I will expose the flank of Moab, beginning at its frontier towns—Beth Jeshimoth, Baal Meon and Kiriathaim—the glory of that land. [10] I will give Moab along with the Ammonites to the people of the East as a possession, so that the Ammonites will not be remembered among the nations; [11] and I will inflict punishment on Moab. Then they will know that I am the LORD.' "

A Prophecy Against Edom

[12] "This is what the Sovereign LORD says: 'Because Edom took revenge on the house of Judah and became very guilty by doing so, [13] therefore this is what the Sovereign LORD says: I will stretch out my hand against Edom and kill its men and their animals. I will lay it waste, and from Teman to Dedan they will fall by the sword. [14] I will take vengeance on Edom by the hand of my people Israel, and they will deal with Edom in accordance with my anger and my wrath; they will know my vengeance, declares the Sovereign LORD.' "

A Prophecy Against Philistia

[15] "This is what the Sovereign LORD says: 'Because the Philistines acted in vengeance and took revenge with malice in their hearts, and with ancient hostility sought to destroy Judah, [16] therefore this is what the Sovereign LORD says: I am about to stretch out my hand against the Philistines, and I will cut off the Kerethites and destroy those remaining along the coast. [17] I will carry out great vengeance on them and punish them in my wrath. Then they will know that I am the LORD, when I take vengeance on them.' "

A Prophecy Against Tyre

26 In the eleventh year, on the first day of the month, the word of the LORD came to me: [2] "Son of man, because Tyre has said of Jerusalem, 'Aha! The gate to the nations is broken, and its doors have swung open to me; now that she lies in ruins I will prosper,' [3] therefore this is what the Sovereign LORD says: I am against you, O Tyre, and I will bring many nations against you, like the sea casting up its waves. [4] They will destroy the walls of Tyre and pull down her towers; I will scrape away her rubble and make her a bare rock. [5] Out in the sea she will become a place to spread fishing nets, for I have spoken, declares the

---

[a] 23 Or *away in*

Sovereign LORD. She will become plunder for the nations, [6]and her settlements on the mainland will be ravaged by the sword. Then they will know that I am the LORD.

[7]"For this is what the Sovereign LORD says: From the north I am going to bring against Tyre Nebuchadnezzar[a] king of Babylon, king of kings, with horses and chariots, with horsemen and a great army. [8]He will ravage your settlements on the mainland with the sword; he will set up siege works against you, build a ramp up to your walls and raise his shields against you. [9]He will direct the blows of his battering-rams against your walls and demolish your towers with his weapons. [10]His horses will be so many that they will cover you with dust. Your walls will tremble at the noise of the war horses, wagons and chariots when he enters your gates as men enter a city whose walls have been broken through. [11]The hoofs of his horses will trample all your streets; he will kill your people with the sword, and your strong pillars will fall to the ground. [12]They will plunder your wealth and loot your merchandise; they will break down your walls and demolish your fine houses and throw your stones, timber and rubble into the sea. [13]I will put an end to your noisy songs, and the music of your harps will be heard no more. [14]I will make you a bare rock, and you will become a place to spread fishing nets. You will never be rebuilt, for I the LORD have spoken, declares the Sovereign LORD.

[15]"This is what the Sovereign LORD says to Tyre: Will not the coastlands tremble at the sound of your fall, when the wounded groan and the slaughter takes place in you? [16]Then all the princes of the coast will step down from their thrones and lay aside their robes and take off their embroidered garments. Clothed with terror, they will sit on the ground, trembling every moment, appalled at you. [17]Then they will take up a lament concerning you and say to you:

" 'How you are destroyed, O city of renown,
   peopled by men of the sea!
You were a power on the seas,
   you and your citizens;
you put your terror
   on all who lived there.
[18]Now the coastlands tremble
   on the day of your fall;
the islands in the sea
   are terrified at your collapse.'

[19]"This is what the Sovereign LORD says: When I make you a desolate city, like cities no longer inhabited, and when I bring the ocean depths over you and its vast waters cover you, [20]then I will bring you down with those who go down to the pit, to the people of long ago. I will make you dwell in the earth below, as in ancient ruins, with those who go down to the pit, and you will not return or take your place[b] in the land of the living. [21]I will bring you to a horrible end and you will be no more. You will be sought, but you will never again be found, declares the Sovereign LORD."

A Lament for Tyre

27 The word of the LORD came to me: [2]"Son of man, take up a lament concerning Tyre. [3]Say to Tyre, situated at the gateway to the sea, merchant of peoples on many coasts, 'This is what the Sovereign LORD says:

" 'You say, O Tyre,
   "I am perfect in beauty."
[4]Your domain was on the high seas;
   your builders brought your beauty to perfection.
[5]They made all your timbers
   of pine trees from Senir;[a]
they took a cedar from Lebanon
   to make a mast for you.
[6]Of oaks from Bashan
   they made your oars;
of cypress wood[b] from the coasts of Cyprus[c]
   they made your deck, inlaid with ivory.
[7]Fine embroidered linen from Egypt was your sail
   and served as your banner;
your awnings were of blue and purple
   from the coasts of Elishah.
[8]Men of Sidon and Arvad were your oarsmen;
   your skilled men, O Tyre, were aboard as your
     seamen.
[9]Veteran craftsmen of Gebal[d] were on board
   as shipwrights to caulk your seams.
All the ships of the sea and their sailors
   came alongside to trade for your wares.

[10]" 'Men of Persia, Lydia and Put
   served as soldiers in your army.
They hung their shields and helmets on your
    walls,
   bringing you splendour.
[11]Men of Arvad and Helech
   manned your walls on every side;
men of Gammad
   were in your towers.
They hung their shields around your walls;
   they brought your beauty to perfection.

[12]" 'Tarshish did business with you because of your great wealth of goods; they exchanged silver, iron, tin and lead for your merchandise.

[13]" 'Greece, Tubal and Meshech traded with you; they exchanged slaves and articles of bronze for your wares.

[14]" 'Men of Beth Togarmah exchanged work horses, war horses and mules for your merchandise.

[15]" 'The men of Rhodes[e] traded with you, and many coastlands were your customers; they paid you with ivory tusks and ebony.

[16]" 'Aram[f] did business with you because of your many products; they exchanged turquoise, purple fabric, embroidered work, fine linen, coral and rubies for your merchandise.

[17]" 'Judah and Israel traded with you; they

---

[a]7 Hebrew *Nebuchadrezzar*, of which *Nebuchadnezzar* is a variant; here and often in Ezekiel and Jeremiah
[b]20 Septuagint; Hebrew *return, and I will give glory*   [a]5 That is, Hermon
[b]6 Targum; the Masoretic Text has a different division of the consonants.   [c]6 Hebrew *Kittim*   [d]9 That is, Byblos
[e]15 Septuagint; Hebrew *Dedan*   [f]16 Most Hebrew manuscripts; some Hebrew manuscripts and Syriac *Edom*

exchanged wheat from Minnith and confections,*
honey, oil and balm for your wares.

18" 'Damascus, because of your many products and
great wealth of goods, did business with you in wine
from Helbon and wool from Zahar.

19" 'Danites and Greeks from Uzal bought your merchandise; they exchanged wrought iron, cassia and
calamus for your wares.

20" 'Dedan traded in saddle blankets with you.

21" 'Arabia and all the princes of Kedar were your
customers; they did business with you in lambs, rams
and goats.

22" 'The merchants of Sheba and Raamah traded
with you; for your merchandise they exchanged the
finest of all kinds of spices and precious stones, and
gold.

23" 'Haran, Canneh and Eden and merchants of
Sheba, Asshur and Kilmad traded with you. 24In your
market-place they traded with you beautiful garments,
blue fabric, embroidered work and multicoloured rugs
with cords twisted and tightly knotted.

25" 'The ships of Tarshish serve
    as carriers for your wares.
You are filled with heavy cargo
    in the heart of the sea.
26Your oarsmen take you
    out to the high seas.
But the east wind will break you to pieces
    in the heart of the sea.
27Your wealth, merchandise and wares,
    your mariners, seamen and shipwrights,
    your merchants and all your soldiers,
    and everyone else on board
will sink into the heart of the sea
    on the day of your shipwreck.
28The shorelands will quake
    when your seamen cry out.
29All who handle the oars
    will abandon their ships;
the mariners and all the seamen
    will stand on the shore.
30They will raise their voice
    and cry bitterly over you;
they will sprinkle dust on their heads
    and roll in ashes.
31They will shave their heads because of you
    and will put on sackcloth.
They will weep over you with anguish of soul
    and with bitter mourning.
32As they wail and mourn over you,
    they will take up a lament concerning you:
"Who was ever silenced like Tyre,
    surrounded by the sea?"
33When your merchandise went out on the seas,
    you satisfied many nations;
with your great wealth and your wares
    you enriched the kings of the earth.
34Now you are shattered by the sea
    in the depths of the waters;
your wares and all your company
    have gone down with you.

35All who live in the coastlands
    are appalled at you;
their kings shudder with horror
    and their faces are distorted with fear.
36The merchants among the nations hiss at you;
    you have come to a horrible end
    and will be no more.' "

A Prophecy Against the King of Tyre

28 The word of the LORD came to me: 2"Son of
man, say to the ruler of Tyre, 'This is what the
Sovereign LORD says:

" 'In the pride of your heart
    you say, "I am a god;
I sit on the throne of a god
    in the heart of the seas."
But you are a man and not a god,
    though you think you are as wise as a god.
3Are you wiser than Daniel?*
    Is no secret hidden from you?
4By your wisdom and understanding
    you have gained wealth for yourself
and amassed gold and silver
    in your treasuries.
5By your great skill in trading
    you have increased your wealth,
and because of your wealth
    your heart has grown proud.

6" 'Therefore this is what the Sovereign LORD says:

" 'Because you think you are wise,
    as wise as a god,
7I am going to bring foreigners against you,
    the most ruthless of nations;
they will draw their swords against your beauty
    and wisdom
    and pierce your shining splendour.
8They will bring you down to the pit,
    and you will die a violent death
    in the heart of the seas.
9Will you then say, "I am a god,"
    in the presence of those who kill you?
You will be but a man, not a god,
    in the hands of those who slay you.
10You will die the death of the uncircumcised
    at the hands of foreigners.

I have spoken, declares the Sovereign LORD.' "

11The word of the LORD came to me: 12"Son of man,
take up a lament concerning the king of Tyre and say
to him: 'This is what the Sovereign LORD says:

" 'You were the model of perfection,
    full of wisdom and perfect in beauty.
13You were in Eden,
    the garden of God;
every precious stone adorned you:
    ruby, topaz and emerald,
    chrysolite, onyx and jasper,
    sapphire,* turquoise and beryl.*

---

*17 The meaning of the Hebrew for this word is uncertain.
*3 Or Danel; the Hebrew spelling may suggest a person other than the prophet Daniel.
*13 Or lapis lazuli   *13 The precise identification of some of these precious stones is uncertain.

Your settings and mountings*d* were made of
    gold;
  on the day you were created they were
    prepared.
[14]You were anointed as a guardian cherub,
  for so I ordained you.
  You were on the holy mount of God;
  you walked among the fiery stones.
[15]You were blameless in your ways
  from the day you were created
    till wickedness was found in you.
[16]Through your widespread trade
  you were filled with violence,
    and you sinned.
So I drove you in disgrace from the mount of
    God,
  and I expelled you, O guardian cherub,
    from among the fiery stones.
[17]Your heart became proud
  on account of your beauty,
  and you corrupted your wisdom
    because of your splendour.
So I threw you to the earth;
  I made a spectacle of you before kings.
[18]By your many sins and dishonest trade
  you have desecrated your sanctuaries.
So I made a fire come out from you,
  and it consumed you,
and I reduced you to ashes on the ground
  in the sight of all who were watching.
[19]All the nations who knew you
  are appalled at you;
you have come to a horrible end
  and will be no more.' "

A Prophecy Against Sidon

[20]The word of the LORD came to me: [21]"Son of man,
set your face against Sidon; prophesy against her [22]and
say: 'This is what the Sovereign LORD says:

" 'I am against you, O Sidon,
  and I will gain glory within you.
They will know that I am the LORD,
  when I inflict punishment on her
  and show myself holy within her.
[23]I will send a plague upon her
  and make blood flow in her streets.
The slain will fall within her,
  with the sword against her on every side.
Then they will know that I am the LORD.

[24]" 'No longer will the people of Israel have malicious neighbours who are painful briers and sharp
thorns. Then they will know that I am the Sovereign
LORD.

[25]" 'This is what the Sovereign LORD says: When I
gather the people of Israel from the nations where they
have been scattered, I will show myself holy among
them in the sight of the nations. Then they will live in
their own land, which I gave to my servant Jacob.
[26]They will live there in safety and will build houses
and plant vineyards; they will live in safety when I
inflict punishment on all their neighbours who
maligned them. Then they will know that I am the
LORD their God.' "

A Prophecy Against Egypt

29 In the tenth year, in the tenth month on the
  twelfth day, the word of the LORD came to me:
[2]"Son of man, set your face against Pharaoh king of
Egypt and prophesy against him and against all Egypt.
[3]Speak to him and say: 'This is what the Sovereign
LORD says:

" 'I am against you, Pharaoh king of Egypt,
  you great monster lying among your streams.
You say, "The Nile is mine;
  I made it for myself."
[4]But I will put hooks in your jaws
  and make the fish of your streams stick to your
    scales.
I will pull you out from among your streams,
  with all the fish sticking to your scales.
[5]I will leave you in the desert,
  you and all the fish of your streams.
You will fall on the open field
  and not be gathered or picked up.
I will give you as food
  to the beasts of the earth and the birds of the
    air.

[6]Then all who live in Egypt will know that I am the
LORD.

" 'You have been a staff of reed for the house of
Israel. [7]When they grasped you with their hands, you
splintered and you tore open their shoulders; when
they leaned on you, you broke and their backs were
wrenched.*a*
[8]" 'Therefore this is what the Sovereign LORD says:
I will bring a sword against you and kill your men and
their animals. [9]Egypt will become a desolate wasteland. Then they will know that I am the LORD.

" 'Because you said, "The Nile is mine; I made it,"
[10]therefore I am against you and against your streams,
and I will make the land of Egypt a ruin and a desolate
waste from Migdol to Aswan, as far as the border of
Cush.*b* [11]No foot of man or animal will pass through
it; no-one will live there for forty years. [12]I will make
the land of Egypt desolate among devastated lands, and
her cities will lie desolate for forty years among ruined
cities. And I will disperse the Egyptians among the
nations and scatter them through the countries.

[13]" 'Yet this is what the Sovereign LORD says: At the
end of forty years I will gather the Egyptians from the
nations where they were scattered. [14]I will bring them
back from captivity and return them to Upper Egypt,*c*
the land of their ancestry. There they will be a lowly
kingdom. [15]It will be the lowliest of kingdoms and will

---

d13 The meaning of the Hebrew for this phrase is uncertain.
a7 Syriac (see also Septuagint and Vulgate); Hebrew *and you caused their backs to stand*   *b10* That is, the upper Nile region
c14 Hebrew *to Pathros*

never again exalt itself above the other nations. I will make it so weak that it will never again rule over the nations. ¹⁶Egypt will no longer be a source of confidence for the people of Israel but will be a reminder of their sin in turning to her for help. Then they will know that I am the Sovereign LORD.' "

¹⁷In the twenty-seventh year, in the first month on the first day, the word of the LORD came to me: ¹⁸"Son of man, Nebuchadnezzar king of Babylon drove his army in a hard campaign against Tyre; every head was rubbed bare and every shoulder made raw. Yet he and his army got no reward from the campaign he led against Tyre. ¹⁹Therefore this is what the Sovereign LORD says: I am going to give Egypt to Nebuchadnezzar king of Babylon, and he will carry off its wealth. He will loot and plunder the land as pay for his army. ²⁰I have given him Egypt as a reward for his efforts because he and his army did it for me, declares the Sovereign LORD.

²¹"On that day I will make a horn*d* grow for the house of Israel, and I will open your mouth among them. Then they will know that I am the LORD."

A Lament for Egypt

30 The word of the LORD came to me: ²"Son of man, prophesy and say: 'This is what the Sovereign LORD says:

" 'Wail and say,
"Alas for that day!"
³For the day is near,
　the day of the LORD is near—
a day of clouds,
　a time of doom for the nations.
⁴A sword will come against Egypt,
　and anguish will come upon Cush.*a*
When the slain fall in Egypt,
　her wealth will be carried away
　and her foundations torn down.

⁵Cush and Put, Lydia and all Arabia, Libya*b* and the people of the covenant land will fall by the sword along with Egypt.

⁶" 'This is what the LORD says:

" 'The allies of Egypt will fall
　and her proud strength will fail.
From Migdol to Aswan
　they will fall by the sword within her,
　　　　　　declares the Sovereign LORD.
⁷" 'They will be desolate
　among desolate lands,
and their cities will lie
　among ruined cities.
⁸Then they will know that I am the LORD,
　when I set fire to Egypt
　and all her helpers are crushed.

⁹" 'On that day messengers will go out from me in ships to frighten Cush out of her complacency. Anguish

will take hold of them on the day of Egypt's doom, for it is sure to come.

¹⁰" 'This is what the Sovereign LORD says:

" 'I will put an end to the hordes of Egypt
　by the hand of Nebuchadnezzar king of Babylon.
¹¹He and his army—the most ruthless of nations—
　will be brought in to destroy the land.
They will draw their swords against Egypt
　and fill the land with the slain.
¹²I will dry up the streams of the Nile
　and sell the land to evil men;
by the hand of foreigners
　I will lay waste the land and everything in it.

I the LORD have spoken.

¹³" 'This is what the Sovereign LORD says:

" 'I will destroy the idols
　and put an end to the images in Memphis.*c*
No longer will there be a prince in Egypt,
　and I will spread fear throughout the land.
¹⁴I will lay waste Upper Egypt,*d*
　set fire to Zoan
　and inflict punishment on Thebes.*e*
¹⁵I will pour out my wrath on Pelusium,*f*
　the stronghold of Egypt,
　and cut off the hordes of Thebes.
¹⁶I will set fire to Egypt;
　Pelusium will writhe in agony.
Thebes will be taken by storm;
　Memphis will be in constant distress.
¹⁷The young men of Heliopolis*g* and Bubastis*h*
　will fall by the sword,
　and the cities themselves will go into captivity.
¹⁸Dark will be the day at Tahpanhes
　when I break the yoke of Egypt;
　there her proud strength will come to an end.
She will be covered with clouds,
　and her villages will go into captivity.
¹⁹So I will inflict punishment on Egypt,
　and they will know that I am the LORD.' "

²⁰In the eleventh year, in the first month on the seventh day, the word of the LORD came to me: ²¹"Son of man, I have broken the arm of Pharaoh king of Egypt. It has not been bound up for healing or put in a splint so as to become strong enough to hold a sword. ²²Therefore this is what the Sovereign LORD says: I am against Pharaoh king of Egypt. I will break both his arms, the good arm as well as the broken one, and make the sword fall from his hand. ²³I will disperse the Egyptians among the nations and scatter them through the countries. ²⁴I will strengthen the arms of the king of Babylon and put my sword in his hand, but I will break the arms of Pharaoh, and he will groan before him like a mortally wounded man. ²⁵I will strengthen the arms of the king of Babylon, but the arms of Pharaoh will fall limp. Then they will know that I am the LORD, when I put my sword into the hand of the king of Babylon and he brandishes it against Egypt. ²⁶I will

---

d21 Horn here symbolises strength.　　　　*a4 That is, the upper Nile region; also in verses 5 and 9*　　*b5 Hebrew Cub*
c13 Hebrew Noph; also in verse 16　　　*d14 Hebrew waste Pathros*　　　*e14 Hebrew No; also in verses 15 and 16*
f15 Hebrew Sin; also in verse 16　　　*g17 Hebrew Awen (or On)*　　　*h17 Hebrew Pi Beseth*

disperse the Egyptians among the nations and scatter them through the countries. Then they will know that I am the LORD."

A Cedar in Lebanon

31 In the eleventh year, in the third month on the first day, the word of the LORD came to me: [2]"Son of man, say to Pharaoh king of Egypt and to his hordes:

" 'Who can be compared with you in majesty?
[3]Consider Assyria, once a cedar in Lebanon,
  with beautiful branches overshadowing the
    forest;
  it towered on high,
    its top above the thick foliage.
[4]The waters nourished it,
  deep springs made it grow tall;
  their streams flowed
    all around its base
  and sent their channels
    to all the trees of the field.
[5]So it towered higher
    than all the trees of the field;
  its boughs increased
    and its branches grew long,
    spreading because of abundant waters.
[6]All the birds of the air
    nested in its boughs,
  all the beasts of the field
    gave birth under its branches;
  all the great nations
    lived in its shade.
[7]It was majestic in beauty,
    with its spreading boughs,
  for its roots went down
    to abundant waters.
[8]The cedars in the garden of God
    could not rival it,
  nor could the pine trees
    equal its boughs,
  nor could the plane trees
    compare with its branches—
  no tree in the garden of God
    could match its beauty.
[9]I made it beautiful
    with abundant branches,
  the envy of all the trees of Eden
    in the garden of God.

[10]" 'Therefore this is what the Sovereign LORD says: Because it towered on high, lifting its top above the thick foliage, and because it was proud of its height, [11]I handed it over to the ruler of the nations, for him to deal with according to its wickedness. I cast it aside, [12]and the most ruthless of foreign nations cut it down and left it. Its boughs fell on the mountains and in all the valleys; its branches lay broken in all the ravines of the land. All the nations of the earth came out from under its shade and left it. [13]All the birds of the air settled on the fallen tree, and all the beasts of the field were among its branches. [14]Therefore no other trees by

the waters are ever to tower proudly on high, lifting their tops above the thick foliage. No other trees so well-watered are ever to reach such a height; they are all destined for death, for the earth below, among mortal men, with those who go down to the pit.

[15]" 'This is what the Sovereign LORD says: On the day it was brought down to the grave[a] I covered the deep springs with mourning for it; I held back its streams, and its abundant waters were restrained. Because of it I clothed Lebanon with gloom, and all the trees of the field withered away. [16]I made the nations tremble at the sound of its fall when I brought it down to the grave with those who go down to the pit. Then all the trees of Eden, the choicest and best of Lebanon, all the trees that were well-watered, were consoled in the earth below. [17]Those who lived in its shade, its allies among the nations, had also gone down to the grave with it, joining those killed by the sword.

[18]" 'Which of the trees of Eden can be compared with you in splendour and majesty? Yet you, too, will be brought down with the trees of Eden to the earth below; you will lie among the uncircumcised, with those killed by the sword.

" 'This is Pharaoh and all his hordes, declares the Sovereign LORD.' "

A Lament for Pharaoh

32 In the twelfth year, in the twelfth month on the first day, the word of the LORD came to me: [2]"Son of man, take up a lament concerning Pharaoh king of Egypt and say to him:

" 'You are like a lion among the nations;
  you are like a monster in the seas
thrashing about in your streams,
  churning the water with your feet
  and muddying the streams.

[3]" 'This is what the Sovereign LORD says:

" 'With a great throng of people
  I will cast my net over you,
  and they will haul you up in my net.
[4]I will throw you on the land
  and hurl you on the open field.
I will let all the birds of the air settle on you
  and all the beasts of the earth gorge themselves
    on you.
[5]I will spread your flesh on the mountains
  and fill the valleys with your remains.
[6]I will drench the land with your flowing blood
  all the way to the mountains,
  and the ravines will be filled with your flesh.
[7]When I snuff you out, I will cover the heavens
  and darken their stars;
I will cover the sun with a cloud,
  and the moon will not give its light.
[8]All the shining lights in the heavens
  I will darken over you;
I will bring darkness over your land,
              declares the Sovereign LORD.

---

[a]15 Hebrew *Sheol*; also in verses 16 and 17

⁹I will trouble the hearts of many peoples
   when I bring about your destruction among the
      nations,
   among[a] lands you have not known.
¹⁰I will cause many peoples to be appalled at you,
   and their kings will shudder with horror
      because of you
   when I brandish my sword before them.
On the day of your downfall
   each of them will tremble
   every moment for his life.

¹¹" 'For this is what the Sovereign LORD says:

" 'The sword of the king of Babylon
   will come against you.
¹²I will cause your hordes to fall
   by the swords of mighty men—
   the most ruthless of all nations.
They will shatter the pride of Egypt,
   and all her hordes will be overthrown.
¹³I will destroy all her cattle
   from beside abundant waters
no longer to be stirred by the foot of man
   or muddied by the hoofs of cattle.
¹⁴Then I will let her waters settle
   and make her streams flow like oil,
                     declares the Sovereign LORD.
¹⁵When I make Egypt desolate
   and strip the land of everything in it,
   when I strike down all who live there,
      then they will know that I am the LORD.'

¹⁶"This is the lament they will chant for her. The
daughters of the nations will chant it; for Egypt and all
her hordes they will chant it, declares the Sovereign
LORD."

¹⁷In the twelfth year, on the fifteenth day of the
month, the word of the LORD came to me: ¹⁸"Son of
man, wail for the hordes of Egypt and consign to the
earth below both her and the daughters of mighty
nations, with those who go down to the pit. ¹⁹Say to
them, 'Are you more favoured than others? Go down
and be laid among the uncircumcised.' ²⁰They will fall
among those killed by the sword. The sword is drawn;
let her be dragged off with all her hordes. ²¹From
within the grave[b] the mighty leaders will say of Egypt
and her allies, 'They have come down and they lie with
the uncircumcised, with those killed by the sword.'
²²"Assyria is there with her whole army; she is surrounded by the graves of all her slain, all who have
fallen by the sword. ²³Their graves are in the depths of
the pit and her army lies around her grave. All who had
spread terror in the land of the living are slain, fallen
by the sword.
²⁴"Elam is there, with all her hordes around her
grave. All of them are slain, fallen by the sword. All
who had spread terror in the land of the living went
down uncircumcised to the earth below. They bear
their shame with those who go down to the pit. ²⁵A bed
is made for her among the slain, with all her hordes
around her grave. All of them are uncircumcised, killed
by the sword. Because their terror had spread in the
land of the living, they bear their shame with those
who go down to the pit; they are laid among the slain.
²⁶"Meshech and Tubal are there, with all their
hordes around their graves. All of them are uncircumcised, killed by the sword because they spread their
terror in the land of the living. ²⁷Do they not lie with
the other uncircumcised warriors who have fallen,
who went down to the grave with their weapons of
war, whose swords were placed under their heads?
The punishment for their sins rested on their bones,
though the terror of these warriors had stalked through
the land of the living.
²⁸"You too, O Pharaoh, will be broken and will lie
among the uncircumcised, with those killed by the
sword.
²⁹"Edom is there, her kings and all her princes;
despite their power, they are laid with those killed by
the sword. They lie with the uncircumcised, with
those who go down to the pit.
³⁰"All the princes of the north and all the Sidonians
are there; they went down with the slain in disgrace
despite the terror caused by their power. They lie
uncircumcised with those killed by the sword and bear
their shame with those who go down to the pit.
³¹"Pharaoh—he and all his army—will see them
and he will be consoled for all his hordes that were
killed by the sword, declares the Sovereign LORD.
³²Although I had him spread terror in the land of the
living, Pharaoh and all his hordes will be laid among
the uncircumcised, with those killed by the sword,
declares the Sovereign LORD."

Ezekiel a Watchman

33 The word of the LORD came to me: ²"Son of
man, speak to your countrymen and say to
them: 'When I bring the sword against a land, and the
people of the land choose one of their men and make
him their watchman, ³and he sees the sword coming
against the land and blows the trumpet to warn the
people, ⁴then if anyone hears the trumpet but does not
take warning and the sword comes and takes his life,
his blood will be on his own head. ⁵Since he heard the
sound of the trumpet but did not take warning, his
blood will be on his own head. If he had taken warning,
he would have saved himself. ⁶But if the watchman
sees the sword coming and does not blow the trumpet
to warn the people and the sword comes and takes the
life of one of them, that man will be taken away
because of his sin, but I will hold the watchman
accountable for his blood.'

33:6   Ezekiel was frequently referred to
as a watchman, and it probably best
described his role in Babylon as the Lord's
representative watching over his people. In
ancient Eastern communities, the watchman
would guard vineyards (a metaphor for
Israel), or warn a city of approaching disaster,
which was also a function of the prophet.

---

[a]9 Hebrew; Septuagint *bring you into captivity among the nations,* / *to*   [b]21 Hebrew *Sheol*; also in verse 27

7"Son of man, I have made you a watchman for the house of Israel; so hear the word I speak and give them warning from me. 8When I say to the wicked, 'O wicked man, you will surely die,' and you do not speak out to dissuade him from his ways, that wicked man will die for*a* his sin, and I will hold you accountable for his blood. 9But if you do warn the wicked man to turn from his ways and he does not do so, he will die for his sin, but you will be saved yourself.

10"Son of man, say to the house of Israel, 'This is what you are saying: "Our offences and sins weigh us down, and we are wasting away because of*b* them. How then can we live?" ' 11Say to them, 'As surely as I live, declares the Sovereign LORD, I take no pleasure in the death of the wicked, but rather that they turn from their ways and live. Turn! Turn from your evil ways! Why will you die, O house of Israel?'

12"Therefore, son of man, say to your countrymen, 'The righteousness of the righteous man will not save him when he disobeys, and the wickedness of the wicked man will not cause him to fall when he turns from it. The righteous man, if he sins, will not be allowed to live because of his former righteousness.' 13If I tell the righteous man that he will surely live, but then he trusts in his righteousness and does evil, none of the righteous things he has done will be remembered; he will die for the evil he has done. 14And if I say to the wicked man, 'You will surely die,' but he then turns away from his sin and does what is just and right — 15if he gives back what he took in pledge for a loan, returns what he has stolen, follows the decrees that give life, and does no evil, he will surely live; he will not die. 16None of the sins he has committed will be remembered against him. He has done what is just and right; he will surely live.

17"Yet your countrymen say, 'The way of the Lord is not just.' But it is their way that is not just. 18If a righteous man turns from his righteousness and does evil, he will die for it. 19And if a wicked man turns away from his wickedness and does what is just and right, he will live by doing so. 20Yet, O house of Israel, you say, 'The way of the Lord is not just.' But I will judge each of you according to his own ways."

Jerusalem's Fall Explained

21In the twelfth year of our exile, in the tenth month on the fifth day, a man who had escaped from Jerusalem came to me and said, "The city has fallen!" 22Now the evening before the man arrived, the hand of the LORD was upon me, and he opened my mouth before the man came to me in the morning. So my mouth was opened and I was no longer silent.

23Then the word of the LORD came to me: 24"Son of man, the people living in those ruins in the land of Israel are saying, 'Abraham was only one man, yet he possessed the land. But we are many; surely the land has been given to us as our possession.' 25Therefore say to them, 'This is what the Sovereign LORD says: Since you eat meat with the blood still in it and look to your idols and shed blood, should you then possess the land? 26You rely on your sword, you do detestable things, and

each of you defiles his neighbour's wife. Should you then possess the land?'

27"Say this to them: 'This is what the Sovereign LORD says: As surely as I live, those who are left in the ruins will fall by the sword, those out in the country I will give to the wild animals to be devoured, and those in strongholds and caves will die of a plague. 28I will make the land a desolate waste, and her proud strength will come to an end, and the mountains of Israel will become desolate so that no-one will cross them. 29Then they will know that I am the LORD, when I have made the land a desolate waste because of all the detestable things they have done.'

30"As for you, son of man, your countrymen are talking together about you by the walls and at the doors of the houses, saying to each other, 'Come and hear the message that has come from the LORD.' 31My people come to you, as they usually do, and sit before you to listen to your words, but they do not put them into practice. With their mouths they express devotion, but their hearts are greedy for unjust gain. 32Indeed, to them you are nothing more than one who sings love songs with a beautiful voice and plays an instrument well, for they hear your words but do not put them into practice.

33"When all this comes true — and it surely will — then they will know that a prophet has been among them."

Shepherds and Sheep

34 The word of the LORD came to me: 2"Son of man, prophesy against the shepherds of Israel; prophesy and say to them: 'This is what the Sovereign LORD says: Woe to the shepherds of Israel who only take care of themselves! Should not shepherds take care of the flock? 3You eat the curds, clothe yourselves with the wool and slaughter the choice animals, but you do not take care of the flock. 4You have not strengthened the weak or healed the sick or bound up the injured. You have not brought back the strays or searched for the lost. You have ruled them harshly and brutally. 5So they were scattered because there was no shepherd, and when they were scattered they became food for all the wild animals. 6My sheep wandered over all the mountains and on every high hill. They were scattered over the whole earth, and no-one searched or looked for them.

7" 'Therefore, you shepherds, hear the word of the LORD: 8As surely as I live, declares the Sovereign LORD, because my flock lacks a shepherd and so has been plundered and has become food for all the wild animals, and because my shepherds did not search for my flock but cared for themselves rather than for my flock, 9therefore, O shepherds, hear the word of the LORD: 10This is what the Sovereign LORD says: I am against the shepherds and will hold them accountable for my flock. I will remove them from tending the flock so that the shepherds can no longer feed themselves. I will rescue my flock from their mouths, and it will no longer be food for them.

11" 'For this is what the Sovereign LORD says: I

a8 Or in; also in verse 9   *b10 Or away in*

myself will search for my sheep and look after them. [12]As a shepherd looks after his scattered flock when he is with them, so will I look after my sheep. I will rescue them from all the places where they were scattered on a day of clouds and darkness. [13]I will bring them out from the nations and gather them from the countries, and I will bring them into their own land. I will pasture them on the mountains of Israel, in the ravines and in all the settlements in the land. [14]I will tend them in a good pasture, and the mountain heights of Israel will be their grazing land. There they will lie down in good grazing land, and there they will feed in a rich pasture on the mountains of Israel. [15]I myself will tend my sheep and make them lie down, declares the Sovereign LORD. [16]I will search for the lost and bring back the strays. I will bind up the injured and strengthen the weak, but the sleek and the strong I will destroy. I will shepherd the flock with justice.

34:16 In contrast to the vision at the beginning of the book, here Ezekiel used a more rugged, down-to-earth image, and he compared God to a shepherd. It is another "guarding" image, like that of the watchman in chapter 33, and this time the shepherds of Israel are the nation's rulers who led God's people in the wrong direction. God, however, is the shepherd who searches out his sheep (his people) and will lead them to safety.

---

[17]" 'As for you, my flock, this is what the Sovereign LORD says: I will judge between one sheep and another, and between rams and goats. [18]Is it not enough for you to feed on the good pasture? Must you also trample the rest of your pasture with your feet? Is it not enough for you to drink clear water? Must you also muddy the rest with your feet? [19]Must my flock feed on what you have trampled and drink what you have muddied with your feet?

[20]" 'Therefore this is what the Sovereign LORD says to them: See, I myself will judge between the fat sheep and the lean sheep. [21]Because you shove with flank and shoulder, butting all the weak sheep with your horns until you have driven them away, [22]I will save my flock, and they will no longer be plundered. I will judge between one sheep and another. [23]I will place over them one shepherd, my servant David, and he will tend them; he will tend them and be their shepherd. [24]I the LORD will be their God, and my servant David will be prince among them. I the LORD have spoken.

[25]" 'I will make a covenant of peace with them and rid the land of wild beasts so that they may live in the desert and sleep in the forests in safety. [26]I will bless them and the places surrounding my hill.[a] I will send down showers in season; there will be showers of blessing. [27]The trees of the field will yield their fruit and the ground will yield its crops; the people will be secure in their land. They will know that I am the LORD, when I break the bars of their yoke and rescue

them from the hands of those who enslaved them. [28]They will no longer be plundered by the nations, nor will wild animals devour them. They will live in safety, and no-one will make them afraid. [29]I will provide for them a land renowned for its crops, and they will no longer be victims of famine in the land or bear the scorn of the nations. [30]Then they will know that I, the LORD their God, am with them and that they, the house of Israel, are my people, declares the Sovereign LORD. [31]You my sheep, the sheep of my pasture, are people, and I am your God, declares the Sovereign LORD.' "

A Prophecy Against Edom

35 The word of the LORD came to me: [2]"Son of man, set your face against Mount Seir; prophesy against it [3]and say: 'This is what the Sovereign LORD says: I am against you, Mount Seir, and I will stretch out my hand against you and make you a desolate waste. [4]I will turn your towns into ruins and you will be desolate. Then you will know that I am the LORD.

[5]" 'Because you harboured an ancient hostility and delivered the Israelites over to the sword at the time of their calamity, the time their punishment reached its climax, [6]therefore as surely as I live, declares the Sovereign LORD, I will give you over to bloodshed and it will pursue you. Since you did not hate bloodshed, bloodshed will pursue you. [7]I will make Mount Seir a desolate waste and cut off from it all who come and go. [8]I will fill your mountains with the slain; those killed by the sword will fall on your hills and in your valleys and in all your ravines. [9]I will make you desolate for ever; your towns will not be inhabited. Then you will know that I am the LORD.

[10]" 'Because you have said, "These two nations and countries will be ours and we will take possession of them," even though I the LORD was there, [11]therefore as surely as I live, declares the Sovereign LORD, I will treat you in accordance with the anger and jealousy you showed in your hatred of them and I will make myself known among them when I judge you. [12]Then you will know that I the LORD have heard all the contemptible things you have said against the mountains of Israel. You said, "They have been laid waste and have been given over to us to devour." [13]You boasted against me and spoke against me without restraint, and I heard it. [14]This is what the Sovereign LORD says: While the whole earth rejoices, I will make you desolate. [15]Because you rejoiced when the inheritance of the house of Israel became desolate, that is how I will treat you. You will be desolate, O Mount Seir, you and all of Edom. Then they will know that I am the LORD.' "

A Prophecy to the Mountains of Israel

36 "Son of man, prophesy to the mountains of Israel and say, 'O mountains of Israel, hear the word of the LORD. [2]This is what the Sovereign LORD says: The enemy said of you, "Aha! The ancient heights have become our possession." ' [3]Therefore prophesy and say, 'This is what the Sovereign LORD says: Because they ravaged and hounded you from every side

---

[a]26 Or I will make them and the places surrounding my hill a blessing

so that you became the possession of the rest of the nations and the object of people's malicious talk and slander, [4]therefore, O mountains of Israel, hear the word of the Sovereign LORD: This is what the Sovereign LORD says to the mountains and hills, to the ravines and valleys, to the desolate ruins and the deserted towns that have been plundered and ridiculed by the rest of the nations around you—[5]this is what the Sovereign LORD says: In my burning zeal I have spoken against the rest of the nations, and against Edom, for with glee and with malice in their hearts they made my land their own possession so that they might plunder its pasture-land.' [6]Therefore prophesy concerning the land of Israel and say to the mountains and hills, to the ravines and valleys: 'This is what the Sovereign LORD says: I speak in my jealous wrath because you have suffered the scorn of the nations. [7]Therefore this is what the Sovereign LORD says: I swear with uplifted hand that the nations around you will also suffer scorn.

[8]" 'But you, O mountains of Israel, will produce branches and fruit for my people Israel, for they will soon come home. [9]I am concerned for you and will look on you with favour; you will be ploughed and sown, [10]and I will multiply the number of people upon you, even the whole house of Israel. The towns will be inhabited and the ruins rebuilt. [11]I will increase the number of men and animals upon you, and they will be fruitful and become numerous. I will settle people on you as in the past and will make you prosper more than before. Then you will know that I am the LORD. [12]I will cause people, my people Israel, to walk upon you. They will possess you, and you will be their inheritance; you will never again deprive them of their children.

[13]" 'This is what the Sovereign LORD says: Because people say to you, "You devour men and deprive your nation of its children," [14]therefore you will no longer devour men or make your nation childless, declares the Sovereign LORD. [15]No longer will I make you hear the taunts of the nations, and no longer will you suffer the scorn of the peoples or cause your nation to fall, declares the Sovereign LORD.' "

[16]Again the word of the LORD came to me: [17]"Son of man, when the people of Israel were living in their own land, they defiled it by their conduct and their actions. Their conduct was like a woman's monthly uncleanness in my sight. [18]So I poured out my wrath on them because they had shed blood in the land and because they had defiled it with their idols. [19]I dispersed them among the nations, and they were scattered through the countries; I judged them according to their conduct and their actions. [20]And wherever they went among the nations they profaned my holy name, for it was said of them, 'These are the LORD's people, and yet they had to leave his land.' [21]I had concern for my holy name, which the house of Israel profaned among the nations where they had gone.

[22]"Therefore say to the house of Israel, 'This is what the Sovereign LORD says: It is not for your sake, O house of Israel, that I am going to do these things, but for the sake of my holy name, which you have profaned among the nations where you have gone. [23]I will show the holiness of my great name, which has been profaned among the nations, the name you have profaned among them. Then the nations will know that I am the LORD, declares the Sovereign LORD, when I show myself holy through you before their eyes.

[24]" 'For I will take you out of the nations; I will gather you from all the countries and bring you back into your own land. [25]I will sprinkle clean water on you, and you will be clean; I will cleanse you from all your impurities and from all your idols. [26]I will give you a new heart and put a new spirit in you; I will remove from you your heart of stone and give you a heart of flesh. [27]And I will put my Spirit in you and move you to follow my decrees and be careful to keep my laws. [28]You will live in the land I gave your forefathers; you will be my people, and I will be your God. [29]I will save you from all your uncleanness. I will call for the corn and make it plentiful and will not bring famine upon you. [30]I will increase the fruit of the trees and the crops of the field, so that you will no longer suffer disgrace among the nations because of famine. [31]Then you will remember your evil ways and wicked deeds, and you will loathe yourselves for your sins and detestable practices. [32]I want you to know that I am not doing this for your sake, declares the Sovereign LORD. Be ashamed and disgraced for your conduct, O house of Israel!

[33]" 'This is what the Sovereign LORD says: On the day I cleanse you from all your sins, I will resettle your towns, and the ruins will be rebuilt. [34]The desolate land will be cultivated instead of lying desolate in the sight of all who pass through it. [35]They will say, "This land that was laid waste has become like the garden of Eden; the cities that were lying in ruins, desolate and destroyed, are now fortified and inhabited." [36]Then the nations around you that remain will know that I the LORD have rebuilt what was destroyed and have replanted what was desolate. I the LORD have spoken, and I will do it.'

[37]"This is what the Sovereign LORD says: Once again I will yield to the plea of the house of Israel and do this for them: I will make their people as numerous as sheep, [38]as numerous as the flocks for offerings at Jerusalem during her appointed feasts. So will the ruined cities be filled with flocks of people. Then they will know that I am the LORD."

The Valley of Dry Bones

37 The hand of the LORD was upon me, and he brought me out by the Spirit of the LORD and set me in the middle of a valley; it was full of bones. [2]He led me to and fro among them, and I saw a great many bones on the floor of the valley, bones that were very dry. [3]He asked me, "Son of man, can these bones live?"

I said, "O Sovereign LORD, you alone know."

[4]Then he said to me, "Prophesy to these bones and say to them, 'Dry bones, hear the word of the LORD! [5]This is what the Sovereign LORD says to these bones: I will make breath[a] enter you, and you will come to life. [6]I will attach tendons to you and make flesh come upon you and cover you with skin; I will put breath in

---

[a]5 The Hebrew for this word can also mean *wind* or *spirit* (see verses 6–14).

you, and you will come to life. Then you will know that I am the LORD.' "

37:6   In this famous passage about the dry bones, Ezekiel recalled the dry bones which were God's people in the cooking pot (chapter 24), and showed how those who were useless now had a new hope and a new future. The idea of newness continues by God breathing life into the bones, just like he did when he first created a man (see Genesis 2:7).

7So I prophesied as I was commanded. And as I was prophesying, there was a noise, a rattling sound, and the bones came together, bone to bone. 8I looked, and tendons and flesh appeared on them and skin covered them, but there was no breath in them.
9Then he said to me, "Prophesy to the breath; prophesy, son of man, and say to it, 'This is what the Sovereign LORD says: Come from the four winds, O breath, and breathe into these slain, that they may live.' " 10So I prophesied as he commanded me, and breath entered them; they came to life and stood up on their feet—a vast army.
11Then he said to me: "Son of man, these bones are the whole house of Israel. They say, 'Our bones are dried up and our hope is gone; we are cut off.' 12Therefore prophesy and say to them: 'This is what the Sovereign LORD says: O my people, I am going to open your graves and bring you up from them; I will bring you back to the land of Israel. 13Then you, my people, will know that I am the LORD, when I open your graves and bring you up from them. 14I will put my Spirit in you and you will live, and I will settle you in your own land. Then you will know that I the LORD have spoken, and I have done it, declares the LORD.' "

One Nation Under One King

15The word of the LORD came to me: 16"Son of man, take a stick of wood and write on it, 'Belonging to Judah and the Israelites associated with him.' Then take another stick of wood, and write on it, 'Ephraim's stick, belonging to Joseph and all the house of Israel associated with him.' 17Join them together into one stick so that they will become one in your hand.
18"When your countrymen ask you, 'Won't you tell us what you mean by this?' 19say to them, 'This is what the Sovereign LORD says: I am going to take the stick of Joseph—which is in Ephraim's hand—and of the Israelite tribes associated with him, and join it to Judah's stick, making them a single stick of wood, and they will become one in my hand.' 20Hold before their eyes the sticks you have written on 21and say to them, 'This is what the Sovereign LORD says: I will take the Israelites out of the nations where they have gone. I will gather them from all around and bring them back into their own land. 22I will make them one nation in

the land, on the mountains of Israel. There will be one king over all of them and they will never again be two nations or be divided into two kingdoms. 23They will no longer defile themselves with their idols and vile images or with any of their offences, for I will save them from all their sinful backsliding,[b] and I will cleanse them. They will be my people, and I will be their God.
24" 'My servant David will be king over them, and they will all have one shepherd. They will follow my laws and be careful to keep my decrees. 25They will live in the land I gave to my servant Jacob, the land where your fathers lived. They and their children and their children's children will live there for ever, and David my servant will be their prince for ever. 26I will make a covenant of peace with them; it will be an everlasting covenant. I will establish them and increase their numbers, and I will put my sanctuary among them for ever. 27My dwelling-place will be with them; I will be their God, and they will be my people. 28Then the nations will know that I the LORD make Israel holy, when my sanctuary is among them for ever.' "

A Prophecy Against Gog

38   The word of the LORD came to me: 2"Son of man, set your face against Gog, of the land of Magog, the chief prince of[a] Meshech and Tubal; prophesy against him 3and say: 'This is what the Sovereign LORD says: I am against you, O Gog, chief prince of[b] Meshech and Tubal. 4I will turn you around, put hooks in your jaws and bring you out with your whole army—your horses, your horsemen fully armed, and a great horde with large and small shields, all of them brandishing their swords. 5Persia, Cush[c] and Put will be with them, all with shields and helmets, 6also Gomer with all its troops, and Beth Togarmah from the far north with all its troops—the many nations with you.
7" 'Get ready; be prepared, you and all the hordes gathered about you, and take command of them. 8After many days you will be called to arms. In future years you will invade a land that has recovered from war, whose people were gathered from many nations to the mountains of Israel, which had long been desolate. They had been brought out from the nations, and now all of them live in safety. 9You and all your troops and the many nations with you will go up, advancing like a storm; you will be like a cloud covering the land.
10" 'This is what the Sovereign LORD says: On that day thoughts will come into your mind and you will devise an evil scheme. 11You will say, "I will invade a land of unwalled villages; I will attack a peaceful and unsuspecting people—all of them living without walls and without gates and bars. 12I will plunder and loot and turn my hand against the resettled ruins and the people gathered from the nations, rich in livestock and goods, living at the centre of the land." 13Sheba and Dedan and the merchants of Tarshish and all her villages[d] will say to you, "Have you come to plunder? Have you gathered your hordes to loot, to carry off

---

b23 Many Hebrew manuscripts (see also Septuagint); most Hebrew manuscripts all their dwelling-places where they sinned
a2 Or the prince of Rosh,   *b3 Or Gog, prince of Rosh,*   *c5 That is, the upper Nile region*   *d13 Or her strong lions*

silver and gold, to take away livestock and goods and to seize much plunder?" '

14"Therefore, son of man, prophesy and say to Gog: 'This is what the Sovereign LORD says: In that day, when my people Israel are living in safety, will you not take notice of it? 15You will come from your place in the far north, you and many nations with you, all of them riding on horses, a great horde, a mighty army. 16You will advance against my people Israel like a cloud that covers the land. In days to come, O Gog, I will bring you against my land, so that the nations may know me when I show myself holy through you before their eyes.

17" 'This is what the Sovereign LORD says: Are you not the one I spoke of in former days by my servants the prophets of Israel? At that time they prophesied for years that I would bring you against them. 18This is what will happen in that day: When Gog attacks the land of Israel, my hot anger will be aroused, declares the Sovereign LORD. 19In my zeal and fiery wrath I declare that at that time there shall be a great earthquake in the land of Israel. 20The fish of the sea, the birds of the air, the beasts of the field, every creature that moves along the ground, and all the people on the face of the earth will tremble at my presence. The mountains will be overturned, the cliffs will crumble and every wall will fall to the ground. 21I will summon a sword against Gog on all my mountains, declares the Sovereign LORD. Every man's sword will be against his brother. 22I will execute judgment upon him with plague and bloodshed; I will pour down torrents of rain, hailstones and burning sulphur on him and on his troops and on the many nations with him. 23And so I will show my greatness and my holiness, and I will make myself known in the sight of many nations. Then they will know that I am the LORD.'

39 "Son of man, prophesy against Gog and say: 'This is what the Sovereign LORD says: I am against you, O Gog, chief prince of[a] Meshech and Tubal. 2I will turn you around and drag you along. I will bring you from the far north and send you against the mountains of Israel. 3Then I will strike your bow from your left hand and make your arrows drop from your right hand. 4On the mountains of Israel you will fall, you and all your troops and the nations with you. I will give you as food to all kinds of carrion birds and to the wild animals. 5You will fall in the open field, for I have spoken, declares the Sovereign LORD. 6I will send fire on Magog and on those who live in safety in the coastlands, and they will know that I am the LORD.

7" 'I will make known my holy name among my people Israel. I will no longer let my holy name be profaned, and the nations will know that I the LORD am the Holy One in Israel. 8It is coming! It will surely take place, declares the Sovereign LORD. This is the day I have spoken of.

9" 'Then those who live in the towns of Israel will go out and use the weapons for fuel and burn them up—the small and large shields, the bows and arrows, the war clubs and spears. For seven years they will use them for fuel. 10They will not need to gather wood from

the fields or cut it from the forests, because they will use the weapons for fuel. And they will plunder those who plundered them and loot those who looted them, declares the Sovereign LORD.

11" 'On that day I will give Gog a burial place in Israel, in the valley of those who travel east towards[b] the Sea.[c] It will block the way of travellers, because Gog and all his hordes will be buried there. So it will be called the Valley of Hamon Gog.[d]

12" 'For seven months the house of Israel will be burying them in order to cleanse the land. 13All the people of the land will bury them, and the day I am glorified will be a memorable day for them, declares the Sovereign LORD.

14" 'Men will be regularly employed to cleanse the land. Some will go throughout the land and, in addition to them, others will bury those that remain on the ground. At the end of the seven months they will begin their search. 15As they go through the land and one of them sees a human bone, he will set up a marker beside it until the gravediggers have buried it in the Valley of Hamon Gog. 16(Also a town called Hamonah[e] will be there.) And so they will cleanse the land.'

17"Son of man, this is what the Sovereign LORD says: Call out to every kind of bird and all the wild animals: 'Assemble and come together from all around to the sacrifice I am preparing for you, the great sacrifice on the mountains of Israel. There you will eat flesh and drink blood. 18You will eat the flesh of mighty men and drink the blood of the princes of the earth as if they were rams and lambs, goats and bulls—all of them fattened animals from Bashan. 19At the sacrifice I am preparing for you, you will eat fat till you are glutted and drink blood till you are drunk. 20At my table you will eat your fill of horses and riders, mighty men and soldiers of every kind,' declares the Sovereign LORD.

21"I will display my glory among the nations, and all the nations will see the punishment I inflict and the hand I lay upon them. 22From that day forward the house of Israel will know that I am the LORD their God. 23And the nations will know that the people of Israel went into exile for their sin, because they were unfaithful to me. So I hid my face from them and handed them over to their enemies, and they all fell by the sword. 24I dealt with them according to their uncleanness and their offences, and I hid my face from them.

25"Therefore this is what the Sovereign LORD says: I will now bring Jacob back from captivity[f] and will have compassion on all the people of Israel, and I will be zealous for my holy name. 26They will forget their shame and all the unfaithfulness they showed towards me when they lived in safety in their land with no-one to make them afraid. 27When I have brought them back from the nations and have gathered them from the countries of their enemies, I will show myself holy through them in the sight of many nations. 28Then they will know that I am the LORD their God, for though I sent them into exile among the nations, I will gather them to their own land, not leaving any behind. 29I will no longer hide my face from them, for I will pour out

a 1 Or Gog, prince of Rosh,   b 11 Or of   c 11 That is, the Dead Sea   d 11 Hamon Gog means hordes of Gog.
e 16 Hamonah means horde.   f 25 Or now restore the fortunes of Jacob

my Spirit on the house of Israel, declares the Sovereign LORD."

The New Temple Area

40 In the twenty-fifth year of our exile, at the beginning of the year, on the tenth of the month, in the fourteenth year after the fall of the city — on that very day the hand of the LORD was upon me and he took me there. [2]In visions of God he took me to the land of Israel and set me on a very high mountain, on whose south side were some buildings that looked like a city. [3]He took me there, and I saw a man whose appearance was like bronze; he was standing in the gateway with a linen cord and a measuring rod in his hand. [4]The man said to me, "Son of man, look with your eyes and hear with your ears and pay attention to everything I am going to show you, for that is why you have been brought here. Tell the house of Israel everything you see."

40:4 In the next chapter, we see Ezekiel's priestly concern with the temple. The description demonstrates the importance that was attached to the place where God was worshipped and where his glory dwelt. Israel could only be considered to be a nation rebuilt when God's glory was worshipped in Jerusalem, at the centre of their national life.

The East Gate to the Outer Court

[5]I saw a wall completely surrounding the temple area. The length of the measuring rod in the man's hand was six long cubits, each of which was a cubit[a] and a handbreadth.[b] He measured the wall; it was one measuring rod thick and one rod high.

[6]Then he went to the gate facing east. He climbed its steps and measured the threshold of the gate; it was one rod deep.[c] [7]The alcoves for the guards were one rod long and one rod wide, and the projecting walls between the alcoves were five cubits thick. And the threshold of the gate next to the portico facing the temple was one rod deep.

[8]Then he measured the portico of the gateway; [9]it[d] was eight cubits deep and its jambs were two cubits thick. The portico of the gateway faced the temple.

[10]Inside the east gate were three alcoves on each side; the three had the same measurements, and the faces of the projecting walls on each side had the same measurements. [11]Then he measured the width of the entrance to the gateway; it was ten cubits and its length was thirteen cubits. [12]In front of each alcove was a wall one cubit high, and the alcoves were six cubits square. [13]Then he measured the gateway from the top of the rear wall of one alcove to the top of the opposite one; the distance was twenty-five cubits from one parapet opening to the opposite one. [14]He measured along the faces of the projecting walls all around the inside of the gateway — sixty cubits. The measurement was up to the portico[e] facing the courtyard.[f] [15]The distance from the entrance of the gateway to the far end of its portico was fifty cubits. [16]The alcoves and the projecting walls inside the gateway were surmounted by narrow parapet openings all round, as was the portico; the openings all round faced inward. The faces of the projecting walls were decorated with palm trees.

The Outer Court

[17]Then he brought me into the outer court. There I saw some rooms and a pavement that had been constructed all round the court; there were thirty rooms along the pavement. [18]It abutted the sides of the gateways and was as wide as they were long; this was the lower pavement. [19]Then he measured the distance from the inside of the lower gateway to the outside of the inner court; it was a hundred cubits on the east side as well as on the north.

The North Gate

[20]Then he measured the length and width of the gate facing north, leading into the outer court. [21]Its alcoves — three on each side — its projecting walls and its portico had the same measurements as those of the first gateway. It was fifty cubits long and twenty-five cubits wide. [22]Its openings, its portico and its palm tree decorations had the same measurements as those of the gate facing east. Seven steps led up to it, with its portico opposite them. [23]There was a gate to the inner court facing the north gate, just as there was on the east. He measured from one gate to the opposite one; it was a hundred cubits.

The South Gate

[24]Then he led me to the south side and I saw a gate facing south. He measured its jambs and its portico, and they had the same measurements as the others. [25]The gateway and its portico had narrow openings all round, like the openings of the others. It was fifty cubits long and twenty-five cubits wide. [26]Seven steps led up to it, with its portico opposite them; it had palm tree decorations on the faces of the projecting walls on each side. [27]The inner court also had a gate facing south, and he measured from this gate to the outer gate on the south side; it was a hundred cubits.

Gates to the Inner Court

[28]Then he brought me into the inner court through the south gate, and he measured the south gate; it had the same measurements as the others. [29]Its alcoves, its

---

[a]5 The common cubit was about 1½ feet (about 0.5 metre).
[b]5 That is, about 3 inches (about 8 centimetres)
[c]6 Septuagint; Hebrew *deep, the first threshold, one rod deep*
[d]8, 9 Many Hebrew manuscripts, Septuagint, Vulgate and Syriac; most Hebrew manuscripts *gateway facing the temple; it was one rod deep.*
[9]*Then he measured the portico of the gateway; it*   [e]14 Septuagint; Hebrew *projecting wall*
[f]14 The meaning of the Hebrew for this verse is uncertain.

projecting walls and its portico had the same measurements as the others. The gateway and its portico had openings all round. It was fifty cubits long and twenty-five cubits wide. 30(The porticoes of the gateways around the inner court were twenty-five cubits wide and five cubits deep.) 31Its portico faced the outer court; palm trees decorated its jambs, and eight steps led up to it.

32Then he brought me to the inner court on the east side, and he measured the gateway; it had the same measurements as the others. 33Its alcoves, its projecting walls and its portico had the same measurements as the others. The gateway and its portico had openings all round. It was fifty cubits long and twenty-five cubits wide. 34Its portico faced the outer court; palm trees decorated the jambs on either side, and eight steps led up to it.

35Then he brought me to the north gate and measured it. It had the same measurements as the others, 36as did its alcoves, its projecting walls and its portico, and it had openings all round. It was fifty cubits long and twenty-five cubits wide. 37Its porticog faced the outer court; palm trees decorated the jambs on either side, and eight steps led up to it.

The Rooms for Preparing Sacrifices

38A room with a doorway was by the portico in each of the inner gateways, where the burnt offerings were washed. 39In the portico of the gateway were two tables on each side, on which the burnt offerings, sin offerings and guilt offerings were slaughtered. 40By the outside wall of the portico of the gateway, near the steps at the entrance to the north gateway were two tables, and on the other side of the steps were two tables. 41So there were four tables on one side of the gateway and four on the other—eight tables in all—on which the sacrifices were slaughtered. 42There were also four tables of dressed stone for the burnt offerings, each a cubit and a half long, a cubit and a half wide and a cubit high. On them were placed the utensils for slaughtering the burnt offerings and the other sacrifices. 43And double-pronged hooks, each a handbreadth long, were attached to the wall all around. The tables were for the flesh of the offerings.

Rooms for the Priests

44Outside the inner gate, within the inner court, were two rooms, oneh at the side of the north gate and facing south, and another at the side of the southi gate and facing north. 45He said to me, "The room facing south is for the priests who have charge of the temple, 46and the room facing north is for the priests who have charge of the altar. These are the sons of Zadok, who are the only Levites who may draw near to the LORD to minister before him."

47Then he measured the court: It was square—a hundred cubits long and a hundred cubits wide. And the altar was in front of the temple.

The Temple

48He brought me to the portico of the temple and measured the jambs of the portico; they were five cubits wide on either side. The width of the entrance was fourteen cubits and its projecting walls werej three cubits wide on either side. 49The portico was twenty cubits wide, and twelvek cubits from front to back. It was reached by a flight of stairs,l and there were pillars on each side of the jambs.

41 Then the man brought me to the outer sanctuary and measured the jambs; the width of the jambs was six cubitsa on each side.b 2The entrance was ten cubits wide, and the projecting walls on each side of it were five cubits wide. He also measured the outer sanctuary; it was forty cubits long and twenty cubits wide.

3Then he went into the inner sanctuary and measured the jambs of the entrance; each was two cubits wide. The entrance was six cubits wide, and the projecting walls on each side of it were seven cubits wide. 4And he measured the length of the inner sanctuary; it was twenty cubits, and its width was twenty cubits across the end of the outer sanctuary. He said to me, "This is the Most Holy Place."

5Then he measured the wall of the temple; it was six cubits thick, and each side room round the temple was four cubits wide. 6The side rooms were on three levels, one above another, thirty on each level. There were ledges all round the wall of the temple to serve as supports for the side rooms, so that the supports were not inserted into the wall of the temple. 7The side rooms all round the temple were wider at each successive level. The structure surrounding the temple was built in ascending stages, so that the rooms widened as one went upward. A stairway went up from the lowest floor to the top floor through the middle floor.

8I saw that the temple had a raised base all round it, forming the foundation of the side rooms. It was the length of the rod, six long cubits. 9The outer wall of the side rooms was five cubits thick. The open area between the side rooms of the temple 10and the ∟priests'⌐ rooms was twenty cubits wide all round the temple. 11There were entrances to the side rooms from the open area, one on the north and another on the south; and the base adjoining the open area was five cubits wide all round.

12The building facing the temple courtyard on the west side was seventy cubits wide. The wall of the building was five cubits thick all round, and its length was ninety cubits.

13Then he measured the temple; it was a hundred cubits long, and the temple courtyard and the building with its walls were also a hundred cubits long. 14The width of the temple courtyard on the east, including the front of the temple, was a hundred cubits.

15Then he measured the length of the building facing the courtyard at the rear of the temple, including its galleries on each side; it was a hundred cubits.

The outer sanctuary, the inner sanctuary and the

---

g37 Septuagint (see also verses 31 and 34); Hebrew jambs   h44 Septuagint; Hebrew were rooms for singers, which were
i44 Septuagint; Hebrew east   j48 Septuagint; Hebrew entrance was   k49 Septuagint; Hebrew eleven
l49 Hebrew; Septuagint Ten steps led up to it   a1 The common cubit was about 1½ feet (about 0.5 metre).
b1 One Hebrew manuscript and Septuagint; most Hebrew manuscripts side, the width of the tent

portico facing the court, [16]as well as the thresholds and the narrow windows and galleries round the three of them — everything beyond and including the threshold was covered with wood. The floor, the wall up to the windows, and the windows were covered. [17]In the space above the outside of the entrance to the inner sanctuary and on the walls at regular intervals all round the inner and outer sanctuary [18]were carved cherubim and palm trees. Palm trees alternated with cherubim. Each cherub had two faces: [19]the face of a man towards the palm tree on one side and the face of a lion towards the palm tree on the other. They were carved all round the whole temple. [20]From the floor to the area above the entrance, cherubim and palm trees were carved on the wall of the outer sanctuary.

[21]The outer sanctuary had a rectangular door-frame, and the one at the front of the Most Holy Place was similar. [22]There was a wooden altar three cubits high and two cubits square;[c] its corners, its base[d] and its sides were of wood. The man said to me, "This is the table that is before the LORD." [23]Both the outer sanctuary and the Most Holy Place had double doors. [24]Each door had two leaves — two hinged leaves for each door. [25]And on the doors of the outer sanctuary were carved cherubim and palm trees like those carved on the walls, and there was a wooden overhang on the front of the portico. [26]On the side walls of the portico were narrow windows with palm trees carved on each side. The side rooms of the temple also had overhangs.

Rooms for the Priests

42 Then the man led me northward into the outer court and brought me to the rooms opposite the temple courtyard and opposite the outer wall on the north side. [2]The building whose door faced north was a hundred cubits[a] long and fifty cubits wide. [3]Both in the section twenty cubits from the inner court and in the section opposite the pavement of the outer court, gallery faced gallery at the three levels. [4]In front of the rooms was an inner passageway ten cubits wide and a hundred cubits[b] long. Their doors were on the north. [5]Now the upper rooms were narrower, for the galleries took more space from them than from the rooms on the lower and middle floors of the building. [6]The rooms on the third floor had no pillars, as the courts had; so they were smaller in floor space than those on the lower and middle floors. [7]There was an outer wall parallel to the rooms and the outer court; it extended in front of the rooms for fifty cubits. [8]While the row of rooms on the side next to the outer court was fifty cubits long, the row on the side nearest the sanctuary was a hundred cubits long. [9]The lower rooms had an entrance on the east side as one enters them from the outer court.

[10]On the south side[c] along the length of the wall of the outer court, adjoining the temple courtyard and opposite the outer wall, were rooms [11]with a passage-

way in front of them. These were like the rooms on the north; they had the same length and width, with similar exits and dimensions. Similar to the doorways on the north [12]were the doorways of the rooms on the south. There was a doorway at the beginning of the passageway that was parallel to the corresponding wall extending eastward, by which one enters the rooms.

[13]Then he said to me, "The north and south rooms facing the temple courtyard are the priests' rooms, where the priests who approach the LORD will eat the most holy offerings. There they will put the most holy offerings — the grain offerings, the sin offerings and the guilt offerings — for the place is holy. [14]Once the priests enter the holy precincts, they are not to go into the outer court until they leave behind the garments in which they minister, for these are holy. They are to put on other clothes before they go near the places that are for the people."

[15]When he had finished measuring what was inside the temple area, he led me out by the east gate and measured the area all around: [16]He measured the east side with the measuring rod; it was five hundred cubits.[d] [17]He measured the north side; it was five hundred cubits[e] by the measuring rod. [18]He measured the south side; it was five hundred cubits by the measuring rod. [19]Then he turned to the west side and measured; it was five hundred cubits by the measuring rod. [20]So he measured the area on all four sides. It had a wall round it, five hundred cubits long and five hundred cubits wide, to separate the holy from the common.

The Glory Returns to the Temple

43 Then the man brought me to the gate facing east, [2]and I saw the glory of the God of Israel coming from the east. His voice was like the roar of rushing waters, and the land was radiant with his glory. [3]The vision I saw was like the vision I had seen when he[a] came to destroy the city and like the visions I had seen by the Kebar River, and I fell face down. [4]The glory of the LORD entered the temple through the gate facing east. [5]Then the Spirit lifted me up and brought me into the inner court, and the glory of the LORD filled the temple.

[6]While the man was standing beside me, I heard someone speaking to me from inside the temple. [7]He said: "Son of man, this is the place of my throne and the place for the soles of my feet. This is where I will live among the Israelites for ever. The house of Israel will never again defile my holy name — neither they nor their kings — by their prostitution[b] and the lifeless idols[c] of their kings at their high places. [8]When they placed their threshold next to my threshold and their doorposts beside my doorposts, with only a wall between me and them, they defiled my holy name by their detestable practices. So I destroyed them in my

---

c22 Septuagint; Hebrew *long*   d22 Septuagint; Hebrew *length*
b4 Septuagint and Syriac; Hebrew *and one cubit*   c10 Septuagint; Hebrew *Eastward*
d16 See Septuagint of verse 17; Hebrew *rods*; also in verses 18 and 19.   e17 Septuagint; Hebrew *rods*
a3 Some Hebrew manuscripts and Vulgate; most Hebrew manuscripts *I*   b7 Or *their spiritual adultery*; also in verse 9
c7 Or *the corpses*; also in verse 9

a2 The common cubit was about 1½ feet (about 0.5 metre).

anger. [9]Now let them put away from me their prostitution and the lifeless idols of their kings, and I will live among them for ever.

[10]"Son of man, describe the temple to the people of Israel, that they may be ashamed of their sins. Let them consider the plan, [11]and if they are ashamed of all they have done, make known to them the design of the temple — its arrangement, its exits and entrances — its whole design and all its regulations[d] and laws. Write these down before them so that they may be faithful to its design and follow all its regulations.

[12]"This is the law of the temple: All the surrounding area on top of the mountain will be most holy. Such is the law of the temple.

The Altar

[13]"These are the measurements of the altar in long cubits, that cubit being a cubit[e] and a handbreadth:[f] Its gutter is a cubit deep and a cubit wide, with a rim of one span[g] around the edge. And this is the height of the altar: [14]From the gutter on the ground up to the lower ledge it is two cubits high and a cubit wide, and from the smaller ledge up to the larger ledge it is four cubits high and a cubit wide. [15]The altar hearth is four cubits high, and four horns project upward from the hearth. [16]The altar hearth is square, twelve cubits long and twelve cubits wide. [17]The upper ledge also is square, fourteen cubits long and fourteen cubits wide, with a rim of half a cubit and a gutter of a cubit all round. The steps of the altar face east."

[18]Then he said to me, "Son of man, this is what the Sovereign LORD says: These will be the regulations for sacrificing burnt offerings and sprinkling blood upon the altar when it is built: [19]You are to give a young bull as a sin offering to the priests, who are Levites, of the family of Zadok, who come near to minister before me, declares the Sovereign LORD. [20]You are to take some of its blood and put it on the four horns of the altar and on the four corners of the upper ledge and all round the rim, and so purify the altar and make atonement for it. [21]You are to take the bull for the sin offering and burn it in the designated part of the temple area outside the sanctuary.

[22]"On the second day you are to offer a male goat without defect for a sin offering, and the altar is to be purified as it was purified with the bull. [23]When you have finished purifying it, you are to offer a young bull and a ram from the flock, both without defect. [24]You are to offer them before the LORD, and the priests are to sprinkle salt on them and sacrifice them as a burnt offering to the LORD.

[25]"For seven days you are to provide a male goat daily for a sin offering; you are also to provide a young bull and a ram from the flock, both without defect. [26]For seven days they are to make atonement for the altar and cleanse it; thus they will dedicate it. [27]At the end of these days, from the eighth day on, the priests are to present your burnt offerings and fellowship offerings[h] on the altar. Then I will accept you, declares the Sovereign LORD."

The Prince, the Levites, the Priests

44 Then the man brought me back to the outer gate of the sanctuary, the one facing east, and it was shut. [2]The LORD said to me, "This gate is to remain shut. It must not be opened; no-one may enter through it. It is to remain shut because the LORD, the God of Israel, has entered through it. [3]The prince himself is the only one who may sit inside the gateway to eat in the presence of the LORD. He is to enter by way of the portico of the gateway and go out the same way."

[4]Then the man brought me by way of the north gate to the front of the temple. I looked and saw the glory of the LORD filling the temple of the LORD, and I fell face down.

[5]The LORD said to me, "Son of man, look carefully, listen closely and give attention to everything I tell you concerning all the regulations regarding the temple of the LORD. Give attention to the entrance of the temple and all the exits of the sanctuary. [6]Say to the rebellious house of Israel, 'This is what the Sovereign LORD says: Enough of your detestable practices, O house of Israel! [7]In addition to all your other detestable practices, you brought foreigners uncircumcised in heart and flesh into my sanctuary, desecrating my temple while you offered me food, fat and blood, and you broke my covenant. [8]Instead of carrying out your duty in regard to my holy things, you put others in charge of my sanctuary. [9]This is what the Sovereign LORD says: No foreigner uncircumcised in heart and flesh is to enter my sanctuary, not even the foreigners who live among the Israelites.

[10]" 'The Levites who went far from me when Israel went astray and who wandered from me after their idols must bear the consequences of their sin. [11]They may serve in my sanctuary, having charge of the gates of the temple and serving in it; they may slaughter the burnt offerings and sacrifices for the people and stand before the people and serve them. [12]But because they served them in the presence of their idols and made the house of Israel fall into sin, therefore I have sworn with uplifted hand that they must bear the consequences of their sin, declares the Sovereign LORD. [13]They are not to come near to serve me as priests or come near any of my holy things or my most holy offerings; they must bear the shame of their detestable practices. [14]Yet I will put them in charge of the duties of the temple and all the work that is to be done in it.

[15]" 'But the priests, who are Levites and descendants of Zadok and who faithfully carried out the duties of my sanctuary when the Israelites went astray from me, are to come near to minister before me; they are to stand before me to offer sacrifices of fat and blood, declares the Sovereign LORD. [16]They alone are to enter my sanctuary; they alone are to come near my table to minister before me and perform my service.

[17]" 'When they enter the gates of the inner court, they are to wear linen clothes; they must not wear any woollen garment while ministering at the gates of the inner court or inside the temple. [18]They are to wear linen turbans on their heads and linen undergarments

[d]11 Some Hebrew manuscripts and Septuagint; most Hebrew manuscripts *regulations and its whole design*
[e]13 The common cubit was about 1½ feet (about 0.5 metre).   [f]13 That is, about 3 inches (about 8 centimetres)
[g]13 That is, about 9 inches (about 23 centimetres)   [h]27 Traditionally *peace offerings*

round their waists. They must not wear anything that makes them perspire. [19]When they go out into the outer court where the people are, they are to take off the clothes they have been ministering in and leave them in the sacred rooms, and put on other clothes, so that they do not consecrate the people by means of their garments.

[20]" 'They must not shave their heads or let their hair grow long, but they are to keep the hair of their heads trimmed. [21]No priest is to drink wine when he enters the inner court. [22]They must not marry widows or divorced women; they may marry only virgins of Israelite descent or widows of priests. [23]They are to teach my people the difference between the holy and the common and show them how to distinguish between the unclean and the clean.

[24]" 'In any dispute, the priests are to serve as judges and decide it according to my ordinances. They are to keep my laws and my decrees for all my appointed feasts, and they are to keep my Sabbaths holy.

[25]" 'A priest must not defile himself by going near a dead person; however, if the dead person was his father or mother, son or daughter, brother or unmarried sister, then he may defile himself. [26]After he is cleansed, he must wait seven days. [27]On the day he goes into the inner court of the sanctuary to minister in the sanctuary, he is to offer a sin offering for himself, declares the Sovereign LORD.

[28]" 'I am to be the only inheritance the priests have. You are to give them no possession in Israel; I will be their possession. [29]They will eat the grain offerings, the sin offerings and the guilt offerings; and everything in Israel devoted[a] to the LORD will belong to them. [30]The best of all the firstfruits and of all your special gifts will belong to the priests. You are to give them the first portion of your ground meal so that a blessing may rest on your household. [31]The priests must not eat anything, bird or animal, found dead or torn by wild animals.

Division of the Land

45 " 'When you allot the land as an inheritance, you are to present to the LORD a portion of the land as a sacred district, 25,000 cubits long and 20,000[a] cubits wide; the entire area will be holy. [2]Of this, a section 500 cubits square is to be for the sanctuary, with 50 cubits around it for open land. [3]In the sacred district, measure off a section 25,000 cubits[b] long and 10,000 cubits[c] wide. In it will be the sanctuary, the Most Holy Place. [4]It will be the sacred portion of the land for the priests, who minister in the sanctuary and who draw near to minister before the LORD. It will be a place for their houses as well as a holy place for the sanctuary. [5]An area 25,000 cubits long and 10,000 cubits wide will belong to the Levites, who serve in the temple, as their possession for towns to live in.[d]

[6]" 'You are to give the city as its property an area 5,000 cubits wide and 25,000 cubits long, adjoining the sacred portion; it will belong to the whole house of Israel.

[7]" 'The prince will have the land bordering each side of the area formed by the sacred district and the property of the city. It will extend westward from the west side and eastward from the east side, running lengthwise from the western to the eastern border parallel to one of the tribal portions. [8]This land will be his possession in Israel. And my princes will no longer oppress my people but will allow the house of Israel to possess the land according to their tribes.

[9]" 'This is what the Sovereign LORD says: You have gone far enough, O princes of Israel! Give up your violence and oppression and do what is just and right. Stop dispossessing my people, declares the Sovereign LORD. [10]You are to use accurate scales, an accurate ephah[e] and an accurate bath.[f] [11]The ephah and the bath are to be the same size, the bath containing a tenth of a homer[g] and the ephah a tenth of a homer; the homer is to be the standard measure for both. [12]The shekel[h] is to consist of twenty gerahs. Twenty shekels plus twenty-five shekels plus fifteen shekels equal one mina.[i]

Offerings and Holy Days

[13]" 'This is the special gift you are to offer: a sixth of an ephah from each homer of wheat and a sixth of an ephah from each homer of barley. [14]The prescribed portion of oil, measured by the bath, is a tenth of a bath from each cor (which consists of ten baths or one homer, for ten baths are equivalent to a homer). [15]Also one sheep is to be taken from every flock of two hundred from the well-watered pastures of Israel. These will be used for the grain offerings, burnt offerings and fellowship offerings[j] to make atonement for the people, declares the Sovereign LORD. [16]All the people of the land will participate in this special gift for the use of the prince in Israel. [17]It will be the duty of the prince to provide the burnt offerings, grain offerings and drink offerings at the festivals, the New Moons and the Sabbaths — at all the appointed feasts of the house of Israel. He will provide the sin offerings, grain offerings, burnt offerings and fellowship offerings to make atonement for the house of Israel.

[18]" 'This is what the Sovereign LORD says: In the first month on the first day you are to take a young bull without defect and purify the sanctuary. [19]The priest is to take some of the blood of the sin offering and put it on the doorposts of the temple, on the four corners of the upper ledge of the altar and on the gateposts of the inner court. [20]You are to do the same on the seventh day of the month for anyone who sins unintentionally or through ignorance; so you are to make atonement for the temple.

[21]" 'In the first month on the fourteenth day you are

---

a29 The Hebrew term refers to the irrevocable giving over of things or persons to the LORD.
a1 Septuagint (see also verses 3 and 5 and 48:9); Hebrew 10,000   b3 That is, about 7 miles (about 11 kilometres)
c3 That is, about 3 miles (about 5 kilometres)   d5 Septuagint; Hebrew temple; they will have as their possession 20 rooms
e10 An ephah was a dry measure.   f10 A bath was a liquid measure.   g11 A homer was a dry measure.
h12 A shekel weighed about ⅔ ounce (about 11.5 grams).   i12 That is, 60 shekels; the common mina was 50 shekels.
j15 Traditionally peace offerings; also in verse 17

to observe the Passover, a feast lasting seven days, during which you shall eat bread made without yeast. ²²On that day the prince is to provide a bull as a sin offering for himself and for all the people of the land. ²³Every day during the seven days of the Feast he is to provide seven bulls and seven rams without defect as a burnt offering to the LORD, and a male goat for a sin offering. ²⁴He is to provide as a grain offering an ephah for each bull and an ephah for each ram, along with a hin^k of oil for each ephah.

²⁵" 'During the seven days of the Feast, which begins in the seventh month on the fifteenth day, he is to make the same provision for sin offerings, burnt offerings, grain offerings and oil.

46 " 'This is what the Sovereign LORD says: The gate of the inner court facing east is to be shut on the six working days, but on the Sabbath day and on the day of the New Moon it is to be opened. ²The prince is to enter from the outside through the portico of the gateway and stand by the gatepost. The priests are to sacrifice his burnt offering and his fellowship offerings.^a He is to worship at the threshold of the gateway and then go out, but the gate will not be shut until evening. ³On the Sabbaths and New Moons the people of the land are to worship in the presence of the LORD at the entrance to that gateway. ⁴The burnt offering the prince brings to the LORD on the Sabbath day is to be six male lambs and a ram, all without defect. ⁵The grain offering given with the ram is to be an ephah,^b and the grain offering with the lambs is to be as much as he pleases, along with a hin^c of oil for each ephah. ⁶On the day of the New Moon he is to offer a young bull, six lambs and a ram, all without defect. ⁷He is to provide as a grain offering one ephah with the bull, one ephah with the ram, and with the lambs as much as he wants to give, along with a hin of oil with each ephah. ⁸When the prince enters, he is to go in through the portico of the gateway, and he is to come out the same way.

⁹" 'When the people of the land come before the LORD at the appointed feasts, whoever enters by the north gate to worship is to go out by the south gate; and whoever enters by the south gate is to go out by the north gate. No-one is to return through the gate by which he entered, but each is to go out by the opposite gate. ¹⁰The prince is to be among them, going in when they go in and going out when they go out.

¹¹" 'At the festivals and the appointed feasts, the grain offering is to be an ephah with a bull, an ephah with a ram, and with the lambs as much as one pleases, along with a hin of oil for each ephah. ¹²When the prince provides a freewill offering to the LORD — whether a burnt offering or fellowship offerings — the gate facing east is to be opened for him. He shall offer his burnt offering or his fellowship offerings as he does on the Sabbath day. Then he shall go out, and after he has gone out, the gate will be shut.

¹³" 'Every day you are to provide a year-old lamb without defect for a burnt offering to the LORD; morning by morning you shall provide it. ¹⁴You are also to provide with it morning by morning a grain offering, consisting of a sixth of an ephah with a third of a hin of oil to moisten the flour. The presenting of this grain offering to the LORD is a lasting ordinance. ¹⁵So the lamb and the grain offering and the oil shall be provided morning by morning for a regular burnt offering.

¹⁶" 'This is what the Sovereign LORD says: If the prince makes a gift from his inheritance to one of his sons, it will also belong to his descendants; it is to be their property by inheritance. ¹⁷If, however, he makes a gift from his inheritance to one of his servants, the servant may keep it until the year of freedom; then it will revert to the prince. His inheritance belongs to his sons only; it is theirs. ¹⁸The prince must not take any of the inheritance of the people, driving them off their property. He is to give his sons their inheritance out of his own property, so that none of my people will be separated from his property.' "

¹⁹Then the man brought me through the entrance at the side of the gate to the sacred rooms facing north, which belonged to the priests, and showed me a place at the western end. ²⁰He said to me, "This is the place where the priests will cook the guilt offering and the sin offering and bake the grain offering, to avoid bringing them into the outer court and consecrating the people."

²¹He then brought me to the outer court and led me round to its four corners, and I saw in each corner another court. ²²In the four corners of the outer court were enclosed^d courts, forty cubits long and thirty cubits wide; each of the courts in the four corners was the same size. ²³Around the inside of each of the four courts was a ledge of stone, with places for fire built all round under the ledge. ²⁴He said to me, "These are the kitchens where those who minister at the temple will cook the sacrifices of the people."

The River From the Temple

47 The man brought me back to the entrance of the temple, and I saw water coming out from under the threshold of the temple towards the east (for the temple faced east). The water was coming down from under the south side of the temple, south of the altar. ²He then brought me out through the north gate and led me round the outside to the outer gate facing east, and the water was flowing from the south side.

³As the man went eastward with a measuring line in his hand, he measured off a thousand cubits^a and then led me through water that was ankle-deep. ⁴He measured off another thousand cubits and led me through water that was knee-deep. He measured off another thousand and led me through water that was up to the waist. ⁵He measured off another thousand, but now it was a river that I could not cross, because the water had risen and was deep enough to swim in — a river that no-one could cross. ⁶He asked me, "Son of man, do you see this?"

Then he led me back to the bank of the river. ⁷When I arrived there, I saw a great number of trees on each side of the river. ⁸He said to me, "This water flows

---

k24 That is, probably about 6 pints (about 4 litres)
b5 That is, probably about ⅗ bushel (about 22 litres)
d22 The meaning of the Hebrew for this word is uncertain.

a2 Traditionally *peace offerings*; also in verse 12
c5 That is, probably about 6 pints (about 4 litres)
a3 That is, about 1,500 feet (about 460 metres)

towards the eastern region and goes down into the Arabah,[b] where it enters the Sea.[c] When it empties into the Sea,[c] the water there becomes fresh. [9]Swarms of living creatures will live wherever the river flows. There will be large numbers of fish, because this water flows there and makes the salt water fresh; so where the river flows everything will live. [10]Fishermen will stand along the shore; from En Gedi to En Eglaim there will be places for spreading nets. The fish will be of many kinds—like the fish of the Great Sea.[d] [11]But the swamps and marshes will not become fresh; they will be left for salt. [12]Fruit trees of all kinds will grow on both banks of the river. Their leaves will not wither, nor will their fruit fail. Every month they will bear, because the water from the sanctuary flows to them. Their fruit will serve for food and their leaves for healing."

The Boundaries of the Land

[13]This is what the Sovereign Lord says: "These are the boundaries by which you are to divide the land for an inheritance among the twelve tribes of Israel, with two portions for Joseph. [14]You are to divide it equally among them. Because I swore with uplifted hand to give it to your forefathers, this land will become your inheritance.

[15]"This is to be the boundary of the land:

"On the north side it will run from the Great Sea by the Hethlon road past Lebo[e] Hamath to Zedad, [16]Berothah[f] and Sibraim (which lies on the border between Damascus and Hamath), as far as Hazer Hatticon, which is on the border of Hauran. [17]The boundary will extend from the sea to Hazar Enan,[g] along the northern border of Damascus, with the border of Hamath to the north. This will be the north boundary.
[18]"On the east side the boundary will run between Hauran and Damascus, along the Jordan between Gilead and the land of Israel, to the eastern sea and as far as Tamar.[h] This will be the east boundary.
[19]"On the south side it will run from Tamar as far as the waters of Meribah Kadesh, then along the Wadi of Egypt, to the Great Sea. This will be the south boundary.
[20]"On the west side, the Great Sea will be the boundary to a point opposite Lebo[i] Hamath. This will be the west boundary.

[21]"You are to distribute this land among yourselves according to the tribes of Israel. [22]You are to allot it as an inheritance for yourselves and for the aliens who have settled among you and who have children. You are to consider them as native-born Israelites; along with you they are to be allotted an inheritance among the tribes of Israel. [23]In whatever tribe the alien settles, there you are to give him his inheritance," declares the Sovereign Lord.

The Division of the Land

48 "These are the tribes, listed by name: At the northern frontier, Dan will have one portion; it will follow the Hethlon road to Lebo[a] Hamath; Hazar Enan and the northern border of Damascus next to Hamath will be part of its border from the east side to the west side.

[2]"Asher will have one portion; it will border the territory of Dan from east to west.
[3]"Naphtali will have one portion; it will border the territory of Asher from east to west.
[4]"Manasseh will have one portion; it will border the territory of Naphtali from east to west.
[5]"Ephraim will have one portion; it will border the territory of Manasseh from east to west.
[6]"Reuben will have one portion; it will border the territory of Ephraim from east to west.
[7]"Judah will have one portion; it will border the territory of Reuben from east to west.
[8]"Bordering the territory of Judah from east to west will be the portion you are to present as a special gift. It will be 25,000 cubits[b] wide, and its length from east to west will equal one of the tribal portions; the sanctuary will be in the centre of it.
[9]"The special portion you are to offer to the Lord will be 25,000 cubits long and 10,000 cubits[c] wide. [10]This will be the sacred portion for the priests. It will be 25,000 cubits long on the north side, 10,000 cubits wide on the west side, 10,000 cubits wide on the east side and 25,000 cubits long on the south side. In the centre of it will be the sanctuary of the Lord. [11]This will be for the consecrated priests, the Zadokites, who were faithful in serving me and did not go astray as the Levites did when the Israelites went astray. [12]It will be a special gift to them from the sacred portion of the land, a most holy portion, bordering the territory of the Levites.
[13]"Alongside the territory of the priests, the Levites will have an allotment 25,000 cubits long and 10,000 cubits wide. Its total length will be 25,000 cubits and its width 10,000 cubits. [14]They must not sell or exchange any of it. This is the best of the land and must not pass into other hands, because it is holy to the Lord.
[15]"The remaining area, 5,000 cubits wide and 25,000 cubits long, will be for the common use of the city, for houses and for pasture-land. The city will be in the centre of it [16]and will have these measurements: the north side 4,500 cubits, the south side 4,500 cubits, the east side 4,500 cubits, and the west side 4,500 cubits. [17]The pasture-land for the city will be 250 cubits on the north, 250 cubits on the south, 250 cubits on the east, and 250 cubits on the west. [18]What remains of the area, bordering on the sacred portion and running the length of it, will be 10,000 cubits on the east side and 10,000 cubits on the west side. Its

---

b8 Or *the Jordan Valley*   c8 That is, the Dead Sea   d10 That is, the Mediterranean; also in verses 15, 19 and 20
e15 Or *past the entrance to*   f15, 16 See Septuagint and Ezekiel 48:1; Hebrew *road to go into Zedad,* 16Hamath, Berothah
g17 Hebrew *Enon,* a variant of *Enan*   h18 Septuagint and Syriac; Hebrew *Israel. You will measure to the eastern sea*
i20 Or *opposite the entrance to*   a1 Or *to the entrance to*   b8 That is, about 7 miles (about 11 kilometres)
c9 That is, about 3 miles (about 5 kilometres)

produce will supply food for the workers of the city. ¹⁹The workers from the city who farm it will come from all the tribes of Israel. ²⁰The entire portion will be a square, 25,000 cubits on each side. As a special gift you will set aside the sacred portion, along with the property of the city.

²¹"What remains on both sides of the area formed by the sacred portion and the city property will belong to the prince. It will extend eastward from the 25,000 cubits of the sacred portion to the eastern border, and westward from the 25,000 cubits to the western border. Both these areas running the length of the tribal portions will belong to the prince, and the sacred portion with the temple sanctuary will be in the centre of them. ²²So the property of the Levites and the property of the city will lie in the centre of the area that belongs to the prince. The area belonging to the prince will lie between the border of Judah and the border of Benjamin.

²³"As for the rest of the tribes: Benjamin will have one portion; it will extend from the east side to the west side.

²⁴"Simeon will have one portion; it will border the territory of Benjamin from east to west.

²⁵"Issachar will have one portion; it will border the territory of Simeon from east to west.

²⁶"Zebulun will have one portion; it will border the territory of Issachar from east to west.

²⁷"Gad will have one portion; it will border the territory of Zebulun from east to west.

²⁸"The southern boundary of Gad will run south from Tamar to the waters of Meribah Kadesh, then along the Wadi ⌊of Egypt⌋ to the Great Sea. ᵈ

²⁹"This is the land you are to allot as an inheritance to the tribes of Israel, and these will be their portions," declares the Sovereign LORD.

The Gates of the City

³⁰"These will be the exits of the city: Beginning on the north side, which is 4,500 cubits long, ³¹the gates of the city will be named after the tribes of Israel. The three gates on the north side will be the gate of Reuben, the gate of Judah and the gate of Levi.

³²"On the east side, which is 4,500 cubits long, will be three gates: the gate of Joseph, the gate of Benjamin and the gate of Dan.

³³"On the south side, which measures 4,500 cubits, will be three gates: the gate of Simeon, the gate of Issachar and the gate of Zebulun.

³⁴"On the west side, which is 4,500 cubits long, will be three gates: the gate of Gad, the gate of Asher and the gate of Naphtali.

³⁵"The distance all around will be 18,000 cubits.

"And the name of the city from that time on will be:

THE LORD IS THERE."

ᵈ28 That is, the Mediterranean

Daniel

A Real Test of Faith

The book of Daniel stands out as something different among the prophetic books of the Bible. Unlike Isaiah and Jeremiah there was no calling and commissioning of the prophet, and he did not obviously preach to his contemporaries, but that does not mean that the book is without prophetic significance. It tells the story of a man who was taken a prisoner by the Babylonians during the sacking of Jerusalem in 605 BC, along with the majority of the population of Jerusalem. It addresses the pressures faced by these Jewish hostages as they tried to keep their faith alive and vibrant in a foreign land where they were persecuted, and where the temptation to give up their faith and take up pagan worship was very strong.

Two Major Episodes

The book is roughly divided into two distinct sections. The first, chapters 1—6, begins by giving a brief account of Nebuchadnezzar's tyrade on Jerusalem, and then tells how Daniel became a court official in Babylon. He refused to defile himself by eating from the king's table (see the note on 1:8), and was able to interpret the king's dreams. The central and most significant part of this episode is the account of the three court officials, Shadrach, Meshach, and Abednigo, being thrown into a blazing hot furnace for refusing to worship the golden idol which Nebuchadnezzar had constructed, and which he had commanded the whole of Babylon to worship. Because of their constancy and faithfulness to God they were spared from their ordeal. They were able to show how, despite such dire circumstances, God shows himself to be sovereign over even the most powerful and seemingly indestructible earthly ruler. This first episode ends by telling how Nebuchadnezzar was succeeded by Belshazzar, and how Daniel bravely foretold the downfall of Babylon to Darius, ruler of the Medes. Daniel continued in the court of Darius, but carried on worshipping God and ended up being thrown into a den of lions for doing so. But God saved Daniel from his ordeal, and showed how his purposes always come to fulfilment for those who trust him.

Out of This World

The second episode of the book is different. It consists of a series of visions, which look forward to the future, using images and language which were familiar to near-Eastern culture. They may strike us as strange, and they sound a bit like scenes from Star Trek, giving an extra-terrestrial vision of nations battling it out to rule the world. Like the first episode of the book, these visions have one overall purpose: to show how God is the sovereign Lord of all the world, and how he is active in the affairs of men and women, and controls the future direction of history. No matter how skilled a nation is on the battlefield, the people must finally be brought down to worship before the Son of Man, a title which was later used in the New Testament to describe Jesus, where they will discover where true strength and sovereignty comes from.

Daniel's Training in Babylon

1 In the third year of the reign of Jehoiakim king of Judah, Nebuchadnezzar king of Babylon came to Jerusalem and besieged it. [2]And the Lord delivered Jehoiakim king of Judah into his hand, along with some of the articles from the temple of God. These he carried off to the temple of his god in Babylonia[a] and put in the treasure-house of his god.

[3]Then the king ordered Ashpenaz, chief of his court officials, to bring in some of the Israelites from the royal family and the nobility — [4]young men without any physical defect, handsome, showing aptitude for every kind of learning, well informed, quick to understand, and qualified to serve in the king's palace. He was to teach them the language and literature of the Babylonians.[b] [5]The king assigned them a daily amount of food and wine from the king's table. They were to be trained for three years, and after that they were to enter the king's service.

[6]Among these were some from Judah: Daniel, Hananiah, Mishael and Azariah. [7]The chief official gave them new names: to Daniel, the name Belteshazzar; to Hananiah, Shadrach; to Mishael, Meshach; and to Azariah, Abednego.

[8]But Daniel resolved not to defile himself with the royal food and wine, and he asked the chief official for permission not to defile himself in this way. [9]Now God had caused the official to show favour and sympathy to Daniel, [10]but the official told Daniel, "I am afraid of my lord the king, who has assigned your[c] food and drink. Why should he see you looking worse than the other young men of your age? The king would then have my head because of you."

1:8   Daniel's refusal to eat the king's food was not just rudeness but a matter of faithfulness to God, because some of the food and wine from the king's table would have been used in pagan sacrifices. It is also highly likely that the food would have consisted of meat, such as pork, that was considered unclean under the Law or food which may not have been slaughtered and prepared according to the Law.

---

[11]Daniel then said to the guard whom the chief official had appointed over Daniel, Hananiah, Mishael and Azariah, [12]"Please test your servants for ten days: Give us nothing but vegetables to eat and water to drink.

[13]Then compare our appearance with that of the young men who eat the royal food, and treat your servants in accordance with what you see." [14]So he agreed to this and tested them for ten days.

[15]At the end of the ten days they looked healthier and better nourished than any of the young men who ate the royal food. [16]So the guard took away their choice food and the wine they were to drink and gave them vegetables instead.

[17]To these four young men God gave knowledge and understanding of all kinds of literature and learning. And Daniel could understand visions and dreams of all kinds.

[18]At the end of the time set by the king to bring them in, the chief official presented them to Nebuchadnezzar. [19]The king talked with them, and he found none equal to Daniel, Hananiah, Mishael and Azariah; so they entered the king's service. [20]In every matter of wisdom and understanding about which the king questioned them, he found them ten times better than all the magicians and enchanters in his whole kingdom.

[21]And Daniel remained there until the first year of King Cyrus.

Nebuchadnezzar's Dream

2 In the second year of his reign, Nebuchadnezzar had dreams; his mind was troubled and he could not sleep. [2]So the king summoned the magicians, enchanters, sorcerers and astrologers[a] to tell him what he had dreamed. When they came in and stood before the king, [3]he said to them, "I have had a dream that troubles me and I want to know what it means."[b]

[4]Then the astrologers answered the king in Aramaic,[c] "O king, live for ever! Tell your servants the dream, and we will interpret it."

2:4   The reference to the astrologers speaking in Aramaic is a significant one as here the entire language of the book changes from Hebrew to Aramaic, until the end of chapter 7. It has been suggested that this linguistic shift is due to the fact that the issues which the writer addresses are of importance to those living beyond the Hebrew-speaking world. The narrative reverts to Hebrew in chapter 8, when the book seems to be responding to issues which specifically concern the Jews.

---

a2 Hebrew Shinar   b4 Or Chaldeans   c10 The Hebrew for your and you in this verse is plural.
a2 Or Chaldeans; also in verses 4, 5 and 10   b3 Or was   c4 The text from here through chapter 7 is in Aramaic.

5The king replied to the astrologers, "This is what I have firmly decided: If you do not tell me what my dream was and interpret it, I will have you cut into pieces and your houses turned into piles of rubble. 6But if you tell me the dream and explain it, you will receive from me gifts and rewards and great honour. So tell me the dream and interpret it for me."

7Once more they replied, "Let the king tell his servants the dream, and we will interpret it."

8Then the king answered, "I am certain that you are trying to gain time, because you realise that this is what I have firmly decided: 9If you do not tell me the dream, there is just one penalty for you. You have conspired to tell me misleading and wicked things, hoping the situation will change. So then, tell me the dream, and I will know that you can interpret it for me."

10The astrologers answered the king, "There is not a man on earth who can do what the king asks! No king, however great and mighty, has ever asked such a thing of any magician or enchanter or astrologer. 11What the king asks is too difficult. No-one can reveal it to the king except the gods, and they do not live among men."

12This made the king so angry and furious that he ordered the execution of all the wise men of Babylon. 13So the decree was issued to put the wise men to death, and men were sent to look for Daniel and his friends to put them to death.

14When Arioch, the commander of the king's guard, had gone out to put to death the wise men of Babylon, Daniel spoke to him with wisdom and tact. 15He asked the king's officer, "Why did the king issue such a harsh decree?" Arioch then explained the matter to Daniel. 16At this, Daniel went in to the king and asked for time, so that he might interpret the dream for him.

17Then Daniel returned to his house and explained the matter to his friends Hananiah, Mishael and Azariah. 18He urged them to plead for mercy from the God of heaven concerning this mystery, so that he and his friends might not be executed with the rest of the wise men of Babylon. 19During the night the mystery was revealed to Daniel in a vision. Then Daniel praised the God of heaven 20and said:

"Praise be to the name of God for ever and ever;
    wisdom and power are his.
21He changes times and seasons;
    he sets up kings and deposes them.
He gives wisdom to the wise
    and knowledge to the discerning.
22He reveals deep and hidden things;
    he knows what lies in darkness,
    and light dwells with him.
23I thank and praise you, O God of my fathers:
    You have given me wisdom and power,
you have made known to me what we asked of
        you,
you have made known to us the dream of the
        king."

Daniel Interprets the Dream

24Then Daniel went to Arioch, whom the king had appointed to execute the wise men of Babylon, and said to him, "Do not execute the wise men of Babylon. Take me to the king, and I will interpret his dream for him."

25Arioch took Daniel to the king at once and said, "I have found a man among the exiles from Judah who can tell the king what his dream means."

26The king asked Daniel (also called Belteshazzar), "Are you able to tell me what I saw in my dream and interpret it?"

27Daniel replied, "No wise man, enchanter, magician or diviner can explain to the king the mystery he has asked about, 28but there is a God in heaven who reveals mysteries. He has shown King Nebuchadnezzar what will happen in days to come. Your dream and the visions that passed through your mind as you lay on your bed are these:

29"As you were lying there, O king, your mind turned to things to come, and the revealer of mysteries showed you what is going to happen. 30As for me, this mystery has been revealed to me, not because I have greater wisdom than other living men, but so that you, O king, may know the interpretation and that you may understand what went through your mind.

31"You looked, O king, and there before you stood a large statue—an enormous, dazzling statue, awesome in appearance. 32The head of the statue was made of pure gold, its chest and arms of silver, its belly and thighs of bronze, 33its legs of iron, its feet partly of iron and partly of baked clay. 34While you were watching, a rock was cut out, but not by human hands. It struck the statue on its feet of iron and clay and smashed them. 35Then the iron, the clay, the bronze, the silver and the gold were broken to pieces at the same time and became like chaff on a threshing-floor in the summer. The wind swept them away without leaving a trace. But the rock that struck the statue became a huge mountain and filled the whole earth.

36"This was the dream, and now we will interpret it to the king. 37You, O king, are the king of kings. The God of heaven has given you dominion and power and might and glory; 38in your hands he has placed mankind and the beasts of the field and the birds of the air. Wherever they live, he has made you ruler over them all. You are that head of gold.

39"After you, another kingdom will rise, inferior to yours. Next, a third kingdom, one of bronze, will rule over the whole earth. 40Finally, there will be a fourth kingdom, strong as iron—for iron breaks and smashes everything—and as iron breaks things to pieces, so it will crush and break all the others. 41Just as you saw that the feet and toes were partly of baked clay and partly of iron, so this will be a divided kingdom; yet it will have some of the strength of iron in it, even as you saw iron mixed with clay. 42As the toes were partly iron and partly clay, so this kingdom will be partly strong and partly brittle. 43And just as you saw the iron mixed with baked clay, so the people will be a mixture and will not remain united, any more than iron mixes with clay.

44"In the time of those kings, the God of heaven will set up a kingdom that will never be destroyed, nor will it be left to another people. It will crush all those kingdoms and bring them to an end, but it will itself endure for ever. 45This is the meaning of the vision of the rock cut out of a mountain, but not by human hands—a rock that broke the iron, the bronze, the clay, the silver and the gold to pieces.

"The great God has shown the king what will take place in the future. The dream is true and the interpretation is trustworthy."

[46]Then King Nebuchadnezzar fell prostrate before Daniel and paid him honour and ordered that an offering and incense be presented to him. [47]The king said to Daniel, "Surely your God is the God of gods and the Lord of kings and a revealer of mysteries, for you were able to reveal this mystery."

[48]Then the king placed Daniel in a high position and lavished many gifts on him. He made him ruler over the entire province of Babylon and placed him in charge of all its wise men. [49]Moreover, at Daniel's request the king appointed Shadrach, Meshach and Abednego administrators over the province of Babylon, while Daniel himself remained at the royal court.

The Image of Gold and the Fiery Furnace

3 King Nebuchadnezzar made an image of gold, ninety feet high and nine feet[a] wide, and set it up on the plain of Dura in the province of Babylon. [2]He then summoned the satraps, prefects, governors, advisers, treasurers, judges, magistrates and all the other provincial officials to come to the dedication of the image he had set up. [3]So the satraps, prefects, governors, advisers, treasurers, judges, magistrates and all the other provincial officials assembled for the dedication of the image that King Nebuchadnezzar had set up, and they stood before it.

[4]Then the herald loudly proclaimed, "This is what you are commanded to do, O peoples, nations and men of every language: [5]As soon as you hear the sound of the horn, flute, zither, lyre, harp, pipes and all kinds of music, you must fall down and worship the image of gold that King Nebuchadnezzar has set up. [6]Whoever does not fall down and worship will immediately be thrown into a blazing furnace."

[7]Therefore, as soon as they heard the sound of the horn, flute, zither, lyre, harp and all kinds of music, all the peoples, nations and men of every language fell down and worshipped the image of gold that King Nebuchadnezzar had set up.

[8]At this time some astrologers[b] came forward and denounced the Jews. [9]They said to King Nebuchadnezzar, "O king, live for ever! [10]You have issued a decree, O king, that everyone who hears the sound of the horn, flute, zither, lyre, harp, pipes and all kinds of music must fall down and worship the image of gold, [11]and that whoever does not fall down and worship will be thrown into a blazing furnace. [12]But there are some Jews whom you have set over the affairs of the province of Babylon — Shadrach, Meshach and Abednego — who pay no attention to you, O king. They neither serve your gods nor worship the image of gold you have set up."

[13]Furious with rage, Nebuchadnezzar summoned Shadrach, Meshach and Abednego. So these men were brought before the king, [14]and Nebuchadnezzar said to them, "Is it true, Shadrach, Meshach and Abednego, that you do not serve my gods or worship the image of gold I have set up? [15]Now when you hear the sound of the horn, flute, zither, lyre, harp, pipes and all kinds of music, if you are ready to fall down and worship the image I made, very good. But if you do not worship it, you will be thrown immediately into a blazing furnace. Then what god will be able to rescue you from my hand?"

[16]Shadrach, Meshach and Abednego replied to the king, "O Nebuchadnezzar, we do not need to defend ourselves before you in this matter. [17]If we are thrown into the blazing furnace, the God we serve is able to save us from it, and he will rescue us from your hand, O king. [18]But even if he does not, we want you to know, O king, that we will not serve your gods or worship the image of gold you have set up."

[19]Then Nebuchadnezzar was furious with Shadrach, Meshach and Abednego, and his attitude towards them changed. He ordered the furnace to be heated seven times hotter than usual [20]and commanded some of the strongest soldiers in his army to tie up Shadrach, Meshach and Abednego and throw them into the blazing furnace. [21]So these men, wearing their robes, trousers, turbans and other clothes, were bound and thrown into the blazing furnace. [22]The king's command was so urgent and the furnace so hot that the flames of the fire killed the soldiers who took up Shadrach, Meshach and Abednego, [23]and these three men, firmly tied, fell into the blazing furnace.

3:19 Nebuchadnezzar's instruction to heat the furnace seven times hotter than usual may give the impression that it worked like a modern thermostat, with careful temperature control. It may well have been that the furnace was heated by two or three bellows, and it could have meant using seven times more bellows than usual. Or it may have been symbolic: in Jewish thought, seven was the "perfect" number and seven times hotter may have meant "completely hot" or "perfectly hot".

---

[24]Then King Nebuchadnezzar leaped to his feet in amazement and asked his advisers, "Weren't there three men that we tied up and threw into the fire?"

They replied, "Certainly, O king."

[25]He said, "Look! I see four men walking around in the fire, unbound and unharmed, and the fourth looks like a son of the gods."

[26]Nebuchadnezzar then approached the opening of the blazing furnace and shouted, "Shadrach, Meshach and Abednego, servants of the Most High God, come out! Come here!"

So Shadrach, Meshach and Abednego came out of the fire, [27]and the satraps, prefects, governors and royal advisers crowded around them. They saw that the fire had not harmed their bodies, nor was a hair of their heads singed; their robes were not scorched, and there was no smell of fire on them.

---

[a]1 Aramaic *sixty cubits high and six cubits wide* (about 27 metres high and 2.7 metres wide)   [b]8 Or *Chaldeans*

28Then Nebuchadnezzar said, "Praise be to the God of Shadrach, Meshach and Abednego, who has sent his angel and rescued his servants! They trusted in him and defied the king's command and were willing to give up their lives rather than serve or worship any god except their own God. 29Therefore I decree that the people of any nation or language who say anything against the God of Shadrach, Meshach and Abednego be cut into pieces and their houses be turned into piles of rubble, for no other god can save in this way."

30Then the king promoted Shadrach, Meshach and Abednego in the province of Babylon.

Nebuchadnezzar's Dream of a Tree

4 King Nebuchadnezzar,

To the peoples, nations and men of every language, who live in all the world:

May you prosper greatly!

2It is my pleasure to tell you about the miraculous signs and wonders that the Most High God has performed for me.

3How great are his signs,
how mighty his wonders!
His kingdom is an eternal kingdom;
his dominion endures from generation to generation.

4I, Nebuchadnezzar, was at home in my palace, contented and prosperous. 5I had a dream that made me afraid. As I was lying in my bed, the images and visions that passed through my mind terrified me. 6So I commanded that all the wise men of Babylon be brought before me to interpret the dream for me. 7When the magicians, enchanters, astrologers*a* and diviners came, I told them the dream, but they could not interpret it for me. 8Finally, Daniel came into my presence and I told him the dream. (He is called Belteshazzar, after the name of my god, and the spirit of the holy gods is in him.)

9I said, "Belteshazzar, chief of the magicians, I know that the spirit of the holy gods is in you, and no mystery is too difficult for you. Here is my dream; interpret it for me. 10These are the visions I saw while lying in my bed: I looked, and there before me stood a tree in the middle of the land. Its height was enormous. 11The tree grew large and strong and its top touched the sky; it was visible to the ends of the earth. 12Its leaves were beautiful, its fruit abundant, and on it was food for all. Under it the beasts of the field found shelter, and the birds of the air lived in its branches; from it every creature was fed.

13"In the visions I saw while lying in my bed, I looked, and there before me was a messenger,*b* a holy one, coming down from heaven. 14He called in a loud voice: 'Cut down the tree and trim off its branches; strip off its leaves and scatter its fruit. Let the animals flee from under it and the birds from its branches. 15But let the stump and its roots, bound with iron and bronze, remain in the ground, in the grass of the field.

" 'Let him be drenched with the dew of heaven, and let him live with the animals among the plants of the earth. 16Let his mind be changed from that of a man and let him be given the mind of an animal, till seven times*c* pass by for him.

17" 'The decision is announced by messengers, the holy ones declare the verdict, so that the living may know that the Most High is sovereign over the kingdoms of men and gives them to anyone he wishes and sets over them the lowliest of men.'

18"This is the dream that I, King Nebuchadnezzar, had. Now, Belteshazzar, tell me what it means, for none of the wise men in my kingdom can interpret it for me. But you can, because the spirit of the holy gods is in you."

Daniel Interprets the Dream

19Then Daniel (also called Belteshazzar) was greatly perplexed for a time, and his thoughts terrified him. So the king said, "Belteshazzar, do not let the dream or its meaning alarm you."

Belteshazzar answered, "My lord, if only the dream applied to your enemies and its meaning to your adversaries! 20The tree you saw, which grew large and strong, with its top touching the sky, visible to the whole earth, 21with beautiful leaves and abundant fruit, providing food for all, giving shelter to the beasts of the field, and having nesting places in its branches for the birds of the air — 22you, O king, are that tree! You have become great and strong; your greatness has grown until it reaches the sky, and your dominion extends to distant parts of the earth.

23"You, O king, saw a messenger, a holy one, coming down from heaven and saying, 'Cut down the tree and destroy it, but leave the stump, bound with iron and bronze, in the grass of the field, while its roots remain in the ground. Let him be drenched with the dew of heaven; let him live like the wild animals, until seven times pass by for him.'

24"This is the interpretation, O king, and this is the decree the Most High has issued against my lord the king: 25You will be driven away from people and will live with the wild animals; you will eat grass like cattle and be drenched with the dew of heaven. Seven times will pass by for you until you acknowledge that the Most High is sovereign over the kingdoms of men and gives them to anyone he wishes. 26The command to leave the stump of the tree with its roots means that your kingdom will be restored to you when you acknowledge that Heaven rules. 27Therefore, O king, be pleased to accept my advice: Renounce your sins by doing what is right, and your wickedness by being kind to the oppressed. It may be that then your prosperity will continue."

a7 Or *Chaldeans*   *b13* Or *watchman*; also in verses 17 and 23   *c16* Or *years*; also in verses 23, 25 and 32

4:26 In accordance with the Jewish custom which forbade anyone saying the divine name of God, "Yahweh", aloud, Daniel used "Heaven" instead of "God". In his Gospel, Matthew adopted a similar stance by saying "the kingdom of heaven" rather than "the kingdom of God".

The Dream Is Fulfilled

²⁸All this happened to King Nebuchadnezzar. ²⁹Twelve months later, as the king was walking on the roof of the royal palace of Babylon, ³⁰he said, "Is not this the great Babylon I have built as the royal residence, by my mighty power and for the glory of my majesty?"

³¹The words were still on his lips when a voice came from heaven, "This is what is decreed for you, King Nebuchadnezzar: Your royal authority has been taken from you. ³²You will be driven away from people and will live with the wild animals; you will eat grass like cattle. Seven times will pass by for you until you acknowledge that the Most High is sovereign over the kingdoms of men and gives them to anyone he wishes."

³³Immediately what had been said about Nebuchadnezzar was fulfilled. He was driven away from people and ate grass like cattle. His body was drenched with the dew of heaven until his hair grew like the feathers of an eagle and his nails like the claws of a bird.

³⁴At the end of that time, I, Nebuchadnezzar, raised my eyes towards heaven, and my sanity was restored. Then I praised the Most High; I honoured and glorified him who lives for ever.

His dominion is an eternal
   dominion;
his kingdom endures from
   generation to generation.
³⁵All the peoples of the earth
are regarded as nothing.
He does as he pleases
   with the powers of heaven
   and the peoples of the earth.
No-one can hold back his hand
   or say to him: "What have you
   done?"

³⁶At the same time that my sanity was restored, my honour and splendour were returned to me for the glory of my kingdom. My advisers and nobles sought me out, and I was restored to my throne and became even greater than before. ³⁷Now I, Nebuchadnezzar, praise and exalt and glorify the King of heaven, because everything he does is right and all his ways are just. And those who walk in pride he is able to humble.

The Writing on the Wall

5 King Belshazzar gave a great banquet for a thousand of his nobles and drank wine with them. ²While Belshazzar was drinking his wine, he gave orders to bring in the gold and silver goblets that Nebuchadnezzar his father[a] had taken from the temple in Jerusalem, so that the king and his nobles, his wives and his concubines might drink from them. ³So they brought in the gold goblets that had been taken from the temple of God in Jerusalem, and the king and his nobles, his wives and his concubines drank from them. ⁴As they drank the wine, they praised the gods of gold and silver, of bronze, iron, wood and stone.

⁵Suddenly the fingers of a human hand appeared and wrote on the plaster of the wall, near the lampstand in the royal palace. The king watched the hand as it wrote. ⁶His face turned pale and he was so frightened that his knees knocked together and his legs gave way.

⁷The king called out for the enchanters, astrologers[b] and diviners to be brought and said to these wise men of Babylon, "Whoever reads this writing and tells me what it means will be clothed in purple and have a gold chain placed around his neck, and he will be made the third highest ruler in the kingdom."

⁸Then all the king's wise men came in, but they could not read the writing or tell the king what it meant. ⁹So King Belshazzar became even more terrified and his face grew more pale. His nobles were baffled.

¹⁰The queen,[c] hearing the voices of the king and his nobles, came into the banquet hall. "O king, live for ever!" she said. "Don't be alarmed! Don't look so pale! ¹¹There is a man in your kingdom who has the spirit of the holy gods in him. In the time of your father he was found to have insight and intelligence and wisdom like that of the gods. King Nebuchadnezzar your father—your father the king, I say—appointed him chief of the magicians, enchanters, astrologers and diviners. ¹²This man Daniel, whom the king called Belteshazzar, was found to have a keen mind and knowledge and understanding, and also the ability to interpret dreams, explain riddles and solve difficult problems. Call for Daniel, and he will tell you what the writing means."

¹³So Daniel was brought before the king, and the king said to him, "Are you Daniel, one of the exiles my father the king brought from Judah? ¹⁴I have heard that the spirit of the gods is in you and that you have insight, intelligence and outstanding wisdom. ¹⁵The wise men and enchanters were brought before me to read this writing and tell me what it means, but they could not explain it. ¹⁶Now I have heard that you are able to give interpretations and to solve difficult problems. If you can read this writing and tell me what it means, you will be clothed in purple and have a gold chain placed around your neck, and you will be made the third highest ruler in the kingdom."

¹⁷Then Daniel answered the king, "You may keep your gifts for yourself and give your rewards to someone else. Nevertheless, I will read the writing for the king and tell him what it means.

---

a2 Or *ancestor*; or *predecessor*; also in verses 11, 13 and 18   b7 Or *Chaldeans*; also in verse 11   c10 Or *queen mother*

18"O king, the Most High God gave your father Nebuchadnezzar sovereignty and greatness and glory and splendour. 19Because of the high position he gave him, all the peoples and nations and men of every language dreaded and feared him. Those the king wanted to put to death, he put to death; those he wanted to spare, he spared; those he wanted to promote, he promoted; and those he wanted to humble, he humbled. 20But when his heart became arrogant and hardened with pride, he was deposed from his royal throne and stripped of his glory. 21He was driven away from people and given the mind of an animal; he lived with the wild donkeys and ate grass like cattle; and his body was drenched with the dew of heaven, until he acknowledged that the Most High God is sovereign over the kingdoms of men and sets over them anyone he wishes.

22"But you his son,d O Belshazzar, have not humbled yourself, though you knew all this. 23Instead, you have set yourself up against the Lord of heaven. You had the goblets from his temple brought to you, and you and your nobles, your wives and your concubines drank wine from them. You praised the gods of silver and gold, of bronze, iron, wood and stone, which cannot see or hear or understand. But you did not honour the God who holds in his hand your life and all your ways. 24Therefore he sent the hand that wrote the inscription.

25"This is the inscription that was written:

MENE, MENE, TEKEL, PARSINe

26"This is what these words mean:

Menef: God has numbered the days of your reign and brought it to an end.
27 Tekelg: You have been weighed on the scales and found wanting.
28Peresh: Your kingdom is divided and given to the Medes and Persians."

29Then at Belshazzar's command, Daniel was clothed in purple, a gold chain was placed around his neck, and he was proclaimed the third highest ruler in the kingdom.

30That very night Belshazzar, king of the Babylonians,i was slain, 31and Darius the Mede took over the kingdom, at the age of sixty-two.

Daniel in the Den of Lions

6 It pleased Darius to appoint 120 satraps to rule throughout the kingdom, 2with three administrators over them, one of whom was Daniel. The satraps were made accountable to them so that the king might not suffer loss. 3Now Daniel so distinguished himself among the administrators and the satraps by his exceptional qualities that the king planned to set him over the whole kingdom. 4At this, the administrators and the satraps tried to find grounds for charges against Daniel in his conduct of government affairs, but they were unable to do so. They could find no corruption in him, because he was trustworthy and neither

corrupt nor negligent. 5Finally these men said, "We will never find any basis for charges against this man Daniel unless it has something to do with the law of his God."

6So the administrators and the satraps went as a group to the king and said: "O King Darius, live for ever! 7The royal administrators, prefects, satraps, advisers and governors have all agreed that the king should issue an edict and enforce the decree that anyone who prays to any god or man during the next thirty days, except to you, O king, shall be thrown into the lions' den. 8Now, O king, issue the decree and put it in writing so that it cannot be altered—in accordance with the laws of the Medes and Persians, which cannot be repealed." 9So King Darius put the decree in writing.

10Now when Daniel learned that the decree had been published, he went home to his upstairs room where the windows opened towards Jerusalem. Three times a day he got down on his knees and prayed, giving thanks to his God, just as he had done before. 11Then these men went as a group and found Daniel praying and asking God for help. 12So they went to the king and spoke to him about his royal decree: "Did you not publish a decree that during the next thirty days anyone who prays to any god or man except to you, O king, would be thrown into the lions' den?"

6:10   Daniel prayed to God by looking towards Jerusalem. It was there, in the temple, that devout Jews believed that God made his holy dwelling place. It was an established custom of the Law for Jews to face Jerusalem when they prayed while outside the city (see 2 Chronicles 6:38).

The king answered, "The decree stands—in accordance with the laws of the Medes and Persians, which cannot be repealed."

13Then they said to the king, "Daniel, who is one of the exiles from Judah, pays no attention to you, O king, or to the decree you put in writing. He still prays three times a day." 14When the king heard this, he was greatly distressed; he was determined to rescue Daniel and made every effort until sundown to save him.

15Then the men went as a group to the king and said to him, "Remember, O king, that according to the law of the Medes and Persians no decree or edict that the king issues can be changed."

16So the king gave the order, and they brought Daniel and threw him into the lions' den. The king said to Daniel, "May your God, whom you serve continually, rescue you!"

17A stone was brought and placed over the mouth of the den, and the king sealed it with his own signet ring and with the rings of his nobles, so that Daniel's situation might not be changed. 18Then the king returned to his palace and spent the night without eating and

---

d22 Or descendant; or successor   e25 Aramaic UPARSIN (that is, AND PARSIN)
f26 Mene can mean numbered or mina (a unit of money).   g27 Tekel can mean weighed or shekel.
h28 Peres (the singular of Parsin) can mean divided or Persia or a half mina or a half shekel.   i30 Or Chaldeans

without any entertainment being brought to him. And he could not sleep.

[19]At the first light of dawn, the king got up and hurried to the lions' den. [20]When he came near the den, he called to Daniel in an anguished voice, "Daniel, servant of the living God, has your God, whom you serve continually, been able to rescue you from the lions?"

[21]Daniel answered, "O king, live for ever! [22]My God sent his angel, and he shut the mouths of the lions. They have not hurt me, because I was found innocent in his sight. Nor have I ever done any wrong before you, O king."

[23]The king was overjoyed and gave orders to lift Daniel out of the den. And when Daniel was lifted from the den, no wound was found on him, because he had trusted in his God.

[24]At the king's command, the men who had falsely accused Daniel were brought in and thrown into the lions' den, along with their wives and children. And before they reached the floor of the den, the lions overpowered them and crushed all their bones.

[25]Then King Darius wrote to all the peoples, nations and men of every language throughout the land:

"May you prosper greatly!

[26]"I issue a decree that in every part of my kingdom people must fear and reverence the God of Daniel.

"For he is the living God
    and he endures for ever;
his kingdom will not be destroyed,
    his dominion will never end.
[27]He rescues and he saves;
    he performs signs and wonders
    in the heavens and on the earth.
He has rescued Daniel
    from the power of the lions."

[28]So Daniel prospered during the reign of Darius and the reign of Cyrus[a] the Persian.

Daniel's Dream of Four Beasts

7 In the first year of Belshazzar king of Babylon, Daniel had a dream, and visions passed through his mind as he was lying on his bed. He wrote down the substance of his dream.

[2]Daniel said: "In my vision at night I looked, and there before me were the four winds of heaven churning up the great sea. [3]Four great beasts, each different from the others, came up out of the sea.

[4]"The first was like a lion, and it had the wings of an eagle. I watched until its wings were torn off and it was lifted from the ground so that it stood on two feet like a man, and the heart of a man was given to it.

[5]"And there before me was a second beast, which looked like a bear. It was raised up on one of its sides, and it had three ribs in its mouth between its teeth. It was told, 'Get up and eat your fill of flesh!'

[6]"After that, I looked, and there before me was another beast, one that looked like a leopard. And on

its back it had four wings like those of a bird. This beast had four heads, and it was given authority to rule.

[7]"After that, in my vision at night I looked, and there before me was a fourth beast—terrifying and frightening and very powerful. It had large iron teeth; it crushed and devoured its victims and trampled underfoot whatever was left. It was different from all the former beasts, and it had ten horns.

[8]"While I was thinking about the horns, there before me was another horn, a little one, which came up among them; and three of the first horns were uprooted before it. This horn had eyes like the eyes of a man and a mouth that spoke boastfully.

[9]"As I looked,

"thrones were set in place,
    and the Ancient of Days took his seat.
His clothing was as white as snow;
    the hair of his head was white like wool.
His throne was flaming with fire,
    and its wheels were all ablaze.
[10]A river of fire was flowing,
    coming out from before him.
Thousands upon thousands attended him;
    ten thousand times ten thousand stood before
        him.
The court was seated,
    and the books were opened.

[11]"Then I continued to watch because of the boastful words the horn was speaking. I kept looking until the beast was slain and its body destroyed and thrown into the blazing fire. [12](The other beasts had been stripped of their authority, but were allowed to live for a period of time.)

[13]"In my vision at night I looked, and there before me was one like a son of man, coming with the clouds of heaven. He approached the Ancient of Days and was led into his presence. [14]He was given authority, glory and sovereign power; all peoples, nations and men of every language worshipped him. His dominion is an everlasting dominion that will not pass away, and his kingdom is one that will never be destroyed.

7:13   The strange son of man figure in Daniel's vision has raised many questions: what, or who, is it supposed to be? It is certainly a figure who is seen in future, heavenly terms; and in Hebrew and Aramaic the phrase "son of man" was understood as an inclusive term for all humanity and, in this case, could simply mean another human being. It was also understood as a figure representing Israel, and within the time that Daniel lived, a figure in a heavenly vision was often described as being "an appearance" or "likeness" of man. There are strong associations with the expectation of a coming Messiah, who is described elsewhere in the Bible as "man" (see Psalm 80:17).

The Interpretation of the Dream

15"I, Daniel, was troubled in spirit, and the visions that passed through my mind disturbed me. 16I approached one of those standing there and asked him the true meaning of all this.

"So he told me and gave me the interpretation of these things: 17'The four great beasts are four kingdoms that will rise from the earth. 18But the saints of the Most High will receive the kingdom and will possess it for ever — yes, for ever and ever.'

19"Then I wanted to know the true meaning of the fourth beast, which was different from all the others and most terrifying, with its iron teeth and bronze claws — the beast that crushed and devoured its victims and trampled underfoot whatever was left. 20I also wanted to know about the ten horns on its head and about the other horn that came up, before which three of them fell — the horn that looked more imposing than the others and that had eyes and a mouth that spoke boastfully. 21As I watched, this horn was waging war against the saints and defeating them, 22until the Ancient of Days came and pronounced judgment in favour of the saints of the Most High, and the time came when they possessed the kingdom.

23"He gave me this explanation: 'The fourth beast is a fourth kingdom that will appear on earth. It will be different from all the other kingdoms and will devour the whole earth, trampling it down and crushing it. 24The ten horns are ten kings who will come from this kingdom. After them another king will arise, different from the earlier ones; he will subdue three kings. 25He will speak against the Most High and oppress his saints and try to change the set times and the laws. The saints will be handed over to him for a time, times and half a time.*a*

26" 'But the court will sit, and his power will be taken away and completely destroyed for ever. 27Then the sovereignty, power and greatness of the kingdoms under the whole heaven will be handed over to the saints, the people of the Most High. His kingdom will be an everlasting kingdom, and all rulers will worship and obey him.'

28"This is the end of the matter. I, Daniel, was deeply troubled by my thoughts, and my face turned pale, but I kept the matter to myself."

Daniel's Vision of a Ram and a Goat

8 In the third year of King Belshazzar's reign, I, Daniel, had a vision, after the one that had already appeared to me. 2In my vision I saw myself in the citadel of Susa in the province of Elam; in the vision I was beside the Ulai Canal. 3I looked up, and there before me was a ram with two horns, standing beside the canal, and the horns were long. One of the horns was longer than the other but grew up later. 4I watched the ram as he charged towards the west and the north and the south. No animal could stand against him, and none could rescue from his power. He did as he pleased and became great.

5As I was thinking about this, suddenly a goat with a prominent horn between his eyes came from the west, crossing the whole earth without touching the ground. 6He came towards the two-horned ram I had seen standing beside the canal and charged at him in great rage. 7I saw him attack the ram furiously, striking the ram and shattering his two horns. The ram was powerless to stand against him; the goat knocked him to the ground and trampled on him, and none could rescue the ram from his power. 8The goat became very great, but at the height of his power his large horn was broken off, and in its place four prominent horns grew up towards the four winds of heaven.

9Out of one of them came another horn, which started small but grew in power to the south and to the east and towards the Beautiful Land. 10It grew until it reached the host of the heavens, and it threw some of the starry host down to the earth and trampled on them. 11It set itself up to be as great as the Prince of the host; it took away the daily sacrifice from him, and the place of his sanctuary was brought low. 12Because of rebellion, the host ⌊of the saints⌋*a* and the daily sacrifice were given over to it. It prospered in everything it did, and truth was thrown to the ground.

13Then I heard a holy one speaking, and another holy one said to him, "How long will it take for the vision to be fulfilled — the vision concerning the daily sacrifice, the rebellion that causes desolation, and the surrender of the sanctuary and of the host that will be trampled underfoot?"

14He said to me, "It will take 2,300 evenings and mornings; then the sanctuary will be reconsecrated."

The Interpretation of the Vision

15While I, Daniel, was watching the vision and trying to understand it, there before me stood one who looked like a man. 16And I heard a man's voice from the Ulai calling, "Gabriel, tell this man the meaning of the vision."

17As he came near the place where I was standing, I was terrified and fell prostrate. "Son of man," he said to me, "understand that the vision concerns the time of the end."

18While he was speaking to me, I was in a deep sleep, with my face to the ground. Then he touched me and raised me to my feet.

8:18 In the Bible, deep sleep is often associated with "other worldly" visions — where a person is felt to have been taken outside him or herself. An example is Genesis 2:21, where God caused Adam to fall into a deep sleep while he took one of his ribs to create woman.

19He said: "I am going to tell you what will happen later in the time of wrath, because the vision concerns the appointed time of the end.*b* 20The two-horned ram that you saw represents the kings of Media and Persia. 21The shaggy goat is the king of Greece, and the

---

a 25 Or for a year, two years and half a year   *a 12 Or rebellion, the armies*
b 19 Or because the end will be at the appointed time

large horn between his eyes is the first king. [22]The four horns that replaced the one that was broken off represent four kingdoms that will emerge from his nation but will not have the same power.

[23]"In the latter part of their reign, when rebels have become completely wicked, a stern-faced king, a master of intrigue, will arise. [24]He will become very strong, but not by his own power. He will cause astounding devastation and will succeed in whatever he does. He will destroy the mighty men and the holy people. [25]He will cause deceit to prosper, and he will consider himself superior. When they feel secure, he will destroy many and take his stand against the Prince of princes. Yet he will be destroyed, but not by human power.

[26]"The vision of the evenings and mornings that has been given you is true, but seal up the vision, for it concerns the distant future."

[27]I, Daniel, was exhausted and lay ill for several days. Then I got up and went about the king's business. I was appalled by the vision; it was beyond understanding.

Daniel's Prayer

9 In the first year of Darius son of Xerxes[a] (a Mede by descent), who was made ruler over the Babylonian[b] kingdom — [2]in the first year of his reign, I, Daniel, understood from the Scriptures, according to the word of the LORD given to Jeremiah the prophet, that the desolation of Jerusalem would last seventy years. [3]So I turned to the Lord God and pleaded with him in prayer and petition, in fasting, and in sackcloth and ashes.

[4]I prayed to the LORD my God and confessed:

9:4   Daniel's prayer of confession has many phrases and words which allude to other parts of the Bible. This was usual Jewish practice within worship at the time, as the people drew upon the hope expressed by the prophets before them, just as today (and throughout history), Jews and Christians use language and images from the Bible as they address God and make known their desires and aspirations in prayer.

"O Lord, the great and awesome God, who keeps his covenant of love with all who love him and obey his commands, [5]we have sinned and have done wrong. We have been wicked and have rebelled; we have turned away from your commands and laws. [6]We have not listened to your servants the prophets, who spoke in your name to our kings, our princes and our fathers, and to all the people of the land.

[7]"Lord, you are righteous, but this day we are covered with shame — the men of Judah and people of Jerusalem and all Israel, both near and far, in all the countries where you have scattered us because of our unfaithfulness to you. [8]O LORD, we and our kings, our princes and our fathers are covered with shame because we have sinned against you. [9]The Lord our God is merciful and forgiving, even though we have rebelled against him; [10]we have not obeyed the LORD our God or kept the laws he gave us through his servants the prophets. [11]All Israel has transgressed your law and turned away, refusing to obey you.

"Therefore the curses and sworn judgments written in the Law of Moses, the servant of God, have been poured out on us, because we have sinned against you. [12]You have fulfilled the words spoken against us and against our rulers by bringing upon us great disaster. Under the whole heaven nothing has ever been done like what has been done to Jerusalem. [13]Just as it is written in the Law of Moses, all this disaster has come upon us, yet we have not sought the favour of the LORD our God by turning from our sins and giving attention to your truth. [14]The LORD did not hesitate to bring the disaster upon us, for the LORD our God is righteous in everything he does; yet we have not obeyed him.

[15]"Now, O Lord our God, who brought your people out of Egypt with a mighty hand and who made for yourself a name that endures to this day, we have sinned, we have done wrong. [16]O Lord, in keeping with all your righteous acts, turn away your anger and your wrath from Jerusalem, your city, your holy hill. Our sins and the iniquities of our fathers have made Jerusalem and your people an object of scorn to all those around us.

[17]"Now, our God, hear the prayers and petitions of your servant. For your sake, O Lord, look with favour on your desolate sanctuary. [18]Give ear, O God, and hear; open your eyes and see the desolation of the city that bears your Name. We do not make requests of you because we are righteous, but because of your great mercy. [19]O Lord, listen! O Lord, forgive! O Lord, hear and act! For your sake, O my God, do not delay, because your city and your people bear your Name."

The Seventy "Sevens"

[20]While I was speaking and praying, confessing my sin and the sin of my people Israel and making my request to the LORD my God for his holy hill — [21]while I was still in prayer, Gabriel, the man I had seen in the earlier vision, came to me in swift flight about the time of the evening sacrifice. [22]He instructed me and said to me, "Daniel, I have now come to give you insight and understanding. [23]As soon as you began to pray, an answer was given, which I have come to tell you, for you are highly esteemed. Therefore, consider the message and understand the vision:

[24]"Seventy 'sevens'[c] are decreed for your people and your holy city to finish[d] transgression, to put an end to sin, to atone for wickedness, to bring in

---

a 1 Hebrew Ahasuerus   b 1 Or Chaldean   c 24 Or 'weeks'; also in verses 25 and 26   d 24 Or restrain everlasting righteousness, to seal up vision and prophecy and to anoint the most holy. *e*

25"Know and understand this: From the issuing of the decree*f* to restore and rebuild Jerusalem until the Anointed One,*g* the ruler, comes, there will be seven 'sevens', and sixty-two 'sevens'. It will be rebuilt with streets and a trench, but in times of trouble. 26After the sixty-two 'sevens', the Anointed One will be cut off and will have nothing.*h* The people of the ruler who will come will destroy the city and the sanctuary. The end will come like a flood: War will continue until the end, and desolations have been decreed. 27He will confirm a covenant with many for one 'seven'.*i* In the middle of the 'seven'*i* he will put an end to sacrifice and offering. And on a wing ‚of the temple‚ he will set up an abomination that causes desolation, until the end that is decreed is poured out on him.*i"k*

Daniel's Vision of a Man

10 In the third year of Cyrus king of Persia, a revelation was given to Daniel (who was called Belteshazzar). Its message was true and it concerned a great war.*a* The understanding of the message came to him in a vision.

2At that time I, Daniel, mourned for three weeks. 3I ate no choice food; no meat or wine touched my lips; and I used no lotions at all until the three weeks were over.

4On the twenty-fourth day of the first month, as I was standing on the bank of the great river, the Tigris, 5I looked up and there before me was a man dressed in linen, with a belt of the finest gold round his waist. 6His body was like chrysolite, his face like lightning, his eyes like flaming torches, his arms and legs like the gleam of burnished bronze, and his voice like the sound of a multitude.

7I, Daniel, was the only one who saw the vision; the men with me did not see it, but such terror overwhelmed them that they fled and hid themselves. 8So I was left alone, gazing at this great vision; I had no strength left, my face turned deathly pale and I was helpless. 9Then I heard him speaking, and as I listened to him, I fell into a deep sleep, my face to the ground.

10A hand touched me and set me trembling on my hands and knees. 11He said, "Daniel, you who are highly esteemed, consider carefully the words I am about to speak to you, and stand up, for I have now been sent to you." And when he said this to me, I stood up trembling.

12Then he continued, "Do not be afraid, Daniel. Since the first day that you set your mind to gain understanding and to humble yourself before your God, your words were heard, and I have come in response to them. 13But the prince of the Persian kingdom resisted me twenty-one days. Then Michael, one of the chief princes, came to help me, because I was detained there

with the king of Persia. 14Now I have come to explain to you what will happen to your people in the future, for the vision concerns a time yet to come."

15While he was saying this to me, I bowed with my face towards the ground and was speechless. 16Then one who looked like a man*b* touched my lips, and I opened my mouth and began to speak. I said to the one standing before me, "I am overcome with anguish because of the vision, my lord, and I am helpless. 17How can I, your servant, talk with you, my lord? My strength is gone and I can hardly breathe."

18Again the one who looked like a man touched me and gave me strength. 19"Do not be afraid, O man highly esteemed," he said. "Peace! Be strong now; be strong."

When he spoke to me, I was strengthened and said, "Speak, my lord, since you have given me strength."

20So he said, "Do you know why I have come to you? Soon I will return to fight against the prince of Persia, and when I go, the prince of Greece will come; 21but first I will tell you what is written in the Book of Truth. (No-one supports me against them except Michael,

11 your prince. 1And in the first year of Darius the Mede, I took my stand to support and protect him.)

The Kings of the South and the North

2"Now then, I tell you the truth: Three more kings will appear in Persia, and then a fourth, who will be far richer than all the others. When he has gained power by his wealth, he will stir up everyone against the kingdom of Greece. 3Then a mighty king will appear, who will rule with great power and do as he pleases. 4After he has appeared, his empire will be broken up and parcelled out towards the four winds of heaven. It will not go to his descendants, nor will it have the power he exercised, because his empire will be uprooted and given to others.

5"The king of the South will become strong, but one of his commanders will become even stronger than he and will rule his own kingdom with great power. 6After some years, they will become allies. The daughter of the king of the South will go to the king of the North to make an alliance, but she will not retain her power, and he and his power*a* will not last. In those days she will be handed over, together with her royal escort and her father*b* and the one who supported her.

7"One from her family line will arise to take her place. He will attack the forces of the king of the North and enter his fortress; he will fight against them and be victorious. 8He will also seize their gods, their metal images and their valuable articles of silver and gold and carry them off to Egypt. For some years he will leave the king of the North alone. 9Then the king of the North will invade the realm of the king of the South but will retreat to his own country. 10His sons will prepare for war and assemble a great army, which will sweep

---

*e*24 Or *Most Holy Place;* or *most holy One*   *f*25 Or *word*   *g*25 Or *an anointed one;* also in verse 26
*h*26 Or *off and will have no-one;* or *off, but not for himself*   *i*27 Or *'week'*   *j*27 Or *it*
*k*27 Or *And one who causes desolation will come upon the pinnacle of the abominable* ‚*temple*‚ *until the end that is decreed is poured out on the desolated* ‚*city*‚   *a*1 Or *true and burdensome*
*b*16 Most manuscripts of the Masoretic Text; one manuscript of the Masoretic Text, Dead Sea Scrolls and Septuagint *Then something that looked like a man's hand*   *a*6 Or *offspring*   *b*6 Or *child* (see Vulgate and Syriac)

on like an irresistible flood and carry the battle as far as his fortress.

[11] "Then the king of the South will march out in a rage and fight against the king of the North, who will raise a large army, but it will be defeated. [12] When the army is carried off, the king of the South will be filled with pride and will slaughter many thousands, yet he will not remain triumphant. [13] For the king of the North will muster another army, larger than the first; and after several years, he will advance with a huge army fully equipped.

[14] "In those times many will rise against the king of the South. The violent men among your own people will rebel in fulfilment of the vision, but without success. [15] Then the king of the North will come and build up siege ramps and will capture a fortified city. The forces of the South will be powerless to resist; even their best troops will not have the strength to stand. [16] The invader will do as he pleases; no-one will be able to stand against him. He will establish himself in the Beautiful Land and will have the power to destroy it. [17] He will determine to come with the might of his entire kingdom and will make an alliance with the king of the South. And he will give him a daughter in marriage in order to overthrow the kingdom, but his plans [c] will not succeed or help him. [18] Then he will turn his attention to the coastlands and will take many of them, but a commander will put an end to his insolence and will turn his insolence back upon him. [19] After this, he will turn back towards the fortresses of his own country but will stumble and fall, to be seen no more.

[20] "His successor will send out a tax collector to maintain the royal splendour. In a few years, however, he will be destroyed, yet not in anger or in battle.

[21] "He will be succeeded by a contemptible person who has not been given the honour of royalty. He will invade the kingdom when its people feel secure, and he will seize it through intrigue. [22] Then an overwhelming army will be swept away before him; both it and a prince of the covenant will be destroyed. [23] After coming to an agreement with him, he will act deceitfully, and with only a few people he will rise to power. [24] When the richest provinces feel secure, he will invade them and will achieve what neither his fathers nor his forefathers did. He will distribute plunder, loot and wealth among his followers. He will plot the overthrow of fortresses — but only for a time.

[25] "With a large army he will stir up his strength and courage against the king of the South. The king of the South will wage war with a large and very powerful army, but he will not be able to stand because of the plots devised against him. [26] Those who eat from the king's provisions will try to destroy him; his army will be swept away, and many will fall in battle. [27] The two kings, with their hearts bent on evil, will sit at the same table and lie to each other, but to no avail, because an end will still come at the appointed time. [28] The king of the North will return to his own country with great wealth, but his heart will be set against the holy covenant. He will take action against it and then return to his own country.

[29] "At the appointed time he will invade the South again, but this time the outcome will be different from what it was before. [30] Ships of the western coastlands [d] will oppose him, and he will lose heart. Then he will turn back and vent his fury against the holy covenant. He will return and show favour to those who forsake the holy covenant.

[31] "His armed forces will rise up to desecrate the temple fortress and will abolish the daily sacrifice. Then they will set up the abomination that causes desolation. [32] With flattery he will corrupt those who have violated the covenant, but the people who know their God will firmly resist him.

[33] "Those who are wise will instruct many, though for a time they will fall by the sword or be burned or captured or plundered. [34] When they fall, they will receive a little help, and many who are not sincere will join them. [35] Some of the wise will stumble, so that they may be refined, purified and made spotless until the time of the end, for it will still come at the appointed time.

The King Who Exalts Himself

[36] "The king will do as he pleases. He will exalt and magnify himself above every god and will say unheard-of things against the God of gods. He will be successful until the time of wrath is completed, for what has been determined must take place. [37] He will show no regard for the gods of his fathers or for the one desired by women, nor will he regard any god, but will exalt himself above them all. [38] Instead of them, he will honour a god of fortresses; a god unknown to his fathers he will honour with gold and silver, with precious stones and costly gifts. [39] He will attack the mightiest fortresses with the help of a foreign god and will greatly honour those who acknowledge him. He will make them rulers over many people and will distribute the land at a price. [e]

[40] "At the time of the end the king of the South will engage him in battle, and the king of the North will storm out against him with chariots and cavalry and a great fleet of ships. He will invade many countries and sweep through them like a flood. [41] He will also invade the Beautiful Land. Many countries will fall, but Edom, Moab and the leaders of Ammon will be delivered from his hand. [42] He will extend his power over many countries; Egypt will not escape. [43] He will gain control of the treasures of gold and silver and all the riches of Egypt, with the Libyans and Nubians in submission. [44] But reports from the east and the north will alarm him, and he will set out in a great rage to destroy and annihilate many. [45] He will pitch his royal tents between the seas at [f] the beautiful holy mountain. Yet he will come to his end, and no-one will help him.

The End Times

12 "At that time Michael, the great prince who protects your people, will arise. There will be a time of distress such as has not happened from the beginning of nations until then. But at that time your people — everyone whose name is found written in the

---

[c] 17 Or but she   [d] 30 Hebrew of Kittim   [e] 39 Or land for a reward   [f] 45 Or the sea and

book—will be delivered. ²Multitudes who sleep in the dust of the earth will awake: some to everlasting life, others to shame and everlasting contempt. ³Those who are wise[a] will shine like the brightness of the heavens, and those who lead many to righteousness, like the stars for ever and ever. ⁴But you, Daniel, close up and seal the words of the scroll until the time of the end. Many will go here and there to increase knowledge."

⁵Then I, Daniel, looked, and there before me stood two others, one on this bank of the river and one on the opposite bank. ⁶One of them said to the man clothed in linen, who was above the waters of the river, "How long will it be before these astonishing things are fulfilled?"

⁷The man clothed in linen, who was above the waters of the river, lifted his right hand and his left hand towards heaven, and I heard him swear by him who lives for ever, saying, "It will be for a time, times and half a time.[b] When the power of the holy people has been finally broken, all these things will be completed."

⁸I heard, but I did not understand. So I asked, "My lord, what will the outcome of all this be?"

⁹He replied, "Go your way, Daniel, because the words are closed up and sealed until the time of the end. ¹⁰Many will be purified, made spotless and refined, but the wicked will continue to be wicked. None of the wicked will understand, but those who are wise will understand.

12:9   Daniel was left asking questions, and experienced one of the many tensions of time within the Bible: that God has declared his purposes, and that it will come to fulfilment at a time when he decides—not when we decide. Until then, we must live life as God intended it, within the expectation of his promises.

---

¹¹"From the time that the daily sacrifice is abolished and the abomination that causes desolation is set up, there will be 1,290 days. ¹²Blessed is the one who waits for and reaches the end of the 1,335 days.

¹³"As for you, go your way till the end. You will rest, and then at the end of the days you will rise to receive your allotted inheritance."

ᵃ3 Or who impart wisdom   ᵇ7 Or a year, two years and half a year

---

Hosea

A Turbulent Time

Hosea began his active ministry as a prophet around 755 BC. It was a turbulent period in the life of God's people: the nation of Israel was divided; the neighbouring nation of Assyria was increasing its influence and represented a great threat to Israel; there was internal moral and religious corruption; and, to top it all off, four kings were murdered in the space of fifteen years. Amos had begun his ministry a few years earlier, and Zechariah was killed around the time that Hosea began his ministry. Into this historical background, the themes of faithfulness and rebellion seem entirely appropriate.

An Unusual Start

Hosea began his ministry with a call from God, but the nature of his call could not be more different from that of Isaiah or Ezekiel. Instead of a vision of God's holiness, Hosea was told to go out and get married—to a prostitute! They were told to have children, and soon Gomer, Hosea's wife, deserted him to return to her trade. Hosea went after her to win her back and they became reconciled to each other. As the book progresses, and Hosea began to proclaim God's word, he used images and language from marriage to describe Israel's relationship with God. And, because he had experienced it for himself, Hosea's words were not empty platitudes; they came from raw, painful experience.

Voicing God's Demands

Hosea, however, is not a "soft" book. The prophet spared no punches in proclaiming God's anger. He confronted the people with their own sinfulness and corruption, and warned them that their moral irresponsibility would be their downfall. Yet God always holds out the possibility of forgiveness and reconciliation. Following the teaching of the other prophets, Hosea stressed that worship of God was useless unless it was put into good practical action, by showing compassion to the poor, and following God's law. In a speech against the corrupt priests, Hosea summed up the message of the whole book:

"For I desire mercy, not sacrifice,
　　and acknowledgement of God rather than burnt offerings." (6:6)

God Always Searches Us Out

Using graphic images from his own experience, Hosea told the sinful people that God had made a covenant with them. This was like the solemn vows exchanged between husband and wife, and although they had broken these vows and cheated on their part of the deal, he would come after them and seek to be reconciled to them like a husband to a wife.

1 The word of the LORD that came to Hosea son of Beeri during the reigns of Uzziah, Jotham, Ahaz and Hezekiah, kings of Judah, and during the reign of Jeroboam son of Joash king of Israel:

Hosea's Wife and Children

2When the LORD began to speak through Hosea, the LORD said to him, "Go, take to yourself an adulterous wife and children of unfaithfulness, because the land is guilty of the vilest adultery in departing from the LORD." 3So he married Gomer daughter of Diblaim, and she conceived and bore him a son.

4Then the LORD said to Hosea, "Call him Jezreel, because I will soon punish the house of Jehu for the massacre at Jezreel, and I will put an end to the kingdom of Israel. 5In that day I will break Israel's bow in the Valley of Jezreel."

6Gomer conceived again and gave birth to a daughter. Then the LORD said to Hosea, "Call her Lo-Ruhamah,a for I will no longer show love to the house of Israel, that I should at all forgive them. 7Yet I will show love to the house of Judah; and I will save them— not by bow, sword or battle, or by horses and horsemen, but by the LORD their God."

8After she had weaned Lo-Ruhamah, Gomer had another son. 9Then the LORD said, "Call him Lo-Ammi,b for you are not my people, and I am not your God.

1:4 In the Bible, people's names meant more than they do now; they often had descriptive and theological significance. The names of Gomer's children carried and reinforced God's message of judgement. Jezreel means "God plants"; Lo-Ruhamah means "Not my loved one"; Lo-Ammi means "Not my people".

10"Yet the Israelites will be like the sand on the seashore, which cannot be measured or counted. In the place where it was said to them, 'You are not my people', they will be called 'sons of the living God'. 11The people of Judah and the people of Israel will be reunited, and they will appoint one leader and will come up out of the land, for great will be the day of Jezreel.

a6 Lo-Ruhamah means not loved.　　b9 Lo-Ammi means not my people.

2 "Say of your brothers, 'My people', and of your sisters, 'My loved one'.

Israel Punished and Restored

2"Rebuke your mother, rebuke her,
  for she is not my wife,
  and I am not her husband.
Let her remove the adulterous look from her face
  and the unfaithfulness from between her
    breasts.
3Otherwise I will strip her naked
  and make her as bare as on the day she was
    born;
I will make her like a desert,
  turn her into a parched land,
  and slay her with thirst.
4I will not show my love to her children,
  because they are the children of adultery.
5Their mother has been unfaithful
  and has conceived them in disgrace.
She said, 'I will go after my lovers,
  who give me my food and my water,
  my wool and my linen, my oil and my drink.'
6Therefore I will block her path with thornbushes;
  I will wall her in so that she cannot find her
    way.
7She will chase after her lovers but not catch
    them;
  she will look for them but not find them.
Then she will say,
  'I will go back to my husband as at first,
  for then I was better off than now.'
8She has not acknowledged that I was the one
  who gave her the grain, the new wine and oil,
who lavished on her the silver and gold—
  which they used for Baal.

9"Therefore I will take away my grain when it
    ripens,
  and my new wine when it is ready.
I will take back my wool and my linen,
  intended to cover her nakedness.
10So now I will expose her lewdness
  before the eyes of her lovers;
  no-one will take her out of my hands.
11I will stop all her celebrations:
  her yearly festivals, her New Moons,
  her Sabbath days—all her appointed feasts.
12I will ruin her vines and her fig-trees,
  which she said were her pay from her lovers;
I will make them a thicket,
  and wild animals will devour them.
13I will punish her for the days
  she burned incense to the Baals;
she decked herself with rings and jewellery,
  and went after her lovers,
  but me she forgot,"
                        declares the LORD.

14"Therefore I am now going to allure her;
  I will lead her into the desert
  and speak tenderly to her.

15There I will give her back her vineyards,
  and will make the Valley of Achor^a a door of
    hope.
There she will sing^b as in the days of her youth,
  as in the day she came up out of Egypt.

2:14 By taking his chosen people back to the desert, God took them back to the very beginnings of his relationship with them before they entered the promised land. Using Hosea's marriage imagery, it was almost like a couple taking a second honeymoon to remember the marriage and vows they once made.

16"In that day," declares the LORD,
  "you will call me 'my husband';
  you will no longer call me 'my master'.^{c}
17I will remove the names of the Baals from her
    lips;
  no longer will their names be invoked.
18In that day I will make a covenant for them
  with the beasts of the field and the birds of the
    air
  and the creatures that move along the ground.
Bow and sword and battle
  I will abolish from the land,
  so that all may lie down in safety.
19I will betroth you to me for ever;
  I will betroth you in^d righteousness and
    justice,
  in^e love and compassion.
20I will betroth you in faithfulness,
  and you will acknowledge the LORD.

21"In that day I will respond,"
    declares the LORD—
  "I will respond to the skies,
  and they will respond to the earth;
22and the earth will respond to the grain,
  the new wine and oil,
  and they will respond to Jezreel.^{f}
23I will plant her for myself in the land;
  I will show my love to the one I called 'Not my
    loved one'.^{g}
I will say to those called 'Not my people',^{h} 'You
    are my people';
  and they will say, 'You are my God.' "

Hosea's Reconciliation With His Wife

3 The LORD said to me, "Go, show your love to your wife again, though she is loved by another and is an adulteress. Love her as the LORD loves the Israelites, though they turn to other gods and love the sacred raisin cakes."

2So I bought her for fifteen shekels^a of silver and about a homer and a lethek^b of barley. 3Then I told her, "You are to live with^c me for many days; you

---

^{a}15 *Achor* means *trouble.* ^{b}15 Or *respond* ^{c}16 Hebrew *baal* ^{d}19 Or *with*; also in verse 20
^{e}19 Or *with* ^{f}22 *Jezreel* means *God plants.* ^{g}23 Hebrew *Lo-Ruhamah* ^{h}23 Hebrew *Lo-Ammi*
^{a}2 That is, about 6 ounces (about 170 grams) ^{b}2 That is, probably about 9 bushels (about 330 litres) ^{c}3 Or *wait for*

must not be a prostitute or be intimate with any man,
and I will live with c you."

4For the Israelites will live for many days without
king or prince, without sacrifice or sacred stones, without
ephod or idol. 5Afterwards the Israelites will return
and seek the LORD their God and David their king.
They will come trembling to the LORD and to his blessings
in the last days.

The Charge Against Israel

4 Hear the word of the LORD, you Israelites,
    because the LORD has a charge to bring
  against you who live in the land:
  "There is no faithfulness, no love,
    no acknowledgment of God in the land.
  2There is only cursing,a lying and murder,
    stealing and adultery;
  they break all bounds,
    and bloodshed follows bloodshed.
  3Because of this the land mourns,b
    and all who live in it waste away;
  the beasts of the field and the birds of the air
    and the fish of the sea are dying.

  4"But let no man bring a charge,
    let no man accuse another,
  for your people are like those
    who bring charges against a priest.
  5You stumble day and night,
    and the prophets stumble with you.
  So I will destroy your mother —
  6 my people are destroyed from lack of
      knowledge.

  "Because you have rejected knowledge,
    I also reject you as my priests;
  because you have ignored the law of your God,
    I also will ignore your children.
  7The more the priests increased,
    the more they sinned against me;
  they exchangedc theird Glory for something
      disgraceful.
  8They feed on the sins of my people
    and relish their wickedness.
  9And it will be: Like people, like priests.
    I will punish both of them for their ways
    and repay them for their deeds.

4:9 Status as a priest will not save anyone.
Everyone had rebelled against God and
no-one would be spared his wrath.

  10"They will eat but not have enough;
    they will engage in prostitution but not
      increase,
  because they have deserted the LORD
    to give themselves 11to prostitution,
  to old wine and new,
    which take away the understanding 12of my
      people.

They consult a wooden idol
    and are answered by a stick of wood.
  A spirit of prostitution leads them astray;
    they are unfaithful to their God.
  13They sacrifice on the mountaintops
    and burn offerings on the hills,
  under oak, poplar and terebinth,
    where the shade is pleasant.
  Therefore your daughters turn to prostitution
    and your daughters-in-law to adultery.

  14"I will not punish your daughters
    when they turn to prostitution,
  nor your daughters-in-law
    when they commit adultery,
  because the men themselves consort with harlots
    and sacrifice with shrine-prostitutes —
  a people without understanding will come to
      ruin!

  15"Though you commit adultery, O Israel,
    let not Judah become guilty.

  "Do not go to Gilgal;
    do not go up to Beth Aven.e
  And do not swear, 'As surely as the LORD lives!'
  16The Israelites are stubborn,
    like a stubborn heifer.
  How then can the LORD pasture them
    like lambs in a meadow?
  17Ephraim is joined to idols;
    leave him alone!
  18Even when their drinks are gone,
    they continue their prostitution;
    their rulers dearly love shameful ways.
  19A whirlwind will sweep them away,
    and their sacrifices will bring them shame.

Judgment Against Israel

5 "Hear this, you priests!
    Pay attention, you Israelites!
  Listen, O royal house!
    This judgment is against you:
  You have been a snare at Mizpah,
    a net spread out on Tabor.
  2The rebels are deep in slaughter.
    I will discipline all of them.
  3I know all about Ephraim;
    Israel is not hidden from me.
  Ephraim, you have now turned to prostitution;
    Israel is corrupt.

  4"Their deeds do not permit them
    to return to their God.
  A spirit of prostitution is in their heart;
    they do not acknowledge the LORD.
  5Israel's arrogance testifies against them;
    the Israelites, even Ephraim, stumble in their
      sin;
    Judah also stumbles with them.
  6When they go with their flocks and herds
    to seek the LORD,

---

a2 That is, to pronounce a curse upon   b3 Or dries up
c7 Syriac and an ancient Hebrew scribal tradition; Masoretic Text I will exchange
d7 Masoretic Text; an ancient Hebrew scribal tradition my
e15 Beth Aven means house of wickedness (a name for Bethel, which means house of God).

they will not find him;
　he has withdrawn himself from them.
[7]They are unfaithful to the LORD;
　they give birth to illegitimate children.
Now their New Moon festivals
　will devour them and their fields.

[8]"Sound the trumpet in Gibeah,
　the horn in Ramah.
Raise the battle cry in Beth Aven;[a]
　lead on, O Benjamin.
[9]Ephraim will be laid waste
　on the day of reckoning.
Among the tribes of Israel
　I proclaim what is certain.
[10]Judah's leaders are like those
　who move boundary stones.
I will pour out my wrath on them
　like a flood of water.
[11]Ephraim is oppressed,
　trampled in judgment,
　intent on pursuing idols.[b]
[12]I am like a moth to Ephraim,
　like rot to the people of Judah.

[13]"When Ephraim saw his sickness,
　and Judah his sores,
then Ephraim turned to Assyria,
　and sent to the great king for help.
But he is not able to cure you,
　not able to heal your sores.
[14]For I will be like a lion to Ephraim,
　like a great lion to Judah.
I will tear them to pieces and go away;
　I will carry them off, with no-one to rescue
　　them.
[15]Then I will go back to my place
　until they admit their guilt.
And they will seek my face;
　in their misery they will earnestly seek me."

6:1　　The people of Israel had been
tempted to trust in the might of Assyria to
save and protect them, but now realized that
God was the source of their wellbeing.

Israel Unrepentant

6 "Come, let us return to the LORD.
　He has torn us to pieces
　but he will heal us;
he has injured us
　but he will bind up our wounds.
[2]After two days he will revive us;
　on the third day he will restore us,
　that we may live in his presence.
[3]Let us acknowledge the LORD;
　let us press on to acknowledge him.
As surely as the sun rises,
　he will appear;
he will come to us like the winter rains,
　like the spring rains that water the earth."

[4]"What can I do with you, Ephraim?
　What can I do with you, Judah?
Your love is like the morning mist,
　like the early dew that disappears.
[5]Therefore I cut you in pieces with my prophets,
　I killed you with the words of my mouth;
　my judgments flashed like lightning upon you.
[6]For I desire mercy, not sacrifice,
　and acknowledgment of God rather than burnt
　　offerings.
[7]Like Adam,[a] they have broken the covenant—
　they were unfaithful to me there.
[8]Gilead is a city of wicked men,
　stained with footprints of blood.
[9]As marauders lie in ambush for a man,
　so do bands of priests;
they murder on the road to Shechem,
　committing shameful crimes.
[10]I have seen a horrible thing
　in the house of Israel.
There Ephraim is given to prostitution
　and Israel is defiled.

[11]"Also for you, Judah,
　a harvest is appointed.

"Whenever I would restore the fortunes of my
　　people,
7 [1]whenever I would heal Israel,
　the sins of Ephraim are exposed
and the crimes of Samaria revealed.
They practise deceit,
　thieves break into houses,
　bandits rob in the streets;
[2]but they do not realise
　that I remember all their evil deeds.
Their sins engulf them;
　they are always before me.

[3]"They delight the king with their wickedness,
　the princes with their lies.
[4]They are all adulterers,
　burning like an oven
whose fire the baker need not stir
　from the kneading of the dough till it rises.
[5]On the day of the festival of our king
　the princes become inflamed with wine,
　and he joins hands with the mockers.
[6]Their hearts are like an oven;
　they approach him with intrigue.
Their passion smoulders all night;
　in the morning it blazes like a flaming fire.
[7]All of them are hot as an oven;
　they devour their rulers.
All their kings fall,
　and none of them calls on me.

[8]"Ephraim mixes with the nations;
　Ephraim is a flat cake not turned over.
[9]Foreigners sap his strength,
　but he does not realise it.

---

[a]8 Beth Aven means house of wickedness (a name for Bethel, which means house of God).
[b]11 The meaning of the Hebrew for this word is uncertain.　　[a]7 Or As at Adam; or Like men

His hair is sprinkled with grey,
  but he does not notice.
10Israel's arrogance testifies against him,
  but despite all this
he does not return to the LORD his God
  or search for him.

11"Ephraim is like a dove,
  easily deceived and senseless—
now calling to Egypt,
  now turning to Assyria.
12When they go, I will throw my net over them;
  I will pull them down like birds of the air.
When I hear them flocking together,
  I will catch them.
13Woe to them,
  because they have strayed from me!
Destruction to them,
  because they have rebelled against me!
I long to redeem them
  but they speak lies against me.
14They do not cry out to me from their hearts
  but wail upon their beds.
They gather together*a* for grain and new wine
  but turn away from me.
15I trained them and strengthened them,
  but they plot evil against me.
16They do not turn to the Most High;
  they are like a faulty bow.
Their leaders will fall by the sword
  because of their insolent words.
For this they will be ridiculed
  in the land of Egypt.

8:2   The prophet confronted the hypocrisy in the land. The people called out, in a
style used in worship, that God was at the
centre of their lives, when, in reality their
lifestyle and values flatly contradicted the
law of God.

Israel to Reap the Whirlwind

8 "Put the trumpet to your lips!
    An eagle is over the house of the LORD
because the people have broken my covenant
  and rebelled against my law.
2Israel cries out to me,
  'O our God, we acknowledge you!'
3But Israel has rejected what is good;
  an enemy will pursue him.
4They set up kings without my consent;
  they choose princes without my approval.
With their silver and gold
  they make idols for themselves
  to their own destruction.
5Throw out your calf-idol, O Samaria!
  My anger burns against them.
How long will they be incapable of purity?
6 They are from Israel!
This calf—a craftsman has made it;
  it is not God.

It will be broken in pieces,
  that calf of Samaria.

7"They sow the wind
  and reap the whirlwind.
The stalk has no head;
  it will produce no flour.
Were it to yield grain,
  foreigners would swallow it up.
8Israel is swallowed up;
  now she is among the nations
  like a worthless thing.
9For they have gone up to Assyria
  like a wild donkey wandering alone.
Ephraim has sold herself to lovers.
10Although they have sold themselves among the
    nations,
  I will now gather them together.
They will begin to waste away
  under the oppression of the mighty king.

11"Though Ephraim built many altars for sin
    offerings,
  these have become altars for sinning.
12I wrote for them the many things of my law,
  but they regarded them as something alien.
13They offer sacrifices given to me
  and they eat the meat,
  but the LORD is not pleased with them.
Now he will remember their wickedness
  and punish their sins:
  They will return to Egypt.
14Israel has forgotten his Maker
  and built palaces;
Judah has fortified many towns.
But I will send fire upon their cities
  that will consume their fortresses."

Punishment for Israel

9 Do not rejoice, O Israel;
    do not be jubilant like the other nations.
For you have been unfaithful to your God;
  you love the wages of a prostitute
  at every threshing-floor.
2Threshing-floors and winepresses will not feed the
    people;
  the new wine will fail them.
3They will not remain in the LORD's land;
  Ephraim will return to Egypt
  and eat unclean*a* food in Assyria.
4They will not pour out wine offerings to the
    LORD,
  nor will their sacrifices please him.
Such sacrifices will be to them like the bread of
    mourners;
  all who eat them will be unclean.
This food will be for themselves;
  it will not come into the temple of the LORD.
5What will you do on the day of your appointed
    feasts,
  on the festival days of the LORD?

---

a 14 Most Hebrew manuscripts; some Hebrew manuscripts and Septuagint *They slash themselves*   *a 3* That is, ceremonially unclean

⁶Even if they escape from destruction,
    Egypt will gather them,
    and Memphis will bury them.
Their treasures of silver will be taken over by
        briers,
    and thorns will overrun their tents.
⁷The days of punishment are coming,
    the days of reckoning are at hand.
Let Israel know this.
Because your sins are so many
    and your hostility so great,
the prophet is considered a fool,
    the inspired man a maniac.
⁸The prophet, along with my God,
    is the watchman over Ephraim,ᵇ
yet snares await him on all his paths,
    and hostility in the house of his God.
⁹They have sunk deep into corruption,
    as in the days of Gibeah.
God will remember their wickedness
    and punish them for their sins.

¹⁰"When I found Israel,
    it was like finding grapes in the desert;
when I saw your fathers,
    it was like seeing the early fruit on the fig-tree.
But when they came to Baal Peor,
    they consecrated themselves to that shameful
        idol
    and became as vile as the thing they loved.
¹¹Ephraim's glory will fly away like a bird—
    no birth, no pregnancy, no conception.
¹²Even if they bring up children,
    I will bereave them of every one.
Woe to them
    when I turn away from them!
¹³I have seen Ephraim, like Tyre,
    planted in a pleasant place.
But Ephraim will bring out
    their children to the slayer."

¹⁴Give them, O LORD—
    what will you give them?
Give them wombs that miscarry
    and breasts that are dry.

¹⁵"Because of all their wickedness in Gilgal,
    I hated them there.
Because of their sinful deeds,
    I will drive them out of my house.
I will no longer love them;
    all their leaders are rebellious.
¹⁶Ephraim is blighted,
    their root is withered,
    they yield no fruit.
Even if they bear children,
    I will slay their cherished offspring."

¹⁷My God will reject them
    because they have not obeyed him;
    they will be wanderers among the nations.

10 Israel was a spreading vine;
       he brought forth fruit for himself.
As his fruit increased,
    he built more altars;
as his land prospered,
    he adorned his sacred stones.
²Their heart is deceitful,
    and now they must bear their guilt.
The LORD will demolish their altars
    and destroy their sacred stones.

³Then they will say, "We have no king
    because we did not revere the LORD.
But even if we had a king,
    what could he do for us?"
⁴They make many promises,
    take false oaths
    and make agreements;
therefore lawsuits spring up
    like poisonous weeds in a ploughed field.
⁵The people who live in Samaria fear
    for the calf-idol of Beth Aven.ᵃ
Its people will mourn over it,
    and so will its idolatrous priests,
those who had rejoiced over its splendour,
    because it is taken from them into exile.
⁶It will be carried to Assyria
    as tribute for the great king.
Ephraim will be disgraced;
    Israel will be ashamed of its wooden idols.ᵇ
⁷Samaria and its king will float away
    like a twig on the surface of the waters.
⁸The high places of wickednessᶜ will be
        destroyed—
    it is the sin of Israel.
Thorns and thistles will grow up
    and cover their altars.
Then they will say to the mountains, "Cover us!"
    and to the hills, "Fall on us!"

⁹"Since the days of Gibeah, you have sinned,
        O Israel,
    and there you have remained.ᵈ
Did not war overtake
    the evildoers in Gibeah?
¹⁰When I please, I will punish them;
    nations will be gathered against them
    to put them in bonds for their double sin.
¹¹Ephraim is a trained heifer
    that loves to thresh;
so I will put a yoke
    on her fair neck.
I will drive Ephraim,
    Judah must plough,
    and Jacob must break up the ground.
¹²Sow for yourselves righteousness,
    reap the fruit of unfailing love,
and break up your unploughed ground;
    for it is time to seek the LORD,
until he comes
    and showers righteousness on you.

ᵇ8 Or *The prophet is the watchman over Ephraim, / the people of my God*
ᵃ5 *Beth Aven* means *house of wickedness* (a name for Bethel, which means *house of God*).   ᵇ6 Or *its counsel*
ᶜ8 Hebrew *aven*, a reference to Beth Aven (a derogatory name for Bethel)   ᵈ9 Or *there a stand was taken*

13But you have planted wickedness,
    you have reaped evil,
    you have eaten the fruit of deception.
Because you have depended on your own strength
    and on your many warriors,
14the roar of battle will rise against your people,
    so that all your fortresses will be devastated—
as Shalman devastated Beth Arbel on the day of
        battle,
    when mothers were dashed to the ground with
        their children.
15Thus will it happen to you, O Bethel,
    because your wickedness is great.
When that day dawns,
    the king of Israel will be completely destroyed.

God's Love for Israel

11 "When Israel was a child, I loved him,
    and out of Egypt I called my son.
2But the more I a called Israel,
    the further they went from me. b
They sacrificed to the Baals
    and they burned incense to images.
3It was I who taught Ephraim to walk,
    taking them by the arms;
but they did not realise
    it was I who healed them.
4I led them with cords of human kindness,
    with ties of love;
I lifted the yoke from their neck
    and bent down to feed them.

11:4 God reminded Israel of the love he
had shown in the past, and (verses 8–11)
went on to tell how he would continue to
show the same love towards his people, if
only they would return to him.

5"Will they not return to Egypt
    and will not Assyria rule over them
    because they refuse to repent?
6Swords will flash in their cities,
    will destroy the bars of their gates
    and put an end to their plans.
7My people are determined to turn from me.
    Even if they call to the Most High,
    he will by no means exalt them.

8"How can I give you up, Ephraim?
    How can I hand you over, Israel?
How can I treat you like Admah?
    How can I make you like Zeboiim?
My heart is changed within me;
    all my compassion is aroused.
9I will not carry out my fierce anger,
    nor will I turn and devastate Ephraim.
For I am God, and not man—
    the Holy One among you.
    I will not come in wrath. c

10They will follow the LORD;
    he will roar like a lion.
When he roars,
    his children will come trembling from the west.
11They will come trembling
    like birds from Egypt,
    like doves from Assyria.
I will settle them in their homes,"
    declares the LORD.

Israel's Sin

12Ephraim has surrounded me with lies,
    the house of Israel with deceit.
And Judah is unruly against God,
    even against the faithful Holy One.

12 1Ephraim feeds on the wind;
    he pursues the east wind all day
    and multiplies lies and violence.
He makes a treaty with Assyria
    and sends olive oil to Egypt.
2The LORD has a charge to bring against Judah;
    he will punish Jacob a according to his ways
    and repay him according to his deeds.
3In the womb he grasped his brother's heel;
    as a man he struggled with God.
4He struggled with the angel and overcame him;
    he wept and begged for his favour.
He found him at Bethel
    and talked with him there—
5the LORD God Almighty,
    the LORD is his name of renown!
6But you must return to your God;
    maintain love and justice,
    and wait for your God always.

7The merchant uses dishonest scales;
    he loves to defraud.
8Ephraim boasts,
    "I am very rich; I have become wealthy.
With all my wealth they will not find in me
    any iniquity or sin."

9"I am the LORD your God,
    who brought you out of b Egypt;
I will make you live in tents again,
    as in the days of your appointed feasts.
10I spoke to the prophets,
    gave them many visions
    and told parables through them."

11Is Gilead wicked?
    Its people are worthless!
Do they sacrifice bulls in Gilgal?
    Their altars will be like piles of stones
    on a ploughed field.
12Jacob fled to the country of Aram; c
    Israel served to get a wife,
    and to pay for her he tended sheep.
13The LORD used a prophet to bring Israel up from
        Egypt,
    by a prophet he cared for him.

---

a2 Some Septuagint manuscripts; Hebrew *they*   b2 Septuagint; Hebrew *them*   c9 Or *come against any city*
a2 *Jacob* means *he grasps the heel* (figuratively, *he deceives*).   b9 Or *God / ever since you were in*
c12 That is, North-west Mesopotamia

14But Ephraim has bitterly provoked him to anger;
   his Lord will leave upon him the guilt of his
      bloodshed
   and will repay him for his contempt.

The LORD's Anger Against Israel

13 When Ephraim spoke, men trembled;
   he was exalted in Israel.
But he became guilty of Baal worship and died.
2Now they sin more and more;
   they make idols for themselves from their silver,
cleverly fashioned images,
   all of them the work of craftsmen.
It is said of these people,
   "They offer human sacrifice
   and kiss[a] the calf-idols."
3Therefore they will be like the morning mist,
   like the early dew that disappears,
   like chaff swirling from a threshing-floor,
   like smoke escaping through a window.

4"But I am the LORD your God,
   who brought you out of[b] Egypt.
You shall acknowledge no God but me,
   no Saviour except me.
5I cared for you in the desert,
   in the land of burning heat.
6When I fed them, they were satisfied;
   when they were satisfied, they became proud;
   then they forgot me.
7So I will come upon them like a lion,
   like a leopard I will lurk by the path.
8Like a bear robbed of her cubs,
   I will attack them and rip them open.
Like a lion I will devour them;
   a wild animal will tear them apart.

9"You are destroyed, O Israel,
   because you are against me, against your helper.
10Where is your king, that he may save you?
   Where are your rulers in all your towns,
   of whom you said,
      'Give me a king and princes'?
11So in my anger I gave you a king,
   and in my wrath I took him away.
12The guilt of Ephraim is stored up,
   his sins are kept on record.
13Pains as of a woman in childbirth come to him,
   but he is a child without wisdom;
when the time arrives,
   he does not come to the opening of the womb.

14"I will ransom them from the power of the
      grave;[c]
   I will redeem them from death.
Where, O death, are your plagues?
   Where, O grave,[c] is your destruction?

"I will have no compassion,
15   even though he thrives among his brothers.
An east wind from the LORD will come,
   blowing in from the desert;
his spring will fail
   and his well dry up.

His storehouse will be plundered
   of all its treasures.
16The people of Samaria must bear their guilt,
   because they have rebelled against their God.
They will fall by the sword;
   their little ones will be dashed to the ground,
   their pregnant women ripped open."

Repentance to Bring Blessing

14 Return, O Israel, to the LORD your God.
   Your sins have been your downfall!
2Take words with you
   and return to the LORD.
Say to him:
   "Forgive all our sins
and receive us graciously,
   that we may offer the fruit of our lips.[a]
3Assyria cannot save us;
   we will not mount war-horses.
We will never again say 'Our gods'
   to what our own hands have made,
   for in you the fatherless find compassion."

14:2   The book of Hosea reflects a great
theme in the prophets: that God wanted not
sacrifice and hollow rituals, but a true
expression of sorrow and repentance. So the
prophet called Israel to come to the Lord
with "words"—but not empty, hollow
words. Only words which truly expressed
their sorrow would be acceptable to God.

4"I will heal their waywardness
   and love them freely,
   for my anger has turned away from them.
5I will be like the dew to Israel;
   he will blossom like a lily.
Like a cedar of Lebanon
   he will send down his roots;
6   his young shoots will grow.
His splendour will be like an olive tree,
   his fragrance like a cedar of Lebanon.
7Men will dwell again in his shade.
   He will flourish like the corn.
He will blossom like a vine,
   and his fame will be like the wine from
      Lebanon.
8O Ephraim, what more have I[b] to do with
      idols?
   I will answer him and care for him.
I am like a green pine tree;
   your fruitfulness comes from me."

9Who is wise? He will realise these things.
   Who is discerning? He will understand
      them.
The ways of the LORD are right;
   the righteous walk in them,
   but the rebellious stumble in them.

---

a2 Or "Men who sacrifice / kiss   b4 Or God / ever since you were in   c14 Hebrew Sheol
a2 Or offer our lips as sacrifices of bulls   b8 Or What more has Ephraim

Joel

A Vivid Picture of Impending Doom

Of all the incidents of "natural disaster" in the Old Testament, the book of Joel is, perhaps, the one which contains the most vivid example and could be a real film director's paradise. The book begins with a solemn warning to the people of Judah that their sinfulness can go on no longer; the day of God's judgement is coming like a massive plague of locusts, causing widespread destruction to their crops, their land, and their economic wellbeing. The prophet did not mince his words, and he spared no punches in getting his message across to the nation of Judah. Throughout the book there are some blunt phrases ("Wake up, you drunkards," 1:5), underlining the fact that things were in a great state of urgency. The only way out of this mess was for the people to repent. Just as God's judgement will be spectacular, so the people's repentance must be deep and heartfelt. Joel told the priests, the establishment figures, to tear their clothes apart and wear rags, and organize a national fast. Only then would God's spirit of healing and forgiveness come upon the land and the people.

A Message for Every Age

Unlike other prophets, it is difficult to locate Joel's ministry within the history of Israel. Some scholars have suggested that he was active during the ninth century BC, just after Elisha and before Jonah. It is also suggested that the different types of locust referred to in the book may be representative of Israel's enemies: Babylonians, Persians, and Assyrians. Others, however, referring to 3:1, have suggested that it may refer to a time when the Babylonian exile was over and Israel was once more restored as a nation. The fact that we cannot date Joel with any certainty is, perhaps, a good thing. It reminds us that sinfulness and evil are always with us, and not just restricted to particular periods of history. Joel's message is universal, calling us to remember that when we sin and turn our backs on God, his judgement will follow. Only by facing up to our sin and repenting can we receive God's spirit of healing and forgiveness.

1

The word of the LORD that came to Joel son of Pethuel.

1:1 Joel began his prophecy with a divine sanction. Unlike other prophets (e.g. Isaiah, Jeremiah, and Hosea), Joel did not seem to have received a long, extended "call"; but he did stress that the words he spoke were not his own, but the words addressed to him by God.

An Invasion of Locusts

²Hear this, you elders;
 listen, all who live in the land.
Has anything like this ever happened in your days
 or in the days of your forefathers?
³Tell it to your children,
 and let your children tell it to their children,
 and their children to the next generation.
⁴What the locust swarm has left
 the great locusts have eaten;
what the great locusts have left
 the young locusts have eaten;
what the young locusts have left
 other locusts ᵃ have eaten.

⁵Wake up, you drunkards, and weep!
 Wail, all you drinkers of wine;
wail because of the new wine,
 for it has been snatched from your lips.
⁶A nation has invaded my land,
 powerful and without number;
 it has the teeth of a lion,
 the fangs of a lioness.
⁷It has laid waste my vines
 and ruined my fig-trees.
It has stripped off their bark
 and thrown it away,
 leaving their branches white.

⁸Mourn like a virgin ᵇ in sackcloth
 grieving for the husband ᶜ of her youth.
⁹Grain offerings and drink offerings
 are cut off from the house of the LORD.
The priests are in mourning,
 those who minister before the LORD.
¹⁰The fields are ruined,
 the ground is dried up; ᵈ
the grain is destroyed,
 the new wine is dried up,
 the oil fails.
¹¹Despair, you farmers,
 wail, you vine growers;
grieve for the wheat and the barley,
 because the harvest of the field is destroyed.
¹²The vine is dried up
 and the fig-tree is withered;

the pomegranate, the palm and the apple tree—
 all the trees of the field—are dried up.
Surely the joy of mankind
 is withered away.

A Call to Repentance

¹³Put on sackcloth, O priests, and mourn;
 wail, you who minister before the altar.
Come, spend the night in sackcloth,
 you who minister before my God;
for the grain offerings and drink offerings
 are withheld from the house of your God.
¹⁴Declare a holy fast;
 call a sacred assembly.
Summon the elders
 and all who live in the land
to the house of the LORD your God,
 and cry out to the LORD.

¹⁵Alas for that day!
 For the day of the LORD is near;
 it will come like destruction from the
 Almighty. ᵉ

¹⁶Has not the food been cut off
 before our very eyes—
joy and gladness
 from the house of our God?
¹⁷The seeds are shrivelled
 beneath the clods. ᶠ
The storehouses are in ruins,
 the granaries have been broken down,
 for the grain has dried up.
¹⁸How the cattle moan!
 The herds mill about
because they have no pasture;
 even the flocks of sheep are suffering.

¹⁹To you, O LORD, I call,
 for fire has devoured the open pastures
 and flames have burned up all the trees of the
 field.
²⁰Even the wild animals pant for you;
 the streams of water have dried up
 and fire has devoured the open pastures.

An Army of Locusts

2

Blow the trumpet in Zion;
 sound the alarm on my holy hill.
Let all who live in the land tremble,
 for the day of the LORD is coming.
It is close at hand—
² a day of darkness and gloom,
 a day of clouds and blackness.
Like dawn spreading across the mountains
 a large and mighty army comes,
such as never was of old
 nor ever will be in ages to come.

³Before them fire devours,
 behind them a flame blazes.

ᵃ4 The precise meaning of the four Hebrew words used here for locusts is uncertain.   ᵇ8 Or *young woman*
ᶜ8 Or *betrothed*   ᵈ10 Or *ground mourns*   ᵉ15 Hebrew *Shaddai*
ᶠ17 The meaning of the Hebrew for this word is uncertain.

Before them the land is like the garden of Eden,
  behind them, a desert waste—
  nothing escapes them.
⁴They have the appearance of horses;
  they gallop along like cavalry.
⁵With a noise like that of chariots
  they leap over the mountaintops,
like a crackling fire consuming stubble,
  like a mighty army drawn up for battle.

⁶At the sight of them, nations are in anguish;
  every face turns pale.
⁷They charge like warriors;
  they scale walls like soldiers.
They all march in line,
  not swerving from their course.
⁸They do not jostle each other;
  each marches straight ahead.
They plunge through defences
  without breaking ranks.
⁹They rush upon the city;
  they run along the wall.
They climb into the houses;
  like thieves they enter through the
    windows.

¹⁰Before them the earth shakes,
  the sky trembles,
the sun and moon are darkened,
  and the stars no longer shine.
¹¹The LORD thunders
  at the head of his army;
his forces are beyond number,
  and mighty are those who obey his
    command.
The day of the LORD is great;
  it is dreadful.
  Who can endure it?

Rend Your Heart

¹²"Even now," declares the LORD,
  "return to me with all your heart,
  with fasting and weeping and mourning."

¹³Rend your heart
  and not your garments.
Return to the LORD your God,
  for he is gracious and compassionate,
slow to anger and abounding in love,
  and he relents from sending calamity.
¹⁴Who knows? He may turn and have pity
  and leave behind a blessing—
grain offerings and drink offerings
  for the LORD your God.

¹⁵Blow the trumpet in Zion,
  declare a holy fast,
  call a sacred assembly.
¹⁶Gather the people,
  consecrate the assembly;
bring together the elders,
  gather the children,
  those nursing at the breast.

Let the bridegroom leave his room
  and the bride her chamber.
¹⁷Let the priests, who minister before the LORD,
  weep between the temple porch and the
    altar.
Let them say, "Spare your people, O LORD.
  Do not make your inheritance an object of
    scorn,
  a byword among the nations.
Why should they say among the peoples,
  'Where is their God?' "

The LORD's Answer

¹⁸Then the LORD will be jealous for his land
  and take pity on his people.

  ¹⁹The LORD will reply[a] to them:

"I am sending you grain, new wine and oil,
  enough to satisfy you fully;
never again will I make you
  an object of scorn to the nations.

²⁰"I will drive the northern army far from you,
  pushing it into a parched and barren land,
with its front columns going into the eastern
    sea[b]
and those in the rear into the western sea.[c]
And its stench will go up;
  its smell will rise."

Surely he has done great things.[d]
²¹ Be not afraid, O land;
  be glad and rejoice.
Surely the LORD has done great things.
²² Be not afraid, O wild animals,
  for the open pastures are becoming green.
The trees are bearing their fruit;
  the fig-tree and the vine yield their riches.
²³Be glad, O people of Zion,
  rejoice in the LORD your God,
for he has given you
  the autumn rains in righteousness.[e]
He sends you abundant showers,
  both autumn and spring rains, as before.
²⁴The threshing-floors will be filled with grain;
  the vats will overflow with new wine and oil.

²⁵"I will repay you for the years the locusts have
    eaten—
  the great locust and the young locust,
  the other locusts and the locust swarm[f]—
my great army that I sent among you.
²⁶You will have plenty to eat, until you are full,
  and you will praise the name of the LORD your
    God,
who has worked wonders for you;
  never again will my people be shamed.
²⁷Then you will know that I am in Israel,
  that I am the LORD your God,
  and that there is no other;
never again will my people be shamed.

---

a 18, 19 Or LORD was jealous . . . / and took pity . . . / ¹⁹ The LORD replied   b 20 That is, the Dead Sea
c 20 That is, the Mediterranean   d 20 Or rise. / Surely it has done great things."   e 23 Or / the teacher for righteousness:
f 25 The precise meaning of the four Hebrew words used here for locusts is uncertain.

The Day of the LORD

28"And afterwards,
  I will pour out my Spirit on all people.
Your sons and daughters will prophesy,
  your old men will dream dreams,
  your young men will see visions.
29Even on my servants, both men and women,
  I will pour out my Spirit in those days.
30I will show wonders in the heavens
  and on the earth,
  blood and fire and billows of smoke.
31The sun will be turned to darkness
  and the moon to blood
before the coming of the great and dreadful day
  of the LORD.
32And everyone who calls
  on the name of the LORD will be saved;
for on Mount Zion and in Jerusalem
  there will be deliverance,
  as the LORD has said,
among the survivors
  whom the LORD calls.

2:28 These words of Joel were quoted by Peter in his sermon on the day of Pentecost (see Acts 2:17–21). The original Hebrew uses the word "flesh" (as compared to "people" in this translation). The Hebrew understanding of flesh was far more than just the physical part; it included the whole personality. God's Spirit is able to enter every part of life — including our breathing and bloodstream.

The Nations Judged

3 "In those days and at that time,
  when I restore the fortunes of Judah and
  Jerusalem,
2I will gather all nations
  and bring them down to the Valley of
  Jehoshaphat.ᵃ
There I will enter into judgment against them
  concerning my inheritance, my people Israel,
for they scattered my people among the nations
  and divided up my land.
3They cast lots for my people
  and traded boys for prostitutes;
they sold girls for wine
  that they might drink.

4"Now what have you against me, O Tyre and Sidon and all you regions of Philistia? Are you repaying me for something I have done? If you are paying me back, I will swiftly and speedily return on your own heads what you have done. 5For you took my silver and my gold and carried off my finest treasures to your temples. 6You sold the people of Judah and Jerusalem to the Greeks, that you might send them far from their homeland.

7"See, I am going to rouse them out of the places to which you sold them, and I will return on your own heads what you have done. 8I will sell your sons and daughters to the people of Judah, and they will sell them to the Sabeans, a nation far away." The LORD has spoken.

9Proclaim this among the nations:
  Prepare for war!
Rouse the warriors!
  Let all the fighting men draw near and attack.
10Beat your ploughshares into swords
  and your pruning hooks into spears.
Let the weakling say,
  "I am strong!"
11Come quickly, all you nations from every side,
  and assemble there.

Bring down your warriors, O LORD!

12"Let the nations be roused;
  let them advance into the Valley of Jehoshaphat,
for there I will sit
  to judge all the nations on every side.
13Swing the sickle,
  for the harvest is ripe.
Come, trample the grapes,
  for the winepress is full
  and the vats overflow—
so great is their wickedness!"

14Multitudes, multitudes
  in the valley of decision!
For the day of the LORD is near
  in the valley of decision.
15The sun and moon will be darkened,
  and the stars no longer shine.
16The LORD will roar from Zion
  and thunder from Jerusalem;
  the earth and the sky will tremble.
But the LORD will be a refuge for his people,
  a stronghold for the people of Israel.

Blessings for God's People

17"Then you will know that I, the LORD your God,
  dwell in Zion, my holy hill.
Jerusalem will be holy;
  never again will foreigners invade her.

18"In that day the mountains will drip new wine,
  and the hills will flow with milk;
  all the ravines of Judah will run with water.
A fountain will flow out of the LORD's house
  and will water the valley of acacias.ᵇ
19But Egypt will be desolate,
  Edom a desert waste,
because of violence done to the people of Judah,
  in whose land they shed innocent blood.
20Judah will be inhabited for ever
  and Jerusalem through all generations.
21Their bloodguilt, which I have not pardoned,
  I will pardon."

The LORD dwells in Zion!

ᵃ2 Jehoshaphat means the LORD judges; also in verse 12.   ᵇ18 Or Valley of Shittim

Amos

The Earliest Record

Amos lived around the middle of the eighth century BC and was the first prophet whose message was recorded for posterity. His home was in Tekoa, about 12 miles south of Jerusalem on the edge of the Judean desert. However his prophetic ministry took place in the Northern Kingdom of Israel, particularly in the city of Bethel and Samaria, the capital.

The Political Background

After the death of Solomon the kingdom had divided into two parts (1 Kings 12): the Northern Kingdom of Israel consisted of the bulk of the land and the Southern Kingdom of Judah was made up of the territories of Benjamin and Judah. Both kingdoms had suffered mixed fortunes, but the external situation was favourable and there was strong rule under Uzziah for Judah (783—742 BC) and Jeroboam II for Israel (786—746 BC). This meant there was a time of such peace and unrivalled prosperity for both kingdoms as had not been experienced since the heady days of the empire under David and Solomon. Some people had never had it so good, but for others it was a different story.

The Social Background to the Message of Amos

The monarchy in both the Northern and Southern Kingdoms had brought great changes in Israelite society and culture. There was a social elite whose primary loyalty was to the king rather than to the local community. He was the source of their livelihood and they were responsible for implementing his domestic policies, which included taxation and forced labour for various projects. One reward for their services was land from the king, a practice which was new to Israel although it was common in neighbouring countries. A widening gulf appeared between the rich, who made their homes in the cities but owned a large proportion of the agricultural land, and the poor, who had great difficulty remaining self-sufficient. When there was agricultural disaster and then debt which led eventually to the loss of their land, they had to become tenant farmers or hired workers on the land of the rich. But it was not just in relation to the land that the poor were suffering at the hands of the rich. Old standards of justice, and the concern to give each member of the community their rights, had been discarded, judges had become corrupt, and the decision of the courts was influenced by financial considerations in favour of the party which offered the largest bribe (5:12). Sharp business practices were rife (8:5,6) especially in the cities, and those who fell into debt to the rich land owners or the merchants found themselves at risk of being sold into slavery (2:6).

It was all a far cry from the days when God had called Israel to be his family, a community who were faithful to him and righteous in their dealings with one another. In theory, the people of Israel were still his and they performed their religious duties in a way they thought was commendable. But according to Amos, God was not at all impressed with outward formality and the observance of religious rituals which were divorced from the social reality of daily living (5:21–24).

The message of Amos has a timeless ring about it and it makes uncomfortable reading for those who really want to live their lives in obedience to God's standards for his people.

---

1 The words of Amos, one of the shepherds of Tekoa—what he saw concerning Israel two years before the earthquake, when Uzziah was king of Judah and Jeroboam son of Jehoash[a] was king of Israel. ²He said:

"The LORD roars from Zion
and thunders from Jerusalem;
the pastures of the shepherds dry up,[b]
and the top of Carmel withers."

Judgment on Israel's Neighbours

³This is what the LORD says:

"For three sins of Damascus,
even for four, I will not turn back ⸤my wrath⸥.
Because she threshed Gilead
with sledges having iron teeth,
⁴I will send fire upon the house of Hazael
that will consume the fortresses of Ben-Hadad.
⁵I will break down the gate of Damascus;
I will destroy the king who is in[c] the Valley of Aven[d]
and the one who holds the sceptre in Beth Eden.
The people of Aram will go into exile to Kir,"
says the LORD.

1:3 The crowd listening to Amos would have loved his opening words as he pronounced God's judgement on one after another of their neighbours. The expression "for three sins . . . even for four" is a figure of speech implying an indefinite number. God had been very patient but enough was enough. They were not judged by the law of God because they did not possess it. Instead they were accountable to the standards of acceptable human behaviour which are common to all. God's judgement is always just because the actions of men and women are assessed in the light of the knowledge they possess.

⁶This is what the LORD says:

"For three sins of Gaza,
even for four, I will not turn back ⸤my wrath⸥.
Because she took captive whole communities
and sold them to Edom,
⁷I will send fire upon the walls of Gaza
that will consume her fortresses.
⁸I will destroy the king[e] of Ashdod
and the one who holds the sceptre in Ashkelon.
I will turn my hand against Ekron,
till the last of the Philistines is dead,"
says the Sovereign LORD.

⁹This is what the LORD says:

"For three sins of Tyre,
even for four, I will not turn back ⸤my wrath⸥.
Because she sold whole communities of captives
to Edom,
disregarding a treaty of brotherhood,
¹⁰I will send fire upon the walls of Tyre
that will consume her fortresses."

¹¹This is what the LORD says:

"For three sins of Edom,
even for four, I will not turn back ⸤my wrath⸥.
Because he pursued his brother with a sword,
stifling all compassion,[f]
because his anger raged continually
and his fury flamed unchecked,
¹²I will send fire upon Teman
that will consume the fortresses of Bozrah."

¹³This is what the LORD says:

"For three sins of Ammon,
even for four, I will not turn back ⸤my wrath⸥.
Because he ripped open the pregnant women of Gilead
in order to extend his borders,
¹⁴I will set fire to the walls of Rabbah
that will consume her fortresses
amid war cries on the day of battle,
amid violent winds on a stormy day.
¹⁵Her king[g] will go into exile,
he and his officials together,"
says the LORD.

---

2 This is what the LORD says:

"For three sins of Moab,
  even for four, I will not turn back ₊my wrath₊.
Because he burned, as if to lime,
  the bones of Edom's king,
²I will send fire upon Moab
  that will consume the fortresses of Kerioth.ª
Moab will go down in great tumult
  amid war cries and the blast of the trumpet.
³I will destroy her ruler
  and kill all her officials with him,"
                                        says the LORD.

⁴This is what the LORD says:

"For three sins of Judah,
  even for four, I will not turn back ₊my wrath₊.
Because they have rejected the law of the LORD
  and have not kept his decrees,
because they have been led astray by false gods,ᵇ
  the godsᶜ their ancestors followed,
⁵I will send fire upon Judah
  that will consume the fortresses of Jerusalem."

Judgment on Israel

⁶This is what the LORD says:

"For three sins of Israel,
  even for four, I will not turn back ₊my wrath₊.
They sell the righteous for silver,
  and the needy for a pair of sandals.
⁷They trample on the heads of the poor
  as upon the dust of the ground
  and deny justice to the oppressed.
Father and son use the same girl
  and so profane my holy name.
⁸They lie down beside every altar
  on garments taken in pledge.
In the house of their god
  they drink wine taken as fines.

⁹"I destroyed the Amorite before them,
  though he was tall as the cedars
  and strong as the oaks.
I destroyed his fruit above
  and his roots below.

2:10 The people of Israel were guilty of ignoring God's faithfulness in the past, and of mocking those who took their religious calling seriously in the present. The Nazirites (verse 11) reminded the people that they were all meant to be holy and live lives that were obedient to God's word.

---

¹⁰"I brought you up out of Egypt,
  and I led you for forty years in the desert
  to give you the land of the Amorites.
¹¹I also raised up prophets from among your sons
  and Nazirites from among your young men.

Is this not true, people of Israel?"
                                        declares the LORD.
¹²"But you made the Nazirites drink wine
  and commanded the prophets not to prophesy.

¹³"Now then, I will crush you
  as a cart crushes when loaded with grain.
¹⁴The swift will not escape,
  the strong will not muster their strength,
  and the warrior will not save his life.
¹⁵The archer will not stand his ground,
  the fleet-footed soldier will not get away,
  and the horseman will not save his life.
¹⁶Even the bravest warriors
  will flee naked on that day,"
                                        declares the LORD.

Witnesses Summoned Against Israel

3 Hear this word the LORD has spoken against you,
  O people of Israel—against the whole family I
brought up out of Egypt:

²"You only have I chosen
  of all the families of the earth;
therefore I will punish you
  for all your sins."

3:2 God had chosen Israel to be his special people, and to enjoy an intimate family relationship with him. They were about to learn the hard way that privilege always brings its own responsibilities.

---

³Do two walk together
  unless they have agreed to do so?
⁴Does a lion roar in the thicket
  when he has no prey?
Does he growl in his den
  when he has caught nothing?
⁵Does a bird fall into a trap on the ground
  where no snare has been set?
Does a trap spring up from the earth
  when there is nothing to catch?
⁶When a trumpet sounds in a city,
  do not the people tremble?
When disaster comes to a city,
  has not the LORD caused it?

⁷Surely the Sovereign LORD does nothing
  without revealing his plan
  to his servants the prophets.

⁸The lion has roared—
  who will not fear?
The Sovereign LORD has spoken—
  who can but prophesy?

⁹Proclaim to the fortresses of Ashdod
  and to the fortresses of Egypt:
"Assemble yourselves on the mountains of
    Samaria;
  see the great unrest within her
  and the oppression among her people."

ª2 Or of her cities   ᵇ4 Or by lies   ᶜ4 Or lies

10"They do not know how to do right," declares the
    LORD,
    "who hoard plunder and loot in their
        fortresses."

11Therefore this is what the Sovereign LORD says:

"An enemy will overrun the land;
    he will pull down your strongholds
    and plunder your fortresses."

12This is what the LORD says:

"As a shepherd saves from the lion's mouth
    only two leg bones or a piece of an ear,
    so will the Israelites be saved,
those who sit in Samaria
    on the edge of their beds
    and in Damascus on their couches."ᵃ

13"Hear this and testify against the house of Jacob,"
declares the Lord, the LORD God Almighty.

14"On the day I punish Israel for her sins,
    I will destroy the altars of Bethel;
the horns of the altar will be cut off
    and fall to the ground.
15I will tear down the winter house
    along with the summer house;
the houses adorned with ivory will be destroyed
    and the mansions will be demolished,"
                            declares the LORD.

Israel Has Not Returned to God

4 Hear this word, you cows of Bashan on Mount
    Samaria,
    you women who oppress the poor and crush
        the needy
    and say to your husbands, "Bring us some
        drinks!"
2The Sovereign LORD has sworn by his holiness:
    "The time will surely come
when you will be taken away with hooks,
    the last of you with fish-hooks.
3You will each go straight out
    through breaks in the wall,
    and you will be cast out towards Harmon,"ᵃ
                            declares the LORD.

4"Go to Bethel and sin;
    go to Gilgal and sin yet more.
Bring your sacrifices every morning,
    your tithes every three years.ᵇ
5Burn leavened bread as a thank-offering
    and brag about your freewill offerings—
boast about them, you Israelites,
    for this is what you love to do,"
                    declares the Sovereign LORD.

6"I gave you empty stomachsᶜ in every city
    and lack of bread in every town,
    yet you have not returned to me,"
                            declares the LORD.

7"I also withheld rain from you
    when the harvest was still three months away.
I sent rain on one town,
    but withheld it from another.
One field had rain;
    another had none and dried up.
8People staggered from town to town for water
    but did not get enough to drink,
    yet you have not returned to me,"
                            declares the LORD.

4:5   The people were proud of their religious achievements but deaf to God's displeasure. The catastrophes that are listed in
4:6–11 were probably regular occurrences
in the people's experience but they are interpreted by the prophet as an appeal by God
to his people to repent and return to him
before it was too late.

9"Many times I struck your gardens and vineyards,
    I struck them with blight and mildew.
Locusts devoured your fig and olive trees,
    yet you have not returned to me,"
                            declares the LORD.

10"I sent plagues among you
    as I did to Egypt.
I killed your young men with the sword,
    along with your captured horses.
I filled your nostrils with the stench of your
        camps,
    yet you have not returned to me,"
                            declares the LORD.

11"I overthrew some of you
    as Iᵈ overthrew Sodom and Gomorrah.
You were like a burning stick snatched from the
        fire,
    yet you have not returned to me,"
                            declares the LORD.

12"Therefore this is what I will do to you, Israel,
    and because I will do this to you,
    prepare to meet your God, O Israel."

13He who forms the mountains,
    creates the wind,
    and reveals his thoughts to man,
he who turns dawn to darkness,
    and treads the high places of the earth—
    the LORD God Almighty is his name.

A Lament and Call to Repentance

5 Hear this word, O house of Israel, this lament I
    take up concerning you:

2"Fallen is Virgin Israel,
    never to rise again,
deserted in her own land,
    with no-one to lift her up."

ᵃ12 The meaning of the Hebrew for this line is uncertain.
ᵃ3 Masoretic Text; with a different word division of the Hebrew (see Septuagint) out, O mountain of oppression
ᵇ4 Or tithes on the third day   ᶜ6 Hebrew you cleanness of teeth   ᵈ11 Hebrew God

³This is what the Sovereign LORD says:

"The city that marches out a thousand strong for
    Israel
  will have only a hundred left;
the town that marches out a hundred strong
  will have only ten left."

⁴This is what the LORD says to the house of Israel:

"Seek me and live;
⁵ do not seek Bethel,
do not go to Gilgal,
  do not journey to Beersheba.
For Gilgal will surely go into exile,
  and Bethel will be reduced to nothing." ᵃ
⁶Seek the LORD and live,
  or he will sweep through the house of Joseph
    like a fire;
it will devour,
  and Bethel will have no-one to quench it.

⁷You who turn justice into bitterness
  and cast righteousness to the ground
⁸(he who made the Pleiades and Orion,
  who turns blackness into dawn
  and darkens day into night,
who calls for the waters of the sea
  and pours them out over the face of the land—
    the LORD is his name—
⁹he flashes destruction on the stronghold
  and brings the fortified city to ruin),
¹⁰you hate the one who reproves in court
  and despise him who tells the truth.

¹¹You trample on the poor
  and force him to give you grain.
Therefore, though you have built stone mansions,
  you will not live in them;
though you have planted lush vineyards,
  you will not drink their wine.
¹²For I know how many are your offences
  and how great your sins.

You oppress the righteous and take bribes
  and you deprive the poor of justice in the
    courts.
¹³Therefore the prudent man keeps quiet in such
    times,
  for the times are evil.

¹⁴Seek good, not evil,
  that you may live.
Then the LORD God Almighty will be with you,
  just as you say he is.
¹⁵Hate evil, love good;
  maintain justice in the courts.
Perhaps the LORD God Almighty will have mercy
  on the remnant of Joseph.

¹⁶Therefore this is what the Lord, the LORD God
Almighty, says:

"There will be wailing in all the streets
  and cries of anguish in every public square.

The farmers will be summoned to weep
  and the mourners to wail.
¹⁷There will be wailing in all the vineyards,
  for I will pass through your midst,"
                                        says the LORD.

The Day of the LORD

¹⁸Woe to you who long
  for the day of the LORD!
Why do you long for the day of the LORD?
  That day will be darkness, not light.
¹⁹It will be as though a man fled from a lion
  only to meet a bear,
as though he entered his house
  and rested his hand on the wall
  only to have a snake bite him.
²⁰Will not the day of the LORD be darkness, not
    light—
  pitch-dark, without a ray of brightness?

5:18   In the popular imagination the "day
of the LORD" was going to be a marvellous
triumph for the people of Israel over all their
enemies when everybody else got what they
deserved. Amos called for a drastic rethink
because when judgement came it would
begin with God's own people, and there
would be no escape.

---

²¹"I hate, I despise your religious feasts;
  I cannot stand your assemblies.
²²Even though you bring me burnt offerings and
    grain offerings,
  I will not accept them.
Though you bring choice fellowship offerings,ᵇ
  I will have no regard for them.
²³Away with the noise of your songs!
  I will not listen to the music of your harps.
²⁴But let justice roll on like a river,
  righteousness like a never-failing stream!

²⁵"Did you bring me sacrifices and offerings
  for forty years in the desert, O house of Israel?
²⁶You have lifted up the shrine of your king,
  the pedestal of your idols,
  the star of your god— ᶜ
which you made for yourselves.
²⁷Therefore I will send you into exile beyond
    Damascus,"
  says the LORD, whose name is God Almighty.

Woe to the Complacent

6 Woe to you who are complacent in Zion,
    and to you who feel secure on Mount Samaria,
you notable men of the foremost nation,
  to whom the people of Israel come!
²Go to Calneh and look at it;
  go from there to great Hamath,
  and then go down to Gath in Philistia.

ᵃ5 Or *grief*; or *wickedness*; Hebrew *aven*, a reference to Beth Aven (a derogatory name for Bethel)   ᵇ22 Traditionally *peace offerings*
ᶜ26 Or *lifted up Sakkuth your king / and Kaiwan your idols, / your star-gods*; Septuagint *lifted up the shrine of Molech / and the star of your
god Rephan, / their idols*

Are they better off than your two kingdoms?
Is their land larger than yours?
3You put off the evil day
and bring near a reign of terror.
4You lie on beds inlaid with ivory
and lounge on your couches.
You dine on choice lambs
and fattened calves.
5You strum away on your harps like David
and improvise on musical instruments.
6You drink wine by the bowlful
and use the finest lotions,
but you do not grieve over the ruin of Joseph.
7Therefore you will be among the first to go into
exile;
your feasting and lounging will end.

6:6   Amos was not against wealth in itself but he did condemn the way in which it was acquired (see 5:11), and the use to which it was put. Self indulgence while others starve doesn't rate very highly with God (6:8).

The LORD Abhors the Pride of Israel

8The Sovereign LORD has sworn by himself—the LORD God Almighty declares:

"I abhor the pride of Jacob
and detest his fortresses;
I will deliver up the city
and everything in it."

9If ten men are left in one house, they too will die. 10And if a relative who is to burn the bodies comes to carry them out of the house and asks anyone still hiding there, "Is anyone with you?" and he says, "No," then he will say, "Hush! We must not mention the name of the LORD."

11For the LORD has given the command,
and he will smash the great house into pieces
and the small house into bits.

12Do horses run on the rocky crags?
Does one plough there with oxen?
But you have turned justice into poison
and the fruit of righteousness into bitterness—
13you who rejoice in the conquest of Lo Debar*a*
and say, "Did we not take Karnaim*b* by our
own strength?"

14For the LORD God Almighty declares,
"I will stir up a nation against you, O house of
Israel,
that will oppress you all the way
from Lebo*c* Hamath to the valley of the
Arabah."

Locusts, Fire and a Plumb-Line

7 This is what the Sovereign LORD showed me: He was preparing swarms of locusts after the king's share had been harvested and just as the second crop was coming up. 2When they had stripped the land clean, I cried out, "Sovereign LORD, forgive! How can Jacob survive? He is so small!"

3So the LORD relented.

"This will not happen," the LORD said.

4This is what the Sovereign LORD showed me: The Sovereign LORD was calling for judgment by fire; it dried up the great deep and devoured the land. 5Then I cried out, "Sovereign LORD, I beg you, stop! How can Jacob survive? He is so small!"

6So the LORD relented.

"This will not happen either," the Sovereign LORD said.

7This is what he showed me: the Lord was standing by a wall that had been built true to plumb, with a plumb-line in his hand. 8And the LORD asked me, "What do you see, Amos?"

"A plumb-line," I replied.

Then the Lord said, "Look, I am setting a plumb-line among my people Israel; I will spare them no longer.

9"The high places of Isaac will be destroyed
and the sanctuaries of Israel will be ruined;
with my sword I will rise against the house of
Jeroboam."

Amos and Amaziah

10Then Amaziah the priest of Bethel sent a message to Jeroboam king of Israel: "Amos is raising a conspiracy against you in the very heart of Israel. The land cannot bear all his words. 11For this is what Amos is saying:

" 'Jeroboam will die by the sword,
and Israel will surely go into exile,
away from their native land.' "

12Then Amaziah said to Amos, "Get out, you seer! Go back to the land of Judah. Earn your bread there and do your prophesying there. 13Don't prophesy any more at Bethel, because this is the king's sanctuary and the temple of the kingdom."

14Amos answered Amaziah, "I was neither a prophet nor a prophet's son, but I was a shepherd, and I also took care of sycamore-fig trees. 15But the LORD took me from tending the flock and said to me, 'Go, prophesy to my people Israel.' 16Now then, hear the word of the LORD. You say,

" 'Do not prophesy against Israel,
and stop preaching against the house of Isaac.'

17"Therefore this is what the LORD says:

" 'Your wife will become a prostitute in the city,
and your sons and daughters will fall by the
sword.
Your land will be measured and divided up,
and you yourself will die in a pagan*a* country.

---

a13 Lo Debar means nothing.   *b13 Karnaim means horns; horn here symbolises strength.*   *c14 Or from the entrance to*
a17 Hebrew an unclean

And Israel will certainly go into exile,
away from their native land.' "

A Basket of Ripe Fruit

8 This is what the Sovereign LORD showed me: a basket of ripe fruit. [2]"What do you see, Amos?" he asked.

"A basket of ripe fruit," I answered.

Then the LORD said to me, "The time is ripe for my people Israel; I will spare them no longer.

[3]"In that day," declares the Sovereign LORD, "the songs in the temple will turn to wailing.[a] Many, many bodies — flung everywhere! Silence!"

[4]Hear this, you who trample the needy
and do away with the poor of the land,

[5]saying,

"When will the New Moon be over
that we may sell grain,
and the Sabbath be ended
that we may market wheat?" —
skimping the measure,
boosting the price
and cheating with dishonest scales,
[6]buying the poor with silver
and the needy for a pair of sandals,
selling even the sweepings with the wheat.

[7]The LORD has sworn by the Pride of Jacob: "I will never forget anything they have done.

[8]"Will not the land tremble for this,
and all who live in it mourn?
The whole land will rise like the Nile;
it will be stirred up and then sink
like the river of Egypt.

[9]"In that day," declares the Sovereign LORD,

"I will make the sun go down at noon
and darken the earth in broad daylight.
[10]I will turn your religious feasts into mourning
and all your singing into weeping.
I will make all of you wear sackcloth
and shave your heads.
I will make that time like mourning for an only
son
and the end of it like a bitter day.

[11]"The days are coming," declares the Sovereign
LORD,
"when I will send a famine through the land —
not a famine of food or a thirst for water,
but a famine of hearing the words of the LORD.
[12]Men will stagger from sea to sea
and wander from north to east,
searching for the word of the LORD,
but they will not find it.

[13]"In that day

"the lovely young women and strong young men
will faint because of thirst.

[14]They who swear by the shame[b] of Samaria,
or say, 'As surely as your god lives, O Dan',
or, 'As surely as the god[c] of Beersheba lives' —
they will fall,
never to rise again."

Israel to Be Destroyed

9 I saw the Lord standing by the altar, and he said:

"Strike the tops of the pillars
so that the thresholds shake.
Bring them down on the heads of all the people;
those who are left I will kill with the sword.
Not one will get away,
none will escape.
[2]Though they dig down to the depths of the
grave,[a]
from there my hand will take them.
Though they climb up to the heavens,
from there I will bring them down.
[3]Though they hide themselves on the top of
Carmel,
there I will hunt them down and seize them.
Though they hide from me at the bottom of the
sea,
there I will command the serpent to bite them.
[4]Though they are driven into exile by their
enemies,
there I will command the sword to slay them.
I will fix my eyes upon them
for evil and not for good."

[5]The Lord, the LORD Almighty,
he who touches the earth and it melts,
and all who live in it mourn —
the whole land rises like the Nile,
then sinks like the river of Egypt —
[6]he who builds his lofty palace[b] in the heavens
and sets its foundation[c] on the earth,
who calls for the waters of the sea
and pours them out over the face of the land —
the LORD is his name.

[7]"Are not you Israelites
the same to me as the Cushites?"[d]
                                        declares the LORD.
"Did I not bring Israel up from Egypt,
the Philistines from Caphtor[e]
and the Arameans from Kir?

[8]"Surely the eyes of the Sovereign LORD
are on the sinful kingdom.
I will destroy it
from the face of the earth —
yet I will not totally destroy
the house of Jacob,"
                                        declares the LORD.
[9]"For I will give the command,
and I will shake the house of Israel
among all the nations
as grain is shaken in a sieve,
and not a pebble will reach the ground.

---

[a]3 Or "the temple singers will wail   [b]14 Or by Ashima; or by the idol   [c]14 Or power   [a]2 Hebrew to Sheol
[b]6 The meaning of the Hebrew for this phrase is uncertain.   [c]6 The meaning of the Hebrew for this word is uncertain.
[d]7 That is, people from the upper Nile region   [e]7 That is, Crete

¹⁰All the sinners among my people
  will die by the sword,
all those who say,
  'Disaster will not overtake or meet us.'

9:8   Amos did not preach the end of God's relationship with Israel, but God's discipline of his people within that relationship. Therefore there was still hope for the future, not because of what Israel was but because of who God is.

Israel's Restoration

¹¹"In that day I will restore
  David's fallen tent.
I will repair its broken places,
  restore its ruins,
  and build it as it used to be,

¹²so that they may possess the remnant of Edom
  and all the nations that bear my name,"ᶠ
                        declares the LORD,
                        who will do these things.

¹³"The days are coming," declares the LORD,

"when the reaper will be overtaken by the
    ploughman
  and the planter by the one treading grapes.
New wine will drip from the mountains
  and flow from all the hills.
¹⁴I will bring back my exiledᵍ people Israel;
  they will rebuild the ruined cities and live in
    them.
They will plant vineyards and drink their
    wine;
  they will make gardens and eat their fruit.
¹⁵I will plant Israel in their own land,
  never again to be uprooted
  from the land I have given them,"
                        says the LORD your God.

ᶠ12 Hebrew; Septuagint *so that the remnant of men / and all the nations that bear my name may seek the Lord,*
ᵍ14 Or *will restore the fortunes of my*

Obadiah

A Small Book With a Big Message

The book of Obadiah is the shortest of the books of Prophets — it has just 21 verses! During this short book, however, we discover something of fundamental importance about God and his relationship with his chosen people, Israel. Israel was God's chosen nation, and he loved the people. He protected them as a parent protects a child: pouring compassion and love on them, and, although they rebelled against him and he punished them, his motives were utterly righteous as he desired Israel's wellbeing. The book of Obadiah is a moving cry from a prophet who called upon God to save his chosen people and deal out vengeance upon the neighbouring nation of Edom who were becoming an increasing political threat to Israel.

Nationalism

Edom is south of the Dead Sea, and its people were descended from Jacob's brother, Esau (see Genesis 25:19—27:45). Esau traded his national inheritance for a meal, and went south to be the founding father of the nation of Edom, while Jacob, the younger of the two, inherited the nation of Israel. Despite the two nations starting out as "blood relatives", they began to distrust each other, and Israel regarded Edom as aggressive and cruel.

Where Were You When We Needed You?

When Israel was invaded and sent into exile by the Babylonians in 586 BC, instead of coming to the help of their close national relation, Edom moved in from the south and took advantage of the situation. The people plundered the Israelites who tried to escape, and then moved into Jerusalem to help in the destruction of the city and the temple; thus helping in the destruction of Israel's national and religious centre.

A Cry for Vengeance From an Exiled People

All these terrible things were still fresh in the memory of the Israelites, and the prophecy of Obadiah may have been composed before they returned to Judah from exile. Obadiah declared that God would punish the Edomites who ravaged and plundered his chosen nation, and all that they did to Israel would happen to them (1–14).

God's Justice Will Triumph

Obadiah ends with a moving prophecy of the day when God will restore his chosen nation, and punish those who have harmed it. Edom will be destroyed, and Israel will enjoy security under God once more (15–21).

---

¹The vision of Obadiah.

This is what the Sovereign LORD says about Edom—

We have heard a message from the LORD:
  An envoy was sent to the nations to say,
"Rise, and let us go against her for battle"—

²"See, I will make you small among the nations;
  you will be utterly despised.
³The pride of your heart has deceived you,
  you who live in the clefts of the rocks*ª*
  and make your home on the heights,
you who say to yourself,
  'Who can bring me down to the ground?'
⁴Though you soar like the eagle
  and make your nest among the stars,
  from there I will bring you down,"
                              declares the LORD.
⁵"If thieves came to you,
  if robbers in the night—
Oh, what a disaster awaits you—
  would they not steal only as much as they
    wanted?
If grape pickers came to you,
  would they not leave a few grapes?
⁶But how Esau will be ransacked,
  his hidden treasures pillaged!
⁷All your allies will force you to the border;
  your friends will deceive and overpower you;
those who eat your bread will set a trap for
    you,*ᵇ*
  but you will not detect it.

⁸"In that day," declares the LORD,
  "will I not destroy the wise men of Edom,
  men of understanding in the mountains of
    Esau?
⁹Your warriors, O Teman, will be terrified,
  and everyone in Esau's mountains
  will be cut down in the slaughter.
¹⁰Because of the violence against your brother
    Jacob,
  you will be covered with shame;
  you will be destroyed for ever.
¹¹On the day you stood aloof
  while strangers carried off his wealth
and foreigners entered his gates
  and cast lots for Jerusalem,
  you were like one of them.
¹²You should not look down on your brother
  in the day of his misfortune,
nor rejoice over the people of Judah
  in the day of their destruction,
nor boast so much
  in the day of their trouble.
¹³You should not march through the gates of
    my people
  in the day of their disaster,
nor look down on them in their calamity
  in the day of their disaster,
nor seize their wealth
  in the day of their disaster.
¹⁴You should not wait at the crossroads
  to cut down their fugitives,
nor hand over their survivors
  in the day of their trouble.

ª3 Or *of Sela*   *ᵇ7* The meaning of the Hebrew for this clause is uncertain.

15"The day of the LORD is near
  for all nations.
As you have done, it will be done to you;
  your deeds will return upon your own head.
16Just as you drank on my holy hill,
  so all the nations will drink continually;
they will drink and drink
  and be as if they had never been.
17But on Mount Zion will be deliverance;
  it will be holy,
and the house of Jacob
  will possess its inheritance.
18The house of Jacob will be a fire
  and the house of Joseph a flame;
the house of Esau will be stubble,
  and they will set it on fire and consume it.
There will be no survivors

from the house of Esau."

The LORD has spoken.

19People from the Negev will occupy
  the mountains of Esau,
and people from the foothills will possess
  the land of the Philistines.
They will occupy the fields of Ephraim and
    Samaria,
  and Benjamin will possess Gilead.
20This company of Israelite exiles who are in
    Canaan
  will possess ,the land, as far as Zarephath;
the exiles from Jerusalem who are in Sepharad
  will possess the towns of the Negev.
21Deliverers will go up on c Mount Zion
  to govern the mountains of Esau.
And the kingdom will be the LORD's.

c21 Or from

Jonah

The Cost of God's Call

Throughout the Bible, God called many different sorts of people for many
different reasons. Sometimes they were skilled diplomats or powerful kings,
sometimes they were unlikely characters who had neither eloquent speech
nor wisdom and experience. But whoever they were, sooner or later, they
discovered that being called by God was a costly and demanding business.
Often, those who were called by God found that cost too much, and turned
against his will, preferring to run away and find life somewhere else. Jonah
is the story of a man who found being called by God too much to cope with,
ran away, and was sent back to preach God's word to the greatest bunch
of undesirables you could ever imagine!

A Nation of Bloodthirsty Torturers

These undesirables were the Assyrians. They were a mighty empire, with
an appalling record of violence and cruelty. Whenever they launched an
invasion, they would leave behind a trail of suffering and destruction, and,
so that no one could forget how barbaric they were, they would even carve
graffiti all over the walls, describing all the gory details.

Mission Impossible

Nineveh was the capital of Assyria, and it was there that God sent Jonah.
Knowing all he did about the Assyrians (and their reputation was widespread!) can you blame Jonah for running in the opposite direction? Surely,
the Assyrians were the last people God wanted to show mercy to. They

were a threat to his chosen people, Israel, and deserved to be destroyed. Why should Jonah, the Lord's prophet, waste his time (and risk his own neck) with these people?

God Continues to Surprise

God, however, would have none of this. The earth is his, and he created everything in it; no one is beyond his love and compassion, not even the undesirable Assyrians. So, as Jonah began to think he had run away from God, and was sailing away into the sunset to safety and a new life, God used his creation to play a series of practical jokes on him and deliver him safely to where he was meant to be in the first place (chapters 1 and 2).

A Safe Delivery

Courtesy of that famous fish, Jonah landed safely in Nineveh, and was amazed by the way the Assyrians repented. His surprise was so great that he even complained to God about how successful his mission had been (chapter 4). Jonah still had some hard lessons to learn about God and his relationship with the world.

God's Love Is Available to Everyone

The book of Jonah is important because it proclaims something important about God. When the book was written, most probably after the exile was over, the people of Israel were especially conscious that they were God's chosen people, that he had brought them out of exile and restored their national identity once more; it was very easy for them to adopt an attitude of racial superiority. By sending Jonah to Nineveh, by showing that the Assyrians turned and repented on such a massive scale (more than the people of Israel had ever done), God demonstrated that his love extends to everyone—even to Israel's greatest enemy.

Jonah Flees From the Lord

1 The word of the Lord came to Jonah son of Amittai: 2"Go to the great city of Nineveh and preach against it, because its wickedness has come up before me."

3But Jonah ran away from the Lord and headed for Tarshish. He went down to Joppa, where he found a ship bound for that port. After paying the fare, he went aboard and sailed for Tarshish to flee from the Lord.

4Then the Lord sent a great wind on the sea, and such a violent storm arose that the ship threatened to break up. 5All the sailors were afraid and each cried out to his own god. And they threw the cargo into the sea to lighten the ship.

But Jonah had gone below deck, where he lay down and fell into a deep sleep. 6The captain went to him and said, "How can you sleep? Get up and call on your god! Maybe he will take notice of us, and we will not perish."

7Then the sailors said to each other, "Come, let us cast lots to find out who is responsible for this calamity." They cast lots and the lot fell on Jonah.

8So they asked him, "Tell us, who is responsible for making all this trouble for us? What do you do? Where do you come from? What is your country? From what people are you?"

9He answered, "I am a Hebrew and I worship the Lord, the God of heaven, who made the sea and the land."

10This terrified them and they asked, "What have you done?" (They knew he was running away from the Lord, because he had already told them so.)

11The sea was getting rougher and rougher. So they asked him, "What should we do to you to make the sea calm down for us?"

12"Pick me up and throw me into the sea," he replied, "and it will become calm. I know that it is my fault that this great storm has come upon you."

13Instead, the men did their best to row back to land. But they could not, for the sea grew even wilder than before. ¹⁴Then they cried to the Lord, "O Lord, please do not let us die for taking this man's life. Do not hold us accountable for killing an innocent man, for you, O Lord, have done as you pleased." ¹⁵Then they took Jonah and threw him overboard, and the raging sea grew calm. ¹⁶At this the men greatly feared the Lord, and they offered a sacrifice to the Lord and made vows to him.

¹⁷But the Lord provided a great fish to swallow Jonah, and Jonah was inside the fish three days and three nights.

Jonah's Prayer

2 From inside the fish Jonah prayed to the Lord his God. ²He said:

"In my distress I called to the Lord,
    and he answered me.
From the depths of the grave^a I called for help,
    and you listened to my cry.
³You hurled me into the deep,
    into the very heart of the seas,
    and the currents swirled about me;
all your waves and breakers
    swept over me.
⁴I said, 'I have been banished
    from your sight;
yet I will look again
    towards your holy temple.'
⁵The engulfing waters threatened me,^b
    the deep surrounded me;
    seaweed was wrapped around my head.
⁶To the roots of the mountains I sank down;
    the earth beneath barred me in for ever.
But you brought my life up from the pit,
    O Lord my God.

⁷"When my life was ebbing away,
    I remembered you, Lord,
and my prayer rose to you,
    to your holy temple.

⁸"Those who cling to worthless idols
    forfeit the grace that could be theirs.
⁹But I, with a song of thanksgiving,
    will sacrifice to you.
What I have vowed I will make good.
    Salvation comes from the Lord."

¹⁰And the Lord commanded the fish, and it vomited Jonah onto dry land.

Jonah Goes to Nineveh

3 Then the word of the Lord came to Jonah a second time: ²"Go to the great city of Nineveh and proclaim to it the message I give you."

³Jonah obeyed the word of the Lord and went to Nineveh. Now Nineveh was a very important city—a visit required three days. ⁴On the first day, Jonah started into the city. He proclaimed: "Forty more days and Nineveh will be overturned." ⁵The Ninevites believed God. They declared a fast, and all of them, from the greatest to the least, put on sackcloth.

⁶When the news reached the king of Nineveh, he rose from his throne, took off his royal robes, covered himself with sackcloth and sat down in the dust. ⁷Then he issued a proclamation in Nineveh:

"By the decree of the king and his nobles:

Do not let any man or beast, herd or flock, taste anything; do not let them eat or drink. ⁸But let man and beast be covered with sackcloth. Let everyone call urgently on God. Let them give up their evil ways and their violence. ⁹Who knows? God may yet relent and with compassion turn from his fierce anger so that we will not perish."

¹⁰When God saw what they did and how they turned from their evil ways, he had compassion and did not bring upon them the destruction he had threatened.

Jonah's Anger at the Lord's Compassion

4 But Jonah was greatly displeased and became angry. ²He prayed to the Lord, "O Lord, is this not what I said when I was still at home? That is why I was so quick to flee to Tarshish. I knew that you are a gracious and compassionate God, slow to anger and abounding in love, a God who relents from sending calamity. ³Now, O Lord, take away my life, for it is better for me to die than to live."

⁴But the Lord replied, "Have you any right to be angry?"

⁵Jonah went out and sat down at a place east of the city. There he made himself a shelter, sat in its shade and waited to see what would happen to the city. ⁶Then the Lord God provided a vine and made it grow up over Jonah to give shade for his head to ease his discomfort, and Jonah was very happy about the vine. ⁷But at dawn the next day God provided a worm, which chewed the vine so that it withered. ⁸When the sun rose, God provided a scorching east wind, and the sun blazed on Jonah's head so that he grew faint. He wanted to die, and said, "It would be better for me to die than to live."

⁹But God said to Jonah, "Do you have a right to be angry about the vine?"

"I do," he said. "I am angry enough to die."

¹⁰But the Lord said, "You have been concerned about this vine, though you did not tend it or make it grow. It sprang up overnight and died overnight. ¹¹But Nineveh has more than a hundred and twenty thousand people who cannot tell their right hand from their left, and many cattle as well. Should I not be concerned about that great city?"

---

^a2 Hebrew *Sheol*   ^b5 Or *waters were at my throat*

Micah

City Life and Country Life

Like London is to the English today (and Paris is to the French, and Tokyo to the Japanese), so Jerusalem was at the heart of the national life of the Jews. It was there that the wealthy lived and went about their daily business, it was there that the country folk travelled to worship at the temple for the Pilgrim Feasts. The city people felt that they were very much at the centre of things, and tended to live the "high life". They were regarded with suspicion by those in the country tended to be much poorer and live on the edges of society.

Micah was from Morosheth, a village in the country region to the west of the Hebron valley. Like Amos, another "country" prophet, Micah was not impressed by life in the city, and the city people found that he was ready to direct some of his fiercest criticism towards them. He was a contemporary of Hosea and later Isaiah, and undertook his prophetic ministry under kings Ahaz and Hezekiah (c. 742—687 BC).

Difficult Times

Micah was active as a prophet during a particularly brutal period of Israel's history, described in 2 Kings 15—20 and 2 Chronicles 26—30. The nation was divided. The Southern Kingdom waged war against the Northern Kingdom, and the Northern Kingdom was besieged by the neighbouring, bloodthirsty Assyrians for three years (see 2 Chronicles 32). The political situation in the area, not unlike the Middle East today, was very insecure. Although Micah was a "country boy" and therefore not likely to be held in very high esteem, he was undaunted, and came into the middle of this situation boldly preaching the word of the Lord.

The Issues of The Day

Micah dealt with several different issues. He focused on God's displeasure with the idolatry, fraud, greed, oppression, murder, and hypocrisy of the citizens of Jerusalem (the capital of the Northern Kingdom) and Samaria (the capital of the Southern Kingdom). Like his contemporaries Hosea and Isaiah, Micah laid great emphasis on the fact that true worship of God goes hand in hand with social justice, and when religion becomes just outward show and the rest of life is corrupt and sinful, a nation's life begins to fall to pieces and destruction is just around the corner.

Prophet of Doom or Hope?

Like all true prophets, Micah did not dodge the real issues, however painful they were. He boldly proclaimed God's judgement, and talked about worldwide destruction, the ruin of Samaria, the towns around the countryside where he lived, and finally, the destruction of Jerusalem itself. To the people of the time, it must have seemed like the end of the world! But all was not lost completely, and Micah had a message of hope.

God always holds out to his people the opportunity to turn, to repent, and to obey his teaching. Even the minority (the "remnant") who have been faithful to God will be saved. In one of the most memorable verses in the whole Bible, Micah summed up what faithfulness to God is: "To act justly and to love mercy and to walk humbly with your God." (6:8)

---

1 The word of the LORD that came to Micah of Moresheth during the reigns of Jotham, Ahaz and Hezekiah, kings of Judah—the vision he saw concerning Samaria and Jerusalem.

²Hear, O peoples, all of you,
listen, O earth and all who are in it,
that the Sovereign LORD may witness against you,
the Lord from his holy temple.

Judgment Against Samaria and Jerusalem

³Look! The LORD is coming from his
dwelling-place;
he comes down and treads the high places of
the earth.
⁴The mountains melt beneath him
and the valleys split apart,
like wax before the fire,
like water rushing down a slope.
⁵All this is because of Jacob's transgression,
because of the sins of the house of Israel.
What is Jacob's transgression?
Is it not Samaria?
What is Judah's high place?
Is it not Jerusalem?

⁶"Therefore I will make Samaria a heap of rubble,
a place for planting vineyards.
I will pour her stones into the valley
and lay bare her foundations.
⁷All her idols will be broken to pieces;
all her temple gifts will be burned with fire;
I will destroy all her images.
Since she gathered her gifts from the wages of
prostitutes,
as the wages of prostitutes they will again be
used."

Weeping and Mourning

⁸Because of this I will weep and wail;
I will go about barefoot and naked.
I will howl like a jackal
and moan like an owl.

⁹For her wound is incurable;
it has come to Judah.
It*a* has reached the very gate of my
people,
even to Jerusalem itself.
¹⁰Tell it not in Gath;*b*
weep not at all.*c*
In Beth Ophrah*d*
roll in the dust.
¹¹Pass on in nakedness and shame,
you who live in Shaphir.*e*
Those who live in Zaanan*f*
will not come out.
Beth Ezel is in mourning;
its protection is taken from you.
¹²Those who live in Maroth*g* writhe in pain,
waiting for relief,
because disaster has come from the LORD,
even to the gate of Jerusalem.
¹³You who live in Lachish,*h*
harness the team to the chariot.
You were the beginning of sin
to the Daughter of Zion,
for the transgressions of Israel
were found in you.
¹⁴Therefore you will give parting gifts
to Moresheth Gath.
The town of Aczib*i* will prove deceptive
to the kings of Israel.
¹⁵I will bring a conqueror against you
who live in Mareshah.*j*
He who is the glory of Israel
will come to Adullam.
¹⁶Shave your heads in mourning
for the children in whom you delight;
make yourselves as bald as the vulture,
for they will go from you into exile.

Man's Plans and God's

2 Woe to those who plan iniquity,
to those who plot evil on their beds!
At morning's light they carry it out
because it is in their power to do it.

*a*9 Or He   *b*10 Gath sounds like the Hebrew for tell.
*c*10 Hebrew; Septuagint may suggest not in Acco. The Hebrew for in Acco sounds like the Hebrew for weep.
*d*10 Beth Ophrah means house of dust.   *e*11 Shaphir means pleasant.   *f*11 Zaanan sounds like the Hebrew for come out.
*g*12 Maroth sounds like the Hebrew for bitter.   *h*13 Lachish sounds like the Hebrew for team.   *i*14 Aczib means deception.
*j*15 Mareshah sounds like the Hebrew for conqueror.

²They covet fields and seize them,
  and houses, and take them.
They defraud a man of his home,
  a fellow-man of his inheritance.

³Therefore, the LORD says:

"I am planning disaster against this people,
  from which you cannot save yourselves.
You will no longer walk proudly,
  for it will be a time of calamity.
⁴In that day men will ridicule you;
  they will taunt you with this mournful
    song:
'We are utterly ruined;
  my people's possession is divided up.
He takes it from me!
  He assigns our fields to traitors.' "

⁵Therefore you will have no-one in the
    assembly of the LORD
  to divide the land by lot.

False Prophets

⁶"Do not prophesy," their prophets say.
  "Do not prophesy about these things;
  disgrace will not overtake us."
⁷Should it be said, O house of Jacob:
  "Is the Spirit of the LORD angry?
  Does he do such things?"

  "Do not my words do good
    to him whose ways are upright?
⁸Lately my people have risen up
  like an enemy.
You strip off the rich robe
  from those who pass by without a care,
  like men returning from battle.
⁹You drive the women of my people
  from their pleasant homes.
You take away my blessing
  from their children for ever.
¹⁰Get up, go away!
  For this is not your resting place,
because it is defiled,
  it is ruined, beyond all remedy.
¹¹If a liar and deceiver comes and says,
  'I will prophesy for you plenty of wine
    and beer,'
  he would be just the prophet for this
    people!

Deliverance Promised

¹²"I will surely gather all of you, O Jacob;
  I will surely bring together the remnant of
    Israel.
I will bring them together like sheep in a pen,
  like a flock in its pasture;
  the place will throng with people.
¹³One who breaks open the way will go up
    before them;
  they will break through the gate and go
    out.
Their king will pass through before them,
  the LORD at their head."

Leaders and Prophets Rebuked

3 Then I said,

"Listen, you leaders of Jacob,
  you rulers of the house of Israel.
Should you not know justice,
² you who hate good and love evil;
who tear the skin from my people
  and the flesh from their bones;
³who eat my people's flesh,
  strip off their skin
  and break their bones in pieces;
who chop them up like meat for the
    pan,
  like flesh for the pot."

⁴Then they will cry out to the LORD,
  but he will not answer them.
At that time he will hide his face from
    them
  because of the evil they have done.

⁵This is what the LORD says:

"As for the prophets
  who lead my people astray,
if one feeds them,
  they proclaim 'peace';
if he does not,
  they prepare to wage war against him.
⁶Therefore night will come over you,
    without visions,
  and darkness, without divination.
The sun will set for the prophets,
  and the day will go dark for them.
⁷The seers will be ashamed
  and the diviners disgraced.
They will all cover their faces
  because there is no answer from
    God."

⁸But as for me, I am filled with power,
  with the Spirit of the LORD,
  and with justice and might,
to declare to Jacob his transgression,
  to Israel his sin.
⁹Hear this, you leaders of the house of
    Jacob,
  you rulers of the house of Israel,
who despise justice
  and distort all that is right;
¹⁰who build Zion with bloodshed,
  and Jerusalem with wickedness.
¹¹Her leaders judge for a bribe,
  her priests teach for a price,
  and her prophets tell fortunes for
    money.
Yet they lean upon the LORD and say,
  "Is not the LORD among us?
  No disaster will come upon us."
¹²Therefore because of you,
  Zion will be ploughed like a field,
Jerusalem will become a heap of rubble,
  the temple hill a mound overgrown with
    thickets.

The Mountain of the LORD

4 In the last days

the mountain of the LORD's temple will be
established
as chief among the mountains;
it will be raised above the hills,
and peoples will stream to it.

²Many nations will come and say,

"Come, let us go up to the mountain of the LORD,
to the house of the God of Jacob.
He will teach us his ways,
so that we may walk in his paths."
The law will go out from Zion,
the word of the LORD from Jerusalem.
³He will judge between many peoples
and will settle disputes for strong nations far
and wide.
They will beat their swords into ploughshares
and their spears into pruning hooks.
Nation will not take up sword against nation,
nor will they train for war any more.
⁴Every man will sit under his own vine
and under his own fig-tree,
and no-one will make them afraid,
for the LORD Almighty has spoken.
⁵All the nations may walk
in the name of their gods;
we will walk in the name of the LORD
our God for ever and ever.

The LORD's Plan

⁶"In that day," declares the LORD,

"I will gather the lame;
I will assemble the exiles
and those I have brought to grief.
⁷I will make the lame a remnant,
those driven away a strong nation.
The LORD will rule over them in Mount Zion
from that day and for ever.
⁸As for you, O watchtower of the flock,
O stronghold*ᵃ* of the Daughter of Zion,
the former dominion will be restored to you;
kingship will come to the Daughter of
Jerusalem."

⁹Why do you now cry aloud—
have you no king?
Has your counsellor perished,
that pain seizes you like that of a woman in
labour?
¹⁰Writhe in agony, O Daughter of Zion,
like a woman in labour,
for now you must leave the city
to camp in the open field.
You will go to Babylon;
there you will be rescued.
There the LORD will redeem you
out of the hand of your enemies.

¹¹But now many nations
are gathered against you.
They say, "Let her be defiled,
let our eyes gloat over Zion!"
¹²But they do not know
the thoughts of the LORD;
they do not understand his plan,
he who gathers them like sheaves to the
threshing-floor.
¹³"Rise and thresh, O Daughter of Zion,
for I will give you horns of iron;
I will give you hoofs of bronze
and you will break to pieces many nations."

You will devote their ill-gotten gains to the LORD,
their wealth to the Lord of all the earth.

A Promised Ruler From Bethlehem

5 Marshal your troops, O city of troops,*ᵃ*
for a siege is laid against us.
They will strike Israel's ruler
on the cheek with a rod.

²"But you, Bethlehem Ephrathah,
though you are small among the clans*ᵇ* of
Judah,
out of you will come for me
one who will be ruler over Israel,
whose origins*ᶜ* are from of old,
from ancient times."*ᵈ*

³Therefore Israel will be abandoned
until the time when she who is in labour gives
birth
and the rest of his brothers return
to join the Israelites.

⁴He will stand and shepherd his flock
in the strength of the LORD,
in the majesty of the name of the LORD his God.
And they will live securely, for then his greatness
will reach to the ends of the earth.
⁵ And he will be their peace.

Deliverance and Destruction

When the Assyrian invades our land
and marches through our fortresses,
we will raise against him seven shepherds,
even eight leaders of men.
⁶They will rule*ᵉ* the land of Assyria with the
sword,
the land of Nimrod with drawn sword.*ᶠ*
He will deliver us from the Assyrian
when he invades our land
and marches into our borders.

⁷The remnant of Jacob will be
in the midst of many peoples
like dew from the LORD,
like showers on the grass,
which do not wait for man
or linger for mankind.

ᵃ8 Or *hill*   *ᵃ1* Or *Strengthen your walls, O walled city*   *ᵇ2* Or *rulers*   *ᶜ2* Hebrew *goings out*
ᵈ2 Or *from days of eternity*   *ᵉ6* Or *crush*   *ᶠ6* Or *Nimrod in its gates*

⁸The remnant of Jacob will be among the nations,
 in the midst of many peoples,
like a lion among the beasts of the forest,
 like a young lion among flocks of sheep,
which mauls and mangles as it goes,
 and no-one can rescue.
⁹Your hand will be lifted up in triumph over your
  enemies,
 and all your foes will be destroyed.

¹⁰"In that day," declares the LORD,

"I will destroy your horses from among you
 and demolish your chariots.
¹¹I will destroy the cities of your land
 and tear down all your strongholds.
¹²I will destroy your witchcraft
 and you will no longer cast spells.
¹³I will destroy your carved images
 and your sacred stones from among you;
you will no longer bow down
 to the work of your hands.
¹⁴I will uproot from among you your Asherah
  poles ᵍ
 and demolish your cities.
¹⁵I will take vengeance in anger and wrath
 upon the nations that have not obeyed me."

The LORD's Case Against Israel

6 Listen to what the LORD says:

"Stand up, plead your case before the mountains;
 let the hills hear what you have to say.
²Hear, O mountains, the LORD's accusation;
 listen, you everlasting foundations of the earth.
For the LORD has a case against his people;
 he is lodging a charge against Israel.

³"My people, what have I done to you?
 How have I burdened you? Answer me.
⁴I brought you up out of Egypt
 and redeemed you from the land of slavery.
I sent Moses to lead you,
 also Aaron and Miriam.
⁵My people, remember
 what Balak king of Moab counselled
 and what Balaam son of Beor answered.
Remember ˌyour journeyˌ from Shittim to Gilgal,
 that you may know the righteous acts of the
  LORD."

⁶With what shall I come before the LORD
 and bow down before the exalted God?
Shall I come before him with burnt offerings,
 with calves a year old?
⁷Will the LORD be pleased with thousands of rams,
 with ten thousand rivers of oil?
Shall I offer my firstborn for my transgression,
 the fruit of my body for the sin of my soul?
⁸He has showed you, O man, what is good.
 And what does the LORD require of you?

To act justly and to love mercy
 and to walk humbly with your God.

Israel's Guilt and Punishment

⁹Listen! The LORD is calling to the city—
 and to fear your name is wisdom—
"Heed the rod and the One who appointed it. ᵃ
¹⁰Am I still to forget, O wicked house,
 your ill-gotten treasures
 and the short ephah, ᵇ which is accursed?
¹¹Shall I acquit a man with dishonest scales,
 with a bag of false weights?
¹²Her rich men are violent;
 her people are liars
 and their tongues speak deceitfully.
¹³Therefore, I have begun to destroy you,
 to ruin you because of your sins.
¹⁴You will eat but not be satisfied;
 your stomach will still be empty. ᶜ
You will store up but save nothing,
 because what you save I will give to the sword.
¹⁵You will plant but not harvest;
 you will press olives but not use the oil on
  yourselves,
 you will crush grapes but not drink the wine.
¹⁶You have observed the statutes of Omri
 and all the practices of Ahab's house,
 and you have followed their traditions.
Therefore I will give you over to ruin
 and your people to derision;
 you will bear the scorn of the nations." ᵈ

Israel's Misery

7 What misery is mine!
 I am like one who gathers summer fruit
 at the gleaning of the vineyard;
there is no cluster of grapes to eat,
 none of the early figs that I crave.
²The godly have been swept from the land;
 not one upright man remains.
All men lie in wait to shed blood;
 each hunts his brother with a net.
³Both hands are skilled in doing evil;
 the ruler demands gifts,
the judge accepts bribes,
 the powerful dictate what they desire—
 they all conspire together.
⁴The best of them is like a brier,
 the most upright worse than a thorn hedge.
The day of your watchmen has come,
 the day God visits you.
Now is the time of their confusion.
⁵Do not trust a neighbour;
 put no confidence in a friend.
Even with her who lies in your embrace
 be careful of your words.
⁶For a son dishonours his father,
 a daughter rises up against her mother,

ᵍ14 That is, symbols of the goddess Asherah   ᵃ9 The meaning of the Hebrew for this line is uncertain.
ᵇ10 An ephah was a dry measure.   ᶜ14 The meaning of the Hebrew for this word is uncertain.
ᵈ16 Septuagint; Hebrew *scorn due to my people*

a daughter-in-law against her mother-in-law—
a man's enemies are the members of his own
household.

[7]But as for me, I watch in hope for the LORD,
I wait for God my Saviour;
my God will hear me.

Israel Will Rise

[8]Do not gloat over me, my enemy!
Though I have fallen, I will rise.
Though I sit in darkness,
the LORD will be my light.
[9]Because I have sinned against him,
I will bear the LORD's wrath,
until he pleads my case
and establishes my right.
He will bring me out into the light;
I will see his righteousness.
[10]Then my enemy will see it
and will be covered with shame,
she who said to me,
"Where is the LORD your God?"
My eyes will see her downfall;
even now she will be trampled underfoot
like mire in the streets.

[11]The day for building your walls will come,
the day for extending your boundaries.
[12]In that day people will come to you
from Assyria and the cities of Egypt,
even from Egypt to the Euphrates
and from sea to sea
and from mountain to mountain.
[13]The earth will become desolate because of its
inhabitants,
as the result of their deeds.

[a] 14 Or in the middle of Carmel

Prayer and Praise

[14]Shepherd your people with your staff,
the flock of your inheritance,
which lives by itself in a forest,
in fertile pasture-lands.[a]
Let them feed in Bashan and Gilead
as in days long ago.

[15]"As in the days when you came out of
Egypt,
I will show them my wonders."

[16]Nations will see and be ashamed,
deprived of all their power.
They will lay their hands on their mouths
and their ears will become deaf.
[17]They will lick dust like a snake,
like creatures that crawl on the ground.
They will come trembling out of their dens;
they will turn in fear to the LORD our
God
and will be afraid of you.
[18]Who is a God like you,
who pardons sin and forgives the
transgression
of the remnant of his inheritance?
You do not stay angry for ever
but delight to show mercy.
[19]You will again have compassion on us;
you will tread our sins underfoot
and hurl all our iniquities into the depths
of the sea.
[20]You will be true to Jacob,
and show mercy to Abraham,
as you pledged on oath to our fathers
in days long ago.

Nahum

Religion and Politics

It is not very easy for a western reader in the twentieth century to
appreciate the strong connection between prophecy and politics. We have
mostly grown up to understand that religion is entirely separate from politics, and those who try and mix the two, as modern prophets like Bishop
Desmond Tutu and Jim Wallace have discovered, find themselves being
strongly criticized. The prophets of Israel would have been absolutely flabbergasted by this. For them, religious faith and the social and political
dimension of life were so bound up with each other that they were insep-
arable. God, they believed, called prophets to bring his word to every aspect
of life, not just the outwardly religious side of it, because the whole of life
was given by him and is subject to his laws and commands.

A Prophet's Job Description

Nahum's task was no easy one. Not only was he called to proclaim God's word during a period of great upheaval, but also to address the word of God to a mighty enemy nation—the Assyrians. About one hundred years earlier, the prophet Jonah had been sent by God to preach and call Assyria's capital city, Nineveh, to repentance. But now the city stood for all that was powerfully brutal, and it represented a great military threat to the small, vulnerable Southern Kingdom of Judah. It was, therefore, only a matter of time before the Assyrians came crashing into Judah. They left behind a trail of destruction, dragging Manasseh, the Judaean king, back to Nineveh, and forcing Judah to pay tribute to Assyria as an annexed state (see 2 Chronicles 33:11). In the face of such great power, Nahum was called to preach to the people of Nineveh and to predict that their city would suffer destruction.

Unusual Qualities Required

By anyone's standards, you have got to be mad to do what God was asking Nahum to do! No one with any regard for their own safety would dare stand up and tell mighty, brutal people that their own destruction is just around the corner. But a prophet is always sent into the heat of the situation, and Nahum had no choice! His confidence in God's justice, and his outrage at blatant oppression, strengthened his resolve to preach the word of God.

Job Satisfaction

Nahum's message was uncompromising: God will judge all who oppose his will and purpose (1:11, 2:1); he will punish all who oppress his chosen people, Israel (1:12,13); and he will bring to destruction to all who destroy other nations (3:17). Nahum was concerned to show that God's concern is universal, and that his justice reaches out to the ends of the earth—a message which is sure to have raised the hopes of a downtrodden nation.

One thing that we never discover in the course of this book is what actually happened to Nahum. The intriguing idea of a humble human being preaching an uncomfortable message to a mighty nation is bound to make us inquisitive: did they capture him, torture him, or kill him even? We are not told. All we know is what Nahum preached, and from this we discover God's will and purpose.

Fulfilment

In 612 BC, not long after Nahum's prophecy, Nineveh was reduced to a pile of rubble, never to rise again. It was a fitting fulfilment of all that the prophet had foretold:

"The LORD is good,
  a refuge in times of trouble.
He cares for those who trust in him,
  but with an overwhelming flood. . .
  he will pursue his foes into darkness."

(1:7–8)

1 An oracle concerning Nineveh. The book of the vision of Nahum the Elkoshite.

The LORD's Anger Against Nineveh

²The LORD is a jealous and avenging God;
   the LORD takes vengeance and is filled with
      wrath.
The LORD takes vengeance on his foes
   and maintains his wrath against his enemies.
³The LORD is slow to anger and great in power;
   the LORD will not leave the guilty unpunished.
His way is in the whirlwind and the storm,
   and clouds are the dust of his feet.
⁴He rebukes the sea and dries it up;
   he makes all the rivers run dry.
Bashan and Carmel wither
   and the blossoms of Lebanon fade.
⁵The mountains quake before him
   and the hills melt away.
The earth trembles at his presence,
   the world and all who live in it.
⁶Who can withstand his indignation?
   Who can endure his fierce anger?
His wrath is poured out like fire;
   the rocks are shattered before him.

⁷The LORD is good,
   a refuge in times of trouble.
He cares for those who trust in him,
⁸ but with an overwhelming flood
he will make an end of ⌊Nineveh⌋;
   he will pursue his foes into darkness.

⁹Whatever they plot against the LORD
   heᵃ will bring to an end;
trouble will not come a second time.
¹⁰They will be entangled among thorns
   and drunk from their wine;
   they will be consumed like dry stubble.ᵇ
¹¹From you, ⌊O Nineveh,⌋ has one come forth
   who plots evil against the LORD
   and counsels wickedness.

¹²This is what the LORD says:

"Although they have allies and are numerous,
   they will be cut off and pass away.
Although I have afflicted you, ⌊O Judah,⌋
   I will afflict you no more.
¹³Now I will break their yoke from your neck
   and tear your shackles away."

¹⁴The LORD has given a command concerning you,
      ⌊Nineveh⌋:
"You will have no descendants to bear your
      name.
I will destroy the carved images and cast idols
   that are in the temple of your gods.
I will prepare your grave,
   for you are vile."

¹⁵Look, there on the mountains,
   the feet of one who brings good news,
   who proclaims peace!
Celebrate your festivals, O Judah,
   and fulfil your vows.
No more will the wicked invade you;
   they will be completely destroyed.

Nineveh to Fall

2 An attacker advances against you, ⌊Nineveh⌋.
   Guard the fortress,
watch the road,
brace yourselves,
marshal all your strength!

²The LORD will restore the splendour of Jacob
   like the splendour of Israel,
though destroyers have laid them waste
   and have ruined their vines.

³The shields of his soldiers are red;
   the warriors are clad in scarlet.
The metal on the chariots flashes
   on the day they are made ready;
   the spears of pine are brandished.ᵃ
⁴The chariots storm through the streets,
   rushing back and forth through the squares.
They look like flaming torches;
   they dart about like lightning.

⁵He summons his picked troops,
   yet they stumble on their way.
They dash to the city wall;
   the protective shield is put in place.
⁶The river gates are thrown open
   and the palace collapses.
⁷It is decreedᵇ that ⌊the city⌋
   be exiled and carried away.
Its slave girls moan like doves
   and beat upon their breasts.
⁸Nineveh is like a pool,
   and its water is draining away.
"Stop! Stop!" they cry,
   but no-one turns back.
⁹Plunder the silver!
   Plunder the gold!
The supply is endless,
   the wealth from all its treasures!
¹⁰She is pillaged, plundered, stripped!
   Hearts melt, knees give way,
   bodies tremble, every face grows pale.

¹¹Where now is the lions' den,
   the place where they fed their young,
where the lion and lioness went,
   and the cubs, with nothing to fear?
¹²The lion killed enough for his cubs
   and strangled the prey for his mate,
filling his lairs with the kill
   and his dens with the prey.

ᵃ9 Or What do you foes plot against the LORD? / He
ᵃ3 Hebrew; Septuagint and Syriac / the horsemen rush to and fro

ᵇ10 The meaning of the Hebrew for this verse is uncertain.
ᵇ7 The meaning of the Hebrew for this word is uncertain.

13"I am against you,"
  declares the LORD Almighty.
"I will burn up your chariots in smoke,
  and the sword will devour your young lions.
I will leave you no prey on the earth.
The voices of your messengers
  will no longer be heard."

Woe to Nineveh

3 Woe to the city of blood,
  full of lies,
full of plunder,
  never without victims!
2The crack of whips,
  the clatter of wheels,
galloping horses
  and jolting chariots!
3Charging cavalry,
  flashing swords
  and glittering spears!
Many casualties,
  piles of dead,
bodies without number,
  people stumbling over the corpses—
4all because of the wanton lust of a harlot,
  alluring, the mistress of sorceries,
who enslaved nations by her prostitution
  and peoples by her witchcraft.

5"I am against you," declares the LORD Almighty.
  "I will lift your skirts over your face.
I will show the nations your nakedness
  and the kingdoms your shame.
6I will pelt you with filth,
  I will treat you with contempt
  and make you a spectacle.
7All who see you will flee from you and say,
  'Nineveh is in ruins—who will mourn for her?'
Where can I find anyone to comfort you?"

8Are you better than Thebes,a
  situated on the Nile,
  with water around her?
The river was her defence,
  the waters her wall.
9Cushb and Egypt were her boundless
    strength;
  Put and Libya were among her allies.

10Yet she was taken captive
  and went into exile.
Her infants were dashed to pieces
  at the head of every street.
Lots were cast for her nobles,
  and all her great men were put in chains.
11You too will become drunk;
  you will go into hiding
  and seek refuge from the enemy.

12All your fortresses are like fig-trees
  with their first ripe fruit;
when they are shaken,
  the figs fall into the mouth of the eater.
13Look at your troops—
  they are all women!
The gates of your land
  are wide open to your enemies;
  fire has consumed their bars.

14Draw water for the siege,
  strengthen your defences!
Work the clay,
  tread the mortar,
  repair the brickwork!
15There the fire will devour you;
  the sword will cut you down
  and, like grasshoppers, consume you.
Multiply like grasshoppers,
  multiply like locusts!
16You have increased the number of your
    merchants
  till they are more than the stars of the sky,
but like locusts they strip the land
  and then fly away.
17Your guards are like locusts,
  your officials like swarms of locusts
  that settle in the walls on a cold day—
but when the sun appears they fly away,
  and no-one knows where.

18O king of Assyria, your shepherdsc slumber;
  your nobles lie down to rest.
Your people are scattered on the mountains
  with no-one to gather them.
19Nothing can heal your wound;
  your injury is fatal.
Everyone who hears the news about you
  claps his hands at your fall,
for who has not felt
  your endless cruelty?

---

a8 Hebrew No Amon   b9 That is, the upper Nile region   c18 Or rulers

Habakkuk

A Big Question

Throughout history, people have asked the question, "Why?" to many things. It is a question of protest: an unwillingness to accept a particular situation, a need to probe deeper, a refusal to let someone else have the last word. It is a question asked by individual people and whole nations of people. The Jews have asked this question with urgency, and the book of Habakkuk is the story of a prophet who asked questions as a way of protesting, and who refused to believe that God could allow his chosen people to suffer in the face of violence and oppression. This is not the only book to concentrate on this subject. The book of Job is probably the supreme example in the Bible, while modern history has painfully shown us how, even in our own century, the Jews have been victims of persecution and genocide on a massive scale in the Nazi death camps of Eastern Europe.

In Turbulent Times

Habakkuk's questions came at a particularly distressing time in the history of Israel. The mighty nation of Babylon was mounting a whole series of invasions and plunderings; Babylonian victory in the Battle of Carchemish in 605 BC had ensured that the notorious Babylonian king, Nebuchadnezzar, was perhaps the most important person in Middle-Eastern politics, and it would only be a matter of time before the Babylonian troops came thundering into Judea. During Habakkuk's ministry, the prophet Daniel was taken by Nebuchadnezzar into captivity in Babylon (at the same time as Jeremiah and Nahum were prophesying). So Habakkuk was active during a particularly turbulent period, probably until the fall of Judah in 586 BC.

Why?

Why, in the face of cruelty and injustice, did God stay silent? Why didn't he do something? God's answer was not the one Habakkuk expected: he would send in the Babylonians—that should put a stop to the activities of the violent Judaeans! Habakkuk did not understand why God could be so rash, when the Babylonians would come in and ransack the whole country. What sort of justice was it that repaid violence with violence? God answered with reassurance: the Babylonians would be punished with the same strength and the same weapons which they had used on others, and would be destroyed as they had destroyed other nations.

The Future Is God's

By asking questions of protest, Habakkuk discovered one essential truth: evil and violence may be around every corner, but as evil grows it turns back on itself and self-destructs (this is the essential meaning of the Greek word, "nemesis"). The questions may baffle us, and God may seem remote and silent, but the future is God's and, despite all the cruelty and hardship, authority lies with him (2:14). It was only by having the confidence to stand up and protest in the first place that Habakkuk eventually discovered that God has the final word. This turned his cries of protest into a song of praise, rejoicing in the faithfulness of God.

---

1 The oracle that Habakkuk the prophet received.

Habakkuk's Complaint

²How long, O LORD, must I call for help,
    but you do not listen?
Or cry out to you, "Violence!"
    but you do not save?
³Why do you make me look at injustice?
    Why do you tolerate wrong?
Destruction and violence are before me;
    there is strife, and conflict abounds.
⁴Therefore the law is paralysed,
    and justice never prevails.
The wicked hem in the righteous,
    so that justice is perverted.

The LORD's Answer

⁵"Look at the nations and watch—
    and be utterly amazed.
For I am going to do something in your days
    that you would not believe,
    even if you were told.
⁶I am raising up the Babylonians,ᵃ
    that ruthless and impetuous people,
who sweep across the whole earth
    to seize dwelling-places not their own.
⁷They are a feared and dreaded people;
    they are a law to themselves
    and promote their own honour.
⁸Their horses are swifter than leopards,
    fiercer than wolves at dusk.
Their cavalry gallops headlong;
    their horsemen come from afar.
They fly like a vulture swooping to devour;
⁹   they all come bent on violence.
Their hordesᵇ advance like a desert wind
    and gather prisoners like sand.
¹⁰They deride kings
    and scoff at rulers.
They laugh at all fortified cities;
    they build earthen ramps and capture them.
¹¹Then they sweep past like the wind and go on—
    guilty men, whose own strength is their god."

Habakkuk's Second Complaint

¹²O LORD, are you not from everlasting?
    My God, my Holy One, we will not die.
O LORD, you have appointed them to execute
    judgment;
O Rock, you have ordained them to punish.
¹³Your eyes are too pure to look on evil;
    you cannot tolerate wrong.
Why then do you tolerate the treacherous?
Why are you silent while the wicked
    swallow up those more righteous than
    themselves?
¹⁴You have made men like fish in the sea,
    like sea creatures that have no ruler.
¹⁵The wicked foe pulls all of them up with hooks,
    he catches them in his net,
he gathers them up in his drag-net;
    and so he rejoices and is glad.
¹⁶Therefore he sacrifices to his net
    and burns incense to his drag-net,
for by his net he lives in luxury
    and enjoys the choicest food.
¹⁷Is he to keep on emptying his net,
    destroying nations without mercy?

2 I will stand at my watch
    and station myself on the ramparts;
I will look to see what he will say to me,
    and what answer I am to give to this
    complaint.ᵃ

The LORD's Answer

²Then the LORD replied:

"Write down the revelation
    and make it plain on tablets
    so that a heraldᵇ may run with it.
³For the revelation awaits an appointed time;
    it speaks of the end
    and will not prove false.
Though it linger, wait for it;
    itᶜ will certainly come and will not delay.

ᵃ6 Or Chaldeans   ᵇ9 The meaning of the Hebrew for this word is uncertain.   ᵃ1 Or and what to answer when I am rebuked
ᵇ2 Or so that whoever reads it   ᶜ3 Or Though he linger, wait for him; / he

4"See, he is puffed up;
   his desires are not upright —
   but the righteous will live by his faith[d] —
5indeed, wine betrays him;
   he is arrogant and never at rest.
Because he is as greedy as the grave[e]
   and like death is never satisfied,
he gathers to himself all the nations
   and takes captive all the peoples.

6"Will not all of them taunt him with ridicule and scorn, saying,

" 'Woe to him who piles up stolen goods
   and makes himself wealthy by extortion!
   How long must this go on?'
7Will not your debtors[f] suddenly arise?
   Will they not wake up and make you tremble?
   Then you will become their victim.
8Because you have plundered many nations,
   the peoples who are left will plunder you.
For you have shed man's blood;
   you have destroyed lands and cities and
     everyone in them.

9"Woe to him who builds his realm by unjust gain
   to set his nest on high,
   to escape the clutches of ruin!
10You have plotted the ruin of many peoples,
   shaming your own house and forfeiting your
     life.
11The stones of the wall will cry out,
   and the beams of the woodwork will echo it.

12"Woe to him who builds a city with bloodshed
   and establishes a town by crime!
13Has not the LORD Almighty determined
   that the people's labour is only fuel for the fire,
   that the nations exhaust themselves for
     nothing?
14For the earth will be filled with the knowledge of
   the glory of the LORD,
   as the waters cover the sea.

15"Woe to him who gives drink to his neighbours,
   pouring it from the wineskin till they are drunk,
   so that he can gaze on their naked bodies.
16You will be filled with shame instead of glory.
   Now it is your turn! Drink and be exposed![g]
The cup from the LORD's right hand is coming
   round to you,
   and disgrace will cover your glory.
17The violence you have done to Lebanon will
   overwhelm you,
   and your destruction of animals will terrify you.
For you have shed man's blood;
   you have destroyed lands and cities and
     everyone in them.

18"Of what value is an idol, since a man has carved
   it?
Or an image that teaches lies?
For he who makes it trusts in his own creation;
   he makes idols that cannot speak.

19Woe to him who says to wood, 'Come to life!'
   Or to lifeless stone, 'Wake up!'
Can it give guidance?
   It is covered with gold and silver;
   there is no breath in it.
20But the LORD is in his holy temple;
   let all the earth be silent before him."

Habakkuk's Prayer

3 A prayer of Habakkuk the prophet. On shigionoth.[a]

2LORD, I have heard of your fame;
   I stand in awe of your deeds, O LORD.
Renew them in our day,
   in our time make them known;
   in wrath remember mercy.

3God came from Teman,
   the Holy One from Mount Paran.   Selah[b]
His glory covered the heavens
   and his praise filled the earth.
4His splendour was like the sunrise;
   rays flashed from his hand,
   where his power was hidden.
5Plague went before him;
   pestilence followed his steps.
6He stood, and shook the earth;
   he looked, and made the nations tremble.
The ancient mountains crumbled
   and the age-old hills collapsed.
   His ways are eternal.
7I saw the tents of Cushan in distress,
   the dwellings of Midian in anguish.

8Were you angry with the rivers, O LORD?
   Was your wrath against the streams?
Did you rage against the sea
   when you rode with your horses
   and your victorious chariots?
9You uncovered your bow,
   you called for many arrows.   Selah
You split the earth with rivers;
10   the mountains saw you and writhed.
Torrents of water swept by;
   the deep roared
   and lifted its waves on high.

11Sun and moon stood still in the heavens
   at the glint of your flying arrows,
   at the lightning of your flashing spear.
12In wrath you strode through the earth
   and in anger you threshed the nations.
13You came out to deliver your people,
   to save your anointed one.
You crushed the leader of the land of
   wickedness,
   you stripped him from head to foot.   Selah
14With his own spear you pierced his head
   when his warriors stormed out to scatter us,
gloating as though about to devour
   the wretched who were in hiding.

¹⁵You trampled the sea with your horses,
  churning the great waters.

¹⁶I heard and my heart pounded,
  my lips quivered at the sound;
decay crept into my bones,
  and my legs trembled.
Yet I will wait patiently for the day of calamity
  to come on the nation invading us.
¹⁷Though the fig-tree does not bud
  and there are no grapes on the vines,
though the olive crop fails

and the fields produce no food,
though there are no sheep in the pen
  and no cattle in the stalls,
¹⁸yet I will rejoice in the LORD,
  I will be joyful in God my Saviour.

¹⁹The Sovereign LORD is my strength;
  he makes my feet like the feet of a
  deer,
  he enables me to go on the heights.

For the director of music. On my stringed
  instruments.

Zephaniah

There's a Light at the End of the Tunnel

Zephaniah was active as a prophet in Judah around the time that Jeremiah was beginning his ministry. It was during the reign of King Josiah who succeeded to the throne in 640 BC at the age of eight (2 Kings 22:1). His father, Amon, had been assassinated by his own officials after only a few months on the throne. Josiah is remembered in Jewish tradition as a very good king who led a religious reform based on a national recommitment to God's law. He revitalized the faith of the nation, restored the temple, and reintroduced Passover celebrations which had been allowed to lapse over the years (2 Kings 23:25). This reform took place during the latter part of his reign and nothing of his earlier rule is recorded in the Old Testament. It is probable that the way of life in Judah changed little in those years from how it had been during the fifty-year reign of Manasseh which had ended in 641 BC.

God's Ways Had Been Forgotten

Manasseh had not been faithful to God. He had worshipped foreign gods and idols, set up altars to star gods in the Jerusalem temple, and permitted all kinds of immoral rituals. He may even have sacrificed his own child in a pagan ritual. The account of his reign in 2 Kings 21:1–18 stresses the evil that he did and tells of how he led the people astray. This was the legacy that Josiah inherited and it is probable that Zephaniah proclaimed his words against this background of religious decadence. His prophecy may have prompted people to start thinking about God and matters of faith once more. If so, he perhaps helped to prepare the way for the reforming work which God wanted to do through Josiah.

A Day of Judgement

The book begins with a warning of God's judgement on the whole earth. This was probably an exaggerated prophecy intended to draw attention to how serious the situation was. Zephaniah then proclaimed harsh words against Judah, condemning all their sinful worship. He spoke repeatedly of a particular day, "the day of the LORD", when God would punish everyone in the land for their sin. No one would escape and the complacent would discover that God was not a disinterested bystander (1:12). The prophet's description of that day developed into a vivid picture of great distress, defeat, and darkness resulting from the anger of God towards his people. Zephaniah used this terrible picture to emphasize the supernatural aspect of the event and the awesome power of God. He offered no hope that the day could be avoided, only a glimmer of hope that the humble might escape its full consequences if they turned back to God and obeyed him (2:3).

The rest of that chapter extends the scope of God's judgement to certain foreign peoples who were neighbours of Judah. They were condemned for a variety of offences against God's people, or for their arrogant rejection of God's sovereignty. The prophet then turned his attention back onto Jerusalem and contrasted the faithlessness of the city with the righteousness of God (3:1–5). God had tried to make his people change from their corrupt ways but they had refused to accept his correction and so he had no option other than to exercise his judgement on the whole world.

Beyond Darkness

Zephaniah then considered what hope lay beyond the day of God's judgement for the nations and for Judah. At this point (3:9) the tone of his words changes dramatically. He did not believe that God in his righteousness would totally destroy his creation, and consequently he envisaged the dawning of a new age. First there was a promise that the nations would be purified and would become worshippers of God. This was followed by a promise that the humble and truthful among God's people would be preserved as a faithful remnant and allowed to live in peace. This is probably the point at which Zephaniah ended his prophecies.

Most people believe that the words in 3:14–20 were added later, perhaps after the exile, by someone who wanted to reinforce the note of hope and joy at the end of Zephaniah's message. These verses picture an age when God's people can rejoice because all their enemies have been defeated and because of God's presence in their midst protecting them and drawing them ever closer to himself. Whatever their origin, these words remain part of the Christian hope and we look forward to their complete fulfilment.

---

1 The word of the LORD that came to Zephaniah son of Cushi, the son of Gedaliah, the son of Amariah, the son of Hezekiah, during the reign of Josiah son of Amon king of Judah:

Warning of Coming Destruction

2 "I will sweep away everything
from the face of the earth,"
                    declares the LORD.

3 "I will sweep away both men and animals;
I will sweep away the birds of the air
and the fish of the sea.
The wicked will have only heaps of rubble[a]
when I cut off man from the face of the
earth,"
                    declares the LORD.

Against Judah

4 "I will stretch out my hand against Judah
and against all who live in Jerusalem.

[a] 3 The meaning of the Hebrew for this line is uncertain.

I will cut off from this place every remnant of
  Baal,
  the names of the pagan and the idolatrous
  priests—
5those who bow down on the roofs
  to worship the starry host,
  those who bow down and swear by the LORD
  and who also swear by Molech,[b]
6those who turn back from following the LORD
  and neither seek the LORD nor enquire of him.
7Be silent before the Sovereign LORD,
  for the day of the LORD is near.
The LORD has prepared a sacrifice;
  he has consecrated those he has invited.
8On the day of the LORD's sacrifice
  I will punish the princes
  and the king's sons
and all those clad
  in foreign clothes.
9On that day I will punish
  all who avoid stepping on the threshold,[c]
who fill the temple of their gods
  with violence and deceit.

10"On that day," declares the LORD,
  "a cry will go up from the Fish Gate,
  wailing from the New Quarter,
  and a loud crash from the hills.
11Wail, you who live in the market district;[d]
  all your merchants will be wiped out,
  all who trade with[e] silver will be ruined.
12At that time I will search Jerusalem with lamps
  and punish those who are complacent,
  who are like wine left on its dregs,
  who think, 'The LORD will do nothing,
  either good or bad.'
13Their wealth will be plundered,
  their houses demolished.
They will build houses
  but not live in them;
they will plant vineyards
  but not drink the wine.

The Great Day of the LORD

14"The great day of the LORD is near—
  near and coming quickly.
Listen! The cry on the day of the LORD will be
  bitter,
  the shouting of the warrior there.
15That day will be a day of wrath,
  a day of distress and anguish,
  a day of trouble and ruin,
  a day of darkness and gloom,
  a day of clouds and blackness,
16a day of trumpet and battle cry
  against the fortified cities
  and against the corner towers.
17I will bring distress on the people
  and they will walk like blind men,
  because they have sinned against the LORD.
Their blood will be poured out like dust
  and their entrails like filth.

18Neither their silver nor their gold
  will be able to save them
  on the day of the LORD's wrath.
In the fire of his jealousy
  the whole world will be consumed,
for he will make a sudden end
  of all who live in the earth."

2 Gather together, gather together,
  O shameful nation,
2before the appointed time arrives
  and that day sweeps on like chaff,
before the fierce anger of the LORD comes upon
  you,
before the day of the LORD's wrath comes upon
  you.
3Seek the LORD, all you humble of the land,
  you who do what he commands.
Seek righteousness, seek humility;
  perhaps you will be sheltered
  on the day of the LORD's anger.

Against Philistia

4Gaza will be abandoned
  and Ashkelon left in ruins.
At midday Ashdod will be emptied
  and Ekron uprooted.
5Woe to you who live by the sea,
  O Kerethite people;
the word of the LORD is against you,
  O Canaan, land of the Philistines.

"I will destroy you,
  and none will be left."

6The land by the sea, where the Kerethites[a]
  dwell,
  will be a place for shepherds and sheep pens.
7It will belong to the remnant of the house of
  Judah;
  there they will find pasture.
In the evening they will lie down
  in the houses of Ashkelon.
The LORD their God will care for them;
  he will restore their fortunes.[b]

Against Moab and Ammon

8"I have heard the insults of Moab
  and the taunts of the Ammonites,
who insulted my people
  and made threats against their land.
9Therefore, as surely as I live,"
  declares the LORD Almighty, the God of Israel,
"surely Moab will become like Sodom,
  the Ammonites like Gomorrah—
a place of weeds and salt pits,
  a wasteland for ever.
The remnant of my people will plunder them;
  the survivors of my nation will inherit their
  land."

b5 Hebrew Malcam, that is, Milcom   c9 See 1 Samuel 5:5.
a6 The meaning of the Hebrew for this word is uncertain.
d11 Or the Mortar   e11 Or in
b7 Or will bring back their captives

¹⁰This is what they will get in return for their
    pride,
  for insulting and mocking the people of the
    LORD Almighty.
¹¹The LORD will be awesome to them
  when he destroys all the gods of the land.
  The nations on every shore will worship him,
  every one in its own land.

Against Cush

¹²"You too, O Cushites,ᶜ
  will be slain by my sword."

Against Assyria

¹³He will stretch out his hand against the north
    and destroy Assyria,
  leaving Nineveh utterly desolate
    and dry as the desert.
¹⁴Flocks and herds will lie down there,
    creatures of every kind.
  The desert owl and the screech owl
    will roost on her columns.
  Their calls will echo through the windows,
    rubble will be in the doorways,
    the beams of cedar will be exposed.
¹⁵This is the carefree city
    that lived in safety.
  She said to herself,
    "I am, and there is none besides me."
  What a ruin she has become,
    a lair for wild beasts!
  All who pass by her scoff
    and shake their fists.

The Future of Jerusalem

3 Woe to the city of oppressors,
    rebellious and defiled!
²She obeys no-one,
    she accepts no correction.
  She does not trust in the LORD,
    she does not draw near to her God.
³Her officials are roaring lions,
    her rulers are evening wolves,
  who leave nothing for the morning.
⁴Her prophets are arrogant;
    they are treacherous men.
  Her priests profane the sanctuary
    and do violence to the law.
⁵The LORD within her is righteous;
    he does no wrong.
  Morning by morning he dispenses his justice,
    and every new day he does not fail,
  yet the unrighteous know no shame.

⁶"I have cut off nations;
    their strongholds are demolished.
  I have left their streets deserted,
    with no-one passing through.
  Their cities are destroyed;
    no-one will be left—no-one at all.

⁷I said to the city,
    'Surely you will fear me
    and accept correction!'
  Then her dwelling would not be cut off,
    nor all my punishments come upon her.
  But they were still eager
    to act corruptly in all they did.
⁸Therefore wait for me," declares the LORD,
    "for the day I will stand up to testify.ᵃ
  I have decided to assemble the nations,
    to gather the kingdoms
  and to pour out my wrath on them—
    all my fierce anger.
  The whole world will be consumed
    by the fire of my jealous anger.

⁹"Then will I purify the lips of the peoples,
    that all of them may call on the name of the
      LORD
    and serve him shoulder to shoulder.
¹⁰From beyond the rivers of Cushᵇ
    my worshippers, my scattered people,
    will bring me offerings.
¹¹On that day you will not be put to shame
    for all the wrongs you have done to me,
  because I will remove from this city
    those who rejoice in their pride.
  Never again will you be haughty
    on my holy hill.
¹²But I will leave within you
    the meek and humble,
  who trust in the name of the LORD.
¹³The remnant of Israel will do no wrong;
    they will speak no lies,
  nor will deceit be found in their mouths.
  They will eat and lie down
    and no-one will make them afraid."

¹⁴Sing, O Daughter of Zion;
    shout aloud, O Israel!
  Be glad and rejoice with all your heart,
    O Daughter of Jerusalem!
¹⁵The LORD has taken away your punishment,
    he has turned back your enemy.
  The LORD, the King of Israel, is with you;
    never again will you fear any harm.
¹⁶On that day they will say to Jerusalem,
    "Do not fear, O Zion;
    do not let your hands hang limp.
¹⁷The LORD your God is with you,
    he is mighty to save.
  He will take great delight in you,
    he will quiet you with his love,
    he will rejoice over you with singing."

¹⁸"The sorrows for the appointed feasts
    I will remove from you;
    they are a burden and a reproach to you.ᶜ
¹⁹At that time I will deal
    with all who oppressed you;
  I will rescue the lame
    and gather those who have been scattered.

ᶜ12 That is, people from the upper Nile region
ᵇ10 That is, the upper Nile region
ᶜ18 Or "I will gather you who mourn for the appointed feasts; / your reproach is a burden to you

ᵃ8 Septuagint and Syriac; Hebrew *will rise up to plunder*

I will give them praise and honour
in every land where they were put to shame.
20At that time I will gather you;
at that time I will bring you home.

I will give you honour and praise
among all the peoples of the earth
when I restore your fortunes*d*
before your very eyes,"
says the LORD.

d20 Or *I bring back your captives*

Haggai

The Prophet Who Was Listened to

The prophet Haggai was active in Jerusalem around the year 520 BC over a period of four months. He was remarkable among the Old Testament prophets because he had a positive response from the people. He spoke at a time of general despondency when nothing was going right for the nation, and there was little sense of real community since individuals were struggling to look after themselves. The people had come back from exile in Babylon about 20 years earlier, with permission from their new Persian rulers to rebuild the temple which had been destroyed by the Babylonians when they sacked Jerusalem and conquered Judah. They had even been given some resources for the task by the Persian king, Cyrus (see Ezra 1—6) but for varied reasons the work had never got properly underway. The people said that the time was not right (1:2), and they concentrated on improving their own standard of living (1:4,9). That and the harsh economic situation (1:6; 2:16,17) contributed to the failure to get on with the work of rebuilding.

A Different Perspective

Haggai viewed the situation in a different way from the ordinary population. He came to the conclusion that the problem was their tendency to be self-reliant—they failed to turn to God and to put his demands first in their lives. He saw the failing crops despite the efforts of the community, he saw the problems they experienced trying to make ends meet, and by logical argument he challenged the people to recognize that they had not got their priorities right. He told them that before everything else they must rebuild the temple.

Why was the temple so important? It was the focal point of their worship. It was understood as the place where God made himself known on earth, it was his home and the place where his presence could be experienced. Although the official rituals and sacrifices could be performed on a makeshift altar perfectly well, Haggai believed that while the temple was allowed to lie in ruins it demonstrated the lack of honour the nation had for God. To show that God really mattered to them it was necessary to construct a worthy temple and to restore it to its central place in the life of the community.

A Wholehearted Response and Renewed Trust

Haggai's words made sense and the people and their leaders obeyed (1:12). Work on the temple began in earnest, and it was completed about four years later. Some of them were rather discouraged during the building (2:3) because the new temple didn't have the magnificence of Solomon's ruined temple, but Haggai reassured them that God was with them in the work and that God would "fill this house with glory" (2:7). The prophet reminded the people that they were required to work hard and to do their best in obedience to God; and then to trust him to fulfil his purposes. It wasn't the beauty of the building in human eyes that mattered, nor the splendour of its furnishings—all the treasures of the earth belonged to God anyway. What mattered was that the temple was completed so that the community could experience the peace which God promised (2:9). The Hebrew word "shalom" which is translated as "peace" means more than the absence of war or disturbance; it indicates all the positive blessings which God can bestow on his people during their earthly life. To a community without belief in life after death (no Jews believed in resurrection until about 400 years later) this was the supreme hope and Haggai proclaimed that the new temple would usher in its fulfilment.

The Promises of God

Haggai didn't promise that material blessings would automatically follow from obeying God's will but he encouraged the people to give careful thought to the overall change in their situation that occurred when they started to get their priorities right (2:15–19). Haggai's final words were about God's plans not only for Israel but for the whole of creation. He proclaimed that God was concerned about and involved in political events of this world as well as in matters of faith and worship, and that ultimately God's will would be done among the nations and his kingdom would be established. This promise still awaits fulfilment but through Christ we are assured that it will one day come to pass.

A Call to Build the House of the LORD

1 In the second year of King Darius, on the first day of the sixth month, the word of the LORD came through the prophet Haggai to Zerubbabel son of Shealtiel, governor of Judah, and to Joshua[a] son of Jehozadak, the high priest:

2This is what the LORD Almighty says: "These people say, 'The time has not yet come for the LORD's house to be built.' "

3Then the word of the LORD came through the prophet Haggai: 4"Is it a time for you yourselves to be living in your panelled houses, while this house remains a ruin?"

5Now this is what the LORD Almighty says: "Give careful thought to your ways. 6You have planted much, but have harvested little. You eat, but never have enough. You drink, but never have your fill. You put on clothes, but are not warm. You earn wages, only to put them in a purse with holes in it."

7This is what the LORD Almighty says: "Give careful thought to your ways. 8Go up into the mountains and bring down timber and build the house, so that I may take pleasure in it and be honoured," says the LORD. 9"You expected much, but see, it turned out to be little. What you brought home, I blew away. Why?" declares the LORD Almighty. "Because of my house, which remains a ruin, while each of you is busy with his own house. 10Therefore, because of you the heavens have withheld their dew and the earth its crops. 11I called for a drought on the fields and the mountains, on the grain, the new wine, the oil and whatever the ground produces, on men and cattle, and on the labour of your hands."

12Then Zerubbabel son of Shealtiel, Joshua son of Jehozadak, the high priest, and the whole remnant of the people obeyed the voice of the LORD their God and the message of the prophet Haggai, because the LORD their God had sent him. And the people feared the LORD.

[13]Then Haggai, the LORD's messenger, gave this message of the LORD to the people: "I am with you," declares the LORD. [14]So the LORD stirred up the spirit of Zerubbabel son of Shealtiel, governor of Judah, and the spirit of Joshua son of Jehozadak, the high priest, and the spirit of the whole remnant of the people. They came and began work on the house of the LORD Almighty, their God, [15]on the twenty-fourth day of the sixth month in the second year of King Darius.

The Promised Glory of the New House

2 On the twenty-first day of the seventh month, the word of the LORD came through the prophet Haggai: [2]"Speak to Zerubbabel son of Shealtiel, governor of Judah, to Joshua son of Jehozadak, the high priest, and to the remnant of the people. Ask them, [3]'Who of you is left who saw this house in its former glory? How does it look to you now? Does it not seem to you like nothing? [4]But now be strong, O Zerubbabel,' declares the LORD. 'Be strong, O Joshua son of Jehozadak, the high priest. Be strong, all you people of the land,' declares the LORD, 'and work. For I am with you,' declares the LORD Almighty. [5]'This is what I covenanted with you when you came out of Egypt. And my Spirit remains among you. Do not fear.'

[6]"This is what the LORD Almighty says: 'In a little while I will once more shake the heavens and the earth, the sea and the dry land. [7]I will shake all nations, and the desired of all nations will come, and I will fill this house with glory,' says the LORD Almighty. [8]'The silver is mine and the gold is mine,' declares the LORD Almighty. [9]'The glory of this present house will be greater than the glory of the former house,' says the LORD Almighty. 'And in this place I will grant peace,' declares the LORD Almighty.'"

2:12 Old Testament law listed many things which were defiled or "unclean" and stated that anyone coming into contact with them became unclean (see Leviticus 11). In contrast the law indicated that consecrated meat—set aside for use in sacrificial worship—could not transmit its "holiness" to anything it touched. It was recognized that evil readily corrupts everything around it whereas good has to persevere to produce its positive results. The people's failure to rebuild the temple defiled them and so everything they did was tainted, even their good deeds.

Blessings for a Defiled People

[10]On the twenty-fourth day of the ninth month, in the second year of Darius, the word of the LORD came to the prophet Haggai: [11]"This is what the LORD Almighty says: 'Ask the priests what the law says: [12]If

a person carries consecrated meat in the fold of his garment, and that fold touches some bread or stew, some wine, oil or other food, does it become consecrated?' "

The priests answered, "No."

[13]Then Haggai said, "If a person defiled by contact with a dead body touches one of these things, does it become defiled?"

"Yes," the priests replied, "it becomes defiled."

[14]Then Haggai said, " 'So it is with this people and this nation in my sight,' declares the LORD. 'Whatever they do and whatever they offer there is defiled.

[15]" 'Now give careful thought to this from this day on[a]—consider how things were before one stone was laid on another in the LORD's temple. [16]When anyone came to a heap of twenty measures, there were only ten. When anyone went to a wine vat to draw fifty measures, there were only twenty. [17]I struck all the work of your hands with blight, mildew and hail, yet you did not turn to me,' declares the LORD. [18]'From this day on, from this twenty-fourth day of the ninth month, give careful thought to the day when the foundation of the LORD's temple was laid. Give careful thought: [19]Is there yet any seed left in the barn? Until now, the vine and the fig-tree, the pomegranate and the olive tree have not borne fruit.

" 'From this day on I will bless you.' "

2:23 Zerubbabel was grandson or great nephew to Jehoiachin, the king of Judah who was captured and taken into exile when the Babylonians defeated the nation. The prophet Jeremiah understood this event as God's rejection of Jehoiachin and the Davidic dynasty. He spoke in terms of "a signet ring" which God had pulled off (Jeremiah 22:24). In the ancient world a signet ring was used to impress a seal to authorize a document, in place of a signature. It conveyed the authority of the person who owned the signet. Haggai was saying that God had again chosen a descendant of David to represent him on earth and to lead his people. Jesus, a descendant of Zerubbabel, was the ultimate fulfilment of this prophecy for he did more than represent God on earth, he actually revealed God with us.

Zerubbabel the LORD's Signet Ring

[20]The word of the LORD came to Haggai a second time on the twenty-fourth day of the month: [21]"Tell Zerubbabel governor of Judah that I will shake the heavens and the earth. [22]I will overturn royal thrones and shatter the power of the foreign kingdoms.

[a]15 Or to the days past

I will overthrow chariots and their drivers; horses and their riders will fall, each by the sword of his brother.

23 " 'On that day,' declares the LORD Almighty, 'I will take you, my servant Zerubbabel son of Shealtiel,' declares the LORD, 'and I will make you like my signet ring, for I have chosen you,' declares the LORD Almighty."

Zechariah

Visions of Hope

The prophet Zechariah addressed the same community as Haggai. His message is dated as beginning a couple of months later than Haggai's, when the work on rebuilding the temple was underway. He apparently prophesied for a longer period, encouraging the people to complete the temple and to establish proper structures for the internal administration of the whole community. It is widely accepted that Zechariah's message is contained in chapters 1 — 8 of the book and that the remaining chapters were written at a later time, probably by people who were following in the same tradition. The second part of the book is written in a different style and is more difficult to understand, but a careful reading, perhaps with the help of a commentary, will enable its message of future judgement and salvation to be understood.

Zechariah was concerned with rebuilding the temple, the city of Jerusalem, and the development of stable and effective leadership among the people of God. After a brief introduction in which the community was reminded about the importance of obeying God, a series of eight symbolic visions experienced by the prophet are described, together with comments on their meaning. These are not as hard to understand as they might at first seem, but they need to be thought about one at a time.

Zechariah's Visions Are Shared

The first vision (1:8–17) assured the people that God was at work among them, caring for them and helping them towards a secure future. The second (1:18–21) represented the defeat of Israel's enemies. The third (2:1–12) promised that Jerusalem would be a great city to which all God's people would be drawn, and that God's presence would be the only security that was necessary. The fourth (3:1–10) depicted the cleansing of the High Priest and symbolized the cleansing of the whole nation of its sin. The fifth (4:1–6a, 10b–14) is interrupted by a prophecy about the temple. The vision refers to a dual leadership which the High Priest and the civil governor would share equally, which Zechariah believed was ordained by God as the appropriate way for his sovereignty to be represented among the people. The sixth (5:1–4) and seventh (5:5–11) visions both refer to the banishment of evil, and the last (6:1–5) reinforces the truth of God's universal concern and rule.

Promise and Responsibility

Chapters 7 and 8 address the quality of life which God intends his people to enjoy. They contain encouraging promises but emphasize that these will come from social justice, reverence for God, and obedience towards him. Zechariah reiterated some of the challenging words of earlier prophets and reminded his hearers of the charitable aspects of God's law. He drew attention to the past and warned the community not to be like their ancestors who suffered the consequences of their behaviour. A change of heart and a new relationship with God was called for, and then the promises would become a reality. The first half of the book ends on a high point—a promise that Israel would have a central role within God's purposes for all the nations, so long as they demonstrated the reality of God's presence with them and so drew others to God.

The Message Continues

The second part of the book may contain the prophecies of several different people and have been written over a long period of time. Although their origins are unknown, their importance for Christian understanding is shown by the frequency with which the Gospel writers quoted from them in the narratives about Jesus' suffering and death. The writer of the book of Revelation also drew on some of the imagery in these chapters, especially chapter 14, for his description of the new heaven and earth.

A Different Style of Leadership

The prophecies relate to the final victory of God and affirm that his final rule will be universal, but much is said about the distress and suffering which God's people have to endure before the great day arrives. The prophecies centre on Israel and on a future leader who will come as the agent of God's rule. People had hopes that the Messiah would be a warrior king who would defeat all their enemies but the prophet said he would be "gentle and riding on a donkey" (9:9). Another passage spoke of the nation's rejection of God's appointed shepherd (a term which means leader) (11:4–17). New Testament writers naturally applied passages like these to Jesus. In accounts of Palm Sunday, Matthew 21:5 and John 12:14 both quote 9:9. The bribe Judas accepted for betraying Jesus was related to 11:12,13. (In Matthew 27:9 the words are wrongly attributed to Jeremiah, which shows that doubt about the authorship of these prophecies existed from early days.) The piercing of Jesus' side on the cross was seen as the fulfilment of 12:10 (John 19:37), and the disciples' desertion of Jesus' arrest was said to fulfil 13:7 (Matthew 26:31). These chapters express confidence in God's final triumph and give an assurance that God would care for his people when their human leaders let them down. Consequently they have proved to be a source of great encouragement to believers in times of crisis through the ages.

A Call to Return to the LORD

1 In the eighth month of the second year of Darius, the word of the LORD came to the prophet Zechariah son of Berekiah, the son of Iddo:

2 "The LORD was very angry with your forefathers.

3 Therefore tell the people: This is what the LORD Almighty says: 'Return to me,' declares the LORD Almighty, 'and I will return to you,' says the LORD Almighty. 4 Do not be like your forefathers, to whom the earlier prophets proclaimed: This is what the LORD

Almighty says: 'Turn from your evil ways and your evil practices.' But they would not listen or pay attention to me, declares the LORD. ⁵Where are your forefathers now? And the prophets, do they live for ever? ⁶But did not my words and my decrees, which I commanded my servants the prophets, overtake your forefathers?

"Then they repented and said, 'The LORD Almighty has done to us what our ways and practices deserve, just as he determined to do.' "

The Man Among the Myrtle Trees

⁷On the twenty-fourth day of the eleventh month, the month of Shebat, in the second year of Darius, the word of the LORD came to the prophet Zechariah son of Berekiah, the son of Iddo.

⁸During the night I had a vision—and there before me was a man riding a red horse! He was standing among the myrtle trees in a ravine. Behind him were red, brown and white horses.

⁹I asked, "What are these, my lord?"

The angel who was talking with me answered, "I will show you what they are."

¹⁰Then the man standing among the myrtle trees explained, "They are the ones the LORD has sent to go throughout the earth."

¹¹And they reported to the angel of the LORD, who was standing among the myrtle trees, "We have gone throughout the earth and found the whole world at rest and in peace."

¹²Then the angel of the LORD said, "LORD Almighty, how long will you withhold mercy from Jerusalem and from the towns of Judah, which you have been angry with these seventy years?" ¹³So the LORD spoke kind and comforting words to the angel who talked with me.

¹⁴Then the angel who was speaking to me said, "Proclaim this word: This is what the LORD Almighty says: 'I am very jealous for Jerusalem and Zion, ¹⁵but I am very angry with the nations that feel secure. I was only a little angry, but they added to the calamity.'

¹⁶"Therefore, this is what the LORD says: 'I will return to Jerusalem with mercy, and there my house will be rebuilt. And the measuring line will be stretched out over Jerusalem,' declares the LORD Almighty.

¹⁷"Proclaim further: This is what the LORD Almighty says: 'My towns will again overflow with prosperity, and the LORD will again comfort Zion and choose Jerusalem.' "

Four Horns and Four Craftsmen

¹⁸Then I looked up—and there before me were four horns! ¹⁹I asked the angel who was speaking to me, "What are these?"

He answered me, "These are the horns that scattered Judah, Israel and Jerusalem."

²⁰Then the LORD showed me four craftsmen. ²¹I asked, "What are these coming to do?"

He answered, "These are the horns that scattered Judah so that no-one could raise his head, but the craftsmen have come to terrify them and throw down

these horns of the nations who lifted up their horns against the land of Judah to scatter its people."

1:18 An agricultural society was dependent on oxen to draw the plough, and the horned bulls were the strongest power known. This probably accounts for the Old Testament writers' frequent use of horns to symbolize invincible strength.

A Man With a Measuring Line

2 Then I looked up—and there before me was a man with a measuring line in his hand! ²I asked, "Where are you going?"

He answered me, "To measure Jerusalem, to find out how wide and how long it is."

³Then the angel who was speaking to me left, and another angel came to meet him ⁴and said to him: "Run, tell that young man, 'Jerusalem will be a city without walls because of the great number of men and livestock in it. ⁵And I myself will be a wall of fire around it,' declares the LORD, 'and I will be its glory within.'

⁶"Come! Come! Flee from the land of the north," declares the LORD, "for I have scattered you to the four winds of heaven," declares the LORD.

⁷"Come, O Zion! Escape, you who live in the Daughter of Babylon!" ⁸For this is what the LORD Almighty says: "After he has honoured me and has sent me against the nations that have plundered you—for whoever touches you touches the apple of his eye—⁹I will surely raise my hand against them so that their slaves will plunder them.ᵇ Then you will know that the LORD Almighty has sent me.

¹⁰"Shout and be glad, O Daughter of Zion. For I am coming, and I will live among you," declares the LORD. ¹¹"Many nations will be joined with the LORD in that day and will become my people. I will live among you and you will know that the LORD Almighty has sent me to you. ¹²The LORD will inherit Judah as his portion in the holy land and will again choose Jerusalem. ¹³Be still before the LORD, all mankind, because he has roused himself from his holy dwelling."

Clean Garments for the High Priest

3 Then he showed me Joshuaᵃ the high priest standing before the angel of the LORD, and Satanᵇ standing at his right side to accuse him. ²The LORD said to Satan, "The LORD rebuke you, Satan! The LORD, who has chosen Jerusalem, rebuke you! Is not this man a burning stick snatched from the fire?"

³Now Joshua was dressed in filthy clothes as he stood before the angel. ⁴The angel said to those who were standing before him, "Take off his filthy clothes."

Then he said to Joshua, "See, I have taken away your sin, and I will put rich garments on you."

⁵Then I said, "Put a clean turban on his head." So

ᵇ8, 9 Or says after . . . eye: ⁹"I . . . plunder them."
ᵇ1 Satan means accuser.

ᵃ1 A variant of Jeshua; here and elsewhere in Zechariah

they put a clean turban on his head and clothed him, while the angel of the LORD stood by.

⁶The angel of the LORD gave this charge to Joshua: ⁷"This is what the LORD Almighty says: 'If you will walk in my ways and keep my requirements, then you will govern my house and have charge of my courts, and I will give you a place among these standing here.

⁸" 'Listen, O high priest Joshua and your associates seated before you, who are men symbolic of things to come: I am going to bring my servant, the Branch. ⁹See, the stone I have set in front of Joshua! There are seven eyes ᶜ on that one stone, and I will engrave an inscription on it,' says the LORD Almighty, 'and I will remove the sin of this land in a single day.

3:8   The term "Branch" had been used by earlier prophets to refer to a future messiah (Isaiah 11:1; Jeremiah 23:5; 33:15). The text is confusing here and it might appear that Zechariah thought that Zerubbabel or Joshua was the Branch. However, the prophet was looking beyond the present to the time when a new leader, chosen by God, would rule with divine majesty.

---

¹⁰" 'In that day each of you will invite his neighbour to sit under his vine and fig-tree,' declares the LORD Almighty."

The Gold Lampstand and the Two Olive Trees

4 Then the angel who talked with me returned and wakened me, as a man is wakened from his sleep. ²He asked me, "What do you see?"

I answered, "I see a solid gold lampstand with a bowl at the top and seven lights on it, with seven channels to the lights. ³Also there are two olive trees by it, one on the right of the bowl and the other on its left."

⁴I asked the angel who talked with me, "What are these, my lord?"

⁵He answered, "Do you not know what these are?"

"No, my lord," I replied.

⁶So he said to me, "This is the word of the LORD to Zerubbabel: 'Not by might nor by power, but by my Spirit,' says the LORD Almighty.

⁷"Whatᵃ are you, O mighty mountain? Before Zerubbabel you will become level ground. Then he will bring out the capstone to shouts of 'God bless it! God bless it!' "

⁸Then the word of the LORD came to me: ⁹"The hands of Zerubbabel have laid the foundation of this temple; his hands will also complete it. Then you will know that the LORD Almighty has sent me to you.

¹⁰"Who despises the day of small things? Men will rejoice when they see the plumb-line in the hand of Zerubbabel.

"(These seven are the eyes of the LORD, which range throughout the earth.)"

¹¹Then I asked the angel, "What are these two olive trees on the right and the left of the lampstand?"

¹²Again I asked him, "What are these two olive branches beside the two gold pipes that pour out golden oil?"

¹³He replied, "Do you not know what these are?"

"No, my lord," I said.

¹⁴So he said, "These are the two who are anointed to ᵇ serve the Lord of all the earth."

The Flying Scroll

5 I looked again—and there before me was a flying scroll!

²He asked me, "What do you see?"

I answered, "I see a flying scroll, thirty feet long and fifteen feet wide." ᵃ

³And he said to me, "This is the curse that is going out over the whole land; for according to what it says on one side, every thief will be banished, and according to what it says on the other, everyone who swears falsely will be banished. ⁴The LORD Almighty declares, 'I will send it out, and it will enter the house of the thief and the house of him who swears falsely by my name. It will remain in his house and destroy it, both its timbers and its stones.' "

The Woman in a Basket

⁵Then the angel who was speaking to me came forward and said to me, "Look up and see what this is that is appearing."

⁶I asked, "What is it?"

He replied, "It is a measuring basket." ᵇ And he added, "This is the iniquity ᶜ of the people throughout the land."

⁷Then the cover of lead was raised, and there in the basket sat a woman! ⁸He said, "This is wickedness," and he pushed her back into the basket and pushed the lead cover down over its mouth.

⁹Then I looked up—and there before me were two women, with the wind in their wings! They had wings like those of a stork, and they lifted up the basket between heaven and earth.

¹⁰"Where are they taking the basket?" I asked the angel who was speaking to me.

¹¹He replied, "To the country of Babylonia ᵈ to build a house for it. When it is ready, the basket will be set there in its place."

Four Chariots

6 I looked up again—and there before me were four chariots coming out from between two mountains—mountains of bronze! ²The first chariot had red horses, the second black, ³the third white, and the fourth dappled—all of them powerful. ⁴I asked the angel who was speaking to me, "What are these, my lord?"

⁵The angel answered me, "These are the four spirits ᵃ of heaven, going out from standing in the presence of the Lord of the whole world. ⁶The one with the

---

ᶜ9 Or facets   ᵃ7 Or Who   ᵇ14 Or two who bring oil and
ᵃ2 Hebrew twenty cubits long and ten cubits wide (about 9 metres long and 4.5 metres wide)
ᵇ6 Hebrew an ephah; also in verses 7–11   ᶜ6 Or appearance   ᵈ11 Hebrew Shinar   ᵃ5 Or winds

black horses is going towards the north country, the one with the white horses towards the west,^b and the one with the dappled horses towards the south."

⁷When the powerful horses went out, they were straining to go throughout the earth. And he said, "Go throughout the earth!" So they went throughout the earth.

⁸Then he called to me, "Look, those going towards the north country have given my Spirit^c rest in the land of the north."

A Crown for Joshua

⁹The word of the LORD came to me: ¹⁰"Take ‚silver and gold‚ from the exiles Heldai, Tobijah and Jedaiah, who have arrived from Babylon. Go the same day to the house of Josiah son of Zephaniah. ¹¹Take the silver and gold and make a crown, and set it on the head of the high priest, Joshua son of Jehozadak. ¹²Tell him this is what the LORD Almighty says: 'Here is the man whose name is the Branch, and he will branch out from his place and build the temple of the LORD. ¹³It is he who will build the temple of the LORD, and he will be clothed with majesty and will sit and rule on his throne. And he will be a priest on his throne. And there will be harmony between the two.' ¹⁴The crown will be given to Heldai,^d Tobijah, Jedaiah and Hen^e son of Zephaniah as a memorial in the temple of the LORD. ¹⁵Those who are far away will come and help to build the temple of the LORD, and you will know that the LORD Almighty has sent me to you. This will happen if you diligently obey the LORD your God."

Justice and Mercy, Not Fasting

7 In the fourth year of King Darius, the word of the LORD came to Zechariah on the fourth day of the ninth month, the month of Kislev. ²The people of Bethel had sent Sharezer and Regem-Melech, together with their men, to entreat the LORD ³by asking the priests of the house of the LORD Almighty and the prophets, "Should I mourn and fast in the fifth month, as I have done for so many years?"

7:3 During the exile people had fasted and mourned on special days to commemorate the seige and destruction of Jerusalem. This was still going on although the exiles had returned and Jerusalem was being rebuilt. They asked Zechariah if it was necessary. His answer was that fasts should be replaced by feasts in thanksgiving to God (8:19). But there was a warning; all religious ceremonies are meaningless unless they comply with God's will.

---

⁴Then the word of the LORD Almighty came to me: ⁵"Ask all the people of the land and the priests, 'When you fasted and mourned in the fifth and seventh months for the past seventy years, was it really for me that you fasted? ⁶And when you were eating and drinking, were you not just feasting for yourselves? ⁷Are these not the words the LORD proclaimed through the earlier prophets when Jerusalem and its surrounding towns were at rest and prosperous, and the Negev and the western foothills were settled?' "

⁸And the word of the LORD came again to Zechariah: ⁹"This is what the LORD Almighty says: 'Administer true justice; show mercy and compassion to one another. ¹⁰Do not oppress the widow or the fatherless, the alien or the poor. In your hearts do not think evil of each other.'

¹¹"But they refused to pay attention; stubbornly they turned their backs and stopped up their ears. ¹²They made their hearts as hard as flint and would not listen to the law or to the words that the LORD Almighty had sent by his Spirit through the earlier prophets. So the LORD Almighty was very angry.

¹³" 'When I called, they did not listen; so when they called, I would not listen,' says the LORD Almighty. ¹⁴'I scattered them with a whirlwind among all the nations, where they were strangers. The land was left so desolate behind them that no-one could come or go. This is how they made the pleasant land desolate.' "

The LORD Promises to Bless Jerusalem

8 Again the word of the LORD Almighty came to me. ²This is what the LORD Almighty says: "I am very jealous for Zion; I am burning with jealousy for her."

³This is what the LORD says: "I will return to Zion and dwell in Jerusalem. Then Jerusalem will be called the City of Truth, and the mountain of the LORD Almighty will be called the Holy Mountain."

⁴This is what the LORD Almighty says: "Once again men and women of ripe old age will sit in the streets of Jerusalem, each with cane in hand because of his age. ⁵The city streets will be filled with boys and girls playing there."

⁶This is what the LORD Almighty says: "It may seem marvellous to the remnant of this people at that time, but will it seem marvellous to me?" declares the LORD Almighty.

⁷This is what the LORD Almighty says: "I will save my people from the countries of the east and the west. ⁸I will bring them back to live in Jerusalem; they will be my people, and I will be faithful and righteous to them as their God."

⁹This is what the LORD Almighty says: "You who now hear these words spoken by the prophets who were there when the foundation was laid for the house of the LORD Almighty, let your hands be strong so that the temple may be built. ¹⁰Before that time there were no wages for man or beast. No-one could go about his business safely because of his enemy, for I had turned every man against his neighbour. ¹¹But now I will not deal with the remnant of this people as I did in the past," declares the LORD Almighty.

¹²"The seed will grow well, the vine will yield its fruit, the ground will produce its crops, and the heavens will drop their dew. I will give all these things as an inheritance to the remnant of this people. ¹³As you have been an object of cursing among the nations, O

---

^b6 Or horses after them   ^c8 Or spirit   ^d14 Syriac; Hebrew Helem   ^e14 Or and the gracious one, the

Judah and Israel, so will I save you, and you will be a blessing. Do not be afraid, but let your hands be strong."

¹⁴This is what the LORD Almighty says: "Just as I had determined to bring disaster upon you and showed no pity when your fathers angered me," says the LORD Almighty, ¹⁵"so now I have determined to do good again to Jerusalem and Judah. Do not be afraid. ¹⁶These are the things you are to do: Speak the truth to each other, and render true and sound judgment in your courts; ¹⁷do not plot evil against your neighbour, and do not love to swear falsely. I hate all this," declares the LORD.

¹⁸Again the word of the LORD Almighty came to me. ¹⁹This is what the LORD Almighty says: "The fasts of the fourth, fifth, seventh and tenth months will become joyful and glad occasions and happy festivals for Judah. Therefore love truth and peace."

²⁰This is what the LORD Almighty says: "Many peoples and the inhabitants of many cities will yet come, ²¹and the inhabitants of one city will go to another and say, 'Let us go at once to entreat the LORD and seek the LORD Almighty. I myself am going.' ²²And many peoples and powerful nations will come to Jerusalem to seek the LORD Almighty and to entreat him."

²³This is what the LORD Almighty says: "In those days ten men from all languages and nations will take firm hold of one Jew by the hem of his robe and say, 'Let us go with you, because we have heard that God is with you.' "

Judgment on Israel's Enemies

An Oracle

9 The word of the LORD is against the land of Hadrach
and will rest upon Damascus —
for the eyes of men and all the tribes of Israel
are on the LORD — ᵃ
²and upon Hamath too, which borders on it,
and upon Tyre and Sidon, though they are very skilful.
³Tyre has built herself a stronghold;
she has heaped up silver like dust,
and gold like the dirt of the streets.
⁴But the Lord will take away her possessions
and destroy her power on the sea,
and she will be consumed by fire.
⁵Ashkelon will see it and fear;
Gaza will writhe in agony,
and Ekron too, for her hope will wither.
Gaza will lose her king
and Ashkelon will be deserted.
⁶Foreigners will occupy Ashdod,
and I will cut off the pride of the Philistines.
⁷I will take the blood from their mouths,
the forbidden food from between their teeth.
Those who are left will belong to our God
and become leaders in Judah,
and Ekron will be like the Jebusites.

⁸But I will defend my house
against marauding forces.
Never again will an oppressor overrun my people,
for now I am keeping watch.

The Coming of Zion's King

⁹Rejoice greatly, O Daughter of Zion!
Shout, Daughter of Jerusalem!
See, your kingᵇ comes to you,
righteous and having salvation,
gentle and riding on a donkey,
on a colt, the foal of a donkey.
¹⁰I will take away the chariots from Ephraim
and the war-horses from Jerusalem,
and the battle-bow will be broken.
He will proclaim peace to the nations.
His rule will extend from sea to sea
and from the Riverᶜ to the ends of the earth.ᵈ
¹¹As for you, because of the blood of my covenant with you,
I will free your prisoners from the waterless pit.
¹²Return to your fortress, O prisoners of hope;
even now I announce that I will restore twice as much to you.
¹³I will bend Judah as I bend my bow
and fill it with Ephraim.
I will rouse your sons, O Zion,
against your sons, O Greece,
and make you like a warrior's sword.

The LORD Will Appear

¹⁴Then the LORD will appear over them;
his arrow will flash like lightning.
The Sovereign LORD will sound the trumpet;
he will march in the storms of the south,
¹⁵   and the LORD Almighty will shield them.
They will destroy
and overcome with slingstones.
They will drink and roar as with wine;
they will be full like a bowl
used for sprinklingᵉ the corners of the altar.
¹⁶The LORD their God will save them on that day
as the flock of his people.
They will sparkle in his land
like jewels in a crown.
¹⁷How attractive and beautiful they will be!
Grain will make the young men thrive,
and new wine the young women.

The LORD Will Care for Judah

10 Ask the LORD for rain in the springtime;
it is the LORD who makes the storm clouds.
He gives showers of rain to men,
and plants of the field to everyone.
²The idols speak deceit,
diviners see visions that lie;
they tell dreams that are false,
they give comfort in vain.

ᵃ1 Or Damascus. / For the eye of the LORD is on all mankind, / as well as on the tribes of Israel.   ᵇ9 Or King
ᶜ10 That is, the Euphrates   ᵈ10 Or the end of the land   ᵉ15 Or bowl, / like

Therefore the people wander like sheep
  oppressed for lack of a shepherd.

3"My anger burns against the shepherds,
  and I will punish the leaders;
for the LORD Almighty will care
  for his flock, the house of Judah,
  and make them like a proud horse in battle.
4From Judah will come the cornerstone,
  from him the tent peg,
  from him the battle-bow,
  from him every ruler.
5Together they[a] will be like mighty men
  trampling the muddy streets in battle.
Because the LORD is with them,
  they will fight and overthrow the horsemen.

6"I will strengthen the house of Judah
  and save the house of Joseph.
I will restore them
  because I have compassion on them.
They will be as though
  I had not rejected them,
for I am the LORD their God
  and I will answer them.
7The Ephraimites will become like mighty men,
  and their hearts will be glad as with wine.
Their children will see it and be joyful;
  their hearts will rejoice in the LORD.
8I will signal for them
  and gather them in.
Surely I will redeem them;
  they will be as numerous as before.
9Though I scatter them among the peoples,
  yet in distant lands they will remember me.
They and their children will survive,
  and they will return.
10I will bring them back from Egypt
  and gather them from Assyria.
I will bring them to Gilead and Lebanon,
  and there will not be room enough for them.
11They will pass through the sea of trouble;
  the surging sea will be subdued
  and all the depths of the Nile will dry up.
Assyria's pride will be brought down
  and Egypt's sceptre will pass away.
12I will strengthen them in the LORD
  and in his name they will walk,"
                            declares the LORD.

11 Open your doors, O Lebanon,
     so that fire may devour your cedars!
2Wail, O pine tree, for the cedar has fallen;
  the stately trees are ruined!
Wail, oaks of Bashan;
  the dense forest has been cut down!
3Listen to the wail of the shepherds:
  their rich pastures are destroyed!
Listen to the roar of the lions;
  the lush thicket of the Jordan is ruined!

Two Shepherds

4This is what the LORD my God says: "Pasture the
flock marked for slaughter. 5Their buyers slaughter

them and go unpunished. Those who sell them say,
'Praise the LORD, I am rich!' Their own shepherds do
not spare them. 6For I will no longer have pity on the
people of the land," declares the LORD. "I will hand
everyone over to his neighbour and his king. They will
oppress the land, and I will not rescue them from their
hands."
  7So I pastured the flock marked for slaughter, particularly the oppressed of the flock. Then I took two
staffs and called one Favour and the other Union, and
I pastured the flock. 8In one month I got rid of the three
shepherds.
  The flock detested me, and I grew weary of them
9and said, "I will not be your shepherd. Let the dying
die, and the perishing perish. Let those who are left eat
one another's flesh."
  10Then I took my staff called Favour and broke it,
revoking the covenant I had made with all the nations.
11It was revoked on that day, and so the afflicted of the
flock who were watching me knew it was the word of
the LORD.
  12I told them, "If you think it best, give me my pay;
but if not, keep it." So they paid me thirty pieces of
silver.
  13And the LORD said to me, "Throw it to the potter" — the handsome price at which they priced me! So
I took the thirty pieces of silver and threw them into
the house of the LORD to the potter.
  14Then I broke my second staff called Union, breaking the brotherhood between Judah and Israel.
  15Then the LORD said to me, "Take again the equipment of a foolish shepherd. 16For I am going to raise
up a shepherd over the land who will not care for the
lost, or seek the young, or heal the injured, or feed the
healthy, but will eat the meat of the choice sheep, tearing off their hoofs.

17"Woe to the worthless shepherd,
  who deserts the flock!
May the sword strike his arm and his right eye!
  May his arm be completely withered,
  his right eye totally blinded!"

Jerusalem's Enemies to Be Destroyed

An Oracle

12 This is the word of the LORD concerning Israel.
     The LORD, who stretches out the heavens,
who lays the foundation of the earth, and who forms
the spirit of man within him, declares: 2"I am going to
make Jerusalem a cup that sends all the surrounding
peoples reeling. Judah will be besieged as well as Jerusalem. 3On that day, when all the nations of the earth
are gathered against her, I will make Jerusalem an
immovable rock for all the nations. All who try to move
it will injure themselves. 4On that day I will strike
every horse with panic and its rider with madness,"
declares the LORD. "I will keep a watchful eye over the
house of Judah, but I will blind all the horses of the
nations. 5Then the leaders of Judah will say in their
hearts, 'The people of Jerusalem are strong, because
the LORD Almighty is their God.'

a4, 5 Or ruler, all of them together. / 5 They

⁶"On that day I will make the leaders of Judah like a brazier in a woodpile, like a flaming torch among sheaves. They will consume right and left all the surrounding peoples, but Jerusalem will remain intact in her place.

⁷"The LORD will save the dwellings of Judah first, so that the honour of the house of David and of Jerusalem's inhabitants may not be greater than that of Judah. ⁸On that day the LORD will shield those who live in Jerusalem, so that the feeblest among them will be like David, and the house of David will be like God, like the Angel of the LORD going before them. ⁹On that day I will set out to destroy all the nations that attack Jerusalem.

Mourning for the One They Pierced

¹⁰"And I will pour out on the house of David and the inhabitants of Jerusalem a spirit[a] of grace and supplication. They will look on[b] me, the one they have pierced, and they will mourn for him as one mourns for an only child, and grieve bitterly for him as one grieves for a firstborn son. ¹¹On that day the weeping in Jerusalem will be great, like the weeping of Hadad Rimmon in the plain of Megiddo. ¹²The land will mourn, each clan by itself, with their wives by themselves: the clan of the house of David and their wives, the clan of the house of Nathan and their wives, ¹³the clan of the house of Levi and their wives, the clan of Shimei and their wives, ¹⁴and all the rest of the clans and their wives.

12:10   Christians see in this passage (verses 10,11) a picture of the events of Jesus' crucifixion. Luke 23:27 mentions the women weeping in Jerusalem and the references to "a firstborn son" and "the one they have pierced" in this passage can easily be applied to Jesus; but it is not an actual prediction about Jesus. The prophet was talking about Israel's need for a new spirit and cleansing from sin (13:1) and proclaiming that this would somehow be connected with death and mourning.

Cleansing From Sin

13   "On that day a fountain will be opened to the house of David and the inhabitants of Jerusalem, to cleanse them from sin and impurity.

²"On that day, I will banish the names of the idols from the land, and they will be remembered no more," declares the LORD Almighty. "I will remove both the prophets and the spirit of impurity from the land. ³And if anyone still prophesies, his father and mother, to whom he was born, will say to him, 'You must die, because you have told lies in the LORD's name.' When he prophesies, his own parents will stab him.

⁴"On that day every prophet will be ashamed of his prophetic vision. He will not put on a prophet's garment of hair in order to deceive. ⁵He will say, 'I am not a prophet. I am a farmer; the land has been my livelihood since my youth.'[a] ⁶If someone asks him, 'What are these wounds on your body?'[b] he will answer, 'The wounds I was given at the house of my friends.'

The Shepherd Struck, the Sheep Scattered

⁷"Awake, O sword, against my shepherd,
    against the man who is close to me!"
    declares the LORD Almighty.
"Strike the shepherd,
    and the sheep will be scattered,
    and I will turn my hand against the little ones.
⁸In the whole land," declares the LORD,
    "two-thirds will be struck down and perish;
    yet one-third will be left in it.
⁹This third I will bring into the fire;
    I will refine them like silver
    and test them like gold.
They will call on my name
    and I will answer them;
I will say, 'They are my people,'
    and they will say, 'The LORD is our God.' "

The LORD Comes and Reigns

14   A day of the LORD is coming when your plunder will be divided among you.

²I will gather all the nations to Jerusalem to fight against it; the city will be captured, the houses ransacked, and the women raped. Half of the city will go into exile, but the rest of the people will not be taken from the city. ³Then the LORD will go out and fight against those nations, as he fights in the day of battle. ⁴On that day his feet will stand on the Mount of Olives, east of Jerusalem, and the Mount of Olives will be split in two from east to west, forming a great valley, with half of the mountain moving north and half moving south. ⁵You will flee by my mountain valley, for it will extend to Azel. You will flee as you fled from the earthquake[a] in the days of Uzziah king of Judah. Then the LORD my God will come, and all the holy ones with him.

⁶On that day there will be no light, no cold or frost. ⁷It will be a unique day, without daytime or night-time—a day known to the LORD. When evening comes, there will be light.

⁸On that day living water will flow out from Jerusalem, half to the eastern sea[b] and half to the western sea,[c] in summer and in winter.

⁹The LORD will be king over the whole earth. On that day there will be one LORD, and his name the only name.

¹⁰The whole land, from Geba to Rimmon, south of Jerusalem, will become like the Arabah. But Jerusalem will be raised up and remain in its place, from the Benjamin Gate to the site of the First Gate, to the Corner

---

a 10 Or the Spirit   b 10 Or to   a 5 Or farmer; a man sold me in my youth   b 6 Or wounds between your hands
a 5 Or 5My mountain valley will be blocked and will extend to Azel. It will be blocked as it was blocked because of the earthquake
b 8 That is, the Dead Sea   c 8 That is, the Mediterranean

Gate, and from the Tower of Hananel to the royal wine-presses. [11]It will be inhabited; never again will it be destroyed. Jerusalem will be secure.

[12]This is the plague with which the LORD will strike all the nations that fought against Jerusalem: Their flesh will rot while they are still standing on their feet, their eyes will rot in their sockets, and their tongues will rot in their mouths. [13]On that day men will be stricken by the LORD with great panic. Each man will seize the hand of another, and they will attack each other. [14]Judah too will fight at Jerusalem. The wealth of all the surrounding nations will be collected — great quantities of gold and silver and clothing. [15]A similar plague will strike the horses and mules, the camels and donkeys, and all the animals in those camps.

[16]Then the survivors from all the nations that have attacked Jerusalem will go up year after year to worship the King, the LORD Almighty, and to celebrate the Feast of Tabernacles. [17]If any of the peoples of the earth do not go up to Jerusalem to worship the King, the LORD Almighty, they will have no rain. [18]If the Egyptian people do not go up and take part, they will have no rain. The LORD[d] will bring on them the plague he inflicts on the nations that do not go up to celebrate the Feast of Tabernacles. [19]This will be the punishment of Egypt

d18 Or part, then the LORD　　　*e21 Or merchant*

and the punishment of all the nations that do not go up to celebrate the Feast of Tabernacles.

14:20　　The priests and temple had always been understood as "holy", or "separate" from the rest of Israel. Indeed, the words HOLY TO THE LORD were fixed to the priests' turbans (Exodus 28:36). The prophet declared that in the future such words would be inscribed on horse bells; and ordinary kitchen utensils would be as holy as sacramental vessels. There would be no separation between the secular and the sacred because everything would be sacred.

---

[20]On that day HOLY TO THE LORD will be inscribed on the bells of the horses, and the cooking pots in the LORD's house will be like the sacred bowls in front of the altar. [21]Every pot in Jerusalem and Judah will be holy to the LORD Almighty, and all who come to sacrifice will take some of the pots and cook in them. And on that day there will no longer be a Canaanite[e] in the house of the LORD Almighty.

Malachi

Faded Hopes and a Weary Faith

Malachi means "my messenger" but, unlike the other prophetic books, it may not indicate the name of the prophet to whom its message is attributed. The book says nothing about the prophet although it is certain that he lived after the Babylonian exile because he referred to the governor (1:8), which was a title used to denote the ruler appointed by the Persians, rather than the king. Since the temple was in use (1:10) he must have prophesied after Haggai and Zechariah, and many years had probably passed because his message suggests that worship had by this time degenerated into wearisome routine (1:13). Many people believe that the prophet addressed the community in Jerusalem shortly before the reforming work of Ezra and Nehemiah, and a date around 460 BC is possible.

Where Was God?

When the people rebuilt the temple they had hoped that God would come to dwell in their midst, bringing in a new era and making Jerusalem the focal point of the world to which all the nations would be drawn (see Haggai 2:6–9 and Zechariah 2:11; 8:20–23). However, life had not been radically changed and Israel continued to be ruled by a foreign power.

Hopes faded and they began to doubt God's promises and their place within them. Where was the evidence that God loved them? What was the point of being religious? Why wasn't there any sign of God's justice? The people grew apathetic towards their faith until they were doing little more than going through the motions of worship. The prophet proclaimed God's word in this situation to reawaken faith and rekindle enthusiasm in the community's worship and lifestyle.

Questions Answered

His message deals with several issues presented in the form of an argument or dialogue, but it is basically concerned with reminding God's people that successful relationships depend on both parties doing their bit. In each section the prophet stated the kind of question or complaint he had heard voiced among them, to which he gave God's response. He began by assuring Israel that God had always loved the people (1:2) and suggested that they compare their situation with the disasters that neighbouring Edom had suffered if they wanted some proof of that.

God's People Have Responsibilities

The prophet challenged the priests and through them all the people over the second-rate offerings they presented to God (1:7,8). If they disobeyed God's commands about bringing perfect animals (e.g. Leviticus 1:3,10; 3:1,6) and failed to honour him, how could they expect God to be pleased with them? When they were not keeping their side of the agreement made with God what right had they to complain? Blame for the substandard worship could be attached to everyone but it was levelled primarily against the priests because it was their responsibility to teach the people about God's will and to help them offer worship which would be acceptable. However, it is a clear warning to all of the sad consequences that can arise if there is a loss of zeal for God among religious leaders.

---

1 An oracle: The word of the LORD to Israel through Malachi.[a]

Jacob Loved, Esau Hated

2"I have loved you," says the LORD.

"But you ask, 'How have you loved us?'

"Was not Esau Jacob's brother?" the LORD says. "Yet I have loved Jacob, 3but Esau I have hated, and I have turned his mountains into a wasteland and left his inheritance to the desert jackals."

4Edom may say, "Though we have been crushed, we will rebuild the ruins."

But this is what the LORD Almighty says: "They may build, but I will demolish. They will be called the Wicked Land, a people always under the wrath of the LORD. 5You will see it with your own eyes and say, 'Great is the LORD — even beyond the borders of Israel!'

Blemished Sacrifices

6"A son honours his father, and a servant his master. If I am a father, where is the honour due to me? If I am a master, where is the respect due to me?" says the LORD Almighty. "It is you, O priests, who show contempt for my name.

"But you ask, 'How have we shown contempt for your name?'

7"You place defiled food on my altar.

"But you ask, 'How have we defiled you?'

"By saying that the LORD's table is contemptible. 8When you bring blind animals for sacrifice, is that not wrong? When you sacrifice crippled or diseased animals, is that not wrong? Try offering them to your governor! Would he be pleased with you? Would he accept you?" says the LORD Almighty.

9"Now implore God to be gracious to us. With such offerings from your hands, will he accept you?" — says the LORD Almighty.

a1 Malachi means my messenger.

[10]"Oh, that one of you would shut the temple doors, so that you would not light useless fires on my altar! I am not pleased with you," says the LORD Almighty, "and I will accept no offering from your hands. [11]My name will be great among the nations, from the rising to the setting of the sun. In every place incense and pure offerings will be brought to my name, because my name will be great among the nations," says the LORD Almighty.

[12]"But you profane it by saying of the Lord's table, 'It is defiled', and of its food, 'It is contemptible.' [13]And you say, 'What a burden!' and you sniff at it contemptuously," says the LORD Almighty.

"When you bring injured, crippled or diseased animals and offer them as sacrifices, should I accept them from your hands?" says the LORD. [14]"Cursed is the cheat who has an acceptable male in his flock and vows to give it, but then sacrifices a blemished animal to the Lord. For I am a great king," says the LORD Almighty, "and my name is to be feared among the nations.

Admonition for the Priests

2 "And now this admonition is for you, O priests. [2]If you do not listen, and if you do not set your heart to honour my name," says the LORD Almighty, "I will send a curse upon you, and I will curse your blessings. Yes, I have already cursed them, because you have not set your heart to honour me.

[3]"Because of you I will rebuke[a] your descendants;[b] I will spread on your faces the offal from your festival sacrifices, and you will be carried off with it. [4]And you will know that I have sent you this admonition so that my covenant with Levi may continue," says the LORD Almighty. [5]"My covenant was with him, a covenant of life and peace, and I gave them to him; this called for reverence and he revered me and stood in awe of my name. [6]True instruction was in his mouth and nothing false was found on his lips. He walked with me in peace and uprightness, and turned many from sin.

2:4 The establishment of this covenant is not recorded in the Old Testament but it is presupposed in Jeremiah 33:21. The blessing of Moses on the tribe of Levi (Deuteronomy 33:8–11) commissioned them for both a priestly and a teaching role. Malachi accused the priests of giving false instruction and of failing to follow God's ways.

---

[7]"For the lips of a priest ought to preserve knowledge, and from his mouth men should seek instruction—because he is the messenger of the LORD Almighty. [8]But you have turned from the way and by your teaching have caused many to stumble; you have violated the covenant with Levi," says the LORD Almighty. [9]"So I have caused you to be despised and humiliated before all the people, because you have not

followed my ways but have shown partiality in matters of the law."

Judah Unfaithful

[10]Have we not all one Father?[c] Did not one God create us? Why do we profane the covenant of our fathers by breaking faith with one another?

[11]Judah has broken faith. A detestable thing has been committed in Israel and in Jerusalem: Judah has desecrated the sanctuary the LORD loves, by marrying the daughter of a foreign god. [12]As for the man who does this, whoever he may be, may the LORD cut him off from the tents of Jacob[d]—even though he brings offerings to the LORD Almighty.

[13]Another thing you do: You flood the LORD's altar with tears. You weep and wail because he no longer pays attention to your offerings or accepts them with pleasure from your hands. [14]You ask, "Why?" It is because the LORD is acting as the witness between you and the wife of your youth, because you have broken faith with her, though she is your partner, the wife of your marriage covenant.

[15]Has not ⸢the LORD⸥ made them one? In flesh and spirit they are his. And why one? Because he was seeking godly offspring.[e] So guard yourself in your spirit, and do not break faith with the wife of your youth.

[16]"I hate divorce," says the LORD God of Israel, "and I hate a man's covering himself[f] with violence as well as with his garment," says the LORD Almighty.

So guard yourself in your spirit, and do not break faith.

The Day of Judgment

[17]You have wearied the LORD with your words.

"How have we wearied him?" you ask.

By saying, "All who do evil are good in the eyes of the LORD, and he is pleased with them" or "Where is the God of justice?"

3 "See, I will send my messenger, who will prepare the way before me. Then suddenly the Lord you are seeking will come to his temple; the messenger of the covenant, whom you desire, will come," says the LORD Almighty.

[2]But who can endure the day of his coming? Who can stand when he appears? For he will be like a refiner's fire or a launderer's soap. [3]He will sit as a refiner and purifier of silver; he will purify the Levites and refine them like gold and silver. Then the LORD will have men who will bring offerings in righteousness, [4]and the offerings of Judah and Jerusalem will be acceptable to the LORD, as in days gone by, as in former years.

[5]"So I will come near to you for judgment. I will be quick to testify against sorcerers, adulterers and perjurers, against those who defraud labourers of their wages, who oppress the widows and the fatherless, and deprive aliens of justice, but do not fear me," says the LORD Almighty.

---

a3 Or *cut off* (see Septuagint)   *b3* Or *will blight your corn*   *c10* Or *father*
d12 Or *12May the LORD cut off from the tents of Jacob anyone who gives testimony on behalf of the man who does this*
e15 Or *15But the one ⸢who is our father⸣, did not do this, not as long as life remained in him. And what was he seeking? An offspring from God*   *f16* Or *his wife*

Robbing God

⁶"I the LORD do not change. So you, O descendants of Jacob, are not destroyed. ⁷Ever since the time of your forefathers you have turned away from my decrees and have not kept them. Return to me, and I will return to you," says the LORD Almighty.

"But you ask, 'How are we to return?'

⁸"Will a man rob God? Yet you rob me.

"But you ask, 'How do we rob you?'

"In tithes and offerings. ⁹You are under a curse — the whole nation of you — because you are robbing me. ¹⁰Bring the whole tithe into the storehouse, that there may be food in my house. Test me in this," says the LORD Almighty, "and see if I will not throw open the floodgates of heaven and pour out so much blessing that you will not have room enough for it. ¹¹I will prevent pests from devouring your crops, and the vines in your fields will not cast their fruit," says the LORD Almighty. ¹²"Then all the nations will call you blessed, for yours will be a delightful land," says the LORD Almighty.

¹³"You have said harsh things against me," says the LORD.

"Yet you ask, 'What have we said against you?'

¹⁴"You have said, 'It is futile to serve God. What did we gain by carrying out his requirements and going about like mourners before the LORD Almighty? ¹⁵But now we call the arrogant blessed. Certainly the evildoers prosper, and even those who challenge God escape.' "

¹⁶Then those who feared the LORD talked with each other, and the LORD listened and heard. A scroll of remembrance was written in his presence concerning those who feared the LORD and honoured his name. ¹⁷"They will be mine," says the LORD Almighty, "in the day when I make up my treasured possession.ᵃ I will spare them, just as in compassion a man spares his son who serves him. ¹⁸And you will again see the distinction between the righteous and the wicked, between those who serve God and those who do not.

The Day of the LORD

4 "Surely the day is coming; it will burn like a furnace. All the arrogant and every evildoer will be stubble, and that day that is coming will set them on fire," says the LORD Almighty. "Not a root or a branch will be left to them. ²But for you who revere my name, the sun of righteousness will rise with healing in its wings. And you will go out and leap like calves released from the stall. ³Then you will trample down the wicked; they will be ashes under the soles of your feet on the day when I do these things," says the LORD Almighty.

⁴"Remember the law of my servant Moses, the decrees and laws I gave him at Horeb for all Israel.

⁵"See, I will send you the prophet Elijah before that great and dreadful day of the LORD comes. ⁶He will turn the hearts of the fathers to their children, and the hearts of the children to their fathers; or else I will come and strike the land with a curse."

ᵃ 17 Or Almighty, "my treasured possession, in the day when I act

THE
NEW TESTAMENT

Matthew

Another Genesis

Someone once worked out that the Hebrew Bible (the Old Testament) has exactly 1,068 chapters, and the Gospel of Matthew exactly 1,068 verses. No one imagines that this is anything other than sheer coincidence: the Bible was not divided into chapters until the thirteenth century, nor into verses until 300 years later. But it is a happy parable. Matthew took up his pen to write his own abbreviated version of the Hebrew Bible. In our modern translation his opening words are "A record of the genealogy. . ." But in the Greek Matthew wrote "The book of genesis", which is the title of the first book of the Bible.

Five Volumes

Genesis is only the first of the five books which form the bedrock of the Hebrew Bible. Together the collection is known as the Pentateuch. So it is interesting that Matthew divided his Gospel into five, and marked the divisions by repeating the same punch line five times: when "Jesus had finished saying these things" (see 7:28; 11:1; 13:53; 19:1; 26:1). He was quite deliberately writing a new Pentateuch. The Jesus of Matthew's Gospel is not just the heroic leader that Mark had wanted to present to the early Christians. He is the Teacher.

Another Moses

Many people were disturbed when they saw the brilliant film *The Gospel according to Matthew* (directed by Pasolini). What they found difficult was the way that Jesus was portrayed. The Jesus they had in mind was, in fact, a composite figure made up from images and stories from all four Gospels. In contrast, this film portrayed Jesus as someone who never stopped talking, even as he strode down the road with his disciples struggling to keep up with him. But here only Matthew's Gospel was presented, and one third of it consists of the teaching of Jesus. Jesus, in fact, was seen as another Moses. He began his teaching, like Moses on Mount Sinai, with a Sermon on the Mount (5:1).

True and False Jews

Matthew's Gospel has a strong Jewish tone, and it refers more to the Old Testament than any of the other Gospels. This comes from the circumstances in which he wrote. In the years AD 75–80, two groups of Jews were fighting for survival. One was composed of the Jews who had fled to Jamnia on the Palestine coast, after the Roman destruction of Jerusalem in AD 70.

Until that time their religious life had revolved around the temple and the priesthood which served it. But with the temple gone, never to be rebuilt, priests no longer had a role to play, and a new kind of leadership arose as the people regrouped around their Rabbis, the Pharisees. Modern Judaism is the direct descendant of this group. The other group was composed of the small band of Jews who had attached themselves to the memory of Jesus of Nazareth. Until a short time before they had never distinguished themselves from the first group of Jews. Now they found themselves excommunicated by them.

Fulfilment

Which of the two groups was truly Jewish? Matthew's answer was unhesitating. The Judaism of the Rabbis, he maintained, had taken the wrong road and not opened itself to the Roman world, as the Jews who were Christians had done. The whole direction and purpose of the Hebrew Bible had been fulfilled in the life of Jesus—he was the true successor of Moses, and remained the only authoritative teacher (see 7:29). Jesus was the long-awaited Messiah, and those who didn't acknowledge him were lost. "God with us" Matthew announced (1:23), and it is repeated in his closing sentence, "I am with you always, to the very end" (28:20). This does not mean that Judaism was abolished. On the contrary, it continues in Christianity, which is precisely what Judaism was meant to become. In Christianity, the kingdom of God (or the "kingdom of the heavens" as the Jewish Matthew preferred to call it out of reverence for God's name) has arrived on earth.

The Church

In order to give the community of Christian Jews a sure foundation, Matthew provided guidelines, rules, and regulations. After all, this is what the rival group of Jews at Jamnia were doing, to establish themselves as "the synagogue". Matthew called his own group "the church".

There is, therefore, a rather institutional and "churchy" tone in Matthew's Gospel. He organized all the teaching of Jesus that he had into five great discourses: the qualifications for membership of the kingdom (the Sermon on the Mount (chapters 5—7)), a list of instructions for missionaries (chapter 11), a series of explanations of the mystery of the kingdom (chapter 13), a handbook of Christian conduct (chapter 18), and a description of God's final vindication of Jesus' teaching (chapters 24, 25).

Repetition

There are some phrases in Matthew which crop up again and again. This repetitious approach may be unfamiliar to some westerners, but it is a style much appreciated by the easterner. Early Christian scholars and Saints wrote more commentaries on it than on any other Gospel. The Church's worship chose more readings from this Gospel than from the others. Matthew's Gospel has in fact been so successful that a huge number of people know his version of the Lord's Prayer by heart (6:9–13). There are few who could repeat Luke's version (Luke 11:2–4).

Roots

Matthew's opposition to the official Judaism of his time was eventually to cause enormous problems for Christians. But that rivalry was secondary to his main concern—to show Christians how deeply rooted they are in Judaism. He was quick to emphasize the Jewishness of Jesus, and to show that if Christians ever denied their roots, or simply forgot them, they would no longer know who they were.

The Genealogy of Jesus

1 A record of the genealogy of Jesus Christ the son of David, the son of Abraham:

[2]Abraham was the father of Isaac,
  Isaac the father of Jacob,
  Jacob the father of Judah and his brothers,
  [3]Judah the father of Perez and Zerah, whose mother was Tamar,
  Perez the father of Hezron,
  Hezron the father of Ram,
  [4]Ram the father of Amminadab,
  Amminadab the father of Nahshon,
  Nahshon the father of Salmon,
  [5]Salmon the father of Boaz, whose mother was Rahab,
  Boaz the father of Obed, whose mother was Ruth,
  Obed the father of Jesse,
  [6]and Jesse the father of King David.

David was the father of Solomon, whose mother had been Uriah's wife,
  [7]Solomon the father of Rehoboam,
  Rehoboam the father of Abijah,
  Abijah the father of Asa,
  [8]Asa the father of Jehoshaphat,
  Jehoshaphat the father of Jehoram,
  Jehoram the father of Uzziah,
  [9]Uzziah the father of Jotham,
  Jotham the father of Ahaz,
  Ahaz the father of Hezekiah,
  [10]Hezekiah the father of Manasseh,
  Manasseh the father of Amon,
  Amon the father of Josiah,
  [11]and Josiah the father of Jeconiah[a] and his brothers at the time of the exile to Babylon.

[12]After the exile to Babylon:
  Jeconiah was the father of Shealtiel,
  Shealtiel the father of Zerubbabel,
  [13]Zerubbabel the father of Abiud,
  Abiud the father of Eliakim,
  Eliakim the father of Azor,
  [14]Azor the father of Zadok,
  Zadok the father of Akim,
  Akim the father of Eliud,
  [15]Eliud the father of Eleazar,

Eleazar the father of Matthan,
  Matthan the father of Jacob,
  [16]and Jacob the father of Joseph, the husband of Mary, of whom was born Jesus, who is called Christ.

[17]Thus there were fourteen generations in all from Abraham to David, fourteen from David to the exile to Babylon, and fourteen from the exile to the Christ.[b]

1:17 Matthew reconstructed a genealogy of Jesus to present him as the descendant not only of Abraham, who was the prototype of all believers, but especially of King David. The Saviour ("Messiah", or "Christ") was looked forward to as another David. Matthew drew attention to three fourteens in his genealogy (see verse 17). Hebrew has no symbols for numbers, and the letters of the alphabet have to be used instead. So the letters DVD not only stand for David, but can also be added up to fourteen $(4+6+4)$. Jesus is therefore presented as the beginning of the fourth fourteen, or the seventh seven. The number seven was regarded as the perfect number.

The Birth of Jesus Christ

[18]This is how the birth of Jesus Christ came about: His mother Mary was pledged to be married to Joseph, but before they came together, she was found to be with child through the Holy Spirit. [19]Because Joseph her husband was a righteous man and did not want to expose her to public disgrace, he had in mind to divorce her quietly.

[20]But after he had considered this, an angel of the Lord appeared to him in a dream and said, "Joseph son of David, do not be afraid to take Mary home as your wife, because what is conceived in her is from the Holy Spirit. [21]She will give birth to a son, and you are to give him the name Jesus,[c] because he will save his people from their sins."

[22]All this took place to fulfil what the Lord had said through the prophet: [23]"The virgin will be with child

---

[a]11 That is, Jehoiachin; also in verse 12
[b]17 Or Messiah. "The Christ" (Greek) and "the Messiah" (Hebrew) both mean "the Anointed One".
[c]21 Jesus is the Greek form of Joshua, which means the LORD saves.

and will give birth to a son, and they will call him Immanuel" [d]—which means, "God with us."

[24]When Joseph woke up, he did what the angel of the Lord had commanded him and took Mary home as his wife. [25]But he had no union with her until she gave birth to a son. And he gave him the name Jesus.

The Visit of the Magi

2 After Jesus was born in Bethlehem in Judea, during the time of King Herod, Magi [a] from the east came to Jerusalem [2]and asked, "Where is the one who has been born king of the Jews? We saw his star in the east [b] and have come to worship him."

2:1 The universal relevance of Jesus is an important feature right from the beginning of Matthew's Gospel. His birth concerns not only the chosen race of the Jews, but outsiders too. Those who imagine that they have a "right" to Jesus must think again.

---

[3]When King Herod heard this he was disturbed, and all Jerusalem with him. [4]When he had called together all the people's chief priests and teachers of the law, he asked them where the Christ [c] was to be born. [5]"In Bethlehem in Judea," they replied, "for this is what the prophet has written:

[6]" 'But you, Bethlehem, in the land of Judah,
are by no means least among the rulers of Judah;
for out of you will come a ruler
who will be the shepherd of my people Israel.' [d]"

[7]Then Herod called the Magi secretly and found out from them the exact time the star had appeared. [8]He sent them to Bethlehem and said, "Go and make a careful search for the child. As soon as you find him, report to me, so that I too may go and worship him." [9]After they had heard the king, they went on their way, and the star they had seen in the east [e] went ahead of them until it stopped over the place where the child was. [10]When they saw the star, they were overjoyed. [11]On coming to the house, they saw the child with his mother Mary, and they bowed down and worshipped him. Then they opened their treasures and presented him with gifts of gold and of incense and of myrrh. [12]And having been warned in a dream not to go back to Herod, they returned to their country by another route.

The Escape to Egypt

[13]When they had gone, an angel of the Lord appeared to Joseph in a dream. "Get up," he said, "take the child and his mother and escape to Egypt. Stay there until I tell you, for Herod is going to search for the child to kill him." [14]So he got up, took the child and his mother during the night and left for Egypt, [15]where he stayed until the death of Herod. And so was fulfilled what the Lord had said through the prophet: "Out of Egypt I called my son." [f]

[16]When Herod realised that he had been outwitted by the Magi, he was furious, and he gave orders to kill all the boys in Bethlehem and its vicinity who were two years old and under, in accordance with the time he had learned from the Magi. [17]Then what was said through the prophet Jeremiah was fulfilled:

[18]"A voice is heard in Ramah,
weeping and great mourning,
Rachel weeping for her children
and refusing to be comforted,
because they are no more." [g]

The Return to Nazareth

[19]After Herod died, an angel of the Lord appeared in a dream to Joseph in Egypt [20]and said, "Get up, take the child and his mother and go to the land of Israel, for those who were trying to take the child's life are dead." [21]So he got up, took the child and his mother and went to the land of Israel. [22]But when he heard that Archelaus was reigning in Judea in place of his father Herod, he was afraid to go there. Having been warned in a dream, he withdrew to the district of Galilee, [23]and he went and lived in a town called Nazareth. So was fulfilled what was said through the prophets: "He will be called a Nazarene."

John the Baptist Prepares the Way

3 In those days John the Baptist came, preaching in the Desert of Judea [2]and saying, "Repent, for the kingdom of heaven is near." [3]This is he who was spoken of through the prophet Isaiah:

"A voice of one calling in the desert,
'Prepare the way for the Lord,
make straight paths for him.' " [a]

[4]John's clothes were made of camel's hair, and he had a leather belt round his waist. His food was locusts and wild honey. [5]People went out to him from Jerusalem and all Judea and the whole region of the Jordan. [6]Confessing their sins, they were baptised by him in the Jordan River.

[7]But when he saw many of the Pharisees and Sadducees coming to where he was baptising, he said to them: "You brood of vipers! Who warned you to flee from the coming wrath? [8]Produce fruit in keeping with repentance. [9]And do not think you can say to yourselves, 'We have Abraham as our father.' I tell you that out of these stones God can raise up children for Abraham. [10]The axe is already at the root of the trees, and every tree that does not produce good fruit will be cut down and thrown into the fire.

[11]"I baptise you with [b] water for repentance. But after me will come one who is more powerful than I, whose sandals I am not fit to carry. He will baptise you with the Holy Spirit and with fire. [12]His winnowing

---

[d]23 Isaiah 7:14   [a]1 Traditionally *Wise Men*   [b]2 Or *star when it rose*   [c]4 Or *Messiah*
[d]6 Micah 5:2   [e]9 Or *seen when it rose*   [f]15 Hosea 11:1   [g]18 Jer. 31:15   [a]3 Isaiah 40:3
[b]11 Or *in*

fork is in his hand, and he will clear his threshing-floor, gathering his wheat into the barn and burning up the chaff with unquenchable fire."

The Baptism of Jesus

[13] Then Jesus came from Galilee to the Jordan to be baptised by John. [14] But John tried to deter him, saying, "I need to be baptised by you, and do you come to me?" [15] Jesus replied, "Let it be so now; it is proper for us to do this to fulfil all righteousness." Then John consented.

[16] As soon as Jesus was baptised, he went up out of the water. At that moment heaven was opened, and he saw the Spirit of God descending like a dove and lighting on him. [17] And a voice from heaven said, "This is my Son, whom I love; with him I am well pleased."

The Temptation of Jesus

4 Then Jesus was led by the Spirit into the desert to be tempted by the devil. [2] After fasting for forty days and forty nights, he was hungry. [3] The tempter came to him and said, "If you are the Son of God, tell these stones to become bread."

[4] Jesus answered, "It is written: 'Man does not live on bread alone, but on every word that comes from the mouth of God.'[a]"

[5] Then the devil took him to the holy city and had him stand on the highest point of the temple. [6] "If you are the Son of God," he said, "throw yourself down. For it is written:

" 'He will command his angels concerning you,
    and they will lift you up in their hands,
so that you will not strike your foot against a
    stone.'[b]"

[7] Jesus answered him, "It is also written: 'Do not put the Lord your God to the test.'[c]"

[8] Again, the devil took him to a very high mountain and showed him all the kingdoms of the world and their splendour. [9] "All this I will give you," he said, "if you will bow down and worship me."

[10] Jesus said to him, "Away from me, Satan! For it is written: 'Worship the Lord your God, and serve him only.'[d]"

[11] Then the devil left him, and angels came and attended him.

Jesus Begins to Preach

[12] When Jesus heard that John had been put in prison, he returned to Galilee. [13] Leaving Nazareth, he went and lived in Capernaum, which was by the lake in the area of Zebulun and Naphtali—[14] to fulfil what was said through the prophet Isaiah:

[15] "Land of Zebulun and land of Naphtali,
    the way to the sea, along the Jordan,
    Galilee of the Gentiles—
[16] the people living in darkness
    have seen a great light;
on those living in the land of the shadow of death
    a light has dawned."[e]

[17] From that time on Jesus began to preach, "Repent, for the kingdom of heaven is near."

4:17   As a devout Jew writing for other Jews Matthew frequently avoided the word "God" and substituted another word, like "heaven". So his "kingdom of heaven" is exactly equivalent to what the other Gospel writers called the kingdom of God. It does not mean another world, but this world once it has accepted and acknowledged the sovereignty of God.

The Calling of the First Disciples

[18] As Jesus was walking beside the Sea of Galilee, he saw two brothers, Simon called Peter and his brother Andrew. They were casting a net into the lake, for they were fishermen. [19] "Come, follow me," Jesus said, "and I will make you fishers of men." [20] At once they left their nets and followed him.

[21] Going on from there, he saw two other brothers, James son of Zebedee and his brother John. They were in a boat with their father Zebedee, preparing their nets. Jesus called them, [22] and immediately they left the boat and their father and followed him.

Jesus Heals the Sick

[23] Jesus went throughout Galilee, teaching in their synagogues, preaching the good news of the kingdom, and healing every disease and sickness among the people. [24] News about him spread all over Syria, and people brought to him all who were ill with various diseases, those suffering severe pain, the demon-possessed, those having seizures, and the paralysed, and he healed them. [25] Large crowds from Galilee, the Decapolis,[f] Jerusalem, Judea and the region across the Jordan followed him.

The Beatitudes

5 Now when he saw the crowds, he went up on a mountainside and sat down. His disciples came to him, [2] and he began to teach them, saying:

[3] "Blessed are the poor in spirit,
    for theirs is the kingdom of heaven.
[4] Blessed are those who mourn,
    for they will be comforted.
[5] Blessed are the meek,
    for they will inherit the earth.
[6] Blessed are those who hunger and thirst for
    righteousness,
    for they will be filled.
[7] Blessed are the merciful,
    for they will be shown mercy.
[8] Blessed are the pure in heart,
    for they will see God.

---

a4 Deut. 8:3   b6 Psalm 91:11,12   c7 Deut. 6:16   d10 Deut. 6:13   e16 Isaiah 9:1,2
f25 That is, the Ten Cities

9Blessed are the peacemakers,
   for they will be called sons of God.
10Blessed are those who are persecuted because of
   righteousness,
   for theirs is the kingdom of heaven.

11"Blessed are you when people insult you, persecute you and falsely say all kinds of evil against you because of me. 12Rejoice and be glad, because great is your reward in heaven, for in the same way they persecuted the prophets who were before you.

Salt and Light

13"You are the salt of the earth. But if the salt loses its saltiness, how can it be made salty again? It is no longer good for anything, except to be thrown out and trampled by men.
14"You are the light of the world. A city on a hill cannot be hidden. 15Neither do people light a lamp and put it under a bowl. Instead they put it on its stand, and it gives light to everyone in the house. 16In the same way, let your light shine before men, that they may see your good deeds and praise your Father in heaven.

The Fulfilment of the Law

17"Do not think that I have come to abolish the Law or the Prophets; I have not come to abolish them but to fulfil them. 18I tell you the truth, until heaven and earth disappear, not the smallest letter, not the least stroke of a pen, will by any means disappear from the Law until everything is accomplished. 19Anyone who breaks one of the least of these commandments and teaches others to do the same will be called least in the kingdom of heaven, but whoever practises and teaches these commands will be called great in the kingdom of heaven. 20For I tell you that unless your righteousness surpasses that of the Pharisees and the teachers of the law, you will certainly not enter the kingdom of heaven.

5:20 Matthew did not want Christians to ignore their Jewish roots. Like Jesus, they must be even more faithful to the Jewish Bible (the Law and the Prophets) than anyone else.

Murder

21"You have heard that it was said to the people long ago, 'Do not murder,a and anyone who murders will be subject to judgment.' 22But I tell you that anyone who is angry with his brotherb will be subject to judgment. Again, anyone who says to his brother, 'Raca,'c is answerable to the Sanhedrin. But anyone who says, 'You fool!' will be in danger of the fire of hell.
23"Therefore, if you are offering your gift at the altar and there remember that your brother has something against you, 24leave your gift there in front of the altar.

First go and be reconciled to your brother; then come and offer your gift.
25"Settle matters quickly with your adversary who is taking you to court. Do it while you are still with him on the way, or he may hand you over to the judge, and the judge may hand you over to the officer, and you may be thrown into prison. 26I tell you the truth, you will not get out until you have paid the last penny.d

Adultery

27"You have heard that it was said, 'Do not commit adultery.'e 28But I tell you that anyone who looks at a woman lustfully has already committed adultery with her in his heart. 29If your right eye causes you to sin, gouge it out and throw it away. It is better for you to lose one part of your body than for your whole body to be thrown into hell. 30And if your right hand causes you to sin, cut it off and throw it away. It is better for you to lose one part of your body than for your whole body to go into hell.

Divorce

31"It has been said, 'Anyone who divorces his wife must give her a certificate of divorce.'f 32But I tell you that anyone who divorces his wife, except for marital unfaithfulness, causes her to become an adulteress, and anyone who marries the divorced woman commits adultery.

Oaths

33"Again, you have heard that it was said to the people long ago, 'Do not break your oath, but keep the oaths you have made to the Lord.' 34But I tell you, Do not swear at all: either by heaven, for it is God's throne; 35or by the earth, for it is his footstool; or by Jerusalem, for it is the city of the Great King. 36And do not swear by your head, for you cannot make even one hair white or black. 37Simply let your 'Yes' be 'Yes', and your 'No', 'No'; anything beyond this comes from the evil one.

An Eye for an Eye

38"You have heard that it was said, 'Eye for eye, and tooth for tooth.'g 39But I tell you, Do not resist an evil person. If someone strikes you on the right cheek, turn to him the other also. 40And if someone wants to sue you and take your tunic, let him have your cloak as well. 41If someone forces you to go one mile, go with him two miles. 42Give to the one who asks you, and do not turn away from the one who wants to borrow from you.

Love for Enemies

43"You have heard that it was said, 'Love your neighbourh and hate your enemy.' 44But I tell you: Love your enemiesi and pray for those who persecute you, 45that you may be sons of your Father in heaven. He causes his sun to rise on the evil and the good, and

---

a21 Exodus 20:13   b22 Some manuscripts brother without cause   c22 An Aramaic term of contempt
d26 Greek kodrantes   e27 Exodus 20:14   f31 Deut. 24:1   g38 Exodus 21:24; Lev. 24:20 and Deut. 19:21
h43 Lev. 19:18   i44 Some late manuscripts enemies, bless those who curse you, do good to those who hate you

sends rain on the righteous and the unrighteous. ⁴⁶If you love those who love you, what reward will you get? Are not even the tax collectors doing that? ⁴⁷And if you greet only your brothers, what are you doing more than others? Do not even pagans do that? ⁴⁸Be perfect, therefore, as your heavenly Father is perfect.

Giving to the Needy

6 "Be careful not to do your 'acts of righteousness' before men, to be seen by them. If you do, you will have no reward from your Father in heaven.

²"So when you give to the needy, do not announce it with trumpets, as the hypocrites do in the synagogues and on the streets, to be honoured by men. I tell you the truth, they have received their reward in full. ³But when you give to the needy, do not let your left hand know what your right hand is doing, ⁴so that your giving may be in secret. Then your Father, who sees what is done in secret, will reward you.

Prayer

⁵"And when you pray, do not be like the hypocrites, for they love to pray standing in the synagogues and on the street corners to be seen by men. I tell you the truth, they have received their reward in full. ⁶But when you pray, go into your room, close the door and pray to your Father, who is unseen. Then your Father, who sees what is done in secret, will reward you. ⁷And when you pray, do not keep on babbling like pagans, for they think they will be heard because of their many words. ⁸Do not be like them, for your Father knows what you need before you ask him.

⁹"This, then, is how you should pray:

" 'Our Father in heaven,
    hallowed be your name,
¹⁰your kingdom come,
    your will be done
        on earth as it is in heaven.
¹¹Give us today our daily bread.
¹²Forgive us our debts,
    as we also have forgiven our debtors.
¹³And lead us not into temptation,
    but deliver us from the evil one.'ᵃ

¹⁴For if you forgive men when they sin against you, your heavenly Father will also forgive you. ¹⁵But if you do not forgive men their sins, your Father will not forgive your sins.

Fasting

¹⁶"When you fast, do not look sombre as the hypocrites do, for they disfigure their faces to show men they are fasting. I tell you the truth, they have received their reward in full. ¹⁷But when you fast, put oil on your head and wash your face, ¹⁸so that it will not be obvious to men that you are fasting, but only to your Father, who is unseen; and your Father, who sees what is done in secret, will reward you.

Treasures in Heaven

¹⁹"Do not store up for yourselves treasures on earth, where moth and rust destroy, and where thieves break in and steal. ²⁰But store up for yourselves treasures in heaven, where moth and rust do not destroy, and where thieves do not break in and steal. ²¹For where your treasure is, there your heart will be also.

²²"The eye is the lamp of the body. If your eyes are good, your whole body will be full of light. ²³But if your eyes are bad, your whole body will be full of darkness. If then the light within you is darkness, how great is that darkness!

²⁴"No-one can serve two masters. Either he will hate the one and love the other, or he will be devoted to the one and despise the other. You cannot serve both God and Money.

Do Not Worry

²⁵"Therefore I tell you, do not worry about your life, what you will eat or drink; or about your body, what you will wear. Is not life more important than food, and the body more important than clothes? ²⁶Look at the birds of the air; they do not sow or reap or store away in barns, and yet your heavenly Father feeds them. Are you not much more valuable than they? ²⁷Who of you by worrying can add a single hour to his life?ᵇ

²⁸"And why do you worry about clothes? See how the lilies of the field grow. They do not labour or spin. ²⁹Yet I tell you that not even Solomon in all his splendour was dressed like one of these. ³⁰If that is how God clothes the grass of the field, which is here today and tomorrow is thrown into the fire, will he not much more clothe you, O you of little faith? ³¹So do not worry, saying, 'What shall we eat?' or 'What shall we drink?' or 'What shall we wear?' ³²For the pagans run after all these things, and your heavenly Father knows that you need them. ³³But seek first his kingdom and his righteousness, and all these things will be given to you as well. ³⁴Therefore do not worry about tomorrow, for tomorrow will worry about itself. Each day has enough trouble of its own.

Judging Others

7 "Do not judge, or you too will be judged. ²For in the same way as you judge others, you will be judged, and with the measure you use, it will be measured to you.

³"Why do you look at the speck of sawdust in your brother's eye and pay no attention to the plank in your own eye? ⁴How can you say to your brother, 'Let me take the speck out of your eye,' when all the time there is a plank in your own eye? ⁵You hypocrite, first take the plank out of your own eye, and then you will see clearly to remove the speck from your brother's eye.

⁶"Do not give dogs what is sacred; do not throw your pearls to pigs. If you do, they may trample them under their feet, and then turn and tear you to pieces.

ᵃ13 Or from evil; some late manuscripts one, / for yours is the kingdom and the power and the glory for ever. Amen.
ᵇ27 Or single cubit to his height

Ask, Seek, Knock

7"Ask and it will be given to you; seek and you will find; knock and the door will be opened to you. 8For everyone who asks receives; he who seeks finds; and to him who knocks, the door will be opened.

9"Which of you, if his son asks for bread, will give him a stone? 10Or if he asks for a fish, will give him a snake? 11If you, then, though you are evil, know how to give good gifts to your children, how much more will your Father in heaven give good gifts to those who ask him! 12So in everything, do to others what you would have them do to you, for this sums up the Law and the Prophets.

The Narrow and Wide Gates

13"Enter through the narrow gate. For wide is the gate and broad is the road that leads to destruction, and many enter through it. 14But small is the gate and narrow the road that leads to life, and only a few find it.

A Tree and Its Fruit

15"Watch out for false prophets. They come to you in sheep's clothing, but inwardly they are ferocious wolves. 16By their fruit you will recognise them. Do people pick grapes from thornbushes, or figs from thistles? 17Likewise every good tree bears good fruit, but a bad tree bears bad fruit. 18A good tree cannot bear bad fruit, and a bad tree cannot bear good fruit. 19Every tree that does not bear good fruit is cut down and thrown into the fire. 20Thus, by their fruit you will recognise them.

21"Not everyone who says to me, 'Lord, Lord,' will enter the kingdom of heaven, but only he who does the will of my Father who is in heaven. 22Many will say to me on that day, 'Lord, Lord, did we not prophesy in your name, and in your name drive out demons and perform many miracles?' 23Then I will tell them plainly, 'I never knew you. Away from me, you evil-doers!'

The Wise and Foolish Builders

24"Therefore everyone who hears these words of mine and puts them into practice is like a wise man who built his house on the rock. 25The rain came down, the streams rose, and the winds blew and beat against that house; yet it did not fall, because it had its foundation on the rock. 26But everyone who hears these words of mine and does not put them into practice is like a foolish man who built his house on sand. 27The rain came down, the streams rose, and the winds blew and beat against that house, and it fell with a great crash."

28When Jesus had finished saying these things, the crowds were amazed at his teaching, 29because he taught as one who had authority, and not as their teachers of the law.

The Man With Leprosy

8 When he came down from the mountainside, large crowds followed him. 2A man with leprosy[a] came and knelt before him and said, "Lord, if you are willing, you can make me clean."

8:1   The second "volume" of Matthew's Gospel begins with a series of miracle stories, and ends with a discourse instructing the disciples to go and heal the sick in the same way (chapter 10). There have been gifted healers throughout history, among believers and unbelievers alike, of course, but the special thing about Jesus' healing ministry was that he saw it as a clear sign that the kingdom of God was breaking in on the world.

3Jesus reached out his hand and touched the man. "I am willing," he said. "Be clean!" Immediately he was cured[b] of his leprosy. 4Then Jesus said to him, "See that you don't tell anyone. But go, show yourself to the priest and offer the gift Moses commanded, as a testimony to them."

The Faith of the Centurion

5When Jesus had entered Capernaum, a centurion came to him, asking for help. 6"Lord," he said, "my servant lies at home paralysed and in terrible suffering."

7Jesus said to him, "I will go and heal him."

8The centurion replied, "Lord, I do not deserve to have you come under my roof. But just say the word, and my servant will be healed. 9For I myself am a man under authority, with soldiers under me. I tell this one, 'Go,' and he goes; and that one, 'Come,' and he comes. I say to my servant, 'Do this,' and he does it."

10When Jesus heard this, he was astonished and said to those following him, "I tell you the truth, I have not found anyone in Israel with such great faith. 11I say to you that many will come from the east and the west, and will take their places at the feast with Abraham, Isaac and Jacob in the kingdom of heaven. 12But the subjects of the kingdom will be thrown outside, into the darkness, where there will be weeping and gnashing of teeth."

13Then Jesus said to the centurion, "Go! It will be done just as you believed it would." And his servant was healed at that very hour.

Jesus Heals Many

14When Jesus came into Peter's house, he saw Peter's mother-in-law lying in bed with a fever. 15He touched her hand and the fever left her, and she got up and began to wait on him.

16When evening came, many who were demon-possessed were brought to him, and he drove out the

---

a2 The Greek word was used for various diseases affecting the skin—not necessarily leprosy.   b3 Greek made clean spirits with a word and healed all the sick. [17]This was to fulfil what was spoken through the prophet Isaiah:

"He took up our infirmities
and carried our diseases." [c]

The Cost of Following Jesus

[18]When Jesus saw the crowd around him, he gave orders to cross to the other side of the lake. [19]Then a teacher of the law came to him and said, "Teacher, I will follow you wherever you go."

[20]Jesus replied, "Foxes have holes and birds of the air have nests, but the Son of Man has nowhere to lay his head."

8:20 Jesus often referred to himself as "Son of Man". This was quite a common expression in the Gospels. Now people sometimes refer to themselves as "one" to avoid the word "I", although it did not have the same affectation. The expression "Son of Man" was often used by the prophets. Ezekiel spoke about the weak and suffering Son of Man, and Daniel about the glorious and heavenly Son of Man (Daniel 7).

---

[21]Another disciple said to him, "Lord, first let me go and bury my father."

[22]But Jesus told him, "Follow me, and let the dead bury their own dead."

Jesus Calms the Storm

[23]Then he got into the boat and his disciples followed him. [24]Without warning, a furious storm came up on the lake, so that the waves swept over the boat. But Jesus was sleeping. [25]The disciples went and woke him, saying, "Lord, save us! We're going to drown!"

[26]He replied, "You of little faith, why are you so afraid?" Then he got up and rebuked the winds and the waves, and it was completely calm.

[27]The men were amazed and asked, "What kind of man is this? Even the winds and the waves obey him!"

The Healing of Two Demon-possessed Men

[28]When he arrived at the other side in the region of the Gadarenes,[d] two demon-possessed men coming from the tombs met him. They were so violent that no-one could pass that way. [29]"What do you want with us, Son of God?" they shouted. "Have you come here to torture us before the appointed time?"

[30]Some distance from them a large herd of pigs was feeding. [31]The demons begged Jesus, "If you drive us out, send us into the herd of pigs."

[32]He said to them, "Go!" So they came out and went into the pigs, and the whole herd rushed down the steep bank into the lake and died in the water. [33]Those tending the pigs ran off, went into the town and reported all this, including what had happened to the demon-possessed men. [34]Then the whole town went out to meet Jesus. And when they saw him, they pleaded with him to leave their region.

Jesus Heals a Paralytic

9 Jesus stepped into a boat, crossed over and came to his own town. [2]Some men brought to him a paralytic, lying on a mat. When Jesus saw their faith, he said to the paralytic, "Take heart, son; your sins are forgiven."

[3]At this, some of the teachers of the law said to themselves, "This fellow is blaspheming!"

[4]Knowing their thoughts, Jesus said, "Why do you entertain evil thoughts in your hearts? [5]Which is easier: to say, 'Your sins are forgiven,' or to say, 'Get up and walk'? [6]But so that you may know that the Son of Man has authority on earth to forgive sins. . . ." Then he said to the paralytic, "Get up, take your mat and go home." [7]And the man got up and went home. [8]When the crowd saw this, they were filled with awe; and they praised God, who had given such authority to men.

The Calling of Matthew

[9]As Jesus went on from there, he saw a man named Matthew sitting at the tax collector's booth. "Follow me," he told him, and Matthew got up and followed him.

9:9 Mark and Luke also tell this story, giving the detested tax collector the name Levi. Was Matthew humbly coming clean that it was really himself under another name? It was to people like him on the margins of society that Jesus proclaimed the good news of God's forgiveness.

---

[10]While Jesus was having dinner at Matthew's house, many tax collectors and "sinners" came and ate with him and his disciples. [11]When the Pharisees saw this, they asked his disciples, "Why does your teacher eat with tax collectors and 'sinners'?"

[12]On hearing this, Jesus said, "It is not the healthy who need a doctor, but the sick. [13]But go and learn what this means: 'I desire mercy, not sacrifice.'[a] For I have not come to call the righteous, but sinners."

Jesus Questioned About Fasting

[14]Then John's disciples came and asked him, "How is it that we and the Pharisees fast, but your disciples do not fast?"

[15]Jesus answered, "How can the guests of the bridegroom mourn while he is with them? The time will come when the bridegroom will be taken from them; then they will fast.

[16]"No-one sews a patch of unshrunk cloth on an old garment, for the patch will pull away from the garment, making the tear worse. [17]Neither do men pour new wine into old wineskins. If they do, the skins will burst, the wine will run out and the wineskins will be ruined.

---

c 17 Isaiah 53:4   *d 28* Some manuscripts *Gergesenes*; others *Gerasenes*   *a 13* Hosea 6:6

No, they pour new wine into new wineskins, and both are preserved."

A Dead Girl and a Sick Woman

18While he was saying this, a ruler came and knelt before him and said, "My daughter has just died. But come and put your hand on her, and she will live." 19Jesus got up and went with him, and so did his disciples.

20Just then a woman who had been subject to bleeding for twelve years came up behind him and touched the edge of his cloak. 21She said to herself, "If I only touch his cloak, I will be healed."

22Jesus turned and saw her. "Take heart, daughter," he said, "your faith has healed you." And the woman was healed from that moment.

23When Jesus entered the ruler's house and saw the flute players and the noisy crowd, 24he said, "Go away. The girl is not dead but asleep." But they laughed at him. 25After the crowd had been put outside, he went in and took the girl by the hand, and she got up. 26News of this spread through all that region.

Jesus Heals the Blind and Mute

27As Jesus went on from there, two blind men followed him, calling out, "Have mercy on us, Son of David!"

28When he had gone indoors, the blind men came to him, and he asked them, "Do you believe that I am able to do this?"

"Yes, Lord," they replied.

29Then he touched their eyes and said, "According to your faith will it be done to you"; 30and their sight was restored. Jesus warned them sternly, "See that no-one knows about this." 31But they went out and spread the news about him all over that region.

32While they were going out, a man who was demon-possessed and could not talk was brought to Jesus. 33And when the demon was driven out, the man who had been mute spoke. The crowd was amazed and said, "Nothing like this has ever been seen in Israel."

34But the Pharisees said, "It is by the prince of demons that he drives out demons."

The Workers Are Few

35Jesus went through all the towns and villages, teaching in their synagogues, preaching the good news of the kingdom and healing every disease and sickness. 36When he saw the crowds, he had compassion on them, because they were harassed and helpless, like sheep without a shepherd. 37Then he said to his disciples, "The harvest is plentiful but the workers are few. 38Ask the Lord of the harvest, therefore, to send out workers into his harvest field."

Jesus Sends Out the Twelve

10 He called his twelve disciples to him and gave them authority to drive out evil[a] spirits and to heal every disease and sickness.

2These are the names of the twelve apostles: first, Simon (who is called Peter) and his brother Andrew; James son of Zebedee, and his brother John; 3Philip and Bartholomew; Thomas and Matthew the tax collector; James son of Alphaeus, and Thaddaeus; 4Simon the Zealot and Judas Iscariot, who betrayed him.

5These twelve Jesus sent out with the following instructions: "Do not go among the Gentiles or enter any town of the Samaritans. 6Go rather to the lost sheep of Israel. 7As you go, preach this message: 'The kingdom of heaven is near.' 8Heal the sick, raise the dead, cleanse those who have leprosy,[b] drive out demons. Freely you have received, freely give. 9Do not take along any gold or silver or copper in your belts; 10take no bag for the journey, or extra tunic, or sandals or a staff; for the worker is worth his keep.

11"Whatever town or village you enter, search for some worthy person there and stay at his house until you leave. 12As you enter the home, give it your greeting. 13If the home is deserving, let your peace rest on it; if it is not, let your peace return to you. 14If anyone will not welcome you or listen to your words, shake the dust off your feet when you leave that home or town. 15I tell you the truth, it will be more bearable for Sodom and Gomorrah on the day of judgment than for that town. 16I am sending you out like sheep among wolves. Therefore be as shrewd as snakes and as innocent as doves.

17"Be on your guard against men; they will hand you over to the local councils and flog you in their synagogues. 18On my account you will be brought before governors and kings as witnesses to them and to the Gentiles. 19But when they arrest you, do not worry about what to say or how to say it. At that time you will be given what to say, 20for it will not be you speaking, but the Spirit of your Father speaking through you.

21"Brother will betray brother to death, and a father his child; children will rebel against their parents and have them put to death. 22All men will hate you because of me, but he who stands firm to the end will be saved. 23When you are persecuted in one place, flee to another. I tell you the truth, you will not finish going through the cities of Israel before the Son of Man comes.

24"A student is not above his teacher, nor a servant above his master. 25It is enough for the student to be like his teacher, and the servant like his master. If the head of the house has been called Beelzebub,[c] how much more the members of his household!

26"So do not be afraid of them. There is nothing concealed that will not be disclosed, or hidden that will not be made known. 27What I tell you in the dark, speak in the daylight; what is whispered in your ear, proclaim from the roofs. 28Do not be afraid of those who kill the body but cannot kill the soul. Rather, be afraid of the One who can destroy both soul and body in hell. 29Are not two sparrows sold for a penny?[d] Yet not one of them will fall to the ground apart from the will of your Father. 30And even the very hairs of your head are all numbered. 31So don't be afraid; you are worth more than many sparrows.

a1 Greek unclean　　b8 The Greek word was used for various diseases affecting the skin—not necessarily leprosy.
c25 Greek Beezeboul or Beelzeboul　　d29 Greek an assarion

³²"Whoever acknowledges me before men, I will also acknowledge him before my Father in heaven. ³³But whoever disowns me before men, I will disown him before my Father in heaven.

³⁴"Do not suppose that I have come to bring peace to the earth. I did not come to bring peace, but a sword. ³⁵For I have come to turn

" 'a man against his father,
    a daughter against her mother,
    a daughter-in-law against her mother-in-law —
³⁶ a man's enemies will be the members of his
        own household.' e

³⁷"Anyone who loves his father or mother more than me is not worthy of me; anyone who loves his son or daughter more than me is not worthy of me; ³⁸and anyone who does not take his cross and follow me is not worthy of me. ³⁹Whoever finds his life will lose it, and whoever loses his life for my sake will find it.

⁴⁰"He who receives you receives me, and he who receives me receives the one who sent me. ⁴¹Anyone who receives a prophet because he is a prophet will receive a prophet's reward, and anyone who receives a righteous man because he is a righteous man will receive a righteous man's reward. ⁴²And if anyone gives even a cup of cold water to one of these little ones because he is my disciple, I tell you the truth, he will certainly not lose his reward."

Jesus and John the Baptist

11 After Jesus had finished instructing his twelve disciples, he went on from there to teach and preach in the towns of Galilee. a

²When John heard in prison what Christ was doing, he sent his disciples ³to ask him, "Are you the one who was to come, or should we expect someone else?"

⁴Jesus replied, "Go back and report to John what you hear and see: ⁵The blind receive sight, the lame walk, those who have leprosy b are cured, the deaf hear, the dead are raised, and the good news is preached to the poor. ⁶Blessed is the man who does not fall away on account of me."

⁷As John's disciples were leaving, Jesus began to speak to the crowd about John: "What did you go out into the desert to see? A reed swayed by the wind? ⁸If not, what did you go out to see? A man dressed in fine clothes? No, those who wear fine clothes are in kings' palaces. ⁹Then what did you go out to see? A prophet? Yes, I tell you, and more than a prophet. ¹⁰This is the one about whom it is written:

" 'I will send my messenger ahead of you,
    who will prepare your way before you.' c

¹¹I tell you the truth: Among those born of women there has not risen anyone greater than John the Baptist; yet he who is least in the kingdom of heaven is greater than he. ¹²From the days of John the Baptist until now, the kingdom of heaven has been forcefully advancing, and forceful men lay hold of it. ¹³For all the Prophets and the Law prophesied until John. ¹⁴And if you are willing to accept it, he is the Elijah who was to come. ¹⁵He who has ears, let him hear.

¹⁶"To what can I compare this generation? They are like children sitting in the market-places and calling out to others:

¹⁷" 'We played the flute for you,
    and you did not dance;
we sang a dirge,
    and you did not mourn.'

¹⁸For John came neither eating nor drinking, and they say, 'He has a demon.' ¹⁹The Son of Man came eating and drinking, and they say, 'Here is a glutton and a drunkard, a friend of tax collectors and "sinners".' But wisdom is proved right by her actions."

Woe on Unrepentant Cities

²⁰Then Jesus began to denounce the cities in which most of his miracles had been performed, because they did not repent. ²¹"Woe to you, Korazin! Woe to you, Bethsaida! If the miracles that were performed in you had been performed in Tyre and Sidon, they would have repented long ago in sackcloth and ashes. ²²But I tell you, it will be more bearable for Tyre and Sidon on the day of judgment than for you. ²³And you, Capernaum, will you be lifted up to the skies? No, you will go down to the depths. d If the miracles that were performed in you had been performed in Sodom, it would have remained to this day. ²⁴But I tell you that it will be more bearable for Sodom on the day of judgment than for you."

Rest for the Weary

²⁵At that time Jesus said, "I praise you, Father, Lord of heaven and earth, because you have hidden these things from the wise and learned, and revealed them to little children. ²⁶Yes, Father, for this was your good pleasure.

²⁷"All things have been committed to me by my Father. No-one knows the Son except the Father, and no-one knows the Father except the Son and those to whom the Son chooses to reveal him.

²⁸"Come to me, all you who are weary and burdened, and I will give you rest. ²⁹Take my yoke upon you and learn from me, for I am gentle and humble in heart, and you will find rest for your souls. ³⁰For my yoke is easy and my burden is light."

Lord of the Sabbath

12 At that time Jesus went through the cornfields on the Sabbath. His disciples were hungry and began to pick some ears of corn and eat them. ²When the Pharisees saw this, they said to him, "Look! Your disciples are doing what is unlawful on the Sabbath."

³He answered, "Haven't you read what David did when he and his companions were hungry? ⁴He entered the house of God, and he and his companions ate the consecrated bread — which was not lawful for them to do, but only for the priests. ⁵Or haven't you

e 36 Micah 7:6   a 1 Greek in their towns
b 5 The Greek word was used for various diseases affecting the skin — not necessarily leprosy.   c 10 Mal. 3:1
d 23 Greek Hades

read in the Law that on the Sabbath the priests in the temple desecrate the day and yet are innocent? ⁶I tell you that one*ᵃ* greater than the temple is here. ⁷If you had known what these words mean, 'I desire mercy, not sacrifice,'*ᵇ* you would not have condemned the innocent. ⁸For the Son of Man is Lord of the Sabbath."

⁹Going on from that place, he went into their synagogue, ¹⁰and a man with a shrivelled hand was there. Looking for a reason to accuse Jesus, they asked him, "Is it lawful to heal on the Sabbath?"

¹¹He said to them, "If any of you has a sheep and it falls into a pit on the Sabbath, will you not take hold of it and lift it out? ¹²How much more valuable is a man than a sheep! Therefore it is lawful to do good on the Sabbath."

¹³Then he said to the man, "Stretch out your hand." So he stretched it out and it was completely restored, just as sound as the other. ¹⁴But the Pharisees went out and plotted how they might kill Jesus.

12:14 What was it that drove people to kill Jesus? The Gospel offers many possibilities: outrage at his disrespect for sacred institutions? envy of his popularity? resentment of his air of authority? opposition to his liberal ideas and fear of what they could lead to? possession by devils? sheer bigotry? Whatever it was, a political charge of treason finally brought about his death (see 27:11,29,37,42).

God's Chosen Servant

¹⁵Aware of this, Jesus withdrew from that place. Many followed him, and he healed all their sick, ¹⁶warning them not to tell who he was. ¹⁷This was to fulfil what was spoken through the prophet Isaiah:

¹⁸"Here is my servant whom I have chosen,
the one I love, in whom I delight;
I will put my Spirit on him,
and he will proclaim justice to the nations.
¹⁹He will not quarrel or cry out;
no-one will hear his voice in the streets.
²⁰A bruised reed he will not break,
and a smouldering wick he will not snuff out,
till he leads justice to victory.
²¹   In his name the nations will put their hope."*ᶜ*

Jesus and Beelzebub

²²Then they brought him a demon-possessed man who was blind and mute, and Jesus healed him, so that he could both talk and see. ²³All the people were astonished and said, "Could this be the Son of David?"

²⁴But when the Pharisees heard this, they said, "It is only by Beelzebub,*ᵈ* the prince of demons, that this fellow drives out demons."

²⁵Jesus knew their thoughts and said to them, "Every kingdom divided against itself will be ruined,

and every city or household divided against itself will not stand. ²⁶If Satan drives out Satan, he is divided against himself. How then can his kingdom stand? ²⁷And if I drive out demons by Beelzebub, by whom do your people drive them out? So then, they will be your judges. ²⁸But if I drive out demons by the Spirit of God, then the kingdom of God has come upon you.

²⁹"Or again, how can anyone enter a strong man's house and carry off his possessions unless he first ties up the strong man? Then he can rob his house.

³⁰"He who is not with me is against me, and he who does not gather with me scatters. ³¹And so I tell you, every sin and blasphemy will be forgiven men, but the blasphemy against the Spirit will not be forgiven. ³²Anyone who speaks a word against the Son of Man will be forgiven, but anyone who speaks against the Holy Spirit will not be forgiven, either in this age or in the age to come.

³³"Make a tree good and its fruit will be good, or make a tree bad and its fruit will be bad, for a tree is recognised by its fruit. ³⁴You brood of vipers, how can you who are evil say anything good? For out of the overflow of the heart the mouth speaks. ³⁵The good man brings good things out of the good stored up in him, and the evil man brings evil things out of the evil stored up in him. ³⁶But I tell you that men will have to give account on the day of judgment for every careless word they have spoken. ³⁷For by your words you will be acquitted, and by your words you will be condemned."

The Sign of Jonah

³⁸Then some of the Pharisees and teachers of the law said to him, "Teacher, we want to see a miraculous sign from you."

³⁹He answered, "A wicked and adulterous generation asks for a miraculous sign! But none will be given it except the sign of the prophet Jonah. ⁴⁰For as Jonah was three days and three nights in the belly of a huge fish, so the Son of Man will be three days and three nights in the heart of the earth. ⁴¹The men of Nineveh will stand up at the judgment with this generation and condemn it; for they repented at the preaching of Jonah, and now one*ᵉ* greater than Jonah is here. ⁴²The Queen of the South will rise at the judgment with this generation and condemn it; for she came from the ends of the earth to listen to Solomon's wisdom, and now one greater than Solomon is here.

⁴³"When an evil*ᶠ* spirit comes out of a man, it goes through arid places seeking rest and does not find it. ⁴⁴Then it says, 'I will return to the house I left.' When it arrives, it finds the house unoccupied, swept clean and put in order. ⁴⁵Then it goes and takes with it seven other spirits more wicked than itself, and they go in and live there. And the final condition of that man is worse than the first. That is how it will be with this wicked generation."

Jesus' Mother and Brothers

⁴⁶While Jesus was still talking to the crowd, his mother and brothers stood outside, wanting to speak

---

ᵃ6 Or *something;* also in verses 41 and 42   *ᵇ7* Hosea 6:6   *ᶜ21* Isaiah 42:1–4
ᵈ24 Greek *Beezeboul* or *Beelzeboul;* also in verse 27   *ᵉ41* Or *something;* also in verse 42   *ᶠ43* Greek *unclean*

to him. [47]Someone told him, "Your mother and brothers are standing outside, wanting to speak to you."[g]

[48]He replied to him, "Who is my mother, and who are my brothers?" [49]Pointing to his disciples, he said, "Here are my mother and my brothers. [50]For whoever does the will of my Father in heaven is my brother and sister and mother."

The Parable of the Sower

13 That same day Jesus went out of the house and sat by the lake. [2]Such large crowds gathered round him that he got into a boat and sat in it, while all the people stood on the shore. [3]Then he told them many things in parables, saying: "A farmer went out to sow his seed. [4]As he was scattering the seed, some fell along the path, and the birds came and ate it up. [5]Some fell on rocky places, where it did not have much soil. It sprang up quickly, because the soil was shallow. [6]But when the sun came up, the plants were scorched, and they withered because they had no root. [7]Other seed fell among thorns, which grew up and choked the plants. [8]Still other seed fell on good soil, where it produced a crop—a hundred, sixty or thirty times what was sown. [9]He who has ears, let him hear."

13:3 Like any good teacher, Jesus taught a lot through stories. They caught the people's attention, and also deliberately shocked the hearers by revealing an aspect of God surprisingly different from what they expected.

---

[10]The disciples came to him and asked, "Why do you speak to the people in parables?"

[11]He replied, "The knowledge of the secrets of the kingdom of heaven has been given to you, but not to them. [12]Whoever has will be given more, and he will have an abundance. Whoever does not have, even what he has will be taken from him. [13]This is why I speak to them in parables:

"Though seeing, they do not see;
    though hearing, they do not hear or understand.

[14]In them is fulfilled the prophecy of Isaiah:

" 'You will be ever hearing but never
        understanding;
    you will be ever seeing but never perceiving.
[15]For this people's heart has become calloused;
    they hardly hear with their ears,
    and they have closed their eyes.
Otherwise they might see with their eyes,
    hear with their ears,
    understand with their hearts
and turn, and I would heal them.'[a]

[16]But blessed are your eyes because they see, and your ears because they hear. [17]For I tell you the truth, many prophets and righteous men longed to see what you see

but did not see it, and to hear what you hear but did not hear it.

[18]"Listen then to what the parable of the sower means: [19]When anyone hears the message about the kingdom and does not understand it, the evil one comes and snatches away what was sown in his heart. This is the seed sown along the path. [20]The one who received the seed that fell on rocky places is the man who hears the word and at once receives it with joy. [21]But since he has no root, he lasts only a short time. When trouble or persecution comes because of the word, he quickly falls away. [22]The one who received the seed that fell among the thorns is the man who hears the word, but the worries of this life and the deceitfulness of wealth choke it, making it unfruitful. [23]But the one who received the seed that fell on good soil is the man who hears the word and understands it. He produces a crop, yielding a hundred, sixty or thirty times what was sown."

The Parable of the Weeds

[24]Jesus told them another parable: "The kingdom of heaven is like a man who sowed good seed in his field. [25]But while everyone was sleeping, his enemy came and sowed weeds among the wheat, and went away. [26]When the wheat sprouted and formed ears, then the weeds also appeared.

[27]"The owner's servants came to him and said, 'Sir, didn't you sow good seed in your field? Where then did the weeds come from?'

[28]" 'An enemy did this,' he replied.

"The servants asked him, 'Do you want us to go and pull them up?'

[29]" 'No,' he answered, 'because while you are pulling the weeds, you may root up the wheat with them. [30]Let both grow together until the harvest. At that time I will tell the harvesters: First collect the weeds and tie them in bundles to be burned; then gather the wheat and bring it into my barn.' "

The Parables of the Mustard Seed and the Yeast

[31]He told them another parable: "The kingdom of heaven is like a mustard seed, which a man took and planted in his field. [32]Though it is the smallest of all your seeds, yet when it grows, it is the largest of garden plants and becomes a tree, so that the birds of the air come and perch in its branches."

[33]He told them still another parable: "The kingdom of heaven is like yeast that a woman took and mixed into a large amount[b] of flour until it worked all through the dough."

[34]Jesus spoke all these things to the crowd in parables; he did not say anything to them without using a parable. [35]So was fulfilled what was spoken through the prophet:

"I will open my mouth in parables,
    I will utter things hidden since the creation of
        the world."[c]

---

g47 Some manuscripts do not have verse 47.   *a15* Isaiah 6:9,10
b33 Greek *three satas* (probably about ⅓ bushel or 22 litres)   *c35* Psalm 78:2

The Parable of the Weeds Explained

36Then he left the crowd and went into the house. His disciples came to him and said, "Explain to us the parable of the weeds in the field."

37He answered, "The one who sowed the good seed is the Son of Man. 38The field is the world, and the good seed stands for the sons of the kingdom. The weeds are the sons of the evil one, 39and the enemy who sows them is the devil. The harvest is the end of the age, and the harvesters are angels.

40"As the weeds are pulled up and burned in the fire, so it will be at the end of the age. 41The Son of Man will send out his angels, and they will weed out of his kingdom everything that causes sin and all who do evil. 42They will throw them into the fiery furnace, where there will be weeping and gnashing of teeth. 43Then the righteous will shine like the sun in the kingdom of their Father. He who has ears, let him hear.

The Parables of the Hidden Treasure and the Pearl

44"The kingdom of heaven is like treasure hidden in a field. When a man found it, he hid it again, and then in his joy went and sold all he had and bought that field.

45"Again, the kingdom of heaven is like a merchant looking for fine pearls. 46When he found one of great value, he went away and sold everything he had and bought it.

The Parable of the Net

47"Once again, the kingdom of heaven is like a net that was let down into the lake and caught all kinds of fish. 48When it was full, the fishermen pulled it up on the shore. Then they sat down and collected the good fish in baskets, but threw the bad away. 49This is how it will be at the end of the age. The angels will come and separate the wicked from the righteous 50and throw them into the fiery furnace, where there will be weeping and gnashing of teeth.

51"Have you understood all these things?" Jesus asked.

"Yes," they replied.

52He said to them, "Therefore every teacher of the law who has been instructed about the kingdom of heaven is like the owner of a house who brings out of his storeroom new treasures as well as old."

A Prophet Without Honour

53When Jesus had finished these parables, he moved on from there. 54Coming to his home town, he began teaching the people in their synagogue, and they were amazed. "Where did this man get this wisdom and these miraculous powers?" they asked. 55"Isn't this the carpenter's son? Isn't his mother's name Mary, and aren't his brothers James, Joseph, Simon and Judas? 56Aren't all his sisters with us? Where then did this man get all these things?" 57And they took offence at him.

But Jesus said to them, "Only in his home town and in his own house is a prophet without honour."

a24 Greek many stadia

58And he did not do many miracles there because of their lack of faith.

John the Baptist Beheaded

14 At that time Herod the tetrarch heard the reports about Jesus, 2and he said to his attendants, "This is John the Baptist; he has risen from the dead! That is why miraculous powers are at work in him."

3Now Herod had arrested John and bound him and put him in prison because of Herodias, his brother Philip's wife, 4for John had been saying to him: "It is not lawful for you to have her." 5Herod wanted to kill John, but he was afraid of the people, because they considered him a prophet.

6On Herod's birthday the daughter of Herodias danced for them and pleased Herod so much 7that he promised with an oath to give her whatever she asked. 8Prompted by her mother, she said, "Give me here on a platter the head of John the Baptist." 9The king was distressed, but because of his oaths and his dinner guests, he ordered that her request be granted 10and had John beheaded in the prison. 11His head was brought in on a platter and given to the girl, who carried it to her mother. 12John's disciples came and took his body and buried it. Then they went and told Jesus.

Jesus Feeds the Five Thousand

13When Jesus heard what had happened, he withdrew by boat privately to a solitary place. Hearing of this, the crowds followed him on foot from the towns. 14When Jesus landed and saw a large crowd, he had compassion on them and healed their sick.

15As evening approached, the disciples came to him and said, "This is a remote place, and it's already getting late. Send the crowds away, so that they can go to the villages and buy themselves some food."

16Jesus replied, "They do not need to go away. You give them something to eat."

17"We have here only five loaves of bread and two fish," they answered.

18"Bring them here to me," he said. 19And he directed the people to sit down on the grass. Taking the five loaves and the two fish and looking up to heaven, he gave thanks and broke the loaves. Then he gave them to the disciples, and the disciples gave them to the people. 20They all ate and were satisfied, and the disciples picked up twelve basketfuls of broken pieces that were left over. 21The number of those who ate was about five thousand men, besides women and children.

Jesus Walks on the Water

22Immediately Jesus made the disciples get into the boat and go on ahead of him to the other side, while he dismissed the crowd. 23After he had dismissed them, he went up on a mountainside by himself to pray. When evening came, he was there alone, 24but the boat was already a considerable distancea from land, buffeted by the waves because the wind was against it.

25During the fourth watch of the night Jesus went out to them, walking on the lake. 26When the disciples saw him walking on the lake, they were terrified. "It's a ghost," they said, and cried out in fear.

27But Jesus immediately said to them: "Take courage! It is I. Don't be afraid."

28"Lord, if it's you," Peter replied, "tell me to come to you on the water."

29"Come," he said.

Then Peter got down out of the boat, walked on the water and came towards Jesus. 30But when he saw the wind, he was afraid and, beginning to sink, cried out, "Lord, save me!"

31Immediately Jesus reached out his hand and caught him. "You of little faith," he said, "why did you doubt?"

32And when they climbed into the boat, the wind died down. 33Then those who were in the boat worshipped him, saying, "Truly you are the Son of God." 34When they had crossed over, they landed at Gennesaret. 35And when the men of that place recognised Jesus, they sent word to all the surrounding country. People brought all their sick to him 36and begged him to let the sick just touch the edge of his cloak, and all who touched him were healed.

Clean and Unclean

15 Then some Pharisees and teachers of the law came to Jesus from Jerusalem and asked, 2"Why do your disciples break the tradition of the elders? They don't wash their hands before they eat!"

3Jesus replied, "And why do you break the command of God for the sake of your tradition? 4For God said, 'Honour your father and mother'a and 'Anyone who curses his father or mother must be put to death.'b 5But you say that if a man says to his father or mother, 'Whatever help you might otherwise have received from me is a gift devoted to God,' 6he is not to 'honour his father'c with it. Thus you nullify the word of God for the sake of your tradition. 7You hypocrites! Isaiah was right when he prophesied about you:

8" 'These people honour me with their lips,
   but their hearts are far from me.
9They worship me in vain;
   their teachings are but rules taught by men.'d "

10Jesus called the crowd to him and said, "Listen and understand. 11What goes into a man's mouth does not make him 'unclean', but what comes out of his mouth, that is what makes him 'unclean'."

12Then the disciples came to him and asked, "Do you know that the Pharisees were offended when they heard this?"

13He replied, "Every plant that my heavenly Father has not planted will be pulled up by the roots. 14Leave them; they are blind guides.e If a blind man leads a blind man, both will fall into a pit."

15Peter said, "Explain the parable to us."

16"Are you still so dull?" Jesus asked them. 17"Don't you see that whatever enters the mouth goes into the stomach and then out of the body? 18But the things that come out of the mouth come from the heart, and these make a man 'unclean'. 19For out of the heart come evil thoughts, murder, adultery, sexual immorality, theft, false testimony, slander. 20These are what make a man 'unclean'; but eating with unwashed hands does not make him 'unclean'."

The Faith of the Canaanite Woman

21Leaving that place, Jesus withdrew to the region of Tyre and Sidon. 22A Canaanite woman from that vicinity came to him, crying out, "Lord, Son of David, have mercy on me! My daughter is suffering terribly from demon-possession."

23Jesus did not answer a word. So his disciples came to him and urged him, "Send her away, for she keeps crying out after us."

24He answered, "I was sent only to the lost sheep of Israel."

25The woman came and knelt before him. "Lord, help me!" she said.

26He replied, "It is not right to take the children's bread and toss it to their dogs."

27"Yes, Lord," she said, "but even the dogs eat the crumbs that fall from their masters' table."

28Then Jesus answered, "Woman, you have great faith! Your request is granted." And her daughter was healed from that very hour.

Jesus Feeds the Four Thousand

29Jesus left there and went along the Sea of Galilee. Then he went up on a mountainside and sat down. 30Great crowds came to him, bringing the lame, the blind, the crippled, the mute and many others, and laid them at his feet; and he healed them. 31The people were amazed when they saw the mute speaking, the crippled made well, the lame walking and the blind seeing. And they praised the God of Israel.

15:29 Like Mark, Matthew told the story of the desert meal twice, with only slight variations. This is presumably how the story stood in their source. Luke and John tell the story only once.

32Jesus called his disciples to him and said, "I have compassion for these people; they have already been with me three days and have nothing to eat. I do not want to send them away hungry, or they may collapse on the way."

33His disciples answered, "Where could we get enough bread in this remote place to feed such a crowd?"

34"How many loaves do you have?" Jesus asked.

"Seven," they replied, "and a few small fish."

35He told the crowd to sit down on the ground. 36Then he took the seven loaves and the fish, and when he had given thanks, he broke them and gave them to the disciples, and they in turn to the people. 37They all

---

a4 Exodus 20:12; Deut. 5:16   b4 Exodus 21:17; Lev. 20:9
d9 Isaiah 29:13   e14 Some manuscripts guides of the blind

c6 Some manuscripts father or his mother

ate and were satisfied. Afterwards the disciples picked up seven basketfuls of broken pieces that were left over. [38]The number of those who ate was four thousand, besides women and children. [39]After Jesus had sent the crowd away, he got into the boat and went to the vicinity of Magadan.

The Demand for a Sign

16 The Pharisees and Sadducees came to Jesus and tested him by asking him to show them a sign from heaven.

[2]He replied,[a] "When evening comes, you say, 'It will be fair weather, for the sky is red,' [3]and in the morning, 'Today it will be stormy, for the sky is red and overcast.' You know how to interpret the appearance of the sky, but you cannot interpret the signs of the times. [4]A wicked and adulterous generation looks for a miraculous sign, but none will be given it except the sign of Jonah." Jesus then left them and went away.

The Yeast of the Pharisees and Sadducees

[5]When they went across the lake, the disciples forgot to take bread. [6]"Be careful," Jesus said to them. "Be on your guard against the yeast of the Pharisees and Sadducees."

[7]They discussed this among themselves and said, "It is because we didn't bring any bread."

[8]Aware of their discussion, Jesus asked, "You of little faith, why are you talking among yourselves about having no bread? [9]Do you still not understand? Don't you remember the five loaves for the five thousand, and how many basketfuls you gathered? [10]Or the seven loaves for the four thousand, and how many basketfuls you gathered? [11]How is it you don't understand that I was not talking to you about bread? But be on your guard against the yeast of the Pharisees and Sadducees." [12]Then they understood that he was not telling them to guard against the yeast used in bread, but against the teaching of the Pharisees and Sadducees.

Peter's Confession of Christ

[13]When Jesus came to the region of Caesarea Philippi, he asked his disciples, "Who do people say the Son of Man is?"

[14]They replied, "Some say John the Baptist; others say Elijah; and still others, Jeremiah or one of the prophets."

[15]"But what about you?" he asked. "Who do you say I am?"

[16]Simon Peter answered, "You are the Christ,[b] the Son of the living God."

[17]Jesus replied, "Blessed are you, Simon son of Jonah, for this was not revealed to you by man, but by my Father in heaven. [18]And I tell you that you are Peter,[c] and on this rock I will build my church, and the gates of Hades[d] will not overcome it.[e] [19]I will give you the keys of the kingdom of heaven; whatever

you bind on earth will be[f] bound in heaven, and whatever you loose on earth will be[f] loosed in heaven." [20]Then he warned his disciples not to tell anyone that he was the Christ.

16:18　　Matthew made much of Peter's profession of faith, which he saw as the foundation stone on which the church was to be built. It is unclear what precise claim was being made here. Is it Peter in person who is the rock? If so, he has no successor. However, if it is Peter's faith on which the church is built, it is a faith shared by all Christians. The rock is not necessarily stable: it can very easily turn into a stumbling-block (verse 23).

Jesus Predicts His Death

[21]From that time on Jesus began to explain to his disciples that he must go to Jerusalem and suffer many things at the hands of the elders, chief priests and teachers of the law, and that he must be killed and on the third day be raised to life.

[22]Peter took him aside and began to rebuke him. "Never, Lord!" he said. "This shall never happen to you!"

[23]Jesus turned and said to Peter, "Get behind me, Satan! You are a stumbling-block to me; you do not have in mind the things of God, but the things of men."

[24]Then Jesus said to his disciples, "If anyone would come after me, he must deny himself and take up his cross and follow me. [25]For whoever wants to save his life[g] will lose it, but whoever loses his life for me will find it. [26]What good will it be for a man if he gains the whole world, yet forfeits his soul? Or what can a man give in exchange for his soul? [27]For the Son of Man is going to come in his Father's glory with his angels, and then he will reward each person according to what he has done. [28]I tell you the truth, some who are standing here will not taste death before they see the Son of Man coming in his kingdom."

The Transfiguration

17 After six days Jesus took with him Peter, James and John the brother of James, and led them up a high mountain by themselves. [2]There he was transfigured before them. His face shone like the sun, and his clothes became as white as the light. [3]Just then there appeared before them Moses and Elijah, talking with Jesus.

[4]Peter said to Jesus, "Lord, it is good for us to be here. If you wish, I will put up three shelters — one for you, one for Moses and one for Elijah."

[5]While he was still speaking, a bright cloud enveloped them, and a voice from the cloud said, "This is my Son, whom I love; with him I am well pleased. Listen to him!"

---

[a]2 Some early manuscripts do not have the rest of verse 2 and all of verse 3.　　　[b]16 Or *Messiah*; also in verse 20
[c]18 *Peter* means *rock*.　　　[d]18 Or *hell*　　　[e]18 Or *not prove stronger than it*　　　[f]19 Or *have been*
[g]25 The Greek word means either *life* or *soul*; also in verse 26.

[6]When the disciples heard this, they fell face down to the ground, terrified. [7]But Jesus came and touched them. "Get up," he said. "Don't be afraid." [8]When they looked up, they saw no-one except Jesus.

[9]As they were coming down the mountain, Jesus instructed them, "Don't tell anyone what you have seen, until the Son of Man has been raised from the dead."

[10]The disciples asked him, "Why then do the teachers of the law say that Elijah must come first?"

[11]Jesus replied, "To be sure, Elijah comes and will restore all things. [12]But I tell you, Elijah has already come, and they did not recognise him, but have done to him everything they wished. In the same way the Son of Man is going to suffer at their hands." [13]Then the disciples understood that he was talking to them about John the Baptist.

The Healing of a Boy With a Demon

[14]When they came to the crowd, a man approached Jesus and knelt before him. [15]"Lord, have mercy on my son," he said. "He has seizures and is suffering greatly. He often falls into the fire or into the water. [16]I brought him to your disciples, but they could not heal him."

[17]"O unbelieving and perverse generation," Jesus replied, "how long shall I stay with you? How long shall I put up with you? Bring the boy here to me." [18]Jesus rebuked the demon, and it came out of the boy, and he was healed from that moment.

[19]Then the disciples came to Jesus in private and asked, "Why couldn't we drive it out?"

[20]He replied, "Because you have so little faith. I tell you the truth, if you have faith as small as a mustard seed, you can say to this mountain, 'Move from here to there' and it will move. Nothing will be impossible for you." [a]

[22]When they came together in Galilee, he said to them, "The Son of Man is going to be betrayed into the hands of men. [23]They will kill him, and on the third day he will be raised to life." And the disciples were filled with grief.

The Temple Tax

[24]After Jesus and his disciples arrived in Capernaum, the collectors of the two-drachma tax came to Peter and asked, "Doesn't your teacher pay the temple tax?" [b]

[25]"Yes, he does," he replied.

When Peter came into the house, Jesus was the first to speak. "What do you think, Simon?" he asked. "From whom do the kings of the earth collect duty and taxes—from their own sons or from others?"

[26]"From others," Peter answered.

"Then the sons are exempt," Jesus said to him. [27]"But so that we may not offend them, go to the lake and throw out your line. Take the first fish you catch; open its mouth and you will find a four-drachma coin. Take it and give it to them for my tax and yours."

The Greatest in the Kingdom of Heaven

18 At that time the disciples came to Jesus and asked, "Who is the greatest in the kingdom of heaven?"

[2]He called a little child and had him stand among them. [3]And he said: "I tell you the truth, unless you change and become like little children, you will never enter the kingdom of heaven. [4]Therefore, whoever humbles himself like this child is the greatest in the kingdom of heaven.

[5]"And whoever welcomes a little child like this in my name welcomes me. [6]But if anyone causes one of these little ones who believe in me to sin, it would be better for him to have a large millstone hung around his neck and to be drowned in the depths of the sea.

[7]"Woe to the world because of the things that cause people to sin! Such things must come, but woe to the man through whom they come! [8]If your hand or your foot causes you to sin, cut it off and throw it away. It is better for you to enter life maimed or crippled than to have two hands or two feet and be thrown into eternal fire. [9]And if your eye causes you to sin, gouge it out and throw it away. It is better for you to enter life with one eye than to have two eyes and be thrown into the fire of hell.

The Parable of the Lost Sheep

[10]"See that you do not look down on one of these little ones. For I tell you that their angels in heaven always see the face of my Father in heaven. [a]

[12]"What do you think? If a man owns a hundred sheep, and one of them wanders away, will he not leave the ninety-nine on the hills and go to look for the one that wandered off? [13]And if he finds it, I tell you the truth, he is happier about that one sheep than about the ninety-nine that did not wander off. [14]In the same way your Father in heaven is not willing that any of these little ones should be lost.

A Brother Who Sins Against You

[15]"If your brother sins against you, [b] go and show him his fault, just between the two of you. If he listens to you, you have won your brother over. [16]But if he will not listen, take one or two others along, so that 'every matter may be established by the testimony of two or three witnesses.' [c] [17]If he refuses to listen to them, tell it to the church; and if he refuses to listen even to the church, treat him as you would a pagan or a tax collector.

[18]"I tell you the truth, whatever you bind on earth will be [d] bound in heaven, and whatever you loose on earth will be [d] loosed in heaven.

[19]"Again, I tell you that if two of you on earth agree about anything you ask for, it will be done for you by my Father in heaven. [20]For where two or three come together in my name, there am I with them."

---

[a]20 Some manuscripts you. 21 But this kind does not go out except by prayer and fasting.   [b]24 Greek the two drachmas
[a]10 Some manuscripts heaven. 11 The Son of Man came to save what was lost.   [b]15 Some manuscripts do not have against you.
[c]16 Deut. 19:15   [d]18 Or have been

The Parable of the Unmerciful Servant

21Then Peter came to Jesus and asked, "Lord, how many times shall I forgive my brother when he sins against me? Up to seven times?"

18:21   Peter's offer was more generous than we realize. He was willing to forgive someone seven times for the same fault. Jesus compared his offer with God's forgiveness, which simply goes on and on and on. Ironically, Peter was to need this endless forgiveness himself.

22Jesus answered, "I tell you, not seven times, but seventy-seven times.*e*

23"Therefore, the kingdom of heaven is like a king who wanted to settle accounts with his servants. 24As he began the settlement, a man who owed him ten thousand talents*f* was brought to him. 25Since he was not able to pay, the master ordered that he and his wife and his children and all that he had be sold to repay the debt.

26"The servant fell on his knees before him. 'Be patient with me,' he begged, 'and I will pay back everything.' 27The servant's master took pity on him, cancelled the debt and let him go.

28"But when that servant went out, he found one of his fellow-servants who owed him a hundred denarii.*g* He grabbed him and began to choke him. 'Pay back what you owe me!' he demanded.

29"His fellow-servant fell to his knees and begged him, 'Be patient with me, and I will pay you back.'

30"But he refused. Instead, he went off and had the man thrown into prison until he could pay the debt. 31When the other servants saw what had happened, they were greatly distressed and went and told their master everything that had happened.

32"Then the master called the servant in. 'You wicked servant,' he said, 'I cancelled all that debt of yours because you begged me to. 33Shouldn't you have had mercy on your fellow-servant just as I had on you?' 34In anger his master turned him over to the jailers to be tortured, until he should pay back all he owed.

35"This is how my heavenly Father will treat each of you unless you forgive your brother from your heart."

Divorce

19 When Jesus had finished saying these things, he left Galilee and went into the region of Judea to the other side of the Jordan. 2Large crowds followed him, and he healed them there.

3Some Pharisees came to him to test him. They asked, "Is it lawful for a man to divorce his wife for any and every reason?"

4"Haven't you read," he replied, "that at the beginning the Creator 'made them male and female',*a* 5and said, 'For this reason a man will leave his father and mother and be united to his wife, and the two will become one flesh'*b*? 6So they are no longer two, but one. Therefore what God has joined together, let man not separate."

7"Why then," they asked, "did Moses command that a man give his wife a certificate of divorce and send her away?"

8Jesus replied, "Moses permitted you to divorce your wives because your hearts were hard. But it was not this way from the beginning. 9I tell you that anyone who divorces his wife, except for marital unfaithfulness, and marries another woman commits adultery."

10The disciples said to him, "If this is the situation between a husband and wife, it is better not to marry."

11Jesus replied, "Not everyone can accept this word, but only those to whom it has been given. 12For some are eunuchs because they were born that way; others were made that way by men; and others have renounced marriage*c* because of the kingdom of heaven. The one who can accept this should accept it."

The Little Children and Jesus

13Then little children were brought to Jesus for him to place his hands on them and pray for them. But the disciples rebuked those who brought them.

14Jesus said, "Let the little children come to me, and do not hinder them, for the kingdom of heaven belongs to such as these." 15When he had placed his hands on them, he went on from there.

The Rich Young Man

16Now a man came up to Jesus and asked, "Teacher, what good thing must I do to get eternal life?"

17"Why do you ask me about what is good?" Jesus replied. "There is only One who is good. If you want to enter life, obey the commandments."

18"Which ones?" the man enquired.

Jesus replied, " 'Do not murder, do not commit adultery, do not steal, do not give false testimony, 19honour your father and mother,'*d* and 'love your neighbour as yourself.'*e*"

20"All these I have kept," the young man said. "What do I still lack?"

21Jesus answered, "If you want to be perfect, go, sell your possessions and give to the poor, and you will have treasure in heaven. Then come, follow me."

22When the young man heard this, he went away sad, because he had great wealth.

23Then Jesus said to his disciples, "I tell you the truth, it is hard for a rich man to enter the kingdom of heaven. 24Again I tell you, it is easier for a camel to go through the eye of a needle than for a rich man to enter the kingdom of God."

25When the disciples heard this, they were greatly astonished and asked, "Who then can be saved?"

26Jesus looked at them and said, "With man this is impossible, but with God all things are possible."

27Peter answered him, "We have left everything to follow you! What then will there be for us?"

e 22 Or seventy times seven   f 24 That is, millions of pounds
b 5 Gen. 2:24   c 12 Or have made themselves eunuchs
e 19 Lev. 19:18

g 28 That is, a few pounds   a 4 Gen. 1:27
d 19 Exodus 20:12–16; Deut. 5:16–20

²⁸Jesus said to them, "I tell you the truth, at the renewal of all things, when the Son of Man sits on his glorious throne, you who have followed me will also sit on twelve thrones, judging the twelve tribes of Israel. ²⁹And everyone who has left houses or brothers or sisters or father or mother*f* or children or fields for my sake will receive a hundred times as much and will inherit eternal life. ³⁰But many who are first will be last, and many who are last will be first.

The Parable of the Workers in the Vineyard

20 "For the kingdom of heaven is like a landowner who went out early in the morning to hire men to work in his vineyard. ²He agreed to pay them a denarius for the day and sent them into his vineyard.

³"About the third hour he went out and saw others standing in the market-place doing nothing. ⁴He told them, 'You also go and work in my vineyard, and I will pay you whatever is right.' ⁵So they went.

"He went out again about the sixth hour and the ninth hour and did the same thing. ⁶About the eleventh hour he went out and found still others standing around. He asked them, 'Why have you been standing here all day long doing nothing?'

⁷" 'Because no-one has hired us,' they answered.

"He said to them, 'You also go and work in my vineyard.'

⁸"When evening came, the owner of the vineyard said to his foreman, 'Call the workers and pay them their wages, beginning with the last ones hired and going on to the first.'

⁹"The workers who were hired about the eleventh hour came and each received a denarius. ¹⁰So when those came who were hired first, they expected to receive more. But each one of them also received a denarius. ¹¹When they received it, they began to grumble against the landowner. ¹²'These men who were hired last worked only one hour,' they said, 'and you have made them equal to us who have borne the burden of the work and the heat of the day.'

¹³"But he answered one of them, 'Friend, I am not being unfair to you. Didn't you agree to work for a denarius? ¹⁴Take your pay and go. I want to give the man who was hired last the same as I gave you. ¹⁵Don't I have the right to do what I want with my own money? Or are you envious because I am generous?'

¹⁶"So the last will be first, and the first will be last."

Jesus Again Predicts His Death

¹⁷Now as Jesus was going up to Jerusalem, he took the twelve disciples aside and said to them, ¹⁸"We are going up to Jerusalem, and the Son of Man will be betrayed to the chief priests and the teachers of the law. They will condemn him to death ¹⁹and will turn him over to the Gentiles to be mocked and flogged and crucified. On the third day he will be raised to life!"

A Mother's Request

²⁰Then the mother of Zebedee's sons came to Jesus with her sons and, kneeling down, asked a favour of him.

²¹"What is it you want?" he asked.

She said, "Grant that one of these two sons of mine may sit at your right and the other at your left in your kingdom."

²²"You don't know what you are asking," Jesus said to them. "Can you drink the cup I am going to drink?"

"We can," they answered.

²³Jesus said to them, "You will indeed drink from my cup, but to sit at my right or left is not for me to grant. These places belong to those for whom they have been prepared by my Father."

²⁴When the ten heard about this, they were indignant with the two brothers. ²⁵Jesus called them together and said, "You know that the rulers of the Gentiles lord it over them, and their high officials exercise authority over them. ²⁶Not so with you. Instead, whoever wants to become great among you must be your servant, ²⁷and whoever wants to be first must be your slave — ²⁸just as the Son of Man did not come to be served, but to serve, and to give his life as a ransom for many."

Two Blind Men Receive Sight

²⁹As Jesus and his disciples were leaving Jericho, a large crowd followed him. ³⁰Two blind men were sitting by the roadside, and when they heard that Jesus was going by, they shouted, "Lord, Son of David, have mercy on us!"

³¹The crowd rebuked them and told them to be quiet, but they shouted all the louder, "Lord, Son of David, have mercy on us!"

³²Jesus stopped and called them. "What do you want me to do for you?" he asked.

³³"Lord," they answered, "we want our sight."

³⁴Jesus had compassion on them and touched their eyes. Immediately they received their sight and followed him.

The Triumphal Entry

21 As they approached Jerusalem and came to Bethphage on the Mount of Olives, Jesus sent two disciples, ²saying to them, "Go to the village ahead of you, and at once you will find a donkey tied there, with her colt by her. Untie them and bring them to me. ³If anyone says anything to you, tell him that the Lord needs them, and he will send them right away."

⁴This took place to fulfil what was spoken through the prophet:

⁵"Say to the Daughter of Zion,
'See, your king comes to you,
gentle and riding on a donkey,
on a colt, the foal of a donkey.' "*a*

⁶The disciples went and did as Jesus had instructed them. ⁷They brought the donkey and the colt, placed their cloaks on them, and Jesus sat on them. ⁸A very

f29 Some manuscripts mother or wife　　　*a5 Zech. 9:9*

large crowd spread their cloaks on the road, while others cut branches from the trees and spread them on the road. ⁹The crowds that went ahead of him and those that followed shouted,

"Hosanna ᵇ to the Son of David!"

"Blessed is he who comes in the name of the
     Lord!" ᶜ

"Hosanna ᵇ in the highest!"

¹⁰When Jesus entered Jerusalem, the whole city was stirred and asked, "Who is this?"
¹¹The crowds answered, "This is Jesus, the prophet from Nazareth in Galilee."

Jesus at the Temple

¹²Jesus entered the temple area and drove out all who were buying and selling there. He overturned the tables of the money-changers and the benches of those selling doves. ¹³"It is written," he said to them, " 'My house will be called a house of prayer,' ᵈ but you are making it a 'den of robbers'. ᵉ"
¹⁴The blind and the lame came to him at the temple, and he healed them. ¹⁵But when the chief priests and the teachers of the law saw the wonderful things he did and the children shouting in the temple area, "Hosanna to the Son of David," they were indignant.
¹⁶"Do you hear what these children are saying?" they asked him.
"Yes," replied Jesus, "have you never read,

" 'From the lips of children and infants
     you have ordained praise' ʄ?"

¹⁷And he left them and went out of the city to Bethany, where he spent the night.

The Fig-Tree Withers

¹⁸Early in the morning, as he was on his way back to the city, he was hungry. ¹⁹Seeing a fig-tree by the road, he went up to it but found nothing on it except leaves. Then he said to it, "May you never bear fruit again!" Immediately the tree withered.
²⁰When the disciples saw this, they were amazed. "How did the fig-tree wither so quickly?" they asked.
²¹Jesus replied, "I tell you the truth, if you have faith and do not doubt, not only can you do what was done to the fig-tree, but also you can say to this mountain, 'Go, throw yourself into the sea,' and it will be done. ²²If you believe, you will receive whatever you ask for in prayer."

The Authority of Jesus Questioned

²³Jesus entered the temple courts, and, while he was teaching, the chief priests and the elders of the people came to him. "By what authority are you doing these things?" they asked. "And who gave you this authority?"
²⁴Jesus replied, "I will also ask you one question. If you answer me, I will tell you by what authority I am

doing these things. ²⁵John's baptism—where did it come from? Was it from heaven, or from men?"
They discussed it among themselves and said, "If we say, 'From heaven', he will ask, 'Then why didn't you believe him?' ²⁶But if we say, 'From men'—we are afraid of the people, for they all hold that John was a prophet."
²⁷So they answered Jesus, "We don't know."
Then he said, "Neither will I tell you by what authority I am doing these things.

The Parable of the Two Sons

²⁸"What do you think? There was a man who had two sons. He went to the first and said, 'Son, go and work today in the vineyard.'
²⁹" 'I will not,' he answered, but later he changed his mind and went.
³⁰"Then the father went to the other son and said the same thing. He answered, 'I will, sir,' but he did not go.
³¹"Which of the two did what his father wanted?"
"The first," they answered.
Jesus said to them, "I tell you the truth, the tax collectors and the prostitutes are entering the kingdom of God ahead of you. ³²For John came to you to show you the way of righteousness, and you did not believe him, but the tax collectors and the prostitutes did. And even after you saw this, you did not repent and believe him.

The Parable of the Tenants

³³"Listen to another parable: There was a landowner who planted a vineyard. He put a wall around it, dug a winepress in it and built a watchtower. Then he rented the vineyard to some farmers and went away on a journey. ³⁴When the harvest time approached, he sent his servants to the tenants to collect his fruit.
³⁵"The tenants seized his servants; they beat one, killed another, and stoned a third. ³⁶Then he sent other servants to them, more than the first time, and the tenants treated them in the same way. ³⁷Last of all, he sent his son to them. 'They will respect my son,' he said.
³⁸"But when the tenants saw the son, they said to each other, 'This is the heir. Come, let's kill him and take his inheritance.' ³⁹So they took him and threw him out of the vineyard and killed him.
⁴⁰"Therefore, when the owner of the vineyard comes, what will he do to those tenants?"
⁴¹"He will bring those wretches to a wretched end," they replied, "and he will rent the vineyard to other tenants, who will give him his share of the crop at harvest time."
⁴²Jesus said to them, "Have you never read in the Scriptures:

" 'The stone the builders rejected
     has become the capstone; ᵍ
the Lord has done this,
     and it is marvellous in our eyes' ʰ?

⁴³"Therefore I tell you that the kingdom of God will be taken away from you and given to a people who will

---

ᵇ9 A Hebrew expression meaning "Save!" which became an exclamation of praise; also in verse 15   ᶜ9 Psalm 118:26
ᵈ13 Isaiah 56:7   ᵉ13 Jer. 7:11   ʄ16 Psalm 8:2   ᵍ42 Or cornerstone   ʰ42 Psalm 118:22,23

produce its fruit. ⁴⁴He who falls on this stone will be broken to pieces, but he on whom it falls will be crushed." *i*

⁴⁵When the chief priests and the Pharisees heard Jesus' parables, they knew he was talking about them. ⁴⁶They looked for a way to arrest him, but they were afraid of the crowd because the people held that he was a prophet.

The Parable of the Wedding Banquet

22 Jesus spoke to them again in parables, saying: ²"The kingdom of heaven is like a king who prepared a wedding banquet for his son. ³He sent his servants to those who had been invited to the banquet to tell them to come, but they refused to come.

⁴"Then he sent some more servants and said, 'Tell those who have been invited that I have prepared my dinner: My oxen and fattened cattle have been slaughtered, and everything is ready. Come to the wedding banquet.'

⁵"But they paid no attention and went off—one to his field, another to his business. ⁶The rest seized his servants, ill-treated them and killed them. ⁷The king was enraged. He sent his army and destroyed those murderers and burned their city.

⁸"Then he said to his servants, 'The wedding banquet is ready, but those I invited did not deserve to come. ⁹Go to the street corners and invite to the banquet anyone you find.' ¹⁰So the servants went out into the streets and gathered all the people they could find, both good and bad, and the wedding hall was filled with guests.

¹¹"But when the king came in to see the guests, he noticed a man there who was not wearing wedding clothes. ¹²'Friend,' he asked, 'how did you get in here without wedding clothes?' The man was speechless.

22:11 It is generally agreed that the story of the wedding clothes was originally separate from the story of the wedding breakfast (verses 2–10), in which the gospel is on free offer to all outcasts whether they are dressed for the occasion or not. It is Matthew who put the two stories together.

---

¹³"Then the king told the attendants, 'Tie him hand and foot, and throw him outside, into the darkness, where there will be weeping and gnashing of teeth.'

¹⁴"For many are invited, but few are chosen."

Paying Taxes to Caesar

¹⁵Then the Pharisees went out and laid plans to trap him in his words. ¹⁶They sent their disciples to him along with the Herodians. "Teacher," they said, "we know you are a man of integrity and that you teach the way of God in accordance with the truth. You aren't swayed by men, because you pay no attention to who they are. ¹⁷Tell us then, what is your opinion? Is it right to pay taxes to Caesar or not?"

¹⁸But Jesus, knowing their evil intent, said, "You hypocrites, why are you trying to trap me? ¹⁹Show me the coin used for paying the tax." They brought him a denarius, ²⁰and he asked them, "Whose portrait is this? And whose inscription?"

²¹"Caesar's," they replied.

Then he said to them, "Give to Caesar what is Caesar's, and to God what is God's."

²²When they heard this, they were amazed. So they left him and went away.

Marriage at the Resurrection

²³That same day the Sadducees, who say there is no resurrection, came to him with a question. ²⁴"Teacher," they said, "Moses told us that if a man dies without having children, his brother must marry the widow and have children for him. ²⁵Now there were seven brothers among us. The first one married and died, and since he had no children, he left his wife to his brother. ²⁶The same thing happened to the second and third brother, right on down to the seventh. ²⁷Finally, the woman died. ²⁸Now then, at the resurrection, whose wife will she be of the seven, since all of them were married to her?"

²⁹Jesus replied, "You are in error because you do not know the Scriptures or the power of God. ³⁰At the resurrection people will neither marry nor be given in marriage; they will be like the angels in heaven. ³¹But about the resurrection of the dead—have you not read what God said to you, ³²'I am the God of Abraham, the God of Isaac, and the God of Jacob'ᵃ? He is not the God of the dead but of the living."

³³When the crowds heard this, they were astonished at his teaching.

The Greatest Commandment

³⁴Hearing that Jesus had silenced the Sadducees, the Pharisees got together. ³⁵One of them, an expert in the law, tested him with this question: ³⁶"Teacher, which is the greatest commandment in the Law?"

³⁷Jesus replied: " 'Love the Lord your God with all your heart and with all your soul and with all your mind.'ᵇ ³⁸This is the first and greatest commandment. ³⁹And the second is like it: 'Love your neighbour as yourself.'ᶜ ⁴⁰All the Law and the Prophets hang on these two commandments."

Whose Son Is the Christ?

⁴¹While the Pharisees were gathered together, Jesus asked them, ⁴²"What do you think about the Christ?ᵈ Whose son is he?"

"The son of David," they replied.

⁴³He said to them, "How is it then that David, speaking by the Spirit, calls him 'Lord'? For he says,

⁴⁴" 'The Lord said to my Lord:
  "Sit at my right hand
  until I put your enemies
    under your feet." 'ᵉ

ⁱ44 Some manuscripts do not have verse 44.   ᵃ32 Exodus 3:6   ᵇ37 Deut. 6:5   ᶜ39 Lev. 19:18
ᵈ42 Or *Messiah*   ᵉ44 Psalm 110:1

45If then David calls him 'Lord', how can he be his son?" 46No-one could say a word in reply, and from that day on no-one dared to ask him any more questions.

Seven Woes

23 Then Jesus said to the crowds and to his disciples: 2"The teachers of the law and the Pharisees sit in Moses' seat. 3So you must obey them and do everything they tell you. But do not do what they do, for they do not practise what they preach. 4They tie up heavy loads and put them on men's shoulders, but they themselves are not willing to lift a finger to move them.

5"Everything they do is done for men to see: They make their phylacteries*a* wide and the tassels on their garments long; 6they love the place of honour at banquets and the most important seats in the synagogues; 7they love to be greeted in the market-places and to have men call them 'Rabbi'.

8"But you are not to be called 'Rabbi', for you have only one Master and you are all brothers. 9And do not call anyone on earth 'father', for you have one Father, and he is in heaven. 10Nor are you to be called 'teacher', for you have one Teacher, the Christ.*b* 11The greatest among you will be your servant. 12For whoever exalts himself will be humbled, and whoever humbles himself will be exalted.

13"Woe to you, teachers of the law and Pharisees, you hypocrites! You shut the kingdom of heaven in men's faces. You yourselves do not enter, nor will you let those enter who are trying to.*c*

15"Woe to you, teachers of the law and Pharisees, you hypocrites! You travel over land and sea to win a single convert, and when he becomes one, you make him twice as much a son of hell as you are.

16"Woe to you, blind guides! You say, 'If anyone swears by the temple, it means nothing; but if anyone swears by the gold of the temple, he is bound by his oath.' 17You blind fools! Which is greater: the gold, or the temple that makes the gold sacred? 18You also say, 'If anyone swears by the altar, it means nothing; but if anyone swears by the gift on it, he is bound by his oath.' 19You blind men! Which is greater: the gift, or the altar that makes the gift sacred? 20Therefore, he who swears by the altar swears by it and by everything on it. 21And he who swears by the temple swears by it and by the one who dwells in it. 22And he who swears by heaven swears by God's throne and by the one who sits on it.

23"Woe to you, teachers of the law and Pharisees, you hypocrites! You give a tenth of your spices — mint, dill and cummin. But you have neglected the more important matters of the law — justice, mercy and faithfulness. You should have practised the latter, without neglecting the former. 24You blind guides! You strain out a gnat but swallow a camel.

25"Woe to you, teachers of the law and Pharisees, you hypocrites! You clean the outside of the cup and dish, but inside they are full of greed and self-indulgence. 26Blind Pharisee! First clean the inside of the cup and dish, and then the outside also will be clean.

27"Woe to you, teachers of the law and Pharisees, you hypocrites! You are like whitewashed tombs, which look beautiful on the outside but on the inside are full of dead men's bones and everything unclean. 28In the same way, on the outside you appear to people as righteous but on the inside you are full of hypocrisy and wickedness.

29"Woe to you, teachers of the law and Pharisees, you hypocrites! You build tombs for the prophets and decorate the graves of the righteous. 30And you say, 'If we had lived in the days of our forefathers, we would not have taken part with them in shedding the blood of the prophets.' 31So you testify against yourselves that you are the descendants of those who murdered the prophets. 32Fill up, then, the measure of the sin of your forefathers!

33"You snakes! You brood of vipers! How will you escape being condemned to hell? 34Therefore I am sending you prophets and wise men and teachers. Some of them you will kill and crucify; others you will flog in your synagogues and pursue from town to town. 35And so upon you will come all the righteous blood that has been shed on earth, from the blood of righteous Abel to the blood of Zechariah son of Barakiah, whom you murdered between the temple and the altar. 36I tell you the truth, all this will come upon this generation.

37"O Jerusalem, Jerusalem, you who kill the prophets and stone those sent to you, how often I have longed to gather your children together, as a hen gathers her chicks under her wings, but you were not willing. 38Look, your house is left to you desolate. 39For I tell you, you will not see me again until you say, 'Blessed is he who comes in the name of the Lord.'*d*"

Signs of the End of the Age

24 Jesus left the temple and was walking away when his disciples came up to him to call his attention to its buildings. 2"Do you see all these things?" he asked. "I tell you the truth, not one stone here will be left on another; every one will be thrown down."

3As Jesus was sitting on the Mount of Olives, the disciples came to him privately. "Tell us," they said, "when will this happen, and what will be the sign of your coming and of the end of the age?"

4Jesus answered: "Watch out that no-one deceives you. 5For many will come in my name, claiming, 'I am the Christ,'*a* and will deceive many. 6You will hear of wars and rumours of wars, but see to it that you are not alarmed. Such things must happen, but the end is still to come. 7Nation will rise against nation, and kingdom against kingdom. There will be famines and earthquakes in various places. 8All these are the beginning of birth-pains.

9"Then you will be handed over to be persecuted and put to death, and you will be hated by all nations because of me. 10At that time many will turn away from

---

*a 5 That is, boxes containing Scripture verses, worn on forehead and arm   *b 10 Or Messiah
*c 13 Some manuscripts to. 14Woe to you, teachers of the law and Pharisees, you hypocrites! You devour widows' houses and for a show make lengthy prayers. Therefore you will be punished more severely.   *d 39 Psalm 118:26   *a 5 Or Messiah; also in verse 23

the faith and will betray and hate each other, [11]and many false prophets will appear and deceive many people. [12]Because of the increase of wickedness, the love of most will grow cold, [13]but he who stands firm to the end will be saved. [14]And this gospel of the kingdom will be preached in the whole world as a testimony to all nations, and then the end will come.

24:3   Matthew, Mark, and Luke all concluded Jesus' teaching with an obscure discourse in the style of an "apocalypse" (an unveiling of the future). The discourse begins with the forthcoming destruction of Jerusalem (which was the end of a world in 70 AD), and becomes a cosmic prediction of the end of the whole world, when the Son of Man will come to judge the world. Matthew's practical conclusion is to care for those in need (chapter 25:31–46); that is the criterion on which people will be judged.

---

[15]"So when you see standing in the holy place 'the abomination that causes desolation',[b] spoken of through the prophet Daniel—let the reader understand—[16]then let those who are in Judea flee to the mountains. [17]Let no-one on the roof of his house go down to take anything out of the house. [18]Let no-one in the field go back to get his cloak. [19]How dreadful it will be in those days for pregnant women and nursing mothers! [20]Pray that your flight will not take place in winter or on the Sabbath. [21]For then there will be great distress, unequalled from the beginning of the world until now—and never to be equalled again. [22]If those days had not been cut short, no-one would survive, but for the sake of the elect those days will be shortened. [23]At that time if anyone says to you, 'Look, here is the Christ!' or, 'There he is!' do not believe it. [24]For false Christs and false prophets will appear and perform great signs and miracles to deceive even the elect—if that were possible. [25]See, I have told you ahead of time. [26]"So if anyone tells you, 'There he is, out in the desert,' do not go out; or, 'Here he is, in the inner rooms,' do not believe it. [27]For as lightning that comes from the east is visible even in the west, so will be the coming of the Son of Man. [28]Wherever there is a carcass, there the vultures will gather. [29]"Immediately after the distress of those days

" 'the sun will be darkened,
    and the moon will not give its light;
the stars will fall from the sky,
    and the heavenly bodies will be shaken.'[c]

[30]"At that time the sign of the Son of Man will appear in the sky, and all the nations of the earth will mourn. They will see the Son of Man coming on the clouds of the sky, with power and great glory. [31]And he will send his angels with a loud trumpet call, and they will gather his elect from the four winds, from one end of the heavens to the other.

[32]"Now learn this lesson from the fig-tree: As soon as its twigs get tender and its leaves come out, you know that summer is near. [33]Even so, when you see all these things, you know that it[d] is near, right at the door. [34]I tell you the truth, this generation[e] will certainly not pass away until all these things have happened. [35]Heaven and earth will pass away, but my words will never pass away.

The Day and Hour Unknown

[36]"No-one knows about that day or hour, not even the angels in heaven, nor the Son,[f] but only the Father. [37]As it was in the days of Noah, so it will be at the coming of the Son of Man. [38]For in the days before the flood, people were eating and drinking, marrying and giving in marriage, up to the day Noah entered the ark; [39]and they knew nothing about what would happen until the flood came and took them all away. That is how it will be at the coming of the Son of Man. [40]Two men will be in the field; one will be taken and the other left. [41]Two women will be grinding with a hand mill; one will be taken and the other left.

[42]"Therefore keep watch, because you do not know on what day your Lord will come. [43]But understand this: If the owner of the house had known at what time of night the thief was coming, he would have kept watch and would not have let his house be broken into. [44]So you also must be ready, because the Son of Man will come at an hour when you do not expect him.

[45]"Who then is the faithful and wise servant, whom the master has put in charge of the servants in his household to give them their food at the proper time? [46]It will be good for that servant whose master finds him doing so when he returns. [47]I tell you the truth, he will put him in charge of all his possessions. [48]But suppose that servant is wicked and says to himself, 'My master is staying away a long time,' [49]and he then begins to beat his fellow-servants and to eat and drink with drunkards. [50]The master of that servant will come on a day when he does not expect him and at an hour he is not aware of. [51]He will cut him to pieces and assign him a place with the hypocrites, where there will be weeping and gnashing of teeth.

The Parable of the Ten Virgins

25   "At that time the kingdom of heaven will be like ten virgins who took their lamps and went out to meet the bridegroom. [2]Five of them were foolish and five were wise. [3]The foolish ones took their lamps but did not take any oil with them. [4]The wise, however, took oil in jars along with their lamps. [5]The bridegroom was a long time in coming, and they all became drowsy and fell asleep.

[6]"At midnight the cry rang out: 'Here's the bridegroom! Come out to meet him!'

[7]"Then all the virgins woke up and trimmed their lamps. [8]The foolish ones said to the wise, 'Give us some of your oil; our lamps are going out.'

[9]" 'No,' they replied, 'there may not be enough for

---

[b]15 Daniel 9:27; 11:31; 12:11   [c]29 Isaiah 13:10; 34:4   [d]33 Or he   [e]34 Or race
[f]36 Some manuscripts do not have nor the Son.

both us and you. Instead, go to those who sell oil and buy some for yourselves.'

¹⁰"But while they were on their way to buy the oil, the bridegroom arrived. The virgins who were ready went in with him to the wedding banquet. And the door was shut.

¹¹"Later the others also came. 'Sir! Sir!' they said. 'Open the door for us!'

¹²"But he replied, 'I tell you the truth, I don't know you.'

¹³"Therefore keep watch, because you do not know the day or the hour.

The Parable of the Talents

¹⁴"Again, it will be like a man going on a journey, who called his servants and entrusted his property to them. ¹⁵To one he gave five talents*a* of money, to another two talents, and to another one talent, each according to his ability. Then he went on his journey. ¹⁶The man who had received the five talents went at once and put his money to work and gained five more. ¹⁷So also, the one with the two talents gained two more. ¹⁸But the man who had received the one talent went off, dug a hole in the ground and hid his master's money.

¹⁹"After a long time the master of those servants returned and settled accounts with them. ²⁰The man who had received the five talents brought the other five. 'Master,' he said, 'you entrusted me with five talents. See, I have gained five more.'

²¹"His master replied, 'Well done, good and faithful servant! You have been faithful with a few things; I will put you in charge of many things. Come and share your master's happiness!'

²²"The man with the two talents also came. 'Master,' he said, 'you entrusted me with two talents; see, I have gained two more.'

²³"His master replied, 'Well done, good and faithful servant! You have been faithful with a few things; I will put you in charge of many things. Come and share your master's happiness!'

²⁴"Then the man who had received the one talent came. 'Master,' he said, 'I knew that you are a hard man, harvesting where you have not sown and gathering where you have not scattered seed. ²⁵So I was afraid and went out and hid your talent in the ground. See, here is what belongs to you.'

²⁶"His master replied, 'You wicked, lazy servant! So you knew that I harvest where I have not sown and gather where I have not scattered seed? ²⁷Well then, you should have put my money on deposit with the bankers, so that when I returned I would have received it back with interest.

²⁸"'Take the talent from him and give it to the one who has the ten talents. ²⁹For everyone who has will be given more, and he will have an abundance. Whoever does not have, even what he has will be taken from him. ³⁰And throw that worthless servant outside, into the darkness, where there will be weeping and gnashing of teeth.'

a 15 A talent was worth several hundred pounds.

The Sheep and the Goats

³¹"When the Son of Man comes in his glory, and all the angels with him, he will sit on his throne in heavenly glory. ³²All the nations will be gathered before him, and he will separate the people one from another as a shepherd separates the sheep from the goats. ³³He will put the sheep on his right and the goats on his left.

³⁴"Then the King will say to those on his right, 'Come, you who are blessed by my Father; take your inheritance, the kingdom prepared for you since the creation of the world. ³⁵For I was hungry and you gave me something to eat, I was thirsty and you gave me something to drink, I was a stranger and you invited me in, ³⁶I needed clothes and you clothed me, I was sick and you looked after me, I was in prison and you came to visit me.'

³⁷"Then the righteous will answer him, 'Lord, when did we see you hungry and feed you, or thirsty and give you something to drink? ³⁸When did we see you a stranger and invite you in, or needing clothes and clothe you? ³⁹When did we see you sick or in prison and go to visit you?'

⁴⁰"The King will reply, 'I tell you the truth, whatever you did for one of the least of these brothers of mine, you did for me.'

⁴¹"Then he will say to those on his left, 'Depart from me, you who are cursed, into the eternal fire prepared for the devil and his angels. ⁴²For I was hungry and you gave me nothing to eat, I was thirsty and you gave me nothing to drink, ⁴³I was a stranger and you did not invite me in, I needed clothes and you did not clothe me, I was sick and in prison and you did not look after me.'

⁴⁴"They also will answer, 'Lord, when did we see you hungry or thirsty or a stranger or needing clothes or sick or in prison, and did not help you?'

⁴⁵"He will reply, 'I tell you the truth, whatever you did not do for one of the least of these, you did not do for me.'

⁴⁶"Then they will go away to eternal punishment, but the righteous to eternal life."

The Plot Against Jesus

26 When Jesus had finished saying all these things, he said to his disciples, ²"As you know, the Passover is two days away—and the Son of Man will be handed over to be crucified."

³Then the chief priests and the elders of the people assembled in the palace of the high priest, whose name was Caiaphas, ⁴and they plotted to arrest Jesus in some sly way and kill him. ⁵"But not during the Feast," they said, "or there may be a riot among the people."

Jesus Anointed at Bethany

⁶While Jesus was in Bethany in the home of a man known as Simon the Leper, ⁷a woman came to him with an alabaster jar of very expensive perfume, which she poured on his head as he was reclining at the table.

⁸When the disciples saw this, they were indignant. "Why this waste?" they asked. ⁹"This perfume could

have been sold at a high price and the money given to the poor."

¹⁰Aware of this, Jesus said to them, "Why are you bothering this woman? She has done a beautiful thing to me. ¹¹The poor you will always have with you, but you will not always have me. ¹²When she poured this perfume on my body, she did it to prepare me for burial. ¹³I tell you the truth, wherever this gospel is preached throughout the world, what she has done will also be told, in memory of her."

Judas Agrees to Betray Jesus

¹⁴Then one of the Twelve—the one called Judas Iscariot—went to the chief priests ¹⁵and asked, "What are you willing to give me if I hand him over to you?" So they counted out for him thirty silver coins. ¹⁶From then on Judas watched for an opportunity to hand him over.

The Lord's Supper

¹⁷On the first day of the Feast of Unleavened Bread, the disciples came to Jesus and asked, "Where do you want us to make preparations for you to eat the Passover?"

¹⁸He replied, "Go into the city to a certain man and tell him, 'The Teacher says: My appointed time is near. I am going to celebrate the Passover with my disciples at your house.'" ¹⁹So the disciples did as Jesus had directed them and prepared the Passover.

²⁰When evening came, Jesus was reclining at the table with the Twelve. ²¹And while they were eating, he said, "I tell you the truth, one of you will betray me."

²²They were very sad and began to say to him one after the other, "Surely not I, Lord?"

²³Jesus replied, "The one who has dipped his hand into the bowl with me will betray me. ²⁴The Son of Man will go just as it is written about him. But woe to that man who betrays the Son of Man! It would be better for him if he had not been born."

²⁵Then Judas, the one who would betray him, said, "Surely not I, Rabbi?"

Jesus answered, "Yes, it is you."ᵃ

²⁶While they were eating, Jesus took bread, gave thanks and broke it, and gave it to his disciples, saying, "Take and eat; this is my body."

²⁷Then he took the cup, gave thanks and offered it to them, saying, "Drink from it, all of you. ²⁸This is my blood of theᵇ covenant, which is poured out for many for the forgiveness of sins. ²⁹I tell you, I will not drink of this fruit of the vine from now on until that day when I drink it anew with you in my Father's kingdom."

³⁰When they had sung a hymn, they went out to the Mount of Olives.

Jesus Predicts Peter's Denial

³¹Then Jesus told them, "This very night you will all fall away on account of me, for it is written:

" 'I will strike the shepherd,
and the sheep of the flock will be scattered.'ᶜ

³²But after I have risen, I will go ahead of you into Galilee."

³³Peter replied, "Even if all fall away on account of you, I never will."

³⁴"I tell you the truth," Jesus answered, "this very night, before the cock crows, you will disown me three times."

³⁵But Peter declared, "Even if I have to die with you, I will never disown you." And all the other disciples said the same.

Gethsemane

³⁶Then Jesus went with his disciples to a place called Gethsemane, and he said to them, "Sit here while I go over there and pray." ³⁷He took Peter and the two sons of Zebedee along with him, and he began to be sorrowful and troubled. ³⁸Then he said to them, "My soul is overwhelmed with sorrow to the point of death. Stay here and keep watch with me."

³⁹Going a little farther, he fell with his face to the ground and prayed, "My Father, if it is possible, may this cup be taken from me. Yet not as I will, but as you will."

⁴⁰Then he returned to his disciples and found them sleeping. "Could you men not keep watch with me for one hour?" he asked Peter. ⁴¹"Watch and pray so that you will not fall into temptation. The spirit is willing, but the body is weak."

⁴²He went away a second time and prayed, "My Father, if it is not possible for this cup to be taken away unless I drink it, may your will be done."

⁴³When he came back, he again found them sleeping, because their eyes were heavy. ⁴⁴So he left them and went away once more and prayed the third time, saying the same thing.

⁴⁵Then he returned to the disciples and said to them, "Are you still sleeping and resting? Look, the hour is near, and the Son of Man is betrayed into the hands of sinners. ⁴⁶Rise, let us go! Here comes my betrayer!"

Jesus Arrested

⁴⁷While he was still speaking, Judas, one of the Twelve, arrived. With him was a large crowd armed with swords and clubs, sent from the chief priests and the elders of the people. ⁴⁸Now the betrayer had arranged a signal with them: "The one I kiss is the man; arrest him." ⁴⁹Going at once to Jesus, Judas said, "Greetings, Rabbi!" and kissed him.

⁵⁰Jesus replied, "Friend, do what you came for."ᵈ

Then the men stepped forward, seized Jesus and arrested him. ⁵¹With that, one of Jesus' companions reached for his sword, drew it out and struck the servant of the high priest, cutting off his ear.

⁵²"Put your sword back in its place," Jesus said to him, "for all who draw the sword will die by the sword. ⁵³Do you think I cannot call on my Father, and he will at once put at my disposal more than twelve legions of

---

ᵃ25 Or "You yourself have said it"   ᵇ28 Some manuscripts the new   ᶜ31 Zech. 13:7
ᵈ50 Or "Friend, why have you come?"

angels? 54But how then would the Scriptures be fulfilled that say it must happen in this way?"

55At that time Jesus said to the crowd, "Am I leading a rebellion, that you have come out with swords and clubs to capture me? Every day I sat in the temple courts teaching, and you did not arrest me. 56But this has all taken place that the writings of the prophets might be fulfilled." Then all the disciples deserted him and fled.

Before the Sanhedrin

57Those who had arrested Jesus took him to Caiaphas, the high priest, where the teachers of the law and the elders had assembled. 58But Peter followed him at a distance, right up to the courtyard of the high priest. He entered and sat down with the guards to see the outcome.

59The chief priests and the whole Sanhedrin were looking for false evidence against Jesus so that they could put him to death. 60But they did not find any, though many false witnesses came forward.

Finally two came forward 61and declared, "This fellow said, 'I am able to destroy the temple of God and rebuild it in three days.' "

62Then the high priest stood up and said to Jesus, "Are you not going to answer? What is this testimony that these men are bringing against you?" 63But Jesus remained silent.

The high priest said to him, "I charge you under oath by the living God: Tell us if you are the Christ,e the Son of God."

64"Yes, it is as you say," Jesus replied. "But I say to all of you: In the future you will see the Son of Man sitting at the right hand of the Mighty One and coming on the clouds of heaven."

65Then the high priest tore his clothes and said, "He has spoken blasphemy! Why do we need any more witnesses? Look, now you have heard the blasphemy. 66What do you think?"

"He is worthy of death," they answered.

67Then they spat in his face and struck him with their fists. Others slapped him 68and said, "Prophesy to us, Christ. Who hit you?"

Peter Disowns Jesus

69Now Peter was sitting out in the courtyard, and a servant girl came to him. "You also were with Jesus of Galilee," she said.

70But he denied it before them all. "I don't know what you're talking about," he said.

71Then he went out to the gateway, where another girl saw him and said to the people there, "This fellow was with Jesus of Nazareth."

72He denied it again, with an oath: "I don't know the man!"

73After a little while, those standing there went up to Peter and said, "Surely you are one of them, for your accent gives you away."

74Then he began to call down curses on himself and he swore to them, "I don't know the man!"

Immediately a cock crowed. 75Then Peter remembered the word Jesus had spoken: "Before the cock crows, you will disown me three times." And he went outside and wept bitterly.

Judas Hangs Himself

27 Early in the morning, all the chief priests and the elders of the people came to the decision to put Jesus to death. 2They bound him, led him away and handed him over to Pilate, the governor.

3When Judas, who had betrayed him, saw that Jesus was condemned, he was seized with remorse and returned the thirty silver coins to the chief priests and the elders. 4"I have sinned," he said, "for I have betrayed innocent blood."

"What is that to us?" they replied. "That's your responsibility."

5So Judas threw the money into the temple and left. Then he went away and hanged himself.

6The chief priests picked up the coins and said, "It is against the law to put this into the treasury, since it is blood money." 7So they decided to use the money to buy the potter's field as a burial place for foreigners. 8That is why it has been called the Field of Blood to this day. 9Then what was spoken by Jeremiah the prophet was fulfilled: "They took the thirty silver coins, the price set on him by the people of Israel, 10and they used them to buy the potter's field, as the Lord commanded me."a

Jesus Before Pilate

11Meanwhile Jesus stood before the governor, and the governor asked him, "Are you the king of the Jews?"

"Yes, it is as you say," Jesus replied.

12When he was accused by the chief priests and the elders, he gave no answer. 13Then Pilate asked him, "Don't you hear the testimony they are bringing against you?" 14But Jesus made no reply, not even to a single charge—to the great amazement of the governor.

15Now it was the governor's custom at the Feast to release a prisoner chosen by the crowd. 16At that time they had a notorious prisoner, called Barabbas. 17So when the crowd had gathered, Pilate asked them, "Which one do you want me to release to you: Barabbas, or Jesus who is called Christ?" 18For he knew it was out of envy that they had handed Jesus over to him.

19While Pilate was sitting on the judge's seat, his wife sent him this message: "Don't have anything to do with that innocent man, for I have suffered a great deal today in a dream because of him."

20But the chief priests and the elders persuaded the crowd to ask for Barabbas and to have Jesus executed.

21"Which of the two do you want me to release to you?" asked the governor.

"Barabbas," they answered.

22"What shall I do, then, with Jesus who is called Christ?" Pilate asked.

They all answered, "Crucify him!"

23"Why? What crime has he committed?" asked Pilate.

e 63 Or Messiah; also in verse 68   a 10 See Zech. 11:12,13; Jer. 19:1–13; 32:6–9.

But they shouted all the louder, "Crucify him!"

[24] When Pilate saw that he was getting nowhere, but that instead an uproar was starting, he took water and washed his hands in front of the crowd. "I am innocent of this man's blood," he said. "It is your responsibility!"

[25] All the people answered, "Let his blood be on us and on our children!"

[26] Then he released Barabbas to them. But he had Jesus flogged, and handed him over to be crucified.

The Soldiers Mock Jesus

[27] Then the governor's soldiers took Jesus into the Praetorium and gathered the whole company of soldiers round him. [28] They stripped him and put a scarlet robe on him, [29] and then twisted together a crown of thorns and set it on his head. They put a staff in his right hand and knelt in front of him and mocked him. "Hail, king of the Jews!" they said. [30] They spat on him, and took the staff and struck him on the head again and again. [31] After they had mocked him, they took off the robe and put his own clothes on him. Then they led him away to crucify him.

The Crucifixion

[32] As they were going out, they met a man from Cyrene, named Simon, and they forced him to carry the cross. [33] They came to a place called Golgotha (which means The Place of the Skull). [34] There they offered Jesus wine to drink, mixed with gall; but after tasting it, he refused to drink it. [35] When they had crucified him, they divided up his clothes by casting lots. [b] [36] And sitting down, they kept watch over him there. [37] Above his head they placed the written charge against him: THIS IS JESUS, THE KING OF THE JEWS. [38] Two robbers were crucified with him, one on his right and one on his left. [39] Those who passed by hurled insults at him, shaking their heads [40] and saying, "You who are going to destroy the temple and build it in three days, save yourself! Come down from the cross, if you are the Son of God!"

[41] In the same way the chief priests, the teachers of the law and the elders mocked him. [42] "He saved others," they said, "but he can't save himself! He's the King of Israel! Let him come down now from the cross, and we will believe in him. [43] He trusts in God. Let God rescue him now if he wants him, for he said, 'I am the Son of God.' " [44] In the same way the robbers who were crucified with him also heaped insults on him.

The Death of Jesus

[45] From the sixth hour until the ninth hour darkness came over all the land. [46] About the ninth hour Jesus cried out in a loud voice, "Eloi, Eloi,[c] lama sabachthani?" —which means, "My God, my God, why have you forsaken me?"[d]

[47] When some of those standing there heard this, they said, "He's calling Elijah."

[48] Immediately one of them ran and got a sponge. He filled it with wine vinegar, put it on a stick, and offered it to Jesus to drink. [49] The rest said, "Now leave him alone. Let's see if Elijah comes to save him."

[50] And when Jesus had cried out again in a loud voice, he gave up his spirit.

[51] At that moment the curtain of the temple was torn in two from top to bottom. The earth shook and the rocks split. [52] The tombs broke open and the bodies of many holy people who had died were raised to life. [53] They came out of the tombs, and after Jesus' resurrection they went into the holy city and appeared to many people.

27:51   Matthew alone mentioned an earthquake in both the crucifixion and resurrection stories. He wanted to explain the earth-shattering significance of these events.

---

[54] When the centurion and those with him who were guarding Jesus saw the earthquake and all that had happened, they were terrified, and exclaimed, "Surely he was the Son[e] of God!"

[55] Many women were there, watching from a distance. They had followed Jesus from Galilee to care for his needs. [56] Among them were Mary Magdalene, Mary the mother of James and Joses, and the mother of Zebedee's sons.

The Burial of Jesus

[57] As evening approached, there came a rich man from Arimathea, named Joseph, who had himself become a disciple of Jesus. [58] Going to Pilate, he asked for Jesus' body, and Pilate ordered that it be given to him. [59] Joseph took the body, wrapped it in a clean linen cloth, [60] and placed it in his own new tomb that he had cut out of the rock. He rolled a big stone in front of the entrance to the tomb and went away. [61] Mary Magdalene and the other Mary were sitting there opposite the tomb.

The Guard at the Tomb

[62] The next day, the one after Preparation Day, the chief priests and the Pharisees went to Pilate. [63] "Sir," they said, "we remember that while he was still alive that deceiver said, 'After three days I will rise again.' [64] So give the order for the tomb to be made secure until the third day. Otherwise, his disciples may come and steal the body and tell the people that he has been raised from the dead. This last deception will be worse than the first."

[65] "Take a guard," Pilate answered. "Go, make the tomb as secure as you know how." [66] So they went and made the tomb secure by putting a seal on the stone and posting the guard.

The Resurrection

28 After the Sabbath, at dawn on the first day of the week, Mary Magdalene and the other Mary went to look at the tomb.

[2] There was a violent earthquake, for an angel of the

---

b 35 A few late manuscripts lots that the word spoken by the prophet might be fulfilled: "They divided my garments among themselves and cast lots for my clothing." (Psalm 22:18)   c 46 Some manuscripts Eli, Eli   d 46 Psalm 22:1   e 54 Or a son

Lord came down from heaven and, going to the tomb, rolled back the stone and sat on it. [3]His appearance was like lightning, and his clothes were white as snow. [4]The guards were so afraid of him that they shook and became like dead men.

[5]The angel said to the women, "Do not be afraid, for I know that you are looking for Jesus, who was crucified. [6]He is not here; he has risen, just as he said. Come and see the place where he lay. [7]Then go quickly and tell his disciples: 'He has risen from the dead and is going ahead of you into Galilee. There you will see him.' Now I have told you."

28:6   Each Gospel writer tells the resurrection story in his own way, and close comparison reveals variations in the content. However, they all agreed that the death of Jesus was not the end of him, and that his friends experienced him as more alive after his death than before. This experience was so real that it changed their lives.

---

[8]So the women hurried away from the tomb, afraid yet filled with joy, and ran to tell his disciples. [9]Suddenly Jesus met them. "Greetings," he said. They came to him, clasped his feet and worshipped him. [10]Then Jesus said to them, "Do not be afraid. Go and tell my brothers to go to Galilee; there they will see me."

The Guards' Report

[11]While the women were on their way, some of the guards went into the city and reported to the chief priests everything that had happened. [12]When the chief priests had met with the elders and devised a plan, they gave the soldiers a large sum of money, [13]telling them, "You are to say, 'His disciples came during the night and stole him away while we were asleep.' [14]If this report gets to the governor, we will satisfy him and keep you out of trouble." [15]So the soldiers took the money and did as they were instructed. And this story has been widely circulated among the Jews to this very day.

The Great Commission

[16]Then the eleven disciples went to Galilee, to the mountain where Jesus had told them to go. [17]When they saw him, they worshipped him; but some doubted. [18]Then Jesus came to them and said, "All authority in heaven and on earth has been given to me. [19]Therefore go and make disciples of all nations, baptising them in[a] the name of the Father and of the Son and of the Holy Spirit, [20]and teaching them to obey everything I have commanded you. And surely I am with you always, to the very end of the age."

28:19   Matthew's Gospel ends with a fine sense of "rounding off". Jesus the Teacher preached his last sermon, like his first, on a mountain in Galilee. He commissioned his followers to become teachers themselves. And the Jesus who embodied the presence of God at the beginning (1:23) promises to be present with his disciples to the end of time.

---

a19 Or into; see Acts 8:16; 19:5; Rom. 6:3; 1 Cor. 1:13; 10:2 and Gal. 3:27.

Mark

Vivid Presentation

You need to read a piece of Mark's Gospel in close parallel with those of Matthew and Luke, and compare each line word by word, in order to realize what a brilliant writer Mark was. Take the story of Jesus and the children, for instance:

Matthew 19:13–15

Then little children were brought to Jesus for him to place his hands on them and pray for them. But the disciples rebuked those who brought them.

Jesus said, "Let the little children come to me, and do not hinder them, for the kingdom of heaven belongs to such as these." When he had placed his hands on them, he went on from there.

Mark 10:13–16

People were bringing little children to Jesus to have him touch them, but the disciples rebuked them. When Jesus saw this, he was *indignant.* He said to them, "Let the little children come to me, and do not hinder them, for the kingdom of God belongs to such as these. I tell you the truth, anyone who will not receive the kingdom of God like a little child will never enter it." And *he took the children in his arms, put his hands on them* and blessed them.

Luke 18:15–17

People were also bringing babies to Jesus to have him touch them. When the disciples saw this, they rebuked them. But Jesus called the children to him and said, "Let the little children come to me, and do not hinder them, for the kingdom of God belongs to such as these. I tell you the truth, anyone who will not receive the kingdom of God like a little child will never enter it."

No one can fail to notice Mark's touch here. Only his version mentions Jesus' awareness, Jesus' anger, Jesus embracing the children, and Jesus pronouncing a blessing on them. Matthew and Luke wrote their Gospels by drawing on Mark's but chose to leave those phrases out. Their Gospels are never as vivid as Mark's.

Mark's Style

It is the same in story after story. If you want the feeling of actually being present at the scene, of hearing the words spoken by Jesus in the original Aramaic—"Ephphatha", "Talitha Cum", "Abba"—go to Mark. If you like hearing stories told in the disjointed, disorderly, and repetitious style of the person in the street, with the past tense easily slipping into the present— "He left there and walked down the road, and this man comes up and says . . ."—go to Mark. If you enjoy the sort of detail which is quite irrelevant to the story but brings it to life, like the cushion in the stern of the boat (4:38), the crowds sitting down "on the green grass" (6:39), the whiteness of Jesus' clothes at the transfiguration "whiter than anyone in the world could bleach them" (9:3),—go to Mark.

Mark's Gospel almost needs to be read in an accent or dialect to get the real flavour of it. Matthew and Luke, when they followed him, found him far too blunt and colloquial: their own Gospels (not to mention their picture of Jesus and the disciples) are far more polished and sophisticated. Translators who put Mark into English hardly dare to give an exact and literal rendering of what he wrote; it wouldn't read like a piece of literature. But in the original Greek, Mark's Gospel is a very rough diamond indeed. He presented a vivid and haphazard succession of scenes from the life of Jesus, using unfinished sentences and a breathless pace. They are thrown up at the reader like a series of images in a pop video. There is little of Jesus' preaching that comes in the other three Gospels. For Mark, Jesus' preaching lay in what he was and what he did.

A Biography?

It might sound as if Mark's main purpose in writing was to provide a biography, that he was concerned to keep an exact record of the events in the life of Jesus before people began to put their own interpretation on those events. But this would be to underrate him. Mark interpreted Jesus quite as boldly as the other Gospel writers did. He said so in his opening line: "The beginning of the gospel about Jesus Christ, the Son of God." What could it possibly mean to be "Son of God"? Mark wrote his Gospel to try to spell out an answer. Notice that this title "Son of God", which crops up frequently throughout the pages of Matthew and Luke, is not given again to Jesus in this Gospel until the last page. Other things proclaimed him Son of God, but no human being did until Jesus was hanging on the cross, only sixteen verses before the end of the story (15:39). According to Mark, you have to wait until then before you really understand what that title means.

Mystery

Is there then some mystery about the title "Son of God" that makes it difficult to understand? Of course there is. Mark underlined the mystery by having people ask again and again, from page one onwards, "Who is this?" When Jesus spoke, people were constantly bowled over, saying they had never heard anything like it. When Jesus healed people, everyone kept saying, "We've never seen anything like this before." Jesus was regularly misunderstood, even by his disciples. People were often seized with fear in his presence. Most strangely of all, the Jesus of Mark's Gospel told people over and over again not to reveal who he was. The phrase comes up so many times that Matthew and Luke, when they followed Mark, found it too prominent and cut it down severely. But Mark insisted that you mustn't come to a conclusion about Jesus too quickly. There is a mystery about him. He is an enigma, a puzzle that can't be solved glibly.

A Gospel for the Persecuted

Mark's gospel was probably written in Rome, round about AD 65–70. Those were years of turmoil, with Rome burnt down in 64, Peter crucified in 65 and Paul beheaded in 67, Nero committing suicide in 68, and four rival generals fighting over the empty throne. These were years in which the small community of Christians in Rome were viciously persecuted by Nero's police. Many of them were martyred. Their friends and relatives must have wondered what was the point of proclaiming Jesus as Lord, or Son of God, if it ended in such pain. Mark wrote his Gospel to explain to the Christians of Rome that, in the kind of world people live in, no one can be a son of God without suffering; Jesus first and then his followers. Jesus' suffering and death were not an unfortunate accident which could have been avoided. They were the very meaning of his life. He was Son of God, not in spite of his death, but because of it. If he had not suffered and died, he would not have been Son of God.

Do You Understand?

This means that until you reach the pages that tell of his suffering, you haven't really grasped who he is. You will have your own expectations about what the Son of God should be like, and you will give Jesus that title because of his appealing teaching or his marvellous healing powers, not imagining that these will get him into trouble. You must not call Jesus "Son of God" until you get to the cross. That is where you will understand what being a son of God is all about. Whether you live in Jerusalem or Rome, in Jarrow or Romford.

First Christian Dramatist

Paul had already written his famous letters to the churches when Mark sat down to write this Gospel. They contain a very similar interpretation of the meaning of Jesus' life and death. But where Paul used theological argument to make his point, Mark used a simple narrative form. Matthew, Luke, and John later found this formula so brilliant that they each adopted it, and like Mark presented the meaning of Jesus through stories. Christians have good reason to be grateful to Mark, the first Christian dramatist.

John the Baptist Prepares the Way

1 The beginning of the gospel about Jesus Christ, the Son of God.[a]

[2]It is written in Isaiah the prophet:

"I will send my messenger ahead of you,
    who will prepare your way"[b]—
[3]"a voice of one calling in the desert,
'Prepare the way for the Lord,
    make straight paths for him.' "[c]

[4]And so John came, baptising in the desert region and preaching a baptism of repentance for the forgiveness of sins. [5]The whole Judean countryside and all the people of Jerusalem went out to him. Confessing their sins, they were baptised by him in the Jordan River. [6]John wore clothing made of camel's hair, with a leather belt round his waist, and he ate locusts and wild honey. [7]And this was his message: "After me will come one more powerful than I, the thongs of whose sandals I am not worthy to stoop down and untie. [8]I baptise you with[d] water, but he will baptise you with the Holy Spirit."

The Baptism and Temptation of Jesus

[9]At that time Jesus came from Nazareth in Galilee and was baptised by John in the Jordan. [10]As Jesus was coming up out of the water, he saw heaven being torn open and the Spirit descending on him like a dove. [11]And a voice came from heaven: "You are my Son, whom I love; with you I am well pleased."

[12]At once the Spirit sent him out into the desert, [13]and he was in the desert for forty days, being tempted

---

a1 Some manuscripts do not have *the Son of God.*   *b2* Mal. 3:1   *c3* Isaiah 40:3   *d8* Or *in* by Satan. He was with the wild animals, and angels attended him.

1:1   Though he was more "primitive" in his style than Matthew or Luke, Mark was not less "theological". He was not writing just a biography of Jesus. His opening line states that he believed him to be the Son of God. Notice that the very first appearance of Jesus is told in resurrection terms (verse 10). Jesus emerged from the waters, which symbolize death, to be declared Son of God, and to reveal that the heavens were open and the Spirit of God made available to all.

The Calling of the First Disciples

¹⁴After John was put in prison, Jesus went into Galilee, proclaiming the good news of God. ¹⁵"The time has come," he said. "The kingdom of God is near. Repent and believe the good news!"

¹⁶As Jesus walked beside the Sea of Galilee, he saw Simon and his brother Andrew casting a net into the lake, for they were fishermen. ¹⁷"Come, follow me," Jesus said, "and I will make you fishers of men." ¹⁸At once they left their nets and followed him.

¹⁹When he had gone a little farther, he saw James son of Zebedee and his brother John in a boat, preparing their nets. ²⁰Without delay he called them, and they left their father Zebedee in the boat with the hired men and followed him.

Jesus Drives Out an Evil Spirit

²¹They went to Capernaum, and when the Sabbath came, Jesus went into the synagogue and began to teach. ²²The people were amazed at his teaching, because he taught them as one who had authority, not as the teachers of the law. ²³Just then a man in their synagogue who was possessed by an evil*ᵉ* spirit cried out, ²⁴"What do you want with us, Jesus of Nazareth? Have you come to destroy us? I know who you are — the Holy One of God!"

²⁵"Be quiet!" said Jesus sternly. "Come out of him!" ²⁶The evil spirit shook the man violently and came out of him with a shriek.

²⁷The people were all so amazed that they asked each other, "What is this? A new teaching — and with authority! He even gives orders to evil spirits and they obey him." ²⁸News about him spread quickly over the whole region of Galilee.

Jesus Heals Many

²⁹As soon as they left the synagogue, they went with James and John to the home of Simon and Andrew. ³⁰Simon's mother-in-law was in bed with a fever, and they told Jesus about her. ³¹So he went to her, took her hand and helped her up. The fever left her and she began to wait on them.

³²That evening after sunset the people brought to Jesus all the sick and demon-possessed. ³³The whole town gathered at the door, ³⁴and Jesus healed many who had various diseases. He also drove out many demons, but he would not let the demons speak because they knew who he was.

Jesus Prays in a Solitary Place

³⁵Very early in the morning, while it was still dark, Jesus got up, left the house and went off to a solitary place, where he prayed. ³⁶Simon and his companions went to look for him, ³⁷and when they found him, they exclaimed: "Everyone is looking for you!"

³⁸Jesus replied, "Let us go somewhere else — to the nearby villages — so that I can preach there also. That is why I have come." ³⁹So he travelled throughout Galilee, preaching in their synagogues and driving out demons.

1:39   Within fewer than forty verses, Mark has already mentioned evil spirits eight times. He saw a world which was in the grip of Satan, and Jesus' ministry as a costly battle to free the human race from the forces of evil, in order to re-establish the kingship of God.

A Man With Leprosy

⁴⁰A man with leprosy*ᶠ* came to him and begged him on his knees, "If you are willing, you can make me clean."

⁴¹Filled with compassion, Jesus reached out his hand and touched the man. "I am willing," he said. "Be clean!" ⁴²Immediately the leprosy left him and he was cured.

⁴³Jesus sent him away at once with a strong warning: ⁴⁴"See that you don't tell this to anyone. But go, show yourself to the priest and offer the sacrifices that Moses commanded for your cleansing, as a testimony to them." ⁴⁵Instead he went out and began to talk freely, spreading the news. As a result, Jesus could no longer enter a town openly but stayed outside in lonely places. Yet the people still came to him from everywhere.

Jesus Heals a Paralytic

2 A few days later, when Jesus again entered Capernaum, the people heard that he had come home. ²So many gathered that there was no room left, not even outside the door, and he preached the word to them. ³Some men came, bringing to him a paralytic, carried by four of them. ⁴Since they could not get him to Jesus because of the crowd, they made an opening in the roof above Jesus and, after digging through it, lowered the mat the paralysed man was lying on. ⁵When Jesus saw their faith, he said to the paralytic, "Son, your sins are forgiven."

⁶Now some teachers of the law were sitting there,

ᵉ23 Greek unclean; also in verses 26 and 27
ᶠ40 The Greek word was used for various diseases affecting the skin — not necessarily leprosy.

thinking to themselves, [7]"Why does this fellow talk like that? He's blaspheming! Who can forgive sins but God alone?"

[8]Immediately Jesus knew in his spirit that this was what they were thinking in their hearts, and he said to them, "Why are you thinking these things? [9]Which is easier: to say to the paralytic, 'Your sins are forgiven,' or to say, 'Get up, take your mat and walk'? [10]But that you may know that the Son of Man has authority on earth to forgive sins . . . ." He said to the paralytic, [11]"I tell you, get up, take your mat and go home." [12]He got up, took his mat and walked out in full view of them all. This amazed everyone and they praised God, saying, "We have never seen anything like this!"

The Calling of Levi

[13]Once again Jesus went out beside the lake. A large crowd came to him, and he began to teach them. [14]As he walked along, he saw Levi son of Alphaeus sitting at the tax collector's booth. "Follow me," Jesus told him, and Levi got up and followed him.

[15]While Jesus was having dinner at Levi's house, many tax collectors and "sinners" were eating with him and his disciples, for there were many who followed him. [16]When the teachers of the law who were Pharisees saw him eating with the "sinners" and tax collectors, they asked his disciples: "Why does he eat with tax collectors and 'sinners'?"

[17]On hearing this, Jesus said to them, "It is not the healthy who need a doctor, but the sick. I have not come to call the righteous, but sinners."

Jesus Questioned About Fasting

[18]Now John's disciples and the Pharisees were fasting. Some people came and asked Jesus, "How is it that John's disciples and the disciples of the Pharisees are fasting, but yours are not?"

[19]Jesus answered, "How can the guests of the bridegroom fast while he is with them? They cannot, so long as they have him with them. [20]But the time will come when the bridegroom will be taken from them, and on that day they will fast.

[21]"No-one sews a patch of unshrunk cloth on an old garment. If he does, the new piece will pull away from the old, making the tear worse. [22]And no-one pours new wine into old wineskins. If he does, the wine will burst the skins, and both the wine and the wineskins will be ruined. No, he pours new wine into new wineskins."

Lord of the Sabbath

[23]One Sabbath Jesus was going through the cornfields, and as his disciples walked along, they began to pick some ears of corn. [24]The Pharisees said to him, "Look, why are they doing what is unlawful on the Sabbath?"

[25]He answered, "Have you never read what David did when he and his companions were hungry and in need? [26]In the days of Abiathar the high priest, he entered the house of God and ate the consecrated bread, which is lawful only for priests to eat. And he also gave some to his companions."

[27]Then he said to them, "The Sabbath was made for man, not man for the Sabbath. [28]So the Son of Man is Lord even of the Sabbath."

2:27   No saying of Jesus is more radical than this, and no one stated it more clearly than Mark. However sacred governments, organizations, systems, institutions, laws, and rules are, they exist for people, not the other way round.

---

3 Another time he went into the synagogue, and a man with a shrivelled hand was there. [2]Some of them were looking for a reason to accuse Jesus, so they watched him closely to see if he would heal him on the Sabbath. [3]Jesus said to the man with the shrivelled hand, "Stand up in front of everyone."

[4]Then Jesus asked them, "Which is lawful on the Sabbath: to do good or to do evil, to save life or to kill?" But they remained silent.

[5]He looked round at them in anger and, deeply distressed at their stubborn hearts, said to the man, "Stretch out your hand." He stretched it out, and his hand was completely restored. [6]Then the Pharisees went out and began to plot with the Herodians how they might kill Jesus.

Crowds Follow Jesus

[7]Jesus withdrew with his disciples to the lake, and a large crowd from Galilee followed. [8]When they heard all he was doing, many people came to him from Judea, Jerusalem, Idumea, and the regions across the Jordan and around Tyre and Sidon. [9]Because of the crowd he told his disciples to have a small boat ready for him, to keep the people from crowding him. [10]For he had healed many, so that those with diseases were pushing forward to touch him. [11]Whenever the evil[a] spirits saw him, they fell down before him and cried out, "You are the Son of God." [12]But he gave them strict orders not to tell who he was.

The Appointing of the Twelve Apostles

[13]Jesus went up on a mountainside and called to him those he wanted, and they came to him. [14]He appointed twelve—designating them apostles[b]—that they might be with him and that he might send them out to preach [15]and to have authority to drive out demons. [16]These are the twelve he appointed: Simon (to whom he gave the name Peter); [17]James son of Zebedee and his brother John (to them he gave the name Boanerges, which means Sons of Thunder); [18]Andrew, Philip, Bartholomew, Matthew, Thomas, James son of Alphaeus, Thaddaeus, Simon the Zealot [19]and Judas Iscariot, who betrayed him.

---

a 11 Greek *unclean*; also in verse 30   *b 14* Some manuscripts do not have *designating them apostles*.

Jesus and Beelzebub

[20]Then Jesus entered a house, and again a crowd gathered, so that he and his disciples were not even able to eat. [21]When his family heard about this, they went to take charge of him, for they said, "He is out of his mind."

[22]And the teachers of the law who came down from Jerusalem said, "He is possessed by Beelzebub![c] By the prince of demons he is driving out demons."

[23]So Jesus called them and spoke to them in parables: "How can Satan drive out Satan? [24]If a kingdom is divided against itself, that kingdom cannot stand. [25]If a house is divided against itself, that house cannot stand. [26]And if Satan opposes himself and is divided, he cannot stand; his end has come. [27]In fact, no-one can enter a strong man's house and carry off his possessions unless he first ties up the strong man. Then he can rob his house. [28]I tell you the truth, all the sins and blasphemies of men will be forgiven them. [29]But whoever blasphemes against the Holy Spirit will never be forgiven; he is guilty of an eternal sin."

[30]He said this because they were saying, "He has an evil spirit."

Jesus' Mother and Brothers

[31]Then Jesus' mother and brothers arrived. Standing outside, they sent someone in to call him. [32]A crowd was sitting around him, and they told him, "Your mother and brothers are outside looking for you."

[33]"Who are my mother and my brothers?" he asked.

[34]Then he looked at those seated in a circle around him and said, "Here are my mother and my brothers! [35]Whoever does God's will is my brother and sister and mother."

The Parable of the Sower

4 Again Jesus began to teach by the lake. The crowd that gathered round him was so large that he got into a boat and sat in it out on the lake, while all the people were along the shore at the water's edge. [2]He taught them many things by parables, and in his teaching said: [3]"Listen! A farmer went out to sow his seed. [4]As he was scattering the seed, some fell along the path, and the birds came and ate it up. [5]Some fell on rocky places, where it did not have much soil. It sprang up quickly, because the soil was shallow. [6]But when the sun came up, the plants were scorched, and they withered because they had no root. [7]Other seed fell among thorns, which grew up and choked the plants, so that they did not bear grain. [8]Still other seed fell on good soil. It came up, grew and produced a crop, multiplying thirty, sixty, or even a hundred times."

[9]Then Jesus said, "He who has ears to hear, let him hear."

[10]When he was alone, the Twelve and the others around him asked him about the parables. [11]He told them, "The secret of the kingdom of God has been given to you. But to those on the outside everything is said in parables [12]so that,

" 'they may be ever seeing but never perceiving, and ever hearing but never understanding; otherwise they might turn and be forgiven!'[a]"

4:12 Why did Jesus use parables? Mark's explanation is fiercer than Matthew's. Jesus taught in parables, not because his hearers did not understand, but so that they would not understand. Mark saw the mysterious parables as part of the mystery of Jesus. They did not make sense to people who were only interested in the superficial, only to those who understood his mission, and were willing to share it.

---

[13]Then Jesus said to them, "Don't you understand this parable? How then will you understand any parable? [14]The farmer sows the word. [15]Some people are like seed along the path, where the word is sown. As soon as they hear it, Satan comes and takes away the word that was sown in them. [16]Others, like seed sown on rocky places, hear the word and at once receive it with joy. [17]But since they have no root, they last only a short time. When trouble or persecution comes because of the word, they quickly fall away. [18]Still others, like seed sown among thorns, hear the word; [19]but the worries of this life, the deceitfulness of wealth and the desires for other things come in and choke the word, making it unfruitful. [20]Others, like seed sown on good soil, hear the word, accept it, and produce a crop—thirty, sixty or even a hundred times what was sown."

A Lamp on a Stand

[21]He said to them, "Do you bring in a lamp to put it under a bowl or a bed? Instead, don't you put it on its stand? [22]For whatever is hidden is meant to be disclosed, and whatever is concealed is meant to be brought out into the open. [23]If anyone has ears to hear, let him hear."

[24]"Consider carefully what you hear," he continued. "With the measure you use, it will be measured to you—and even more. [25]Whoever has will be given more; whoever does not have, even what he has will be taken from him."

The Parable of the Growing Seed

[26]He also said, "This is what the kingdom of God is like. A man scatters seed on the ground. [27]Night and day, whether he sleeps or gets up, the seed sprouts and grows, though he does not know how. [28]All by itself the soil produces corn—first the stalk, then the ear, then the full grain in the ear. [29]As soon as the grain is ripe, he puts the sickle to it, because the harvest has come."

The Parable of the Mustard Seed

[30]Again he said, "What shall we say the kingdom of God is like, or what parable shall we use to describe it? [31]It is like a mustard seed, which is the smallest seed you plant in the ground. [32]Yet when planted, it grows

---

[c]22 Greek Beezeboul or Beelzeboul   [a]12 Isaiah 6:9,10

and becomes the largest of all garden plants, with such big branches that the birds of the air can perch in its shade."

[33]With many similar parables Jesus spoke the word to them, as much as they could understand. [34]He did not say anything to them without using a parable. But when he was alone with his own disciples, he explained everything.

Jesus Calms the Storm

[35]That day when evening came, he said to his disciples, "Let us go over to the other side." [36]Leaving the crowd behind, they took him along, just as he was, in the boat. There were also other boats with him. [37]A furious squall came up, and the waves broke over the boat, so that it was nearly swamped. [38]Jesus was in the stern, sleeping on a cushion. The disciples woke him and said to him, "Teacher, don't you care if we drown?"

[39]He got up, rebuked the wind and said to the waves, "Quiet! Be still!" Then the wind died down and it was completely calm.

[40]He said to his disciples, "Why are you so afraid? Do you still have no faith?"

[41]They were terrified and asked each other, "Who is this? Even the wind and the waves obey him!"

The Healing of a Demon-possessed Man

5 They went across the lake to the region of the Gerasenes.[a] [2]When Jesus got out of the boat, a man with an evil[b] spirit came from the tombs to meet him. [3]This man lived in the tombs, and no-one could bind him any more, not even with a chain. [4]For he had often been chained hand and foot, but he tore the chains apart and broke the irons on his feet. No-one was strong enough to subdue him. [5]Night and day among the tombs and in the hills he would cry out and cut himself with stones.

[6]When he saw Jesus from a distance, he ran and fell on his knees in front of him. [7]He shouted at the top of his voice, "What do you want with me, Jesus, Son of the Most High God? Swear to God that you won't torture me!" [8]For Jesus had said to him, "Come out of this man, you evil spirit!"

[9]Then Jesus asked him, "What is your name?"

"My name is Legion," he replied, "for we are many." [10]And he begged Jesus again and again not to send them out of the area.

[11]A large herd of pigs was feeding on the nearby hillside. [12]The demons begged Jesus, "Send us among the pigs; allow us to go into them." [13]He gave them permission, and the evil spirits came out and went into the pigs. The herd, about two thousand in number, rushed down the steep bank into the lake and were drowned. [14]Those tending the pigs ran off and reported this in the town and countryside, and the people went out to see what had happened. [15]When they came to Jesus, they saw the man who had been possessed by the legion of demons, sitting there, dressed and in his right mind; and they were afraid. [16]Those who had seen it told the people what had happened to the demon-possessed man—and told about the pigs as well. [17]Then the people began to plead with Jesus to leave their region.

[18]As Jesus was getting into the boat, the man who had been demon-possessed begged to go with him. [19]Jesus did not let him, but said, "Go home to your family and tell them how much the Lord has done for you, and how he has had mercy on you." [20]So the man went away and began to tell in the Decapolis[c] how much Jesus had done for him. And all the people were amazed.

A Dead Girl and a Sick Woman

[21]When Jesus had again crossed over by boat to the other side of the lake, a large crowd gathered round him while he was by the lake. [22]Then one of the synagogue rulers, named Jairus, came there. Seeing Jesus, he fell at his feet [23]and pleaded earnestly with him, "My little daughter is dying. Please come and put your hands on her so that she will be healed and live." [24]So Jesus went with him.

A large crowd followed and pressed around him. [25]And a woman was there who had been subject to bleeding for twelve years. [26]She had suffered a great deal under the care of many doctors and had spent all she had, yet instead of getting better she grew worse. [27]When she heard about Jesus, she came up behind him in the crowd and touched his cloak, [28]because she thought, "If I just touch his clothes, I will be healed." [29]Immediately her bleeding stopped and she felt in her body that she was freed from her suffering.

[30]At once Jesus realised that power had gone out from him. He turned around in the crowd and asked, "Who touched my clothes?"

[31]"You see the people crowding against you," his disciples answered, "and yet you can ask, 'Who touched me?' "

[32]But Jesus kept looking around to see who had done it. [33]Then the woman, knowing what had happened to her, came and fell at his feet and, trembling with fear, told him the whole truth. [34]He said to her, "Daughter, your faith has healed you. Go in peace and be freed from your suffering."

[35]While Jesus was still speaking, some men came from the house of Jairus, the synagogue ruler. "Your daughter is dead," they said. "Why bother the teacher any more?"

[36]Ignoring what they said, Jesus told the synagogue ruler, "Don't be afraid; just believe."

[37]He did not let anyone follow him except Peter, James and John the brother of James. [38]When they came to the home of the synagogue ruler, Jesus saw a commotion, with people crying and wailing loudly. [39]He went in and said to them, "Why all this commotion and wailing? The child is not dead but asleep." [40]But they laughed at him.

After he put them all out, he took the child's father and mother and the disciples who were with him, and went in where the child was. [41]He took her by the hand

---

[a]1 Some manuscripts *Gadarenes*; other manuscripts *Gergesenes*　　　[b]2 Greek *unclean*; also in verses 8 and 13
[c]20 That is, the Ten Cities

and said to her, "*Talitha koum!*" (which means, "Little girl, I say to you, get up!"). [42]Immediately the girl stood up and walked around (she was twelve years old). At this they were completely astonished. [43]He gave strict orders not to let anyone know about this, and told them to give her something to eat.

A Prophet Without Honour

6 Jesus left there and went to his home town, accompanied by his disciples. [2]When the Sabbath came, he began to teach in the synagogue, and many who heard him were amazed.

"Where did this man get these things?" they asked. "What's this wisdom that has been given him, that he even does miracles! [3]Isn't this the carpenter? Isn't this Mary's son and the brother of James, Joseph,[a] Judas and Simon? Aren't his sisters here with us?" And they took offence at him.

[4]Jesus said to them, "Only in his home town, among his relatives and in his own house is a prophet without honour." [5]He could not do any miracles there, except lay his hands on a few sick people and heal them. [6]And he was amazed at their lack of faith.

6:5 Matthew said that the reason Jesus did not do any miracles in his home town was because of the people's lack of faith. Mark says that he could not. It is simply impossible to reveal the hand of God to minds that are closed.

Jesus Sends Out the Twelve

Then Jesus went round teaching from village to village. [7]Calling the Twelve to him, he sent them out two by two and gave them authority over evil[b] spirits.

[8]These were his instructions: "Take nothing for the journey except a staff—no bread, no bag, no money in your belts. [9]Wear sandals but not an extra tunic. [10]Whenever you enter a house, stay there until you leave that town. [11]And if any place will not welcome you or listen to you, shake the dust off your feet when you leave, as a testimony against them."

[12]They went out and preached that people should repent. [13]They drove out many demons and anointed many sick people with oil and healed them.

John the Baptist Beheaded

[14]King Herod heard about this, for Jesus' name had become well known. Some were saying,[c] "John the Baptist has been raised from the dead, and that is why miraculous powers are at work in him."

[15]Others said, "He is Elijah."

And still others claimed, "He is a prophet, like one of the prophets of long ago."

[16]But when Herod heard this, he said, "John, the man I beheaded, has been raised from the dead!"

[17]For Herod himself had given orders to have John arrested, and he had him bound and put in prison. He did this because of Herodias, his brother Philip's wife, whom he had married. [18]For John had been saying to Herod, "It is not lawful for you to have your brother's wife." [19]So Herodias nursed a grudge against John and wanted to kill him. But she was not able to, [20]because Herod feared John and protected him, knowing him to be a righteous and holy man. When Herod heard John, he was greatly puzzled;[d] yet he liked to listen to him.

[21]Finally the opportune time came. On his birthday Herod gave a banquet for his high officials and military commanders and the leading men of Galilee. [22]When the daughter of Herodias came in and danced, she pleased Herod and his dinner guests.

The king said to the girl, "Ask me for anything you want, and I'll give it to you." [23]And he promised her with an oath, "Whatever you ask I will give you, up to half my kingdom."

[24]She went out and said to her mother, "What shall I ask for?"

"The head of John the Baptist," she answered.

[25]At once the girl hurried in to the king with the request: "I want you to give me right now the head of John the Baptist on a platter."

[26]The king was greatly distressed, but because of his oaths and his dinner guests, he did not want to refuse her. [27]So he immediately sent an executioner with orders to bring John's head. The man went, beheaded John in the prison, [28]and brought back his head on a platter. He presented it to the girl, and she gave it to her mother. [29]On hearing of this, John's disciples came and took his body and laid it in a tomb.

Jesus Feeds the Five Thousand

[30]The apostles gathered round Jesus and reported to him all they had done and taught. [31]Then, because so many people were coming and going that they did not even have a chance to eat, he said to them, "Come with me by yourselves to a quiet place and get some rest."

[32]So they went away by themselves in a boat to a solitary place. [33]But many who saw them leaving recognised them and ran on foot from all the towns and got there ahead of them. [34]When Jesus landed and saw a large crowd, he had compassion on them, because they were like sheep without a shepherd. So he began teaching them many things.

[35]By this time it was late in the day, so his disciples came to him. "This is a remote place," they said, "and it's already very late. [36]Send the people away so that they can go to the surrounding countryside and villages and buy themselves something to eat."

[37]But he answered, "You give them something to eat."

They said to him, "That would take eight months of a man's wages![e] Are we to go and spend that much on bread and give it to them to eat?"

[38]"How many loaves do you have?" he asked. "Go and see."

When they found out, they said, "Five—and two fish."

---

[a]3 Greek *Joses*, a variant of *Joseph*   [b]7 Greek *unclean*   [c]14 Some early manuscripts *He was saying*
[d]20 Some early manuscripts *he did many things*   [e]37 Greek *take two hundred denarii*

[39]Then Jesus directed them to have all the people sit down in groups on the green grass. [40]So they sat down in groups of hundreds and fifties. [41]Taking the five loaves and the two fish and looking up to heaven, he gave thanks and broke the loaves. Then he gave them to his disciples to set before the people. He also divided the two fish among them all. [42]They all ate and were satisfied, [43]and the disciples picked up twelve basketfuls of broken pieces of bread and fish. [44]The number of the men who had eaten was five thousand.

Jesus Walks on the Water

[45]Immediately Jesus made his disciples get into the boat and go on ahead of him to Bethsaida, while he dismissed the crowd. [46]After leaving them, he went up on a mountainside to pray.

[47]When evening came, the boat was in the middle of the lake, and he was alone on land. [48]He saw the disciples straining at the oars, because the wind was against them. About the fourth watch of the night he went out to them, walking on the lake. He was about to pass by them, [49]but when they saw him walking on the lake, they thought he was a ghost. They cried out, [50]because they all saw him and were terrified.

Immediately he spoke to them and said, "Take courage! It is I. Don't be afraid." [51]Then he climbed into the boat with them, and the wind died down. They were completely amazed, [52]for they had not understood about the loaves; their hearts were hardened.

[53]When they had crossed over, they landed at Gennesaret and anchored there. [54]As soon as they got out of the boat, people recognised Jesus. [55]They ran throughout that whole region and carried the sick on mats to wherever they heard he was. [56]And wherever he went—into villages, towns or countryside—they placed the sick in the market-places. They begged him to let them touch even the edge of his cloak, and all who touched him were healed.

Clean and Unclean

7 The Pharisees and some of the teachers of the law who had come from Jerusalem gathered round Jesus and [2]saw some of his disciples eating food with hands that were "unclean", that is, unwashed. [3](The Pharisees and all the Jews do not eat unless they give their hands a ceremonial washing, holding to the tradition of the elders. [4]When they come from the marketplace they do not eat unless they wash. And they observe many other traditions, such as the washing of cups, pitchers and kettles.[a])

[5]So the Pharisees and teachers of the law asked Jesus, "Why don't your disciples live according to the tradition of the elders instead of eating their food with 'unclean' hands?"

[6]He replied, "Isaiah was right when he prophesied about you hypocrites; as it is written:

" 'These people honour me with their lips,
    but their hearts are far from me.

[7]They worship me in vain;
    their teachings are but rules taught by men.'[b]

[8]You have let go of the commands of God and are holding on to the traditions of men."

[9]And he said to them: "You have a fine way of setting aside the commands of God in order to observe[c] your own traditions! [10]For Moses said, 'Honour your father and your mother,'[d] and, 'Anyone who curses his father or mother must be put to death.'[e] [11]But you say that if a man says to his father or mother: 'Whatever help you might otherwise have received from me is Corban' (that is, a gift devoted to God), [12]then you no longer let him do anything for his father or mother. [13]Thus you nullify the word of God by your tradition that you have handed down. And you do many things like that."

[14]Again Jesus called the crowd to him and said, "Listen to me, everyone, and understand this. [15]Nothing outside a man can make him 'unclean' by going into him. Rather, it is what comes out of a man that makes him 'unclean'."[f]

[17]After he had left the crowd and entered the house, his disciples asked him about this parable. [18]"Are you so dull?" he asked. "Don't you see that nothing that enters a man from the outside can make him 'unclean'? [19]For it doesn't go into his heart but into his stomach, and then out of his body." (In saying this, Jesus declared all foods "clean".)

[20]He went on: "What comes out of a man is what makes him 'unclean'. [21]For from within, out of men's hearts, come evil thoughts, sexual immorality, theft, murder, adultery, [22]greed, malice, deceit, lewdness, envy, slander, arrogance and folly. [23]All these evils come from inside and make a man 'unclean'."

The Faith of a Syro-Phoenician Woman

[24]Jesus left that place and went to the vicinity of Tyre.[g] He entered a house and did not want anyone to know it; yet he could not keep his presence secret. [25]In fact, as soon as she heard about him, a woman whose little daughter was possessed by an evil[h] spirit came and fell at his feet. [26]The woman was a Greek, born in Syrian Phoenicia. She begged Jesus to drive the demon out of her daughter.

[27]"First let the children eat all they want," he told her, "for it is not right to take the children's bread and toss it to their dogs."

[28]"Yes, Lord," she replied, "but even the dogs under the table eat the children's crumbs."

[29]Then he told her, "For such a reply, you may go; the demon has left your daughter."

[30]She went home and found her child lying on the bed, and the demon gone.

The Healing of a Deaf and Mute Man

[31]Then Jesus left the vicinity of Tyre and went through Sidon, down to the Sea of Galilee and into the region of the Decapolis.[i] [32]There some people

---

[a]4 Some early manuscripts *pitchers, kettles and dining couches*   [b]6,7 Isaiah 29:13   [c]9 Some manuscripts *set up*
[d]10 Exodus 20:12; Deut. 5:16   [e]10 Exodus 21:17; Lev. 20:9
[f]15 Some early manuscripts *'unclean'*. [16]*If anyone has ears to hear, let him hear."*   [g]24 Many early manuscripts *Tyre and Sidon*
[h]25 Greek *unclean*   [i]31 That is, the Ten Cities

brought to him a man who was deaf and could hardly talk, and they begged him to place his hand on the man. [33]After he took him aside, away from the crowd, Jesus put his fingers into the man's ears. Then he spat and touched the man's tongue. [34]He looked up to heaven and with a deep sigh said to him, "*Ephphatha!*" (which means, "Be opened!"). [35]At this, the man's ears were opened, his tongue was loosened and he began to speak plainly.

[36]Jesus commanded them not to tell anyone. But the more he did so, the more they kept talking about it. [37]People were overwhelmed with amazement. "He has done everything well," they said. "He even makes the deaf hear and the mute speak."

Jesus Feeds the Four Thousand

8 During those days another large crowd gathered. Since they had nothing to eat, Jesus called his disciples to him and said, [2]"I have compassion for these people; they have already been with me three days and have nothing to eat. [3]If I send them home hungry, they will collapse on the way, because some of them have come a long distance."

[4]His disciples answered, "But where in this remote place can anyone get enough bread to feed them?"

[5]"How many loaves do you have?" Jesus asked.

"Seven," they replied.

[6]He told the crowd to sit down on the ground. When he had taken the seven loaves and given thanks, he broke them and gave them to his disciples to set before the people, and they did so. [7]They had a few small fish as well; he gave thanks for them also and told the disciples to distribute them. [8]The people ate and were satisfied. Afterwards the disciples picked up seven basketfuls of broken pieces that were left over. [9]About four thousand men were present. And having sent them away, [10]he got into the boat with his disciples and went to the region of Dalmanutha.

[11]The Pharisees came and began to question Jesus. To test him, they asked him for a sign from heaven. [12]He sighed deeply and said, "Why does this generation ask for a miraculous sign? I tell you the truth, no sign will be given to it." [13]Then he left them, got back into the boat and crossed to the other side.

The Yeast of the Pharisees and Herod

[14]The disciples had forgotten to bring bread, except for one loaf they had with them in the boat. [15]"Be careful," Jesus warned them. "Watch out for the yeast of the Pharisees and that of Herod."

[16]They discussed this with one another and said, "It is because we have no bread."

[17]Aware of their discussion, Jesus asked them: "Why are you talking about having no bread? Do you still not see or understand? Are your hearts hardened? [18]Do you have eyes but fail to see, and ears but fail to hear? And don't you remember? [19]When I broke the five loaves for the five thousand, how many basketfuls of pieces did you pick up?"

"Twelve," they replied.

[20]"And when I broke the seven loaves for the four thousand, how many basketfuls of pieces did you pick up?"

They answered, "Seven."

[21]He said to them, "Do you still not understand?"

The Healing of a Blind Man at Bethsaida

[22]They came to Bethsaida, and some people brought a blind man and begged Jesus to touch him. [23]He took the blind man by the hand and led him outside the village. When he had spat on the man's eyes and put his hands on him, Jesus asked, "Do you see anything?"

[24]He looked up and said, "I see people; they look like trees walking around."

[25]Once more Jesus put his hands on the man's eyes. Then his eyes were opened, his sight was restored, and he saw everything clearly. [26]Jesus sent him home, saying, "Don't go into the village." [a]

Peter's Confession of Christ

[27]Jesus and his disciples went on to the villages around Caesarea Philippi. On the way he asked them, "Who do people say I am?"

[28]They replied, "Some say John the Baptist; others say Elijah; and still others, one of the prophets."

[29]"But what about you?" he asked. "Who do you say I am?"

Peter answered, "You are the Christ."[b]

[30]Jesus warned them not to tell anyone about him.

8:29   This is the first time since the opening line of Mark's Gospel that the title "Christ" (or "Messiah") is given to Jesus. The question repeatedly asked in the previous chapters, "Who is this man?", is here given the answer. For Mark, this forms the climax of his story. From here on, enormous implications must be opened out.

Jesus Predicts His Death

[31]He then began to teach them that the Son of Man must suffer many things and be rejected by the elders, chief priests and teachers of the law, and that he must be killed and after three days rise again. [32]He spoke plainly about this, and Peter took him aside and began to rebuke him.

[33]But when Jesus turned and looked at his disciples, he rebuked Peter. "Get behind me, Satan!" he said. "You do not have in mind the things of God, but the things of men."

[34]Then he called the crowd to him along with his disciples and said: "If anyone would come after me, he must deny himself and take up his cross and follow me. [35]For whoever wants to save his life[c] will lose it, but whoever loses his life for me and for the gospel will save it. [36]What good is it for a man to gain the whole

---

[a]26 Some manuscripts *Don't go and tell anyone in the village*
[b]29 Or *Messiah*. "The Christ" (Greek) and "the Messiah" (Hebrew) both mean "the Anointed One".
[c]35 The Greek word means either *life* or *soul*; also in verse 36.

world, yet forfeit his soul? [37]Or what can a man give in exchange for his soul? [38]If anyone is ashamed of me and my words in this adulterous and sinful generation, the Son of Man will be ashamed of him when he comes in his Father's glory with the holy angels."

9 And he said to them, "I tell you the truth, some who are standing here will not taste death before they see the kingdom of God come with power."

The Transfiguration

[2]After six days Jesus took Peter, James and John with him and led them up a high mountain, where they were all alone. There he was transfigured before them. [3]His clothes became dazzling white, whiter than anyone in the world could bleach them. [4]And there appeared before them Elijah and Moses, who were talking with Jesus.

[5]Peter said to Jesus, "Rabbi, it is good for us to be here. Let us put up three shelters—one for you, one for Moses and one for Elijah." [6](He did not know what to say, they were so frightened.)

[7]Then a cloud appeared and enveloped them, and a voice came from the cloud: "This is my Son, whom I love. Listen to him!"

[8]Suddenly, when they looked round, they no longer saw anyone with them except Jesus.

[9]As they were coming down the mountain, Jesus gave them orders not to tell anyone what they had seen until the Son of Man had risen from the dead. [10]They kept the matter to themselves, discussing what "rising from the dead" meant.

[11]And they asked him, "Why do the teachers of the law say that Elijah must come first?"

[12]Jesus replied, "To be sure, Elijah does come first, and restores all things. Why then is it written that the Son of Man must suffer much and be rejected? [13]But I tell you, Elijah has come, and they have done to him everything they wished, just as it is written about him."

The Healing of a Boy With an Evil Spirit

[14]When they came to the other disciples, they saw a large crowd around them and the teachers of the law arguing with them. [15]As soon as all the people saw Jesus, they were overwhelmed with wonder and ran to greet him.

[16]"What are you arguing with them about?" he asked.

[17]A man in the crowd answered, "Teacher, I brought you my son, who is possessed by a spirit that has robbed him of speech. [18]Whenever it seizes him, it throws him to the ground. He foams at the mouth, gnashes his teeth and becomes rigid. I asked your disciples to drive out the spirit, but they could not."

[19]"O unbelieving generation," Jesus replied, "how long shall I stay with you? How long shall I put up with you? Bring the boy to me."

[20]So they brought him. When the spirit saw Jesus, it immediately threw the boy into a convulsion. He fell to the ground and rolled around, foaming at the mouth.

[21]Jesus asked the boy's father, "How long has he been like this?"

"From childhood," he answered. [22]"It has often thrown him into fire or water to kill him. But if you can do anything, take pity on us and help us."

[23]" 'If you can'?" said Jesus. "Everything is possible for him who believes."

[24]Immediately the boy's father exclaimed, "I do believe; help me overcome my unbelief!"

[25]When Jesus saw that a crowd was running to the scene, he rebuked the evil[a] spirit. "You deaf and mute spirit," he said, "I command you, come out of him and never enter him again."

[26]The spirit shrieked, convulsed him violently and came out. The boy looked so much like a corpse that many said, "He's dead." [27]But Jesus took him by the hand and lifted him to his feet, and he stood up.

[28]After Jesus had gone indoors, his disciples asked him privately, "Why couldn't we drive it out?"

[29]He replied, "This kind can come out only by prayer."[b]

[30]They left that place and passed through Galilee. Jesus did not want anyone to know where they were, [31]because he was teaching his disciples. He said to them, "The Son of Man is going to be betrayed into the hands of men. They will kill him, and after three days he will rise." [32]But they did not understand what he meant and were afraid to ask him about it.

9:32 Jesus' mission being misunderstood is a prominent theme in these chapters: for example Peter's plan to avoid trouble in Jerusalem (8:32), and the argument about rank (9:34). Mark was again stressing that what is entailed in being a son of God is so difficult to grasp that even Jesus' closest friends got it wrong.

Who Is the Greatest?

[33]They came to Capernaum. When he was in the house, he asked them, "What were you arguing about on the road?" [34]But they kept quiet because on the way they had argued about who was the greatest.

[35]Sitting down, Jesus called the Twelve and said, "If anyone wants to be first, he must be the very last, and the servant of all."

[36]He took a little child and had him stand among them. Taking him in his arms, he said to them, [37]"Whoever welcomes one of these little children in my name welcomes me; and whoever welcomes me does not welcome me but the one who sent me."

Whoever Is Not Against Us Is for Us

[38]"Teacher," said John, "we saw a man driving out demons in your name and we told him to stop, because he was not one of us."

[39]"Do not stop him," Jesus said. "No-one who does a miracle in my name can in the next moment say anything bad about me, [40]for whoever is not against us is

---

[a]25 Greek *unclean*   [b]29 Some manuscripts *prayer and fasting*

for us. [41]I tell you the truth, anyone who gives you a cup of water in my name because you belong to Christ will certainly not lose his reward.

Causing to Sin

[42]"And if anyone causes one of these little ones who believe in me to sin, it would be better for him to be thrown into the sea with a large millstone tied around his neck. [43]If your hand causes you to sin, cut it off. It is better for you to enter life maimed than with two hands to go into hell, where the fire never goes out.[c] [45]And if your foot causes you to sin, cut it off. It is better for you to enter life crippled than to have two feet and be thrown into hell.[d] [47]And if your eye causes you to sin, pluck it out. It is better for you to enter the kingdom of God with one eye than to have two eyes and be thrown into hell, [48]where

" 'their worm does not die,
and the fire is not quenched.'[e]

[49]Everyone will be salted with fire. [50]"Salt is good, but if it loses its saltiness, how can you make it salty again? Have salt in yourselves, and be at peace with each other."

Divorce

10 Jesus then left that place and went into the region of Judea and across the Jordan. Again crowds of people came to him, and as was his custom, he taught them.

[2]Some Pharisees came and tested him by asking, "Is it lawful for a man to divorce his wife?"

[3]"What did Moses command you?" he replied.

[4]They said, "Moses permitted a man to write a certificate of divorce and send her away."

[5]"It was because your hearts were hard that Moses wrote you this law," Jesus replied. [6]"But at the beginning of creation God 'made them male and female'.[a] [7]'For this reason a man will leave his father and mother and be united to his wife,[b] [8]and the two will become one flesh.'[c] So they are no longer two, but one. [9]Therefore what God has joined together, let man not separate."

[10]When they were in the house again, the disciples asked Jesus about this. [11]He answered, "Anyone who divorces his wife and marries another woman commits adultery against her. [12]And if she divorces her husband and marries another man, she commits adultery."

The Little Children and Jesus

[13]People were bringing little children to Jesus to have him touch them, but the disciples rebuked them. [14]When Jesus saw this, he was indignant. He said to them, "Let the little children come to me, and do not hinder them, for the kingdom of God belongs to such

as these. [15]I tell you the truth, anyone who will not receive the kingdom of God like a little child will never enter it." [16]And he took the children in his arms, put his hands on them and blessed them.

The Rich Young Man

[17]As Jesus started on his way, a man ran up to him and fell on his knees before him. "Good teacher," he asked, "what must I do to inherit eternal life?"

[18]"Why do you call me good?" Jesus answered. "No-one is good — except God alone. [19]You know the commandments: 'Do not murder, do not commit adultery, do not steal, do not give false testimony, do not defraud, honour your father and mother.'[d]"

[20]"Teacher," he declared, "all these I have kept since I was a boy."

[21]Jesus looked at him and loved him. "One thing you lack," he said. "Go, sell everything you have and give to the poor, and you will have treasure in heaven. Then come, follow me."

[22]At this the man's face fell. He went away sad, because he had great wealth.

[23]Jesus looked around and said to his disciples, "How hard it is for the rich to enter the kingdom of God!"

[24]The disciples were amazed at his words. But Jesus said again, "Children, how hard it is[e] to enter the kingdom of God! [25]It is easier for a camel to go through the eye of a needle than for a rich man to enter the kingdom of God."

[26]The disciples were even more amazed, and said to each other, "Who then can be saved?"

[27]Jesus looked at them and said, "With man this is impossible, but not with God; all things are possible with God."

[28]Peter said to him, "We have left everything to follow you!"

[29]"I tell you the truth," Jesus replied, "no-one who has left home or brothers or sisters or mother or father or children or fields for me and the gospel [30]will fail to receive a hundred times as much in this present age (homes, brothers, sisters, mothers, children and fields — and with them, persecutions) and in the age to come, eternal life. [31]But many who are first will be last, and the last first."

Jesus Again Predicts His Death

[32]They were on their way up to Jerusalem, with Jesus leading the way, and the disciples were astonished, while those who followed were afraid. Again he took the Twelve aside and told them what was going to happen to him. [33]"We are going up to Jerusalem," he said, "and the Son of Man will be betrayed to the chief priests and teachers of the law. They will condemn him to death and will hand him over to the Gentiles, [34]who will mock him and spit on him, flog him and kill him. Three days later he will rise."

---

[c]43 Some manuscripts out, 44where / " 'their worm does not die, / and the fire is not quenched.'
[d]45 Some manuscripts hell, 46where / " 'their worm does not die, / and the fire is not quenched.'   [e]48 Isaiah 66:24
[a]6 Gen. 1:27   [b]7 Some early manuscripts do not have and be united to his wife.   [c]8 Gen. 2:24
[d]19 Exodus 20:12–16; Deut. 5:16–20   [e]24 Some manuscripts is for those who trust in riches

The Request of James and John

³⁵Then James and John, the sons of Zebedee, came to him. "Teacher," they said, "we want you to do for us whatever we ask."

³⁶"What do you want me to do for you?" he asked.

³⁷They replied, "Let one of us sit at your right and the other at your left in your glory."

³⁸"You don't know what you are asking," Jesus said. "Can you drink the cup I drink or be baptised with the baptism I am baptised with?"

³⁹"We can," they answered.

Jesus said to them, "You will drink the cup I drink and be baptised with the baptism I am baptised with, ⁴⁰but to sit at my right or left is not for me to grant. These places belong to those for whom they have been prepared."

⁴¹When the ten heard about this, they became indignant with James and John. ⁴²Jesus called them together and said, "You know that those who are regarded as rulers of the Gentiles lord it over them, and their high officials exercise authority over them. ⁴³Not so with you. Instead, whoever wants to become great among you must be your servant, ⁴⁴and whoever wants to be first must be slave of all. ⁴⁵For even the Son of Man did not come to be served, but to serve, and to give his life as a ransom for many."

Blind Bartimaeus Receives His Sight

⁴⁶Then they came to Jericho. As Jesus and his disciples, together with a large crowd, were leaving the city, a blind man, Bartimaeus (that is, the Son of Timaeus), was sitting by the roadside begging. ⁴⁷When he heard that it was Jesus of Nazareth, he began to shout, "Jesus, Son of David, have mercy on me!"

⁴⁸Many rebuked him and told him to be quiet, but he shouted all the more, "Son of David, have mercy on me!"

⁴⁹Jesus stopped and said, "Call him."

So they called to the blind man, "Cheer up! On your feet! He's calling you." ⁵⁰Throwing his cloak aside, he jumped to his feet and came to Jesus.

⁵¹"What do you want me to do for you?" Jesus asked him.

The blind man said, "Rabbi, I want to see."

⁵²"Go," said Jesus, "your faith has healed you." Immediately he received his sight and followed Jesus along the road.

The Triumphal Entry

11 As they approached Jerusalem and came to Bethphage and Bethany at the Mount of Olives, Jesus sent two of his disciples, ²saying to them, "Go to the village ahead of you, and just as you enter it, you will find a colt tied there, which no-one has ever ridden. Untie it and bring it here. ³If anyone asks you, 'Why are you doing this?' tell him, 'The Lord needs it and will send it back here shortly.' "

⁴They went and found a colt outside in the street, tied at a doorway. As they untied it, ⁵some people standing there asked, "What are you doing, untying that colt?" ⁶They answered as Jesus had told them to, and the people let them go. ⁷When they brought the colt to Jesus and threw their cloaks over it, he sat on it. ⁸Many people spread their cloaks on the road, while others spread branches they had cut in the fields. ⁹Those who went ahead and those who followed shouted,

"Hosanna!" ᵃ

"Blessed is he who comes in the name of the Lord!" ᵇ

11:9   The words "Blessed is he who comes" are so much part of the normal greetings given to pilgrims that they are still used in Israel today. On feast days all pilgrims were welcomed into Jerusalem, as Jesus is here, with palm branches known as "hosannas".

---

¹⁰"Blessed is the coming kingdom of our father David!"

"Hosanna in the highest!"

¹¹Jesus entered Jerusalem and went to the temple. He looked around at everything, but since it was already late, he went out to Bethany with the Twelve.

Jesus Clears the Temple

¹²The next day as they were leaving Bethany, Jesus was hungry. ¹³Seeing in the distance a fig-tree in leaf, he went to find out if it had any fruit. When he reached it, he found nothing but leaves, because it was not the season for figs. ¹⁴Then he said to the tree, "May no-one ever eat fruit from you again." And his disciples heard him say it.

¹⁵On reaching Jerusalem, Jesus entered the temple area and began driving out those who were buying and selling there. He overturned the tables of the money-changers and the benches of those selling doves, ¹⁶and would not allow anyone to carry merchandise through the temple courts. ¹⁷And as he taught them, he said, "Is it not written:

" 'My house will be called
    a house of prayer for all nations'ᶜ?

But you have made it 'a den of robbers'. ᵈ"

¹⁸The chief priests and the teachers of the law heard this and began looking for a way to kill him, for they feared him, because the whole crowd was amazed at his teaching.

¹⁹When evening came, theyᵉ went out of the city.

The Withered Fig-Tree

²⁰In the morning, as they went along, they saw the fig-tree withered from the roots. ²¹Peter remembered

---

ᵃ⁹ A Hebrew expression meaning "Save!" which became an exclamation of praise; also in verse 10.   ᵇ⁹ Psalm 118:25,26   ᶜ¹⁷ Isaiah 56:7   ᵈ¹⁷ Jer. 7:11   ᵉ¹⁹ Some early manuscripts he and said to Jesus, "Rabbi, look! The fig-tree you cursed has withered!"

22"Have*f* faith in God," Jesus answered. 23"I tell you the truth, if anyone says to this mountain, 'Go, throw yourself into the sea,' and does not doubt in his heart but believes that what he says will happen, it will be done for him. 24Therefore I tell you, whatever you ask for in prayer, believe that you have received it, and it will be yours. 25And when you stand praying, if you hold anything against anyone, forgive him, so that your Father in heaven may forgive you your sins."*g*

The Authority of Jesus Questioned

27They arrived again in Jerusalem, and while Jesus was walking in the temple courts, the chief priests, the teachers of the law and the elders came to him. 28"By what authority are you doing these things?" they asked. "And who gave you authority to do this?"

29Jesus replied, "I will ask you one question. Answer me, and I will tell you by what authority I am doing these things. 30John's baptism—was it from heaven, or from men? Tell me!"

31They discussed it among themselves and said, "If we say, 'From heaven,' he will ask, 'Then why didn't you believe him?' 32But if we say, 'From men' . . . ." (They feared the people, for everyone held that John really was a prophet.)

33So they answered Jesus, "We don't know."

Jesus said, "Neither will I tell you by what authority I am doing these things."

The Parable of the Tenants

12 He then began to speak to them in parables: "A man planted a vineyard. He put a wall around it, dug a pit for the winepress and built a watchtower. Then he rented the vineyard to some farmers and went away on a journey. 2At harvest time he sent a servant to the tenants to collect from them some of the fruit of the vineyard. 3But they seized him, beat him and sent him away empty-handed. 4Then he sent another servant to them; they struck this man on the head and treated him shamefully. 5He sent still another, and that one they killed. He sent many others; some of them they beat, others they killed.

6"He had one left to send, a son, whom he loved. He sent him last of all, saying, 'They will respect my son.'

7"But the tenants said to one another, 'This is the heir. Come, let's kill him, and the inheritance will be ours.' 8So they took him and killed him, and threw him out of the vineyard.

9"What then will the owner of the vineyard do? He will come and kill those tenants and give the vineyard to others. 10Haven't you read this scripture:

" 'The stone the builders rejected
      has become the capstone;*a*
11the Lord has done this,
      and it is marvellous in our eyes'*b*?"

12Then they looked for a way to arrest him because they knew he had spoken the parable against them. But they were afraid of the crowd; so they left him and went away.

Paying Taxes to Caesar

13Later they sent some of the Pharisees and Herodians to Jesus to catch him in his words. 14They came to him and said, "Teacher, we know you are a man of integrity. You aren't swayed by men, because you pay no attention to who they are; but you teach the way of God in accordance with the truth. Is it right to pay taxes to Caesar or not? 15Should we pay or shouldn't we?"

But Jesus knew their hypocrisy. "Why are you trying to trap me?" he asked. "Bring me a denarius and let me look at it." 16They brought the coin, and he asked them, "Whose portrait is this? And whose inscription?"

"Caesar's," they replied.

17Then Jesus said to them, "Give to Caesar what is Caesar's and to God what is God's."

And they were amazed at him.

Marriage at the Resurrection

18Then the Sadducees, who say there is no resurrection, came to him with a question. 19"Teacher," they said, "Moses wrote for us that if a man's brother dies and leaves a wife but no children, the man must marry the widow and have children for his brother. 20Now there were seven brothers. The first one married and died without leaving any children. 21The second one married the widow, but he also died, leaving no child. It was the same with the third. 22In fact, none of the seven left any children. Last of all, the woman died too. 23At the resurrection*c* whose wife will she be, since the seven were married to her?"

24Jesus replied, "Are you not in error because you do not know the Scriptures or the power of God? 25When the dead rise, they will neither marry nor be given in marriage; they will be like the angels in heaven. 26Now about the dead rising—have you not read in the book of Moses, in the account of the bush, how God said to him, 'I am the God of Abraham, the God of Isaac, and the God of Jacob'*d*? 27He is not the God of the dead, but of the living. You are badly mistaken!"

The Greatest Commandment

28One of the teachers of the law came and heard them debating. Noticing that Jesus had given them a good answer, he asked him, "Of all the commandments, which is the most important?"

29"The most important one," answered Jesus, "is this: 'Hear, O Israel, the Lord our God, the Lord is one.*e* 30Love the Lord your God with all your heart and with all your soul and with all your mind and with all your strength.'*f* 31The second is this: 'Love your

---

*f*22 Some early manuscripts *If you have*
*g*25 Some manuscripts *sins.* 26*But if you do not forgive, neither will your Father who is in heaven forgive your sins.*
*a*10 Or *cornerstone*   *b*11 Psalm 118:22,23   *c*23 Some manuscripts *resurrection, when men rise from the dead,*
*d*26 Exodus 3:6   *e*29 Or *the Lord our God is one Lord*   *f*30 Deut. 6:4,5

neighbour as yourself.'ᵍ There is no commandment greater than these."

³²"Well said, teacher," the man replied. "You are right in saying that God is one and there is no other but him. ³³To love him with all your heart, with all your understanding and with all your strength, and to love your neighbour as yourself is more important than all burnt offerings and sacrifices."

³⁴When Jesus saw that he had answered wisely, he said to him, "You are not far from the kingdom of God." And from then on no-one dared ask him any more questions.

Whose Son Is the Christ?

³⁵While Jesus was teaching in the temple courts, he asked, "How is it that the teachers of the law say that the Christʰ is the son of David? ³⁶David himself, speaking by the Holy Spirit, declared:

" 'The Lord said to my Lord:
   "Sit at my right hand
   until I put your enemies
   under your feet." 'ⁱ

³⁷David himself calls him 'Lord'. How then can he be his son?"

The large crowd listened to him with delight.

³⁸As he taught, Jesus said, "Watch out for the teachers of the law. They like to walk around in flowing robes and be greeted in the market-places, ³⁹and have the most important seats in the synagogues and the places of honour at banquets. ⁴⁰They devour widows' houses and for a show make lengthy prayers. Such men will be punished most severely."

The Widow's Offering

⁴¹Jesus sat down opposite the place where the offerings were put and watched the crowd putting their money into the temple treasury. Many rich people threw in large amounts. ⁴²But a poor widow came and put in two very small copper coins,ʲ worth only a fraction of a penny.ᵏ

⁴³Calling his disciples to him, Jesus said, "I tell you the truth, this poor widow has put more into the treasury than all the others. ⁴⁴They all gave out of their wealth; but she, out of her poverty, put in everything—all she had to live on."

Signs of the End of the Age

13 As he was leaving the temple, one of his disciples said to him, "Look, Teacher! What massive stones! What magnificent buildings!"

²"Do you see all these great buildings?" replied Jesus. "Not one stone here will be left on another; every one will be thrown down."

³As Jesus was sitting on the Mount of Olives opposite the temple, Peter, James, John and Andrew asked him privately, ⁴"Tell us, when will these things happen? And what will be the sign that they are all about to be fulfilled?"

⁵Jesus said to them: "Watch out that no-one deceives you. ⁶Many will come in my name, claiming, 'I am he,' and will deceive many. ⁷When you hear of wars and rumours of wars, do not be alarmed. Such things must happen, but the end is still to come. ⁸Nation will rise against nation, and kingdom against kingdom. There will be earthquakes in various places, and famines. These are the beginning of birth-pains.

⁹"You must be on your guard. You will be handed over to the local councils and flogged in the synagogues. On account of me you will stand before governors and kings as witnesses to them. ¹⁰And the gospel must first be preached to all nations. ¹¹Whenever you are arrested and brought to trial, do not worry beforehand about what to say. Just say whatever is given you at the time, for it is not you speaking, but the Holy Spirit.

¹²"Brother will betray brother to death, and a father his child. Children will rebel against their parents and have them put to death. ¹³All men will hate you because of me, but he who stands firm to the end will be saved.

¹⁴"When you see 'the abomination that causes desolation'ᵃ standing where itᵇ does not belong—let the reader understand—then let those who are in Judea flee to the mountains. ¹⁵Let no-one on the roof of his house go down or enter the house to take anything out. ¹⁶Let no-one in the field go back to get his cloak. ¹⁷How dreadful it will be in those days for pregnant women and nursing mothers! ¹⁸Pray that this will not take place in winter, ¹⁹because those will be days of distress unequalled from the beginning, when God created the world, until now—and never to be equalled again. ²⁰If the Lord had not cut short those days, no-one would survive. But for the sake of the elect, whom he has chosen, he has shortened them. ²¹At that time if anyone says to you, 'Look, here is the Christ!'ᶜ or, 'Look, there he is!' do not believe it. ²²For false Christs and false prophets will appear and perform signs and miracles to deceive the elect—if that were possible. ²³So be on your guard; I have told you everything ahead of time.

²⁴"But in those days, following that distress,

" 'the sun will be darkened,
   and the moon will not give its light;
²⁵the stars will fall from the sky,
   and the heavenly bodies will be shaken.'ᵈ

²⁶"At that time men will see the Son of Man coming in clouds with great power and glory. ²⁷And he will send his angels and gather his elect from the four winds, from the ends of the earth to the ends of the heavens.

²⁸"Now learn this lesson from the fig-tree: As soon as its twigs get tender and its leaves come out, you know that summer is near. ²⁹Even so, when you see these things happening, you know that it is near, right at the door. ³⁰I tell you the truth, this generationᵉ will certainly not pass away until all these things have happened. ³¹Heaven and earth will pass away, but my words will never pass away.

ᵍ31 Lev. 19:18   ʰ35 Or Messiah   ⁱ36 Psalm 110:1
ᵃ14 Daniel 9:27; 11:31; 12:11   ᵇ14 Or he; also in verse 29
ᵉ30 Or race   ʲ42 Greek two lepta   ᶜ21 Or Messiah   ᵏ42 Greek kodrantes   ᵈ25 Isaiah 13:10; 34:4

The Day and Hour Unknown

32"No-one knows about that day or hour, not even the angels in heaven, nor the Son, but only the Father. 33Be on guard! Be alert![f] You do not know when that time will come. 34It's like a man going away: He leaves his house and puts his servants in charge, each with his assigned task, and tells the one at the door to keep watch.

35"Therefore keep watch because you do not know when the owner of the house will come back— whether in the evening, or at midnight, or when the cock crows, or at dawn. 36If he comes suddenly, do not let him find you sleeping. 37What I say to you, I say to everyone: 'Watch!'"

Jesus Anointed at Bethany

14 Now the Passover and the Feast of Unleavened Bread were only two days away, and the chief priests and the teachers of the law were looking for some sly way to arrest Jesus and kill him. 2"But not during the Feast," they said, "or the people may riot."

14:1 All the Gospels emphasize the story of Jesus' passion and death. It occupies a third of Mark's Gospel; the rest is really no more than a long prologue. Here the "secret" about Jesus is finally unveiled.

3While he was in Bethany, reclining at the table in the home of a man known as Simon the Leper, a woman came with an alabaster jar of very expensive perfume, made of pure nard. She broke the jar and poured the perfume on his head.

4Some of those present were saying indignantly to one another, "Why this waste of perfume? 5It could have been sold for more than a year's wages[a] and the money given to the poor." And they rebuked her harshly.

6"Leave her alone," said Jesus. "Why are you bothering her? She has done a beautiful thing to me. 7The poor you will always have with you, and you can help them any time you want. But you will not always have me. 8She did what she could. She poured perfume on my body beforehand to prepare for my burial. 9I tell you the truth, wherever the gospel is preached throughout the world, what she has done will also be told, in memory of her."

10Then Judas Iscariot, one of the Twelve, went to the chief priests to betray Jesus to them. 11They were delighted to hear this and promised to give him money. So he watched for an opportunity to hand him over.

The Lord's Supper

12On the first day of the Feast of Unleavened Bread, when it was customary to sacrifice the Passover lamb, Jesus' disciples asked him, "Where do you want us to go and make preparations for you to eat the Passover?" 13So he sent two of his disciples, telling them, "Go into the city, and a man carrying a jar of water will meet you. Follow him. 14Say to the owner of the house he enters, 'The Teacher asks: Where is my guest room, where I may eat the Passover with my disciples?' 15He will show you a large upper room, furnished and ready. Make preparations for us there."

16The disciples left, went into the city and found things just as Jesus had told them. So they prepared the Passover.

17When evening came, Jesus arrived with the Twelve. 18While they were reclining at the table eating, he said, "I tell you the truth, one of you will betray me—one who is eating with me."

19They were saddened, and one by one they said to him, "Surely not I?"

20"It is one of the Twelve," he replied, "one who dips bread into the bowl with me. 21The Son of Man will go just as it is written about him. But woe to that man who betrays the Son of Man! It would be better for him if he had not been born."

22While they were eating, Jesus took bread, gave thanks and broke it, and gave it to his disciples, saying, "Take it; this is my body."

23Then he took the cup, gave thanks and offered it to them, and they all drank from it.

24"This is my blood of the[b] covenant, which is poured out for many," he said to them. 25"I tell you the truth, I will not drink again of the fruit of the vine until that day when I drink it anew in the kingdom of God."

26When they had sung a hymn, they went out to the Mount of Olives.

Jesus Predicts Peter's Denial

27"You will all fall away," Jesus told them, "for it is written:

" 'I will strike the shepherd,
    and the sheep will be scattered.'[c]

28But after I have risen, I will go ahead of you into Galilee."

29Peter declared, "Even if all fall away, I will not."

30"I tell you the truth," Jesus answered, "today— yes, tonight—before the cock crows twice[d] you yourself will disown me three times."

31But Peter insisted emphatically, "Even if I have to die with you, I will never disown you." And all the others said the same.

Gethsemane

32They went to a place called Gethsemane, and Jesus said to his disciples, "Sit here while I pray." 33He took Peter, James and John along with him, and he began to be deeply distressed and troubled. 34"My soul is overwhelmed with sorrow to the point of death," he said to them. "Stay here and keep watch."

35Going a little farther, he fell to the ground and prayed that if possible the hour might pass from him. 36"Abba,[e] Father," he said, "everything is possible for you. Take this cup from me. Yet not what I will, but what you will."

---

f33 Some manuscripts *alert and pray*   a5 Greek *than three hundred denarii*   b24 Some manuscripts *the new*
c27 Zech. 13:7   d30 Some early manuscripts do not have *twice*.   e36 Aramaic for *Father*

[37]Then he returned to his disciples and found them sleeping. "Simon," he said to Peter, "are you asleep? Could you not keep watch for one hour? [38]Watch and pray so that you will not fall into temptation. The spirit is willing, but the body is weak."

[39]Once more he went away and prayed the same thing. [40]When he came back, he again found them sleeping, because their eyes were heavy. They did not know what to say to him.

[41]Returning the third time, he said to them, "Are you still sleeping and resting? Enough! The hour has come. Look, the Son of Man is betrayed into the hands of sinners. [42]Rise! Let us go! Here comes my betrayer!"

Jesus Arrested

[43]Just as he was speaking, Judas, one of the Twelve, appeared. With him was a crowd armed with swords and clubs, sent from the chief priests, the teachers of the law, and the elders. [44]Now the betrayer had arranged a signal with them: "The one I kiss is the man; arrest him and lead him away under guard. [45]Going at once to Jesus, Judas said, "Rabbi!" and kissed him. [46]The men seized Jesus and arrested him. [47]Then one of those standing near drew his sword and struck the servant of the high priest, cutting off his ear.

[48]"Am I leading a rebellion," said Jesus, "that you have come out with swords and clubs to capture me? [49]Every day I was with you, teaching in the temple courts, and you did not arrest me. But the Scriptures must be fulfilled." [50]Then everyone deserted him and fled.

[51]A young man, wearing nothing but a linen garment, was following Jesus. When they seized him, [52]he fled naked, leaving his garment behind.

Before the Sanhedrin

[53]They took Jesus to the high priest, and all the chief priests, elders and teachers of the law came together. [54]Peter followed him at a distance, right into the courtyard of the high priest. There he sat with the guards and warmed himself at the fire.

[55]The chief priests and the whole Sanhedrin were looking for evidence against Jesus so that they could put him to death, but they did not find any. [56]Many testified falsely against him, but their statements did not agree.

[57]Then some stood up and gave this false testimony against him: [58]"We heard him say, 'I will destroy this man-made temple and in three days will build another, not made by man.'" [59]Yet even then their testimony did not agree.

[60]Then the high priest stood up before them and asked Jesus, "Are you not going to answer? What is this testimony that these men are bringing against you?" [61]But Jesus remained silent and gave no answer.

Again the high priest asked him, "Are you the Christ,[f] the Son of the Blessed One?"

[62]"I am," said Jesus. "And you will see the Son of Man sitting at the right hand of the Mighty One and coming on the clouds of heaven."

[63]The high priest tore his clothes. "Why do we need any more witnesses?" he asked. [64]"You have heard the blasphemy. What do you think?"

They all condemned him as worthy of death. [65]Then some began to spit at him; they blindfolded him, struck him with their fists, and said, "Prophesy!" And the guards took him and beat him.

Peter Disowns Jesus

[66]While Peter was below in the courtyard, one of the servant girls of the high priest came by. [67]When she saw Peter warming himself, she looked closely at him.

"You also were with that Nazarene, Jesus," she said.

[68]But he denied it. "I don't know or understand what you're talking about," he said, and went out into the entrance.[g]

[69]When the servant girl saw him there, she said again to those standing around, "This fellow is one of them." [70]Again he denied it.

After a little while, those standing near said to Peter, "Surely you are one of them, for you are a Galilean." [71]He began to call down curses on himself, and he swore to them, "I don't know this man you're talking about."

[72]Immediately the cock crowed the second time.[h] Then Peter remembered the word Jesus had spoken to him: "Before the cock crows twice[i] you will disown me three times." And he broke down and wept.

Jesus Before Pilate

15 Very early in the morning, the chief priests, with the elders, the teachers of the law and the whole Sanhedrin, reached a decision. They bound Jesus, led him away and turned him over to Pilate.

[2]"Are you the king of the Jews?" asked Pilate.

"Yes, it is as you say," Jesus replied.

[3]The chief priests accused him of many things. [4]So again Pilate asked him, "Aren't you going to answer? See how many things they are accusing you of."

[5]But Jesus still made no reply, and Pilate was amazed.

[6]Now it was the custom at the Feast to release a prisoner whom the people requested. [7]A man called Barabbas was in prison with the insurrectionists who had committed murder in the uprising. [8]The crowd came up and asked Pilate to do for them what he usually did.

[9]"Do you want me to release to you the king of the Jews?" asked Pilate, [10]knowing it was out of envy that the chief priests had handed Jesus over to him. [11]But the chief priests stirred up the crowd to have Pilate release Barabbas instead.

[12]"What shall I do, then, with the one you call the king of the Jews?" Pilate asked them.

[13]"Crucify him!" they shouted.

[14]"Why? What crime has he committed?" asked Pilate.

But they shouted all the louder, "Crucify him!"

[15]Wanting to satisfy the crowd, Pilate released

---

f61 Or *Messiah*   *g68* Some early manuscripts *entrance and the cock crowed*
h72 Some early manuscripts do not have *the second time.*   *i72* Some early manuscripts do not have *twice.*

Barabbas to them. He had Jesus flogged, and handed him over to be crucified.

The Soldiers Mock Jesus

16The soldiers led Jesus away into the palace (that is, the Praetorium) and called together the whole company of soldiers. 17They put a purple robe on him, then twisted together a crown of thorns and set it on him. 18And they began to call out to him, "Hail, king of the Jews!" 19Again and again they struck him on the head with a staff and spat on him. Falling on their knees, they paid homage to him. 20And when they had mocked him, they took off the purple robe and put his own clothes on him. Then they led him out to crucify him.

The Crucifixion

21A certain man from Cyrene, Simon, the father of Alexander and Rufus, was passing by on his way in from the country, and they forced him to carry the cross. 22They brought Jesus to the place called Golgotha (which means The Place of the Skull). 23Then they offered him wine mixed with myrrh, but he did not take it. 24And they crucified him. Dividing up his clothes, they cast lots to see what each would get.
25It was the third hour when they crucified him. 26The written notice of the charge against him read: THE KING OF THE JEWS. 27They crucified two robbers with him, one on his right and one on his left.a 29Those who passed by hurled insults at him, shaking their heads and saying, "So! You who are going to destroy the temple and build it in three days, 30come down from the cross and save yourself!"
31In the same way the chief priests and the teachers of the law mocked him among themselves. "He saved others," they said, "but he can't save himself! 32Let this Christ,b this King of Israel, come down now from the cross, that we may see and believe." Those crucified with him also heaped insults on him.

The Death of Jesus

33At the sixth hour darkness came over the whole land until the ninth hour. 34And at the ninth hour Jesus cried out in a loud voice, "Eloi, Eloi, lama sabachthani?" —which means, "My God, my God, why have you forsaken me?"c
35When some of those standing near heard this, they said, "Listen, he's calling Elijah."
36One man ran, filled a sponge with wine vinegar, put it on a stick, and offered it to Jesus to drink. "Now leave him alone. Let's see if Elijah comes to take him down," he said.
37With a loud cry, Jesus breathed his last.
38The curtain of the temple was torn in two from top to bottom. 39And when the centurion, who stood there in front of Jesus, heard his cry andd saw how he died, he said, "Surely this man was the Sone of God!"
40Some women were watching from a distance. Among them were Mary Magdalene, Mary the mother

of James the younger and of Joses, and Salome. 41In Galilee these women had followed him and cared for his needs. Many other women who had come up with him to Jerusalem were also there.

The Burial of Jesus

42It was Preparation Day (that is, the day before the Sabbath). So as evening approached, 43Joseph of Arimathea, a prominent member of the Council, who was himself waiting for the kingdom of God, went boldly to Pilate and asked for Jesus' body. 44Pilate was surprised to hear that he was already dead. Summoning the centurion, he asked him if Jesus had already died. 45When he learned from the centurion that it was so, he gave the body to Joseph. 46So Joseph bought some linen cloth, took down the body, wrapped it in the linen, and placed it in a tomb cut out of rock. Then he rolled a stone against the entrance of the tomb. 47Mary Magdalene and Mary the mother of Joses saw where he was laid.

The Resurrection

16 When the Sabbath was over, Mary Magdalene, Mary the mother of James, and Salome bought spices so that they might go to anoint Jesus' body. 2Very early on the first day of the week, just after sunrise, they were on their way to the tomb 3and they asked each other, "Who will roll the stone away from the entrance of the tomb?"
4But when they looked up, they saw that the stone, which was very large, had been rolled away. 5As they entered the tomb, they saw a young man dressed in a white robe sitting on the right side, and they were alarmed.
6"Don't be alarmed," he said. "You are looking for Jesus the Nazarene, who was crucified. He has risen! He is not here. See the place where they laid him. 7But go, tell his disciples and Peter, 'He is going ahead of you into Galilee. There you will see him, just as he told you.' "
8Trembling and bewildered, the women went out and fled from the tomb. They said nothing to anyone, because they were afraid.

16:8   As the footnote points out, in most of the oldest manuscripts Mark's Gospel ends here. Verses 9–21 are extracts from Matthew, Luke, and John put together. Mark himself seemed to have wanted to end his Gospel with the observation that anyone who had finally seen the death of Jesus would also be bewildered like the women, and silent.

---

a27 Some manuscripts left, 28and the scripture was fulfilled which says, "He was counted with the lawless ones" (Isaiah 53:12)
b32 Or Messiah   c34 Psalm 22:1   d39 Some manuscripts do not have heard his cry and.   e39 Or a son

[The most reliable early manuscripts and other ancient witnesses do not have Mark 16:9–20.]

⁹When Jesus rose early on the first day of the week, he appeared first to Mary Magdalene, out of whom he had driven seven demons. ¹⁰She went and told those who had been with him and who were mourning and weeping. ¹¹When they heard that Jesus was alive and that she had seen him, they did not believe it.

¹²Afterwards Jesus appeared in a different form to two of them while they were walking in the country. ¹³These returned and reported it to the rest; but they did not believe them either.

¹⁴Later Jesus appeared to the Eleven as they were eating; he rebuked them for their lack of faith and their stubborn refusal to believe those who had seen him after he had risen.

¹⁵He said to them, "Go into all the world and preach the good news to all creation. ¹⁶Whoever believes and is baptised will be saved, but whoever does not believe will be condemned. ¹⁷And these signs will accompany those who believe: In my name they will drive out demons; they will speak in new tongues; ¹⁸they will pick up snakes with their hands; and when they drink deadly poison, it will not hurt them at all; they will place their hands on sick people, and they will get well."

¹⁹After the Lord Jesus had spoken to them, he was taken up into heaven and he sat at the right hand of God. ²⁰Then the disciples went out and preached everywhere, and the Lord worked with them and confirmed his word by the signs that accompanied it.

Luke

Luke's Good News

Anyone wanting to know what sort of a book Luke's Gospel is should compare the closing lines with Mark's. (Note that the early and most reliable manuscripts of Mark's Gospel end at 16:8.)

Mark: "Trembling and bewildered, the women went out and fled from the tomb. They said nothing to anyone, because they were afraid."

Luke: "Then they worshipped him and returned to Jerusalem with great joy. And they stayed continually at the temple, praising God."

The opening and closing lines set the tone of the whole book. Against the background of Mark, it was important to stress the fearful responsibility of being a Christian. Luke's background persuaded him to draw attention to the joy to be found in the gospel, the good news of Jesus Christ.

The Christian Humanist

A comparison of Luke with Matthew is equally enlightening. Someone said that turning from Matthew to Luke is like coming out of the church into the market-place. There is a feeling of leisurely ease and spaciousness in Luke's Gospel. It is, after all, only the first of two volumes, of which the second (the book of Acts) takes us into a world the other Gospels don't dream of — from Jerusalem into Samaria, Syria, Turkey, and Greece, and eventually to Rome itself, the centre of the civilized world. Luke's Gospel is not about dying for your faith (Mark), nor about preserving it behind locked doors (Matthew). It is about living your faith in the ordinary world of men and women. For Luke, Christianity was not a cause for martyrs or a set of regulations for members, but a message of common sense for everyone. If Mark can be called the first Christian dramatist, then Luke is the first Christian humanist.

Orderliness

Luke's Gospel, like that of Mark and Matthew, was dictated by the circumstances in which he wrote. In the years 80–90 AD, the Christian community was expanding rapidly into the Greek-speaking Roman world. This world needed a gospel which was attuned to the Greek mind, which demanded not only thoroughness, moderation, and universality, but above all order. Mark's Gospel, for all its brilliance, was too haphazard for such a mentality, and its use of Greek almost barbaric. Even Matthew's Gospel, which has its own order of repetition, was too Jewish for the Greek mind. Luke, who was himself a Greek and therefore able to write in a style rather kinder to the Greek language, also understood the Greek passion for orderliness. Look, for example, at his version of Jesus' birth. The last of the prophets, John the Baptist, is depicted as a kind of mirror image of the first prophet, Samuel, so that both can throw light on Jesus as the fulfilment of the prophets' hopes. Look at his author's preface: "I myself have carefully investigated everything from the beginning . . . to write an orderly account" (1:3), and then check this statement with chapters 10—19, where he has done his own thing and collected a vast amount of material which is not found in Mark or Matthew. He presented this mass of material as one long journey to Jerusalem. There are pointers to Jerusalem twelve times in this section, so that the reader will see Jerusalem as not only the starting point but also the finishing point of the gospel, which in Acts will spread from Jerusalem to the rest of the world. Greek readers would have loved this sense of orderliness.

Sense of Proportion

They would also warm to Luke's sense of proportion. The Greeks did not like extremes; "moderation in all things" was their ideal. So in Luke's Gospel, the mind-blowing mystery of Mark is a much more leisurely and urbane story of a man who went about doing good. The Jesus who spoke from mountain tops in Matthew is here more usually found speaking to friends at table. The disciples are no longer crudely reproached for their stupidity, and even Jesus no longer demands divine perfection (Matthew 5:48), but simply endless compassion (Luke 6:36). Even the final shocking cry of dereliction "My God, my God, why have you forsaken me?" (Matthew 27:46) is toned down to the much calmer, "Father, into your hands I commit my spirit" (Luke 23:46). There is a sense of composure, of soberness, of cooling down, and of smoothing off the rough edges, in order to commend this Gospel to the civilized world.

Openness

The Greeks were specially opposed to narrow-mindedness and self-interest. Their views were worldwide. So were Luke's. His genealogy traces Jesus back beyond the Hebrew Abraham (where Matthew stopped) to Adam, the forefather of the whole human race. Nor did Jesus restrict his ministry to the Jews as he did in Matthew's Gospel: he went to foreign Samaritan territory (9:52), and happily told a story of a foreigner showing far more practical charity than the Jewish clergy (10:30ff). This openness to the whole world comes across most strongly in Luke's treatment of women and others who were outcasts in the Jewish world of the first century AD. If we only had Mark and Matthew, we would never have heard of Elizabeth, John the Baptist's mother (1:5), Anna the prophetess (2:36), the widow of Nain (7:12), the women who went with the first disciples (8:2), Mary (10:38), the crippled woman (13:11), the distraught housewife (15:8), and hardly at all of Mary the mother of Jesus (chapters 1, 2), who has no speaking part in Matthew, and no part at all in Mark. But they all appear in Luke's Gospel. He knew that the good news concerned women as well as men. And it concerns, above all, the poor, the wretched, and the outcasts. Luke's Gospel is above all the story of people like Joseph and Mary, the shepherds, Zacchaeus, the prodigal son, the tax-collector, and the penitent criminal. These, he emphasized, will be the first, not the last, to benefit from the good news proclaimed by Jesus.

Joy

The joy which shines out of this Gospel is no afterthought. It is Luke's trademark. Mark had underlined the awesome fear inspired by Jesus. Luke regularly changed the word to joy, or added the refrain, "Do not be afraid". He saw the story of Jesus as the "good news of great joy . . . for all people" (2:10).

Introduction

1 Many have undertaken to draw up an account of the things that have been fulfilled[a] among us, [2]just as they were handed down to us by those who from the first were eye-witnesses and servants of the word. [3]Therefore, since I myself have carefully investigated everything from the beginning, it seemed good also to me to write an orderly account for you, most excellent Theophilus, [4]so that you may know the certainty of the things you have been taught.

The Birth of John the Baptist Foretold

[5]In the time of Herod king of Judea there was a priest named Zechariah, who belonged to the priestly division of Abijah; his wife Elizabeth was also a descendant of Aaron. [6]Both of them were upright in the sight of God, observing all the Lord's commandments and regulations blamelessly. [7]But they had no children, because Elizabeth was barren; and they were both well on in years.

[8]Once when Zechariah's division was on duty and he was serving as priest before God, [9]he was chosen by lot, according to the custom of the priesthood, to go into the temple of the Lord and burn incense. [10]And when the time for the burning of incense came, all the assembled worshippers were praying outside.

[11]Then an angel of the Lord appeared to him, standing at the right side of the altar of incense. [12]When Zechariah saw him, he was startled and was gripped with fear. [13]But the angel said to him: "Do not be afraid, Zechariah; your prayer has been heard. Your wife Elizabeth will bear you a son, and you are to give him the name John. [14]He will be a joy and delight to you, and many will rejoice because of his birth, [15]for he will be great in the sight of the Lord. He is never to take wine or other fermented drink, and he will be filled with the Holy Spirit even from birth.[b] [16]Many of the people of Israel will he bring back to the Lord their God. [17]And he will go on before the Lord, in the spirit and power of Elijah, to turn the hearts of the fathers to their children and the disobedient to the wisdom of the righteous — to make ready a people prepared for the Lord."

[18]Zechariah asked the angel, "How can I be sure of this? I am an old man and my wife is well on in years."

[19]The angel answered, "I am Gabriel. I stand in the presence of God, and I have been sent to speak to you and to tell you this good news. [20]And now you will be silent and not able to speak until the day this happens, because you did not believe my words, which will come true at their proper time."

[21]Meanwhile, the people were waiting for Zechariah and wondering why he stayed so long in the temple. [22]When he came out, he could not speak to them. They realised he had seen a vision in the temple, for he kept making signs to them but remained unable to speak.

[23]When his time of service was completed, he returned home. [24]After this his wife Elizabeth became pregnant and for five months remained in seclusion. [25]"The Lord has done this for me," she said. "In these days he has shown his favour and taken away my disgrace among the people."

The Birth of Jesus Foretold

[26]In the sixth month, God sent the angel Gabriel to Nazareth, a town in Galilee, [27]to a virgin pledged to be married to a man named Joseph, a descendant of David. The virgin's name was Mary. [28]The angel went to her and said, "Greetings, you who are highly favoured! The Lord is with you."

[29]Mary was greatly troubled at his words and wondered what kind of greeting this might be. [30]But the angel said to her, "Do not be afraid, Mary, you have found favour with God. [31]You will be with child and give birth to a son, and you are to give him the name Jesus. [32]He will be great and will be called the Son of the Most High. The Lord God will give him the throne of his father David, [33]and he will reign over the house of Jacob for ever; his kingdom will never end."

1:31 For easterners, names are not simply labels. They say a lot about a person. The name Jesus means "God has come to save us".

---

[34]"How will this be," Mary asked the angel, "since I am a virgin?"

[35]The angel answered, "The Holy Spirit will come upon you, and the power of the Most High will overshadow you. So the holy one to be born will be called[c] the Son of God. [36]Even Elizabeth your relative is going to have a child in her old age, and she who was said to be barren is in her sixth month. [37]For nothing is impossible with God."

[38]"I am the Lord's servant," Mary answered. "May it be to me as you have said." Then the angel left her.

---

a1 Or been surely believed   b15 Or from his mother's womb   c35 Or So the child to be born will be called holy,

Mary Visits Elizabeth

39At that time Mary got ready and hurried to a town in the hill country of Judea, 40where she entered Zechariah's home and greeted Elizabeth. 41When Elizabeth heard Mary's greeting, the baby leaped in her womb, and Elizabeth was filled with the Holy Spirit. 42In a loud voice she exclaimed: "Blessed are you among women, and blessed is the child you will bear! 43But why am I so favoured, that the mother of my Lord should come to me? 44As soon as the sound of your greeting reached my ears, the baby in my womb leaped for joy. 45Blessed is she who has believed that what the Lord has said to her will be accomplished!"

Mary's Song

46And Mary said:

1:46 The Magnificat (Mary's song) can provide a comfortable and soothing background when sung to traditional music in church. In the raw, it is a revolutionary statement close to Luke's heart: God has chosen to be with the humble and the hungry.

"My soul glorifies the Lord
47 and my spirit rejoices in God my Saviour,
48for he has been mindful
   of the humble state of his servant.
From now on all generations will call me blessed,
49 for the Mighty One has done great things for me —
   holy is his name.
50His mercy extends to those who fear him,
   from generation to generation.
51He has performed mighty deeds with his arm;
   he has scattered those who are proud in their inmost thoughts.
52He has brought down rulers from their thrones
   but has lifted up the humble.
53He has filled the hungry with good things
   but has sent the rich away empty.
54He has helped his servant Israel,
   remembering to be merciful
55to Abraham and his descendants for ever,
   even as he said to our fathers."

56Mary stayed with Elizabeth for about three months and then returned home.

The Birth of John the Baptist

57When it was time for Elizabeth to have her baby, she gave birth to a son. 58Her neighbours and relatives heard that the Lord had shown her great mercy, and they shared her joy.

59On the eighth day they came to circumcise the child, and they were going to name him after his father Zechariah, 60but his mother spoke up and said, "No! He is to be called John."

d69 Horn here symbolises strength.

61They said to her, "There is no-one among your relatives who has that name."

62Then they made signs to his father, to find out what he would like to name the child. 63He asked for a writing tablet, and to everyone's astonishment he wrote, "His name is John." 64Immediately his mouth was opened and his tongue was loosed, and he began to speak, praising God. 65The neighbours were all filled with awe, and throughout the hill country of Judea people were talking about all these things. 66Everyone who heard this wondered about it, asking, "What then is this child going to be?" For the Lord's hand was with him.

Zechariah's Song

67His father Zechariah was filled with the Holy Spirit and prophesied:

68"Praise be to the Lord, the God of Israel,
   because he has come and has redeemed his people.
69He has raised up a horn d of salvation for us
   in the house of his servant David
70(as he said through his holy prophets of long ago),
71salvation from our enemies
   and from the hand of all who hate us —
72to show mercy to our fathers
   and to remember his holy covenant,
73 the oath he swore to our father Abraham:
74to rescue us from the hand of our enemies,
   and to enable us to serve him without fear
75 in holiness and righteousness before him all our days.

76And you, my child, will be called a prophet of the Most High;
   for you will go on before the Lord to prepare the way for him,
77to give his people the knowledge of salvation
   through the forgiveness of their sins,
78because of the tender mercy of our God,
   by which the rising sun will come to us from heaven
79to shine on those living in darkness
   and in the shadow of death,
   to guide our feet into the path of peace."

80And the child grew and became strong in spirit; and he lived in the desert until he appeared publicly to Israel.

The Birth of Jesus

2 In those days Caesar Augustus issued a decree that a census should be taken of the entire Roman world. (2This was the first census that took place while Quirinius was governor of Syria.) 3And everyone went to his own town to register.

4So Joseph also went up from the town of Nazareth in Galilee to Judea, to Bethlehem the town of David, because he belonged to the house and line of David. 5He went there to register with Mary, who was pledged to be married to him and was expecting a child. [6]While they were there, the time came for the baby to be born, [7]and she gave birth to her firstborn, a son. She wrapped him in cloths and placed him in a manger, because there was no room for them in the inn.

The Shepherds and the Angels

[8]And there were shepherds living out in the fields near by, keeping watch over their flocks at night. [9]An angel of the Lord appeared to them, and the glory of the Lord shone around them, and they were terrified. [10]But the angel said to them, "Do not be afraid. I bring you good news of great joy that will be for all the people. [11]Today in the town of David a Saviour has been born to you; he is Christ[a] the Lord. [12]This will be a sign to you: You will find a baby wrapped in cloths and lying in a manger."

2:8 Matthew narrated how the infant Jesus was visited by wise men from the east. In Luke they are shepherds, the outcasts of Jewish society. Luke again underlined Jesus' interest in the poor.

---

[13]Suddenly a great company of the heavenly host appeared with the angel, praising God and saying,

[14]"Glory to God in the highest,
  and on earth peace to men on whom his favour
      rests."

[15]When the angels had left them and gone into heaven, the shepherds said to one another, "Let's go to Bethlehem and see this thing that has happened, which the Lord has told us about."

[16]So they hurried off and found Mary and Joseph, and the baby, who was lying in the manger. [17]When they had seen him, they spread the word concerning what had been told them about this child, [18]and all who heard it were amazed at what the shepherds said to them. [19]But Mary treasured up all these things and pondered them in her heart. [20]The shepherds returned, glorifying and praising God for all the things they had heard and seen, which were just as they had been told.

Jesus Presented in the Temple

[21]On the eighth day, when it was time to circumcise him, he was named Jesus, the name the angel had given him before he had been conceived.

[22]When the time of their purification according to the Law of Moses had been completed, Joseph and Mary took him to Jerusalem to present him to the Lord [23](as it is written in the Law of the Lord, "Every firstborn male is to be consecrated to the Lord"[b]), [24]and to offer a sacrifice in keeping with what is said in the Law of the Lord: "a pair of doves or two young pigeons".[c]

[25]Now there was a man in Jerusalem called Simeon, who was righteous and devout. He was waiting for the consolation of Israel, and the Holy Spirit was upon him.

[26]It had been revealed to him by the Holy Spirit that he would not die before he had seen the Lord's Christ. [27]Moved by the Spirit, he went into the temple courts. When the parents brought in the child Jesus to do for him what the custom of the Law required, [28]Simeon took him in his arms and praised God, saying:

[29]"Sovereign Lord, as you have promised,
  you now dismiss[d] your servant in peace.
[30]For my eyes have seen your salvation,
[31] which you have prepared in the sight of all
          people,
[32]a light for revelation to the Gentiles
  and for glory to your people Israel."

[33]The child's father and mother marvelled at what was said about him. [34]Then Simeon blessed them and said to Mary, his mother: "This child is destined to cause the falling and rising of many in Israel, and to be a sign that will be spoken against, [35]so that the thoughts of many hearts will be revealed. And a sword will pierce your own soul too."

[36]There was also a prophetess, Anna, the daughter of Phanuel, of the tribe of Asher. She was very old; she had lived with her husband seven years after her marriage, [37]and then was a widow until she was eighty-four.[e] She never left the temple but worshipped night and day, fasting and praying. [38]Coming up to them at that very moment, she gave thanks to God and spoke about the child to all who were looking forward to the redemption of Jerusalem.

[39]When Joseph and Mary had done everything required by the Law of the Lord, they returned to Galilee to their own town of Nazareth. [40]And the child grew and became strong; he was filled with wisdom, and the grace of God was upon him.

The Boy Jesus at the Temple

[41]Every year his parents went to Jerusalem for the Feast of the Passover. [42]When he was twelve years old, they went up to the Feast, according to the custom. [43]After the Feast was over, while his parents were returning home, the boy Jesus stayed behind in Jerusalem, but they were unaware of it. [44]Thinking he was in their company, they travelled on for a day. Then they began looking for him among their relatives and friends. [45]When they did not find him, they went back to Jerusalem to look for him. [46]After three days they found him in the temple courts, sitting among the teachers, listening to them and asking them questions. [47]Everyone who heard him was amazed at his understanding and his answers. [48]When his parents saw him, they were astonished. His mother said to him, "Son, why have you treated us like this? Your father and I have been anxiously searching for you."

[49]"Why were you searching for me?" he asked. "Didn't you know I had to be in my Father's house?" [50]But they did not understand what he was saying to them.

[51]Then he went down to Nazareth with them and was obedient to them. But his mother treasured all

---

[a]11 Or Messiah. "The Christ" (Greek) and "the Messiah" (Hebrew) both mean "the Anointed One"; also in verse 26.
[b]23 Exodus 13:2,12   [c]24 Lev. 12:8   [d]29 Or promised, / now dismiss   [e]37 Or widow for eighty-four years

these things in her heart. [52]And Jesus grew in wisdom and stature, and in favour with God and men.

John the Baptist Prepares the Way

3 In the fifteenth year of the reign of Tiberius Caesar—when Pontius Pilate was governor of Judea, Herod tetrarch of Galilee, his brother Philip tetrarch of Iturea and Traconitis, and Lysanias tetrarch of Abilene—[2]during the high priesthood of Annas and Caiaphas, the word of God came to John son of Zechariah in the desert. [3]He went into all the country around the Jordan, preaching a baptism of repentance for the forgiveness of sins. [4]As is written in the book of the words of Isaiah the prophet:

"A voice of one calling in the desert,
'Prepare the way for the Lord,
    make straight paths for him.
[5]Every valley shall be filled in,
    every mountain and hill made low.
The crooked roads shall become straight,
    the rough ways smooth.
[6]And all mankind will see God's salvation.' " [a]

[7]John said to the crowds coming out to be baptised by him, "You brood of vipers! Who warned you to flee from the coming wrath? [8]Produce fruit in keeping with repentance. And do not begin to say to yourselves, 'We have Abraham as our father.' For I tell you that out of these stones God can raise up children for Abraham. [9]The axe is already at the root of the trees, and every tree that does not produce good fruit will be cut down and thrown into the fire."

[10]"What should we do then?" the crowd asked.

[11]John answered, "The man with two tunics should share with him who has none, and the one who has food should do the same."

[12]Tax collectors also came to be baptised. "Teacher," they asked, "what should we do?"

[13]"Don't collect any more than you are required to," he told them.

[14]Then some soldiers asked him, "And what should we do?"

He replied, "Don't extort money and don't accuse people falsely—be content with your pay."

[15]The people were waiting expectantly and were all wondering in their hearts if John might possibly be the Christ.[b] [16]John answered them all, "I baptise you with[c] water. But one more powerful than I will come, the thongs of whose sandals I am not worthy to untie. He will baptise you with the Holy Spirit and with fire. [17]His winnowing-fork is in his hand to clear his threshing-floor and to gather the wheat into his barn, but he will burn up the chaff with unquenchable fire." [18]And with many other words John exhorted the people and preached the good news to them.

[19]But when John rebuked Herod the tetrarch because of Herodias, his brother's wife, and all the other evil things he had done, [20]Herod added this to them all: He locked John up in prison.

The Baptism and Genealogy of Jesus

[21]When all the people were being baptised, Jesus was baptised too. And as he was praying, heaven was opened [22]and the Holy Spirit descended on him in bodily form like a dove. And a voice came from heaven: "You are my Son, whom I love; with you I am well pleased."

[23]Now Jesus himself was about thirty years old when he began his ministry. He was the son, so it was thought, of Joseph,

the son of Heli, [24]the son of Matthat,
the son of Levi, the son of Melki,
the son of Jannai, the son of Joseph,
[25]the son of Mattathias, the son of Amos,
the son of Nahum, the son of Esli,
the son of Naggai, [26]the son of Maath,
the son of Mattathias, the son of Semein,
the son of Josech, the son of Joda,
[27]the son of Joanan, the son of Rhesa,
the son of Zerubbabel, the son of Shealtiel,
the son of Neri, [28]the son of Melki,
the son of Addi, the son of Cosam,
the son of Elmadam, the son of Er,
[29]the son of Joshua, the son of Eliezer,
the son of Jorim, the son of Matthat,
the son of Levi, [30]the son of Simeon,
the son of Judah, the son of Joseph,
the son of Jonam, the son of Eliakim,
[31]the son of Melea, the son of Menna,
the son of Mattatha, the son of Nathan,
the son of David, [32]the son of Jesse,
the son of Obed, the son of Boaz,
the son of Salmon,[d] the son of Nahshon,
[33]the son of Amminadab, the son of Ram,[e]
the son of Hezron, the son of Perez,
the son of Judah, [34]the son of Jacob,
the son of Isaac, the son of Abraham,
the son of Terah, the son of Nahor,
[35]the son of Serug, the son of Reu,
the son of Peleg, the son of Eber,
the son of Shelah, [36]the son of Cainan,
the son of Arphaxad, the son of Shem,
the son of Noah, the son of Lamech,
[37]the son of Methuselah, the son of Enoch,
the son of Jared, the son of Mahalalel,
the son of Kenan, [38]the son of Enosh,
the son of Seth, the son of Adam,
the son of God.

The Temptation of Jesus

4 Jesus, full of the Holy Spirit, returned from the Jordan and was led by the Spirit in the desert, [2]where for forty days he was tempted by the devil. He ate nothing during those days, and at the end of them he was hungry.

[3]The devil said to him, "If you are the Son of God, tell this stone to become bread."

[4]Jesus answered, "It is written: 'Man does not live on bread alone.' [a]"

---

[a]6 Isaiah 40:3–5   [b]15 Or Messiah   [c]16 Or in   [d]32 Some early manuscripts Sala
[e]33 Some manuscripts Amminadab, the son of Admin, the son of Arni; other manuscripts vary widely.   [a]4 Deut. 8:3

5The devil led him up to a high place and showed him in an instant all the kingdoms of the world. 6And he said to him, "I will give you all their authority and splendour, for it has been given to me, and I can give it to anyone I want to. 7So if you worship me, it will all be yours."

8Jesus answered, "It is written: 'Worship the Lord your God and serve him only.'*b*"

9The devil led him to Jerusalem and had him stand on the highest point of the temple. "If you are the Son of God," he said, "throw yourself down from here. 10For it is written:

" 'He will command his angels concerning you
   to guard you carefully;
11they will lift you up in their hands,
   so that you will not strike your foot against a
      stone.'*c*"

12Jesus answered, "It says: 'Do not put the Lord your God to the test.'*d*"

13When the devil had finished all this tempting, he left him until an opportune time.

Jesus Rejected at Nazareth

14Jesus returned to Galilee in the power of the Spirit, and news about him spread through the whole countryside. 15He taught in their synagogues, and everyone praised him.

16He went to Nazareth, where he had been brought up, and on the Sabbath day he went into the synagogue, as was his custom. And he stood up to read. 17The scroll of the prophet Isaiah was handed to him. Unrolling it, he found the place where it is written:

18"The Spirit of the Lord is on me,
   because he has anointed me
   to preach good news to the poor.
He has sent me to proclaim freedom for the
      prisoners
   and recovery of sight for the blind,
   to release the oppressed,
19 to proclaim the year of the Lord's favour."*e*

4:18   As Luke told it, Jesus explained his manifesto (his intentions) the first time he preached in public. Like his mother's Magnificat, it was addressed to the poor, the oppressed, and the insignificant. They will be the first to recognize his gospel as good news.

20Then he rolled up the scroll, gave it back to the attendant and sat down. The eyes of everyone in the synagogue were fastened on him, 21and he began by saying to them, "Today this scripture is fulfilled in your hearing."

22All spoke well of him and were amazed at the gracious words that came from his lips. "Isn't this Joseph's son?" they asked.

23Jesus said to them, "Surely you will quote this proverb to me: 'Physician, heal yourself! Do here in your home town what we have heard that you did in Capernaum.' "

24"I tell you the truth," he continued, "no prophet is accepted in his home town. 25I assure you that there were many widows in Israel in Elijah's time, when the sky was shut for three and a half years and there was a severe famine throughout the land. 26Yet Elijah was not sent to any of them, but to a widow in Zarephath in the region of Sidon. 27And there were many in Israel with leprosy*f* in the time of Elisha the prophet, yet not one of them was cleansed — only Naaman the Syrian."

28All the people in the synagogue were furious when they heard this. 29They got up, drove him out of the town, and took him to the brow of the hill on which the town was built, in order to throw him down the cliff. 30But he walked right through the crowd and went on his way.

Jesus Drives Out an Evil Spirit

31Then he went down to Capernaum, a town in Galilee, and on the Sabbath began to teach the people. 32They were amazed at his teaching, because his message had authority.

33In the synagogue there was a man possessed by a demon, an evil*g* spirit. He cried out at the top of his voice, 34"Ha! What do you want with us, Jesus of Nazareth? Have you come to destroy us? I know who you are — the Holy One of God!"

35"Be quiet!" Jesus said sternly. "Come out of him!" Then the demon threw the man down before them all and came out without injuring him.

36All the people were amazed and said to each other, "What is this teaching? With authority and power he gives orders to evil spirits and they come out!" 37And the news about him spread throughout the surrounding area.

Jesus Heals Many

38Jesus left the synagogue and went to the home of Simon. Now Simon's mother-in-law was suffering from a high fever, and they asked Jesus to help her. 39So he bent over her and rebuked the fever, and it left her. She got up at once and began to wait on them.

40When the sun was setting, the people brought to Jesus all who had various kinds of sickness, and laying his hands on each one, he healed them. 41Moreover, demons came out of many people, shouting, "You are the Son of God!" But he rebuked them and would not allow them to speak, because they knew he was the Christ.*h*

42At daybreak Jesus went out to a solitary place. The people were looking for him and when they came to where he was, they tried to keep him from leaving them. 43But he said, "I must preach the good news of the kingdom of God to the other towns also, because that is why I was sent." 44And he kept on preaching in the synagogues of Judea.*i*

---

*b*8 Deut. 6:13   *c*11 Psalm 91:11,12   *d*12 Deut. 6:16   *e*19 Isaiah 61:1,2
*f*27 The Greek word was used for various diseases affecting the skin — not necessarily leprosy.   *g*33 Greek *unclean*; also in verse 36
*h*41 Or *Messiah*   *i*44 Or *the land of the Jews*; some manuscripts *Galilee*

The Calling of the First Disciples

5 One day as Jesus was standing by the Lake of Gennesaret,[a] with the people crowding round him and listening to the word of God, [2]he saw at the water's edge two boats, left there by the fishermen, who were washing their nets. [3]He got into one of the boats, the one belonging to Simon, and asked him to put out a little from shore. Then he sat down and taught the people from the boat.

[4]When he had finished speaking, he said to Simon, "Put out into deep water, and let down[b] the nets for a catch."

[5]Simon answered, "Master, we've worked hard all night and haven't caught anything. But because you say so, I will let down the nets."

[6]When they had done so, they caught such a large number of fish that their nets began to break. [7]So they signalled to their partners in the other boat to come and help them, and they came and filled both boats so full that they began to sink.

[8]When Simon Peter saw this, he fell at Jesus' knees and said, "Go away from me, Lord; I am a sinful man!" [9]For he and all his companions were astonished at the catch of fish they had taken, [10]and so were James and John, the sons of Zebedee, Simon's partners.

Then Jesus said to Simon, "Don't be afraid; from now on you will catch men." [11]So they pulled their boats up on shore, left everything and followed him.

The Man With Leprosy

[12]While Jesus was in one of the towns, a man came along who was covered with leprosy.[c] When he saw Jesus, he fell with his face to the ground and begged him, "Lord, if you are willing, you can make me clean."

[13]Jesus reached out his hand and touched the man. "I am willing," he said. "Be clean!" And immediately the leprosy left him.

[14]Then Jesus ordered him, "Don't tell anyone, but go, show yourself to the priest and offer the sacrifices that Moses commanded for your cleansing, as a testimony to them."

[15]Yet the news about him spread all the more, so that crowds of people came to hear him and to be healed of their sicknesses. [16]But Jesus often withdrew to lonely places and prayed.

Jesus Heals a Paralytic

[17]One day as he was teaching, Pharisees and teachers of the law, who had come from every village of Galilee and from Judea and Jerusalem, were sitting there. And the power of the Lord was present for him to heal the sick. [18]Some men came carrying a paralytic on a mat and tried to take him into the house to lay him before Jesus. [19]When they could not find a way to do this because of the crowd, they went up on the roof and lowered him on his mat through the tiles into the middle of the crowd, right in front of Jesus.

[20]When Jesus saw their faith, he said, "Friend, your sins are forgiven."

[21]The Pharisees and the teachers of the law began thinking to themselves, "Who is this fellow who speaks blasphemy? Who can forgive sins but God alone?"

[22]Jesus knew what they were thinking and asked, "Why are you thinking these things in your hearts? [23]Which is easier: to say, 'Your sins are forgiven,' or to say, 'Get up and walk'? [24]But that you may know that the Son of Man has authority on earth to forgive sins. . . ." He said to the paralysed man, "I tell you, get up, take your mat and go home." [25]Immediately he stood up in front of them, took what he had been lying on and went home praising God. [26]Everyone was amazed and gave praise to God. They were filled with awe and said, "We have seen remarkable things today."

The Calling of Levi

[27]After this, Jesus went out and saw a tax collector by the name of Levi sitting at his tax booth. "Follow me," Jesus said to him, [28]and Levi got up, left everything and followed him.

[29]Then Levi held a great banquet for Jesus at his house, and a large crowd of tax collectors and others were eating with them. [30]But the Pharisees and the teachers of the law who belonged to their sect complained to his disciples, "Why do you eat and drink with tax collectors and 'sinners'?"

[31]Jesus answered them, "It is not the healthy who need a doctor, but the sick. [32]I have not come to call the righteous, but sinners to repentance."

Jesus Questioned About Fasting

[33]They said to him, "John's disciples often fast and pray, and so do the disciples of the Pharisees, but yours go on eating and drinking."

[34]Jesus answered, "Can you make the guests of the bridegroom fast while he is with them? [35]But the time will come when the bridegroom will be taken from them; in those days they will fast."

[36]He told them this parable: "No-one tears a patch from a new garment and sews it on an old one. If he does, he will have torn the new garment, and the patch from the new will not match the old. [37]And no-one pours new wine into old wineskins. If he does, the new wine will burst the skins, the wine will run out and the wineskins will be ruined. [38]No, new wine must be poured into new wineskins. [39]And no-one after drinking old wine wants the new, for he says, 'The old is better.' "

Lord of the Sabbath

6 One Sabbath Jesus was going through the cornfields, and his disciples began to pick some ears of corn, rub them in their hands and eat the grain. [2]Some of the Pharisees asked, "Why are you doing what is unlawful on the Sabbath?"

[3]Jesus answered them, "Have you never read what David did when he and his companions were hungry? [4]He entered the house of God, and taking the

a[1] That is, Sea of Galilee   b[4] The Greek verb is plural.
c[12] The Greek word was used for various diseases affecting the skin—not necessarily leprosy.

consecrated bread, he ate what is lawful only for priests to eat. And he also gave some to his companions." [5]Then Jesus said to them, "The Son of Man is Lord of the Sabbath."

[6]On another Sabbath he went into the synagogue and was teaching, and a man was there whose right hand was shrivelled. [7]The Pharisees and the teachers of the law were looking for a reason to accuse Jesus, so they watched him closely to see if he would heal on the Sabbath. [8]But Jesus knew what they were thinking and said to the man with the shrivelled hand, "Get up and stand in front of everyone." So he got up and stood there.

[9]Then Jesus said to them, "I ask you, which is lawful on the Sabbath: to do good or to do evil, to save life or to destroy it?"

[10]He looked round at them all, and then said to the man, "Stretch out your hand." He did so, and his hand was completely restored. [11]But they were furious and began to discuss with one another what they might do to Jesus.

The Twelve Apostles

[12]One of those days Jesus went out to a mountainside to pray, and spent the night praying to God. [13]When morning came, he called his disciples to him and chose twelve of them, whom he also designated apostles: [14]Simon (whom he named Peter), his brother Andrew, James, John, Philip, Bartholomew, [15]Matthew, Thomas, James son of Alphaeus, Simon who was called the Zealot, [16]Judas son of James, and Judas Iscariot, who became a traitor.

6:12   Luke presented Jesus as a man of prayer more than the other Gospel writers did. At all the key moments of his life he turned to his Father in prayer. In Acts we see how his first disciples put this into practice.

Blessings and Woes

[17]He went down with them and stood on a level place. A large crowd of his disciples was there and a great number of people from all over Judea, from Jerusalem, and from the coast of Tyre and Sidon, [18]who had come to hear him and to be healed of their diseases. Those troubled by evil[a] spirits were cured, [19]and the people all tried to touch him, because power was coming from him and healing them all.

[20]Looking at his disciples, he said:

"Blessed are you who are poor,
   for yours is the kingdom of God.
[21]Blessed are you who hunger now,
   for you will be satisfied.
Blessed are you who weep now,
   for you will laugh.
[22]Blessed are you when men hate you,
   when they exclude you and insult you
   and reject your name as evil,
   because of the Son of Man.

[23]"Rejoice in that day and leap for joy, because great is your reward in heaven. For that is how their fathers treated the prophets.

[24]"But woe to you who are rich,
   for you have already received your comfort.
[25]Woe to you who are well fed now,
   for you will go hungry.
Woe to you who laugh now,
   for you will mourn and weep.
[26]Woe to you when all men speak well of you,
   for that is how their fathers treated the false
      prophets.

Love for Enemies

[27]"But I tell you who hear me: Love your enemies, do good to those who hate you, [28]bless those who curse you, pray for those who ill-treat you. [29]If someone strikes you on one cheek, turn to him the other also. If someone takes your cloak, do not stop him from taking your tunic. [30]Give to everyone who asks you, and if anyone takes what belongs to you, do not demand it back. [31]Do to others as you would have them do to you.

6:27   In a country under occupation by enemy troops, Jesus' command, "Love your enemies" must have come as a great shock. Yet the God whom Jesus knew was totally undiscriminating in his love. His kingdom cannot be established unless people treat everyone with compassion, regardless of who they are or what they have done.

---

[32]"If you love those who love you, what credit is that to you? Even 'sinners' love those who love them. [33]And if you do good to those who are good to you, what credit is that to you? Even 'sinners' do that. [34]And if you lend to those from whom you expect repayment, what credit is that to you? Even 'sinners' lend to 'sinners', expecting to be repaid in full. [35]But love your enemies, do good to them, and lend to them without expecting to get anything back. Then your reward will be great, and you will be sons of the Most High, because he is kind to the ungrateful and wicked. [36]Be merciful, just as your Father is merciful.

Judging Others

[37]"Do not judge, and you will not be judged. Do not condemn, and you will not be condemned. Forgive, and you will be forgiven. [38]Give, and it will be given to you. A good measure, pressed down, shaken together and running over, will be poured into your lap. For with the measure you use, it will be measured to you."

[39]He also told them this parable: "Can a blind man lead a blind man? Will they not both fall into a pit? [40]A student is not above his teacher, but everyone who is fully trained will be like his teacher. [41]"Why do you look at the speck of sawdust in your brother's eye and pay no attention to the plank in your

---

[a]18 Greek *unclean*

own eye? [42]How can you say to your brother, 'Brother, let me take the speck out of your eye,' when you yourself fail to see the plank in your own eye? You hypocrite, first take the plank out of your eye, and then you will see clearly to remove the speck from your brother's eye.

A Tree and Its Fruit

[43]"No good tree bears bad fruit, nor does a bad tree bear good fruit. [44]Each tree is recognised by its own fruit. People do not pick figs from thorn-bushes, or grapes from briers. [45]The good man brings good things out of the good stored up in his heart, and the evil man brings evil things out of the evil stored up in his heart. For out of the overflow of his heart his mouth speaks.

The Wise and Foolish Builders

[46]"Why do you call me, 'Lord, Lord,' and do not do what I say? [47]I will show you what he is like who comes to me and hears my words and puts them into practice. [48]He is like a man building a house, who dug down deep and laid the foundation on rock. When the flood came, the torrent struck that house but could not shake it, because it was well built. [49]But the one who hears my words and does not put them into practice is like a man who built a house on the ground without a foundation. The moment the torrent struck that house, it collapsed and its destruction was complete."

The Faith of the Centurion

7 When Jesus had finished saying all this in the hearing of the people, he entered Capernaum. [2]There a centurion's servant, whom his master valued highly, was sick and about to die. [3]The centurion heard of Jesus and sent some elders of the Jews to him, asking him to come and heal his servant. [4]When they came to Jesus, they pleaded earnestly with him, "This man deserves to have you do this, [5]because he loves our nation and has built our synagogue." [6]So Jesus went with them.

He was not far from the house when the centurion sent friends to say to him: "Lord, don't trouble yourself, for I do not deserve to have you come under my roof. [7]That is why I did not even consider myself worthy to come to you. But say the word, and my servant will be healed. [8]For I myself am a man under authority, with soldiers under me. I tell this one, 'Go', and he goes; and that one, 'Come', and he comes. I say to my servant, 'Do this', and he does it."

[9]When Jesus heard this, he was amazed at him, and turning to the crowd following him, he said, "I tell you, I have not found such great faith even in Israel." [10]Then the men who had been sent returned to the house and found the servant well.

Jesus Raises a Widow's Son

[11]Soon afterwards, Jesus went to a town called Nain, and his disciples and a large crowd went along with him. [12]As he approached the town gate, a dead person was being carried out—the only son of his mother, and she was a widow. And a large crowd from the town was with her. [13]When the Lord saw her, his heart went out to her and he said, "Don't cry."

[14]Then he went up and touched the coffin, and those carrying it stood still. He said, "Young man, I say to you, get up!" [15]The dead man sat up and began to talk, and Jesus gave him back to his mother.

[16]They were all filled with awe and praised God. "A great prophet has appeared among us," they said. "God has come to help his people." [17]This news about Jesus spread throughout Judea[a] and the surrounding country.

Jesus and John the Baptist

[18]John's disciples told him about all these things. Calling two of them, [19]he sent them to the Lord to ask, "Are you the one who was to come, or should we expect someone else?"

[20]When the men came to Jesus, they said, "John the Baptist sent us to you to ask, 'Are you the one who was to come, or should we expect someone else?' "

[21]At that very time Jesus cured many who had diseases, sicknesses and evil spirits, and gave sight to many who were blind. [22]So he replied to the messengers, "Go back and report to John what you have seen and heard: The blind receive sight, the lame walk, those who have leprosy[b] are cured, the deaf hear, the dead are raised, and the good news is preached to the poor. [23]Blessed is the man who does not fall away on account of me."

[24]After John's messengers left, Jesus began to speak to the crowd about John: "What did you go out into the desert to see? A reed swayed by the wind? [25]If not, what did you go out to see? A man dressed in fine clothes? No, those who wear expensive clothes and indulge in luxury are in palaces. [26]But what did you go out to see? A prophet? Yes, I tell you, and more than a prophet. [27]This is the one about whom it is written:

" 'I will send my messenger ahead of you,
    who will prepare your way before you.'[c]

[28]I tell you, among those born of women there is no-one greater than John; yet the one who is least in the kingdom of God is greater than he."

([29]All the people, even the tax collectors, when they heard Jesus' words, acknowledged that God's way was right, because they had been baptised by John. [30]But the Pharisees and experts in the law rejected God's purpose for themselves, because they had not been baptised by John.)

[31]"To what, then, can I compare the people of this generation? What are they like? [32]They are like children sitting in the market-place and calling out to each other:

" 'We played the flute for you,
    and you did not dance;
  we sang a dirge,
    and you did not cry.'

[33]For John the Baptist came neither eating bread nor

---

[a]17 Or the land of the Jews   [b]22 The Greek word was used for various diseases affecting the skin—not necessarily leprosy.
[c]27 Mal. 3:1

drinking wine, and you say, 'He has a demon.' 34The Son of Man came eating and drinking, and you say, 'Here is a glutton and a drunkard, a friend of tax collectors and "sinners".' 35But wisdom is proved right by all her children."

Jesus Anointed by a Sinful Woman

36Now one of the Pharisees invited Jesus to have dinner with him, so he went to the Pharisee's house and reclined at the table. 37When a woman who had lived a sinful life in that town learned that Jesus was eating at the Pharisee's house, she brought an alabaster jar of perfume, 38and as she stood behind him at his feet weeping, she began to wet his feet with her tears. Then she wiped them with her hair, kissed them and poured perfume on them.

39When the Pharisee who had invited him saw this, he said to himself, "If this man were a prophet, he would know who is touching him and what kind of woman she is—that she is a sinner."

40Jesus answered him, "Simon, I have something to tell you."

"Tell me, teacher," he said.

41"Two men owed money to a certain moneylender. One owed him five hundred denarii,d and the other fifty. 42Neither of them had the money to pay him back, so he cancelled the debts of both. Now which of them will love him more?"

43Simon replied, "I suppose the one who had the bigger debt cancelled."

"You have judged correctly," Jesus said.

44Then he turned towards the woman and said to Simon, "Do you see this woman? I came into your house. You did not give me any water for my feet, but she wet my feet with her tears and wiped them with her hair. 45You did not give me a kiss, but this woman, from the time I entered, has not stopped kissing my feet. 46You did not put oil on my head, but she has poured perfume on my feet. 47Therefore, I tell you, her many sins have been forgiven—for she loved much. But he who has been forgiven little loves little."

48Then Jesus said to her, "Your sins are forgiven."

49The other guests began to say among themselves, "Who is this who even forgives sins?"

50Jesus said to the woman, "Your faith has saved you; go in peace."

The Parable of the Sower

8 After this, Jesus travelled about from one town and village to another, proclaiming the good news of the kingdom of God. The Twelve were with him, 2and also some women who had been cured of evil spirits and diseases: Mary (called Magdalene) from whom seven demons had come out; 3Joanna the wife of Chuza, the manager of Herod's household; Susanna; and many others. These women were helping to support them out of their own means.

4While a large crowd was gathering and people were coming to Jesus from town after town, he told this parable: 5"A farmer went out to sow his seed. As he was scattering the seed, some fell along the path; it was trampled on, and the birds of the air ate it up. 6Some fell on rock, and when it came up, the plants withered because they had no moisture. 7Other seed fell among thorns, which grew up with it and choked the plants. 8Still other seed fell on good soil. It came up and yielded a crop, a hundred times more than was sown."

When he said this, he called out, "He who has ears to hear, let him hear."

9His disciples asked him what this parable meant. 10He said, "The knowledge of the secrets of the kingdom of God has been given to you, but to others I speak in parables, so that,

" 'though seeing, they may not see;
though hearing, they may not understand.'a

11"This is the meaning of the parable: The seed is the word of God. 12Those along the path are the ones who hear, and then the devil comes and takes away the word from their hearts, so that they may not believe and be saved. 13Those on the rock are the ones who receive the word with joy when they hear it, but they have no root. They believe for a while, but in the time of testing they fall away. 14The seed that fell among thorns stands for those who hear, but as they go on their way they are choked by life's worries, riches and pleasures, and they do not mature. 15But the seed on good soil stands for those with a noble and good heart, who hear the word, retain it, and by persevering produce a crop.

8:11   The explanation of the parable has a pessimistic flavour, as if only a part of what is sown bears fruit. Yet Jesus' own telling of it must have been much more optimistic—as sowing is in real life. The losses a farmer suffers in sowing are compensated for by the abundant harvest; if they weren't, all farmers would stop sowing. This parable is not simply a lesson in perseverance either. The seed is the word which God has always sown abundantly and generously, and as a result it has had unending success in spreading.

A Lamp on a Stand

16"No-one lights a lamp and hides it in a jar or puts it under a bed. Instead, he puts it on a stand, so that those who come in can see the light. 17For there is nothing hidden that will not be disclosed, and nothing concealed that will not be known or brought out into the open. 18Therefore consider carefully how you listen. Whoever has will be given more; whoever does not have, even what he thinks he has will be taken from him."

Jesus' Mother and Brothers

19Now Jesus' mother and brothers came to see him, but they were not able to get near him because of the

---

d41 A denarius was a coin worth about a day's wages.   a10 Isaiah 6:9

crowd. [20]Someone told him, "Your mother and brothers are standing outside, wanting to see you."

[21]He replied, "My mother and brothers are those who hear God's word and put it into practice."

Jesus Calms the Storm

[22]One day Jesus said to his disciples, "Let's go over to the other side of the lake." So they got into a boat and set out. [23]As they sailed, he fell asleep. A squall came down on the lake, so that the boat was being swamped, and they were in great danger.

[24]The disciples went and woke him, saying, "Master, Master, we're going to drown!"

He got up and rebuked the wind and the raging waters; the storm subsided, and all was calm. [25]"Where is your faith?" he asked his disciples.

In fear and amazement they asked one another, "Who is this? He commands even the winds and the water, and they obey him."

The Healing of a Demon-possessed Man

[26]They sailed to the region of the Gerasenes,[b] which is across the lake from Galilee. [27]When Jesus stepped ashore, he was met by a demon-possessed man from the town. For a long time this man had not worn clothes or lived in a house, but had lived in the tombs. [28]When he saw Jesus, he cried out and fell at his feet, shouting at the top of his voice, "What do you want with me, Jesus, Son of the Most High God? I beg you, don't torture me!" [29]For Jesus had commanded the evil[c] spirit to come out of the man. Many times it had seized him, and though he was chained hand and foot and kept under guard, he had broken his chains and had been driven by the demon into solitary places.

[30]Jesus asked him, "What is your name?"

"Legion," he replied, because many demons had gone into him. [31]And they begged him repeatedly not to order them to go into the Abyss.

[32]A large herd of pigs was feeding there on the hillside. The demons begged Jesus to let them go into them, and he gave them permission. [33]When the demons came out of the man, they went into the pigs, and the herd rushed down the steep bank into the lake and was drowned.

[34]When those tending the pigs saw what had happened, they ran off and reported this in the town and countryside, [35]and the people went out to see what had happened. When they came to Jesus, they found the man from whom the demons had gone out, sitting at Jesus' feet, dressed and in his right mind; and they were afraid. [36]Those who had seen it told the people how the demon-possessed man had been cured. [37]Then all the people of the region of the Gerasenes asked Jesus to leave them, because they were overcome with fear. So he got into the boat and left.

[38]The man from whom the demons had gone out begged to go with him, but Jesus sent him away, saying, [39]"Return home and tell how much God has done for you." So the man went away and told all over the town how much Jesus had done for him.

A Dead Girl and a Sick Woman

[40]Now when Jesus returned, a crowd welcomed him, for they were all expecting him. [41]Then a man named Jairus, a ruler of the synagogue, came and fell at Jesus' feet, pleading with him to come to his house [42]because his only daughter, a girl of about twelve, was dying.

As Jesus was on his way, the crowds almost crushed him. [43]And a woman was there who had been subject to bleeding for twelve years,[d] but no-one could heal her. [44]She came up behind him and touched the edge of his cloak, and immediately her bleeding stopped.

[45]"Who touched me?" Jesus asked.

When they all denied it, Peter said, "Master, the people are crowding and pressing against you."

[46]But Jesus said, "Someone touched me; I know that power has gone out from me."

[47]Then the woman, seeing that she could not go unnoticed, came trembling and fell at his feet. In the presence of all the people, she told why she had touched him and how she had been instantly healed. [48]Then he said to her, "Daughter, your faith has healed you. Go in peace."

[49]While Jesus was still speaking, someone came from the house of Jairus, the synagogue ruler. "Your daughter is dead," he said. "Don't bother the teacher any more."

[50]Hearing this, Jesus said to Jairus, "Don't be afraid; just believe, and she will be healed."

[51]When he arrived at the house of Jairus, he did not let anyone go in with him except Peter, John and James, and the child's father and mother. [52]Meanwhile, all the people were wailing and mourning for her. "Stop wailing," Jesus said. "She is not dead but asleep."

[53]They laughed at him, knowing that she was dead. [54]But he took her by the hand and said, "My child, get up!" [55]Her spirit returned, and at once she stood up. Then Jesus told them to give her something to eat. [56]Her parents were astonished, but he ordered them not to tell anyone what had happened.

Jesus Sends Out the Twelve

9 When Jesus had called the Twelve together, he gave them power and authority to drive out all demons and to cure diseases, [2]and he sent them out to preach the kingdom of God and to heal the sick. [3]He told them: "Take nothing for the journey — no staff, no bag, no bread, no money, no extra tunic. [4]Whatever house you enter, stay there until you leave that town. [5]If people do not welcome you, shake the dust off your feet when you leave their town, as a testimony against them." [6]So they set out and went from village to village, preaching the gospel and healing people everywhere.

[7]Now Herod the tetrarch heard about all that was going on. And he was perplexed, because some were saying that John had been raised from the dead, [8]others that Elijah had appeared, and still others that one of the prophets of long ago had come back to life. [9]But Herod

---

[b]26 Some manuscripts *Gadarenes*; other manuscripts *Gergesenes*; also in verse 37
[d]43 Many manuscripts *years, and she had spent all she had on doctors*
[c]29 Greek *unclean*

said, "I beheaded John. Who, then, is this I hear such things about?" And he tried to see him.

Jesus Feeds the Five Thousand

[10]When the apostles returned, they reported to Jesus what they had done. Then he took them with him and they withdrew by themselves to a town called Bethsaida, [11]but the crowds learned about it and followed him. He welcomed them and spoke to them about the kingdom of God, and healed those who needed healing.

[12]Late in the afternoon the Twelve came to him and said, "Send the crowd away so they can go to the surrounding villages and countryside and find food and lodging, because we are in a remote place here."

[13]He replied, "You give them something to eat."

They answered, "We have only five loaves of bread and two fish — unless we go and buy food for all this crowd." [14](About five thousand men were there.)

9:13   Whether it happened once or twice, what is the reality behind the feeding of the thousands? Was it really a case of magical multiplication? Did Jesus have a store of bread secretly available in the desert? Were people shamed into sharing the sandwiches they had brought so that there was enough for everyone? Did Jesus literally break each loaf into a thousand pieces and in the circumstances everyone felt satisfied? The truth is that the evidence we possess no longer allows us to tell. What is important is that no one would tell such a story of someone *unable* to satisfy the hunger of thousands.

But he said to his disciples, "Make them sit down in groups of about fifty each." [15]The disciples did so, and everybody sat down. [16]Taking the five loaves and the two fish and looking up to heaven, he gave thanks and broke them. Then he gave them to the disciples to set before the people. [17]They all ate and were satisfied, and the disciples picked up twelve basketfuls of broken pieces that were left over.

Peter's Confession of Christ

[18]Once when Jesus was praying in private and his disciples were with him, he asked them, "Who do the crowds say I am?"

[19]They replied, "Some say John the Baptist; others say Elijah; and still others, that one of the prophets of long ago has come back to life."

[20]"But what about you?" he asked. "Who do you say I am?"

Peter answered, "The Christ[a] of God."

[21]Jesus strictly warned them not to tell this to anyone. [22]And he said, "The Son of Man must suffer many things and be rejected by the elders, chief priests and teachers of the law, and he must be killed and on the third day be raised to life."

[23]Then he said to them all: "If anyone would come after me, he must deny himself and take up his cross daily and follow me. [24]For whoever wants to save his life will lose it, but whoever loses his life for me will save it. [25]What good is it for a man to gain the whole world, and yet lose or forfeit his very self? [26]If anyone is ashamed of me and my words, the Son of Man will be ashamed of him when he comes in his glory and in the glory of the Father and of the holy angels. [27]I tell you the truth, some who are standing here will not taste death before they see the kingdom of God."

The Transfiguration

[28]About eight days after Jesus said this, he took Peter, John and James with him and went up onto a mountain to pray. [29]As he was praying, the appearance of his face changed, and his clothes became as bright as a flash of lightning. [30]Two men, Moses and Elijah, [31]appeared in glorious splendour, talking with Jesus. They spoke about his departure, which he was about to bring to fulfilment at Jerusalem. [32]Peter and his companions were very sleepy, but when they became fully awake, they saw his glory and the two men standing with him. [33]As the men were leaving Jesus, Peter said to him, "Master, it is good for us to be here. Let us put up three shelters — one for you, one for Moses and one for Elijah." (He did not know what he was saying.)

9:29   Jesus was seen in a brilliant light, like the glory of heaven, in this remarkable experience on the mountain. Luke's observation that it happened to Jesus as "he was praying" almost suggests that it could happen to anyone else who prayed.

---

[34]While he was speaking, a cloud appeared and enveloped them, and they were afraid as they entered the cloud. [35]A voice came from the cloud, saying, "This is my Son, whom I have chosen; listen to him." [36]When the voice had spoken, they found that Jesus was alone. The disciples kept this to themselves, and told no-one at that time what they had seen.

The Healing of a Boy With an Evil Spirit

[37]The next day, when they came down from the mountain, a large crowd met him. [38]A man in the crowd called out, "Teacher, I beg you to look at my son, for he is my only child. [39]A spirit seizes him and he suddenly screams; it throws him into convulsions so that he foams at the mouth. It scarcely ever leaves him and is destroying him. [40]I begged your disciples to drive it out, but they could not."

[41]"O unbelieving and perverse generation," Jesus replied, "how long shall I stay with you and put up with you? Bring your son here."

[42]Even while the boy was coming, the demon threw him to the ground in a convulsion. But Jesus rebuked the evil[b] spirit, healed the boy and gave him back to his father. [43]And they were all amazed at the greatness of God.

---

[a]20 Or *Messiah*   [b]42 Greek *unclean*

While everyone was marvelling at all that Jesus did, he said to his disciples, 44"Listen carefully to what I am about to tell you: The Son of Man is going to be betrayed into the hands of men." 45But they did not understand what this meant. It was hidden from them, so that they did not grasp it, and they were afraid to ask him about it.

Who Will Be the Greatest?

46An argument started among the disciples as to which of them would be the greatest. 47Jesus, knowing their thoughts, took a little child and made him stand beside him. 48Then he said to them, "Whoever welcomes this little child in my name welcomes me; and whoever welcomes me welcomes the one who sent me. For he who is least among you all — he is the greatest."

49"Master," said John, "we saw a man driving out demons in your name and we tried to stop him, because he is not one of us."

50"Do not stop him," Jesus said, "for whoever is not against you is for you."

Samaritan Opposition

51As the time approached for him to be taken up to heaven, Jesus resolutely set out for Jerusalem. 52And he sent messengers on ahead, who went into a Samaritan village to get things ready for him; 53but the people there did not welcome him, because he was heading for Jerusalem. 54When the disciples James and John saw this, they asked, "Lord, do you want us to call fire down from heaven to destroy them?"*c* 55But Jesus turned and rebuked them, 56and*d* they went to another village.

9:51   Jesus' mystical experience on the mountain, according to Luke, had been to do with his departure (Greek "exodus") in Jerusalem (9:31). What would happen to him there would bring about another sort of freedom for God's people. Hence his resolute journey. The theme is continued in Luke, with repeated reminders, over the next ten chapters.

The Cost of Following Jesus

57As they were walking along the road, a man said to him, "I will follow you wherever you go."

58Jesus replied, "Foxes have holes and birds of the air have nests, but the Son of Man has nowhere to lay his head."

59He said to another man, "Follow me."

But the man replied, "Lord, first let me go and bury my father."

60Jesus said to him, "Let the dead bury their own dead, but you go and proclaim the kingdom of God."

61Still another said, "I will follow you, Lord; but first let me go back and say good-bye to my family."

62Jesus replied, "No-one who puts his hand to the plough and looks back is fit for service in the kingdom of God."

Jesus Sends Out the Seventy-two

10 After this the Lord appointed seventy-two*a* others and sent them two by two ahead of him to every town and place where he was about to go. 2He told them, "The harvest is plentiful, but the workers are few. Ask the Lord of the harvest, therefore, to send out workers into his harvest field. 3Go! I am sending you out like lambs among wolves. 4Do not take a purse or bag or sandals; and do not greet anyone on the road.

5"When you enter a house, first say, 'Peace to this house.' 6If a man of peace is there, your peace will rest on him; if not, it will return to you. 7Stay in that house, eating and drinking whatever they give you, for the worker deserves his wages. Do not move around from house to house.

8"When you enter a town and are welcomed, eat what is set before you. 9Heal the sick who are there and tell them, 'The kingdom of God is near you.' 10But when you enter a town and are not welcomed, go into its streets and say, 11'Even the dust of your town that sticks to our feet we wipe off against you. Yet be sure of this: The kingdom of God is near.' 12I tell you, it will be more bearable on that day for Sodom than for that town.

13"Woe to you, Korazin! Woe to you, Bethsaida! For if the miracles that were performed in you had been performed in Tyre and Sidon, they would have repented long ago, sitting in sackcloth and ashes. 14But it will be more bearable for Tyre and Sidon at the judgment than for you. 15And you, Capernaum, will you be lifted up to the skies? No, you will go down to the depths.*b*

16"He who listens to you listens to me; he who rejects you rejects me; but he who rejects me rejects him who sent me."

17The seventy-two returned with joy and said, "Lord, even the demons submit to us in your name."

18He replied, "I saw Satan fall like lightning from heaven. 19I have given you authority to trample on snakes and scorpions and to overcome all the power of the enemy; nothing will harm you. 20However, do not rejoice that the spirits submit to you, but rejoice that your names are written in heaven."

21At that time Jesus, full of joy through the Holy Spirit, said, "I praise you, Father, Lord of heaven and earth, because you have hidden these things from the wise and learned, and revealed them to little children. Yes, Father, for this was your good pleasure.

22"All things have been committed to me by my Father. No-one knows who the Son is except the Father, and no-one knows who the Father is except the Son and those to whom the Son chooses to reveal him."

23Then he turned to his disciples and said privately, "Blessed are the eyes that see what you see. 24For I tell

---

c54 Some manuscripts *them, even as Elijah did*
d55,56 Some manuscripts *them. And he said, "You do not know what kind of spirit you are of, for the Son of Man did not come to destroy men's lives, but to save them." 56And*   *a1* Some manuscripts *seventy*; also in verse 17   *b15* Greek *Hades*

you that many prophets and kings wanted to see what you see but did not see it, and to hear what you hear but did not hear it."

The Parable of the Good Samaritan

25On one occasion an expert in the law stood up to test Jesus. "Teacher," he asked, "what must I do to inherit eternal life?"

26"What is written in the Law?" he replied. "How do you read it?"

27He answered: " 'Love the Lord your God with all your heart and with all your soul and with all your strength and with all your mind';c and, 'Love your neighbour as yourself.'d"

10:27 Luke's parable, read superficially, is a simple lesson in neighbourliness. But Jesus would not have needed to use a priest or Levite, less still a despised Samaritan heretic, if that was all it was about. His point was that neighbourly love is more likely to arise from ordinary human feeling than from religion which is tied up with taboos (touching dead bodies made these people ritually impure). Followers of Jesus often need to break religious taboos.

28"You have answered correctly," Jesus replied. "Do this and you will live."

29But he wanted to justify himself, so he asked Jesus, "And who is my neighbour?"

30In reply Jesus said: "A man was going down from Jerusalem to Jericho, when he fell into the hands of robbers. They stripped him of his clothes, beat him and went away, leaving him half-dead. 31A priest happened to be going down the same road, and when he saw the man, he passed by on the other side. 32So too, a Levite, when he came to the place and saw him, passed by on the other side. 33But a Samaritan, as he travelled, came where the man was; and when he saw him, he took pity on him. 34He went to him and bandaged his wounds, pouring on oil and wine. Then he put the man on his own donkey, brought him to an inn and took care of him. 35The next day he took out two silver coinse and gave them to the innkeeper. 'Look after him,' he said, 'and when I return, I will reimburse you for any extra expense you may have.'

36"Which of these three do you think was a neighbour to the man who fell into the hands of robbers?"

37The expert in the law replied, "The one who had mercy on him."

Jesus told him, "Go and do likewise."

At the Home of Martha and Mary

38As Jesus and his disciples were on their way, he came to a village where a woman named Martha opened her home to him. 39She had a sister called Mary, who sat at the Lord's feet listening to what he said. 40But Martha was distracted by all the preparations that had to be made. She came to him and asked, "Lord, don't you care that my sister has left me to do the work by myself? Tell her to help me!"

41"Martha, Martha," the Lord answered, "you are worried and upset about many things, 42but only one thing is needed.f Mary has chosen what is better, and it will not be taken away from her."

Jesus' Teaching on Prayer

11 One day Jesus was praying in a certain place. When he finished, one of his disciples said to him, "Lord, teach us to pray, just as John taught his disciples."

2He said to them, "When you pray, say:

" 'Father,a
hallowed be your name,
your kingdom come.b
3Give us each day our daily bread.
4Forgive us our sins,
for we also forgive everyone who sins against us.c
And lead us not into temptation.' "d

5Then he said to them, "Suppose one of you has a friend, and he goes to him at midnight and says, 'Friend, lend me three loaves of bread, 6because a friend of mine on a journey has come to me, and I have nothing to set before him.'

7"Then the one inside answers, 'Don't bother me. The door is already locked, and my children are with me in bed. I can't get up and give you anything.' 8I tell you, though he will not get up and give him the bread because he is his friend, yet because of the man's boldnesse he will get up and give him as much as he needs.

9"So I say to you: Ask and it will be given to you; seek and you will find; knock and the door will be opened to you. 10For everyone who asks receives; he who seeks finds; and to him who knocks, the door will be opened.

11"Which of you fathers, if your son asks forf a fish, will give him a snake instead? 12Or if he asks for an egg, will give him a scorpion? 13If you then, though you are evil, know how to give good gifts to your children, how much more will your Father in heaven give the Holy Spirit to those who ask him!"

Jesus and Beelzebub

14Jesus was driving out a demon that was mute. When the demon left, the man who had been mute spoke, and the crowd was amazed. 15But some of them

---

c27 Deut. 6:5   d27 Lev. 19:18   e35 Greek *two denarii*
f42 Some manuscripts *but few things are needed—or only one*   a2 Some manuscripts *Our Father in heaven*
b2 Some manuscripts *come. May your will be done on earth as it is in heaven.*   c4 Greek *everyone who is indebted to us*
d4 Some manuscripts *temptation but deliver us from the evil one*   e8 Or *persistence*
f11 Some manuscripts *for bread, will give him a stone; or if he asks for*

said, "By Beelzebub,⁸ the prince of demons, he is driving out demons." ¹⁶Others tested him by asking for a sign from heaven.

¹⁷Jesus knew their thoughts and said to them: "Any kingdom divided against itself will be ruined, and a house divided against itself will fall. ¹⁸If Satan is divided against himself, how can his kingdom stand? I say this because you claim that I drive out demons by Beelzebub. ¹⁹Now if I drive out demons by Beelzebub, by whom do your followers drive them out? So then, they will be your judges. ²⁰But if I drive out demons by the finger of God, then the kingdom of God has come to you.

²¹"When a strong man, fully armed, guards his own house, his possessions are safe. ²²But when someone stronger attacks and overpowers him, he takes away the armour in which the man trusted and divides up the spoils.

²³"He who is not with me is against me, and he who does not gather with me, scatters.

²⁴"When an evil ʰ spirit comes out of a man, it goes through arid places seeking rest and does not find it. Then it says, 'I will return to the house I left.' ²⁵When it arrives, it finds the house swept clean and put in order. ²⁶Then it goes and takes seven other spirits more wicked than itself, and they go in and live there. And the final condition of that man is worse than the first."

²⁷As Jesus was saying these things, a woman in the crowd called out, "Blessed is the mother who gave you birth and nursed you."

²⁸He replied, "Blessed rather are those who hear the word of God and obey it."

The Sign of Jonah

²⁹As the crowds increased, Jesus said, "This is a wicked generation. It asks for a miraculous sign, but none will be given it except the sign of Jonah. ³⁰For as Jonah was a sign to the Ninevites, so also will the Son of Man be to this generation. ³¹The Queen of the South will rise at the judgment with the men of this generation and condemn them; for she came from the ends of the earth to listen to Solomon's wisdom, and now one ⁱ greater than Solomon is here. ³²The men of Nineveh will stand up at the judgment with this generation and condemn it; for they repented at the preaching of Jonah, and now one greater than Jonah is here.

The Lamp of the Body

³³"No-one lights a lamp and puts it in a place where it will be hidden, or under a bowl. Instead he puts it on its stand, so that those who come in may see the light. ³⁴Your eye is the lamp of your body. When your eyes are good, your whole body also is full of light. But when they are bad, your body also is full of darkness. ³⁵See to it, then, that the light within you is not darkness. ³⁶Therefore, if your whole body is full of light, and no part of it dark, it will be completely lighted, as when the light of a lamp shines on you."

Six Woes

³⁷When Jesus had finished speaking, a Pharisee invited him to eat with him; so he went in and reclined at the table. ³⁸But the Pharisee, noticing that Jesus did not first wash before the meal, was surprised.

³⁹Then the Lord said to him, "Now then, you Pharisees clean the outside of the cup and dish, but inside you are full of greed and wickedness. ⁴⁰You foolish people! Did not the one who made the outside make the inside also? ⁴¹But give what is inside ₍the dish,ʲ to the poor, and everything will be clean for you.

⁴²"Woe to you Pharisees, because you give God a tenth of your mint, rue and all other kinds of garden herbs, but you neglect justice and the love of God. You should have practised the latter without leaving the former undone.

⁴³"Woe to you Pharisees, because you love the most important seats in the synagogues and greetings in the market-places.

⁴⁴"Woe to you, because you are like unmarked graves, which men walk over without knowing it."

⁴⁵One of the experts in the law answered him, "Teacher, when you say these things, you insult us also."

⁴⁶Jesus replied, "And you experts in the law, woe to you, because you load people down with burdens they can hardly carry, and you yourselves will not lift one finger to help them.

⁴⁷"Woe to you, because you build tombs for the prophets, and it was your forefathers who killed them. ⁴⁸So you testify that you approve of what your forefathers did; they killed the prophets, and you build their tombs. ⁴⁹Because of this, God in his wisdom said, 'I will send them prophets and apostles, some of whom they will kill and others they will persecute.' ⁵⁰Therefore this generation will be held responsible for the blood of all the prophets that has been shed since the beginning of the world, ⁵¹from the blood of Abel to the blood of Zechariah, who was killed between the altar and the sanctuary. Yes, I tell you, this generation will be held responsible for it all.

⁵²"Woe to you experts in the law, because you have taken away the key to knowledge. You yourselves have not entered, and you have hindered those who were entering."

⁵³When Jesus left there, the Pharisees and the teachers of the law began to oppose him fiercely and to besiege him with questions, ⁵⁴waiting to catch him in something he might say.

Warnings and Encouragements

12 Meanwhile, when a crowd of many thousands had gathered, so that they were trampling on one another, Jesus began to speak first to his disciples, saying: "Be on your guard against the yeast of the Pharisees, which is hypocrisy. ²There is nothing concealed that will not be disclosed, or hidden that will not be made known. ³What you have said in the dark will be heard in the daylight, and what you have whispered in

---

⁸15 Greek *Beezeboul* or *Beelzeboul*; also in verses 18 and 19   ʰ24 Greek *unclean*   ⁱ31 Or *something*; also in verse 32
ʲ41 Or *what you have*

the ear in the inner rooms will be proclaimed from the roofs.

4"I tell you, my friends, do not be afraid of those who kill the body and after that can do no more. 5But I will show you whom you should fear: Fear him who, after the killing of the body, has power to throw you into hell. Yes, I tell you, fear him. 6Are not five sparrows sold for two pennies?ª Yet not one of them is forgotten by God. 7Indeed, the very hairs of your head are all numbered. Don't be afraid; you are worth more than many sparrows.

8"I tell you, whoever acknowledges me before men, the Son of Man will also acknowledge him before the angels of God. 9But he who disowns me before men will be disowned before the angels of God. 10And everyone who speaks a word against the Son of Man will be forgiven, but anyone who blasphemes against the Holy Spirit will not be forgiven. 11"When you are brought before synagogues, rulers and authorities, do not worry about how you will defend yourselves or what you will say, 12for the Holy Spirit will teach you at that time what you should say."

The Parable of the Rich Fool

13Someone in the crowd said to him, "Teacher, tell my brother to divide the inheritance with me."

14Jesus replied, "Man, who appointed me a judge or an arbiter between you?" 15Then he said to them, "Watch out! Be on your guard against all kinds of greed; a man's life does not consist in the abundance of his possessions."

16And he told them this parable: "The ground of a certain rich man produced a good crop. 17He thought to himself, 'What shall I do? I have no place to store my crops.'

18"Then he said, 'This is what I'll do. I will tear down my barns and build bigger ones, and there I will store all my grain and my goods. 19And I'll say to myself, "You have plenty of good things laid up for many years. Take life easy; eat, drink and be merry." '

20"But God said to him, 'You fool! This very night your life will be demanded from you. Then who will get what you have prepared for yourself?'

21"This is how it will be with anyone who stores up things for himself but is not rich towards God."

Do Not Worry

22Then Jesus said to his disciples: "Therefore I tell you, do not worry about your life, what you will eat; or about your body, what you will wear. 23Life is more than food, and the body more than clothes. 24Consider the ravens: They do not sow or reap, they have no storeroom or barn; yet God feeds them. And how much more valuable you are than birds! 25Who of you by worrying can add a single hour to his life?ᵇ 26Since you cannot do this very little thing, why do you worry about the rest?

27"Consider how the lilies grow. They do not labour or spin. Yet I tell you, not even Solomon in all his splendour was dressed like one of these. 28If that is how God clothes the grass of the field, which is here today, and tomorrow is thrown into the fire, how much more will he clothe you, O you of little faith! 29And do not set your heart on what you will eat or drink; do not worry about it. 30For the pagan world runs after all such things, and your Father knows that you need them. 31But seek his kingdom, and these things will be given to you as well.

32"Do not be afraid, little flock, for your Father has been pleased to give you the kingdom. 33Sell your possessions and give to the poor. Provide purses for yourselves that will not wear out, a treasure in heaven that will not be exhausted, where no thief comes near and no moth destroys. 34For where your treasure is, there your heart will be also.

Watchfulness

35"Be dressed ready for service and keep your lamps burning, 36like men waiting for their master to return from a wedding banquet, so that when he comes and knocks they can immediately open the door for him. 37It will be good for those servants whose master finds them watching when he comes. I tell you the truth, he will dress himself to serve, will have them recline at the table and will come and wait on them. 38It will be good for those servants whose master finds them ready, even if he comes in the second or third watch of the night. 39But understand this: If the owner of the house had known at what hour the thief was coming, he would not have let his house be broken into. 40You also must be ready, because the Son of Man will come at an hour when you do not expect him."

41Peter asked, "Lord, are you telling this parable to us, or to everyone?"

42The Lord answered, "Who then is the faithful and wise manager, whom the master puts in charge of his servants to give them their food allowance at the proper time? 43It will be good for that servant whom the master finds doing so when he returns. 44I tell you the truth, he will put him in charge of all his possessions. 45But suppose the servant says to himself, 'My master is taking a long time in coming,' and he then begins to beat the menservants and maidservants and to eat and drink and get drunk. 46The master of that servant will come on a day when he does not expect him and at an hour he is not aware of. He will cut him to pieces and assign him a place with the unbelievers.

47"That servant who knows his master's will and does not get ready or does not do what his master wants will be beaten with many blows. 48But the one who does not know and does things deserving punishment will be beaten with few blows. From everyone who has been given much, much will be demanded; and from the one who has been entrusted with much, much more will be asked.

Not Peace but Division

49"I have come to bring fire on the earth, and how I wish it were already kindled! 50But I have a baptism to undergo, and how distressed I am until it is completed! 51Do you think I came to bring peace on earth?

ª6 Greek two assaria   ᵇ25 Or single cubit to his height

No, I tell you, but division. ⁵²From now on there will be five in one family divided against each other, three against two and two against three. ⁵³They will be divided, father against son and son against father, mother against daughter and daughter against mother, mother-in-law against daughter-in-law and daughter-in-law against mother-in-law."

12:51 There are different kinds of peace. Peace that simply covers up underlying turmoil is useless. The turmoil will eventually have to be dealt with, even if it means trouble. Christianity is not about people being nice to each other. It is about a radical lifestyle, and to live like Jesus is to ask for trouble. To insist that peace should be built on genuine justice is to ask for a baptism of fire.

Interpreting the Times

⁵⁴He said to the crowd: "When you see a cloud rising in the west, immediately you say, 'It's going to rain,' and it does. ⁵⁵And when the south wind blows, you say, 'It's going to be hot,' and it is. ⁵⁶Hypocrites! You know how to interpret the appearance of the earth and the sky. How is it that you don't know how to interpret this present time?

⁵⁷"Why don't you judge for yourselves what is right? ⁵⁸As you are going with your adversary to the magistrate, try hard to be reconciled to him on the way, or he may drag you off to the judge, and the judge turn you over to the officer, and the officer throw you into prison. ⁵⁹I tell you, you will not get out until you have paid the last penny." ᶜ

Repent or Perish

13 Now there were some present at that time who told Jesus about the Galileans whose blood Pilate had mixed with their sacrifices. ²Jesus answered, "Do you think that these Galileans were worse sinners than all the other Galileans because they suffered this way? ³I tell you, no! But unless you repent, you too will all perish. ⁴Or those eighteen who died when the tower in Siloam fell on them—do you think they were more guilty than all the others living in Jerusalem? ⁵I tell you, no! But unless you repent, you too will all perish."

⁶Then he told this parable: "A man had a fig-tree, planted in his vineyard, and he went to look for fruit on it, but did not find any. ⁷So he said to the man who took care of the vineyard, 'For three years now I've been coming to look for fruit on this fig-tree and haven't found any. Cut it down! Why should it use up the soil?'

⁸" 'Sir,' the man replied, 'leave it alone for one more year, and I'll dig round it and fertilise it. ⁹If it bears fruit next year, fine! If not, then cut it down.' "

A Crippled Woman Healed on the Sabbath

¹⁰On a Sabbath Jesus was teaching in one of the synagogues, ¹¹and a woman was there who had been crippled by a spirit for eighteen years. She was bent over and could not straighten up at all. ¹²When Jesus saw her, he called her forward and said to her, "Woman, you are set free from your infirmity." ¹³Then he put his hands on her, and immediately she straightened up and praised God.

¹⁴Indignant because Jesus had healed on the Sabbath, the synagogue ruler said to the people, "There are six days for work. So come and be healed on those days, not on the Sabbath."

¹⁵The Lord answered him, "You hypocrites! Doesn't each of you on the Sabbath untie his ox or donkey from the stall and lead it out to give it water? ¹⁶Then should not this woman, a daughter of Abraham, whom Satan has kept bound for eighteen long years, be set free on the Sabbath day from what bound her?"

¹⁷When he said this, all his opponents were humiliated, but the people were delighted with all the wonderful things he was doing.

The Parables of the Mustard Seed and the Yeast

¹⁸Then Jesus asked, "What is the kingdom of God like? What shall I compare it to? ¹⁹It is like a mustard seed, which a man took and planted in his garden. It grew and became a tree, and the birds of the air perched in its branches."

²⁰Again he asked, "What shall I compare the kingdom of God to? ²¹It is like yeast that a woman took and mixed into a large amount ᵃ of flour until it worked all through the dough."

The Narrow Door

²²Then Jesus went through the towns and villages, teaching as he made his way to Jerusalem. ²³Someone asked him, "Lord, are only a few people going to be saved?"

He said to them, ²⁴"Make every effort to enter through the narrow door, because many, I tell you, will try to enter and will not be able to. ²⁵Once the owner of the house gets up and closes the door, you will stand outside knocking and pleading, 'Sir, open the door for us.'

"But he will answer, 'I don't know you or where you come from.'

²⁶"Then you will say, 'We ate and drank with you, and you taught in our streets.'

²⁷"But he will reply, 'I don't know you or where you come from. Away from me, all you evildoers!'

²⁸"There will be weeping there, and gnashing of teeth, when you see Abraham, Isaac and Jacob and all the prophets in the kingdom of God, but you yourselves thrown out. ²⁹People will come from east and west and north and south, and will take their places at the feast in the kingdom of God. ³⁰Indeed there are those who are last who will be first, and first who will be last."

ᶜ59 Greek *lepton*   ᵃ21 Greek *three satas* (probably about ⅗ bushel or 22 litres)

Jesus' Sorrow for Jerusalem

31 At that time some Pharisees came to Jesus and said to him, "Leave this place and go somewhere else. Herod wants to kill you."

32 He replied, "Go tell that fox, 'I will drive out demons and heal people today and tomorrow, and on the third day I will reach my goal.' 33 In any case, I must keep going today and tomorrow and the next day — for surely no prophet can die outside Jerusalem!

34 "O Jerusalem, Jerusalem, you who kill the prophets and stone those sent to you, how often I have longed to gather your children together, as a hen gathers her chicks under her wings, but you were not willing! 35 Look, your house is left to you desolate. I tell you, you will not see me again until you say, 'Blessed is he who comes in the name of the Lord.' *b*"

Jesus at a Pharisee's House

14 One Sabbath, when Jesus went to eat in the house of a prominent Pharisee, he was being carefully watched. 2 There in front of him was a man suffering from dropsy. 3 Jesus asked the Pharisees and experts in the law, "Is it lawful to heal on the Sabbath or not?" 4 But they remained silent. So taking hold of the man, he healed him and sent him away.

5 Then he asked them, "If one of you has a son *a* or an ox that falls into a well on the Sabbath day, will you not immediately pull him out?" 6 And they had nothing to say.

7 When he noticed how the guests picked the places of honour at the table, he told them this parable: 8 "When someone invites you to a wedding feast, do not take the place of honour, for a person more distinguished than you may have been invited. 9 If so, the host who invited both of you will come and say to you, 'Give this man your seat.' Then, humiliated, you will have to take the least important place. 10 But when you are invited, take the lowest place, so that when your host comes, he will say to you, 'Friend, move up to a better place.' Then you will be honoured in the presence of all your fellow guests. 11 For everyone who exalts himself will be humbled, and he who humbles himself will be exalted."

12 Then Jesus said to his host, "When you give a luncheon or dinner, do not invite your friends, your brothers or relatives, or your rich neighbours; if you do, they may invite you back and so you will be repaid. 13 But when you give a banquet, invite the poor, the crippled, the lame, the blind, 14 and you will be blessed. Although they cannot repay you, you will be repaid at the resurrection of the righteous."

The Parable of the Great Banquet

15 When one of those at the table with him heard this, he said to Jesus, "Blessed is the man who will eat at the feast in the kingdom of God."

16 Jesus replied: "A certain man was preparing a great banquet and invited many guests. 17 At the time of the banquet he sent his servant to tell those who had been invited, 'Come, for everything is now ready.'

18 "But they all alike began to make excuses. The first said, 'I have just bought a field, and I must go and see it. Please excuse me.'

19 "Another said, 'I have just bought five yoke of oxen, and I'm on my way to try them out. Please excuse me.'

20 "Still another said, 'I have just got married, so I can't come.'

21 "The servant came back and reported this to his master. Then the owner of the house became angry and ordered his servant, 'Go out quickly into the streets and alleys of the town and bring in the poor, the crippled, the blind and the lame.'

22 " 'Sir,' the servant said, 'what you ordered has been done, but there is still room.'

23 "Then the master told his servant, 'Go out to the roads and country lanes and make them come in, so that my house will be full. 24 I tell you, not one of those men who were invited will get a taste of my banquet.' "

The Cost of Being a Disciple

25 Large crowds were travelling with Jesus, and turning to them he said: 26 "If anyone comes to me and does not hate his father and mother, his wife and children, his brothers and sisters — yes, even his own life — he cannot be my disciple. 27 And anyone who does not carry his cross and follow me cannot be my disciple.

14:26   Luke, out of character, omitted to translate his eastern source into western language. The easterner tended to speak in black and white, and would say, "I like this and hate that", where the westerner would say, "I like this more than that". Even so, Jesus' demand is costly: discipleship must take priority over everything, even family ties.

---

28 "Suppose one of you wants to build a tower. Will he not first sit down and estimate the cost to see if he has enough money to complete it? 29 For if he lays the foundation and is not able to finish it, everyone who sees it will ridicule him, 30 saying, 'This fellow began to build and was not able to finish.'

31 "Or suppose a king is about to go to war against another king. Will he not first sit down and consider whether he is able with ten thousand men to oppose the one coming against him with twenty thousand? 32 If he is not able, he will send a delegation while the other is still a long way off and will ask for terms of peace. 33 In the same way, any of you who does not give up everything he has cannot be my disciple.

34 "Salt is good, but if it loses its saltiness, how can it be made salty again? 35 It is fit neither for the soil nor for the manure heap; it is thrown out.

"He who has ears to hear, let him hear."

b35 Psalm 118:26   *a5* Some manuscripts *donkey*

The Parable of the Lost Sheep

15 Now the tax collectors and "sinners" were all gathering round to hear him. ²But the Pharisees and the teachers of the law muttered, "This man welcomes sinners, and eats with them."

15:1 The three stories in this chapter celebrate the endless and unconditional love of God. They are only found in Luke, and act as a counterbalance to the more severe stories in chapter 14, also only in Luke.

---

³Then Jesus told them this parable: ⁴"Suppose one of you has a hundred sheep and loses one of them. Does he not leave the ninety-nine in the open country and go after the lost sheep until he finds it? ⁵And when he finds it, he joyfully puts it on his shoulders ⁶and goes home. Then he calls his friends and neighbours together and says, 'Rejoice with me; I have found my lost sheep.' ⁷I tell you that in the same way there will be more rejoicing in heaven over one sinner who repents than over ninety-nine righteous persons who do not need to repent.

The Parable of the Lost Coin

⁸"Or suppose a woman has ten silver coins*a* and loses one. Does she not light a lamp, sweep the house and search carefully until she finds it? ⁹And when she finds it, she calls her friends and neighbours together and says, 'Rejoice with me; I have found my lost coin.' ¹⁰In the same way, I tell you, there is rejoicing in the presence of the angels of God over one sinner who repents."

The Parable of the Lost Son

¹¹Jesus continued: "There was a man who had two sons. ¹²The younger one said to his father, 'Father, give me my share of the estate.' So he divided his property between them.

¹³"Not long after that, the younger son got together all he had, set off for a distant country and there squandered his wealth in wild living. ¹⁴After he had spent everything, there was a severe famine in that whole country, and he began to be in need. ¹⁵So he went and hired himself out to a citizen of that country, who sent him to his fields to feed pigs. ¹⁶He longed to fill his stomach with the pods that the pigs were eating, but no-one gave him anything.

¹⁷"When he came to his senses, he said, 'How many of my father's hired men have food to spare, and here I am starving to death! ¹⁸I will set out and go back to my father and say to him: Father, I have sinned against heaven and against you. ¹⁹I am no longer worthy to be called your son; make me like one of your hired men.' ²⁰So he got up and went to his father.

"But while he was still a long way off, his father saw him and was filled with compassion for him; he ran to his son, threw his arms around him and kissed him.

²¹"The son said to him, 'Father, I have sinned against heaven and against you. I am no longer worthy to be called your son.'*b*

²²"But the father said to his servants, 'Quick! Bring the best robe and put it on him. Put a ring on his finger and sandals on his feet. ²³Bring the fattened calf and kill it. Let's have a feast and celebrate. ²⁴For this son of mine was dead and is alive again; he was lost and is found.' So they began to celebrate.

²⁵"Meanwhile, the older son was in the field. When he came near the house, he heard music and dancing. ²⁶So he called one of the servants and asked him what was going on. ²⁷'Your brother has come,' he replied, 'and your father has killed the fattened calf because he has him back safe and sound.'

²⁸"The older brother became angry and refused to go in. So his father went out and pleaded with him. ²⁹But he answered his father, 'Look! All these years I've been slaving for you and never disobeyed your orders. Yet you never gave me even a young goat so I could celebrate with my friends. ³⁰But when this son of yours who has squandered your property with prostitutes comes home, you kill the fattened calf for him!'

³¹" 'My son,' the father said, 'you are always with me, and everything I have is yours. ³²But we had to celebrate and be glad, because this brother of yours was dead and is alive again; he was lost and is found.' "

The Parable of the Shrewd Manager

16 Jesus told his disciples: "There was a rich man whose manager was accused of wasting his possessions. ²So he called him in and asked him, 'What is this I hear about you? Give an account of your management, because you cannot be manager any longer.'

³"The manager said to himself, 'What shall I do now? My master is taking away my job. I'm not strong enough to dig, and I'm ashamed to beg—⁴I know what I'll do so that, when I lose my job here, people will welcome me into their houses.'

⁵"So he called in each one of his master's debtors. He asked the first, 'How much do you owe my master?'

⁶" 'Eight hundred gallons*a* of olive oil,' he replied.

"The manager told him, 'Take your bill, sit down quickly, and make it four hundred.'

⁷"Then he asked the second, 'And how much do you owe?'

" 'A thousand bushels*b* of wheat,' he replied.

"He told him, 'Take your bill and make it eight hundred.'

⁸"The master commended the dishonest manager because he had acted shrewdly. For the people of this world are more shrewd in dealing with their own kind than are the people of the light. ⁹I tell you, use worldly wealth to gain friends for yourselves, so that when it is gone, you will be welcomed into eternal dwellings. ¹⁰Whoever can be trusted with very little can also be trusted with much, and whoever is dishonest with very little will also be dishonest with much. ¹¹So if you have not been trustworthy in handling worldly wealth, who will trust you with true riches? ¹²And if you have

---

a8 Greek *ten drachmas*, each worth about a day's wages
a6 Greek *one hundred batous* (probably about 3 kilolitres)
b21 Some early manuscripts *son. Make me like one of your hired men.*
b7 Greek *one hundred korous* (probably about 35 kilolitres)

not been trustworthy with someone else's property, who will give you property of your own?

¹³"No servant can serve two masters. Either he will hate the one and love the other, or he will be devoted to the one and despise the other. You cannot serve both God and Money."

16:13   Luke was concerned with wealth and its dangers. His Gospel has many references to the theme, compared with Mark's five, and Matthew's only one.

---

¹⁴The Pharisees, who loved money, heard all this and were sneering at Jesus. ¹⁵He said to them, "You are the ones who justify yourselves in the eyes of men, but God knows your hearts. What is highly valued among men is detestable in God's sight.

Additional Teachings

¹⁶"The Law and the Prophets were proclaimed until John. Since that time, the good news of the kingdom of God is being preached, and everyone is forcing his way into it. ¹⁷It is easier for heaven and earth to disappear than for the least stroke of a pen to drop out of the Law.

¹⁸"Anyone who divorces his wife and marries another woman commits adultery, and the man who marries a divorced woman commits adultery.

The Rich Man and Lazarus

¹⁹"There was a rich man who was dressed in purple and fine linen and lived in luxury every day. ²⁰At his gate was laid a beggar named Lazarus, covered with sores ²¹and longing to eat what fell from the rich man's table. Even the dogs came when the beggar died and licked his sores.

²²"The time came when the beggar died and the angels carried him to Abraham's side. The rich man also died and was buried. ²³In hell,ᶜ where he was in torment, he looked up and saw Abraham far away, with Lazarus by his side. ²⁴So he called to him, 'Father Abraham, have pity on me and send Lazarus to dip the tip of his finger in water and cool my tongue, because I am in agony in this fire.'

²⁵"But Abraham replied, 'Son, remember that in your lifetime you received your good things, while Lazarus received bad things, but now he is comforted here and you are in agony. ²⁶And besides all this, between us and you a great chasm has been fixed, so that those who want to go from here to you cannot, nor can anyone cross over from there to us.'

²⁷"He answered, 'Then I beg you, father, send Lazarus to my father's house, ²⁸for I have five brothers. Let him warn them, so that they will not also come to this place of torment.'

²⁹"Abraham replied, 'They have Moses and the Prophets; let them listen to them.'

³⁰" 'No, father Abraham,' he said, 'but if someone from the dead goes to them, they will repent.'

³¹"He said to him, 'If they do not listen to Moses and the Prophets, they will not be convinced even if someone rises from the dead.' "

Sin, Faith, Duty

17 Jesus said to his disciples: "Things that cause people to sin are bound to come, but woe to that person through whom they come. ²It would be better for him to be thrown into the sea with a millstone tied round his neck than for him to cause one of these little ones to sin. ³So watch yourselves.

"If your brother sins, rebuke him, and if he repents, forgive him. ⁴If he sins against you seven times in a day, and seven times comes back to you and says, 'I repent,' forgive him."

⁵The apostles said to the Lord, "Increase our faith!"

⁶He replied, "If you have faith as small as a mustard seed, you can say to this mulberry tree, 'Be uprooted and planted in the sea,' and it will obey you.

⁷"Suppose one of you had a servant ploughing or looking after the sheep. Would he say to the servant when he comes in from the field, 'Come along now and sit down to eat'? ⁸Would he not rather say, 'Prepare my supper, get yourself ready and wait on me while I eat and drink; after that you may eat and drink'? ⁹Would he thank the servant because he did what he was told to do? ¹⁰So you also, when you have done everything you were told to do, should say, 'We are unworthy servants; we have only done our duty.' "

Ten Healed of Leprosy

¹¹Now on his way to Jerusalem, Jesus travelled along the border between Samaria and Galilee. ¹²As he was going into a village, ten men who had leprosyᵃ met him. They stood at a distance ¹³and called out in a loud voice, "Jesus, Master, have pity on us!"

¹⁴When he saw them, he said, "Go, show yourselves to the priests." And as they went, they were cleansed.

¹⁵One of them, when he saw he was healed, came back, praising God in a loud voice. ¹⁶He threw himself at Jesus' feet and thanked him—and he was a Samaritan.

¹⁷Jesus asked, "Were not all ten cleansed? Where are the other nine? ¹⁸Was no-one found to return and give praise to God except this foreigner?" ¹⁹Then he said to him, "Rise and go; your faith has made you well."

The Coming of the Kingdom of God

²⁰Once, having been asked by the Pharisees when the kingdom of God would come, Jesus replied, "The kingdom of God does not come with your careful observation, ²¹nor will people say, 'Here it is,' or 'There it is,' because the kingdom of God is withinᵇ you."

²²Then he said to his disciples, "The time is coming when you will long to see one of the days of the Son of Man, but you will not see it. ²³Men will tell you, 'There he is!' or 'Here he is!' Do not go running off after them. ²⁴For the Son of Man in his dayᶜ will be like the lightning, which flashes and lights up the sky from one

---

ᶜ23 Greek *Hades*   ᵃ12 The Greek word was used for various diseases affecting the skin—not necessarily leprosy.
ᵇ21 Or *among*   ᶜ24 Some manuscripts do not have *in his day.*

end to the other. 25But first he must suffer many things and be rejected by this generation.

26"Just as it was in the days of Noah, so also will it be in the days of the Son of Man. 27People were eating, drinking, marrying and being given in marriage up to the day Noah entered the ark. Then the flood came and destroyed them all.

28"It was the same in the days of Lot. People were eating and drinking, buying and selling, planting and building. 29But the day Lot left Sodom, fire and sulphur rained down from heaven and destroyed them all.

30"It will be just like this on the day the Son of Man is revealed. 31On that day no-one who is on the roof of his house, with his goods inside, should go down to get them. Likewise, no-one in the field should go back for anything. 32Remember Lot's wife! 33Whoever tries to keep his life will lose it, and whoever loses his life will preserve it. 34I tell you, on that night two people will be in one bed; one will be taken and the other left. 35Two women will be grinding grain together; one will be taken and the other left." d

37"Where, Lord?" they asked.

He replied, "Where there is a dead body, there the vultures will gather."

The Parable of the Persistent Widow

18 Then Jesus told his disciples a parable to show them that they should always pray and not give up. 2He said: "In a certain town there was a judge who neither feared God nor cared about men. 3And there was a widow in that town who kept coming to him with the plea, 'Grant me justice against my adversary.'

4"For some time he refused. But finally he said to himself, 'Even though I don't fear God or care about men, 5yet because this widow keeps bothering me, I will see that she gets justice, so that she won't eventually wear me out with her coming!' "

6And the Lord said, "Listen to what the unjust judge says. 7And will not God bring about justice for his chosen ones, who cry out to him day and night? Will he keep putting them off? 8I tell you, he will see that they get justice, and quickly. However, when the Son of Man comes, will he find faith on the earth?"

The Parable of the Pharisee and the Tax Collector

9To some who were confident of their own righteousness and looked down on everybody else, Jesus told this parable: 10"Two men went up to the temple to pray, one a Pharisee and the other a tax collector. 11The Pharisee stood up and prayed about a himself: 'God, I thank you that I am not like other men — robbers, evildoers, adulterers — or even like this tax collector. 12I fast twice a week and give a tenth of all I get.'

13"But the tax collector stood at a distance. He would not even look up to heaven, but beat his breast and said, 'God, have mercy on me, a sinner.'

14"I tell you that this man, rather than the other, went home justified before God. For everyone who exalts himself will be humbled, and he who humbles himself will be exalted."

18:9   Chapters 18 and 19 are full of stories about people who lived on the margins of society: widows, tax-collectors, children, beggars, the blind. The famous parable of the Pharisee and the tax-collector is perhaps the most provocative and shocking of all. What does it mean to say that a hated schemer and extortioner can be closer to God's heart than the most pious religious people of the land?

The Little Children and Jesus

15People were also bringing babies to Jesus to have him touch them. When the disciples saw this, they rebuked them. 16But Jesus called the children to him and said, "Let the little children come to me, and do not hinder them, for the kingdom of God belongs to such as these. 17I tell you the truth, anyone who will not receive the kingdom of God like a little child will never enter it."

The Rich Ruler

18A certain ruler asked him, "Good teacher, what must I do to inherit eternal life?"

19"Why do you call me good?" Jesus answered. "No-one is good — except God alone. 20You know the commandments: 'Do not commit adultery, do not murder, do not steal, do not give false testimony, honour your father and mother.' b"

21"All these I have kept since I was a boy," he said.

22When Jesus heard this, he said to him, "You still lack one thing. Sell everything you have and give to the poor, and you will have treasure in heaven. Then come, follow me."

23When he heard this, he became very sad, because he was a man of great wealth. 24Jesus looked at him and said, "How hard it is for the rich to enter the kingdom of God! 25Indeed, it is easier for a camel to go through the eye of a needle than for a rich man to enter the kingdom of God."

26Those who heard this asked, "Who then can be saved?"

27Jesus replied, "What is impossible with men is possible with God."

28Peter said to him, "We have left all we had to follow you!"

29"I tell you the truth," Jesus said to them, "no-one who has left home or wife or brothers or parents or children for the sake of the kingdom of God 30will fail to receive many times as much in this age and, in the age to come, eternal life."

---

d35 Some manuscripts left. 36Two men will be in the field; one will be taken and the other left.   a11 Or to
b20 Exodus 20:12–16; Deut. 5:16–20

Jesus Again Predicts His Death

[31]Jesus took the Twelve aside and told them, "We are going up to Jerusalem, and everything that is written by the prophets about the Son of Man will be fulfilled. [32]He will be turned over to the Gentiles. They will mock him, insult him, spit on him, flog him and kill him. [33]On the third day he will rise again."

[34]The disciples did not understand any of this. Its meaning was hidden from them, and they did not know what he was talking about.

A Blind Beggar Receives His Sight

[35]As Jesus approached Jericho, a blind man was sitting by the roadside begging. [36]When he heard the crowd going by, he asked what was happening. [37]They told him, "Jesus of Nazareth is passing by."

[38]He called out, "Jesus, Son of David, have mercy on me!"

[39]Those who led the way rebuked him and told him to be quiet, but he shouted all the more, "Son of David, have mercy on me!"

[40]Jesus stopped and ordered the man to be brought to him. When he came near, Jesus asked him, [41]"What do you want me to do for you?"

"Lord, I want to see," he replied.

[42]Jesus said to him, "Receive your sight; your faith has healed you." [43]Immediately he received his sight and followed Jesus, praising God. When all the people saw it, they also praised God.

Zacchaeus the Tax Collector

19 Jesus entered Jericho and was passing through. [2]A man was there by the name of Zacchaeus; he was a chief tax collector and was wealthy. [3]He wanted to see who Jesus was, but being a short man he could not, because of the crowd. [4]So he ran ahead and climbed a sycamore-fig tree to see him, since Jesus was coming that way.

[5]When Jesus reached the spot, he looked up and said to him, "Zacchaeus, come down immediately. I must stay at your house today." [6]So he came down at once and welcomed him gladly.

[7]All the people saw this and began to mutter, "He has gone to be the guest of a 'sinner'."

[8]But Zacchaeus stood up and said to the Lord, "Look, Lord! Here and now I give half of my possessions to the poor, and if I have cheated anybody out of anything, I will pay back four times the amount."

[9]Jesus said to him, "Today salvation has come to this house, because this man, too, is a son of Abraham. [10]For the Son of Man came to seek and to save what was lost."

The Parable of the Ten Minas

[11]While they were listening to this, he went on to tell them a parable, because he was near Jerusalem and the people thought that the kingdom of God was going to appear at once. [12]He said: "A man of noble birth went to a distant country to have himself appointed king and then to return. [13]So he called ten of his servants and gave them ten minas.[a] 'Put this money to work,' he said, 'until I come back.'

[14]"But his subjects hated him and sent a delegation after him to say, 'We don't want this man to be our king.'

[15]"He was made king, however, and returned home. Then he sent for the servants to whom he had given the money, in order to find out what they had gained with it.

[16]"The first one came and said, 'Sir, your mina has earned ten more.'

[17]" 'Well done, my good servant!' his master replied. 'Because you have been trustworthy in a very small matter, take charge of ten cities.'

[18]"The second came and said, 'Sir, your mina has earned five more.'

[19]"His master answered, 'You take charge of five cities.'

[20]"Then another servant came and said, 'Sir, here is your mina; I have kept it laid away in a piece of cloth. [21]I was afraid of you, because you are a hard man. You take out what you did not put in and reap what you did not sow.'

[22]"His master replied, 'I will judge you by your own words, you wicked servant! You knew, did you, that I am a hard man, taking out what I did not put in, and reaping what I did not sow? [23]Why then didn't you put my money on deposit, so that when I came back, I could have collected it with interest?'

[24]"Then he said to those standing by, 'Take his mina away from him and give it to the one who has ten minas.'

[25]" 'Sir,' they said, 'he already has ten!'

[26]"He replied, 'I tell you that to everyone who has, more will be given, but as for the one who has nothing, even what he has will be taken away. [27]But those enemies of mine who did not want me to be a king over them — bring them here and kill them in front of me.' "

The Triumphal Entry

[28]After Jesus had said this, he went on ahead, going up to Jerusalem. [29]As he approached Bethphage and Bethany at the hill called the Mount of Olives, he sent two of his disciples, saying to them, [30]"Go to the village ahead of you, and as you enter it, you will find a colt tied there, which no-one has ever ridden. Untie it and bring it here. [31]If anyone asks you, 'Why are you untying it?' tell him, 'The Lord needs it.' "

[32]Those who were sent ahead went and found it just as he had told them. [33]As they were untying the colt, its owners asked them, "Why are you untying the colt?"

[34]They replied, "The Lord needs it."

[35]They brought it to Jesus, threw their cloaks on the colt and put Jesus on it. [36]As he went along, people spread their cloaks on the road.

[37]When he came near the place where the road goes down the Mount of Olives, the whole crowd of disciples began joyfully to praise God in loud voices for all the miracles they had seen:

---

a 13 A mina was about three months' wages.

38"Blessed is the king who comes in the name of the Lord!"*b*

"Peace in heaven and glory in the highest!"

39Some of the Pharisees in the crowd said to Jesus, "Teacher, rebuke your disciples!"

40"I tell you," he replied, "if they keep quiet, the stones will cry out."

41As he approached Jerusalem and saw the city, he wept over it 42and said, "If you, even you, had only known on this day what would bring you peace — but now it is hidden from your eyes. 43The days will come upon you when your enemies will build an embankment against you and encircle you and hem you in on every side. 44They will dash you to the ground, you and the children within your walls. They will not leave one stone on another, because you did not recognise the time of God's coming to you."

Jesus at the Temple

45Then he entered the temple area and began driving out those who were selling. 46"It is written," he said to them, " 'My house will be a house of prayer';*c* but you have made it 'a den of robbers'.*d*"

47Every day he was teaching at the temple. But the chief priests, the teachers of the law and the leaders among the people were trying to kill him. 48Yet they could not find any way to do it, because all the people hung on his words.

The Authority of Jesus Questioned

20 One day as he was teaching the people in the temple courts and preaching the gospel, the chief priests and the teachers of the law, together with the elders, came up to him. 2"Tell us by what authority you are doing these things," they said. "Who gave you this authority?"

3He replied, "I will also ask you a question. Tell me, 4John's baptism — was it from heaven, or from men?"

5They discussed it among themselves and said, "If we say, 'From heaven', he will ask, 'Why didn't you believe him?' 6But if we say, 'From men', all the people will stone us, because they are persuaded that John was a prophet."

7So they answered, "We don't know where it was from."

8Jesus said, "Neither will I tell you by what authority I am doing these things."

The Parable of the Tenants

9He went on to tell the people this parable: "A man planted a vineyard, rented it to some farmers and went away for a long time. 10At harvest time he sent a servant to the tenants so they would give him some of the fruit of the vineyard. But the tenants beat him and sent him away empty-handed. 11He sent another servant, but that one also they beat and treated shamefully and sent away empty-handed. 12He sent still a third, and they wounded him and threw him out.

13"Then the owner of the vineyard said, 'What shall I do? I will send my son, whom I love; perhaps they will respect him.'

14"But when the tenants saw him, they talked the matter over. 'This is the heir,' they said. 'Let's kill him, and the inheritance will be ours.' 15So they threw him out of the vineyard and killed him.

"What then will the owner of the vineyard do to them? 16He will come and kill those tenants and give the vineyard to others."

When the people heard this, they said, "May this never be!"

17Jesus looked directly at them and asked, "Then what is the meaning of that which is written:

" 'The stone the builders rejected
has become the capstone'*a,b*?

18Everyone who falls on that stone will be broken to pieces, but he on whom it falls will be crushed."

19The teachers of the law and the chief priests looked for a way to arrest him immediately, because they knew he had spoken this parable against them. But they were afraid of the people.

Paying Taxes to Caesar

20Keeping a close watch on him, they sent spies, who pretended to be honest. They hoped to catch Jesus in something he said so that they might hand him over to the power and authority of the governor. 21So the spies questioned him: "Teacher, we know that you speak and teach what is right, and that you do not show partiality but teach the way of God in accordance with the truth. 22Is it right for us to pay taxes to Caesar or not?"

23He saw through their duplicity and said to them, 24"Show me a denarius. Whose portrait and inscription are on it?"

25"Caesar's," they replied.

He said to them, "Then give to Caesar what is Caesar's, and to God what is God's."

26They were unable to trap him in what he had said there in public. And astonished by his answer, they became silent.

The Resurrection and Marriage

27Some of the Sadducees, who say there is no resurrection, came to Jesus with a question. 28"Teacher," they said, "Moses wrote for us that if a man's brother dies and leaves a wife but no children, the man must marry the widow and have children for his brother. 29Now there were seven brothers. The first one married a woman and died childless. 30The second 31and then the third married her, and in the same way the seven died, leaving no children. 32Finally, the woman died too. 33Now then, at the resurrection whose wife will she be, since the seven were married to her?"

34Jesus replied, "The people of this age marry and are given in marriage. 35But those who are considered worthy of taking part in that age and in the resurrection from the dead will neither marry nor be given in marriage, 36and they can no longer die; for they are like the angels. They are God's children, since they are

b38 Psalm 118:26   *c46* Isaiah 56:7   *d46* Jer. 7:11   *a17* Or *cornerstone*   *b17* Psalm 118:22

children of the resurrection. ³⁷But in the account of the bush, even Moses showed that the dead rise, for he calls the Lord 'the God of Abraham, and the God of Isaac, and the God of Jacob'.ᶜ ³⁸He is not the God of the dead, but of the living, for to him all are alive."

³⁹Some of the teachers of the law responded, "Well said, teacher!" ⁴⁰And no-one dared to ask him any more questions.

Whose Son Is the Christ?

⁴¹Then Jesus said to them, "How is it that they say the Christᵈ is the Son of David? ⁴²David himself declares in the Book of Psalms:

" 'The Lord said to my Lord:
"Sit at my right hand
⁴³until I make your enemies
a footstool for your feet." 'ᵉ

⁴⁴David calls him 'Lord'. How then can he be his son?"

⁴⁵While all the people were listening, Jesus said to his disciples, ⁴⁶"Beware of the teachers of the law. They like to walk around in flowing robes and love to be greeted in the market-places and have the most important seats in the synagogues and the places of honour at banquets. ⁴⁷They devour widows' houses and for a show make lengthy prayers. Such men will be punished most severely."

The Widow's Offering

21 As he looked up, Jesus saw the rich putting their gifts into the temple treasury. ²He also saw a poor widow put in two very small copper coins.ᵃ ³"I tell you the truth," he said, "this poor widow has put in more than all the others. ⁴All these people gave their gifts out of their wealth; but she out of her poverty put in all she had to live on."

Signs of the End of the Age

⁵Some of his disciples were remarking about how the temple was adorned with beautiful stones and with gifts dedicated to God. But Jesus said, ⁶"As for what you see here, the time will come when not one stone will be left on another; every one of them will be thrown down."

⁷"Teacher," they asked, "when will these things happen? And what will be the sign that they are about to take place?"

⁸He replied: "Watch out that you are not deceived. For many will come in my name, claiming, 'I am he,' and 'The time is near.' Do not follow them. ⁹When you hear of wars and revolutions, do not be frightened. These things must happen first, but the end will not come right away."

¹⁰Then he said to them: "Nation will rise against nation, and kingdom against kingdom. ¹¹There will be great earthquakes, famines and pestilences in various places, and fearful events and great signs from heaven. ¹²"But before all this, they will lay hands on you and persecute you. They will deliver you to synagogues and prisons, and you will be brought before kings and governors, and all on account of my name. ¹³This will result in your being witnesses to them. ¹⁴But make up your mind not to worry beforehand how you will defend yourselves. ¹⁵For I will give you words and wisdom that none of your adversaries will be able to resist or contradict. ¹⁶You will be betrayed even by parents, brothers, relatives and friends, and they will put some of you to death. ¹⁷All men will hate you because of me. ¹⁸But not a hair of your head will perish. ¹⁹By standing firm you will gain life.

²⁰"When you see Jerusalem being surrounded by armies, you will know that its desolation is near. ²¹Then let those who are in Judea flee to the mountains, let those in the city get out, and let those in the country not enter the city. ²²For this is the time of punishment in fulfilment of all that has been written. ²³How dreadful it will be in those days for pregnant women and nursing mothers! There will be great distress in the land and wrath against this people. ²⁴They will fall by the sword and will be taken as prisoners to all the nations. Jerusalem will be trampled on by the Gentiles until the times of the Gentiles are fulfilled.

²⁵"There will be signs in the sun, moon and stars. On the earth, nations will be in anguish and perplexity at the roaring and tossing of the sea. ²⁶Men will faint from terror, apprehensive of what is coming on the world, for the heavenly bodies will be shaken. ²⁷At that time they will see the Son of Man coming in a cloud with power and great glory. ²⁸When these things begin to take place, stand up and lift up your heads, because your redemption is drawing near."

²⁹He told them this parable: "Look at the fig-tree and all the trees. ³⁰When they sprout leaves, you can see for yourselves and know that summer is near. ³¹Even so, when you see these things happening, you know that the kingdom of God is near.

³²"I tell you the truth, this generationᵇ will certainly not pass away until all these things have happened. ³³Heaven and earth will pass away, but my words will never pass away.

³⁴"Be careful, or your hearts will be weighed down with dissipation, drunkenness and the anxieties of life, and that day will close on you unexpectedly like a trap. ³⁵For it will come upon all those who live on the face of the whole earth. ³⁶Be always on the watch, and pray that you may be able to escape all that is about to happen, and that you may be able to stand before the Son of Man."

³⁷Each day Jesus was teaching at the temple, and each evening he went out to spend the night on the hill called the Mount of Olives, ³⁸and all the people came early in the morning to hear him at the temple.

Judas Agrees to Betray Jesus

22 Now the Feast of Unleavened Bread, called the Passover, was approaching, ²and the chief priests and the teachers of the law were looking for some way to get rid of Jesus, for they were afraid of the people. ³Then Satan entered Judas, called Iscariot, one of the Twelve. ⁴And Judas went to the chief priests and the officers of the temple guard and discussed with

ᶜ37 Exodus 3:6   ᵈ41 Or Messiah   ᵉ43 Psalm 110:1   ᵃ2 Greek *two lepta*   ᵇ32 Or *race* them how he might betray Jesus. [5]They were delighted and agreed to give him money. [6]He consented, and watched for an opportunity to hand Jesus over to them when no crowd was present.

The Last Supper

[7]Then came the day of Unleavened Bread on which the Passover lamb had to be sacrificed. [8]Jesus sent Peter and John, saying, "Go and make preparations for us to eat the Passover."

[9]"Where do you want us to prepare for it?" they asked.

[10]He replied, "As you enter the city, a man carrying a jar of water will meet you. Follow him to the house that he enters, [11]and say to the owner of the house, 'The Teacher asks: Where is the guest room, where I may eat the Passover with my disciples?' [12]He will show you a large upper room, all furnished. Make preparations there."

[13]They left and found things just as Jesus had told them. So they prepared the Passover.

[14]When the hour came, Jesus and his apostles reclined at the table. [15]And he said to them, "I have eagerly desired to eat this Passover with you before I suffer. [16]For I tell you, I will not eat it again until it finds fulfilment in the kingdom of God."

[17]After taking the cup, he gave thanks and said, "Take this and divide it among you. [18]For I tell you I will not drink again of the fruit of the vine until the kingdom of God comes."

[19]And he took bread, gave thanks and broke it, and gave it to them, saying, "This is my body given for you; do this in remembrance of me."

[20]In the same way, after the supper he took the cup, saying, "This cup is the new covenant in my blood, which is poured out for you. [21]But the hand of him who is going to betray me is with mine on the table. [22]The Son of Man will go as it has been decreed, but woe to that man who betrays him." [23]They began to question among themselves which of them it might be who would do this.

[24]Also a dispute arose among them as to which of them was considered to be greatest. [25]Jesus said to them, "The kings of the Gentiles lord it over them; and those who exercise authority over them call themselves Benefactors. [26]But you are not to be like that. Instead, the greatest among you should be like the youngest, and the one who rules like the one who serves. [27]For who is greater, the one who is at the table or the one who serves? Is it not the one who is at the table? But I am among you as one who serves. [28]You are those who have stood by me in my trials. [29]And I confer on you a kingdom, just as my Father conferred one on me, [30]so that you may eat and drink at my table in my kingdom and sit on thrones, judging the twelve tribes of Israel.

[31]"Simon, Simon, Satan has asked to sift you[a] as wheat. [32]But I have prayed for you, Simon, that your faith may not fail. And when you have turned back, strengthen your brothers."

[33]But he replied, "Lord, I am ready to go with you to prison and to death."

22:27   Mark and Matthew placed these sayings of Jesus earlier in the Gospel. Luke put them here because he found them more appropriate in the context of the Christian Eucharist (Holy Communion). John even omitted all mention of the bread and wine at the Last Supper in order to focus on Jesus as the servant, who washed his disciples' feet.

---

[34]Jesus answered, "I tell you, Peter, before the cock crows today, you will deny three times that you know me."

[35]Then Jesus asked them, "When I sent you without purse, bag or sandals, did you lack anything?"

"Nothing," they answered.

[36]He said to them, "But now if you have a purse, take it, and also a bag; and if you don't have a sword, sell your cloak and buy one. [37]It is written: 'And he was numbered with the transgressors';[b] and I tell you that this must be fulfilled in me. Yes, what is written about me is reaching its fulfilment."

[38]The disciples said, "See, Lord, here are two swords."

"That is enough," he replied.

Jesus Prays on the Mount of Olives

[39]Jesus went out as usual to the Mount of Olives, and his disciples followed him. [40]On reaching the place, he said to them, "Pray that you will not fall into temptation." [41]He withdrew about a stone's throw beyond them, knelt down and prayed, [42]"Father, if you are willing, take this cup from me; yet not my will, but yours be done." [43]An angel from heaven appeared to him and strengthened him. [44]And being in anguish, he prayed more earnestly, and his sweat was like drops of blood falling to the ground.[c]

[45]When he rose from prayer and went back to the disciples, he found them asleep, exhausted from sorrow. [46]"Why are you sleeping?" he asked them. "Get up and pray so that you will not fall into temptation."

Jesus Arrested

[47]While he was still speaking a crowd came up, and the man who was called Judas, one of the Twelve, was leading them. He approached Jesus to kiss him, [48]but Jesus asked him, "Judas, are you betraying the Son of Man with a kiss?"

[49]When Jesus' followers saw what was going to happen, they said, "Lord, should we strike with our swords?" [50]And one of them struck the servant of the high priest, cutting off his right ear.

[51]But Jesus answered, "No more of this!" And he touched the man's ear and healed him.

[52]Then Jesus said to the chief priests, the officers of the temple guard, and the elders, who had come for him, "Am I leading a rebellion, that you have come

---

a 31 The Greek is plural.   *b 37* Isaiah 53:12   *c 44* Some early manuscripts do not have verses 43 and 44.

with swords and clubs? ⁵³Every day I was with you in the temple courts, and you did not lay a hand on me. But this is your hour—when darkness reigns."

Peter Disowns Jesus

⁵⁴Then seizing him, they led him away and took him into the house of the high priest. Peter followed at a distance. ⁵⁵But when they had kindled a fire in the middle of the courtyard and had sat down together, Peter sat down with them. ⁵⁶A servant girl saw him seated there in the firelight. She looked closely at him and said, "This man was with him."

⁵⁷But he denied it. "Woman, I don't know him," he said.

⁵⁸A little later someone else saw him and said, "You also are one of them."

"Man, I am not!" Peter replied.

⁵⁹About an hour later another asserted, "Certainly this fellow was with him, for he is a Galilean."

⁶⁰Peter replied, "Man, I don't know what you're talking about!" Just as he was speaking, the cock crowed. ⁶¹The Lord turned and looked straight at Peter. Then Peter remembered the word the Lord had spoken to him: "Before the cock crows today, you will disown me three times." ⁶²And he went outside and wept bitterly.

The Guards Mock Jesus

⁶³The men who were guarding Jesus began mocking and beating him. ⁶⁴They blindfolded him and demanded, "Prophesy! Who hit you?" ⁶⁵And they said many other insulting things to him.

Jesus Before Pilate and Herod

⁶⁶At daybreak the council of the elders of the people, both the chief priests and teachers of the law, met together, and Jesus was led before them. ⁶⁷"If you are the Christ,"ᵈ they said, "tell us."

Jesus answered, "If I tell you, you will not believe me, ⁶⁸and if I asked you, you would not answer. ⁶⁹But from now on, the Son of Man will be seated at the right hand of the mighty God."

⁷⁰They all asked, "Are you then the Son of God?"

He replied, "You are right in saying I am."

⁷¹Then they said, "Why do we need any more testimony? We have heard it from his own lips."

23 Then the whole assembly rose and led him off to Pilate. ²And they began to accuse him, saying, "We have found this man subverting our nation. He opposes payment of taxes to Caesar and claims to be Christ,ᵃ a king."

³So Pilate asked Jesus, "Are you the king of the Jews?"

"Yes, it is as you say," Jesus replied.

⁴Then Pilate announced to the chief priests and the crowd, "I find no basis for a charge against this man."

⁵But they insisted, "He stirs up the people all over Judeaᵇ by his teaching. He started in Galilee and has come all the way here."

⁶On hearing this, Pilate asked if the man was a Galilean. ⁷When he learned that Jesus was under Herod's jurisdiction, he sent him to Herod, who was also in Jerusalem at that time.

⁸When Herod saw Jesus, he was greatly pleased, because for a long time he had been wanting to see him. From what he had heard about him, he hoped to see him perform some miracle. ⁹He plied him with many questions, but Jesus gave him no answer. ¹⁰The chief priests and the teachers of the law were standing there, vehemently accusing him. ¹¹Then Herod and his soldiers ridiculed and mocked him. Dressing him in an elegant robe, they sent him back to Pilate. ¹²That day Herod and Pilate became friends—before this they had been enemies.

¹³Pilate called together the chief priests, the rulers and the people, ¹⁴and said to them, "You brought me this man as one who was inciting the people to rebellion. I have examined him in your presence and have found no basis for your charges against him. ¹⁵Neither has Herod, for he sent him back to us; as you can see, he has done nothing to deserve death. ¹⁶Therefore, I will punish him and then release him."ᶜ

¹⁸With one voice they cried out, "Away with this man! Release Barabbas to us!" (¹⁹Barabbas had been thrown into prison for an insurrection in the city, and for murder.)

²⁰Wanting to release Jesus, Pilate appealed to them again. ²¹But they kept shouting, "Crucify him! Crucify him!"

²²For the third time he spoke to them: "Why? What crime has this man committed? I have found in him no grounds for the death penalty. Therefore I will have him punished and then release him."

²³But with loud shouts they insistently demanded that he be crucified, and their shouts prevailed. ²⁴So Pilate decided to grant their demand. ²⁵He released the man who had been thrown into prison for insurrection and murder, the one they asked for, and surrendered Jesus to their will.

The Crucifixion

²⁶As they led him away, they seized Simon from Cyrene, who was on his way in from the country, and put the cross on him and made him carry it behind Jesus. ²⁷A large number of people followed him, including women who mourned and wailed for him. ²⁸Jesus turned and said to them, "Daughters of Jerusalem, do not weep for me; weep for yourselves and for your children. ²⁹For the time will come when you will say, 'Blessed are the barren women, the wombs that never bore and the breasts that never nursed!' ³⁰Then

" 'they will say to the mountains, "Fall on us!"
and to the hills "Cover us!" ' ᵈ

³¹For if men do these things when the tree is green, what will happen when it is dry?"

³²Two other men, both criminals, were also led out with him to be executed. ³³When they came to the place called the Skull, there they crucified him, along

---

ᵈ67 Or Messiah   ᵃ2 Or Messiah; also in verses 35 and 39   ᵇ5 Or over the land of the Jews
ᶜ16 Some manuscripts him." ¹⁷Now he was obliged to release one man to them at the Feast.   ᵈ30 Hosea 10:8

with the criminals—one on his right, the other on his left. [34]Jesus said, "Father, forgive them, for they do not know what they are doing." [e] And they divided up his clothes by casting lots.

23:34   These words of Jesus on the cross, and his words to the terrorist crucified with him (verse 43), are to be found only in Luke. Luke presented the dying Jesus as a way into God, who puts no limits on his forgiveness.

---

[35]The people stood watching, and the rulers even sneered at him. They said, "He saved others; let him save himself if he is the Christ of God, the Chosen One."

[36]The soldiers also came up and mocked him. They offered him wine vinegar [37]and said, "If you are the king of the Jews, save yourself."

[38]There was a written notice above him, which read: THIS IS THE KING OF THE JEWS.

[39]One of the criminals who hung there hurled insults at him: "Aren't you the Christ? Save yourself and us!"

[40]But the other criminal rebuked him. "Don't you fear God," he said, "since you are under the same sentence? [41]We are punished justly, for we are getting what our deeds deserve. But this man has done nothing wrong."

[42]Then he said, "Jesus, remember me when you come into your kingdom.[f]"

[43]Jesus answered him, "I tell you the truth, today you will be with me in paradise."

Jesus' Death

[44]It was now about the sixth hour, and darkness came over the whole land until the ninth hour, [45]for the sun stopped shining. And the curtain of the temple was torn in two. [46]Jesus called out with a loud voice, "Father, into your hands I commit my spirit." When he had said this, he breathed his last.

[47]The centurion, seeing what had happened, praised God and said, "Surely this was a righteous man." [48]When all the people who had gathered to witness this sight saw what took place, they beat their breasts and went away. [49]But all those who knew him, including the women who had followed him from Galilee, stood at a distance, watching these things.

Jesus' Burial

[50]Now there was a man named Joseph, a member of the Council, a good and upright man, [51]who had not consented to their decision and action. He came from the Judean town of Arimathea and he was waiting for the kingdom of God. [52]Going to Pilate, he asked for Jesus' body. [53]Then he took it down, wrapped it in linen cloth and placed it in a tomb cut in the rock, one in which no-one had yet been laid. [54]It was Preparation Day, and the Sabbath was about to begin.

[55]The women who had come with Jesus from Galilee followed Joseph and saw the tomb and how his body was laid in it. [56]Then they went home and prepared spices and perfumes. But they rested on the Sabbath in obedience to the commandment.

The Resurrection

24 On the first day of the week, very early in the morning, the women took the spices they had prepared and went to the tomb. [2]They found the stone rolled away from the tomb, [3]but when they entered, they did not find the body of the Lord Jesus. [4]While they were wondering about this, suddenly two men in clothes that gleamed like lightning stood beside them. [5]In their fright the women bowed down with their faces to the ground, but the men said to them, "Why do you look for the living among the dead? [6]He is not here; he has risen! Remember how he told you, while he was still with you in Galilee: [7]'The Son of Man must be delivered into the hands of sinful men, be crucified and on the third day be raised again.' " [8]Then they remembered his words.

[9]When they came back from the tomb, they told all these things to the Eleven and to all the others. [10]It was Mary Magdalene, Joanna, Mary the mother of James, and the others with them who told this to the apostles. [11]But they did not believe the women, because their words seemed to them like nonsense. [12]Peter, however, got up and ran to the tomb. Bending over, he saw the strips of linen lying by themselves, and he went away, wondering to himself what had happened.

On the Road to Emmaus

[13]Now that same day two of them were going to a village called Emmaus, about seven miles[a] from Jerusalem. [14]They were talking with each other about everything that had happened. [15]As they talked and discussed these things with each other, Jesus himself came up and walked along with them; [16]but they were kept from recognising him.

[17]He asked them, "What are you discussing together as you walk along?"

They stood still, their faces downcast. [18]One of them, named Cleopas, asked him, "Are you only a visitor to Jerusalem and do not know the things that have happened there in these days?"

[19]"What things?" he asked.

"About Jesus of Nazareth," they replied. "He was a prophet, powerful in word and deed before God and all the people. [20]The chief priests and our rulers handed him over to be sentenced to death, and they crucified him; [21]but we had hoped that he was the one who was going to redeem Israel. And what is more, it is the third day since all this took place. [22]In addition, some of our women amazed us. They went to the tomb early this morning [23]but didn't find his body. They came and told us that they had seen a vision of angels, who said he was alive. [24]Then some of our companions went to the

---

[e]34 Some early manuscripts do not have this sentence.
[a]13 Greek *sixty stadia* (about 11 kilometres)   [f]42 Some manuscripts *come with your kingly power*

tomb and found it just as the women had said, but him they did not see." 25He said to them, "How foolish you are, and how slow of heart to believe all that the prophets have spoken! 26Did not the Christ[b] have to suffer these things and then enter his glory?" 27And beginning with Moses and all the Prophets, he explained to them what was said in all the Scriptures concerning himself.

28As they approached the village to which they were going, Jesus acted as if he were going further. 29But they urged him strongly, "Stay with us, for it is nearly evening; the day is almost over." So he went in to stay with them.

30When he was at the table with them, he took bread, gave thanks, broke it and began to give it to them. 31Then their eyes were opened and they recognised him, and he disappeared from their sight. 32They asked each other, "Were not our hearts burning within us while he talked with us on the road and opened the Scriptures to us?"

24:30   Of all the resurrection stories, that of the Emmaus pilgrims has always been recognized as the most sensitive, with its blend of the mysterious and the ordinary, of the unknown and the familiar. It is a reminder that the risen Christ can be perceived by the senses, and yet remains mysterious and cannot be fully grasped.

33They got up and returned at once to Jerusalem. There they found the Eleven and those with them, assembled together 34and saying, "It is true! The Lord has risen and has appeared to Simon." 35Then the two told what had happened on the way, and how Jesus was recognised by them when he broke the bread.

Jesus Appears to the Disciples

36While they were still talking about this, Jesus himself stood among them and said to them, "Peace be with you."

37They were startled and frightened, thinking they saw a ghost. 38He said to them, "Why are you troubled, and why do doubts rise in your minds? 39Look at my hands and my feet. It is I myself! Touch me and see; a ghost does not have flesh and bones, as you see I have."

40When he had said this, he showed them his hands and feet. 41And while they still did not believe it because of joy and amazement, he asked them, "Do you have anything here to eat?" 42They gave him a piece of broiled fish, 43and he took it and ate it in their presence.

44He said to them, "This is what I told you while I was still with you: Everything must be fulfilled that is written about me in the Law of Moses, the Prophets and the Psalms."

45Then he opened their minds so they could understand the Scriptures. 46He told them, "This is what is written: The Christ will suffer and rise from the dead on the third day, 47and repentance and forgiveness of sins will be preached in his name to all nations, beginning at Jerusalem. 48You are witnesses of these things. 49I am going to send you what my Father has promised; but stay in the city until you have been clothed with power from on high."

The Ascension

50When he had led them out to the vicinity of Bethany, he lifted up his hands and blessed them. 51While he was blessing them, he left them and was taken up into heaven. 52Then they worshipped him and returned to Jerusalem with great joy. 53And they stayed continually at the temple, praising God.

[b]26 Or Messiah; also in verse 46

John

A Different Book

You'll only need to read a couple of chapters of John's Gospel to realize how different it is from the other three. It is not just the style and language that are in contrast. John's Gospel has relatively little material in common with Matthew, Mark, and Luke, and what it does have is approached from a very different angle.

The contrast is clear from the start. The writer doesn't include an account of Jesus' birth, nor does he launch straight into Jesus' ministry. Instead he gives us the famous "prologue", so familiar from Christmas services, in which he describes Jesus as the Word made flesh (1:1–18). This rather more developed idea about Jesus permeates the whole Gospel. Instead of fairly short sections found in the other three Gospels, in John there are more extended passages which develop the real significance of an event and put it in a more theological perspective. For example, John has accounts of seven miracles (only two of which are found in Matthew, Mark, or Luke), but each is called a "sign", a pointer to a deeper reality, and some are incorporated into much larger passages explaining their significance, for example Jesus healing a blind man (chapter 9).

Early and Late

Some scholars believe that John was written much later than the other three Gospels because it is more advanced in its theology, and seems to have been intended for Greek readership. This is because the author understood the significance of Jesus in a much more developed way than the other three Gospel writers. He did not rely so heavily on "Jewish" ideas about Jesus being a fulfilment of ancient prophets, but tended towards the idea of "incarnation" (compare the openings of Mark and John). This idea about gods coming to earth in human form was rooted in Greek philosophy. But although the ideas in the Gospel are more advanced, it is an early book. The author knew Jerusalem well before the Romans destroyed it in AD 70. His knowledge of the temple, his familiarity with Jewish feasts and festivals, his description of streets—like Gabbatha in the crucifixion narrative—which were destroyed as part of the overthrow of Jerusalem, all point to this. The early church was also right to associate the Gospel with the disciple John. He was around with Jesus and knew about the life of the city. If he did not actually write it himself, it is very likely that he was behind the material used.

Truth and Belief

Gnosticism is a general term for a wide range of beliefs which arose during the first century. It was based on Greek philosophy, and contained a mixture of beliefs, but its unique distinguishing feature was the conviction that the physical world was inferior to knowledge. By learning knowledge a person became enlightened to be able to escape from the confines of the physical world and become part of a superior (heavenly) world. This knowledge was revealed only to an elite group, whose souls would be released from their bodily "prison". As a result, Gnostics could not accept that Jesus the man was also the Christ, the anointed Son of God. Instead, they argued that he only appeared to be human, but was actually a "sub god". This meant that he couldn't have died or been raised from death, and thus denied the heart of the Christian faith preached by the apostles. Jesus' humanity is graphically described by this writer, as is his relationship with his heavenly Father. He is the Word made flesh.

A Different Type of Teaching

Unlike the other Gospel writers, the author of John's Gospel conveyed Jesus' teaching not in parables, but in dialogues and lengthy discourses. Sometimes he addressed a crowd, sometimes he talked with an individual. Perhaps the best known teachings on John are the seven "I am" sayings, which focus on Jesus' identity and mission. Some are based on passages which develop a particular symbol: "I am the bread of life" (6:35); "I am the light of the world" (8:12); "I am the good shepherd" (10:11); "I am the gate for the sheep" (10:7); and "I am the true vine" (15:1). "I am the resurrection and the life" (11:25) comes in the account of Lazarus being raised from death. All of them are summed up in the words "I am the way and the truth and the life" (14:6).

A Dramatic End

Almost half of John's Gospel is involved with the last week of Jesus' life. From 12:1 onwards we see Jesus' inevitable procession to the cross. The "farewell discourses" (chapters 14—17) take up some of this, but even the action narratives contain theological reflection. For John's Gospel, the cross is the crowning glory of Jesus' life, the supreme achievement of his mission. His work was to fulfil his Father's plan for the salvation of humankind, and so, in a complete paradox, Jesus' glory is seen fully as he dies on the cross.

Why was this Gospel written? The answer is clear in 20:31. The author could have chosen from many events in Jesus' life, and from a large amount of his teachings. But he chose the selection he did to persuade people to believe that Jesus is who he claimed to be, and above all, to enjoy the new life he came to bring.

The Word Became Flesh

1 In the beginning was the Word, and the Word was with God, and the Word was God. [2]He was with God in the beginning.

[3]Through him all things were made; without him nothing was made that has been made. [4]In him was life, and that life was the light of men. [5]The light shines in the darkness, but the darkness has not understood[a] it.

[6]There came a man who was sent from God; his name was John. [7]He came as a witness to testify concerning that light, so that through him all men might believe. [8]He himself was not the light; he came only as a witness to the light. [9]The true light that gives light to every man was coming into the world.[b]

a 5 Or darkness, and the darkness has not overcome
b 9 Or This was the true light that gives light to every man who comes into the world

[10]He was in the world, and though the world was made through him, the world did not recognise him. [11]He came to that which was his own, but his own did not receive him. [12]Yet to all who received him, to those who believed in his name, he gave the right to become children of God—[13]children born not of natural descent,[c] nor of human decision or a husband's will, but born of God.

1:1 "Logos" is the Greek for "word". It has many shades of meaning, but only here and in 1 John does it refer to Jesus. The writer of this prologue used a Greek secular term to help people understand a Christian truth.

---

[14]The Word became flesh and made his dwelling among us. We have seen his glory, the glory of the One and Only,[d] who came from the Father, full of grace and truth. [15]John testifies concerning him. He cries out, saying, "This was he of whom I said, 'He who comes after me has surpassed me because he was before me.' " [16]From the fulness of his grace we have all received one blessing after another. [17]For the law was given through Moses; grace and truth came through Jesus Christ. [18]No-one has ever seen God, but God the One and Only,[e,f] who is at the Father's side, has made him known.

John the Baptist Denies Being the Christ

[19]Now this was John's testimony when the Jews of Jerusalem sent priests and Levites to ask him who he was. [20]He did not fail to confess, but confessed freely, "I am not the Christ."[g]

[21]They asked him, "Then who are you? Are you Elijah?"

He said, "I am not."

"Are you the Prophet?"

He answered, "No."

[22]Finally they said, "Who are you? Give us an answer to take back to those who sent us. What do you say about yourself?"

[23]John replied in the words of Isaiah the prophet, "I am the voice of one calling in the desert, 'Make straight the way for the Lord.'[h]"

[24]Now some Pharisees who had been sent [25]questioned him, "Why then do you baptise if you are not the Christ, nor Elijah, nor the Prophet?"

[26]"I baptise with[i] water," John replied, "but among you stands one you do not know. [27]He is the one who comes after me, the thongs of whose sandals I am not worthy to untie."

[28]This all happened at Bethany on the other side of the Jordan, where John was baptising.

Jesus the Lamb of God

[29]The next day John saw Jesus coming towards him and said, "Look, the Lamb of God, who takes away the sin of the world! [30]This is the one I meant when I said, 'A man who comes after me has surpassed me because he was before me.' [31]I myself did not know him, but the reason I came baptising with water was that he might be revealed to Israel."

[32]Then John gave this testimony: "I saw the Spirit come down from heaven as a dove and remain on him. [33]I would not have known him, except that the one who sent me to baptise with water told me, 'The man on whom you see the Spirit come down and remain is he who will baptise with the Holy Spirit.' [34]I have seen and I testify that this is the Son of God."

Jesus' First Disciples

[35]The next day John was there again with two of his disciples. [36]When he saw Jesus passing by, he said, "Look, the Lamb of God!"

[37]When the two disciples heard him say this, they followed Jesus. [38]Turning round, Jesus saw them following and asked, "What do you want?"

They said, "Rabbi" (which means Teacher), "where are you staying?"

[39]"Come," he replied, "and you will see."

So they went and saw where he was staying, and spent that day with him. It was about the tenth hour.

[40]Andrew, Simon Peter's brother, was one of the two who heard what John had said and who had followed Jesus. [41]The first thing Andrew did was to find his brother Simon and tell him, "We have found the Messiah" (that is, the Christ). [42]And he brought him to Jesus.

Jesus looked at him and said, "You are Simon son of John. You will be called Cephas" (which, when translated, is Peter[j]).

Jesus Calls Philip and Nathanael

[43]The next day Jesus decided to leave for Galilee. Finding Philip, he said to him, "Follow me."

[44]Philip, like Andrew and Peter, was from the town of Bethsaida. [45]Philip found Nathanael and told him, "We have found the one Moses wrote about in the Law, and about whom the prophets also wrote—Jesus of Nazareth, the son of Joseph."

[46]"Nazareth! Can anything good come from there?" Nathanael asked.

"Come and see," said Philip.

[47]When Jesus saw Nathanael approaching, he said of him, "Here is a true Israelite, in whom there is nothing false."

[48]"How do you know me?" Nathanael asked.

Jesus answered, "I saw you while you were still under the fig-tree before Philip called you."

[49]Then Nathanael declared, "Rabbi, you are the Son of God; you are the King of Israel."

---

[c]13 Greek *of bloods*   [d]14 Or *the Only Begotten*   [e]18 Or *the Only Begotten*
[f]18 Some manuscripts *but the only* (or *only begotten*) *Son*
[g]20 Or *Messiah*. "The Christ" (Greek) and "the Messiah" (Hebrew) both mean "the Anointed One"; also in verse 25.
[h]23 Isaiah 40:3   [i]26 Or *in*; also in verses 31 and 33   [j]42 Both *Cephas* (Aramaic) and *Peter* (Greek) mean *rock*.

[50]Jesus said, "You believe[k] because I told you I saw you under the fig-tree. You shall see greater things than that." [51]He then added, "I tell you[l] the truth, you[l] shall see heaven open, and the angels of God ascending and descending on the Son of Man."

Jesus Changes Water to Wine

2 On the third day a wedding took place at Cana in Galilee. Jesus' mother was there, [2]and Jesus and his disciples had also been invited to the wedding. [3]When the wine was gone, Jesus' mother said to him, "They have no more wine."

[4]"Dear woman, why do you involve me?" Jesus replied. "My time has not yet come."

[5]His mother said to the servants, "Do whatever he tells you."

[6]Nearby stood six stone water jars, the kind used by the Jews for ceremonial washing, each holding from twenty to thirty gallons.[a]

[7]Jesus said to the servants, "Fill the jars with water"; so they filled them to the brim.

[8]Then he told them, "Now draw some out and take it to the master of the banquet."

They did so, [9]and the master of the banquet tasted the water that had been turned into wine. He did not realise where it had come from, though the servants who had drawn the water knew. Then he called the bridegroom aside [10]and said, "Everyone brings out the choice wine first and then the cheaper wine after the guests have had too much to drink; but you have saved the best till now."

[11]This, the first of his miraculous signs, Jesus performed at Cana in Galilee. He thus revealed his glory, and his disciples put their faith in him.

Jesus Clears the Temple

[12]After this he went down to Capernaum with his mother and brothers and his disciples. There they stayed for a few days.

[13]When it was almost time for the Jewish Passover, Jesus went up to Jerusalem. [14]In the temple courts he found men selling cattle, sheep and doves, and others sitting at tables exchanging money. [15]So he made a whip out of cords, and drove all from the temple area, both sheep and cattle; he scattered the coins of the money-changers and overturned their tables. [16]To those who sold doves he said, "Get these out of here! How dare you turn my Father's house into a market!"

[17]His disciples remembered that it is written: "Zeal for your house will consume me."[b]

[18]Then the Jews demanded of him, "What miraculous sign can you show us to prove your authority to do all this?"

[19]Jesus answered them, "Destroy this temple, and I will raise it again in three days."

[20]The Jews replied, "It has taken forty-six years to build this temple, and you are going to raise it in three days?" [21]But the temple he had spoken of was his body. [22]After he was raised from the dead, his disciples recalled what he had said. Then they believed the Scripture and the words that Jesus had spoken.

2:18 The running dispute between Jesus and the Jewish leaders about his authority and power to teach and preach as he did, and to perform "signs and wonders" to demonstrate the truth of what he said, is a recurring theme in John's Gospel.

---

[23]Now while he was in Jerusalem at the Passover Feast, many people saw the miraculous signs he was doing and believed in his name.[c] [24]But Jesus would not entrust himself to them, for he knew all men. [25]He did not need man's testimony about man, for he knew what was in a man.

Jesus Teaches Nicodemus

3 Now there was a man of the Pharisees named Nicodemus, a member of the Jewish ruling council. [2]He came to Jesus at night and said, "Rabbi, we know you are a teacher who has come from God. For no-one could perform the miraculous signs you are doing if God were not with him."

[3]In reply Jesus declared, "I tell you the truth, no-one can see the kingdom of God unless he is born again."[a]

[4]"How can a man be born when he is old?" Nicodemus asked. "Surely he cannot enter a second time into his mother's womb to be born!"

[5]Jesus answered, "I tell you the truth, no-one can enter the kingdom of God unless he is born of water and the Spirit. [6]Flesh gives birth to flesh, but the Spirit[b] gives birth to spirit. [7]You should not be surprised at my saying, 'You[c] must be born again.' [8]The wind blows wherever it pleases. You hear its sound, but you cannot tell where it comes from or where it is going. So it is with everyone born of the Spirit."

[9]"How can this be?" Nicodemus asked.

[10]"You are Israel's teacher," said Jesus, "and do you not understand these things? [11]I tell you the truth, we speak of what we know, and we testify to what we have seen, but still you people do not accept our testimony. [12]I have spoken to you of earthly things and you do not believe; how then will you believe if I speak of heavenly things? [13]No-one has ever gone into heaven except the one who came from heaven—the Son of Man.[d] [14]Just as Moses lifted up the snake in the desert, so the Son of Man must be lifted up, [15]that everyone who believes in him may have eternal life.[e]

3:14 This is a reference to Numbers 21:4–9. The bronze serpent erected by Moses was a symbol of healing and salvation—all who looked at it were restored, and drawn back to God. Similarly, Jesus will be "lifted up" on the cross, and draw people to himself to receive healing and salvation.

---

[k]50 Or Do you believe . . . ?　　[l]51 The Greek is plural.　　[a]6 Greek two to three metretes (probably about 75 to 115 litres)
[b]17 Psalm 69:9　　[c]23 Or and believed in him　　[a]3 Or born from above; also in verse 7　　[b]6 Or but spirit
[c]7 The Greek is plural　　[d]13 Some manuscripts Man, who is in heaven　　[e]15 Or believes may have eternal life in him

16"For God so loved the world that he gave his one and only Son,ᶠ that whoever believes in him shall not perish but have eternal life. 17For God did not send his Son into the world to condemn the world, but to save the world through him. 18Whoever believes in him is not condemned, but whoever does not believe stands condemned already because he has not believed in the name of God's one and only Son.ᵍ 19This is the verdict: Light has come into the world, but men loved darkness instead of light because their deeds were evil. 20Everyone who does evil hates the light, and will not come into the light for fear that his deeds will be exposed. 21But whoever lives by the truth comes into the light, so that it may be seen plainly that what he has done has been done through God."ʰ

John the Baptist's Testimony About Jesus

22After this, Jesus and his disciples went out into the Judean countryside, where he spent some time with them, and baptised. 23Now John also was baptising at Aenon near Salim, because there was plenty of water, and people were constantly coming to be baptised. 24(This was before John was put in prison.) 25An argument developed between some of John's disciples and a certain Jewⁱ over the matter of ceremonial washing. 26They came to John and said to him, "Rabbi, that man who was with you on the other side of the Jordan — the one you testified about — well, he is baptising, and everyone is going to him."

27To this John replied, "A man can receive only what is given him from heaven. 28You yourselves can testify that I said, 'I am not the Christʲ but am sent ahead of him.' 29The bride belongs to the bridegroom. The friend who attends the bridegroom waits and listens for him, and is full of joy when he hears the bridegroom's voice. That joy is mine, and it is now complete. 30He must become greater; I must become less.

31"The one who comes from above is above all; the one who is from the earth belongs to the earth, and speaks as one from the earth. The one who comes from heaven is above all. 32He testifies to what he has seen and heard, but no-one accepts his testimony. 33The man who has accepted it has certified that God is truthful. 34For the one whom God has sent speaks the words of God, for Godᵏ gives the Spirit without limit. 35The Father loves the Son and has placed everything in his hands. 36Whoever believes in the Son has eternal life, but whoever rejects the Son will not see life, for God's wrath remains on him."ˡ

Jesus Talks With a Samaritan Woman

4 The Pharisees heard that Jesus was gaining and baptising more disciples than John, 2although in fact it was not Jesus who baptised, but his disciples. 3When the Lord learned of this, he left Judea and went back once more to Galilee.

4Now he had to go through Samaria. 5So he came to a town in Samaria called Sychar, near the plot of ground Jacob had given to his son Joseph. 6Jacob's well was there, and Jesus, tired as he was from the journey, sat down by the well. It was about the sixth hour.

4:5 Samaria was the old capital of the northern part of the divided kingdom of Israel. Those from the Southern Kingdom of Judah (Jerusalem was the capital) thought very badly of Samaritans. For Jesus to talk to a Samaritan was a scandal, let alone to a woman who had a history of broken marriages.

7When a Samaritan woman came to draw water, Jesus said to her, "Will you give me a drink?" 8(His disciples had gone into the town to buy food.)

9The Samaritan woman said to him, "You are a Jew and I am a Samaritan woman. How can you ask me for a drink?" (For Jews do not associate with Samaritans.ᵃ)

10Jesus answered her, "If you knew the gift of God and who it is that asks you for a drink, you would have asked him and he would have given you living water."

11"Sir," the woman said, "you have nothing to draw with and the well is deep. Where can you get this living water? 12Are you greater than our father Jacob, who gave us the well and drank from it himself, as did also his sons and his flocks and herds?"

13Jesus answered, "Everyone who drinks this water will be thirsty again, 14but whoever drinks the water I give him will never thirst. Indeed, the water I give him will become in him a spring of water welling up to eternal life."

15The woman said to him, "Sir, give me this water so that I won't get thirsty and have to keep coming here to draw water."

16He told her, "Go, call your husband and come back."

17"I have no husband," she replied.

Jesus said to her, "You are right when you say you have no husband. 18The fact is, you have had five husbands, and the man you now have is not your husband. What you have just said is quite true."

19"Sir," the woman said, "I can see that you are a prophet. 20Our fathers worshipped on this mountain, but you Jews claim that the place where we must worship is in Jerusalem."

4:20 One of the big arguments between Jews and Samaritans was over where true worship should take place. The Jews believed that worship was only acceptable to God in Jerusalem and the temple. Jesus stated that true worship is not restricted to one place — God is more concerned with a sincere heart and mind.

21Jesus declared, "Believe me, woman, a time is coming when you will worship the Father neither on

---

ᶠ16 Or *his only begotten Son*   ᵍ18 Or *God's only begotten Son*
ⁱ25 Some manuscripts *and certain Jews*   ʲ28 Or *Messiah*
ˡ36 Some interpreters end the quotation after verse 30.
ʰ21 Some interpreters end the quotation after verse 15.
ᵏ34 Greek *he*
ᵃ9 Or *do not use dishes Samaritans have used*

this mountain nor in Jerusalem. ²²You Samaritans worship what you do not know; we worship what we do know, for salvation is from the Jews. ²³Yet a time is coming and has now come when the true worshippers will worship the Father in spirit and truth, for they are the kind of worshippers the Father seeks. ²⁴God is spirit, and his worshippers must worship in spirit and in truth."

²⁵The woman said, "I know that Messiah" (called Christ) "is coming. When he comes, he will explain everything to us."

²⁶Then Jesus declared, "I who speak to you am he."

The Disciples Rejoin Jesus

²⁷Just then his disciples returned and were surprised to find him talking with a woman. But no-one asked, "What do you want?" or "Why are you talking with her?"

²⁸Then, leaving her water jar, the woman went back to the town and said to the people, ²⁹"Come, see a man who told me everything I ever did. Could this be the Christ?" ᵇ ³⁰They came out of the town and made their way towards him.

³¹Meanwhile his disciples urged him, "Rabbi, eat something."

³²But he said to them, "I have food to eat that you know nothing about."

³³Then his disciples said to each other, "Could someone have brought him food?"

³⁴"My food," said Jesus, "is to do the will of him who sent me and to finish his work. ³⁵Do you not say, 'Four months more and then the harvest'? I tell you, open your eyes and look at the fields! They are ripe for harvest. ³⁶Even now the reaper draws his wages, even now he harvests the crop for eternal life, so that the sower and the reaper may be glad together. ³⁷Thus the saying 'One sows and another reaps' is true. ³⁸I sent you to reap what you have not worked for. Others have done the hard work, and you have reaped the benefits of their labour."

Many Samaritans Believe

³⁹Many of the Samaritans from that town believed in him because of the woman's testimony, "He told me everything I ever did." ⁴⁰So when the Samaritans came to him, they urged him to stay with them, and he stayed two days. ⁴¹And because of his words many more became believers.

⁴²They said to the woman, "We no longer believe just because of what you said; now we have heard for ourselves, and we know that this man really is the Saviour of the world."

Jesus Heals the Official's Son

⁴³After the two days he left for Galilee. ⁴⁴(Now Jesus himself had pointed out that a prophet has no honour in his own country.) ⁴⁵When he arrived in Galilee, the Galileans welcomed him. They had seen all that he had done in Jerusalem at the Passover Feast, for they also had been there.

⁴⁶Once more he visited Cana in Galilee, where he had turned the water into wine. And there was a certain royal official whose son lay sick at Capernaum. ⁴⁷When this man heard that Jesus had arrived in Galilee from Judea, he went to him and begged him to come and heal his son, who was close to death.

4:47   This account of a "sign" has obvious similarities with the accounts of the healing of the centurion's servant in Luke 7:2–10 and Matthew 8:5–13. It may be the same incident described here, but the variations between the reports highlight the different things that John wanted to emphasize.

---

⁴⁸"Unless you people see miraculous signs and wonders," Jesus told him, "you will never believe."

⁴⁹The royal official said, "Sir, come down before my child dies."

⁵⁰Jesus replied, "You may go. Your son will live."

The man took Jesus at his word and departed. ⁵¹While he was still on the way, his servants met him with the news that his boy was living. ⁵²When he enquired as to the time when his son got better, they said to him, "The fever left him yesterday at the seventh hour."

⁵³Then the father realised that this was the exact time at which Jesus had said to him, "Your son will live." So he and all his household believed.

⁵⁴This was the second miraculous sign that Jesus performed, having come from Judea to Galilee.

The Healing at the Pool

5 Some time later, Jesus went up to Jerusalem for a feast of the Jews. ²Now there is in Jerusalem near the Sheep Gate a pool, which in Aramaic is called Bethesdaᵃ and which is surrounded by five covered colonnades. ³Here a great number of disabled people used to lie—the blind, the lame, the paralysed. ᵇ ⁵One who was there had been an invalid for thirty-eight years. ⁶When Jesus saw him lying there and learned that he had been in this condition for a long time, he asked him, "Do you want to get well?"

⁷"Sir," the invalid replied, "I have no-one to help me into the pool when the water is stirred. While I am trying to get in, someone else goes down ahead of me."

⁸Then Jesus said to him, "Get up! Pick up your mat and walk." ⁹At once the man was cured; he picked up his mat and walked.

The day on which this took place was a Sabbath, ¹⁰and so the Jews said to the man who had been healed, "It is the Sabbath; the law forbids you to carry your mat."

¹¹But he replied, "The man who made me well said to me, 'Pick up your mat and walk.' "

ᵇ29 Or *Messiah*   ᵃ2 Some manuscripts *Bethzatha*; other manuscripts *Bethsaida*
ᵇ3 Some less important manuscripts *paralysed—and they waited for the moving of the waters.* ⁴*From time to time an angel of the Lord would come down and stir up the waters. The first one into the pool after each such disturbance would be cured of whatever disease he had.*

[12]So they asked him, "Who is this fellow who told you to pick it up and walk?"

[13]The man who was healed had no idea who it was, for Jesus had slipped away into the crowd that was there.

[14]Later Jesus found him at the temple and said to him, "See, you are well again. Stop sinning or something worse may happen to you." [15]The man went away and told the Jews that it was Jesus who had made him well.

Life Through the Son

[16]So, because Jesus was doing these things on the Sabbath, the Jews persecuted him. [17]Jesus said to them, "My Father is always at his work to this very day, and I, too, am working." [18]For this reason the Jews tried all the harder to kill him; not only was he breaking the Sabbath, but he was even calling God his own Father, making himself equal with God.

[19]Jesus gave them this answer: "I tell you the truth, the Son can do nothing by himself; he can do only what he sees his Father doing, because whatever the Father does the Son also does. [20]For the Father loves the Son and shows him all he does. Yes, to your amazement he will show him even greater things than these. [21]For just as the Father raises the dead and gives them life, even so the Son gives life to whom he is pleased to give it. [22]Moreover, the Father judges no-one, but has entrusted all judgment to the Son, [23]that all may honour the Son just as they honour the Father. He who does not honour the Son does not honour the Father, who sent him.

[24]"I tell you the truth, whoever hears my word and believes him who sent me has eternal life and will not be condemned; he has crossed over from death to life. [25]I tell you the truth, a time is coming and has now come when the dead will hear the voice of the Son of God and those who hear will live. [26]For as the Father has life in himself, so he has granted the Son to have life in himself. [27]And he has given him authority to judge because he is the Son of Man.

[28]"Do not be amazed at this, for a time is coming when all who are in their graves will hear his voice [29]and come out—those who have done good will rise to live, and those who have done evil will rise to be condemned. [30]By myself I can do nothing; I judge only as I hear, and my judgment is just, for I seek not to please myself but him who sent me.

Testimonies About Jesus

[31]"If I testify about myself, my testimony is not valid. [32]There is another who testifies in my favour, and I know that his testimony about me is valid.

[33]"You have sent to John and he has testified to the truth. [34]Not that I accept human testimony; but I mention it that you may be saved. [35]John was a lamp that burned and gave light, and you chose for a time to enjoy his light.

[36]"I have testimony weightier than that of John. For the very work that the Father has given me to finish, and which I am doing, testifies that the Father has sent me. [37]And the Father who sent me has himself testified concerning me. You have never heard his voice nor seen his form, [38]nor does his word dwell in you, for you do not believe the one he sent. [39]You diligently study[c] the Scriptures because you think that by them you possess eternal life. These are the Scriptures that testify about me, [40]yet you refuse to come to me to have life.

[41]"I do not accept praise from men, [42]but I know you. I know that you do not have the love of God in your hearts. [43]I have come in my Father's name, and you do not accept me; but if someone else comes in his own name, you will accept him. [44]How can you believe if you accept praise from one another, yet make no effort to obtain the praise that comes from the only God?[d]

[45]"But do not think I will accuse you before the Father. Your accuser is Moses, on whom your hopes are set. [46]If you believed Moses, you would believe me, for he wrote about me. [47]But since you do not believe what he wrote, how are you going to believe what I say?"

Jesus Feeds the Five Thousand

6 Some time after this, Jesus crossed to the far shore of the Sea of Galilee (that is, the Sea of Tiberias), [2]and a great crowd of people followed him because they saw the miraculous signs he had performed on the sick. [3]Then Jesus went up on a mountainside and sat down with his disciples. [4]The Jewish Passover Feast was near.

[5]When Jesus looked up and saw a great crowd coming towards him, he said to Philip, "Where shall we buy bread for these people to eat?" [6]He asked this only to test him, for he already had in mind what he was going to do.

[7]Philip answered him, "Eight months' wages[a] would not buy enough bread for each one to have a bite!"

[8]Another of his disciples, Andrew, Simon Peter's brother, spoke up, [9]"Here is a boy with five small barley loaves and two small fish, but how far will they go among so many?"

[10]Jesus said, "Make the people sit down." There was plenty of grass in that place, and the men sat down, about five thousand of them. [11]Jesus then took the loaves, gave thanks, and distributed to those who were seated as much as they wanted. He did the same with the fish.

[12]When they had all had enough to eat, he said to his disciples, "Gather the pieces that are left over. Let nothing be wasted." [13]So they gathered them and filled twelve baskets with the pieces of the five barley loaves left over by those who had eaten.

[14]After the people saw the miraculous sign that Jesus did, they began to say, "Surely this is the Prophet who is to come into the world." [15]Jesus, knowing that they intended to come and make him king by force, withdrew again to a mountain by himself.

---

[c]39 Or *Study diligently* (the imperative)   [d]44 Some early manuscripts *the Only One*   [a]7 Greek *two hundred denarii*

Jesus Walks on the Water

[16]When evening came, his disciples went down to the lake, [17]where they got into a boat and set off across the lake for Capernaum. By now it was dark, and Jesus had not yet joined them. [18]A strong wind was blowing and the waters grew rough. [19]When they had rowed three or three and a half miles,[b] they saw Jesus approaching the boat, walking on the water; and they were terrified. [20]But he said to them, "It is I; don't be afraid." [21]Then they were willing to take him into the boat, and immediately the boat reached the shore where they were heading.

6:15   The people assumed the coming Messiah would be a political figure, who could free them from the oppression of the Romans. Jesus knew he was not supposed to be their leader in this sense.

[22]The next day the crowd that had stayed on the opposite shore of the lake realised that only one boat had been there, and that Jesus had not entered it with his disciples, but that they had gone away alone. [23]Then some boats from Tiberias landed near the place where the people had eaten the bread after the Lord had given thanks. [24]Once the crowd realised that neither Jesus nor his disciples were there, they got into the boats and went to Capernaum in search of Jesus.

Jesus the Bread of Life

[25]When they found him on the other side of the lake, they asked him, "Rabbi, when did you get here?"
[26]Jesus answered, "I tell you the truth, you are looking for me, not because you saw miraculous signs but because you ate the loaves and had your fill. [27]Do not work for food that spoils, but for food that endures to eternal life, which the Son of Man will give you. On him God the Father has placed his seal of approval."
[28]Then they asked him, "What must we do to do the works God requires?"
[29]Jesus answered, "The work of God is this: to believe in the one he has sent."
[30]So they asked him, "What miraculous sign then will you give that we may see it and believe you? What will you do? [31]Our forefathers ate the manna in the desert; as it is written: 'He gave them bread from heaven to eat.'[c]"

6:31   The story about the people receiving manna is in Exodus 16. Jesus' hearers would have been very familiar with this story, and he used it to help them understand a bit more about who he was.

[32]Jesus said to them, "I tell you the truth, it is not Moses who has given you the bread from heaven, but it is my Father who gives you the true bread from heaven. [33]For the bread of God is he who comes down from heaven and gives life to the world."
[34]"Sir," they said, "from now on give us this bread."
[35]Then Jesus declared, "I am the bread of life. He who comes to me will never go hungry, and he who believes in me will never be thirsty. [36]But as I told you, you have seen me and still you do not believe. [37]All that the Father gives me will come to me, and whoever comes to me I will never drive away. [38]For I have come down from heaven not to do my will but to do the will of him who sent me. [39]And this is the will of him who sent me, that I shall lose none of all that he has given me, but raise them up at the last day. [40]For my Father's will is that everyone who looks to the Son and believes in him shall have eternal life, and I will raise him up at the last day."
[41]At this the Jews began to grumble about him because he said, "I am the bread that came down from heaven." [42]They said, "Is this not Jesus, the son of Joseph, whose father and mother we know? How can he now say, 'I came down from heaven'?"
[43]"Stop grumbling among yourselves," Jesus answered. [44]"No-one can come to me unless the Father who sent me draws him, and I will raise him up at the last day. [45]It is written in the Prophets: 'They will all be taught by God.'[d] Everyone who listens to the Father and learns from him comes to me. [46]No-one has seen the Father except the one who is from God; only he has seen the Father. [47]I tell you the truth, he who believes has everlasting life. [48]I am the bread of life. [49]Your forefathers ate the manna in the desert, yet they died. [50]But here is the bread that comes down from heaven, which a man may eat and not die. [51]I am the living bread that came down from heaven. If anyone eats of this bread, he will live for ever. This bread is my flesh, which I will give for the life of the world."
[52]Then the Jews began to argue sharply among themselves, "How can this man give us his flesh to eat?"
[53]Jesus said to them, "I tell you the truth, unless you eat the flesh of the Son of Man and drink his blood, you have no life in you. [54]Whoever eats my flesh and drinks my blood has eternal life, and I will raise him up at the last day. [55]For my flesh is real food and my blood is real drink. [56]Whoever eats my flesh and drinks my blood remains in me, and I in him. [57]Just as the living Father sent me and I live because of the Father, so the one who feeds on me will live because of me. [58]This is the bread that came down from heaven. Your forefathers ate manna and died, but he who feeds on this bread will live for ever." [59]He said this while teaching in the synagogue in Capernaum.

6:53   Most scholars agree that this passage (verses 53–58) is a reference to Holy Communion. Notice how there are constant references to eternal life.

[b]19 Greek rowed twenty-five or thirty stadia (about 5 or 6 kilometres)
[d]45 Isaiah 54:13
[c]31 Exodus 16:4; Neh. 9:15; Psalm 78:24,25

Many Disciples Desert Jesus

⁶⁰On hearing it, many of his disciples said, "This is a hard teaching. Who can accept it?"

⁶¹Aware that his disciples were grumbling about this, Jesus said to them, "Does this offend you? ⁶²What if you see the Son of Man ascend to where he was before! ⁶³The Spirit gives life; the flesh counts for nothing. The words I have spoken to you are spirit^e and they are life. ⁶⁴Yet there are some of you who do not believe." For Jesus had known from the beginning which of them did not believe and who would betray him. ⁶⁵He went on to say, "This is why I told you that no-one can come to me unless the Father has enabled him."

⁶⁶From this time many of his disciples turned back and no longer followed him.

⁶⁷"You do not want to leave too, do you?" Jesus asked the Twelve.

⁶⁸Simon Peter answered him, "Lord, to whom shall we go? You have the words of eternal life. ⁶⁹We believe and know that you are the Holy One of God."

⁷⁰Then Jesus replied, "Have I not chosen you, the Twelve? Yet one of you is a devil!" ⁷¹(He meant Judas, the son of Simon Iscariot, who, though one of the Twelve, was later to betray him.)

Jesus Goes to the Feast of Tabernacles

7 After this, Jesus went around in Galilee, purposely staying away from Judea because the Jews there were waiting to take his life. ²But when the Jewish Feast of Tabernacles was near, ³Jesus' brothers said to him, "You ought to leave here and go to Judea, so that your disciples may see the miracles you do. ⁴No-one who wants to become a public figure acts in secret. Since you are doing these things, show yourself to the world." ⁵For even his own brothers did not believe in him.

⁶Therefore Jesus told them, "The right time for me has not yet come; for you any time is right. ⁷The world cannot hate you, but it hates me because I testify that what it does is evil. ⁸You go to the Feast. I am not yet^a going up to this Feast, because for me the right time has not yet come." ⁹Having said this, he stayed in Galilee.

¹⁰However, after his brothers had left for the Feast, he went also, not publicly, but in secret. ¹¹Now at the Feast the Jews were watching for him and asking, "Where is that man?"

¹²Among the crowds there was widespread whispering about him. Some said, "He is a good man."

Others replied, "No, he deceives the people." ¹³But no-one would say anything publicly about him for fear of the Jews.

Jesus Teaches at the Feast

¹⁴Not until halfway through the Feast did Jesus go up to the temple courts and begin to teach. ¹⁵The Jews were amazed and asked, "How did this man get such learning without having studied?"

¹⁶Jesus answered, "My teaching is not my own. It comes from him who sent me. ¹⁷If anyone chooses to do God's will, he will find out whether my teaching comes from God or whether I speak on my own. ¹⁸He who speaks on his own does so to gain honour for himself, but he who works for the honour of the one who sent him is a man of truth; there is nothing false about him. ¹⁹Has not Moses given you the law? Yet not one of you keeps the law. Why are you trying to kill me?"

²⁰"You are demon-possessed," the crowd answered. "Who is trying to kill you?"

²¹Jesus said to them, "I did one miracle, and you are all astonished. ²²Yet, because Moses gave you circumcision (though actually it did not come from Moses, but from the patriarchs), you circumcise a child on the Sabbath. ²³Now if a child can be circumcised on the Sabbath so that the law of Moses may not be broken, why are you angry with me for healing the whole man on the Sabbath? ²⁴Stop judging by mere appearances, and make a right judgment."

Is Jesus the Christ?

²⁵At that point some of the people of Jerusalem began to ask, "Isn't this the man they are trying to kill? ²⁶Here he is, speaking publicly, and they are not saying a word to him. Have the authorities really concluded that he is the Christ?^b ²⁷But we know where this man is from; when the Christ comes, no-one will know where he is from."

²⁸Then Jesus, still teaching in the temple courts, cried out, "Yes, you know me, and you know where I am from. I am not here on my own, but he who sent me is true. You do not know him, ²⁹but I know him because I am from him and he sent me."

³⁰At this they tried to seize him, but no-one laid a hand on him, because his time had not yet come. ³¹Still, many in the crowd put their faith in him. They said, "When the Christ comes, will he do more miraculous signs than this man?"

³²The Pharisees heard the crowd whispering such things about him. Then the chief priests and the Pharisees sent temple guards to arrest him.

³³Jesus said, "I am with you for only a short time, and then I go to the one who sent me. ³⁴You will look for me, but you will not find me; and where I am, you cannot come."

³⁵The Jews said to one another, "Where does this man intend to go that we cannot find him? Will he go where our people live scattered among the Greeks, and teach the Greeks? ³⁶What did he mean when he said, 'You will look for me, but you will not find me,' and 'Where I am, you cannot come'?"

³⁷On the last and greatest day of the Feast, Jesus stood and said in a loud voice, "If anyone is thirsty, let him come to me and drink. ³⁸Whoever believes in me, as^c the Scripture has said, streams of living water will flow from within him." ³⁹By this he meant the Spirit, whom those who believed in him were later to receive. Up to that time the Spirit had not been given, since Jesus had not yet been glorified.

---

^e63 Or *Spirit*   ^a8 Some early manuscripts do not have *yet.*   ^b26 Or *Messiah*; also in verses 27, 31, 41 and 42
^c37, 38 Or *If anyone is thirsty, let him come to me. / And let him drink,* ³⁸*who believes in me. / As*

40On hearing his words, some of the people said, "Surely this man is the Prophet."

7:38   The Feast of Tabernacles is described in Leviticus 23:33–43. It was a reminder to the Israelites of their time in the desert after leaving Egypt. Part of the ritual of this festival was to fill a golden flagon with water from the pool of Siloam. Jesus used this symbolic action to underline the significance of his own coming.

41Others said, "He is the Christ."

Still others asked, "How can the Christ come from Galilee? 42Does not the Scripture say that the Christ will come from David's family*d* and from Bethlehem, the town where David lived?" 43Thus the people were divided because of Jesus. 44Some wanted to seize him, but no-one laid a hand on him.

Unbelief of the Jewish Leaders

45Finally the temple guards went back to the chief priests and Pharisees, who asked them, "Why didn't you bring him in?"

46"No-one ever spoke the way this man does," the guards declared.

47"You mean he has deceived you also?" the Pharisees retorted. 48"Has any of the rulers or of the Pharisees believed in him? 49No! But this mob that knows nothing of the law—there is a curse on them."

50Nicodemus, who had gone to Jesus earlier and who was one of their own number, asked, 51"Does our law condemn a man without first hearing him to find out what he is doing?"

52They replied, "Are you from Galilee, too? Look into it, and you will find that a prophet*e* does not come out of Galilee."

[The earliest and most reliable manuscripts and other ancient witnesses do not have John 7:53–8:11.]

53Then each went to his own home.

8 But Jesus went to the Mount of Olives. 2At dawn he appeared again in the temple courts, where all the people gathered round him, and he sat down to teach them. 3The teachers of the law and the Pharisees brought in a woman caught in adultery. They made her stand before the group 4and said to Jesus, "Teacher, this woman was caught in the act of adultery. 5In the Law Moses commanded us to stone such women. Now what do you say?" 6They were using this question as a trap, in order to have a basis for accusing him.

But Jesus bent down and started to write on the ground with his finger. 7When they kept on questioning him, he straightened up and said to them, "If any one of you is without sin, let him be the first to throw a stone at her." 8Again he stooped down and wrote on the ground.

9At this, those who heard began to go away one at a time, the older ones first, until only Jesus was left, with the woman still standing there. 10Jesus straightened up and asked her, "Woman, where are they? Has no-one condemned you?"

8:3   The most reliable early manuscripts omit this account (7:53 – 8:11). It certainly wasn't an original part of the Gospel and was added later, maybe when the punishment for adultery was less severe than at that time. The irony is that the Pharisees were also guilty of breaking the Law, since they had not brought both the people involved in the affair (see Leviticus 20:10).

11"No-one, sir," she said.

"Then neither do I condemn you," Jesus declared. "Go now and leave your life of sin."

The Validity of Jesus' Testimony

12When Jesus spoke again to the people, he said, "I am the light of the world. Whoever follows me will never walk in darkness, but will have the light of life."

13The Pharisees challenged him, "Here you are, appearing as your own witness; your testimony is not valid."

14Jesus answered, "Even if I testify on my own behalf, my testimony is valid, for I know where I came from and where I am going. But you have no idea where I come from or where I am going. 15You judge by human standards; I pass judgment on no-one. 16But if I do judge, my decisions are right, because I am not alone. I stand with the Father, who sent me. 17In your own Law it is written that the testimony of two men is valid. 18I am one who testifies for myself; my other witness is the Father, who sent me."

19Then they asked him, "Where is your father?"

"You do not know me or my Father," Jesus replied. "If you knew me, you would know my Father also." 20He spoke these words while teaching in the temple area near the place where the offerings were put. Yet no-one seized him, because his time had not yet come.

21Once more Jesus said to them, "I am going away, and you will look for me, and you will die in your sin. Where I go, you cannot come."

22This made the Jews ask, "Will he kill himself? Is that why he says, 'Where I go, you cannot come'?"

23But he continued, "You are from below; I am from above. You are of this world; I am not of this world. 24I told you that you would die in your sins; if you do not believe that I am ˌthe one I claim to beˌ,*a* you will indeed die in your sins."

25"Who are you?" they asked.

"Just what I have been claiming all along," Jesus replied. 26"I have much to say in judgment of you. But he who sent me is reliable, and what I have heard from him I tell the world."

---

*d*42 Greek *seed*   *e*52 Two early manuscripts *the Prophet*   *a*24 Or *I am he*; also in verse 28

27They did not understand that he was telling them about his Father. 28So Jesus said, "When you have lifted up the Son of Man, then you will know that I am ˌthe one I claim to beˌ and that I do nothing on my own but speak just what the Father has taught me. 29The one who sent me is with me; he has not left me alone, for I always do what pleases him." 30Even as he spoke, many put their faith in him.

The Children of Abraham

31To the Jews who had believed him, Jesus said, "If you hold to my teaching, you are really my disciples. 32Then you will know the truth, and the truth will set you free."

33They answered him, "We are Abraham's descendants b and have never been slaves of anyone. How can you say that we shall be set free?"

34Jesus replied, "I tell you the truth, everyone who sins is a slave to sin. 35Now a slave has no permanent place in the family, but a son belongs to it for ever. 36So if the Son sets you free, you will be free indeed. 37I know you are Abraham's descendants. Yet you are ready to kill me, because you have no room for my word. 38I am telling you what I have seen in the Father's presence, and you do what you have heard from your father." c

39"Abraham is our father," they answered.

"If you were Abraham's children," said Jesus, "then you would d do the things Abraham did. 40As it is, you are determined to kill me, a man who has told you the truth that I heard from God. Abraham did not do such things. 41You are doing the things your own father does."

"We are not illegitimate children," they protested. "The only Father we have is God himself."

The Children of the Devil

42Jesus said to them, "If God were your Father, you would love me, for I came from God and now am here. I have not come on my own; but he sent me. 43Why is my language not clear to you? Because you are unable to hear what I say. 44You belong to your father, the devil, and you want to carry out your father's desire. He was a murderer from the beginning, not holding to the truth, for there is no truth in him. When he lies, he speaks his native language, for he is a liar and the father of lies. 45Yet because I tell the truth, you do not believe me! 46Can any of you prove me guilty of sin? If I am telling the truth, why don't you believe me? 47He who belongs to God hears what God says. The reason you do not hear is that you do not belong to God."

The Claims of Jesus About Himself

48The Jews answered him, "Aren't we right in saying that you are a Samaritan and demon-possessed?"

49"I am not possessed by a demon," said Jesus, "but I honour my Father and you dishonour me. 50I am not seeking glory for myself; but there is one who seeks it,

and he is the judge. 51I tell you the truth, if anyone keeps my word, he will never see death."

52At this the Jews exclaimed, "Now we know that you are demon-possessed! Abraham died and so did the prophets, yet you say that if anyone keeps your word, he will never taste death. 53Are you greater than our father Abraham? He died, and so did the prophets. Who do you think you are?"

54Jesus replied, "If I glorify myself, my glory means nothing. My Father, whom you claim as your God, is the one who glorifies me. 55Though you do not know him, I know him. If I said I did not, I would be a liar like you, but I do know him and keep his word. 56Your father Abraham rejoiced at the thought of seeing my day; he saw it and was glad."

57"You are not yet fifty years old," the Jews said to him, "and you have seen Abraham!"

58"I tell you the truth," Jesus answered, "before Abraham was born, I am!" 59At this, they picked up stones to stone him, but Jesus hid himself, slipping away from the temple grounds.

Jesus Heals a Man Born Blind

9 As he went along, he saw a man blind from birth. 2His disciples asked him, "Rabbi, who sinned, this man or his parents, that he was born blind?"

9:2   The Jews assumed that blindness, or any other handicap, was the result of sin. The disciples were only interested in whose sin had caused this man to suffer but the blindness in this case was not a result of sin. Jesus saw the man's blindness in a positive light — an opportunity for God to heal the man, and for his power to be seen. Jesus also drew the contrast between light and darkness, and between spiritual sight and blindness.

3"Neither this man nor his parents sinned," said Jesus, "but this happened so that the work of God might be displayed in his life. 4As long as it is day, we must do the work of him who sent me. Night is coming, when no-one can work. 5While I am in the world, I am the light of the world."

6Having said this, he spat on the ground, made some mud with the saliva, and put it on the man's eyes. 7"Go," he told him, "wash in the Pool of Siloam" (this word means Sent). So the man went and washed, and came home seeing.

8His neighbours and those who had formerly seen him begging asked, "Isn't this the same man who used to sit and beg?" 9Some claimed that he was.

Others said, "No, he only looks like him."

But he himself insisted, "I am the man."

10"How then were your eyes opened?" they demanded.

11He replied, "The man they call Jesus made some mud and put it on my eyes. He told me to go to Siloam and wash. So I went and washed, and then I could see."

b33 Greek seed; also in verse 37   c38 Or presence. Therefore do what you have heard from the Father.
d39 Some early manuscripts "If you are Abraham's children," said Jesus, "then

¹²"Where is this man?" they asked him.
"I don't know," he said.

The Pharisees Investigate the Healing

¹³They brought to the Pharisees the man who had been blind. ¹⁴Now the day on which Jesus had made the mud and opened the man's eyes was a Sabbath. ¹⁵Therefore the Pharisees also asked him how he had received his sight. "He put mud on my eyes," the man replied, "and I washed, and now I see."

¹⁶Some of the Pharisees said, "This man is not from God, for he does not keep the Sabbath."

But others asked, "How can a sinner do such miraculous signs?" So they were divided.

¹⁷Finally they turned again to the blind man, "What have you to say about him? It was your eyes he opened."

The man replied, "He is a prophet."

¹⁸The Jews still did not believe that he had been blind and had received his sight until they sent for the man's parents. ¹⁹"Is this your son?" they asked. "Is this the one you say was born blind? How is it that now he can see?"

²⁰"We know he is our son," the parents answered, "and we know he was born blind. ²¹But how he can see now, or who opened his eyes, we don't know. Ask him. He is of age; he will speak for himself." ²²His parents said this because they were afraid of the Jews, for already the Jews had decided that anyone who acknowledged that Jesus was the Christ*a* would be put out of the synagogue. ²³That was why his parents said, "He is of age; ask him."

²⁴A second time they summoned the man who had been blind. "Give glory to God,"*b* they said. "We know this man is a sinner."

²⁵He replied, "Whether he is a sinner or not, I don't know. One thing I do know. I was blind but now I see!"

²⁶Then they asked him, "What did he do to you? How did he open your eyes?"

²⁷He answered, "I have told you already and you did not listen. Why do you want to hear it again? Do you want to become his disciples, too?"

²⁸Then they hurled insults at him and said, "You are this fellow's disciple! We are disciples of Moses! ²⁹We know that God spoke to Moses, but as for this fellow, we don't even know where he comes from."

³⁰The man answered, "Now that is remarkable! You don't know where he comes from, yet he opened my eyes. ³¹We know that God does not listen to sinners. He listens to the godly man who does his will. ³²Nobody has ever heard of opening the eyes of a man born blind. ³³If this man were not from God, he could do nothing."

³⁴To this they replied, "You were steeped in sin at birth; how dare you lecture us!" And they threw him out.

Spiritual Blindness

³⁵Jesus heard that they had thrown him out, and when he found him, he said, "Do you believe in the Son of Man?"

³⁶"Who is he, sir?" the man asked. "Tell me so that I may believe in him."

³⁷Jesus said, "You have now seen him; in fact, he is the one speaking with you."

³⁸Then the man said, "Lord, I believe," and he worshipped him.

³⁹Jesus said, "For judgment I have come into this world, so that the blind will see and those who see will become blind."

⁴⁰Some Pharisees who were with him heard him say this and asked, "What? Are we blind too?"

⁴¹Jesus said, "If you were blind, you would not be guilty of sin; but now that you claim you can see, your guilt remains.

The Shepherd and His Flock

10 "I tell you the truth, the man who does not enter the sheep pen by the gate, but climbs in by some other way, is a thief and a robber. ²The man who enters by the gate is the shepherd of his sheep. ³The watchman opens the gate for him, and the sheep listen to his voice. He calls his own sheep by name and leads them out. ⁴When he has brought out all his own, he goes on ahead of them, and his sheep follow him because they know his voice. ⁵But they will never follow a stranger; in fact, they will run away from him because they do not recognise a stranger's voice." ⁶Jesus used this figure of speech, but they did not understand what he was telling them.

⁷Therefore Jesus said again, "I tell you the truth, I am the gate for the sheep. ⁸All who ever came before me were thieves and robbers, but the sheep did not listen to them. ⁹I am the gate; whoever enters through me will be saved.*a* He will come in and go out, and find pasture. ¹⁰The thief comes only to steal and kill and destroy; I have come that they may have life, and have it to the full.

¹¹"I am the good shepherd. The good shepherd lays down his life for the sheep. ¹²The hired hand is not the shepherd who owns the sheep. So when he sees the wolf coming, he abandons the sheep and runs away. Then the wolf attacks the flock and scatters it. ¹³The man runs away because he is a hired hand and cares nothing for the sheep.

10:11 This passage is very reminiscent of Ezekiel 34, which compares the priests of that time with bad shepherds. God is often described as a shepherd (see Psalm 23) and his people are his "sheep". Jesus developed the idea further, pointing out that the thief kills the sheep, but the good shepherd will give his own life for them.

---

¹⁴"I am the good shepherd; I know my sheep and my sheep know me — ¹⁵just as the Father knows me and I know the Father — and I lay down my life for the sheep. ¹⁶I have other sheep that are not of this sheep pen. I must bring them also. They too will listen to my voice, and there shall be one flock and one shepherd. ¹⁷The

*a*22 Or *Messiah*   *b*24 A solemn charge to tell the truth (see Joshua 7:19)   *a*9 Or *kept safe* reason my Father loves me is that I lay down my life — only to take it up again. [18]No-one takes it from me, but I lay it down of my own accord. I have authority to lay it down and authority to take it up again. This command I received from my Father."

[19]At these words the Jews were again divided. [20]Many of them said, "He is demon-possessed and raving mad. Why listen to him?"

[21]But others said, "These are not the sayings of a man possessed by a demon. Can a demon open the eyes of the blind?"

The Unbelief of the Jews

[22]Then came the Feast of Dedication [b] at Jerusalem. It was winter, [23]and Jesus was in the temple area walking in Solomon's Colonnade. [24]The Jews gathered round him, saying, "How long will you keep us in suspense? If you are the Christ, [c] tell us plainly."

[25]Jesus answered, "I did tell you, but you do not believe. The miracles I do in my Father's name speak for me, [26]but you do not believe because you are not my sheep. [27]My sheep listen to my voice; I know them, and they follow me. [28]I give them eternal life, and they shall never perish; no-one can snatch them out of my hand. [29]My Father, who has given them to me, is greater than all; [d] no-one can snatch them out of my Father's hand. [30]I and the Father are one."

[31]Again the Jews picked up stones to stone him, [32]but Jesus said to them, "I have shown you many great miracles from the Father. For which of these do you stone me?"

[33]"We are not stoning you for any of these," replied the Jews, "but for blasphemy, because you, a mere man, claim to be God."

[34]Jesus answered them, "Is it not written in your Law, 'I have said you are gods' [e]? [35]If he called them 'gods', to whom the word of God came — and the Scripture cannot be broken — [36]what about the one whom the Father set apart as his very own and sent into the world? Why then do you accuse me of blasphemy because I said, 'I am God's Son'? [37]Do not believe me unless I do what my Father does. [38]But if I do it, even though you do not believe me, believe the miracles, that you may know and understand that the Father is in me, and I in the Father." [39]Again they tried to seize him, but he escaped their grasp.

[40]Then Jesus went back across the Jordan to the place where John had been baptising in the early days. Here he stayed [41]and many people came to him. They said, "Though John never performed a miraculous sign, all that John said about this man was true." [42]And in that place many believed in Jesus.

The Death of Lazarus

11 Now a man named Lazarus was sick. He was from Bethany, the village of Mary and her sister Martha. [2]This Mary, whose brother Lazarus now lay sick, was the same one who poured perfume on the Lord and wiped his feet with her hair. [3]So the sisters sent word to Jesus, "Lord, the one you love is sick."

[4]When he heard this, Jesus said, "This sickness will not end in death. No, it is for God's glory so that God's Son may be glorified through it." [5]Jesus loved Martha and her sister and Lazarus. [6]Yet when he heard that Lazarus was sick, he stayed where he was two more days.

[7]Then he said to his disciples, "Let us go back to Judea."

[8]"But Rabbi," they said, "a short while ago the Jews tried to stone you, and yet you are going back there?"

[9]Jesus answered, "Are there not twelve hours of daylight? A man who walks by day will not stumble, for he sees by this world's light. [10]It is when he walks by night that he stumbles, for he has no light."

[11]After he had said this, he went on to tell them, "Our friend Lazarus has fallen asleep; but I am going there to wake him up."

[12]His disciples replied, "Lord, if he sleeps, he will get better." [13]Jesus had been speaking of his death, but his disciples thought he meant natural sleep.

[14]So then he told them plainly, "Lazarus is dead, [15]and for your sake I am glad I was not there, so that you may believe. But let us go to him."

[16]Then Thomas (called Didymus) said to the rest of the disciples, "Let us also go, that we may die with him."

Jesus Comforts the Sisters

[17]On his arrival, Jesus found that Lazarus had already been in the tomb for four days. [18]Bethany was less than two miles [a] from Jerusalem, [19]and many Jews had come to Martha and Mary to comfort them in the loss of their brother. [20]When Martha heard that Jesus was coming, she went out to meet him, but Mary stayed at home.

[21]"Lord," Martha said to Jesus, "if you had been here, my brother would not have died. [22]But I know that even now God will give you whatever you ask."

[23]Jesus said to her, "Your brother will rise again."

[24]Martha answered, "I know he will rise again in the resurrection at the last day."

[25]Jesus said to her, "I am the resurrection and the life. He who believes in me will live, even though he dies; [26]and whoever lives and believes in me will never die. Do you believe this?"

[27]"Yes, Lord," she told him, "I believe that you are the Christ, [b] the Son of God, who was to come into the world."

[28]And after she had said this, she went back and called her sister Mary aside. "The Teacher is here," she said, "and is asking for you." [29]When Mary heard this, she got up quickly and went to him. [30]Now Jesus had not yet entered the village, but was still at the place where Martha had met him. [31]When the Jews who had been with Mary in the house, comforting her, noticed how quickly she got up and went out, they followed her, supposing she was going to the tomb to mourn there.

[32]When Mary reached the place where Jesus was

---

[b]22 That is, Hanukkah   [c]24 Or *Messiah*   [d]29 Many early manuscripts *What my Father has given me is greater than all*
[e]34 Psalm 82:6   [a]18 Greek *fifteen stadia* (about 3 kilometres)   [b]27 Or *Messiah*

and saw him, she fell at his feet and said, "Lord, if you had been here, my brother would not have died."

[33]When Jesus saw her weeping, and the Jews who had come along with her also weeping, he was deeply moved in spirit and troubled. [34]"Where have you laid him?" he asked.

"Come and see, Lord," they replied.

[35]Jesus wept.

[36]Then the Jews said, "See how he loved him!"

[37]But some of them said, "Could not he who opened the eyes of the blind man have kept this man from dying?"

Jesus Raises Lazarus From the Dead

[38]Jesus, once more deeply moved, came to the tomb. It was a cave with a stone laid across the entrance. [39]"Take away the stone," he said.

"But, Lord," said Martha, the sister of the dead man, "by this time there is a bad odour, for he has been there four days."

[40]Then Jesus said, "Did I not tell you that if you believed, you would see the glory of God?"

[41]So they took away the stone. Then Jesus looked up and said, "Father, I thank you that you have heard me. [42]I knew that you always hear me, but I said this for the benefit of the people standing here, that they may believe that you sent me."

[43]When he had said this, Jesus called in a loud voice, "Lazarus, come out!" [44]The dead man came out, his hands and feet wrapped with strips of linen, and a cloth around his face.

Jesus said to them, "Take off the grave clothes and let him go."

11:44   This is perhaps the greatest of the signs Jesus performed. It is the climax to the first part of John, and leads into the drama of Jesus' trial and crucifixion. The Pharisees firmly believed in a resurrection, and Martha also believed in it. However, despite her clear statement of faith (verse 27), she did not believe that her brother really would be brought back to life, there and then. The miracle itself is astonishing and the account stops very abruptly. What else is there to be said?

The Plot to Kill Jesus

[45]Therefore many of the Jews who had come to visit Mary, and had seen what Jesus did, put their faith in him. [46]But some of them went to the Pharisees and told them what Jesus had done. [47]Then the chief priests and the Pharisees called a meeting of the Sanhedrin.

"What are we accomplishing?" they asked. "Here is this man performing many miraculous signs. [48]If we let him go on like this, everyone will believe in him, and then the Romans will come and take away both our place[c] and our nation."

[49]Then one of them, named Caiaphas, who was high priest that year, spoke up, "You know nothing at all! [50]You do not realise that it is better for you that one man die for the people than that the whole nation perish."

[51]He did not say this on his own, but as high priest that year he prophesied that Jesus would die for the Jewish nation, [52]and not only for that nation but also for the scattered children of God, to bring them together and make them one. [53]So from that day on they plotted to take his life.

[54]Therefore Jesus no longer moved about publicly among the Jews. Instead he withdrew to a region near the desert, to a village called Ephraim, where he stayed with his disciples.

[55]When it was almost time for the Jewish Passover, many went up from the country to Jerusalem for their ceremonial cleansing before the Passover. [56]They kept looking for Jesus, and as they stood in the temple area they asked one another, "What do you think? Isn't he coming to the Feast at all?" [57]But the chief priests and Pharisees had given orders that if anyone found out where Jesus was, he should report it so that they might arrest him.

Jesus Anointed at Bethany

12 Six days before the Passover, Jesus arrived at Bethany, where Lazarus lived, whom Jesus had raised from the dead. [2]Here a dinner was given in Jesus' honour. Martha served, while Lazarus was among those reclining at the table with him. [3]Then Mary took about a pint[a] of pure nard, an expensive perfume; she poured it on Jesus' feet and wiped his feet with her hair. And the house was filled with the fragrance of the perfume.

[4]But one of his disciples, Judas Iscariot, who was later to betray him, objected, [5]"Why wasn't this perfume sold and the money given to the poor? It was worth a year's wages."[b] [6]He did not say this because he cared about the poor but because he was a thief; as keeper of the money bag, he used to help himself to what was put into it.

[7]"Leave her alone," Jesus replied. "It was intended that she should save this perfume for the day of my burial. [8]You will always have the poor among you, but you will not always have me."

[9]Meanwhile a large crowd of Jews found out that Jesus was there and came, not only because of him but also to see Lazarus, whom he had raised from the dead. [10]So the chief priests made plans to kill Lazarus as well, [11]for on account of him many of the Jews were going over to Jesus and putting their faith in him.

The Triumphal Entry

[12]The next day the great crowd that had come for the Feast heard that Jesus was on his way to Jerusalem. [13]They took palm branches and went out to meet him, shouting,

---

[c]48 Or *temple*   [a]3 Greek *a litra* (probably about 0.5 litre)   [b]5 Greek *three hundred denarii*

"Hosanna!" *c*

"Blessed is he who comes in the name of the Lord!" *d*

"Blessed is the King of Israel!"

[14]Jesus found a young donkey and sat upon it, as it is written,

[15]"Do not be afraid, O Daughter of Zion;
see, your king is coming,
seated on a donkey's colt." *e*

[16]At first his disciples did not understand all this. Only after Jesus was glorified did they realise that these things had been written about him and that they had done these things to him.

[17]Now the crowd that was with him when he called Lazarus from the tomb and raised him from the dead continued to spread the word. [18]Many people, because they had heard that he had given this miraculous sign, went out to meet him. [19]So the Pharisees said to one another, "See, this is getting us nowhere. Look how the whole world has gone after him!"

Jesus Predicts His Death

[20]Now there were some Greeks among those who went up to worship at the Feast. [21]They came to Philip, who was from Bethsaida in Galilee, with a request. "Sir," they said, "we would like to see Jesus." [22]Philip went to tell Andrew; Andrew and Philip in turn told Jesus.

[23]Jesus replied, "The hour has come for the Son of Man to be glorified. [24]I tell you the truth, unless a grain of wheat falls to the ground and dies, it remains only a single seed. But if it dies, it produces many seeds. [25]The man who loves his life will lose it, while the man who hates his life in this world will keep it for eternal life. [26]Whoever serves me must follow me; and where I am, my servant also will be. My Father will honour the one who serves me.

[27]"Now my heart is troubled, and what shall I say? 'Father, save me from this hour'? No, it was for this very reason I came to this hour. [28]Father, glorify your name!"

Then a voice came from heaven, "I have glorified it, and will glorify it again." [29]The crowd that was there and heard it said it had thundered; others said an angel had spoken to him.

[30]Jesus said, "This voice was for your benefit, not mine. [31]Now is the time for judgment on this world; now the prince of this world will be driven out. [32]But I, when I am lifted up from the earth, will draw all men to myself." [33]He said this to show the kind of death he was going to die.

[34]The crowd spoke up, "We have heard from the Law that the Christ *f* will remain for ever, so how can you say, 'The Son of Man must be lifted up'? Who is this 'Son of Man'?"

[35]Then Jesus told them, "You are going to have the light just a little while longer. Walk while you have the light, before darkness overtakes you. The man who walks in the dark does not know where he is going. [36]Put your trust in the light while you have it, so that you may become sons of light." When he had finished speaking, Jesus left and hid himself from them.

The Jews Continue in Their Unbelief

[37]Even after Jesus had done all these miraculous signs in their presence, they still would not believe in him. [38]This was to fulfil the word of Isaiah the prophet:

"Lord, who has believed our message
and to whom has the arm of the Lord been revealed?" *g*

[39]For this reason they could not believe, because, as Isaiah says elsewhere:

[40]"He has blinded their eyes
and deadened their hearts,
so they can neither see with their eyes,
nor understand with their hearts,
nor turn—and I would heal them." *h*

[41]Isaiah said this because he saw Jesus' glory and spoke about him.

[42]Yet at the same time many even among the leaders believed in him. But because of the Pharisees they would not confess their faith for fear they would be put out of the synagogue; [43]for they loved praise from men more than praise from God.

12:42   Following Jesus was risky. Towards the end of the first century AD there was a large excommunication of Jewish Christians from synagogues, but even before Jesus' death his followers seem to have feared such treatment.

---

[44]Then Jesus cried out, "When a man believes in me, he does not believe in me only, but in the one who sent me. [45]When he looks at me, he sees the one who sent me. [46]I have come into the world as a light, so that no-one who believes in me should stay in darkness.

[47]"As for the person who hears my words but does not keep them, I do not judge him. For I did not come to judge the world, but to save it. [48]There is a judge for the one who rejects me and does not accept my words; that very word which I spoke will condemn him at the last day. [49]For I did not speak of my own accord, but the Father who sent me commanded me what to say and how to say it. [50]I know that his command leads to eternal life. So whatever I say is just what the Father has told me to say."

Jesus Washes His Disciples' Feet

13 It was just before the Passover Feast. Jesus knew that the time had come for him to leave this world and go to the Father. Having loved his own who were in the world, he now showed them the full extent of his love. *a*

[2]The evening meal was being served, and the devil had already prompted Judas Iscariot, son of Simon, to betray Jesus. [3]Jesus knew that the Father had put all

---

c 13 A Hebrew expression meaning "Save!" which became an exclamation of praise *d 13* Psalm 118:25,26   *e 15* Zech. 9:9
f 34 Or *Messiah*   *g 38* Isaiah 53:1   *h 40* Isaiah 6:10   *a 1* Or *he loved them to the last*

things under his power, and that he had come from God and was returning to God; ⁴so he got up from the meal, took off his outer clothing, and wrapped a towel round his waist. ⁵After that, he poured water into a basin and began to wash his disciples' feet, drying them with the towel that was wrapped round him.

⁶He came to Simon Peter, who said to him, "Lord, are you going to wash my feet?"

⁷Jesus replied, "You do not realise now what I am doing, but later you will understand."

⁸"No," said Peter, "you shall never wash my feet." Jesus answered, "Unless I wash you, you have no part with me."

⁹"Then, Lord," Simon Peter replied, "not just my feet but my hands and my head as well!"

¹⁰Jesus answered, "A person who has had a bath needs only to wash his feet; his whole body is clean. And you are clean, though not every one of you." ¹¹For he knew who was going to betray him, and that was why he said not every one was clean.

¹²When he had finished washing their feet, he put on his clothes and returned to his place. "Do you understand what I have done for you?" he asked them. ¹³"You call me 'Teacher' and 'Lord', and rightly so, for that is what I am. ¹⁴Now that I, your Lord and Teacher, have washed your feet, you also should wash one another's feet. ¹⁵I have set you an example that you should do as I have done for you. ¹⁶I tell you the truth, no servant is greater than his master, nor is a messenger greater than the one who sent him. ¹⁷Now that you know these things, you will be blessed if you do them.

Jesus Predicts His Betrayal

¹⁸"I am not referring to all of you; I know those I have chosen. But this is to fulfil the scripture: 'He who shares my bread has lifted up his heel against me.'[b]

¹⁹"I am telling you now before it happens, so that when it does happen you will believe that I am He. ²⁰I tell you the truth, whoever accepts anyone I send accepts me; and whoever accepts me accepts the one who sent me."

²¹After he had said this, Jesus was troubled in spirit and testified, "I tell you the truth, one of you is going to betray me."

²²His disciples stared at one another, at a loss to know which of them he meant. ²³One of them, the disciple whom Jesus loved, was reclining next to him. ²⁴Simon Peter motioned to this disciple and said, "Ask him which one he means."

²⁵Leaning back against Jesus, he asked him, "Lord, who is it?"

²⁶Jesus answered, "It is the one to whom I will give this piece of bread when I have dipped it in the dish." Then, dipping the piece of bread, he gave it to Judas Iscariot, son of Simon. ²⁷As soon as Judas took the bread, Satan entered into him.

"What you are about to do, do quickly," Jesus told him, ²⁸but no-one at the meal understood why Jesus said this to him. ²⁹Since Judas had charge of the money, some thought Jesus was telling him to buy what was needed for the Feast, or to give something to the poor. ³⁰As soon as Judas had taken the bread, he went out. And it was night.

13:26 Unlike the other Gospel writers, the writer here did not include what is called the "institution narrative" (e.g. Luke 22:19,20), at the point when Jesus distributed the bread and wine. Instead he described the washing of the disciples' feet, and emphasized the servant attitude of Jesus. There is also what appears to be an eyewitness account of Judas' departure into the darkness of the night, and out of the light of Jesus' presence.

Jesus Predicts Peter's Denial

³¹When he was gone, Jesus said, "Now is the Son of Man glorified and God is glorified in him. ³²If God is glorified in him,[c] God will glorify the Son in himself, and will glorify him at once.

³³"My children, I will be with you only a little longer. You will look for me, and just as I told the Jews, so I tell you now: Where I am going, you cannot come.

³⁴"A new command I give you: Love one another. As I have loved you, so you must love one another. ³⁵By this all men will know that you are my disciples, if you love one another."

³⁶Simon Peter asked him, "Lord, where are you going?"

Jesus replied, "Where I am going, you cannot follow now, but you will follow later."

³⁷Peter asked, "Lord, why can't I follow you now? I will lay down my life for you."

³⁸Then Jesus answered, "Will you really lay down your life for me? I tell you the truth, before the cock crows, you will disown me three times!

Jesus Comforts His Disciples

14 "Do not let your hearts be troubled. Trust in God;[a] trust also in me. ²In my Father's house are many rooms; if it were not so, I would have told you. I am going there to prepare a place for you. ³And if I go and prepare a place for you, I will come back and take you to be with me that you also may be where I am. ⁴You know the way to the place where I am going."

Jesus the Way to the Father

⁵Thomas said to him, "Lord, we don't know where you are going, so how can we know the way?"

⁶Jesus answered, "I am the way and the truth and the life. No-one comes to the Father except through me. ⁷If you really knew me, you would know[b] my Father as well. From now on, you do know him and have seen him."

---

b18 Psalm 41:9   c32 Many early manuscripts do not have If God is glorified in him.   a1 Or You trust in God
b7 Some early manuscripts If you really have known me, you will know

8Philip said, "Lord, show us the Father and that will be enough for us."

9Jesus answered: "Don't you know me, Philip, even after I have been among you such a long time? Anyone who has seen me has seen the Father. How can you say, 'Show us the Father'? 10Don't you believe that I am in the Father, and that the Father is in me? The words I say to you are not just my own. Rather, it is the Father, living in me, who is doing his work. 11Believe me when I say that I am in the Father and the Father is in me; or at least believe on the evidence of the miracles themselves. 12I tell you the truth, anyone who has faith in me will do what I have been doing. He will do even greater things than these, because I am going to the Father. 13And I will do whatever you ask in my name, so that the Son may bring glory to the Father. 14You may ask me for anything in my name, and I will do it.

Jesus Promises the Holy Spirit

15"If you love me, you will obey what I command. 16And I will ask the Father, and he will give you another Counsellor to be with you for ever — 17the Spirit of truth. The world cannot accept him, because it neither sees him nor knows him. But you know him, for he lives with you and will be c in you. 18I will not leave you as orphans; I will come to you. 19Before long, the world will not see me any more, but you will see me. Because I live, you also will live. 20On that day you will realise that I am in my Father, and you are in me, and I am in you. 21Whoever has my commands and obeys them, he is the one who loves me. He who loves me will be loved by my Father, and I too will love him and show myself to him."

22Then Judas (not Judas Iscariot) said, "But, Lord, why do you intend to show yourself to us and not to the world?"

23Jesus replied, "If anyone loves me, he will obey my teaching. My Father will love him, and we will come to him and make our home with him. 24He who does not love me will not obey my teaching. These words you hear are not my own; they belong to the Father who sent me.

25"All this I have spoken while still with you. 26But the Counsellor, the Holy Spirit, whom the Father will send in my name, will teach you all things and will remind you of everything I have said to you. 27Peace I leave with you; my peace I give you. I do not give to you as the world gives. Do not let your hearts be troubled and do not be afraid.

28"You heard me say, 'I am going away and I am coming back to you.' If you loved me, you would be glad that I am going to the Father, for the Father is greater than I. 29I have told you now before it happens, so that when it does happen you will believe. 30I will not speak with you much longer, for the prince of this world is coming. He has no hold on me, 31but the world must learn that I love the Father and that I do exactly what my Father has commanded me.

"Come now; let us leave.

The Vine and the Branches

15 "I am the true vine, and my Father is the gardener. 2He cuts off every branch in me that bears no fruit, while every branch that does bear fruit he prunes a so that it will be even more fruitful. 3You are already clean because of the word I have spoken to you. 4Remain in me, and I will remain in you. No branch can bear fruit by itself; it must remain in the vine. Neither can you bear fruit unless you remain in me.

15:1 In the Old Testament the Israelites were often compared to a vine or vineyard (e.g. Isaiah 5:1–7). Here, as elsewhere, Jesus took a familiar image and gave it a far wider significance. Unlike Israel, the unfruitful vine, Jesus is the true vine, the source of life for all who remain with him (verse 4). The seven "I am" sayings are of great importance. "I AM" was the name of God that Jews were not allowed to speak (Exodus 3:14). Jesus' use of it indicated his own divine nature and authority.

5"I am the vine; you are the branches. If a man remains in me and I in him, he will bear much fruit; apart from me you can do nothing. 6If anyone does not remain in me, he is like a branch that is thrown away and withers; such branches are picked up, thrown into the fire and burned. 7If you remain in me and my words remain in you, ask whatever you wish, and it will be given you. 8This is to my Father's glory, that you bear much fruit, showing yourselves to be my disciples.

9"As the Father has loved me, so have I loved you. Now remain in my love. 10If you obey my commands, you will remain in my love, just as I have obeyed my Father's commands and remain in his love. 11I have told you this so that my joy may be in you and that your joy may be complete. 12My command is this: Love each other as I have loved you. 13Greater love has no-one than this, that he lay down his life for his friends. 14You are my friends if you do what I command. 15I no longer call you servants, because a servant does not know his master's business. Instead, I have called you friends, for everything that I learned from my Father I have made known to you. 16You did not choose me, but I chose you and appointed you to go and bear fruit — fruit that will last. Then the Father will give you whatever you ask in my name. 17This is my command: Love each other.

The World Hates the Disciples

18"If the world hates you, keep in mind that it hated me first. 19If you belonged to the world, it would love you as its own. As it is, you do not belong to the world, but I have chosen you out of the world. That is why the world hates you. 20Remember the words I spoke to you: 'No servant is greater than his master.' b If they persecuted me, they will persecute you also. If they

---

c17 Some early manuscripts *and is*   a2 The Greek for *prunes* also means *cleans*.   b20 John 13:16

obeyed my teaching, they will obey yours also. 21They will treat you this way because of my name, for they do not know the One who sent me. 22If I had not come and spoken to them, they would not be guilty of sin. Now, however, they have no excuse for their sin. 23He who hates me hates my Father as well. 24If I had not done among them what no-one else did, they would not be guilty of sin. But now they have seen these miracles, and yet they have hated both me and my Father. 25But this is to fulfil what is written in their Law: 'They hated me without reason.'c

26"When the Counsellor comes, whom I will send to you from the Father, the Spirit of truth who goes out from the Father, he will testify about me. 27And you also must testify, for you have been with me from the beginning.

16 "All this I have told you so that you will not go astray. 2They will put you out of the synagogue; in fact, a time is coming when anyone who kills you will think he is offering a service to God. 3They will do such things because they have not known the Father or me. 4I have told you this, so that when the time comes you will remember that I warned you. I did not tell you this at first because I was with you.

The Work of the Holy Spirit

5"Now I am going to him who sent me, yet none of you asks me, 'Where are you going?' 6Because I have said these things, you are filled with grief. 7But I tell you the truth: It is for your good that I am going away. Unless I go away, the Counsellor will not come to you; but if I go, I will send him to you. 8When he comes, he will convict the world of guilta in regard to sin and righteousness and judgment: 9in regard to sin, because men do not believe in me; 10in regard to righteousness, because I am going to the Father, where you can see me no longer; 11and in regard to judgment, because the prince of this world now stands condemned.

16:7   Only John's Gospel refers to the Holy Spirit as the "Paraclete". This is a legal term in Greek which means an "advocate". Here it means both "one who exhorts" and "one who consoles". The Spirit would only come when Jesus' work was completed and he had returned to his Father.

12"I have much more to say to you, more than you can now bear. 13But when he, the Spirit of truth, comes, he will guide you into all truth. He will not speak on his own; he will speak only what he hears, and he will tell you what is yet to come. 14He will bring glory to me by taking from what is mine and making it known to you. 15All that belongs to the Father is mine. That is why I said the Spirit will take from what is mine and make it known to you.

16"In a little while you will see me no more, and then after a little while you will see me."

The Disciples' Grief Will Turn to Joy

17Some of his disciples said to one another, "What does he mean by saying, 'In a little while you will see me no more, and then after a little while you will see me,' and 'Because I am going to the Father'?" 18They kept asking, "What does he mean by 'a little while'? We don't understand what he is saying."

19Jesus saw that they wanted to ask him about this, so he said to them, "Are you asking one another what I meant when I said, 'In a little while you will see me no more, and then after a little while you will see me'? 20I tell you the truth, you will weep and mourn while the world rejoices. You will grieve, but your grief will turn to joy. 21A woman giving birth to a child has pain because her time has come; but when her baby is born she forgets the anguish because of her joy that a child is born into the world. 22So with you: Now is your time of grief, but I will see you again and you will rejoice, and no-one will take away your joy. 23In that day you will no longer ask me anything. I tell you the truth, my Father will give you whatever you ask in my name. 24Until now you have not asked for anything in my name. Ask and you will receive, and your joy will be complete.

25"Though I have been speaking figuratively, a time is coming when I will no longer use this kind of language but will tell you plainly about my Father. 26In that day you will ask in my name. I am not saying that I will ask the Father on your behalf. 27No, the Father himself loves you because you have loved me and have believed that I came from God. 28I came from the Father and entered the world; now I am leaving the world and going back to the Father."

29Then Jesus' disciples said, "Now you are speaking clearly and without figures of speech. 30Now we can see that you know all things and that you do not even need to have anyone ask you questions. This makes us believe that you came from God."

31"You believe at last!"b Jesus answered. 32"But a time is coming, and has come, when you will be scattered, each to his own home. You will leave me all alone. Yet I am not alone, for my Father is with me. 33"I have told you these things, so that in me you may have peace. In this world you will have trouble. But take heart! I have overcome the world."

Jesus Prays for Himself

17 After Jesus said this, he looked towards heaven and prayed:

"Father, the time has come. Glorify your Son, that your Son may glorify you. 2For you granted him authority over all people that he might give eternal life to all those you have given him. 3Now this is eternal life: that they may know you, the only true God, and Jesus Christ, whom you have sent. 4I have brought you glory on earth by completing the work you gave me to do. 5And now,

c25 Psalms 35:19; 69:4   a8 Or will expose the guilt of the world   b31 Or "Do you now believe?"

Father, glorify me in your presence with the glory I had with you before the world began.

Jesus Prays for His Disciples

⁶"I have revealed you[a] to those whom you gave me out of the world. They were yours; you gave them to me and they have obeyed your word. ⁷Now they know that everything you have given me comes from you. ⁸For I gave them the words you gave me and they accepted them. They knew with certainty that I came from you, and they believed that you sent me. ⁹I pray for them. I am not praying for the world, but for those you have given me, for they are yours. ¹⁰All I have is yours, and all you have is mine. And glory has come to me through them. ¹¹I will remain in the world no longer, but they are still in the world, and I am coming to you. Holy Father, protect them by the power of your name—the name you gave me—so that they may be one as we are one. ¹²While I was with them, I protected them and kept them safe by that name you gave me. None has been lost except the one doomed to destruction so that Scripture would be fulfilled.

¹³"I am coming to you now, but I say these things while I am still in the world, so that they may have the full measure of my joy within them. ¹⁴I have given them your word and the world has hated them, for they are not of the world any more than I am of the world. ¹⁵My prayer is not that you take them out of the world but that you protect them from the evil one. ¹⁶They are not of the world, even as I am not of it. ¹⁷Sanctify[b] them by the truth; your word is truth. ¹⁸As you sent me into the world, I have sent them into the world. ¹⁹For them I sanctify myself, that they too may be truly sanctified.

17:20   The Gospels often mention Jesus' prayers, but rarely the contents of those prayers. This (17:1–26) is by far the longest of Jesus' recorded prayers. It is known as the "high priestly" prayer, and is one of the most profound passages in the Bible. In it Jesus prayed for himself as he approached the cross (verses 1–5), for his disciples (6–19), and for all believers (20–26). There is an emphasis on unity among Christians as a reflection of the unity of Jesus and his Father.

Jesus Prays for All Believers

²⁰"My prayer is not for them alone. I pray also for those who will believe in me through their message, ²¹that all of them may be one, Father, just as you are in me and I am in you. May they also be in us so that the world may believe that you have sent me. ²²I have given them the glory that you gave me, that they may be one as we are one:

²³I in them and you in me. May they be brought to complete unity to let the world know that you sent me and have loved them even as you have loved me.

²⁴"Father, I want those you have given me to be with me where I am, and to see my glory, the glory you have given me because you loved me before the creation of the world. ²⁵Righteous Father, though the world does not know you, I know you, and they know that you have sent me. ²⁶I have made you known to them, and will continue to make you known in order that the love you have for me may be in them and that I myself may be in them."

Jesus Arrested

18 When he had finished praying, Jesus left with his disciples and crossed the Kidron Valley. On the other side there was an olive grove, and he and his disciples went into it.

²Now Judas, who betrayed him, knew the place, because Jesus had often met there with his disciples. ³So Judas came to the grove, guiding a detachment of soldiers and some officials from the chief priests and Pharisees. They were carrying torches, lanterns and weapons.

⁴Jesus, knowing all that was going to happen to him, went out and asked them, "Who is it you want?"

⁵"Jesus of Nazareth," they replied.

"I am he," Jesus said. (And Judas the traitor was standing there with them.) ⁶When Jesus said, "I am he," they drew back and fell to the ground.

⁷Again he asked them, "Who is it you want?"

And they said, "Jesus of Nazareth."

⁸"I told you that I am he," Jesus answered. "If you are looking for me, then let these men go." ⁹This happened so that the words he had spoken would be fulfilled: "I have not lost one of those you gave me."[a]

¹⁰Then Simon Peter, who had a sword, drew it and struck the high priest's servant, cutting off his right ear. (The servant's name was Malchus.)

¹¹Jesus commanded Peter, "Put your sword away! Shall I not drink the cup the Father has given me?"

Jesus Taken to Annas

¹²Then the detachment of soldiers with its commander and the Jewish officials arrested Jesus. They bound him ¹³and brought him first to Annas, who was the father-in-law of Caiaphas, the high priest that year. ¹⁴Caiaphas was the one who had advised the Jews that it would be good if one man died for the people.

Peter's First Denial

¹⁵Simon Peter and another disciple were following Jesus. Because this disciple was known to the high priest, he went with Jesus into the high priest's courtyard, ¹⁶but Peter had to wait outside at the door. The other disciple, who was known to the high priest, came back, spoke to the girl on duty there and brought Peter in.

---

a6 Greek *your name*; also in verse 26   b17 Greek *hagiazo* (*set apart for sacred use* or *make holy*); also in verse 19
a9 John 6:39

17"You are not one of his disciples, are you?" the girl at the door asked Peter.

He replied, "I am not."

18It was cold, and the servants and officials stood round a fire they had made to keep warm. Peter also was standing with them, warming himself.

The High Priest Questions Jesus

19Meanwhile, the high priest questioned Jesus about his disciples and his teaching.

20"I have spoken openly to the world," Jesus replied. "I always taught in synagogues or at the temple, where all the Jews come together. I said nothing in secret. 21Why question me? Ask those who heard me. Surely they know what I said."

22When Jesus said this, one of the officials near by struck him in the face. "Is this the way you answer the high priest?" he demanded.

23"If I said something wrong," Jesus replied, "testify as to what is wrong. But if I spoke the truth, why did you strike me?" 24Then Annas sent him, still bound, to Caiaphas the high priest. b

Peter's Second and Third Denials

25As Simon Peter stood warming himself, he was asked, "You are not one of his disciples, are you?"

He denied it, saying, "I am not."

26One of the high priest's servants, a relative of the man whose ear Peter had cut off, challenged him, "Didn't I see you with him in the olive grove?" 27Again Peter denied it, and at that moment a cock began to crow.

Jesus Before Pilate

28Then the Jews led Jesus from Caiaphas to the palace of the Roman governor. By now it was early morning, and to avoid ceremonial uncleanness the Jews did not enter the palace; they wanted to be able to eat the Passover. 29So Pilate came out to them and asked, "What charges are you bringing against this man?"

30"If he were not a criminal," they replied, "we would not have handed him over to you."

31Pilate said, "Take him yourselves and judge him by your own law."

"But we have no right to execute anyone," the Jews objected. 32This happened so that the words Jesus had spoken indicating the kind of death he was going to die would be fulfilled.

33Pilate then went back inside the palace, summoned Jesus and asked him, "Are you the king of the Jews?"

34"Is that your own idea," Jesus asked, "or did others talk to you about me?"

35"Am I a Jew?" Pilate replied. "It was your people and your chief priests who handed you over to me. What is it you have done?"

36Jesus said, "My kingdom is not of this world. If it were, my servants would fight to prevent my arrest by the Jews. But now my kingdom is from another place."

37"You are a king, then!" said Pilate.

Jesus answered, "You are right in saying I am a king. In fact, for this reason I was born, and for this I came into the world, to testify to the truth. Everyone on the side of truth listens to me."

18:36 There are a number of differences between this account of Jesus' trial and crucifixion and those in the other Gospels. One of the most striking is the emphasis here on Jesus' kingship and authority. As Pilate seemed to realize, now more than ever, Jesus could be seen as a king.

38"What is truth?" Pilate asked. With this he went out again to the Jews and said, "I find no basis for a charge against him. 39But it is your custom for me to release to you one prisoner at the time of the Passover. Do you want me to release 'the king of the Jews'?"

40They shouted back, "No, not him! Give us Barabbas!" Now Barabbas had taken part in a rebellion.

Jesus Sentenced to be Crucified

19 Then Pilate took Jesus and had him flogged. 2The soldiers twisted together a crown of thorns and put it on his head. They clothed him in a purple robe 3and went up to him again and again, saying, "Hail, king of the Jews!" And they struck him in the face.

4Once more Pilate came out and said to the Jews, "Look, I am bringing him out to you to let you know that I find no basis for a charge against him." 5When Jesus came out wearing the crown of thorns and the purple robe, Pilate said to them, "Here is the man!"

6As soon as the chief priests and their officials saw him, they shouted, "Crucify! Crucify!"

But Pilate answered, "You take him and crucify him. As for me, I find no basis for a charge against him."

7The Jews insisted, "We have a law, and according to that law he must die, because he claimed to be the Son of God."

8When Pilate heard this, he was even more afraid, 9and he went back inside the palace. "Where do you come from?" he asked Jesus, but Jesus gave him no answer. 10"Do you refuse to speak to me?" Pilate said. "Don't you realise I have power either to free you or to crucify you?"

11Jesus answered, "You would have no power over me if it were not given to you from above. Therefore the one who handed me over to you is guilty of a greater sin."

12From then on, Pilate tried to set Jesus free, but the Jews kept shouting, "If you let this man go, you are no friend of Caesar. Anyone who claims to be a king opposes Caesar."

13When Pilate heard this, he brought Jesus out and sat down on the judge's seat at a place known as the Stone Pavement (which in Aramaic is Gabbatha). 14It was the day of Preparation of Passover Week, about the sixth hour.

"Here is your king," Pilate said to the Jews.

---

b 24 Or (Now Annas had sent him, still bound, to Caiaphas the high priest.)

[15]But they shouted, "Take him away! Take him away! Crucify him!"

"Shall I crucify your king?" Pilate asked.

"We have no king but Caesar," the chief priests answered.

[16]Finally Pilate handed him over to them to be crucified.

The Crucifixion

So the soldiers took charge of Jesus. [17]Carrying his own cross, he went out to the place of the Skull (which in Aramaic is called Golgotha). [18]Here they crucified him, and with him two others — one on each side and Jesus in the middle.

[19]Pilate had a notice prepared and fastened to the cross. It read: JESUS OF NAZARETH, THE KING OF THE JEWS. [20]Many of the Jews read this sign, for the place where Jesus was crucified was near the city, and the sign was written in Aramaic, Latin and Greek. [21]The chief priests of the Jews protested to Pilate, "Do not write 'The King of the Jews', but that this man claimed to be king of the Jews."

[22]Pilate answered, "What I have written, I have written."

[23]When the soldiers crucified Jesus, they took his clothes, dividing them into four shares, one for each of them, with the undergarment remaining. This garment was seamless, woven in one piece from top to bottom. [24]"Let's not tear it," they said to one another. "Let's decide by lot who will get it."

This happened that the scripture might be fulfilled which said,

"They divided my garments among them
    and cast lots for my clothing." [a]

So this is what the soldiers did.

[25]Near the cross of Jesus stood his mother, his mother's sister, Mary the wife of Clopas, and Mary Magdalene. [26]When Jesus saw his mother there, and the disciple whom he loved standing near by, he said to his mother, "Dear woman, here is your son," [27]and to the disciple, "Here is your mother." From that time on, this disciple took her into his home.

The Death of Jesus

[28]Later, knowing that all was now completed, and so that the Scripture would be fulfilled, Jesus said, "I am thirsty." [29]A jar of wine vinegar was there, so they soaked a sponge in it, put the sponge on a stalk of the hyssop plant, and lifted it to Jesus' lips. [30]When he had received the drink, Jesus said, "It is finished." With that, he bowed his head and gave up his spirit.

[31]Now it was the day of Preparation, and the next day was to be a special Sabbath. Because the Jews did not want the bodies left on the crosses during the Sabbath, they asked Pilate to have the legs broken and the bodies taken down. [32]The soldiers therefore came and broke the legs of the first man who had been crucified with Jesus, and then those of the other. [33]But when they came to Jesus and found that he was already dead,

they did not break his legs. [34]Instead, one of the soldiers pierced Jesus' side with a spear, bringing a sudden flow of blood and water. [35]The man who saw it has given testimony, and his testimony is true. He knows that he tells the truth, and he testifies so that you also may believe. [36]These things happened so that the scripture would be fulfilled: "Not one of his bones will be broken," [b] [37]and, as another scripture says, "They will look on the one they have pierced." [c]

19:28 The writer was concerned that people would understand how these events fulfilled what was written in the Old Testament. Here there is a reference to Psalm 69:21.

The Burial of Jesus

[38]Later, Joseph of Arimathea asked Pilate for the body of Jesus. Now Joseph was a disciple of Jesus, but secretly because he feared the Jews. With Pilate's permission, he came and took the body away. [39]He was accompanied by Nicodemus, the man who earlier had visited Jesus at night. Nicodemus brought a mixture of myrrh and aloes, about seventy-five pounds. [d] [40]Taking Jesus' body, the two of them wrapped it, with the spices, in strips of linen. This was in accordance with Jewish burial customs. [41]At the place where Jesus was crucified, there was a garden, and in the garden a new tomb, in which no-one had ever been laid. [42]Because it was the Jewish day of Preparation and since the tomb was near by, they laid Jesus there.

The Empty Tomb

20 Early on the first day of the week, while it was still dark, Mary Magdalene went to the tomb and saw that the stone had been removed from the entrance. [2]So she came running to Simon Peter and the other disciple, the one Jesus loved, and said, "They have taken the Lord out of the tomb, and we don't know where they have put him!"

[3]So Peter and the other disciple started for the tomb. [4]Both were running, but the other disciple outran Peter and reached the tomb first. [5]He bent over and looked in at the strips of linen lying there but did not go in. [6]Then Simon Peter, who was behind him, arrived and went into the tomb. He saw the strips of linen lying there, [7]as well as the burial cloth that had been around Jesus' head. The cloth was folded up by itself, separate from the linen. [8]Finally the other disciple, who had reached the tomb first, also went inside. He saw and believed. [9](They still did not understand from Scripture that Jesus had to rise from the dead.)

Jesus Appears to Mary Magdalene

[10]Then the disciples went back to their homes, [11]but Mary stood outside the tomb crying. As she wept, she bent over to look into the tomb [12]and saw two angels

[a]24 Psalm 22:18   [b]36 Exodus 12:46; Num. 9:12; Psalm 34:20   [c]37 Zech. 12:10
[d]39 Greek a hundred litrai (about 34 kilograms)

in white, seated where Jesus' body had been, one at the head and the other at the foot.

¹³They asked her, "Woman, why are you crying?"

"They have taken my Lord away," she said, "and I don't know where they have put him." ¹⁴At this, she turned round and saw Jesus standing there, but she did not realise that it was Jesus.

¹⁵"Woman," he said, "why are you crying? Who is it you are looking for?"

Thinking he was the gardener, she said, "Sir, if you have carried him away, tell me where you have put him, and I will get him."

¹⁶Jesus said to her, "Mary."

She turned towards him and cried out in Aramaic, "Rabboni!" (which means Teacher).

¹⁷Jesus said, "Do not hold on to me, for I have not yet returned to the Father. Go instead to my brothers and tell them, 'I am returning to my Father and your Father, to my God and your God.'"

20:17   Jesus told Mary Magdalene not to touch him. Although he had been raised from death, he was different. The writer wanted to emphasize that the resurrection, far from being the end, was the beginning of a whole new story. From now on the Christian life must be lived by faith.

---

¹⁸Mary Magdalene went to the disciples with the news: "I have seen the Lord!" And she told them that he had said these things to her.

Jesus Appears to His Disciples

¹⁹On the evening of that first day of the week, when the disciples were together, with the doors locked for fear of the Jews, Jesus came and stood among them and said, "Peace be with you!" ²⁰After he said this, he showed them his hands and side. The disciples were overjoyed when they saw the Lord.

²¹Again Jesus said, "Peace be with you! As the Father has sent me, I am sending you." ²²And with that he breathed on them and said, "Receive the Holy Spirit. ²³If you forgive anyone his sins, they are forgiven; if you do not forgive them, they are not forgiven."

Jesus Appears to Thomas

²⁴Now Thomas (called Didymus), one of the Twelve, was not with the disciples when Jesus came. ²⁵So the other disciples told him, "We have seen the Lord!"

But he said to them, "Unless I see the nail marks in his hands and put my finger where the nails were, and put my hand into his side, I will not believe it."

²⁶A week later his disciples were in the house again, and Thomas was with them. Though the doors were locked, Jesus came and stood among them and said, "Peace be with you!" ²⁷Then he said to Thomas, "Put your finger here; see my hands. Reach out your hand and put it into my side. Stop doubting and believe."

²⁸Thomas said to him, "My Lord and my God!"

²⁹Then Jesus told him, "Because you have seen me, you have believed; blessed are those who have not seen and yet have believed."

³⁰Jesus did many other miraculous signs in the presence of his disciples, which are not recorded in this book. ³¹But these are written that you may ª believe that Jesus is the Christ, the Son of God, and that by believing you may have life in his name.

Jesus and the Miraculous Catch of Fish

21 Afterwards Jesus appeared again to his disciples, by the Sea of Tiberias.ª It happened this way: ²Simon Peter, Thomas (called Didymus), Nathanael from Cana in Galilee, the sons of Zebedee, and two other disciples were together. ³"I'm going out to fish," Simon Peter told them, and they said, "We'll go with you." So they went out and got into the boat, but that night they caught nothing.

⁴Early in the morning, Jesus stood on the shore, but the disciples did not realise that it was Jesus.

⁵He called out to them, "Friends, haven't you any fish?"

"No," they answered.

⁶He said, "Throw your net on the right side of the boat and you will find some." When they did, they were unable to haul the net in because of the large number of fish.

⁷Then the disciple whom Jesus loved said to Peter, "It is the Lord!" As soon as Simon Peter heard him say, "It is the Lord," he wrapped his outer garment around him (for he had taken it off) and jumped into the water. ⁸The other disciples followed in the boat, towing the net full of fish, for they were not far from shore, about a hundred yards.ᵇ ⁹When they landed, they saw a fire of burning coals there with fish on it, and some bread.

¹⁰Jesus said to them, "Bring some of the fish you have just caught."

¹¹Simon Peter climbed aboard and dragged the net ashore. It was full of large fish, 153, but even with so many the net was not torn. ¹²Jesus said to them, "Come and have breakfast." None of the disciples dared ask him, "Who are you?" They knew it was the Lord. ¹³Jesus came, took the bread and gave it to them, and did the same with the fish. ¹⁴This was now the third time Jesus appeared to his disciples after he was raised from the dead.

Jesus Reinstates Peter

¹⁵When they had finished eating, Jesus said to Simon Peter, "Simon son of John, do you truly love me more than these?"

"Yes, Lord," he said, "you know that I love you." Jesus said, "Feed my lambs."

¹⁶Again Jesus said, "Simon son of John, do you truly love me?"

He answered, "Yes, Lord, you know that I love you." Jesus said, "Take care of my sheep."

¹⁷The third time he said to him, "Simon son of John, do you love me?"

Peter was hurt because Jesus asked him the third

ª31 Some manuscripts *may continue to*   ª1 That is, Sea of Galilee   ᵇ8 Greek *about two hundred cubits* (about 90 metres) time, "Do you love me?" He said, "Lord, you know all things; you know that I love you."

21:15 Jesus' three questions to Peter reflect Peter's three denials of his Lord. In a sense Jesus was reinstating him after what he had done. It is quite clear throughout the Gospel that those who love Jesus will suffer as he did.

Jesus said, "Feed my sheep. [18]I tell you the truth, when you were younger you dressed yourself and went where you wanted; but when you are old you will stretch out your hands, and someone else will dress you and lead you where you do not want to go." [19]Jesus said this to indicate the kind of death by which Peter would glorify God. Then he said to him, "Follow me!"

[20]Peter turned and saw that the disciple whom Jesus loved was following them. (This was the one who had leaned back against Jesus at the supper and had said, "Lord, who is going to betray you?") [21]When Peter saw him, he asked, "Lord, what about him?"

[22]Jesus answered, "If I want him to remain alive until I return, what is that to you? You must follow me." [23]Because of this, the rumour spread among the brothers that this disciple would not die. But Jesus did not say that he would not die; he only said, "If I want him to remain alive until I return, what is that to you?"

[24]This is the disciple who testifies to these things and who wrote them down. We know that his testimony is true.

[25]Jesus did many other things as well. If every one of them were written down, I suppose that even the whole world would not have room for the books that would be written.

Acts

How Christ Works Through His Followers

The very first verse of Acts tells us that it is the continuation of a story which has already begun. The first volume is the Gospel of Luke, which records the earthly ministry, death, and resurrection of Jesus, and closes with a brief mention of his ascension. In the second volume Luke resumed the story with a fuller account of the ascension, and Jesus' promise to the waiting disciples that they would receive the Holy Spirit. As a result they would be enabled to share their faith in him with people throughout the world (Acts 1:8). When Luke wrote Acts—probably about AD 70—a number of Christian congregations had already been established in various parts of the Roman empire. Theophilus, to whom both the third Gospel and Acts are addressed, was probably an educated member of the congregation in Rome itself. It would be natural enough for Theophilus, and others like him, to want to know how a movement which had begun with a crucified preacher in far-away Palestine had become a new religion which had spread to the heart of the empire.

A History and a Witness

Acts is, therefore, a history of the early Christian Church. It records how congregations were planted and tells about the Church's early leaders, preachers, and missionaries. From Acts we learn how the first Christian congregations organized their lives, and also something of the difficult questions of belief and practice which needed to be settled. Yet Acts is not merely a factual account of what happened, it is also a witness to the truth of the Christian faith. The key to understanding Acts lies in remembering that very early on (chapter 2), God's Holy Spirit came upon the disciples. The result of this event, which is called Pentecost, was that the followers of Jesus were given the strength to continue his work. The work which Jesus began to do in his earthly ministry was now entrusted to the first believers, along with the power and authority by which it could be done. The history in Acts is not just an account of human activity, it is the story of God at work through his people. As we read it we can sometimes sense Luke's amazement and gratitude that so much had been achieved despite great difficulties.

A Brief Outline

For practical purposes Acts can be divided into two parts. The first twelve chapters recount the struggles and joys of the early Church in Jerusalem, and in the surrounding areas of Samaria and Judaea. Peter, one of the twelve disciples of Jesus, played an important part in those days, though others, James and Philip especially, also had crucial roles in the story. We are introduced to a man called Saul and told how he became a Christian believer. This proved to be one of the most significant events in the life of the early Church for, under his new name Paul, he became one of the most influential of Christian preachers. The last sixteen chapters of Acts are largely devoted to his missionary journeys, in the course of which he planted a number of churches, and to his arrest and various court appearances. The book ends with Paul under house arrest in Rome, but still free to preach and teach about Jesus to any who came (28:31). In this way Acts traces the spread of the Christian faith from a small group of people in Palestine to the capital city itself. Luke planned his book in a way which makes it quite clear that Christianity was intended to be a faith for the whole world.

Problems to be Overcome

The life and work of the early Church was not free from problems. Persecution was, of course, to be expected—Jesus had told his friends that (see Mark 13:9), and Acts records a number of instances of such persecution. There were also, however, "internal" problems to be sorted out. For instance, despite the close fellowship of the early Christian community, there were people who tried to lie and cheat. Acts 5:1–10 records one particularly scandalous story. Or again, as the Church grew, it became necessary to set up a formal system to make sure that its charitable work was fairly run (see Acts 6:1–6).

The Greatest Problem

The greatest problem of all, however, was whether Gentiles (non-Jews) could become Christians and, if so, on what terms. Jesus and the first disciples were all Jewish and it seems that the first converts were Jewish too, either by birth or conversion. At first, becoming a Christian was seen as something which a person added to their Jewish faith. But what if a person heard the apostle's preaching about Jesus and believed it, but had never been a Jew in the first place? Were they required to go through the ceremonies (which involved lengthy instruction, ritual purification and, in the case of men, circumcision) to become Jews? The question became particularly acute when Saul was converted and God told Ananias that this new convert had been chosen for missionary work which would involve witnessing to the Gentiles (Acts 9:15). Acts relates how this problem was worked through, first by the conversion of a God-fearing Gentile, Cornelius, and the vision given to Peter that he must not call anything which God had made unclean (Acts 10), and then by the way the Jewish-born leaders of the Church responded to what had happened (Acts 11:18). Despite this, some believers still wanted to impose Jewish customs on all Gentile converts, and Acts 15 is about a council of the Church which had to be called to settle the problem once and for all. In this way Acts is a reminder that there were disagreements and difficulties in the early Church just as there are in the Church today, and that they must be settled by discussion and reflection, and by openness to the Holy Spirit.

Jesus Taken Up Into Heaven

1 In my former book, Theophilus, I wrote about all that Jesus began to do and to teach ²until the day he was taken up to heaven, after giving instructions through the Holy Spirit to the apostles he had chosen. ³After his suffering, he showed himself to these men and gave many convincing proofs that he was alive. He appeared to them over a period of forty days and spoke about the kingdom of God. ⁴On one occasion, while he was eating with them, he gave them this command: "Do not leave Jerusalem, but wait for the gift my Father promised, which you have heard me speak about. ⁵For John baptised with ª water, but in a few days you will be baptised with the Holy Spirit."

⁶So when they met together, they asked him, "Lord, are you at this time going to restore the kingdom to Israel?"

⁷He said to them: "It is not for you to know the times or dates the Father has set by his own authority. ⁸But you will receive power when the Holy Spirit comes on you; and you will be my witnesses in Jerusalem, and in all Judea and Samaria, and to the ends of the earth."

⁹After he said this, he was taken up before their very eyes, and a cloud hid him from their sight.

¹⁰They were looking intently up into the sky as he was going, when suddenly two men dressed in white stood beside them. ¹¹"Men of Galilee," they said, "why do you stand here looking into the sky? This same Jesus, who has been taken from you into heaven, will come back in the same way you have seen him go into heaven."

Matthias Chosen to Replace Judas

¹²Then they returned to Jerusalem from the hill called the Mount of Olives, a Sabbath day's walk ᵇ from the city. ¹³When they arrived, they went upstairs to the room where they were staying. Those present were Peter, John, James and Andrew; Philip and Thomas, Bartholomew and Matthew; James son of Alphaeus and Simon the Zealot, and Judas son of James. ¹⁴They all joined together constantly in prayer, along with the women and Mary the mother of Jesus, and with his brothers.

¹⁵In those days Peter stood up among the believers ᶜ (a group numbering about a hundred and twenty) ¹⁶and said, "Brothers, the Scripture had to be fulfilled which the Holy Spirit spoke long ago through the mouth of David concerning Judas, who served as guide for those who arrested Jesus — ¹⁷he was one of our number and shared in this ministry."

¹⁸(With the reward he got for his wickedness, Judas bought a field; there he fell headlong, his body burst open and all his intestines spilled out. ¹⁹Everyone in Jerusalem heard about this, so they called that field in their language Akeldama, that is, Field of Blood.)

²⁰"For," said Peter, "it is written in the Book of Psalms,

" 'May his place be deserted;
let there be no-one to dwell in it,' ᵈ

and,

" 'May another take his place of leadership.' ᵉ

²¹Therefore it is necessary to choose one of the men who have been with us the whole time the Lord Jesus went in and out among us, ²²beginning from John's baptism to the time when Jesus was taken up from us. For one of these must become a witness with us of his resurrection."

²³So they proposed two men: Joseph called Barsabbas (also known as Justus) and Matthias. ²⁴Then they prayed, "Lord, you know everyone's heart. Show us which of these two you have chosen ²⁵to take over this apostolic ministry, which Judas left to go where he belongs." ²⁶Then they cast lots, and the lot fell to Matthias; so he was added to the eleven apostles.

The Holy Spirit Comes at Pentecost

2 When the day of Pentecost came, they were all together in one place. ²Suddenly a sound like the blowing of a violent wind came from heaven and filled the whole house where they were sitting. ³They saw what seemed to be tongues of fire that separated and came to rest on each of them. ⁴All of them were filled with the Holy Spirit and began to speak in other tongues ª as the Spirit enabled them.

⁵Now there were staying in Jerusalem God-fearing Jews from every nation under heaven. ⁶When they heard this sound, a crowd came together in bewilderment, because each one heard them speaking in his own language. ⁷Utterly amazed, they asked: "Are not all these men who are speaking Galileans? ⁸Then how is it that each of us hears them in his own native language? ⁹Parthians, Medes and Elamites; residents of Mesopotamia, Judea and Cappadocia, Pontus and Asia, ¹⁰Phrygia and Pamphylia, Egypt and the parts of Libya near Cyrene; visitors from Rome ¹¹(both Jews and converts to Judaism); Cretans and Arabs — we hear them declaring the wonders of God in our own tongues!" ¹²Amazed and perplexed, they asked one another, "What does this mean?"

¹³Some, however, made fun of them and said, "They have had too much wine." ᵇ

Peter Addresses the Crowd

¹⁴Then Peter stood up with the Eleven, raised his voice and addressed the crowd: "Fellow Jews and all of you who live in Jerusalem, let me explain this to you; listen carefully to what I say. ¹⁵These men are not drunk, as you suppose. It's only nine in the morning! ¹⁶No, this is what was spoken by the prophet Joel:

¹⁷" 'In the last days, God says,
    I will pour out my Spirit on all people.
  Your sons and daughters will prophesy,
    your young men will see visions,
    your old men will dream dreams.
¹⁸Even on my servants, both men and women,
    I will pour out my Spirit in those days,
    and they will prophesy.

ª5 Or in   ᵇ12 That is, about ¾ of a mile (about 1,100 metres)   ᶜ15 Greek brothers   ᵈ20 Psalm 69:25
ᵉ20 Psalm 109:8   ª4 Or languages; also in verse 11   ᵇ13 Or sweet wine

[19]I will show wonders in the heaven above
  and signs on the earth below,
  blood and fire and billows of smoke.
[20]The sun will be turned to darkness
  and the moon to blood
  before the coming of the great and glorious day
    of the Lord.
[21]And everyone who calls
  on the name of the Lord will be saved.'[c]

[22]"Men of Israel, listen to this: Jesus of Nazareth was a man accredited by God to you by miracles, wonders and signs, which God did among you through him, as you yourselves know. [23]This man was handed over to you by God's set purpose and foreknowledge; and you, with the help of wicked men,[d] put him to death by nailing him to the cross. [24]But God raised him from the dead, freeing him from the agony of death, because it was impossible for death to keep its hold on him. [25]David said about him:

" 'I saw the Lord always before me.
  Because he is at my right hand,
  I will not be shaken.
[26]Therefore my heart is glad and my tongue
    rejoices;
  my body also will live in hope,
[27]because you will not abandon me to the grave,
  nor will you let your Holy One see decay.
[28]You have made known to me the paths of life;
  you will fill me with joy in your presence.'[e]

[29]"Brothers, I can tell you confidently that the patriarch David died and was buried, and his tomb is here to this day. [30]But he was a prophet and knew that God had promised him on oath that he would place one of his descendants on his throne. [31]Seeing what was ahead, he spoke of the resurrection of the Christ,[f] that he was not abandoned to the grave, nor did his body see decay. [32]God has raised this Jesus to life, and we are all witnesses of the fact. [33]Exalted to the right hand of God, he has received from the Father the promised Holy Spirit and has poured out what you now see and hear. [34]For David did not ascend to heaven, and yet he said,

" 'The Lord said to my Lord:
  "Sit at my right hand
[35]until I make your enemies
  a footstool for your feet." '[g]

[36]"Therefore let all Israel be assured of this: God has made this Jesus, whom you crucified, both Lord and Christ."

[37]When the people heard this, they were cut to the heart and said to Peter and the other apostles, "Brothers, what shall we do?"

[38]Peter replied, "Repent and be baptised, every one of you, in the name of Jesus Christ for the forgiveness of your sins. And you will receive the gift of the Holy Spirit. [39]The promise is for you and your children and for all who are far off — for all whom the Lord our God will call."

[40]With many other words he warned them; and he pleaded with them, "Save yourselves from this corrupt generation." [41]Those who accepted his message were baptised, and about three thousand were added to their number that day.

2:36   Peter was speaking to Jews in this sermon. Other sermons in Acts have different starting points — compare it with Paul's sermon in Athens (Acts 17:22–31). However, the main point of the preaching was always the same: God had raised the crucified Jesus from the dead and made him Lord. That was the heart of the Christian gospel from the very beginning.

The Fellowship of the Believers

[42]They devoted themselves to the apostles' teaching and to the fellowship, to the breaking of bread and to prayer. [43]Everyone was filled with awe, and many wonders and miraculous signs were done by the apostles. [44]All the believers were together and had everything in common. [45]Selling their possessions and goods, they gave to anyone as he had need. [46]Every day they continued to meet together in the temple courts. They broke bread in their homes and ate together with glad and sincere hearts, [47]praising God and enjoying the favour of all the people. And the Lord added to their number daily those who were being saved.

Peter Heals the Crippled Beggar

3 One day Peter and John were going up to the temple at the time of prayer — at three in the afternoon. [2]Now a man crippled from birth was being carried to the temple gate called Beautiful, where he was put every day to beg from those going into the temple courts. [3]When he saw Peter and John about to enter, he asked them for money. [4]Peter looked straight at him, as did John. Then Peter said, "Look at us!" [5]So the man gave them his attention, expecting to get something from them.

[6]Then Peter said, "Silver or gold I do not have, but what I have I give you. In the name of Jesus Christ of Nazareth, walk." [7]Taking him by the right hand, he helped him up, and instantly the man's feet and ankles became strong. [8]He jumped to his feet and began to walk. Then he went with them into the temple courts, walking and jumping, and praising God. [9]When all the people saw him walking and praising God, [10]they recognised him as the same man who used to sit begging at the temple gate called Beautiful, and they were filled with wonder and amazement at what had happened to him.

Peter Speaks to the Onlookers

[11]While the beggar held on to Peter and John, all the people were astonished and came running to them in the place called Solomon's Colonnade. [12]When Peter

---

c21 Joel 2:28–32   *d23* Or *of those not having the law* (that is, Gentiles)   *e28* Psalm 16:8–11
f31 Or *Messiah.* "The Christ" (Greek) and "the Messiah" (Hebrew) both mean "the Anointed One"; also in verse 36.
g35 Psalm 110:1

saw this, he said to them: "Men of Israel, why does this surprise you? Why do you stare at us as if by our own power or godliness we had made this man walk? [13]The God of Abraham, Isaac and Jacob, the God of our fathers, has glorified his servant Jesus. You handed him over to be killed, and you disowned him before Pilate, though he had decided to let him go. [14]You disowned the Holy and Righteous One and asked that a murderer be released to you. [15]You killed the author of life, but God raised him from the dead. We are witnesses of this. [16]By faith in the name of Jesus, this man whom you see and know was made strong. It is Jesus' name and the faith that comes through him that has given this complete healing to him, as you can all see.

[17]"Now, brothers, I know that you acted in ignorance, as did your leaders. [18]But this is how God fulfilled what he had foretold through all the prophets, saying that his Christ[a] would suffer. [19]Repent, then, and turn to God, so that your sins may be wiped out, that times of refreshing may come from the Lord, [20]and that he may send the Christ, who has been appointed for you — even Jesus. [21]He must remain in heaven until the time comes for God to restore everything, as he promised long ago through his holy prophets. [22]For Moses said, 'The Lord your God will raise up for you a prophet like me from among your own people; you must listen to everything he tells you. [23]Anyone who does not listen to him will be completely cut off from among his people.'[b]

[24]"Indeed, all the prophets from Samuel on, as many as have spoken, have foretold these days. [25]And you are heirs of the prophets and of the covenant God made with your fathers. He said to Abraham, 'Through your offspring all peoples on earth will be blessed.'[c] [26]When God raised up his servant, he sent him first to you to bless you by turning each of you from your wicked ways."

Peter and John Before the Sanhedrin

4 The priests and the captain of the temple guard and the Sadducees came up to Peter and John while they were speaking to the people. [2]They were greatly disturbed because the apostles were teaching the people and proclaiming in Jesus the resurrection of the dead. [3]They seized Peter and John, and because it was evening, they put them in jail until the next day. [4]But many who heard the message believed, and the number of men grew to about five thousand.

[5]The next day the rulers, elders and teachers of the law met in Jerusalem. [6]Annas the high priest was there, and so were Caiaphas, John, Alexander and the other men of the high priest's family. [7]They had Peter and John brought before them and began to question them: "By what power or what name did you do this?"

[8]Then Peter, filled with the Holy Spirit, said to them: "Rulers and elders of the people! [9]If we are being called to account today for an act of kindness shown to a cripple and are asked how he was healed, [10]then know this, you and all the people of Israel: It is by the name of Jesus Christ of Nazareth, whom you crucified but whom God raised from the dead, that this man stands before you healed. [11]He is

" 'the stone you builders rejected,
  which has become the capstone.'[a,b]

[12]Salvation is found in no-one else, for there is no other name under heaven given to men by which we must be saved."

[13]When they saw the courage of Peter and John and realised that they were unschooled, ordinary men, they were astonished and they took note that these men had been with Jesus. [14]But since they could see the man who had been healed standing there with them, there was nothing they could say. [15]So they ordered them to withdraw from the Sanhedrin and then conferred together. [16]"What are we going to do with these men?" they asked. "Everybody living in Jerusalem knows they have done an outstanding miracle, and we cannot deny it. [17]But to stop this thing from spreading any further among the people, we must warn these men to speak no longer to anyone in this name."

[18]Then they called them in again and commanded them not to speak or teach at all in the name of Jesus. [19]But Peter and John replied, "Judge for yourselves whether it is right in God's sight to obey you rather than God. [20]For we cannot help speaking about what we have seen and heard."

4:18   Peter and John had been given courage by the Holy Spirit to speak out as they did. There are times when preaching the gospel or witnessing to the Christian faith involves disobeying orders given by authority. This is a real dilemma for Christians in countries where those in authority are hostile to Christianity.

---

[21]After further threats they let them go. They could not decide how to punish them, because all the people were praising God for what had happened. [22]For the man who was miraculously healed was over forty years old.

The Believers' Prayer

[23]On their release, Peter and John went back to their own people and reported all that the chief priests and elders had said to them. [24]When they heard this, they raised their voices together in prayer to God. "Sovereign Lord," they said, "you made the heaven and the earth and the sea, and everything in them. [25]You spoke by the Holy Spirit through the mouth of your servant, our father David:

" 'Why do the nations rage
  and the peoples plot in vain?
[26]The kings of the earth take their stand
  and the rulers gather together
against the Lord
  and against his Anointed One.'[c,d]

---

[a]18 Or Messiah; also in verse 20   [b]23 Deut. 18:15,18,19   [c]25 Gen. 22:18; 26:4   [a]11 Or cornerstone
[b]11 Psalm 118:22   [c]26 That is, Christ or Messiah   [d]26 Psalm 2:1,2

²⁷Indeed Herod and Pontius Pilate met together with the Gentiles and the people*e* of Israel in this city to conspire against your holy servant Jesus, whom you anointed. ²⁸They did what your power and will had decided beforehand should happen. ²⁹Now, Lord, consider their threats and enable your servants to speak your word with great boldness. ³⁰Stretch out your hand to heal and perform miraculous signs and wonders through the name of your holy servant Jesus."

³¹After they prayed, the place where they were meeting was shaken. And they were all filled with the Holy Spirit and spoke the word of God boldly.

The Believers Share Their Possessions

³²All the believers were one in heart and mind. No-one claimed that any of his possessions was his own, but they shared everything they had. ³³With great power the apostles continued to testify to the resurrection of the Lord Jesus, and much grace was upon them all. ³⁴There were no needy persons among them. For from time to time those who owned lands or houses sold them, brought the money from the sales ³⁵and put it at the apostles' feet, and it was distributed to anyone as he had need.

³⁶Joseph, a Levite from Cyprus, whom the apostles called Barnabas (which means Son of Encouragement), ³⁷sold a field he owned and brought the money and put it at the apostles' feet.

Ananias and Sapphira

5 Now a man named Ananias, together with his wife Sapphira, also sold a piece of property. ²With his wife's full knowledge he kept back part of the money for himself, but brought the rest and put it at the apostles' feet.

³Then Peter said, "Ananias, how is it that Satan has so filled your heart that you have lied to the Holy Spirit and have kept for yourself some of the money you received for the land? ⁴Didn't it belong to you before it was sold? And after it was sold, wasn't the money at your disposal? What made you think of doing such a thing? You have not lied to men but to God."

⁵When Ananias heard this, he fell down and died. And great fear seized all who heard what had happened. ⁶Then the young men came forward, wrapped up his body, and carried him out and buried him.

⁷About three hours later his wife came in, not knowing what had happened. ⁸Peter asked her, "Tell me, is this the price you and Ananias got for the land?"

"Yes," she said, "that is the price."

⁹Peter said to her, "How could you agree to test the Spirit of the Lord? Look! The feet of the men who buried your husband are at the door, and they will carry you out also."

¹⁰At that moment she fell down at his feet and died. Then the young men came in and, finding her dead, carried her out and buried her beside her husband. ¹¹Great fear seized the whole church and all who heard about these events.

The Apostles Heal Many

¹²The apostles performed many miraculous signs and wonders among the people. And all the believers used to meet together in Solomon's Colonnade. ¹³No-one else dared join them, even though they were highly regarded by the people. ¹⁴Nevertheless, more and more men and women believed in the Lord and were added to their number. ¹⁵As a result, people brought the sick into the streets and laid them on beds and mats so that at least Peter's shadow might fall on some of them as he passed by. ¹⁶Crowds gathered also from the towns around Jerusalem, bringing their sick and those tormented by evil*a* spirits, and all of them were healed.

The Apostles Persecuted

¹⁷Then the high priest and all his associates, who were members of the party of the Sadducees, were filled with jealousy. ¹⁸They arrested the apostles and put them in the public jail. ¹⁹But during the night an angel of the Lord opened the doors of the jail and brought them out. ²⁰"Go, stand in the temple courts," he said, "and tell the people the full message of this new life."

²¹At daybreak they entered the temple courts, as they had been told, and began to teach the people.

When the high priest and his associates arrived, they called together the Sanhedrin—the full assembly of the elders of Israel—and sent to the jail for the apostles. ²²But on arriving at the jail, the officers did not find them there. So they went back and reported, ²³"We found the jail securely locked, with the guards standing at the doors; but when we opened them, we found no-one inside." ²⁴On hearing this report, the captain of the temple guard and the chief priests were puzzled, wondering what would come of this.

²⁵Then someone came and said, "Look! The men you put in jail are standing in the temple courts teaching the people." ²⁶At that, the captain went with his officers and brought the apostles. They did not use force, because they feared that the people would stone them.

²⁷Having brought the apostles, they made them appear before the Sanhedrin to be questioned by the high priest. ²⁸"We gave you strict orders not to teach in this name," he said. "Yet you have filled Jerusalem with your teaching and are determined to make us guilty of this man's blood."

²⁹Peter and the other apostles replied: "We must obey God rather than men! ³⁰The God of our fathers raised Jesus from the dead—whom you had killed by hanging him on a tree. ³¹God exalted him to his own right hand as Prince and Saviour that he might give repentance and forgiveness of sins to Israel. ³²We are witnesses of these things, and so is the Holy Spirit, whom God has given to those who obey him."

³³When they heard this, they were furious and wanted to put them to death. ³⁴But a Pharisee named Gamaliel, a teacher of the law, who was honoured by all the people, stood up in the Sanhedrin and ordered that the men be put outside for a little while. ³⁵Then

---

e 27 The Greek is plural.   *a 16* Greek *unclean*

he addressed them: "Men of Israel, consider carefully what you intend to do to these men. [36]Some time ago Theudas appeared, claiming to be somebody, and about four hundred men rallied to him. He was killed, all his followers were dispersed, and it all came to nothing. [37]After him, Judas the Galilean appeared in the days of the census and led a band of people in revolt. He too was killed, and all his followers were scattered. [38]Therefore, in the present case I advise you: Leave these men alone! Let them go! For if their purpose or activity is of human origin, it will fail. [39]But if it is from God, you will not be able to stop these men; you will only find yourselves fighting against God."

5:34   Gamaliel once taught Paul (Acts 22:3), and was a very respected rabbi. Here God used his wisdom to save the lives of the apostles. Gamaliel's advice illustrates the best of the tradition of the Pharisees: God is sovereign and he will fulfil his purposes without our being over zealous to defend his honour.

---

[40]His speech persuaded them. They called the apostles in and had them flogged. Then they ordered them not to speak in the name of Jesus, and let them go. [41]The apostles left the Sanhedrin, rejoicing because they had been counted worthy of suffering disgrace for the Name. [42]Day after day, in the temple courts and from house to house, they never stopped teaching and proclaiming the good news that Jesus is the Christ. [b]

The Choosing of the Seven

6 In those days when the number of disciples was increasing, the Grecian Jews among them complained against the Hebraic Jews because their widows were being overlooked in the daily distribution of food. [2]So the Twelve gathered all the disciples together and said, "It would not be right for us to neglect the ministry of the word of God in order to wait on tables. [3]Brothers, choose seven men from among you who are known to be full of the Spirit and wisdom. We will turn this responsibility over to them [4]and will give our attention to prayer and the ministry of the word."
[5]This proposal pleased the whole group. They chose Stephen, a man full of faith and of the Holy Spirit; also Philip, Procorus, Nicanor, Timon, Parmenas and Nicolas from Antioch, a convert to Judaism. [6]They presented these men to the apostles, who prayed and laid their hands on them.
[7]So the word of God spread. The number of disciples in Jerusalem increased rapidly, and a large number of priests became obedient to the faith.

Stephen Seized

[8]Now Stephen, a man full of God's grace and power, did great wonders and miraculous signs among the people. [9]Opposition arose, however, from members of the Synagogue of the Freedmen (as it was called) — Jews of Cyrene and Alexandria as well as the provinces of Cilicia and Asia. These men began to argue with Stephen, [10]but they could not stand up against his wisdom or the Spirit by whom he spoke.
[11]Then they secretly persuaded some men to say, "We have heard Stephen speak words of blasphemy against Moses and against God."
[12]So they stirred up the people and the elders and the teachers of the law. They seized Stephen and brought him before the Sanhedrin. [13]They produced false witnesses, who testified, "This fellow never stops speaking against this holy place and against the law. [14]For we have heard him say that this Jesus of Nazareth will destroy this place and change the customs Moses handed down to us."
[15]All who were sitting in the Sanhedrin looked intently at Stephen, and they saw that his face was like the face of an angel.

Stephen's Speech to the Sanhedrin

7 Then the high priest asked him, "Are these charges true?"
[2]To this he replied: "Brothers and fathers, listen to me! The God of glory appeared to our father Abraham while he was still in Mesopotamia, before he lived in Haran. [3]'Leave your country and your people,' God said, 'and go to the land I will show you.'[a]
[4]"So he left the land of the Chaldeans and settled in Haran. After the death of his father, God sent him to this land where you are now living. [5]He gave him no inheritance here, not even a foot of ground. But God promised him that he and his descendants after him would possess the land, even though at that time Abraham had no child. [6]God spoke to him in this way: 'Your descendants will be strangers in a country not their own, and they will be enslaved and ill-treated for four hundred years. [7]But I will punish the nation they serve as slaves,' God said, 'and afterwards they will come out of that country and worship me in this place.'[b] [8]Then he gave Abraham the covenant of circumcision. And Abraham became the father of Isaac and circumcised him eight days after his birth. Later Isaac became the father of Jacob, and Jacob became the father of the twelve patriarchs.
[9]"Because the patriarchs were jealous of Joseph, they sold him as a slave into Egypt. But God was with him [10]and rescued him from all his troubles. He gave Joseph wisdom and enabled him to gain the goodwill of Pharaoh king of Egypt; so he made him ruler over Egypt and all his palace.
[11]"Then a famine struck all Egypt and Canaan, bringing great suffering, and our fathers could not find food. [12]When Jacob heard that there was grain in Egypt, he sent our fathers on their first visit. [13]On their second visit, Joseph told his brothers who he was, and Pharaoh learned about Joseph's family. [14]After this, Joseph sent for his father Jacob and his whole family, seventy-five in all. [15]Then Jacob went down to Egypt, where he and our fathers died. [16]Their bodies were brought back to Shechem and placed in the tomb that Abraham had

---

[b]42 Or *Messiah*   [a]3 Gen. 12:1   [b]7 Gen. 15:13,14

bought from the sons of Hamor at Shechem for a certain sum of money.

17 "As the time drew near for God to fulfil his promise to Abraham, the number of our people in Egypt greatly increased. 18 Then another king, who knew nothing about Joseph, became ruler of Egypt. 19 He dealt treacherously with our people and oppressed our forefathers by forcing them to throw out their newborn babies so that they would die.

20 "At that time Moses was born, and he was no ordinary child.c For three months he was cared for in his father's house. 21 When he was placed outside, Pharaoh's daughter took him and brought him up as her own son. 22 Moses was educated in all the wisdom of the Egyptians and was powerful in speech and action.

23 "When Moses was forty years old, he decided to visit his fellow Israelites. 24 He saw one of them being ill-treated by an Egyptian, so he went to his defence and avenged him by killing the Egyptian. 25 Moses thought that his own people would realise that God was using him to rescue them, but they did not. 26 The next day Moses came upon two Israelites who were fighting. He tried to reconcile them by saying, 'Men, you are brothers; why do you want to hurt each other?'

27 "But the man who was ill-treating the other pushed Moses aside and said, 'Who made you ruler and judge over us? 28 Do you want to kill me as you killed the Egyptian yesterday?'d 29 When Moses heard this, he fled to Midian, where he settled as a foreigner and had two sons.

30 "After forty years had passed, an angel appeared to Moses in the flames of a burning bush in the desert near Mount Sinai. 31 When he saw this, he was amazed at the sight. As he went over to look more closely, he heard the Lord's voice: 32 'I am the God of your fathers, the God of Abraham, Isaac and Jacob.'e Moses trembled with fear and did not dare to look.

33 "Then the Lord said to him, 'Take off your sandals; the place where you are standing is holy ground. 34 I have indeed seen the oppression of my people in Egypt. I have heard their groaning and have come down to set them free. Now come, I will send you back to Egypt.'f

35 "This is the same Moses whom they had rejected with the words, 'Who made you ruler and judge?' He was sent to be their ruler and deliverer by God himself, through the angel who appeared to him in the bush. 36 He led them out of Egypt and did wonders and miraculous signs in Egypt, at the Red Seag and for forty years in the desert.

37 "This is that Moses who told the Israelites, 'God will send you a prophet like me from your own people.'h 38 He was in the assembly in the desert, with the angel who spoke to him on Mount Sinai, and with our fathers; and he received living words to pass on to us.

39 "But our fathers refused to obey him. Instead, they rejected him and in their hearts turned back to Egypt. 40 They told Aaron, 'Make us gods who will go before

us. As for this fellow Moses who led us out of Egypt—we don't know what has happened to him!'i 41 That was the time they made an idol in the form of a calf. They brought sacrifices to it and held a celebration in honour of what their hands had made. 42 But God turned away and gave them over to the worship of the heavenly bodies. This agrees with what is written in the book of the prophets:

" 'Did you bring me sacrifices and offerings
       for forty years in the desert, O house of Israel?
43 You have lifted up the shrine of Molech
       and the star of your god Rephan,
       the idols you made to worship.
Therefore I will send you into exile'j beyond
       Babylon.

44 "Our forefathers had the tabernacle of the Testimony with them in the desert. It had been made as God directed Moses, according to the pattern he had seen. 45 Having received the tabernacle, our fathers under Joshua brought it with them when they took the land from the nations God drove out before them. It remained in the land until the time of David, 46 who enjoyed God's favour and asked that he might provide a dwelling-place for the God of Jacob.k 47 But it was Solomon who built the house for him.

48 "However, the Most High does not live in houses made by men. As the prophet says:

49 " 'Heaven is my throne,
       and the earth is my footstool.
What kind of house will you build for me?
                                          says the Lord.
Or where will my resting place be?
50 Has not my hand made all these things?'l

51 "You stiff-necked people, with uncircumcised hearts and ears! You are just like your fathers: You always resist the Holy Spirit! 52 Was there ever a prophet your fathers did not persecute? They even killed those who predicted the coming of the Righteous One. And now you have betrayed and murdered him—53 you who have received the law that was put into effect through angels but have not obeyed it."

The Stoning of Stephen

54 When they heard this, they were furious and gnashed their teeth at him. 55 But Stephen, full of the Holy Spirit, looked up to heaven and saw the glory of God, and Jesus standing at the right hand of God. 56 "Look," he said, "I see heaven open and the Son of Man standing at the right hand of God."

57 At this they covered their ears and, yelling at the top of their voices, they all rushed at him, 58 dragged him out of the city and began to stone him. Meanwhile, the witnesses laid their clothes at the feet of a young man named Saul.

59 While they were stoning him, Stephen prayed, "Lord Jesus, receive my spirit." 60 Then he fell on his

---

c20 Or was fair in the sight of God   d28 Exodus 2:14   e32 Exodus 3:6   f34 Exodus 3:5,7,8,10
g36 That is, Sea of Reeds   h37 Deut. 18:15   i40 Exodus 32:1   j43 Amos 5:25-27
k46 Some early manuscripts the house of Jacob   l50 Isaiah 66:1,2

knees and cried out, "Lord, do not hold this sin against them." When he had said this, he fell asleep.

8 And Saul was there, giving approval to his death.

7:59 Stephen, one of those appointed to look after the food distribution (6:5), paid the penalty for such a direct and bold speech before the Jewish leaders. He was the first person to die for his belief, and as he died he had a vision of Jesus. His words at that point were similar to some of Jesus' words (Luke 23:46).

The Church Persecuted and Scattered

On that day a great persecution broke out against the church at Jerusalem, and all except the apostles were scattered throughout Judea and Samaria. [2]Godly men buried Stephen and mourned deeply for him. [3]But Saul began to destroy the church. Going from house to house, he dragged off men and women and put them in prison.

Philip in Samaria

[4]Those who had been scattered preached the word wherever they went. [5]Philip went down to a city in Samaria and proclaimed the Christ[a] there. [6]When the crowds heard Philip and saw the miraculous signs he did, they all paid close attention to what he said. [7]With shrieks, evil[b] spirits came out of many, and many paralytics and cripples were healed. [8]So there was great joy in that city.

Simon the Sorcerer

[9]Now for some time a man named Simon had practised sorcery in the city and amazed all the people of Samaria. He boasted that he was someone great, [10]and all the people, both high and low, gave him their attention and exclaimed, "This man is the divine power known as the Great Power." [11]They followed him because he had amazed them for a long time with his magic. [12]But when they believed Philip as he preached the good news of the kingdom of God and the name of Jesus Christ, they were baptised, both men and women. [13]Simon himself believed and was baptised. And he followed Philip everywhere, astonished by the great signs and miracles he saw.

[14]When the apostles in Jerusalem heard that Samaria had accepted the word of God, they sent Peter and John to them. [15]When they arrived, they prayed for them that they might receive the Holy Spirit, [16]because the Holy Spirit had not yet come upon any of them; they had simply been baptised into[c] the name of the Lord Jesus. [17]Then Peter and John placed their hands on them, and they received the Holy Spirit.

[18]When Simon saw that the Spirit was given at the laying on of the apostles' hands, he offered them money [19]and said, "Give me also this ability so that everyone on whom I lay my hands may receive the Holy Spirit."

[20]Peter answered: "May your money perish with you, because you thought you could buy the gift of God with money! [21]You have no part or share in this ministry, because your heart is not right before God. [22]Repent of this wickedness and pray to the Lord. Perhaps he will forgive you for having such a thought in your heart. [23]For I see that you are full of bitterness and captive to sin."

[24]Then Simon answered, "Pray to the Lord for me so that nothing you have said may happen to me."

[25]When they had testified and proclaimed the word of the Lord, Peter and John returned to Jerusalem, preaching the gospel in many Samaritan villages.

Philip and the Ethiopian

[26]Now an angel of the Lord said to Philip, "Go south to the road — the desert road — that goes down from Jerusalem to Gaza." [27]So he started out, and on his way he met an Ethiopian[d] eunuch, an important official in charge of all the treasury of Candace, queen of the Ethiopians. This man had gone to Jerusalem to worship, [28]and on his way home was sitting in his chariot reading the book of Isaiah the prophet. [29]The Spirit told Philip, "Go to that chariot and stay near it."

[30]Then Philip ran up to the chariot and heard the man reading Isaiah the prophet. "Do you understand what you are reading?" Philip asked.

[31]"How can I," he said, "unless someone explains it to me?" So he invited Philip to come up and sit with him.

[32]The eunuch was reading this passage of Scripture:

"He was led like a sheep to the slaughter,
    and as a lamb before the shearer is silent,
    so he did not open his mouth.
[33]In his humiliation he was deprived of justice.
    Who can speak of his descendants?
    For his life was taken from the earth."[e]

[34]The eunuch asked Philip, "Tell me, please, who is the prophet talking about, himself or someone else?" [35]Then Philip began with that very passage of Scripture and told him the good news about Jesus.

[36]As they travelled along the road, they came to some water and the eunuch said, "Look, here is water. Why shouldn't I be baptised?"[f] [38]And he gave orders to stop the chariot. Then both Philip and the eunuch went down into the water and Philip baptised him. [39]When they came up out of the water, the Spirit of the Lord suddenly took Philip away, and the eunuch did not see him again, but went on his way rejoicing. [40]Philip, however, appeared at Azotus and travelled about, preaching the gospel in all the towns until he reached Caesarea.

---

[a]5 Or *Messiah*   [b]7 Greek *unclean*   [c]16 Or *in*   [d]27 That is, from the upper Nile region
[e]33 Isaiah 53:7,8
[f]36 Some late manuscripts *baptised?" [37]Philip said, "If you believe with all your heart, you may." The eunuch answered, "I believe that Jesus Christ is the Son of God."*

Saul's Conversion

9 Meanwhile, Saul was still breathing out murderous threats against the Lord's disciples. He went to the high priest [2]and asked him for letters to the synagogues in Damascus, so that if he found any there who belonged to the Way, whether men or women, he might take them as prisoners to Jerusalem. [3]As he neared Damascus on his journey, suddenly a light from heaven flashed around him. [4]He fell to the ground and heard a voice say to him, "Saul, Saul, why do you persecute me?"

9:4   Saul was enthusiastic about persecuting Christians. He was a loyal Jew and regarded it as his religious duty to wipe out what he saw as a heretical and dangerous sect. Jesus, when addressing Saul, made it plain that in persecuting the believers Saul was really persecuting him.

---

[5]"Who are you, Lord?" Saul asked.

"I am Jesus, whom you are persecuting," he replied. [6]"Now get up and go into the city, and you will be told what you must do."

[7]The men travelling with Saul stood there speechless; they heard the sound but did not see anyone. [8]Saul got up from the ground, but when he opened his eyes he could see nothing. So they led him by the hand into Damascus. [9]For three days he was blind, and did not eat or drink anything.

[10]In Damascus there was a disciple named Ananias. The Lord called to him in a vision, "Ananias!"

"Yes, Lord," he answered.

[11]The Lord told him, "Go to the house of Judas on Straight Street and ask for a man from Tarsus named Saul, for he is praying. [12]In a vision he has seen a man named Ananias come and place his hands on him to restore his sight."

[13]"Lord," Ananias answered, "I have heard many reports about this man and all the harm he has done to your saints in Jerusalem. [14]And he has come here with authority from the chief priests to arrest all who call on your name."

[15]But the Lord said to Ananias, "Go! This man is my chosen instrument to carry my name before the Gentiles and their kings and before the people of Israel. [16]I will show him how much he must suffer for my name."

[17]Then Ananias went to the house and entered it. Placing his hands on Saul, he said, "Brother Saul, the Lord—Jesus, who appeared to you on the road as you were coming here—has sent me so that you may see again and be filled with the Holy Spirit." [18]Immediately, something like scales fell from Saul's eyes, and he could see again. He got up and was baptised, [19]and after taking some food, he regained his strength.

Saul in Damascus and Jerusalem

Saul spent several days with the disciples in Damascus. [20]At once he began to preach in the synagogues that Jesus is the Son of God. [21]All those who heard him were astonished and asked, "Isn't he the man who caused havoc in Jerusalem among those who call on this name? And hasn't he come here to take them as prisoners to the chief priests?" [22]Yet Saul grew more and more powerful and baffled the Jews living in Damascus by proving that Jesus is the Christ.[a]

[23]After many days had gone by, the Jews conspired to kill him, [24]but Saul learned of their plan. Day and night they kept close watch on the city gates in order to kill him. [25]But his followers took him by night and lowered him in a basket through an opening in the wall.

[26]When he came to Jerusalem, he tried to join the disciples, but they were all afraid of him, not believing that he really was a disciple. [27]But Barnabas took him and brought him to the apostles. He told them how Saul on his journey had seen the Lord and that the Lord had spoken to him, and how in Damascus he had preached fearlessly in the name of Jesus. [28]So Saul stayed with them and moved about freely in Jerusalem, speaking boldly in the name of the Lord. [29]He talked and debated with the Grecian Jews, but they tried to kill him. [30]When the brothers learned of this, they took him down to Caesarea and sent him off to Tarsus.

[31]Then the church throughout Judea, Galilee and Samaria enjoyed a time of peace. It was strengthened; and encouraged by the Holy Spirit, it grew in numbers, living in the fear of the Lord.

Aeneas and Dorcas

[32]As Peter travelled about the country, he went to visit the saints in Lydda. [33]There he found a man named Aeneas, a paralytic who had been bedridden for eight years. [34]"Aeneas," Peter said to him, "Jesus Christ heals you. Get up and tidy up your mat." Immediately Aeneas got up. [35]All those who lived in Lydda and Sharon saw him and turned to the Lord.

[36]In Joppa there was a disciple named Tabitha (which, when translated, is Dorcas[b]), who was always doing good and helping the poor. [37]About that time she became sick and died, and her body was washed and placed in an upstairs room. [38]Lydda was near Joppa; so when the disciples heard that Peter was in Lydda, they sent two men to him and urged him, "Please come at once!"

[39]Peter went with them, and when he arrived he was taken upstairs to the room. All the widows stood around him, crying and showing him the robes and other clothing that Dorcas had made while she was still with them.

[40]Peter sent them all out of the room; then he got down on his knees and prayed. Turning towards the dead woman, he said, "Tabitha, get up." She opened her eyes, and seeing Peter she sat up. [41]He took her by the hand and helped her to her feet. Then he called the believers and the widows and presented her to them alive. [42]This became known all over Joppa, and many people believed in the Lord. [43]Peter stayed in Joppa for some time with a tanner named Simon.

---

[a]22 Or *Messiah*   [b]36 Both *Tabitha* (Aramaic) and *Dorcas* (Greek) mean *gazelle*.

Cornelius Calls for Peter

10 At Caesarea there was a man named Cornelius, a centurion in what was known as the Italian Regiment. [2]He and all his family were devout and God-fearing; he gave generously to those in need and prayed to God regularly. [3]One day at about three in the afternoon he had a vision. He distinctly saw an angel of God, who came to him and said, "Cornelius!"

[4]Cornelius stared at him in fear. "What is it, Lord?" he asked.

The angel answered, "Your prayers and gifts to the poor have come up as a memorial offering before God. [5]Now send men to Joppa to bring back a man named Simon who is called Peter. [6]He is staying with Simon the tanner, whose house is by the sea."

[7]When the angel who spoke to him had gone, Cornelius called two of his servants and a devout soldier who was one of his attendants. [8]He told them everything that had happened and sent them to Joppa.

Peter's Vision

[9]About noon the following day as they were on their journey and approaching the city, Peter went up on the roof to pray. [10]He became hungry and wanted something to eat, and while the meal was being prepared, he fell into a trance. [11]He saw heaven opened and something like a large sheet being let down to earth by its four corners. [12]It contained all kinds of four-footed animals, as well as reptiles of the earth and birds of the air. [13]Then a voice told him, "Get up, Peter. Kill and eat."

[14]"Surely not, Lord!" Peter replied. "I have never eaten anything impure or unclean."

[15]The voice spoke to him a second time, "Do not call anything impure that God has made clean."

[16]This happened three times, and immediately the sheet was taken back to heaven.

[17]While Peter was wondering about the meaning of the vision, the men sent by Cornelius found out where Simon's house was and stopped at the gate. [18]They called out, asking if Simon who was known as Peter was staying there.

[19]While Peter was still thinking about the vision, the Spirit said to him, "Simon, three[a] men are looking for you. [20]So get up and go downstairs. Do not hesitate to go with them, for I have sent them."

[21]Peter went down and said to the men, "I'm the one you're looking for. Why have you come?"

[22]The men replied, "We have come from Cornelius the centurion. He is a righteous and God-fearing man, who is respected by all the Jewish people. A holy angel told him to have you come to his house so that he could hear what you have to say." [23]Then Peter invited the men into the house to be his guests.

Peter at Cornelius' House

The next day Peter started out with them, and some of the brothers from Joppa went along. [24]The following day he arrived in Caesarea. Cornelius was expecting them and had called together his relatives and close friends. [25]As Peter entered the house, Cornelius met him and fell at his feet in reverence. [26]But Peter made him get up. "Stand up," he said, "I am only a man myself."

[27]Talking with him, Peter went inside and found a large gathering of people. [28]He said to them: "You are well aware that it is against our law for a Jew to associate with a Gentile or visit him. But God has shown me that I should not call any man impure or unclean. [29]So when I was sent for, I came without raising any objection. May I ask why you sent for me?"

[30]Cornelius answered: "Four days ago I was in my house praying at this hour, at three in the afternoon. Suddenly a man in shining clothes stood before me [31]and said, 'Cornelius, God has heard your prayer and remembered your gifts to the poor. [32]Send to Joppa for Simon who is called Peter. He is a guest in the home of Simon the tanner, who lives by the sea.' [33]So I sent for you immediately, and it was good of you to come. Now we are all here in the presence of God to listen to everything the Lord has commanded you to tell us."

[34]Then Peter began to speak: "I now realise how true it is that God does not show favouritism [35]but accepts men from every nation who fear him and do what is right. [36]You know the message God sent to the people of Israel, telling the good news of peace through Jesus Christ, who is Lord of all. [37]You know what has happened throughout Judea, beginning in Galilee after the baptism that John preached — [38]how God anointed Jesus of Nazareth with the Holy Spirit and power, and how he went around doing good and healing all who were under the power of the devil, because God was with him.

[39]"We are witnesses of everything he did in the country of the Jews and in Jerusalem. They killed him by hanging him on a tree, [40]but God raised him from the dead on the third day and caused him to be seen. [41]He was not seen by all the people, but by witnesses whom God had already chosen — by us who ate and drank with him after he rose from the dead. [42]He commanded us to preach to the people and to testify that he is the one whom God appointed as judge of the living and the dead. [43]All the prophets testify about him that everyone who believes in him receives forgiveness of sins through his name."

[44]While Peter was still speaking these words, the Holy Spirit came on all who heard the message. [45]The circumcised believers who had come with Peter were astonished that the gift of the Holy Spirit had been poured out even on the Gentiles. [46]For they heard them speaking in tongues[b] and praising God.

Then Peter said, [47]"Can anyone keep these people from being baptised with water? They have received the Holy Spirit just as we have." [48]So he ordered that they be baptised in the name of Jesus Christ. Then they asked Peter to stay with them for a few days.

Peter Explains His Actions

11 The apostles and the brothers throughout Judea heard that the Gentiles also had received the word of God. [2]So when Peter went up to

---

[a]19 One early manuscript *two*; other manuscripts do not have the number.   [b]46 Or *other languages*

Jerusalem, the circumcised believers criticised him ³and said, "You went into the house of uncircumcised men and ate with them."

⁴Peter began and explained everything to them precisely as it had happened: ⁵"I was in the city of Joppa praying, and in a trance I saw a vision. I saw something like a large sheet being let down from heaven by its four corners, and it came down to where I was. ⁶I looked into it and saw four-footed animals of the earth, wild beasts, reptiles, and birds of the air. ⁷Then I heard a voice telling me, 'Get up, Peter. Kill and eat.'

⁸"I replied, 'Surely not, Lord! Nothing impure or unclean has ever entered my mouth.'

⁹"The voice spoke from heaven a second time, 'Do not call anything impure that God has made clean.' ¹⁰This happened three times, and then it was pulled up to heaven again.

¹¹"Right then three men who had been sent to me from Caesarea stopped at the house where I was staying. ¹²The Spirit told me to have no hesitation about going with them. These six brothers also went with me, and we entered the man's house. ¹³He told us how he had seen an angel appear in his house and say, 'Send to Joppa for Simon who is called Peter. ¹⁴He will bring you a message through which you and all your household will be saved.'

¹⁵"As I began to speak, the Holy Spirit came on them as he had come on us at the beginning. ¹⁶Then I remembered what the Lord had said: 'John baptised with ᵃ water, but you will be baptised with the Holy Spirit.' ¹⁷So if God gave them the same gift as he gave us, who believed in the Lord Jesus Christ, who was I to think that I could oppose God?"

¹⁸When they heard this, they had no further objections and praised God, saying, "So then, God has granted even the Gentiles repentance unto life."

The Church in Antioch

¹⁹Now those who had been scattered by the persecution in connection with Stephen travelled as far as Phoenicia, Cyprus and Antioch, telling the message only to Jews. ²⁰Some of them, however, men from Cyprus and Cyrene, went to Antioch and began to speak to Greeks also, telling them the good news about the Lord Jesus. ²¹The Lord's hand was with them, and a great number of people believed and turned to the Lord.

²²News of this reached the ears of the church at Jerusalem, and they sent Barnabas to Antioch. ²³When he arrived and saw the evidence of the grace of God, he was glad and encouraged them all to remain true to the Lord with all their hearts. ²⁴He was a good man, full of the Holy Spirit and faith, and a great number of people were brought to the Lord.

²⁵Then Barnabas went to Tarsus to look for Saul, ²⁶and when he found him, he brought him to Antioch. So for a whole year Barnabas and Saul met with the church and taught great numbers of people. The disciples were called Christians first at Antioch.

²⁷During this time some prophets came down from Jerusalem to Antioch. ²⁸One of them, named Agabus, stood up and through the Spirit predicted that a severe famine would spread over the entire Roman world. (This happened during the reign of Claudius.) ²⁹The disciples, each according to his ability, decided to provide help for the brothers living in Judea. ³⁰This they did, sending their gift to the elders by Barnabas and Saul.

11:26   The word "Christ" is a Greek word which is a translation of the Hebrew word "Messiah", and means "anointed one". The pagans of Antioch, who had never heard of the Jewish Messiah, took it to be the name of a person rather than an actual title. So the believers in Jesus the Messiah acquired the name Christians.

Peter's Miraculous Escape From Prison

12 It was about this time that King Herod arrested some who belonged to the church, intending to persecute them. ²He had James, the brother of John, put to death with the sword. ³When he saw that this pleased the Jews, he proceeded to seize Peter also. This happened during the Feast of Unleavened Bread. ⁴After arresting him, he put him in prison, handing him over to be guarded by four squads of four soldiers each. Herod intended to bring him out for public trial after the Passover.

⁵So Peter was kept in prison, but the church was earnestly praying to God for him.

⁶The night before Herod was to bring him to trial, Peter was sleeping between two soldiers, bound with two chains, and sentries stood guard at the entrance. ⁷Suddenly an angel of the Lord appeared and a light shone in the cell. He struck Peter on the side and woke him up. "Quick, get up!" he said, and the chains fell off Peter's wrists.

⁸Then the angel said to him, "Put on your clothes and sandals." And Peter did so. "Wrap your cloak around you and follow me," the angel told him. ⁹Peter followed him out of the prison, but he had no idea that what the angel was doing was really happening; he thought he was seeing a vision. ¹⁰They passed the first and second guards and came to the iron gate leading to the city. It opened for them by itself, and they went through it. When they had walked the length of one street, suddenly the angel left him.

¹¹Then Peter came to himself and said, "Now I know without a doubt that the Lord sent his angel and rescued me from Herod's clutches and from everything the Jewish people were anticipating."

¹²When this had dawned on him, he went to the house of Mary the mother of John, also called Mark, where many people had gathered and were praying. ¹³Peter knocked at the outer entrance, and a servant girl named Rhoda came to answer the door. ¹⁴When she recognised Peter's voice, she was so overjoyed she ran back without opening it and exclaimed, "Peter is at the door!"

ᵃ16 Or in

15"You're out of your mind," they told her. When she kept insisting that it was so, they said, "It must be his angel."

16But Peter kept on knocking, and when they opened the door and saw him, they were astonished. 17Peter motioned with his hand for them to be quiet and described how the Lord had brought him out of prison. "Tell James and the brothers about this," he said, and then he left for another place.

18In the morning, there was no small commotion among the soldiers as to what had become of Peter. 19After Herod had a thorough search made for him and did not find him, he cross-examined the guards and ordered that they be executed.

Herod's Death

Then Herod went from Judea to Caesarea and stayed there a while. 20He had been quarrelling with the people of Tyre and Sidon; they now joined together and sought an audience with him. Having secured the support of Blastus, a trusted personal servant of the king, they asked for peace, because they depended on the king's country for their food supply.

21On the appointed day Herod, wearing his royal robes, sat on his throne and delivered a public address to the people. 22They shouted, "This is the voice of a god, not of a man." 23Immediately, because Herod did not give praise to God, an angel of the Lord struck him down, and he was eaten by worms and died.

24But the word of God continued to increase and spread.

25When Barnabas and Saul had finished their mission, they returned from[a] Jerusalem, taking with them John, also called Mark.

Barnabas and Saul Sent Off

13 In the church at Antioch there were prophets and teachers: Barnabas, Simeon called Niger, Lucius of Cyrene, Manaen (who had been brought up with Herod the tetrarch) and Saul. 2While they were worshipping the Lord and fasting, the Holy Spirit said, "Set apart for me Barnabas and Saul for the work to which I have called them." 3So after they had fasted and prayed, they placed their hands on them and sent them off.

13:2   It was a decisive moment in the life of the Church when Saul and Barnabas were commissioned and set apart for their special work. Appropriately, such an important act was performed in the context of prayer and fasting.

On Cyprus

4The two of them, sent on their way by the Holy Spirit, went down to Seleucia and sailed from there to Cyprus. 5When they arrived at Salamis, they proclaimed the word of God in the Jewish synagogues. John was with them as their helper.

6They travelled through the whole island until they came to Paphos. There they met a Jewish sorcerer and false prophet named Bar-Jesus, 7who was an attendant of the proconsul, Sergius Paulus. The proconsul, an intelligent man, sent for Barnabas and Saul because he wanted to hear the word of God. 8But Elymas the sorcerer (for that is what his name means) opposed them and tried to turn the proconsul from the faith. 9Then Saul, who was also called Paul, filled with the Holy Spirit, looked straight at Elymas and said, 10"You are a child of the devil and an enemy of everything that is right! You are full of all kinds of deceit and trickery. Will you never stop perverting the right ways of the Lord? 11Now the hand of the Lord is against you. You are going to be blind, and for a time you will be unable to see the light of the sun."

Immediately mist and darkness came over him, and he groped about, seeking someone to lead him by the hand. 12When the proconsul saw what had happened, he believed, for he was amazed at the teaching about the Lord.

In Pisidian Antioch

13From Paphos, Paul and his companions sailed to Perga in Pamphylia, where John left them to return to Jerusalem. 14From Perga they went on to Pisidian Antioch. On the Sabbath they entered the synagogue and sat down. 15After the reading from the Law and the Prophets, the synagogue rulers sent word to them, saying, "Brothers, if you have a message of encouragement for the people, please speak."

16Standing up, Paul motioned with his hand and said: "Men of Israel and you Gentiles who worship God, listen to me! 17The God of the people of Israel chose our fathers; he made the people prosper during their stay in Egypt, with mighty power he led them out of that country, 18he endured their conduct[a] for about forty years in the desert, 19he overthrew seven nations in Canaan and gave their land to his people as their inheritance. 20All this took about 450 years.

"After this, God gave them judges until the time of Samuel the prophet. 21Then the people asked for a king, and he gave them Saul son of Kish, of the tribe of Benjamin, who ruled for forty years. 22After removing Saul, he made David their king. He testified concerning him: 'I have found David son of Jesse a man after my own heart; he will do everything I want him to do.'

23"From this man's descendants God has brought to Israel the Saviour Jesus, as he promised. 24Before the coming of Jesus, John preached repentance and baptism to all the people of Israel. 25As John was completing his work, he said: 'Who do you think I am? I am not that one. No, but he is coming after me, whose sandals I am not worthy to untie.'

26"Brothers, children of Abraham, and you God-fearing Gentiles, it is to us that this message of salvation has been sent. 27The people of Jerusalem and their rulers did not recognise Jesus, yet in condemning him

---

a25 Some manuscripts to   a18 Some manuscripts and cared for them they fulfilled the words of the prophets that are read every Sabbath. 28Though they found no proper ground for a death sentence, they asked Pilate to have him executed. 29When they had carried out all that was written about him, they took him down from the tree and laid him in a tomb. 30But God raised him from the dead, 31and for many days he was seen by those who had travelled with him from Galilee to Jerusalem. They are now his witnesses to our people.

32"We tell you the good news: What God promised our fathers 33he has fulfilled for us, their children, by raising up Jesus. As it is written in the second Psalm:

" 'You are my Son;
today I have become your Father.' b,c

34The fact that God raised him from the dead, never to decay, is stated in these words:

" 'I will give you the holy and sure blessings
promised to David.' d

35So it is stated elsewhere:

" 'You will not let your Holy One see decay.' e

36"For when David had served God's purpose in his own generation, he fell asleep; he was buried with his fathers and his body decayed. 37But the one whom God raised from the dead did not see decay.

38"Therefore, my brothers, I want you to know that through Jesus the forgiveness of sins is proclaimed to you. 39Through him everyone who believes is justified from everything you could not be justified from by the law of Moses. 40Take care that what the prophets have said does not happen to you:

41" 'Look, you scoffers,
wonder and perish,
for I am going to do something in your days
that you would never believe,
even if someone told you.' f"

42As Paul and Barnabas were leaving the synagogue, the people invited them to speak further about these things on the next Sabbath. 43When the congregation was dismissed, many of the Jews and devout converts to Judaism followed Paul and Barnabas, who talked with them and urged them to continue in the grace of God.

44On the next Sabbath almost the whole city gathered to hear the word of the Lord. 45When the Jews saw the crowds, they were filled with jealousy and talked abusively against what Paul was saying.

46Then Paul and Barnabas answered them boldly: "We had to speak the word of God to you first. Since you reject it and do not consider yourselves worthy of eternal life, we now turn to the Gentiles. 47For this is what the Lord has commanded us:

" 'I have made you g a light for the Gentiles,
that you g may bring salvation to the ends of
the earth.' h"

48When the Gentiles heard this, they were glad and honoured the word of the Lord; and all who were appointed for eternal life believed.

49The word of the Lord spread through the whole region. 50But the Jews incited the God-fearing women of high standing and the leading men of the city. They stirred up persecution against Paul and Barnabas, and expelled them from their region. 51So they shook the dust from their feet in protest against them and went to Iconium. 52And the disciples were filled with joy and with the Holy Spirit.

In Iconium

14 At Iconium Paul and Barnabas went as usual into the Jewish synagogue. There they spoke so effectively that a great number of Jews and Gentiles believed. 2But the Jews who refused to believe stirred up the Gentiles and poisoned their minds against the brothers. 3So Paul and Barnabas spent considerable time there, speaking boldly for the Lord, who confirmed the message of his grace by enabling them to do miraculous signs and wonders. 4The people of the city were divided; some sided with the Jews, others with the apostles. 5There was a plot afoot among the Gentiles and Jews, together with their leaders, to ill-treat them and stone them. 6But they found out about it and fled to the Lycaonian cities of Lystra and Derbe and to the surrounding country, 7where they continued to preach the good news.

In Lystra and Derbe

8In Lystra there sat a man crippled in his feet, who was lame from birth and had never walked. 9He listened to Paul as he was speaking. Paul looked directly at him, saw that he had faith to be healed 10and called out, "Stand up on your feet!" At that, the man jumped up and began to walk.

11When the crowd saw what Paul had done, they shouted in the Lycaonian language, "The gods have come down to us in human form!" 12Barnabas they called Zeus, and Paul they called Hermes because he was the chief speaker. 13The priest of Zeus, whose temple was just outside the city, brought bulls and wreaths to the city gates because he and the crowd wanted to offer sacrifices to them.

14:11 It was perhaps understandable that the people of Lystra, seeing the remarkable healing which had been performed, thought that Paul and Barnabas were gods in human form. However it had to be made plain that as Christians they were working to bring glory to God, not to themselves.

14But when the apostles Barnabas and Paul heard of this, they tore their clothes and rushed out into the crowd, shouting: 15"Men, why are you doing this? We too are only men, human like you. We are bringing you good news, telling you to turn from these worthless things to the living God, who made heaven and earth

---

b33 Or have begotten you   c33 Psalm 2:7   d34 Isaiah 55:3   e35 Psalm 16:10   f41 Hab. 1:5
g47 The Greek is singular.   h47 Isaiah 49:6

and sea and everything in them. [16]In the past, he let all nations go their own way. [17]Yet he has not left himself without testimony: He has shown kindness by giving you rain from heaven and crops in their seasons; he provides you with plenty of food and fills your hearts with joy." [18]Even with these words, they had difficulty keeping the crowd from sacrificing to them.

[19]Then some Jews came from Antioch and Iconium and won the crowd over. They stoned Paul and dragged him outside the city, thinking he was dead. [20]But after the disciples had gathered round him, he got up and went back into the city. The next day he and Barnabas left for Derbe.

The Return to Antioch in Syria

[21]They preached the good news in that city and won a large number of disciples. Then they returned to Lystra, Iconium and Antioch, [22]strengthening the disciples and encouraging them to remain true to the faith. "We must go through many hardships to enter the kingdom of God," they said. [23]Paul and Barnabas appointed elders[a] for them in each church and, with prayer and fasting, committed them to the Lord, in whom they had put their trust. [24]After going through Pisidia, they came into Pamphylia, [25]and when they had preached the word in Perga, they went down to Attalia.

[26]From Attalia they sailed back to Antioch, where they had been committed to the grace of God for the work they had now completed. [27]On arriving there, they gathered the church together and reported all that God had done through them and how he had opened the door of faith to the Gentiles. [28]And they stayed there a long time with the disciples.

The Council at Jerusalem

15 Some men came down from Judea to Antioch and were teaching the brothers: "Unless you are circumcised, according to the custom taught by Moses, you cannot be saved." [2]This brought Paul and Barnabas into sharp dispute and debate with them. So Paul and Barnabas were appointed, along with some other believers, to go up to Jerusalem to see the apostles and elders about this question. [3]The church sent them on their way, and as they travelled through Phoenicia and Samaria, they told how the Gentiles had been converted. This news made all the brothers very glad. [4]When they came to Jerusalem, they were welcomed by the church and the apostles and elders, to whom they reported everything God had done through them.

[5]Then some of the believers who belonged to the party of the Pharisees stood up and said, "The Gentiles must be circumcised and required to obey the law of Moses."

[6]The apostles and elders met to consider this question. [7]After much discussion, Peter got up and addressed them: "Brothers, you know that some time ago God made a choice among you that the Gentiles might hear from my lips the message of the gospel and

believe. [8]God, who knows the heart, showed that he accepted them by giving the Holy Spirit to them, just as he did to us. [9]He made no distinction between us and them, for he purified their hearts by faith. [10]Now then, why do you try to test God by putting on the necks of the disciples a yoke that neither we nor our fathers have been able to bear? [11]No! We believe it is through the grace of our Lord Jesus that we are saved, just as they are."

[12]The whole assembly became silent as they listened to Barnabas and Paul telling about the miraculous signs and wonders God had done among the Gentiles through them. [13]When they finished, James spoke up: "Brothers, listen to me. [14]Simon[a] has described to us how God at first showed his concern by taking from the Gentiles a people for himself. [15]The words of the prophets are in agreement with this, as it is written:

[16]" 'After this I will return
    and rebuild David's fallen tent.
  Its ruins I will rebuild,
    and I will restore it,
[17]that the remnant of men may seek the Lord,
    and all the Gentiles who bear my name,
  says the Lord, who does these things'[b]
[18] that have been known for ages.[c]

[19]"It is my judgment, therefore, that we should not make it difficult for the Gentiles who are turning to God. [20]Instead we should write to them, telling them to abstain from food polluted by idols, from sexual immorality, from the meat of strangled animals and from blood. [21]For Moses has been preached in every city from the earliest times and is read in the synagogues on every Sabbath."

The Council's Letter to Gentile Believers

[22]Then the apostles and elders, with the whole church, decided to choose some of their own men and send them to Antioch with Paul and Barnabas. They chose Judas (called Barsabbas) and Silas, two men who were leaders among the brothers. [23]With them they sent the following letter:

The apostles and elders, your brothers,

To the Gentile believers in Antioch, Syria and Cilicia:

Greetings.

[24]We have heard that some went out from us without our authorisation and disturbed you, troubling your minds by what they said. [25]So we all agreed to choose some men and send them to you with our dear friends Barnabas and Paul — [26]men who have risked their lives for the name of our Lord Jesus Christ. [27]Therefore we are sending Judas and Silas to confirm by word of mouth what we are writing. [28]It seemed good to the Holy Spirit and to us not to burden you with anything beyond

---

[a]23 Or Barnabas ordained elders; or Barnabas had elders elected   [a]14 Greek Simeon, a variant of Simon; that is, Peter
[b]17 Amos 9:11,12   [c]17,18 Some manuscripts things'— / [18]known to the Lord for ages is his work

the following requirements: [29]You are to abstain from food sacrificed to idols, from blood, from the meat of strangled animals and from sexual immorality. You will do well to avoid these things.

Farewell.

[30]The men were sent off and went down to Antioch, where they gathered the church together and delivered the letter. [31]The people read it and were glad for its encouraging message. [32]Judas and Silas, who themselves were prophets, said much to encourage and strengthen the brothers. [33]After spending some time there, they were sent off by the brothers with the blessing of peace to return to those who had sent them.[d] [35]But Paul and Barnabas remained in Antioch, where they and many others taught and preached the word of the Lord.

Disagreement Between Paul and Barnabas

[36]Some time later Paul said to Barnabas, "Let us go back and visit the brothers in all the towns where we preached the word of the Lord and see how they are doing." [37]Barnabas wanted to take John, also called Mark, with them, [38]but Paul did not think it wise to take him, because he had deserted them in Pamphylia and had not continued with them in the work. [39]They had such a sharp disagreement that they parted company. Barnabas took Mark and sailed for Cyprus, [40]but Paul chose Silas and left, commended by the brothers to the grace of the Lord. [41]He went through Syria and Cilicia, strengthening the churches.

Timothy Joins Paul and Silas

16 He came to Derbe and then to Lystra, where a disciple named Timothy lived, whose mother was a Jewess and a believer, but whose father was a Greek. [2]The brothers at Lystra and Iconium spoke well of him. [3]Paul wanted to take him along on the journey, so he circumcised him because of the Jews who lived in that area, for they all knew that his father was a Greek. [4]As they travelled from town to town, they delivered the decisions reached by the apostles and elders in Jerusalem for the people to obey. [5]So the churches were strengthened in the faith and grew daily in numbers.

16:3 It seems strange that shortly after the Church had formally decided that it was not necessary for converts to be circumcised, Paul should circumcise Timothy before taking him on a missionary journey. He did so, not because it was necessary, but because it would gain a more ready acceptance for Timothy among those he would minister to. Paul's overriding principle was to commend the good news by every means possible (see 1 Corinthians 9:20).

Paul's Vision of the Man of Macedonia

[6]Paul and his companions travelled throughout the region of Phrygia and Galatia, having been kept by the Holy Spirit from preaching the word in the province of Asia. [7]When they came to the border of Mysia, they tried to enter Bithynia, but the Spirit of Jesus would not allow them to. [8]So they passed by Mysia and went down to Troas. [9]During the night Paul had a vision of a man of Macedonia standing and begging him, "Come over to Macedonia and help us." [10]After Paul had seen the vision, we got ready at once to leave for Macedonia, concluding that God had called us to preach the gospel to them.

Lydia's Conversion in Philippi

[11]From Troas we put out to sea and sailed straight for Samothrace, and the next day on to Neapolis. [12]From there we travelled to Philippi, a Roman colony and the leading city of that district of Macedonia. And we stayed there several days.

[13]On the Sabbath we went outside the city gate to the river, where we expected to find a place of prayer. We sat down and began to speak to the women who had gathered there. [14]One of those listening was a woman named Lydia, a dealer in purple cloth from the city of Thyatira, who was a worshipper of God. The Lord opened her heart to respond to Paul's message. [15]When she and the members of her household were baptised, she invited us to her home. "If you consider me a believer in the Lord," she said, "come and stay at my house." And she persuaded us.

Paul and Silas in Prison

[16]Once when we were going to the place of prayer, we were met by a slave girl who had a spirit by which she predicted the future. She earned a great deal of money for her owners by fortune-telling. [17]This girl followed Paul and the rest of us, shouting, "These men are servants of the Most High God, who are telling you the way to be saved." [18]She kept this up for many days. Finally Paul became so troubled that he turned round and said to the spirit, "In the name of Jesus Christ I command you to come out of her!" At that moment the spirit left her.

[19]When the owners of the slave girl realised that their hope of making money was gone, they seized Paul and Silas and dragged them into the market-place to face the authorities. [20]They brought them before the magistrates and said, "These men are Jews, and are throwing our city into an uproar [21]by advocating customs unlawful for us Romans to accept or practise."

[22]The crowd joined in the attack against Paul and Silas, and the magistrates ordered them to be stripped and beaten. [23]After they had been severely flogged, they were thrown into prison, and the jailer was commanded to guard them carefully. [24]Upon receiving such orders, he put them in the inner cell and fastened their feet in the stocks.

[25]About midnight Paul and Silas were praying and singing hymns to God, and the other prisoners were

---

[d]33 Some manuscripts *them,* 34*but Silas decided to remain there*

listening to them. [26]Suddenly there was such a violent earthquake that the foundations of the prison were shaken. At once all the prison doors flew open, and everybody's chains came loose. [27]The jailer woke up, and when he saw the prison doors open, he drew his sword and was about to kill himself because he thought the prisoners had escaped. [28]But Paul shouted, "Don't harm yourself! We are all here!"

[29]The jailer called for lights, rushed in and fell trembling before Paul and Silas. [30]He then brought them out and asked, "Sirs, what must I do to be saved?"

[31]They replied, "Believe in the Lord Jesus, and you will be saved—you and your household." [32]Then they spoke the word of the Lord to him and to all the others in his house. [33]At that hour of the night the jailer took them and washed their wounds; then immediately he and all his family were baptised. [34]The jailer brought them into his house and set a meal before them; he was filled with joy because he had come to believe in God—he and his whole family.

[35]When it was daylight, the magistrates sent their officers to the jailer with the order: "Release those men." [36]The jailer told Paul, "The magistrates have ordered that you and Silas be released. Now you can leave. Go in peace."

[37]But Paul said to the officers: "They beat us publicly without a trial, even though we are Roman citizens, and threw us into prison. And now do they want to get rid of us quietly? No! Let them come themselves and escort us out."

[38]The officers reported this to the magistrates, and when they heard that Paul and Silas were Roman citizens, they were alarmed. [39]They came to appease them and escorted them from the prison, requesting them to leave the city. [40]After Paul and Silas came out of the prison, they went to Lydia's house, where they met with the brothers and encouraged them. Then they left.

In Thessalonica

17 When they had passed through Amphipolis and Apollonia, they came to Thessalonica, where there was a Jewish synagogue. [2]As his custom was, Paul went into the synagogue, and on three Sabbath days he reasoned with them from the Scriptures, [3]explaining and proving that the Christ[a] had to suffer and rise from the dead. "This Jesus I am proclaiming to you is the Christ,"[a] he said. [4]Some of the Jews were persuaded and joined Paul and Silas, as did a large number of God-fearing Greeks and not a few prominent women.

[5]But the Jews were jealous; so they rounded up some bad characters from the market-place, formed a mob and started a riot in the city. They rushed to Jason's house in search of Paul and Silas in order to bring them out to the crowd.[b] [6]But when they did not find them, they dragged Jason and some other brothers before the city officials, shouting: "These men who have caused trouble all over the world have now come here, [7]and Jason has welcomed them into his house. They are all defying Caesar's decrees, saying that there

is another king, one called Jesus." [8]When they heard this, the crowd and the city officials were thrown into turmoil. [9]Then they put Jason and the others on bail and let them go.

In Berea

[10]As soon as it was night, the brothers sent Paul and Silas away to Berea. On arriving there, they went to the Jewish synagogue. [11]Now the Bereans were of more noble character than the Thessalonians, for they received the message with great eagerness and examined the Scriptures every day to see if what Paul said was true. [12]Many of the Jews believed, as did also a number of prominent Greek women and many Greek men.

[13]When the Jews in Thessalonica learned that Paul was preaching the word of God at Berea, they went there too, agitating the crowds and stirring them up. [14]The brothers immediately sent Paul to the coast, but Silas and Timothy stayed at Berea. [15]The men who escorted Paul brought him to Athens and then left with instructions for Silas and Timothy to join him as soon as possible.

In Athens

[16]While Paul was waiting for them in Athens, he was greatly distressed to see that the city was full of idols. [17]So he reasoned in the synagogue with the Jews and the God-fearing Greeks, as well as in the market-place day by day with those who happened to be there. [18]A group of Epicurean and Stoic philosophers began to dispute with him. Some of them asked, "What is this babbler trying to say?" Others remarked, "He seems to be advocating foreign gods." They said this because Paul was preaching the good news about Jesus and the resurrection. [19]Then they took him and brought him to a meeting of the Areopagus, where they said to him, "May we know what this new teaching is that you are presenting? [20]You are bringing some strange ideas to our ears, and we want to know what they mean." [21](All the Athenians and the foreigners who lived there spent their time doing nothing but talking about and listening to the latest ideas.)

[22]Paul then stood up in the meeting of the Areopagus and said: "Men of Athens! I see that in every way you are very religious. [23]For as I walked around and looked carefully at your objects of worship, I even found an altar with this inscription: TO AN UNKNOWN GOD. Now what you worship as something unknown I am going to proclaim to you.

[24]"The God who made the world and everything in it is the Lord of heaven and earth and does not live in temples built by hands. [25]And he is not served by human hands, as if he needed anything, because he himself gives all men life and breath and everything else. [26]From one man he made every nation of men, that they should inhabit the whole earth; and he determined the times set for them and the exact places where they should live. [27]God did this so that men would seek him and perhaps reach out for him and find him, though he is not far from each one of us. [28]'For

a3 Or *Messiah*   *b5* Or *the assembly of the people*

in him we live and move and have our being.' As some of your own poets have said, 'We are his offspring.' 29"Therefore since we are God's offspring, we should not think that the divine being is like gold or silver or stone—an image made by man's design and skill. 30In the past God overlooked such ignorance, but now he commands all people everywhere to repent. 31For he has set a day when he will judge the world with justice by the man he has appointed. He has given proof of this to all men by raising him from the dead." 32When they heard about the resurrection of the dead, some of them sneered, but others said, "We want to hear you again on this subject." 33At that, Paul left the Council. 34A few men became followers of Paul and believed. Among them was Dionysius, a member of the Areopagus, also a woman named Damaris, and a number of others.

17:32   Athens was a cultivated and sophisticated city, and Paul preached in a different style than usual. Even so, although he tailored the gospel to the capacity of his hearers, he still emphasized the reality of the resurrection, despite the fact that his hearers found it a difficult idea.

In Corinth

18 After this, Paul left Athens and went to Corinth. 2There he met a Jew named Aquila, a native of Pontus, who had recently come from Italy with his wife Priscilla, because Claudius had ordered all the Jews to leave Rome. Paul went to see them, 3and because he was a tentmaker as they were, he stayed and worked with them. 4Every Sabbath he reasoned in the synagogue, trying to persuade Jews and Greeks.

5When Silas and Timothy came from Macedonia, Paul devoted himself exclusively to preaching, testifying to the Jews that Jesus was the Christ.[a] 6But when the Jews opposed Paul and became abusive, he shook out his clothes in protest and said to them, "Your blood be on your own heads! I am clear of my responsibility. From now on I will go to the Gentiles."

7Then Paul left the synagogue and went next door to the house of Titius Justus, a worshipper of God. 8Crispus, the synagogue ruler, and his entire household believed in the Lord; and many of the Corinthians who heard him believed and were baptised.

9One night the Lord spoke to Paul in a vision: "Do not be afraid; keep on speaking, do not be silent. 10For I am with you, and no-one is going to attack and harm you, because I have many people in this city." 11So Paul stayed for a year and a half, teaching them the word of God.

12While Gallio was proconsul of Achaia, the Jews made a united attack on Paul and brought him into court. 13"This man," they charged, "is persuading the people to worship God in ways contrary to the law."

14Just as Paul was about to speak, Gallio said to the Jews, "If you Jews were making a complaint about some misdemeanour or serious crime, it would be reasonable for me to listen to you. 15But since it involves questions about words and names and your own law— settle the matter yourselves. I will not be a judge of such things." 16So he had them ejected from the court. 17Then they all turned on Sosthenes the synagogue ruler and beat him in front of the court. But Gallio showed no concern whatever.

Priscilla, Aquila and Apollos

18Paul stayed on in Corinth for some time. Then he left the brothers and sailed for Syria, accompanied by Priscilla and Aquila. Before he sailed, he had his hair cut off at Cenchrea because of a vow he had taken. 19They arrived at Ephesus, where Paul left Priscilla and Aquila. He himself went into the synagogue and reasoned with the Jews. 20When they asked him to spend more time with them, he declined. 21But as he left, he promised, "I will come back if it is God's will." Then he set sail from Ephesus. 22When he landed at Caesarea, he went up and greeted the church and then went down to Antioch.

23After spending some time in Antioch, Paul set out from there and travelled from place to place throughout the region of Galatia and Phrygia, strengthening all the disciples.

24Meanwhile a Jew named Apollos, a native of Alexandria, came to Ephesus. He was a learned man, with a thorough knowledge of the Scriptures. 25He had been instructed in the way of the Lord, and he spoke with great fervour[b] and taught about Jesus accurately, though he knew only the baptism of John. 26He began to speak boldly in the synagogue. When Priscilla and Aquila heard him, they invited him to their home and explained to him the way of God more adequately.

27When Apollos wanted to go to Achaia, the brothers encouraged him and wrote to the disciples there to welcome him. On arriving, he was a great help to those who by grace had believed. 28For he vigorously refuted the Jews in public debate, proving from the Scriptures that Jesus was the Christ.

Paul in Ephesus

19 While Apollos was at Corinth, Paul took the road through the interior and arrived at Ephesus. There he found some disciples 2and asked them, "Did you receive the Holy Spirit when[a] you believed?"

They answered, "No, we have not even heard that there is a Holy Spirit."

3So Paul asked, "Then what baptism did you receive?"

"John's baptism," they replied.

4Paul said, "John's baptism was a baptism of repentance. He told the people to believe in the one coming after him, that is, in Jesus." 5On hearing this, they were baptised into[b] the name of the Lord Jesus. 6When Paul placed his hands on them, the Holy Spirit came on them, and they spoke in tongues[c] and prophesied. 7There were about twelve men in all.

---

a5 Or Messiah; also in verse 28   b25 Or with fervour in the Spirit   a2 Or after   b5 Or in
c6 Or other languages

8Paul entered the synagogue and spoke boldly there for three months, arguing persuasively about the kingdom of God. 9But some of them became obstinate; they refused to believe and publicly maligned the Way. So Paul left them. He took the disciples with him and had discussions daily in the lecture hall of Tyrannus. 10This went on for two years, so that all the Jews and Greeks who lived in the province of Asia heard the word of the Lord.

11God did extraordinary miracles through Paul, 12so that even handkerchiefs and aprons that had touched him were taken to the sick, and their illnesses were cured and the evil spirits left them.

13Some Jews who went around driving out evil spirits tried to invoke the name of the Lord Jesus over those who were demon-possessed. They would say, "In the name of Jesus, whom Paul preaches, I command you to come out." 14Seven sons of Sceva, a Jewish chief priest, were doing this. 15One day, the evil spirit answered them, "Jesus I know, and I know about Paul, but who are you?" 16Then the man who had the evil spirit jumped on them and overpowered them all. He gave them such a beating that they ran out of the house naked and bleeding.

17When this became known to the Jews and Greeks living in Ephesus, they were all seized with fear, and the name of the Lord Jesus was held in high honour. 18Many of those who believed now came and openly confessed their evil deeds. 19A number who had practised sorcery brought their scrolls together and burned them publicly. When they calculated the value of the scrolls, the total came to fifty thousand drachmas.*d* 20In this way the word of the Lord spread widely and grew in power.

21After all this had happened, Paul decided to go to Jerusalem, passing through Macedonia and Achaia. "After I have been there," he said, "I must visit Rome also." 22He sent two of his helpers, Timothy and Erastus, to Macedonia, while he stayed in the province of Asia a little longer.

The Riot in Ephesus

23About that time there arose a great disturbance about the Way. 24A silversmith named Demetrius, who made silver shrines of Artemis, brought in no little business for the craftsmen. 25He called them together, along with the workmen in related trades, and said: "Men, you know we receive a good income from this business. 26And you see and hear how this fellow Paul has convinced and led astray large numbers of people here in Ephesus and in practically the whole province of Asia. He says that man-made gods are no gods at all. 27There is danger not only that our trade will lose its good name, but also that the temple of the great goddess Artemis will be discredited, and the goddess herself, who is worshipped throughout the province of Asia and the world, will be robbed of her divine majesty."

28When they heard this, they were furious and began shouting: "Great is Artemis of the Ephesians!" 29Soon the whole city was in an uproar. The people

seized Gaius and Aristarchus, Paul's travelling companions from Macedonia, and rushed as one man into the theatre. 30Paul wanted to appear before the crowd, but the disciples would not let him. 31Even some of the officials of the province, friends of Paul, sent him a message begging him not to venture into the theatre.

19:26 Ephesus was a dangerous place to preach the gospel. Much of its prosperity came from the cult of the goddess Artemis. The success of the Christian preaching threatened not only the local religion but some people's livelihoods as well, and it is no wonder that there was a riot. It is also significant that the church Paul founded became an important one.

32The assembly was in confusion: Some were shouting one thing, some another. Most of the people did not even know why they were there. 33The Jews pushed Alexander to the front, and some of the crowd shouted instructions to him. He motioned for silence in order to make a defence before the people. 34But when they realised he was a Jew, they all shouted in unison for about two hours: "Great is Artemis of the Ephesians!"

35The city clerk quietened the crowd and said: "Men of Ephesus, doesn't all the world know that the city of Ephesus is the guardian of the temple of the great Artemis and of her image, which fell from heaven? 36Therefore, since these facts are undeniable, you ought to be quiet and not do anything rash. 37You have brought these men here, though they have neither robbed temples nor blasphemed our goddess. 38If, then, Demetrius and his fellow craftsmen have a grievance against anybody, the courts are open and there are proconsuls. They can press charges. 39If there is anything further you want to bring up, it must be settled in a legal assembly. 40As it is, we are in danger of being charged with rioting because of today's events. In that case we would not be able to account for this commotion, since there is no reason for it." 41After he had said this, he dismissed the assembly.

Through Macedonia and Greece

20 When the uproar had ended, Paul sent for the disciples and, after encouraging them, said good-bye and set out for Macedonia. 2He travelled through that area, speaking many words of encouragement to the people, and finally arrived in Greece, 3where he stayed three months. Because the Jews made a plot against him just as he was about to sail for Syria, he decided to go back through Macedonia. 4He was accompanied by Sopater son of Pyrrhus from Berea, Aristarchus and Secundus from Thessalonica, Gaius from Derbe, Timothy also, and Tychicus and Trophimus from the province of Asia. 5These men went on ahead and waited for us at Troas. 6But we sailed from Philippi after the Feast of Unleavened Bread, and five days later joined the others at Troas, where we stayed seven days.

d19 A drachma was a silver coin worth about a day's wages.

Eutychus Raised From the Dead at Troas

[7] On the first day of the week we came together to break bread. Paul spoke to the people and, because he intended to leave the next day, kept on talking until midnight. [8] There were many lamps in the upstairs room where we were meeting. [9] Seated in a window was a young man named Eutychus, who was sinking into a deep sleep as Paul talked on and on. When he was sound asleep, he fell to the ground from the third storey and was picked up dead. [10] Paul went down, threw himself on the young man and put his arms around him. "Don't be alarmed," he said. "He's alive!" [11] Then he went upstairs again and broke bread and ate. After talking until daylight, he left. [12] The people took the young man home alive and were greatly comforted.

Paul's Farewell to the Ephesian Elders

[13] We went on ahead to the ship and sailed for Assos, where we were going to take Paul aboard. He had made this arrangement because he was going there on foot. [14] When he met us at Assos, we took him aboard and went on to Mitylene. [15] The next day we set sail from there and arrived off Kios. The day after that we crossed over to Samos, and on the following day arrived at Miletus. [16] Paul had decided to sail past Ephesus to avoid spending time in the province of Asia, for he was in a hurry to reach Jerusalem, if possible, by the day of Pentecost.

[17] From Miletus, Paul sent to Ephesus for the elders of the church. [18] When they arrived, he said to them: "You know how I lived the whole time I was with you, from the first day I came into the province of Asia. [19] I served the Lord with great humility and with tears, although I was severely tested by the plots of the Jews. [20] You know that I have not hesitated to preach anything that would be helpful to you but have taught you publicly and from house to house. [21] I have declared to both Jews and Greeks that they must turn to God in repentance and have faith in our Lord Jesus.

[22] "And now, compelled by the Spirit, I am going to Jerusalem, not knowing what will happen to me there. [23] I only know that in every city the Holy Spirit warns me that prison and hardships are facing me. [24] However, I consider my life worth nothing to me, if only I may finish the race and complete the task the Lord Jesus has given me — the task of testifying to the gospel of God's grace.

[25] "Now I know that none of you among whom I have gone about preaching the kingdom will ever see me again. [26] Therefore, I declare to you today that I am innocent of the blood of all men. [27] For I have not hesitated to proclaim to you the whole will of God. [28] Keep watch over yourselves and all the flock of which the Holy Spirit has made you overseers. [a] Be shepherds of the church of God, [b] which he bought with his own blood. [29] I know that after I leave, savage wolves will come in among you and will not spare the flock. [30] Even from your own number men will arise and distort the truth in order to draw away disciples after them. [31] So be on your guard! Remember that for three years I never stopped warning each of you night and day with tears.

[32] "Now I commit you to God and to the word of his grace, which can build you up and give you an inheritance among all those who are sanctified. [33] I have not coveted anyone's silver or gold or clothing. [34] You yourselves know that these hands of mine have supplied my own needs and the needs of my companions. [35] In everything I did, I showed you that by this kind of hard work we must help the weak, remembering the words the Lord Jesus himself said: 'It is more blessed to give than to receive.' "

20:35   Paul stayed longer in Ephesus than anywhere else in his ministry and accomplished some of his best work there. His farewell speech shows that close bonds had been forged between him and the congregation. He quoted some words of Jesus (which are not found in the Gospels) and indicated that he had tried to make his actions match up to his preaching.

---

[36] When he had said this, he knelt down with all of them and prayed. [37] They all wept as they embraced him and kissed him. [38] What grieved them most was his statement that they would never see his face again. Then they accompanied him to the ship.

On to Jerusalem

21 After we had torn ourselves away from them, we put out to sea and sailed straight to Cos. The next day we went to Rhodes and from there to Patara. [2] We found a ship crossing over to Phoenicia, went on board and set sail. [3] After sighting Cyprus and passing to the south of it, we sailed on to Syria. We landed at Tyre, where our ship was to unload its cargo. [4] Finding the disciples there, we stayed with them seven days. Through the Spirit they urged Paul not to go on to Jerusalem. [5] But when our time was up, we left and continued on our way. All the disciples and their wives and children accompanied us out of the city, and there on the beach we knelt to pray. [6] After saying goodbye to each other, we went aboard the ship, and they returned home.

[7] We continued our voyage from Tyre and landed at Ptolemais, where we greeted the brothers and stayed with them for a day. [8] Leaving the next day, we reached Caesarea and stayed at the house of Philip the evangelist, one of the Seven. [9] He had four unmarried daughters who prophesied.

[10] After we had been there a number of days, a prophet named Agabus came down from Judea. [11] Coming over to us, he took Paul's belt, tied his own hands and feet with it and said, "The Holy Spirit says, 'In this way the Jews of Jerusalem will bind the owner of this belt and will hand him over to the Gentiles.' "

[12] When we heard this, we and the people there pleaded with Paul not to go up to Jerusalem. [13] Then Paul answered, "Why are you weeping and breaking

---

a 28 Traditionally *bishops*   *b 28* Many manuscripts *of the Lord* my heart? I am ready not only to be bound, but also to die in Jerusalem for the name of the Lord Jesus." ¹⁴When he would not be dissuaded, we gave up and said, "The Lord's will be done."

¹⁵After this, we got ready and went up to Jerusalem. ¹⁶Some of the disciples from Caesarea accompanied us and brought us to the home of Mnason, where we were to stay. He was a man from Cyprus and one of the early disciples.

Paul's Arrival at Jerusalem

¹⁷When we arrived at Jerusalem, the brothers received us warmly. ¹⁸The next day Paul and the rest of us went to see James, and all the elders were present. ¹⁹Paul greeted them and reported in detail what God had done among the Gentiles through his ministry.

²⁰When they heard this, they praised God. Then they said to Paul: "You see, brother, how many thousands of Jews have believed, and all of them are zealous for the law. ²¹They have been informed that you teach all the Jews who live among the Gentiles to turn away from Moses, telling them not to circumcise their children or live according to our customs. ²²What shall we do? They will certainly hear that you have come, ²³so do what we tell you. There are four men with us who have made a vow. ²⁴Take these men, join in their purification rites and pay their expenses, so that they can have their heads shaved. Then everybody will know there is no truth in these reports about you, but that you yourself are living in obedience to the law. ²⁵As for the Gentile believers, we have written to them our decision that they should abstain from food sacrificed to idols, from blood, from the meat of strangled animals and from sexual immorality."

²⁶The next day Paul took the men and purified himself along with them. Then he went to the temple to give notice of the date when the days of purification would end and the offering would be made for each of them.

Paul Arrested

²⁷When the seven days were nearly over, some Jews from the province of Asia saw Paul at the temple. They stirred up the whole crowd and seized him, ²⁸shouting, "Men of Israel, help us! This is the man who teaches all men everywhere against our people and our law and this place. And besides, he has brought Greeks into the temple area and defiled this holy place." ²⁹(They had previously seen Trophimus the Ephesian in the city with Paul and assumed that Paul had brought him into the temple area.)

³⁰The whole city was aroused, and the people came running from all directions. Seizing Paul, they dragged him from the temple, and immediately the gates were shut. ³¹While they were trying to kill him, news reached the commander of the Roman troops that the whole city of Jerusalem was in an uproar. ³²He at once took some officers and soldiers and ran down to the crowd. When the rioters saw the commander and his soldiers, they stopped beating Paul.

³³The commander came up and arrested him and ordered him to be bound with two chains. Then he asked who he was and what he had done. ³⁴Some in the crowd shouted one thing and some another, and since the commander could not get at the truth because of the uproar, he ordered that Paul be taken into the barracks. ³⁵When Paul reached the steps, the violence of the mob was so great he had to be carried by the soldiers. ³⁶The crowd that followed kept shouting, "Away with him!"

21:28   When Paul was on Jewish territory he was careful not to give unnecessary offence. In the Jerusalem temple Gentiles were only allowed to go into the outer court, and it was a capital offence to go into the inner courts. People knew that Paul had brought Gentile companions with him to Jerusalem and these Jews assumed, without proof, that Paul had taken one of them into the forbidden areas.

Paul Speaks to the Crowd

³⁷As the soldiers were about to take Paul into the barracks, he asked the commander, "May I say something to you?"

"Do you speak Greek?" he replied. ³⁸"Aren't you the Egyptian who started a revolt and led four thousand terrorists out into the desert some time ago?"

³⁹Paul answered, "I am a Jew, from Tarsus in Cilicia, a citizen of no ordinary city. Please let me speak to the people."

⁴⁰Having received the commander's permission, Paul stood on the steps and motioned to the crowd. When they were all silent, he said to them in Aramaic*: ¹"Brothers and fathers, listen now to my defence."

²When they heard him speak to them in Aramaic, they became very quiet.

Then Paul said: ³"I am a Jew, born in Tarsus of Cilicia, but brought up in this city. Under Gamaliel I was thoroughly trained in the law of our fathers and was just as zealous for God as any of you are today. ⁴I persecuted the followers of this Way to their death, arresting both men and women and throwing them into prison, ⁵as also the high priest and all the Council can testify. I even obtained letters from them to their brothers in Damascus, and went there to bring these people as prisoners to Jerusalem to be punished.

⁶"About noon as I came near Damascus, suddenly a bright light from heaven flashed around me. ⁷I fell to the ground and heard a voice say to me, 'Saul! Saul! Why do you persecute me?'

⁸" 'Who are you, Lord?' I asked.

" 'I am Jesus of Nazareth, whom you are persecuting,' he replied. ⁹My companions saw the light, but they did not understand the voice of him who was speaking to me.

¹⁰" 'What shall I do, Lord?' I asked.

---

a40 Or possibly Hebrew; also in 22:2

" 'Get up,' the Lord said, 'and go into Damascus. There you will be told all that you have been assigned to do.' ¹¹My companions led me by the hand into Damascus, because the brilliance of the light had blinded me.

¹²"A man named Ananias came to see me. He was a devout observer of the law and highly respected by all the Jews living there. ¹³He stood beside me and said, 'Brother Saul, receive your sight!' And at that very moment I was able to see him.

¹⁴"Then he said: 'The God of our fathers has chosen you to know his will and to see the Righteous One and to hear words from his mouth. ¹⁵You will be his witness to all men of what you have seen and heard. ¹⁶And now what are you waiting for? Get up, be baptised and wash your sins away, calling on his name.'

¹⁷"When I returned to Jerusalem and was praying at the temple, I fell into a trance ¹⁸and saw the Lord speaking. 'Quick!' he said to me. 'Leave Jerusalem immediately, because they will not accept your testimony about me.'

¹⁹" 'Lord,' I replied, 'these men know that I went from one synagogue to another to imprison and beat those who believe in you. ²⁰And when the blood of your martyr[a] Stephen was shed, I stood there giving my approval and guarding the clothes of those who were killing him.'

²¹"Then the Lord said to me, 'Go; I will send you far away to the Gentiles.' "

Paul the Roman Citizen

²²The crowd listened to Paul until he said this. Then they raised their voices and shouted, "Rid the earth of him! He's not fit to live!"

²³As they were shouting and throwing off their cloaks and flinging dust into the air, ²⁴the commander ordered Paul to be taken into the barracks. He directed that he be flogged and questioned in order to find out why the people were shouting at him like this. ²⁵As they stretched him out to flog him, Paul said to the centurion standing there, "Is it legal for you to flog a Roman citizen who hasn't even been found guilty?"

22:25   Roman citizenship was a privilege. To have flogged a Roman citizen in this way would have been a serious offence. Some of the Roman emperors sold their privilege to raise money, and this is what the army commander seems to have been involved in (verse 28). Paul, however, had acquired it by birth, which means that his father had held citizenship before him.

---

²⁶When the centurion heard this, he went to the commander and reported it. "What are you going to do?" he asked. "This man is a Roman citizen."

²⁷The commander went to Paul and asked, "Tell me, are you a Roman citizen?"

"Yes, I am," he answered.

²⁸Then the commander said, "I had to pay a big price for my citizenship."

"But I was born a citizen," Paul replied.

²⁹Those who were about to question him withdrew immediately. The commander himself was alarmed when he realised that he had put Paul, a Roman citizen, in chains.

Before the Sanhedrin

³⁰The next day, since the commander wanted to find out exactly why Paul was being accused by the Jews, he released him and ordered the chief priests and all the Sanhedrin to assemble. Then he brought Paul and had him stand before them.

23 Paul looked straight at the Sanhedrin and said, "My brothers, I have fulfilled my duty to God in all good conscience to this day." ²At this the high priest Ananias ordered those standing near Paul to strike him on the mouth. ³Then Paul said to him, "God will strike you, you whitewashed wall! You sit there to judge me according to the law, yet you yourself violate the law by commanding that I be struck!"

⁴Those who were standing near Paul said, "You dare to insult God's high priest?"

⁵Paul replied, "Brothers, I did not realise that he was the high priest; for it is written: 'Do not speak evil about the ruler of your people.'[a]"

⁶Then Paul, knowing that some of them were Sadducees and the others Pharisees, called out in the Sanhedrin, "My brothers, I am a Pharisee, the son of a Pharisee. I stand on trial because of my hope in the resurrection of the dead." ⁷When he said this, a dispute broke out between the Pharisees and the Sadducees, and the assembly was divided. ⁸(The Sadducees say that there is no resurrection, and that there are neither angels nor spirits, but the Pharisees acknowledge them all.)

⁹There was a great uproar, and some of the teachers of the law who were Pharisees stood up and argued vigorously. "We find nothing wrong with this man," they said. "What if a spirit or an angel has spoken to him?" ¹⁰The dispute became so violent that the commander was afraid Paul would be torn to pieces by them. He ordered the troops to go down and take him away from them by force and bring him into the barracks.

¹¹The following night the Lord stood near Paul and said, "Take courage! As you have testified about me in Jerusalem, so you must also testify in Rome."

The Plot to Kill Paul

¹²The next morning the Jews formed a conspiracy and bound themselves with an oath not to eat or drink until they had killed Paul. ¹³More than forty men were involved in this plot. ¹⁴They went to the chief priests and elders and said, "We have taken a solemn oath not to eat anything until we have killed Paul. ¹⁵Now then, you and the Sanhedrin petition the commander to bring him before you on the pretext of wanting more accurate information about his case. We are ready to kill him before he gets here."

---

a 20 Or *witness*   a 5 Exodus 22:28

16But when the son of Paul's sister heard of this plot, he went into the barracks and told Paul.

17Then Paul called one of the centurions and said, "Take this young man to the commander; he has something to tell him." 18So he took him to the commander.

The centurion said, "Paul, the prisoner, sent for me and asked me to bring this young man to you because he has something to tell you."

19The commander took the young man by the hand, drew him aside and asked, "What is it you want to tell me?"

20He said: "The Jews have agreed to ask you to bring Paul before the Sanhedrin tomorrow on the pretext of wanting more accurate information about him. 21Don't give in to them, because more than forty of them are waiting in ambush for him. They have taken an oath not to eat or drink until they have killed him. They are ready now, waiting for your consent to their request."

22The commander dismissed the young man and cautioned him, "Don't tell anyone that you have reported this to me."

Paul Transferred to Caesarea

23Then he called two of his centurions and ordered them, "Get ready a detachment of two hundred soldiers, seventy horsemen and two hundred spearmen*b* to go to Caesarea at nine tonight. 24Provide mounts for Paul so that he may be taken safely to Governor Felix."

25He wrote a letter as follows:

26Claudius Lysias,

To His Excellency, Governor Felix:

Greetings.

27This man was seized by the Jews and they were about to kill him, but I came with my troops and rescued him, for I had learned that he is a Roman citizen. 28I wanted to know why they were accusing him, so I brought him to their Sanhedrin. 29I found that the accusation had to do with questions about their law, but there was no charge against him that deserved death or imprisonment. 30When I was informed of a plot to be carried out against the man, I sent him to you at once. I also ordered his accusers to present to you their case against him.

31So the soldiers, carrying out their orders, took Paul with them during the night and brought him as far as Antipatris. 32The next day they let the cavalry go on with him, while they returned to the barracks. 33When the cavalry arrived in Caesarea, they delivered the letter to the governor and handed Paul over to him. 34The governor read the letter and asked what province he was from. Learning that he was from Cilicia, 35he said, "I will hear your case when your accusers get here." Then he ordered that Paul be kept under guard in Herod's palace.

The Trial Before Felix

24 Five days later the high priest Ananias went down to Caesarea with some of the elders and a lawyer named Tertullus, and they brought their charges against Paul before the governor. 2When Paul was called in, Tertullus presented his case before Felix: "We have enjoyed a long period of peace under you, and your foresight has brought about reforms in this nation. 3Everywhere and in every way, most excellent Felix, we acknowledge this with profound gratitude. 4But in order not to weary you further, I would request that you be kind enough to hear us briefly.

5"We have found this man to be a troublemaker, stirring up riots among the Jews all over the world. He is a ringleader of the Nazarene sect 6and even tried to desecrate the temple; so we seized him. 8By*a* examining him yourself you will be able to learn the truth about all these charges we are bringing against him."

24:5 The Romans, who ruled Palestine and much else of the known world, were noted for their fairness and their firmness. On the whole they were not troubled what religion people professed, provided they obeyed the laws of the land. Paul's enemies would not have succeeded in getting him tried for his beliefs, so they had to use the argument that in preaching this new religion he was causing civil unrest.

9The Jews joined in the accusation, asserting that these things were true.

10When the governor motioned for him to speak, Paul replied: "I know that for a number of years you have been a judge over this nation; so I gladly make my defence. 11You can easily verify that no more than twelve days ago I went up to Jerusalem to worship. 12My accusers did not find me arguing with anyone at the temple, or stirring up a crowd in the synagogues or anywhere else in the city. 13And they cannot prove to you the charges they are now making against me. 14However, I admit that I worship the God of our fathers as a follower of the Way, which they call a sect. I believe everything that agrees with the Law and that is written in the Prophets, 15and I have the same hope in God as these men, that there will be a resurrection of both the righteous and the wicked. 16So I strive always to keep my conscience clear before God and man.

17"After an absence of several years, I came to Jerusalem to bring my people gifts for the poor and to present offerings. 18I was ceremonially clean when they found me in the temple courts doing this. There was no crowd with me, nor was I involved in any disturbance. 19But there are some Jews from the province of Asia, who ought to be here before you and bring charges if they have anything against me. 20Or these who are here should state what crime they found in me

---

b 23 The meaning of the Greek for this word is uncertain. *a 6–8* Some manuscripts *him and wanted to judge him according to our law.* 7But the commander, Lysias, came and with the use of much force snatched him from our hands 8and ordered his accusers to come before you. By when I stood before the Sanhedrin—²¹unless it was this one thing I shouted as I stood in their presence: 'It is concerning the resurrection of the dead that I am on trial before you today.' "

²²Then Felix, who was well acquainted with the Way, adjourned the proceedings. "When Lysias the commander comes," he said, "I will decide your case." ²³He ordered the centurion to keep Paul under guard but to give him some freedom and permit his friends to take care of his needs.

²⁴Several days later Felix came with his wife Drusilla, who was a Jewess. He sent for Paul and listened to him as he spoke about faith in Christ Jesus. ²⁵As Paul discoursed on righteousness, self-control and the judgment to come, Felix was afraid and said, "That's enough for now! You may leave. When I find it convenient, I will send for you." ²⁶At the same time he was hoping that Paul would offer him a bribe, so he sent for him frequently and talked with him.

²⁷When two years had passed, Felix was succeeded by Porcius Festus, but because Felix wanted to grant a favour to the Jews, he left Paul in prison.

The Trial Before Festus

25 Three days after arriving in the province, Festus went up from Caesarea to Jerusalem, ²where the chief priests and Jewish leaders appeared before him and presented the charges against Paul. ³They urgently requested Festus, as a favour to them, to have Paul transferred to Jerusalem, for they were preparing an ambush to kill him along the way. ⁴Festus answered, "Paul is being held at Caesarea, and I myself am going there soon. ⁵Let some of your leaders come with me and press charges against the man there, if he has done anything wrong."

⁶After spending eight or ten days with them, he went down to Caesarea, and the next day he convened the court and ordered that Paul be brought before him. ⁷When Paul appeared, the Jews who had come down from Jerusalem stood around him, bringing many serious charges against him, which they could not prove.

⁸Then Paul made his defence: "I have done nothing wrong against the law of the Jews or against the temple or against Caesar."

⁹Festus, wishing to do the Jews a favour, said to Paul, "Are you willing to go up to Jerusalem and stand trial before me there on these charges?"

¹⁰Paul answered: "I am now standing before Caesar's court, where I ought to be tried. I have not done any wrong to the Jews, as you yourself know very well. ¹¹If, however, I am guilty of doing anything deserving death, I do not refuse to die. But if the charges brought against me by these Jews are not true, no-one has the right to hand me over to them. I appeal to Caesar!"

¹²After Festus had conferred with his council, he declared: "You have appealed to Caesar. To Caesar you will go!"

Festus Consults King Agrippa

¹³A few days later King Agrippa and Bernice arrived at Caesarea to pay their respects to Festus. ¹⁴Since they were spending many days there, Festus discussed Paul's case with the king. He said: "There is a man here whom Felix left as a prisoner. ¹⁵When I went to Jerusalem, the chief priests and elders of the Jews brought charges against him and asked that he be condemned.

¹⁶"I told them that it is not the Roman custom to hand over any man before he has faced his accusers and has had an opportunity to defend himself against their charges. ¹⁷When they came here with me, I did not delay the case, but convened the court the next day and ordered the man to be brought in. ¹⁸When his accusers got up to speak, they did not charge him with any of the crimes I had expected. ¹⁹Instead, they had some points of dispute with him about their own religion and about a dead man named Jesus whom Paul claimed was alive. ²⁰I was at a loss how to investigate such matters; so I asked if he would be willing to go to Jerusalem and stand trial there on these charges. ²¹When Paul made his appeal to be held over for the Emperor's decision, I ordered him to be held until I could send him to Caesar."

²²Then Agrippa said to Festus, "I would like to hear this man myself."

He replied, "Tomorrow you will hear him."

Paul Before Agrippa

²³The next day Agrippa and Bernice came with great pomp and entered the audience room with the high ranking officers and the leading men of the city. At the command of Festus, Paul was brought in. ²⁴Festus said: "King Agrippa, and all who are present with us, you see this man! The whole Jewish community has petitioned me about him in Jerusalem and here in Caesarea, shouting that he ought not to live any longer. ²⁵I found he had done nothing deserving of death, but because he made his appeal to the Emperor I decided to send him to Rome. ²⁶But I have nothing definite to write to His Majesty about him. Therefore I have brought him before all of you, and especially before you, King Agrippa, so that as a result of this investigation I may have something to write. ²⁷For I think it is unreasonable to send on a prisoner without specifying the charges against him."

26 Then Agrippa said to Paul, "You have permission to speak for yourself."

So Paul motioned with his hand and began his defence: ²"King Agrippa, I consider myself fortunate to stand before you today as I make my defence against all the accusations of the Jews, ³and especially so because you are well acquainted with all the Jewish customs and controversies. Therefore, I beg you to listen to me patiently.

⁴"The Jews all know the way I have lived ever since I was a child, from the beginning of my life in my own country, and also in Jerusalem. ⁵They have known me for a long time and can testify, if they are willing, that according to the strictest sect of our religion, I lived as a Pharisee. ⁶And now it is because of my hope in what God has promised our fathers that I am on trial today. ⁷This is the promise our twelve tribes are hoping to see fulfilled as they earnestly serve God day and night. O King, it is because of this hope that the Jews are accusing me. ⁸Why should any of you consider it incredible that God raises the dead?

⁹"I too was convinced that I ought to do all that was

possible to oppose the name of Jesus of Nazareth. [10]And that is just what I did in Jerusalem. On the authority of the chief priests I put many of the saints in prison, and when they were put to death, I cast my vote against them. [11]Many a time I went from one synagogue to another to have them punished, and I tried to force them to blaspheme. In my obsession against them, I even went to foreign cities to persecute them.

[12]"On one of these journeys I was going to Damascus with the authority and commission of the chief priests. [13]About noon, O King, as I was on the road, I saw a light from heaven, brighter than the sun, blazing around me and my companions. [14]We all fell to the ground, and I heard a voice saying to me in Aramaic,[a] 'Saul, Saul, why do you persecute me? It is hard for you to kick against the goads.'

[15]"Then I asked, 'Who are you, Lord?'

" 'I am Jesus, whom you are persecuting,' the Lord replied. [16]'Now get up and stand on your feet. I have appeared to you to appoint you as a servant and as a witness of what you have seen of me and what I will show you. [17]I will rescue you from your own people and from the Gentiles. I am sending you to them [18]to open their eyes and turn them from darkness to light, and from the power of Satan to God, so that they may receive forgiveness of sins and a place among those who are sanctified by faith in me.'

[19]"So then, King Agrippa, I was not disobedient to the vision from heaven. [20]First to those in Damascus, then to those in Jerusalem and in all Judea, and to the Gentiles also, I preached that they should repent and turn to God and prove their repentance by their deeds. [21]That is why the Jews seized me in the temple courts and tried to kill me. [22]But I have had God's help to this very day, and so I stand here and testify to small and great alike. I am saying nothing beyond what the prophets and Moses said would happen— [23]that the Christ[b] would suffer and, as the first to rise from the dead, would proclaim light to his own people and to the Gentiles."

[24]At this point Festus interrupted Paul's defence. "You are out of your mind, Paul!" he shouted. "Your great learning is driving you insane."

[25]"I am not insane, most excellent Festus," Paul replied. "What I am saying is true and reasonable. [26]The king is familiar with these things, and I can speak freely to him. I am convinced that none of this has escaped his notice, because it was not done in a corner. [27]King Agrippa, do you believe the prophets? I know you do."

[28]Then Agrippa said to Paul, "Do you think that in such a short time you can persuade me to be a Christian?"

[29]Paul replied, "Short time or long—I pray God that not only you but all who are listening to me today may become what I am, except for these chains."

[30]The king rose, and with him the governor and Bernice and those sitting with them. [31]They left the room, and while talking with one another, they said, "This man is not doing anything that deserves death or imprisonment."

[32]Agrippa said to Festus, "This man could have been set free if he had not appealed to Caesar."

Paul Sails for Rome

27 When it was decided that we would sail for Italy, Paul and some other prisoners were handed over to a centurion named Julius, who belonged to the Imperial Regiment. [2]We boarded a ship from Adramyttium about to sail for ports along the coast of the province of Asia, and we put out to sea. Aristarchus, a Macedonian from Thessalonica, was with us.

[3]The next day we landed at Sidon; and Julius, in kindness to Paul, allowed him to go to his friends so they might provide for his needs. [4]From there we put out to sea again and passed to the lee of Cyprus because the winds were against us. [5]When we had sailed across the open sea off the coast of Cilicia and Pamphylia, we landed at Myra in Lycia. [6]There the centurion found an Alexandrian ship sailing for Italy and put us on board. [7]We made slow headway for many days and had difficulty arriving off Cnidus. When the wind did not allow us to hold our course, we sailed to the lee of Crete, opposite Salmone. [8]We moved along the coast with difficulty and came to a place called Fair Havens, near the town of Lasea.

[9]Much time had been lost, and sailing had already become dangerous because by now it was after the Fast.[a] So Paul warned them, [10]"Men, I can see that our voyage is going to be disastrous and bring great loss to ship and cargo, and to our own lives also." [11]But the centurion, instead of listening to what Paul said, followed the advice of the pilot and of the owner of the ship. [12]Since the harbour was unsuitable to winter in, the majority decided that we should sail on, hoping to reach Phoenix and winter there. This was a harbour in Crete, facing both south-west and north-west.

The Storm

[13]When a gentle south wind began to blow, they thought they had obtained what they wanted; so they weighed anchor and sailed along the shore of Crete. [14]Before very long, a wind of hurricane force, called the "north-easter", swept down from the island. [15]The ship was caught by the storm and could not head into the wind; so we gave way to it and were driven along. [16]As we passed to the lee of a small island called Cauda, we were hardly able to make the lifeboat secure. [17]When the men had hoisted it aboard, they passed ropes under the ship itself to hold it together. Fearing that they would run aground on the sand-bars of Syrtis, they lowered the sea anchor and let the ship be driven along. [18]We took such a violent battering from the storm that the next day they began to throw the cargo overboard. [19]On the third day, they threw the ship's tackle overboard with their own hands. [20]When neither sun nor stars appeared for many days and the storm continued raging, we finally gave up all hope of being saved.

[21]After the men had gone a long time without food, Paul stood up before them and said: "Men, you should have taken my advice not to sail from Crete; then you

---

a 14 Or *Hebrew*   *b 23* Or *Messiah*   *a 9* That is, the Day of Atonement (Yom Kippur) would have spared yourselves this damage and loss. [22]But now I urge you to keep up your courage, because not one of you will be lost; only the ship will be destroyed. [23]Last night an angel of the God whose I am and whom I serve stood beside me [24]and said, 'Do not be afraid, Paul. You must stand trial before Caesar; and God has graciously given you the lives of all who sail with you.' [25]So keep up your courage, men, for I have faith in God that it will happen just as he told me. [26]Nevertheless, we must run aground on some island."

27:13   A number of passages in Acts make it plain that from time to time Luke was one of Paul's travelling companions. Here, as in other places, the use of language (such as the references to "we") and the vividness of the writing make it plain that it is a first-hand testimony.

The Shipwreck

[27]On the fourteenth night we were still being driven across the Adriatic[b] Sea, when about midnight the sailors sensed they were approaching land. [28]They took soundings and found that the water was one hundred and twenty feet[c] deep. A short time later they took soundings again and found it was ninety feet[d] deep. [29]Fearing that we would be dashed against the rocks, they dropped four anchors from the stern and prayed for daylight. [30]In an attempt to escape from the ship, the sailors let the lifeboat down into the sea, pretending they were going to lower some anchors from the bow. [31]Then Paul said to the centurion and the soldiers, "Unless these men stay with the ship, you cannot be saved." [32]So the soldiers cut the ropes that held the lifeboat and let it fall away.

[33]Just before dawn Paul urged them all to eat. "For the last fourteen days," he said, "you have been in constant suspense and have gone without food — you haven't eaten anything. [34]Now I urge you to take some food. You need it to survive. Not one of you will lose a single hair from his head." [35]After he said this, he took some bread and gave thanks to God in front of them all. Then he broke it and began to eat. [36]They were all encouraged and ate some food themselves. [37]Altogether there were 276 of us on board. [38]When they had eaten as much as they wanted, they lightened the ship by throwing the grain into the sea.

[39]When daylight came, they did not recognise the land, but they saw a bay with a sandy beach, where they decided to run the ship aground if they could. [40]Cutting loose the anchors, they left them in the sea and at the same time untied the ropes that held the rudders. Then they hoisted the foresail to the wind and made for the beach. [41]But the ship struck a sand-bar and ran aground. The bow stuck fast and would not move, and the stern was broken to pieces by the pounding of the surf.

[42]The soldiers planned to kill the prisoners to prevent any of them from swimming away and escaping.

[43]But the centurion wanted to spare Paul's life and kept them from carrying out their plan. He ordered those who could swim to jump overboard first and get to land. [44]The rest were to get there on planks or on pieces of the ship. In this way everyone reached land in safety.

Ashore on Malta

28 Once safely on shore, we found out that the island was called Malta. [2]The islanders showed us unusual kindness. They built a fire and welcomed us all because it was raining and cold. [3]Paul gathered a pile of brushwood and, as he put it on the fire, a viper, driven out by the heat, fastened itself on his hand. [4]When the islanders saw the snake hanging from his hand, they said to each other, "This man must be a murderer; for though he escaped from the sea, Justice has not allowed him to live." [5]But Paul shook the snake off into the fire and suffered no ill effects. [6]The people expected him to swell up or suddenly fall dead, but after waiting a long time and seeing nothing unusual happen to him, they changed their minds and said he was a god.

[7]There was an estate near by that belonged to Publius, the chief official of the island. He welcomed us to his home and for three days entertained us hospitably. [8]His father was sick in bed, suffering from fever and dysentery. Paul went in to see him and, after prayer, placed his hands on him and healed him. [9]When this had happened, the rest of the sick on the island came and were cured. [10]They honoured us in many ways and when we were ready to sail, they furnished us with the supplies we needed.

Arrival at Rome

[11]After three months we put out to sea in a ship that had wintered in the island. It was an Alexandrian ship with the figurehead of the twin gods Castor and Pollux. [12]We put in at Syracuse and stayed there three days. [13]From there we set sail and arrived at Rhegium. The next day the south wind came up, and on the following day we reached Puteoli. [14]There we found some brothers who invited us to spend a week with them. And so we came to Rome. [15]The brothers there had heard that we were coming, and they travelled as far as the Forum of Appius and the Three Taverns to meet us. At the sight of these men Paul thanked God and was encouraged. [16]When we got to Rome, Paul was allowed to live by himself, with a soldier to guard him.

Paul Preaches at Rome Under Guard

[17]Three days later he called together the leaders of the Jews. When they had assembled, Paul said to them: "My brothers, although I have done nothing against our people or against the customs of our ancestors, I was arrested in Jerusalem and handed over to the Romans. [18]They examined me and wanted to release

---

[b]27 In ancient times the name referred to an area extending well south of Italy.   [c]28 Greek *twenty orguias* (about 37 metres)
[d]28 Greek *fifteen orguias* (about 27 metres)

me, because I was not guilty of any crime deserving death. ¹⁹But when the Jews objected, I was compelled to appeal to Caesar—not that I had any charge to bring against my own people. ²⁰For this reason I have asked to see you and talk with you. It is because of the hope of Israel that I am bound with this chain."

²¹They replied, "We have not received any letters from Judea concerning you, and none of the brothers who have come from there has reported or said anything bad about you. ²²But we want to hear what your views are, for we know that people everywhere are talking against this sect."

²³They arranged to meet Paul on a certain day, and came in even larger numbers to the place where he was staying. From morning till evening he explained and declared to them the kingdom of God and tried to convince them about Jesus from the Law of Moses and from the Prophets. ²⁴Some were convinced by what he said, but others would not believe. ²⁵They disagreed among themselves and began to leave after Paul had made this final statement: "The Holy Spirit spoke the truth to your forefathers when he said through Isaiah the prophet:

²⁶" 'Go to this people and say,
"You will be ever hearing but never
   understanding;
you will be ever seeing but never perceiving."
²⁷For this people's heart has become calloused;
   they hardly hear with their ears,
   and they have closed their eyes.
Otherwise they might see with their eyes,
   hear with their ears,
   understand with their hearts
and turn, and I would heal them.' ᵃ

²⁸"Therefore I want you to know that God's salvation has been sent to the Gentiles, and they will listen!" ᵇ

³⁰For two whole years Paul stayed there in his own rented house and welcomed all who came to see him. ³¹Boldly and without hindrance he preached the kingdom of God and taught about the Lord Jesus Christ.

ᵃ27 Isaiah 6:9,10   ᵇ28 Some manuscripts listen!" ²⁹After he said this, the Jews left, arguing vigorously among themselves.

Romans

Explaining the Faith

In the world of the first century AD it was almost literally true that all roads led to Rome. It was a capital of commerce and culture, and a cosmopolitan city. A number of people who belonged to what today we would call minority groups—including a sizeable Jewish community—made it their home and it attracted many visitors.

Establishing the Faith

That, probably, is how the church in Rome began. We have no firm evidence about its origins although one thing is certain; it was not started through the preaching of the apostle Paul. By the time Paul came to write his letter to the Roman Christians the church had evidently been established for some time. When Luke listed those who heard the Christian believers speaking in their own languages in Jerusalem at Pentecost he included visitors from Rome (Acts 2:10). Although Luke did not specifically say that these particular visitors were among the three thousand who responded to Peter's sermon by becoming Christians (Acts 2:41), it would seem likely that this was the case. Given the amount of business travel which took place between Rome and various parts of the empire, it was only a matter of time before some of those travellers would be Jewish Christians, anxious to tell others about their new faith. In such a way the church was founded: a reminder to us of the importance of ordinary Christians sharing their faith with those they meet.

A Journey Cut Short

In AD 57 Paul finished a ten year period of church planting in the main cities of four different Roman provinces. After a visit to Jerusalem he planned something rather different; a visit to Spain. It would be a long and difficult journey, but he could break it to pay a visit to the church in Rome. Many of the Christians Paul had met elsewhere had moved to Rome and he no doubt wished to see them again. Such a visit would, however, be very different from the kind he normally made. He was a pioneer whose task was to take the good news of Jesus where none had heard it. This, of course, was not the case in Rome, where the church was already well established, so the character of Paul's visit would be rather different. In fact the visit did not actually take place as planned, and when he eventually reached Rome he was not on his way to preach the gospel in Spain; he was in chains, awaiting the final outcome of a trial under Roman law (Acts 28:16).

A Letter of Belief

The letter to the Romans was written to prepare the church for his arrival. If they understood the nature of the gospel which Paul preached they would understand him too. Romans is, therefore, a systematic setting out of what we might call "the Gospel according to Paul". In some of his other letters Paul wrote passionately about particular issues, often to those whom he himself had brought to Christian faith, and did so as if he were wrestling for their souls. There is no lack of passion in Romans, because Paul felt deeply about the truth of the gospel, but he addressed the central and abiding issues of the Christian faith rather than the concerns of the moment.

Major Themes

Because Romans is the outcome of Paul's reflections on his Christian belief, the major themes with which it deals follow on from one another in a logical order. Even for today's readers, who sometimes find particular ideas and expressions difficult to grasp, the main thrust of the arguments is clear enough. Above all, Romans is concerned to answer the question: "How can I find a God who is gracious?"

Made Right With God

Romans begins, after the preliminary greetings, with a grim picture of a sinful world without God. Paul declared that people who behave in such ways deserve death (1:32). Like many of his readers, he had been brought up as a Jew and, as such, taught to believe that if he kept the Law which had been given through Moses he could find a right relationship with God. By the time he wrote Romans he had come to realize that though there were many advantages in having been brought up a Jew, salvation could not be found that way. All the Law did was to make him even more conscious of his sin (3:20). However, there was no reason for despair. There was another way for people to come into a right relationship with God; through faith in Christ. Paul found the principle of faith at work in the Jewish Scriptures, the Old Testament, and used the life of Abraham (4:1–3) as an illustration. This is what has happened to all those who have become Christians: they have been put right with God through their faith, and this gives them peace, joy, and hope (5:1–11). Such faith in Christ also brings freedom, and Paul also wrote about freedom from sin, from the false bondage of the Law, and from the power of death.

A Right Relationship With God

Having set out such a wonderful story, the logical question for Paul (as perhaps for us) was, "Why doesn't everyone believe it?", and, in particular, "Why do so many of God's own people, the Jews, not believe it?" Paul also wrestled with the difficult question: "If this is what I believe, then how should I act?" The final chapters of Romans are concerned, therefore, with practical questions of Christian living which arise from the character of the gospel itself. These chapters deal with such matters as relationships between Christians, duty to the state, and the true meaning of Christian liberty. Romans is the ultimate answer to those who say: "It does not matter what you believe as long as you do good." Paul showed that we cannot do good unless we are in a right relationship with God and also that if we are in such a relationship it will show in the quality of our living.

---

1 Paul, a servant of Christ Jesus, called to be an apostle and set apart for the gospel of God — ²the gospel he promised beforehand through his prophets in the Holy Scriptures ³regarding his Son, who as to his human nature was a descendant of David, ⁴and who through the Spirit*a* of holiness was declared with power to be the Son of God, *b* by his resurrection from the dead: Jesus Christ our Lord. ⁵Through him and for his name's sake, we received grace and apostleship to call people from among all the Gentiles to the obedience that comes from faith. ⁶And you also are among those who are called to belong to Jesus Christ.

⁷To all in Rome who are loved by God and called to be saints:

Grace and peace to you from God our Father and from the Lord Jesus Christ.

Paul's Longing to Visit Rome

⁸First, I thank my God through Jesus Christ for all of you, because your faith is being reported all over the world. ⁹God, whom I serve with my whole heart in preaching the gospel of his Son, is my witness how constantly I remember you ¹⁰in my prayers at all times; and I pray that now at last by God's will the way may be opened for me to come to you. ¹¹I long to see you so that I may impart to you some spiritual gift to make you strong — ¹²that is, that you and I may be mutually encouraged by each other's faith. ¹³I do not want you to be unaware, brothers, that I planned many times to come to you (but have been prevented from doing so until now) in order that I might have a harvest among you, just as I have had among the other Gentiles.

¹⁴I am bound both to Greeks and non-Greeks, both to the wise and the foolish. ¹⁵That is why I am so eager to preach the gospel also to you who are at Rome.

¹⁶I am not ashamed of the gospel, because it is the power of God for the salvation of everyone who believes: first for the Jew, then for the Gentile. ¹⁷For in the gospel a righteousness from God is revealed, a righteousness that is by faith from first to last,*c* just as it is written: "The righteous will live by faith."*d*

God's Wrath Against Mankind

¹⁸The wrath of God is being revealed from heaven against all the godlessness and wickedness of men who suppress the truth by their wickedness, ¹⁹since what may be known about God is plain to them, because God has made it plain to them. ²⁰For since the creation of the world God's invisible qualities — his eternal power and divine nature — have been clearly seen, being understood from what has been made, so that men are without excuse.

1:18   Many people find it difficult to believe that God can be angry. Perhaps this is because we usually regard anger as a bad quality and so cannot associate it with God. In the Bible, however, God's anger is part of his holiness and it means that he will not rest content until his people are the best they can be.

---

²¹For although they knew God, they neither glorified him as God nor gave thanks to him, but their thinking became futile and their foolish hearts were darkened. ²²Although they claimed to be wise, they became fools ²³and exchanged the glory of the immortal God for images made to look like mortal man and birds and animals and reptiles.

²⁴Therefore God gave them over in the sinful desires of their hearts to sexual impurity for the degrading of their bodies with one another. ²⁵They exchanged the truth of God for a lie, and worshipped and served created things rather than the Creator — who is for ever praised. Amen.

²⁶Because of this, God gave them over to shameful lusts. Even their women exchanged natural relations for unnatural ones. ²⁷In the same way the men also abandoned natural relations with women and were inflamed with lust for one another. Men committed indecent acts with other men, and received in themselves the due penalty for their perversion.

²⁸Furthermore, since they did not think it worth while to retain the knowledge of God, he gave them over to a depraved mind, to do what ought not to be done. ²⁹They have become filled with every kind of wickedness, evil, greed and depravity. They are full of envy, murder, strife, deceit and malice. They are gossips, ³⁰slanderers, God-haters, insolent, arrogant and boastful; they invent ways of doing evil; they disobey their parents; ³¹they are senseless, faithless, heartless, ruthless. ³²Although they know God's righteous decree that those who do such things deserve death, they not only continue to do these very things but also approve of those who practise them.

God's Righteous Judgment

2 You, therefore, have no excuse, you who pass judgment on someone else, for at whatever point you judge the other, you are condemning yourself, because you who pass judgment do the same things. ²Now we know that God's judgment against those who

---

a4 Or who as to his spirit   *b4 Or was appointed to be the Son of God with power*   *c17 Or is from faith to faith*
d17 Hab. 2:4

do such things is based on truth. [3]So when you, a mere man, pass judgment on them and yet do the same things, do you think you will escape God's judgment? [4]Or do you show contempt for the riches of his kindness, tolerance and patience, not realising that God's kindness leads you towards repentance?

[5]But because of your stubbornness and your unrepentant heart, you are storing up wrath against yourself for the day of God's wrath, when his righteous judgment will be revealed. [6]God "will give to each person according to what he has done".[a] [7]To those who by persistence in doing good seek glory, honour and immortality, he will give eternal life. [8]But for those who are self-seeking and who reject the truth and follow evil, there will be wrath and anger. [9]There will be trouble and distress for every human being who does evil: first for the Jew, then for the Gentile; [10]but glory, honour and peace for everyone who does good: first for the Jew, then for the Gentile. [11]For God does not show favouritism.

[12]All who sin apart from the law will also perish apart from the law, and all who sin under the law will be judged by the law. [13]For it is not those who hear the law who are righteous in God's sight, but it is those who obey the law who will be declared righteous. [14](Indeed, when Gentiles, who do not have the law, do by nature things required by the law, they are a law for themselves, even though they do not have the law, [15]since they show that the requirements of the law are written on their hearts, their consciences also bearing witness, and their thoughts now accusing, now even defending them.) [16]This will take place on the day when God will judge men's secrets through Jesus Christ, as my gospel declares.

The Jews and the Law

[17]Now you, if you call yourself a Jew; if you rely on the law and brag about your relationship to God; [18]if you know his will and approve of what is superior because you are instructed by the law; [19]if you are convinced that you are a guide for the blind, a light for those who are in the dark, [20]an instructor of the foolish, a teacher of infants, because you have in the law the embodiment of knowledge and truth — [21]you, then, who teach others, do you not teach yourself? You who preach against stealing, do you steal? [22]You who say that people should not commit adultery, do you commit adultery? You who abhor idols, do you rob temples? [23]You who brag about the law, do you dishonour God by breaking the law? [24]As it is written: "God's name is blasphemed among the Gentiles because of you."[b]

[25]Circumcision has value if you observe the law, but if you break the law, you have become as though you had not been circumcised. [26]If those who are not circumcised keep the law's requirements, will they not be regarded as though they were circumcised? [27]The one who is not circumcised physically and yet obeys the law will condemn you who, even though you have the[c] written code and circumcision, are a law-breaker.

[28]A man is not a Jew if he is only one outwardly, nor is circumcision merely outward and physical. [29]No, a man is a Jew if he is one inwardly; and circumcision is circumcision of the heart, by the Spirit, not by the written code. Such a man's praise is not from men, but from God.

God's Faithfulness

3 What advantage, then, is there in being a Jew, or what value is there in circumcision? [2]Much in every way! First of all, they have been entrusted with the very words of God.

[3]What if some did not have faith? Will their lack of faith nullify God's faithfulness? [4]Not at all! Let God be true, and every man a liar. As it is written:

"So that you may be proved right when you speak
  and prevail when you judge."[a]

[5]But if our unrighteousness brings out God's righteousness more clearly, what shall we say? That God is unjust in bringing his wrath on us? (I am using a human argument.) [6]Certainly not! If that were so, how could God judge the world? [7]Someone might argue, "If my falsehood enhances God's truthfulness and so increases his glory, why am I still condemned as a sinner?" [8]Why not say — as we are being slanderously reported as saying and as some claim that we say — "Let us do evil that good may result"? Their condemnation is deserved.

No-one Is Righteous

[9]What shall we conclude then? Are we any better?[b] Not at all! We have already made the charge that Jews and Gentiles alike are all under sin. [10]As it is written:

"There is no-one righteous, not even one;
[11] there is no-one who understands,
    no-one who seeks God.
[12]All have turned away,
    they have together become worthless;
  there is no-one who does good,
    not even one."[c]
[13]"Their throats are open graves;
    their tongues practise deceit."[d]
"The poison of vipers is on their lips."[e]
[14] "Their mouths are full of cursing and
      bitterness."[f]
[15]"Their feet are swift to shed blood;
[16] ruin and misery mark their ways,
[17]and the way of peace they do not know."[g]
[18] "There is no fear of God before their eyes."[h]

[19]Now we know that whatever the law says, it says to those who are under the law, so that every mouth may be silenced and the whole world held accountable to God. [20]Therefore no-one will be declared righteous in his sight by observing the law; rather, through the law we become conscious of sin.

---

a6 Psalm 62:12; Prov. 24:12   b24 Isaiah 52:5; Ezek. 36:22
b9 Or worse   c12 Psalms 14:1–3; 53:1–3; Eccles. 7:20
f14 Psalm 10:7   g17 Isaiah 59:7,8   h18 Psalm 36:1

c27 Or who, by means of a   a4 Psalm 51:4
d13 Psalm 5:9   e13 Psalm 140:3

Righteousness Through Faith

21But now a righteousness from God, apart from law, has been made known, to which the Law and the Prophets testify. 22This righteousness from God comes through faith in Jesus Christ to all who believe. There is no difference, 23for all have sinned and fall short of the glory of God, 24and are justified freely by his grace through the redemption that came by Christ Jesus. 25God presented him as a sacrifice of atonement,*i* through faith in his blood. He did this to demonstrate his justice, because in his forbearance he had left the sins committed beforehand unpunished 26 — he did it to demonstrate his justice at the present time, so as to be just and the one who justifies those who have faith in Jesus.

3:20   When Paul talked about "the law" he did not mean the law of the nation or state. He was referring to the Law of Moses which, as a Jew, he tried to keep to make himself acceptable to God. Is this perhaps similar to some people today who believe that God will love them if they behave well?

27Where, then, is boasting? It is excluded. On what principle? On that of observing the law? No, but on that of faith. 28For we maintain that a man is justified by faith apart from observing the law. 29Is God the God of Jews only? Is he not the God of Gentiles too? Yes, of Gentiles too, 30since there is only one God, who will justify the circumcised by faith and the uncircumcised through that same faith. 31Do we, then, nullify the law by this faith? Not at all! Rather, we uphold the law.

Abraham Justified by Faith

4 What then shall we say that Abraham, our forefather, discovered in this matter? 2If, in fact, Abraham was justified by works, he had something to boast about — but not before God. 3What does the Scripture say? "Abraham believed God, and it was credited to him as righteousness."*a*

4Now when a man works, his wages are not credited to him as a gift, but as an obligation. 5However, to the man who does not work but trusts God who justifies the wicked, his faith is credited as righteousness. 6David says the same thing when he speaks of the blessedness of the man to whom God credits righteousness apart from works:

7"Blessed are they
   whose transgressions are forgiven,
   whose sins are covered.
8Blessed is the man
   whose sin the Lord will never count against
       him."*b*

9Is this blessedness only for the circumcised, or also for the uncircumcised? We have been saying that Abraham's faith was credited to him as righteousness. 10Under what circumstances was it credited? Was it after he was circumcised, or before? It was not after, but before! 11And he received the sign of circumcision, a seal of the righteousness that he had by faith while he was still uncircumcised. So then, he is the father of all who believe but have not been circumcised, in order that righteousness might be credited to them. 12And he is also the father of the circumcised who not only are circumcised but who also walk in the footsteps of the faith that our father Abraham had before he was circumcised.

13It was not through law that Abraham and his offspring received the promise that he would be heir of the world, but through the righteousness that comes by faith. 14For if those who live by law are heirs, faith has no value and the promise is worthless, 15because law brings wrath. And where there is no law there is no transgression.

16Therefore, the promise comes by faith, so that it may be by grace and may be guaranteed to all Abraham's offspring — not only to those who are of the law but also to those who are of the faith of Abraham. He is the father of us all. 17As it is written: "I have made you a father of many nations."*c* He is our father in the sight of God, in whom he believed — the God who gives life to the dead and calls things that are not as though they were.

18Against all hope, Abraham in hope believed and so became the father of many nations, just as it had been said to him, "So shall your offspring be."*d* 19Without weakening in his faith, he faced the fact that his body was as good as dead — since he was about a hundred years old — and that Sarah's womb was also dead. 20Yet he did not waver through unbelief regarding the promise of God, but was strengthened in his faith and gave glory to God, 21being fully persuaded that God had power to do what he had promised. 22This is why "it was credited to him as righteousness." 23The words "it was credited to him" were written not for him alone, 24but also for us, to whom God will credit righteousness — for us who believe in him who raised Jesus our Lord from the dead. 25He was delivered over to death for our sins and was raised to life for our justification.

Peace and Joy

5 Therefore, since we have been justified through faith, we*a* have peace with God through our Lord Jesus Christ, 2through whom we have gained access by faith into this grace in which we now stand. And we*a* rejoice in the hope of the glory of God. 3Not only so, but we*a* also rejoice in our sufferings, because we know that suffering produces perseverance; 4perseverance, character; and character, hope. 5And hope does not disappoint us, because God has poured out his love into our hearts by the Holy Spirit, whom he has given us.

6You see, at just the right time, when we were still powerless, Christ died for the ungodly. 7Very rarely will anyone die for a righteous man, though for a good man someone might possibly dare to die. 8But God

---

i25 Or *as the one who would turn aside his wrath, taking away sin*
b8 Psalm 32:1,2   *c17* Gen. 17:5   *d18* Gen. 15:5

a3 Gen. 15:6; also in verse 22
a1,2,3 Or *let us*

demonstrates his own love for us in this: While we were still sinners, Christ died for us.

5:8   This verse expresses the heart of Paul's gospel message. God in Christ does not wait for us to become good before he loves us. Rather, he loves us even though we do not deserve it, and shows that love through the death of Christ.

---

[9]Since we have now been justified by his blood, how much more shall we be saved from God's wrath through him! [10]For if, when we were God's enemies, we were reconciled to him through the death of his Son, how much more, having been reconciled, shall we be saved through his life! [11]Not only is this so, but we also rejoice in God through our Lord Jesus Christ, through whom we have now received reconciliation.

Death Through Adam, Life Through Christ

[12]Therefore, just as sin entered the world through one man, and death through sin, and in this way death came to all men, because all sinned — [13]for before the law was given, sin was in the world. But sin is not taken into account when there is no law. [14]Nevertheless, death reigned from the time of Adam to the time of Moses, even over those who did not sin by breaking a command, as did Adam, who was a pattern of the one to come.

[15]But the gift is not like the trespass. For if the many died by the trespass of the one man, how much more did God's grace and the gift that came by the grace of the one man, Jesus Christ, overflow to the many! [16]Again, the gift of God is not like the result of the one man's sin: The judgment followed one sin and brought condemnation, but the gift followed many trespasses and brought justification. [17]For if, by the trespass of the one man, death reigned through that one man, how much more will those who receive God's abundant provision of grace and of the gift of righteousness reign in life through the one man, Jesus Christ.

[18]Consequently, just as the result of one trespass was condemnation for all men, so also the result of one act of righteousness was justification that brings life for all men. [19]For just as through the disobedience of the one man the many were made sinners, so also through the obedience of the one man the many will be made righteous.

[20]The law was added so that the trespass might increase. But where sin increased, grace increased all the more, [21]so that, just as sin reigned in death, so also grace might reign through righteousness to bring eternal life through Jesus Christ our Lord.

Dead to Sin, Alive in Christ

6   What shall we say, then? Shall we go on sinning, so that grace may increase? [2]By no means! We died to sin; how can we live in it any longer? [3]Or don't you know that all of us who were baptised into Christ Jesus were baptised into his death? [4]We were therefore

buried with him through baptism into death in order that, just as Christ was raised from the dead through the glory of the Father, we too may live a new life.

6:4   Paul's imagery here is strong. Baptism is a symbolic burial in which the old life comes to its end and is followed by life lived with Christ and based on hope in the resurrection. This is how baptism is to be interpreted whenever it takes place and however it is administered.

---

[5]If we have been united with him like this in his death, we will certainly also be united with him in his resurrection. [6]For we know that our old self was crucified with him so that the body of sin might be done away with,[a] that we should no longer be slaves to sin — [7]because anyone who has died has been freed from sin.

[8]Now if we died with Christ, we believe that we will also live with him. [9]For we know that since Christ was raised from the dead, he cannot die again; death no longer has mastery over him. [10]The death he died, he died to sin once for all; but the life he lives, he lives to God.

[11]In the same way, count yourselves dead to sin but alive to God in Christ Jesus. [12]Therefore do not let sin reign in your mortal body so that you obey its evil desires. [13]Do not offer the parts of your body to sin, as instruments of wickedness, but rather offer yourselves to God, as those who have been brought from death to life; and offer the parts of your body to him as instruments of righteousness. [14]For sin shall not be your master, because you are not under law, but under grace.

Slaves to Righteousness

[15]What then? Shall we sin because we are not under law but under grace? By no means! [16]Don't you know that when you offer yourselves to someone to obey him as slaves, you are slaves to the one whom you obey — whether you are slaves to sin, which leads to death, or to obedience, which leads to righteousness? [17]But thanks be to God that, though you used to be slaves to sin, you wholeheartedly obeyed the form of teaching to which you were entrusted. [18]You have been set free from sin and have become slaves to righteousness.

[19]I put this in human terms because you are weak in your natural selves. Just as you used to offer the parts of your body in slavery to impurity and to ever-increasing wickedness, so now offer them in slavery to righteousness leading to holiness. [20]When you were slaves to sin, you were free from the control of righteousness. [21]What benefit did you reap at that time from the things you are now ashamed of? Those things result in death! [22]But now that you have been set free from sin and have become slaves to God, the benefit you reap leads to holiness, and the result is eternal life. [23]For the wages of sin is death, but the gift of God is eternal life in[b] Christ Jesus our Lord.

---

[a]6 Or be rendered powerless   [b]23 Or through

An Illustration From Marriage

7 Do you not know, brothers—for I am speaking to men who know the law—that the law has authority over a man only as long as he lives? [2]For example, by law a married woman is bound to her husband as long as he is alive, but if her husband dies, she is released from the law of marriage. [3]So then, if she marries another man while her husband is still alive, she is called an adulteress. But if her husband dies, she is released from that law and is not an adulteress, even though she marries another man.

[4]So, my brothers, you also died to the law through the body of Christ, that you might belong to another, to him who was raised from the dead, in order that we might bear fruit to God. [5]For when we were controlled by the sinful nature,[a] the sinful passions aroused by the law were at work in our bodies, so that we bore fruit for death. [6]But now, by dying to what once bound us, we have been released from the law so that we serve in the new way of the Spirit, and not in the old way of the written code.

Struggling With Sin

[7]What shall we say, then? Is the law sin? Certainly not! Indeed I would not have known what sin was except through the law. For I would not have known what coveting really was if the law had not said, "Do not covet."[b] [8]But sin, seizing the opportunity afforded by the commandment, produced in me every kind of covetous desire. For apart from law, sin is dead. [9]Once I was alive apart from law; but when the commandment came, sin sprang to life and I died. [10]I found that the very commandment that was intended to bring life actually brought death. [11]For sin, seizing the opportunity afforded by the commandment, deceived me, and through the commandment put me to death. [12]So then, the law is holy, and the commandment is holy, righteous and good.

[13]Did that which is good, then, become death to me? By no means! But in order that sin might be recognised as sin, it produced death in me through what was good, so that through the commandment sin might become utterly sinful.

[14]We know that the law is spiritual; but I am unspiritual, sold as a slave to sin. [15]I do not understand what I do. For what I want to do I do not do, but what I hate I do. [16]And if I do what I do not want to do, I agree that the law is good. [17]As it is, it is no longer I myself who do it, but it is sin living in me. [18]I know that nothing good lives in me, that is, in my sinful nature.[c] For I have the desire to do what is good, but I cannot carry it out. [19]For what I do is not the good I want to do; no, the evil I do not want to do—this I keep on doing. [20]Now if I do what I do not want to do, it is no longer I who do it, but it is sin living in me that does it.

[21]So I find this law at work: When I want to do good, evil is right there with me. [22]For in my inner being I delight in God's law; [23]but I see another law at work in the members of my body, waging war against the law of my mind and making me a prisoner of the law of sin at work within my members. [24]What a wretched man I am! Who will rescue me from this body of death? [25]Thanks be to God—through Jesus Christ our Lord!

So then, I myself in my mind am a slave to God's law, but in the sinful nature a slave to the law of sin.

7:23   In this chapter Paul wrote about the way in which sin pervades every part of human nature. Even when we know what we ought to do, we are often powerless to do it. Whether Paul was writing here about his pre Christian or Christian experience is not certain. What matters is his reminder that the impulse to sin remains strong in all human beings.

Life Through the Spirit

8 Therefore, there is now no condemnation for those who are in Christ Jesus,[a] [2]because through Christ Jesus the law of the Spirit of life set me free from the law of sin and death. [3]For what the law was powerless to do in that it was weakened by the sinful nature,[b] God did by sending his own Son in the likeness of sinful man to be a sin offering.[c] And so he condemned sin in sinful man,[d] [4]in order that the righteous requirements of the law might be fully met in us, who do not live according to the sinful nature but according to the Spirit.

[5]Those who live according to the sinful nature have their minds set on what that nature desires; but those who live in accordance with the Spirit have their minds set on what the Spirit desires. [6]The mind of sinful man[e] is death, but the mind controlled by the Spirit is life and peace; [7]the sinful mind[f] is hostile to God. It does not submit to God's law, nor can it do so. [8]Those controlled by the sinful nature cannot please God.

[9]You, however, are controlled not by the sinful nature but by the Spirit, if the Spirit of God lives in you. And if anyone does not have the Spirit of Christ, he does not belong to Christ. [10]But if Christ is in you, your body is dead because of sin, yet your spirit is alive because of righteousness. [11]And if the Spirit of him who raised Jesus from the dead is living in you, he who raised Christ from the dead will also give life to your mortal bodies through his Spirit, who lives in you.

[12]Therefore, brothers, we have an obligation—but it is not to the sinful nature, to live according to it. [13]For if you live according to the sinful nature, you will die; but if by the Spirit you put to death the misdeeds of the body, you will live, [14]because those who are led by the Spirit of God are sons of God. [15]For you did not receive a spirit that makes you a slave again to fear, but you received the Spirit of sonship.[g] And by him we cry, "Abba,[h] Father." [16]The Spirit himself testifies with our spirit that we are God's children. [17]Now if we are

---

a 5 Or the flesh; also in verse 25   b 7 Exodus 20:17; Deut. 5:21   c 18 Or my flesh
a 1 Some later manuscripts Jesus, who do not live according to the sinful nature but according to the Spirit,
b 3 Or the flesh; also in verses 4, 5, 8, 9, 12 and 13   c 3 Or man, for sin   d 3 Or in the flesh
e 6 Or mind set on the flesh   f 7 Or the mind set on the flesh   g 15 Or adoption   h 15 Aramaic for Father

children, then we are heirs—heirs of God and co-heirs with Christ, if indeed we share in his sufferings in order that we may also share in his glory.

Future Glory

[18]I consider that our present sufferings are not worth comparing with the glory that will be revealed in us. [19]The creation waits in eager expectation for the sons of God to be revealed. [20]For the creation was subjected to frustration, not by its own choice, but by the will of the one who subjected it, in hope [21]that[i] the creation itself will be liberated from its bondage to decay and brought into the glorious freedom of the children of God.

[22]We know that the whole creation has been groaning as in the pains of childbirth right up to the present time. [23]Not only so, but we ourselves, who have the firstfruits of the Spirit, groan inwardly as we wait eagerly for our adoption as sons, the redemption of our bodies. [24]For in this hope we were saved. But hope that is seen is no hope at all. Who hopes for what he already has? [25]But if we hope for what we do not yet have, we wait for it patiently.

[26]In the same way, the Spirit helps us in our weakness. We do not know what we ought to pray for, but the Spirit himself intercedes for us with groans that words cannot express. [27]And he who searches our hearts knows the mind of the Spirit, because the Spirit intercedes for the saints in accordance with God's will.

More Than Conquerors

[28]And we know that in all things God works for the good of those who love him,[j] who[k] have been called according to his purpose. [29]For those God foreknew he also predestined to be conformed to the likeness of his Son, that he might be the firstborn among many brothers. [30]And those he predestined, he also called; those he called, he also justified; those he justified, he also glorified.

8:28 There is a difference between naive optimism and faith. Naive optimism believes that everything will turn out for the best and is too superficial to take account of the real difficulties and agonies through which humans sometimes go. Faith, by contrast, is the trust that even though the problems are real ones, God is at work in them seeking to bring good out of evil.

---

[31]What, then, shall we say in response to this? If God is for us, who can be against us? [32]He who did not spare his own Son, but gave him up for us all—how will he not also, along with him, graciously give us all things? [33]Who will bring any charge against those whom God

has chosen? It is God who justifies. [34]Who is he that condemns? Christ Jesus, who died—more than that, who was raised to life—is at the right hand of God and is also interceding for us. [35]Who shall separate us from the love of Christ? Shall trouble or hardship or persecution or famine or nakedness or danger or sword? [36]As it is written:

"For your sake we face death all day long;
we are considered as sheep to be
slaughtered."[l]

[37]No, in all these things we are more than conquerors through him who loved us. [38]For I am convinced that neither death nor life, neither angels nor demons,[m] neither the present nor the future, nor any powers, [39]neither height nor depth, nor anything else in all creation, will be able to separate us from the love of God that is in Christ Jesus our Lord.

God's Sovereign Choice

9 I speak the truth in Christ—I am not lying, my conscience confirms it in the Holy Spirit—[2]I have great sorrow and unceasing anguish in my heart. [3]For I could wish that I myself were cursed and cut off from Christ for the sake of my brothers, those of my own race, [4]the people of Israel. Theirs is the adoption as sons; theirs the divine glory, the covenants, the receiving of the law, the temple worship and the promises. [5]Theirs are the patriarchs, and from them is traced the human ancestry of Christ, who is God over all, for ever praised![a] Amen.

[6]It is not as though God's word had failed. For not all who are descended from Israel are Israel. [7]Nor because they are his descendants are they all Abraham's children. On the contrary, "It is through Isaac that your offspring will be reckoned."[b] [8]In other words, it is not the natural children who are God's children, but it is the children of the promise who are regarded as Abraham's offspring. [9]For this was how the promise was stated: "At the appointed time I will return, and Sarah will have a son."[c]

[10]Not only that, but Rebekah's children had one and the same father, our father Isaac. [11]Yet, before the twins were born or had done anything good or bad—in order that God's purpose in election might stand: [12]not by works but by him who calls—she was told, "The older will serve the younger."[d] [13]Just as it is written: "Jacob I loved, but Esau I hated."[e]

[14]What then shall we say? Is God unjust? Not at all! [15]For he says to Moses,

"I will have mercy on whom I have mercy,
and I will have compassion on whom I have
compassion."[f]

[16]It does not, therefore, depend on man's desire or effort, but on God's mercy. [17]For the Scripture says to Pharaoh: "I raised you up for this very purpose, that I

---

i20,21 Or subjected it in hope. *21 For*
j28 Some manuscripts And we know that all things work together for good to those who love God
k28 Or works together with those who love him to bring about what is good—with those who   *l36 Psalm 44:22*
m38 Or nor heavenly rulers
a5 Or Christ, who is over all. God be for ever praised! Or Christ. God who is over all be for ever praised!   *b7 Gen. 21:12*
c9 Gen. 18:10,14   *d12 Gen. 25:23*   *e13 Mal. 1:2,3*   *f15 Exodus 33:19*

might display my power in you and that my name might be proclaimed in all the earth."*g* 18Therefore God has mercy on whom he wants to have mercy, and he hardens whom he wants to harden.

19One of you will say to me: "Then why does God still blame us? For who resists his will?" 20But who are you, O man, to talk back to God? "Shall what is formed say to him who formed it, 'Why did you make me like this?' "*h* 21Does not the potter have the right to make out of the same lump of clay some pottery for noble purposes and some for common use?

22What if God, choosing to show his wrath and make his power known, bore with great patience the objects of his wrath—prepared for destruction? 23What if he did this to make the riches of his glory known to the objects of his mercy, whom he prepared in advance for glory—24even us, whom he also called, not only from the Jews but also from the Gentiles? 25As he says in Hosea:

"I will call them 'my people' who are not my
        people;
and I will call her 'my loved one' who is not
        my loved one,"*i*

26and,

"It will happen that in the very place where it
        was said to them,
'You are not my people,'
they will be called 'sons of the living God'."*j*

27Isaiah cries out concerning Israel:

"Though the number of the Israelites be like the
        sand by the sea,
only the remnant will be saved.
28For the Lord will carry out
his sentence on earth with speed and
        finality."*k*

29It is just as Isaiah said previously:

"Unless the Lord Almighty
had left us descendants,
we would have become like Sodom,
we would have been like Gomorrah."*l*

Israel's Unbelief

30What then shall we say? That the Gentiles, who did not pursue righteousness, have obtained it, a righteousness that is by faith; 31but Israel, who pursued a law of righteousness, has not attained it. 32Why not? Because they pursued it not by faith but as if it were by works. They stumbled over the "stumbling-stone". 33As it is written:

"See, I lay in Zion a stone that causes men to
        stumble
and a rock that makes them fall,
and the one who trusts in him will never be put
        to shame."*m*

10 Brothers, my heart's desire and prayer to God for the Israelites is that they may be saved. 2For I can testify about them that they are zealous for God, but their zeal is not based on knowledge. 3Since they did not know the righteousness that comes from God and sought to establish their own, they did not submit to God's righteousness. 4Christ is the end of the law so that there may be righteousness for everyone who believes.

5Moses describes in this way the righteousness that is by the law: "The man who does these things will live by them."*a* 6But the righteousness that is by faith says: "Do not say in your heart, 'Who will ascend into heaven?'*b*" (that is, to bring Christ down) 7"or 'Who will descend into the deep?'*c*" (that is, to bring Christ up from the dead). 8But what does it say? "The word is near you; it is in your mouth and in your heart,"*d* that is, the word of faith we are proclaiming: 9That if you confess with your mouth, "Jesus is Lord," and believe in your heart that God raised him from the dead, you will be saved. 10For it is with your heart that you believe and are justified, and it is with your mouth that you confess and are saved. 11As the Scripture says, "Anyone who trusts in him will never be put to shame."*e* 12For there is no difference between Jew and Gentile—the same Lord is Lord of all and richly blesses all who call on him, 13for, "Everyone who calls on the name of the Lord will be saved."*f*

14How, then, can they call on the one they have not believed in? And how can they believe in the one of whom they have not heard? And how can they hear without someone preaching to them? 15And how can they preach unless they are sent? As it is written, "How beautiful are the feet of those who bring good news!"*g*

16But not all the Israelites accepted the good news. For Isaiah says, "Lord, who has believed our message?"*h* 17Consequently, faith comes from hearing the message, and the message is heard through the word of Christ. 18But I ask: Did they not hear? Of course they did:

"Their voice has gone out into all the earth,
their words to the ends of the world."*i*

19Again I ask: Did Israel not understand? First, Moses says,

"I will make you envious by those who are not a
        nation;
I will make you angry by a nation that has no
        understanding."*j*

20And Isaiah boldly says,

"I was found by those who did not seek me;
I revealed myself to those who did not ask for
        me."*k*

21But concerning Israel he says,

"All day long I have held out my hands
to a disobedient and obstinate people."*l*

---

g17 Exodus 9:16   *h20* Isaiah 29:16; 45:9   *i25* Hosea 2:23   *j26* Hosea 1:10   *k28* Isaiah 10:22,23
i29 Isaiah 1:9   *m33* Isaiah 8:14; 28:16   *a5* Lev. 18:5   *b6* Deut. 30:12   *c7* Deut. 30:13
d8 Deut. 30:14   *e11* Isaiah 28:16   *f13* Joel 2:32   *g15* Isaiah 52:7   *h16* Isaiah 53:1
i18 Psalm 19:4   *j19* Deut. 32:21   *k20* Isaiah 65:1   *l21* Isaiah 65:2

The Remnant of Israel

11 I ask then: Did God reject his people? By no means! I am an Israelite myself, a descendant of Abraham, from the tribe of Benjamin. [2]God did not reject his people, whom he foreknew. Don't you know what the Scripture says in the passage about Elijah— how he appealed to God against Israel: [3]"Lord, they have killed your prophets and torn down your altars; I am the only one left, and they are trying to kill me"[a]? [4]And what was God's answer to him? "I have reserved for myself seven thousand who have not bowed the knee to Baal."[b] [5]So too, at the present time there is a remnant chosen by grace. [6]And if by grace, then it is no longer by works; if it were, grace would no longer be grace.[c]

11:1 If the Jews have not accepted the gospel, does that mean that God has turned his back on them? Paul wrestled with this question in these chapters. His conclusion was that far from rejecting Israel, God still had a purpose for them and that one day that purpose would be seen. The basis of Paul's argument is that God is too faithful to break his promises.

---

[7]What then? What Israel sought so earnestly it did not obtain, but the elect did. The others were hardened, [8]as it is written:

"God gave them a spirit of stupor,
    eyes so that they could not see
    and ears so that they could not hear,
to this very day."[d]

[9]And David says:

"May their table become a snare and a trap,
    a stumbling-block and a retribution for them.
[10]May their eyes be darkened so they cannot see,
    and their backs be bent for ever."[e]

Ingrafted Branches

[11]Again I ask: Did they stumble so as to fall beyond recovery? Not at all! Rather, because of their transgression, salvation has come to the Gentiles to make Israel envious. [12]But if their transgression means riches for the world, and their loss means riches for the Gentiles, how much greater riches will their fulness bring!

[13]I am talking to you Gentiles. Inasmuch as I am the apostle to the Gentiles, I make much of my ministry [14]in the hope that I may somehow arouse my own people to envy and save some of them. [15]For if their rejection is the reconciliation of the world, what will their acceptance be but life from the dead? [16]If the part of the dough offered as firstfruits is holy, then the whole batch is holy; if the root is holy, so are the branches.

[17]If some of the branches have been broken off, and you, though a wild olive shoot, have been grafted in among the others and now share in the nourishing sap from the olive root, [18]do not boast over those branches. If you do, consider this: You do not support the root, but the root supports you. [19]You will say then, "Branches were broken off so that I could be grafted in." [20]Granted. But they were broken off because of unbelief, and you stand by faith. Do not be arrogant, but be afraid. [21]For if God did not spare the natural branches, he will not spare you either.

[22]Consider therefore the kindness and sternness of God: sternness to those who fell, but kindness to you, provided that you continue in his kindness. Otherwise, you also will be cut off. [23]And if they do not persist in unbelief, they will be grafted in, for God is able to graft them in again. [24]After all, if you were cut out of an olive tree that is wild by nature, and contrary to nature were grafted into a cultivated olive tree, how much more readily will these, the natural branches, be grafted into their own olive tree!

All Israel Will Be Saved

[25]I do not want you to be ignorant of this mystery, brothers, so that you may not be conceited: Israel has experienced a hardening in part until the full number of the Gentiles has come in. [26]And so all Israel will be saved, as it is written:

"The deliverer will come from Zion;
    he will turn godlessness away from Jacob.
[27]And this is[f] my covenant with them
    when I take away their sins."[g]

[28]As far as the gospel is concerned, they are enemies on your account; but as far as election is concerned, they are loved on account of the patriarchs, [29]for God's gifts and his call are irrevocable. [30]Just as you who were at one time disobedient to God have now received mercy as a result of their disobedience, [31]so they too have now become disobedient in order that they too may now[h] receive mercy as a result of God's mercy to you. [32]For God has bound all men over to disobedience so that he may have mercy on them all.

Doxology

[33]Oh, the depth of the riches of the wisdom and[i]
        knowledge of God!
    How unsearchable his judgments,
        and his paths beyond tracing out!
[34]"Who has known the mind of the Lord?
        Or who has been his counsellor?"[j]
[35]"Who has ever given to God,
        that God should repay him?"[k]
[36]For from him and through him and to him are all
        things.
    To him be the glory for ever! Amen.

---

a3 1 Kings 19:10,14   b4 1 Kings 19:18
c6 Some manuscripts by grace. But if by works, then it is no longer grace; if it were, work would no longer be work.
d8 Deut. 29:4; Isaiah 29:10   e10 Psalm 69:22,23   f27 Or will be   g27 Isaiah 59:20,21; 27:9; Jer. 31:33,34
h31 Some manuscripts do not have now.   i33 Or riches and the wisdom and the   j34 Isaiah 40:13
k35 Job 41:11

Living Sacrifices

12 Therefore, I urge you, brothers, in view of God's mercy, to offer your bodies as living sacrifices, holy and pleasing to God—this is your spiritual[a] act of worship. [2]Do not conform any longer to the pattern of this world, but be transformed by the renewing of your mind. Then you will be able to test and approve what God's will is—his good, pleasing and perfect will.

12:1 The word "therefore" appears a number of times in the later chapters of Romans. It was Paul's reminder to his readers of the intimate connection between belief and action, and faith and ethics. If the gospel he has outlined is true, then the whole of a Christian's life must reflect that—in fact it must become a spiritual sacrifice to God.

---

[3]For by the grace given me I say to every one of you: Do not think of yourself more highly than you ought, but rather think of yourself with sober judgment, in accordance with the measure of faith God has given you. [4]Just as each of us has one body with many members, and these members do not all have the same function, [5]so in Christ we who are many form one body, and each member belongs to all the others. [6]We have different gifts, according to the grace given us. If a man's gift is prophesying, let him use it in proportion to his[b] faith. [7]If it is serving, let him serve; if it is teaching, let him teach; [8]if it is encouraging, let him encourage; if it is contributing to the needs of others, let him give generously; if it is leadership, let him govern diligently; if it is showing mercy, let him do it cheerfully.

Love

[9]Love must be sincere. Hate what is evil; cling to what is good. [10]Be devoted to one another in brotherly love. Honour one another above yourselves. [11]Never be lacking in zeal, but keep your spiritual fervour, serving the Lord. [12]Be joyful in hope, patient in affliction, faithful in prayer. [13]Share with God's people who are in need. Practise hospitality.

[14]Bless those who persecute you; bless and do not curse. [15]Rejoice with those who rejoice; mourn with those who mourn. [16]Live in harmony with one another. Do not be proud, but be willing to associate with people of low position.[c] Do not be conceited.

[17]Do not repay anyone evil for evil. Be careful to do what is right in the eyes of everybody. [18]If it is possible, as far as it depends on you, live at peace with everyone. [19]Do not take revenge, my friends, but leave room for God's wrath, for it is written: "It is mine to avenge; I will repay,"[d] says the Lord. [20]On the contrary:

"If your enemy is hungry, feed him;
  if he is thirsty, give him something to drink.

In doing this, you will heap burning coals on his head."[e]

[21]Do not be overcome by evil, but overcome evil with good.

Submission to the Authorities

13 Everyone must submit himself to the governing authorities, for there is no authority except that which God has established. The authorities that exist have been established by God. [2]Consequently, he who rebels against the authority is rebelling against what God has instituted, and those who do so will bring judgment on themselves. [3]For rulers hold no terror for those who do right, but for those who do wrong. Do you want to be free from fear of the one in authority? Then do what is right and he will commend you. [4]For he is God's servant to do you good. But if you do wrong, be afraid, for he does not bear the sword for nothing. He is God's servant, an agent of wrath to bring punishment on the wrongdoer. [5]Therefore, it is necessary to submit to the authorities, not only because of possible punishment but also because of conscience.

[6]This is also why you pay taxes, for the authorities are God's servants, who give their full time to governing. [7]Give everyone what you owe him: If you owe taxes, pay taxes; if revenue, then revenue; if respect, then respect; if honour, then honour.

Love, for the Day Is Near

[8]Let no debt remain outstanding, except the continuing debt to love one another, for he who loves his fellow-man has fulfilled the law. [9]The commandments, "Do not commit adultery," "Do not murder," "Do not steal," "Do not covet,"[a] and whatever other commandment there may be, are summed up in this one rule: "Love your neighbour as yourself."[b] [10]Love does no harm to its neighbour. Therefore love is the fulfilment of the law.

[11]And do this, understanding the present time. The hour has come for you to wake up from your slumber, because our salvation is nearer now than when we first believed. [12]The night is nearly over; the day is almost here. So let us put aside the deeds of darkness and put on the armour of light. [13]Let us behave decently, as in the daytime, not in orgies and drunkenness, not in sexual immorality and debauchery, not in dissension and jealousy. [14]Rather, clothe yourselves with the Lord Jesus Christ, and do not think about how to gratify the desires of the sinful nature.[c]

The Weak and the Strong

14 Accept him whose faith is weak, without passing judgment on disputable matters. [2]One man's faith allows him to eat everything, but another man, whose faith is weak, eats only vegetables. [3]The man who eats everything must not look down on him who does not, and the man who does not eat everything must not condemn the man who does, for God has accepted him. [4]Who are you to judge someone

---

else's servant? To his own master he stands or falls. And he will stand, for the Lord is able to make him stand.

14:1 Paul referred to some of the differences of opinion which existed between Christians on such matters as food laws and special days. What he said is worth reflecting upon because it is about such matters that Christian communities are often still divided. Paul commended mutual respect for different positions, and also recognized that there are "disputable matters" which can result in different opinions.

---

⁵One man considers one day more sacred than another; another man considers every day alike. Each one should be fully convinced in his own mind. ⁶He who regards one day as special, does so to the Lord. He who eats meat, eats to the Lord, for he gives thanks to God; and he who abstains, does so to the Lord and gives thanks to God. ⁷For none of us lives to himself alone and none of us dies to himself alone. ⁸If we live, we live to the Lord; and if we die, we die to the Lord. So, whether we live or die, we belong to the Lord. ⁹For this very reason, Christ died and returned to life so that he might be the Lord of both the dead and the living. ¹⁰You, then, why do you judge your brother? Or why do you look down on your brother? For we will all stand before God's judgment seat. ¹¹It is written:

" 'As surely as I live,' says the Lord,
'Every knee will bow before me;
every tongue will confess to God.' " ᵃ

¹²So then, each of us will give an account of himself to God.

¹³Therefore let us stop passing judgment on one another. Instead, make up your mind not to put any stumbling-block or obstacle in your brother's way. ¹⁴As one who is in the Lord Jesus, I am fully convinced that no food ᵇ is unclean in itself. But if anyone regards something as unclean, then for him it is unclean. ¹⁵If your brother is distressed because of what you eat, you are no longer acting in love. Do not by your eating destroy your brother for whom Christ died. ¹⁶Do not allow what you consider good to be spoken of as evil. ¹⁷For the kingdom of God is not a matter of eating and drinking, but of righteousness, peace and joy in the Holy Spirit, ¹⁸because anyone who serves Christ in this way is pleasing to God and approved by men.

¹⁹Let us therefore make every effort to do what leads to peace and to mutual edification. ²⁰Do not destroy the work of God for the sake of food. All food is clean, but it is wrong for a man to eat anything that causes someone else to stumble. ²¹It is better not to eat meat or drink wine or to do anything else that will cause your brother to fall.

²²So whatever you believe about these things keep between yourself and God. Blessed is the man who does not condemn himself by what he approves. ²³But the man who has doubts is condemned if he eats, because his eating is not from faith; and everything that does not come from faith is sin.

15 We who are strong ought to bear with the failings of the weak and not to please ourselves. ²Each of us should please his neighbour for his good, to build him up. ³For even Christ did not please himself but, as it is written: "The insults of those who insult you have fallen on me." ᵃ ⁴For everything that was written in the past was written to teach us, so that through endurance and the encouragement of the Scriptures we might have hope.

⁵May the God who gives endurance and encouragement give you a spirit of unity among yourselves as you follow Christ Jesus, ⁶so that with one heart and mouth you may glorify the God and Father of our Lord Jesus Christ.

⁷Accept one another, then, just as Christ accepted you, in order to bring praise to God. ⁸For I tell you that Christ has become a servant of the Jews ᵇ on behalf of God's truth, to confirm the promises made to the patriarchs ⁹so that the Gentiles may glorify God for his mercy, as it is written:

"Therefore I will praise you among the Gentiles;
I will sing hymns to your name." ᶜ

¹⁰Again, it says,

"Rejoice, O Gentiles, with his people." ᵈ

¹¹And again,

"Praise the Lord, all you Gentiles,
and sing praises to him, all you peoples." ᵉ

¹²And again, Isaiah says,

"The Root of Jesse will spring up,
one who will arise to rule over the nations;
the Gentiles will hope in him." ᶠ

¹³May the God of hope fill you with all joy and peace as you trust in him, so that you may overflow with hope by the power of the Holy Spirit.

Paul the Minister to the Gentiles

¹⁴I myself am convinced, my brothers, that you yourselves are full of goodness, complete in knowledge and competent to instruct one another. ¹⁵I have written to you quite boldly on some points, as if to remind you of them again, because of the grace God gave me ¹⁶to be a minister of Christ Jesus to the Gentiles with the priestly duty of proclaiming the gospel of God, so that the Gentiles might become an offering acceptable to God, sanctified by the Holy Spirit.

¹⁷Therefore I glory in Christ Jesus in my service to God. ¹⁸I will not venture to speak of anything except what Christ has accomplished through me in leading the Gentiles to obey God by what I have said and done — ¹⁹by the power of signs and miracles, through the power of the Spirit. So from Jerusalem all the way round to Illyricum, I have fully proclaimed the gospel

---

ᵃ*11* Isaiah 45:23   ᵇ*14* Or *that nothing*   ᵃ*3* Psalm 69:9   ᵇ*8* Greek *circumcision*
ᶜ*9* 2 Samuel 22:50; Psalm 18:49   ᵈ*10* Deut. 32:43   ᵉ*11* Psalm 117:1   ᶠ*12* Isaiah 11:10

of Christ. [20]It has always been my ambition to preach the gospel where Christ was not known, so that I would not be building on someone else's foundation. [21]Rather, as it is written:

"Those who were not told about him will see,
and those who have not heard will
understand." [g]

[22]This is why I have often been hindered from coming to you.

Paul's Plan to Visit Rome

[23]But now that there is no more place for me to work in these regions, and since I have been longing for many years to see you, [24]I plan to do so when I go to Spain. I hope to visit you while passing through and to have you assist me on my journey there, after I have enjoyed your company for a while. [25]Now, however, I am on my way to Jerusalem in the service of the saints there. [26]For Macedonia and Achaia were pleased to make a contribution for the poor among the saints in Jerusalem. [27]They were pleased to do it, and indeed they owe it to them. For if the Gentiles have shared in the Jews' spiritual blessings, they owe it to the Jews to share with them their material blessings. [28]So after I have completed this task and have made sure that they have received this fruit, I will go to Spain and visit you on the way. [29]I know that when I come to you, I will come in the full measure of the blessing of Christ.

15:25 For some time Paul had been collecting money from his Gentile converts to relieve the needs of the Christians in Jerusalem who had fallen on hard times, possibly as a result of their experiment in communal living (Acts 4:32–35). This is a reminder of the responsibility Christians have for one another.

---

[30]I urge you, brothers, by our Lord Jesus Christ and by the love of the Spirit, to join me in my struggle by praying to God for me. [31]Pray that I may be rescued from the unbelievers in Judea and that my service in Jerusalem may be acceptable to the saints there, [32]so that by God's will I may come to you with joy and together with you be refreshed. [33]The God of peace be with you all. Amen.

Personal Greetings

16 I commend to you our sister Phoebe, a servant[a] of the church in Cenchrea. [2]I ask you to receive her in the Lord in a way worthy of the saints and to give her any help she may need from you, for she has been a great help to many people, including me.

[3]Greet Priscilla[b] and Aquila, my fellow-workers in Christ Jesus. [4]They risked their lives for me. Not only I but all the churches of the Gentiles are grateful to them.

[5]Greet also the church that meets at their house.
Greet my dear friend Epenetus, who was the first convert to Christ in the province of Asia.
[6]Greet Mary, who worked very hard for you.
[7]Greet Andronicus and Junias, my relatives who have been in prison with me. They are outstanding among the apostles, and they were in Christ before I was.
[8]Greet Ampliatus, whom I love in the Lord.
[9]Greet Urbanus, our fellow-worker in Christ, and my dear friend Stachys.
[10]Greet Apelles, tested and approved in Christ.
Greet those who belong to the household of Aristobulus.
[11]Greet Herodion, my relative.
Greet those in the household of Narcissus who are in the Lord.
[12]Greet Tryphena and Tryphosa, those women who work hard in the Lord.
Greet my dear friend Persis, another woman who has worked very hard in the Lord.
[13]Greet Rufus, chosen in the Lord, and his mother, who has been a mother to me, too.
[14]Greet Asyncritus, Phlegon, Hermes, Patrobas, Hermas and the brothers with them.
[15]Greet Philologus, Julia, Nereus and his sister, and Olympas and all the saints with them.
[16]Greet one another with a holy kiss.
All the churches of Christ send greetings.

[17]I urge you, brothers, to watch out for those who cause divisions and put obstacles in your way that are contrary to the teaching you have learned. Keep away from them. [18]For such people are not serving our Lord Christ, but their own appetites. By smooth talk and flattery they deceive the minds of naïve people. [19]Everyone has heard about your obedience, so I am full of joy over you; but I want you to be wise about what is good, and innocent about what is evil.
[20]The God of peace will soon crush Satan under your feet.
The grace of our Lord Jesus be with you.
[21]Timothy, my fellow-worker, sends his greetings to you, as do Lucius, Jason and Sosipater, my relatives.
[22]I, Tertius, who wrote down this letter, greet you in the Lord.
[23]Gaius, whose hospitality I and the whole church here enjoy, sends you his greetings.
Erastus, who is the city's director of public works, and our brother Quartus send you their greetings.[c]
[25]Now to him who is able to establish you by my gospel and the proclamation of Jesus Christ, according to the revelation of the mystery hidden for long ages past, [26]but now revealed and made known through the prophetic writings by the command of the eternal God, so that all nations might believe and obey him — [27]to the only wise God be glory for ever through Jesus Christ! Amen.

---

g21 Isaiah 52:15   *a1* Or *deaconess*   *b3* Greek *Prisca*, a variant of *Priscilla*
c23 Some manuscripts *their greetings.* *24May the grace of our Lord Jesus Christ be with all of you. Amen.*

1 Corinthians

The Beginning of the Story

The Christian faith came to Corinth through the preaching of the apostle Paul, although it seems that he had not particularly intended to preach in that area. In the course of his second preaching tour, or "missionary journey" as it is sometimes called, he had spread the gospel in the Roman province of Macedonia. Churches were started in several places, including Philippi and Thessalonica, but the work had often been difficult and Paul was worried about their wellbeing. He described his feelings as he arrived in Corinth as ". . . weakness and fear, and with much trembling" (1 Corinthians 2:3). This does not seem a very promising start to a programme of evangelization, and indeed the indications are that Paul had no intention of preaching in Corinth at all. He had returned to his trade as a tentmaker and found employment with a couple called Aquila and Priscilla. They were Jewish Christians who had only recently arrived in Corinth from Rome. Their friendship evidently did much to encourage Paul and, despite many difficulties, he began to preach the gospel again. The city in which he arrived in despair proved to be the scene of one of his most successful preaching ministries. He stayed there about eighteen months, and when he left there was a vigorous and growing church. Luke records the most important incidents of that period in Acts 18.

Why the Church Had Problems

One major difference between the church in Corinth and other churches that Paul founded was that most of his converts in Corinth were Gentiles — people who had never been Jews. Everything about the faith was therefore entirely new to them, and this caused problems which did not occur elsewhere. The situation was not helped by the environment in which these new Christians had to live. Corinth was an important seaport. It was materially prosperous and a centre for the worship of the goddess Aphrodite. In the ancient world Corinth also had a well deserved reputation for being a centre of sexual immorality. Knowledge of this background helps us to understand some of the things Paul needed to say to his Corinthian converts which did not need to be said elsewhere. Even so, it is not always easy for us to work out exactly why Paul wrote to the Corinthians as he did. In various places in his letters he was evidently dealing with problems which had arisen in the church, and giving advice concerning questions he had been asked. We, of course, have only Paul's letter to go on, and we do not always know precisely the nature of the problems involved or the exact reasons why he had been asked certain questions.

A Missing Letter

Unfortunately we do not even have all of Paul's correspondence with the Corinthian Church. Paul said, "I have written to you in my letter . . ." (1 Corinthians 5:9), but that previous letter has almost certainly been completely lost. Some time after it was written Paul received news of problems and divisions within the church, and in response he wrote the opening chapters of 1 Corinthians, adding the rest after he had received requests for spiritual guidance on a range of important matters.

Themes of the Letter

After initial greetings and thanksgiving, Paul dealt with reports that there were divisions within the church (1:10–17). He reminded the people that however grateful they were for their spiritual leaders, what mattered most was that all belonged to Christ (3:23). Then Paul reflected on the nature of his calling as an apostle and the hardships it involved, reminding them that he was their spiritual father (4:15). Paul also dealt with further reports which had reached him about immorality in the church. Some of the Corinthian Christians had failed to understand that if they were united by faith to Christ they had to live by different moral standards from other people. Similarly, they needed to recognize that their Christian faith gave them a fellowship which should enable them to settle disputes among themselves without going to the law courts.

Getting Down to Specifics

Paul had been asked specific questions in a letter from the church at Corinth. In a city where sexual immorality was so widespread it was inevitable that matters of marriage, divorce, and singleness would crop up, and Paul answered their questions (chapter 7). In the same way, in a city where pagan worship was strong, inevitable difficulties arose about how far Christians could engage in quite ordinary social relationships which might, for example, involve sharing a meal where the food had previously been offered in pagan sacrifices. It is against the background of social customs in Corinth that we should read what seems to us to be the difficult advice on the role of women in the church in 11:2–16 and 14:33–35.

There Must Be Love

The disorder which characterized much of the church life in Corinth extended to the gatherings for worship too, and Paul gave directions about this (11:17–33). This is the earliest account of the Lord's Supper (this letter was written before any of the Gospels), and makes it plain that from the earliest times the Lord's Supper was central to Christian worship. Paul then dealt with another kind of disorder. Some of the Corinthian Christians possessed the gift known as "speaking in tongues". That in itself was not a problem, but difficulty arose when some of them claimed that their spiritual gifts made them superior Christians. Paul's advice about this contains one of the most famous passages in the whole Bible; chapter 13. There he made it plain that love, following Christ's example, must be the beginning and the end of Christian life and nothing can take its place.

Resurrection—the Key to Salvation

The last major theme to be dealt with in this letter is a matter of belief, and it concerns the resurrection. Evidently Paul had been asked a number of questions about this, including whether it was necessary to believe in it at all. He argued at length that belief in the resurrection is not an optional extra for Christians. If there is no resurrection there is no salvation.

---

1 Paul, called to be an apostle of Christ Jesus by the will of God, and our brother Sosthenes,

2To the church of God in Corinth, to those sanctified in Christ Jesus and called to be holy, together with all those everywhere who call on the name of our Lord Jesus Christ—their Lord and ours:

3Grace and peace to you from God our Father and the Lord Jesus Christ.

Thanksgiving

4I always thank God for you because of his grace given you in Christ Jesus. 5For in him you have been enriched in every way—in all your speaking and in all your knowledge—6because our testimony about Christ was confirmed in you. 7Therefore you do not lack any spiritual gift as you eagerly wait for our Lord Jesus Christ to be revealed. 8He will keep you strong to the end, so that you will be blameless on the day of our Lord Jesus Christ. 9God, who has called you into fellowship with his Son Jesus Christ our Lord, is faithful.

Divisions in the Church

10I appeal to you, brothers, in the name of our Lord Jesus Christ, that all of you agree with one another so that there may be no divisions among you and that you may be perfectly united in mind and thought. 11My brothers, some from Chloe's household have informed me that there are quarrels among you. 12What I mean is this: One of you says, "I follow Paul"; another, "I follow Apollos"; another, "I follow Cephas";[a] still another, "I follow Christ."

1:12 Apollos was a wise Jew who was instructed in the faith by Paul's friends Aquila and Priscilla. He then went to Corinth and was a strong evangelist amongst his fellow Jews—see Acts 18:28. Some members of the Corinthian church formed themselves into groupings with opposing viewpoints and each claimed to be loyal to one Christian leader or another. This is dealt with further in 3:3–5.

13Is Christ divided? Was Paul crucified for you? Were you baptised into[b] the name of Paul? 14I am thankful that I did not baptise any of you except Crispus and Gaius, 15so no-one can say that you were baptised into my name. (16Yes, I also baptised the household of Stephanas; beyond that, I don't remember if I baptised anyone else.) 17For Christ did not send me to baptise, but to preach the gospel—not with words of human wisdom, lest the cross of Christ be emptied of its power.

Christ the Wisdom and Power of God

18For the message of the cross is foolishness to those who are perishing, but to us who are being saved it is the power of God. 19For it is written:

"I will destroy the wisdom of the wise;
   the intelligence of the intelligent I will
      frustrate."[c]

20Where is the wise man? Where is the scholar? Where is the philosopher of this age? Has not God made foolish the wisdom of the world? 21For since in the wisdom of God the world through its wisdom did not know him, God was pleased through the foolishness of what was preached to save those who believe. 22Jews demand miraculous signs and Greeks look for wisdom, 23but we preach Christ crucified: a stumbling-block to Jews and foolishness to Gentiles, 24but to those whom God has called, both Jews and Greeks, Christ the power of God and the wisdom of God. 25For the foolishness of God is wiser than man's wisdom, and the weakness of God is stronger than man's strength.

26Brothers, think of what you were when you were called. Not many of you were wise by human standards; not many were influential; not many were of noble birth. 27But God chose the foolish things of the world to shame the wise; God chose the weak things of the world to shame the strong. 28He chose the lowly things of this world and the despised things—and the things that are not—to nullify the things that are, 29so that no-one may boast before him. 30It is because of him that you are in Christ Jesus, who has become for us wisdom from God—that is, our righteousness, holiness and redemption. 31Therefore, as it is written: "Let him who boasts boast in the Lord."[d]

2 When I came to you, brothers, I did not come with eloquence or superior wisdom as I proclaimed to you the testimony about God.[a] 2For I resolved to know nothing while I was with you except Jesus Christ and him crucified. 3I came to you in

---

a12 That is, Peter   b13 Or in; also in verse 15   c19 Isaiah 29:14   d31 Jer. 9:24
a1 Some manuscripts as I proclaimed to you God's mystery

weakness and fear, and with much trembling. [4]My message and my preaching were not with wise and persuasive words, but with a demonstration of the Spirit's power, [5]so that your faith might not rest on men's wisdom, but on God's power.

Wisdom From the Spirit

[6]We do, however, speak a message of wisdom among the mature, but not the wisdom of this age or of the rulers of this age, who are coming to nothing. [7]No, we speak of God's secret wisdom, a wisdom that has been hidden and that God destined for our glory before time began. [8]None of the rulers of this age understood it, for if they had, they would not have crucified the Lord of glory. [9]However, as it is written:

"No eye has seen,
    no ear has heard,
no mind has conceived
    what God has prepared for those who love
        him"[b]—

[10]but God has revealed it to us by his Spirit.

The Spirit searches all things, even the deep things of God. [11]For who among men knows the thoughts of a man except the man's spirit within him? In the same way no-one knows the thoughts of God except the Spirit of God. [12]We have not received the spirit of the world but the Spirit who is from God, that we may understand what God has freely given us. [13]This is what we speak, not in words taught us by human wisdom but in words taught by the Spirit, expressing spiritual truths in spiritual words.[c] [14]The man without the Spirit does not accept the things that come from the Spirit of God, for they are foolishness to him, and he cannot understand them, because they are spiritually discerned. [15]The spiritual man makes judgments about all things, but he himself is not subject to any man's judgment:

[16]"For who has known the mind of the Lord
    that he may instruct him?"[d]

But we have the mind of Christ.

2:14   In this passage human wisdom is contrasted with God's wisdom. Paul did not mean that human knowledge is of no value (he used his own Jewish education often enough in the course of his preaching tours). Rather, he was concerned to stress that being wise in the usual sense of that term does not lead anyone to faith: only openness to the Holy Spirit can do that.

On Divisions in the Church

3 Brothers, I could not address you as spiritual but as worldly—mere infants in Christ. [2]I gave you milk, not solid food, for you were not yet ready for it. Indeed, you are still not ready. [3]You are still worldly.

For since there is jealousy and quarrelling among you, are you not worldly? Are you not acting like mere men? [4]For when one says, "I follow Paul," and another, "I follow Apollos," are you not mere men?

[5]What, after all, is Apollos? And what is Paul? Only servants, through whom you came to believe—as the Lord has assigned to each his task. [6]I planted the seed, Apollos watered it, but God made it grow. [7]So neither he who plants nor he who waters is anything, but only God, who makes things grow. [8]The man who plants and the man who waters have one purpose, and each will be rewarded according to his own labour. [9]For we are God's fellow-workers; you are God's field, God's building.

[10]By the grace God has given me, I laid a foundation as an expert builder, and someone else is building on it. But each one should be careful how he builds. [11]For no-one can lay any foundation other than the one already laid, which is Jesus Christ. [12]If any man builds on this foundation using gold, silver, costly stones, wood, hay or straw, [13]his work will be shown for what it is, because the Day will bring it to light. It will be revealed with fire, and the fire will test the quality of each man's work. [14]If what he has built survives, he will receive his reward. [15]If it is burned up, he will suffer loss; he himself will be saved, but only as one escaping through the flames.

[16]Don't you know that you yourselves are God's temple and that God's Spirit lives in you? [17]If anyone destroys God's temple, God will destroy him; for God's temple is sacred, and you are that temple.

[18]Do not deceive yourselves. If any one of you thinks he is wise by the standards of this age, he should become a "fool" so that he may become wise. [19]For the wisdom of this world is foolishness in God's sight. As it is written: "He catches the wise in their craftiness";[a] [20]and again, "The Lord knows that the thoughts of the wise are futile."[b] [21]So then, no more boasting about men! All things are yours, [22]whether Paul or Apollos or Cephas[c] or the world or life or death or the present or the future—all are yours, [23]and you are of Christ, and Christ is of God.

Apostles of Christ

4 So then, men ought to regard us as servants of Christ and as those entrusted with the secret things of God. [2]Now it is required that those who have been given a trust must prove faithful. [3]I care very little if I am judged by you or by any human court; indeed, I do not even judge myself. [4]My conscience is clear, but that does not make me innocent. It is the Lord who judges me. [5]Therefore judge nothing before the appointed time; wait till the Lord comes. He will bring to light what is hidden in darkness and will expose the motives of men's hearts. At that time each will receive his praise from God.

[6]Now, brothers, I have applied these things to myself and Apollos for your benefit, so that you may learn from us the meaning of the saying, "Do not go beyond what is written." Then you will not take pride

---

[b]9 Isaiah 64:4   [c]13 Or *Spirit, interpreting spiritual truths to spiritual men*   [d]16 Isaiah 40:13
[a]19 Job 5:13   [b]20 Psalm 94:11   [c]22 That is, Peter

in one man over against another. 7For who makes you different from anyone else? What do you have that you did not receive? And if you did receive it, why do you boast as though you did not?

8Already you have all you want! Already you have become rich! You have become kings—and that without us! How I wish that you really had become kings so that we might be kings with you! 9For it seems to me that God has put us apostles on display at the end of the procession, like men condemned to die in the arena. We have been made a spectacle to the whole universe, to angels as well as to men. 10We are fools for Christ, but you are so wise in Christ! We are weak, but you are strong! You are honoured, we are dishonoured! 11To this very hour we go hungry and thirsty, we are in rags, we are brutally treated, we are homeless. 12We work hard with our own hands. When we are cursed, we bless; when we are persecuted, we endure it; 13when we are slandered, we answer kindly. Up to this moment we have become the scum of the earth, the refuse of the world.

4:8   In this passage Paul wrote with heavy irony. Some people in the church had been comparing their strength and riches with Paul's weakness and poverty, and had come to the conclusion that God's blessing was theirs rather than his. In reply, Paul stressed that those who share the hardships of the Christian life are the ones who are truly blessed. This is what Jesus said to his followers (see Matthew 5:10–12).

14I am not writing this to shame you, but to warn you, as my dear children. 15Even though you have ten thousand guardians in Christ, you do not have many fathers, for in Christ Jesus I became your father through the gospel. 16Therefore I urge you to imitate me. 17For this reason I am sending to you Timothy, my son whom I love, who is faithful in the Lord. He will remind you of my way of life in Christ Jesus, which agrees with what I teach everywhere in every church.

18Some of you have become arrogant, as if I were not coming to you. 19But I will come to you very soon, if the Lord is willing, and then I will find out not only how these arrogant people are talking, but what power they have. 20For the kingdom of God is not a matter of talk but of power. 21What do you prefer? Shall I come to you with a whip, or in love and with a gentle spirit?

Expel the Immoral Brother!

5 It is actually reported that there is sexual immorality among you, and of a kind that does not occur even among pagans: A man has his father's wife. 2And you are proud! Shouldn't you rather have been filled with grief and have put out of your fellowship the man who did this? 3Even though I am not physically present, I am with you in spirit. And I have already passed judgment on the one who did this, just as if I were present. 4When you are assembled in the name of our Lord Jesus and I am with you in spirit, and the power of our Lord Jesus is present, 5hand this man over to Satan, so that the sinful nature[a] may be destroyed and his spirit saved on the day of the Lord.

6Your boasting is not good. Don't you know that a little yeast works through the whole batch of dough? 7Get rid of the old yeast that you may be a new batch without yeast—as you really are. For Christ, our Passover lamb, has been sacrificed. 8Therefore let us keep the Festival, not with the old yeast, the yeast of malice and wickedness, but with bread without yeast, the bread of sincerity and truth.

9I have written to you in my letter not to associate with sexually immoral people—10not at all meaning the people of this world who are immoral, or the greedy and swindlers, or idolaters. In that case you would have to leave this world. 11But now I am writing to you that you must not associate with anyone who calls himself a brother but is sexually immoral or greedy, an idolater or a slanderer, a drunkard or a swindler. With such a man do not even eat.

12What business is it of mine to judge those outside the church? Are you not to judge those inside? 13God will judge those outside. "Expel the wicked man from among you."[b]

Lawsuits Among Believers

6 If any of you has a dispute with another, dare he take it before the ungodly for judgment instead of before the saints? 2Do you not know that the saints will judge the world? And if you are to judge the world, are you not competent to judge trivial cases? 3Do you not know that we will judge angels? How much more the things of this life! 4Therefore, if you have disputes about such matters, appoint as judges even men of little account in the church![a] 5I say this to shame you. Is it possible that there is nobody among you wise enough to judge a dispute between believers? 6But instead, one brother goes to law against another—and this in front of unbelievers!

7The very fact that you have lawsuits among you means you have been completely defeated already. Why not rather be wronged? Why not rather be cheated? 8Instead, you yourselves cheat and do wrong, and you do this to your brothers.

9Do you not know that the wicked will not inherit the kingdom of God? Do not be deceived: Neither the sexually immoral nor idolaters nor adulterers nor male prostitutes nor homosexual offenders 10nor thieves nor the greedy nor drunkards nor slanderers nor swindlers will inherit the kingdom of God. 11And that is what some of you were. But you were washed, you were sanctified, you were justified in the name of the Lord Jesus Christ and by the Spirit of our God.

Sexual Immorality

12"Everything is permissible for me"—but not everything is beneficial. "Everything is permissible for me"—but I will not be mastered by anything. 13"Food

---

a5 Or that his body; or that the flesh   b13 Deut. 17:7; 19:19; 21:21; 22:21,24; 24:7
a4 Or matters, do you appoint as judges men of little account in the church?

for the stomach and the stomach for food"—but God will destroy them both. The body is not meant for sexual immorality, but for the Lord, and the Lord for the body. [14]By his power God raised the Lord from the dead, and he will raise us also. [15]Do you not know that your bodies are members of Christ himself? Shall I then take the members of Christ and unite them with a prostitute? Never! [16]Do you not know that he who unites himself with a prostitute is one with her in body? For it is said, "The two will become one flesh."[b] [17]But he who unites himself with the Lord is one with him in spirit.

6:15 Some of the Corinthians turned their Christian liberty into a licence to do whatever they liked, assuming that it did not matter because they were saved through faith. This verse summarizes the basis of Paul's thinking about Christian behaviour: believers behave well not because a religious rulebook tells them to, but because they are spiritually united with Christ.

---

[18]Flee from sexual immorality. All other sins a man commits are outside his body, but he who sins sexually sins against his own body. [19]Do you not know that your body is a temple of the Holy Spirit, who is in you, whom you have received from God? You are not your own; [20]you were bought at a price. Therefore honour God with your body.

Marriage

7 Now for the matters you wrote about: It is good for a man not to marry.[a] [2]But since there is so much immorality, each man should have his own wife, and each woman her own husband. [3]The husband should fulfil his marital duty to his wife, and likewise the wife to her husband. [4]The wife's body does not belong to her alone but also to her husband. In the same way, the husband's body does not belong to him alone but also to his wife. [5]Do not deprive each other except by mutual consent and for a time, so that you may devote yourselves to prayer. Then come together again so that Satan will not tempt you because of your lack of self-control. [6]I say this as a concession, not as a command. [7]I wish that all men were as I am. But each man has his own gift from God; one has this gift, another has that.

[8]Now to the unmarried and the widows I say: It is good for them to stay unmarried, as I am. [9]But if they cannot control themselves, they should marry, for it is better to marry than to burn with passion.

[10]To the married I give this command (not I, but the Lord): A wife must not separate from her husband. [11]But if she does, she must remain unmarried or else be reconciled to her husband. And a husband must not divorce his wife.

[12]To the rest I say this (I, not the Lord): If any brother has a wife who is not a believer and she is willing to live with him, he must not divorce her. [13]And

if a woman has a husband who is not a believer and he is willing to live with her, she must not divorce him. [14]For the unbelieving husband has been sanctified through his wife, and the unbelieving wife has been sanctified through her believing husband. Otherwise your children would be unclean, but as it is, they are holy.

[15]But if the unbeliever leaves, let him do so. A believing man or woman is not bound in such circumstances; God has called us to live in peace. [16]How do you know, wife, whether you will save your husband? Or, how do you know, husband, whether you will save your wife?

[17]Nevertheless, each one should retain the place in life that the Lord assigned to him and to which God has called him. This is the rule I lay down in all the churches. [18]Was a man already circumcised when he was called? He should not become uncircumcised. Was a man uncircumcised when he was called? He should not be circumcised. [19]Circumcision is nothing and uncircumcision is nothing. Keeping God's commands is what counts. [20]Each one should remain in the situation which he was in when God called him. [21]Were you a slave when you were called? Don't let it trouble you—although if you can gain your freedom, do so. [22]For he who was a slave when he was called by the Lord is the Lord's freedman; similarly, he who was a free man when he was called is Christ's slave. [23]You were bought at a price; do not become slaves of men. [24]Brothers, each man, as responsible to God, should remain in the situation God called him to.

[25]Now about virgins: I have no command from the Lord, but I give a judgment as one who by the Lord's mercy is trustworthy. [26]Because of the present crisis, I think that it is good for you to remain as you are. [27]Are you married? Do not seek a divorce. Are you unmarried? Do not look for a wife. [28]But if you do marry, you have not sinned; and if a virgin marries, she has not sinned. But those who marry will face many troubles in this life, and I want to spare you this.

7:25 The whole discussion of marriage and singleness in this chapter may sound strange. This is because the social background was quite different to now. Although some of Paul's specific advice does not apply in situations today, the principles which underlie it do. Note how Paul was careful to distinguish between advice he gave on the command of the Lord (verse 10), and that which he gives on his own authority (verses 12 and 25).

---

[29]What I mean, brothers, is that the time is short. From now on those who have wives should live as if they had none; [30]those who mourn, as if they did not; those who are happy, as if they were not; those who buy something, as if it were not theirs to keep; [31]those who use the things of the world, as if not engrossed in

---

[b]16 Gen. 2:24   [a]1 Or "It is good for a man not to have sexual relations with a woman."

them. For this world in its present form is passing away.

[32] I would like you to be free from concern. An unmarried man is concerned about the Lord's affairs — how he can please the Lord. [33] But a married man is concerned about the affairs of this world — how he can please his wife — [34] and his interests are divided. An unmarried woman or virgin is concerned about the Lord's affairs: Her aim is to be devoted to the Lord in both body and spirit. But a married woman is concerned about the affairs of this world — how she can please her husband. [35] I am saying this for your own good, not to restrict you, but that you may live in a right way in undivided devotion to the Lord.

[36] If anyone thinks he is acting improperly towards the virgin he is engaged to, and if she is getting on in years and he feels he ought to marry, he should do as he wants. He is not sinning. They should get married. [37] But the man who has settled the matter in his own mind, who is under no compulsion but has control over his own will, and who has made up his mind not to marry the virgin — this man also does the right thing. [38] So then, he who marries the virgin does right, but he who does not marry her does even better.[b]

[39] A woman is bound to her husband as long as he lives. But if her husband dies, she is free to marry anyone she wishes, but he must belong to the Lord. [40] In my judgment, she is happier if she stays as she is — and I think that I too have the Spirit of God.

Food Sacrificed to Idols

8 Now about food sacrificed to idols: We know that we all possess knowledge.[a] Knowledge puffs up, but love builds up. [2] The man who thinks he knows something does not yet know as he ought to know. [3] But the man who loves God is known by God.

[4] So then, about eating food sacrificed to idols: We know that an idol is nothing at all in the world and that there is no God but one. [5] For even if there are so-called gods, whether in heaven or on earth (as indeed there are many "gods" and many "lords"), [6] yet for us there is but one God, the Father, from whom all things came and for whom we live; and there is but one Lord, Jesus Christ, through whom all things came and through whom we live.

[7] But not everyone knows this. Some people are still so accustomed to idols that when they eat such food they think of it as having been sacrificed to an idol, and since their conscience is weak, it is defiled. [8] But food does not bring us near to God; we are no worse if we do not eat, and no better if we do.

[9] Be careful, however, that the exercise of your freedom does not become a stumbling-block to the weak. [10] For if anyone with a weak conscience sees you who have this knowledge eating in an idol's temple, won't he be emboldened to eat what has been sacrificed to idols? [11] So this weak brother, for whom Christ died, is destroyed by your knowledge. [12] When you sin against

your brothers in this way and wound their weak conscience, you sin against Christ. [13] Therefore, if what I eat causes my brother to fall into sin, I will never eat meat again, so that I will not cause him to fall.

The Rights of an Apostle

9 Am I not free? Am I not an apostle? Have I not seen Jesus our Lord? Are you not the result of my work in the Lord? [2] Even though I may not be an apostle to others, surely I am to you! For you are the seal of my apostleship in the Lord.

[3] This is my defence to those who sit in judgment on me. [4] Don't we have the right to food and drink? [5] Don't we have the right to take a believing wife along with us, as do the other apostles and the Lord's brothers and Cephas?[a] [6] Or is it only I and Barnabas who must work for a living?

[7] Who serves as a soldier at his own expense? Who plants a vineyard and does not eat of its grapes? Who tends a flock and does not drink of the milk? [8] Do I say this merely from a human point of view? Doesn't the Law say the same thing? [9] For it is written in the Law of Moses: "Do not muzzle an ox while it is treading out the grain."[b] Is it about oxen that God is concerned? [10] Surely he says this for us, doesn't he? Yes, this was written for us, because when the ploughman ploughs and the thresher threshes, they ought to do so in the hope of sharing in the harvest. [11] If we have sown spiritual seed among you, is it too much if we reap a material harvest from you? [12] If others have this right of support from you, shouldn't we have it all the more?

But we did not use this right. On the contrary, we put up with anything rather than hinder the gospel of Christ. [13] Don't you know that those who work in the temple get their food from the temple, and those who serve at the altar share in what is offered on the altar? [14] In the same way, the Lord has commanded that those who preach the gospel should receive their living from the gospel.

[15] But I have not used any of these rights. And I am not writing this in the hope that you will do such things for me. I would rather die than have anyone deprive me of this boast. [16] Yet when I preach the gospel, I cannot boast, for I am compelled to preach. Woe to me if I do not preach the gospel! [17] If I preach voluntarily, I have a reward; if not voluntarily, I am simply discharging the trust committed to me. [18] What then is my reward? Just this: that in preaching the gospel I may offer it free of charge, and so not make use of my rights in preaching it.

[19] Though I am free and belong to no man, I make myself a slave to everyone, to win as many as possible. [20] To the Jews I became like a Jew, to win the Jews. To those under the law I became like one under the law (though I myself am not under the law), so as to win those under the law. [21] To those not having the law I became like one not having the law (though I am not free from God's law but am under Christ's law), so as

---

[b] 36–38 Or [36] If anyone thinks he is not treating his daughter properly, and if she is getting on in years, and he feels she ought to marry, he should do as he wants. He is not sinning. He should let her get married. [37] But the man who has settled the matter in his own mind, who is under no compulsion but has control over his own will, and who has made up his mind to keep the virgin unmarried — this man also does the right thing. [38] So then, he who gives his virgin in marriage does right, but he who does not give her in marriage does even better.
[a] 1 Or "We all possess knowledge," as you say   [a] 5 That is, Peter   [b] 9 Deut. 25:4

to win those not having the law. ²²To the weak I became weak, to win the weak. I have become all things to all men so that by all possible means I might save some. ²³I do all this for the sake of the gospel, that I may share in its blessings.

9:22   We are inclined to think of people who are "all things to all men" as lacking in principles. What Paul meant was that his overriding principle was to win people for Christ. Provided he was not required to compromise any essential truths of the Christian faith, he was prepared to go along with other people's way of life in order not to place stumbling blocks to faith in their way.

---

²⁴Do you not know that in a race all the runners run, but only one gets the prize? Run in such a way as to get the prize. ²⁵Everyone who competes in the games goes into strict training. They do it to get a crown that will not last; but we do it to get a crown that will last for ever. ²⁶Therefore I do not run like a man running aimlessly; I do not fight like a man beating the air. ²⁷No, I beat my body and make it my slave so that after I have preached to others, I myself will not be disqualified for the prize.

Warnings From Israel's History

10 For I do not want you to be ignorant of the fact, brothers, that our forefathers were all under the cloud and that they all passed through the sea. ²They were all baptised into Moses in the cloud and in the sea. ³They all ate the same spiritual food ⁴and drank the same spiritual drink; for they drank from the spiritual rock that accompanied them, and that rock was Christ. ⁵Nevertheless, God was not pleased with most of them; their bodies were scattered over the desert.

⁶Now these things occurred as examples[a] to keep us from setting our hearts on evil things as they did. ⁷Do not be idolaters, as some of them were; as it is written: "The people sat down to eat and drink and got up to indulge in pagan revelry."[b] ⁸We should not commit sexual immorality, as some of them did—and in one day twenty-three thousand of them died. ⁹We should not test the Lord, as some of them did—and were killed by snakes. ¹⁰And do not grumble, as some of them did—and were killed by the destroying angel.

¹¹These things happened to them as examples and were written down as warnings for us, on whom the fulfilment of the ages has come. ¹²So, if you think you are standing firm, be careful that you don't fall! ¹³No temptation has seized you except what is common to man. And God is faithful; he will not let you be tempted beyond what you can bear. But when you are tempted, he will also provide a way out so that you can stand up under it.

Idol Feasts and the Lord's Supper

¹⁴Therefore, my dear friends, flee from idolatry. ¹⁵I speak to sensible people; judge for yourselves what I say. ¹⁶Is not the cup of thanksgiving for which we give thanks a participation in the blood of Christ? And is not the bread that we break a participation in the body of Christ? ¹⁷Because there is one loaf, we, who are many, are one body, for we all partake of the one loaf.

¹⁸Consider the people of Israel: Do not those who eat the sacrifices participate in the altar? ¹⁹Do I mean then that a sacrifice offered to an idol is anything, or that an idol is anything? ²⁰No, but the sacrifices of pagans are offered to demons, not to God, and I do not want you to be participants with demons. ²¹You cannot drink the cup of the Lord and the cup of demons too; you cannot have a part in both the Lord's table and the table of demons. ²²Are we trying to arouse the Lord's jealousy? Are we stronger than he?

The Believer's Freedom

²³"Everything is permissible"—but not everything is beneficial. "Everything is permissible"—but not everything is constructive. ²⁴Nobody should seek his own good, but the good of others.

²⁵Eat anything sold in the meat market without raising questions of conscience, ²⁶for, "The earth is the Lord's, and everything in it."[c]

²⁷If some unbeliever invites you to a meal and you want to go, eat whatever is put before you without raising questions of conscience. ²⁸But if anyone says to you, "This has been offered in sacrifice," then do not eat it, both for the sake of the man who told you and for conscience' sake[d]—²⁹the other man's conscience, I mean, not yours. For why should my freedom be judged by another's conscience? ³⁰If I take part in the meal with thankfulness, why am I denounced because of something I thank God for?

³¹So whether you eat or drink or whatever you do, do it all for the glory of God. ³²Do not cause anyone to stumble, whether Jews, Greeks or the church of God—³³even as I try to please everybody in every way. For I am not seeking my own good but the good of many,

11 so that they may be saved. ¹Follow my example, as I follow the example of Christ.

Propriety in Worship

²I praise you for remembering me in everything and for holding to the teachings,[a] just as I passed them on to you.

³Now I want you to realise that the head of every man is Christ, and the head of the woman is man, and the head of Christ is God. ⁴Every man who prays or prophesies with his head covered dishonours his head. ⁵And every woman who prays or prophesies with her head uncovered dishonours her head—it is just as though her head were shaved. ⁶If a woman does not cover her head, she should have her hair cut off; and if it is a disgrace for a woman to have her hair cut or shaved off, she should cover her head. ⁷A man ought

---

a6 Or *types*; also in verse 11   b7 Exodus 32:6   c26 Psalm 24:1
d28 Some manuscripts *conscience' sake, for "the earth is the Lord's and everything in it"*   a2 Or *traditions*

not to cover his head,[b] since he is the image and glory of God; but the woman is the glory of man. [8]For man did not come from woman, but woman from man; [9]neither was man created for woman, but woman for man. [10]For this reason, and because of the angels, the woman ought to have a sign of authority on her head.

[11]In the Lord, however, woman is not independent of man, nor is man independent of woman. [12]For as woman came from man, so also man is born of woman. But everything comes from God. [13]Judge for yourselves: Is it proper for a woman to pray to God with her head uncovered? [14]Does not the very nature of things teach you that if a man has long hair, it is a disgrace to him, [15]but that if a woman has long hair, it is her glory? For long hair is given to her as a covering. [16]If anyone wants to be contentious about this, we have no other practice—nor do the churches of God.

The Lord's Supper

[17]In the following directives I have no praise for you, for your meetings do more harm than good. [18]In the first place, I hear that when you come together as a church, there are divisions among you, and to some extent I believe it. [19]No doubt there have to be differences among you to show which of you have God's approval. [20]When you come together, it is not the Lord's Supper you eat, [21]for as you eat, each of you goes ahead without waiting for anybody else. One remains hungry, another gets drunk. [22]Don't you have homes to eat and drink in? Or do you despise the church of God and humiliate those who have nothing? What shall I say to you? Shall I praise you for this? Certainly not!

[23]For I received from the Lord what I also passed on to you: The Lord Jesus, on the night he was betrayed, took bread, [24]and when he had given thanks, he broke it and said, "This is my body, which is for you; do this in remembrance of me." [25]In the same way, after supper he took the cup, saying, "This cup is the new covenant in my blood; do this, whenever you drink it, in remembrance of me." [26]For whenever you eat this bread and drink this cup, you proclaim the Lord's death until he comes.

11:23   The words translated here "received" and "passed on" are technical terms which refer to the passing on of a tradition. It was not Paul's or anyone else's idea to observe a sacramental meal which they called the Lord's Supper. Rather, the church worshipped in this way because the tradition came from Jesus himself and he commanded his followers to do it (Luke 22:19).

---

[27]Therefore, whoever eats the bread or drinks the cup of the Lord in an unworthy manner will be guilty of sinning against the body and blood of the Lord. [28]A man ought to examine himself before he eats of the bread and drinks of the cup. [29]For anyone who eats and drinks without recognising the body of the Lord eats and drinks judgment on himself. [30]That is why many among you are weak and sick, and a number of you have fallen asleep. [31]But if we judged ourselves, we would not come under judgment. [32]When we are judged by the Lord, we are being disciplined so that we will not be condemned with the world.

[33]So then, my brothers, when you come together to eat, wait for each other. [34]If anyone is hungry, he should eat at home, so that when you meet together it may not result in judgment.

And when I come I will give further directions.

Spiritual Gifts

12 Now about spiritual gifts, brothers, I do not want you to be ignorant. [2]You know that when you were pagans, somehow or other you were influenced and led astray to mute idols. [3]Therefore I tell you that no-one who is speaking by the Spirit of God says, "Jesus be cursed," and no-one can say, "Jesus is Lord," except by the Holy Spirit.

[4]There are different kinds of gifts, but the same Spirit. [5]There are different kinds of service, but the same Lord. [6]There are different kinds of working, but the same God works all of them in all men.

[7]Now to each one the manifestation of the Spirit is given for the common good. [8]To one there is given through the Spirit the message of wisdom, to another the message of knowledge by means of the same Spirit, [9]to another faith by the same Spirit, to another gifts of healing by that one Spirit, [10]to another miraculous powers, to another prophecy, to another distinguishing between spirits, to another speaking in different kinds of tongues,[a] and to still another the interpretation of tongues.[a] [11]All these are the work of one and the same Spirit, and he gives them to each one, just as he determines.

One Body, Many Parts

[12]The body is a unit, though it is made up of many parts; and though all its parts are many, they form one body. So it is with Christ. [13]For we were all baptised by[b] one Spirit into one body—whether Jews or Greeks, slave or free—and we were all given the one Spirit to drink.

[14]Now the body is not made up of one part but of many. [15]If the foot should say, "Because I am not a hand, I do not belong to the body," it would not for that reason cease to be part of the body. [16]And if the ear should say, "Because I am not an eye, I do not belong to the body," it would not for that reason cease to be part of the body. [17]If the whole body were an eye, where would the sense of hearing be? If the whole body were an ear, where would the sense of smell be? [18]But in fact God has arranged the parts in the body, every one of them, just as he wanted them to be. [19]If

---

[b] 4–7 Or [4]Every man who prays or prophesies with long hair dishonours his head. [5]And every woman who prays or prophesies with no covering of hair on her head dishonours her head—she is just like one of the "shorn women". [6]If a woman has no covering, let her be for now with short hair, but since it is a disgrace for a woman to have her hair shorn or shaved, she should grow it again. [7]A man ought not to have long hair   [a] 10 Or languages; also in verse 28   [b] 13 Or with; or in

they were all one part, where would the body be? 20As it is, there are many parts, but one body. 21The eye cannot say to the hand, "I don't need you!" And the head cannot say to the feet, "I don't need you!" 22On the contrary, those parts of the body that seem to be weaker are indispensable, 23and the parts that we think are less honourable we treat with special honour. And the parts that are unpresentable are treated with special modesty, 24while our presentable parts need no special treatment. But God has combined the members of the body and has given greater honour to the parts that lacked it, 25so that there should be no division in the body, but that its parts should have equal concern for each other. 26If one part suffers, every part suffers with it; if one part is honoured, every part rejoices with it.

27Now you are the body of Christ, and each one of you is a part of it. 28And in the church God has appointed first of all apostles, second prophets, third teachers, then workers of miracles, also those having gifts of healing, those able to help others, those with gifts of administration, and those speaking in different kinds of tongues. 29Are all apostles? Are all prophets? Are all teachers? Do all work miracles? 30Do all have gifts of healing? Do all speak in tongues?c Do all interpret? 31But eagerly desired the greater gifts.

12:28 The list of gifts the Spirit gives is not intended to be an exhaustive one, although it is clear from the way Paul wrote that apostles, prophets, and teachers were seen as the most important ministries. In different times and places the Spirit may give different gifts to people within the church: Paul's overall point was that all the different gifts are needed to make up the work of the church, and therefore people should honour one another's gifts.

Love

And now I will show you the most excellent way. 13 If I speak in the tonguesa of men and of angels, but have not love, I am only a resounding gong or a clanging cymbal. 2If I have the gift of prophecy and can fathom all mysteries and all knowledge, and if I have a faith that can move mountains, but have not love, I am nothing. 3If I give all I possess to the poor and surrender my body to the flames,b but have not love, I gain nothing.

4Love is patient, love is kind. It does not envy, it does not boast, it is not proud. 5It is not rude, it is not self-seeking, it is not easily angered, it keeps no record of wrongs. 6Love does not delight in evil but rejoices with the truth. 7It always protects, always trusts, always hopes, always perseveres.

8Love never fails. But where there are prophecies, they will cease; where there are tongues, they will be stilled; where there is knowledge, it will pass away. 9For we know in part and we prophesy in part, 10but when perfection comes, the imperfect disappears. 11When I was a child, I talked like a child, I thought like a child, I reasoned like a child. When I became a man, I put childish ways behind me. 12Now we see but a poor reflection as in a mirror; then we shall see face to face. Now I know in part; then I shall know fully, even as I am fully known.

13And now these three remain: faith, hope and love. But the greatest of these is love.

Gifts of Prophecy and Tongues

14 Follow the way of love and eagerly desire spiritual gifts, especially the gift of prophecy. 2For anyone who speaks in a tonguea does not speak to men but to God. Indeed, no-one understands him; he utters mysteries with his spirit.b 3But everyone who prophesies speaks to men for their strengthening, encouragement and comfort. 4He who speaks in a tongue edifies himself, but he who prophesies edifies the church. 5I would like every one of you to speak in tongues,c but I would rather have you prophesy. He who prophesies is greater than one who speaks in tongues,c unless he interprets, so that the church may be edified.

14:1 The gift of tongues (speaking or praying in a language not known to humans) was evidently highly honoured in Corinth. While not forbidding it, Paul made it clear that the gift of prophecy is more important. Prophecy in the New Testament was the gift of declaring the mind and will of God for those who heard it, and not, as we might imagine, looking into the future. Thus contemporary preaching can fulfil a prophetic role.

6Now, brothers, if I come to you and speak in tongues, what good will I be to you, unless I bring you some revelation or knowledge or prophecy or word of instruction? 7Even in the case of lifeless things that make sounds, such as the flute or harp, how will anyone know what tune is being played unless there is a distinction in the notes? 8Again, if the trumpet does not sound a clear call, who will get ready for battle? 9So it is with you. Unless you speak intelligible words with your tongue, how will anyone know what you are saying? You will just be speaking into the air. 10Undoubtedly there are all sorts of languages in the world, yet none of them is without meaning. 11If then I do not grasp the meaning of what someone is saying, I am a foreigner to the speaker, and he is a foreigner to me. 12So it is with you. Since you are eager to have spiritual gifts, try to excel in gifts that build up the church.

13For this reason anyone who speaks in a tongue should pray that he may interpret what he says. 14For

c30 Or other languages   d31 Or But you are eagerly desiring   a1 Or languages
b3 Some early manuscripts body that I may boast   a2 Or another language; also in verses 4, 13, 14, 19, 26 and 27
b2 Or by the Spirit   c5 Or other languages; also in verses 6, 18, 22, 23 and 39

if I pray in a tongue, my spirit prays, but my mind is unfruitful. [15]So what shall I do? I will pray with my spirit, but I will also pray with my mind; I will sing with my spirit, but I will also sing with my mind. [16]If you are praising God with your spirit, how can one who finds himself among those who do not understand[d] say "Amen" to your thanksgiving, since he does not know what you are saying? [17]You may be giving thanks well enough, but the other man is not edified.

[18]I thank God that I speak in tongues more than all of you. [19]But in the church I would rather speak five intelligible words to instruct others than ten thousand words in a tongue.

[20]Brothers, stop thinking like children. In regard to evil be infants, but in your thinking be adults. [21]In the Law it is written:

"Through men of strange tongues
    and through the lips of foreigners
I will speak to this people,
    but even then they will not listen to me,"[e]
says the Lord.

[22]Tongues, then, are a sign, not for believers but for unbelievers; prophecy, however, is for believers, not for unbelievers. [23]So if the whole church comes together and everyone speaks in tongues, and some who do not understand[f] or some unbelievers come in, will they not say that you are out of your mind? [24]But if an unbeliever or someone who does not understand[g] comes in while everybody is prophesying, he will be convinced by all that he is a sinner and will be judged by all, [25]and the secrets of his heart will be laid bare. So he will fall down and worship God, exclaiming, "God is really among you!"

Orderly Worship

[26]What then shall we say, brothers? When you come together, everyone has a hymn, or a word of instruction, a revelation, a tongue or an interpretation. All of these must be done for the strengthening of the church. [27]If anyone speaks in a tongue, two — or at the most three — should speak, one at a time, and someone must interpret. [28]If there is no interpreter, the speaker should keep quiet in the church and speak to himself and God.

[29]Two or three prophets should speak, and the others should weigh carefully what is said. [30]And if a revelation comes to someone who is sitting down, the first speaker should stop. [31]For you can all prophesy in turn so that everyone may be instructed and encouraged. [32]The spirits of prophets are subject to the control of prophets. [33]For God is not a God of disorder but of peace.

As in all the congregations of the saints, [34]women should remain silent in the churches. They are not allowed to speak, but must be in submission, as the Law says. [35]If they want to enquire about something, they should ask their own husbands at home; for it is disgraceful for a woman to speak in the church.

[36]Did the word of God originate with you? Or are you the only people it has reached? [37]If anybody thinks he is a prophet or spiritually gifted, let him acknowledge that what I am writing to you is the Lord's command. [38]If he ignores this, he himself will be ignored.[h]

[39]Therefore, my brothers, be eager to prophesy, and do not forbid speaking in tongues. [40]But everything should be done in a fitting and orderly way.

The Resurrection of Christ

15 Now, brothers, I want to remind you of the gospel I preached to you, which you received and on which you have taken your stand. [2]By this gospel you are saved, if you hold firmly to the word I preached to you. Otherwise, you have believed in vain.

[3]For what I received I passed on to you as of first importance:[a] that Christ died for our sins according to the Scriptures, [4]that he was buried, that he was raised on the third day according to the Scriptures, [5]and that he appeared to Peter,[b] and then to the Twelve. [6]After that, he appeared to more than five hundred of the brothers at the same time, most of whom are still living, though some have fallen asleep. [7]Then he appeared to James, then to all the apostles, [8]and last of all he appeared to me also, as to one abnormally born.

[9]For I am the least of the apostles and do not even deserve to be called an apostle, because I persecuted the church of God. [10]But by the grace of God I am what I am, and his grace to me was not without effect. No, I worked harder than all of them — yet not I, but the grace of God that was with me. [11]Whether, then, it was I or they, this is what we preach, and this is what you believed.

The Resurrection of the Dead

[12]But if it is preached that Christ has been raised from the dead, how can some of you say that there is no resurrection of the dead? [13]If there is no resurrection of the dead, then not even Christ has been raised. [14]And if Christ has not been raised, our preaching is useless and so is your faith. [15]More than that, we are then found to be false witnesses about God, for we have testified about God that he raised Christ from the dead. But he did not raise him if in fact the dead are not raised. [16]For if the dead are not raised, then Christ has not been raised either. [17]And if Christ has not been raised, your faith is futile; you are still in your sins. [18]Then those also who have fallen asleep in Christ are lost. [19]If only for this life we have hope in Christ, we are to be pitied more than all men.

[20]But Christ has indeed been raised from the dead, the firstfruits of those who have fallen asleep. [21]For since death came through a man, the resurrection of the dead comes also through a man. [22]For as in Adam all die, so in Christ all will be made alive. [23]But each in his own turn: Christ, the firstfruits; then, when he comes, those who belong to him. [24]Then the end will come, when he hands over the kingdom to God the Father after he has destroyed all dominion, authority and power. [25]For he must reign until he has put all his

---

d16 Or *among the enquirers*   *e21* Isaiah 28:11,12   *f23* Or *some enquirers*   *g24* Or *or some enquirer*
h38 Some manuscripts *If he is ignorant of this, let him be ignorant*   *a3* Or *you at the first*   *b5* Greek *Cephas*

enemies under his feet. [26]The last enemy to be destroyed is death. [27]For he "has put everything under his feet".[c] Now when it says that "everything" has been put under him, it is clear that this does not include God himself, who put everything under Christ. [28]When he has done this, then the Son himself will be made subject to him who put everything under him, so that God may be all in all.

[29]Now if there is no resurrection, what will those do who are baptised for the dead? If the dead are not raised at all, why are people baptised for them? [30]And as for us, why do we endanger ourselves every hour? [31]I die every day—I mean that, brothers—just as surely as I glory over you in Christ Jesus our Lord. [32]If I fought wild beasts in Ephesus for merely human reasons, what have I gained? If the dead are not raised,

"Let us eat and drink,
for tomorrow we die."[d]

[33]Do not be misled: "Bad company corrupts good character." [34]Come back to your senses as you ought, and stop sinning; for there are some who are ignorant of God—I say this to your shame.

The Resurrection Body

[35]But someone may ask, "How are the dead raised? With what kind of body will they come?" [36]How foolish! What you sow does not come to life unless it dies. [37]When you sow, you do not plant the body that will be, but just a seed, perhaps of wheat or of something else. [38]But God gives it a body as he has determined, and to each kind of seed he gives its own body. [39]All flesh is not the same: Men have one kind of flesh, animals have another, birds another and fish another. [40]There are also heavenly bodies and there are earthly bodies; but the splendour of the heavenly bodies is one kind, and the splendour of the earthly bodies is another. [41]The sun has one kind of splendour, the moon another and the stars another; and star differs from star in splendour.

[42]So will it be with the resurrection of the dead. The body that is sown is perishable, it is raised imperishable; [43]it is sown in dishonour, it is raised in glory; it is sown in weakness, it is raised in power; [44]it is sown a natural body, it is raised a spiritual body.

15:44 Some people find the idea of a future resurrection unbelievable because, they say, bodies perish after they have been buried. Paul used the analogy of the seed that is sown and the plant that springs up from it to explain how the resurrection can be understood. It is the person we are which will be raised, and the body will not be a physical but a spiritual one.

If there is a natural body, there is also a spiritual body. [45]So it is written: "The first man Adam became a living being";[e] the last Adam, a life-giving spirit.

[46]The spiritual did not come first, but the natural, and after that the spiritual. [47]The first man was of the dust of the earth, the second man from heaven. [48]As was the earthly man, so are those who are of the earth; and as is the man from heaven, so also are those who are of heaven. [49]And just as we have borne the likeness of the earthly man, so shall we[f] bear the likeness of the man from heaven.

[50]I declare to you, brothers, that flesh and blood cannot inherit the kingdom of God, nor does the perishable inherit the imperishable. [51]Listen, I tell you a mystery: We will not all sleep, but we will all be changed— [52]in a flash, in the twinkling of an eye, at the last trumpet. For the trumpet will sound, the dead will be raised imperishable, and we will be changed. [53]For the perishable must clothe itself with the imperishable, and the mortal with immortality. [54]When the perishable has been clothed with the imperishable, and the mortal with immortality, then the saying that is written will come true: "Death has been swallowed up in victory."[g]

[55]"Where, O death, is your victory?
Where, O death, is your sting?"[h]

[56]The sting of death is sin, and the power of sin is the law. [57]But thanks be to God! He gives us the victory through our Lord Jesus Christ.

[58]Therefore, my dear brothers, stand firm. Let nothing move you. Always give yourselves fully to the work of the Lord, because you know that your labour in the Lord is not in vain.

The Collection for God's People

16 Now about the collection for God's people: Do what I told the Galatian churches to do. [2]On the first day of every week, each one of you should set aside a sum of money in keeping with his income, saving it up, so that when I come no collections will have to be made. [3]Then, when I arrive, I will give letters of introduction to the men you approve and send them with your gift to Jerusalem. [4]If it seems advisable for me to go also, they will accompany me.

Personal Requests

[5]After I go through Macedonia, I will come to you—for I will be going through Macedonia. [6]Perhaps I will stay with you awhile, or even spend the winter, so that you can help me on my journey, wherever I go. [7]I do not want to see you now and make only a passing visit; I hope to spend some time with you, if the Lord permits. [8]But I will stay on at Ephesus until Pentecost, [9]because a great door for effective work has opened to me, and there are many who oppose me.

[10]If Timothy comes, see to it that he has nothing to fear while he is with you, for he is carrying on the work of the Lord, just as I am. [11]No-one, then, should refuse to accept him. Send him on his way in peace so that

c27 Psalm 8:6   d32 Isaiah 22:13   e45 Gen. 2:7   f49 Some early manuscripts so let us
g54 Isaiah 25:8   h55 Hosea 13:14

he may return to me. I am expecting him along with the brothers.

12Now about our brother Apollos: I strongly urged him to go to you with the brothers. He was quite unwilling to go now, but he will go when he has the opportunity.

13Be on your guard; stand firm in the faith; be men of courage; be strong. 14Do everything in love.

15You know that the household of Stephanas were the first converts in Achaia, and they have devoted themselves to the service of the saints. I urge you, brothers, 16to submit to such as these and to everyone who joins in the work, and labours at it. 17I was glad when Stephanas, Fortunatus and Achaicus arrived, because they have supplied what was lacking from you.

18For they refreshed my spirit and yours also. Such men deserve recognition.

Final Greetings

19The churches in the province of Asia send you greetings. Aquila and Priscilla[a] greet you warmly in the Lord, and so does the church that meets at their house. 20All the brothers here send you greetings. Greet one another with a holy kiss.

21I, Paul, write this greeting in my own hand.

22If anyone does not love the Lord—a curse be on him. Come, O Lord![b]

23The grace of the Lord Jesus be with you.

24My love to all of you in Christ Jesus. Amen.[c]

a19 Greek Prisca, a variant of Priscilla   b22 In Aramaic the expression Come, O Lord is Marana tha.
c24 Some manuscripts do not have Amen.

2 Corinthians

Dealing With Painful Questions

Paul wrote his first letter to the Corinthians to deal with a crisis which had taken place and to offer some advice in response to questions they had asked him. However, that was not the end of the story. Further trouble then occurred in the church at Corinth. We do not know the exact nature of this, but it seems likely that Christians came from elsewhere and taught the Corinthians to despise Paul because they saw him as weak and suffering. Paul therefore paid a personal visit to them which he described as "painful" (2 Corinthians 2:1). His purpose was a direct confrontation with those church leaders who were defying his authority. Unfortunately the visit was not a success and on his return he sent a very strong letter in which he defended his life and work in vigorous terms (see 2 Corinthians 2:4). This letter may well be what we now know as 2 Corinthians 10–13, although some students of the Bible believe that, like Paul's first letter to Corinth, that letter is now lost. However it seems to have had the desired effect and Paul's correspondence with this troublesome church closed on a much happier note with a letter which we know as 2 Corinthians chapters 1–9. If, therefore, we want to read what Paul wrote in the order in which he wrote it, we probably ought to read chapters 10–13 first, and then begin on chapters 1–9! The abrupt change of mood and style between the two sections is quite startling.

A Question of Understanding

It is understandable that much of the content of this letter is concerned with Paul's own authority as an apostle, given the challenges to that authority in Corinth. We should not think that it has no relevance for the rest of us. Quite the contrary; in the course of his writing Paul touched on many things which concern the essential nature of the Christian faith and which, in somewhat different forms, still trouble the church today.

Themes of the Letter

Paul's defence of his authority as an apostle, commissioned to preach by the risen Jesus himself, is a major theme of the letter, and so we ought to note the concern which lies behind this defence. Sometimes when we are personally attacked or criticized for what we have done, or not done, we react very badly. In such a case we respond out of a feeling of personal hurt. Paul's writing leaves us in no doubt that he did feel very hurt by some of the things which had been said and done, but his underlying motive for responding as he did lay much deeper.

A Caring Ministry

Paul had a true pastor's heart. He felt deeply for the needs of his converts (11:29). After all, it was he who had first brought the gospel to Corinth, and he regarded the Corinthians as his spiritual children, even if they were rebellious and difficult. He wanted the best for them, and it grieved him to see them continuing to live immoral lives and dividing the church into factions. Above all he was conscious that God had given him a special commission to preach the good news about Jesus well beyond the boundaries of Palestine (10:13). That commission gave him authority to build up the life of the church and encourage it to be spiritually healthy (10:8). This in turn involved opposing those who would lead the church astray.

A Divine Commission

Including among those were some who called themselves "super apostles", but whose understanding of the Christian faith was clearly quite different from that which Paul had taught (11:4–5). Since Paul's preaching, unimpressive though it may have been in human terms, was at the command of the risen Lord, he had no option but to try and convince the Corinthians of the error of these "super apostles". He therefore gave the Corinthians an impressive list of his credentials as a preacher, things he had endured for Christ (11:21–28). Indeed, he went further. If these "super apostles" lay claim to have had special revelations from the Lord, he could claim them too, even though he would rather not have to have done so (12:1–6). Far from his personal weakness being a sign that he was not a real apostle, it was really a sign that strength comes from God alone (12:9–10). However, even if others regarded him as a weak and unimpressive person, Paul was conscious that the Lord he served now lived by God's power (13:4). If he needed to exercise the authority Christ had given him, he would do so (13:2).

Jesus as Lord

The success of his heartfelt appeal meant that when Paul sent the Corinthians his final letter he could consider these earlier matters much more calmly. He wrote about ministry, and he even described the Corinthians as a recommendation to others of his own ministry (3:1–3). What is the church's ministry all about? It is to preach "Jesus Christ as Lord, and ourselves as your servants for Jesus' sake" (4:5), and to appeal for people to be reconciled to God (5:20). Of course, Christians have their weaknesses and frailties because they are human, but that only makes plainer that the truth of the gospel comes not from them but from God himself (4:7). Christians ought not to stand on their spiritual dignity too much. Those in the church at Corinth who had been so difficult had been given the grace to repent, and Paul wrote movingly of the joy this restoration of mutual confidence gave to him.

Practical Action

For some years Paul had been organizing a collection amongst his converts. The purpose of this was to help the church in Jerusalem which had fallen on hard times. The Corinthians had already contributed to this (8:10), but Paul was anxious to encourage them to do more (8:11). In the process he set out principles of Christian giving which still make sense today. Christians should give to God's work cheerfully, in proportion to what they can afford, knowing that God will supply all their needs (9:6–11). Paul wrote to a church which had caused him so much heartache and distress in a very practical manner. It had all been worthwhile, because the generosity of the Corinthians would be clear proof of the wonderful grace that God had given to them (9:14). Perhaps above all, 2 Corinthians teaches us that when relationships between Christians become difficult, as they sometimes do, people should never give up on each other, but must instead work for the time when they shall be able to see God's grace in each other.

---

1 Paul, an apostle of Christ Jesus by the will of God, and Timothy our brother,

To the church of God in Corinth, together with all the saints throughout Achaia:

²Grace and peace to you from God our Father and the Lord Jesus Christ.

The God of All Comfort

³Praise be to the God and Father of our Lord Jesus Christ, the Father of compassion and the God of all comfort, ⁴who comforts us in all our troubles, so that we can comfort those in any trouble with the comfort we ourselves have received from God. ⁵For just as the sufferings of Christ flow over into our lives, so also through Christ our comfort overflows. ⁶If we are distressed, it is for your comfort and salvation; if we are comforted, it is for your comfort, which produces in you patient endurance of the same sufferings we suffer. ⁷And our hope for you is firm, because we know that just as you share in our sufferings, so also you share in our comfort.

⁸We do not want you to be uninformed, brothers, about the hardships we suffered in the province of Asia. We were under great pressure, far beyond our ability to endure, so that we despaired even of life.

⁹Indeed, in our hearts we felt the sentence of death. But this happened that we might not rely on ourselves but on God, who raises the dead. ¹⁰He has delivered us from such a deadly peril, and he will deliver us. On him we have set our hope that he will continue to deliver us, ¹¹as you help us by your prayers. Then many will give thanks on our[a] behalf for the gracious favour granted us in answer to the prayers of many.

1:8 We do not know what these hardships were; perhaps illness, or the work of enemies of the gospel. What matters is that although Paul said that it was beyond his ability to endure them, he testified to God's deliverance and, as he looked back on the experience, was encouraged to have hope for the future.

Paul's Change of Plans

¹²Now this is our boast: Our conscience testifies that we have conducted ourselves in the world, and especially in our relations with you, in the holiness and sincerity that are from God. We have done so not according to worldly wisdom but according to God's grace. ¹³For we do not write to you anything you

---

cannot read or understand. And I hope that, [14]as you have understood us in part, you will come to understand fully that you can boast of us just as we will boast of you in the day of the Lord Jesus.

[15]Because I was confident of this, I planned to visit you first so that you might benefit twice. [16]I planned to visit you on my way to Macedonia and to come back to you from Macedonia, and then to have you send me on my way to Judea. [17]When I planned this, did I do it lightly? Or do I make my plans in a worldly manner so that in the same breath I say, "Yes, yes" and "No, no"?

[18]But as surely as God is faithful, our message to you is not "Yes" and "No". [19]For the Son of God, Jesus Christ, who was preached among you by me and Silas[b] and Timothy, was not "Yes" and "No", but in him it has always been "Yes." [20]For no matter how many promises God has made, they are "Yes" in Christ. And so through him the "Amen" is spoken by us to the glory of God. [21]Now it is God who makes both us and you stand firm in Christ. He anointed us, [22]set his seal of ownership on us, and put his Spirit in our hearts as a deposit, guaranteeing what is to come.

[23]I call God as my witness that it was in order to spare you that I did not return to Corinth. [24]Not that we lord it over your faith, but we work with you for your joy, because it is by faith you stand firm. 2 [1]So I made up my mind that I would not make another painful visit to you. [2]For if I grieve you, who is left to make me glad but you whom I have grieved? [3]I wrote as I did so that when I came I should not be distressed by those who ought to make me rejoice. I had confidence in all of you, that you would all share my joy. [4]For I wrote to you out of great distress and anguish of heart and with many tears, not to grieve you but to let you know the depth of my love for you.

Forgiveness for the Sinner

[5]If anyone has caused grief, he has not so much grieved me as he has grieved all of you, to some extent—not to put it too severely. [6]The punishment inflicted on him by the majority is sufficient for him. [7]Now instead, you ought to forgive and comfort him, so that he will not be overwhelmed by excessive sorrow. [8]I urge you, therefore, to reaffirm your love for him. [9]The reason I wrote to you was to see if you would stand the test and be obedient in everything. [10]If you forgive anyone, I also forgive him. And what I have forgiven—if there was anything to forgive—I have forgiven in the sight of Christ for your sake, [11]in order that Satan might not outwit us. For we are not unaware of his schemes.

Ministers of the New Covenant

[12]Now when I went to Troas to preach the gospel of Christ and found that the Lord had opened a door for me, [13]I still had no peace of mind, because I did not find my brother Titus there. So I said good-bye to them and went on to Macedonia.

[14]But thanks be to God, who always leads us in triumphal procession in Christ and through us spreads everywhere the fragrance of the knowledge of him. [15]For we are to God the aroma of Christ among those who are being saved and those who are perishing. [16]To the one we are the smell of death; to the other, the fragrance of life. And who is equal to such a task? [17]Unlike so many, we do not peddle the word of God for profit. On the contrary, in Christ we speak before God with sincerity, like men sent from God.

3 [1]Are we beginning to commend ourselves again? Or do we need, like some people, letters of recommendation to you or from you? [2]You yourselves are our letter, written on our hearts, known and read by everybody. [3]You show that you are a letter from Christ, the result of our ministry, written not with ink but with the Spirit of the living God, not on tablets of stone but on tablets of human hearts.

[4]Such confidence as this is ours through Christ before God. [5]Not that we are competent in ourselves to claim anything for ourselves, but our competence comes from God. [6]He has made us competent as ministers of a new covenant—not of the letter but of the Spirit; for the letter kills, but the Spirit gives life.

3:6   This is the contrast between Paul's former religion of Judaism and his Christian faith. The letter (the written code of conduct) led to death because it demanded moral perfection but did not provide the power to achieve it, and the Spirit of life set him free from the law of sin and death (see Romans 8:2).

The Glory of the New Covenant

[7]Now if the ministry that brought death, which was engraved in letters on stone, came with glory, so that the Israelites could not look steadily at the face of Moses because of its glory, fading though it was, [8]will not the ministry of the Spirit be even more glorious? [9]If the ministry that condemns men is glorious, how much more glorious is the ministry that brings righteousness! [10]For what was glorious has no glory now in comparison with the surpassing glory. [11]And if what was fading away came with glory, how much greater is the glory of that which lasts!

[12]Therefore, since we have such a hope, we are very bold. [13]We are not like Moses, who would put a veil over his face to keep the Israelites from gazing at it while the radiance was fading away. [14]But their minds were made dull, for to this day the same veil remains when the old covenant is read. It has not been removed, because only in Christ is it taken away. [15]Even to this day when Moses is read, a veil covers their hearts. [16]But whenever anyone turns to the Lord, the veil is taken away. [17]Now the Lord is the Spirit, and where the Spirit of the Lord is, there is freedom. [18]And we, who with unveiled faces all reflect[a] the Lord's glory, are being transformed into his likeness with ever-increasing glory, which comes from the Lord, who is the Spirit.

---

[b]19 Greek *Silvanus*, a variant of *Silas*   [a]18 Or *contemplate*

Treasures in Jars of Clay

4 Therefore, since through God's mercy we have this ministry, we do not lose heart. [2]Rather, we have renounced secret and shameful ways; we do not use deception, nor do we distort the word of God. On the contrary, by setting forth the truth plainly we commend ourselves to every man's conscience in the sight of God. [3]And even if our gospel is veiled, it is veiled to those who are perishing. [4]The god of this age has blinded the minds of unbelievers, so that they cannot see the light of the gospel of the glory of Christ, who is the image of God. [5]For we do not preach ourselves, but Jesus Christ as Lord, and ourselves as your servants for Jesus' sake. [6]For God, who said, "Let light shine out of darkness," [a] made his light shine in our hearts to give us the light of the knowledge of the glory of God in the face of Christ.

[7]But we have this treasure in jars of clay to show that this all-surpassing power is from God and not from us. [8]We are hard pressed on every side, but not crushed; perplexed, but not in despair; [9]persecuted, but not abandoned; struck down, but not destroyed. [10]We always carry around in our body the death of Jesus, so that the life of Jesus may also be revealed in our body. [11]For we who are alive are always being given over to death for Jesus' sake, so that his life may be revealed in our mortal body. [12]So then, death is at work in us, but life is at work in you.

[13]It is written: "I believed; therefore I have spoken." [b] With that same spirit of faith we also believe and therefore speak, [14]because we know that the one who raised the Lord Jesus from the dead will also raise us with Jesus and present us with you in his presence. [15]All this is for your benefit, so that the grace that is reaching more and more people may cause thanksgiving to overflow to the glory of God.

[16]Therefore we do not lose heart. Though outwardly we are wasting away, yet inwardly we are being renewed day by day. [17]For our light and momentary troubles are achieving for us an eternal glory that far outweighs them all. [18]So we fix our eyes not on what is seen, but on what is unseen. For what is seen is temporary, but what is unseen is eternal.

Our Heavenly Dwelling

5 Now we know that if the earthly tent we live in is destroyed, we have a building from God, an eternal house in heaven, not built by human hands. [2]Meanwhile we groan, longing to be clothed with our heavenly dwelling, [3]because when we are clothed, we will not be found naked. [4]For while we are in this tent, we groan and are burdened, because we do not wish to be unclothed but to be clothed with our heavenly dwelling, so that what is mortal may be swallowed up by life. [5]Now it is God who has made us for this very purpose and has given us the Spirit as a deposit, guaranteeing what is to come.

[6]Therefore we are always confident and know that as long as we are at home in the body we are away from the Lord. [7]We live by faith, not by sight. [8]We are confident, I say, and would prefer to be away from the body and at home with the Lord. [9]So we make it our goal to please him, whether we are at home in the body or away from it. [10]For we must all appear before the judgment seat of Christ, that each one may receive what is due to him for the things done while in the body, whether good or bad.

5:5   Paul saw the Holy Spirit as a pledge, or guarantee ("down payment" would translate Paul's Greek word very well), of the eternal life which is to come.

The Ministry of Reconciliation

[11]Since, then, we know what it is to fear the Lord, we try to persuade men. What we are is plain to God, and I hope it is also plain to your conscience. [12]We are not trying to commend ourselves to you again, but are giving you an opportunity to take pride in us, so that you can answer those who take pride in what is seen rather than in what is in the heart. [13]If we are out of our mind, it is for the sake of God; if we are in our right mind, it is for you. [14]For Christ's love compels us, because we are convinced that one died for all, and therefore all died. [15]And he died for all, that those who live should no longer live for themselves but for him who died for them and was raised again.

[16]So from now on we regard no-one from a worldly point of view. Though we once regarded Christ in this way, we do so no longer. [17]Therefore, if anyone is in Christ, he is a new creation; the old has gone, the new has come! [18]All this is from God, who reconciled us to himself through Christ and gave us the ministry of reconciliation: [19]that God was reconciling the world to himself in Christ, not counting men's sins against them. And he has committed to us the message of reconciliation. [20]We are therefore Christ's ambassadors, as though God were making his appeal through us. We implore you on Christ's behalf: Be reconciled to God. [21]God made him who had no sin to be sin [a] for us, so that in him we might become the righteousness of God.

6 As God's fellow-workers we urge you not to receive God's grace in vain. [2]For he says,

"In the time of my favour I heard you,
    and in the day of salvation I helped you." [a]

I tell you, now is the time of God's favour, now is the day of salvation.

Paul's Hardships

[3]We put no stumbling-block in anyone's path, so that our ministry will not be discredited. [4]Rather, as servants of God we commend ourselves in every way: in great endurance; in troubles, hardships and distresses; [5]in beatings, imprisonments and riots; in hard work, sleepless nights and hunger; [6]in purity, understanding, patience and kindness; in the Holy Spirit and in sincere love; [7]in truthful speech and in the power of God; with weapons of righteousness in the right

---

a6 Gen. 1:3   *b13* Psalm 116:10   *a21* Or *be a sin offering*   *a2* Isaiah 49:8

hand and in the left; [8]through glory and dishonour, bad report and good report; genuine, yet regarded as impostors; [9]known, yet regarded as unknown; dying, and yet we live on; beaten, and yet not killed; [10]sorrowful, yet always rejoicing; poor, yet making many rich; having nothing, and yet possessing everything.

[11]We have spoken freely to you, Corinthians, and opened wide our hearts to you. [12]We are not withholding our affection from you, but you are withholding yours from us. [13]As a fair exchange—I speak as to my children—open wide your hearts also.

Do Not Be Yoked With Unbelievers

[14]Do not be yoked together with unbelievers. For what do righteousness and wickedness have in common? Or what fellowship can light have with darkness? [15]What harmony is there between Christ and Belial?[b] What does a believer have in common with an unbeliever? [16]What agreement is there between the temple of God and idols? For we are the temple of the living God. As God has said: "I will live with them and walk among them, and I will be their God, and they will be my people."[c]

[17]"Therefore come out from them
  and be separate,
                              says the Lord.
Touch no unclean thing,
  and I will receive you."[d]
[18]"I will be a Father to you,
  and you will be my sons and daughters,
                        says the Lord Almighty."[e]

7 Since we have these promises, dear friends, let us purify ourselves from everything that contaminates body and spirit, perfecting holiness out of reverence for God.

Paul's Joy

[2]Make room for us in your hearts. We have wronged no-one, we have corrupted no-one, we have exploited no-one. [3]I do not say this to condemn you; I have said before that you have such a place in our hearts that we would live or die with you. [4]I have great confidence in you; I take great pride in you. I am greatly encouraged; in all our troubles my joy knows no bounds.

[5]For when we came into Macedonia, this body of ours had no rest, but we were harassed at every turn—conflicts on the outside, fears within. [6]But God, who comforts the downcast, comforted us by the coming of Titus, [7]and not only by his coming but also by the comfort you had given him. He told us about your longing for me, your deep sorrow, your ardent concern for me, so that my joy was greater than ever.

[8]Even if I caused you sorrow by my letter, I do not regret it. Though I did regret it—I see that my letter hurt you, but only for a little while—[9]yet now I am happy, not because you were made sorry, but because your sorrow led you to repentance. For you became sorrowful as God intended and so were not harmed in any way by us. [10]Godly sorrow brings repentance that leads to salvation and leaves no regret, but worldly sorrow brings death. [11]See what this godly sorrow has produced in you: what earnestness, what eagerness to clear yourselves, what indignation, what alarm, what longing, what concern, what readiness to see justice done. At every point you have proved yourselves to be innocent in this matter. [12]So even though I wrote to you, it was not on account of the one who did the wrong or of the injured party, but rather that before God you could see for yourselves how devoted to us you are. [13]By all this we are encouraged.

In addition to our own encouragement, we were especially delighted to see how happy Titus was, because his spirit has been refreshed by all of you. [14]I had boasted to him about you, and you have not embarrassed me. But just as everything we said to you was true, so our boasting about you to Titus has proved to be true as well. [15]And his affection for you is all the greater when he remembers that you were all obedient, receiving him with fear and trembling. [16]I am glad I can have complete confidence in you.

Generosity Encouraged

8 And now, brothers, we want you to know about the grace that God has given the Macedonian churches. [2]Out of the most severe trial, their overflowing joy and their extreme poverty welled up in rich generosity. [3]For I testify that they gave as much as they were able, and even beyond their ability. Entirely on their own, [4]they urgently pleaded with us for the privilege of sharing in this service to the saints. [5]And they did not do as we expected, but they gave themselves first to the Lord and then to us in keeping with God's will. [6]So we urged Titus, since he had earlier made a beginning, to bring also to completion this act of grace on your part. [7]But just as you excel in everything—in faith, in speech, in knowledge, in complete earnestness and in your love for us[a]—see that you also excel in this grace of giving.

[8]I am not commanding you, but I want to test the sincerity of your love by comparing it with the earnestness of others. [9]For you know the grace of our Lord Jesus Christ, that though he was rich, yet for your sakes he became poor, so that you through his poverty might become rich.

8:9   Paul explained the incarnation of Christ as the supreme example of generosity. He expanded on this thought in Philippians 2:6–7 where he wrote about how Christ "made himself nothing" for people.

---

[10]And here is my advice about what is best for you in this matter: Last year you were the first not only to give but also to have the desire to do so. [11]Now finish the work, so that your eager willingness to do it may be matched by your completion of it, according to your means. [12]For if the willingness is there, the gift is

---

[b]15 Greek *Beliar*, a variant of *Belial*   [c]16 Lev. 26:12; Jer. 32:38; Ezek. 37:27   [d]17 Isaiah 52:11; Ezek. 20:34,41
[e]18 2 Samuel 7:14; 7:8   [a]7 Some manuscripts *in our love for you*

acceptable according to what one has, not according to what he does not have.

13Our desire is not that others might be relieved while you are hard pressed, but that there might be equality. 14At the present time your plenty will supply what they need, so that in turn their plenty will supply what you need. Then there will be equality, 15as it is written: "He who gathered much did not have too much, and he who gathered little did not have too little."b

Titus Sent to Corinth

16I thank God, who put into the heart of Titus the same concern I have for you. 17For Titus not only welcomed our appeal, but he is coming to you with much enthusiasm and on his own initiative. 18And we are sending along with him the brother who is praised by all the churches for his service to the gospel. 19What is more, he was chosen by the churches to accompany us as we carry the offering, which we administer in order to honour the Lord himself and to show our eagerness to help. 20We want to avoid any criticism of the way we administer this liberal gift. 21For we are taking pains to do what is right, not only in the eyes of the Lord but also in the eyes of men.

22In addition, we are sending with them our brother who has often proved to us in many ways that he is zealous, and now even more so because of his great confidence in you. 23As for Titus, he is my partner and fellow-worker among you; as for our brothers, they are representatives of the churches and an honour to Christ. 24Therefore show these men the proof of your love and the reason for our pride in you, so that the churches can see it.

9 There is no need for me to write to you about this service to the saints. 2For I know your eagerness to help, and I have been boasting about it to the Macedonians, telling them that since last year you in Achaia were ready to give; and your enthusiasm has stirred most of them to action. 3But I am sending the brothers in order that our boasting about you in this matter should not prove hollow, but that you may be ready, as I said you would be. 4For if any Macedonians come with me and find you unprepared, we—not to say anything about you—would be ashamed of having been so confident. 5So I thought it necessary to urge the brothers to visit you in advance and finish the arrangements for the generous gift you had promised. Then it will be ready as a generous gift, not as one grudgingly given.

Sowing Generously

6Remember this: Whoever sows sparingly will also reap sparingly, and whoever sows generously will also reap generously. 7Each man should give what he has decided in his heart to give, not reluctantly or under compulsion, for God loves a cheerful giver. 8And God is able to make all grace abound to you, so that in all things at all times, having all that you need, you will abound in every good work. 9As it is written:

"He has scattered abroad his gifts to the poor;
  his righteousness endures for ever."a

10Now he who supplies seed to the sower and bread for food will also supply and increase your store of seed and will enlarge the harvest of your righteousness. 11You will be made rich in every way so that you can be generous on every occasion, and through us your generosity will result in thanksgiving to God. 12This service that you perform is not only supplying the needs of God's people but is also overflowing in many expressions of thanks to God. 13Because of the service by which you have proved yourselves, men will praise God for the obedience that accompanies your confession of the gospel of Christ, and for your generosity in sharing with them and with everyone else. 14And in their prayers for you their hearts will go out to you, because of the surpassing grace God has given you. 15Thanks be to God for his indescribable gift!

9:12   The Corinthian Christians were told by Paul that if they gave generously towards the collection for the church in Jerusalem, the people there would be grateful to God. We can compare this with the instruction of Jesus to his disciples that they should let people see their good deeds in order that the glory might come to God (Matthew 5:16).

Paul's Defence of His Ministry

10 By the meekness and gentleness of Christ, I appeal to you—I, Paul, who am "timid" when face to face with you, but "bold" when away! 2I beg you that when I come I may not have to be as bold as I expect to be towards some people who think that we live by the standards of this world. 3For though we live in the world, we do not wage war as the world does. 4The weapons we fight with are not the weapons of the world. On the contrary, they have divine power to demolish strongholds. 5We demolish arguments and every pretension that sets itself up against the knowledge of God, and we take captive every thought to make it obedient to Christ. 6And we will be ready to punish every act of disobedience, once your obedience is complete.

7You are looking only on the surface of things.a If anyone is confident that he belongs to Christ, he should consider again that we belong to Christ just as much as he. 8For even if I boast somewhat freely about the authority the Lord gave us for building you up rather than pulling you down, I will not be ashamed of it. 9I do not want to seem to be trying to frighten you with my letters. 10For some say, "His letters are weighty and forceful, but in person he is unimpressive and his speaking amounts to nothing." 11Such people should realise that what we are in our letters when we are absent, we will be in our actions when we are present.

---

b15 Exodus 16:18   a9 Psalm 112:9   a7 Or Look at the obvious facts

[12]We do not dare to classify or compare ourselves with some who commend themselves. When they measure themselves by themselves and compare themselves with themselves, they are not wise. [13]We, however, will not boast beyond proper limits, but will confine our boasting to the field God has assigned to us, a field that reaches even to you. [14]We are not going too far in our boasting, as would be the case if we had not come to you, for we did get as far as you with the gospel of Christ. [15]Neither do we go beyond our limits by boasting of work done by others.[b] Our hope is that, as your faith continues to grow, our area of activity among you will greatly expand, [16]so that we can preach the gospel in the regions beyond you. For we do not want to boast about work already done in another man's territory. [17]But, "Let him who boasts boast in the Lord."[c] [18]For it is not the one who commends himself who is approved, but the one whom the Lord commends.

Paul and the False Apostles

11 I hope you will put up with a little of my foolishness; but you are already doing that. [2]I am jealous for you with a godly jealousy. I promised you to one husband, to Christ, so that I might present you as a pure virgin to him. [3]But I am afraid that just as Eve was deceived by the serpent's cunning, your minds may somehow be led astray from your sincere and pure devotion to Christ. [4]For if someone comes to you and preaches a Jesus other than the Jesus we preached, or if you receive a different spirit from the one you received, or a different gospel from the one you accepted, you put up with it easily enough. [5]But I do not think I am in the least inferior to those "super-apostles". [6]I may not be a trained speaker, but I do have knowledge. We have made this perfectly clear to you in every way.

[7]Was it a sin for me to lower myself in order to elevate you by preaching the gospel of God to you free of charge? [8]I robbed other churches by receiving support from them so as to serve you. [9]And when I was with you and needed something, I was not a burden to anyone, for the brothers who came from Macedonia supplied what I needed. I have kept myself from being a burden to you in any way, and will continue to do so. [10]As surely as the truth of Christ is in me, nobody in the regions of Achaia will stop this boasting of mine. [11]Why? Because I do not love you? God knows I do! [12]And I will keep on doing what I am doing in order to cut the ground from under those who want an opportunity to be considered equal with us in the things they boast about.

[13]For such men are false apostles, deceitful workmen, masquerading as apostles of Christ. [14]And no wonder, for Satan himself masquerades as an angel of light. [15]It is not surprising, then, if his servants masquerade as servants of righteousness. Their end will be what their actions deserve.

Paul Boasts About His Sufferings

[16]I repeat: Let no-one take me for a fool. But if you do, then receive me just as you would a fool, so that I may do a little boasting. [17]In this self-confident boasting I am not talking as the Lord would, but as a fool. [18]Since many are boasting in the way the world does, I too will boast. [19]You gladly put up with fools since you are so wise! [20]In fact, you even put up with anyone who enslaves you or exploits you or takes advantage of you or pushes himself forward or slaps you in the face. [21]To my shame I admit that we were too weak for that!

11:9   Paul made it clear in 1 Corinthians 9:14 that those who preach the gospel have the right to receive their living from it. Nevertheless, Paul himself did not always choose to exercise that right. In Corinth he supported himself at first by working as a tent maker and later, when he began preaching full time, he received necessary support from believers in other places, most notably in Macedonia.

What anyone else dares to boast about — I am speaking as a fool — I also dare to boast about. [22]Are they Hebrews? So am I. Are they Israelites? So am I. Are they Abraham's descendants? So am I. [23]Are they servants of Christ? (I am out of my mind to talk like this.) I am more. I have worked much harder, been in prison more frequently, been flogged more severely, and been exposed to death again and again. [24]Five times I received from the Jews the forty lashes minus one. [25]Three times I was beaten with rods, once I was stoned, three times I was shipwrecked, I spent a night and a day in the open sea, [26]I have been constantly on the move. I have been in danger from rivers, in danger from bandits, in danger from my own countrymen, in danger from Gentiles; in danger in the city, in danger in the country, in danger at sea; and in danger from false brothers. [27]I have laboured and toiled and have often gone without sleep; I have known hunger and thirst and have often gone without food; I have been cold and naked. [28]Besides everything else, I face daily the pressure of my concern for all the churches. [29]Who is weak, and I do not feel weak? Who is led into sin, and I do not inwardly burn?

[30]If I must boast, I will boast of the things that show my weakness. [31]The God and Father of the Lord Jesus, who is to be praised for ever, knows that I am not lying. [32]In Damascus the governor under King Aretas had the city of the Damascenes guarded in order to arrest me. [33]But I was lowered in a basket from a window in the wall and slipped through his hands.

Paul's Vision and His Thorn

12 I must go on boasting. Although there is nothing to be gained, I will go on to visions and revelations from the Lord. [2]I know a man in Christ

---

b 13–15 Or 13 We, however, will not boast about things that cannot be measured, but we will boast according to the standard of measurement that the God of measure has assigned us—a measurement that relates even to you. 14 . . . 15 Neither do we boast about things that cannot be measured in regard to the work done by others.   c 17 Jer. 9:24 who fourteen years ago was caught up to the third heaven. Whether it was in the body or out of the body I do not know — God knows. [3]And I know that this man — whether in the body or apart from the body I do not know, but God knows — [4]was caught up to paradise. He heard inexpressible things, things that man is not permitted to tell. [5]I will boast about a man like that, but I will not boast about myself, except about my weaknesses. [6]Even if I should choose to boast, I would not be a fool, because I would be speaking the truth. But I refrain, so no-one will think more of me than is warranted by what I do or say.

[7]To keep me from becoming conceited because of these surpassingly great revelations, there was given me a thorn in my flesh, a messenger of Satan, to torment me. [8]Three times I pleaded with the Lord to take it away from me. [9]But he said to me, "My grace is sufficient for you, for my power is made perfect in weakness." Therefore I will boast all the more gladly about my weaknesses, so that Christ's power may rest on me. [10]That is why, for Christ's sake, I delight in weaknesses, in insults, in hardships, in persecutions, in difficulties. For when I am weak, then I am strong.

12:7   There has been much speculation about what this was, but there is no way of knowing for certain. What matters more is how Paul dealt with it. He asked the Lord three times for it to be taken away, but his prayer was not answered in the way he hoped. Instead, he had to learn to live with it and trust God's grace to cover his weakness. Being a Christian does not offer freedom from distressing conditions.

Paul's Concern for the Corinthians

[11]I have made a fool of myself, but you drove me to it. I ought to have been commended by you, for I am not in the least inferior to the "super-apostles", even though I am nothing. [12]The things that mark an apostle — signs, wonders and miracles — were done among you with great perseverance. [13]How were you inferior to the other churches, except that I was never a burden to you? Forgive me this wrong!

[14]Now I am ready to visit you for the third time, and I will not be a burden to you, because what I want is not your possessions but you. After all, children should not have to save up for their parents, but parents for their children. [15]So I will very gladly spend for you everything I have and expend myself as well. If I love you more, will you love me less? [16]Be that as it may, I have not been a burden to you. Yet, crafty fellow that I am, I caught you by trickery! [17]Did I exploit you through any of the men I sent you? [18]I urged Titus to

go to you and I sent our brother with him. Titus did not exploit you, did he? Did we not act in the same spirit and follow the same course?

[19]Have you been thinking all along that we have been defending ourselves to you? We have been speaking in the sight of God as those in Christ; and everything we do, dear friends, is for your strengthening. [20]For I am afraid that when I come I may not find you as I want you to be, and you may not find me as you want me to be. I fear that there may be quarrelling, jealousy, outbursts of anger, factions, slander, gossip, arrogance and disorder. [21]I am afraid that when I come again my God will humble me before you, and I will be grieved over many who have sinned earlier and have not repented of the impurity, sexual sin and debauchery in which they have indulged.

Final Warnings

13 This will be my third visit to you. "Every matter must be established by the testimony of two or three witnesses."[a] [2]I already gave you a warning when I was with you the second time. I now repeat it while absent: On my return I will not spare those who sinned earlier or any of the others, [3]since you are demanding proof that Christ is speaking through me. He is not weak in dealing with you, but is powerful among you. [4]For to be sure, he was crucified in weakness, yet he lives by God's power. Likewise, we are weak in him, yet by God's power we will live with him to serve you.

[5]Examine yourselves to see whether you are in the faith; test yourselves. Do you not realise that Christ Jesus is in you — unless, of course, you fail the test? [6]And I trust that you will discover that we have not failed the test. [7]Now we pray to God that you will not do anything wrong. Not that people will see that we have stood the test but that you will do what is right even though we may seem to have failed. [8]For we cannot do anything against the truth, but only for the truth. [9]We are glad whenever we are weak but you are strong; and our prayer is for your perfection. [10]This is why I write these things when I am absent, that when I come I may not have to be harsh in my use of authority — the authority the Lord gave me for building you up, not for tearing you down.

13:14   Despite all the controversies and difficulties in the church, Paul ended his letter with a characteristic benediction (divine blessing). He wanted the people to have the quality of relationships which only the Holy Spirit can create. Those who claim to have the Spirit of God in their lives must recognize that one of the main outcomes is true fellowship with other people.

---

a 1 Deut. 19:15

Final Greetings

[11] Finally, brothers, good-bye. Aim for perfection, listen to my appeal, be of one mind, live in peace. And the God of love and peace will be with you.

[12] Greet one another with a holy kiss. [13] All the saints send their greetings.

[14] May the grace of the Lord Jesus Christ, and the love of God, and the fellowship of the Holy Spirit be with you all.

Galatians

Right up to Date

At first glance, Paul's letter to the Galatians is out of date for most readers in the late twentieth century. Paul was writing about the Jewish law and food codes that most people now know little about. However, it is one of the most apt letters for Christians to read because it warns people away from telling others that they have to fulfil strict moral and religious laws to be saved. In fact, Christ will change people's lives because the fruits of the Spirit—love, joy, peace, patience, kindness, goodness, faithfulness, gentleness, and self control—are shown in moral and upright lives. If all the fruits are there then the law is no longer required.

Do We Need to Prove Ourselves?

So in this letter Paul warned the people not to prove themselves by their actions. Ironically, in letters to the Corinthians he warned the people not to treat their actions as totally unconnected with themselves. Paul was clear: actions are limited in what they can do. Christianity had grown within Judaism and as a Jew he lived with its laws, and the Rabbis' codes for living. In this letter he wrote about how he kept every one of the laws and was legally near perfect. It was not enough, however, because it was the intentions that really mattered. No one was able to fulfil the law all the time, in all their thoughts and their faith.

No Distinctions

When Christianity entered the Gentile communities there was the problem of whether a person needed to be Jewish to be a Christian, and whether they needed to live as a Jew—obeying their food laws, as well as their ceremonies (such as circumcision)—and then be baptized. Some said you needed to become a Jew or at least live like one; others said you did not have to, but that it was the better life to live anyway. Paul and others said that Christ had changed everything. Old divisions like Jew or Gentile, slave or free, male or female, have no place in Christianity. It is the effect of Christ on the world, on individuals, and on faith that makes the old ways of the Law, and particularly legalism, out of date. Sometimes they can even lead to division.

1 Paul, an apostle — sent not from men nor by man, but by Jesus Christ and God the Father, who raised him from the dead — ²and all the brothers with me,

To the churches in Galatia:

³Grace and peace to you from God our Father and the Lord Jesus Christ, ⁴who gave himself for our sins to rescue us from the present evil age, according to the will of our God and Father, ⁵to whom be glory for ever and ever. Amen.

No Other Gospel

⁶I am astonished that you are so quickly deserting the one who called you by the grace of Christ and are turning to a different gospel — ⁷which is really no gospel at all. Evidently some people are throwing you into confusion and are trying to pervert the gospel of Christ. ⁸But even if we or an angel from heaven should preach a gospel other than the one we preached to you, let him be eternally condemned! ⁹As we have already said, so now I say again: If anybody is preaching to you a gospel other than what you accepted, let him be eternally condemned!

¹⁰Am I now trying to win the approval of men, or of God? Or am I trying to please men? If I were still trying to please men, I would not be a servant of Christ.

Paul Called by God

¹¹I want you to know, brothers, that the gospel I preached is not something that man made up. ¹²I did not receive it from any man, nor was I taught it; rather, I received it by revelation from Jesus Christ.

¹³For you have heard of my previous way of life in Judaism, how intensely I persecuted the church of God and tried to destroy it. ¹⁴I was advancing in Judaism beyond many Jews of my own age and was extremely zealous for the traditions of my fathers. ¹⁵But when God, who set me apart from birth[a] and called me by his grace, was pleased ¹⁶to reveal his Son in me so that I might preach him among the Gentiles, I did not consult any man, ¹⁷nor did I go up to Jerusalem to see those who were apostles before I was, but I went immediately into Arabia and later returned to Damascus.

¹⁸Then after three years, I went up to Jerusalem to get acquainted with Peter[b] and stayed with him fifteen days. ¹⁹I saw none of the other apostles — only James, the Lord's brother. ²⁰I assure you before God that what I am writing to you is no lie. ²¹Later I went to Syria and Cilicia. ²²I was personally unknown to the churches of Judea that are in Christ. ²³They only heard the report: "The man who formerly persecuted us is now preaching the faith he once tried to destroy." ²⁴And they praised God because of me.

Paul Accepted by the Apostles

2 Fourteen years later I went up again to Jerusalem, this time with Barnabas. I took Titus along also. ²I went in response to a revelation and set before them the gospel that I preach among the Gentiles. But I did this privately to those who seemed to be leaders, for fear that I was running or had run my race in vain. ³Yet not even Titus, who was with me, was compelled to be circumcised, even though he was a Greek. ⁴This matter arose, because some false brothers had infiltrated our ranks to spy on the freedom we have in Christ Jesus and to make us slaves. ⁵We did not give in to them for a moment, so that the truth of the gospel might remain with you.

⁶As for those who seemed to be important — whatever they were makes no difference to me; God does not judge by external appearance — those men added nothing to my message. ⁷On the contrary, they saw that I had been entrusted with the task of preaching the gospel to the Gentiles,[a] just as Peter had been to the Jews.[b] ⁸For God, who was at work in the ministry of Peter as an apostle to the Jews, was also at work in my ministry as an apostle to the Gentiles. ⁹James, Peter[c] and John, those reputed to be pillars, gave me and Barnabas the right hand of fellowship when they recognised the grace given to me. They agreed that we should go to the Gentiles, and they to the Jews. ¹⁰All they asked was that we should continue to remember the poor, the very thing I was eager to do.

Paul Opposes Peter

¹¹When Peter came to Antioch, I opposed him to his face, because he was clearly in the wrong. ¹²Before certain men came from James, he used to eat with the Gentiles. But when they arrived, he began to draw back and separate himself from the Gentiles because he was afraid of those who belonged to the circumcision group. ¹³The other Jews joined him in his hypocrisy, so that by their hypocrisy even Barnabas was led astray.

2:11 Paul seems to have had problems with some Christians not thinking of him as a true apostle who had any right to speak as he did. He pointed out that the other apostles accepted him, and so he was able to question Peter and James over how the early church could contain both Jews and Gentiles. Peter and James seemed to have tried a compromise that favoured the Jewish Christians and would have denied the ministry to the Gentiles by restoring the Law to a primary position. As Paul argued, the Law was now unnecessary for all people.

---

¹⁴When I saw that they were not acting in line with the truth of the gospel, I said to Peter in front of them all, "You are a Jew, yet you live like a Gentile and not like a Jew. How is it, then, that you force Gentiles to follow Jewish customs?

¹⁵"We who are Jews by birth and not 'Gentile sinners' ¹⁶know that a man is not justified by observing the law, but by faith in Jesus Christ. So we, too, have

---

a 15 Or *from my mother's womb*   *b 18* Greek *Cephas*   *a 7* Greek *uncircumcised*
b 7 Greek *circumcised*; also in verses 8 and 9   *c 9* Greek *Cephas*; also in verses 11 and 14

put our faith in Christ Jesus that we may be justified by faith in Christ and not by observing the law, because by observing the law no-one will be justified.

[17]"If, while we seek to be justified in Christ, it becomes evident that we ourselves are sinners, does that mean that Christ promotes sin? Absolutely not! [18]If I rebuild what I destroyed, I prove that I am a law-breaker. [19]For through the law I died to the law so that I might live for God. [20]I have been crucified with Christ and I no longer live, but Christ lives in me. The life I live in the body, I live by faith in the Son of God, who loved me and gave himself for me. [21]I do not set aside the grace of God, for if righteousness could be gained through the law, Christ died for nothing!"[d]

Faith or Observance of the Law

3 You foolish Galatians! Who has bewitched you? Before your very eyes Jesus Christ was clearly portrayed as crucified. [2]I would like to learn just one thing from you: Did you receive the Spirit by observing the law, or by believing what you heard? [3]Are you so foolish? After beginning with the Spirit, are you now trying to attain your goal by human effort? [4]Have you suffered so much for nothing—if it really was for nothing? [5]Does God give you his Spirit and work miracles among you because you observe the law, or because you believe what you heard?

[6]Consider Abraham: "He believed God, and it was credited to him as righteousness."[a] [7]Understand, then, that those who believe are children of Abraham. [8]The Scripture foresaw that God would justify the Gentiles by faith, and announced the gospel in advance to Abraham: "All nations will be blessed through you."[b] [9]So those who have faith are blessed along with Abraham, the man of faith.

[10]All who rely on observing the law are under a curse, for it is written: "Cursed is everyone who does not continue to do everything written in the Book of the Law."[c] [11]Clearly no-one is justified before God by the law, because, "The righteous will live by faith."[d] [12]The law is not based on faith; on the contrary, "The man who does these things will live by them."[e] [13]Christ redeemed us from the curse of the law by becoming a curse for us, for it is written: "Cursed is everyone who is hung on a tree."[f] [14]He redeemed us in order that the blessing given to Abraham might come to the Gentiles through Christ Jesus, so that by faith we might receive the promise of the Spirit.

The Law and the Promise

[15]Brothers, let me take an example from everyday life. Just as no-one can set aside or add to a human covenant that has been duly established, so it is in this case. [16]The promises were spoken to Abraham and to his seed. The Scripture does not say "and to seeds", meaning many people, but "and to your seed",[g] meaning one person, who is Christ. [17]What I mean is this: The law, introduced 430 years later, does not set aside the covenant previously established by God and

thus do away with the promise. [18]For if the inheritance depends on the law, then it no longer depends on a promise; but God in his grace gave it to Abraham through a promise.

3:17 Paul was a Pharisee, and very familiar with Scripture. He used the fact that God had made his promises to Abraham a long time (Paul says 430 years) before Moses came with the Law. Abraham's righteousness did not come from the Law. We cannot gain God's love by earning it ourselves; we need his grace which came in Christ, who fulfilled the Law.

[19]What, then, was the purpose of the law? It was added because of transgressions until the Seed to whom the promise referred had come. The law was put into effect through angels by a mediator. [20]A mediator, however, does not represent just one party; but God is one.

[21]Is the law, therefore, opposed to the promises of God? Absolutely not! For if a law had been given that could impart life, then righteousness would certainly have come by the law. [22]But the Scripture declares that the whole world is a prisoner of sin, so that what was promised, being given through faith in Jesus Christ, might be given to those who believe.

[23]Before this faith came, we were held prisoners by the law, locked up until faith should be revealed. [24]So the law was put in charge to lead us to Christ[h] that we might be justified by faith. [25]Now that faith has come, we are no longer under the supervision of the law.

Sons of God

[26]You are all sons of God through faith in Christ Jesus, [27]for all of you who were baptised into Christ have clothed yourselves with Christ. [28]There is neither Jew nor Greek, slave nor free, male nor female, for you are all one in Christ Jesus. [29]If you belong to Christ, then you are Abraham's seed, and heirs according to the promise.

4 What I am saying is that as long as the heir is a child, he is no different from a slave, although he owns the whole estate. [2]He is subject to guardians and trustees until the time set by his father. [3]So also, when we were children, we were in slavery under the basic principles of the world. [4]But when the time had fully come, God sent his Son, born of a woman, born under law, [5]to redeem those under law, that we might receive the full rights of sons. [6]Because you are sons, God sent the Spirit of his Son into our hearts, the Spirit who calls out, "Abba,[a] Father." [7]So you are no longer a slave, but a son; and since you are a son, God has made you also an heir.

---

[d]21 Some interpreters end the quotation after verse 14.   [a]6 Gen. 15:6   [b]8 Gen. 12:3; 18:18; 22:18
[c]10 Deut. 27:26   [d]11 Hab. 2:4   [e]12 Lev. 18:5   [f]13 Deut. 21:23   [g]16 Gen. 12:7; 13:15; 24:7
[h]24 Or *charge until Christ came*   [a]6 Aramaic for *Father*

Paul's Concern for the Galatians

[8]Formerly, when you did not know God, you were slaves to those who by nature are not gods. [9]But now that you know God—or rather are known by God—how is it that you are turning back to those weak and miserable principles? Do you wish to be enslaved by them all over again? [10]You are observing special days and months and seasons and years! [11]I fear for you, that somehow I have wasted my efforts on you.

[12]I plead with you, brothers, become like me, for I became like you. You have done me no wrong. [13]As you know, it was because of an illness that I first preached the gospel to you. [14]Even though my illness was a trial to you, you did not treat me with contempt or scorn. Instead, you welcomed me as if I were an angel of God, as if I were Christ Jesus himself. [15]What has happened to all your joy? I can testify that, if you could have done so, you would have torn out your eyes and given them to me. [16]Have I now become your enemy by telling you the truth?

4:15   At times in this letter Paul put forward highly complex theological arguments, at other times he was obviously arguing from his heart. He was most concerned that the people were going to reject Christ in favour of legalism, and he felt this personally, even saying he was "in the pains of childbirth" about it (verse 19).

---

[17]Those people are zealous to win you over, but for no good. What they want is to alienate you ‚from us‚, so that you may be zealous for them. [18]It is fine to be zealous, provided the purpose is good, and to be so always and not just when I am with you. [19]My dear children, for whom I am again in the pains of childbirth until Christ is formed in you, [20]how I wish I could be with you now and change my tone, because I am perplexed about you!

Hagar and Sarah

[21]Tell me, you who want to be under the law, are you not aware of what the law says? [22]For it is written that Abraham had two sons, one by the slave woman and the other by the free woman. [23]His son by the slave woman was born in the ordinary way; but his son by the free woman was born as the result of a promise. [24]These things may be taken figuratively, for the women represent two covenants. One covenant is from Mount Sinai and bears children who are to be slaves: This is Hagar. [25]Now Hagar stands for Mount Sinai in Arabia and corresponds to the present city of Jerusalem, because she is in slavery with her children. [26]But the Jerusalem that is above is free, and she is our mother. [27]For it is written:

> "Be glad, O barren woman,
>   who bears no children;
> break forth and cry aloud,
>   you who have no labour pains;

because more are the children of the desolate woman
>   than of her who has a husband."[b]

[28]Now you, brothers, like Isaac, are children of promise. [29]At that time the son born in the ordinary way persecuted the son born by the power of the Spirit. It is the same now. [30]But what does the Scripture say? "Get rid of the slave woman and her son, for the slave woman's son will never share in the inheritance with the free woman's son."[c] [31]Therefore, brothers, we are not children of the slave woman, but of the free woman.

Freedom in Christ

5 It is for freedom that Christ has set us free. Stand firm, then, and do not let yourselves be burdened again by a yoke of slavery.

[2]Mark my words! I, Paul, tell you that if you let yourselves be circumcised, Christ will be of no value to you at all. [3]Again I declare to every man who lets himself be circumcised that he is required to obey the whole law. [4]You who are trying to be justified by law have been alienated from Christ; you have fallen away from grace. [5]But by faith we eagerly await through the Spirit the righteousness for which we hope. [6]For in Christ Jesus neither circumcision nor uncircumcision has any value. The only thing that counts is faith expressing itself through love.

[7]You were running a good race. Who cut in on you and kept you from obeying the truth? [8]That kind of persuasion does not come from the one who calls you. [9]"A little yeast works through the whole batch of dough." [10]I am confident in the Lord that you will take no other view. The one who is throwing you into confusion will pay the penalty, whoever he may be. [11]Brothers, if I am still preaching circumcision, why am I still being persecuted? In that case the offence of the cross has been abolished. [12]As for those agitators, I wish they would go the whole way and emasculate themselves!

[13]You, my brothers, were called to be free. But do not use your freedom to indulge the sinful nature;[a] rather, serve one another in love. [14]The entire law is summed up in a single command: "Love your neighbour as yourself."[b] [15]If you keep on biting and devouring each other, watch out or you will be destroyed by each other.

Life by the Spirit

[16]So I say, live by the Spirit, and you will not gratify the desires of the sinful nature. [17]For the sinful nature desires what is contrary to the Spirit, and the Spirit what is contrary to the sinful nature. They are in conflict with each other, so that you do not do what you want. [18]But if you are led by the Spirit, you are not under law.

[19]The acts of the sinful nature are obvious: sexual immorality, impurity and debauchery; [20]idolatry and witchcraft; hatred, discord, jealousy, fits of rage, selfish ambition, dissensions, factions [21]and envy; drunkenness, orgies, and the like. I warn you, as I did before,

---

b27 Isaiah 54:1   *c30* Gen. 21:10   *a13* Or *the flesh*; also in verses 16, 17, 19 and 24   *b14* Lev. 19:18

that those who live like this will not inherit the kingdom of God.

²²But the fruit of the Spirit is love, joy, peace, patience, kindness, goodness, faithfulness, ²³gentleness and self-control. Against such things there is no law. ²⁴Those who belong to Christ Jesus have crucified the sinful nature with its passions and desires. ²⁵Since we live by the Spirit, let us keep in step with the Spirit. ²⁶Let us not become conceited, provoking and envying each other.

Doing Good to All

6 Brothers, if someone is caught in a sin, you who are spiritual should restore him gently. But watch yourself, or you also may be tempted. ²Carry each other's burdens, and in this way you will fulfil the law of Christ. ³If anyone thinks he is something when he is nothing, he deceives himself. ⁴Each one should test his own actions. Then he can take pride in himself, without comparing himself to somebody else, ⁵for each one should carry his own load.

6:2 Christians should help one another to fulfil Christ's law, and there should be an attitude of forgiveness towards those who fail. Despite the problems the Galatians were having, they should not give up but should strive to do good.

ᵃ8 Or *his flesh, from the flesh*   ᵇ14 Or *whom*

⁶Anyone who receives instruction in the word must share all good things with his instructor.

⁷Do not be deceived: God cannot be mocked. A man reaps what he sows. ⁸The one who sows to please his sinful nature, from that natureᵃ will reap destruction; the one who sows to please the Spirit, from the Spirit will reap eternal life. ⁹Let us not become weary in doing good, for at the proper time we will reap a harvest if we do not give up. ¹⁰Therefore, as we have opportunity, let us do good to all people, especially to those who belong to the family of believers.

Not Circumcision but a New Creation

¹¹See what large letters I use as I write to you with my own hand!

¹²Those who want to make a good impression outwardly are trying to compel you to be circumcised. The only reason they do this is to avoid being persecuted for the cross of Christ. ¹³Not even those who are circumcised obey the law, yet they want you to be circumcised that they may boast about your flesh. ¹⁴May I never boast except in the cross of our Lord Jesus Christ, through whichᵇ the world has been crucified to me, and I to the world. ¹⁵Neither circumcision nor uncircumcision means anything; what counts is a new creation. ¹⁶Peace and mercy to all who follow this rule, even to the Israel of God.

¹⁷Finally, let no-one cause me trouble, for I bear on my body the marks of Jesus.

¹⁸The grace of our Lord Jesus Christ be with your spirit, brothers. Amen.

Ephesians

Ephesus—the Cultural Capital

Two thousand years ago, Ephesus was the city to go to. It was a port in what is now Turkey, and was well known for its riches and its patron goddess Diana. It was a busy trading city and was thought of as a place of fun, a kind of Blackpool or Brighton. Like all those sorts of places, it had a great number of problems and lonely people.

A Sense of Belonging

The letter to the Ephesians sets out to show that because of what God and Christ are, Christians are not alone but part of a new family. Being part of God's family carries with it responsibilities, but also new joys and hopes. This was principally a letter of encouragement. Everyone could belong to the community of believers, regardless of their background. It was all possible because God had raised Jesus from the dead and placed him above all the earthly rulers. At the time when the letter was written these rulers would have been thought of as Caesar and the Roman empire, who had imprisoned Paul.

Good News for Everyone

Paul saw himself as the speaker for, and to, the Gentiles (the non-Jewish world). Through Christ, he saw no need for the old divide of Jew and Gentile. People are all fellow citizens and no longer foreigners and aliens. This concept would have been appropriate in a letter to a port where a large number of the people would be foreigners. Everyone is a child of God, and needs to grow up in a relationship with God. Paul prayed that the Spirit of God would strengthen the church to make an adult body. This also implied that the people should try and live good lives, not in order to win God's favour, but because of God's grace and Spirit living in them.

Love and Respect

Towards the end of the letter, Paul talked about the family in specific terms and not just as the general family of God. He did this to tell the people something about God's love for his church. It also challenged the view of the time that wives and children were property, and did not exist in their own right. Christ had changed this by loving all people, so the people's response should be to love and respect everyone. He finished with an analogy of the Christian as a soldier prepared for battle and protected by armour. This is not physical armour like the Roman soldiers wore, but God's armour of truth, righteousness, peace, faith, and salvation. These were for protection against attack, and the sword of the Spirit was both for protection and attack. It is an analogy that Paul used often, and is a clear and vibrant one.

1

Paul, an apostle of Christ Jesus by the will of God,

To the saints in Ephesus,[a] the faithful[b] in Christ Jesus:

[2]Grace and peace to you from God our Father and the Lord Jesus Christ.

Spiritual Blessings in Christ

[3]Praise be to the God and Father of our Lord Jesus Christ, who has blessed us in the heavenly realms with every spiritual blessing in Christ. [4]For he chose us in him before the creation of the world to be holy and blameless in his sight. In love [5]he[c] predestined us to be adopted as his sons through Jesus Christ, in accordance with his pleasure and will — [6]to the praise of his glorious grace, which he has freely given us in the One he loves. [7]In him we have redemption through his blood, the forgiveness of sins, in accordance with the riches of God's grace [8]that he lavished on us with all

wisdom and understanding. [9]And he[d] made known to us the mystery of his will according to his good pleasure, which he purposed in Christ, [10]to be put into effect when the times will have reached their fulfilment — to bring all things in heaven and on earth together under one head, even Christ.

1:7　　Paul, who was once a Pharisee and kept all the Jewish laws, now insisted that salvation did not actually come from just keeping rules and regulations. However, good works should be a part of a person's life as they grow in the love of Christ.

---

[11]In him we were also chosen,[e] having been predestined according to the plan of him who works out everything in conformity with the purpose of his will, [12]in order that we, who were the first to hope in Christ, might be for the praise of his glory. [13]And you also were

---

a 1 Some early manuscripts do not have *in Ephesus.*　　*b 1* Or *believers who are*　　*c 4,5* Or *sight in love. 5 He*
d 8,9 Or *us. With all wisdom and understanding,* 9*he*　　*e 11* Or *were made heirs*

included in Christ when you heard the word of truth, the gospel of your salvation. Having believed, you were marked in him with a seal, the promised Holy Spirit, [14]who is a deposit guaranteeing our inheritance until the redemption of those who are God's possession — to the praise of his glory.

Thanksgiving and Prayer

[15]For this reason, ever since I heard about your faith in the Lord Jesus and your love for all the saints, [16]I have not stopped giving thanks for you, remembering you in my prayers. [17]I keep asking that the God of our Lord Jesus Christ, the glorious Father, may give you the Spirit[f] of wisdom and revelation, so that you may know him better. [18]I pray also that the eyes of your heart may be enlightened in order that you may know the hope to which he has called you, the riches of his glorious inheritance in the saints, [19]and his incomparably great power for us who believe. That power is like the working of his mighty strength, [20]which he exerted in Christ when he raised him from the dead and seated him at his right hand in the heavenly realms, [21]far above all rule and authority, power and dominion, and every title that can be given, not only in the present age but also in the one to come. [22]And God placed all things under his feet and appointed him to be head over everything for the church, [23]which is his body, the fulness of him who fills everything in every way.

Made Alive in Christ

2 As for you, you were dead in your transgressions and sins, [2]in which you used to live when you followed the ways of this world and of the ruler of the kingdom of the air, the spirit who is now at work in those who are disobedient. [3]All of us also lived among them at one time, gratifying the cravings of our sinful nature[a] and following its desires and thoughts. Like the rest, we were by nature objects of wrath. [4]But because of his great love for us, God, who is rich in mercy, [5]made us alive with Christ even when we were dead in transgressions — it is by grace you have been saved. [6]And God raised us up with Christ and seated us with him in the heavenly realms in Christ Jesus, [7]in order that in the coming ages he might show the incomparable riches of his grace, expressed in his kindness to us in Christ Jesus. [8]For it is by grace you have been saved, through faith — and this not from yourselves, it is the gift of God — [9]not by works, so that no one can boast. [10]For we are God's workmanship, created in Christ Jesus to do good works, which God prepared in advance for us to do.

One in Christ

[11]Therefore, remember that formerly you who are Gentiles by birth and called "uncircumcised" by those who call themselves "the circumcision" (that done in the body by the hands of men) — [12]remember that at that time you were separate from Christ, excluded from citizenship in Israel and foreigners to the covenants of the promise, without hope and without God

in the world. [13]But now in Christ Jesus you who once were far away have been brought near through the blood of Christ.

[14]For he himself is our peace, who has made the two one and has destroyed the barrier, the dividing wall of hostility, [15]by abolishing in his flesh the law with its commandments and regulations. His purpose was to create in himself one new man out of the two, thus making peace, [16]and in this one body to reconcile both of them to God through the cross, by which he put to death their hostility. [17]He came and preached peace to you who were far away and peace to those who were near. [18]For through him we both have access to the Father by one Spirit.

2:14 The majority of the inhabitants of the Roman empire were Gentiles. There were relatively few Jews and in order to preserve their identity, especially when they were dispersed all over the empire, they kept various cultural and religious barriers. In the temple in Jerusalem non-Jews could not go beyond a certain wall. However, Paul believed that this wall of division was destroyed by Christ and that God had given everyone equal opportunity to meet him.

---

[19]Consequently, you are no longer foreigners and aliens, but fellow-citizens with God's people and members of God's household, [20]built on the foundation of the apostles and prophets, with Christ Jesus himself as the chief cornerstone. [21]In him the whole building is joined together and rises to become a holy temple in the Lord. [22]And in him you too are being built together to become a dwelling in which God lives by his Spirit.

Paul the Preacher to the Gentiles

3 For this reason I, Paul, the prisoner of Christ Jesus for the sake of you Gentiles —
[2]Surely you have heard about the administration of God's grace that was given to me for you, [3]that is, the mystery made known to me by revelation, as I have already written briefly. [4]In reading this, then, you will be able to understand my insight into the mystery of Christ, [5]which was not made known to men in other generations as it has now been revealed by the Spirit to God's holy apostles and prophets. [6]This mystery is that through the gospel the Gentiles are heirs together with Israel, members together of one body, and sharers together in the promise in Christ Jesus.

[7]I became a servant of this gospel by the gift of God's grace given me through the working of his power. [8]Although I am less than the least of all God's people, this grace was given me: to preach to the Gentiles the unsearchable riches of Christ, [9]and to make plain to everyone the administration of this mystery, which for ages past was kept hidden in God, who created all things. [10]His intent was that now, through the church, the manifold wisdom of God should be made known to the rulers and authorities in the heavenly realms,

---

f17 Or a spirit   *a3 Or our flesh*

[11]according to his eternal purpose which he accomplished in Christ Jesus our Lord. [12]In him and through faith in him we may approach God with freedom and confidence. [13]I ask you, therefore, not to be discouraged because of my sufferings for you, which are your glory.

A Prayer for the Ephesians

[14]For this reason I kneel before the Father, [15]from whom his whole family[a] in heaven and on earth derives its name. [16]I pray that out of his glorious riches he may strengthen you with power through his Spirit in your inner being, [17]so that Christ may dwell in your hearts through faith. And I pray that you, being rooted and established in love, [18]may have power, together with all the saints, to grasp how wide and long and high and deep is the love of Christ, [19]and to know this love that surpasses knowledge — that you may be filled to the measure of all the fulness of God.

3:16   This letter does not spend time working over urgent problems as the ones to Corinth and Galatia do. It seems to be encouraging the church to grow. Some scholars have suggested that it could possibly have been a general letter sent to a number of churches and that the one to the Ephesians is the one that survived.

---

[20]Now to him who is able to do immeasurably more than all we ask or imagine, according to his power that is at work within us, [21]to him be glory in the church and in Christ Jesus throughout all generations, for ever and ever! Amen.

Unity in the Body of Christ

4 As a prisoner for the Lord, then, I urge you to live a life worthy of the calling you have received. [2]Be completely humble and gentle; be patient, bearing with one another in love. [3]Make every effort to keep the unity of the Spirit through the bond of peace. [4]There is one body and one Spirit — just as you were called to one hope when you were called — [5]one Lord, one faith, one baptism; [6]one God and Father of all, who is over all and through all and in all.

[7]But to each one of us grace has been given as Christ apportioned it. [8]This is why it[a] says:

"When he ascended on high,
    he led captives in his train
    and gave gifts to men."[b]

[9](What does "he ascended" mean except that he also descended to the lower, earthly regions?[c] [10]He who descended is the very one who ascended higher than all the heavens, in order to fill the whole universe.) [11]It was he who gave some to be apostles, some to be prophets, some to be evangelists, and some to be pastors and teachers, [12]to prepare God's people for works of service, so that the body of Christ may be built up

[13]until we all reach unity in the faith and in the knowledge of the Son of God and become mature, attaining to the whole measure of the fulness of Christ.

[14]Then we will no longer be infants, tossed back and forth by the waves, and blown here and there by every wind of teaching and by the cunning and craftiness of men in their deceitful scheming. [15]Instead, speaking the truth in love, we will in all things grow up into him who is the Head, that is, Christ. [16]From him the whole body, joined and held together by every supporting ligament, grows and builds itself up in love, as each part does its work.

Living as Children of Light

[17]So I tell you this, and insist on it in the Lord, that you must no longer live as the Gentiles do, in the futility of their thinking. [18]They are darkened in their understanding and separated from the life of God because of the ignorance that is in them due to the hardening of their hearts. [19]Having lost all sensitivity, they have given themselves over to sensuality so as to indulge in every kind of impurity, with a continual lust for more.

[20]You, however, did not come to know Christ that way. [21]Surely you heard of him and were taught in him in accordance with the truth that is in Jesus. [22]You were taught, with regard to your former way of life, to put off your old self, which is being corrupted by its deceitful desires; [23]to be made new in the attitude of your minds; [24]and to put on the new self, created to be like God in true righteousness and holiness.

[25]Therefore each of you must put off falsehood and speak truthfully to his neighbour, for we are all members of one body. [26]"In your anger do not sin"[d]: Do not let the sun go down while you are still angry, [27]and do not give the devil a foothold. [28]He who has been stealing must steal no longer, but must work, doing something useful with his own hands, that he may have something to share with those in need.

[29]Do not let any unwholesome talk come out of your mouths, but only what is helpful for building others up according to their needs, that it may benefit those who listen. [30]And do not grieve the Holy Spirit of God, with whom you were sealed for the day of redemption. [31]Get rid of all bitterness, rage and anger, brawling and slander, along with every form of malice. [32]Be kind and compassionate to one another, forgiving each other, just as in Christ God forgave you.

5 Be imitators of God, therefore, as dearly loved children [2]and live a life of love, just as Christ loved us and gave himself up for us as a fragrant offering and sacrifice to God.

[3]But among you there must not be even a hint of sexual immorality, or of any kind of impurity, or of greed, because these are improper for God's holy people. [4]Nor should there be obscenity, foolish talk or coarse joking, which are out of place, but rather thanksgiving. [5]For of this you can be sure: No immoral, impure or greedy person — such a man is an idolater — has any inheritance in the kingdom of Christ and of

---

[a]15 Or whom all fatherhood   [a]8 Or God   [b]8 Psalm 68:18   [c]9 Or the depths of the earth
[d]26 Psalm 4:4

God.[a] [6]Let no-one deceive you with empty words, for because of such things God's wrath comes on those who are disobedient. [7]Therefore do not be partners with them.

[8]For you were once darkness, but now you are light in the Lord. Live as children of light [9](for the fruit of the light consists in all goodness, righteousness and truth) [10]and find out what pleases the Lord. [11]Have nothing to do with the fruitless deeds of darkness, but rather expose them. [12]For it is shameful even to mention what the disobedient do in secret. [13]But everything exposed by the light becomes visible, [14]for it is light that makes everything visible. This is why it is said:

"Wake up, O sleeper,
    rise from the dead,
and Christ will shine on you."

[15]Be very careful, then, how you live — not as unwise but as wise, [16]making the most of every opportunity, because the days are evil. [17]Therefore do not be foolish, but understand what the Lord's will is. [18]Do not get drunk on wine, which leads to debauchery. Instead, be filled with the Spirit. [19]Speak to one another with psalms, hymns and spiritual songs. Sing and make music in your heart to the Lord, [20]always giving thanks to God the Father for everything, in the name of our Lord Jesus Christ.

[21]Submit to one another out of reverence for Christ.

5:21   Christ is part of every relationship, and there is no excuse for the manipulation of fellow human beings, whether they are slaves, children, or wives. There is a responsibility to love as Christ loves, and people should behave with a mixture of submission and love in all their relationships.

Wives and Husbands

[22]Wives, submit to your husbands as to the Lord. [23]For the husband is the head of the wife as Christ is the head of the church, his body, of which he is the Saviour. [24]Now as the church submits to Christ, so also wives should submit to their husbands in everything.

[25]Husbands, love your wives, just as Christ loved the church and gave himself up for her [26]to make her holy, cleansing[b] her by the washing with water through the word, [27]and to present her to himself as a radiant church, without stain or wrinkle or any other blemish, but holy and blameless. [28]In this same way, husbands ought to love their wives as their own bodies. He who loves his wife loves himself. [29]After all, no-one ever hated his own body, but he feeds and cares for it, just as Christ does the church — [30]for we are members of his body. [31]"For this reason a man will leave his father and mother and be united to his wife, and the two will become one flesh."[c] [32]This is a profound mystery —

but I am talking about Christ and the church. [33]However, each one of you also must love his wife as he loves himself, and the wife must respect her husband.

Children and Parents

6 Children, obey your parents in the Lord, for this is right. [2]"Honour your father and mother" — which is the first commandment with a promise — [3]"that it may go well with you and that you may enjoy long life on the earth."[a]

[4]Fathers, do not exasperate your children; instead, bring them up in the training and instruction of the Lord.

Slaves and Masters

[5]Slaves, obey your earthly masters with respect and fear, and with sincerity of heart, just as you would obey Christ. [6]Obey them not only to win their favour when their eye is on you, but like slaves of Christ, doing the will of God from your heart. [7]Serve wholeheartedly, as if you were serving the Lord, not men, [8]because you know that the Lord will reward everyone for whatever good he does, whether he is slave or free.

[9]And masters, treat your slaves in the same way. Do not threaten them, since you know that he who is both their Master and yours is in heaven, and there is no favouritism with him.

The Armour of God

[10]Finally, be strong in the Lord and in his mighty power. [11]Put on the full armour of God so that you can take your stand against the devil's schemes. [12]For our struggle is not against flesh and blood, but against the rulers, against the authorities, against the powers of this dark world and against the spiritual forces of evil in the heavenly realms. [13]Therefore put on the full armour of God, so that when the day of evil comes, you may be able to stand your ground, and after you have done everything, to stand. [14]Stand firm then, with the belt of truth buckled round your waist, with the breastplate of righteousness in place, [15]and with your feet fitted with the readiness that comes from the gospel of peace. [16]In addition to all this, take up the shield of faith, with which you can extinguish all the flaming arrows of the evil one. [17]Take the helmet of salvation and the sword of the Spirit, which is the word of God. [18]And pray in the Spirit on all occasions with all kinds of prayers and requests. With this in mind, be alert and always keep on praying for all the saints.

[19]Pray also for me, that whenever I open my mouth, words may be given me so that I will fearlessly make known the mystery of the gospel, [20]for which I am an ambassador in chains. Pray that I may declare it fearlessly, as I should.

Final Greetings

[21]Tychicus, the dear brother and faithful servant in the Lord, will tell you everything, so that you also may know how I am and what I am doing. [22]I am sending

---

[a] 5 Or kingdom of the Christ and God   [b] 26 Or having cleansed   [c] 31 Gen. 2:24   [a] 3 Deut. 5:16

him to you for this very purpose, that you may know how we are, and that he may encourage you. 23Peace to the brothers, and love with faith from God the Father and the Lord Jesus Christ. 24Grace to all who love our Lord Jesus Christ with an undying love.

Philippians

Joy From Prison

Paul sounds as if he was tired of being in prison, and missed his friends in Philippi. He thought about his fellow Christians who competed with each other and who put him down as a failure because he was in prison. In many ways this could be a letter of despair. Yet because of the way Paul saw Christ in all his sufferings, it is nowhere near a letter of despair; it is in fact one of great and lasting joy. This was not a superficial joy but the manifestation of a real happiness that came through despite all his pain and suffering.

Suffering Transformed Into Joy

We get the impression that Paul loved the church at Philippi deeply. He still warned them of the same things as the other churches; the problem of pride, and the split into groups of Jewish and Gentile Christians, and he answered those who questioned his ministry. Yet this letter is more gentle and less urgent than some of his others. He praised the people for their generosity and their kindness towards him, both physical and spiritual. The letter is all about how God's love can transform suffering into joy.

---

1 Paul and Timothy, servants of Christ Jesus,

To all the saints in Christ Jesus at Philippi, together with the overseersᵃ and deacons:

2Grace and peace to you from God our Father and the Lord Jesus Christ.

Thanksgiving and Prayer

3I thank my God every time I remember you. 4In all my prayers for all of you, I always pray with joy 5because of your partnership in the gospel from the first day until now, 6being confident of this, that he who began a good work in you will carry it on to completion until the day of Christ Jesus.

7It is right for me to feel this way about all of you, since I have you in my heart; for whether I am in chains or defending and confirming the gospel, all of you share in God's grace with me. 8God can testify how I long for all of you with the affection of Christ Jesus.

9And this is my prayer: that your love may abound more and more in knowledge and depth of insight, 10so that you may be able to discern what is best and may be pure and blameless until the day of Christ, 11filled with the fruit of righteousness that comes through Jesus Christ—to the glory and praise of God.

Paul's Chains Advance the Gospel

12Now I want you to know, brothers, that what has happened to me has really served to advance the gospel. 13As a result, it has become clear throughout the whole palace guardᵇ and to everyone else that I am in chains for Christ. 14Because of my chains, most of

ᵃ1 Traditionally bishops   ᵇ13 Or whole palace

the brothers in the Lord have been encouraged to speak the word of God more courageously and fearlessly.

[15]It is true that some preach Christ out of envy and rivalry, but others out of goodwill. [16]The latter do so in love, knowing that I am put here for the defence of the gospel. [17]The former preach Christ out of selfish ambition, not sincerely, supposing that they can stir up trouble for me while I am in chains.[c] [18]But what does it matter? The important thing is that in every way, whether from false motives or true, Christ is preached. And because of this I rejoice.

Yes, and I will continue to rejoice, [19]for I know that through your prayers and the help given by the Spirit of Jesus Christ, what has happened to me will turn out for my deliverance.[d] [20]I eagerly expect and hope that I will in no way be ashamed, but will have sufficient courage so that now as always Christ will be exalted in my body, whether by life or by death. [21]For to me, to live is Christ and to die is gain. [22]If I am to go on living in the body, this will mean fruitful labour for me. Yet what shall I choose? I do not know! [23]I am torn between the two: I desire to depart and be with Christ, which is better by far; [24]but it is more necessary for you that I remain in the body. [25]Convinced of this, I know that I will remain, and I will continue with all of you for your progress and joy in the faith, [26]so that through my being with you again your joy in Christ Jesus will overflow on account of me.

[27]Whatever happens, conduct yourselves in a manner worthy of the gospel of Christ. Then, whether I come and see you or only hear about you in my absence, I will know that you stand firm in one spirit, contending as one man for the faith of the gospel [28]without being frightened in any way by those who oppose you. This is a sign to them that they will be destroyed, but that you will be saved — and that by God. [29]For it has been granted to you on behalf of Christ not only to believe on him, but also to suffer for him, [30]since you are going through the same struggle you saw I had, and now hear that I still have.

Imitating Christ's Humility

2 If you have any encouragement from being united with Christ, if any comfort from his love, if any fellowship with the Spirit, if any tenderness and compassion, [2]then make my joy complete by being likeminded, having the same love, being one in spirit and purpose. [3]Do nothing out of selfish ambition or vain conceit, but in humility consider others better than yourselves. [4]Each of you should look not only to your own interests, but also to the interests of others.

[5]Your attitude should be the same as that of Christ Jesus:

[6]Who, being in very nature[a] God,
   did not consider equality with God something to
      be grasped,
[7]but made himself nothing,
   taking the very nature[b] of a servant,
   being made in human likeness.

[8]And being found in appearance as a man,
   he humbled himself
   and became obedient to death — even death on
      a cross!
[9]Therefore God exalted him to the highest place
   and gave him the name that is above every
      name,
[10]that at the name of Jesus every knee should bow,
   in heaven and on earth and under the earth,
[11]and every tongue confess that Jesus Christ is
      Lord,
   to the glory of God the Father.

2:6   This is an ancient hymn. It celebrates Christ's humility and suffering, and praises his victory over death. Some scholars think that Paul might have been quoting it from an earlier tradition, others that he wrote it himself. Either way, it is in some way a very early creed (statement of belief).

Shining as Stars

[12]Therefore, my dear friends, as you have always obeyed — not only in my presence, but now much more in my absence — continue to work out your salvation with fear and trembling, [13]for it is God who works in you to will and to act according to his good purpose.

2:13   Paul praised the Philippians for their continuing work for God, and encouraged them to keep going as they grew in the faith. He acknowledged that a relationship with God is very much a two-way thing.

---

[14]Do everything without complaining or arguing, [15]so that you may become blameless and pure, children of God without fault in a crooked and depraved generation, in which you shine like stars in the universe [16]as you hold out[c] the word of life — in order that I may boast on the day of Christ that I did not run or labour for nothing. [17]But even if I am being poured out like a drink offering on the sacrifice and service coming from your faith, I am glad and rejoice with all of you. [18]So you too should be glad and rejoice with me.

Timothy and Epaphroditus

[19]I hope in the Lord Jesus to send Timothy to you soon, that I also may be cheered when I receive news about you. [20]I have no-one else like him, who takes a genuine interest in your welfare. [21]For everyone looks out for his own interests, not those of Jesus Christ. [22]But you know that Timothy has proved himself, because as a son with his father he has served with me in the work of the gospel. [23]I hope, therefore, to send him as soon as I see how things go with me. [24]And I am confident in the Lord that I myself will come soon.

[25]But I think it is necessary to send back to you

---

c 16,17 Some late manuscripts have verses 16 and 17 in reverse order.   d 19 Or salvation   a 6 Or in the form of
b 7 Or the form   c 16 Or hold on to

Epaphroditus, my brother, fellow-worker and fellow-soldier, who is also your messenger, whom you sent to take care of my needs. 26For he longs for all of you and is distressed because you heard he was ill. 27Indeed he was ill, and almost died. But God had mercy on him, and not on him only but also on me, to spare me sorrow upon sorrow. 28Therefore I am all the more eager to send him, so that when you see him again you may be glad and I may have less anxiety. 29Welcome him in the Lord with great joy, and honour men like him, 30because he almost died for the work of Christ, risking his life to make up for the help you could not give me.

2:25 The Philippians had sent Epaphroditus to Paul in prison, a journey of some 700 miles to Rome, because they had heard that he was in need. He had probably brought some money for Paul (Philippi was one of the few places from which Paul accepted financial help). Epaphroditus' illness and then homesickness when he heard about their concern for him meant that Paul sent him back, probably with this letter.

No Confidence in the Flesh

3 Finally, my brothers, rejoice in the Lord! It is no trouble for me to write the same things to you again, and it is a safeguard for you.

2Watch out for those dogs, those men who do evil, those mutilators of the flesh. 3For it is we who are the circumcision, we who worship by the Spirit of God, who glory in Christ Jesus, and who put no confidence in the flesh—4though I myself have reasons for such confidence.

If anyone else thinks he has reasons to put confidence in the flesh, I have more: 5circumcised on the eighth day, of the people of Israel, of the tribe of Benjamin, a Hebrew of Hebrews; in regard to the law, a Pharisee; 6as for zeal, persecuting the church; as for legalistic righteousness, faultless.

7But whatever was to my profit I now consider loss for the sake of Christ. 8What is more, I consider everything a loss compared to the surpassing greatness of knowing Christ Jesus my Lord, for whose sake I have lost all things. I consider them rubbish, that I may gain Christ 9and be found in him, not having a righteousness of my own that comes from the law, but that which is through faith in Christ—the righteousness that comes from God and is by faith. 10I want to know Christ and the power of his resurrection and the fellowship of sharing in his sufferings, becoming like him in his death, 11and so, somehow, to attain to the resurrection from the dead.

Pressing on Towards the Goal

12Not that I have already obtained all this, or have already been made perfect, but I press on to take hold of that for which Christ Jesus took hold of me.

13Brothers, I do not consider myself yet to have taken hold of it. But one thing I do: Forgetting what is behind and straining towards what is ahead, 14I press on towards the goal to win the prize for which God has called me heavenwards in Christ Jesus.

15All of us who are mature should take such a view of things. And if on some point you think differently, that too God will make clear to you. 16Only let us live up to what we have already attained.

17Join with others in following my example, brothers, and take note of those who live according to the pattern we gave you. 18For, as I have often told you before and now say again even with tears, many live as enemies of the cross of Christ. 19Their destiny is destruction, their god is their stomach, and their glory is in their shame. Their mind is on earthly things. 20But our citizenship is in heaven. And we eagerly await a Saviour from there, the Lord Jesus Christ, 21who, by the power that enables him to bring everything under his control, will transform our lowly bodies so that they will be like his glorious body.

4 Therefore, my brothers, you whom I love and long for, my joy and crown, that is how you should stand firm in the Lord, dear friends!

Exhortations

2I plead with Euodia and I plead with Syntyche to agree with each other in the Lord. 3Yes, and I ask you, loyal yokefellow,a help these women who have contended at my side in the cause of the gospel, along with Clement and the rest of my fellow-workers, whose names are in the book of life.

4:2 Many people think that Paul hated women, but he did encourage women in the church at a time when they would not have been allowed into the synagogues. Here he encouraged two of the women to sort out their differences and continue working within the church.

4Rejoice in the Lord always. I will say it again: Rejoice! 5Let your gentleness be evident to all. The Lord is near. 6Do not be anxious about anything, but in everything, by prayer and petition, with thanksgiving, present your requests to God. 7And the peace of God, which transcends all understanding, will guard your hearts and your minds in Christ Jesus.

8Finally, brothers, whatever is true, whatever is noble, whatever is right, whatever is pure, whatever is lovely, whatever is admirable—if anything is excellent or praiseworthy—think about such things. 9Whatever you have learned or received or heard from me, or seen in me—put it into practice. And the God of peace will be with you.

Thanks for Their Gifts

10I rejoice greatly in the Lord that at last you have renewed your concern for me. Indeed, you have been concerned, but you had no opportunity to show it.

a3 Or loyal Syzygus

[11]I am not saying this because I am in need, for I have learned to be content whatever the circumstances. [12]I know what it is to be in need, and I know what it is to have plenty. I have learned the secret of being content in any and every situation, whether well fed or hungry, whether living in plenty or in want. [13]I can do everything through him who gives me strength.

[14]Yet it was good of you to share in my troubles. [15]Moreover, as you Philippians know, in the early days of your acquaintance with the gospel, when I set out from Macedonia, not one church shared with me in the matter of giving and receiving, except you only; [16]for even when I was in Thessalonica, you sent me aid again and again when I was in need. [17]Not that I am looking for a gift, but I am looking for what may be credited to your account. [18]I have received full payment and even more; I am amply supplied, now that I have received from Epaphroditus the gifts you sent. They are a fragrant offering, an acceptable sacrifice, pleasing to God. [19]And my God will meet all your needs according to his glorious riches in Christ Jesus.

[20]To our God and Father be glory for ever and ever. Amen.

Final Greetings

[21]Greet all the saints in Christ Jesus. The brothers who are with me send greetings. [22]All the saints send you greetings, especially those who belong to Caesar's household.

[23]The grace of the Lord Jesus Christ be with your spirit. Amen. [b]

[b]23 Some manuscripts do not have *Amen*.

Colossians

Christ Is Sufficient

Paul was concerned that the people were being affected too much by outward things. Their desire to know more about God was affecting the simplicity of their faith, and all sorts of rules and philosophies had been introduced. The thing that is important is that God is accessible to everyone through Christ. Paul did not waste time in arguing every point with the false philosophies or ideas, instead he sought to show that Christ is sufficient and shows us God without any grand systems or human constructions.

---

1 Paul, an apostle of Christ Jesus by the will of God, and Timothy our brother,

[2]To the holy and faithful[a] brothers in Christ at Colosse:

Grace and peace to you from God our Father. [b]

Thanksgiving and Prayer

[3]We always thank God, the Father of our Lord Jesus Christ, when we pray for you, [4]because we have heard of your faith in Christ Jesus and of the love you have for all the saints— [5]the faith and love that spring from the hope that is stored up for you in heaven and that you have already heard about in the word of truth, the gospel [6]that has come to you. All over the world this gospel is bearing fruit and growing, just as it has been doing among you since the day you heard it and understood God's grace in all its truth. [7]You learned it from Epaphras, our dear fellow-servant, who is a faithful minister of Christ on our[c] behalf, [8]and who also told us of your love in the Spirit.

[9]For this reason, since the day we heard about you, we have not stopped praying for you and asking God to fill you with the knowledge of his will through all spiritual wisdom and understanding. [10]And we pray this in order that you may live a life worthy of the Lord and may please him in every way: bearing fruit in every good work, growing in the knowledge of God, [11]being strengthened with all power according to his glorious might so that you may have great endurance and patience, and joyfully [12]giving thanks to the Father, who has qualified you[d] to share in the inheritance of the saints in the kingdom of light. [13]For he has rescued us from the dominion of darkness and brought us into the kingdom of the Son he loves, [14]in whom we have redemption,[e] the forgiveness of sins.

[a]2 Or *believing*   [b]2 Some manuscripts *Father and the Lord Jesus Christ*
[c]7 Some manuscripts *your*   [d]12 Some manuscripts *us*   [e]14 A few late manuscripts *redemption through his blood*

The Supremacy of Christ

15He is the image of the invisible God, the firstborn over all creation. 16For by him all things were created: things in heaven and on earth, visible and invisible, whether thrones or powers or rulers or authorities; all things were created by him and for him. 17He is before all things, and in him all things hold together. 18And he is the head of the body, the church; he is the beginning and the firstborn from among the dead, so that in everything he might have the supremacy. 19For God was pleased to have all his fulness dwell in him, 20and through him to reconcile to himself all things, whether things on earth or things in heaven, by making peace through his blood, shed on the cross.

1:15　This passage (verses 15–20) is like a hymn. Like Philippians 2:6–11, some scholars think it was used by Christians before Paul wrote it down. It celebrates Christ's role in creation.

21Once you were alienated from God and were enemies in your minds because of*f* your evil behaviour. 22But now he has reconciled you by Christ's physical body through death to present you holy in his sight, without blemish and free from accusation — 23if you continue in your faith, established and firm, not moved from the hope held out in the gospel. This is the gospel that you heard and that has been proclaimed to every creature under heaven, and of which I, Paul, have become a servant.

Paul's Labour for the Church

24Now I rejoice in what was suffered for you, and I fill up in my flesh what is still lacking in regard to Christ's afflictions, for the sake of his body, which is the church. 25I have become its servant by the commission God gave me to present to you the word of God in its fulness — 26the mystery that has been kept hidden for ages and generations, but is now disclosed to the saints. 27To them God has chosen to make known among the Gentiles the glorious riches of this mystery, which is Christ in you, the hope of glory.

28We proclaim him, admonishing and teaching everyone with all wisdom, so that we may present everyone perfect in Christ. 29To this end I labour, struggling with all his energy, which so powerfully works in me.

2 I want you to know how much I am struggling for you and for those at Laodicea, and for all who have not met me personally. 2My purpose is that they may be encouraged in heart and united in love, so that they may have the full riches of complete understanding, in order that they may know the mystery of God, namely, Christ, 3in whom are hidden all the treasures of wisdom and knowledge. 4I tell you this so that no-one may deceive you by fine-sounding arguments. 5For though I am absent from you in body, I am present with you in spirit and delight to see how orderly you are and how firm your faith in Christ is.

Freedom From Human Regulations Through Life With Christ

6So then, just as you received Christ Jesus as Lord, continue to live in him, 7rooted and built up in him, strengthened in the faith as you were taught, and overflowing with thankfulness.

8See to it that no-one takes you captive through hollow and deceptive philosophy, which depends on human tradition and the basic principles of this world rather than on Christ.

9For in Christ all the fulness of the Deity lives in bodily form, 10and you have been given fulness in Christ, who is the Head over every power and authority. 11In him you were also circumcised, in the putting off of the sinful nature,*a* not with a circumcision done by the hands of men but with the circumcision done by Christ, 12having been buried with him in baptism and raised with him through your faith in the power of God, who raised him from the dead.

13When you were dead in your sins and in the uncircumcision of your sinful nature,*b* God made you*c* alive with Christ. He forgave us all our sins, 14having cancelled the written code, with its regulations, that was against us and that stood opposed to us; he took it away, nailing it to the cross. 15And having disarmed the powers and authorities, he made a public spectacle of them, triumphing over them by the cross.*d*

16Therefore do not let anyone judge you by what you eat or drink, or with regard to a religious festival, a New Moon celebration or a Sabbath day. 17These are a shadow of the things that were to come; the reality, however, is found in Christ. 18Do not let anyone who delights in false humility and the worship of angels disqualify you for the prize. Such a person goes into great detail about what he has seen, and his unspiritual mind puffs him up with idle notions. 19He has lost connection with the Head, from whom the whole body, supported and held together by its ligaments and sinews, grows as God causes it to grow.

2:16　Paul warned the people that they must not be seduced into thinking that these things were ways to holiness. New life was entirely due to Christ, and they should follow him and live a heavenly life, not in order to win God's favour but as a response to what he had done for them. If this all sounds familiar, it is no surprise. Paul's letters were written to Christian communities in the very early days of Christianity, and all would have had similar problems, especially with regard to moral living and avoiding Judaistic legalism. The interesting thing is how Paul's letters are still very applicable to Christian communities two thousand years later!

---

f21 Or minds, as shown by　　*a11 Or the flesh*　　*b13 Or your flesh*　　*c13 Some manuscripts us*
d15 Or them in him

²⁰Since you died with Christ to the basic principles of this world, why, as though you still belonged to it, do you submit to its rules: ²¹"Do not handle! Do not taste! Do not touch!"? ²²These are all destined to perish with use, because they are based on human commands and teachings. ²³Such regulations indeed have an appearance of wisdom, with their self-imposed worship, their false humility and their harsh treatment of the body, but they lack any value in restraining sensual indulgence.

Rules for Holy Living

3 Since, then, you have been raised with Christ, set your hearts on things above, where Christ is seated at the right hand of God. ²Set your minds on things above, not on earthly things. ³For you died, and your life is now hidden with Christ in God. ⁴When Christ, who is your^a life, appears, then you also will appear with him in glory.

⁵Put to death, therefore, whatever belongs to your earthly nature: sexual immorality, impurity, lust, evil desires and greed, which is idolatry. ⁶Because of these, the wrath of God is coming.^b ⁷You used to walk in these ways, in the life you once lived. ⁸But now you must rid yourselves of all such things as these: anger, rage, malice, slander and filthy language from your lips. ⁹Do not lie to each other, since you have taken off your old self with its practices ¹⁰and have put on the new self, which is being renewed in knowledge in the image of its Creator. ¹¹Here there is no Greek or Jew, circumcised or uncircumcised, barbarian, Scythian, slave or free, but Christ is all, and is in all.

¹²Therefore, as God's chosen people, holy and dearly loved, clothe yourselves with compassion, kindness, humility, gentleness and patience. ¹³Bear with each other and forgive whatever grievances you may have against one another. Forgive as the Lord forgave you. ¹⁴And over all these virtues put on love, which binds them all together in perfect unity.

¹⁵Let the peace of Christ rule in your hearts, since as members of one body you were called to peace. And be thankful. ¹⁶Let the word of Christ dwell in you richly as you teach and admonish one another with all wisdom, and as you sing psalms, hymns and spiritual songs with gratitude in your hearts to God. ¹⁷And whatever you do, whether in word or deed, do it all in the name of the Lord Jesus, giving thanks to God the Father through him.

Rules for Christian Households

¹⁸Wives, submit to your husbands, as is fitting in the Lord.

¹⁹Husbands, love your wives and do not be harsh with them.

²⁰Children, obey your parents in everything, for this pleases the Lord.

²¹Fathers, do not embitter your children, or they will become discouraged.

²²Slaves, obey your earthly masters in everything; and do it, not only when their eye is on you and to win their favour, but with sincerity of heart and reverence for the Lord. ²³Whatever you do, work at it with all your heart, as working for the Lord, not for men, ²⁴since you know that you will receive an inheritance from the Lord as a reward. It is the Lord Christ you are serving. ²⁵Anyone who does wrong will be repaid for his wrong, and there is no favouritism.

4 Masters, provide your slaves with what is right and fair, because you know that you also have a Master in heaven.

Further Instructions

²Devote yourselves to prayer, being watchful and thankful. ³And pray for us, too, that God may open a door for our message, so that we may proclaim the mystery of Christ, for which I am in chains. ⁴Pray that I may proclaim it clearly, as I should. ⁵Be wise in the way you act towards outsiders; make the most of every opportunity. ⁶Let your conversation be always full of grace, seasoned with salt, so that you may know how to answer everyone.

Final Greetings

⁷Tychicus will tell you all the news about me. He is a dear brother, a faithful minister and fellow-servant in the Lord. ⁸I am sending him to you for the express purpose that you may know about our^a circumstances and that he may encourage your hearts. ⁹He is coming with Onesimus, our faithful and dear brother, who is one of you. They will tell you everything that is happening here.

¹⁰My fellow-prisoner Aristarchus sends you his greetings, as does Mark, the cousin of Barnabas. (You have received instructions about him; if he comes to you, welcome him.) ¹¹Jesus, who is called Justus, also sends greetings. These are the only Jews among my fellow-workers for the kingdom of God, and they have proved a comfort to me. ¹²Epaphras, who is one of you and a servant of Christ Jesus, sends greetings. He is always wrestling in prayer for you, that you may stand firm in all the will of God, mature and fully assured. ¹³I vouch for him that he is working hard for you and for those at Laodicea and Hierapolis. ¹⁴Our dear friend Luke, the doctor, and Demas send greetings. ¹⁵Give my greetings to the brothers at Laodicea, and to Nympha and the church in her house.

¹⁶After this letter has been read to you, see that it is also read in the church of the Laodiceans and that you in turn read the letter from Laodicea.

¹⁷Tell Archippus: "See to it that you complete the work you have received in the Lord."

¹⁸I, Paul, write this greeting in my own hand. Remember my chains. Grace be with you.

---

^a4 Some manuscripts *our*   ^b6 Some early manuscripts *coming on those who are disobedient*
^a8 Some manuscripts *that he may know about your*

1 Thessalonians

An Early Letter

Most scholars believe that this is one of the earliest of Paul's letters, written about 20 years after Christ's death, resurrection, and ascension. Paul was not a full-time minister of the gospel when he was in Thessalonica. The small church there could not have afforded to put him up so he worked, probably as a tentmaker, at the same time as teaching about Christ. He remembered fondly those whose faith he had helped nurture and how they had gone on encouraging others to turn to Jesus Christ. Even when he was away from Thessalonica and was unable to return, he sent Timothy who reported back that despite many trials their faith was fine.

Difficult Times

In many ways 1 Thessalonians deals with problems similar to those of 1 Corinthians. Paul warned the people about immorality and not living holy lives, and urged them that outsiders would respect them for living a "quiet life" and would learn more about Christ that way than if they were lazy or immoral. He also dealt with the problem of people who had "died in Christ"—what would happen to them at the last day? The political and religious times were very turbulent and some kept saying that the end was near and that Christ would return very soon. Paul, like Jesus, taught them to live in the light of Christ, to be always ready, but not to ask when the end was going to be. This meant that they should live in the world, working for a living just like Paul did when he was staying with them, and encouraging and helping each other in their lives and faith.

---

1 Paul, Silas[a] and Timothy,

To the church of the Thessalonians in God the Father and the Lord Jesus Christ:

Grace and peace to you.[b]

Thanksgiving for the Thessalonians' Faith

[2]We always thank God for all of you, mentioning you in our prayers. [3]We continually remember before our God and Father your work produced by faith, your labour prompted by love, and your endurance inspired by hope in our Lord Jesus Christ.

[4]For we know, brothers loved by God, that he has chosen you, [5]because our gospel came to you not simply with words, but also with power, with the Holy Spirit and with deep conviction. You know how we lived among you for your sake. [6]You became imitators of us and of the Lord; in spite of severe suffering, you welcomed the message with the joy given by the Holy Spirit. [7]And so you became a model to all the believers in Macedonia and Achaia. [8]The Lord's message rang out from you not only in Macedonia and Achaia—your faith in God has become known everywhere. Therefore we do not need to say anything about it, [9]for they themselves report what kind of reception you gave us. They tell how you turned to God from idols to serve the living and true God, [10]and to wait for his Son from heaven, whom he raised from the dead—Jesus, who rescues us from the coming wrath.

---

a 1 Greek Silvanus, a variant of Silas   b 1 Some early manuscripts you from God our Father and the Lord Jesus Christ

Paul's Ministry in Thessalonica

2 You know, brothers, that our visit to you was not a failure. [2]We had previously suffered and been insulted in Philippi, as you know, but with the help of our God we dared to tell you his gospel in spite of strong opposition. [3]For the appeal we make does not spring from error or impure motives, nor are we trying to trick you. [4]On the contrary, we speak as men approved by God to be entrusted with the gospel. We are not trying to please men but God, who tests our hearts. [5]You know we never used flattery, nor did we put on a mask to cover up greed—God is our witness. [6]We were not looking for praise from men, not from you or anyone else.

As apostles of Christ we could have been a burden to you, [7]but we were gentle among you, like a mother caring for her little children. [8]We loved you so much that we were delighted to share with you not only the gospel of God but our lives as well, because you had become so dear to us. [9]Surely you remember, brothers, our toil and hardship; we worked night and day in order not to be a burden to anyone while we preached the gospel of God to you.

2:9 Paul worked very hard so that he would not be a burden to the people. It also showed that he was not making a profit from his spiritual work.

---

[10]You are witnesses, and so is God, of how holy, righteous and blameless we were among you who believed. [11]For you know that we dealt with each of you as a father deals with his own children, [12]encouraging, comforting and urging you to live lives worthy of God, who calls you into his kingdom and glory.

[13]And we also thank God continually because, when you received the word of God, which you heard from us, you accepted it not as the word of men, but as it actually is, the word of God, which is at work in you who believe. [14]For you, brothers, became imitators of God's churches in Judea, which are in Christ Jesus: You suffered from your own countrymen the same things those churches suffered from the Jews, [15]who killed the Lord Jesus and the prophets and also drove us out. They displease God and are hostile to all men [16]in their effort to keep us from speaking to the Gentiles so that they may be saved. In this way they always heap up their sins to the limit. The wrath of God has come upon them at last.[a]

2:14 The church in Thessalonica was being persecuted. Paul had had to leave earlier than he wished because some people were following him and stirring the synagogue against him and what he was teaching.

Paul's Longing to See the Thessalonians

[17]But, brothers, when we were torn away from you for a short time (in person, not in thought), out of our intense longing we made every effort to see you. [18]For we wanted to come to you—certainly I, Paul, did, again and again—but Satan stopped us. [19]For what is our hope, our joy, or the crown in which we will glory in the presence of our Lord Jesus when he comes? Is it not you? [20]Indeed, you are our glory and joy.

3 So when we could stand it no longer, we thought it best to be left by ourselves in Athens. [2]We sent Timothy, who is our brother and God's fellow-worker[a] in spreading the gospel of Christ, to strengthen and encourage you in your faith, [3]so that no-one would be unsettled by these trials. You know quite well that we were destined for them. [4]In fact, when we were with you, we kept telling you that we would be persecuted. And it turned out that way, as you well know. [5]For this reason, when I could stand it no longer, I sent to find out about your faith. I was afraid that in some way the tempter might have tempted you and our efforts might have been useless.

3:4 Yet again Paul had to defend his ministry. A lot of people thought that he must have some other motives for what he did and that he was not a proper teacher. He was unhappy about the fact that he had been unable to return to see them again.

Timothy's Encouraging Report

[6]But Timothy has just now come to us from you and has brought good news about your faith and love. He has told us that you always have pleasant memories of us and that you long to see us, just as we also long to see you. [7]Therefore, brothers, in all our distress and persecution we were encouraged about you because of your faith. [8]For now we really live, since you are standing firm in the Lord. [9]How can we thank God enough for you in return for all the joy we have in the presence of our God because of you? [10]Night and day we pray most earnestly that we may see you again and supply what is lacking in your faith.

[11]Now may our God and Father himself and our Lord Jesus clear the way for us to come to you. [12]May the Lord make your love increase and overflow for each other and for everyone else, just as ours does for you. [13]May he strengthen your hearts so that you will be blameless and holy in the presence of our God and Father when our Lord Jesus comes with all his holy ones.

Living to Please God

4 Finally, brothers, we instructed you how to live in order to please God, as in fact you are living. Now we ask you and urge you in the Lord Jesus to do this more and more. [2]For you know what instructions we gave you by the authority of the Lord Jesus.

---

[a]16 Or *them fully*   [a]2 Some manuscripts *brother and fellow-worker*; other manuscripts *brother and God's servant*

³It is God's will that you should be sanctified: that you should avoid sexual immorality; ⁴that each of you should learn to control his own body[a] in a way that is holy and honourable, ⁵not in passionate lust like the heathen, who do not know God; ⁶and that in this matter no-one should wrong his brother or take advantage of him. The Lord will punish men for all such sins, as we have already told you and warned you. ⁷For God did not call us to be impure, but to live a holy life. ⁸Therefore, he who rejects this instruction does not reject man but God, who gives you his Holy Spirit.

⁹Now about brotherly love we do not need to write to you, for you yourselves have been taught by God to love each other. ¹⁰And in fact, you do love all the brothers throughout Macedonia. Yet we urge you, brothers, to do so more and more.

¹¹Make it your ambition to lead a quiet life, to mind your own business and to work with your hands, just as we told you, ¹²so that your daily life may win the respect of outsiders and so that you will not be dependent on anybody.

The Coming of the Lord

¹³Brothers, we do not want you to be ignorant about those who fall asleep, or to grieve like the rest of men, who have no hope. ¹⁴We believe that Jesus died and rose again and so we believe that God will bring with Jesus those who have fallen asleep in him. ¹⁵According to the Lord's own word, we tell you that we who are still alive, who are left till the coming of the Lord, will certainly not precede those who have fallen asleep. ¹⁶For the Lord himself will come down from heaven, with a loud command, with the voice of the archangel and with the trumpet call of God, and the dead in Christ will rise first. ¹⁷After that, we who are still alive and are left will be caught up together with them in the clouds to meet the Lord in the air. And so we will be with the Lord for ever. ¹⁸Therefore encourage each other with these words.

4:13 Paul answered their questions about what would happen to those who died before Christ's return. He reassured them that all people who believed would rise from the dead.

---

5 Now, brothers, about times and dates we do not need to write to you, ²for you know very well that the day of the Lord will come like a thief in the night. ³While people are saying, "Peace and safety", destruction will come on them suddenly, as labour pains on a pregnant woman, and they will not escape.

⁴But you, brothers, are not in darkness so that this day should surprise you like a thief. ⁵You are all sons of the light and sons of the day. We do not belong to the night or to the darkness. ⁶So then, let us not be like others, who are asleep, but let us be alert and self-controlled. ⁷For those who sleep, sleep at night, and those who get drunk, get drunk at night. ⁸But since we belong to the day, let us be self-controlled, putting on faith and love as a breastplate, and the hope of salvation as a helmet. ⁹For God did not appoint us to suffer wrath but to receive salvation through our Lord Jesus Christ. ¹⁰He died for us so that, whether we are awake or asleep, we may live together with him. ¹¹Therefore encourage one another and build each other up, just as in fact you are doing.

Final Instructions

¹²Now we ask you, brothers, to respect those who work hard among you, who are over you in the Lord and who admonish you. ¹³Hold them in the highest regard in love because of their work. Live in peace with each other. ¹⁴And we urge you, brothers, warn those who are idle, encourage the timid, help the weak, be patient with everyone. ¹⁵Make sure that nobody pays back wrong for wrong, but always try to be kind to each other and to everyone else.

¹⁶Be joyful always; ¹⁷pray continually; ¹⁸give thanks in all circumstances, for this is God's will for you in Christ Jesus.

¹⁹Do not put out the Spirit's fire; ²⁰do not treat prophecies with contempt. ²¹Test everything. Hold on to the good. ²²Avoid every kind of evil.

²³May God himself, the God of peace, sanctify you through and through. May your whole spirit, soul and body be kept blameless at the coming of our Lord Jesus Christ. ²⁴The one who calls you is faithful and he will do it.

²⁵Brothers, pray for us. ²⁶Greet all the brothers with a holy kiss. ²⁷I charge you before the Lord to have this letter read to all the brothers.

²⁸The grace of our Lord Jesus Christ be with you.

^a4 Or *learn to live with his own wife*; or *learn to acquire a wife*

2 Thessalonians

Keeping the Faith Under Trial

Times were hard. The church in Thessalonica was being persecuted for its faith. Someone was misrepresenting Paul and claiming he had said things that he hadn't. Everything seemed to be on trial. But Paul pointed out that the suffering the people were going through was temporary, and that at the end all would be put right. Those who had been seduced into lawlessness would be shown for what they were. He prayed for the weak who might be misguided, and reminded them that Christ was present in all their problems.

Playing Your Part

As a letter, 2 Thessalonians deals with the same issues as 1 Thessalonians. Things seem to have got more difficult for the people, so Paul had to deal with some of the issues more strongly. Some of them were still not pulling their weight. Their attitude seemed to be one of "if the world is about to end, why bother working?" This was obviously a problem Paul had come up against when he was there before, as he reminded them of a strict teaching that he had given them: "If a man will not work, he shall not eat." (3:10) This was to encourage everyone in the community to play their part to the best of their abilities. Note that it was idleness he was warning against, which is very different from being unable to work because of poor health or the absence of job opportunities.

1

Paul, Silas[a] and Timothy,

To the church of the Thessalonians in God our Father and the Lord Jesus Christ:

[2]Grace and peace to you from God the Father and the Lord Jesus Christ.

Thanksgiving and Prayer

[3]We ought always to thank God for you, brothers, and rightly so, because your faith is growing more and more, and the love every one of you has for each other is increasing. [4]Therefore, among God's churches we boast about your perseverance and faith in all the persecutions and trials you are enduring.

[5]All this is evidence that God's judgment is right, and as a result you will be counted worthy of the kingdom of God, for which you are suffering. [6]God is just: He will pay back trouble to those who trouble you [7]and give relief to you who are troubled, and to us as well. This will happen when the Lord Jesus is revealed from heaven in blazing fire with his powerful angels. [8]He will punish those who do not know God and do not obey the gospel of our Lord Jesus. [9]They will be punished with everlasting destruction and shut out from the presence of the Lord and from the majesty of his power [10]on the day he comes to be glorified in his holy people and to be marvelled at among all those who have believed. This includes you, because you believed our testimony to you.

[11]With this in mind, we constantly pray for you, that our God may count you worthy of his calling, and that by his power he may fulfil every good purpose of yours and every act prompted by your faith. [12]We pray this so that the name of our Lord Jesus may be glorified in

you, and you in him, according to the grace of our God and the Lord Jesus Christ.[b]

The Man of Lawlessness

2 Concerning the coming of our Lord Jesus Christ and our being gathered to him, we ask you, brothers, [2]not to become easily unsettled or alarmed by some prophecy, report or letter supposed to have come from us, saying that the day of the Lord has already come. [3]Don't let anyone deceive you in any way, for that day will not come, until the rebellion occurs and the man of lawlessness[a] is revealed, the man doomed to destruction. [4]He will oppose and will exalt himself over everything that is called God or is worshipped, so that he sets himself up in God's temple, proclaiming himself to be God.

[5]Don't you remember that when I was with you I used to tell you these things? [6]And now you know what is holding him back, so that he may be revealed at the proper time. [7]For the secret power of lawlessness is already at work; but the one who now holds it back will continue to do so till he is taken out of the way. [8]And then the lawless one will be revealed, whom the Lord Jesus will overthrow with the breath of his mouth and destroy by the splendour of his coming. [9]The coming of the lawless one will be in accordance with the work of Satan displayed in all kinds of counterfeit miracles, signs and wonders, [10]and in every sort of evil that deceives those who are perishing. They perish because they refused to love the truth and so be saved. [11]For this reason God sends them a powerful delusion so that they will believe the lie [12]and so that all will be condemned who have not believed the truth but have delighted in wickedness.

2:7 This is a very difficult passage and people have interpreted it in many different ways. It talks of the chaos that will be around before the last days and the "lawless one" whom Jesus will crush.

Stand Firm

[13]But we ought always to thank God for you, brothers loved by the Lord, because from the beginning God chose you[b] to be saved through the sanctifying work of the Spirit and through belief in the truth. [14]He called you to this through our gospel, that you might share in the glory of our Lord Jesus Christ. [15]So then, brothers, stand firm and hold to the teachings[c] we

passed on to you, whether by word of mouth or by letter.

[16]May our Lord Jesus Christ himself and God our Father, who loved us and by his grace gave us eternal encouragement and good hope, [17]encourage your hearts and strengthen you in every good deed and word.

Request for Prayer

3 Finally, brothers, pray for us that the message of the Lord may spread rapidly and be honoured, just as it was with you. [2]And pray that we may be delivered from wicked and evil men, for not everyone has faith. [3]But the Lord is faithful, and he will strengthen and protect you from the evil one. [4]We have confidence in the Lord that you are doing and will continue to do the things we command. [5]May the Lord direct your hearts into God's love and Christ's perseverance.

Warning Against Idleness

[6]In the name of the Lord Jesus Christ, we command you, brothers, to keep away from every brother who is idle and does not live according to the teaching[a] you received from us. [7]For you yourselves know how you ought to follow our example. We were not idle when we were with you, [8]nor did we eat anyone's food without paying for it. On the contrary, we worked night and day, labouring and toiling so that we would not be a burden to any of you. [9]We did this, not because we do not have the right to such help, but in order to make ourselves a model for you to follow. [10]For even when we were with you, we gave you this rule: "If a man will not work, he shall not eat."

[11]We hear that some among you are idle. They are not busy; they are busybodies. [12]Such people we command and urge in the Lord Jesus Christ to settle down and earn the bread they eat. [13]And as for you, brothers, never tire of doing what is right.

[14]If anyone does not obey our instruction in this letter, take special note of him. Do not associate with him, in order that he may feel ashamed. [15]Yet do not regard him as an enemy, but warn him as a brother.

Final Greetings

[16]Now may the Lord of peace himself give you peace at all times and in every way. The Lord be with all of you.

[17]I, Paul, write this greeting in my own hand, which is the distinguishing mark in all my letters. This is how I write.

[18]The grace of our Lord Jesus Christ be with you all.

---

b12 Or God and Lord, Jesus Christ   a3 Some manuscripts sin
b13 Some manuscripts because God chose you as his firstfruits   c15 Or traditions   a6 Or tradition

The Pastoral Letters

Choosing Pastors

Paul's two letters to Timothy and his letter to Titus are together often referred to as the "Pastoral Letters". These three letters were written at a time when it was necessary to choose and train new leaders for the young churches. The first generation of apostles was dying out, and Christian communities were becoming bigger and more widespread. These letters give specific instructions about what sort of people should be chosen as pastors, and how they should take care of their communities. They were addressed to particular people, who were faced with particular problems.

Who Were They for?

In books about the Bible you will find discussions about whether these letters were actually written by the apostle Paul, and whether or not Timothy and Titus are the same people who are mentioned elsewhere as two of Paul's most loyal followers. Certainly, these letters are not as fiery as could be expected from Paul, although some people say that this may be because they were written for him by a secretary—possibly Luke (see 2 Timothy 4:11). For the purpose of faith, what matters is that believers have always accepted these letters as authentic Christian teaching in the tradition of Paul. It is obvious that the writer had authority and regarded his readers as his spiritual children. More importantly, the writer was driven by faith in Jesus Christ and expected the same of his readers.

A Job Description

The writer gave instructions in the duties of pastors. These duties were to include teaching, governing, and administration in a society quite different from ours. They were to preach the gospel tirelessly, keeping themselves and their listeners faithful to the truth which they had received from the apostles. They were to supervise worship and take care in selecting other church leaders. In addition they were also to be responsible for the discipline of their communities, and for obtaining practical help, including money for those in need.

1 Timothy

Ministers and Ministry

An Irish missionary arrived in a remote village in Africa and went around introducing himself. He was dismayed to discover that every time he mentioned his home country he was asked, "Why are the Protestants and Catholics in Ireland fighting each other?" Few of these people could have identified Ireland on a map or given any further information about that country. But they listened to the news on the radio and knew that there was a place called Ireland where there was violence between groups of Christians. No doubt their understanding of the situation was oversimplified and the media reports distorted, but they were scandalized. Unfortunately the "scandal" does not begin or end in Ireland. The scandal is that there are so many denominations and rival factions in the church of Christ. The word "scandal" means stumbling block, something that causes people to fall. We know from experience that many people fall away from faith in God into apathy or cynicism because they are shocked by the attitude and behaviour of supposedly Christian people.

Learning From Differences

Yet, although there is no room for hatred and rivalry between groups of Christians, a careful study of the Pastoral Letters will show some reasons why there are different traditions within the church. Denominations differ in the way they conduct their public worship. They differ in the titles that they give to their ministers: deacons, priests, presbyters, bishops, superintendents. They also differ in the degree to which they include women in ministry. Sometimes the differences are simply a matter of words, but there are also important differences of understanding—a difference of theology. All denominations can learn from each other, and, most importantly, all can benefit from an open and honest study of what the apostles said and did in the early church. In the next three letters you will find different terms to describe ministers; words like deacon, overseer, and bishop. The words did not mean exactly the same as they do today, and the problems they were asked to solve are also different.

Today

If you want to "do theology" as you read these letters, try to think what advice you would give to a minister in a modern city parish where there are some people who are unemployed and poor, some who are very wealthy, some divorced, some homeless, many pensioners and children, and some criminals. Remember the minister's aim: that all must "be saved and come to a knowledge of the truth" (1 Timothy 2:4). You will immediately realize that there is much to do, many opinions about how to go about it, and no room for fighting or rivalry between those who have been called to this vital task.

---

1 Paul, an apostle of Christ Jesus by the command of God our Saviour and of Christ Jesus our hope,

[2]To Timothy my true son in the faith:

Grace, mercy and peace from God the Father and Christ Jesus our Lord.

Warning Against False Teachers of the Law

[3]As I urged you when I went into Macedonia, stay there in Ephesus so that you may command certain men not to teach false doctrines any longer [4]nor to devote themselves to myths and endless genealogies. These promote controversies rather than God's work—which is by faith. [5]The goal of this command is love, which comes from a pure heart and a good conscience and a sincere faith. [6]Some have wandered away from these and turned to meaningless talk. [7]They want to be teachers of the law, but they do not know what they are talking about or what they so confidently affirm.

[8]We know that the law is good if one uses it properly. [9]We also know that law[a] is made not for the righteous but for lawbreakers and rebels, the ungodly and sinful, the unholy and irreligious; for those who kill their fathers or mothers, for murderers, [10]for adulterers and perverts, for slave traders and liars and perjurers—and for whatever else is contrary to the sound doctrine [11]that conforms to the glorious gospel of the blessed God, which he entrusted to me.

The Lord's Grace to Paul

[12]I thank Christ Jesus our Lord, who has given me strength, that he considered me faithful, appointing me to his service. [13]Even though I was once a blasphemer and a persecutor and a violent man, I was shown mercy because I acted in ignorance and unbelief. [14]The grace of our Lord was poured out on me abundantly, along with the faith and love that are in Christ Jesus. [15]Here is a trustworthy saying that deserves full acceptance: Christ Jesus came into the world to save sinners—of whom I am the worst. [16]But for that very reason I was shown mercy so that in me, the worst of sinners, Christ Jesus might display his unlimited patience as an example for those who would believe on him and receive eternal life. [17]Now to the King eternal, immortal, invisible, the only God, be honour and glory for ever and ever. Amen.

[18]Timothy, my son, I give you this instruction in keeping with the prophecies once made about you, so that by following them you may fight the good fight, [19]holding on to faith and a good conscience. Some have rejected these and so have shipwrecked their faith. [20]Among them are Hymenaeus and Alexander, whom I have handed over to Satan to be taught not to blaspheme.

Instructions on Worship

2 I urge, then, first of all, that requests, prayers, intercession and thanksgiving be made for everyone—[2]for kings and all those in authority, that we may live peaceful and quiet lives in all godliness and holiness. [3]This is good, and pleases God our Saviour, [4]who wants all men to be saved and to come to a knowledge of the truth. [5]For there is one God and one mediator between God and men, the man Christ Jesus, [6]who gave himself as a ransom for all men—the testimony given in its proper time. [7]And for this purpose I was appointed a herald and an apostle—I am telling the truth, I am not lying—and a teacher of the true faith to the Gentiles.

2:6   Paul had an international outlook. He was a Jew immersed in Greek culture and a citizen of the Roman empire. He was the Apostle to the Gentiles, and disagreed with those who wanted converts to become Jews before becoming Christians. Here he taught that Christ Jesus gave himself as a ransom for everyone. Christian faith cannot be reserved to one sect or nation: it must be universal.

---

[8]I want men everywhere to lift up holy hands in prayer, without anger or disputing.

[9]I also want women to dress modestly, with decency and propriety, not with braided hair or gold or pearls or expensive clothes, [10]but with good deeds, appropriate for women who profess to worship God.

[11]A woman should learn in quietness and full submission. [12]I do not permit a woman to teach or to have authority over a man; she must be silent. [13]For Adam was formed first, then Eve. [14]And Adam was not the one deceived; it was the woman who was deceived and became a sinner. [15]But women[a] will be saved[b] through childbearing—if they continue in faith, love and holiness with propriety.

Overseers and Deacons

3 Here is a trustworthy saying: If anyone sets his heart on being an overseer,[a] he desires a noble task. [2]Now the overseer must be above reproach, the husband of but one wife, temperate, self-controlled, respectable, hospitable, able to teach, [3]not given to drunkenness, not violent but gentle, not quarrelsome, not a lover of money. [4]He must manage his own family well and see that his children obey him with proper

---

respect. [5](If anyone does not know how to manage his own family, how can he take care of God's church?) [6]He must not be a recent convert, or he may become conceited and fall under the same judgment as the devil. [7]He must also have a good reputation with outsiders, so that he will not fall into disgrace and into the devil's trap.

[8]Deacons, likewise, are to be men worthy of respect, sincere, not indulging in much wine, and not pursuing dishonest gain. [9]They must keep hold of the deep truths of the faith with a clear conscience. [10]They must first be tested; and then if there is nothing against them, let them serve as deacons.

[11]In the same way, their wives[b] are to be women worthy of respect, not malicious talkers but temperate and trustworthy in everything.

[12]A deacon must be the husband of but one wife and must manage his children and his household well. [13]Those who have served well gain an excellent standing and great assurance in their faith in Christ Jesus.

[14]Although I hope to come to you soon, I am writing you these instructions so that, [15]if I am delayed, you will know how people ought to conduct themselves in God's household, which is the church of the living God, the pillar and foundation of the truth. [16]Beyond all question, the mystery of godliness is great:

He[c] appeared in a body,[d]
    was vindicated by the Spirit,
was seen by angels,
    was preached among the nations,
was believed on in the world,
    was taken up in glory.

Instructions to Timothy

4 The Spirit clearly says that in later times some will abandon the faith and follow deceiving spirits and things taught by demons. [2]Such teachings come through hypocritical liars, whose consciences have been seared as with a hot iron. [3]They forbid people to marry and order them to abstain from certain foods, which God created to be received with thanksgiving by those who believe and who know the truth. [4]For everything God created is good, and nothing is to be rejected if it is received with thanksgiving, [5]because it is consecrated by the word of God and prayer.

[6]If you point these things out to the brothers, you will be a good minister of Christ Jesus, brought up in the truths of the faith and of the good teaching that you have followed. [7]Have nothing to do with godless myths and old wives' tales; rather, train yourself to be godly. [8]For physical training is of some value, but godliness has value for all things, holding promise for both the present life and the life to come.

[9]This is a trustworthy saying that deserves full acceptance [10](and for this we labour and strive), that we have put our hope in the living God, who is the Saviour of all men, and especially of those who believe.

[11]Command and teach these things. [12]Don't let anyone look down on you because you are young, but set an example for the believers in speech, in life, in love, in faith and in purity. [13]Until I come, devote yourself

to the public reading of Scripture, to preaching and to teaching. [14]Do not neglect your gift, which was given you through a prophetic message when the body of elders laid their hands on you.

4:6 This letter was written when the first leaders of the church, the apostles, were dying or had already all died. It was necessary to choose worthy ministers to take their place, and Paul described the sort of qualities needed in a pastor. Further on (4:14), he mentioned that Timothy was assigned his role as a community leader in a ceremony in which the elders laid their hands on him.

---

[15]Be diligent in these matters; give yourself wholly to them, so that everyone may see your progress. [16]Watch your life and doctrine closely. Persevere in them, because if you do, you will save both yourself and your hearers.

Advice About Widows, Elders and Slaves

5 Do not rebuke an older man harshly, but exhort him as if he were your father. Treat younger men as brothers, [2]older women as mothers, and younger women as sisters, with absolute purity.

5:1 One of Paul's favourite themes is that faith in Jesus radically alters all human relationships. All people, regardless of age, sex, or status, are to be treated as brothers and sisters in Christ. We must support those who are not able to care for themselves, and those who direct the work of the church. He also cautioned the readers about lazy, unscrupulous people who take advantage of charity when they could be earning their own living.

---

[3]Give proper recognition to those widows who are really in need. [4]But if a widow has children or grandchildren, these should learn first of all to put their religion into practice by caring for their own family and so repaying their parents and grandparents, for this is pleasing to God. [5]The widow who is really in need and left all alone puts her hope in God and continues night and day to pray and to ask God for help. [6]But the widow who lives for pleasure is dead even while she lives. [7]Give the people these instructions, too, so that no-one may be open to blame. [8]If anyone does not provide for his relatives, and especially for his immediate family, he has denied the faith and is worse than an unbeliever.

[9]No widow may be put on the list of widows unless she is over sixty, has been faithful to her husband,[a] [10]and is well known for her good deeds, such as bringing up children, showing hospitality, washing the feet of the saints, helping those in trouble and devoting herself to all kinds of good deeds.

---

b 11 Or way, deaconesses   *c 16 Some manuscripts God*   *d 16 Or in the flesh*   *a 9 Or has had but one husband*

[11]As for younger widows, do not put them on such a list. For when their sensual desires overcome their dedication to Christ, they want to marry. [12]Thus they bring judgment on themselves, because they have broken their first pledge. [13]Besides, they get into the habit of being idle and going about from house to house. And not only do they become idlers, but also gossips and busybodies, saying things they ought not to. [14]So I counsel younger widows to marry, to have children, to manage their homes and to give the enemy no opportunity for slander. [15]Some have in fact already turned away to follow Satan.

[16]If any woman who is a believer has widows in her family, she should help them and not let the church be burdened with them, so that the church can help those widows who are really in need.

[17]The elders who direct the affairs of the church well are worthy of double honour, especially those whose work is preaching and teaching. [18]For the Scripture says, "Do not muzzle the ox while it is treading out the grain,"[b] and "The worker deserves his wages."[c] [19]Do not entertain an accusation against an elder unless it is brought by two or three witnesses. [20]Those who sin are to be rebuked publicly, so that the others may take warning.

[21]I charge you, in the sight of God and Christ Jesus and the elect angels, to keep these instructions without partiality, and to do nothing out of favouritism. [22]Do not be hasty in the laying on of hands, and do not share in the sins of others. Keep yourself pure.

[23]Stop drinking only water, and use a little wine because of your stomach and your frequent illnesses.

[24]The sins of some men are obvious, reaching the place of judgment ahead of them; the sins of others trail behind them. [25]In the same way, good deeds are obvious, and even those that are not cannot be hidden.

6 All who are under the yoke of slavery should consider their masters worthy of full respect, so that God's name and our teaching may not be slandered. [2]Those who have believing masters are not to show less respect for them because they are brothers. Instead, they are to serve them even better, because those who benefit from their service are believers, and dear to them. These are the things you are to teach and urge on them.

Love of Money

[3]If anyone teaches false doctrines and does not agree to the sound instruction of our Lord Jesus Christ and to godly teaching, [4]he is conceited and understands nothing. He has an unhealthy interest in controversies and quarrels about words that result in envy, strife, malicious talk, evil suspicions [5]and constant friction between men of corrupt mind, who have been robbed of the truth and who think that godliness is a means to financial gain.

[6]But godliness with contentment is great gain. [7]For we brought nothing into the world, and we can take nothing out of it. [8]But if we have food and clothing, we will be content with that. [9]People who want to get rich fall into temptation and a trap and into many foolish and harmful desires that plunge men into ruin and destruction. [10]For the love of money is a root of all kinds of evil. Some people, eager for money, have wandered from the faith and pierced themselves with many griefs.

6:7   Two verses in this chapter may well be familiar. This one is almost a direct quotation from Job (see 1:20) and is often quoted today. More often than not, 6:10 is misquoted. It warns that the desire for profit, the love of money, can tempt us away from things of greater and more lasting value. It is not money itself which is necessarily evil.

Paul's Charge to Timothy

[11]But you, man of God, flee from all this, and pursue righteousness, godliness, faith, love, endurance and gentleness. [12]Fight the good fight of the faith. Take hold of the eternal life to which you were called when you made your good confession in the presence of many witnesses. [13]In the sight of God, who gives life to everything, and of Christ Jesus, who while testifying before Pontius Pilate made the good confession, I charge you [14]to keep this command without spot or blame until the appearing of our Lord Jesus Christ, [15]which God will bring about in his own time — God, the blessed and only Ruler, the King of kings and Lord of lords, [16]who alone is immortal and who lives in unapproachable light, whom no-one has seen or can see. To him be honour and might for ever. Amen.

[17]Command those who are rich in this present world not to be arrogant nor to put their hope in wealth, which is so uncertain, but to put their hope in God, who richly provides us with everything for our enjoyment. [18]Command them to do good, to be rich in good deeds, and to be generous and willing to share. [19]In this way they will lay up treasure for themselves as a firm foundation for the coming age, so that they may take hold of the life that is truly life.

[20]Timothy, guard what has been entrusted to your care. Turn away from godless chatter and the opposing ideas of what is falsely called knowledge, [21]which some have professed and in so doing have wandered from the faith.

Grace be with you.

---

[b]18 Deut. 25:4   [c]18 Luke 10:7

2 Timothy

The Breath of God

Spirit is something intangible and difficult to describe. Many people who do not deny the existence of spirits do reject silly images of spooks and ghosts which come from popular films and books. In the Bible the word "spirit" is often equated with breath—the breath of God. So when we say that the Bible is inspired we mean, as Paul told Timothy in this letter, that God has breathed into it (3:16).

Ministers and Missionaries

Paul was a very wholehearted character. As a young man he went about zealously persecuting followers of Jesus of Nazareth. Then, suddenly and dramatically on the road to Damascus, he was converted. Immediately he dedicated himself fervently to preaching the good news about the death and resurrection of Jesus. Nothing could dampen his enthusiasm. He travelled long distances in arduous conditions, constantly at risk from robbers. He was whipped, beaten with sticks, jailed, but he never faltered (see 2 Corinthians 11:23–29).

Preaching the Good News

The image of Paul in 2 Timothy is of a weary old man in prison who knew that he was near to death either by execution or from old age. He was lonely and felt rejected and abandoned because Christians had not rallied to his side. But he knew that he was in prison for preaching the Good News and so he confidently placed his trust in Christ. He recalled with affection his mission days with Timothy. He exhorted Timothy not to allow fear to prevent him from preaching. But new and reliable leaders had to be found for the church and the young communities had to be protected from falsehood.

An Inspired Message

In biblical times there were no printing machines or copyright laws. The attitude to books and letters was quite different from today. Authors did not guard their writing jealously as though it were a precious possession. Some scholars say that this letter was not written by Paul, but by someone else who was thoroughly immersed in the gospel and who was equally concerned for the future of the church. Using the name of Paul would not have been regarded as fraudulent unless the message deviated from the good news of Jesus Christ. The approach to this letter does not have to be that of the forensic scientist who wants to check if it is Paul's handwriting—we can be confident that God has breathed into it.

---

1 Paul, an apostle of Christ Jesus by the will of God, according to the promise of life that is in Christ Jesus,

[2]To Timothy, my dear son:

Grace, mercy and peace from God the Father and Christ Jesus our Lord.

Encouragement to Be Faithful

[3]I thank God, whom I serve, as my forefathers did, with a clear conscience, as night and day I constantly remember you in my prayers. [4]Recalling your tears, I long to see you, so that I may be filled with joy. [5]I have been reminded of your sincere faith, which first lived in your grandmother Lois and in your mother Eunice and, I am persuaded, now lives in you also. [6]For this reason I remind you to fan into flame the gift of God, which is in you through the laying on of my hands. [7]For God did not give us a spirit of timidity, but a spirit of power, of love and of self-discipline.

1:6 Paul was a fiery person: we could even say hot-headed. Here he described the Spirit of God as a fire which is lit inside those who are chosen to be ministers, through the laying on of hands. This transforms the most mild and timid persons—like Timothy himself—into disciplined leaders and courageous preachers.

---

[8]So do not be ashamed to testify about our Lord, or ashamed of me his prisoner. But join with me in suffering for the gospel, by the power of God, [9]who has saved us and called us to a holy life—not because of anything we have done but because of his own purpose and grace. This grace was given us in Christ Jesus before the beginning of time, [10]but it has now been revealed through the appearing of our Saviour, Christ Jesus, who has destroyed death and has brought life and immortality to light through the gospel. [11]And of this gospel I was appointed a herald and an apostle and a teacher. [12]That is why I am suffering as I am. Yet I am not ashamed, because I know whom I have believed, and am convinced that he is able to guard what I have entrusted to him for that day.

[13]What you heard from me, keep as the pattern of sound teaching, with faith and love in Christ Jesus. [14]Guard the good deposit that was entrusted to you— guard it with the help of the Holy Spirit who lives in us.

[15]You know that everyone in the province of Asia has deserted me, including Phygelus and Hermogenes. [16]May the Lord show mercy to the household of Onesiphorus, because he often refreshed me and was not ashamed of my chains. [17]On the contrary, when he was in Rome, he searched hard for me until he found me. [18]May the Lord grant that he will find mercy from the Lord on that day! You know very well in how many ways he helped me in Ephesus.

2 You then, my son, be strong in the grace that is in Christ Jesus. [2]And the things you have heard me say in the presence of many witnesses entrust to reliable men who will also be qualified to teach others. [3]Endure hardship with us like a good soldier of Christ Jesus. [4]No-one serving as a soldier gets involved in civilian affairs—he wants to please his commanding officer. [5]Similarly, if anyone competes as an athlete, he does not receive the victor's crown unless he competes according to the rules. [6]The hardworking farmer should be the first to receive a share of the crops. [7]Reflect on what I am saying, for the Lord will give you insight into all this.

[8]Remember Jesus Christ, raised from the dead, descended from David. This is my gospel, [9]for which I am suffering even to the point of being chained like a criminal. But God's word is not chained. [10]Therefore I endure everything for the sake of the elect, that they too may obtain the salvation that is in Christ Jesus, with eternal glory.

2:8 Paul never deviated from the basic message of his faith: that Jesus Christ died a cruel death on the cross and rose again. Those who want to be followers of Jesus must also accept suffering, death, and resurrection. Here there is an extract from an early Christian hymn which expresses this concept very well.

---

[11]Here is a trustworthy saying:

If we died with him,
we will also live with him;
[12]if we endure,
we will also reign with him.
If we disown him,
he will also disown us;
[13]if we are faithless,
he will remain faithful,
for he cannot disown himself.

A Workman Approved by God

[14]Keep reminding them of these things. Warn them before God against quarrelling about words; it is of no value, and only ruins those who listen. [15]Do your best to present yourself to God as one approved, a workman who does not need to be ashamed and who correctly handles the word of truth. [16]Avoid godless chatter, because those who indulge in it will become more and more ungodly. [17]Their teaching will spread like

gangrene. Among them are Hymenaeus and Philetus, [18]who have wandered away from the truth. They say that the resurrection has already taken place, and they destroy the faith of some. [19]Nevertheless, God's solid foundation stands firm, sealed with this inscription: "The Lord knows those who are his,"[a] and, "Everyone who confesses the name of the Lord must turn away from wickedness."

[20]In a large house there are articles not only of gold and silver, but also of wood and clay; some are for noble purposes and some for ignoble. [21]If a man cleanses himself from the latter, he will be an instrument for noble purposes, made holy, useful to the Master and prepared to do any good work.

[22]Flee the evil desires of youth, and pursue righteousness, faith, love and peace, along with those who call on the Lord out of a pure heart. [23]Don't have anything to do with foolish and stupid arguments, because you know they produce quarrels. [24]And the Lord's servant must not quarrel; instead, he must be kind to everyone, able to teach, not resentful. [25]Those who oppose him he must gently instruct, in the hope that God will grant them repentance leading them to a knowledge of the truth, [26]and that they will come to their senses and escape from the trap of the devil, who has taken them captive to do his will.

Godlessness in the Last Days

3 But mark this: There will be terrible times in the last days. [2]People will be lovers of themselves, lovers of money, boastful, proud, abusive, disobedient to their parents, ungrateful, unholy, [3]without love, unforgiving, slanderous, without self-control, brutal, not lovers of the good, [4]treacherous, rash, conceited, lovers of pleasure rather than lovers of God — [5]having a form of godliness but denying its power. Have nothing to do with them.

[6]They are the kind who worm their way into homes and gain control over weak-willed women, who are loaded down with sins and are swayed by all kinds of evil desires, [7]always learning but never able to acknowledge the truth. [8]Just as Jannes and Jambres opposed Moses, so also these men oppose the truth — men of depraved minds, who, as far as the faith is concerned, are rejected. [9]But they will not get very far because, as in the case of those men, their folly will be clear to everyone.

3:8　These names, not mentioned in the Old Testament, were handed down in Jewish tradition as the names of the Egyptian magicians who opposed Moses during the ten plagues against Egypt (Exodus 7:11; 9:11).

Paul's Charge to Timothy

[10]You, however, know all about my teaching, my way of life, my purpose, faith, patience, love, endurance, [11]persecutions, sufferings — what kinds of things

happened to me in Antioch, Iconium and Lystra, the persecutions I endured. Yet the Lord rescued me from all of them. [12]In fact, everyone who wants to live a godly life in Christ Jesus will be persecuted, [13]while evil men and impostors will go from bad to worse, deceiving and being deceived. [14]But as for you, continue in what you have learned and have become convinced of, because you know those from whom you learned it, [15]and how from infancy you have known the holy Scriptures, which are able to make you wise for salvation through faith in Christ Jesus. [16]All Scripture is God-breathed and is useful for teaching, rebuking, correcting and training in righteousness, [17]so that the man of God may be thoroughly equipped for every good work.

4 In the presence of God and of Christ Jesus, who will judge the living and the dead, and in view of his appearing and his kingdom, I give you this charge: [2]Preach the Word; be prepared in season and out of season; correct, rebuke and encourage — with great patience and careful instruction. [3]For the time will come when men will not put up with sound doctrine. Instead, to suit their own desires, they will gather around them a great number of teachers to say what their itching ears want to hear. [4]They will turn their ears away from the truth and turn aside to myths. [5]But you, keep your head in all situations, endure hardship, do the work of an evangelist, discharge all the duties of your ministry.

4:3　Paul's repeated challenge for Christians to accept suffering and death so that they might rise with Christ is very difficult. It should not be surprising that many believers want to hear an easier message. However, we are warned several times in this letter that easier messages carry empty promises. If we want to live with Christ we must first die with Christ.

---

[6]For I am already being poured out like a drink offering, and the time has come for my departure. [7]I have fought the good fight, I have finished the race, I have kept the faith. [8]Now there is in store for me the crown of righteousness, which the Lord, the righteous Judge, will award to me on that day — and not only to me, but also to all who have longed for his appearing.

Personal Remarks

[9]Do your best to come to me quickly, [10]for Demas, because he loved this world, has deserted me and has gone to Thessalonica. Crescens has gone to Galatia, and Titus to Dalmatia. [11]Only Luke is with me. Get Mark and bring him with you, because he is helpful to me in my ministry. [12]I sent Tychicus to Ephesus. [13]When you come, bring the cloak that I left with Carpus at Troas, and my scrolls, especially the parchments.

---

[a]*19* Num. 16:5 (see Septuagint)

[14]Alexander the metalworker did me a great deal of harm. The Lord will repay him for what he has done. [15]You too should be on your guard against him, because he strongly opposed our message.

[16]At my first defence, no-one came to my support, but everyone deserted me. May it not be held against them. [17]But the Lord stood at my side and gave me strength, so that through me the message might be fully proclaimed and all the Gentiles might hear it. And I was delivered from the lion's mouth. [18]The Lord will rescue me from every evil attack and will bring me safely to his heavenly kingdom. To him be glory for ever and ever. Amen.

Final Greetings

[19]Greet Priscilla[a] and Aquila and the household of Onesiphorus. [20]Erastus stayed in Corinth, and I left Trophimus sick in Miletus. [21]Do your best to get here before winter. Eubulus greets you, and so do Pudens, Linus, Claudia and all the brothers.

[22]The Lord be with your spirit. Grace be with you.

[a]19 Greek *Prisca*, a variant of *Priscilla*

Titus

The Universal Church

A newly-appointed vicar of a London church was puzzled by the fact that almost all of his congregation were white although the church was in an area populated by people of many races and colours. The churchgoers were all apparently friendly and tolerant and gave no evidence of being closed to newcomers. The vicar enlisted a few friends to make discreet enquiries and learned that many people of different ethnic groups said that they would like to come to church, and they would like to be active in the parish, but that they felt excluded by the white parishioners. Over a period of time, the vicar persuaded his regular churchgoers to reflect on what was happening. Gradually they realized that when someone was needed for any church project, they always looked around at the same few people. At any parish social events the food, the music, and the activities reflected an English way of life. Without being malicious or conscious of any discrimination, they had come to accept that Christians were people like them: people who shared their tastes in food, music, clothing, and sport.

A Universal Message

That church had a problem that was similar to one in the early church. The earliest followers of Jesus Christ were all Jews. The teaching of Jesus was rooted in the Jewish Scriptures and his parables were drawn from a Hebrew way of life. Jesus' message was, however, indisputably universal. He proclaimed a new covenant which replaced the old covenant made with the Jews. Paul understood this and proclaimed it loudly, but many Jews did not understand this at first, and looked for their converts among people like themselves.

Lessons for Titus

Titus was one of the first non-Jewish Christians. He had been one of Paul's most trusted companions, and the bearer of Paul's severe letter to

Corinth (see 2 Corinthians 7:6). He had collected money in Corinth to support poor Christians in Jerusalem as proof that the Gentile and Jewish Christians were indeed brothers and sisters in Christ. Like the other two Pastoral Letters (1 and 2 Timothy), this one gives a very clear command about holding fast to the message that Paul had passed on. It also gives precise instructions about the type of people who are to be appointed as pastors (1:5–16), and what sort of behaviour the pastors are to encourage in the people under their care (2:1–10).

A Lot of Teaching

Although the letter is brief, it contains several very condensed summaries of Paul's theology. You will find some paragraphs that are so packed with ideas that you will have to read them over several times. The opening greeting to Titus gives us plenty to think about, including the fact that faith rests on a promise of eternal life given by God, who does not lie. In the second chapter (verses 11–4) we are reminded that the grace of God is universal—not limited to one tribe or sect—and are reminded of how we must behave in expectation of the second coming of Christ. The final chapter summarizes the story of salvation in a few verses (4–8) that are well worth pondering on because 'these things are excellent and profitable for everyone."

1 Paul, a servant of God and an apostle of Jesus Christ for the faith of God's elect and the knowledge of the truth that leads to godliness — ²a faith and knowledge resting on the hope of eternal life, which God, who does not lie, promised before the beginning of time, ³and at his appointed season he brought his word to light through the preaching entrusted to me by the command of God our Saviour,

⁴To Titus, my true son in our common faith:

Grace and peace from God the Father and Christ Jesus our Saviour.

Titus' Task on Crete

⁵The reason I left you in Crete was that you might straighten out what was left unfinished and appoint*ᵃ* elders in every town, as I directed you. ⁶An elder must be blameless, the husband of but one wife, a man whose children believe and are not open to the charge of being wild and disobedient. ⁷Since an overseer*ᵇ* is entrusted with God's work, he must be blameless — not overbearing, not quick-tempered, not given to drunkenness, not violent, not pursuing dishonest gain. ⁸Rather he must be hospitable, one who loves what is good, who is self-controlled, upright, holy and disciplined. ⁹He must hold firmly to the trustworthy message as it has been taught, so that he can encourage others by sound doctrine and refute those who oppose it.

1:15 "To the pure, all things are pure,"—one of the many biblical sayings that is used in everyday conversation. But the message of this passage is quite serious. Paul said that it is not enough for us just to say that we believe, or to join the right church. We must be converted, and our behaviour must improve.

¹⁰For there are many rebellious people, mere talkers and deceivers, especially those of the circumcision group. ¹¹They must be silenced, because they are ruining whole households by teaching things they ought not to teach—and that for the sake of dishonest gain. ¹²Even one of their own prophets has said, "Cretans are always liars, evil brutes, lazy gluttons." ¹³This testimony is true. Therefore, rebuke them sharply, so that they will be sound in the faith ¹⁴and will pay no attention to Jewish myths or to the commands of those who reject the truth. ¹⁵To the pure, all things are pure, but to those who are corrupted and do not believe, nothing is pure. In fact, both their minds and consciences are corrupted. ¹⁶They claim to know God, but by their actions they deny him. They are detestable, disobedient and unfit for doing anything good.

ᵃ5 Or *ordain*   *ᵇ7* Traditionally *bishop*

What Must Be Taught to Various Groups

2 You must teach what is in accord with sound doctrine. [2]Teach the older men to be temperate, worthy of respect, self-controlled, and sound in faith, in love and in endurance.

[3]Likewise, teach the older women to be reverent in the way they live, not to be slanderers or addicted to much wine, but to teach what is good. [4]Then they can train the younger women to love their husbands and children, [5]to be self-controlled and pure, to be busy at home, to be kind, and to be subject to their husbands, so that no-one will malign the word of God.

[6]Similarly, encourage the young men to be self-controlled. [7]In everything set them an example by doing what is good. In your teaching show integrity, seriousness [8]and soundness of speech that cannot be condemned, so that those who oppose you may be ashamed because they have nothing bad to say about us.

[9]Teach slaves to be subject to their masters in everything, to try to please them, not to talk back to them, [10]and not to steal from them, but to show that they can be fully trusted, so that in every way they will make the teaching about God our Saviour attractive.

[11]For the grace of God that brings salvation has appeared to all men. [12]It teaches us to say "No" to ungodliness and worldly passions, and to live self-controlled, upright and godly lives in this present age, [13]while we wait for the blessed hope—the glorious appearing of our great God and Saviour, Jesus Christ, [14]who gave himself for us to redeem us from all wickedness and to purify for himself a people that are his very own, eager to do what is good.

[15]These, then, are the things you should teach. Encourage and rebuke with all authority. Do not let anyone despise you.

Doing What Is Good

3 Remind the people to be subject to rulers and authorities, to be obedient, to be ready to do whatever is good, [2]to slander no-one, to be peaceable and considerate, and to show true humility towards all men.

[3]At one time we too were foolish, disobedient, deceived and enslaved by all kinds of passions and pleasures. We lived in malice and envy, being hated and hating one another. [4]But when the kindness and love of God our Saviour appeared, [5]he saved us, not because of righteous things we had done, but because of his mercy. He saved us through the washing of rebirth and renewal by the Holy Spirit, [6]whom he poured out on us generously through Jesus Christ our Saviour, [7]so that, having been justified by his grace, we might become heirs having the hope of eternal life. [8]This is a trustworthy saying. And I want you to stress these things, so that those who have trusted in God may be careful to devote themselves to doing what is good. These things are excellent and profitable for everyone.

[9]But avoid foolish controversies and genealogies and arguments and quarrels about the law, because these are unprofitable and useless. [10]Warn a divisive person once, and then warn him a second time. After that, have nothing to do with him. [11]You may be sure that such a man is warped and sinful; he is self-condemned.

3:9 The difference between thinking and daydreaming is that thought is limited and guided by the truth. Likewise, the difference between discussion and empty argument is that discussion is kept within the bounds of what is true. Paul warned here, as in other places, to avoid foolish discussions that do not lead to the truth, but divide the church.

Final Remarks

[12]As soon as I send Artemas or Tychicus to you, do your best to come to me at Nicopolis, because I have decided to winter there. [13]Do everything you can to help Zenas the lawyer and Apollos on their way and see that they have everything they need. [14]Our people must learn to devote themselves to doing what is good, in order that they may provide for daily necessities and not live unproductive lives.

[15]Everyone with me sends you greetings. Greet those who love us in the faith.

Grace be with you all.

Philemon

Slavery

Many people use the past tense when they talk about slavery. They say that it was a serious injustice that was eliminated some years ago. But there are still many slaves in the world. Slaves are people who are bought and sold as property. They have no property of their own, and are not free to come and go as they wish. In many parts of the world today there are people who are so poor that, to survive, they have no choice but to sell themselves. In many third world countries, there are gangs of child thieves who are owned by their masters. Other people are forced to sell themselves in prostitution. These people are treated as property; they have no freedom and no belongings of their own. They are easy prey for unscrupulous wealthy people.

Letter to a Slave Owner

Imagine writing to someone who is a wealthy modern-day slave dealer and who claims to be a Christian. Imagine asking them to treat the poor not as property, but as sisters and brothers. It would be a very startling challenge, but that is what Paul did in this letter. It is written to Philemon, a wealthy man, whom Paul had converted to Christ. It is a very personal letter, but was not intended to be private because it is also addressed to the Christian community. Onesimus, a slave, had escaped from Philemon. While on the run, he met Paul and was converted. Onesimus was afraid to return because he expected to be punished publicly by being flogged or even killed. Paul asked Philemon to accept Onesimus back without punishment, saying that the slave was so valuable that Christ had died for him. He pointed out that because he converted the two of them, he was the spiritual father of both the slave owner and the slave. He urged them, in Christ, to regard each other as brothers.

True Freedom

The argument is made more interesting by the fact that it was written when Paul was himself in prison in Rome (AD 61–63). He described himself as a prisoner of Christ, not as a prisoner of the Romans. He could have meant two things by this. Firstly, he had been taken captive by Jesus, his master, and felt bound to work zealously on his behalf. Secondly, his fervent work of preaching the good news had led to his imprisonment. All the Christian life is concerned with freedom: freedom from slavery, from sin, from addictions, and from compulsions. Doing "what we like" is not freedom, but slavery to our whims. The message of the gospel is that true freedom comes from doing the will of God.

[1]Paul, a prisoner of Christ Jesus, and Timothy our brother,

To Philemon our dear friend and fellow-worker, [2]to Apphia our sister, to Archippus our fellow-soldier and to the church that meets in your home:

[3]Grace to you and peace from God our Father and the Lord Jesus Christ.

Thanksgiving and Prayer

[4]I always thank my God as I remember you in my prayers, [5]because I hear about your faith in the Lord Jesus and your love for all the saints. [6]I pray that you may be active in sharing your faith, so that you will have a full understanding of every good thing we have in Christ. [7]Your love has given me great joy and encouragement, because you, brother, have refreshed the hearts of the saints.

Paul's Plea for Onesimus

[8]Therefore, although in Christ I could be bold and order you to do what you ought to do, [9]yet I appeal to you on the basis of love. I then, as Paul—an old man and now also a prisoner of Christ Jesus—[10]I appeal to you for my son Onesimus,[a] who became my son while I was in chains. [11]Formerly he was useless to you, but now he has become useful both to you and to me.

[12]I am sending him—who is my very heart—back to you. [13]I would have liked to keep him with me so that he could take your place in helping me while I am in chains for the gospel. [14]But I did not want to do anything without your consent, so that any favour you do will be spontaneous and not forced. [15]Perhaps the reason he was separated from you for a little while was that you might have him back for good—[16]no longer as a slave, but better than a slave, as a dear brother. He is very dear to me but even dearer to you, both as a man and as a brother in the Lord.

[17]So if you consider me a partner, welcome him as you would welcome me. [18]If he has done you any wrong or owes you anything, charge it to me. [19]I, Paul, am writing this with my own hand. I will pay it back—not to mention that you owe me your very self. [20]I do wish, brother, that I may have some benefit from you in the Lord; refresh my heart in Christ. [21]Confident of your obedience, I write to you, knowing that you will do even more than I ask.

[22]And one thing more: Prepare a guest room for me, because I hope to be restored to you in answer to your prayers.

[23]Epaphras, my fellow-prisoner in Christ Jesus, sends you greetings. [24]And so do Mark, Aristarchus, Demas and Luke, my fellow-workers.

[25]The grace of the Lord Jesus Christ be with your spirit.

---

[a] 10 Onesimus means useful.

Hebrews

Tempted to Give Up?

Many Christians experience a desire to give up their faith at some time in their lives. Their commitment is under increasing pressure, both from the attraction of old ways of life, and from the influence of the world about them. The first flush of enthusiasm in the early days of their faith gives way to uncertainty as believing becomes costly. Despite the evidence of Christ working in their lives, despite all that they have gone through, it comes to decision time. The choice is whether to go forward with Christ, or to turn back. This book was written for just these people to encourage them not to lose heart but to press on.

The Author and His Audience

We have no real clue about who wrote the letter, and no firm idea who it was written to. The title "Hebrews" would suggest a whole nation was being addressed but this probably was not the case. The addition of a title came some time after the letter was written, and there are enough references in the letter to show that the author was writing to a definite group of people. They had gone through persecution and there was an expectation that they had been believers long enough to be able to teach others but they had not yet achieved maturity (5:12); the writer hoped to visit them again (13:19); his mention of the release of Timothy (13:23) suggests his readers knew who he was referring to and that the group was part of a larger Christian community (10:25; 13:7). There is no clear evidence of who the group were but any group receiving this letter would have needed a broad knowledge of the Jewish religion and the writings that we know as the Old Testament. This had led to the belief that the community was made up of people who had converted from Judaism to Christianity. It would explain all the warnings about falling back into the old ways of Judaism and the emphasis on the fact that Christ fulfilled the promises that God had made to his people. To turn away from Christ was to turn away from God's purpose for his people.

Main Purpose

The main purpose of the letter was to warn Jewish Christians against returning to their old faith. It begins by asserting the uniqueness of Christ. He was both fully God (1:3) and fully man (2:17) at the same time. He existed before the world began and it was through him that the world was created (1:2). In the past God had spoken to his people through his prophets, but now he showed himself in the life, death, and resurrection of Christ. Christ was superior to the angels (1:4), but while he was on earth he shared in the weakness of humankind (2:14) even though he was perfect and without sin (4:15). Jesus was also greater than Moses, the larger-than-life Old Testament character who had led the people of Israel out of slavery (3:3). Jesus was called the great high priest because he was superior to all human priests. Finally, God made a new covenant (or promise) with his people through Jesus Christ over the old covenant made with Moses. The strength of the new covenant lay in the quality of the mediator (9:15) between God and humankind. It was only Christ who was able to set people free from their sins by his own sacrifice on the cross.

Encouragement

Having stated the arguments for the superiority of Christ over Judaism, the writer encouraged the believers to continue in their Christian faith because of the uniqueness of Christ to warn them of the dangers if they denied Christ (10:29), and to remind them of all they had come through in the service of Christ (10:32). He sought to encourage them by recording examples of faithful men and women who had less reason for hope than them, but who endured greater hardships for God (11:39). Jesus Christ is cited as the supreme example to follow because of what he endured (12:2). If the lessons of the letter were to be taken to heart they would affect the people's lives in practical ways, such as relationships, marriages, materialism, and obedience.

Christ—the True Way of Life

The people to whom this was addressed needed to make that final break with their old life. Christians in every generation have the same struggle to let go of their former lives and begin a new life totally committed to Christ. It is not possible to keep a foot in both camps. The writer of Hebrews makes a strong case for following Christ rather than following old habits of life and religion.

The Son Superior to Angels

1 In the past God spoke to our forefathers through the prophets at many times and in various ways, ²but in these last days he has spoken to us by his Son, whom he appointed heir of all things, and through whom he made the universe. ³The Son is the radiance of God's glory and the exact representation of his being, sustaining all things by his powerful word. After he had provided purification for sins, he sat down at the right hand of the Majesty in heaven. ⁴So he became as much superior to the angels as the name he has inherited is superior to theirs.

1:3 This emphasizes the difference between the prophets, who merely spoke what God wanted them to say, and Jesus who shares the nature of God and so is able to reveal God's inmost thoughts.

---

⁵For to which of the angels did God ever say,

"You are my Son;
today I have become your Father" [a,b]?

Or again,

"I will be his Father,
and he will be my Son" [c]?

⁶And again, when God brings his firstborn into the world, he says,

"Let all God's angels worship him." [d]

⁷In speaking of the angels he says,

"He makes his angels winds,
his servants flames of fire." [e]

⁸But about the Son he says,

"Your throne, O God, will last for ever and ever,
and righteousness will be the sceptre of your kingdom.

---

[a]5 Or have begotten you   [b]5 Psalm 2:7   [c]5 2 Samuel 7:14; 1 Chron. 17:13
[d]6 Deut. 32:43 (see Dead Sea Scrolls and Septuagint)   [e]7 Psalm 104:4

9You have loved righteousness and hated
    wickedness;
therefore God, your God, has set you above
    your companions
by anointing you with the oil of joy."*f*

10He also says,

"In the beginning, O Lord, you laid the
    foundations of the earth,
and the heavens are the work of your hands.
11They will perish, but you remain;
    they will all wear out like a garment.
12You will roll them up like a robe;
    like a garment they will be changed.
But you remain the same,
    and your years will never end."*g*

13To which of the angels did God ever say,

"Sit at my right hand
until I make your enemies
    a footstool for your feet"*h*?

14Are not all angels ministering spirits sent to serve
those who will inherit salvation?

Warning to Pay Attention

2 We must pay more careful attention, therefore, to
what we have heard, so that we do not drift away.
2For if the message spoken by angels was binding, and
every violation and disobedience received its just punishment, 3how shall we escape if we ignore such a
great salvation? This salvation, which was first
announced by the Lord, was confirmed to us by those
who heard him. 4God also testified to it by signs, wonders and various miracles, and gifts of the Holy Spirit
distributed according to his will.

Jesus Made Like His Brothers

5It is not to angels that he has subjected the world
to come, about which we are speaking. 6But there is
a place where someone has testified:

"What is man that you are mindful of him,
    the son of man that you care for him?
7You made him a little*a* lower than the angels;
    you crowned him with glory and honour
8   and put everything under his feet."*b*

In putting everything under him, God left nothing that
is not subject to him. Yet at present we do not see
everything subject to him. 9But we see Jesus, who was
made a little lower than the angels, now crowned with
glory and honour because he suffered death, so that by
the grace of God he might taste death for everyone.
10In bringing many sons to glory, it was fitting that
God, for whom and through whom everything exists,
should make the author of their salvation perfect
through suffering. 11Both the one who makes men holy
and those who are made holy are of the same family.
So Jesus is not ashamed to call them brothers. 12He
says,

"I will declare your name to my brothers;
    in the presence of the congregation I will sing
    your praises."*c*

13And again,

"I will put my trust in him."*d*

And again he says,

"Here am I, and the children God has given
    me."*e*

14Since the children have flesh and blood, he too
shared in their humanity so that by his death he might
destroy him who holds the power of death — that is, the
devil — 15and free those who all their lives were held
in slavery by their fear of death. 16For surely it is not
angels he helps, but Abraham's descendants. 17For this
reason he had to be made like his brothers in every
way, in order that he might become a merciful and
faithful high priest in service to God, and that he might
make atonement for*f* the sins of the people. 18Because
he himself suffered when he was tempted, he is able
to help those who are being tempted.

2:14 Here is the purpose behind Christ's
work on earth. He came to destroy the
power of the devil, and only by sharing in the
weakness of humanity could he achieve his
purpose. That was why it was important for
the writer to emphasize the humanity of
Christ and deny any suggestion that Christ
did not suffer pain and death on the cross.
The very fact of Christ's humanity encourages our belief that we have a God who fully
understands us because he has been one of
us.

Jesus Greater Than Moses

3 Therefore, holy brothers, who share in the heavenly calling, fix your thoughts on Jesus, the
apostle and high priest whom we confess. 2He was
faithful to the one who appointed him, just as Moses
was faithful in all God's house. 3Jesus has been found
worthy of greater honour than Moses, just as the builder of a house has greater honour than the house itself.
4For every house is built by someone, but God is the
builder of everything. 5Moses was faithful as a servant
in all God's house, testifying to what would be said in
the future. 6But Christ is faithful as a son over God's
house. And we are his house, if we hold on to our courage and the hope of which we boast.

Warning Against Unbelief

7So, as the Holy Spirit says:

"Today, if you hear his voice,
8   do not harden your hearts
    as you did in the rebellion,

---

*f*9 Psalm 45:6,7   *g*12 Psalm 102:25–27   *h*13 Psalm 110:1   *a*7 Or *him for a little while*; also in verse 9
*b*8 Psalm 8:4–6   *c*12 Psalm 22:22   *d*13 Isaiah 8:17   *e*13 Isaiah 8:18
*f*17 Or *and that he might turn aside God's wrath, taking away*

during the time of testing in the desert,
[9]where your fathers tested and tried me
    and for forty years saw what I did.
[10]That is why I was angry with that generation,
    and I said, 'Their hearts are always going astray,
    and they have not known my ways.'
[11]So I declared on oath in my anger,
    'They shall never enter my rest.' "[a]

[12]See to it, brothers, that none of you has a sinful, unbelieving heart that turns away from the living God. [13]But encourage one another daily, as long as it is called Today, so that none of you may be hardened by sin's deceitfulness. [14]We have come to share in Christ if we hold firmly till the end the confidence we had at first. [15]As has just been said:

"Today, if you hear his voice,
  do not harden your hearts
  as you did in the rebellion."[b]

[16]Who were they who heard and rebelled? Were they not all those Moses led out of Egypt? [17]And with whom was he angry for forty years? Was it not with those who sinned, whose bodies fell in the desert? [18]And to whom did God swear that they would never enter his rest if not to those who disobeyed?[c] [19]So we see that they were not able to enter, because of their unbelief.

A Sabbath-rest for the People of God

4 Therefore, since the promise of entering his rest still stands, let us be careful that none of you be found to have fallen short of it. [2]For we also have had the gospel preached to us, just as they did; but the message they heard was of no value to them, because those who heard did not combine it with faith.[a] [3]Now we who have believed enter that rest, just as God has said,

"So I declared on oath in my anger,
  'They shall never enter my rest.' "[b]

And yet his work has been finished since the creation of the world. [4]For somewhere he has spoken about the seventh day in these words: "And on the seventh day God rested from all his work."[c] [5]And again in the passage above he says, "They shall never enter my rest."

[6]It still remains that some will enter that rest, and those who formerly had the gospel preached to them did not go in, because of their disobedience. [7]Therefore God again set a certain day, calling it Today, when a long time later he spoke through David, as was said before:

"Today, if you hear his voice,
  do not harden your hearts."[d]

[8]For if Joshua had given them rest, God would not have spoken later about another day. [9]There remains, then, a Sabbath-rest for the people of God; [10]for anyone who enters God's rest also rests from his own work, just as God did from his. [11]Let us, therefore, make every effort

to enter that rest, so that no-one will fall by following their example of disobedience.

4:9 In the previous chapter (3:7–11) the writer reminded his readers of the "rest" which God had promised to his people. The people of Israel had never found this rest because of their disobedience. Believers still have the promise of the Sabbath rest that is eternal life.

---

[12]For the word of God is living and active. Sharper than any double-edged sword, it penetrates even to dividing soul and spirit, joints and marrow; it judges the thoughts and attitudes of the heart. [13]Nothing in all creation is hidden from God's sight. Everything is uncovered and laid bare before the eyes of him to whom we must give account.

Jesus the Great High Priest

[14]Therefore, since we have a great high priest who has gone through the heavens,[e] Jesus the Son of God, let us hold firmly to the faith we profess. [15]For we do not have a high priest who is unable to sympathise with our weaknesses, but we have one who has been tempted in every way, just as we are — yet was without sin. [16]Let us then approach the throne of grace with confidence, so that we may receive mercy and find grace to help us in our time of need.

4:14 The theme of the "high priest" is one that dominates the letter to the Hebrews. A priest was responsible for representing the people before God, and representing God before the people. It was necessary for him to make sacrifices on behalf of the people, in order to win God's favour and put right any wrong that had been done. The writer showed how Christ was able to fulfil the role of priest more than any human. Christ himself was the sacrifice which enables him to represent people to God, and because Christ shares the nature of God, he can perfectly represent God to humans.

---

5 Every high priest is selected from among men and is appointed to represent them in matters related to God, to offer gifts and sacrifices for sins. [2]He is able to deal gently with those who are ignorant and are going astray, since he himself is subject to weakness. [3]This is why he has to offer sacrifices for his own sins, as well as for the sins of the people.

[4]No-one takes this honour upon himself; he must be called by God, just as Aaron was. [5]So Christ also did not

---

[a]11 Psalm 95:7–11   [b]15 Psalm 95:7,8   [c]18 Or *disbelieved*
[a]2 Many manuscripts *because they did not share in the faith of those who obeyed*   [b]3 Psalm 95:11; also in verse 5
[c]4 Gen. 2:2   [d]7 Psalm 95:7,8   [e]14 Or *gone into heaven*

take upon himself the glory of becoming a high priest. But God said to him,

"You are my Son;
today I have become your Father." [a,b]

6And he says in another place,

"You are a priest for ever,
in the order of Melchizedek." [c]

7During the days of Jesus' life on earth, he offered up prayers and petitions with loud cries and tears to the one who could save him from death, and he was heard because of his reverent submission. 8Although he was a son, he learned obedience from what he suffered 9and, once made perfect, he became the source of eternal salvation for all who obey him 10and was designated by God to be high priest in the order of Melchizedek.

Warning Against Falling Away

11We have much to say about this, but it is hard to explain because you are slow to learn. 12In fact, though by this time you ought to be teachers, you need someone to teach you the elementary truths of God's word all over again. You need milk, not solid food! 13Anyone who lives on milk, being still an infant, is not acquainted with the teaching about righteousness. 14But solid food is for the mature, who by constant use have trained themselves to distinguish good from evil.

6 Therefore let us leave the elementary teachings about Christ and go on to maturity, not laying again the foundation of repentance from acts that lead to death, [a] and of faith in God, 2instruction about baptisms, the laying on of hands, the resurrection of the dead, and eternal judgment. 3And God permitting, we will do so.

4It is impossible for those who have once been enlightened, who have tasted the heavenly gift, who have shared in the Holy Spirit, 5who have tasted the goodness of the word of God and the powers of the coming age, 6if they fall away, to be brought back to repentance, because [b] to their loss they are crucifying the Son of God all over again and subjecting him to public disgrace.

7Land that drinks in the rain often falling on it and that produces a crop useful to those for whom it is farmed receives the blessing of God. 8But land that produces thorns and thistles is worthless and is in danger of being cursed. In the end it will be burned.

9Even though we speak like this, dear friends, we are confident of better things in your case — things that accompany salvation. 10God is not unjust; he will not forget your work and the love you have shown him as you have helped his people and continue to help them. 11We want each of you to show this same diligence to the very end, in order to make your hope sure. 12We do not want you to become lazy, but to imitate those who through faith and patience inherit what has been promised.

The Certainty of God's Promise

13When God made his promise to Abraham, since there was no-one greater for him to swear by, he swore by himself, 14saying, "I will surely bless you and give you many descendants." [c] 15And so after waiting patiently, Abraham received what was promised.

16Men swear by someone greater than themselves, and the oath confirms what is said and puts an end to all argument. 17Because God wanted to make the unchanging nature of his purpose very clear to the heirs of what was promised, he confirmed it with an oath. 18God did this so that, by two unchangeable things in which it is impossible for God to lie, we who have fled to take hold of the hope offered to us may be greatly encouraged. 19We have this hope as an anchor for the soul, firm and secure. It enters the inner sanctuary behind the curtain, 20where Jesus, who went before us, has entered on our behalf. He has become a high priest for ever, in the order of Melchizedek.

Melchizedek the Priest

7 This Melchizedek was king of Salem and priest of God Most High. He met Abraham returning from the defeat of the kings and blessed him, 2and Abraham gave him a tenth of everything. First, his name means "king of righteousness"; then also, "king of Salem" means "king of peace". 3Without father or mother, without genealogy, without beginning of days or end of life, like the Son of God he remains a priest for ever.

7:1　　　Melchizedek the king—priest gets very little mention in the Old Testament (see Genesis 14:18), but here the writer used him as an example of what Christ has done for humans. The name means "king of righteousness" and his title "king of Salem" means "king of peace". Both these titles aptly describe Christ. Using this character shows the superiority of Christ over the traditional priests.

4Just think how great he was: Even the patriarch Abraham gave him a tenth of the plunder! 5Now the law requires the descendants of Levi who become priests to collect a tenth from the people — that is, their brothers — even though their brothers are descended from Abraham. 6This man, however, did not trace his descent from Levi, yet he collected a tenth from Abraham and blessed him who had the promises. 7And without doubt the lesser person is blessed by the greater. 8In the one case, the tenth is collected by men who die; but in the other case, by him who is declared to be living. 9One might even say that Levi, who collects the tenth, paid the tenth through Abraham, 10because when Melchizedek met Abraham, Levi was still in the body of his ancestor.

a5 Or have begotten you　　　b5 Psalm 2:7　　　c6 Psalm 110:4　　　a1 Or from useless rituals
b6 Or repentance while　　　c14 Gen. 22:17

Jesus Like Melchizedek

[11]If perfection could have been attained through the Levitical priesthood (for on the basis of it the law was given to the people), why was there still need for another priest to come — one in the order of Melchizedek, not in the order of Aaron? [12]For when there is a change of the priesthood, there must also be a change of the law. [13]He of whom these things are said belonged to a different tribe, and no-one from that tribe has ever served at the altar. [14]For it is clear that our Lord descended from Judah, and in regard to that tribe Moses said nothing about priests. [15]And what we have said is even more clear if another priest like Melchizedek appears, [16]one who has become a priest not on the basis of a regulation as to his ancestry but on the basis of the power of an indestructible life. [17]For it is declared:

"You are a priest for ever,
in the order of Melchizedek."[a]

[18]The former regulation is set aside because it was weak and useless [19](for the law made nothing perfect), and a better hope is introduced, by which we draw near to God.

[20]And it was not without an oath! Others became priests without any oath, [21]but he became a priest with an oath when God said to him:

"The Lord has sworn
and will not change his mind:
'You are a priest for ever.' "[b]

[22]Because of this oath, Jesus has become the guarantee of a better covenant.

[23]Now there have been many of those priests, since death prevented them from continuing in office; [24]but because Jesus lives for ever, he has a permanent priesthood. [25]Therefore he is able to save completely[c] those who come to God through him, because he always lives to intercede for them.

[26]Such a high priest meets our need — one who is holy, blameless, pure, set apart from sinners, exalted above the heavens. [27]Unlike the other high priests, he does not need to offer sacrifices day after day, first for his own sins, and then for the sins of the people. He sacrificed for their sins once for all when he offered himself. [28]For the law appoints as high priests men who are weak; but the oath, which came after the law, appointed the Son, who has been made perfect for ever.

The High Priest of a New Covenant

8 The point of what we are saying is this: We do have such a high priest, who sat down at the right hand of the throne of the Majesty in heaven, [2]and who serves in the sanctuary, the true tabernacle set up by the Lord, not by man.

[3]Every high priest is appointed to offer both gifts and sacrifices, and so it was necessary for this one also to have something to offer. [4]If he were on earth, he would not be a priest, for there are already men who offer the gifts prescribed by the law. [5]They serve at a sanctuary that is a copy and shadow of what is in heaven. This is why Moses was warned when he was about to build the tabernacle: "See to it that you make everything according to the pattern shown you on the mountain."[a] [6]But the ministry Jesus has received is as superior to theirs as the covenant of which he is mediator is superior to the old one, and it is founded on better promises.

[7]For if there had been nothing wrong with that first covenant, no place would have been sought for another. [8]But God found fault with the people and said:[b]

"The time is coming, declares the Lord,
    when I will make a new covenant
with the house of Israel
    and with the house of Judah.
[9]It will not be like the covenant
    I made with their forefathers
when I took them by the hand
    to lead them out of Egypt,
because they did not remain faithful to my
        covenant,
    and I turned away from them,
                    declares the Lord.
[10]This is the covenant I will make with the house
        of Israel
    after that time, declares the Lord.
I will put my laws in their minds
    and write them on their hearts.
I will be their God,
    and they will be my people.
[11]No longer will a man teach his neighbour,
    or a man his brother, saying, 'Know the
        Lord,'
because they will all know me,
    from the least of them to the greatest.
[12]For I will forgive their wickedness
    and will remember their sins no more."[c]

[13]By calling this covenant "new", he has made the first one obsolete; and what is obsolete and ageing will soon disappear.

8:13 The need for a new covenant between God and his people did not mean that God had made a mistake with the old one. The grace and mercy with which he created the old agreement continued, but the people had come to understand the covenant as a series of rules and regulations which had to be obeyed, rather than as an expression of God's love for his people. So God promised a new covenant which was not based on laws but on the nature and work of Christ.

---

[a]17 Psalm 110:4   [b]21 Psalm 110:4   [c]25 Or for ever
[b]8 Some manuscripts may be translated fault and said to the people.

[a]5 Exodus 25:40
[c]12 Jer. 31:31–34

Worship in the Earthly Tabernacle

9 Now the first covenant had regulations for worship and also an earthly sanctuary. ²A tabernacle was set up. In its first room were the lampstand, the table and the consecrated bread; this was called the Holy Place. ³Behind the second curtain was a room called the Most Holy Place, ⁴which had the golden altar of incense and the gold-covered ark of the covenant. This ark contained the gold jar of manna, Aaron's staff that had budded, and the stone tablets of the covenant. ⁵Above the ark were the cherubim of the Glory, overshadowing the atonement cover.ᵃ But we cannot discuss these things in detail now.

⁶When everything had been arranged like this, the priests entered regularly into the outer room to carry on their ministry. ⁷But only the high priest entered the inner room, and that only once a year, and never without blood, which he offered for himself and for the sins the people had committed in ignorance. ⁸The Holy Spirit was showing by this that the way into the Most Holy Place had not yet been disclosed as long as the first tabernacle was still standing. ⁹This is an illustration for the present time, indicating that the gifts and sacrifices being offered were not able to clear the conscience of the worshipper. ¹⁰They are only a matter of food and drink and various ceremonial washings — external regulations applying until the time of the new order.

The Blood of Christ

¹¹When Christ came as high priest of the good things that are already here,ᵇ he went through the greater and more perfect tabernacle that is not man-made, that is to say, not a part of this creation. ¹²He did not enter by means of the blood of goats and calves; but he entered the Most Holy Place once for all by his own blood, having obtained eternal redemption. ¹³The blood of goats and bulls and the ashes of a heifer sprinkled on those who are ceremonially unclean sanctify them so that they are outwardly clean. ¹⁴How much more, then, will the blood of Christ, who through the eternal Spirit offered himself unblemished to God, cleanse our consciences from acts that lead to death,ᶜ so that we may serve the living God!

¹⁵For this reason Christ is the mediator of a new covenant, that those who are called may receive the promised eternal inheritance — now that he has died as a ransom to set them free from the sins committed under the first covenant.

¹⁶In the case of a will,ᵈ it is necessary to prove the death of the one who made it, ¹⁷because a will is in force only when somebody has died; it never takes effect while the one who made it is living. ¹⁸This is why even the first covenant was not put into effect without blood. ¹⁹When Moses had proclaimed every commandment of the law to all the people, he took the blood of calves, together with water, scarlet wool and branches of hyssop, and sprinkled the scroll and all the people. ²⁰He said, "This is the blood of the covenant, which God has commanded you to keep."ᵉ ²¹In the same way, he sprinkled with the blood both the tabernacle and everything used in its ceremonies. ²²In fact, the law requires that nearly everything be cleansed with blood, and without the shedding of blood there is no forgiveness.

²³It was necessary, then, for the copies of the heavenly things to be purified with these sacrifices, but the heavenly things themselves with better sacrifices than these. ²⁴For Christ did not enter a man-made sanctuary that was only a copy of the true one; he entered heaven itself, now to appear for us in God's presence. ²⁵Nor did he enter heaven to offer himself again and again, the way the high priest enters the Most Holy Place every year with blood that is not his own. ²⁶Then Christ would have had to suffer many times since the creation of the world. But now he has appeared once for all at the end of the ages to do away with sin by the sacrifice of himself. ²⁷Just as man is destined to die once, and after that to face judgment, ²⁸so Christ was sacrificed once to take away the sins of many people; and he will appear a second time, not to bear sin, but to bring salvation to those who are waiting for him.

Christ's Sacrifice Once for All

10 The law is only a shadow of the good things that are coming — not the realities themselves. For this reason it can never, by the same sacrifices repeated endlessly year after year, make perfect those who draw near to worship. ²If it could, would they not have stopped being offered? For the worshippers would have been cleansed once for all, and would no longer have felt guilty for their sins. ³But those sacrifices are an annual reminder of sins, ⁴because it is impossible for the blood of bulls and goats to take away sins.

⁵Therefore, when Christ came into the world, he said:

"Sacrifice and offering you did not desire,
  but a body you prepared for me;
⁶with burnt offerings and sin offerings
  you were not pleased.
⁷Then I said, 'Here I am — it is written about me
  in the scroll —
I have come to do your will, O God.' "ᵃ

⁸First he said, "Sacrifices and offerings, burnt offerings and sin offerings you did not desire, nor were you pleased with them" (although the law required them to be made). ⁹Then he said, "Here I am, I have come to do your will." He sets aside the first to establish the second. ¹⁰And by that will, we have been made holy through the sacrifice of the body of Jesus Christ once for all.

¹¹Day after day every priest stands and performs his religious duties; again and again he offers the same sacrifices, which can never take away sins. ¹²But when this priest had offered for all time one sacrifice for sins, he sat down at the right hand of God. ¹³Since that time he waits for his enemies to be made his footstool,

---

ᵃ5 Traditionally *the mercy seat*   ᵇ11 Some early manuscripts *are to come*   ᶜ14 Or *from useless rituals*
ᵈ16 Same Greek word as *covenant*; also in verse 17   ᵉ20 Exodus 24:8   ᵃ7 Psalm 40:6–8 (see Septuagint)

¹⁴because by one sacrifice he has made perfect for ever those who are being made holy.

¹⁵The Holy Spirit also testifies to us about this. First he says:

¹⁶"This is the covenant I will make with them
   after that time, says the Lord.
 I will put my laws in their hearts,
   and I will write them on their minds." ᵇ

¹⁷Then he adds:

"Their sins and lawless acts
   I will remember no more." ᶜ

¹⁸And where these have been forgiven, there is no longer any sacrifice for sin.

A Call to Persevere

¹⁹Therefore, brothers, since we have confidence to enter the Most Holy Place by the blood of Jesus, ²⁰by a new and living way opened for us through the curtain, that is, his body, ²¹and since we have a great priest over the house of God, ²²let us draw near to God with a sincere heart in full assurance of faith, having our hearts sprinkled to cleanse us from a guilty conscience and having our bodies washed with pure water. ²³Let us hold unswervingly to the hope we profess, for he who promised is faithful. ²⁴And let us consider how we may spur one another on towards love and good deeds. ²⁵Let us not give up meeting together, as some are in the habit of doing, but let us encourage one another — and all the more as you see the Day approaching.

10:20   The holiest place in the temple in Jerusalem was cut off from the rest of the temple by a curtain which was a symbol of the great gulf between God and humankind. The Gospel of Mark records that when Christ died the curtain was torn in two, and so those who trusted in Christ could have access to God.

---

²⁶If we deliberately keep on sinning after we have received the knowledge of the truth, no sacrifice for sins is left, ²⁷but only a fearful expectation of judgment and of raging fire that will consume the enemies of God. ²⁸Anyone who rejected the law of Moses died without mercy on the testimony of two or three witnesses. ²⁹How much more severely do you think a man deserves to be punished who has trampled the Son of God under foot, who has treated as an unholy thing the blood of the covenant that sanctified him, and who has insulted the Spirit of grace? ³⁰For we know him who said, "It is mine to avenge; I will repay," ᵈ and again, "The Lord will judge his people." ᵉ ³¹It is a dreadful thing to fall into the hands of the living God.

³²Remember those earlier days after you had received the light, when you stood your ground in a great contest in the face of suffering. ³³Sometimes you were publicly exposed to insult and persecution; at other times you stood side by side with those who were so treated. ³⁴You sympathised with those in prison and joyfully accepted the confiscation of your property, because you knew that you yourselves had better and lasting possessions.

³⁵So do not throw away your confidence; it will be richly rewarded. ³⁶You need to persevere so that when you have done the will of God, you will receive what he has promised. ³⁷For in just a very little while,

"He who is coming will come and will not delay.
³⁸ But my righteous one ᶠ will live by faith.
 And if he shrinks back,
   I will not be pleased with him." ᵍ

³⁹But we are not of those who shrink back and are destroyed, but of those who believe and are saved.

By Faith

11 Now faith is being sure of what we hope for and certain of what we do not see. ²This is what the ancients were commended for.

³By faith we understand that the universe was formed at God's command, so that what is seen was not made out of what was visible.

⁴By faith Abel offered God a better sacrifice than Cain did. By faith he was commended as a righteous man, when God spoke well of his offerings. And by faith he still speaks, even though he is dead.

⁵By faith Enoch was taken from this life, so that he did not experience death; he could not be found, because God had taken him away. For before he was taken, he was commended as one who pleased God. ⁶And without faith it is impossible to please God, because anyone who comes to him must believe that he exists and that he rewards those who earnestly seek him.

⁷By faith Noah, when warned about things not yet seen, in holy fear built an ark to save his family. By his faith he condemned the world and became heir of the righteousness that comes by faith.

⁸By faith Abraham, when called to go to a place he would later receive as his inheritance, obeyed and went, even though he did not know where he was going. ⁹By faith he made his home in the promised land like a stranger in a foreign country; he lived in tents, as did Isaac and Jacob, who were heirs with him of the same promise. ¹⁰For he was looking forward to the city with foundations, whose architect and builder is God.

¹¹By faith Abraham, even though he was past age — and Sarah herself was barren — was enabled to become a father because he ᵃ considered him faithful who had made the promise. ¹²And so from this one man, and he as good as dead, came descendants as numerous as the stars in the sky and as countless as the sand on the seashore.

¹³All these people were still living by faith when they died. They did not receive the things promised; they only saw them and welcomed them from a distance. And they admitted that they were aliens and

ᵇ16 Jer. 31:33   ᶜ17 Jer. 31:34   ᵈ30 Deut. 32:35
ᶠ38 One early manuscript But the righteous   ᵍ38 Hab. 2:3,4   ᵉ30 Deut. 32:36; Psalm 135:14
ᵃ11 Or By faith even Sarah, who was past age, was enabled to bear children because she

strangers on earth. [14]People who say such things show that they are looking for a country of their own. [15]If they had been thinking of the country they had left, they would have had opportunity to return. [16]Instead, they were longing for a better country—a heavenly one. Therefore God is not ashamed to be called their God, for he has prepared a city for them.

[17]By faith Abraham, when God tested him, offered Isaac as a sacrifice. He who had received the promises was about to sacrifice his one and only son, [18]even though God had said to him, "It is through Isaac that your offspring[b] will be reckoned." [c] [19]Abraham reasoned that God could raise the dead, and figuratively speaking, he did receive Isaac back from death.

[20]By faith Isaac blessed Jacob and Esau in regard to their future.

[21]By faith Jacob, when he was dying, blessed each of Joseph's sons, and worshipped as he leaned on the top of his staff.

[22]By faith Joseph, when his end was near, spoke about the exodus of the Israelites from Egypt and gave instructions about his bones.

[23]By faith Moses' parents hid him for three months after he was born, because they saw he was no ordinary child, and they were not afraid of the king's edict.

[24]By faith Moses, when he had grown up, refused to be known as the son of Pharaoh's daughter. [25]He chose to be ill-treated along with the people of God rather than to enjoy the pleasures of sin for a short time. [26]He regarded disgrace for the sake of Christ as of greater value than the treasures of Egypt, because he was looking ahead to his reward. [27]By faith he left Egypt, not fearing the king's anger; he persevered because he saw him who is invisible. [28]By faith he kept the Passover and the sprinkling of blood, so that the destroyer of the firstborn would not touch the firstborn of Israel.

[29]By faith the people passed through the Red Sea[d] as on dry land; but when the Egyptians tried to do so, they were drowned.

[30]By faith the walls of Jericho fell, after the people had marched around them for seven days.

[31]By faith the prostitute Rahab, because she welcomed the spies, was not killed with those who were disobedient.[e]

[32]And what more shall I say? I do not have time to tell about Gideon, Barak, Samson, Jephthah, David, Samuel and the prophets, [33]who through faith conquered kingdoms, administered justice, and gained what was promised; who shut the mouths of lions, [34]quenched the fury of the flames, and escaped the edge of the sword; whose weakness was turned to strength; and who became powerful in battle and routed foreign armies. [35]Women received back their dead, raised to life again. Others were tortured and refused to be released, so that they might gain a better resurrection. [36]Some faced jeers and flogging, while still others were chained and put in prison. [37]They were stoned;[f] they were sawn in two; they were put to death by the sword. They went about in sheepskins and goatskins, destitute, persecuted and ill-treated— [38]the world was not worthy of them. They wandered in deserts and mountains, and in caves and holes in the ground.

[39]These were all commended for their faith, yet none of them received what had been promised. [40]God had planned something better for us so that only together with us would they be made perfect.

God Disciplines His Sons

12 Therefore, since we are surrounded by such a great cloud of witnesses, let us throw off everything that hinders and the sin that so easily entangles, and let us run with perseverance the race marked out for us. [2]Let us fix our eyes on Jesus, the author and perfecter of our faith, who for the joy set before him endured the cross, scorning its shame, and sat down at the right hand of the throne of God. [3]Consider him who endured such opposition from sinful men, so that you will not grow weary and lose heart.

[4]In your struggle against sin, you have not yet resisted to the point of shedding your blood. [5]And you have forgotten that word of encouragement that addresses you as sons:

"My son, do not make light of the Lord's discipline,
    and do not lose heart when he rebukes you,
[6]because the Lord disciplines those he loves,
    and he punishes everyone he accepts as a son."[a]

[7]Endure hardship as discipline; God is treating you as sons. For what son is not disciplined by his father? [8]If you are not disciplined (and everyone undergoes discipline), then you are illegitimate children and not true sons. [9]Moreover, we have all had human fathers who disciplined us and we respected them for it. How much more should we submit to the Father of our spirits and live! [10]Our fathers disciplined us for a little while as they thought best; but God disciplines us for our good, that we may share in his holiness. [11]No discipline seems pleasant at the time, but painful. Later on, however, it produces a harvest of righteousness and peace for those who have been trained by it.

12:7 This argues for an entirely different view on suffering which results from the faithful witness to Christ. It is seen not as something to be avoided at all costs but to be endured with the knowledge that God disciplines us through it and helps us to reach full maturity.

---

[12]Therefore, strengthen your feeble arms and weak knees! [13]"Make level paths for your feet,"[b] so that the lame may not be disabled, but rather healed.

Warning Against Refusing God

[14]Make every effort to live in peace with all men and to be holy; without holiness no-one will see the Lord. [15]See to it that no-one misses the grace of God and that

b18 Greek seed   c18 Gen. 21:12   d29 That is, Sea of Reeds   e31 Or unbelieving
f37 Some early manuscripts stoned; they were put to the test;   a6 Prov. 3:11,12   b13 Prov. 4:26

no bitter root grows up to cause trouble and defile many. [16]See that no-one is sexually immoral, or is godless like Esau, who for a single meal sold his inheritance rights as the oldest son. [17]Afterwards, as you know, when he wanted to inherit this blessing, he was rejected. He could bring about no change of mind, though he sought the blessing with tears.

[18]You have not come to a mountain that can be touched and that is burning with fire; to darkness, gloom and storm; [19]to a trumpet blast or to such a voice speaking words that those who heard it begged that no further word be spoken to them, [20]because they could not bear what was commanded: "If even an animal touches the mountain, it must be stoned."[c] [21]The sight was so terrifying that Moses said, "I am trembling with fear."[d]

[22]But you have come to Mount Zion, to the heavenly Jerusalem, the city of the living God. You have come to thousands upon thousands of angels in joyful assembly, [23]to the church of the firstborn, whose names are written in heaven. You have come to God, the judge of all men, to the spirits of righteous men made perfect, [24]to Jesus the mediator of a new covenant, and to the sprinkled blood that speaks a better word than the blood of Abel.

[25]See to it that you do not refuse him who speaks. If they did not escape when they refused him who warned them on earth, how much less will we, if we turn away from him who warns us from heaven? [26]At that time his voice shook the earth, but now he has promised, "Once more I will shake not only the earth but also the heavens."[e] [27]The words "once more" indicate the removing of what can be shaken — that is, created things — so that what cannot be shaken may remain.

[28]Therefore, since we are receiving a kingdom that cannot be shaken, let us be thankful, and so worship God acceptably with reverence and awe, [29]for our "God is a consuming fire."[f]

Concluding Exhortations

13 Keep on loving each other as brothers. [2]Do not forget to entertain strangers, for by so doing some people have entertained angels without knowing it. [3]Remember those in prison as if you were their fellow-prisoners, and those who are ill-treated as if you yourselves were suffering.

[4]Marriage should be honoured by all, and the marriage bed kept pure, for God will judge the adulterer and all the sexually immoral. [5]Keep your lives free from the love of money and be content with what you have, because God has said,

"Never will I leave you;
never will I forsake you."[a]

[6]So we say with confidence,

"The Lord is my helper; I will not be afraid.
What can man do to me?"[b]

[7]Remember your leaders, who spoke the word of God to you. Consider the outcome of their way of life and imitate their faith. [8]Jesus Christ is the same yesterday and today and for ever.

[9]Do not be carried away by all kinds of strange teachings. It is good for our hearts to be strengthened by grace, not by ceremonial foods, which are of no value to those who eat them. [10]We have an altar from which those who minister at the tabernacle have no right to eat.

[11]The high priest carries the blood of animals into the Most Holy Place as a sin offering, but the bodies are burned outside the camp. [12]And so Jesus also suffered outside the city gate to make the people holy through his own blood. [13]Let us, then, go to him outside the camp, bearing the disgrace he bore. [14]For here we do not have an enduring city, but we are looking for the city that is to come.

13:13 Jesus suffered disgrace and death outside the walls of Jerusalem. The encouragement for people to join this is not in the sense that they can in any way add to the work of Christ, but that they should identify with Christ in his suffering. Such identifying may well be costly in terms of a worldly position, but ultimately rewarding in terms of eternal life.

---

[15]Through Jesus, therefore, let us continually offer to God a sacrifice of praise — the fruit of lips that confess his name. [16]And do not forget to do good and to share with others, for with such sacrifices God is pleased.

[17]Obey your leaders and submit to their authority. They keep watch over you as men who must give an account. Obey them so that their work will be a joy, not a burden, for that would be of no advantage to you.

[18]Pray for us. We are sure that we have a clear conscience and desire to live honourably in every way. [19]I particularly urge you to pray so that I may be restored to you soon.

[20]May the God of peace, who through the blood of the eternal covenant brought back from the dead our Lord Jesus, that great Shepherd of the sheep, [21]equip you with everything good for doing his will, and may he work in us what is pleasing to him, through Jesus Christ, to whom be glory for ever and ever. Amen.

[22]Brothers, I urge you to bear with my word of exhortation, for I have written you only a short letter. [23]I want you to know that our brother Timothy has been released. If he arrives soon, I will come with him to see you.

[24]Greet all your leaders and all God's people. Those from Italy send you their greetings.

[25]Grace be with you all.

[c]20 Exodus 19:12,13   [d]21 Deut. 9:19   [e]26 Haggai 2:6   [f]29 Deut. 4:24   [a]5 Deut. 31:6
[b]6 Psalm 118:6,7

James

Cultural Forms

In parts of Indonesia there is a form of theatre in which large puppets are made to act out folk stories and drama. Many Indian people who live in other parts of the world try to keep in touch with their roots by watching musical films from their home country. In the Scottish islands the people gather around the fire on winter evenings to sing Celtic songs. Every culture in every age has its own ways of expressing itself. It is not only the content of the stories and songs that is different in each culture, but also the mode of expression. We tend to think of our way of expressing ourselves as natural and obvious, but this is not the case. Consider, for example, how we take novels for granted. We think that the novel is an obvious way of telling a story or exploring ideas, but the English language had been written down for centuries before the first English novels were written.

Understanding the Strangeness

The books of the Bible are written in different styles, some of which are unfamiliar to us. For this reason the letter of James may seem a little strange. Unlike Paul's letters it was not intended for one particular person or community; it makes no reference to particular times and places; it contains no personal greetings; and it mentions no firsthand account of meeting his readers. Like the Old Testament book of Proverbs it consists of many sayings and instructions, almost like a preacher's notebook. This was not a traditional form of writing for the Jews, but it was very familiar to the Greeks. It was the style often used for teaching ethics. It is also written as though it were addressed to a second person, sometimes as though the writer were in vigorous debate with someone else, but no other person is named. Some of the phrases may be quotations from Greek writings. We can conclude, therefore, that the intended readers were Greek, but the message is decidedly Christian.

Lessons for All Seasons

James (or Jacob) was one of the most common names of the time. It is possible that the writer was a relative of Jesus, one of those who did not at first believe in him (see John 7:3–8), but who later became an important leader in the church. In any case, the writer described himself as a servant of God and it is clear that he spoke with authority. His message contains many elements of the teaching of Jesus, especially of the Sermon on the Mount (see Matthew 5—7).

Because this letter, unlike those of Paul, does not mention particular people, times, and places, it can very readily be applied to our day. Many of the images and metaphors are universal because they are taken from nature. The tone is very direct, even blunt, and there can seldom be any doubt about what the writer meant.

Faith and Works

However, over the centuries there has often been a dispute in the churches about what James said about faith and deeds. He said it was not enough just to listen to the word, but that it should also be put into practice (1:22). He also asked if it is possible to be a believer without doing good (2:14). A careful reading of the text will show that James was saying that believers are transformed by the living word of God within them. This leads, inevitably, to an improvement in the way that they behave so that they show their concern for others in practical ways.

1 James, a servant of God and of the Lord Jesus Christ,

To the twelve tribes scattered among the nations:

Greetings.

Trials and Temptations

²Consider it pure joy, my brothers, whenever you face trials of many kinds, ³because you know that the testing of your faith develops perseverance. ⁴Perseverance must finish its work so that you may be mature and complete, not lacking anything. ⁵If any of you lacks wisdom, he should ask God, who gives generously to all without finding fault, and it will be given to him. ⁶But when he asks, he must believe and not doubt, because he who doubts is like a wave of the sea, blown and tossed by the wind. ⁷That man should not think he will receive anything from the Lord; ⁸he is a double-minded man, unstable in all he does.

⁹The brother in humble circumstances ought to take pride in his high position. ¹⁰But the one who is rich should take pride in his low position, because he will pass away like a wild flower. ¹¹For the sun rises with scorching heat and withers the plant; its blossom falls and its beauty is destroyed. In the same way, the rich man will fade away even while he goes about his business.

¹²Blessed is the man who perseveres under trial, because when he has stood the test, he will receive the crown of life that God has promised to those who love him.

¹³When tempted, no-one should say, "God is tempting me." For God cannot be tempted by evil, nor does he tempt anyone; ¹⁴but each one is tempted when, by his own evil desire, he is dragged away and enticed. ¹⁵Then, after desire has conceived, it gives birth to sin; and sin, when it is full-grown, gives birth to death.

¹⁶Don't be deceived, my dear brothers. ¹⁷Every good and perfect gift is from above, coming down from the Father of the heavenly lights, who does not change like shifting shadows. ¹⁸He chose to give us birth through the word of truth, that we might be a kind of firstfruits of all he created.

Listening and Doing

¹⁹My dear brothers, take note of this: Everyone should be quick to listen, slow to speak and slow to become angry, ²⁰for man's anger does not bring about the righteous life that God desires. ²¹Therefore, get rid of all moral filth and the evil that is so prevalent, and humbly accept the word planted in you, which can save you.

1:19 We are reminded that we must not be arrogant and self-righteous. We must be ready to listen to the Scriptures and to others, and if we pay attention, the word of God will be planted in us. If we then nurture it and allow it to blossom it will bear fruit. This will transform us and our behaviour will improve, and we will then do what the word tells us.

---

²²Do not merely listen to the word, and so deceive yourselves. Do what it says. ²³Anyone who listens to the word but does not do what it says is like a man who looks at his face in a mirror ²⁴and, after looking at himself, goes away and immediately forgets what he looks like. ²⁵But the man who looks intently into the perfect law that gives freedom, and continues to do this, not forgetting what he has heard, but doing it — he will be blessed in what he does.

²⁶If anyone considers himself religious and yet does not keep a tight rein on his tongue, he deceives himself and his religion is worthless. ²⁷Religion that God our Father accepts as pure and faultless is this: to look after orphans and widows in their distress and to keep oneself from being polluted by the world.

Favouritism Forbidden

2 My brothers, as believers in our glorious Lord Jesus Christ, don't show favouritism. ²Suppose a man comes into your meeting wearing a gold ring and fine clothes, and a poor man in shabby clothes also comes in. ³If you show special attention to the man wearing fine clothes and say, "Here's a good seat for

you," but say to the poor man, "You stand there" or "Sit on the floor by my feet," 4have you not discriminated among yourselves and become judges with evil thoughts?

2:1   Luke's Gospel makes it clear that Jesus was born in poverty and that the first people to acknowledge him were humble shepherds (see Luke 2). Here, in his characteristically blunt language, James made it clear that followers of Jesus are not to fall into the trap of treating the rich with greater respect than the poor. God has chosen the poor to be rich in faith.

5Listen, my dear brothers: Has not God chosen those who are poor in the eyes of the world to be rich in faith and to inherit the kingdom he promised those who love him? 6But you have insulted the poor. Is it not the rich who are exploiting you? Are they not the ones who are dragging you into court? 7Are they not the ones who are slandering the noble name of him to whom you belong?

8If you really keep the royal law found in Scripture, "Love your neighbour as yourself,"ᵃ you are doing right. 9But if you show favouritism, you sin and are convicted by the law as law-breakers. 10For whoever keeps the whole law and yet stumbles at just one point is guilty of breaking all of it. 11For he who said, "Do not commit adultery,"ᵇ also said, "Do not murder."ᶜ If you do not commit adultery but do commit murder, you have become a law-breaker.

12Speak and act as those who are going to be judged by the law that gives freedom, 13because judgment without mercy will be shown to anyone who has not been merciful. Mercy triumphs over judgment!

Faith and Deeds

14What good is it, my brothers, if a man claims to have faith but has no deeds? Can such faith save him? 15Suppose a brother or sister is without clothes and daily food. 16If one of you says to him, "Go, I wish you well; keep warm and well fed," but does nothing about his physical needs, what good is it? 17In the same way, faith by itself, if it is not accompanied by action, is dead.

18But someone will say, "You have faith; I have deeds."

Show me your faith without deeds, and I will show you my faith by what I do. 19You believe that there is one God. Good! Even the demons believe that—and shudder.

20You foolish man, do you want evidence that faith without deeds is useless?ᵈ 21Was not our ancestor Abraham considered righteous for what he did when he offered his son Isaac on the altar? 22You see that his faith and his actions were working together, and his faith was made complete by what he did. 23And the scripture was fulfilled that says, "Abraham believed God, and it was credited to him as righteousness,"ᵉ

and he was called God's friend. 24You see that a person is justified by what he does and not by faith alone.

25In the same way, was not even Rahab the prostitute considered righteous for what she did when she gave lodging to the spies and sent them off in a different direction? 26As the body without the spirit is dead, so faith without deeds is dead.

Taming the Tongue

3 Not many of you should presume to be teachers, my brothers, because you know that we who teach will be judged more strictly. 2We all stumble in many ways. If anyone is never at fault in what he says, he is a perfect man, able to keep his whole body in check.

3When we put bits into the mouths of horses to make them obey us, we can turn the whole animal. 4Or take ships as an example. Although they are so large and are driven by strong winds, they are steered by a very small rudder wherever the pilot wants to go. 5Likewise the tongue is a small part of the body, but it makes great boasts. Consider what a great forest is set on fire by a small spark. 6The tongue also is a fire, a world of evil among the parts of the body. It corrupts the whole person, sets the whole course of his life on fire, and is itself set on fire by hell.

7All kinds of animals, birds, reptiles and creatures of the sea are being tamed and have been tamed by man, 8but no man can tame the tongue. It is a restless evil, full of deadly poison.

9With the tongue we praise our Lord and Father, and with it we curse men, who have been made in God's likeness. 10Out of the same mouth come praise and cursing. My brothers, this should not be. 11Can both fresh water and saltᵃ water flow from the same spring? 12My brothers, can a fig-tree bear olives, or a grapevine bear figs? Neither can a salt spring produce fresh water.

Two Kinds of Wisdom

13Who is wise and understanding among you? Let him show it by his good life, by deeds done in the humility that comes from wisdom. 14But if you harbour bitter envy and selfish ambition in your hearts, do not boast about it or deny the truth. 15Such "wisdom" does not come down from heaven but is earthly, unspiritual, of the devil. 16For where you have envy and selfish ambition, there you find disorder and every evil practice.

17But the wisdom that comes from heaven is first of all pure; then peace-loving, considerate, submissive, full of mercy and good fruit, impartial and sincere. 18Peacemakers who sow in peace raise a harvest of righteousness.

Submit Yourselves to God

4 What causes fights and quarrels among you? Don't they come from your desires that battle within you? 2You want something but don't get it. You

---

ᵃ8 Lev. 19:18   ᵇ11 Exodus 20:14; Deut. 5:18   ᶜ11 Exodus 20:13; Deut. 5:17   ᵈ20 Some early manuscripts *dead*
ᵉ23 Gen. 15:6   ᵃ11 Greek *bitter* (see also verse 14)

kill and covet, but you cannot have what you want. You quarrel and fight. You do not have, because you do not ask God. ³When you ask, you do not receive, because you ask with wrong motives, that you may spend what you get on your pleasures.

⁴You adulterous people, don't you know that friendship with the world is hatred towards God? Anyone who chooses to be a friend of the world becomes an enemy of God. ⁵Or do you think Scripture says without reason that the spirit he caused to live in us envies intensely?ª ⁶But he gives us more grace. That is why Scripture says:

"God opposes the proud
but gives grace to the humble."ᵇ

⁷Submit yourselves, then, to God. Resist the devil, and he will flee from you. ⁸Come near to God and he will come near to you. Wash your hands, you sinners, and purify your hearts, you double-minded. ⁹Grieve, mourn and wail. Change your laughter to mourning and your joy to gloom. ¹⁰Humble yourselves before the Lord, and he will lift you up.

4:7   People who are not self-seeking may be called do-gooders; peace-makers may be ridiculed as timid. Society encourages us to be proud, selfish, and aggressive, though perhaps without actually using these words. The problems that James faced in his time still exist today, so his reminder is still valid: "God opposes the proud but gives grace to the humble."

---

¹¹Brothers, do not slander one another. Anyone who speaks against his brother or judges him speaks against the law and judges it. When you judge the law, you are not keeping it, but sitting in judgment on it. ¹²There is only one Lawgiver and Judge, the one who is able to save and destroy. But you—who are you to judge your neighbour?

Boasting About Tomorrow

¹³Now listen, you who say, "Today or tomorrow we will go to this or that city, spend a year there, carry on business and make money." ¹⁴Why, you do not even know what will happen tomorrow. What is your life? You are a mist that appears for a little while and then vanishes. ¹⁵Instead, you ought to say, "If it is the Lord's will, we will live and do this or that." ¹⁶As it is, you boast and brag. All such boasting is evil. ¹⁷Anyone, then, who knows the good he ought to do and doesn't do it, sins.

Warning to Rich Oppressors

5 Now listen, you rich people, weep and wail because of the misery that is coming upon you. ²Your wealth has rotted, and moths have eaten your clothes. ³Your gold and silver are corroded. Their corrosion will testify against you and eat your flesh like fire. You have hoarded wealth in the last days. ⁴Look! The wages you failed to pay the workmen who mowed your fields are crying out against you. The cries of the harvesters have reached the ears of the Lord Almighty. ⁵You have lived on earth in luxury and self-indulgence. You have fattened yourselves in the day of slaughter.ª ⁶You have condemned and murdered innocent men, who were not opposing you.

Patience in Suffering

⁷Be patient, then, brothers, until the Lord's coming. See how the farmer waits for the land to yield its valuable crop and how patient he is for the autumn and spring rains. ⁸You too, be patient and stand firm, because the Lord's coming is near. ⁹Don't grumble against each other, brothers, or you will be judged. The Judge is standing at the door!

¹⁰Brothers, as an example of patience in the face of suffering, take the prophets who spoke in the name of the Lord. ¹¹As you know, we consider blessed those who have persevered. You have heard of Job's perseverance and have seen what the Lord finally brought about. The Lord is full of compassion and mercy.

5:10   Suffering tempts many faithful people to abandon their trust in God. On the other hand, many who have forgotten their faith only turn to God when they are sick. James reminds us that the church has a particularly important ministry to care for the sick. Praying over the sick is a widespread Christian custom, and some traditions also continue the practice of anointing with oil (verse 14).

---

¹²Above all, my brothers, do not swear—not by heaven or by earth or by anything else. Let your "Yes" be yes, and your "No", no, or you will be condemned.

The Prayer of Faith

¹³Is any one of you in trouble? He should pray. Is anyone happy? Let him sing songs of praise. ¹⁴Is any one of you sick? He should call the elders of the church to pray over him and anoint him with oil in the name of the Lord. ¹⁵And the prayer offered in faith will make the sick person well; the Lord will raise him up. If he has sinned, he will be forgiven. ¹⁶Therefore confess your sins to each other and pray for each other so that you may be healed. The prayer of a righteous man is powerful and effective.

¹⁷Elijah was a man just like us. He prayed earnestly that it would not rain, and it did not rain on the land for three and a half years. ¹⁸Again he prayed, and the

---

ª5 Or that God jealously longs for the spirit that he made to live in us; or that the Spirit he caused to live in us longs jealously
ᵇ6 Prov. 3:34   ª5 Or yourselves as in a day of feasting

heavens gave rain, and the earth produced its crops. ¹⁹My brothers, if one of you should wander from the truth and someone should bring him back, ²⁰remember

this: Whoever turns a sinner from the error of his way will save him from death and cover over a multitude of sins.

1 Peter

Peter

Both the weight of evidence and Church tradition point to the author of this letter being the apostle Peter. We are given a clear indication of who was intended to receive the letter; Christians who lived in the provinces in the north of Asia Minor (1:1). There seems to have been a wide social mix among the Christian churches, with both slaves and masters worshipping in the same church. Judging from the comments Peter makes about the believers' past lives (1:14), the churches would appear to be largely made up of Gentiles (non Jews), although in these regions there were large Jewish communities and it is likely that there were converts from Judaism in the churches as well.

A Letter to Encourage

Peter set out the main purpose for his letter in 5:12: to encourage the churches to hold fast to their hope in the middle of persecution and an unfriendly world. Peter was just the person to encourage the faint hearted. His warmth and affection for these churches and his experience of suffering made his message very powerful. The hope the believers should cling to needed to be shown in their daily lives by their attitudes to each other in the fellowship, and their attitudes to the society in which they lived.

Scattered and Scared

Peter was writing to a scared people. Because of their beliefs they were regarded as strangers (1:1; 2:11) in a world with different values to their own (4:4); they were scattered away from each other (1:1) and so suffered a sense of isolation; they were suffering persecution (3:17) at the hands of people they lived with (2:12), and probably the beginnings of state persecution at the hands of the authorities in the regions as well. There was fear among the believers (3:14). The danger for them was twofold: either they would be crushed by fear and oppression or they would begin to behave like the society around them and lose the distinctiveness they had as Christians.

The Promises of Christ

Peter began by building the people up, encouraging them to hold on to the hope that they first had. Though they felt scattered and lonely, they were a chosen people, a people who belonged to God (2:9); despite the discouragement of daily life, they could still trust in the hope which Christ promised (1:21); though they suffered, the promise of salvation still held true for them (1:9); indeed the very suffering which they were enduring had a purpose: to refine them (1:7) and build up their faith (2:5). Finally, they could cling to the promise that Christ would restore them in the end (5:10) and that the end time was not very far away (4:7). Until then they could pray to God who would share their suffering with them (5:7).

A Practical Faith

It was not enough for Peter that the churches knew that hope. The people should also live it out in very practical ways; in their relationships with each other and with the world. If they had hope, they should live in that hope. Just as in the letters Paul wrote, there is a strong connection between theology and practical faith. In a world which showed little love, the believers were to love one another (1:22; 2:17) so that there would be harmony among them (3:8; 4:8); they had to accept that they were strangers in the world (1:17) because their lifestyles were very different from those around them. They were not to copy the ways of the world (2:11) but show restraint (4:7) and live holy lives which would leave no room for others to criticize (2:15) and would give God glory (2:12). This holy way of life was to extend to the different relationships which made up the body of believers: slaves (2:18), wives (3:1), husbands (3:7), elders (5:1) and the young men of the church (5:5). For modern readers the message is the same. If we possess the hope that we have in Jesus Christ then that will not only sustain us through difficult times but also radically transform the way we live our lives. No matter what the circumstances, our Christianity should be evident in our lives, and in our relationships. That is the challenge for Christian living which Peter still faces us with today.

1 Peter, an apostle of Jesus Christ,

To God's elect, strangers in the world, scattered throughout Pontus, Galatia, Cappadocia, Asia and Bithynia, 2who have been chosen according to the foreknowledge of God the Father, through the sanctifying work of the Spirit, for obedience to Jesus Christ and sprinkling by his blood:

Grace and peace be yours in abundance.

Praise to God for a Living Hope

3Praise be to the God and Father of our Lord Jesus Christ! In his great mercy he has given us new birth into a living hope through the resurrection of Jesus Christ from the dead, 4and into an inheritance that can never perish, spoil or fade — kept in heaven for you, 5who through faith are shielded by God's power until the coming of the salvation that is ready to be revealed in the last time. 6In this you greatly rejoice, though now for a little while you may have had to suffer grief in all kinds of trials. 7These have come so that your faith — of greater worth than gold, which perishes even though refined by fire — may be proved genuine and may result in praise, glory and honour when Jesus Christ is revealed. 8Though you have not seen him, you love him; and even though you do not see him now,

you believe in him and are filled with an inexpressible and glorious joy, 9for you are receiving the goal of your faith, the salvation of your souls.

1:5   In the midst of suffering it may seem inappropriate to talk about salvation at the end of time, but to a suffering people the knowledge that the present life was not everything was a source of inspiration. It also reminds us that we should live each moment as if the end of the world is only a short time away. The possibility of the end of our sufferings makes them bearable.

10Concerning this salvation, the prophets, who spoke of the grace that was to come to you, searched intently and with the greatest care, 11trying to find out the time and circumstances to which the Spirit of Christ in them was pointing when he predicted the sufferings of Christ and the glories that would follow. 12It was revealed to them that they were not serving themselves but you, when they spoke of the things that have now been told you by those who have preached the gospel to you by the Holy Spirit sent from heaven. Even angels long to look into these things.

Be Holy

13Therefore, prepare your minds for action; be self-controlled; set your hope fully on the grace to be given you when Jesus Christ is revealed. 14As obedient children, do not conform to the evil desires you had when you lived in ignorance. 15But just as he who called you is holy, so be holy in all you do; 16for it is written: "Be holy, because I am holy." [a]

17Since you call on a Father who judges each man's work impartially, live your lives as strangers here in reverent fear. 18For you know that it was not with perishable things such as silver or gold that you were redeemed from the empty way of life handed down to you from your forefathers, 19but with the precious blood of Christ, a lamb without blemish or defect. 20He was chosen before the creation of the world, but was revealed in these last times for your sake. 21Through him you believe in God, who raised him from the dead and glorified him, and so your faith and hope are in God.

22Now that you have purified yourselves by obeying the truth so that you have sincere love for your brothers, love one another deeply, from the heart. [b] 23For you have been born again, not of perishable seed, but of imperishable, through the living and enduring word of God. 24For,

"All men are like grass,
   and all their glory is like the flowers of the
      field;
the grass withers and the flowers fall,
25 but the word of the Lord stands for ever." [c]

And this is the word that was preached to you.

2 Therefore, rid yourselves of all malice and all deceit, hypocrisy, envy, and slander of every kind. 2Like newborn babies, crave pure spiritual milk, so that by it you may grow up in your salvation, 3now that you have tasted that the Lord is good.

The Living Stone and a Chosen People

4As you come to him, the living Stone — rejected by men but chosen by God and precious to him — 5you also, like living stones, are being built into a spiritual house to be a holy priesthood, offering spiritual sacrifices acceptable to God through Jesus Christ. 6For in Scripture it says:

"See, I lay a stone in Zion,
   a chosen and precious cornerstone,
and the one who trusts in him
   will never be put to shame." [a]

7Now to you who believe, this stone is precious. But to those who do not believe,

"The stone the builders rejected
   has become the capstone," [b,c]

8and,

"A stone that causes men to stumble
   and a rock that makes them fall." [d]

They stumble because they disobey the message — which is also what they were destined for.

2:4   The word for "stone" means one that is shaped or dressed for the purpose of building, rather than any piece of rock. Just as Christ was made to be the foundation of a spiritual building, so we are made to be part of that same building, the church of God. Just as each brick is important to the strength of the building, so the members of the church depend upon each other.

9But you are a chosen people, a royal priesthood, a holy nation, a people belonging to God, that you may declare the praises of him who called you out of darkness into his wonderful light. 10Once you were not a people, but now you are the people of God; once you had not received mercy, but now you have received mercy.

11Dear friends, I urge you, as aliens and strangers in the world, to abstain from sinful desires, which war against your soul. 12Live such good lives among the pagans that, though they accuse you of doing wrong, they may see your good deeds and glorify God on the day he visits us.

Submission to Rulers and Masters

13Submit yourselves for the Lord's sake to every authority instituted among men: whether to the king, as the supreme authority, 14or to governors, who are sent by him to punish those who do wrong and to commend those who do right. 15For it is God's will that by doing good you should silence the ignorant talk of foolish men. 16Live as free men, but do not use your freedom as a cover-up for evil; live as servants of God. 17Show proper respect to everyone: Love the brotherhood of believers, fear God, honour the king.

18Slaves, submit yourselves to your masters with all respect, not only to those who are good and considerate, but also to those who are harsh. 19For it is commendable if a man bears up under the pain of unjust suffering because he is conscious of God. 20But how is it to your credit if you receive a beating for doing wrong and endure it? But if you suffer for doing good and you endure it, this is commendable before God. 21To this you were called, because Christ suffered for you, leaving you an example, that you should follow in his steps.

22"He committed no sin,
   and no deceit was found in his mouth." [e]

23When they hurled their insults at him, he did not retaliate; when he suffered, he made no threats. Instead, he entrusted himself to him who judges justly. 24He himself bore our sins in his body on the tree, so that we might die to sins and live for righteousness; by his wounds you have been healed. 25For you were like sheep going astray, but now you have returned to the Shepherd and Overseer of your souls.

---

a16 Lev. 11:44,45; 19:2; 20:7   b22 Some early manuscripts *from a pure heart*   c25 Isaiah 40:6–8
a6 Isaiah 28:16   b7 Or *cornerstone*   c7 Psalm 118:22   d8 Isaiah 8:14   e22 Isaiah 53:9

Wives and Husbands

3 Wives, in the same way be submissive to your husbands so that, if any of them do not believe the word, they may be won over without words by the behaviour of their wives, ²when they see the purity and reverence of your lives. ³Your beauty should not come from outward adornment, such as braided hair and the wearing of gold jewellery and fine clothes. ⁴Instead, it should be that of your inner self, the unfading beauty of a gentle and quiet spirit, which is of great worth in God's sight. ⁵For this is the way the holy women of the past who put their hope in God used to make themselves beautiful. They were submissive to their own husbands, ⁶like Sarah, who obeyed Abraham and called him her master. You are her daughters if you do what is right and do not give way to fear.

3:1 Some people may have difficulty with the idea of wives being submissive to their husbands, but here Peter encouraged them to behave in this way so that their unbelieving husbands might come to faith through the example set by their wives. This is still a difficulty for many Christian wives and husbands today.

---

⁷Husbands, in the same way be considerate as you live with your wives, and treat them with respect as the weaker partner and as heirs with you of the gracious gift of life, so that nothing will hinder your prayers.

Suffering for Doing Good

⁸Finally, all of you, live in harmony with one another; be sympathetic, love as brothers, be compassionate and humble. ⁹Do not repay evil with evil or insult with insult, but with blessing, because to this you were called so that you may inherit a blessing. ¹⁰For,

"Whoever would love life
  and see good days
must keep his tongue from evil
  and his lips from deceitful speech.
¹¹He must turn from evil and do good;
  he must seek peace and pursue it.
¹²For the eyes of the Lord are on the righteous
  and his ears are attentive to their prayer,
but the face of the Lord is against those who do
  evil." [a]

¹³Who is going to harm you if you are eager to do good? ¹⁴But even if you should suffer for what is right, you are blessed. "Do not fear what they fear; [b] do not be frightened." [c] ¹⁵But in your hearts set apart Christ as Lord. Always be prepared to give an answer to everyone who asks you to give the reason for the hope that you have. But do this with gentleness and respect, ¹⁶keeping a clear conscience, so that those who speak maliciously against your good behaviour in Christ may be ashamed of their slander. ¹⁷It is better, if it is God's will, to suffer for doing good than for doing evil. ¹⁸For Christ died for sins once for all, the righteous for the unrighteous, to bring you to God. He was put to death in the body but made alive by the Spirit, ¹⁹through whom [d] also he went and preached to the spirits in prison ²⁰who disobeyed long ago when God waited patiently in the days of Noah while the ark was being built. In it only a few people, eight in all, were saved through water, ²¹and this water symbolises baptism that now saves you also — not the removal of dirt from the body but the pledge [e] of a good conscience towards God. It saves you by the resurrection of Jesus Christ, ²²who has gone into heaven and is at God's right hand — with angels, authorities and powers in submission to him.

Living for God

4 Therefore, since Christ suffered in his body, arm yourselves also with the same attitude, because he who has suffered in his body is done with sin. ²As a result, he does not live the rest of his earthly life for evil human desires, but rather for the will of God. ³For you have spent enough time in the past doing what pagans choose to do — living in debauchery, lust, drunkenness, orgies, carousing and detestable idolatry. ⁴They think it strange that you do not plunge with them into the same flood of dissipation, and they heap abuse on you. ⁵But they will have to give account to him who is ready to judge the living and the dead. ⁶For this is the reason the gospel was preached even to those who are now dead, so that they might be judged according to men in regard to the body, but live according to God in regard to the spirit.

⁷The end of all things is near. Therefore be clear minded and self-controlled so that you can pray. ⁸Above all, love each other deeply, because love covers over a multitude of sins. ⁹Offer hospitality to one another without grumbling. ¹⁰Each one should use whatever gift he has received to serve others, faithfully administering God's grace in its various forms. ¹¹If anyone speaks, he should do it as one speaking the very words of God. If anyone serves, he should do it with the strength God provides, so that in all things God may be praised through Jesus Christ. To him be the glory and the power for ever and ever. Amen.

Suffering for Being a Christian

¹²Dear friends, do not be surprised at the painful trial you are suffering, as though something strange were happening to you. ¹³But rejoice that you participate in the sufferings of Christ, so that you may be overjoyed when his glory is revealed. ¹⁴If you are insulted because of the name of Christ, you are blessed, for the Spirit of glory and of God rests on you. ¹⁵If you suffer, it should not be as a murderer or thief or any other kind of criminal, or even as a meddler. ¹⁶However, if you suffer as a Christian, do not be ashamed, but praise God that you bear that name. ¹⁷For it is time for judgment to begin with the family of God; and if it begins with

---

us, what will the outcome be for those who do not obey the gospel of God? [18]And,

> "If it is hard for the righteous to be saved,
> what will become of the ungodly and the
> sinner?"[a]

[19]So then, those who suffer according to God's will should commit themselves to their faithful Creator and continue to do good.

To Elders and Young Men

5 To the elders among you, I appeal as a fellow-elder, a witness of Christ's sufferings and one who also will share in the glory to be revealed: [2]Be shepherds of God's flock that is under your care, serving as overseers — not because you must, but because you are willing, as God wants you to be; not greedy for money, but eager to serve; [3]not lording it over those entrusted to you, but being examples to the flock. [4]And when the Chief Shepherd appears, you will receive the crown of glory that will never fade away.

[5]Young men, in the same way be submissive to those who are older. All of you, clothe yourselves with humility towards one another, because,

> "God opposes the proud
> but gives grace to the humble."[a]

[6]Humble yourselves, therefore, under God's mighty

hand, that he may lift you up in due time. [7]Cast all your anxiety on him because he cares for you.

[8]Be self-controlled and alert. Your enemy the devil prowls around like a roaring lion looking for someone to devour. [9]Resist him, standing firm in the faith, because you know that your brothers throughout the world are undergoing the same kind of sufferings.

[10]And the God of all grace, who called you to his eternal glory in Christ, after you have suffered a little while, will himself restore you and make you strong, firm and steadfast. [11]To him be the power for ever and ever. Amen.

Final Greetings

[12]With the help of Silas,[b] whom I regard as a faithful brother, I have written to you briefly, encouraging you and testifying that this is the true grace of God. Stand fast in it.

5:13　　Peter is likely to be referring to the church in Rome.

---

[13]She who is in Babylon, chosen together with you, sends you her greetings, and so does my son Mark. [14]Greet one another with a kiss of love.

Peace to all of you who are in Christ.

[a]18 Prov. 11:31　　　[a]5 Prov. 3:34　　　[b]12 Greek *Silvanus*, a variant of *Silas*

2 Peter

"... to stimulate you to wholesome thinking ..."

The wholesome thinking that Peter wanted the church to be indulging in concerned the judgement of God which would come with Christ's return. Christians were to live their daily lives in the light of that judgement, and so once again theological teaching was accompanied by advice on how they should live. But this letter was much more than an encouragement to the church. It also sought to counter the influence of the doubters and heretics (those who depart from the accepted beliefs of the church).

Maintaining True Faith

We can work out what the opponents of truth were saying from Peter's counter-arguments. Some members of the church were denying the truths which Peter and others had been teaching. They questioned whether Christ would come again, considering that nothing had happened yet despite all the warnings (3:4); they claimed that the teaching on the second coming and judgement was made up on (1:16); they also denied the prophetic words which had been spoken concerning the final judgement (1:20–21). They were sceptical of the idea that God would intervene in the world in such a dramatic way, and believed that life would go on as it always had done (3:4) forgetting the teaching of the Scriptures (3:5ff.). Because these people did not believe in judgement, it followed that what they did with their lives would have no effect on their relationship with God. It was as if they believed that Peter and others had invented the idea of judgement in order to scare believers into living respectable and enslaved lives. These same "false teachers" had even tried to find a basis for their beliefs within Paul's teaching (3:15ff.) and taught and encouraged others to follow their example (2:2; 2:18).

The Power of Christ

Peter's answer was to emphasize again the certainty of the coming of Christ in judgement. The day of judgement would come suddenly when least expected (3:10a) and would be dramatic (3:10b–11). The basis for Peter's teaching was his own knowledge and experience of the power and majesty of Christ. He had seen Christ in all his glory and knew that this same king would return in power (1:16ff.). He addressed the problem about the delay of the second coming by arguing that if God was delaying the judgement it was because he wanted everyone to have the chance to turn back to him (3:9). His strongest words were ones of condemnation for those who were leading others astray by their false teaching and sinful lives (2:17). The inevitable result of such sinfulness would be destruction for them at the day of judgement.

Future Reward and Present Actions

However, to those who remained true to the teaching of the Church, and believed in the promises that Peter wrote about, there was the promise of a new heaven and a new earth (3:13) and their own salvation (3:15). Peter was not content with simply pointing out the reward for faithfulness, but made the connection between future reward and present actions. It is because of God's promises that believers have the opportunity of breaking free from the evil and corruption of the world (1:4). They have the opportunity to grow in faith and spiritual maturity (1:5ff.) so that they will not lose their reward of eternal life (3:17). Such was the fate of the false teachers and all who followed their teaching.

What Type of Judgement?

How should we regard judgement day, especially considering it has still not come to pass? Do we deny or neglect the future and concentrate on our enjoyment of the present like the false teachers of 2 Peter? Does the coming judgement affect our lives and determine the way we live? Peter argued that it has to if we are to mature as Christians and if we don't want to run the risk of losing the inheritance which God has promised for all those who truly believe in him. We must take heed of Peter's final encouragement: "grow in the grace and knowledge of our Lord and Saviour Jesus Christ."

1

Simon Peter, a servant and apostle of Jesus Christ,

To those who through the righteousness of our God and Saviour Jesus Christ have received a faith as precious as ours:

[2]Grace and peace be yours in abundance through the knowledge of God and of Jesus our Lord.

Making One's Calling and Election Sure

[3]His divine power has given us everything we need for life and godliness through our knowledge of him who called us by his own glory and goodness. [4]Through these he has given us his very great and precious promises, so that through them you may participate in the divine nature and escape the corruption in the world caused by evil desires.

1:4 One of the startling claims of Christianity is that by the grace of God people can take on more of Christ's nature day by day. To enter into the nature of God is not the end of the Christian journey, but very much part of the daily walk from the beginning.

---

[5]For this very reason, make every effort to add to your faith goodness; and to goodness, knowledge; [6]and to knowledge, self-control; and to self-control, perseverance; and to perseverance, godliness; [7]and to godliness, brotherly kindness; and to brotherly kindness, love. [8]For if you possess these qualities in increasing measure, they will keep you from being ineffective and unproductive in your knowledge of our Lord Jesus Christ. [9]But if anyone does not have them, he is shortsighted and blind, and has forgotten that he has been cleansed from his past sins.

[10]Therefore, my brothers, be all the more eager to make your calling and election sure. For if you do these things, you will never fall, [11]and you will receive a rich welcome into the eternal kingdom of our Lord and Saviour Jesus Christ.

Prophecy of Scripture

[12]So I will always remind you of these things, even though you know them and are firmly established in the truth you now have. [13]I think it is right to refresh your memory as long as I live in the tent of this body, [14]because I know that I will soon put it aside, as our Lord Jesus Christ has made clear to me. [15]And I will make every effort to see that after my departure you will always be able to remember these things.

[16]We did not follow cleverly invented stories when we told you about the power and coming of our Lord Jesus Christ, but we were eye-witnesses of his majesty. [17]For he received honour and glory from God the Father when the voice came to him from the Majestic Glory, saying, "This is my Son, whom I love; with him I am well pleased."[a] [18]We ourselves heard this voice that came from heaven when we were with him on the sacred mountain.

[19]And we have the word of the prophets made more certain, and you will do well to pay attention to it, as to a light shining in a dark place, until the day dawns and the morning star rises in your hearts. [20]Above all, you must understand that no prophecy of Scripture came about by the prophet's own interpretation. [21]For prophecy never had its origin in the will of man, but men spoke from God as they were carried along by the Holy Spirit.

False Teachers and Their Destruction

2

But there were also false prophets among the people, just as there will be false teachers among you. They will secretly introduce destructive heresies, even denying the sovereign Lord who bought them — bringing swift destruction on themselves. [2]Many will follow their shameful ways and will bring the way of truth into disrepute. [3]In their greed these teachers will exploit you with stories they have made up. Their condemnation has long been hanging over them, and their destruction has not been sleeping.

[4]For if God did not spare angels when they sinned, but sent them to hell,[a] putting them into gloomy dungeons[b] to be held for judgment; [5]if he did not spare the ancient world when he brought the flood on its ungodly people, but protected Noah, a preacher of righteousness, and seven others; [6]if he condemned the cities of Sodom and Gomorrah by burning them to ashes, and made them an example of what is going to happen to the ungodly; [7]and if he rescued Lot, a righteous man, who was distressed by the filthy lives of lawless men [8](for that righteous man, living among them day after day, was tormented in his righteous soul by the lawless deeds he saw and heard) — [9]if this is so, then the Lord knows how to rescue godly men from trials and to hold the unrighteous for the day of judgment, while continuing their punishment.[c] [10]This is especially true of those who follow the corrupt desire of the sinful nature[d] and despise authority.

Bold and arrogant, these men are not afraid to slander celestial beings; [11]yet even angels, although they are stronger and more powerful, do not bring slanderous accusations against such beings in the presence of the Lord. [12]But these men blaspheme in matters they do not understand. They are like brute beasts, creatures of instinct, born only to be caught and destroyed, and like beasts they too will perish.

[13]They will be paid back with harm for the harm they have done. Their idea of pleasure is to carouse in broad daylight. They are blots and blemishes, revelling in their pleasures while they feast with you.[e] [14]With eyes full of adultery, they never stop sinning; they seduce the unstable; they are experts in greed — an accursed brood! [15]They have left the straight way and wandered off to follow the way of Balaam son of Beor, who loved the wages of wickedness. [16]But he was rebuked for his wrongdoing by a donkey — a beast without speech — who spoke with a man's voice and restrained the prophet's madness.

[17]These men are springs without water and mists

---

a 17 Matt. 17:5; Mark 9:7; Luke 9:35   a 4 Greek *Tartarus*   b 4 Some manuscripts *into chains of darkness*
c 9 Or *unrighteous for punishment until the day of judgment*   d 10 Or *the flesh*   e 13 Some manuscripts *in their love feasts*

driven by a storm. Blackest darkness is reserved for them. ¹⁸For they mouth empty, boastful words and, by appealing to the lustful desires of sinful human nature, they entice people who are just escaping from those who live in error. ¹⁹They promise them freedom, while they themselves are slaves of depravity—for a man is a slave to whatever has mastered him. ²⁰If they have escaped the corruption of the world by knowing our Lord and Saviour Jesus Christ and are again entangled in it and overcome, they are worse off at the end than they were at the beginning. ²¹It would have been better for them not to have known the way of righteousness, than to have known it and then to turn their backs on the sacred command that was passed on to them. ²²Of them the proverbs are true: "A dog returns to its vomit,"ᶠ and, "A sow that is washed goes back to her wallowing in the mud."

The Day of the Lord

3 Dear friends, this is now my second letter to you. I have written both of them as reminders to stimulate you to wholesome thinking. ²I want you to recall the words spoken in the past by the holy prophets and the command given by our Lord and Saviour through your apostles.

³First of all, you must understand that in the last days scoffers will come, scoffing and following their own evil desires. ⁴They will say, "Where is this 'coming' he promised? Ever since our fathers died, everything goes on as it has since the beginning of creation." ⁵But they deliberately forget that long ago by God's word the heavens existed and the earth was formed out of water and by water. ⁶By these waters also the world of that time was deluged and destroyed. ⁷By the same word the present heavens and earth are reserved for fire, being kept for the day of judgment and destruction of ungodly men.

3:8 Here Peter encouraged the people to see the history of the world not through human eyes but from God's perspective. This is not an excuse to explain the delay in the second coming but to end speculation about when it will happen. Instead it is important to live life in the knowledge that it will indeed come.

---

⁸But do not forget this one thing, dear friends: With the Lord a day is like a thousand years, and a thousand years are like a day. ⁹The Lord is not slow in keeping his promise, as some understand slowness. He is patient with you, not wanting anyone to perish, but everyone to come to repentance.

¹⁰But the day of the Lord will come like a thief. The heavens will disappear with a roar; the elements will be destroyed by fire, and the earth and everything in it will be laid bare.ᵃ

¹¹Since everything will be destroyed in this way, what kind of people ought you to be? You ought to live holy and godly lives ¹²as you look forward to the day of God and speed its coming.ᵇ That day will bring about the destruction of the heavens by fire, and the elements will melt in the heat. ¹³But in keeping with his promise we are looking forward to a new heaven and a new earth, the home of righteousness.

¹⁴So then, dear friends, since you are looking forward to this, make every effort to be found spotless, blameless and at peace with him. ¹⁵Bear in mind that our Lord's patience means salvation, just as our dear brother Paul also wrote to you with the wisdom that God gave him. ¹⁶He writes the same way in all his letters, speaking in them of these matters. His letters contain some things that are hard to understand, which ignorant and unstable people distort, as they do the other Scriptures, to their own destruction.

3:16 It is comforting to know that the problem of some passages of Scripture having obscure meanings is not new to the church. Even Peter found problems with understanding some of Paul's ideas. He alerted his readers to the danger of taking difficult passages out of context and using them to build their own theories. We must measure any interpretation of a passage against the whole of God's Word.

---

¹⁷Therefore, dear friends, since you already know this, be on your guard so that you may not be carried away by the error of lawless men and fall from your secure position. ¹⁸But grow in the grace and knowledge of our Lord and Saviour Jesus Christ. To him be glory both now and for ever! Amen.

---

1 John

A Writer's Style

A great writer can usually be distinguished by their instantly recognizable style. It is true of novels by Austen and Hardy, poetry by Browning and Milton, and plays by Chekhov, Shakespeare, and Brecht. They could never be confused with anyone else's work.

A Letter of Authority

The first letter of John does not actually mention who wrote it, but its similarities with John's Gospel have led many theologians to believe that both were written by the same person. It is not just that there is a distinctive style, or a lot of words common to both. More important, there are many common theme and points. The tradition of the early Church said that this letter was indeed written by John, the disciple of Jesus; quite apart from which there is strong internal evidence that suggests the same. The author claimed to have been an eyewitness of the events of Jesus' life, death, and resurrection (1 John 1:1-4)—if this weren't true, it doesn't seem likely that the Christians to whom this letter was written would have accepted what it said. In addition, the author wrote from a strong position of authority, which suggests that he would have been regarded as an apostle (2:1,7,12-14). Like most of the New Testament letters, this one was probably written to be read aloud during worship, and would have been circulated among several churches. The writer had a very close relationship with his readers, and his authority seems related to his care for them—they would have recognized him as their spiritual leader.

A Warning

The leaders of the church in the early Christian centuries following John's letter (often known as the Church Fathers) were also concerned with issues of right and wrong belief, and this letter was probably used by them as they set about establishing right belief (or orthodoxy) over and against wrong belief (heresy) as some of the problems encountered in Gnosticism were still present. (See the introduction to John's Gospel for an explanation of Gnosticism.) The Fathers often told a story about John, whom they associated with the city of Ephesus, to bring home the point about remaining within orthodoxy. The story tells how John went to the public baths, only to discover that a noted Gnostic teacher, Cerinthus, whom he had frequently opposed in public, was there too. John refused to stay under the same roof as the heretic teacher, and would certainly not bathe with him, as he was so concerned to keep his true faith pure from any association with heresy.

It serves to remind us how important it is not to associate with beliefs that confuse and discredit true faith in Christ.

Tests for Faith

In 1885 the Scottish theologian Robert Law wrote a commentary on 1 John called "The Tests of Faith". He said that in this letter John provided three tests to check out what was authentic Christianity. There is the doctrinal test: Is what is being taught in accordance with right beliefs about God, the Father, the Son and the Holy Spirit? Then there is the moral test: Is our behaviour in everyday life in accordance with those beliefs? Finally there is the social test: Is our behaviour characterized by the love of Jesus seen in our lives? All these are summarized in 5:1–5: what we believe affects the way we behave, which determines our relationships with other people.

A Reassuring Letter

The author's motive for writing is made clear in 5:13 — "that you may know that you have eternal life." In contrast to the sort of "knowledge" the Gnostics advocated and preached, the writer wanted his readers to know the truth about Christ and about eternal life. They could be certain that Jesus was the Christ not only from the historical data and eyewitnesses, but also by the anointing of the Holy Spirit, who guides everyone into all truth (John 16:13). They are "in him", "know him" and "belong to him", which is the basis for being sure about Christ and about eternal life. That was the writer's main aim (5:13). Even in the twentieth century these tests and assurances hold as true for us as they did for the first readers of this letter.

The Word of Life

1 That which was from the beginning, which we have heard, which we have seen with our eyes, which we have looked at and our hands have touched — this we proclaim concerning the Word of life. ²The life appeared; we have seen it and testify to it, and we proclaim to you the eternal life, which was with the Father and has appeared to us. ³We proclaim to you what we have seen and heard, so that you also may have fellowship with us. And our fellowship is with the Father and with his Son, Jesus Christ. ⁴We write this to make our^a joy complete.

Walking in the Light

⁵This is the message we have heard from him and declare to you: God is light; in him there is no darkness at all. ⁶If we claim to have fellowship with him yet walk in the darkness, we lie and do not live by the truth. ⁷But if we walk in the light, as he is in the light, we have fellowship with one another, and the blood of Jesus, his Son, purifies us from all^b sin. ⁸If we claim to be without sin, we deceive ourselves and the truth is not in us. ⁹If we confess our sins, he

is faithful and just and will forgive us our sins and purify us from all unrighteousness. ¹⁰If we claim we have not sinned, we make him out to be a liar and his word has no place in our lives.

2 My dear children, I write this to you so that you will not sin. But if anybody does sin, we have one who speaks to the Father in our defence — Jesus Christ, the Righteous One. ²He is the atoning sacrifice for our sins, and not only for ours but also for^a the sins of the whole world.

³We know that we have come to know him if we obey his commands. ⁴The man who says, "I know him," but does not do what he commands is a liar, and the truth is not in him. ⁵But if anyone obeys his word, God's love^b is truly made complete in him. This is how we know we are in him: ⁶Whoever claims to live in him must walk as Jesus did.

⁷Dear friends, I am not writing you a new command but an old one, which you have had since the beginning. This old command is the message you have heard. ⁸Yet I am writing you a new command; its truth is seen in him and you, because the darkness is passing and the true light is already shining.

⁹Anyone who claims to be in the light but hates his

---

^{a}4 Some manuscripts *your* ^{b}7 Or *every*
^{a}2 Or *He is the one who turns aside God's wrath, taking away our sins, and not only ours but also* ^{b}5 Or *word, love for God*

brother is still in the darkness. [10]Whoever loves his brother lives in the light, and there is nothing in him[c] to make him stumble. [11]But whoever hates his brother is in the darkness and walks around in the darkness; he does not know where he is going, because the darkness has blinded him.

[12]I write to you, dear children,
because your sins have been forgiven on
account of his name.
[13]I write to you, fathers,
because you have known him who is from the
beginning.
I write to you, young men,
because you have overcome the evil one.
I write to you, dear children,
because you have known the Father.
[14]I write to you, fathers,
because you have known him who is from the
beginning.
I write to you, young men,
because you are strong,
and the word of God lives in you,
and you have overcome the evil one.

Do Not Love the World

[15]Do not love the world or anything in the world. If anyone loves the world, the love of the Father is not in him. [16]For everything in the world—the cravings of sinful man, the lust of his eyes and the boasting of what he has and does—comes not from the Father but from the world. [17]The world and its desires pass away, but the man who does the will of God lives for ever.

Warning Against Antichrists

[18]Dear children, this is the last hour; and as you have heard that the antichrist is coming, even now many antichrists have come. This is how we know it is the last hour. [19]They went out from us, but they did not really belong to us. For if they had belonged to us, they would have remained with us; but their going showed that none of them belonged to us. [20]But you have an anointing from the Holy One, and all of you know the truth.[d] [21]I do not write to you because you do not know the truth, but because you do know it and because no lie comes from the truth. [22]Who is the liar? It is the man who denies that Jesus is the Christ. Such a man is the antichrist—he denies the Father and the Son. [23]No-one who denies the Son has the Father; whoever acknowledges the Son has the Father also.

[24]See that what you have heard from the beginning remains in you. If it does, you also will remain in the Son and in the Father. [25]And this is what he promised us—even eternal life.

[26]I am writing these things to you about those who are trying to lead you astray. [27]As for you, the anointing you received from him remains in you, and you do not need anyone to teach you. But as his anointing teaches you about all things and as that anointing is real, not counterfeit—just as it has taught you, remain in him.

Children of God

[28]And now, dear children, continue in him, so that when he appears we may be confident and unashamed before him at his coming.

[29]If you know that he is righteous, you know that everyone who does what is right has been born of him. **3** How great is the love the Father has lavished on us, that we should be called children of God! And that is what we are! The reason the world does not know us is that it did not know him. [2]Dear friends, now we are children of God, and what we will be has not yet been made known. But we know that when he appears,[a] we shall be like him, for we shall see him as he is. [3]Everyone who has this hope in him purifies himself, just as he is pure.

[4]Everyone who sins breaks the law; in fact, sin is lawlessness. [5]But you know that he appeared so that he might take away our sins. And in him is no sin. [6]No-one who lives in him keeps on sinning. No-one who continues to sin has either seen him or known him.

[7]Dear children, do not let anyone lead you astray. He who does what is right is righteous, just as he is righteous. [8]He who does what is sinful is of the devil, because the devil has been sinning from the beginning. The reason the Son of God appeared was to destroy the devil's work. [9]No-one who is born of God will continue to sin, because God's seed remains in him; he cannot go on sinning, because he has been born of God. [10]This is how we know who the children of God are and who the children of the devil are: Anyone who does not do what is right is not a child of God; nor is anyone who does not love his brother.

Love One Another

[11]This is the message you heard from the beginning: We should love one another. [12]Do not be like Cain, who belonged to the evil one and murdered his brother. And why did he murder him? Because his own actions were evil and his brother's were righteous. [13]Do not be surprised, my brothers, if the world hates you. [14]We know that we have passed from death to life, because we love our brothers. Anyone who does not love remains in death. [15]Anyone who hates his brother is a murderer, and you know that no murderer has eternal life in him.

[16]This is how we know what love is: Jesus Christ laid down his life for us. And we ought to lay down our lives for our brothers. [17]If anyone has material possessions and sees his brother in need but has no pity on him, how can the love of God be in him? [18]Dear children, let us not love with words or tongue but with actions and in truth. [19]This then is how we know that we belong to the truth, and how we set our hearts at rest in his presence [20]whenever our hearts condemn us. For God is greater than our hearts, and he knows everything.

[21]Dear friends, if our hearts do not condemn us, we have confidence before God [22]and receive from him anything we ask, because we obey his commands and do what pleases him. [23]And this is his command: to believe in the name of his Son, Jesus Christ, and to love

---

_c10_ Or it   _d20_ Some manuscripts _and you know all things_   _a2_ Or _when it is made known_ one another as he commanded us. ²⁴Those who obey his commands live in him, and he in them. And this is how we know that he lives in us: We know it by the Spirit he gave us.

Test the Spirits

4 Dear friends, do not believe every spirit, but test the spirits to see whether they are from God, because many false prophets have gone out into the world. ²This is how you can recognise the Spirit of God: Every spirit that acknowledges that Jesus Christ has come in the flesh is from God, ³but every spirit that does not acknowledge Jesus is not from God. This is the spirit of the antichrist, which you have heard is coming and even now is already in the world.

⁴You, dear children, are from God and have overcome them, because the one who is in you is greater than the one who is in the world. ⁵They are from the world and therefore speak from the viewpoint of the world, and the world listens to them. ⁶We are from God, and whoever knows God listens to us; but whoever is not from God does not listen to us. This is how we recognise the Spirit^a of truth and the spirit of falsehood.

God's Love and Ours

⁷Dear friends, let us love one another, for love comes from God. Everyone who loves has been born of God and knows God. ⁸Whoever does not love does not know God, because God is love. ⁹This is how God showed his love among us: He sent his one and only Son^b into the world that we might live through him. ¹⁰This is love: not that we loved God, but that he loved us and sent his Son as an atoning sacrifice for^c our sins. ¹¹Dear friends, since God so loved us, we also ought to love one another. ¹²No-one has ever seen God; but if we love one another, God lives in us and his love is made complete in us.

¹³We know that we live in him and he in us, because he has given us of his Spirit. ¹⁴And we have seen and testify that the Father has sent his Son to be the Saviour of the world. ¹⁵If anyone acknowledges that Jesus is the Son of God, God lives in him and he in God. ¹⁶And so we know and rely on the love God has for us.

God is love. Whoever lives in love lives in God, and God in him. ¹⁷In this way, love is made complete among us so that we will have confidence on the day of judgment, because in this world we are like him. ¹⁸There is no fear in love. But perfect love drives out fear, because fear has to do with punishment. The one who fears is not made perfect in love.

¹⁹We love because he first loved us. ²⁰If anyone says, "I love God," yet hates his brother, he is a liar. For anyone who does not love his brother, whom he has seen, cannot love God, whom he has not seen. ²¹And

he has given us this command: Whoever loves God must also love his brother.

Faith in the Son of God

5 Everyone who believes that Jesus is the Christ is born of God, and everyone who loves the father loves his child as well. ²This is how we know that we love the children of God: by loving God and carrying out his commands. ³This is love for God: to obey his commands. And his commands are not burdensome, ⁴for everyone born of God overcomes the world. This is the victory that has overcome the world, even our faith. ⁵Who is it that overcomes the world? Only he who believes that Jesus is the Son of God.

⁶This is the one who came by water and blood — Jesus Christ. He did not come by water only, but by water and blood. And it is the Spirit who testifies, because the Spirit is the truth. ⁷For there are three that testify: ⁸the^a Spirit, the water and the blood; and the three are in agreement. ⁹We accept man's testimony, but God's testimony is greater because it is the testimony of God, which he has given about his Son. ¹⁰Anyone who believes in the Son of God has this testimony in his heart. Anyone who does not believe God has made him out to be a liar, because he has not believed the testimony God has given about his Son. ¹¹And this is the testimony: God has given us eternal life, and this life is in his Son. ¹²He who has the Son has life; he who does not have the Son of God does not have life.

Concluding Remarks

¹³I write these things to you who believe in the name of the Son of God so that you may know that you have eternal life. ¹⁴This is the confidence we have in approaching God: that if we ask anything according to his will, he hears us. ¹⁵And if we know that he hears us — whatever we ask — we know that we have what we asked of him.

¹⁶If anyone sees his brother commit a sin that does not lead to death, he should pray and God will give him life. I refer to those whose sin does not lead to death. There is a sin that leads to death. I am not saying that he should pray about that. ¹⁷All wrongdoing is sin, and there is sin that does not lead to death.

¹⁸We know that anyone born of God does not continue to sin; the one who was born of God keeps him safe, and the evil one cannot harm him. ¹⁹We know that we are children of God, and that the whole world is under the control of the evil one. ²⁰We know also that the Son of God has come and has given us understanding, so that we may know him who is true. And we are in him who is true — even in his Son Jesus Christ. He is the true God and eternal life.

²¹Dear children, keep yourselves from idols.

---

^a6 Or *spirit*   ^b9 Or *his only begotten Son*   ^c10 Or *as the one who would turn aside his wrath, taking away*
^a7,8 Late manuscripts of the Vulgate *testify in heaven: the Father, the Word and the Holy Spirit, and these three are one.* ⁸*And there are three that testify on earth: the* (not found in any Greek manuscript before the sixteenth century)

2 John

The Same John?

The relationship between 1 John and the other two letters attributed to him is rather complex. There are certainly many similarities of language and style, as well as common themes, but the writer of both 2 and 3 John called himself "the elder" (a title used normally by apostles or those in authority). Even in the early church there was a belief that this John was not the one who wrote the Gospel or 1 John. The connections are close enough, however, to maintain that if there were different authors, they would have known each other well. The answer may be that there was a "school" of thinking in Ephesus based around the apostle John. He would have been the teacher and motivator for this group of Christians, but the letters and Gospel as we now have them may have been reworkings of his material by them. 2 John is essentially a warning to Christians who might be tempted to welcome itinerant false prophets into their fellowship (verses 7–11). Many scholars think this dates the letter before 1 John because it indicates that the heretics had already been excluded (1 John 2:19).

¹The elder,

To the chosen lady and her children, whom I love in the truth — and not I only, but also all who know the truth — ²because of the truth, which lives in us and will be with us for ever:

³Grace, mercy and peace from God the Father and from Jesus Christ, the Father's Son, will be with us in truth and love.

⁴It has given me great joy to find some of your children walking in the truth, just as the Father commanded us. ⁵And now, dear lady, I am not writing you a new command but one we have had from the beginning. I ask that we love one another. ⁶And this is love: that we walk in obedience to his commands. As you have heard from the beginning, his command is that you walk in love.

⁷Many deceivers, who do not acknowledge Jesus Christ as coming in the flesh, have gone out into the world. Any such person is the deceiver and the antichrist. ⁸Watch out that you do not lose what you have worked for, but that you may be rewarded fully. ⁹Anyone who runs ahead and does not continue in the teaching of Christ does not have God; whoever continues in the teaching has both the Father and the Son. ¹⁰If anyone comes to you and does not bring this teaching, do not take him into your house or welcome him. ¹¹Anyone who welcomes him shares in his wicked work.

¹²I have much to write to you, but I do not want to use paper and ink. Instead, I hope to visit you and talk with you face to face, so that our joy may be complete.

¹³The children of your chosen sister send their greetings.

3 John

A Personal Letter

Whereas 2 John was written by "the elder" to a church (the most likely meaning of the "chosen lady and her children") this is a personal letter to a believer called Gaius, commending him, and warning him about the man Diotrephes. It is not clear what John had against him, but it appears not to be a theological disagreement. More likely, by the time this letter was written, there were new patterns of church government. Diotrephes was probably one of the emerging leaders, whose authoritarian and heavy handed approach was causing concern. There is nothing new about church disputes!

---

¹The elder,

To my dear friend Gaius, whom I love in the truth.

²Dear friend, I pray that you may enjoy good health and that all may go well with you, even as your soul is getting along well. ³It gave me great joy to have some brothers come and tell about your faithfulness to the truth and how you continue to walk in the truth. ⁴I have no greater joy than to hear that my children are walking in the truth.

⁵Dear friend, you are faithful in what you are doing for the brothers, even though they are strangers to you. ⁶They have told the church about your love. You will do well to send them on their way in a manner worthy of God. ⁷It was for the sake of the Name that they went out, receiving no help from the pagans. ⁸We ought therefore to show hospitality to such men so that we may work together for the truth.

⁹I wrote to the church, but Diotrephes, who loves to be first, will have nothing to do with us. ¹⁰So if I come, I will call attention to what he is doing, gossiping maliciously about us. Not satisfied with that, he refuses to welcome the brothers. He also stops those who want to do so and puts them out of the church.

¹¹Dear friend, do not imitate what is evil but what is good. Anyone who does what is good is from God. Anyone who does what is evil has not seen God. ¹²Demetrius is well spoken of by everyone—and even by the truth itself. We also speak well of him, and you know that our testimony is true.

¹³I have much to write to you, but I do not want to do so with pen and ink. ¹⁴I hope to see you soon, and we will talk face to face.

Peace to you. The friends here send their greetings. Greet the friends there by name.

Jude

Take Care!

If someone wants to drive a taxi in London they must first spend months learning the names of the districts, streets, and major buildings. A cab driver must be able to find the way from one place to another without wasting passengers' time and money. Only after they have passed an examination of their knowledge are they given a licence. If you met someone who lives in Scotland and who never visits London but has a detailed knowledge of that city's streets, you would consider them a little eccentric. Of course, there are people who memorize large amounts of apparently useless information just for a challenge or to demonstrate the capacity of their memory.

Living Word or Test Book of Facts?

There is a temptation for Christians who read the Bible regularly, and who know the text quite well, to forget why they read it. They may get into empty disputes in which they try to outdo others in the number of texts that they can quote. They may be proud of the fact that they have a better memory than someone else. The Bible, however, is the living word of God and we should read it with this in mind. We go to the Scriptures in the same frame of mind that we visit a close friend; listening with an open heart.

A Direction in Life

In the Bible we do not find detailed directions as in a street map, but we do learn what direction to take in life. Without this guidance we should be lost. On the other hand, if we know which direction we should take but go another way, then we will also be lost. The letter of Jude warns us against this danger.

Keep to the Right Road

Jude actually wanted to write an encouraging letter about salvation (verse 3). He was writing to Christians whose faith was not fully formed, and who were in danger of being led astray by troublemakers. He did not say exactly who the troublemakers were, but it is possible that they were people who denied that Jesus was truly human. Jude urgently reminded his readers that they should not be led astray. They should be clear about what they actually believed and hold on to it confidently. There was no room for unclear thinking or feeble faith. The teaching which had been given to them by the apostles was not useless information, but was intended for their guidance.

You can read the whole of this letter in a few minutes: it is a lot like James and 2 Peter. But to understand the full force of Jude's argument you will need to look up the various Old Testament references. (The account of the archangel Michael disputing with the devil occurs in The Assumption of Moses, and verse 14 refers to the book of Enoch, two Jewish books that are not accepted as part of the Bible.)

An Expression of Praise

The letter closes with a doxology (an expression of praise) which is often used by Christians today: "to the only God our Saviour be glory, majesty, power and authority, through Jesus Christ our Lord, before all ages, now and for evermore! Amen."

---

[1]Jude, a servant of Jesus Christ and a brother of James,

To those who have been called, who are loved by God the Father and kept by[a] Jesus Christ:

[2]Mercy, peace and love be yours in abundance.

The Sin and Doom of Godless Men

[3]Dear friends, although I was very eager to write to you about the salvation we share, I felt I had to write and urge you to contend for the faith that was once for all entrusted to the saints. [4]For certain men whose condemnation was written about[b] long ago have secretly slipped in among you. They are godless men, who change the grace of our God into a licence for immorality and deny Jesus Christ our only Sovereign and Lord.

[5]Though you already know all this, I want to remind you that the Lord[c] delivered his people out of Egypt, but later destroyed those who did not believe. [6]And the angels who did not keep their positions of authority but abandoned their own home—these he has kept in darkness, bound with everlasting chains for judgment on the great Day. [7]In a similar way, Sodom and Gomorrah and the surrounding towns gave themselves up to sexual immorality and perversion. They serve as an example of those who suffer the punishment of eternal fire.

[8]In the very same way, these dreamers pollute their own bodies, reject authority and slander celestial beings. [9]But even the archangel Michael, when he was disputing with the devil about the body of Moses, did not dare to bring a slanderous accusation against him, but said, "The Lord rebuke you!" [10]Yet these men speak abusively against whatever they do not understand; and what things they do understand by instinct, like unreasoning animals—these are the very things that destroy them.

[11]Woe to them! They have taken the way of Cain; they have rushed for profit into Balaam's error; they have been destroyed in Korah's rebellion. [12]These men are blemishes at your love feasts, eating with you without the slightest qualm—shepherds who feed only themselves. They are clouds without rain, blown along by the wind; autumn trees, without fruit and uprooted—twice dead. [13]They are wild waves of the sea, foaming up their shame; wandering stars, for whom blackest darkness has been reserved for ever.

[14]Enoch, the seventh from Adam, prophesied about these men: "See, the Lord is coming with thousands upon thousands of his holy ones [15]to judge everyone, and to convict all the ungodly of all the ungodly acts they have done in the ungodly way, and of all the harsh words ungodly sinners have spoken against him." [16]These men are grumblers and fault-finders; they follow their own evil desires; they boast about themselves and flatter others for their own advantage.

A Call to Persevere

[17]But, dear friends, remember what the apostles of our Lord Jesus Christ foretold. [18]They said to you, "In the last times there will be scoffers who will follow their own ungodly desires." [19]These are the men who divide you, who follow mere natural instincts and do not have the Spirit.

[20]But you, dear friends, build yourselves up in your most holy faith and pray in the Holy Spirit. [21]Keep yourselves in God's love as you wait for the mercy of our Lord Jesus Christ to bring you to eternal life.

[22]Be merciful to those who doubt; [23]snatch others from the fire and save them; to others show mercy, mixed with fear—hating even the clothing stained by corrupted flesh.

Doxology

[24]To him who is able to keep you from falling and to present you before his glorious presence without fault and with great joy—[25]to the only God our Saviour be glory, majesty, power and authority, through Jesus Christ our Lord, before all ages, now and for evermore! Amen.

---

[a]1 Or for; or in   [b]4 Or men who were marked out for condemnation   [c]5 Some early manuscripts Jesus

Revelation

A Strange Book!

At first glance the style of writing, the language, and the strange thought patterns of this book present an imposing barrier to understanding. It is tempting at first to dismiss this book as a fairy tale, or as something which may have had a use once but not in our modern, scientific society. It may well be the least read of the New Testament books and yet it has a big influence on many aspects of our Christian life. If we dismiss this book as being of little importance, we do not do justice to the claim set out in the first verse. We are told that this is "The revelation of Jesus Christ, which God gave him to show his servants what must soon take place." We would do better to take to heart the words of encouragement in 1:3: "Blessed is the one who reads the words of this prophecy, and blessed are those who hear it and take to heart what is written in it".

Visions

The word "revelation" means "unveiling". It is as if there is a curtain between us and God's ultimate destiny for the world, and thanks to the revelation, we catch a fleeting glimpse of that ultimate destiny. Mere language can hardly describe the picture revealed and so the revelation is painted in a series of visions, rich pictures, and colourful language which present the main themes of the book again and again. The language appears strange to us, but through it we catch a glimpse of God's judgement and his ultimate victory over evil and sin. The victory which Christ won on the cross is realized in full for the whole of creation.

Tradition has it that the person who received the revelation and wrote it down was the apostle John. That is the same person who wrote the Gospel of John and probably the three letters which bear his name. Whoever did write it certainly had authority in the Christian communities in Asia and was respected and listened to. It would seem likely that only one of the original followers of Jesus, such as John, would have the necessary authority over the churches to write in the terms he did.

Addressing Specific Problems

The book was written to specific churches with specific problems in mind. The intended receivers of the letter were seven churches in the province of Asia Minor (modern day Turkey). The churches were not necessarily in the most important towns of the region but appear to have been chosen for their links with John. The letter is a circular one which would have been intended to be read out to the congregations in turn. Each of the churches was presented with both a challenge and an encouragement. The challenge was for them to turn away from bad attitudes and practices which had been allowed to creep into their churches, and which were limiting their effectiveness for Christ. The letter gave credit where it was due in order to encourage the young churches in the right direction. In fact the theme of encouragement dominates the whole of Revelation.

A Wide Message

Although the book was intended as a circular letter to the seven churches, it has a much wider application with its twin message of hope in the face of persecution and God's final judgement on both Christ's followers and his enemies. Such a message would have been welcomed and valued over a wider area than these seven communities. Its influence was not just over churches when it was first written, but in the Christian Church for centuries to come. As is so often the case with the Bible, what began as a set of specific instructions to specific problems has become relevant to the whole Church.

A Call for Repentance

The book would appear to have several purposes. John dealt with particular problems at the various churches, such as a lack of spirituality, the influence of an immoral society, false teaching from within the church, and the impact of material prosperity on the church members. He demanded a return to the lessons learned at the setting up of the Christian communities; a getting back to Christian basics. It is a call to repentance, a turning away from sin and turning to Christ. That was the challenge to the churches if they wanted to find their health and vitality as Christian communities again.

Persecution

The book also deals with the fears caused by the heavy atmosphere of persecution which dominated at this time. The churches and their members were under constant threat from the state. Such persecution could lead to loss of jobs, of home, of position in society, of possessions, and even of life. John put the suffering and the pain of persecution into the wider context of God's redeeming work in Jesus Christ. There would be suffering and at times it would appear as if the devil and evil were all-conquering but ultimately Christ, here referred to as "the Lamb", would have the victory. That was the hope to cling onto in a world which increasingly represented hatred and injustice.

Judgement

Such teaching encouraged the readers to look at their present circumstances in the light of the inevitability of what was to come — God's judgement for all, when the righteous would be rewarded for their sufferings with the blessing of a new heaven and a new earth over which Christ would reign, and the evil would perish along with the devil. The writer's strong teaching on the judgement to come is a reminder to see all of history in the context of God's judgement; to live one's life in the knowledge of such judgement.

Challenge and Encouragement

That is why the message of Revelation, despite its obscure language, is so vital for Christians today. Christians need the challenge and encouragement of this book just as much today. There is always the danger that Christian witness may be watered down by the pressures of the society or by the growth of false teaching or slack ways from within fellowships. Christians are still suffering for their beliefs today and are just as much in need of the encouragement that this book can give. Today, many need to know the assurance that their suffering is not in vain and that ultimately God's truth and justice will win the day and Christ will have the victory. We need to be reminded that one day we must answer for the way we have lived our lives, and we should live in the light of the judgement which is to come. We can only understand and interpret what is happening now in the light of what has gone before and what is to happen in the future. It is God's ultimate victory over evil that gives meaning to our lives.

Prologue

1 The revelation of Jesus Christ, which God gave him to show his servants what must soon take place. He made it known by sending his angel to his servant John, ²who testifies to everything he saw—that is, the word of God and the testimony of Jesus Christ. ³Blessed is the one who reads the words of this prophecy, and blessed are those who hear it and take to heart what is written in it, because the time is near.

Greetings and Doxology

⁴John,

To the seven churches in the province of Asia:

Grace and peace to you from him who is, and who was, and who is to come, and from the seven spirits*a* before his throne, ⁵and from Jesus Christ, who is the faithful witness, the firstborn from the dead, and the ruler of the kings of the earth.

To him who loves us and has freed us from our sins by his blood, ⁶and has made us to be a kingdom and priests to serve his God and Father—to him be glory and power for ever and ever! Amen.

⁷Look, he is coming with the
clouds,
and every eye will see him,
even those who pierced him;
and all the peoples of the
earth will mourn because
of him.
So shall it be! Amen.

⁸"I am the Alpha and the Omega," says the Lord God, "who is, and who was, and who is to come, the Almighty."

One Like a Son of Man

⁹I, John, your brother and companion in the suffering and kingdom and patient endurance that are ours in Jesus, was on the island of Patmos because of the word of God and the testimony of Jesus. ¹⁰On the Lord's Day I was in the Spirit, and I heard behind me a loud voice like a trumpet, ¹¹which said: "Write on a scroll what you see and send it to the seven churches: to Ephesus, Smyrna, Pergamum, Thyatira, Sardis, Philadelphia and Laodicea."

1:9 Revelation was written down about 90 AD, and John, who had been condemned to hard labour in the quarries of Patmos, would have been about eighty years old at the time. His message of ultimate hope came out of his own experience of persecution.

---

¹²I turned round to see the voice that was speaking to me. And when I turned I saw seven golden lampstands, ¹³and among the lampstands was someone "like a son of man",*b* dressed in a robe reaching down to his feet and with a golden sash round his chest. ¹⁴His head and hair were white like wool, as white as snow, and his eyes were like blazing fire. ¹⁵His feet were like bronze glowing in a furnace, and his voice was like the sound of rushing waters. ¹⁶In his right hand he held seven stars, and out of his mouth came a sharp double-edged sword. His face was like the sun shining in all its brilliance.

¹⁷When I saw him, I fell at his feet as though dead. Then he placed his right hand on me and said: "Do not be afraid. I am the First and the Last. ¹⁸I am the Living One; I was dead, and behold I am alive for ever and ever! And I hold the keys of death and Hades. ¹⁹"Write, therefore, what you have seen, what is now and what will take place later. ²⁰The mystery of

e seven stars that you saw in my right hand and of
the seven golden lampstands is this: The seven stars
are the angels[c] of the seven churches, and the seven
lampstands are the seven churches.

To the Church in Ephesus

2 "To the angel[a] of the church in Ephesus write:

These are the words of him who holds the
seven stars in his right hand and walks among the
seven golden lampstands: [2]I know your deeds,
your hard work and your perseverance. I know
that you cannot tolerate wicked men, that you
have tested those who claim to be apostles but are
not, and have found them false. [3]You have persevered and have endured hardships for my name,
and have not grown weary.

[4]Yet I hold this against you: You have forsaken
your first love. [5]Remember the height from which
you have fallen! Repent and do the things you did
at first. If you do not repent, I will come to you and
remove your lampstand from its place. [6]But you
have this in your favour: You hate the practices of
the Nicolaitans, which I also hate.

2:6   Nothing is known about the Nicolaitans, but we can presume they were another
group which was weakening the church
from within.

---

[7]He who has an ear, let him hear what the
Spirit says to the churches. To him who overcomes, I will give the right to eat from the tree of
life, which is in the paradise of God.

To the Church in Smyrna

[8]"To the angel of the church in Smyrna write:

These are the words of him who is the First and
the Last, who died and came to life again. [9]I know
your afflictions and your poverty—yet you are
rich! I know the slander of those who say they are
Jews and are not, but are a synagogue of Satan.
[10]Do not be afraid of what you are about to suffer.
I tell you, the devil will put some of you in prison
to test you, and you will suffer persecution for ten
days. Be faithful, even to the point of death, and
I will give you the crown of life.

[11]He who has an ear, let him hear what the
Spirit says to the churches. He who overcomes
will not be hurt at all by the second death.

To the Church in Pergamum

[12]"To the angel of the church in Pergamum write:

These are the words of him who has the sharp,
double-edged sword. [13]I know where you live—
where Satan has his throne. Yet you remain true
to my name. You did not renounce your faith
in me, even in the days of Antipas, my faithful

witness, who was put to death in your city—
where Satan lives.

[14]Nevertheless, I have a few things against you:
You have people there who hold to the teaching
of Balaam, who taught Balak to entice the Israelites to sin by eating food sacrificed to idols and by
committing sexual immorality. [15]Likewise you
also have those who hold to the teaching of the
Nicolaitans. [16]Repent therefore! Otherwise, I will
soon come to you and will fight against them with
the sword of my mouth.

[17]He who has an ear, let him hear what the
Spirit says to the churches. To him who overcomes, I will give some of the hidden manna. I
will also give him a white stone with a new name
written on it, known only to him who receives it.

To the Church in Thyatira

[18]"To the angel of the church in Thyatira write:

These are the words of the Son of God, whose
eyes are like blazing fire and whose feet are like
burnished bronze. [19]I know your deeds, your love
and faith, your service and perseverance, and that
you are now doing more than you did at first.

[20]Nevertheless, I have this against you: You tolerate that woman Jezebel, who calls herself a
prophetess. By her teaching she misleads my servants into sexual immorality and the eating of food
sacrificed to idols. [21]I have given her time to
repent of her immorality, but she is unwilling.
[22]So I will cast her on a bed of suffering, and I will
make those who commit adultery with her suffer
intensely, unless they repent of her ways. [23]I will
strike her children dead. Then all the churches
will know that I am he who searches hearts and
minds, and I will repay each of you according to
your deeds. [24]Now I say to the rest of you in Thyatira, to you who do not hold to her teaching and
have not learned Satan's so-called deep secrets (I
will not impose any other burden on you): [25]Only
hold on to what you have until I come.

[26]To him who overcomes and does my will to
the end, I will give authority over the nations—

[27]'He will rule them with an iron sceptre;
    he will dash them to pieces like
      pottery'[b]—

just as I have received authority from my Father.
[28]I will also give him the morning star. [29]He who
has an ear, let him hear what the Spirit says to the
churches.

To the Church in Sardis

3 "To the angel[a] of the church in Sardis write:

These are the words of him who holds the
seven spirits[b] of God and the seven stars. I know
your deeds; you have a reputation of being alive,
but you are dead. [2]Wake up! Strengthen what
remains and is about to die, for I have not found

---

[c]20 Or *messengers*   [a]1 Or *messenger*; also in verses 8, 12 and 18   [b]27 Psalm 2:9
[a]1 Or *messenger*; also in verses 7 and 14   [b]1 Or *the sevenfold Spirit*

your deeds complete in the sight of my God. [3]Remember, therefore, what you have received and heard; obey it, and repent. But if you do not wake up, I will come like a thief, and you will not know at what time I will come to you.

3:1 There were other cities in Asia Minor with Christian communities but the choice of seven as the number would suggest that those chosen cities were representative of the whole church.

---

[4]Yet you have a few people in Sardis who have not soiled their clothes. They will walk with me, dressed in white, for they are worthy. [5]He who overcomes will, like them, be dressed in white. I will never blot out his name from the book of life, but will acknowledge his name before my Father and his angels. [6]He who has an ear, let him hear what the Spirit says to the churches.

To the Church in Philadelphia

[7]"To the angel of the church in Philadelphia write:

These are the words of him who is holy and true, who holds the key of David. What he opens no-one can shut, and what he shuts no-one can open. [8]I know your deeds. See, I have placed before you an open door that no-one can shut. I know that you have little strength, yet you have kept my word and have not denied my name. [9]I will make those who are of the synagogue of Satan, who claim to be Jews though they are not, but are liars—I will make them come and fall down at your feet and acknowledge that I have loved you. [10]Since you have kept my command to endure patiently, I will also keep you from the hour of trial that is going to come upon the whole world to test those who live on the earth.

[11]I am coming soon. Hold on to what you have, so that no-one will take your crown. [12]Him who overcomes I will make a pillar in the temple of my God. Never again will he leave it. I will write on him the name of my God and the name of the city of my God, the new Jerusalem, which is coming down out of heaven from my God; and I will also write on him my new name. [13]He who has an ear, let him hear what the Spirit says to the churches.

To the Church in Laodicea

[14]"To the angel of the church in Laodicea write:

These are the words of the Amen, the faithful and true witness, the ruler of God's creation. [15]I know your deeds, that you are neither cold nor hot. I wish you were either one or the other! [16]So, because you are lukewarm—neither hot nor cold—I am about to spit you out of my mouth. [17]You say, 'I am rich; I have acquired wealth and do not need a thing.' But you do not realise that you are wretched, pitiful, poor, blind and naked.

[18]I counsel you to buy from me gold refined in the fire, so that you can become rich; and white clothes to wear, so that you can cover your shameful nakedness; and salve to put on your eyes, so that you can see.

[19]Those whom I love I rebuke and discipline. So be earnest, and repent. [20]Here I am! I stand at the door and knock. If anyone hears my voice and opens the door, I will come in and eat with him, and he with me.

[21]To him who overcomes, I will give the right to sit with me on my throne, just as I overcame and sat down with my Father on his throne. [22]He who has an ear, let him hear what the Spirit says to the churches."

The Throne in Heaven

4 After this I looked, and there before me was a door standing open in heaven. And the voice I had first heard speaking to me like a trumpet said, "Come up here, and I will show you what must take place after this." [2]At once I was in the Spirit, and there before me was a throne in heaven with someone sitting on it. [3]And the one who sat there had the appearance of jasper and carnelian. A rainbow, resembling an emerald, encircled the throne. [4]Surrounding the throne were twenty-four other thrones, and seated on them were twenty-four elders. They were dressed in white and had crowns of gold on their heads. [5]From the throne came flashes of lightning, rumblings and peals of thunder. Before the throne, seven lamps were blazing. These are the seven spirits[a] of God. [6]Also before the throne there was what looked like a sea of glass, clear as crystal.

4:4 Numbers play an important part in Revelation. They are more likely to be symbolic rather than provide an accurate series of statistics. The most significant numbers in Revelation are 4, 7, and 12 and their multiples. The 24 would appear to represent the whole church of God as represented by the 12 tribes of Israel of the Old Testament, and the 12 apostles from the New. Seven is a number which occurs often in the Bible and traditionally it has been taken to mean perfection or completeness. The 4 may symbolize the created world, reminding us of the four points of the compass.

In the centre, around the throne, were four living creatures, and they were covered with eyes, in front and behind. [7]The first living creature was like a lion, the second was like an ox, the third had a face like a man, the fourth was like a flying eagle. [8]Each of the four living creatures had six wings and was covered with eyes all around, even under his wings. Day and night they never stop saying:

[a]5 Or the sevenfold Spirit

"Holy, holy, holy
is the Lord God Almighty,
who was, and is, and is to come."

9 Whenever the living creatures give glory, honour and thanks to him who sits on the throne and who lives for ever and ever, 10 the twenty-four elders fall down before him who sits on the throne, and worship him who lives for ever and ever. They lay their crowns before the throne and say:

11 "You are worthy, our Lord and God,
to receive glory and honour and power,
for you created all things,
and by your will they were created
and have their being."

The Scroll and the Lamb

5 Then I saw in the right hand of him who sat on the throne a scroll with writing on both sides and sealed with seven seals. 2 And I saw a mighty angel proclaiming in a loud voice, "Who is worthy to break the seals and open the scroll?" 3 But no-one in heaven or on earth or under the earth could open the scroll or even look inside it. 4 I wept and wept because no-one was found who was worthy to open the scroll or look inside. 5 Then one of the elders said to me, "Do not weep! See, the Lion of the tribe of Judah, the Root of David, has triumphed. He is able to open the scroll and its seven seals."

5:6   The picture of the sacrificial Lamb recalls Christ's sacrifice on the cross. Lambs brought for sacrifice were without blemish just as Christ was without sin. It is this same Lamb who receives the honour and worship of the 24 elders. It echoes the Christian mystery of how Christ's victory was won on the cross.

---

6 Then I saw a Lamb, looking as if it had been slain, standing in the centre of the throne, encircled by the four living creatures and the elders. He had seven horns and seven eyes, which are the seven spirits[a] of God sent out into all the earth. 7 He came and took the scroll from the right hand of him who sat on the throne. 8 And when he had taken it, the four living creatures and the twenty-four elders fell down before the Lamb. Each one had a harp and they were holding golden bowls full of incense, which are the prayers of the saints. 9 And they sang a new song:

"You are worthy to take the scroll
and to open its seals,
because you were slain,
and with your blood you purchased men for
God
from every tribe and language and people and
nation.
10 You have made them to be a kingdom and priests
to serve our God,
and they will reign on the earth."

11 Then I looked and heard the voice of many angels, numbering thousands upon thousands, and ten thousand times ten thousand. They encircled the throne and the living creatures and the elders. 12 In a loud voice they sang:

"Worthy is the Lamb, who was slain,
to receive power and wealth and wisdom and
strength
and honour and glory and praise!"

13 Then I heard every creature in heaven and on earth and under the earth and on the sea, and all that is in them, singing:

"To him who sits on the throne and to the Lamb
be praise and honour and glory and power,
for ever and ever!"

14 The four living creatures said, "Amen", and the elders fell down and worshipped.

The Seals

6 I watched as the Lamb opened the first of the seven seals. Then I heard one of the four living creatures say in a voice like thunder, "Come!" 2 I looked, and there before me was a white horse! Its rider held a bow, and he was given a crown, and he rode out as a conqueror bent on conquest.

6:1   The whole course of human history is portrayed in the first five seals which the Lamb breaks. Humanity will suffer and those in the church will not escape that suffering, but the Lamb, Christ, is still in control. Nothing occurs until each seal is broken by him. The history of humankind moves inevitably towards its conclusion with the breaking of the sixth seal which pictures the end of the world. We are told virtually nothing about the seventh seal but its existence shows that there is another world to come of which we know very little.

---

3 When the Lamb opened the second seal, I heard the second living creature say, "Come!" 4 Then another horse came out, a fiery red one. Its rider was given power to take peace from the earth and to make men slay each other. To him was given a large sword.
5 When the Lamb opened the third seal, I heard the third living creature say, "Come!" I looked, and there before me was a black horse! Its rider was holding a pair of scales in his hand. 6 Then I heard what sounded like a voice among the four living creatures, saying, "A quart[a] of wheat for a day's wages,[b] and three quarts of barley for a day's wages,[b] and do not damage the oil and the wine!"
7 When the Lamb opened the fourth seal, I heard the voice of the fourth living creature say, "Come!" 8 I looked, and there before me was a pale horse! Its rider was named Death, and Hades was following close

---

a 6 Or the sevenfold Spirit   a 6 Greek a choinix (probably about a litre)   b 6 Greek a denarius behind him. They were given power over a fourth of the earth to kill by sword, famine and plague, and by the wild beasts of the earth.

⁹When he opened the fifth seal, I saw under the altar the souls of those who had been slain because of the word of God and the testimony they had maintained. ¹⁰They called out in a loud voice, "How long, Sovereign Lord, holy and true, until you judge the inhabitants of the earth and avenge our blood?" ¹¹Then each of them was given a white robe, and they were told to wait a little longer, until the number of their fellow-servants and brothers who were to be killed as they had been was completed.

¹²I watched as he opened the sixth seal. There was a great earthquake. The sun turned black like sackcloth made of goat hair, the whole moon turned blood red, ¹³and the stars in the sky fell to earth, as late figs drop from a fig-tree when shaken by a strong wind. ¹⁴The sky receded like a scroll, rolling up, and every mountain and island was removed from its place.

¹⁵Then the kings of the earth, the princes, the generals, the rich, the mighty, and every slave and every free man hid in caves and among the rocks of the mountains. ¹⁶They called to the mountains and the rocks, "Fall on us and hide us from the face of him who sits on the throne and from the wrath of the Lamb! ¹⁷For the great day of their wrath has come, and who can stand?"

144,000 Sealed

7 After this I saw four angels standing at the four corners of the earth, holding back the four winds of the earth to prevent any wind from blowing on the land or on the sea or on any tree. ²Then I saw another angel coming up from the east, having the seal of the living God. He called out in a loud voice to the four angels who had been given power to harm the land and the sea: ³"Do not harm the land or the sea or the trees until we put a seal on the foreheads of the servants of our God." ⁴Then I heard the number of those who were sealed: 144,000 from all the tribes of Israel.

7:4   The 144,000 with God's seal on them represent the whole church which will survive the sufferings of the world. This is the assurance that whatever the present circumstances, Christians can be certain of eternal life.

---

⁵From the tribe of Judah 12,000 were sealed,
from the tribe of Reuben 12,000,
from the tribe of Gad 12,000,
⁶from the tribe of Asher 12,000,
from the tribe of Naphtali 12,000,
from the tribe of Manasseh 12,000,
⁷from the tribe of Simeon 12,000,
from the tribe of Levi 12,000,
from the tribe of Issachar 12,000,
⁸from the tribe of Zebulun 12,000,
from the tribe of Joseph 12,000,
from the tribe of Benjamin 12,000.

The Great Multitude in White Robes

⁹After this I looked and there before me was a great multitude that no-one could count, from every nation, tribe, people and language, standing before the throne and in front of the Lamb. They were wearing white robes and were holding palm branches in their hands. ¹⁰And they cried out in a loud voice:

"Salvation belongs to our God,
who sits on the throne,
and to the Lamb."

¹¹All the angels were standing round the throne and around the elders and the four living creatures. They fell down on their faces before the throne and worshipped God, ¹²saying:

"Amen!
Praise and glory
and wisdom and thanks and honour
and power and strength
be to our God for ever and ever.
Amen!"

¹³Then one of the elders asked me, "These in white robes — who are they, and where did they come from?"

¹⁴I answered, "Sir, you know."

And he said, "These are they who have come out of the great tribulation; they have washed their robes and made them white in the blood of the Lamb. ¹⁵Therefore,

"they are before the throne of God
and serve him day and night in his temple;
and he who sits on the throne will spread his
tent over them.
¹⁶Never again will they hunger;
never again will they thirst.
The sun will not beat upon them,
nor any scorching heat.
¹⁷For the Lamb at the centre of the throne will be
their shepherd;
he will lead them to springs of living water.
And God will wipe away every tear from their
eyes."

The Seventh Seal and the Golden Censer

8 When he opened the seventh seal, there was silence in heaven for about half an hour.

²And I saw the seven angels who stand before God, and to them were given seven trumpets.

³Another angel, who had a golden censer, came and stood at the altar. He was given much incense to offer, with the prayers of all the saints, on the golden altar before the throne. ⁴The smoke of the incense, together with the prayers of the saints, went up before God from the angel's hand. ⁵Then the angel took the censer, filled it with fire from the altar, and hurled it on the earth; and there came peals of thunder, rumblings, flashes of lightning and an earthquake.

The Trumpets

⁶Then the seven angels who had the seven trumpets prepared to sound them.

⁷The first angel sounded his trumpet, and there

came hail and fire mixed with blood, and it was hurled down upon the earth. A third of the earth was burned up, a third of the trees were burned up, and all the green grass was burned up.

8:6 The message of Revelation is often emphasized by telling the same story with different pictures. The scene with the trumpets is a reference to the same events as the breaking of seals.

8The second angel sounded his trumpet, and something like a huge mountain, all ablaze, was thrown into the sea. A third of the sea turned into blood, 9a third of the living creatures in the sea died, and a third of the ships were destroyed.

10The third angel sounded his trumpet, and a great star, blazing like a torch, fell from the sky on a third of the rivers and on the springs of water — 11the name of the star is Wormwood.a A third of the waters turned bitter, and many people died from the waters that had become bitter.

12The fourth angel sounded his trumpet, and a third of the sun was struck, a third of the moon, and a third of the stars, so that a third of them turned dark. A third of the day was without light, and also a third of the night.

13As I watched, I heard an eagle that was flying in mid-air call out in a loud voice: "Woe! Woe! Woe to the inhabitants of the earth, because of the trumpet blasts about to be sounded by the other three angels!"

9 The fifth angel sounded his trumpet, and I saw a star that had fallen from the sky to the earth. The star was given the key to the shaft of the Abyss. 2When he opened the Abyss, smoke rose from it like the smoke from a gigantic furnace. The sun and sky were darkened by the smoke from the Abyss. 3And out of the smoke locusts came down upon the earth and were given power like that of scorpions of the earth. 4They were told not to harm the grass of the earth or any plant or tree, but only those people who did not have the seal of God on their foreheads. 5They were not given power to kill them, but only to torture them for five months. And the agony they suffered was like that of the sting of a scorpion when it strikes a man. 6During those days men will seek death, but will not find it; they will long to die, but death will elude them.

7The locusts looked like horses prepared for battle. On their heads they wore something like crowns of gold, and their faces resembled human faces. 8Their hair was like women's hair, and their teeth were like lions' teeth. 9They had breastplates like breastplates of iron, and the sound of their wings was like the thundering of many horses and chariots rushing into battle. 10They had tails and stings like scorpions, and in their tails they had power to torment people for five months. 11They had as king over them the angel of the Abyss, whose name in Hebrew is Abaddon, and in Greek, Apollyon.a

12The first woe is past; two other woes are yet to come.

13The sixth angel sounded his trumpet, and I heard a voice coming from the hornsb of the golden altar that is before God. 14It said to the sixth angel who had the trumpet, "Release the four angels who are bound at the great river Euphrates." 15And the four angels who had been kept ready for this very hour and day and month and year were released to kill a third of mankind. 16The number of the mounted troops was two hundred million. I heard their number.

17The horses and riders I saw in my vision looked like this: Their breastplates were fiery red, dark blue, and yellow as sulphur. The heads of the horses resembled the heads of lions, and out of their mouths came fire, smoke and sulphur. 18A third of mankind was killed by the three plagues of fire, smoke and sulphur that came out of their mouths. 19The power of the horses was in their mouths and in their tails; for their tails were like snakes, having heads with which they inflict injury.

20The rest of mankind that were not killed by these plagues still did not repent of the work of their hands; they did not stop worshipping demons, and idols of gold, silver, bronze, stone and wood — idols that cannot see or hear or walk. 21Nor did they repent of their murders, their magic arts, their sexual immorality or their thefts.

The Angel and the Little Scroll

10 Then I saw another mighty angel coming down from heaven. He was robed in a cloud, with a rainbow above his head; his face was like the sun, and his legs were like fiery pillars. 2He was holding a little scroll, which lay open in his hand. He planted his right foot on the sea and his left foot on the land, 3and he gave a loud shout like the roar of a lion. When he shouted, the voices of the seven thunders spoke. 4And when the seven thunders spoke, I was about to write; but I heard a voice from heaven say, "Seal up what the seven thunders have said and do not write it down."

5Then the angel I had seen standing on the sea and on the land raised his right hand to heaven. 6And he swore by him who lives for ever and ever, who created the heavens and all that is in them, the earth and all that is in it, and the sea and all that is in it, and said, "There will be no more delay! 7But in the days when the seventh angel is about to sound his trumpet, the mystery of God will be accomplished, just as he announced to his servants the prophets."

8Then the voice that I had heard from heaven spoke to me once more: "Go, take the scroll that lies open in the hand of the angel who is standing on the sea and on the land."

9So I went to the angel and asked him to give me the little scroll. He said to me, "Take it and eat it. It will turn your stomach sour, but in your mouth it will be as sweet as honey." 10I took the little scroll from the angel's hand and ate it. It tasted as sweet as honey in my mouth, but when I had eaten it, my stomach turned sour. 11Then I was told, "You must prophesy again about many peoples, nations, languages and kings."

---

a11 That is, Bitterness   a11 Abaddon and Apollyon mean Destroyer.   b13 That is, projections

The Two Witnesses

11 I was given a reed like a measuring rod and was told, "Go and measure the temple of God and the altar, and count the worshippers there. ²But exclude the outer court; do not measure it, because it has been given to the Gentiles. They will trample on the holy city for 42 months. ³And I will give power to my two witnesses, and they will prophesy for 1,260 days, clothed in sackcloth." ⁴These are the two olive trees and the two lampstands that stand before the Lord of the earth. ⁵If anyone tries to harm them, fire comes from their mouths and devours their enemies. This is how anyone who wants to harm them must die. ⁶These men have power to shut up the sky so that it will not rain during the time they are prophesying; and they have power to turn the waters into blood and to strike the earth with every kind of plague as often as they want.

⁷Now when they have finished their testimony, the beast that comes up from the Abyss will attack them, and overpower and kill them. ⁸Their bodies will lie in the street of the great city, which is figuratively called Sodom and Egypt, where also their Lord was crucified. ⁹For three and a half days men from every people, tribe, language and nation will gaze on their bodies and refuse them burial. ¹⁰The inhabitants of the earth will gloat over them and will celebrate by sending each other gifts, because these two prophets had tormented those who live on earth.

¹¹But after the three and a half days a breath of life from God entered them, and they stood on their feet, and terror struck those who saw them. ¹²Then they heard a loud voice from heaven saying to them, "Come up here." And they went up to heaven in a cloud, while their enemies looked on.

¹³At that very hour there was a severe earthquake and a tenth of the city collapsed. Seven thousand people were killed in the earthquake, and the survivors were terrified and gave glory to the God of heaven. ¹⁴The second woe has passed; the third woe is coming soon.

The Seventh Trumpet

¹⁵The seventh angel sounded his trumpet, and there were loud voices in heaven, which said:

"The kingdom of the world has become the
    kingdom of our Lord and of his Christ,
and he will reign for ever and ever."

¹⁶And the twenty-four elders, who were seated on their thrones before God, fell on their faces and worshipped God, ¹⁷saying:

"We give thanks to you, Lord God Almighty,
    the One who is and who was,
because you have taken your great power
    and have begun to reign.
¹⁸The nations were angry;
    and your wrath has come.
The time has come for judging the dead,
    and for rewarding your servants the prophets

and your saints and those who reverence your
    name,
    both small and great—
and for destroying those who destroy the earth."

¹⁹Then God's temple in heaven was opened, and within his temple was seen the ark of his covenant. And there came flashes of lightning, rumblings, peals of thunder, an earthquake and a great hailstorm.

The Woman and the Dragon

12 A great and wondrous sign appeared in heaven: a woman clothed with the sun, with the moon under her feet and a crown of twelve stars on her head. ²She was pregnant and cried out in pain as she was about to give birth. ³Then another sign appeared in heaven: an enormous red dragon with seven heads and ten horns and seven crowns on his heads. ⁴His tail swept a third of the stars out of the sky and flung them to the earth. The dragon stood in front of the woman who was about to give birth, so that he might devour her child the moment it was born. ⁵She gave birth to a son, a male child, who will rule all the nations with an iron sceptre. And her child was snatched up to God and to his throne. ⁶The woman fled into the desert to a place prepared for her by God, where she might be taken care of for 1,260 days.

12:4   The dragon, the woman, and the child are not literal characters but symbols with much deeper significance. The dragon represents Satan, the deceiver; the woman is the church (the people of God), and the child is Christ, born into a dangerous world, but now ascended into heaven.

---

⁷And there was war in heaven. Michael and his angels fought against the dragon, and the dragon and his angels fought back. ⁸But he was not strong enough, and they lost their place in heaven. ⁹The great dragon was hurled down—that ancient serpent called the devil, or Satan, who leads the whole world astray. He was hurled to the earth, and his angels with him.

¹⁰Then I heard a loud voice in heaven say:

"Now have come the salvation and the power and
    the kingdom of our God,
    and the authority of his Christ.
For the accuser of our brothers,
    who accuses them before our God day and
    night,
    has been hurled down.
¹¹They overcame him
    by the blood of the Lamb
    and by the word of their testimony;
they did not love their lives so much
    as to shrink from death.
¹²Therefore rejoice, you heavens
    and you who dwell in them!
But woe to the earth and the sea,
    because the devil has gone down to you!

He is filled with fury,
   because he knows that his time is short."

[13]When the dragon saw that he had been hurled to the earth, he pursued the woman who had given birth to the male child. [14]The woman was given the two wings of a great eagle, so that she might fly to the place prepared for her in the desert, where she would be taken care of for a time, times and half a time, out of the serpent's reach. [15]Then from his mouth the serpent spewed water like a river, to overtake the woman and sweep her away with the torrent. [16]But the earth helped the woman by opening its mouth and swallowing the river that the dragon had spewed out of his mouth. [17]Then the dragon was enraged at the woman and went off to make war against the rest of her offspring — those who obey God's commandments and hold to the testimony of Jesus. [1]And the dragon[a] stood on the shore of the sea.

13

13:1   For John, the beast represented the Roman empire, but every generation of Christians sees the beast as representing any power which seeks to destroy the church.

The Beast out of the Sea

And I saw a beast coming out of the sea. He had ten horns and seven heads, with ten crowns on his horns, and on each head a blasphemous name. [2]The beast I saw resembled a leopard, but had feet like those of a bear and a mouth like that of a lion. The dragon gave the beast his power and his throne and great authority. [3]One of the heads of the beast seemed to have had a fatal wound, but the fatal wound had been healed. The whole world was astonished and followed the beast. [4]Men worshipped the dragon because he had given authority to the beast, and they also worshipped the beast and asked, "Who is like the beast? Who can make war against him?"

[5]The beast was given a mouth to utter proud words and blasphemies and to exercise his authority for forty-two months. [6]He opened his mouth to blaspheme God, and to slander his name and his dwelling-place and those who live in heaven. [7]He was given power to make war against the saints and to conquer them. And he was given authority over every tribe, people, language and nation. [8]All inhabitants of the earth will worship the beast — all whose names have not been written in the book of life belonging to the Lamb that was slain from the creation of the world.[b]

[9]He who has an ear, let him hear.

[10]If anyone is to go into captivity,
   into captivity he will go.
If anyone is to be killed[c] with the sword,
   with the sword he will be killed.

This calls for patient endurance and faithfulness on the part of the saints.

The Beast out of the Earth

[11]Then I saw another beast, coming out of the earth. He had two horns like a lamb, but he spoke like a dragon. [12]He exercised all the authority of the first beast on his behalf, and made the earth and its inhabitants worship the first beast, whose fatal wound had been healed. [13]And he performed great and miraculous signs, even causing fire to come down from heaven to earth in full view of men. [14]Because of the signs he was given power to do on behalf of the first beast, he deceived the inhabitants of the earth. He ordered them to set up an image in honour of the beast who was wounded by the sword and yet lived. [15]He was given power to give breath to the image of the first beast, so that it could speak and cause all who refused to worship the image to be killed. [16]He also forced everyone, small and great, rich and poor, free and slave, to receive a mark on his right hand or on his forehead, [17]so that no-one could buy or sell unless he had the mark, which is the name of the beast or the number of his name.

13:11   The new beast has all the hallmarks of "false religion". It has authority and power, encourages worship, and performs miracles but is in fact a counterfeit.

---

[18]This calls for wisdom. If anyone has insight, let him calculate the number of the beast, for it is man's number. His number is 666.

The Lamb and the 144,000

14   Then I looked, and there before me was the Lamb, standing on Mount Zion, and with him 144,000 who had his name and his Father's name written on their foreheads. [2]And I heard a sound from heaven like the roar of rushing waters and like a loud peal of thunder. The sound I heard was like that of harpists playing their harps. [3]And they sang a new song before the throne and before the four living creatures and the elders. No-one could learn the song except the 144,000 who had been redeemed from the earth. [4]These are those who did not defile themselves with women, for they kept themselves pure. They follow the Lamb wherever he goes. They were purchased from among men and offered as firstfruits to God and the Lamb. [5]No lie was found in their mouths; they are blameless.

The Three Angels

[6]Then I saw another angel flying in mid-air, and he had the eternal gospel to proclaim to those who live on the earth — to every nation, tribe, language and people. [7]He said in a loud voice, "Fear God and give him glory, because the hour of his judgment has come. Worship him who made the heavens, the earth, the sea and the springs of water."

[8]A second angel followed and said, "Fallen! Fallen is

---

a 1 Some late manuscripts *And I*
b 8 Or *written from the creation of the world in the book of life belonging to the Lamb that was slain*
c 10 Some manuscripts *anyone kills*

Babylon the Great, which made all the nations drink the maddening wine of her adulteries."

[9]A third angel followed them and said in a loud voice: "If anyone worships the beast and his image and receives his mark on the forehead or on the hand, [10]he, too, will drink of the wine of God's fury, which has been poured full strength into the cup of his wrath. He will be tormented with burning sulphur in the presence of the holy angels and of the Lamb. [11]And the smoke of their torment rises for ever and ever. There is no rest day or night for those who worship the beast and his image, or for anyone who receives the mark of his name." [12]This calls for patient endurance on the part of the saints who obey God's commandments and remain faithful to Jesus.

[13]Then I heard a voice from heaven say, "Write: Blessed are the dead who die in the Lord from now on."

"Yes," says the Spirit, "they will rest from their labour, for their deeds will follow them."

The Harvest of the Earth

[14]I looked, and there before me was a white cloud, and seated on the cloud was one "like a son of man" [a] with a crown of gold on his head and a sharp sickle in his hand. [15]Then another angel came out of the temple and called in a loud voice to him who was sitting on the cloud, "Take your sickle and reap, because the time to reap has come, for the harvest of the earth is ripe." [16]So he who was seated on the cloud swung his sickle over the earth, and the earth was harvested.

[17]Another angel came out of the temple in heaven, and he too had a sharp sickle. [18]Still another angel, who had charge of the fire, came from the altar and called in a loud voice to him who had the sharp sickle, "Take your sharp sickle and gather the clusters of grapes from the earth's vine, because its grapes are ripe." [19]The angel swung his sickle on the earth, gathered its grapes and threw them into the great winepress of God's wrath. [20]They were trampled in the winepress outside the city, and blood flowed out of the press, rising as high as the horses' bridles for a distance of 1,600 stadia.[b]

Seven Angels With Seven Plagues

15 I saw in heaven another great and marvellous sign: seven angels with the seven last plagues—last, because with them God's wrath is completed. [2]And I saw what looked like a sea of glass mixed with fire and, standing beside the sea, those who had been victorious over the beast and his image and over the number of his name. They held harps given them by God [3]and sang the song of Moses the servant of God and the song of the Lamb:

"Great and marvellous are your deeds,
  Lord God Almighty.
Just and true are your ways,
  King of the ages.
[4]Who will not fear you, O Lord,
  and bring glory to your name?

For you alone are holy.
All nations will come
  and worship before you,
for your righteous acts have been revealed."

[5]After this I looked and in heaven the temple, that is, the tabernacle of the Testimony, was opened. [6]Out of the temple came the seven angels with the seven plagues. They were dressed in clean, shining linen and wore golden sashes round their chests. [7]Then one of the four living creatures gave to the seven angels seven golden bowls filled with the wrath of God, who lives for ever and ever. [8]And the temple was filled with smoke from the glory of God and from his power, and no-one could enter the temple until the seven plagues of the seven angels were completed.

The Seven Bowls of God's Wrath

16 Then I heard a loud voice from the temple saying to the seven angels, "Go, pour out the seven bowls of God's wrath on the earth."

[2]The first angel went and poured out his bowl on the land, and ugly and painful sores broke out on the people who had the mark of the beast and worshipped his image.

[3]The second angel poured out his bowl on the sea, and it turned into blood like that of a dead man, and every living thing in the sea died.

[4]The third angel poured out his bowl on the rivers and springs of water, and they became blood. [5]Then I heard the angel in charge of the waters say:

"You are just in these judgments,
  you who are and who were, the Holy One,
  because you have so judged;
[6]for they have shed the blood of your saints and
    prophets,
  and you have given them blood to drink as they
    deserve."

[7]And I heard the altar respond:

"Yes, Lord God Almighty,
  true and just are your judgments."

[8]The fourth angel poured out his bowl on the sun, and the sun was given power to scorch people with fire. [9]They were seared by the intense heat and they cursed the name of God, who had control over these plagues, but they refused to repent and glorify him.

[10]The fifth angel poured out his bowl on the throne of the beast, and his kingdom was plunged into darkness. Men gnawed their tongues in agony [11]and cursed the God of heaven because of their pains and their sores, but they refused to repent of what they had done.

[12]The sixth angel poured out his bowl on the great river Euphrates, and its water was dried up to prepare the way for the kings from the East. [13]Then I saw three evil[a] spirits that looked like frogs; they came out of the mouth of the dragon, out of the mouth of the beast and out of the mouth of the false prophet. [14]They are spirits of demons performing miraculous signs, and they go out to the kings of the whole world, to gather

them for the battle on the great day of God Almighty.

[15]"Behold, I come like a thief! Blessed is he who stays awake and keeps his clothes with him, so that he may not go naked and be shamefully exposed."

[16]Then they gathered the kings together to the place that in Hebrew is called Armageddon.

16:16 Armageddon represents the decisive conflict which will happen between God and the forces of evil.

---

[17]The seventh angel poured out his bowl into the air, and out of the temple came a loud voice from the throne, saying, "It is done!" [18]Then there came flashes of lightning, rumblings, peals of thunder and a severe earthquake. No earthquake like it has ever occurred since man has been on earth, so tremendous was the quake. [19]The great city split into three parts, and the cities of the nations collapsed. God remembered Babylon the Great and gave her the cup filled with the wine of the fury of his wrath. [20]Every island fled away and the mountains could not be found. [21]From the sky huge hailstones of about a hundred pounds each fell upon men. And they cursed God on account of the plague of hail, because the plague was so terrible.

The Woman on the Beast

17 One of the seven angels who had the seven bowls came and said to me, "Come, I will show you the punishment of the great prostitute, who sits on many waters. [2]With her the kings of the earth committed adultery and the inhabitants of the earth were intoxicated with the wine of her adulteries."

[3]Then the angel carried me away in the Spirit into a desert. There I saw a woman sitting on a scarlet beast that was covered with blasphemous names and had seven heads and ten horns. [4]The woman was dressed in purple and scarlet, and was glittering with gold, precious stones and pearls. She held a golden cup in her hand, filled with abominable things and the filth of her adulteries. [5]This title was written on her forehead:

MYSTERY
BABYLON THE GREAT
THE MOTHER OF PROSTITUTES
AND OF THE ABOMINATIONS OF THE EARTH.

[6]I saw that the woman was drunk with the blood of the saints, the blood of those who bore testimony to Jesus.

When I saw her, I was greatly astonished. [7]Then the angel said to me: "Why are you astonished? I will explain to you the mystery of the woman and of the beast she rides, which has the seven heads and ten horns. [8]The beast, which you saw, once was, now is not, and will come up out of the Abyss and go to his destruction. The inhabitants of the earth whose names have not been written in the book of life from the creation of the world will be astonished when they see the beast, because he once was, now is not, and yet will come.

[9]"This calls for a mind with wisdom. The seven

heads are seven hills on which the woman sits. [10]They are also seven kings. Five have fallen, one is, the other has not yet come; but when he does come, he must remain for a little while. [11]The beast who once was, and now is not, is an eighth king. He belongs to the seven and is going to his destruction.

[12]"The ten horns you saw are ten kings who have not yet received a kingdom, but who for one hour will receive authority as kings along with the beast. [13]They have one purpose and will give their power and authority to the beast. [14]They will make war against the Lamb, but the Lamb will overcome them because he is Lord of lords and King of kings—and with him will be his called, chosen and faithful followers."

[15]Then the angel said to me, "The waters you saw, where the prostitute sits, are peoples, multitudes, nations and languages. [16]The beast and the ten horns you saw will hate the prostitute. They will bring her to ruin and leave her naked; they will eat her flesh and burn her with fire. [17]For God has put it into their hearts to accomplish his purpose by agreeing to give the beast their power to rule, until God's words are fulfilled. [18]The woman you saw is the great city that rules over the kings of the earth."

The Fall of Babylon

18 After this I saw another angel coming down from heaven. He had great authority, and the earth was illuminated by his splendour. [2]With a mighty voice he shouted:

"Fallen! Fallen is Babylon the Great!
  She has become a home for demons
and a haunt for every evil[a] spirit,
  a haunt for every unclean and detestable bird.
[3]For all the nations have drunk
  the maddening wine of her adulteries.
The kings of the earth committed adultery with her,
  and the merchants of the earth grew rich from her excessive luxuries."

18:2 Much has been written about the possible identity of Babylon. It has been identified both with Rome and Jerusalem. It is easier to understand such references as representing all kingdoms or powers which seek to destroy the church. The encouragement is in the fact that such powers will be destroyed.

---

[4]Then I heard another voice from heaven say:

"Come out of her, my people,
  so that you will not share in her sins,
  so that you will not receive any of her plagues;
[5]for her sins are piled up to heaven,
  and God has remembered her crimes.
[6]Give back to her as she has given;
  pay her back double for what she has done.
  Mix her a double portion from her own cup.

[a]2 Greek *unclean*

⁷Give her as much torture and grief
   as the glory and luxury she gave herself.
In her heart she boasts,
   'I sit as queen; I am not a widow,
   and I will never mourn.'
⁸Therefore in one day her plagues will overtake
   her:
   death, mourning and famine.
She will be consumed by fire,
   for mighty is the Lord God who judges her.

⁹"When the kings of the earth who committed adultery with her and shared her luxury see the smoke of
her burning, they will weep and mourn over her. ¹⁰Ter-
rified at her torment, they will stand far off and cry:

" 'Woe! Woe, O great city,
   O Babylon, city of power!
   In one hour your doom has come!'

¹¹"The merchants of the earth will weep and mourn
over her because no-one buys their cargoes any
more — ¹²cargoes of gold, silver, precious stones and
pearls; fine linen, purple, silk and scarlet cloth; every
sort of citron wood, and articles of every kind made of
ivory, costly wood, bronze, iron and marble; ¹³cargoes
of cinnamon and spice, of incense, myrrh and frankincense, of wine and olive oil, of fine flour and wheat;
cattle and sheep; horses and carriages; and bodies and
souls of men.
¹⁴"They will say, 'The fruit you longed for is gone
from you. All your riches and splendour have vanished,
never to be recovered.' ¹⁵The merchants who sold
these things and gained their wealth from her will
stand far off, terrified at her torment. They will weep
and mourn ¹⁶and cry out:

" 'Woe! Woe, O great city,
   dressed in fine linen, purple and scarlet,
   and glittering with gold, precious stones and
      pearls!
¹⁷In one hour such great wealth has been brought
   to ruin!'

"Every sea captain, and all who travel by ship, the
sailors, and all who earn their living from the sea, will
stand far off. ¹⁸When they see the smoke of her burning, they will exclaim, 'Was there ever a city like this
great city?' ¹⁹They will throw dust on their heads, and
with weeping and mourning cry out:

" 'Woe! Woe, O great city,
   where all who had ships on the sea
   became rich through her wealth!
In one hour she has been brought to ruin!
²⁰Rejoice over her, O heaven!
   Rejoice, saints and apostles and prophets!
God has judged her for the way she treated
      you.' "

²¹Then a mighty angel picked up a boulder the size
of a large millstone and threw it into the sea, and said:

"With such violence
   the great city of Babylon will be thrown down,
   never to be found again.

²²The music of harpists and musicians, flute players
      and trumpeters,
   will never be heard in you again.
No workman of any trade
   will ever be found in you again.
The sound of a millstone
   will never be heard in you again.
²³The light of a lamp
   will never shine in you again.
The voice of bridegroom and bride
   will never be heard in you again.
Your merchants were the world's great men.
   By your magic spell all the nations were led
      astray.
²⁴In her was found the blood of prophets and of the
      saints,
   and of all who have been killed on the earth."

Hallelujah!

19 After this I heard what sounded like the roar
      of a great multitude in heaven shouting:

"Hallelujah!
Salvation and glory and power belong to our God,
² for true and just are his judgments.
He has condemned the great prostitute
   who corrupted the earth by her adulteries.
He has avenged on her the blood of his servants."

³And again they shouted:

"Hallelujah!
The smoke from her goes up for ever and ever."

⁴The twenty-four elders and the four living creatures
fell down and worshipped God, who was seated on the
throne. And they cried:

"Amen, Hallelujah!"

⁵Then a voice came from the throne, saying:

"Praise our God,
   all you his servants,
you who fear him,
   both small and great!"

⁶Then I heard what sounded like a great multitude,
like the roar of rushing waters and like loud peals of
thunder, shouting:

"Hallelujah!
   For our Lord God Almighty reigns.
⁷Let us rejoice and be glad
   and give him glory!
For the wedding of the Lamb has come,
   and his bride has made herself ready.
⁸Fine linen, bright and clean,
   was given her to wear."
(Fine linen stands for the righteous acts of the saints.)

⁹Then the angel said to me, "Write: 'Blessed are
those who are invited to the wedding supper of the
Lamb!' " And he added, "These are the true words of
God."
¹⁰At this I fell at his feet to worship him. But he said
to me, "Do not do it! I am a fellow-servant with you and
with your brothers who hold to the testimony of Jesus.

Worship God! For the testimony of Jesus is the spirit of prophecy."

The Rider on the White Horse

[11]I saw heaven standing open and there before me was a white horse, whose rider is called Faithful and True. With justice he judges and makes war. [12]His eyes are like blazing fire, and on his head are many crowns. He has a name written on him that no-one knows but he himself. [13]He is dressed in a robe dipped in blood, and his name is the Word of God. [14]The armies of heaven were following him, riding on white horses and dressed in fine linen, white and clean. [15]Out of his mouth comes a sharp sword with which to strike down the nations. "He will rule them with an iron sceptre."[a] He treads the winepress of the fury of the wrath of God Almighty. [16]On his robe and on his thigh he has this name written:

KING OF KINGS AND LORD OF LORDS.

[17]And I saw an angel standing in the sun, who cried in a loud voice to all the birds flying in mid-air, "Come, gather together for the great supper of God, [18]so that you may eat the flesh of kings, generals, and mighty men, of horses and their riders, and the flesh of all people, free and slave, small and great."

[19]Then I saw the beast and the kings of the earth and their armies gathered together to make war against the rider on the horse and his army. [20]But the beast was captured, and with him the false prophet who had performed the miraculous signs on his behalf. With these signs he had deluded those who had received the mark of the beast and worshipped his image. The two of them were thrown alive into the fiery lake of burning sulphur. [21]The rest of them were killed with the sword that came out of the mouth of the rider on the horse, and all the birds gorged themselves on their flesh.

The Thousand Years

20 And I saw an angel coming down out of heaven, having the key to the Abyss and holding in his hand a great chain. [2]He seized the dragon, that ancient serpent, who is the devil, or Satan, and bound him for a thousand years. [3]He threw him into the Abyss, and locked and sealed it over him, to keep him from deceiving the nations any more until the thousand years were ended. After that, he must be set free for a short time.

[4]I saw thrones on which were seated those who had been given authority to judge. And I saw the souls of those who had been beheaded because of their testimony for Jesus and because of the word of God. They had not worshipped the beast or his image and had not received his mark on their foreheads or their hands. They came to life and reigned with Christ for a thousand years. [5](The rest of the dead did not come to life until the thousand years were ended.) This is the first resurrection. [6]Blessed and holy are those who have part in the first resurrection. The second death has no power over them, but they will be priests of God and of Christ and will reign with him for a thousand years.

Satan's Doom

[7]When the thousand years are over, Satan will be released from his prison [8]and will go out to deceive the nations in the four corners of the earth — Gog and Magog — to gather them for battle. In number they are like the sand on the seashore. [9]They marched across the breadth of the earth and surrounded the camp of God's people, the city he loves. But fire came down from heaven and devoured them. [10]And the devil, who deceived them, was thrown into the lake of burning sulphur, where the beast and the false prophet had been thrown. They will be tormented day and night for ever and ever.

The Dead Are Judged

[11]Then I saw a great white throne and him who was seated on it. Earth and sky fled from his presence, and there was no place for them. [12]And I saw the dead, great and small, standing before the throne, and books were opened. Another book was opened, which is the book of life. The dead were judged according to what they had done as recorded in the books. [13]The sea gave up the dead that were in it, and death and Hades gave up the dead that were in them, and each person was judged according to what he had done. [14]Then death and Hades were thrown into the lake of fire. The lake of fire is the second death. [15]If anyone's name was not found written in the book of life, he was thrown into the lake of fire.

The New Jerusalem

21 Then I saw a new heaven and a new earth, for the first heaven and the first earth had passed away, and there was no longer any sea. [2]I saw the Holy City, the new Jerusalem, coming down out of heaven from God, prepared as a bride beautifully dressed for her husband. [3]And I heard a loud voice from the throne saying, "Now the dwelling of God is with men, and he will live with them. They will be his people, and God himself will be with them and be their God. [4]He will wipe every tear from their eyes. There will be no more death or mourning or crying or pain, for the old order of things has passed away."

[5]He who was seated on the throne said, "I am making everything new!" Then he said, "Write this down, for these words are trustworthy and true."

[6]He said to me: "It is done. I am the Alpha and the Omega, the Beginning and the End. To him who is thirsty I will give to drink without cost from the spring of the water of life. [7]He who overcomes will inherit all this, and I will be his God and he will be my son. [8]But the cowardly, the unbelieving, the vile, the murderers, the sexually immoral, those who practise magic arts, the idolaters and all liars — their place will be in the fiery lake of burning sulphur. This is the second death."

[9]One of the seven angels who had the seven bowls full of the seven last plagues came and said to me, "Come, I will show you the bride, the wife of the Lamb." [10]And he carried me away in the Spirit to a mountain great and high, and showed me the Holy

a 15 Psalm 2:9

City, Jerusalem, coming down out of heaven from God. [11]It shone with the glory of God, and its brilliance was like that of a very precious jewel, like a jasper, clear as crystal. [12]It had a great, high wall with twelve gates, and with twelve angels at the gates. On the gates were written the names of the twelve tribes of Israel. [13]There were three gates on the east, three on the north, three on the south and three on the west. [14]The wall of the city had twelve foundations, and on them were the names of the twelve apostles of the Lamb.

[15]The angel who talked with me had a measuring rod of gold to measure the city, its gates and its walls. [16]The city was laid out like a square, as long as it was wide. He measured the city with the rod and found it to be 12,000 stadia[a] in length, and as wide and high as it is long. [17]He measured its wall and it was 144 cubits[b] thick,[c] by man's measurement, which the angel was using. [18]The wall was made of jasper, and the city of pure gold, as pure as glass. [19]The foundations of the city walls were decorated with every kind of precious stone. The first foundation was jasper, the second sapphire, the third chalcedony, the fourth emerald, [20]the fifth sardonyx, the sixth carnelian, the seventh chrysolite, the eighth beryl, the ninth topaz, the tenth chrysoprase, the eleventh jacinth, and the twelfth amethyst.[d] [21]The twelve gates were twelve pearls, each gate made of a single pearl. The great street of the city was of pure gold, like transparent glass.

[22]I did not see a temple in the city, because the Lord God Almighty and the Lamb are its temple. [23]The city does not need the sun or the moon to shine on it, for the glory of God gives it light, and the Lamb is its lamp. [24]The nations will walk by its light, and the kings of the earth will bring their splendour into it. [25]On no day will its gates ever be shut, for there will be no night there. [26]The glory and honour of the nations will be brought into it. [27]Nothing impure will ever enter it, nor will anyone who does what is shameful or deceitful, but only those whose names are written in the Lamb's book of life.

22:1   The final chapters recall the beauty and perfection of the Garden of Eden which the Bible opens with in Genesis. The old world which had been spoiled by humanity has now been made new. It is the hope of a new heaven and a new earth that will sustain the suffering church through its persecutions.

The River of Life

22 Then the angel showed me the river of the water of life, as clear as crystal, flowing from the throne of God and of the Lamb [2]down the middle of the great street of the city. On each side of the river stood the tree of life, bearing twelve crops of fruit, yielding its fruit every month. And the leaves of the tree are for the healing of the nations. [3]No longer will there be any curse. The throne of God and of the Lamb will be in the city, and his servants will serve him. [4]They will see his face, and his name will be on their foreheads. [5]There will be no more night. They will not need the light of a lamp or the light of the sun, for the Lord God will give them light. And they will reign for ever and ever.

[6]The angel said to me, "These words are trustworthy and true. The Lord, the God of the spirits of the prophets, sent his angel to show his servants the things that must soon take place."

Jesus Is Coming

[7]"Behold, I am coming soon! Blessed is he who keeps the words of the prophecy in this book."

[8]I, John, am the one who heard and saw these things. And when I had heard and seen them, I fell down to worship at the feet of the angel who had been showing them to me. [9]But he said to me, "Do not do it! I am a fellow-servant with you and with your brothers the prophets and of all who keep the words of this book. Worship God!"

[10]Then he told me, "Do not seal up the words of the prophecy of this book, because the time is near. [11]Let him who does wrong continue to do wrong; let him who is vile continue to be vile; let him who does right continue to do right; and let him who is holy continue to be holy."

[12]"Behold, I am coming soon! My reward is with me, and I will give to everyone according to what he has done. [13]I am the Alpha and the Omega, the First and the Last, the Beginning and the End.

[14]"Blessed are those who wash their robes, that they may have the right to the tree of life and may go through the gates into the city. [15]Outside are the dogs, those who practise magic arts, the sexually immoral, the murderers, the idolaters and everyone who loves and practises falsehood.

[16]"I, Jesus, have sent my angel to give you[a] this testimony for the churches. I am the Root and the Offspring of David, and the bright Morning Star."

[17]The Spirit and the bride say, "Come!" And let him who hears say, "Come!" Whoever is thirsty, let him come; and whoever wishes, let him take the free gift of the water of life.

[18]I warn everyone who hears the words of the prophecy of this book: If anyone adds anything to them, God will add to him the plagues described in this book. [19]And if anyone takes words away from this book of prophecy, God will take away from him his share in the tree of life and in the holy city, which are described in this book.

[20]He who testifies to these things says, "Yes, I am coming soon."

Amen. Come, Lord Jesus.

[21]The grace of the Lord Jesus be with God's people. Amen.

---

[a]16 That is, about 1,400 miles (about 2,200 kilometres)   [b]17 That is, about 200 feet (about 65 metres)
[c]17 Or high   [d]20 The precise identification of some of these precious stones is uncertain.   [a]16 The Greek is plural.

TABLE OF WEIGHTS AND MEASURES

	Approximate Biblical Unit	Approximate Imperial Unit	Metric Equivalent
Weights			
talent	*60 minas*	75 pounds	34 kilograms
mina	*50 shekels*	1¼ pounds	0.6 kilogram
shekel	*2 bekas*	⅖ ounce	11.5 grams
pim	*⅔ shekel*	¼ ounce	7.7 grams
beka	*10 gerahs*	⅕ ounce	5.8 grams
gerah		¹⁄₅₀ ounce	0.6 gram
Length			
cubit		18 inches	0.5 metre
span		9 inches	23 centimetres
handbreadth		3 inches	8 centimetres
Capacity: Dry Measure			
cor [homer]	*10 ephahs*	6 bushels	220 litres
lethek	*5 ephahs*	3 bushels	110 litres
ephah	*10 omers*	⅗ bushel	22 litres
seah	*⅓ ephah*	13 pints	7.3 litres
omer	*¹⁄₁₀ ephah*	4 pints	2 litres
cab	*¹⁄₁₈ ephah*	2 pints	1 litre
Capacity: Liquid Measure			
bath	*1 ephah*	5 gallons	22 litres
hin	*⅙ bath*	7 pints	4 litres
log	*¹⁄₇₂ bath*	½ pint	0.3 litre

The figures of the table are calculated on the basis of a shekel equalling 11.5 grams, a cubit equalling 18 inches and an ephah equalling 22 litres. It is based upon the best available information, but it is not intended to be mathematically precise; like the measurement equivalents in the footnotes, it merely gives approximate amounts and distances. Weights and measures differed somewhat at various times and places in the ancient world. There is uncertainty particularly about the ephah and the bath; further discoveries may give more light on these units of capacity.

WORD LIST

Aaron   brother of Moses and the first high priest
dealings with Moses, Exodus 4:10—12:50
consecration as a priest, Exodus 29
building of golden calf, Exodus 32
death, Numbers 20:1–12; 33:38,39

Abba   word used by Jesus to address God
Mark 14:36
Romans 8:15
Galatians 4:6

Abednigo   one of the young men to be deported to Babylon, along with Daniel and Shedrach
deportation, Daniel 1:1–6
refusal to eat the king's food, Daniel 1:8–20
in the burning furnace, Daniel 3:13–30

Abel   second son of Adam
life story, Genesis 4:1–9

Abraham   the founder of the Jewish nation
called by God, Genesis 11:26—12:20
life story, Genesis 11:26—25:11
covenant with God, Genesis 15, 17
sacrifices Isaac, Genesis 22

Abstinence   doing without, or refraining from
sexual relationships, Exodus 19:15
wine and strong drink, Numbers 6:3
evil desires, 1 Peter 2:11

Adam   the first man created by God
life story, Genesis 1:26—5:5
fall, Genesis 3

Angels   God's messengers (from the Greek "angelos")
helping, Genesis 24

bringing God's message, Luke 1:26–38; 2:8–15
worshipping before God, Revelation 8, 9

Ahab   king of Israel
life story, 1 Kings 16:28—22:40

Ahaz   king of Judah
life story, 2 Kings 16

Antichrist   an evil or fraudulant person, claiming to be God's anointed
foretelling his coming, Daniel 11:36–45
what he will be like, 1 John 2:18–23; 4:1–6
seen in the future, Revelation 11—13

Apollos   Jewish teacher, acknowledged by Paul in his letters
Acts 18:24–28
1 Corinthians 3:1–9

Apostles   a collective name given to the followers of Jesus who founded the early church
being sent to preach, Matthew 28:16–20
anointed with the Holy Spirit, Acts 2

Areopagus   place of learning in Athens, where Paul taught
Acts 17:19–34

Ark of the Covenant   the place where the tablets of stone containing the Law were kept
being given, Exodus 25:10–22
symbol of authority, 1 Samuel 4, 5
return to Jerusalem by David, 2 Samuel 6:1–15

Ascension   Jesus' return to God in heaven
Acts 1:1–11

Baal a god worshipped by the Canaanites and Phoenicians
1 Kings 16:29–34
1 Kings 18
2 Kings 17:7–23

Baasha a king of Israel
life story, 1 Kings 15:16—16:7

Babylon a mighty nation which conquered and took Israel into captivity
sorrow of the Jews, Psalm 137
condemnation of, Jeremiah 29:10

Balaam dubious character sent by the Moabites to condemn Israel
life story, Numbers 22—24
death of, Numbers 31:1–24

Baptism a sign of conversion, first used in the Bible by John the Baptist
baptism of Jesus, Matthew 3:1–12
command from Jesus, Matthew 28:16–20
use in the church, Acts 8:26–39

Barabbas local terrorist in Jerusalem at the time of Jesus' death
crowd demanded his release in place of Jesus, Matthew 27:11–26

Blood as source of life
in priestly sacrifice, Exodus 29
as an offering for sin, Leviticus 3, 4
of Christ, Matthew 26:27–29

Breath as source of life
in creation, Genesis 2:7
at the end of Jesus' death on the cross, Mark 15:37
at the giving of the Holy Spirit, John 20:22

Cain first son of Adam
life story, Genesis 4:1–26

Calvary the hill on which Jesus was crucified
Luke 23:26–43

Canaan land which God promised to his people
Genesis 15:12–21
Joshua 1—12

Capernaum town in Galilee where Jesus lived
Matthew 4:13

Circumcision a ritual carried out on all new-born males as a sign of the covenant
Genesis 17:9–14

Covenant the solemn promise of faithfulness made between God and his people
with Noah, Genesis 9:1–17
with Abraham, Genesis 15; 17:1–14
with the Israelites, Exodus 29
with David, 2 Samuel 7:1–17
the new covenant in Christ, 2 Corinthians 2:12—3:8

Cross instrument of the execution during Roman occupancy of Israel, on which Jesus died
as a metaphor, Mark 8:31—9:1
Luke 23:26–49

David king of Israel
life story, 1 Samuel 16—1 Kings 2

Deacon a serving office in the church
1 Timothy 3:8–12

Deborah a judge and prophet of Israel
life story, Judges 4, 5

Disciples those called to follow and learn from a teacher, especially Jesus
Luke 14:25–34

Divorce to break marriage vows
Law of Moses, Deuteronomy 24:1–4
teaching of Jesus, Matthew 19:1–12
teaching of Paul, 1 Corinthians 7:10–16

Eli a priest and teacher of Samuel
life story, 1 Samuel 1—4

Elijah one of the prophets active during the reign of the Kings
life story, 1 Kings 17—19

Elisha Elijah's successor
life story, 2 Kings 2—13

Esau older brother of Jacob
life story, Genesis 25:19—28:9

Eve the first woman created by God
life story, Genesis 1:26—5:2

Evil the opposite of goodness and truth
how it all began, Genesis 3:1–24

Ezra the prophet who led the Jews out of exile and back to Jerusalem
life story, Ezra 7—10; Nehemiah 8, 12

Fasting giving up food for a period of time for spiritual reasons
a real motive, Isaiah 58

Jesus' understanding of, Matthew 6:16

Feasts *and* Festivals   days which punctuated the year, recalling God's saving activity in the life of his people
Exodus 12
Deuteronomy 16

Gabriel   one of the angels of God who carried God's message to his people, especially Mary
with Daniel, Daniel 8, 9
with Zechariah, Luke 1:5–25
with Mary, Luke 1:26–38

Gad   Son of Jacob and brother of Joseph
life story, Genesis 30:9–11

Gehazi   servant and companion of Elijah
life story, 2 Kings 4:12—5:27

God
as creator, Genesis 1, 2
known by name, Exodus 3
incarnate in Christ, John 1:1–18

Gethsemane   place where Jesus prayed on the night before his arrest
Matthew 26:36

Gideon   leader of Israel, during the period of the Judges, who delivered Israel from the Midianites
life story, Judges 6—8

Golgotha   the hill outside Jerusalem (known as the place of the skull) where Jesus was crucified
Matthew 27:33
John 19:17

Grace   the love and kindness from God, offered freely
Romans 5
Ephesians 2

Habakkuk   Judean prophet who protested at the success of the enemies of Judah
outline of the main themes of preaching, Habukkuk 1, 2

Hagar   servant and wife of Abraham, and mother of Ishmael
life story, Genesis 16:1–16

Haggai   prophet of Israel, who encouraged the establishment of Jerusalem and the temple as the focal point of

Israel's worship, after the return from exile
life story, Haggai 1, 2

Healing   bringing peace and wholeness to every part of life
prayers answered, 1 Kings 17:7–24; 2 Kings 5
by Jesus, Luke 4:38–41
when to do it, James 5:13–18

Hell   absence from God, usually referring to a time after death
a place to avoid, Matthew 5:21–30; Romans 8:1–16
as punishment, 2 Thessalonians 1:3–12

Hezekiah   king of Judah
life story, 2 Kings 18—20

Holy Spirit   the presence of God in the life of his people
comforter, John 14:15–31
its coming, Acts 2
giver of life, Romans 8:1–17

Idols   false gods, worshipped and put in place of the living God
Exodus 20:3–6
Isaiah 44:6–23

Isaac   only son of Sarah and Abraham
God's command to Abraham to sacrifice him, Genesis 22:1–29
life story, Genesis 24, 27, 25:16–29

Jacob   son of Isaac and younger brother of Esau
life story, Genesis 25—49

James   son of Zebedee, one of the twelve apostles
Matthew 4:18–22
Matthew 17:1–13

Jehoahaz   son of Josiah, king of Judah
2 Kings 23:31–34

Jeremiah   prophet of Judah
life story, Jeremiah 1, 2, 11, 28, 36, 37, 43

John the Baptist   last of the prophets and forerunner to Jesus
birth, Luke 1:5–25,57–80
ministry, Luke 3:1–20
death, Mark 6:14–29

Joseph   son of Jacob and Rachel
life story, Genesis 37—50

Judas Iscariot   one of the twelve disciples, betrayed Jesus to the authorities
Matthew 26:47–56
death, Matthew 27:1–10

Justification by Faith   freedom in God and freedom from sin
Romans 3:21–31
Galatians 2:15–21

Korah   a Levite who led the people of God to rebel against Moses
life story, Numbers 16

Lamb of God   title given to Jesus by John the Baptist, and to the exalted Christ in Revelation
John 1:29–42
Revelation 5

Law   the commandments of God, particularly those given to Moses
Exodus 19:1—24:8

Lazarus   close friend of Jesus, brother of Mary and Martha, who was raised from the dead by Jesus
John 11:1–44

Levites   descendants of Levi, many of whom served as priests in the temple
duties, Numbers 3; 1 Chronicles 23, 24

Lion   description of Christ in Revelation
Revelation 5:1–5

Lord's Prayer   prayer Jesus taught to his followers
Matthew 6:5–15

Lord's Supper   the last meal Jesus shared with his disciples before his death, and which is still celebrated by Christians today to remember his death and resurrection
Jesus' meal, Luke 22:7–23
instructions, 1 Corinthians 11:17–34

Martha   close friend of Jesus, sister of Mary and Lazarus
John 11

Mary   mother of Jesus and wife of Joseph
life story, Matthew 1:18—2:23
Luke 1:26–56; 2
John 2:1–11; 19:16–27

Melchizidek   priest, king, and first of the patriarchs
gives his blessing to Abram, Genesis 14:17–20

Michael   archangel, protecting and bringing God's message to Israel
Daniel 10, 12
Revelation 12

Moses   servant of God and leader of the nation of Israel
life story, Exodus, Numbers, Deuteronomy

Nebuchadnezzar   Babylonian ruler who plundered Jerusalem, and held the Jews in captivity
2 Kings 25:1–26
Daniel 1—4

Nicodemus   pharisee who was impressed by Jesus
John 3:1–21; 19:38–42

Noah   faithful servant of God, saved from a worldwide flood
Genesis 6—9

Parable   symbolic story, especially used by Jesus to describe God and the nature of his kingdom
Matthew 13:10–17

Paul   zealous Jew who persecuted Christ's followers, was later converted to Christ and spread the message of the gospel through his letters and travels
conversion, Acts 9:1–31
missionary journeys, Acts 13:1—14:28; Acts 15:36—19:41
Rome, Acts 27:1—28:31

Pentecost   Jewish festival, instituted in Leviticus, but celebrated by Christians as the day to commemorate the sending of the Holy Spirit
Leviticus 23:15–21
Acts 2

Peter   disciple of Jesus, and one of the twelve apostles
Matthew 4:18–22; 26:31–75
Acts 10:1—11:18

Pharisees   a group of devout Jews who observed the Law with particular rigour and piety
Matthew 23

Luke 11:37–54

Philistines an enemy of Israel
Judges 13:1—16:31
1 Samuel 17:1–58

Pontius Pilate Roman governor of Judea, responsible for passing the death sentence on Jesus
John 18:28—19:22

Predestination God's choice of those who are to be saved
Romans 8:28–30
Ephesians 1:3–14

Rahab a prostitute who played a part in the downfall of Jericho
Joshua 2, 6

Rebekah mother of Esau and Jacob, and wife of Isaac
Genesis 24, 25:19–34; 27:1—28:9

Redeemer one who rescues, a title given to Jesus as the one who saves us from sin
Isaiah 54:1–8
Hebrews 9:11–14

Resurrection Christ's rising from death
Matthew 27:57—28:20
John 20, 21
1 Corinthians 15

Sabbath day on which God rested after creation, traditionally the day when God's people rest from their work
Ezekiel 20:1–29
Mark 2:23—3:6

Sadducees a group of the Jewish religious establishment at the time of Jesus, who did not believe in life after death
Matthew 16:1–12
Acts 4:1–22
Acts 23:1–11

Samson one of the last Judges of Israel
life story, Judges 13—16

Samuel the last Judge of Israel
life story, 1 Samuel 1:1—3:21; 5:1—8:22; 9:1—15:35; 16:1–13

Sanhedrin the religious and political court with the highest powers during the Roman occupation of Palestine, at the time of Jesus
John 18
Acts 4:1–22; 23:1–11

Sarah wife of Abraham and mother of Isaac
life story, Genesis 11:29—12:20; 16:1—18:15; 21:1–21; 23:1–20

Satan the fallen angel, often referred to as the devil, Lucifer, or Beelzebub
Matthew 4:1–11
John 8:42–47
1 Peter 5:8–11
Revelation 20

Saul the first Israelite king
life story, 1 Samuel 9—15

Saul the Jewish official who persecuted the church, and who, upon his conversion, became Paul the apostle
Acts 8:1–3; 9:1–31

Saviour the one who saves his people from defeat; a title given to Christ
Christ foretold, Isaiah 59:15–21
Christ proclaimed as, Acts 13:13–52

Sinai the mountain where God gave Moses the Law
Exodus 19

Solomon the last king of a united Israel
life story, 1 Kings 1:1—4:34; 5:1—9:9; 11:1–43

Stephen the first Christian to die for his faith
life story, Acts 6:1—8:3

Tabernacle the place where the Israelites worshipped God, when they were in the wilderness, and before they had settled in the promised land.
Exodus 25, 26

Temple the central place of worship for the Jews, in Jerusalem
1 Kings 5—8
Ezra 1—6
Ezekiel 40—43
John 2:12–25
Revelation 21:22

Ten Commandments another name given to the Law which God gave to Moses on Sinai
Exodus 19, 20

Deuteronomy 5

Thomas   one of the twelve disciples
John 11:1–16
John 20:19–31

Timothy   a companion and disciple of
Paul, who also undertook leadership
of the church in Ephesus
Acts 16:1–5

Tithe   an offering of a peron's goods
and income to God, usually one
tenth of all that a person owns
Leviticus 27:30–33

Vine *and* Vineyard   metaphors for the
kingdom of God, used in both Old
and New Testaments
Isaiah 5:1–7
John 15:1–17

Widow   a woman who survives her
husband. The status of widowhood is
significant in the Old Testament, because it brought disposession and
powerlessness
Exodus 22:22–24
Deuteronmomy 24:17–22
1 Corinthians 7:8,9

Zacchaeus   a tax collector from Jericho
meeting Jesus, Luke 19:1–10

Zion   one of the hills on which Jerusalem was built. It was often used to
refer to Jerusalem in general, as
God's holy mountain and the place
where he dwelt
2 Samuel 5:6–16
Hebrews 12:22–29